45°E
60°E
75°E
Black Sea
Caspian Sea
Aral Sea
Aras River
Amu Darya (Oxus River)
Toros Dağlari
Cyprus
Mesopotamia
Tigris River
Euphrates River
Kuhha-ye Zāgros
Reshteh-ye Alborz
Hindu Kush
Dasht-e Kavor (Salt Desert)
Iranian Plateau
Dasht-e Lut (Sand Desert)
Syrian Desert
Jordan River
Dead Sea
Sinai
Nafud
Persian Gulf
Nile River
Najd
al-Hijaz
Red Sea
Gulf of Oman
Arabian Peninsula
Nubian Desert
al-Rub al-Khali
Atbara River
Blue Nile River
Arabian Sea
Gulf of Aden
Socotra
Nile River
INDIAN OCEAN
N
0 200 400 mi.
0 200 400 km
D1788564

ENCYCLOPEDIA OF THE MODERN MIDDLE EAST & NORTH AFRICA

SECOND EDITION

Editor in Chief

Philip Mattar
United States Institute of Peace

Associate Editors

Charles E. Butterworth
University of Maryland

Neil Caplan
Vanier College, Montreal, Canada

Michael R. Fischbach
Randolph-Macon College, Ashland, Virginia

Eric Hooglund
Institute for Palestine Studies, Washington, DC

Laurie King-Irani
University of Victoria, British Columbia, Canada

John Ruedy
Georgetown University

Consultant Editor

Don Peretz
State University of New York

ENCYCLOPEDIA OF THE MODERN MIDDLE EAST & NORTH AFRICA

SECOND EDITION

VOLUME 4

Shammar – Zurayk
Index

Philip Mattar
EDITOR IN CHIEF

MACMILLAN REFERENCE USA
An imprint of Thomson Gale, a part of The Thomson Corporation

THOMSON
GALE

Detroit • New York • San Francisco • San Diego • New Haven, Conn. • Waterville, Maine • London • Munich

THOMSON
GALE

The Encyclopedia of the Modern Middle East and North Africa, 2nd Edition

Philip Mattar

© 2004 Thomson Gale, a part of The Thomson Corporation.

Thomson, Star Logo and Macmillan Reference USA are trademarks and Gale is a registered trademark used herein under license.

For more information, contact
Macmillan Reference USA
27500 Drake Rd.
Farmington Hills, MI 48331-3535
Or you can visit our internet site at
http://www.gale.com.

ALL RIGHTS RESERVED
No part of this work covered by the copyright hereon may be reproduced or used in any form or by any means—graphic, electronic, or mechanical, including photocopying, recording, taping, Web distribution, or information storage retrieval systems—without the written permission of the publisher.

For permission to use material from this product, submit your request via Web at http://www.gale-edit.com/permissions, or you may download our Permissions Request form and sumbit your request by fax or mail to:

Thomson Gale
27500 Drake Rd.
Farmington Hills, MI 48331-3535
Permissions Hotline:
248-699-8006 or 800-877-4253, ext. 8006
Fax: 248-699-8074 or 800-762-4058

Cover photographs reproduced by permission of Corbis, and AP/Wide World Photos.

Since this page cannot legibly accommodate all copyright notices, the acknowledgements constitute an extension of the copyright notice.

While every effort has been made to ensure the reliability of the information presented in this publication, Thomson Gale does not guarantee the accuracy of the data contained herein. Thomson Gale accepts no payment for listing; and inclusion in the publication of any organization, agency, institution, publication, service, or individual does not imply endorsement of the editors or publisher. Errors brought to the attention of the publisher and verified to the satisfaction of the publisher will be corrected in future editions.

LIBRARY OF CONGRESS CATALOGING-IN-PUBLICATION DATA

Encyclopedia of the modern Middle East and North Africa / edited by Philip Mattar.— 2nd ed.
p. cm.
Includes bibliographical references and index.
ISBN 0-02-865769-1 (set : alk. paper) — ISBN 0-02-865770-5 (v. 1 : alk. paper) — ISBN 0-02-865771-3 (v. 2 : alk. paper) — ISBN 0-02-865772-1 (v. 3 : alk. paper) — ISBN 0-02-865773-X (v. 4 : alk. paper)
1. Middle East—Encyclopedias. 2. Africa, North—Encyclopedias. I. Mattar, Philip, 1944-

DS43.E53 2004
956'.003—dc22 2004005650

This title is also avalable as an e-book.
ISBN 0-02-865987-2 (set)
Contact your Gale sales representative for ordering information.

Printed in the United States of America
10 9 8 7 6 5 4 3 2 1

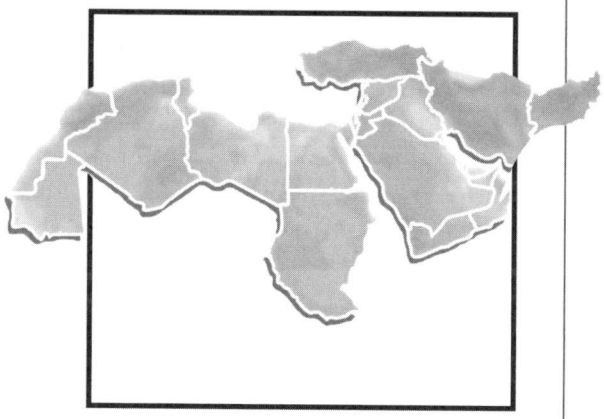

S

(*Continued*)

SHAMMAR

See TRIBES AND TRIBALISM: SHAMMAR

SHAMMAS, ANTON

[1950–]

Israeli Palestinian novelist, poet, journalist, translator, and nonfiction writer.

Anton Shammas was born to a Christian family in Fassuta, Galilee; he defines himself as an atheist, as a Palestinian citizen of Israel, and as one who identifies with Islamic culture. He studied art history and English and Arabic literature at Hebrew University of Jerusalem from 1968 to 1972, edited the literary journal *al-Sharq* from 1970 to 1975, and produced Arabic television shows in Israel from 1976 to 1986 at the same time that he worked as a freelance journalist.

Shammas writes in Hebrew and English, and his works are characterized by an attempt to challenge the definition and test the tolerance of the Israeli discourse from within the Hebrew language. His highly praised first novel *Arabeshot* (1986; *Arabesques,* 1988) was written in Hebrew and deals with the residents of his native village and, more specifically, with the Shammas family. Interwoven with their lives are historical events and associations that highlight the conditions of the Arabs residing in Israel.

He moved to the United States in 1987 and has been teaching at the University of Michigan since 1988.

See also HEBREW UNIVERSITY OF JERUSALEM.

Bibliography

Fischbach, Michael R. "Anton Shammas." In *Encyclopedia of the Palestinians,* edited by Philip Mattar. New York: Facts On File, 2000.

Shammas, Anton. *Arabesques,* translated from the Hebrew by Vivian Eden. New York: Harper & Row, 1988.

ANN KAHN
UPDATED BY MICHAEL R. FISCHBACH

SHAPIRA, HAYYIM MOSHE

[1902–1970]

Israeli political leader; active in the Ze'irei ha-Mizrahi Zionist movement.

Born in Russia, Hayyim Moshe Shapira studied at the Grodno Yeshiva in Russia and at the Hildesheimer Rabbinical Seminary in Berlin. He attended the fourteenth Zionist Congress and later was elected to the Zionist General Council as a representative of ha Poʿel ha-Mizrahi. In 1925, he emigrated to Palestine, where he became a leader in the Zionist Executive.

After the Anschluss of Austria and Germany in 1938, Shapira went to evacuate Austrian Jews to Palestine. Throughout his life, he sought to facilitate the emigration of religious Jews to Israel. From the time the state of Israel was proclaimed in 1948 until his death, Shapira was a minister in the Israeli cabinet as part of the National Religious party.

Bryan Daves

SHARABATI, AHMAD AL-

[1905–]

Syrian politician.

Ahmad al-Sharabati, the son of nationalist Damascene merchant Uthman al-Sharabati, studied engineering at the American University of Beirut and at the Massachusetts Institute of Technology. He started his career by running a tobacco factory for his father and later became involved in the import trade, especially of motor vehicles. His political career started in the early 1930s when he joined the National Action League, a pan-Arabist movement that was anticommunist. Harassed by the French Mandatory authorities in Syria, Sharabati fled to Transjordan (now Jordan), where he stayed for several years. In 1943, he became a member of the Syrian parliament, running as a nationalist. In 1945, he became minister of education and then minister of national economy in the ministry of Faris al-Khuri. After his resignation from the cabinet that year, in 1946 he was appointed minister of national defense in the cabinet of Jamil Mardam. In 1948 he resigned as a result of the poor performance of the Syrian army in the Arab-Israel War. In 1951, he was implicated in a conspiracy against Adib Shishakli, the military ruler in Syria, and was sentenced to two years and four months in prison.

Bibliography

Khoury, Philip. *Syria and the French Mandate: The Politics of Arab Nationalism, 1920–1945.* Princeton, NJ: Princeton University Press, 1987.

Seale, Patrick. *The Struggle for Syria: A Study of Post-War Arab Politics, 1945–1958.* New Haven, CT: Yale University Press, 1987.

Abdul-Karim Rafeq

SHAʿRAWI, HUDA AL-

[1879–1947]

Egyptian feminist.

A native of Minya, Huda al-Shaʿrawi was born to a prominent and prosperous politician-landowner and a Circassian mother. She was raised in an elite household, where domestic life was still centered on the cloistered *harim* (harem), although transitionally so during the late nineteenth century. She describes this experience in her memoirs, dictated to her secretary during the 1940s but published only in 1981; this section of the memoir has appeared in English as *Harem Years.* Shaʿrawi grew up studying with tutors at home, as was typical for elite girls of the time, and was taught in Arabic, Persian, Turkish, and French. Her marriage to her much older cousin and guardian, Ali Shaʿrawi, also a prominent politician, was arranged by the family and took place when she was thirteen. Some seven years later she managed to obtain a separation. Her interest in women's issues developed gradually out of her experiences and her awareness of women's activism in Europe. She was one of the founders of the 1914 Intellectual Association of Egyptian Women. As a wealthy patron as well as an organizer, she was active in charity organizing, a province open to upper-class women. But Shaʿrawi was unusual in moving from behind-the-scenes work into a highly visible, public political role. She spearheaded the Wafdist Women's Central Committee (1919) and was a leader of the famous first women's nationalist demonstration in March 1919. However, disagreement over women's appropriate political roles and particularly over whether women's demands should be admitted to discussions leading to the Egyptian constitution caused a rift with the Wafd, Egypt's nationalist party. Shaʿrawi went on to found, with a group of women, al-Ittihad al-nisa'i al-Misri (Egyptian Feminist Union; EFU) in 1923. She presided over it until her death. The EFU founded two journals, the French-language *L'Egyptienne* (1925), for which Shaʿrawi wrote editorials, and *al-Misriyya* in Arabic over a decade later (1937), when a broader audience fueled the need for a journal in the indigenous language. Shaʿrawi's writing appeared here, too, though she probably played less of a role in the journal. Shaʿrawi and two colleagues attended the 1923 International Women Suffrage Alliance in Rome and was responsible for a famous symbolic moment when, on her return, she publicly lifted her veil at Cairo's main railway station. She gradually became more involved in regional and international feminist organizing, becoming vice president of the International Alliance of Women for Suffrage and Equal Citizenship in 1935 and leading a move to found the Arab Feminist Union in 1945.

See also ARAB FEMINIST UNION; CIRCASSIANS; EGYPT; EGYPTIAN FEMINIST UNION; GENDER: GENDER AND EDUCATION; GENDER: GENDER AND LAW; GENDER: GENDER AND POLITICS; WAFDIST WOMEN'S CENTRAL COMMITTEE.

Bibliography

Badran, Margot. *Feminists, Islam, and Nation: Gender and the Making of Modern Egypt.* Princeton, NJ: Princeton University Press, 1995.

Shaarawi, Huda. *Harem Years: The Memoirs of an Egyptian Feminist (1879–1924),* translated, edited, and introduced by Margot Badran. London: Virago, 1986; New York: Feminist Press, City University of New York, 1987.

DAVID WALDNER
UPDATED BY MARILYN BOOTH

SHAʿRAWI, MUHAMMAD MUTWALLI AL-
[1911–1998]

Egyptian cleric.

Muhammad Mutwalli al-Shaʿrawi was born in Daqadus, Egypt, in 1911. He originally wanted to devote his career to farming, but his father encouraged him to study in Cairo. In 1937 he joined the faculty of Arabic language of al-Azhar. He was active in student politics and served time in jail. Shaʿrawi came to prominence as a cleric during the presidency of Anwar al-Sadat. He was famous for his utilization of modern media (television, audio- and videocassettes, pamphlets, and books) to disseminate his religious message. He was a firm believer in Islamic fundamentalism, but did not address political questions directly for fear of embarrassing his friend and protector, Sadat. He served as minister of Waqf from 1976 to 1978, but he was more famous for his televised religious sermons. As minister, he was behind the establishment of the Faysal Bank, the first Islamic bank in Egypt. Shaʿrawi never wavered from his loyalty to Sadat, which led his critics to accuse him of serving as the "sultan's cleric." Shaʿrawi has been credited (or blamed) for convincing a few well-known Egyptian actresses and singers—most famously, Shadya and Shams al-Barudi—to veil themselves and withdraw from show business.

See also SADAT, ANWAR AL-.

Bibliography

Shaʿrawi, Muhammad Mutwalli. *How Allah Provides.* Cairo: Dar At-Taqwa, 1995.

AS'AD ABUKHALIL

SHAREF, ZE'EV
[1906–1984]

Israeli political leader.

Having emigrated from Romania in 1924, Ze'ev Sharef became secretary of the central committee of the Haganah. After Israeli statehood he served in various capacities in the government, including as secretary of the political department of the Jewish Agency, secretary of the Emergency Committee and the National Administration (which established the Israeli civil service), and secretary of the Cabinet from 1948 to 1957.

Sharef played a unique role in Israeli history by transporting the Proclamation of Statehood from the Jewish National Fund Building (where it was typed) to David Ben-Gurion at the Tel Aviv Museum on the afternoon the State of Israel was declared, 14 May 1948. After Ben-Gurion read the Proclamation Sharef read out the names of the members of the National Council to sign the document.

From 1948 to 1957 Sharef was the first secretary of the Israeli government. From 1957 to 1959 he was director general of the Prime Minister's Office. He served as director of state revenues, and administrator of the Weizmann Institute. From 1965 to 1974 he was a member of the Knesset, serving as minister of commerce and industry in 1966, as minister of finance in 1968, and as minister of housing from 1969 to 1974.

Bibliography

Jerusalem Center for Public Affairs. "Israel's Early Diplomatic Struggles: From the Debates of the First Knesset." In *Glossary of Israeli Parties and Personalities—1948–1981.* Available from <http://www.jcpa.org/art>.

Jewish Agency for Israel, Department for Jewish Zionist Education. "Israel & the UN: A Resolution of Support, About the Declaration of Independence." Available from <http://www.jajz-ed.org.il>.

Sharef, Ze'ev. *Three Days,* translated by Julian Louis Meltzer. Garden City, NY: Doubleday, 1962.

Wohlgelernter, Elli. "One Day that Shook the World." *Jerusalem Post* (30 April 1998).

BRYAN DAVES
UPDATED BY GREGORY S. MAHLER

SHARETT, MOSHE

[1894–1965]

Israel's first foreign minister and second prime minister.

Moshe Sharett was born Moshe Shertok. His family migrated from Russia to Palestine in 1906. He attended school in Herzliyya and Tel Aviv, and after graduating in 1913, he entered the University of Istanbul to study law. When World War I broke out, he was drafted into the Turkish army.

At the end of the war, Sharett attended the London School of Economics, graduating in 1924. He returned to Palestine and became a journalist; from 1929 to 1931 he was editor of *Davar,* a daily newspaper in Tel Aviv.

In 1931 Sharett became political secretary of the Jewish Agency Executive. In 1935 he was named director of its political department, and began laying the foundations for what was later to become Israel's Ministry of Foreign Affairs. Sharett had a long-time working partnership with David Ben-Gurion in the Jewish Agency Executive, and after 1948, in Israel's first cabinets.

In 1946 he participated unofficially in talks in London to negotiate Zionist goals. Sharett was a representative of the Jewish Agency in the 1947 negotiations with the United Nations (UN) Special Committee on Palestine. He sought UN support for the creation of an independent state for the Jews in Palestine. In December 1947 he was among Jewish leaders lobbying for American support in the UN.

Moshe Sharett (1894–1965) in the 1950s. Sharett was an influential member of the Zionist movement and played an important role in the creation of the state of Israel in 1948. He was Israel's first foreign minister, and in January 1954 became the second man to serve as premier. © BETTMANN/CORBIS. REPRODUCED BY PERMISSION.

In May 1948, Sharett (who had hebraized the name Shertok at the time of the creation of the state of Israel) was named foreign minister in the Jewish provisional administration. In that capacity he negotiated support for Israel's statehood with U.S. Secretary of State George Marshall.

Once the state of Israel was in existence, Sharett became its first foreign minister, a position he held until 1956. In that post he emphasized that proceeds from the sale of lands belonging to absentee Arabs would be applied to a fund to resettle the refugees elsewhere, not to repatriate them in Israel. He argued that the problems of the Palestinian refugees were just like the problems of refugees around the world. In that sense, there was no legal precedent requiring their repatriation to the lands they had occupied before the war.

In March 1949, Sharett introduced the "principle of nonidentification" to indicate that Israel would not be aligned with either the East or the West. Israel's intention was to work with all nations to develop peaceful links and support for its existence. By 1951, however, it had become clear that the Soviet Union would support the Arab bloc against Israel, and Israel's foreign policy became clearly aligned with the West.

Prime Minister Ben-Gurion resigned in December 1953, and Sharett became prime minister. In June 1955 his cabinet was overturned by the withdrawal of the General Zionist Party from the coalition. He remained as acting prime minister until the scheduled elections for the third Knesset took place. After the elections, Ben-Gurion returned to the prime ministership with a new cabinet in November 1955.

In 1956 tensions increased between Ben-Gurion and Sharett over the appropriate response to Egypt's actions in and around the Suez Canal. Sharett argued that Israel should act with great restraint, while Ben-Gurion was in favor of a more provocative strategy. When Ben-Gurion felt that the tensions were growing too great, he asked for Sharett's resignation as foreign minister in June 1956, replacing him with Golda Meir.

See also BEN-GURION, DAVID; JEWISH AGENCY FOR PALESTINE; KNESSET; MEIR, GOLDA; NEWSPAPERS AND PRINT MEDIA: ISRAEL.

Bibliography

Ben-Gurion, David. *Israel: A Personal History,* translated by Nechemia Meyers and Uzy Nystar. New York: Funk and Wagnalls, 1971.

Sachar, Howard M. *A History of Israel: From the Rise of Zionism to Our Time,* 2d edition. New York: Knopf, 1996.

Sheffer, Gabriel. *Moshe Sharett: Biography of a Political Moderate.* Oxford and New York: Clarendon Press, 1996.

GREGORY S. MAHLER

SHARIʿA

Arabic for "the trodden path leading to a water hole." In Islam, the regulations of God's law as transmitted through a prophet; the dominant law in Islamic societies.

Muslims, Christians, and Jews each have "a law (*shirʿa*) and a normative way to follow," the Qurʾan attests (verse 48). In the Middle Ages, Islamic discourse referred not only to this strict definition of *Shariʿa* as law but also to all that which Allah has revealed—whether it pertained to actual religious practice or to belief. In Islam, those aspects relating to practice belong to the province of law (*fiqh*); those that concern belief belong to theology (*ilm al-kalam or ilm al-tawhid*). Law, however, depends on theology, since the contents and validity of law rest on textual sources, whose divine origins and truth are known. Furthermore, all sciences that are used to attain a knowledge of law and theology are considered *Shariʿa* sciences, even if their subject matter is not legal or theological. Therefore, the Arabic language, *hadith* (verbal statements of Prophetic traditions), exegesis (interpretations), and even logic are deemed *Shariʿa*—even if designating logic this way has always been controversial.

The use of the term *Shariʿa* has actually, in practice, been restricted to the realm of law, and particularly to those aspects that bear upon the conduct of the individual in both worldly and religious matters. *Shariʿa* may be equated, therefore, with *fiqh* in both its components: (1) positive law (*furu*) and (2) legal theory (*usul*). Positive law delineates legal obligations, ranging from rituals to personal and penal law; contracts; sales; hunting; and more. Legal theory demonstrates how positive law is derived through legal reasoning and interpretation, which results in the law stipulating the legal and moral responsibility thrust upon Muslims.

The legal and moral elements in the *Shariʿa* are evident in the individual rulings classified in accordance with five norms (*ahkam*): (1) the obligatory (*wajib*), (2) the recommended (*mandub*), (3) the permissible or indifferent (*mubah*), (4) the prohibited (*haram*), and (5) the repugnant (*makruh*). The obligatory represents an act whose performance entails reward and whose omission entails punishment. It is commonly divided into those acts that are binding on all and those that are binding on the Muslim community as a whole but which are discharged once a sufficient number of individuals perform them. The recommended act requires a reward for performance but does not involve a punishment for omission. In the permissible, both omission and commission are equally legitimate. The prohibited is an act that entails punishment upon commission. The repugnant act is rewarded when omitted but not punished when committed.

The nature of reward and punishment supports the permeating moral element in Islamic law. Reward is always bestowed in the hereafter; punishment—in rituals and in several other spheres of the law—is nothing but divine punishment to be meted out at the resurrection. As a comprehensive system of law, imbued with religious mores, the rules of the *Shariʿa* are not always enforceable.

As a system of legal rights and obligations that governs public and private life, *Shariʿa* has always been the dominant law in Islamic societies. No doubt secular organs of justice, such as the early and medieval *mazalim* courts and the *qanun* of the Ottoman Empire, have always supplemented *Shariʿa*; however, their jurisdiction was confined mainly to administrative and penal law, and they were, more often than not, run by *Shariʿa* judges and jurists.

Judges and jurisconsults (muftis) have played the central role of developing *Shariʿa* since the first century of Islam. Immediately after the death of the Prophet Muhammad in 632 C.E., the Qurʾan provided the main source of the law that may be considered Islamic. To be sure, customary Arabian law and the later Umayyad dynasty's administrative practices supplemented Qurʾanic legislation, but these were not yet imbued with a religious character. The Prophet's *sunna* (his utterances and idealized practice as expressed in *hadith*) was to gain importance as a source of law only gradually. It was not until the end of Islam's first century (c. 700 C.E.) that his *sunna* became a source of law, supplementing the Qurʾan and the still prevailing popular and administrative practices of the Umayyads. Islam's second century (ending c. 800 C.E.) witnessed a gradual yet definite process whereby these practices were idealized as the consensus of the geographical schools—a consensus seen to reflect the ideal practice of the Prophet Muhammad and the early caliphs who succeeded him. Thus imbued with a religious element, these practices, expressed through verbal statements of *hadith*, were gradually and constantly projected back to the earlier generations until they have come to be connected with the Prophet himself. By the beginning of Islam's third century (the ninth century C.E.), the process of back-projection was virtually completed, and the law, now elaborated to its fullness, was recognized to have been exclusively derived from the Qurʾan and the *sunna* and sanctioned by the authoritative instrument of consensus *(ijma)*.

By the eighth and ninth centuries, the body of *Shariʿa* law was elaborated by a variety of legal schools, ranging from those that resorted to free reasoning and expediency in elaborating their positive law—such as the Hanafi school of law—to those standing on the other end of the spectrum, such as the Zahiris, who interpreted the texts literally. Such radical tendencies and their schools, including the Zahiri, soon disappeared; but liberal tendencies were not sufficient to bring the Hanafi school to extinction. Nevertheless, they had to be rationalized and modified to be admitted by mainstream jurisprudence. A classical example of this process of adjustment may be seen in the concept of *istihsan*, which represented to the eighth-century Hanafis a means of formulating law on the basis of practical considerations, without being restricted by the imperatives of the religious texts. Whereas problems of law solved by *istihsan* were largely accepted, even in later centuries, the procedure of *istihsan* had to be, and indeed was, restructured by the likes of Dabusi and Sarakhsi—this was based on the proposition that the *sunna* and the Qurʾan were the ultimate sources of the law and that no human intervention can be allowed in the unraveling of divine law.

The Sunni schools of law thus came finally to acknowledge a common legal theory, though differences among them continued to exist—partly as a reflection of the legacy they inherited from their early development within differing geographical schools. Be that as it may, in addition to the Shiʿa schools, only four Sunni schools survive and they provide, in effect, a comprehensive system of *Shariʿa*.

Shariʿa continued to dominate the life of Muslims until the nineteenth century, when, because of influences and pressures from the West, changes in the law were deemed necessary. Formally, the most notable legal change was the introduction of the code system, which was foreign to *Shariʿa*, a law based on interpretation of religious doctrine. Substantively, several attempts were made to wholly substitute European codes for a number of *Shariʿa* laws. Thus, during the Ottoman Empire, commercial and penal codes based on their French counterparts were promulgated in 1850 and 1858, respectively. A more important codification of this period was the Mejelle (1876), which represented the first attempt ever to codify Islamic law. Selectively codified, Hanafi law was restricted to contracts, some torts, and a law of procedure. The last part, however, was soon replaced by the Code of Civil Procedure (1880), again based on French law.

A more drastic set of reforms was adopted in Egypt in 1875. In addition to new penal, commercial, and procedural codes based on French law, a new court structure was introduced. It incorporated into the Egyptian court system the Mixed Courts, with a majority of non-Egyptian judges, one of whom presided over the bench.

In 1917, the first attempt at reforming family law was made by the Ottomans, without resorting to European codes. It promulgated the *Ottoman Law of Family Rights,* which regulated matters of personal status and was based on a comprehensive amalgamation of legal doctrines belonging to the Maliki, Shafiʿi, and Hanbali schools of law, and sometimes weak authorities from the Hanafi school. One of the main concerns in this promulgation was the improvement of the legal status of married women.

Legal reforms, introduced by national legislation, have become an ongoing process in the Muslim states since the beginning of the twentieth century (based on Sunni and Shiʿite principles). In these reforms, *Shariʿa* law was to some extent preserved in the area of family matters, but even here it was applied in a new system of courts and administered through a modern law of procedure. With these sweeping changes, the officials of the traditional court virtually disappeared, and the traditional role of the qadi (judge) has been drastically diminished.

See also FIQH; HADITH; HANAFI SCHOOL OF LAW; HANBALI SCHOOL OF LAW; MALIKI SCHOOL OF LAW; MIXED COURTS; MUHAMMAD; QANUN; QURʾAN; SHAFIʿI SCHOOL OF LAW.

Bibliography

Anderson, Norman. *Law Reform in the Muslim World.* London: Athlone Press, 1976.

Fyzee, A. A. *Outlines of Muhammadan Law,* 2d edition. London and New York: Oxford University Press, 1955.

Khadduri, Majid, and Liebesny, Herbert J., eds. *Law in the Middle East.* Washington, DC: Middle East Institute, 1955.

Schacht, Joseph. *An Introduction to Islamic Law.* Oxford and New York: Clarendon, 1982.

Schacht, Joseph. *The Origins of Muhammadan Jurisprudence.* Oxford: Clarendon, 1953.

Smith, Wilfred Cantwell. "The Concept of Shariʿa among Some Mutakallimun." In *Arabic and Islamic Studies in Honor of Hamilton A. R. Gibb,* edited by George Makdisi. Cambridge, MA: Harvard University Press, 1965.

WAEL B. HALLAQ

SHARIʿATI, ALI

[1933–1977]

Iranian Islamic ideologue, whose lectures and writings on secularly educated youth helped prepare the way for the Islamic Revolution of 1978/79.

Ali Shariʿati was born in the village of Mazinan in northeastern Iran but soon moved with his father, Mohammad Taqi Shariʿati, a reformist cleric of Islam, to the city of Mashhad. There he attended high school and teachers' training college as well as pursuing a religious education under the aegis of his father. He then began working as a teacher, studying at the same time at the Mashhad Faculty of Letters and beginning his long career of oppositional activity; his first arrest came in 1957. After a year's delay, he was permitted to travel to Paris in 1960 for his doctoral studies. While in France, he came under the influence of scholars and thinkers, such as Louis Massignon and Jacques Berque, became politically involved in the struggle for Algerian independence and the organization of Iranian students in Europe, and, most importantly, acquired the ideological orientation that was essential to his thought.

Immediately on his return to Iran in 1964, Shariʿati was arrested and detained for several months before being allowed to take up a post at the University of Mashhad. His tenure there was short-lived, and it was outside the academic environment that he exercised the greatest influence. Moving to Tehran, he began lecturing on Islam in a variety of settings, most importantly the Hosayniyeh-ye Ershad, a modernist religious institution established in 1969 that attracted large crowds to its functions. Shariʿati's name became virtually synonymous with the institution, and when it was closed by the government in 1973, he was arrested for a third time. Released in 1975, he spent two years under house arrest in his native village before being allowed to leave for England. He died there on 19 June 1977, soon after his arrival, under circumstances that led to widespread suspicion of involvement by the Iranian secret police. His body was taken to Damascus for burial.

Central to Shariʿati's understanding and presentation of Islam were an emphasis on the social and civilizational functions of religion; an impatience with the niceties and abstractions of traditional Iranian Islamic culture; and a bold if often unconvincing use of themes and terms eclectically derived from non-Islamic sources. His legacy has been varyingly assessed in postrevolutionary Iran, being sometimes denounced for its syncretic nature and its implicitly anticlerical message.

Bibliography

Shariʿati, Ali. *On the Sociology of Islam,* translated by Hamid Algar. Berkeley, CA: Mizan Press, 1979.

HAMID ALGAR

SHARIATMADARI, KAZEM

[1904–1986]

One of Iran's most important clerics.

Ayatollah Sayyid Kazem Shariatmadari, born in Azerbaijan, was a *marja al-taqlid* (source of emulation) from 1962 until his death in 1986.

Ayatollah Shariatmadari was not inclined to political activism. But throughout the Pahlavi period, the scholars affiliated with his Center for Islamic Study and Publication rivaled Ayatollah Ruhollah Khomeini's more activist followers. Shariatmadari was briefly imprisoned in 1963, following the June uprisings. In general, he viewed the Pahlavi regime as dictatorial and favored restoration of constitutional rule in Iran. With the triumph of the Islamic Revolution in 1979, Shariatmadari again called for restraint and the rule of law, denouncing the revolutionary tribunals and summary executions of the early days of the revolution. He also confronted the regime on the issue of a referendum to decide the form of the post-Pahlavi state. Rather than a simple vote of yes or no on an Islamic republic, Shariatmadari, as well as most secular parties, supported at the least a choice between an Islamic, democratic, or just simple and plain republic. Shariatmadari was also associated with the Islamic People's Republican party (IPRP), the main contender to Khomeini's Islamic Republican party. The IPRP favored collective rule of the *ulama* (Islamic clergy), a more democratic constitution, and an elected rather than an appointed assembly of experts empowered to draft the constitution of the nascent Islamic republic. The IPRP was dissolved in 1980, over the first presidential elections, a victory for Khomeini and the Islamic Republican party.

Shariatmadari continued to oppose the excesses of the Khomeini regime and, in 1982, was implicated in a coup against the Islamic republic, organized by Sadeq Qotbzadeh, was stripped of his title of *marja al-taqlid,* and was placed under house arrest, where he remained a marginal player in the political life of his country until his death in 1986.

See also KHOMEINI, RUHOLLAH; MARJA AL-TAQLID; PAHLAVI, MOHAMMAD REZA; QOTBZADEH, SADEQ.

Bibliography

Akhavi, Shahrough. *Religion and Politics in Contemporary Iran: Clergy-State Relations in the Pahlavi Period.* Albany: State University of New York Press, 1980.

Bakhash, Shaul. *The Reign of the Ayatollahs: Iran and the Islamic Revolution,* revised edition. New York: Basic Books, 1990.

NEGUIN YAVARI

SHARIF

An Arabic word that literally means "noble" or "illustrious," especially by virtue of one's lineage.

In the first few centuries of the Muslim era, *sharif* (pl., *ashraf* or *shurafa*) was used to refer to members of the prominent Arab families that made up the typically landed aristocracy of the expanding Muslim domains. Much like its rough equivalent *sayyid,* however, use of *sharif* as an honorific was gradually limited to scions of the clan of the prophet Muhammad (that is, the Banu Hashim), and eventually was further restricted to Muhammad's direct descendants through his grandsons Hasan and Husayn. In Mecca, Medina, and their environs, the custom developed of applying the title *sharif* almost exclusively to descendants of Hasan, with *sayyid* referring to descendents of Husayn. Under Ottoman rule the senior member of the Arabian sharifs was recognized as the semiautonomous governor of Mecca and the keeper of its sacred sanctuary.

See also MUHAMMAD.

SCOTT ALEXANDER

SHARIF, AZIZ

[1904–]

Iraqi politician.

Born in Ana and educated at Baghdad Law College, Aziz Sharif founded the People's Party in 1943 and subsequently joined the Communist Party. He was a candidate member of its central committee (1958–1963), and secretary-general of the Partisans of Peace, a pro-Soviet umbrella organization. Sharif was minister of justice under the Baʿth government (1970–1971) and a key intermediary in the Baʿth-Kurdish negotiations. Sharif served as minister without portfolio until 1976.

MARION FAROUK-SLUGLETT
UPDATED BY MICHAEL R. FISCHBACH

SHARIF-EMAMI, JAʿFAR

[1910–1998]

Iranian prime minister and statesman.

Jaʿfar Sharif-Emami was the son of Hajj Mohammad Hasan (known as Sharif), a member of the religious establishment who worked as an aide to Sayyid Mohammad Emami, the leader of Friday prayers in Tehran. Sharif-Emami attended college in Germany and worked at the Railroad Office of the Ministry of Roads. In 1943 the British forces accused him of belonging to a German fifth column in Iran and incarcerated him for one year. He was elected to the senate as a deputy from Tehran in 1953 and became minister of industries and mines in 1957 and prime minister in 1960. In 1961 he was made head of the Pahlavi Foundation, the largest corporation in the country; he amassed a great fortune in that capacity. In 1962 he also was appointed speaker of the senate. It was widely believed that Sharif-Emami led the German Freemasonry Lodge in Iran. In an effort to quell the Islamic Revolution by choosing a leader with some degree of credibility with the clerical establishment, Mohammad Reza Shah Pahlavi reappointed him premier in August 1978. Sharif-Emami failed in his mandate, however, and the military government of General Gholam Reza Azhari was declared in November 1978. Sharif-Emami left Iran in 1979 and died in New York on 16 June 1998.

Bibliography

Ladjevardi, Habib, ed. *Memoirs of Jafar Sharif-Emami, Prime Minister of Iran (1960–1961 & 1978).* Cambridge, MA: Center for Middle Eastern Studies, Harvard University Press, 1999.

NEGUIN YAVARI

SHARIFIAN DYNASTIES

Rulers of Morocco since the sixteenth century, when the modern principle was first established that they be sharifs—descendants of the prophet Muhammad, founder of Islam.

The cult of the Sharif was introduced in Morocco under Idris II in the early ninth century but went into abeyance. Sharifism became established in Morocco as a response to the crises of the sixteenth century—occasioned by Christian efforts to extend the *reconquista* (reconquest) of the Iberian Peninsula into Morocco; large-scale tribal migrations in North Africa; the fragmentation of the Moroccan polity following the decline of the Merinid dynasty; the rise of regional Sufi powers; and the conquest of Algeria in 1517 by the Ottoman Empire.

Both the Saʿdians (1548–1641) and the Alawi (1668–present) were Alids, and traced their descent to Muhammad through his son-in-law Ali, but they were Sunni rather than followers of Shiʿism. Both assembled powerful political coalitions that combined tribal solidarities, rural Sufism, and Sharifism. Both rose to power after first securing control over southern Morocco and then conquered the cities and Atlantic plains. Both were responses to the long-term crisis of legitimization caused by the fragmentation of Islam's power in the Maghrib (North Africa) and al-Andalus (Iberian province) and especially to the threat posed by the Spanish and Portuguese, who had driven the Moors from the Iberian Peninsula and unified their countries under Catholic monarchs.

The Saʿdians emerged in the period 1514–1548 as opponents of the Portuguese in southern Morocco and revivers of Islam. Under Muhammad al-Shaykh, they defeated the reigning Wattasids, conquered Fez and Marrakech, and stabilized Morocco's frontiers at roughly their present borders. Under Ahmad al-Mansur (1578–1603), the state was reorganized along Ottoman principles, including notably a force of musketeers, financed by the production of sugar for export on royal estates. The conquest of Timbuktu in 1591 briefly gave Morocco direct access to the salt and gold of the sub-Saharan zone. With the help of an alliance with Elizabethan merchant adventurers, the Saʿdians were able to defeat the Iberians and confine them to a few coastal enclaves. Following the death of Ahmad in 1603, the Saʿdians went into a long decline, as the result of dynastic conflict, a resurgence of Iberian threat, and the reemergence of regional power centers of which the *zawiya* (community) of Dila in the Middle Atlas mountains and the Andalusian corsair republic of Sala were the most important.

The rise of the Alawis, cousins of the Saʿdians, took place under Muhammad al-Sharif and Rashid, who were able to defeat the Dila Marabouts and assert their control over Morocco by 1668. The consolidator of the dynasty was Ismaʿil (1672–1727), a remarkable ruler who by incessant warfare and systematic organization was able to bring the disparate regions of the state under control. Ismaʿil restructured the army around a contingent of musket-wielding black slaves, defeated the Sufi brotherhoods, and imposed a system of heavy taxation. He expelled foreign occupiers, notably the Spanish from Larache and the British from Tangier. Henceforth, Moroccan sultans styled themselves as "Commander of the Faithful," an implicit claim to the caliphate otherwise also claimed by the Ottomans. Following Ismaʿil's death, however, the army revolted, and power once again fragmented.

After the turbulent reign of Abdullah, who was deposed five times between 1727 and 1757, the state was reorganized under Muhammad III (1757–1790), the architect of "modern," that is, precolonial, Morocco. By de-emphasizing the tax on agricultural produce and increasing trade (and thus customs revenues), Muhammad III provided an alternate basis for the state finances without disturbing the potentially volatile rural populations. The port of Essaouira was founded in 1767 to place the foreign trade of the Atlantic coast of Morocco under government control.

By emphasizing the religious aspects of his leadership as sultan, caliph, and sharif, Muhammad III sought to counter the reassertion of the maraboutic forces in the countryside. By constant diplomatic negotiation with foreign powers and constant bargaining with local authorities, he devised a precarious balance for the Moroccan state. Its dependence upon foreign commerce made it vulnerable to foreign intervention, however, while the absence of a strong army deprived it of any means to reassert its control over the population.

Under Sulayman (1792–1822) and Abd al-Rahman ibn Hisham (1822–1859), Morocco entered into a precolonial phase, increasingly dependent upon foreign trade and increasingly vulnerable to European pressure, notably signing after 1856 a series of treaties granting most-favored nation status to leading European powers. In retaliation for Moroccan support of the Algerian resistance leader Abd al-Qadir, Moroccan ports were shelled by the French navy, and a Moroccan army was defeated at Isly in 1844. A war with Spain in 1859–1860 over the city of Tetuan was settled only after Morocco agreed to pay a sizable indemnity and make other concessions.

Hassan I (1873–1894) sought to reverse the decline, with mixed results. His military and administrative reforms failed to survive his death, although his adroit diplomacy managed to buy time for Morocco in the face of rising European imperialist ambitions. His successors Abd al-Aziz and Abd al-Hafid also sought to introduce needed reforms and to play off the European powers, but with less success. The Moroccan Question (1900–1912) marks a period of increase in European rivalries over Morocco. In 1912 the Treaty of Fes with France and the Spanish–Moroccan accords marked the formal end of Moroccan independence.

The protectorates of France and Spain lasted from 1912 to 1956. During this period, Moroccan sultans Mulay Youssef (1912–1927) and Muhammad V (1927–1961) were formally incorporated into the French colonial administration, their titles confirmed, but their powers largely alienated to the European occupiers and their local Moroccan agents through a factional delegation. With the rise of nationalism in the 1930s and 1940s, Muhammad V began increasingly to show his sympathy for the nationalists. In 1946 he publicly broke with the French and assumed leadership of the nationalist movement.

Since 1956, independent Morocco has continued to be governed by the Alawite dynasty. The present sultan, Hassan II, assumed power in 1961 upon the death of his father.

See also ABD AL-AZIZ IBN AL-HASSAN; ABD AL-HAFID IBN AL-HASSAN; ABD AL-QADIR; ABD AL-RAHMAN IBN HISHAM; ALAWI; ALAWITE DYNASTY; FES, TREATY OF (1912); HASSAN I; HASSAN II; MOROCCAN QUESTION; MUHAMMAD; MUHAMMAD V; SUFISM AND THE SUFI ORDERS; SULEIMAN, MULAY; YOUSSEF, MULAY.

Bibliography

Abun-Nasr, Jamil M. *A History of the Maghrib,* 2d edition. Cambridge, U.K., and New York: Cambridge University Press, 1975.

Julien, Charles André. *History of North Africa,* translated by John Petrie. New York: Praeger, 1970.

Laroui, Abdullah. *The History of the Maghrib,* translated by Ralph Manheim. Princeton, NJ: Princeton University Press, 1977.

Pennell, C. R. *Morocco since 1830: A History.* New York: New York University Press, 2000.

EDMUND BURKE III

SHARIF OF MECCA

The local, hereditary rulers of Mecca from about 965 to 1916.

Although the sharifs never enjoyed complete independence from distant powers, their remoteness from the imperial capitals of Cairo and Constantinople (now Istanbul) helped them maintain effective rule in Mecca, as did their claimed descent from the prophet Muhammad. The last sharif, Husayn ibn Ali (1852–1931), tried to establish an independent Arabian kingdom, leading the Arab Revolt in 1916 against the Turks in the Hijaz, but he was overthrown by the Saudis in 1925. Founder of the modern Arab Hashimite dynasty, Husayn died in Amman, the capital of his son Abdullah, then ruler of Transjordan (now Jordan). His third son, Faisal I, founded the royal line of Iraq.

See also ABDULLAH I IBN HUSSEIN; ARAB REVOLT (1916); FAISAL I IBN HUSSEIN; HASHIMITE HOUSE (HOUSE OF HASHIM); HUSAYN IBN ALI.

Bibliography

De Gaury, Gerald. *Rulers of Mecca.* London: Harrap, 1951.

KHALID Y. BLANKINSHIP

SHARIF, OMAR

[1932–]

Egyptian movie star.

The son of a wealthy merchant of Lebanese descent, Omar (also Umar) Sharif was born Michel Chalhoub on 10 April 1932. Educated at Victoria College in Alexandria, he converted from Christianity to Islam and changed his name to Omar Sharif before making his Egyptian film debut in *The Blazing Sun* in 1953. Between 1953 and 1958, he appeared in twenty-four Arabic-language films. On the set of his first film, Sharif became bored during the long pauses between his scenes and took up the game of bridge to while away the time. Sharif became internationally known after playing a lead role in the film *Lawrence of Arabia,* a part for which he received an Academy Award nomination for best supporting actor. Sharif has appeared in many English-language films, including *Doctor Zhivago* and *Funny Girl.* He won the Golden Lion lifetime achievement award for fifty years in films in 2003 after a comeback in the film *Mr. Ibrahim,* in which he plays the role of an old Arab man in Paris who adopts a young Jewish boy. He also pursued his interest in bridge, becoming one of the world's leading authorities on the game and authoring several books on the subject.

Bibliography

Katz, Ephraim. *The Film Encyclopedia.* New York: Crowell, 1979.

DAVID WALDNER
UPDATED BY ROXANNE VARZI

SHARJAH

One of seven shaykhdoms making up the United Arab Emirates.

Sharjah is the third largest emirate in the United Arab Emirates (U.A.E.), with an area of 1,000 square miles. Seventy-five percent of its 400,000 inhabitants (2001 estimate) live in the capital city of the same name on the Persian Gulf coast, just north of Dubai. Three exclaves on the Gulf of Oman coast—Dibba, Kalba, and Khor Fakkan—belong to Sharjah and make it the only one of the seven emirates to share borders with all the others. It has the extreme summer heat and aridity of its neighbors, but agriculture is possible in the Dhayd Oasis and in the exclave territories.

In the late-eighteenth and early nineteenth centuries Sharjah and its northern neighbor, Ra'S al-Khayma, formed the most powerful state of the lower Gulf under the al-Qasimi family, which is still the ruling clan in each emirate. The al-Qasimi state was defeated by Britain in an 1819 naval battle. Subsequently, the al-Qasimi ruler signed the General Treaty of Peace (1820), which began the process by which the area became a protectorate of Britain. During the 1840s and 1850s the al-Qasimi gradually were eclipsed by the Banu Yas tribal confederation of Abu Dhabi—then, as now, led by the Al Nahayyan family. Following the death of Shaykh Sultan bin Saqr al-Qasimi, one of his sons set up an "independent" state at Ra'S al-Khayma; this state formally split from Sharjah in 1869, but it did not gain formal British recognition as a separate emirate until 1921.

Sharjah enjoyed moderate prosperity in the early twentieth century, boosted by the presence of a Royal Air Force base from the 1930s until 1955. In the early 1950s Sharjah's creek became silted, and with the decline of maritime commerce, it lost its position of importance in the lower Gulf. In 1971, on the eve of independence, Britain pressured Sharjah to agree to shared sovereignty with Iran of the island of Abu Musa. This agreement precipitated a coup attempt in Sharjah (1972) during which the ruler, Shaykh Khalid ibn Muhammad, was killed.

Oil and gas discoveries in 1973 and 1980 brought prosperity, as did the development of several factories in a specially created industrial zone in the western part of Sharjah city. Sharjah also has developed a successful tourist industry. Reflecting the academic bent of the ruler, who holds a doctorate from Exeter University, Sharjah leads the U.A.E. in the development of arts, literature, and museums.

See also ABU MUSA ISLAND; QASIMI FAMILY OF SHARJAH, AL-; UNITED ARAB EMIRATES.

Bibliography

Hooglund, Eric, and Toth, Anthony B. "United Arab Emirates." In *Persian Gulf States: Country Studies,* edited by Helen Chapin Metz. Washington, DC: Library of Congress, 1994.

Peck, Malcolm C. *The United Arab Emirates: A Venture in Unity.* Boulder, CO: Westview Press, 1986.

MALCOLM C. PECK
UPDATED BY ERIC HOOGLUND

SHARM AL-SHAYKH

Strategic town opposite Tiran island, near the southern tip of the Sinai Peninsula.

The cove and town of Sharm al-Shaykh control maritime access to the Strait of Tiran from the Gulf of Aqaba. In 1954 Egypt fortified the cove to block Israeli shipping from the port of Elat, but in the Arab–Israel War (1956) Israel captured it along with the rest of the peninsula. The United States later persuaded Israel to withdraw its forces in return for assurances of free passage through the Tiran Strait. When the Sinai was restored to Egyptian control in 1957, the United Nations Emergency Force was based at Sharm al-Shaykh until 1967, when Egypt asked it to leave. Its removal was one of the events precipitating the 1967 Arab–Israel War. Occupied by Israel during that conflict, the site became the Israeli naval and air base of Ophira. Restored to Egypt in 1982, the town has become a major tourist resort and frequently serves as the site of high-profile meetings of Middle Eastern and world leaders, notably the Anti-terrorism Summit of 1996 and one phase of the Israeli-Palestinian negotiations in 2000.

See also AQABA, GULF OF; ARAB–ISRAEL WAR (1956); ARAB–ISRAEL WAR (1967); TIRAN, STRAIT OF.

Bibliography

Fry, Michael, and Hochstein, Miles. "The Forgotten Middle East Crisis of 1957: Gaza and Sharm el Sheikh." *International History Review* 15 (1993): 46–83.

ZACHARY KARABELL
UPDATED BY ARTHUR GOLDSCHMIDT

SHARON, ARIEL
[1928–]

Israeli prime minister and army commander.

Ariel Sharon was born on 27 February 1928 into a family of stubbornly independent pioneer farmers in Kfar Malal. He joined the Haganah in 1945 and took part in the 1948 Arab–Israel War as a platoon commander and intelligence officer. He served in Jerusalem and the northern Negev, making his mark as an inspirational leader. In 1952 he formed Unit 101, a special commando force geared for unconventional retaliatory operations in enemy territory. In 1953 it raided the Palestinian village of Qibya, destroying forty-five houses and killing sixty-nine villagers, half of them women and children. Unit 101 set the standard for the elite commando units of the Israel Defense Force (IDF). In 1954 it was integrated into the paratroop regiment, with Sharon as commander. In 1956 he was appointed to command a paratroop corps, which executed Israel's defense strategy of inflicting retaliatory blows more severe than the original provocations.

Sharon's performance as military strategist during the 1956 Arab-Israel War earned him a reputation as one of IDF's most brilliant field commanders. At the same time, his activism made him a controversial figure and drew criticism from his superiors. He disobeyed orders and sent paratroopers into the Mitla Pass, deep in the Sinai desert. This ended disastrously, with thirty-eight Israelis dead. As a major general commanding an armored division during the 1967 Arab-Israel War, Sharon revealed a new talent for orchestrating huge, set-piece battles. In 1969 he was appointed chief of the Southern Command. He ruthlessly demolished thousands of homes in Gaza refugee camps to open roads for antiterror patrols, and deported hundreds of young men to Jordan and Lebanon. The number of sabotage attacks dropped dramatically.

Sharon retired from the army in June 1972 after he recognized that he was not going to be promoted chief of the general staff. He entered politics as a member of the Liberal party and was influential in merging it with the right-wing Herut and two smaller parties to form the Likud. He was called back to military service for the 1973 Arab–Israel War, during which he led Israeli forces in penetrating Egyptian defenses to cross the Suez Canal. During this period, in a bitter dispute with the military high command over tactics, he was accused of insubordination but was not relieved of his command. Elected in December 1973 to the Knesset, he resigned after a year to accept an emergency appointment with the IDF. From June 1975 to March 1976, he served as Prime Minister Yitzhak Rabin's special adviser on terrorism. He founded a new political party, Shlomzion, which gained two Knesset seats in the 1977 elections. Shortly thereafter, he rejoined the Likud, which had won the elections, and was appointed minister of agriculture.

Israeli prime minister Ariel Sharon (b. 1928) is a veteran of the Israeli military and achieved his first seat in government in 1973. He was elected prime minister in a special election on 6 February 2001. © AP/Wide World Photos. Reproduced by permission.

Sharon spearheaded Jewish settlement expansion in the occupied territories. Yet he supported returning Sinai to Egypt under the 1979 peace treaty and initiated and administered the destruction of the Jewish settlements there. In 1981 he was appointed defense minister in Menachem Begin's government. He planned and led Israel's invasion of Lebanon, which began in June 1982, and was accused of extending the war's objectives far beyond those originally approved by the government. The war destroyed the Palestine Liberation Organization's infrastructure and drove its leaders into exile in Tunis, but it left Israeli troops mired in guerrilla warfare in Lebanon for the next eighteen years. The Kahan Commission concluded that Sharon was culpable for not preventing the slaughter of hundreds of Palestinians by Israel's Lebanese Christian allies at the Sabra and Shatila refugee camps. As a consequence, he was forced to resign the defense ministry but allowed to remain in the cabinet. In 1984, and again in 1988, he was appointed industry and trade minister in a National Unity government. From 1990 to 1992 he served as housing and construction minister under Yitzhak Shamir and as chairman of the ministerial committee on immigration and absorption. After the collapse of the Soviet Union, he built homes for hundreds of thousands of immigrants.

When the Likud returned to office, Benjamin Netanyahu appointed Sharon national infrastructure minister in 1996, and foreign minister two years later. Following the election of Labor's Ehud Barak as prime minister in May 1999, Sharon succeeded Netanyahu as Likud leader. His visit to the Temple Mount in Jerusalem in September 2000 sparked Muslims riots, which grew into a second, more bloody, Palestinian intifada.

Sharon was elected prime minister in February 2001 following the collapse of Barak's peace policy and his failure to control the violence. After a suicide bomber killed thirty Jews celebrating Passover in a Netanya resort hotel in March 2002, Sharon invaded and reoccupied West Bank cities, destroying buildings and killing and capturing hundreds of Palestinian fighters. Although the bloodshed continued, albeit on a reduced scale, the voters endorsed his aggressive strategy and confirmed him in the premiership by a landslide in January 2003. Sharon declared the Palestinian leader Yasir Arafat "irrelevant" and isolated him in the ruins of his Ramallah headquarters.

Under United States pressure, Arafat appointed Mahmud Abbas as the first Palestinian prime minister. Sharon opened negotiations with him and accepted a "performance-based road map to a permanent two-state solution," drafted by the United States, the European Union, Russia, and the United Nations. Abandoning his earlier contention that "Jordan is Palestine" and that the Jews had a right to all of the land west of the River Jordan, Sharon surprised many observers when he labeled the West Bank and Gaza territories as "occupied" and declared that Israel could not go on ruling 3.5 million Palestinians. After Abbas was replaced by Ahmad Qurai, Sharon gave the new prime minister a chance to prove that he could curb the Palestinian militias and bring the two sides back to the negotiating table. Sharon showed himself more pragmatic than his party, but his premiership was shadowed by police investigations of alleged financial irregularities.

See also ABBAS, MAHMUD; AQSA INTIFADA, AL-; ARAFAT, YASIR; BEGIN, MENACHEM; HAGANAH; ISRAEL; ISRAELI SETTLEMENTS; KAHAN COMMISSION (1983); LIKUD; QURAI, AHMAD SULAYMAN; SABRA AND SHATILA MASSACRES.

Bibliography

Benziman, Uzi. *Sharon: An Israeli Caesar,* translated by Louis Rousso. New York: Adama, 1985.

Miller, Anita; Miller, Jordan; and Zetouni, Sigalit. *Sharon: Israel's Warrior-Politician.* Chicago: Academy Chicago, Olive, 2002.

Sharon, Ariel (with David Chanoff). *Warrior: The Autobiography of Ariel Sharon,* 2d Touchstone edition. New York: Simon & Schuster, 2001.

YAAKOV SHAVIT
UPDATED BY ERIC SILVER

SHARQI FAMILY, AL-

Ruling family of Fujayra, one of the members of the United Arab Emirates.

Fujayra's ruling family's Sharqiyyin tribe inhabits the Hajjar Mountains and the coastal region of the Shimailiyya district on the Gulf of Oman. The current ruler's family, the Sharqi, came to power in 1876 with the accession of Hamad ibn Abdullah al-Sharqi, who was part of the Qasimi tribal federation that ruled Sharjah. In 1902 the ruler declared independence from Sharjah and was recognized by the other emirates, but not by Britain. Hamad's son Muhammad continued the family's rule and its insistence on independence, which the British finally recognized in 1952. The current ruler, Hamad ibn Muhammad al-Sharqi, came to power in 1974 after his father's death. Born in 1948, he was educated at Mons Military Academy and Hendon Police College.

See also FUJAYRA.

Bibliography

Abdullah, Muhammad Morsy. *The United Arab Emirates: A Modern History.* New York: Barnes and Noble; London: Croom Helm, 1978.

Heard-Bey, Frauke. *From Trucial States to United Arab Emirates: A Society in Transition.* New York: Longman, 1982.

Reich, Bernard, ed. *Political Leaders of the Contemporary Middle East and North Africa: A Biographical Dictionary.* Westport, CT: Greenwood Press, 1990.

M. MORSY ABDULLAH
UPDATED BY ANTHONY B. TOTH

SHARQI, HAMAD IBN MUHAMMAD AL-

See SHARQI FAMILY, AL-

SHAS

See ISRAEL: POLITICAL PARTIES IN

SHASHILIK

See FOOD: SHASHILIK

SHATT AL-ARAB

The narrow waterway that forms the southern border between Iran and Iraq.

The Shatt al-Arab, or Arvandrud in Persian, provides Iraq with its only means of access to the Persian Gulf. Issues of joint sovereignty over the waterway have long been a source of contention between Iran and Iraq. In 1975 Mohammad Reza Shah Pahlavi of Iran and Vice President Saddam Hussein of Iraq signed the Algiers Agreement, which demarcated the *thalweg* (middle) line along the Shatt al-Arab as the border between the two states. In September 1980 Iraq launched an offensive against the Islamic Republic of Iran, declaring one of its intentions to be the restoration of the Shatt al-Arab to sole Iraqi sovereignty. Hostilities were brought to an end in 1988, but a peace agreement remains to be signed between the two countries. UN Resolution 598 has not been implemented other than to establish a cease-fire; sovereignty of and navigation rights in the Shatt al-Arab remain unresolved. Since Iraq's massive defeat at the hands of the United States in the Gulf War of 1991, borders have reverted to the 1975 demarcations, albeit unofficially.

See also ALGIERS AGREEMENT (1975).

Bibliography

Sirriyeh, Hoseyn. "Development of the Iraqi–Iranian Dispute, 1847–1975." *Journal of Contemporary History* 20, no. 3 (1985): 483–492.

NEGUIN YAVARI

SHA'UL, ANWAR

[1904–1984]

Iraqi Jewish writer and journalist.

Anwar Sha'ul was born into a Jewish family in the city of al-Hilla in southern Iraq; they moved to Baghdad when he was in his early teens. He studied at the Alliance Israélite Universelle and later obtained a law degree. Between 1924 and 1938 he was a journalist, first editing the Jewish weekly *al-Misbah* (The lantern) and in 1929 launching his own weekly magazine, *al-Hasid* (The reaper).

Sha'ul's knowledge of foreign languages enabled him to translate literary works from English and French. A volume of original and translated fiction appeared in 1922 under the title *al-Hisad al-Awwal* (The first harvest). It was followed in 1955 by *Fi Zi-ham al-Madina* (In the crowded city) and in 1956 by a volume of poetry, *Hamasat al-Zaman* (Whispers of time).

Sha'ul stayed in Iraq after the mass exodus of its Jewish community in 1951 and 1952. In 1971 he left Baghdad and settled in Kiron, near Tel Aviv. In 1981 he published his collected poetry in *Wa Bazagha Fajr Jadid* (And a new dawn has risen). He also published an autobiography, *Qissat Hayati fi Wadi al-Rafidayn* (My life in Mesopotamia), in 1980.

Bibliography

Somekh, Sasson. "Lost Voices: Jewish Authors in Modern Arabic Literature." In *Jews among Arabs: Contacts and Boundaries,* edited by Mark R. Cohen and Abraham L. Udovitch. Princeton, NJ: Darwin Press, 1989.

SASSON SOMEKH

SHAWA, LAILA

[1940–]

Palestinian artist and illustrator.

A native of Gaza, Laila Shawa (Layla Shawwa) is an oil painter, a silk-screen artist, and an illustrator of children's books who has also done sculpture. She studied in Cairo, at two arts academies in Rome, and in Austria with Oskar Kokoschka. She has also worked on United Nations children's art programs in Gaza. Shawa's famous silk-screen installation *Walls of Gaza* (1992–1995) exemplifies her ongoing interest in political struggle and oppression, and in children who live with war and deprivation. Her photographs of children and graffiti-laden walls in Gaza are juxtaposed on large panels to make the viewer confront the effects of conflict and violence on generations of children. Other works examine breast cancer as a metaphor for other eruptions and invasions, such as the 1991 Gulf War, and atomic bombs, linking the body with the land—a strategy adopted by other Palestinian artists. Shawa's paintings on a variety of subjects, including the restrictions on Middle Eastern women, are reminiscent of Henri Rousseau in style and color. Her works have been exhibited throughout the Middle East, in England, and in the United States.

See also ART; GENDER: GENDER AND EDUCATION.

Bibliography

Ali, Wijdan. *Modern Islamic Art: Development and Continuity.* Gainesville: University Press of Florida, 1997.

Lloyd, Fran, ed. *Contemporary Arab Women's Art: Dialogues of the Present.* London: Women's Art Library, 1999.

Shawa, Laila. Available at <http://www.lailashawa.com>.

Shawa, Laila. *Laila Shawa Works 1964–1996.* Cyprus: MCS Publications, 1997.

JESSICA WINEGAR

SHAWARMA

See FOOD: SHAWARMA

SHAW COMMISSION

A British commission of inquiry into a 1929 disturbance in Palestine.

A commission of inquiry, led by Sir Walter Shaw, was sent to Palestine by the British government to investigate the August 1929 Western Wall Disturbances, which caused the deaths of 249 Jews and Arabs. The commission's report, issued in March 1930, stated that the fundamental cause of the political violence was "the Arab feeling of animosity and hostility towards the Jews consequent upon the disappointment of their political and national aspirations and fear for their economic future." The Palestinians feared that by "Jewish immigration and land purchases they may be deprived of their livelihood and placed under the economic domination of the Jews." The commission's report called for an explicit policy regulating land and immigration that would have, in effect, curtailed the Zionist program in Palestine. The British government, however, postponed consideration of any change in policy until after another commission, which it appointed in May 1930 under Sir John Hope-Simpson, had studied land settlement, immigration, and development.

See also WESTERN WALL DISTURBANCES.

Bibliography

Palestine Government. *A Survey of Palestine for the Information of the Anglo-American Committee of Inquiry.* 2 vols. Jerusalem, 1946. Reprint, Washington, DC: Institute for Palestine Studies, 1991.

Smith, Charles D. *Palestine and the Arab-Israeli Conflict,* 4th edition. Boston: Bedford/St. Martin's, 2001.

PHILIP MATTAR

SHAWQI, AHMAD

[1868–1932]

Foremost Arab neoclassical poet.

In the course of his poetic career of forty years, Ahmad Shawqi both renovated the language of Arabic poetry and endowed it with the genre that had been missing in it, namely, the verse drama. After receiving a thorough Arabic and Islamic education in Cairo, he was sent by Khedive Tawfiq to France, where he spent three years, 1891 to 1893, during which he immersed himself in French literature, especially the Romantic Trio: Alfred de Musset, Lamartine, and Victor Hugo. This was the decisive influence on Shawqi—his window into Western literary art, through which he was able to rejuvenate modern Arabic poetry.

On his return to Egypt, he became in 1893 the court poet of Khedive Abbas Hilmi II. This marked the first phase of his poetic career, which lasted until 1914, when the First World War broke out. During this period, he composed odes on the khedive and the Alawi Dynasty and on Egyptian history, and he emerged as the poet of Islam and the Islamic Caliphate (then the Ottoman Empire). He also wrote a number of historical novels, perhaps inspired by his model, Victor Hugo. In 1898 he published his collected poems as a *diwan* titled *al-Shawqiyyat,* and this immediately established his reputation as the leading poet of his generation in the entire Arab world.

In 1914 his patron, the khedive, was deposed by Britain, and Shawqi was sent into exile. He chose Spain, where he spent the second phase of his poetic career, four years (1915–1919) in Barcelona, devoting his time to reading and contemplation. These four years witnessed the composition of splendid odes in which he remembered the glories of Spanish Islam.

The third phase of Shawqi's poetic career began in 1919 on his return to Egypt and lasted until his death in 1932. Shawqi was free from involvement with the court and court life, and with the abolishment of the caliphate in 1924, he became more interested in Arab nationalist aspirations, especially in Egypt and Syria, which inspired his memorable odes with pan-Arab overtones. It was also in this period that he composed his verse dramas, the most striking of which are *Majnun Layla* and *Masra Cleopatra.*

Shawqi did not limit his themes to the Arab and Islamic world. He is the poet of the Mediterranean par excellence and of pharaonic Egypt. His odes on both, hardly known in Europe and the United States, stand well in comparison with the best in world literature. Four years before his death, his preeminence as a poet was recognized when delegates from the Arab world travelled to Cairo, fêted him, and saluted him as *Amir al-Shuʿara* ("Prince of Poets").

See also LITERATURE: ARABIC.

Bibliography

"The Arab Mirror." In *Napoleon: One Image, Ten Mirrors,* edited by John Hirsh and Roberto Severino. Washington, DC: Georgetown University, 2002.

Shawqi, Ahmad. *Al-Mawsuʾa al-Shawqiyya,* vols. 1–9, edited by I. al-Abyari, Dar al-Kitab al-Arabi. Beirut: 1994–1995.

IRFAN SHAHÎD

SHAYKH

A general title of respect.

The term *shaykh* (also sheikh), can be applied to an elderly man, a tribal chief, a ruler of a shaykhdom along the Persian Gulf, a village chief, a religious scholar, a senator, or a Sufi master. The early caliphs were known as shaykhs. Shaykh al-Islam was the title given to the chief *mufti* (jurist) of the Ottoman Empire, who had direct access to the sultan and served as the highest-ranking legal administrator.

See also SHAYKH AL-ISLAM.

MARILYN HIGBEE

SHAYKH AL-ISLAM

Honorary title for Muslim jurists.

Shaykh al-Islam (literally, Elder of Islam) is an honorific title that has been historically applied to prominent Muslim jurists, theologians, and spiritual masters in recognition of outstanding knowledge and/or piety. In the early medieval period (c. 800–1200), the title was quasi-official and conferred on an elite few through acclamation by disciples or peers. Over time, however, the title was adopted by certain highly trained jurists (that is, muftis, or "jurisconsults"), who could legitimately claim the authority to issue a formal legal opinion *(fatwa).* In fact, although the more elitist, quasi-official usage of this title has continued into the modern period (particularly in the form of posthumous conferral), the later medieval and early modern periods witnessed an increasingly widespread attachment of the title to official positions in state-controlled judicial administrations.

The office of Shaykh al-Islam seems to have reached its apex as part of the Ottoman imperial establishment. By the time of Süleyman I (ruled 1520–1566), the chief jurisconsult of Constantinople (now Istanbul) was designated as the unique Shaykh al-Islam and recognized as the highest-ranking and most powerful member of the extensive imperial judiciary with exclusive direct access to the sultan himself. In 1916, however, the Committee for Union and Progress transferred much of the power of the former Ottoman Shaykh al-Islam to a secular Ministry of Justice, and by 1924 the new Turkish republic completely abolished the office. It is important to note that the office of Shaykh al-Islam has been much more widely and systematically instituted in Twelver Shiʿa contexts than in Sunni contexts. It was first introduced into the Iranian Shiʿite judicial system by the Safavid Shah Abbas I (ruled 1588–1629) and remains today the official title of the presidents of municipal religious courts in the Shiʿa communities of Iran and the former Soviet Union.

See also COMMITTEE FOR UNION AND PROGRESS; SHAYKH.

Bibliography

Gilsenan, Michael. *Recognizing Isla: Religion and Society in the Modern Middle East.* London and New York: Tauris, 2000.

Wheeler, Brannon M. *Teaching Islam.* New York: Oxford University Press, 2003.

SCOTT ALEXANDER

SHAYKH, HANAN AL-

[1945–]

Arab writer.

Hanan al-Shaykh is undisputedly one of the most important Arab women writers at the beginning of the twenty-first century. Born and raised in Lebanon, al-Shaykh first distinguished herself by writing prose fiction that exposed some of the repressive patriarchal traditions of her society. She did so by introducing characters, often women, who unabashedly explored themselves, their families, and their communities. She faced brief periods of censorship and occasional negative reviews. Although some of her fiction is set in the broader Arab world, two of her most prominent novels are situated in Lebanon during the Civil War of 1975 through 1990. Al-Shaykh has become an important voice in critical studies of the war itself. The renowned *Hikayat Zahra* (The Story of Zahra, 1980) is a relentless psychosexual drama that manages, primarily through its complex protagonist, to narrate an insane society in violent civil disarray. Al-Shaykh's stark imagery and gripping plot mesmerized readers. Her follow-up novel, *Barid Bayrut* (Beirut blues, 1992), structured as a series of letters by another memorable female protagonist, extends the depiction of the Lebanese wars and fortifies the ideology of nonpartisanship, as every militia, army, confessional (religious/ethnic), and national group is subject to critique and to ridicule. Al-Shaykh's focus is on nuanced reactions, complex relationships, and multiple points of view. Her war novels offered new ways of imagining Lebanon in this destructive era.

Al-Shaykh spent her early school years in Lebanon and Egypt and later lived in Saudi Arabia. Since the early 1980s, she has lived in London and has participated in local productions of her experimental plays. One of her publications, *Only in London* (2001), explores some of the issues of Arab émigrés in Europe. With a keen sense of humor and a fresh Arabic writing style, al-Shaykh's works have extended the possibilities for Arab women writers. Because of good translations into English and other languages, Al-Shaykh's readership is growing outside the Arab world.

See also GENDER: GENDER AND EDUCATION; LEBANESE CIVIL WAR (1958); LEBANESE CIVIL WAR (1975–1990); LEBANON; LITERATURE: ARABIC.

Bibliography

Cooke, Miriam. *War's Other Voices: Women Writers on the Lebanese Civil War.* Cambridge, U.K.: Cambridge University Press, 1988.

Salem, Elise. *Constructing Lebanon: A Century of Literary Narratives.* Gainesville: University Press of Florida, 2003.

Zeidan, Joseph. *Arab Women Novelists: The Formative Years and Beyond.* New York: New York University Press, 1995.

ELISE SALEM

SHAYKHI

Follower of Shaykh Ahmad al-Ahsaʿi (1753–1826), a Twelver Shiʿite Islamic thinker who emphasized the esoteric and intuitional aspects of the religion.

Shaykh Ahmad cultivated followers in al-Hasa in eastern Arabia, Bahrain, and Iraq, as well as in Yazd and Kermanshah in Iran. A separate school of Shiʿism did not coalesce around his name until after his death, when he was succeeded by Sayyid Kazim Rashti (d. 1844) in Karbala; for a time, esoteric Shaykhism offered a challenge to the scholastic orthodoxy of the Usuli school.

After Rashti's death, though many Shaykhis became Babis, important Shaykhi communities continued to exist in the Persian Gulf, and in Kerman and Tabriz. The Tabriz Shaykhis diminished their doctrinal and ritual differences with the majority Usuli school, and played a progressive role during Iran's Constitutional Revolution (1905–1911). The Kerman Shaykhis, led by the Qajar noble Karim Khan Kermani (1810–1871) and his descendants, remained esoteric. Some among the Qajar nobility, as well as Mozaffar al-Din Shah (r. 1896–1906), converted to this school. Kerman Shaykhism proved conservative and often was supported by local governors. This privileged position helped to provoke Shaykhi-Usuli riots in 1905.

In the twentieth century Shaykhism became marginalized as a Shiʿite sect and Shaykhis suffered persecution under the Islamic Republic of Iran after 1979. Shaykhi communities persist in Kerman and elsewhere. The Ihqaqi family (based in Kuwait but originally from Tabriz) now produces most Shaykhi publications and claims many followers in southern Iraq. The movement also has been prominent in recent decades in Pakistan, where debates have raged over its orthodoxy and a Shaykhi Institute was founded in Faisalabad.

See also BABIS.

Bibliography

Amir-Moezzi, Mohammad Ali. "An Absence Filled with Presences: Shaykhiyya Hermeneutics of the Occultation." In *The Twelver Shiʿa in Modern Times: Religious Culture and Political History,* edited by Rainer Brunner and Werner Ende. Boston; Leiden, Netherlands: Brill, 2001.

Bayat, Mangol. *Mysticism and Dissent: Socioreligious Thought in Qajar Iran.* Syracuse, NY: Syracuse University Press, 1982.

Cole, Juan R. I. "Casting Away the Self: The Mysticism of Shaykh Ahmad al-Ahsaʾi." In *The Twelver Shiʿa in Modern Times: Religious Culture and Political History,* edited by Rainer Brunner and Werner Ende. Boston and Leiden, Netherlands: Brill, 2001.

Naqvi, Syed Hussain Arif. "The Controversy about the Shaykhiyya Tendency among Shiʿa 'Ulama' of Pakistan." In *The Twelver Shiʿa in Modern Times: Religious Culture and Political History,* edited by Rainer Brunner and Werner Ende. Boston and Leiden, Netherlands: Brill, 2001.

JUAN R. I. COLE

SHAZAR, SHNEOUR ZALMAN

[1898–1974]

Third Israeli president.

Shneour Zalman Shazar's last name is actually an acronym for Shneour Zalman Rubashov, his original name. Shazar was born in Minsk, Russia, and raised in Stabsty where he was educated in a Habad Heder, a Lubovitch Hasidic school. He joined the Poʿalei Zion (Labor Zionist) movement in 1905. In 1911, Shazar went to Palestine for the first time and worked on Kibbutz Merhavia, but he did not emigrate there until 1924. He became a member of the Secretariat of the Histadrut (General Federation of Labor) and was on the editorial board of its newspaper, *Davar.*

In 1947, he served as a member of the Jewish Agency delegation to the United Nations. After statehood Shazar ran and was elected on the MAPAI (Labor) list for the Knesset in 1949 and served there until 1957. He was appointed to be the minister of education and culture in 1949, and two years later he became a member of the executive of the Jewish Agency. In 1963 he was elected Israel's third president, to succeed Yizhak Ben-Zvi, and served two terms.

See also BEN-ZVI, YIZHAK; HISTADRUT; ISRAEL: POLITICAL PARTIES IN; JEWISH AGENCY FOR PALESTINE; KNESSET; LABOR ZIONISM; NEWSPAPERS AND PRINT MEDIA: ISRAEL.

Bibliography

Winer, Gershon. *The Founding Fathers of Israel.* New York: Bloch, 1971.

BRYAN DAVES

SHAZLI, SAʿD AL-DIN AL-

[1922–]

Egyptian military officer and opposition politician.

Saʿd al-Din al-Shazli (also Shadhili, Shazly) was educated at Cairo University and the Military and Staff colleges in Cairo, and received training at the infantry school at Fort Benning in the United States. Shazli was chief of staff of Egyptian armed forces during the 1973 Arab–Israel War. Al-Shazli broke with President Anwar al-Sadat over Sadat's 1977 peace initiative with Israel, and was sent as ambassador to the United Kingdom and to Portugal. In 1978, he called for the overthrow of Sadat. In 1980, he went into exile in Algeria, where he formed an opposition party. Al-Shazli has published books on military strategy and the Arab–Israeli conflict.

See also ARAB–ISRAEL WAR (1973); SADAT, ANWAR AL-.

Bibliography

El Shazly, Saad. *The Arab Military Option.* San Francisco, CA: American Mideast Research, 1986.

El Shazly, Saad. *The Crossing of the Suez.* San Francisco, CA: American Mideast Research, 1986.

DAVID WALDNER

SHEKEL

Name of Israeli currency.

The word *shekel* derives from biblical times, when coins were called shekels. *Shekel* was the term used by leaders of the Zionist movement to denote the price of membership. For the purpose of designating this cost of membership, attendees at the First Zionist Congress pegged the shekel to a fixed rate of certain major Western currencies.

Until 1970, the Israeli currency was called the lira or pound. In 1984, following a steep devaluation, the name of the currency was changed to the new Israeli shekel (NIS).

BRYAN DAVES

SHENHAR, YITZHAK

[1902–1957]

Hebrew writer.

Yitzhak Shenhar was born in Ukraine and became active in the ha-Halutz movement before moving to Palestine in 1921. He published his first poetry in 1924 and held a number of manual labor jobs until he began his literary career. In the 1930s, he worked as a writer, editor, and translator for the Schocken publishing house. He wrote short stories and poems about the life of Jews in Eastern Europe and in Palestine.

BRYAN DAVES

SHENOUDA III

[1923–]

Patriarch of the Coptic Orthodox Church.

Few Coptic patriarchs have had as much experience in both secular and ecclesiastical affairs prior to their election as Shenouda III. Born near Asyut and originally named Nazir Jayyid, he graduated from Cairo University in 1947 and fought in the 1948 Arab-Israel War. He earned a bachelor of divinity degree in 1950 from the Coptic Orthodox Theological Seminary. He became a leader in the lay-dominated Sunday School movement, editing its monthly magazine, and took holy orders in 1954. Within the church, he was successively a monk, a secretary to Cyril VI, and a bishop. He became a professor of Old Testament studies at the Coptic Seminary and the editor of its journal. Elected patriarch in 1971, Shenouda is the highest-ranking cleric of the Coptic Orthodox Church, the Middle East's largest Christian denomination. He has traveled frequently to North America, Europe, and Australia in order to maintain contact with expatriate Copts worldwide.

Shenouda was among the more than 1,500 Egyptians who were accused by President Anwar al-Sadat in September 1981 of extremist religious activity. Exiled and replaced by a council of five bishops, Shenouda fled to the desert monastery of Anba Bishoi in Wadi Natrun, northwest of Cairo. The reasons for his arrest and exile were unclear. Although religious turmoil had increased in the late 1970s and early 1980s (mainly instigated by Muslims opposed to Sadat's peace treaty with Israel), the president's charges, including those against Shenouda, could not be proven. Some Copts and Muslims punished by Sadat were active in religious professions and thus superficially gave credence to his allegations, but others had secular occupations—lawyers, writers, journalists, broadcasters, politicians—and appear to have been guilty only of disagreeing with the president.

Sadat's actions may have been a delayed response to Shenouda's September 1977 protest against the proposed imposition of Islamic law (*shariʿa*) in Egypt. The proposal would have made apostasy—in this case, conversion from Islam—a capital offense. Shenouda had feared that the law would discriminate against Egyptian Christians and other non-Muslims. He succeeded temporarily, for Sadat's recommendation was withdrawn, only to be reintroduced in 1980. Because Muslim fundamentalists then unleashed a murderous round of terror against the Copts, Shenouda ordered a series of demonstrations that enraged many Muslims and caused them to accuse the patriarch of engaging in politics. Sadat turned down Shenouda's repeated requests for a meeting, and so in 1981 the patriarch refused to accept the government's Easter greeting, humiliating Sadat, who may have taken revenge by the September arrest. Some Copts believed that Shenouda's dismissal was a political move to balance Sadat's incarceration of many Muslims. Another possible explanation is that, during a 1980 meeting between Sadat and U.S. president Ronald Reagan in Washington, D.C., a group of Coptic expatriates staged a protest, which Sadat wrongly blamed on Shenouda.

The censure of Shenouda for "sectarian sedition" was both ironic and unfortunate. Although he had vigorously defended the Coptic Church and struck back against Muslim fundamentalists, he has never been antagonistic toward Islam per se. Throughout his career, he has been sympathetic to Muslim causes and to Egyptian national interests. Some of his theological writings, particularly his major 1967 work *al-Khalas fi al-Mafhum al-Urthuduksi* (Salvation in Orthodox understanding), are as critical of aspects of Protestantism as of Islamic fundamentalism. Shenouda has specifically denounced the intrusion of religion as a divisive force in political affairs. One result of his historic meeting with the Roman Catholic Pope Paul VI in May 1973 (the first visit by an Egyptian pope to his Roman counterpart since 325 C.E.) was a joint statement of concern about the Palestinian problem. In May 1986 Shenouda sent a representative to the funeral of a leader of the Muslim Brotherhood.

Shenouda's plight improved slowly after Sadat's assassination in October 1981. However, in 1983 an administrative court upheld Sadat's actions against Shenouda and ordered the Coptic Orthodox Church to hold a new papal election; only in January 1985 did a decree from President Husni Mubarak allow Shenouda to regain his office.

Shenouda reaffirmed his policy against politicizing religion by opposing an initiative by the Ibn Khaldun Center to host a conference in 1994 on minorities in the Arab world and efforts by the U.S. Congress in 1997 to pass legislation that would have barred aid to Egypt as long as it allowed discrimination against Copts. He attacked Israel's administration of Christian holy places and vowed not to visit Jerusalem until it was freed from Jewish control. He also condemned U.S. policy toward Iraq. Generally, his strategy has been to align Egypt's Copts closely with their Muslim counterparts in the interest of preserving national unity. He received UNESCO's prize for tolerance in October 1995. He is a past president of the World Council of Churches and headed for many years the Middle Eastern Council of Churches.

See also CHRISTIANS IN THE MIDDLE EAST; COPTS; SADAT, ANWAR AL-.

Bibliography

Abu-Saif, Leila. *Middle East Journal: A Woman's Journey into the Heart of the Arab World.* New York: Scribner, 1990.

Fernandez, Alberto M. "The Coptic Orthodox Salvation Theology of Anba Shenouda III." M.A. thesis, University of Arizona, 1983.

Goldschmidt, Arthur, Jr. "Shinuda III, al-Baba." In *Biographical Dictionary of Modern Egypt,* edited by Arthur Goldschmidt, Jr. Boulder, CO: Lynne Rienner, 2000.

Hirst, David, and Beeson, Irene. *Sadat.* London: Faber and Faber, 1981.

Pennington, J. D. "The Copts in Modern Egypt." *Middle Eastern Studies* 18 (1982): 158–179.

"Shenouda III." In *Coptic Encyclopedia.* New York: Macmillan, 1991.

Tincq, Henri. "Siege Mentality Grips the Copts of Egypt." *Guardian.* 21 February 1988.

DONALD SPANEL
UPDATED BY ARTHUR GOLDSCHMIDT

SHEPHEARD'S HOTEL

British gathering place in Cairo from 1841 to 1952.

In 1841 a British farmer's son named Samuel Shepheard built Shepheard's Hotel in Cairo. As Britain became more involved with the finances of khedival Egypt and especially after the establishment of an informal British protectorate in 1882, Shepheard's became the center of British social life in Cairo. Renovated in 1891, 1899, 1904, 1909, and 1927, the hotel was famous for its opulence.

British officers and administrators often retired to the bar at Shepheard's at the end of the day, and the Moorish Hall attracted tourists from Europe and America. After World War II, the relationship between Britain and Egypt deteriorated and, on Saturday, 26 January 1952, riots erupted in Cairo, which led to the destruction of numerous British and foreign establishments. Singled out by the crowd for particular attention was Shepheard's Hotel. The hotel was destroyed in an explosion, and although rebuilt on another site in 1957, it never regained its former stature.

Bibliography

Hopwood, Derek. *Egypt: Politics and Society, 1945–1990*, 3d edition. London and New York: Routledge, 1987.

ZACHARY KARABELL

SHESHBESH

One of several names for a board game, known in the West as backgammon, played with two dice and thirty pieces (fifteen per side).

Sheshbesh pieces are usually black for one player and white for the other. The origins of the game are obscure; while some experts argue for its invention in Persia, others suggest that it originated in southwest Asia. In 1927, Sir Leonard Wooley discovered a board game in the ruined city of Ur that was marked off into elaborately inlaid squares (twenty in all) accompanied by two sets of dice and two sets of discs, seven white and seven black. This places sheshbesh variants in Sumeria as early as 2600 B.C.E. Although it is not known how this game was played, experts assume that movement of the pieces over the board was governed by rolling the dice. The Ur game appears somewhat related to modern ludo, which in turn is related to backgammon.

The traditional game consists of balancing the elements of skill and chance while playing on a board marked with twenty-four chevrons in alternating colors of black and white. The pieces, fifteen to a player, are arranged on the trays according to a specific pattern, or are held off the board. Entry or movement begins according to the roll of the dice. The pieces move the full distance around the board in a race to the home tray, and are then borne off. Most commonly, players try to prevent and delay one's opponent from bearing off. If a hit has been made the player will attempt to block the entry of the piece by making homes—covering a chevron with a minimum of two pieces. Shesbesh is known by a large variety of names. These include *takht-e nard* in Iran, *plakato* and *tawali* in Greece, *tric-trac* in France and Germany, tables *reales* in Italy and Spain, *mahbusa, yahudiyya farahjiyya,* or *tawlat al-zahr* in Syria and Arabia, and *bula* in Egypt.

Bibliography

Grosvenor, N. *Modern Backgammon.* New York: Holt, 1928.

CYRUS MOSHAVER

SHIBERGHAN

City in northern Afghanistan.

The capital of the Afghan province of Jowzjan, Shiberghan is located approximately 80 miles west of Mazar-e Sharif. The city has about 30,000 inhabitants, but the number is only a rough approximation. The official 1979 census showed a population of 19,000, but by 2003 estimates held that it might be as high as 40,000. Most of Shiberghan's population is Uzbek, although the city also has a sizable Turkmen and Tajik population. After natural gas was discovered in 1931, Shiberghan was developed with Soviet aid into a modern city. The city became a focal point in the battle between the Taliban and Afghanistan's Northern Alliance. Shiberghan is the location of a prison used by the Northern Alliance, and it has been alleged that several hundred Taliban and al-Qaʿida prisoners were killed at the prison.

Bibliography

Adamec, Ludwig. *Historical Dictionary of Afghanistan*, 2d edition. Lanham, MD: Scarecrow Press, 1997.

GRANT FARR

SHID, NAHID

[1953–]

Iranian lawyer.

Nahid Shid was born in 1953. She graduated from Tehran University law school and pursued religious education with Ayatollah Mar'ashi-Najafi. She has been an attorney since 1980, specializing in women's affairs, employment, and social insurance. She also is an expert at the Social Welfare organization and a consultant at the High Council of the Cultural Revolution. She initiated several amendments to the insurance law and divorce law, especially the principles of *ojrat-ol misl* and the reevaluation of dowry. The amendment to *ojrat-ol misl,* which was promulgated in 1993, stipulates that when a man files for divorce his wife can ask to be compensated for the housework she did during the marriage. The change to dowry, promulgated in 1996, stipulates that the amount of dowry should be calculated according to its current value, taking into account inflation. Shid argues that most religious laws should be changed because they are based on secondary principles and do not take account of social change. She maintains that blood money cannot be functional in a society in which women are medical doctors, university professors, and the like, and concludes that blood money should be the same for men and women. She presented her candidacy for the Fifth Parliament elections (1996) but was disqualified by the Council of Guardians.

Bibliography

Interview with Nahid Shid. *Zanan* 5, no. 28 (March 1996): 18–19.

AZADEH KIAN-THIÉBAUT

SHIDYAQ, AHMAD FARIS AL-

[1804–1887]

Lebanese writer, linguist, and literary critic who played a leading role in the Arabic literary revival of the mid-to-late nineteenth century.

A Maronite who converted to Protestantism in 1826 after witnessing the Maronite clergy's persecution of his brother As'ad, Faris al-Shidyaq was sent to Egypt by the American Protestant missionaries in Lebanon so that he could pursue his studies in Cairo. From 1834 to 1848, he taught at the American Protestant mission school in Malta, undertook a new Arabic translation of the Bible, and edited the publications of the American press there. For several years afterward, he traveled widely through Europe and the Near East, and worked as editor of the official Tunisian journal *al-Ra'id al-Tunisi* between 1854 and 1860. He converted to Islam during his stay in Tunis and adopted the name Ahmad Faris. In 1860, he relocated to Istanbul at the invitation of the Ottoman authorities. While there, he undertook his most important project: the publication of the Arabic-language newspaper *al-Jawa'ib,* a mouthpiece for Ottomanism which soon became a leading forum for the discussion of the political and cultural issues of the time and can be considered a pioneer of modern Arabic journalism. In addition to the many pieces of literary criticism that he wrote for this journal and others, Ahmad Faris al-Shidyaq is also remembered for his own writings in prose and verse and for his travel writing. A writer whose influence was felt throughout the region, he was one of the architects of modern literary Arabic.

See also OTTOMANISM.

Bibliography

Salibi, Kamal. *The Modern History of Lebanon.* New York: Praeger, 1965.

Sharabi, Hisham. *Arab Intellectuals and the West: The Formative Years, 1875–1914.* Baltimore, MD: Johns Hopkins Press, 1970.

GUILAIN P. DENOEUX

SHIHABI, ZLIKHA AL-

[1903–1992]

Palestinian women's activist.

Zlikha (also Zulaykha) Ishaq al-Shihabi was born in Jerusalem and educated at the Sisters of Zion School there. Her education was supplemented by private lessons. In 1929 she was a member of the Arab Women's Executive Committee, which convened the Palestine Arab Women's Conference in Jerusalem, and directed the Palestinian women's movement during the Mandate period. Shihabi was elected president of the Arab Women's Union (AWU) in Jerusalem in 1937, a position she held until her death. In the 1940s the AWU founded a sports club with its own playground and tennis courts, and in 1946 it opened a clinic near Bab al-Zahira, a gate of the Old City of Jerusalem. She represented Palestinian women and spoke at the Eastern Women's Conference on Palestine (Cairo, 1938), and the Arab Women's Conference (Cairo, 1944), as well as other international conferences. In 1964 she was president of the preparatory committee that founded the General Union of Palestinian Women in Jerusalem, which was subsequently banned by both the Jordanian authorities and then the Israeli government after Jerusalem was captured in 1967. Because of her political activities the Israelis deported Shihabi to Jordan in 1969, but she managed to return to Jerusalem after a few months and continued her work with the AWU there until her death.

See also GAZA STRIP; GENDER: GENDER AND LAW; GENDER: GENDER AND POLITICS; GENERAL UNION OF PALESTINIAN WOMEN'S COMMITTEES (GUPWC); JERUSALEM; PALESTINE; PALESTINE LIBERATION ORGANIZATION (PLO); WEST BANK.

Bibliography

Fleischmann, Ellen. *The Nation and Its "New" Women: The Palestinian Women's Movement, 1920–1948.* Berkeley: University of California Press, 2003.

Kawar, Amal. *Daughters of Palestine: Leading Women of the Palestinian National Movement.* Albany: State University of New York Press, 1996.

ELLEN L. FLEISCHMANN

SHIʿISM

Branch of Islam that traces its leadership to Ali ibn Abi Talib, cousin of Muhammad.

The Shiʿa constitute the largest Islamic community after the Sunnis, numbering close to 90 million worldwide. Iran is the only predominantly Shiʿite country; significant Shiʿite minorities exist in Iraq, India, Pakistan, Afghanistan, Yemen, Kuwait, Bahrain, eastern Saudi Arabia, Lebanon, and various Western countries. Shiʿism rests on a belief that the right of succession to political and religious leadership of the community belongs solely to the prophet Muhammad's cousin, Ali ibn Abi Talib, and his progeny. The Prophet was first succeeded by three of his companions—Abu Bakr, Umar, and Uthman—who ruled successively (632–656). Ali's rule (656–661) was almost immediately contested by Muʿawiyya, who succeeded him and founded the Umayyad dynasty. Upon Muʾawiyya's death, Ali's son Husayn revolted against Yazid, the successor and son of Muʾawiyya. For the followers of Ali, Husayn's death in battle at Karbala became symbolic of the hostility between them and those linked with Sunni Islam. The battle, especially the martyrdom of Husayn, continues to be commemorated by Shiʿa.

Origins

The assassination of Uthman in 656 opened a split in the Islamic community. Soon after the accession of Ali to the caliphate, Muʿawiya, governor of Syria, kinsman of Uthman, and among the last generation of companions of the Prophet, declared his opposition to Ali's leadership. His opposition soon gained support among tribal groups in Syria and Mesopotamia. In response, Ali moved the Islamic capital to Kufa (in southern Iraq) and engaged Muʿawiya in a protracted rivalry that ended in an armistice known as *al-Tahkim,* which left Muʿawiya sovereign in Syria, Egypt, and northern Mesopotamia, while Ali ruled the Arabian peninsula and the east. Those who supported Ali were known as *Shiʿat Ali* (the partisans of Ali); hence the name Shiʿism. Ali was assassinated in 661; subsequently, Muʿawiya consolidated his rule over the territories formerly under Ali and moved to make the line of political succession that of his family, the Umayyads. Since Ali's martyrdom the city of al-Najaf, where he is buried, has become a place of pilgrimage for Shiʿa.

Ali had two sons, Hasan and Husayn (or Hussein), from his marriage to the Prophet's daughter, Fatima. They quickly inherited Ali's leadership and attracted the loyalty of the Shiʿa. Exasperated by the political deadlock, Hasan abandoned his claim to succession, leaving Muʿawiya free to extend his control. Muʿawiya was succeeded in 680 by his son Yazid, who lacked the political acumen of his father. Yazid's hereditary route to power upset an Islamic community accustomed to having a strong consultative element in political election and viewing senior companions of the Prophet as worthier candidates to rule.

In 680 the residents of Kufa invited Husayn, who lived in Medina, to assert his right to succeed his father, and they pledged to support him. Husayn left Medina with his family and close associates, but before he could reach Kufa, an Umayyad force attacked and killed him and most of his family. This unprovoked attack on the youngest of the Prophet's grandchildren increased opposition to the Umayyads.

The cause of Shiʿism then expanded to include other branches of the larger family of the Prophet, the Banu Hashim, or Hashimites. There were a number of Hashimite revolts, primarily in Iraq and the east. Pivotal revolts were those of Zayd ibn Ali ibn al-Husayn in Kufa (743), and of his son Yahya in Transoxiania. Zayd's movement formed an early current of Shiʿism that espoused political activity to further the Alid cause, and did not restrict the imamate to one particular branch of the Alid family. (The Zaydi sect still survives in Yemen.)

In 750 a broadly based movement originating in Khorasan toppled the Umayyad caliphate. Succession to the caliphate passed to the Abbasids, a Hashimite branch named after Abbas, an uncle of the Prophet. Feeling betrayed, the Alids staged several revolts, the most notable of which was the one in Medina by Muhammad al-Nafs al-Zakiyya (762), a descendant of Hasan. By then, however, the Abbasids had consolidated their control.

The Abbas Mosque, located in Kerbala, Iraq. © AFP/Corbis. Reproduced by permission.

Theology

Shiʿism originated as a political movement supporting the rights of Ali to the caliphate. Since leadership in the early Islamic community was associated to a great extent with religious merit, Ali was considered the rightful ruler not only because of his early conversion to Islam and close family ties to the Prophet, but also because of his religious knowledge. Shiʿite tradition states that the Prophet always referred to Ali as the preeminent expert on spiritual matters among his companions, and that at Ghadir Khumm, Muhammad reportedly declared to his companions that Ali was his *waliyy* (rightful and trusted successor) and blessed him with special prayers. The earliest concrete evidence of Shiʿism as a spiritual sect, however, did not appear until the 750s or 760s. In the era immediately following the revolution, a divergence emerged among those supporting the cause of Ali's family. Shiʿism came to be associated increasingly with descendants of Husayn, and in particular, the sixth descendant, Jaʿfar al-Sadiq.

Although little historical fact is known about Jaʿfar al-Sadiq, it is generally believed that it was during his time that the rudiments of Shiʿite theology were first formed. These consisted of the beliefs that the imam (presumably from the Husaynid line) holds the secrets of religious knowledge *(maʿrifa)*, that he has the authority to pass on this knowledge to a designated successor through a process of investment known as *wasiyya*, and that the followers of the imam must not challenge the authority of the established state in support of the Alid imamate until the imam declares the historically assigned time for such a political revolution. From the time of Jaʿfar al-Sadiq, the Shiʿa became closely clustered around the line of his descendants. However, a significant division took place within his lifetime. Jaʿfar's son Ismaʿil was supposed to be the spiritual successor to his father, and thus began to attract followers. Either because Ismaʿil died during his father's lifetime or because during his last years Jaʿfar decided to transfer the succession to another of his

The Hussein Mosque, located in Kerbala, Iraq. © CHARLES & JOSETTE LENARS/CORBIS. REPRODUCED BY PERMISSION.

sons, Musa, another group began to recognize Musa as his only successor.

This latter group continued to recognize the transmission of the authority of the imamate in a line of twelve successors, the last of whom, a child, is believed to have disappeared in the city of Samarra in 873. Shiʿa believe that the last of the twelve imams will one day reveal himself as the leading religious and political guide (the Mahdi), reestablish his leadership over the whole Islamic community, and usher in an age of justice and righteousness. Recognition of twelve descendants of Ali as imams led to this larger Shiʿite community being known as Twelver (also Thaʿashar) Shiʿa, or Imamis. The other group, which refused to accept Musa as successor and maintained its religous loyalty to Ismaʿil, the seventh imam, is hence known as Ismaʿilis, or Seveners. Like the Twelvers, some Ismaʿilis believe in occulation *(ghayba)*, but they consider Ismaʿil to be the vanished imam destined to usher in a righteous age.

The Growth of Shiʿism

In the late ninth century competing Shiʿite missions emerged. For some time, Ismaʿili *daʿwa* (mission, propaganda) had its strongest support in North Africa, where it was the religious affiliation of the Fatimid dynasty (909–1171), which came to rule North Africa, Egypt, Hijaz, and Syria. Establishing the city of Cairo (969) as their capital, the Fatimids hoped to turn Egypt into the center of Ismaʿili propaganda, and for this purpose they founded al-Azhar seminary. The Fatimids' religious enterprise had little success because the majority of their subjects adhered to Sunni schools of thought; Ismaʿilism became the ideology of the state and of a minority in society. Elsewhere in the Islamic world, the Buyid dynasty, which ruled Iran and Iraq between 932 and 1062, declared its loyalty to Shiʿism but chose to follow the Twelver branch. Although Shiʿism did not become the religious affiliation of the majority under Buyid rule, the dynasty did much to promote it. For example, Husayn's murder was commemorated with public ceremonies on the tenth of Muharram, the events at Ghadir Khumm were celebrated, and steps were taken to protect Shiʿism.

The next stage of substantial elaboration of Twelver Shiʿite thought occurred in the sixteenth century under the Safavid dynasty in Iran. Until their arrival, Iran had been primarily a Sunni region. Locked in a mortal conflict with two Sunni dynasties—the Ottomans to the west and the Uzbeks in Transoxiania to the east—Ismaʿil al-Safawi (1494–1524), founder of the dynasty, found it politically helpful to underline the ideological particularity of his government by adopting Shiʿism as the state religion. At the time, Safavid Shiʿism consisted largely of an affiliation to Sufi movements in Azerbaijan. Under Safawi's successor, Tahmasp (1524–1576), however, the state moved toward a more institutional and hierarchical structure guided by a clergy and an established law, rather than by the esoteric propensity of Sufi masters. This change fostered the alliance between the state and the clergy, the latter bolstering the legitimacy of the state and the former supporting Shiʿite propaganda. The Safavids sought to make Shiʿism the law of the land and the only religious affiliation in society. Under Abbas I (1588–1629) they built theological seminaries and attracted renowned scholars from Iraq, southern Lebanon, and Bahrain to help systematize Shiʿite learning. Sunni Islam was all but eliminated in the Safavid territories.

Shiʿite Scholars and Differences with Sunnism

The idea of the occultation of the imam deprived Shiʿism of binding authority in spiritual matters. This inevitably called for the presence of religious scholars who could guide the community. Kufa was the earliest center of Shiʿite thought, and in later times Qom in Iran emerged as a preeminent center of Shiʿite learning. Among the most prominent of scholars in Qom were Abu Jaʿfar al-Kulayni (d. 941) and Ibn Babawayh al-Saduq (d. 991). Noted scholars in the later theological schools of Baghdad were Shaykh al-Mufid (d. 1022) and Sharif Murtada Alam al-Huda (d. 1067). The greatest Shiʿite scholar, however, was perhaps al-Majlisi (d. 1699), who contributed the most toward changing a Sufi form of Shiʿism to a dogmatic and formal legislative form. Beginning in the nineteenth century there was a debate between two main currents in Shiʿism: the Akhbari, which seeks to establish Shiʿite jurisprudence on the authority of tradition *(akhbar)*, and the Usuli, which emphasizes the primacy of rationalist principles *(usul)* and the need to exercise *ijtihad* (reasoned speculation). Since the debate has been resolved in favor of the Usuli current in the twentieth century, the authority of the *mujtahid* (expert scholar capable of exercising reasoned speculation) has taken on greater importance. Although Shiʿa and Sunnis agree on core matters of ritual, dogma, and law, they differ on details. Whereas Sunnis, for instance, permit the occasional practice of wiping the foot covering with water *(al-mash ala al-khuffayn)* during ablution, Shiʿa reject the practice. The institution of temporary marriage *(mutʿa)*, accepted under Shiʿite law, is rejected in Sunnism. The most prominent area of difference, however, remains historical. The Shiʿa's rejection of the caliphate of the first successors to the Prophet—viewed as equals according to Sunni historical reading—and their insistence on the sole right of Ali ibn Abi Talib to the succession has long formed the most visible difference between the two communities.

See also AKHBARI; AZHAR, AL-; ISLAM; ISMAʿILI SHIʿISM; KARBALA; MAHDI; MUHAMMAD; NAJAF, AL-; SUNNI ISLAM; USULI; ZAYDISM.

Bibliography

Algar, Hamid. *Religion and State in Iran, 1785–1906: The Role of the Ulama in the Qajar Period.* Berkeley: University of California Press, 1980.

Arjomand, Said Amir. *Authority and Political Culture in Shiʿism.* Albany: State University of New York Press, 1988.

Arjomand, Said Amir. *The Shadow of God and the Hidden Imam: Religion, Political Order, and Societal Change in Shiʿite Iran from the Beginning to 1890.* Chicago: University of Chicago Press, 1984.

Chelkowski, P. J. *Taʿziyeh: Ritual and Drama in Iran.* New York: New York University Press, 1979.

Dabashi, Hamid. *Theology of Discontent: The Ideological Foundation of the Islamic Revolution in Iran.* New York: New York University Press, 1993.

Daftary, Farhad. *The Ismaʿilis: Their History and Doctrines.* Cambridge, U.K.: Cambridge University Press, 1990.

Keddie, Nikki. *Religion and Politics in Iran: Shiʿism from Quietism to Revolution.* New Haven, CT: Yale University Press, 1983.

Momen, Moojan. *An Introduction to Shiʿi Islam.* New Haven, CT: Yale University Press, 1985.

Moosa, Matti. *Extremist Shiʿites: The Ghulat Sects.* Syracuse, NY: Syracuse University Press, 1988.

Sachedina, A. A. *Islamic Messianism: The Idea of the Mahdi in Twelver Shiʿism.* Albany: State University of New York Press, 1981.

TAYEB EL-HIBRI
UPDATED BY ROXANNE VARZI

SHILLUK

Non-Muslim Sudanese people.

The Shilluk are a linguistic group belonging to the Western Nilotic subgroup of the Eastern Sudanic branch of the Nilo-Saharan family. They are concentrated along the west bank of the White Nile in southern Sudan. Because Shilluk political organization is centered around the king *(reth)*, the Shilluk have experienced greater unity than other tribes in the region. Enjoying access to good agricultural land along the Nile, the Shilluk are more settled than other tribes and rely more on cultivation and fishing than on cattle raising. The Shilluk numbered about 150,000 persons according to the 1983 census.

Bibliography

Voll, John Obert. *Historical Dictionary of the Sudan.* Metuchen, NJ: Scarecrow Press, 1978.

DAVID WALDNER

SHILOAH, REUVEN
[1909–1959]

Israeli intelligence official, strategist, and diplomat.

Born Reuven Zaslani in Jerusalem, Shiloah served in the SHAI (the Haganah intelligence service) in the 1930s and worked with the Jewish community in Iraq. He headed the Arab section of the political department of the Jewish Agency under Moshe Shertok (Sharett). He was liaison officer with British and U.S. intelligence services during World War II. Shiloah held many secret meetings with King Abdullah of Transjordan before and after the 1948 war.

He was the first director of the political department of the Israeli Foreign Ministry and headed the Israeli delegation to the Lausanne peace talks in 1949. He was also the first head of the Mossad (1949–1952), but was worn down by the disastrous collapse of the Israeli spy network in Iraq, by a serious road accident, and by constant feuding with Isser Harel, the first head of the Shin Bet and Shiloah's successor as Mossad chief.

Shiloah resigned his chairmanship of the intelligence services coordinating committee to serve under ambassador Abba Eban as a minister at the Israeli embassy in Washington, D.C. (1953–1957). While there he forged close ties with the U.S. intelligence community.

As a senior adviser to Golda Meir, the foreign minister, Shiloah was instrumental in forging Israel's "periphery doctrine" of responding to the Cold War and Nasserism by seeking closer links with non-Arab regimes such as Turkey, Iran, and Ethiopia. He attempted but failed to establish an Israeli relationship with NATO. Shiloah was widely described as a workaholic; this trait contributed to his poor health and his premature death.

See also EBAN, ABBA (AUBREY); HAREL, ISSER; MOSSAD; SHIN BET.

Bibliography

Black, Ian, and Morris, Benny. *Israel's Secret Wars: A History of Israel's Intelligence Services.* New York: Grove Press, 1991.

Eshed, Haggai. *Reuven Shiloah: The Man Behind the Mossad.* London: Frank Cass, 1997.

IAN BLACK

SHIMʿUN, MAR

[1908–1975]

Patriarch of the Assyrian (Nestorian) community.

Ishai Mar Shimʿun XXIII was born in the Ottoman Empire (now Turkey) and educated in England in the 1920s. In 1918 and 1919, some 20,000 Assyrians (Nestorians) who had fled southeastern Turkey were settled in Iraq by the British authorities. Fearing the consequences of British withdrawal in 1932, the Mar Shimʿun attempted to set up a separate enclave for his people with himself as politico-spiritual leader. The Assyrians were told that they should either become assimilated as Iraqis or leave, and in a confrontation between the community and the Iraqi army in August 1933, at least 600 Assyrians were killed. The Mar Shimʿun left Iraq, eventually reaching the United States; though he returned briefly to Iraq in 1970, he died in the United States in 1975.

See also ASSYRIANS.

PETER SLUGLETT

SHIN BET

Israel's General Security Service (G.S.S. or Shabak), responsible for preventing hostile activity.

The Shin Bet was created in 1948 to counter espionage, subversion, and sabotage. Its early preoccupations were Soviet-bloc espionage and monitoring Israel's Arab minority. Its first head was Isser Harel, who was succeeded by Amos Manor in 1954.

The Shin Bet expanded greatly after the 1967 war, becoming the leading civilian agency for controlling the Palestinians in the newly occupied territories, recruiting informers and collaborators and working with the Mossad to penetrate resistance groups such as al-Fatah and the Popular Front for the Liberation of Palestine.

The Shabak affair (1984–1986) brought unwelcome exposure of Shin Bet practices. Two Palestinians who hijacked an Israeli bus were said by the authorities to have died during the rescue. Photographs showed them leaving the bus alive, and it became clear that they had been deliberately killed by Shin Bet personnel while in custody. Israel's attorney general recommended that Avraham Shalom, head of the Shin Bet, be dismissed, but amid accusations of a cover-up, President Chaim Herzog pardoned Shalom and eleven other Shin Bet officers. A new committee investigated Shin Bet procedures, including interrogation methods that some human-rights experts said constituted torture.

The Shin Bet struggled to cope with the Palestinian uprising after 1987 and saw its effectiveness weakened when Israel withdrew from the Gaza Strip and large parts of the West Bank after the Oslo Accords. Its reputation was damaged by its failure to prevent the assassination of Yitzhak Rabin by a right-wing Jew in 1995 and by the Palestinian suicide bombings that accompanied the second intifada that began in 2000.

See also HAREL, ISSER; MOSSAD; SHILOAH, REUVEN.

Bibliography

Black, Ian, and Morris, Benny. *Israel's Secret Wars: A History of Israel's Intelligence Services.* New York: Grove Press, 1991.

Raviv, Dan, and Melman, Yossi. *Every Spy a Prince.* Boston: Houghton Mifflin, 1990.

JULIE ZUCKERMAN
UPDATED BY IAN BLACK

SHIRAZ

Ancient city and provincial capital in southwestern Iran.

Shiraz, the capital of Fars, probably dates back to Achemenid times (c. 550–330 B.C.E.). During the Sassanian dynasty (c. 226–642 C.E.), it developed into an important commercial center and military base, a position it has retained for more than 1,300 years. During the medieval period, two of Iran's greatest poets, Saʿdi and Hafez, lived in the city. Shiraz flourished in the late eighteenth century as the capital of the Zand dynasty (1750–1794).

During the nineteenth century Shiraz was an important center for the distribution of foreign trade, much of which passed through the Persian Gulf port of Bushehr (Bushire), about 125 miles west of the city. The development of ports in Khuzestan in the early twentieth century, and especially the building of the Trans-Iranian Railway, which bypassed both Shiraz and Bushehr, led to the decline of this trade. Beginning in the 1930s, however, modern industries were developed in Shiraz, initially textile factories, but increasingly more diversified manufacturing after 1965. Industrialization brought a major influx of rural migrants, and the city's population increased nearly sixfold in 40 years, from 179,000 in 1956 to 1,053,000 by 1996.

Bibliography

Fisher, W. B. "Physical Geography." In *The Cambridge History of Iran,* vol. 1, edited by W. B. Fisher. Cambridge, U.K.: Cambridge University Press, 1968.

NEGUIN YAVARI
UPDATED BY ERIC HOOGLUND

SHIRAZI, MIRZA HASAN
[1815–1897]

Nineteenth-century Iranian cleric.

Born in Shiraz to a well-established clerical family, Mirza Hasan Shirazi embarked on vigorous religious training that took him first to Isfahan and then Iraq. He has become most notable for a religious decree *(fatwa)* in 1892 against the use of tobacco. The decree read as follows: "In the name of God the merciful, the usage of tobacco in any way is equal to denouncing God and fighting against the divinely guided messianic leader [that is, the Mahdi, the Imam of the Age]." Shirazi's decision to issue such a proclamation is said to have stemmed from the allocation of exclusive rights of tobacco production and sales to the British by Naser al-Din Shah and his prime minister. The effect of the decree was that the government was forced to annul its agreement with the British. It is said that even the wives of the shah refused to use and serve tobacco during the period of the decree.

See also TOBACCO REVOLT.

Bibliography

Algar, Hamid. *Mirza Malkum Khan: A Study in the History of Iranian Modernism.* Berkeley: University of California Press, 1973.

FARHAD ARSHAD

SHIRAZ UNIVERSITY

A private university established in 1956 in Shiraz, Iran.

The Pahlavi University of Shiraz, Iran, was established by a special law passed by the parliament in 1956 as a nongovernment university under the trust of the king, the queen, and the crown prince. Its name was changed to Shiraz University after the 1979 Iranian Revolution. It began with nine colleges or faculties and by 1977 had 648 faculty members and 5,129 students. It was one of the first Middle Eastern universities created on the U.S. model, offering courses in English and including among its faculty a number of foreigners. Its curriculum includes courses in literature, natural sciences, medicine, agriculture, and engineering. It had 12,600 students and 360 teachers in 2002.

PARVANEH POURSHARIATI

SHISH KEBAB

See FOOD: SHISH KEBAB

SHITREET, BEKHOR

[1897–1967]

Israeli Mizrahi leader.

Bekhor Shitreet (also Shitrit) was born in Tiberias into a family that had emigrated from Morocco to Palestine in the eighteenth century. He was educated as a rabbi and taught Hebrew, Arabic, and French in the Alliance (French) school system in Tiberias. An organizer of the police force set up in Palestine by the British in 1919, he later was a police commander in lower Galilee and head of the Tel Aviv police force in 1927. After the founding of the State of Israel in 1948, he was elected to the Knesset as a member of the MAPAI party and served as minister of police. During his lifetime Shitreet sought to improve relations between religious minorities in Israel.

See also ISRAEL: POLITICAL PARTIES IN; KNESSET.

BRYAN DAVES

SHLONSKY, AVRAHAM

[1900–1973]

Hebrew poet, literary critic, editor, and translator.

Avraham Shlonsky was the main leader and proponent of modern Hebrew poetry in the evolving Jewish community of British mandatory Palestine and the State of Israel. Born in 1900 in the tsarist Ukraine, he was sent at age thirteen by his Zionist parents to study at the prestigious Herzliya Gymnasia (high school) in Tel Aviv, but had to return to Russia during World War I. In 1921 he emigrated to Palestine and joined a new kibbutz and for a while worked as a *halutz* (pioneer) in road paving, construction, and agriculture. His early poems appeared in 1922, and he was soon drawn to the burgeoning cultural life in Tel Aviv. During a visit to Paris, Shlonsky was influenced by modern French poetry, especially by the symbolists and the expressionists, but also by the Russian avant-garde poetry that flourished during the Russian Revolution and in the early days of the Soviet Union.

During the 1920s Shlonsky became a leading figure in the literary revolt against the rhetorical-didactic style of Hayyim Nahman Bialik, the towering and authoritative king of early Hebrew and Zionist poetry. Shlonsky edited the literary pages of *Davar,* the daily paper of the labor movement, and from 1926 edited *Ketuvim* (Writings) and from 1933 *Turim* (Columns), the literary journals of the rebellious young opposition to the literary establishment. In the late 1930s he became active in the Marxist left wing of the labor movement (ha-Shomer ha-Tzaʿir and later MAPAM), founded its *Sifriyat ha-Poʿalim* (Workers Library) publishing house, and edited the party's literary supplements and journals. In the late 1940s and early 1950s Shlonsky edited *Orlogin,* the home for what was then called Progressive Culture, which sympathized with the Soviet Union in the Cold War. During the 1950s he was active in the Moscow-influenced World Peace Movement, but after the revelations of Stalin's antisemitic tendencies Shlonsky became critical of the attitude of the Soviet regime toward the Jews and Zionism.

Shlonsky was acclaimed for his agility with the Hebrew language. Beside his influential "serious" poetry, he was widely admired for his light poetry, satires, and children's verse. A prolific translator, he introduced the young Hebrew-speaking generation to the world classics (Shakespeare, Molière, Romain Rolland, De Coster) and in particular to Russian poetry and prose (Pushkin, Gogol, Chekhov, Mayakovsky, and Tolstoy). In addition to the nine major collections of poetry that he published, Shlonsky also translated more than seventy major European works into Hebrew. In 1967 Shlonsky was awarded the prestigious Israel Prize. He died in 1973.

See also BIALIK, HAYYIM NAHMAN; LITERATURE: HEBREW; NEWSPAPERS AND PRINT MEDIA: ISRAEL.

Bibliography

Burnshaw, Stanley, Carmi, T., and Spicehandler, Ezra, eds. *The Modern Hebrew Poem Itself,* updated edition. Cambridge, MA: Harvard University Press, 1989.

Spicehandler, Ezra. "The Fiction of the 'Generation of the Land.'" In *Israel: The First Decade of Independence,* edited by S. Ilan Troen and Noah Lucas. Albany: State University of New York Press, 1995.

MORDECHAI BAR-ON

SHOCHAT, MANYA
[1879–1961]

Leading Zionist pioneer, advocate for Russian Jewry, feminist, mother of the kibbutz movement, and founder of the League of Arab-Jewish Rapprochement.

Born near Grodno, Russia, Manya Wilbushevitz Shochat (also Shohat) reacted to the Kishinev pogrom of 1903 by distancing herself from the Russian revolutionary movement in favor of Jewish self-defense and nonrevolutionary socialist movements. For supporting an attempt to assassinate the Russian interior minister, Shochat was imprisoned. She persuaded the secret police to release her, then fled when her police contact fell from office. Arriving in Ottoman Palestine in 1904, Shochat established the first collective, Kibbutz Sejera, and was a founding member of the Jewish self-defense movement, Ha-Shomer. She undertook a number of overseas fundraising missions on behalf of Palestinian Jewish workers and Russian Jewry and attempted to foster dialogue with local Arabs while also smuggling arms to Jewish communities, which led to her arrest by the Turkish authorities. Under the British Mandate in Palestine, Shochat was prominent in the kibbutz movement and the newly established Haganah (Jewish defense force). After rioting resulted in the death of Jews across the country in 1929, she helped to found the small League of Arab-Jewish Rapprochement while continuing to support Jewish immigration and defense efforts—a combination she pursued through the subsequent war, believing that respect could win peace while survival demanded self-reliance.

See also HAGANAH; HA-SHOMER.

Bibliography

Ben-Zvi, Rahel Yanait. *Before Golda: Manya Shochat: A Biography,* translated by Sandra Shurin. New York: Biblio Press, 1989.

Bernstein, Deborah, ed. *Pioneers and Homemakers: Jewish Women in Pre-State Israel.* Albany: State University of New York, 1992.

Shepherd, Naomi. *A Price below Rubies: Jewish Women as Rebels and Radicals.* Cambridge MA: Harvard University Press, 1993.

GEORGE R. WILKES

SHORFA

North African title for all descendants of the prophet Muhammad.

In Morocco, since the rule of the Idrisid dynasty, descent from the prophet Muhammad became a source of legitimacy for establishing political power. All the founders of the religious brotherhoods claimed such origin to gain authority and credit among disciples. A genealogical tree linking the shorfa to the Prophet would assess the claim. The Saʿdi (sixteenth century) and Alawi (seventeenth century to the present) dynasties that ruled or have ruled Morocco are considered shorfa dynasties.

See also ALAWI; IDRISIDS; SHARIF.

RAHMA BOURQIA

SHUF

Region of Lebanon.

The Shuf is the district (*qada*) located in southern Lebanon between the Jizzin and al-Matn districts, and between the Mediterranean Sea and the Biqa valley. It has more than 220 towns. The main city is the predominantly Druze town of Baʿaklin, which was, for a while, the seat of government for the Maʿnids. The Shuf was made part of the governorate of Mount Lebanon because a sectarian balance between Maronite Christians and Druze was desired. Historically, the electoral battles in the region were between the candidates of Kamal Jumblatt and those of Camille Chamoun, but the presence of a number of sects in the region forced both leaders to seek support among nonaligned sects to win the election. For example, the Shuf had a Sunni Muslim seat, and even the Maronite Chamoun had to field a Sunni candidate to win the election. Druze leader Walid Jumblatt has been demanding the division of the Mount Lebanon governorate into two sections to achieve a degree of sectarian parity. He does not feel he should have to seek support among the Maronites, who constitute a majority in the northern part of the governorate. By the early 2000s, however, Jumblatt—whose traditional pro-Syrian stance had shifted—began making political alliances with Christian candidates.

See also BIQA VALLEY; CHAMOUN, CAMILLE; JUMBLATT, KAMAL; JUMBLATT, WALID.

Bibliography

AbuKhalil, As'ad. *Historical Dictionary of Lebanon.* Lanham, MD: Rowman and Littlefield, 1998.

AS'AD ABUKHALIL
UPDATED BY MICHAEL R. FISCHBACH

SHUFMAN, GERSHON
[1880–1972]

Hebrew writer.

Born in Belorussia, Gershon Shufman received a traditional Yeshiva education and taught himself Hebrew and Russian. In 1902, he enlisted in the Russian army, which coincided with the publication of his first collection of short stories. From 1913 to 1938 he lived in Austria and from there emigrated to Palestine. His brief articles and short stories are his best literary creations. They describe life in Galicia, Austria, and in Israel, and focus on day-to-day experiences that, in turn, reflect reality.

Shufman's writings are considered forerunners of modern Hebrew literature. A four-volume revised version of his collected works appeared between 1946 and 1952, and a fifth volume was added in 1960. He received the Israel Prize for literature in 1957.

ANN KAHN

SHUKRI, MOHAMMAD
[1935–]

Moroccan novelist.

Mohammad Shukri was born in Beni Shiker in the Nadhor region of Morocco. He learned to read and write only at the age of twenty. He lives in Tangier.

Shukri's first autobiographical novel, *al-Khubz al-Hafi Sira Riwa'iyya, 1935–1956* (For bread alone), details his difficult childhood and stirs the admiration of the reader for his efforts to overcome his circumstances. The extreme realism of Shukri's writings, reproducing the life of hunger, theft, drugs, and prostitution he experienced or observed around him, delayed the publication of his novel in Arabic for many years—the English translation by Paul Bowles, *For Bread Alone* (1973), appeared first. Shukri's collection of short stories *Majnun al-Ward* (1979; Enamored of roses) depicts city life in Morocco with the same harsh realism and a camera-eye technique; the words are even more poignant than the situations they describe, and have a stronger impact on the reader.

The second volume of Shukri's autobiography, *Zaman al-Akhta* (The time of mistakes) was published in 1992; its fourth edition has a different title, *Al-Shuttar* (2000; Streetwise). Abandoning the fictionalized narrative of *For Bread Alone,* Shukri stays closer to reality made vibrant through the use of the present tense, and the forthrightness in speech that characterized his earlier book reappears. Autobiographical information also figures in Shukri's fiction works such as *al-Suq al-Dakhili* (1985; The inner market), where he evokes with his usual blunt and uninhibited style the intimate details of day and night life in Tangier.

Shukri's oeuvre extends beyond the novel. His account of Jean Genet and Tennessee Williams's visit to Tangier was later translated into French by Mohammed el-Ghoulabzouri under the title *Jean Genet et Tennessee Williams à Tangier* (1992). His literary assessment of his contemporary Arab and Western authors (as well as his own work) is found in *Ghiwayat al-Shahrur al-Abyad* (1998; The seduction of the white sparrow). Shukri has also published two plays, *al-Talqa al-Akhira* (1980; The last bullet) and *al-Sa'ada* (1994; Happiness).

See also LITERATURE: ARABIC, NORTH AFRICAN.

Bibliography

Allen, Roger. "Shukri, Muhammad." In *Encyclopedia of Arabic Literature,* edited by Julie Scott Meisami and Paul Starkey. London and New York: Routledge, 1998.

Williams, Malcolm, and Watterson, Gavin, trans. *Anthology of Moroccan Short Stories.* Tangier, Morocco: King Fahd School of Translation, 1995.

AIDA A. BAMIA

SHULTZ, GEORGE

[1920–]

U.S. secretary of state, 1982 to 1989.

George Shultz was born in New York City on 13 December 1920. He earned an economics B.A. from Princeton in 1942, and a Ph.D. from the Massachusetts Institute of Technology (MIT) in 1949. During World War II he joined the Marine Corps Reserve. Shultz pursued an academic career at MIT, as a member of the U.S. Senate staff, and at the University of Chicago. In the late 1960s he started his political career as secretary of labor and then director of the Office of Management and Budget.

While secretary of the treasury in the administration of U.S. president Richard Nixon, George Shultz was confronted with the Oil Crisis. During a business career he established a solid economic knowledge of the Middle East. Following Alexander Haig as the second secretary of state of the administration of Ronald Reagan, Shultz had to tackle the aftermath of the Iranian Revolution and the Israeli invasion within the Lebanese civil war. His time in office as secretary of state was marked by the final stages of the Cold War, from a deterioration of relations up to the beginning of the U.S.–Soviet honeymoon in the short period before the collapse of the Soviet Union.

Despite Israeli–U.S. tensions that flared over the Reagan Plan, which linked Palestinian self-rule with Jordan, and escalated during the Lebanon invasion and the Pollard spy case, bilateral relations between Israel and the United States were largely improved as—due to the political wills of Shultz and Reagan—Israel was declared a strategic ally.

The Iran-Contra Affair and the clandestine U.S. involvement in the anti-Soviet resistance in Afghanistan were not shaped by Shultz. New approaches in engaging an Arab-Israeli peace process were only possible shortly after his term in office, when the end of the Cold War and the Kuwait crisis profoundly reshaped the political landscape of the Middle East.

See also ARAB–ISRAEL WAR (1982); REAGAN, RONALD.

Bibliography

Shultz, George P. *Turmoil and Triumph: My Years as Secretary of State.* New York: Charles Scribner's Sons, 1993.

OLIVER BENJAMIN HEMMERLE

SHUMAYYIL, SHIBLI

[1850–1917]

Syrian medical scholar and intellectual.

Born in Syria to a Christian family, Shibli Shumayyil was one of the first graduates of the Syrian Protestant College's medical school in Beirut. He completed his medical studies in Paris and settled in Egypt to practice medicine and write numerous articles on medicine and on social and scientific theories. He was particularly influenced by Charles Darwin, using the evolutionist's ideas to formulate his ideas on the unity of being and natural laws in human society. He denounced despotism as unnatural and false. Also influenced by the thought of philosophers Herbert Spencer and Ludwig Büchner, Shumayyil criticized nationalism and all forms of exclusive solidarity because they divided human society. He preached universalism and liberalism and so gave measured support to the Young Turk movement. Like his contemporary, the Lebanese Farah Antun, Shumayyil sought the theoretical basis for a secular state that would promote a society where Christians and Muslims would be equal.

Bibliography

Hourani, Albert. *Arabic Thought in the Liberal Age, 1789–1939.* Cambridge, U.K., and New York: Cambridge University Press, 1983.

ELIZABETH THOMPSON

SHUQAYRI, AHMAD

[1908–1980]

Diplomat, activist, and first head of the Palestine Liberation Organization.

Ahmad Shuqayri was a Palestinian born in Tibnin, Lebanon, while his father, the Islamic judge Shaykh As^cad Shuqayri, was living there in exile. Ahmad returned to the family's home town of Acre in 1916. After studies there and in Jerusalem, he entered the American University of Beirut in 1926 but was expelled by French Mandate authorities the following year for Arab nationalist activities. Following his return to Palestine, he studied law and wrote for a newspaper; after graduating from college, he went to work in the law offices of the nationalist figure Awni Abd al-Hadi and became involved in the pan-Arab nationalist Istiqlal Party. During the 1930s,

Shuqayri put his legal skills to work on behalf of Palestinians charged by the British with security offenses. He fled Palestine for Cairo following the end of the Palestine Arab Revolt, returning only at the end of World War II. During the late 1940s, he was appointed head of the Arab Higher Committee's Arab Information Office in Washington and later headed the central Arab Information Office in Jerusalem. He fled to Lebanon during the 1948 fighting.

In exile, Shuqayri rose to become a leading Arab diplomatic figure during the 1950s and early 1960s. He served in the Syrian delegation to the United Nations from 1949 to 1950 before being appointed assistant general secretary of the League of Arab States (Arab League) from 1950 to 1957. He then served the government of Saudi Arabia as minister of state for UN affairs and as its UN representative until he was dismissed in 1963 for disagreeing with the Saudis over Egyptian intervention in the first Yemeni Civil War. Shuqayri began to play a major role in Palestinian nationalist affairs in September 1963, when he was asked to serve as the representative of Palestine at the Arab League. At the Arab summit of January 1964, he was asked to begin investigating the possibility of creating a uniquely Palestinian organization. That February, Shuqayri called for the convening of a Palestine National Council in East Jerusalem. At that meeting the Palestine Liberation Organization (PLO) was created, with Shuqayri as its head. The PLO sought to mobilize Palestinians politically and militarily. It established offices in several Arab countries and worked to raise men to serve in the PLO's fighting force, the Palestine Liberation Army, brigades of which were attached to the armies of Syria, Iraq, and Egypt.

Shuqayri and the PLO remained close to Egyptian president Gamal Abdel Nasser and the Arab regimes. Far from a revolutionary organization, the PLO consisted of conservatives and nationalists willing to work with the regimes in liberating Palestine in coordination with overall Arab strategies toward Israel. Younger Palestinian militants, such as those in the al-Fatah organization, believed instead in a policy of independent, guerrilla-style struggle. Israel's massive defeat of Arab forces during the Arab–Israel War of June 1967 rendered the policies of the Arab states and the PLO bankrupt in the eyes of many Palestinians. For them, Shuqayri's elegant and sometimes heated rhetoric about liberation contrasted starkly with his failure and that of the established Arab elites. Associated with Nasser and the catastrophe of defeat, and facing criticism for his administration of the PLO, Shuqayri resigned on 24 December 1967.

He lived thereafter in Cairo until his opposition to the 1978 Camp David Accords prompted him to leave Egypt and move to Tunisia. He died in Amman, Jordan, while receiving medical treatment there on 25 February 1980, and was buried in the Jordan Valley just across the cease-fire line from his native country.

See also ABD AL-HADI FAMILY; ARAB HIGHER COMMITTEE (PALESTINE); ARAB–ISRAEL WAR (1967); CAMP DAVID ACCORDS (1978); FATAH, AL-; ISTIQLAL PARTY: PALESTINE; LEAGUE OF ARAB STATES; NASSER, GAMAL ABDEL; PALESTINE LIBERATION ORGANIZATION (PLO); PALESTINE NATIONAL COUNCIL; SHUQAYRI FAMILY.

Bibliography

Cobban, Helena. *The Palestinian Liberation Organization: People, Power, and Politics.* Cambridge, U.K.: Cambridge University Press, 1984.

Lesch, Ann Mosely. *Arab Politics in Palestine, 1917–1939: The Frustration of a Nationalist Movement.* Ithaca, NY: Cornell University Press, 1979.

MICHAEL R. FISCHBACH

SHUQAYRI, AS'AD AL-

See SHUQAYRI FAMILY

SHUQAYRI FAMILY

Prominent Palestinian family from Acre.

In the late nineteenth century, the Shuqayris emerged among the elites of Acre, one of the fastest-growing Palestinian cities of the time. They were landowners, Ottoman administrators, and religious officials. The family's prominence continued into the twentieth century. As'ad Shuqayri (1860–1940), mufti of Acre, served on the Shari'a Inquiries Court at Istanbul and as mufti for the Fourth Army during World War I. Opposed to the anti-Zionist movement, As'ad sold several hundred *dunums* of the family's land near Haifa to Zionists in the 1930s.

The family was associated with the Nashashibi-led National Defense party. Another member of the family, Dr. Anwar al-Shuqayri (?–1939), was assassinated by members of the opposing Husayni party in 1939. As'ad's son Ahmad Shuqayri (1908–1980), a lawyer, edited the newspaper *Mir'at al-Sharq* for two years and was a founder of the Istiqlal Party in 1931. In the 1940s Ahmad became known as a feisty nationalist, taking on several leading political roles. In the 1950s he represented Syria and Saudi Arabia at the United Nations and in the 1960s was chosen Palestinian delegate to the Arab League. He founded the Palestine Liberation Organization (PLO) in 1964.

See also ISTIQLAL PARTY: PALESTINE; SHUQAYRI, AHMAD.

Bibliography

Khalaf, Issa. *Politics in Palestine: Arab Factionalism and Social Disintegration, 1939–1948.* Albany: State University of New York Press, 1991.

Mandel, Neville J. *The Arabs and Zionism before World War I.* Berkeley University of California Press, 1976.

Muslih, Muhammad Y. *The Origins of Palestinian Nationalism.* New York: Columbia University Press, 1988.

ELIZABETH THOMPSON

SHURA

A consultative council.

The first recorded *shura* in Islamic history was called by Caliph Umar in 644 to choose his successor. The choice of later caliphs, although usually designated by their predecessor, was customarily ratified by a *shura* of family members and political leaders. The *shura* soon became generalized as an Islamic tradition of leaders consulting members of a community or family and asking them to reach consensus on troublesome issues.

The term *shura* has been used throughout the Middle East in the nineteenth and twentieth centuries to confer traditional legitimacy on a variety of modern representative councils. The Ottomans applied the term to many of the administrative councils created by the nineteenth-century Tanzimat reforms. Political groups in twentieth-century Arab states, particularly around the Gulf, have based their demands for representative bodies on injunctions in the Qur'an that men should conduct their affairs through *shura*, or consultation, with others.

Bibliography

Lapidus, Ira M. *A History of Islamic Societies,* 2d edition. Cambridge, U.K., and New York: Cambridge University Press, 2002.

Peterson, J. E. *The Arab Gulf States: Steps toward Political Participation.* New York: Praeger, 1988.

ELIZABETH THOMPSON

SHUSTER, W. MORGAN

[1877–1960]

Financial adviser to Persia in the early twentieth century.

W. Morgan Shuster, an American publisher, financier, and lawyer, was born in Washington, D.C. After attending Columbia College and Law School, Shuster worked for the War Department and the Cuban Customs Service from 1898 to 1901. He then served in a variety of posts in the Philippines from 1901 to 1909, after which he became a banker. From May 1911 to January 1912, he was treasurer general and financial adviser in Persia (now Iran). In 1915 Shuster became president of the Century Corporation in New York City, a post he held until 1933 when he became the president and chief executive officer of Appleton-Century-Croft. In an effort to rationalize Persia's finances, the Majles (legislature) hired Shuster upon the recommendation of the U.S. State Department and with the consent of Russia. Described by some as lacking in tact and courtesy, Shuster immediately organized a Treasury Gendarmerie to collect taxes, some from prominent Russian officials. Shuster chose Major C. B. Stokes, a devoted friend of Persia and former British military attaché, to head this new treasury police force. The Russian legation opposed this appointment, leading the British to post Stokes to India. Shuster's successful opposition to the Russian-supported restoration of Muhammad Ali as shah earned him additional enmity from that quarter.

The British also viewed Shuster's activities as hostile to Anglo-Russian understandings regarding

Persia, dating from the agreement of 1907. This opposition came to a head in November 1911 when Shuster ordered the confiscation of property owned by the former shah's brother, Shoa al-Saltana, then living in exile in Russia. The Russian consul general, claiming that Saltana's assets were owed to the Russian bank, sent an armed force often Russian-trained Persian cossacks to prevent Shuster from taking control of the property. Shuster responded with a larger force. This led to the Russian demand of 5 November for an apology; Persia apologized, but then Russia demanded Shuster's removal. For a time the Majles rejected this demand, and Persian nationalists attacked Russian troops in Tabriz and Rasht. There was also a boycott of Russian goods and the assassination of a pro-Russian minister. Russia responded with force, hanging a number of nationalists and sending troops to Tehran. In early December, the Majles again rejected the demand of Shuster's removal, but it finally yielded to Russian pressure and that of the powerful Bakhtiari tribe on 20 December. Shuster left Persia in January 1912 to pursue his other interests.

Bibliography

Shuster, W. Morgan. *The Strangling of Persia: A Story of the European Diplomacy and Oriental Intrigue that Resulted in the Denationalization of Twelve Million Mohammedans–A Personal Narrative.* New York: Century, 1912; reprint, Washington, DC: Mage Publishers, 1987.

DANIEL E. SPECTOR

SHUTTLE DIPLOMACY

See GLOSSARY

SIB, TREATY OF (1920)

Treaty between the sultanate and imamate in Oman.

A British-mediated undertaking signed 25 September 1920, by the rival sultanate and imamate governments in Oman. Ending seven years of warfare, it recognized both regimes' mutual autonomy and initiated a peace lasting until 1955. Subsequently, it was used unsuccessfully to justify the creation of a fully independent imamate in Oman's interior.

Bibliography

Landen, Robert G., *Oman since 1856: Disruptive Modernization in a Traditional Arab Society.* Princeton, NJ: Princeton University Press 1967.

ROBERT G. LANDEN

SIDARA

See GLOSSARY

SIDERA, ZINEB

[1963–]

London-based multimedia artist of Algerian origin.

Sidera's video installations and photographic work center on displacement and exile; they draw on her own experience being born in France to immigrant Algerian parents and moving to Britain. She trained at the Slade School of Art, Central Saint Martin's School of Art, and Royal College of Art in England, where she lives and works. Women, the veil, the gaze, and memory are some of the themes that emerge in her artistic exploration of the shifting subject positions that are part of the immigrant and exile experience, especially among Muslim and Arab women living in the West. Like many other artists from Arab countries living in exile, Sidera is particularly concerned with capturing the personal and political paradoxes and contradictions of living within and between cultures and finds the veil a useful way to do so. In many of her works, she examines the ways in which veiling has carried multiple meanings—from the history and legacy of the Algerian encounter with French colonialism to its place within individual and family life. Sidera also explores what she has called "the veiling of the mind"—the process of censorship and self-censorship within individuals and societies. Through photographs of herself veiled and veiling, or photographs of her own gaze (marked off by obscuring the edges of the work as if it were being seen by a veiled viewer), she challenges stereotypes of the submissive veiled woman while at the same time showing how the veil becomes a sign of backwardness and a vehicle of submission. The ambiguous meanings of visible and invisible veiling are a metaphor for her own restless experience of migration and exile, and for the complicated questions she has encountered therein.

See also ALGERIA: OVERVIEW; ART.

Bibliography

Lloyd, Fran, ed. *Contemporary Arab Women's Art: Dialogues of the Present.* London: WAL, 1999.

Lloyd, Fran, ed. *Displacement and Difference: Contemporary Arab Visual Culture in the Diaspora.* London: Saffron Books, 2001.

JESSICA WINEGAR

SIDON

Syrian seaport city.

Sidon (in Arabic, Sayda, Saida, or Sayida) was an ancient Mediterranean seaport city founded by the Phoenicians during the third millennium B.C.E. and ruled in turn by Assyrians, Babylonians, Persians, Alexandrian Greeks, Syrian Seleucids, Egyptian Ptolemys, Romans, Arabs, Crusaders, and Ottomans. Located on the coast of present-day southwestern Lebanon, its name derives from *sayd* (*fishing* in Semitic languages), referring to murex marine snail *(Murex brandaris)* fishing, from which the famous purple dye was extracted. Sidon is mentioned in ancient writings, including the Egyptian Amarna letters, inscriptions in the city of Ugarit, and in Homer's *Iliad.* The city's golden age was during the seventeenth century C.E., under Amir Fakhr al-Din II, when Sidon became a dynastic capital and a center for the dyeing and silk industries. Fakhr al-Din built castles, gardens, and inns to house foreign tradesmen. During this period, religious coexistence among Christians and Muslims was marked, and it is still reflected in Sidon's Great Mosque of Umar and the Maronite church, whose foundations date to Roman times. Rebuilt after a disastrous 1837 earthquake, Sidon remains a commercial, fishing, and agricultural market center for citrus fruit and vegetables. A petroleum refinery plant, light industry, and fishing provide important sources of livelihood for Sidon's 140,000 inhabitants (as of 2000), the majority of whom are Sunni Muslims.

GEORGE E. IRANI
UPDATED BY CHARLES C. KOLB

SIDQI, BAKR

[1885–1937]

Iraqi soldier and government official.

Bakr Sidqi carried out the first military coup in the period between the two world wars in the Arab Middle East. Sidqi fought in the Ottoman army in World War I and joined the Iraqi army in 1921. In August 1933, he gained national prominence as the commander of an army unit that killed some six hundred Assyrian villagers in Sumayl.

Sidqi's ruthlessness and decisiveness in putting down the Rumaytha Rebellion in 1935 served to enhance his prestige further. At the same time, he formed a secret alliance between himself and Yasin al-Hashimi's main rivals, Jamaʿat al-Ahali, the Ahali Group, led principally by Hikmat Sulayman. This culminated in a coup d'état, organized by Sidqi and Sulayman, which forced Yasin's government out of office on 29 October 1936. Sulayman became prime minister and appointed a largely Ahali or pro-Ahali cabinet, while Sidqi remained the power behind the regime. However, Sidqi's dictatorial style gradually lost him the confidence of al-Ahali, most of whom had resigned by May 1937. By this time, Sidqi had also managed to alienate many of his colleagues in the army, who organized his assassination at Mosul in northern Iraq on 11 August 1937.

See also AHALI GROUP; HASHIMI, YASIN AL-; SULAYMAN, HIKMAT.

PETER SLUGLETT

SIDQI, ISMAʿIL

[1875–1949]

Egyptian politician and prime minister.

Ismaʿil Sidqi was born into a bourgeois family in Alexandria. His father was a high government official. Sidqi graduated from the School of Law in Cairo, and began a career in government. He was a colleague of Saʿd Zaghlul, the leader of the Wafd party favoring autonomy for Egypt, and was exiled with the other Wafdists in 1919, but soon broke with Zaghlul and joined the Liberal Constitutionalist party in 1924.

When King Fuʾad dismissed the Wafd government in 1930, Sidqi was asked to form a new government. Sidqi quickly renounced his membership in the Liberal Constitutionalist party, suspended parliament, instituted press censorship, and abrogated the 1923 constitution, replacing it with a more conservative constitution. He next formed his own political party, al-Shaʿb (The People), which he used to run in the 1931 elections. The Wafd and other liberal parties boycotted these elections in protest of Sidqi's autocratic rule. Throughout Sidqi's term as prime minister, there were frequent protest by nationalist politicians demanding the restoration of the 1923 constitution. Sidqi's policies, combined with the effects of the 1929 depression, made his rule very unpopular in Egypt, but the lack of unity among his opponents kept him in office.

By 1933, King Fuʾad felt that he had sufficiently weakened the Wafd and strengthened his own power that he could rule without Sidqi. Sidqi stepped down in September of 1933 and immediately joined the National Front, which called for the reinstatement of the 1923 constitution.

In February of 1946, Sidqi was again invited to form a government, which lasted until December of 1946, when he resigned on the grounds of bad health. During this year, Sidqi conducted negotiations with Britain about troop withdrawals. These negotiations were widely condemned by nationalists, particularly with regard to the threat to Egypt's position in the Sudan.

DAVID WALDNER

SIDRA, GULF OF

A body of water on the coast of Libya.

The Gulf of Sidra is located on the Mediterranean cost of Libya. Its coastline, 310 miles (500 km) of barren desert, forms an important geographical boundary between Libya's two major populated areas: Tripolitania, the western coastal region that shares many historical features with the Maghrib, and Cyrenaica, the eastern coastal region that has been more closely associated with the Arab states of the Middle East. This gulf then provides an important dividing line for the culture of the Maghrib and that of the Mashriq.

See also MAGHRIB.

STUART J. BORSCH

SILK

Fiber taken from the wrapping of silkworm cocoons.

Silk became an important textile product and luxury commodity in the Middle East from antiquity. Silk textiles came into the Middle East by trade from India and China. While Indian and Arab merchants sailed the Indian Ocean, Chinese merchants sent the fine cloth along the famous 4,000 mile (6,400 km) Silk Road—through central Asia and northern Iran to Europe. (Except for a few traders, rarely did any travel more than a short distance of the entire route.)

In the sixth century C.E., the Byzantines smuggled Chinese silk cocoons to Istanbul to begin their own mulberry groves and silkworm industry. Lebanon, Iran, and Iraq cultivated mulberry trees and silkworms as well. Parts of the Ottoman Empire, Bursa and Mount Lebanon, were important centers of silk-cocoon farming, and their fine silk textiles were loomed throughout the empire for both trade and imperial use. In the late nineteenth and early twentieth centuries, many Middle Eastern silk weavers lost their trade because of French intervention during the mandate period and the appearance of increasingly inexpensive silk goods that were being produced in the industrialized nations and in Asia for world markets.

See also OTTOMAN EMPIRE; TEXTILE INDUSTRY; TRADE.

Bibliography

Owen, Roger. *The Middle East in the World Economy, 1800–1914.* London and New York: Methuen, 1981.

Quataert, Donald. "The Silk Industry of Bursa, 1880–1914." In *Contributions à l'histoire economique et sociale de l'empire ottoman.* Louvain, Belgium: Editions Peeters, 1983.

"Silk Route." *Encyclopedia of Asian History.* 4 vols. New York: Scribner; London: Collier Macmillan, 1988.

ELIZABETH THOMPSON

SILVER, ABBA HILLEL
[1893–1963]

American Jewish leader.

Abba Hillel Silver was born in Lithuania. He was brought to the United States as a small child and raised in New York City's Yiddish-speaking immigrant milieu. He later studied at the University of Cincinnati and the Hebrew Union College, the seminary of U.S. Reform Judaism. In 1917, Silver assumed the pulpit of The Temple—Tifereth Israel in Cleveland, Ohio, a position he maintained until his death.

During the 1930s, Silver was among the first U.S. Jewish leaders to denounce the Nazi Party in Germany, and he joined with Rabbi Stephen S. Wise in organizing a countrywide anti-Nazi boycott. With the escalation of violence against the Jews of Central Europe, Silver emerged as a spokesman for U.S. Zionism's militant camp. He publicly challenged the Franklin Roosevelt administration to do more to intervene on behalf of European Jews. After the outbreak of World War II, he emerged as U.S. Zionism's undisputed leader.

Silver brought energy and vigor to Zionist lobbying efforts in Washington, D.C., during the 1940s. He campaigned tirelessly for bipartisan support of a Jewish state in postwar Palestine and skillfully deployed U.S. Jewry's political leverage to advance Zionist interests. His efforts to increase public pressure on the Roosevelt and Harry S. Truman administrations marked a dramatic shift in U.S. Jewish policymaking.

MIA BLOOM
UPDATED BY MARK A. RAIDER

SIMAVI, SEDAT
[1896–1953]

Turkish newspaper and magazine publisher.

Sedat Simavi, born in Istanbul, was the son of a governor of Samsun and was descended on both sides of his family from grand viziers of the Ottoman Empire. After graduating from Galatasaray Lycée, he worked as a teacher for a few years, then in 1917 made two of Turkey's earliest films, *The Claw* and *The Spy*. He began his publishing career in 1916, with magazines like the political-humor weekly *Hande* and, in 1919, the slick, progressive monthly women's magazine *Inci*. Simavi published a variety of popular magazines between 1918 and 1939 on women, fashion, health, humor, and cinema.

Simavi is best known for founding the daily newspaper *Hürriyet*, in 1948. The first of the boulevard-type newspapers, emphasizing slick style, sensation, and personal stories, it reached a circulation of 30,000 in its first year and by the 1950s was Turkey's largest paper (it had supported the winner—the new Democrat party—in the 1950 elections). While *Hürriyet*'s circulation approached 700,000 in the 1970s, it declined in the 1980s to about 450,000, with stiff competition from newer newspapers like Sabah and the Simavi-owned *Günaydin*. After Simavi's death, his son Erol became editor of the paper. With other family members, including grandson Sedat Simavi, he heads a publishing empire that includes several top daily newspapers and magazines.

See also HÜRRIYET.

Bibliography

Özkök, Ertuğrul. "The Turkish Press, 150 Years of Controversy." In *The Transformation of Turkish Culture*, edited by Günsel Renda and C. Max Kortepeter. Princeton, NJ: Kingston Press, 1986.

ELIZABETH THOMPSON

SINAI PENINSULA

Triangular peninsula between the Mediterranean and Red seas.

The Sinai is the desert area of northeast Egypt that forms the land bridge between Africa and Asia. In the north it is a flat and sandy dune sheet. Rugged mountains, including the al-Tih Plateau and Egma Escarpment as well as Sinai Massif surrounding Gabal Musa, dominate the central and southern regions. The peninsula is bordered on the east by the State of Israel and the Gulf of Aqaba and on the west by the Suez Canal and the Gulf of Suez. To the north it is bordered by the Mediterranean and in the south it comes to a point extending into the Red Sea. The Sinai is hot year round: it has average highs of about 90°F (32°C) and average lows of about 60°F (15°C), but temperatures tend to be lower in the mountains of the south.

The term *Sinai* is an ancient one, derived possibly from the name of the Semitic moon god Sin. The peninsula has generally come under Egyptian domination since ancient times. According to the Bible, it was the area in which the Israelites wandered for forty years after their deliverance from slavery in Egypt, and the site of Mount Sinai, where Moses received the Ten Commandments. During the reign of the Byzantine Emperor Justinian (527–565), the Eastern Orthodox Monastery of Saint Catherine was built at the foot of the legendary Mount Sinai, known as Gabal Musa (Mount Moses), in central Sinai. It remains an important attraction for pilgrims and tourists.

During the Middle Ages, the area was settled primarily by nomadic Bedouin tribes and loosely controlled by successive empires. It fell under the Ottoman Turks from 1517 until 1840. After Muhammad Ali broke with the Ottoman Empire, the Treaty of London gave Muhammad Ali control over Egypt, but the Sinai remained under Ottoman administration. The British Colonial Office exerted its own rule over Egypt from 1882 and clashed with the Ottomans over specific areas of the Sinai. They managed to establish the eastern boundary as a line from al-Arish or Rafah to Aqaba. A line from Rafah to Aqaba became the southern boundary of the British Mandate territory of Palestine from 1922 to 1948. It remained the international border between Egypt and the new state of Israel from 1949 through June 1967, when Israel occupied the Sinai. During Israel's occupation, Jewish settlements were established in the Sinai, two major air force bases were constructed, and the Alma Oil Field was discovered and developed.

Under the 1978 Camp David Accords, phased Israeli withdrawals were undertaken in 1980 and 1982. The territory of Sinai was divided between four demilitarized zones, three in Egypt and one on the Israeli side of the border. Under the Egypt-Israel Peace Treaty of 1979, the Multinational Force and Observers (MFO), headquartered in the area of al-Gorah in northeast Sinai, has been established to observe and verify force reductions in the eastern zone, and to ensure free navigation through the Strait of Tiran.

The Sinai is now primarily divided between the two Egyptian governorates of North and South Sinai, with portions of the region abutting the Suez Canal attached to the governorates of Bur Saʿid, Ismailiyya, and Suez. The population of the peninsula was estimated at about 38,000 in 1948, mainly Bedouin; it had grown to about 140,000 by 1970, with the development of petroleum and manganese deposits plus the influx of Palestinian refugees. By 1994 the population of the peninsula had grown to approximately 270,000. Aggressive plans for resettlement and development of the region, most importantly the Salam Canal project in the north, have contributed to a rapidly increasing population base.

Along the northeastern coast of North Sinai is the city of al-Arish, the largest settlement in the Sinai with a population of well over 75,000. Along the southern coasts, several small resorts have emerged as important local centers, including Taba, Nuwayba, and Dahab on the coast of the Gulf of Aqaba, and the port of Sharm al-Shaykh on the Red Sea coast at the extreme southern end of the peninsula. The latter has played host to several high-level negotiations and Middle East summits since the early 1990s. It is also renowned as a diving resort for its spectacular coral reef and variety of tropical fish. The environmental significance of the area was recognized with the creation of nearby Ras Muhammed National Park in 1983.

Bibliography

Greenwood, Ned H. *The Sinai: A Physical Geography.* Austin: University of Texas Press, 1997.

Saad el Din, Mursi; Taher, Ayman; and Romano, Luciano. *Sinai: The Site and the History.* New York: New York University Press, 1998.

Siliotti, Alberto. *Guide to Exploration of the Sinai.* Shrewsbury, U.K.: Swan Hill, 1994.

ELIZABETH THOMPSON
UPDATED BY PAUL S. ROWE

ŞINASI, İBRAHIM

[1826–1871]

Ottoman intellectual.

İbrahim Şinasi's father was an army officer for the Ottoman Empire, and Şinasi himself became an army scribe after completing elementary school. He learned French, and in 1849 he was sent to Europe by the leading Tanzimat reformer, Mustafa Reşid Paşa. There he was influenced by such luminaries as Ernest Renan and Albert Lamartine, but when he returned to Turkey, he was unable to advance in the government and devoted himself to literary endeavors. The author of several plays and books of poetry, he was also a prominent journalist and the editor of *Tasvir-i Efkar* (Description of ideas), which began in 1862 and acted as a clearinghouse for the liberal Young Ottoman ideas then in vogue. Like many of the Young Ottomans, Şinasi found himself at odds with the more autocratic Tanzimat officials of the day, including Ali Paşa and Fuad Paşa, and he was forced to leave Istanbul in 1864. He remained in Paris until his return to Istanbul shortly before his death.

Bibliography

Lewis, Bernard. *The Emergence of Modern Turkey,* 3d edition. New York: Oxford University Press, 2002.

Mardin, Serif. *The Genesis of Young Ottoman Thought: A Study in the Modernization of Turkish Political Ideas.* Princeton, NJ: Princeton University Press, 1962.

Shaw, Stanford J., and Shaw, Ezel Kural. *History of the Ottoman Empire and Modern Turkey.* 2 vols. Cambridge, U.K., and New York: Cambridge University Press, 1976–1977.

ZACHARY KARABELL

ŞIRKET-I HAYRIYE

Nineteenth-century Istanbul ferryboat company for the Bosporus Straits.

This was the first substantial joint-stock company established in the Ottoman Empire. It was founded in 1849 with two thousand shares and sixty thousand Turkish lire in capital with the support of Mustafa Reşid Paşa, one of the leaders of the mid-nineteenth-century reforms called Tanzimat. Created to provide ferry transport on the Bosporus in Istanbul, the company bought its boats for seven thousand Turkish lire each from a British company.

The company was promoted by Reşid Paşa as an example of new economic forms. To demonstrate the security of joint-stock companies, he encouraged several other government officials to invest in the ferryboat firm. Similar companies were soon founded in the 1850s, including the Bank-ı Osmani, the Aydin-İzmir Railroad, and Şirket-i Osmaniyyesi.

Bibliography

Lewis, Bernard. *The Emergence of Modern Turkey,* 3d edition. New York: Oxford University Press, 2002.

ELIZABETH THOMPSON

SIRRY, GAZBIA

[1925–]

Egyptian painter.

Gazbia Sirry (also Jadhbiya Sirri) is one of the most prominent and influential painters in Egypt. Sirry trained at the Faculty of Fine Arts in Cairo and received additional tutelage in Paris under Marcel Gromaire as well as at the Slade School of Art in London. A prolific painter as well as an art educator, she has held more than fifty solo exhibitions, received many prizes both in Egypt and abroad, and established a fund in her name to support young Egyptian artists. Throughout her career, she has been concerned with the fusion of the personal with the social or political, describing her work as embodying her "sensual relationship with color" and her "obsession with the human condition." Sirry was a member of the Group of Modern Art in the 1950s, which adopted the ideology of modernization. Sirry's contribution was to portray nationalist subjects (e.g., martyrdom against British occupation; peasant mothers) in a figurative style inspired by pharaonic representation and also international Expressionism. With the increasing problems of the Nasserist regime and the Arab defeat in the 1967 war, Sirry took on grim subjects such as imprisonment, grief, and racial discrimination. In the 1970s and 1980s, her concerns shifted to crowded urban environments and, in contrast, the sparse landscapes of the desert and the sea. The changes in Sirry's subjects and styles parallel the ebbs and flows in the general outlook of Egyptian intellectuals toward politics and society during her career.

See also EFFLATOUN, INJI; GENDER: GENDER AND EDUCATION.

Bibliography

El-Din, Mursi Saad. *Gazbia Sirry: Lust for Color.* Cairo: American University in Cairo Press, 1998.

Karnouk, Liliane. *Contemporary Egyptian Art.* Cairo: American University in Cairo Press, 1995.

JESSICA WINEGAR

SISCO, JOSEPH

[1919–]

U.S. diplomat at the heart of Henry Kissinger's shuttle diplomacy.

Educated in Illinois, Joseph Sisco gained his Ph.D. (University of Chicago) between periods of service in the army (1941–1945) and in the CIA (1950–1951). From 1951 to 1968 he worked at the State Department on UN affairs, then was appointed assistant secretary for Near East and South Asian affairs in 1968 and undersecretary of state for political affairs in 1974. By that time, Sisco was Secretary of State Henry Kissinger's key adviser on the Middle East, and third in seniority in the State Department. From 1968 to 1976 Sisco played a key role in attempts to mediate between Israel and neighboring Arab states, notably the series of interim peace settlements reached through U.S. *shuttle diplomacy*—a term Kissinger attributed to Sisco underscoring the role of American mediators flying between enemies that refuse to meet.

Sisco had not served in the Middle East and did not speak Arabic, and he began his term as assistant secretary for Near East affairs with a personnel reshuffle that some saw as marginalizing its "Arabist" diplomats. Both Arab and Israeli critics claimed that Sisco's attempts to forge realistic interpretations of UN Resolution 242 were biased, but the shuttles nevertheless proved crucial in the 1974 and 1975 disengagement agreements between Egypt and Israel.

Sisco later became a member of several company and university boards, president of American University, chairman of the American Academy of Diplomacy, and a partner in the management consultancy Sisco Associates. He coauthored a Trilateral Commission report on the peace process in 1981, and was a regular commentator on Mideast policy thereafter.

See also KISSINGER, HENRY.

Bibliography

American Enterprise Institute for Public Policy Research. *Middle East Negotiations: A Conversation with Joseph Sisco.* Washington, DC: Author, 1980.

Kissinger, Henry. *Years of Upheaval.* London: Phoenix, 1982.

Oren, Nissan. *Intellectuals in Politics.* Jerusalem: Magnes Press, 1984.

Sisco, Joseph. "Middle East—Progress or Lost Opportunity?" *Foreign Affairs* 61, 3 (1983): 611–640.

GEORGE R. WILKES

SISTAN AND BALUCHISTAN

Province in the southeast of Iran.

The formerly separate provinces of Sistan and Baluchistan united in 1959 to form one administrative unit (Baluchistan is also a contiguous Pakistani province). The region is fertile but has a hot, arid climate. The Helmand is the principal river and the source for agriculture in the region. Major cities include Zahedan (the capital), Zabol, and Iranshahr. Although each province has a separate but intertwined history, the ethnic groups residing in each are distinct. The population of Baluchistan is composed mainly of Baluchi tribespeople who speak Baluchi, a western Iranian language now heavily influenced by eastern regional languages. Standard Persian is more common in Sistan, but the eastern language known as Sistani is still spoken to some extent. According to the 1996 census, the population of the combined province was 1,722,579.

See also BALUCHISTAN.

Bibliography

Barthold, W. *An Historical Geography of Iran,* edited by C. E. Bosworth, translated by Svat Soucek. Princeton, NJ: Princeton University Press, 1984.

PARVANEH POURSHARIATI

SISTANI, ALI AL-

[1930–]

Leading Shiʿite cleric in Iraq.

The most senior Shiʿite cleric in Iraq by early 2004, Ali al-Husayni al-Sistani is actually an Iranian who, despite having lived in Iraq for decades, speaks Arabic with a heavy Persian accent. Al-Sistani was born in Mashhad, Iran, to a family of well-known Shiʿite religious figures. His father was Mohammad Baqir, and his grandfather was a famous cleric known as Sayyid Ali. Al-Sistani studied theology in Qom, Iran, and first traveled to al-Najaf, Iraq, in 1951 to continue his studies. He lived in al-Najaf for most of the rest of his life.

By 1960 he had been certified as a *mujtahid,* one of the few Shiʿa permitted to interpret Islamic practice. Al-Sistani eventually obtained the rank of grand ayatullah *(ayatullah uzma).* After the death of Grand Ayatullah Abu al-Qasim al-Kho'i (1899–1992) in 1992, al-Sistani was the unquestioned leading Shiʿite in Iraq. He also became the sold surviving *marja al-taqlid* (source of imitation) for Shiʿa worldwide.

The breakdown of security in Iraq following the American invasion in March 2003 led to the death of two potential rivals for influence among Iraq's Shiʿa. Ayatullah Muhammad Baqir al-Hakim (1939–2003), leader of the Supreme Council for the Islamic Revolution in Iraq, returned from two decades of exile in Iran only to be killed in a massive bombing in al-Najaf in August 2003. Another potential rival was killed earlier in April 2003: Abd al-Majid al-Kho'i (1962–2003), son of the Grand Ayatullah Abu al-Qasim al-Kho'i.

The clear leading figure among Iraqi Shiʿa by late 2003, al-Sistani was in a position to influence the United States' attempt to politically reconstruct the country. Unlike some of his contemporaries, including Iran's late Ayatollah Ruhollah Khomeini, with whom he studied when they were both young, al-Sistani called for maintaining the separation of politics and religion. Although he made it clear that he wanted U.S. forces to leave the country as soon as possible, he urged the Shiʿa not to resist them. Since then he has pointedly refused to meet with U.S. government representatives, but has granted audiences to others from his secluded residence. It was his opinion that prompted the U.S. to allow the UN a greater role in Iraq's reconstruction as well as to allow a constitution to be written prior to elections (which he urged be held as soon as possible). Al-Sistani's influence was also what prompted a last-minute delay in the signing of the new, interim Iraqi constitution in early March 2004.

See also KHOMEINI, RUHOLLAH; MARJA AL-TAQLID; NAJAF, AL-; QOM; WAR IN IRAQ (2003).

MICHAEL R. FISCHBACH

SITRA

One of the thirty-three islands in the Bahrain archipelago.

Sitra lies in the Persian (Arabian) Gulf, just off the northeast corner of Bahrain, the main island, to which it is connected by a short bridge. On Sitra are located the petroleum loading terminal and tank farm belonging to the Bahrain Petroleum Company, as well as a small number of date palm gardens and a limited amount of cropland at the northern end of its eleven square miles (28 sq. km).

Bibliography

Clarke, Angela. *The Islands of Bahrain: An Illustrated Guide to Their Heritage.* Manama: Bahrain Historical and Archaeological Society, 1981.

FRED H. LAWSON

SITT

See GLOSSARY

SIVAS CONFERENCE (1919)

Convened (4–11 September 1919) to resist plans of the Triple Entente to dismember the Ottoman Empire; a significant step in the progression of events leading to the Turkish revolution.

The official communiqué issued by the Sivas Conference was the first Turkish declaration against the partitioning of lands under Ottoman sovereignty that had taken place when the Mudros Armistice was signed. The same document summoned the sultan to call for a general election and announced the creation of the Association for the Defense of the Rights of Anatolia and Rumelia, whose Representative Committee was designated to act as a provisional government in Anatolia until May 1920.

AHMET KUYAS

SIWA OASIS

Oasis in northwest Egypt.

The Siwa oasis, 186 miles (300 km) west of Marsa Matruh, had an estimated population of 23,000 in 2002. In ancient times Siwa was the seat of the oracle of Jupiter Ammon, visited by Alexander the Great in 331 B.C.E. It has historically served as both Egypt's western boundary and the easternmost area inhabited by Berbers. The spoken Siwan dialect is a Berber language heavily influenced by Arabic. In the nineteenth century it was one of the centers of the Sanusi Order, and some fighting took place there during World War I. The people of Siwa pride themselves on their differences from other Egyptians and their ability to resolve disputes without resort to bloodshed. The oasis is a center for date palm agriculture. Formerly isolated, it has become accessible by motor transport and is now being developed for tourism. Siwa is also the name of a town in the southern part of the oasis.

See also SANUSI ORDER.

Bibliography

Fakhry, Ahmed. *Siwa Oasis.* Cairo: American University in Cairo Press, 1990.

Sears, Constance S. "The Oasis of Siwa: Visited and Revisited." *Newsletter of the American Research Center in Egypt* 165 (spring/summer 1994): 1–10.

Souryal, Sam S. "Social Control in the Oasis of Siwa: A Study in Natural Justice and Conflict Resolution." *International Criminal Justice Review* 11 (2001): 82–103.

Vivian, Cassandra. *Siwa Oasis: Its History, Sites, and Crafts.* Ma'adi, Egypt, 1991.

ARTHUR GOLDSCHMIDT

SLAVE TRADE

The buying and selling of humans for servitude was an old tradition in the Middle East as in many other parts of the world.

Since antiquity, slavery was an integral part of the various societies that inhabited the Middle East. Men, women, and children were enslaved within these lands or imported into them from neighboring and faraway regions. From the early sixteenth to the early twentieth centuries, the Middle East was part of the Ottoman Empire, in which slavery was legal and the slave trade active. The traffic in slaves was substantially reduced toward the end of the nineteenth century, and slavery died out in most of the Middle East during the first decade of the twentieth. In certain parts of Arabia, the practice lingered on well into the second half of this century, and various forms of slavery continue to exist even today.

"Slavery" in Middle Eastern—and other—societies can be difficult to define. Some attempts to answer the question "who is a slave?" have resulted in "one whose labor is controlled and whose freedom is withheld," a person "in a state of legal and actual servility or [who is] of slave origins," or a "natally alienated and generally dishonored person" under "permanent, violent domination." In Islamic legal terms, slavery grants one person ownership over another person, which means that the owner has rights to the slave's labor, property, and sexuality and that the slave's freedoms are severely restricted. But in sociocultural terms, slavery sometimes meant high social status, or political power, for male slaves in the military and bureaucracy (Mamluks and *kuls*) and female slaves in elite harems. Even ordinary domestic slaves were often better fed, clothed, and protected than many free men and women. In any event, slavery was an important, albeit involuntary, channel of recruitment and socialization into the elite and a major—though forced—means of linking into patronage networks.

Slavery gradually became a differentiated and broadly defined concept in many Islamic societies since the introduction of military slaves into the Abbasid Caliphate in the ninth century. In the Ottoman Empire, military-administrative servitude, better known as the *kul* system, coexisted with other types of slavery: harem (quite different from Western fantasy), domestic, and agricultural (on a rather limited scale). While the latter types of slavery remained much the same until late in the nineteenth century, the *kul* system underwent profound changes.

From its inception, the *kul* system was nourished on periodical levies of the unmarried, able-bodied, male children of the sultan's Orthodox Christian subjects, mostly from the Balkans. This child levy was known as the *devşirme.* The children were reduced to slavery, converted to Islam, and rigorously socialized at the palace school into various government roles, carrying elite status. However, freeborn Muslims gradually entered government service, and the *kul* system evolved to accommodate this change. Ultimately, the child levy was abandoned during the seventeenth century, the palace school lost its monopoly on the reproduction of military-administrative slaves, and a new, *kul*-type recruitment-cum-socialization pattern came to prevail.

With the evolution of the *kul* system, the classification of *kuls* as slaves was gradually becoming irrelevant. Ottoman officials of *kul* origins and training held elevated, powerful positions with all rights, privileges, and honors, and cases in which the sultan confiscated their property or took their life became increasingly rare. Whereas *kuls* and non-*kuls* were subject to the sultan's "whims" to the same extent, the intimacy and mutual reliance of the master-slave relationship often provided the *kul* with greater protection than that enjoyed by free officials. Harem women of slave origins were in much the same predicament, playing a major role in the reproduction of the Ottoman elite. Toward the nineteenth century, the servility of persons in the *kul*/harem category becomes more a symbol of their high status and less a practical or legal disability. All that has led some scholars to question the very use of the term "slaves" for such men and women. In any event, the Hatt-i Serif of Gülhane of 1839 freed government officials from the last vestiges of servility attached to their status.

In the Ottoman Middle East, and with local modifications also in other Muslim societies, there was a continuum of various degrees of servility rather than a dichotomy between slave and free. At one end of that continuum were domestic and agricultural slaves, the "real slaves" in Ottoman society, while at the other were officeholders in the army and bureaucracy, with little to tie them to actual slavery. In between, but close to officeholders and far from domestic and agricultural slaves, came officials of slave origins (*kul*-type) and then harem ladies of slave origins.

The overwhelming majority of the slaves living in the Middle East during the Ottoman period were female, black, and domestic; they served in menial jobs in households across a broad social spectrum. A smaller number of white female slaves also worked in similar circumstances, as did a number of black and white male slaves. African male slaves were employed in the Red Sea, Persian/Arabian Gulf, and Indian Ocean as pearl divers, oarsmen, and crew members in sailboats, in Arabia as agricultural laborers (in date, coffee, and other plantations) and outdoor servants, and in Egypt as cotton pickers in the 1860s. African men were used as soldiers in scattered instances in Yemen and other parts of Arabia, as in Egypt where the experiment of Muhammad Ali Pasha to recruit Sudanese slave soldiers failed. *Kul* and harem slaves were a relatively small minority among Middle Eastern slaves in the nineteenth century.

At the time, a fairly steady stream of about eleven thousand to thirteen thousand slaves per year entered the region from central Africa and the Sudan, from western Ethiopia, and from Circassia, Abkhazia, and Georgia. They were brought in by caravan and boat via the Sahara desert routes, the Ethiopian plateau, the Red Sea, the Nile river valley, the Mediterranean, the Persian Gulf, the Black Sea, and the pilgrimage routes to and from Arabia. After raids, sales, and resales, they reached their final destinations in the great urban centers of the Middle East, where they were sold in markets or in private homes of slave dealers.

Whereas slaveholding was still legal at the beginning of the twentieth century, the slave trade into the region had already been prohibited by law for several decades. The traffic in Africans and Caucasians practically died down, although it would pick up from time to time on a small scale. Slavery was gradually being transformed into free forms of service-cum-patronage, such as raising freeborn children (mostly female) in the household, socializing them into lower- or upper-class roles—as talent and need determined—and later marrying them off and setting them up in life. Ottoman elite culture was articulating a negative attitude toward the practice and gradually disengaging from it on moral grounds. This was a significant development, given the fact that slavery enjoyed Islamic legitimacy and wide social acceptance in the Middle East and that, except for cases of cruelty and ill-usage, it was a matter over which no serious moral debate ever arose.

The profound change that occurred was part of a major reform program introduced into the Middle East during the nineteenth century. Much of this happened during the Tanzimat (loosely covering the 1830s to the 1880s), generally regarded as a period of change in many areas of Ottoman life, although it is not certain how deeply the reforms affected the over-whelming majority of the population or even the peripheral groups within the Ottoman elite. Visible changes in the army, the bureaucracy, the economy, law and justice, education, communication, transportation, and public health went along with the reinvigoration of central authority. This was the work of a strongly motivated, Ottoman-centered group of reformers, who implemented their own program and political agenda and were not merely the tools of Western influence. While the government came to possess more efficient means of repression, its reforms also sowed the seeds of political change, giving rise to a strong constitutional movement, although the extent to which Western ideas—not just technology and fashion—were assimilated into Middle Eastern culture is still under debate.

Having abolished slavery by the end of the first third of the nineteenth century, the powers of Europe now turned their zeal to slavery in the Americas. But in the 1840s, the British government and public opinion were already beginning to take an interest in the abolition of slavery in the Ottoman Middle East. Attempts to induce Istanbul to adopt measures to that effect soon proved futile. Instead—and as an alternative method that would ultimately choke slavery for want of supply—a major effort was launched to suppress the slave trade into the region. The essence of that long-term British drive was to extract from the Ottomans, on humanitarian grounds, edicts forbidding the trade in Africans and Caucasians. The implementation of such edicts was then carefully monitored by British diplomatic and commercial representatives throughout the Middle East and reported back to London. In turn, London would press Istanbul to enforce the edicts, and so on.

This pattern yielded the prohibition of the slave trade in the Gulf in 1847, the temporary prohibition of the traffic in Circassians and Georgians in 1854–1855, the general prohibition of the African slave trade in 1857, the Anglo-Egyptian convention for the suppression of the slave trade in 1877, and the Anglo-Ottoman one in 1880. The campaign reached its climax in the Brussels Act against the slave trade, which the Ottoman government signed in 1890. From the mid-1850s onward, Caucasian slavery and slave trade were excluded from the realm of Anglo-Ottoman relations. In that area, the Ottomans initiated some major changes, acting alone and according to their own views.

One of the most important factors that shaped Ottoman policy toward Caucasian slavery was the large number of Circassian refugees—estimates run from 500,000 to 1 million—who entered Ottoman territory from the mid-1850s to the mid-1860s. That Russian-forced migration contained about 10 percent unfree agricultural population, which put the question of non-African slavery into a different perspective. Increased tensions between refugee owners and slaves, at times causing violence and disturbance of public order, induced the Ottoman government in 1867 to design a special program for slaves who wished to obtain their freedom. Using an Islamic legal device, the government granted the slaves the land they were cultivating in order to purchase manu-mission from their own masters.

In 1882, the authorities moved further in the same method to facilitate the conscription of Circassian and Georgian slaves. Such a step was necessary because only free men could be drafted into the army. Measures were also taken from the mid-1860s onward to restrict the traffic in Circassian and Georgian children, mostly young girls. Thus, by the last decade of the nineteenth century, the trade in Caucasian slaves was considerably reduced. The remaining demand was maintained only by the harems of the imperial family and the households of well-to-do elite members. The imperial harem at the time contained about 400 women in a wide array of household positions quite different from those consigned to them by Western fantasy. Those harems also continued to employ eunuchs, and as late as 1903, the Ottoman family alone owned 194 of them. In the nineteenth century, a perceived decline occurred in their political influence, both as individuals and as a distinct corps in court politics. Whether officially abolished by the 1908 revolution, or only later by the new Turkish republic, Ottoman slavery died piecemeal, not abruptly, with the end of the empire.

Except for the issue of equality for non-Muslims, the call for the abolition of slavery was perhaps the most sensitive and culturally loaded topic processed in the Tanzimat period. Although it was rarely debated in the open, this was a matter of daily and personal concern, for both the public and private spheres of elite life were permeated by slaves on all levels. Faced with British diplomatic pressure to suppress the slave trade into the Middle East and with the zeal of Western abolitionism, Ottoman reformers and thinkers responded on both the political and the ideological planes. However, that response came when slavery was already on the wane, doomed to disappear with other obsolete institutions.

See also MAMLUKS; TANZIMAT.

Bibliography

Baer, Gabriel. "Slavery and Its Abolition." In *Studies in the Social History of Modern Egypt,* by Gabriel Baer. Chicago: University of Chicago Press, 1969.

Lewis, Bernard. *Race and Slavery in the Middle East: An Historical Enquiry.* New York: Oxford University Press, 1990.

Peirce, Leslie P. *The Imperial Harem: Women and Sovereignty in the Ottoman Empire.* New York: Oxford University Press, 1993.

Toledano, Ehud R. "The Imperial Eunuchs of Istanbul: From Africa to the Heart of Islam." *Middle Eastern Studies* 20, no. 3 (1984): 379–390.

Toledano, Ehud R. "Ottoman Concepts of Slavery in the Period of Reform (1830s to 1880s)." In *Breaking the Chains: Slavery, Bondage and Emancipation in Modern Africa and Asia,* edited by Martin A. Klein. Madison: University of Wisconsin Press, 1993.

Toledano, Ehud R. *The Ottoman Slave Trade and Its Suppression, 1840–1890.* Princeton, NJ: Princeton University Press, 1982.

Toledano, Ehud R. "Slave Dealers, Women, Pregnancy, and Abortion: The Story of a Circassian Slave-Girl in Mid-Nineteenth-Century Cairo." *Slavery and Abolition* 2, no. 1 (1980): 53–68.

EHUD R. TOLEDANO

SMILANSKY, MOSHE

[1874–1953]

Israeli author, peace advocate, and agricultural pioneer.

Moshe Smilansky was born in Kiev province in Russian Ukraine to a family of farmers. He emigrated to Palestine in 1891 and helped to found the Hadera settlement, farming in various places before settling in Rehovot in 1893. There he spent the remainder of his life as a citrus plantation owner, writer, and agricultural leader (heading the Histadrut ha-Ikarim, or Farmers' Association). A disciple of Ahad Ha-Am, he took issue with Theodor Herzl's political Zionism and sought coexistence with Arabs throughout his career, gaining prominence among the binationalists after the 1936 Arab uprising.

Smilansky's Hebrew stories depicting Arab life, written under the pseudonym Khawaja Musa, were collected in a single volume entitled *Benei Arav* (1964; Arab sons). Through his writing, Smilansky hoped to show the benefits of cooperation between Arabs and Jewish pioneers. His most famous works on the pioneers are the six-volume *Perakim be-Toledot ha-Yishuv* (1959; Chapters in the history of the Yishuv) and the four-volume *Mishpahat ha-Adamah* (1943–1953; Family of the soil). His works were highly criticized at the time, but have had greater impact on students of Hebrew literature since. His son is the noted writer S. Yizhar.

Bibliography

Domb, Risa. "The Arab in Fact and Fiction as Reflected in the Works of Moshe Smilansky (1874–1953)." *Jewish Quarterly* 29, no. 4 (1982): 3–7.

Ramras-Rauch, Gila. *The Arab in Israeli Literature.* Bloomington: Indiana University Press, 1989.

ANN KAHN
UPDATED BY GEORGE R. WILKES

SNEH, MOSHE

[1909–1972]

Israeli politician and statesman.

Born in Poland where he became an active Zionist, Moshe Sneh emigrated to Israel in 1940. He was active against British anti-Zionist policy, and was chief of the Haganah high command from 1941 to 1946. Between 1945 and 1946 Sneh was a member of the Jewish Agency's executive committee, but he resigned in 1946 when they decided to refrain from further sabotage against the British occupation forces in Palestine. He served as director of the Jewish Agency's European office from 1946 to 1947. Sneh was also a physician active in the Zionist movement in its early years, and later in the MAPAM party. From 1949 to 1965 he was a member of the Knesset from Maki, the Israeli communist party, and editor of its daily newspaper. In the Knesset Sneh advocated self-determination for the Palestinian nation and recognition of Palestinian rights to a state of their own. After being out of the Knesset from 1965 to 1969 he was reelected in 1969 and served until his death in 1972.

See also ISRAEL: POLITICAL PARTIES IN.

Bibliography

Ben-Gurion, David. *Israel: A Personal History.* New York: Funk and Wagnalls, 1971.

WALTER F. WEIKER
UPDATED BY GREGORY S. MAHLER

SOBOL, YEHOSHUA

[1939–]

Israeli playwright.

The plays of Yehoshua Sobol reflect common Israeli themes, including the Holocaust, the Zionist state-building enterprise, and the Arab-Israel conflict. A graduate of the Sorbonne in Paris, Sobol has worked as artistic director of the Haifa Municipal Theater since 1984, and most of his plays have premiered there. His most famous work is *Ghetto* (1984), one of three related plays about the Vilna ghetto. Other works include *Soul of a Jew* (1982), *The Days to Come* (1971), and *Shooting Magda,* or *The Palestinian Girl* (1985). Sobol has made it his artistic mission to explore the problematic roots of the Zionist project, as he did most forcefully in his 1977 production, *Night of the Twentieth,* and to show the consequences for both Jews and Arabs of succumbing to political interests rather than fulfilling nationalist ideals. Many of his later plays, such as *Kefar* (1996), have also probed the difficulties of trying to assimilate personal lives into paradigms created by historical developments. Looking at history as a way of examining contemporary Israeli society, Sobol is particularly interested in the intersection between the personal—even the emotional—and the political. His plays emphasize that while Zionist ideals could not extinguish personal desires, they did complicate the formation of strong, secure individual identities. *Almah* (1999) extends his focus on individual personality by meditating on the life of Alma Mahler Gropius Werfel and her torturous efforts to form an authentic, creative public life. Sobol's plays, always sensitive to the morally problematic compromises imposed upon by history and circumstance, have been produced all over the world and in many languages.

Bibliography

Abramson, Glenda. *Drama and Ideology in Modern Israel.* Cambridge, U.K.: Cambridge University Press, 1998.

Ben-Zvi, Linda, ed. *Theater in Israel.* Ann Arbor: University of Michigan Press, 1996.

Sobol, Yehoshua. *Ghetto,* translated from the Hebrew by Miriam Shlesinger. Tel Aviv: Institute for the Translation of Hebrew Literature, 1986.

Taub, Michael. *Israeli Holocaust Drama.* Syracuse, NY: Syracuse University Press, 1996.

Taub, Michael. *Modern Israeli Drama in Translation.* Portsmouth, NH: Heinemann, 1992.

JULIE ZUCKERMAN
UPDATED BY DONNA ROBINSON DIVINE

SOCIAL DEMOCRATIC PARTY OF AZERBAIJAN

Political party in Iranian Azerbaijan.

The Firqa-ye Ijtimaʿiyun-e Ammiyun (Social democratic party), also called *Mujahid,* was active mainly in Iranian Azerbaijan. It may have been an offshoot of the Adalat (Justice) party, a nominally social democratic, but actually anticolonial, organization formed in 1904/05 by Azerbaijanis in Baku (on the Caspian Sea) who were involved in the social democratic party Hümmet (Endeavor). Adalat was created for workers from Iran employed in the Baku petroleum industry.

In August or September 1906, members of the founding committee of the party established a "secret center" in Tabriz, then cells in Ardebil, Rasht, and Enzeli; these organizations apparently remained under the direction of a central committee in Baku. The party program demanded a constitution in Iran, ministerial responsibility to the Majles (Iran's legislature), establishment of universal suffrage, and civil liberties. It pointed to Qurʾanic precedents and the example of "every civilized state of Europe and Asia."

The party was apparently suppressed around 1909 but served as a model to the later Communist Tudeh Party.

See also ADALAT PARTY; TUDEH PARTY.

Bibliography

Bayat, Mangol. *Iran's First Revolution: Shiʿism and Constitutional Revolution of 1905–1909.* New York: Oxford University Press, 1991.

Swietochowski, Tadeusz, and Collins, Brian C. *Historical Dictionary of Azerbaijan.* Lanham, MD: Scarecrow Press, 1999.

AUDREY L. ALTSTADT

SOCIAL DEMOCRATIC POPULIST PARTY

Center-left political party in Turkey, 1985 to 1998.

The Social Democratic Populist Party (Sosyal Demokrat Halkçi Partisi, or SHP) was formed in November 1985 as a result of the merger of two left-of-center parties, the Social Democratic Party (SDP), founded in 1983 by Erdal İnönü, and Necdet Calp's Populist Party, which also was founded in 1983. In the parliamentary elections of November 1983 the Populist Party had won the second largest number of seats in the Turkish Grand National Assembly. The SDP had been banned from participating in those elections, but the National Security Council did allow it take part in the 1984 local elections, and it emerged at the local level as the main opposition to the ruling Motherland Party of Turgut Özal. The Populist Party received less than 10 percent of the vote in the local elections and thus won no seats on the municipal councils, although it remained the main opposition to the Motherland Party within the National Assembly. Because they espoused a similar political ideology and appealed to the same voting constituency, the two parties joined to form the SHP. İnönü became the chair of the SHP, which presented itself as an heir to the Republican People's Party (CHP), which had been founded by his father, İsmet İnönü, and Mustafa Kemal Atatürk. In the 1991 parliamentary elections the SHP emerged as the third largest party in the National Assembly, with 88 seats. Subsequently, it joined with the True Path Party of Süleyman Demirel as the junior partner in a coalition government. The SHP's participation in this coalition became controversial because a small group of SHP deputies charged that the True Path Party sanctioned civil-rights abuses, especially in the Kurdish areas, and that these violations compromised democratic practices and also Turkey's chances for membership in the European Union. Most prominent among these dissidents was Deniz Baykal, who left the SHP in 1992 and announced that he was reactivating the CHP. Although several of its deputies in parliament defected to the CHP, the SHP remained in the coalition government until the 1996 parliamentary elections, when it lost many seats. Subsequently, the SHP entered into negotiations with the CHP and merged with it following the February 1997 "soft coup" by the military against the Refah Party–dominated coalition government of Prime Minister Necmeddin Erbakan.

See also ATATÜRK, MUSTAFA KEMAL; DEMIREL, SÜLEYMAN; ERBAKAN, NECMEDDIN; İNÖNÜ, ERDAL; MOTHERLAND PARTY; NATIONAL SECURITY COUNCIL (TURKEY); ÖZAL, TURGUT; REFAH PARTISI; REPUBLICAN PEOPLE'S PARTY (RPP); TRUE PATH PARTY; TURKISH GRAND NATIONAL ASSEMBLY.

Bibliography

Hooglund, Eric. "Government and Politics." In *Turkey: A Country Study,* edited by Helen Chapin Metz. Washington, DC: GPO for Library of Congress, 1996.

FRANK TACHAU
UPDATED BY M. HAKAN YAVUZ

SOCOTRA

Largest island of Yemen.

Measuring 1,200 square miles, Socotra (also Suqutra) Island is located in the Arabian Sea, about 500 miles from Aden and less than 200 miles from Somalia. The sparsely populated island has a mountainous interior and most of its population engages in farming or fishing; the most striking feature of this isolated place is its biodiversity and the great number of unique flora and fauna. The ruler of the Mahra Sultanate of Qishn and Socotra resided there under British rule during much of the nineteenth and twentieth centuries. The island became a part of South Yemen in 1967 and, with Yemeni unification in 1990, it became a part of the Republic of Yemen (ROY). Given its location near the sea lanes, Socotra was long thought to be of strategic value by Western imperial powers. During the latter half of the Cold War, South Yemen allowed the Soviet Union to maintain a submarine base and other military facilities there; Russia continues to maintain a modest naval presence. During the late 1990s there were rumors about a deal between the United States and the ROY over military facilities on the island, but the complicated, if not strained, relations between the two countries, beginning with the bombing of the U.S.S. *Cole* in Aden in 2000, squelched this talk. The considerable activities regarding Socotra now focus on its development as a tourist destination featuring and protecting its unique biodiversity.

See also YEMEN.

Bibliography

Miller, Anthony G., and Morris, M. J. *An Ethnoflora of the Socotra Archipelago.* Edinburgh: Royal Botanic Garden, 2004.

Wranik, Wolfgang. *A Field Guide to the Fauna of the Socotra Archipelago.* Rostock, Ger.: University of Rostock, 2004.

ROBERT D. BURROWES

SOHEYLI, ALI

[?–1954]

Iranian politician.

Ali Soheyli was born in Tabriz and studied at the military school in Tehran. After several cabinet positions, he was named minister of foreign affairs in 1937 and served three times as prime minister during the tenure of Mohammad Reza Shah Pahlavi. In 1947, because of pressure from the parliamentary faction loyal to Mohammad Mossadegh, Soheyli, a royalist, was put on trial. He was charged with mishandling of public funds, illegal intervention in elections in the south of the country, disrespect for the constitutional provision of free speech and a free press, and conspiracy against the nationalist government. After being acquitted of all charges, Soheyli resumed political activity as a minister without portfolio. Famous for his skill in handling foreign diplomats in Iran, he enjoyed amicable relations with both the Russian and the British legations in Tehran. In 1953, he sought appointment as prime minister but failed to get it. The shah appointed him ambassador to Britain, where he died of leukemia.

See also MOSSADEGH, MOHAMMAD; PAHLAVI, MOHAMMAD REZA.

NEGUIN YAVARI

SOKOLOW, NAHUM

[1859–1936]

Hebrew journalist, author, Zionist diplomat and leader.

Born and educated in Poland, Nahum Sokolow was a journalist for the Hebrew language newspaper *ha-Tzfira,* becoming editor in 1885. Sokolow published numerous books on the sciences, Hebrew literature, and the historical roots of Zionism, among other topics, writing in six languages. He was a strong supporter of Theodor Herzl and a principal spokesman for Zionism in eastern Europe. He was appointed secretary-general of the World Zionist Organization (WZO) in 1906, whereupon he established the WZO's official newspaper, *ha-Olam.*

In 1911 Sokolow was given the political portfolio on the Zionist Executive, and he traveled extensively as a diplomat for the Zionist cause, meeting with leaders throughout Europe and with Arab leaders in Lebanon and Syria. He chaired the committee that drafted the Balfour Declaration in 1917, and in 1919 led the Zionist delegation to the Paris Peace Conference. In 1929 he became chairman of the expanded Zionist Executive. At the 17th Zionist Congress in 1931, Chaim Weizmann was defeated in his reelection bid for the presidency of the WZO after a bitter challenge from Vladimir Jabotinsky and the Revisionists. Sokolow, a broadly respected Zionist leader, took Weizmann's place and was reelected president at the 18th Congress in 1933. When the Revisionists withdrew from the WZO in 1935, Weizmann resumed the presidency. Sokolow died in London the following year.

See also BALFOUR DECLARATION (1917); WEIZMANN, CHAIM; WORLD ZIONIST ORGANIZATION (WZO).

Bibliography

Laqueur, Walter. *A History of Zionism.* New York: Schocken, 2003.

PIERRE M. ATLAS

SOLTANI, ABDELLATIF

[1904–1983]

Islamic religious scholar in Algeria.

Shaykh Abdellatif Soltani was a highly respected, independent religious scholar and a staunch critic of the socialist orientation of the postindependence Algerian regime. Soltani was born in 1904 in Biskra, northeast of Algiers, and received a religious education at the Zaytouna mosque in Tunisia. He became closely associated with the Islamic reformer Abdelhamid Ibn Badis, the founder of the Association of Algerian Scholars, which was established in 1931 to promote Arabic and Islamic teachings and to reassert the Algerian identity. Soltani worked as an educator and as an imam in a number of mosques that became bastions of Islamic activism. He taught religious subjects to young Algerians, some of whom later became leaders of the Islamic Salvation Front, the main Islamic opposition party in Algeria.

In 1974 Soltani published a book, *Mazdaqism Is the Origin of Socialism,* that was published in Morocco and banned in Algeria, in which he scathingly criticized the country's ruling elite and secular intellectuals for their deviation from the true Islamic principles and for their adoption instead of foreign ideologies. He also criticized the regime for its intolerance of dissent and defended the country's scholars against attempts to marginalize them. His other two books were *Arrows of Islam* and *Toward Islamic Doctrine.*

Following the eruption of violent clashes in 1982 between Islamist and communist students at the main campus of the University of Algiers, Soltani, along with Abbasi al-Madani and Ahmed Sahnoun, issued a statement, "The Statement of Advice," in which they criticized the secular policies of the state and demanded the promotion of Islam in government and society. Soltani was placed under house arrest until his death in 1983.

See also ALGERIA; ARABIZATION POLICIES; BENDJEDID, CHADLI; BOUYALI, MOUSTAFA; FRONT DE LIBERATION NATIONALE (FLN); FRONT ISLAMIQUE DU SALUT (FIS); SAHNOUN, AHMED.

Bibliography

Shahin, Emad Eldin. *Political Ascent: Contemporary Islamic Movements in North Africa.* Boulder, CO: Westview Press, 1998.

EMAD ELDIN SHAHIN

SOMIKH, ABDULLAH
[1813–1880]

Iraqi rabbi.

Somikh, one of the most venerated rabbinic authorities in Baghdad in the nineteenth century, was instrumental in renewing Jewish religious studies in that city. In 1840 he established its first modern rabbinic seminary, Bet Zilkha. He wrote a commentary on Shulhan Arukh and a number of volumes of responsa that often addressed problems arising from the incursion of technology and modern education into the life of the Mizrahi (Jews of Middle Eastern, North African, and Western Asian origin) —for instance, whether a telegraphic message can be used as evidence in a Torah court. Somikh often dealt with religious questions addressed to him by Iraqi Jews who had settled in India, China, and other Far Eastern nations. In the 1860s, when the Alliance Israélite Universelle was established in Baghdad, he sent his son to study there, ignoring the protestations of conservative rabbis who strongly disapproved of secular education. Somikh died in Baghdad during a plague epidemic.

See also ADOT HA-MIZRAH; ALLIANCE ISRAÉLITE UNIVERSELLE (AIU).

Bibliography

Cohen, Hayyim J. *The Jews of the Middle East, 1860–1972.* New York: Wiley, 1973.

SASSON SOMEKH
UPDATED BY MICHAEL R. FISCHBACH

SONATRACH

Holding company for the state's interests in Algeria's hydrocarbon sector.

In the events leading up to the independence of Algeria in 1962, the French government attempted to create a number of arrangements for continued access to Algerian oil, which had been discovered in the Sahara regions of the country a few years earlier. As part of its strategy to put the proceeds from oil sales into industrialization, the government of Algeria formed SONATRACH (Société Nationale de Transport et de Commercialisation des Hydrocarbures). It was headed initially by Abdessalam Belaid, who would become the country's head of centrally guided industrialization—a strategy in which SONATRACH was seen as the financial cornerstone.

The initial difficulty faced by SONATRACH was that all production and marketing of hydrocarbons in the country had been geared toward the requirements of France's economy, a goal now incompatible with the socialist and inward-oriented new development strategy of the Algerian government. Initially restricted to pipeline development and marketing abroad in an effort to break the French monopoly, SONATRACH eventually branched out into all aspects of oil exploration, refining, and marketing, often entering into joint ventures with foreign oil companies for exploration and production. By the early 1970s SONATRACH had become a giant state enterprise and the single largest employer in the country. It not only exercised control over the recovery of oil but managed the major refineries in Algiers, Arzew, and Skikda, and it was the domestic distributor for Algerian oil. In addition, the state enterprise also controlled a large number of oil-related subsidiaries that fueled much of the country's industrialization drive.

Because Algeria was estimated to possess the fourth-largest gas reserves in the world, the Algerian government under President Houari Boumédienne (1965–1978) attempted to index the price of natural gas to that of petroleum. At the same time SONATRACH increased its exploration activities substantially, at a time when the world demand for Algerian natural gas was stagnant or declining. The strategy necessitated heavy investments, among other items, in liquefaction plants built on the Algerian coast, for which the country borrowed extensively on the international market, starting in the mid-1970s. Neither the indexing nor the investments proved sound decisions, and by the early 1980s SONATRACH was forced to renegotiate most of its major contracts and accept lower prices for its natural gas exports. By 1970 SONATRACH directly controlled an estimated 30 percent of Algerian oil production, which accounted for some 34 percent of the country's gross domestic product. By 1977, after a series of nationalizations that ended in 1971, its participation had increased to approximately 75 percent.

The death of President Boumédienne in 1978 brought to a halt the socialist experiment that Algeria had adopted after independence. The June 1980 party congress, guided by the new president, Chadli Bendjedid, stressed the need for increased privatization and liberalization in the Algerian economy. Bendjedid advocated a reorganization of the huge national enterprise to make it more competitive and efficient. A decentralization process thus began, and the giant company was divided into smaller companies, each of which would compete for clients.

Since the early 1990s international companies have been allowed to work in existing oil fields, but the state-owned company still controls the industry. A new hydrocarbon investment law was drafted in 1991, but SONATRACH's complete privatization stalled as it faced staunch opposition from trade unions and, most important, from certain factions within the regime that resisted losing control over the most valuable resource of political and economic power in Algeria. As of 2003, SONATRACH continued to provide the Algerian economy with over 90 percent of its foreign currency revenues.

Bibliography

Entelis, John P. "Sonatrach: The Political Economy of an Algerian State Institution." *Middle East Journal* 53, no. 1 (1999): 9–27.

Dirk Vandewalle
Updated by Ana Torres-Garcia

SOROUSH, ABDOLKARIM
[1944–]

Iranian religious reformer and author who became internationally known during the 1990s for his liberal interpretation of Islam.

AbdolKarim Soroush was born Farajollah Dabbagh in Tehran in 1944. After being educated at a religious high school and at Tehran University, he went to England for graduate studies in pharmacology and philosophy. Returning to Iran in 1979, he became a vocal advocate of the newly inaugurated Islamic Republic of Iran. Adopting the name *Soroush* (meaning angel, especially the archangel Gabriel, in Persian), he became a major promoter of Islamic ideology, mainly writing against and debating Marxists, who were seen as ideological rivals. In the early 1980s Soroush was involved in the Cultural Revolution, a project that imposed "Islamic" curricula on Iranian universities and purged them of dissidents—mostly leftist students and professors—many of whom were imprisoned or executed.

However, as the Islamic Republic faced mounting problems in its second decade, Soroush emerged as a leader in a movement of loyal dissidents calling themselves "religious intellectuals." In numerous books, essays, and public lectures, he argued against turning religion into a political ideology and urged that Islam was open to a plurality of interpretations. Eclectically drawing on philosophy of science, modern hermeneutics, rationalist theology, and mysticism, Soroush holds that humans are able to understand and appreciate revelation according to their rational faculties and cultural limitations. His constant challenge to the clergy's claim to binding religious authority thus prompts some to portray him as something of a Muslim "Protestant." Similarly, his controversial proposal for a "democratic religious government" is a challenge to the Shiʿite clergy's hold on political power in Iran.

Soroush's ideas gained further attention during the first presidential term of another "religious intellectual," Mohammad Khatami (1997–2001). However, during Khatami's second term (2001–present), the limitations of "Islamic democracy" as envisioned by Soroush and his like-minded colleagues became more evident as clerical hard-liners contained the movement to reform the Islamic Republic from within.

See also IRANIAN REVOLUTION (1979); KHATAMI, MOHAMMAD.

Bibliography

Boroujerdi, Mehrzad. *Iranian Intellectuals and the West: The Tormented Triumph of Nativism.* Syracuse, NY: Syracuse University Press, 1996.

Matin-asgari, Afshin. "Abdolkarim Sorush and the Secularization of Islamic Thought in Iran." *Iranian Studies* 30, nos. 1–2 (Winter–Spring 1997).

Vahdat, Farzin. *God and Juggernaut.* Syracuse, NY: Syracuse University Press, 2002.

Vala, Vakili. *Debating Religion and Politics in Iran: The Political Thought of Abdolkarim Sorush.* New York: Council on Foreign Relations, 1996.

AFSHIN MATIN-ASGARI

SOUSSE

Northeast coastal town in Tunisia on the Gulf of Hammamet.

Sousse (also Susa; ancient Hadrumetum) was founded as a Phoenician commercial post and became the center of Sousse province under French colonialism (after the protectorate of 1881). After the independence of Tunisia in 1956, it was made the center of the Sousse governorate. In 2002, its estimated population was 177,450. It is a busy port, handling mostly phosphates and olive oil, and the tourist trade centers on a well-preserved medieval Islamic fortress.

MATTHEW S. GORDON

SOUSTELLE, JACQUES

[1912–1990]

French statesman.

A faithful adherent of General Charles de Gaulle, Jacques Soustelle was governor-general of Algeria (1955–1956), where he combined social reforms with harsh repression of the Front de Libération Nationale (FLN; National Liberation Front). He broke with de Gaulle in 1960 over concessions to the FLN, and following the failed army coup of 1961, Soustelle left France under the threat of arrest because of his hard-line *pied noir* sympathies. He remained in exile until 1968.

See also DE GAULLE, CHARLES; FRONT DE LIBÉRATION NATIONALE (FLN).

Bibliography

Horne, Alistair. *A Savage War of Peace: Algeria 1954–1962,* revised edition. New York: Penguin, 1987.

ZACHARY KARABELL

SOUTH ARABIAN ARMED FORCES

Short-lived army of the Federation of South Arabia.

The armed forces of the ill-fated Federation of South Arabia were created by the merger of the Federal National Guard and the Federal Regular Army in mid-1967, on the eve of South Yemen's rushed independence. By this time, however, the national struggle had rendered these forces unreliable, and they were to play no real part in the collapse of the federation and the transfer of power from the British to the National Liberation Front (NLF).

ROBERT D. BURROWES

SOUTH ARABIAN LEAGUE

Group promoting independence of Britain's protectorates in southern Arabia.

The South Arabian League was the oldest (founded 1950) of the major nationalist groups created to change the status of Britain's possessions in southern Arabia. Its goal was to unite the various principalities of Aden and the Protectorate States into an independent state, to be called South Arabia.

The league's politics tended to be reformist and conservative, and it received much of its support from Saudi Arabia during the 1960s, when the conflict over the future of the protectorates and Aden became a major issue. In 1967, they became part of South Yemen.

See also YEMEN.

MANFRED W. WENNER

SOUTHEASTERN ANATOLIA PROJECT

A massive integrated regional development scheme for the Euphrates and Tigris river basins in Turkey (in Turkish, Güney Anadolu Projesi, or GAP).

The project area covers about 27,000 square miles (70,000 sq. km) in six provinces of the Anatolia region of Turkey, lying between the Anti-Taurus mountains and the border with Syria: Adiyaman, Diyarbakir, Gaziantep, Mardin, Sanliurfa, and Siirt. The project is designed to create economic, social, and spatial changes through the construction and integration of dams, hydroelectric power plants, and irrigation projects, and infrastructural improvements in transportation, health, education, and nonagricultural employment opportunities. Estimated completion is in 2013.

GAP is composed of thirteen subprojects, of which seven are on the Euphrates and six on the Tigris. These comprise fifteen dams, fourteen hydroelectric power stations, and nineteen irrigation projects. The completed project will also incorporate the already completed Keban Dam and will vastly increase the extent of irrigated land in what has been the most economically depressed region of Turkey. As of the early 1990s, only some 315,000 acres (about 127,000 ha) were irrigated in this region—or about 4 percent of the total irrigated land in Turkey. Upon completion, almost 5 million acres (some 2 million ha) will be irrigated. The project will also double Turkey's electrical output by generating 22 billion kilowatt-hours of electricity each year.

The World Bank refused to provide project loans until an agreement had been reached with Syria and Iraq on sharing the water of the two rivers. Because foreign currency has been in great shortage in Turkey, international contractors who had been awarded contracts were replaced by Turkish firms. Since Turkish firms have proven themselves capable of completing the project, international financial circles have been persuaded to make loans. In 1985, the Export-Import Bank of New York and Manufacturers-Hanover Trust lent Turkey 111 million U.S. dollars for the Atatürk Dam, and European banks are providing another 440 million dollars for equipment purchases.

GAP has caused friction with Turkey's neighbors. The Euphrates and Tigris rivers are important sources of water for both Syria and Iraq, and the governments of both countries have expressed reservations about the project. The official Turkish position is that year-long regulation of the flow of the rivers will increase the amount of water available to Syria and Iraq. In July 1984, Turkey and Iraq signed a protocol guaranteeing a minimum flow of 654 cubic yards (500 cu. m) per second, which did not include Syria. In July 1987, a similar agreement was signed with Syria, and further negotiations were held in March 1991. The agreements have not ended the political tensions created by GAP: Turkish forces stood guard in January of 1990 when the Euphrates river was cut to divert water into the reservoir for the Atatürk Dam, which reduced the flow of water into Syria and Iraq by 75 percent.

A number of problems have delayed completion of the project. Because the dam sites are located in remote mountainous areas, roads, worker accommodations, and other infrastructure services must be provided. There are also shortages of skilled labor and engineers. Finally, the reservoirs created by the two Karakaya and Atatürk dams alone will force the relocation of an estimated seventy thousand people, with more relocations to come in the future.

See also WATER.

Bibliography

Kolars, John R., and Mitchell, William A. *The Euphrates River and the Southeast Anatolia Development Project.* Carbondale: Southern Illinois University Press, 1991.

Pitman, Paul M., III. *Turkey: A Country Study,* 4th edition. Washington, DC: U.S. Government Printing Office, 1988.

DAVID WALDNER

SOUTH LEBANON ARMY

Israeli-supported militia in southern Lebanon.

Renegade Lebanese army Major Saʿd Haddad founded the Free Lebanon Militia (FLM) to combat the Palestine Liberation Organization (PLO) in southern Lebanon during Lebanon's civil war (1975–1990) and made common cause with Israel when it invaded Lebanon in March 1978 to drive PLO guerrillas away from the Israeli border. Israel withdrew from Lebanon in June 1978 and turned over to Haddad a buffer zone three to six miles (5 to 10 km) wide along the Lebanese side of the border. Israel funded and trained Haddad's renamed South Lebanon Army (SLA) in return for SLA efforts to prevent the return of elements hostile to Israel to the area.

Israel's 1982 invasion of Lebanon to rout the PLO deepened the relationship between the Israel Defense Force (IDF) and the SLA. Headquartered in Marjayoun, Lebanon, the SLA's twenty-five hundred fighters were Maronite Christians (40%) and Shiʿa Muslims (60%), although Christians predominated among the officers. Haddad died in January 1984 and General Antoine Lahad replaced him. In 1985 Israel withdrew from Lebanon, leaving behind a small force to advise the SLA. The rise of Hizbullah, a Shiʿite militia created to liberate southern Lebanon from Israel and its SLA client, provoked SLA-Hizbullah battles and drew IDF troops back into Lebanon. By the late 1990s IDF fatalities in Lebanon led to an Israeli grass-roots campaign for a unilateral withdrawal. When the IDF withdrew from Lebanon suddenly on 24 March 2000, the SLA disintegrated, and its members either surrendered to Hizbullah or to the Lebanese army, returned quietly to their villages, or sought emergency refuge, along with their families, in Israel. Military courts in Beirut sentenced hundreds of SLA members to prison terms ranging from months to years for collaborating with the enemy, while SLA commanders tried in absentia received death sentences. SLA families struggled to adjust to Israeli society; most returned to Lebanon or moved to other countries within several years of the SLA's collapse.

See also HADDAD, SAʿD; LAHAD, ANTOINE.

Bibliography

Hamizrachi, Beate. *The Emergence of the South Lebanon Security Belt: Major Saʿad Haddad and the Ties with Israel, 1975–1978.* New York: Praeger, 1988.

Schiff, Zeʾev, and Yaʾari, Ehud. *Israel's Lebanon War.* New York: Simon & Schuster, 1984.

ELIZABETH THOMPSON
UPDATED BY LAURA ZITTRAIN EISENBERG

SOUTH PERSIA RIFLES

British-organized paramilitary unit in Iran during World War I.

The South Persia Rifles was a largely indigenous, paramilitary force of about 8,000 men trained and paid by Britain. Its headquarters was in Shiraz, with secondary bases in Abadeh and Kerman. Britain dispatched Major (later Brigadier General) Sir Percy Molesworth Sykes (1867–1945) to southern Iran in 1916 to organize a military force to counter the presumed pro-German sentiments of the Swedish-officered gendarmerie in Fars and Kerman provinces. It thus could protect British interests—southern Iran was adjacent to British India—from perceived threats by agents of Germany, Britain's enemy during World War I (1914–1918). The reluctance of the Iranian government to recognize the South Persia Rifles encouraged the largest and most militarily powerful tribal confederation in southern Iran, the Qashqa'i, to attack the force in May 1918. Sykes and his troops were besieged for several weeks at Shiraz before they finally defeated the Qashqa'i tribesmen. Following the 1921 coup d'état in Tehran, Minister of War Reza Khan, the future Reza Shah Pahlavi, ordered the disbanding of the South Persia Rifles.

See also PAHLAVI, REZA.

Bibliography

Sykes, Percy Molesworth. *A History of Persia,* vol. 2, 2d edition. London: Macmillan, 1921.

JACK BUBON
UPDATED BY ERIC HOOGLUND

SPAIN AND THE MIDDLE EAST

The Kingdom of Spain, located in southwest Europe, has ties with the Middle East and North Africa that go back to the early medieval period.

Between 711 and 1492, the Iberian Peninsula witnessed the growth of several Islamic administrations, which ruled over a multiethnic and multireligious population in a space that would be known as *al-Andalus.* The arrival of Berber troops under Arab leadership in 711 was followed by the establishment of a governorate dependent on the Umayyad caliphate based in Damascus (711–756). With the onset of the Abbasid revolution in the east, the Umayyad Abd al-Rahman I established an independent emirate based in Cordova (756–929). In 929, Abd al-Rahman III proclaimed himself caliph and turned Cordova into the most important cultural and intellectual center of Western Europe (929–1008). Cordovese splendor lasted for a century, after which the Christian kingdoms of the north began pushing southward, conquering Muslim territory while taking advantage of the weakness of the petty kingdoms (1031–1086). An invasion by North African Berber tribes (Almoravids and Almohads; 1086–1232) temporarily halted the Christian advance. The Nasrid kingdom of Granada (1232–1492), last Muslim stronghold in the peninsula, fell in 1492 to the armies of the Catholic monarchs of Castile and Aragon, Isabella and Ferdinand. The monarchs decreed that Iberian Jews must either convert or be expelled; in 1502, Castilian Muslims were forced to convert to Christianity, and Aragonese Muslims were forced to do so in 1525. Zealous religious authorities were suspicious of the fidelity of new Christians (Jewish *conversos* and Muslim *moriscos*), who fell under the scrutiny of the Inquisition. Morisco rebelliousness against the abuses of the old Christian settlers led to the uprising of the Alpujarras (1568–1571). In 1609, Phillip III decreed the mass expulsion of the remaining *moriscos.* Throughout the sixteenth century, the rivalry between imperial Spain and the Ottoman Empire led to the Spanish occupation of several North African ports—Oran, Budjia, Algiers, Tripoli, and Tunis—under Charles V. The diminution of the rivalry with the Ottoman Empire, the economic crisis that affected the Spanish Empire in the seventeenth century, and Spain's colonial enterprise in the Americas put a hold on Spanish incursions in North Africa.

In 1859–1860, Spain waged war against Morocco. Franco-Spanish rivalry in North Africa led to the establishment of a Spanish protectorate in northern Morocco (1912–1956) and the Western Sahara (1884–1975); Spanish troops fiercely repressed the Berber liberation movement of the Rif region (1921–1927). After the Spanish Civil War (1936–1939), General Francisco Franco maintained an official policy of "friendship" toward Arab countries. In 1975, King Hassan II of Morocco organized the Green March toward Western Sahara and occupied the former Spanish protectorate. The signing of the Madrid Agreements (1975), in which Spain ceded the territory to Morocco and Mauritania, ignored the wishes of the inhabitants of the region and was opposed by POLISARIO; almost thirty years after the signing of the Madrid Agreements, the Saharan conflict is pending resolution under UN supervision. Upon joining the European Economic Community (E.E.C.) in 1986, Spain—then under a democratic socialist government—established diplomatic ties with Israel. In 1991, the socialist government supported the international coalition against Iraq. That same year, Spain hosted the Madrid Peace Conference. Subsequently, Spain became an important mediator in the Palestinian-Israeli conflict. Throughout the last quarter of the twentieth century, Spain and Morocco maintained a bitter contest over the sovereignty of the Spanish cities of Ceuta and Melilla and over fishing rights along the Moroccan coast.

Under the Conservative government of Prime Minister José María Aznar (1996–2003), Spain aligned itself with the policies of the United States. In the aftermath of the 11 September 2001 attacks on the United States, Aznar was a staunch ally of U.S. policies in the Middle East and became one of the international anchors of the war against Iraq in 2003. Despite widespread popular opposition—90 percent of the population opposed military intervention in Iraq—the Spanish government supported the U.S. occupation and stationed troops in the Diwaniyah region.

See also GREEN MARCH; POLISARIO; WAR IN IRAQ (2003); WESTERN SAHARA.

Bibliography

Castro, Américo. *The Structure of Spanish History.* Princeton, NJ: Princeton University Press, 1954.

Hess, Andrew. *The Forgotten Frontier: A History of the Sixteenth Century Ibero-African Frontier.* Chicago: University of Chicago Press, 1978.

Menocal, Maria Rosa. *The Ornament of the World: How Muslims, Jews, and Christians Created a Culture of Tolerance in Medieval Spain.* Boston: Little, Brown, 2002

VANESA CASANOVA-FERNANDEZ

SPANISH MOROCCO

Portions of northwest Africa held by Spain from the 1500s until 1975.

The presence of Spain along the coast of northwest Africa was initially manifested during the 1400s and 1500s—after centuries of Muslim rule in the Iberian Peninsula had been overturned by warfare and the Moors retreated to North Africa. The Mediterranean port cities of Melilla and Ceuta came under Spanish rule in 1496 and 1578, respectively, and remain so today, as do three tiny islands off the Mediterranean coast of Morocco. In the late nineteenth century, Spain joined the European scramble for overseas territories. Spain expanded its Ceuta and Melilla enclaves, asserted itself militarily in the Rif mountains, and temporarily occupied Tetuan in 1860; an 1860 treaty committed Morocco to ceding land along its southern coast for the establishment of Spanish fisheries, eventually resulting in Spain staking claim to Ifni. Further south, Spain established coastal trading stations at Villa Cisneros (Dakhla), Cintra, and Cape Blanca. In December 1884, a Spanish protectorate was declared along the Saharan coast, a claim recognized by the Berlin Conference in 1885.

Spanish holdings in both the north and south were expanded by three treaties between Spain and France, the last in 1912. Spain then nominally held full sovereignty over Saguia el-Hamra and Rio de Oro (Spanish Sahara, now Western Sahara), 102,703 square miles (266,000 sq km) of territory, below the twenty-seventh parallel, wedged in between the Atlantic Ocean and what are today the internationally recognized boundaries of Morocco, Algeria, and Mauritania. Implementation of Spanish authority came in stages: Control of Tarfaya, north of the twenty-seventh parallel, was taken in 1916; La Guera, in the extreme south of Rio de Oro, in 1920; the 580-square-mile (1,502 sq km) Ifni zone, between Tarfaya and Agadir, in 1934; and Smara, in the Saharan interior, also in 1934. Spanish Sahara and the Ifni and Tarfaya areas were governed between 1934 and 1958 as parts of Spanish West Africa, whose military governor was based in Ifni.

Part of the "Green March" moves into Spanish Morocco in November 1975. During the Green March, hundreds of thousands of Moroccan civilians marched across their border into Spanish Morocco at the behest of King Hassan II, as part of an effort to assert Morocco's claim to the territory. © ALAIN NOGUES/CORBIS SYGMA. REPRODUCED BY PERMISSION.

The Spanish protectorate in the north, established in 1912, was one-twentieth the size of the French zone. Tangier was made part of the Spanish zone from 1940 to 1945, but then reverted to its previous international regime. The Spanish zone's population in 1955, including Europeans, was about one million, nearly 10 percent of Morocco's total population. Economic resources were few and the area underwent little development, constituting an economic liability to Spain.

Spain was both a competitor and sometimes junior partner of France, often working in tandem politically and militarily—the latter during the Rif rebellion led by Muhammad ibn Abd al-Karim al-Khattabi from 1921 to 1926; in the southern campaigns in 1934; and again in 1957–1958 against the irregular Moroccan Army of Liberation, following Morocco's achieving independence in 1956. Nonetheless, Spanish rule was both weaker and often less dominating than that of France. Spain returned Tarfaya and its surroundings to Morocco in 1958 and the Ifni enclave in 1969.

Phosphates were first discovered in Spanish Sahara during the 1940s, and proved to be of high grade and large quantity. Exports began in the early 1970s. By 1975, exports stood at 2.6 million tons (2.36 million metric tons), the sixth largest in the world. In 1974, the Spanish presence numbered just over 26,000; a 1974 census of the native Sahrawi population counted 73,497 persons, most of whom had been sedentarized from their nomadic life.

In 1973, Spain decided to introduce internal self-government, to deflect international pressure for decolonization. But by mid-1974, following the collapse of Portugal's Africa empire, Madrid promised to implement United Nations calls for a referendum in the territory during the first half of 1975. In September 1975, Spain's foreign minister and POLISARIO representatives agreed on a mutual release of prisoners and the principle of an independent Sahrawi state in return for fishing and phosphate concessions to Spain. But following Morocco's Green March in the Western Sahara War, and with Spain's Generalissimo Francisco Franco on his deathbed, Spain, Morocco, and Mauritania signed a tripartite agreement in Madrid on 14 November 1975, administratively dividing the region into Moroccan and Mauritanian zones and setting up a transitional tripartite administration. The final Spanish departure from its Saharan colony came on 26 February 1975.

See also GREEN MARCH; KHATTABI, MUHAMMAD IBN ABD AL-KARIM AL-; POLISARIO; RIF WAR.

Bibliography

Hodges, Tony. *Western Sahara: The Roots of a Desert War.* Westport, CT: L. Hill, 1983.

Mercer, John. *Spanish Sahara.* London: Allen and Unwin, 1976.

Pennell, C. R. *Morocco since 1830: A History.* New York: New York University Press, 2000.

BRUCE MADDY-WEITZMAN

SPECIAL FORCES OF THE LEVANT

Military group under the French mandate in Lebanon.

After France gained control of Lebanon through the mandate from the League of Nations, it formed the Troupes Spéciales du Levant, which recruited Lebanese and Syrian soldiers and was commanded almost exclusively by French officers. It was devised to legitimize French police and military activities in the region and to give the impression of local rule. The percentage of officers who were Lebanese or Syrian increased over the years although the power of command and control remained in French hands. By 1945, 90 percent of the officers in the 14,000-strong Special Forces were Arabs.

During World War II, Lebanese Special Forces troops were ordered to fight on the side of the Vichy French against the British and Free French. When the Vichy forces in the Middle East surrendered in 1941, volunteers from the Special Forces were recruited by the Free French to fight actively in North Africa, Italy, and southern France. In 1945 three thousand Lebanese troops in the Special Forces formed the nucleus of the Lebanese Army.

AS'AD ABUKHALIL

SPHINX

Mythological human-headed lion carved from rock at the pyramids of Giza.

The Sphinx is 190 feet (27 m) long and 66 feet (20 m) tall at its highest. It probably represents the pharaoh Khafre (c. 2550 B.C.E.), whose pyramid is nearby. Arabs called it Abu al-Hawl, "father of terror." Like the pyramids, it has become a symbol of Egypt, first appearing on postage stamps in 1867 and replacing the bust of King Farouk (1936–1952) on coins in the 1950s.

Bibliography

Hassan, Selim. *The Sphinx: Its History in the Light of Recent Excavations.* Cairo: Government Press, 1949.

DONALD MALCOLM REID

SPRINZAK, JOSEPH

[1885–1959]

Israeli political leader.

Born in Moscow, Joseph Sprinzak was one of the founders of Tze'irei Zion in Russia (1905) and was a delegate to Zionist Congresses.

He began medical school at the American University in Beirut but then settled in Palestine in 1908, where he was an early activist in the Labor movement. He was a founder of the Histadrut and the MAPAI party and served in leadership positions in both organizations. Unanimously elected speaker of the first Knesset in 1949, he served in that capacity until his death. He also was acting president of Israel while Chaim Weizmann was ill and after Weizmann's death (1952), until the election of Yizhak Ben-Zvi.

See also HISTADRUT; ISRAEL: POLITICAL PARTIES IN.

Bibliography

Merhav, Peretz. *The Israeli Left: History, Problems, Documents.* San Diego, CA: A. S. Barnes, 1980.

BRYAN DAVES

SRVANTZIANTS, GAREGIN
[1840–1892]

Armenian ecclesiastical leader, ethnographer, and folklorist.

Garegin Srvantziants was born in Van and educated in local parochial schools. He became a teacher and was ordained a celibate priest in 1867. While assigned ecclesiastical responsibilities in Van, Erzurum, Bitlis, and Harput, he organized a number of schools and was the assistant prior of the Armenian monastery of Surp Karapet (Holy Precursor), one of the most hallowed sites of Armenian religious pilgrimage, at Moosh. After his investiture as a bishop in 1886, he was appointed prior of Surp Karapet. A fervent preacher and exponent of Armenian emancipation, he was removed from office and placed under surveillance in Istanbul.

Well before his confinement to the Ottoman capital, Srvantziants had published what in the aggregate may be considered the most important ethnographic data on the Armenians yet gathered at the time. As an associate of Mkrtich Khrimian, he had traveled with the later catholicos through the Armenian provinces in 1860 and 1861. Recognized much like his mentor for the kinship he felt with his own people, Srvantziants was instructed by the Armenian patriarch of Istanbul, Nerses Vazhapetian, to investigate and report on the condition of the Armenian communities in eastern Anatolia after the Russian–Ottoman War of 1877 and 1878, while Khrimian prepared to plead the Armenian cause at the Congress of Berlin.

During these trips, and at all other opportunities, Srvantziants tirelessly recorded the folklore of the Armenian rustic population. He released the results of his expeditions in a series of works issued in the 1870s and 1800s. In *Grots u brots* (The written and the spoken, 1874), he published popular Armenian folk stories and traditions. In *Hnots yev norots* (From the old and the new, 1874), he published Armenian stories from manuscript records. *Manana* (Manna, 1876) included proverbs, riddles, songs, and epigraphs from the Van region. In *Hamov-hotov* (The flavorful and the colorful, 1884), he described the topography, climate, and monuments of Armenia. The most significant of his discoveries was the first cycle of what was later recognized as the Armenian national folk epic *Sasna Tsrrer* (The daredevils of Sasun), more popularly known by the name of its hero. Srvantziants recorded the section called "Sasuntsi Davit kam Mheri tur" (David of Sasun, or the Gate of Mher). Srvantziants also published important studies on the subjects he recorded and was elected an honorary member of the Imperial Academy of Antiquities in Saint Petersburg. He died in Istanbul.

See also BERLIN, CONGRESS AND TREATY OF; KHRIMIAN, MKRTICH; RUSSIAN–OTTOMAN WARS; VAZHAPETIAN, NERSES.

ROUBEN P. ADALIAN

STACK, LEE
[1868–1924]

Governor-general of the Sudan and sirdar (commander) of the Egyptian army.

Sir Lee Stack was assassinated in Cairo as part of an Egyptian nationalist campaign to gain complete independence from Great Britain. He had joined the Anglo-Egyptian army in the Sudan in 1899 (when it became an Anglo-Egyptian condominium after its conquest, 1896–1898). As governor-general, he contributed to the economic and political development of the Sudan.

Bibliography

Marlowe, John. *Anglo-Egyptian Relations, 1800–1956,* 2d edition. London: F. Cass, 1965.

OLES M. SMOLANSKY

STANHOPE, HESTER

[1776–1839]

English aristocrat and traveler.

Hester Stanhope was the eldest of three daughters of Charles, third earl of Stanhope, and Lady Hester Pitt, sister of William Pitt the Younger. She emerged in London society as hostess and private secretary to her uncle, the prime minister, and was known for her satiric tongue. After Pitt's death in 1803, dissatisfied with a quiet life in London, she tried Wales but left for the eastern Mediterranean in 1810. By 1818 she had settled in Lebanon, befriending the Druze Amir Bashir al-Shihabi, whom she later opposed. She built an elaborate manor with lush tropical gardens on a hilltop above the village of Jun (7 miles northeast of Sidon), where she maintained a large pool of servants and a camel caravan to supply the manor with drinking water. Known as *al-Sitt* (the lady), she was both imperious and generous to the local population; some believed her to have special spiritual powers. She seems to have had considerable influence, since Ibrahim Pasha, about to invade Ottoman Syria in 1832, is said to have wanted her to declare neutrality.

Stanhope visited mosques in Damascus dressed as a young male Arab and organized a lavish procession to Palmyra, where the Bedouin apparently called her "the second Queen Zenobia." To maintain her estate, she fell into heavy debt to local moneylenders, despite the pension the British government had given her after Pitt's death, and she died poor. She was buried on her estate but her remains were transferred to a British cemetery near Beirut in 1989. Not only her own memoirs but remembrances by Charles Kingslake and Alphonse de Lamartine enhanced her notoriety; early twentieth-century Arab feminists memorialized her as a negative exemplar.

See also BELL, GERTRUDE; COLONIALISM IN THE MIDDLE EAST; GENDER: GENDER AND EDUCATION.

Bibliography

Booth, Marilyn. *May Her Likes Be Multiplied: Biography and Gender Politics in Egypt.* Berkeley: University of California Press, 2001.

Haslip, Joan. *Lady Hester Stanhope: A Biography.* New York: Frederick A. Stokes, 1936.

Meryon, Charles Lewis, ed. *Memoirs of the Lady Hester Stanhope, As Related By Herself in Conversations with Her Physician, Comprising Her Opinions and Anecdotes of Some of the Most Remarkable Persons of Her Time,* 3 vols. London: H. Colburn, 1845.

Meryon, Charles Lewis, ed. *Travels of Lady Hester Stanhope, Forming the Completion of Her Memoirs, Narrated by Her Physician,* 3 vols. London: H. Colburn, 1846.

MARILYN BOOTH

STARK, FREYA

[1893–1993]

British author and explorer.

Born in Paris into an expatriate English family and raised largely in Italy, Freya Madeleine Stark moved to England in 1911 to study English and history at Bedford College. When World War I interrupted her studies, she returned to the Continent, where she volunteered as a nurse. After the war, Stark studied Arabic in London, followed by a more intensive course in the Levant. The Arab world became her passion, and in 1927 she began extensive travels in the region, publishing newspaper articles in the *Baghdad Times* and elsewhere about the Middle East.

Stark's visit to the remote castles of the Assassins in western Iran in 1930 and 1931 led to the publication of her first book, *The Valleys of the Assassins* (1934). It brought instant recognition, together with financial success; its photographic observations set the style for her future work. Stark next journeyed south to Arabia in 1935, which resulted in the publication of *The Southern Gates of Arabia* (1935), followed by *Winter in Arabia* (1940). Stark spoke English, French, German, and Italian in addition to Arabic, Persian, and Turkish. Her knowledge of languages greatly facilitated her travels across the eastern Mediterranean and over much of the Asian continent.

Stark's remarkable life spanned almost the entire twentieth century. She mapped remote regions of the Arab world, and her cartographic accomplishments were honored by the Royal Geographic Society. However, it is as an author that she is most remembered. Freya Stark was the most gifted and widely read female travel writer of her time. She published more than thirty books, most of which were highly personal travel adventures and many of which remain in print.

See also BELL, GERTRUDE; COLONIALISM IN THE MIDDLE EAST; GENDER: GENDER AND EDUCATION; STANHOPE, HESTER.

Bibliography

Geniesse, Jane Fletcher. *Passionate Nomad: The Life of Freya Stark.* New York: Random House, 1999.

Ruthven, Malise, ed. *Freya Stark in Southern Arabia.* Reading, U.K.: Garnet Publishing, 1995.

Stark, Freya. *The Southern Gates of Arabia: A Journey in the Hadhramaut.* New York: Modern Library, 2001.

Stark, Freya. *The Valleys of the Assassins and Other Persian Travels.* New York: Modern Library, 2001.

RONALD BRUCE ST JOHN

STAR OF NORTH AFRICA

The first Algerian political movement to call openly for independence.

The Star of North Africa, also known as the Etoile Nord-Africaine (ENA) was founded in 1926 in Paris by Hadj Ali Abd al-Qadir and Messali al-Hadj. With a base in the large Algerian immigrant community that was influenced by the Communist-dominated French labor movement, it also propounded a leftist social and economic agenda.

The movement was banned in 1929 but grew clandestinely until it reappeared in reorganized form in 1933. Messali al-Hadj returned to Algeria in the summer of 1936 to address the Algerian Muslim Congress that was designing a program of reforms within the Colonial framework. Before that audience, he became the first individual to speak openly of independence within Algeria itself. He then turned to organizing ENA cells across the country. Authorities in January 1937 banned the ENA. Its successor was the Parti du Peuple Algérien (PPA), which was outlawed, in its turn, in September 1939.

See also HADJ, MESSALI AL-.

JOHN RUEDY

STATE PLANNING ORGANIZATION (SPO)

Organization set up in Turkey in 1960 to administer national economic development.

Turkey first experimented with central planning in the 1930s, but with the focus only on industrialization. Between 1950 and 1960, the Democratic Party governments were criticized for their opposition to any kind of economic planning. The agricultural sector was virtually tax exempt. After the military intervention of May 1960, planning became a priority. Accordingly, the principle of indicative, not compulsory, planning was written into the 1961 constitution. The State Planning Organization (SPO) was created to draw up five-year plans covering all aspects of economic development, as well as long-term plans and annual programs. The institutional structure of the SPO was designed to create a degree of independence and security for the technical experts charged with preparing the plans and to facilitate cooperation between them and political authorities. The final authority was supposed to lie with the High Planning Council.

During the discussion of the first five-year plan, there were differences of opinion between planners and military bureaucrats. In contrast to the planners' liberal-productive conception of the state, the military bureaucrats remained loyal to an etatist patrimonial tradition that gave priority to social justice and full employment over economic growth and efficiency. With the transition to civilian rule in October 1961, the climate changed radically. The Justice Party viewed the SPO as a political tool of a military-cum-bureaucratic elite, to which they were opposed by both interest and instinct. Although the party had to implement the constitutional requirement, the party leadership was anxious to limit the planners' power.

After 1965 representatives of the private sector, who had been virtually excluded from the preparation of the first plan, were fully consulted on the second, which was to run from 1967 to 1972. The new constitution of 1982 endorsed planning, and a decree of 1984 reorganized the SPO and attached it to the office of the prime minister.

The SPO is headed by an undersecretary. It consists of eight departments: Economic Planning; Social Planning; Coordination; Priority Regional

Development; Relations with the European Union; Credit Allocation; Foreign Capital Investment; and Evaluation of Yearly Programs. The SPO also maintains permanent representatives in international economic organizations and major foreign capitals. In spite of its elaborate organizational structure and its constitutionally defined task, the state bureaucracy regards the suggestions and recommendations of the SPO as a hindrance to its administrative tasks.

The most important achievement of the SPO is the realization of the Southeastern Anatolia Project (GAP). This project is a multisector and integrated regional development effort approached in the context of sustainable development. The project covers nine administrative provinces established in the basin of the Euphrates and Tigris Rivers. The program envisages the construction of 22 dams and 19 hydraulic power plants and irrigation of 1.7 million hectares. The total cost is estimated at $32 billion (in 1997 prices). The GAP represents a major part of the Eighth Five-Year Development Plan (2001–2006). The SPO also is involved in the preparation of the pre-accession structural changes required by the European Union.

Bibliography

Hale, William. *The Political and Economic Development of Modern Turkey.* London: Croom Helm, 1981.

Milor, Vedat. "The Genesis of Planning in Turkey." *New Perspectives on Turkey,* 4 (1990): 1–30.

Pamuk, Şevket, and Owen, Roger. *A History of the Middle East Economies in the Twentieth Century.* Cambridge, MA: Harvard University Press, 1998.

NERMIN ABADAN-UNAT

STERN, ABRAHAM
[1907–1942]

Jewish underground leader during the British mandate of Palestine.

Abraham Stern (nicknamed Ya'ir) was born in Poland but spent many of his formative years in Russia. He moved to Palestine in 1924 where he studied Latin and Greek at Hebrew University and later began to study for his doctorate in Florence, Italy. Stern served in the Haganah starting in 1929 but broke off in 1931 to form the Irgun Zva'i Le'umi (IZL), through which he smuggled weapons into Palestine and established contacts with the Polish military. In 1934 he gave up his academic interests to devote himself fully to the underground.

Stern returned to Palestine in 1939, following the publication of the British White Paper, to organize resistance to the British. He was detained by the British for ten months, until his friends in the Revisionist movement arranged for his release. In 1940 he broke with the Irgun and its leader, David Raziel, and formed a new group, Lohamei Herut Yisrael, also known as Lehi, or the Stern Gang, because he did not feel the Irgun was militaristic enough. His ideological manifesto, "Eighteen Principles of Renaissance," included many controversial ideas, including that the new Zionist goals should be a land of Israel extending from the Nile to the Euphrates Rivers.

During World War II, unaware of the realities of the Holocaust, Stern sought links with Fascist Italy and Nazi Germany, although they did not result in anything. Stern, who appeared on British "wanted" posters for bank robbery and murder, was found and killed by British policemen in 1942.

See also HAGANAH; HOLOCAUST; IRGUN ZVA'I LE'UMI (IZL); LOHAMEI HERUT YISRAEL; WHITE PAPERS ON PALESTINE.

Bibliography

Heller, Joseph. *The Stern Gang: Ideology, Politics, and Terror.* London and Portland, OR: F. Cass, 1995.

JULIE ZUCKERMAN

STOCK MARKET

Middle Eastern stock markets are small and often closed to foreign investors.

The stock markets of the Middle East tend to remain relatively small relative to the respective economies of each country, and except in Turkey and Israel are not used by entrepreneurs to fund their operations.

Even in countries where economic liberalism is embedded in the economic life, such as Saudi Arabia, capital markets are heavily regulated and have not had any major influence in helping non-government firms raise capital from the public at large. Exchanges suffer from a lack of reliable information on and from the companies, insider trading is often a problem, and accounting practices are not reliable enough for private investors and funds to make adequate judgment on the value of the companies. Governments tend to interfere with the markets, either to limit their expansion through overregulation or to limit the losses in downtrends, as was the case in Kuwait in 1982. In most countries the markets have little depth and are closed to foreign investors. Since 1998 there have been some efforts to use the markets to improve privatization efforts. Foreign investors have been welcomed in some bourses, such as those of Egypt, Lebanon, and Israel. However, most other markets have limited foreigners to investment through small mutual funds managed by local banks, as in Saudi Arabia. The Saudi market has the largest capitalization of the Arab world, at about US$100 billion.

Major stock markets within the Middle East, 2003

Country traded	Number of companies	Capitalization (in millions of U.S. $)
Israel	617	40,900
Turkey	262	33,800
Saudi Arabia	68	100,000
Kuwait	93	35,100
Jordan	76	1,664
Iran	324	65,000
Egypt	1,110	18,400

SOURCE: Zawya, online at http://www.zawya.com; Tehran Stock Exchange, online at http://www.tse.or.ir; Istanbul Stock Exchange, online at http://www.ise.org; Tel Aviv Stock Exchange, online at http://www.tase.co.il; *Middle East Economic Survey*; Saudi Arabian Monetary Agency, online at http://www.sama.gov.sa

TABLE BY GGS INFORMATION SERVICES, THE GALE GROUP.

Bahrain

The market in Bahrain is still very small and highly regulated. However, it is beginning to open up to foreign investors if they reside in Bahrain. Each foreign investor is limited to a maximum 1 percent stake in a company. If markets become more deregulated in Bahrain and if Saudi Arabia—the main center for private industrial ventures—approves, this stock market could become an important place for Persian (Arabian) Gulf industries to raise capital.

Iran

In the liberalization of 1992 the Iranian stock market was expected to be the transmission belt between Iranian capital at home and abroad and the companies to be denationalized. Foreign capital was permitted to buy minority positions. However, the move toward liberalization seems to have stalled, and the market is not very active.

Israel

The Israeli stock exchange is located in Tel Aviv. It lists about 654 companies and has a capitalization of US$41 billion. The market is open to foreign investors. Technically, the market is quite advanced, with computer support similar to that of U.S. markets. However, volumes traded are relatively low, in the average range of $36 million per day in 2002. The market tends to be somewhat volatile due to the low number of buyers and sellers. The progress of the markets is marked by the TASE index.

Jordan

The Jordanian market, which was started in 1977, is still small in terms of volume but has a good reputation among investors. Foreign investors need to be approved by the government, which greatly limits the liquidity of the shares and the potential growth of the market.

Kuwait

Until 1982 the Kuwaiti capital markets were the largest in the Middle East. After the crash of the Suq al-Manakh, the government enforced old regulations and introduced new ones. The number of brokers, the number of companies eligible to be traded, and the daily volumes are limited. The 1991 Gulf War, which caused many industrial companies to disappear, limited the number of tradable issues to the financial institutions. Kuwaiti-owned companies based in Bahrain and elsewhere in the Gulf also are traded. No foreigners are allowed to trade in Kuwaiti shares, except Gulf Cooperation Council nationals.

Saudi Arabia

Saudi Arabia, despite having the largest volume of shares traded in the Gulf, does not have a stock exchange or trading floor. All shares are exchanged

The Istanbul Stock Exchange was established in 1986 and is an autonomous organization that provides trading in equities, bonds and bills, revenue-sharing certificates, private sector bonds, foreign securities, real estate certificates, and international securities. © AP/WIDEWORLD PHOTOS. REPRODUCED BY PERMISSION.

and cleared through the banks. To have shares traded, companies must be registered as Sharikat al-Musahama, a registration somewhat similar to a U.S. Corporation C. To obtain this status, companies must be vetted by the Saudi Arabian Monetary Agency and, until 1992, also needed approval by the king. Only firms not involved in defense or oil are allowed to register. Thus, Saudi firms have a very difficult time raising money directly from the public through the stock market. No foreign capital is allowed to trade in Saudi shares, except in limited circumstances if originating from within the Gulf Cooperation Council. Since 11 September 2001, the Saudi stock market index has become more popular. The number of shares traded has increased from 691 million in 2001 to 1736 million in 2002. In an overall declining world market, TASI, the Saudi stock exchange index, increased 5.7 percent between 2001 and February 2003.

Turkey

The stock exchange in Turkey got its impetus from a 1989 law on investments. The law strongly restricts insider trading, provides for proper financial reporting by companies, and authorizes foreigners to invest. By 1993 the Turkish market had become one of the leading emerging markets, with investments from many U.S. and European mutual funds.

JEAN-FRANÇOIS SEZNEC

STORRS, RONALD

[1881–1955]

British colonial official.

After studying classics at Pembroke College, Cambridge, Ronald Storrs served as Lord Horatio Kitchener's Oriental secretary in Egypt prior to and during World War I. In this capacity, he met with Amir Abdullah ibn Hussein in April 1914, one of the Hashimites' early attempts to determine Britain's attitude toward their ambitions. Storrs later played an important role in the Anglo–Hashimite dialogue and the Arab Revolt, traveling from Egypt to the Hijaz on several occasions in 1916, including a journey with T. E. Lawrence, to cement Britain's relationship with the Hashimites.

In December 1917, Storrs was appointed the first military governor of Jerusalem after Allied troops entered the city. He believed that the role of Britain's military government in Palestine was simply to administer the country, not to introduce fundamental social or political changes. Britain, however, had pledged to support Zionist settlements in Palestine through the Balfour Declaration. In April 1918, Storrs formally received the Zionist commission, headed by Chaim Weizmann, which had traveled to Jerusalem to begin making arrangements for implementing the Balfour Declaration. He felt that the commission's dismay at the negative attitude displayed toward it and Zionism in general betrayed a fundamental naïveté about the Palestinians and their understanding of Zionism.

Palestinian nationalist frustrations were manifested in the Nabi Musa disturbances (April 1920). As governor of Jerusalem, Storrs subsequently dismissed the mayor of Jerusalem, Musa Kazim al-Husayni, for his role in the affair. Husayni went on to become the senior Palestinian nationalist figure in the 1920s, as head of the Arab Executive.

Storrs took an interest in cultural preservation in Jerusalem, forming the Pro-Jerusalem Society to restore historic monuments in the city. He arranged for Armenian artisans to produce tiles for the Islamic shrines at the Haram al-Sharif as part of these efforts.

Following the introduction of civil rule in Palestine in the mid-1920s, Storrs was Jerusalem's first civilian governor. After leaving service in Palestine, he became governor of Cyprus in 1926 and of Northern Rhodesia in 1932. He retired from colonial service in 1934.

See also ABDULLAH I IBN HUSSEIN; BALFOUR DECLARATION (1917); HARAM AL-SHARIF; HUSAYNI, MUSA KAZIM AL-; KITCHENER, HORATIO HERBERT; LAWRENCE, T. E.; NABI MUSA PILGRIMAGE; WEIZMANN, CHAIM.

Bibliography

Storrs, Ronald. *Orientations: The Memories of Sir Ronald Storrs.* London: Nicholson and Watson, 1943.

Wasserstein, Bernard. *The British in Palestine,* 2d edition. Oxford and Cambridge, MA: B. Blackwell, 1991.

MICHAEL R. FISCHBACH

STRAITS CONVENTION

International agreement, signed in 1841, on access to the Black Sea; it denied passage in peacetime to non-Ottoman warships through the Straits connecting the Mediterranean and Black seas.

Until 1774, when the Russian Empire under Catherine the Great acquired territory on the north shore of the Black Sea, there was no question concerning passage of ships between the Black and Mediterranean seas because the Black Sea was essentially an internal Ottoman sea. After 1774 access to the Straits presented a persistent problem in international affairs. Russia sought to ensure its right to passage while opposing similar rights for other maritime powers; Britain, in particular, wanted to restrict Russian access to the Mediterranean as a threat to its aspirations in the Levant. The Ottoman Empire considered its control of the Straits essential to its sovereignty and a guarantee of its security and independence.

The Straits Convention of 1841 resulted from internal Ottoman problems and imperial rivalries. The Ottoman Empire had been wracked by the aspirations of Greece for independence and the threat posed by Muhammad Ali of Egypt in his efforts to establish control over Syria and possibly to replace the Ottomans as head of the empire. Russia and most other European powers supported the Greek cause. France supported Muhammad Ali in hopes of reaping benefits as his ally. Russia wanted unhampered access to the Mediterranean and acknowledgment of its claim of protection over Christian Orthodox subjects of the Ottoman Empire. Britain and Austria-Hungary were suspicious of Russian designs.

Muhammad Ali originally supported the Ottomans in their struggle against the Greeks seeking independence; he sent his son Ibrahim ibn Muhammad Ali with an army to help the Ottomans subdue the Greeks in 1825. The venture was not successful, and by 1828 Ibrahim's army had withdrawn from Greece. Muhammad Ali then turned his attention to Syria in an attempt to expand his control of the eastern Mediterranean, launching an army led by Ibrahim against the Ottomans in the first Syrian war (1831–1833). France tacitly supported this effort; Britain, distracted by other international problems (particularly Belgium), did not; the Russians supported the Ottomans. Ibrahim's forces came within 150 miles of Constantinople, but in February 1833 Russia sent a naval force and troops to support the Ottoman defense of the city. France and Britain, fearing the prospect of Russian influence in the Ottoman Empire, called for mediation. The Convention of Kütahya (8 April 1833) conceded Ottoman Syria to Egypt but prevented Egyptian control of the empire as a whole. Because of its support, Russia retained its position as the Ottomans' principal ally. This was reflected in the Treaty of Hunkar-Iskelesi (8 July 1833), in which Russia and the Ottoman Empire pledged mutual support in any future conflict. The treaty also called for closure of the Straits to any naval forces threatening Russia.

The agreements of 1833 did not last long. In 1839 Sultan Mahmud II decided to deal with Muhammad Ali's threat by sending a military force against his son, Ibrahim, in Syria; thus began the second Syrian war. In spite of a force developed by Helmuth von Moltke of Prussia, the Ottomans were defeated at Nesib on 24 June and the Ottoman fleet defected to Egypt. Fearing that the breakup of the Ottoman Empire would not be in the best interests of Britain, Lord Palmerston, foreign minister and later prime minister, called for talks with Russia, Austria, and Prussia in London in 1840. In July the ambassadors of the four powers persuaded the Ottomans to recognize Muhammad Ali as hereditary pasha of Egypt and grant him control of Palestine (southern Syria) in return for a cease-fire within ten days. France, although now under a government more favorable to Britain, was noncommittal, and Muhammad Ali refused the compromise. The British, with help from Austria, occupied Beirut and Acre in October and November and helped the Ottomans defeat Ibrahim's forces in Syria. Muhammad Ali, no longer counting on French help, was forced to accept Egypt as a hereditary domain and return the Ottoman fleet to the control of Constantinople.

Russia, Austria, Prussia, Britain, and France then signed the Treaty of London on 13 July 1841, ratifying these agreements. Appended to the treaty was an agreement on the Straits question: "Warships of foreign powers have always been forbidden to enter the Straits of the Dardanelles and of the Bosporus." Lord Palmerston had succeeded in strengthening Britain's position in the Middle East, preventing France from gaining influence in Syria, and containing Russian advances in the Ottoman Empire. That empire was thus preserved for a time, its existence now guaranteed by the five major European powers. Muhammad Ali remained in control of Egypt, with special rights in the Sudan. Although all parties seemed to have gained something, the stage was set for continued jockeying for position in the Middle East.

See also HUNKAR-ISKELESI, TREATY OF (1833); IBRAHIM IBN MUHAMMAD ALI; KÜTAHYA, PEACE OF; MAHMUD II; MOLTKE, HELMUTH VON; MUHAMMAD ALI; PALMERSTON, LORD HENRY JOHN TEMPLE; STRAITS, TURKISH.

Bibliography

Arnakis, George G. *The Near East in Modern Times,* Vol. 1: *The Ottoman Empire and the Balkan States to 1900.* Austin, TX: Pemberton Press, 1969–1973.

Hurewitz, J. C. *Diplomacy in the Near and Middle East,* Vol. 1: *1535–1914.* Princeton, NJ: Van Nostrand, 1956.

DANIEL E. SPECTOR

STRAITS, TURKISH

A strategic 200-mile (320 km) natural waterway that joins the Black and Aegean seas.

Less than 30 percent of the length of the Straits—the Bosporus, starting in the Black Sea, and the Dardanelles, ending in the Aegean—are natural straits; between them lies the inland Sea of Marmara. So long as the Black Sea was Ottoman and the only approaches flowed through the sultan's domain, he alone decided what ships might visit what parts of his realm. Foreign naval vessels did not enter Ottoman inland waters except on calls of courtesy or for repairs—unless in time of war they sought to breach the sultan's naval defenses. At the Straits and in the Ottoman-dominated river mouths of the Black Sea, attempting such a breach would have entailed over-whelming risks. The fact that at its southern end the Bosporus divided the imperial capital between Europe and Asia enhanced the Ottoman security planners' sensitivity to the movement of foreign vessels through the Straits. By the eighteen century, commercial ships arriving from the Mediterranean were permitted into the Sea of Marmara only as far as Constantinople. From that point north, all trade with Black Sea ports moved on Ottoman ships.

MAP BY XNR PRODUCTIONS, INC. THE GALE GROUP.

Once Russia captured primary river outlets to the Black Sea (such as the Dnieper and the Don—the latter connected to the Black Sea by the Sea of Azov), and thus could validly claim riparian status, the situation changed. The Treaty of Kuçuk Kaynarja, which in 1774 ended a six-year war with the

Ottoman Empire, opened all water lanes with outlets on the Black Sea to Russian commercial shipping. The Ottomans subsequently bestowed the privilege of free merchant navigation through the Straits upon other seafaring powers of Europe and even the United States. This was done by separate act for any Western state enjoying capitulatory (extraterritorial) privileges that requested it. The Ottoman government in 1822 notified all powers that "the passage of the Bosporus is closed to the ships of nations to whom the Porte never accorded the right of entry to . . . [the Black] sea." Not until the Treaty of Paris in 1856 was commercial freedom conferred on all flags.

The transit of war vessels was also resolved by international agreement, starting with the Straits Convention, signed in London on 13 July 1841. Article 1 expressed the sultan's firm resolve "to maintain . . . the principle . . . [whereby] it has . . . been prohibited for the Ships of War of Foreign Powers to enter the Straits . . .; and . . . so long as the Porte is at peace . . . [to] admit no foreign Ship of War into the said Straits." In the same article the powers of Europe pledged "to respect this determination." In Article 2 the sultan reserved "to himself . . . to deliver f[e]rmans [edicts] of passage for light vessels under flag of war . . . employed . . . in the services of the Missions of foreign powers."

The defeat in World War I of the Ottoman imperial government ended the 1841 agreement. Under the Armistice of Mudros in 1918, the victors (chiefly Britain, France, and Italy) imposed a naval occupation on the Sublime Porte, and in 1922 on its successor, the Republic of Turkey. The powers of Europe assumed the role of Straits traffic regulator until the ratification in 1923 of the Treaty of Lausanne. For a dozen years, an International Straits Commission oversaw the flow of all Straits traffic. In 1936 the Montreux Convention restored sovereign authority to the Republic of Turkey.

In conferences with Britain and the United States at Tehran in 1943 and at Yalta in 1945, the Soviet Union declared the Montreux Convention prejudicial to its security interests. It acknowledged that in wartime Turkey had acted with goodwill in defense of the Straits. Nevertheless, Moscow demanded revision of the 1936 convention to assure its warships free movement through the Straits at all times.

When the issue was reviewed at Potsdam in mid-1945, the Western powers agreed that each of the Big Three would hold talks with the Turkish government on revising the 1936 instrument "to meet present-day conditions." After a year of diplomatic exchanges, Moscow's insistence on sharing in the defense of the Straits led to a stalemate in August 1946. The Soviet Union refused to modify its demands, and Britain and the United States gave full support to Turkey. Seven months later, President Harry Truman promulgated the U.S. strategy for the global containment of the Soviet Union "and international communism" thereby marking the formal start of the Cold War.

See also CAPITULATIONS; LAUSANNE, TREATY OF (1923); MONTREUX CONVENTION (1936); STRAITS CONVENTION.

Bibliography

Hurewitz, J. C. *The Middle East and North Africa in World Politics: A Documentary Record.* 2 vols. New Haven, CT: Yale University Press, 1975–1979.

Hurewitz, J. C. "Russia and the Turkish Straits: A Revaluation of the Origins of the Problem." *World Politics* (July 1962): 605–632.

Shotwell, James Thomson, and Deák, Francis. *Turkey at the Straits: A Short History.* New York: Macmillan, 1940.

J. C. HUREWITZ

STRUMA

Ship on which Jewish World War II refugees died, in part because of Britain's wartime refugee policy.

In October 1941, the 180-ton Romanian coastal vessel *Struma,* which normally carried one hundred passengers, sailed for Haifa with almost one thousand Jewish refugees. The ship broke down at Istanbul on 16 December because of overloading, a leaking hull, and defective engines. Turkey would not permit the passengers to land without British certificates for Palestine, but the British refused to issue them.

Since the refugees could not go forward and could not return to Romania, the *Struma* remained in port for ten weeks. The British refused the appeal of the Jewish Agency to permit the refugees entrance to Palestine—if only for later transport to Mauritius, an island in the Indian Ocean. On 24

February, Turkey towed the *Struma* with its passengers out to sea, where six miles from shore it sank; it is not known whether it capsized, struck a mine, or was hit by a torpedo. Some 70 children, 269 women, and 428 men drowned—only 2 swam to safety.

This event became the symbol for the Jewish community in Palestine (the Yishuv) of Britain's unrelenting World War II policy toward the Jewish refugees of Nazi-occupied Europe.

See also YISHUV.

Bibliography

Morse, Arthur D. *While Six Million Died: A Chronicle of American Apathy.* New York: Random House, 1968.

Sachar, Howard M. *A History of Israel: From the Rise of Zionism to Our Time,* 2d revised and updated edition. New York: Knopf, 1996.

MIRIAM SIMON

STUDENTS IN THE LINE OF THE IMAM

An organization of Iranian students that held U.S. hostages for over one year.

Students in the Line of the Imam was a militant group formed after the Iranian Revolution (1979). It advocated radical policies that its members insisted were supported by the revolution's leader, Ayatollah Ruhollah Khomeini, whom they called *imam.* The group acquired domestic and international attention when it seized the U.S. embassy in Tehran in November 1979 and announced that captured U.S. diplomatic personnel would be held until the United States extradited the deposed shah, Mohammad Reza Pahlavi, to Iran for trial. This action began the most dramatic of regional hostage crises, one that would not be resolved for 444 days. During the crisis, the students pasted together shredded secret documents pertaining to U.S. policy that they found in the embassy compound. They published the U.S. documents in several volumes and also used the material in the documents to discredit moderate politicians mentioned in them. Although the Students in the Line of the Imam group gradually was relegated to the margins of Iranian politics after the hostage crisis was resolved in January 1981, several of its leaders subsequently played important roles. Abbas Abdi, for example, became an influential editor and champion of the reform movement in the 1990s. Maryam Ebtehar, media spokesperson for the Students in the Line of the Imam, became Iran's first woman vice president in 1997.

See also HOSTAGE CRISES; IRANIAN REVOLUTION (1979); KHOMEINI, RUHOLLAH; PAHLAVI, MOHAMMAD REZA.

Bibliography

Bakhash, Shaul. *The Reign of the Ayatollahs: Iran and the Islamic Revolution.* New York: Basic Books, 1986.

Iran Research Group. *Who's Who in Iran.* Meckenheim, Germany, 1990.

NEGUIN YAVARI
UPDATED BY ERIC HOOGLUND

SUARÈS FAMILY

Prominent Sephardic family, influential in Egyptian society and economy.

The Suarès family settled in Livorno, Italy, then went to Egypt during the first half of the nineteenth century. Menachem Suarès della Pegna settled in Alexandria while his brother Isaac settled in Cairo. In the mid-1870s Isaac's sons—Joseph (1837–1900), Félix (1844–1906), and Raphael (1846–1902)—created the Banque Suarès, which until 1906 served as mediator for European capital investment in Egypt. Given Raphael Suarès's connections with British industrial investors, he channeled British investments into such enterprises as the construction of the first Aswan Dam, the National Bank of Egypt, and the khedivial estates *(al-da'ira al-saniyya).* The Suarès family was not only involved in banking and finance but also transportation, establishing in Cairo the first public transportation company and building railway lines between Cairo and Helwan, Qina and Aswan. Members of the family owned real estate in the heart of Cairo where Suarès Square bore Félix Suarès's name (Maydan Suarès was renamed, in 1939, Maydan Mustafa Kamil).

One family member, Edgar Suarès, was involved with a major shareholders' company. Owing to his initiative, vast areas of land—several thousand *feddan* (a *feddan* is approximately one acre)—were purchased in Upper and Lower Egypt. Edgar Suarès reclaimed them and introduced modern irrigation facilities for large-scale agricultural development. He subsequently sold the land as small holdings to rural Egyptians at low prices and long-term credit. The Suarèses were not very active in Jewish communal affairs; only Edgar Suarès served very briefly as president of Alexandria's Jewish community during World War I. Their influence in Egyptian society and the economy declined after the 1930s.

Bibliography

Krämer, Gudrun. *The Jews in Modern Egypt, 1914–1952.* Seattle: University of Washington Press, 1989.

Mizrahi, Maurice. "The Role of Jews in Economic Development." In *The Jews of Egypt: A Mediterranean Society in Modern Times,* edited by Shimon Shamir. Boulder, CO: Westview Press, 1987.

MICHAEL M. LASKIER

SUBLIME PORTE

Residence/office of the Ottoman sultan.

In the Ottoman Empire, the sultan would appoint a grand vizier to head the government. Just as the prime minister of Great Britain resides at 10 Downing Street, the grand vizier of the Ottoman Empire lived and worked in the Sublime Porte. This term is a French translation of *al-Bab al-Ali,* which means literally "the High Door." In the nineteenth century, it became common to refer to the entire Ottoman government as "the Sublime Porte," as it is common today to refer to the U.S. government as "the White House."

Bibliography

Lewis, Bernard. *The Emergence of Modern Turkey,* 3d edition. New York: Oxford University Press, 2002.

ZACHARY KARABELL

SUDAN

A country in northeast Africa located south of Egypt on the Nile.

Known in the past as *bilad al-sudan* (the land of the black people), Sudan is the largest country in Africa, covering one million square miles. Its nearly thirty million residents, who live scattered across the wide expanse, differ along lines of ethnicity, language, and religion. The country's political instability is, in part, a result of this diversity. Moreover, given its geostrategic location astride the Nile, it has been vulnerable to foreign pressure.

Omdurman is the largest city and chief commercial center of Sudan. It is located across the White Nile from Khartoum, the country's capital. © CORBIS. REPRODUCED BY PERMISSION.

Peoples

Sudan contains more than fifty ethnic groups, which are subdivided into at least 570 tribes. The principal groups in the north are Arab, Beja, Nuba, Nubian, and Fur. Nearly half the population identifies itself as Arab, generally meaning peoples who speak Arabic and reflect its cultural heritage. The Arabs along the northern and central Nile valley tend to dominate Sudanese political and economic life. The Beja, who comprise 6 to 7 percent of the population, are concentrated in the east along the Red Sea and coastal mountain ranges; they are Muslim but speak a distinct language. The Nuba, residing in the Nuba mountains of southern Kordofan, are 5 percent of the population and also speak their own

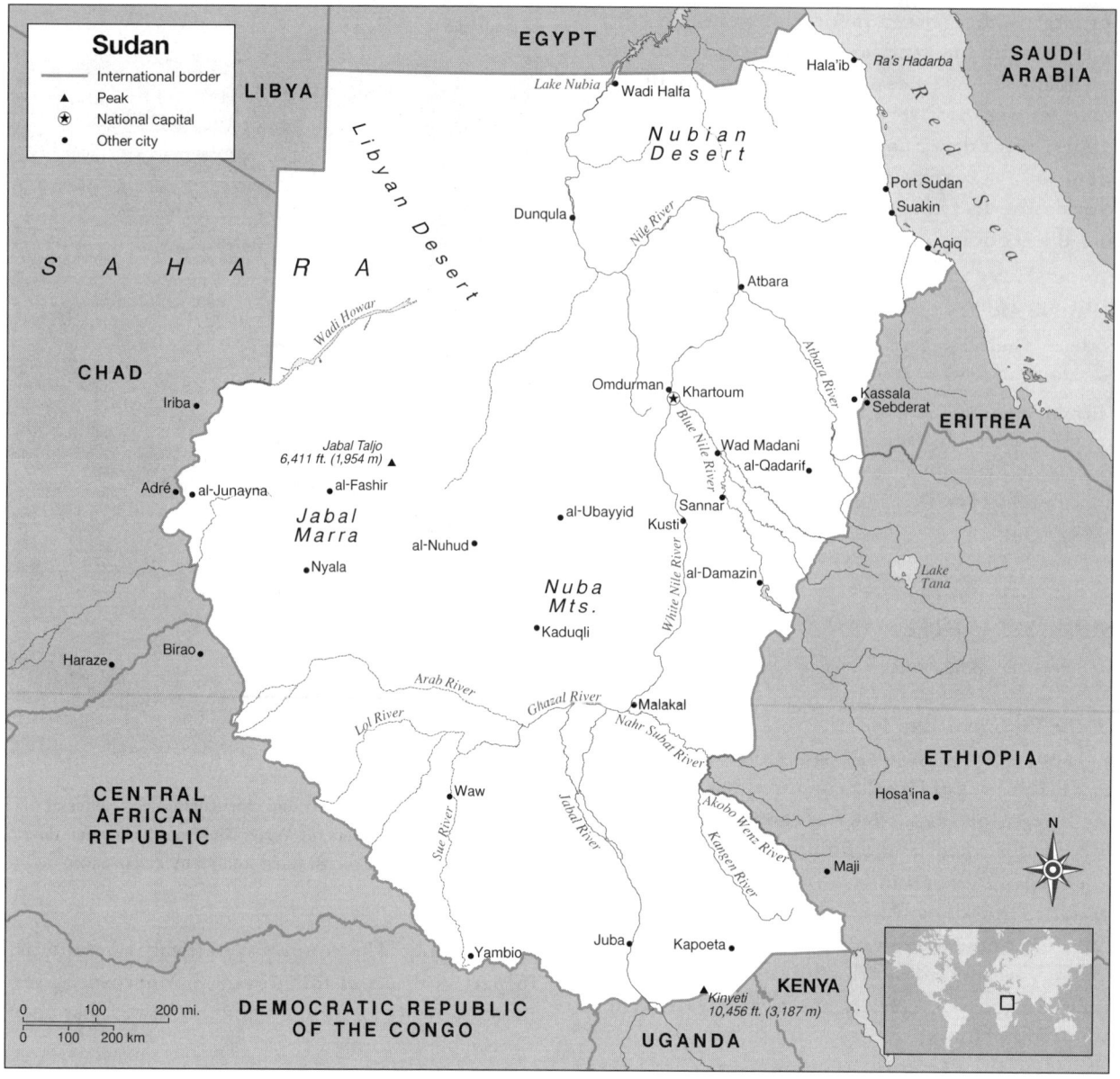

MAP BY XNR PRODUCTIONS, INC. THE GALE GROUP.

languages, not Arabic; some are Muslim, others Christian or adherents of traditional African religious beliefs. About 3 percent are Nubians, who traditionally lived along the northern reaches of the Nile, merging into Egypt. In the early 1960s, many Nubians were relocated to Khashm al-Ghirba in central Sudan when the construction of the Aswan High Dam flooded their homes. They speak their own ancient languages; they were early converts to Christianity but converted to Islam several centuries ago. The Fur, 2 percent of the population, live in the far west; like the Nubians, they have a tradition of independent kingdoms. The Sultanate of Fur lasted from the fifteenth century until the early 1890s. Many other non-Arab peoples live in villages in the west, notably the Berti, Zaghawa, Borgu, and Massalit.

In the southern third of Sudan, the Dinka are 40 percent of the population, or 12 percent of the Sudanese as a whole. The Nuer are 5 percent of the whole Sudanese people, and the Shilluk are 1 percent. None of those groups are homogeneous, and they compete for territory, cattle, and trade routes.

The numerous groups that live in Equatoria, the southernmost area, differ in language, customs, and religion. Overall, the ethnic fragmentation in the south is greater than in the north.

In addition to those indigenous groups, 6 percent of the Sudanese are migrants from West Africa who settled in western and central Sudan in search of employment or on their way to or from Mecca, the most important site for Muslim pilgrims. Known by the pejorative term *fellata,* they lack many of the legal and economic protections accorded to full Sudanese citizens.

Language overlaps with ethnicity as a basic distinguishing trait among the Sudanese. Half the population speaks Arabic as its native tongue. At most, half the adults are literate (far fewer than that in the wartorn south and Nuba Mountains), and indigenous languages remain important. Arabic serves as the lingua franca among the educated classes in the north. Although residents of the south resisted learning Arabic and were taught English in the missionary schools, Arabic has made inroads there in recent decades.

Religion also divides the population—65 to 70 percent are Muslim, 20 to 25 percent follow traditional beliefs, and 5 to 10 percent are Christian. The north is overwhelmingly Muslim, with pockets of Christians in the Nuba Mountains and in urban areas. Many Muslims belong to the networks of Sufi *tariqas* (brotherhoods) that formed around holy men and serve economic, social, and political as well as religious functions. The brotherhoods cut across tribal and ethnic allegiances: For example, many Beja belong to the Khatmiyya order, which is led by the Arab riverain Mirghani family. Otherwise, most of the divisions reinforce cleavages, particularly the Arab/Muslim separation from the African/non-Muslim.

Geography and Economy

Sudan is predominantly rural, with a third of the population living in urban areas. (That share is growing as people flee famine in the outlying provinces.) Two-thirds of the labor force works in agriculture or herding, and a third of the gross national product was derived from agriculture until the advent of oil exports in 1999. Northern Sudan is largely flat savannah and desert where cattle,

Men in Rashayda build a mud hut. In many areas of Sudan, there is little building material to work with other than what nature has provided. Even some government facilities, such as immigration and customs centers, are wattle-and-daub structures. © CORBIS. REPRODUCED BY PERMISSION.

camels, and sheep are raised, sorghum and sesame are grown, and gum arabic is harvested. Meat and grains are sold in large amounts to oil-rich states in Arabia, and gum arabic is exported to Europe and the United States for use in soft drinks. Along the Blue and White Nile, south of Khartoum, cotton and peanuts are grown for export on large-scale agricultural holdings called *schemes.* Rains are heavier in the tropical south than in the north, but development in the south has been hampered by civil war and difficult conditions, such as the vast swamp known as the Sudd (barrier). The north suffers from severe deforestation: The forest cover diminished annually by one percent in the 1980s and 1990s due to overgrazing, charcoal burning, and drought.

Industry is based on agriculture, and its products are consumed within the country. Manufactures include sugar refining, flour milling, vegetable oil processing, canning, and textiles. Cement, tire, and cigarette production is also important for the domestic market.

There are substantial untapped deposits of copper and other minerals in Sudan. Chinese and French joint ventures export gold from the Red Sea Hills. Oil has now become the most important resource.

In 1979 the Chevron Oil Company discovered oil in Bentiu (Upper Nile) and Muglad (southern Kordofan). Extraction was blocked by the civil war that resumed in 1983. Chevron sold out its share to the Sudanese government in 1984. In the mid-1990s the government resumed exploration, utilizing the skills of a consortium of Canadian, European, Chinese, and Malaysian oil companies. Export began in August 1999, when the pipeline to Port Sudan was completed. Since then Sudan has become self-sufficient in oil. It exports increasing amounts of crude and refined oil, particularly to East Africa and Asia. The Canadian Talisman company sold its share to the Indian state oil company in 2002 after widespread protests by human-rights groups against the government's expulsion of Nuer from Upper Nile in order to ensure central control over this vital resource.

Oil exports have enabled Sudan to have a positive balance of trade for the first time in decades and to start to reduce its heavy debt burden. That burden is estimated at $23 billion, most of which is long in arrears. U.S. government sanctions, imposed in November 1997, ban U.S. companies from conducting transactions in Sudan, with the exception of those for gum Arabic.

Urban Areas

The urban population is centered in the Three Towns—Khartoum, Omdurman, and Khartoum North—which serve as the political and economic capital and together house at least 1.2 million people. Port Sudan (pop. 300,000), built by the British in 1910, remains the only port on the Red Sea, although efforts have been made to revive the historic port at Sawakin. Kassala (pop. 235,000) and Qadarif (pop. 190,000) are the main towns in the grain-growing east, and Wad Madani (pop. 220,000) is the capital of the cotton-growing Gezira area. In the west, al-Ubayyad (pop. 230,000) serves as the capital of Kordofan, and al-Fashir—on the border with Chad—is the capital of Darfur; both are important trading centers. Juba (pop. 115,000), the capital of Equatoria, was the capital of the south when it was unified from 1972 to 1983; it has been isolated from the surrounding countryside by the rebel forces of the Sudan Peoples Liberation Army (SPLA) since 1985.

History since 1821

The territory that now comprises Sudan was not unified until the Turco-Egyptian invasion of 1821, which imposed centralized control over most of the north relatively quickly. The Turco-Egyptian forces did not conquer Darfur until 1874 and never subdued the southern tribes. Their raiders seized gold, ivory, and slaves from the south, deeply alienating those African peoples.

The indigenous politico-religious movement called the Mahdiyya overthew the Turco-Egyptian government in 1885 and ruled until 1898. Muhammad Ahmad ibn Abdullah called himself the *mahdi* (messiah) in 1881, gathering his followers on Aba Island (White Nile) and later in Kordofan, from which he launched attacks against the Turco-Egyptian army. The mahdi died shortly afterward. His successor *(khalifa)* Abdullahi al-Ta'isha consolidated control over northern Sudan and attempted to seize territory from Ethiopia and Egypt. He established a religious-based government that continued to raid into the southern areas, seizing slaves and promoting Islam.

British forces, marching south from Egypt, overran the country in 1898 to 1899 and imposed the Anglo-Egyptian condominium. Messianic anticolonial revolts broke out in the west and center, and were finally subdued in 1912. Sultan Ali Dinar was not defeated in Darfur until 1916. In the early 1920s nationalist outbreaks called for Sudan's independence, or for its linking with Egypt: Those two strands persisted in the northern nationalist movement until Egypt renounced its claim to Sudan in the 1950s. One enduring legacy of British rule was the virtual separation of the south from the north; from 1922 to 1946 the southern provinces and Nuba Mountains were isolated from the rest of the country. Meanwhile, considerable economic and educational development took place in the north, centered on the Gezira agricultural scheme (opened in 1925) and Gordon Memorial College (opened in 1903). In 1938 the graduates formed the Graduates Congress, which lobbied for independence during World War II. By then, several northern political parties also competed for influence. Britain established a legislative assembly in 1948; this led to self-government in 1952 and the election of the first parliament in the next year. Sudanization of the army and administration began in 1954. Those measures primarily benefited the north; the south was compelled to accept a subordinate position at the Juba Conference (1947) and hardly benefited from Sudanization.

When Sudan gained independence on 1 January 1956, parliamentary rule was established. The two leading religious orders—the Ansar and the Khatmiyya—predominated in the new governments, although secular nationalists, communists, and southerners gained token positions in the parliament. The democratic institutions had not had taken root by the time General Ibrahim Abbud instituted military rule on 17 November 1958. His rule lasted until November 1964, when a popular uprising led to a renewed democracy. That, too, proved unstable as the traditional politicians jockeyed for power, were challenged from the religious right by Hasan al-Turabi's Islamist Party, and failed to deal with the rebellion that had accelerated in the south during Abbud's era.

Young officers led by Muhammad Jaʿfar Numeiri launched a coup d'état on 25 May 1969 and crushed the traditional political groups. Numeiri turned against his left-wing allies in 1971 but mollified the south by granting regional autonomy in 1972. He instituted major economic development programs in the mid-1970s, backed by the party, the Sudan Socialist Union. Economic development remained hampered by poor planning, high-level corruption, and skyrocketing oil prices. In 1977 to 1978 Numeiri sought to widen his base of support by reconciling with the traditional and fundamentalist religious forces. That led to the gradual Islamization of the political system. Numeiri instituted Islamic criminal punishments in September 1983, which he enforced against widespread opposition by draconian emergency measures. By spring 1985 Numeiri's support was confined to Turabi's Islamic movement—northern secularists, the banned political forces, and the southerners (who resumed their civil war in 1983 under the banner of the Sudan People's Liberation Movement) actively sought to overthrow him.

In April 1985 a popular uprising led to a bloodless coup and the installation of a one-year Transitional Military Council. Elections were held in April 1986, and northern religious-oriented political movements won 85 percent of the seats. Turabi's National Islamic Front (NIF) won 20 percent of those seats. African (southern and Nuba) and northern secularist (communist) parties controlled only 15 percent of the parliamentary seats. Al-Sadiq al-Mahdi, leader of the Umma Party and the Ansar religious order, became prime minister. Despite his pledges to institute a liberal government and to negotiate an end to the fighting, he failed to cancel Numeiri's Islamic laws. Instead, he announced that he would not enforce them in the south, a move that alienated the southerners as well as northern secularists. Mahdi's rival Muhammad Uthman al-Mirghani, leader of the Khatmiyya Sufi order and head of the Democratic Unionist Party (DUP), won acclaim for reaching an agreement with the SPLM to freeze the Islamic laws pending the convening of a constitutional conference. Mahdi and Turabi joined to force the DUP out of the government, but the senior army officers then compelled Mahdi to endorse Mirghani's agreement and negotiate with the SPLM.

On 30 June 1989, hours before the government could finalize the freezing of Islamic law, Brigadier Umar Hasan Ahmad al-Bashir overthrew the government. The coup d'état was orchestrated by Turabi's NIF, which vehemently opposed the annulment of Islamic law. Once again, constitutional institutions were banned: Bashir closed the parliament, banned political parties and trade unions, and shut down independent newspapers. The government accelerated the fighting in the south and in the Nuba mountains. The civil war was redefined as a jihad (holy war) against infidels and apostates. The regime instituted Islamic legal codes in 1991 and an Islamic constitution in 1999. In the late 1990s it reintroduced carefully controlled parliamentary elections and a direct presidential election, which Bashir won handily. In late 1999 Bashir and Turabi had a major falling-out after Turabi sought to sideline Bashir. Bashir, using his power as president and commander of the military and security services, decreed emergency rule and closed down the parliament. From early 2001 until late 2003, Bashir kept Turabi either in jail or under house arrest.

The political and trade union groups that had benefited from the short-lived parliamentary system formed the National Democratic Alliance (NDA) in October 1989. NDA members inside Sudan attempted to mount protests and petitions, which were crushed by the military regime. Most of the leaders fled into exile, from which they continued to try to overthrow the government and reinstitute democracy. The NDA attempted to mount military operations in eastern Sudan, but it lacked the strength to bring down the regime either militarily or politically. The government even attracted Mahdi back to Khartoum in 2000, but it failed to provide him with a significant political position.

Sudan Today

The geostrategic location of Sudan contributes to its sociopolitical instability. Located astride the Nile River, which flows north from Ethiopia and Uganda into Sudan and through Egypt to the Mediterranean Sea, Sudan has been the object of contention by those neighbors as well as external powers. Egypt cannot tolerate the presence of a hostile government in Khartoum, because the Egyptian economy depends on the Nile waters. Sudan and Egypt worry that Ethiopia might dam the Blue Nile and deprive them both of water. Sudan also borders the Red Sea, a major artery of international trade, and adjoins nine countries (Egypt, Libya, Chad, Central African Republic, Congo, Uganda, Kenya, Ethiopia, and Eritrea). Lacking the capacity to police its remote desert borders and its lengthy coast along the Red Sea, Sudan is vulnerable to incursion. Refugees from neighboring civil wars and famines find haven in Sudan, and hostile governments support rebellious Sudanese groups. Sudanese governments have meddled in the politics of such neighbors as Ethiopia, Chad, and Uganda, although those countries can easily undertake reprisals.

Some view Sudan as a *terra media,* lying between and linking Africa and the Arab world; others see it as lying on the fault line between the two peoples, torn between them and unable to unite. Nearly fifteen years after achieving independence, Sudan's national identity and political system are still violently contested.

See also ABBUD, IBRAHIM; ANSAR, AL-; BEJA; DINKA; KHARTOUM; KORDOFAN; NUBIANS; NUER; NUMEIRI, MUHAMMAD JAʿFAR; OMDURMAN; SHILLUK; SUDANESE CIVIL WARS; TURABI, HASAN AL-; UMMA PARTY.

Bibliography

Abdel Rahim, Muddathir. *Imperialism and Nationalism in the Sudan.* Oxford, U.K.: Clarendon Press, 1969.

Bechtold, Peter K. *Politics in the Sudan: Parliamentary and Military Rule in an Emerging African Nation.* New York: Praeger, 1976.

Beshir, Mohamed Omer. *Revolution and Nationalism in the Sudan.* London: Rex Collings, 1974.

Khalid, Mansour. *The Government They Deserve: The Role of the Elite in Sudan's Political Evolution.* London: Kegan Paul, 1990.

Lesch, Ann M. *The Sudan: Contested National Identities.* Bloomington: Indiana University Press, 1998.

Lobban, Richard A., Jr.; Kramer, Robert S.; and Fluehr-Lobban, Carolyn. *Historical Dictionary of the Sudan,* 3d edition. Lanham, MD: Scarecrow Press, 2002.

Mahmoud, Fatima Babiker. *The Sudanese Bourgeoisie: Vanguard of Development?* London: Zed Books, 1984.

Voll, John Obert, and Voll, Sarah Potts. *The Sudan: Unity and Diversity in a Multicultural State.* Boulder, CO: Westview Press, 1985.

Woodward, Peter. *Sudan, 1898–1989: The Unstable State.* Boulder, CO: Westview Press, 1990.

ANN M. LESCH

SUDANESE CIVIL WARS

Two wars fought since the independence of Sudan in 1956.

There have been two prolonged civil wars in Sudan since independence in 1956. The first lasted from August 1955 to March 1972, and the second began in May 1983. Although both wars have been fought largely in the southern third of the country, their aims have diverged. The first aimed at independence, or at least autonomy for the south, whereas the second primarily aimed at restructuring the central political institutions and devolving power on marginalized areas. Secession is the fallback position should restructuring fail.

The background for the wars lay in the tension between north and south Sudan, the former largely Arabic speaking and Muslim and the latter home to diverse African peoples who adhered to traditional religions or converted to Christianity. Southern peoples had resisted Turco-Egyptian and Mahdist slave raids in the nineteenth century; the British did not manage to subdue them until the 1920s. Britain then imposed the Closed Districts Act (1925) and other measures that banned northern traders and Muslim preachers from the south and even banned Arab-style dress and the use of the Arabic language in government offices and schools. Britain failed to promote education and economic development in the south, leaving it far behind the north when the two parts were merged at independence under a centralized system that placed power in the hands of northerners. Many southerners felt that they had not gained independence but had, instead, exchanged one foreign ruler for another.

First Civil War, 1955–1972

The first civil war was triggered by the Torit mutiny (August 1955) of the Southern Defence Force and was heightened by the northern politicians' rejection of federalism. Under the parliamentary system (1956–1958), the south was marginalized politically. Under the military rule of General Ibrahim Abbud (1958–1964), the religious and ethnic norms that predominate in the north were imposed on the south: Arabic became the language of government and education, Islam was promoted and Christianity repressed, and increasingly harsh military means were used to quell the revolt. The return to civilian rule in late 1964 did not, in itself, end the conflict. Although the Roundtable Conference of March 1965 examined southern grievances, the ruling northern political parties still sought to establish an Islamic state, which was anathema to southerners and northern secularists. Only after Muhammad Jaʿfar Numeiri seized power in May 1969 was an effort made to recognize the inherent ethnic and religious diversity in Sudan and negotiate with the Anya-Nya rebels. The Addis Ababa Accord of 27 February 1972, which ended the first war, was implemented through the Regional Self-Government Act for the Southern Provinces (promulgated on 3 March 1972) and incorporated into the permanent constitution of 1973. The three southern provinces became one large region with its own regional assembly and High Executive Council (HEC). The south gained considerable autonomy in the social and economic fields. Religious discrimination was prohibited, and English was recognized as the principal language in the south because it had been the common language used in schools. Efforts were made to reintegrate the refugees who had fled the country during the seventeen years of fighting and to absorb the Anya-Nya into the regular armed forces.

Despite constitutional safeguards against altering provisions of the Addis Ababa Accord, Numeiri interfered continually in the implementation of the accord. At times, he dissolved the regional assembly, dismissed the HEC, and tried to prevent potential oil revenue from accruing to the south. Finally, he decreed on 5 June 1983 the redivision of the south into its three original provinces. That illegal action completed the dismemberment of the accord. By then, members of the absorbed Anya-Nya forces had engaged in sporadic mutinies, culminating in mutinies in Bor and Pibor in spring 1983. When Numeiri sent troops to crush the mutineers, they fled to the bush, where they were joined by Colonel John Garang de Mabior, head of the army research center in Khartoum.

Second Civil War, 1983

By midsummer 1983 Garang had molded the Sudan People's Liberation Army (SPLA) and its political wing, the Sudan People's Liberation Movement (SPLM) into a militant force that supported the continued unity of Sudan, but on a new basis, requiring proportional sharing of power among the various peoples and regions; special attention to the socioeconomic needs of the deprived east, west, and south; and nondomination by any one religious or racial group over the others. The SPLM gained support as Numeiri's policies led to economic ruin and his institution of Islamic law in September 1983 alienated a wide array of citizens. Numeiri's overthrow in April 1985 did not, however, end the rebellion. The transitional government (April 1985 to April 1986) and the elected government under Prime Minister al-Sadiq al-Mahdi (May 1986 through June 1989) failed to respond to the underlying demands of the SPLM and SPLA. The governments sought to modify, rather than annul, Islamic laws, and they treated the SPLM merely as a southern movement. Nonetheless, in spring 1989 the high command of the armed forces compelled the politicians to negotiate an accord with the SPLM that involved canceling Islamic laws until a constitutional conference could resolve the issue of the legal basis of rule. By then, the SPLA controlled nearly 90 percent of the countryside in the south and had made inroads into areas in the north. Fighting had spread into the Nuba Mountains and the southern Blue Nile Province, where the Ingessana people held economic and political grievances against their Arab overlords.

The Sudan People's Liberation Army fought for a unified Sudan during the country's second civil war. © AP/WIDE WORLD PHOTOS. REPRODUCED BY PERMISSION.

That effort to negotiate a solution was undermined abruptly by the coup d'état on 30 June 1989—the coup's leaders rejected the agreement to hold the constitutional conference and insisted that Islamic laws be retained. A comprehensive Islamic legal system was instituted in the north and the south was fragmented into ten provinces. After the coup, the SPLM aligned with the exiled opposition National Democratic Alliance in March 1990 and gained the support of the ousted high command of the armed forces in September 1990. The SPLM became the most militarily active element in the nationalist opposition to the Islamist military government. By 1991 the SPLA controlled nearly all the south. However, the fall of Mengistu's government in Ethiopia, which had provided essential support for the SPLA, deepened internal tensions inside the SPLA. Commanders in Upper Nile defected in August 1991, thereby enabling the armed forces to recapture many garrisons and to put the SPLA on the defensive.

Prospects for a negotiated solution seemed to vanish. At negotiations in Abuja, Nigeria, in 1992 and 1993, the SPLM proposed establishing a confederal system, just short of secession, but the government responded that "secession will come at the barrel of the gun" (Wondu and Lesch, p. 51). The Organization of African Unity's East African Intergovernmental Authority on Drought and Desertification (IGADD) initiated negotiations in 1994. IGADD called for the formation of a secular state in Sudan; absent a secular, democratic system, the south should have the right to secede. This position pleased the SPLM but infuriated the government in Khartoum. Only in 1997 did the government allow the issue of self-determination to be an agenda item in the negotiations. Soon after, Khartoum's incentive to negotiate diminished: The export of oil from Upper Nile, which began in August 1999, enabled the government to double its arms purchases within two years and establish military industries. The expulsion of the indigenous (largely Nuer) population from the oil fields area accelerated in the late 1990s and early 2000s. This deepened the already severe humanitarian crisis on the south.

After 11 September 2001, the government began to respond to U.S. pressure to negotiate. It reengaged in negotiations (the African body having been renamed the Intergovernmental Authority on Development—IGAD) and signed a potentially breakthrough accord with the SPLM at Machakos (Kenya) in July 2002. This accord called for the formation of a confederation between the north and south that would last for a transitional six years. Negotiations during the winter of 2002 to 2003 over the specifics of power and resource sharing and the relation of religion to the state remained acrimonious and it remained uncertain whether a fundamental accord was possible. The future status of the other marginalized areas also remained uncertain.

The two civil wars sought to deal with the underlying problem of Sudan—how to build unity in a multiethnic and multireligious country. The first war proposed regionalism as the means to give each community a degree of autonomy; the second war proposed restructuring power in the center so that regional autonomy could be secure. Sudanese politicians still grapple with that fundamental problem.

See also ABBUD, IBRAHIM; GARANG, JOHN; NUMEIRI, MUHAMMAD JAʿFAR; SUDAN.

Bibliography

Alier, Abel. *Southern Sudan: Too Many Agreements Dishonoured.* Exeter, U.K.: Ithaca Press, 1990.

Beshir, Mohammed Omer. *The Southern Sudan: Background to Conflict.* London: Hurst, 1968.

Deng, Francis. *War of Visions: Conflict of Identities in the Sudan.* Washington, DC: Brookings Institution Press, 1995.

Garang, John. *John Garang Speaks,* edited by Mansour Khalid. London: Kegan Paul, 1987.

Jok, Jok Madut. *War and Slavery in Sudan.* Philadelphia: University of Pennsylvania Press, 2001.

Lesch, Ann M. *The Sudan: Contested National Identities.* Bloomington: Indiana University Press, 1998.

Wondu, Steven, and Lesch, Ann. *Battle for Peace in Sudan: An Analysis of the Abuja Conferences, 1992–1993.* Lanham, MD: University Press of America, 2000.

ANN M. LESCH

SUDANESE WOMEN'S UNION

Women's-rights organization.

The Sudanese Women's Union (SWU), an affiliate of the Sudanese Communist Party and an heir of the Educated Girls' Association and the Association of Sudanese Women as well as other organizations of the 1940s, was founded in 1952. Its first executive committee was composed of Fatima Talib, Khalda Zahir, and Fatima Ahmed Ibrahim.

The SWU was active during the late nationalist period (1952–1956). It reached its zenith in 1965, when it had branches throughout the country and a successful monthly publication, *Sawt al-Marʾa* (Woman's voice), and had made gains in women's rights such as suffrage, equal pay, and maternity leave. In addition, its president, Fatima Ibrahim, was the first woman elected to parliament. Under Ibrahim's leadership, the SWU gained prominence as one of the largest and most effective women's organizations on the African continent, boasting some 15,000 members at its peak.

Political repression under successive military governments took a toll on the SWU. Ultimately, with the Islamist military coup d'etat in 1989, the SWU was forced underground and Ibrahim into exile in London. Nonetheless, in the 1990s Amnesty International and the United Nations presented the SWU with human-rights awards for its history of struggle and its efforts in exile.

See also GENDER: GENDER AND LAW; GENDER: GENDER AND POLITICS; IBRAHIM, FATIMA AHMED; SUDAN; SUDANESE CIVIL WARS.

Bibliography

Fluehr-Lobban, Carolyn. "Women and Social Liberation: The Sudan Experience." In *Three Studies on National Integration in the Arab World.* North Dartmouth, MA: Association of Arab-American University Graduates, 1974.

Hale, Sondra. *Gender Politics in Sudan: Islamism, Socialism, and the State.* Boulder, CO: Westview Press, 1996.

Hall, Marjorie, and Ismail, Bakhita Amin. *Sisters under the Sun: The Story of Sudanese Women.* London: Longman, 1981.

Mahmoud, Fatima Babiker. *The Role of the Sudanese Women's Movement in Sudanese Politics.* Unpublished M.A. dissertation, University of Khartoum, 1971.

Niblock, Tim. *Class and Power in Sudan.* Albany: State University of New York Press, 1987.

Sanousi, Magda M. el-, and Amin, Nafissa Ahmed el-. "The Women's Movement, Displaced Women, and Rural Women in Sudan." In *Women and Politics Worldwide,* edited by Barbara Nelson and Najma Chowdhury. New Haven, CT: Yale University Press, 1994.

SONDRA HALE

SUDD

Great swamps of the Upper Nile.

Sudd (in Arabic, *sadd,* or barrier) was the word used by European and Arab merchants to describe the largest swamps in the world, which are situated on the Upper Nile in Sudan. It had prevented passage up the Nile River until 1841, when Salim Qapudan, acting on the orders of Muhammad Ali Pasha, viceroy of Egypt, was the first person to pass through its labyrinthine channels. Although open to navigation, the Sudd continues to present a formidable barrier to the passage of water from the equatorial lakes to Sudan and Egypt. Its size expands and contracts depending on the amount of water from the lakes, and its slope, only a few inches per mile, spreads any additional water across the Nilotic plain. The average annual amount of water flowing into the Sudd in the twentieth century is 33 billion cubic meters, of which only half, some 16 billion cubic meters, leaves the Sudd for Sudan and Egypt. In 1976 the French Compagnie de Constructions Internationales (CCI) began the excavation of the Jonglei Canal to permit water from the Lake Plateau to bypass the swamps. The excavation of the 225-mile canal past the Sudd threatened to disrupt the seasonal movement of livestock and the migrations of great herds of African wildlife. When the Sudan People's Liberation Movement/Army (SPLM/A), led by John Garang de Mabior, revolted against the Sudan government in May 1983, his forces terminated the canal's construction at mile 166. It has never been resumed.

See also NILE RIVER.

Bibliography

Collins, Robert. *The Nile.* New Haven, CT: Yale University Press, 2002.

Howell, Paul P.; Lock, M.; and Cobb, S. *The Jonglei Canal: Impact and Opportunity.* Cambridge, U.K.: Cambridge University Press, 1988.

ROBERT O. COLLINS

SUEZ CANAL

Channel built from 1856 to 1869 that links the Mediterranean Sea to the Red Sea.

Several early rulers of Egypt constructed canals for the passage of seagoing ships, usually linking the Nile River to the Gulf of Suez. The followers of Saint-Simon, the French utopian socialist (Claude Henri de Rouvray, Comte de Saint-Simon, 1760–1825), proposed building a canal linking the Mediterranean to the Red Sea in the early nineteenth century. The entrepreneur who actually carried out this scheme was Ferdinand de Lesseps, a former French diplomat who was on friendly terms with Muhammad Saʿid Pasha. As soon as Saʿid became Egypt's viceroy in 1854, de Lesseps described to him his plan for constructing and financing this waterway, which would be the largest public-works project in Egypt since the pyramids. Saʿid consented, but it took some time for de Lesseps to secure approval from the sultan of the Ottoman

The Suez Canal was inaugurated on 17 November 1869. The waterway, which extends one hundred miles and has been enlarged twice since its completion, is used to transport 41 percent of goods and cargo that reach the Persian/Arab Gulf ports and 14 percent of total world trade. © BETTMANN/CORBIS. REPRODUCED BY PERMISSION.

Empire and the European powers (Britain was strongly opposed to a canal that might imperil its defense of India) and to raise the necessary capital.

The construction cost, estimated at more than 450 million French francs (worth about $100 million at that time), was borne mainly by Egyptian taxpayers and by thousands of unpaid or underpaid Egyptian peasants who were forced into corvée labor until the European powers and the Ottoman government enjoined the Universal Maritime Suez Canal Company to stop this practice.

When the 100-mile waterway was opened in 1869, it was 30 feet deep and 100 feet wide, adequate for most oceangoing vessels at the time. It soon became a main trade route for steam-driven passenger and cargo ships because it reduced travel time between Europe and East Africa, South Asia, China, Japan, and the East Indies. The canal was supposed to be open to ships of all nations in war or peace, but Britain made sure that it was closed to shipping for Germany and its allies in both world wars, and Egypt barred its use to Israel and to other countries' ships carrying goods for Israel until 1975. The canal was administered by the Canal Company until it was nationalized by Egypt under Gamal Abdel Nasser in 1956. Since then it has been admin-

Suez Canal

	No. of transits		Net ship tonnage in thousands of tons	
	2000	2001	2000	2001
Tankers	2,563	2,764	105,237	117,014
Other vessels	11,578	11,222	333,725	339,099
Total	14,141	13,986	438,962	456,113

SOURCE: MEES 45:18, 6 May 2002.

TABLE BY GGS INFORMATION SERVICES, THE GALE GROUP.

istered by the Suez Canal Authority. It was closed from 1956 to 1967 and from 1967 to 1975 because of the Arab-Israel conflict.

The canal was enlarged from 1960 to 1964 and from 1975 to 1980 to accommodate larger oil tankers, which have become its main users; in 1992, it was 590 feet wide at its narrowest point and had a maximum draught of 53 feet. Transit time is now 15 hours, and 80 ships can transit per day. The Suez Canal is a major route for transport of crude oil from the Persian Gulf. In 2000 the northbound tankers from the Gulf carried 28.2 million tons of crude oil (about 580,000 barrels per day) and in 2001 28.8 million tons (about 592,000 barrels per day).

The transit rates are established by the Suez Canal Authority. They are computed to keep the canal transit fees attractive to shippers. For example, in January 2002, the fee for the transport of crude oil for very large tankers was $1.21 per ton above the first 30,000 tons. Such a rate would amount to approximately $190,000 for a 150,000-ton oil tanker.

See also LESSEPS, FERDINAND DE; NASSER, GAMAL ABDEL; SAʿID PASHA; SUEZ CRISIS (1956–1957).

Bibliography

Beatty, Charles. *De Lesseps of Suez.* New York: Harper, 1956.

Kyle, Keith. *Suez: Britain's End of Empire in the Middle East.* New York: I.B. Tauris, 2003.

Marlowe, John. *The Making of the Suez Canal.* London: Cresset Press, 1964.

Schonfield, Hugh J. *The Suez Canal in Peace and War.* Coral Gables, FL: University of Miami Press, 1969.

ARTHUR GOLDSCHMIDT
UPDATED BY JEAN-FRANÇOIS SEZNEC

SUEZ CANAL UNIVERSITY

Public university founded in Ismaʿilia, Egypt, in 1976.

Egypt's President Anwar al-Sadat (1970–1981) founded Suez Canal University as part of his plan to rebuild and symbolically reclaim the war-damaged Suez Canal cities. In 1975 he had reopened the canal, which had been blocked since the June 1967 Arab–Israel War. With five colleges in Ismaʿilyya and two each in al-Arish and Suez, the university has a teaching staff of 638, 12,312 undergraduates, and 1,588 graduate students.

Bibliography

Suez Canal University. Available from <http://www.suez.edu.eg>.

The World of Learning 2004. London, Europa Publications, 2004: pp. 492–93.

DONALD MALCOLM REID

SUEZ CRISIS (1956–1957)

The British and French challenging of Egyptian President Nasser's nationalization of the Suez Canal, also involving Israel, and ending in the achievement of control of the Canal by Egypt.

On 26 July 1956, before 100,000 Egyptians in the main square of Alexandria, Egyptian President Gamal Abdul Nasser announced his decision to nationalize the Suez Canal Company. This came as a rebuff to the recent withdrawal of the United States and Great Britain from their pledge to finance the construction of a high dam across the Nile River near Aswan. The Suez Canal lay formally under Egyptian sovereignty, but the implementation of these sovereign rights was regulated by an international convention agreed upon by Egypt and several maritime powers in 1888 in Constantinople. The revenue and daily administration of navigation through the canal were handled by an international company based in Paris and owned mainly by British and French shareholders. There was nothing illegal in the act of nationalization, since Nasser promised to compensate the shareholders faithfully and ensure there was no disruption of navigation. But Great Britain and France saw in Nasser's act a defiant blow to their prestige and political standing in the Middle East and North Africa.

Within hours the British and French decided jointly to make every effort, including the use of military action if necessary, to regain control of the Canal. They ordered their chiefs of staff to plan an invasion of Egypt. Under the command of British general Sir Charles Keightley and French admiral Pierre Barjot, a large force assembled in several Mediterranean ports and operative plans were laid out for an operation code-named "Musketeer." The U.S. administration, while in agreement on the need to ensure the international nature of the Canal, made clear from the outset its strong objection to the use of force for this purpose. Also, considering the support Nasser was allegedly giving to Arab rebels in Algeria, French public opinion supported its government's hard-lined intention. Public opinion in Britain, even within the ruling Conservative Party, was, however, divided.

In order to overcome these difficulties and save the time needed for the preparation of the military operation, some preliminary diplomatic measures had to be taken. While British Prime Minister Sir Anthony Eden and French Prime Minister Guy Mollet interpreted these measures as preparation of the military operation, American Secretary of State John Foster Dulles took them as an opportunity to calm his allies and forestall any resort to force. As expected, the Soviet Union and several "neutral" states led by India unequivocally supported Egypt's position. A conference was held between 18 and 23 August in London, at the end of which a resolution signed by eighteen of the participating maritime states was presented to President Nasser by Australian Prime Minister Sir Robert Menzies. The resolution demanded that Egypt agree to the empowerment of a new international agency that represented the interests of the canal users and took over the administration of canal affairs.

The French and British, having almost completed their military preparations, were ready to take the next diplomatic step of bringing the issue before the United Nations (UN) Security Council. But Dulles feared that such a move would lead to an impasse and precipitate the use of force. He persuaded his allies and several other maritime states to convene once more on 19 September for a second conference in London. On 21 September the group announced the formation of a Suez Canal Users' Association (SCUA), which was supposed to deal with matters of finance and administration of the canal on a practical level and uphold the users' rights. But SCUA was stillborn, since in the meantime Nasser had replaced all the old company's navigators and arranged for uninterrupted operation of the canal under Egyptian management. Prudently, Nasser decided at this stage not to force the issue of payments for the passage in the canal, rendering SCUA nothing more than a paper declaration.

At the end of September Britain and France, becoming restless as their assembled invasion force began to exact a heavy burden, filed a formal complaint in the Security Council. Dag Hammarskjöld, the UN secretary-general, tried to mediate a compromise in private meetings with foreign secretaries Selwyn Lloyd (Great Britain), Christian Pineau (France), and Mahmud Fawzi (Egypt), and formulated a six-point draft proposal to be elaborated at a later stage. But France and Great Britain were not looking for a compromise in defeating Nasser. Despite the fact that the Security Council voted favorably on Hammarskjöld's "Six Points," Lloyd and Pineau insisted on another formal Security Council resolution that would condemn and nullify the nationalization act. This proposal was defeated by a Soviet veto and the council disbanded without a practical solution to the crisis.

From the British and French standpoint, by the middle of October 1956 all diplomatic measures were exhausted and the time was ripe for the "Musketeer" operation. But in view of the smooth operation of the canal, mounting opposition inside Britain, and repeated warnings of the American administration against the use of force, Eden procrastinated. It seemed that he had lost a clear and compelling casus belli.

From the beginning of the crisis the British, knowing of the warm relations developing between France and Israel over recent months, had insisted on a strict separation between their quarrel with Nasser and the Arab–Israeli conflict. Israel, Britain maintained, should be left outside the imbroglio. Despite having many grievances against Egypt and despite the disruption of the balance of power introduced in September 1955 by a huge Soviet-Egyptian arms deal, Israel preferred to concentrate all its energies on absorbing the large quantities of armaments acquired from France since the end of June. The French, on the other hand, whose part in "Musketeer" was to operate on the east bank the Canal, sought to examine the possibility of getting tactical assistance from Israeli forces, if they could press the Egyptians in the Sinai Peninsula from the east. By the end of September, recognizing Eden's hesitations, the French had begun to consider triggering the entire situation by inducing Israel to take the initiative and attack Nasser first.

Invited by the French, Golda Meir, Israel's minister of foreign affairs, together with General Moshe Dayan, the Israel Defense Force (IDF) chief of staff, and Shimon Peres, the director-general of the Ministry of Defense, arrived in Paris on 30 September for exploratory talks. The St. Germain Conference did not yield any definitive military plans, however, since the situation at the UN was not resolved and Britain's position remained unclear. Under the assumption that Israel might be invited at some point to participate in the war, further French armaments were rapidly shipped to Israel and a group of high-ranking French officers, headed by Major General Maurice Challe, proceeded to Tel Aviv to explore operations possibilities. Having become better acquainted with Israel's capabilities, Challe conceived a new plan: Israel would initiate an assault on the Sinai, and the French and British would issue an ultimatum to Israel and Egypt to withdraw so that French and British forces could occupy the canal and assure free and secure navigation. Assuming that Nasser would reject the demand, the road for "Musketeer" was open.

Eden was persuaded to join in this collusion, under the strict condition that it not look as if Great Britain had invited Israel's attack, and that Great Britain appeared to be reacting to a new situation provoked by Israel. Prime Minister of Israel David Ben-Gurion considered the proposal humiliating; he also did not trust the British intention to fulfill their share of the "scenario." To unravel the complex situation, a highly confidential meeting took place between 20 and 23 October at a small private villa in Sèvres, outside Paris. A series of meetings involving Ben-Gurion, Moshe Dayan, and Shimon Peres from Israel; Guy Mollet, Christian Pineau, and Maurice Bourges-Maunoury, the French minister of defense, and briefly also involving Selwyn Lloyd of Great Britain, took place. After the group reached agreement on slight changes in the Challe scenario, and the French assured Israel of military reinforcement, the Sèvres Protocol was signed by Ben-Gurion, Pineau, and Patrick Dean, a senior British official.

On 29 October, an Israeli parachute battalion was dropped east of the Mitla Pass, about forty miles east of Port Suez, and Israeli armor and infantry began to push west into the heart of Sinai. In accordance with the Sèvres Protocol, the next day an appeal was made jointly by the French and British governments demanding that the belligerent parties clear the canal zone. Israel, not intending to reach the banks of the canal anyway, acceded to the request. Nasser, as expected, declined. Thirty-six hours later, on the evening of 31 October, the British and French launched heavy air attacks on Egyptian airports and other military and supply installations, operating from their bases in Cyprus and from aircraft carriers off the shore of Egypt, and started the six-day naval voyage of their invasion forces from Malta, Toulon, and Algiers.

The thinly disguised deception and the unwarranted attack on Egypt incensed President Eisenhower who started, in concert with the Soviet Union and almost the entire international community, to put pressure on the colluding parties. Because British and French vetoes would be used to stymie the Security Council, a special emergency session of the General Assembly convened under the "Uniting for Peace" formula (which had been used during the Korean crisis in 1950). On 5 November French and British paratroopers dropped near the towns of Port Said and Port Tawfiq at the northern edge of the canal, while Israel had by this point already completed the conquest of the entire Sinai Peninsula. The landing from the sea of further troops the next day completed the capture of Port Saʿid, but their advance was arrested about thirty miles to the south. The mounting pressure of the UN, threats of the Soviet Union, and heavy pressure of public opinion in Great Britain opposing the war, were all factors that moved Eden to order a cease-fire.

Following a proposal devised by Lester Pearson, the Canadian minister of foreign affairs, the UN established a special Emergency Force (UNEF) under the command of Canadian general E. L. M Burns. The invading parties now succumbed to international pressure and withdrew their forces from the Canal on 22 December, assuming that UNEF would take responsibility for the management of the areas they evacuated. But, acting on their sovereign prerogatives, the Egyptians immediately took over those territories and UNEF moved eastward into Sinai to shadow the gradually retreating Israeli forces. By the middle of February 1957, after the IDF completed the evacuation of almost the entire peninsula, a crisis developed because Israel had hoped to hold on to the Gaza Strip and to the entrance to the Gulf of Aqaba (Elat) at Sharm al-Shaykh. Heavy American pressure and the threat of UN sanctions moved Ben-Gurion to withdraw Israeli forces to the old armistice demarcation lines by 6 March 1957. The UN force was newly deployed along the Egyptian side of the Egyptian-Israeli frontier, but the Egyptians refrained from returning to the Sinai Peninsula and the Gaza Strip with more than token forces. Both these measures put an end, at least for the following ten years, to the many frictions that had inflamed relations along those frontiers before the war, and left the Straits of Tiran open to Israeli navigation.

The 1956 Suez War is commonly considered a major blunder in modern international relations and a watershed leading to the final demise of British and French colonialism. Within a few years both Great Britain and France lost their positions in the Middle East and North Africa, and their status as first-rate powers waned while dependence on U.S. power grew. The Eisenhower Doctrine of January 1957 gave a symbolic imprimatur to the evolving new situation in the Middle East. The main winner of the entire affair was President Nasser, who not only achieved nationalization of the Suez Company and expelled the last vestiges of British presence along the canal, but also emerged as the uncontested leader of the Arab people and became, along with India's Jawaharlal Nehru and Yugoslavia's Josef Broz Tito, one of the outstanding leaders of the neutralist bloc of nations.

See also ARAB–ISRAEL WAR (1956); LONDON CONFERENCE (1956); SÈVRES PROTOCOL.

Bibliography

Bar-On, Mordechai. *The Gates of Gaza: Israel's Road to Suez and Back, 1955–1957.* New York: St. Martin's, 1994.

Burns, E. L. M. *Between Arab and Israeli.* London: G. G. Harrap, 1962.

Fawzi, Mahmoud. *Suez 1956, an Egyptian Perspective.* London: Shorouk International, 1986.

Golani, Motti. *Israel in Search of a War: The Sinai Campaign, 1955–1956.* Brighton and Portland, OR: Sussex Academic Press, 1998.

Kyle, Keith. *Suez.* London: Weidenfeld and Nicolson, 1991.

Love, Kennett. *Suez— The Twice-Fought War: A History.* New York: McGraw-Hill, 1969.

Lucas, W. Scott. *Divided We Stand: Britain, the US, and the Suez Crisis.* London: Hodder & Stoughton, 1991.

Nutting, Anthony. *No End of a Lesson: The Story of Suez.* London: Constable, 1967.

Pineau, Christian. *1956 Suez.* Paris: R. Laffont, 1976.

MORDECHAI BAR-ON

SUEZ–MEDITERRANEAN PIPELINE

Pipeline linking the Red and Mediterranean seas.

The Suez–Mediterranean Pipeline (SUMED) was opened in 1977. It consists of two pipelines 210 miles long and 42 inches in diameter. It has a capacity of 2.4 million barrels per day. SUMED allows the Persian Gulf oil-producing states to bypass the Suez Canal, which cannot accommodate tankers larger than 200,000 tons. The pipeline can provide an alternative route to Gulf exporters if the Suez canal is blocked, as happened in 1973. Half of the pipeline is owned by the Egyptian General Petroleum Company. The balance is divided among PETROMIN of Saudi Arabia, the Abu Dhabi Oil Company, and the Qatar General Petroleum Company.

SUMED is designed to allow easy transshipment and dispatch to numerous destinations with minimal disruption. It can transport different grades of crude oil with minimal contamination. The terminals at Ayn Sukhna, on the Red Sea, and at Sidi Krayr, near Alexandria, can accommodate both very small tankers and those over 500,000 tons. Many tankers too large to use the Suez Canal can unload a portion of their oil in Ayn Sukhna, sail through the canal, and reload in Sidi Krayr.

Seventy-three percent of the oil transported by SUMED is destined for Europe. The pipeline has more than forty clients. The main ones are the major oil companies, Arabian American Oil Company, and the National Iranian Oil Company.

See also PETROLEUM, OIL, AND NATURAL GAS; PETROMIN.

JEAN-FRANÇOIS SEZNEC

SUFISM AND THE SUFI ORDERS

Islamic mysticism.

The word *Sufi* is generally assumed to derive from *suf* (wool), in reference to the simple clothing of the early ascetic mystics. It refers to the practice and philosophical tradition in Islam that relates to spiritualism and mysticism.

Theological and Philosophical Basis

Mysticism in Islam has two distinct origins. The first is the Qur'an itself, which postulates an intensely personal and direct relationship between the individual and God. This fervent devotion was expressed in the early practice of Hasan al-Basri (d. 728) and the poetry of Rabiʿa al-Adawiyya (d. 801) and gave rise to spiritual Sufism. Practiced by preachers who embraced a simple—almost ascetic—life, it also included celibacy and extensive religious worship and contemplation carried out individually or, more often, in a *halaqa,* or circle of devotees.

The second source is the mystical doctrines of other religious traditions, including gnosticism, Christianity, Zoroastrianism, and Hinduism, which converts to Islam brought into their new faith, giving rise to theosophical Sufism. These traditions had elaborate theosophical doctrines, at the heart of which lay the concept of the unity with the divine, the ultimate goal of the mystic. However, the principle of *tawhid* (divine unity), the cornerstone of orthodox Islamic belief, establishes God's absolute unity and absolute transcendence, thereby precluding any possibility of the creature joining with the Creator.

Theosophical Sufism eventually resolved this contradiction through the elaboration of a number of paradoxical concepts that maintain at once unity and difference, annihilation of self into the divine *(fana)* and self-persistence *(baqa),* presence and absence, intoxication and sobriety. The analogy of seeing God in a mirror image of oneself is often used to explain this unity with the divine. The reinterpretation of *tawhid* as unity of being, according to which the mystic could claim unity with divine existence or attributes while preserving the transcendence of divine essence, allowed Sufism to claim adherence to fundamental orthodox Islamic dogma and gave Islamic mysticism its distinctive flavor.

Idris I (1889–1983) became king of Libya in 1951, when the country declared its independence. He ruled until 1969, when he traveled to Turkey for medical treatment and Muammar al-Qaddafi overthrew the monarchy. © HULTON-DEUTSCH COLLECTION/CORBIS. REPRODUCED BY PERMISSION.

On the basis of this new interpretation, divine truth *(haqiqa)* became the ultimate object of the Sufi gnosis, which was called *maʿrifa* (intuitive knowledge) to set it apart from the rational and exoteric discourse of the law; the law itself became secondary—either a mere step to reach unity with the divine or a hindrance that could be dismissed after a certain level of illumination. Knowledge of the divine

Iraqi Sufis practice a mystical form of Islam that focuses heavily on enlightening the soul through internal holiness, rather than external surroundings. Pictured is a group of Sufis praying at their shrine in Baghdad. © BENJAMIN LOWY/CORBIS. REPRODUCED BY PERMISSION.

nature was called *kashf* and was considered to be infallible, a characteristic that in orthodox Islam is attributed only to Prophetic revelation. The concept of the unity of being was tied to the Hellenistic understanding of God as a First Intellect from whose self-contemplation the world emanates, and that was reinforced by the Greek-inspired Muslim philosophers, who adopted that understanding against the dogma of the Muslim theological schools. The articulation of theosophical Sufism and its harmonization with the *shariʿa* (Islamic law) was carried out by Muhyi al-Din ibn al-Arabi (d. 1240), who systematized a sainthood hierarchy that culminated in a "seal of sainthood" parallel to the Qurʾanic "seal of prophecy" that he attributed to himself.

Although at first fought by the orthodox, this process of presenting the theosophical concepts in Islamic terms and justifying them through the esoteric interpretation of the Qurʾan eventually made Sufism legitimate. The process was furthered by the elaboration of a body of Sufi prophetic sayings (*hadith*) that justified Sufi practice (although that led to the elaboration of anti-Sufi *hadith*.) The full adherence by theosophical Sufism to the *shariʿa* and the nominal adherence to the concept of *tawhid* met the main legal requirement of the faith. In addition, the materialism that accompanied the economic, technological, and cultural expansion of the Islamic empire in Umawi and Abbassid times, as well as the tendency among literalist jurists and theologians to reduce the law and the faith to a numbing amalgam of rules and rituals, helped the spread of Sufism by causing a popular reaction against these trends. In the eleventh century, Abu Hamid al-Ghazzali (d. 1111), who dominated the orthodox movement with his powerful intellect, strongly defended the spiritual dimension in Sufism against the impoverished literalist views of its most vocal opponents and integrated it into the theological expression of the faith; and although he opposed the unity of being and the asceticism and withdrawal preached by some Sufis, the stature of al-Ghazzali helped validate Sufism. Sufism could now spread unimpeded in all its various expression, although any unambiguous claim of having achieved unity with the divine met with retribution or persecution from the orthodox theologians (as happened to Husayn bin Mansur al-Hallaj, executed for heresy in 922.)

Sufi Orders

Partly because orthodox resistance precluded its integration in the theological disciplines and partly because of its very nature, Sufism did not become an organized discipline and came to refer to anything from intense piety to specific devotional steps to mystical philosophy. Most often, however, a Sufi cell (called *tariqa* or *zawiya* or *ribat*) was formed around a teacher, and spiritual doctrine and practice could vary widely from one cell to another. Generally, the Sufi experience centers on a number of practices (including *dhikr* or recitation of the Qur'an, contemplation, prayer, singing, dancing, and fasting) prescribed by the Sufi shaykh, who determines the progress of the disciple through the *maqamat* (stages of spiritual development, codified by Dhu Nun, d. 859.) Sufism contributed greatly to Islamic art in poetry (that of Jalal al-Din al-Rumi, d. 1273, is the best known in the Muslim world as well as in the West) and in literature and music.

By the middle of the ninth century, Sufi orders had established schools throughout the Muslim world. Since any teacher could establish a cell, these were innumerable. However, the main Sufi schools established a *silsila* (chain) through which the master's teachings were transmitted from teacher to disciple, and a loose lineage was traced back either to Abu al-Qasim al-Junayd (d. 910) in the Arab world or to Abu Yazid al-Bistami (d. 874) in Central Asia and Iran. Within the Arab tradition, the Rifa'iyya (Ahmad al-Rifa'i, d. 1182), became know for some wild practices and spread widely until overtaken in the fifteenth century by the Qadiriyya (Abd al-Qadir al-Jilani, d. 1166), whose orthodox bent and more flexible teachings became popular. Less famous because of its emphasis on strict mystical discipline was the Suhrawardiyya (al-Suhrawardi, d. 1168), which gained favor with the upper classes. Within Central Asia and Anatolia, were the Mawlawiyya (also Mevlevis; Jalal al-Din al-Rumi, d. 1258), an introspective order known for its use of chanting and its dancing dervishes, the nomadic Yasawiyya (Ahmad al-Yisavi, d. 1166), and the powerful and orthodox Naqshbandiyya (Muhammad Baha' al-Din al Naqshabandi, d. 1389), which was popular with the elite in India and Central Asia. Also popular in the Indian subcontinent was the Chishtiyya (Mu'in al-Din Chishti, d. 1236). In Africa, the Badawiyya in Egypt (Ahmad al-Badawi, d. 1276) and the Shadhiliyya (Abu al-Hassan al-Shadhili, d. 1258) had emerged from the Rifa'iyya, though the latter was more insistent on following the Sunna (tradition of the Prophet) and discouraged asceticism. The Tijaniyya (Ahmad al-Tijani, d. 1815) became very active in fighting European colonization in Northern Africa in the nineteenth century. Amongst the Shi'a, the most popular orders were the Safawiyya (Safiy al-Din, d. 1334), which originally had been a Sunni movement, and the Ni'matullah (Ni'matullah bin 'Abdullah, d. 1431). The orders shared the same general structure, an initiation ceremony during which the disciple (or the affiliate) was inducted in a similar path, marked with individual and collective rituals that focused on total obedience to the Sufi master.

These orders contributed greatly to the spread of Islam and often served as social protest movements, through their association with craft and commercial guilds, against state authority and abuses of power. But the veneration of the saints and the belief in their power to perform miracles (a claim that was eventually sanctioned by orthodoxy) slowly degenerated in popular practice into a muddle of saint worship, fatalism, superstition, and magic and cultic practices. This was accentuated by the excesses of the more extreme Sufi organizations, which demanded profession of faith in the saints as part of the *shahada* (Muslim creed); other organizations allowed followers to use illicit substances and disregard the law in the pursuit of the loftier goal of achieving knowledge of the divine; still others preached extreme asceticism and withdrawal from the world. Such excesses had always met with strong disapproval from orthodox jurists, although all of the jurists accepted the spiritual dimension of Sufism, but it was not until the reform movements of the eighteenth century that a reaction against these excesses took place. Building on the criticism of theosophical Sufism by Taqiyy al-Din ibn Taymiyya, Muhammad ibn Abd al-Wahhab (d. 1792) introduced a strict return to the pristine sources of Islam, namely the Qur'an and the *Sunna* (the Prophet's tradition), and condemned the morally lax practices and quasi-worship of the saints and the Prophet that were practiced by Sufis.

In India and North Africa, reform was also under way, although for different reasons. The Sufi movements, whose active preaching had brought massive conversions to Islam in those areas, had adopted beliefs and practices from their converts that were at times clearly in opposition to Islamic belief and to the *shari'a*. Alarmed by this syncretism, Sufi masters including Muhammad al-Baqi Billah and Ahmad Sirhindi in India and Muhammad ibn Idris in North Africa initiated a move to restore orthodoxy and in the process reinterpreted the Sufi concepts and shifted their content from unity of being to unity of witnessing God *(wahdat al-shuhud)* and from a traditional Sufi path *(tariqa)* centered on a saint to a *tariqa Muhammadiyya* (the Prophet's *tariqa*) centered on the emulation of the Prophet through strict and active observation of the *shari'a*. But the threat that European colonialism posed to the Muslim movements transformed their efforts from religious and social reform to a national jihad against the invaders, which only hastened the disintegration of a Sufi worldview based on otherworldliness and ascetic withdrawal. Modern Muslim movements facing many of the same political challenges have generally been critical of Sufism and have espoused more and more a legalistic interpretation of the faith. However, despite the decline of the Sufi orders in recent history, many of the Sufi rituals and traditions survive today in individual and communal practice.

The Muslim world's understanding of its faith has constantly oscillated between the poles of excessive spiritualism and legalistic interpretation, although the existence of these poles has kept Islam from falling permanently into one or the other extreme, in the one case by preserving the spiritual dimension of the faith and preventing the reification of religious consciousness and in the other by grounding the faith in textual sources and moral activism. The great jurists and theologians have attempted to maintain a balance between these two dimensions of Islam, and despite opposition to certain elements in it, Sufism is generally seen as part of normal religious commitment. Thus, it was considered perfectly acceptable during the 1980s for the vice president of Cairo University, a noted scholar in Arabic-Islamic philosophy, to serve as the leader of Sufi circles in Egypt. Popular religion, however, has generally swung from one extreme to the other.

See also HADITH; MEVLEVI BROTHERHOOD; NAQSHBANDI; QADIRIYYA ORDER; QUR'AN; *SHARI'A;* SUNNA.

Bibliography

Nasr, Sayyed Hossein. *Three Muslim Sages: Avicenna, Suhrawardi, ibn Arabi.* Cambridge, MA: Harvard University Press, 1964.

Rahman, Fazlur. *Islam,* 2d edition. Chicago: University of Chicago Press, 1979.

Trimingham, J. Spencer. *The Sufi Orders in Islam.* Oxford: Clarendon, 1971.

MAYSAM J. AL FARUQI

SUISSA, ALBERT

[1959–]

Israeli author.

Suissa was born in Casablanca, Morocco, and emigrated to Israel in 1963. He grew up in Jerusalem, where he studied in an Orthodox school. Later he moved to Paris and studied mime, taught theater, and performed with a mime troupe. He now lives in Paris and Jerusalem.

Akud (The bound, 1990), Suissa's only book, consists of novellas that cumulatively form a variation of a bildungsroman. The protagonist is a child of an immigrant North African family uprooted and replanted on the outskirts of Jerusalem—for that matter, on the margins of Israeli society. Rich with ornamental details, fantasy, and ethnic authenticity, the novel relates the development of a child whose disintegrating family has had its very foundations undermined by its transplantation. Pitted against the slogans of Eastern European Zionism and mainstream Israeli culture, the impotence and irrelevance of the family is portrayed boldly. Both the original home and the new home seem to be driven by violence and oppression, which breed a devastating alienation. Suissa's language and the structure of the novel are arabesque in pattern and logic, baroque in style, and modern in psychological sensitivities.

Bibliography

Gover, Yerach. *Zionism: The Limits of Moral Discourse in Israeli Hebrew Fiction.* Minneapolis: University of Minnesota Press, 1994.

Shaked, Gershon, ed. *Hebrew Writers: A General Directory.* Israel: Institute for the Translation of Hebrew Literature, 1993.

ZVIA GINOR
DONNA ROBINSON DIVINE

SULAYMAN, HIKMAT
[1889–1946]

Iraqi government official.

Hikmat Sulayman held various senior administrative positions and ministerial posts in Iraq in the 1920s and 1930s. Associated first with Yasin al-Hashimi and Rashid Ali al-Kaylani, he fell out with them in 1935. His friendship with Bakr Sidqi led to his becoming prime minister after the latter's coup in October 1936, a post he held until Sidqi's overthrow in August 1937.

PETER SLUGLETT

SULAYMANIYA

Town in northeastern Iraq, capital of Iraqi Kurdistan.

A market town in Kurdistan, Iraq, 60 miles (96.5 km) east of Kirkuk, Sulaymaniya is bounded on the east and south by Iran. Its name was linked to Süleyman Paşa, *wali* of Baghdad when the town was founded in 1781. Surrounded by mountains, the town has cold winters and mild summers. It has archaeological sites (some in caves) that date to about fifty thousand years ago.

Most of the population are Kurds. Dokan Dam, 37 miles (60 km) northwest of the town, has a hydroelectric station.

Bibliography

Harris, George L. *Iraq: Its People, Its Society, Its Culture.* New Haven, CT: HRAF Press, 1958.

Hassani, Abdul Razzak, Al-. *The History of Modern Iraq.* Baghdad, 1980.

NAZAR AL-KHALAF

SULEIMAN, MULAY

Alawi sultan of Morocco, 1792–1822.

Heir to the badly divided government of his brother and predecessor, Mulay Yazid (ruled 1790–1792), Suleiman also faced provincial unrest and a weakened tax base. He brought much of coastal and central Morocco under *makhzan* control, although his capture and subsequent release by Berber forces in the central Atlas mountains in 1819 underscored the limits of the crown's control over large provinces of Morocco. Suleiman is also known for his bid to suppress popular Sufism and other local socioreligious activities. In the face of growing European pressures, Suleiman adopted a generally hostile and insular stance.

See also ALAWI; SUFISM AND THE SUFI ORDERS.

Bibliography

Burke, Edmund, III. *Prelude to Protectorate in Morocco: Precolonial Protest and Resistance, 1860–1912.* Chicago: University of Chicago, 1976.

Pennell, C. R. *Morocco since 1830: A History.* New York: New York University Press, 2000.

MATTHEW S. GORDON

SULH, KAZEM AL-
[1909–1977]

Lebanese politician, diplomat, and journalist; former ambassador to Iraq; member of parliament, 1960–1964.

Kazem al-Sulh (also al-Solh) was born into a prestigious Sunni family that was active in the Arab nationalist movement at the turn of the century. He emerged in the 1930s as one of the most articulate advocates of an independent, sovereign Lebanon that would be free from French control but would also remain separate from Syria. In defending the territorial boundaries that the French mandatory power had established, he went against the dominant opinion of people in his community, who still favored reintegrating into Syria those regions the French had annexed to Mount Lebanon in 1920.

Unlike many of his Muslim contemporaries, Kazem al-Sulh understood very early on that independence from France could only be gained by reaching out to moderate Christians, particularly Maronites. He argued that the Maronites would more easily loosen their ties to France and join the nationalist cause if they could be reassured that independence would not be followed by absorption into Syria, or by policies that would undermine Lebanon's political autonomy vis-à-vis other Arab countries. He aspired to create an independent Lebanon based on Muslim-Christian accommodation. It would be possible to achieve this goal, he believed, if the Sunnis agreed to a historic compromise: if they would shed their traditional demand for reunification with Syria in exchange for the Maronites' abandoning their call for a Christian Lebanon and renouncing French protection and interference in Lebanese affairs.

To promote these ideas, Kazem al-Sulh created a group called al-Nida al-Qawmi (The National Appeal), which attracted moderate Sunnis and became a political party in 1945. Although it never was able to develop a mass following, the group played an important role in mobilizing Sunni support for an independent Lebanon. It also strengthened the hand of Maronite leaders like Bishara al-Khuri who were arguing within their own communities for the very kind of cross-confessional compromise that Kazem al-Sulh and like-minded Sunni notables and intellectuals were advocating. Some measure of the influence of Kazem al-Sulh and groups such as al-Nida al-Qawmi can be gotten by noting that the aspirations they articulated were eventually embodied in the 1943 National Pact. Kazem and his brother Taki al-Din are usually credited with facilitating the conversion of their first cousin Riyad al-Sulh to the cause of an independent, sovereign Lebanon managed through a Maronite-Sunni partnership.

Although his ideas had a critical impact on the course of Lebanese history, Kazem al-Sulh played only a marginal role in post-independence Lebanese politics. Although he was a gifted writer and political thinker, he never was a particularly effective politician. By the late 1950s, al-Nida al-Qawmi had ceased to function, a victim to the rising tide of Arab nationalism. Kazem al-Sulh's politics had always been based on compromise, tolerance, and conciliation, and this approach had become increasingly inappropriate in the context of an Arab world that, caught in the ferment of the 1950s and 1960s, witnessed the radicalization of the Sunni masses. Kazem al-Sohl served as Lebanese ambassador to Iraq during the 1940s and 1950s, and he was criticized by pan-Arab intellectuals and politicians for the part it was alleged he played in designing the ill-fated Baghdad Pact. Thanks to Christian votes, he was elected a Sunni representative from Zahle to the parliament (1960–1964). Kazem al-Sulh ended his career as a relatively uninfluential politician, largely discredited within his own community.

See also BAGHDAD PACT (1955); NATIONAL PACT (LEBANON); SULH, RIYAD AL-.

Bibliography

Goria, Wader R. *Sovereignty and Leadership in Lebanon, 1943–1976.* London: Ithaca Press, 1985.

Hudson, Michael C. *The Precarious Republic: Political Modernization in Lebanon.* Boulder, CO: Westview Press, 1985.

Johnson, Michael. *Class and Client in Beirut: The Sunni Muslim Community and the Lebanese State, 1840–1985.* London: Ithaca Press, 1986.

GUILAIN P. DENOEUX

SULH, RASHID AL-

[1926–]

Lebanese politician; prime minister, 1974–1975 and 1992.

Rashid al-Sulh (also Solh), born into a minor branch of the prestigious Sunni Sulh family, was brought up in the house of former prime minister Sami al-Sulh. After studying at the College of the Christian Brothers and al-Maqasid College, he received his LL.B. from Saint Joseph University in Beirut and became a lawyer and a judge. Elected deputy for Beirut in 1964 and 1972, he inherited the political mantle of Sami al-Sulh following the latter's death in 1968. Considered a moderate among Sunni leaders in the 1970s, Sulh nevertheless developed a reputation as a champion of the working class and maintained a close relationship with Kamal Jumblatt. While still a relative newcomer among Sunni political bosses, he was chosen as prime minister by President Sulayman Franjiyya in October 1974; he held the premiership until May 1975, when he resigned. He thus presided over the outbreak of the Lebanese Civil War, which he was unable to prevent or stop. Before stepping down, Sulh denounced the inertia of Lebanon's society and the political and administrative corruption and nepotism that, he claimed, had thwarted the implementation of his reforms. He warned that unless the entire political system was overhauled, the country was headed toward political chaos and disintegration.

In May 1992, Sulh became prime minister again, following the demonstrations and riots that brought down the government of Umar Karami. He held the position until October, when he was replaced by Rafiq Hariri. During his short tenure, he was frequently criticized for subservience to Syria. In particular, his insistence on proceeding with parliamentary elections in the summer of 1992 alienated many Lebanese, who opposed the timing of these elections. Beirut's electorate severely punished him for this and other decisions that were seen as bowing to Syria's wishes. The electoral list he headed was soundly defeated by that led by Salim al-Hoss. Although he managed to win a seat in parliament, Sulh received the fewest votes (11,428) of any Sunni elected, and no other Sunni on his list was elected (three Armenian Orthodox candidates and one Armenian Catholic were).

See also FRANJIYYA, SULAYMAN; HARIRI, RAFIQ BAHA'UDDIN AL-; HOSS, SALIM AL-; JUMBLATT, KAMAL.

Bibliography

Johnson, Michael. *Class and Client in Beirut: The Sunni Muslim Community and the Lebanese State, 1840–1985.* Atlantic Highlands, NJ: Ithaca Press, 1986.

GUILAIN P. DENOEUX
UPDATED BY MICHAEL R. FISCHBACH

SULH, RIYAD AL-
[1894–1951]

Lebanese politician; prime minister, 1943–1945 and 1946–1951.

Riyad al-Sulh (second from right) was the first prime minister of independent Lebanon. He played an instrumental role in ending French control of the region and in establishing Lebanon's sectarian political system. He is shown here at a meeting of the Arab League in Aley, Lebanon, 1947. © HULTON-DEUTSCH COLLECTION/CORBIS. REPRODUCED BY PERMISSION.

Riyad al-Sulh (also al-Solh) was born into a prominent Sunni family that had played a major role in the Arab nationalist movement during the last decades of the Ottoman Empire. Unlike many other aristocratic families in Beirut, whose concerns revolved around parochial issues, the Sulhs were known for their cosmopolitanism, sophistication, and wide-ranging contacts throughout the empire. His father, Rida, had served as governor *(mutasarrif)* in Salonika and in 1909 had been elected one of Beirut's two representatives in the Ottoman parliament at Constantinople.

Sulh studied law at the University of Istanbul and at St. Joseph University in Beirut. After World War I, he and his father were elected to the National Congress of Syria, which proclaimed Amir Faisal king of an independent Syria. Following the military defeat of Faisal by France in July 1920, and the establishment of Greater Lebanon two months later, he became a vocal opponent of France's mandate. Forced to flee Lebanon, he was sentenced to death in absentia and spent most of the 1920s in exile, primarily in Paris and Geneva, where he worked closely with other Arab nationalists. In 1929, Sulh was allowed to return to Lebanon after Emile Eddé intervened on his behalf with the government of Charles Dabbas. From then on, except for another brief period of exile in 1935, he lived in Beirut. By the early 1930s, he had become one of the most influential Arab nationalist politicians, despite France's efforts to contain his power.

In the late 1930s, Sulh was progressively converted to the concept of an independent Lebanon that would be free of France's control and separate from Syria. This position, which he adopted in part under the influence of his cousins Kazem al-Sulh and Taki al-Din al-Sulh, reflected the growing recognition among large segments of the Sunni community that their interests lay in the preservation of existing boundaries and an alliance with moderate Maronite leaders.

The outbreak of World War II made possible the Christian-Muslim alliance that Sulh had advocated. The war weakened France's influence and prestige in Lebanon and thus undermined those in the Maronite community, led by Eddé, who insisted on a Christian Lebanon closely aligned with France. By the same token, it strengthened the hand of those Maronites, led by Bishara al-Khuri and his Constitutional Bloc, who called for an independent and sovereign Lebanon based on Muslim-Christian accommodation. Taking advantage of this changing balance of power within the Maronite community and of active support for Lebanese independence by Britain and the United States, Khuri and Riyad al-Sulh formed an alliance that led the movement for an end to France's mandate.

After parliament elected him president of Lebanon in September 1943, Khuri immediately chose Sulh as his prime minister. The two quickly concluded the informal agreement known as the National Pact, which embodied the "historical compromise" between Muslims and Christians that they had supported for some time. Because of his role in the National Pact, which became the backbone of postindependence politics in Lebanon, Sulh can be regarded as one of the founding fathers of independent Lebanon. His pragmatism and tolerance made him ideally suited to play a leading role in designing a system based on interconfessional accommodation, while his charisma, dynamism, and political skills ensured that he could deliver the support of his community. His vision of a secular, sovereign Lebanon based on a cross-confessional understanding and open to the outside world continued to inspire generations of Lebanese politicians long after his death, and despite its shortcomings, it permitted Lebanon to experience several decades of political stability, remarkable economic growth, and rapid modernization. It is important to note that Sulh appears to have been aware of the limits of the political formula embodied in the National Pact, which called for the distribution of positions in the government and the bureaucracy among the country's various sects. He saw this confessional system as only a temporary expedient that would have to be eliminated in the long run. He once described political sectarianism as "an obstacle to national progress, impeding the representation of the national will and poisoning the good relations between diverse elements of the Lebanese population."

One of the first decisions of Sulh's government was to abrogate the parts of the 1926 constitution that limited Lebanon's sovereignty to the benefit of France. The mandate authorities responded by arresting Khuri, Sulh, and all but two members of the cabinet. Strikes and widespread demonstrations and riots ensued; together with pressure by Britain and the United States on the government of Free France, they forced the latter to reverse its policy and reinstate Khuri and Sulh on 22 November 1943. This date effectively marks the emergence of independent Lebanon.

Until the beginning of Khuri's second term in 1949, Sulh maintained a close working relationship with the president. Between 1943 and 1951, he headed six cabinets for a total of some sixty-five months. For most of his tenure as prime minister, he was involved in all important decisions and was widely seen as almost an equal of Khuri, for whom he was a precious ally because of the weight his opinions carried with the Sunni masses. Following Khuri's reelection, however, strains developed between the two men, largely as a result of the president's increasing tendency to bypass the cabinet and rely instead on a group of cronies, influence peddlers, and advisers headed by his brother Salim. Sulh resigned on 14 February 1951. He was assassinated on 16 July by a member of the Syrian Social Nationalist Party (SSNP), who killed him at the airport in Amman, Jordan, in revenge for Lebanon's 1949 execution of Antun Saʿada, the SSNP's founder and leader.

See also EDDÉ, EMILE; KHURI, BISHARA AL-; NATIONAL PACT (LEBANON); SULH, KAZEM

AL-; SULH, TAKI AL-DIN AL.; SYRIAN SOCIAL NATIONALIST PARTY.

Bibliography

Binder, Leonard, ed. *Politics in Lebanon.* New York: Wiley, 1966.

Goria, Wade R. *Sovereignty and Leadership in Lebanon, 1943–1976.* London: Ithaca Press, 1986.

Hudson, Michael C. *The Precarious Republic: Political Modernization in Lebanon.* Boulder, CO: Westview Press, 1985.

Johnson, Michael. *Class and Client in Beirut: The Sunni Muslim Community and the Lebanese State, 1840–1985.* London: Ithaca Press, 1986.

GUILAIN P. DENOEUX

SULH, SAMI AL-

[1890–1968]

Lebanese Muslim politician.

Sami al-Sulh (also al-Solh), born to a prominent Sunni Muslim family, studied in Beirut and earned a law degree from Istanbul. He went to France to obtain a doctorate in law but returned to Lebanon before completing his studies. He claimed that while in Istanbul he had joined Arab secret societies working against the government of the Ottoman Empire, but no documentation supports his claims. He is accused of having supported the Ottoman government when other educated Arabs were struggling for Arab independence. He was a judge from 1920 to 1942, and, with French support, he was appointed prime minister in 1942. He represented Beirut in the Chamber of Deputies from 1943 to 1960 and from 1964 to 1968 and was prime minister seven times between 1945 and 1958.

The most controversial aspect of al-Sulh's political career was his support for Camille Chamoun. During the 1958 civil war he refused to criticize Chamoun, opposing the tide of Muslim public opinion. Al-Sulh was seen as a weak prime minister who did not stand up to President Chamoun. Chamoun used al-Sulh as a token Muslim because al-Sulh did not object to Chamoun's pro-Western foreign policy. His close association with Chamoun earned him the wrath of the Muslim masses, and his house in Beirut was burned down. He fled Lebanon for several months, then settled in the predominantly Christian area of Beirut. Al-Sulh surprised all those who had prematurely written his political obituary by returning to public life in 1964 after winning a parliamentary seat from Beirut. Christian support in his district of course helped make his victory possible, but within a few years he was able to win the backing of some Muslims who had declared him a traitor in 1958. He spent the rest of his life defending his position in 1958, writing two memoirs to vindicate himself. He claimed that he never opposed President Gamal Abdel Nasser of Egypt, and that he was a staunch defender of the Palestinian cause. He blamed Nasser's supporters in Lebanon for the anti-Nasser reputation that was associated with his name after 1958.

Being the oldest deputy made al-Sulh president protem of the parliament. Members of the Christian establishment saw al-Sulh as demonstrating how Muslim politicians should conduct themselves. His support for Chamoun was viewed by the Phalange party, which supported him, as evidence of his patriotism. He was nicknamed Abu al-Faqir (Father of the Poor) because he championed the common people.

AS'AD ABUKHALIL

SULH, TAKI AL-DIN AL-

[1909–1988]

Lebanese journalist and politician.

A first cousin of Riyad al-Sulh, Taki al-Din al-Sulh (also al-Solh, Taqi al-Din or Takidedine) was born in Beirut and educated at the American University of Beirut, where he studied literature and history. During the 1930s, he worked as a journalist, literature teacher, and director of the Ministry of Information. With his brother Kazem, he founded the al-Nida al-Qawmi (The National Appeal), a group of moderate Sunni politicians and intellectuals who advocated a free and sovereign Lebanon, independent from the French and separate from Syria. A traditional, nonideological politician, al-Sulh proved either unwilling or unable to build a strong political machine and consequently did not develop a wide base of popular support. He nevertheless—because of his connection to a prestigious family—occupied several important political positions in the 1960s: he was a member of parliament (1964–1968) and a minister of the interior (1964–1965).

Al-Sulh's early career reached its zenith in July 1973 when President Sulayman Franjiyya called upon him to become prime minister. During his fifteen months in office, he was unable to prevent Lebanon's slide toward political disintegration. His tenure was marked by economic crisis and political turmoil, student and labor unrest, a growing rift between Muslims and Christians, repeated clashes between the Lebanese army and Palestinian commandos, and numerous Israeli raids in southern Lebanon. He resigned in September 1974 and was replaced by Sa'ib Salam, but served as prime minister again in 1980.

See also AMERICAN UNIVERSITY OF BEIRUT (AUB); FRANJIYYA, SULAYMAN; SALAM, SA'IB; SULH, RIYAD AL-.

Bibliography

Hudson, Michael C. *The Precarious Republic: Political Modernization in Lebanon.* Boulder, CO: Westview, 1985.

Salibi, Kamal S. *Crossroads to Civil War: Lebanon, 1958–1976.* Delmar, NY: Caravan Books, 1976.

GUILAIN P. DENOEUX
UPDATED BY MICHAEL R. FISCHBACH

SULTAN

Title implying political power; a king or sovereign, especially of a Muslim state.

The title of sultan came to prominence around 1000 C.E., after the political position of the caliphate (office of the leader of Islam) had eroded around the time of the establishment of the Seljuk sultanate. Turko–Iranian dynasts used the title as an equivalent of the Eurasian steppe title khan. Later, it was used generally in Islamic lands by many states large and small. In some cases, for example, in Persia (now Iran), from 1500 on, the term was further devalued to denote a governor, not even a petty ruler.

In the Ottoman Empire, sultan, along with *padishah* and khan, was one of the titles of the sovereign (for example, Sultan Süleyman Khan), as well as the other members of the ruling family. The ruler's sons and grandsons, who served as governors and thus shared political power in the steppe manner, were all styled sultan. In the case of the female members of the ruling house, the title followed the personal name of the main designation—for example, Hürrem Sultan, *valide sultan* (dowager queen), *khasseki sultan* (favorite consort), or Mihrimah Sultan, who was a princess. The sultanate of the Ottoman Empire was abolished in 1922, just before the Republic of Turkey was founded.

I. METIN KUNT

SULTAN AHMET MOSQUE

Ottoman mosque.

Popularly known as the Blue mosque because of the predominantly turquoise-colored faience tile panels that embellish its vast prayer hall, the mosque of Sultan Ahmet I (1590–1617) stands next to Istanbul's Hippodrome. Supporting a domed, cruciform superstructure and six slender minarets, it is the major work of the architect Sedefkar Mehmet Ağa.

Bibliography

Goodwin, Godfrey. *A History of Ottoman Architecture.* London: Thames and Hudson, 1971.

APTULLAH KURAN

SULTAN HASAN MOSQUE

One of the finest examples of Arab Egyptian architecture; situated below the citadel in Cairo.

Sultan Hasan mosque was built for the Mamluk Sultan Hasan al-Nasir in 1356–1363. The ground plan of the mosque takes the form of an irregular pentagon and occupies 9,450 square yards (7,800 sq m). It boasts a 267-foot (88 m) minaret in its south corner, the tallest in Cairo, and a massive main door at the north corner that is almost 85 feet (26 m) high. The exterior walls echo an ancient Egyptian temple, with large expanses of stone that are relieved by blind niches and double round arched windows. Stalactitic cornices, heavily restored, crown the facades. The mausoleum, which extends from the southeast wall, carries a 180-foot-high (55 m) dome of the Arab Turkish style that was almost completely rebuilt in the eighteenth century.

Bibliography

Berhens-Abuseif, D. *Islamic Architecture in Cairo: An Introduction.* Leiden, Netherlands, and New York: Brill, 1989.

Rogers, J. M. "Seljuk Influence in the Monuments of Cairo." *Kunst des Orients* 7 (1970–1971): 40 ff.

RAYMOND WILLIAM BAKER

SULTANI SCHOOLS

Ottoman intermediate schools.

Sultani lycées were higher secondary schools funded by the sultan's personal treasury. The first and most famous of these was Lycée Galatasaray (also called Mekteb-i Sultani), founded in 1868 in Istanbul and modeled on the French lycée. An 1869 educational reform law provided for one sultani lycée in each provincial capital. In an expansion of the humanist education offered at these schools, in 1908 ten former İdadi schools, whose curriculum had partly overlapped that of the lycées, were renamed sultani schools. By 1914 there were 8,380 students, mostly from elite backgrounds, enrolled in twenty-four sultani schools across the Ottoman Empire.

See also İDADI SCHOOLS.

Bibliography

Kazamias, Andreas M. *Education and the Quest for Modernity in Turkey.* Chicago: University of Chicago Press, 1966.

ELIZABETH THOMPSON

SUMUD

Principle adopted by the Palestinian national movement of clinging to the soil of the homeland.

The Sumud (Steadfastness) Fund was established at the Baghdad Arab Summit in 1978 to discourage Palestinian emigration from the territories occupied by Israel in 1967. The annual budget of $150 million was to be administered by the Joint Committee, composed of members from the Palestine Liberation Organization (PLO) and the government of Jordan. Funds were distributed to Palestinian leaders, trade unions, universities, newspapers, and cooperatives. Sumud paid unemployment benefits and pensions for retirees and granted interest-free housing loans. In the early 1980s, about $87 million per year was transferred to the occupied territories. Funds dried up in the mid-1980s as oil-rich Arab countries defaulted on their contributions.

In the late 1980s, the principle of *sumud* was revived in an altered form by Palestinian residents of the Gaza Strip, Golan Heights, and West Bank who resented their passive role as welfare recipients. Under the leadership of Dr. Hisham Awartani, an economist at al-Najah University in Nablus, *sumud* was transformed into a call for Palestinian residents to think and act for themselves.

See also BAGHDAD SUMMIT (1978); PALESTINE LIBERATION ORGANIZATION (PLO).

Bibliography

Benvenisti, Meron. *The West Bank Handbook: A Political Lexicon.* Jerusalem: Jerusalem Post, 1986.

Cobban, Helena. *The Palestinian Liberation Organisation: People, Power, and Politics.* Cambridge, U.K., and New York: Cambridge University Press, 1984.

Schiff, Ze'ev, and Ya'ari, Ehud. *Intifada: The Palestinian Uprising—Israel's Third Front,* translated by Ina Friedman. New York: Simon and Schuster, 1990.

Shehadeh, Raja. *Samed: Journal of a West Bank Palestinian.* New York: Adama Books, 1984.

ELIZABETH THOMPSON

SUNAY, CEVDET

[1899–1982]

Turkish military officer and politician; president of Turkey, 1966–1973.

Cevdet Sunay was born in Trabzon, the son of a village effendi in the Ottoman Empire. He attended the Küleli military high school and fought in Palestine in World War I. In the Turkish War of Independence (1921–1922), Sunay fought on the Maraş, Gaziantep, and Western fronts, finally chasing enemy armies to İzmir. He became a staff officer for the new Republic of Turkey in 1930, after completing studies at the War Academy; he was promoted to general in 1958. In 1961, he was appointed chief of staff, following the military coup, although he apparently did not play a direct role in the plot against Adnan Menderes.

Sunay resigned his office to become president of Turkey in 1966 in an alliance between the Justice party and military interests. He served as president through the 1971 coup, in which some observers said he played a key role. Sunay's presidency ended in 1973, when his bid for an extended term fell one vote short in the assembly. His term in office is associated with the continued penetration of the military into Turkish politics.

Bibliography

Lewis, Geoffrey. *Modern Turkey,* 4th edition. New York: Praeger, 1974.

ELIZABETH THOMPSON

SUN LANGUAGE THEORY

A 1930s movement that claimed Turkish was the mother of all languages.

H. F. Kvergic is credited with inventing this theory in 1935, although numerous others contributed to its general formulation. The theory draws its name from Kvergic's initial proposition that a Turkish man was first inspired to create language while looking at the sun. Others, such as Ibrahim Necmi Dilmen, presented charts of concept groups drawn from the sun—for example, light/beauty, fire/excitement, and motion/time. Supporters of the theory held that since Turks inhabited the so-called cradle of civilization, central Asia, their language was the origin for later languages, such as those of the Hittites, Arabs, and Europeans.

Although criticized for fantastic speculations, the theory attracted interest in the mid-1930s for several reasons. Some supporters, including Atatürk, used it to stem the drastic expurgation from the modern Turkish language of foreign words by language reformers. Supporters argued that since foreign words were derived from Turkish, they should remain in use. Others found in the theory justification for radical nationalist Turkist ideologies in their vaunting of the Turks' ancient heritage. They also used its link to the Hittites to establish a long history for the Turks in Anatolia. By World War II, interest in the theory faded, although Atatürk's support of it is occasionally evoked today by opponents of the direction of Turkish-language reform.

Bibliography

Lewis, Geoffrey. *Modern Turkey,* 4th edition. New York: Praeger, 1974.

ELIZABETH THOMPSON

SUNNA

Literally, trodden path, *meaning* norm *or* practice.

The *Sunna* refers to the divine physical and moral laws set out in the universe and in the Qurʾan. However, the term is used most commonly in reference to the example and customary practice of the prophet Muhammad. The Prophet's *Sunna* has more than one usage in Muslim tradition. As a technical term used in the *shariʿa* (Islamic law), it refers to the binding rules derived from the Prophet's sayings, or *hadith.* The *Sunna* then represents the laws that can be extracted from the *hadith.* As such, it is the second most important source of law after the Qurʾan. In a more general meaning, often used by jurists and theologians, the *Sunna* refers also to all the customs and habits of the Prophet, including his everyday life practices, that are not considered by the *shariʿa* as obligatory. Hence the term *Sunna* is often used in the sense of *recommended* or *good practice.* Examples of this are the supererogatory prayers and fasting the Prophet performed over and above the prescribed rituals. These are referred to as *Sunna* prayers or *Sunna* fasting. Certain very strict Muslim movements make the nonbinding *Sunna* obligatory, and extreme Muslim parties have, at times, after seizing power, imposed it on all Muslims and made practices such as wearing beards mandatory, although the enforcement of any practice that is not legally binding is considered illegitimate in Islamic law.

See also HADITH; MUHAMMAD; QURʾAN; *SHARIʿA.*

Bibliography

Kamali, Mohammad Hashim. *Principles of Islamic Jurisprudence,* revised edition. Cambridge, U.K.: Islamic Texts Society, 1991

SCOTT ALEXANDER
UPDATED BY MAYSAM J. AL FARUQI

SUNNI ISLAM

The largest branch in Islam, sometimes referred to as "orthodox Islam"; its full name is ahl al-Sunna wa al-jamaʿa *(the people of* Sunna *and consensus), and it represents about 90 percent of the world Muslim population.*

The Sunni movement can be identified in terms of its differences with the second largest division of Islam, the Shiʿite, with whom it shares the fundamental creed of Islam. After the death of the Prophet, the political issue of how leadership was to be chosen split the new community. The Shiʿa of

Ali (literally, the party of Ali) insisted that the Prophet had intended for his cousin Ali to succeed him, while the majority of Muslims maintained that the caliph should be elected and did not have to belong to the Prophet's family. The Sunnis maintained that since the Prophet had not clearly designated a successor, his *Sunna* (example, custom), by which they were to abide (hence their name), mandated elections. Of course, the Shiʿa also consider the *Sunna* of the Prophet as binding and second only to the Qurʾan in authority, but they differ on the actual content of the *Sunna* in regard to the matter of the divinely appointed leaders from the Prophet's family (imams), who in their view are the legitimate rulers. In addition to the concept of divinely appointed leadership, the Sunnis also reject the notion of a *mahdi* (messiah) as an integral part of the creed, and they emphasize exoteric interpretation of the Qurʾan over the esoteric approach followed by the Shiʿa.

The Sunni Schools of Law

In addition to the Qurʾan and the *Sunna* as primary sources of Islamic law, Sunni jurists also admit *ijma* (consensus) and *qiyas* (personal parallel reasoning) as legitimate sources for legal judgment. *Qiyas,* the fourth source of law, is a form of *ijtihad* (exercising personal judgment in legal interpretation). All schools of law generally admit *ijtihad,* but with different definitions and restrictions. At first, *raʾy* (personal opinion issued without justification) was exercised, but its unrestricted use was deemed too arbitrary and it was eliminated in favor of *qiyas,* a form of reasoning that identifies an *illah (ratio legis)* parallel or similar to another already established by the Qurʾan or the *Sunna.*

Ijma, or consensus, constitutes the third source of law and it takes precedence over *qiyas.* There was disagreement among the Sunni schools of law as to the nature of consensus. While all jurists accept the consensus of the companions of the Prophet, the more liberal schools will also admit of the consensus of the schools of law at any given time. The more conservative schools will only accept a global community consensus, which cannot be easily achieved, so in effect the Sunni schools of law did build the legal system on the basis of juristic consensus. However, the right to dissent *(ikhtilaf)* was scrupulously maintained by all schools. In contrast, the Shiʿa eschew *ijma* in favor of the *ijtihad* of the imam or his representative. That the Sunnis consider the law to be a matter of consensus (whether juristic or communal) is underscored in their name, *ahl al-Sunna wa al-jamaʿa.*

Over time, the various Sunni schools of law coalesced into four major schools: the Hanafi (founded by Abu Hanifa, d. 767), the Maliki (founded by Malik ibn Anas, d. 795), the Shafiʿi (founded by Shafiʿi, d. 820) and the Hanbali school (founded by ibn Hanbal, d. 855). The most widespread is the Hanafi, which was favored by various Muslim governments, most notably by the Ottomans, since it was not as strict as the other schools in its acceptance and use of less rigorous tools of legal interpretation. The Hanafis can be found throughout the Muslim world, while the Malikis are mostly found in Egypt and North Africa, the Shafiʿis in Southeast Asia, and the Hanbalis in the Arabian Peninsula.

Historical and Modern Developments

Tensions between Sunnis and Shiʿa (especially with the sectarian movements derived from the Shiʿa, such as the Ismaʿilis) were very high in early Muslim history as Shiʿite groups tried to destabilize the Sunni caliphate and ensure leadership to the followers of the imams. The problems subsided after the decisive victory of the Ayyubids over the Shiʿite regimes of Egypt and the Near East in the late twelfth century and the subsequent coming to power of the Ottoman Turks, who had always been staunch Sunnis. Tension still exists between local Sunni and Shiʿite groups, although most of it is due more to ethnic and tribal strife than to religious divisions, as can be seen in Lebanon and Pakistan. However, the rise among the Sunnis of strict reform movements (such as the Wahhabi movement), which came to oppose any deviation from their interpretation of the Islamic creed, has exacerbated existing tensions with the Shiʿa in the Persian Gulf area and wherever Wahhabism has spread.

The theological and juristic views on which the four major Sunni schools agree are considered to form the core of orthodox Islam. Although some of these views have coalesced into dogma, others have been subject to changes of interpretation through the years. Specifically, the eventual reliance by

Sunni jurists on *taqlid* (imitation or continuation of established past consensus) led to a reification of thought and law that gave rise to reform movements in the eighteenth century. Taking a stand against past consensus and building on the thought of the Hanbali ibn Taymiyya, the reform movements (the Wahhabis of Arabia, the Sanusis of North Africa, and the followers of Sirhindi in India), rejected *ijma* and emphasized *ijtihad,* considering themselves *ghayr muqallidin* (against imitation) and underscoring the need for new thought in Islamic law. Today, however, and after most Muslim countries have adopted the secular constitutions imposed on them by colonial powers in the nineteenth and early twentieth centuries, the major concern of the various contemporary Sunni Muslim movements is how to restore Islamic law and make it compatible with the demands of modern life.

See also ISLAM; MUWAHHIDUN; SANUSI ORDER; SHIʿISM.

Bibliography

Kamali, Mohammad Hashim. *Principles of Islamic Jurisprudence.* Cambridge, U.K.: Islamic Texts Society, 1991.

Makdisi, George. *Religion, Law, and Learning in Classical Islam.* Aldershot, U.K.; Brookfield, VT: Variorum, 1991.

Rahman, Fazlur. *Islam,* 2d edition. Chicago: University of Chicago Press, 1979.

TAYEB EL-HIBRI
UPDATED BY MAYSAM J. AL FARUQI

SUPHI EZGI
[1869–1962]

Turkish composer and musicologist.

Suphi Ezgi was born in Istanbul and attended the Military Medical Academy. At the same time, he was studying music with Turkish masters like Dede Zekai. Between 1913 and 1920, Suphi Ezgi, along with Sadeddin Arel and Rauf Yekta Bey, created modern Turkish musicology. Suphi Ezgi was also an accomplished singer and tanbur player and composed more than seven hundred pieces. The most important of this fourteen books on musicology is the five-volume *Nazari ve ameli Türk musikisi* (Turkish music in theory and practice).

DAVID WALDNER

SUPREME MUSLIM COUNCIL

Muslim institution in Palestine, 1921–1948.

During Ottoman rule in Palestine (1516–1917), Muslim *waqf* (plural, *awqaf*) and *shariʿa* courts were headed by the Shaykh al-Islam, and in the nineteenth century they were administered by the Ministry of Awqaf in Constantinople (now Istanbul). The British occupation of Palestine, which started in 1917, severed all ties with Constantinople, and these Muslim institutions were placed under British officials. Palestinian Muslims were alarmed at the prospect of their religious affairs being controlled by a Christian power headed by Zionists: Sir Herbert Samuel, the first high commissioner, and Norman Bentwich, legal secretary in charge of the *awqaf* and *shariʿa* courts. The Muslims complained of religious discrimination and demanded control over their affairs. Anxious lest the 1921 anti-Zionist disturbances recur and wanting to provide the Palestinians with autonomous institutions that the Zionists were granted, Samuel proposed that the Muslim secondary electors to the last Ottoman parliament choose a higher body that would control the affairs of the Muslim community.

Samuel issued an order in December 1921 establishing a Supreme Muslim Council (SMC) constituted for "the control and management of Moslem awqaf and Shariʿa affairs in Palestine." It was to consist of a president and four members, two of whom were to represent the district of Jerusalem and the remaining two to represent the districts of Nablus and Acre. All were to be paid from government and *awqaf* funds. In the first election, held on 9 January 1922, the mufti of Jerusalem, Hajj Amin al-Husayni, was elected president; his budget was 50,000 British pounds.

Husayni initiated an Islamic cultural revival in Palestine in the 1920s. Through the SMC, he established an orphanage, supported schools, expanded welfare and health clinics, and renovated religious buildings. The most ambitious and impressive project was the renovation of the two dilapidated mosques within the Haram al-Sharif, the third holiest shrine of Islam. The restored structures enhanced the importance of Jerusalem in the Muslim and Arab worlds and asserted Jerusalem's centrality within Palestine. By the end of the decade, the mufti had consolidated his religious power and had increased his political influence throughout Palestine. He used his enhanced political position to advocate Palestinian self-determination. After he led the Palestine Arab Revolt (1936–1939), however, the British dismissed him and dissolved the SMC in 1937.

See also BENTWICH, NORMAN; HUSAYNI, MUHAMMAD AMIN AL-; PALESTINE ARAB REVOLT (1936–1939); SAMUEL, HERBERT LOUIS; *SHARIʿA*; WAQF.

Bibliography

Mattar, Philip. *The Mufti of Jerusalem: Al-Hajj Amin al-Husayni and the Palestinian National Movement,* revised edition. New York: Columbia University Press, 1992.

Palestine Government. *A Survey of Palestine for the Information of the Anglo-American Committee of Inquiry.* Jerusalem, 1947. Reprint, Washington, DC: Institute for Palestine Studies, 1991.

PHILIP MATTAR

SURSOCK, LADY COCHRANE

Lebanese cultural official.

Yvonne, Lady Cochrane Sursock is the daughter of Alfred Bey Sursock, a Levantine aristocrat who came to Lebanon from Turkey at the beginning of the twentieth century, and Donna Maria Theresa Serra diCassano, daughter of Francesco Serra, seventh Duke of Cassano. She is the wife of Sir Desmond Cochrane, whom she married in 1946. She has played an active public role in Lebanon since her young adulthood, particularly in the arts. She was president of the committee and general manager of the Nicolas Sursock Museum in Beirut (1960–1966) and founder and president of the Association for the Protection of the Natural Sites and Ancient Buildings (APSAD; Association pour la protection des sites et anciennes demeures) in Lebanon (1960–2002). She is currently involved in projects to stem the exodus of Lebanese by rerooting them in their villages of origin and creating jobs in the fields of agriculture, textiles, and handcrafts. Lady Cochrane has been a pioneer in the protection of the environment and in developing Lebanese citizens' awareness of the unique architectural and cultural heritage of Lebanon.

See also ARCHITECTURE; ART; GENDER AND EDUCATION; HARIRI, RAFIQ BAHAʾUDDIN AL-; LEBANESE CIVIL WAR (1958); LEBANESE CIVIL WAR (1975–1990); LEBANON.

MONA TAKIEDDINE AMYUNI

SURSUQ FAMILY

Prominent Lebanese landowning business family.

One of the wealthiest Greek Orthodox families in Beirut, the Sursuqs (also Sursock or Sursok) benefited from the 1858 Ottoman land reform to acquire large tracts of fertile land in northern Palestine. They were also bankers who controlled cotton and grain trade in Acre. The family was associated with controversial land sales to Zionists before and after World War I.

Various family members were active in Beirut politics before World War I, with Albert Sursuq a leading member of the Beirut Reform Society and Michel Sursuq a member of the Ottoman parliament. After the war, the family became a target of anti-Zionist criticism when their land sales to Jews in the Jezreel valley and at Lake Hula displaced hundreds of peasants. The family remained prominent among Beirut's Europeanized elite after World War II. In the 1960s, the family villa was turned into the Nicolas Sursuq Museum.

Bibliography

Abboushi, W. F. *The Unmaking of Palestine.* Wisbech, U.K.: Middle East and North African Studies Press; Boulder, CO: L. Rienner, 1985.

ELIZABETH THOMPSON

SUWAYDI FAMILY

Iraqi family prominent in religious affairs and politics.

The Suwaydi family of al-Karth district of Baghdad traces its origins to Abbas, the uncle of the Prophet Muhammad, whose descendants founded the Abbasid dynasty that ruled Baghdad from 750 to 1258. A well-known member was Shaykh Abdullah al-Suwaydi, a Sunni jurist who took part in the famous theological conference at al-Najaf in 1773 that sought to bring about reconciliation between the Sunni and Shiʿa sects.

The Suwaydi family also has played a leading role in the affairs of modern Iraq. For example,

Yusuf Suwaydi (1854–1925), a *sharʿia* (religious) judge, played a leading role in the Arab movement against the Ottoman Empire. He was imprisoned in 1913 and 1914 for his political activities and later released. He also was involved in the revolt against the British in 1920.

Two of Yusuf's children, Naji and Tawfiq, completed their legal training in Istanbul in the early part of the twentieth century and helped to draft Iraq's constitution. Both of them were elected deputy and senator, and both served as prime minister. Naji advocated pan-Arabism and resented British interference in Iraq. He participated in the 1941 uprising against the British. When the uprising failed, he was exiled to Rhodesia, where he died in 1945. Tawfiq was a pro-British activist. After the revolution of 1958, he was sentenced to life imprisonment but was released in 1962. Tawfiq moved to Lebanon where he died in 1968.

See also SUWAYDI, TAWFIQ AL-.

Bibliography

Khadduri, Majid. *Independent Iraq, 1932–1958: A Study in Iraqi Politics,* 2d edition. London and New York: Oxford University Press, 1960.

Longrigg, Stephen Hemsley. *Iraq, 1900 to 1950: A Political, Social, and Economic History.* London and New York: Oxford University Press, 1953.

AYAD AL-QAZZAZ

SUWAYDI, TAWFIQ AL-

[c. 1889–1968]

Iraqi politician.

Tawfiq al-Suwaydi, a pro-British moderate, was born in Baghdad to an influential Sunni family. His origins trace back to Abbas, the uncle of the Prophet Muhammed, whose descendants established the Abbasid dynasty that ruled Baghdad from 750 to 1258. Suwaydi attended school in Baghdad and studied law in Istanbul and France. He was elected to parliament and served in various government capacities: minister of education (1928), ambassador to Iran (1931), minister of justice (1935), and minister of foreign affairs (1934, 1937, 1941). Suwaydi was prime minister three times (1929, 1946, 1950). During his second term he legalized previously banned political parties. In his last term, he initiated negotiations for a new oil agreement, established the Board of Development to improve economic conditions, and enacted a law permitting Iraqi Jews to leave the country, provided they gave up their citizenship and property. In the aftermath of the 1958 revolution, Suwaydi was sentenced to life imprisonment. In 1962 he was permitted to leave Iraq for Lebanon, where he died.

See also SUWAYDI FAMILY.

Bibliography

Khadduri, Majid. *Independent Iraq, 1932–1958: A Study in Iraqi Politics,* 2d edition. London and New York: Oxford University Press, 1960.

AYAD AL-QAZZAZ

SUWAYDIYA OIL FIELDS

Largest oil field in Syria, with a yearly output of 1 million tons (907,000 t).

The first Suwaydiya oil well was discovered toward the end of 1960 by the German company Concordia at a depth of 5,617 feet (1,712 m). This well is located southeast of Qarah Shuk in al-Jazira plateau in northeastern Syria. It was the second oil field to be discovered in Syria after the Qarah Shuk field, which was discovered in 1958 and contained nine wells. Between 1960 and 1962, the Concordia Company's field showed minimal progress. Three more wells were drilled in the Suwaydiya field, capable of production from the upper Cretaceous rock layer, with average depths of 5,000 feet (1,525 m). But the heaviness of the crude oil produced was discouraging, unless it was blended with lighter crudes from Iraq, in which case the Homs refinery could handle it. At that time, the Suwaydiya reserves were assessed at about 35 million tons (31.7 million t). The Suwaydiya fields were then thought capable of producing 12,000 barrels per day. In 1964, Concordia, which had begun a deep test-well a year earlier, had its license suspended when the Syrian government nationalized the oil industry. The Syrian Petroleum Authority, which was attached to the Ministry of Industry, undertook drilling with assistance from Soviet geophysicists and drillers.

In 1965, the Suwaydiya oil fields were considered commercial. Toward the end of 1974, a ministry for oil and mineral resources was established in Syria. It became responsible for concerting efforts with foreign oil companies for oil drilling, which has intensified since then. Compared with the Qarah Shuk, the Rumayla, and the Tayyim oil fields, the Suwaydiya fields are the largest, with an established reserve of 410 million tons (372 million t) and a yearly output of 1 million tons (907,000 t).

See also HOMS; PETROLEUM, OIL, AND NATURAL GAS; SYRIA.

Bibliography

Longrigg, Stephen H. *Syria and Lebanon under French Mandate.* London and New York: Oxford University Press, 1958.

ABDUL-KARIM RAFEQ

SUWAYHLI, RAMADAN AL-

[?–1920]

Tripolitanian nationalist.

Ramadan al-Suwayhli was a member of a prominent Arab family from the eastern Tripolitanian coastal town of Misurata. They opposed the interests of the other leading family, the Muntasirs.

Suwayhli had been tried and acquitted of murdering Abd al-Qasim Muntasir shortly after the Young Turk Revolution of 1908, when Tripolitania was part of the Ottoman Empire. Suwayhli had played a vital role in supporting the Ottomans against Italian and Sanusi incursions. After the Treaty of Ouchy (1912), which ended the war between Italy and the Ottoman Empire, Suwayhli sought an independent Tripolitania. He had been instrumental in founding the short-lived Tripolitanian republic in 1917, which had not been recognized by Italy but was tolerated (even after the laws of 1919, the *Legge Fondamentale,* when alternative administrative structures were established). Its members, including Ramadan al-Suwayhli, were paid large stipends by the Italian authorities until the structure of the republic collapsed. Italy then connived in Suwayhli's death, at the hands of the Muntasir family (who still held him responsible for Abd al-Qasim's murder) and Abd al-Nabi Bilhayr, leader of the Warfalla (who had fallen out with him concerning the republic).

See also MUNTASIR FAMILY; TRIPOLITANIA.

Bibliography

Anderson, Lisa S. "The Tripoli Republic, 1917–1922." In *Social and Economic Development of Libya,* edited by E. G. H. Joffe and K. S. McLachlan. Wisbech, U.K.: Middle East and North African Studies Press; Boulder, CO: Westview Press, 1982.

GEORGE JOFFE

SYKES, MARK

[1879–1919]

British soldier, orientalist, politician, and emissary.

An artistocrat, Mark Sykes first visited the Ottoman Empire as a boy and returned there as a Cambridge undergraduate. As an honorary consul in Constantinople who was sympathetic to the old Ottoman regime, he rode on horseback through many regions that the British would occupy after defeating the Turks in World War I. Sykes served as an officer in the Boer War. In two books and several articles, he revealed his preference for the religious, rural, and traditional elements of the East over the materialism and cosmopolitanism he so disliked in its cities. Sir Mark became a conservative member of Parliament in 1911.

After serving briefly on the Western front in World War I, Sykes was attached to the general staff of Lord Kitchener. Kitchener sent Sykes to the Middle East and India, where he found poor communication and little coordination among British officers and officials. To deal with these problems, he founded the Arab Bureau in Cairo after he returned to London and then made comprehensive plans for the postwar Middle East. Sykes advocated a large, loose Arab confederation under Husayn, the Sharif of Mecca, except for an international area around Jerusalem, holy to Christians, Muslims, and Jews. Sykes and his French counterpart, François Georges-Picot, negotiated a secret wartime agreement that was signed by tsarist Russia, but later repudiated by the Bolsheviks. Sykes was deeply impressed by Zionism in Russia, where he believed Jews would fight for Zion if not the tsar.

In the last two years of the war, when Sykes was attached to the War Cabinet Secretariat, he drafted various statements for the British entry into Jerusalem,

Baghdad, and Damascus that were in line with the anti-imperialism and self-determination favored by the United States, which had not declared war against the Turks. His third wartime mission to the Middle East failed to get any consensus among Arabs, Armenians, and Jews. Sykes then attended the peace conference at Paris, where he contracted influenza and died.

See also SYKES–PICOT AGREEMENT (1916).

Bibliography

Adelson, Roger. *Mark Sykes: Portrait of an Amateur.* London: Cape, 1975.

Fromkin, David. *A Peace to End All Peace: Creating the Modern Middle East, 1914–1922.* New York: H. Holt, 1989.

ZACHARY KARABELL
UPDATED BY ROGER ADELSON

SYKES, PERCY MOLESWORTH

See SOUTH PERSIA RIFLES

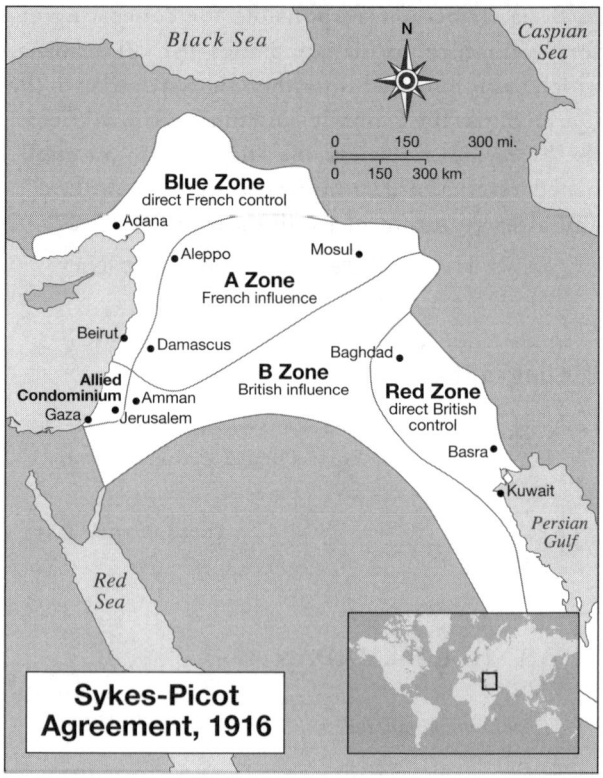

MAP BY XNR PRODUCTIONS, INC. THE GALE GROUP.

SYKES–PICOT AGREEMENT (1916)

World War I document of 1916 that would have divided the Middle East into British and French spheres.

The Sykes–Picot Agreement was one of the pivotal diplomatic documents of World War I concerning the Middle East. It was negotiated in secret at the end of 1915 by Sir Mark Sykes of Great Britain and Georges François Picot of France, with full knowledge by their respective foreign ministries. It provided for a partition of the Middle East into French and British spheres.

The French were to have direct control of Syria, Lebanon, and Cilicia plus a zone of influence extending east from Damascus and Aleppo through Mosul. The British were granted direct control of the Mesopotamian provinces (now Iraq) of Baghdad and Basra as well as a zone of influence extending from Basra to Palestine. Palestine was itself to be placed under international administration.

Under the subsequent Anglo–Russian–French Agreement of 1916, the Russians adhered to Sykes–Picot after extensive discussions between Sykes and the Russian foreign minister, Sergei Sazanov. In return for their support, the Russians were granted direct control over much of eastern Anatolia. In a successful attempt at embarrassing the coalition, the terms of the Anglo–Russian–French Agreement were made public by the Bolsheviks in the spring of 1918. The Arabs claimed that Sykes–Picot contradicted promises made to them by the Hussein–McMahon Correspondence, and the Jews claimed that it contravened the Balfour Declaration. U.S. President Woodrow Wilson wished to annul Sykes–Picot, and even Sykes soon repudiated the agreement. Nonetheless, though the French renounced their claim to Mosul and Britain won control of Palestine, the Middle East treaties framed at the Paris Peace Settlements after World War I closely mirrored the Sykes–Picot Agreement.

See also BALFOUR DECLARATION (1917); HUSAYN–MCMAHON CORRESPONDENCE (1915–1916); PARIS PEACE SETTLEMENTS (1918–1923); SYKES, MARK; WILSON, WOODROW.

Bibliography

Anderson, Matthew S. *The Eastern Question.* New York: St. Martin's, 1966.

Fromkin, David. *A Peace to End All Peace.* New York: Henry Holt, 1989.

Hurewitz, J. C., ed. *The Middle East and North Africa in World Politics.* New Haven, CT: Yale University Press, 1979.

Khalidi, Rashid. *British Policy towards Syria and Palestine, 1906–1914: A Study of the Antecedents of the Hussein–the [sic] McMahon Correspondence, the Sykes–Picot Agreement, and the Balfour Declaration.* London: Ithaca Press, 1980.

ZACHARY KARABELL

The world-renowned Great Mosque was constructed in the eighth century, when Damascus was the seat of the Umayyad dynasty. Most Syrians are Sunnis, with far smaller numbers of other Muslims as well as a sizable minority of Christians, primarily Greek Orthodox and Armenian Gregorian. Islamic fundamentalists are active but not in a position of power; the socialist Baʿth Party violently suppressed an uprising of the Muslim Brotherhood in 1982. © CORBIS. REPRODUCED BY PERMISSION.

SYRIA

Formally, the Syrian Arab Republic (al-Jumhuriyya al-Arabiyya al-Suriyya).

Syria's 71,500 square miles include a narrow plain along the Mediterranean between Turkey to the north and Lebanon to the south, which contains the ports of Latakia and Tartus; fertile highlands between the capital, Damascus, and the border with Jordan, called the Hawran (Hauran); an extensive central plain, in which are situated the cities of Homs, Hama, and Aleppo; the Euphrates River valley, in which are the cities of al-Raqqa (Rakka) and Dayr al-Zawr; an eastern plateau bounded by Turkey to the north and Iraq to the east, whose major centers are al-Hasaka and al-Qamishli; and a large southeastern desert adjacent to Iraq and Jordan, whose oases contain the ruins of ancient fortifications and trading posts.

Syria has three major rivers. The largest, the Euphrates, enters from Turkey and is joined by the Khabur and the Balikh before crossing into Iraq southeast of Al Bu Kamal. The Euphrates system is regulated by the Euphrates Dam at Tabaqa, just west of al-Raqqa, which stores water for use in irrigation and power generation. Running south from mountains in the pre-1920 Syrian province of Iskenderun (now the Turkish province of Hatay), through the fertile Ghab basin and past the cities of Hama and Homs, is the Orontes river (Nahr al-Asi). The Yarmuk river, across which small irrigation dams were constructed during the 1980s, defines the border between Syria and Jordan. At current rates of use, Syria's groundwater reserves are expected to run dry by 2010, leaving the country entirely dependent on river water.

Population

The total population is estimated to be 17.6 million (2002) with Damascus and Aleppo the major population centers. Population growth averaged over 3 percent annually for much of the second half of the twentieth century but then slowed to 2.45 percent (2002). On the other hand, the death rate plunged from 21 deaths per 1,000 during the early 1950s to 5 per 1,000 in 2002. Several thousand Armenians moved to Syria from the Soviet Union in 1945–1946, and founded a sizable community in Aleppo. After the establishment of the state of Israel, virtually all of the Syrian Jewish population emigrated, and about 100,000 Palestinians fleeing Israel's takeover of the Galilee in 1948 ended up in camps on the fringes of Damascus.

Muslims make up 85–90 percent of the population; approximately 75 percent of this number are Sunnis, 13–15 percent are Alawis, about 1 percent are Ismaʿilis, and less than 1 percent are Twelver Shiʿites. Some 3 percent of Syrians are Druze, a sect

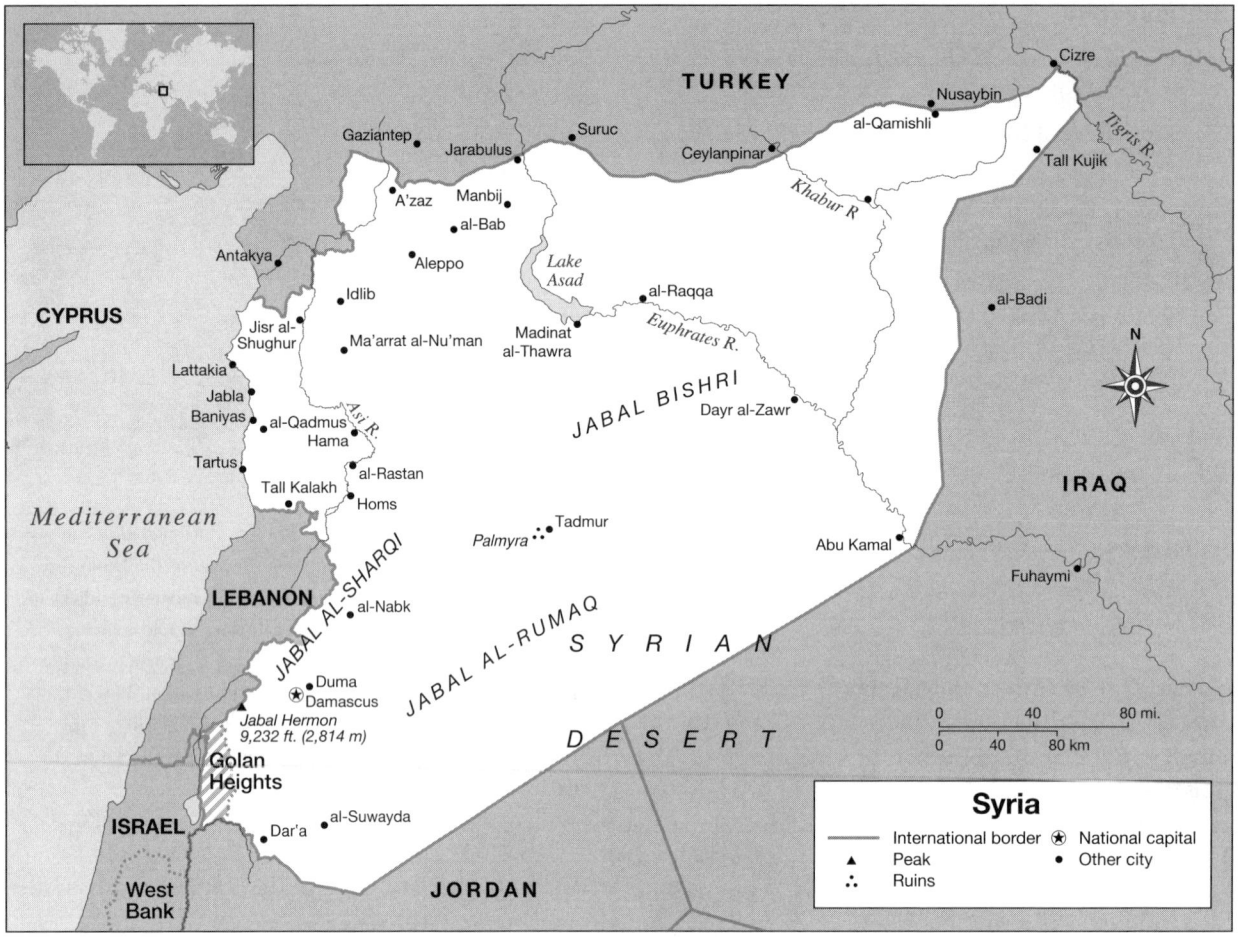

MAP BY XNR PRODUCTIONS, INC. THE GALE GROUP.

that follows a mixture of Christian and Shiʿa doctrines. Isolated pockets of Yazidis exist in the hills outside Aleppo and northeast of al-Qamishli. About 10 percent of the population are Christians, divided among at least a dozen sects. The Greek Orthodox and Armenian Gregorian communities are the largest and most influential.

Administration

Syria's governmental structure is highly centralized and strictly hierarchical, concentrating power primarily in the hands of the president and secondarily with the top leadership of the Baʿth party. This system was developed after March 1963, when military supporters of the Baʿth overthrew the parliamentary order that had reappeared following the dissolution of the union with Egypt in 1961. In November 1970, Gen. Hafiz al-Asad, minister of defense and head of the Baʿth party's military wing, seized power. He served as head of state, commander in chief, and secretary-general of the Regional (Syrian) Command of the Baʿth until his death in June 2000. Shortly after coming to power, the new regime appointed a representative body, the People's Council, to draft a permanent constitution. This document, approved in March 1973, provides for a seven-year presidential term of office; it empowers the president to appoint and remove the vice presidents, the prime minister, and other cabinet ministers. In addition, it grants the president the authority to dissolve the People's Council and call national plebiscites to ratify legislative measures not adopted by the parliament. Upon the death of Hafiz al-Asad, his second son, Bashshar al-Asad, was elected president in July 2000.

Syria consists of thirteen provinces, each administered by a governor. Each governor is advised by a provincial council, one-fourth of whose members are appointed and the remainder of whom are elected by popular balloting. Since 1970, these councils have exercised little decision-making autonomy. Municipal councils provide public services, license businesses, and supervise the collection of local taxes. Each municipal council is headed by a mayor. Damascus city constituted a separate governorate until 1987, when it merged with the surrounding province of Damascus to form a single administrative unit.

Economy

Syria's economy expanded dramatically during the 1940s, due to a combination of restrictions on imports and heightened spending by British and French occupation forces. The Korean War perpetuated the boom by creating greater demand for Syrian cotton on world markets. Private enterprise provided the main impetus for economic growth until the union with Egypt in 1958, when state officials introduced an extensive program of land reform, nationalization of industry, and regulation of commercial transactions. The short-lived parliamentary regime that seceded from the union in 1961 attempted to resurrect the private sector, but the Baʿth-affiliated officers who overthrew the civilian regime in March 1963 gradually extended government control over most sectors of the economy. State intervention peaked with the nationalization of industry, banking, and trade that began in January 1965. Under the regime of Salah Jadid (1966–1970), extensive state control accompanied the establishment of a network of production and distribution cooperatives, state farms, and Baʿth-affiliated popular-front organizations.

By the end of the 1960s, Syria's public-sector enterprises were experiencing severe financial difficulties. The government responded by relaxing restrictions on the activities of private business, particularly in construction and trade. Private enterprise quickly moved into agriculture and manufacturing as well, supported both by the return of large amounts of local capital that had fled the country during the late 1950s and by an influx of investment from the oil-producing Arab Gulf states. Government spending jumped from around 29 percent of gross domestic product (GDP) in 1972 to some 37 percent of GDP in 1987. This rise was not matched by an increase in current revenues, resulting in large budget deficits. The shortfalls resulted primarily from sharp increases in military spending; by 1987, support for the armed forces accounted for 39 percent of total state outlays. With an imbalance of this magnitude sustainable only through heavy reliance on the Communist bloc and Arab oil states, the implosion of the Soviet Union during the early 1990s forced the Syrian government to take austerity measures.

The economy grew at a rate of more than 9 percent per year during the 1970s, slowed to around 2.2 percent during the 1980s, rebounded to more than 5 percent during the 1990s, and continued to grow at an annual rate of 2.5 to 3.5 percent during the early years of the twenty-first century. Income per capita was approximately $1,000 (2002). With the growth in population approximating 2.5 percent, the World Bank has estimated that Syria would need real economic growth of more than 5 percent to improve the welfare of its people. Major distortions contribute to the overall weak performance of the Syrian economy, including multiple exchange rate and exchange controls, restrictions on private sector activity, price controls, major agricultural subsidies, an inefficient state-owned financial system, and the dominance of state-owned enterprises.

The Syrian government implemented limited economic reforms after 2000, permitting Syrians to hold foreign currency and licensing the first public banks, an essential step in modernizing the state-dominated economy. However, the far-reaching economic reforms required to modernize the economy were put on hold for fear that widespread economic change could lead to calls for concomitant political reform and democratization. As a result, sweeping economic reform remains the number one priority in the Syrian domestic agenda.

Education

Since 1967, Syria's schools, technical institutes, and universities have been supervised by the Ministry of Education or the Ministry of Higher Education. Successive Baʿth regimes have expanded the education system, and have taken steps to reduce illiteracy by establishing adult and women's education programs. Elementary education is free and compulsory. Secondary education, which consists of three years of preparatory school and three years of high school, is free but not compulsory. The great majority of children attend public schools; several private schools in Damascus serve foreign nationals and the elite. The Ministry of Education regulates textbooks, curricula, and teacher certification.

Syria has four universities. The largest and most prestigious is Damascus University, founded in 1923, which had some 60,000 students by 2002. The University of Aleppo, chartered in 1958, serves around 30,000 students. Tishrin University in Latakia and al-Baʿth University in Homs offer limited curricula. The University of Aleppo operates a faculty of agriculture in Dayr al-Zawr. Technical institutes are scattered throughout the country. The language of instruction is Arabic, although English and French are required as second languages by many faculties.

History

Syria's modern history began with the end of the Egyptian occupation (1831–1840). After the reassertion of Ottoman control, European manufactured goods flooded the country, ruining the textile industry and leading urban merchants to invest in agricultural land. The trend toward private estate ownership was reinforced by the Ottoman land law of 1858, which allowed landholders to convert nominally state-owned communal lands in the villages into private property. At the end of the nineteenth century, French enterprises won numerous concessions in exchange for loans to the Ottoman authorities. French firms invested in ports, railroads, and highways, opening the cities of the interior to the outside world. As manufacturing continued to contract, to the evident benefit of Syria's well-connected minority communities, anti-Christian and anti-European riots, like the 1860 massacres in Damascus, erupted. These drew European governments into local politics, and growing outside interference generated rising disaffection with Ottoman authority among Syria's Arab elite.

During the 1890s, clubs advocating Syrian independence formed in Aleppo, Damascus, and Beirut. These coalesced into political parties after the 1908 revolution that brought the Committee of Union and Progress (CUP) to power in Constantinople (now Istanbul). Members of an underground CUP branch in Damascus led popular demonstrations in support of the coup, prompting prominent religious notables to form an organization of their own, the Muslim Union. Candidates sympathetic to the latter won the parliamentary elections of 1909. Liberal opponents of the CUP openly denounced the regime in Constantinople, setting the stage for new elections in 1912, which were rigged to ensure that only CUP supporters won seats in parliament.

Following the balloting, influential Syrian liberals emigrated to Cairo, where they formed the Ottoman Party of Administrative Decentralization to seek greater autonomy for the empire's Arabic-speaking provinces. The publication of its program accompanied widespread anti-CUP agitation orchestrated by secret societies including the Constantinople-based Qahtan society, the Paris-based Young Arab Society (al-Fatat), and the Iraq- and Syria-based Society of the Covenant (Jamʿiyyat al-Ahd). The seeds of Arab nationalism germinated among these societies prior to World War I.

Nationalist sentiment blossomed during the war, and when Faisal I ibn Hussein of the Hijaz led an Arab army into Damascus in October 1918, he was welcomed as a liberator and Damascus declared itself an autonomous Arab administration for the whole of greater Syria. Faisal attempted to consolidate popular support by calling elections in mid-1919, but CUP sympathizers won most of the seats representing Damascus. Members of the Young Arab Society dominated the rest of the assembly, and in the fall of 1919 this organization formed the Committee of National Defense to resist Faisal's alleged willingness to capitulate to French demands. Faisal responded by forming the National Party, whose platform called for the establishment of a constitutional monarchy with French assistance. The assembly, led by Hashim al-Atasi of Homs, acclaimed Faisal king of an independent Syria. His acquiescence in the declaration led France to occupy Damascus in 1920, establishing a tutelary regime that governed the country for the next quarter-century.

After independence in 1946, the armed forces became a major means of advancement for Syria's minority communities, particularly poorer Alawis and Druze, who entered the military academy in rapidly growing numbers. There they encountered radical political ideas, including those of the Baʿth and the local communist party. Rising disaffection within the ranks prompted the military high com-

Markets remain a focus of life in Syria. Agriculture, like construction, trade, and manufacturing, has benefited from an influx of private capital since the 1960s. © Cory Langley. Reproduced by permission.

mand to champion social reform programs and solidarity with nationalists in neighboring Arab states. Popular and parliamentary discontent over Syria's defeat in Palestine persisted through the winter of 1948–1949, and in March 1949 a clique of commanders led by Col. Husni al-Zaʿim overthrew the elected government. Zaʿim abrogated the 1930 constitution, suppressed all political parties, and ruled by decree. That June he was assassinated by rival officers, who restored civilian rule and called for elections to a popular assembly to frame a new constitution. The assembly fragmented along regional lines, and in December a group of junior officers led by Col. Adib Shishakli seized power. Shishakli's regime adopted a revised constitution in 1950 but soon resorted to severe tactics to control the resurgent labor unions and peasant movement, and was ousted in 1954.

The new military-civilian coalition restored the 1950 constitution and held parliamentary elections, in which the Arab Baʿth Socialist party won a substantial number of seats. Leftist forces were unable to form a coalition cabinet, and the liberal People's party took over the government. This development sparked renewed militancy among workers and peasants, convincing the cabinet to implement wide-ranging agricultural and industrial reforms. Startled by the reforms, as well as by demands for greater change from the Baʿth and the communists, conservatives in parliament mobilized support for former President Shukri al-Quwatli, who won the presidency in 1955. By 1957 escalating tensions among pro–United States, pro-Egypt, and Syrian nationalist politicians led to a postponement of local elections while military intelligence officers uncovered an elaborate plot by agents of Iraq to undermine the government. These developments sent Chief of Staff Afif al-Bizri to Cairo to request immediate union with Egypt. In 1958 President Quwatli announced the creation of the United Arab Republic.

Downtown Damascus shows clear signs of Syria's efforts since the 1980s to modernize its economy, with some additional reforms taking effect after 2000. Many sectors of the economy, however, have long been run by the state; the country has been firmly under the centralized, hierarchical control of the Baʿth party, with the backing of the military, since 1963. © AP/WIDEWORLD PHOTOS. REPRODUCED BY PERMISSION.

Efforts to unify the two countries eventually provoked widespread unrest in Syria. When the cabinet nationalized and redistributed the assets of private enterprises during the summer of 1961, largely in response to problems in Egypt, merchants and tradespeople in Syria's cities agitated for dissolution of the union. A group of military officers and civilian politicians orchestrated secession that September. Over the next two years, Syria's politics consisted of jockeying among socialists, who favored continued state control over key sectors of the economy; large landholders and rich merchants, who advocated the restoration of private property and parliamentary rule; and moderates, including a wing of the Baʿth party led by Michel Aflaq, who supported maintaining a mixed economy. In 1962, a compromise government supported by the military high command took steps to dismantle the public sector and remove doctrinaire socialists from the armed forces, moves that precipitated both resistance among Baʿth and communist officers and growing Islamist opposition. Spurred by threats to the position of radicals within the military and by burgeoning popular unrest, members of the military committee of the Baʿth carried out a coup in 1963, ushering in a period of Baʿth party–military rule.

Gen. Hafiz al-Asad, who played a major role in the 1963 coup, was promoted to commander of the air force in 1964, serving also as a senior leader in the Baʿthist military command. Mastering the survival techniques necessary in the factional politics plaguing Syria, he seized control of the government in November 1970, dismissing or purging opponents and initiating three decades of rule. Characterized by internal political stability and continuity, the Asad regime ushered in a new chapter in both domestic and foreign policies. On the domestic front, it stressed the need for reconciliation and national unity, built stable state institutions, and courted disenchanted social classes with measures of economic and political liberalization. At the same time, it tolerated no opposition, attacking the Muslim Brotherhood and viciously suppressing an uprising in Hama in February 1982. In addition to the army, the institutional pillars of the regime were a multilayered intelligence network, formal state structures, and revitalized Baʿth party congresses.

In foreign policy, the Asad regime succeeded in transforming Syria into a regional middle power out of all proportion to its size, population, and economic resources. The regime began by moving quickly to end Syrian isolation in the Arab world, focusing on Egypt, Jordan, and Saudi Arabia. Accepting UN Security Council Resolutions 242 and 338, it agreed to a May 1974 disengagement agreement with Israel in the wake of the 1973 Arab-Israel War, but then worked to kill the 1983 Israel-Lebanon accord. Syrian military power expanded steadily in this period; by 1986, it had a very large military force for a state of its size. Personal animosity, together with geopolitical rivalry and a Baʿth party schism, separated Asad's Syria from Saddam Hussein's Iraq. Syria sided with Iran during the Iran-Iraq War and adhered to the Western-led anti-Iraq coalition during the Gulf War. A new entente with Egypt, and Syria's subsequent involvement in the U.S.–sponsored Middle East peace process that started with the Madrid Conference in October 1991, led the Syrian government for the first time into face-to-face negotiations with Israel. Stalled in 1996, talks with Israel again foundered in 1999. However, the positions of the two protagonists were closer than ever before, and a future agreement seemed possible.

President Hafiz al-Asad died of natural causes on 10 June 2000 and was replaced by his son, Bashshar al-Asad, on 17 July 2000. Dual themes of continuity and change characterized the early policies of the new regime. Bashshar al-Asad cautiously promoted limited socioeconomic change to stimulate the economy and generate popular support, but delayed broader economic reforms out of fear they would cause political destabilization. In foreign affairs, he maintained his father's commitment to a just and lasting Middle East peace in which Syria would regain all occupied lands. However, the Israeli-Palestinian struggle, the U.S. occupation of Iraq, and Syria's uncertain place in the war on terrorism combined to limit Bashshar al-Asad's scope for regional and international initiatives.

See also AFLAQ, MICHEL; ASAD, BASHSHAR AL-; ASAD, HAFIZ AL-; BAʿTH; DAMASCUS; HAMA; IRAN–IRAQ WAR (1980–1988); JADID, SALAH; MUSLIM BROTHERHOOD.

Bibliography

Batatu, Hanna. *Syria's Peasantry, the Descendants of Its Lesser Rural Notables, and Their Politics.* Princeton, NJ: Princeton University Press, 1999.

Deeb, Marius. *Syria's Terrorist War on Lebanon and the Peace Process.* New York: Palgrave Macmillan, 2003.

Hinnebusch, Raymond A. *Authoritarian Power and State Formation in Baʿthist Syria: Army, Party, and Peasant.* Boulder, CO: Westview Press, 1990.

Hinnebusch, Raymond A. *Syria: Revolution from Above.* London: Taylor & Francis, 2002.

Khoury, Philip S. *Syria and the French Mandate: The Politics of Arab Nationalism, 1920–1945.* Princeton, NJ: Princeton University Press, 1987.

Kienle, Eberhard, ed. *Contemporary Syria: Liberalization between Cold War and Cold Peace.* London: British Academic Press, 1994.

Longrigg, Stephen Hemsley. *Syria and Lebanon under the French Mandate.* New York; London: Oxford University Press, 1958.

Perthes, Volker. *The Political Economy of Syria under Asad.* New York; London: I. B. Tauris, 1995.

Pipes, Daniel. *Greater Syria: The History of an Ambition.* New York: Oxford University Press, 1990.

Seale, Patrick. *Asad: The Struggle for the Middle East.* Berkeley: University of California Press, 1995.

Seale, Patrick. *The Struggle for Syria: A Study of Post-War Arab Politics, 1945–1958.* New York; London: Oxford University Press, 1965.

Van Dam, Nikolaos. *The Struggle for Power in Syria: Politics and Society under Asad and the Baʿth Party.* New York; London: I. B. Tauris, 1996.

Wedeen, Lisa. *Ambiguities of Domination: Politics, Rhetoric, and Symbols in Contemporary Syria.* Chicago: University of Chicago Press, 1999.

FRED H. LAWSON
UPDATED BY RONALD BRUCE ST JOHN

SYRIAN DESERT

A huge stretch of mostly barren land covering parts of four countries: Syria, Iraq, Jordan, and Saudi Arabia.

Known in Arabic as *Badiyat al-Sham* after the nomadic bedouin (Badu, hence Badiya) who roam its parts in search of pasture, it is also known as the Greater Badiyat al-Sham (Badiyat al-Sham al-Kubra) because it extends between the desert of al-Nufud on the Arabian peninsula and the Euphrates river. Badiyat al-Sham covers about two-thirds—about 52,000 square miles (130,000 sq. km)—of the overall area of Syria. It is divided into two parts: the first, in the northeast, is called Badiyat al-Jazira, and the second, in the southeast, is called al-Shamiyya or Badiyat al-Sham, that is, the Syrian desert. This desert begins at the Syro-Jordanian border, skirts the frontier of settlement toward the north at a line east of Jabal Druze, al-Ghuta oasis of Damascus and its *marj* (meadow), then up along the Qalamun mountains, then east of al-Jabbul, the finally ends at Meskene on the Euphrates.

The Syrian desert, in turn, is divided into two parts, which differ in their surface structure. The first, a plateau in the southwest, is more elevated than the other part and also much drier. The part to the northeast starts at lower elevation in the south—2,208 feet (673 m)—and ends at 623 feet (190 m) in the north. This part is dry and has dry river channels (wadis) exposed to flooding. These wadis range in length from 93 to 186 miles (150–300 km) and in width from 0.3 to 0.6 miles (0.5 to 1 km). Annual precipitation in the Syrian desert does not exceed 5.85 inches (150 mm).

The few plants and animals of the Syrian desert are of the type that can withstand a subtropical climate. The nomads raise sheep and camels, and they move according to the seasons, from one region to the other across political frontiers seeking pasture. Phosphates, oil, and butane gas have been discovered in this desert, and modern network of roads and railways makes the exploitation of the desert much easier than before.

ABDUL-KARIM RAFEQ

SYRIAN SOCIAL NATIONALIST PARTY

Political party established in Lebanon in 1932 with the aim of uniting the Syrian nation.

Syrian Social Nationalist Party militia watch over the streets of Beirut. After decades of division and weakness, the radical party reached a more pragmatic accommodation with the Syrian government of Hafiz al-Asad in the 1980s. © SAMER MOHDAD/CORBIS. REPRODUCED BY PERMISSION.

The Syrian Social Nationalist Party (SSNP) was founded in Beirut by Antun Khalil Saʿada, a Greek Orthodox intellectual, in November 1932. He served as the party's leader until his death in 1949, and the organization reflects his personality and ideas. The SSNP had a strong political influence on the twentieth-century history of the two states, Lebanon and Syria, where it was the most active. It was the first political party in the region to embrace radical, secular ideas which later had an impact on virtually every radical group organized in the two countries, especially the Baʿth Party. The SSNP offered minorities, particularly Greek Orthodox Christians, a vehicle for political action. Its ideology also influenced the development of Pan-Arabism, defining inter-Arab relations in the Levant.

The party's ideology, as defined by Saʿada, was grounded in three related tenets: radical social reform along secular lines, fascist-style rituals and organization, and a Pan-Syrian doctrine. Best known for its Pan-Syrian approach, emphasizing Syrian history and culture but opposing Arab unity, the SSNP called for the creation of a "Greater Syria," encompassing Cyprus, Jordan, Lebanon, and Palestine, in addition to Syria. In one of his publications, Saʿada wrote: "[The] Syrian homeland is that geographic environment in which the Syrian nation evolved. It has natural boundaries which separate it from other countries, extending from the Taurus range in the north-west and the Zagros in the northeast to the Suez Canal and the Red Sea in the south and including the Sinai peninsula and the Gulf of Aqaba, and from the Syrian Sea (Mediterranean) in the west, including the island of Cyprus, to the arch of the Arabian desert and Persian Gulf in the east. (This region is also called the Syrian Fertile Crescent, the island of Cyprus being its star.)" While this Pan-Syrian emphasis was the most prominent aspect of SSNP ideology, its appeal and influence also stemmed from its fascist qualities and emphasis on radical social reform.

Saʿada argued that Lebanon did not constitute a separate entity but was instead part of the Syrian nation. This philosophy led to clashes with Lebanese authorities. In 1949 Saʿada declared an armed revolt against the government and called on his supporters to carry weapons and attack police stations. With the help of Syrian leader Husni al-Zaʿim, Lebanese authorities retaliated and arrested Saʿada. He was executed in July 1949. Saʿada's death led to the overthrow of Zaʿim in Syria and to increased popularity for the SSNP in the 1950s. The killing of a major Baʿth party official and the adversarial relationship between SSNP members and Arab nationalists later caused the party to lose its support in Syria.

In the Lebanese upheaval of 1958, the SSNP allied itself with President Camille Chamoun against pro-Arab nationalist forces in Lebanon. Under attack in Syria, the leaders of the SSNP rightly feared that a victory of the government's opponents would close Lebanon to them. At the end of 1961, the SSNP was involved in an unsuccessful coup against the Lebanese government. As a result, the party was banned in Lebanon as well as in Syria. Many of the party leaders were arrested, and the other party members dispersed or left the organization.

During the Lebanese civil war (1975–1976), the SSNP regained some strength but remained a divided party. One faction retained Saʿada's original ideology. Another group, led by Inʿam Raad, believed it possible to combine Marxist doctrine with the ideology of the SSNP. This group also considered violence a legitimate means of achieving political aims. Raad and his group split from the original SSNP and joined the Lebanese National Movement. In September 1977 a third splinter of the SSNP was formed for the purpose of unifying the party.

Militia members of the Syrian Social Nationalist Party (SSNP) in Beirut, Lebanon, birthplace of the movement in 1932. The party, whose radical secular ideology is centered around the concept of a "Greater Syria," comprising not only Syria and Lebanon but also Cyprus, Jordan, Iraq, Kuwait, and Palestine. © SAMER MOHDAD/CORBIS. REPRODUCED BY PERMISSION.

Syrian president Hafiz al-Asad's government later co-opted Pan-Syrianism into what has been characterized as Syro-centric Arabism, and the Baʿth Party and SSNP cooperated as never before. Several factors helped to explain the reconciliation that took place. Asad grew up in a time and place in which SSNP ideology enjoyed great strength; the family of his wife had close ties to the party; and Asad saw practical, political advantage in accommodating the SSNP. Following decades of competition, they thus reached a mutually beneficial accommodation in which the SSNP became a client of the Syrian state. Even though it remained discredited in its pure, ideological form, a reborn, pragmatic Pan-Syrianism became more significant during the 1980s and after than at any time since the 1920s. For example, in the 1990 and 1994 elections, an SSNP member was elected to the Syrian parliament, albeit standing formally as an independent.

The Syrian Social Nationalist Party has had a profound impact on politics in Lebanon and Syria, introducing a variety of new ideas to the region, including the ideological party, fascist leadership, complete political secularism, and the destruction of existing borders between states. Its repeated challenges to the Lebanese state also served to undermine the power and prestige of the Beirut government. Finally, it led the way in the use of violence to destroy the existing political order, with virtually every radical group in the region adopting aspects of its program.

See also ASAD, HAFIZ AL-; PAN-ARABISM; RAAD, IN'AM; SA'ADA, ANTUN.

Bibliography

Pipes, Daniel. *Greater Syria: The History of an Ambition.* New York: Oxford University Press, 1990.

Suleiman, Michael W. *Political Parties in Lebanon: The Challenge of a Fragmented Political Culture.* Ithaca, NY: Cornell University Press, 1967.

RONALD BRUCE ST JOHN

SYRKIN, NACHMAN
[1867–1924]

Early Socialist Zionist.

Nachman (also spelled Nahman) Syrkin wrote a brochure in German, "The Jewish Problem and the Socialist Jewish State," under the pseudonym Ben Elieser, in Switzerland in 1898. The pamphlet was his considered opinion on solving the Jewish problem with Socialist Zionism. Born a Russian Jew who subsequently went to the West for an education, Syrkin drew on his experience of both Russian socialism and the misery and suffering of Russian Jewish life. He was one of the first to do so.

He attended the first Zionist Congress in 1897 and remained in the World Zionist Organization until 1905, when at the seventh Zionist Congress it was clear that the British offer of Uganda as a place for a Jewish state was impossible. He moved to the United States in 1907 to continue as an official of the Labor Zionist movement and worked as a territorialist (a member of Israel Zangwill's Jewish Territorial Organization [ITO], willing for the Jewish people to settle any unpopulated area). He also wrote and edited journals in Yiddish and Hebrew in support of his views.

Syrkin's socialism was utopian and ethical, not Marxist. At the base was his view that the common people would realize a Jewish state, not the successful or wealthy; and the state was necessary, since even a new socialist order would not integrate the Jewish minority. He reasoned that modern antisemitism was different from historical forms that had been unleashed in earlier eras, since it stemmed from dislocations of modernization.

Bibliography

Hertzberg, Arthur, ed. *The Zionist Idea: A Historical Analysis and Reader.* Philadelphia: Jewish Publication Society, 1997.

Syrkin, Marie, ed. *Nachman Syrkin: Socialist Zionist.* New York: Herzl Press, 1960.

DONNA ROBINSON DIVINE

SZOLD, HENRIETTA
[1860–1945]

Founder of Hadassah, the largest Jewish women's organization.

Henrietta Szold was the daughter of a modernist rabbi from Baltimore. After visiting Palestine in 1909, she resolved to bring modern medical care and hygiene to the area and to establish a health-care system to meet the needs of the Jewish community there. Szold was the first director of the Youth Aliyah.

See also YOUTH ALIYAH.

Bibliography

Dash, Joan. *Summoned to Jerusalem: The Life of Henrietta Szold.* New York: Harper and Row, 1979.

Geller, L. D., ed. *The Henrietta Szold Papers in the Hadassah Archives, 1875–1965.* New York: Hadassah, 1982.

MIA BLOOM

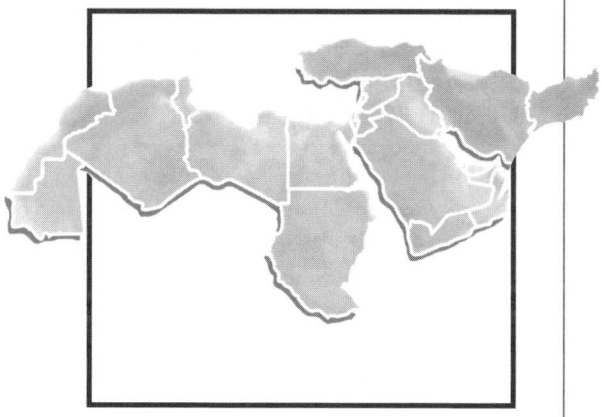

T

TABA

A piece of land disputed by Egypt and Israel.

Taba is a 250-acre patch of land that juts into the Gulf of Aqaba, a dozen miles south of Elat. When the Israeli and Egyptian governments finalized terms on 19 January 1982 for the return of the entire Sinai peninsula to Egypt, Israeli negotiators claimed that Taba should remain within Israel. They based their claim on alleged ambiguities in the physical description of Taba in the 1 October 1906 accord that demarcated the administrative border between Palestine and Egypt. Israel reinforced that claim by constructing two hotels, after spring 1982, within the Taba zone. Article 7 of the Egypt-Israel peace treaty of 1979 provided for mediation or arbitration of such differences if direct negotiations failed to resolve them. Egypt urged the formation of an international arbitration team, but the Israeli cabinet did not agree to the principle of arbitration until 13 January 1986. The membership and terms of the arbitration team were agreed upon by 12 September 1986. The three-person panel was empowered to decide on the location of the boundary pillars as of 1948, the end of the Palestine Mandate, and its rulings were final and binding on both parties. On 29 September 1988, the panel ruled in favor of Egypt. Israel evacuated Taba on 15 March 1989. Egyptian sovereignty was restored over Taba and over the hotels that Israel had constructed. However, Israelis could visit the enclave without obtaining an Egyptian visa, and Israel continued to supply Taba's water and electricity from Elat. The Taba accord was a rare example of the resolution of a contentious issue through judicial means.

Bibliography

Lesch, Ann M. "The Egyptian-Israeli Accord to Submit the Dispute over Taba to International Arbitration." In *The Middle East and North Africa: Essays in Honor of J. C. Hurewitz*, edited by Reeva S. Simon. New York: Middle East Institute, 1990.

Ann M. Lesch

TABA ACCORDS

See Taba; Taba Negotiations (1995, 2001)

TABA NEGOTIATIONS (1995, 2001)

Two separate Israeli-Palestinians negotiations that led to an accord on interim arrangements in 1995, and to bridging differences on the final status issues in 2001.

The Taba resort in Egypt was the site of the Israeli-PLO negotiations that concluded with the Israeli-Palestinian Interim Agreement, West Bank–Gaza Strip, also known as the Taba Accords or Oslo II, which was signed in Washington, D.C., on 28 September 1995. The agreement dealt with such issues as civil affairs, economic relations, legal matters, the Palestinian election of an 88-member Palestinian Legislative Council, and security arrangements. The West Bank was divided into areas A, B, and C. In area A, Israel was to redeploy from six cities, whose overall security would be placed in Palestinian hands. In area B, Palestinian towns and villages, Israel would be responsible for security and the Palestinians for public order. In area C, unpopulated areas, Israel would maintain full control. Negotiations for permanent status of the territories were to begin in May 1996, but were delayed for four years.

Five years after the first Taba negotiations, President Bill Clinton convened a summit on 11 through 24 July 2000 at Camp David between Israeli Prime Minister Ehud Barak and PLO Chairman Yasir Arafat and their teams to negotiate the final status issues, but the parties failed to reach an agreement. More negotiations took place, especially at Bolling Air Force Base in December 2000; these ended on 23 December with Clinton issuing what became known as the Clinton proposals or parameters. These meetings and Clinton's intervention set the stage for the last Israeli-Palestinian meeting of the Oslo peace process, which took place at Taba between 21 and 27 January 2001.

Thanks to the Clinton proposals the two parties at Taba were able to narrow their differences on final status issues, though, since there was no official note taking, there are conflicting accounts about the extent of the progress. Both sides made unprecedented concessions. The Israelis reportedly agreed to withdraw from 100 percent of the Gaza Strip and 92 percent of the West Bank, coupled with a 3 percent land swap. The Palestinians accepted Israeli annexation of clusters of settlements but were seeking sovereignty over 98 percent so as to have maximum contiguity in the West Bank. These figures are in dispute, since both sides do not agree on how to calculate withdrawal percentage, especially on whether East Jerusalem, parts of the Jordan Valley, and other parts should count as part of the West Bank. When these parts are counted, the withdrawal figures are smaller than those cited above. On Jerusalem, the Palestinians conceded the Jewish Quarter, including the Western Wall, and Israel agreed to return noncontiguous parts of East Jerusalem. The parties discussed the return of 100,000 to 150,000 Palestinian refugees, out of some 3.7 million, to what is now Israel, but they remained apart on this and other issues.

While the Israeli offer was far-reaching, it was not enough for the Palestinians, because it would not have allowed for a contiguous capital in East Jerusalem, the settlement clusters that Israel wanted to annex would have reduced contiguity in the West Bank, and Palestinian inability to control their borders and air space would have negated Palestinian sovereignty. The two sides needed more time to bridge their differences, but time ran out. The negotiations were interrupted by the departure from office of Clinton on 20 January 2001, and by the defeat of Barak in the Israeli elections of 6 February 2001. But the narrowing of differences at Taba in 2001 had been significant and was hailed by several of the negotiators as representing the closest the two sides had ever come to an agreement.

See also CLINTON, WILLIAM JEFFERSON; OLSO ACCORD (1993).

Bibliography

Enderlin, Charles. *Shattered Dreams: The Failure of the Peace Process in the Middle East, 1995–2002.* New York: Other Press, 2002.

The Moratinos Document. Available at <http://disarm.igc.org/morotinosdocument1.htm>.

PHILIP MATTAR

TABAQA DAM

Dam on the Euphrates river built to irrigate Syria.

Started in 1968, the dam was finished in 1973 with Soviet assistance, at a total cost of US$600 million. It forms Lake Asad on the Euphrates, above Raqqa, Syria. It is intended to irrigate 1.5 million acres (640,000 ha) by the year 2005 and produce six hundred megawatts of electricity. By the mid-1980s, only about 187,500 acres (75,000 ha) were under irrigation and five of the eight power generators were not operating.

When all projects are completed, the dam will take seven billion cubic meters of the thirty billion cubic meters of water that once entered Iraq each year. Iraq complains of this and that the upstream irrigation projects lower Iraq's water quality by raising salinity levels. Turkey also has ambitious irrigation projects under way at Keban and Karababa, which will reduce Iraq's share to eleven billion cubic meters. Syria has protested to Turkey about excessive use of Euphrates water and tried in 1984 to block Arab oil states from making loans to Turkey for construction of the Karababa dam. No treaty exists for sharing the flow, thus this serious dispute has no foreseeable prospect of resolution.

Bibliography

Drysdale, Alasdair, and Blake, Gerald H. *The Middle East and North Africa: A Political Geography.* New York: Oxford University Press, 1985.

JOHN R. CLARK

TABATABA'I, MOHAMMAD
[1841–1920]

Persian religious scholar; one of the principal leaders of the Constitutional Revolution, 1905–1909.

Born in Karbala in 1841 to a family with illustrious scholarly antecedents, Mohammad Tabataba'i spent his early childhood in Hamadan in the care of Aqa Sayyed Mehdi, his paternal grandfather, before moving to Tehran, the capital, where his father, Sayyed Sadeq, was firmly established as a leading religious authority. There he studied jurisprudence with his father and other prominent scholars, philosophy with Mirza Abul-Hasan Jelve, and—most significant for his political activity in later years—ethics with Shaykh Hadi Najmabadi, many of whose opinions were regarded as subversively liberal. At the same time, through reading newspapers and closely questioning returning travelers, Tabataba'i began taking an interest in the affairs of Europe, which was atypical for the religious scholars of his time.

In 1882, Tabataba'i set out from Tehran with the intention of making the pilgrimage to Mecca. He took a circuitous route, traveling via Russia, Anatolia, and Istanbul, meeting new scholars and men of state wherever he alighted, and he arrived in Mecca too late for the pilgrimage. Cholera was raging in the Hijaz, so he left promptly for the area that is now Iraq, where he joined the circle of the great scholar Mirza Hasan Shirazi in Samarra. He spent more than ten years with Shirazi, perfecting his command of Shi'ite jurisprudence and acting as the trusted adviser of his teacher in political matters. It was in this capacity that he was addressed a letter by the celebrated Jamal al-Din Asadabadi (Afghani), then resident in London, calling on him to make greater political use of Shirazi's prestige, which had been inaugurated by the Tobacco Revolt and boycott of 1891.

Despite the oppositional tendencies that Asadabadi correctly perceived in him, Tabataba'i's return to Tehran was due to an initiative of Naser al-Din Shah. The monarch wished to create in Tehran a counterweight to Mirza Hasan Ashtiani, a cleric whose prestige had grown considerably in the course of the tobacco boycott, and he accordingly suggested to Shirazi that he should send one of his prominent disciples to Tehran. Shirazi selected Tabataba'i, who arrived back in Tehran in the fall of 1893. His father had died almost a decade before, but Tabataba'i fell heir to his influence in the Iranian capital with little difficulty. The shah's expectations of Tabataba'i were disappointed; not only did he establish cordial relations with Mirza Hasan Ashtiani, but he also emerged as an implacable critic of the corruption and tyranny of the court. Indeed, in 1911 he claimed to have begun working for the cause of constitutional government immediately after his return from Samarra, preaching from the pulpit on the need for establishing a consultative assembly. On another occasion, he stated frankly that he and his colleagues in the clerical class had no direct acquaintance with the concept of constitutionalism, having learned of it from those with experience of Europe. During the decade leading up to the Constitutional Revolution he deepened both his understanding of con stitutional government and his contacts with secular intellectuals working for the same goal.

The beginnings of the revolution may be dated to an alliance concluded by Tabataba'i with another leading cleric of Tehran, Sayyed Abdollah Behbahani, on 23 November 1905, initially for the purpose of obtaining the dismissal of Ayn al-Dowleh, the prime minister. Soon thereafter, the two clerics joined a group of bazaar merchants who had taken sanctuary in the Shah Mosque in Tehran to protest government policies. After Tehran's *imam jomeh* (the highest-ranking paid government-appointed cleric) had the group forcibly evicted from the mosque, Tabataba'i and the clerics led a migration of their colleagues and supporters to the shrine of Shah Abd al-Azim, south of Tehran, where they formulated the demand for an *adalat-khaneh* (house of justice) as a condition of their return. Their demand was formally accepted, and on 12 January 1906 Tabataba'i and Behbahani returned to the capital in triumph. Ayn al-Dowleh remained in office, however, and he stalled implementing the royal decree for convening a house of justice. The tensions that persisted between him and the constitutionalists led to a new and more significant migration of Tabataba'i, Behbahani, and their associates, this time to Qom, on 15 July 1906. They demanded the dismissal of Ayn al-Dowleh, in addition to the establishment of a consultative assembly. Their demands were accepted, and on 18 August 1906 Tabataba'i and Behbahani were able to reenter Tehran. Tabataba'i exercised great influence in the *majles* (assembly) that was convened soon thereafter, attempting to preserve the alliance of personalities and interests that had made possible the introduction of constitutional government. His success was limited, however, and the majles was in a state of chronic dissension when its debates were brought abruptly to an end by the royal coup of 23 June 1908. Tabataba'i was arrested and taken in chains to the garrison at Bagh-e Shah. After a spell of imprisonment, he lived in seclusion in Shemiran, north of Tehran, before being banished to Mashhad. He returned to Tehran on 24 August 1909, one month after the restoration of the constitution, but thereafter tired of direct political involvement. He spent the rest of his life in Tehran, with the exception of a journey in 1917 to the shrine cities of Iraq.

Tabataba'i stands out above all as the most prominent religious leader of his time to have understood fully and accepted the far-reaching implications of constitutionalism for Iranian society, recognizing, for example, that it required a modernization of the educational system. This broadness of outlook may have been connected to the Freemasons' affiliations he had inherited from his father, which led him also to join the Masonic Lodge Reveil de l'Iran, the first Iranian lodge officially affiliated to the Grand Orient of France.

See also AFGHANI, JAMAL AL-DIN AL-; SHIRAZI, MIRZA HASAN.

Bibliography

Browne, Edward. *The Persian Revolution of 1905–1909.* Cambridge, U.K.: Cambridge University Press, 1910.

Hairi, Abdul-Hadi. *Shi'ism and Constitutionalism in Iran.* Leiden, Netherlands: Brill, 1977.

HAMID ALGAR
UPDATED BY ERIC HOOGLUND

TABATABA'I, ZIYA

[c. 1889–1969]

Anglophile Iranian politician and journalist.

Born in Iran, in the southeastern city of Yazd, Ziya Tabataba'i began his public career as a journalist in Shiraz, publishing a series of newspapers—*Islam Sharq* (The east), and *Barq* (Lightning)—in which he supported the causes of constitutional government and social reform. He next moved to Tehran, where during World War I he published *Ra'd* (Thunder), a journal staunchly supporting British policy in Iran. This earned him favorable standing with the British, enabling him to act as a go-between for Iranian notables who wanted their checks cashed by the British-owned Imperial Bank of Persia, which in turn gained for him considerable influence in Tehran society. In 1919, Tabataba'i traveled to Baku (in Azerbaijan) to negotiate on behalf of Iran a political and commercial treaty with the temporarily independent states of the south Caucasus, taking advantage of the opportunity to impress other members of the delegation with his political acumen. In 1920 and 1921, he was active in the Anjoman-e Pulad (Steel Committee), a reformist political committee that was the offshoot of a similar organization established by the British in Isfahan and sought to bring together politicians and military officers to initiate change. At the same time, he maintained close links with the head of the British military mission in Iran. These relations with the British enabled him, together with Reza Khan (later Reza Shah

Pahlavi), then a commander of the Iranian Cossack Brigade, to launch a coup d'état on 21 February 1921, that resulted in the appointment of Tabataba'i as prime minister.

The real significance of this coup was that it marked the first stage in the rise of Reza Khan to supreme power and the replacement of the Qajar dynasty by the Pahlavis, and the premiership of Tabataba'i did not last long. He began energetically enough, banning newspapers hostile to his government and imprisoning many of the titled landowners for whom he nurtured a lifelong enmity. He then concluded a treaty of friendship with the Soviet Union and formally abrogated the already moribund Anglo-Iranian Agreement of 1919. His intention, as he privately informed the British minister in Tehran, was to "throw dust in the eyes of the Bolsheviks and native malcontents" (*Documents on British Foreign Policy,* 1919–1939, London, 1963, vol. 13, p. 731). However, differences soon arose. Over the objections of Tabataba'i, on 6 May 1921, Reza Khan succeeded in bringing the gendarmerie under the control of the Ministry of War and then, some two weeks later, in obtaining the dismissal of the British officers who had been seconded to the Iranian army. The swift erosion of Tabataba'i's position became fully apparent on 24 May, when most of the enemies he had had arrested were released without his permission; the following day he went into exile.

Tabataba'i spent the next nine years in Switzerland, moving in 1930 to Palestine, where he lived for thirteen years under the protection of the British mandate government. In the course of World War II Reza Khan was deposed by the Allies (1941), and in September 1943 Tabataba'i was able to return to Iran—in the face of strong objections from the Iranian court, the Soviet Union, and the United States, which were overcome only by the energetic representations of the British.

Embarking on the second half of his political career, Tabataba'i first aligned himself with the Patriotic Caucus (Fraksiun-e Mihan), a pro-British grouping in the Majles (Iran's legislature). Soon, however, he founded his own party, the Fatherland party (Hezb-e Vatan), which early in 1944 was reorganized along authoritarian lines and renamed the National Will party (Hezb-e Erade-ye Melli). He launched yet another newspaper, *Ra'd-e Emruz* (Today's thunder), in which he denounced the remnants of the military dictatorship established by Reza Khan, the continued hold on national life of the landowning oligarchy, and the growing influence of the communist Tudeh party. Tabataba'i's views won him the support of many bazaar merchants and guild leaders, as well as some lesser-ranking religious scholars, but his National Will party did not contest parliamentary elections. Nonetheless, he was elected to the Majles as deputy from Yazd, under the auspices of the Patriotic Caucus. He opposed a whole series of prime ministers, including most notably Qavam al-Dowleh, who had him arrested for several months in 1946, probably to placate the Soviet Union, the patron of the Tudeh party. Despite his rooted aversion to the Tudeh party, Tabataba'i sided with it in 1948 when efforts were under way to wrest control of the army from the shah. This tactical alliance did not last long, and it was in part because of a growing dependence on the Tudeh party that Tabataba'i opposed the government of Mohammad Mossadegh from 1951 onward (his continued alignment with the British was, no doubt, a more important factor in this regard).

Tabataba'i appears to have withdrawn from active political involvement even before the royalist coup of August 1953 that restored full-fledged autocracy to Iran. He spent the remaining years of his life in the village of Sa'adatabad, dying there in 1969. Notwithstanding his earlier hostility to the Pahlavis, he is said to have become a trusted consultant of the shah during the last phase of his life, meeting with him regularly at least once a week.

See also PAHLAVI, REZA.

Bibliography

Abrahamian, Ervand. *Iran between Two Revolutions.* Princeton, NJ: Princeton University Press, 1982.

Avery, P. W. *Modern Iran.* New York: Praeger, 1965.

HAMID ALGAR

TABBULA

See FOOD: TABBULA

TABRIZ

Provincial capital in northwestern Iran.

Tabriz, the capital of East Azerbaijan, is Iran's fourth largest city, with 1,191,000 inhabitants according to the 1996 census. The city dates back to the Parthian period (approximately 238 B.C.E. to 224 C.E.). The Blue Mosque, built in the fifteenth century, and the Rubʿe Rashidi, constructed by the famous Mongol vizier Rashid al-Din Fazl Allah, are among its archaeological sites. In 1295 the Mongol ruler Ghazan Khan made Tabriz the capital of his empire. In the fourteenth century Tamerlane conquered Tabriz. The Safavid Shah Ismaʿil I made it his capital in 1501. At that time, Tabriz, with a population estimated at 250,000, was one of the world's largest cities. Most of the city was destroyed in the massive earthquake of 1721, which left it devastated, and according to some accounts, caused 80,000 to 100,000 casualties. In the Qajar period (between 1779 and 1925) Tabriz was the seat of the crown prince and a major military headquarters against the Russian frontier. During the Constitutional Revolution (1905–1911) it was a site of antigovernment activity, and Russians occupied the city from 1911 to 1917. Soviet troops occupied the city in 1941 and in 1945 supported the Autonomous Government of Azerbaijan, a secessionist movement headed by Jaʿfar Pishevari. The Soviets withdrew in 1946, and subsequently Iranian forces occupied Tabriz and put an end to Pishevari's government. As an important commercial center, Tabriz also played a prominent role in the revolution of 1979.

Tabriz is one of Iran's most important centers for manufacturing industries, producing chemicals, metals, machinery, and textiles. Hand-knotted carpets made in the city have had an international reputation for quality and design for more than a century. Agricultural products from the Tabriz region include wheat, barley, potatoes, and onions; this region is also a considerable producer of fruits and nuts exported from Iran. The variety of agricultural products has contributed to Tabriz becoming a major food-processing center.

See also AZERBAIJAN.

NEGUIN YAVARI

TABRIZ UNIVERSITY

University in Tabriz, Iran.

Established in 1949 as the University of Azerbaijan, the University of Tabriz had 5,187 students by 1970. It includes schools of literature, agriculture, science, and engineering, as well as an institute for advanced studies. The faculty of literature and philosophy publishes a journal with a solid reputation. According to the university's own statistics, the total student population in 2002 exceeded 10,000, and the faculty numbers about 500, with some 900 administrative personnel.

PARVANEH POURSHARIATI

TAGGER, SIONEH

[1900–1988]

Israeli artist.

Sioneh Tagger was born at the turn of the century in Jaffa to Sephardic Jews who had settled there in the nineteenth century. Her parents helped to found the modern city of Tel Aviv. She studied art at the Herzliya Gymnasium in 1919/20 with a Russian sculptor, Joseph Constant, who introduced her to cubism and European modernism. In 1921 she moved to Jerusalem to study at Bezalel on condition that she live with her grandfather's family, who were religious people. Her works from this period include drawings of elderly Jews and "Oriental types" of Jews, as well as decorative metalwork and painting of miniatures. In 1924 she went to study in Paris, where she learned to build her drawings based on simple geometric structures. Tagger was influenced by several painters from the Jewish School of Paris, as well as by André Derain and Picasso, whose influence can be seen in *Clown* (1925) and *Harlequin* (1901). Later in life, Tagger painted on plexiglass, inspired by memories of glass paintings decorating quotations from the Qurʾan hanging in Arab homes in Jaffa (she, though, used Jewish themes).

JULIE ZUCKERMAN

TAHA, MAHMUD MUHAMMAD

[c.1909–1985]

Founder of the Republican Brotherhood.

Mahmud Muhammad Taha was born in Rufaʿa, in central Sudan, in either 1909 or 1911. He graduated from Gordon Memorial College (now the University of Khartoum) in 1936 and practiced agricultural engineering in the Gazira, where his interest in local and nationalist politics grew. Taha founded the New Islamic Mission or Republican Brotherhood in 1945. His first arrest was in 1946, for leading a demonstration for the release of a midwife detained for performing a circumcision on a young girl just after the British had outlawed the practice. Taha's point was that the colonial authorities had no legitimacy to legislate morality that could only change with the equality of women in society.

Taha was both theologian and political leader. The Republican Brotherhood movement was one of the many nationalist movements that agitated for the independence of Sudan from British colonialism. In addition, Taha's "second message" of Islam was among the earliest of the liberal Muslim reformist movements now called "progressive Islam." He argued for a scientific understanding in Islam rendering it capable of resolving the problems of modern life. He argued against the application of the *hadd* punishments of amputation for theft as a violation of *shariʿa* and of Islam because their imposition presupposes a level of education and social justice that are lacking in today's society. He also argued for equal rights for women in marriage in Islamic law. The community of "Republicans," which included significant numbers of women, put into practice the egalitarian ideas of the movement. The movement was also notable for its emphasis on the rights of non-Muslims in predominantly Muslim Sudan, especially recognizing the oppressed southern masses whose resistance has been manifested in decades of protracted civil war.

Taha and the Republican movement opposed the imposition of *shariʿa* as state law in September 1983 because it divided Muslims from the large non-Muslim Sudanese population and thus was contrary to national unity. They argued that non-Muslims should enjoy full rights as citizens and called for repeal of the "September laws." As a result of this protest, Taha was tried by the Islamist government of Jaʿfar Nimeiri for apostasy. He was found guilty and hanged by the regime on 18 January 1985.

See also GENDER: GENDER AND EDUCATION; GENDER: GENDER AND LAW; GENDER: GENDER AND POLITICS; NUMEIRI, MUHAMMAD JAʿFAR; *SHARIʿA;* SUDAN; SUDANESE CIVIL WARS.

Bibliography

Howard, W. Stephen. "Mahmoud Mohamed Taha." In *Historical Dictionary of the Sudan,* edited by Richard A. Lobban, Jr., Robert S. Kramer, and Carolyn Fluehr-Lobban. Lanham, MD: Scarecrow Press, 2002.

Taha, Mahmoud Mohammed. *The Second Message of Islam,* translated by Abdullahi Ahmed An-Naʿim. Syracuse, NY: Syracuse University Press, 1987.

CAROLYN FLUEHR-LOBBAN

TAHA YASIN RAMADAN

See RAMADAN, TAHA YASIN

TAHINA

See FOOD: TAHINA

TAHIR, KEMAL

[1910–1973]

Turkish novelist.

The son of a naval officer, Kemal Tahir was born Ismail Kemalettin Demir in Istanbul and attended the prestigious Galatasaray Lycée (secondary school), though he did not graduate. In 1932, he began writing for newspapers and periodicals, as well as historical novels that glorified the Ottoman past. Between 1938 and 1950, he was imprisoned, along with the poet Nazim Hikmet, by the government of Turkey because of his ideological views and political convictions. During his incarceration, Tahir collected the observations of villagers who were in prison with him; he used these as the basis for a series of novels that authentically depicted the mentality, social structure, and mode of life in the villages of central Anatolia. He was released from prison in 1950 as part of a general amnesty.

Tahir's novels and his political-cultural theories influenced many Turkish authors, known collectively as Tahiris. His influence spread beyond the realm of literature into cinema, inspiring filmmakers to create films rooted in popular Turkish culture, not Western masterpieces. One of Tahir's last novels, *Mother State,* which took as its subject the founding of the Ottoman Empire in the thirteenth century, signaled a transition in Turkish literature from portraying social realities to searching for new models for change.

Bibliography

Ertop, Konur. "Trends and Characteristics of Contemporary Turkish Literature." In *The Transformation of Turkish Culture: The Atatürk Legacy,* edited by Günsel Renda and C. Max Kortepeter. Princeton, NJ: Kingston Press, 1986.

Halman, Talat Sait, ed. *Contemporary Turkish Literature: Fiction and Poetry.* Rutherford, NJ: Fairleigh Dickinson University Press, 1982.

DAVID WALDNER

TAHTAWI, RIFAʿA AL-RAFI AL

[c. 1801–1873]

Egyptian writer and educator and the founder of the translation movement; precursor of modern Arab secular thought.

Rifaʿa al-Rafi al-Tahtawi was born in Tanta, in upper Egypt, into a family of rural notables with a religious learning tradition, whose genealogy went back to al-Husayn ibn Fatima, grandson of the prophet Muhammad. In his early childhood, his family was exposed to pecuniary difficulties following the confiscation by Muhammad Ali of the *iltizamat* (tax farms).

Education

He was educated in al-Azhar in the traditional range of religious and linguistic studies, but was exposed there to the influence of the unconventional Shaykh Hasan al-Attar who advocated a broader out-look to *ilm* (knowledge) than the range to which al-Azhar was confined. His career was further inspired in Paris (1826–1831), where he was attached to the first mission of students from Egypt, initially as an imam (prayer leader) but soon as the mission's only translation student. Tahtawi read in a wide range of subjects, became acquainted with French liberal tradition, established direct contacts with leading French orientalists and noted the institutionalization of Arabic studies in L'Ecole Spéciale des Langues Orientales Vivantes. He also followed closely the 1830 revolution, studied the structure of the French political system and keenly observed Parisian social life and manners. He provided in great detail the first documented Arabic account of modern encounters with Western life and society in his *Takhlis al-Ibriz fi Talkhis Bariz* (The extraction of gold in the summary of Paris, 1935).

Institutional Career

Tahtawi's institutional career thrived during the reigns of Muhammad Ali and Ismaʿil in two distinct and separate phases. In each phase, he held several positions, all at the same time. The first of these phases (1837–1849), started toward the end of Muhammad Ali's expansion of education and continued up to the large-scale closure of schools at the time of Abbas (1848–1854). During that phase, Tahtawi directed the newly established *Madrasat al-Alsun* (School of languages), then founded and headed *Qalam al-Tarjama* (Translation department) and became chief editor of *al-Waqa'i al-Misriyya* newspaper in 1842. The second phase (1863–1873), corresponds to the reign of Ismaʿil (1863–1879), during which new activity in translation and education was initiated. In this second phase, Tahtawi headed the reinstated Qalam al-Tarjama, participated in *Qumisyun al-Taʿlim* (a central commission for educational planning), and was chief editor of a new fortnightly *(Rawdat al-Madaris al-Misriyya).* He continued to hold these positions until his death in 1873. During the long interlude between these phases (1849–1863), a general trend of reductions in education, and hence translation, prevailed under Abbas (1848–1854) and Saʿid (1854–1863). Tahtawi, virtually exiled to the Sudan for four years (1850–1854), was kept from institutional channels of influence, not-withstanding a relatively short-lived assignment to run a new military school with wide-ranging departments from its opening in 1855 to its closure in 1860.

Educational Agenda and Influence

Tahtawi practically founded the translation movement in Egypt. Works translated by Tahtawi and his pupils into Arabic and Turkish number more than two thousand, many of them geared to a wide variety of educational and general policy requirements. As an educator, he was equipped to run an integrated syllabus of studies. When initial contractions in Muhammad Ali's military establishment forced retrenchments in education, several schools were amalgamated in 1842 into a single institute under Tahtawi's directorship. He ran in that expanded domain the first curriculum that offered a combination of Islamic studies—including law—and European studies, in an educational milieu which had been characterized by strict dualism. These orientations earned Tahtawi the resentment of the *ulama,* whose traditional positions (that is, as judges) were being threatened by his pupils. During the reign of Ismaʿil, Tahtawi cosubmitted a project *(Makatib al-Milla)* for the establishment of a new educational administration to promote and supervise an integrated syllabus in existing elementary schools of traditional learning *(Katatib),* and to sponsor the opening of a network of similarly oriented government elementary schools.

Towards the end of his life, Tahtawi articulated prescriptive reformist views on knowledge, education and the political order in *Manahij al-Albab al-Misriyya fi Mabahij al-Adab al-Asriyya* (The paths of Egyptian minds to the joys of modern manners, 1869) and *al-Murshid al-Amin fi Tarbiyyat al-Banat wa al-Banin* (The honest guide in the upbringing of girls and boys, 1874). Within the context of a dominating traditional heritage, Tahtawi challenged traditional notions on knowledge and education in effective support for state-managed change. He preached that any branch of learning which contributed to human welfare fell within the realm of necessary ilm, that civilization had a material component acquired through adoption of rational sciences from advanced sources in Europe by appropriately prepared calibers, and that education should therefore be aimed at producing new men of knowledge capable of making such adoptions. On these premises, the existing state of al-Azhar *ulama* was criticized and education reforms were advocated, including girls' education, a call that coincided with the opening of the first girls' school in Egypt at the time of Ismaʿil.

Political Perspective

Tahtawi's prescriptions for political reform involved a blend of traditional Islamic and modern secular orientations. He referred to Egypt as a distinct and historically continuous entity, and perceived of the community in terms of a social and political order pertinent to a territorial nation *(watan)* whose members were bound by the common tie of nation-hood and were equally entitled to freedom of belief. He recognized that the social order could be organized on the basis of a man-made law equally applied to all members in the national community *(al-jamʿiyya),* that the political order involved three distinct functional organs, including a legislative organ, and that its role in binding the community made it a necessity to include basic political education in schools' syllabi. But the inherent secular and liberal orientations were constrained by traditional premises and dimensions. Religion was maintained as a determinant within the political community by the perception that a common religious law was among the binding elements for a nation and by preaching equal civil rights of non-Muslims on an appeal to tolerance and justice based on *shariʿa* (Islamic law) rather than on the implications of equality inherent in nation-hood. The absolute authority of the monarch was maintained by requiring that absolute obedience was due to him, that he was not held accountable to his subjects, and that the parliamentary organ's functions were only consultative and supportive. It is on the basis of his general exposure of the Arab mind to reform issues, rather than on the specific positions taken on each, that the origin of modern Arab secular thought is identified with Tahtawi.

Analysis of His Role

His role through state-sponsored institutions, as well as the congruence and timing of specific elements of his thought with specific policy measures, prompted a perception of him as an etatistic ideologue. The mix of reformist and conservative notions in his writings is interpreted accordingly by Israel Altman. Based on this perception, Tahtawi's thought is seen to have reflected a blend of vested interests in educational reform, intellectual commitment to the cause, and self-assertion vis-à-vis the Turco-Circassian bureaucratic superiors, all characteristic of Egyptian officials who participated in state reform policies between 1830 and 1880.

The Western influence on Tahtawi is generally emphasized. However, the contention that his thought was largely a process of acculturation to the West was recently challenged, and it was shown that Tahtawi's work involved "the reestablishment of direct contact with certain elements of classical Islamic [rationalist] tradition." The genuine and indigenous elements in Tahtawi's thought, and in the Arab "renascence" in general, are accordingly highlighted and emphasized.

Tahtawi produced over thirty publications of translations and original works, including Fénelon's *Les aventures de Télémaque* (1867), the first translation into Arabic of a work of Western literature. Among his other important original writings were two attempts made to simplify the teaching of Arabic grammar, the second of which, *al-Tuhfa al-Maktabiyya li-Taqrib al-Lughat al-Arabiyya* (The bookshelves' [or library's] Antique [*sic*] for the Simplification of Arabic Language, 1869) involved a departure from the prose-memorizing method applied then to the presentation of rules in a tabulated and systematic form. As chief editor of *al-Waqa'i al-Misriyya,* he introduced the newspaper article as a new genre of writing through various commentaries on current affairs. He wrote in serial form, in *Rawdat al-Madaris al-Misriyya,* the first sira (prophet's biography) in modern times, later published as *Nihayat al-Ijaz fi Sirat Sakin al-Hijaz* (The ultimate brief on the biography of the resident of Hijaz, 1876).

Notwithstanding the specific differences in interpreting his role and in classifying his political thought, Tahtawi's contributions to the policies and notions of cultural change, as well as his contributions to Arab secular thought, continue to be recognized. More than a century after Tahtawi's death, he remains relevant to contemporary endeavors. During Nasser's era, the widely circulating Egyptian daily *al-Ahram* used his words as epigraph for its opinion page: "Let the watan, the fatherland, be a place for our common happiness, which we build with freedom, intellect, and factories."

Bibliography

Altman, Israel. "The Political Thought of Rifaʿa Rafi' at-Tahtawi, A Nineteenth Century Egyptian Reformer." Ph.D. diss., University of California at Los Angeles, 1976.

Cole, Juan R. "Rifaʿa al-Tahtawi and the Revival of Practical Philosophy." *The Muslim World* 70 (1980): 29–46.

Heyworth-Dunne, J. "Rifaʿa Badawi Rafi' at-Tahtawi: The Egyptian Revivalist." *Bulletin of the School of Oriental and African Studies* 9 (1937–1939): 961–967; and 10 (1939–1942): 399–415.

Husry, Khaldun S., Al- *Origins of Modern Arab Political Thought.* Delmar, NY: Caravan Books, 1980.

Abdel Aziz EzzelArab

TA'IF ACCORD

Agreement ending the civil war in Lebanon, 1989.

In July 1989, the Arab Tripartite Committee (Morocco, Saudi Arabia, and Algeria) made recommendations to resolve Lebanon's civil war: expanded Lebanese sovereignty, a pullback of Syria's forces, and formalization of Syria and Lebanon's relationship with Israel. Syria promptly rejected them. In September, in the city of Taʾif, Saudi Arabia, representatives of the various Lebanese factions accepted a new National Unity charter. Under it, Syria would restrain Shiʿite groups backed by Iran in exchange for recognition of its dominance in Lebanon and the isolation of the Christian military figure Michel Aoun; vacant parliamentary seats would be filled by the new government before holding elections; Syria was empowered to become involved in reconstituting national governmental authority; redeployment of its forces left Syria firmly in control of territory strategically important for access to Beirut; and the governments of Syria and Lebanon were permitted to conclude secret agreements. The Taʾif Accord came under heavy criticism because several of its clauses were never implemented. Foremost was the issue of Syrian troops' presence in Lebanon. In 2002 and 2003, the Syrian regime implemented symbolic minor withdrawals from some areas in Lebanon, including Beirut. As of today, there are still more than 25,000 Syrian troops in Lebanon.

Bryan Daves
Updated by George E. Irani

TA'IF, AL-

A highland city in Saudi Arabia's al-Hijaz region.

Al-Taʾif is about 75 miles southeast of the holy city of Mecca. Although located on a sandy plain, it possesses plentiful water, making it an important agricultural center serving Mecca and Jidda. Many inhabitants are immigrants or the descendants of immigrants from throughout the Islamic world, especially Yemen, the Indian subcontinent, and central Asia. Al-Taʾif was the first city of al-Hijaz to fall to the Al Saʿud in 1924, and the Ikhwan armies that first entered the city plundered it and massacred many of its inhabitants. It has long served as a summer residence for kings and wealthy Meccans, who are a mainstay of its economy, along with several Saudi military bases. Estimates in the early twenty-first century placed its permanent population at about 350,000, with a seasonal increase to 500,000. The nearby district of al-Shafa is a popular summer resort.

See also AL SAʿUD FAMILY; IKHWAN; SAUDI ARABIA.

Bibliography

Hogarth, David George. *Hejaz before World War I: A Handbook,* 1917. Reprint, New York: Oleander, 1978.

Peterson, J. E. *Historical Dictionary of Saudi Arabia,* 2d edition. Landover, MD: Scarecrow Press, 2003.

J. E. PETERSON

TAʾIF, TREATY OF AL-

Treaty that concluded the 1933–1934 border war between Saudi Arabia and Yemen.

The treaty that ended the border war between Saudi Arabia and Yemen and set up a framework for peaceful relations was signed in al-Taʾif (Hijaz) in May 1934. After Saudi Arabia's occupation of the port city of Hodeida, Yemen—and under pressure from Great Britain and Italy, which were wary of the extension of Saudi Arabia's power nearer their colonies (Aden and Eritrea, respectively)—King Abd al-Aziz (Ibn Saʿud) and Imam Yahya agreed to settle the border issue. Yemen recognized Saudi Arabia's sovereignty over Asir and the towns of Najran and Jizan and agreed to pay Saudi Arabia an indemnity of 100,000 pounds sterling in gold. In exchange, Saudi Arabia evacuated its forces from Hodeidah and other areas of Yemen it had captured. The border area was to be demilitarized, and its demarcation was outlined from the Red Sea coast to just east of Najran; beyond that point it was undefined. A committee was to be established in order to work out the limits of tribal areas. In addition, the treaty called for the renewal of its terms in twenty years. Its terms were reaffirmed and expanded in a June 2000 international border treaty between the two countries.

See also ABD AL-AZIZ IBN SAʿUD AL SAʿUD; HODEIDA; YEMEN.

Bibliography

Tuson, Penelope, and Quick, Emma, eds. *Arabian Treaties, 1600–1960.* Volume 4. Slough, U.K.: Archives Editions, 1992.

F. GREGORY GAUSE III
UPDATED BY ANTHONY B. TOTH

TAʿIZ

Province and largest city in the south of North Yemen.

Taʿiz Province is, along with Ibb Province, the heart of the Shafiʿi south of North Yemen. It embraces the Hujariyya region, and the city of Taʿiz is its soul. The southern uplands of Taʿiz Province, at a few thousand feet, have a more temperate climate and more rainfall than do the northern highlands, and the agriculture of the province has in the past supported a larger, denser population than that of provinces farther north. In the past, the city of Taʿiz was an important center of power in North Yemen, especially under the Rasulids from the mid-thirteenth to the mid-fifteenth centuries; more recently, Imam Ahmad insisted on residing there between 1948 and 1962. Linked since the late nineteenth century to British Aden by an increasing stream of workers, merchants, and students, and then linked through Aden to the outside world, Taʿiz became a part of world commerce and was in touch with the modern world and its ideas far more than was Sanʿa; by the 1940s, it had become the hotbed of modernist, republican, and even revolutionary ideas in the Yemen ruled by the imams. Thus, through the 1970s, Taʿiz was compared favorably to Sanʿa, and especially by many southerners.

By the 1980s, however, Sanʿa had outstripped it in size and political importance and Hodeida had outstripped it in commercial importance; its basic infrastructure—including electricity, water, and roads—was allowed to degrade. Still, Taʿiz remained in the 1990s and thereafter a major center of business and light industry; its links to Aden, and the new economic role of the latter, may enhance the position of Taʿiz in unified Yemen, or unification may lead to a bypassing of Taʿiz. In any case, the Taʿiz of old is no more. Within defining walls and highlighted by great whitewashed mosque minarets and domes, its back pressed against the cloud-topped mountain named Jabal Sabr, which towers over it, the old Taʿiz was a jewel of a small Arab Islamic city. The Ta'iz of today has burst its walls, and unattractive modern construction has replaced, crowded out, and hidden most of the old. The population of Ta'iz and the villages it has absorbed is about 700,000.

See also SAN'A; YEMEN; YEMEN ARAB REPUBLIC.

Bibliography

Burrowes, Robert. *Historical Dictionary of Yemen.* Lanham, MD: Scarecrow Press, 1995.

Carapico, Sheila. *Civil Society in Yemen: The Political Economy of Activism in Modern Arabia.* New York and Cambridge, U.K.: Cambridge University Press, 1998.

Dresch, Paul. *A History of Modern Yemen.* New York and Cambridge, U.K.: Cambridge University Press, 2000.

ROBERT D. BURROWES

TAJIKS

People of Central Asia; the original Iranian population of Afghanistan and historic Turkistan.

The Tajiks are Muslim people of Central Asia living in the countries of Afghanistan, Tajikistan, and Uzbekistan. Their population is thought to be about 10 million, with more living outside of Tajikistan than within. About 3.5 million live in Afghanistan. Although their history is not well known, Tajiks are thought to be the original inhabitants of Central Asia, perhaps the direct descendants of the ancient Aryans. Their language, Tajiki, is a dialect of Persian.

Tajiks in Afghanistan live primarily in the northern and western provinces, where they are mainly settled farmers and landowners. Most Tajiks in Afghanistan, like most Afghans, identify with their local village or valley and are not always aware of their ethnic name. In fact, *Tajik* is sometimes used to describe any Persian speaker in Central Asia, whether or not the people themselves so identify.

In Afghanistan the Tajiks played an important role in the civil war of the 1980s and 1990s, especially those in the Panjsher Valley. The famous Afghan resistance leader Ahmad Shah Masoud was a Panjsher Tajik.

Although historically the Tajiks have not played an important role in the governance of Afghanistan, their position changed after 11 September 2001. The Northern Alliance, which had strong Tajik leadership, took control of Afghanistan in November 2001. Tajiks occupied a number of key Afghan ministries in the government of Hamid Karzai, including foreign affairs and defense. They have continued to play a dominant role in the Karzai government.

See also AFGHANISTAN; KARZAI, HAMID.

Bibliography

Ewans, Martin. *Afghanistan: A New History.* London: Curzon Press, 2001.

GRANT FARR

TAJIN

See FOOD: TAJIN

TAKFIR WA AL-HIJRA, AL-

Egyptian Islamic fundamentalist organization.

Al-Takfir wa al-Hijra is one of the most notorious radical Egyptian fundamentalist organizations. Its real name is the Society of Muslims (Jama'at al-Muslimin). The group was formed in 1969 by Shukri Mustafa, who had been arrested in 1965 and served prison time with the influential Sayyid Qutb (an Egyptian who came to be considered the most radical fundamentalist thinker in the Arab world). Mustafa argued that the Egyptian society is living in a corrupt, decadent, and non-Islamic state of paganism *(jahiliyya).* His solution for the group was to withdraw itself from society and forge a new, purely Islamic society, in the unpopulated hinterland off the Nile River Valley. Though the group did spend some time living in caves, for most of its existence members lived in shared apartments in the poor neighborhood of Cairo. When the government arrested and detained several members in 1977, the organization responded by kidnapping, and ultimately murdering, a former minister for religious endowments. After a large-scale shootout with the police, several hundred members of the group were arrested and tried. Shukri Mustafa and four other leaders were sentenced to death, and others received prison sentences ranging from five to twenty-five years. Today, the group is considered to be part of the Arab Afghans and is led by Ahmad al-Jazaʾiri.

At the ideological level, Mustafa delineates two stages for the organization: First, the stage of weakness *(istiddʿaf)*, during which the group builds itself; and second, the stage of action *(tamkin)*, during which the group attacks the *jahili* society. Hence the group's popular names *al-takfir* (excommunication) and *al-hijra* (migration). Furthermore, the group rejects mainstream doctrines accepted by traditional scholars and moderate fundamentalists. Thus, it does not believe in the validity of consensus *(ijma)* or independent reasoning *(ijtihad)*—it only believes in the literal validity of the Qurʾan and the *Sunna* of the Prophet, which are the basis of constructing divine governance *(hakimiyya)* and destroying worldly paganism. The group adheres to a militant view of jihad (holy war) and makes the whole world its enemy; thus, the United States, the United Nations, and Israel as well as the Islamic states are viewed as illegitimate systems of government that should be toppled.

Bibliography

Kepel, Gilles. *Muslim Extremism in Egypt: The Prophet and Pharaoh.* Berkeley: University of California Press, 1985.

Moussalli, Ahmad. *Historical Dictionary of Islamic Fundamentalist Movements in the Arab World, Iran, and Turkey.* Lanham, MD: Scarecrow Press, 1999.

DAVID WALDNER
UPDATED BY AHMAD S. MOUSSALLI

TAKVIM-I VEKAYI

See NEWSPAPERS AND PRINT MEDIA: TURKEY

TALABANI, JALAL

[1934–]

Kurdish leader.

Leader of one of the two main Iraqi Kurdish political parties, Jalal Talabani was born in 1934 near Koi Sanjaq, in Iraqi Kurdistan. The son of a Qadiri (Sufi) *murshid* (teacher) belonging to a very famous Kurdish family, Talabani studied law in Baghdad. In 1962 he joined General Mustafa Barzani in the armed struggle of the Kurds against the Arabs. The bright leftist intellectual Talabani could not get along with the more traditional, conservative Barzani, and from 1966 until 1970 Talabani led a group of government mercenaries *(jash)* fighting against the Kurdistan Democratic Party (KDP). After the 11 March 1970 autonomy agreement between General Barzani and Iraq's then vice president Saddam Hussein, Talabani lived in exile in Beirut and Damascus. After the collapse of Barzani's movement (caused by the Algiers Agreement in March 1975), Talabani founded in 1977 the Patriotic Union of Kurdistan (PUK). Since then he has competed with Masʿud al-Barzani (the general's son) for the leadership of the Iraqi Kurdish movement. After the Gulf War (1990–1991) and the formation of the Kurdish Autonomous Zone, Talabani shared power with Masʿud al-Barzani from the elections of May 1992 until May 1994, when fighting resumed between the two leaders. In 1996 Talabani established his own Kurdish Regional Government in Sulaymaniyya. Since the Washington Agreement of September 1998, Talabani has coexisted with Barzani, and on 8 September 2002 he signed the agreement of Sari Rash, which paved the way for the first full session of the Kurdish Parliament on 4 October 2002 and the normalization of the relations between the KDP and PUK. In 2003, after the fall of Saddam Hussein, Talabani was appointed a member of the Iraqi Governing Council.

See also BARZANI FAMILY; KURDISH AUTONOMOUS ZONE; PATRIOTIC UNION OF KURDISTAN (PUK).

Bibliography

McDowall, David. *A Modern History of Kurds.* London: I. B. Tauris, 1996.

Randal, Jonathan C. *After Such Knowledge, What Forgiveness?: My Encounters with Kurdistan.* New York: Farrar, Straus, and Giroux, 1997.

CHRIS KUTSCHERA

TALAL IBN ABDULLAH

[1909–1972]

King of Jordan who, during his brief reign, encouraged democracy.

Talal ibn Abdullah assumed the duties of king at a critical period of transition in Jordan's history. When King Abdullah I ibn Hussein was assassinated

Talal ibn Abdullah, crown prince of Jordan, stands to the left of his father King Abdullah bin Al-Hussein in the Palace Gardens of Amman, Jordan, 1948. Talal became king on 5 September 1951 after the assassination of his father, but due to his poor mental health he was forced to abdicate in favor of his son on 11 August 1952. © BETTMANN/CORBIS. REPRODUCED BY PERMISSION.

on 20 July 1951, a group of Jordanian royalists determined that King Abdullah's chosen successor, his grandson Prince Hussein ibn Talal, was too young to govern. The only way to ensure the legitimacy of transition to Hussein was for Crown Prince Talal, who suffered from acute depression and paranoia, to be crowned king. The alternatives were either to crown Prince Na'if, the regent and Talal's half-brother, or to accede to some form of union with Iraq, in which case a member of the Iraqi branch of the Hashimite dynasty would succeed to the Jordanian throne. Hence, Talal was considered an interim figure, yet he became significantly more during his tenure.

On 5 September 1951, the cabinet proclaimed Talal king, and the newly elected parliament confirmed Talal on the throne on receipt of a medical report by Minister of Health Jamil Tutunji. Prince Na'if, the regent, flew to Switzerland to escort his brother home.

The most notable legacy of King Talal's brief reign was to transform Jordan into a true democracy. Under Talal's instructions, the veteran prime minister, Tawfiq Abu al-Huda, won a vote of confidence in parliament on 24 September 1951. A new constitution was promulgated, declaring the people the source of all power. Citizens were guaranteed individual liberty and equality before the law. The constitution was approved by the lower and upper houses and was signed by King Talal on 1 January 1952. It enshrined the freedom of opinion, the right to hold public meetings and form political parties and trade unions, the freedom of conscience and worship, compulsory free education, as well as the right to own property. The new constitution made the cabinet collectively and individually responsible to parliament. Ministers could be impeached. The king could dissolve parliament, but new elections had to be held within four months, otherwise the old parliament would be reinstated. According to Article 93, parliament could override the king's veto over legislation by a two-thirds majority. Parliament was empowered to ratify treaties and could assemble without being called to do so by the king, but the king could declare martial law by decree with the consent of the cabinet.

The king's foreign minister declared in September 1951 that Jordan was not seeking union with Iraq. In December 1951, the king visited Saudi Arabia and made clear his desire for good relations with the house of Sa'ud. He was skeptical of Western alliances, and in January 1952, he led Jordan into acceptance of the Arab Collective Security Pact.

Despite his popularity, after eight months the king's psychological troubles returned. While vacationing in Europe in May 1952, the cabinet transformed the Regency Council into a Crown Council, which exercised the powers of head of state for the rest of Talal's reign. On 11 August 1952, parliament deposed him and proclaimed Prince Hussein king. King Talal accepted gracefully. The duties of king were assumed by a Regency Council until Hussein came of age.

The deposed king moved to Egypt then took up residence in Turkey, where he died twenty years later. Talal was the first king of Jordan to graduate from the Royal Military College at Sandhurst, an English school, and while there had absorbed democratic ideals. Sir John Bagot Glubb recalls in his memoir, *A Soldier with the Arabs*: "The tragedy of King Talal seemed to be rendered more poignant by the fact that, apart from his insanity, he appeared so ideally fit to be king. . . . He was of acute intelligence, outstanding personal charm, faultless private morals, and inspired by a deeply conscious wish to serve his country and his people, with no selfish motives."

See also ABDULLAH I IBN HUSSEIN; ABU AL-HUDA, TAWFIQ; GLUBB, JOHN BAGOT; HUSSEIN IBN TALAL.

Bibliography

Abidi, Aqil Hyder Hasan. *Jordan: A Political Study, 1948–1957.* New York: Asia, 1965.

Glubb, John Bagot. *A Soldier with the Arabs.* New York: Hodder and Staughton, 1957.

JENAB TUTUNJI

TALAT, MEHMET

[1874–1921]

Turkish statesman.

Born in Edirne, Mehmet Talat Bey became chief administrator of the telegraph and postal office in Salonika in the Ottoman Empire. There, he became part of the secret Committee for Union and Progress. After the Young Turk revolution, he went to Istanbul in December 1908 to assume a leading position in the Young Turk government, rising to minister of interior. After 1913 and until the Ottoman defeat in World War I, Talat Paşa, Enver Paşa, and Cemal Paşa comprised the unofficial triumvirate that controlled the Ottoman Empire. While Enver was a military leader and Cemal was famous for his ruthlessness, Talat was a sophisticated diplomat and a consummate politician. In February 1917, Talat became grand vizier and held that position until 8 October 1918, just before the armistice of Mudros, which signaled the Ottoman surrender to the Allies. On 2 November, three days after the armistice was signed, Talat left Istanbul on a German ship and was murdered in Berlin in 1921.

Bibliography

Lewis, Bernard. *The Emergence of Modern Turkey,* 3d edition. New York: Oxford University Press, 2002.

Ramsaur, E. E. *The Young Turks: Prelude to the Revolution of 1908.* Princeton, NJ: Princeton University Press, 1957.

Shaw, Stanford J., and Shaw, Ezel Kural. *History of the Ottoman Empire and Modern Turkey.* 2 vols. Cambridge, U.K., and New York: Cambridge University Press, 1976–1977.

ZACHARY KARABELL

TALEQANI, AZAM

[1943–]

Iranian advocate for women's rights, social justice, and democracy.

Azam Taleqani, daughter of the radical cleric Ayatollah Mahmud Taleqani, was born in 1943 in Tehran. She obtained her B.A. degree in Persian literature and was a schoolteacher and principal. She was politically active before Iran's Islamic Revolution and a political prisoner under the shah. After the revolution she was elected to the first parliament (1980–1984). Her quest for social justice led her to focus on the plight of women. In 1979 she founded the Iranian Islamic Women's Institute and started publishing a magazine, *Payam-i Hajar,* which has been closed down temporarily several times. Along with the members of her institute, she assists urban poor and rural women, providing them with legal advice, organizing conferences on women's problems, and creating jobs for women carpet weavers, tailors, and the like. *Payam-i Hajar* was the first journal to publish an article (in 1992) that refuted the legal basis of polygyny and men's superiority and proposed a new interpretation of the Qur'anic verse *al-Nisa* (Women) founded on Iranian social, demographic, and cultural realities. Taleqani registered to run as a candidate in the 1997 presidential elections in order to challenge the traditional views on women. She and seven other women candidates were disqualified by the Council of Guardians, which provided no reason for their disqualification. She also was disqualified in the 1999 municipal elections. She criticizes personal enrichment on the part of the power elite and the widening gap between the rich and the poor, and continues to advocate social justice and democracy.

AZADEH KIAN-THIÉBAUT

TALFA, ADNAN KHAYR ALLAH
[1940–1989]

Iraqi government official; relative of Saddam Hussein.

Adnan Khayr Allah Talfa was Saddam Hussein's brother-in-law and a maternal cousin; Saddam is married to Talfa's sister Sajida. Talfah was born in Tikrit and combined military and political careers in Iraq. In 1977, when still a colonel, through Saddam Hussein's pressure he became a member of the Regional Leadership of the Baʿth party and of the Revolutionary Command Council, as well as minister of defense. During the Iran-Iraq War (1980–1988), he played a major role in mediating between the civilian leadership and the military. In 1988 his relations with Saddam Hussein became strained through a family dispute. In May 1989 he was killed in a helicopter crash amid rumors of foul play on the part of Saddam.

See also HUSSEIN, SADDAM.

Bibliography

Baram, Amatzia. "The Ruling Political Elite in Baʿthi Iraq, 1968–1986." *International Journal of Middle East Studies* 21 (1989): 447–493.

AMATZIA BARAM

TALIʿA, AL-

See NEWSPAPERS AND PRINT MEDIA: ARAB COUNTRIES

TALIBAN

Islamic fundamentalist group in Afghanistan.

The Taliban appeared in Afghanistan in late 1994. In September 1996 they took Kabul and hanged Najibullah, Afghanistan's Soviet-sponsored president. Subsequently, they banned female access to education and employment, and imposed draconian Islamic laws that called for severe punishments, including the stoning to death of proven adulterers and the amputating of thieves' hands and feet. The Taliban's Islamic fundamentalism was a kind of transnational street force that had the potential to topple established governments through agitation, or to terrorize even much larger nations. Increasingly, fear of Islamic fundamentalism replaced the old dread of communism in the United States.

The term *taliban* is derived from the Persian and Pashtun plural of the Arabic word *talib* ("seeker of knowledge"). Before 1947, Afghan religious students studied in India, and when it was partitioned, they went to Pakistan. Their favorite *madrasa* in India was the Dar al-Ulum (House of Sciences) of the University of Deoband in Uttar Pradesh, which was established in 1862. It was known for its anti-Western orientation and stood for the independence of a united India. The Deoband Dar al-Ulum trained young, working- and lower-middle-class Muslims, who received a traditional religious education and joined the ranks of "big" and "small" mullahs in *masajid* (mosques).

Intellectually, the Taliban are heirs to the traditional affinity between the Deoband Dar al-Ulum and the Afghan *ulama* (Islamic scholars). After 1947, *ulama* in Pakistan established Houses of Science (Diyar al-Ulum) in all the provinces of Pakistan. The number of graduates of different levels of education from these institutions, especially from 1982 to 1987, was impressive. The Taliban leaders were the product of these theological seminaries. Their education is frozen in time: All Sunni theological institutions' curricula are based upon the curriculum established by the eighteenth-century scholar Mullah Nizam-ud-Din, who flourished during the period of Aurangzeb (d. 1707). This curriculum comprises:

1. Arabic grammar;
2. syntax;
3. rhetoric;
4. philosophy of logic;
5. dialectical theology *(ilm al-kalam)*;
6. Qurʾanic exegesis *(tafsir)*;
7. Islamic jurisprudence *(fiqh)*;
8. roots of Islamic jurisprudence *(usul al-fiqh)*;
9. accounts of sayings and deeds by the Prophet and immediate followers *(hadith)*; and
10. some mathematics.

The Taliban's educational system emphasized *taqlid*, the following of traditional Islam, which neglected modern scientific training. They divided the world into *Dar al-Islam* (the Muslim states, especially Saudi Arabia, the United Arab Emirates, and Pakistan, which had recognized their rule) and *Dar al-Harb* (the non-Muslim states, which were projected as the enemies of Islam and Muslims). This bifurcation of the world into external enemies and permanent friends generated an exceptionally intolerant mind-set, which distinguished the Taliban's educational system.

The Taliban's political structure was based, according to them, on that of the four "rightly guided" caliphs (632–662) who succeeded the prophet Muhammad. The Taliban were "committed to establishing an exemplary Islamic rule" for the world, and especially for the Muslim states. Emulating the early caliphate, the Taliban created a supreme council (Majles al-Shura) of twenty individuals. Almost 1,500 Sunni *ulama* who represented various ethnic tribes elected young Mullah Muhammad Omar *amir al-mu'minin* ("commander of the faithful"). The majority of the council members were Pashtuns; fourteen of them had suffered corporeal loss while fighting against the Soviet Union (Mullah Omar, for example, lost an eye). Because of the Pashtun ethnic origin of the Taliban, their jihad became a struggle for power against the Tajiks in the Panjsher Valley and the Uzbeks in the north.

During the 1980s, Osama bin Ladin established guerrilla warfare bases in Afghanistan against the Soviet Union. After the Soviet withdrawal from Afghanistan in 1989, bin Ladin turned his attention to the United States. On 11 September 2001 his terrorists attacked the World Trade Center in New York City and the Pentagon outside Washington, D.C. In retaliation, the United States invaded Afghanistan, eliminated the Taliban's rule, and destroyed bin Ladin's terror infrastructure.

See also AFGHANISTAN; BIN LADIN, OSAMA; DAR AL-ULUM; NAJIBULLAH; OMAR, MUHAMMAD (MULLAH); SUNNI ISLAM.

Bibliography

Kamal, Matinuddin. *The Taliban Phenomenon: Afghanistan, 1994–1997.* Oxford, U.K.: Oxford University Press, 1999.

Marsden, Peter. *The Taliban: War, Religion, and the New Order in Afghanistan.* London: Zed Books, 1998.

Rashid, Ahmed. *Taliban: Militant Islam, Oil, and Fundamentalism in Central Asia.* New Haven, CT: Yale University Press, 2000.

HAFEEZ MALIK

TALLAL, CHAIBIA

[1929–]

Moroccan painter.

Chaibia Tallal is a self-taught painter who was "discovered" and encouraged by Pierre Gaudibert, director of the Museum of Modern Art in Grenoble, France. She gained recognition in Europe and in the Arab world for her bright paintings, done in what has been called a naive style. Chaibia (who is known by her first name) was born in the village of Chtouka and came to the suburbs of Casablanca as a girl but counts her experience in the village as formative. Her memories of being unusual in her community, of making things with flowers and covering herself with them, and of a dream that motivated her to paint help explain how a woman who was not born into the urban life of art and intellectuals came to be an internationally celebrated artist. Chaibia is primarily a colorist who has been described as capturing the vibrancy of Moroccan life and landscape. Like Matisse's Moroccan work, her paintings feature human figures and flora and fauna rendered in expressive, often broad, brushstrokes and fields of rich color. Chaibia has exhibited throughout Europe, mainly in Paris, and also participated in the Havana Biennial. In 1984 one of her paintings served as the poster for the Contemporary Women's International Art Exhibition in France.

See also ART; GENDER: GENDER AND EDUCATION; MOROCCO.

Bibliography

Tallal, Chaibia. "My Life." In *Opening the Gates: A Century of Arab Feminist Writing,* edited by Margot Badran and Miriam Cook. Bloomington: Indiana University Press, 1990.

JESSICA WINEGAR

TALL AL-ZAʿTAR REFUGEE CAMP

Refugee camp in East Beirut, Lebanon.

Built in 1950 by UNRWA (United National Relief and Works Agency for Palestinian Refugees in the Near East), Tall al-Zaʿtar's Palestinian and South Lebanese population exceeded thirty thousand refugees by the early 1970s. In perhaps the bloodiest battle of the Lebanese Civil War that started in

1975, members of the Christian Phalange laid siege to the camp 22 June 1976. Thousands of residents are believed to have been killed during the siege and the mass killings that followed the Phalangist victory 12 August. The remaining population of the camp was transferred to West Beirut. The Phalangists' intent is believed to have been the expulsion of all non-Christians, and particularly the Palestine Liberation Organization (PLO), from East Beirut. The Christian militias had largely avoided direct confrontations with the PLO until the Syrian army entered the war in Lebanon on the Christian side 31 May 1976. The PLO defended the camp for fifty-two days before it fell with the help of Syrian artillery.

See also PHALANGE.

Bibliography

Petran, Tabitha. *The Struggle over Lebanon.* New York: Monthly Review Press, 1987.

Smith, Pamela Ann. *Palestine and the Palestinians, 1876–1983.* New York: St. Martin's, 1984.

ELIZABETH THOMPSON

TALL, MUSTAFA WAHBI AL-
[1899–1949]

Jordan's most famous poet.

Mustafa Wahbi al-Tall's use of colloquial expressions in his poetry plus mentions of geographical places helped establish a unique Jordanian literary tradition in the Arabic language. Despite numerous positions in the government of Jordan, his populist politics and anti-establishment behavior landed him in prison or exile on several occasions. He is also the father of the Jordanian politician Wasfi al-Tall.

See also TALL, WASFI AL-.

Bibliography

Tall, Mustafa Wahbi. *Mustafa's Journey: A Verse of Arar, Poet of Jordan.* Irbid, Jordan: Yarmouk University Publications, 1988.

MICHAEL R. FISCHBACH

TALL, WASFI AL-
[1920–1971]

Prime minister of Jordan (1962–1963, 1965–1967, 1970–1971).

Wasfi al-Tall was born in Irbid, in northern Jordan. After being educated at the American University of Beirut, he served as an officer in Britain's army (1942–1945), then joined Jordan's civil service, rising to the rank of ambassador to Iraq (1961–1962). Tall was expelled from Baghdad for alleged subversive activities against the regime of Abd al-Karim Qasim; he was also channeling funds to the anti-Nasser Syrian Social Nationalist party in Lebanon.

Tall formed his first cabinet in January 1962 and embarked on an efficiency campaign in the civil service and attempted to promote economic development. He also launched a policy designed to show that Jordan was the true repository of Palestinian aspirations; it was a failure.

A Jordan–Saudi Arabia summit in August 1962 resulted in an agreement to coordinate foreign policy. When a coup took place in Yemen in October 1962, resulting in the proclamation of the Yemen Arab Republic, Jordan and Saudi Arabia backed the insurgents under Imam al-Badr. In November 1962, Tall supervised parliamentary elections in which political parties were banned. Baʿathist coups in Baghdad in February 1963 and in Damascus in March 1963 led Iraq and Syria to launch unity talks with Egypt. A shift in policy was required, so Tall resigned at the end of March.

In February 1965, Tall began his second term as prime minister. He helped King Hussein ibn Talal reactivate the entente with Saudi Arabia, and on 9 August 1965, a treaty was signed delimiting borders between the two countries. Jordan joined an alliance of Islamic states organized by Saudi Arabia and directed against Egypt, Syria, and Iraq.

Al-Fatah raids into Israel began. Under pressure from the Arab League, Jordan agreed to set up "summer camps for military training and moral guidance" for Palestinian recruits. In June 1966, King Hussein said there could be no cooperation with the Palestine Liberation Organization (PLO), and Tall prevented elections for the PLO National Council.

Tall closed the PLO office in Amman and expelled Ahmad Shuqayri, head of the PLO. In retaliation for an operation by al-Fatah guerrillas supported by Syria, Israel launched a raid against

Jordan, demolishing the village of Sammu on 13 November 1966. Residents of the West Bank and refugee camps hated Tall because of his disbanding of the National Guard, which had been stationed in frontier villages. Under the press law of 1 February 1967, instigated by Tall, all existing papers and periodicals were closed down, and newly licensed publications had to have 25 percent government ownership. Tall resigned in March 1967 and was appointed chief of the royal court, in which position he tried unsuccessfully to keep Jordan out of the Arab–Israel War of 1967.

Tall began his third term as prime minister on 26 September 1970. The following day, King Hussein and PLO chairman Yasir Arafat signed an agreement in Cairo that called for the withdrawal of Palestinian guerrillas from the cities but allowed them to continue the battle against Israel from the countryside. Tall and the military, however, devised a plan to drive the guerrillas out of Amman, Irbid, Jarash, and Ajlun. It was all over by 18 June 1971. In revenge, during a visit to Cairo in September 1971, Tall was assassinated by the Black September Group.

See also ARAB–ISRAEL WAR (1967); ARAFAT, YASIR; BLACK SEPTEMBER; FATAH, AL-; HUSSEIN IBN TALAL; JORDANIAN CIVIL WAR (1970–1971); LEAGUE OF ARAB STATES; PALESTINE LIBERATION ORGANIZATION (PLO); QASIM, ABD AL-KARIM; SHUQAYRI, AHMAD.

Bibliography

Amos, John W., II. *Palestinian Resistance: Organization of a Nationalist Movement.* New York: Pergamon, 1980.

Dann, Uriel. *King Hussein and the Challenge of Arab Radicalism: Jordan, 1955–1967.* New York: Oxford University Press in cooperation with the Moshe Dayan Center for Middle Eastern and African Studies, Tel Aviv University, 1989.

Iyad, Abu, with Rouleau, Eric. *My Home, My Land: A Narrative of the Palestinian Struggle,* translated by Linda Butler Koseoglu. New York: Times Books, 1978.

Lunt, James. *Hussein of Jordan: Searching for a Just and Lasting Peace.* New York: W. Morrow, 1989.

Susser, Asher. *On Both Banks of the Jordan: A Political Biography of Wasfi al-Tall.* Newberry Park, U.K., and Portland, OR: F. Cass, 1994.

JENAB TUTUNJI

TALMUD

The Jewish teachings of the sages.

The Pentateuch *(Torah),* Prophets *(Nevi'im),* and Hagiographa *(Ketuvim)* constitute the written law of Judaism. Over the years, that law was discussed, interpreted, and transferred. These teachings of the sages are known as the oral law. Eventually, the oral law *(torah she-b'al peh)* was written down and formed the basis of the Talmud. While *torah* refers only to the written law and *talmud* to the oral law, both terms essentially carry the same meaning: teaching or study. Since it is incumbent upon the children of Israel to follow the path of their ancestors, it is necessary for the Jewish people to continually teach and study the law until they understand and follow it completely.

Scholars differ as to when the Talmud began to be written down and whether it was based on notes or recorded upon its completion. It is generally accepted that Rabbi Yehuda ha-Nasi (170–219 C.E.) compiled and edited the first section of the Talmud, the Mishnayot (pl. of *mishna,* or teaching, to distinguish it from Torah) from a multitude of manuscripts, perhaps in different dialects and languages.

The Mishnayot are organized into six sections, or *sedarim,* each dealing with a particular subject. The sections are then subdivided into tracts (or *mesekhtot,* singular *mesekhta*) that deal with matters relating to those sections. The sections are: Seeds (or *Zera'im,* which includes laws relating to vegetables; offerings; tithes; and *shmitta,* the sabbatical year); Festivals (or *Mo'ed,* holidays; the Sabbath; and more general laws affected by the festivals); Women (or *Nashim,* including marriage and divorce); Damages (or *Nezikin,* laws of property; penalties; and morals); Sacred Things (or *Kodashim,* sacrifices; laws of the first born; and slaughtering); Purifications (or *Tohorot,* defilement and purification in general; and defilement of vessels, tents, and menstruating women).

The Mishnayot were imparted with a degree of sanctity that dictated that nothing could be added to or subtracted from them. Upon their completion, religious colleges were established in Palestine and Babylonia to explain their meaning and to extrapolate the laws that emanated from them. This task was complicated by contradictory Mishnayot and by the discovery of new texts that had not been incorporated in the Mishnayot. The body of knowledge that developed from the discussions and the explanations of the Mishna came to be called *Gemara* (Aramaic for *teaching*). The tractates of the Gemara are arranged like the sections of the Mishnayot. The Mishna opens the tractate and is followed by the Gemara. The Mishna and the Gemara together constitute the Talmud.

At the time of Rabbi Yehuda ha-Nasi's death, the Roman-dominated Middle East was characterized by political strife, which led many Jews to leave Galilee for Persian-ruled Babylon. The development of the Talmud continued there. The Palestinian Talmud, also known as the Jerusalem Talmud *(Talmud Yerushalmi)*, was finalized in about 400 C.E. (although it might have been much later). The Babylonian Talmud (*Talmud Bavli*, which might have developed without its formulators knowing about the Jerusalem Talmud) was finalized in about 500 C.E. Although the Jerusalem Talmud includes more tracts (thirty-nine to the Babylonian's thirty-seven), it is considerably smaller (about one-fourth the size) and less elaborate, especially in the field of religious law *(Halakhah)*. It is stronger in *Aggadah*, a collection of legends and stories, proverbs, parables, and mystic and veiled religious wisdom. The Babylonian Talmud, with its emphasis on religious law, became the dominant focus of study. This was partially determined by the political situation, which allowed the Jews in exile to study the Talmud to a greater degree than Jews could in Palestine. It is the Babylonian Talmud that continues to dominate today.

Talmudic rulings have served as the basis for religious law in Judaism throughout the generations. A vast rabbinic literature now exists based on discussions and analyses stemming from Talmudic discourse. Whereas elementary school education includes the study of the Pentateuch and Prophets, advanced religious education in higher *yeshivot* (Torah seminaries) concentrates on the study of the Talmud. Religious traditionalists reject the scientific approach to the study of the Talmud, which has developed in the university. Many similarly reject the desire of a small but increasing number of Orthodox women who wish to take part in intensive religious study, believing that only men are allowed to learn this sacred text.

Bibliography

Gilbert, Martin, ed. *The Illustrated Atlas of Jewish Civilization: 4,000 Years of Jewish History.* New York: Macmillan, 1990.

Benjamin Joseph
Updated by Ephraim Tabory

TAMI

See Israel: Political Parties in

TAMIMAHS

Paramount shaykhs of larger Omani tribal groupings.

Tamimahs are selected from an elite family within the tribe, and their main functions are to resolve disputes and provide a focus of leadership among lineages within the tribe. The title implies complete or total authority to the extent that the bearer has the power to impose the death penalty on a tribesman, although this is rarely the case at the tribal level in Oman.

Calvin H. Allen, Jr.

TAMIMI, AMIN AL-

[1892–1944]

Palestinian politician.

Born to a Muslim family in Nablus, Palestine, Amin al-Tamimi studied in Istanbul, where he encountered Arab literary and political circles before World War I. After the war, he served as an adviser to the regime of the Syrian king, Faisal I ibn Hussein, in Damascus and joined delegations to Istanbul and to Lausanne in 1922 to seek Turkish support for Arab independence. He was a leader of the Nablus Muslim–Christian Association, and a member of the Supreme Muslim Council of the *mufti* (interpreter of the law of Islam) in Jerusalem from 1926 to 1938.

Tamimi went to Iraq in 1939 and participated in the 1941 Rashid Ali al-Kaylani revolt of pan-Arabism against Britain. The British then interned him in Rhodesia, where he died. He was proclaimed a martyr in the streets of Jerusalem. His son Adnan, an Iraqi citizen, was a United Nations official until 1983.

See also FAISAL I IBN HUSSEIN; KAYLANI, RASHID ALI AL-; PAN-ARABISM.

Bibliography

Hurewitz, J. C. *The Struggle for Palestine.* New York: Norton, 1950.

Porath, Yehoshua. *The Emergence of the Palestinian-Arab National Movement, 1918–1929.* London: Frank Cass, 1974.

Porath, Yehoshua. *Palestinian-Arab National Movement, 1929–1939: From Riots to Rebellion.* London and Totowa, NJ: Frank Cass, 1977.

ELIZABETH THOMPSON

TAMIR, SHMUEL

[1923–]

Israeli politician and attorney.

Shmuel Tamir was born in Jerusalem as Shmuel Katsnelson. He was influenced by the 1929 Hebron massacre, during which sixty Orthodox Jews were murdered by Arab rioters. The rioters were themselves reacting to a demonstration by Jews who demanded access to the Western Wall in Jerusalem, At age fifteen he joined Irgun Zvaʾi Leʾumi. He was arrested in 1947 and deported to Kenya, where he was allowed to take his final law examinations. Returning to Israel after it became a state, he changed his name to Shmuel Tamir (his underground name) and was active in the Herut movement, where he was viewed as a natural heir to Menachem Begin.

He established a reputation as an outstanding attorney and was involved in some well-known cases, including the Kasztner trial in 1954, in which Reszo Kasztner brought suit against Malkiel Grunwald, who had accused Kasztner of being a traitor and causing the deaths of many Jews by negotiating with the Nazis. As Grunwald's attorney, Tamir framed the trial as being about Kasztner rather than Grunwald. The judge, Benjamin Halevi, accepted most of Tamir's arguments and accused Kasztner of having "sold his soul to the devil." Before the verdict was handed down, Kasztner was murdered by nationalist extremists who took Halevi's words literally. In the end, the court exonerated Kasztner on all charges except that he had helped Nazis escape from justice.

Tamir was a member of sixth through ninth Knessets, representing several different parties, including Gahal, the Free Center, Likud, and the Democratic Movement for Change. In 1977, when Tamir joined the Democratic Movement for Change, he was appointed minister of justice under Begin. In 1981, he left politics and returned to his legal practice.

See also BEGIN, MENACHEM; IRGUN, ZVAʾI LEʾUMI (IZL); ISRAEL: POLITICAL PARTIES IN; LIKUD.

Bibliography

Bell, J. Bowyer. *Terror out of Zion: Irgun Zvai Leumi, LEHI, and the Palestine Underground, 1929–1949.* New York: St. Martin's, 1977.

"Kasztner, Reszo." Museum of Tolerance. Available from <http://motlc.wiesenthal.com/text/x12/xm1230.html>.

Segev, Tom. *The Seventh Million: The Israelis and the Holocaust,* translated by Haim Watzman. New York: Hill and Wang, 1993.

JULIE ZUCKERMAN
UPDATED BY GREGORY MAHLER

TAMMUZ, BENYAMIN

[1919–1989]

Israeli novelist and journalist.

Benyamin Tammuz was born in Kharkov, in the Ukraine, and emigrated to Palestine in 1924. Throughout his life he worked for various newspapers, including *Haaretz.* Tammuz was a founding member of the Canaanite movement, which advocated the creation of a Hebrew, rather than a Jewish, state in Israel. This association undoubtedly influenced his earlier works, which were republished as *Angioxyl, Terufah Nedirah* (1973; A rare cure, 1981). He left the movement following a stay in Europe, which brought him into close contact with European Jews. Tammuz served as cultural attaché at the Israeli embassy in London in 1971.

In his works, Tammuz criticizes Israeli society's loss of soul and its lack of normalcy. *Requiem Le-Naʿaman* (1978; Requiem for Naʿaman, 1982) is considered his most forceful work. He deals with the seemingly intractable Arab-Israel conflict in his metaphorical *Ha-Pardes* (1971; The orchard, 1984) and in *Taharut Sehiya* (1952; Swimming race, 1953). In his *Mishlei Baqbuqim* (1975, Proverbs of bottles), Tammuz addresses Israel's lack of spirituality, while in *Pundaqo Shel Yirmiyahu* (1984, Jeremiah's inn), he satirizes the involvement of the ultra-orthodox in Israeli politics.

ANN KAHN

TAN

See NEWSPAPERS AND PRINT MEDIA: TURKEY

TANBURI CEMIL

[1871–1916]

Ottoman Turkish musician and composer.

Tanburi Cemil was born in Istanbul into a family of musicians. He enrolled in the Mulukhiyya but left before finishing his studies and began to study music. By his death at the age of forty-five, he was considered the foremost Turkish virtuoso. Although he was most well known for playing the *tanbur* (guitar), an instrument he had mastered as a child, Tanburi Cemil was equally proficient on the *kemençe* (a small three-stringed violin) and the *lavta* (lute). Tanburi Cemil's compositions, characterized by a refined sensitivity, are considered among the masterpieces of Turkish music. Among his best-known works are *Ferahfeza Saz Semaisi, Mahur Peşrevi, Muhayyer Saz Semaisi,* and *Hicazkar Saz Semaisi.*

DAVID WALDNER

TANER, HALDUN

[1916–1986]

Turkish writer.

The son of a university professor, Haldun Taner was born in Istanbul, where he attended Galatasaray Lycée. He studied political science at Heidelberg University in 1938 and later studied literature in Istanbul. He then taught literature and art history for a number of years at the Journalism Institute and at the Ankara Language, History, and Geography School. Taner became popular in the 1950s for his short stories about the urban middle class, which have been translated from Turkish into more than a dozen languages. He worked as a journalist and in 1960 became editor-in-chief of the Istanbul daily *Tercüman.*

Taner also made his mark in the theater world, joining a young generation of playwrights in the 1950s who addressed the tensions between traditional values and the demands of modern life. He drew on the epic traditions of Turkey for his play *The Ballad of Ali from Keshan,* which was also made into a film. He won a prize with Orhan Kemal in 1957 for their screenplay *Ferhat, the Mountain Lover.* Taner also founded a private theater, the Devekusu Kabare Tiyatrosu.

Bibliography

Renda, Günsel, and Kortepeter, C. Max, eds. *The Transformation of Turkish Culture.* Princeton, NJ: Kingston Press, 1986.

ELIZABETH THOMPSON

TANGIER, TREATY OF

Franco-Moroccan agreement of 10 September 1844.

The Treaty of Tangier followed the defeat of the Moroccan army at the Battle of Isly by a French force pursuing the Algerian resistance leader Abd al-Qadir, who had frequently sought refuge in Moroccan territory. The treaty obligated the Moroccan government to consider Abd al-Qadir an outlaw and to offer him no assistance.

See also ABD AL-QADIR.

KENNETH J. PERKINS

TANIN

See NEWSPAPERS AND PRINT MEDIA: TURKEY

TANPINAR, AHMED HAMDI

[1901–1962]

Turkish professor and author.

The son of a *qadi* (judge), Ahmed Hamdi Tanpinar was born in Istanbul and moved with his father to various cities of the Ottoman Empire. He graduated from the Antalya secondary school and studied at the Faculty of Literature, where he was a student of Yahya Kemal. After graduating in 1923, he taught at secondary schools, including the Fine Arts Academy, until 1939, when he was appointed professor of modern Turkish Literature at Istanbul University.

He wrote a major volume on post-Tanzimat-era Turkish literature, a monograph on Tevfik Fikret, and a series of critical essays.

Tanpinar also wrote poetry, novels, and short stories. In his novels, he studied the era from the Crimean War (1854) to World War II (1939), portraying developments within Turkish society and the fate of traditional ties in a modernizing society. In 1942, Tanpinar was elected to the parliament, representing Maraş.

Bibliography

Ertop, Konur. "Trends and Characteristics of Contemporary Turkish Literature." In *The Transformation of Turkish Culture: The Atatürk Legacy,* edited by Günsel Renda and C. Max Kortepeter. Princeton, NJ: Kingston Press, 1986.

DAVID WALDNER

TANTAWI, MUHAMMAD SAYYID AL-

[1928–]

Shaykh of al-Azhar.

Born in Suhaj in Upper Egypt, Muhammad Sayyid al-Tantawi earned a Ph.D. in Qur'anic Exegesis and *Hadith* (sayings of the Prophet) from al-Azhar University in 1966. In 1976 he became a professor; ten years later he became dean of the Islamic and Arabic Studies faculty and was appointed the grand mufti, Egypt's highest religious juristic authority. In 1996 he was appointed shaykh of al-Azhar, making him the forty-third shaykh of al-Azhar. Muslims seek his advice on new controversial matters.

As a mufti, Tantawi issued opinions representing the views of the government. His *fatawa* (legal opinions) have mostly been at odds with those of al-Azhar. But once he became shaykh of al-Azhar, he began oscillating between the opinions he issued as mufti and pronouncements more faithful to al-Azhar. He is under constant pressure from religious scholars to follow al-Azhar's conservative line of thinking. Many civil and human-rights organizations welcomed the appointment of this liberal shaykh to the top religious post in Egypt, but his *fatwa* prohibiting the boycott of U.S. goods brought about major protests by Christians as well as Muslims. The powerful and conservative Front for the Scholars of al-Azhar, founded in 1946, had been critical of Tantawi since he became mufti, challenging him on his giving permission to deal with banks based on interest, his prohibition of suicide attacks committed by HAMAS in Palestine, his meeting the chief rabbi of Israel, and his reduction of secondary education to three years. He was able to get the government to dissolve the Front in 1998, and he fired many outspoken scholars from al-Azhar.

On the touchy issue of female circumcision, Tantawi, as the mufti, argued against its validity. However, as shaykh of al-Azhar he gave in to the Azharite establishment. Later, when the Ministry of Health banned the practice, Tantawi changed his view again. Also, as a mufti, Tantawi viewed the *hijab* (head cover) as a woman's choice, but as shaykh, he upheld the Azhar view that it was mandatory. But on the issue of organ transplants, he held to his original position, and promised to donate his own organs after his death. On the political level, when Tantawi became shaykh, his political views became more obvious. For instance, he asked Muslims to launch jihad (holy war) against Israel to prevent the Judaization of Jerusalem, and to defuse religious sectarian tensions in Egypt, he met with Pope Shenouda III and other Christian personalities. These changes of opinion seem to be the result of both political expediency and an attempt to serve the interests of the Egyptian government.

See also AZHAR, AL-.

AHMAD S. MOUSSALLI

TANZIMAT

Mid-nineteenth-century Ottoman reform movement.

The Tanzimat-i Hayriye (Auspicious Reorganization) was a series of governmental reforms between 1839 and 1876 that sought to centralize and rationalize Ottoman rule and capture more tax revenues for the military defense of the empire. The Tanzimat period is usually associated with particular personalities in the central government: the sultans Abdülmecit II and Abdülaziz, and the high-ranking bureaucrats Mustafa Reşid Paşa, Ali Paşa, and Fuad Paşa. The Tanzimat was preceded by earlier reform efforts since the eighteenth century, particularly by Abdülmecit I and Abdülaziz's father, Mahmud II, between 1808 and 1839. And it would be followed by reforms in the early reigns of Abdülhamit II and the Young Turks.

Order and Justice

The thirty-seven years of the Tanzimat period are significant in this long process for establishing the basic principles and the governmental apparatus of reform. The bywords of the movement were justice and order, which were seen as prerequisites to effecting substantial social and economic change. The major product of the movement was a huge increase in the power of the central state. The major edicts of the Tanzimat significantly enlarged the scope of government activity by creating new fiscal, legal, and administrative instruments. For example, the edict that inaugurated the Tanzimat, the 1839 Hatt-i Şerif of Gülhane, proposed replacing inefficient tax farms with a centralized revenue service and establishing a new imperial council, the Meclis-i Vala, to formulate and direct reform policy. Subsequent edicts sought to promote justice and confidence in government, such as those of 1840, 1850, and 1870 to 1876 that laid out uniform codes of law for commerce, civil transactions, and criminal cases. A series of provincial reforms culminating in the 1864 Vilayet Law regularized the structure of local government and strengthened lines of authority to Constantinople (now Istanbul). And in the capital itself, government was reorganized into formal departments and specialized ministries. During the Tanzimat period, the Ottoman state also began to intervene in society in new ways. The 1839 Gülhane edict and other laws expanded military conscription. And the state established new elite secular schools. The 1869 Regulation of Public Instruction introduced an empire-wide school system intended to produce bureaucrats and military officers at every level of government equipped with the skills necessary to implement policy.

Defense and International Affairs

But the Tanzimat was not solely a project of administrative reform. Its goals of order and justice were often ancillary to other, more immediate goals. The 1839 Gülhane edict was issued when the Ottomans were fighting to regain territory captured by Egypt in 1832. Greece had already won its independence in 1839, and in the Crimean War (1853–1856) the Ottomans would again go to war with Russia. Hence, the 1839 edict would promise to continue the military buildup begun by Mahmud II to defend the empire from external threats. The military was reorganized in 1842 and 1869, producing a larger, more unified structure under the *serasker,* a combined chief of staff and war minister. And many other reforms were explicitly intended to raise more revenue for defense.

Tanzimat goals were further complicated by international affairs with the growing influence of France and England in the empire. The Ottomans sought European alliances for protection against Russian and Egyptian invasions. This alliance was bought at a price. For their own domestic reasons, and to further their interests in the empire, France and England pushed another set of often contradictory goals. While the Europeans advocated equal rights and democratic participation in the empire, they also acted to protect the privileges and separate status of non-Muslim millets. So, while the Gülhane edict and the 1856 Hatt-i Hümayun proclaimed equality of all citizens regardless of religion, and new secular courts were established to offset any prejudice in *shariʿa* (Islamic law) courts, in fact, society remained divided by religion in subcommunities with separate legal and social institutions.

Economic Concerns

Missing from the great initiatives of the Tanzimat was serious fiscal and economic reform. Roger Owen explains the neglect of economic reform thus: "Limited financial resources, the lack of competent administrators, the growing technological gap between Europe and the rest of the world, and the constraints imposed by Turkey's social structure and weakened international position all combined to set strict limits on the types of economic politics pursued" (Owen, p. 116). Restricted in their development of policy, the Ottomans were also plagued by the misfortune that they were attempting reform precisely during a period of economic boom in France and England.

The Tanzimat coincided with the first wave of industrial imperialism. France and England used their diplomatic influence in Constantinople to facilitate imperialist expansion at the expense of economic reform within the empire. For example, the

1838 Anglo-Turkish commercial convention, which preceded British support in fighting Egypt, promoted the spread of European imports in Ottoman markets. In the 1850s and 1860s, the British and French established new kinds of investment banks equipped to funnel domestic savings into overseas loans and projects. These banks played no small part in encouraging Ottoman indebtedness. The first foreign loan was taken out in 1854, for 3 million British pounds, to pay war expenses. Twenty years later, the Ottoman government would devote more than half of its budget to servicing foreign loans totaling 242 million British pounds.

The Tanzimat reforms had not yet produced a government apparatus capable of mounting an economic defense. For example, attempts to increase collection of taxes (and avoid foreign loans) faltered without trained personnel until well after 1859, when the Mekteb-i Mülkiye school to train bureaucrats was established. And although the 1858 land code sought to encourage more efficient exploitation of agriculture by promoting private land ownership, poor administration derailed it. In many areas, wealthy absentee landowners succeeded in registering large tracts of land, taking control away from the peasants who, if they had owned the land, might have found incentive to improve efficiency in cultivation. Instead, sharecropping discouraged investment in the land.

This is not to say that there was no effort at economic development, but rather that these efforts were overwhelmed by external factors. The Tanzimat period saw the first boom in building roads, ports, and other economic infrastructure that facilitated the transport of goods. But the tariff structure made the new transport more profitable to foreign traders than domestic merchants. While Ottoman exports increased nearly 500 percent between 1840 and the 1870s, these exports represented less than 10 percent of total production in the empire and were largely in the form of raw agricultural materials sent to England and France. In the meantime, the empire's terms of trade with Europe actually worsened. Ottoman industry, especially textiles, was undermined by unprecedented foreign competition. Although Ottoman officials established an industrial reform commission in the 1860s, they produced no significant industrial policy. So while Ottoman port cities boomed in this period, producing the first bloom of bourgeois culture, their wealth came from the profits of international trade, not from local production. The empire still relied overwhelmingly on an agricultural economy, and peasants remained as destitute as ever. And despite pockets of prosperity, the empire as a whole would sink so far into debt that it would declare bankruptcy in 1875.

It would be misguided, however, to conclude that the Tanzimat was the handmaiden of European imperialism. Older theories that it was primarily European pressure that forced the Tanzimat on the "sick man of Europe" have been substantially revised. Scholars like Shaw and Ortayli have suggested that the main impetus for reform came from bureaucrats, most prominently Mustafa Reşid Paşa, author of the 1839 edict. They acted from alarm at internal corruption and weakness, as well as from the desire to advance their own interests and protect their rights against the power of the sultan. Hence the 1839 edict abolished the sultan's right to confiscate property, commonly practiced on bureaucrats. Disenchanted bureaucrats led a second reform movement, the Young Ottomans, who in the 1860s and 1870s advocated liberalization and curtailment of the sultan's power. This led to a coup in 1876 that established a short-lived constitution and parliament.

European Influences and Internal Motivations

European influence, while not a primary motive of reform, was nonetheless significant. French and British diplomats repeatedly contributed to drafts of the various Tanzimat reform edicts, particularly those issued in times of war, as in the 1839 expulsion of the Egyptians and in 1856, at the end of the Crimean War. And Ottoman reformers often turned to European institutions for inspiration, as in the 1864 restructuring of provincial administration, the 1868 Council of State, and the 1869 Education Law, all modeled on French institutions.

Finally, a motive for reform came from the peoples of the empire. Dissatisfaction with Ottoman military weakness and a growing perception of alternatives to the current regime promoted unrest. This included not only the often cited Balkan nationalist movements, but smaller intermittent outbreaks, like the 1860 riots in Mount Lebanon and in Damascus that grew out of economic upheaval. Religious leaders, too, organized protest, as in the 1859 Küeli Incident in Constantinople. And religious minorities agitated against the oppressive and often corrupt rule of their state-sponsored patriarchs, leading to reform of the millets in the 1860s. Provincial notables used the local councils established in 1840 as a forum for protest and as a vehicle for negotiating the path of reform.

Design and Implementation of Efforts

In assessing the success of the Tanzimat, it is important to recognize that it was not a coherent, prefabricated plan; the Gülhane proclamation was not a blueprint. The Tanzimat took shape through efforts in Constantinople and in the provinces of Ottoman officials and notables to reconcile the many pressures on the empire. In Istanbul, the MecIİs-İ Vala, in concert with the grand vizier and sultan, had to weigh a variety of simultaneous and often conflicting interests, including military challengers like the Russians, Egyptians, and separatist movements in the Balkans; entrenched interests like those of landowners and the religious hierarchy; and the expanding aims of France and England. In the provinces, local representative councils and governors faced their own spectrum of interests to satisfy: landowners, *ulama* (Islamic clergy) who resented the new secular courts and schools, artisans hurt by European imports, and peasants who could not pay the new taxes.

Tanzimat goals were thus formulated and implemented through bargains made among opposing forces. Policy steered between the simultaneous aims of central control and provincial autonomy, between the ideal of a universal and equal Ottoman citizenry and reality of divisive religious social structures and nationalist particularisms, between the need to appease international challenges and the need to protect domestic interests, and between the efficacy of autocratic, top-down reform and the equally necessary participation of the public in effecting change.

Summary of Accomplishments

In the end, the reform program succeeded most in its goal of order: reorganizing the central and provincial bureaucracy, restructuring the military, and building infrastructure for trade and transport. Less auspicious was its progress toward justice; while law codes were rationalized and venality in office reduced through improved salaries, economic inequalities increased and political participation remained minimal. The concentration of power in Constantinople lent itself to abuse. The Tanzimat period would conclude with a far more effective administrative and legal apparatus, but one that would be commandeered by an autocratic sultan, with the accession of Abdülhamit II in 1876. And in some ways, the Tanzimat was too little, too late. Efforts to strengthen the military and to integrate a population riven with religious and ethnic differences would not proceed quickly enough to avert the dismemberment of the Balkan provinces and the disastrous Russo-Turkish War of 1877/78.

The Tanzimat was, however, a bold and often impressive attempt to restructure the Ottoman polity; it simply did not have the time or opportunity by 1876 to effect significant social and economic change. Much of what the Tanzimat started, however, would bear fruit under Abdülhamit, who continued the Tanzimat's pursuit of order. And while Abdülhamit would leave behind other significant aspects of the Tanzimat, like justice and political participation, these would be taken up again with the rise of a new generation trained in the Tanzimat's schools and the 1908 constitutional revolution.

See also MILLET SYSTEM; YOUNG OTTOMANS.

Bibliography

Davison, Roderic H. *Reform in the Ottoman Empire, 1856–1876.* Princeton, NJ: Princeton University Press 1963.

Lewis, Bernard. *The Emergence of Modern Turkey,* 3d edition. New York: Oxford University Press, 2002.

Owen, Roger. *The Middle East in the World Economy, 1800–1914.* New York: Methuen, 1981.

Pamuk, Şevket. *The Ottoman Empire and European Capitalism, 1820–1913: Trade, Investment, and Production.* Cambridge, U.K., and New York: Cambridge University Press, 1987.

Shaw, Stanford J., and Shaw, Ezel Kural. *History of the Ottoman Empire and Modern Turkey,* Vol. 2: *Reform, Revolution, and Republic: The Rise of Modern Turkey, 1808-1975.* Cambridge, U.K., and New York: Cambridge University Press, 1977.

Thompson, Elizabeth. "Ottoman Reform in the Provinces: The Damascus Advisory Council,

1844–1845." *International Journal of Middle East Studies* 25, no. 3 (August 1993).

ELIZABETH THOMPSON

TAQLA, PHILIPPE

[1915–]

Lebanese politician and banker.

Philippe Taqla was born into a well-established Greek Catholic family with a long history of involvement in Lebanese politics. His father, Salim Taqla, was a minister in the cabinet that amended the Lebanese constitution and was, as a result, jailed by the French on 8 November 1943. He was released on 22 November 1943. A member of Bishara al-Khuri's Constitutional Bloc party, Philippe Taqla became a minister for the first time in 1946, the year his father died. In 1947, he was elected to parliament, and he held several ministerial positions between 1946 and 1952. His opposition to President Camille Chamoun (1952–1958) kept him out of power for several years, although he was again elected to parliament in 1957.

Under presidents Fu'ad Chehab (1958–1964) and Charles Hilu (1964–1970), he was minister of foreign affairs in eight separate cabinets, for a total of some fifty-seven months—a record by Lebanese standards. From 1965 to 1966, he was head of the Bank of Lebanon. In 1967, he became the permanent representative of Lebanon to the United Nations, and from 1968 to 1971 he was the ambassador to France. During his public career, which spanned the three decades from 1946 to 1976, he belonged to more cabinets than any other Lebanese politician except the late Prince Majid Arslan. From 1975 to 1976, he was a member of the Syrian-sponsored National Dialogue Committee, which unsuccessfully sought to put an end to the civil war that had just broken out. The war ended Taqla's public career. Since the end of the Lebanese civil war, Taqla has been serving on the board of one of Lebanon's largest commercial banks, BLOM Bank (Banque du Liban et d'Outre-Mer).

See also CHEHAB, FU'AD; CONSTITUTIONAL BLOC; HILU, CHARLES; KHURI, BISHARA AL-; LEBANESE CIVIL WAR (1975–1990); LEBANON.

Bibliography

Goria, Wade. *Sovereignty and Leadership in Lebanon, 1943–1976.* London: Ithaca Press, 1985.

Khazen, Farid el. *The Breakdown of the Lebanese State, 1967–1976.* London: I.B. Tauris, 1999.

Salameh, Ghassan. "Is a Lebanese Foreign Policy Possible?" In *Toward a Viable Lebanon,* edited by Halim Barakat. London: Croom Helm, 1988.

GUILIAN P. DENOEUX
UPDATED BY KHALIL GEBARA

TAQLID

See GLOSSARY

TARBUSH

See CLOTHING

TARHAN, ABDÜLHAK HAMIT

[1852–1937]

Turkish poet, diplomat, and politician.

Abdülhak Hamit Tarhan was born into a wealthy Istanbul family; his grandfather was physician to the sultan of the Ottoman Empire. He was privately tutored, then enrolled in a French school, and after a tour of Europe became one of the first Muslim students to enroll at Robert College (now part of Bosporus University). In 1871, he married into an aristocratic family and served in the empire's embassy in Paris. In 1878, his play *Nestren* was deemed subversive, and he was dismissed. In 1881, he was readmitted to the Ottoman foreign service and was posted abroad (in Paris, Bombay, London, and Belgium) until 1921. This was also his most active period of literary production. In 1922, he returned to Turkey, where he was soon elected to represent Istanbul in the new Turkish Grand National Assembly.

Tarhan was a major writer of the Tanzimat era. His participation in the *Servet-i Fünun* (Wealth of Sciences) movement, with its concern for technique and its valorization of art for its own sake, helped to prepare an environment for the flowering of modern literature in Turkey. The sheer extent of his output—the drama *Finten* is five hundred pages—is more remarkable than the quality of his prose, with its mixed meters and bombastic language. Tarhan is not widely read today.

Bibliography

Ertop, Konur. "Trends and Characteristics of Contemporary Turkish Literature." In *The Transformation of Turkish Culture: The Atatürk Legacy,* edited by Günsel Renda and C. Max Kortepeter. Princeton, NJ: Kingston Press, 1986.

Mitler, Louis. *Ottoman Turkish Writers: A Bibliographical Dictionary of Significant Figures in Pre-Republican Turkish Literature.* New York: P. Lang, 1988.

DAVID WALDNER

TARIKH TOLANA

The Afghan Historical Society.

Tarikh Tolana (Long History) is the Afghan name for the Historical Society of Afghanistan. Tarikh Tolana was founded in 1941 by Zahir Shah to promote the historical study of Afghanistan. Tarikh Tolana produced many publications, including the journals *Aryana* and *Afghanistan. Aryana* appeared in Pushto and Dari from 1942 to 1985, and *Afghanistan,* also in Dari and Pushto, from 1945 to 1975. The society later became part of the Afghan Academy of Science. The society fell into disarray as Afghanistan disintegrated in civil war in the 1980s and although it has never officially been disbanded, it no longer functions.

Bibliography

Adamec, Ludwig. *Historical Dictionary of Afghanistan,* 2d edition. Lanham, MD: Scarecrow Press, 1997.

GRANT FARR

TARIKI, ABDULLAH

[1919–]

Cofounder of the Organization of Petroleum Exporting Countries and prominent Saudi government minister during the 1950s and 1960s.

Born in 1919 in the Najd town of Zilfi and educated in Cairo and at the University of Texas, Abdullah Tariki was a prominent figure among Saudi Arabia's first generation of technocrats. He became head of the Directorate of Oil and Mining Affairs in 1955 and was instrumental in guiding Saudi domestic and international oil policies. In 1959, Tariki met with Juan Pablo Pérez Alfonso of Venezuela and representatives of Iran, Iraq, and Kuwait in order to establish a consultative commission designed to regulate oil prices, establish national companies, and oppose the fifty-fifty participation agreements with Western oil companies that characterized oil concessions of the day. This informal group coalesced into the Organization of Petroleum Exporting Countries (OPEC) on 14 September 1960, after Western oil companies initiated a price cut without consulting with nationals of the oil-producing countries.

Because of his opposition to the often overbearing and exploitative practices of U.S. oil companies in Saudi Arabia and his strong support for Arab nationalism, including that of Egypt's Gamal Abdel Nasser, Tariki's detractors called him "the Red Shaykh." In 1962, Crown Prince Faisal replaced him with Ahmad Zaki Yamani. From 1962 to 1976, Tariki remained politically active, writing articles and serving as a consultant for petroleum-producing countries, including Muammar al-Qaddafi's Libya. His nationalism and populism led him to denounce Western oil companies and urge Arabs to take full control over their natural resources so they could better advance their societies.

See also NASSER, GAMAL ABDEL; ORGANIZATION OF PETROLEUM EXPORTING COUNTRIES (OPEC); QADDAFI, MUAMMAR AL-.

Bibliography

Duguid, S. "A Biographical Approach to the Study of Social Change in the Middle East: Abdullah Tariki as a New Man." *International Journal of Middle East Studies* 1 (1970): 195–220.

Peterson, J. E. *Historical Dictionary of Saudi Arabia.* Metuchen, NJ: Scarecrow Press, 1993.

Yergin, Daniel. *The Prize: The Epic Quest for Oil, Money, and Power.* New York: Simon & Schuster, 1991.

LES ORDEMAN
UPDATED BY ANTHONY B. TOTH

TASHILHIT LANGUAGE

Berber dialect spoken in the south of Morocco.

The Berber language as a whole is composed of three dialects: Tashilhit, used in the region of Agadir and

Sous (southwest of Marrakech); Tamazight, widespread in the Middle Atlas and High Atlas mountains in the heart of Morocco; and Tarifit, spoken in the Rif, a region in the north of Morocco. *Tifinagh* is the name given to the writing of Tashilhit.

RAHMA BOURQIA

TAURUS MOUNTAINS

Major mountain chain of southern Turkey.

The Taurus chain is composed of several parallel limestone ranges rimming and reaching the Mediterranean, for about 930 miles (1,500 km), from Muğla in the west to Lake Van in the east. The summits often exceed 10,000 feet (3,000 m), the highest nonvolcanic peak being 12,323 feet (3,756 m)—the Aladağ—north of Adana. The average width of the range is 95 miles (150 km), and it forms a barrier to the Anatolian plateau but provides a valuable source of water for irrigation, forest products, and summer pasture. The most important pass is north of Tarsus, called the Cilician Gates. To the northeast is the extension of the range, called the Anti-Taurus.

Bibliography

Fisher, Sydney N. *The Middle East: A History*, 3d edition. New York: Knopf, 1979.

JOHN R. CLARK

TAX FARMING

Means of managing agrarian revenues, as well as of financing governmental programs.

Similar to the contemporary concept of privatization, tax farming is a poorly understood phenomenon in Middle Eastern history. It is often linked to the abuse of state power and debates on the institutional causes of the fall of premodern Islamic states. In essence, however, tax farming refers to any type of tax collection conducted by private individuals rather than salaried state personnel. These individuals acquire the right, often by auction, to collect a defined revenue for a specific period of time. From the Umayyads onward, Islamic states contracted out collection of taxes in proximate and more distant provinces. Tax farming allowed administrators a degree of flexibility and an opportunity to strike a compromise between the old and the new. Indeed, the earliest Islamic administrators of Egypt awarded contracts to Copts and women. Although the powers of tax farmers were contingent on the type of revenue collected, the status of taxpayers, and the degree of state oversight, Islamic governments found ways to curb abuse and default of contract by requiring financial guarantors and subdividing responsibilities. As this form of collection falls under the legal notions of contract, Islamic lawyers usually separate the discussion of tax farming from the actual fiscal responsibilities of Muslim and non-Muslim subjects in terms of alms *(zakat)*, tithes *(ushr)*, and poll taxes *(jizya)*.

There are few comprehensive studies of tax farming during the period between the Abbasids and the Mongols, though Middle Eastern states contracted out to private agents many types of taxes, both those that were Islamically recognized and those that were not. More than an institutional or legal question, tax farming may be regarded as a window on the evolving structure of premodern Islamic states and its relation to society. Because most of the Islamic schools of law regarded conquered land of non-Muslim populations *(kharaj)* to be, effectively, state land, tax farming was utilized alongside the *iqta* or tax fief, a form of resident administration, as an important means of managing agrarian revenues. Pending further research, one may speculate that the alternation between military and privatized forms of tax collection preceding and after the thirteenth-century Mongol invasions was not only the result of corruption of institutions or abuse of office, as the private auction of tax fiefs during the later Mamluk period in Egypt suggests, but also a means of coping with the dislocation of agrarian populations, greater demand for cash revenues, and changing land-use patterns.

Although the forms of tax farming in the Middle East after the sixteenth century have similar legal bases, the practices coincide with new worldwide trends, namely the escalating costs of warfare and expanding global trade. In the Ottoman Empire, for example, tax farming before the sixteenth century had been largely limited to certain commercial revenues and tariffs, and many of the tax farmers were non-Muslims. But as participants in the "gunpowder revolution" and the battle for Europe and

West Asia, the Ottomans required ever greater sources of cash to pay their infantries. Auctions of revenue contracts were a means of borrowing: They allowed the state to anticipate future tax receipts, albeit at a certain loss. Although the Ottoman state continued to administer many taxes directly, over the seventeenth century, many Muslim Ottoman officers and civilians bid for rights to collect taxes on the extensive crown and vizierial domains, tariffs, and manufacturing and tribal taxes, as well as to hold certain offices. A 1695 decree gave Muslim tax farmers the right to hold contracts for life *(malikane mukataa)* and to pass these holdings on to male heirs. Although this extensive use of tax farming produced many problems, it also reinforced the loyalty of Muslim tax farmers, if only by dint of self-interest, to the state, which awarded and recognized these rights.

Since the French Revolution, social scientists have tended to regard fiscal decentralization as one of the ancien régime's greatest evils as did the Ottoman state planners who tried to restrict and then eliminate tax farming in the early decades of the nineteenth century. Despite good intentions, Middle Eastern reformers were frustrated by chronic fiscal shortfalls and lack of administrative staff. No such compunctions about modern statecraft burdened the French colonial regime in Algeria, however. Well into mid-century, French imperialists continued to adapt an older tax-farming system to new political and fiscal purposes.

Bibliography

Cuno, Kenneth M. *The Pasha's Peasants: Land, Society, and Economy in Lower Egypt, 1740–1858.* Cambridge, U.K., and New York: Cambridge University Press, 1992.

Frantz-Murphy, Gladys. "Land Tenure and Social Transformation in Early Islamic Egypt." In *Land Tenure and Social Transformation in the Middle East,* edited by Tarif Khalidi. Beirut: American University of Beirut, 1984.

Johansen, Baber. *The Islamic Law on Land Tax and Rent.* London and New York: Croon Helm, 1988.

Morony, Michael G. "Land Holding and Social Change: Lower al-Iraq in the Early Islamic Period." In *Land Tenure and Social Transformation in the Middle East,* edited by Tarif Khalidi. Beirut: American University of Beirut, 1984.

Salzmann, Ariel. "An Ancien Régime Revisited: Privatization and Political Economy in the Eighteenth-Century Ottoman Empire." *Politics & Society* 21, no. 4 (1993): 393–423.

ARIEL SALZMANN

TCHERNICHOVSKY, SAUL
[1875–1943]

Hebrew poet, translator, and physician.

Saul Tchernichovsky (also Tsharnikhousky) was born in Mikhailovka, a village bordering on the Ukraine and Crimea. The most versatile of Hebrew poets, he was instrumental in the development, both in form and content, of Hebrew poetry. He published his first poem, *Ba-Halomi* (1892; In My Dream), at seventeen in the U.S. Hebrew paper *Ha-Pisgah.* His first book of poetry, *Hezyonot U-Manginot* (1898; Visions and Melodies), is romantic in style and deals with love and nature. From 1899 to 1906, he studied medicine in Heidelberg and Lausanne. During this period he wrote the first of his "Greek" poems—an indictment of Judaism's weakness vis-à-vis the vitality of Greek culture. The most powerful of these poems is *Lenokhah Pesel Apollo* (In the Presence of Apollo's Statue). In 1906 he returned to Russia, and until World War I, he held various positions as a doctor. The turbulent period in Russia following the war is described in his collection *Sonnetot Krim* (Crimean Sonnets). His *Lashemesh* (To the Sun), a series of sonnets written beginning in 1919, is in stark contrast to the surrounding darkness. In 1922 he left Russia but, failing to reach Palestine, he settled in Berlin where he translated such classical writers as Goethe, Molière, Shakespeare, and Homer. In 1929 he began to publish a ten-volume jubilee edition of his poetry, short stories, plays, and translations.

In 1931, at the invitation of Dr. A. M. Masie's family, Tchernichovsky arrived in Palestine to complete and edit a medical dictionary begun by the deceased doctor. The result was a trilingual work in Latin, English, and Hebrew, *Sefer Ha-Munahim Li-Refuah U-Lemadaei Ha-Tev'a* (1934, A Book of Terminologies in Medicine and the Natural Sciences). Tchernichovsky first resided in Tel Aviv and then moved to Jerusalem, where he wrote his final works of poetry. In 1937 he published *Kol Shirei Shaul Tcher-*

nichovsky (The Poems of Saul Tchernichovsky). In 1942 the Tel Aviv municipality established a prize in his name for translations of classics and world classical literature with Tchernichovsky as its first recipient. Once in Palestine, his poems became strongly nationalistic, and in the resettlement of Eretz Yisrael, he saw the redemption and rejuvenation of pre-exilic Judaism. He expressed all these sentiments in ballad form, such as in *Amma Dedhahaba* (1943; The Golden People). Tchernichovsky died after a long illness and was buried in Tel Aviv's old cemetery.

ANN KAHN

TEA

A drink for social occasions and after meals.

In the Middle East, tea is a popular drink brewed with the leaves and water in a kettle (although tea bags are becoming more common). Hot tea is strained into small glasses, often set in decorative metal holders, and served with various additions depending on region and personal taste. These include sugar, honey, lemon, apple flavoring, and mint. (Mint tea is also a very popular digestive drink; it is made solely from mint leaves of the genus *Mentha,* which grow throughout the Mediterranean region and Eurasia.)

Tea is imported to the Middle East from the Asian tea plantations of China, Japan, India, Sri Lanka, and islands of the East Indies. It is also cultivated along Iran's Caspian Sea coast and Turkey's Black Sea coast. Originally it came into the region by way of ancient caravan routes along the Silk Road (from China to Iran to the Black Sea and Constantinople) or ship routes from the South China Sea and the Indian Ocean into the Arabian Sea, the Persian Gulf, and the Red Sea.

Bibliography

Hartel, Herbert, et al. *Along the Ancient Silk Routes.* New York: Metropolitan Museum of Art, 1982.

CLIFFORD A. WRIGHT
UPDATED BY ERIC HOOGLUND

TEBU TRIBE

See TRIBES AND TRIBALISM: TEBU TRIBE

TECHNION-ISRAEL INSTITUTE OF TECHNOLOGY

Israeli university.

The Technion-Israel Institute of Technology, located in Haifa, was founded because of the lack of opportunities for technical studies for Jews in places such as Russia. This void meant that Jews were excluded from technical professions and pushed into urban commercial occupations. While the cornerstone was laid in 1912, World War I delayed the opening. The first classes were held in 1924. Hebrew became the language of instruction only after a long "language conflict" over whether German or Hebrew should be used.

There are faculties and departments in aeronautical engineering, agricultural engineering, architecture and town planning, chemical engineering, chemistry, civil engineering, electrical engineering, food and biotechnology, general studies, industrial and management engineering, materials engineering, mathematics, mechanical engineering, mechanics, nuclear sciences, physics, and teacher training. The number of undergraduate and graduate students enrolled in 1999/2000 was 12,700.

MIRIAM SIMON

TEHIYA

See ISRAEL: POLITICAL PARTIES IN

TEHRAN

Capital of Iran since the late eighteenth century.

In 1800, Tehran was a small city with an estimated population of 20,000; it was surrounded by twenty-foot mud walls with four gates. The wall was encircled by a moat, which was up to 40 feet wide and between 20 and 30 feet deep. Although several new buildings were constructed during the reign of Fath Ali Shah Qajar (1797–1834), the first major expansion of Tehran dates from the reign of Naser al-Din Shah (1848–1896), the third Qajar monarch. The old walls were pulled down, plans for an octagonal wall on a French model were followed, and twelve gates were built. New grounds were added to the city compound, as well as large boulevards and imposing public and private buildings, designed with many European features. The city had a small railway leading to a place of pilgrimage in the south, and the summer resorts in the Alborz Mountains in the north were developed and became popular with richer Tehranis. In 1852, a first census and a count of all the buildings were made, which show how small the city still was: It had only 12,772 buildings, 8,697 houses, and 4,220 shops. The second census, prepared in 1869, gave the population as 150,000.

Tehran's second phase of development dates to the reign (1926–1941) of Reza Shah Pahlavi, founder of the Pahlavi dynasty. The city was expanded outside its old walls, especially to the north and the northwest. A notable feature was the neoclassical buildings, designed mainly by European architects, especially exiles fleeing the Russian Revolution but also Iranians who had studied abroad. Houses began to be built facing outward, to the street, instead of inward, to the courtyard, and streets were planned for the passage of automobiles. The ornate gates, a special feature of old Tehran, were pulled down, as were many buildings of the Qajar dynasty period.

Tehran's third phase of development dates to the early 1950s, when a new generation of Iranian architects and technocrats, who had studied in U.S. universities, returned to erase many of the remaining features of the old city. Tehran began expanding rapidly and haphazardly, because of the petroleum industry, oil-induced construction, and the industrialization boom of the 1960s and 1970s. Between 1956 and 1976, the city's population tripled, from 1.5 million to 4.5 million. Despite the economic, political, and social upheavals caused by the Iranian Revolution (1979) and the Iran–Iraq War (1980–1988), Tehran's population continued to grow at an average annual rate of 3.5 percent from the mid-1970s to the late 1980s. Thereafter, population growth declined by about 1 percent per year within the city, but nearby towns and rural areas experienced rapid growth as they were developed as suburban communities to the east, south, and west of Tehran. According to the 1996 census, a total of 6,759,000 people lived in the city of Tehran; more than 1.3 million lived in suburbs, including the densely populated communities of Islamshahr and Karaj.

See also FATH ALI SHAH QAJAR; IRANIAN REVOLUTION (1979); IRAN–IRAQ WAR (1980–1988); NASER AL-DIN SHAH; PAHLAVI, REZA.

Bibliography

Adamec, Ludwig W., ed. *Historical Gazetteer of Iran, Vol. 1, Tehran and Northwestern Iran.* Graz, Austria: Akademische Drucku, 1976.

Ettehadieh, Mansoureh. "Patterns in Urban Development: The Growth of Tehran, 1852–1903." In *Qajar Iran: Political, Social and Cultural Change, 1800–1925,* edited by Edmund Bosworth and Carole Hillenbrand. Edinburgh, U.K.: Edinburgh University Press, 1983.

Firoozi, Ferydoon. "Tehran: A Demographic and Economic Analysis." *Middle Eastern Studies* 10, no. 1 (Jan. 1974): 60–67.

MANSOUREH ETTEHADIEH
UPDATED BY ERIC HOOGLUND

TEKELI, ŞIRIN

[1940–]

A feminist activist in Turkey.

Şirin Tekeli is the foremost feminist author and activist of second-wave feminism in Turkey. Born in 1944, she is the only child of two philosophy teachers. She received her high school education in Ankara and completed her college education in political science in Lausanne University, Switzerland. She studied the work of David Easton for her Ph.D. in political science in Istanbul University, where she was employed as an assistant professor. The thesis she wrote in 1978 for promotion to associate professor was on women's political participation, and prompted her feminist activism. Published in 1982 as a book called *Kadınlar ve Siyasal-Toplumsal Hayat* (Women and political-social life), this study was the first serious and comprehensive discussion of women's marginalization in sociopolitical life written in Turkish and from a predominantly Marxist perspective. Her interviews with Turkish women parliamentarians, which she included in the book, exposed their striking marginality and problems in political life. The book was widely read, moving beyond a narrow academic circle, and had immediate and long-lasting influence in shaping a feminist culture in Turkey.

Tekeli resigned from her position as an associate professor in 1981 and began her career as a feminist activist, translating and editing books. She engaged in organizing consciousness-raising groups and feminist publication circles in early 1980s and initiated the founding of the Kadın Eserleri Kütüphanesi ve Bilgi Merkezi (Women's Library and Information Center) and Mor Çatı Kadın Sığınağı (Purple Roof Women's Shelter) Foundations with her friends in 1990. She worked as a volunteer in the Women's Library between 1990 and 1996 and helped the institution develop into a vital organ of feminist dialogue. In 1997, she responded to the hunger strikes that were staged in prisons by deciding to work for women's entry into the parliament. She founded KADER, Kadın Adayları Destekleme ve Eğitme Derneği (Association to support and educate women candidates) in 1997 and served as its president between 1997 and 1999. The French government presented her with the award of *Officier* of *l'Ordre des Palmes Academiques* in 1996.

See also GENDER: GENDER AND LAW; GENDER: GENDER AND POLITICS; TURKEY; WOMEN'S LIBRARY AND INFORMATION CENTER.

YEŞIM ARAT

TEKKE

Local headquarters for Sufi orders.

Tekke is the Turkish word for the local meeting and living center of a Sufi fraternity. The Persian equivalent, *khangah,* is commonly used in most non-Turkic contexts, while *zawiya* (Arabic) functions as a distinctively North African synonym.

The late tenth and eleventh centuries saw a rise in the popularity of Sufi teachings and charismatic leaders, as well as the concurrent evolution of various Sufi organizations or "fraternities." As they expanded, these fraternities began to establish special living quarters for their members, as well as space for the various ritual, scholarly, and social service activities conducted by the local chapters of what gradually grew into international Sufi orders. In different contexts, either the state or private citizens endowed a vast network of tekke and khangah complexes designed to serve as regional headquarters for the fraternities. Many of these were composed of residence cells, a large kitchen-refectory for members and guests, a Qur'an school for local youth, a library for advanced study, a tomb-shrine of a deceased spiritual master, and a mosque. Partly because the money used to endow tekkes and khangahs was often invested in local business and agriculture, a number of them throughout the late medieval and early modern Muslim world (c. 1200–1900) functioned as important economic, cultural, and political centers. In fact in some regions—particularly southern Asia, western North Africa, and the Balkans—tekkes and khangahs played a role in the Islamization of local peoples and cultures. Although the institution of the tekke generally flourished under Ottoman patronage, the stridently secularist vision of Mustafa Kemal Atatürk and his regime led to the 1925 closing of all the great Anatolian tekkes—including that of the Mevlevi Brotherhood (the famed "whirling dervishes") in Konya—and the subsequent abolishment of nearly all institutional Sufi activity in the new Turkish republic.

See also SUFISM AND THE SUFI ORDERS.

Bibliography

Trimingham, J. Spencer. *The Sufi Orders in Islam.* New York: Oxford University Press, 1998.

SCOTT ALEXANDER

TEL AVIV

Coastal city founded in Ottoman Palestine in 1909; capital of Israel, 1948–1950.

Tel Aviv is a sprawling metropolis surrounded by suburbs; it was the first city to be established by Jews in the modern era. As numerous Jewish settlers arrived in Palestine in the late nineteenth century, they had increasing difficulties finding accommodations at affordable prices in the overcrowded residential areas of Jerusalem and Jaffa. In both cities, Jews began to purchase land and build new suburbs.

Jaffa is adjacent to, and today part of, Tel Aviv because Ahuzat Bayit, the building society, purchased beachfront property and underwrote the construction of Tel Aviv's first sixty houses in 1909—initially intended as a new suburb of Jaffa. Important differences between this project and other suburbs could be immediately discerned. Architects and engineers helped design the arrangement of houses and streets; individual land grants were large; all connecting roads and streets were paved; and running water was supplied to each house. Ahuzat Bayit became the most spacious and comfortable suburb in all Palestine. The building society changed the name to Tel Aviv in 1910, marking both a biblical text (Ezekiel 3:15) where the name appears and mention in Nahum Sokolow's translation of Zionist leader Theodor Herzl's *Alteneuland* (The Old New Land). Initially planned as a residential suburb, all of Tel Aviv's first settlers worked in Jaffa. Many of Tel Aviv's founders had private capital; they owned businesses and worked in the free professions. Jewish engineers and contractors built the city's first houses with supplies furnished by Jewish factories. Symbol of the New Yishuv (Jewish community), Tel Aviv's relatively rapid expansion paused during World War I, but resumed and intensified during the British mandate (1923–1948).

Although Zionism stressed agricultural settlement, and donated funds subsidized the cost of collective and communal settlements, most immigrants chose to live in cities and many selected Tel Aviv. By 1935, the population had grown from 2,000 to 120,000 and Tel Aviv became the political, economic, and cultural center of the Jewish National Home. Factories and businesses stood alongside the Histadrut (Jewish Labor Federation) and military headquarters. Publishing firms, major newspapers, several dance and theater companies, the symphony, and an important museum were founded. Transport and roads radiated out to other cities and the countryside.

In May 1948, David Ben-Gurion proclaimed the independence of the State of Israel at a meeting held in the Tel Aviv Museum. In 1950, the commercial port city of Jaffa was incorporated with Tel Aviv, forming the twin city of Tel Aviv-Jaffa. Tel Aviv-Jaffa has benefited from Israel's rapid economic growth, today numbering more than 350,000 residents. (The population of Tel Aviv and its outskirts numbers 2.5 million.) The Histadrut headquarters no longer dominates the skyline or the city's economy. Art, music, and drama flourish in galleries and theaters, and there is an impressive array of shops, cabarets, and restaurants (both kosher and nonkosher). Much of Tel Aviv's cosmopolitan core now remains open on the Jewish Sabbath, presenting an urban profile that differs in scale and tone from that projected by Jerusalem.

Bibliography

Kark, Ruth. *Jaffa: A City in Evolution, 1799–1917,* translated by Gila Brand. Jerusalem: Yad Izhak Ben-Zvi Press, 1990.

Katz, Yossi. "Ideology and Urban Development: Zionism and the Origins of Tel Aviv, 1906–1914." *Journal of Historical Geography* 12 (1986): 402–424.

Orni, Efraim, and Elisha Efrat. *Geography of Israel,* 4th revised edition. Jerusalem: Israel Universities Press, 1980.

DONNA ROBINSON DIVINE

TEL AVIV UNIVERSITY

Israeli university.

In 1953 the city of Tel Aviv founded the university to meet the higher education needs of the populous, developing area.

The university offers programs in the arts and sciences within the nine faculties of engineering, exact sciences, humanities, law, life sciences, management, medicine, social sciences, and visual and performing arts, as well as schools of dental medicine, social work, education, and environmental studies. In 2002 the student population was approximately 26,000.

MIRIAM SIMON

TELEVISION

See RADIO AND TELEVISION

TEL HAI

Pioneer Jewish settlement in Palestine that became a national symbol.

Tel Hai is a Jewish settlement founded in 1918 in Galilee, on the northern frontier of Palestine, as an attempt to influence the drawing of the boundary between British and French colonial possessions. After the British gave up responsibility for Syria and Lebanon at the end of World War I, and before the French Mandate began, a hiatus in authority led to irregular warfare endangering Jewish settlements in the undefined upper Galilee/northern border area. Many Zionist leaders, among them Vladimir Ze'ev Jabotinsky, advised the small number of settlers at Tel Hai to withdraw because a reasonable defense could not be mounted. They remained, and six Jews died in the final attack in 1920, among them the military hero Yosef Trumpeldor, who had been sent to organize their defense. Tel Hai became a national symbol of the determination of Zionists to hold on to settlements at all costs and a metaphor for the principle that Jewish national life in Palestine required personal sacrifice.

See also TRUMPELDOR, YOSEF.

Bibliography

Zerubavel, Yael. "The Historic, the Legendary, and the Incredible: Invented Tradition and Collective Memory in Israel." In *Commemorations: The Politics of National Identity,* edited by John R. Gillis. Princeton, NJ: Princeton University Press, 1994.

Zerubavel, Yael. *Recovered Roots: Collective Memory and the Making of Israeli National Tradition.* Chicago: University of Chicago Press, 1995.

DONNA ROBINSON DIVINE

TELL

See GLOSSARY

TEMPLARS

German evangelical settlers in Palestine in the late nineteenth century.

The Temple Society (Tempelgesellschaft) was founded in the mid-nineteenth century in the Kingdom of Württemberg. Pietistic Evangelicals, the Templars criticized the church and decided at first to settle and found colonies and, later, to improve the land in Palestine as they awaited the imminent Kingdom of Heaven. They established a colony in Haifa in 1868 and brought modern European methods of agriculture. They also established the carriage trade from Jaffa to Jerusalem, exported wine, and established settlements in Jaffa, Haifa, Sarone (part of modern Tel Aviv), Jerusalem, Wilhelma, Galilen Bethlehem, and Waldheim. Individuals settled in Jerusalem and founded a German colony there that, although denied official support by the German government, numbered some 1,200 people by 1914.

Deported as enemy aliens by the British from 1917 to 1918, as German nationals they kept a low profile after they were permitted to return during the Palestine Mandate. Their religious fervor had decreased by the third generation and, as Germans, many were receptive to National Socialism, even though there was no official advocacy of support for the Nazi Party. Many sympathetic members were allowed to join the party; they also enlisted their children in the Nazi Youth and disseminated Nazi propaganda. With the outbreak of World War II, there were approximately 1,500 Germans of Templar origin who were interned, and afterward they were repatriated to Germany in exchange for Palestinians who had fallen into German hands. Some were deported to Australia. In 1948 their property was taken over by the Israeli government and placed under the Guardian of German Property; it was later taken into account during the negotiations over Nazi Holocaust reparations conducted by the World Jewish Congress and the West German government.

See also GERMANY AND THE MIDDLE EAST; HAIFA; JAFFA; JERUSALEM; WEST GERMAN REPARATIONS AGREEMENT.

Bibliography

Carmel, Alex. "The German Settlers in Palestine and Their Relations with the Local Arab Population and the Jewish Community, 1868–1918." In *Studies on Palestine during the Ottoman Empire,* edited by Moshe Ma'oz. Jerusalem: Magnes Press, 1975.

Thalmann, Naftali. "Introducing Modern Agriculture into Nineteenth Century Palestine: The German Templers." In *The Land that Became Israel: Studies in Historical Geography,* edited by Ruth Kark. New Haven, CT: Yale University Press, 1990.

Yazbak, Mahmoud. "Templars as 'Proto-Zionists': The 'German Colony' in Late Ottoman Haifa." *Journal of Palestine Studies* xx, no. 112 (Summer 1999): 40–45.

REEVA S. SIMON
UPDATED BY MICHAEL R. FISCHBACH

TEMPLE, HENRY JOHN

See PALMERSTON, LORD HENRY JOHN TEMPLE

TEMPLE MOUNT AND HARAM AL-SHARIF

See HARAM AL-SHARIF

TEMPORARY MARRIAGE

See ZIWAJ MUTʿA

TERAKKI

See NEWSPAPERS AND PRINT MEDIA: TURKEY

TERCÜMAN-I AHVAL

See NEWSPAPERS AND PRINT MEDIA: TURKEY

TERCÜMAN-I HAKIKAT

See NEWSPAPERS AND PRINT MEDIA: TURKEY

TERRORISM

Violence directed primarily and randomly against civilians with the aim of intimidating them, achieving political goals, or exacting revenge for perceived grievances.

Since the 11 September 2001 terrorist attacks that destroyed the twin World Trade Center skyscrapers in New York City and killed nearly 2,800 persons, terrorism arising out of conflicts in the Middle East has been a focus of international media attention. Concern about violence undertaken by groups and states it considered to be terrorists prompted the United States to declare a war on terrorism, two manifestations of which have been the wars in Afghanistan and Iraq. Despite this close association of terrorism with the Middle East, with the notable exception of the year 2001, the majority of terrorist incidents committed worldwide and the majority of victims of terrorism have been outside of or unrelated to political conflicts in the Middle East. Nevertheless, it is true that civilians somewhere in the Middle East have been victims of politically motivated violence every year since at least 1992.

Defining Terrorism

In trying to assess the significance of terrorism, the most difficult problem is the lack of an agreed-upon understanding of what the word *terrorism* means. Political scientists tend to restrict terrorism to acts of violence carried out by nonstate actors against civilians. Historians, sociologists, and experts in international humanitarian law, however, tend to use a broader definition that includes all premeditated acts of violence against civilians, whether carried out by nonstate political groups or by states. Governments—especially those confronting armed opposition groups—and the media generally use the political-science definition of terrorism, often expanding it to include violent acts against military as well as civilian victims. In contrast, the nonstate perpetrators of violence consider their actions to be legitimate forms of resistance to state terrorism aimed at suppressing self-determination, even though they may be directed against civilians (Kimmerling, p. 23). The notion of a legitimate right to resist state oppression is controversial, and no international legal convention addresses this matter. Nonstate groups generally cite the 1960 United Nations General Assembly Resolution on the Granting of Independence to Colonial Countries and Peoples as recognizing their right of resistance. Indeed, that resolution declares, "forcible resistance to forcible denial of self-determination . . . is legitimate," and it says that nonstate groups may receive external support from other governments.

Giving a measure of international legitimacy to resistance struggles has complicated the problem of defining terrorism because it essentially has become a political decision whether a nonstate actor is deemed a terrorist or a genuine national liberation movement fighting for independence from foreign control or occupation. During the Cold War rivalry between the Soviet Union and the United States (1947–1991), such decisions tended to be based more on ideological factors than on objective assessments of the goals and motives of particular nonstate groups. For example, the Soviet Union provided clandestine support for the South Yemen independence movement (1963–1967) and for the Dhufar liberation movement in Oman (1965–1971) primarily because both areas at the time were under the control of Britain, a major U.S. ally. Similarly, the United States provided covert assistance to the Kurds in Iraq (1970–1975) and the Mojahedin in Afghanistan (1979–1989) primarily because in both cases the nonstate groups were fighting for independence from Soviet client regimes. The Soviet Union and the United States condemned as

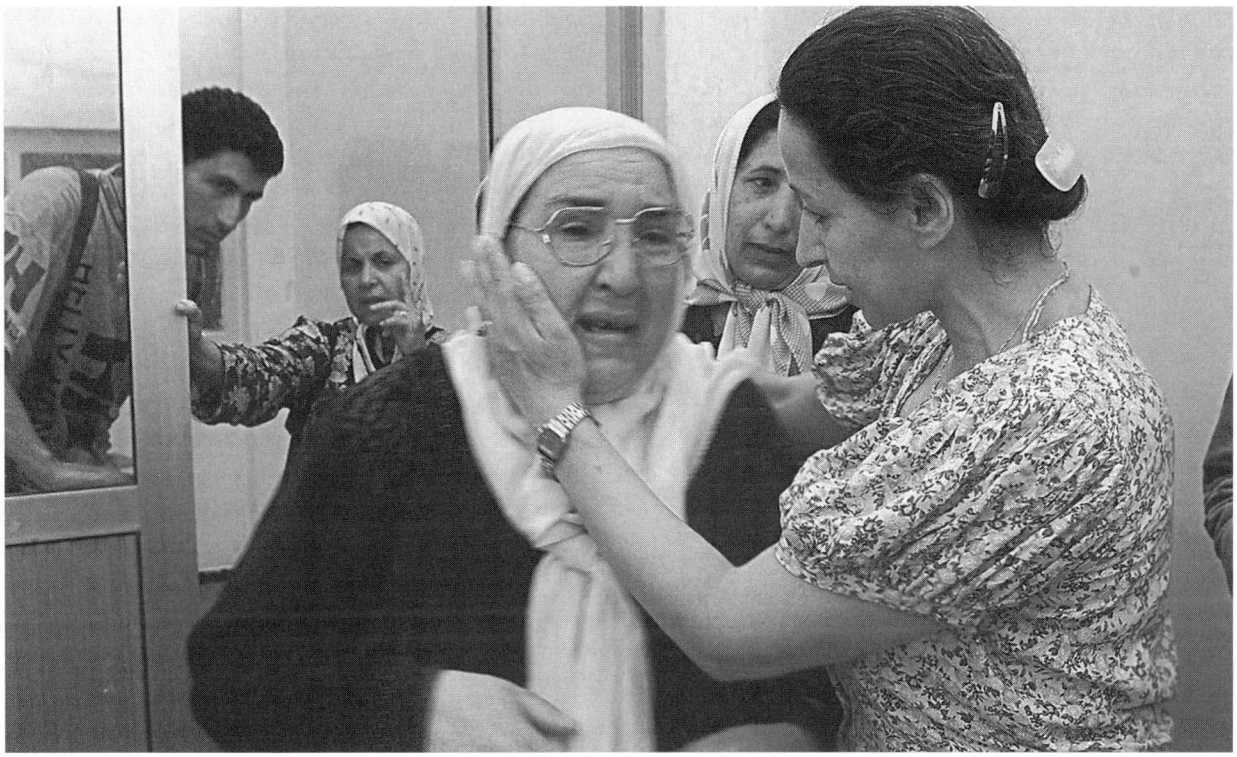

Social worker Farida Djefel (right) comforts Khalti Taous at the offices of the National Association for the Families of Terrorism Victims in Algiers, Algeria, in 1999. Taous's son, a policeman, was killed by suspected Islamic militants in 1994. © AP/WIDE WORLD PHOTOS. REPRODUCED BY PERMISSION.

terrorists those nonstate groups that were fighting against regimes the other country favored, and they praised as national resistance heroes those groups fighting against governments they opposed.

Over time, a special vocabulary of terrorism emerged. For instance, the term *state terrorism* came to be used for violent acts used by disfavored states to suppress resistance movements. The Soviet Union used this term to describe the policies of two U.S. allies: Israel, for the repression of Palestinians in the occupied West Bank and Gaza Strip after 1967; and Turkey, for the repression of its Kurdish minority after 1984. The United States, in turn, used *state terrorism* as early as the mid-1970s to describe the repressive domestic policies of states it considered to be Soviet allies, such as Iraq, Syria, and South Yemen. During the 1980s another term, *state sponsor of terrorism,* emerged to describe the support for nonstate groups provided by countries that clearly were not allied to either the Soviet Union or the United States. Iran and Libya were identified as the main state sponsors of terrorism, the former because of its assistance after 1982 to Hizbullah in Lebanon. In the case of Libya, the United States accused that country of supporting Palestinian groups that targeted U.S. and Israeli interests in Europe and of assisting several terrorist groups operating in north and central Africa.

Origins of Terrorism in the Arab–Israel Conflict

The superpower rivalry in and rhetoric about the Middle East tended both to obscure the local origins of terrorism and to frustrate efforts to address the multifaceted consequences of violence. This problem is best revealed in the Arab–Israel conflict, which began in 1948 separately from but in tandem with the Cold War and still continues unresolved even though the superpower conflict has ended. One significant legacy of the Cold War relationship to the Arab–Israel conflict has been a great volume of partisan literature, especially in the years after the formation of the Palestine Liberation Organization (PLO) in 1964. The Israeli–Palestinian struggle over pre-1948 Palestine (which became Israel plus the territories of the Gaza Strip and the West Bank in 1948) is the core of the Arab–Israel conflict. The literature on this aspect of the conflict illustrates the controversies in trying to achieve any relatively objective consensus on what groups merit designation as terrorists and what kinds of violent acts constitute terrorism. For this reason, it is a useful case to study.

For nearly thirty years prior to the signing of the Oslo Accord in September 1993, the State of Israel proclaimed the PLO and the various Palestinian resistance groups that comprised its membership to be terrorist organizations. Inevitably, there emerged a body of writings that supported the Israeli position, not just in Israel but also in Europe and North America. Although some of these studies were sophisticated and scholarly analyses of the PLO's goals and methods, other accounts were merely polemical denunciations of PLO tactics. Beginning in 1968 and continuing for more than a decade, armed Palestinian groups known as *fidaʾiyyun* (guerrillas) carried out numerous, violent operations that resulted in the deaths of civilians. Many of their actions were sensational incidents that attracted considerable media attention—a PLO objective, as the guerrillas hoped publicity would further their cause. The several international airplane hijackings, for example, culminated in September 1970 (known as Black September) with the hijacking of four planes in as many days, precipitating a civil war between the PLO and the army of Jordan. Attacks on Israeli interests abroad culminated in the seizing of Israeli athletes as hostages at the 1972 Olympic games in Munich, an incident that left eleven athletes dead. Sporadic cross-border raids into Israel (from Jordan and Lebanon) culminated in the temporary seizure of buildings in the northern Israeli towns of Kiryat Shmona and Maʿalot (April and May 1974) and the deaths of thirty-eight civilians, including many children. Rather than winning sympathy for the Palestinians as the perpetrators expected, such incidents created and reinforced a public image of the PLO as a terrorist organization.

In contrast to the official Israeli and U.S. views, the PLO saw itself as a national liberation movement dedicated to achieving Palestinian rights and resisting what it termed Israeli state terrorism. Its fighters were lauded as heroes and martyrs, and its operations against Israeli civilians were justified as defense of, or reprisals for, Israeli attacks on Palestinian refugee camps and assassinations of PLO leaders. The Soviet Union, the primary international backer of the PLO after 1968, tended to remain silent about many of the more sensational acts of violence by Palestinian guerrillas, but it continued to promote the PLO as a national liberation movement. Soviet support was especially significant after 1974 when Moscow encouraged diplomatic recognition of the PLO as the legitimate representative of the Palestinian people. Quite separate from the Soviet backing for the PLO, a few academic studies and advocacy articles appeared that were sympathetic to Palestinian claims and rights. Although these writings were scarcer than the volumes of pro-Israeli literature and never achieved a similar impact on the mainstream U.S. media, they did have some influence on intellectuals in Africa, Asia, and Europe.

The Israeli–PLO conflict affected both regional and international politics by the late 1970s. This is because the PLO used Lebanon, where a large number of Palestinian refugees had lived since 1948, as a base for operations against Israel throughout the 1970s, and Israel responded with retaliatory raids against what it termed "terrorist nests"—suspected PLO facilities in refugee camps. Many Lebanese and Palestinian civilians died in these raids, and their deaths were described officially as "collateral damage" in a larger operation against "terrorist infrastructure." The PLO condemned Israeli air strikes as further evidence of state terror and also cited them as justification for its own continuing attacks across the Lebanon-Israel border. The escalating cycle of attacks and reprisals contributed to the civil war in Lebanon (1975–1989) and also led to an Israeli invasion of southern Lebanon in 1978. Israeli forces occupied a 6-mile-wide security strip, ostensibly to prevent attacks into Israel; this occupation lasted until 2000. A second Israeli invasion of Lebanon in 1982 resulted in a war with the PLO, its forced withdrawal from Lebanon under international protection, and the Israeli occupation of Beirut and all of southern Lebanon. However, almost as soon as the threat from the PLO seemed to be contained, Israel faced a new source of terrorism that stemmed directly from its occupation of Lebanon (which lasted until 1985).

A Lebanese group, Hizbullah, was formed in late 1982 with the initial aim of expelling Israeli forces from Lebanon. Hizbullah's tactics, which included suicide bombings against French and U.S. military forces in 1983 and, beginning in 1984, the kidnapping of European civilians to use as hostages for the release of its members held in Israeli jails, earned it an international reputation as a terrorist organization. Hizbullah, however, neither sought nor received any support from the Soviet Union. Like the revolutionary government that assumed power in Iran in 1979, Hizbullah was equally hostile to Soviet and U.S. policies in the Middle East. Although its objectives were first and foremost political, Hizbullah also was inspired by its own interpretation of Shiʿite Islam. Its frequent use of religious rhetoric to explain or to justify its actions tended to alienate the Soviet Union even more than its direct criticisms did. Thus, Hizbullah became one of the first major nonstate groups in the Middle East to lack a superpower patron. Despite or perhaps because of this status, Hizbullah succeeded in establishing a permanent presence in Lebanon's politics and in becoming a nonstate group whose actions Israel neither could control nor ignore.

Meanwhile, the removal of the PLO to Tunisia did not end its political influence among Palestinians, and when an intifada (uprising) erupted in December 1987 among Palestinians living under Israeli occupation in the West Bank and Gaza Strip, the PLO gradually emerged as a main coordinating force for the resistance. New groups unaffiliated with the PLO also emerged during the intifada, principally HAMAS and Islamic Jihad. Unlike the PLO, which claimed to be inspired by secular ideas, HAMAS and Islamic Jihad cited religious ideals and percepts as at least partial justification for their resistance against Israeli rule. Concern about the increasing influence of groups such as HAMAS and Islamic Jihad may have prompted the leaders of Israel's Labor Party to begin negotiations with the PLO to end the long conflict. The political rapprochement between Israel and the PLO in 1993 not only was unexpected, but it also necessitated a re-evaluation of the negative ways each side had depicted the other. However, the years of intellectual and emotional investment in the terrorism paradigm made it difficult for some people on both sides to view formerly hated terrorists as legitimate partners in peace negotiations. Thus, from the outset of the Oslo peace process, some Israelis and Palestinians were skeptical of the agreement and even were determined to overturn it. The assassination of Israeli prime minister Yitzhak Rabin in November 1995 (by an Israeli opposed to the Oslo Accord) and the first suicide bombings undertaken in 1996 by HAMAS were significant terrorist incidents that led to multiple actions and reprisals that cumulatively undermined popular support for the peace process among both Israelis and Palestinians.

A 1999 wanted poster for Osama bin Ladin, leader of the al-Qaʿida terrorist network. The poster depicts the carnage from bombings of the U.S. embassies in Kenya and Tanzania on 7 August 1998, an act that the United States blamed on bin Ladin. The terrorist attacks of 11 September 2001 would bring far greater infamy to bin Ladin in the future. © CORBIS. REPRODUCED BY PERMISSION.

It was in this increasingly tense atmosphere that Israeli politician Ariel Sharon intervened in a manner that would have the effect (albeit at the time, unforeseen) of overturning the peace process. Sharon was one of those Israelis who distrusted and even opposed the Oslo Accord, and it is plausible that he never had changed his conviction that the PLO was a terrorist organization. When in September 2000 he led a group of Knesset members, under armed escort, into the Muslim religious complex in Jerusalem known as al-Haram al-Sharif, his intention was to assert Israeli sovereignty over a site that Jews claim is the Temple Mount—the location of their ancient temple destroyed by the Romans more than 2,000 years ago—and thus to prevent its possible return to Palestinian sovereignty, which had been proposed by some members of the Labor Party. The incident provoked clashes with Palestinian worshipers, and the next day Israeli police killed four protesting Palestinians as they emerged from Friday prayers at the al-Aqsa Mosque in al-Haram al-Sharif complex. The situation escalated rapidly as Palestinian policemen, in an effort to protect civilians, clashed with Israeli soldiers at checkpoints in the West Bank. The al-Aqsa intifada thus began, and subsequently its characteristic features included targeted assassinations of suspected Palestinian resistance leaders by Israel and retaliatory Palestinian suicide bombings at crowded civilian sites inside Israeli cities. By early 2001, Israel and its supporters were labeling all acts of violence from the Palestinian side as terrorism.

The U.S. "War on Terrorism"

Middle East terrorism, except for incidents such as the attack at the Munich Olympic games in 1972, generally has stayed within the region. However, Middle East–related terrorism acquired a global dimension with the 11 September 2001 attacks in the United States by nineteen members of the al-Qaʿida network. Al-Qaʿida is a political organization founded by Saudi Arabian national Osama bin Ladin, and its objectives after 1991 were to attack the United States and its interests because it viewed the U.S. government as the main sponsor of regimes that it defined as "unjust," oppressive, and illegitimate. Ironically, bin Ladin collaborated with U.S. officials during the 1980s when he and the United States shared the same goal of forcing the Soviet Union to withdraw its troops from Afghanistan. But when the United States dispatched troops to Saudi Arabia in 1990, bin Ladin viewed this development as being no different from the situation of Soviet troops in Afghanistan—in both cases the army of an "imperialist" superpower occupying a weaker and Muslim country. Furthermore, the presence of U.S. military forces in Saudi Arabia meant that a non-Muslim army for the first time in more than 1,400 years was occupying the religiously sacred land in which were located Islam's two holiest sites, the cities of Mecca and Medina. Even though bin Ladin believed and practiced a very conservative interpretation of Sunni Islam, his primary objectives vis-à-vis the United States are political, not religious. Beginning with the bombing in the underground parking garage of the World Trade Center in 1993, persons close to his al-Qaʿida organization were implicated in several terrorist attacks. The most sensational incidents included suicide bombings outside the barracks housing U.S. military personnel in Saudi Arabia in 1996 and outside two U.S. embassies in East Africa in 1998. The 2001 attacks prompted the United States to declare a "war on terrorism," and the Taliban regime in Afghanistan became the first target because it provided sanctuary to al-Qaʿida and rejected requests for the extradition of bin Ladin and other leaders.

Its war on terrorism policy led the United States to focus on groups it designated as terrorist to an unprecedented extent. One consequence of this new preoccupation was that after 2001 Washington accepted the argument of Israeli prime minister Sharon that PLO chairman and Palestinian Authority president Yasir Arafat was condoning terrorist actions by groups such as HAMAS, Islamic Jihad, and his own Al-Fatah movement. When in spring 2002 the Israeli army reoccupied West Bank towns and villages that were supposed to be under the control of the Palestinian Authority, the United States effectively did not protest. Thus, the peace process between Israel and the PLO, seriously ailing since fall 2000, became an indirect but fatal casualty of the war on terrorism.

The war on terrorism is cause for concern among legal experts in the field of international humanitarian law, especially because states identified as sponsors of terrorism, such as Iraq, become legitimate targets for attack because they are thought to possess weapons of mass destruction that they might provide to terrorist groups. The experts believe that civilians, who have been the primary victims of violent conflicts since the early 1990s, will be the main victims again, and they cite statistics that demonstrate that this has been the case in both Afghanistan and Iraq.

The phenomenon of terrorism has prompted the drafting of several conventions, most notably the Rome Statute, that would make the intentional killing of civilians a war crime, no matter who is responsible (i.e., a government or a nonstate group). The intent is to criminalize violence against civilians so that individuals can be prosecuted. The European Union generally, and its member states such as Belgium specifically, have made the most progress in terms of accepting the idea that violence against civilians, whether undertaken by a state or nonstate organization, is terrorism and needs to be punished. Other states, including major countries such as China, Israel, Russia, and the United States, reject categorically the notion of state terrorism and insist that international laws pertaining to terrorism must limit definitions to nonstate groups that target civilians. Ultimately, one of the most effective ways of reducing terrorism is for states to identify and remove the causes that motivates terrorists, such as the denial of freedom and political participation, repressive political occupation, and poverty and despair.

See also AQSA INTIFADA, AL-; ARAFAT, YASIR; BIN LADIN, OSAMA; BLACK SEPTEMBER; FIDA'IYYUN; HAMAS; HIZBULLAH; HOSTAGE CRISES; ISLAMIC JIHAD; PALESTINE LIBERATION ORGANIZATION (PLO); POPULAR FRONT FOR THE LIBERATION OF PALESTINE; QA'IDA, AL-.

Bibliography

Davis, Joyce M. *Martyrs: Innocence, Vengeance, and Despair in the Middle East.* New York: Palgrave, 2003.

Falk, Richard. "Azmi Bishara, the Right of Resistance, and the Palestinian Ordeal." *Journal of Palestine Studies* 31, no. 2 (Winter 2002): 19–33.

Hirst, David. *The Gun and the Olive Branch: The Roots of Violence in the Middle East,* 3d edition. New York: Thunder Mouth's Press/Nation Books, 2004.

Picco, Giandomenico. *Man without a Gun: One Diplomat's Secret Struggle to Free the Hostages, Fight Terrorism, and End a War.* New York: Times Books/Random House, 1999.

Ron, James. *Frontiers and Ghettos: State Violence in Serbia and Israel.* Berkeley: University of California Press, 2003.

Shlaim, Avi. *The Iron Wall: Israel and the Arab World.* New York: Norton, 2000.

Stern, Jessica. *Terror in the Name of God: Why Religious Militants Kill.* New York: Ecco, 2003.

Victor, Barbara. *Army of Roses: Inside the World of Palestinian Women Suicide Bombers.* Emmaus, PA: Rodale, 2003.

ERIC HOOGLUND

TETUAN

Provincial capital of Morocco's northern Rif region.

Tetuan, with a population of about 466,000 (projection for 2001 based on 1994 census number of 363,813), was founded (1306–1307) by the Maranid sultan to serve as a base for attacks against Ceuta. It was destroyed by Henry III of Castile in 1400, and rebuilt around 1492. Tetuan was occupied by Spain on 6 February 1860, after they had defeated the Anjar tribesmen.

As the first part of Morocco to be occupied by Europeans in two centuries, Tetuan symbolized the threat from Christian Europe. Pressure by Britain and rethinking within Spain's leadership resulted in Spain's agreement to evacuate the city (2 May 1862) in return for a lower indemnity payment. In 1906, Spain was given responsibility for policing the port of Tetuan by a thirteen-nation conference called to maintain the balance of power between European states in Morocco, and to institute economic reforms and an open door policy. Three years later, Spain began its conquest of northern Morocco and built road links to Tetuan. It was made the capital of the Spanish protectorate in 1913, and remained so until Morocco attained independence in 1956 and Spain evacuated the area.

BRUCE MADDY-WEITZMAN

TEVFIK FIKRET

[1867–1915]

Ottoman Turkish poet and editor.

Tevfik Fikret, the son of a bureaucrat in the foreign service, was born Mehmet Tevfik in Istanbul. He studied literature at the prestigious Galatasaray lycée, where his teachers included Muallim Naci and Recaizade Mahmud Ekrem. At the age of fifteen, he published his first poetry in the newspaper *Tercüman-i Hakikat* under the name Nazmi. He entered the civil service but later resigned, drawing public attention when he donated his salary to the refugee commission, saying that it was "a disgrace to accept so much money for so little work." In 1896, he became the editor of *Servet-i Fünun,* the main journal of the new literary movement. At this time, he became known as Tevfik Fikret. Under the influence of the French Parnassian school, his pre-1901 poetry emphasizes art for its own sake, preferring form and technique over content, and poetry over prose. Generally written in the *aruz* meter, Fikret's poetry draws from scenes of everyday life, as in the poems "Hasta çocuk" (The sick child), "Balikçilar" (The fishermen), and "Bir içim su" (A drink of water). In 1899, Fikret became professor of literature at Robert College. Following the Young Turk Revolution in 1908, he joined with Hüseyin Cahit Yalçin in establishing the newspaper *Tanin* (The echo).

Bibliography

Mitler, Louis. *Ottoman Turkish Writers: A Bibliographical Dictionary of Significant Figures in Pre-Republican Turkish Literature.* New York: P. Lang, 1988.

Shaw, Stanford, and Shaw, Ezel Kural. *History of the Ottoman Empire and Modern Turkey,* Vol. 2: *Reform, Revolution, and Republic: The Rise of Modern Turkey, 1808–1975.* Cambridge, U.K., and New York: Cambridge University Press, 1977.

DAVID WALDNER

TEXTILE INDUSTRY

Production of fibers, filaments, and yarns used in making woven or knitted cloth for domestic or foreign trade is widespread in the Middle East.

The oldest textile materials produced and used in the Middle East—linen and wool—go back to remote antiquity. Cotton and silk, which originated in India and China, respectively, came into the region during the Roman Empire, in the early centuries of the Christian era. By the early Middle Ages, quantities of flax (for linen) were exported to Europe, chiefly from Egypt; of raw cotton from Syria and Egypt; of silk thread from Iran, Syria, and the Bursa region (northwest Turkey); and of mohair from Turkey. Flax and silk fibers and fabrics were traded to Europe for many centuries, but flax was gradually produced in many European nations, and the silks of India, China, and Japan competed with Middle Eastern silks and cottons as well as with cottons from the newly colonized Americas and from India. In the nineteenth century, however, the introduction of long-staple cotton made Egypt an important producer, and in the twentieth century, Egypt was joined by Turkey, Syria, Sudan, and Israel. In the 1990s, the Middle East produced 75 percent of the world output of long-staple cotton but only about 8 percent of the total world output of all cottons.

Although the preeminence of the Middle East in the manufacture of handloomed textiles goes back to antiquity, by the late Middle Ages, European products—woolens, fine silks, and linens—were fine enough to be imported by the Middle East. Until the middle of the eighteenth century, the Middle East continued to export cotton cloth and yarn to Europe, but European protective tariffs soon restricted even that trade. With the Industrial Revolution, European machine-loomed fabrics overwhelmed Middle Eastern handmade products and local markets. The number of Middle Eastern handlooms and

Textiles are the major export for the Turkish economy. Pictured is a Turkish woman weaving a carpet. © JOSÉ F. POBLETE/ CORBIS. REPRODUCED BY PERMISSION.

their total output declined sharply; for example, in Bursa, output of cloth fell from 20,000 pieces in 1843 to 3,000 in 1863. In Aleppo and Damascus combined, the number of looms dropped from about 12,000 in the 1820s to some 2,500 in the 1840s. Middle Eastern weavers were able to recover by using improved looms, importing cheaper and better European yarns, concentrating on inexpensive products, and drastically reducing wages. Handcrafted fabrics continued to form a large proportion of the textile output until after World War II. In Syria, in the 1930s, there were some 40,000 handweavers, and in Egypt in the 1940s, some 50,000. In Turkey and Iran, carpetmaking was greatly stimulated by rising foreign demand, lower freights that reduced export costs, and some foreign capital investments in the industry. Just before World War I, in 1913, Turkey exported 1,500 tons of carpets, then worth three million U.S. dollars, but the subsequent world wars devastated the industry. Persian carpet exports in 1914 were then worth five million U.S. dollars, and by the 1950s Iran's rugweaving and carpetmaking employed some 130,000 people—with exports of 5,000 tons, then worth twenty-five million U.S. dollars, the carpets accounted for 16 percent of Iran's non-oil exports.

Mills

Textile factories, or mills, were first used in the Middle East in the 1830s, in the modernizing program of Muhammad Ali's Egypt. The mills exported large amounts of cotton textiles, but they did not survive his death. A few small factories were also set up in Turkey in the nineteenth century, and by World War I, several textile centers had been developed in Turkey—notably in Adana, İzmir, and in the Salonika region. Egypt also had cotton-spinning mills in Alexandria and Cairo. Iran had a small spinning mill in Tehran, but other unsuccessful mills had closed. In Syria, one small mill, founded in Damascus in the 1860s, was operating, but two others, in Beirut and Antioch, had failed. Some two hundred small silk-reeling factories were set up in Lebanon, with others in Bursa, İzmir, and other silk-growing regions of Turkey. In Iran, there was a mill in Gilan.

After World War I, the textile industry wove rayon as well as cotton and wool and expanded greatly, especially after the tariff reforms. Table 1 shows the situation in the cotton industry in 1939, at the outbreak of World War II. By then, textile factories had been built in all the main towns and cities of the Middle East, and local production of cotton yarn and fabrics met 35 to 50 percent of total domestic demand within the larger countries.

During World War II, the region's textile industry expanded by about 50 percent, and the expansion continues—with several additional countries,

Middle East cotton industry in 1939

	Spindles (thousands)	Power looms (thousands)	Output of yarn (thousands of metric tons)	Output of cloth (million square meters)
Egypt	250	15	24	100
Iran	188	4	—	—
Iraq	—	1	—	—
Lebanon	14	1	1	—
Palestine	12	2	1	4
Syria	10	4	1	—
Turkey	189	6	23	152
Total	**663**	**33**	**50**	**256**

SOURCE: United Nations, *Review of Economic Conditions in the Middle East, 1951–52* (New York, 1953).

TABLE BY GGS INFORMATION SERVICES, THE GALE GROUP.

Middle East textile output in 1987

	Cotton		Wool		Silk
	Yarn[2]	Fabrics[3]	Yarn[2]	Fabrics[3]	Fabrics[3]
Egypt	251	694	19	24	5
Iran[1]	88	140	16	26	—
Israel	16	—	4	—	—
Jordan	—	2	—	—	—
Syria	39	180	2	1	—
Turkey	332	399	51	27	1
Total	**726**	**1,415**	**92**	**78**	**6**
World	15,091	47,360	2,223	3,484	2,248

[1]1981
[2]In million metric tons
[3]In million square meters

SOURCE: United Nations. *Industrial Statistical Yearbook* (New York, 1988).

TABLE BY GGS INFORMATION SERVICES, THE GALE GROUP.

with diversification, and with improvement in quality, especially in the finishing processes. Foreign investments have been gradually taken over, and the industry is now owned mainly by the state or local citizens. Turkey, Israel, Egypt, and Lebanon now export significant textile lots to worldwide markets. The second table shows recent figures.

Bibliography

Issawi, Charles. *An Economic History of the Middle East and North Africa.* New York: Columbia University Press, 1982.

CHARLES ISSAWI

THAALBI, ABD AL-AZIZ

[1874–1944]

Tunisian political leader and founder of the Destour party.

Abd al-Aziz Thaalbi's father was a notary whose family had emigrated to Tunis following the French occupation of Algeria in 1830. During his studies at Zaytuna University, Thaalbi became conversant with Salafiyya concepts. For a year following his graduation from Zaytuna in 1895, he published a religious journal called *Sabil al-Rashid* (the Proper Path). When the French authorities suspended the journal, Thaalbi left the country and traveled in Libya, Egypt, and India until 1902. Soon after his return to Tunis, he was imprisoned by a beylical tribunal for making a reformist attack on the local saints, who formed an important part of popular religious practices. In 1904, he published, in both an Arabic and a French edition, *L'esprit libérale du Coran* (The liberal spirit of the Qur'an), which criticized the religious establishment. At this time, Thaalbi established links with the Young Tunisians. He became the editor of the Arabic edition of its newspaper, *Le Tunisien,* in 1909 and participated in all of its political activities until his expulsion from Tunisia in 1912. He returned to the country at the start of World War I.

At the end of the war, Thaalbi joined a delegation of former Young Tunisians that went to Versailles to petition the Allies for a relaxation of French control. Frustrated by France's unwillingness to make concessions, Thaalbi wrote *La Tunisie martyre* (Tunisia martyred) in early 1920. In this book, he stressed the need for restoration of the Tunisian constitution of 1861, the creation of an elected assembly and an independent judiciary, the development of education, and the safeguarding of individual liberties. He also urged that the establishment of the protectorate had stalled Tunisian development. Thaalbi was arrested and brought back to Tunisia. Upon his release in 1921, he assumed the leadership of a group of middle-class merchants, artisans, and lower level *ulama,* many of them formerly affiliated with the Young Tunisians, that had evolved into a political party, the Destour, based on the program elaborated in *La Tunisie martyre.*

In response to Destour demands, France introduced a series of limited reforms in 1922. Thaalbi guided Destour's rejection of these changes, arguing that they fell too far short of Tunisian requirements to merit consideration. The death in 1923 of the Tunisian ruler Nasir Bey, who had sympathized with Destour, and the growing impatience of the protectorate authorities with the party convinced Thaalbi that his political activism would not be tolerated much longer, and he fled the country in the same year.

After fourteen years of exile in Egypt, Iraq, and India, he returned in 1937, when the relative liberalism of the French Popular Front government created a more congenial atmosphere for the expression of nationalist grievances. By that time, however, the remnants of Thaalbi's Destour party had given way to the Neo-Destour, whose youthful, dynamic, and secular leaders had little use for Thaalbi or for the traditional Arab-Islamic values he stressed. Finding support among only a small segment of the population and encountering opposition from Neo-Destour militants who disrupted his public appearances, Thaalbi attempted to revive Destour but failed miserably, though the party survived in moribund form until his death in 1944.

See also SALAFIYYA MOVEMENT.

KENNETH J. PERKINS

THALWEG LINE

See GLOSSARY

THARTHAR PROJECT

Reservoir constructed in eastern Iraq to control flooding and provide irrigation.

The Wadi al-Tharthar is a vast natural depression forty-two miles (68 km) southwest of Samarra and one hundred miles (160 km) north of Baghdad between the Tigris and Euphrates rivers. The Iraqi Development Board, on the recommendation of the International Bank for Reconstruction and Development, created an enormous storage reservoir in the Wadi al-Tharthar depression to drain runoff from the Tigris and thereby protect Baghdad from flooding. Staged construction of the reservoir, the largest earth-moving project of its kind in the Middle East, began in 1952. A regulator built on the Tigris near Samarra diverted excess water into the reservoir, which was also connected by a channel with the Euphrates. By 1972, with a capacity of 110 billion cubic yards (85 billion cu. m) when filled to a height of 200 feet (60 m) above sea level, the water contained in the reservoir could be used to irrigate nearly half a million acres (200,000 ha) of land.

Bibliography

Salter, Lord. *The Development of Iraq: A Plan of Action.* London, 1955.

ALBERTINE JWAIDEH

THARWAT, ABD AL-KHALIQ
[1873–1928]

Egyptian politician.

A graduate of the School of Law in Cairo, Abd al-Khaliq Tharwat was one of the first Egyptian nationalist leaders and a founder of the Liberal Constitutionalist Party. His negotiations with Britain's high commissioner for Egypt, Edmund Allenby, led to the declaration of Egyptian independence from Britain in 1922. Tharwat supported the declaration, even though it guaranteed the maintenance of British influence in Egypt, because he believed that it made possible the drafting of a constitution and the establishment of parliamentary politics. He formed the first government following the declaration and helped to draft the post-independence constitution. Tharwat was opposed by Sultan Fu'ad, who objected to being reduced to a constitutional monarch, and by the Wafd party, which objected to the preservation of British control. Tharwat resigned as prime minister in November 1922. He formed a second ministry in April 1927, but again confronted opposition from Fu'ad—who had taken the title of king in 1922—and the Wafd. He resigned in February 1928.

See also LIBERAL CONSTITUTIONALIST PARTY.

Bibliography

Sayyid-Marsot, Afaf Lutfi al-. *Egypt's Liberal Experiment, 1922–1936.* Berkeley: University of California Press, 1977.

DAVID WALDNER

THAWRA, AL- (IRAQ)

See NEWSPAPERS AND PRINT MEDIA: ARAB COUNTRIES

THAWRA, AL- (SYRIA)

See NEWSPAPERS AND PRINT MEDIA: ARAB COUNTRIES

THEATER

Overview of the region's numerous traditional and indigenous dramatic art forms and performances.

The Middle East comprises four regions: The Arab world (22 countries), Iran, Turkey, and Israel. This area did not know theater (in the Western sense of a space containing stage and auditorium, and dramas with the three unities of time, space, and plot) in its pre-modern periods. However, the whole region had numerous traditional and indigenous dramatic art forms and performances. Through colonialism and cultural exchanges with Europe in the early nineteenth century, theater as a space and a mode of writing and presenting found its way into the various Middle Eastern cultures. In the modern period, as a form of cultural identity, many Middle Eastern theater artists have tried to honor their traditional art forms and rituals by incorporating aspects of them with their stage events. This endeavor is a prevalent feature, and an ongoing trend, in Middle Eastern theater.

Arab Theater

The ancient Arab literary tradition did not encompass dramatic texts; however, the countries that constitute today's Arab world have always incorporated dramatic and mimetic arts within their performance and literary traditions. Among the various Arab performance arts that thrived throughout the premodern periods are *al-hakawati* (storytellers), dance, ritual reenactments, shadow plays, puppetry, poetry recitations, *maqama* (outdoor dramatic enactments in poetry and prose), street performance by traveling troupes called *al-muhabizun,* and *al-samir* (village gatherings that included dramatizations). Many of these art forms continue, albeit in a state of decline, but others have died away as a result of competing modern entertainment.

In the nineteenth century, contact with the European theatrical tradition through colonialism, educational exchanges, and translations sparked a theatrical movement in the Arab world. In 1848, the Lebanese writer Marun al-Naqqash (d. 1855) mounted in his own home performances of plays based on Molière's dramas as well as adaptations of tales from *A Thousand and One Nights.* This process was continued in Damascus by Abu Khalil al-Qabbani (d. 1902), whose attempts to stage dramatic performances aroused the opposition of the religious establishment. Al-Qabbani moved to Egypt, where artists were able to exercise more freedom.

In Egypt, Yaʿqub Sanu (d. 1912), considered by many the father of Egyptian theater, formed a troupe of actors and in 1870 opened the first Egyptian playhouse under the auspices of the khedive. Sanu wrote and directed his own plays and introduced women to the Egyptian stage for the first time. His theater was an immediate success but was closed down by the authorities in 1873 on the grounds that his plays were politically subversive.

By the turn of the century, many theater troupes were presenting musicals, dramatic adaptations, and Arabizations of world drama, but no original plays in Arabic. A number of Egyptian poets wrote verse dramas; among them was the poet laureate of Egypt, Ahmad Shawqi. However, those plays were not stage successes, since their poetic merit exceeded their dramatic construction.

The towering figure of prose drama in Egypt and the Arab world is Tawfiq al-Hakim (1898–1986). His family sent him to France to obtain a doctorate in law. Instead, he spent his time there learning the Western theater tradition. When he returned to Egypt, he took up writing for the stage. His dearest wish was to establish a modern Egyptian dramatic tradition based on Western notions of the unity of space, time, and action. He spent five decades of his life working to enrich the Arab dramatic tradition, and enrich it he did. He wrote more than seventy plays of exceptional variety, experimenting with dramatic form and offering various dramatic styles. He also presented a variety of dramatic themes, some of which he categorized as the theater of ideas, the theater of social themes, and the theater of the absurd.

During the second half of the nineteenth century, many young playwrights emerged, theaters were built, and theater troupes were established around the Arab world. The 1960s is regarded as the golden age of Arabic theater for its impressive theatrical movement, which gave rise to great playwrights, actors, and directors throughout the region, including Nuʿman Ashur, Yusuf Idris, Alfred Farag, Mikhaʾil Ruman, and Najib Surur in Egypt; Saʿdallah Wannus, Walid Ikhlassi, and Yusuf al-Ani in Syria and Iraq; Isam Mahfuz and Roger Assaf in Lebanon; and Izz al-Din al-Madani, Ahmad al-Ilj, and al-Tayyib al-Siddiqi in the Maghrib.

In Palestine, under the watchful eye of the Israeli armed forces, theater troupes like the Balalin and Hakawati have produced highly experimental dramas that comment on the plight of their fellow countrymen. Alongside the male dramatists, directors, and critics, a large number of Arab women have contributed to the modern Arab stage, including playwrights Fathiyya al-Assal, Nehad Gad, Andre Chided, and Nawal al-Saadawi; director Nidal al-Ashqar; and critic Nehad Selaiha.

Israeli Theater

The Israeli theater is essentially modern; whereas pre-1960s theater was heavily influenced by Russian social realism, in the 1960s it diverged and presented experimental drama. Until the early 1970s, most of the theatrical repertoire in Israel continued to be European classics and modern plays. However, in the 1970s and 1980s, playwrights focused more on the contemporary Israeli's predicament and identity. From the 1980s onward a shift became noticeable in the Hebrew stage, from a commitment to the ideology of the Jewish national

The courtyard and entrance to the Jerusalem Center for the Performing Arts in Jerusalem, Israel. © DAVE G. HOUSER/CORBIS. REPRODUCED BY PERMISSION.

movement to debates over secularization and cultural identity.

After the 1948 war, two Israeli playwrights rose to prominence in the newly established state. In 1949, Moshe Shamir wrote *Hu Halah Basdot* (He walked in the fields), and Yigal Mossinsohn produced *Be'arvot Hanegev* (In the plains of the Negev). The first is a stage adaptation of a novel—a prevalent practice in late 1940s and 1950s Israel due to the limited number of playwrights. The second is a war story that tries to uphold the ideals of the new Israeli society; its success was based more on audience reaction then than on artistic excellence.

In the 1950s, Israeli theater focused on realism and produced plays concerned with the social realities of Israel after the 1948 war. One of the major themes that preoccupied dramatists was the realities of coexistence between early and new immigrants, and between Palestinians and Israelis. Some of the playwrights who tackled these issues were Ephraim Kishon, Yigal Mossinsohn, and Hanoch Bar-Tov.

In the 1960s, Israeli theater departed from realism and created a non-mimetic experimental theater, opening itself to the influence of modern European drama as well as to new themes, forms, and theatrical devices. Using techniques from the Theater of the Absurd, Israeli playwrights set out to depict the grotesque and absurd in their society. Without reference to particulars, their criticism was conveyed through abstractions, symbolism, and distancing techniques. Among the most talented playwrights of that decade are Nessim Aloni (b. 1921), Ben-Zion Tomer (b. 1928), Yosef Bar-Yosef (b. 1933), and A. B. Yehoshua (b. 1936). Their efforts propelled Israeli theater away from a provincial outlook to universal themes.

In the 1970s, Israeli theater became self-reflective and began expressing doubts about the means of realizing the Zionist dream. For some, those were introspective years of self-reevaluation. Two new stars became the focus of the Israeli stage: Yehoshua Sobol (b. 1939) and Hanoch Levin (b. 1943). Sobol's writing style is naturalistic. Some of his earlier works are semifictitious and based on documentary material. Levin, on the other hand, is famous for his biting satire and tendency to break taboos. He continues to be one of the most provocative and controversial figures in Israeli theater.

The following decades show a variety of dramatic themes and approaches, from social and political disillusionment, as many Israelis call for an alternative to war, to fears about the demise of the Zionist dream. Common themes include nationhood, selfhood, and secularization. In addition, many theaters continue to present world classics and modern comedies. At the top of the list of thriving theater companies in Israel are the Habima (also ha-Bima), the Cameri, and the Haifa Municipal Theaters.

Persian Theater

Persian theater can be divided into three categories: traditional, which comprises ritual reenactments, puppetry, and improvised street theater; modern, which is primarily modeled on Western paradigms; and diasporic, which laments the separation from the homeland after the 1979 revolution.

The most famous traditional Persian theater is Taʿziyeh, which encompasses cycles of passion plays intended not for entertainment but rather to console the devout Shiʿite population by reenacting the events that led to the martyrdom of their beloved imam (spiritual leader) Husayn, grandson of the Prophet. The house of Husayn in its entirety was decimated in the city of Karbala, in Iraq, by Muʿawiyah, the governor of Syria, who the Shiʿa believe usurped the throne from Ali, Husayn's father, closest cousin and confidant of the Prophet. The suffering and death of this holy family is the central theme of elaborate mourning rites, in Iran and wherever there is a considerable Shiʿite population. Those rites take place on the tenth day of Muharram, the first month of the Islamic calendar.

Two categories of Taʿziyeh plays deal with the tragic events of Karbala, and others refer to those events indirectly. However, those dealing with the martyrdom of Husayn and his family are the most popular and moving. Taʿziyeh is written in verse by anonymous writers and its stagecraft is extremely simple, with virtually no scenery. Settings are indicated symbolically, and men play the women's roles. The most important component of these plays is the music: Players chant and sing, and musical instruments are used to heighten the mood. Although professional Taʿziyeh players exist, the plays are frequently presented by amateurs as an act of piety.

By the turn of the twentieth century, and as a result of Western impact, Taʿziyeh went into a decline. Today, there is a great deal of interest in the performance and study of Taʿziyeh, both inside and outside of Iran.

During the early nineteenth century, Western drama found its way into Persian culture in the form of translations of European and Turkish plays. This was followed by a period of Persian dramatic and satirical composition that took reform as its main subject matter. During the first half of the twentieth century, a number of didactic dramas upholding the modernizing and educational efforts of Reza Shah Pahlavi were on the rise. Among the most popular playwrights of this period are Sayyed Ali Nasr (1893–1965), who founded and headed the Komedi-e Iran in 1918, and Sadegh Hedayat (1903–1951).

The second half of the twentieth century was characterized by severe censorship, which led playwrights to find refuge in symbolism, Theater of the Absurd, and psychological themes. Gifted playwrights emerged during this period and produced exciting works. Among them are Ali Nasirian, Gholamhossein Saʿedi (working under the pseudonym Gowhar Morad), and Bahram Beyzai.

After the 1979 revolution, a number of artists, disillusioned by the new regime, left the country with no intention of returning. Living in exile, they write dramas that are inherently Iranian and intensely nostalgic for the homeland. Among those is Parviz Sayyad, who continues to produce plays that have been categorized as theater of diaspora.

Turkish Theater

The first Western-style Turkish play performed in Istanbul was *Vatan yahut Silistre* (Fatherland), by Namik Kemal, in 1873. From that date onward theater in

Turkey following the Western paradigm was a vital element in the country's cultural life.

Turkey has been home to a wide array of popular performance arts and entertainments since the thirteenth century, including dances, peasant plays, pageants, rites, processions, mock fights, festival acts, acrobatics, mime, puppetry, marionette performances, clowning, juggling, and magic. The most dramatic and popular of all are the *meddahs* (who are panegyrists, storytellers, and comedians), *karagoz* (shadow plays), and *ortaoyunus* (improvised plays). *Meddahs* were solo performers who told traditional tales of heroism and religious narratives. *Karagoz,* have the longest history and continued to be practiced until the 1940s. They are being resurrected in many contemporary plays. They were essentially a one-man act. The presenter manipulated flat leather figures behind a linen screen and played all characters. *Ortaoyunu,* the indigenous Turkish theater-in-the-round, is the most mimetic premodern performance art form. It borrowed many of its basic plots and characters from the *karagoz,* and the actors performed in the middle of a circle of spectators. The characters were presented as stereotypes, depending on wordplay and comic situations. All three ancient art forms had declined severely by the early twentieth century due to competition from Western-style theater and cinema.

The second half of the nineteenth century introduced Western theater into Turkey. A number of local theater troupes were created, mainly by Armenians, and they presented European plays in both their original languages and in translation. The first Turkish play published was *Shair Evlenmesi* (The poet's marriage, in 1860), by Ibrahim Shinasi, and the first produced on stage was *Fatherland.* In spite of the quick strides that playwrights made by the late nineteenth century, severe censorship by the sultan slowed the progress of Turkish drama. However, theater was given new vigor in 1908 by an era of political freedom under a constitutional government. Until 1923, Turkish theater featured a variety of new naturalistic and satirical plays reflecting social problems and expressing a need for political reform. One of the most celebrated playwrights of that period was Abdulhak Hamit (1852–1937), who produced verse and history plays. In 1916, the government-subsidized City Theater in Istanbul was established; it remained a vital core of Turkey's theatrical scene until the 1950s.

With the founding of the Turkish Republic under Mustafa Kemal Atatürk, theater received greater government support and funding. Mushin Ertuğrul, artistic director of the City Theater, shaped the modern theater movement in Turkey by creating a children's theater, encouraging young playwrights, and establishing a network of regional theaters. In 1936 the State Conservatory for Music and Drama was inaugurated, and in the 1940s the State Opera. Since the 1960s Turkey has established twenty-six state theaters in sixteen provinces, and state theaters are continually opening in Istanbul. In the 1950s and 1960s a number of private theaters were established in both Istanbul and Ankara.

In the 1960s, a number of excellent playwrights contributed to the Turkish stage, including Turan Oflazoglu, Necati Cumali, Gunger Dilmen, and Haldun Taner. In the 1970s and 1980s, the varying strengths and weaknesses of the Turkish theatrical scene reflected the political and economic situation. During the following two decades Turkish theater witnessed a rising number of experimental plays by a younger generation wishing to explore new ground and possibilities.

See also HAKIM, TAWFIQ AL-; HEDAYAT, SADEGH; IDRIS, YUSUF; IKHLASSI, WALID; SAADAWI, NAWAL AL-; SAʿEDI, GHOLAMHOSSEIN; SANU, YAʿQUB; SHAMIR, MOSHE; SHAWQI, AHMAD; SOBOL, YEHOSHUA; TANER, HALDUN.

Bibliography

Allen, Roger. *An Introduction to Arabic Literature.* Cambridge, U.K.: Cambridge University Press, 2000.

And, Metin. *A History of Theatre and Popular Entertainment in Turkey.* Ankara: Forum Yayinlan, 1963.

And, Metin. *Karagoz: Turkish Shadow Theatre.* Ankara: Dost Yayinlari, 1975.

Badawi, Muhammad Mustafa. *Early Arabic Drama.* Cambridge, U.K.: Cambridge University Press, 1988.

Badawi, Muhammad Mustafa. *Modern Arabic Drama in Egypt.* Cambridge, U.K.: Cambridge University Press, 1987.

Ben-Zvi, Linda, ed. *Theater in Israel.* Ann Arbor: University of Michigan Press, 1996.

Chelkowsky, Peter, ed. *Ta'ziyeh, Ritual and Drama in Iran.* New York: New York University Press, 1979.

Gouryh, Admer. "Recent Trends in Syrian Drama." *World Literature Today* 60, No. 2 (spring 1986): 216–221.

Halman, Talat Sait, ed. *Modern Turkish Drama: An Anthology of Plays in Translation.* Minneapolis, MN: Bibliotheca Islamica, 1976.

Jaffery, Yunus, ed. *History of Persian Literature.* Delhi: Triveni, 1981.

Khozai, Mohamed A. al-. *The Development of Early Arabic Drama, 1847–1900.* London: Longman, 1984.

Offer, Rita. *Literature in Pre-Revolutionary Iran: Golshiri's Prose Fiction,* 1983.

Ricks, Thomas, ed. *Critical Perspectives on Modern Persian Literature.* Washington, DC: Three Continents, 1984.

Sayyad, Parviz. *Theater of Diaspora: Two Plays, The Ass and The Rex Cinema Trial,* edited by Hamid Dabashi. Costa Mesa, CA: Mazda, 1992.

Urian, Dan. *The Arab in Israeli Drama and Theater,* translated by Naomi Paz. Amsterdam: Harwood, 1997.

Urian, Dan. *The Judaic Nature of Israeli Theatre: A Search for Identity,* translated by Naomi Paz. Amsterdam: Harwood, 2000.

DINA AMIN

THEATER, ARAB

See THEATER

THEATER, ISRAELI

See THEATER

TIBERIAS

Town located on the eastern shore of Lake Tiberias (also referred to as the Sea of Galilee or Kinneret) in northern Israel.

The town of Tiberias was founded by Herod Antipas (c. 20 C.E.) and named for the Roman emperor Tiberius. It was an important center of Jewish learning, law, and religion from the second through fifth centuries. Over the course of its history, Tiberias was controlled by Arabs, Crusaders, and Ottoman Turks. Early Zionist pioneers set up kibbutzim in this area around the turn of the twentieth century. The city's population quadrupled after the establishment of the state of Israel in 1948. In the 1948 Arab-Israel War, fighting broke out with an Arab attack on Jews in the older sections of the town. Jewish fighters were able to push out their Arab adversaries, and eventually the Arab inhabitants fled.

Tiberias, which has a relatively warm climate in winter, is a favorite tourist site, featuring boating, lakefront hotels, and a hot springs spa. Its 2004 population was about 43,000, the majority of them immigrants from North African and Eastern European countries.

BRYAN DAVES

TIGRIS AND EUPHRATES RIVERS

River systems that join to drain into the Persian Gulf.

The Tigris (Arabic, *Shatt Dijla*; Turkish, *Dicle*) rises in a lake in the mountains north of Diyarbakir, in southeastern Turkey. It picks up major tributaries, the Zab rivers, downstream from Mosul, then the Diyala, just past Baghdad—flowing some 1,180 miles (1,900 km). It ends at the confluence of the Euphrates, in southeast Iraq, to form the Shatt al-Arab, which empties into the Gulf. With its short tributaries flowing directly from the mountains, it floods in April, about one month before the Euphrates, and with about 50 percent greater flow.

The Euphrates (Arabic, *Furat*; Turkish, *Firat*) also originates in Turkey, from a spring in the Taurus mountains. It flows for 1,740 miles (2,800 km), passing through northern Syria and providing that country with an important water source. In 1973, Syria completed construction of the large Euphrates Dam. From Syria, the Euphrates flows into Iraq, where it joins the Tigris.

Since the Sumerian era (3500 B.C.E.), canals have connected tributaries to the Tigris-Euphrates confluence area, although the lower course was farther west at that time. The capitals of great empires—Ashur, Nineveh, Seleucia, Ctesiphon, and Baghdad—were built on or near its banks. In 1990, Turkey completed the Atatürk Dam, the first of twenty-two dams, as well as a series of hydroelectric power stations, planned for the Tigris and Euphrates. Turkey's huge diversion of water may pose serious problems for countries such as Syria and Iraq. Most of Iraq's future irrigation schemes rely on Tigris water.

Bibliography

Shapland, Greg. *Rivers of Discord: International Water Disputes in the Middle East.* New York: St. Martin's, 1997.

JOHN R. CLARK

TIKRIT

Iraqi city on the Tigris River northwest of Baghdad, on the main road to Mosul.

Tikrit (also Takrit) is located in north-central Iraq, some 100 miles north-northwest of Baghdad. The fortress around which the city was built was constructed by a Sassanid Persian king as a border post against the Byzantines. The first dwellers of the city belonged to the Banu Iyad tribe of Christian Arabs, and its name is believed to have honored the tribal chief's daughter. It was conquered by Muslims in the mid-600s C.E. Tikrit's population is now mainly Sunni Arab, with some Kurds. The Kurdish Muslim hero Salah al-Din al-Ayyubi (Saladin, 1137–1193) was born in Tikrit.

With the decline in sales of *kalaks* (rafts of inflated skins), for which the city was noted, many people moved to Baghdad during the nineteenth century. Under the monarchy, some entered the military academy with the help of an influential Tikriti. After the 1968 coup by the Baʿth party, Tikritis became the single most powerful group in Iraq's senior officer corps and in the civilian flank of the party. Both Ahmad Hasan al-Bakr and Saddam Hussein were from Tikrit, so they invested large sums in modernizing the city. In 2003, its population numbered about 30,000.

See also BAKR, AHMAD HASAN AL-; BAʿTH, AL-; HUSSEIN, SADDAM.

Bibliography

Batatu, Hanna. *The Old Social Classes and the Revolutionary Movements of Iraq: A Study of Iraq's Old Landed and Commercial Classes and of Its Communists, Baʿthists, and Free Officers.* Princeton, NJ: Princeton University Press, 1978.

AMATZIA BARAM
UPDATED BY MICHAEL R. FISCHBACH

TIKRITI FAMILIES

Iraqi families from Tikrit.

The Tikriti trace their origins to the city of Tikrit in Iraq. Tikrit is located on the Tigris River halfway between Baghdad and Mosul, and has a rich history that goes back to the Assyrian empire. The famous Muslim leader Saladin, who defeated the Crusaders, was born in Tikrit. In recent history, Tikrit was a small, sleepy town with a few thousand inhabitants.

The military coup of 1963 temporarily brought to power a few people who were born in Tikrit. Hasan al-Bakr, who became prime minister, and Hardan al-Tikriti, who became a defense minister, were born in Tikrit. The coup of 1968 brought to power more people from Tikrit, who controlled and shaped Iraqi politics from 1968 until the U.S. invasion of Iraq in March 2003.

The most prominent one was Saddam Hussein, who dominated Iraqi politics after 1968, and was born on 28 April 1937 in the small village of al-Awja, a village that belongs to the city of Tikrit. Like many other Tikritis, he belonged to the Al Abu Nasir tribe. He was vice president of Iraq until 1979, when he became president. He was removed from office when the United States invaded Iraq in 2003.

Hussein relied heavily on his immediate family, close relatives, and members of his tribe to govern the country, putting them into top positions in the bureaucracy, the armed forces, the police forces, and the local governments. In most cases, they were chosen mainly for their loyalty rather than for their skills and qualifications. During the Hussein regime, Tikrit was transformed into a large modern city with a university, modern facilities, and services. It also became the capital of the newly established province of Salah al-Din in the early 1980s.

See also BAKR, AHMAD HASAN AL-; HUSSEIN, SADDAM; TIKRIT; TIKRITI, HARDAN AL-.

Bibliography

Marr, Phebe. *The Modern History of Iraq,* 2d edition. Boulder, CO: Westview Press, 1985.

Tripp, Charles. *A History of Iraq.* Cambridge, U.K.: Cambridge University Press, 2000.

AYAD AL-QAZZAZ

TIKRITI, HARDAN AL-

[1925–1971]

Iraqi military officer and official of the Baʿth party.

Born in Tikrit to the family of a Sunni Arab police officer, Hardan al-Tikriti graduated from both flight and staff academies. He also joined the Baʿth party in 1961. After the Ramadan Revolution, from February to November 1963, he commanded the Iraqi air force. After the second Baʿthist coup of July 1968, he served as deputy commander in chief of the armed forces, deputy prime minister, minister of defense, and member of the Revolutionary Command Council. In 1970, after a power struggle with his two distant relatives, Ahmad Hasan al-Bakr and Saddam Hussein, he was dismissed from his posts and promoted to the ceremonial position of vice president. He was then formally dismissed and exiled. He was assassinated in Kuwait in 1971 by Hussein's agents.

See also BAKR, AHMAD HASAN AL-; BAʿTH, AL-; HUSSEIN, SADDAM.

Bibliography

Batatu, Hanna. *The Old Social Classes and the Revolutionary Movements of Iraq: A Study of Iraq's Old Landed and Commercial Classes and of its Communists, Baʿthists, and Free Officers.* Princeton, NJ: Princeton University Press, 1978.

AMATZIA BARAM
UPDATED BY MICHAEL R. FISCHBACH

TIMAR

Land rights earned in exchange for service to the Ottoman state.

The *timar* system began under Murad I (1359–1389), who granted land rights as payment to his military officers. In the fifteenth and sixteenth centuries timars became the primary means of financing the Ottoman military. The typical timar holder was a provincial cavalry officer who contributed troops and supplies when called up for battle. He financed these through his timar, a state grant of nonhereditary rights over land, usually in the village where he lived. The officer kept a set amount of the tax revenue as his salary and delivered the remainder to the central state.

With economic and technological change in the late sixteenth and seventeenth centuries, tax farms gradually supplanted timars. The state confiscated timars from officers who died or could no longer afford to send troops, and reassigned them to notables who would contract to collect taxes in exchange for monetary compensation. Although they contributed less and less to imperial tax revenues, timars continued to exist on a small scale through the nineteenth century.

Bibliography

Karpat, Kemal H. "The Land Regime, Social Structure, and Modernization in the Ottoman Empire." In *The Beginnings of Modernization in the Middle East: The Nineteenth Century,* edited by William R. Polk and Richard L. Chambers. Chicago: University of Chicago Press, 1968.

Keyder, Çağlar, and Tabak, Faruk, eds. *Landholding and Commercial Agriculture in the Middle East.* Albany: State University of New York Press, 1991.

ELIZABETH THOMPSON
UPDATED BY ERIC HOOGLUND

TINDOUF

A strategically important Saharan town in western Algeria, situated near large mineral deposits.

Tindouf is close to Algeria's borders with Mauritania, Morocco, and Western Sahara. It was an administrative outpost built largely by the French colonial government and became a political and economic hub in the years after Algeria gained independence from France in 1962. Rich deposits of phosphates and iron ore dominate the region, particularly at Gara Djebilet, 93 miles (150 km) to the southeast. Tindouf became the capital of the Western Saharan government-in-exile after Morocco's invasion of what was then the Spanish Sahara in 1975 and 1976. Both Algeria and Libya assisted POLISARIO (Frente Popular para la Liberación de Saguia el Hamra y Río de Oro) in its bid for an independent state, which froze relations between Algeria and Morocco throughout the 1980s and 1990s. Since then, oil and natural gas deposits discovered nearby have increased Tindouf's importance in regional politics and economic development. The Algerian government signed exploratory agreements with major European energy companies in the early 2000s for the Tindouf basin, and Morocco signed similar agreements with American energy companies for Western Sahara. This heightened competition over natural resources threatened what had been improving relations between Algeria and Morocco as well as the fragile cease-fire agreement between Morocco and POLISARIO.

The 1998 Algerian census estimated Tindouf's population at 27,000. However, this figure does not include the nearby refugee camps, which are estimated to house 180,000 Reguibat refugees from Western Sahara.

See also ALGERIA: OVERVIEW; ARAB MAGHREB UNION; POLISARIO; WESTERN SAHARA; WESTERN SAHARA WAR.

Bibliography

Hodges, Tony. *Western Sahara: The Roots of a Desert War.* Westport, CT: L. Hill, 1983.

DAVID GUTELIUS

TIRAN, STRAIT OF

A strategic strait connecting the Gulf of Aqaba and the Red Sea.

The Strait of Tiran is barely 2.5 miles wide at one point; it provides narrow passage for ships traveling from the Red Sea to the Jordanian port of Aqaba and the Israeli port of Elat. Near the coast of the Sinai Peninsula at the mouth of the strait are several islands, including Tiran and Sanafir, that Saudi Arabia permitted Egypt to claim in 1949. Egypt subsequently asserted that its territorial waters extended across the strait, and closed the passage to ships bound for Elat on two occasions as part of its political and military conflict with Israel. The first instance, in the early 1950s, was one of the reasons for Israel's attack on the Sinai in 1956. The second blockade was established in May 1967 and precipitated the 1967 War. Israel occupied the islands and reopened the straits to its ships after the war. As a result of the peace treaty between Egypt and Israel in 1979, the Strait of Tiran was recognized as an international waterway. Israel relinquished the islands to Egypt in 1982 as part of its withdrawal from the territories it had occupied in the Sinai in 1967.

See also SUEZ CRISIS (1956–1957).

Bibliography

Drysdale, Alasdair, and Blake, Gerald H. *The Middle East and North Africa: A Political Geography.* New York: Oxford University Press, 1985.

ANTHONY B. TOTH

TISHRIN

See GLOSSARY

TIWIZI

See GLOSSARY

TLAS, MUSTAFA

[1932–]

Syrian military officer and politician.

Born in al-Rastan, near Homs, Mustafa Abd al-Qadir Tlas attended Syria's military academy in Homs (1952–1954). Commissioned in the tank corps, he served in Egypt (1959–1961) during the period of the United Arab Republic.

Tlas joined the Baʿth Party in 1947. The Baʿthist military committee that overthrew Syria's government in 1963 brought him into its ranks after the coup. Tlas was granted important positions through which he proved his loyalty to the party and the military committee. He was elected to the Regional Council of the Baʿth Party in 1965 and headed courts trying persons accused of plotting against the regime, including the regime established following the 1964 anti-Baʿthist violence in Hama. As commander of the garrison at Homs in 1965, Tlas was associated with the "radical" faction of the Baʿth during the period of growing intra-Baʿthist friction. Removed from his post in December 1965 after trying to dismiss officers loyal to President Amin al-Hafiz, Tlas returned to the military after Salah Jadid's "radical Baʿth" coup in 1966.

Tlas's most important contribution in Syrian history, however,lies in his long-standing and loyal association with the powerful Baʿthist figure Hafiz al-Asad. Tlas and Asad studied together in the military academy and came from similar backgrounds. Although Tlas was a Sunni Muslim and Asad an Alawi, both were of humble village origins and both supported the secular, pan-Arab socialist ideology of the Baʿth. As Asad's confidant, Tlas quickly rose to high positions in the military and the regime. While defense minister, Asad appointed Tlas chief of staff and deputy defense minister (1968). When Baʿthist rivals tried to depose the two in 1970, Asad seized power, and he appointed Tlas defense minister in 1972. Tlas has been Syria's defense minister since then, overseeing tremendous growth in the size and technological sophistication of the nation's military through Soviet assistance in the 1970s and 1980s. In 1972, he attended staff training at Voroshilov Academy in Moscow. Elected to the Baʿth central committee in 1980, he remained a key member of the Asad regime until Asad's death in 2000, after which he continued as defense minister under Syria's new president, Asad's son Bashshar.

Tlas is known as an outspoken hard-liner in Syria's frosty relationship with the Palestine Liberation Organization (PLO) and its chairman, Yasir Arafat, since the mid-1970s. Tlas and Syria's military had assisted guerrillas from Arafat's al-Fatah movement in the 1960s and during the PLO's conflict with Jordan in 1970, but he became increasingly hostile to Arafat after Syria intervened against the PLO in Lebanon's civil war in 1976 and the bitter Syria-PLO relations that followed.

Tlas runs a publishing house, Dar al-Tlas, in Damascus, and has written numerous books on military science, literature, and other topics.

See also ALAWI; ARAFAT, YASIR; ASAD, BASHSHAR AL-; ASAD, HAFIZ AL-; BAʿTH, AL-; FATAH, AL-; HAFIZ, AMIN AL-; HAMA; HOMS; JADID, SALAH; PALESTINE LIBERATION ORGANIZATION (PLO); SUNNI ISLAM; UNITED ARAB REPUBLIC (UAR).

Bibliography

Batatu, Hanna. *Syria's Peasantry, the Descendants of Its Rural Notables, and Their Politics.* Princeton, NJ: Princeton University Press, 1999.

Seale, Patrick. *Asad: The Struggle for the Middle East.* Berkeley: University of California Press, 1988.

MICHAEL R. FISCHBACH

TLATLI, MOUFIDA

[1947–]

Tunisian film director, editor, and screenwriter.

Moufida Tlatli was born in 1947 in picturesque Sidi Bou Said, Tunisia. Following her graduation from the Institut des Hautes Etudes Cinématographiques (IDHEC) in Paris, Tlatli worked as a writer and production manager for the Office de la Radiodiffusion-Télévision Française (ORTF) from 1968 to 1972. Returning to Tunisia, Tlatli edited and wrote screenplays for a number of important Arab films, such as Allouache's *Omar Gatlato,* Ben Ammar's *Aziza,* Louhichi's *L'ombre de la terre,* and Boughedir's *Halfaouine.* Tlatli's own award-winning first film, *Les Silences du palais* (Samt al Qusur, 1994), which takes place on the eve of independence from the French in the 1950s, traces the systemic and internalized oppression suffered by generations of servant women working in the kitchens of the Bey's relatives. Like *Silences,* Tlatli's second film, *La saison des hommes* (2000), set on the island of Djerba, focuses on mothers and daughters confronting patriarchal traditions, now exacerbated by economic pressures that have made their husbands internal migrants who come home one month a year. Tlatli's rich, sensuous imagery, slow rhythms, and retrospective narrative structures translate unspoken feelings of isolation and desire into the body language of women who long to emancipate themselves—not from Tunisian men or Arab culture, but from the everyday practices and social systems, both local and global, that entrap them.

See also FILM; GENDER: GENDER AND EDUCATION.

LAURA RICE

TLEMCEN

City near the Moroccan border in eastern Algeria.

Situated on a high ridge of the Little Atlas mountains thirty miles (50 km) inland from the Mediterranean Sea, Tlemcen has a population of 155,000 (1998). The Almoravids founded Tlemcen in the eleventh century, on an ancient Berber, Phoenician, and Roman site. It was an important trade and political center in the Middle Ages, as capital of the Arab sultanate, and was Abd al-Qadir's capital from 1837 to 1842, when it came under French colonial rule. Tlemcen had received many of the Moors expelled from Spain after 1492. The city came under the Ottoman Empire in 1555 and was attached to Algeria in 1942.

LAURENCE MICHALAK

TLILI, MUSTAFA

[1937–]

Tunisian novelist.

Mustafa Tlili was born in Fériana, Tunisia. He attended the *madrasa* (traditional school) in his native city and later received a bilingual education at the Sorbonne, where he received a *diplôme d'études supérieurs de philosophie.* He also studied at the UN Institute for Training and Research and worked for almost thirteen years at the UN offices in New York. He moved to France in 1980, and he was made a Knight of the French Order of Arts and Letters.

Tlili has published four novels, all written in French. Each reflects in its own way the writer's preoccupation with life's meaning. He is determined to denounce corruption, especially among the aristocracy, whether in the Arabian Peninsula, as revealed in *Gloire des sables* (1982; Glory of the sands); in Paris, as described in *La rage aux tripes* (1975; Visceral anger); or in New York, as in *Le bruit dort* (1978; The noise sleeps). Tlili's fourth and last novel, *La montagne du lion* (1988; Lion mountain), centers on corruption in Tunisia. Tlili's language reflects a playful anger and humorous cynicism toward the upper classes of society.

In spite of Tlili's global outlook, he remains strongly linked to the Maghrib. His multilingual and multicultural background enhances his novels and reflects a new trend among Maghribi writers who write in French: Instead of being confined to two cultures—Arabic and French—as their predecessors were, they are expanding their horizons. With Tlili it is possible to speak of the beginning of the cultural liberation of the French-educated Maghribi writers.

See also LITERATURE: ARABIC, NORTH AFRICAN.

Bibliography

Jack, Belinda. *Francophone Literatures. An Introductory Survey.* New York: Oxford University Press, 1996.

Mortimer, Mildred, ed. *Maghrebian Mosaic.* Boulder, CO, and London: Lynne Rienner Publishers, 2001.

AIDA A. BAMIA

TOBACCO REVOLT

A popular rebellion (1891–1892) in Iran that defeated a tobacco monopoly granted to British interests.

One of the most controversial concessions that Iran's Qajar monarchy granted to foreign nationals in exchange for monetary compensation was a complete monopoly on the production, domestic sales, and export of tobacco. This was granted to Major G. F. Talbot of Britain and was registered in March 1890 as the Imperial Tobacco Corporation of Persia. Talbot agreed to pay 25,000 pounds immediately for the concession and to provide an annual payment of 15,000 pounds to the Imperial Treasury. This payment was to be accompanied by a 25 percent share of the net profits after deduction of a 5 percent shareholder's dividend. The arrangement was to be maintained for a period of fifty years.

Beginning in the spring of 1891 the implications of the monopoly became apparent to merchants and the Iranian population at large, the majority of whom consumed some form of tobacco on a daily basis, arousing nationalistic fervor. The void in leadership prompted the politicization of the intellectuals and the clergy. As the events of 1891 unfolded, the *ulama* (the clergy) successfully mobilized crowds against the government and its foreign policies. Under the leading *ulama,* protests began in Shiraz and Tabriz, principal market centers for domestic tobacco production, and then spread throughout the rest of the country. In Isfahan two leading *ulama,* Aqa Najafi and his brother Shaykh Muhammad Ali, pronounced the use of tobacco unclean as their followers took to the streets and broke all visible water pipes in the bazaars. In December the most prominent *mujtahid* (expert on Shiʿite Islamic law), Mirza Muhammad Hasan Shirazi, who resided in Ottoman Iraq, issued a *fatwa* (legal opinion) forbidding all forms of smoking until the tobacco concession was abolished. Shops throughout the bazaars closed and smoking was completely abandoned, even in the shah's own palace.

The value of the shares paid to the Imperial Bank was reduced by 50 percent. On Christmas Day, placards were hung throughout the Isfahan bazaar threatening a jihad against Europeans. Three days later, the shah announced the conditional withdrawal of the tobacco concession and requested that the population resume smoking. The suspicious crowds awaited word from Shirazi that the *fatwa* had been rescinded, but it did not arrive. The agitated shah, Naser al-Din, sent a personal letter to Tehran's leading *mujtahid,* Mirza Hasan Ashtiani, demanding that he immediately resume smoking or leave the country. As the news of the shah's message spread through the capital, the enraged crowds occupied the streets surrounding the shah's palace.

Fearing for the safety of the shah, the government's troops opened fire on the rioters, killing seven people, including the *sayyid* who originally had led the crowds. With the help of the merchants, Ashtiani and other *ulama* sent a strong message to Naser al-Din Shah and his prime minister, Amin al-Soltan. Realizing the severity of the situation, the shah in January 1892 abolished the concession completely, agreed to pay compensation to the families of those killed, and pardoned all leaders of the revolt. Shirazi telegraphed a few days later to say that Muslims could resume smoking.

See also SHIRAZI, MIRZA HASAN.

Bibliography

Browne, Edward G. *The Persian Revolution of 1905–1909.* Cambridge, U.K.: Cambridge University Press, 1910.

Keddie, Nikki. *Religion and Rebellion in Iran: The Tobacco Protest of 1891–1892.* London: Frank Cass, 1966.

Keddie, Nikki. *Sayyid Jamal ad-Din al-Afghani.* Berkeley: University of California Press, 1972.

Lambton, Ann K. S. "The Tobacco Regie: Prelude to Revolution." *Studia Islamica* 23 (1965): 71–90; 119–157.

ROSHANAK MALEK
UPDATED BY ERIC HOOGLUND

TOBRUK

Small Libyan seaport west of the Egyptian border; scene of fierce fighting during World War II.

Tobruk had been occupied by General Erwin Rommel's Afrika Korps but fell to British forces under General Archibald Wavell on 22 January 1941 during World War II. In April 1941, Rommel's counteroffensive left Tobruk under siege until December, when it was retaken by the British. Rommel's drive into Egypt in May 1942 led to the surrender of 25,000 troops at Tobruk on 21 June, after a one-day assault. Tobruk remained in German hands until liberated by General Bernard Law Montgomery's Eighth Army, after Britain's successful conclusion to the battle of al-Alamayn in November 1942.

In the 1960s, port facilities in the town were expanded to provide links to nearby oil fields. The population of Tobruk in 2004 was estimated at 157,800.

Bibliography

Pitt, Barrie. *The Crucible of War.* London: Cassell, 2001.

DANIEL E. SPECTOR

TOMAN

See GLOSSARY

TOPKAPI PALACE

Governmental seat of the Ottoman Empire.

The New Palace (Saray-Cedid), now known as the Topkapi Palace (in reference to the eighteenth-century royal summer residence next to the seaside Cannon Gate), occupied the site of Byzantium's ancient acropolis in what was then the city of Constantinople (now Istanbul). Enclosed by protective walls, the Topkapi Palace stood in the middle of a vast woodland. It served for nearly four centuries as the principal center of governance for the entire Ottoman Empire.

The administrative functions of the government were located in the outer *(birun)* court of the fortress-palace, and the inner *(enderun)* court included space for the royal pavilions and the palace school. The quarters for the sultan's pages surrounded the inner court; the harem quarters were behind its northern wall, overlooking the section of Istanbul known as the Golden Horn.

The Topkapi Palace lost its importance when the court moved to the Dolmabahçe Palace in 1854. After that date, aside from certain ceremonial occasions involving the holy relics of Islam (kept in the privy chamber), it hardly ever was used. Since its renovation in the 1930s, the Topkapi Palace has been a museum.

Bibliography

Necipoğlu, Gülrü. *Architecture, Ceremonial, and Power: The Topkapi Palace in the Fifteenth and Sixteenth Centuries.* New York: Architectural History Foundation, 1991.

APTULLAH KURAN
UPDATED BY ERIC HOOGLUND

TOUMI, KHALIDA

[1958–]

One of the pioneers of the feminist movement in Algeria.

Khalida Toumi was known as Khalida Messaoudi before she reclaimed her maiden name. She was born in 1958 in Sidi Ali Moussa, a village in the Kabylie region, and entered the University of Algiers in 1977 to pursue a degree in mathematics. After graduating from the École Normale Supérieure, she taught mathematics until 1993. In 1981, she founded the Collectif féminin (Women's Grouping) not only to oppose the ministerial interdiction on Algerian women leaving the country unless accompanied by a male family member, but also to oppose state endorsement of the discriminatory Family Code, which the National Assembly eventually adopted in 1984. Following the adoption of this code, Toumi presided over the Association for Equality between Men and Women, founded by a group of Trotskyite militants. In 1985, she cofounded and became a member of the executive committee of the Algerian League of Human Rights. She later distanced herself from the Trotskyite militants and in 1990 founded the Independent Association for the Triumph of Women's Rights. She staunchly opposed Islamist ideology and endorsed cancellation of the January 1992 legislative elections, which the Islamic Salvation Front (FIS) was poised to win. She considered the FIS to display "absolutely all the classic ingredients of totalitarian populist movements." During the years of terrorism in Algeria, she traveled to Western countries to provide an anti-Islamist perspective. A member of the Rassemblement pour la Culture et la Démocratie (RCD), she won a seat in the assembly and served as the RCD's national vice president for human rights and women's issues. After profound disagreements with the RCD's president Said Sadi, she severed relations with the RCD in January 2001, at the peak of the crisis in her native Kabylie; she was subsequently expelled from the RCD. In May 2002, she became minister of culture and communication, as well as the government's spokesperson, the first woman ever to hold that job. Khalida Toumi has in recent years lost her credibility as a staunch proponent of democracy because of her loyalty to President Abdelaziz Bouteflika, harshly criticized today for his authoritarianism and alliance with Islamists. The independent press and most advocates of democracy do not wish to see Bouteflika re-elected in April 2004.

See also ALGERIA: OVERVIEW; GENDER: GENDER AND POLITICS; KABYLIA; RASSEMBLEMENT POUR LA CULTURE ET LA DÉMOCRATIE (RCD); SADI, SAID.

Bibliography

Messaoudi, Khalida, with Schemla, Elisabeth. *Unbowed: An Algerian Woman Confronts Islamic Fundamentalism*, translated by Anne C. Vila. Philadelphia: University of Pennsylvania Press, 1998.

YAHIA ZOUBIR

TOURISM

An economic and social activity that has widely varying manifestations in the Middle East and North Africa.

Since the rise of civilization, the Middle East has been rich in notable sights and sites, and people have been visiting them for millennia. The Great Pyramids, the Hanging Gardens of Babylon, and places of religious significance such as Jerusalem and Mecca were drawing visitors long before the invention of the word *tourism*. And while travel for the purpose of seeing religious sites or carrying out religious obligations may be rightly termed "pilgrimage," the social and economic effects of this sort of travel are essentially indistinguishable from travel for purely secular reasons. If one accepts a broad definition of tourism, then it has been going on for centuries, on a large scale, to the region's many religious destinations. If one defines tourism more narrowly, as secular travel for the purposes of sightseeing and leisure on a scale large enough to be economically significant, then tourism, especially by Europeans, became important in the region only in the second half of the nineteenth century, when transportation methods improved and leisure time increased along with disposable income.

Europe's interest in the region historically had a religious component: Its Christians and Jews were keenly aware of the Holy Land, and much of the literature of European travelers to Palestine is intertwined with religious themes. Colonialism also drove European curiosity. The French and British occupations of parts of Egypt brought a flood of information about the land of the pharaohs. And with

Tourists take in the sights of Istanbul. Tourism is Turkey's second-largest source of foreign currency earnings, bringing in approximately US$10 billion a year. Upwards of thirteen million people typically visit Turkey annually, though recent terrorist activity in the country has severely curtailed those numbers. © DAVID KEATON/CORBIS. REPRODUCED BY PERMISSION.

the coming of steamship travel and the wealth and leisure generated by the industrial revolution in Europe, tourism as an organized industry spread from Europe to the Middle East. The first tours of Egypt from England were organized by Thomas Cook in 1868, and the first editions of Baedeker's guides for Palestine, Syria, and Egypt were published a few years later, first in German and later in French and English.

Early tourists were drawn by the region's sites of religious and historical importance, and today many still flock to such world treasures as the Great Pyramids at Giza, the Blue Mosque of Istanbul, and the old medina of Fez. As modern governments and private investors attempt to increase tourism revenues, they are adopting new strategies to attract visitors and keep them entertained. Egypt, Syria, Morocco, and some Persian Gulf countries have been developing waterfront resorts. Turkey, long a summertime destination for many Europeans, has begun to develop mountain areas for winter tourism. Bahrain expanded its International Exhibition Centre in 1999 and plans to construct facilities for international-caliber formula-one auto racing. Dubai, in the United Arab Emirates, has for years been hosting international tennis and golf tournaments. Several countries have built large exhibition and convention facilities, new sports venues, and a variety of resorts, from Tunisia's Saharan winter resorts to beach complexes on the Mediterranean, Red Sea, Persian Gulf, and Gulf of Oman and Indian Ocean coasts.

Turkey has the largest volume of annual tourist arrivals in the region, with about 11.6 million visitors recorded in 2001. Tunisia also has an active tourism sector, with an average of about 5 million visitors between 1999 and 2001. Morocco, where tourism is important in the country's development strategy, averaged more than 2 million arrivals between 1999 and 2001. Countries with the least tourist activity were Algeria, Iraq, Oman, Qatar, and Yemen.

The political and security situations in a country can have a markedly negative impact on tourism. Periods of prolonged conflict can cut the number of visitors drastically, even in places where tourism often is encouraged. For example, despite a highly developed and well-funded tourism infrastructure and an active Ministry of Tourism, tourist arrivals in Israel dropped from 2.3 million in 1999 to 1.2 million in 2001, due in large part to continuing violence. The fact that arrivals in Algeria, a country with tremendous tourist potential, numbered fewer than 200,000 between 1998 and 2000 can be attributed in large part to the unsettled security situation there. Violent groups sometimes attempt to make a political statement by attacking tourists or other foreigners. This was the case in Egypt when Islamists carried out a number of deadly attacks in the late 1990s. The government responded by increasing security measures, including the hiring of special "tourist police." In Yemen it has been the practice of some tribes to put pressure on the government by taking hostages, often foreign tourists. After the events of 11 September 2001, security became more perilous as the government, in cooperation with the United States, attempted to capture or kill al-Qaʿida members and sympathizers.

Bibliography

Compendium of Tourism Statistics, 2001 Edition. Madrid: World Tourism Organization, 2001.

ANTHONY B. TOTH

TRACHOMA

See DISEASES

TRADE

The geographical position of the Middle East has made the region part of far-flung trade networks, as both market and supplier, since antiquity.

The Middle East is the cradle of civilization, the place where agriculture and urban life are thought to have originated. The region was economically vibrant and a center of trade in early antiquity, and it connected far-flung markets across the Eastern Hemisphere during Roman times. The collapse of the Roman Empire fragmented governing institutions in northwestern Europe, dividing its markets from the rest of the world. The rise of Islam during the seventh century C.E. and its subsequent diffusion spread Arabic and a common legal system (*shariʿa*) across the southern Mediterranean and as far east as what now is Indonesia. Trade was reinvigorated and, following the Mongol conquest and consolidation in east and west Asia, overland trade between the Middle East and China along the Silk Road also thrived.

Trade before the Modern Period

Before the modern period, the Middle East exported mainly high-quality manufactured products to Europe and Africa, with which it generally enjoyed a trade surplus. Raw materials and manufactured products went to Asia but, like others trading with this region, Middle Eastern merchants often ran deficits with their east Asian partners.

The area around the Indian Ocean was a main market and supplier of goods to the Middle East. Pepper and spices came from the East Indies and were re-exported as well as consumed locally. Teak for ship construction and other tropical woods were imported from India; porcelain and silk came from China. After silkworms were smuggled out of China during the sixth century C.E., the Middle East also became a producer and exporter of silk cloth. Arab and Iranian shipping dominated the Indian Ocean as far as the Straits of Malacca, where Chinese junks took over, sailing to Guangzhou (Canton) and other Chinese ports to sell carpets, linens, cotton and wool fabrics, metalwork, iron ore, pearls, and ivory.

Overland trade with the Baltic region went via the Volga and other Russian rivers. Along these routes, Middle Eastern traders exchanged manufactured goods for furs, wax, amber, and slaves. The ancient sea trade with East Africa expanded greatly with the spread of Islam and with the establishment of branches of family trading concerns by Arabs and Iranians down the East African coast. Middle Eastern traders exchanged cloth, glassware, weapons, and trinkets for Africa's wood, ivory, palm oil, and gold. Slaves were sent from Africa to the Middle East in large numbers, most remaining in the countries bordering the Red Sea and Persian Gulf, but some going as far as India and China. The trans-Sahara trade blossomed following the introduction of caravans between Egypt, North African ports, and tropical Africa, exchanging African gold, ivory, pepper, and slaves for salt, weapons, copper, textiles, glassware, and trinkets.

Trade with Europe eventually would come to dominate Middle Eastern exchange relations, but Europe's lagging development following the sack of Rome confined most European exports to the Middle East to raw materials such as wood, iron, furs, and slaves. In exchange, Europeans received the high-quality manufactures for which the Middle East had long been famous: glassware, metal goods, and fabrics. As corruption eroded Egypt's competitive position during the fourteenth century, manufactures brought by Venetian traders began to displace local products. During the first half of the sixteenth century, Portugal invaded and took control of the Indian Ocean trade, constructing fortifications in ports like Bahrain and charging protection rents to merchants for allowing their goods to pass. The Dutch then displaced the Portuguese from much of their empire, and Portuguese interference with

Dubai, the chief commercial center of the United Arab Emirates, boasts the world's largest man-made harbor, Jabal Ali Port. It is the most frequented port outside of the United States, with sixty-seven berths and an impressive dry-dock facility. © PETER BLAKELY/CORBIS SABA. REPRODUCED BY PERMISSION.

local shipping waned. Shipbuilding thrived in the Persian Gulf during the eighteenth century, and merchant families grew rich from pearling and long-distance trade. Gulf-based merchants carried a wide variety of goods—including live horses—east to South Asia and west to the African coast. Their predominance in their own region was challenged and gradually eroded during the nineteenth century. In mid-century, competition from British steam-powered ships began taking business from Arab shippers who relied on wind-powered dhows and boums. Near the end of the century, the British navy established protectorates over the smaller emirates near the mouth of the Gulf and soon dominated that sea.

During the nineteenth century, the terms of trade between the Middle East and Europe gradually shifted as Europeans penetrated Middle Eastern markets and pressed governments for changes favoring imports over articles produced locally. High value-added products (i.e., manufactured or processed goods rather than raw materials) increasingly came from Europe rather than being produced at home. For example, Morocco had been famous for its refined sugar, but its Middle Eastern markets were overtaken by sugar from southern Europe and by sugar from the New World that had been refined in Europe. A similar displacement occurred later with respect to coffee. Manufactured goods were similarly displaced as fine silk and woolen fabrics, high-quality paper, and glass, which formerly had gone from the Middle East to Europe, began to flow from Europe to the Middle East. New European products, such as clocks, spectacles, and weapons, entered Middle Eastern markets without local competition. Although yarn exports to Europe continued until the end of the eighteenth century, it was clear by the time of the industrial revolution that the Middle East was becoming a peripheral actor in world trade, exporting mostly primary products and importing mostly manufactured and processed goods from the industrializing European core.

Shifting trade patterns accelerated during the nineteenth-century era of globalization, which ended with World War I. Total world trade rose from some $1.7 billion in 1800 to $42 billion in 1913. During this period, the share of world trade going to the Middle East was halved, falling from about 3 percent in 1800 to 1.5 percent in 1913. The slope of the upsurge in trade reflected European investment in steamships and railroads, and what economists like John Gallagher and Ronald Robinson called "the imperialism of free trade": in the name of open markets, Britain forced weaker trading partners to abolish monopolies and local trade regulations and to adopt low uniform tariffs on imports. Referred to as *capitulations,* these institutional changes ensured that the market effects of competition from an industrializing Europe on artisan production in the Middle East (and elsewhere) would not be moderated by the state. This virtually guaranteed that the region would be incorporated into the global trading system as a dependent exporter of raw materials: tobacco, dried fruits, and cotton from Turkey; silk and opium from Iran; wheat, barley, and dates from Syria and Iraq; silk from Lebanon; oranges from Palestine; and coffee beans from Yemen.

Foreign investment and loans were key elements changing the terms of trade and fostering trade dependency. Egyptian overinvestment in cotton production during the U.S. Civil War displaced local food production and, when cotton prices collapsed, increased Egypt's foreign debt. The protection of foreign creditors served as a justification for imposing on the Egyptian government a joint British-French commission in 1876. Britain used this

Sacks of figs being prepared for shipping from Smyrna. Turkey is one of the world's leading exporting countries of dried figs, raisins, and dried apricots. © UNDERWOOD & UNDERWOOD/CORBIS. REPRODUCED BY PERMISSION.

opportunity to take control of the Suez Canal and, in 1882, of Egypt itself. Trade deficits combined with heavy foreign borrowing caused the Ottoman Empire to declare bankruptcy in 1875 and, six years later, led to the establishment of the Ottoman Debt Commission. This essentially parallel ministry of finance represented the interests of the Ottoman Empire's creditors, and imposed an early version of conditionality (i.e., the surrender of control over fiscal policy to an agent of foreign creditors) to ensure that they would be repaid.

The Modern Period

The discovery of oil in Iran at the turn of the twentieth century confirmed the position of the Middle East as a supplier of raw materials, defining its position in world trade for the next century. Competition between France and Britain for control of Iraqi oil influenced the way the defeated Ottoman Empire was divided into mandates governed by these two victors after World War I. During the interwar period, oil was found in Bahrain, Kuwait, and Saudi Arabia, while the Iraqi oil industry became the balance wheel regulating the development of production capacity in the region via the Red Line Agreement of 1928. During World War II, trade volume declined regionally and globally owing to blockades, dangers to shipping, and shut-in oil production. Afterward, the production and sale of petroleum came to dominate interregional trade. Starting in 1960, the Organization of Petroleum

Foreign trade of some Middle East Countries *

	1938	1948	1963	1977	1984	2000
Egypt						
Imports	190	700	900	4,800	10,300	14,010
Exports	150	600	500	1,700	3,200	4,641
Israel						
Imports	56	300	700	4,700	8,400	35,750
Exports	29	40	300	3,000	4,900	31,404
Turkey						
Imports	120	300	700	5,700	10,800	53,499
Exports	115	200	400	1,800	7,100	26,572
Iran						
Imports	—	200	500	13,800	11,500	14,296
Exports	—	500	900	24,200	13,200	28,345
Iraq						
Imports	50	—	300	3,900	19,900	n/a
Exports	—	—	800	9,700	9,800	n/a
Kuwait						
Imports	—	—	300	4,500	8,300	7,157
Exports	—	—	1,100	9,800	10,600	19,436
Saudi Arabia						
Imports	—	—	—	14,700	39,200	30,237
Exports	—	300	1,100	43,500	46,900	77,583
United Arab Emirates						
Imports	—	—	—	4,600	9,400	38,139
Exports	—	—	—	9,500	14,400	n/a
Total						
Imports	**400**	**1,500**	**4,300**	**58,500**	**123,400**	**179,687**
Exports	**400**	**1,500**	**5,700**	**106,000**	**119,700**	**268,495**
Middle East as percentage of the world						
Imports	1.6	2.4	2.6	5.2	6.2	2.9
Exports	1.7	2.6	3.7	9.4	6.3	4.4

* In millions of U.S. dollars, rounded.

SOURCE: United Nations, *Statistical Yearbook* (New York: United Nations, 1986); for 2000, United Nation, *Statistical Yearbook* (New York: United Nations, 2003), 667-677.

TABLE BY GGS INFORMATION SERVICES, THE GALE GROUP.

Exporting Countries (OPEC) struggled to reverse the unfavorable terms of trade that had beset its Middle Eastern members since the nineteenth century by halting and then reversing the incipient decline in real oil prices that threatened to erode oil-exporter income.

Oil exports altered economic positions intraregionally. Until 1948, Egypt and Turkey accounted for the majority of Middle Eastern trade. After that, the oil-producing countries captured an enormous proportion of total regional trade, especially exports. Attempts to foster intraregional trade through common markets and regional organizations such as the Gulf Cooperation Council mostly foundered on the shoals of economies deformed by dependent development—that is, development strategies emphasizing oil and gas production rather than goods and services aimed primarily at domestic and regional markets. Local industrial development also was affected by what is sometimes called "Dutch disease" (because the same situation affected Holland during the heyday of its exploitation of the riches of the East Indies), oil export–induced monetary inflation that decreased the competitiveness of local goods as compared to imports. Dutch disease makes domestic production uncompetitive, even at home, further discouraging economic diversification.

The Arab League trade boycott, imposed against Israel after its creation in 1948 and still in effect in a number of Arab countries, was another factor retarding the development of local industries in Arab countries; it also deprived Israeli farms and factories of a nearby market for their products and increased Israel's already massive dependence on foreign assistance. Together, these outcomes increased the power of government over civil society, both in Israel and in the Arab states, by diminishing the capacity of domestic business interests to exercise checks on the state. The boycott also aggravated a conflict that all the region's governments used to their advantage to discourage if not repress domestic dissent.

Middle Eastern trade oscillates in response to political crises and wars, many connected to the Arab–Israeli conflict. In general, crises tend to depress Middle Eastern oil exports, either through oil embargoes or as a result of war-induced oil price increases. For example, the global position of Arab oil exporters was gravely damaged by consumer efforts to find other sources of hydrocarbon imports following the 1973 Arab-Israel war and the Arab oil embargo, which enabled OPEC to raise crude oil prices to what then were unheard-of levels. Ten years later, the volume of oil exports from OPEC countries was half what it had been in 1973. (Oil income did not fall in proportion because of further oil price increases during that period.) Other conflicts, such as the revolution in Iran and the subsequent U.S. trade sanctions against it, and the three Gulf Wars in which Iraq was a major belligerent (1980–1988; 1990–1991; and 2003), also affected regional trade. The first Gulf War, between Iran and Iraq, was fought in part with oil exports. Iraqi exports were occasionally halted by Iranian attacks but Iraq continued to receive oil income from Saudi and Kuwaiti sales of oil from the former Neutral Zone. Meanwhile, Iran suffered under U.S. trade sanctions, which depressed its export income.

As regards the balance of trade overall, oil-exporting-country revenues usually have exceeded the cost of imported goods and services. Non-oil exporters, such as Egypt, Israel, Syria, Jordan, Yemen, and Turkey, ran trade deficits, some incurred to pay for oil imports. The deficits were covered by foreign aid and loans, leading to large foreign debts. These macro-level effects mask significant changes in non-oil-exporting economies. For most, the composition of exports has changed. Traditional raw-material exports like cotton and grain have declined owing to greater processing and consumption at home. A growing export trade in manufactured goods, such as high-tech equipment and finished textiles, is bringing new trade income to Israel, Turkey, Egypt, Syria, and Lebanon. On the import side, rising incomes from oil exports have trickled down to non-oil-exporting neighbors via labor migration and, prior to the collapse in oil prices in 1986, through intraregional foreign aid. This allowed imports of foodstuffs, durable consumer goods, industrial and transport machinery, and raw materials to rise.

The most disturbing component of Middle Eastern trade is armaments. Higher oil prices in the 1970s were offset by the aggressive marketing of weapons to Middle Eastern Muslim countries. The motives of arms buyers were diverse. Some, such as Iran, Iraq, and Saudi Arabia, sought arms from external patrons as a way to assert their political and religious authority in the region. Others felt themselves to be at a disadvantage as compared to their neighbors, especially Israel, with its virtually First World military industries and its ability to acquire weapons and advanced military technologies, mostly free, from the United States. The overall decline in the world economy following the 1973 Arab-Israeli war made trade-surplus oil exporters attractive targets of marketing efforts by arms exporters from throughout the world. Britain, France, China, and Russia joined the United States in building arms export markets in the Middle East. Beginning in the 1980s, when U.S. policy shifted toward greater marketization of supporting strategic industries by encouraging them to market weapons abroad, then expanding during the 1990s, following the collapse of the Soviet Union, even materials for so-called weapons of mass destruction became widely available for import into the Middle East and elsewhere.

See also GULF COOPERATION COUNCIL; ORGANIZATION OF PETROLEUM EXPORTING COUNTRIES (OPEC); RED LINE AGREEMENT.

Bibliography

Gallagher, John, and Robinson, Ronald. "The Imperialism of Free Trade." *Economic History Review,* 2d series, no. 6 (1953): 1–15.

Issawi, Charles. *An Economic History of the Middle East and North Africa.* New York: Columbia University Press, 1982.

Nitzan, Jonathan, and Bichler, Shimshon. *The Global Political Economy of Israel.* Sterling, VA; London: Pluto Press, 2002.

Schwartz, Herman M. *States Versus Markets: The Emergence of a Global Economy.* 2d edition. New York and Basingstoke, U.K.: Palgrave, 2000.

CHARLES ISSAWI
UPDATED BY MARY ANN TÉTREAULT

TRAD, PETRO
[1876–1947]

Lebanese politician.

Petro Trad was born to a Greek Orthodox family in Beirut and received a law degree from the University of Paris. Known for his eloquent presentations, he was one of a handful of wealthy lawyers who monopolized law practice in Beirut. Trad was also involved in politics; he was one of six signatories to a petition presented to the French Foreign Ministry in 1913 on behalf of Christian sects in Beirut, that demanded an end to Ottoman control of Syria (including Palestine and Lebanon) and called for a separate entity run by "French specialists." This petition so angered Cemal Paşa against Arabs in general and Christians in particular that he asked the War Council in Alayh to execute the six signatories. They fled Lebanon.

After the World War I, Trad returned to Beirut as an ally of the French and founded the League of Christian Sects, which comprised the elite of Beirut society and demanded a French mandate over Syria and Lebanon. His law firm attained fame throughout the region, partly because he would defend poor persons who could not afford his fees. He was elected deputy from Beirut in 1925, with both Arab and French support. Trad served in the parliament for much of the 1920s and 1930s, either elected or appointed by the French authorities. He was a member of the parliamentary committee that worked on the French-Lebanese treaty of 1936. The French rewarded his support by appointing him speaker of parliament in 1937, a post he held until September 1939.

Trad could not stay neutral in the political feud between the staunchly pro-French Emile Eddé and the moderately pro-French Bishara al-Khuri. In his memoirs al-Khuri accuses Trad of supporting Eddé. In fact, Trad believed that both al-Khuri and Eddé were incapable of winning the presidency. He promoted himself as a consensus candidate.

Trad became president by default. He was briefly appointed by the French government, to oversee the election of a new president by members of an appointed parliament. The election of al-Khuri made it clear to him that his chances of winning the presidency were nil. He died in Beirut.

See also CEMAL PAŞA; EDDÉ, EMILE; KHURI, BISHARA AL-.

AS'AD ABUKHALIL

TRANS-ARABIAN PIPELINE

Pipeline transporting crude oil from Saudi Arabia to the Mediterranean.

The Trans-Arabian Pipeline (Tapline) was constructed by the Arabian American Oil Company (ARAMCO) to carry crude oil from Abqaiq, Saudi Arabia, to the Mediterranean coast. As originally conceived during World War II, the line was to follow a great circular route running northwest through Saudi Arabia and Jordan, which would have located the Mediterranean terminus at Haifa, then part of the British Mandate of Palestine. The postwar conflict over the disposition of Palestine ended in the Arab–Israel War (1948) that put Haifa in the new state of Israel. Tapline's route, more than 1,000 miles long, was altered to run through Syria and site its western terminus a few miles south of Sidon, Lebanon.

The construction of Tapline was hastened by the end of the Red Line Agreement, which brought a new infusion of capital into ARAMCO as the result of the removal of the restriction preventing Standard Oil of New Jersey (now Exxon) and Socony Vacuum (now Mobil; both combined as Exxon Mobil) from joining the partnership then composed of SOCAL (now Chevron) and Texaco. Capital was not the only requirement in short supply. Steel was also scarce following the end of World War II, and its allocation was controlled by the U.S. government. A second important factor speeding the construction of Tapline was support from the administration of U.S. president Harry S. Truman, which regarded Middle Eastern oil as crucial to the success of the Marshall Plan.

When Tapline was built, it was the world's largest privately financed construction project. At the peak of construction, it employed more than sixteen thousand men. Towns were constructed at Qaysumah, Rafha, Badana, and Turayf, where the four main pumping stations in Saudi Arabia were located. Initial capacity was 320,000 barrels per day. In 1957 auxiliary pumping stations were installed, raising capacity to 450,000 barrels per day. Tapline's capacity in 2003 was 500,000 barrels per day.

Tapline increased ARAMCO's capacity to export crude oil and reduced its oil-transport expenses. This prompted the government of Saudi Arabia to demand 50 percent of Tapline's profits under the fifty-fifty profit-sharing agreement that governed oil production. ARAMCO argued that transport was not covered under the profit-sharing agreement and claimed that Tapline was not an affiliate of ARAMCO but a separate company. After years of negotiations, the company agreed in 1963 to pay Saudi Arabia half the difference, after costs were deducted, between the price of petroleum at Ra'ṣ Tannūrah and the price at Sidon. The agreement, retroactive to 1953, netted the government $93 million in arrears.

Tapline and other pipelines in the region not only reduce transport costs and increase oil-export capacity but also provide alternatives to shipping from the Persian Gulf or through the Suez Canal. However, pipelines have security problems. Syria halted the passage of oil through Tapline for twenty-four hours in October 1956 during the Arab–Israel War, and in Syria a tractor ruptured Tapline in May 1970, just as Libya was restricting the production of Occidental Petroleum during the early days of the "squeeze." This blocked the transit of 500,000 barrels of crude from Saudi Arabia to the Mediterranean, triggering an immediate threefold rise in oil-tanker rates. The vulnerability of Tapline was highlighted by several incidents of sabotage in 1973, including an armed attack on the Sidon terminal and attacks on the pipeline itself in Syria and in Saudi Arabia.

In order to counter some of the strategic liabilities of relying so heavily on Tapline for pipeline transport, Saudi Arabia constructed a 720-mile crude-oil pipeline, Petroline, from the eastern oil fields to Yanbu, on the Red Sea, in 1981. A parallel line, connected to a spur running from Iraq's southern oil fields, was constructed to enable Iraq to export oil from Saudi Arabia during its war with Iran. This line was closed under United Nations sanctions following Iraq's invasion of Kuwait. The Saudis seized ownership in June 2001. Petroline, located entirely within Saudi Arabia, carried a maximum of 5 million barrels per day at its peak. In 2003 utilization was about half this capacity to accommodate the conversion of the line to carry natural gas. Like Tapline, Petroline increases the kingdom's export flexibility and demonstrates its commitment to a secure supply of hydrocarbon fuels to consumers.

See also ARABIAN AMERICAN OIL COMPANY (ARAMCO); PETROLEUM, OIL, AND NATURAL GAS; PETROLEUM RESERVES AND PRODUCTION; RED LINE AGREEMENT.

Bibliography

Nawwab, Ismail I.; Speers, Peter C.; and Hoye, Paul F.; eds. *ARMACO and Its World: Arabia and the Middle East.* Dhahran, Saudi Arabia: ARMACO Dhahran, 1980.

Yergin, Daniel. *The Prize: The Epic Quest for Oil, Money, and Power.* New York: Simon & Schuster, 1991.

MARY ANN TÉTREAULT

TRANS-IRANIAN RAILWAY

North-south railroad completed in 1938, which links Caspian ports in the north to Tehran and Persian/Arabian Gulf ports in the south.

The Trans-Iranian railway, one of the great engineering feats of the twentieth century, was commissioned by Reza Shah Pahlavi after his consolidation of power in Iran in 1925. Preliminary planning and construction efforts were contracted with KAMPSAX, a Scandinavian syndicate, in 1933. With the hub at Tehran, single tracklines were laid north and south through mountain and desert terrain to newly constructed ports on the Caspian Sea and Persian Gulf coasts. The 865-mile (1,392-km) railroad became operational in 1938, with 190 tunnels, totaling 47 miles (76 km), and traversing mountain passess higher than 7,000 feet (2,135 m).

The railway symbolized the new regime's goals of nationalism, independence, and modernization. To avoid foreign exploitation, particularly from English and Russian interests, it was financed by taxes on the popular subsistence items of tea and sugar. Ironically, during World War II, the railroad was commandeered by the Allies as a major supply route to the Soviet Union.

Bibliography

Millspaugh, Arthur C. *Americans in Persia.* Washington, DC: Brookings Institution, 1946.

JACK BUBON

TRANSJORDAN FRONTIER FORCE

Military group established to defend Palestine and Transjordan (1926–1948).

The Transjordan Frontier Force (TJFF) was organized by the high commissioner for Palestine to fulfill Britain's responsibility under terms of the mandate treaty. The TJFF should not be confused with the Arab Legion, from which it was entirely separate.

Confusion arose out of the TJFF's having a name identifying it with Transjordan but being a part of the imperial forces in Palestine and thus a Palestinian responsibility. In the end, the British treasury agreed to have Palestine pay five-sixths of the cost of the TJFF and Transjordan pay one-sixth, following the line of reasoning that security in Transjordan contributed to security in Palestine.

Further disagreement arose over the need for a force to undertake responsibilities many believed could be handled by the Arab Legion. The high commissioner for Palestine, Lord Plumer, considered that the frontiers with Syria and Saudi Arabia were vulnerable. The latter frontier was regarded as particularly open to the possibility of expansion efforts by Abd al-Aziz ibn Saʿud Al Saʿud, who had proclaimed himself king of the Hijaz in January 1926 and conceivably would seek to expand into areas controlled by the Hashimites, particularly Transjordan. The TJFF proved incapable of patrolling the desert of Transjordan and retired across the Jordan river to Palestine in 1930 when John Bagot Glubb created the Desert Mobile Force, which became the nucleus of the Arab Legion, and took over responsibility for the frontiers.

When the TJFF was formed, its recruits came from the disbanded Palestine gendarmeries, including noncommissioned officers and enlisted men who had had five years of experience. Some 70 percent of the recruits were Arabs from Palestine, mainly literate fallahin from the villages. In addition, there was a camel company of Sudanese enlisted men; it was replaced in 1933 by a mechanized unit. Some Jews and town Arabs served in administrative and technical services. Before 1935, about 25 percent of the force were Circassians.

The TJFF was under direct control of the high commissioner in Jerusalem, and above him the War Office in London. Non-British officers were not to attain command positions that gave them seniority over British personnel. Therefore, the officer corps and squadron commanders (majors or above) were British. Troop commanders (captains) and below included Palestinians, Syrians, Sudanese, Circassians, and a few Jews.

Initially the TJFF had three squadrons of two companies each, plus one camel company. In 1930, a mechanized company was added, bringing the total to eight companies. After the camel corps was replaced by a mechanized company, the TJFF consisted of three squadrons and two mechanized companies until the TJFF was disbanded.

All in all, there were some one thousand officers and men in the TJFF. Command headquarters, al-Zarqa, near Amman, was headed by a British lieutenant colonel. By 1935, there were twenty-four British officers in command of the TJFF: the commanding officer, seven majors, and sixteen captains. This complement remained more or less constant.

See also ABD AL-AZIZ IBN SAʿUD AL SAʿUD; ARAB LEGION.

Bibliography

Dann, Uriel. *Studies in the History of Transjordan, 1920–1949: The Making of a State.* Boulder, CO: Westview Press, 1984.

Vatikiotis, P. J. *Politics and the Military in Jordan: A Study of the Arab Legion, 1921–1957.* New York: Praeger, 1967.

JENAB TUTUNJI

TRANSPORT

Ships, caravans, railroads, and pipelines carry Middle Eastern goods to market.

Until the twentieth century, and in many places until the middle of that century, people, animals, and water were the primary modes of transport in the Middle East.

Shipping

Waterways are few and not always navigable, but coastal navigation has always been important. Of the various river systems, only two were navigable—the Nile and the Tigris and Euphrates system. All were used for irrigation as well as transport, and canal systems were built to extend their benefits. The Nile runs north through East Africa, emptying across a broad delta into the eastern Mediterranean Sea. The longest river in the world, it flows from Lake Victoria through Uganda, Sudan, and Egypt. Since the prevailing winds are northerly, boats without motors can sail upstream and float downstream. The Tigris and Euphrates rivers are less suited to navigation, since their currents are swifter, their levels vary, and they often change course before merging into the Shatt al-Arab, which drains into the Persian Gulf. Because of these means of access to the sea, both areas have long transported bulk goods by water and built seaports that accommodated goods from other coastal trading areas, such as Turkey and Syria. Since antiquity, the coastal people of the Mediterranean have traded, traveled, and warred among themselves over the riches of one another's lands.

Caravans

For the local movement of goods to rivers or seaports, and even for long-distance overland journeys, caravans were relied on. Caravans of mules and, especially, camels, took over from wheeled traffic at the end of the Roman era. Camel loads varied, generally ranging from 550 to 660 pounds; the speed of a caravan was 2.5 to 3 miles per hour; the usual daily stage was 15 to 20 miles. Caravans differed greatly in size, depending on need and the availability of people and animals: In 1820, before the Suez Canal was built, the Suez caravan had about 500 camels; in 1847, the Baghdad–Damascus caravan had some 1,500 to 2,000 camels; and the Damascus–Baghdad caravan, some 800 to 1,200. During the 1870s, some 15,000 pack animals made three round trips a year on the Tabriz–Trabzon route (Iran to Turkey), carrying the equivalent of the contents of seven or eight sailing ships each way. Boats and pack animals were adequate for the relatively small volume of traffic under traditional conditions before the advent of the industrial revolution and the expansion of European trade and imperialism into the Middle East.

After an agreement was negotiated between French engineer Ferdinand de Lesseps and the Egyptian government, construction of the Suez Canal began in 1859 and continued for ten years. The canal links two oceans and two seas, and transports 14 percent of total world trade. © PETER TURNLEY/CORBIS. REPRODUCED BY PERMISSION.

Steamships

During the nineteenth century, transport was revolutionized. During the 1820s and 1830s, regular steamer lines linked the Middle East with Europe

In the 1830s, the East India Company began to use steamships to travel between Bombay and Suez. In these early days, ports were inadequate for loading and unloading, and cargo had to be ferried out to the ships in smaller boats. © JACK FIELDS/CORBIS. REPRODUCED BY PERMISSION.

across the Mediterranean, with Russia and Austria across the Black Sea, and with India through the Red Sea. Later, services were established in the Caspian Sea and the gulf. By the closing decades of that century, the bulk of the region's foreign trade was carried on steamships, and freight costs were drastically reduced. Starting in the 1830s, steam tugs and steamboats were used on the Nile and on the Euphrates, soon carrying a large portion of domestic trade. Since no port improvements had occurred since Roman times, the steamers were loaded and unloaded by lighters, which were boats used to carry cargo from ships to ports. The first modern port facilities were installed in Alexandria in 1818 (followed by later improvements), at Suez in 1866, in İzmir in 1875, in Aden in 1888, in Beirut in 1895, and in Istanbul in 1902. Except for Alexandria and Suez, all these harbors were built with European capital. The opening of the Suez Canal in 1869 by a French company was a major advance for world navigation.

Railroads

The first railway in the Middle East was begun in 1851, at British insistence, to link Alexandria with Cairo and Suez, speeding transport on the Mediterranean–India route. Like all Egypt's main lines, it was financed by the government. Soon after, British capital built two lines from İzmir in Turkey to the countryside. The Ottoman Empire, however, wanted a railroad that linked Istanbul with their provinces of Anatolia, Syria, and Iraq; following the completion of the Vienna–Istanbul line in 1888 (which became the Orient Express), it gave a concession to a German company for an Istanbul–Ankara line, later extended to Basra. This Berlin–Baghdad Railway aroused much international controversy, which was settled just before the outbreak of World War I. When the war ended in 1918, the line reached Aleppo in northern Syria, and a small stretch had been built in Iraq. Other foreign-owned short lines were built in Palestine, Lebanon, and Syria. The Hijaz Railroad (1903–1908), linking Damascus, in Syria, to Medina, in western Saudi Arabia (near Mecca), was financed by contributions from Muslims throughout the world. During World War I, the British army built extensive rail lines in Iraq and Palestine and put the Arabian section of the Hijaz railroad out of service. In Iran, the Russians built a line to Tabriz. After the war, Turkey doubled its mileage and Iran built a railroad between the Caspian Sea and the Persian Gulf. Since then, important lines have been built in Iran, Saudi Arabia, and Syria. Table 1 shows the length of rail lines built from 1870 to 2000. Rail service reduced both the time and costs of transport. On the Ankara–Istanbul route, the rate per ton-mile fell from 10 cents to 1 cent; on the Damascus–Beirut line, from 4.5 cents to 1.5 cents; the journey from Damascus to Cairo was reduced from 25 days to 18 hours. In some areas, telegraph lines accompanied or preceded the railroads.

Length of rail service (in kilometers)

Country	1870	1890	1914	1939	1948	1975	2000
Egypt	1,400	1,797	4,314	5,606	6,092	4,856	8,600
Iran	—	—	—	1,700	3,180	4,944	6,600
Iraq	—	—	132	1,304	1,555	2,203	2,000
Jordan	—	—	—	332	332	420	700
Lebanon	—	—	—	232	423	417	200
Palestine/Israel (as of 1948)	—	—	—	1,188	1,225	902	n.d
Saudi Arabia	—	—	800	—	—	612	700
Sudan	—	—	2,396	3,206	3,242	4,556	5,000
Syria	—	—	—	854	867	1,761	2,400
Turkey	230	1,443	3,400	7,324	7,634	8,138	10,300
Total	**1,630**	**3,240**	**11,042**	**21,746**	**24,550**	**28,809**	**36,500**

SOURCE: *The International Year Book and Statesmen's Who's Who, 2003.* East Grinstead, U.K.: CSA, 2002. *Africa South of the Sahara, 2003.* London: Europa Publications, 2002. *The Middle East and North Africa, 2003.* London: Europa Publications, 2002. *Statistical Yearbook 1999.* New York: United Nations, 2002.

TABLE BY GGS INFORMATION SERVICES, THE GALE GROUP.

Modern means of transport, as of 2003

	Paved Roads (thousands of km)	Passenger Motor Vehicles (thousands)	Commercial Motor Vehicles (thousands)	Ships (thousands of grt/tons)*	Airlines (millions of passenger/km)
Egypt	39.0	1,154	554	1,350	8,036
Iran	93.5	1,793	235	3,943	8,539
Iraq	39.9	773	323	240	20
Israel	16.5	1,460	371	611	12,418
Jordan	5.5	245	112	42	4,065
Kuwait	3.8	747	140	2,291	6,207
Lebanon	6.2	1,299	92	301	1,504
Saudi Arabia	47.3	2,762	2,340	1,133	18,820
Sudan	3.9	285	53	43	148
Syria	43.3	138	322	498	1,410
Turkey	62.6	4,539	1,590	5,896	n.d.
United Arab Emirates	3.3	346	89	746	15,633

* grt is gross registered tons
Note: The dates for the figures in this table range from 1993 to 2001. n.d. = no data available.

SOURCE: *The International Year Book and Statesmen's Who's Who, 2003.* East Grinstead, U.K.: CSA, 2002. *Africa South of the Sahara, 2003.* London: Europa Publications, 2002. *The Middle East and North Africa, 2003.* London: Europa Publications, 2002. *Statistical Yearbook 1999.* New York: United Nations, 2002.

TABLE BY GGS INFORMATION SERVICES, THE GALE GROUP.

Modern Services

From the mid-1900s on, the Middle East has been served by an extensive network of telegraph and telephone lines, which extend to all cities and towns, and to almost all villages. Computer, electronic mail, and Internet and fax services exist in main centers as well.

Modern roadways were first built during the late nineteenth century; except for those in northern Iran and Lebanon, they played no significant role in the transport system of the period. After World War I, and then again after World War II, they were greatly expanded and improved. Motor vehicles, which came to the Middle East before World War I, carry the bulk of inland transport. Air transport has a similar history: every country has its own airline and the region has become a hub of air traffic, connecting North America and Europe with Africa, India, and Asia.

Because of the Suez Canal, the Middle East plays an important part in world navigation. Just before Egypt nationalized the canal in 1956, it carried 13 percent of world shipping but 20 percent of oil tankers. The canal has been repeatedly enlarged and deepened to accommodate increasingly larger tankers and supertankers. During the 1990s, most petroleum producers maintained a large fleet of tankers, and oil-refining and consumer nations had sizeable merchant and tanker fleets; still, the share of the Middle East in world shipping was only 1 percent, and its share in world tankers only 3 percent. Nationalization of all transport facilities has been a fact of Middle Eastern life, beginning with Turkey's railways during the 1920s.

Oil has brought another form of transport to the region: pipelines. The first, opened in 1934, carried Iraq's oil to the Mediterranean. Since then, far longer and larger pipelines have been built to transport Saudi Arabian and Iraqi oil through Syria to the Mediterranean, as well as Iraqi oil through Turkey and Saudi Arabia. Many pipelines no longer operate due to various political conflicts. Oil-producing countries also have extensive networks of internal pipelines that transport crude petroleum to refineries.

See also BERLIN–BAGHDAD RAILWAY; HIJAZ RAILROAD; PERSIAN (ARABIAN) GULF; SHATT AL-ARAB.

Bibliography

American Automobile Manufacturers Association. *World Motor Vehicles Data.* Detroit, 1989.

Earle, Edward. *Turkey, the Great Powers, and the Bagdad Railway: A Study in Imperialism.* New York: Macmillan, 1923.

International Air Transport Association. *World Air Transport Statistics.* Montréal: Author, 1991.

Issawi, Charles. *An Economic History of the Middle East and North Africa.* New York: Columbia University Press, 1982.

Kark, Ruth. "The Pilgrimage to Budding Tourism: The Role of Thomas Cook in the Rediscovery of the Holy Land." *Travellers in the Levant: Voyagers and Visionaries,* edited by Sarah Searight and Malcolm Wagstaff. Durham, U.K.: Astene, 2001.

CHARLES ISSAWI
UPDATED BY ANTHONY B. TOTH

TRANS-TURKEY PIPELINE

Oil pipeline connecting fields in Iraq and Turkey.

The Iraq-Turkey pipeline connects the rich oil fields around Kirkuk, Iraq, to the Mediterranean port of Yumurtalik in Turkey. It consists of two parallel pipes, 584 miles (941 km) long (398 miles or 641 km in Turkey), with a total capacity of 14 million barrels of crude oil. The first line was opened in 1977; the second, in 1987. It is operated jointly by the national oil companies of Iraq and Turkey. Oil flows through the pipeline ceased in 1991, in accordance with UN sanctions against Iraq after its invasion of Kuwait.

NIYAZI DALYANCI

TREATY OF 1815

Agreement between the United States and the ruler of Algiers that ended U.S. annual tribute payments.

In 1815, after the *dey* (ruler) of Algiers had declared war on the United States and began to tolerate corsair attacks on American shipping in the Mediterranean Sea, Washington dispatched to the area a ten-ship squadron under the command of naval hero Stephen Decatur (1779–1820). Decatur's objective was to punish Algiers and to assert freedom of the seas for trade. Decatur defeated the Algiers fleet and threatened to bombard the city unless the dey signed a new treaty promising to protect American ships and seamen from corsairs. The treaty signed on 30 June 1815 abolished U.S. indemnity payments, freed all U.S. prisoners without any ransom, and granted U.S. ships trading privileges in ports that recognized the suzerainty of Algiers.

See also CORSAIRS.

Bibliography

Chidsey, Donald B. *The Wars in Barbary: Arab Piracy and the Birth of the United States.* New York: Crown, 1971.

ERIC HOOGLUND

TREATY OF PROTECTION (1886)

British treaty made with south Arabian rulers.

This formal treaty of friendship and protection between Britain and the rulers of Qishn and Socotra in 1886 was followed by similar treaties with the rulers of the other states along the southern coast of the Arabian Peninsula and with the major tribal shaykhs of the interior that were deemed crucial to the security and commerce of Aden. Designed to end growing threats posed by the Ottoman Turks in North Yemen and by other European imperial powers, these treaties were a major step toward the creation of the Aden Protectorates and the binding of Aden to the interior territories in modern times. The local rulers traded control of foreign policy for British protection and modest subsidies. Between 1886 and 1895, Britain signed treaties with the Aqrabis, Lower Aulaqis, Fadhlis, Hawshabis, Alawis, Lower Yafais, and some of the Wahidis.

ROBERT D. BURROWES

TRIBALISM

See TRIBES AND TRIBALISM

TRIBES AND TRIBALISM

This entry consists of the following articles:

ARABIAN PENINSULA
BUTAYNA TRIBE
DAWASIR TRIBE
FADAN KHARASA TRIBE
GUISH TRIBES
HASSANA TRIBE
MATAWIRAH TRIBE
MUNTAFIQ TRIBE
MURRAH, AL-

MUTAYR TRIBE
QASHQA'I
QURAYSH TRIBE
SHAMMAR
TEBU TRIBE
UTAYBA TRIBE
YAZIDIS
YEMINI

ARABIAN PENINSULA

In the peninsula, a tribe is a group defined by perceived descent from a common male ancestor.

The word *qabila* (tribe) refers not only to a kinship group but also to a status category: *qabili* families claim descent from one of two eponymous Arab ancestors, Adnan or Qahtan, and feel themselves to be distinct from and superior to the nontribal *khadiri,* freeborn people who cannot claim such descent. The *khadiri* included most of the tradesmen, artisans, merchants, and scholars of pre-oil Arabia.

People of *qabili* status divide themselves into superior and inferior tribes, with the former able to claim purity in blood and origin *(asl).* The most prominent of the superior tribes of Arabia are the Aniza, Shammar, Harb, Mustayr, Ajman, Dhafir, Banu Khalid, Banu Hajir, al-Murrah, Qahtan, Utayba, Dawasir, Sahul, Manasir, Banu Yas, Sibay, Qawasim, Banu Yam, Za'ab, and Banu Tamim. The main tribes considered inferior are the Awazim, Rashayda, Hutaym, Aqayl, and Sulubba. The Sulubba, who traveled the desert as tinkers and metalworkers in service to the more affluent bedouin, were at the bottom of the tribal social scale.

Marriage between individuals of *qabila* and *khadiri* status, and between individuals of superior and inferior tribes, is frowned upon. Since the *qabili* claim to status is dependent upon purity of descent through the paternal line, the children of such a marriage would suffer the taint of mixed blood and reflect on the status of the tribe as a whole. These status barriers to marriage are beginning to break down in contemporary Saudi Arabia as access to education and economic advantage have created new status categories, which are beginning to compete with tribal affiliation and are undermining its importance in the social hierarchy.

The proportion of the population of Saudi Arabia that claims a tribal affiliation is unknown. Nearly all nomadic people are organized in tribal associations, and in 1950 Saudi Arabia's nomadic population was estimated at 50 percent. Since, historically, branches of tribal groups have lived in agricultural settlements at least part of the year or were permanently settled in towns, an estimate (according to a study done in the late 1970s) that the proportion of the population who claim a tribal affiliation could be as high as 80 percent would seem reasonable. A more recent study, however, suggests that the bulk of the settled population in Najd were nontribal *khadiri,* many of whom intermarried with the *abd,* or black slaves. Since the major cities of the Hijaz—Jidda and Mecca—and the towns of the Persian (Arabian) Gulf have long attracted foreigners, it is likely that the proportion of the contemporary Saudi population claiming a tribal affiliation is far smaller.

Structurally, nomadic tribal groups are organized by patrilineal descent, which unites individuals in increasingly larger segments. The smallest functional unit is the *hamula* (lineage), which consists of three to seven generations of one family related through the paternal line. Since lineage members are patrilineal cousins, the *hamula* is also referred to as one's *ibn amm* (father's brother's son), or *ahl* (people). The residential unit within the lineage is the *bayt* (house or tent), usually consisting of members of a nuclear family, including wife or wives and children.

Members of a single lineage usually camp close to one another and herd their animals as a unit. The lineage shares joint responsibility for avenging wrongs suffered by its members and pays compensation for any caused by its members. Although tribes may differ in status, all lineages within a given tribe are considered equals. Water wells, aside from the newer deep wells drilled by the government, are held in common by lineages. Among nomads, lineage membership is the basis of summer camps, and all animals, though they are owned by individual households, bear the lineage's brand. In terms of social relationships, access to government bureaucracy, and economic well-being, connection with the lineage is the most important relationship for the individual member of a tribe.

Bedouin nomads gather to eat at a camp in the Sahara Desert of Tunisia. © CORBIS. REPRODUCED BY PERMISSION.

Above the level of lineage there are larger segments that together make up the tribe. The *fakhd* (thigh) consists of a number of lineages that together control pasture and wells in the tribal area, while the *ashira* (plural *asha'ir*) consisting of numerous *fakhds,* is the largest segment below the tribe. While the system allows lineages to locate themselves genealogically relative to other groups in the same tribe, in general the larger the tribal segment, the smaller its function in the daily life of the individual.

In eastern Arabia, there is a recognized division among tribal groups based on perceived origin: the Yamani (or Qahtani) who predominate in Oman are believed to have emigrated in ancient times from Yemen in the south, while the Adnani (or Nizari) tribes—settled in northern Oman, the Trucial coast, Bahrain, and Qatar—are believed to have come from the north and are considered racially less "pure" than those from the south. Most of the tribal groups in Qatar, despite their common origin, are also located throughout eastern Arabia. The ruling family of the State of Qatar are the Al Thani, originally part of the Banu Tamim tribe of central Arabia who arrived in Qatar in the early seventeenth century. The Manasir, one of the most widespread tribes of eastern Arabia, are mostly bedouin and range from the al-Buraymi oasis across the United Arab Emirates to Qatar and al-Hasa in the west, with some residing in Sharjah and Ra's al-Khayma, and in the al-Shafra and al-Liwa oases in western Abu Dhabi. Some sections of the formerly powerful al-Na'im tribe of Oman reside in Qatar as well as in the rest of eastern Arabia. The Quabysat section of the Banu Yas Tribe tried unsuccessfully in the early twentieth century to settle at Khawar al-Udayd, a marshy inlet at the eastern base of the Qatar peninsula.

In Saudi Arabia, a new national consciousness to compete with tribal identities is starting to emerge as the centralized state undercuts tribal autonomy, sedentarization undermines the economic benefits of tribal organization, and children are exposed to a common government-imposed school curriculum. Tribal affiliation, however, especially for nomadic people, plays a pivotal role in relations between individuals and the central government. Since the mid-1980s, the central government has assumed the right to officially designate tribal leaders who may act as representatives on behalf of tribal members' interests. These leaders are expected to work through district amirs and governors and to deal with such issues as education, agricultural development, assistance in legal matters, transportation and communication improvement, welfare and social assistance, and helping to attain citizenship privileges.

For many tribal groups such as the al-Murrah, the National Guards have institutionalized tribal solidarity and strengthened tribal ties to the central government. Membership in individual National Guards units is based on tribal affiliation, and leadership of each tribal unit can be synonymous with traditional tribal leadership. Through the National Guards, former nomads receive training and the potential for higher-level careers, instruction in military sciences, housing, and health and social services for dependents and families.

For those tribal people who continue to live as bedouins, the government also provides water taps; market areas in cities, towns, and villages that are used in marketing livestock; veterinary services; subsidized fodder; and buildings for storage. It has been estimated that only 5 percent of the Saudi population today remain wholly nomadic.

Most tribes are affiliated with the House of Saʿud through marriage ties as the product of Ibn Saʿud's deliberate policy of cementing ties between himself and the tribal groups. Today the political alliance between tribe and state is being reinforced through marriage between tribal women and government officials as well as Saudi princes. Among the al-Saʿar bedouin in southern Arabia, for example, these marriages are encouraged by tribal leaders as a means of ensuring ongoing access to governmental leaders.

See also ABD AL-AZIZ IBN SAʿUD AL SAʿUD; AJMAN; AL THANI FAMILY; NAJD.

Bibliography

Anthony, John Duke. *Historical and Cultural Dictionary of the Sultanate of Oman and the Emirates of Eastern Arabia.* Metuchen, NJ: Scarecrow, 1976.

Dahlan, Ahmed Massan, ed. *Politics, Administration and Development in Saudi Arabia.* Jidda, Saudi Arabia: Dar al-Shorouq, 1990.

Dickson, Harold. *The Arab of the Desert.* London: Allen and Unwin, 1949.

Doughty, Charles. *Travels in Arabia Deserta.* Reprint, New York: Dover, 1980.

Hopkins, Nicholas. "Class and State in Rural Arab Communities." In *Beyond Coercion,* edited by Adeed Dawisha and I. Zartman. London and New York: Croom Helm, 1980.

Kingdom of Saudi Arabia. *Fifth Plan.* N.d.

ELEANOR ABDELLA DOUMATO

BUTAYNA TRIBE

One of two major factions within the Sibaʿa (also Asbiʿa) tribe of Syria.

The Sibaʿa is a major tribe of the Anaza confederation of tribes. The other faction is al-Abda tribe. Both factions were divided into clans. Those clans spend the summer season north of al-Salamiyya in Syria, to the east of Hama, and also east of Homs.

The Sibaʿa tribe as a whole numbered about 4,000 households *(bayt)* in the early 1930s. A *bayt* or *khayma* (tent) numbered about 5 persons, according to the Ottoman *Salname* (yearbook). Thus the Sibaʿa would total 20,000 persons. It is not known what percentage of this total the Butayna tribe represented.

ABDUL-KARIM RAFEQ

DAWASIR TRIBE

A sharif tribe of central Saudi Arabia, centered in the Wadi al-Dawasir south of Riyadh.

The Dawasir are notable for their great success as landowners and oil contractors and for their maintenance of tribal solidarity. The Al Sudayri family is the most famous to have come from the tribe; through it the tribe's influence has been felt throughout Saudi Arabia.

See also AL SUDAYRI FAMILY.

ELEANOR ABDELLA DOUMATO

Fadan Kharasa Tribe

Kharasa is one of two factions of the Fadan, which is a major tribe in the Anaza confederation of tribes.

The other faction is the Fadan Waʿad. The Kharasa numbered 1,500 *bayt* (household) or *khayma* (tent) in the early 1930s. According to the Ottoman *Salname,* which gives the size of the *khayma* as equal to about five persons, the total number of the Kharasa would have been 7,500 inhabitants. The Kharasa spread in the summer season along the Balikh and the Euphrates rivers in Syria; they are not allowed by the Syrian authorities to cross both rivers to the west. In winter, they go eastward into Iraq, especially during the years of drought. The Kharasa are divided into smaller clans, and they are on the whole warlike tribes.

ABDUL-KARIM RAFEQ

Guish Tribes

Tribes in the military service of the Makhzen in precolonial Morocco.

The most important of the Guish tribes were the Sherarda, Sheraga, and Udayay. Guish tribes were distinguished from the Naiba tribes, which were occasionally recruited to serve the Makhzen militarily. They lived on a plot of land offered by the sultan and did not pay taxes. Most of the administrators of the Makhzen were recruited from the Guish tribes.

RAHMA BOURQIA

Hassana Tribe

A major tribe of the Anaza confederation of Arab tribes who were known for their bravery.

In the second half of the eighteenth century, the Hassana tribe headed towards Syria from Najd, pushed by the Wahhabis. They reached the confines of Homs and Hama and clashed with the Mawali bedouin in control there. The weakened Mawali relinquished their positions and retreated towards Salamiyya and Maʿarrat al-Nuʿman. The Hassana numbered 400 *bayts* (households), that is, about 2,000 persons (the *bayt* or the *khayma* [tent], according to the Ottoman *Salname,* included about five persons). The Hassana additionally had 300 *bayts* of followers.

ABDUL-KARIM RAFEQ

Matawirah Tribe

One of four major tribal confederations into which the Alawite community of Syria is divided.

The other three Alawite confederations are the Khayyatin, the Haddadin, and the Kalbiyya. Each of these confederations is made up of a number of clans, each of which carries a specific name. A case in point is the Numaylatiyya clan, which is part of the Matawirah tribe.

Bibliography

Khuri, Fuad. "The Alawis of Syria: Religion, Ideology and Organization." In *Syria, Society, Culture, and Polity,* edited by Richard Antoun and Donald Quataert. Albany: State University of New York Press, 1991.

ABDUL-KARIM RAFEQ

Muntafiq Tribe

A tribal confederation in southern Iraq.

Muntafiq designates a 300,000-member tribal confederation of settled, seminomadic, and nomadic tribes, including the Ajwad, Bani Malik, Bani Saʿid, Dhafir, and Jashaʿam. They occupied the banks of the Euphrates from Chabaish to Darraji, and the Shatt al-Gharraf as far as Kut al-Hay. Led by the al-Saʿdun family, they were independent from the Ottomans, who relied upon them to defend lower Iraq against the Wahhabis and the Persians. Before and during the Mamluk period (1749–1831), they contested the court of Baghdad for power over Basra. After 1831, the policy of Iltizam, which required tribal shaykhs to collect government duties and revenues, eroded tribal relationships as the leaders demanded ever-increasing taxes on behalf of the government. When the Saʿdun became Ottoman landlords and government officials in 1870, reducing their tribes from landholders to tenants, the intense sense of betrayal further undermined their authority and weakened tribal power.

See also MAMLUKS; SAʿDUN FAMILY, AL-.

Bibliography

Longrigg, Stephen Hemsley. *Four Centuries of Modern Iraq.* Oxford: Clarendon Press, 1925.

ALBERTINE JWAIDEH

MURRAH, AL-

A bedouin tribe of Saudi Arabia.

The al-Murrah inhabit the Empty Quarter (Rub al-Khali), southern Najd, south-central al-Hasa, and as far west as the Najran oasis. Considered to be a Sharif tribe (one claiming noble descent), they are renowned both for their utilization of the Empty Quarter for grazing camels and for skills of desert tracking, and have therefore been called the "nomads of the nomads." Although the majority still remain nomadic, in recent years al-Murrah households have begun to build permanent housing near traditional watering places, replacing camel herding with herding sheep and goats, and to derive part of their income from urban occupations and service in the Saudi National Guard.

See also RUB AL-KHALI; SHARIF.

ELEANOR ABDELLA DOUMATO

MUTAYR TRIBE

A tribe of northeastern Arabia.

The Mutayr cover an area that ranges from Kuwait in the north to al-Dahna, the sand belt in the south. The Mutayr were active in the Ikhwan movement in the first quarter of the twentieth century. Among the first to be induced to settle under the movement's influence, Mutayr tribespeople in 1912 built al-Artawiya, an Ikhwan settlement that achieved fame for its zealotry in attempting to create a religious community living by God's laws, and for trying to convert others to the same goal. Some of the Mutayr, such as Faysal al-Duwish, led the Ikhwan rebellion against King Ibn Saʿud in 1929/1930.

See also IKHWAN.

ELEANOR ABDELLA DOUMATO

QASHQAʾI

Turkic-speaking (western Oghuz Turkic) tribal people of the southern Zagros Mountains of southwestern Iran, in the vicinity of the city of Shiraz.

The Qashqaʾi form a historically important tribal confederacy that originated in the late eighteenth century. Until the 1960s, the majority of Qashqaʾi were nomadic pastoralists. In the 1990s, many Qashqaʾi continue to rely on nomadism (increasingly by motorized vehicles) for a livelihood. Many have settled in villages, some for part of the year, and agriculture plays an increasingly important economic role.

Qashqaʾi territory is ecologically rich and diverse. Low-altitude winter pastures near the Persian Gulf and high-altitude summer pastures to the north and northeast are separated by hundreds of miles, and the migrations of spring and autumn each last from two to three months. The people follow Shiʿism and numbered approximately 600,000 in 1990. The Qashqaʾi have a strong sense of ethnic and national-minority identity, especially because of periodic repression of them by Iranian state rulers.

Bibliography

Beck, Lois. *Nomad: A Year in the Life of a Qashqaʾi Tribesman in Iran.* Berkeley: University of California Press, 1991.

Beck, Lois. *The Qashqaʾi of Iran.* New Haven, CT: Yale University Press, 1986.

LOIS BECK

QURAYSH TRIBE

The tribe of the Prophet Muhammad and the leading tribe of Mecca in the Prophet's time.

Before being converted to Islam, the Quraysh provided the strongest opposition to Muhammad, because the monotheism preached by the Prophet appeared to undermine tribal wealth derived from the pilgrimage to the Kaʿba, then a house of idolworship. In classical theory it was held that the leadership of the Muslim *umma* (community) should be held only by a descendant of the Quraysh tribe, and this idea has been used by political opposition groups in contemporary Saudi Arabia to challenge the legitimacy of the Al Saʿud family, who are of the Anaza tribe. It has also been used to strengthen the legitimacy of the Sharifian dynasty of Morocco, which claims descent from the Quraysh.

See also KAʿBA.

ELEANOR ABDELLA DOUMATO

SHAMMAR

A tribe of north-central Saudi Arabia.

The Shammar are a sharif tribe (a tribe claiming noble descent), centered in northern Najd in the region of Ha'il, Jabal Shammar, and the Nafud. The Shammar are led by the Al Rashid family, former rulers of Ha'il who captured Riyadh in 1891 and were ousted by Ibn Sa'ud in 1902. Divided into four sections—Abda, Aslam, Al Sinjara, and Tuman—the Shammar tribe was primarily camel-herding bedouin. Some few lineages live in farming villages. Many of their lineages, including the ruling Al Rashid, were seminomadic, maintaining oasis gardens during part of the year and grazing their animals in the desert in the wake of winter rains. In the nineteenth century, the Al Rashid were active proponents of the Muwahhidun reform movement, though they opposed the extension of Al Sa'ud family rule into their territory, encouraged Qur'anic education for boys and girls, and required Friday attendance in the mosque by men. In the twentieth century, the Shammar intermarried with the Al Sa'ud family and benefit today from the patronage of the ruling family, although they have been generally excluded from governing posts.

ELEANOR ABDELLA DOUMATO

TEBU TRIBE

Group of black Africans of unknown origin centered in the Tibesti mountains of the Sahara.

The Tebu are located in both southern Libya and northern Chad. Their language is part of the Nilo-Saharan family. The Tebu are Muslims, their form of Islam strongly influenced by the Libyan Sanusi movement of the nineteenth century. Their economy is a combination of pastoralism, farming, and date cultivation.

Bibliography

Metz, Helen Chapin, ed. *Libya: A Country Study*, 4th ed. Washington, DC: U.S. Government Printing Office, 1989.

STUART J. BORSCH

UTAYBA TRIBE

The most powerful tribe in central Arabia.

The Utayba (also Otayba) were wealthy in camels and horses, which were sold on the international market, and strong in arms. In nobility, the Utayba were second only to the Anaza tribe of the Al Sa'ud, and they ranged from the eastern Hijaz to central Najd. In the nineteenth century, there were settled villages of Utayba as well as large, fully nomadic confederations. The Utayba joined the Ikhwan in the early years of the twentieth century, with some sections of the tribe settling in Artawiya and Ghatghat, the most fervent of the Muwahhidun religious settlements. The religious zealot who led the attempt to seize the Grand Mosque at Mecca in 1979, Juhaiman al-Utaybi, was a member of the Utayba.

ELEANOR ABDELLA DOUMATO

YAZIDIS

Kurdish tribe.

A Kurdish tribal group of nomadic clans numbering 60,000 to 70,000 persons indigenous to the area of northern Iraq (Mosul) and eastern Turkey (Diyarbekir), they practice a heterodox religion incorporating Islamic, Christian, Jewish, and pagan elements. These include baptism, dualism, the prohibition of certain foods, circumcision, fasting, pilgrimage, interpretation of dreams, and transmigration of souls. Though they possess two sacred books—*Kitab al-Jilwa* (Book of revelation) and *Mashaf Rash* (Black book)—written in Arabic, they are not accorded the status of Ahl al-Kitab (protected minority status).

The Yazidis (the name does not seem to be related to *Yazid* but probably to the Persian word *ized* or angel) refer to themselves as Dasin or Dawasin (possibly from the name of an old Nestorian diocese). They believe themselves to be a unique people; not, for instance, descended directly from Adam and Eve like the rest of humanity. They practice a form of dualism between God and the peacock angel, with whom Shaykh Adi (to whose tomb annual devotional pilgrimages are made) was united through transmigration. Figures of peacocks made of bronze or iron are ritual devotional objects. There is a hierarchy of clerics, tribal shaykhs, and lesser priests, headed by a religious chief shaykh and a lay leader, Mirza Beg.

Pejoratively labeled "devil worshipers" or associated with the Caliph Yazid, they were branded as heretics, and numerous unsuccessful attempts by Turks and Kurds were made to convert or completely annihilate them.

Bibliography

Held, Colbert C. *Middle East Patterns: Places, Peoples, and Politics,* 3d edition. Boulder, CO: Westview, 1994.

REEVA S. SIMON

YEMINI

Yemeni tribes, rather than being mere vestiges of the past, are vital forces that continue to play determinant roles in the political, social, and cultural spheres.

Despite the tendency to characterize the highlands of Northern Yemen as "tribal" and southern Yemen as "peasant," tribes and tribalism are part of the cultural, social, and political landscape of nearly all regions of Yemen, even the Tihama coast and Wadi Hadramawt. For centuries, however, what has distinguished the northern highlands from the other regions of the country is the importance of the tribe as a unit of identification and action and the great extent to which tribes can be mobilized and organized into larger confederations when the interests of the tribe or tribal system are at stake. Although many residents of the southern uplands and the Hadramawt claim a tribal lineage, this often seems to be less important as a basis of personal identity than does place of origin—a village, valley, or region—or some other attribute. By contrast, many men of the highlands define themselves primarily in terms of their tribes, and many of these northern highland tribes with their present names were in existence at least a thousand years ago.

The majority of tribesmen in most parts of Yemen are sedentary farmers who grow sorghum, but the sparsely populated arid land on the edge of the Rub al-Khali (Empty Quarter) and the Ramlat al-Sabatayn is home to nomadic tribes principally engaged in animal husbandry. These bedouin populations have declined in recent years, in part because they were forced to give up their traditional roles as guardians and pillagers of the old trade routes, and now constitute a tiny portion of the total population of unified Yemen.

ROBERT D. BURROWES

TRIPARTITE DECLARATION (1950)

Declaration issued by the United States, Britain, and France guaranteeing borders in Middle Eastern states.

On 25 May 1950 the United States, Britain, and France jointly issued the Tripartite Declaration, which guaranteed the territorial status quo determined by Arab–Israeli armistice agreements and stipulated close consultation among the three powers with a view to limiting the Arab–Israeli arms race. The aim of the Western powers was to contain the Arab–Israeli conflict in order to focus the attention of the states of the Middle East on anti-Soviet defense plans.

In June 1952 the Western powers set up the Near East Arms Coordinating Committee (NEACC), through which they coordinated their arms sales to all parties in the conflict. In fact, the United States sold virtually no arms in the Middle East, leaving those markets to Britain and France. Despite fierce Anglo-French competition, the NEACC functioned reasonably well for more than three years. Both Britain and France periodically withheld arms from the rivals in the Arab–Israeli dispute, primarily when those states took action that threatened British or French regional interests. The Czech arms deal of September 1955, by means of which the Soviet Union agreed to sell Egypt $250 million worth of modern weaponry, made irrelevant Western efforts to limit the flow of arms. In April 1956 France began to transfer large quantities of modern arms to Israel.

See also ARMS AND ARMAMENTS IN THE MIDDLE EAST.

Bibliography

Levey, Zach. *Israel and the Western Powers, 1952–1960.* Chapel Hill: University of North Carolina Press, 1997.

Safran, Nadav. *From War to War: The Arab–Israeli Confrontation, 1948–1967; A Study of the Conflict from the Perspective of Coercion in the Context of Inter-Arab and Big Power Relations.* New York: Pegasus, 1969.

Slonim, Shlomo. "Origins of the 1950 Tripartite Declaration on the Middle East." *Middle Eastern Studies* 23 (1987): 135–149.

ZACH LEVEY

TRIPARTITE TREATY OF ALLIANCE

Agreement regulating Allied occupation of Iran during World War II.

Following the German invasion of the Soviet Union in June 1941, the British and Soviet governments jointly demanded that Iran, which bordered the southern Soviet Union, expel an estimated 2,000 Germans working on various projects there. Dissatisfied with the pace of Iran's response, British and Soviet military forces jointly invaded Iran on 25 August 1941, routed its armed forces within days, and occupied the country. To harmonize the occupation with the aims of the Atlantic Charter, which had been promulgated by Britain and the United States less than two weeks before the invasion, Britain and the Soviet Union signed a Tripartite Treaty of Alliance with Iran on 29 January 1942. Under the terms of this agreement, the Allies pledged to respect the territorial integrity, sovereignty, and political independence of Iran, and to withdraw all their military forces from the country within six months after the cessation of all hostilities.

Bibliography

Avery, Peter. *Modern Iran.* New York: Praeger, 1965.

ERIC HOOGLUND

TRIPOLI

City on the Mediterranean coast of northwest Libya.

Tripoli is the capital, largest city, and chief seaport of Libya. The city was founded by the Phoenicians on a small, rocky promontory. Known by the Romans as Oea, it formed (with Sabrata and Leptis Magna) the *tripolis* (Greek, three towns) from which its modern name derives. (In Arabic Tripoli is known as *Tarablus al-Gharb*—Tripoli of the West—to distinguish it from Lebanon's Tripoli.) Tripoli owed its preeminence to a fair harbor on the short sea route to Malta, Sicily, and Italy; to good water supplies and a moderately productive oasis and hinterland; and to domination of the northern ends of the shortest trade routes from the Mediterranean to central Africa via Fezzan.

After a history of foreign and local rule, prosperity declined by the end of the nineteenth century with the demise of Barbary Pirates and Mediterranean corsairing as well as the collapse of the trans-Saharan trade system. In 1911, the population was estimated at some 20,000, when Tripoli was the prime objective of the Italian invasion. It remained in Italian hands throughout the varying fortunes of Italy's presence in Libya. Under Italian rule, and especially during the post-1922 Fascist era, Tripoli was developed outside the walled Old City and acquired modern municipal services and the appearance of an Italian provincial town. In 1934, it became the capital of the colony of Libya, combining Tripolitania and Cyrenaica. During World War II, Tripoli fell, with little damage, to the invading British Eighth Army in January 1943 and became the seat of the British military administration that ruled Tripolitania until Libya's UN-supervised independence in 1951. On independence, Tripoli became joint capital of the Libyan federal kingdom, with Benghazi.

The oil boom of the 1950s and 1960s brought commercial expansion and increased population, with development into the outlying villages of the oasis. Shantytowns—which housed migrants from the countryside—proliferated on the outskirts. The United States had a large air base at Wheelus (al-Mallaha) to the east of the city, and the international airport was developed at the Royal Air Force base at Idris, near Gasr ben Gashir to the south. After the 1969 revolution, Tripoli became the sole capital of Libya and, following expulsion of its remaining Italian and Jewish communities, took on a more overtly Arab and Muslim character. Shanty towns were cleared and large public-housing schemes and commercial developments spread in a six-to-ten mile (10–15 km) radius from the city center. The population doubled between 1973 and 1984.

Attempts by the royalist regime to create a new capital at Baida and move the central administration to the central Libyan oases did little to diminish Tripoli's political, commercial, and social preeminence. It dominates one of Libya's main agricultural and industrial regions, and its port, airport, and roads to Tunisia, Fezzan, and Cyrenaica make it a key communications and transshipment center.

In 1986 the United States bombed Tripoli because of Libya's involvement in international terrorism. Some of the city was destroyed. Its population in 2003 was estimated at 1,775,000.

Bibliography

Wright, John. *Libya.* New York: Praeger, 1969.

JOHN L. WRIGHT

TRIPOLI CONFERENCE (1977)

Conference of Arab leaders in Tripoli, Libya.

The Tripoli Conference was convened 2 December 1977 in response to Egyptian President Anwar Sadat's trip to Jerusalem the previous month. It established the Steadfastness and Confrontation Front to oppose Sadat's peace initiative toward Israel. The front was joined by all of the attending heads of state, from Libya, Syria, Algeria, and South Yemen, and by leaders of Palestine Liberation Organization (PLO) factions.

Iraq, which sent a minor delegate, refused to join. On 5 December, Sadat broke diplomatic relations with all countries that attended the conference. A second result of the conference was the brief reunion of feuding PLO factions under Syria's sponsorship.

Bibliography

Cobban, Helena. *The Palestinian Liberation Organisation: People, Power, and Politics.* Cambridge, U.K., and New York: Cambridge University Press, 1984.

ELIZABETH THOMPSON

TRIPOLI PROGRAMME (1962)

Document representing the first comprehensive endeavor to define an identity and direction for independent Algeria.

At the end of the Algerian War of Independence, the Tripoli Programme, one of the most important documents in modern Algerian history, was introduced, the product of the meeting in Libya of Algeria's Front de Libération Nationale (National Liberation Front, FLN). This occasion in June 1962 marked the last time the wartime FLN convened before the intraelite conflict of that summer, which established the new government under Ahmed Ben Bella.

The program proposed a "socialist option" for Algeria's development. According to its chief authors, Redha Malek, Mohamed Bedjaoui, and Mohamed Benyahia, the quest for democracy necessitated class conflict and economic transformation. It projected the nationalization of foreign interests, the establishment of an industrial economy, and the inauguration of agricultural cooperatives. Stridently anticolonial, the program viewed the recently signed Evian agreements with France as neocolonialist. The Tripoli Programme was complemented in April 1964 by the Algiers Charter and by Algeria's National Charter (1976; 1986).

See also ALGIERS CHARTER.

PHILLIP C. NAYLOR

TRIPOLITANIA

A region in Libya.

The three historic North African regions of Tripolitania, Cyrenaica, and the Fezzan combine to make up the modern state of Libya, which is officially known as the Great Socialist People's Libyan Arab Jamahiriya. Tripolitania is the most populous of the three regions, with almost 80 percent of the country's five million people. It is located in the northwestern part of the country and covers an area of approximately 140,000 square miles (365,000 sq. km). Bordered on the north by the Mediterranean Sea, its boundaries stretch east to the Gulf of Sidra and Cyrenaica, west to Tunisia, and south into the Saharan Desert, where it adjoins the Fezzan.

In classical times, three ancient cities, Leptis Magna, Oea, and Sabratah, flourished on the northern coast of Tripolitania. Founded by Phoenician colonists, each was situated at the end of a long caravan route winding south into the heart of sub-Saharan Africa. All three cities enjoyed naturally safe harbors; lying at the end of ancient routes to the south, what began as primitive trading posts soon turned into flourishing caravan centers.

During the Roman period, Leptis Magna developed into one of the finest examples of an African city. A key factor in its development was its location on the Mediterranean Sea, sheltered by a promontory at the mouth of the Wadi Lebda, and near the relatively well watered hinterland of Tripolitania. Leptis, over time, became much more important as a commercial center than either Oea or Sabratah. Leptis Magna is the most impressive archaeological site in Tripolitania, and in Libya as well. The Severan Arch, erected in honor of a visit from Emperor Septimius Severus in 203 C.E., and the Hadrianic Baths complex are particularly noteworthy.

Tripolitania shares a common history and close ties with the Maghrib, the western Islamic world traditionally comprising Algeria, Morocco, and Tunisia. It is a part, both geographically and culturally, of the Maghrib and is sometimes included in descriptions of that region. Libyan migration from Tripolitania to Tunisia, in particular, has been commonplace for centuries. Cross-border migration was especially heavy during the Italian occupation, which began in 1911, as many Tripolitanians fled Libya to escape the Italian invaders. In consequence, many Tunisians are of Libyan descent, and related families are often found on opposite sides of the Libya-Tunisia border.

At the outset of the twentieth century, the Italian occupation of Libya stimulated political consciousness throughout Tripolitania. Consequently, it was from this region that the strongest impulses supporting unification with Cyrenaica and the Fezzan developed. The ill-fated Tripoli Republic, proclaimed in the fall of 1918, was the first republican government formally created in the Arab world. However, the creation of the Tripoli Republic, together with a declaration of independence and subsequent attempts to promote Libyan independence at the 1919 Paris Peace Conference, stirred little enthusiasm among the major powers of the world. By 1923 the Tripoli Republic had disintegrated.

Following World War II, a wide variety of political groups and parties were formed in Libya, and especially in Tripolitania. All of them favored a free and united Libya with membership in the Arab League. However, they differed widely in their choice of leadership for an independent Libya. When the foreign powers charged with determining Libya's future were unable to reach agreement, the traditional elites in Tripolitania, together with their peers in Cyrenaica and the Fezzan, agreed in 1950 to form a federal government, known as the United Kingdom of Libya, under the leadership of King Idris I. The monarchy was later replaced by a revolutionary government headed by Muammar al-Qaddafi in September 1969.

Located on the site of the ancient city of Oea, Tripoli is the capital of Tripolitania as well as the de facto capital of Libya. The area surrounding Tripoli as far south as the Jabal Nafusa is rich agricultural land with large groves of fruit and olive trees as well as date palms. Much of Libya's food comes from this region. South of the Jabal Nafusa, the desert begins, providing spectacular scenery most of the way to the Fezzan. Tripolitania also includes limited oil reserves and scattered iron ore deposits.

See also LIBYA; MAGHRIB; QADDAFI, MUAMMAR AL-; TRIPOLI.

Bibliography

Nelson, Harold D., ed. *Libya: A Country Study,* 3d edition. Washington, DC: U.S. Government Printing Office, 1979.

St John, Ronald Bruce. *Historical Dictionary of Libya,* 3d edition. Lanham, MD: Scarecrow Press, 1998.

Wright, John. *Libya: A Modern History.* Baltimore, MD: Johns Hopkins University Press, 1982.

RONALD BRUCE ST JOHN

TRUCIAL COAST

Colonial precursor of the United Arab Emirates.

The Trucial Coast was known to Europeans as the Pirate Coast in the late eighteenth and early nineteenth centuries, when the powerful federation of the Qawasim, operating primarily from the port of Ra'ʾs al-Khayma, ravaged shipping in the lower Persian (Arabian) Gulf. The government of British India sent several expeditions against them, finally subduing them in 1819. In the following year, Britain through the General Treaty of Peace, imposed a truce that condemned piracy and implied Britain's obligation to maintain peace in the Gulf. Subsequent treaties (truces) made the agreements more explicit, and the territories ruled by the shaykhs who were signatories to them became, in European usage, the Trucial Coast. The terms "Trucial States" and, confusingly, "Trucial Oman" were also used.

Fear of European rivals led Britain to establish "exclusive agreements" with these shaykhs in 1892. These engagements made Great Britain, through the colonial government in Delhi, responsible for the foreign relations of these shaykhdoms and, by implication, for their protection. The British, interested primarily in the security of the Gulf, kept their involvement on land to a minimum. Their intervention however, tended to freeze political relationships. This situation remained essentially unaltered until the interwar period, when the British government forced the rulers to deal only with prospecting oil companies of which it approved. Britain's simultaneous establishment of an air route across the Gulf began to open the area to the outside world, especially Sharjah, where an Imperial Airways airfield was established. Moreover, oil concession agreements created the need for the novel concept of fixed borders, which the British began to establish.

After World War II, Britain was much more fully involved in the affairs of the Trucial States. After 1947, with India's independence, the states became the responsibility of the Foreign Office in London. Britain's representative in the Trucial States was a permanent political officer assigned to Sharjah in 1948 (upgraded to political agent in 1953), and several state institutions were established. In 1951 the Trucial Oman Levies, a small force with British officers, was created to keep order in the Trucial States. Expanded and renamed the Trucial Oman Scouts in the mid-1950s, it became the nucleus of the United Arab Emirates, armed forces in 1971. In 1952 the Trucial States Council was created; though limited to a consultative role, it provided the first forum in which the rulers of the seven shaykhdoms could discuss common concerns. From 1965 until independence a Development Office, operating under the aegis of the Council, carried out infrastructure projects financed through a development fund to which Britain, Kuwait, Bahrain, Qatar, and Abu Dhabi contributed; Abu Dhabi carried the lion's share as its oil income expanded from the mid-1960s.

In December 1968, Britain's Labor government, beset by a balance-of-payments crisis, decided to withdraw military forces and relinquish responsibilities in the Gulf by the end of 1971. Though some of the rulers viewed Britain's withdrawal with alarm, Shaykh Zayid of Abu Dhabi and Shaykh Rashid of Dubai, the wealthiest of the seven Trucial States, agreed, as early as February 1968, to form a federation that would include Bahrain and Qatar. Despite British encouragement of this venture, it had foundered by early 1971. On 2 December 1971, a few months after Bahrain and Qatar had become separately independent, Sharjah, Umm al-Qaywayn, Ajman, and Fujayra joined Abu Dhabi and Dubai in the federation of the United Arab Emirates. In February 1972, Ra's al-Khayma belatedly joined the United Arab Emirates.

See also SHARJAH; UNITED ARAB EMIRATES.

Bibliography

Anthony, John Duke. *Arab States of the Lower Gulf: People, Politics, Petroleum.* Washington, DC: Middle East Institute, 1975.

Heard-Bey, Frauke. *From Trucial States to United Arab Emirates: A Society in Transition.* New York: Longman, 1982.

Peck, Malcolm C. *The United Arab Emirates: A Venture in Unity.* Boulder, CO: Westview Press, 1986.

MALCOLM C. PECK

TRUE PATH PARTY

A major centrist political party in Turkey from the late 1980s to the end of the 1990s.

The True Path Party (Doğru Yol Partisi, or DYP) was founded in 1983 by former members of the Justice Party. The military's National Security Council had banned former Justice Party chair Süleyman Demirel from active participation in politics until 1987; nevertheless, he was the behind-the-scenes driving force for the organization of the DYP. After his political activity ban had been lifted, Demirel became DYP's chair and led it to victory in the 1991 parliamentary elections. DYP won the largest number of seats, but not an absolute majority, and so formed a coalition government with the Social Democratic Populist Party (SHP). Upon the sudden death of President Turgut Özal in 1993, the Turkish Grand National Assembly voted for Demirel to be the new chief of state, and he resigned as the party's chair. DYP then chose Tansu Çiller as its leader, and she subsequently formed a new coalition government with SHP as Turkey's first woman prime minister. DYP lost its parliamentary plurality to the Refah Party in the 1995 elections. It formed a brief coalition with its rival, the Motherland Party, in early 1996, then joined Refah in a coalition from June 1996 to June 1997. Nevertheless, DYP's appeal continued to erode, and in the 1999 parliamentary elections it secured just 15 percent of seats. In the 2002 elections DYP fared even worse, receiving less than 10 percent of the overall nationwide vote and thus no seats in the parliament.

See also ÇILLER, TANSU; DEMIREL, SÜLEYMAN; JUSTICE PARTY; MOTHERLAND PARTY; NATIONAL SECURITY COUNCIL (TURKEY); REFAH PARTISI; SOCIAL DEMOCRATIC POPULIST PARTY; TURKISH GRAND NATIONAL ASSEMBLY.

Bibliography

Hooglund, Eric. "Government and Politics." In *Turkey: A Country Study,* edited by Helen Chapin Metz. Washington, DC: U.S. Government Printing Office, 1996.

FRANK TACHAU
UPDATED BY M. HAKAN YAVUZ

TRUMAN, HARRY S.
[1884–1972]

Thirty-third president of the United States.

At the end of World War II, the Middle East was not among the United States' strategic priorities. Even after the Iranian crisis of 1945 and 1946 and following the promulgation of the Truman Doctrine in 1947, the American administration seemed reluctant to involve the United States in an area that had been part of the British, and partially French, sphere of influence. Indeed, Truman and his assistants hoped that, even after the British withdrawal from Greece and Turkey, London would be able to retain control of the Middle Eastern "inner core" and to resist any threat of Soviet infiltration into the area. Although members of the Truman administration held negative opinions about the effects of British (and French) colonialism on emerging Arab nationalism, nevertheless geostrategic necessities led the United States to favor some continuation of British influence in the region.

This inconsistency also applied to American policy on the "Zionist question." The foundation of a Jewish state in Palestine became one of the main issues of Truman's worldview, although the U.S. president was annoyed by Zionist importunity and influenced by the State Department's negative opinion. However, advised above all by his special counselor, Clark Clifford, and by David Niles, Truman believed that the birth of Israel would represent a strategic asset for Washington's Middle East policy. So the United States favored the new Jewish state, with the negative repercussion that its relations with the Arab Middle East became problematic. Fearing that some Arab countries would be drawn into the Soviet orbit, Truman tried to implement a policy of appeasement toward the Arabs. In this connection, he attempted to find a solution (via the UN Conciliation Commission for Palestine) to the question of the Palestinian refugees of the 1948 Arab-Israel War. This issue was not resolved and, along with other unresolved questions, became the inheritance of Truman's successor, Dwight D. Eisenhower, and Secretary of State John Foster Dulles.

Bibliography

Cohen, Michael J. *Fighting World War Three from the Middle East: Allied Contingency Plans, 1945–1954.* London: Cass, 1997.

Cohen, Michael J. *Truman and Israel.* Berkeley: University of California Press, 1990.

Druks, Herbert. *The Uncertain Friendship: The U.S. and Israel from Roosevelt to Kennedy.* Westport, CT: Greenwood Press, 2001.

Lesch, David W., ed. *The Middle East and the United States: A Historical and Political Reassessment.* Boulder, CO: Westview Press, 2003.

ANTONIO DONNO

TRUMPELDOR, YOSEF
[1880–1920]

Zionist leader and military organizer in Palestine.

Born in the northern Caucasus in Russia, Yosef Trumpeldor served in the tsar's army during the Russo–Japanese War (1904–1905). He was wounded and lost an arm but returned to combat, which earned him decorations and promotion as the first Jewish officer in the Russian army.

Ardent about Zionism and an advocate of agricultural settlements, he organized Jewish self-defense groups in Russia (for emigration) and later in Ottoman Palestine, where he immigrated. During World War I he lobbied for the creation of a British-backed Jewish Legion, serving as second-in-command in what became the Zion Mule Corps. After the war he was affiliated with ha-Halutz (the agricultural pioneers) and encouraged Russian Jewish youth to go to Palestine to create agricultural and industrial settlements. Just before the British and French mandates took effect in the Middle East, he was sent to organize the defenses of Tel Hai, a pioneer Jewish settlement in northern Galilee. He died defending it on 1 March 1920. His last words, reported as "never mind, it is good to die for our country," initially became the motto of a nationalist myth and more recently have been material for humorous subversions of the legend that both signify and contribute to the erosion of classical Zionist ideology in Israel.

See also HA-HALUTZ; JEWISH LEGION; TEL HAI.

Bibliography

Zerubavel, Yael. "The Politics of Interpretation: Tel Hai in Israel's Collective Memory." *American Jewish Studies Review* 16 (1991): 133–160.

Zerubavel, Yael. *Recovered Roots: Collective Memory and the Making of Israeli National Tradition.* Chicago: University of Chicago Press, 1995.

DONNA ROBINSON DIVINE

TSEMEL, LEAH

[1945–]

Israeli lawyer and human rights activist.

Leah Tsemel was born in Haifa in 1945. Her mother and father were Jewish émigrés from Russia and Poland, respectively. Tsemel graduated from the Hebrew University of Jerusalem with a degree in criminal law in 1968. While at university she joined Matzpen, a radical left group a of the 1960s and 1970s that opposed Zionism and occupation.

Her distinguished legal career reflects a passionate and uncompromising commitment to human rights and progressive political positions, including support for establishing an independent state of Palestine with the 1967 Green Line as its borders, a unified Jerusalem as the capital of both Israel and Palestine, and the recognition in principle of the right of return of Palestinian refugees.

Since the 1970s, Tsemel has represented Palestinians in legal cases involving identity card confiscation, family reunification, house demolitions, deportations, political prisoners and administrative detainees, accused suicide bombers, and land confiscation. Her efforts to contest the use of torture on Palestinians are internationally recognized. In 1996, she received the Human Rights Award of the French Republic on behalf of the Public Action Committee against Torture in Israel. Tsemel was instrumental in a landmark Israeli Supreme Court decision of 6 September 1999 prohibiting the use of torture in interrogations by the Israeli General Security Services.

In 1972, Tsemel married Michael Warshavsky, a journalist and peace activist. They have two children.

See also GREEN LINE; REFUGEES: PALESTINIAN.

Bibliography

Salokar, Rebecca Mae, and Volcansek, Mary L., eds. *Women in Law: A Bio-Bibliographical Sourcebook.* Westport, CT: Greenwood Press, 1996.

MONA GHALI

TUBI, TAWFIQ

[1922–1994]

Israeli Palestinian politician.

Born in Haifa, Tawfiq Tubi was educated at the Mt. Zion school in Jerusalem. He joined the Palestine Communist party in 1941 and later was one of the founders of the League for National Liberation, which originally opposed partition of Palestine but later came to accept it, after the Soviet Union indicated that it would support partition. After the state of Israel was proclaimed (1948), he became a member of the Knesset on the Maki (Israel Communist

Party) list and a member of the Central Committee. In 1976, he was elected secretary general of the Hadash political faction. He was also the editor of *al-Ittihad.*

Bibliography

Rolef, Susan Hattis, ed. *Political Dictionary of the State of Israel,* 2d edition. New York: Macmillan, 1993.

BRYAN DAVES

TUDEH PARTY

The main orthodox Communist organization in contemporary Iran.

The Tudeh Party (Hezb-e Tudeh-ye Iran; the Party of the Iranian Masses) was formed in 1941 in Iran by members of the famous Fifty-three, who had been arrested in 1937 but were released immediately on the British-Soviet occupation of Iran during World War II. The Fifty-three were predominantly young, university-educated Marxist intellectuals from middle-class and Persian-speaking families. The Tudeh Party quickly grew to become the organization of the masses in reality as well as in name. It did so in part because its labor unions mobilized a significant portion of the wage-earning population; in part because it attracted many civil servants, professionals, and intellectuals; and in part because it successfully portrayed itself as the champion of patriotism and constitutional liberties against foreign imperialism and the threat of royal dictatorship. By 1945, the list of Tudeh sympathizers read like a Who's Who of Iran's intelligentsia.

After 1945, however, the Tudeh suffered a series of setbacks. Its patriotic credentials were undermined when it supported the Soviet-sponsored revolt in Azerbaijan, echoed the demands of the Soviet Union's Josef Stalin for an oil concession, and failed to give full backing to Mohammad Mossadegh's campaign to nationalize the petroleum industry. Its constitutional and democratic credentials were brought into question once it declared itself a Marxist-Leninist party and became a formal member of the Soviet-led Communist movement. Moreover, its ability to function was drastically curtailed—first in 1949, when the party was banned after an attempt was made on the life of Mohammad Reza Shah Pahlavi; and second after the 1953 coup, when SAVAK, the secret police, helped by the U.S. Central Intelligence Agency, vigorously unearthed its underground network. Over forty Tudeh members were executed in the 1950s.

The Tudeh was further weakened by two major internal disputes. In the aftermath of the Azerbaijan revolt, a number of intellectuals left the party and in later years joined Mosaddegh's National Front (Jebhe-ye Melli). In the 1960s, at the height of the Sino-Soviet dispute, a number of younger activists, denouncing the Tudeh leadership as reformist and revisionist, formed their own pro-Chinese Sazman-e Engelab-e Hezb-e Tudeh-ye Iran (Revolutionary Organization of the Tudeh Party of Iran).

By the time of the Iranian Revolution (1979), little remained of the Tudeh within Iran. Despite this, the party tried a comeback; it instructed its cadres to return and elected as its first secretary Nur al-Din Kianuri, the proponent of an alliance with Ayatollah Ruhollah Khomeini. The previous first secretary, Iraj Iskandari, had favored the secular liberals, especially the National Front. From 1978 until 1983, the Tudeh supported the Islamic Republic of Iran, even when much of the left denounced the regime as a medieval theocracy.

This support ended abruptly in 1983, in the midst of the Iran–Iraq War, after Khomeini ordered Iranian troops to cross the border into Iraq. As soon as the Tudeh criticized this action, most of the party's leaders and cadres were arrested and tortured into confessing that they were "spies and traitors plotting to overthrow the Islamic Republic." The most extensive recantation came from Ehsan Tabari, a member of the Fifty-three and the most important intellectual in the Tudeh leadership. Tabari died in prison from heart failure, but 163 of his colleagues were killed—some under torture, others by hanging. A few party leaders escaped to Western Europe, where they continue to be active. They publish a biweekly, *Nameh-ye Mardom* (People's newsletter) and a periodical, *Donya* (The world), and run a clandestine radio station. They held a party congress in 1998 in Germany and often send delegates to international communist meetings.

See also AZERBAIJAN CRISIS; IRANIAN REVOLUTION (1979); IRAN–IRAQ WAR (1980–1988); KHOMEINI, RUHOLLAH; KIANURI, NUR AL-

DIN; MOSSADEGH, MOHAMMAD; NATIONAL FRONT, IRAN; PAHLAVI, MOHAMMAD REZA.

Bibliography

Abrahamian, Ervand. *Iran between Two Revolutions.* Princeton, NJ: Princeton University Press, 1982.

Raffat, Donné. *The Prison Papers of Bozorg Alavi: A Literary Odyssey.* Syracuse, NY: Syracuse University Press, 1985.

Zabih, Sepehr. *The Communist Movement in Iran.* Berkeley: University of California Press, 1966.

ERVAND ABRAHAMIAN

TUHAMI AL-GLAWI

[1879–1956]

Pasha of Marrakech under the French protectorate in Morocco, 1912–1956.

The younger brother of Madani al-Glawi, who established the power of the family, Tuhami ibn Muhammad al-Mazwari al-Glawi first served as pasha of Marrakech under Morocco's Sultan Abd al-Hafid from 1908 to 1911. He then benefited from Madani's alliance with the protectorate government of France in 1912, and following Madani's death in 1918 Tuhami was named pasha of Marrakech. A staunch supporter of the French protectorate and a wily politician, he accumulated enormous wealth and power as viceroy of southern Morocco and gained a reputation of being greedy and oppressive. His leadership of the movement to depose Sultan Muhammad V (1953), part of a pro-French effort to prevent the collapse of the protectorate, gained him much notoriety among Moroccan nationalists. He died in 1956, after the independence of Morocco.

See also GLAWI FAMILY, AL-.

Bibliography

Pascon, Paul. *Capitalism and Agriculture in the Haouz of Marrakesh.* London: KPI; New York: Routledge and Kegan Paul, 1986.

EDMUND BURKE III

TUMAN BEY

[1473–1517]

The last independent Mamluk sultan of Egypt.

After the death of Qansuh al-Ghuri al-Ashrafi in the battle of Marj Dabiq near Aleppo (August 1516), the Mamluks selected his viceroy, Tuman Bey, to continue the struggle against the invasion of Sultan Selim the Grim.

Superior Ottoman tactics and weaponry forced the Egyptian ruler to hurriedly manufacture cannons and raise an infantry corps that used muskets similar to those used by the janissaries. He rejected an offer to submit to Ottoman suzerainty in exchange for being allowed to remain governor of Egypt. The two armies met in Raydaniyya, near Cairo, on 22 January 1517. The Mamluk cavalry again suffered defeat, and Selim entered the capital in triumph. On 28 January, Tuman Bey launched a surprise night attack against the Ottomans in Bulaq. The battle raged for four days, with both sides displaying extreme ferocity, but the Mamluks finally withdrew to the haven of Upper Egypt. There, Tuman Bey raised an army composed of a combination of Arab bedouins and Mamluks, and he returned, on 2/3 April, to attack Selim near Giza. After another defeat, Tuman Bey escaped north to a village near Damanhur, where he was captured by Ottoman troops. He was hanged a fortnight later in Cairo.

Bibliography

Glubb, John Bagot. *Soldiers of Fortune: The Story of the Mamlukes.* New York: Stein and Day, 1973.

BASSAM NAMANI

TUNB ISLANDS

Islands near the entrance to the Persian Gulf that are controlled by Iran and claimed by the United Arab Emirates.

The Greater and Lesser Tunbs are two small islands in the Persian (Arabian) Gulf close to the Strait of Hormuz. Greater Tunb, 17 miles (27 km) southwest of the large Iranian island of Qeshm, has a total area of about 3 square miles (7.5 sq. km). There are no permanent freshwater sources on the island and historically no permanent settlements, although it was occupied seasonally. Lesser Tunb, about 5 miles (8 km) east of Greater Tunb, is less than 2 square miles (5 sq. km) in area and has no fresh water or inhabitants.

Historical evidence for the ownership of the Tunbs prior to the mid-nineteenth century is sketchy, but by the mid-1880s, both Iran and the shaykhdom of Ra's al-Khayma were claiming sovereignty over the islands. Ra's al-Khayma was a British protectorate, and in 1904 Britain sided with its dependency by expelling the Iranian customs officers from Greater Tunb. Iran protested the action and periodically asserted its claim to the Tunbs, most notably in 1968 after Britain announced that it would recognize the full independence of its Persian Gulf protectorates. Britain mediated an agreement for shared sovereignty over the nearby island of Abu Musa, but the ruler of Ra's al-Khayma declined to accept such an arrangement for the Tunbs. Consequently, one day before the British treaty of protection with Ra's al-Khayma was due to expire, Iran forcibly occupied the Tunbs (30 November 1971); Britain took no action. After the shaykhdom joined the new United Arab Emirates (UAE), the dispute with Iran remained dormant for twenty years. The UAE raised the issue of Iran's occupation in 1992, in conjunction with the dispute over Abu Musa. Since then, the Tunbs have been a source of contention between Iran and the UAE.

Bibliography

Mirfendereski, Guive. "The Ownership of the Tonb Islands: A Legal Analysis." In *Small Islands, Big Politics: the Tonbs and Abu Musa in the Persian Gulf,* edited by Hooshang Amirahamdi. New York: St. Martin's Press, 1996.

MALCOLM C. PECK
UPDATED BY ERIC HOOGLUND

TUNIS

Capital of the Republic of Tunisia.

Tunis is the largest city in Tunisia. The population of the greater Tunis urban area is estimated at 2,083,000 (2001), more than one-quarter of the country's total population of 9,673,000. (In 1984 the population of the city itself was estimated at about 600,000.)

In 1160, Tunis became the provincial capital of the Moroccon-based Almohad dynasty. The Almohads built the *qasba* (citadel) that remained the seat of political power in the city until France's protectorate (1881). In the thirteenth century, under the Hafsid dynasty, Tunis became the national capital, a distinction it has retained ever since.

Tunis had only one congregational mosque, that of al-Zaytuna, until 1252, when the mosque of al-Tawfiq was constructed. Subsequently congregational mosques were built throughout the city. Following their seizure of Tunis in 1574, the Ottomans converted the mosques of the qasba and al-Qasr to follow the Hanafi usage, the school of Islamic law to which they adhered. In the seventeenth and eighteenth centuries, the Tunis skyline was altered by construction of new mosques, including those of Yusuf Dey (1612), Hammuda Pasha (1655), and Sidi Mahriz (1692), and the New Mosque of Husayn (1726).

Corsair wealth of the deys and beys transformed Tunis into a cosmopolitan complex dominated by mosques, madrasas (Islamic secondary schools), *zawiyas* (Islamic mystic centers), palaces, and elegant homes. The Turks also constructed a *maristan* (hospital) in the seventeenth century.

Prior to 1858, Tunis was organized into a quarter system centered on major mosques. The gates between quarters were locked at night and whenever public disturbances occurred. Each quarter was self-sufficient, with its own bread ovens, markets, bathhouses, wells, cisterns, Qur'anic schools *(kuttab),* and prayer mosques *(masjid).* Daytime security was provided by the *dawlatli* (a position directly descended from the dey). The *shaykh al-madina* (chief guild leader, akin to city mayor) controlled nighttime security patrols.

This loose administration ended in 1858, when Muhammad Bey established the City Council *(al-majlis al-baladi).* He appointed the shaykh al-madina to head this council of fifteen members. Today the shaykh al-madina is president of the City Council and is appointed by the country's president.

France's protectorate (1881–1956) brought changes to Tunis. A deep-water channel was constructed that made it possible for oceangoing vessels to dock in the port of Tunis, near the modern city's downtown area. A causeway beside this channel connects Tunis and its suburbs of La Goulette (now Halq al-Wadi), Carthage, Sidi Bou Said, and La Marsa. France also drained the swamp that separated the walled old city from the Lake of Tunis and built there a new European-style city with parks, broad avenues, cathedrals, an embassy, and modern housing.

In the twentieth century, Tunis became the major destination of rural-to-urban migration because of its being the political, social, educational, economic, and entertainment center of Tunisia. It is the seat of the national government and the national headquarters of the government party, the Constitutional Democratic Rally (Ralliement Constitutionel Démocratique; RCD), and the site of the national university.

LARRY A. BARRIE

TUNISIA

This entry consists of the following articles:

TUNISIA: OVERVIEW
TUNISIA: PERSONAL STATUS CODE
TUNISIA: POLITICAL PARTIES IN

OVERVIEW

Arab republic in central North Africa.

Tunisia is bordered by Algeria on the west, the Mediterranean on the north and east, and Libya on the southeast. It includes the Kerkenna Islands off the east coast and the island of Djerba in the southeast. In 1993, Algeria and Tunisia settled a border dispute that had been under negotiation since 1983.

Geography and Climate

Tunisia's landmass comprises 59,984 square miles (155,360 sq. km); the total area is 63,170 square miles (163,610 sq. km). The country has three distinct regions: the northern Tell or high plains; the central steppes; and the arid south, characterized by date palm oases and numerous *shatts* (salt marshes), the largest of which is the Shatt al-Jarid.

The Dorsale massif, an extension of the Atlas Mountains, limits rainfall on the central steppes. The highest point in the chain is Mount Chambi (1,544 meters; 5,066 feet). The mountains enter Tunisia northwest of Fernania and veer northeast across Cape Bon before plummeting into the Mediterranean near El Haouaria.

One of Tunisia's few perennial rivers, the Medjerda, rises in Algeria, crosses northern Tunisia, and empties into the Gulf of Tunis. Most other Tunisian streams, except the Miliana, dry up during the summer. Since antiquity the Medjerda valley has contained Tunisia's richest farmland.

The central steppes are high near the border with Algeria and low near the coast, then merge into the Sahel (coast), an area lying between Hammamet (near Cape Bon) and Sfax. Farther south lies the Sahara.

The north and the Sahel are the most urbanized and most densely populated regions of Tunisia. Tunis is the largest city and the national capital. The second largest city, Sfax, has half as many inhabitants as greater Tunisia (2 million). Other important cities are Qairawan (an important religious center and the first Arab town in the country, founded in 670 C.E.), Sousse, Gafsa, and Bizerte.

Tunisia's natural resources include phosphate mines near Gafsa and a developing natural gas and petroleum industry. Foreign companies compete for oil concessions and continue to explore for new fields. Tunisia also produces small quantities of iron ore, lead, zinc, and salt. The Sahel region is a rich olive-growing area, and the southern oases contain extensive date-palm groves.

Northern Tunisia has a Mediterranean climate with cool, damp winters and warm, humid summers. Precipitation declines south of the Dorsale along the coast and is minimal in the interior steppes and Sahara, where winter days are mild but nights can be bitterly cold. Summer daytime temperatures in the interior steppes and southern desert can be very high. Temperatures at Tunis range from 6°C (43°F) to 33°C (91°F). Precipitation averages 60 inches in the north and 8 inches in the Sahara.

The People, the Language, and Religion

Tunisia's 8.4 million people are concentrated in the north, in the Sahel, and in regional urban centers such as Qairawan and Gafsa. More than half the population lives in the northern Tell and the Sahel, on about 20 percent of Tunisia's total land surface. About 53 percent (4,452,000) of Tunisians live in cities. Population density is 133 persons per square mile. Family planning programs in the 1970s and 1980s managed to lower the population growth rate from over 3 percent to about 2.1 percent by 1992; 38 percent of Tunisians were under age fifteen in that year. Many Tunisians engage in agricultural pursuits, but a growing number are in the tourist industry, humanities and professions, commercial sector, and government.

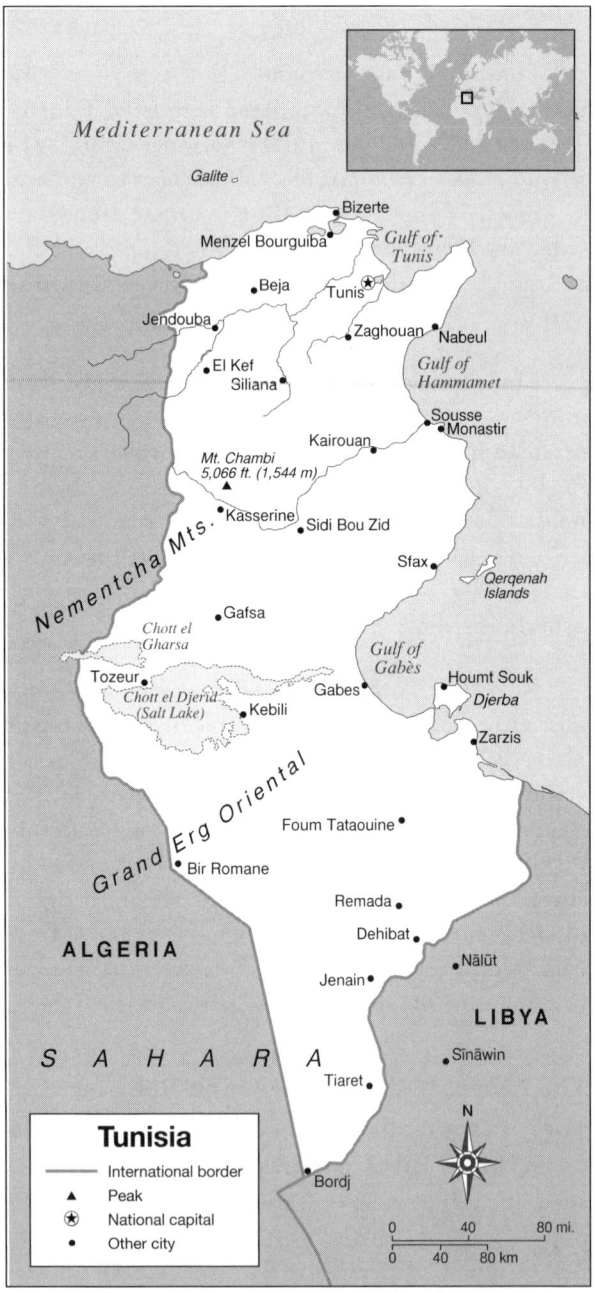

MAP BY XNR PRODUCTIONS, INC. THE GALE GROUP.

Tunisia's ethnic base is primarily mixed Arab-Berber or Arabized Berber. There are a few Berber speakers in isolated regions of the south. A tiny Jewish minority still exists; most Tunisian Jews left the country after 1957. Some European Christians live in Tunisia, primarily in the capital.

Tunisia's national language is Arabic (the first language of at least 98 percent of the people); French is the major second language as well as the dominant language of commerce and education. Although the print and audiovisual media use standard Arabic, most Tunisians speak their own dialect, which has three variations: an urban dialect, a rural village and small-town dialect, and a Bedouin dialect. Knowledge of the Egyptian dialect has been increasing since the 1970s because of Egypt's domination of the Arab cinema and television soap operas.

Islam is the official state religion. At least 98 percent of the population are Sunni Muslims. The island of Djerba harbors many Khariji Muslims. In the 1980s the Islamic Tendency Movement (Mouvement de Tendance Islamique; MTI) was formed, with Rached Ghannushi and Abdelfattah Mourou as its ideological leaders. Observance of Islamic rituals increased considerably in Tunisia during the 1980s and early 1990s. In recognition of this fact, and to thwart the designs of Islamists, the government sought to control all mosque appointments and to encourage moderation in religion. The government has grown more outwardly Islamic, following such traditional practices as waiting for the new moon before announcing the start of the Ramadan fast, and the firing of cannon to herald the first and last days of Ramadan.

The Economy

Tunisia's economy has improved due to good harvests (since 1990), economic restructuring, a growing manufacturing industry, a developing oil and gas sector, remittances from expatriates (an estimated 400,000 Tunisians work overseas), and a healthy tourist trade. Economic growth since 1988 has averaged about 4.2 percent, peaking at 8.6 percent in 1992. Unemployment ranges from the official 15 percent to a high of 20 to 50 percent in informal sectors of the economy. High rural unemployment has caused many young people to mi-

Habib Bourguiba is carried on the shoulders of his supporters as they celebrate the signing of the Franco-Tunisian Common Protocol in 1950. © CORBIS. REPRODUCED BY PERMISSION.

grate to urban centers in search of work, causing deterioration of public services and the taxing of city resources, especially in Tunis.

Tunisia's gross domestic product is about US$10 billion, and per capita income is about US$1,235. Agriculture comprises some 16 percent of the gross domestic product, and industry accounts for about 38 percent. The workforce is estimated at 2,250,000, with 34 percent in industry, 26 percent in agriculture, and 40 percent in services. Women make up just under 25 percent of the workforce (probably a much higher percentage of the rural "informal" sector). Labor unions have organized between 11 and 20 percent of the working class. The General Union of Tunisian Workers (Union Générale des Travailleurs Tunisiens; UGTT), headed by Ismail Sahbani, collaborates closely with the government and the Tunisian Union of Industrialists, Businessmen, and Artisans (Union Tunisienne des Industrialistes, Compagnies, et Artisans; UTICA).

History

Tunisia's geographic openness has made its history one of periodic invasions. Berber peoples settled the country in the fifth and fourth millennia B.C.E. The first outside civilization to make an impact came from Phoenicia, when émigrés from Tyre founded Carthage in 814 B.C.E. Carthage developed a maritime empire in the western Mediterranean and in the third century B.C.E. confronted Rome for control of the western Mediterranean. Three conflicts ensued that came to be known collectively as the Punic Wars. In the final battle of the Second Punic War (Zama, 202 B.C.E.), Rome's Scipio Africanus defeated Carthage's Hannibal. Rome now supplanted Carthage as mistress of the Mediterranean and dominated North Africa until the Vandal invasion of 429 C.E. Following the Vandals, the Byzantines in 533 extended their hegemony over Tunisia.

The most enduring historical legacy for Tunisia derives from the Arab invasions of the late seventh century. From 643 until 698, the Arabs struggled to defeat the Berbers and impose the Arabic language and Islam upon them. Qairawan was the capital for most medieval Tunisian dynasties. Founded in 670, it survived for centuries as the main garrison town and political and religious center.

The Aghlabid dynasty (800–909) ruled from Qairawan. The Shiʿite Fatimids (909–969) moved their capital to Mahdiya, then Egypt, founding a new imperial capital at Cairo. They left their lieutenants, the Zirids, in charge of North Africa. In 1049 the Zirids broke with the Fatimids who, in retaliation, unleashed the Banu Hilal nomads. They disrupted the countryside, intensified the renomadization of the steppes, and introduced a new dialect. Their defeat at Haidaran in 1052 and the sack of Qairawan in 1057 led the Zirids to move to Mahdiya.

The Almoravids, a Tuareg puritanical religious group, swept out of the western Sahara in the eleventh century. In the middle of the twelfth century, the Berber Almohads came down from the High Atlas and extended their domains into Tunisia.

By 1250, Almohad power had waned to such a degree that a successor dynasty, the Hafsids, emerged in Tunisia to rule for the next three centuries with Tunis as their capital. In 1574, an Ottoman Turkish fleet under Sinan Pasha landed forces at La Goulette (now Halq al-Wadi). Following a brief siege, those forces seized Tunis and laid the foundations for Ottoman control that continued until the imposition of a protectorate by France in 1881. To collect taxes and to maintain security, the Ottomans established a rudimentary administration. Initially an Ottoman *bulukbash* (commander) was placed in charge of the janissary garrison *(ocak)*. In 1590, rebel janissaries formed a government dominated by the deys, who ran the country through the *diwan* (council). After 1640, an important tax-collecting official, the bey, emerged, and the powerful

Tunis, the capital of Tunisia. Tunis is built near the site of Carthage, an ancient enemy of Rome that was later incorporated into its empire. Buildings that date back to Carthage's time as one of the major cities of the Roman Empire can be seen here on Byrsa Hill. © LAURE COMMUNICATIONS. REPRODUCED BY PERMISSION.

Muradid family exercised considerable control over the government. During a civil war from 1702 to 1705, Ibrahim al-Sharif seized power. In 1705 an associate of al-Sharif, Husayn ibn Ali Turki, proclaimed himself bey of Tunis. In 1710 the Ottoman sultan officially recognized Husayn and legitimized his rule. The Husaynid dynasty ruled the country independently until 1881, and thereafter under France's control until 1956.

In the nineteenth century, the Husaynids accepted the suzerainty of the Ottoman Empire while pursuing their own reform agendas and independent foreign policies vis-à-vis Europe. Misguided military reforms in the 1840s, financial mismanagement in the 1860s, and increasing pressures from Europe in the 1870s culminated in France's protectorate based on the treaty of Bardo (1881) and the La Marsa Convention (1883).

The protectorate authorities speeded up the economic development of Tunisia, built a physical infrastructure, reformed the educational system, and imposed a political administration while retaining the bey as figurehead ruler. Simultaneously they heeded settler demands for land, sweeping aside informal tribal and village ownership agreements. Arabs were excluded from participation in politics. French settlers dominated the political structures, the courts, and the media.

Although there had been armed resistance to the French occupation from southern tribal elements, most of it was crushed by the end of 1883. The first stage of Tunisian nationalism was an intellectual elitist movement known as the Young Tunisians, which aimed to assimilate to the civilization of France so they could eventually rule their own country. They agitated for equal treatment because of their accomplishments, but the French did not take them seriously. A more serious stage in protonationalist agitation occurred just before and just after World War I in a movement led by Abd al-Aziz Thaalbi. The third stage came in the 1930s when a young lawyer, Habib Bourguiba, broke with the Destour Party and proclaimed the Neo-Destour.

World War II slowed the development of nationalism in Tunisia. After the war, however, Bourguiba followed a staged process, arguing that its cumulative effect would result in political independence. By late 1955, Algeria violently challenged France's rule through a war of national liberation. France therefore agreed to Tunisia's autonomy in 1955 and to its independence in March 1956. In 1957 the Republic of Tunisia proclaimed Bourguiba its first president.

In Tunisia's first decades of independence, continued dominance of the Neo-Destour, which became the Socialist Destour in 1964, and the government's antireligious attitude tarnished the nation's image. Police intimidated those who sought to chant the Qur'an in public, often beating and imprisoning them. In protest, pious intellectuals organized the Society for the Preservation of the Qur'an and, in the early 1980s, created the MTI.

Bourguiba's anti-Islam policies led to Zayn al-Abidine Ben Ali's palace coup of 7 November 1987. Ben Ali tried to co-opt the Islamists for the promised elections of 1989. To demonstrate his piety, he appeared on television participating in Ramadan rites at al-Zaytuna mosque in Tunis. In the spring of 1989, however, Ben Ali hedged on his promise to recognize the MTI if they removed religious terminology from their name. As the April elections approached and MTI changed its name to the Renaissance party, the government refused to recognize it.

Ben Ali's regime considers the Islamists to be the major challenge to its survival, equating them with terrorists. Ben Ali announced in late 1993 that national elections would be held in March 1994. He promised that seats would be set aside for minority party candidates. Ben Ali then announced his candidacy for a second presidential term.

Tunisia's "regime of change" has tamed the Islamist movement for the moment, has modestly improved its human-rights and democratic credentials, and has continued economic restructuring and privatization. The economy is functioning reasonably well, harvests continue to be good, tourism has rebounded dramatically, and the immediate prospects for the future appear good.

See also BEN ALI, ZAYN AL-ABIDINE; BERBER; BIZERTE; BOURGUIBA, HABIB; LA MARSA CONVENTION; QAIRAWAN; SFAX; SOUSSE; SUNNI ISLAM; THAALBI, ABD AL-AZIZ; TUNIS; UNION GÉNÉRALE DES TRAVAILLEURS

TUNISIENS (UGTT); UNION TUNISIENNE DES INDUSTRIALISTES, COMPAGNIES, ARTISANS (UTICA).

Bibliography

Abun-Nasr, Jamil. "The Beylicate in Seventeenth Century Tunisia." *International Journal of Middle East Studies* 6 (1975): 70–93.

Anderson, Lisa. *The State and Social Transformation in Tunisia and Libya, 1830–1980.* Princeton, NJ: Princeton University Press, 1986.

Barrie, Larry A. "Tunisia: The Era of Reformism, 1837–1877." Master's thesis, Harvard University, 1966.

Entelis, John P. *Comparative Politics of North Africa: Algeria, Morocco, and Tunisia.* Syracuse, NY: Syracuse University Press, 1980.

Perkins, Kenneth J. *Tunisia: Crossroads of the Islamic and European Worlds.* Boulder, CO: Westview Press, 1986.

Valensi, Lucette. *On the Eve of Colonialism: North Africa before the French Conquest.* New York: Africana, 1977.

Zartman, I. William, ed. *Tunisia: The Political Economy of Reform.* Boulder, CO: L. Rienner, 1991.

Zussman, Mira. *Development and Disenchantment in Rural Tunisia: The Bourguiba Years.* Boulder, CO: Westview Press, 1992.

LARRY A. BARRIE

TUNISIA: PERSONAL STATUS CODE

Set of family laws that reduced gender inequality in Tunisia.

On 13 August 1956, less than five months after the proclamation of independence from French colonial rule, the Republic of Tunisia promulgated the Code of Personal Status (CPS). A set of laws regulating marriage, divorce, custody, and inheritance, the code profoundly changed family law and the legal status of women. Together with the Turkish civil code of 1926, the Tunisian CPS of 1956 represented a pioneering body of legislation that reduced gender inequality before the law in an Islamic country.

A reform from above, the CPS was initiated by the political leadership in the absence of a feminist grassroots mass movement. Although it expanded women's rights, the CPS should not be seen as a response from the state to pressures from women's protest groups. Individual women had participated in the struggle for national liberation and espoused a nationalist ideology, but no women's mass movement defending women's causes had developed in Tunisia in the 1950s. The initiators of the CPS described it primarily as an instrument of change, a way of bringing about a transformation in kinship patterns and family life, which they saw as a necessary condition for broader social, political, and economic changes.

The Tunisian code is called the *majalla* in Arabic. Several amendments further equalizing the legal status of men and women have been made and the text has been regularly updated since 1956. The CPS altered regulations on marriage, divorce, alimony, custody, adoption, and to a lesser extent inheritance, leaving few, if any, aspects of family life untouched. The best known and most daring reforms embodied in the CPS concern polygamy, or the man's right to have as many as four wives, and repudiation, or the unilateral right of the husband to end the marriage at will. The *majalla* outlawed polygamy altogether. It stated unequivocally that polygamy was forbidden. An attempt at marrying again while one was still married was punished with imprisonment of a year and a fine of approximately $500, which represented the equivalent of a year's income for many Tunisians when the CPS was promulgated in 1956. The CPS also abolished repudiation and changed regulations on divorce in fundamental ways. A divorce could now only take place in court. The wife and husband were equally entitled to file for divorce, and they could do so by mutual consent. One of them could also file alone, in which case the judge would determine whether compensation should be given by one spouse to the other and what the amount ought to be. A woman was liable to pay compensation to her husband if the judge estimated that it was the husband who had been wronged.

Among other innovations, the CPS made the wife responsible for contributing to the expenses of the household and to the financial support of children, if she had to means to do so. It expanded the right of mothers to have custody of their children. It made the registration of marriages and divorces mandatory, something that was not systematically the case earlier. It made adoption legally valid. It somewhat modified the rules on inheritance by favoring the spouse and female descendants over male cousins in some specific kinship configurations.

The CPS gave women greater rights by increasing the range of options available to them in their private lives. It also gave them greater obligations, as for example in the case of divorce and with respect to the financial responsibility for the household. Some aspects of the CPS overtly maintained gender inequality, however. The code left unaltered the general rule according to which women inherit half as much as men. The 1956 text required a wife to obey her husband; this was later debated and changed in the 1990s.

The reforms of the CPS can be seen as an effort to reshape kinship in Tunisian society in the aftermath of independence from colonial rule. The CPS replaced the vision of the family as an extended kinship group built on strong ties crisscrossing a community of male relatives with the vision of a conjugal unit in which ties between spouses and between parents and children are prominent. The elite in power in the 1950s treated family law reform as part of the transformation of society necessary for the development of a modern state.

See also GENDER: GENDER AND LAW.

MOUNIRA M. CHARRAD

TUNISIA: POLITICAL PARTIES IN

Tunisia has eleven active political parties.

There are eight legal political parties in Tunisia, including the government party. There are also three parties that have not been authorized: the Popular Unity Movement (Mouvement de L'Unité Populaire; MUP), a socialist party founded by Ahmed Ben Salah, former planning minister who fled Tunisia in 1973; the Tunisian Communist Workers Party (Parti Ouvrier Communiste Tunisien; POCT), a Maoist group; and the Renaissance Party (Hizb al-Nahda in Arabic), the party of Islamists, founded by Rashid Ghannushi. The legal parties are the Constitutional Democratic Rally (Ralliement Constitutionnel Démocratique; RCD), the Movement of Socialist Democrats (Mouvement des Dèmocrates Socialistes; MDS), the Popular Unity Party (Parti D'Unité Populaire; PUP), the Movement of Renewal (Harakat al-Tajdid), the Progressive Democratic Party (Parti démocrate progressiste; PDP), the Unionist Democratic Union (Union Démocratique Unioniste; UDU), the Socialist Liberal Party (Parti Socialiste Liberale; PSL), and the Democratic Forum for Labor and Freedoms (Forum démocratique pour le travail et les libertés; FDTL).

Tunisian president Zayn al-Abidine Ben Ali (b. 1936) came to power in 1987 when previous leader Habib Bourguiba was dismissed on grounds of failing mental capabilities. Once in power, Ben Ali changed the Destourian Socialist Party to the Democratic Constitutional Rally, and he easily retained his office in the country's first free elections in 1989. © AFP/CORBIS. REPRODUCED BY PERMISSION.

RCD

The RCD has dominated all governmental institutions since Tunisia's independence in 1956. The party was founded by Habib Bourguiba and others in 1934 as the Neo-Destour. They broke away from the Destour (Constitution) Party, established by Abd al-Aziz Thaalbi in 1920. Bourguiba's group felt that the Destour had become too elitist and sought to build a grassroots party that could appeal to the rural and small-town folk that the Destour failed to represent. In 1964 the party changed its name to Socialist Destour Party (Parti Socialist Destourien; PSD). The party's final name change occurred in 1988, when the party congress adopted the name Constitutional Democratic Rally. This expressed the new direction of the government party following a coup that replaced Bourguiba with Zayn al-Abidine

Ben Ali. Moderate and pragmatic, the RCD has opened up the political system to multiple parties and has attempted to refashion a market economy to replace the earlier centralized socialist planning system. President Ben Ali is party president, and Ali Chaouch occupies the post of secretary-general. The party claims over 1.5 million members, distributed in thousands of cells nationwide. It controls the national parliament (Chamber of Deputies).

MDS

Ahmad Mestiri, formerly a member of the ruling party, founded the MDS in 1978 and welded the new party into the largest opposition to the RCD. With its forty thousand members, the MDS offers almost the same program as the RCD, except that it is more Arab nationalist and socialist. Ismaïl Boulahya is secretary-general.

PUP

Headed by Mohamed Belhaj Amor, the PUP offers a nationalist and socialist program. It splintered off from the MUP in 1981 and in 1985 it was renamed the Parti d'Unité Populaire (PUP). Amor was succeeded in 2000 by Mohamed Bouchiha.

Movement of Renewal

Secretary-General Mohamed Harmel is a longtime Communist Party activist. The Movement adopted the name Mouvement Ettajdid (Arabic, Harakat al-Tajdid) in 1993, dropping the name Tunisian Communist Party (Parti Communiste Tunisien; PCT). It now follows a leftist, non-Marxist ideology that offers an alternative for leftists and intellectuals. It remains a small party whose membership numbers somewhere in the low thousands.

PDP

Nejib Chebbi, a lawyer, heads the Progressive Democratic Party, the former Socialist Progressive Rally (RSP), which has a nationalist and socialist emphasis. PDP leaders are willing to accommodate all nonviolent political viewpoints in national elections. The PDP seeks a broader role for Tunisia in Arab politics. Regarded as the most critical of the opposition parties, it did not gain any seats to the Chamber of Deputies in the legislative elections of 1999.

UDU

Abderrahmane Tlili founded the Unionist Democratic Union (UDU). It has close ties with the Union Générale des Travailleurs Tunisiens (UGTT), the country's largest labor union. A high concentration of union members makes up UDU's constituency. UDU espouses both Arab nationalism and Israel-PLO peace talks.

PSL

In 1993 the Social Party for Progress (PSP) became the Socialist Liberal Party (PSL). Led by Mounir Beji, a lawyer, the PSL supports liberalism, economic privatization, and American foreign policy interests in the region. Despite being considered the weakest legal party, it obtained two deputies in the 1999 legislative elections.

FDTL

Founded in 1994, the Democratic Forum for Labor and Freedoms (FDTL) was legalized in 2002. Its secretary-general, Mustapha Ben Jaafar, a former leader of the MDS, defines its ideology as social-democratic.

Since 1993, new laws have been implemented aimed at encouraging political pluralism. Accordingly, and as of 2003, the legal opposition parties share 34 seats, out of 182, in the Chamber of Deputies. The results of the legislative elections of 1999 were as follows: RCD, 148 deputies; MDS, 13; PUP, 7; UDU, 7; Ettajdid, 5; PSL, 2; PDP, 0.

Bibliography

Murphy, Emma. *Economic and Political Change in Tunisia: From Bourguiba to Ben Ali.* New York: St. Martin's Press in association with University of Durham, 1999.

Nelson, Harold D., ed. *Tunisia: A Country Study,* 3d edition. Washington, DC: U.S. Government Printing Office, 1986.

Perkins, Kenneth J. *Historical Dictionary of Tunisia.* Metuchen, NJ: Scarecrow Press, 1989.

Zartman, I. William, ed. *Tunisia: The Political Economy of Reform.* Boulder, CO: L. Rienner, 1991.

LARRY A. BARRIE
UPDATED BY ANA TORRES-GARCÍA

TUNISI, BAYRAM AL-
[1893–1961]

Egyptian poet.

Born into a small merchant family in a popular quarter of Alexandria, Bayram al-Tunisi studied at religious schools but learned the form of poetry called *zajal* by memorizing oral poetry. In 1919, he began to publish poetry critical of Egypt's monarchy and of the British occupation, in the journal *Issues,* leading to a long period of exile in France and Tunisia. After his return to Egypt in 1938, al-Tunisi published poetry in various Egyptian newspapers.

DAVID WALDNER

TUQAN, FADWA
[1917–2003]

Palestinian poet.

Fadwa Tuqan was born to the eminent Tuqan family of Nablus, one of the leading traditional families of central Palestine, which produced several notable figures in Palestinian education, literature, and politics. Like her elder brother, Ibrahim, she became one of the most influential poets in modern Palestinian literature, publishing her first collection of poetry, *Wahdi ma al-Ayyam* (Along with the days), in 1952.

Her work is noted for having broken with traditional Arabic poetic styles, introducing, for example, free verse into modern Arabic poetry. Tuqan's poetry is also noteworthy for discussing sensual themes, as well as for depicting the social conditions facing Palestinians, especially Palestinian women. Her 1985 autobiography, *Rihla Jabaliyya, Rihla Sa'ba* (A mountainous journey, a difficult journey), provides a forceful discussion of the plight of women in Palestine prior to the first Arab–Israel War and the creation of Israel in 1948. Starting with the Israeli occupation of her native West Bank in June 1967, Tuqan also began writing poetry with nationalist themes. Some of her poems were printed in the underground nationalist publication *Filastin* in the mid-1970s. Israeli general and politician Moshe Dayan once remarked that the power of just one of her poems, like her famous "The Freedom Fighter and the Land," was equal to that of several Palestinian guerrilla fighters. She was not above participating in secret Arab-Israeli contacts, however. Dayan met with her twice in late 1968, when he was Israel's defense minister, as part of his secret effort to strike up a dialogue with Arab leaders. Tuqan once passed along a message from Dayan to Egyptian President Gamal Abdel Nasser, and offered to contact Yasir Arafat, leader of the al-Fatah movement.

In 1990 she was awarded the Palestine Liberation Organization's Jerusalem Award for Culture and Arts, as well as the Honorary Palestine Prize for Poetry in 1996. Fadwa Tuqan died in Nablus, where she had lived all her life, on 13 December 2003. A line from one of her poems sums up her wish to be buried in her native Palestine: "Enough for me to die on her earth, be buried in her, to melt and vanish into her soil."

See also ARAFAT, YASIR; DAYAN, MOSHE; FATAH, AL-; NASSER, GAMAL ABDEL; WEST BANK.

Bibliography

Fischbach, Michael R. "Fadwa Tuqan." In *Encyclopedia of the Palestinians,* edited by Philip Mattar. New York: Facts On File, 2000.

Jayyusi, Salma, ed. *Anthology of Modern Palestinian Literature.* New York: Columbia University Press, 1995.

Tuqan, Fadwa. *A Mountainous Journey: An Autobiography,* translated by Olive Kenny and Naomi Shihab Nye. St. Paul, MN: Graywolf Press, 1990.

ABLA M. AMAWI
UPDATED BY MICHAEL R. FISCHBACH

TUQAN FAMILY

Prominent Palestinian family from Nablus.

Descended from an ancient Arabian tribe, the Tuqans settled in Nablus during the twelfth century. Through the nineteenth century, they were associated with other Qaysi tribes in rivalry with the local Yemeni federation. By the 1800s they had amassed great wealth, owning an imposing palace as well as a number of villas in Nablus. They shared the post of governor with the Abd al-Hadi family and used their land and tax-farm wealth to build up Nablus's famed soap and olive oil industries. Their political dominance in Nablus lasted through the

1970s as various family members gained posts under the rule of Jordan.

Prominent family members include Hafiz, a late-nineteenth-century banker; Ahmad (1903–1981), a Cambridge University graduate who was prominent in education under the British Mandate and Jordanian rule; Sulayman (1893–1958), mayor of Nablus from 1925 to 1948 and a leader of resistance to Zionism; Fadwa (1917–2003) and Ibrahim (1905–1941), sister and brother who became noted poets; Qadri (1911–1971), an educator and writer who sat in the Jordanian parliament from 1951 to 1955 and became Jordan's foreign minister in 1964; Baha al-Din (1910–1998), a historian and politician in the Jordanian government; and Aliya (1948–1977), daughter of Baha al-Din who became the third wife of Jordan's King Hussein ibn Talal from December 1972 until her death in a helicopter crash in February 1977.

See also ABD AL-HADI FAMILY; HUSSEIN IBN TALAL; NABLUS; TUQAN, FADWA.

Bibliography

Fischbach, Michael R. "Tuqan Family." In *Encyclopedia of the Palestinians,* edited by Philip Mattar. New York: Facts On File, 2000.

Muslih, Muhammad Y. *The Origins of Palestinian Nationalism.* New York: Columbia University Press, 1988.

ELIZABETH THOMPSON
UPDATED BY MICHAEL R. FISCHBACH

TURABI, HASAN AL-

[1932–]

Fundamentalist Islamic thinker.

Born in the city of Kasla in Sudan to a family of religious learning and traditions, Hasan al-Turabi earned a B.A. in law from the University of Khartoum, an M.A. in law from the University of London, and a doctorate in constitutional law from the Sorbonne in Paris. He became dean of the University of Khartoum Law School in 1964, then attorney general in 1979, and a member of the Sudanese parliament in 1965. In 1977 he became a minister of justice.

Turabi is the leader of the Sudanese branch of the Muslim Brotherhood, which was transformed into the National Islamic Front (NIF) in 1985 under his leadership. In 1988 the NIF joined the coalition government of Sadiq al-Mahdi, and Turabi served first as minister of foreign affairs and later as deputy prime minister. He was the ideological power behind the military regime of Hasan al-Bashir in Sudan in 1989. In 1996 Turabi became the speaker of the parliament, and his influence spread throughout the state organization and political parties. He fell out of favor with President al-Bashir's regime and since 2000 has been either in prison or under house arrest. However, Turabi's importance lies not in his statesmanship, but in his intellectual and ideological developments as well as his impact on Islamism in North Africa in particular and the Arab world in general.

Turabi is a fundamentalist Islamic thinker because he views Islam as the ultimate ideological and political authority for both the state and society. He views Islam as containing all the necessary elements for the creation of a viable and modern civilization and culture. Rather than a return to earlier Islamic social and political practices, Turabi advocates a progressive Islamic revival that incorporates into Islam the best of traditional Islam and Western culture. He argues that the state's only purpose is to set rules to enable society to conduct its affairs, and that it must allow society, the primary institution in Islam, to freely pursue its interests. The *shariʿa* and the Islamist jurists ensure that the role of the state remains limited. Because any society has the right to exercise *shura* (consultation) and *ijma* (consensus), and because this requires producing *ijtihad* (opinions), pluralism is necessary to enable society to identify which policies best serve its interests. As such, Turabi argues, *democracy* is simply a Western term identical to Islam's *shura* and *ijma.* Although ultimate sovereignty belongs to God, practical and political sovereignty belong to the people. Society, therefore, always remains free to choose its rulers and representatives. In this fashion, Islam can bring the best of its own civilization along with other civilizations.

Turabi distinguishes the conditions of contemporary life from those present during the rise of Islam in the seventh century. Because Muslims are living in a world much different from the one that Islamic jurisprudence legislated, they must look toward radical social and political reforms in order to

In 1964, Hasan al-Turabi participated in a revolt in Khartoum, the capital of Sudan, fighting for the formation of an Islamic government. He fought alongside, and became the leader of, the Muslim Brotherhood. He helped the group grow and gain power, and it eventually became the National Islamic Front. Turabi would then go on to help install President Omar Hassan al-Bashir, who vowed to rule the country under Islamic law. © AP/WIDE WORLD PHOTOS. REPRODUCED BY PERMISSION.

bring about the necessary Islamic revival. The historical development of Islamic jurisprudence must be rejected in favor of a process that depends on free thinking, and the state must establish a new circle of *ulama* (Islamic clergy) while continuing to derive its jurisprudence from the people. Any democratic developments in Islam must extend to the institutions of society and the family, each segment of which must work to further Islamic revival in both public and private life. Political freedom is an original part of creed and nature because freedom is what distinguishes man from animal. This includes the freedom of expression, which is stipulated in the *shariʿa*.

As for the individual, Turabi notes that man is not forced to worship God, but chooses to do so. Individual freedom is essential and cannot be taken away by the state, institutions, or society. This freedom, he argues, must be embodied in a constitution to ensure that the strength of any political leader may be checked by representative councils. Because institutionalization of freedom inevitably leads to its destruction, individual freedoms are bound and protected by Islam.

Turabi's views and writings on Islam seem to place him in the category of moderate Islamist thinkers, but the practice of his authority in Sudan suggests otherwise. Although he has called for freedom of association and multiparty representative bodies, the current Sudanese government has systematically destroyed most civic associations and remains one of the most oppressive regimes and egregious human-rights violators in the Middle East.

See also SUDAN.

Bibliography

El-Effendi, Abdelwahab. *Turabi's Revolution: Islam and Power in Sudan.* London: Grey Seal, 1991.

Moussalli, Ahmad. *Moderate and Radical Islamic Fundamentalism: The Quest for Modernity, Legitimacy, and the Islamic State.* Gainesville: University of Florida Press, 1999.

Turabi, Hasan al-. "Islam, Democracy, the State and the West: Summary of a Lecture and Roundtable Discussion with Hasan al-Turabi," prepared by Louis Cantori and Arthur Lowrie. *Middle East Policy* 1, no. 3 (1992): 52–54.

JILLIAN SCHWEDLER
UPDATED BY AHMAD S. MOUSSALLI

TURABI, WISAL AL-MAHDI

[?–]

Supporter of women's rights in Sudan.

Wisal al-Mahdi Turabi, a member of the large landowning al-Mahdi aristocracy, is the wife of Hasan al-Turabi, founder of the Sudanese Muslim Brotherhood and architect of the National Islamic Front (NIF) takeover of Sudan by military coup d'etat in 1989. Her brother, Sadiq al-Mahdi, is a leader of the influential Umma Party who has twice been prime minister of Sudan. Although the Umma Party and the NIF have been rivals, they both support Muslim women's activism, in which Wisel al-Mahdi has played a prominent role.

When the NIF seized power in 1989, the activist band of Islamists mobilized its female adherents. Wisal al-Mahdi became a spokeswoman for NIF policies such as mandatory veiling and the removal of women from "humiliating" public jobs, such as waitresses and gas station attendants. She upheld the right of women to hold high-status positions, such as judges and government ministers, and she supported *shariʿa* as state law.

Although a trained lawyer, Wisal al-Mahdi has not practiced law and appears to adhere to a conservative Muslim role for women, maintaining a proper *Shariʿ* home and providing support for her husband's national and international roles as a leading figure in the global Islamist movement. Nevertheless, some of her public comments reveal a radical Islamist feminism, blaming Arab patriarchy for the oppression of women in Sudan and elsewhere.

See also GENDER: GENDER AND LAW; GENDER: GENDER AND POLITICS; SUDAN; TURABI, HASAN AL-.

Bibliography

Hale, Sondra. *Gender Politics in Sudan: Islamism, Socialism, and the State.* Boulder, CO: Westview Press, 1996.

CAROLYN FLUEHR-LOBBAN

TURBAN

See CLOTHING

TÜRKES, ALPARSLAN

[1917–1997]

Turkish military officer and leader of the ultrapatriotic National Action Party.

Alparslan Türkes was born in Cyprus and graduated from the Turkish military academy. Due to his involvement in pan-Turkish propaganda during World War II, he was arrested in 1944 but released after an investigation. During the 1950s he served on the general staff and with NATO. He emerged as a key player in Turkey's 1960 military coup, and in its aftermath he was a member of the National Unity Committee (NUC) that was in charge of the government. Due to his radicalism, he was removed from the NUC in November 1960 and sent to New Delhi as a military attaché. After his return to Turkey in 1963 he became active in politics, eventually becoming the leader of the Republican Peasants Nation Party in 1965. He developed the doctrine of Nine Lights, which stressed nationalism and order in society. Under his leadership, the party transformed itself into the ultrapatriotic Nationalist Action Party (1969–1980). He served as vice-premier in Süleyman Demirel's National Front governments of 1975 and 1977. After the 1980 coup, Türkes was arrested and the party was banned; he reentered the political arena in 1983, became the leader of the Nationalist Worker Party, and entered parliament in 1991.

See also NATIONALIST ACTION PARTY.

Bibliography

Zürcher, Erik J. *Turkey: A Modern History,* revised edition. London: I. B. Tauris, 1997.

FRANK TACHAU
UPDATED BY M. HAKAN YAVUZ

TURKEY

Modern republic formed from the central regions of the Ottoman Empire.

The Republic of Turkey (Türkiye Cumhuriyeti) was established in 1923. Its government was an authoritarian, one-party state until 1946, when the first competitive elections were held. In subsequent decades there have been three military coups, and one instance of military pressure that forced a civilian government to resign.

According to the 2000 census, Turkey's population was 67,844,903, an increase of 18.34 percent over the population of 56,473,035 enumerated in October 1990. In 2000 the population distribution was 65 percent urban and 35 percent rural.

The total area of Turkey is 300,948 square miles (779,456 sq. km). The Asian portion of Turkey, Anatolia (historically Asia Minor), comprises 291,773 square miles (755,693 sq. km), or about 97 percent of the total; the section located on the European continent totals 9,175 square miles (23,763 sq. km). The European portion of Turkey is separated from the Asian by the Sea of Marmara, which in turn is connected to two larger bodies of water by two narrow straits. In the northeast, the Bosporus Strait connects the Sea of Marmara to the Black Sea, while in the southwest, the Dardanelles Strait connects it to the Aegean Sea. Turkey borders the Aegean Sea and Greece on the west, Bulgaria on the northwest, the Black Sea on the north,

Georgia on the northeast, Armenia on the east, Iran and Iraq on the southeast, and Syria and the Mediterranean Sea on the south.

The capital of Turkey, Ankara, is located in the central Anatolian plains; a small market town in 1923, Ankara today is home to more than 3.5 million people. The largest city, Istanbul, straddles the European and Asian sides of Turkey and has a population of 9.1 million. An important historical city, Istanbul (formerly Byzantium, then Constantinople) was first the capital of the Byzantine Empire and later the capital of the Ottoman Empire. Today, it is the cultural and business capital of Turkey. The third-largest city is İzmir (English, Smyrna), a major industrial center with a population of 2 million. Other major cities, each with populations over 1 million, include Adana, Bursa, and Konya.

Geographically, Turkey consists of a ring of mountains that enclose a series of plateaus that lie between 2,625 and 6,560 feet (800 and 2,000 m) above sea level. The highest mountains are in the east, with Mount Ararat reaching 16,945 feet (5,165 m). In the west, the highest mountain, Mount Erciyas, reaches 12,800 feet (3,900 m). The coastal regions on the south, west, and north are extremely narrow. Most of the coastal regions receive adequate rainfall; as much as 100 inches (254 cm) falls annually on the eastern Black Sea coast, and almost as much on the Aegean coast. The central plateau, on the other hand, is sheltered by its ring of mountains and receives little rainfall, generally under 10 inches (250 mm) annually. There are extensive expanses of arid steppe and even desert. Turkey's two major rivers, the Tigris and Euphrates, are both in the east. There are many lakes, both salt and freshwater; the largest is Lake Van, which covers 1,100 square miles (2,850 sq. km). Climate in the central plain ranges from severe winters with temperatures often dropping to minus 22 degrees Fahrenheit (minus 30 degrees Celsius) to hot and dry summers, with temperatures ranging from highs of 85 to 110 degrees Fahrenheit (30 to 43 degrees Celsius) in the southeast. In the western region, winters are relatively mild, hovering around freezing, and summers are hot. The Aegean coast is mild in winter and temperate in summer.

Turkey is divided into seventy-three provinces, each administered by a governor. According to the

Suleimaniye Mosque is one of the highlights of Istanbul. Turkey is overwhelmingly Muslim, but the military has determinedly kept religion out of government. Istanbul, formerly Constantinople, Turkey's largest city was the capital of the Eastern Roman, or Byzantine, Empire for more than 1,000 years and then of the Ottoman Empire for another 450 years. © CORBIS. REPRODUCED BY PERMISSION.

1982 constitution, legislative power is vested in a unicameral Grand National Assembly composed of 400 deputies elected by universal adult suffrage and serving five-year terms. In 1987 the number of deputies was raised to 450. Executive power is vested in the office of the prime minister and in the office of the president, who is elected to a seven-year term by the assembly. Although the prime minister heads the government, the president has the power to appoint a prime minister, senior civil servants, and senior members of the judiciary; submit constitutional amendments for popular referenda; challenge the constitutionality of laws by submitting them to the constitutional court; call for new elections; declare martial law; and order the armed forces into action domestically or internationally. In addition, the National Security Council—composed of the president; prime minister; chief of staff; heads of the army, navy, air force, and police; and

The ancient city wall still stands in Alanya, southern Turkey, along the Mediterranean Sea opposite Cyprus. A significant link between Europe and Asia, Turkey has roots dating back many millennia. © CORBIS. REPRODUCED BY PERMISSION.

ministers of interior, foreign affairs, and defense—has the power to present compulsory orders to the government in matters of national security.

There are no official census data on the ethnic, religious, and linguistic composition of the population of Turkey. The majority of Turks are native Turkish speakers. Ethnically, they trace their roots back to central Asia, although many Turks are Caucasians, particularly Circassians and Georgians. There is also a significant population of Kurds, a people of Indo-European descent who speak Kurdish, a language closely related to Persian. Kurds comprise an estimated 15 to 20 percent of Turkey's total population. Kurds are concentrated in the east and southeast and along the Syrian and Iraqi borders, but significant numbers have migrated to major cities in western Turkey. A large number of Arabs inhabit the region of Hatay, a small territory formerly part of Syria but ceded by the French to Turkey in 1939. The large populations of Greeks and Armenians in the nineteenth century were reduced by war and deportations during and after World War I to relatively small numbers living in Istanbul: roughly 6,000 Greeks and 60,000 Armenians. The vast majority of Turkish citizens are Muslim. Most Kurds and Turks are Sunni Muslims, but an estimated 20 to 30 percent of the population are Shiʿite Muslims, primarily of the Alevi sect. There are also small numbers of Jews (22,000), Greek Orthodox, Armenian Orthodox, and Assyrian Christians.

Agriculture and Industry

Turkey's major agricultural products are cereals, cotton, tobacco, grapes, figs, olives, hazelnuts, oilseeds, and tea. Until 1980 agricultural products, particularly cotton, provided the bulk of exports. Despite continued government attention to raising agricultural output, growth has been slow, limited by the lack of irrigated land and the low rainfall on the central plateau. Only about one-third of all land is cultivated, mostly on family-size plots, with larger farms in the coastal regions. Agriculture provides about 20 percent of the gross national product.

The Turkish government initiated a strategy of state-led industrialization in the 1930s, when a series of public enterprises were established. After 1950 increasing support was given to the private sector, so that by 1970, private-sector industrial output and investment was almost equal to that of the public sector. In 1980 the government launched a program of liberalization, designed to diminish state economic intervention and increase the role of market forces. Since 1987 the government has been privatizing some state economic enterprises, though progress has been slow. The largest industry is textiles, providing about one-third of output and export earnings. Turkey's production and export of iron and steel have increased rapidly, as has production of cement and paper products. Motor vehicle production began in the 1950s but consists mostly of assembly industries; because production has been spread out over a large number of small plants, production costs are high and exports have been negligible. Turkey's petrochemical industry produces fertilizers and a range of industrial inputs.

MAP BY XNR PRODUCTIONS, INC. THE GALE GROUP.

Other manufacturing industries include tobacco, chemicals, pharmaceuticals, glassware, and engineering.

Turkey has a large mining industry, mostly in the public sector, employing over 200,000 workers. Important mineral resources include bauxite, borax, chromium, copper, iron ore, manganese, and sulfur. The center of coal mining is at Zonguldak, on the Black Sea coast. Oil was discovered in 1950 in the southeast, but production is limited, accounting for about 10 percent of domestic consumption; the remainder is imported. In 1990 petroleum products accounted for about 15 percent of all imports. Of Turkey's natural mineral resources, only borates and petroleum products are exported, in small quantities.

Imperial History

Urban culture in Asia Minor dates to the second millennium B.C.E. In 330 C.E., the Roman emperor Constantine founded the city of Constantinople (now Istanbul), which became the capital of the Eastern Roman, or Byzantine, Empire. In the eleventh century, Ghuzz Turks who had established the Seljuk empire in the area that is today Iran and Iraq began to migrate into Anatolia, conquering territory from the Byzantine Empire. By the thirteenth century, independent princedoms were established in Anatolia, including the principality of the House of Osman, or Othman, in the northwest. Over the next several centuries, the Ottoman (from Othman) Empire conquered all of the Byzantine Empire, capturing Constantinople in 1453, as well as much of eastern Europe and the Middle East.

By the year 1800, however, several European states as well as the Russian Empire had become stronger than the Ottoman Empire. Throughout the nineteenth century, the government undertook various reform efforts to strengthen the Ottoman military, administration, political organization, and economy in order to meet the competition presented by rivals.

In the course of the nineteenth century, a middle class emerged in the Ottoman Empire. Educated in the new schools of the empire, members of the middle class had a vision of a liberal society ruled by a constitutional government and formed movements to achieve their goal, such as the Young Ottomans and later the Young Turks. These groups alternately were supported by reformist governments or suppressed by autocratic governments. In 1908, the Committee of Union and Progress (CUP) overthrew Abdülhamit II and restored the constitution. The CUP government initially enjoyed widespread popular support. But subsequent opposition to its modernizing reforms, combined with foreign wars, led the CUP to establish its own dictatorship. In 1914 the CUP formed an alliance with the Central Powers and entered World War I. After four years of fighting a bitter defensive war against the Allies on many fronts, the empire was defeated; Allied armies captured the Middle Eastern territories of Palestine, Syria, and Iraq; and Allied forces occupied Istanbul. On 30 October 1918 the Turks signed an armistice at Mudros.

Birth of the Modern Republic

On 15 May 1919, Greek forces invaded western Turkey, triggering the formation of a new Turkish army that would defeat the Greeks and then establish the modern Turkish republic. The leader of the Turkish war of liberation was Mustafa Kemal, later given the name Atatürk (Turkish: "father of the Turks"). On 23 July 1919 Kemal convened a nationalist congress in Erzurum, delegates to which later issued the National Pact (Mithaq al-Watani), a declaration calling for the dissolution of the empire and control over non-Turkish provinces, the end of foreign occupation, and the independence of all areas inhabited by Turks. Pulling together an army, the independence movement succeeded in defeating the Greek army and negotiating a withdrawal of Allied forces. The Treaty of Mudanya recognizing Turkish sovereignty was signed on 24 July 1923. On 29 October 1923 Turkey was declared a republic with Kemal as its first president and Ankara as its capital.

Modernization

The next two decades were years of reform, as Kemal and his associates attempted to complete the now 100-year-old project of modernizing Turkey. The 1924 constitution created an elected parliament as the sole repository of sovereignty and a presidency exercising executive power. In practice, however, Kemal's government was a dictatorship. A single party, the Republican People's Party (RPP), was formed as the agent of central government rule and control. In 1924 the caliphate, the highest religious office, was abolished, and in 1928 Turkey was declared a secular state. The old legal codes were annulled and replaced with civil and criminal codes adopted from Europe. The fez, the trademark Ottoman headgear adopted in the nineteenth century, was considered a symbol of the old order and was declared illegal, while the Arabic alphabet was replaced with a Roman one.

In 1929, with the onset of the Great Depression and the lapsing of the Treaty of Lausanne, which had imposed a laissez-faire trade policy on Turkey, Kemal launched a program of state-led economic development. Influenced by the Soviet experiment with its five-year development plans, in 1934 the government formulated its own five-year plan for industrial investment. Completed in 1939, the plan introduced heavy industry into Turkey while allowing the country to weather the depression with a trade surplus.

During the 1930s Kemal transformed the RPP on the model of European fascist parties. The distinction between party members and government officials was blurred, as all public officials were expected to work to implement the new ideology of the party. This ideology, officially adopted in 1931 and known as Kemalism, emphasized six themes: republicanism, nationalism, populism, statism, secularism, and *devrimçilik,* which was interpreted by moderates as reformism and by radicals as revolutionism. In 1938 Kemal Atatürk died and was replaced as president by his lieutenant, Ismet Inönü. Although Inönü kept Turkey neutral during World War II, a number of government policies on resource mobilization created widespread economic austerity, alienating large sectors of the population including those businessmen who opposed the policy of state-led economic development.

Political Reforms and Military Coups

The post–World War II period was a new era for the Turkish republic. Responding to the dissatisfaction of wartime economic policies and feeling the need to win American support against Soviet encroachments, Inönü announced the resumption of multiparty politics and competitive elections. There had been two experiments with a second party in the 1920s, but in both cases the opposition party was closed down after a short life. This time, the commitment to political pluralism was greater, and in the general elections of May 1950, the chief opposition, the Democrat Party (DP), won an overwhelming victory. The DP had campaigned on a platform of economic and cultural liberalism and increased political freedoms. Its new economic policies, based on import-substituting industrialization and the encouragement of agriculture, increased the standard of living of wide sectors of the population, particularly peasants. The DP permitted more freedom of religion than the Kemalists, who were militantly hostile to religion. But the DP increased the role of the state in the economy instead of reducing it; as the 1950s passed, the party showed signs of becoming dictatorial. A combination of incipient economic crisis and antidemocratic measures prompted a military coup on 27 May 1960.

Mustafa Kemal (who later took the name Atatürk, or "father of the Turks") led the Turkish war of independence in 1919, marking an end to the long-declining Ottoman Empire and the birth of the Republic of Turkey in 1923. As its first president, Kemal forcefully transformed the Islamic country into a modernized, secular, authoritarian state before his death in 1938. © BETTMANN/CORBIS. REPRODUCED BY PERMISISON.

The new military rulers formed a thirty-seven-member National Unity Committee (NUC) and convened a constitutional convention, dominated by supporters of the RPP. A new constitution was promulgated in 1961, and it included several liberal provisions. The NUC also allowed political parties to resume their activities. The two principal parties, the RPP—still led by Inönü—and the Justice Party (JP), the successor to the DP, formed a series of short-lived coalition governments, first together, and later between the RPP and several smaller parties, and then the JP with smaller parties. In October 1965 the JP, led by Süleyman Demirel, won a majority. The Turkish economy, now supervised by the State Planning Organization, which issued five-year development plans, grew at a rapid rate during the 1960s. But political instability came from two sources: numerous defections of members from existing parties and the proliferation of smaller parties; and the eruption of street violence as radical students and organizations on the left clashed with extremist students and organizations on the right.

On 12 March 1971 the military leadership accused the government of allowing the country to slip into anarchy and called for the creation of a stable government. The Demirel government resigned, and subsequently martial law was declared. After martial law was finally lifted in September 1973, Turkey was ruled by a series of weak coalition governments as economic conditions deteriorated. By the end of the decade, the economy was in critical condition; beginning in 1978, political violence once again erupted in the streets. On 12 September 1980 the military intervened for the third time in two decades. All existing political parties were banned, and their members prohibited from engaging in politics. A new constitution, promulgated in 1982, reversed some of the liberal measures of the 1961 constitution by enhancing the authority of the president and the cabinet vis-a-vis parliament and placing restrictions on political activity.

Party Politics

In 1983 elections were held among three new parties. The winning party was the Motherland Party (Anavatan Partisi; ANAP), led by Turgut Özal, a technocrat who had designed the January 1980 measures. Özal formed a new government and accelerated the strategy of economic liberalization and encouraging exports. Despite some success at economic liberalization, persistent government deficits resulted in high inflation and eroded popular support for the government. New parties emerged to rival ANAP: the True Path Party (TPP; Doğru Yol Partisi), a continuation of the Justice Party, led by Süleyman Demirel after 1987; the Social Democratic Populist Party (Sosyal Demokrat Halkci Parti; SHP), a continuation of the RPP under the leadership of Erdal Inönü, the son of Ismet Inönü; and the Refah Party, the continuation of the National Salvation Party. In 1989 Özal was elected president. In the 1991 elections ANAP, now led by Mesut Yilmaz, came in third, and the top two parties, the TPP and the SHP, formed a coalition government. On 17 April 1993 Özal died, and Demirel replaced him as president. On 13 June 1993 Tansu Çiller, an American-trained economist and former professor at Bosporus University, became the new head of the TPP and prime minister. Çiller was the first woman to serve as prime minister of Turkey.

In the 1995 parliamentary elections, the Refah Party obtained the largest number, but not a majority, of parliamentary seats, the first time an avowedly religious party had done so well since the establishment of the republic more than seventy years earlier. In 1996 Necmeddin Erbakan formed a coalition government, but the military effectively forced him to resign one year later. During the next five years, a series of coalition governments that purposefully excluded Refah and its successor failed to implement programs to deal with the country's economic problems. In the fall 2002 elections, the Justice Party and the Development Party, one of the successor parties to Refah, won an overwhelming majority of parliamentary seats in an election that saw the virtual elimination of ANAP and TTP from politics.

See also ABDÜLHAMIT II; ADANA; ALEVI; ANATOLIA; ANKARA; ATATÜRK, MUSTAFA KEMAL; BURSA; ÇILLER, TANSU; COMMITTEE FOR UNION AND PROGRESS; DEMIREL, SÜLEYMAN; DEMOCRAT PARTY; ERBAKAN, NECMEDDIN; ERZURUM; INÖNÜ, ERDAL; INÖNÜ, İSMET; ISTANBUL; İZMIR; KEMALISM; KONYA; KURDS; NATIONAL UNITY COMMITTEE (TURKEY); ÖZAL, TURGUT; YOUNG OTTOMANS; YOUNG TURKS.

Bibliography

Ahmad, Feroz. *The Making of Modern Turkey.* New York: Routledge, 1993.

Bianchi, Robert. *Interest Groups and Political Development in Turkey.* Princeton, NJ: Princeton University Press, 1984.

Findley, Carter V. *Bureaucratic Reform in the Ottoman Empire: The Sublime Porte, 1789–1922.* Princeton, NJ: Princeton University Press, 1980.

Fisher, W. B. *The Middle East: A Physical, Social, and Regional Geography,* 7th edition. London: Methuen, 1978.

Tapper, Richard, ed. *Islam in Modern Turkey: Religion, Politics, and Literature in a Secular State.* London: I. B. Tauris, 1991.

Waldner, David. *State Building and Late Development.* Ithaca, NY: Cornell University Press, 1999.

DAVID WALDNER
UPDATED BY ERIC HOOGLUND

TURKI, FAWAZ

[1940–]

Palestinian writer.

Fawaz (also Fawwaz) Turki was born in Haifa, Palestine, but grew up as a refugee in Beirut after his family fled Palestine during the Arab–Israel War of 1948. He later worked in Saudi Arabia, has taught in Europe and in Australia, and has traveled widely in India, the Middle East, and the United States. Turki has written several personal accounts dealing with aspects of Palestinian struggle and identity, including his acclaimed *The Disinherited: Journal of a Palestinian in Exile.* His later book, *Exile's Return,* was noteworthy for its criticism of Palestinian society.

His style is noteworthy for his exceptional and forceful command of English, and his ability to offer a penetrating view of Palestinian life for an English-speaking audience. His writings include poetry and newspaper columns as well as novels.

See also LITERATURE: ARABIC.

Bibliography

Turki, Fawaz. *The Disinherited: Journal of a Palestinian in Exile.* New York: Monthly Review Press, 1972.

Turki, Fawaz. *Exile's Return: The Making of a Palestinian American.* New York: Free Press, 1994.

JENAB TUTUNJI
UPDATED BY MICHAEL R. FISCHBACH

TURKISH–AFGHAN TREATY (1928)

Agreement between Turkey and Afghanistan designed to secure their independence from Soviet and British influence.

The Turkish–Afghan treaty, signed 28 May 1928, was the third in a series of bilateral agreements between Turkey and Afghanistan, non-Arab Muslim states bordering the Soviet Union. While the treaty did not include a mutual defense pact, it did proclaim peaceful relations between the two countries, barred either party from entering into a hostile alliance against the other, and called for mutual consultations in the event of threat of aggression from third parties.

Bibliography

Hurewitz, J. C. *The Middle East and North Africa in World Politics: A Documentary Record,* 2d edition. 2 vols. New Haven, CT: Yale University Press, 1975–1979.

DAVID WALDNER

TURKISH FILM

See FILM

TURKISH GRAND NATIONAL ASSEMBLY

The legislative body of Turkey.

The first parliament in Ottoman/Turkish history was convened in 1876 and was short lived. The second attempt, in 1908, also lasted for only a brief period. After the collapse of the Ottoman Empire, the Turkish Grand National Assembly (Türkiye Büyük Millet Meclisi) was founded on 23 April 1921, at the outset of the Turkish War of Independence; it proclaimed the republic on 29 October 1923. The assembly functioned as a legislature with one party until 1946; a transition to multiparty politics was initiated by the original party, the Republican People's Party (RPP; or Cumhuriyet Halk Partisi, CHP).

Two-Party Politics

According to the constitution, the assembly represented the expression of national sovereignty. Its function was to legislate, control the executive via the budget, and elect the head of state. From 1950 to 1957 the assembly was headed by the Democrat Party. In the 1950, 1954, and 1957 elections, the two major parties collectively received more than 90 percent of the total votes and controlled 98 percent of the parliamentary seats. The traditional center-periphery or elite-mass cleavage that the Turkish Republic inherited from the Ottoman Empire shaped the emerging political dualism. The Democrat Party projected the image of representing the interests of the periphery, including their religious aspirations, while the RPP was identified with the elitist and secularist orientation of the political center. Institutional factors also proved to be important. The simple plurality electoral system with multimember districts worked to the advantage of the two strongest parties.

Financial and economic crises and the electoral losses of the Democrat Party in 1957 led to the adoption of authoritarian policies and laws, which brought about the military coup of 1960. The activities of the assembly were suspended for a year; all the deputies and cabinet members of the Democrat Party were prosecuted and parliament was dissolved.

1961 Constitution

The 1961 constitution, drafted by a constituent assembly, placed importance on the division of powers and broadened civil liberties. Broadcasting and higher education were granted autonomy. Numerous checks and balances were introduced, aimed at controlling arbitrary executive rule. A bicameral legislature was formed. The lower house, the National Assembly (Millet Meclisi), had 400 members elected for four-year terms. The upper house, the Republican Senate (Cumhuriyet Senatosu), consisted of 150 members elected for six-year terms, plus fifteen additional senators appointed by the president of the republic on the basis of merit, a varying number of ex-officio life members who belonged to the National Unity Committee of the interim military government, and former presidents of the republic. The legislative powers of the Senate remained limited and subordinate to the National Assembly. Joint sessions of the two assemblies constituted the new Turkish Grand National Assembly (TGNA). After the military coup of 1980, the Senate was abolished. On 12 September 1980, the legislature was dissolved and all political parties banned. The interim regime lasted two years. An appointed consultative assembly prepared a new constitution.

Yalim Erez (in the background, at left), the minister for industry and an independent deputy in the Turkish Grand National Assembly, formed a new Turkish government in 1998. It was one of several coalition governments established between 1996 and 2002 in an effort to deal with serious economic problems. © ABC AJANSI/CORBIS SYGMA. REPRODUCED BY PERMISSION.

1982 Constitution

The 1982 constitution was approved by a referendum on 9 November 1982. It vests legislative power in a unicameral assembly, elected by universal adult suffrage (the age at which one could vote was at first twenty-one but in 1995 was lowered to eighteen) for a maximum of five years. By-elections are to be held once between elections unless the number of vacancies reaches 5 percent of the parliament. The president of the republic is elected by the TGNA from among its members or from among candidates who have a higher education and are over forty. The president serves for a single term of seven years; a successor must be elected within thirty days. If no successor can be elected by the fourth ballot, parliament must dissolve itself. After the presidencies of Turgut Özal and Süleyman Demirel, in 2000 the TGNA elected Ahmet Necdet Nezer, former chair of the Constitutional Court. The prerogatives of the president are more extensive than in the previous constitution; they include the power to dissolve parliament. The 1987 elections enlarged the membership of the TGNA from 400 to 450; in 1995, the number of seats was raised to 550. The main functions of the TGNA are enacting, amending, and repealing laws; supervising the Council of Ministers; authorizing the Council of Ministers to issue governmental decrees that have the force of law; approving the budget; declaring war; ratifying international agreements; and proclaiming amnesties and pardons. Legislators exercise control in the form of written questions, investigation, and interpellation. Members of parliament are granted parliamentary immunity with regard to freedom of speech and, under certain circumstances, freedom from arrest.

As of 1993, constitutional amendments require a two-thirds majority. If no quorum is achieved, the president of the republic can return the amendment to parliament or refer the amendment to a popular vote. The state monopoly on television was eliminated, opening television to national and international channels; the right of government officials to organize unions was granted; prisoners were given the right to vote; political parties were permitted to establish women's and youth branches; discretionary power was allocated to the executive to declare early local elections or to postpone them. In the summer of 2002, new amendments legalized Kurdish-language radio and television, private-school education in Kurdish, and the abolition of capital punishment.

Under the current electoral rules, a party must receive 10 percent of the vote to gain representation in parliament. After 1987, this threshold was increased by adding a district-level quota (calculated by a simple proportion of the valid votes) to the parliamentary seats per district. This practice left a number of parties out of parliament. The Kurdish parties were eliminated despite their high regional return because their nationwide vote was less than 10 percent. Parties that do receive 10 percent of the national note win a proportionally higher share of parliamentary seats. For example, the Justice and Development Party (Adalet ve Kalkınma Partisi) under the leadership of Tayyip Erdoğan received 34.2 percent of the votes but 363 seats, eliminating all competing parties with the exception of the RPP, which received 19.3 percent of the votes and 178 seats. With the phasing out of sixteen political parties, 45.3 percent of the voters remained without representation. This brought Turkish politics back to a dual party system. In parliament, 89 percent of the members were newcomers. More than 80 percent of the parliamentarians had a higher education; they were predominantly lawyers, engineers, businessmen, and economists. The representation of women registered a slow gain. Despite the active support of women's organizations, the number of women parliamentarians registered only a slight increase, from 23 in 1999 to 24 in 2002.

Realignment

Looking at the political composition of the TGNA, a significant voter realignment can be seen, and high volatility in Turkey's major parties. Beginning in the 1980s and continuing in the 1990s, the moderate right parties registered a steady decline. Özal's party, the Motherland Party (Anavatan Partisi), winner of the 1983 elections, fell from having 292 representatives in 1987 to having 88 in 1999. On the moderate left, a similar phenomenon took place. The RPP was left out of parliament in 1999 with 8.7 percent of the votes and returned in 2002 with 19.3 percent; Bülent Ecevit's party, the Democratic Left Party (Demokratik Sol Partisi), gained 22.2 percent in 1999 but was eliminated with 1.2 percent in 2002.

This realignment pushed the extreme right, exemplified by the ultra-right-wing Nationalist Action Party (Milliyetçi Hareket Partisi) and the much smaller nationalist Great Unity Party (Büyük Birlik Partisi), into the political spectrum. The Islamist Welfare Party (Refah Partisi) and its successor the Virtue Party (Fazilet Partisi) also benefited from this realignment. The coalition governments of the 1990s were dominated by these political groups. The results of the 2002 election indicate that the center-periphery cleavage has lost its determining relevance. Instead, protest voting seems to have gained ascendancy.

The performance of Turkey's parliamentary system offers an important example of how electoral processes have played a critical role in opening the political system after each military intervention. Another new aspect of Turkish political life is the growing importance of local elections. With the increasing weight of large cities and metropolitan areas, urban problems influence electoral choice at the local and national level. The recent electoral success of the Justice and Development Party is partly due to the reputation Erdoğan, the former mayor of Istanbul, acquired. Major conflicts in national politics, such as those over secularism, affect voting patterns at both levels. Although Turkey's democratization started during the late 1940s, democracy has not been fully achieved, but the country's relatively long and continuous experience with democratic politics in twenty-two national elections represents a significant achievement.

See also AKP (JUSTICE AND DEVELOPMENT PARTY); DEMIREL, SÜLEYMAN; DEMOCRAT PARTY; ERDOĞAN, TAYYIP; MOTHERLAND PARTY; NATIONALIST ACTION PARTY; OTTOMAN EMPIRE; ÖZAL, TURGUT; REFAH PARTISI; REPUBLICAN PEOPLE'S PARTY (RPP).

Bibliography

Heper, Metin, and Evin, Ahmet, eds. *State, Democracy, and the Military: Turkey in the 1980s.* New York; Berlin: W. de Gruyter, 1988.

Özbudun, Ergun. *Contemporary Turkish Politics: Challenges to Democratic Consolidation.* Boulder, CO: Lynne Rienner, 2000.

Zürcher, Erik J. *Turkey: A Modern History,* new revised edition. New York and London: I. B. Tauris, 1998.

NERMIN ABADAN-UNAT

TURKISH HEARTH ASSOCIATION

Group formed to promote Turkish nationalism.

Toward the end of the Ottoman Empire, Ziya Gökalp and other Turkish intellectuals founded the Turkish Hearth Association (Türk Ocaği) in 1911 to promote nationalism, especially Gökalp's synthesis of Turkism, Islamism, and modernism. The association provided the Union and Progress political party with ideological direction. With government support, this private association sponsored nationalistic publications, speeches, sports, health, and economic development projects. By 1930, the association had 254 branches in cities and towns across Turkey. In 1931/32, the Republican People's party dissolved the association, took over its property, and established the People's Houses *(Halk Evleri)* in its place.

See also GÖKALP, ZIYA; PEOPLE'S HOUSES.

Bibliography

Lewis, Bernard. *The Emergence of Modern Turkey,* 3d edition. New York: Oxford University Press, 2002.

PAUL J. MAGNARELLA

TURKISH HISTORICAL SOCIETY

Academy dedicated to the study of Turkish history.

The forerunner to this society was the Turkish Historical Committee of the Turkish Hearth (Türk Ocaği Türk Tarih Heyeti) formed on 4 June 1930. This committee was reorganized as the Society for the Study of Turkish History (Türk Tarihi Tetkik Cemiyeti) on 12 April 1931 (officially recognized on 15 April 1931), and renamed the Turkish Historical Society (Türk Tarih Kurumu) on 3 October 1935. On 7 November 1982, the society was made subordinate to the Atatürk Kültür, Dil ve Tarih Yüksek Kurumu that now oversees the cultural, linguistic, and historical societies. The society has convened historical congresses (the first one, held 2-10 July 1932), publishes the journal *Belleten,* as well as monograph series devoted to all periods of the history of Turkey from the civilizations of ancient Anatolia to the modern day. It also serves as an academy for historical sciences honoring Turkish and foreign scholars.

ULI SCHAMILOGLU

TURKISH–ITALIAN WAR (1911–1912)

War launched by Italy against Turkey for control of Libya.

The Turkish–Italian War (29 September 1911 to 8 October 1912) was initiated by Italy in Libya as a step toward acquiring a modern empire. The diplomatic ground for this move was prepared by reaching secret bilateral agreements with Britain, France, Germany, Austria-Hungary, and Russia, all of which gave Italy a free hand in Libya in exchange for reciprocity elsewhere. This was in violation of the Congress and Treaty of Berlin (1878), in which the European powers guaranteed the sovereignty and territorial integrity of the Ottoman Empire.

Italy sent an ultimatum to the Ottoman government on 26 September 1911, declaring that it would occupy Libya within twenty-four hours unless the Ottoman Empire undertook immediate measures to protect the security of Italian citizens residing in Libya and also their property. Italy also said that Istanbul's dispatch of weapons to Libya was a provocation because these would be used against "peaceful" Italian colonists. When its demands were not met, Italy declared war against the Ottoman Empire (29 September), placed a blockade on the Libyan coast, and started landing in Tripoli (4 October). The conquest of the coastal towns was swift: Tripoli (12 October), Derna (18 October), Benghazi and Khoms (21 October), and the smaller towns soon after.

The Ottoman military force in Libya was small and much below standard. When war broke out, the Ottomans could not forward military support to

Libya due to the Italian sea blockade and the decision of Britain and France to prevent the passage of military reinforcements to the belligerents through Egypt or Tunisia.

As a result of these conditions, the Ottoman authorities in Istanbul allowed volunteers to infiltrate into Libya. (Among them were Enver Paşa, who later became the minister of war, and Mustafa Kemal Atatürk, the founder of the Turkish republic.) They left the actual direction of the war to the Ottoman military command in Libya, which decided to retreat from the coast—where the Italians had a clear military advantage owing to the size and quality of their forces. An Ottoman-Libyan force was established, composed of tribal soldiers, Ottoman professionals, and a mixed Ottoman-tribal command, which in Cyrenaica was connected with the Sanusi leadership and network of *zawiyas* (religious compounds).

The Italian invading forces were the first to make military use of airplanes (for reconnaissance and bombing). They made no meaningful gains after their initial conquests because they attempted to fight a trench war against the resistance, which engaged in guerrilla warfare and took advantage of the hilly or desert terrain and the support of the population. Failing to advance into the hinterland, the Italians widened the scope of the war to the eastern Mediterranean to put more pressure on the Ottomans. During April and May 1912, Italy occupied the Dodecanese islands, tried to enter forcibly the Dardanelles channel connecting Istanbul to the Aegean Sea, and bombarded some Ottoman ports, including Beirut. These operations caused the Ottomans heavy damage, aroused strong apprehension among the European powers, and provoked international efforts to solve the crisis.

In the Balkans, increasing unrest led to the outbreak of the first Balkan War on 8 October 1912. Unable to fight on two major fronts, and perceiving the Balkans as more important to the empire than Libya, the Ottoman government decided to end the war in Libya. The Treaty of Peace, concluded in October 1912, stipulated that Ottoman forces were to depart Libya, but that the Ottomans could send Muslim religious representatives there. The Ottoman withdrawal was to be followed by an Italian evacuation of the Dodecanese. The issue of sovereignty was not settled conclusively: Although Italy regarded Libya as part of the Italian homeland following its declaration on the extension of Italian law over Libya (5 November 1911, only one month after the war had started and before any peace treaty had been concluded), the Ottomans told the local population that they were being granted autonomy under Ottoman rule. Most Ottoman forces left Tripolitania, but many remained in Cyrenaica, and reinforcements also were sent later, especially during World War I. Until then, Italy managed to occupy most of Tripolitania and prevented the functioning of the Ottoman-chosen religious representation.

Bibliography

Childs, Timothy W. *Italo-Turkish Diplomacy and the War over Libya, 1911–1912*. New York; Leiden, Netherlands: Brill, 1990.

Simon, Rachel. *Libya between Ottomanism and Nationalism: Ottoman Involvement in Libya during the War with Italy (1911–1919)*. Berlin: K. Schwarz, 1987.

RACHEL SIMON
UPDATED BY ERIC HOOGLUND

TURKISH LANGUAGE

Türkçe; official language of the Republic of Turkey.

Turkish is one of the Turkic languages of the Altaic language family, one of the world's major language families. Turkic, Mongolian, and Manchu-Tungus constitute the Altaic language family, which originated around the Altai mountain ranges in central Asia, straddling Mongolia, China, and Russia. Altaic languages usually are grouped with the Uralic languages—for example, Samoyed, Finnish, and Hungarian. Debates continue about whether the typological and lexical similarities between the two language families signal a common ancestor language or prolonged contact.

The Turkic Languages

The Turkic language group includes most of the languages and dialects spoken along a wide Eurasian belt that extends from eastern Siberia to eastern Europe and the Balkans. The major representative Turkic languages are (starting in the east) Yakut, Altai, Khakas, Uygur, Kyrgyz, Kazakh, Uzbek,

Turkmen, Bashkir, Tatar, Chuvash, Azeri, and Turkish. With the exception of Turkish, all of these languages are spoken in the republics and territories of the former Soviet Union or in northwestern China.

Turkish, Azeri (also referred to as Azerbaijani Turkish), and Turkmen are the major members of the southwestern, or Oghuz, branch of the Turkic languages. In demographic terms, this branch is the most important Turkic group. The Azeri language is spoken in the Republic of Azerbaijan and in northwestern Iran. Turkmen is spoken in the Republic of Turkmenistan and in adjoining territories in northern Iran and Afghanistan, as well as in Iraq. Lesser-known members of the southwestern branch are Gagauz, spoken in the Balkan states of Bulgaria and Moldavia, and Qashqa'i, spoken in parts of southwestern Iran. The languages of this branch are closely related and have a relatively high degree of mutual intelligibility. What interferes with the complete comprehension of written material is mainly vocabulary, which was developed or acquired by each language while functioning in different historical and cultural spheres, and the different alphabets they use (Arabic and Latin). In oral communication, differences in pronunciation slow down comprehension.

Turkish was introduced to the Middle East with the westward migration of various Turkish tribes, who had converted to Islam by the ninth century, from the western regions of central Asia. By the end of the eleventh century, these Muslim Turks had conquered Asia Minor, and the Turkish language began to be established in Anatolia. As the official administrative language of the Ottoman Turks, Turkish spread further with the continuing Ottoman conquests, into the Balkans and central Europe to the north and into the Arab lands and North Africa to the south. Turkish became the lingua franca in many of these regions, and the impact of Turkish on the indigenous languages after centuries of contact is clearly discernible today.

Old Anatolian, Ottoman, and Modern Turkish

The earliest written Anatolian Turkish materials are in Arabic script and date from the thirteenth century. Three basic periods are recognized for the historical development of the Turkish language, based on written data: (1) Old Anatolian Turkish for the thirteenth through fifteenth centuries; (2) Ottoman Turkish for the fifteenth through the early twentieth centuries; (3) Modern Turkish since 1928. The linguistic base remained remarkably stable, particularly for the spoken language, so that some poetry, including early hymns of Sufism and Sufi orders from the fourteenth century still can be understood and appreciated by a general audience. However, in the process of adapting to Islam and the Arab-Persian culture, Turkish gradually acquired many words and some syntactic elements from Arabic and Persian. As the Ottoman Turks became the standard-bearers for the Islamic world, borrowings from both Arabic and Persian accelerated to such an extent that by the nineteenth century an official or literary Ottoman Turkish text could be understood only by an educated elite conversant in Turkish, Persian, and Arabic.

By the start of the twentieth century—and hastened by the post–World War I disintegration of the Ottoman Empire—nationalistic notions about a distinct Turkish identity inspired moves to rid the language of excessive foreign elements. The Alphabet Reform of 1928 abandoned the Arabic script and mandated a phonetic Turkish script based on the Latin alphabet; this was a crucial factor in the emergence of Modern Turkish. The new writing system was tailored exclusively to the vowel-rich Turkish sound system, eventually setting up a well-defined modern national standard for Turkish based on the dialect of Istanbul, the old capital of the Ottoman Empire and the educational, cultural, and intellectual center of the country.

The Turkish language shares a core vocabulary with the other Turkic languages and exhibits characteristic common features: vowel harmony, agglutination, and, on the syntactic level, left-branching. Turkish has eight vowels, four pairs with corresponding front/back, high/low, and rounded/unrounded sounds, which form the basis for vowel harmony. According to vowel harmony rules, vowels of suffixes must have the same properties as the vowel in the last syllable: either front/back or rounded/unrounded. Twenty-one letters represent the consonants. Agglutination in Turkish takes the form of suffixes attached to the end of a word, whether noun or verb. Suffixes add to the word's meaning and/or mark its grammatical function. Turkish does not have a definite article, nor does it have gender pronouns (one word signifies *he, she, or it*). Sentence construction follows the subject-object-verb pattern. As a left-branching language, all modifiers precede the element modified.

A lexical inventory of Modern Turkish clearly shows that the Turkish language has enriched itself by borrowing freely from other languages and continues to do so. In 1931 the Turkish Linguistic Society undertook reforms that effectively resulted in eliminating Arabic and Persian words not fully assimilated into the Turkish language. However, these words were replaced with neologisms or borrowings from European languages.

See also ANATOLIA; AZERI LANGUAGE AND LITERATURE; ISTANBUL; LITERATURE: TURKISH; OTTOMAN EMPIRE; SUFISM AND THE SUFI ORDERS; TRIBES AND TRIBALISM: QASHQA'I; TURKISH LINGUISTIC SOCIETY; TURKISH SCRIPT.

Bibliography

Boeschoten, Hendrik, and Verhoeven, Ludo, eds. *Turkish Linguistics Today.* New York; Leiden, Netherlands: E. J. Brill, 1991.

Kowalski, T. "Ottoman Turkish Dialects." In *Encyclopaedia of Islam,* Vol. 4. Leiden, Netherlands: E. J. Brill.

Lewis, G. L. *Turkish Grammar.* Oxford: Clarendon Press, 1967.

Slobin, Dan Isaac, and Zimmer, Karl, eds. *Studies in Turkish Linguistics.* Philadelphia; Amsterdam: J. Benjamins, 1986.

ERIKA GILSON
UPDATED BY ERIC HOOGLUND

TURKISH LAW ON THE PROTECTION OF THE FAMILY (1998)

Turkish law to protect women.

The Law on the Protection of the Family primarily aims to improve the handling of domestic violence cases. Before its enactment, such cases were tried in accordance with the Criminal Code, thus requiring victims to appeal to the police and to obtain a report from a state hospital. Women's organizations have claimed that such requirements inhibit women's appeal to legal recourse, because police and doctors are usually more interested in the "reconciliation" of spouses than in initiating legal action. With the introduction of the law, the complaint of the victim or the decision of the public prosecutor suffices to order immediate removal of the abuser from the domicile or imprisonment for up to six months.

The issue of domestic violence is central to Turkey's post-1980 feminism, and the enactment of the law illustrates a successful collaboration between activists and the state. Among many others, three organizations—the Purple Roof Foundation, the Altındağ Women's Solidarity Foundation, and Women for Women's Rights—have closely worked with the General Directorate on the Status and Problems of Women to secure support from parliamentarians, jurists, and the media.

The impact of the law on social attitudes is, however, questionable. The number of reported cases of domestic violence did not decrease significantly in the five years after passage of the law, and, according to a study conducted among college students, most males still approve of wife beating.

See also GENDER: GENDER AND LAW; GENDER: GENDER AND POLITICS; TURKEY.

Bibliography

Arat, Yeşim. "Feminist Institutions and Democratic Aspirations: The Case of the Purple Roof Women's Shelter Foundation." In *Deconstructing the Images of "The Turkish Woman,"* edited by Z. Arat. New York: St. Martin's Press, 1998.

Sakallı, Nuray. "Beliefs about Wife Beating among Turkish College Students: The Effects of Patriarchy, Sexism, and Sex Differences." *Sex Roles* 44, nos. 9–10 (2001): 599–610.

BURÇAK KESKIN-KOZAT

TURKISH LINGUISTIC SOCIETY

Organization devoted to the study of Turkish and the Turkic languages.

The Society for the Study of the Turkish Language (Türk Dili Tetkik Cemiyeti) was founded on 12 July 1932, on the model of a similar society that already existed for the study of Turkish history. In 1934, its name was updated to the Türk Dili Araştirma Kurumu reflecting the society's interest in purging the Turkish Language of its numerous borrowed Arabic and Persian words. In 1936, the name was changed again to the Turkish Linguistic Society (Türk Dil Kurumu). On 7 November 1982, the society was made subordinate to the Atatürk Kültür, Dil ve Tarih Yüksek Kurumu that now oversees the cultural, linguistic, and historical societies. The society has convened linguistic congresses (the first congress opened in 1932), publishes the journal *Türk Dili,* and publishes dictionaries and other works related to Turkish and all the other Turkic languages. In contrast to other such societies in Turkey, the activities of the Turkish Linguistic Society have not been led by scholars of the Turkish language, and one result has been that the society's activities have assumed a populist character. The society has also been at the center of recurring and intense national debates over language reform, most recently over the degree to which vast numbers of neologisms (new words or word forms adopted from foreign words) should be introduced into the Turkish language (often over the objections of many politicians and scholars).

See also TURKISH LANGUAGE.

Bibliography

Heyd, Uriel. *Language Reform in Modern Turkey.* Jerusalem: Israel Oriental Society, 1954.

ULI SCHAMILOGLU

TURKISH NATIONAL PACT

A resolution that stated the goal of political independence for Turkey.

This resolution adopted by the Ottoman parliament in Istanbul on 17 February 1920, declared support for the demands of the nationalist movement led by Mustafa Kemal Pasha (Atatürk). It included: the integrity of all territories inhabited by "an Ottoman Islamic majority"; popular plebiscites to determine the future of territories whose status was in doubt (Kars, Ardahan, and Batum in the Caucasus; western Thrace; and areas with Arab majorities); "protection" of the city of Istanbul and the Sea of Marmara and negotiation regarding trade and commerce in the Bosporus and the Dardanelles; recognition of minority rights provided reciprocal rights were extended to Muslim minorities in other countries; and recognition of full independence and sovereignty for "the country." This was essentially the program implemented in the wake of the defeat of the Greek army in western Anatolia and the withdrawal of British power from Istanbul and its environment in 1922. Functionally, the national pact served as a declaration of independence by nationalist Turkey.

Bibliography

Shaw, Stanford J., and Shaw, Ezel Kural. *History of the Ottoman Empire and Modern Turkey,* Vol. 2: *Reform, Revolution, and Republic: The Rise of Modern Turkey, 1808-1975.* Cambridge, U.K., and New York: Cambridge University Press, 1977.

FRANK TACHAU

TURKISH NEWS AGENCY

See NEWSPAPERS AND PRINT MEDIA: TURKEY

TURKISH SCRIPT

Latin alphabet used predominantly in Turkey to write Turkish.

Contemporary Turkish is written in the Roman alphabet; the Turkish script is composed of eight vowels and twenty-one consonants, which are marked by various diacriticals. The first writings in Turkic language date to about 700 C.E. and use a runic alphabet. Later, Turkish came to be written in the Arabic alphabet. The earliest writings of Turkish in the Arabic script date to the thirteenth century and show strong Arabo-Persian linguistic influences. The fourteenth and fifteenth centuries show a boom in textual production. The literary Ottoman Turkish of this period was far removed from the spoken language. Beginning in the eighteenth century, with the decline of the Ottoman Empire, movements in favor of a language with stronger Turkish and less Ottoman characteristics gained momentum. In 1909, the Turkish Club began promoting a simpler Turkish, comprehensible across social strata. Mustafa Kemal Atatürk later founded the Turkish Language Academy. As part of Atatürk's sweeping reforms, the Turkish script was officially switched from the Arabic to the Roman alphabet in 1928.

See also ATATÜRK, MUSTAFA KEMAL; TURKISH LANGUAGE.

Bibliography

Campbell, George. *Compendium of the World's Languages*, vol. 2, 2d edition. London: Routledge, 2000.

NOAH BUTLER

TURKISH WORKERS PARTY

Turkish political party, 1961–1971.

This first avowedly socialist group to make a significant impact on the Turkish party system was founded in February of 1961. Its emergence signified the relative liberalism of the political order in the wake of the military intervention of 27 May 1960. The party competed successfully in the elections of 1965 and 1969, polling about 3 percent of the vote and gaining fifteen seats in the former and two in the latter election (the difference is attributable to changes in the electoral law). Its presence on the scene may have pulled the centrist Republican People's party (RPP) to the left. The party was subject to official and mob harassment, including violent attacks on its facilities and members. It was dissolved by order of the constitutional court in July 1971 on grounds that its leaders had encouraged communism and ethnic divisiveness (specifically, Kurdish separatism).

Bibliography

Ahmad, Feroz. *The Turkish Experiment in Democracy, 1950–1975*. Boulder, CO: Westview Press, 1977.

FRANK TACHAU

TURKISM

Political and cultural movement that emerged in the late nineteenth century and helped to form the new Turkish republic.

A movement of many tendencies, Turkism evolved largely in response to European nationalism and to the perceived failure of Ottomanism, as the empire was rocked by minority nationalist movements in the Balkans and Armenia. Sentiments of Turkish nationalist feeling can be traced to historical writings of the mid-nineteenth century, such as those of Ahmet Vefik Paşa (1823–1891). The first Ottoman Turcologist was Necib Asim (1861–1935). Politically, Turkism was most prominently expressed by the Young Turk movement, first in exile in the 1890s in Europe and Egypt and later in Anatolia after the 1908 Young Turk revolution. Competing tendencies included Anatolian nationalism, which traced Turkish roots in the territory to ancient times, and pan-Turkism, espoused especially by Turkish refugees from Russia and central Asia. The political manifesto of pan-Turkism is considered Russian-born Yusuf Akçura's 1904 essay, "Üç Tarz-i Siyaset" (Three Kinds of Policy), which rejected Ottomanism and Islam as bases of national identity and policy.

A major Turkish literary movement appeared in the early twentieth century, with groups like the Genç Kalemler (Young Pens) founded in 1911 in Salonika and the Türk Deneği (Turkish Society) founded in 1908 in Constantinople (now Istanbul). These and other groups were devoted to reviving Turkish folklore, studying the roots and branches of the various Turkic languages, and purifying the Ottoman language of non-Turkish words. The most important ideologue of the Young Turk era was the pan-Turkist writer and sociologist, Ziya Gökalp (1876–1924), who developed a populist vision of the rebirth of Turkish society. Eventually, Anatolian-based Turkism would prevail, with Mustafa Kemal's revolution and war of independence, beginning in 1919.

See also AHMET VEFIK; GENÇ KALEMLER; GÖKALP, ZIYA.

Bibliography

Lewis, Bernard. *The Emergence of Modern Turkey*, 3d edition. New York: Oxford University Press, 2002.

Shaw, Stanford J., and Shaw, Ezel Kural. *History of the Ottoman Empire and Modern Turkey*, Vol. 2: *Reform, Revolution, and Republic: The Rise of Modern Turkey, 1808–1975*. Cambridge, U.K., and New York: Cambridge University Press, 1977.

ELIZABETH THOMPSON

TURKMANCHAI, TREATY OF (1828)

Treaty by which Iran ceded its territories in the Caucasus to Russia.

The Treaty of Turkmanchai concluded a war between Iran and Russia that Iran initiated in 1826 with the aim of recovering territory in the Caucasus region that it had lost to Russia in 1813. The war went very badly for Iran, which was forced to accept unfavorable peace terms in the treaty signed in the village of Turkmanchai, about 80 miles southeast of Tabriz, on 21 February 1828. Under the treaty, Iran ceded its remaining provinces north of the Aras River (Yerevan and Nakhichevan) to Russia; extended preferential trade rights to Russian subjects; recognized Russia's exclusive naval rights in the Caspian Sea; accepted the application of Russian law to Russian subjects in Iran involved in civil or criminal legal cases; and agreed to pay Russia an indemnity of 20 million rubles.

Bibliography

Lambton, Ann K. S. "Persian Trade under the Early Qajars." In *Islam and the Trade of Asia: A Colloquium*, edited by D. S. Richards. Philadelphia: University of Pennsylvania Press, 1970.

FARHAD SHIRZAD
UPDATED BY ERIC HOOGLUND

TURKMEN

See GLOSSARY

TURKO–IRANIAN WAR (1821–1823)

The final war between the Qajar Persians and the Ottoman Turks.

This conflict began in 1821 when the Persian governor of Erzerum gave protection to tribes fleeing Azerbaijan. Actually, the conflict was instigated by Russia, which was anxious to weaken the Ottoman position in the Greek Revolution. The Russians induced Abbas Mirza, son of Fath Ali Shah Qajar, to invade Ottoman Turkey. He did, occupying Kurdistan and all the districts adjacent to Azerbaijan. As a counter move, the Ottoman viceroy of Baghdad invaded Persia but was defeated and chased back to Baghdad. In retaliation, Fath Ali Shah Qajar's oldest son, Mohammad Ali Mirza, laid siege to that city; his illness, and later death, lifted the siege, and the action shifted to the north. In the battle of Erzurum (1821) Abbas Mirza's army of 30,000 men defeated an Ottoman army of over 50,000. An epidemic of cholera precluded further action in the south, and the two powers ended hostilities with the Treaty of Erzurum on 28 July 1823. This treaty involved no change in territorial borders, but it did guarantee Persia access to the holy places in Iraq and Arabia; Ottoman suppression of Kurdish raids on Persian territory; release of the possessions of Persian merchants in Turkey; and an exchange of ambassadors.

Bibliography

Sykes, Percy Molesworth. *A History of Persia* (1915). London: Routledge and K. Paul, 1969.

DANIEL E. SPECTOR

TURKOLOGY

The academic study of the languages and civilization of the Turkic peoples with a traditional emphasis on sources written in Turkic languages.

The modern Turkic languages include Turkish, Uzbek, Kazakh, Azeri, Kazan Tatar, Turkmen, Kirghiz, Chuvash, Bashkir, Karakalpak, Yakut, Kumik, Crimean Tatar, Uighur, Tuvan, Gagauz, Karachay, Balkar, Xakas, Noghay, Altay, Shor, Dolgan, Karaim, and Tofalar. Native scholars have been writing descriptions of the Turkic dialects since the eleventh century. In the West, the earliest works on Turkey appeared in the fifteenth and sixteenth centuries, and the first descriptions of the Turkish language were published in the seventeenth century. The formal study of Turkish and other Turkic languages was introduced in Europe in the eighteenth century, and by the end of the nineteenth century, there were prominent centers of Turkology at universities in Paris, Moscow, Saint Petersburg, Kazan, Budapest, and Vienna. Today Turkology is widely taught in modern political units representing individual Turkic peoples: the Turkish republic, the Turkic republics of the former USSR, and the Uighur Autonomous Region in the People's Republic of China, where it is synonymous with the study of the local national culture. Turkology is also offered at major universities in Europe and North America, though the study of the language and civilization of the Turkish republic is far better represented than the study of the Turkic peoples as a whole.

Bibliography

Menges, Karl H. *The Turkic Languages and Peoples: An Introduction to Turkic Studies,* 2nd revised edition. Wiesbaden: Harrassowitz, 1995.

Poppe, Nicholas. *Introduction to Altaic Linguistics.* Wiesbaden: Harrassowitz, 1965.

ULI SCHAMILOGLU

TURKS

Ethnic group living in Turkey; also used to refer to Turkic-language speakers in Central Asia.

Turks are an ethnolinguistic group living in a broad geographic expanse extending from southeastern Europe through Anatolia and the Caucasus Mountains and throughout Central Asia. Thus Turks include the Turks of Turkey, the Azeris of Azerbaijan, and the Kazakhs, Kyrgyz, Tatars, Turkmen, and Uzbeks of Central Asia, as well as many smaller groups in Asia speaking Turkic languages. In a legal sense, however, *Turks* refers only to citizens of Turkey, even those (up to 20% of the population) who are not ethnically Turkish.

Nomadic Turks began infiltrating into Iran from Central Asia as early as the eighth century. Although the initial contacts generally were peaceful, by the tenth century large groups of Turks were invading Iran, and in the eleventh century they began invading Anatolia. First the Seljuk Turks and subsequently the Ottoman Turks established kingdoms in Anatolia. The Ottomans conquered the Byzantine imperial capital Constantinople (now Istanbul) in 1453, and this city then became the center of the Ottoman Empire, which at its height in the sixteenth and seventeenth centuries spanned three continents. Although the Ottoman Empire was multiethnic, Europeans often referred to its subjects as Turks and used "Ottoman Empire" synonymously with "Turkey."

During the nineteenth century, some Ottoman/Turkish intellectuals began to advocate pan-Turanism, a movement to unite all Turkic-language peoples under the Ottoman Empire. After the establishment of the Republic of Turkey in 1923, the government rejected pan-Turanism as an official policy. Nevertheless, interest in the cultural, if not political, unity of Turkic peoples has been a strong current among intellectuals in Turkey and has been revitalized since the collapse of the Soviet Union in 1991 and the emergence in Central Asia of several new Turkic-speaking countries.

See also ANATOLIA; ISTANBUL; TURKEY; TURKISH LANGUAGE.

Bibliography

Yavuz, M. Hakan. "Turkish Identity Politics and Central Asia." In *Islam and Central Asia: An Enduring Legacy or an Evolving Threat?* edited by Roland Sagdeev and Susan Eisenhower. Washington, DC: Center for Political and Strategic Studies, 2000.

ERIC HOOGLUND

TÜRK YURDU

See NEWSPAPERS AND PRINT MEDIA: TURKEY

TWAREG

Berber-speaking people of the Sahara, mostly in Algeria.

Twareg is an apparently non-Berber plural; the singular is *targui* or *targi.* Twareg (also Tuareg) call themselves, according to the region, *amahagh, amaiagh,* or *amashagh,* all reflexes of *amazigh,* the term more widely used for Berber in the rest of North Africa. It is estimated that there are 400,000 to 500,000 Twareg-language/dialect speakers. Most are fair-skinned Europids, although many are descendants of or mixed with negroid populations (of whom most were slaves). Twareg traditionally distinguish socially between the "noble" clans, camel nomads who in the past could range far and wide, wage war, and claim a share of the resources of groups they dominated (and whose protection they assured), and "vassal" clans, also nomadic but essentially herdsmen (mainly goats, but also camels belonging to the nobles, and cattle in some places), subjects of the noble clans. Other groups often are counted as Twareg, notably sedentary former slave populations (now primarily agriculturalists in the oases and artisans).

The requirements of modern states—fixed borders, schooling of children, control of territory and citizens—and the industrial exploitation of resources have placed extreme pressures on the nomadic existence and traditions dear to the Twareg. They nonetheless maintain such traditional cultural traits as a strong matrilineal principle (in much of their inheritance of property, succession to chieftainship, rights and obligations toward vassal groups, etc.) and the strict veiling of men (women, however, typically are not veiled).

See also BERBER.

THOMAS G. PENCHOEN

TWAYNI, GHASSAN

[1926–]

Lebanon's best-known journalist and publisher; former minister, ambassador, and representative from Lebanon to the United Nations.

A Greek Orthodox born in Beirut, Ghassan Twayni (also Tueni) has been one of the most influential figures in post–World War II Lebanon. His impressive and multifaceted career as academic, journalist, businessman, politician, diplomat, and man of letters has made him a prime shaper of public opinion in his country and one of the most respected commentators on Lebanese and Arab affairs throughout the United States and Europe.

He received a bachelor of arts degree in philosophy from the American University of Beirut (AUB) in 1945 and a master of arts degree in political science from Harvard University in 1947. After a year as a lecturer in political science at AUB (1947–1948), he became editor in chief of the daily newspaper *al-Nahar* in 1948, a position he occupied until he turned it over to his son, Jubran, in December 1999. He worked in journalism and publishing most of his life, and was active as the founder and chairman (from 1960 onwards) of Press Cooperative S.A.L. publishing group, editor-publisher of the *al-Nahar* S.C.P.A. Publishing Company after 1963, publisher and editor in chief of the French-language dailies *Le jour* (1965) and *L'orient-Le jour* (1970–1991), and chairman of the board of the Société Générale de la Presse et d'Edition (1985–1991).

In 1951, embarking on a political career, Twayni won a parliamentary seat after running successfully in Mount Lebanon as a candidate of the Socialist National Front, a loose coalition of politicians headed by Camille Chamoun and Kamal Jumblatt that called for the resignation of President Bishara al-Khuri, whose second term in office had become tainted with charges of nepotism, administrative corruption, and heavy-handed tactics. Twayni was reelected in 1953 and 1957, both times as a representative for Beirut, and was deputy speaker of parliament between 1953 and 1957. By then, he had established himself as one of the most prominent and competent members of a new generation of young, well-educated, reform-minded professionals who had become active in politics in an effort to modernize the Lebanese state. It was this reputation that led to his appointment in October 1970 as deputy prime minister and minister of information and education in President Sulayman Franjiyya's first cabinet (the so-called Youth Cabinet, headed by Sa'ib Salam and composed predominantly of young technocrats recruited from outside parliament). Twayni resigned in January 1971, however, in protest against the president's and the prime minister's unwillingness to support the educational reforms he had proposed. He was subsequently appointed minister of labor and social affairs, tourism, and industry and oil in a cabinet headed by Rashid Karame (July 1975 to December 1976).

After the 1960s Twayni frequently represented his country abroad, both in official and unofficial positions. Following the Arab–Israel War (1967), he was ambassador-at-large and personal representative of President Charles Hilu on a special mission to the United States. In December 1976 he was President Ilyas Sarkis's special emissary to Washington, D.C. His diplomatic skills and achievements eventually led to his appointment in September 1977 as ambassador and permanent representative of Lebanon to the United Nations, a position he held until September 1982. Between 1982 and 1988 he served as special adviser to President Amin Jumayyil. His responsibilities during this period included coordinating negotiations for the withdrawal of foreign forces from Lebanon. In the early 1990s he was president of Balamand University, and he remains on the board of trustees of AUB. He continues to shuttle back and forth between Lebanon, Europe, and the United States.

See also AMERICAN UNIVERSITY OF BEIRUT (AUB); ARAB–ISRAEL WAR (1967); CHAMOUN, CAMILLE; FRANJIYYA, SULAYMAN; HILU, CHARLES; JUMAYYIL, AMIN; JUMBLATT,

KAMAL; KARAME, RASHID; KHURI, BISHARA AL-; SARKIS, ILYAS.

Bibliography

Hudson, Michael C. *The Precarious Republic: Political Modernization in Lebanon.* Boulder, CO: Westview Press, 1985.

Petran, Tabitha. *The Struggle over Lebanon.* New York: Monthly Review Press, 1987.

GUILAIN P. DENOEUX
UPDATED BY MICHAEL R. FISCHBACH

TWIN PILLARS POLICY

U.S. policy to promote Iran and Saudi Arabia as local guardians of U.S. interests in the Persian Gulf region.

The decision by Great Britain in the late 1960s to withdraw its military forces from the Persian Gulf and to grant independence to its ten protectorates along the east coast of the Arabian Peninsula confronted the United States with a strategic dilemma. It was the height of Cold War rivalry with the Soviet Union, and the United States was deeply involved in Vietnam. Consequently, the United States decided instead of direct intervention to build up its two regional allies, Iran and Saudi Arabia, as local powers that could protect the region from the spread of Soviet influence. As the "twin pillars" of U.S. policy, both countries were encouraged to acquire billions of dollars of the most advanced arms during the 1970s. Iran embraced the twin pillars policy more enthusiastically than Saudi Arabia and intervened militarily, with U.S. approbation, in Iraq and Oman. The policy collapsed suddenly in 1979, when the shah (king) of Iran was overthrown in a revolution that brought to power a republican regime opposed to U.S. influence in the region.

See also UNITED STATES OF AMERICA AND THE MIDDLE EAST.

Bibliography

Hooglund, Eric. "The Persian Gulf." In *Intervention into the 1990s: U.S. Foreign Policy in the Third World,* edited by Peter Schraeder. Boulder, CO: Lynne Rienner, 1992.

ZACHARY KARABELL
UPDATED BY ERIC HOOGLUND

TYRE

Historic coastal city in south Lebanon on the Mediterranean Sea.

Throughout its history, Tyre (now Sur), which is located fifty-two miles (83 km) from Beirut, has known several invasions and occupations. In the eighth century B.C.E., Tyre rebelled against the Assyrians, and in the sixth century B.C.E., the population of Tyre organized a revolt against the Chaldeans. In 333 B.C.E., following his defeat of the Persians, Alexander the Great was welcomed by all Phoenician cities with the exception of Tyre.

Tyre has also had a golden age (especially under the Romans) because of its flourishing glass and purple dye manufacturing. It was under the Romans that Christianity reached Tyre in the person of Saint Paul, who visited the city and stayed for ten days. In 638 C.E., Tyre fell under the control of the Fatimids, where it remained until 1124. In that year Tyre was besieged by the Crusaders and was incorporated in the kingdom of Jerusalem, as a part of which it grew prosperous. The city was recaptured and destroyed by the Mamluks in 1291.

Oranges, citrus, bananas, and sugar cane are the major fruits and vegetables produced in Tyre. Some of the inhabitants of the city and the surrounding region also make their living as fishermen. The old Phoenician city today has a large number of banks and financial institutions, several educational and humanitarian institutions, and hospitals and health centers to serve its population of 30,000 (1996). In a city that also has an active sport life, soccer clubs are especially popular.

GEORGE E. IRANI

TZOMET

See ISRAEL: POLITICAL PARTIES IN

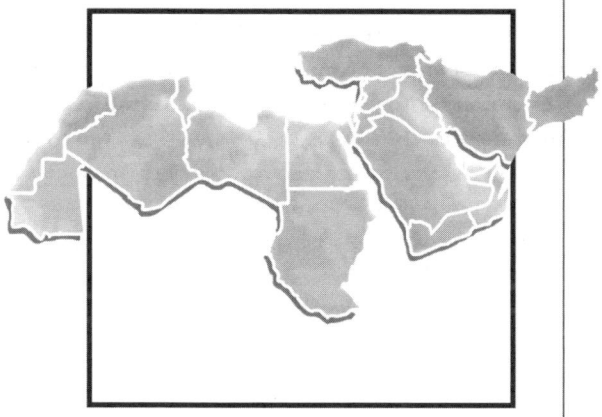

U

UGANDA PROJECT

Proposal for a Jewish state in British territory in East Africa.

In 1902 Theodor Herzl petitioned the Royal Commission for Alien Immigration in London for assistance in alleviating the plight of Jews. In the summer of 1903, the British colonial secretary informed the World Zionist Organization of Great Britain's agreement in principle that East Africa could serve as a potential Jewish homeland. The apparent motivation for this plan, which became known as the Uganda Project or Uganda Scheme, was a desire to help the Jews as well as to develop the area for further colonization and perhaps to minimize further Jewish immigration to Great Britain.

The Sixth Zionist Congress met shortly thereafter, and Herzl presented the Uganda Scheme (it was actually Kenya), urging its acceptance as a temporary measure. Max Nordau, Eliezer Ben-Yehuda, Nachman Syrkin, and Rabbi Yitzhak Yaacov Reines supported it, whereas Menachem Ussishkin and Ber Borochov, as well as Vladimir Ze'ev Jabotinsky, staunchly opposed it. The proposal became the subject of one of the fiercest debates in Zionist history. When Herzl won, and the Congress voted, 295 to 178, in favor of a proposal to investigate the plan's viability, the opposition stormed out and agreed to return only after Herzl assured them of his allegiance to Palestine as the ultimate objective of Zionism.

In spring 1904 the British government withdrew its offer. Herzl died before the Seventh Zionist Congress, in 1905, at which the scheme was overwhelmingly rejected by a majority of the 497 delegates.

See also HERZL, THEODOR; WORLD ZIONIST ORGANIZATION (WZO).

Bibliography

Heymann, Michael, ed. *The Uganda Controversy: Minutes of the Zionist General Council,* 2 vols. Tel Aviv and Jerusalem: Tel Aviv University, Institute for Zionist Research and the Zionist Library, 1970–1977.

Shimoni, Gideon. *The Zionist Ideology.* Hanover, NH: University Press of New England, 1995.

CHAIM I. WAXMAN

ULAMA

Muslim religious scholars.

The term *ulama* literally means those who possess knowledge (*ilm*), particularly of Islam. The *ulama* emerged as the first interpreters of the Qur'an and transmitters of *hadith,* the words and deeds of the prophet Muhammad. These scholars also became the first to outline and elaborate the basic principles of Islamic law (*shari'a*). The *ulama* were central to Islamic education in the premodern Middle East. They regulated instruction at all levels and were instrumental in the process of training Islamic scholars in *madrasas* (residential colleges), which were established by the eleventh century. These medieval institutions developed a rigorous curriculum centered around instruction in the law, training future jurists, theologians, and state functionaries. This system of higher education was the first in a series of successful attempts to link the *ulama* to political authority in the Islamic world. Members of the *ulama* might also participate in Islamic mysticism as members—even leaders—of organized Sufi fraternities.

Now under the leadership of Ayatollah Seyed Ali Khamenei, the Shi'ite *ulama,* or cultural elite acting as guardians and interpreters of Islamic faith, have exercised unequaled political as well as religious authority in Iran since the revolution of 1979. This is in contrast to the deep divides over the authority of the *ulama* in the Sunni world. © AP/WIDEWORLD PHOTOS. REPRODUCED BY PERMISSION.

The *ulama* are often defined as a class when in fact the socioeconomic status of their membership remained quite varied. Lawyers and judges were key members of the *ulama*; their legal skills were critical to the regulation of Islamic society in social and commercial matters such as wills, marriage, and trade. The *ulama* also included theologians, prayer leaders, and teachers, many of whom continued to participate in the economy as traders or artisans. Until the mid-nineteenth century, state bureaucracies in the Middle East employed members of the *ulama* as tax collectors, scribes, secretaries, and market inspectors. The *ulama* formed a cultural elite and retained the admiration and respect of the Muslim masses because they, not the rulers, were perceived as the true guardians and interpreters of the Islamic faith. As long as the *ulama* remained independent of state control, they continued to represent a base of potential support or opposition to ruling elites.

The advent of secularism and nationalism in the Middle East aroused the resistance of the *ulama,* who, increasingly, were perceived as obstacles to modernism and reform. The traditional power of the Sunni *ulama* over law, education, and bureaucracy was stripped away in the nineteenth century throughout the Ottoman Empire and in Egypt. Confiscation of *Waqf* properties, the traditional means of economic support for the *ulama,* increased their reliance on government authority for economic maintenance and served to compromise the group's independent religious and political influence. In the late nineteenth century individual members of the *ulama,* such as Muhammad Abduh, directed their influence in educational and religious reform through Egypt's famed Sunni theological center al-Azhar. More recent twentieth-century Islamic political movements in Egypt, such as the Muslim Brotherhood, successfully circumvented what was perceived as the compromised model of the traditional *ulama.*

The problem for the contemporary Sunni *ulama* rests in the definition and scope of their authority. Challenges to the sole Sunni legal authority of al-Azhar have arisen in Saudi Arabia with its state-sponsored Permanent Council for Scientific Research and Legal Opinions. Hanbali jurists who issue *fatawa* (sing.: *fatwa*) through this medium are able to affect much of the Arabic-speaking world through the power of electronic communication. The tendency toward such authoritarian discourses in the Sunni world has been challenged by individuals who wish to assert the egalitarian possibilities of a more accessible *ulama*. Sudanese President Hasan al-Turabi has argued that the *ulama* should consist of all devout, educated Muslims, not only those strictly trained in legal and theological matters. Such populist assertions undermine premodern precedent and underscore the deep divide within Sunni Muslim society today over the definition of religious and legal authority. The continued power and legitimacy of the *ulama* as leaders for the Sunni Muslim majority worldwide remains a matter of heated debate.

In contrast, the role of the *ulama* in Shiʿite Iran has reached new heights of political and religious authority since the Iranian Revolution of 1979. Under the weak Safavid and Qajar dynasties the strength of the *ulama* increased. Beginning in 1925, despite the Pahlavi regime's attempts at secular government and bringing the *ulama* under state control, the scholars remained a potentially potent source of opposition. The *ulama* assumed leadership in the organized resistance to the shah, which culminated in the 1979 revolution and the formation of the Islamic Republic of Iran. The Shiʿite *ulama* in Iran successfully utilized their religious prestige as the only legitimate interpreters of Islam as a revolutionary weapon against a modern secular government.

See also ABDUH, MUHAMMAD; AZHAR, AL-; IRANIAN REVOLUTION (1979); MUSLIM BROTHERHOOD; *SHARIʿA*; SHIʿISM; SUNNI ISLAM; WAQF.

Bibliography

Abou el Fadl, Khaled. *Speaking in God's Name: Islamic Law, Authority, and Women.* London: Oneworld Press, 2001.

Mottahedeh, Roy P. *The Mantle of the Prophet: Religion and Politics in Iran.* New York: Pantheon, 1985.

Zaman, Muhammad Qasim. *The Ulama in Contemporary Islam: Custodians of Change.* Princeton, NJ: Princeton University Press, 2002.

DENISE A. SPELLBERG

UMAR, MADIHA

[1908–]

Syrian painter.

Madiha Umar was born in Syria. She is widely regarded as a pioneer in using the abstract elements of Arabic calligraphy in modernist painting. This innovation, turning an element of historical Islamic art into a recognized modernist form, was later to emerge as a major trend in contemporary art throughout the Arab world and in other majority-Muslim countries. Although some artists have focused on the Arabic word as communicative of spiritual power (a concept in Islam), Umar concentrates on the beauty of individual letters, including their formal possibilities and their figurative associations. This interest in letters originally stems from her early fascination with the Arabic calligraphy on mosque domes and minarets. During the 1930s, Umar trained in England and also spent time in Iraq, taking classes and teaching. She completed her M.F.A. at the Corcoran School of Art in Washington, D.C. Her works were exhibited in the United States as early as the 1940s.

See also ART.

Bibliography

Ali, Wijdan. *Modern Islamic Art: Development and Continuity.* Gainesville: University Press of Florida, 1997

JESSICA WINEGAR

UMAYYAD MOSQUE

Mosque established in Damascus by the Umayyad Caliph Walid ibn Abd al-Malik (705–715).

To construct and decorate the mosque, Walid employed the best craftsmen from Constantinople (now Istanbul) and from the Umayyad Empire. The design included a large open courtyard, a covered area on the side closest to the *qibla* (the direction of Mecca), and walls covered with elaborate mosaics. The mosque was one of the spectacular results of the building program of the Umayyads, who made Damascus the capital of their empire. The Umayyad mosque is one of the most monumental artistic structures in modern Syria.

MUHAMMAD MUSLIH

UMMA

See GLOSSARY

UMM AL-QAYWAYN

The emirate in the United Arab Emirates with the smallest population.

Umm al-Qaywayn lies south of Ra'ʾs al-Khayma, the northern-most emirate, and north of Sharjah on the coast of the Persian (Arabian) Gulf. It possesses the second-smallest territory, approximately 300 square miles, and its population was estimated in 1997 to be about 39,000. The capital town of the same name, which contains most of the emirate's population, was established on a sand spit for physical security. Only Abu Dhabi shares Umm al-Qaywayn's advantage of being located in a single contiguous territory.

Along with Ajman and Fujayra, Umm al-Qaywayn is one of the poorest of the United Arab Emirates and is heavily dependent on development funds from Abu Dhabi. It has very modest gas production, and few industries, the most important being cement production. Like Dubai, the emirate has established a free zone to attract overseas investment in manufacturing and trade. Nonetheless, much of Umm al-Qaywayn's population engages in the traditional pursuits of fishing and shipbuilding.

The ruling family is the Muʿalla, sometimes referred to as the Al Ali. The current amir, Shaykh Rashid ibn Ahmad, has ruled since 1981, when he succeeded his father, Shaykh Ahmad ibn Rashid al-Muʿalla, whose rule had begun in 1929.

See also MUʿALLA FAMILY, AL-; UNITED ARAB EMIRATES.

Bibliography

Anthony, John Duke. *Arab States of the Lower Gulf: People, Politics, Petroleum.* Washington, DC: Middle East Institute, 1975.

Ghareeb, Edmund, and Abed, Ibrahim al-, eds. *Perspectives on the United Arab Emirates.* London: Trident Press, 1997.

Metz, Helen Chapin, ed. *Persian Gulf States: Country Studies,* 3d edition. Washington, DC: Library of Congress, 1994.

Peck, Malcolm C. *The United Arab Emirates: A Venture in Unity.* Boulder, CO: Westview Press; London: Croom Helm, 1986.

Taryam, Abdullah Omran. *The Establishment of the United Arab Emirates, 1950–1985.* New York; London: Croom Helm, 1987.

MALCOLM C. PECK
UPDATED BY ANTHONY B. TOTH

UMM AL-QURA UNIVERSITY

Saudi Arabian university.

King Abd al-Aziz University was founded in Jidda in 1967 as a private college. Later taken over by the Saudi state, it opened branches in Mecca and Medina; the former became independent as Umm al-Qura ("The Mother of Villages," a name for Mecca) University in 1979. It opened another campus at al-Ta'if in 1981. Umm al-Qura University offers programs in the sciences, Islamic studies, Arabic language, education, and agriculture. Student enrollment numbers more than 20,000. King Abd al-Aziz University employs more than 2,000 teachers and has a student population of more than 39,000.

KHALID Y. BLANKINSHIP

UMMA PARTY

Political party in Sudan founded by Abd al-Rahman al-Mahdi in 1945.

Sayyid Abd al-Rahman al-Mahdi (1885–1959), the posthumous son of Muhammad Ahmad Abdullah al-Mahdi (1848–1885), used his wealth acquired by his loyalty to the British during World War I and his religious influence as the leader of the Ansar to enhance his political ambitions by launching a newspaper, *al-Umma.* Then, in February 1945, he mobilized his followers, the Ansar, to establish the Umma political party. The name refers to the community of Islam *(umma).* Its political platform, however, promotes a Sudan for the Sudanese, evoking the legacy of the Mahdist State, founded by his father, which was hostile to the imperial ambitions of Egypt. The founding members included prominent Mahdists. Although Abd al-Rahman publicly remained aloof, he provided the funds and spiritual guidance for the party, which alienated many non-Mahdist Sudanese who were deeply suspicious that he was using the party to further his monarchical ambitions. The opposition gravitated to the Ashiqqa (Brothers) Party founded by Isma'il al-Azhari (1900–1969), which advocated the union of the Nile Valley with Egypt.

Frequent attempts to reconcile the unionists and the Umma failed when Azhari broadened his narrow political base to found the National Unionist Party (NUP) with Sayyid Ali al-Mirghani and his Khatmiyya Brotherhood, bitter rivals of the Ansar and historically pro-Egyptian. The Umma lost the elections in 1952 to the NUP, and Azhari declared the Sudan independent on 1 January 1956. The Umma Party continued to play a powerful role in the first parliamentary government (1956–1958) and even under the military regimes of Major-General Ibrahim Abbud (1958–1964) and Colonel Muhammad Ja'far Numeiri (1969–1985), when political parties were officially proscribed. It sustained an intense rivalry with the Democratic Unionist Party (the former NUP), whose patrons, the Mirghani family, played a role similar to that of the descendants of Sayyid Abd al-Rahman—his son Siddiq al-Mahdi and grandson Sadiq al- Mahdi—in the Umma Party.

The Umma Party was not without internal rivalry, particularly among the more conservative Ansar, who were led by Imam al-Hadi until he was killed in the suppression of the Ansar by Numeiri in 1970. Since then, Sadiq al-Mahdi, the great-grandson of the Mahdi, has led the Umma Party. He served as prime minister in all the coalition governments between 1986 and 1989, after which he was placed under arrest by Brigadier Umar Hasan Ahmad al-Bashir, who seized control of the government in his coup d'état of June 1989. Although all political parties except Bashir's National Islamic Front (NIF) were proscribed, the organization of the Umma Party in the Sudan remained in place and its leadership joined the other opposition parties in exile who had formed the National Democratic Alliance (NDA) in Asmara, Eritrea.

In December 1996 Sadiq made a spectacular escape from house arrest to join the NDA in Asmara. Thereafter, he played an ambiguous role, seeking control of the NDA on the one hand and a rapprochement with the Bashir government on the other, both of which weakened the authority of the NDA. He failed to dominate the NDA; but when President Bashir permitted political parties to once again be openly active in Sudan, Sadiq signed the Djibouti Agreement with President Bashir in November 1999 and was able to return to lead the Umma as an opposition party. Although a body of the Umma leadership defected from the Umma to join the government, Sadiq remained in Khartoum and was confirmed leader of the opposition Umma Party in April 2003 at its first general conference in fifteen years.

See also ANSAR, AL-; AZHARI, ISMA'IL; *MAHDI*; MAHDIST STATE; SUDAN.

Bibliography

Khalid, Mansour. *The Government They Deserve: The Role of the Elite in Sudan's Political Evolution.* London: Kegan Paul, 1990.

Khalid, Mansour. *War and Peace in Sudan: A Tale of Two Countries.* London: Kegan Paul, 2003.

Mahjoub, M. A. *Democracy on Trial.* London: Andre Deutsch, 1974.

Niblock, Tim. *Class and Power in the Sudan: The Dynamics of Sudanese Politics, 1898–1985.* Albany: State University of New York Press, 1987.

Woodward, Peter. *Sudan: The Unstable State.* Boulder, CO: Lynne Rienner, 1990.

ROBERT O. COLLINS

UMM KULTHUM

[c. 1904–1975]

The most famous Arab singer of the twentieth century.

Umm Kulthum performed for more than fifty years, beginning in the villages and towns of the Egyptian delta in the early twentieth century and continuing until her final illness in 1973. In the course of her long career, Umm Kulthum recorded over three hundred songs and appeared in six films. She performed throughout the Arab world and is often considered the most accomplished singer of her time.

The Egyptian singer Umm Kulthum, photographed in Cairo in 1968, enjoyed immense popularity throughout the Arab world from the 1920s until her death in 1975. She supported Arab culture through her performances of populist songs derived from Arab music and poetry, as well as by speaking out for government support of such music and the musicians who played it. © BETTMANN/CORBIS. REPRODUCED BY PERMISSION.

She was born in the Egyptian village of Tammay al-Zahayra in the province of Daqhaliya to Shaykh Ibrahim al-Sayyid al-Baltaji (died 1932), the imam of the village mosque, and his wife, Fatima al-Maliji (died 1947). Her father augmented his income by singing religious songs for local celebrations. Umm Kulthum learned the songs while listening to him train her brother Khalid as his accompanist. Impressed with the power of his young daughter's voice, Shaykh Ibrahim eventually included her along with Khalid and their cousin Sabr in his performances.

The young girl with the very strong voice became the family's star attraction. To protect her reputation, the father had her wear a boy's coat and head covering, and he conducted all business on her behalf. By 1917, the family began to consider a serious singing career for Umm Kulthum and in about 1922 they moved to Cairo to launch her in the commercial music business. In Cairo, Umm Kulthum was not an immediate success. Compared with the women already established as successful performers and recording stars, including Munira al-Mahdiyya and Fathiyya Ahmad, she was viewed as unsophisticated and countrified. She engaged music teachers and endeavored to copy the manners of the elite women in whose homes she sang. Like other aspiring performers, she was aided and schooled by a number of mentors, including singer Shaykh Abu al-Ilah Muhammad, poet Ahmad Rami, and the amateur musician Amin al-Mahdi. By 1928, she surpassed the popularity of her competitors and remained at the top of musical society for the remainder of her career.

Umm Kulthum began to make commercial recordings in 1924. Although recording companies were usually conservative and disinclined to take a chance on an unknown singer, they vied with each other for the largest possible share of the market; as a result the relatively unknown Umm Kulthum was recruited by Odeon Records and recorded fourteen songs in 1924 and 1925. These were immediately successful, for, as she later explained, her long years of performing in the delta provided her with a larger audience outside Cairo than most other singers. This experience awakened Umm Kulthum to the nature of her potential audience. During the late 1920s and the 1930s she began her lifelong involvement with the mass media: commercial recording (1924), radio (1934), film (1934), and television (1960). Commercial recordings had been circulating in Egypt since about 1904 and, despite the relatively high cost of phonograph players and records, were widely accessible. They were installed in public places, such as coffee houses, where even those who could not afford the equipment could hear the records. (Later, radios, televisions, and cassette players were similarly shared.) From 1937 until her final illness, her concerts on the first Thursday of each month were broadcast live to an ever growing audience. These concerts were certainly her best-known professional activity and allowed Umm Kulthum to count among her audience millions of listeners beyond the ticket-buying audience in Cairo.

She started with a repertoire of traditional, predominantly religious songs as a child; in the late 1920s and 1930s, she began to sing new virtuosic songs, often composed for her by Muhammad al-Qasabji on the romantic poetry then in vogue by Ahmad Rami. During her golden age in the 1940s and 1950s, she sang colloquial songs of populist expression written by Zakariyya Ahmad and Bayram al-Tunisi and serious neoclassical songs by Riyadh al-Sunbati and Ahmad Shawqi; these have become her best known. In the late 1950s and 1960s, she commissioned new love songs by younger poets and composers and finally collaborated with her colleague and rival, Muhammad Abd al-Wahhab; they produced ten songs, which retain great popularity to the present day.

In her later years, she was recognized as an important public figure, in general, and a symbol of authentically Egyptian and Arab culture and art. She served seven terms as president of the musicians' union and as a member of the selection committee for radio and of several national commissions on the arts. After the Egyptian defeat in the Arab-Israel War (1967), she initiated a series of benefit concerts in Egypt and throughout the Arab world designed to replenish the Egyptian treasury. She appeared in Morocco, Libya, Sudan, Lebanon, Abu Dhabi, and Tunisia, and her trips to these countries took on the character of diplomatic visits.

Health problems that had plagued Umm Kulthum for much of her life worsened as she aged, and she spent most of the last year of her life under medical treatment. She died on 3 February 1975.

See also ABD AL-WAHHAB, MUHAMMAD; MUSIC; SHAWQI, AHMAD.

Bibliography

Awad, Mahmud. "Umm Kulthum: Allati la ya'rifuha ahad" (The Umm Kulthum Nobody Knows). In *Middle Eastern Muslim Women Speak,* edited and translated by Elizabeth Warnock Fernea and Basima Qattan Bezirgan. Austin: University of Texas Press, 1977.

Danielson, Virginia. "Shaping Tradition in Arab Song: The Career and Repertory of Umm Kulthum." Ph.D. diss., University of Illinois, 1991.

Danielson, Virginia. *The Voice of Egypt: Umm Kulthum, Arabic Song, and Egyptian Society in the Twentieth Century*. Chicago: University of Chicago Press, 1997.

VIRGINIA DANIELSON

UMM NAʿSAN

Second largest of the thirty-three islands in the archipelago that constitutes the State of Bahrain.

Umm Naʿsan occupies some 8.5 square miles (22 sq. km) and lies approximately 2.5 miles (4 km) off the western coast of the main island of Bahrain, the largest in the archipelago. It is reserved for the private use of the ruler. Several small springs provide water for a limited pastureland, and date palm gardens grow along its western shore, gardens planted and stocked with deer and gazelle by Shaykh Hamad ibn Isa Al Khalifa during the 1930s. Ruins dot the surface of the island, lending credence to local legends that it was the seat of the ancient rulers. The causeway from Saudi Arabia to the main island, Bahrain, passes through Umm Naʿsan.

Bibliography

Cottrell, Alvin J., ed. *The Persian Gulf States: A General Survey.* Baltimore, MD: Johns Hopkins University Press, 1980.

FRED H. LAWSON

UNION DÉMOCRATIQUE DU MANIFESTE ALGÉRIEN (UDMA)

A moderate Algerian organization whose goals changed from autonomy within the colonial system to full independence.

The Union Démocratique du Manifeste Algérien (UDMA; Democratic Union of the Algerian Manifesto) was founded by Ferhat ABBAS during the spring of 1946 and ceased to exist in April 1956 when Abbas, in Cairo, announced his alliance with the Front de Libération Nationale (FLN; National Liberation Front). It grew out of the moderate wing of the Algerian political spectrum, which in the 1930s had sought reform within the colonial system. When the colons refused such reform, it moved in the 1940s toward Algerian autonomy.

Winning eleven of the thirteen Algerian seats in the second French Constituent Assembly in 1946, Abbas proposed an autonomous Algeria within the framework of the French Union. When this program failed to carry, the party was diminished considerably in influence. Representing mainly educated, middle-class levels of society, the party had some three thousand members by 1950 and participated actively in the Algerian Assembly established by the Organic Law in 1947.

After joining the FLN, Abbas and other UDMA leaders served in the Conseil National de la Révolution Algérienne (CNRA; National Council of the Algerian Revolution) and subsequently in the Provisional Government of the Algerian Republic (Gouvernement Provisoire de la République Algérienne; GPRA).

Bibliography

Quandt, William B. *Revolution and Political Leadership: Algeria, 1954–1958.* Cambridge, MA: MIT Press, 1969.

JOHN RUEDY

UNION GÉNÉRALE DES ÉTUDIANTS TUNISIENS (UGET)

See GENERAL TUNISIAN UNION OF STUDENTS (UGTE)

UNION GÉNÉRALE DES TRAVAILLEURS MAROCAINS (UGTM)

Moroccan labor union.

The Istiqlal Party founded the General Union of Moroccan Workers (UGTM) in 1959 to compete with the Moroccan Labor Union (Union Marocaine du Travail, UMT), then associated with the National Union of Popular Forces (Union Nationale des Forces Populaires, UNFP). The UGTM represents the labor branch of the Istiqlal Party, which emphasizes nationalistic, pro-Islamic, and pan-Arab policies. The UGTM takes a pragmatic stance toward the government, not hesitating to support its policies. This was particularly true when the Istiqlal Party was represented in the cabinet (1977–1984). During the 1980s the UGTM gained ascendancy within various sectors, but especially in the rural milieu and agriculture.

The UGTM competed with the UMT in the 1970s and with the Democratic Confederation of Labor (CDT), created in 1978, in the 1980s. However, in the 1990s the UGTM joined forces with the CDT. The socioeconomic situation of the country had been steadily worsening since the 1980s, and both unions called for strikes during the 1990s to force the government into a dialogue with labor representatives. Similar tactics were repeated in 2002 under the government of Abderrahmane Youssoufi. The strikes concluded the following month with a social pact negotiated by the government, the employers, the CDT, and the UGTM.

As of 2003, the modification of the current Labor Code, which could represent a limitation on the right to strike, is an issue of great concern to both unions. UGTM's secretary general is Abderrazak Afilal.

See also UNION MAROCAINE DU TRAVAIL (UMT); YOUSSOUFI, ABDERRAHMANE.

LARRY A. BARRIE
UPDATED BY ANA TORRES-GARCIA

UNION GÉNÉRALE DES TRAVAILLEURS TUNISIENS (UGTT)

Tunisian labor union.

The Union Générale des Travailleurs Tunisiens (General Union of Tunisian Workers) is the strongest labor union in Tunisia. Founded in 1946 by Ferhat Hached, the union was the first indigenous attempt to organize Tunisia's workers. Hached broke with the French, communist-led General Confederation of Workers (*Confédération Générale des Travailleurs*; CGT). The new union worked closely with the nationalist movement in Tunisia. Consequently, members of the French resistance organization Red Hand assassinated Hached in 1952.

From 1952 until 1969, the union was under the influence of Ahmed Ben Salah and his socialist economic policies. The fall of Ben Salah in 1970 led to its reorganization and reemergence in 1976 under the charismatic leadership of Habib Achour, who dominated the UGTT until 1989. From the late 1970s to the early 1980s, the union exerted a fierce opposition to the government. The UGTT tended to oppose economic liberalization because this would lessen its control of the labor movement and adversely affect workers. Achour signed the Social Contract of 1977, which stipulated that the union would control labor unrest. Deteriorating economic conditions, however, caused Achour to break this pact. A wildcat work stoppage at Qsar Hellal in October 1977 led to a confrontation between the army and striking workers, the first time the government had used the army to suppress labor. In early January 1978, the UGTT issued a resolution extremely critical of the economic policies of Habib Bourguiba's regime. On 26 January 1978, called "Black Thursday," a bloody clash left 150 people dead. The government declared a state of emergency and arrested UGTT leaders. Achour was tried for sedition and sentenced to ten years in jail. The regime imposed a new executive bureau on the union and weakened it as a force of opposition to the government's economic policies.

Pardoned in 1981, Achour returned to the post of UGTT president, with leftist Taieb Baccouche as secretary-general. Privatization measures of the mid-1980s eroded the UGTT's clout. In January 1984, riots broke out as a result of an increase in the price of bread. The ensuing violence led the union to harden its stance toward the government. By 1985, the UGTT had again run afoul of the government by threatening to strike if the decline in workers' real wages was not reversed. In December, the government again disbanded the union and jailed its leadership on various charges.

The 1987 palace coup of Zayn al-Abidine Ben Ali led to improved relations between the government and the UGTT. Internal dissent, exemplified by the split that in the early 1980s created the National Union of Tunisian Workers (*Union Nationale des Travailleurs Tunisiens;* UNTT), had weakened the organization as the main opposition force. The union, therefore, started to lose its role as the country's leading social movement to the Tunisian League for the Defense of Human Rights (LTDH).

In 1989, encouraged by the government, the reunification of the UGTT and the UNTT was made official and the union leaders were substituted. Achour was replaced by Ismail Sahbani and Ali Romdhane. In late December 1993, Sahbani consolidated his position and expelled his chief opponents from the UGTT's executive bureau.

The union's nineteenth congress, held in April 1999, elected Sahbani as secretary general for the third time. There was, however, increasing discontent among the UGTT membership over his authoritarian leadership style and his conciliatory attitude toward the regime. Forced to resign, Sahbani was replaced by Abdessalem Jerad in September 2000.

See also ACHOUR, HABIB.

Bibliography

Murphy, Emma. *Economic and Political Change in Tunisia: From Bourguiba to Ben Ali.* New York: St. Martin's Press in association with University of Durham, 1999.

Nelson, Harold D., ed. *Tunisia: A Country Study,* 3d edition. Washington, DC: American University, 1988.

LARRY A. BARRIE
UPDATED BY ANA TORRES-GARCIA

UNION MAROCAINE DU TRAVAIL (UMT)

Morocco's oldest trade union.

The Moroccan Labor Union (Union Marocaine du Travail, UMT) was formed in 1955 with the help of the nationalist Istiqlal Party. It reportedly had a membership of over 600,000 in the early years of Morocco's independence, becoming the nation's largest labor organization. It enjoyed a monopoly of Moroccan unionism until the Istiqlal Party founded the General Union of Moroccan Workers (Union Générale des Travailleurs Marocains, UGTM) in 1959, which took over 10 percent of its membership.

Although affiliated with the National Union of Popular Forces (Union Nationale des Forces Populaires, UNFP) from 1959 to 1962, the UMT declared its autonomy from political parties at its Third Congress (1963). In the 1960s the government declared a state of emergency, during which political and union activity was restricted for several years. During this period the UMT saw its membership decline sharply. The state of emergency ended in July 1970, prompting a rapid rise in labor unrest soon afterward. Nevertheless, the UMT remained weak, affected by organizational and leadership problems.

By the mid-1970s internal dissent had emerged within the organization. Some criticized the union leadership for inaction and subordination to the state. Mahjoub Ben Seddiq has been its secretary general since 1955. In 1978 the USFP founded the Democratic Confederation of Labor (Confédération Démocratique du Travail, CDT), an organization that soon attracted former UMT union members. In the 1990s UMT's political activism was surpassed by the CDT, which, in alliance with the UGTM, has become the leader of trade union militancy in Morocco.

See also UNION GÉNÉRALE DES TRAVAILLEURS MAROCAINS (UGTM).

Bibliography

Clement, Jean-François, and Paul, Jim. "Trade Unions and Moroccan Politics." *Merip Reports* 127 (October 1984): 19–24.

BRADFORD DILLMAN
UPDATED BY ANA TORRES-GARCIA

UNION NATIONALE DES ETUDIANTS MAROCAINS (UNEM)

Originally left-wing opposition group in Morocco that came to be dominated by Islamists in the 1990s.

The Union Nationale des Etudiants Marocains (UNEM), originally supported by teachers and high school students, was involved in extralegal and radical activities against the monarchy and its governments during the 1960s and 1970s, when it was associated with the progressive faction of the Istiqlal Party and the Union Nationale des Forces Populaires (UNFP). Its agenda was redress of political, social, economic, and educational grievances. In July 1963 Hamid Berrada, secretary-general of the UNEM, was condemned to death for allegedly plotting against the state in support of Mehdi Ben Barka. He fled the country and, with Ben Barka and Muhammad al-Basri, initiated a campaign to denounce the monarchy. One year later, UNEM's president, Muhammad Halaoui, was arrested for having criticized Berrada's sentencing. Between 1963 and 1973 UNEM leaders were repeatedly arrested and imprisoned for organizing strikes and engaging in subversion. The peak of the government's crackdown came in April 1972 with a mass trial of eighty-one student leaders on charges of treason. Twenty-eight received long jail sentences.

The UNEM was dissolved in 1973 and reconstituted in 1978. The new leadership initiated a number of demonstrations between 1979 and 1981 that resulted in further clashes with the authorities, but in general the political calm in Morocco during the 1980s was reflected in the UNEM's relatively low profile. In 1991 clashes on university campuses between leftists and Islamists were related, in part, to their respective attempts to gain control of the UNEM. Mostly affiliated with Jamiʿat al-Adl wa al-Ihsan (Justice and Charity Group), the leading Islamist extraparliamentary movement, Islamist students came to control most of the country's student organizations by the end of the decade, including the UNEM, and found themselves in periodic confrontations with the authorities.

See also BEN BARKA, MEHDI; ISTIQLAL PARTY: MOROCCO; UNION NATIONALE DES FORCES POPULAIRES (UNFP).

Bibliography

Waterbury, John. *The Commander of the Faithful.* London: Weidenfeld and Nicolson, 1970.

BRUCE MADDY-WEITZMAN

UNION NATIONALE DES FORCES POPULAIRES (UNFP)

One of Morocco's leading leftist political parties.

The Union Nationale des Forces Populaires (National Union of Popular Forces, UNFP) was founded in December 1959 by progressive and leftist elements of the Istiqlal Party, Morocco's most important nationalist force. Among its founders were Mehdi Ben Barka; Abdullah Ibrahim (prime minister from 1959 to 1960); Mahjoub Ben Seddiq (secretary-general of the Union Marocaine du Travail [Moroccan Labor Union], UMT); Abderrahmane Youssoufi; Mohamed Fqih Basri; and Abderrahim Bouabid. Following two failed coup attempts in 1971 and 1972, the government arrested many UNFP members and placed them on trial. In 1972, internal disputes led to the emergence of two blocs within the party: the Casablanca group led by Ibrahim, and the Rabat section led by Bouabid. During 1973, a series of detentions forced the Rabat group to put its activities on hold for a period of four months. The political turmoil led to severe divisions within the party, causing the UNFP section in the city of Rabat to split from the party and found a new party, the Union Socialiste des Forces Populaires (Socialist Union of Socialist Forces, USFP), in 1974. Because most of the UNFP's members joined the USFP, the remnant UNFP headed by Ibrahim became an insignificant party under the guidance of the UMT. The UNFP boycotted the 1977 elections and the municipal and parliamentary elections of 1983 and 1984.

The ideology of the UNFP was socialist, calling for a transformation of the social structure, nationalization of the means of production, greater rewards for workers, and land reform. It consistently opposed the leadership of King Hassan II and called for the creation of a representative democracy. In the international arena, the UNFP supported Arab unity within a socialist democratic framework, favored developing nation revolutionary movements, and opposed Western involvement in the national economy. Strongly nationalist, the party and its successor, the USFP, unconditionally supported the government line in Western Sahara and refused to agree to any form of settlement that would relinquish Moroccan sovereignty rights over the territory.

Ben Barka served as the UNFP's general secretary until his assassination in France in 1965. The party's principal leadership structure consisted of a central committee, an administrative commission, and a general secretariat. In 1967, the UNFP created a political bureau composed of Bouabid, Ibrahim, and Ben Seddiq, which the party's administrative commission dissolved in 1972. The leadership of the UNFP was often divided. The party held its second and last national congress in 1963. The UMT provided most of the party's infrastructure at the local level.

After briefly heading the government in 1959 and 1960, the UNFP joined the opposition. At the height of its power during the early 1960s, it won 414 out of 765 seats in the 1960 local elections and 28 out of 144 seats in the 1963 parliamentary elections. Severe repression after 1962 and a split with the UMT caused it to lose much of its strength during the late 1960s.

The UNFP had a diverse membership united more by a commonality of interests than a common ideology. Second-generation nationalists from the Istiqlal with modest family backgrounds and French educations held top positions. Professionals, teachers, and government workers composed much of the party's middle-level hierarchy. Rank and file members were largely trade union members and students. Wealthy members of the UNFP provided most of its financing. It had a diverse constituency, attracting its greatest support from workers living in Atlantic coast cities and from government cadres, students, and traders in the Sousse region.

See also BEN BARKA, MEHDI; BOUABID, ABDERRAHIM; IBRAHIM, ABDULLAH; ISTIQLAL PARTY: MOROCCO; UNION SOCIALISTE DES FORCES POPULAIRES (USFP); YOUSSOUFI, ABDERRAHMANE.

Bibliography

Waterbury, John. *The Commander of the Faithful: The Moroccan Political Elite—A Study in Segmented Politics.* New York: Columbia University Press; London: Weidenfeld & Nicolson, 1970.

BRADFORD DILLMAN
UPDATED BY VANESA CASANOVA-FERNANDEZ

UNION OF TUNISIAN WOMEN

The largest and oldest women's organization in Tunisia.

In 1956, L'Union Nationale des Femmes Tunisiennes (Union of Tunisian Women; UNFT) was formed with the explicit goal of elevating the cultural, social, economic, and political status of Tunisian women. As a women's auxiliary of the national Neo-Destour Party, the UNFT was primarily responsible for communicating, supporting, and implementing the Neo-Destour Party's initiatives and policies. Among its early initiatives were literacy and education campaigns and awareness-raising programs about the personal status code and women's rights. The UNFT became a prominent organization in the years after independence, with nearly 14,000 members in 1960 and more than 38,000 in 1969. By 2000, the UNFT had grown to a membership of more than 135,000, with regional offices and regional delegates in each of Tunisia's twenty-three governorates.

The UNFT has been primarily dedicated to women's advocacy at the national level, urging the implementation of state-sponsored programs. With the goal of promoting women's interests in all areas of society, the UNFT has sponsored and implemented projects relating to business, culture, science, health, and education. The social condition of women and the elimination of poverty continue to be of particular concern to the organization, and the UNFT works with both governmental and nongovernmental organizations to address women's needs and represent women's interests.

See also GENDER: GENDER AND EDUCATION; GENDER: GENDER AND LAW; GENDER: GENDER AND POLITICS; TUNISIA.

ANGEL M. FOSTER

UNION SOCIALISTE DES FORCES POPULAIRES (USFP)

Moroccan Socialist political party.

The Union Socialiste des Forces Populaires (Socialist Union of Popular Forces, USFP) was formed in 1974 by a large breakaway faction of the Union Nationale des Forces Populaires (National Union of Popular Forces, UNFP) led by Abderrahim Bouabid. A member of the Socialist International and strongly nationalist, the USFP supports the Moroccan government's stand on Western Sahara and it has consistently opposed the United Nations referendum plan for the region. The position of general secretary has been held by Bouabid (1974–1992) and Abderrahmane Youssoufi (1992–). Most of its members—primarily teachers, students, and government workers—come from urban middle-class backgrounds. During the 1990s the party, which in the past had a strong constituency among students, workers, and the unemployed, lost ground in favor of Morocco's Islamist parties, mainly the moderate Justice et Développement Party (Justice and Development, PJD) and the now illegal Al-Adl wa'l Ihsan (Justice and Charity Organization) headed by Abdessalam Yassine. The USFP is closely allied with the Democratic Labor Confederation, one of Morocco's leading trade unions.

Following the establishment of a bicameral system in 1997 and the elections that took place amid wide accusations of fraud, King Hassan II appointed Youssoufi prime minister in February 1998. Together with the Istiqlal Party, the USFP formed the core of the new government. The USFP won the legislative elections of 27 September 2002, which were marked by low participation (51.5%) and the success of the Islamist PJD. After the elections, the USFP announced that it would not form a cabinet with the PJD but would instead resuscitate its alliance with the Istiqlal Party. Despite the victory of the USFP, the king appointed Driss Jetou of the Istiqlal Party prime minister in October 2002, amid protests from the USFP and other parties. Differences over the USFP's role after 1998 have caused strains in relations with other member parties of the national democratic bloc, or Kutla. In the municipal elections of September 2003, which took place in the aftermath of bomb attacks that killed forty-five people in Casablanca and severely restricted the participation of Islamist parties, the USFP ranked second after the Istiqlal party, winning 14.2 percent of the vote and 3,373 of the total 23,689 local council seats.

See also ISTIQLAL PARTY: MOROCCO; UNION NATIONALE DES FORCES POPULAIRES (UNFP); WESTERN SAHARA; YOUSSOUFI, ABDERRAHMANE.

Bibliography

Hughes, Stephen O. *Morocco under King Hassan.* Reading, U.K.: Ithaca, 2001.

VANESA CASANOVA-FERNANDEZ

UNION TUNISIENNE DES INDUSTRIALISTES, COMPAGNIES, ARTISANS (UTICA)

Tunisian federation of employers.

The Tunisian Union of Industrialists, Businessmen, and Artisans (UTICA) was created during the third congress of the Neo-Destour Party on 17 October 1948. Initially called Union Tunisienne de l'Industrie et du Commerce (Tunisian Union of Industry and Commerce) and later the Union Tunisienne de l'Industrie, du Commerce, et de l'Artisanat (Tunisian Federation of Industry, Commerce, and Handicrafts), the union represents the interests of Tunisian employers as signatories of pacts regarding wages and work conditions in the Tunisian market. As of 2003, Hédi Djilani became the president of the union.

UTICA regularly negotiates wages and working conditions with the government and the Union Générale des Travailleurs Tunisiens (General Union of Tunisian Workers; UGTT). Based on these negotiations, the government sets annual wages for the labor force. The 1956 labor code guarantees a minimum wage, provides for arbitration to settle disputes, authorizes union membership, sets the work week and other labor standards, and provides for social security and disability insurance payments. The government also seeks to ensure that wages do not lag behind inflation. In May 1999, the Tunisian government increased minimum monthly wages in the public and private sectors by between 3.3 percent and 3.7 percent. Amendments to the labor code in 1994 and 1996 allowed firms to consider an employee's productivity when evaluating salary, to set working hours according to their needs, and to base part of an employee's salary on productivity; it also allowed layoffs based on economic or technological needs.

Since 1986, Tunisia's economic restructuring program has led to the privatization of a number of public conglomerates, the reduction of food subsidies, and a general liberalization of the economy. Tunisia's economic liberalization is linked to structural adjustment policies under the patronage of the International Monetary Fund and the World Bank, upon which the country depends for financial support. The liberalization of Tunisia's economy has taken place within the framework of a structural adjustment program (1986); adherence to the General Agreement on Terms of Trade (GATT) in 1989 and membership in the World Trade Organization since 1994; and the signing of a free-trade agreement with the European Union in 1995.

UTICA supported the construction in 1999 of the Elgazala Technology Park in Ariana (a city north of Tunis). The union views the transfer of technology and automation to Tunisia as a key to the country's economic diversification and a necessary step toward attracting foreign investment.

In the international sphere, UTICA has become prominent in strengthening economic ties between the Tunisian government and other developing nations. In March 2003, UTICA signed a series of agreements with its Moroccan counterpart, the Confédération Générale des Enterprises du Maroc (General Confederation of Enterprises in Morocco), to promote the integration of both economic regions. The two organizations called for the implementation of the Moroccan-Tunisian free-trade agreement, the creation of a databank of joint industrial projects, and the deregulation of customs duties. Outside the Arab world, UTICA has played a prominent role in the strengthening of commercial ties between Tunisia and Pakistan. In October 2002, UTICA signed an agreement with its Pakistani counterpart to set up a joint business council between their respective national chambers of commerce.

See also UNION GÉNÉRALE DES TRAVAILLEURS TUNISIENS (UGTT).

Bibliography

Nelson, Harold D., ed. *Tunisia: A Country Study*, 3d edition. Washington, DC: U.S. Government Printing Office, 1988.

UTICA. Available from <http://www.utica.org.tn/>.

LARRY A. BARRIE
UPDATED BY VANESA CASANOVA-FERNANDEZ

UNITED ARAB EMIRATES

Federation of seven shaykhdoms at the southern end of the Persian Gulf.

The United Arab Emirates (U.A.E.) is bounded on the north by a small portion of Qatar, the Persian (Arabian) Gulf, and a detached segment of Oman. The country shares a long, undefined border with Saudi Arabia (west and south) and Oman (east). It has an area of just over 32,000 square miles, about the size of the state of Maine. Abu Dhabi occupies nearly 87 percent of the total; Dubai, less than 5 percent; and Sharjah, just more than 3 percent. The emirates of Ra'ʾs al-Khayma, Fujayra, Umm al-Qaywayn, and Ajman occupy the remainder. The country has a flat coastal plain; an interior desert, part of the Empty Quarter (Rub al-Khali); an elevated plateau; and the Hajar Mountains, shared with Oman. Principal oasis regions are Liwa and Buraymi. Rainfall is highly seasonal, localized, and scanty. Summer temperatures often reach 115°F on the humid coast, and higher in the dry interior. From October to March the weather is mild and pleasant.

The U.A.E.'s population has risen from about 180,000 in 1968 to approximately 3.1 million in 2000; the influx of expatriate workers and their dependents account for most of the growth and some 80 percent of the total population. The U.A.E. is overwhelmingly urban, and the largest cities are (in descending order) Dubai, Abu Dhabi, Sharjah, and Ra'ʾs al-Khaymah. Nearly all U.A.E. nationals and expatriates are Muslims; significant exceptions include some Indians, Filipinos, and Westerners. Sunnis account for about 85 percent of all Muslims. Tribal affiliation remains very important among Emiratis, whose rulers are drawn from the leading families of the dominant tribes.

History

Most of the current ruling families took power in the early part of the nineteenth century when Great Britain imposed a general truce after a series of violent clashes with the Qawasim seafaring forces who had opposed Britain's military and commercial ascendancy in the lower Persian Gulf. A series of treaties between these rulers and Britain codified Britain's predominant position and gave rise to the region being called the Trucial Coast or Trucial Oman. The area was known as Sahil Oman (Oman Coast) by Arabic-speakers. These treaties had a tendency to reinforce the leading role of the local rulers and create a powerful political status quo. However, local politics, mainly in the form of family disputes and alliances, have resulted in some changes. For example, Dubai became independent of Abu Dhabi in 1833, Ra'ʾs al-Khayma seceded from Sharjah in 1869, and Fujayra gained independence from Sharjah in 1952. A treaty in 1892 further codified British power in the region, prohibiting rulers from engaging in diplomacy with non-British powers or ceding their territories to outsiders without British approval. In the nineteenth and early twentieth century, fishing, pearling, trade, and agriculture were the main sources of income for the inhabitants of the emirates. However, the world depression of the 1930s and the collapse of the Persian Gulf pearl market plunged the region into great poverty, forcing many to migrate elsewhere.

Traditions, including camel races in the desert, and tribal affiliations remain important elements of life in the United Arab Emirates, even as this federation of seven shaykhdoms experiences widespread change thanks to its oil wealth. © ALAIN LE GARSMEUR/CORBIS. REPRODUCED BY PERMISSION.

Britain instigated the first efforts at federation when it established the Trucial Council in 1952, an administrative body made up of the seven rulers. However, rivalries and philosophical differences prevented the rulers from joining in federation until 1971, when all but Ra'ʾs al-Khaymah formed the U.A.E. (Ra'ʾs al-Khaymah joined the federation the following year.) The ruler of Abu Dhabi, the largest and wealthiest emirate, Shaykh Zayid ibn Sultan al-Nahayyan, became president of the U.A.E., and Dubai's Shaykh Rashid ibn Saʿid al-Maktum became vice president. While much of the political history of the emirates has revolved around relations among the ruling families, it also has been affected by interactions with regional powers such as Oman, the rulers of Najd (later Saudi Arabia), Bahrain, Qatar, and Iran. At its inception Abu Dhabi's dispute with Saudi Arabia and Oman over the Buraymi (al-Ayn) Oasis remained unresolved; traditional rivalries among the seven amirs threatened the federation's viability; and Iran coerced Sharjah into a joint occupation of Abu Musa island (which contributed to a coup attempt that took the life of Sharjah's ruler, Shaykh Khalid ibn Muhammad), and forcibly seized the Tunb Islands from Ra'ʾs al-Khayma.

Economy

Since the early 1960s, when Abu Dhabi began exporting oil, the U.A.E. economy has been dominated by this sector. The country's proven oil reserves, 94 percent of which were located in Abu

Dubai, the largest city in the United Arab Emirates, has undergone considerable and almost continuous transformation since this late 20th-century photograph along Dubai Creek. Although Abu Dhabi has by far the most land and greatest amount of oil and natural gas reserves of the U.A.E.'s seven shaykhdoms, Dubai has a vital function with its extensive port facilities and free-trade zone. © CHRISTINE OSBORNE/CORBIS. REPRODUCED BY PERMISSION.

Dhabi emirate, amounted to some 98 billion barrels in 2001, more than 9 percent of the world's total. Dubai possesses 4 billion barrels; Sharjah, 1.5 billion; and Ra'ʾs al-Khayma, 100 million. Abu Dhabi also has the bulk of the country's 212 trillion cubic feet of natural gas reserves. The gap in economic development between Abu Dhabi, Dubai, and Sharjah, on the one hand, and the rest of the emirates is considerable, though it is moderated by federal government spending on infrastructure, with most of the funding from Abu Dhabi. Dubai, long the major trading center of the lower Gulf, is the region's leading entrepôt with the most extensive port facilities. Its Jabal Ali free zone has helped expand the U.A.E.'s nonoil sector to 60 percent of total GDP. Promotion of traditional economic activities, including agriculture and fishing, has created employment opportunities in the poorer emirates and achieved significant import substitution.

Government and Politics

The U.A.E.'s constitution provides for federal legislative, executive, and judicial institutions. The political system is a mix of presidential and parliamentary features, with the greatest power in the executive Federal Supreme Council, whose members are the rulers of the seven member states. Zayid has been president since independence, and Rashid served as both prime minister and vice president, posts assumed by his son Maktum in 1986, following Rashid's incapacitation. The legislature, called the Federal National Council, has only consultative powers, despite being given a somewhat greater role in the 1990s. Its forty members are appointed by the rulers: eight each from Abu Dhabi and Dubai,

MAP BY XNR PRODUCTIONS, INC. THE GALE GROUP.

six each from Sharjah and Ra's al-Khayma, and four apiece from the remaining emirates. Real legislative authority resides in the Council of Ministers, which initiates most laws, oversees implementation of federal laws, and prepares the federal budget.

Considerable powers are left to the individual emirates, each governed in an essentially traditional manner by a hereditary ruler. Even in foreign affairs, defense, and finance, theoretically federal concerns under the constitution, the individual emirates act autonomously. Each emirate has pursued its own oil policy. Dubai and Sharjah maintained business as usual with Iran while the federal government tilted toward Iraq during the Iran-Iraq War (1980–1988). Zayid has championed a centralized U.A.E., whereas others, especially his former rival, Rashid, have favored the loose federal arrangement.

Foreign Relations

The U.A.E. maintains generally friendly relations with its neighbors, although these can be complicated by the independent actions of various emirates. It has played an active role in the Gulf Cooperation Council (GCC), which promotes economic and security ties to the other five conservative Gulf Arab states. Zayid has assumed a major role in the Arab world as a force for moderation, as in his efforts to promote Egypt's reintegration into the Arab League. Relations with the United States have been friendly, though sometimes strained because of what is seen as a one-sided American policy toward the Arab-Israel conflict. The United States, Japan, and the United Kingdom are the U.A.E.'s major trading partners. After the Iraqi occupation of Kuwait, the U.A.E. cooperated closely with the United States and other members of the anti-Iraq coalition. However, during the late 1990s the country modified its stance, sending food and medicine to Iraq, and opposing a U.S. attack on the country. In a dramatic break from precedent among countries in the Arab League, the U.A.E. suggested in early 2003 that Saddam Hussein step down as leader of Iraq as a way to avoid imminent war with the United States.

See also ABU DHABI; AJMAN; BURAYMI OASIS DISPUTE; DUBAI; FUJAYRA; RA'S AL-KHAYMA; RUB AL-KHALI; SHARJAH; TRUCIAL COAST; UMM AL-QAYWAYN.

Bibliography

Anthony, John Duke. *Arab States of the Lower Gulf: People, Politics, Petroleum.* Washington, DC: Middle East Institute, 1975.

Ghareeb, Edmund, and Abed, Ibrahim al-, eds. *Perspectives on the United Arab Emirates.* London: Trident Press, 1997.

Heard-Bey, Frauke. *From Trucial States to United Arab Emirates: A Society in Transition.* New York; London: Longman, 1982.

Lienhardt, Peter. *Shaikhdoms of Eastern Arabia,* edited by Ahmed Al-Shahi. New York; Houndmills, U.K.: Palgrave, 2001.

Metz, Helen Chapin, ed. *Persian Gulf States: Country Studies,* 3d edition. Washington, DC: Library of Congress, 1994.

Peck, Malcolm C. *The United Arab Emirates: A Venture in Unity.* Boulder, CO: Westview Press; London: Croom Helm, 1986.

Taryam, Abdullah Omran. *The Establishment of the United Arab Emirates, 1950–1985.* New York; London: Croom Helm, 1987.

MALCOLM C. PECK
UPDATED BY ANTHONY B. TOTH

UNITED ARAB REPUBLIC (UAR)

Union of Syria and Egypt, 1958–1961.

By the late 1950s, Egypt was the most powerful Arab state. Many Arabs were enamored of President Gamal Abdel Nasser's advocacy of pan-Arab unity under Egypt's leadership. Syria, which shared Egypt's anti-Western stance, was considerably weaker, facing both external threats and an unstable internal political situation. For some Syrians, particularly members of the Baʿth party, union with Egypt offered hope for resolving a host of problems. As early as November 1957, Syria's National Assembly called for union with Egypt. Nasser agreed, but only on his terms: full union (not a federation) under his leadership. On 1 February 1958, he joined Syria's president, Shukri al-Quwatli, in announcing the formation of the United Arab Republic (UAR). A referendum on union and Nasser's presidency was approved on 21 February.

New governmental institutions were created in March 1958. Four vice presidents were appointed: two Egyptians (Abd al-Hakim Amir and Abd al-Latif al-Baghdadi) and two Syrians (Akram al-Hawrani and Sabri al-Asali). Amir also was commander of the joint UAR military. A regional council of ministers was established for each province, as was a unified cabinet (whose members were appointed in October). In March 1960, a new National Assembly was created. Nasser appointed its delegates—a higher proportion of whom were Egyptians—who first met that July. He also imposed Egypt's one-party system on Syria. Only the National Union, established in Egypt in May 1957, was allowed to function.

Formation of the UAR threatened the West with the prospect of Arab unity under Nasser's leadership. That the UAR immediately tried to draw in other states furthered this perception. In March 1958, the United Arab States was forged with Yemen and would last until December 1961. More significantly, cooperation talks were held between the UAR and the government that came to power during the July 1958 revolution in Iraq. Although the two never unified, Britain and the United States were unsettled by the prospect. Formation of the UAR, the civil war in pro-Western Lebanon, and the revolution in Iraq, formerly the West's leading Arab client, prompted the dispatch of U.S. troops to Lebanon and British troops to Jordan in July 1958, to bolster anti-UAR Arab governments.

Syria soon became disappointed with the UAR. Baʿthists were angered at being barred from power in a union that some Syrians felt more closely approached Egypt's occupation of Syria. By late 1959, major Baʿthists had been dismissed from the government. The powerful Syrian bourgeoisie was alienated by Nasser's state-managed economic policies, especially limits on landholdings and the 1961 socialist decrees. In August 1961, Nasser strengthened his centralized control by abolishing the two councils of ministers and the cabinet, and adding three new vice presidents, for a total of seven (only two of whom were Syrians).

Syria's units of the UAR army in Damascus launched a secessionist coup on 28 September 1961. Following limited fighting, Nasser decided against enforcing union militarily. The breakup of the UAR was a tremendous blow to Nasser's prestige and the dream of pan-Arab unity. Egypt used the name United Arab Republic until 1971, when it became the Arab Republic of Egypt.

See also AMIR, ABD AL-HAKIM; BAGHDADI, ABD AL-LATIF AL-; BAʿTH, AL-; HAWRANI, AKRAM AL-; NASSER, GAMAL ABDEL; NATIONAL UNION (EGYPT); QUWATLI, SHUKRI AL-.

Bibliography

Jankowski, James. *Nassers' Egypt, Arab Nationalism and the United Arab Republic.* Boulder, CO: Lynne Rienner Publishers, 2001.

MICHAEL R. FISCHBACH

UNITED JEWISH APPEAL (UJA)

The main organization through which U.S. Jews support Jews abroad.

In 1939 the United Palestine Appeal joined with the American Jewish Joint Distribution Committee and the National Refugee Service to form the United Jewish Appeal (UJA). Most of what it raises goes to what is now called the United Israel Appeal, which operates through the Jewish Agency in Israel. Funds are also given to support Jewish communities in other parts of the world. The UJA operates through hundreds of federations and welfare funds in the United States.

Between 1939 and 1967 the UJA raised an estimated $1.925 billion, including $147 million in 1948, the year that the state of Israel was created, and $250 million in 1967, when the 1967 War occurred. Nearly $1 billion was distributed to the UJA and its predecessor, the United Palestine Appeal (UPA).

In 1999 the UJA, the United Israel Appeal (UIA), and the Council of Jewish Federations merged to form the United Jewish Communities (UJC). In the same year the UJC was reported to have raised $524 million, making it the seventh-largest charity in the United States. The UJA Federation of New York was reported to have raised $157 million.

See also JEWISH AGENCY FOR PALESTINE.

Bibliography

American Jewish Yearbook, 2000. Scranton, PA: American Jewish Committee and Publication Society, 2000.

United Jewish Communities. Available from <http://www.ujc.org>.

PAUL RIVLIN

UNITED NATIONS AND THE MIDDLE EAST

The United Nations (UN) has played a prominent role in the Middle East, passing resolutions, facilitating negotiations, and organizing peacekeeping operations.

The world organization's most important contributions since 1948 are discussed in chronological order.

Arab–Israel War (1948)

The problem of Palestine was brought before the United Nations in April 1947. In May, the General Assembly set up the United Nations Special Committee on Palestine. In its August report, the majority recommended a plan of partition. On 29 November 1947, the General Assembly adopted one and decided that the British Mandate over Palestine should be terminated not later than 1 August 1948. The Jewish Agency accepted the partition plan, but the Arab Higher Committee and all Arab states rejected it.

On 14 May 1948, the British Mandate over Palestine expired. The Jewish Agency proclaimed the State of Israel on the territory allotted to the Jewish community under the partition plan. On the following day, the Arab states instituted armed action in Palestine. On 21 May, the Security Council appointed Folke Bernadotte the United Nations mediator for Palestine.

Fighting ended in June with a truce, which was followed by the dispatch of a military observer mission, the United Nations Truce Supervision Organization (UNTSO), the first UN peacekeeping operation. Bernadotte's mediation activities were cut short when he was assassinated in Jerusalem on 17 September 1948 by the Stern gang (LEHI). His work was immediately resumed by Ralph Bunche. On 11 December 1948, the General Assembly set up the UN Conciliation Commission for Palestine (France, Turkey, and the United States).

Between February and July 1949, Israel concluded armistice agreements with Egypt, Lebanon, Jordan, and Syria under Bunche's auspices; he was awarded the 1950 Nobel Peace Prize for his efforts. The agreements gave temporary control of the Gaza Strip to Egypt; of the West Bank, including East Jerusalem, to Jordan; and of the remaining parts of Palestine to Israel. With three of the four armistice agreements signed, Israel was admitted to the United Nations on 11 May 1949.

In December 1949, the General Assembly established the United Nations Relief and Works Agency to provide assistance to Palestinian refugees. The Trusteeship Council drafted a statute for the internationalization of Jerusalem in April 1950; it was rejected by Israel and Jordan.

After the conclusion of the armistice agreements, the responsibility for promoting a final settlement of the Palestine problem fell on the Conciliation Commission, but no progress was achieved. Despite the efforts of UNTSO, the situation along the armistice demarcation lines remained tense. Palestinian *fidaʾiyyun* (freedom fighters) carried out frequent raids against Israel, which were invariably followed by harsh retaliation by Israel's armed forces.

Suez Crisis

Tension in the region rose to a critical level in 1956, when Egypt's Gamal Abdel Nasser nationalized the Suez Canal Company, which was controlled by British and French interests. While UN secretary-general Dag Hammarskjöld endeavored to work out a compromise solution, Israel's troops invaded Egypt on 28 October 1956 and within a few days occupied the Gaza Strip and most of the Sinai Peninsula, while an Anglo-French force landed in the Suez Canal Zone. To help resolve the crisis, the Security Council established the United Nations Emergency Force (UNEF) to separate Egyptian and Israeli forces along the Gaza and Sinai frontiers.

Six-Day War

On 18 May 1967, UNEF was withdrawn at Egypt's request. Three weeks later, war broke out. Hostilities started on the Egyptian front on 5 June and soon thereafter spread to the Jordanian and Syrian fronts. The war ended on 10 June with a cease-fire. By that time, Israel had taken Sinai and the Gaza Strip from Egypt, the West Bank (including East Jerusalem) from Jordan, and the Golan Heights from Syria.

On 22 November 1967, the Security Council unanimously adopted Resolution 242, known as the land for peace resolution, which remains the basis for a negotiated settlement. It called on the parties to seek a comprehensive settlement in the Middle East and stipulated that the establishment of a just and lasting peace should be based on the withdrawal of Israel's armed forces from territories occupied in June 1967 and the recognition of the right of all states in the region to live in peace within secure boundaries. Gunnar Jarring, special representative of the secretary-general, began a mediation mission in December 1967, but little progress was made. The mission lapsed in early 1973.

October 1973 War

War broke out on 6 October 1973, when Egypt's and Syria's forces launched simultaneous attacks against Israel's posts in the Suez Canal Zone and on the Golan Heights in order to liberate their occupied territories. As fighting intensified, especially on the Egyptian front, the Security Council met on 22 October and adopted Resolution 338, which called on belligerents to cease fighting and begin negotiations to establish a just and durable peace on the basis of Resolution 242.

Count Folke Bernadotte (1895–1948) was sent by the UN, in 1948, to the newly formed nation of Israel, in order to assist in mediating the conflict between Israel and surrounding Arab countries. While in Israel, Bernadotte was assassinated by Jewish terrorists. © NATIONAL ARCHIVES/USHMM PHOTO ARCHIVES. REPRODUCED BY PERMISSION.

But the fighting continued. At the request of President Anwar al-Sadat of Egypt, the Soviet Union agreed to send troops to the area, a move that the United States strongly opposed. On 25 October 1973, the Security Council ordered an immediate cease-fire and established the second United Nations Emergency Force (UNEF II) to supervise it.

A peace conference convened in Geneva under U.S. and Soviet sponsorship in December 1973. Chaired by UN secretary-general Kurt Waldheim, it was attended by Egypt, Israel, and Jordan. Syria refused to participate, and the Palestine Liberation Organization (PLO) was not invited. The conference lasted only two days, but it paved the way for U.S. mediation, which led to military disengagement agreements between Israel and Egypt and Syria.

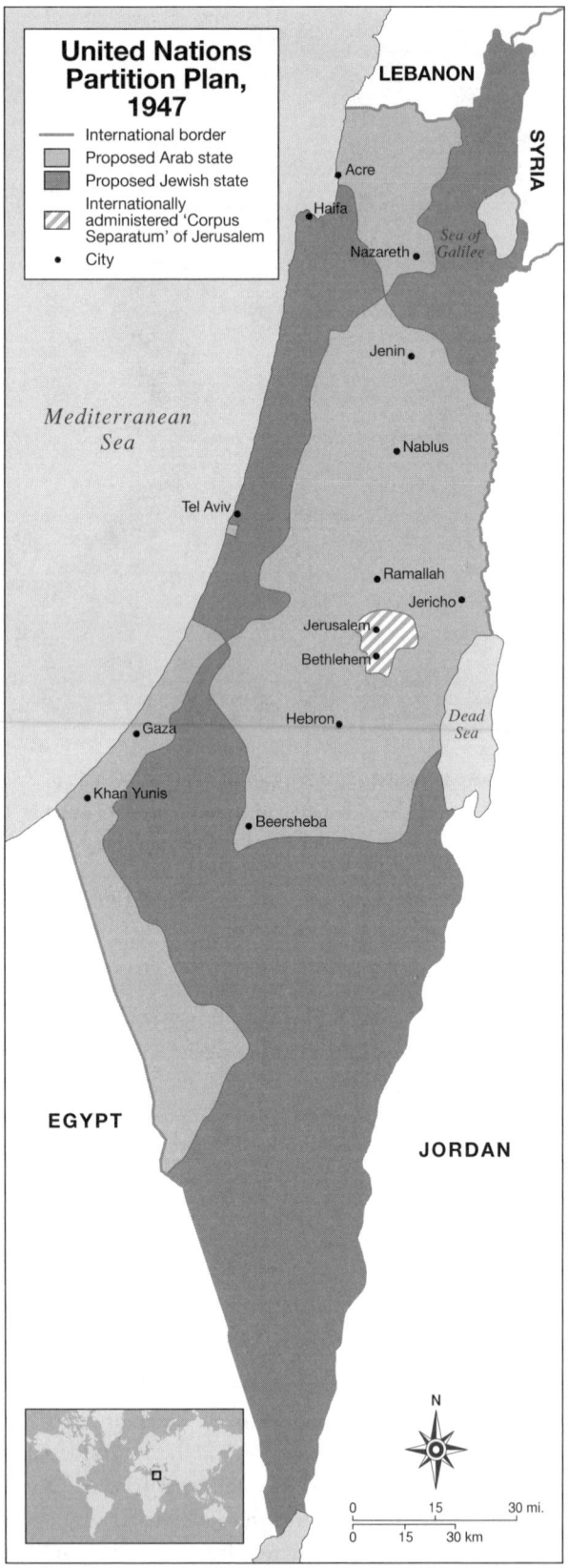

MAP BY XNR PRODUCTIONS, INC. THE GALE GROUP.

The Camp David Accords and the Egypt–Israel Peace Treaty

The peace process was revived in November 1977, when President Sadat traveled to Jerusalem. His visit was followed by direct negotiations between Egypt and Israel under U.S. auspices, which led to the Camp David Accords in September 1978 and the peace treaty between Egypt and Israel in March 1979. Sadat and Israeli Prime Minister Menachem Begin shared the 1978 Nobel Peace Prize.

It was the clear intention of the parties to the peace treaty to use UNEF II and UNTSO military observers for peacekeeping along the border, but the Soviet Union, which strongly opposed the peace treaty, made it clear that it would veto an extension of UNEF II. The Security Council therefore decided to let the UNEF's mandate lapse. The U.S. later organized and financed the Multinational Force and Observers to carry out the peacekeeping functions that the UNEF II had been expected to perform.

Israel's Invasions of Lebanon

Although relations between Egypt and Israel were normalized with the peace treaty, other aspects of the Arab–Israel conflict deteriorated after Israel's invasion of Lebanon in March 1978, following a terrorist raid against Israel by PLO fighters based in southern Lebanon. On 19 March, the Security Council called on Israel to withdraw from Lebanon's territory and established the UN Interim Force in Lebanon (UNIFIL) to confirm the withdrawal process. UNIFIL was unable to fulfill its mandate, however. In 1982, Israel again invaded Lebanon. In 1985, Israel's forces withdrew from most of the occupied territory but continued to hold a border area known as the security zone. UNIFIL remains in southern Lebanon.

Resumption of the Peace Process

The Madrid Peace Conference on the Middle East was convened in November 1991 by the United States and the Soviet Union to promote a comprehensive settlement of the Arab–Israel conflict on the basis of Security Council Resolutions 242 and 338. On 13 September 1993, Israel and the PLO signed the Declaration of Principles for interim self-government for the Gaza Strip and Jericho. Although the agreement is known as the Oslo Accord because of the secret negotiations held there, the PLO and Israel actually signed the text in Washington. The Oslo Accord was renegotiated in 1995 (known as Oslo 2). The United Nations played a marginal role in negotiating and implementing these agreements, but the world body's ability to continue virtually came to a halt during the second intifada early in September 2000 (see below). It has, however, been active in international assistance supporting the implementation of the declaration of principles.

The United Nations maintains three peacekeeping operations in the area: the UN Disengagement Observer Force on the Golan Heights, UNIFIL, and UNTSO. UNRWA assists about 3.2 million Palestinian refugees in Gaza, the West Bank, and neighboring Arab states.

The Rebellion in Lebanon

In May 1958, a rebellion by armed Muslims broke out in Lebanon when President Camille Chamoun, a Christian Maronite, announced his intention to seek a constitutional amendment that would enable him to stand for a second term. Lebanon's government brought the matter before the Security Council, charging that the United Arab Republic (formed temporarily by the union of Egypt and Syria under Nasser) was supporting the rebellion.

By Resolution 128 of 11 June 1958, the Security Council decided to dispatch the UN Observation Group in Lebanon (UNOGIL). By August 1958, General Fu'ad Chehab, the Maronite commander of the army, had been elected president of Lebanon, effectively removing the question of a second term for Chamoun. In November 1958, Lebanon's government informed the Security Council that cordial and close relations had been reestablished between Lebanon and the United Arab Republic. UNOGIL was terminated the following month.

Yemen

In September 1962, a rebellion led by the army overthrew Imam Muhammad al-Badr and proclaimed the Yemen Arab Republic. Following his overthrow, the imam rallied the tribes in the northern part of the country and, with financial and material support from Saudi Arabia, the royalists fought a fierce guerrilla war against republican forces. At the beginning of October 1962, Egyptian troops were dispatched to Yemen at the request of the revolutionary government. After the 1962 session of the General Assembly, UN Secretary-General U Thant undertook a peace initiative. In April 1963, Egypt, Saudi Arabia, and the Yemen Arab Republic accepted his disengagement plan. Saudi Arabia would terminate all support to the Yemeni royalists and Egypt would withdraw its troops from Yemen. A demilitarized zone would be established on each side of the border between Saudi Arabia and Yemen, and impartial observers would monitor the disengagement.

The UN Observation Mission in Yemen (UNYOM) began operations in July 1963. Following the conference of Arab heads of state at Cairo in mid-January 1964, relations between Egypt and Saudi Arabia improved markedly. UNYOM was withdrawn on 4 September 1964.

Economic and Social Commission for Western Asia (ESCWA)

On 9 August 1973, Economic and Social Council (ECOSOC) Resolution 1818 established the Economic Commission for Western Asia as the successor to the United Nations Economic and Social Office in Beirut to facilitate development within and outside the region. Largely because of the awkwardness of excluding Israel from the "region," this was the last UN regional commission to be created (the first began in 1947), and on 26 July 1985 ECOSOC added social aspects to the commission's work and changed its title to the Economic and Social Commission for Western Africa (ESCWA). As a result of insecurity, the headquarters were relocated temporarily from Beirut to Amman, and then to Baghdad in 1982. After the beginning of the Gulf War, the headquarters were relocated to Amman once again in 1991. In July 1994, the General Assembly decided that the commission would return to Beirut; and UN secretary-general Kofi Annan inaugurated the permanent headquarters in March 1998.

Cyprus

Following the outbreak of fighting between the Greek and Turkish communities on Cyprus in December 1963, the conflict was brought before the

The United Nations grants admission to Israel, 1949. © HULTON-DEUTSCH COLLECTION/CORBIS. REPRODUCED BY PERMISSION.

Security Council. By Resolution 186 of 4 March 1964, the council established the UN Peacekeeping Force in Cyprus (UNFICYP) to prevent a recurrence of fighting and to return normal conditions to the island. UNFICYP became operational on 13 March. After August 1964, quiet was restored, and it lasted until July 1974, when supporters of *enosis* (union of Cyprus with Greece) staged a coup d'état against the Cyprus government. Turkey launched an extensive military operation on the island. The fighting ended in August 1974. By that time, Turkey's army controlled about 38 percent of northern Cyprus. To prevent a recurrence of fighting, UNFICYP established a zone across the island between the Cyprus National Guard to the south and the Turkish and Turkish Cypriot forces to the north.

Resolution 186 also asked the UN secretary-general to appoint a mediator to promote a peaceful settlement of the Cyprus problem. The first mediator, Galo Plaza Lasso, reported in April 1965 that a settlement could best be achieved on the basis of a unitary government with adequate protection and guarantees for individual and minority rights. His report was rejected by the Turkish side and Plaza Lasso resigned in December 1965. Intercommunal talks began in 1968 under the auspices of the UN secretary-general, but they made little progress.

In February 1975, the Turkish Cypriot leadership announced the establishment of the Turkish Federated State of Cyprus in the northern part of the island. Known after 1983 as the Turkish Republic of North Cyprus, it failed to receive international recognition. UN-sponsored intercommunal negotiations finally resulted, in February 2004, in an agreement to have a unified island become a member of the European Union in May 2004. UNFICYP, whose mandate has been repeatedly extended, continues to deploy military personnel.

Bahrain

Bahrain, which until 1970 had "special treaty relations" with the former colonial power, Britain, was claimed by Iran because the island had been under its sovereign jurisdiction before 1783. Britain announced its intention to withdraw from East of Suez in 1968, and in early 1969 Iran and Britain asked Secretary-General U Thant to help resolve the disputed territory. Following nearly one year of negotiations, an agreement was reached under which U Thant would appoint a personal representative to ascertain the wishes of the people of Bahrain.

A resulting April 1970 report affirmed that the overwhelming majority of the people of Bahrain wished it to be a fully independent and sovereign state. On 11 May 1970, the Security Council endorsed the findings. Shortly thereafter, Bahrain gained its independence; it became a UN member in September 1971.

Afghanistan

On 27 December 1979, the Soviet Union entered Afghanistan to assist the communist-led government in its fight against insurgent movements. It was soon embroiled in a guerrilla war with the fighters of the Afghan resistance, known as Mojahedin, who received substantial financial and material support from Pakistan and the United States. During the hostilities, some 3 million refugees fled to Pakistan and about 2 million to Iran.

On 14 January 1980, the General Assembly adopted a resolution that called for the withdrawal of all foreign troops from Afghanistan. In February 1981, UN secretary-general Kurt Waldheim appointed Javier Pérez de Cuéllar as his personal representative to deal with the situation. When Pérez de Cuéllar succeeded Waldheim as secretary-general in January 1982, the mission was taken over by Diego Cordovez.

Afghanistan and Pakistan agreed in 1982 to engage in indirect negotiations, with Cordovez as intermediary. Those negotiations led to the conclusion, in Geneva, of the April 1988 Agreements on the Settlement of the Situation relating to Afghanistan. Both Afghanistan and Pakistan undertook not to interfere in the internal affairs of the other state, and the Soviet Union and the United States agreed not

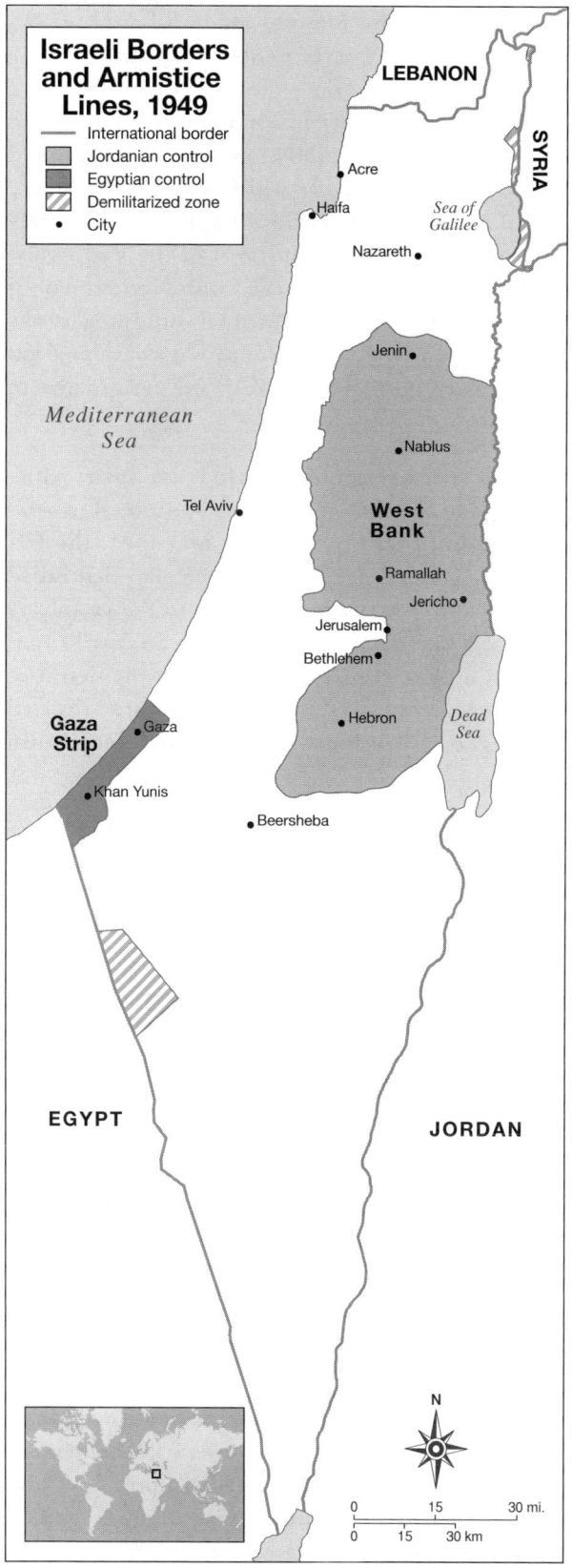

MAP BY XNR PRODUCTIONS, INC. THE GALE GROUP.

to interfere in the internal affairs of Afghanistan and Pakistan. The agreements also provided for a phased withdrawal of Soviet forces from Afghanistan by 15 February 1989 and for the establishment of the UN Good Offices Mission in Afghanistan and Pakistan (UNGOMAP), which was set up at the end of April 1988, to monitor implementation. Besides monitoring the withdrawal of the Red Army, UNGOMAP assisted in the voluntary return of refugees to Afghanistan. The final withdrawal of the Soviet Union's 100,300 troops was completed on 12 February 1989. UNGOMAP was terminated in March 1990.

The civil war continued after the Soviet withdrawal, and the two superpowers continued to send weapons until January 1991. In May 1991, the UN secretary-general proposed a peace plan that called for free and fair elections leading to the establishment of a broad-based government. In April 1992, the communist regime collapsed with the defeat of the government forces, but this did not stop the civil war; fighting continued between rival Mojahedin factions.

In September 1996, the Taliban, a group comprised of Afghans trained in religious schools in Pakistan and former Mojahedin fighters, captured Kabul with the stated aim of setting up a pure Islamic state. Following an American attack (see below), the Taliban was ousted from power on 17 November 2001, and in December the Afghan Interim Authority (AIA) was established after a number of prominent Afghans met under UN auspices in Bonn, Germany, led by Special Representative of the Secretary-General Lakhdar Brahimi. The AIA was inaugurated on 22 December 2001, with a six-month mandate, to be followed by a two-year transitional authority.

Iran–Iraq War

On 22 September 1980, the armed forces of Iraq invaded Iran and soon occupied a sizable portion of its territory. By Resolution 479 of 28 September 1980, the Security Council called upon Iran and Iraq to refrain from further use of force and to settle their dispute by peaceful means, but Iran rejected the resolution as one-sided. On 11 November, Secretary-General Waldheim appointed Olof Palme as his special representative to promote a peace settlement. Palme made some initial progress, but a peace settlement remained elusive.

During the initial phase of the war, Iraq's forces advanced inside Iran. In December 1980, Iranian forces stopped the advance, and by late 1982 they had pushed the Iraqi troops back in some areas beyond the border. Then fighting settled into a stalemate. Both parties engaged in frequent air attacks against military and oil installations and urban civilian areas.

Facilitated by the waning of the Cold War, on 20 July 1987 the Security Council adopted Resolution 598, which demanded that Iran and Iraq observe an immediate cease-fire and withdraw their forces to the international border. Intensive diplomatic negotiations lasted until 8 August 1988, when both parties formally accepted the cease-fire arrangements.

The next day, the Security Council established the UN Iran–Iraq Military Observer Group (UNIIMOG) to supervise the cease-fire and the withdrawal process. The mission began operations in mid-August with 400 military observers and about 500 military support personnel. After the cessation of hostilities, Iran and Iraq began direct talks to settle outstanding issues. On 15 August 1990, shortly after its invasion of Kuwait, Iraq lifted its claim over the Shatt al-Arab, thus removing a major cause of conflict with Iran. UNIIMOG was terminated on 28 February 1991.

Following the war, Pérez de Cuéllar used the close relationship he had developed with Iran's leaders to obtain the release of hostages in Beirut. After securing Iran's cooperation in 1989, he asked Giandomenico Picco to deal with this matter in a one-man secret mission. Almost four years later, the mission resulted in the release of eleven Western hostages detained in Beirut and of ninety-one Lebanese held by kidnap groups.

Western Sahara

In 1985, Secretary-General Pérez de Cuéllar and the chairman of the Organization of African Unity sought to promote a peaceful settlement of the conflict between Morocco and POLISARIO (Frente Popular para la Liberación de Saguia al-Hamra y Río de Oro) over Western Sahara. In August 1988, the two warring parties accepted the settlement proposals in principle. Those proposals envisaged a

The United Nations tours the Jenin refugee camp in Palestine, surveying the damage from an Israeli military strike. © AP/World Wide Photos. Reproduced by permission.

cease-fire followed by a referendum that would enable the people of Western Sahara to choose between independence and continued union with Morocco.

In April 1991, the secretary-general submitted to the Security Council a detailed plan for implementing the settlement proposals. It provided for the establishment of the UN Mission for the Referendum in Western Sahara (MINURSO) and contained a tentative timetable for the operation, according to which the referendum would be held twenty weeks after the ceasefire. On 29 April 1991, the Security Council approved the implementation plan and established MINURSO, and on 24 May the secretary-general announced that the cease-fire would enter into effect on 6 September 1991. As an interim measure, military observers were sent to Western Sahara to monitor the ceasefire.

MINURSO's Identification Commission was established in May 1993, and registration of voters began in August 1994 and was completed in December 1999. A crucial issue in the process involved the identification of applicants from three contested tribal groups. Although divergent views still exist between the parties and elections are yet to be held, the situation in Western Sahara has been generally quiet.

The Gulf Crisis and its Aftermath

On 2 August 1990, Iraq invaded Kuwait, quickly occupied the country, and annexed it. On the same day, the Security Council condemned the invasion and demanded the immediate withdrawal of Iraq's forces. When Iraq failed to comply, the council met again on 6 August and imposed economic sanctions. On 29 November, it adopted Resolution 678, which authorized member states cooperating with Kuwait to use all necessary measures to implement its resolutions if Iraq failed to withdraw by 15 January 1991.

On 16 January 1991, coalition forces led by the United States launched military operations against Iraq. The United Nations was on the sidelines during the Gulf War, but it played a key role again after the military operations were suspended on 28 February. At that time, coalition forces had driven Iraq's troops from Kuwait and had occupied southern Iraq.

On 2 March 1991, the Security Council demanded that Iraq implement all its resolutions and specified the measures to be taken to end the hostilities. The next day, an informal cease-fire was signed by military commanders in the field. On 3 April 1991, the Security Council adopted Resolution 687, which laid down in detail the specific terms that Iraq must accept in order to obtain a formal cease-fire. After receiving Iraq's official acceptance, the Security Council established the UN Iraq-Kuwait Observation Mission to supervise the cease-fire and monitor a demilitarized zone between Iraq and Kuwait.

In the aftermath of the Gulf War, the Kurdish population in northern Iraq and the Shiʿites in the south rebelled against the government, which took harsh actions to suppress the rebellions. By Resolution 688 of 5 April 1991, the Security Council demanded that Iraq immediately end the repression and give international humanitarian organizations access to all those in need of assistance within its territory. A UN humanitarian operation to provide food and essential relief supplies in all parts of Iraq, especially in the northern Kurdish area, was launched. Indeed, this was the first in a series of military interventions in the 1990s to foster humanitarian values as the theme of "sovereignty as responsibility" gained resonance.

Sanctions were not lifted by the Security Council until May 2003 (see below) because Iraq under Saddam Hussein never fully complied with the conditions of the initial resolutions to end the war or with the thirteen subsequent ones passed by the Security Council between 1991 and 2002. The negative impact of sanctions on the lives of Iraqis became controversial even after the institution of an oil-for-food program. An innovation approved by the Security Council in Resolution 687 was the UN Special Commission (UNSCOM), which from 1991 to 1998 sought to find and eliminate Iraq's weapons of mass destruction. Iraq's lack of compliance and the eventual rejection of UNSCOM would later become an issue in the United States–United Kingdom invasion of Iraq in March 2003 (see below).

After 11 September 2001: Wars in Afghanistan and Iraq

The attack by al-Qaʿida operatives on the World Trade Center and on the Pentagon on 11 September 2001 altered substantially the security equation in the Middle East and around the world. On 12 September, the Security Council adopted the strong condemnatory Resolution 1368, which termed these assaults a threat to international peace and security and referred to the right of self-defense. Later that same month, Resolution 1373 obliged member states under Chapter VII of the UN charter to cooperate in the fight against terrorism and also created the Counter-Terrorism Committee. Also in September, the General Assembly condemned the devastating attacks. Citing the provisions for self-defense under UN Charter Article 51, the United States began military operations against Afghanistan on 7 October 2001 and overthrew the Taliban government in November (see above). With the United Nations playing a substantial role in helping to rebuild political structures, almost 10,000 U.S. troops remained in the country along with the UN-approved International Security Assistance Force (ISAF) under NATO auspices. ISAF maintained security around Kabul but resisted pressures to deploy elsewhere until late 2003, when a decision was made to do so. At the same time, the security situation remained tenuous, with al-Qaʿida's leader, Osama bin Ladin, apparently at large.

In the fall of 2002, the United States opened a new front in its war on terrorism and weapons of mass destruction with an attack on the regime of Saddam Hussein in Iraq. In December 1999, the Security Council had created the UN Monitoring, Verification, and Inspection Committee (UNMOVIC) to replace UNSCOM; in October 2002, resolution 1441, which had unanimous support, granted UNMOVIC unconditional and unrestricted access to locations in Iraq, including those previously termed sensitive sites. UNMOVIC's mandate was to disarm Iraq of its weapons of mass destruction and to mon-

A United Nations convoy travels through Lebanon. © AFP/CORBIS. REPRODUCED BY PERMISSION.

itor conformity with its obligations not to reacquire the weapons prohibited by the Security Council. Citing Iraq's lack of compliance with UN resolutions, the United States and the United Kingdom went to war in Iraq on 23 March 2003 without Security Council approval. They had withdrawn a draft resolution following a heated debate that reflected divisions not only among Western states but throughout the world. One of the main points of contention was the need to permit more time for inspections. Saddam Hussein's regime fell on 9 April 2003 and U.S. president George W. Bush declared victory on 1 May, although substantial resistance continued.

Security Council Resolution 1483 brought the United Nations back into the picture and led to the end of sanctions and the beginning of the world organization's involvement on the ground. U.S. insistence on maintaining political and military control inside occupied Iraq prevented a more diverse international presence. The attack on the UN's Baghdad headquarters on 19 August 2003 led to the highest death toll in the history of the organization, killing twenty-two people, including the special representative of the secretary-general, Sergio Vieira de Mello.

The United States and the United Kingdom returned to the United Nations in the hope of securing more international military and financial support for the war's aftermath. The Security Council passed Resolution 1511 on 16 October 2003, which appeared to have been helpful in securing modest financial pledges at a donors' conference held shortly thereafter in Madrid. However, the resolution did not secure substantial military forces from other states, which sought a clearer role for the United Nations. At the outset of 2004, there was still no evidence that Iran had either weapons of mass destruction or links to al-Qaʿida, which were the main reasons the administrations of U.S. president George W. Bush and U.K. prime minister Tony Blair had cited for going to war.

Ongoing Israeli–Palestinian Conflict

The second armed intifada, or uprising, began in September 2000 after a near-breakthrough in the final days of the administration of President Bill Clinton, who had sought to bridge the divide between Israeli prime minister Ehud Barak and Palestine Authority president Yasir Arafat. Following the election of Ariel Sharon as prime minister of Israel, violence involving Palestinian suicide bombings of Israeli civilians and harsh Israeli repression and assassinations continued and worsened. A suicide bombing at a Netanya hotel during the Passover holiday led to a massive Israeli attack against the Jenin refugee camp in April 2002, and a fierce battle ensued. In response to Palestinian accusations of a massacre, the Security Council asked the United Nations to investigate the events in Jenin, but Israel, after having initially agreed to permit access, did not do so. Under pressure after widespread criticism of its unilateral approach to Iraq and to international relations more generally, in April 2003 the Bush administration published a "road map" to encourage a break in the violence and eventual political negotiations for the creation of a Palestinian state. The road map was created by a quartet, whose members were the United States, the United Nations, Russia, and the European Union.

See also AFGHANISTAN: U.S. INTERVENTION IN; ANNAN, KOFI A.; AQSA INTIFADA, AL-; ARAB HIGHER COMMITTEE (PALESTINE); ARAB–ISRAEL WAR (1948); ARAB–ISRAEL WAR (1967); ARAB–ISRAEL WAR (1973); BAHRAIN; BERNADOTTE, FOLKE; BIN LADIN, OSAMA; BUNCHE, RALPH J.; FIDA'IYYUN; GULF CRISIS (1990–1991); HAMMARSKJÖLD, DAG; IRAN–IRAQ WAR (1980–1988); JEWISH AGENCY FOR PALESTINE; MANDATE SYSTEM; OSLO ACCORD (1993); PAKISTAN AND THE MIDDLE EAST; PALESTINE LIBERATION ORGANIZATION (PLO); PARTITION PLANS (PALESTINE); PÉREZ DE CUÉLLAR, JAVIER; POLISARIO; QA'IDA, AL-; SANCTIONS, IRAQI; SUEZ CRISIS (1956–1957); TALIBAN; UNITED NATIONS EMERGENCY FORCE; UNITED NATIONS INTERIM FORCE IN LEBANON; UNITED NATIONS RELIEF AND WORKS AGENCY FOR PALESTINE REFUGEES IN THE NEAR EAST (UNRWA); UNITED NATIONS SPECIAL COMMITTEE ON PALESTINE, 1947 (UNSCOP); WAR IN IRAQ (2003); WESTERN SAHARA WAR; YEMEN CIVIL WAR.

Bibliography

Annual Report of the Secretary-General on the Work of the Organization. New York: United Nations.

Boudreault, Jody, ed. *United Nations Resolutions on Palestine and the Arab–Israeli Conflict,* Vol 4: *1987–1991.* Washington, DC: Institute for Palestine Studies, 1993.

Krasno, Jean E., and Sutterlin, James S. *The United Nations and Iraq: Defanging the Viper.* Westport, CT: Praeger, 2003.

Sherif, Regina S., ed. *United Nations Resolutions on Palestine and the Arab–Israeli Conflict Vol. 2, 1975–1981.* Washington, DC: Institute for Palestine Studies, 1988.

Simpson, Michael, ed. *United Nations Resolutions on Palestine and the Arab–Israeli Conflict Vol. 3, 1982–1986.* Washington, DC: Institute for Palestine Studies, 1987.

Tomeh, George J. *United Nations Resolutions on Palestine and the Arab–Israeli Conflict, 1947–1974.* Washington, DC: Institute for Palestine Studies, 1988.

United Nations. *The Blue Helmets: A Review of United Nations Peace-Keeping.* New York: United Nations, 1996.

United Nations Yearbook. New York: United Nations, 1947–1996.

Urquhart, Brian. *Ralph Bunche: An American Life.* New York: Norton, 1993.

Weiss, Thomas G.; Forsythe, David P.; and Coate, Roger A. *The United Nations and Changing World Politics,* 4th edition. Boulder, CO: Westview Press 2004.

F. T. LIU
UPDATED BY THOMAS G. WEISS

UNITED NATIONS CONCILIATION COMMISSION FOR PALESTINE (UNCCP)

Commission appointed to deal with the problem of dislocated Palestinians and to help reach a comprehensive peace settlement after the 1948 Arab–Israel War.

Following debate on the Bernadotte report, a UN General Assembly resolution on 11 December 1948 established the Conciliation Commission for Palestine, instructing it "to take steps to assist the parties concerned to achieve a final comprehensive peace settlement of all questions outstanding between them" and to facilitate the repatriation or resettlement with compensation of the Palestinian refugees. The commission was composed of representatives from France, Turkey, and the United States. The commissioners began with a round of shuttle diplomacy in Middle Eastern capitals, held a conference with Arab representatives in Beirut, and then convened a major conference, meeting separately with Arab and Israeli representatives, in Lausanne between April and August 1949. These meetings, along with a further series of discussions in Geneva in 1950, produced little apart from declarations of good intention (including the Lausanne Protocol), preparations to unblock frozen Arab bank accounts in Israel, and a scheme for family reunification.

At a conference of Arab and Israeli delegates in Paris in late 1951, the commission tried but failed to achieve agreement on specific proposals for a peace settlement. After the breakdown of the conference, the commission, convinced that the parties were not yet prepared to make peace, confined its efforts to dealing with the Palestinian refugee problem. Even then, it was able to make only limited progress, mainly on background studies of the technical aspects regarding future compensation. Despite the lack of progress, the commission still exists and the General Assembly still continues to pass annual resolutions calling on it to continue its efforts to carry out its original mandate.

See also LAUSANNE CONFERENCE (1949).

Bibliography

Azcárate, Pablo de. *Mission in Palestine, 1948–1952.* Washington, DC: Middle East Institute, 1966.

Caplan, Neil. *Futile Diplomacy,* Vol. 3: *The United Nations, the Great Powers and Middle East Peacemaking, 1948–1954.* Totowa, NJ, and London: Frank Cass, 1997.

Fischbach, Michael R. *Records of Dispossession: Palestinian Refugee Property and the Arab–Israeli Conflict.* New York: Columbia University Press, 2003.

Forsythe, David P. *United Nations Peacemaking: The Conciliation Commission for Palestine.* Baltimore, MD: Johns Hopkins University Press, 1972.

Hamzeh, Fuad Said. *United Nations Conciliation Commission for Palestine, 1949–1967.* Beirut: Institute for Palestine Studies, 1968.

Morris, Benny. *The Birth of the Palestinian Refugee Problem, 1947–1949.* New York; Cambridge, U.K.: Cambridge University Press, 1987.

FRED J. KHOURI
UPDATED BY NEIL CAPLAN

UNITED NATIONS ECONOMIC SURVEY MISSION (1949)

Mission to recommend effects of 1948 Arab–Israeli war and origins of UNRWA.

On 23 August 1949 the United Nations Conciliation Commission for Palestine (UNCCP) established the Economic Survey Mission, instructing it to recommend a program to assist in the recovery of the countries affected by the 1948 Arab-Israel War. The principal impetus for the creation of the mission was the failure of the UNCCP to make progress toward a political solution of the Palestinian refugee problem, but the UNCCP appointed Gordon R. Clapp, former director of the U.S. Tennessee Valley Authority, to chair the mission, thus focusing instead upon fostering the economic conditions requisite to a peace settlement. Within three months the mission concluded that the large-scale undertakings it hoped would fully reintegrate the refugees, such as Arab-Israeli cooperation in a development project for the Jordan River, were politically unfeasible.

In mid-November 1949 the mission recommended that the United Nations General Assembly both adopt a more circumspect program of public works as a first step toward rehabilitating the refugees, and assist needy individuals. On 8 December 1949 the General Assembly responded by passing Resolution 302, thereby creating the United Nations Relief and Works Agency. The agency coordinated its activities with the local governments and allocated $49 million for eighteen months of operations, but it continued to function after that in order to prevent a further deterioration of the refugees' conditions.

See also UNITED NATIONS AND THE MIDDLE EAST; UNITED NATIONS RELIEF AND WORKS AGENCY FOR PALESTINE REFUGEES IN THE NEAR EAST (UNRWA).

Bibliography

Fischbach, Michael R. *Records of Dispossession: Palestinian Refugee Property and the Arab–Israel Conflict.* New York: Columbia University Press, 2003.

Hurewitz, J.C. *The Struggle for Palestine.* New York: Greenwood Press, 1968.

Khouri, Fred J. *The Arab–Israeli Dilemma,* 2d edition. Syracuse, NY: Syracuse University Press, 1976.

ZACH LEVEY

UNITED NATIONS EMERGENCY FORCE

Peacekeeping operation established during the Suez crisis.

The Suez crisis, during which Israel, France, and Britain invaded Egypt and occupied sizable portions of its territory, was brought before the United Nations (UN) General Assembly in early November 1956. Secretary General Dag Hammarskjöld submitted a plan for setting up an emergency UN force to supervise the cessation of hostilities on 5 November. The General Assembly then authorized the establishment of the United Nations Emergency Force (UNEF), the first UN peacekeeping force.

UNEF was composed of contingents provided by member states. Troops from the five permanent members of the Security Council and any countries that might have a special interest in the conflict were excluded. UNEF's establishment in the conflict area required the consent of all parties concerned. Its soldiers had light defensive weapons but were not authorized to use force except in self-defense.

UNEF, operational by mid-November 1956, initially had about 6,000 troops from Brazil, Canada, Colombia, Denmark, Finland, India, Indonesia, Norway, Sweden, and Yugoslavia. Its first commander was Major General E. L. M. Burns of Canada. As the troops were deployed to supervise the cease-fire, negotiations were being carried out for the withdrawal of the occupation forces. A phased withdrawal began under the supervision and with the assistance of UNEF. The withdrawal of Britain's and France's forces was completed by 22 December 1956, and that of Israel's forces in March 1957.

After the withdrawal, UNEF was deployed along the Egypt–Israel border and maintained a post at Sharm al-Shaykh, which controlled access to the Gulf of Aqaba. By 1967 UNEF had been reduced to about 3,400 troops.

In May 1967, as tension arose again to a critical level in the Middle East and, despite Secretary General U Thant's appeal, President Gamal Abdel Nasser of Egypt requested the withdrawal of UNEF. UNEF therefore discontinued its operations on 18 May 1967. Three weeks later there was a new war in the Middle East.

See also ARAB–ISRAEL WAR (1956); HAMMARSKJÖLD, DAG; NASSER, GAMAL ABDEL; SUEZ CRISIS (1956–1957); UNITED NATIONS AND THE MIDDLE EAST.

Bibliography

Burns, E. L. M. *Between Arab and Israeli.* Toronto: Clarke, Irwin, 1962.

Thant, U. *A View from the UN.* Garden City, NY: Doubleday, 1978.

F. T. LIU

UNITED NATIONS INTERIM FORCE IN LEBANON

UN force in Lebanon to confirm Israeli withdrawal and assist the Lebanese government with restoring order and security.

Israel's invasion of southern Lebanon in March 1978, at a crucial stage in negotiations between Egypt and Israel, caused the United States to insist on rapid United Nations Security Council action. Resolution 425 of 19 March called on Israel to withdraw its forces and established a United Nations Interim Force in Lebanon (UNIFIL) to confirm Israel's withdrawal, restore peace and security, and assist the Lebanese government in regaining its authority. The force, initially 4,000 strong, later increasing to 6,000, began to arrive in early April 1978.

UNIFIL had no mandate to deal with the various Palestine Liberation Organization (PLO) groups and Israel's proxy South Lebanon Army, irregular forces that dominated the region. The Lebanese government had no wish to reestablish its authority in the area. Southern Lebanon was a peacekeepers nightmare.

Despite humiliations, including being swept aside during Israel's 1982 invasion, and sustaining almost 250 casualties, UNIFIL remained in place because it provided some measure of security, stability, and humanitarian protection in an extremely volatile border area. When Israel finally withdrew in May 2000, UNIFIL deployed to the border. The Lebanese government, deaf to all exhortations, left the radical Shiʿite movement Hizbullah in control of the border area, and many incidents resulted. In

2002 UNIFIL was restructured as a 2,000-strong armed observer force with contingents from France, Ghana, India, Italy, Nepal, Poland, and Ukraine. Its mandate ran to July 2003.

See also HIZBULLAH; PALESTINE LIBERATION ORGANIZATION (PLO); SOUTH LEBANON ARMY; UNITED NATIONS AND THE MIDDLE EAST.

Bibliography

Skogmo, Bjørn. *UNIFIL: International Peacekeeping in Lebanon, 1978–1988.* Boulder, CO: Lynne Rienner, 1989.

UNIFIL–United Nations Web site. Available from <http://www.un.org/depts/dpko/missions/unifil>.

AS'AD ABUKHALIL
UPDATED BY BRIAN URQUHART

UNITED NATIONS RELIEF AND WORKS AGENCY FOR PALESTINE REFUGEES IN THE NEAR EAST (UNRWA)

Organization that aids Palestine refugees.

The United Nations Relief and Works Agency for Palestine Refugees in the Near East (UNRWA) was created by UN General Assembly Resolution 302 (IV) on 8 December 1949, with the mandate to provide humanitarian assistance and emergency relief to Palestine refugees who had lost their homes and livelihood as a result of the Arab–Israel War of 1948. Palestine refugees within the purview of UNRWA are persons whose normal residences were in Palestine for a minimum of two years before the 1948 war, and their descendants. In 1949 UNRWA extended assistance to some 750,000 refugees, practically all of them Palestinian Arabs. By 2001 UNRWA had 3,874,738 registered refugees on its rolls, and was present in 59 refugee camps in the Middle East.

UNRWA's humanitarian activities have centered on three major programs: an educational program that ran 647 elementary and preparatory schools and vocational centers with 457,349 students in 1999; a health program with a network of units and medical staff that registered 7,163,056 patient visits in 1999; and a relief and social services program to assist disadvantaged groups. UNRWA also has set up special programs to improve the living conditions in refugee camps, especially housing and environmental sanitation, and to respond to emergencies. UNRWA has often had to carry out its mission in the midst of civil strife and military conflict. During the Arab–Israel War of 1967, more than 350,000 Palestinians fled from the territories seized by Israel; these included 200,000 refugees from the 1948 war, who were displaced for a second time. Later, the 1970 fighting between Jordan's army and the armed elements of the Palestine Liberation Organization (PLO) stationed in Jordan, another Arab–Israel War (October 1973), the Lebanese civil war that started in 1975, Israel's invasions of Lebanon in 1978 and in 1982, the Palestinian uprising (Intifada) and Israel's response to it, and more recently, Iraq's invasion of Kuwait and the Gulf Crisis (1990–1991) all had serious effects on the conditions of Palestine refugees and the work of UNRWA. The organization was long headquartered in Beirut, but due to the Lebanese civil war it moved to Vienna in 1978. In 1994 it announced that it was moving to Gaza, to territory controlled by the Palestinian Authority. The move was completed by July 1996.

UNRWA's budget is funded 95 percent by voluntary contributions. In 2002 the UN General Assembly approved a cash and in-kind budget of $326.2 million, of which UNRWA actually received $305.9 million. With the significant increases in costs associated with the wide-scale destruction wrought during the al-Aqsa Intifada that began in October 2000, the agency's budgetary needs have increased considerably. Yet the shortfall had to be made up by cutbacks. Actual expenditures during 2002 were $293.8 million, $32.3 million less than had been budgeted for by the General Assembly. By early 2003, UNRWA was facing a dire financial situation, and had made six emergency appeals for additional funding within a year.

See also AQSA INTIFADA, AL-; ARAB–ISRAEL WAR (1948); ARAB–ISRAEL WAR (1967); ARAB–ISRAEL WAR (1973); GAZA (CITY); GULF CRISIS (1990–1991); INTIFADA (1987–1991); PALESTINE LIBERATION ORGANIZATION (PLO); PALESTINIAN AUTHORITY; REFUGEES: PALESTINIAN.

Bibliography

UNRWA web site. Available from <www.un.org/unrwa>.

Viorst, Milton. *Reaching for the Olive Branch: UNRWA and Peace in the Middle East.* Washington, DC: Middle East Institute, 1989.

F. T. LIU
UPDATED BY MICHAEL R. FISCHBACH

UNITED NATIONS SPECIAL COMMISSION (UNSCOM)

Commission charged with eliminating Iraq's weapons of mass destruction.

After the end of the first Gulf War (1991), the United Nations Security Council passed several resolutions concerning Iraq. Resolution 687, which was passed on 3 April 1991, was the most important one. It set forth the continuation of the sanctions and the embargo on Iraq until it dismantled its weapons of mass destruction (WMD) program, which included all ballistic missiles with a range of 90 miles (150 km), and all chemical, biological, and nuclear facilities. Resolution 687 also banned the development of such weapons in the future. A related resolution, 715, adopted on 11 October 1991, called for the establishment of a long-term comprehensive monitoring system covering all current and future facilities related to weapons of mass destruction.

The United Nations Security Council created a special commission, the United Nations Special Commission (UNSCOM), which it charged with eliminating Iraq's nonnuclear WMD covered by Resolution 687. Also, UNSCOM would assist with the International Atomic Energy Agency (IAEA) inspections in the nuclear area. UNSCOM was given sweeping powers to do on-site inspections of Iraq's biological, chemical, and missile capacities, to remove and render harmless all chemical and biological weapons, to supervise the destruction of all ballistic missiles with a range exceeding 90 miles (150 km), and to verify Iraq's compliance with Resolution 687.

With a great deal of reluctance, the Iraqi government accepted Resolution 687 in May 1991. The government did not have much choice, as the resolution had passed the Security Council unanimously. Furthermore, the United States and Britain were ready to implement it and they were willing to use force if necessary.

UNSCOM operations lasted about eight years. The commission was first chaired by Rolf Ekeus, a Swedish career diplomat. From the beginning, the relationship between UNSCOM and Iraq was strained and shrouded in suspicion. On many occasions, Iraq acted in bad faith by delaying and hesitating to fulfill both the letter and the spirit of Resolutions 689 and 715. When Iraq tried to prevent UNSCOM inspectors from using their aircraft for security and political reasons, the UN Security Council adopted Resolution 707 on 15 August 1991, calling for Iraq to give full access to UNSCOM inspectors, full disclosure of weapons programs, and full disclosure of all suppliers' names. UNSCOM team members came from various countries, but the majority of the members were American and British.

The tension continued between Iraq and UNSCOM throughout the commission's operation in the country. Several confrontations between the parties prompted the United States to launch short military operations against targets inside Iraq. In July 1997 Ekeus was replaced by Richard Butler, an Australian disarmament expert who lacked diplomatic finesse, and who began to work more closely with the U.S. government. After a series of confrontations in 1997 and 1998 between Iraq and UNSCOM, the United States launched Operation Desert Fox in December 1998. The operation lasted for four days and consisted of aerial bombardments of military targets. It put an end to UNSCOM inspections, because Iraq refused further cooperation. The United Nations Security Council struggled for a year to come up with a new arms inspection formula that was acceptable to the members of the council. In January 2000 the UN adopted Resolution 1284, which formed a new commission, the United Nations Monitoring, Verification, and Inspection Commission (UNMOVIC). For two years Iraq refused to deal with the new commission.

Both Iraq and UNSCOM were responsible for confrontations. To Iraq, Resolution 687 and the commission it created impinged on Iraqi sovereignty, because Iraq's weapons program was one of the mainstays of Saddam's power, both domestically and regionally. Iraq accused the inspectors of trying to strip the nation of its industrial and technological capacity, and it objected to UNSCOM's intrusive and confrontational approach. In addition, Iraq accused the United States of using and subverting UNSCOM to gather intelligence in order to change the government in Iraq.

UNSCOM, on the other hand, allowed itself to be used by the United States government to collect intelligence data by the U.S. members of the inspection teams, according to Dilip Hiro (pp. 97, 107, and 119). The United States started to subvert UNSCOM operations as early as 1992 by using its intelligence agents and technicians trained in handling communications and bugging devices to intercept microwave transmissions sent by the Iraqi military. In the aftermath of Operation Desert Fox, several damaging revelations appeared in the U.S. press about the infiltration of UNSCOM by U.S. intelligence agencies.

By 1998, despite the tension between Iraq and UNSCOM, the commission had accomplished most of its job of discovering WMD, destroying them, and establishing a comprehensive remote monitoring system. According to Scott Ritter, the bulldog of UNSCOM, Iraq no longer possessed any meaningful quantities of chemical or biological agents, if it had possessed any at all (*New York Times,* 3 July 2000). In the spring of 2003 U.S. armed forces invaded and occupied Iraq; despite intense searching, as of the following spring they had failed to discover any weapons of mass destruction.

See also GULF WAR (1991); IRAQ; WAR IN IRAQ (2003).

Bibliography

Hiro, Dilip. *Iraq in the Eye of the Storm.* New York: Thunder's Mouth Press, 2002.

Ritter, Scott. *Frontier Justice: Weapons of Mass Destruction and the Bushwhacking of America.* New York: Context Books, 2003.

AYAD AL-QAZZAZ

UNITED NATIONS SPECIAL COMMITTEE ON PALESTINE, 1947 (UNSCOP)

Committee created in 1947 to deal with the future government of Palestine.

Following the end of World War II the Arab-Zionist conflict in Palestine was internationalized, and greater efforts were made to resolve it. After a few unsuccessful Anglo-American endeavors, in February 1947 the British handed over the Palestine problem to the United Nations.

In May 1947 the UN General Assembly created a Special Committee on Palestine (UNSCOP) with eleven members—Australia, Canada, Czechoslovakia, Guatemala, India, Iran, the Netherlands, Peru, Sweden (chair), Uruguay, and Yugoslavia. It was mandated to investigate all matters relevant to the Palestine problem and to submit a report, including proposals for a solution, to the General Assembly.

The committee visited Palestine and heard testimonies from Jewish representatives, and it witnessed the dramatic capture by the British of the ship *Exodus,* which carried 4,500 European Jewish refugees. The Palestinian Arab leadership refused to testify, but the committee nevertheless met in Lebanon with representatives of the Arab states. Members of the committee also met Jewish inmates of displaced persons camps in Europe.

The UNSCOP Report, submitted on 31 August 1947, unanimously supported the termination of the British mandate in Palestine. The representatives of Iran, India, and Yugoslavia supported a federal solution (known as the minority plan) that envisaged Arab and Jewish regions within a federal union with Jerusalem as its capital. The representatives of the other states (except Australia) favored a partition into two separate independent states (the majority plan) with Jerusalem as a *corpus separatum* under an international regime.

On 29 November 1947 the General Assembly adopted Resolution 181, based on the UNSCOP majority plan, by a 33–13 vote, with 10 abstentions. The Jewish Agency accepted the resolution, and the Arab Higher Committee rejected it.

See also EXODUS (1947).

Bibliography

Garcia-Granados, Jorge. *The Birth of Israel: The Drama As I Saw It.* New York: Knopf, 1948.

Louis, William Roger, and Stookey, Robert W., eds. *The End of the Palestine Mandate.* Austin: University of Texas Press; London: IB Tauris, 1986.

Wilson, Evan. *Decision on Palestine: How the U.S. Came to Recognize Israel.* Stanford, CA: Hoover Institution Press, 1979.

F. T. LIU
UPDATED BY JOSEPH NEVO

UNITED NATIONS TRUCE SUPERVISION ORGANIZATION (UNTSO)

United Nations (UN) peacekeeping machinery in Israel and neighboring Arab countries.

The United Nations Truce Supervision Organization (UNTSO) was created through several UN resolutions to oversee the Security Council truce agreement between Israel and the Arab states that went into effect on 11 June 1948. Unarmed UN military observers were first sent to Cairo and throughout Palestine. After hostilities in the 1948–1949 Arab-Israel war ended, UNTSO was expanded and charged with overseeing the signatories' application of the four armistice agreements. Its observers were stationed along armistice lines between Israel and Egypt, Syria, Lebanon, and Jordan. Observers remained in the region through the 1956 Suez crisis and were supported by the new and more broadly empowered UN Emergency Force. In June 1967 UNTSO demarcated the cease-fire lines between Israel and Syria, supervised the cease-fire, and oversaw renegotiations for observers along the Suez Canal. UNTSO observers assist other armed peacekeeping operations in the Middle East, such as the UN Interim Force in Lebanon. In March 1996 UNTSO had 178 observers, down from its maximum strength of 572 observers in 1948; 28 have died in service since 1948. UNTSO is headquartered in Jerusalem and has offices in Beirut and Damascus.

See also ARAB–ISRAELI GENERAL ARMISTICE AGREEMENTS (1949).

Bibliography

Burns, E. L. M. *Between Arab and Israeli.* New York: Ivan Obolensky, 1963.

Higgins, Rosalyn. *United Nations Peacekeeping: Documents and Commentary.* 4 vols. New York; Oxford, U.K.: Oxford University Press, 1969–1981.

United Nations. *The Blue Helmets: A Review of United Nations Peace-keeping,* 3d edition. New York: United Nations Deptartment of Public Information, 1996.

CHARLES U. ZENZIE
UPDATED BY NEIL CAPLAN

UNITED STATES OF AMERICA AND THE MIDDLE EAST

The Middle East has been an area of vital interest to the United States since World War II.

Although U.S. interest in the Middle East can be traced to the early years of the American republic, the region has been a principal focus of U.S. foreign policy since World War II. Oil investments and the special U.S. relationship with Israel were the chief reasons for U.S. involvement in that area of confrontation between the United States and the Soviet Union during the Cold War.

U.S.–Middle East Relations

U.S. contacts with the Middle East started in about 1800 in North Africa. U.S. naval forces defeated the Barbary pirates in 1816, but most relations in the nineteenth century were educational and commercial in nature. Protestant missionaries established several schools, medical facilities, and colleges in Egypt, Turkey, Syria, and Lebanon.

In 1919 President Woodrow Wilson sent the King–Crane Commission to inquire into the wishes of the Syrian and Palestinian people as to their political future. In the 1920s and 1930s U.S. oil companies invested heavily in Iran, Iraq, Bahrain, Saudi Arabia, and Kuwait. During World War II, the United States participated in the Allied battles for North Africa and established the Persian Gulf Command to transport lend-lease materials from the Gulf, through Iran, to the Soviet Union. By 1945 several U.S. air bases, supply depots, and transportation facilities were operating throughout the Middle East. From the end of World War II until the collapse of the USSR in the early 1990s, a major objective of U.S. foreign policy was to prevent Soviet penetration of the Middle East. When British political and military commitments in the area diminished, several Middle Eastern countries signed agreements with the United States, and the region became the recipient of the greatest portion of U.S. military and economic aid.

Soviet pressure on Turkey and Iran marked the beginning of the Cold War, and the Truman Doctrine of 1947 represented one of the first efforts in the new "containment" policy to halt Soviet expansion. Responding to feared Soviet encroachments in Greece, Turkey, and Iran, the United States, under the Truman Doctrine, sent $400 million in aid to Greece and Turkey, and helped modernize Turkey's armed forces. U.S. advisers were also sent to Iran.

Founded in 1948 with U.S. support and, by the 1960s, viewed as an important strategic asset, Israel became the largest single recipient of U.S. economic and military assistance. Close ties with Israel were reinforced by humanitarian impulses inspired by knowledge of the Holocaust. The assistance to Israel made it difficult for the United States to establish closer ties with the surrounding Arab nations. During the 1950s Egypt refused to join a Middle East defense organization proposed by the United States, Great Britain, and France. Instead, the Northern Tier or Baghdad Pact, which was based on a military alliance between Turkey, Iraq, Iran, and Pakistan, was devised. The pact was linked with other containment alliances through Turkey's membership in the North Atlantic Treaty Organization in the West and Pakistan's affiliation with the Southeast Asia Treaty Organization in the East.

U.S. secretary of state Madeleine Albright listened in as Palestinian leader Yasir Arafat talked with President William J. Clinton by telephone from Arafat's office in Gaza in September 1999. Despite initial progress toward final settlement of disputes about Palestine, Clinton's efforts to achieve Camp David Accords of his own in summer 2000 ultimately collapsed and were soon followed by a new and bloody Palestinian uprising against Israel. © REUTERS NEWMEDIA INC./CORBIS. REPRODUCED BY PERMISSION.

Efforts by Western countries to keep Soviet influence out of the Middle East were undermined by the events leading up to the Arab–Israel War of 1956. Attempts by the United States to cultivate better relations with Egypt were subverted when the United States refused to provide Egypt with aid to construct the Aswan High Dam; as a consequence, President Gamal Abdel Nasser nationalized the Suez Canal in July 1956. Despite the strain in relations between the two countries, the Eisenhower administration strongly opposed the invasion of Egypt by Britain, France, and Israel in October 1956, and joined the Soviet Union in condemning the attack.

Following the war, unrest throughout the Middle East and the spread of nationalist doctrines that the U.S. government perceived as leftist led in January 1957 to the Eisenhower Doctrine, whereby military and economic assistance was dispensed to the Middle East and the use of U.S. forces was provided to protect countries in the region "against overt aggression from any nation controlled by international Communism." The doctrine was tested in April 1957 when the U.S. Sixth Fleet was sent to the eastern Mediterranean to support Jordan's King Hussein. After the 1958 revolution in Iraq, Lebanon's President Camille Chamoun also called on the United States for assistance to protect his regime from revolutionary forces, and President Eisenhower responded by sending 14,000 marines. They were withdrawn a few weeks after a truce was arranged, through intervention of the United States, between the various conflicting Lebanese parties.

The United States's efforts to resolve the Arab–Israel dispute during the Eisenhower administration centered on the Arab refugee problem and projects intended to achieve the economic reconstruction of the Middle East through cooperative development of the region's water resources. Although he was successful in achieving a de facto regional water-sharing accord, Eric Johnston, Eisenhower's special representative, failed to obtain agreement for proposals to resettle the refugees. During 1955 and 1956 the United States also joined Britain in a secret operation, code-named "Alpha," which was designed to coerce Egypt and Israel into direct talks. The operation ended in failure when another Eisenhower emissary, Robert Anderson, returned to Washington in March 1956 after a fruitless round of shuttle diplomacy. The Kennedy administration sought to promote good relations with

U.S. deputy secretary of defense Paul Wolfowitz, addressing a pro-Israel rally on 15 April 2002 in front of the U.S. Capitol, expressed President George W. Bush's "solidarity" with Israel. The United States supported the creation of Israel in 1948 and developed closer ties, including large amounts of economic and military aid, beginning in the late 1960s—which in turn often strained its relationship with Arab nations. © AFP/CORBIS. REPRODUCED BY PERMISSION.

"progressive" Middle Eastern countries concerning containment. Kennedy also approved the first U.S. sale of a major weapons system to Israel.

UN Resolutions

After the Arab–Israel War of 1967 between Israel and Egypt, Syria, and Jordan, UN Security Council Resolution 242, drafted with U.S. help, became the basis for U.S. policy in the Arab–Israel conflict. Its requirement that Israeli forces withdraw from territories occupied during the war hinged on the achievement of a comprehensive peace settlement. The Nixon administration's Rogers Plan, which was based on Resolution 242, called for Israel to withdraw to its pre-June 1967 borders (with minor exceptions). After the 1967 war, Egypt and Syria were rearmed by the Soviet Union, with whom they signed defensive alliances. In 1968, when the British announced their planned withdrawal from the Persian Gulf, the United States decided to build up the military forces of Saudi Arabia and Iran. Ties between Israel and the United States were greatly strengthened after the 1967 war when Israel demonstrated its potential as a strategic ally by shipping great quantities of captured Soviet-made weapons to the United States for close analysis. Ties were also aided by a strong pro-Israel lobby that influenced Congress, the White House, and the media. During the Reagan administration a memorandum of understanding was signed between Israel and the United States calling for cooperation to "deter all threats from the Soviet Union to the region." The pact provided for joint military exercises and working groups for cooperation in development and in the defense trade. In 1987 the U.S. Congress formally designated Israel a "major non-NATO ally." Israel was considered a special case in U.S. efforts to curb the expansion of nuclear powers and was not pressured to join the Nuclear Nonproliferation Treaty.

During the 1973 October War between Israel and Egypt and Syria, U.S.–Soviet relations worsened. Moscow and Washington provided their respective clients with billions of dollars in arms; a threat by the Soviets to send troops to assist Egypt and nuclear alert by the United States brought the two countries to the brink of war. After the outbreak of the war in late October, the Arab oil-producing nations imposed an oil embargo that created an energy crisis in the United States and Western Europe. A peace conference at Geneva in December 1973 broke up after two days without settling the conflict, but Secretary of State Henry Kissinger subsequently initiated step-by-step negotiations that resulted in disengagement agreements between Israel, Syria, and Egypt and provided for Israel's withdrawal from parts of Sinai and the Golan area.

Relations between Egypt and the United States improved after 1973 as Egypt's President Anwar al-Sadat shifted from relying on Soviet aid to being receptive to U.S. influence. Hoping to capitalize on the improved diplomatic climate, President Jimmy Carter attempted to reconvene the Geneva Peace Conference in 1977, but Sadat flew to Jerusalem in November to start direct negotiations with Israel.

U.S. president Jimmy Carter (center) engaged in intensive diplomacy with President Anwar al-Sadat (left) of Egypt and Prime Minister Menachem Begin of Israel in 1978 to bring about the Camp David Accords, for which the two Middle Eastern leaders were awarded the Nobel Peace Prize. The agreement resulted in the Israeli return of the occupied Sinai Peninsula to Egypt and Egyptian recognition of Israel, but it did not lead to an overall settlement of the Arab–Israel conflict. COURTESY OF JIMMY CARTER LIBRARY.

Sadat's dramatic initiative began a new peace process based on direct bilateral contacts between Egypt and Israel. When bitter disagreements between the two adversaries threatened to disrupt negotiations, Carter intervened personally. He invited Sadat and Israel's Prime Minister Menachem Begin to Camp David, where two frameworks for peace were hammered out—one dealing with Egyptian–Israeli relations and the other with the Palestinian issue. Under Carter's guidance, the Camp David Accords were shaped into the Egyptian–Israeli peace treaty that was signed in Washington, D.C., in March 1979. At the Camp David summit Carter persuaded Begin to include establishment of a Palestinian "self-governing authority" in the final accords. "Palestinian homeland" and "Palestinian rights" were accepted for the first time as legitimate concepts by the U.S. government.

Elsewhere in the Middle East, Carter's policy of containing Soviet influence in the Persian Gulf was undermined when his close ally Mohammad Reza Pahlavi, the shah of Iran, was overthrown in 1979. The president's efforts to obtain the release of U.S. hostages held by the new revolutionary government in Tehran took over a year to resolve successfully, and this delay was a factor in his loss of the 1980 presidential election.

An American soldier in Baghdad, Iraq, looks for the enemy after a rocket-propelled grenade hit a U.S. Army vehicle, killing three other soldiers and a translator. U.S., British, and other forces rapidly took control of Iraq and ousted Saddam Hussein as its ruler in April 2003, but the occupation was marked by numerous daily attacks on American and coalition troops, as well as civilian supporters and aid workers, which continued after the capture of Saddam in December. © AP/WIDEWORLD PHOTOS. REPRODUCED BY PERMISSION.

Presidents Ronald Reagan and George H. W. Bush continued the containment policies of their predecessors and also became deeply involved in the Arab–Israel conflict. During the Lebanese war in 1982, Reagan sent the Sixth Fleet and the U.S. Marines to Beirut as part of a multinational peacekeeping force. Lebanese militias attacked the marines, inflicting heavy casualties, and the marines were withdrawn soon after. The Reagan plan for Middle East peace envisioned "self-government by the Palestinians . . . in association with Jordan" as the "best chance for a durable, just, and lasting peace." Bush's attempts to continue negotiations based on the Reagan plan and Resolution 242 were stymied until 1991, when the Madrid Conference convened. Cosponsored by the United States and Russia, the new peace process provided for bilateral talks between Israel and Syria, Lebanon, and joint Jordanian–Palestinian delegations. It also included a series of multilateral meetings on such substantive issues as security, environment, economic development, water, and refugees.

President Bush involved the United States in its largest foreign military operation since Vietnam when in 1991 he sent U.S. forces to drive Iraq from Kuwait. From a military perspective, the operation was a success because the United States and the allied forces sustained only minor casualties. Bush was sharply criticized, however, because Iraq's President Saddam Hussein remained in power despite his defeat on the battlefield.

Post–Cold War Policy

When the Soviet Union collapsed in 1991, a new phase of U.S. foreign policy began; containment was no longer the principal objective. Instead, Russia and the United States cooperated in regard to the Middle East. As Soviet influence in the region declined, the United States became the dominant power, and its influence was paramount. This situation greatly facilitated Washington's goal of maintaining the political status quo through its support of friendly regimes. It also made it easier to intervene when U.S. concerns such as assured access to oil and the security of Israel appeared to be threatened.

Initial attempts by President William J. Clinton to resolve the Arab–Israel conflict seemed encouraging, but the failure of an Israeli–Palestinian summit at Camp David in July 2000 contributed to a second Palestinian intifada (uprising) against Israel's occupation of the West Bank and Gaza. By 2003 hostilities degenerated into a low-intensity war between Israel and Palestinians that threatened U.S. policies aimed at maintaining stability in the region through support for the status quo.

An attack by Middle Eastern terrorists destroyed the World Trade Center in New York and severely damaged the Pentagon in Virginia on 11 September 2001, resulting in thousands of casualties. The September attack intensified President George W. Bush's war on terrorism, leading to a U.S.-led attack on Afghanistan. The war in Afghanistan resulted in expulsion of the Taliban government in Kabul and establishment of a new regime allied with the United States. Bush renewed efforts to overthrow Saddam Hussein in 2002 and 2003, charging that he was a threat to international peace and that he had developed weapons of mass destruction in violation of UN Security Council resolutions. U.S. forces were assembled in surrounding countries, and invaded Iraq in March 2003.

See also CAMP DAVID ACCORDS (1978); CAMP DAVID SUMMIT (2000); GULF CRISIS (1990–1991); KING–CRANE COMMISSION (1919); MADRID CONFERENCE (1991); TWIN PILLARS POLICY; WAR IN IRAQ (2003).

Bibliography

Bialer, Uri. *Oil and the Arab–Israeli Conflict, 1948–63.* London: Macmillan, and New York: St. Martin's Press, 1999.

Carter, Jimmy. *The Blood of Abraham.* Boston: Houghton Mifflin, 1985.

Clawson, Patric, and Gedal, Zoe Danon. *Dollars and Diplomacy: The Impact of U.S. Economic Initiatives on Arab–Israeli Negotiations.* Washington, DC: Washington Institute for Near East Policy, 1999.

Cristol, A. J. *The Liberty Incident: The 1967 Israeli Attack on the U.S. Navy Spy Ship.* Washington, DC: Brassey's, 2002.

Davidson, Lawrence. *America's Palestine: Popular and Official Perceptions from Balfour to Israeli Statehood.* Gainesville: University Press of Florida, 2001.

Gerges, Fawaz A. *America and Political Islam: Clash of Cultures or Clash of Interests?* Cambridge, U.K.: Cambridge University Press, 1999.

Hart, Parker T. *Saudi Arabia and the United States: Birth of a Security Partnership.* Bloomington: Indiana University Press, 1999.

Obenzinger, Hilton. *American Palestine: Melville, Twain and the Holy Land Mania.* Princeton, NJ: Princeton University Press, 1999.

Quandt, William B. *Peace Process: American Diplomacy and the Arab–Israeli Conflict,* revised edition. Washington, DC: Brookings Institution Press; Los Angeles: University of California Press, 2001.

Sick, Gary. *All Fall Down: America's Tragic Encounter with Iran.* New York: Penguin Books, 1985.

Spiegel, Steven. *The Other Arab–Israeli Conflict: Making America's Middle East Policy, from Truman to Reagan.* Chicago: University of Chicago Press, 1985.

Stein, Kenneth W. *Heroic Diplomacy: Sadat, Kissinger, Carter, Begin and the Quest for Arab–Israeli Peace.* New York: Routledge, 1999.

Telhami, Shibley. *The Stakes: America and the Middle East.* Boulder, CO: Westview Press, 2002.

Touval, Saadia. *The Peace Brokers: Mediators in the Arab–Israeli Conflict, 1948–1979.* Princeton, NJ: Princeton University Press, 1982.

DON PERETZ

UNITY PARTY

Turkish political party, active in the 1960s and 1970s.

The Unity party came to be identified with the Shiʿite Alevi minority community. It changed its name to the Turkish Unity party in November of 1971, perhaps to overcome this image. With the outlawing of the Turkish Workers Party, eight of its former members were allowed to run as independents on the Unity party's election list in 1973, giving it a distinct leftist inclination. It polled only 1 percent of the vote and gained only one seat, however, compared to nearly 3 percent and eight seats in 1969. In 1977 it did even less well, failing to win any seats at all.

See also ALEVI; TURKISH WORKERS PARTY.

Bibliography

Weiker, Walter F. *The Modernization of Turkey: From Ataturk to the Present Day.* New York: Holmes and Meier, 1981.

FRANK TACHAU

UNIVERSITY OF JORDAN

The main public university in Jordan.

The University of Jordan was established in 1962 on a picturesque hillside in the western outskirts of Amman that formerly was the site of an agricultural research station. The university comprises eighteen faculties, including arts, sciences, economics and commerce, *shariʿa* (Islamic law), medical sciences (including general medicine, nursing, and pharmacy), education, agriculture, engineering and technology, law, and physical education, and as of 2003 boasted 961 faculty members. It awards both undergraduate and graduate diplomas, and also has a teaching hospital. As with all public universities in Jordan, students pay nominal tuition and are able to buy books and materials at subsidized prices. In 2003, the university student population stood at 25,000, eighty-eight percent of which came from Jordan.

Bibliography

Gubser, Peter. *Jordan: Crossroads of Middle Eastern Events.* Boulder, CO: Westview, 1983.

JENAB TUTUNJI
UPDATED BY MICHAEL R. FISCHBACH

UNIVERSITY OF KHARTOUM

A Sudanese institution established in 1902.

Horatio Herbert Kitchener, Lord Kitchener of Khartoum, established the Gordon Memorial College in the memory of the British general Charles George Gordon, who died at Khartoum in 1885, to establish a formal seat of learning in the Sudan. Kitchener opened the college on 8 November 1902. During the first half of the twentieth century, Gordon Memorial College was transformed from a secondary school to a college with a more sophisticated curriculum and a more renowned faculty. Most graduates during these years became civil servants in the British administration of the Sudan.

Its function as a vocational training institute was substantively changed when the college was affiliated with London University in 1945 to grant equivalent degrees; in 1951 the Gordon Memorial College and Kitchener School of Medicine were combined to create the University College of Khartoum. Upon Sudan's independence in 1956 the University College abandoned its connections with the University of London to become the University of Khartoum. Since then it has expanded to include numerous research institutes and a variety of schools.

As the campus lies in the heart of Khartoum, the university's faculty, staff, and particularly its students have played a significant role in the political life of Sudan. Its graduates organized and led the Graduates' General Congress in 1938, which played a dynamic role in the evolution of Sudanese nationalism and in Sudan's governments after independence. After the coup d'état of 30 June 1989 by Umar Hasan Ahmad al-Bashir, the National Islamic Front (NIF) government reoriented the university's curriculum and purged the Western-educated Sudanese and expatriate faculty, replacing them with instructors more suitable to the NIF's Islamist ideology. At the same time the government launched a dramatic expansion of the university, so that in 2002 there were 17,000 undergraduates, 6,000 graduate students, and an academic staff of more than 1,000.

Bibliography

Beshir, Mohamed Omer. *Educational Development in the Sudan, 1898–1956.* Oxford, U.K.: Clarendon Press, 1969.

ROBERT O. COLLINS

UNIVERSITY OF TEHRAN

The first modern university in Iran.

In May 1934, the Majles (national assembly) passed a law to incorporate five existing public colleges as a new University of Tehran. The original faculties included law, literature, medicine, science, and technology (engineering). Reza Shah Pahlavi officially inaugurated the University of Tehran in February 1935 by laying the foundation stone for its campus in an area northwest of the then new administrative and commercial district. Subsequently, faculties of agriculture, fine arts, and theology were added, as well as a printing press and a central library.

In 1943, the university became independent of the ministry of education and a board of directors was organized. Elected by the faculty, the new governing body also elected the dean. This independence was undermined after 1953, when the election of the dean became a formality, since the new dean had to be approved by the shah. By the late 1960s, the shah was making appointments from among politicians instead of academics, further undermining the university's academic integrity. These efforts at political control, however, did not prevent the University of Tehran from becoming the nurturing ground for all the opposition movements against Mohammad Reza Shah Pahlavi's regime, including the opposition that eventually led to the Iranian Revolution (1979).

The 1979 revolution and the Iran–Iraq War slowed the development of the university, but since 1989 it has continued to develop and expand, adding several new faculties and institutes. Despite the establishment of other universities in both Tehran and other Iranian cities, the University of Tehran has an unrivaled reputation in the country for academic excellence. During the early 2000s, the annual enrollment was about 30,000 students, over 60 percent of whom were female; the faculty exceeded 1,500. The administration of the university is still based on the pattern established during the previous regime.

See also IRANIAN REVOLUTION (1979); IRAN–IRAQ WAR (1980–1988); PAHLAVI, MOHAMMAD REZA; PAHLAVI, REZA.

Bibliography

Banani, Amin. "Educational Reforms." In *The Modernization of Iran, 1921–1941.* Stanford, CA: Stanford University Press, 1961.

MANSOUREH ETTEHADIEH
UPDATED BY ERIC HOOGLUND

UQBI, TAYYIB AL-
[1888–1960]

Prominent member of the Algerian Association of Reformist Ulama.

Born near Biskra in Algeria, Tayyib al-Uqbi (also Tayeb el-Okbi) studied in Medina and was influenced by the Muwahhidun movement of Islam. He was known as an eloquent and controversial Islamic scholar. In 1936 al-Uqbi was accused of planning the murder of the *mufti* (canon lawyer) of Algiers but was acquitted in 1939. Al-Uqbi criticized Shaykh Abd al-Hamid Ben Badis's political involvements and left the association in 1938; he preferred discussion of religious and spiritual questions as disclosed by his journal, al-Islah.

See also MUWAHHIDUN.

Bibliography

Naylor, Phillip C., and Heggoy, Alf. *Historical Dictionary of Algeria,* 2d edition. Metuchen, NJ: Scarecrow Press, 1994.

PHILLIP C. NAYLOR

URABI, AHMAD
[1841–1911]

Egyptian nationalist leader and army officer.

Ahmad Urabi, the son of a village shaykh of Iraqi Arab origin, studied for two years at al-Azhar in Cairo and then entered the Cairo military academy at the behest of Saʿid Pasha in 1854/55 and soon earned his commission. After the deposition of Khedive Ismaʿil in 1879, he is said to have supported the emerging National Party of Egypt, but his first proven act was to represent a group of discontented ethnic Egyptian officers who were protesting against the favoritism shown to Turkish and Circassian officers by War Minister Uthman Rifqi. Khedive Tawfiq and Prime Minister Riyadh intended to dismiss Urabi and his group for insubordination, but other Egyptian officers seized control of the war office and rescued Urabi in February 1881. Subsequently, the khedive agreed to replace Rifqi with Mahmud Sami al-Barudi as war minister. On 9 September fearing a khedival counterplot, the Egyptian officers surrounded Abdin Palace, confronted Tawfiq, and obliged him to set up a constitutionalist government with Muhammad Sharif as prime minister and to increase the size of the Egyptian army.

As Britain and especially France—concerned about the safety of the Suez Canal, their investments, and their citizens in Egypt—became increasingly hostile to the Urabist movement, the Nationalists replaced Premier Sharif with Mahmud Sami al-Barudi in February 1882, and Urabi became war minister. The Nationalists continued to fear a khedival counterplot and took steps to weaken the Turks and Circassians within the officer corps, also stirring up popular feeling against the European powers. Riots broke out in Alexandria in June 1882, and many European residents fled. Britain and France threatened military intervention to support the khedive (whose relationship with the Nationalists seems to have been ambivalent) and to protect their citizens. They demanded that the Egyptian army remove all fortifications from Alexandria, and, when Urabi did not comply quickly enough, British ships began bombarding them, leading to the outbreak of fires in Alexandria. British troops (unaided by France, which had withdrawn because of a ministerial crisis) landed at Alexandria and later at Isma'ilia to restore order. Urabi and the Egyptian army continued to resist the British, even after the khedive had gone over to their side, until their crushing defeat at al-Tall al-Kabir on 13 September 1882. Once the British entered Cairo, Urabi surrendered, was put on trial for treason against the khedive, but was not executed. He was exiled to Ceylon—until he was allowed by Khedive Abbas Hilmi II to return in 1901. He played no part in the later National party of Mustafa Kamil, died in obscurity, and was generally scorned by educated Egyptians until the 1952 revolution. Since then he has been rehabilitated by Gamal Abdel Nasser and his fellow officers—whose occupational and class backgrounds paralleled his own. Now he is generally considered a patriot who resisted the British, the khedive, and the aristocracy in favor of constitutional government and the welfare of Egypt's common people.

His writings include *Kashf al-Sitar an Sirr al-Asrar,* published in two volumes (Cairo, 1925).

Bibliography

Baring, Evelyn, Earl of Cromer. *Modern Egypt.* London: Macmillan, 1908; reprint, London and New York: Routledge, 2000.

Blunt, Wilfrid S. *Secret History of the English Occupation of Egypt.* London: Unwin, 1907.

Mayer, Thomas. *The Changing Past: Egyptian Historiography of the Urabi Revolt, 1882–1983.* Gainesville: University of Florida Press, 1988.

Schölch, Alexander. *Egypt for the Egyptians! The Socio-Political Crisis in Egypt, 1878–1882.* London: Ithaca Press, 1981.

ARTHUR GOLDSCHMIDT

URBANIZATION

The growth of cities and the social and physical transformations arising from this phenomenon.

The Middle East is home to the world's first cities as well as some of its most notable ones. The first cities, which developed in southern Mesopotamia (now in Iraq) about 3500 B.C.E., had small populations by modern standards—not exceeding about 20,000 inhabitants. By 3000 B.C.E. cities also grew along the Nile in Egypt. From these early centers, urban life spread throughout the world.

Until about 1800 most of the great cities such as Babylon, Alexandria, Ctesiphon, Constantinople (now Istanbul), Baghdad, and Cairo could grow large because they had access to water transport and income from an imperial tax base. Industry and trade were the main sources of income for smaller cities, including Tyre, Sidon, Beirut, Carthage, Tabriz, Palmyra, and Mecca. The development of some cities was heavily influenced by their religious significance; these include Jerusalem, Karbala, Mashhad, Mecca, Medina, and Qom. The proportion of the total population living in cities in what became known as the Middle East seldom exceeded 15 percent before the nineteenth century.

New factors contributed to the growth of cities after 1800, including modern transportation, new trade patterns, and European penetration. Following World War I and the fall of the Ottoman Empire, nationalist regimes were established, first in Iran and Turkey, later in Iraq, Jordan, and Syria. These focused development inward. East of Libya, the capitals of the large countries are all inland (Ankara, Cairo, Damascus, Baghdad, Riyadh, San'a, Tehran) and since their development policies were statist, these cities expanded. After World War II, rail and road networks that centered on the capitals were extended, facilitating migration to them. At the same time, rapid rural population growth and the mechanization of agriculture, largely implemented after 1945, pushed farmers from the land. Millions of people in the region moved to cities in search of jobs, education, and other services.

Israel was established in 1948 after a period of conflict, and its urban growth—mainly Tel Aviv and Haifa—was fueled by an influx of Jewish immigrants. Palestinians left or were expelled by Israeli forces in 1948, swelling cities in neighboring countries including Lebanon (Tyre, Sidon, and Beirut), Jordan (Amman), and Kuwait, as well as the territories of the West Bank and the Gaza Strip.

Oil boomtowns (Abadan, Abu Dhabi, Dhahran, Kuwait City) grew rapidly for short periods, but they never became as large as the major political and commercial centers. In the larger countries (Algeria, Egypt, Iran, Morocco, Turkey) close to 50 percent of the population was urban by the mid-1990s. In some of the smaller countries (Israel, Lebanon, Kuwait, the United Arab Emirates) the proportion is as high as 90 percent.

See also URBAN PLANNING.

Bibliography

Blake, G. H., and Lawless, R. I., eds. *The Changing Middle Eastern City.* New York: Barnes & Noble; London: Croom Helm, 1980.

Bonine, Michael, ed. *Population, Poverty, and Politics in Middle East Cities.* Gainesville: University Press of Florida, 1997.

Brown, L. Carl, ed. *From Madina to Metropolis: Heritage and Change in the Near Eastern City.* Princeton, NJ: Darwin Press, 1973.

Saqqaf, Abdulaziz Y., ed. *The Middle East City: Ancient Traditions Confront a Modern World.* New York: Paragon House, 1987.

JOHN R. CLARK
UPDATED BY ANTHONY B. TOTH

URBAN PLANNING

Effect on city organization of colonialism and petroleum wealth.

In the modern period two major influences have shaped contemporary urban planning in the Middle East: colonialism and petroleum. These two influences, and a host of other minor factors, have had different roles during three phases of constructing urban landscapes: the colonial period (c. 1800–1945), a transitional period (c. 1945–1972), and the oil-boom era (post-1972). Within these three stages, urban planning has shifted from being primarily involved in physical planning and urban design to integrating socioeconomic and physical planning.

The Colonial Period (1800–1945)

Although not all countries in the Middle East were colonized at the same time or in the same pattern, a common thread connects the urban-planning process. Europeans used urban planning successfully to establish and maintain the colonial extractive system. Physical segregation was the main tool used in implementing this policy. Urban planning in this period was dominated by physical land-use planning and urban design, which chiefly concerned the arrangement of urban infrastructure and land use. The colonial use of physical planning established and maintained a trading network and facilitated a suitable living environment for European colonial administrators, workers, and their households.

European colonialists built port cities to collect and ship goods (for example, Aden, Casablanca, Tunis, Suez, Hormuz, and Port Saʿid). They also built interior towns to serve as military centers, local administrative capitals, or collection points for regional resources, and they built infrastructure, such as roads and railways, to connect interior cities to ports. This trade-related settlement system became the new colonial urban hierarchy that is still common all over the Middle East.

Urban planning then played its second major role in this period by maintaining and servicing the influx of European military personnel, administrators, businesspeople, settlers, and fortune seekers. Planning was utilized to build the segregated city, in which a European, upper-class quarter was separated from the rest of the city. French Morocco offers the most vivid example of this kind of city planning: European quarters were built separate from the old medinas; important urban cultural sites were preserved; and the European part of the city utilized the most up-to-date urban-planning techniques. Similar practices were followed in Algeria, Tunisia, Libya, and Egypt. These urban plans segregated Europeans, along with some local resident minority groups (such as Coptic Christians and Jews) and a small community of the native rich, from the indigenous population, resulting in a dual city. A parallel but noninstitutionalized development in Palestine was the building of Tel Aviv as a Jewish city adjacent to Arab Jaffa.

In the dual city, a disproportionate share of the urban revenue was spent on the European quarters, even though taxes were raised mostly from the native quarters. As a result, the European neighborhoods had large residential plots, low densities of population, and broad tree-lined roads and streets. They were also better connected to urban amenities like water, electricity, and sewage facilities. These low-density residential quarters with their superior facilities and other urban benefits provided healthier environments for their residents. In addition, they provided the Europeans with a culturally familiar environment, making them more interested in working in colonies and thus maintaining the colonial system.

In countries where local rulers had more autonomy or colonialism was not officially present, rulers tried to copy European styles of design and urban planning. In Egypt before British control began in 1882, Khedive Ismaʿil (r. 1863–1879), influenced by his visit to Paris, tried to follow for Cairo the urban plans of Baron Georges-Eugène Haussmann. Later, in Iran, Reza Pahlavi Shah (r. 1925–1941) promoted a grid design for Tehran and constructed wide avenues through the old quarters of the city, and a "modern" city along the lines of the European model was built in north Tehran, where the rich began to reside. It was thought that copying Western urban form would lead to modernization, but the end result was the growth of dual cities similar to those that developed in colonized countries. Indeed, the internal structure of most Middle Eastern cities still can be traced back to this period.

The Transitional Period (1945–1972)

Urban planing assumed a lesser role in the Middle East during this politically active period. Since most of the countries in this region either had just become politically independent or were in the process of becoming so, urban planning was less important than ongoing political struggles and social movements. In the immediate postcolonial period, a spontaneous population movement occurred within some major Middle Eastern cities. In particular, the space formerly occupied by Europeans was taken over by the indigenous elites. In countries such as Morocco and Tunisia, this transition occurred in a peaceful and orderly fashion, but in a few countries, most notably Algeria, the rapid exodus of foreign settlers resulted in more diverse economic classes taking over the quarters formerly occupied by colonialists. Nevertheless, most Middle Eastern cities maintained their dual character.

Major concerns for urban planners were to provide housing for new migrants from rural areas and to bridge the gap between the former European and traditional quarters. To consolidate power, new rulers provided various social groups with land, housing, and urban amenities in return for their political support. In Israel, for example, the Labor Party provided temporary housing in the 1950s for Jews immigrating from postwar Europe and from other areas of the Middle East. Later, these immigrants were resettled in new urban neighborhoods and in newly established development towns in less populous areas.

Urban planning also began to develop in a new direction, emphasizing company-town building, master-plan technique, and economic development. This aspect was particularly evident in the Persian Gulf states of Iran, Iraq, Kuwait, Qatar, and Saudi Arabia. The steady growth of oil revenues beginning in the late 1950s encouraged governments to devise long-term economic development plans or to invest in industrial projects. These policies had a major impact on developing urban planning into an integrated physical-economic approach.

U.S. and British oil companies also established company towns for their workers. The Arabian-American Oil Company (ARAMCO), for example, used Western planners and engineers to lay out company towns such as Dhahran and Abqaiq using a system of blocks with a grid pattern. Similarly in Iran, British planners modeled the city of Abadan on the landscape of suburban England. Middle Eastern countries depended on the West for qualified planners and consultants to carry out urban planning. Consequently, a planning technique then common in the West, the master plan, was imported to the Middle East and soon became ubiquitous throughout the region. Most plans were end-state master plans, in that the ultimate look of the city in the future was already predetermined. Most plans were also unclear about the process of city planning or procedures for implementation. Additionally, the plans were usually static and design-oriented, with little consideration for the social and economic needs of the majority. Although very few master plans actually were implemented, the process of designing master plans proved to be a positive development for urban planning.

The Oil-Boom Era (1973 to the Present)

In the 1970s the role of urban planning underwent a rapid transformation, particularly in the oil-producing countries, where the rise in oil revenues enabled governments to embark on a variety of grandiose urban projects. A major focus was on comprehensive planning, which involved the private sector and considered spatial development concerns. The construction of new towns absorbed considerable investment. Three major goals prompted the building of new towns: to relieve the population pressures on the major cities by drawing migrants away from already overcrowded cities; to accommodate the growing population of industrial workers and to facilitate industrialization; and to accommodate military bases throughout the region. Primarily, Western firms have undertaken the planning of these new towns, especially those in oil-rich countries. Although efforts to incorporate aspects of indigenous culture into the design of these towns have been made, such efforts have not been fully successful. Most of these towns have used zoning to isolate economic activities, in contrast with the mixed-use tradition in the region, and their layouts are designed for the use of the automobile.

With the oil wealth–fueled economic growth of the Persian Gulf countries serving as a catalyst, the rejection of end-state master plans soon became common all over the Middle East in favor of new city plans that give more consideration to social and economic factors. In addition, the new plans were integrated into broader regional and national planning strategies based on large urban centers in such countries as Egypt, Iran, Morocco, and Saudi Arabia. The new dynamic style of planning is also evident in the use of Integrated Urban Development Projects (IUDPs) among local planners and planning consultants. The emphasis of IUDPs is on the sectoral and spatial integration of projects, operating alongside, although often effectively replacing, comprehensive master planning. For example, the IUDP for Baghdad consisted of three integrated plans for central Iraq, greater Baghdad, and Baghdad the city. Three models—urban corridors, growth poles, and dispersed settlements—were used to develop comprehensive alternative strategies based on future scenarios. After evaluating the scenarios, a hybrid of all three models applicable to Iraq's needs was adopted.

Although the focus of making plans had changed, the tools for implementing them remained inadequate in most Middle Eastern countries. The reasons include a lack of cooperation among decision makers, a lack of enforcement legislation, and the conflict between the beautification and modernization of the city and the meeting of basic needs of the inhabitants. Thus, urban planning in the Middle East still is grappling with numerous problems. One major issue in large cities of oil-rich countries is how to allocate resources between immigrants and the native population. These immigrants, often from other Middle Eastern countries, are not granted citizenship or the right to own property, placing a heavy burden on the rental markets. In addition, a new form of segregation is taking place: Housing estates are planned so as to minimize contact between immigrants and the indigenous population. For example, in the new towns of Jubail (Saudi Arabia) and Umm Said (Qatar), dormitory-style housing for single expatriate workers secludes them from the native population.

Perhaps the most important issue for city planning is rapid population growth and urbanization. At approximately 3 percent per annum, the region's population growth rate is higher than the figure for any other world region with the exception of sub-Saharan Africa. The urbanization rate, at more than 4.5 percent for most countries in the Middle East, is also among the fastest in the developing world. Most large cities of the region suffer from overcrowding; squatter settlements; housing shortages; poverty; unemployment; lack of adequate urban infrastructure, services, and amenities; and escalating environmental degradation, including unbearable pollution. These and other urban problems are placing increasing stress on the budgets, resources, and planning capacities of municipal governments, forcing planners and policy makers to seek new ways of managing urban growth. In fact, this need to cope with many intertwined urban problems often has led to planning being used as a tool to anticipate future problems and merely manage current ones, rather than solve them. A more preventive approach to urban planning must take the place of the existing curative approach.

See also ARCHITECTURE; COLONIALISM; URBANIZATION.

Bibliography

Abu-Lughod, Janet L. "Moroccan Urbanization: Some New Questions." In *Development of Urban Systems in Africa,* edited by R. A. Obudho and Salah El-Shakhs. New York: Praeger Publishers, 1979.

Amirahmadi, Hooshang. "Regional Planning in Iran: A Survey of Problems and Policies." *Journal of Developing Areas* 20, no. 4 (1987): 501–530.

Amirahmadi, Hooshang, and El-Shakhs, Salah S., eds. *Urban Development in the Muslim World.* New Brunswick, NJ: Center for Urban Policy Research, 1993.

Brown, Kenneth, et al., eds. *Middle Eastern Cities in Comparative Perspective: Points de vue sur les villes du Maghreb et du Machrek: Franco-British Symposium, London 10–14 May 1984.* Atlantic Highlands, NJ; London: Ithaca Press, 1986.

Denither, Jean. "Evolution of Concepts of Housing, Urbanism, and Country Planning in a Developing Country: Morocco, 1900–1972." In *From Madina to Metropolis: Heritage and Change in the Near Eastern City,* edited by L. Carl Brown. Princeton, NJ: Darwin Press, 1973.

Zaim, Sabahaddin. "Urbanization Trends in Turkey." In *The Middle East City: Ancient Traditions Confront a Modern World,* edited by Abdulaziz Y. Saqqaf. New York: Paragon, 1987.

HOOSHANG AMIRAHMADI
UPDATED BY ERIC HOOGLUND

URF

See GLOSSARY

URWA AL-WUTHQA, AL-

Anti-British Muslim newspaper.

Edited from Paris by Jamal al-Din al-Afghani and Muhammad Abduh, *al-Urwa al-Wuthqa* was published between March and October 1884. The title, meaning "the firmest bond," alludes to the Qur'an; it had been used by Afghani in 1883 to refer to the pan-Islamic caliphate of the Ottoman sultan. After eighteen issues had appeared in 1884, the paper suddenly ceased publication, probably owing to lack of funds. (The closing is usually atributed to the British banning the paper from entering India and Egypt, but since it was distributed free throughout the Muslim world, this measure should not have stopped it.) The financing of *al-Urwa al-Wuthqa* is unclear, although documents suggest that a Tunisian general, probably Wilfrid Blunt, and possibly the former Egyptian Khedive Isma'il were involved. Subsidization afforded wide distribution, which helped to enhance the reputation of the paper and its editors.

Most of the political articles in the paper championed the struggle against British imperialism in Muslim lands. The more theoretical articles were mainly devoted to an activist reinterpretation of Islamic ideas and to a call for unity among Muslims. *Al-Urwa al-Wuthqa,* which contributed to the fame of its editors in the Muslim world, was the first forum in which Afghani stressed Muslim unity, or pan-Islam, the ideology with which he is most associated.

See also ABDUH, MUHAMMAD; AFGHANI, JAMAL AL-DIN AL-.

NIKKI KEDDIE

UŞAKLIĞIL, HALIT ZIYA

[c. 1866–1945]

Turkish novelist, journalist, and poet.

Halit Ziya Uşakliğil was born in Istanbul, the son of a businessman from a prestigious İzmir family. When he was fourteen years old, the family returned to İzmir, where in 1884 he published the city's first daily newspaper, *Nevruz.* He started up other İzmir newspapers while working in Istanbul as a French teacher and bank employee. In the 1890s, he became active in the Servet-i Fünun (Wealth of Knowledge) literary movement and began writing novels. In 1909, he became a professor of literary history and aesthetics at Istanbul University.

Uşakliğil is considered a top Turkish novelist who bridged the nineteenth-century Tanzimat (reform) and twentieth-century republican periods, combining the complex storylines and heightened rhetoric of the former period with the cosmopolitan tastes and psychological realism of the later one. In the 1920s, he turned from novels to other forms, particularly short stories, and published about two hundred. He also published poetry, several plays, literary studies, and memoirs.

Bibliography

Mitler, Louis. *Ottoman Turkish Writers: A Bibliographical Dictionary of Significant Figures in Pre-Republican Turkish Literature.* New York: P. Lang, 1988.

ELIZABETH THOMPSON

ÜSKÜDAR

The oldest and largest district of Asian Istanbul.

Situated across the Bosporus from the walled city of Constantinople, Üsküdar was called Chrysopolis in ancient times and Scutari in the Byzantine era. In the period of Ottoman rule, Üsküdar became more integrated into the life of the capital city, as it became the center of several dervish orders and tekkes, military barracks, and, in the nineteenth century, textile and other factories. In the 1860s, it was formally incorporated into the municipal government of Constantinople (now Istanbul). It was in Üsküdar that Florence Nightingale set up her famed hospital during the Crimean War (1853–1856). And in the late nineteenth century, Russian Turks established the first center of Turkic studies in the empire in an Üsküdar *tekke.* The district, known for its fine gardens, in recent years has become a large residential quarter of the city with a population over 200,000.

See also TEKKE.

Bibliography

Shaw, Stanford J., and Shaw, Ezel Kural. *History of the Ottoman Empire and Modern Turkey,* Vol. 2: *Reform, Revolution, and Republic: The Rise of Modern Turkey, 1808–1975.* Cambridge, U.K., and New York: Cambridge University Press, 1977.

ELIZABETH THOMPSON

USS *COLE*

See COLE, USS

USSISHKIN, MENAHEM

[1863–1941]

Zionist leader.

Menahem Ussishkin, engineer and leader of the Russian-based Zionist movement Hibbat Zion, was a spokesman for a practical Zionism favoring land settlement, diaspora activities to aid distressed communities, and cultural autonomy, even after the World Zionist Organization insisted on suspending such actions until a political charter recognizing Jewish national rights in Palestine was secured. Ussishkin replaced Chaim Weizmann as head of the short-lived Zionist Commission after the end of World War I and later served as chairman of the Jewish National Fund until his death in 1941. A fervent advocate of expanding Jewish land ownership as a tool for strengthening Zionism's political claims, he was equally passionate about reviving Hebrew as a spoken language and expanding educational institutions in Palestine.

See also HIBBAT ZION.

Bibliography

Luz, Ehud. *Parallels Meet: Religion and Nationalism in the Early Zionist Movement (1882–1904).* Philadelphia: Jewish Publication Society, 1988.

DONNA ROBINSON DIVINE

USS *LIBERTY*

See LIBERTY, USS

U.S.S.R.

See RUSSIA AND THE MIDDLE EAST

USTADH

See GLOSSARY

USULI

Philosophy of Islamic law.

The Usuli school of Shiʿite jurisprudence, developed in contrast to the Akhbari (traditionalist) school, argues for the primacy of the *ulama* as interpreters of Islamic law and prophetic and imami traditions. The Usulis favor the legitimacy of reasoning (*aql*) and interpretation (*ijtihad*) of traditions of the Prophet and the imams as sources for the derivation of Islamic law. Thus, they allow for the emulation of prominent Shiʿite *ulama* by the believers, who are incapable themselves of interpreting the Qurʾan or the teachings of the Prophet and the imams. In addition, the Usulis believe in critical readings of the contents of major Shiʿite compilations of prophetic and imami traditions. They also prohibit the emulation of past masters of religion, so that the centrality of living *ulama* as interpreters of Shiʿite jurisprudence is preserved. Rivalry between the two schools heightened in the Safavid period, with the Usulis emerging as the ultimate victors by the eighteenth century.

Shiʿite *ulama* were able to play a prominent role in the constitutional movement of Iran (1905–1911), drawing on elements of Usuli thought to justify both the ratification of the constitution and the participation of clergymen in political affairs. The evolution of the Usuli doctrine of a hierarchical clerical establishment made for the creation of clerical ranks such as *hujjat al-islam, ayatollah,* and the *marja al-taqlid* (source of emulation) in contemporary Shiʿism. In addition, Usuli discourse made for the legitimation of the doctrine of *velayat-e faqih,* or governance of the jurisconsult, in post-1979 Iran.

See also SHIʿISM.

Bibliography

Amanat, Abbas. "In Between the Madrasah and the Marketplace: The Designation of Clerical Leadership in Modern Shiʿism." In *Authority and Political Culture in Shiʿism,* edited by S. A. Arjomand. Albany: State University of New York Press, 1988.

Hairi, Abdolhadi. *Shiʿism and Constitutionalism in Iran.* Leiden, Netherlands: Brill, 1977.

Newman, Andrew J. "The Nature of the Akhbari/Usuli Dispute in Late Safawid Iran." *Bulletin of the School of Oriental and African Studies* 55, 1–2 (1990): 22–51; 250–261.

NEGUIN YAVARI

UTAYBA TRIBE

See TRIBES AND TRIBALISM: UTAYBA TRIBE

UTAYBI, JUHAYMAN AL-

[c. 1940–1980]

Saudi ideologue and leader of the Mecca insurrection, 1979.

Utaybi was born in a bedouin settlement at Qasim in central Saudi Arabia. It is unclear whether he received any formal education during his childhood. Utaybi served in the National Guards for about eighteen years, and toward the end of this period he studied at the Islamic University in Medina.

The year 1974 seems to have marked Utaybi's break with formal state institutions. The circumstances under which he left the National Guards are unknown; his departure from the university resulted from his disagreement with his teachers' applied interpretation of Islamic law in relation to the Saudi regime. He began a period of self-education and preaching, drawing a circle of followers. His first *risala* (treatise), "Al-imara wa al-bayʿa wa al-taʿa" (Rulership, allegiance, and obedience), appeared in 1974. Utaybi was arrested with ninety-eight others in 1978; all were released without trial.

At least eleven *risalas* by Utaybi were printed between 1974 and 1979. His writings combined a strict application of the Wahhabi (Muwahhidun) doctrine with widely accepted traditions having a messianic dimension. He accused the Saudi rulers of doctrinal deviation, greed, and corruption. He also accused the religious establishment of complicity and preached that it was the duty of Muslims to combat the evils of the regime.

Utaybi anticipated that the regime would pursue and persecute its puritan opponents, whose sole and ultimate refuge would be the Kaʿba (the holy shrine inside the Grand Mosque at Mecca). There, the *mahdi's* (messiah's) appearance would be established, armed resistance would start, and the Muslims would be victorious in the Arabian Peninsula and beyond. On 22 November 1979 Utaybi led a heavily armed group, estimated at between 500 and 2,000, who seized the Kaʿba. They were ousted two weeks later. For their crime, Utaybi and sixty-two others were beheaded on 9 January 1980.

See also IKHWAN; MUWAHHIDUN.

Bibliography

Kechichian, Joseph. "Islamic Revivalism and Change in Saudi Arabia: Juhayman al-Utaybi's 'Letters' to the Saudi People." *Muslim World* 80, no. 1 (1990): 1–16.

ABDEL AZIZ EZZELARAB
UPDATED BY ERIC HOOGLUND

UTHMAN, MUHAMMAD ALI

[c. 1908–1973]

North Yemen political leader.

Muhammad Ali Uthman was a Yemeni nationalist and republican, a strong supporter of both the 1962 revolution that resulted in the Yemen Arab Republic (YAP) and the 1967 coup that replaced the al-Sallal regime with that of Qadi Abd al-Rahman al-Iryani. He was a member of the Republican Council, the plural executive created by the al-Iryani regime, from 1967 until his assassination in 1973. His murder, the result of a local dispute, was at the time attributed wrongly to leftist dissidents supported by the revolutionary regime in South Yemen; it was seized upon by the government as an excuse to crack down on leftists. Uthman was a traditional local notable and landowner, and a Sunni Muslim of the Shafiʿi sect, with much influence in part of the Hujariyya, Jabal Sabr, and the lower elevations south of Taʿiz City. He is memorialized in a very good English-language school in Taʿiz (grades 1 through 12), which was named after him shortly after his death.

See also PEOPLE'S DEMOCRATIC REPUBLIC OF YEMEN; TAʿIZ; YEMEN; YEMEN ARAB REPUBLIC.

Bibliography

Bidwell, Robin. *The Two Yemens.* Boulder, CO: Westview; Harlow, U.K.: Longman, 1983.

ROBERT D. BURROWES

UTHMAN, UTHMAN AHMAD
[1917–1999]

Egyptian civil engineer, construction magnate, and cabinet minister.

Born in Ismaʿiliyya and educated at Cairo University, Uthman Ahmad Uthman founded a civil engineering company soon after graduation instead of entering government service. But he quickly discovered that the booming oil industry in Saudi Arabia offered him better opportunities for advancement than did Egypt. His construction firm, the Arab Contractors, founded in 1940, expanded until it was able to bid on multimillion-dollar projects in the United Arab Emirates (then called Trucial Oman), Iraq, Kuwait, and Libya. Although his company was sequestered by Gamal Abdel Nasser in 1961, Uthman remained in control and played a major role in constructing the Aswan High Dam.

He became highly visible in Egyptian public life during the period of the Infitah policy of Anwar al-Sadat, building a new bridge across the Nile River and various traffic flyways in downtown Cairo. His firm also deepened the Suez Canal and built the Dhahran International Airport, the Kuwait Municipal Building, the Benghazi (Libya) sewer system, the Kirkuk (Iraq) feeder canal, and a first-class hotel in Khartoum (Sudan). He became minister for reconstruction in 1973, adding housing to his portfolio in 1974. His son married one of Sadat's daughters.

During the Sadat era, Uthman accumulated power and wealth in ways that aroused widespread suspicion, in part by being both a minister who could issue tenders on contracts and a contractor who could bid on them. Under Husni Mubarak he became vulnerable to criticism by journalists, the Engineers' Syndicate, and even his son, but his firm has remained prominent in Egypt, other Arab states, and other African countries. Although he was a fervent advocate of free-enterprise capitalism, Uthman's personal success depended on his political connections as much as on his intelligence and hard work.

See also ASWAN HIGH DAM; INFITAH.

Bibliography

Baker, Raymond William. *Sadat and After: Struggles for Egypt's Political Soul.* Cambridge, MA: Harvard University Press, 1990.

Beattie, Kirk J. *Egypt during the Sadat Years.* New York: Palgrave, 2000.

Goldschmidt, Arthur. *Biographical Dictionary of Modern Egypt.* Boulder, CO: Westview, 2000.

Heikal, Mohamed. *Autumn of Fury: The Assassination of Sadat.* New York: Random House, 1983.

Springborg, Robert. *Mubarak's Egypt: Fragmentation of the Political Order.* Boulder, CO: Westview, 1989.

ARTHUR GOLDSCHMIDT

UZBEKS

A Central Asian people.

In the 1920s and 1930s, before the Soviet Union implemented language and nationalities policies, the Uzbek language, an eastern Turkic language of the Altaic family generally known as Turki (Chaghatai), was written in Arabic script and was the principal literary language for all Turkic-speaking central Asians. When they were forced to adopt Cyrillic script (i.e., the Russian and Slavic alphabet), Uzbeks and other central Asian Turks were denied easy access to their rich literary heritage, which dates to the fifteenth century.

Uzbeks practice Islam; they are Sunni Hanafi Muslims. Originally pastoral nomads, by the early part of the twentieth century they were predominantly sedentary subsistence farmers, herders, or inhabitants of small towns engaged in producing and marketing crafts. Until the mid-nineteenth century, the Uzbeks were politically the preeminent force in the region. From the 1860s to 1991, the Uzbeks and other central Asian Muslims suffered colonial occupation of their lands by czarist Russia and its successor, the Soviet Union. As of 2001, Uzbeks constitute more than 80 percent of the population of the independent state of Uzbekistan; about 15 million Uzbeks speak the Northern Uzbek language. Uzbeks are also one of the larger ethnic minority groups in neighboring Tajikistan and in the northern part of the Islamic State of Afghanistan, where Southern Uzbek, a related but distinct language, is spoken.

Bibliography

Allworth, Edward A. *The Modern Uzbeks: From the Fourteenth Century to the Present: A Cultural History.* Stanford, CA: Hoover Institution Press, 1990.

M. Nazif Shahrani

UZI

See Glossary

V

VAʿAD LEʾUMI

National Council of the Jews in Mandatory Palestine.

The Vaʿad Leʾumi (VL) was the supreme executive authority and representative organ of the Yishuv (Jewish community in Palestine) between 1920 and 1948. Functioning much like a cabinet, each Vaʿad Leʾumi was composed of members of an Asefat ha-Nivharim (elected assembly), and its day-to-day operations were largely in the hands of a chairman and a smaller executive committee. For most of the Mandate period the executive was headed by a praesidium of Yizhak Ben-Zvi, Yaakov Thon, and David Yellin.

One of the main functions of the VL was to act as official representative for the heterogeneous, highly politicized Jewish community in Palestine. The VL served as a high-level public forum for debating the divergent viewpoints and conflicting interests of religious versus secular Jews; farmers and employers versus organized labor; and native versus newly arrived immigrant groups having differing traditions (e.g., Sephardim versus Ashkenazim). The Palestine Royal Commission Report (1937) credited the VL and its local educational system with counteracting these divisive forces by the forging of a "national self-consciousness of unusual intensity."

The VL was frequently beset by organizational difficulties and jurisdictional squabbles with the Palestine Zionist Executive and the Jewish Agency Executive (both responsible to the World Zionist Organization). While most matters of high policy were decided by Zionist leaders and organs in Palestine and abroad, the VL was able to exercise its autonomy mainly in the spheres of education and local communal affairs. After 14 May 1948 the functions and departments of the VL and those of certain sections of the Jewish Agency came under the authority of a provisional state council of the State of Israel.

See also BEN-ZVI, YIZHAK.

Bibliography

Burstein, Mosh. *Self-Government of the Jews in Palestine since 1900.* Tel Aviv: Hapoel Hatzair, 1934.

Caplan, Neil. *Palestine Jewry and the Arab Question, 1917–1925.* London: Frank Cass, 1978.

Shaw, J. V. W., ed. *A Survey of Palestine: Prepared in December 1945 and January 1946 for the Information of the Anglo-American Committee of Inquiry* (1946), 2 vols. Washington, DC: Institute for Palestine Studies, 1991.

NEIL CAPLAN

VAKA-I HAYRIYE

Turkish for "the beneficial event"; the end of the janissary corps in 1826.

The term *vaka-i hayriye* has been used by Turkish historians to describe the government-ordered destruction of the Ottoman Empire's military unit, the janissary corps, on 15 June 1826. This momentous event resulted in considerable bloodshed (6,000 dead, according to conservative estimates) and was received with dismay and mixed emotions by large segments of the populace. In an attempt to gain public approval, Mahmud II's regime, using the services of the *ulama* (Islamic scholars), presented the incident as unavoidable and necessary to protect the very survival of Islam and the Ottoman Empire. Immediately following the destruction of the janissary corps, Mahmud II ordered the court chronicler, Mehmet Esad Efendi (c. 1789–1848), to record the official version of events, *Üss-i Zafer* (Foundation of victory), which was printed in Istanbul in 1828 and served as the main source for every other Ottoman account of this period.

See also JANISSARIES; MAHMUD II.

Bibliography

Levy, Avigdor. "The Ottoman Ulama and the Military Reforms of Sultan Mahmud II." *Asian and African Studies* 7 (1971): 13–39.

AVIGDOR LEVY
UPDATED BY ERIC HOOGLUND

VALENSI, ALFRED
[1878–1944]

Tunisian Zionist.

Alfred Valensi, a member of the Sephardic Jewish elite, was one of the founders and leaders of the Tunisian Zionist Federation. While still a law student in France, he became a disciple of Max Nordau. Valensi was a contributor to major European journals.

A brilliant theoretician and organizer, he represented Tunisian Zionists at international gatherings in London and Carlsbad with his associate Rabbi Joseph Brami. In 1926, he settled in Paris, where he was later arrested and transported by the Nazis in 1944 to his death.

See also NORDAU, MAX.

Bibliography

Stillman, Norman A. *The Jews of Arab Lands in Modern Times.* Philadelphia: Jewish Publication Society, 1991.

NORMAN STILLMAN

VALI

See GLOSSARY

VANCE, CYRUS
[1917–2002]

U.S. lawyer and government official.

Cyrus Vance, born in Clarksburg, West Virginia, received a bachelor of arts degree from Yale University in 1939 and a law degree in 1942. After serving as a junior naval gunnery officer in the Pacific Theater in World War II and practicing law, he served in a number of government positions, including general counsel for the Department of Defense (1961–1962), secretary of the army (1962–1963), deputy secretary of defense (1964–1967), and secretary of state (1977–1980). He continued to be active in international affairs after his resignation in 1980. His work with Middle Eastern and Eastern European problems included service as President Lyndon Baines Johnson's special representative on Cyprus in 1967, helping to ensure that Greece and Turkey would not be drawn into war over the conflict. He received the Medal of Freedom from the U.S. president for his work. Before returning to federal service, Vance and Daniel Yankelovich founded the respected Public Agenda, a nonprofit and nonpartisan research organization in New York. His most prominent role in the Middle East was as secretary of state under President Jimmy Carter, during which he had a leading role in the Camp David Accords: He held extensive consultations with Israeli prime minister Menachem Begin and Egyptian president Anwar al-Sadat at Camp

David, Maryland, which led to the September 1978 peace agreement between the two countries. Vance resigned from the Carter administration in 1980 because he disagreed with the president's decision to use force to rescue the U.S. citizens held hostage in Teheran. Widely respected for his integrity and range of international contacts, Vance worked with the United Nations to secure the cease-fire in Croatia in 1991, and later helped to resolve creditor claims in a real estate case in New York in 1993. Vance died in 2002 after an extended bout with Alzheimer's disease.

See also CAMP DAVID ACCORDS (1978).

Bibliography

McClellan, David S. *Cyrus Vance.* Totowa, NJ: Rowman and Allanheld, 1985.

Quandt, William B. *Camp David: Peacemaking and Politics.* Washington, DC: Brookings Institute, 1986.

Vance, Cyrus. *Hard Choices: Critical Years in America's Foreign Policy.* New York: Simon and Schuster, 1983.

DANIEL E. SPECTOR

VAN, LAKE

Salt lake in eastern Turkey.

Lake Van is the largest lake in Turkey, some 5,600 feet (1,600 m) above sea level, with a surface area of 1,400 square miles (3,700 sq. km). Having no outlet, its waters evaporate and concentrate salts, including carbonates and sulphates of soda; the resulting blue-green color creates a startling, austere beauty. Lake Van is stocked with darek, a herring-like fish consumed locally.

Bibliography

Fisher, Sydney N. *The Middle East: A History,* 3d edition. New York: Knopf, 1979.

JOHN R. CLARK

VANUNU AFFAIR

A controversy over divulging Israeli nuclear information to a British newspaper.

In October 1986, Mordechai Vanunu (1954–), a former employee of the Dimona nuclear reactor in Israel, provided the *Sunday Times* of London with information and photographs of the plant, claiming Israel was producing nuclear arms and that it had stockpiled between one hundred and two hundred nuclear weapons. Israel denied the charges and stated that it did not possess nuclear weapons and would not be the first Middle Eastern country to introduce nuclear arms to the region.

Vanunu was kidnapped in Italy by the Mossad and returned to Israel, where he underwent a seven-month-long secret trial for treason and espionage against the state. The three-judge court's sixty-page verdict was almost completely classified; only one sentence was made public: "We decided the defendant is guilty on all three counts." The three counts involved espionage, the unauthorized transmission of information, and helping Israel's enemies in a time of war.

Vanunu was widely portrayed in the Israeli press as a traitor and as mentally deranged. His prison sentence at times included solitary confinement, and his cause was taken up by human rights and disarmament groups and scientists around the world. European disarmament groups claimed that he was a hero and he was nominated for the Nobel Peace Prize. World opinion was that the bulk of Vanunu's story and data was accurate, demonstrating that Israel did indeed have a substantial nuclear arsenal.

See also DIMONA; MOSSAD; NUCLEAR CAPABILITY AND NUCLEAR ENERGY.

Bibliography

Gaffney, Mark. *Dimona, the Third Temple?: The Story behind the Vanunu Revelation.* Brattleboro, VT: Amana Books, 1989.

Israel's First Bomb, The First Victim: The Case of Mordechai Vanunu. Nottingham, U.K.: Bertrand Russell Peace Foundation, 1988.

"Israel: Vanunu Convicted, Given 18 Years." Facts On File. Available from <www.2facts.com/stories/temp/77635temp1988009410.asp>.

JULIE ZUCKERMAN
UPDATED BY GREGORY S. MAHLER

VARLIK VERGISI

Capital tax levied in Turkey during World War II.

Adopted in November 1942 to finance Turkey's emergency military expenditures during World War

II, the Varlik Vergisi was heavily criticized as confiscatory and discriminatory. It was abolished in March 1944. Justified as a social equalization measure against those who profiteered during the war, up to 75 percent of net profits were collected as tax from trade companies. Istanbul merchants and non-Muslims were taxed far more heavily than Muslims and farmers. The tax produced long-term political effects in the fear of government as a threat to private property and in highlighting the dangers of one-party rule.

Bibliography

Lewis, Bernard. *The Emergence of Modern Turkey,* 3d edition. New York: Oxford University Press, 2002.

ELIZABETH THOMPSON

VATAN

See NEWSPAPERS AND PRINT MEDIA: TURKEY

VATICAN AND THE MIDDLE EAST

The Roman Catholic Church struggles to maintain its presence in the Middle East.

The presence of the Roman Catholic Church in the Middle East goes back to the Roman and Byzantine empires, to the Crusades, and to European imperialism and colonialism. Following the Second Vatican Council (1962–1965), Vatican diplomacy in the Middle East focused on three goals: preserving Christianity and a Christian presence in what Christians term the Holy Land, fostering peace with justice between Israel and the Palestinians, and maintaining Lebanon as an example of coexistence between Christians and Muslims.

The Vatican faces problems of demographic changes in the Middle East, especially in Jerusalem and the West Bank, where Christian Arabs are leaving because of their minority status; the resurgence of Islamic and Jewish fundamentalisms; and unstable economic and political situations. The relationship between the Vatican and Israel is a mixture of theological prejudice and political pragmatism. In recent years, however, the Holy See has established diplomatic relations with Israel (December 1993) and with the Hashemite Kingdom of Jordan (April 1994), and in 2000 the Vatican signed a Basic Agreement with the Palestine Liberation Organization (PLO). This agreement called for the resolution of the Israeli-Palestinian conflict on the basis of the various relevant UN resolutions. In March 2000 Pope John Paul II undertook a historic trip to Israel and the Palestinian-controlled territories, only the second time since 1964 that a sovereign pontiff set foot in the Holy Land. Throughout the Oslo peace process and the al-Aqsa Intifada the Vatican used its influence to ensure that the papacy's concerns and interests in Jerusalem and Christian holy sites were taken into consideration by U.S. president Bill Clinton, Israeli prime minister Ehud Barak, and PLO chairman Yasir Arafat.

The Lebanese Civil War (1975–1989) was a major challenge to the papacy. Several mediation missions were dispatched by both Pope Paul VI and Pope John Paul II, and in 1995 the latter convened in Rome a synod of Roman Catholic bishops, with Muslim and Orthodox Christian observers, for the express purpose of addressing the Lebanese situation. It is clear that if Lebanon were to fail as an example of coexistence, the Vatican's position in the region would be weakened.

See also CHRISTIANS IN THE MIDDLE EAST; HOLY LAND.

Bibliography

Dumper, Michael. *The Politics of Sacred Space: The Old City of Jerusalem in the Middle East Conflict.* Boulder, CO: Lynne Rienner, 2002.

Irani, George E. *The Papacy and the Middle East.* South Bend, IN: University of Notre Dame Press, 1989.

GEORGE E. IRANI

VAZHAPETIAN, NERSES
[1837–1884]

Armenian patriarch of Istanbul, 1873–1884.

Born in Istanbul, Nerses Vazhapetian spent his entire life in or near the Ottoman capital. Although deprived of a formal education at the age of fifteen after the death of his father, Vazhapetian became a teacher and joined the clergy of the Armenian Apostolic Church. Anointed a celibate priest in 1858, he was a bishop by 1862. Active in the administrative affairs of the Armenian Millet, Vazhapetian had a hand in drafting the so-called Armenian national constitution by which the Armenian Church and millet were regulated in the Ottoman Empire. In 1873, at age thirty-seven, he was elected Armenian partiarch of Istanbul.

The Russo-Ottoman War of 1877–1878, partly waged over the Armenian-populated provinces of eastern Anatolia, brought the issue of the Armenians to the fore of the diplomatic contest for influence in the Ottoman Empire. When the extent of the Kurdish predations over the Armenian communities became known, Vazhapetian, who had issued an encyclical supporting the Ottoman war effort, was authorized by the Armenian national assembly to appeal to Grand Duke Nicholas at San Stefano for consideration of local self-government in the areas of Armenian concentration. In the formal Treaty of San Stefano, signed on 3 March 1878, by the Ottomans and Russians, Article 16 provided for reforms and security under Russian trusteeship in the so-called Armenian provinces.

While Russian withdrawal from these areas was conditional on implementation of the reforms, the Congress of Berlin revised the terms of the treaty. The Armenian delegation sent by Vazhapetian to Berlin received no hearing, and Article 61 of the Treaty of Berlin, signed 13 July 1878, provided only for reforms as those territories were returned to the Ottomans. Still Armenians expected an international treaty to prove more binding on the Ottomans than mere promises. The failure of the European powers to require Sultan Abdülhamit II to proceed with reforms became the source of disillusionment. By the time of Vazhapetian's death in Istanbul, small groups of provincial Armenians had began to resort to self-defense in the face of continued insecurity in what became known as the Armenian Revolutionary Movement.

See also ARMENIAN MILLET; BERLIN, CONGRESS AND TREATY OF; SAN STEFANO, TREATY OF (1878).

Bibliography

Nalbandian, Louise. *The Armenian Revolutionary Movement: The Development of Armenian Political Parties through the Nineteenth Century.* Berkeley: University of California Press, 1967.

Walker, Christopher J. *Armenia: The Survival of a Nation,* revised 2d edition. New York: St. Martin's, 1990.

ROUBEN P. ADALIAN

VAZIR AFKHAM, SOLTAN ALI KHAN
[1867–1918]

Iranian courtier of the Qajar period.

Soltan Ali Khan was in the service of Mozaffar al-Din Qajar from the time the latter became crown prince in Tabriz. Upon the shah's ascension to power, Soltan Ali Khan was first appointed head of the Royal Correspondence Office and then minister of revenues, and in 1901 he received the title Vazir Afkham. In 1907, he was made prime minister and minister of interior under Mohammad Ali Qajar and headed the first Iranian cabinet after the Constitutional Revolution. Opposed by the Constitutionalists, he was deposed in 1909 and died in 1918, the same year his oldest son was killed in a romantic feud.

See also CONSTITUTIONAL REVOLUTION; MOHAMMAD ALI SHAH QAJAR; MOZAFFAR AL-DIN QAJAR.

NEGUIN YAVARI

VAZIRI, QAMAR AL-MOLUK
[1905–1959]

Considered the first professional female singer in Iran.

Qamar al-Moluk Vaziri was born to a middle-class family in the city of Kashan, Iran, in 1905. Raised by her grandmother, a religiously inclined woman who performed as a eulogist in women's gatherings, Qamar accompanied her to these events, where she herself also performed eulogies. She later studied under masters of Persian classical music and acquired fame as a singer. Numerous recordings were made of her songs. The singer died in 1959 from heart disease and was buried in Dhahir al-Dowleh cemetery in northern Tehran.

PARVANEH POURSHARIATI

VELAYAT-E FAQIH

Theory of governance in Shiʿite Islam.

From the Arabic term for "the authority, or governance, of the jurist," the doctrine of *velayat-e faqih* was associated particularly with Iran's Ayatollah Ruhollah Khomeini. It holds that those scholars of Shiʿite Islam most qualified in terms of piety and erudition are to exercise the governmental functions of the Twelfth Imam during his major occultation (absence from the terrestrial plane), which began in 939 C.E. and still continues. Even before the occultation, the imams would delegate certain of their functions, particularly in the judicial sphere, to qualified members of the Shiʿite Islam community as a matter of practical necessity. It was therefore natural that after the beginning of the occultation, other executive functions of the imam also should be assigned to the Shiʿite jurists, including, for example, the collection and disbursement of religiously mandated taxes (*zakat* and *khoms*), but not the waging of offensive jihad (holy war) or (according to some jurists) the holding of Friday prayers. This led to the crystallization of the theory of the *niyabat-e amma* (general deputyship) of the jurists, a process that was complete by the middle of the sixteenth century. Already in the Safavid period (1501–1702) the general deputyship occasionally was interpreted to include all the prerogatives of rule that in principle had belonged to the imams, but no special emphasis was placed on this. Similarly, although *velayat-e faqih* began to be discussed as a distinct legal topic in the nineteenth century, against a background of enhanced social authority for the Shiʿite jurists, no concrete political conclusions were drawn from the concept.

It was left to Ayatollah Khomeini to claim, in typically radical and comprehensive fashion, the right or even duty of the leading Shiʿite scholars to rule. He did this in his first published work (*Kashf al-Asrar,* 1944), again in a technical work on Shiʿite jurisprudence, and most fully and importantly, in a series of lectures delivered in 1970 during his exile in Iraq; these lectures were published under the title *Hokumat-e Islami* (Islamic government).

Khomeini's arguments in the lectures are both scriptural and rational, traditional and revolutionary. Asserting that Islamic government differs from all other forms of rule by being based on the implementation of divine law, Khomeini attributes the disarray of the Islamic world in general and Iran in particular to the prevalence of arbitrary rule and its concomitant man-made laws. He then demonstrates the centrality of government to the Islamic worldview and ridicules the opinion that the validity of the laws contained in the Qurʾan (the holy book of Islam) and other sources should have been restricted to the first few centuries of the Islamic era. Next, he reviews in great detail the Qurʾanic verses and traditions of the prophet Muhammad and the imams, which, in his estimation, support the thesis of *velayat-e faqih*; cites the opinions of previous, mostly recent, Shiʿite scholars on the subject; and reaches the conclusion that "the same governance that was exercised by the Most Noble Messenger and by the Imams is also the prerogative of the jurists" (Khomeini).

In the last of the lectures, Khomeini laments the prevalence of the "pseudo-saintly" in the religious institution, and it was indeed several years before a sizable number of Khomeini's colleagues came to accept his thesis. It was the repressive policies of the shah of Iran, Mohammad Reza Pahlavi (ruled 1941–1979), that impelled the religious scholars to conceive of broad and radical aims and enabled them to gain a favorable response from much of the Iranian public. Nonetheless, although by the autumn of 1978 a clear majority of Iranians had come to favor the institution of an Islamic government under the leadership of Khomeini, it cannot be said that *velayat-e faqih* was a prominent slogan of the Iranian Revolution. Khomeini himself made no mention of it in the proclamations he issued during the revolution.

Not until the constitution of the Islamic Republic of Iran was elaborated by the Assembly of Experts that convened in the fall of 1979 did *velayat-e faqih* emerge as the pillar of the new order. It was enshrined in the preamble to the constitution in Article Five ("During the Occultation of the Lord of the Age [that is, the Hidden Imam], the governance and leadership of the nation devolve upon the pious and just jurist who is acquainted with the circumstances of his age; courageous, resourceful, and possessed of administrative ability; and recognized and accepted as leader by the majority of the people"); and in Articles 107 to 112, which specify the procedure for selecting the leader and list his constitutional functions.

Khomeini's own view was that these provisions did not do justice to *velayat-e faqih,* and in February 1988 he propounded the theory of *velayat-e motlaqa-ye faqih* ("the absolute authority of the jurist"). He declared obedience to the ruling jurist to be as incumbent on the believer as the performance of prayer, and his powers to extend even to the temporary suspension of such essential rites of Islam as the hajj (pilgrimage to Mecca). Although this formulation of the theory might appear to be an ideal prescription for theocratic absolutism, in fact, Khomeini was not seeking to extend his control of Iranian affairs (which in any event was far less than absolute). Rather, he was seeking to provide theoretical justification for government attempts to break the stalemate on controversial items of social and economic legislation.

The actual implementation of *velayat-e faqih,* moreover, was destined to change in a quite different direction. When Ayatollah Hosainali Montazeri was compelled in March 1989 to resign as designated successor to Khomeini, none of the other senior religious scholars seemed qualified for the position. When Khomeini died on 4 June of the same year, it was therefore Hojjat al-Islam Ali Khamenehi—a relatively junior figure in the religious hierarchy, despite his political prominence—who was chosen as leader of the Islamic Republic. This necessitated the modification of Article 109 of the constitution to remove scholarly seniority from the qualifications of the leader, a change that was approved in a referendum held in August 1989. It has been argued credibly that the resulting disjunction of political leadership from seniority in the learned hierarchy of Iranian Shiʿism effectively brings the implementation of *velayat-e faqih* to an end. If this is true, *velayat-e faqih* must be designated as a theory that was, to a degree, workable only because of the unique qualities and appeal of Khomeini, and that falls short of being a permanent solution to the problem of governance in a Shiʿite Muslim society.

Bibliography

Khomeini, Ruhollah. *Islam and Revolution: Writings and Declarations of Imam Khomeini,* translated by Hamid Algar. Berkeley, CA: Mizan Press, 1981.

Sachedina, Abdulaziz Abdulhussein. *The Just Ruler in Shiʿite Islam.* Oxford, U.K.: Oxford University Press, 1988.

HAMID ALGAR
UPDATED BY ERIC HOOGLUND

VELAYATI, ALI AKBAR

[1945–]

Foreign minister of Iran, 1981–1997.

Born in Tehran in 1945, Ali Akbar Velayati received a doctorate in pediatrics from Tehran University in 1971. After completing postgraduate work, he left for further studies in the United States, where he joined the Organization of Iranian Moslem Students. Returning home, he taught at his alma mater and was appointed deputy health minister in the first government appointed by Ayatollah Ruhollah Khomeini in 1979. He also served in the first parliament in 1980.

Before the Iranian revolution, Velayati was a member of the Hojjatieh group, an anti-Bahai conservative group that eventually challenged the dominance of the Islamic Republican Party (IRP). He left the group in 1983 when Khomeini denounced its activities, and he joined the Jamʿiat Motalefeh Islami (Islamic Society, or JME), a group very close to the conservative *ulama* and bazaari merchants. In 1980 the IRP and JME unsuccessfully had pressed Iran's current president, Abolhasan Bani Sadr, to appoint Velayati as a foreign minister. In 1981 President Hojatoleslam Seyed Ali Khamenehi nominated Velayati for premier but could not win support from the parliament. Khamenehi accepted the parliament's choice of Mir Hossein Mousavi as prime minister if Velayati were appointed as foreign minister—a position Velayati held for more than sixteen years and through four administrations until 1997.

Velayati is a conservative pragmatist who helped to move Iran out of its revolutionary isolation and temper its adventurist foreign policies of the early 1980s. However, he opposed ties with the United States as an archenemy of the Islamic Republic and regards Israel as an illegitimate state in the heartland of Islam. He helped Iran to join international organizations and favored developing ties with Europe and developing countries.

Internally, his tenure in the foreign ministry has been criticized for putting more emphasis on loyalty than on professional qualifications. He is regarded as a nonclerical protégé of the religious elite who owes his long presence in Iranian politics to his loyalty to the supreme leader, Ayatollah Khamenehi. In 1997 he was named by a German court as a member of the Special Operations Committee that approved the 1992 assassinations of three Kurdish

Democratic Party leaders in the Mykonos Restaurant in Berlin.

Since his departure from the foreign ministry, Velayati has been a member of the Expediency Council, serves as an adviser on international affairs to Ayatollah Khamenehi and conducts foreign policy assignments, and continues to teach in the university and write articles and books on the history of Iran and the Iranian revolution for government publication. He also serves as the secretary-general of the Ahlul Bayt World Assembly—a religious institution named after the descendants of the prophet Muhammad and established to advance the Shiʿite cause around the world.

See also IRANIAN REVOLUTION (1979); IRAN–IRAQ WAR (1980–1988); KHAMENEHI, ALI; KHOMEINI, RUHOLLAH.

Bibliography

Moslem, Mehdi. *Factional Politics in Post-Khomeini Iran.* Syracuse, NY: Syracuse University Press, 2002.

ALI AKBAR MAHDI

VERSAILLES, TREATY OF (1920)

Treaty ending World War I; it established the mandate system for the governance and eventual independence of the Central Powers' former colonies.

The armistices of October and November 1918 ending hostilities in World War I were followed by the Conference of Paris at which World War I victors and associated powers determined the terms for dealing with Germany and her allies during the war. The conference, which officially began on 18 January 1919, resulted in five treaties. The Treaty of Versailles, signed on 28 June at Versailles, France, and ratified on 20 January 1920, addressed the terms of peace with Germany. The treaties of Sèvres, Neuilly, St. Germain, and Trianon dealt with the Ottoman Empire, Bulgaria, Austria, and Hungary, respectively. Besides setting forth the terms for dealing with Germany after World War I, the Treaty of Versailles established the League of Nations and the mandate system for governing territories surrendered by Germany. This treaty included the Covenant of the League of Nations as Part I, with Article 22 giving the league the power to supervise mandated territories consisting of former German colonies. The other treaties included the covenant in their texts.

The armistice with Germany and the Conference of Paris were both predicated on U.S. President Woodrow Wilson's Fourteen Points for peace enunciated in his address to Congress on 8 January 1918. In addition to his vision of a League of Nations, these included an adjustment of all colonial claims giving equal weight to the interests of colonial populations and to those of countries with colonial claims. This led many to believe that the peace conference would lead to the independence of the Arab portions of the Ottoman Empire. Based on this, Prince Faisal I ibn Hussein arrived in Paris in January 1919 as head of the Hijaz delegation and with the objective of securing an independent Arab state. At first the French opposed recognition of the Hijaz delegation based on the fact that the Hijaz was not one of the Allied belligerent states. The British, however, intervened, and the Hijaz delegation was recognized. On 29 January Faisal submitted a statement to the conference defining Arab claims. He requested recognition as "independent sovereign peoples" for those Arab-speaking peoples of Asia from the Alexandretta–Diyarbekir line south to the Indian Ocean. Essentially, this included what is now Syria, Lebanon, Israel, Jordan, and Iraq. Faisal exempted the Hijaz as already independent, as well as British Aden. The prince addressed the conference on 6 February, stressing the principle of the consent of the governed. He then proposed a commission to visit Syria and Palestine and ascertain the wishes of the populace. The French were not inclined to support this, but pressure by Wilson resulted, on 25 March, in the approval of a commission, later known as the King–Crane Commission.

Despite the sincere desires of Wilson to forge a new world in which all peoples would be the ultimate determiners of their national destinies and the eloquent arguments of Faisal and others on behalf of the Arabs, the Conference of Paris yielded to the imperial interests of Britain and France and, to a lesser extent, to those of Italy and Japan. The colonial territories of Germany and the Arab portions of the Ottoman Empire were assigned to members of the League of Nations under the mandate system established in the covenant. In the case of the Middle East, agreements made during World War I played a large role in distribution of mandates. The secret Anglo–Franco–Russian agreement of 16 May 1916, commonly known as the Sykes–Picot Agreement, divided the Arab dominions of the Ottoman Empire between Britain and France. Britain received the areas that are now Iraq, Jordan, and Israel; France got what is now Syria and Lebanon. The Balfour Declaration of 2 November 1917, also played a role in the disposition of Arab territories by the Conference of Paris. This was a letter from Lord Balfour, British foreign secretary, to Lord (Edmond de) Rothschild, a prominent British Zionist, that supported the establishment of a national home for the Jewish people in Palestine. These two documents, more than anything else, shaped the fate of the Middle East in the post–World War I era. The San Remo Conference of April 1920 awarded Syria, including Lebanon, as a Class A mandate to France; Iraq and Palestine, including Transjordan, became Class A mandates under British supervision. The mandate for Palestine endorsed the provisions of the Balfour Declaration. In 1921 Britain separated Transjordan from Palestine, exempting it from the provisions of the Balfour Declaration. As Class A mandates, all three were to be given independence when it was determined that they were able to stand on their own. In the case of Iraq and Transjordan, Arab dignitaries were given royal status in preparation for the eventual independence of these areas. Prince Faisal became the king of Iraq, and Prince Abdullah I ibn Hussein became the amir of Transjordan. The League of Nations confirmed these mandates in 1922, some of which outlived the international organization under which they were formed. The first mandate to obtain independence was Iraq, in 1932, followed by Syria and Lebanon in 1941. Transjordan, now Jordan, gained its independence in 1946. Palestine, much of which is now Israel, gained independence in 1948.

See also ABDULLAH I IBN HUSSEIN; ALEXANDRETTA; BALFOUR DECLARATION (1917); DIYARBAKIR; FAISAL I IBN HUSSEIN; HIJAZ; KING–CRANE COMMISSION (1919); ROTHSCHILD, EDMOND DE; SAN REMO CONFERENCE (1920); SÈVRES, TREATY OF (1920); SYKES–PICOT AGREEMENT (1916); WILSON, WOODROW; WORLD WAR I.

Bibliography

Antonius, George. *The Arab Awakening: The Story of the Arab National Movement.* London: H. Hamilton, 1938.

Sontag, Raymond J. *A Broken World, 1919–1939.* New York: Harper and Row, 1971.

DANIEL E. SPECTOR

VICTORIA COLLEGE

British-style public school in Alexandria, Egypt.

Victoria College was founded in 1901 on the initiative of eight resident merchants, bankers, and shipping magnates, six of whom were British, one Syrian, and one the Austro-Hungarian president of the Jewish Community of Alexandria. The makeup of the entering classes of 1902 reflected the cosmopolitanism that was to characterize the institution up to the mid-1950s—eight of the students were Syrian, including George Antonius and his three brothers, three were Greek, three were Egyptian Muslims, one was English, and ten were identified in the language of the time as "Israelite." In those early decades the language of instruction was English, but the study of Arabic and French was mandatory. The school also placed a strong emphasis on cricket, soccer, and hockey. Under the leadership (1901–1922) of its first headmaster, Charles Lias of King's College, Cambridge University, Victoria adopted the Oxford and Cambridge Joint Board Examination, the qualifying exam for English medical and engineering schools as well as for Oxford and Cambridge. Victoria boys obtained outstanding exam results, and the school became a breeding ground for university education in England and elsewhere. For example, between 1908 and 1913, thirty-three Victoria graduates attended European or U.S. universities, including nine at Cambridge, four at Toulouse, and one at the University of Edinburgh Medical School.

In 1906 the campus moved from downtown to the city's eastern suburbs. There its stately buildings and spacious playing fields stood out as an Alexandrian landmark and were the envy of other, less privileged schools. For more than half a century, Victoria College played an important role in providing a first-rate European education along British public-school lines to successive generations of well-born Egyptians—Muslims, Copts, and Jews—as well as foreign residents in Egypt, whatever their race, color, or creed. Primary identification with the school blurred ethnic and religious differences and created an atmosphere of tolerance within the tightly knit student body. The school's prestige extended well beyond Egypt under its second headmaster, R. W. G. Reed of Oxford, and it began to attract the scions of the English-speaking ruling elite in the rest of the region: Thus, King Hussein ibn Talal of Jordan and his brother, Prince Hassan; the last Hashimite king of Iraq, Faisal II ibn Ghazi, and his uncle, the regent Abd al-Ilah; the former sultan of Zanzibar; and the king of Albania were students at Victoria.

Along with all other foreign schools, Victoria was nationalized by Gamal Abdel Nasser in the wake of the Suez War in 1956 and now survives as a pale reflection of its former self, under the label of Victory College. In the 1990s, as a coeducational institution, its 6,000 students were jammed into a campus originally built for 500.

Bibliography

Atiyah, Edward. *An Arab Tells His Story: A Study in Loyalties.* London: John Murray, 1947.

Hamouda, Sahar, and Clement, Colin, eds. *Victoria College: A History Revealed.* Cairo: American University in Cairo Press, 2002.

ALAIN SILVERA
UPDATED BY WILLIAM L. CLEVELAND

VILAYET

See GLOSSARY

VILLAGE INSTITUTES

Turkish institutes for training primary-school teachers.

The Village Institutes (Köy Enstitüleri) of Turkey represented a short-lived (1940–1950) but highly innovative experiment in primary-school teacher training. In the 1930s, over 75 percent of Turkey's people lived in some 35,000 villages, and over 80 percent of these villagers were illiterate. Only a small proportion of villages had primary schools, and most of their urban-born teachers had difficulty coping with rural conditions. After the dissolution of the Ottoman Empire and the establishment of the Republic of Turkey in 1923, Mustafa Kemal (Atatürk) and his ruling Republican People's Party (RPP) planned to design a national system of compulsory secular education to enculturate a new generation of Turks in the principles of modern science and Turkish nationalism. Educational reform and a cadre of new, secular teachers were to spread Kemalism and lift the masses from the depths of poverty and ignorance. While impressive educational gains were achieved in the cities, most villages remained without schools.

Ismail Hakki Tonguç, the director general of primary education, and his colleagues designed a plan they hoped would produce teachers capable of living in the villages and able to make a comprehensive impact on them. The plan called for creating special teacher-training institutes, recruiting village students to them, teaching these students general subjects plus useful village technology, and then sending them back to the villages to teach in five-year primary schools.

Shortly after the Turkish Grand National Assembly passed the necessary legislation in 1940, fourteen Village Institutes opened their doors to eager recruits. Actually, many of the institutes' facilities were incomplete, so teachers and students worked side by side building classrooms, dining halls, and dormitories. In the process, students acquired useful carpentry, masonry, and other construction skills.

The ministry of education intentionally located the institutes in rural areas, so that students could practice farming, plant orchards, develop water and sanitation systems, and generally confront typical village problems with modern skills and science. Youths of both sexes, between the ages of twelve and sixteen, who were graduated by a five-year village primary school, qualified for admission to a village institute. The government offered this education free to students who pledged to teach in an assigned village for twenty years after graduation.

Twenty-five percent of the Institute's five-year curriculum was devoted to agriculture (crop production, zootechnology, apiculture [beekeeping], and silkworm culture); 25 percent was devoted to technology (carpentry, construction, blacksmithing, health, and childcare for female students); and 50 percent dealt with general education (the Turkish language, history, literature, geography, math, biology, and civics). In 1950, the curriculum was expanded to six years. As village teachers, institute graduates were expected to teach general education subjects to children, adult-literacy classes, scientific farming and animal husbandry, and handicrafts; they were obligated to play a central role in the community and generally awaken the civic conscience of the rural population.

The institutes provided some of the most idealistic and dedicated rural teachers in Turkey's history. These young men and women inspired many villagers to continue their educations beyond primary school; some even went to the university. A number of village teachers, such as Mahmut Makal (author of *Bizim Köy,* translated as *A Village in Anatolia*), became famous writers who pioneered a new literary genre that focused on peasant life.

From their inception, however, the Village Institutes were subject to controversy. Political opponents described them as indoctrination agencies of the ruling party. Some educators claimed they failed to prepare students adequately for their exhaustive duties as rural teachers. Very conservative villagers complained that institute graduates preached revolutionary and antireligious ideas in their villages. More extreme opponents accused the institutes of teaching communism.

When the new opposition party, the Democrat party (DP), came to power in 1950, they removed institute supporters from the ministry of education and abolished the twenty-one existing institutes by transforming them into ordinary teacher-training schools. Before their demise, the institutes had graduated 15,767 men and 1,395 women.

Bibliography

Stone, Frank A. "Rural Revitalization and the Village Institutes in Turkey: Sponsors and Critics." *Comparative Education Review* 18 (1974): 419–429.

Vexliard, Alexandre, and Aytac, Kemal. "The Village Institutes in Turkey." *Comparative Education Review* 8 (1964): 41–47.

PAUL J. MAGNARELLA

VIZIER

See GLOSSARY

VOICE OF LEBANON

See RADIO AND TELEVISION: ARAB COUNTRIES

VOICE OF PALESTINE

See NEWSPAPERS AND PRINT MEDIA: ARAB COUNTRIES; RADIO AND TELEVISION: ARAB COUNTRIES

VOLPI, GIUSEPPE

Governor of Libya from 1922 to 1925, after a short period as governor of Tripolitania.

Giuseppe Volpi abandoned the policy of trying to govern Libya through Libyan representatives in the aftermath of the first Italo–Sanusi War. This had involved recognizing a Sanusi amir in Cyrenaica or trying to use the leaders of the Tripolitanian republic in Tripolitania.

Instead, Volpi gave a free hand to the military commanders on the spot, Rodolfo Graziani and Pietro Badoglio. His new policy was enthusiastically endorsed by the Fascists when they came to power in October 1922. It had been signaled the previous April, when he sanctioned an attack on Misurata, and achieved its fullest expression with the outbreak of the second Italo–Sanusi War in early 1923.

Volpi's three-year tenure as governor also marked the introduction of an intensive colonization scheme. He sought to increase the amount of state funds made available for it, alienated to the state all uncultivated land and all rebel-held land, once it was conquered, and provided tax-relief schemes to attract investment funding. By doing this, he prepared the way for the legislation introduced by Emilio de Bono, who actually began the process of large-scale Italian peasant migration into Libya.

See also GRAZIANI, RODOLFO; ITALY IN THE MIDDLE EAST.

Bibliography

Lombardi, P. "Italian Agrarian Policy during the Fascist Per iod." In *Social and Economic Development of Libya,* edited by E. G. H. Joffe and K. S. McLachlan. Wisbech, U.K.: Middle East and North African Studies Press, 1982.

GEORGE JOFFE

VOZUQ AL-DOWLEH, MIRZA HASAN KHAN

[1873–1950]

Iranian politician.

Mirza Hasan Khan was the nephew of Mirza Ali Khan Amin al-Dowleh, the famous prime minister under Mozaffar al-Din Qajar, and he was also the brother of Ahmad Qavam al-Saltaneh. In 1892, he replaced his father as tax collector of Azerbaijan, and four years later he was granted the title Vozuq al-Dowleh. He was elected to the first parliament from Tehran (1906), and, after holding several ministerial posts, he was appointed prime minister and minister of foreign affairs (1916). In 1918, he was reappointed prime minister for the purpose of forming a cabinet, and he headed the ministry of the interior. It was during his tenure as premier that the infamous Anglo-Iranian Agreement of 1919, transforming Iran into a British protectorate, was ratified. Following the conclusion of the agreement, Vozuq al-Dowleh received 60,000 pounds from the British government, but he was forced to return the sum to the Iranian government after Reza Shah Pahlavi took office. In 1921, Vozuq al-Dowleh was appointed minister of finance by the prime minister. After Reza Shah was forced by the Allied powers to abdicate in 1941, Vozuq al-Dowleh returned to private life as a land speculator.

See also AMIN AL-DOWLEH, MIRZA ALI KHAN; ANGLO-IRANIAN AGREEMENT (1919); MOZAFFAR AL-DIN QAJAR; PAHLAVI, REZA.

NEGUIN YAVARI

W

WADI

See GLOSSARY

WADI HADRAMAWT

Great valley in eastern Yemen.

Wadi Hadramawt is a 400-mile-long (640 km), well-watered valley east of Aden that constitutes one of the most agriculturally rich areas in Yemen. It produces millet, cotton, wheat, qat, and a variety of fruits and vegetables. The wadi dissects and drains the high plateau of eastern Yemen and is at the center of the Hadramawt, a distinctive geographic and sociopolitical region that was a famous trading state in ancient, pre-Islamic times.

See also HADRAMAWT.

ROBERT D. BURROWES

WADI NATRUN

Principal site of Coptic monasteries in Egypt.

Wadi Natrun is an elongated valley in Egypt's western desert near the Cairo-Alexandria road. As many as 500 Coptic monasteries, once housing up to 50,000 monks, were built there beginning in the fourth century, Four are currently in use: Dayr al-Baramus, Dayr Abu Maqar (St. Macarius), Dayr Anba Bishoi, and Dayr al-Surian. Dayr Anba Bishoi was the site of the enforced exile of Pope Shenouda III by President Anwar al-Sadat in 1981; he was released in 1985. Dayr Abu Maqar has witnessed a revival of Coptic monasticism since it was reopened by a dozen hermit monks in 1969. Since that date, rising numbers of Egyptian Christians have elected to spend part of their lives at Wadi Natrun's monasteries. Several are also open to tourism.

See also COPTS; SHENOUDA III.

Bibliography

Butler, Alfred J. *The Ancient Coptic Churches of Egypt,* 2 vols. Oxford: Clarendon, 1884; reprint, 1970.

Cannuyer, Christian. *Coptic Egypt: The Christians of the Nile.* New York: Abrams, 2000.

Evelyn-White, Hugh G. *The Monasteries of the Wadi 'n Natrun*, 3 vols. New York: Arno Press, 1973.

Kamil, Jill. *Coptic Egypt: History and Guide.* Cairo: American University in Cairo Press, 1987.

Meinardus, Otto F. A. *Two Thousand Years of Coptic Christianity.* Cairo: American University in Cairo Press, 1999.

RAYMOND WILLIAM BAKER
UPDATED BY ARTHUR GOLDSCHMIDT

WAFD

Major Egyptian nationalist party organized in 1919.

The Wafd Party took its name from the delegation (in Arabic, *wafd*) composed of Saʿd Zaghlul and other notables who called for the complete independence *(istiqlal tamm)* of Egypt from the British immediately after World War I. When Britain refused to negotiate with the Wafd and exiled its leaders, Egypt launched a full-scale rebellion in 1919. A sophisticated network of organizers in key cities and villages allowed the Wafd to dominate the political scene.

Mustafa al-Nahhas (right), seen here with President Giuseppe Motta of Switzerland at a conference in 1937, was president of the Wafd Party, which fought for years after World War I to achieve Egyptian independence from Great Britain. He became prime minister in 1941, but the Wafd lost popular support as he worked with the British during World War II. © BETTMANN/ CORBIS. REPRODUCED BY PERMISSION.

The Wafd did not become a formal political party until 1924, six years after its inception. The party was organized along hierarchical lines, with an executive council. Although the party enjoyed the support of a cross section of the Egyptian populace, its leaders were predominantly urban, upper- and middle-class, modern, and secular. The highly charismatic Zaghlul served as its president until his death in 1927. The Wafdist leadership also included both Muslims and Copts, notably Makram Ubayd. Women, particularly Zaghlul's wife, Safiyya, and Huda al-Shaʿrawi, became leaders in the struggle for women's voting rights, acting on the principle that the struggle against imperialism had to be accompanied by a similar struggle for gender equality. Between the two world wars, the Wafd engaged in a three-way struggle with the British and the Egyptian monarchy. Seeking to undercut Egypt's demands for independence, Britain unilaterally declared Egypt independent in 1922 and promulgated a constitutional monarchy in 1923. As the only party to enjoy widespread popular support for its anti-British stand, the Wafd won the 1924 elections and all subsequent elections that were not manipulated or rigged by King Ahmad Fuʾad or his son Farouk.

Following Zaghlul's death, Mustafa al-Nahhas became president of the party and continued its struggle against the British. In 1936 he signed the Anglo-Egyptian Treaty, which formalized Egyptian and British relations but permitted both the continuation of a British military presence along the Suez Canal zone and British control over the Sudan.

This failure to secure complete independence, coupled with allegations of nepotism and corruption within the party, undermined some of its popular support. In the 1930s many Egyptian youths joined various fascist and radical groups, and the Wafd countered by creating the Blue Shirts, a paramilitary youth organization. In 1941, fearing a pro-Nazi Egyptian government, Britain's ambassador Miles Lampson (later Lord Killearn) forced King Farouk to accept Nahhas as prime minister. Nahhas's willingness to work with the British throughout

World War II further undercut the Wafd's credibility as a nationalist and anti-imperialist party.

Following the 1952 military coup that deposed Farouk, the Wafd was formally disbanded (1953); some of its leaders were then tried for corruption and crimes against the state. In 1976, when Anwar al-Sadat announced the return to a multiparty system, the Wafd was revived under the leadership of Fuʾad Siraj al-Din. The New Wafd called for a parliamentary, multiparty system and the dismantling of socialist measures that had been enacted under Egypt's former president, Gamal Abdel Nasser. In a short time, the Wafd gathered a notable degree of support, particularly among Copts and in the richer urban areas. The Wafd voted to disband in reaction to Sadat's political crackdown in late 1978, but it was revived after Sadat's assassination by Islamists in 1981. In the 1984 elections the New Wafd cooperated with the Muslim Brotherhood and won 58 seats in parliament. By 1990 the New Wafd opposed the government and the continuation of the state of emergency, and it boycotted the 1993 elections. Its newspaper, *al-Wafd,* remained one of the few opposition publications. Following Siraj al-Din's death in 2000, Nʿuman Jumaʿa, a university professor, was elected the new leader in a notably open and transparent election. Representing the new generation, Jumaʿa pushed for political and economic changes; but without grassroots support, the Wafd remained a minority party in parliament.

See also NAHHAS, MUSTAFA AL-; NEW WAFD; SHAʿRAWI, HUDA AL-; ZAGHLUL, SAʿD.

Bibliography

Deeb, Marius. *Party Politics in Egypt: The Wafd and Its Rivals, 1919–1939.* London: Ithaca Press, 1979.

Terry, Janice J. *The Wafd, 1919–1952: Cornerstone of Egyptian Power.* London: Third World Centre for Research and Publishing, 1982.

JANICE J. TERRY

WAFDIST WOMEN'S CENTRAL COMMITTEE

Egyptian women's committee of the early Wafd party.

Early in the twentieth century Egypt took steps toward forming a *wafd,* or delegation, to demand independence from British rule. In 1910 the National Party (al-Hizb al-Watani) held a congress in Brussels, where Inshirah Shawqi's appeal for independence was read by a man because Egyptian gender conventions prevented her from speaking publicly. Later, Indian nationalist Bhikaji Cama confronted the Wafdist men on the issue of women's participation in the Egyptian nationalist movement. Women's participation in Egyptian civil society became a mobilizing component of the fight for independence, a struggle in which women played a key role.

As women began to enter the Egyptian public sphere, so too did they begin to enter the realm of politics. Wafd members' wives and other women took up the national cause and established the Wafdist Women's Central Committee (Lajnat al-Wafd al-Markaziyya lil-Sayyidat, WWCC) on 12 January 1920 in a meeting at St. Mark's Cathedral. When Wafd leader Saʿd Zaghlul was deported to the Seychelles in 1921, the WWCC continued to work for the nationalist cause in his absence. They coordinated embargoes against British goods and managed the financial side of the nationalist movement. Huda al-Shaʿrawi was elected president of the committee, and other founding members included Ulfat Ratib, Regina Habib Khayyat, Wissa Wasif, Ahmad Abu Usba, Sharifa Riyad, Ester Fahmi Wissa, Louise Majorelle Wasif Ghali, Ihsan al-Qusi, and Fikriyya Husni. Most came from large land-owning families, although some were middle-class Cairenes. The WWCC solidified links between various women's associations in Cairo in the nationalist cause, such as the New Women Society (Jamʿiyat al-Marʾa al-Jadida, founded by Shaʿrawi in 1919), the Society of the Renaissance of the Egyptian Woman (Jamʿiyyat Nahdat al-Sayyidat al-Misriyyat), and the Society of Mothers of the Future (Jamʿiyyat Ummuhat al-Mustaqbal). In addition, women from the WWCC helped to found women's organizations outside Cairo in Minya, Asyut, and Tanta.

Before the WWCC was a year old, members were bitterly disappointed when Saʿd Zaghlul and other Wafdist men did not consult them on a proposal for independence. They published a critique of the Wafdist men's actions and eventually founded the Egyptian Feminist Union (al-Ittihad al-Nisaʾi al-Misri). When Shaʿrawi left, other Wafdist women renamed their group the Committee of Saʿdist Women (al-Lajna al-Saʿdiyya lil-Sayyidat) and remained loyal to Zaghlul. Shaʿrawi and other women went on to dedicate their efforts to the feminist movement while the Wafd Party's role of serving as a vehicle for women's concerns diminished.

See also EGYPT; EGYPTIAN FEMINIST UNION; GENDER: GENDER AND LAW; GENDER: GENDER AND POLITICS; SHAʿRAWI, HUDA AL-; WAFD; ZAGHLUL, SAʿD.

Bibliography

Badran, Margo. *Feminists, Islam, and Nation: Gender and the Making of Modern Egypt.* Princeton, NJ: Princeton University Press, 1995.

Sharawi, Huda. *Harem Years: Memoirs of an Egyptian Feminist,* edited and translated by Margo Badran. London: Virago Press, 1986.

MARIA F. CURTIS

WAHDA DAM, AL-

See MAQARIN DAM

WAHHABI

See MUWAHHIDUN

WAHRHAFTIG, ZERAH

[1906–2002]

Israeli legal expert and politician.

Zerah Wahrhaftig (Warhaftig) was born in Belorussia and emigrated to Israel in 1947 via Poland, Lithuania, Japan, and the United States. Before his death in September 2002 at age 96 he was one of the last two living signers of the Israel's Declaration of Independence. As a young man he was active in the National Religious Front. He was a member of the Provisional Council of State, and after being elected to the first Knesset was continuously reelected to the Knesset through the ninth Knesset in 1981. Wahrhaftig served as deputy minister of religious affairs from 1952 to 1958 and as minister of religious affairs in three governments, from 1961 to 1974. He was a member of the National Religious Party's moderate wing.

Wahrhaftig was an expert on the legal and constitutional system of Israel. As chairman of the Knesset Committee, he helped to draft legislation creating rabbinical courts and religious councils, enforcing sabbath law, the Israel Lands Law, and the 1950 Law of Return, which allowed Jews to settle in Israel. After the 1967 war, Wahrhaftig wrote a decree guaranteeing religious autonomy for Jews, Muslims, and Christians in the newly Israeli-administered Jerusalem, and drafted a constitutionally binding edict protecting respective holy sites.

See also ISRAEL: POLITICAL PARTIES IN.

BRYAN DAVES
UPDATED BY GREGORY S. MAHLER

WALLACH, YONA

[1944–1985]

Israeli poet.

Yona Wallach was born in Kiryat Uno, near Tel Aviv, to a veteran pioneer family. Her father was killed in the War of Independence when she was four, a trauma that haunted Wallach throughout her short life. Her widowed mother owned the only local cinema, where the impressionable Wallach absorbed the new-wave films that later echoed in her writing. A misfit in her small town and a high school dropout, Wallach, who wrote her first poem when she was seven, studied art, joined the Tel Aviv Circle of Poets, and published in their avant-garde periodicals.

Seeking relief from her emotional unrest, she turned to mental institutions and drugs, diving uninhibitedly into intense experiences. Life and writing became one, and when her first book, *Devarim* (Words, or Things, 1966), appeared, it shook the Israeli literary world with its inner demons, imaginary and absurd situations, surreal connections, bold depictions of sexuality, and fluid, violent, and seemingly unstructured diction.

In the five books that followed, Wallach took on the feminine revolution in Hebrew writing. She subverted religious and national preconceptions unprecedentedly and often used sexual encounters as the arena for examining issues of social injustice. Her poems blur boundaries between female and male, conscious and subconscious, horror and beauty, sensuality and spirituality. The self is shattered, and its components become separate entities.

Wallach, a precursor of postmodernism, led Israeli literature to uncharted lands. She died of cancer at the age of forty-one.

Bibliography

Kuvovi, Miri. "Violence in Wallach's Poetry." *Proceedings of the Eleventh World Congress of Jewish Studies,* Division C, vol. 3. Jerusalem: Ha-Igud ha-'olami le-madaè ha-Yahadut, 1994.

NILI GOLD

WAQF

An Islamic endowment created by its founder to dedicate specific property for the benefit of a particular public good (waqf khayri) *and/or the donor's family* (waqf ahli).

A *waqf* (Arabic plural, *awqâf*) may be composed of any kind of durable property whose use or income provides communal benefits, including mosques, hospitals, libraries, schools, canals, roads, and water fountains. The donor will write the charter for the administration of the *waqf* and appoint its initial trustees. The *ka'ba* in Mecca, the center of the Muslim pilgrimage, is the archetype of a *waqf.*

The first *waqf* established by Muhammad's community was the mosque at Quba in Medina. Charitable *waqfs* were established soon after when Muhammad dedicated seven orchards inherited from a follower to provide for the poor and needy. During the caliphate of Umar some donors established family *waqfs,* dedicating the income from their estates first to provide for their own descendents, with the surplus going to the poor. In the classical period of Islamic civilization the *waqfs* were an integral part of the economic and civil society infrastructure.

In the nineteenth and twentieth centuries, after the colonial powers had, to varying degrees, marginalized the *waqfs,* the secular states that succeeded them dismantled or appropriated them to a significant degree throughout most of the Muslim world. Motivations were partly economic (that the permanent nature of *waqfs* tied up resources that might be more effectively reallocated), but mainly political, aiming to increase state function, authority, and wealth at the expense of the civil (especially, the religious) sector. After appropriation of *waqf* lands for the benefit of multinational corporations by the shah of Iran, for example, migration of evicted tenant farmers to the cities contributed to the discontent leading to the revolution that established the Islamic Republic in 1979.

Despite the diminution in their properties, size, and autonomy, the *waqf* remains a significant element of Islamic society. In recent years they have experienced a resurgence, especially in Lebanon, Turkey, Jordan, and Algeria.

See also KA'BA.

Bibliography

Makdisi, George. *The Rise of Colleges: Institutions of Learning in Islam and the West.* Edinburgh, U.K.: Edinburgh University Press, 1981.

DENISE A. SPELLBERG
UPDATED BY IMAD-AD-DEAN AHMAD

WAR IN IRAQ (2003)

Controversial U.S.-led invasion and occupation of Iraq.

During the decade following the Gulf War of 1991, U.S.–Iraqi relations remained tense. At issue was the extent to which Iraq was cooperating with international monitors looking for evidence that the country was free of any weapons of mass destruction (chemical, biological, nuclear weapons). The United States was the leading force within the UN Security Council urging that the crippling international economic sanctions against Iraq that had been in place since August 1990 be continued until the United Nations Special Commission (UNSCOM) could certify Iraqi compliance. Several times during the administration of U.S. president William J. (Bill) Clinton, the situation deteriorated into crisis, including the December 1998 U.S. attack on Iraq known in the United States as Operation Desert Fox. Shortly thereafter, Iraq announced that UNSCOM's mission was over altogether.

Hardening of U.S–Iraq Relations under George W. Bush

The administration of President George W. Bush brought about a marked hardening of U.S. attitudes toward Iraq once he took office in January 2001. Bush, son of former president George H.W. Bush, who had led the 1991 Gulf War against Iraqi president Saddam Hussein, filled his administration with many veterans of his father's war with Iraq. These included Secretary of State Colin L. Powell, who had been chairman of the joint chiefs of staff of the U.S. military at the time of the Gulf War, and Vice President Richard Cheney, who had been secretary of defense for the elder Bush. The attacks carried out by al-Qaʿida on 11 September 2001, and Bush's decision to invade Afghanistan in October 2001, only hardened his resolve to confront Iraq. In his 30 January 2002 state of the union address, Bush included Iraq along with Iran and North Korea in what he called an "Axis of Evil." He pointed to what he claimed was evidence of Iraq's noncompliance with UN Security Council resolutions calling for disarmament, including a document purporting to show that Iraq had attempted to purchase 500 tons of uranium from Niger in 2000 (the International Atomic Energy Agency later proclaimed the document to be counterfeit). After months of claiming that Saddam Hussein constituted a clear threat to the United States, Bush convinced the U.S. congress to authorize him to use force against Iraq. The U.S. media offered no serious challenge to the administration's agenda.

Iraq agreed to allow UN weapons inspectors to return in September 2002, but an international debate over how to proceed ensued. The Bush administration encountered significant difficulties when it tried to convince other nations to support the use of force against Iraq if it failed to comply fully with UN resolutions. Not only did Bush face opposition from traditional rivals such as Russia and China, but he also had problems with longstanding U.S. allies within the North Atlantic Treaty Organization (NATO), including Germany and France. Those four nations, all of which sat on the UN Security Council at that time (Russia, China, and France as permanent members), remained adamant that the weapons inspectors be allowed to resume their activities before they would countenance any talk of war. Among U.S. allies, only Britain and Spain offered their full support to the U.S. hard line.

On 8 November 2002 the UN Security Council finally passed Resolution 1441, which demanded that Iraq allow the return of weapons inspectors. Iraq accepted, and officials of the United Nations Monitoring, Verification, and Inspection Commission (UNMOVIC), created in December 1999 to replace UNSCOM, began their work on 27 November. In a 27 January 2003 report, chief inspectors Hans Blix and Muhammad El Baradei generally praised Iraqi cooperation and noted that they had not uncovered any evidence of weapons of mass destruction in the approximately 300 inspections that UNMOVIC had carried out to that date. The United States and Britain continued to make the case that Iraq had such weapons and constituted an immediate threat. On 3 February British prime minister Tony Blair posted a document on his official Web site that he claimed showed Iraqi weapons violations, based in part on British intelligence (parts of the document were later shown to have been plagiarized from open sources, not intelligence reports). U.S. secretary of state Colin Powell addressed the Security Council five days later, using props such as intercepted audiotapes of Iraqi military commanders' conversations, to convince the council that Iraq continued to disregard the international community. The U.S. administration also shifted its rationale for war during late 2002 and early 2003, mentioning banned weapons, then discussing possible Iraqi links to the al-Qaʿida network, then discussing the need to liberate Iraqis from Saddam's Hussein's dictatorial rule.

During the weeks of this debate there was unprecedented popular global opposition to waging war against Iraq. Demonstrations were held on all seven continents in early 2003, including at the McMurdo scientific research station in Antarctica. It has been estimated that 30 million people worldwide participated in antiwar demonstrations in 600 cities in dozens of countries during a weekend of global protest from 14 to 16 February. Countries whose governments supported the war—Britain, Spain, Italy, and the United States—were the scenes of what were perhaps their nations' largest ever public rallies. Huge demonstrations were held in Italy, where Pope John Paul II appealed for peace from the hawks. A January 2003 demonstration in freezing temperatures in Washington, D.C., was called the largest demonstration in the United States since the era of the Vietnam war protests.

Undeterred by such massive global opposition, including from longstanding U.S. allies, the United

States tried twice, in late February and early March, to convince the Security Council to adopt a resolution stating that Iraq had failed to comply with Resolution 1441 and calling for "serious consequences." These attempts failed. On 15 March UN Secretary-General Kofi Annan weighed into the debate by saying that an attack on Iraq absent a new resolution would constitute a violation of the UN charter. Bush, however, gave a televised speech the following day in which he demanded that Saddam Hussein and his sons Uday and Qusay leave Iraq within 48 hours or face attack. They refused. In Britain, the House of Commons voted two days after that, on 18 March, to support war.

The war commenced on 20 March with aerial bombing of Baghdad. Ground forces of a U.S.-led coalition invaded from Kuwait the next day while airborne troops based secretly in Jordan captured air bases in western Iraq. In addition to 255,000 Americans, this coalition eventually included 45,000 British troops, 2,000 Australians, and 200 each from Poland, Slovakia, and the Czech Republic. Fighting was fierce, but Iraqi forces were doomed from the start. By 6 April U.S.forces had captured Karbala and British troops had entered Basra. By 9 April U.S. forces had entered Baghdad as Saddam's regime crumbled. There were scenes of wild jubilation in parts of Baghdad at Saddam's downfall, as, for example, when crowds (and a U.S. tank) pulled down a huge statue of the deposed leader that had stood in Firdaws Square in downtown Baghdad. Tragically, the looting that swept through the city spread to some of Iraq's most important archaeological museums. The National Museum in Baghdad was sacked between 9 and 12 April, and both common pilferers and professional art thieves stole nearly 15,000 artifacts, some of them priceless treasures. Working with INTERPOL, U.S. officials worked to track down stolen artifacts that had been smuggled out of Iraq. By September 2003 more than 3,400 items from the National Museum had been recovered in Iraq, Jordan, Italy, and elsewhere. There was at least one case in which members of the U.S. forces themselves took an artifact from an Iraqi museum: The helmet of an Israeli aviator shot down over Iraq in June 1967 was taken from a display in a Baghdad military museum and given to Israeli authorities in Jordan in August 2003.

In the north, Kurdish forces joined the fight and helped to capture Mosul and Kirkuk. Saddam Hussein and other leading Iraqi officials went into hiding. The fighting was largely over by 16 April, and Bush declared on 1 May that "major combat operations" were over. At that point, U.S. and British military deaths in combat totaled 120. Iraqi deaths during that time, both civilian and military, were much more difficult to ascertain; estimates range from between 5,000 to 7,000 civilians killed, and 4,800 to 6,300 Iraqi soldiers. Saddam Hussein's sons Uday and Qusay were killed in a shootout with U.S. troops in Mosul on 22 July. Saddam himself was eventually captured by U.S. forces near Tikrit on 14 December.

Occupation of Iraq

To administer the occupied country, the United States created the Office for Reconstruction and Humanitarian Assistance. On 21 April 2003 former U.S. army general Jay Garner (1938–) was appointed as its head. Garner served as the civilian governor of occupied Iraq until he was replaced on 6 May by former U.S. State Department official L. Paul Bremer III (1941–). Bremer was named the administrator of the new Coalition Provisional Authority (CPA; in Arabic, Sultat al-I'tilaf al-Mu'aqqata), a division of the U.S. Department of Defense. As a result, Bremer became the civilian head of a U.S. military occupation administration. Through Security Council Resolution 1483 of 22 May 2003, the UN formally recognized the United States and Britain as occupying powers and lifted the sanctions imposed on Iraq, even though UNMOVIC had not yet certified Iraqi disarmament, as required by the sanctions resolutions. U.S. officials stated that the occupation was costing the United States approximately $1 billion per week, although some of those costs included items such as military salaries that would have been paid anyway. The United States also dispatched former secretary of state James Baker on an international campaign to convince Iraq's creditors to forgive the country's debts that had been accumulated by Saddam.

On 13 July 2003 Bremer created the Iraqi Governing Council (IGC) as an advisory body. The IGC included representatives from Iraq's main ethnic and religious groups, opposition politicians such as the Kurdish leaders Jalal Talabani and Mas'ud

Barzani, and returned exiles such as former diplomat Adnan Pachachi and Ahmad Chalabi, founder of the Iraqi National Congress. The IGC was allowed to form a cabinet, but final authority lay with Bremer, who retained veto powers over the IGC's decisions.

Armed resistance to the occupation escalated in the summer of 2003, as did attacks on a variety of Iraqi political and religious figures and foreign officials. On 19 August a car bomb at UN headquarters in Baghdad killed the top UN envoy to Iraq, Brazilian Sergio Vieira de Mello (1948–2003). Ten days later, on 29 August, leading Shiʿite cleric Ayatullah Muhammad Baqir al-Hakim (1939–2003) was assassinated in a massive bomb explosion in al-Najaf. By early 2004 guerrillas were carrying out increasingly more sophisticated bombings and other attacks on U.S. and other occupation troops, which had expanded by early 2004 to include combat and noncombat forces from thirty additional countries besides those that originally participated in the war. These attacks became an almost daily occurrence, not so much in the Shiʿite and Kurdish regions of Iraq as in the "Sunni Triangle" north of Baghdad, near towns such as Falluja and Tikrit. In addition, numerous car bombings killed scores of Iraqi civilians and officers of the reconstructed Iraqi police. On 2 March 2004, over 140 Iraqi Shiʿa were killed during attacks in Baghdad and Karbala that came during the important Shiʿite religious celebration of Ashura. By late February 2004, 548 U.S. soldiers had died in Iraq since the beginning of the war, 337 as a result of hostile activity. Iraqi civilian deaths since the war began ranged somewhere between 8,000 and 10,000.

Controversy continued to swirl after the onset of the occupation. Although the presence of weapons of mass destruction was the major ostensible reason for going to war, by early 2004 occupation authorities had still not found any such stockpiles, a situation that eventually led President Bush, in January 2004, to call for a formal inquiry into prewar U.S. intelligence failures. In late 2003 in Britain, Prime Minister Blair was also engulfed in a controversy over the accuracy of his government's handling of intelligence. Paul Bremer was adamant by early 2004 that the CPA would turn over "sovereignty" to the Iraqi people on 30 June 2004, although coalition troops would remain in the country. There were conflicting opinions about the shape of the new governmental system. Bremer's proposals for regional caucuses as the basis for constructing a new Iraqi legislature and interim government were rejected by most Iraqis, and he backed away from the idea in mid-February 2004. The leading Shiʿite cleric, Ayatullah Ali al-Husayni al-Sistani (1930–), wanted direct elections held as soon as possible. Iraq's Shiʿite Arabs and Kurds were much better organized politically than other ethnic and religious groups, including Sunni Arabs, Turkmen, Assyrians, and others, who were fearful that such quick elections could produce a Shiʿite-dominated country. In addition, the fact that al-Sistani is originally an Iranian (who came to Iraq decades ago) has raised some Sunni suspicions about Iranian influence. UN Secretary-General Kofi Annan sent special envoy Lakhdar Brahimi to Iraq to produce a recommendation for how to proceed, and stated in late February that it was not feasible to hold direct elections prior to the handover of sovereignty on 30 June. Fearing the possibility that Iraqis might draft a constitution that proclaimed *shariʿa* to be the basis for legislation in the new Iraq, Bremer announced on 16 February that he would veto any such proposal coming from the IGC. On 8 March 2004, the IGC signed a provisional constitution for a federal Iraq that granted the Kurds a considerable voice in government. The constitution also called *shariʿa* "a source" of legislation, as opposed to "the source."

See also ANNAN, KOFI A.; BAKER, JAMES A.; BARZANI FAMILY; BUSH, GEORGE HERBERT WALKER; BUSH, GEORGE WALKER; CHALABI, AHMAD; CLINTON, WILLIAM JEFFERSON; GULF CRISIS (1990–1991); GULF WAR (1991); HUSSEIN, SADDAM; IRAQ; IRAQI NATIONAL CONGRESS; POWELL, COLIN L.; QAʿIDA, AL-; SANCTIONS, IRAQI.

Bibliography

Cordesman, Anthony H. *The Iraq War: Strategy, Tactics, and Military Lessons.* New York: Praeger, 2003.

Mahajan, Rahul. *Full Spectrum Dominance: U.S. Power in Iraq and Beyond.* New York: Seven Stories Press, 2003.

Official web site of the Coalition Provisional Authority: Authority. Official web site available from <http://cpa-iraq.org>.

Smith, Ray L., and West, Bing. *The March Up: Taking Baghdad with the First Marine Division.* New York: Bantam, 2003.

MICHAEL R. FISCHBACH

WARNIER LAW

Law passed by France's National Assembly in 1873 to establish individual titles on previously undivided lands held by families and tribes in Algeria.

The Warnier Law greatly facilitated land purchases by European settlers and appropriations by the state domain. It also hastened the appearance of small and dispersed properties insufficient to support the indigenous rural population.

PETER VON SIVERS

WAR OF ATTRITION (1969–1970)

Egypt's unsuccessful campaign to drive Israel back from the Suez Canal.

After the Arab–Israel War in 1967, fighting continued along the borders of the new territories captured by Israel, particularly along the Suez Canal. Violations of the cease-fire proliferated in September 1968, when Egypt concentrated some 150,000 troops along the west side of the canal. Heavy fighting took place on 8 and 9 March 1969, causing the death of Egypt's chief of staff, General Abd al-Munʿim Riyad. On 23 July of that year, President Gamal Abdel Nasser formally declared a war of attrition. He stated that, although his country was incapable of regaining the Sinai Peninsula by force, it could and would wear Israel out—hoping that Egyptian artillery barrages would make Israel withdraw its troops from the Suez Canal. Israel responded by building a system of thirty strongholds along the canal, known as the Bar-Lev Line.

On 31 October 1968 Israel had destroyed a power station at Naj Hamadi in upper Egypt, but it was not until July 1969 that it began regular aerial attacks that devastated Egyptian cities along the canal and turned their residents into refugees. In early 1970 Egypt received substantial amounts of Soviet military aid, including surface-to-air missile batteries that could down Israeli aircraft. After a number of aerial battles between Israeli planes and Russian-flown MiG fighters, the United States introduced its Rogers Plan and pressed Egypt and Israel for a new cease-fire, which went into effect on 7 August 1970.

Some controversy exists among military scholars as to which country actually won the war of attrition. Israel certainly proved its military superiority, especially in aerial dogfights with Egyptian pilots, but Egypt gained a diplomatic victory in persuading the Soviet Union to provide military assistance and in moving SAM missile batteries, which Egypt used in the 1973 Arab–Israel War, close to the Suez Canal. The long-term effect of the war of attrition has been to make Israel more suspicious of international peace proposals and Egypt more precise in its strategic military planning.

See also ARAB–ISRAEL WAR (1967); ARAB–ISRAEL WAR (1973); BAR-LEV, HAIM; ROGERS, WILLIAM PIERCE.

Bibliography

Bar-Siman-Tov, Yaacov. *The Israeli-Egyptian War of Attrition, 1969–1970: A Case Study of Limited Local War.* New York: Columbia University Press, 1980.

Herzog, Chaim. *The Arab–Israeli Wars: War and Peace in the Middle East,* revised edition. New York: Vintage, 1984.

Korn, David A. *Stalemate: The War of Attrition and Great Power Diplomacy in the Middle East, 1967–1970.* Boulder, CO: Westview, 1992.

BENJAMIN JOSEPH
UPDATED BY ARTHUR GOLDSCHMIDT

WATER

Because of its scarcity, water plays a central role in Middle Eastern politics and society.

Nowhere in the world is water more important than in the Middle East and North Africa. In no other region do so many people strive so hard for economic growth on the basis of so little water: here is found 5 percent of the world's population but only 1 percent of its fresh water. Of the ten nations with the least water per capita, six are in this region. No wonder that both Jewish and Muslim scriptures are full of references to water.

The Dead Sea is the lowest point on earth and the culmination of the Jordan River. Its high concentration of mineral salts makes this body of water lifeless but also makes its visitors buoyant, creating a popular tourist attraction along the border between Israel and Jordan. © RICHARD T. NOWITZ/CORBIS. REPRODUCED BY PERMISSION.

Role of Climate

The more heavily populated parts of the Middle East are semiarid, with rainfall of 10 to 29 inches (250 to 750 mm) per year. However, low rainfall is less of a problem than variability in rainfall. The great bulk of the rain falls in four winter months, with none falling during the rest of the year. Rainfall also changes rapidly with distance, from more than 20 inches (500 mm) on the coast of Lebanon to 8 inches (200 mm) in the Biqa, only an hour away by road but across the Lebanon mountains.

Seasonal and spatial variations in rainfall are sharp but predictable. What makes planning difficult is the sharp variation from one year to the next. Reliable flow in the rivers (the flow that can be expected nine years out of ten) is only 10 percent of the average. In northern latitudes, water planning can be built around statistical averages; here, it must be built around extremes.

This already difficult water situation will likely get worse. Population growth rates are high, and most climate change models suggest higher temperatures, lower rainfall, and more frequent droughts for the region.

Role of History

Development in the Middle East and North Africa has always been more dependent on water than on any other resource, including oil. By the fourth millennium B.C.E., the Sumerians had built a paradise in what is now Iraq through intricate canals for irrigating crops; two millennia later it had largely collapsed because of salinization of the soil. Ancient cities, such as Palmyra in Syria, were possible only because of carefully engineered tunnels, called *qanats* (*foggaras* in Iran), to bring water from springs tens of kilometers away.

Over the years, the peoples of the Middle East have made water a preoccupation, and each nation has a central agency, typically a full ministry, to deal with water. Many of the principles for good water management were worked out in the Middle East—although just as often they were ignored for political, financial, or social reasons.

Water Sources

The Middle East includes two of the mightiest river systems in the world. The Nile has two main branches: The White Nile originates in Uganda, and the larger Blue Nile (together with the Atbara) originates in Ethiopia; they join near Khartoum and flow northward through Egypt to the Mediterranean. The Tigris and Euphrates both originate in Turkey and flow south-southeastward through Syria and Iraq before joining and flowing into the Persian Gulf via the Shatt al-Arab, at the Iranian border.

The region also includes numerous medium-sized rivers, such as the Jordan, which flows from three springs through the Sea of Galilee (one of the few natural lakes in the region) and into the Dead Sea, 415 meters below sea level. Only Turkey has an

Atatürk Dam, built across the Euphrates River in southeastern Turkey and in use since 1990, is one of the largest dams of its kind (earth and rock fill) in the world. Dams such as these are not only expensive but are also costly in terms of reducing the flow of water to countries lying downstream, contributing to a growing shortage of fresh water in much of the region. © Ed Kashi/Corbis. Reproduced by permission.

abundance of river water, but its big rivers are only found in the eastern part of the nation. Finally, there are small coastal rivers (many of them ephemeral), and a few major wetlands, such as the marshlands in southern Iraq and the Sudd swamp in southern Sudan.

The construction of new dams and pipelines to deliver water from major rivers in the Middle East will cost two or three times as much per unit of water as current supplies, and if construction occurs in upstream countries, such as Ethiopia and Turkey, it will reduce flows downstream. Therefore, the region will increasingly shift toward the use of underground water, which has the great advantage of not evaporating. (Lakes and reservoirs in the region lose meters of water per year to evaporation.)

Historically, underground water was tapped by shallow wells dug in unconsolidated materials to get small flows of water. Today, much larger volumes of water are extracted from wells drilled tens to hundreds of meters into aquifers, which are rock layers with pores that contain water. Renewable aquifers are replenished (generally slowly) by rainfall; nonrenewable, or fossil, aquifers contain water trapped in sediments laid down millions of years ago.

Just more than 10 percent of the water supply for the region comes from aquifers, but in Israel and Jordan the share approaches 50 percent, and in Kuwait and parts of the Arabian Peninsula it approaches 100 percent (apart from desalination). Libya's Great Man-Made River pumps water from fossil aquifers in the south of the country and moves it 930 miles (1,500 km) to farms and cities in the north.

The third most important source of water in the Middle East is recycled sewage, which is treated and reused, mainly for irrigation. Despite common

Lake Van, a salt lake in eastern Turkey near the border with Iran, is the largest lake in the country. Turkey is the source of the Tigris and Euphrates as well as numerous lesser rivers, and it is one of only a handful of nations in the region where water is abundant. © ADAM WOOLFITT/CORBIS. REPRODUCED BY PERMISSION.

belief (shared by both Muslims and non-Muslims), there is no objection in Islamic law to the reuse of sewer water provided it is properly treated.

More than half of the world's desalination capacity is found in the region, mainly in the oil-producing nations of the Arabian peninsula with lots of by-product natural gas that was formerly flared. (Desalination is an energy-intensive process.) Costs for desalination have fallen to a level that makes it feasible as a source of potable water but still too expensive for irrigation.

Other sources of water are individually small but collectively provide sizable amounts of water. Water harvesting gathers rain that falls over a wide area and directs it to one field through small channels and micro-barrages. The technique can allow crops in areas where rainfall is only 4 inches (100 mm) per year. Rainwater is also collected from rooftops and stored in cisterns. If handled carefully, rooftop water can be used for drinking.

Uses of Water

By far the largest share of water in the region goes to agriculture—as much as 90 percent of total water use in some countries, and 60 percent in the more industrialized countries.

Drinking requires only a relatively small volume of water, but it must meet higher standards than that used for irrigation. Thirty liters of potable water per person-day is generally regarded as the minimum for drinking, cooking, and washing.

Industrial water use is low. Food and beverage processing are the largest industrial consumers. More is withdrawn for cooling but most of this water is recycled or returned to the watercourse.

A hidden but critical amount of water must be left in place to support fisheries and hydropower, as well as to protect habitat. This use is typically neglected by governments when they drain swamps, canalize rivers, or extend land. As a result, not only has the environment been degraded, but fish catches have declined and the salinity of groundwater has increased.

Problems

The nations of the Middle East all face three overlapping sources of stress in their water management: 1) quantity, which has been a source of stress since history began; 2) quality, which is a newer stress but increasingly important; and 3) equity, which occurs when the same water is subject to competing demands.

Quantity. Iran, Iraq, Lebanon, Sudan, Syria, and Turkey are fairly well endowed with water, with more than 1 million cubic meters (Mcm) per capita; Algeria, Egypt, Israel, Morocco, and Palestine form a middle group; and Jordan, Libya, Tunisia, and the countries of the Arabian Peninsula are least well endowed, with less than 500 Mcm per capita. However, water availability is declining in every nation, which means that current patterns of water use are not sustainable. Some projections for the Jordan River basin suggest that by 2025 household and industrial uses will require all the fresh water, leaving none for farmers. Most nations are also drawing down their renewable aquifers and mining fossil ones. Some have annual water deficits of several thousand Mcm.

Water quantity problems in the region can be resolved in small part by exploiting additional

Freshwater withdrawals by country and sector

Estimates for 2000

Country	Total	Per capita	Use (%)	(cubic km/a) Domestic	(cubic km/a) Industry	% with safe (cubic m/p) drinking water
Afghanistan	26.1	1,020	1	0	99	13
Algeria	4.5	142	25	15	60	94
Bahrain	0.2	387	39	4	56	100
Egypt	55.1	809	6	8	86	95
Iran	70.0	916	6	2	92	95
Iraq	42.8	1,852	5	3	92	85
Israel	1.7	280	36	11	51*	100
Jordan	1.0	155	22	3	75	96
Lebanon	1.3	393	28	4	68	100
Libya	4.6	720	11	2	87	72
Morocco	11.1	381	5	3	92	82
Oman	1.2	450	5	2	94	39
Saudi Arabia	17.0	786	9	1	90	95
Sudan	17.8	597	4	1	94	75
Syria	14.4	894	4	2	94	80
Tunisia	3.1	313	32	8	60	99
Turkey	31.6	481	16	11	72	83
Yemen	2.9	162	7	1	92	69

* Percentage by sector adjusted by author on basis of estimates by the Planning Department of the Israeli Water Commission. All data for Israel based on estimates by the author.

SOURCE: Gleick, Peter, et al, ed. *The World's Water: The Biennial Report in Freshwater Resources, 2002–2003* (Washington, D.C., Island Press, 2002).

TABLE BY GGS INFORMATION SERVICES, THE GALE GROUP.

sources of supply but in much larger part by better use of the water that is already available. People in the region use less water than those elsewhere in the world, but as a result of poor management and misguided economic policies conservation here (as in most other parts of the world) remains far short of its potential. Many nations lose half the water put into municipal systems to leaks, and they typically deliver piped water at low (or no) price. Cost-effective savings of 25 to 50 percent are possible in most uses.

Moreover, every country in the region provides water to farmers at highly subsidized prices. Under the influence of higher prices, Israeli scientists developed drip irrigation systems that have cut water use per hectare by 40 percent. However, drip irrigation is expensive and not appropriate for all crops. Lower-cost sprinkler systems, used at night to minimize evaporation, can also increase irrigation efficiency, as can irrigating only at times critical to plant growth.

Most analysts find that water is tens of times more valuable in industrial or household uses than in agriculture. Therefore, crops grown in the region will gradually be replaced by imports. It takes roughly a thousand tons of water to produce one ton of wheat. Using that ratio, Middle Eastern nations already import grains with a virtual water content equal to the flow of the Nile.

Quality. Much of the limited fresh water in the Middle East is polluted from growing volumes of human, industrial, and agricultural waste. Three problems stand out: 1) Overpumping of wells causes a decline in the water table—by as much as a meter a year in some areas. This decline adds to pumping costs and permits lower-quality water (or, if near the coast, seawater) to flow inward and contaminate the aquifer. The only way to avoid the problem is to match pumping rates to inflow. 2) Agricultural runoff is the major non-point source of water pollution—mainly sediment, phosphorus, nitrogen, and pesticides. Better farming methods, such as conservation tillage, contour planting, and terracing can control soil erosion and cut pollution by half or more. 3) Urban sewage systems have either begun to deteriorate or cannot handle the growing loads placed on them. Large investments are needed to improve their physical infrastructure.

Equity. Most of the larger rivers in the region cross an international border—some cross several borders—or form a border. No tabulation exists for aquifers that underlie national borders, but there are many.

Despite many statements suggesting that the next war in the Middle East will be over fresh water, there is little evidence for this. Not a single war has been fought over water for hundreds of years, but many treaties dealing with water have been signed. Water will be a source of conflict, but the conflicts will mainly be intranational rather than international. Likely sources of conflict include rural and urban users contending for the same water and rising demands from poor farmers, who are often disadvantaged in their access to water, and from women, who typically want more water for their households while men prefer to use it to grow cash crops. Israeli control of water in the West Bank is contentious, but even here experts have shown that compromise is feasible.

None of the three stresses on water in the Middle East will be easily resolved. Most of the nations in the region have already reached or are fast approaching the limits of their indigenous water supplies. Although higher prices for water and technological advances may defer the crisis, the only long-term solutions involve much greater efficiency in use, full reuse of wastewater, and gradual shifts of water from agriculture to other sectors. All of the nations of the Middle East and North Africa must revise their water policies to provide for a sustainable future, and they must find equitable ways to share water within and between nations.

Bibliography

Amery, Hussein A., and Wolf, Aaron T., eds. *Water in the Middle East: A Geography of Peace.* Austin: University of Texas Press, 2000.

Beaumont, Peter. "Water Policies for the Middle East in the Twenty-first Century: The New Economic Realities." *International Journal of Water Resources Development* 18, no. 2 (2002): 315–334.

Brooks, David B., and Mehmet, Ozay, eds. *Water Balances in the Eastern Mediterranean.* Ottawa: International Development Research Centre, 2000.

Kolars, John. "The Spatial Attributes of Water Negotiation: The Need for a River Ethic and River Advocacy in the Middle East." In *Water in the Middle East: A Geography of Peace,* edited by Hussein A. Amery and Aaron T. Wolf. Austin: University of Texas Press, 2000.

Lonergan, Stephen C., and Brooks, David B. *Watershed: The Role of Fresh Water in the Israeli-Palestinian Conflict.* Ottawa: International Development Research Centre, 1994.

Postel, Sandra. *Pillar of Sand: Can the Irrigation Miracle Last?* New York: Norton, 1999.

Rogers, Peter, and Lydon, Peter, eds. *Water in the Arab World: Perspectives and Prognoses.* Cambridge, MA: Division of Applied Sciences, Harvard University, 1994.

Shapland, Greg. *Rivers of Discord: International Water Disputes in the Middle East.* New York: St. Martin's Press; London: Hurst, 1997.

Waterbury, John. *The Nile Basin: National Determinants of Collective Action.* New Haven, CT: Yale University Press, 2002.

Wolf, Aaron T. "Transboundary Fresh Water Database." Department of Geosciences, Oregon State University. Available from <http://www.transboundarywaters.orst.edu>.

DAVID B. BROOKS

WATTAR, AL-TAHER

[1936–]

Algerian novelist, short-story writer, and journalist.

Al-Taher Wattar (also spelled Tahar Ouettar and Tahir Watter) was born in Sedrata (department of Souk Ahras, eastern Algeria). His studies, exclusively in Arabic schools, took him to the Ibn Badis Intitute of Constantine and then to the Zeitouna University of Tunis in 1954. In 1955–1956 he published his first short stories in newspapers and joined the Civil Organization of the FLN (Front de Libération Nationale). After the war, he edited two periodicals in Tunisia and Algeria: *al-Jamahir* (The masses) from 1962 to 1963 and *al-Ahrar* (Free people) from 1972 to 1974. He also served as a civil servant of the FLN and general director of Algerian Radio. Since 1989, Wattar has served as president of *al-Jahidhiya,* the Algerian literary and cultural association. An important figure in Algerian literature, he is one of the few novelists who have attempted to make up for the lack of conventional types in the Arabic novel.

His writings present a panorama of Algeria's postindependence history, with a look back at the Algerian War of Independence and a subtle treatment of postcolonial Algerian politics, culture, and society. His nationalistic works defend the socialist ideology and the role played by the communists in the Algerian War of Independence. His novel *L'As* (1974; The genius), in particular, reveals the communists' involvement in the fighting; Wattar used this book as a first step to indict those in power for their many failures. His *al-Shamʿa wa ad-Dahalib* (1995; The candle and dark tunnels), addresses the fall of the Soviet Union and its aftermath.

The symbolic novel *al-Hawwat wa al-Qasr* (1980; The fisherman and the palace) reveals the disappointments of the people with the political agenda of independent Algeria. Another controversial subject Wattar raises is the abuses by the opportunists who benefited from both war and peace. His novels *al-Zilzal* (1974; The earthquake) and *Urs Baghl* (1978; A mule's wedding) are primarily allegorical writings with a deep vein of satire and provide insight into Algerian culture, politics, society, and psychology. His novel *al-Wali al-Tahir yaʿud ila Maqamihi al-Zaki* (1999; Saint Tahir returns to his holy shrine), deals with the Islamic renaissance. Wattar's *al-Shuhada Yaʿudun Hatha al-Usbu* (1980; Martyrs come back this week), a collection of seven linked short stories, dramatically portrays the national betrayal of the memory of the martyrs of the War of Independence.

The novel *al-Ishq wa al-Mawt fi al-Zaman al-Harrashi* (1980; Love and death in the Harrashi time) expresses Wattar's great optimism during the rule of President Houari Boumedienne. But changes on the political scene ended his dreams, and the novel *Tajribatun fi al-Ishq* (1994; An experience in passion) is the cry of a disappointed man.

See also LITERATURE: ARABIC, NORTH AFRICAN.

Bibliography

Allen, Roger, ed. *Modern Arabic Literature.* New York: Ungar, 1987.

Cox, Debbie. "Marginality as Resistance to Incorporation in Algeria's Arabic Literature: An Approach to Tahar Wattar's 'Urs Baghal.'" *Journal of Algerian Studies* 1, no. 1 (1998).

Cox, Debbie. "The Novels of Taher Watter: Command and Critique?" *Research in African Literature* 28, no. 3 (fall 1997): 94–109.

Cox, Debbie. *Politics, Language and Gender in the Algerian Arabic Novel.* London: Edwin Mellen Press, 2002.

Granara, William. "Mythologising the Algerian War of Independence: Tahir Wattar and the Contemporary Algerian Novel." *Journal of North African Studies* 4, no. 3 (1999).

AIDA A. BAMIA
UPDATED BY AZZEDINE G. MANSOUR

WAUCHOPE, ARTHUR
[1874–1947]

British high commissioner in Palestine and Transjordan, 1931–1938.

Sir Arthur Grenfell Wauchope, a Scotsman, was a professional soldier who served in the Second Boer War and, from 1903 to 1914, in India. During the first two years of World War I he served on the western front. In 1916 he was transferred to Mesopotamia in command of the Highland Battalion and was wounded at the battle of Shaykh Saʿd. After the war he served in Germany, Great Britain, and Northern Ireland. He retired from the army as a lieutenant-general in 1931 and was appointed high commissioner of Palestine and Transjordan. The prime minister, Ramsay MacDonald, said that Wauchope was "a general who does it with his head, not his feet." As high commissioner, Wauchope compared the difficulty of dealing with the Arabs and Jews to that of a circus performer riding two horses at once. The early years of his tenure were marked by unprecedented levels of Jewish immigration and by growing political tension. Wauchope's proposal in 1935 for the establishment of an elected legislative council was rejected by Arabs and Jews as well as by the British parliament. In 1936 the three-year-long countrywide Palestine Arab revolt broke out. At first Wauchope urged restraint, but when clashes between British forces and Arab rebels intensified, he recommended the use of large-scale armed force to quell disorder. He retired on grounds of ill health in February 1938, before completing his second five-year term.

See also PALESTINE ARAB REVOLT (1936–1939).

Bibliography

Sykes, Christopher. *Cross Roads to Israel.* London: Collins, 1965.

KAREN A. THORNSVARD
UPDATED BY BERNARD WASSERSTEIN

WAVELL, ARCHIBALD PERCIVAL
[1883–1950]

Commander in chief of British forces in the Middle East; British general in World War II; Viceroy of India, 1943–1947.

Archibald Percival Wavell was born in Colchester, England, and graduated from Sandhurst, the British military academy. He served under General Edmund Allenby in Palestine in World War I. In 1937 he was again sent to Palestine to deal with the unrest between the Arabs and Jews. He successfully quelled the Palestine Arab Revolt and returned to Britain in 1938. In 1939, he became commander in chief for all British forces in the Middle East, where he defeated the Italian forces in North and East Africa (1940–1941). He was not successful in preventing the fall of Greece and Crete, and when he succumbed to General Erwin Rommel's Afrika Korps in 1941, he was reassigned to Southeast Asia. Wavell concluded his career as viceroy of India (1943–1947), the last viceroy before Lord Mountbatten, who helped ease India into independence from the British Empire.

See also PALESTINE ARAB REVOLT (1936–1939).

Bibliography

Collins, Robert J. *Lord Wavell.* London, 1947.

DANIEL E. SPECTOR

WAZIR, INTISAR AL- (UMM JIHAD)
[1941–]

Palestinian political figure.

Intisar al-Wazir was born in 1941 in Gaza city. In 1965 she married Khalil al-Wazir (Abu Jihad) a cofounder of al-Fatah and leader of the first Palestinian uprising, who was assassinated by Israeli commandos in Tunisia in early 1988. In 1965 she also participated in founding the General Union for Palestinian Women (GUPW) to support Palestinian women socially, economically, and legally. She served as the secretary-general of the GUPW between 1980 and 1985.

Al-Wazir founded numerous centers for women that focused on literacy training and rehabilitation, including the Social Affairs Committee, the Martyrs' Families Organization, and the Committee for Prisoners and the Injured. Upon the creation of the Palestinian Authority, al-Wazir served as the first Palestinian minister for social affairs between 1996 and 2003.

In addition to her prominent role in social activism, al-Wazir has held important political positions since the early days of her public career. She joined al-Fatah in 1959 as its first female member. She has been a member of the Palestinian National Council since 1974 and a member of the Fatah Central Committee since 1987. In 1983 she served as the deputy secretary-general of the Fatah Revolutionary Council.

Al-Wazir lived in exile for thirty years, returning to the Gaza Strip in 1995. She was elected to the Palestinian Legislative Council (PLC) in 1996.

See also WAZIR, KHALIL AL-.

Bibliography

Kawar, Amal. *Daughters of Palestine: Leading Women of the Palestinian National Movement.* Albany: State University of New York Press, 1996.

KHALED ISLAIH

WAZIR, KHALIL AL-
[1935–1988]

Also known as Abu Jihad, one of the founding members of al-Fatah.

Khalil Ibrahim al-Wazir was born on 10 October 1935 to a Palestinian Sunni Muslim shopkeeper in Ramla in Mandatory Palestine. When its inhabitants were summarily expelled by Israeli forces in July 1948, al-Wazir made his way to Gaza City, where he resumed his education at a United Nations Relief and Works Agency school.

Al-Wazir first became politically active in 1953, covertly receiving military training in the Egyptian-administered Gaza Strip. Probably affiliated with the Muslim Brotherhood at this time, he formed his own commando unit, whose activities led to his brief imprisonment by the Egyptian authorities in 1954. In 1954 he also first met the future Palestine Liberation Organization (PLO) chairman, Yasir Arafat, beginning a lifelong partnership and friendship, which, in association with future PLO deputy chairman Salah Khalaf (Abu Iyad), was to form the resilient core leadership of the contemporary Palestinian national movement.

After completing his studies in Cairo, where he had moved in September 1956, al-Wazir left in 1957 for Kuwait as a schoolteacher. His meeting there with Arafat that fall, a meeting of minds regarding the need to establish an independent, armed Palestinian movement, sowed the seeds for the formation of the Palestine National Liberation Movement (al-Fatah) in 1959. Al-Wazir would serve on its Central Committee and the subsequently established Revolutionary Council for the rest of his life.

Among al-Fatah's founders, al-Wazir alone had prior experience in forming a guerrilla organization and played a leading role in its development. In 1963 he went to Algiers to open al-Fatah's first diplomatic mission and organize military training for its recruits. He used this post to establish relations with China (al-Fatah's first non-Arab source of arms), North Korea, and Vietnam; meet guerrilla theoretician Che Guevara; and participate in the 1964 Palestine National Council, which founded the PLO. During this period he also remained, with Arafat, the leading advocate within al-Fatah's Central Committee for an immediate start to military operations. When the debate was resolved in late 1964, al-Wazir was appointed deputy commander in chief of al-Fatah's military wing, al-Asifa (The Storm).

After the PLO came under the control of al-Fatah and other guerrilla organizations in 1968–1969, al-Wazir additionally assumed the post of deputy commander in chief of PLO military forces. Although this position gave him only limited authority over non-Fatah forces, al-Fatah's preponderance within the PLO ensured that he played a central role in PLO military affairs until his death. He firmly believed armed struggle was legitimate and consistently sought to escalate it. He also did not hesitate to attack or retaliate against civilian targets when he thought this necessary but opposed the use of violence outside the region.

Khalil al-Wazir (right) with George Habash at the 16th Palestinian National Council Meeting in 1983. Al-Wazir was one of the original members of the Palestinian Liberation Organization and played an important role in many of its operations up until his assassination in 1988. © Alain Nogues/Corbis Sygma. Reproduced by permission.

Al-Wazir, who furthermore directed al-Fatah's Department of the Occupied Homeland, was also among the first of his colleagues to grasp the importance of complementing armed struggle in Gaza and the West Bank with political mobilization. Particularly after the PLO's evacuation from Beirut in 1982, he worked hard to develop al-Fatah's political infrastructure in the West Bank and Gaza Strip, thus helping prepare the ground for the popular uprising, or Intifada, which erupted in December 1987. It was primarily on account of his leading role in assisting the uprising's clandestine leadership and channeling support to the West Bank and Gaza that he was assassinated by an Israeli commando squad (which filmed the event) in Tunis on 16 April 1988. His death precipitated the most serious disturbances the West Bank and Gaza Strip had witnessed since 1967, and his funeral in Damascus was attended by hundreds of thousands, including representatives from all Palestinian factions. He is survived by his wife, prominent Fatah militant Intisar al-Wazir, and four of their five children.

Along with Khalaf, Khalil al-Wazir was the most important PLO and Fatah leader after Arafat and, in internal debates, consistently Arafat's closest ally. The achievements and failures of these organizations and of the Palestinian people generally during his time are therefore equally his.

A straightforward nationalist whose mind was attuned to practical action and organizational matters, al-Wazir was among Palestinians respected in life and venerated in death. Though denounced as a reactionary by more radical elements during the 1970s for his conservative positions, he enjoyed extensive contacts among other factions and later emerged as a prominent mediator. As with all Palestinian nationalist leaders during his lifetime, he was viewed by Israel as a terrorist, and Israel rejected his support of a negotiated settlement.

Neither an intellectual nor an orator, al-Wazir does not have any writings to his name and gave fewer press statements than his colleagues.

See also ARAFAT, YASIR; FATAH, AL-; INTIFADA (1987–1991); KHALAF, SALAH; MUSLIM BROTHERHOOD; PALESTINE LIBERATION ORGANIZATION (PLO); WAZIR, INTISAR AL- (UMM JIHAD).

Bibliography

Cobban, Helena. *The Palestinian Liberation Organisation: People, Power, and Politics.* Cambridge, U.K., and New York: Cambridge University Press, 1984.

Hart, Alan. *Arafat, Terrorist or Peacemaker?* London: Sidgwick and Jackson, 1984.

Sayid, Yezid. "Death of the 'Quiet Man.'" *Middle East International* 324 (30 April 1988):9.

MOUIN RABBANI

WAZZANI, MUHAMMAD HASSAN AL-

[1910–1978]

Moroccan nationalist.

In the early 1930s, Muhammad Hassan al-Wazzani, a native of Fez, was a leader of the Comité d'Action Marocaine (CAM). He was elected secretary-general of the Bloc d'Action Nationale in October 1936, but the following year founded the Parti Démocratique Constitutionnel (PDC). Wazzani was imprisoned for nine years (1937–1946) on political charges. Periodically, he cooperated with the Istiqlal, and from 1953 to 1954, he and his followers joined the National Front. Wazzani was named minister of state without portfolio in King Hassan's 1961 coalition government. He was among those wounded in 1971 in the attempted coup against the king.

See also PARTI DÉMOCRATIQUE CONSTITUTIONNEL (PDC).

BRUCE MADDY-WEITZMAN

WEIZMAN, EZER

[1924–]

Israeli politician and soldier; president of Israel (1993–2000).

Born in Haifa, Ezer Weizman is the nephew of Chaim Weizmann, Israel's first president. In 1942 Weizman joined the Royal Air Force and served in Rhodesia, Egypt, and India. In 1946 and 1947 he studied aeronautics in Britain. From 1946 to 1948 he was a member of the prestate underground Irgun Zvaʾi Leʾumi.

Weizman was one of the founding fathers of the Israeli Air Force (IAF). Following the United Nations vote to partition Palestine, he worked in the Air Service, the IAF's predecessor, and during the 1948 war he commanded an IAF squadron. In 1950 he became IAF chief of operations, and in 1956 commander. In 1967 he became chief of the general staff.

In 1969 Weizman entered politics. He served as leader of the GAHAL Party and was minister of transportation in Levi Eshkol's Government of National Unity. He resigned from the government in 1970 and went into private business, but continued on the Herut Executive Committee. In 1977, when the Likud (formed from the merger of Herut, Gahal, and other right-of-center parties) won its first national election, Weizman was campaign manager.

Having been appointed minister of defense by the new prime minister, Menachem Begin, Weizman supervised the invasion of Lebanon in 1978; he also was a moderating influence in the Camp David peace talks in September 1978. Although he was perceived as a hawk when he joined the Begin government, Weizman increasingly argued for a more moderate approach; this led to conflicts with other members of the Likud. In May 1980 he resigned from the cabinet; six months later he voted against the government on a no-confidence vote, charging that Begin was intentionally frustrating the peace process.

In 1984 Weizman's political party, Yahad, won three seats in the Eleventh Knesset. Following the elections, Weizman was appointed minister of science in a National Unity government. In 1986 Yahad officially joined the Labor Party. In 1987 Weizman was the first member of the Labor Party in the Knesset to call for negotiations with the Palestine Liberation Organization (PLO). In 1990 he was accused of undertaking secret meetings with PLO officials (illegal at the time), but charges were never filed. He resigned his seat in the Knesset before the 1992 election, ostensibly because he was frustrated with the slow pace of peace negotiations, and in March 1993 the Labor Party nominated him as its candidate for president. He became the president of Israel on 14 May 1993 and was reelected to a second term as president in 1998.

Weizman introduced the modern presidency to Israel, breaking from the traditional model in which "nonpolitical" presidents avoided partisan politics. He was unapologetic about taking controversial positions, and on several occasions his actions caused political disruption. He resigned his presidency in July 2000. An investigation by the attorney general found that Weizman had received more than $300,000 from a French Jewish businessman between 1987 and 1993; the scandal resulted in his being the first Israeli president to be the subject of police investigation, and the first president to resign.

See also ISRAEL: POLITICAL PARTIES IN; WEIZMANN, CHAIM.

Bibliography

American-Israeli Cooperative Enterprise. "Ezer Weizman." In *Jewish Virtual Library.* Available from <http://www.us-israel.org/jsource/biography>.

State of Israel Ministry of Foreign Affairs. "Ezer Weizman." In *Personalities.* Available from <http://www.israel-mfa.gov.il/mfa>.

Weizman, Ezer. *The Battle for Peace.* New York: Bantam, 1981.

Weizman, Ezer. *On Eagles' Wings.* New York: Macmillan, 1976.

GREGORY S. MAHLER

WEIZMANN, CHAIM

[1874–1952]

Zionist leader; first president of Israel, 1948–1952.

Chaim (also Hayyim) Weizmann was born in the Jewish community of Motol, near Pinsk, in Belorussia, part of the Pale of Settlement, the region into which Jews were largely confined by the Russian empire. His father, a moderately prosperous timber merchant, educated his twelve children in the modern style. Chaim went to a Russian secondary school in Pinsk, studied in Germany, and earned his doctorate in chemistry in Geneva in 1899. From 1900 to 1904 he taught at the University of Geneva.

From his earliest youth Weizmann was a convinced Zionist. Committed to the promotion of Haskalah (secular modern Hebrew literature and culture), he encouraged a group of young Zionists, called the Democratic Fraction, to challenge the cautious policies of established Zionist leadership. Their initial project, the creation of a Jewish university in Palestine, widened the rift between secular and religious Zionists. In 1904 Weizmann took a position at the University of Manchester in England. He continued to participate in Zionist activities and, in the course of election campaigns in Manchester, met Arthur Balfour and Winston Churchill.

The outbreak of World War I dislocated the World Zionist Organization (WZO). Weizmann accepted a government appointment to supervise the synthetic production of acetone, a vital necessity for the production of mortar shells. As the war progressed, Weizmann's professional and political standing grew. Helped by C. P. Scott, editor of the *Manchester Guardian* and a sympathizer with Zionism, he met David Lloyd George, Herbert Samuel, and other Liberal ministers. Without the formal authorization of any official Zionist agency, Weizmann was instrumental in persuading British politicians to support Zionist aims. He argued that a British-sponsored Zionist entity in Palestine would enhance British strategic interests in the Middle East and secure imperial lines of communication to India. The Balfour Declaration of 2 November 1917, which promised British support for the establishment in Palestine of a Jewish National Home, was Weizmann's great diplomatic achievement and a turning point in modern Jewish history.

Chaim Weizmann (right) stands with U.S. president Harry Truman, holding the Torah, at the White House on 25 May 1948. Weizmann, serving as the president of the New Jewish State of Israel, met with the U.S. president to discuss Palestinian affairs. © BETTMANN/CORBIS. REPRODUCED BY PERMISSION.

In 1918 Weizmann headed the Zionist Commission, which visited Palestine and established a basis for cooperation with the British military administration there. He led the Zionist delegation to the Paris Peace Conference signalling the end of World War I 1919 and helped to secure confirmation of the British Mandate for Palestine. The terms of this document, which he negotiated in 1920 to 1922, established the legal basis for the Jewish National Home in Palestine. As president of the WZO from 1920 to 1931 and 1935 to 1946, Weizmann championed policies that strengthened the Jewish presence in Palestine without antagonizing the British. He called the alliance between Zionism and Britain the "Rock of Gibraltar" of his policy.

In spite of his diplomatic achievements, Weizmann was disappointed by the slow pace of Zionist development in Palestine in the 1920s. His energy was dissipated in quarrels with other Zionist leaders, in particular Louis D. Brandeis and Vladimir Ze'ev Jabotinsky, as well as in fundraising to meet the chronic financial difficulties of the WZO. Weizmann's Union of General Zionists adopted a moderate, centrist position on most issues. Although he was not a socialist, Weizmann formed an alliance with the more militant socialist-Zionists in Palestine. He promoted pioneer agricultural communities as an effective way of attracting Jews to Palestine.

Increasingly concerned with the need to broaden the basis of the Zionist movement, Weizmann pushed through a proposal in 1929 to include leaders of non-Zionist organizations in the Jewish Agency, the official liaison with British authorities in Palestine. The Palestine riots of 1929 and the subsequent wavering in British support for Zionism led Weizmann to resign in protest from his joint presidency of the WZO and the Jewish Agency, but his skillful lobbying in London induced the prime minister, J. Ramsay MacDonald, to issue a clarifying letter in 1931 that reaffirmed Britain's commitment to the Balfour Declaration. Weizmann failed, however, to be reelected president of the WZO, which was headed from 1931 to 1935 by his close colleague Nahum Sokolow.

Weizmann returned to leadership of the movement in 1935. In the following year he gave powerful evidence to the Palestine Royal Commission, headed by Earl Peel. Weizmann's testimony and his subsequent private discussions with the commission helped bring about its recommendation for the partition of Palestine. In 1937 he succeeded in persuading a majority within a reluctant Zionist Congress to accept partition in principle. But the British government, which had initially approved the concept, changed its mind and in May 1939 issued a White Paper strictly limiting Jewish immigration and land purchase in Palestine.

Britain's shift in policy away from Zionism, and the consequent growth of Zionist hostility to Britain, weakened Weizmann's authority and diminished his stature. After the outbreak of World War II, the Palestinian labor-Zionist leader David Ben-Gurion superseded him as the dominant figure in the movement. By the end of the war Weizmann's paramount influence with the British and within Zionist circles was all but spent. His stern denunciation of Jewish terrorism earned him many enemies in the movement. Weizmann's tenure as president of the WZO ended in 1946, but out of respect for him no successor was named. He remained politically active and helped to persuade U.S. president Harry S. Truman to support the establishment of Israel upon the termination of the British Mandate in 1948. Weizmann served as first president of Israel, but he was frustrated by the largely ceremonial nature of the position. He lived on the grounds of the scientific institute at Rehovot, which was later named after him, until his death in November 1952.

See also BALFOUR DECLARATION (1917); CHURCHILL, WINSTON S.; HASKALAH; JABOTINSKY, VLADIMIR ZE'EV; JEWISH AGENCY FOR PALESTINE; LLOYD GEORGE, DAVID; PEEL COMMISSION REPORT (1937); SAMUEL, HERBERT LOUIS; SOKOLOW, NAHUM; WHITE PAPERS ON PALESTINE; WORLD ZIONIST ORGANIZATION (WZO); ZIONIST COMMISSION FOR PALESTINE.

Bibliography

Berlin, Isaiah. *Personal Impressions.* Oxford, U.K.: Oxford University Press, 1982.

Reinharz, Jehuda. *Chaim Weizmann: The Making of a Zionist Leader.* New York: Oxford University Press, 1985.

Weizmann, Chaim. *Trial and Error.* London: Hamish Hamilton, 1949.

BERNARD WASSERSTEIN

WEIZMANN INSTITUTE OF SCIENCE

A center of scientific research and graduate study in Israel.

Founded in 1934, the Weizmann Institute of Science is located in Rehovot, Israel. Dr. Chaim Weizmann, a world-renowned chemist, was the first president of the institute and later became Israel's first president. He organized the institute to pursue "pure" science while also dealing with practical problems facing the country and its economy. In the 1930s, Weizmann started work on projects relating to the citrus industry, dairy farming, and medicine. The institute was formally dedicated 2 November 1949.

The Weizmann Institute has nineteen departments grouped into five faculties: biology, biochemistry, chemistry, physics, and mathematics and computer science. It also encompasses several multidisciplinary research centers and institutes. In 2002, 2,500 scientists, technicians, and students were engaged in study and research at the Weizmann Institute.

See also WEIZMANN, CHAIM.

MIRIAM SIMON

WEST BANK

Territory disputed between Israel and the Palestinians, demarcated by the Green Line to the west and the Jordan River to the east.

The West Bank refers to the territory situated west of the Jordan River that was not included as part of Israel following the establishment of the state after the Arab–Israel War of 1948. The West Bank's total area is 2,270 square miles (5,880 sq. km), smaller than the area that was originally allocated to a future Arab state by the United Nations partition resolution of November 1947. It is demarcated by the Green Line (the armistice line set by the 1949 Jordanian-Israeli talks at Rhodes) in the west and the Jordan River in the east.

The West Bank occupies a place in the international consciousness far larger than its geography would suggest. The term acquired greater political significance and only came into common usage after the 1967 Arab-Israel War, when the area was separated from the rest of the Kingdom of Jordan (the East Bank). Many Israelis—and in particular the settlers—use the biblical term "Judea and Samaria" (Hebrew, Yehuda ve Shomron) to describe this region.

King Abdullah I ibn Hussein annexed the area to Jordan in April 1950 but, with only Great Britain and Pakistan recognizing this move, the region has remained without any clear status in international

At an Israeli checkpoint, Palestinians are held back while attempting to cross from Bethlehem into Jerusalem. © SHAUL SCHWARZ/CORBIS. REPRODUCED BY PERMISSION.

MAP BY XNR PRODUCTIONS, INC. THE GALE GROUP.

law. During the 1967 Arab-Israel War, Israel captured the region, occupying it fully until 1994, and parts of it thereafter. Since 1994, parts of the West Bank have been transferred to the Palestinian Authority under the terms of the 1993 Oslo Accord. The region forms the core of a possible future sovereign Palestinian state.

According to international law, Israel has administered the West Bank since June 1967 as a belligerent occupant. On 7 June 1967 Israel's area commander for the West Bank issued a military proclamation declaring the assumption by the Israel Defense Force (IDF) area commander of all governmental, legislative, appointive, and administrative power over the region and its inhabitants. Palestinian inhabitants of the West Bank continued until 1995 to be ruled under this system of military government. Municipal governments and village councils administered local services. As the occupying power, Israel both permitted and canceled scheduled elections for local governments and appointed and dismissed elected and appointed Palestinians as officials.

The region has been subject to widespread Israeli settlement activity since 1967. The settlements are administered under a municipal system separate from that of the Palestinian towns and villages. In 1992 the Israeli settlement of Ma'ale Adumim, with a population of 15,000, became the first Israeli city in the West Bank.

On 27 June 1967 Israeli law, jurisdiction, and public administration were extended over a 28-square-mile (73 sq. km) area of the West Bank, including the 2.3 square miles (6 sq. km) that had constituted the municipal boundaries of East Jerusalem under Jordanian rule. This de facto annexation placed East Jerusalem and its Palestinian inhabitants under Israeli sovereignty. East Jerusalem is now considered by Israel an indivisible part of its capital city. Palestinians view East Jerusalem as the capital of their future state.

Other cities in the West Bank include Hebron, Bethlehem, Ramallah, Nablus, Jenin, and Jericho. The total population of the region in 2003 consisted of some 2 million Palestinians in the West Bank, with a further 180,000 Palestinians in East Jerusalem. Over 200,000 Israeli settlers lived in the West Bank and a further 170,000 Israelis in East Jerusalem.

In 1967 the Palestinian population of the region was largely agricultural, but under Israeli rule many left agriculture to find employment in the Israeli cities as menial laborers. Following the onset of the first intifada in 1987, most of the Palestinians were excluded from the Israeli labor market, giving rise to widespread unemployment and severe poverty. In early 2003 the economic situation of the population was worse than it had ever been since 1967.

In September 1993 the signing of the Oslo Accord marked the beginning of a transition to Palestinian self-rule. The West Bank was divided into Areas A, B, and C, with the Palestinian Authority taking over full administration in Area A, including all of the major urban centers, and partial control in Area B, including most of the Palestinian villages, while Israel retained full control in Area C, including most of the Jordan Valley, the areas in close proximity to the Green Line boundary, and around Jerusalem. Following the al-Aqsa Intifada, which began in September 2000, the Sharon government sent the IDF to reoccupy some Palestinian towns. The status of the West Bank was still awaiting resolution when a package of proposals, known as the "Road Map," was drawn up and sponsored by "the Quartet"—the United States, the European Union, Russia, and the United Nations—in 2003.

See also ISRAELI SETTLEMENTS; PALESTINIAN AUTHORITY.

Bibliography

Aronson, Geoffrey. *Israel, Palestinians, and the Intifada: Creating Facts in the West Bank.* London and New York: Kegan Paul, 1990.

Benvenisti, Meron. *The West Bank Data Project.* Washington, DC: American Enterprise Institute for Public Policy Research, 1984.

Benvenisti, Meron, and Khayat, Shlomo. *The West Bank and Gaza Atlas.* Boulder, CO: Westview Press, 1988.

Newman, David. "The Evolution of a Political Landscape: Geographical and Territorial Implications of Jewish Colonization in the West Bank." *Middle Eastern Studies* 21, no. 2 (1985): 192–205.

Newman, David. *Population, Settlement and Conflict: Israel and the West Bank.* Update Series in Contemporary Geographical Issues. New York: Cambridge University Press, 1991.

Shehadeh, Raja. *Occupier's Law: Israel and the West Bank.* Washington, DC: Institute for Palestine Studies, 1985.

Shehadeh, Raja, and Kuttab, Jonathan. *The West Bank and the Rule of Law.* Geneva and New York: International Commission of Jurists, 1980.

GEOFFREY ARONSON
UPDATED BY DAVID NEWMAN

WESTERNIZATION

The relatively uncritical adoption of first European and then North America cultural and sociopolitical attitudes and practices on the part of the non-European and non–North American world.

Westernization is sometimes inaccurately equated with modernization, and by extension with modernization theory, a construct very much in vogue in "development" and foreign aid circles between the 1950s and 1970s. In spite of a certain estrangement in the early modern period, and because of its geographical location, the Middle East never entirely lost the contacts that it had had with Europe in the high Middle Ages. However, the Arab, Iranian, and Turkish world did not experience the European humanist Renaissance, or any equivalent of the European Reformation, and by the sixteenth and seventeenth centuries had lost most of the preeminence in science and technology that it had enjoyed earlier.

More regular contacts between the West and the Middle East were reestablished at the end of the eighteenth century, partly as a result of Napoleon's expedition to Egypt in 1798, although the Ottoman Empire was probably as much if not more affected by the territorial losses inflicted upon it by Austro-Hungarian and Russian military superiority earlier in the century. By this time, the West was clearly "ahead" in economic, material, political, and scientific terms, so that the relationship became one of dependency, by the Middle Eastern "periphery" on the Western "center." Between 1798 and 1914, much of the region became politically subject to Britain and France (and to a lesser extent to Italy, Russia, and Spain), and the areas that were not directly colonized became part of the "informal empire," that is, part of the orbit of the capitalist West.

In the course of the nineteenth century, many of the states in the region, particularly Egypt, Qajar Iran, the Ottoman Empire, and Tunisia, underwent programs of administrative, educational, judicial, and finally constitutional reform. To some extent these programs reflected pressures from Europe and incorporated deliberate borrowings from European models, but they were also responses to widely felt local needs to achieve greater administrative efficiency and consistency, to reduce arbitrariness and despotism, and to introduce concepts of legal equality and citizenship into public life. Thus the *Hatt-i Şerif* of Gülhane of November 1839, one of the key texts of the Ottoman *Tanzimat* reforms, declares that all Ottoman subjects should have complete security for life, honor, and property, and that they shall be taxed and conscripted fairly and equitably, but also that "these imperial concessions extend to all our subjects, of whatever religion or sect they may be."

The extent and speed of the changes that took place in the nineteenth and twentieth centuries often introduced considerable confusion into the lives and thought of those involved. For example, the growing secularism of late nineteenth- and twentieth-century Europe has not been easily transposed to the Middle East, with the result that the relationship between Islam and modernity, or the West, has never been satisfactorily worked out. It has proved almost impossible for believing Muslims to apply the same critical-historical methodology to Islamic history as most Christians or Jews would apply to discussions of Christian or Jewish history. At the same time, some Western social attitudes, especially those concerned with consumerism, dress, the consumption of alcohol, and the social mixing of the sexes, have either been vigorously embraced or equally vigorously rejected by Middle Easterners. The Persian author Jalal Al-e Ahmad coined the phrase *Gharbzadagi,* or "Westoxification" to describe this awkward and often disturbing ambiguity. In general, the notion that the Middle East simply copied everything from the West is too simplistic; the reality is far more complex and nuanced.

Bibliography

Abrahamian, Ervand. *Iran between Two Revolutions.* Princeton, NJ: Princeton University Press, 1982.

Anderson, Lisa. *The State and Social Transformation in Tunisia and Libya, 1830–1980.* Princeton, NJ: Princeton University Press, 1986.

Deringil, Selim. *The Well-Protected Domain.* London: I. B. Tauris, 1998.

Hourani, Albert. *Arabic Thought in the Liberal Age, 1798–1939.* London and New York: Oxford University Press, 1962.

Hunter, F. Robert. *Egypt under the Khedives, 1805–1879.* Pittsburgh, PA: University of Pittsburgh Press, 1984.

Martin, Vanessa. *Islam and Modernism: The Iranian Revolution of 1906.* London: I. B. Tauris, 1989.

PETER SLUGLETT

WESTERN SAHARA

Former Spanish colony in northwest Africa; once called Spanish Sahara.

This area of some 102,700 square miles (266,000 sq km) is bordered by Morocco, Algeria, Mauritania, and the Atlantic Ocean. It has been the subject of a dispute involving the POLISARIO (Frente Popular para la Liberación de Saguia el-Hamra y de Río de Oro; Popular Front for the Liberation of Saguia el-Hamra and Río de Oro) independence movement, Morocco, Algeria, Mauritania, and Libya. In 2003 Western Sahara remained the last colonial territory on the African continent whose political status had not been definitively determined and legitimized by the international community. To rectify this, the United Nations has been attempting since 1986, when the Western Sahara War was still raging, to negotiate and implement a referendum among the inhabitants.

Geography and Population

The Western Sahara territory is part of the Sahara desert and consists of *hammada* (mostly barren rocky plateaus), coarse gravel, and sandy plains. It is extremely arid, receiving an average of less than 2 inches (5.1 cm) of rainfall annually, but rich in natural resources such as phosphates, minerals, and coastal fishing grounds. It is sparsely populated—Spain's 1974 census counted 73,497 persons, which was probably an underestimate; a U.S. Central Intelligence Agency publication placed the 1991 population at 196,737, including, presumably, the tens of thousands of Moroccans who have settled there since 1976. The annual growth rate was put at 2.6 percent. The capital is Laayoune (El-Aiun or al-Ayun).

The indigenous Sahrawi population is a mixture of Berber tribes (whose presence in the region dates from at least the first century B.C.E.) and thirteenth-century Arab migrants from southern Arabia. Until the twentieth century, social organization was tribal, along the lines of confederations, factions, and subfactions. Linguistically, the Hasaniyya dialect of Arabic, brought by the Arabian tribes, gradually supplanted Berber dialects. Economically and socially, the tribes were entirely nomadic. Calling themselves the "sons of the clouds," the Sahrawis roamed constantly in search of grazing land and water for their herds, traded with neighboring sedentary groups, engaged in livestock raiding from one another, and participated in the trans-Saharan caravan trade. Since the nineteenth century, the Reguibat have been the largest tribal grouping.

The nomadic way of life did not fit comfortably with European-introduced notions of fixed territorial delimitations. When coupled with twentieth-century events—prolonged droughts, fighting against French and Spanish colonialism, gradual sedentarization, economic change, and, finally, the outbreak of war following Spain's departure—probably as many Sahrawis came to live in neighboring countries (whose boundaries were themselves of twentieth-century origin) as within Western Sahara.

Political History

The political status of the area was rarely defined, since it belonged to what is known in Moroccan history as *bilad al-siba,* the lands of dissidence, as opposed to *bilad al-makhzan,* the areas of central, sultanic authority. (Ironically, the Almoravid Empire, the first dynasty to unite Morocco during the eleventh century, originated in Western Sahara and Mauritania.) Political linkages and affiliations with Moroccan sultans in the north varied, depending on the relative strength of the sultan and the various tribes, the relations between individual tribes and the government in the north, and relations among the tribes themselves.

King Muhammad VI visited Western Sahara in 2001 to reassert Moroccan authority in the region. Morocco has occupied most of the disputed territory since Mauritania relinquished its claim on the southern portion in 1979. © AP/WIDEWORLD PHOTOS. REPRODUCED BY PERMISSION.

Spain proclaimed a protectorate over part of the region in 1884. The Moroccan nationalist movement, which first emerged in the 1930s, claimed the area as part of its natural patrimony (along with Mauritania and parts of Algeria and Mali as well). The area's status was changed by Spain in 1958 from colony to overseas province. From the late 1950s, the newly emerging state of Mauritania also claimed it, partly to deflect Morocco's threat against Mauritania itself. POLISARIO's emergence in 1973 linked for the first time the notions of decolonization and independence for the territory, setting the stage for conflict. Spain agreed to relinquish the area in 1975, and it was divided between the two neighboring claimants, Mauritania and Morocco. Mauritania gave up its claim in 1979. Morocco has occupied the bulk of the territory since then.

In 1976, the POLISARIO established the Sahrawi Arab Democratic Republic (SADR) and organized a government-in-exile. During the following years, with Algeria's support, dozens of states, mainly developing and nonaligned countries, recognized the republic. After war broke out between Morocco and the POLISARIO, between 50,000 and 150,000 Sahrawi refugees fled to the Algerian Tindouf region, and as of 2003 remained there under the administration of the POLISARIO.

From the mid-1970s on, in his effort to fully integrate the Saharan provinces into Morocco, King Hassan II launched investment projects aimed at promoting the economic development of the territory and attracted settlement with special incentives. Civilian and military expenditures related to Western Sahara represented a considerable burden for Morocco's state budget, particularly from the late 1970s to the mid-1980s.

Morocco's claim over the Saharan territory helped King Hassan II build a national consensus in a period of internal instability. At the regional level, however, it has severely affected Moroccan relations with neighboring Algeria, which was a staunch supporter of the Sahrawis' right to self-determination. Consequently, the process of regional integration, which had been inaugurated with great fanfare in 1989 with the creation of the Arab Maghreb Union (UMA), remained stalled as of 2003.

Toward a Negotiated Settlement

It was not until 1991 that the parties officially accepted a UN-sponsored ceasefire, allowing it to set up MINURSO (United Nations Mission for the Referendum in Western Sahara). Besides monitoring the ceasefire, the objective of this UN mission was to prepare a list of people eligible to vote in the referendum on self-determination, which it would oversee, that would put an end to the conflict. According to the original settlement plan, the referendum should have taken place in 1992. Morocco and the POLISARIO, however, disagreed over voter eligibility criteria.

The situation remained deadlocked until 1997, when UN Secretary-General Kofi Annan, in an attempt to break the stalemate, appointed former U.S. Secretary of State James A. Baker as his personal envoy to try to settle the differences between the parties in conflict. After four rounds of negotiations, Baker managed to get an agreement between Morocco and the POLISARIO to resume the voter identification process, as well as a code of conduct to govern the parties during the referendum campaign.

However, the voter identification process still encountered serious difficulties, forcing continued postponement of the referendum and a continued presence for MINURSO in the disputed territories. When in early 2000 the UN mission finally made public the official list of voters, Morocco expressed its disagreement because a low percentage of its proposed candidates was accepted. The ensuing appeals process again delayed the referendum. The UN secretary-general subsequently concluded that the settlement plan was not a viable solution and suggested exploring other ways of ending the dispute.

Overall, the incompatibility of Morocco's discourse on territorial integrity and the POLISARIO's defense of the Sahrawi right to self-determination, coupled with geopolitical developments, had, as of 2003, left the dispute unresolved. Baker's latest UN-sponsored plan was to establish a transitional autonomous regime over a period of five years, at the end of which a referendum on self-determination would be scheduled. Participation was to include at least some of the Moroccans who had settled in the area. After considerable Algerian prodding, POLISARIO accepted the plan. Morocco, however, rejected the idea, fearing that its claim to sovereignty would be undermined.

See also BAKER, JAMES A.; POLISARIO; WESTERN SAHARA WAR.

Bibliography

Damis, John. *Conflict in Northwest Africa: The Western Sahara Dispute.* Stanford, CA: Hoover Institution Press, 1983.

Hodges, Tony. *Historical Dictionary of Western Sahara.* Metuchen, NJ: Scarecrow Press, 1982.

Hodges, Tony. *Western Sahara: The Roots of a Desert War.* Westport, CT: L. Hill, 1983.

Zoubir, Yahia H., and Volman, Daniel. *International Dimensions of the Western Sahara Conflict.* Westport, CT: Praeger, 1993.

BRUCE MADDY-WEITZMAN
UPDATED BY ANA TORRES-GARCIA

WESTERN SAHARA WAR

Conflict over control of Western Sahara, a former Spanish colony in northwest Africa.

Contention over the control of Western Sahara began on the eve of Spain's withdrawal in February 1976. The main protagonists were Morocco, which claimed the territory as an integral part of its historical patrimony, and the Algerian-backed POLISARIO independence movement. Algeria's patronage of POLISARIO was rooted in its larger geopolitical and ideological clash with Morocco. The dispute poisoned their bilateral relations and for a time held out the specter of Algerian–Moroccan fighting. Mauritania, the weakest of the states bordering Western Sahara, initially occupied part of the territory as well but was forced to disengage and then maintain a vulnerable neutrality.

Internationally, both the United States and France had strong strategic, political, and economic interests in North Africa. The conflict did not become an arena for Cold War competition because the Soviet Union adopted a low, pragmatic profile. The Organization of African Unity (OAU) was actively involved in attempting to mediate the dispute between 1976 and 1981 but then became an additional arena for it, resulting in temporary organizational paralysis. Beginning in the late 1980s, successive UN secretaries-general energetically promoted a diplomatic solution, albeit without success, as of 2003.

Outbreak of War

The parameters of the conflict took shape in the fall of 1975. The International Court of Justice issued an advisory ruling regarding the legal status of the territory that was ambiguous, but tilted away from Morocco's position. In response, Morocco's King Hassan II seized the initiative by dispatching hundreds of thousands of unarmed Moroccans in a great spectacle of nationalist and religious fervor across the Moroccan–Spanish Sahara frontier. This "Green March" catalyzed the transfer of Spanish control of the territory to Morocco and Mauritania, enshrined in the tripartite Madrid Accords of 14 November 1975. Spain's formal termination of control came on 26 February 1976. Moroccan troops immediately completed their takeover of the northern two-thirds of Western Sahara, and Mauritania took the southern third.

Meanwhile, fighting had already begun between Moroccan forces and POLISARIO units. On one occasion, Algerian forces assisting POLISARIO clashed with Moroccan troops. Concurrently, there was a large-scale civilian exodus (35–65% of the population) to camps in the Tindouf region of Algeria.

Militarily, POLISARIO's small units could not hope to block Morocco's advance. POLISARIO thus redirected its military efforts to focus on Mauritania, the weaker of its adversaries. Between 1976 and 1979, POLISARIO attacks helped to destabilize the regime of President Mokhtar Ould Daddah, who was overthrown in July 1978. After renewed pressure, the new Mauritanian military junta agreed in August 1979 to cede their portion of Western Sahara, Tiris al-Gharbia, to POLISARIO. However, the Moroccan army immediately preempted POLISARIO and took control itself.

The next few years witnessed fierce fighting. Morocco was on the defensive against highly motivated and tactically superior POLISARIO mobile units, which conducted a war of attrition against Moroccan forces within Western Sahara and southern Morocco. POLISARIO's goal was to render the economic and political cost too great for Morocco to bear. Morocco responded by tripling the size of its armed forces to approximately 150,000, stationing more than half of them in Western Sahara, and conducting large-scale sweeps of its own. It also threatened to invoke, but never implemented, the right of hot pursuit against POLISARIO sanctuaries situated in both Algeria and Mauritania.

In the fall of 1980 Morocco began constructing a system of defensive sand walls (berms) studded with fortified positions, observation points, and early warning equipment. By 1987 the sixth wall was completed, the network ran over 2,000 miles in length, and POLISARIO had been effectively closed off from 80 percent of the territory. No longer could its Land Rovers traverse the trackless territory from Algeria to the Atlantic; POLISARIO was increasingly limited to sporadic raids along the wall. Concurrently, Morocco poured hundreds of millions of dollars into the region, building schools, hospitals, and telecommunications facilities, staffed by tens of thousands of Moroccan civilians. Morocco's consolidation of its presence was made possible by generous military and civilian aid from France, the United States, and Saudi Arabia.

Whereas POLISARIO's military fortunes declined by the mid-1980s, politically it achieved a number of successes: diplomatic recognition from more than seventy countries for its government in exile, the Saharan Arab Democratic Republic (SADR), and full membership in the OAU. On the other hand, Algeria gradually reduced its aid to POLISARIO and retired to a mere supporting role for the UN secretary-general's renewed diplomatic efforts. The overall result by the late 1980s was a stalemated conflict, with neither side able to impose its will. By the beginning of 1990 POLISARIO was almost completely dependent on the UN-sponsored process. As of 2003 more than ten countries had withdrawn their earlier diplomatic recognition of SADR.

During the first years of the conflict POLISARIO had believed that time was on its side, and therefore refused to countenance any solution that fell short of full independence. King Hassan II, for his part, had staked his throne on the issue, making it the glue by which he consolidated and reinforced his political authority at home. Strategically, he never wavered in his goal to incorporate Western Sahara into his kingdom. Tactically, he showed great

A refugee camp, located at Polisario, houses 40,000 Sahrawi refugees. These people seek protection after having been displaced from their homes during the Western Sahara War. © NOGUES ALAIN/CORBIS SYGMA. REPRODUCED BY PERMISSION.

flexibility and skill. For example, in 1981, operating from a position of relative weakness, he demonstratively accepted the principle of a referendum among the Sahrawi population during an OAU summit at Nairobi and thus bought much-needed time. By 1990, while still negotiating the details of the proposed UN-sponsored referendum, Morocco was operating from a position of strength, as regional and international constellations had shifted in its favor.

UN Efforts at Diplomacy

In April 1991 the UN Security Council authorized the establishment of a combined military and civilian force, the United Nations Mission for t he Referendum in the Western Sahara (MINURSO), to organize and implement a referendum process between September 1991 and January 1992. Eligible Sahrawis were to choose between independence for the territory, necessitating immediate Moroccan withdrawal, and union with Morocco, necessitating the disbanding of POLISARIO. The 6 September 1991 cease-fire called for in the UN plan came into effect, but the timetable for full deployment of MINURSO and implementation of the referendum was repeatedly delayed. This was due to continuing disagreement over the question of voter eligibility. The Spanish census of 1974 served as the basis for the voter registration list—numbering around 74,000—prepared by UN officials. Morocco, however, insisted on major changes to include up to 150,000 persons who it said belonged to Western Saharan tribes but had migrated north during previous decades for economic or political reasons. POLISARIO wanted small-scale modifications to include more of its supporters.

The efforts of the UN secretary-general's personal representative, former U.S. secretary of state James Baker, generated renewed diplomatic momentum. In 1997 Baker hosted four separate rounds of talks between Moroccan and POLISARIO representatives, the last in Houston, Texas in September. A number of outstanding issues pertinent to the organization of the referendum were resolved, and the laborious process of identifying eligible voters was reinvigorated. However, by the beginning of 2000, hopes for holding the long-delayed referendum faded. The provisional list of eligible voters was approximately 90,000 only, while 140,000 other applicants, nearly all from the Moroccan side, had been rejected. Morocco, fearing electoral defeat, was determined to block the referendum and therefore insisted on appealing the rejections, a lengthy process that would take years. The UN Security Council, led by France and the United States, was unwilling to force Morocco to accept a UN *diktat.* Consequently, Baker floated variations of an old-new "third way" proposal that would bypass the referendum and create an autonomous Saharan entity federated to Morocco in all or part of the territory, or, alternatively, postpone the issue of sovereignty for anywhere between five and thirty years. The protagonists continued to meet periodically under Baker's good offices and even engaged in occasional confidence-building measures such as the release of prisoners of war. But as of 2003 a solution remained out of reach. SADR's political successes internationally had not paved the way to independence, marking a major departure from prevailing patterns of decolonization in developing nations. Morocco still desired de jure legitimation of its incorporation of Western Sahara, but its de facto rule there seemed to be accepted as unalterable by a large portion of the international community. The unresolved question continued to be the single most divisive issue between Morocco and Algeria.

See also BAKER, JAMES A.; DADDAH, MOKHTAR OULD; GREEN MARCH; ORGANIZATION OF AFRICAN UNITY (OAU); WESTERN SAHARA.

Bibliography

Damis, John. *Conflict in Northwest Africa: The Western Sahara Dispute.* Palo Alto, CA: Hoover Institution Press, 1983.

Damis, John. "Morocco and the Western Sahara." *Current History* 89 (April 1990): 165–168, 184–186.

Hodges, Tony. *Western Sahara: The Roots of a Desert War.* Westport, CT: Lawrence Hill, 1983.

Maddy-Weitzman, Bruce. "Conflict and Conflict Management in the Western Sahara: Is the Endgame Near?" *Middle East Journal* 45 (Autumn 1991): 596.

Maddy-Weitzman, Bruce. "Conflict Resolution in the New World Order: The UN and the Western Sahara." *Asian and African Studies* 26, no. 2 (July 1992).

Maddy-Weitzman, Bruce. "Inter-Arab Relations," and "Morocco." Annual chapters in *Middle East Contemporary Survey* (1977–2002).

Pazzanita, Anthony G., and Hodges, Tony. *Historical Dictionary of Western Sahara.* Metuchen, NJ: Scarecrow Press, 1982.

Zoubir, Yahia H., and Volman, Daniel, eds. *International Dimensions of the Western Sahara Conflict.* Westport, CT: Praeger Publishers, 1993.

BRUCE MADDY-WEITZMAN

WESTERN WALL

The extant part of the retaining wall surrounding the Temple of Solomon; a Jerusalem landmark and a holy prayer site for Jews.

The Hebrew Ha-Kotel Ha-Maʿaravi refers to the western retaining wall surrounding Jerusalem's Temple Mount. Sometimes called the "Wailing Wall," since Jews pray and cry near it, it is built of large limestones hewn for the Second Temple, which was enlarged during the reign of Herod (37–4 B.C.E.), king of Judea. It was destroyed by the Romans in 70 C.E.

Since then, the remaining wall has stood as a reminder and symbol of lost glory and the redemption to come; Jews turn toward it when they pray. By tradition, notes to heaven are placed in its cracks. During the British mandate, Jews had limited access in bringing religious appurtenances, which had to adhere to certain rules (e.g., using a curtain to separate men and women) or else were banned. During Jordanian rule, Jews' access to the wall was denied. After the reunification of Jerusalem in 1967, the area was excavated and became again a place of public prayer and assembly. The surrounding plaza is also the site of many national assemblies and civil religious events.

Bibliography

Heilman, Samuel. *A Walker in Jerusalem.* Philadelphia: Jewish Publication Society, 1995.

Meir, Ben Dov; Naor, Mordechai; and Aner, Zeev. *The Western Wall,* translated by Raphael Posner. Tel Aviv: Ministry of Defence, 1983.

SAMUEL C. HEILMAN

WESTERN WALL DISTURBANCES

A September 1928 dispute over Jewish religious rights at the Western Wall that led to political violence in August 1929.

The Western, or Wailing, Wall has been holy to Muslims because it is the western part of the Temple Mount and Haram al-Sharif where, Muslims believe, the prophet Muhammad tethered his "fabulous steed," al-Buraq, while on a nocturnal journey to heaven. The wall is also the holiest shrine of Judaism because it is the remnant of the western exterior of the Temple of Herod, built on the site of Solomon's temple. Jews placed a screen at the wall to separate men and women on 23 September 1928, the eve of the Day of Atonement. The Palestinians protested that the screen violated the status quo ante; the British authorities agreed and forcibly removed it. The incident was politicized by both communities over the next few months, a response that led to tensions and events such as a Revisionist Zionist demonstration on 15 August 1929 and a Palestinian counterdemonstration the following day.

Violence began in Jerusalem on 23 August when Palestinians attacked Jews in Meah She^carim. The rioters attacked the largely non-Zionist religious communities of Hebron and Safed, killing sixty-four and twenty-six people, respectively. Jewish rioters in turn killed Palestinians in a number of cities, but most were shot—some of them indiscriminately—by British troops and police suppressing the disturbances. The violence took the lives of 133 Jews and at least 116 Palestinians.

The Shaw Commission, which investigated the disturbances, determined that the immediate cause of the riots was the Jewish and Arab demonstrations of 15 and 16 August and that the ultimate cause was Palestinian fear that Jewish immigration and land purchase would lead to Jewish domination.

See also HARAM AL-SHARIF; SHAW COMMISSION; WESTERN WALL.

Bibliography

Mattar, Philip. "The Role of the Mufti of Jerusalem in the Political Struggle over the Western Wall, 1928–1929." *Middle Eastern Studies* 19, no. 1 (January 1983): 104–118.

Palestine Government. *A Survey of Palestine for the Information of the Anglo-American Committee of Inquiry.* 2 vols. Jerusalem, 1946. Reprint, Washington, DC: Institute for Palestine Studies, 1991.

PHILIP MATTAR

WEST GERMAN REPARATIONS AGREEMENT

Accord with Israel following World War II.

In September 1945 Chaim Weizmann, on behalf of the Jewish Agency, asked the governments that occupied Germany at the end of World War II—the United States, the Soviet Union, the United Kingdom, and France—to secure financial compensation for the Jewish people.

On 10 September 1952 the government of the Federal Republic of Germany (West Germany) agreed to pay 3.45 billion German marks ($845 million) in the form of goods to Israel, in installments between 1953 and 1966. The Conference on Jewish Material Claims against Germany was to allocate 450 million marks ($110 million). Thirty percent of the funds were allocated for the purchase of oil in the United Kingdom and 70 percent for goods bought directly by the Israeli government. These funds played an important role in the development of Israel's economy in the 1950s.

The agreement was the result of an Israeli claim for US$1 billion in compensation from West Germany (and a claim for $500 million from East Germany, which was never submitted because the powers occupying Germany refused to deal with the claim) to cover the cost of absorbing 500,000 victims of Nazi persecution, estimated at US$3,000 each.

The signing of the agreement led to serious political divisions in Israel; riots broke out on 7 to 9 January 1952 in Jerusalem outside the Knesset. The government favored a pragmatic policy toward Germany that would bring much-needed foreign currency to Israel; the opposition, led by Menachem

Begin, was ideologically opposed to reconciliation with Germany.

See also GERMANY AND THE MIDDLE EAST; WEIZMANN, CHAIM.

Bibliography

Brecher, Michael. *Decisions in Israel's Foreign Policy.* New Haven, CT: Yale University Press, 1975.

Deutschkron, Inge. *Bonn and Jerusalem: The Strange Coalition.* Philadelphia: Chilton Books, 1970.

Patinkin, Don. *The Israeli Economy in the First Decade.* Jerusalem: The Maurice Falk Project for Economic Research in Israel, 1959.

PAUL RIVLIN

WHEELUS AIR FORCE BASE

U.S. Air Force base located near Tripoli, Libya.

Wheelus was established as an American military installation in 1954. In return for base rights, the regime of King Idris received military assistance grants and the right to purchase excess stocks of U.S. weapons.

In 1964, Arab nationalism and anti-Western sentiment forced King Idris to call for a withdrawal of Britain's and America's forces. Following the overthrow of Idris in 1969, the United States completed its planned withdrawal and turned the facility over to Libya on 11 June 1970. Libyan pilots subsequently trained there under the guidance of French instructors. Since 1970, 11 June has been a national holiday in Libya.

Bibliography

Metz, Helen Chapin, ed. *Libya: A Country Study,* 4th edition. Washington, DC: U.S. Government Printing Office, 1989.

STUART J. BORSCH

WHITE FLAG LEAGUE

Sudanese nationalist movement founded in 1924.

Ali Abd al-Latif founded the White Flag League when the Sudan was governed by the Anglo-Egyptian Condominium Agreement. The group consisted of about 150 minor officials and junior officers in the Egyptian army. Representing an alliance of Sudanese and Egyptian nationalists, it advocated the union of the entire Nile valley under the Egyptian crown.

The White Flag League was largely responsible for the 1924 revolt against the British. Events reached a crisis following the assassination of Sir Lee Stack in Cairo; Britain's Field Marshal Edmund Allenby demanded the immediate withdrawal of Egyptian units from the Sudan. Refusing to obey the order to evacuate, the Egyptian and Sudanese league troops mutinied in Khartoum. When Egypt ordered its units to withdraw, however, they complied. The Sudanese were left to confront the British on their own; their defeat marked the end of the revolt and also that of the White Flag League.

See also CONDOMINIUM AGREEMENT (1899).

KENNETH S. MAYERS

WHITE PAPERS ON PALESTINE

British policy statements about mandatory Palestine issued from 1922 to 1939.

The British government, which ruled Palestine from 1917/1918 to 1948 under a League of Nations mandate, issued periodic policy statements called white papers that related to the tensions and recurring violence between the Arab and Jewish communities there.

Two precursors to the series of white papers on Palestine were the Palin Commission Report (1 July 1920) and Haycraft Report (Command 1540, 21 October 1921), which concluded that the Palestinian Arabs' feelings of "hostility to the Jews were due to political and economic causes, and connected with Jewish immigration and with their conception of Zionist policy" as leading to a Jewish state in which Palestinians would be subjugated.

Subsequently, the Churchill White Paper of June 1922 (Command 1700) attempted to placate both communities. It stated that the Jewish national home existed by right, but that the Palestinians should not be subordinated to the Jewish community. It declared that all Palestinians were equal before the law and described the Jewish national home as simply "a center in which the Jewish people as a whole may take, on grounds of religion and race, an interest and a pride." Jews would have the right to immigrate to Palestine, but their immigration must not exceed "the economic capacity of the country at the time to absorb new arrivals." Moreover, London aimed to establish full self-government in Palestine in "gradual stages" and would hold elections for a legislative council. The white paper thus reassured Arabs that they would have a political role and that Jewish im migration would be limited. Nonetheless, the Arab Executive objected to the reaffirmation of the Balfour Declaration (1917), which had supported the establishment of a Jewish home in Palestine, and rejected the legislative council as not guaranteeing majority rights. The World Zionist Organization criticized the limits on immigration and the proposed legislative council, which it wanted to postpone until the Jewish population was larger.

The colonial secretary issued the next white paper (Command 3229) on 19 November 1928, as Muslim-Jewish tension escalated over mutual claims at the Western (Wailing) Wall in Jerusalem. The white paper affirmed that no benches or screens could be brought to the wall by Jews, since they had not been allowed during Ottoman rule. Tension escalated, leading to Palestinian attacks against Jews at the wall and in several other towns in August 1929.

Four white papers issued in 1930 tried to defuse the conflict. The Shaw Commission of Inquiry (Command 3530, 30 March 1930) found that Jewish immigration and land purchases were immediate causes of "the Arab feeling of disappointment of their political and national aspirations and fear for their economic future," and that these were the underlying causes of the violence. The report declared that the government must issue clear statements safeguarding Arab rights and regulating Jewish immigration and land purchase. Another white paper (Command 3682, 27 May 1930) reaffirmed those findings, welcomed an investigation by an international commission of the conflicting claims to the Western Wall, and recommended appointing a special commission to assess the problems facing landless Palestinian peasants and the prospects for expanded agricultural cultivation.

Sir John Hope-Simpson's report, dated 30 August 1930 (Command 3686), was published simultaneously with the Passfield White Paper (Command 3692) of 21 October 1930. Hope-Simpson recommended a drastic reduction in the volume of Jewish immigration because of insufficient cultivable Palestinian land and widespread Palestinian unemployment. He criticized the Jewish National Fund, the Zionist Organization's land-purchasing agency, for forbidding Jews from reselling land to Arabs and banning Arab laborers on Jewish farms. The white paper concurred that stricter controls should be placed on Jewish immigration and land purchase, and asserted—for the first time—that the British government had obligations "of equal weight" to both communities and that it must renew the effort to establish the legislative council proposed in 1922.

The Arab Executive was pleased with these British policy recommendations because they acknowledged Arab concerns. But Chaim Weizmann, head of the Jewish Agency, resigned in protest when the Passfield White Paper was issued. London then backtracked. Zionist officials helped to draft a letter, signed by Prime Minister Ramsay MacDonald, to Weizmann on 14 February 1931 that expunged all damaging aspects of the Passfield White Paper and upheld the primacy of the government's promises to the Jewish community. Mollified, Weizmann withdrew his resignation, but the MacDonald "Black Letter," as it became known, infuriated the Arabs.

The white paper of 17 May 1939 (Command 6019) followed three years of Arab rebellion. The Peel Commission had recommended on 7 July 1937 that territorial partition between Arab and Jewish states was the only solution because Arab and Jewish aspirations were irreconcilable. Nonetheless, the Woodhead Partition Commission concluded on 9 November 1938 that partition was not feasible. The British government then convened the London Conference, which brought together the Jewish Agency, Arab governments, and Palestinian Arabs in lengthy but fruitless discussions. Afterwards, London issued a white paper that repudiated partition and proposed to create self-governing institutions over a ten-year period. Authority over the eventual independent state would be shared by its Arab and Jewish citizens. The white paper limited Jewish immigration to 75,000 over five years; subsequent immigration would require Arab approval. Jews' purchase of land would be limited in some parts of Palestine and forbidden in others.

Jewish and Palestinian Arab nationalisms were too intense and too antagonistic for this plan to succeed. The Zionists viewed the Balfour Declaration as a pledge to establish a Jewish state. When the white paper of 1939 withdrew the Peel Commission's partition proposal, their reaction was strongly hostile, particularly because the restrictions on immigration occurred just as Jews sought to flee Nazi persecution in Europe. Palestinians were relieved that London had set aside partition and would restrict Jewish immigration and land purchase, but were skeptical that London would fulfill its pledges. The MacDonald white paper remained mostly unimplemented, apart from the enforcement of immigration restrictions.

See also CHURCHILL WHITE PAPER (1922); HAYCRAFT COMMISSION (1921); MACDONALD, RAMSAY; PALIN COMMISSION REPORT (1920).

Bibliography

Government of Palestine. *A Survey of Palestine,* Vol. 1. Jerusalem: Government Printer, 1946.

Ingrams, Doreen. *Palestine Papers, 1917–1922: Seeds of Conflict.* New York: George Braziller, 1972.

Lesch, Ann Mosely. *Arab Politics in Palestine, 1917–1939: The Frustration of a Nationalist Movement.* Ithaca, NY: Cornell University Press, 1979.

Stein, Kenneth W. *The Land Question in Palestine, 1917–1939.* Chapel Hill: University of North Carolina Press, 1984.

ANN M. LESCH

WHITE REVOLUTION (1961–1963)

Program of reforms initiated by the shah of Iran in 1963.

Iran's ruler, Mohammad Reza Shah Pahlavi (r. 1941–1979), in January 1963 launched a series of reform policies that he called the White Revolution. The domestic aim was to undermine the political appeal of an influential but diffuse opposition movement by appropriating programs such as land tenure reform that it long had advocated. There also was an international objective: to win favor with Iran's principal foreign ally, the United States, which then was a major source of economic and military assistance. During the administration of John F. Kennedy (1961–1963), U.S. policy supported economic and social reforms in countries such as Iran as a means of undercutting the appeal of antiregime movements that were perceived as being allied with the Soviet Union. Thus the major element of the shah's White Revolution was a land reform program (actually begun a year earlier) that eventually would redistribute about one-half of private agricultural land to peasants holding traditional sharecropping rights (approximately one-half of all village families).

Five other programs also comprised the White Revolution at its outset. These included the nationalization of forests; sales of shares in (some) government-owned industries; plans for workers to share in profits of large factories; voting rights for women; and the formation within the army of a literacy corps of draftees assigned to villages as teachers. Later, the literacy corps model was extended to a health corps (for draftees who had college-level training in medicine) and a development corps (for college graduate draftees). By the mid-1970s the White Revolution comprised a total of eighteen programs.

The results of the White Revolution were mixed. On the positive side, about half a million peasants obtained adequate land under the land reform program to engage in profitable farming, primary schools were established in several hundred villages that previously had none, and small towns and rural areas benefited from various government development initiatives. On the negative side, perhaps the most serious deficiency of the White Revolution was the raising of popular expectations that remained unfulfilled. With respect to land reform, for example, one-half of all rural families received no land at all; among those obtaining land, about 73 percent got less than six hectares, an amount sufficient only for subsistence farming. The net result was the creation of widespread disillusionment in villages. This pattern—some benefits accruing to a minority but overall disappointment for the majority—characterized many of the White Revolution programs by the early 1970s. At the same time, a class devoted to the White Revolution became part of the required curriculum in Iran's high schools. Criticism of the White Revolution—or any other policy of the shah—came to be regarded as a punishable political offense. As expressing praise for the White Revolution came to be associated with professing loyalty to the shah's regime, and, conversely, criticizing it came to be associated with opposition, any objective assessment of its actual achievements and failings in the years leading up to the 1979 Iranian Revolution became virtually impossible.

See also IRANIAN REVOLUTION (1979); KENNEDY, JOHN FITZGERALD; LAND REFORM; PAHLAVI, MOHAMMAD REZA.

Bibliography

Hooglund, Eric. *Land and Revolution in Iran, 1960–1980.* Austin: University of Texas Press, 1982.

ERIC HOOGLUND

WIFAQ, AL-

An organization formed in Morocco to cultivate Muslim–Jewish relations.

Al-Wifaq (French, *Entente*) was an organization founded under the aegis of the Istiqlal Party in Rabat in January 1956 to promote Muslim–Jewish rapprochement on the eve of Moroccan independence. The organizers included a number of Moroccan Jewish political activists, among them Marc Sabah, a protégé of Mehdi Ben Barka, and Albert Aflalo, Sabah's nephew and an employee of the U.S. embassy.

The movement enjoyed little success because of the indifference of the Muslim elite, the apprehensions of the Jewish community at large, and increased tensions caused by events in the Middle East.

See also BEN BARKA, MEHDI; ISTIQLAL PARTY: MOROCCO.

Bibliography

Stillman, Norman A. *The Jews of Arab Lands in Modern Times.* Philadelphia: Jewish Publication Society, 1991.

NORMAN STILLMAN

WIJDAN

See ALI, WIJDAN

WILLIAM FOXWELL ALBRIGHT INSTITUTE FOR ARCHEOLOGICAL RESEARCH IN JERUSALEM

See ARCHAEOLOGY IN THE MIDDLE EAST

WILSON, ARNOLD T.

[1884–1940]

British soldier, explorer, colonial administrator, oil company executive, author, and politician.

Sir Arnold Talbot Wilson spent the first part of his career in the Persian/Arabian Gulf and Mesopotamia (now Iraq), transferring from the Indian Army to the Indian Political Department in 1909. He was British consul in various parts of southwest Persia (now Iran) between 1907 and 1914 and carried out the earliest cartographic surveys of the area (*South-West Persia: A Political Officer's Diary, 1940*). He was also a member of the commission to delineate the frontier between the Ottoman Empire and Persia in 1913–1914.

For most of the next six years, Wilson was an administrator in Mesopotamia, first as deputy chief political officer to the Indian Expeditionary Force, then as deputy civil commissioner, serving under Sir Percy Cox in both capacities. In Cox's absence in Tehran between 1918 and October 1920, Wilson was appointed acting civil commissioner in Mesopotamia and the crown's political resident in the Gulf. Comparatively young for such responsibilities, Wilson proved an energetic and tireless administrator and inspired intense loyalty in his subordinates (although not in the Civil Commission's oriental secretary, Gertrude Bell). Nevertheless, a combination of temperament and political inclinations made it difficult for him to accept that Britain could not continue to exercise direct colonial control over Iraq as part of any postwar settlement. His refusal to make any concessions to nationalist sentiment was an important, though by no means the only, factor in precipitating the Iraqi revolution against British rule in the summer and autumn of 1920.

Wilson resigned from his post in Baghdad just before Cox's return to the city in October 1920 and spent the next twelve years working for the Anglo–Persian Oil Company, first in Persia and then in London. He was elected to Parliament as a Conservative in 1933 and 1935 and chaired several parliamentary committees. He published two books about his experiences in Iraq (*Loyalties: Mesopotamia, 1914–1917* [1930] and *Mesopotamia, 1917–1920: A Clash of Loyalties* [1931]). They were colored by his anger at what he saw as the failings of British policy and perhaps as the betrayal of his own ideals.

See also ANGLO–IRANIAN OIL COMPANY; BELL, GERTRUDE; COX, PERCY.

Bibliography

Marlowe, John. *Late Victorian: The Life of Sir Arnold Talbot Wilson.* London: Cresset, 1967.

PETER SLUGLETT

WILSON, WOODROW
[1856–1924]

U.S. president, 1913–1921.

Woodrow Wilson led the United States into World War I with his Fourteen Points as war aims. Among them was the promise of self-determination for the peoples of enemy states, including the Ottoman Empire. Self-determination reflected American idealism, but it conflicted with the imperial ambitions of Britain and France, the nation's wartime allies.

At the Paris Peace Conference held in 1919, the Hashimite leaders of Arabia sought a sovereign Arab state (including Palestine). This had been promised to them by the British in return for their revolt against the Turks. This state was supported by U.S. Protestant missionaries who had been resident for decades in the Ottoman territories. Also, the leaders of the Zionist movement sought access to Palestine for Jewish immigration based on a promise (the Balfour Declaration) made to them by the British in return for wartime support.

President Wilson led the U.S. delegation to the Paris Peace Conference. There he came under pressure from both Zionists and those supporting an Arab state. One result of this situation was the creation of the King-Crane Commission, the mission of which was to determine the popular will of the people of "Greater Syria." At the same time the president came under pressure to modify his support for self-determination so as to accommodate the imperial designs of his allies. The compromise realized here was a "mandate system" under the auspices of the League of Nations. It was Wilson's belief in the "backward" nature of non-European populations that allowed him to accept the mandate system. The King-Crane Commission report was shelved, leaving imperialism triumphant in the guise of mandates.

Bibliography

Heckscher, August. *Woodrow Wilson.* New York: Scribner, 1991.

Schulte Nordholt, Jan Willem. *Woodrow Wilson: A Life for World Peace,* translated by Herbert H. Rowen. Berkeley: University of California Press, 1991.

ZACHARY KARABELL
UPDATED BY LAWRENCE DAVIDSON

WINGATE, CHARLES ORDE
[1903–1944]

British military officer who supported Zionism.

A Scot fluent in Arabic, Charles Orde Wingate was sent to Palestine in 1936 as an intelligence officer in the British army, where he translated his Protestant millenarian sentiments into support for Zionism. Ordered by the commander of British forces in Palestine, General Sir Archibald Wavell, to train mixed British and Zionist units in night fighting and guerrilla tactics during the Arab revolt (1936–1939), Wingate implemented the doctrine of "active defense." His "special night squads" were organized to protect the Iraq Petroleum Company pipeline. They inflicted casualties on the rebels and attacked guerrilla villages in Syria and Lebanon.

Heroic to the Zionists and ruthless to the Arabs, Wingate's actions appeared to cement a British–Zionist alliance. Wingate was removed from Palestine in 1939 by the British, who considered his Zionist sympathies an embarrassment. During World War II he served as a brigadier in Ethiopia and Burma. He died in an airplane crash in Burma.

See also IRAQ PETROLEUM COMPANY (IPC); PALESTINE ARAB REVOLT (1936–1939); WAVELL, ARCHIBALD PERCIVAL.

Bibliography

Bierman, John, and Smith, Colin. *Fire in the Night: Wingate of Burma, Ethiopia, and Zion.* New York: Random House, 2000.

Mead, Peter. *Orde Wingate and the Historians.* Braunton, U.K.: Merlin, 1987.

Rossetto, Arthur L. *Major General Orde Charles Wingate and the Development of Long-Range Penetration.* Lexington, VA: Military Affairs, 1982.

Royle, Trevor. *Orde Wingate: Irregular Soldier.* London: Weidenfeld and Nicolson, 1995.

Tulloch, Derek. *Wingate in Peace and War.* London: Macdonald and Co., 1972.

REEVA S. SIMON

WINGATE, REGINALD
[1861–1953]

Sirdar (commander in chief) and governor-general of the Sudan, 1899–1916; high commissioner in Egypt, 1916–1919.

Sir Francis Reginald Wingate was educated at the Royal Military Academy, Woolwich, England, and attained the rank of general in the British army. He served in India and participated as director of military intelligence in the campaign led by Lord Kitchener to conquer the Sudan (1896–1898).

During his seventeen-year term as governor-general of the Sudan, Wingate, who spoke Arabic and had detailed knowledge of the country, earned a reputation for competence and hard work. He was an ardent supporter of the Arab Revolt (1916) during World War I and consistently urged additional British monetary and military aid for the effort. In 1916, he was appointed high commissioner in Egypt.

With his extensive knowledge of the country, Wingate recognized the rise of Egyptian nationalism, caused in part by increased British military presence and controls during the war. Even before it ended, he advised the British Foreign Office and the British government to make some conciliatory gestures toward Egyptian nationalist feelings. After meeting with the nationalist delegation (Arabic, *wafd*), in November 1918, Wingate recommended that Wafd members be allowed to travel to London for direct negotiations; but Wingate lacked sufficient influence, and his recommendations were curtly rebuffed.

In the face of mounting violence and nationalist demonstrations in Egypt, Wingate was hastily removed from office while vacationing in Britain in 1919; he was replaced by the popular war hero Field Marshal Viscount Edmund Allenby.

See also ALLENBY, EDMUND HENRY; ARAB REVOLT (1916); KITCHENER, HORATIO HERBERT; WAFD.

Bibliography

Wingate, Ronald. *Wingate of the Sudan: The Life and Times of General Sir Reginald Wingate, Maker of the Anglo–Egyptian Sudan.* London: Murray, 1955.

JANICE J. TERRY

WISE, STEPHEN S.
[1874–1949]

U.S. Jewish leader.

Stephen S. Wise was born in Hungary and was brought to the United States as a small child. He received rabbinical training from Adolf Jellinek in Vienna and earned a doctorate at Columbia University. At the turn of the century, Wise was among a handful of card-carrying Zionists in the United States. In 1898 he served as a delegate to the Second Zionist Congress and subsequently helped to establish the Federation of American Zionists (later renamed the Zionist Organization of America [ZOA]). In 1907 Wise founded the Free Synagogue in New York City. Thereafter, his political activity brought him into close contact with U.S. Progressives and the left wing of the Democratic party. He developed close ties to Woodrow Wilson, Louis D. Brandeis, Felix Frankfurter, and Franklin D. Roosevelt.

Wise's public activity included the cofounding of the National Association for the Advancement of Colored People (1909); the establishment of the American Jewish Congress during World War I; securing U.S. support for the Balfour Declaration of 1917; serving as a Zionist spokesman at the Paris Peace Conference after World War I; cofounding the American Civil Liberties Union (1920); leading the ZOA, the United Palestine Appeal, and the American Zionist Emergency Council during the 1930s and 1940s; founding the Jewish Institute of Religion (1922); creating the U.S. anti-Nazi boycott of the 1930s and the World Jewish Congress (1936); and co-founding the American Jewish Conference (1943).

During World War II, Wise emerged as a champion of Roosevelt's wartime strategy. At Roosevelt's request, he even suppressed initial reports of the Holocaust. Wise's stance conflicted with Rabbi Abba Hillel Silver, a right-wing U.S. Jewish leader who advocated Zionist militancy and immediate U.S. intervention on behalf of European Jewry. In 1943 the Wise-Silver clash reached a climax, and Silver displaced Wise as American Zionism's undisputed leader.

See also SILVER, ABBA HILLEL.

MARK RAIDER

WIZO

See WOMEN'S INTERNATIONAL ZIONIST ORGANIZATION

WOLFF, HENRY DRUMMOND
[1830–1908]

British mission head who gained economic concessions from Iran.

Sir Henry Drummond Wolff was the head of a special British mission sent to Iran (then Persia) after 1881, when, under a conservative government, the British started actively to support concessions. He was instrumental in obtaining important economic and financial concessions from the Persian government and was sent to Persia in 1888 as British envoy. As a result of Wolff's pressure, the Qajar dynasty monarch, Naser al-Din Shah, opened Persia's only navigable river, the Karun, to international navigation. Wolff, with Baron Julius de Reuter's son, was instrumental in settling claims to the Reuter Concession obtained in 1872. One concession granted by Persia was the right to establish a national bank, the Imperial Bank of Persia, which gave the concessionaires exclusive rights to issue bank notes and other negotiable papers. In 1890, Wolff obtained from the shah for British financiers a monopoly over the production, sale, and export of Iranian tobacco. This concession triggered one of the first successful mass demonstrations in the modern history of Iran, the Tobacco Revolt, and so the concession was abandoned.

See also TOBACCO REVOLT.

Bibliography

Keddie, Nikki. *Roots of Revolution: An Interpretive History of Modern Iran.* New Haven, CT: Yale University Press, 1981.

PARVANEH POURSHARIATI

WOMEN AND FAMILY AFFAIRS CENTER

An independent Palestinian women's organization.

In 1988, empowered by the Palestinian women's movement during the first Intifada, the Women's Affairs Center was established at the initiative of the novelist Sahar Khalifa. Other independent women's organizations followed, staying outside the control of Palestinian political parties. The center's founding committee included Rita Giacaman, Rema Hammami, Islah Jad, Sahar Khalifa, and Amal Nashashibi. The board include some prominent educated women, mainly from Nablus city. The center was established as a women's research and training organization. In 1991, it opened a branch under the same name in Gaza City. In 1994, the steering committee formally separated the two centers and the Nablus center became the Women and Family Affairs Center. Another branch was opened in Amman (Jordan) but did not last long. The center produced a few issues of a journal, *Women's Affairs,* before it ceased publication. The center works to promote women's rights and gender equality within Palestinian society, and its main mandate is in the city of Nablus. It has no relations with Israelis. It focuses on training and advocacy to promote women's rights. It is difficult to measure the impact of its efforts due to the political instability of the times. The center coordinates some of its activities with other nongovernmental organizations in Nablus, but it has no formal links with the Palestinian Authority and depends on external funding.

See also GAZA STRIP; GENDER: GENDER AND EDUCATION; INTIFADA (1987–1991); OSLO ACCORD (1993); PALESTINE; PALESTINIAN AUTHORITY; WEST BANK.

ISLAH JAD

WOMEN IN BLACK

Israeli movement in support of the first Intifada (1987–1991), promoting a network of women's peace activities in Israel, the Occupied Territories, and the world.

In 1988, a small group of Israeli women responded to the outbreak of the first Palestinian Intifada by protesting in the streets of cities and towns across the country, dressed in black as a sign of mourning. Their regular vigils have inspired protest groups across the Western world. The Women in Black have worked together with other feminist and nonfeminist peace groups in protests against all aspects of the military occupation of the West Bank and Gaza and have given their name and support to groups of women opposed to engagement in other military conflicts as well. In Israel, they are opposed by Women in Green and other right-wing settler movements riled by the apparent success of the women's peace movements in capturing public attention.

The first Jewish Women in Black movement was organized against the oppression of Soviet Jews in the 1970s; it was, in turn, inspired by South African women who stood silently, wearing black sashes, in protest against apartheid. Both the Jewish and the South African groups, often made up of middle aged and middle-class women, successfully demonstrated the power of activism by women's groups standing against the compromise and complacency of the largely male establishments in South Africa and the Jewish community.

Israeli women's groups have drafted a series of peace platforms, formed committees to monitor the treatment of civilians, and engaged from the outset—at first illegally—in dialogues with Palestinian women. The Israeli Women in Black have sought to maintain the spontaneous nature of their demonstrations, aiming to draw together women of different political beliefs and from different organizations. Their efforts were reinvigorated in the late 1990s by the success of the Four Mothers movement in shifting public opinion in favor of Israel's withdrawal from South Lebanon. The Four Mothers movement was founded by four Israeli mothers who had sons serving in Lebanon in 1997, after a helicopter crash in that country that left seventy-three soldiers dead.

See also GAZA STRIP; INTIFADA (1987–1991); WEST BANK.

Bibliography

Women in Black. Available from <http://www.womeninblack.net>.

GEORGE R. WILKES

WOMEN'S AFFAIRS CENTER (GAZA)

A Palestinian women's organization in Gaza.

The Women's Affairs Center is a Palestinian nongovernmental research and training center that promotes women's rights and gender equality within Palestinian society. It was established in Gaza City in August 1991; the founding committee included (alphabetically) Rita Giacaman, Rema Hammami, Sahar Khalifa, Islah Jad, I'timad Muhanna and Amal Nashashibi. In 1994, the center separated from a similar organization in Nablus and a change in the board followed to include prominent educated men and women, mainly from Gaza. In 1995, another change in board membership took place. The center aims at empowering women in Gaza through advocacy and research, and through training women in professional and technical skills in research, media, and management. Its goal is gender equity. It is difficult to assess its impact on women, but the center has managed to train some women in research and media skills. The center has no formal links with the Palestinian Authority and has wide networks of relations with other women's organizations in Gaza, the West Bank, and the Arab world; it has no relations with Israelis. The center depends on external nongovernmental funding and since the second Intifada, in September 2000, has faced financial difficulties.

See also AQSA INTIFADA, AL-; GAZA STRIP; GENDER: GENDER AND EDUCATION; INTIFADA (1987–1991); PALESTINE; WEST BANK.

ISLAH JAD

WOMEN'S CENTRE FOR LEGAL AID AND COUNSELING

Women's organization based in Jerusalem.

The Women's Centre for Legal Aid and Counseling was established in 1991, during the first Intifada, as a unit of the Women's Action Committee, a branch of the Democratic Front for the Liberation of Palestine, at the initiative of Siham Barghouthi, Amal al-Jua'aba, and Zahira Kamal. A board was formed, including Lamis Alami, Siham Barghouthi, Rawda el-Basir, Arham el-Damen, Samar Hawash, Zahira Kamal, Rana Nashashibi, Mukarram Qassrawi, and Lamia Quttineh. After a split with the

Popular Front, the center became an independent organization in 1992. It is based in Jerusalem, with one branch in the Old City of Jerusalem and one in Khalil/Hebron. It works to advance the legal and social status of Palestinian women through programs advocating women's legal rights, and through research and advocacy based on the international principles of human rights. The center's activities encourage the Palestinian Authority to adopt the Convention for the Elimination of All Forms of Discrimination against Women. The center has a wide network of relations with local, regional, and international organizations, including Israeli organizations, as well as with the Palestinian Authority.

See also GENDER: GENDER AND LAW; INTIFADA (1987–1991); POPULAR FRONT; WOMEN AND FAMILY AFFAIRS CENTER; WOMEN'S AFFAIRS CENTER (GAZA).

Bibliography

Women's Centre for Legal Aid and Counseling (WCLAC). *Annual Report,* 1999–2001.

ISLAH JAD

WOMEN'S FORUM FOR RESEARCH AND TRAINING (YEMEN)

A women's forum in Yemen.

The Women's Forum for Research and Training (Multaqa al-mar'a lil-dirasat, wa al-Tadrib, WFRT) was established in 2000 to mobilize women's and human-rights organizations to work together for empowering women. The forum's main objective is to advance the rule of law regarding women's issues and rights and to build consensus in society at large on the urgency of incorporating gender dimensions in all fields of development and law. The forum's work recognizes that even though Yemeni legislation on human rights is among the best in the Arab world, women's rights are regularly violated and women lack knowledge of their rights. To accomplish its goals, the forum works on several levels, including arranging workshops for state officials, introducing human-rights issues to key figures in nongovernmental organizations and development agencies, and arranging training courses for grassroots activists. The forum has its office in Ta'iz, and its staff includes very young people. The initiator and manager of WFRT, Su'ad al-Qadasr is one of the most prominent Yemeni human rights activists. Prior to founding WFRT she was the chairperson of the Yemeni Women's Union Ta'iz branch and a leading figure in Human Rights Information and Training Centre. WFRT publications include research and surveys (*Street Children Phenomenon in Yemen,* 2003), the periodical *Multaqa* (Forum), and the leaflet "Su'al wa jawab" (Questions and answers). WFRT is located on the Internet at <www.geocities.com/taralws/wfrt.htm>.

SUSANNE DAHLGREN

WOMEN'S INTERNATIONAL ZIONIST ORGANIZATION

Organization founded to address the needs of women immigrants in Palestine.

Established in London on 11 July 1920 by the Federation of Women Zionists of the United Kingdom, the Women's International Zionist Organization (WIZO) focused on agricultural training for women immigrants in Palestine, and on these women's role as citizens and as primary providers of education to children. The founders and leaders of the movement were Vera Weizmann, Edith Eder, Romana Goodman, Henrietta Irwell, and Rebecca Sieff, who served as the first president of WIZO until her death in 1966.

Initially headquartered in London, the organization established a network of federations throughout the world (except in the United States and the USSR). A member of both the World Zionist Organization and the World Jewish Congress, WIZO is now based in Israel, where it supports numerous institutions, such as baby homes for children of preschool age, youth clubs, summer camps and kindergartens for schoolchildren, secondary and agricultural schools, and community centers in border settlements and development towns.

See also WORLD ZIONIST ORGANIZATION (WZO).

Bibliography

Marder, Lucy, and Avner, Yossi. *Speaking for Women.* Tel Aviv, 1990.

SHIMON AVISH

WOMEN'S LIBRARY AND INFORMATION CENTER (ISTANBUL)

Istanbul foundation established for the preservation of the history of women.

The Women's Library and Information Center (Kadin Eserleri Kütüphanesi ve Bilgi Merkezi) was established in Istanbul as a foundation by Asli Davaz Mardin, Sirin Tekeli, Jale Baysal, Füsun Akatli, and Füsun Ertug-Yaras. It opened on 14 April 1990 in a historic building owned by the Istanbul municipality and overlooking the Golden Horn. The foundation declaration stated that the purpose of the library was "to gather knowledge about the history of women, to present this information in an organized way to those who do research today, and to preserve the written documents of the past and of today for future generations." A general board administers the library and an executive board, elected annually, directs its activities. The library has a collection of more than 8,500 books written by or about women; Ottoman, Turkish, and some foreign-language periodicals on women; more than 1,300 articles in women's studies; a collection of newspaper clippings since 1990; a collection of ephemera; a special collection to preserve the personal documents of women, including those presented by Hasene Ilgaz, Müfide Ilhan, and Süreyya Agaoglu; a collection on women artists and their works; a collection on women authors; an audio-visual collection; and an oral-history collection.

The library operates as a center of feminist activism, organizing women's exhibitions and special events, and cultivating international links to extend its feminist networks. It has helped to legitimize and institutionalize second-wave feminism in Turkey. In 1991 the library organized the First International Symposium of Women's Libraries in Istanbul. It has generated projects on women's oral history and women's publications.

The library is financed by donations made by its members and by the sale of its publications and annual diaries. It has cultivated amicable relations with different political parties that came to power in the Istanbul municipality, including the pro-Islamists, and has received some support on certain projects from the Turkish government and the Global Fund for Women.

See also GENDER: GENDER AND EDUCATION; TEKELI, SIRIN; TURKEY.

Bibliography

Davaz-Mardin, Asli. "The Women's Library in Istanbul." *Gender and History* 12 (2000): 448–466.

YESIM ARAT

WOMEN'S ORGANIZATION OF IRAN (WOI)

Iranian women's activist organization.

The Women's Organization of Iran (WOI) emerged in 1966, reflecting decades of Iranian women's activism. During the 1950s, as their awareness of progress elsewhere grew, Iranian women formed numerous organizations and sought the right to vote. Princess Ashraf Pahlavi, the shah's sister, bolstered these organizations, forming a committee in 1959 to prepare the articles of association for the High Council of Women's Organizations in Iran. An umbrella group, the high council coordinated the election of a 5,000-member assembly of women representatives approving the WOI's charter on 19 November 1966 in Tehran. A nonprofit institution run mostly by volunteers, the WOI had local branches receiving charitable donations and benefited from national fundraising. By 1975, the International Year of the Woman, the WOI had established 349 branches, 120 women's centers, and a center for research. The centers provided literacy classes and vocational training, family-planning information, and legal advice. The WOI supported the international feminist movement, formulating a national plan of action that resembled the United Nations General Assembly's World Plan of Action. Although anxious to avoid conflict with the religious authorities, the WOI with its successes nevertheless alienated senior clerics. Ironically, the political awareness gained through WOI projects enabled increased and effective women's participation in the Islamic revolution, which ultimately undid the WOI.

See also IRANIAN REVOLUTION (1979); PAHLAVI, MOHAMMAD REZA.

Bibliography

Afary, Janet. *The Iranian Constitutional Revolution, 1906–1911: Grassroots Democracy, Social Democracy, and the Origins of Feminism.* New York: Columbia University Press, 1996.

Afkhami, Mahnaz. "The Women's Organization of Iran: Evolutionary Politics and Revolutionary Change." 2003.

Najmabadi, Afsaneh. "Hazards of Modernity and Morality: Women, State and Ideology in Contemporary Iran." In *Women, Islam, and the State,* edited by Deniz Kandiyoti. Philadelphia: Temple University Press; London: Macmillan, 1991.

Nashat, Guity, ed. *Women and Revolution in Iran.* Boulder, CO: Westview Press, 1983.

Paidar, Parvin. *Women and the Political Process in Twentieth-Century Iran.* New York and Cambridge, U.K.: Cambridge University Press, 1995.

HALEH VAZIRI

WOMEN'S PEOPLE'S PARTY (1923)

The first and the only women's party founded in the Republic of Turkey.

The Kadinlar Halk Firkasi (Women's People's Party) was founded on 16 June 1923 in Istanbul. Among its founders were the leading feminists of the time, including Nezihe Muhittin (president), Nimet Remide (vice president), Şüküfe Nihal (general secretary), and Latife Bekir (party spokesperson). The Istanbul Provincial Administration rejected their petition for authorization, stipulating that women did not have the right to vote and hence could not establish a political party. The real reason for the rejection, however, was preparation for the Kemalist Republican People's Party (RPP), which was then being formed and which ruled the country single handedly until 1950.

Undiscouraged, the women established the Kadinlar Birliği (Women's Federation) on 7 February 1924, with the same leadership and objectives but a less political name, which did not intimidate the Kemalists. The federation intended to ameliorate rural women's conditions and, more importantly, to achieve woman suffrage. The latter was very much contingent upon the Kemalist cadre's wishes and did not happen until the eve of the twelfth congress of the International Women's Union, which was held in 1935 in Istanbul. Ten days after the congress, the federation dissolved itself under strong pressure from the RPP that it had fulfilled its primary task.

See also GENDER: GENDER AND LAW; GENDER: GENDER AND POLITICS; TURKEY.

Bibliography

Arat, Yeşim. "From Emancipation to Liberation: The Changing Role of Women in Turkey's Public Realm." *Journal of International Affairs* 54, no. 1 (2000): 107–125.

BURÇAK KESKIN-KOZAT

WOMEN'S RELIGIOUS RITUALS

In addition to observing their formal religious duties, women of various religious communities have developed their own rituals to meet their spiritual needs and personal aspirations.

Traditionally, women in all the major religious communities in the Middle East and North Africa have had less access to religious learning than have their male counterparts; they have been excluded from the formal clerical hierarchy, and their active role in official and public communal rituals has been, to different degrees, limited. Muslim women's access to the mosque has been restricted, as has that of Jewish women to the synagogue, and these restrictions are sometimes more the result of tradition than of religious law. At the same time, women have created their own rituals, which allow their active involvement in gender-segregated settings, often in the private sphere.

Rituals at Home and outside the Home

One woman-dominated activity is visiting neighborhood shrines and other holy sites—a practice common among Muslims, Jews, Christians, and Zoroastrians. Women use these occasions to pray, ask intercession, and find support from other pilgrims. Some of these shrines are dedicated to female holy figures, such as Rachel's tomb in Bethlehem and the shrine of Zaynab in Damascus; a number are guarded by women and visited solely by female believers. In North Africa, the veneration of *marabouts,* holy men and women, living and deceased, plays a central role. Their graves and their descendants are frequented by women for blessings *(baraka)* and guidance.

Many women's rituals take place at home, transforming domestic spaces into places of worship. In addition to individual prayers of petition *(duʿa),* Muslim women sponsor collective rituals, like prayer meetings of gratitude or entreaty, and gatherings to

Women in chadors pass in front of a mosque in Iraq. As with other monotheistic religious faith communities in the Middle East, Muslim women—whose access to mosques have been restricted—have developed a variety of rituals, performed in the home and elsewhere. © PETER TURNLEY/CORBIS. REPRODUCED BY PERMISSION.

read the Qur'an, chiefly during the month of Ramadan. The Prophet's birthday is celebrated with the chanting of poems about his life. Shi'a women especially partake in a great variety of religious rituals. The days of birth and martyrdom of the imams, as well as significant dates in the lives of some of their female relatives, are commemorated with either festive gatherings or recitals about their sufferings and ritual crying. Women from Iran and Central Asia also prepare and offer a *sofreh,* a ritual meal dedicated to a holy figure.

For Christian women in the Arab world, the month of May is a special time of religious devotion, processions, prayer services, and reflection. This is the month of the Virgin Mary, a period during which women ask special favors, make pledges *(nadhr),* and attend daily prayer gatherings and special masses in church. May is also a time of religious processions to shrines to Mary, in which members of other faith communities frequently participate, as in the procession to the church at Harissa in Jounieh, Lebanon.

Food and cooking play a central role in women's ritual activities throughout the Middle East. In addition to the religious obligation of lighting the Sabbath candles, Orthodox Jewish women are responsible for kosher cooking. Zoroastrian women prepare the food offerings for the religious ceremonies, and during Ramadan Muslim women prepare special meals for their families and guests to share after sunset to break the daily fast. A common ritual is the distribution of votive dishes.

Vows, Cults, and Holy Women

Vows are an integral part of women's religious rituals. In personal or collective prayers, they ask God for favors, or petition a saint to intercede with God on their behalf, promising to fulfill some kind of return service—for example to help the poor. The assistance of supernatural forces is sought for problems over which women have little control: illness, infertility, the lost love of a husband, financial problems, or worries about children. In times of crisis women also contact local ritual experts—religious authorities, holy women and men, healers, midwives—for amulets, divination, and cures. Many rituals concern the individual life cycle. Prayers, recitations from the holy book, and amulets serve to ensure a quick conception, a safe pregnancy, or an easy delivery, or to ward off evil influences harmful to the mother and newborn child or to a newly married couple. Muslim women gather at weddings, chanting religious songs. They gather for the formal naming of a child and for a circumcision. They perform the lament for deceased family members at home and recite prayers for their souls.

Particularly in North Africa, Egypt, Sudan, the countries around the Persian Gulf, and Yemen, Muslim women also take part in spirit possession and healing cults, most commonly referred to as *zar.* Ritual masters, who are often women, try by means of trance and dance to pacify the spirits that have afflicted the women who consult them. They are sometimes also consulted by Christian women. By claiming to be possessed by a malevolent spirit, women can overstep the boundaries of acceptable behavior and demand, in the name of the spirit, concessions from their husbands.

Women may also become members of Sufi orders. Especially in North Africa, Turkey, and Pakistan the *zikr* (remembrance of God) includes ecstatic chanting, dancing, and drumming. These rituals are sometimes connected to a healing cult.

In addition to their religious importance, rituals serve to gain merit for a woman in the next world and to secure the well-being of women and their family members—living as well as deceased. The women sometimes perform the ritual in the name of a male relative or a child, acting as representatives to the supernatural. In all Middle Eastern religious communities, women have played a central role as preservers and transmitters of faith. Further, at collective rituals, women can establish emotional and supportive bonds with others not family members. For traditional women, these rituals often represent the only socially accepted activity outside the house. Excluded from the male religious hierarchy, women find in rituals the possibility of acting as religious experts, thereby gaining esteem, income, and mobility.

Women have developed a great variety of rituals, which differ from country to country and change with historical circumstances. Some are performed by women as well as men, others exclude men. Urban women generally have developed a richer religious life than village and nomad women. Popular rituals are the sphere in which the boundaries between the different religions are most fluid. Zoroastrian women display *sofreh* like Shiʿa women, and in Egypt and Lebanon Muslim women may in times of crisis visit a church or consult a priest. Many women's religious rituals have an ambiguous status and are dismissed by the religious orthodoxy. In Saudi Arabia under the Wahhabis, most Muslim women's rituals have been forbidden. In Soviet Central Asia, women's domestic rituals played an important role in the survival of religious beliefs. With increasing literacy and access to religious learning, women have begun to renegotiate their role within the religious tradition and their activities have become more visible. At the same time Muslim women's less orthodox traditional rituals have become a point of attack by Islamic revivalists, male as well as female, who regard them as superstition.

See also GENDER: GENDER AND EDUCATION; MARABOUT; MUWAHHIDUN; SUFISM AND THE SUFI ORDERS.

Bibliography

Beck, Lois. "The Religious Lives of Muslim Women." In *Women in Contemporary Muslim Societies,* edited by Jane Smith. Lewisburg, PA: Bucknell University Press; London: Associated University Press, 1980.

Doumato, Eleanor Abdella. *Getting God's Ear: Women, Islam, and Healing in Saudi Arabia and the Gulf.* New York: Columbia University Press, 2000.

Fernea, R. and Fernea, E. "Variations in Religious Observances among Islamic Women." In *Women in the Muslim World,* edited by Lois Beck and Nikki Keddie. Cambridge, MA: Harvard University Press, 1978.

Hegland, Mary E. "Gender and Religion in the Middle East and South Asia: Women's Voices Rising." In *Social History of Women and Gender in the Modern Middle East,* edited by Margaret L. Meriwether and Judith E. Tucker. Boulder, CO: Westview Press, 1999.

Mazumdar, Shampa, and Mazumdar, Sanjoy. "Ritual Lives of Muslim Women: Agency in Everyday Life." *Journal of Ritual Studies* 13, no. 2 (1999): 58–70

Sered, Susan Starr. *Women as Ritual Experts: The Religious Lives of Elderly Jewish Women in Jerusalem.* New York and Oxford, U.K.: Oxford University Press, 1992

SABINE KALINOCK

WOMEN'S RENAISSANCE CLUB

The first women's association in Iraq.

The Women's Renaissance Club was established on 24 November 1923, mainly by wives of leading politicians and women from socially prominent families. Its aim was to promote women's welfare by emphasizing charity, education, and the arts. The club worked to increase the number of schools for girls, raise women's educational levels through literacy and sewing classes, and provide for the education and care for orphans. It worked to "combat unacceptable customs that are rejected by all God's precepts, and social customs that violate honor and goodness, and hinder the economy of the country."

The club was essentially a charitable organization to assist less fortunate women. Although it did not fight for the removal of the veil, it considered the veil an issue that could be resolved by social education. This incurred the wrath of conservatives, particularly Muslim conservatives, who felt that the club would corrupt family morals and bring Westernization. Although it was no more than a social club for upper-class women, its advocacy of education for girls was enough that it was forced to close in 1925 under pressure from conservatives.

See also ARAB NATIONALISM; ART; GENDER: GENDER AND EDUCATION; GENDER: GENDER AND LAW; GENDER: GENDER AND POLITICS.

JACQUELINE ISMAEL

WOMEN'S SERVICES

Services available to women in Turkey.

The Turkish parliament's confirmation of the United Nations convention against discrimination based on sex in October 1980 formed the legal basis for the government's providing services to women. It started with the establishment of a Women's Unit within the State Planning Organization in 1985. It was followed by the creation of the General Directorate of Women's Affairs (Kadının Statüsü ve Sorunları Genel Müdürlüğü) within the Ministry of Labor and Social Security in 1990. This directorate was to collect data concerning the status of women in Turkey and their major problems. It was transferred in 1991 to the office of the prime minister.

In 1993, an independent undersecretary for women's affairs and social services (Başbakanlik Kadin ve Sosyal Hizmetler Müsteşarlığı) was created within the office of the prime minister, and the general directorate came under the supervision of this undersecretary. In 1991, the directorate had a staff of five; in 1994, the staff had grown to forty-two. The provincial network has not yet been established. In 1994, its budget was about 0.002 percent of the national budget.

Special women's units have been set up in the ministries of Health, Labor and Social Security, and National Education. In 1993 the State Statistical Institute created a data bank for women's issues.

Several Turkish universities have established women's studies centers that offer graduate courses and M.A. degrees:

1. Istanbul University Women's Studies Center (Istanbul Üniversitesi Kadin Sorunları Araştırma ve Uygulama Merkezi), in 1990
2. Marmara University Women's Labor Force and Employment Center (Marmara Üniversitesi Kadın İşgücü İstihdamı Araştırma ve Uygulama Merkezi), in 1990
3. Ankara University Women's Studies Center (Ankara Üniversitesi Kadın Sorunları Araştırma ve Uygulama Merkezi), in 1993
4. The Middle East Technical University Women's Studies Graduate Program (ODTÜ Kadın Çalışmaları Yüksek Lisans Programı), in 1994

In 1980 local governments started to sponsor literacy courses, legal-advice centers, and occupational orientation services for women. However, these programs remained confined to municipalities in the metropolitan areas. In 1993 labor unions began to establish women's commissions in order to acquaint female workers with their legal rights. Almost all major political parties also have women's commissions as well.

Nongovernment organizations concerned with women's issues number 211. Their major endeavors have been to increase women's visibility on the national level and create favorable public opinion regarding legislative and administrative initiatives that benefit women. They are instrumental in raising consciousness and establishing various types of platforms, particularly combating sexual harassment and violence in the family. The Women's Library and Data Bank (Kadın Eserleri Kütüphanesi ve Bilgi Merkezi Vakfi), which is supported by a foundation and the city of Istanbul, has been active in collecting oral histories of women leaders and artists and creating an archive for historical records.

NERMIN ABADAN-UNAT

WOMEN'S STUDIES CENTER (JERUSALEM)

A women's organization in Jerusalem.

The Women's Studies Center was established at the initiative of the Women's Action Committee (the women's branch of the Democratic Front for the Liberation of Palestine) in 1989. The founding members were Siham Barghouthi, Penny Johnson, Amal el-Jua'abeh, Zahira Kamal, Randa Siniora, and Lisa Taraki. In 1992, the center declared itself an independent nongovernmental organization. It works to promote women's rights and improve their social status through research, training, advocacy, and media research and training. The center has a wide network or relations with local, regional, and international women's organizations and was the coordinator for the Arab Women's Network for many years. It has no relations with Israelis. The center depends on external funding. Due to financial problems it was in the process of being integrated into the Palestinian Agricultural Relief Committees in 2003.

See also GAZA STRIP; GENDER: GENDER AND EDUCATION; INTIFADA (1987–1991); OSLO ACCORD (1993); PALESTINE; PALESTINIAN AUTHORITY; WEST BANK.

ISLAH JAD

WOODHEAD COMMISSION (1938)

British investigatory commission to Palestine.

The commission, led by Sir John Woodhead, was formed in March 1938 in response to dissension within the British government over the July 1937 Peel partition plan for Palestine and the re-ignition of the Arab revolt that had followed its promulgation. The new commission was instructed to gather evidence from the various parties and to recommend boundaries for two self-sufficient states, one Arab and one Jewish, to replace the British Mandate.

The Arab and Jewish positions were irreconcilable. All Palestinian Arab factions and the surrounding Arab states were unified in their opposition to partition and demanded the creation of an independent Arab state on the entire Mandate territory. The Jewish Agency proposed an increase in the territory designated for the Jewish state by Lord Peel. On 9 November 1938 the Woodhead Commission issued its report, which stated that two independent states would be impracticable on financial and administrative grounds. It called for a conference of all relevant parties in London to work out a compromise. The parties met at the St. James Round Table Conference in February/March 1939, which ended in deadlock. In order to enhance its security and improve its position with Arab states on the eve of war, the government then issued the MacDonald White Paper of 17 May 1939.

Bibliography

Galnoor, Itzhak. *The Partition of Palestine: Decision Crossroads in the Zionist Movement.* Albany: State University of New York Press, 1995.

BENJAMIN JOSEPH
UPDATED BY PIERRE M. ATLAS

WORLD BANK

The international organization lends to developing countries of the Middle East.

The World Bank is based in Washington, D.C. It includes the International Bank for Reconstruction and Development (IBRD) and the International Development Agency (IDA). IBRD has two affiliates, the International Finance Corporation (IFC) and the Multilateral Guarantee Agency (MIGA).

IBRD was established in 1945 and is owned by 152 countries. The bank's resources come from its capital, retained earnings, and very large loans from the world financial markets (US$8.9 billion in 1994). Its high creditworthiness allows it to borrow

Statement of subscriptions to the capital stock and voting power of Middle Eastern countries

Country	Capital subscribed*	Capital paid*	% of vote
Algeria	1,116.10	67.10	0.59
Bahrain	133.10	5.70	0.08
Egypt	857.50	50.90	0.46
Iran	2,857.42	175.80	1.48
Iraq	338.70	27.10	0.19
Israel	573.00	33.20	0.31
Jordan	167.40	7.80	0.10
Kuwait	1,602.00	97.40	0.84
Lebanon	41.00	1.10	0.04
Libya	945.80	57.00	0.50
Morocco	599.90	34.80	0.32
Oman	188.30	9.10	0.11
Qatar	132.20	9.00	0.08
Saudi Arabia	5,404.80	335.00	2.79
Syria	265.60	14.00	0.15
U.A.E.	287.70	22.60	0.16
Total	**15,539.50**	**926.60**	**8.20**

*In millions of dollars.

SOURCE: *World Bank Annual Report, 2001.* Washington, D.C.: World Bank, 2001.

TABLE BY GGS INFORMATION SERVICES, THE GALE GROUP.

Loans to Middle East Countries by the World Bank in 2001

Country	IBRD† loans	IBRD loan amounts*	IDA‡ loan amounts*
Algeria	2	41.70	
Egypt	0	0	
Jordan	1	120.00	
Lebanon	1	20.00	
Morocco	2	97.60	
Tunisia	3	75.90	
Yemen			142.30
Total	**9**	**355.20**	**142.30**

*In millions of dollars
†International Bank for Reconstruction and Development
‡International Development Association

SOURCE: *World Bank Annual Report, 2001*. Washington, D.C.: World Bank, 2001.

TABLE BY GGS INFORMATION SERVICES, THE GALE GROUP.

Relative voting strength on the World Bank board of Middle East countries

Members on the executive board	% Votes in International Bank for Reconstruction and Development	% Votes in International Development Association
Algeria	.51	.21
Saudi Arabia	2.79	3.57
Kuwait	.84	.59
Total	**4.14**	**4.37**

SOURCE: World Bank, February 25, 2003.

TABLE BY GGS INFORMATION SERVICES, THE GALE GROUP.

at the most competitive rates. IBRD lends to the more advanced developing countries on creditworthy and productive projects. Pricing is based on the cost of funds to the bank. Loans are made to governments or are guaranteed by governments. Total IBRD loans made in 1994 totaled US$20,836 million. IFC, established in 1956, and MIGA, established in 1984, deal with the private sectors of the developing countries. MIGA is mandated to encourage private equity investments by providing noncommercial risk guarantees. IDA lends interest free to the very poor countries with an annual per capital GNP of US$650 or less per year. The loans have very long maturities and up to a ten-year grace period.

The World Bank's executive board is responsible for the general operations of the bank. The board approves projects, funding programs, and general management of both the IBRD and the IDA. The board is composed of twenty-four members. Each member represents and votes for his country as per its percentage contribution to the capital of either IBRD or IDA. Certain countries also will represent blocs of smaller members and vote on their behalf. The largest vote belongs to the United States, which contributes 17.42 percent of IBRD capital and 15.67 percent of IDA capital. Saudi Arabia has the largest single Arab state representation on the World Bank board with 2.79 percent of the votes of the IBRD.

In the Middle East, the World Bank's stated goals are "to emphasize sustained commitment to operations and analytical work, to promote employment-led growth, to foster human resources development, and to improve natural resource management." The bank provides support to countries that agree to implement stabilization and structural reform. These conditions imply substantial efforts to reduce budget deficits, cut subsidies, allow currencies to reach their market levels, and privatize the economy.

Bibliography

Kapur, Daves; Lewis, John P.; and Webb, Richard. *The World Bank: Its First Half Century*. Washington, DC: The Brookings Institute, 1997.

JEAN-FRANÇOIS SEZNEC

WORLD FEDERATION OF SEPHARDI COMMUNITIES

Organization to support Sephardic settlement in Palestine/Israel.

The organization was founded at a conference of Sephardic communities in Vienna in 1925, prior to the Fourteenth Zionist Congress. The creation of Sephardic settlements at Kfar Hittim, Tzur Moshe, and Bet Hannan followed. After the establishment of the State of Israel, the Sephardi World Congress was convened in Paris in 1951 to renew the organization's activities on behalf of the Sephardic population in Israel, in the areas of education, housing, welfare, and preservation of their heritage. A second congress was held in Jerusalem in 1954. Now known as The World Sephardi Federation, its activities in Israel have been concentrated in education and in helping economically underprivileged Sephardic communities. It also works to promote the bond between Diaspora and Israeli Sephardic communities.

Bibliography

World Sephardi Federation. Available from <http://www.jafi.org.il/wsf>.

MIA BLOOM

WORLD ORGANIZATION OF JEWS FROM ARAB COUNTRIES (WOJAC)

International organization created in 1975.

WOJAC's charter states that Jews from Arab lands can and should form a bridge of understanding between the Arab countries and Israel. Its spokesmen stress that United Nations Resolution 242, which spells out "the necessity for a just settlement of the refugee problem," refers to all refugees, Jews and Palestinian Arabs alike; thus the legitimate rights of post-1948 Jewish refugees from Arab countries will be acknowledged. These Jews or their descendants would then be entitled to indemnification for immovable assets they left behind in their former lands.

WOJAC credits the State of Israel for its efforts to absorb the Jews from Arab lands, despite the difficulties and discriminatory policies these refugees encountered, socially and economically, during their integration processes. On the other hand, it claims that, whereas Israel solved the problem of Jewish refugees from Arab lands, the Arab states are to be faulted for failing to rehabilitate the Palestinians after 1948, rendering the latter eternal refugees as well as political pawns in inter-Arab politics.

Until 1992, when Syria finally allowed Syrian Jews to emigrate freely, WOJAC actively supported Israel's and the Jewish Agency's position that the regime permit all Jews who wished to emigrate to do so. This was in accordance with the promise made by the late Syrian president Hafiz al-Asad to then–U.S. president Jimmy Carter at Geneva in 1977.

See also BEN-PORAT, MORDECHAI.

MICHAEL M. LASKIER

WORLD WAR I

War involving the Central powers (Germany, Austria-Hungary, Bulgaria, and the Ottoman Empire) against the Allies (Britain, France, Russia, Belgium, Greece, Romania, Italy, Portugal, Serbia, Montenegro, Japan, and the United States).

World War I (then called the Great War) began on 28 July 1914, when Austria declared war on Serbia (ostensibly because a Serbian nationalist assassinated the heir to the throne, Austrian Archduke Franz Ferdinand, and his wife on 28 June); on 1 August, Germany declared war on Russia; on 3 August, Germany declared war on France; on 4 August, Germany invaded Belgium.

In retaliation and to aid an ally, Britain declared war on Germany on 4 August. The Russians crossed their western border at the Ukraine to enter Austro-Hungarian Galicia and pressed on to battle Germany, losing the Battle of Tannenberg (26–30 August), on what came to be called the Eastern Front. Germany marched on France in late August but was stopped in the First Battle of the Marne (6–10 September) on what came to be called the Western Front; here trench warfare ensued until March 1918.

In the Middle East, the leadership of the Ottoman Empire was divided among those who desired neutrality, those who wanted to join the Allies, and those who preferred to join the Central powers. The last group, led by Minister of War Enver Paşa prevailed. The Ottoman cabinet signed a secret alliance with Germany on 2 August. The next week the Ottomans purchased the German cruisers *Goeben* and *Breslau,* replacing two Turkish ships (being built by Britain but confiscated by Britain at the outbreak of war). Renamed *Sultan Selim Yavuz* and *Midilli,* they shelled Sevastopol and Odessa, Russian cities on the Black Sea, 28 October, bringing the Ottoman Empire into the war; Russia declared war on the Ottomans 4 November; Britain and France declared war on them 5 November. Germany dominated Ottoman military actions, with General Otto Liman von Sanders directing the army and Admiral Wilhelm Souchon, the navy.

In November 1914, a British naval contingent bombarded the entrance to the Dardanelles, and in January 1915 the British organized to break through

An Australian soldier carries a wounded comrade to a field hospital on the beaches of Gallipoli, Turkey, during World War I (1914–1918). The Allies began an assault on the Gallipoli Penninsula in April 1915, as the first step in a plan to overtake the Ottoman Empire's capital, Constantinople. The plan failed and the Allies were forced to evacuate Gallipoli by the end of the year. © CORBIS. REPRODUCED BY PERMISSION.

the Turkish Straits (from the Mediterranean into the Black Sea at the Bosporus and Dardanelles). Britain's First Lord of the Admiralty Winston Churchill convinced the war cabinet that an amphibious attack could accomplish this, thereby taking the Ottomans out of the war and opening a supply route to Russia. Britain's War Secretary Lord Kitchener sabotaged the plan by refusing to send the necessary land troops. Britain's navy unsuccessfully attacked in February and March; in April an Anglo-French army landed on the Gallipoli peninsula, where the Ottoman Turks caused heavy casualties to the Allies, which by then included Italian forces. The British-French-Italian forces almost broke through twice, but the lack of cooperation by the Russians at the Bosporus end of the Straits, faulty intelligence and, most of all, skillful tactics by the Turks and Germans led to a stalemate. The Allies withdrew from the Straits in January 1916.

Another area of major Middle Eastern hostilities was Egypt, under British protection since 18 December 1914. Khedive Abbas Hilmi II was deposed, and the British appointed Sharif Husayn ibn Ali to be sultan of Egypt. Cemal Paşa, Ottoman minister of marine, took over the Fourth Ottoman army—thereby controlling Syria, including Palestine. He sent his forces to make a surprise attack on the Suez Canal in February 1915; they crossed the Negev desert without detection. The Turkish forces could not hold the eastern bank of the canal and retired to the Sinai desert, maintaining bases in Maʿan, Beersheba, and Gaza. Cemal continued to raid the Suez Canal by air, forcing the British to keep a large force there, but in the end the British prevailed. A second assault on the canal was delayed until the summer of 1916 and failed totally. The Turco-German forces were on the defensive there until the end of the war, although in March and April 1917 they withstood a heavy British attack at Gaza, and moved to the offensive in the Yilderim Operation commanded by General Erich von Falkenhayn. But the Turko-German forces were defeated by a combination of factors, including the troops of British General Edmund Allenby (commander of the Egyptian Expeditionary Force), failure of some of their transport, and sabotage.

Major battles were fought in Russia, where in late 1914 the Turks attempted to take Kars and Batum. In the battles of 1915 and 1916 the Russians took Erzerum, Van, Trabzon, and Erzinjan. They were aided by Armenians—revolutionaries and irregulars. In 1916, Mustafa Kemal (Atatürk), commander of the Second Ottoman Army, joined the Third Army on the Caucasus front, but little was accomplished due to scarce ammunition, impossible conditions for transportation, and rampant disease. The two revolutions in Russia also affected the Caucasus front, as the Russian troops (except the Armenian and Georgian divisions) withdrew and went home to attend to domestic affairs in 1917. The Turks then occupied Kars, Ardahan, and Batum, but Georgian and German forces retook Batum. A Bolshevik-Armenian coup in Baku and the killing of ten thousand Turks there produced a Turkish drive to recapture the city in September 1918 and to kill many Armenians. At the end of the war, the Caucasus became the Allies' problem.

Iraq was the scene for the major hostilities of the Mesopotamia Campaign. British forces from India seized Basra before Turkey declared war. Traveling up to the confluence of the Tigris and Euphrates rivers, the Anglo-Indian forces under General Sir Charles Townshend took Kut al-Amara in 1915. In November, his army was defeated south of Baghdad and surrendered to the Sixth Turkish Army at Kut al-Amara in April 1916. Halil Paşa erred in allowing the Anglo-Indian forces to remain in the south, for they reestablished their hold there, built a railroad, and under Britain's General Sir Frederick Stanley Maude, retook Kut al-Amara in March 1917. Baghdad fell immediately after, and the Anglo-Indian forces headed north to Mosul (on the west bank of the Tigris), which they failed to reach by the time of the Mudros Armistice (30 October 1918).

Enver Pasha, Minister of War and Commander-in-Chief of the Ottoman military during World War I (1914–1918). Enver Pasha was instrumental in bringing the Ottoman Empire into the war on the side of the Central Powers, a decision that eventually led to his downfall and the end of the Ottoman Empire. COURTESY OF THE LIBRARY OF CONGRESS.

Two national groups within the Ottoman Empire openly aided the enemy during the war: the Arabs and the Armenians. The Armenians followed the orders of the head of the Armenian Orthodox Church (who lived in Yerevan in the Caucasus) that the Russian czar was the protector of all Armenians. Some Armenians rebelled; in the region of Van and Erzurum, Armenians openly battled the Turks proclaiming an Armenian government in Van, April 1915—which touched off the Armenian deportations and the massive killing of Armenian civilians by the Turks in 1915/16.

Cemal Paşa's actions in Syria—in arresting and hanging about thirty Arabs in Beirut and Damascus 1915/16, many from prominent families, as well as his refusal to share grain with the starving Lebanese in 1916—pushed many Arabs to desire independence from Ottoman Turkey. This desire was furthered by the proclamation of Arab independence by Sharif Husayn ibn Ali of the Hijaz in June 1916. Husayn's action was part of the outcome of the secret Husayn-McMahon Correspondence.

Another secret negotiation over the division of the Arab Middle East was the Sykes-Picot Agreement between France, Britain, and Russia. An open negotiation between the Zionists and the British had led to the issuance of the November 1917 pro-Zionist Balfour Declaration, concerning a "Jewish national home" in Palestine.

The failure of the German-Turkish campaigns led to the buildup of British troops in Egypt and their move into Palestine. General Allenby led his Egyptian Expeditionary Forces west of the Jordan river, and Jerusalem fell to them in December 1917. Joined by French military detachments, he moved north to take Lebanon, while Hijazi forces, aided by Colonel T. E. Lawrence (of Arabia), Colonel C. C. Wilson, and Sir Reginald Wingate, paralleled Allenby's actions east of the Jordan River. Damascus fell in October 1918—and although Mustafa Kemal (Atatürk) and the Seventh Turkish Army held Aleppo, the armistice at Mudros ended all fighting, 30 October 1918.

Four years of war had devastated Ottoman Turkey, and the old order died. A new period for the Middle East began with the peace treaties, the rise to power in Turkey of Mustafa Kemal, the fall of empires, and the creation of new nation-states and spheres of influence.

See also BALFOUR DECLARATION (1917); HUSAYN–MCMAHON CORRESPONDENCE (1915–1916); SYKES–PICOT AGREEMENT (1916).

Bibliography

Barker, A. J. *The Bastard War: The Mesopotamian Campaign of 1914–1918.* New York: Dial Press, 1967.

Kedourie, Elie. *England and the Middle East: The Destruction of the Ottoman Empire, 1914–1921.* Hassocks, U.K.: Harvester Press, 1978.

Lewis, Bernard. *The Emergence of Modern Turkey,* 3d edition. New York: Oxford University Press, 2002.

SARA REGUER

WORLD WAR II

War involving the Axis (Germany, Italy, Japan, Hungary, Romania, and Bulgaria) against the Allies (Britain, France, the United States, the Soviet Union, Australia, Belgium, Brazil, Canada, China, Denmark, Greece, the Netherlands, New Zealand, Norway, Poland, South Africa, and Yugoslavia).

When World War II began on 1 September 1939, the Middle East consisted of independent, semi-independent, and colonial states. From east to west they included the following: Iran and Turkey were independent, with Iran under Reza Shah Pahlavi and Turkey a republic. Syria and Lebanon were republics but under French control. Transjordan and Iraq were monarchies but under British control. Palestine was a League of Nations mandate under British control. The Arabian peninsula consisted of Saudi Arabia and Yemen, both independent, and Oman and a variety of Persian/Arabian Gulf states within the British sphere of influence. Egypt (with the strategic Suez Canal) and the Sudan were nominally independent but really under British control. Libya was an Italian colony. The French effectively controlled the rest of North Africa—Tunisia, Algeria, and Morocco—except for the western regions under Spanish rule.

In World War II, Britain and France were allied against Germany and Italy. All except Germany had significant imperial holdings and interests in the Middle East. Germany wanted not only the defeat of Britain and France, but German gains in this region. As the war began, the Axis powers controlled only a small part of the Middle East—Libya and some other Italian territory taken during the Ethiopian annexation in 1935. The fall of France to Germany in May 1940 and the establishment of the quasi-independent Vichy republic in June 1940 dramat-

British soldiers salute as the Union Jack is raised over Benghazi, Libya, after its capture from the Italians in 1943. North Africa was the scene of heavy fighting during the middle stages of World War II (1939–1945). © CORBIS. REPRODUCED BY PERMISSION.

ically altered the balance of power: In addition to Italy's territories being in their sphere of influence, the Axis powers had acquired France's territories.

North and East African Campaigns

The British initiated their first military action in the Middle East by an attack on French naval vessels at Oran, Algeria, 3 July 1940—which crippled the French fleet there (and resulted in 1,300 French dead). This was part of an effort to ensure that the Axis powers could not use the French fleet; the French squadron at Alexandria was disarmed while two French submarines in British ports joined the Free French forces fighting with the British. The next day, Italian forces from Ethiopia occupied border towns in the Sudan, and within six weeks they penetrated British Kenya and seized British Somaliland. On 13 September, Italian forces under Rodolfo Graziani invaded Egypt; they penetrated some sixty miles (90 km) within a week, and dug in along a fifty-mile (80 km) front from the coast to Sidi Barrani.

Since the threat to the Suez Canal was of primary importance, the British countered first against Graziani's army of 200,000. General Sir Archibald Wavell launched a surprise attack with an army of 63,000 on 6 December and drove through the Italian lines at Sidi Barrani, capturing 40,000 Italian troops by 12 December. The campaign continued for two months, ending with Italian surrender at Benghazi, Libya, on 7 February 1941. With advance units at al-Agheila, the British had advanced about five hundred miles (800 km), captured 130,000 Italian soldiers, and taken four hundred tanks and one thousand guns.

On 15 January 1941 the British launched an attack against Italian forces in East Africa, from the Sudan. Mogadiscio, capital of Italian Somaliland, fell on 26 February, followed by Neguelli in southern

Ethiopia on 22 March; the capital, Addis Ababa, fell on 6 April.

These British successes were soon to be reversed. Germany had not yet committed her forces to Operation Barbarossa, the invasion of Russia (22 June 1941), and in February and March was able to reinforce the Italians in western Libya with two divisions under General Erwin Rommel. In the meantime, the British had turned their attention to the defense of Greece, diverting troops from North Africa.

Rommel opened his attack on 3 April, and the British retreated from their recent gains in Libya. The Axis forces drove the British back to the Egyptian frontier by 29 May. The tables then turned when Germany diverted troops from North Africa for the invasion of Russia. The British launched an offensive on 11 December and were able to drive into Libya as far as Benghazi by 25 December. A reinforced Rommel was able to begin a drive on Egypt on 22 May 1942 that did not end until checked at al-Alamayn (El Alamein), just eighty miles (127 km) from Alexandria. General Montgomery's offensive from al-Alamayn began on 23 October, resulting in expulsion of Axis forces from Egypt by 12 November and the end of the threat to Egypt and the Suez Canal.

General Erwin Rommel with soldiers of the 15th Panzer Division in 1941, in Libya between Tobruk and Sidi Omar. Rommel earned the nickname "the Desert Fox" for his skillful leadership of Axis forces in North Africa during World War II (1939–1945). NATIONAL ARCHIVES—STILL PICTURE REFERENCE (NWCS-STILLS REFERENCE) NWDNS-242-EAPC-6-M713A. REPRODUCED BY PERMISSION.

At about the same time, on 8 November, a British-American force under U.S. General Dwight D. Eisenhower began Operation Torch, the invasion of North Africa. Allied forces disembarking in French Morocco and Algeria faced some opposition from Vichy forces, but by 11 November, the two sides had reached an armistice. Pressed by Montgomery's Eighth Army in Libya and the new threat from the west, Rommel concentrated the Axis forces in Tunisia. Into 1943, bitter fighting continued, particularly at the Kasserine Pass, but by 12 May all German and Italian resistance had ended. The Axis powers had 950,000 men dead or captured and had lost 8,000 aircraft and 2.4 million tons of shipping.

Southwest Asia and Turkey

While the significant fighting of World War II in the Middle East was in Africa, the British still faced serious threats in Southwest Asia. The regimes in both Iran and Iraq flirted with support of the Axis powers as a means of diminishing British influence over their affairs. On 2 May 1941, pro-Axis sympathizers in Iraq tried to seize power. British forces intervened and put down all resistance by 31 May. Fearing that Reza Shah Pahlavi might take Iran into the German camp in the summer of 1941, British and Soviet forces entered Iran in late August and forced him to abdicate in favor of his son, Muhammad Reza Pahlavi, on 16 September. These actions effectively secured Iraq and Iran for the Allies.

The fall of France in June 1940 threatened to bring Syria and Lebanon into the Axis sphere of influence. Quick action by the British and Free French forces prevented this. On 8 June these forces occupied Syria and Lebanon. On 16 September Syria was proclaimed an independent nation, as was Lebanon on 26 November. Both remained loyal to the Allies during World War II, but soon after the end of hostilities they were able to assert their independence and obtain the withdrawal of Allied forces from their territory.

World War I had led to the disintegration of the Ottoman Empire and the creation of the Turkish republic under Kemal Atatürk. Turkey then faced pressure from both sides and from within as World War II loomed on the horizon. Atatürk and his successor, İsmet İnönü, favored the British as the power they believed would ultimately win. Other Turks feared Britain's ally, the Soviet Union, as a traditional enemy and realized that by June 1941 German troops were within 100 miles (160 km) of Istanbul. Still others remembered the disastrous decision of October 1914, when the Ottomans joined the Central Powers in World War I.

Shortly after the beginning of World War II, on 19 October 1939, Britain and France concluded a fifteen-year mutual assistance pact with Turkey. German success in 1940 and the invasion of Russia in 1941, however, led many Turkish leaders to favor the Axis. Thus, on 1 November 1940, İnönü declared it to be Turkish policy to remain a nonbelligerent in the war, while maintaining friendly ties with both Britain and the Soviet Union. The Allies, of course, continued to pressure Turkey for support, and on 3 December 1941, just before the United States declared war, the American Lend-Lease program was extended to Turkey. İnönü still pursued a neutral course but by 1943 realized that the Axis would lose. In August 1944, Turkey broke diplomatic relations with Germany, and on 23 February 1945 it formally declared war to comply with requirements for participation in the UN conference to be held in San Francisco in April.

Palestine

The Jewish and Arab populations of Palestine greeted World War II with mixed emotions. Neither was content with British rule. The Arabs resented the rule of their country by a European power pledged to uphold the Balfour Declaration (sanctioning Palestine as a haven for persecuted Jews from all parts of the world). The Jewish population, the Yishuv, suspected British commitment to the Balfour Declaration, especially since the British banned Jewish immigration into Palestine after 1939.

In light of the antisemitism of Nazi Germany and its extermination of European Jewry as a matter of state policy, the Yishuv had little recourse but to support the Allies. The resources of the Jewish community in Palestine were put at the disposal of the British, and efforts (often resisted by British authorities) were made to raise Jewish military units to support the war effort. Early in the war the Yishuv devised the Carmel Plan, to create a Jewish enclave on the Palestine coast, near Haifa, to resist a German landing and occupation. Fortunately, this never became necessary.

A small minority of Jews did continue to resist British control of Palestine. The LEHI (Stern Gang), under Abraham Stern, urged rebellion against the British and even approached the German representatives in Vichy-controlled Syria with an offer of support against the British in Palestine. Even after this offer was rejected and Stern killed in confrontation with British authorities in early 1942, this splinter group continued to resist the British; other Jewish groups then began to oppose the British as the war progressed, since British support of the Zionist cause seemed less than enthusiastic.

Some Arabs viewed Germany as an instrument to rid themselves of British rule. The mufti of Jerusalem, Hajj Amin al-Husayni, lent his support to the Nazi cause, and when fleeing from Jerusalem in 1937 and from Beirut in October 1939 to Baghdad, he established contact with the German ambassador to Turkey, Franz von Papen, offering Arab support. After an anti-British revolt in 1941, the British reestablished control of Iraq in May 1941. Hajj Amin, who participated in the revolt, left for Turkey and later for Rome and Berlin to support the Axis powers after they promised to free the Arab world and support its independence and unity. He was able to generate some support for the Axis among the Arabs, but the defeat of the Italians and Germans in North Africa prevented this from becoming a factor in the war.

The War's Effect on the Middle East

World War II ended with British and French control of most of the Middle East. The war did, however, shatter the aura of the invincibility of their arms. Consequently, rapid changes occurred in the region—Arab states asserted their independence, and the Jewish population of Palestine declared the State of Israel in 1948. Iran and Turkey insisted on full partnership in the international community. The European powers would no longer have undisputed control over the fates of the peoples in this region.

With the end of the war the United States emerged the premier Western power, but the challenge of the Cold War with the Soviet Union would soon have its own impact on the oil-rich Middle East.

See also ALAMAYN, AL-; ATATÜRK, MUSTAFA KEMAL; HUSAYNI, MUHAMMAD AMIN AL-; İNÖNÜ, İSMET; MONTGOMERY, BERNARD LAW; PAHLAVI, REZA; ROMMEL, ERWIN; STERN, ABRAHAM; WAVELL, ARCHIBALD PERCIVAL; YISHUV.

Bibliography

Hourani, Albert. *A History of the Arab Peoples.* Cambridge, MA: Belknap Press, 1991.

Keegan, John. *The Second World War.* New York: Penguin, 1990.

Lewis, Bernard. *The Emergence of Modern Turkey,* 3d edition. New York: Oxford University Press, 2002.

Peretz, Don. *The Middle East Today,* 6th edition. Westport, CT: Praeger, 1994.

Sachar, Howard M. *A History of Israel: From the Rise of Zionism to Our Time,* 2d revised and updated edition. New York: Knopf, 1996.

Time-Life Books. *WW II: Time-Life Books History of the Second World War.* New York: Prentice Hall, 1989.

DANIEL E. SPECTOR

WORLD ZIONIST ORGANIZATION (WZO)

Organization that transformed the Zionist idea of establishing a Jewish state into reality.

Founded in 1897 by Theodor Herzl at the first Zionist Congress in Basel, Switzerland, the Zionist Organization, as it was originally known, was created to serve as the organizational framework for the Zionist movement. It was to be composed of "all Jews who accept the Zionist program and pay the shekel (a nominal membership fee, differing from country to country)."

The Zionist Congress was established as the supreme governing body of the WZO. Before 1948 congresses were held in many European cities; thereafter, beginning with the twenty-third congress in 1951, all congresses were held in Jerusalem. At first they were held every one or two years; more recently they have been convened every four years. Herzl, the first president of the WZO, chaired its first five congresses. After his death in 1904 the movement was headed by lackluster figures until the election of Chaim Weizmann as its president in 1920.

Between congresses, the movement was guided by a Greater Actions Committee, or General Council, and a Smaller Actions Committee, or Executive. Under the aegis of the WZO, the Jewish Colonial Trust was formed at the second Zionist Congress to serve as the bank of the Zionist movement. The Jewish National Fund was initiated at the fifth Zionist Congress to act as a land-purchasing agent in Palestine for the Jewish people.

Membership in the World Zionist Organization was initially on a regional basis, but as ideological differences emerged the membership structure splintered along ideological lines. Distinct political parties were formed, of which the most important were the Labor Zionists, the General Zionists (liberal centrists), the Mizrahi (religious Zionists), and (after 1925) the Revisionists (right-wing nationalists). The latter, led by Vladimir Ze'ev Jabotinsky, split from the WZO altogether in 1935 and formed the New Zionist Organization.

During the period of British mandatory rule in Palestine between 1920 and 1948 the WZO assumed many of the powers of a quasi-government of the Jewish community in the country. Article 4 of the Mandate provided for the establishment of a Jewish Agency, which "shall be recognized as a public body for the purpose of advising and cooperating with the administration of Palestine in such economic, social, and other matters as may affect the establishment of the Jewish national home and the interests of the Jewish population in Palestine." Until 1929 the WZO acted as the Jewish Agency for Palestine; thereafter, the agency was enlarged to include non-Zionists, but the WZO remained the dominant power within the new body. The political department of the Jewish Agency functioned, in effect, as the foreign ministry of the WZO throughout this period.

After the establishment of the State of Israel in 1948 the WZO gradually evolved into a foreign propaganda and political mobilization arm of the Israeli government. Many of the WZO's functions were assumed by the new government, but the Jewish Agency was not dismantled. In 1952 the Law of the Status of the WZO-Jewish Agency was promulgated whereby primary responsibility was assigned to the Jewish Agency for the development and settlement of the land and for the absorption of immigrants. In 1960 the WZO adopted a new constitution under which individuals were denied eligibility for membership, which was thereafter reserved for organizations.

See also HERZL, THEODOR; JABOTINSKY, VLADIMIR ZE'EV; JEWISH AGENCY FOR PALESTINE; JEWISH COLONIAL TRUST; JEWISH NATIONAL FUND; LABOR ZIONISM; WEIZMANN, CHAIM.

Bibliography

Laqueur, Walter. *A History of Zionism.* London: Weidenfeld and Nicolson, 1972.

BERNARD WASSERSTEIN

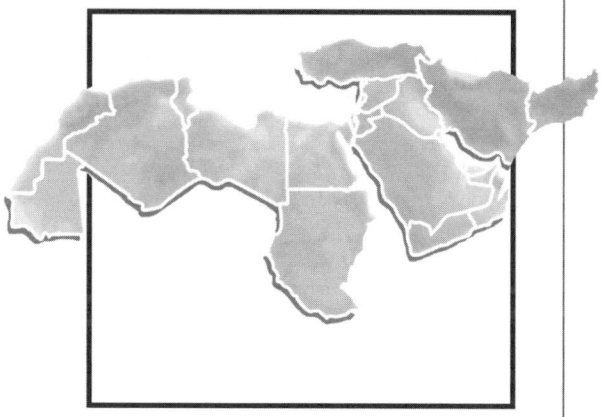

Y

YA'ARI, ME'IR

[1897–1987]

Israeli political leader.

Born in Galicia, Me'ir Ya'ari was educated at the Vienna Academy of Agriculture and the University of Vienna. During World War I, he served as an officer in the Austro-Hungarian army. In Vienna, he was a leader of the ha-Shomer ha-Tzaʿir youth movement before emigrating to Palestine in 1919. Founder of the first kibbutz of ha-Shomer ha-Tzaʿir and the Histadrut, Ya'ari was also an early leader of the Kibbutz Artzi of the ha-Shomer ha-Tzaʿir movement in Israel and abroad. He was elected to the first Israeli Knesset, in which he remained until 1973, and served as general secretary of MAPAM. A prolific writer on Zionist ideology, Ya'ari was a principal intellectual force in the MAPAM movement.

See also ISRAEL: POLITICAL PARTIES IN.

BRYAN DAVES

YACINE, ABDESSALAME

[1928–]

Islamic intellectual and spiritual leader in Morocco.

Abdessalame Yacine is one of the foremost Islamic intellectuals in Morocco and the spiritual leader of the al-Adl wa al-Ihsan (Justice and Charity) movement. A former teacher and school principal, Yacine became an Islamic activist in the early 1970s after having been religiously awakened by an encounter with Sufism. Following his bold criticism of King Hassan II in an open letter entitled "Islam or the Deluge" in 1974, Yacine was jailed on a few occasions, and ultimately put under house arrest between 1989 and 2000. Besides this clash with the monarchy, he has mostly distinguished himself through a prolific literary production and the originality of his philosophy. Deeply influenced by his short Sufi experience, Yacine developed a nonviolent Islamism based on spiritual regeneration. His major works in Arabic and French underline the importance of spiritual guidance (*tarbiya*), proper companionship (*suhbah*), and prayer. In doing so, Yacine invites Muslims to reach a higher stage of consciousness called *ihsan* in order to become truly benevolent and build a better society. Yacine thus wishes to instill justice, honesty, and responsibility within various spheres, from family life to politics. His emphasis on spiritual growth, which he attempts to reconcile with the dryness of Islamic law, sets him apart from the more rigorist Islamists in Morocco and elsewhere. Nevertheless, al-Adl wa al-Ihsan, officially founded in 1987, is currently one of the most important Islamic organizations in the country. Although Yacine continues to criticize the Moroccan monarchy and government within acceptable limits, he has so far eschewed direct political involvement.

See also ADL WA AL-IHSAN AL-; HASSAN II; MOROCCO: OVERVIEW; MOROCCO: POLITICAL PARTIES IN; MUHAMMAD VI.

Bibliography

Shahin, Emad Eldin. "Secularism and Nationalism: The Political Discourse of ʿAbd al-Salam Yassin," in *Islamism and Secularism in North Africa,* edited by John Ruedy. New York: St. Martin's Press, 1994: 167–186.

HENRI LAUZIÈRE

YACOUBI, RACHIDA

[1946–]

Moroccan writer.

Rachida Yacoubi's first novel, *Ma vie, mon cri* (My life, my scream; 1995) described the poor condition of women in Moroccan society and caused a shock both in Morocco and abroad. Based partly on her own experience, the book tells the story of a woman whose husband is an alcoholic. She divorces him to stay alone with four children in a shantytown. This was almost the first time that a story so violently against male domination of society was published in Morocco. It was a great success and Yacoubi was invited to Europe on many occasions to speak about the condition of women.

Before Yacoubi's book, the condition of women in Morocco had been addressed only by male novelists (Tahar Ben-Jelloun, Driss Chraibi, Abdelhak Serhane) or by researchers (Souad Filal, Fatima Mernissi, Soumaya Naamane-Guessous). Following the publication of Yacoubi's novel, other Moroccan women published books about gender issues in Morocco. They include Halima Benhaddou (*Aïcha la rebelle,* 1982), Leila Houari (*Zeida de nulle part,* 1985), Nafissa Sbaï (*L'enfant endormi,* 1987), and Fatiha Boucetta (*Anissa captive,* 1991). In 2002, Yacoubi published an essay about the time she spent in prison ("Je dénonce"; I denounce), showing the inequality of men and woman before the judicial system in Morocco

See also HASSAN II; MOROCCO: OVERVIEW; MOROCCO: POLITICAL PARTIES IN; MOUDAWANA, AL-; MUHAMMAD VI.

RABIA BEKKAR

YADIN, YIGAEL

[1917–1984]

Israeli archaeologist, general, and politician.

Born in Jerusalem, the son of the archaeologist E. L. Sukenik, Yigael Yadin studied archaeology and Semitic languages at Hebrew University (1935–1945), later earning his Ph.D. (1955) studying the Dead Sea Scrolls. He joined the Haganah and adopted the personal code name Yadin, which later became his surname. Yadin was chief operations officer in the 1948 war and later chief of staff (1949–1952); he is credited with creating the principles of Israel's citizens' army reserve system. He resigned from the chief-of-staff position in 1952 because of budgetary disputes and joined the Hebrew University faculty in 1953, where he was appointed professor of archaeology in 1963. In 1976 he was a founder of the centrist Democratic Movement for Change, and from 1977 to 1981 he was a member of the Knesset and deputy prime minister. In 1981 he returned to Hebrew University. Yadin followed his father in studying the Dead Sea Scrolls. With Nahman Avigad, he published *Genesis Apocryphon* (1956), *Ben Sira from Masada* (1965), and *Temple Scroll* (1977). His most important archaeological achievements were the large-scale excavations at Hazor, the Cave of Letters in the Judaean desert, Masada, Megiddo, and Bet She'an.

See also ARCHAEOLOGY IN THE MIDDLE EAST.

Bibliography

Astor, D.; Barnett, R. D.; Kane, J.; et al. "The Yigael Yadin Memorial Lecture." *Bulletin of the Anglo-Israel Archaeological Society* (1984–1985): 9–23.

Greenfield, J. "Bibliography of Yigal Yadin." *Journal of Jewish Studies* 33 (1982): 11–16.

Jerusalem Center for Public Affairs. "Yadin (Sukenik), Yigael." In *Glossary of Israeli Parties and Personalities: 1948–1981.* Available from <http://www.jcpa.org/art/knesset8.htm>.

Jewish Agency for Israel, Department for Jewish Zionist Education."Yigal Yadin." In *Our Gallery of People.* Available from <http://www.jajz-ed.org.il/100/PEOPLE>.

MIA BLOOM
UPDATED BY GREGORY S. MAHLER

YAD MORDEKHAI

Kibbutz that was the site of an important battle in the Arab–Israel War (1948).

Yad Mordekhai, named for Mordekhai Anilewitz, commander of the Warsaw Ghetto uprising, is located between Gaza and Ashkelon on the road to Tel Aviv. Founded in 1943, the kibbutz was attacked by Egypt's army on May 19, 1948. It held out for four days without relief; on the fifth day, the survivors broke through Egypt's lines to the settlement of Gvar Am. The attackers suffered 300 casualties.

Today the kibbutz has 700 inhabitants. The kibbutz supports itself through agriculture; industry, especially bee products from its apiary; and tourism, with visitors to a reconstructed battlefield from the 1948 war and a museum devoted to the Holocaust, Jewish resistance in Europe, the immigration of Holocaust survivors to Palestine during the British Mandate, and Israel's War of Independence.

Bibliography

Allon, Yigal. *Shield of David: The Story of Israel's Armed Forces.* New York: Random House, 1970.

Elon, Amos. *The Israelis: Founders and Sons.* New York: Penguin, 1983.

JON JUCOVY

YAD VASHEM

The Holocaust Martyrs' and Heroes' Remembrance Authority, as well as a site in Israel dedicated to commemorating the Jewish victims of Nazi persecution and extermination.

Established on the authority of the 1945 London Zionist Congress, Yad Vashem (from Isaiah 56:5) includes a museum of the Holocaust, facilities for conferences and memorial gatherings (Holocaust Remembrance Day ceremonies are held there on 27 Nisan), and a research institute. Yad Vashem is a feature of foreign dignitaries' official visits to Israel.

Yad Vashem's task is to perpetuate the legacy of the Holocaust to future generations so that the world never forgets the horrors and cruelty of the Holocaust. Its principal missions are commemoration and documentation of the events of the Holocaust; collection, examination, and publication of testimonies to the Holocaust; the collection and memorialization of the names of Holocaust victims; and research and education.

See also HOLOCAUST.

Bibliography

Young, James Edward. *The Texture of Memory: Holocaust Memorials and Meaning.* New Haven, CT: Yale University Press, 1993.

JON JUCOVY

YAHYA IBN MUHAMMAD HAMID AL-DIN [1867–1948]

Imam of Yemen, 1904–1948; king of Yemen, 1918–1948.

Yahya ibn Muhammad Hamid al-Din took the patronymic al-Mutawakkil ala Allah on becoming imam in 1904. He succeeded to the imamate upon the death of his father Muhammad ibn Yahya, who had inaugurated a new period of rebellion against the rule of the Ottoman Empire in the highlands of Yemen in 1891.

Although Yahya was sometimes amenable to concessions and negotiations with the Ottoman authorities, he approved of the desire of the Zaydi people to be free of Ottoman rule. When Yahya received the *bayʿa* (oath of allegiance), he immediately called for a full-scale revolt against the Ottomans; his major motivation appears to have been the May 1904 boundary agreement about Yemen's southern borders, signed between the Ottomans and British, since he considered himself to be the legitimate ruler of both "north" Yemen and the territories held by the British in "south" Yemen.

Imam Yahya continued to lead the revolt against the Ottomans throughout the period before World

War I. His political shrewdness as well as his ability to wage irregular war against the Ottoman state forced it to negotiate with him, most importantly in the Treaty of Da'an in 1919, which granted most of his demands and gave him an almost free hand in matters of taxation, religious affairs, and judicial appointments.

During World War I, however, the imam sided with the Ottomans as fellow Muslims—the only Arab regime to do so. At the end of the war, the Ottomans departed Yemen and officially recognized Yahya as ruler there. For Imam Yahya, however, this was only the first step in creating the Yemen he perceived to be the patrimony of the Zaydi imams.

Yahya's primary policy objectives in the postwar period appear to have been: (1) to bring all of Yemen under his direct control; (2) to make Yemen completely independent of the influence and/or control of other states (to have complete autarky); (3) to weaken the cohesion and power of the tribes (to prevent them from developing a common front against the central government and resisting its policy objectives); and (4) to establish the ascendancy of Islamic law *(Shari'a)* throughout Yemen.

The methods Yahya employed to bring about his goals were diverse, and some were, in today's light, brutal. At first he paid subsidies and bribes to various tribal elements; later, when the treasury could clearly not support the demands of these payments, he sent military units to quell uprisings against his decisions, and also employed a traditional Yemeni technique—he took hostages from the tribes, typically the sons of the tribal Shaykhs. These hostages were kept in the imam's fortresses (where they were also educated) to guarantee the good behavior of their own tribes or tribal alliances. Yahya was assassinated in 1948.

Bibliography

Fisher, Sydney N. *The Middle East: A History*, 3d edition. New York: Knopf, 1979.

MANFRED W. WENNER

YAMANI, AHMAD ZAKI

[1930–]

Saudi official influential in world petroleum politics in the 1960s and 1970s.

Born in Mecca in 1930, Ahmad Zaki Yamani was educated at Cairo, New York, and Harvard universities. He began working for the government of Saudi Arabia in 1958 and rose to become minister of petroleum and mineral resources in 1962, a post he held until 1986. He is noted for his success in asserting Saudi control over the country's oil resources, helping to establish the Organization of Arab Petroleum Exporting Countries (OAPEC), and increasing the profits of oil-producing countries through asserting their rights to set production and pricing policies. He was instrumental in establishing the General Petroleum and Mineral Organization (PETROMIN), a Saudi company created to develop oil resources, and the College of Petroleum and Minerals in Dhahran. In response to Israel's victory in the October 1973 War, Yamani succeeded in leading an embargo of oil shipments by Arab producers to the United States and other supporters of Israel. He served as secretary-general of OAPEC in 1968 and 1969 and was seen as a prominent voice for moderation in the organization. In 1986 he established the Centre for Global Energy Studies.

See also ORGANIZATION OF ARAB PETROLEUM EXPORTING COUNTRIES (OAPEC).

ANTHONY B. TOTH

YANBU

A port on Saudi Arabia's Red Sea coast.

Located in the Hijaz region, Yanbu traditionally served the city of Medina. Originally Yanbu was divided into the port itself, Yanbu al-Bahr, and the inland agricultural settlement of Yanbu al-Nakhl. In the 1970s, along with al-Jubayl on the Persian Gulf, Yanbu became the center of a massive industrial development scheme that included oil refining, petrochemical industries, and heavy manufacturing complexes based on hydrocarbon fuels. Yanbu was planned as the smaller of the two sites, with two petroleum refineries, a natural gas processing plant, a petrochemical complex, other light industries, an industrial port, and a new city of 100,000 inhabitants. Energy for these projects was to be supplied via oil and gas pipelines from the Eastern Province, and the terminus of the Iraqi pipeline across Saudi Arabia was located nearby; the Iraqi pipeline was closed after Iraq's invasion of Kuwait in 1990, but the capacity of the Saudi east-west pipeline was later increased to nearly five million barrels per day. By 1999 Yanbu's population was about 70,000.

Bibliography

Farsy, Fouad al-. *Modernity and Tradition: The Saudi Equation.* London: Kegan Paul International, 1991.

J. E. PETERSON

YARIV, AHARON
[1920–1994]

Israeli career officer, cabinet minister and defense analyst.

Born in Russia in 1920, Aharon Yariv moved to Palestine at the age of fifteen and joined the Haganah in 1939. During World War II, Yariv fought in the British army, helping to liberate concentration camps. He was the first Israeli to attend the French Military Command and Staff School.

Yariv served in many positions in the Israel Defense Forces (IDF), including commander of the IDF Command and Staff School (1954), head of Central Command (1956–1957), commander of the Golani Brigade (1960–1961), and most significantly as chief of the Intelligence branch (Aman; 1964–1973) during which he provided the intelligence information responsible for the Israeli victory in 1967. From 1957 to 1960, he served as military attaché in Washington, D.C. Yariv left the Intelligence branch shortly before the 1973 Arab–Israel War, although he served as head of the Israeli delegation during the Kilometer 101 disengagement talks.

Elected to the eighth Knesset on the Labor Alignment ticket, Yariv became minister of transport under Golda Meir and later minister of information under Yitzhak Rabin. Together with another minister, Yariv wrote a formula for peace negotiations that recommended Israel carry out negotiations with any Palestinian faction that would recognize Israel's right to exist and that would not engage in terrorism. Yariv founded the Center for Strategic Studies at Tel Aviv University in 1977 and served as its head until his death.

See also ARAB–ISRAEL WAR (1973); HAGANAH; KNESSET; MEIR, GOLDA; RABIN, YITZHAK.

JULIE ZUCKERMAN

YARMUK RIVER

Tributary of the Jordan river.

The Yarmuk river forms boundaries between Jordan, Syria, and Israel, all of which have contested its use as a water source. About fifty miles (80 km) long, the Yarmuk rises in southern Syria and flows westward through a deep gorge along the Jordanian border of the Golan Heights region of Syria annexed by Israel in 1981. It empties into the Jordan river four miles (6.4 km) south of the Sea of Galilee. Although much smaller than the Euphrates (in Turkey, north Syria, and Iraq) or even the Litani (in Lebanon), the Yarmuk supplies up to 50 percent of the water flow in the lower Jordan river.

The Yarmuk shares a long and storied past with the Jordan river valley, as recounted in archaeological evidence, holy scripture and medieval chronicles. A Roman fortress town was built at the junction of the two rivers, and ruins of Roman- and Byzantine-era synagogues have been found nearby. In the early seventh century, it was through the Yarmuk gorge that Arab armies invaded the Jordan valley.

The Yarmuk's strategic importance has continued into the modern era. Today, it is the only undeveloped tributary of the Jordan river, in a region that now exploits the maximum capacity of existing water sources. Its only significant exploitation has been Jordan's East Ghawr Canal, built in 1964 to irrigate thirty thousand acres (12,150 ha) of farmland east of the Jordan river. Jordan plans to extend the nearly 50-mile (80-km) canal and build a 328-foot (100-m) dam at Maqarin to store the Yarmuk's waters for agriculture and for the cities of Irbid and Amman. Syria plans a series of small dams on the upper Yarmuk to benefit agriculture in the Hawran region.

But these plans require agreement from all parties enjoying riparian rights to the river—not just Syria and Jordan, but also Israel. Israeli interest in the Yarmuk began shortly after World War I, when Chaim Weizmann, later Israel's first president, proposed borders for Palestine that would include the river. In 1932, the Palestine Electric Corporation (now the Israel Electric Corporation) built a hydroelectric generating plant at the junction of the Yarmuk and Jordan rivers. It was destroyed by the Arab Legion in the 1948 war, but Israel has continued to claim the water rights to the Yarmuk granted by the British mandate.

Since 1948, the contest for the Yarmuk has at times been violent. Efforts in the 1950s to coordinate joint use of the Jordan river basin, like the 1953 Johnston Plan, failed to gain agreement from all sides. While Jordan pursued its unilateral East Ghawr Canal, Israel, between 1953 and 1964, built its National Water Carrier, which diverts the Jordan's water from north of the Sea of Galilee to Tel Aviv and the Negev desert. In response, the Arab League in 1960 coordinated a plan to develop the Yarmuk for the benefit of Jordan, Syria, and Lebanon. The project, begun in 1964, was to divert the Jordan's northern headwaters to the Yarmuk, where a dam on the Syrian-Jordanian border would also be built. In 1965 and 1966 Israel attacked bulldozers and facilities at construction sites in Syria. Israel's 1967 occupation of the Golan Heights put a final halt to the project. In 1969 Israeli raids destroyed part of Jordan's East Ghawr Canal, which was subsequently repaired.

After years of opposition, in 2003 Syria finally agreed to allow Jordan to begin construction of the Maqarin dam.

See also JOHNSTON PLAN (1953); MAQARIN DAM; WATER.

Bibliography

Farid, Abdel Majid, and Sirriyeh, Hussein, eds. *Israel and Arab Water: An International Symposium.* London: Ithaca Press, 1985.

Khouri, Fred J. *The Arab-Israeli Dilemma,* 3d edition. Syracuse, NY: Syracuse University Press, 1985.

Starr, Joyce R., and Stoll, Daniel, eds. *The Politics of Scarcity: Water in the Middle East.* Boulder, CO: Westview Press, 1988.

ELIZABETH THOMPSON

YARMUK UNIVERSITY

A public university in Jordan.

Established in 1976 on the outskirts of Irbid in northwest Jordan, Yarmuk University was the kingdom's second public university, opened in response to the rapidly increasing demands for higher education. The main campus of the university was built over a fifteen-year period and includes faculties of arts, economics, education and fine arts, engineering, Islamic studies, law, science, and an institute for archaeology and anthropology, as well as centers in various disciplines. At its inception, Yarmuk University pioneered new programs, including a center for Jordanian studies, a department of communications and journalism, a department of continuing education, a school for public health, and a department of computer science. In the 1999/2000 academic year, student enrollment was 17,800.

Bibliography

Gubser, Peter. *Historical Dictionary of the Hashemite Kingdom of Jordan.* Metuchen, NJ: Scarecrow Press, 1991.

JENAB TUTUNJI

YARMULKE

See GLOSSARY

YASAR KEMAL

[c. 1923–]

Long despised by Turkish intellectuals, who considered his "popular frescoes" as second-rate literature, Yasar Kemal is today Turkey's most famous living fiction writer.

Yasar Kemal's family was from Ercis, a small town near Van, in the Kurdish region of Turkey. During World War I, his father settled in the plain of Tchukurova, near Adana, where Yasar was born around 1923. He does not know his exact date of birth, but it was probably after 1923 because he was named Mustafa Kemal, after the founder of the Turkish Republic. During his childhood, he experienced considerable violence—an atmosphere that permeates his books, which are full of bandits and honor killings. Yasar Kemal's maternal uncle was one of Turkey's most renowned bandits, and Yasar Kemal himself was hardly five when his father was murdered in a mosque by his adoptive son.

After his father's death, his family was destitute and Yasar Kemal went to work on other people's land. During this time he observed nature, which he describes at length in his books. The land and its transformations as the seasons change are an important part of his novels. He also describes the poor peasants' fight for land that has been confiscated by rapacious *aghas* and *beys* (landowners)

At seventeen, Yasar Kemal became a leftist political activist. He was introduced to Marxism by Arif and Abidine Dino, two brothers who had been exiled to Adana, and he later became a member of the Central Committee of the Turkish Communist Party. After many menial jobs, he became a journalist, working for *Cumhuriyet* from 1951 to 1963 while writing his first three novels. From 1963 onwards he earned his living as a novelist, writing full-time.

Among his more than twenty-five books, the most famous are *Murder in the Ironsmith Market; Iron Earth, Copper Sky; The Wind from the Plain; The Undying Grass*; and his most famous, *Memed, My Hawk.* Most of them were translated into English by his wife, Thilda. During the early years of the twenty-first century, Yasar Kemal worked on a trilogy about the 1923 exchange of Greek and Turkish populations after the dismembering of the Ottoman Empire, and on his memoirs.

Although many of the secondary characters in his novels are Kurdish, Yasar Kemal used to deny that he was a Kurd. Since the 1990s, however, he has claimed his Kurdish identity, saying, "I am writing in Turkish, I never wrote a line in Kurdish, but I am a Kurd."

See also KURDS; LITERATURE: TURKISH.

KATHLEEN R. F. BURRILL
UPDATED BY CHRIS KUTSCHERA

YASHMAK

See CLOTHING

YASIN, AHMAD ISMA'IL

[1936–2004]

Founder of HAMAS.

Ahmad Isma'il Yasin was born in 1936 in the village of al-Jurah, south of Gaza. His family moved to the Gaza Strip after the 1948 Arab–Israel War. He had an accident in his youth (while playing sports) that resulted in his paralysis. He studied Arabic language and religion, became a teacher in both fields, and rose in prominence as a militant preacher in the mosques of Gaza. He headed the Islamic-oriented al-Mujamma al-Islami. In 1983 Yasin was arrested and charged with possession of weapons, then was released in 1985 during a famous prisoner exchange between Israel and the Popular Front for the Liberation of Palestine–General Command.

Yasin was the key founder and leader of HAMAS (acronym for the Arabic name of the Islamic Resistance Movement), which was officially begun in 1987. HAMAS's ideology is a militant and more violent version of the Muslim Brotherhood, and it analyzes the Arab–Israeli conflict in purely religious terms. Palestine is seen as a religious waqf land that belongs to Muslims, and enmity is expressed toward Jews. The movement calls for armed struggle, but unlike the secular Palestinian organizations of the 1960s and 1970s, it considers this struggle to be obligatory jihad. HAMAS played a key role in the Palestinian Intifada of 1987, and Yasin was arrested in 1989 and sentenced to life in prison. He was released in 1997, when Israel had a deal with Jordan's King Hussein after a failed assassination attempt in Jordan against the head of the Political Bureau of HAMAS, Khalid Mish'al. Despite Yasin's feeble physical state, he provided a strong leadership for the movement. He had a weak voice and a variety of ailments (some resulting from torture and mistreatment in Israeli jails), but he could inspire the masses. Although he left military decisions to the military branch of HAMAS, he legitimized the suicide attacks that characterized the second (al-Aqsa) Intifada of 2000. Yasin succeeded in turning HAMAS into the second most important Palestinian organization after Yasir Arafat's al-Fatah movement. His militancy did not prevent him from reaching pragmatic agreements with Palestinian organizations, including Marxist groups, and he had a large following in the Persian Gulf region, where he raised much of the money for HAMAS before U.S. pressures led Gulf governments to curtail fundraising for the movement. In 2003 Yasin survived an Israeli bomb attack on a house he was thought to inhabit. Yasin was assassinated outside a Gaza mosque on 22 March 2004 by a missile fired from an Israeli helicopter.

AS'AD ABUKHALIL

YATA, ALI
[1920–1997]

Moroccan journalist and left-wing politician.

Ali Yata was the first Muslim secretary-general of the Moroccan Communist Party. He served until it was banned in 1959. Later he established the party of Liberty and Socialism (1968) and the party of Progress and Socialism (1974, as its secretary-general). He also founded the newspaper *al-Bayane.* Yata was elected deputy in the 1977 elections saying that democratic progress had begun, but he demanded annulment of the 1983 local elections alleging fraud. He participated in the 1984 legislative elections. Yata supported Moroccan claims to the Sahara in the 1960s and to the Western Sahara in the 1970s and 1980s.

See also COMMUNISM IN THE MIDDLE EAST.

C. R. PENNELL

YAZD

Ancient Iranian city located in an oasis in the central desert region.

Yazd is the name of a province and its capital city in central Iran. The province, which extends over an area of 27,027 square miles (70,000 sq km), is largely desert, with the great salt desert known as the Kavir in the north merging into the great sand and stone desert (the Lut) of southeastern Iran. The province has lead and zinc deposits, many of which are sites of major commercial mining operations.

The city of Yazd was an important Zoroastrian religious center during the Sassanian dynasty (226–642 C.E.) and has remained a stronghold of Zoroastrianism up to the present, although adherents of this faith comprise less than 10 percent of the city's population. In the early 2000s, about one-half of all Zoroastrians in Iran lived in Yazd, and the fire temples there and in some surrounding villages had become historic pilgrimage sites. Between the thirteenth and nineteenth centuries, the city was internationally renowned for its silk, cotton, and woolen textiles, but these handicrafts declined dramatically after 1850 as the volume of European manufactured textiles imported into Iran increased. By the mid-twentieth century, entrepreneurs had established modern cotton and woolen textile mills in the city, and Yazd gradually recovered its status as a regional commercial and production center. The railroad from Tehran to the Gulf of Oman port of Bandar-e Abbas, completed in 1995, passes through Yazd; its construction helped stimulate development in and migration to the city. Between 1976 and 1996, the population of Yazd increased more than 140 percent (an average of 7 percent per annum), from 135,925 to 326,776.

See also ZOROASTRIANISM.

Bibliography

Boyce, Mary. *A Persian Stronghold of Zoroastrianism.* Oxford, U.K.: Clarendon Press, 1977.

ERIC HOOGLUND

YAZDI, IBRAHIM
[1931–]

Iranian politician.

Born in Qazvin, where his father made his living as a retailer, Ibrahim Yazdi studied pharmacology at Tehran University and emerged as one of the leaders of the Muslim Student Association. In 1952 he galvanized student support in favor of Mohammad Mossadegh's oil nationalization platform. He co-edited two journals, *Forugh-e Elm* (The resplendence of knowledge) and *Ganj-e Shayegan* (The magnificent treasure), and was employed at the Worker Social Security Organization. Following the CIA-sponsored coup that ousted Mossadegh in 1953, Yazdi joined the newly formed National Resistance Movement. The movement was effectively crushed in 1957 but resurfaced in 1960 as the National Front, of which the Liberation Movement of Iran (formed in 1961 by the more religiously minded members of the original nationalist coalition) was a splinter group. Yazdi was a member of the nascent Liberation Movement of Iran, and after he left Iran for the United States in about 1960 was instrumental in organizing its opposition activities abroad, both in the United States and elsewhere. He also studied for his doctoral degree in the United States.

In 1978 he frequented Ayatollah Ruhollah Khomeini's headquarters in France. When he returned to Iran in 1979, he was appointed deputy prime minister, and in 1980 he became foreign minister in the cabinet of Mehdi Bazargan's provisional government. He was among the group of Bazargan's friends who constituted the nonclerical, moderate figures in the Islamic movement and who cooperated closely with the Revolutionary Guards. He also headed the nationalized Kayhan Publishing Group, which produced a daily newspaper whose circulation rate exceeded that of all the other Tehran dailies. He was elected to the Islamic parliament as a deputy from Tehran (1980–1984). In the falling-out between the moderates and the more radical Islamic Republican Party affiliates (1979–1981), the latter won. After falling from political favor, Yazdi devoted his energies to revitalizing the Liberation Movement of Iran, which now functioned as the only tolerated—albeit eventually officially banned—opposition party in the political landscape of Iran.

During the late 1980s and early 1990s, Yazdi's activities consisted primarily of criticizing the government's economic policies and its failure to deliver the political rights promised by the revolutionaries in 1979. Taking advantage of the liberalizing policies of President Ali Akbar Hashemi Rafsanjani, Yazdi in this period advocated—in various speeches, articles, and manifestos—fiscal reform, equitable distribution of income, and the normalization of ties with the United States. In 1995, after the death of Mehdi Bazargan, Yazdi emerged as the leader of the Liberation Movement of Iran. In 1996, he made an unsuccessful bid in the parliamentary elections as the Liberation Movement of Iran candidate for a seat from Tehran. In 1997 he was arrested for a short while after signing a letter protesting maltreatment by Ayatollah Khamenehi, the leader of Iran, of Grand Ayatollah Hosayn Montazeri, Ayatollah Khomeini's designated successor until he fell out with the regime in 1989, shortly before Khomeini's death. The judiciary arrested all senior members of the Liberation Movement of Iran in 2000, but Yazdi escaped arrest because he was in the United States undergoing treatment for prostate cancer. He was charged with antigovernment activity when he returned but was allowed to remain free after posting bail. His trial was still continuing at the end of 2003, although there were periods of several months' duration during which no court sessions were scheduled.

See also BAZARGAN, MEHDI; KHAMENEHI, ALI; MONTAZERI, HOSAYN ALI; MOSSADEGH, MOHAMMAD; RAFSANJANI, ALI AKBAR HASHEMI; REVOLUTIONARY GUARDS.

Bibliography

Chehabi, H. E. *Iranian Politics and Religious Modernism: The Liberation Movement of Iran under the Shah and Khomeini.* Ithaca, NY: Cornell University Press, 1990.

Milani, Mohsen M. *The Making of Iran's Islamic Revolution: From Monarchy to Islamic Republic,* 2d edition, Boulder, CO: Westview Press, 1994.

NEGUIN YAVARI

YAZIDIS

See TRIBES AND TRIBALISM: YAZIDIS

YAZIJI, IBRAHIM

[1847–1906]

A leading figure in the Arabic literary revival of the nineteenth century.

Ibrahim Yaziji was a Greek Catholic poet, grammarian, and man of letters from Mount Lebanon. Following in the footsteps of his father, Nasif, who had done pioneer work in rediscovering the Arabic literary heritage, he made a significant contribution to the Arab cultural and political awakening of the late nineteenth century. Like his father, he maintained a close relationship with the American and British Protestant missionaries in Beirut and played an important role in the revitalization of Arabic as a literary language. A member of the Syrian Scientific Society, an early secret society made up of Arab intellectuals and military officers who agitated for Arab independence from the Ottoman Empire, Yaziji is best remembered for an ode, first recited at a secret meeting of the society, which called upon Arabs to remember their past greatness and shake off Turkish rule. This ode and several other poems of his were memorized by a generation of Arab nationalists and inspired the incipient political movement for Arab independence.

See also ARAB NATIONALISM.

Bibliography

Antonius, George. *The Arab Awakening: The Story of the Arab National Movement.* London: H. Hamilton, 1938.

Salibi, Kamal. *A House of Many Mansions: The History of Lebanon Reconsidered.* Berkeley: University of California Press, 1988.

GUILAIN P. DENOEUX

YAZIJI, NASIF
[1800–1871]

Lebanese Christian scholar and author.

Nasif Yaziji played a significant role in revitalizing Arabic literary traditions. He was employed by Bashir Chehab, the amir of Lebanon, and moved to Beirut in 1840 to help U.S. missionaries prepare Arabic text-books for use in Christian mission schools. Yaziji appreciated classical Arabic literature and campaigned to eliminate the corruptions that had been absorbed into the language. His writings helped revive practices of classical scholarship and made classical literature important in contemporary Arab culture.

MARK MECHLER

YEHOSHUA, AVRAHAM B.
[1936–]

Israeli novelist, essayist, and professor of literature.

Avraham Yehoshua was born in Jerusalem into a fifth-generation Sephardic family and now lives in Haifa, where he teaches literature at the University of Haifa. A peace activist and a staunch defender of the Zionist project in his essays, he is best known as one of Israel's foremost novelists. Although he has published both plays and collections of short stories, the latter in his early writings, his greatest works are his seven novels, all of which have been translated into English. His novels are complex, full of humor and compassion, at times highly innovative in style, steeped in the classical modernist tradition, and always crafted with the highest literary skill. Recurrent themes in his novels are love and identity, history and choice, dialogue, and desire, all of which are embedded in the drama of the Jewish people and modern Israel. His masterpiece, *Mr. Mani,* highlights his skill at its finest, rivaling the best of world literature produced in the twentieth century. Israel's equivalent of U.S. novelist William Faulkner, Yehoshua has been the recipient of many prizes: the Brenner Prize in 1983, the Alterman Prize in 1986, the Bialik Prize in 1988, and the American Prize for the Best Jewish Book in 1990 and 1993. He was the inaugural winner of the Israeli Booker Prize in 1991 and in 1995 he received Israel's highest literary honor, the Israel Prize. His books have been translated into many languages. They have also been made into movies and adapted for the stage, television, and radio.

See also LITERATURE: HEBREW.

Bibliography

Yehoshua, A. B. *Between Right and Right,* translated by Arnold Schwartz. Garden City, NY: Doubleday, 1981.

Yehoshua, A. B. *Five Seasons,* translated by Hillel Halkin. New York: Doubleday, 1989.

Yehoshua, A. B. *A Journey to the End of the Millennium,* translated by Nicholas De Lange. New York: Doubleday, 1999.

Yehoshua, A. B. *A Late Divorce,* translated by Hillel Halkin. Garden City, NY: Doubleday, 1984.

Yehoshua, A. B. *The Liberated Bride,* translated by Hillel Halkin. Orlando, FL: Harcourt, 2003.

Yehoshua, A. B. *The Lover,* translated by Philip Simpson. Garden City, NY: Doubleday, 1977.

Yehoshua, A. B. *Mr. Mani,* translated by Hillel Halkin. New York: Doubleday, 1992.

Yehoshua, A. B. *Open Heart,* translated by Dalya Bilu. New York: Doubleday, 1996.

ANN KAHN
UPDATED BY STEPHEN SCHECTER

YELLIN-MOR, NATAN
[1913–1980]

Israeli underground leader.

Born Nathan Friedman-Yellin in Grodno, Poland, Yellin-Mor was an activist in the Polish branch of Betar and the Irgun Zva'i Le'umi. He was co-editor, along with Abraham (Yair) Stern, of *Di Tat,* the Irgun's Polish newspaper. He followed Stern to Palestine and became a major figure in Stern's virulently anti-British underground, Lohamei Herut Yisrael (LEHI: Freedom Fighters of Israel). In December 1941 he attempted to reach neutral Turkey via Syria to negotiate with Nazi representatives for a mass release of Jews from Eastern Europe in exchange for LEHI's cooperation in fighting Britain.

Upon his return he was imprisoned by the British but escaped in 1943. After Stern's death, Yellin-Mor became a member of the LEHI triumvirate, along with Israel Eldad and Yitzhak Shamir. In 1949 he was tried and convicted for the September 1948 assassination of United Nations emissary Count Folke Bernadotte, but the sentence was commuted in exchange for an oath to desist from any further violent activities. He led the left-wing faction of both LEHI and its post-statehood political entity, the Fighters Party, and he was elected to the First Knesset (1949–1951). In the ensuing years he moved increasingly to the left. He renounced Zionism and advocated a pro-Soviet foreign policy and the creation of a single Arab-Jewish socialist state in all of what had been Mandatory Palestine.

See also BERNADOTTE, FOLKE; SHAMIR, YITZHAK; STERN, ABRAHAM.

Bibliography

Heller, Joseph. *The Stern Gang: Ideology, Politics, and Terror, 1940–1949.* Portland, OR; London: Frank Cass, 1995.

BRYAN DAVES
UPDATED BY PIERRE M. ATLAS

YEMEN

A state on the southwestern corner of the Arabian Peninsula.

The Republic of Yemen was created in May 1990 as a result of the merger of the two previous states that used the name Yemen: the Yemen Arab Republic (YAR; often called North Yemen) and the People's Democratic Republic of Yemen (PDRY; often called South Yemen). The merger brought together two disparate political systems: the North had been governed by a military/tribal elite, which supported a free-market economy, whereas the South had been governed by a Marxist-Leninist political elite, which had introduced one of the most centrally directed economies in the modern world. After a transition period, the president of the North, Ali Abdullah Salih, was made president of the new unified state.

Population

In 2000, the population was estimated at 17.5 million, not including an indeterminate number of Yemenis living and working abroad, primarily in Arabian Peninsula states. Yemen has one of the highest birthrates in the world, as well as a high infant mortality rate; the net rate of annual increase is estimated at 3.6 percent.

Area and Borders

Since Yemen is one of the few states in the modern world without completely demarcated borders, it is not possible to give a precise figure for its total area. The northeast and east still have no internationally (or even locally) accepted borders. This has led to numerous border disputes and even wars between Saudi Arabia and both of the previously existing Yemens since the 1920s. The border with Saudi Arabia was demarcated as far as the Najran oasis after the Saudi-Yemeni War of 1934; this conflict also gave control of the Asir region to the Saudi state through a treaty renewed every twenty years, creating continued difficulties in relations between the two states. In the northeast, the generally recognized end of Yemeni sovereignty lies east of Ma'rib; with the discovery of oil and gas deposits in this area, however, new conflicts over the border between the two states arose in this area in the late 1980s and early 1990s. The demarcation of the border with Oman was officially completed in 1995, but despite repeated memoranda of agreement with Saudi Arabia in the 1990s, as well as a contract with a German firm to undertake its delineation in 2001, that process has yet to be completed. In the mid-1990s, a new set of border disagreements arose; these involved numerous islets in the Red Sea, the ownership of which was disputed with Eritrea as well as Saudi Arabia. A UN arbitration panel awarded the islands to Yemen in 1999, but the agreement specifically avoided defining the maritime boundary in a way that would offend the claims of Saudi Arabia. To the south, Yemen lies on the Gulf of Aden. The old border between the North and South—created by the Ottoman and the British empires in the early years of the twentieth century and technically abolished as a result of the union of 1990—nevertheless continues to be of some political importance.

Major Cities

San'a is the most important, largest, and probably the oldest city in Yemen—it is mentioned in the Bible under its old name, Uzal. By 2000, its population was considerably more than 1 million. It has been the capital city of Yemen for most of the past two millennia (with the exception of the reign of Imam Ahmad, 1948–1962, in which he moved the capital to Ta'iz) and became the administrative (political) capital of the new republic after unification. Its old city has been placed on the list of World Heritage Sites because of its unique architecture and historical importance; many of the buildings are more than 800 years old.

Aden, the capital of the former PDRY, has the best port on the Arabian Peninsula. For more than a century, until the late 1960s, it was a major British military and commercial possession. After unification, it was made the economic and commercial capital of the country, but its role in the civil war of 1994 and subsequent events caused it to lose some of its significance.

Hodeida (al-Hudayda) is the major port of the former North Yemen. Its facilities were extensively modernized by the Soviet Union in the 1960s. Consequently, it grew rapidly from a sleepy Red Sea fishing port handling primarily local trade to a major metropolitan area.

Ta'iz, the major city of the southern highlands of the former North Yemen, is located in one of the richest agricultural areas. Its population, predominantly of the Islamic Shafi'i sect, had the longest and best-developed contacts with the outside world during the reigns of Imams Yahya and Ahmad in the twentieth century.

Although the country has a few smaller cities (e.g., Ibb, Dhamar, Sa'ada and Zabid in the north, and Mukalla, Tarim, and Shibam in the south), the vast majority of the population lives in villages, each with an average population of fewer than 200 people. Yemen probably has the most decentralized population of any contemporary state.

Geography and Climate

Yemen's location, combined with its geographical characteristics, gives it the most favorable climate and agricultural resources of any country on the Arabian Peninsula. The country is divided into a number of relatively clear zones: The first of these, along the Red Sea and the Arabian Sea coasts, is hot and humid; from there, the land slopes upward into the first range of hills and low mountains, where the climate is considerably more temperate; eventually, after a series of high plains, the peaks of the cen-

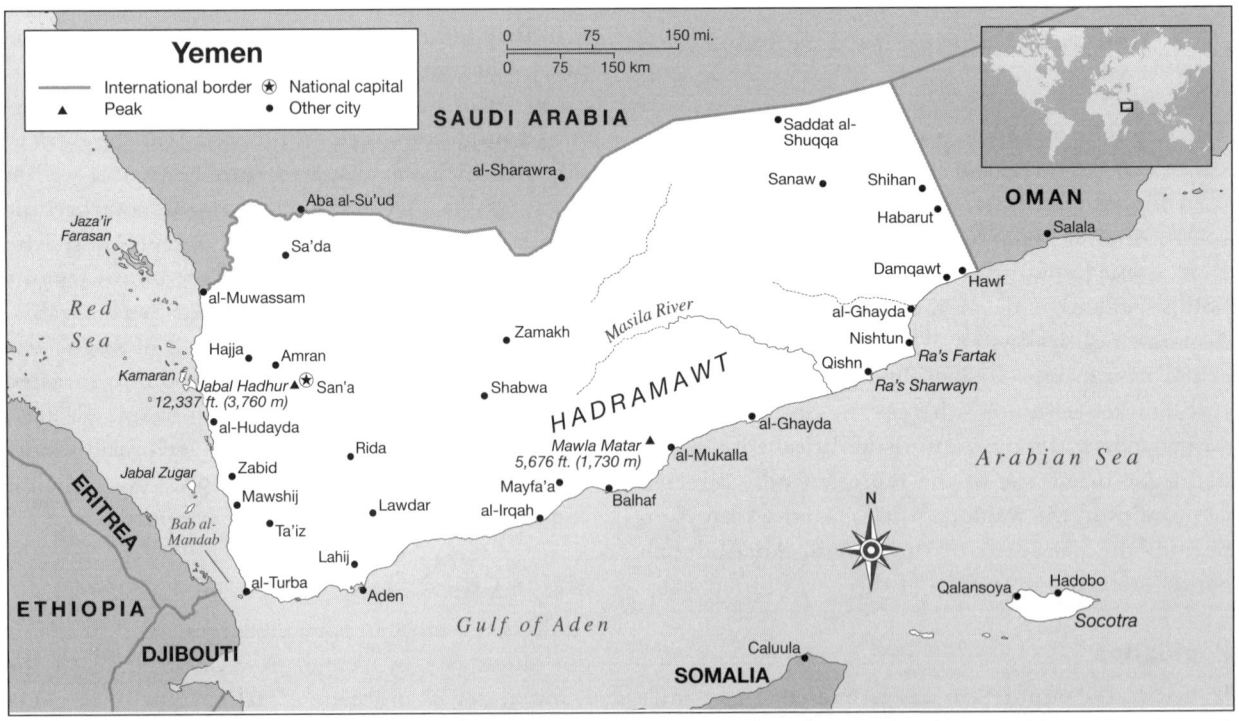

MAP BY XNR PRODUCTIONS, INC. THE GALE GROUP.

The Qubbat Talha Mosque, which sits in Yemen's capital city of San'a. © CHRIS LISLE/CORBIS. REPRODUCED BY PERMISSION.

tral massif reach between 11,000 and 13,000 feet (3,355–3,965 m). These mountains have been terraced from time immemorial, and a vast array of fruits, vegetables, and grains (and the infamous qat plant) can be raised in the many microclimates created by this geography. In the central mountains, the humidity is low and the temperatures moderate, although in the winter it is not unusual to find temperatures below freezing and the occasional snow or ice storm. Over the centuries, the Yemenis have developed plant strains to occupy the many microclimates. On the other side of the central massif and away from the monsoons, which deliver the rain that makes extensive agriculture possible on the westward side, the land slopes away into the great central desert of Arabia, the Rub al-Khali, broken only by the great Hadramawt Valley, the home of numerous towns exploiting the limited water resources found there. The rainfall that the various mountain ranges wring out of the prevailing winds varies widely—from less than 3 inches (7.62 cm) per year in the deserts and northern reaches of the country to about 38 inches (96.52 cm) per year in some of the areas around Ta'iz—about the same as in Seattle, New York, or Chicago.

Political Subdivisions

Administratively, the two preunification Yemeni states varied considerably. The units into which the two states were organized were frequently modified, sometimes as the result of political expediency and at other times due to the nature of the personnel available for major administrative duties. For example, in the PDRY, the first administrative reorganization sought to get rid of the old tribally organized political entities, which had been called the protectorates. Later, the state undertook to recreate some of these entities under new names to regain popular support. In the North, after the revolution, the number of administrative units (governorates) rose with the growth in the population as well as with the increasing number and variety of demands for governmental services. In the immediate aftermath of reunification, the number and characteristics of the administrative subunits within the two separate entities were largely retained. On the other hand, electoral districts have been substantially increased and modified over the years.

The Economy

The natural resource base of Yemen has begun to be developed, largely because it was not until the 1960s that either the North or the South had the opportunity to assess that base or attempt its development. The most important contemporary resources are oil and gas deposits, which were discovered in both North and South Yemen prior to unification and which contributed significantly to the push for unification. The majority of the population of Yemen continues to be employed in the agricultural sector, although productivity is not adequate to the requirements of the population. The multiplicity of microclimates makes it possible to grow just about any fruit or vegetable, from the citrus fruits, bananas, and cotton of the hot coastal plain, through the coffee, grains, and qat (a small tree valued for the alkaloids contained in its leaves) of the middle highlands, to the pears, grapes, and nuts of the high mountains.

Although industrial development has been a priority in both North and South Yemen since independence, it has not reached the stage where industry is a significant factor in the economy of either region. In fact, Yemen operates a monumental deficit in its current accounts because it has few exportable resources. Until 1991, the most important positive element in its balance of payments was the remittances of its large workforce in the various Gulf states and in other countries. Following the 1991 Gulf War, however, the majority of Yemenis abroad were forced to return home (some 800,000 from Saudi Arabia alone), creating a massive social and economic problem. Since then, a variety of international loans and development assistance funds have helped to ameliorate the continuing economic problems.

Culture

The population of Yemen is ethnically Arab, although of different origins. The majority is descended from the ancient south Arabian peoples, and the remainder immigrated from the Fertile Crescent area more than a thousand years ago.

Arabic is the official language. Although everyone speaks it, there are substantial differences in dialect from region to region. In some of the more remote areas of the island of Socotra (located in the Gulf of Aden) Mahri is still spoken.

The overwhelming majority of Yemenis are Muslims. They are, however, divided into different sects: In the northern areas, the Zaydis, members of a branch of Shiʿism, predominate; in the southern areas, the Shafiʿis, who follow a branch of Sunni Islam, are in the majority. There are, in addition, Ismaʿilis, members of another branch of Shiʿism, in the northern mountains; in and around Saʿada there are also small settlements of Jews.

The educational infrastructure is in a state of flux. Until the revolution of 1962, an insignificant number of people received any formal education. After the revolution, the government embarked on a major program to establish educational institutions, from primary schools to universities, of which there are several, including those at Sanʿa, Taʿiz, and Aden; these were, in the overwhelming majority of cases, coeducational. In the 1990s, however, Islamists gained increasing political power and began to impose their views on the educational establishment. Owing to several incidents in which the government saw the hand of Islamic extremists, the government began to implement earlier legislation intended to bring independent religious institutions under the control of the Ministry of Education, closing many, eventually even the private al-Iman University, operated by perhaps the most extreme Islamic leader in Yemen, Shaykh Abd al-Majid al-Zindani, and considered the center of Islamic extremism.

Government

Yemen is governed under a constitution that was approved by the parliaments of the two Yemens in 1990 and by popular referendum in 1991. This constitution declares Yemen to be a parliamentary democracy, with an executive appointed by and responsible to the parliament (the Council of Deputies). In 1994, Ali Abdullah Salih was elected by the coun-

A woman carries a child through an alley in San'a, Yemen. © CHRIS LISLE/CORBIS. REPRODUCED BY PERMISSION.

cil to a five-year term as president. In 1999, due to changes in the law, the first direct elections to the presidency were held; Salih was overwhelmingly elected to a seven-year term. His only real opponent was the son of the former leader of the PDRY, Najib Qahtan al-Sha'abi, although there were two additional candidates.

Elections to the new parliament were held in April 1993, with some eight parties and a sizable number of independents taking seats. Three parties dominated the outcome: the General People's Congress (GPC), formerly dominant in the North and associated with Ali Abdullah Salih; the Islah, now commonly referred to as the Yemeni Islah Party (YIP), a coalition of tribal and Islamic interests led by the second most influential political figure in the country, Shaykh Abdullah al-Ahmar of the Hashid Tribal Confederation; and the Yemeni Socialist Party (YSP), formerly dominant in the South and led by Ali Salim al-Baydh, who had become vice president of the new state. Other parties exist, including a Nasserist party. The second election to the Council of Deputies took place in 1997; the aftermath of the 1994 civil war, however, meant that the role and influence of the YSP was considerably reduced, and the YSP boycotted the elections (al-Baydh went into exile). Consequently, the GPC gained 187 of the 301 seats, with its only serious competition, the YIP, gaining only 53. In the next round of elections, in April 2003, the GPC's margin of victory increased to 238 of 301 seats; the YIP could only manage 46 seats, and the YSP was reduced to 8 seats.

History

Some 2,000 years ago, Yemen (known as Arabia Felix to the Roman geographers) was famous and its city-states (e.g., Saba/Sheba, Ma'in), grew powerful and wealthy due to their monopoly over the trade in frankincense and myrrh. Once this monopoly was broken, Yemen retreated from the world stage. It was not until coffee became an important international trade commodity in the sixteenth through eighteenth centuries that Yemen once again achieved renown. However, its early monopoly over coffee was broken by foreign traders and governments, and it once again became a little-known province of various empires on the Red Sea.

The contemporary state of Yemen was created by two states with different historical experiences during the past two centuries. Although occasionally united in the past, they had not been so since 1728. Developments in the nineteenth century, however, are most important to an understanding of the events that led to the reunification of North and South Yemen in 1990.

In 1839, the British took the city of Aden in South Yemen in order to have a major port in the western Indian Ocean and to forestall further expansion by other parties in the Arabian Peninsula. Over the years, British interests continued to grow, and they eventually established extensive links with the multitude of principalities located in Aden's (Yemeni) hinterland.

Meanwhile, the Ottoman Empire, which had occupied Yemen for a variety of strategic and economic reasons but which had departed in the early seventeenth century, decided to return. One motive was to play a role in the Red Sea trade, as it had in the past, although there were other factors; this goal increased in importance with the completion of the Suez Canal in 1869. Eventually, British and Ottoman interests in southwestern Arabia clashed; the two powers decided to negotiate a frontier between their zones of influence and interest. Beginning in 1902, they agreed to demarcate a border between them; the agreement that was eventually signed in 1914 created the frontier between the Ottoman possession that became the Kingdom of Yemen (North Yemen) after World War I and the British Aden Protectorates, which became South Yemen.

Under the reigns of Imams Yahya and Ahmad (1918–1962), North Yemen remained largely cut off from the rest of the world, while Aden and the protectorates in the south received British subsidies and Aden developed into one of the world's busiest ports. Both states, however, had political movements that sought change. In 1962, a revolution broke out in North Yemen, which sought to create a republic and remove the conservative Zaydi imam(s) from power. After an eight-year civil war, the two major factions compromised and created the Yemen Arab Republic. Imam Muhammad al-Badr, the titular head of the effort to restore the imamate, fled to Saudi Arabia and eventually died in exile in Great Britain. Shortly after the revolution broke out in North Yemen, various groups in South Yemen began to work for independence from Great Britain. After a lengthy and often violent conflict, the British agreed to withdraw from Aden and its protectorates in 1967. The group to which they ceded power, the National Front for the Liberation of South Yemen, created the People's Republic of South Yemen (later the People's Democratic Republic of Yemen).

Although both Yemens spoke of the goal of reunification, relations between them were often extraordinarily poor, due largely to their different economic and political systems. The North was governed by a military elite, which was tied to the West and permitted an almost unrestricted, though underdeveloped, capitalist economy to operate; in the South, a Marxist-Leninist political elite took power and tied the country to the communist bloc. Relations between the two states deteriorated into two separate wars—in 1972 and 1979.

In the late 1980s, oil (and later natural gas) was discovered in both Yemens; more importantly, it was found in the disputed border areas between them. The effort to develop these deposits without wasting further resources in fruitless wars largely overlapped with the decline of the Soviet Union (and some of its satellites that had provided important assistance to South Yemen). As a result, the potential benefits of a unified effort to develop their oil and gas deposits overcame the mutual suspicions and frictions that had characterized the previous twenty-five years, leading to the unity agreement of 1990. Friction between the North and the South did not disappear, however. Disputes within the original coalition government of the General People's Congress and the Yemeni Socialist Party led to a civil war from May through July 1994. The South suffered a complete defeat, which resulted in the forced exile of its leaders and the concomitant ascent of the Islah Party (YIP).

Perhaps the most important development of the 1990s, however, was the increase in Islamist sentiment and support. Fearful of its growing influence, the GPC (and Salih) undertook various measures to limit Islamist power, including seeking a rapprochement with a truncated YSP. The growing influence of the Islamists in Yemen was most dramatically illustrated by the attack, in 2000, by allies and supporters of al-Qaʿida against the USS *Cole* while it was refueling in Aden. Numerous incidents of political violence involving previously unknown groups (e.g., the Sympathizers of al-Qaʿida) heightened fears in Yemen and the West that the country had become a major breeding and training ground for radical Islamist groups. Salih's government had to walk a fine line between recognizing the increased Islamist sentiment in the population and accommodating the interests and concerns of its grantors of financial and political support, including the United States. The fact that the government did not control all of its territory and that its borders were porous did nothing to assuage the fears of the United States and Europe.

See also ADEN; *COLE,* USS; HADRAMAWT; HODEIDA; ISMAʿILI SHIʿISM; MAʾRIB; PEOPLE'S DEMOCRATIC REPUBLIC OF YEMEN; QAʿIDA, AL-; SALIH, ALI ABDULLAH; SANʿA; SOCOTRA; TAʿIZ; YEMEN ARAB REPUBLIC; YEMEN CIVIL WAR; YEMEN DYNASTIES; ZAYDISM.

Bibliography

Burrowes, Robert. *The Yemen Arab Republic: The Politics of Development, 1967–1986.* Boulder, CO: Westview Press, 1987.

Carapico, Sheila. *Civil Society in Yemen: The Political Economy of Activism in Modern Arabia.* Cambridge, U.K.: Cambridge University Press, 1998.

Dresch, Paul. *A History of Modern Yemen.* Cambridge, U.K.: Cambridge University Press, 2000.

Halliday, Fred. *Revolution and Foreign Policy: The Case of South Yemen, 1967–1987.* Cambridge, U.K.: Cambridge University Press, 1990.

Joffe, E.G.H.; Hachemi, M.J.; and Watkins, E.W. *Yemen Today: Crisis and Solutions: Proceedings of a Two-Day Conference Held at the School of Oriental and African Studies, University of London, November 25 and 26, 1995.* London: Caravel, 1997.

Wenner, Manfred. *The Yemen Arab Republic: Development and Change in an Ancient Land.* Boulder, CO: Westview Press, 1991.

MANFRED W. WENNER

YEMEN ARAB REPUBLIC

The official name of North Yemen from 1962 until its 1990 merger with South Yemen.

The emergence of North Yemen as a single political unit in modern times was largely a function of both the reoccupation of the country by the Ottomans in 1849 and the Yemeni resistance to this presence that coalesced around the imamate near the turn of the century. Defeat in World War I forced the Ottomans to withdraw in 1918, and a resurgent imamate state seized the opportunity. From 1918 until 1962, Yahya ibn Muhammad Hamid al-Din and his son Ahmad ibn Yahya Hamid al-Din acted to forge a monarchy much as the kings of England and France had done centuries earlier. The two imams strengthened the state, thereby securing Yemen's borders and pacifying the interior to degrees rarely known over the past millennium.

The imams used the strengthened imamate to revive North Yemen's traditional Islamic culture and society, this at a time when traditional societies around the world were crumbling under the weight of modernity backed by imperial power. They were aided in their efforts to insulate Yemen by the degree to which its agricultural economy was self-contained and self-sufficient. The result was a "backward" Yemen, though a small but increasing number of Yemenis exposed to the modern world wanted change and blamed the imamate for its absence. This produced a fateful chain of events: the birth of the Free Yemeni movement in the mid-1940s; the aborted 1948 revolution that left Imam Yahya dead; the failed 1955 coup against Imam Ahmad; and, finally, the 1962 revolution that yielded the Yemen Arab Republic (YAR).

Major Eras

In retrospect, the history of the YAR can best be divided into three periods. (1) The Sallal era (1962–1967), the wrenching first five years under President Abdullah al-Sallal, was marked by the revolution that began it, the long civil war and Egyptian

The Dar al-Hajar, or Rock Palace, in Wadi Dhahr, Yemen. This palace was built for Imam Yahya in the 1930s. After the fall of the Ottoman Empire in 1918, Imam Yahya assumed control over North Yemen. His family ruled the country until revolutionaries ended their authoritarian rule and created the Yemen Arab Republic in 1962. © EARL & NAZIMA KOWALL/CORBIS. REPRODUCED BY PERMISISON.

intervention that quickly followed, and—above all—the rapid and irreversible opening of the country to the modern world. (2) A ten-year transition period (1967–1977) was marked by the end of the civil war, the republican-royalist reconciliation under President Abd al-Rahman al-Iryani, and the attempt by President Ibrahim al-Hamdi to strengthen the state and restructure politics. (3) The Salih era (1978–1990) is identified with both the long tenure of President Ali Abdullah Salih and the change from political weakness and economic uncertainty at the outset to relative political stability, the discovery of oil, and the prospect of oil-based development and prosperity in more recent years.

Of the many important changes that took place in the YAR since its birth in 1962, most of the positive ones have been compressed into the years since its fifteenth anniversary in 1977. Nevertheless, the previous decade was important, a transition in which much-needed time was bought by a few modest but pivotal acts and, most important, by economic good fortune. Global and regional economic events over which the YAR had no control facilitated a huge flow of funds into the country in the form of both foreign aid and remittances from Yemenis working abroad. This period of transition was necessary because the changes that had buffeted Yemen in the five years following the 1962 revolution had left it both unable to retreat into the past and ill-equipped to go forward. The ability to advance rapidly in the 1980s seems very much the result of the possibility afforded for a breather in the 1970s.

Establishing Sovereignty

Given the isolation and the decentralized nature of North Yemeni society, much of the YAR's first quarter-century was taken up with the effort to establish sovereignty over the land and people. The Yemenis who made the revolution in 1962 were preoccupied from the outset with the need to create a state with the capacity to maintain public security and provide services. The long civil war that came on the heels of the revolution both increased this need and interfered with meeting it. Yemeni state-building was more hindered than helped by the fact that the new state was largely built and staffed by Egyptians and by the fact that Egyptian forces did most of the fighting on behalf of the Yemenis.

The balance of power between the tribal periphery and the state at the center tipped back toward the tribes during the civil war. As a result, the reach of the YAR extended little beyond the triangle in the southern half of the country that was traced by the roads linking the cites of San^ca, Ta^ciz, and Hodeida (al-Hudayda).

State-Building Efforts

The YAR created in 1962 lacked modern political organization. A major theme of its first twenty-five years consisted of attempts to fashion the ideas and organization needed to channel support and demands from society to the regime and, conversely, to channel information, appeals, and directives from the regime to society. The civil war strained and even deformed the new republic, deferring any major effort at political construction under President al-Sallal. Egypt's heavy-handed tutelage left little room for Yemeni national politics and politicians to develop.

As with other late-developing countries, the tasks of state-building in the new YAR went beyond the maintenance of order and security to include the creation of a capacity to influence, if not control, the rate and direction of socioeconomic change. The wrenching effects of the sudden end of isolation and of virtual self-sufficiency made it obvious that state-building in all of its aspects was desperately needed. No less than the viability and survival of Yemen in its new external environment depended upon it, just as the civil war and the political weakness of the YAR made it unlikely.

The Egyptian exodus in 1967 led to the quick overthrow of President al-Sallal and the republican-royalist reconciliation that finally ended the civil war in 1970. Some state-building of importance was achieved thereafter by the regime headed by President al-Iryani. A modern constitution was adopted in 1970, and some of the ministries and other agencies erected after the revolution were strengthened. Economic needs as well as political constraints caused Yemeni leaders during the al-Iryani era to focus on financial and economic institutions; only halting first steps were taken toward reform of the civil service and the armed forces, matters of great political sensitivity. President al-Hamdi, who forced President al-Iryani into exile in 1974, believed in the modern state and worked to realize it. He promoted efforts to build institutions at the center, initiated the first major reform and upgrading of the armed forces, and fostered the idea of exchanging the benefits of state-sponsored development for allegiance to the state.

The results of efforts by the Iryani and Hamdi regimes at political construction were modest. The price of the reconciliation was the first-time granting of office and influence in the state to leading tribal shaykhs and the expulsion of the modernist Left from the body politic—prices that weakened the position of all advocates of a strong state. The result was the narrowly based center-right republican regime, which, with changes, persisted from the late 1960s until at least the early 1980s. The chief institutional focus of politics during the Iryani era was the Consultative Council, which first convened after elections in early 1971. However, political parties were banned and, in the absence of explicit organizational and ideological ties, the council functioned as an assembly of local notables, especially the shaykhs.

President al-Hamdi was unable to strengthen his position by translating his great popularity into political organization. Indeed, his major political achievement actually narrowed the political base of his regime and shortened the reach of the state. Aware that the shaykhs were using their new positions to protect the tribal system, al-Hamdi moved swiftly to drive them from the Consultative Council and from other state offices. To this end, he dissolved the council and suspended the 1970 constitution. The tribes responded with virtual rebellion. Al-Hamdi's efforts to make up for this loss of support by reincorporating the modernist Left were hesitant. In addition to maintaining ties to old leftist friends, he launched both the Local Development Association (LDA) movement and the Correction movement. Despite their initial promise, al-Hamdi seems to have had second thoughts and to have pulled back from efforts to use these two initiatives as bases for a broad, popular political movement. His subsequent plans for a general people's congress ended with his assassination in 1977. Frustrated by his failure to grant them reentry into the polity, several leftist groups in 1976 created the National Democratic Front (NDF), which a few years later became the basis of the rebellion that challenged the Salih regime.

Socioeconomic Development of the 1970s

The civil war finally behind it, the YAR in the 1970s did undergo significant socioeconomic development based upon the rapid creation of a modest capacity to absorb generous amounts of economic and technical assistance from abroad and, most important, from the massive inflow of workers' remittances that fostered unprecedented consumption and prosperity. Whereas the remittances largely flowed through the private sector, the modest strengthening of state institutions and the increase in their capacities were the critical factors in Yemen's ability to absorb significantly increased foreign aid. By the late 1970s, work on a broad array of state-sponsored, foreign-assisted infrastructure, agricultural, and human resource development projects existed side by side with high levels of remittance-fueled consumption and economic activity in the private sector.

The Salih Regime

President Salih's long term in office, beginning in 1978, was witness to major gains in state-building. After a shaky start, the Salih regime slowly increased the capacity of the state in the provinces as well as in the cities, for the first time making the republican state more than just a nominal presence in the countryside. The armed forces were upgraded again in 1979 and, more recently, in 1986 and 1988. Modest efforts were made to improve the functioning of the civil service, ministries, and other agencies.

The Salih regime increased its dominance over lands controlled by the tribes, especially the large area that fans out north and east from San'a, the capital. However, the best evidence of the growing ability of the YAR to exercise power within its own borders was the political-military defeat of the NDF. With its origins in the expulsion of the Left from the republic in 1968, the NDF rebellion had finally burst into flame over a wide area by early 1980. This uprising was extinguished in 1982, and the state was able at last to establish a real presence in lands bordering South Yemen.

In 1979, the Salih regime had little political support outside the armed forces. After the failure of ad hoc efforts to change this, the regime put in place an impressive program of political construction during the first half of the 1980s. This phased, sequential program began in early 1980 with the drafting of the National Pact. The pact then became the subject of a long national dialogue and local plebiscites orchestrated by the National Dialogue Committee. Elections to the General People's Congress (GPC), and its several-day session, were held in mid-1982 to review and then to adopt the National Pact. This done, the GPC declared itself a permanent political organization, which would be selected every four years, meet biennially and be led by a seventy-five-member Standing Committee headed by President Salih.

The key to the success of the Salih regime's political effort lay in the flexible, step-by-step process by which it moved the Yemeni polity from where it was in 1979 to the holding of the GPC in 1982. By design and a bit of luck, moreover, this sustained initiative also provided a political process largely managed by the regime into which elements of the Yemeni left could be safely incorporated when, in 1982, the NDF rebellion was quelled. Two dialogues, the one between the regime and the NDF as well as the more public one between the regime and the rest of the nation, converged in a structure that facilitated a second national reconciliation.

Although President Salih insisted that the GPC was not a political party, its activities were clearly aimed at consensus-building, guidance, and control—typical functions of a party. In fact, the GPC did become an umbrella party, a loose organization of organizations in a society that was not well organized politically for many of the tasks of the modern world. The Salih regime was also buttressed by constitutional change during the 1980s. The 1970 constitution, suspended by al-Hamdi in 1974, had been reinstated confusingly in 1978 without its centerpiece, the Consultative Council, and with an amendment that formally created the presidency. Clarity and closure on a number of issues were not achieved until July 1988 when a new Consultative Council was finally chosen in accordance with the constitution. The council elections, the first since 1971, were hotly contested and relatively fair and open; despite the ban on parties, much partisanship was in evidence. In mid-July, the new council elected President Salih to a new term and then gave approval to the composition and program of the new government. As a result, for the first time since the Iryani regime was ousted in 1974, the head of state and the government were selected in accordance with the 1970 constitution, that is, by a properly chosen Consultative Council.

Oil and the Economy

The modest prosperity that the YAR enjoyed after the mid-1970s was paralleled by the modern sector's increasing vulnerability to negative economic and political forces, domestic and external. Political uncertainty early in the Salih era threatened the limited capacity of the state to foster and manage development, and this was followed by the fall in oil prices and worldwide recession that led to sharp drops in aid and remittances to Yemen. Faced with economic crises, the regime in the early 1980s adopted austerity measures, and these had some success in forcing the country to live within more modest means in a less generous world.

The YAR's long-term development prospects improved abruptly when oil was discovered in commercial quantities in 1984. This event also placed severe demands on the still very limited capacities of the state. With the oil find, the twin tasks facing the Salih regime were to maintain the new discipline and austerity of the past few years and to gear up to absorb efficiently the oil revenues that were expected to start flowing in late 1987. Despite the politically difficult combination of rising expectations and continued hard times, the regime during this period of transition was able to limit imports and government expenditures. Changes in organization and the appointment of top technocrats to key posts contributed to the modest success of the transition. Although oil for export did begin to flow in late 1987, the regime was forced in 1989 to reimpose austerity measures that it had relaxed prematurely the previous year. Nevertheless, at the same time that it wrestled with these politically hard choices, the government proceeded as fast as financing would allow with development of the oil and gas sector as well as with key infrastructure and agricultural projects.

Development in the 1980s

In the 1980s, the increasing capacity of the Yemeni state for development also helped it to perform its more traditional functions and was partly understood and justified in these terms. This was especially the case when the regime stepped up efforts to extend its reach into NDF-influenced and tribal areas. Certain development efforts made the periphery more accessible and made possible the delivery of basic services to places where the state was regarded with suspicion or scorn. Hence the emphasis on pushing roads into such areas as soon as they were pacified. President Salih came to justify development efforts in terms of nation-state building—in terms of national integration—as well as economic gains. The development activities of the second half of the 1980s, as well as the content of the third Five-Year Development Plan adopted in 1988, reflected the continuing influence of these ideas.

This third period of YAR history, spanning the 1980s, ended with the creation of the Republic of Yemen, headed by President Salih. It was the political and economic turnaround of the YAR after the 1970s, as well as the sudden weakening of South Yemen in the late 1980s, that made possible the YAR-initiated merger.

See also AHMAD IBN YAHYA HAMID AL-DIN; FREE YEMENIS; YAHYA IBN MUHAMMAD HAMID AL-DIN.

Bibliography

Burrowes, Robert D. *Historical Dictionary of Yemen.* Lanham, MD: Scarecrow Press, 1995.

Burrowes, Robert D. *The Yemen Arab Republic: The Politics of Development, 1962–1986.* Boulder, CO: Westview Press, 1987.

Dresch, Paul. *Tribes, Government, and History in Yemen.* Oxford: Clarendon, 1989.

Stookey, Robert W. *Yemen: The Politics of the Yemen Arab Republic.* Boulder, CO: Westview Press, 1978.

Wenner, Manfred W. *The Yemen Arab Republic: Development and Change in an Ancient Land.* Boulder, CO: Westview Press, 1991.

ROBERT D. BURROWES

YEMEN CIVIL WAR

The long, bitter, and costly struggle in North Yemen fought by the republicans and royalists between 1962 and 1970.

The Yemen Civil War began with the 1962 revolution and dragged on intermittently until 1970. The second half of the war coincided with a long drought, and the two forces in combination caused hunger, economic hardship, social dislocation, and many deaths in most parts of the country. Without a doubt, the struggle remains as one of a few defining memories of one if not two generations of Yemenis.

In addition, the civil war forced the deferral of most major efforts at political and socioeconomic development in what would become the Yemen Arab Republic (YAR) until the 1970s. Indeed, it was not until after reconciliation that the Yemenis could really begin to take the destiny of Yemen into their own hands. At the height of the struggle, the republicans, who were committed to creating a modern state and using it to overcome the weakness and "backwardness" of Yemen, controlled little more than the third of the country defined by the triangle formed by the roads connecting San'a, Ta'iz, and Hodeida (al-Hudayda)—and much within the triangle was outside their effective control. Another third was controlled by the royalists and their tribal allies, and the last third by tribes and others either concerned with their own autonomy or willing to go either way if the price were right. If anything, the balance between the tribes and the state during these years was more in favor of the former than had been the case under the imamate just before the revolution.

The young imam Muhammad al-Badr survived the revolution on 26 September 1962, escaped from San'a, and went on to rally many of the northern tribes and other allies of the imamate for an assault upon the new republic. The civil war was quickly regionalized when Egypt came in strongly on the side of the republicans and Saudi Arabia sided with the imam and the royalists; it was internationalized when the Soviet Union and Eastern Europe supported Egypt and the new YAR, and the United States and the United Kingdom deferred to the Saudis and their interests. As a result, the Yemen Civil War became a microcosmic battleground for the "Arab cold war" between revolutionary Arab nationalist republicans and conservative monarchists and, to a lesser extent, between the Soviet Union and its socialist bloc and the Free World.

The Egyptians, who clearly saved the republic in those first years, took control of fighting the civil war and came to look over time more and more like an occupier; bogged down, they came to call the Yemeni civil war "our Vietnam." Seen as a puppet of Egypt's President Gamal Abdel Nasser, the regime headed by President Abdullah al-Sallal lost credibility and legitimacy. When Nasser withdrew his forces from Yemen on the occasion of the Arab-Israel War of 1967 (the Six-Day War), the Sallal regime collapsed in a matter of weeks, opening the way to the republican-royalist reconciliation that took another two years to consummate.

Although it put much state-building as well as socioeconomic development on hold and exacted a terrible price in human suffering, the civil war did open up an isolated and insulated Yemen to a flood of new ideas, institutions, and practices. The Yemen of the 1970s and later was able to grasp and utilize many of these new elements in a way that was impossible in the 1960s.

See also BADR, MUHAMMAD AL-; YEMEN; YEMEN ARAB REPUBLIC.

Bibliography

Burrowes, Robert D. *The Yemen Arab Republic: The Politics of Development, 1962–1986.* Boulder, CO: Westview Press, 1987.

Dresch, Paul. *Tribes, Government, and History in Yemen.* Oxford: Clarendon, 1989.

ROBERT D. BURROWES

YEMEN DYNASTIES

Ruling families of the area known today as Yemen.

The Zaydi imamate in Yemen has its origins in 897, when al-Hadi ila al-Haqq Yahya became the first Zaydi imam (with his seat in Sa'da). His fame as an intellectual as well as a leader led to the invitation to Yemen; there he developed a multitude of policies that eventually became the basic guidelines for the religious as well as political characteristics of Yemeni Zaydism.

Yahya, however, was not able to consolidate his rule in all of Yemen; there were revolts as well as segments of the population that did not accept his pretensions to religio-political rule. Although he did not succeed in establishing any permanent administrative infrastructure, Yahya's descendants became the local aristocracy, and it is from among them that the imams of Yemen were selected for the next one thousand years.

Yemen throughout most of that period was only rarely a unified political entity; in fact, what was included within its frontiers varied widely, and it has not been governed consistently or uniformly by any single set of rulers. It existed as a part of a number of different political systems/ruling dynasties between the ninth and sixteenth centuries, after which it became a part of the Ottoman Empire.

After Imam Yahya's death, a multitude of smaller dynasties and families established themselves in the Tihama (the low coastal plain) as well as in the highlands. Among the better known of these are the Sulayhids, the Hatims, the Zuray'ids, and the Yu'firids. It was during this period, when the Fatimid state was influential, that a portion of the population was converted to Ismaʿili Shiʿism.

Beginning with the conquest of Yemen by the family of Salah al-Din ibn Ayyub (Saladin) in 1174, a series of dynasties exercised a modicum of control and administration in Yemen for roughly the next 400 years; these are, in chronological sequence, the Ayyubids, from 1173/74 to 1228; the Rasulids, from 1228 to 1454; the Tahirids, from 1454 to 1517; and the Mamluks, from 1517 to 1538, when the Ottoman Empire took the Yemeni Tihama.

During most of this period, the dynasties and their rulers were primarily engaged in familial, regional, and occasionally sectarian disputes. Ironically, the Sunni Rasulids, who eventually concentrated their rule in southern Yemen for precisely that reason, were the dynasty under which the region experienced the greatest economic growth and political stability.

Very little is known about the Zaydi imams and their efforts to establish themselves and develop some form of administration (including tax collection), or their success in promoting Zaydi goals during this period. From the available evidence, there was very little continuity and a great deal of competition among the Zaydi families and clans. For example, in a presumably representative two-hundred-year period from the thirteenth to the fifteenth centuries, there appear to have been more than twenty different candidates for the imamate, representing more than ten distinct clans.

Eventually, as the Europeans entered the Middle East, specifically the Portuguese and then others in the effort to control the Red Sea trade, Yemen and its Zaydi imams were increasingly unable to maintain their independence. It was not until the ascendancy of Imam Qasim ibn Muhammad and his son al-Mu'ayyad Muhammad in the early seventeenth century that the Zaydi Yemenis were able to resist the Ottoman Empire's forces and become an independent political entity.

See also ISMAʿILI SHIʿISM; ZAYDISM.

MANFRED W. WENNER

YEMEN HUNT OIL COMPANY

U.S. company that first discovered and developed oil in Yemen.

The Yemen Hunt Oil Company (YHOC), a subsidiary of the Hunt Oil Company of Dallas, was the first foreign company to discover and develop oil in North Yemen; the location was the Ma'ib al-Jawf basin, on the edge of the desert in the eastern part of the country, and the year was 1984. Partnering with Exxon and a Korean oil company, the company rapidly developed the production-for-export capacity of that basin and built a pipeline to a terminus on the Red Sea; crude oil began to flow in 1987. YHOC also discovered very sizable natural gas deposits in the area, as yet undeveloped. In addition, it was the operator in another consortium that discovered, developed, and then began producing oil during the 1990s in what, prior to Yemeni unification, was the neutral zone between the Ma'ib al-Jawf basin in North Yemen and the Shabwa region of South Yemen. Called the Jannah field, this area became an important contributor to oil production in unified Yemen. Hailed from the mid-1980s to the mid-1990s as the ally and economic savior of Yemen, the YHOC in recent years has become something of a whipping boy over such issues as "Yemenization" and allegedly questionable accounting procedures.

Bibliography

Burrowes, Robert. *Historical Dictionary of Yemen.* Lanham, MD: Scarecrow Press, 1995.

Burrowes, Robert. *The Yemen Arab Republic: The Politics of Development, 1962–1986.* Boulder, CO: Westview Press, 1987.

ROBERT D. BURROWES

YEMENI SOCIALIST PARTY

Yemeni political party.

Created in October 1978 as the "vanguard party" required by Marxist-Leninist theory, the Yemeni Socialist Party (YSP) superseded the United Political Organization of the National Front, which in turn had replaced the National Front for the Liberation of Occupied South Yemen (the National Front), created in 1963. The latter, which was made up of seven smaller groupings, including the Arab Nationalist movement, eventually emerged as the strongest and best organized of the various groups competing for leadership of Aden and the protectorates in opposition to the British presence.

As the sole party in the People's Democratic Republic of Yemen (PDRY), it was the organization that arranged the union of the People's Democratic Republic of Yemen with the Yemen Arab Republic (YAR) in 1990. Thereafter, it became one of the three major parties in the unified state. However, the elections of 1993 led to a civil war between the former PDRY and YAR, with the leaders of the YSP declaring a new Democratic Republic of Yemen in the South in May 1994. Soundly defeated by the central government, the party's leaders went into exile. Thereafter, the party's northern branch elected a new leadership, none of whose members had participated in the Democratic Republic of Yemen.

Tensions between the other two major parties in the unified Yemen, and the YSP's continued significant support in the South, resulted in a desire to return the YSP to some role in the central government in the late 1990s. Although the YSP boycotted the 1997 elections, some of its members were elected as independents. By the time of the 1999 presidential election, northern members of the YSP had been reintegrated into the political system, and although the actual head of the YSP was disqualified as a candidate, Najib Qahtan al-Shaʿabi, the son of the first president of South Yemen, was approved. In 2000, the YSP joined a bloc of opposition parties to create the Supreme Opposition Council, and in 2003 it participated in the parliamentary elections, gaining 8 percent of the seats.

See also PEOPLE'S DEMOCRATIC REPUBLIC OF YEMEN; YEMEN; YEMEN CIVIL WAR.

Bibliography

Gause, F. Gregory. *Saudi-Yemeni Relations, 1962–1982.* New York: Columbia University Press, 1990.

Halliday, Fred. *Revolution and Foreign Policy: The Case of South Yemen, 1967–1987.* Cambridge, U.K.: Cambridge University Press, 1990.

Joffe, E. G. H.; Hachemi, M. J.; and Watkins, E. W. *Yemen Today: Crisis and Solutions: Proceedings of a Two-Day Conference Held at the School of Oriental and African Studies, University of London, November 25 and 26, 1995.* London: Caravel, 1997.

Mundy, Martha. *Domestic Government: Kinship, Community, and Polity in North Yemen.* Cambridge, U.K.: Cambridge University Press, 1995.

Suwaidi, Jamal al-, ed. *The Yemeni War of 1994: Causes and Consequences.* Emirates Center for Strategic Studies and Research, 1996.

Wenner, Manfred. *The Yemen Arab Republic: Development and Change in an Ancient Land.* Boulder, CO: Westview Press, 1991.

MANFRED W. WENNER

YEMENI WOMEN'S UNION

Oldest women's organization in Yemen.

The Yemeni Women's Union (YWU; Ittihad Nisa al-Yaman) is the oldest women's organization in Yemen, with roots in the preindependence era. The present organization was formed in 1990 by combining the northern and southern branches following the unification of Yemen. In the north, the Yemeni Women's Association (YWA) was established in 1965 with branches in the biggest towns. Without official recognition, the main task of the YWA was to promote literacy and job skills among women. In the south, the General Union of Yemeni Women was formed in 1968 to continue the work of two women's organizations (the Arab Women's Club and the Aden Women's Association) established during the British colonial era. It played a vital role in empowering women and promoting the politics of women's emancipation. Soon after unification, the YWU lost official backing, its funding was minimized, and it faced problems in harmonizing its activities. Whereas the southern branch was dominated by socialists, the Sanaa branch in the north was run by women from the Islah Party. The membership of the united organization is around 4,000. The YWU aims at attaining rights and legitimacy for women, gender equity, and women's advocacy. The union has played an important role in promoting women's increased participation in elections. YWU branches are found today in most governorates, with projects funded by foreign donors. These include microcredit schemes, basic health-care services, and job-skills training for women. The union is an active participant in fighting violence against women, the goal that unites most Yemeni nongovernmental organizations.

See also GENDER: GENDER AND EDUCATION; GENDER: GENDER AND POLITICS; YEMEN.

Bibliography

Dahlgren, Susanne. "Women in the Republic of Yemen." In *The Greenwood Encyclopedia of Women's Issues Worldwide,* Volume 4: *The Middle East,* edited by Bahira Sherif. Westport, CT: Greenwood Publishing, 2003.

SUSANNE DAHLGREN

YENI MECMUA

See NEWSPAPERS AND PRINT MEDIA: TURKEY

YESHIVA

A school in which the Talmud, Jewish legal codes, and rabbinic literature and commentaries are the primary subjects of study.

Although *semikha* (rabbinic ordination) may be an outcome of yeshiva study, yeshivas are institutions intended for all Jewish males who wish to advance their study of Judaism. Originally, it was the local place to sit and study texts. Yeshivas became places where scholars gathered, where each famous and learned teacher attracted his own students. In eighteenth-century Lithuania, where the modern form was developed, yeshivas drew students from a variety of European localities and provided the students with a formal curriculum, a place to stay, and often a stipend as well.

Yeshiva education consists of endless hours of vocal and intensive review of texts with fellow students *(khavruseh).* Usually once a day, after posting a bibliography and a series of textual glosses that students must explore in advance, a teacher will give a *shiur* (lesson in Talmud). Some modern yeshivas include secular studies as well (they are often called day schools in North America and *yeshivot tikhoniyot* in Israel).

In Israel, yeshivas are numerous; some embrace the ideals of religious Zionism, and some deny them. The former encompass *hesder* yeshivas, whose students combine military service with study; the latter have students who are exempted from military service. Among the most prominent of the former are the Etzion Yeshiva, Merkaz ha-Rav Kook, and Kerem b'Yavneh. Among the latter are the Ponovez Yeshiva, in B'nei B'rak, and the Mir Yeshiva, in Jerusalem. The greatest growth has been in yeshivas connected with Sephardim.

Bibliography

Helmreich, William B. *The World of the Yeshiva: An Intimate Portrait of Orthodox Jewry,* augmented edition. Hoboken, NJ: Ktav, 2000.

SAMUEL C. HEILMAN

YIDDISH

A vernacular language used by Ashkenazic Jews.

A language based on Germanic dialects infused with Hebrew and loanwords from areas in Europe in which it was spoken, Yiddish is the vernacular used by Ashkenazic Jews since the European Middle Ages. As Hebrew became primarily the language of liturgy and religious scholarship, Yiddish, by the end of the eighteenth century, emerged as the vehicle for the expression of secular literature, drama, poetry, and popular literature. By the nineteenth century, Yiddish was established as the la nguage of a secular European Jewish culture found mainly in Eastern Europe.

The Zionist ideology that stressed the return to Palestine and the use of Hebrew as the language of the Jewish nation was instrumental in the revival of Hebrew. In the language controversy that ensued in the early part of the twentieth century, Hebrew gained prominence over Yiddish and became the official language of the Yishuv and, later, the State of Israel. Yiddish increasingly became identified with Jews and Jewish culture of the diaspora. In response to the Holocaust and the liquidation of Yiddish culture under Soviet rule there has been a resurgent interest in the Yiddish language both in Israel and in North America. As a spoken language Yiddish has become the established vernacular of Orthodox Haredi and Hasidic Jews.

Bibliography

Rosten, Leo. *The Joys of Yiddish: A Related Lexicon of Yiddish, Hebrew and Yinglish Words Often Encountered in English . . . From the Days of the Bible to Those of the Beatnik.* New York: McGraw-Hill, 1968.

Weinstein, Miriam. *Yiddish: A Nation of Words.* South Royalton, VT: Steerforth Press, 2001.

REEVA S. SIMON
UPDATED BY NEIL CAPLAN

YILDIRIM ARMY

Special Ottoman strike force, also known as the Thunderbolt, or Seventh Army.

The army was organized in early 1917 by Enver Paşa to defend the Eastern Front in World War I. It comprised fourteen Ottoman divisions headed by German General Erich von Falkenhayn and included six thousand German soldiers and sixty-five top Ottoman officers, including General Mustafa Kemal (Atatürk). Enver Paşa had originally planned this special army to recapture Iraq but, in March 1917, sent it to block the new British and Arab campaign in Palestine, where they joined the Fourth Army at Gaza and won an initial victory.

The Ottoman-German effort, however, was weakened by conflicts over jurisdiction, by Turkish nationalist dissent toward the German leadership, and by matériel disadvantages. In the autumn of 1917, the British and Arab offensive forced an Ottoman withdrawal to Damascus, with heavy losses on 27 December. The Allied drive resumed the next autumn, and, on 1 October 1918, British General Edmund Allenby and the Arab nationalist revolt forced the Ottomans to evacuate the Syrian capital. Allenby's troops, aided by French forces landing at Beirut, nearly annihilated the Yildirim Army as the Ottomans were driven back to Alexandretta within two weeks. General Otto Liman von Sanders gave command of the Yildirim to Mustafa Kemal after the Mudros Armistice took effect 31 October, and Kemal surrendered at Adana on 13 November 1918.

Bibliography

Shaw, Stanford J., and Shaw, Ezel Kural. *History of the Ottoman Empire and Modern Turkey.* 2 vols. Cambridge, U.K., and New York: Cambridge University Press, 1976–1977.

ELIZABETH THOMPSON

YISHUV

The Jewish community in Palestine from the Ottoman period through the British Mandate.

Yishuv refers to the Jewish population—including the pre-Zionist Jewish community known as the Old Yishuv—living in Palestine before the State of Israel was proclaimed in 1948. The Old Yishuv had its roots in a religious revival among Jews in Eastern Europe at the end of the eighteenth century, which inspired increasing numbers to journey to Ottoman Palestine and settle in what they deemed the holy cities of Tiberias, Safed, Hebron, and Jerusalem. Motivated by a desire to observe Jewish religious commandments, scholars and pious men came to pray and study as preconditions to salvation. Palestine's Jewish population steadily increased from approximately 4,200 in 1806 to 26,000 on the eve of the first Zionist-sponsored immigration in 1882.

The Old and the New Yishuv

Concerned Jews in Europe sent financial aid to these pious communities as a way of sharing in the holiness of living and studying in the land of Israel. The collection and distribution of this aid (in Hebrew, *halukkah*) to support pious Jews and their religious institutions in Palestine was institutionalized in 1810 by a wealthy Dutch Jew, Rabbi Zvi Hirsch Lehren, who founded the Pekidim and Amarkalim of Eretz Yisrael (Officials of the Land of Israel) in Amsterdam.

Even with a sophisticated system of external funding, as the numbers of Jews in the Old Yishuv increased, their economic lot deteriorated. A few enjoyed economic security, but most lived in poverty. The religious schools *(kollelim)* provided their own subsidies, sometimes offering rent, health care, and support for widows and orphans, but all charitable services depended on budgetary circumstances and on the intellectual status of the scholars, with those from the wealthiest diaspora communities receiving the highest payments.

By 1882, Zionism had emerged in Europe, and Zionists began to sponsor immigration into Ottoman Palestine. Their goal was a self-supporting secular, egalitarian society based on productive labor and a Hebrew cultural renaissance; they named their community the New Yishuv. Proclaiming the need for social change, economic transformation, and

A ship filled with Jewish refugees docks in Haifa Port in 1945. Between 1945 and 1948, 69,000 Jews relocated from Europe to Palestine. Many did not successfully complete the journey and ended up in British detention camps in Cyprus. © PHOTOGRAPH BY ZOLTAN KLUGER. GOVERNMENT PRESS OFFICE (GPO) OF ISRAEL. REPRODUCED BY PERMISSION.

political reform, Zionist activities ruptured traditional patterns of pious Jewish life in Palestine and triggered intense competition for diaspora charity.

In Zionist historiography, the differences between Old and New Yishuv have been described as immense. In fact, there was some overlap. A generation of Jews who matured in Jerusalem during the Ottoman reform era of the 1860s responded to the challenge of meeting daily needs as well as to the spirit of the age by calling for the creation of a productive Jewish economy. Yosef Rivlin, Yoel Moshe Salomon, and Israel Dov Frumkin, prominent cultural and religious figures, became builders of new neighborhoods and founders of a new Jewish infrastructure. Among the housing projects outside the

Old City that they developed or supported were Nahalat Shiva, Mea She'arim, Mishkenot Israel, Kiryah Ne'emana, and Bet Ya'akov. By 1880, 2,000 Jews lived outside the Old City and 16,000 lived within the walls. A similar impulse drove Jaffa's Jewish leaders to establish the new suburbs of Neve Shalom, Yefe Nof, and Ahva. Some also advocated educational reform and contributed to the revival of Hebrew.

As for the Zionists, some came from traditional backgrounds and never gave up their faith or observance of religious ritual. Permanent alliances across the two communities were generally short lived, however; they often split over religious stipulations constraining the establishment of a modern Jewish society.

Zionism

Although immigrants driven by piety continued to arrive alongside Zionists, it was the Zionist vision that created Palestine's new institutions. Between 1882 and 1948, the Zionist movement established about 250 towns, villages, and cities designed by a corps of planners and officials pursuing national political goals. Schools, libraries, newspapers, workshops, and cultural and commercial enterprises were established—even in Jerusalem, the heart of the Old Yishuv.

After World War I and the dissolution of the Ottoman Empire, the British, under a mandate from the League of Nations, ruled Palestine. British doctrine recognized the Yishuv as one of Palestine's religious communities but in practice provided it with the opportunity to operate national-style institutions. Zionists brought their political parties with them to Palestine. From the early years of the twentieth century, a number of Zionist-Socialist parties (Po'alei Zion, ha-Po'el ha-Tza'ir, Left Po'alei Zion) as well as Mizrahi, the religious Zionist movement, had adherents and activists in Palestine. Political parties opened employment offices and founded agricultural collectives, soup kitchens, loan funds, newspapers, and schools. They provided recreational and cultural activities for members. Many of these activities were absorbed in 1920 by the Histadrut, which became one of the central vehicles of state-building for the Yishuv. Histadrut operations—labor exchanges, construction companies, and an underground army—were crucial in helping Jewish immigrants find work and community in their new homeland. The Histadrut became the base of power for David Ben-Gurion, who used his position as secretary-general to bring together several of labor's political parties in 1930 to form MAPAI, dominant in Yishuv politics and eventually in the World Zionist Organization. With backing from both the Histadrut and MAPAI, Ben-Gurion was able to outmaneuver political rivals such as Vladimir Ze'ev Jabotinsky and Chaim Weizmann.

Palestine's Jewish community organized itself in explicitly political structures, beginning with an assembly (Knesset Yisrael) elected by people who were more than twenty years old and had at least three months' residence in the region. Between sessions, the assembly delegated its powers to the Va'ad Le'umi (National Council), appointed from its ranks. The council nominated from among its members an executive charged with the actual administration of the community. Policies generated by the self-governing institutions of the Yishuv covered matters of health, social welfare, defense, and education. Without the authority to tax, however, Knesset Israel and its constituent institutions had limited power. Its funding depended on allocations from the World Zionist Organization. Some of Palestine's Orthodox Jewish residents remained aloof from the organization and did not participate in elections, since they objected to female suffrage and to the secular aims of Zionism. They insisted on their organizational separateness and retained an allegiance to the principles of the Old Yishuv.

Palestine was governed as a colony, but significant policies were often formulated by England's highest elected officials, including the prime minister and parliament. Yishuv politicians such as Ben-Gurion understood the pressing need to influence policymakers in London as well as those implementing regulations in Palestine. Hence, much power was assigned to international Zionist agencies and to their leaders, who attained global stature (e.g., Weizmann).

Until the creation of an expanded Jewish Agency in 1929, the Zionist executive's political department was also the central mechanism for creating contacts with Arab leaders within and outside of Palestine. Founded and directed by Chaim Kalvaryski, this department initiated contacts with Palestinian personalities willing to sit with Jews in institutions established on the basis of the Mandate's political framework. The department extended funds to village shaykhs, municipal leaders, newspapers, and movements deemed moderate on the issue of a Jewish national home in Palestine. In 1929, the Jewish Agency and the National Council set up the Joint Bureau to handle relations with the League of Nations and with Britain in both London and Palestine.

Two developments in the 1930s augmented the authority of Yishuv institutions. The first was an increase in the number of Jewish immigrants, who were now fleeing fascist Europe. This increased the number of people who participated in elections and other voluntary political activities. The second was the outbreak of the Arab Revolt in 1936 and the need for a larger Yishuv defense force. The Yishuv assumed responsibility for helping fund such a force through a voluntary tax levy. Yishuv institutions still drew their authority primarily from the networks created with various political movements and the leadership of the Jewish Agency, but as the legitimacy of these institutions strengthened they also began to function more effectively on their own.

When British rule began in Palestine, there were 56,000 Jews in a total population of 640,000. By the end of Britain's political tenure, the Jewish population had increased to 650,000, with substantial immigration occurring in the Mandate's last decade. Undoubtedly, the rise of Nazism and the threat of war expanded both interest in immigration and the actual numbers of Jewish immigrants, despite Britain's attempts to control the number of Jews entering Palestine.

The outbreak of the war in 1939 and the genocidal policies of the Nazis created enormous difficulty for the Yishuv. On the one hand, these policies substantiated the Zionist claim that diaspora Jewry lived in fragile, untenable conditions; on the other hand, by slaughtering the movement's potential population, they threatened the possibility of achieving the Zionist dream of sovereignty. However, World War II ended with the beginning of the Cold War, and the dramatic shift in the balance of world power helped the Yishuv win the international support necessary for Jewish statehood, especially from those interested in the dismantling of Great Britain's empire.

See also BEN-GURION, DAVID; ERETZ YISRAEL; HISTADRUT; ISRAEL: POLITICAL PARTIES IN; WEIZMANN, CHAIM; ZIONISM.

Bibliography

Caplan, Neil. *Palestine Jewry and the Arab Question, 1917–1925.* Totowa, NJ; London: Frank Cass, 1978.

Halper, Jeff. *Between Redemption and Revival: The Jewish Yishuv of Jerusalem in the Nineteenth Century.* Boulder, CO: Westview Press, 1991.

Halpern, Ben, and Reinharz, Jehuda. *Zionism and the Creation of a New Society.* New York: Oxford University Press, 1998.

Horowitz, Dan, and Lissak, Moshe. *Origins of the Israeli Polity: Palestine under the Mandate,* translated by Charles Hoffman. Chicago: University of Chicago Press, 1978.

Hurewitz, J. C. *The Struggle for Palestine.* New York: Norton, 1950.

McCarthy, Justin. *The Population of Palestine: Population History and Statistics of the Late Ottoman Period and the Mandate.* New York: Columbia University Press, 1990.

Parfitt, Tudor. *The Jews in Palestine: 1800-1882.* Wolfeboro, NH; Woodbridge, U.K.: Boydell Press; London: Royal Historical Society, 1987.

Troen, S. Ilan. *Imagining Zion: Dreams, Designs, and Realities in a Century of Jewish Settlement.* New Haven, CT: Yale University Press, 2003.

DONNA ROBINSON DIVINE

YIZHAR, S.

[1916–]

Israeli novelist.

The grandnephew of Israeli author Moshe Smilansky (1874–1953), S. Yizhar was born in 1969 in Rehovot, Israel. Yizhar's most famous novel, *Yeme Ziklag* (1958), is considered a work of great literary distinction. It describes seven days of battle during the Arab–Israel War of 1948 and underscores the burdens imposed on a society trying to fulfill the Zionist mission. His language and detailed descriptions of the land have influenced all subsequent generations of Israeli writers. His later novel, *Mikdamot* (Foretellings, 1992), views the Zionist pioneering enterprise through the eyes of a child. Yizhar served in the Knesset from 1949 to 1967 as a representative of the mainstream labor movement and also taught school for many years.

Bibiliography

Shaked, Gershon. *Modern Hebrew Fiction,* translated by Yael Lotan. Bloomington: Indiana University Press, 2000.

Yizhar, S. *Midnight Convoy and Other Stories.* Jerusalem: Institute for the Translation of Hebrew Literature, 1969.

Bryan Daves
Updated by Donna Robinson Divine

YÖN

See Newspapers and Print Media: Turkey

YOSEF, OVADIAH

[1920–]

Israeli religious and political leader.

Ovadiah Yosef, Israel's most prominent Mizrahi religious leader, was born in Baghdad but has lived in Palestine since infancy. He was educated at the Sephardic Porat Yosef yeshiva in Jerusalem, and he was recognized as a brilliant scholar with a phenomenal memory from an early age. A rabbi by the age of twenty, he was deputy chief rabbi of Cairo when the state of Israel was founded in 1948. He returned to Israel in 1950, where he became a religious judge. In 1968 he was appointed chief rabbi of Tel Aviv. He served as the Sephardic chief rabbi of Israel from 1973 to 1983—a tenure marred by bickering with the Asheknazic chief rabbi, Shlomo Goren. His religious authority and personal charisma led his followers to continue to accord him higher status than that given to the Sephardic chief rabbis who followed him in that post. His weekly Saturday night talks are broadcast by satellite around the world. These talks are followed closely by Israeli journalists, who are eager to report his often provocative and colorfully worded statements and rulings. These included his declaration that the six million Holocaust victims were "reincarnations of the souls of sinners. . . They had been reincarnated in order to atone."

Yosef's biography includes a series of frustrations and personal slights. He was never invited to join the Ashkenazic Council of Torah Sages of the Agudat Israel party—then the highest political and spiritual authority in the ultra-Orthodox world. In Ashkenazic circles he was dismissed as a person who memorized texts rather than an original thinker. His own religious mentor, Rabbi Eliezer Schach, announced that, because they still needed to follow Ashkenazic guidance, "the time has not yet come for Sephardim to take positions of leadership." Yosef was thus induced to support the first ultra-Orthodox Sephardi SHAS (derived from *Sephardim Shomrei Torah,* or Sephardi Torah Guardians) party, founded in 1983 by disaffected members of the Ashkenazic dominated Agudat Israel party. SHAS won 11 of the 120 parliamentary seats in the 2003 elections (down from 17 in 1999). Yosef's intended purpose is to restore the "crown of glory" to Sephardic Judaism—to reestablish the dominance of the Halakhah in accordance with Sephardic custom in Israel. He is now the ruling force behind the SHAS party, instructing the elected Knesset members how to vote in parliamentary issues.

Yosef's most famous work, *Yabiah Omer,* deals with halakhic problems in daily life. His religious rulings have been original, but also at times controversial, as when he recognized Ethiopian Jews as being fully Jewish during the 1970s. His leniency in religious ruling is sensitive to the diversity of religious observance among Sephardic Jews. He generally seeks accommodation rather than confrontation in Jewish-Arab issues, even as he sometimes uses abusive language (for example, "beasts of prey") to describe his enemies and those of Israel.

See also Adot ha-Mizrah.

Julie Zuckerman
Updated by Ephraim Tabory

YOUNG ALGERIANS

A group of French-educated men who, early in the twentieth century, became the first Algerians to attempt reform within the colonial political system.

Estimated to number between 1,000 and 1,200, the Young Algerians *(Jeunes Algériens)* included intellectuals, members of the liberal professions, and individuals who had succeeded within French business circles. Most prominent among the group's members were Dr. Benthami Ould Hamida, Omar Bouderba, Fekar Ben Ali, Chérif Benhabylès, and—beginning in 1913—Khaled ibn Hashimi ibn Hajj Abd al-Qadir, grandson of Algerian patriot Abd al-Qadir.

While there were differences in the emphases of the Young Algerians, most were attempting to win for themselves rights approximating those of Frenchmen. Their agenda, before World War I, included exemption of at least some Algerians from the exceptive Code de l'Indigénat, more equitable distribution of taxes, easier access to French citizenship, and greater political participation for the educated. The agenda also included programs for the masses, including greater access to education, opening of grazing and forest lands, protections for property, and more careful monitoring of government abuse.

Despite support from many liberals in France, attempts to negotiate concessions failed in 1913 and 1914, largely because of colon opposition. During World War I, when thousands of Algerians served in the French armed forces, a grateful Prime Minister Georges Clemenceau promised reform. The resulting Jonnart Law of 4 February 1919, however, was viewed by most Young Algerians as being very far from what they had been promised. For a few years after the war, Khaled ibn Hashimi ibn Hajj Abd al-Qadir continued to lead the movement for reform within the system, but, by 1923, he gave up the effort and went into exile in the Near East.

See also CODE DE L'INDIGÉNAT.

JOHN RUEDY

YOUNG EGYPT

A patriotic association of Egyptian youth established in October 1933.

In 1937, Young Egypt (Misr al-Fatat) became a formal political party in Egypt; in 1940, the name was changed to the Islamic Nationalist party (al-Hizb al-Watani al-Islami); in 1949, it became the Socialist party of Egypt (Hizb Misr al-Ishtiraki).

The dominant figure in Young Egypt throughout its history was the lawyer/politician Ahmad Husayn. In the 1930s, the movement's program combined a vehement, anti-British Egyptian nationalism, an antiparliamentary outlook, an emphasis on the paramilitary training and mobilization of youth, and a call for greater social justice. Politically opposed to the Wafd, Young Egypt aligned itself with the anti-Wafdist forces centered around the Egyptian palace; its paramilitary squads of Green Shirts periodically fought with the Blue Shirts of the Wafd.

Although it was suppressed during World War II, it afterward dropped its paramilitary features while retaining, but relabeling, much of its prewar populism. Like all Egyptian political parties, it was abolished in January 1953, after the Free Officers, led by General Muhammad Naguib, seized power from the monarchy of King Farouk.

Bibliography

Jankowski, James. *Egypt's Young Rebels: "Young Egypt," 1933–1952.* Stanford, CA: Hoover Institution Press, 1975.

JAMES JANKOWSKI

YOUNG OTTOMANS

Ottoman intellectuals and bureaucrats who constituted the first organized opposition to the pro-West modernizing elite of the Tanzimat.

Members of the group called themselves New Ottomans, while contemporary European observers referred to them as Young Turks. The latter term came to be used more specifically in reference to the next generation of liberal opponents of Sultan Abdülhamit as distinct from Young Ottomans, which has become the synonym of New Ottomans.

The Young Ottomans began their activities in Constantinople (now Istanbul). They faced repression and were forced into exile in Europe and other parts of the Ottoman Empire. Prominent Young Ottoman leaders were Namik Kemal (1840–1888), İbrahim Şinasi (1824–1871), Agha Efendi (1832–1885), Abdülhamit Ziya Paşa (1825–1880), and Ali Suavi (1838–1878). The group received important financial and moral support from a disaffected member of the Egyptian khedival family who had entered the Ottoman service, Mustafa Fazil Paşa (1829–1875). While these leaders were united in their opposition to the Tanzimat elite, and to the autocratic ministry of Paşas Fu'ad and Ali, they had hardly been bystanders to the Tanzimat. They had matured intellectually and professionally during the Tanzimat period. Many had served in the Translation Bureau, a breeding ground for Tanzimat bureaucrats. Some were stimulated by the frustration of their career ambitions under the Tanzimat regime.

The Young Ottomans differed in social and professional background. Ziya Paşa, the oldest in the group, was a writer and poet and had served as third secretary to Sultan Abdülmecit II. Namik Kemal, also poet and writer, came from a distinguished bureaucratic family. Şinasi, an army captain's son who held a post in the imperial arsenal before he was sent to Paris to study finance, was the most innovative and versatile from a literary point of view. Ali Suavi was a middle-school teacher and a religious-minded writer, even agitator.

The forerunner of the group was the Alliance of Fidelity or Patriotic Alliance, a loose group consisting of literary men and functionaries, which first met in Constantinople in June 1865. Organization was secret and conspiratorial, apparently modeled along the Carbonari of Italy, Spain, and France and led by a French-educated agitator, Mehmet Bey. The group did not publicize a program. The members were motivated by recent Ottoman setbacks in the Balkans and Lebanon and fear of disintegration. They felt constitutional government was necessary to preserve the empire and to ward off Europe's economic domination and diplomatic interventions. The group's expanding membership included bureaucrats, *ulama* (Islamic clergy), and army officers.

In 1866/67 Namik Kemal and Ali Suavi published newspapers *(Tasvir-i Efkar* and *Muhbir)* in which they vehemently criticized the government's policy regarding the insurrection in Crete and the impending surrender of Serbia. They published an open letter from Mustafa Fazil, who had left the empire over issues pertaining to his political ambitions in Egypt, which addressed the sultan and amounted to a liberal manifesto. The government ordered Namik Kemal, Ziya, and Ali Suavi to domestic exile and closed their newspapers. Instead, they accepted an invitation from Mustafa Fazil Paşa and fled to Paris. At this time, the government also uncovered the group's contacts with top security officials in preparation for a coup against Abdülaziz that was organized by Mehmet Bey.

The regrouping of the liberal-minded elements of the Patriotic Alliance as New Ottomans occurred in exile at the end of May 1867. In Paris and later London, they published the newspaper *Hürriyet,* edited by Namik Kemal and Ziya Paşa with financial support from Mustafa Fazil. They promoted liberal political principles and demanded a parliament. At the same time, they denounced liberal economic policies and advocated measures to buttress indigenous trade and to promote industry.

Despite considerable variation in their outlook on politics, society, and religion, the Young Ottomans projected an Islamic modernist synthesis. They opposed Western political and economic interference and wholesale adoption of Western thought and culture. Nevertheless, they were sympathetic to Western political institutions. Their thought was premised on the existence in Islamic political traditions of the concepts and institutions fundamental to a liberal political system based on representative principles. The Young Ottomans reinterpreted and popularized the concept of *watan* (homeland) to advance a political allegiance to the Ottoman state. They sought a contractual relationship between the subjects and the ruler, based on the Islamic principles of *shura* (consultation) and *ijma* (consensus), within the framework of an Ottoman watan. These views represented the first systematic expression of Islamic modernist ideas in the Muslim world.

The Young Ottoman movement was not the first expression of political protest against the Tanzimat. As early as 1859, a group of *ulama* and army officers had led a coup d'état aimed at Abdülmecit in resentment of Tanzimat policies that enhanced the status of the non-Muslim minorities vis-à-vis the Muslims, and—perhaps more importantly—had left the payment of officers in arrears (the Küleli Incident). The Young Ottomans constituted the first opposition group that attempted to offer alternative programs, inspired by Western thought but consistent with Islamic political ideals.

The movement signifies the beginnings of a campaign for social mobilization and the forging of a public opinion in the Ottoman Empire, even though the group's propaganda remained restricted to a literate Turkish-speaking intelligentsia. Their ideas appealed to disfranchised Westernized groups, students, Muslim commercial associations, and religious conservative opponents of the Tanzimat. They propagated their views through newspapers and literature utilizing a simplified Ottoman-Turkish. They were influenced by contemporary Turkish discoveries, which reinforced the Islamist and anti-imperialist outlook, especially in the pen of Ali Suavi.

The Young Ottomans pioneered journalism and introduced new genres and themes to Ottoman literature. Indeed, future members of the group began their oppositional activity in the first privately published Ottoman journals that appeared in the early 1860s (such as *Tercüman-i Ahval* and *Tasvir-i Efkar*). They introduced the genres of the novel and the drama to Ottoman literature, popularized them, and effectively used them as vehicles of political propaganda. The pioneer in this journalistic and literary activity was Şinasi. The Young Ottomans also translated into Turkish the works of European Enlightenment philosophers and authors such as Rousseau, Montesquieu, Voltaire, Molière, and Lamartine.

The Young Ottomans did not constitute a party organization despite their espousal of political propaganda and promotion of political agendas. After the early 1870s, the group lost its cohesion. Ideological and personal differences led to estrangement in European exile. Several leaders, including the benefactor Mustafa Fazil Paşa, accepted Abdülaziz's amnesty offer to return to Constantinople. Following the death of their nemesis, Ali Paşa, in 1871 the movement went into disarray in the capital. However, under the duress of the political and financial crises of the 1870s, progressive Ottoman statesmen started to look with favor upon Young Ottoman ideas about constitutional government. Midhat Paşa, known as the architect of the Ottoman constitution and parliament, emerged as the leading proponent of change and set out to give concrete expression to Young Ottoman ideas on constitutional government, drawing also on the services of Young Ottoman leaders. Namik Kemal and Ziya Paşa were members of the committee that drafted the Ottoman constitution of 1876. Namik Kemal's long struggle to promote the Young Ottoman cause, his refusal to compromise, his passionately patriotic poetry and drama, and his lucid political writings stressing the notion of popular sovereignty gave him a reputation as the most influential Young Ottoman activist and author, as well as making him a source of inspiration for later constitutionalists.

Due to the absence of a party organization and their dependence on literary forms for the propagation of their ideas, the Young Ottomans had no direct impact on non-Turkish-speaking parts of the empire. For instance, their Islamic modernist ideas did not have an appreciable influence on later and similar currents in the Arab-populated areas. The Young Ottoman movement, however, was the ideological forerunner and inspiration of the later and more broadly based Young Turk movement. The Young Ottomans may not have offered a coherent political philosophy, but they were the precursors of most modern intellectual and political movements in the Middle East.

See also ALI SUAVI; MUSTAFA FAZIL; NAMIK KEMAL; ŞINASI, İBRAHIM; TANZIMAT; YOUNG TURKS; ZIYA, ABDÜLHAMIT.

Bibliography

Davison, Roderic H. *Reform in the Ottoman Empire, 1856–1876.* Princeton, NJ: Princeton University Press, 1963.

Mardin, Serif. *The Genesis of Young Ottoman Thought: A Study in the Modernization of Turkish Political Ideas.* Princeton, NJ: Princeton University Press, 1962.

HASAN KAYALI

YOUNG TUNISIANS

Tunisian reform movement that championed Tunisian rights during the French protectorate.

The imposition of the French protectorate over Tunisia in 1881 propelled a group of reform-minded urban elites, known as the Young Tunisians, to challenge the traditional order that it blamed for the country's economic and political misfortunes. The Young Tunisians initially acquiesced to French oversight as a practical step toward the modernization of state and society, but they were also intent on reforming native institutions in order to maintain and renew the Muslim heritage and identity of

Tunisia, and to this end, they founded the Khaldunniyya School in 1896. The nucleus of the Young Tunisian movement thus included modernists from the religious notability, such as Abd al-Aziz al-Thaalbi, as well as graduates of French universities or of the European-inspired Sadiqiyya College, such as Bashir Sfar, Ali Bash Hamba, and Hassan Gallati. By 1900, however, growing frustration with their political and economic marginalization was leading many Young Tunisians to intensify their criticism of the protectorate and its various forms of discrimination.

In 1907 Sfar, Bash Hamba, and al-Thaalbi launched French and Arabic editions of the journal *Le Tunisien* to promote and champion indigenous rights. The movement was radicalized further between 1911 and 1912 by the Italian invasion of Libya, and by the Protectorate's use of disproportionate military force against civilian demonstrators in November 1911 (the Jallaz Incident), and again in February 1912 against striking tramway workers. The authorities accused the Young Tunisians of instigating popular unrest, and deported al-Thaalbi, Sfar, Gallati, and Bash Hamba. Thus, on the eve of World War I, the Young Tunisian movement had been effectively decapitated and driven underground, but its popular anticolonial platform was soon resurrected in the 1920s by the Destour Party and its calls for Tunisian self-determination.

See also BOURGUIBA, HABIB; KHALDUNNIYYA; THAALBI, ABD AL-AZIZ; TUNISIA: POLITICAL PARTIES IN.

Bibliography

Abun-Nasr, Jamil. *A History of the Maghrib in the Islamic Period.* Cambridge, U.K.: Cambridge University Press, 1987.

O. W. ABI-MERSHED

YOUNG TURKS

Name given to groups in Ottoman society who demanded and strove for political and social change in the last several decades of the Ottoman Empire.

"Young Turk" is an expression coined in Europe that invokes three distinct phases of the Ottoman constitutionalist movement: the anti-Tanzimat current better known to historians as the "Young Ottoman" movement; the constitutionalist opposition to Sultan Abdülhamit; and the Second Constitutional Period introduced by the reinstitution of the constitutional regime in 1908. There was at no point a distinct organization called the Young Turks; nor did the groups recognized as Young Turks generally embrace this name. Nevertheless, historians identify the last three decades of the empire in reference to Young Turks, while "the Young Turk period" corresponds more precisely to the decade of their political predominance from 1908 to 1918.

Young Turk activity began in the late 1880s. Until the revolution of 1908, their opposition to Abdülhamit manifested itself both within the empire and abroad. The two spheres of activity were linked together only loosely. When a group of medical students in Constantinople (now Istanbul) founded in 1889 the secret cells of what would develop into the Committee for Union and Progress (CUP), individual intellectuals in exile had already launched a political and journalistic campaign against the Hamitian regime. The best known in the latter group was Khalil Ghanim, a Syrian Christian, who published a journal called *La jeune Turquie (Young Turkey).*

The Constantinople secret committee spread rapidly in the capital's higher schools and soon became known to the authorities. Reprisals forced many to exile, whereupon an expatriate liberal opposition came together around Ahmet Riza, a French-educated official in the Ministry of Agriculture. Influenced by European positivists, he failed to return from a mission in 1889 and turned into a vocal critic of the Hamitian regime. In 1895, he joined Khalil Ghanim, Alber Fua (a Jew), and Aristidi Paşa (a Greek) to publish *Meşveret,* which became the leading voice of Young Turks.

The next year, a member of the Constantinople secret committee, Murat Bey, fled to Cairo and later to Geneva. A Russian Turk who taught at the influential Mülkiye (civil service) school, Murat Bey was better connected with the liberal currents in Constantinople. His *Mizan* outshone *Meşveret,* both of which were smuggled into the empire. Murat was an Islamist-Turkist revolutionary, in contrast to Ahmet Riza's elitist and gradualist outlook. The two men were united in their anti-imperialism and denunciation of the Hamitian autocracy. Murat, however, joined Abdülhamit in 1897. Rivalries within the Young Turk movement in exile continued with the publication in Geneva of *Osmanh* by İshak Süküti and Ahmet Cevdet Paşa, founding members of the CUP in Constantinople. As repression increased in the empire, Young Turk activity shifted almost entirely to Europe and Egypt for a decade. The flight of Damad Mahmud Paşa, the brother-in-law of the sultan, to join the Young Turks in Europe opened a new phase in Young Turk activities.

Under the moral guidance and financial support of ailing Mahmud Paşa and the presidency of his son Sabahettin, the Young Turks held a conference in Paris in February 1902, which crystallized the divisions within the movement. Representatives of all major religious groups in the empire attended. The meeting revealed the separatist inclinations of Christian factions, while two groups around Ahmet Riza and Sabahettin divided over the suitability of centralist versus decentralist policies in achieving the ultimate aim of preserving the integrity of the empire. Subsequently, Sabahettin formed the Society of Administrative Decentralization and Private Initiative, modeled along the teachings of economist Frédéric Le Play and Edmond Demolins and as a rival to the CUP. A second conference in 1907 aimed at a reconciliation failed to bring Greek, Albanian, and some Armenian factions to the table.

Meanwhile, domestic opposition and conspiracy against the Hamitian regime regrouped in Macedonia. Different oppositional groups coalesced to revitalize the CUP, which in 1907 contacted the Ahmet Riza group in Europe. However, the exile communities had no role in the immediate circumstances that led to the Young Turk Revolution. If international events like the Japanese victory over Russia and the Russian and Iranian revolutions energized Young Turks everywhere, the nationalist activity among the Balkan peoples and the perceived threat to the empire by enhanced relations between Britain and Russia impelled the unionists in Salonika and Monastir to action.

Due to the role they played in the revolution, leaders of the Macedonian branches of the CUP eclipsed the other factions after 1908. They were, however, too inexperienced to take the helm of government and too insecure to embrace other Young Turk groups, including the CUP leadership in Europe. The differences within the Young Turk movement were now expressed in multiparty politics. The decentralists under Sabahettin formed the Liberal party before the 1908 elections. Even though they failed to block the election of a large majority of CUP candidates to parliament, the decentralists became an increasingly more potent opposition to the CUP, supported by autonomy-minded minority groups. Other parties that formed in 1910 and 1911 soon merged in the Ottoman Liberty and Entente party. The CUP's attempts to manipulate the elections to retain power undermined parliamentary rule, eliciting an ultimatum from a group of military

Ahmet Riza circa 1910. Riza was one of the leaders of the Committee for Union and Progress, one of several groups that collectively came to be known as the Young Turks. The Young Turks sought to reform and modernize the Ottoman Empire. They succeeded in taking control of the government in 1908 but fell from power after defeat in World War I (1914–1918).
© RYKOFF COLLECTION/CORBIS. REPRODUCED BY PERMISSION.

officers called Saviors. Coupled with foreign preoccupations such as the Italian and Balkan wars, the Young Turk governments gave way to governments led by old-school politicians in 1912. In 1913 the CUP wrested power with a coup d'état. Despite conciliatory measures to the liberals, the CUP remained as that faction within the Young Turk movement that dominated Ottoman politics until the end of the empire.

The Young Turks promoted the ideology of Ottomanism in an attempt to foster in all peoples of the empire a commitment to the Ottoman homeland within the framework of a constitutional government. There were organizational similarities, some ideological continuity, and shared political goals between the Young Ottomans and Young Turks. Despite what the ethnocentric term "Young Turk" suggests, the movement represented ethnically and religiously a much more diverse group than the Young Ottomans.

The Young Turk movement embraced varied ideological orientations (Westernism, Islamism, Turkism, positivism, centralism, decentralism), socio-economic backgrounds (lower middle-class students and officers, high officials, members of Ottoman and Egyptian royal households), and ethnic-religious affiliations. It was unified in the conviction for the necessity of reform designed to preserve the empire. The Young Turks were responsible for instituting the beginnings of modern politics in the Middle East, for expanding education and journalism, and for realizing economic, social, and administrative reforms. The movement provided the political nuclei for the successor states of the Ottoman Empire.

See also AHMET RIZA; COMMITTEE FOR UNION AND PROGRESS; OTTOMANISM; TANZIMAT; YOUNG OTTOMANS.

Bibliography

Ahmad, Feroz. *The Young Turks: The Committee of Union and Progress in Turkish Politics, 1908–1914.* Oxford: Clarendon, 1969.

Ramsaur, Ernest E. *The Young Turks: Prelude to the Revolution of 1908.* Princeton, NJ: Princeton University Press, 1957.

HASAN KAYALI

YOUSSEF, MULAY

Alawi sultan of Morocco, 1912–1927.

The ouster by France of Youssef's predecessor, Mulay Abd al-Hafiz, signaled the subordination of the Moroccan sultanate to French colonialism and a serious loss of prestige by the Moroccan ruling house. Mulay Youssef's reign was marked largely by the implementation of the Treaty of Fes (March 1912) and the aggressive administration of French rule by the resident general, Marshal Louis Lyautey, who held office from 1912 to 1925. The period of Youssef's reign also witnessed several significant movements against colonial rule, the most important of which was that of Abd al-Karim (al-Khattabi) in the Rif region from 1919 to 1926.

See also FES, TREATY OF (1912); KHATTABI, MUHAMMAD IBN ABD AL-KARIM AL-; LYAUTEY, LOUIS-HUBERT GONZALVE.

Bibliography

Burke, Edmund, III. *Prelude to Protectorate in Morocco.* Chicago: University of Chicago Press, 1976.

Rinehart, Robert, et al. *Morocco: A Country Survey.* Washington, DC, 1985.

MATTHEW S. GORDON

YOUSSOUFI, ABDERRAHMANE

[1924–]

Moroccan prime minister, 1998–2002.

Abderrahmane Youssoufi was the first opposition politician to occupy the position of Moroccan prime minister since 1958. Born into a Berber- and French-speaking family from the international zone of Tangiers, Youssoufi joined the Istiqlal Party when it was founded in 1944. His European education led him to cultivate personal and ideological ties with Mehdi Ben Barka and the leftist wing of the Istiqlal. In 1959, along with Ben Barka, Youssoufi became one of the founders of the socialist-oriented National Union of Popular Forces (Union Nationale des Forces Populaires, UNFP). Arrested in 1963 during the first major wave of repression against leftist militants, he served eighteen months in prison for his alleged participation in a plot against the monarchy. Pardoned, he left Morocco after the murder of Ben Barka in 1965. During his fifteen-year exile in

France, Youssoufi was a particularly active advocate for human rights. He returned to Morocco in 1980, resumed political action within the Socialist Union of Popular Forces (Union Socialiste des Forces Populaires, USFP), which was created in 1975, and became its secretary-general in 1992. To enhance the credibility of the kingdom's reforms, Hassan II named Youssoufi prime minister in 1998. Youssoufi uneasily presided over a coalition government whose key ministries were reserved for the king's collaborators. Such restrictions limited Youssoufi's capacity to further the democratization process and to address social issues. Priority was given to the creation of a suitable environment for private investors, particularly through a campaign against the corruption of civil servants and court officials. Accused of lacking initiative and compromising with the palace, Youssoufi was replaced by Driss Jettou in November 2002.

See also BEN BARKA, MEHDI; HASSAN II; MOROCCO.

HENRI LAUZIÈRE

YOUTH ALIYAH

Organization that benefits immigrant youth in Israel.

Even before Hitler became Germany's chancellor in 1933, Youth Aliyah (in Hebrew, *Aliyat ha-Noar*), a project that brought Jewish children to Palestine and provided them with vocational training, had been established by Recha Freier in response to the deteriorating condition of Jews in Germany. It was organized in Palestine by Henrietta Szold, with the cooperation of the Jewish Agency, the Vaʿad Le'umi (National Council), and the kibbutz movement. Originally, parents paid for their own children's transportation to Palestine and their room and board. For a number of years, British authorities did not count these children in the official immigration quota for Palestine.

During the mid-1930s the organization expanded its activities and rescued increasing numbers of children from Nazi Germany and later from Austria. Starting in 1939 with the outbreak of World War II, Youth Aliyah brought children from the battle zones to Great Britain, Scandinavia, Belgium, the Netherlands, and even Palestine (such as the Polish children called "the Tehran children," who traveled in 1943 via the Soviet Union and Iran). From 1945 to 1948, Youth Aliyah located orphaned children of the Holocaust and brought some 15,000 to Palestine as "illegals." With the establishment of the State of Israel in 1948, Youth Aliyah focused on rehabilitating needy immigrant children from countries of the Middle East and on helping adolescents in distress and/or in dire poverty. Youth Aliyah programs, mostly financed by the Jewish Agency, have helped integrate more than 300,000 children into Israeli society.

Bibliography

Chinitz, Zelig. *Common Agenda: The Reconstitution of the Jewish Agency for Israel.* Jerusalem: Jerusalem Center for Public Affairs, 1985.

Gelber, Yoav. "The Origins of Youth Aliya." *Zionism* 9 (1988): 147–172.

DONNA ROBINSON DIVINE

YOUTH MOVEMENTS

Social and political groupings and organizations formed for Middle Eastern adolescents and young adults.

Youth movements have played an important role in Middle Eastern politics and society. Until the late nineteenth century, the defense of neighborhoods was frequently ensured by *futuwwa* and other informal associations of young men operating as local militias. These "gangs" provided internal order and protection against outside threats and were often engaged in welfare and charitable activities; however, they sometimes preyed on the people instead.

Although in the twentieth century most of these groups disbanded, new kinds of youth movements developed that transcended residential loyalties. Between the two world wars, scouting and Young Men's Muslim associations made their appearance in many Middle Eastern countries. These nonpolitical youth groups frequently provided the nucleus from which full-fledged political movements developed. Initially, for example, the Muslim Brotherhood relied heavily on the scouting movement to spread its religious message.

In the 1930s, several Middle Eastern countries spawned right-wing paramilitary youth associations and sporting clubs that were inspired by Hitler's

Germany, Mussolini's Italy, and Franco's Spain. These intensely nationalistic groups recruited primarily among newly educated middle-class students disillusioned with Western-style liberal democracy. They drew their appeal from an admiration of fascist discipline, unity, militancy, organization, and power—and from the hope that Germany and Italy might eliminate Franco-British influence in the Middle East. Members of these groups wore uniforms and followed rituals patterned after those of the Hitler Youth and Franco's Falange. The Phalange party (al-Kata'ib) and the Helpers (al-Najjada), in Lebanon, and Young Egypt (Misr al-Fatat) developed out of such paramilitary groups. The youth groups called Betar, which played an influential role in the development of revisionist Zionism in Europe and in Palestine under the British mandate, were also influenced in their organization and methods by the fascist youth movements.

In Palestine, from 1922 until the early years of the State of Israel, youth movements affiliated with the major Zionist political parties, the National Religious party (NRP) and the Histadrut (Israeli Federation of Labor Unions), played key roles as vehicles of socialization and integration into the Zionist polity and as agents of elite recruitment. Ha-Halutz (The Pioneer), a Zionist farming organization, trained young European Jews to join the agricultural movement in Palestine. The role of the youth branches of Israel's major political parties declined after the mid-1950s, except for B'nei Akivah, the NRP's youth branch, whose regular expansion since 1960 has contributed to the growth of religious nationalism in Israel.

In other Middle Eastern countries, governments have tried to prevent the development of autonomous youth movements. In one-party regimes, the ruling party usually has its own youth section. The most developed example of this is probably the Federation of Iraqi Youth, attached to the Iraqi Baʿth party. Under the auspices of athletic and cultural activities, the federation (which is itself divided into several programs catering to specific age groups) tries to diffuse the party's views among Iraq's younger generation.

Throughout the region, youth movements fueled by rapid population growth have played a leading role in antiregime activities. Student activism was a recurrent feature of political life in the 1970s and 1980s in countries as different as Morocco, Egypt, Lebanon, Iran, Turkey, Sudan, and Tunisia, where student associations sometimes joined forces with other social groups to participate in riots against the government. In particular, through a variety of Marxist and Islamic-leftist organizations, young people were actively involved in the 1979 downfall of the shah of Iran. More generally, the Islamic resurgence of the 1970s and 1980s has been primarily a movement of disaffected youth (particularly high school and university students of provincial origins and middle- and lower-middle-class backgrounds) who have organized themselves through informal religious associations.

Youth associations also contributed to the turmoil of the 1970s in Turkey, where the ultranationalist far-right National Action party used youth groups to spread its message and carry out its actions. Similarly, some of the organizational roots of the Intifada, the uprising of Palestinians that broke out in December 1987 in the Israeli-occupied territories, can be found in youth clubs formed in the 1970s and 1980s. These groups were initially created for cultural, social, and athletic activities, but they rapidly developed into a political movement of resistance to Israel's administration. Youth associations enabled a new generation—often the youth of Palestinian refugee camps, who had known only Israeli rule but who, unlike their elders, could no longer bear to live under such control and felt they had little to lose—to vent its anger, frustration, and hatred.

Middle Eastern youth movements also include scouting and Young Men's/Women's Christian associations in Egypt, Lebanon, Jordan, and the Israeli-ruled territories. In Israel, a Young Men's/Women's Hebrew Association is similar. In the 1970s, a Young Men's and a Young Women's Muslim Association were formed in the West Bank. Like scouting, these associations are concerned with organizing social, cultural, self-help, charitable, skill-training, and athletic activities.

See also FUTUWWA; MUSLIM BROTHERHOOD; PHALANGE; YOUNG EGYPT.

Bibliography

Mardin, Serif. "Youth and Violence in Turkey." *European Journal of Sociology* 19 (1978): 229–254.

El-Messiri, Sawsan. *Ibn al-Balad: A Concept of Egyptian Identity.* Leiden: Brill, 1978.

Munson, Henry. *Islam and Revolution in the Middle East.* New Haven, CT: Yale University Press, 1988.

Peretz, Don. *Intifada: The Palestinian Uprising.* Boulder, CO: Westview Press, 1990.

GUILAIN P. DENOEUX

YÜCEL, HASAN ALI
[1897–1961]

Turkish educator, publisher, and writer.

Born in Istanbul, Hasan Ali Yücel obtained a degree in philosophy from Istanbul University in 1921. After teaching philosophy for a few years, he worked in the new Republic of Turkey's education directorate and published poetry and books on Turkish literature in the late 1920s and 1930s. He also joined the Turkish language-reform movement and eventually became a protégé of Atatürk. Yücel served as minister of education between 1938 and 1946, when he became known as an active reformer and supervised the publication of hundreds of translations of world classics. He also fostered the development of Village Institutes, which trained local teachers. President İsmet İnönü promoted his strict and controversial language reforms in school text-books.

In 1946, Yücel was accused by retired general Fevzi Çakmak of harboring communists in the Village Institutes. Although Yücel's name was cleared by a libel suit, during the trial accusations by Islam's religious right—that he supported subversive literature—cast a pall of self-censorship over public debate, and his successor undid many of his reforms. In the 1950s, Yücel worked for a publishing house and returned to writing, producing poetry and books of prose on citizenship, England, and Cyprus.

Bibliography

Heyd, Uriel. *Language Reform in Modern Turkey.* Jerusalem: Israel Oriental Society, 1954.

ELIZABETH THOMPSON

YÜKSEK ÖĞRETIM KURULU (YOK)

The Turkish Council of Higher Education, a policy-making and planning body.

The Yüksek Öğretim Kurulu originally was established in 1973, but in 1975 Turkey's Constitutional Court found its mandate to be incompatible with academic freedom and in conflict with the administrative autonomy of the universities. However, constitutional amendments after the 1980 military coup enabled its resurrection. Since then it has served as a liaison among the state, government, and universities. Its primary functions are to coordinate all resources allocated to higher education and to regulate academic activities. Its chairperson and some of its members are directly appointed by the president of the republic. The remaining members are appointed by the president from among candidates nominated by the government, the chief of the general staff, and the university senates.

Both in 1973 and much more urgently in 1981, the bureaucratic-military elite felt the need to depoliticize higher education. To this end, YOK ended the tradition of individual university senates electing deans and rectors. Instead, YOK gives the president a list of candidates it deems appropriate. Many political party leaders criticize YOK as an antidemocratic organization that restrains academic freedom, both directly and indirectly. Since the mid-1960s, numerous pieces of proposed legislation have sought to curb YOK's authority to intervene in academic issues.

YOK sought to standardize higher education in the early 1980s by determining the curricula to be followed in all universities, and soon became the target of widespread protests. Its position on the practice of veiling on university campuses also met with vociferous criticism. In 1983, it introduced the first nationwide prohibition against female students attending classes and taking examinations while wearing the veil. The Parliament overruled this ban in 1988 with a law that allowed "the covering of the head and the body on the basis of religious faith," but this law was annulled by the Turkish Constitutional Court. When the escalating Islamist mobilization in the 1990s rendered secularism the most crucial issue, and YOK its most reliable vanguard, the Council's authoritarian decisions went unobjected to by the state elites, despite vehement social opposition.

With the pro-religious Justice and Development Party's accession to the government in November

2002, a proposal to reform YOK's mandate was reinvigorated. This proposal endorsed a maximum of four years of service for Council members and rectors; selection of the chairperson by the Council; appointment of rectors by the President upon the recommendations by the university senates; nullification of all disciplinary charges against the faculty and students; and pardoning of students that dropped out because of academic absence. In this respect, the proposal attempted to restrict the YOK's administrative powers and to restore educational rights to veiled students who had been dismissed from the university. Although almost all social groups agree on the democratization of YOK's mandate, the proposal is regarded, especially by secularists, as hastily prepared and as an attempt to expel its current chairperson, Kemal Gürüz, rather than to initiate real reform.

See also TURKEY.

Bibliography

Bollag, Burton. "Clash of Turkish Leaders Stalls Higher-Education Reform." *Chronicle of Higher Education* 48, no. 45 (July 19, 2002): A 35.

Özdalga, Elisabeth. *The Veiling Issue: Official Secularism, and Popular Islam in Modern Turkey.* Richmond, U.K.: Curzon Press, 1998.

YOK. Available from <http://www.yok.gov.tr/english/index_en.htm>.

I. METIN KUNT
UPDATED BY BURÇAK KESKIN-KOZAT

YUNIS JABIR, ABU BAKR
[1940–]

Libyan general.

A brigadier general and de facto chairman of the joint chiefs of staff, Abu Bakr Yunis Jabir was born in 1940. Educated at the military college in Benghazi, he was a classmate of Muammar al-Qaddafi and a founding member of the Free Unionist Officers movement. Yunis Jabir participated in the September 1969 coup that overthrew King Idris and was one of the original members of the Revolutionary Command Council (1969–1977). He has served the Qaddafi regime in a variety of military positions since 1969, most recently as chief military commander.

See also LIBYA; QADDAFI, MUAMMAR AL-; REVOLUTIONARY COMMAND COUNCIL (LIBYA).

Bibliography

El-Kikhia, Mansour O. *Libya's Qaddafi: The Politics of Contradiction.* Gainesville: University Press of Florida, 1997.

St John, Ronald Bruce. *Historical Dictionary of Libya,* 3d edition. Lanham, MD: Scarecrow Press, 1998.

RONALD BRUCE ST JOHN

YURDAKUL, MEHMET EMIN
[1869–1944]

Turkish poet and politician.

Known as the "national poet" for his patriotic verses (he published a famous collection in 1897, *Türkçe Şiirler*), Mehmet Emin Yurdakul was born in Istanbul during the Ottoman Empire, the son of a ship captain. He entered the civil service and was appointed governor of the Hijaz.

In 1912, Mehmet Emin was a founding member of Türk Ocaği (Turkish Hearth), and during World War I he joined the National Turkish party. After the war he became a member of parliament in the new Republic of Turkey, taking the surname Yurdakul (slave to the homeland). Although he was an admirer of Atatürk, Mehmet Emin expressed several disagreements with the ideology of the new government. His poetry, still memorized today by Turkish schoolchildren, was characterized by an unadorned style and unabashed praise for the Turkish nation.

Bibliography

Mitler, Louis. *Ottoman Turkish Writers: A Bibliographical Dictionary of Significant Figures in Pre-Republican Turkish Literature.* New York: P. Lang, 1988.

DAVID WALDNER

YUSUFIAN, BOGHOS
[1775–1844]

Armenian minister of commerce and foreign affairs in Egypt in the 1820s and 1830s.

Boghos Yusufian, better known as Boghos Bey, was born in İzmir to a family well connected to the Armenian merchant class involved with overseas commerce. He made his money in Egypt as a customs official and trader. He was skilled in languages and served the British as an interpreter in the campaign against the French. He was first hired by Muhammad Ali as an interpreter and rapidly progressed to the position of personal secretary. Consolidating his rule in Egypt, Muhammad Ali found in Boghos an instrument for pursuing policies independent of his Ottoman sovereigns. Having earned Muhammad Ali's trust during his service in the palace in Cairo, Boghos was made minister of commerce in 1826. He ran his office from Alexandria and proved an adept intermediary between Egyptian economic policy and European commercial interests. In a reorganization of the government in 1837, Muhammad Ali created the joint ministry of commerce and foreign affairs and appointed Boghos Bey head of the department, leading many foreigners to assume that Boghos was the "prime minister" of Egypt.

To help modernize the administration of the country and improve its economy, Muhammad Ali became a great patron of the Armenians. In his early bid for power in Egypt, Muhammad Ali, then a small tobacco merchant of no military repute, had found an Armenian, Yeghiazar Amira, who was willing to give him a loan. Muhammad Ali repaid Amira many times over. He also encouraged Armenian settlement in Egypt. With Boghos Bey as its leading figure, the Armenian community in Egypt grew from a few dozen to two thousand. Among them were many relatives of Boghos whom he had brought over from İzmir, including the Nubar and Abro families. Arakel Bey Nubar (1826–1859) followed in his uncle's footsteps and became Egypt's minister of commerce. Boghos Bey's more famous nephew, however, was Nubar Pasha, who served three terms as prime minister of Egypt in the last quarter of the nineteenth century. Dicran Pasha d'Abro was minister of foreign affairs in the 1890s.

Among his many assignments, Boghos had also been entrusted by Muhammad Ali with training new and capable administrators. Charged with sending the most promising to Europe for further education with the approval of the pasha, Boghos also sponsored the education of the sons of many Armenian merchants in the service of Muhammad Ali. Among them was his successor to the ministry of commerce and foreign affairs, Artin Chrakian (1804–1859), whom Muhammad Ali appointed upon Boghos's death. It is reported that Boghos Bey died a man of modest means, all his resources having been placed in the service of his master.

See also CHRAKIAN, ARTIN; MUHAMMAD ALI.

Bibliography

Adalian, Rouben. "The Armenian Colony of Egypt during the Reign of Muhammad Ali, 1805–1848." *Armenian Review* 33, no. 2 (1980): 115–144.

Sayyid-Marsot, Afaf Lutfi al-. *Egypt in the Reign of Muhammad Ali.* Cambridge, U.K., and New York: Cambridge University Press, 1984.

ROUBEN P. ADALIAN

YUSUF, YUSUF SALMAN

[1901–1949]

Secretary-general of Iraq's Communist party, 1941–1949.

Yusuf Salman Yusuf, known as Comrade Fahd, was a Chaldean Christian. He attended the KUTV in Moscow (1935–1937). On his return to Iraq in 1938, he became a member of the Central Committee of the Communist party; he became its secretary-general in 1941. In 1947 he was condemned to death, but the sentence was commuted to penal servitude. He ran the party from prison until his retrial and execution in February 1949.

MARION FAROUK-SLUGLETT

YZERNITSKY, YITZHAK

See SHAMIR, YITZHAK

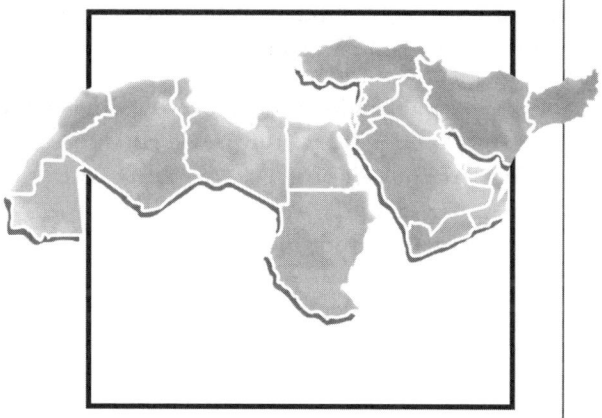

Z

ZAB RIVERS

Great Zab of Turkey and Iraq and Little Zab of Iran and Iraq; major tributaries of the Tigris river.

The Great Zab rises in the mountains of southeast Turkey and runs for 260 miles (420 km), flowing southwest into the Tigris below Mosul, Iraq. The Little Zab rises in the Zagros mountains and flows for about 230 miles (368 km) southwest into the Tigris, some 50 miles (80 km) below the Great Zab. Their violent seasonal spring flow contributes about half the flood crest of the Tigris.

Bibliography

Fisher, Sydney N. *The Middle East: A History,* 3d edition. New York: Knopf, 1979.

JOHN R. CLARK

ZABUL

Afghan province.

Zabul is the name of both a province in Afghanistan and an Iranian city. The Afghan province of Zabul is located in southeastern Afghanistan, bordering Pakistan on the south and the province of Kandahar on the west. Zabul province has a population of approximately 200,000, most of whom are Pushtun, though some Hazara live in the north. The provincial capital is Kalat, which lies along the main highway from Kabul to Kandahar. Zabul, which is famous for its almonds, is in a very dry and windy region, where agriculture is limited to a few irrigated valleys. The drought of the late 1990s and early 2000s hit this area particularly hard. Many of the tribes in Zabul province were strong supporters of the Taliban movement, and security remains problematic in this area.

The Iranian city of Zabul is in the Sistan-Baluchistan province and is situated near the Afghan border across from the Afghan city of Zaranj. The population of Zabul in 2001 was 126,000.

Bibliography

Adamec, Ludwig W. *Historical Dictionary of Afghanistan.* Metuchen, NJ: Scarecrow Press, 1991.

Iranian Statistical Year Book: 1380 (2001–2002). Tehran: Statistical Centre of Iran, 2002.

Rubin, Barnett R. *The Fragmentation of Afghanistan: State Formation and Collapse in the International System,* 2d edition. New Haven, CT: Yale University Press, 2002.

GRANT FARR

ZACH, NATAN

[1930–]

Israeli poet and critic.

Zach, one of the best known Israeli poets abroad, has been called "the most articulate and insistent spokesman of the modernist movement in Hebrew poetry." He had a profound influence on Israeli poetry and literature during the 1950s and 1960s. Zach was born in Berlin and emigrated to Palestine in 1935. He studied at the Hebrew University in Jerusalem and later at the University of Essex, England, where he wrote his doctoral dissertation. After returning to Israel, he lectured at Tel Aviv University and was later appointed professor at Haifa University. He also served as chairman of the repertoire board of two of Israel's leading theaters, the Ohel and the Cameri. In addition to his poems, Zach published critical essays and edited several literary publications. Nationally and internationally acclaimed, Zach was awarded the prestigious Bialik and Israel prizes as well as the Feronia Prize (Rome).

In 1967, together with the late Palestinian-Israeli poet Rashid Husayn, he assembled and translated the first collection of Palestinian folk poems. Individual poems of his have been published in Afrikaans, Arabic, Czech, Dutch, English, Estonian, French, German, Greek, Hungarian, Italian, Japanese, Polish, Portuguese, Russian, Serbo-Croatian, Spanish, Yiddish, and Vietnamese.

One of Zach's most instrumental contributions to the national literature was his conscious rejection of the national symbolism and ethnic sentimentality of mainstream Israeli poetry prior to 1948. Zach's early poems, *First Poems* and *Different Poems* (in Hebrew), exhibit a marked disassociation with the specifics of time and place, expressing instead the voice of the individual. Through emphasizing the more morbid aspects of human existence, Zach sought to undermine both the form and content of traditional Israeli poetry. To achieve that, he introduced new and unique poetic forms into Hebrew, including rhythm, rhyme, language, and metaphor. Other hallmarks of Zach's poetry are its intellectual detachment, emotional restraint, and subtle irony, all of which are employed against the excessive sentimentality and pathos of his predecessors. Zach influenced Hebrew poetry as well through his articulate and vociferous writings on its behalf. He published numerous essays promoting his modernist literary agenda both as a critic and as literary editor.

Zach's publications (in Hebrew) include *First Poems* (1955), *Other Poems* (1960), *All the Milk and Honey* (1966), *Northeasterly* (1979), *Anti-erasure* (1984), *Dog and Bitch Poems* (1990), *Because I'm Around* (1996), and *Death of My Mother* (1997).

Bibliography

Negev, Eilat, with an introduction by Risa Domb. *Close Encounters with Twenty Israeli Writers.* London and Portland, OR: Vallentine Mitchell, 2003.

YARON PELEG
UPDATED BY ADINA FRIEDMAN

ZAGHLUL, SAʿD

[1857–1927]

Egyptian nationalist and leader of the Wafd, the nationalist party founded in Egypt in 1919.

A lawyer by profession, Saʿd Zaghlul served as Egypt's minister of education (1906), earning the praise of Lord Cromer. As vice-president of the Legislative Assembly (1913), Zaghlul attracted attention with his charismatic oratory. His wife, Safia, known in Egypt as "Mother of the People," was the daughter of Egypt's wealthy and pro-British prime minister, Mustafa Fahmi.

After World War I, Zaghlul led a delegation (Arabic, *wafd*) to Cairo to ask Britain's High Commissioner Reginald Wingate for permission to argue the case for Egypt's independence directly before the British government in London. Britain refused and in 1919 deported Zaghlul and other leading members of the wafd to Malta. The deportations precipitated the 1919 uprisings, when Egyptians of all classes, throughout the nation, boycotted British goods and sometimes violently attacked British installations and personnel. In an attempt to halt the rioting, the British reluctantly permitted Zaghlul and others to present the Egyptian nationalist case to the great powers attending the Paris Peace Settlements.

Although he enjoyed the support of the vast majority of Egyptians, Zaghlul failed to achieve independence from the British in these and subsequent negotiations. When he continued to demand the abolition of the protectorate over Egypt and nationalist agitation increased, the British deported Zaghlul again in 1921. The deportations only strengthened the Wafd and contributed to Zaghlul's popularity.

After the British had unilaterally declared the independence of Egypt in 1922 and King Fu'ad had signed the new constitution in 1923, Zaghlul was permitted to return to Egypt where he promptly resumed leadership of the Wafdist nationalist forces. Following the Wafd's overwhelming victory in free elections, Zaghlul became prime minister in 1924.

Zaghlul's triumph was short-lived, for in November 1924 Sir Lee Stack, *sirdar* (commander in chief of the Egyptian army) and governor-general of the Sudan, was assassinated while visiting Cairo. The assassination, coupled with Britain's demands for apologies and reparations, precipitated a government crisis and forced Zaghlul's resignation. Although Zaghlul remained the most popular Egyptian leader, he was prevented by the British from becoming prime minister in subsequent governments. In 1927, he died quietly in his home.

See also PARIS PEACE SETTLEMENTS (1918–1923); WAFD.

JANICE J. TERRY

ZAGROS

Mountain range in Iran.

The Zagros mountain range is the largest in Iran, stretching for 1,400 miles (2,253 km) from Armenia in the former U.S.S.R. in the northwest to the Persian Gulf in the south, and thence eastward to Baluchistan. It consists of a number of parallel ranges, the highest peak of which rises to 14,000 feet (4,270 m). It separates the Iranian plateau from the plains of Mesopotamia and Iraq in the west and the Persian Gulf in the south. Together with the Elburz (also known as Alborz) ranges in the north, the Zagros was formed from the Paleozoic to the Pliocene period.

Bibliography

Wilber, Donald N. *Iran: Past and Present—From Monarchy to Islamic Republic,* 9th edition. Princeton, NJ: Princeton University Press, 1981.

PARVANEH POURSHARIATI

ZAHAWI, JAMIL SIDQI AL-

[1863–1936]

Prominent Iraqi poet, philosopher, and educator, known for his defense of women's rights.

Jamil Sidqi al-Zahawi was born in Baghdad. During the Ottoman era, he held numerous positions: as a member of the Baghdad education council, where he championed education for women; as editor of the only newspaper in Baghdad, *al-Zawra*; as a member of the Supreme Court in Yemen and in Istanbul; as a professor of Islamic philosophy at the Royal University; and as a professor of literature at the College of Arts in Istanbul. After Iraq's independence in 1921, he was elected to parliament twice and appointed to the upper chamber for one term.

He was one of the leading writers in the Arab world, publishing in the major newspapers and journals of Beirut, Cairo, and Baghdad. Describing his life in a collection of his poems, he wrote, "In my childhood I was thought of as eccentric because of my unusual gestures; in my youth, as feckless because of my ebullient nature, lack of seriousness, and excessive playfulness; in my middle age as courageous for my resistance to tyranny; and in my old age as an apostate because I propounded my philosophical views" (Najim, p. 173, translated by author). In the 1930s, because of his political views, he was marginalized by the political establishment.

See also GENDER: GENDER AND EDUCATION; IRAQ.

Bibliography

Najim, Mohammed Yusif, editor. *Diwan Jamil Sidqi al-Zahawi,* Vol. 1. Beirut: Dar al-Kitab al-Arabi, 1971.

JACQUELINE ISMAEL

ZAHEDAN

Main city of southeastern Iran and administrative center of Sistan and Baluchistan province.

Zahedan occupies an upland plateau (4,718 ft./1,438 m in elevation) north of Mount Taftan, an active volcano in southeast Iran. It is just south of the area where the borders of Afghanistan, Iran, and Pakistan meet and 60 miles (96 km) northwest of Mirjaveh, the Iranian customs and passport control checkpoint on the border with Pakistan. Zahedan is a modern city that developed in the twentieth century. During the nineteenth century, the agricultural village of Duzhab occupied the site, one of the few areas in extremely arid Baluchistan with adequate groundwater for irrigated cultivation. During World War I, when Pakistan was part of British India, the British extended the imperial railway from Calcutta to Quetta westward to Duzhab. Later, during the reign of Reza Shah Pahlavi (r. 1926–1941), the village was officially renamed Zahedan after the medieval capital of Sistan, which had been destroyed by the Mongols, and the administrative center for Sistan and Baluchistan was moved here from Khash.

Zahedan had developed into a small town of 17,500 inhabitants by 1956. After Iran and Pakistan joined the U.S.-sponsored Central Treaty Organization in 1958, Zahedan, as a frontier town, became a site for military facilities and related infrastructure projects that spurred rapid growth. By 1976 the population had quintupled to 93,740. However, the ethnic composition of the population also changed, from a majority of local Baluchis and Persian-speaking Sistanis to a majority of migrants from the central areas of Iran. In the 1980s thousands of refugees from Afghanistan resettled in the city. By 1996 Zahedan's population had reached 419,500.

Population growth has spurred the establishment of small and medium-size businesses, including cotton textile manufacturing, woven and knotted carpet production, reed mat and basket making, leather processing, food processing, livestock feed production, ceramics, brick kilns, and grain milling. Zahedan is a large market for foreign goods, a significant proportion of which are smuggled over the border with Pakistan. Zahedan also is believed to be a major center for the illegal processing of opium—smuggled into Iran from Afghanistan and Pakistan—into illicit narcotics.

See also BALUCHIS; CENTRAL TREATY ORGANIZATION (CENTO); SISTAN AND BALUCHISTAN.

ERIC HOOGLUND

ZAHIR SHAH

[1914–]

King of Afghanistan, 1933–1973.

Born in Kabul, the capital of Afghanistan, Zahir attended Habibia and Istiqlal schools (1920–1924), then accompanied his father, Mohammad Nadir Khan, to France, where he continued his studies. Zahir's father was the second eldest and most influential of five Musahiban brothers, members of the Muhammadzai royal clan of the Barakzai Pashtun tribe, who enjoyed considerable power in court during the 1910s and 1920s. During the turbulent rule of the modernizing King Amanullah Barakzai (1919–1929), the Musahiban brothers fell into disfavor. In 1929, when popular rebellions forced Amanullah's abdication, followed by a nine-month interregnum of rule by a rural Tajik, Amir Habibullah, Zahir's father returned to eastern Afghanistan from France. With assistance from the British in India, Pashtun tribesmen, and religious leaders, Nadir Khan claimed the Afghan throne, declaring himself Muhammad Nadir Shah on 15 October 1929—thereby establishing the Musahiban dynasty.

Zahir returned to Kabul in October 1930 and attended the Infantry Officers School for one year. In 1931, he married the daughter of Ahmad Shah, a court minister. The only surviving son of Nadir Shah, Crown Prince Zahir at age seventeen was appointed assistant war minister (1932), then minister of education (1933). On 8 November 1933, following the assassination of his father, he was proclaimed King Mohammad Zahir Shah, with the religious title al-Mutawakkil ala Allah (he who puts his faith in Allah). To ensure the continuation of Musahiban rule, his accession to the throne was unopposed by his three surviving uncles. For the next thirty years, Zahir Shah simply reigned while two of his strong-willed and autocratic uncles held actual power as prime ministers—Sardar (Prince) Muhammad Hashim Khan (1933–1947) and Sardar Shah

Mahmud Khan (1947–1953), followed by Zahir Shah's cousin and brother-in-law, the dictatorial prime minister Sardar Muhammad Daud (1953–1963). During this period, although Afghanistan was officially a constitutional monarchy, power and decision making were monopolized by a few elder members of the Musahiban oligarchy; they maintained family unity through intermarriage, assuring continuation of their rule by stifling liberal expression and political freedoms with an oppressive police state.

Following a rift with Daud and his resignation as prime minister, Zahir Shah took power into his own hands in 1963 by appointing a nonrelative as prime minister. He then launched his program of Demokrasy-i Now (New Democracy)—a period of experimentation with democratic liberalization that lasted for a decade. During this decade, he encouraged the development of a new liberal constitution, supported relatively free elections, extended freedom of the press, and tolerated the formation of many political movements with diverse orientations. Indecisiveness and inaction on the passage of legislation governing political parties and his inability to prevent government interference by family members and friends undermined the democratic experiments. In 1973, while receiving medical treatment in Europe, Zahir Shah was overthrown in a military coup led by his paternal cousin (and sister's husband), Daud. Zahir Shah remained in foreign exile in Italy with his family, and Daud established a republic.

Zahir Shah is considered a mild-mannered, soft-spoken kindly gentleman who lacks energy and is devoid of initiative. He abdicated his throne and passively watched the people's struggles opposing Soviet occupation, communist rule, and civil strife that began in Afghanistan in 1978. Zahir Shah's written statement welcoming the initial fall of Mazar-e Sharif to Taliban in 1997 deeply saddened the peoples of northern Afghanistan. However, some of his former associates and officials also living in exile advocate his return to Afghanistan and possible restoration of the monarchy especially after the fall of the Marxist regime in 1992 and again after the fall of the Taliban regime in 2001. One of Zahir Shah's delegates to the Bonne Conference (December 2001), Hamid Karzai, was appointed chairperson of the interim post-Taliban government. In April 2002 he ended his exile in Rome and returned to his palace in Kabul, renouncing all claims to the throne. The emergency Loya Jerga of June 2002, which he officially opened, gave him the title of "Father of the Nation." His title was reaffirmed by the Constitutional Loya Jerga of December 2003.

Zahir Shah in his residence in Rome, 2001. Zahir was the last king of Afghanistan, reigning from 1933 until he was deposed in a bloodless coup in 1973. After more than 25 years in exile, he acquired a reputation as an elder statesman and was given the symbolic title "Father of the Nation" upon his return in 2002. © REUTERS NEWMEDIA INC./CORBIS. REPRODUCED BY PERMISSION.

Bibliography

Dupree, Louis. *Afghanistan.* Princeton, NJ: Princeton University Press, 1980.

Shahrani, M. Nazif. "State Building and Social Fragmentation in Afghanistan: A Historical Perspective." In *The State, Religion, and Ethnic Politics: Afghanistan, Iran, and Pakistan,* edited by Ali Banuazizi and Myron Weiner. Syracuse, NY: Syracuse University Press, 1986.

M. NAZIF SHAHRANI
UPDATED BY ERIC HOOGLUND

ZAHLA

The capital of Lebanon's Biqa valley and the center of its economic activity.

Under the mandate, Zahla (also Zahleh) was a small town growing silkworms for export to France; it has developed into a major economic hub for the Biqa Valley, with a population of 55,000 (2002). The city's geographic location makes it an important station for commercial trucks coming into or leaving Lebanon. Zahla's main economic activity centers around the farming and poultry industries.

See also BIQA VALLEY.

GEORGE E. IRANI

ZAʿIM

See GLOSSARY

ZAʿIM, HUSNI AL-

[1894–1949]

Syrian military officer and politician.

Born in Aleppo to a Kurdish business family, Husni al-Zaʿim was captured by the British while serving in the Ottoman army and later joined the Troupes Spéciales in the French Mandate forces. Promoted to lieutenant colonel in 1941, he was charged with embezzlement by the Vichy government and was later arrested by the Free French. He was promoted from director of public security to chief of staff of the army in May 1948. As a precursor to his coup d'état, al-Zaʿim defied President Shukri al-Quwatli's order to arrest Col. Antoine Bustani, the scapegoat of a minor scandal, and gave him a position in the defense ministry instead. In the spring of 1949, Colonel al-Zaʿim overthrew the government of Khalid al-Azm and arrested President al-Quwatli.

Encouraged by the local representatives of U.S. intelligence in Damascus, and supported by the future Syrian president Adib Shishakli, the Zaʿim coup marked the first comprehensive takeover by the military in regional politics. The Syrian military would never be far from control of the political institutions. Al-Zaʿim's short rule sought to forcibly strip many traditional customs that appeared to inhibit progress. He even tried to explore the possibility of achieving a peace agreement with Israel. But his inconsistent foreign and domestic policy cost him the support of neighboring Arab regimes and of Syrian public opinion. His regime was overthrown on 14 August 1949 by Sami al-Hinnawi, and al-Zaʿim was executed. It is believed that Zaʿim paid with his life for his betrayal of Antun Saʿada, the leader of the Syrian Social Nationalist Party, whom al-Zaʿim backed at first but then handed over to the Lebanese authorities, who sentenced him to death in July 1949.

See also SAʿADA, ANTUN.

Bibliography

Rathmell, Andrew. *Secret War in the Middle East: The Covert Struggle for Syria, 1949–1961.* New York; London: I. B. Tauris, 1995.

Seale, Patrick. *The Struggle for Syria: A Study of Post-War Arab Politics, 1945–1958.* London: I. B. Tauris, 1986.

CHARLES U. ZENZIE
UPDATED BY EYAL ZISSER

ZAKAT

See GLOSSARY

ZAMIR, ZVI

See MOSSAD

ZAMZAM

The famous well of Mecca.

According to Muslim legend, Zamzam was opened by the angel Gabriel to provide for Hagar and Ismaʿil, who were in danger of dying of thirst after Abraham deposited them in what was then an unpopulated desert valley. History suggests that it was the coexistence of this well and the adjacent shrine (Kaʿba) that led to the emergence of Mecca as an important commercial and cultural center in pre-Islamic Arabia. For centuries Muslims have cherished the brackish water of Zamzam as sacred and have sought to benefit from its reputed blessings. To this day, pilgrims to the Meccan sanctuary descend the enclosed staircase to the well and either draw water for themselves to drink, or bottle it and take it home for a relative or friend who is ill.

See also KAʿBA.

SCOTT ALEXANDER

ZANA, LEYLA

[1961–]

Kurdish member of Turkey's parliament sentenced to jail for defending the rights of the Kurdish people.

Leyla Zana was born in 1961 in a Kurdish village near the town of Silvan in eastern Turkey. When she was fourteen her father married her to his cousin, Mehdi Zana, a political activist. In 1976 the couple moved to the Kurdish city of Diyarbakir, where Mehdi was elected mayor a year later. Arrested during the 1980 military coup d'état, he was sentenced to thirty years in prison.

Defending the rights of her husband as a political prisoner, Zana became an activist, and organized other women visiting their jailed family members. Meanwhile, she studied on her own, obtained a high school diploma, and engaged in journalistic and human rights activism, which led to her arrest in 1988.

In 1991 she became the first Kurdish woman elected to the parliament, and the first to break the ban on speaking in Kurdish in the parliament. She advocated in her native tongue for fraternal relations between Kurdish and Turkish peoples. Declared a "separatist," "traitor," and member of an illegal party, she was tried, convicted, and sentenced to fifteen years in jail in 1994. Since her imprisonment she has received several peace awards, including the European Parliament's Sakharov Prize for Freedom of Thought, and was nominated for a Nobel Peace Prize. In 1998 she was sentenced to two more years in jail for writing an article about the Kurdish new year *(Newroz)*. In April 2003, a retrial convened under pressure from the European Union (which Turkey aspires to join) did not lead to her release.

Bibliography

Leyla Zana. Directed by Kudret Güneş. Artefilm, 2002.

Zana, Leyla. *Writings from Prison,* translated by Kendal Nezan and Harriet Lutzky. Watertown, MA: Blue Crane Books, 1999.

SHAHRZAD MOJAB

ZANAN MAGAZINE

An independent Iranian women's magazine.

The first issue of the monthly magazine *Zanan* (Women) appeared in February 1992 under the editorship and management of Shahla Sherkat. Fired after ten years of working in the editorial board of *Zan-i Ruz* (Today's woman) because of her "growing modernist, Western, and feminist tendencies" (Sherkat, 2003, p.4), Sherkat launched *Zanan* as an independent feminist journal. Although initially produced in a small room borrowed from the office of *Kian,* a reform-oriented journal, and with limited resources and the cooperation of only a couple of journalists, *Zanan* has grown into a professionally produced magazine with about thirty staff members and several freelance contributors; it has its office in an independent office building. *Zanan*'s survival (104 issues published as of December 2003) against financial odds and political pressures is a remarkable record of success in the history of Iran's usually short-lived independent publications in general and of its women's publications in particular.

Zanan represents a gradual shift among numerous Muslim women activists from radical Islamism or conservative patriarchal traditionalism to a liberal spiritualism and modernist egalitarian reformism that is described by some as Islamic feminism. This evolution, occurring within the context of widespread ideological disillusionment with militant and totalitarian Islamism, represents the gender dimension of a growing reform movement toward democracy, pluralism, secularism, and civil rights in Iranian society at large.

Zanan has played a pioneering role in Islamic women's rethinking of gender and reconstruction of womanhood. With significant contributions by Muslim feminist theologians such as Seyyed Mohsen Saʿidzadeh and secular lawyers such as Mehrangiz Kar, *Zanan* began challenging the patriarchal presuppositions that have shaped the dominant interpretations of Islam and the construction of *shariʿa* law and policy concerning women's rights, male-female relationships, sexual mores, and gender roles under the Islamic Republic of Iran.

Believing that *ijtihad* (reasoning from faith) is an obligation of every responsible adult, *Zanan* has expanded the domain of modern Islamic interpretation. It has embarked on a thorough and radical project aimed at "decentering the clergy and placing woman as interpreter and her needs as ground for interpretation" (Najmabadi, 1998, p. 71).

Zanan's agenda has not been limited to the reinterpretation of the Islamic canon. Each issue includes sections addressing social problems and contentious issues; theoretical debates, interviews, and cultural studies; critique of law and legal advice; feminist critique of literature and films; health issues, sports, and leisure; and new books and news. It also carries advertisements, which are not always free of stereotypical marketing techniques geared toward modern homemakers. Some *Zanan*'s writers, especially the younger ones such as Parastu Dokoohaki, Shadi Sadr, and Roya Karimi-Majd, have produced courageous and provocative reports highlighting not only oppressive and sexist traditions but also modern social ills affecting girls and the younger generation of women, including poverty, prostitution, drug abuse, addiction, and violence. Although it is circulated in different parts of Iran and in some diaspora circles, *Zanan*'s readers are primarily in the modern middle class and for the most part are middle-aged urban women.

In the 1997 presidential elections and the subsequent parliamentary elections, *Zanan* played a considerable role in mobilizing women's votes for Mohammad Khatami and moderate candidates for the Iranian parliament, the majlis. Yet through its critical monthly reports on the works of the majlis deputies and the policies of Khatami's government, and especially through challenging interviews and panel discussions, *Zanan* also took the reformers to task by highlighting their shortcomings and failures to safeguard women's rights and achieve progress on gender issues.

Adopting a nonviolent, spiritual, Sufi-like language in its editorials, *Zanan* has emphasized "autonomy and choice as the first pillar of freedom" (Sherkat, 1992, pp. 2–3). By inviting contributions from Iranian secular and Islamic feminists, living inside as well as outside the country, *Zanan* has provided a nonsectarian and inclusive forum for dialogue between secular and faith-based feminists. Its openness, however, is constrained by censorship as well as by the ideological and political constraints imposed by the regime. By introducing feminist theories, reports on women's status and movements in other parts of the world, and translations of Western feminist literature, *Zanan* has avoided a reactive gender conservatism and a phobia about Western ideas, weaving textual, artistic, and intellectual connections between Muslim women and Western feminism. *Zanan* has altered the terms of the debate and dialogue not only among Islamic women activists, but also between Islamic and secular feminists.

See also KAR, MEHRANGIZ; SAʿIDZADEH, SEYYED MOHSEN; *SHARIʿA*.

Bibliography

Karimian, Ramim, and Bahrampour, Shaʾbanali. "Iranian Press Update." Middle East Report no. 212 (fall 1999). Available from <http://www.merip.org/mer/mer212/212_press-update.html>.

Najmabadi, Afsaneh. "Feminism in an Islamic Republic: 'Years of Hardship, Years of Growth.'" In *Islam, Gender, and Social Change,* edited by Y. Y. Haddad and J. L. Esposito. New York: Oxford University Press, 1998.

Tohidi, Nayereh. *Globalization, Gender, and Religion: The Politics of Women's Rights in Catholic and Muslim Contexts,* edited by Jane H. Bayes and Nayereh Tohidi. New York: Palgrave, 2001.

NAYEREH TOHIDI

ZAN-E RUZ

See NEWSPAPERS AND PRINT MEDIA: IRAN

ZANGWILL, ISRAEL
[1864–1926]

British novelist and playwright; early Zionist.

Israel Zangwill was a sophisticated British wit whose reputation was established with his novel *Children of the Ghetto* (1892), which depicted Jewish immigrant life in the East London ghetto. He joined in the Zionist cause of Theodor Herzl in 1895, arranging for Herzl a series of community meetings with prominent members of English Jewish society. He introduced Herzl to the Maccabeans, a society of Jewish authors, artists, and professionals, and helped organize the Maccabean Pilgrimage to Palestine in 1897. He also helped and employed the wandering Hebrew poet Naphtali Herz Imber, author of the

Zionist anthem "Hatikvah," during his stay in England (1889–1892) and made him famous as a character in his writings.

During the period of the Uganda Project, Zangwill founded and led the Jewish Territorial Organization for the Settlement of the Jews within the British Empire (1905–1925); it pursued the possibility of an East African province for a Jewish settlement, a so-called provincial Palestine. Zangwill felt that "any territory which was Jewish [and] under a Jewish flag, saves the Jew's body and the Jew's soul." Many Zionists broke with him over this issue, since his group did not acknowledge any organic connection between Zionism and Palestine.

During the early 1900s, Zangwill scored tremendous success as a playwright in England and in the United States. He also continued to write novels and produced his last play, *We Moderns* (1924), in New York City.

See also HERZL, THEODOR; UGANDA PROJECT.

Bibliography

Laqueur, Walter. *A History of Zionism.* New York: Holt, Rinehart, 1972.

Vital, David. *The Origins of Zionism.* Oxford: Clarendon Press, 1975.

Vital, David. *Zionism, the Formative Years.* Oxford: Clarendon Press, 1982.

MIRIAM SIMON

ZANZIBAR

Islands and coastal land in East Africa.

From the tenth century, many Arabs emigrated to Zanzibar, the 640-square-mile (1,658 sq. km) island of that name (also neighboring islands and the adjacent coast of East Africa). In 1698 Oman seized Zanzibar from the Portuguese, and in 1841 Oman's ruler, Shaykh Sayyid Saʿid, permanently moved his capital there from Muscat. Wealthy Omanis established an extensive plantation economy centered on clove production using African slave labor. After Saʿid's death in 1856, contention between his sons led to Britain's Canning Award (1861), splitting Oman and Zanzibar into separate sultanates. The latter declined, partly because of British suppression of the slave trade in 1873, and became a British protectorate in 1890.

Following Zanzibar's independence (1963) and union with Tanganyika (1964), the Arab population was severely mistreated by the Africans. Several thousand emigrated, mostly to the capital area of Muscat in Oman, after the accession of Sultan Qabus in 1970. In Zanzibar in 2000 and 2001, political tensions and violence followed elections that observers denounced as irregular. The major political parties signed an agreement in October 2001 calling for electoral reforms.

Bibliography

Bennett, Norman R. *A History of the Arab State of Zanzibar.* London: Methuen, 1978.

MALCOLM C. PECK

ZAQAZIQ UNIVERSITY

University in the eastern Nile delta.

Zaqaziq University was founded in 1974 in Zaqaziq, the capital of the eastern Nile delta province of Sharqiyya, from branch faculties of Ain Shams University in Cairo. In 2001, on its main campuses in Zaqaziq and its branch campus at Banha, the university had nearly 6,000 teaching staff and assistants and 146,816 students.

See also AIN SHAMS UNIVERSITY.

Bibliography

The World of Learning 2004. London: Europa Publications, 2004.

DONALD MALCOLM REID

ZARANIQ CONFEDERATION

Tribal grouping on North Yemen's largely nontribal coastal desert, the Tihama.

The Zaraniq, the largest and most formidable tribal grouping of the Tihama, stood in the way of efforts by Imam Yahya to extend control of the imamate state and were compelled to submit to the imam only after a savage two-year campaign in the late 1920s. An important part of the history of the Tihama for many centuries, the Zaraniq were known in the past as the Ma'aziba tribe and, like other tribes on the Tihama, claimed descent from the Akk tribe.

See also YAHYA IBN MUHAMMAD HAMID AL-DIN.

ROBERT D. BURROWES

ZARQA, AL-

Jordanian city.

Lying some 14 miles (23 km) northeast of Jordan's capital, Amman, al-Zarqa is Jordan's second-largest city (pop. 421,000 in 2002). The village witnessed tremendous growth beginning in the 1950s through the presence of a major military base, the development of industry and a free trade zone, and the influx of Palestinian refugees (who constitute some 60 to 70 percent of the population).

ABLA M. AMAWI

ZAWIYA

See GLOSSARY

ZAYDAN, JURJI

[1861–1914]

Early pan-Arab nationalist, author, and publisher.

Jurji Zaydan (also spelled Gurgi Zaidan) was born into a poor Greek Orthodox family in Beirut and, through self-education, obtained entry to the Syrian Protestant College in 1881. After a year in the medical school, he participated in a student strike and was expelled. As did many of his contemporaries, he went to Cairo, where he embarked on a career as a journalist, publisher, novelist, scholar, and pronationalist intellectual. He was a major contributor to Arab literature. During the thirty years of his life in Cairo, he produced twenty-one historical novels dealing with Arab history; a five-volume history of Islamic civilization (*Tarikh al-Tamaddun al-Islami,* Cairo, 1901–1906); a four-volume history of Arabic literature (*Tarikh Adab al-Lugha al-Arabiyya,* Cairo, 1910–1913); and a dozen other books on history, language, and literature. In 1892, he founded the magazine *al-Hilal,* which he authored, published, and distributed for the next twenty-two years practically single-handedly. With *al-Muqtataf,* it became the most important forum of the Arab Nahda (Renaissance) for the discussion of history, nationalism, secularism, modern sciences, and political institutions. In addition, Zaydan was also the author of the first autobiography in Arabic, *Mudhakkirat Jurji Zaydan.*

At the end of the nineteenth century the European presence in the Middle East became ubiquitous and overwhelming in all its cultural, intellectual, political, and economic aspects. The task of the Arab intellectual was to respond to a twofold challenge: to adapt to life in the modern Europe-dominated world while continuing to assert the independent identity and viability of Arab society. It was exactly this twofold challenge that Zaydan made his life task to tackle. Less the political activist than the educator of the nation, he aimed at informing his Arab compatriots about the modern world as well as about their own past and national identity. Even as he familiarized his Arab readers with modern Europe and introduced them to European thought, he established the foundations for a pan-Arab national identity. He was the first to try in a scholarly and systematic fashion to reconstruct a history of the Arabs separate from Islamic history. By incorporating pre-Islamic Arabian and even Babylonian history into Arab history, Islam became only one phase. This perspective also made possible a future for the Arab nation independent from Islam. On the popular level, he tried to spread this idea along with national identity through his historical novels—a genre that he introduced to Arabic literature.

In addition to history, language assumed a central place in Zaydan's thinking. It was the symbol of national identity, a means of achieving such identity, and an expression of one's national culture and heritage. For him, the vitality of the language meant the viability of the nation. Drawing on concepts of evolution and progress, he attacked the classicist ideal and the religious rigor of archaic literary Arabic and insisted that developments and changes in the language were positive, proving its vitality. Especially through his magazine, *al-Hilal,* he contributed greatly to the simplification in style of formal literary Arabic and popularized new terms and concepts that reflected modern thought and knowledge.

His unceasing and successful effort to establish an Arab national identity defined by history and language created the foundations of political pan-Arab nationalism as it arose after the collapse of the Ottoman Empire.

Bibliography

Philipp, Thomas. *Gurgi Zaidan: His Life and Thought.* Wiesbaden, Germany: Steiner, 1979.

Zaydan, Jurji. *The Autobiography of Jurji Zaidan,* edited and translated by Thomas Philipp. Washington, DC: Three Continents Press, 1990.

THOMAS PHILIPP

ZAYDISM

The sect of Shiʿite Islam that prevails in the northern highlands of North Yemen and the political system that has existed to defend and advance that sect almost continuously since the late ninth century.

The Zaydi sect takes its name from Zayd ibn Ali Zayn al-Abidin, the fifth Shiʿite imam and the grandson of Husayn, who was one of the two sons of Ali and Fatima, the cousin and daughter of the prophet Muhammad. (Because Zayd was the fifth imam, Zaydis are sometimes called Fiver Shiʿa.) The doctrine of the sect as developed by Zayd and his followers was pragmatic, rational, and open to extension by critical examination and interpretation; and it rejected such features of other Shiʿite sects as the ideas of a "hidden" imam, an occult explanation of the Qurʾan, systematic dissimulation, and mysticism. Often referred to as the "fifth school" of Sunni Islam, Zaydism differs from Sunni orthodoxy primarily in its insistence on the institution of the imamate and the right of the descendants of Ali and Fatima to rule the world of Islam through that religio-political institution.

The founder of the Zaydi imamate in Yemen was al-Hadi ila al-Haqq Yahya ibn Husayn. He did so in the year 897 after being invited by tribes in the area around Saʿda to come from his native Medina to mediate their disputes and govern them. Al-Hadi's fourteen-year reign established in the highlands of North Yemen the Zaydi imamate, a state and political system that was to persist with numerous changes of fortune and breaks in continuity for over one thousand years into the 1960s, all the while maintaining many of the features that he and his immediate successors had decreed for it. The strong imams of the first decades of the twentieth century, Imam Yahya and his son, Imam Ahmad ibn Yahya, served as the spiritual leaders, temporal rulers, and defenders of the community of Islam much as had their predecessors a millennium earlier. The Zaydi imamate was abolished on the occasion of the 1962 revolution that created the Yemen Arab Republic, but northern Yemen, and Saʿda in particular, is still known for its Zaydi population.

See also AHMAD IBN YAHYA HAMID AL-DIN; QURʾAN; YAHYA IBN MUHAMMAD HAMID AL-DIN.

Bibliography

Halliday, Fred. *Nation and Religion in the Middle East.* Boulder, CO: Lynne Rienner Publishers, 2000.

Serjeant, R. B. *Society and Trade in South Arabia,* edited by G. Rex Smith. Brookfield, VT: Variorum, 1996.

ROBERT D. BURROWES

ZAYTUNA UNIVERSITY

Prominent university in Tunis.

Built as a mosque in the eighth century, Zaytuna was enlarged by the Aghlabids in 864 when the Abbasid caliph al-Muʿtasim ordered the addition of a wing. It continues to serve as a school mosque and houses a huge library that in the fourteenth century was administered by the Malikite theologian Muhammad ibn Arafa. One of Zaytuna's students was Abd al-Rahman ibn Khaldun, the well-known Arab historian and philosopher. In modern times alumni include the leader of the Tunisian Destour party, Abd al-Aziz Thaʿlabi. In addition many Zaytuna graduates staffed the cadres of the Neo-Destour party.

Although at first traditional, teaching at Zaytuna was gradually modernized. The last reform came in 1933, at the hands of its students. Upon Tunisia's independence the Zaytuna became the *shariʿa* (Islamic law) school of the University of Tunis.

In 1945, Zaytuna had five branches in various cities of Tunisia and three thousand students in the secondary and college levels combined. The regional branches were not very active, and their ties with Tunis were very weak. With the appointment of al-Taher ben Ashour as the director of Zaytuna, new branches were opened in Tunisia and even in Algeria, raising their number to twenty-five. All became very active. The number of students in the main and the regional branches jumped to 20,000.

The growing national role of Zaytuna University in opposing French colonialism and the leadership of its graduates in the nationalist movement, caused it to become the target of the French colonial government. The university gradually found itself at odds with the political powers, and its activities were curtailed. The great cultural support Tunisia received from the Arab League allowed it to pursue the spread of Arabic culture and language teaching through Zaytuna University as well as other centers of learning, thus counteracting the colonial cultural policy of promoting French at the expense of Arabic. Zaytuna University was instrumental in safeguarding Arabic culture in Tunisia and also helped its neighbor Algeria, a country that did not have a similar cultural center.

See also LEAGUE OF ARAB STATES.

Bibliography

Abu-Nasr, Jamil M. *A History of the Maghrib.* Cambridge, U.K.: Cambridge University Press, 1971.

Hourani, Albert. *A History of the Arab Peoples.* Cambridge, MA: Belknap Press of Harvard University Press, 1991.

AIDA A. BAMIA

ZAYYAT, LATIFA

[1923–1996]

Egyptian university professor, literary critic, political activist, essayist, and fiction writer.

Latifa Zayyat was a cultural icon of nationalist and feminist commitment. Born in the Delta city of Dimyat (Damietta), she received her university education and in 1957 her doctoral degree in English literature from Ain Shams University, Cairo. She taught there from 1952 until her retirement and was briefly director of the Arts Academy in Cairo during the 1970s.

Throughout her life she remained politically active. Involved in nationalist and student politics in the 1940s, she was a leader of the National Committee of Students and Workers. From 1979 until her death she chaired the Committee for the Defense of National Culture, formed to counter the possible cultural effects of Anwar al-Sadat's normalization policy toward Israel and his *infitah* ("Open Door") economic policy; along with many other activist intellectuals, Zayyat was arrested in 1981—not her first experience as an Egyptian political prisoner.

The activism of the 1940s forms the historical backdrop to her novel *al-Bab al-maftuh* (*The Open Door,* 1960), a landmark work of Arab feminist literature, narrating the physical, social, and political awakening of a middle-class Egyptian girl. After a long hiatus, Zayyat published additional novels, short stories, and a play; her short story collection *al-Shaykhukha wa qisas ukhra* (Old age and other stories, 1986) was notable for its focus on aging and its cross-genre formal experimentation. She also published critical studies in Arabic and English, and translations into Arabic of T. S. Eliot's essays and other texts. In 1992, she published a controversially frank memoir, *Hamlat taftish: Awraq shakhsiyya* (Arrest/search campaign: personal papers). She was awarded Egypt's State Prize for Literature in 1996, a few months before her death.

See also BAKR, SALWA; GENDER: GENDER AND EDUCATION; GENDER: GENDER AND LAW; GENDER: GENDER AND POLITICS; LITERATURE: ARABIC.

Bibliography

Booth, Marilyn. "Translator's Introduction." In *The Open Door,* by Latifa al-Zayyat. New York; Cairo: American University in Cairo Press, 2000.

Zayyat, Latifa. *The Search: Personal Papers,* translated by Sophie Bennett. London: Quartet Books, 1996.

Zayyat, Latifa al-. *The Open Door,* translated by Marilyn Booth. New York; Cairo: American University in Cairo Press, 2000.

MARILYN BOOTH

ZBIRI, TAHAR

[1930–]

Algerian officer.

Born in the Annaba region, Tahar Zbiri supported Messali al-Hadj before joining the Armée de Libération Nationale (ALN). He had a distinguished record during the Algerian War of Independence (1954–1962), participating in the initial attacks of 1 November 1954, escaping with "historic chief" Moustafa Ben Boulaid from the French, and breaching the Morice Line in 1960. Although he served as chief of staff of the Armée Nationale Populaire (ANP) under President Ahmed Ben Bella, Zbiri's loyalties were to Houari Boumédienne, and he arrested Ben Bella during the June 1965 coup. Zbiri remained chief of staff but opposed Boumédienne's increasing authoritarianism. In 1967 he organized a military revolt that failed, resulting in his arrest and exile. President Chadli Bendjedid pardoned Zbiri in 1980 and he returned to Algeria. Immediately after the suppression of the October 1988 riots, Zbiri and other prominent veterans and ex-ministers urged Bendjedid to convene a national conference to organize a new, democratic Algeria. The president rejected this proposal and Zbiri aligned with the anti-Bendjedid faction within the Front de Libération Nationale (FLN). Zbiri was selected to preside over a commission to monitor the parliamentary elections of May 1997. He is also identified with Algeria's liberalizing economy as a supporter of the private Khalifa group, a controversial conglomerate that collapsed in 2003.

See also ALGERIAN WAR OF INDEPENDENCE; BOUMÉDIENNE, HOUARI.

Bibliography

Naylor, Phillip C. *The Historical Dictionary of Algeria,* 3d edition. Lanham, MD: Scarecrow Press, 2003.

PHILLIP C. NAYLOR

ZEID, FAHRALNISSA

[1901–1991]

Turkish artist.

Fahralnissa Zeid was the daughter of a prominent Turkish general. Like many Middle Eastern artists of the early twentieth century, she came from an elite family of politicians and intellectuals. Zeid studied under Namik Ismail at the Academy of Fine Arts in Istanbul and then at the Académie Ranson in Paris, starting in 1927. She later returned to Turkey to join the famed D Group of contemporary artists, who attempted to develop Turkish art along the European model in line with the new Turkish republic. Zeid married the Hashimite ambassador to Turkey and assisted him in diplomatic posts throughout Europe. She was one of the first Middle Eastern artists to show her work in the West, including exhibits in London, New York, and the Salon des Réalités Nouvelles in Paris as early as the 1940s. In the 1970s she went to Amman and founded the Fahralnissa Zeid Institute of Fine Arts, thereby influencing generations of future Jordanian and Palestinian artists. Zeid's work was influenced by Byzantine portraiture, medieval stained glass patterns, and the tradition of Turkish miniature paintings. Her cubist-inspired abstract art was the first art of its kind to gain wide exposure in Jordan, as her openings garnered extensive media coverage. She also did fanciful scenes and portrait painting, working in oil, collage, and stained glass.

Bibliography

Ali, Wijdan. *Modern Islamic Art: Development and Continuity.* Gainesville: University of Florida Press, 1997.

JESSICA WINEGAR

ZELDA

[1914–1984]

Israeli poet.

Born Zelda Shneurson and also known as Zelda Mishkovsky, she signed her poems with her first name only. A devout Hasidic Jew, she was well versed in ancient sacred and traditional Jewish texts. In 1926 she emigrated to Israel from her native Ukraine. Her first book, *Leisure,* was published in 1968. Zelda published six other volumes of poetry: *The Invisible Carmel, Be Not Far, Neither Mountain nor Fire, Tiny Poems, The Spectacular Difference,* and *Beyond All Distance.* Her work is acclaimed by secular Israeli readers for its gentle, transcendental, mystic quality. Her poem "Each Person Has a Name" describes the characteristics acquired by individuals through the names assigned them and has been embraced by Israelis as an expression of their own collective and personal experiences with trauma and loss. The melancholy underlying her worldview is lightened by a sense of acceptance, a faith in the possibility of glory, and an enchantment with the beauty and sanctity of life.

Bibliography

Carmi, T. *The Penguin Book of Hebrew Verse.* New York: Viking, 1981.

ZVIA GINOR
UPDATED BY DONNA ROBINSON DIVINE

ZELL AL-SOLTAN, MAS'UD MIRZA
[1850–1918]

The eldest son of Persia's Naser al-Din Shah.

Mas'ud Mirza Zell al-Soltan (Shadow of the Sovereign) was excluded from succeeding Naser al-Din because his mother was not of the Qajar dynasty. He became governor of Isfahan in 1874 and from 1881 to 1887 was the powerful and oppressive ruler of much of southern Iran. He had a large private army and kept the local tribesmen under control, killing an important Bakhtiari chief in 1882. He had contempt for the *ulama* (Islamic clergy). The rival of his half-brother and future monarch, Mozaffar al-Din, governor of Azerbaijan, Zell al-Soltan was opposed at court in Tehran by Ali-Asghar Amin al-Soltan. In 1888, because of his excesses, his power was restricted to Isfahan. During the Constitutional Revolution, he hoped to replace Mohammad Ali as shah and, consequently, aided the revolutionaries by supplying some financial support.

Bibliography

Curzon, George Nathaniel. *Persia and the Persian Question* (1892). London: Cass, 1966.

LAWRENCE G. POTTER

ZEROUAL, LIAMINE
[1943–]

President of Algeria, 1994–1999.

Born in Batna, Liamine Zeroual (also al-Amin Zirwal) joined Algeria's National Liberation Army (ALN) at the age of sixteen. Later he attended a military school in the Soviet Union and France's Ecole de Guerre. Upon his return, he took over the military school of the National Popular Army (ANP) in Batna. Zeroual held various operational jobs within the ANP, including that of commander of the prestigious Military Academy in Cherchell. He earned the rank of general in 1988 and commanded the Land Forces. Zeroual resigned from the ANP in 1989 because of a conflict with President Chadli Bendjedid about the restructuring of the military. He was appointed ambassador to Romania in 1990. In 1991 he retired to Batna.

After Bendjedid was deposed in 1992, Algeria was ruled by the High State Council. In 1993 General Khaled Nezzar, a powerful member of the Council, called Zeroual back from retirement as his replacement as minister of defense. In January 1994, with the dissolution of the Council, Zeroual was appointed president of Algeria. In November 1995 he was elected president with 60 percent of the popular vote in the country's first pluralist presidential election. His mission was to reestablish peace and security, to build legitimate state institutions, and to break with the old regime. Zeroual was able to build an institutional edifice. A political party, the Rassemblement National Démocratique (RND), was created in February 1997 to support his policies. The party obtained the majority in the June 1997 legislative elections. In a surprise move, Zeroual announced on 11 September 1998 that he would step down in February 1999. In April 1999 Abdelaziz Bouteflika, following a controversial election, became his successor.

See also ALGERIA: OVERVIEW; ALGERIA: POLITICAL PARTIES IN; BENDJEDID, CHADLI; BOUTEFLIKA, ABDELAZIZ; HIGH STATE COUNCIL (ALGERIA).

Bibliography

Quandt, William B. *Between Ballots and Bullets: Algeria's Transition from Authoritarianism.* Washington, DC: Brookings Institution Press, 1998.

Zoubir, Yahia H. "The Algerian Political Crisis: Origins and Prospects for Democracy." *Journal of North African Studies* 3, no. 1 (spring 1998).

Zoubir, Yahia H., and Youcef Bouandel. "Algeria's Elections: Prelude to Democratization?" *Third World Quarterly* 19, no. 2 (June 1998): 177–190.

MIA BLOOM
UPDATED BY YAHIA ZOUBIR

ZIADEH, MAY
[1886–1941]

Poet, translator, orator, essayist, and critic.

Marie Ziadeh (also Ziyada) was born in Nazareth to a Lebanese father and a Palestinian mother. After her family emigrated to Cairo in 1908, Ziadeh began her writing career, which was facilitated by her father becoming editor of the Cairo weekly *al-Mahrusa.* After initially writing under pseudonyms, she changed her name from Marie to May (or Mayy), and quickly distinguished herself as a prolific poet, translator, orator, essayist, and critic. She studied at the Egyptian University, mastered five languages, cooperated with early feminist groups such as the one led by Huda Shaʿrawi, and as early as 1913 started a literary salon in her parents' house.

Ziadeh's early work is characterized by romanticism, but increasingly her writing took on sociopolitical themes relating to socialism, colonialism, freedom of the press, and especially women's rights. Among her groundbreaking publications are her biographical accounts of the pioneer women writers Warda al-Yaziji, Aʾisha Taymur, and Bahithat al-Badiya. Ziadeh was also associated with the *mahjar* (émigré) Arab writers, particularly Kahlil Gibran, with whom she had an intense, lengthy correspondence. Although they never met, there has been much speculation on the nature of their relationship, and much written about her as his muse. Her articles on Gibran were widely read in the Arab world and helped make him famous, while also establishing her as a critic.

Ziadeh is most famous for her literary salon, which met weekly for over twenty years. Unlike other salons, hers was open to men and women of mixed religious, national, and social backgrounds. It drew some of the most prominent intellectuals of Egypt and provided her with a platform for both social acceptability and intellectual opposition.

After her parents died, the salon dissolved, and Ziadeh's final years were enmeshed in accusations of insanity and conjecture about her enigmatic life. In recent years, her work has received considerable attention, and she is now acknowledged to be one of the Arab world's most prominent emancipators.

See also EGYPT; GENDER: GENDER AND EDUCATION; LITERATURE: ARABIC; SYRIA.

ELISE SALEM

ZIKHRON YAʿAKOV

Village located 19 miles (31 km) south of Haifa.

In 1882, Romanian Jews founded Zikhron Yaʿakov, one of the early settlements of the Hovevei Zion (Hibbat Zion) movement. Financially supported in part by the Baron Edmond de Rothschild, the settlement, shortly after its founding, was given its present name in memory of the baron's father, Jacob (Zikhron Yaʿakov means "The Memory of Jacob"). Baron de Rothschild promoted the planting of grapes, and vineyards were established in the settlement as well as one of the largest wine cellars in Israel. In 1954, Baron de Rothschild and his wife were buried in Zikhron Yaʿakov. Located in the foothills of Mount Carmel, the village (pop. 12,000 in 2002) is a tourist site that draws visitors to the Rothschild mausoleum, botanical garden, and winery.

See also HIBBAT ZION.

Bibliography

Schama, Simon. *The Two Rothschilds and the Land of Israel.* New York: Knopf, 1978.

BRYAN DAVES

ZILI, RIDHA

[1942–]

Tunisian poet and photographer.

Ridha Zili was born in Monastir, Tunisia. He received a bilingual (Arabic and French) education but writes in French only. Zili's writing is greatly influenced by his work as a photographer, especially in his concept of the image. His only published collection of poetry, *Ifrikiya, ma pensée* (1967; Africa in my thoughts), describes his love of peace and his search for happiness. Zili rejects sadness and the nonsensical violence in the world and values his Tunisian African roots.

See also LITERATURE: ARABIC, NORTH AFRICAN.

AIDA A. BAMIA

ZIONISM

Movement for the establishment of an independent state in Palestine for the Jewish people.

Zionism may be seen as a national liberation movement for a Jewish homeland based on a nineteenth-century European political model. It defined Jews as a nation whose collective future depended upon the establishment of a national territorial entity in

Eretz Yisrael (in Hebrew, "the land of Israel"), from which most Jews had been dispersed by the Roman Empire at the beginning of the second century C.E. The movement's name was coined by the Viennese Jewish writer Nathan Birnbaum in 1885 and derives from *Zion,* one of the biblical names for Jerusalem, the focus of worldwide Judaism.

Zionists believed that antisemitism was endemic to the diaspora; thus, the achievement of national and civil rights in host nations, while desirable, was insufficient to secure economic and cultural interests for Jews in the long run. Few Zionists believed that the diaspora would be swept away (as was attempted a century later by Hitler's Nazi Germany), but a Jewish homeland—which would serve as a cultural and political model and as a magnet for its finest sons and daughters—could help to secure a future for Jews.

Foundations of Zionism

Through the centuries of exile, ritual, prayer, and the study of sacred texts preserved for Jews the knowledge that Judaism had developed in Eretz Yisrael and Zion. In nineteenth-century Europe during the Haskalah (the Jewish Enlightenment), revival of the Hebrew language as a nonreligious, literary medium transmitted secular works and secularized versions of sacred histories to assimilated generations losing faith in religion and religious authority. If Zionism were to ensure the survival of the Jewish people, it could do so only by going through the modern European Jewish experience, not by denying it. Zionists were Jews who believed that only in Zion could Jewish culture and the Jewish people be re-established and secure. At that time, however, Zion was located in Palestine, within the Ottoman Empire, and was populated by Arabs under Ottoman jurisdiction.

A "proto-Zionism" had existed in fact before it was fully defined or before the word itself was coined. As a way of helping the indigent and scholarly Jewish populations in Ottoman Palestine, Western European philanthropists such as Edmond de Rothschild and Sir Moses Montefiore proffered aid to projects that later would come to be associated with the Zionist movement—the purchase of land for settlements, farms, and businesses from Ottoman officials and Arab landlords; the building of schools for vocational training; and the opening of medical facilities.

Jewish emigration to Eretz Yisrael also antedated the emergence of a Zionist movement. Jewish religious leaders had always endorsed the idea of living in the Holy Land as a means of discharging religious duties, and had actively promoted the expansion of Jewish communities in Safed, Tiberias, Hebron, and Jerusalem, creating financial mechanisms to meet the immigrants' material needs.

The wave of pogroms that followed the assassination of Russia's Czar Alexander II in 1881 turned an attachment for Zion into an ideology embraced by some of Russia's secular Jewish leaders and intellectuals. Newly promulgated regressive legislation and the resuscitation of antisemitic rhetoric dashed the hopes of those who had believed Russia's polity would evolve into a democracy, with basic rights granted to its population and the ideals of tolerance espoused. Although emigration to the United States and Britain was a popular way of escaping the immediate disabilities imposed by Russian policies, some educated Jews saw that moving to another land would neither end antisemitism nor secure a Jewish future. They argued that only a purposeful immigration with the goal of establishing a Jewish majority in a territory would achieve international respectability for Jewry and help protect Jews everywhere against discrimination. For those who called on Jews to liberate themselves, the Zionist idea supplanted the ideal of assimilation. Zionism was presented as resolving the Jewish problem by normalizing the conditions of Jewish existence.

Development of Zionist Organizations

Although many rabbinical authorities opposed Zionism for its secular and humanistic principles, many rabbis—most notably Samuel Mohilever and Isaac Jacob Reines—welcomed Zionism; they affiliated with Hibbat Zion, the first international Zionist organization to be founded, partly because they reasoned that in Eretz Yisrael a social and cultural environment could be created that was conducive to religious observance.

The Orthodox rabbinate did not, however, establish an entirely harmonious relationship with the secular leadership in Hibbat Zion. Many Orthodox

Theodor Herzl addresses a meeting of the Zionist Congress in Basel, Switzerland. The Zionist Congress was dedicated to establishing institutions necessary for the support of a Jewish state. © ISRAEL GOVERNMENT PRESS OFFICE (GPO) OF ISRAEL. REPRODUCED BY PERMISSION.

rabbis could not abide the dynamics of a political struggle that effected compromises between the demands of Zionism's secular and religious constituencies. Nor were the Orthodox entirely comfortable in an organization that did not acknowledge the primacy of religious law and rabbinic authority. The first nonsecular Zionist group, the Mizrahi, opened its office in 1893, but most rabbis, though comfortable with the nationalist claims of Zionism, were unwilling to accede to Zionist demands to share power and resources in local Jewish communities. As a consequence of the frustrating handicaps under which Hibbat Zion labored in the 1880s and 1890s, Zionism was at an impasse when Theodor Herzl undertook to lead the struggle for a Jewish state.

Unaware of developments in Eastern Europe, Herzl, a Viennese journalist, championed the idea of Jewish nationhood in response to the outbreak of antisemitism in France during the fraudulent espionage trial of Alfred Dreyfus (1894–1895). In 1896 Herzl published *Der Judenstaat (The Jewish State)*, a book that set forth the argument that both the world and the Jews needed a Jewish state. In 1897 Herzl succeeded in drawing together representatives from the local and regional Hibbat Zion organizations in eastern Europe and Jews from western Europe, establishing and becoming president of a new Zionist framework, the World Zionist Organization (WZO). Authorized by the WZO to secure international recognition for Zionist political goals, Herzl pursued in the capitals of Europe and in the Ottoman capital, Istanbul, official sanction for Jewish colonization in Palestine, but his efforts, albeit feverish and intense, were unsuccessful. The Ottoman sultan Abdülhamit II was not persuaded that a larger Jewish population in Palestine was consistent with his imperial political objectives or that such a population would promote economic development.

Theodor Herzl (1860–1904) was the founder and first president of the World Zionist Organization, a group whose purpose was to establish a Jewish homeland in Palestine. © LIBRARY OF CONGRESS. REPRODUCED BY PERMISSION.

Herzl's leadership did broaden the popularity of Zionism in western and eastern Europe and enlarge its Orthodox membership. Herzl focused the activities of the WZO on diplomacy and finances. This approach mobilized the support of a number of Orthodox rabbis concerned with easing the economic hardships in Palestine for eastern European immigrants and hopefuls, as well as with the creation of a hospitable political climate there. By permitting groups to shift the mode of their representation from regional affiliation to ideological, the WZO was also used advantageously by the Orthodox to influence the direction of policies and, for a number of years, to exclude Jewish culture from the scope of Zionist activities.

Zionism's preoccupation with political solutions and stratagems triggered opposition. Against the political orientation associated with the leadership of Hibbat Zion, the writer Ahad Ha-Am argued that the purpose of Zionism ought to be to revive a modern Jewish culture through the medium of the Hebrew language and a renewed interpretation of classic religious texts; a new Jewish state could only be founded with new artifacts of Jewish culture. Cultural Zionist Ahad Ha-Am's insights on the problems besetting the Jewish people and the Zionist movement helped to inspire a group opposing Herzl's leadership and political Zionism—the Democratic Faction. This group, led by the scientist Chaim Weizmann, did not repudiate political methods or consider them insignificant; rather, they insisted that just as legal titles (to land) could facilitate resettlement, so could settlement lead to concrete political gains. Insisting that the structure of the WZO must be reformed to increase popular participation and broaden its agenda, the Democratic Faction defined its own priorities as the investigation of the physical, political, and social conditions of Palestine for purposes of increasing Jewish immigration.

Creating a Jewish community in Palestine was not simply the solution to continuing antisemitism but also the opportunity to establish a whole and vigorous modern Jewish life. In the early years of the twentieth century, efforts to create a youth movement and to popularize Zionism among the young led several Zionist leaders to synthesize socialism with Zionism. No longer would Jews have to choose between socialism (popular in Russia and in the Pale of Settlement) and Zionism. Some Socialist-Zionists promoted a non-Marxist socialism, emphasizing social welfare and justice; others insisted that even the Marxist version of socialism could be combined with Zionism. Branches of the first Labor Zionist party, Poʿalei Zion, founded in 1906, opened in many towns and cities of eastern Europe, attracting many educated Jewish teenagers. Ha-Halutz, the young pioneer farm movement, was nonpartisan and attracted many capable Austro-Hungarian Jewish youth, especially when it was funded by the WZO after World War I.

Before the conclusion of World War I, Zionists were unable to engage openly in mass mobilization in many countries. In the United States and western Europe, where organizations could operate freely, Zionism did not hold the imagination of most immigrants, who were struggling to work their way out of grinding poverty. In Russia, where the majority of Jews presumably felt sympathy with Zionist aims, Zionist activities were hobbled by the Russian Revolution, Soviet dictatorship, and persecution.

Establishment of the Jewish State in Palestine

With the issuance of the Balfour Declaration in 1917 and the Sèvres Treaty of 1920, Britain became formally committed to the establishment in Palestine of a Jewish national home. This gave Zionism its first major political victory. World War I had changed the map of Eastern Europe as well as that of the Middle East, thereby providing Zionists an opportunity to engage in grassroots political organization among previously isolated Jewish communities. Youth groups expanded, and camps were created to offer vocational and Hebrew-language training to prepare Jews for life and work in Palestine.

Throughout its history, the Zionist movement has had to make crucial choices among several options: Eretz Yisrael (Palestine) versus another territory, such as Uganda, Canada, Australia; a national home versus a cultural center for world Jewry; a Jewish nation-state versus a binational state in which Jews and Arabs might share political power; neutrality during World War I versus pro-British cooperation; high political profile versus quiet political lobbying; and uniformity versus diversity in political goals. Each decision was made after great debate during and outside of Zionist congresses, often triggering enmity, hard feelings, and the creation of new splinters and factions. One of the most serious splits occurred when Vladimir (Ze'ev) Jabotinsky left the WZO to create his own Revisionist Zionist movement.

With increasing knowledge of the extent of the Holocaust during World War II, the Zionist movement chose Jewish survival over acquiescence in British restrictions on immigration, which resulted in an anti-British militancy aimed at gaining free entry for Jewish refugees into Palestine from 1944 until 1948. With the establishment of the State of Israel in May 1948, the fulfilment of one of Zionism's goals was endorsed by international consensus—majority support at the United Nations, official recognition by many of the world's nations, and acceptance by most Jews (religious Jews excepted). The Arab and Muslim world remained outside this consensus. Post-1948 Zionism evolved into a movement dedicated to immigration (aliyah) for as many Jews as possible, land purchase for continued settlement, and political and economic support for Israel through institutionalized activity. Despite the recent "post-Zionist" intellectual trend that urges a redefinition of Israel as an inclusive state for all its citizens and detaches it from its special diaspora Jewish connections, many Jews continue to consider themselves Zionists in affirming this connection and the importance of Israel in sustaining their Jewish identity.

See also ABDÜLHAMIT II; AHAD HA-AM; ALIYAH; ANTISEMITISM; DIASPORA; DREYFUS AFFAIR; ERETZ YISRAEL; HA-HALUTZ; HASKALAH; HERZL, THEODOR; HIBBAT ZION; HOLY LAND; JABOTINSKY, VLADIMIR ZE'EV; JERUSALEM; LABOR ZIONISM; MIZRAHI MOVEMENT; MOHILEVER, SAMUEL; MONTEFIORE, MOSES; POGROM; ROTHSCHILD, EDMOND DE; WEIZMANN, CHAIM; WORLD ZIONIST ORGANIZATION (WZO); ZIONIST COMMISSION FOR PALESTINE; ZIONIST ORGANIZATION OF AMERICA; ZIONIST REVISIONIST MOVEMENT.

Bibliography

Avineri, Shlomo. *The Making of Modern Zionism: Intellectual Origins of the Jewish State.* New York: Basic Books, 1981.

Dowty, Alan. *The Jewish State: A Century Later.* Berkeley: University of California Press, 1998.

Halpern, Ben. *The Idea of the Jewish state.* Cambridge, MA: Harvard University Press, 1969.

Hertzberg, Arthur. *The Fate of Zionism: A Secular Future for Israel and Palestine.* San Francisco: HarperSanFrancisco, 2003.

Hertzberg, Arthur, ed. *The Zionist Idea: A Historical Analysis and Reader.* Philadelphia: Jewish Publication Society, 1997.

Laqueur, Walter. *A History of Zionism: From the French Revolution to the Establishment of the State of Israel.* New York: Schocken Books, 2003.

Rubinstein, Amnon. *From Herzl to Rabin: The Changing Image of Zionism.* New York: Holmes and Meier, 2000.

Sternhell, Zeev. *The Founding Myths of Israel: Nationalism, Socialism, and the Making of the Jewish State,* translated by David Maisel. Princeton, NJ: Princeton University Press, 1998.

Vital, David. *Zionism: The Crucial Phase.* Oxford, U.K.: Clarendon Press, 1987; New York: Oxford University Press, 1987.

Donna Robinson Divine
Updated by Neil Caplan

ZIONIST COMMISSION FOR PALESTINE

Official representative of the World Zionist Organization in Palestine until 1921; a precursor of the Jewish Agency Executive.

The Zionist Commission was an informal group established by Chaim Weizmann as president of the World Zionist Organization (WZO) to advise the British on policies regarding the establishment of the Jewish national home. It carried out initial surveys of Palestine and aided the repatriation of Jews sent into exile by the Ottoman Turks during World War I.

It expanded the WZO's Palestine office (established 1907) into small departments for agriculture, settlement, education, land, finance, immigration, and statistics. In 1921, the commission became the Palestine Zionist Executive, which acted as the Jewish Agency, designated to advise the British mandate authorities on the development of the country in matters of Jewish interest.

See also Jewish Agency for Palestine; Weizmann, Chaim; World Zionist Organization (WZO).

Bibliography

Caplan, Neil. *Palestine Jewry and the Arab Question, 1917–1925.* London and Totowa, NJ: F. Cass, 1978.

Donna Robinson Divine

ZIONIST ORGANIZATION OF AMERICA

U.S. organization supporting Zionism.

The Zionist Organization of America (ZOA) traces its origins to the 1898 founding of the Federation of American Zionists (FAZ) one year after Theodor Herzl created the World Zionist Organization (WZO). The FAZ sought to mobilize support for Herzl's plan "to create for the Jewish people a national home in Palestine secured by public law" (Basle Program, 1897). At first, the U.S. Zionist organization encountered great difficulty in attracting adherents within a mainly immigrant community concerned about its own integration into mainstream America. Indeed, in its early years, the FAZ, forerunner of the Zionist Organization of America, was perceived as a minor, fringe organization within the U.S. Jewish community. However, during World War I, a combination of factors—the plight of two-thirds of world Jewry in war-torn zones; the decision of the prominent U.S. Jew Louis Brandeis to head the FAZ; and the issuance of Great Britain's Balfour Declaration, which "view[ed] with favour the establishment in Palestine a national home for the Jewish people"—enabled the ZOA (FAZ's successor) to increase its membership from less than 12,000 in 1914 to 180,000 in 1918.

After unsuccessfully challenging the leadership and direction of the World Zionist Organization immediately following the war, the ZOA continued U.S. Zionists' erstwhile policy of loyally supporting the policies of the world Zionist movement and, since 1948, the State of Israel. At times, however, leaders emerged who challenged the policies and directions of the Zionist movement and Israeli government. During the Holocaust, ZOA leader Rabbi Abba Hillel Silver urged the WZO to stop trying to reach a modus vivendi with the British Mandate for Palestine and to seek instead to replace the Mandate Authorities with a Jewish State.

Led by its president Morton A. Klein, in 2003 the ZOA had 50,000 members in more than twelve local chapters. It actively advocates for Israel by combating what it views as "the anti-Israel bias of the media" and by promoting pro-Israel legislation on Capitol Hill. Sometimes, however, the Zionist Organization of America finds its advocacy at odds with the Israeli government itself; it opposes, for instance, former prime minister Yitzhak Rabin's signing of the Oslo Peace Process Agreement and Ehud Barak's negotiations with the Palestinian Authority.

See also Balfour Declaration (1917); Herzl, Theodor; Silver, Abba Hillel; World Zionist Organization (WZO); Zionism.

Bryan Daves
Updated by Jerry Kutnick

ZIONIST REVISIONIST MOVEMENT

The political party that represented the revisionist oppositional trend in Zionism; led by Ze'ev Jabotinsky from the 1920s through the 1940s.

The Zionist Revisionist Movement sometimes referred only to the political party (Ha-Zohar; Union of Zionist-Revisionists) and sometimes to various subsidiary bodies and institutions that expressed the revisionist ideology and accepted the leadership of Vladimir Ze'ev Jabotinsky, in particular the Betar youth movement, an avant-garde mass movement of youth and incipient army founded in 1923. Hence, a distinction must be made between, on the one hand, any discussion of the political history of the union and, on the other hand, the history of Betar, the National Labor Federation, and Brit ha-Hayyal (a union of Polish army veterans)—all of which were part of the Revisionist Movement (although they preferred to regard themselves as belonging to the "national movement" or to the "Jabotinsky movement").

The union itself was founded in 1925 in Paris by a group of veteran Zionists, most of them Russians, to propose a "revision" in the aims of Zionism, which basically meant a return to the principles of political Zionism espoused by Theodor Herzl. It found its greatest support among the Jewish communities of Eastern Europe (Poland and the Baltic states), but it had branches worldwide. It grew rapidly; in the elections for the 1927 Zionist Congress, it drew 8,446 votes and in the 1933 elections, 99,729 votes. Consequently, its representation grew at the Zionist Congress and in the Asefat ha-Nivharim (the parliament of the Jewish Yishuv in Palestine), and it became the major opposition party, taking on the image of the Zionist Right or even Zionist fascism, from the end of the 1920s. This electoral growth and development of revisionist institutions led to a number of controversies between the revisionists and the labor movement and the "official" Zionism. This division was often expressed in acts of violence, leaving a deep imprint on the political history and political culture of Zionism and the Yishuv. An internal conflict also existed between moderate elements that wanted to remain within the Zionist Federation and those that demanded that the union break away. It was resolved in 1933 when the moderates seceded from the union and founded a small independent party called the Jewish State Party.

Ze'ev Jabotinsky (bottom right) meets with Betar leaders in Warsaw, Poland, 1936. Jabotinsky founded the Zionist Revisionist Movement and its related organizations such as Betar in order to bring greater pressure to bear on Great Britain and mainstream Zionists to create a large and well-defended Jewish state in Palestine. © GOVERNMENT PRESS OFFICE (GPO) OF ISRAEL. REPRODUCED BY PERMISSION.

A specific point of controversy with official Zionism was the union's "independent diplomacy." This was expressed in various activities, primarily in attempts to obtain the support of European countries, in particular of Poland, to pressure Britain in the Mandate Council of the League of Nations in Geneva. In 1934 the union organized a mass petition denouncing British policy, and after the rise of the Nazis to power, it organized a boycott against German goods. From the mid-1930s, it began disseminating propaganda (and engaging in clandestine activity) to encourage a mass emigration of 700,000 to 1.5 million Jews from Europe to Palestine within a ten-year period (the Evacuation Plan and the Ten-Year Plan). It also was active in organizing illegal immigration to Palestine.

In 1935, the union broke away from the Zionist Federation and set up the New Zionist Federation (NZO) that met with wide popular support. In 1945, it rejoined the Zionist Federation. The union maintained an extensive organizational system with centers in Paris, London, and Warsaw. In Palestine, the Ha-Zohar was the second-largest political party. After establishment of the state, the Irgun Zvaʾi Leʾumi (IZL) founded an independent party while veteran members of the union had their own Revisionist Party, which never attained any representation, so most of its members finally joined the new party.

The movement's platform reflected Jabotinsky's program and ideology: the future establishment of a Jewish state on both sides of the Jordan river under Jewish sovereignty. As an interim measure, a colonization regime would be set up to create the conditions necessary to achieve a demographic Jewish majority—a prerequisite for a state. For this purpose, it called on the mandatory government to adopt an economic and settlement policy that would foster Jewish immigration and settlement. It also demanded that the Jewish Legion be reinstated, i.e., that Jewish military units be activated as an integral part of the British garrison in Palestine.

The official program relating to socioeconomic matters was a combination of etatism (state socialism) and liberalism: on the one hand, support for the private sector and on the other a demand for involvement by the mandatory government and the Jewish Agency in the creation of infrastructure, in providing assistance to the private sector, and in setting up legal arrangements to prevent strikes. The union viewed Palestinian Arabs as citizens with equal rights, on condition that they do nothing to impair the national character of the Jewish state. The revisionists believed that cooperation with the mandatory government and with Britain was essential. But to prevent Britain from reneging on its commitments, they thought it necessary to bring political and propaganda pressure to bear on Britain. In their view, the strategic cooperation in Palestine and Britain's readiness to help Europe's Jews in their distress were the basis for such cooperation. The party was not monolithic, and various views came to the fore. In the 1930s, its dominant mood was that of the "radical nationalists," who called for a more activist policy toward the British, beginning in 1930 but in particular after the events of 1936 (the revisionists opposed the partition plan recommended by the Peel Commission Report in July 1937).

As a result of the internal disputes, there was a great deal of tension in the movement, particularly between the union and Betar and various maximalist groups. This internal strife led to the creation of new organizations, weakly linked organizationally to the union (in particular, the IZL).

See also HERZL, THEODOR; IRGUN ZVAʾI LEʾUMI (IZL); JABOTINSKY, VLADIMIR ZEʾEV; JEWISH AGENCY FOR PALESTINE; JEWISH LEGION; PEEL COMMISSION REPORT (1937); YISHUV; ZIONISM.

Bibliography

Jabotinsky, Vladimir. *The Political and Social Philosophy of Zeʾev Jabotinsky: Selected Writings,* edited by Mordechai Sarig; translated by Shimshon Feder. Portland, OR: Vallentine Mitchell, 1998.

Katz, Shmuel. *Lone Wolf: A Biography of Vladimir (Zeʾev) Jabotinsky.* New York: Barricade Books, 1996.

Schechtman, J., and Ben Ari, Y. *History of the Revisionist Movement,* Vol. 1. Tel Aviv: Hadar, 1970.

Shavit, Yaakov. *Jabotinsky and the Revisionist Movement, 1925–1948.* London, U.K., and Totawa, NJ: Frank Cass, 1988.

YAAKOV SHAVIT

ZIWAJ MUTʿA

Temporary marriage.

Temporary marriage *(ziwaj mutʿa),* which was practiced in early Islamic Arabia, is a contract between a man and an unmarried woman for a particular duration of time. A man can marry numerous temporary wives in addition to his permanent wife or wives. Umar (r. 634–644), the second caliph, outlawed temporary marriage, but Shiʿites did not find his position legally binding because the Prophet and the Qurʾan permitted *mutʿa* marriage. Even a few Sunni societies continued to practice certain forms of *mutʿa* marriage.

Social and economic circumstances shaping modern Shiʿite societies led to the emergence of new and at times arbitrary forms of temporary marriage. After the rise of the Iranian Islamic Republic in 1979, temporary marriage became popular, particularly among the urban lower classes. It also surfaced in Lebanon and other Arab Shiʿite communities. Shiʿite jurists debated several conditions relating to temporary marriage, but the law remained vague and ambivalent about women's rights. It is rare for a woman to negotiate a share of her husband's inheritance. A man is expected to provide for his children from a temporary marriage, but there are no institutional guarantees. A temporary marriage can be terminated by mutual consent before the end of the stipulated period. Overall, men have greater legal rights and control over the conditions of *mutaʿa* than women.

See also GENDER: GENDER AND HEALTH; GENDER: GENDER AND LAW; *SHARIʿA;* SHIʿISM.

Bibliography

Haeri, Shahla. *Law of Desire: Temporary Marriage in Shiʿi Iran.* Syracuse, NY: Syracuse University Press, 1989.

Khomeini, Ayatullah Ruhullah. "Non-Permanent Marriage." *Mahjubih* 2, no. 5 (1982): 38–40.

RULA JURDI ABISAAB

ZIYA, ABDÜLHAMIT

[1825–1880]

Young Ottoman writer.

The son of a customs clerk, Ziya Paşa was educated in one of the first secular Ruşdiye schools in Istanbul. He began work in the translation office and, through the support of Tanzimat reformer Reşit Pasa in 1854, became a secretary to Sultan Abdülmecit I. He lost his palace job in 1861 with the accession of Sultan Abdülaziz and held several minor posts in the 1860s. By 1866 he had joined the Young Ottoman Society in Europe and, with Namik Kemal and İbrahim Şinasi, became a leading intellectual of the period. Under Abdülaziz's rule, Ziya's political satires and other writings were banned as seditious, and he was posted as governor of Syria, in virtual exile.

Ziya Paşa's greatest influence was through his writings. He warned against blind imitation of Europe and criticized autocracy and poor policies such as the growing Ottoman debt. In 1868 he wrote a famous article, "Poetry and Prose" (Şiir ve Inşa), in which he criticized Ottoman literature as mere imitation of Arabic and Persian traditions and called on writers to seek inspiration in Turkish folk literature.

Bibliography

Davison, Roderic H. *Reform in the Ottoman Empire, 1856–1876.* Princeton, NJ: Princeton University Press, 1963.

Lewis, Bernard. *The Emergence of Modern Turkey,* 3d edition. New York: Oxford University Press, 2002.

Shaw, Stanford J., and Shaw, Ezel Kural. *History of the Ottoman Empire and Modern Turkey,* Vol. 2: *Reform, Revolution, and Republic: The Rise of Modern Turkey, 1808–1975.* Cambridge, U.K., and New York: Cambridge University Press, 1977.

ELIZABETH THOMPSON

ZOHAR, URI

[1935–]

Israeli actor and comedian who became a rabbi and teacher.

Uri Zohar began his professional acting career in 1953 and quickly rose to fame as a satirist and humorist. He starred in Israeli films in the 1960s, including *A Hole in the Moon* and *Every Bastard a King.* He was the first cinema artist to win the Israel Prize (which he refused), in 1976.

In the 1970s he became a sectarian Orthodox Jew and a rabbi and teacher in a yeshiva (religious school). He is active in the movement to attract secular Jews to religious orthodoxy, and uses his entertainment skills to promote this objective. He wrote an account of his religious transformation, *Ubaharta bahaim,* (1983)—which was subsequently translated as *Waking Up Jewish* (1985)—as well as several other volumes that espouse his views on secular Israeli society. In 1999 Zohar directed a widely distributed videotape and CD, titled *Ani Me-ashim* (I accuse) in which the former Shas political party leader Arye Deri alleged that the fraud charges of which he was accused (and for which he was imprisoned) were an Ashkenazic-elitist conspiracy against not only him but also the Sephardim as a group.

CHAIM I. WAXMAN

ZOHRAB, KRIKOR

[1861–1915]

Armenian writer and deputy in the Ottoman parliament.

Krikor Zohrab, also known as Grigor Zohrap, was born in Istanbul. He was educated in his birthplace and practicing law by 1883. He distinguished himself as an attorney who defended cases against the government until he was deprived of his license in 1905 and went abroad to France and Egypt. With the end of the Hamidian autocracy and the restoration of the Ottoman constitution, Zohrab returned to Istanbul. From 1908 to 1915, he was a member of the Armenian National Assembly. He also was elected a deputy to the Ottoman parliament where he defended the cause of universal social justice and gained distinction as an orator. Shocked by the 1909 mass killings of Armenians in Adana, he published his findings in Paris under the pseudonym of Marcel Leart as *La Question Arménienne à la Lumière des Documents.*

Zohrab also earned fame as an author of short stories and novellas in the realist style. The subjects of social inequality, injustice, and prejudice preoccupied him. His more important works include *Anhetatsads Serunt Me* (A vanished generation, 1887), *Khghjmdanki Tzayner* (Voices of conscience, 1909), *Kyanke Inchpes Vor e* (Life as it is, 1911), and *Lur Tsaver* (Silent sorrows, 1911). He also published essays on literature, politics, and the Armenian community. Before his own demise, he protested to Talat, the Young Turk minister of the interior, the summary arrest on the night of 24 April 1915, and subsequent execution of the Istanbul Armenian community leaders. His own immunity as a parliamentary deputy did not spare him from being arrested on 3 June, deported, and killed near Diyarbekir.

Bibliography

Baliozian, Ara. *The Armenians: Their History and Culture,* 2d edition. New York: Ararat Press, 1980.

ROUBEN P. ADALIAN

ZONNENFELD, YOSEF HAYYIM
[1849–1932]

Rabbi; leader of ultra-Orthodox Jerusalem community.

Yosef Hayyim Zonnenfeld was born in Verbo, Slovakia, and educated in the yeshiva in Pressburg. Settling in Jerusalem in 1873, he actively opposed secular Zionist educational activities and became a leader of the Old City Jewish community, assisting in the founding of the Meah She'arim community and others. A staunch sectarian, he opposed all cooperation between the Orthodox and non-Orthodox Jewish communities. He was one of the founders of the separatist rabbinic court in Jerusalem, and in 1920 he was elected rabbi of the separatist Orthodox community of Jerusalem. He was also a founder of the Agudat Israel in Palestine. Despite their warm personal relationship, he opposed Rabbi Abraham Isaac Hacohen Kook as rabbi in Jerusalem and, subsequently, as chief rabbi of Palestine. Nevertheless, Zonnenfeld was a strong supporter of Jewish settlement in Eretz Yisrael.

See also AGUDAT ISRAEL; ERETZ YISRAEL; KOOK, ABRAHAM ISAAC HACOHEN; MEAH SHE'ARIM.

Bibliography

Danziger, Hillel. *Guardian of Jerusalem: The Life and Times of Yosef Chaim Sonnenfeld.* Brooklyn, NY: Mesorah Publications, 1983.

CHAIM I. WAXMAN

ZOROASTRIANISM

Pre-Islamic religion founded by the Iranian prophet Zarathushtra (Zoroaster).

Founded as early as 1400 to 1200 B.C.E., Zoroastrianism spread from central Asia to Iran around the ninth century B.C.E., where it was propagated by priests called the *magi*, or *mobeds.* Zoroastrianism remained the major faith in Iran until the Sassanian state fell to the Arabs in 651 C.E. Thereafter, the religion lost many followers through conversion to Islam between the eighth and the thirteenth centuries. Zoroastrianism reached India in the tenth century, when some Zoroastrians migrated from Iran to avoid adopting Islam. Descendants of these immigrants are called the *Parsis* (Parsees). Those who remained behind sought refuge from Islam by moving to sparsely populated regions in central Iran. By the thirteenth century, extensive contact between Parsis and Persian Zoroastrians had recommenced. In 1854, when the Parsis sent an emissary to the Qajar court, the poll tax levied on Iranian Zoroastrians by the Muslim state was abolished. The community in India flourished, and in the mid-1990s it numbered around 72,000.

Zoroastrians in Iran encountered less success, though there was a respite from financial hardship and pressure to practice Islam during the Pahlavi dynasty (1925–1979). Since the Iranian Revolution, despite being recognized as an official minority of about 30,000, Zoroastrians are offered little protection from their Muslim neighbors, and many have fled Iran. International dispersion during the twentieth century has produced Zoroastrian communities in Pakistan (3,700), England (7,000), Australia (1,000), the United States and Canada (10,000), and other countries. By the early 1990s, low birthrates together with widespread nonacceptance of converts contributed to an overall decline in the number of Zoroastrians.

The faith's central canon is the Avesta (Pure instruction), a scripture that includes the Gathas (Songs), which were probably composed by Zarathushtra himself. Prayers recited by the laity in daily religious observances are compiled in a text known as the Khorde Avesta (Shorter Avesta). Next in importance are religious exegeses written in Pahlavi, a Middle Iranian language; among these are the Zand, a commentary on the Avesta, and the Bundahishn (Book of creation). There are more recent Zoroastrian texts in the New Persian, Gujarati, and English languages that transmit tenets of the faith and the meanings of rituals to believers who no longer understand the Avestan and Pahlavi languages.

The religion proposes an ethical dualism—which later became a cosmic dualism—between righteousness and falsehood, personified by a pair of primal spirits: Ahura Mazda (Ohrmazd), the Lord Wisdom, and Angra Mainyu (Ahreman), the Destructive Spirit. Ahura Mazda, the supreme deity, is believed to have created the spiritual and material worlds completely pure. Evil, disease, pollution, and death are attributed to Angra Mainyu, the devil. According to Zoroastrianism, Ahura Mazda created six *amesha spentas,* or beneficent spiritual beings, and other minor good spirits to assist him in protecting the material creations. Angra Mainyu produced numerous *daevas,* or demons, to defile the spiritual and material worlds. Zoroastrian texts claim that human beings were created by Ahura Mazda as allies in the struggle against Angra Mainyu, and that humans entered into a covenant with their creator to combat the forces of evil through daily good deeds.

Between the ages of seven and twelve, each Zoroastrian child undergoes initiation into the religion.

A Zoroastrian priest in London officiates at an initiation ceremony for children between seven and twelve years old. Founded more than 3,000 years ago in central Asia, Zoroastrianism was the major religion in Iran until the emergence of Islam. During the past 200 years, thousands of its adherents have established communities in India and, in much smaller numbers, in the West. © TIM PAGE/CORBIS. REPRODUCED BY PERMISSION.

The ritual, which symbolizes a spiritual rebirth, is termed *sedra pushun* in Iran and *navjote* in India. Every initiate dons a white undershirt called the *sedra,* or *sudra,* and ties a sacred girdle known as the *kashti,* or *kusti,* around the waist. The girdle, which most Zoroastrians continue to wear, should be untied and retied with the recitation of prayers on awakening each morning, and prior to performing worship. Many rituals, such as the *jashan,* or thanksgiving ceremony, are conducted within buildings known as fire temples. Fire is one of the seven sacred creations; the others are water, earth, metal, plants, animals, and human beings. Moreover, fire is believed to destroy evil, and thus it became the religion's icon. Sacred fires burn constantly in altars at major temples at Sharifabad, near Yazd, in Iran and at Surat, Navsari, and Bombay in India. Smaller temples in Iran and India and elsewhere do not maintain constantly burning fires; rather, a fire is lit in an altar prior to acts of worship. Because impurity is thought to arise from evil, Zoroastrians undergo elaborate rituals to ensure their spiritual purity. In addition to rituals of worship and purification, other acts of devotion include seven feasts, such as that celebrating Nav Ruz, the new year.

Zoroastrian doctrine holds that earth, fire, and water are polluted if a corpse is buried, cremated, or placed in water. Consequently, corpses are washed, then placed in a *dakhma* (funerary tower), which is open to the sky and accessible to birds of prey. Thereafter, the bones are collected and disposed of. Exposure of corpses has been phased out in Iran since the 1940s, replaced with interment (burial), but many Parsis in India and Pakistan continue the tradition of exposing bodies in funerary towers, particularly at Bombay and Karachi. Most Zoroastrians elsewhere follow their Iranian coreligionists' adaptation. Certain Zoroastrian communities, particularly those in North America, now perform cremation. Zoroastrians believe that after death each individual's soul is judged by a triad of gods—Mithra, the keeper of covenants; Rashnu, the judge; and Sraosha, the messenger—at the Bridge of the Separator, which connects earth to heaven over the pit of hell. If the soul's good deeds are greater than its evil deeds, it is led across the bridge into paradise. When its evil deeds outweigh the good, the soul is cast into hell until the day of universal judgment. In cases where a soul's good and evil deeds are equal, it is consigned to limbo. The faithful believe that at the end of time a savior *(saoshyant)* will resurrect the dead. Thereafter, Ahura Mazda will descend to earth and separate the righteous individuals from the evil ones. Each sinner will be purified of his or her transgressions and granted immortality. Then Angra Mainyu will be forced back into hell, and the world will become free of evil and impurity forever.

Bibliography

Boyce, Mary. *A Persian Stronghold of Zoroastrianism.* Oxford, U.K.: Clarendon Press, 1977. Reprint edition, Lanham, MD: University Press of America, 1994.

Choksy, Jamsheed K. *Purity and Pollution in Zoroastrianism: Triumph over Evil.* Austin: University of Texas Press, 1989.

Writer, Rashna. *Contemporary Zoroastrians: An Unstructured Nation.* Lanham, MD: University Press of America, 1994.

Zaehner, Robert C. *The Teachings of the Magi: A Compendium of Zoroastrian Beliefs.* New York: Macmillan; London: Allen and Unwin, 1956. Reprint, London: Sheldon, 1975.

JAMSHEED K. CHOKSY
UPDATED BY ERIC HOOGLUND

ZUBAYRI, QA'ID MUHAMMAD MAHMUD AL-

[1919–1965]

Yemeni political reformer.

Born in San'a, Qa'id Muhammad Mahmud al-Zubayri left North Yemen after a brief career as a government official. With Ahmad Muhammad Nu'man, he began his lifelong effort to reform Yemen's imamic government. He participated in the founding of the Liberal party and the Free Yemeni movement. At this time, his poetry, in particular, earned him a literary reputation. Zubayri strongly supported the revolution of 1962 but quickly became disillusioned with the policies of Abdullah al-Sallal. He founded the "Third Force" as an alternative to the royalists and republicans but was assassinated in 1965.

MANFRED W. WENNER

ZU'BI, MAHMUD AL-

[1938–2000]

Syrian politician and long-serving prime minister.

Hailing from a Sunni family in the southern village of Khirbat al-Ghazala, al-Zu'bi was a Ba'th party member in high school and studied agronomy in Cairo. He ascended in the party's agricultural bureaucracy to become head of the general authority for development of the Euphrates river basin from 1973 to 1976 and, from 1980 to 1981, director of the *maktab al-fallahin* (the peasants' office). In January 1980 he became a member of the Ba'th Regional (Syrian) Command. Al-Zu'bi was continually responsive to agrarian concerns in his capacity as he rose in government, both as speaker of parliament (1981–1987) and, later, as long-time prime minister (1987–2000) during the presidency of Hafiz al-Asad. He was dismissed in March 2000 and accused of corruption, after which he committed suicide on 31 May 2000.

Bibliography

Batatu, Hanna. *Syria's Peasantry, the Descendants of Its Lesser Rural Notables, and Their Politics.* Princeton, NJ: Princeton University Press, 1999.

Hinnebusch, Raymond A. *Authoritarian Power and State Formation in Baʿthist Syria: Army, Party, and Peasant.* Boulder, CO: Westview Press, 1990.

CHARLES U. ZENZIE
UPDATED BY MICHAEL R. FISCHBACH

ZURAYK, CONSTANTINE
[1909–2000]

Syrian intellectual and educator.

Constantine Zurayk (also Qustantin Zurayq) was born in Damascus. He received a B.A. from the American University of Beirut (AUB) in 1928, an M.A. from the University of Chicago in 1929, and a Ph.D. from Princeton University in 1930. He was an assistant professor of history at AUB (1930–1945) and later distinguished professor (1958-1977). He also served as counselor to the Syrian legation and then as minister to the United States (1945–1947), AUB vice president (1947–1949, 1952–1954), rector of the Syrian University in Damascus (1949–1952), and AUB acting president (1954–1957).

Zurayk, a prominent Arab intellectual, wrote *Maʿna al-Nakba* (1948; The meaning of the disaster), the first substantial critique of Arab society in light of the 1948 defeat in Palestine. An advocate of rationalism, scientific and cultural progress, and secular nationalism, he produced many other influential works, including *Nahnu wa al-Taʾrikh* (1959; Facing history), *Fi Maʿrakat al-Hadara* (1964; In the battle for civilization), and *Nahnu wa al-Mustaqbal* (1977; Facing the future), as well as translations and editions of European and Arabic works on cultural history. In 1963 he helped found the Institute for Palestine Studies, and served as its chairman until 1984. Zurayk died in Beirut on 12 August 2000.

See also AMERICAN UNIVERSITY OF BEIRUT (AUB); DAMASCUS; INSTITUTE FOR PALESTINE STUDIES.

Bibliography

Atiyeh, George N., and Oweiss, Ibrahim M. *Arab Civilization—Challenges and Responses: Studies in Honor of Constantine K. Zurayk.* Albany: State University of New York Press, 1988.

Nashabé, Hisham, ed. *Studia Palaestina: Studies in Honour of Constantine K. Zurayk.* Beirut: Institute for Palestine Studies, 1988.

CHARLES U. ZENZIE
UPDATED BY MICHAEL R. FISCHBACH

Synoptic Outline of Entries

The synoptic outline of entries provides a general overview of the conceptual scheme of the encyclopedia. Because the section headings are not mutually exclusive, certain entries are listed in more than one section.

Arab-Israel Conflict

Acheson, Dean
Alpha, Operation
Anglo–American Committee of Inquiry (1946)
Aqsa Intifada, al-
Arab Boycott
Arab Bureau (Cairo)
Arab–Israel Conflict
Arab–Israeli General Armistice Agreements (1949)
Arab–Israel War (1948)
Arab–Israel War (1956)
Arab–Israel War (1967)
Arab–Israel War (1973)
Arab–Israel War (1982)
Arab League Summits
Arafat, Yasir
Ard, al-
Arms and Armaments in the Middle East
Avnery, Uri
Azzam, Abd al-Rahman al-
Baker, James A.
Barak, Ehud
Barghuthi, Marwan
Bar-Lev, Haim
Begin, Menachem
Ben-Gurion, David
Benvenisti, Meron
Bernadotte, Folke
Black September
Bunche, Ralph J.
Camp David Accords (1978)
Dahlan, Muhammad
Dayan, Moshe
Dayr Yasin
Eban, Abba (Aubrey)
Egyptian–Israeli Peace Treaty (1979)
Fahd Plan (1981)
Fatah, al-
Gaza (City)
Gaza Strip
Geneva Peace Conference (1973)
Green Line
Habib, Philip Charles
Hammarskjöld, Dag
Institute for Palestine Studies
Israel: Overview
Israel: Military and Politics
Israeli Settlements
Jarring, Gunnar
Jericho Congress (1948)

Jerusalem
Jews in the Middle East
Johnston Plan (1953)
Jordanian Civil War (1970–1971)
Jordanian Option
Kahan Commission (1983)
Karama, Battle of (1968)
Lausanne Conference (1949)
Lavon Affair
Liberty, USS
Litani Operation (1978)
Litani River
London Conference (1956)
Madrid Conference (1991)
Meir, Golda
Michael, Sami
Mossad
Nakba, al- (1948–1949)
Nasser, Gamal Abdel
Netanyahu, Benjamin
Peace Now
Peres, Shimon
Qaddumi, Faruq
Rabin, Yitzhak
Rajub, Jibril
Reagan Plan (1982)
Refugees: Jewish
Refugees: Palestinian
Rogers, William Pierce
Rusk, Dean
Sabra and Shatila Massacres
Sadat, Anwar al-
Sasson, Eliyahu
Saunders, Harold
Sèvres Protocol (1956)
Shabʿa Farms
Shamir, Yitzhak
Sharett, Moshe
Sharon, Ariel
Shiloah, Reuven
Shultz, George
Sisco, Joseph
Suez Crisis (1956–1957)
Taba
Taba Negotiations (1995, 2001)
Tripartite Declaration (1950)
Truman, Harry S.
United Nations and the Middle East
United Nations Conciliation Commission for Palestine(UNCCP)
United Nations Economic Survey Mission (1949)
United Nations Emergency Force
United Nations Interim Force in Lebanon
United Nations Special Committee on Palestine, 1947 (UNSCOP)
United Nations Truce Supervision Organization (UNTSO)
United States of America and the Middle East
Vanunu Affair
Weizman, Ezer
Weizmann, Chaim
West Bank
Western Wall
Yadin, Yigael
Yad Mordekhai
Yehoshua, Avraham B.
Zaʿim, Husni al-
Zionism

BIOGRAPHIES

Aaronsohn Family
Abbas Hilmi I
Abbas Mirza, Naʾeb al-Saltaneh
Abbas, Mahmud
Abd al-Aziz ibn Saʿud Al Saʿud
Abd al-Ghani, Abd al-Aziz
Abd al-Hadi Family
Abd al-Ilah ibn Ali
Abd al-Maguid, Esmat
Abd al-Quddus, Ihsan
Abd al-Rahman al-Mahdi
Abd al-Rahman Khan
Abd al-Rahman, Umar
Abd al-Sabur, Salah
Abdülaziz
Abdülhamit II
Abdülmecit I
Abdülmecit II
Abduh, Muhammad
Abdul-Aziz Bin Baz, Shaykh
Abdullah I ibn Hussein
Abdullah II ibn Hussein
Abdullahi, Muhammad Turshain
Abu al-Huda, Tawfiq
Abu Nuwwar, Ali
Acheson, Dean
Adamiyat, Abbasquli
Adenauer, Konrad
Adivar, Abdulhak Adnan
Adivar, Halide Edib
Afghani, Jamal al-Din al-
Ahad Ha-Am
Ahmad Durrani
Ahmad ibn Yahya Hamid al-Din
Ahmad Qajar
Ahmad Shah Masʿud

Ahmar, Abdullah ibn Husayn al-
Ahmet Ihsan To'kgoz
Ahmet Izzet
Ahmet Riza
Ahsaʿi, Ahmad al-
Akçura, Yusuf
Akhondzadeh, Mirza Fath Ali
Akkad, Mustafa
Al al-Shaykh Family
Al Bu Saʿid Family and Tribe of Oman
Al Bu Saʿid, Qabus ibn Saʿid
Al Bu Saʿid, Saʿid ibn Taymur
Al Khalifa Family
Al Nahayyan Family
Al Rashid Family
Al Saʿud Family
Al Saʿud, Saʿud ibn Abd al-Aziz
Al Sabah Family
Al Sabah, Mubarak
Al Saqr Family
Al Sudayri Family
Al Sudayri, Hassa bint Ahmad
Al Thani Family
Al Thani, Hamad ibn Khalifa
Al Thunayyan Family
Ala, Hoseyn
Alam, Amir Asadollah
Alami Family, al-
Alavi, Bozorg
Al-e Ahmad, Jalal
Ali Nasir Muhammad al-Hasani
Ali Riza
Ali Suavi
Allon, Yigal
Alterman, Natan
Altinay, Ahmed Refik
Amanollah Khan
Amichai, Yehuda
Amin al-Dowleh, Mirza Ali Khan
Amin al-Soltan, Ali-Asghar
Amin al-Zarb, Mohammad Hasan
Amin, Hafizullah
Amini, Ali
Amini, Fatemeh
Amir Kabir, Mirza Taqi Khan
Amir-Entezam, Abbas
Amit, Meir
Amri, Hasan al-
Anawati, Georges Chehata
Andranik Ozanian
Annan, Kofi A.
Antar, Ali Ahmad Nasir
Antun, Farah
Aoun, Michel
Aql, Saʿid
Arafat, Yasir
Aral, &Obreveθz
Arens, Moshe
Arfa, Hasan
Arif, Arif al-
Arkoun, Mohammed
Arlosoroff, Chaim
Asad, Bashshar al-
Asad, Hafiz al-
Ashmawi, Muhammad Abd al-Rahman Salih al-
Ashmawi, Muhammad Saʿid al-
Askari, Jaʿfar al-
Asmar, Fawzi al-
Atasi, Nur al-Din al-
Atatürk, Mustafa Kemal
Atay, Salih Rifki
Attas, Haydar Abu Bakr al-
Attlee, Clement
Avnery, Uri
Awad, Louis
Ayn al-Dowleh, Abd al-Majid Mirza
Ayni, Muhsin al-
Aziz, Tariq
Azm, Sadiq al-
Azuri, Najib
Azzam, Abd al-Rahman al-
Badr, Muhammad al-
Baghdadi, Abd al-Latif al-
Bahar, Mohammad Taqi
Bakdash, Khalid
Baker, James A.
Bakhtiar, Shapur
Bakhtiar, Timur
Bakhtiari, Najaf Qoli Khan Samsam al-Soltaneh
Balyan Family
Bani Sadr, Abolhasan
Banna, Hasan al-
Banna, Sabri al-
Baraheni, Reza
Barak, Ehud
Barghuthi Family
Barghuthi, Marwan
Baring, Evelyn
Bar-Lev, Haim
Barzani Family
Basma bint Talal
Bayar, Celal
Bayat, Mortaza Qoli
Baydh, Ali Salim al-
Bayrakdar, Mustafa
Bazargan, Mehdi
Begin, Menachem
Behar, Nissim

Beheshti, Mohammad
Behrangi, Samad
Beja
Belgrave, Charles Dalrymple
Bell, Gertrude
Ben-Aharon, Yitzhak
Ben-Gurion, David
Ben-Porat, Mordechai
Bentwich, Norman
Benvenisti, Meron
Ben-Yehuda, Eliezer
Ben-Zvi, Yizhak
Bernadotte, Folke
Bevin, Ernest
Bialik, Hayyim Nahman
bin Ladin, Osama
Bint al-Shati
Bishara, Abdullah
Bitar, Salah al-Din al-
Bliss, Howard
Borochov, Ber
Borujerdi, Hosayn
Boutros-Ghali, Boutros
Brenner, Yosef Hayyim
Brezhnev, Leonid Ilyich
Browne, Edward Granville
Buber, Martin
Bunche, Ralph J.
Burg, Avraham
Burg, Yosef
Burla, Yehuda
Burton, Richard Francis
Bush, George Herbert Walker
Bush, George Walker
Carter, Jimmy
Cattan, Henry
Cemal Paşa
Cevdet, Abdullah
Cevdet, Ahmet
Chalabi, Ahmad
Chamchian, Mikayel
Chamran, Mostafa
Chehab, Bashir
Chubak, Sadeq
Churchill, William
Çiller, Tansu
Civil Code of 1926
Clayton, Gilbert
Clinton, William Jefferson
Clot, Antoine Barthélémy
Cohen, Ge'ula
Cox, Percy
Crane, Charles R.
Creech Jones, Arthur
Crossman, Richard
Curiel Family
Curzon, George Nathaniel
Dağlarca, Fazil Hüsnü
Dabbagh, Marzieh
Daftari, Ahmad Matin
Dahlan, Muhammad
Daneshvar, Simin
Darwaza, Muhammad Izzat
Darwish, Mahmud
Dashti, Ali
Daud, Muhammad
Dayan, Moshe
De Haan, Ya'akov Yisrael
De Menasce Family
Dede Zekai
Deedes, Wyndham
Dehkhoda, Ali Akbar
Dellalzade İsmail
Demirel, Süleyman
Dentz, Henri-Fernand
Derakhshandeh, Puran
Devrim, Izzet Melih
Diba, Farah
Dost Mohammad Barakzai
Doughty, Charles
Dowlatabadi, Mahmoud
Dulles, John Foster
Durrani Dynasty
Ebadi, Shirin
Eban, Abba (Aubrey)
Ebtekar, Ma'sumeh
Ecevit, Bülent
Eddé, Emile
Eddé, Raymond
Eisenhower, Dwight David
Eitan, Rafael
Eldem, Sedad Hakki
Enver Paşa
Eqbal, Manouchehr
Erbakan, Necmeddin
Erbil, Leyla
Erdoğan, Tayyip
Ersoy, Mehmet Akif
Ertuğrul, Muhsin
Esendal, Memduh Şevket
Esfandiary, Fereydun
Eshkol, Levi
Esmati-Wardak, Masuma
Etemadi, Saleha Faruq
Evren, Kenan
Eyüboğlu, Bedri Rahmi
Fadlallah, Shaykh Husayn
Fahd ibn Abd al-Aziz Al Sa'ud

Fahmi, Mahmud Pasha
Faisal ibn Abd al-Aziz Al Saʿud
Farhad, Ghulam Muhammad
Farmanfarma, Abd al-Hoseyn Mirza
Farrokhzad, Forugh
Fassih, Ismail
Fath Ali Shah Qajar
Faysal ibn Turki Al Saʿud
Ferit, Damat Mehmet
Flapan, Simha
Forughi, Mirza Mohammad Ali Khan Zaka al-Molk
Franjiyya Family
Franjiyya, Sulayman
Gökalp, Ziya
Gülbenkian, Calouste
Gülen, Fetullah
Güney, Yilmaz
Gürpinar, Hüseyin Rahmi
Gürsel, Cemal
Gailani, Ahmad
Ganim, Halil
Ganji, Akbar
Garang, John
Gaspirali, Ismail Bey
Geagea, Samir
Ghali, Boutros
Ghanim, al-
Ghanim, Fathi
Ghashmi, Ahmad Husayn
Ghassemlou, Abdul Rahman
Ghazali, Muhammad al-
Ghorbal, Ashraf
Ghuri, Emile al-
Gilboa, Amir
Glubb, John Bagot
Goldberg, Leah
Goldmann, Nahum
Golestan, Ebrahim
Golshiri, Houshang
Gordon, Aaron David
Greenberg, Uri Zvi
Grivas, Georgios Theodoros
Gur, Mordechai
Guri, Chaim
Habash, George
Habib, Philip Charles
Habibi, Emile
Habibollah Khan
Ha-Cohen, Mordechai
Haddad, Wadi
Hafiz, Amin al-
Hajir, Abd al-Hoseyn
Hajri, Abdullah al-
Hakim, Adnan al-
Hamama, Faten
Hamdi, Ibrahim al-
Hammarskjöld, Dag
Hammer, Zevulun
Hanafi, Hasan
Hananu, Ibrahim
Harel, Isser
Hareven, Shulamit
Hariri, Rafiq Bahaʾuddin al-
Harkabi, Yehoshafat
Hasan, Hani al-
Hasan, Khalid al-
Hashemi, Faezeh
Hashim, Ibrahim
Hashimi, Yasin al-
Hashimite House (House of Hashim)
Hatim Sultans of Hamdan
Hawatma, Nayif
Haykal, Muhammad Hasanayn
Hazaz, Hayyim
Hedayat, Sadegh
Hekmatyar, Golbuddin
Herzl, Theodor
Herzog, Chaim
Herzog, Yaʿacov David
Heskayl, Sasson
Hess, Moses
High Commissioners (Palestine)
Hillel, Shlomo
Hilmi, Ahmad
Hilu, Pierre
Hirawi, Ilyas al-
Hobeika, Elie
Hoffman, Yoel
Hoss, Salim al-
Hourani, Albert
Hoveyda, Amir Abbas
Husari, Sati al-
Husayn ibn Ali
Husayni, Husayn al-
Husayni, Jamal al-
Husayni, Muhammad Amin al-
Husayni, Musa Kazim al-
Hussein ibn Talal
Hussein, Saddam
Hut, Shafiq al-
Ibrahim, Saʿad al-Din
Ilaysh, Muhammad
İnönü, Erdal
İnönü,İsmet
İpekci, Abdi
Iqbal, Muhammad
Iryani, Abd al-Rahman al-
Ismaʿil, Abd al-Fattah

Jabotinsky, Vladimir Ze'ev
Jadid, Salah
Jamali, Muhammad Fadhil al-
Jamalzadeh, Mohammad Ali
Jarring, Gunnar
Jibril, Ahmad
Jinnah, Muhammad Ali
Joseph, Dov
Jumayyil, Amin
Jumayyil, Bashir
Jumblatt Family
Jumblatt, Walid
Kadivar, Mohsen
Kahane, Meir
Kalvaryski, Chaim Margaliut-
Kamal, Ahmad
Kamil, Kibrish Mehmet
Kanafani, Ghassan
Kaniuk, Yoram
Kar, Mehrangiz
Karacan, Ali Naci
Karbaschi, Gholamhosain
Karmal, Babrak
Karzai, Hamid
Kasap, Teodor
Kashani, Abu al-Qasem
Kasravi, Ahmad
Katznelson, Berl
Keinan, Amos
Kemalettin Bey
Kenaz, Yehoshua
Kennedy, John Fitzgerald
Kenter, Yildiz
Kessar, Israel
Khaddam, Abd al-Halim
Khalaf, Abdulhadi
Khalid ibn Abd al-Aziz Al Sa'ud
Khalid, Khalid Muhammad
Khalidi, Ahmad al-Samih al-
Khalidi, Husayn Fakhri al-
Khalidi, Walid
Khamenehi, Ali
Kharrazi, Kamal
Khatami, Mohammad
Khaz'al Khan
Khomeini, Ruhollah
Khrimian, Mkrtich
Khuri, Bishara al-
Khyber, Mir Akbar
Kianuri, Nur al-Din
Kiarostami, Abbas
Kimche, David
Kirkbride, Alec Seath
Kisakürek, Necip Fazil
Kissinger, Henry
Koç, Vehbi
Kol, Moshe
Kollek, Teddy
Kook, Zvi Yehuda
Koprülü, Mehmet Fuat
Kovner, Abba
Kuchek Khan-e Jangali
Kudsi, Nazim al-
Lahad, Antoine
Lahhud, Emile
Lavon, Pinhas
Lawrence, T. E.
Leibowitz, Yeshayahu
Levin, Hanoch
Levinger, Moshe
Levy, David
Lloyd George, David
Luke, Harry
Luz, Kadish
Ma'rufi, Abbas
MacDonald, Malcolm
MacDonald, Ramsay
MacMichael, Harold
Madkour, Ibrahim
Magnes, Judah
Mahd-e Ulya, Malek Jahan Khanum
Mahfuz, Najib
Mahmud Durrani
Mahmud II
Mahmud, Muhammad
Mahmud, Mustafa
Maimon, Yehudah Leib Hacohen
Majali Family
Makhmalbaf Family
Makhmalbaf, Mohsen
Makki, Hasan Muhammad
Maksoud, Clovis
Maktum Family, al-
Malik, Charles Habib
Malkom Khan, Mirza
Maspéro, Gaston
Mawdudi, Abu al-A'la al-
Meged, Aharon
Mehmet Rauf
Mehmet V Reşat
Meir, Golda
Menderes, Adnan
Meushi, Paul Peter
Michael, Sami
Midhat Paşa
Millspaugh, Arthur
Minz, Benjamin
Moda'i, Yitzhak

Mohajerani, Ataollah
Mohammad Ali Shah Qajar
Mohammadi, Maulawi Mohammad Nabi
Mojaddedi, Sebghatullah
Mojtahed-Shabestari, Mohammad
Mond, Alfred Moritz
Montazeri, Hosayn Ali
Mossadegh, Mohammad
Motahhari, Mortaza
Mozaffar al-Din Qajar
Muʿalla Family, al-
Muasher, Marwan
Mubarak, Husni
Muhammad, Aziz
Muhtar, Gazi Ahmet
Muhyi al-Din, Khalid
Muhyi al-Din, Zakariyya
Munif, Abdel Rahman
Musavi, Mir-Hosain
Musavi-Ardebili, AbdolKarim
Mustafa Reşid
Mustafa Suphi
Nabavi, Behzad
Nabi Salih, al-
Nabizade Nazim
Nadi, Yunus
Nadir Barakzai, Mohammad
Najibullah
Namik Kemal
Namir, Mordekhai
Naser al-Din Shah
Nashashibi Family
Nasir, Hanna
Nasrallah, Hasan
Nasser, Gamal Abdel
Nateq-Nuri, Ali Akbar
Navon, Yizhak
Nazif, Süleyman
Neʾeman, Yuval
Nerval, Gérard de
Nesin, Nüsret Aziz
Netanyahu, Benjamin
Nissim, Isaac
Nordau, Max
Nuʿaymi Family, al-
Numeiri, Muhammad Jaʿfar
Nuri, Abd al-Malik
Nuri, Fazlollah
Nursi, Said
Nusayba Family
Omar, Muhammad (Mullah)
Ormanian, Maghakia
Ormsby-Gore, William George Arthur
Oufkir, Muhammad
Ouled Sidi Cheikh
Ouziel, Ben Zion Meir Hai
Özal, Turgut
Oz, Amos
Pérez de Cuéllar, Javier
Pagis, Dan
Pahlavi, Mohammad Reza
Pahlavi, Reza
Palmerston, Lord Henry John Temple
Parsipur, Shahrnush
Peled, Mattityahu
Pelt, Adrian
Peres, Shimon
Pharaon, Rashad
Philby, Harry St. John
Plumer, Herbert Charles Onslow
Politi, Elie
Pollard Affair
Powell, Colin L.
Qabbani, Nizar
Qaddumi, Faruq
Qafih, Yihye ben Solomon
Qajar Dynasty
Qajar, Abdullah Mirza
Qajar, Agha Mohammad
Qaradawi, Yusuf al-
Qasimi Family of Raʾs al-Khayma, al-
Qasimi Family of Sharjah, al-
Qassam, Izz al-Din al-
Qotbzadeh, Sadeq
Qurai, Ahmad Sulayman
Qutb, Sayyid
Raab, Esther
Rabbani, Burhanuddin
Rabin, Yitzhak
Rabiyya Ali, Salim
Rafsanjani, Ali Akbar Hashemi
Rahnavard, Zahra
Rajavi, Masud
Rajub, Jibril
Ramadan, Taha Yasin
Ratebzad, Anahita
Ratosh, Yonatan
Ravikovitch, Dahlia
Reagan, Ronald
Recaizade Mahmud Ekrem
Richmond, Ernest T.
Rifaʿi, Zaid al-
Rogers, William Pierce
Roosevelt, Franklin Delano
Roosevelt, Kermit
Rubinstein, Amnon
Ruppin, Arthur
Rusk, Dean

Rutenberg, Pinhas
Saʿada, Antun
Saʿedi, Gholamhossein
Saʿid, Nuri al-
Saʿid Pasha
Saʿidzadeh, Seyyed Mohsen
Saade, George
Saba Family
Sabbagh, Hasib
Sadat, Anwar al-
Sadat, Jihan al-
Sadr, Muhammad Baqir al-
Sadr, Muhsin
Safveti Ziya
Said, Edward
Salam Family
Salam, Saʾib
Salih, Ali Abdullah
Salih, Teyib
Salim, Ali
Salim, Jawad
Sallal, Abdullah al-
Samuel, Herbert Louis
Sane'i, Yusef
Sapir, Pinhas
Sarid, Yossi
Sasson, Eliyahu
Saunders, Harold
Saygun, Ahmed Adnan
Sayyab, Badr Shakir al-
Sediq, Sohaila
Şeker Ahmet
Selçuk, Munir Nurettin
Selim III
Sepehri, Sohrab
Seri, Dan-Benaya
Şevket, Mahmut
Sezer, Ahmet
Sfeir, Nasrallah
Shaʿbi Family
Shaʿrawi, Muhammad Mutwalli al-
Shaʾul, Anwar
Shahada, George
Shahbandar, Abd al-Rahman
Shahin, Tanyos
Shahin, Yusuf
Shaltut, Muhammad
Shami, Ahmad Muhammad al-
Shami, Muhammad Abdullah al-
Shamir, Moshe
Shamir, Yitzhak
Shamlu, Ahmad
Shammas, Anton
Shapira, Hayyim Moshe
Sharabati, Ahmad al-
Sharef, Zeʾev
Sharett, Moshe
Shariʿati, Ali
Shariatmadari, Kazem
Sharif, Aziz
Sharif, Omar
Sharif-Emami, Jaʿfar
Sharon, Ariel
Sharqi Family, al-
Shawqi, Ahmad
Shenouda III
Shid, Nahid
Shiloah, Reuven
Shirazi, Mirza Hasan
Shitreet, Bekhor
Shlonsky, Avraham
Shultz, George
Shuqayri, Ahmad
Shuster, W. Morgan
Silver, Abba Hillel
Simavi, Sedat
Şinasi, İbrahim
Sisco, Joseph
Sistani, Ali al-
Smilansky, Moshe
Sneh, Moshe
Sobol, Yehoshua
Soheyli, Ali
Sokolow, Nahum
Somikh, Abdullah
Soroush, AbdolKarim
Stark, Freya
Stern, Abraham
Storrs, Ronald
Suissa, Albert
Sulayman, Hikmat
Sulh, Rashid al-
Sulh, Taki al-Din al-
Sunay, Cevdet
Suwaydi Family
Suwayhli, Ramadan al-
Sykes, Mark
Türkes, Alparslan
Tabatabaʾi, Mohammad
Tabatabaʾi, Ziya
Tahir, Kemal
Talabani, Jalal
Talal ibn Abdullah
Talat, Mehmet
Taleqani, Azam
Tall, Wasfi al-
Tamimi, Amin al-
Tamir, Shmuel

Tammuz, Benyamin
Tanburi Cemil
Taner, Haldun
Tanpinar, Ahmed Hamdi
Tantawi, Muhammad Sayyid al-
Taqla, Philippe
Tarhan, Abdülhak Hamit
Tariki, Abdullah
Tevfik Fikret
Tikriti, Hardan al-
Tlas, Mustafa
Truman, Harry S.
Trumpeldor, Yosef
Tsemel, Leah
Tuqan, Fadwa
Tuqan Family
Turabi, Hasan al-
Turki, Fawaz
Twayni, Ghassan
Uşakliğil, Halit Ziya
Urabi, Ahmad
Ussishkin, Menahem
Utaybi, Juhayman al-
Uthman, Muhammad Ali
Uthman, Uthman Ahmad
Vance, Cyrus
Vanunu Affair
Vazir Afkham, Soltan Ali Khan
Vaziri, Qamar al-Moluk
Velayati, Ali Akbar
Volpi, Giuseppe
Vozuq al-Dowleh, Mirza Hasan Khan
Wahrhaftig, Zerah
Wattar, al-Taher
Wauchope, Arthur
Wazir, Khalil al-
Weizman, Ezer
Weizmann, Chaim
Wilson, Arnold T.
Wilson, Woodrow
Wingate, Charles Orde
Wise, Stephen S.
Wolff, Henry Drummond
Yücel, Hasan Ali
Yadin, Yigael
Yahya ibn Muhammad Hamid al-Din
Yamani, Ahmad Zaki
Yariv, Aharon
Yasar Kemal
Yasin, Ahmad Ismaʿil
Yazdi, Ibrahim
Yaziji, Nasif
Yehoshua, Avraham B.
Yellin-Mor, Natan
Yizhar, S.
Yosef, Ovadiah
Yunis Jabir, Abu Bakr
Yurdakul, Mehmet Emin
Zaʿim, Husni al-
Zach, Natan
Zahir Shah
Zana, Leyla
Zelda
Zell al-Soltan, Masʿud Mirza
Ziya, Abdülhamit
Zohar, Uri
Zohrab, Krikor
Zuʿbi, Mahmud al-
Zurayk, Constantine

COUNTRIES: AFGHANISTAN

Afghanistan: Overview
Afghanistan: Islamic Movements in
Afghanistan: Political Parties in
Afghanistan: Soviet Intervention in
Afghanistan: U.S. Intervention in
Amu Darya
Anglo–Afghan Treaty (1855)
Anglo–Afghan Wars
Bamyan
Barakzai Dynasty
Bost
Durand Line
Hazara
Helmand River
Herat
Kabul
Kandahar
Khyber Pass
Mazar-e Sharif
Omar, Muhammad (Mullah)
Pushtun
Refugees: Afghan
Shiberghan
Tajiks
Uzbeks

COUNTRIES: ARABIAN PENINSULA

Abu Dhabi
Abu Musa Island
Aden
Ajman
Al Bu Saʿid Family and Tribe of Oman
Anglo–Omani Treaties
Anjoman
Arabian Horses

Arabian Mission
Arabian Peninsula
As-Is Agreement
Ayn, al-
Baharina
Bahrain
Bahraini–Qatari Wars
Bahrain Order in Council
Bubiyan Island
Buraymi Oasis Dispute
Dammam, al-
Dhahran
Dhufar
Dhufar Rebellion
Doha
Dubai
Fao Peninsula
Free Officers, Yemen
Fujayra
Grand Mosque
Gulf Crisis (1990–1991)
Gulf of Oman
Hadramawt
Hamid al-Din Family
Hasa, al-
Hijaz
Hijaz Railroad
Hodeida
Jabal al-Akhdar, Oman
Jabal Shammar
Jazeera, al-
Jidda
Jubayl, al-
Khubar, al-
Kuwait
Kuwait City
Manama
Ma'rib
Maritime Peace in Perpetuity, Treaty of (1853)
Masira Island
Matrah
Mecca
Medina
Muharraq
Muscat
Nafud Desert
Najd
Neutral Zone
Oman
Persian (Arabian) Gulf
Protectorate States
Qatar
Ra's al-Khayma
Riyadh
Rub al-Khali
Saudi Arabia
Sharjah
Sib, Treaty of (1920)
Sitra
Socotra
South Arabian League
Ta'if, al-
Ta'if, Treaty of al-
Tiran, Strait of
Trans-Arabian Pipeline
Tribes and Tribalism: Yemeni
Trucial Coast
Tunb Islands
Umm al-Qaywayn
Umm Na'san
United Arab Emirates
Wadi Hadramawt
Yanbu
Yemen Arab Republic
Yemen Civil War
Yemen Dynasties

Countries: Central Asia

Hindu Kush Mountains
Pamir Mountains

Countries: Egypt

Alexandria
Alexandria University
American University in Cairo (AUC)
Aswan High Dam
Azhar, al-
Cairo
Cairo University
Coptic Museum
Damanhur
Dar al-Kutub al-Misriyya
Dar al-Ulum
Delta Barrages
Egypt
Egyptian Museum
Gezira Sporting Club
Infitah
Institut d'Égypte
Mahmudiyya Canal
Majlis Shura al-Nuwwab
Nasser, Lake
National Party (Egypt)
New Wafd
Nile River
Nubians

People's Assembly
Pharaonicism
Philae
Port Saʿid
Pyramids
Qusayr, al-
Saint Catherine's Monastery
Saint Mark's Cathedral
Satellite Cities Development
Sayyidna Husayn Mosque
Sharm al-Shaykh
Shepheard's Hotel
Sinai Peninsula
Siwa Oasis
Sphinx
Suez Canal University
Suez–Mediterranean Pipeline
Takfir wa al-Hijra, al-
Victoria College
Wadi Natrun
Wafd
Waqf
War of Attrition (1969–1970)
Zaqaziq University

COUNTRIES: IRAN

Abadan
Ahvaz
Algiers Agreement (1975)
Anglo–Iranian Agreement (1919)
Anglo–Iranian Oil Company
Anglo–Persian War (1856)
Anglo–Russian Agreement (1907)
Azerbaijan
Azerbaijan Crisis
Bakhtiari
Baluchis
Baluchistan
Bisitun
Constitutional Revolution
Cossack Brigade
Golestan Palace
Hamadan
Iran
Iran–Contra Affair
Iranian Revolution (1979)
Iran–Iraq War (1980–1988)
Iran Novin Party
Isfahan
Jangali
Jehad-e Sazandegi
Kerman
Kharg Island
Khorasan
Khuzistan
Kurdistan
Kurds
Lurs
Mashhad
Persian Cats
Qom
Revolutionary Guards
Shatt al-Arab
Shiraz
Sistan and Baluchistan
Social Democratic Party of Azerbaijan
South Persia Rifles
Students in the Line of the Imam
Tabriz
Tehran
Tobacco Revolt
Trans-Iranian Railway
Tripartite Treaty of Alliance
Turkmanchai, Treaty of (1828)
Turko–Iranian War (1821–1823)
White Revolution (1961–1963)
Yazd
Zabul
Zagros
Zahedan

COUNTRIES: IRAQ

Abd al-Ilah ibn Ali
Ahali Group
Askari, Jaʿfar al-
Assyrians
Aziz, Tariq
Baghdad
Barzani Family
Basra
Baʿth, al-
Bitar, Salah al-Din al-
Chalabi, Ahmad
Churchill, Winston S.
Cox, Percy
Gulf Crisis (1990–1991)
Hashimi, Taha al-
Husari, Sati al-
Husayn ibn Ali
Hussein, Saddam
Iran–Iraq War (1980–1988)
Iraq
Iraqi National Congress
Iraq Petroleum Company (IPC)
Jamali, Muhammad Fadhil al-
Kurdish Autonomous Zone

Mosul
Muhammad, Aziz
Najaf, al-
Patriotic Union of Kurdistan (PUK)
Ramadan, Taha Yasin
Refugees: Kurdish
Saʿid, Nuri al-
Salim, Jawad
Samarra
Sanctions, Iraqi
Sharif, Aziz
Somikh, Abdullah
Sulaymaniya
Talabani, Jalal
Tikrit
Tikriti Families

COUNTRIES: ISRAEL

Acheson, Dean
Aliyah
Allon, Yigal
Alpha, Operation
Alterman, Natan
American Israel Public Affairs Committee
American Jewish Committee
American Jewish Congress
Amichai, Yehuda
Amit, Meir
Arab Boycott
Arab–Israel Conflict
Arab–Israeli General Armistice Agreements (1949)
Arab–Israel War (1948)
Arab–Israel War (1956)
Arab–Israel War (1967)
Arab–Israel War (1973)
Arab–Israel War (1982)
Ard, al-
Arens, Moshe
Avnery, Uri
Barak, Ehud
Bar-Ilan University
Bar-Lev, Haim
Begin, Menachem
Ben-Aharon, Yitzhak
Ben-Gurion, David
Ben-Porat, Mordechai
Benvenisti, Meron
Ben-Zvi, Yizhak
Bialik, Hayyim Nahman
Black Panthers
Burg, Avraham
Burg, Yosef
Burla, Yehuda
Cohen, Geʾula
Dayan, Moshe
Eban, Abba (Aubrey)
Egyptian–Israeli Peace Treaty (1979)
Eitan, Rafael
Entebbe Operation
Eretz Yisrael
Flapan, Simha
Galilee
Galilee, Sea of
Gilboa, Amir
Golan Heights
Goldberg, Leah
Goldmann, Nahum
Greenberg, Uri Zvi
Guri, Chaim
Gur, Mordechai
Gush Emunim
Haifa
Haifa University
Hammer, Zevulun
Harel, Isser
Hareven, Shulamit
Harkabi, Yehoshafat
Ha-Shomer Ha-Tzaʿir
"Ha-Tikva"
Hazaz, Hayyim
Hebrew
Hebrew University of Jerusalem
Herzl, Theodor
Herzog, Chaim
Herzog, Yaʿacov David
Heskayl, Sasson
Hillel, Shlomo
Histadrut
Hoffman, Yoel
Holocaust
Hula Swamps
Intifada (1987–1991)
Irgun Zvaʾi Leʾumi (IZL)
Israel: Overview
Israel: Military and Politics
Israel: Overview of Political Parties in
Israeli Settlements
Jaffa
Jerusalem
Jewish Agency for Palestine
Jewish National Fund
Jews in the Middle East
Johnston Plan (1953)
Joint Distribution Committee
Jordanian Option
Joseph, Dov
Kafr Qasim

Kahan Commission (1983)
Kahane, Meir
Kaniuk, Yoram
Karp Report (1984)
Keinan, Amos
Kenaz, Yehoshua
Keren Hayesod
Kessar, Israel
Kibbutz
Kimche, David
King David Hotel
Kiryat Arba
Knesset
Kollek, Teddy
Kol, Moshe
Kook, Zvi Yehuda
Kovner, Abba
Labor Zionism
Land Day
Lavon Affair
Lavon, Pinhas
Law of Return
Leibowitz, Yeshayahu
Levinger, Moshe
Levin, Hanoch
Levy, David
Liberty, USS
Litani Operation (1978)
Litani River
Literature: Hebrew
London Conference (1956)
Luz, Kadish
Lydda
Maʿa lot
Maʿbarah
Madrid Conference (1991)
Magen David Adom (MDA)
Magic Carpet Operation
Maimon, Yehudah Leib Hacohen
Masada
Matzpen
Meah Sheʿarim
Meged, Aharon
Meir, Golda
Michael, Sami
Mimouna Festival
Minz, Benjamin
Modaʾi, Yitzhak
Moshav
Mossad
Nahalal
Namir, Mordekhai
National Water System (Israel)
Nazareth
Neʾeman, Yuval
Negev
Netanyahu, Benjamin
Neturei Karta
Newspapers and Print Media: Israel
Nissim, Isaac
Oslo Accord (1993)
Ouziel, Ben Zion Meir Hai
Oz, Amos
Oz ve Shalom (Netivot shalom)
Pagis, Dan
Palestinian Citizens of Israel
Palestinians
Palmah
Partition Plans (Palestine)
Peace Now
Peled, Mattityahu
Peres, Shimon
Petah Tikvah
Pollard Affair
Potash Industry
Raab, Esther
Rabin, Yitzhak
Radio and Television: Israel
Ramla
Ravikovitch, Dahlia
Refugees: Jewish
Rishon le-Zion
Rubinstein, Amnon
Sabra
Safed
Samaritans
Sapir, Pinhas
Sarid, Yossi
Sasson, Eliyahu
Seri, Dan-Benaya
Sèvres Protocol (1956)
Shamir, Moshe
Shamir, Yitzhak
Shammas, Anton
Shapira, Hayyim Moshe
Sharef, Zeʾev
Sharett, Moshe
Sharon, Ariel
Shaʾul, Anwar
Shekel
Shiloah, Reuven
Shin Bet
Shitreet, Bekhor
Shlonsky, Avraham
Silver, Abba Hillel
Sneh, Moshe
Sobol, Yehoshua
Suez Crisis (1956–1957)

Suissa, Albert
Taba
Tamir, Shmuel
Tammuz, Benyamin
Technion-Israel Institute of Technology
Tel Aviv
Tel Aviv University
Tel Hai
Terrorism
Tiberias
United Jewish Appeal (UJA)
United Nations and the Middle East
United Nations Emergency Force
United Nations Truce Supervision Organization (UNTSO)
Vaʿad Leʾumi
Wahrhaftig, Zerah
Weizman, Ezer
Weizmann, Chaim
Weizmann Institute of Science
West Bank
Western Wall
West German Reparations Agreement
World Federation of Sephardi Communities
World Organization of Jews from Arab Countries (WOJAC)
World Zionist Organization (WZO)
Yadin, Yigael
Yad Mordekhai
Yad Vashem
Yariv, Aharon
Yehoshua, Avraham B.
Yellin-Mor, Natan
Yishuv
Yizhar, S.
Yosef, Ovadiah
Youth Aliyah
Zach, Natan
Zelda
Zikhron Yaʿakov
Zionism
Zionist Organization of America
Zohar, Uri

COUNTRIES: JORDAN

Abdullah I ibn Hussein
Abdullah II ibn Hussein
Abu al-Huda, Tawfiq
Amman
Aqaba
Arab Legion
Basma bint Talal
Churchill, William
Circassians
Hussein ibn Talal
Hussein, Saddam
Irbid
Islamic Action Front
Jordan
Jordan River
Karak, al-
Majali Family
Muasher, Marwan
Petra
Rifaʿi, Zaid al-
Salt, al-
University of Jordan
Yarmuk River
Yarmuk University
Zarqa, al-

COUNTRIES: LEBANON

AMAL
American University of Beirut (AUB)
Antun, Farah
Aoun, Michel
Aql, Saʿid
Baʿalbak
Beirut
Berri, Nabi
Biqa Valley
Council for Development and Reconstruction (CDR)
Eddé, Raymond
Franjiyya Family
Franjiyya, Sulayman
Geagea, Samir
Hariri, Rafiq Bahaʾuddin al-
Hilu, Pierre
Hirawi, Ilyas al-
Hizbullah
Hobeika, Elie
Hoss, Salim al-
Husayni, Husayn al-
Jumayyil, Amin
Jumayyil, Bashir
Jumblatt Family
Jumblatt, Walid
Lahad, Antoine
Lahhud, Emile
Lebanese Forces
Lebanese University
Lebanon
Malik, Charles Habib
Nasrallah, Hasan
Parliamentary Democratic Front
Phalange

Phoenicianism
Progressive Socialist Party
Raad, Inʿam
Saʿada, Antun
Saade, George
Salam Family
Salam, Saʾib
Sfeir, Nasrallah
Shahada, George
Shuf
South Lebanon Army
Special Forces of the Levant
Sulh, Rashid al-
Sulh, Taki al-Din al-
Syrian Social Nationalist Party
Taʿif Accord
Twayni, Ghassan
Tyre
Yaziji, Nasif
Zahla

COUNTRIES: SUDAN

Khartoum
Nuer
Omdurman
Sudan
Sudanese Civil Wars
Sudd
Umma Party
University of Khartoum

COUNTRIES: SYRIA

Akkad, Mustafa
Asad, Bashshar al-
Asad, Hafiz al-
Atasi, Nur al-Din al-
Bakdash, Khalid
Baʿth, al-
Bitar, Salah al-Din al-
British–French Oil Agreement
Chehab, Bashir
Chehab, Fuʾad
Circassians
Damascus
Damascus Affair (1840)
Damascus University
Dayr al-Zawr Province
Hafiz, Amin al-
Hama
Hananu, Ibrahim
Husayn ibn Ali
Jadid, Salah
Khaddam, Abd al-Halim
Kudsi, Nazim al-
Latakia
National Bloc
National Progressive Front (Syria)
Qabbani, Nizar
Saʿada, Antun
Shahbandar, Abd al-Rahman
Syria
Syrian Social Nationalist Party
Tlas, Mustafa
Zuʿbi, Mahmud al-
Zurayk, Constantine

COUNTRIES: TURKEY

Alexandretta
Anatolia
Ankara
Ankara, Treaty of (1930)
Antakya
Ararat, Mount
Armenian Genocide
Armenian Millet
Black Sea
Bodrum
Bogazköy
Bursa
Caylak
Cilicia
Diyarbakir
Edirne
Ege University
Erzurum
Erzurum Congress (1919)
Euphrates Dam
Gecekondu
Genç Kalemler
Hacettepe University
Hürriyet
Istanbul
İzmir
İzmir Economic Congress
Justice Party
Kemalism
Konya
Kurds
Lausanne, Treaty of (1923)
People's Houses
Rumelia
Sivas Conference (1919)
Social Democratic Populist Party
Southeastern Anatolia Project
Trans-Turkey Pipeline

Turkey
Turkish–Afghan Treaty (1928)
Turkish Grand National Assembly
Turko–Iranian War (1821–1823)
Üsküdar
Van, Lake
Varlik Vergisi
Village Institutes

COUNTRIES: YEMEN

Islah Party
National Democratic Front (NDF)
National Front for the Liberation of South Yemen
People's Socialist Party
Perim
San'a
San'a University
Tribes and Tribalism: Yemeni
Yemen
Yemen Hunt Oil Company
Yemeni Socialist Party

CULTURE AND SOCIETY

Abu Zeid, Layla
Adham, Soraya
Adnan, Etel
Adot Ha-Mizrah
Agriculture
Akhavan-Saless, Mehdi
Akkad, Mustafa
Al-e Ahmad, Jalal
Algerian Family Code (1984)
Ali, Wijdan
Alizadeh, Ghazaleh
Alliance Israélite Universelle (AIU)
Al-Suswa, Amat al-Alim
Alterman, Natan
AMAL
Amichai, Yehuda
Amrouche, Fadhma At Mansour
Ani, Jannane al-
Anis Al-Jalis Magazine
Antisemitism
Arab College of Jerusalem
Arab Nationalism
Archaeological Museum (Istanbul)
Archaeology in the Middle East
Architecture
Art
Ashkenazim
Attar, Nejat al-
Attar, Suad al-
Avnery, Uri
Aya Sofya
Azeri Language and Literature
Ba'albak
Ba'albakki, Layla
Bahar, Mohammad Taqi
Ba'th, al-
Badr, Liana
Baghdad University
Bahithat al-Lubnaniyyat, al-
Bakkar, Jalillah
Bani-Etemad, Rakhsan
Banking
Baraheni, Reza
Bazaars and Bazaar Merchants
Behar, Nissim
Behbehani, Simin
Behrangi, Samad
Beirut College for Women (BCW)
Ben-Aharon, Yitzhak
Ben-Gurion University of the Negev
Ben-Yehuda, Eliezer
Berlin–Baghdad Railway
Bethlehem
Bialik, Hayyim Nahman
Bir Zeit University
Biret, Idil
Birth Control
Bitton, Simone
Brenner, Yosef Hayyim
Buber, Martin
Burla, Yehuda
Cairo Family Planning Association
Caland, Huguette
Camels
Ceramics
Chédid, Andrée
Chubak, Sadeq
Circumcision
Clothing
Colonialism in the Middle East
Crimes of Honor
Dance
Daneshvar, Simin
Dead Sea Scrolls
Dhow
Diaspora
Diseases
Djebar, Assia
Dönme
Dowlatabadi, Mahmoud
Economic and Military Aid
Economics
Education

Efflatoun, Inji
8 Mars Newspaper
Elites
Eskinazi, Roza
Ethiopian Jews
Faqir, Fadia
Farrokhzad, Forugh
Farès, Nabile
Fayruz
Female Genital Mutilation
Film
Fish and Fishing
Gamal, Samiyah
Gecekondu
Gender: Gender and Education
Ghoussoub, Mai
Gilboa, Amir
Giza
Goldberg, Leah
Golshiri, Houshang
Government
Greenberg, Uri Zvi
Guri, Chaim
Ha-Cohen, Mordechai
Haifa
Hajji Baba of Ispahan
Halukka
Hanafi School of Law
Hareven, Shulamit
"Ha-Tikva"
Hatoum, Mona
Haza, Ofra
Hazaz, Hayyim
Hebrew University of Jerusalem
Hebrew
Histadrut
Holocaust
Human Rights
Imperialism in the Middle East and North Africa
Incense
Industrialization
Infitah
Iranian Languages
Islamic Countries Women Sport Solidarity Games (1992 and 1997)
Israel: Overview of Political Parties in
Israel: Overview
Jababdi, Latifa
Jacir, Emily
Jewish National Fund
Jews in the Middle East
Joint Distribution Committee
Kaʿba
Kanafani, Ghassan
Kaniuk, Yoram
Kenaz, Yehoshua
Keren Hayesod
Kessar, Israel
Khal, Helen
Khalidi, Ahmad al-Samih al-
Khalidi, Walid
Khalifa, Sahar
Kibbutz
King David Hotel
Kovner, Abba
Law, Modern
Lata'if al-Musawwara Magazine
Lebanese University
Levin, Hanoch
Literature: Hebrew
Literature: Persian
Literature: Turkish
Luxor
Maʿbarah
Magen David Adom (MDA)
Magic Carpet Operation
Magnes, Judah
Majles al-Shura
Makdashi, Hesna
Malaʾika, Nazik al-
Maliki School of Law
Marʿi, Mariam
Maronites
Marriage and Family
Masada
Masri, Mai
Medicine and Public Health
Meged, Aharon
Mernissi, Fatema
Michael, Sami
Military in the Middle East
Mimouna Festival
Minz, Benjamin
Moshav
Musa, Nabawiyya
Nabi Musa Pilgrimage
Nasir, Hanna
Nasrallah, Emily
Nasruddin Hoca
National Water System (Israel)
Nazareth
Neʾeman, Yuval
Negev
Newspapers and Print Media: Arab Countries
Newspapers and Print Media: Iran
Newspapers and Print Media: Israel
Newspapers and Print Media: Turkey
Nissim, Isaac

Nuun Magazine
Ordinances on Veiling
Orientalism
Oz, Amos
Pagis, Dan
Palestine Exploration Fund
Palestine Land Development Company
Palestine
Palestinian Citizens of Israel
Palestinians
Persian Script
Persian
Pharaonicism
Potash Industry
Protocols of the Elders of Zion
Pyramids
Qaʿwar, Widad
Qabbani, Nizar
Qurʾan
Raab, Esther
Radio and Television: Arab Countries
Radio and Television: Israel
Radio and Television: Turkey
Ramses College for Girls
Ratosh, Yonatan
Ravikovitch, Dahlia
Refugees: Jewish
Rockefeller Museum
Romanization
Ruppin, Arthur
Rutenberg, Pinhas
Sabbagh, Hasib
Sabbagh, Salah al-Din al-
Sabra
Saʿedi, Gholamhossein
Safed
Saint Catherine's Monastery
Saint Joseph University
Salim, Jawad
Samaritans
Saudi, Mona
Sayyidna Husayn Mosque
School for Hakīmāt
Seri, Dan-Benaya
Shaʾul, Anwar
Shamir, Moshe
Shamlu, Ahmad
Shammas, Anton
Sharif
Shawa, Laila
Shaykh
Shekel
Shin Bet
Shlonsky, Avraham
Sirry, Gazbia
Slave Trade
Smilansky, Moshe
Sobol, Yehoshua
Suez Canal University
Suissa, Albert
Sultan Ahmet Mosque
Sultan Hasan Mosque
Sursock, Lady Cochrane
Tammuz, Benyamin
Tax Farming
Tea
Technion-Israel Institute of Technology
Tel Aviv University
Templars
Textile Industry
Theater
Tlatli, Moufida
Tourism
Trade
Transport
Tuqan, Fadwa
Turki, Fawaz
Turkish Historical Society
Turkish Language
Turkish Script
Turkism
Turks
Umar, Madiha
Urban Planning
Urbanization
Waqf
Water
Weizmann Institute of Science
West German Reparations Agreement
Westernization
Women and Family Affairs Center
Women's Affairs Center (Gaza)
Women's Centre for Legal Aid and Counseling
Women's International Zionist Organization
World Federation of Sephardi Communities
World Organization of Jews from Arab Countries (WOJAC)
Yad Vashem
Yehoshua, Avraham B.
Yeshiva
Yiddish
Yishuv
Yizhar, S.
Youth Aliyah
Zach, Natan
Zanan Magazine
Zaqaziq University
Zayyat, Latifa

Zelda
Ziadeh, May
Zionist Organization of America
Ziwaj Mutʿa
Zohar, Uri

ORGANIZATIONS

Advisory Council (Palestine)
Afghan Women's Council
Ahram Center for Political and Strategic Studies, al-
AISHA: Arab Women's Forum
Alliance Israélite Universelle (AIU)
Al-Suswa, Amat al-Alim
AMAL
American Council for Judaism
American Israel Public Affairs Committee
American Jewish Committee
American Jewish Congress
Anglo–American Committee of Inquiry (1946)
Anglo–Iranian Oil Company
Ankara University
Arab Boycott
Arab Bureau (Cairo)
Arab Feminist Union
Arab Higher Committee (Palestine)
Arab League Summits
Arab Socialist Union
Arab Women's Association of Palestine
Arab Women's Congress
Arab Women's Executive Committee
Arab Women's Solidarity Association International
Arabian American Oil Company (ARAMCO)
Ard, al-
Association des Femmes Tunisiennes pour la Recherche et le Développement (AFTURD)
Association for the Protection of Women's Rights (Afghanistan)
Atatürk University
Awakened Youth
B'nai B'rith
Baʿth, al-
Baghdad Pact (1955)
Bahithat al-Lubnaniyyat, al-
Bahrain Nationalist Movement
Bar-Ilan University
Beirut College for Women (BCW)
Ben-Gurion University of the Negev
Ben-Zvi, Rahel Yanait
Bilkent University
bin Ladin, Osama
Black Panthers
Bludan Conferences (1937, 1946)
Boğaziçi (Bosporus) University
Bouhired, Jamila
Brichah
Bund
Cairo Family Planning Association
Central Intelligence Agency (CIA)
Central Treaty Organization (CENTO)
Centre de Recherches, d'Études, de Documentation et d'Information sur la Femme (CREDIF)
Committee for Defense of Freedom and Human Rights
Committee for the Defense of Legitimate Rights
Confederation of Iranian Students
Confederation of Turkish Trade Unions
Council for Development and Reconstruction (CDR)
Dar al-Fonun
Dar al-Moʿallamin
Democrat Party
Democratic Organization of Afghan Women (1965)
Democratic Party of Azerbaijan
Democratic Party of Kurdistan (Iran; KDP)
Democratic Women's Association (Tunisia)
Egyptian Feminist Union
Fatah, al-
Fedaʾiyan-e Khalq
Fidaʾiyyun
Foreign Office, Great Britain
Free Officers, Egypt
General Federation of Iraqi Women
General Union of Palestinian Women's Committees (GUPWC)
General Women's Union of Syria
Gezira Sporting Club
Gozanski, Tamar
Grossman, Haika
Gulf Cooperation Council
Gush Emunim
Haganah
Ha-Halutz
Haifa University
HAMAS
Ha-Shomer Ha-Tzaʿir
Ha-Shomer
Hibbat Zion
Histadrut
Hizbullah
Husseini, Rana
İdadi Schools
Institut d'Égypte
Institute for Palestine Studies
International Monetary Fund
Iranian Bureau of Women's Affairs
Iraq Petroleum Company (IPC)
Iraqi Women's Union
Irbid

Irgun Zva'i Le'umi (IZL)
Isfahan University
Islah Party
Islamic Action Front
Islamic Countries Women Sport Solidarity Games (1992 and 1997)
Islamic Jihad
Islamic University of Medina
Israel: Overview of Political Parties in
Istanbul Technical University
Istanbul University
Jehad-e Sazandegi
Jenin
Jewish Agency for Palestine
Jewish Legion
Jewish National Fund
Joint Distribution Committee
Kabul University
Kamal, Zahira
Karak, al-
Keren Hayesod
KGB
Khaled, Leila
Khalil, Samiha Salama
Kibbutz
King Saʿud University
Knesset
Kuwait Fund for Arab Economic Development
Kuwait Petroleum Corporation
Kuwait University
Labor Zionism
Lebanese Women's Council
Legislative Council (Palestine)
Livnat, Limor
Lohamei Herut Yisrael
Magen David Adom (MDA)
Mahalle Schools
Majles al-Shura
Makdashi, Hesna
Marmara University
Matzpen
Middle East Technical University
Milli İstihbarat Teşkilati
Mogannam, Matiel
Mojahedin-e Khalq
Moshav
Mossad
Muslim Brotherhood
Muslim Sisters Organization
Naʿamaat
Najaf, al-
National Democratic Front (NDF)
National Party (Egypt)
National Security Council (Turkey)
National Unity Committee (Turkey)
National Women's Committee (Yemen)
Neturei Karta
Nizamiye Courts
North Atlantic Treaty Organization (NATO)
Nuun Magazine
Organization for the Liberation of the Occupied South
Oz ve Shalom (Netivot shalom)
Palestine Exploration Fund
Palestine Land Development Company
Palestine Liberation Organization (PLO)
Palestine National Charter (1968)
Palestine National Council
Palestine National Covenant (1964)
Palestinian Arab Congresses
Palestinian Authority
Palestinian Citizens of Israel
Palmah
Peace Now
People's Assembly
People's Socialist Party
Permanent Mandates Commission
Phalange
Popular Front for the Liberation of Palestine–General Command
Popular Front for the Liberation of Palestine
Princess Basma Women's Resource Center
Progressive Socialist Party
Qaʿida, al-
Qatar Petroleum
Rejection Front
Republican Brotherhood
Revolutionary Association of the Women of Afghanistan (RAWA)
Revolutionary Guards
Ruşdiye Schools
Saʿiqa, al-
Sabbagh, Salah al-Din al-
Salt, al-
Samar, Sima
School for Hakīmāt
Shaʿrawi, Huda al-
Shiraz University
Şirket-i Hayriye
South Arabian Armed Forces
State Planning Organization (SPO)
Stock Market
Straits Convention
Straits, Turkish
Sudanese Women's Union
Sultani Schools
Supreme Muslim Council
Syrian Social Nationalist Party
Tabriz University

Taliban
Technion-Israel Institute of Technology
Tel Aviv University
Turkish Hearth Association
Turkish Linguistic Society
Umm al-Qura University
Umma Party
Union of Tunisian Women
United Jewish Appeal (UJA)
United Nations and the Middle East
United Nations Conciliation Commission for Palestine (UNCCP)
United Nations Economic Survey Mission (1949)
United Nations Emergency Force
United Nations Interim Force in Lebanon
United Nations Relief and Works Agency for Palestine Refugees in the Near East (UNRWA)
United Nations Special Committee on Palestine, 1947 (UNSCOP)
United Nations Truce Supervision Organization (UNTSO)
University of Tehran
Vaʿad Leʾumi
Victoria College
Wafd
Wafdist Women's Central Committee
Weizmann Institute of Science
Women and Family Affairs Center
Women in Black
Women's Affairs Center (Gaza)
Women's Forum for Research and Training (Yemen)
Women's Library and Information Center (Istanbul)
Women's Organization of Iran (WOI)
Women's People's Party (1923)
Women's Religious Rituals
Women's Renaissance Club
Women's Studies Center (Jerusalem)
World Bank
World Federation of Sephardi Communities
World Organization of Jews from Arab Countries (WOJAC)
World Zionist Organization (WZO)
Yüksek Öğretim Kurulu (YOK)
Yarmuk University
Yemen Hunt Oil Company
Yemeni Socialist Party
Yemeni Women's Union
Yeshiva
Yishuv
Youth Aliyah
Youth Movements
Zaraniq Confederation
Zarqa, al-
Zionism
Zionist Commission for Palestine
Zionist Organization of America
Zionist Revisionist Movement

Ottoman Empire

Bedel-i Askeri
Civil Service School (Ottoman)
Congress of Ottoman Liberals (1902)
Dardanelles, Treaty of the (1809)
Darülfünün
Dashnak Party
Dolmabahçe Palace
Dragomans
Erzurum, Treaty of (1823)
Galata
Galatasaray Lycée
Gallipoli
Greco–Turkish War (1897)
Hunkar-Iskelesi, Treaty of (1833)
Janissaries
Konya, Battle of
Land Code of 1858
Millet System
Musa Dagh
Nizip, Battle of (1839)
Ottoman Empire: Overview
Ottoman Empire: Civil Service
Ottoman Empire: Debt
Ottomanism
Ottoman Liberal Union Party
Ottoman Military: Army
Ottoman Military: Navy
Ottoman Parliament
Russian–Ottoman Wars
Salonika
San Stefano, Treaty of (1878)
Sèvres, Treaty of (1920)
Srvantziants, Garegin
Sublime Porte
Sultan
Tanzimat
Topkapi Palace
Turkish–Italian War (1911–1912)
Vaka-i Hayriye
Vazhapetian, Nerses
Yildirim Army
Young Ottomans
Young Turks

Palestine Problem

Abbas, Mahmud
Abd al-Hadi Family

Advisory Council (Palestine)
Ahad Ha-Am
Alami Family, al-
Anglo–American Committee of Inquiry (1946)
Aqsa Intifada, al-
Arab Boycott
Arab College of Jerusalem
Arab Higher Committee (Palestine)
Arab–Israel Conflict
Arab–Israel War (1948)
Arab–Israel War (1956)
Arab–Israel War (1967)
Arab–Israel War (1973)
Arab–Israel War (1982)
Arab League Summits
Arafat, Yasir
Ard, al-
Attlee, Clement
Avnery, Uri
Azuri, Najib
Azzam, Abd al-Rahman al-
Balfour Declaration (1917)
Banna, Sabri al-
Barak, Ehud
Ben-Gurion, David
Bentwich, Norman
Benvenisti, Meron
Bernadotte, Folke
Bevin, Ernest
Biltmore Program (1942)
Binationalism
Bir Zeit University
Black September
Bludan Conferences (1937, 1946)
Bunche, Ralph J.
Camp David Summit (2000)
Cattan, Henry
Crossman, Richard
Darwaza, Muhammad Izzat
Dayr Yasin
Exodus (1947)
Fahd Plan (1981)
Fidaʾiyyun
Gaza (City)
Gaza Strip
Ghuri, Emile al-
Green Line
Gush Emunim
Habash, George
Haddad, Wadi
Haganah
HAMAS
Hasan, Hani al-
Hasan, Khalid al-
Ha-Shomer Ha-Tzaʿir
Hawatma, Nayif
Haycraft Commission (1921)
Hebron
High Commissioners (Palestine)
Hope-Simpson Commission (1930)
Husayni, Jamal al-
Husayni, Muhammad Amin al-
Husayni, Musa Kazim al-
Husayn–McMahon Correspondence (1915–1916)
Hut, Shafiq al-
Intifada (1987–1991)
Islamic Jihad
Israeli Settlements
Jabal al-Khalil
Jabal Nablus
Jabotinsky, Vladimir Zeʾev
Jaffa
Jericho
Jericho Congress (1948)
Jerusalem
Jewish Agency for Palestine
Jews in the Middle East
Jibril, Ahmad
Jordanian Option
Kafr Qasim
Kahane, Meir
Kalvaryski, Chaim Margaliut-
Kanafani, Ghassan
Karama, Battle of (1968)
Karp Report (1984)
Khalidi, Ahmad al-Samih al-
Khalidi, Walid
King David Hotel
Kiryat Arba
Land Day
Lausanne Conference (1949)
Law of Return
Legislative Council (Palestine)
Levinger, Moshe
Lohamei Herut Yisrael
London (Roundtable) Conference (1939)
Luke, Harry
Lydda
Maʿa lot
MacDonald, Ramsay
MacMichael, Harold
Madrid Conference (1991)
Magnes, Judah
Meir, Golda
Mond, Alfred Moritz
Morrison–Grady Plan (1946)
Mossad
Nabi Musa Pilgrimage

Nablus
Nashashibi Family
Nazareth
Nusayba Family
Ormsby-Gore, William George Arthur
Oslo Accord (1993)
Oz ve Shalom (Netivot shalom)
Palestine
Palestine Arab Revolt (1936–1939)
Palestine Exploration Fund
Palestine Land Development Company
Palestine Liberation Organization (PLO)
Palestine National Charter (1968)
Palestine National Council
Palestine National Covenant (1964)
Palestine Research Center
Palestinian Arab Congresses
Palestinian Authority
Palestinian Citizens of Israel
Palestinians
Palin Commission Report (1920)
Partition Plans (Palestine)
Peace Now
Peel Commission Report (1937)
Peled, Mattityahu
Peres, Shimon
Permanent Mandates Commission
Philby, Harry St. John
Plumer, Herbert Charles Onslow
Popular Front for the Liberation of Palestine
Popular Front for the Liberation of Palestine–General Command
Qalqiliya
Qurai, Ahmad Sulayman
Rabin, Yitzhak
Ramallah
Ramla
Reagan Plan (1982)
Rejection Front
Richmond, Ernest T.
Roosevelt, Franklin Delano
Ruppin, Arthur
Rusk, Dean
Rutenberg, Pinhas
Sabbagh, Hasib
Sabra and Shatila Massacres
Safed
Saʿiqa, al-
Samuel, Herbert Louis
Sasson, Eliyahu
Saunders, Harold
Shamir, Yitzhak
Sharett, Moshe
Sharon, Ariel
Shaw Commission
Shuqayri, Ahmad
Silver, Abba Hillel
Stern, Abraham
Storrs, Ronald
Struma
Sumud
Sykes, Mark
Taba
Tamimi, Amin al-
Tel Hai
Terrorism
Tiberias
Truman, Harry S.
Trumpeldor, Yosef
Turki, Fawaz
United Nations and the Middle East
United Nations Conciliation Commission for Palestine (UNCCP)
United Nations Economic Survey Mission (1949)
United Nations Special Committee on Palestine, 1947 (UNSCOP)
United Nations Truce Supervision Organization (UNTSO)
United States of America and the Middle East
Vaʿad Leʾumi
Wauchope, Arthur
Wazir, Khalil al-
Weizman, Ezer
Weizmann, Chaim
West Bank
Western Wall
White Papers on Palestine
Wilson, Woodrow
Wingate, Charles Orde
Woodhead Commission (1938)
Yehoshua, Avraham B.
Yellin-Mor, Natan
Zionism
Zionist Commission for Palestine

POLITICS

Adalat Party
Afghanistan: Political Parties in
AKP (Justice and Development Party)
Anglo–Egyptian Treaty (1954)
Arab Bureau (Cairo)
Arab Higher Committee (Palestine)
Arab League Summits
Arab Nationalism
Arab Socialism
Arab–Israel Conflict
Arab–Israeli General Armistice Agreements (1949)

Arafat, Yasir
Arens, Moshe
Arlosoroff, Chaim
Armenian Revolutionary Movement
Arms and Armaments in the Middle East
Attlee, Clement
Avnery, Uri
Aazerbaijan Crisis
Azuri, Najib
Azzam, Abd al-Rahman al-
Baghdad Pact (1955)
Baker, James A.
Balfour Declaration (1917)
Bandung Conference (1955)
Banna, Sabri al-
Barak, Ehud
Barghuthi, Marwan
Bar-Lev, Haim
Begin, Menachem
Ben-Gurion, David
Ben-Porat, Mordechai
Ben-Zvi, Yizhak
Bevin, Ernest
Boutros-Ghali, Boutros
Brookings Report (1975)
Burg, Avraham
Burg, Yosef
Cairo Conference (1921)
Camp David Accords (1978)
Camp David Summit (2000)
Carter, Jimmy
Churchill White Paper (1922)
Colonial Office, Great Britain
Committee for Union and Progress
Communism in the Middle East
Creech Jones, Arthur
Crossman, Richard
Darwaza, Muhammad Izzat
Decentralization Party
Dreyfus Affair
Dulles, John Foster
Eban, Abba (Aubrey)
Eisenhower, Dwight David
Eitan, Rafael
Eshkol, Levi
Fahd Plan (1981)
Feda'iyan-e Islam
Foreign Office, Great Britain
Forqan
Free Republican Party
Free Yemenis
Freedom Movement (Nezhat-e Azadi Iran)
Freedom Party
Front for the Liberation of South Yemen
Geneva Peace Conference (1973)
Goldmann, Nahum
Golsorkhi, Khosrow
Gulf Crisis (1990–1991)
Gulf War (1991)
Gur, Mordechai
Ha-avarah Agreement
Hammarskjöld, Dag
Hammer, Zevulun
Ha-Shomer Ha-Tza'ir
Haycraft Commission (1921)
Herzog, Chaim
Herzog, Ya'acov David
Hezb-e Islami
Hillel, Shlomo
Histadrut
Hope-Simpson Commission (1930)
Hostage Crises
Husayn–McMahon Correspondence (1915–1916)
Husayni, Jamal al-
Husayni, Musa Kazim al-
Hut, Shafiq al-
Iradeh-ye Melli Party
Iran Novin Party
Islah Taleban Party
Israel: Military and Politics
Israel: Overview of Political Parties in
Israel: Overview
Israel: Political Parties in
Jabotinsky, Vladimir Ze'ev
Jami'at-e Islami
Jangali
Jericho
Jewish Agency for Palestine
Johnston Plan (1953)
Joseph, Dov
Justice Party
Kahan Commission (1983)
Karp Report (1984)
Katznelson, Berl
Kemalism
Kennedy, John Fitzgerald
Kessar, Israel
Knesset
Kol, Moshe
Kollek, Teddy
Kurdish Revolts
Kurdistan Workers Party (PKK)
Labor Zionism
Lausanne Conference (1949)
Lavon Affair
Legislative Council (Palestine)
Levinger, Moshe
Levy, David

Lloyd George, David
Liberty, USS
London (Roundtable) Conference (1939)
London Conference (1956)
London Convention
London, Treaty of (1913)
Madrid Conference (1991)
Maimon, Yehudah Leib Hacohen
Mansure Army
Mardom Party
Maritime Peace in Perpetuity, Treaty of (1853)
Matzpen
Meir, Golda
Moda'i, Yitzhak
Mojahedin
Mojahedin-e Khalq
Montreux Convention (1936)
Morrison–Grady Plan (1946)
Motherland Party
Namir, Mordekhai
Nasser, Gamal Abdel
National Front, Iran
National Liberation Front (Bahrain)
National Salvation Party
Nationalism
Nationalist Action Party
Navon, Yizhak
Ne'eman, Yuval
Netanyahu, Benjamin
Neturei Karta
Nissim, Isaac
North Atlantic Treaty Organization (NATO)
Ormsby-Gore, William George Arthur
Oslo Accord (1993)
Palestine
Palestinian Authority
Palestinian Citizens of Israel
Parcham
Paris Peace Settlements (1918–1923)
Paris, Treaty of (1857)
Peled, Mattityahu
People's Democratic Party of Afghanistan
People's Democratic Republic of Yemen
Peres, Shimon
Popular Front for the Liberation of the Occupied Arabian Gulf
Qurai, Ahmad Sulayman
Rabin, Yitzhak
Reagan Plan (1982)
Reagan, Ronald
Red Line Agreement
Refah Partisi
Refugees: Jewish
Rejection Front
Republican People's Party (RPP)
Rogers, William Pierce
Rome, Treaty of (1935)
Roosevelt, Franklin Delano
Rubinstein, Amnon
Rusk, Dean
Russia and the Middle East
Rutenberg, Pinhas
Sèvres Protocol (1956)
Sadat, Anwar al-
Samuel, Herbert Louis
Sapir, Pinhas
Sarid, Yossi
Sasson, Eliyahu
Saunders, Harold
Shamir, Yitzhak
Shapira, Hayyim Moshe
Sharef, Ze'ev
Sharett, Moshe
Sharif of Mecca
Sharon, Ariel
Shiloah, Reuven
Shitreet, Bekhor
Shultz, George
Shuqayri, Ahmad
Shura
Silver, Abba Hillel
Sisco, Joseph
Sneh, Moshe
Sokolow, Nahum
Stern, Abraham
Storrs, Ronald
Suez Crisis (1956–1957)
Sykes–Picot Agreement (1916)
Sykes, Mark
Tamir, Shmuel
Treaty of 1815
Treaty of Protection (1886)
Tripartite Declaration (1950)
True Path Party
Truman, Harry S.
Tudeh Party
Turkish National Pact
Turkish Workers Party
Twin Pillars Policy
United Arab Republic (UAR)
United Nations and the Middle East
United Nations Special Committee on Palestine, 1947 (UNSCOP)
United States of America and the Middle East
Unity Party
Ussishkin, Menahem
Versailles, Treaty of (1920)
Wahrhaftig, Zerah

Wazir, Khalil al-
Weizman, Ezer
Weizmann, Chaim
West German Reparations Agreement
White Revolution (1961–1963)
White Papers on Palestine
Wilson, Woodrow
Wise, Stephen S.
Woodhead Commission (1938)
World War I
World War II
World Zionist Organization (WZO)
Yadin, Yigael
Yellin-Mor, Natan
Yosef, Ovadiah
Zaʿim, Husni al-
Zionist Revisionist Movement

RELIGION

Afghani, Jamal al-Din al-
Afghanistan: Islamic Movements in
Ahl-e Haqq
Akhbari
Al al-Shaykh Family
Alevi
Allah
Arab Nationalism
Armenian Community of Jerusalem
Armenians in the Middle East
Assyrians
Bab, al-
Babis
Bahaʾi Faith
Bast
bin Ladin, Osama
Burg, Yosef
Caliphate
Christians in the Middle East
Copts
Damascus Affair (1840)
Dead Sea Scrolls
Druze
Fedaʿiyan-e Khalq
Forqan
Grand Mosque
Halakhah
Hammer, Zevulun
Hanafi School of Law
Hanbali School of Law
Haram al-Sharif
Hasidim
Hezb-e Islami
Hijab
Holy Land
Holy Sepulchre, Church of the
Husayni, Muhammad Amin al-
Ibadiyya
Ikhwan
İlmiyye
Jerusalem
Jews in the Middle East
Kahane, Meir
Kalemiyye
Kook, Zvi Yehuda
Law of Return
Leibowitz, Yeshayahu
Levinger, Moshe
Maimon, Yehudah Leib Hacohen
Maliki School of Law
Marja al-Taqlid
Meah Sheʿarim
Mecca
Medina
Mevlevi Brotherhood
Milli Görüş Hareketi
Nabi Musa Pilgrimage
Nazareth
Neturei Karta
Ouziel, Ben Zion Meir Hai
Rabbi
Sabbath
Saint Catherine's Monastery
Saint Mark's Cathedral
Samaritans
Sayyidna Husayn Mosque
Shafiʿi School of Law
Shapira, Hayyim Moshe
Shariʿa
Sharif of Mecca
Shaykh al-Islam
Shaykhi
Shimʿun, Mar
Shirazi
Shura
Sistani, Ali al-
Sunna
Supreme Muslim Council
Takfir wa al-Hijra, al-
Talmud
Taurus Mountains
Tekke
Templars
Vatican and the Middle East
Velayat-e Faqih
Yeshiva
Yosef, Ovadiah
Zamzam

Zaydism
Zoroastrianism

RELIGION: ISLAM

Afghanistan: Islamic Movements in
Alawi
Allah
Azhar, al-
Dar al Daʿwa wa al-Irshad
Dhimma
Druze
Fatwa
Fiqh
Hadith
Islam
Islamic Congresses
Islamic Salvation Army (AIS)
Jamiʿa al-Islamiyya, al-
Jihad
Kaʿba
Muwahhidun
Qurʾan
Shiʿism
Sufism and the Sufi Orders
Sunni Islam
Takfir wa al-Hijra, al-
Taliban
Ulama
Usuli
Waqf

WOMEN

Abu Zayd, Hikmat
Abu Zeid, Layla
Adham, Soraya
Adnan, Etel
Afghan Women's Council
AISHA: Arab Women's Forum
Algerian Family Code (1984)
Alia, Queen
Ali, Wijdan
Aliyer, Fatimah
Aloni, Shulamit
Al-Suswa, Amat al-Alim
Amari, Raja
Amer, Ghada
Amrouche, Fadhma At Mansour
Amrouche, Mary Louise (a.k.a. Marguerite Taos)
Ani, Jannane al-
Anis Al-Jalis Magazine
Arab Feminist Union
Arab Women's Association of Palestine
Arab Women's Executive Committee
Arab Women's Solidarity Association International
Araz, Nezihe
Ashour, Radwa
Association des Femmes Tunisiennes pour la Recherche et le Développement (AFTURD)
Attar, Nejat al-
Attar, Suad al-
Awadhi, Badria A. al-
Baʿalbakki, Layla
Badr, Liana
Bahithat al-Lubnaniyyat, al-
Bakkar, Jalillah
Bakr, Salwa
Bani-Etemad, Rakhsan
Barakat, Hoda
Baya
Behbehani, Simin
Behrouzi, Maryam
Beirut College for Women (BCW)
Ben Bouali, Hassiba
Ben-Zvi, Rahel Yanait
Biret, Idil
Birth Control
Bishara, Suha
Bitton, Simone
Bouhired, Jamila
Bouih, Fatna el-
Cairo Family Planning Association
Caland, Huguette
Centre de Recherches, d'Études, de Documentation et d'Information sur la Femme (CREDIF)
Chazan, Naomi
Chédid, Andrée
Constitutional Revolution, Impact on Women
Crimes of Honor
Dayan, Yael
Democratic Women's Association (Tunisia)
Djebar, Assia
Dorner, Dalia
Ecevit, Rahşan
Efflatoun, Inji
Egyptian Feminist Union
8 Mars Newspaper
Eskinazi, Roza
Faqir, Fadia
Faraj, Maysaloun
Farʾa, Wahiba
Farès, Nabile
Farid, Nagwa Kamal
Farmanfarmian, Settareh
Fawwaz, Zaynab
Fayruz
Faysal, Tujan

Female Genital Mutilation
Freier, Recha
Gamal, Samiyah
Gebeyli, Claire
Gencer, Leyla
Gender: Gender and the Economy
Gender: Gender and Education
Gender: Gender and Law
Gender: Gender and Politics
Gender: Study of
General Directorate on the Status and Problems of Women
General Federation of Iraqi Women
General Union of Palestinian Women's Committees (GUPWC)
General Women's Union of Syria
Ghanmi, Azza
Ghazali, Zaynab al-
Ghoussoub, Mai
Gozanski, Tamar
Grossman, Haika
Gülhane Imperial Edict (1839)
Hanoune, Louisa
Harem
Hass, Amira
Hatoum, Mona
Haza, Ofra
Husayni, Hind al-
Husseini, Rana
Ibrahim, Fatima Ahmed
Idlibi, Ulfat al-
Institute for Women's Studies in the Arab World (Lebanon)
Institute of Women's Studies of Bir Zeit University
International, Dana
Iranian Bureau of Women's Affairs
Iraqi Women's Union
Irshad An-Niswaan
Ishaaq, Kamala Ibrahim
Islamic Countries Women Sport Solidarity Games (1992 and 1997)
Jababdi, Latifa
Jacir, Emily
Kadri, Mufide
Kamal, Zahira
Kan, Suna
Kariyuka, Tahiya
Karnouk, Liliane
Kashwar Kamal, Meena
Kateb, Yacine
Khader, Asma
Khaled, Leila
Khal, Helen
Khalidi, Wahida al-
Khalifa, Sahar
Khalil, Samiha Salama
Khemir, Sabiha
Khidhir, Zahra
Lahiji, Shahla
Langer, Felicia
Lata'if al-Musawwara Magazine
Lebanese Women's Council
Livnat, Limor
Mabarrat Muhammad Ali
Makdashi, Hesna
Malaʾika, Nazik al-
Marʿi, Mariam
Marriage and Family
Masri, Mai
Medicine and Public Health
Mernissi, Fatema
Milani, Tahmineh
Mogannam, Matiel
Moghaizel, Laure
Mostaghanemi, Ahlam
Mouʿawwad, Naila
Musa, Nabawiyya
Muslim Sisters Organization
Naʿamaat
Namir, Orah
Nasrallah, Emily
Nassar, Sadhij
Nassif, Malak Hifni
National Women's Committee (Yemen)
Nawfal, Hind
Neshat, Shirin
Niati, Houria
Noor al-Hussein (Queen Noor)
Nuun Magazine
Ordinances on Veiling
Princess Basma Women's Resource Center
Qaʿwar, Widad
Queen Surraya
Ramses College for Girls
Rania al-Abdullah (Queen Rania)
Rateb, Aisha
Rauf Ezzat, Heba
Revolutionary Association of the Women of Afghanistan (RAWA)
Rifaat, Alifa
Saadawi, Nawal al-
Sabah, Rasha al-
Sabah, Suad al-
Sabbagh, Salah al-Din al-
Sadr, Sitt Rabab al- (Charafeddine)
Saʿid, Amina al-
Samar, Sima
Samman, Ghada

Saudi, Mona
School for Hakīmāt
Sebbar, Leila
Shalvi, Alice
Shaʿrawi, Huda al-
Shawa, Laila
Shaykh, Hanan al-
Shihabi, Zlikha al-
Shochat, Manya
Sidera, Zineb
Sirry, Gazbia
Stanhope, Hester
Sudanese Women's Union
Sursock, Lady Cochrane
Taha, Mahmud Muhammad
Tallal, Chaibia
Tekeli, Şirin
Tlatli, Moufida
Toumi, Khalida
Tsemel, Leah
Tuqan, Fadwa
Turabi, Wisal al-Mahdi
Turkish Law on the Protection of the Family (1998)
Umar, Madiha
Union of Tunisian Women
Wafdist Women's Central Committee
Wazir, Intisar al- (Umm Jihad)
Women and Family Affairs Center
Women in Black
Women's Affairs Center (Gaza)
Women's Centre for Legal Aid and Counseling
Women's Forum for Research and Training (Yemen)
Women's Library and Information Center (Istanbul)
Women's Organization of Iran (WOI)
Women's People's Party (1923)
Women's Religious Rituals
Women's Renaissance Club
Women's Services
Women's Studies Center (Jerusalem)
Yemeni Women's Union
Zahawi, Jamil Sidqi al-
Zanan Magazine
Zayyat, Latifa
Zeid, Fahralnissa
Ziadeh, May
Ziwaj Mutʿa

ZIONISM

Aaronsohn Family
Ahad Ha-Am
Aliyah
Alterman, Natan
American Council for Judaism
Arab–Israel Conflict
Arlosoroff, Chaim
Azuri, Najib
Balfour Declaration (1917)
Begin, Menachem
Ben-Aharon, Yitzhak
Ben-Gurion, David
Ben-Porat, Mordechai
Bentwich, Norman
Ben-Zvi, Yizhak
Bialik, Hayyim Nahman
Biltmore Program (1942)
Binationalism
Borochov, Ber
Brenner, Yosef Hayyim
De Haan, Yaʿakov Yisrael
Dreyfus Affair
Eretz Yisrael
Exodus (1947)
Flapan, Simha
Goldmann, Nahum
Gordon, Aaron David
Ha-avarah Agreement
Ha-Cohen, Mordechai
Haganah
Ha-Halutz
Ha-Shomer
Ha-Shomer Ha-Tzaʿir
Herzl, Theodor
Hess, Moses
Hibbat Zion
Hillel, Shlomo
Histadrut
Holocaust
Irgun Zvaʾi Leʾumi (IZL)
Israel: Overview
Israeli Settlements
Jabotinsky, Vladimir Zeʾev
Jerusalem
Jewish Agency for Palestine
Jewish Brigade
Jewish Legion
Jewish National Fund
Jews in the Middle East
Joseph, Dov
Kahane, Meir
Kalvaryski, Chaim Margaliut-
Katznelson, Berl
Keren Hayesod
Kibbutz
Kiryat Arba
Kollek, Teddy
Kook, Zvi Yehuda
Kovner, Abba

Labor Zionism
Law of Return
Leibowitz, Yeshayahu
Literature: Hebrew
Lohamei Herut Yisrael
London (Roundtable) Conference (1939)
Magic Carpet Operation
Magnes, Judah
Masada
Matzpen
Meir, Golda
Mond, Alfred Moritz
Morrison–Grady Plan (1946)
Moshav
Mossad
Nahalal
Neturei Karta
Nordau, Max
Palestine Land Development Company
Palmah
Permanent Mandates Commission
Petah Tikvah
Ratosh, Yonatan
Rishon le-Zion
Rubinstein, Amnon
Ruppin, Arthur
Rutenberg, Pinhas
Sabra
Saison
Samuel, Herbert Louis
Sasson, Eliyahu
Shamir, Yitzhak
Shapira, Hayyim Moshe
Sharett, Moshe
Shiloah, Reuven
Shlonsky, Avraham
Silver, Abba Hillel
Smilansky, Moshe
Sneh, Moshe
Sokolow, Nahum
Stern, Abraham
Struma
Sykes, Mark
Tel Hai
Trumpeldor, Yosef
Uganda Project
United Jewish Appeal (UJA)
Ussishkin, Menahem
Vaʿad Leʾumi
Weizmann, Chaim
Western Wall
White Papers on Palestine
Wilson, Woodrow
Wingate, Charles Orde
Wise, Stephen S.
Women's International Zionist Organization
World Federation of Sephardi Communities
World Organization of Jews from Arab Countries (WOJAC)
World Zionist Organization (WZO)
Yadin, Yigael
Yehoshua, Avraham B.
Yellin-Mor, Natan
Yiddish
Youth Aliyah
Zelda
Zikhron Yaʿakov
Zionism
Zionist Commission for Palestine
Zionist Organization of America
Zionist Revisionist Movement

List of Maps

Volume 1

The Middle East and North Africa, Physical . . . *front endsheet*
Afghanistan, c. 2003 54
Algeria, c. 2003 121
Gulf of Aqaba 218
Israeli and Occupied Territories, 1967 247
Bahrain, c. 2003 368
The Middle East and North Africa, Political . . . *back endsheet*

Volume 2

The Dead Sea 685
Desalinization in Saudi Arabia, Bahrain, Qatar, United Arab Emirates, Yemen, and Oman 699
Egypt, c. 2003 764
Galilee 865
Gaza Strip 870
Golan Heights 925
Green Line Dividing the West Bank from Israel 942
Al-Haram al-Sharif (Temple Mount) 991
Iran, c. 2003 1112
Iraq, c. 2003 1133
Israel, West Bank, and Gaza Strip, c. 2000 1159
Israeli Settlements in the West Bank and Gaza Strip 1192
Jordan, c. 2003 1241
Khuzistan 1317
Kuwait, c. 2003 1347

Volume 3

Lebanon, c. 2003 1398
Libya, c. 2003 1413
The Litani River 1418
Mauritania, c. 2003 1502
Morocco, c. 2003 1568
Oman, c. 2003 1709
The Ottoman Empire, c. 1700 1731
The Ottoman Empire, c. 1914 1732
Ottoman Palestine and Syria, 1915 1733
Israeli Borders and Armistice Lines, 1949 1760
British Mandate for Palestine 1762
Palestine, Peel Commission Plan, 1937 1765
Israel, West Bank, and Gaza Strip, c. 2000 1768
Qatar, c. 2003 1876
Saudi Arabia, c. 2003 1996

VOLUME 4

The Turkish Straits 2094
Sudan, c. 2003 2098
Sykes–Picot Agreement, 1916 2128
Syria, c. 2003 2130
Tunisia, c. 2003 2226
Turkey, c. 2003 2239
United Arab Emirates, c. 2003 2272
United Nations Partition Plan, 1947 2276
Israeli Borders and Armistice Lines, 1949 2279
The West Bank 2340
Yemen, c. 2003 2386

List of Entries

A

Aaronsohn Family
Chaim I. Waxman

Abadan
Parvaneh Pourshariati

Abbas, Ferhat
Phillip C. Naylor (1996)

Abbas Hilmi I
Arthur Goldschmidt (1996)

Abbas Hilmi II
Arthur Goldschmidt (1996)

Abbas, Mahmud
Michael R. Fischbach
Steve Tamari (1996)

Abbas Mirza, Naʾeb al-Saltaneh
Eric Hooglund
Mansoureh Ettehadieh (1996)

Abbud, Ibrahim
Ann M. Lesch (1996)

Abd al-Aziz ibn al-Hassan
Edmund Burke III (1996)

Abd al-Aziz ibn Saʿud Al Saʿud
Malcolm C. Peck (1996)

Abd al-Ghani, Abd al-Aziz
Robert D. Burrowes

Abd al-Hadi Family
Ann M. Lesch

Abd al-Hadi, Tarab
Ellen L. Fleischmann

Abd al-Hafid ibn al-Hassan
Edmund Burke III (1996)

Abd al-Ilah ibn Ali
Peter Sluglett (1996)

Abd al-Maguid, Esmat
Arthur Goldschmidt

Abd al-Qadir
Byron Cannon (1996)

Abd al-Quddus, Ihsan
David Waldner (1996)

Abd al-Rahman al-Mahdi
Robert O. Collins (1996)

Abd al-Rahman ibn Hisham
Edmund Burke III (1996)

Abd al-Rahman Khan
Ashraf Ghani (1996)

Abd al-Rahman, Umar
Ahmed H. Ibrahim

Abd al-Raziq, Ali
Arthur Goldschmidt (1996)

Abd al-Sabur, Salah
David Waldner (1996)

Abd al-Wahhab, Muhammad ibn
Ali Jihad Racy (1996)

Abdelghani, Mohamed Benahmed
Phillip C. Naylor

Abdesselam, Belaid
Phillip C. Naylor

Abduh, Muhammad
Arthur Goldschmidt (1996)

Abdülaziz
Justin McCarthy (1996)

Abdul-Aziz Bin Baz, Shaykh
Anthony B. Toth

Abdülhamit II
Justin McCarthy (1996)

Abdullah I ibn Hussein
Jenab Tutunji (1996)

Abdullah II ibn Hussein
Michael R. Fischbach

Abdullahi, Muhammad Turshain
Robert O. Collins (1996)

Abdülmecit I
Burçak Keskin-Kozat
I. Metin Kunt (1996)

Abdülmecit II
Eric Hooglund
Elizabeth Thompson (1996)

Abidin, Dino
David Waldner (1996)

Abu al-Huda, Tawfiq
Michael R. Fischbach
Jenab Tutunji (1996)

Abu al-Timman, Jaʿfar
Mahmoud Haddad (1996)

Abu Dhabi
Anthony B. Toth
Malcolm C. Peck (1996)

Abuhatzeira, Aharon
Martin Malin (1996)

Abu Himara
Edmund Burke III (1996)

Abu Musa Island
Eric Hooglund
M. Morsy Abdullah (1996)

Abu Nuwwar, Ali
Michael R. Fischbach
Jenab Tutunji (1996)

Abu Qir, Battle of (1798)
David Waldner (1996)

Abu Risha, Umar
Muhammad Muslih (1996)

Abu Zayd, Hikmat
Mona Russell

Abu Zeid, Layla
Marilyn Booth

Acheson, Dean
Zachary Karabell (1996)

Achour, Habib
Vanesa Casanova-Fernandez
Matthew S. Gordon (1996)

Adalat Party
Parvaneh Pourshariati (1996)

Adamiyat, Abbasquli
Mansoor Moaddel (1996)

Adamiyat, Fereydun
Mansoor Moaddel (1996)

Adana
John R. Clark (1996)

Adana Conference
Zachary Karabell (1996)

Aden
F. Gregory Gause, III (1996)

Adenauer, Konrad
Michael R. Fischbach
Zachary Karabell (1996)

Adham, Soraya
Maria F. Curtis

Adivar, Abdulhak Adnan
Kathleen R. F. Burrill (1996)

Adivar, Halide Edib
Kathleen R. F. Burrill (1996)

Adli
Donald Malcolm Reid (1996)

Adl wa al-Ihsan, al-
Henri Lauzière

Adnan, Etel
Elise Salem

Adonis
Kamal Abu-Deeb (1996)

Adot Ha-Mizrah
Shlomo Deshen (1996)

Advisory Council (Palestine)
Philip Mattar

Aegean Sea
John R. Clark (1996)

Afghani, Jamal al-Din al-
Nikki Keddie (1996)

Afghanistan: Overview
Eric Hooglund

Afghanistan: Islamic Movements in
Eric Hooglund
M. Nazif Shahrani (1996)

Afghanistan: Political Parties in
Grant Farr

Afghanistan: Soviet Intervention in
Robert L. Canfield
Henry S. Bradsher (1996)

Afghanistan: U.S. Intervention in
Grant Farr

Afghan Women's Council
Senzil Nawid

Aflaq, Michel
C. Ernest Dawn (1996)

Agadir Crisis
Jon Jucovy (1996)

Agam, Yaacov
Ann Kahn (1996)

Agnon, Shmuel Yosef
Yaron Peleg (1996)

Agop, Gullu
Elizabeth Thompson (1996)

Agriculture
Vincent Battesti
Alan R. Richards (1996)

Agudat Israel
Chaim I. Waxman (1996)

Ahad Ha-Am
Steven Zipperstein (1996)

Ahali Group
Michael R. Fischbach
Ayad al-Qazzaz (1996)

Ahardane, Majoub
Ana Torres-Garcia
Matthew S. Gordon (1996)

Ahd, al-
Mahmoud Haddad (1996)

Ahdut ha-Avodah
Walter F. Weiker (1996)

Ahl-e Haqq
Ziba Mir-Hosseini

Ahmad al-Jazzar
Steve Tamari (1996)

Ahmad Bey Husayn
Larry A. Barrie (1996)

Ahmad Bey of Constantine
Peter von Sivers (1996)

Ahmad Durrani
Ashraf Ghani (1996)

Ahmad Hibat Allah
Edmund Burke III (1996)

Ahmad ibn Muhammad al-Raysuni
Edmund Burke III (1996)

Ahmad ibn Yahya Hamid al-Din
Manfred W. Wenner (1996)

Ahmad, Muhammad
Ann M. Lesch (1996)

Ahmad Qajar
Mansoureh Ettehadieh (1996)

Ahmad Shah Masʿud
Grant Farr
Barnett R. Rubin (1996)

Ahmar, Abdullah ibn Husayn al-
Maysam J. al Faruqi

Ahmet İhsan Toʾkgoz
David Waldner (1996)

Ahmet İzzet
Elizabeth Thompson (1996)

Ahmet Rasim
David Waldner (1996)

Ahmet Riza
Elizabeth Thompson (1996)

Ahmet Vefik
Zachary Karabell (1996)

Ahram Center for Political and Strategic Studies, al-
Donald Malcolm Reid

Ahsaʿi, Ahmad al-
Juan R. I. Cole (1996)

Ahvaz
Parvaneh Pourshariati

Aicha, Lalla
Rabia Bekkar

Ain Shams University
Donald Malcolm Reid
Ali E. Hillal Dessouki (1996)

AISHA: Arab Women's Forum
Mirna Lattouf

Ait Ahmed, Hocine
Phillip C. Naylor

Ajman
Karen Hunt Ahmed

Akbulut, Ahmet Ziya
David Waldner (1996)

Akçura, Yusuf
Elizabeth Thompson (1996)

Akhavan-Saless, Mehdi
Pardis Minuchehr (1996)

Akhbari
Neguin Yavari (1996)

Akhondzadeh, Mirza Fath Ali
Hamid Algar (1996)

Akkad, Mustafa
Waleed Hazbun

AKP (Justice and Development Party)
M. Hakan Yavuz

Akrad, Hayy al-
Abdul-Karim Rafeq (1996)

Ala, Hoseyn
Neguin Yavari (1996)

Al al-Shaykh Family
J. E. Peterson
Malcolm C. Peck (1996)

Alam, Amir Asadollah
Neguin Yavari (1996)

Alamayn, al-
Daniel E. Spector (1996)

Alami Family, al-
Ann M. Lesch

Alavi, Bozorg
Eric Hooglund

Alawi
Zouhair Ghazzal
Majed Halawi (1996)

Alawite Dynasty
Michael M. Laskier
Donna Lee Bowen (1996)

Al Bu Saʿid Family and Tribe of Oman
J. E. Peterson

Al Bu Saʿid, Qabus ibn Saʿid
J. E. Peterson

Al Bu Saʿid, Saʿid ibn Taymur
J. E. Peterson (1996)

Alcohol
Richard W. Bulliet (1996)

Al-e Ahmad, Jalal
Michael C. Hillmann (1996)

Aleppo
Abraham Marcus (1996)

Alevi
Ruth Mandel

Alexandretta
Noah Butler
John R. Clark (1996)

Alexandria
Donald Malcolm Reid
Jean-Marc R. Oppenheim (1996)

Alexandria Convention
Zachary Karabell (1996)

Alexandria University
Donald Malcolm Reid

Algeciras Conference (1906)
Jon Jucovy (1996)

Algeria: Overview
John Ruedy

Algeria: Constitution
Phillip C. Naylor

Algeria: Political Parties in
Michael M. Laskier

Algerian Family Code (1984)
Rabia Bekkar

Algerian War of Independence
John Ruedy (1996)

Algiers
Peter von Sivers

Algiers Agreement (1975)
Eric Hooglund
Mia Bloom (1996)

Algiers, Battle of (1956–1957)
Matthew S. Gordon (1996)

Algiers Charter
John Ruedy (1996)

Alia, Queen
Tamara Sonn

Ali Nasir Muhammad al-Hasani
Robert D. Burrowes

Ali Riza
David Waldner (1996)

Alishan, Ghevond
Rouben P. Adalian (1996)

Ali Suavi
Zachary Karabell (1996)

Ali, Wijdan
Jessica Winegar

Aliyah
Chaim I. Waxman

Aliyer, Fatimah
Ayse Durakbasa Tarhan

Alizadeh, Ghazaleh
Babak Rahimi

Alkalai, Judah ben Solomon Hai
Martin Malin (1996)

Al Khalifa Family
Fred H. Lawson

Allah
Scott Alexander (1996)

Allenby, Edmund Henry
Jon Jucovy (1996)

Alliance Israélite Universelle (AIU)
Michael M. Laskier

Allied Middle East Command
Daniel E. Spector (1996)

Allon, Yigal
Gregory S. Mahler (1996)

All-Palestine Government
Avi Shlaim (1996)

Al Nahayyan Family
Anthony B. Toth
M. Morsy Abdullah (1996)

Aloni, Shulamit
Meron Medzini

Alpha, Operation
Iris Borowy

Al Rashid Family
Anthony B. Toth
Malcolm C. Peck (1996)

Al Sabah Family
Mary Ann Tétreault

Al Sabah, Mubarak
Mary Ann Tétreault (1996)

Al Saqr Family
Mary Ann Tétreault

Al Saʿud Family
Anthony B. Toth

Al Saʿud, Saʿud ibn Abd al-Aziz
Malcolm C. Peck (1996)

Al Sudayri Family
J. E. Peterson
Malcolm C. Peck (1996)

Al Sudayri, Hassa bint Ahmad
Malcolm C. Peck (1996)

Al-Suswa, Amat al-Alim
Susanne Dahlgren

Altalena
Yaakov Shavit (1996)

Alterman, Natan
Zvia Ginor (1996)

Al Thani Family
Anthony B. Toth

Al Thani, Hamad ibn Khalifa
F. Gregory Gause, III (1996)

Al Thunayyan Family
J. E. Peterson
Malcolm C. Peck (1996)

Altinay, Ahmed Refik
Elizabeth Thompson (1996)

Alusi, Mahmud Shukri al-
Amatzia Baram (1996)

AMAL
As'ad AbuKhalil

Amanollah Khan
Ashraf Ghani (1996)

Amari, Raja
Laura Rice

Amer, Ghada
Jessica Winegar

American Council for Judaism
George R. Wilkes

American Israel Public Affairs Committee
Mark A. Raider

American Jewish Committee
Jerry Kutnick
Mia Bloom (1996)

American Jewish Congress
Jerry Kutnick

American University in Cairo (AUC)
Donald Malcolm Reid

American University of Beirut (AUB)
As'ad AbuKhalil

Amichai, Yehuda
Nili Gold (1996)

Amiens, Treaty of
Jon Jucovy (1996)

Amin, Ahmad
William Shepard (1996)

Amin al-Dowleh, Mirza Ali Khan
Lawrence G. Potter (1996)

Amin al-Soltan, Ali-Asghar
Lawrence G. Potter (1996)

Amin al-Zarb, Mohammad Hasan
Lawrence G. Potter (1996)

Amin Bey, al-
Matthew S. Gordon (1996)

Amin, Hafizullah
Grant Farr (1996)

Amini, Ali
Neguin Yavari (1996)

Amini, Fatemeh
Azadeh Kian-Thiébaut

Amin, Qasim
Juan R. I. Cole (1996)

Amir, Abd al-Hakim
Karen A. Thornsvard (1996)

Amir, Eli
Yarom Peleg (1996)

Amir-Entezam, Abbas
Eric Hooglund
Neguin Yavari (1996)

Amir Kabir, Mirza Taqi Khan
Lawrence G. Potter (1996)

Amis du Manifeste et de la Liberté
Phillip C. Naylor (1996)

Amit, Meir
Meron Medzini
Martin Malin (1996)

Amman
Michael R. Fischbach
Peter Gubser (1996)

Amri, Hasan al-
Robert D. Burrowes

Amrouche, Fadhma At Mansour
Jane E. Goodman

Amrouche, Jean
Phillip C. Naylor (1996)

Amrouche, Mary Louise (a.k.a. Marguerite Taos)
Jane E. Goodman

Amu Darya
Grant Farr (1996)

Anatolia
Eric Hooglund

Anawati, Georges Chehata
Charles E. Butterworth

Andranik Ozanian
Rouben P. Adalian (1996)

Anglo–Afghan Treaty (1855)
Grant Farr (1996)

Anglo–Afghan Wars
Ashraf Ghani (1996)

Anglo–American Committee of Inquiry (1946)
Amikam Nachmani
Steve Tamari (1996)

Anglo–Egyptian Treaty (1954)
Mordechai Bar-On

Anglo–Iranian Agreement (1919)
Eric Hooglund
Mansoor Moaddel (1996)

Anglo–Iranian Oil Company
Mansoor Moaddel (1996)

Anglo–Iraqi Treaties
Peter Sluglett (1996)

Anglo–Omani Treaties
Robert G. Landen (1996)

Anglo–Persian War (1856)
Eric Hooglund (1996)

Anglo–Russian Agreement (1907)
Eric Hooglund (1996)

Ani, Jananne al-
Jessica Winegar

Anis Al-Jalis Magazine
Mona Russell

Anjoman
Nikki Keddie (1996)

Ankara
Eric Hooglund
John R. Clark (1996)

Ankara, Treaty of (1930)
Burçak Keskin-Kozat
Elizabeth Thompson (1996)

Ankara University
Eric Hooglund
I. Metin Kunt (1996)

Annaba
Dirk Vandewalle (1996)

Annan, Kofi A.
Michael R. Fischbach

Ansar, al-
Ann M. Lesch (1996)

Antakya
Eric Hooglund

Antar, Ali Ahmad Nasir
Robert D. Burrowes

Antisemitism
Neil Caplan

Antonius, George
William L. Cleveland (1996)

Antun, Farah
Michael R. Fischbach
Zachary Karabell (1996)

Aoun, Michel
As'ad AbuKhalil

Aozou Strip
George Joffe (1996)

Appelfeld, Aharon
Nili Gold (1996)

Aqaba
Jenab Tutunji (1996)

Aqaba, Gulf of
Michael R. Fischbach
Jenab Tutunji (1996)

Aqaba Incident
Elizabeth Thompson (1996)

Aql, Sa'id
Michael R. Fischbach
Guilain P. Denoeux (1996)

Aqqad, Umar Abd al-Fattah al-
Steve Tamari (1996)

Aqsa Intifada, al-
Philip Mattar

Arab
Carolyn Fluehr-Lobban
Arthur Goldschmidt (1996)

Arab Academy of Damascus
Fred H. Lawson (1996)

Arab Boycott
Michael R. Fischbach
George E. Gruen (1996)

Arab Bureau (Cairo)
Roger Adelson

Arab Club
Muhammad Muslih (1996)

Arab College of Jerusalem
Hisham Nashabi (1996)

Arab Feminist Union
Maria F. Curtis

Arab Higher Committee (Palestine)
Ann M. Lesch

Arabian American Oil Company (ARAMCO)
Mary Ann Tétreault

Arabian Horses
Lisa M. Lacy

Arabian Mission
Malcolm C. Peck (1996)

Arabian Peninsula
Martha Imber-Goldstein (1996)

Arabic
Carolyn Killean (1996)

Arabic Script
Elizabeth M. Bergman (1996)

Arab–Israel Conflict
Don Peretz

Arab–Israeli General Armistice Agreements (1949)
Mordechai Bar-On

Arab–Israel War (1948)
Don Peretz (1996)

Arab–Israel War (1956)
Don Peretz
Reeva S. Simon (1996)

Arab–Israel War (1967)
Don Peretz

Arab–Israel War (1973)
Don Peretz

Arab–Israel War (1982)
Philip Mattar

Arabization Policies
Rabia Bekkar
John Ruedy (1996)

Arab League Summits
Philip Mattar

Arab Legion
Curtis R. Ryan
Jenab Tutunji (1996)

Arab Liberation Army
Steve Tamari (1996)

Arab Liberation Front
Elizabeth Thompson (1996)

Arab Maghreb Union
David Gutelius

Arab Nationalism
Rashid Khalidi (1996)

Arab National Movement (ANM)
Malcolm C. Peck (1996)

Arab Revolt (1916)
Don Peretz (1996)

Arab Socialism
George E. Irani

Arab Socialist Union
Arthur Goldschmidt
Ali E. Hillal Dessouki (1996)

Arab Women's Association of Palestine
Ellen L. Fleischmann

Arab Women's Congress
Steve Tamari (1996)

Arab Women's Executive Committee
Ellen L. Fleischmann

Arab Women's Solidarity Association International
Rita Stephan

Arafat, Yasir
Michael R. Fischbach
Michael Dunn (1996)

Aʿraj, Wasini al-
Aida A. Bamia (1996)

Aral, Oğuz
Elizabeth Thompson (1996)

Ararat, Mount
David Waldner (1996)

Araz, Nezihe
Ayse Durakbasa Tarhan

Arch
Azzedine G. Mansour

Archaeological Museum (Istanbul)
Karen Pinto (1996)

Archaeology in the Middle East
Michael R. Fischbach
Reeva S. Simon (1996)

Architecture
Azzedine G. Mansour
Walter Denny (1996)

Ard, al-
Michael R. Fischbach
Bryan Daves (1996)

Arens, Moshe
Martin Malin (1996)

Arfa, Hasan
Eric Hooglund

Arfa, Muhammad ibn
Matthew S. Gordon (1996)

Argoud, Antoine
Phillip C. Naylor

Arif, Abd al-Rahman
Amatzia Baram (1996)

Arif, Abd al-Salam
Amatzia Baram (1996)

Arif, Arif al-
Michael R. Fischbach
Steve Tamari (1996)

Arish, Convention of al- (1800)
Zachary Karabell (1996)

Arkoun, Mohammed
As'ad AbuKhalil

Arlosoroff, Chaim
Chaim I. Waxman
Neil Caplan

Armée de Libération Nationale (ALN)
John Ruedy (1996)

Armenian Community of Jerusalem
Rouben P. Adalian
Abraham Terian (1996)

Armenian Genocide
Rouben P. Adalian

Armenian Millet
Rouben P. Adalian (1996)

Armenian Revolutionary Movement
Rouben P. Adalian (1996)

Armenians in the Middle East
Rouben P. Adalian

Arms and Armaments in the Middle East
Zach Levey

Arseven, Celal Esat
Elizabeth Thompson (1996)

Arslan, Adil
C. Ernest Dawn (1996)

Arslan Family
As'ad AbuKhalil (1996)

Arslan, Shakib
William L. Cleveland (1996)

Arsuzi, Zaki al-
C. Ernest Dawn (1996)

Art
Jessica Winegar
Walter Denny (1996)

Asʿad, Ahmad
As'ad AbuKhalil (1996)

Asad, Bashshar al-
Ronald Bruce St John

Asʿad Family
As'ad AbuKhalil (1996)

Asad, Hafiz al-
Ronald Bruce St John
Muhammed Muslih (1996)

Asʿad, Kamil
As'ad AbuKhalil (1996)

Asʿad Wali
As'ad AbuKhalil (1996)

Ashkenazim
Arnold Blumberg (1996)

Ashmawi, Muhammad Abd al-Rahman Salih al-
Ahmad S. Moussalli

Ashmawi, Muhammad Saʿid al-
As'ad AbuKhalil

Ashour, Radwa
Marilyn Booth

As-Is Agreement
Mary Ann Tétreault (1996)

Askari, Jaʿfar al-
Ahmad Abdul A. R. Shikara (1996)

Asmahan
Virginia Danielson (1996)

Asmar, Fawzi al-
Philip Mattar
Jenab Tutunji (1996)

Association des Femmes Tunisiennes pour la Recherche et le Développement (AFTURD)
Laura Rice

Association for the Protection of Women's Rights (Afghanistan)
Senzil Nawid

Association of Algerian Muslim Ulama (AUMA)
John Ruedy (1996)

Assyrians
Charles C. Kolb

Aswan
Arthur Goldschmidt (1996)

Aswan High Dam
Gregory B. Baecher
David Waldner (1996)

Atabat
Neguin Yavari (1996)

Atasi, Hashim al-
Muhammad Muslih (1996)

Atasi, Jamal al-
George E. Irani (1996)

Atasi, Nur al-Din al-
Michael R. Fischbach
Muhammed Muslih (1996)

Atatürk, Mustafa Kemal
Ahmet Kuyas (1996)

Atatürk University
I. Metin Kunt (1996)

Atay, Salih Rifki
Elizabeth Thompson (1996)

Atlas Mountains
Will D. Swearingen (1996)

Atrash, Farid al-
Virginia Danielson (1996)

Atrash, Sultan Pasha al-
Muhammad Muslih (1996)

Attar, Nejat al-
Khalil Gebara

Attar, Suad al-
Jessica Winegar

Attas, Haydar Abu Bakr al-
Robert D. Burrowes

Attlee, Clement
Joseph Nevo
Jenab Tutunji (1996)

Austria–Hungary and the Middle East
Zachary Karabell (1996)

Avnery, Uri
Mordechai Bar-On
Martin Malin (1996)

Awadhi, Badria A. al-
Mary Ann Tétreault

Awad, Louis
Charles E. Butterworth
David Waldner (1996)

Awakened Youth
Grant Farr (1996)

Awali, al-
Emile A. Nakhleh (1996)

Ayan
Elizabeth Thompson (1996)

Aya Sofya
Zachary Karabell (1996)

Ayn, al-
Anthony B. Toth

Ayn al-Dowleh, Abd al-Majid Mirza
Neguin Yavari (1996)

Ayni, Muhsin al-
F. Gregory Gause, III (1996)

Ayn, Ras al-
Abdul-Karim Rafeq (1996)

Ayyub, Dhu al-Nun
Amatzia Baram (1996)

Ayyubi, Ali Jawdat al-
Ahmad Abdul A. R. Shikara (1996)

Azerbaijan
Neguin Yavari

Azerbaijan Crisis
Eric Hooglund (1996)

Azeri Language and Literature
Uli Schamiloglu (1996)

Azhar, al-
Donald Malcolm Reid
A. Chris Eccel (1996)

Azhari, Isma'il
Robert O. Collins (1996)

Azib
Rahma Bourqia (1996)

Aziz, Tariq
Michael R. Fischbach
Amatzia Baram (1996)

Azm, Sadiq al-
As'ad AbuKhalil

Azuri, Najib
Muhammad Muslih (1996)

Azzam, Abd al-Rahman al-
Mahmoud Haddad (1996)

B

Baʿalbak
Guilain P. Denoeux (1996)

Baʿalbakki, Layla
Laurie King-Irani

Bab, al-
Juan R. I. Cole (1996)

Bab al-Mandab
Robert D. Burrowes (1996)

Baban Family
Mamoon A. Zaki (1996)

Babis
Juan R. I. Cole (1996)

Baccouche, Hedi
Ana Torres-Garcia
Matthew S. Gordon (1996)

Badran, Mudar
Jenab Tutunji (1996)

Badr, Liana
George R. Wilkes

Badr, Muhammad al-
Emile A. Nakhleh (1996)

Baghdad
Ayad Al-Qazzaz

Baghdadi, Abd al-Latif al-
Donald Malcolm Reid
Arthur Goldschmidt (1996)

Baghdad Pact (1955)
William L. Cleveland
Zachary Karabell (1996)

Baghdad Summit (1978)
Michael R. Fischbach (1996)

Baghdad University
John J. Donohue (1996)

Bahaʾi Faith
Juan R. I. Cole (1996)

Baharina
Anthony B. Toth
Emile A. Nakhleh (1996)

Bahariya
Arthur Goldschmidt (1996)

Bahar, Mohammad Taqi
Michael C. Hillmann (1996)

Bahithat al-Lubnaniyyat, al-
Elise Salem

Bahrain
Fred H. Lawson

Bahraini–Qatari Wars
Fred H. Lawson

Bahrain Nationalist Movement
Fred H. Lawson (1996)

Bahrain National Oil Company (BANOCO)
Emile A. Nakhleh (1996)

Bahrain Order in Council
Emile A. Nakhleh (1996)

Bahr al-Abyad
Robert O. Collins (1996)

Bahr al-Arab
Robert O. Collins (1996)

Bahr al-Ghazal
Robert O. Collins (1996)

Bahr al-Jabal
Robert O. Collins (1996)

Baida
John L. Wright (1996)

Bakdash, Khalid
Garay Menicucci

Baker, James A.
Michael R. Fischbach (1996)

Bakhtiari
Eric Hooglund
Lois Beck (1996)

Bakhtiari, Najaf Qoli Khan Samsam al-Soltaneh
Neguin Yavari (1996)

Bakhtiar, Shapur
Ahmed H. Ibrahim

Bakhtiar, Timur
Neguin Yavari (1996)

Bakil Tribal Confederation
Manfred W. Wenner (1996)

Bakkar, Jalillah
Laura Rice

Bakr, Ahmad Hasan al-
Amatzia Baram (1996)

Bakr, Salwa
Caroline Seymour-Jorn

Balaclava, Battle of
Jean-Marc R. Oppenheim (1996)

Balafrej, Ahmed
Matthew S. Gordon (1996)

Balbo, Italo
George Joffe (1996)

Balfour Declaration (1917)
Philip Mattar

Balkan Crises (1870s)
John Micgiel (1996)

Balkans
John Micgiel (1996)

Balkan Wars (1912–1913)
Hasan Kayali (1996)

Balta Liman, Convention of (1838)
Zachary Karabell (1996)

Baluchis
Charles C. Kolb

Baluchistan
Neguin Yavari (1996)

Balyan Family
Rouben P. Adalian
Aptullah Kuran (1996)

Bamyan
Grant Farr

Bandung Conference (1955)
Zachary Karabell (1996)

Bani-Etemad, Rakhsan
Roxanne Varzi

Bani Sadr, Abolhasan
Neguin Yavari

Banking
Clement Moore Henry

Banna, Hasan al-
Ahmad S. Moussalli
Ali E. Hillal Dessouki (1996)

Banna, Sabri al-
Michael R. Fischbach
Steve Tamari (1996)

Bannis, Mohammad
Aida A. Bamia

Baqri Family
Norman Stillman (1996)

Baraheni, Reza
Eric Hooglund
Michael C. Hillman (1996)

Barakat, Hoda
Elise Salem

Barak, Ehud
Mordechai Bar-On

Barakzai Dynasty
Eric Hooglund
Ashraf Ghani (1996)

Barbary States
Jerome Bookin-Wiener (1996)

Barbary Wars
Jerome Bookin-Wiener (1996)

Barghuthi Family
Michael R. Fischbach
Steve Tamari (1996)

Barghuthi, Marwan
Michael R. Fischbach

Bar-Ilan University
Paul Rivlin
Miriam Simon (1996)

Baring, Evelyn
Arthur Goldschmidt
Robert L. Tignor (1996)

Barkan, Ömer Lutfi
I. Metin Kunt (1996)

Bar-Lev, Haim
Meron Medzini
Martin Malin (1996)

Baron, Dvora
Zvia Ginor (1996)

Barzani Family
Michael R. Fischbach
Chris Kutschera (1996)

Basic People's Congresses
John L. Wright (1996)

Başiretci, Ali
David Waldner (1996)

Basma bint Talal
Michael R. Fischbach

Basra
Nazar al-Khalaf (1996)

Bast
Neguin Yavari (1996)

Baʿth, al-
Peter Sluglett
Reeva S. Simon (1996)

Baya
Jessica Winegar

Bayar, Celal
Walter F. Weiker (1996)

Bayati, Abd al-Wahhab al-
Amatzia Baram (1996)

Bayat, Mortaza Qoli
Mansoureh Ettehadieh (1996)

Baydh, Ali Salim al-
Robert D. Burrowes

Bayrakdar, Mustafa
Elizabeth Thompson (1996)

Bayram V, Muhammad
Larry A. Barrie (1996)

Bazaars and Bazaar Merchants
Ahmad Ashraf

Bazargan, Mehdi
Mansoor Moaddel (1996)

Bazzaz, Abd al-Rahman al-
Ayad al-Qazzaz (1996)

Beaufort, Charles-Marie-Napoléon d'Hautpoul de
Bassam Namani (1996)

Bedel-i Askeri
Elizabeth Thompson (1996)

Beersheba
Steve Tamari (1996)

Begin, Menachem
Eric Silver

Behar, Nissim
Zachary Karabell (1996)

Behbehani, Simin
Roxanne Varzi

Beheshti, Mohammad
Hamid Algar (1996)

Behrangi, Samad
Eric Hooglund

Behrouzi, Maryam
Cherie Taraghi

Beirut
As'ad AbuKhalil

Beirut College for Women (BCW)
Mirna Lattouf

Beitaddin Declaration
George E. Irani (1996)

Beja
Khalid M. El-Hassan
Robert O. Collins (1996)

Bejerano, Maya
Yarom Peleg (1996)

Bekir, Fahri
David Waldner (1996)

Bektashis
Maria F. Curtis
John D. Norton (1996)

Belgrave, Charles Dalrymple
Fred H. Lawson (1996)

Belhadj, Ali
Emad Eldin Shahin

Belkacem, Cherif
Phillip C. Naylor

Bell, Gertrude
Zachary Karabell (1996)

Bellounis, Muhammad
Phillip C. Naylor (1996)

Ben-Aharon, Yitzhak
Gregory S. Mahler
Zachary Karabell (1996)

Ben Ali, Zayn al-Abidine
Maria F. Curtis
Matthew S. Gordon (1996)

Ben Ammar, Tahar
Matthew S. Gordon (1996)

Ben Badis, Abd al-Hamid
Phillip C. Naylor (1996)

Ben Barka, Mehdi
Donna Lee Bowen (1996)

Ben Bella, Ahmed
Phillip C. Naylor

Ben Bouali, Hassiba
Rabia Bekkar

Ben Boulaid, Moustafa
Phillip C. Naylor (1996)

Bendjedid, Chadli
Phillip C. Naylor

Benflis, Ali
Phillip C. Naylor

Benghazi
John L. Wright (1996)

Ben-Gurion, David
Gregory S. Mahler

Ben-Gurion University of the Negev
Miriam Simon (1996)

Ben Jelloun, Umar
Bruce Maddy-Weitzman (1996)

Ben Khedda, Ben Youssef
Phillip C. Naylor (1996)

Ben M'hidi, Muhammad Larbi
Phillip C. Naylor (1996)

Bennabi, Malek
Yahia Zoubir

Ben-Porat, Mordechai
Gregory S. Mahler
Nissim Rejwan (1996)

Ben Salah, Ahmed
Emad Eldin Shahin
Kenneth J. Perkins (1996)

Ben Seddiq, Mahjoub
Bruce Maddy-Weitzman

Ben Simeon, Raphael Aaron
Norman Stillman (1996)

Bentwich, Norman
Bernard Wasserstein

Benvenisti, Meron
Zachary Karabell (1996)

Ben-Yehuda, Eliezer
Martin Malin (1996)

Ben Yousouf, Salah
Kenneth J. Perkins (1996)

Ben-Zvi, Rahel Yanait
Meron Medzini

Ben-Zvi, Yizhak
Donna Robinson Divine (1996)

Berber
Thomas G. Penchoen (1996)

Berber Dahir
Dale F. Eickelman (1996)

Berber Spring
Paul Silverstein

Berkowitz, Yizhak
Ann Kahn (1996)

Berlin–Baghdad Railway
Francis R. Nicosia (1996)

Berlin, Congress and Treaty of
Arnold Blumberg (1996)

Bernadotte, Folke
Amitzur Ilan

Berrada, Mohammed
Aida A. Bamia

Berri, Nabi
As'ad AbuKhalil

Bethlehem
Michael R. Fischbach
Benjamin Joseph (1996)

Bevin, Ernest
Lawrence Tal (1996)

Bevin–Sforza Plan
George Joffe (1996)

Beyoglu Protocol
Zachary Karabell (1996)

Bezalel Academy of Arts and Design
Ann Kahn (1996)

Bialik, Hayyim Nahman
George R. Wilkes
Nili Gold (1996)

Bidonville
Dirk Vandewalle (1996)

Bilhayr, Abd al-Nabi
George Joffe (1996)

Bilkent University
Burçak Keskin-Kozat
I. Metin Kunt (1996)

Biltmore Program (1942)
Neil Caplan

Binationalism
Neil Caplan

Bin Diyaf, Muhsen
Aida A. Bamia

bin Ladin, Osama
As'ad AbuKhalil

Bint al-Shati
Sabah Ghandour

Biqa Valley
Fred H. Lawson

Biret, Idil
Filiz Ali

Birth Control
Laurie King-Irani
Donna Lee Bowen (1996)

Bir Zeit University
Lawrence Tal (1996)

Bishara, Abdullah
Mary Ann Tétreault
Les Ordeman (1996)

Bishara, Suha
As'ad AbuKhalil

Bisitun
A. Shapur Shahbazi (1996)

Bitar, Salah al-Din al-

Bitat, Rabah
Phillip C. Naylor (1996)

Bittari, Zoubida
Aida A. Bamia (1996)

Bitton, Simone
George R. Wilkes

Bizerte
Kenneth J. Perkins (1996)

Bizerte Crisis (1961)
Kenneth J. Perkins (1996)

Black Panthers
Shlomo Deshen (1996)

Black Sea
Zachary Karabell (1996)

Black September
Michael R. Fischbach
Steve Tamari (1996)

Black Spring
Paul Silverstein

Black Thursday (1978)
Matthew S. Gordon (1996)

Bled al-Siba/Bled al-Makhzan
C. R. Pennell (1996)

Bliss, Daniel
Guilain P. Denoeux (1996)

Bliss, Howard
Karen Pinto

Bludan Conferences (1937, 1946)
Joseph Nevo
Elizabeth Thompson (1996)

Blum–Viollette Plan
Phillip C. Naylor (1996)

B'nai B'rith
Vanesa Casanova-Fernandez
Norman Stillman (1996)

Bodrum
Maria F. Curtis
Karen Pinto (1996)

Boğaziçi (Bosporus) University
Burçak Keskin-Kozat
I. Metin Kunt (1996)

Bogazköy
Elizabeth Thompson (1996)

Bonaparte, Napoléon
Jean-Marc R. Oppenheim (1996)

Boratav, Pertev Naili
Burçak Keskin-Kozat
Kathleen R. F. Burrill (1996)

Borochov, Ber
Chaim I. Waxman

Borujerdi, Hosayn
Neguin Yavari (1996)

Bost
Grant Farr

Bouabid, Abderrahim
Ana Torres-Garcia
Matthew S. Gordon (1996)

Boucetta, Muhammad
Matthew S. Gordon (1996)

Boudiaf, Mohamed
Phillip C. Naylor

Boudjedra, Rachid
Phillip C. Naylor

Bouhired, Jamila
Rabia Bekkar

Bouih, Fatna el-
Maria F. Curtis

Boumédienne, Houari
Dirk Vandewalle (1996)

Bourguiba, Habib
Michael M. Laskier
Lisa Anderson (1996)

Bouteflika, Abdelaziz
Phillip C. Naylor

Boutros-Ghali, Boutros
Bryan Daves (1996)

Bouyali, Moustafa
Henri Lauzière

Brahimi, Abdelhamid
Phillip C. Naylor

Brenner, Yosef Hayyim
George R. Wilkes
Ann Kahn (1996)

Brezhnev, Leonid Ilyich
Oles M. Smolansky (1996)

Brichah
Ann Kahn (1996)

Britain and the Middle East from 1914 to the Present
Bernard Wasserstein (1996)

Britain and the Middle East up to 1914
J. C. Hurewitz (1996)

British–French Oil Agreement
Ibrahim M. Oweiss
Zachary Karabell (1996)

Brookings Report (1975)
George R. Wilkes

Browne, Edward Granville
John R. Perry (1996)

Buber, Martin
Paul Mendes-Flohr

Bubiyan Island
Emile A. Nakhleh (1996)

Bucharest, Treaty of (1812)
Zachary Karabell (1996)

Budapest Convention (1877)
Zachary Karabell (1996)

Bugeaud de la Piconnerie, Thomas-Robert
Kenneth J. Perkins (1996)

Bu Hamara
Matthew S. Gordon (1996)

Buhayra
Arthur Goldschmidt (1996)

Bulgarian Horrors
John Micgiel (1996)

Bunche, Ralph J.
Brian Urquhart

Bund
Chaim I. Waxman

Buraymi Oasis Dispute
Anthony B. Toth
Malcolm C. Peck (1996)

Burckhardt, Johann Ludwig
Benjamin Braude (1996)

Bureau of Translation
Carter V. Findlay (1996)

Bureaux Arabes
Phillip C. Naylor (1996)

Burg, Avraham
Gregory S. Mahler

Burg, Yosef
Gregory S. Mahler
Zachary Karabell (1996)

Burla, Yehuda
Ann Kahn (1996)

Bursa
Burçak Keskin-Kozat
I. Metin Kunt (1996)

Burton, Richard Francis
George R. Wilkes
Benjamin Braude (1996)

Bush, George Herbert Walker
Michael R. Fischbach

Bush, George Walker
Michael R. Fischbach

Busnach Family
Norman Stillman (1996)

Bustani, Sulayman
Mahmoud Haddad (1996)

C

Cairo
Donald Malcolm Reid

Cairo Conference (1921)
Zachary Karabell (1996)

Cairo Family Planning Association
Angel M. Foster

Cairo University
Donald Malcolm Reid

Caland, Huguette
Jessica Winegar

Caliphate
Hasan Kayali

Calligraphy
Muhammad Zakariya (1996)

Cambon–Lansdowne Agreement (1904)
Rémy Leveau (1996)

Camels
Mia Bloom (1996)

Camp David Accords (1978)
Laurie Z. Eisenberg
Don Peretz (1996)

Camp David Summit (2000)
Philip Mattar

Camus, Albert
Phillip C. Naylor (1996)

Canning, Stratford
Benjamin Braude (1996)

Cantonnement/Refoulement
Dirk Vandewalle (1996)

Capitulations
C. Max Kortepeter (1996)

Carpets, Persian
Michael C. Hillmann (1996)

Carter, Jimmy
Laurie Z. Eisenberg
Mia Bloom (1996)

Casablanca
C. R. Pennell (1996)

Catroux, Georges
Phillip C. Naylor (1996)

Cattan, Henry
Philip Mattar
Lawrence Tal (1996)

Caylak
David Waldner (1996)

Cemal Paşa
Rouben P. Adalian
Hasan Kayali (1996)

Central Intelligence Agency (CIA)
Michael R. Fischbach
Kathleen M. Christison (1996)

Central Treaty Organization (CENTO)
Zachary Karabell (1996)

Centre de Recherches, d'Études, de Documentation et d'Information sur la Femme (CREDIF)
Laura Rice

Ceramics
Charles C. Kolb
Elizabeth Thompson (1996)

Çerkes Hasan Incident
David Waldner (1996)

Ceuta
C. R. Pennell (1996)

Cevdet, Abdullah
David Waldner (1996)

Cevdet, Ahmed
Carter V. Findley (1996)

Chalabi, Ahmad
Karim Hamdy

Challe, Maurice
Phillip C. Naylor (1996)

Chamchian, Mikayel
Rouben P. Adalian (1996)

Chamoun, Camille
Guilain P. Denoeux (1996)

Chamoun, Dany
Guilain P. Denoeux (1996)

Champollion, Jean-François
Donald Malcolm Reid (1996)

Chamran, Mostafa
Neguin Yavari (1996)

Chazan, Naomi
George R. Wilkes

Chédid, Andrée
Nabil Boudraa

Chehab, Bashir
As'ad AbuKhalil (1996)

Chehab Family
As'ad AbuKhalil (1996)

Chehab, Fu'ad
As'ad AbuKhalil (1996)

Chehab, Khalid
Guilain P. Denoeux (1996)

Chenik, Muhammad
Matthew S. Gordon (1996)

China and the Middle East
P. R. Kumaraswamy
Kazuo Takahashi (1996)

Chraibi, Driss
Aida A. Bamia

Chrakian, Artin
Rouben P. Adalian (1996)

Christians in the Middle East
George E. Irani
Dale L. Bishop (1996)

Chubak, Sadeq
Pardis Minuchehr (1996)

Churchill White Paper (1922)
Philip Mattar (1996)

Churchill, William
Elizabeth Thompson (1996)

Churchill, Winston S.
Martin Gilbert (1996)

Cilicia
Elizabeth Thompson (1996)

Çiller, Tansu
Burçak Keskin-Kozat
Nermin Abadan-Unat (1996)

Circassians
Seteney Shami

Circumcision
Ephraim Tabory

Civil Code of 1926
Nermin Abadan-Unat (1996)

Civil Service School (Ottoman)
David Waldner (1996)

Clark–Darlan Agreement (1942)
Zachary Karabell (1996)

Clayton, Gilbert
Jenab Tutunji (1996)

Clemenceau, Georges
O. W. Abi-Mershed
Zachary Karabell (1996)

Climate
John F. Kolars (1996)

Clinton, William Jefferson
Michael R. Fischbach

Clot, Antoine Barthélémy
David Waldner (1996)

Clothing
Faegheh Shirazi

Club National Israélite
Norman Stillman (1996)

Code de I'lndigénat
Phillip C. Naylor (1996)

Cohen, Ge'ula
Gregory S. Mahler
Yaakov Shavit (1996)

Cole, USS
George R. Wilkes

Colonialism in the Middle East
Peter Sluglett

Colonial Office, Great Britain
Bernard Wasserstein

Colons
John Ruedy (1996)

Comité d'Action Marocaine (CAM)
Bruce Maddy-Weitzman (1996)

Comité de Coordination et d'Exécution
John Ruedy (1996)

Comité Juif Algérien d'études Sociales
Norman Stillman (1996)

Comité Révolutionnaire d'Unité et d'Action (CRUA)
John Ruedy (1996)

Commercial and Navigation Treaties
David Waldner (1996)

Committee for Defense of Freedom and Human Rights
Neguin Yavari (1996)

Committee for the Defense of Legitimate Rights
Anthony B. Toth

Committee for Union and Progress
Hasan Kayali (1996)

Communication
Michael R. Fischbach
Arthur Goldschmidt (1996)

Communism in the Middle East
Joel S. Beinin

Compagnie Française des Pétroles (CFP)
Zachary Karabell (1996)

Condominium Agreement (1899)
Ali E. Hillal Dessouki (1996)

Confédération Démocratique du Travail (CDT)
Bruce Maddy-Weitzman (1996)

Confederation of Iranian Students
Afshin Matin-asgari

Confederation of Turkish Trade Unions
Frank Tachau (1996)

Congress of Ottoman Liberals (1902)
David Waldner (1996)

Conseil National de la Révolution Algérienne (CNRA)
John Ruedy (1996)

Constantine
Dirk Vandewalle (1996)

Constantinople
Paul S. Rowe

Constitutional Bloc
As'ad AbuKhalil (1996)

Constitutional Democratic Rally
Vanesa Casanova-Fernandez

Constitutional Revolution
Eric Hooglund (1996)

Constitutional Revolution, Impact on Women
Mangol Bayat

Coordination des Archs (Algeria)
Robert Mortimer

Coptic Museum
Donald Malcolm Reid
Donald Spanel (1996)

Copts
Milad Hanna
Gawdat Gabra
Donald Spanel (1996)

Corcos Family
Norman Stillman (1996)

Corsairs
Jerome Bookin-Weiner (1996)

Cossack Brigade
Jack Bubon (1996)

Cotton
Richard W. Bulliet (1996)

Council for Development and Reconstruction (CDR)
As'ad AbuKhalil
George E. Irani (1996)

Cox, Percy
Michael R. Fischbach
Peter Sluglett (1996)

Crane, Charles R.
William L. Cleveland
Mia Bloom (1996)

Creech Jones, Arthur
Bernard Wasserstein

Crémieux Decree
Kenneth J. Perkins (1996)

Crimean War
C. Max Kortepeter (1996)

Crimes of Honor
Lynn Welchman

Crossman, Richard
Bernard Wasserstein

Curiel Family
Michael M. Laskier (1996)

Curzon, George Nathaniel
Eric Hooglund (1996)

Cyprus
Alexander Kitroeff (1996)

Cyprus Convention (1878)
Zachary Karabell (1996)

Cyrenaica
Ronald Bruce St John
John L. Wright (1996)

Cyril IV
Donald Spanel (1996)

Cyril V
Donald Spanel (1996)

Cyril VI
Donald Spanel (1996)

D

Dabbagh, Marzieh
Janet Afary

Dabbas, Charles
As'ad AbuKhalil (1996)

Daddah, Mokhtar Ould
Bruce Maddy-Weitzman

Daftari, Ahmad Matin
Neguin Yavari (1996)

Dağlarca, Fazil Hüsnü
Kathleen R. F. Burrill (1996)

Dahlan, Muhammad
Michael R. Fischbach

Damanhur
Arthur Goldschmidt (1996)

Damascus
Fred H. Lawson (1996)

Damascus Affair (1840)
Michael R. Fischbach
Jane Gerber (1996)

Damascus University
Abdul-Karim Rafeq (1996)

Dammam, al-
J. E. Peterson

Dance
Maria F. Curtis

Daneshvar, Simin
Eric Hooglund
Michael C. Hillmann (1996)

Dar al Daʿwa wa al-Irshad
Donald Malcolm Reid (1996)

Dar al-Fonun
Parvaneh Pourshariati (1996)

Dar al-Islam
Cyrus Moshaver (1996)

Dar al-Kutub al-Misriyya
Donald Malcolm Reid

Dar al-Moʿallamin
Grant Farr

Dar al-Ulum
Donald Malcolm Reid

D'Arcy Concession (1901)
Eric Hooglund
Daniel E. Spector (1996)

Dardanelles, Treaty of the (1809)
Daniel E. Spector (1996)

Darülfünün
Zachary Karabell (1996)

Darwaza, Muhammad Izzat
Michael R. Fischbach (1996)

Darwish, Ishaq
Elizabeth Thompson (1996)

Darwish, Mahmud
Robyn Creswell
Kamal Boullatta (1996)

Darwish, Sayyid
Virginia Danielson (1996)

Dashnak Party
Rouben P. Adalian

Dashti, Ali
Eric Hooglund
Michael C. Hillmann (1996)

Dates
Albertine Jwaideh (1996)

Daud, Muhammad
M. Nazif Shahrani (1996)

Daʾud Pasha
As'ad AbuKhalil (1996)

Daʿwa al-Islamiyya, al-
Maysam J. al Faruqi

Dayan, Moshe
Nathan Yanai (1996)

Dayan, Yael
Meron Medzini

Dayr al-Zawr Province
Abdul-Karim Rafeq (1996)

Dayr Yasin
Don Peretz

Dead Sea
Peter Gubser (1996)

Dead Sea Scrolls
Mia Bloom (1996)

De Bunsen, Maurice
Zachary Karabell (1996)

Decentralization Party
Hasan Kayali (1996)

Declaration of La Celle St. Cloud
Zachary Karabell (1996)

Dede Zekai
David Waldner (1996)

Deedes, Wyndham
Elizabeth Thompson (1996)

De Gaulle, Charles
John P. Spagnolo (1996)

De Haan, Ya'akov Yisrael
Bryan Daves (1996)

Dehkhoda, Ali Akbar
Michael C. Hillmann (1996)

Dellalzade İsmail
David Waldner (1996)

Delouvrier, Paul
Phillip C. Naylor

Delta
Arthur Goldschmidt (1996)

Delta Barrages
Gregory B. Baecher
David Waldner (1996)

De Menasce Family
Michael M. Laskier (1996)

Demetrius II
Donald Spanel (1996)

Demirel, Süleyman
Burçak Keskin-Kozat
Nermin Abadan-Unat (1996)

Democratic Organization of Afghan Women (1965)
Senzil Nawid

Democratic Party of Azerbaijan
Audrey L. Altstadt (1996)

Democratic Party of Kurdistan (Iran; KDP)
Parvaneh Pourshariati

Democratic Party of Kurdistan (Iraq)
Chris Kutschera

Democratic Women's Association (Tunisia)
Angel M. Foster

Democrat Party
David Waldner (1996)

Denktash, Rauf
Pierre Oberling (1996)

Dentz, Henri-Fernand
George R. Wilkes

Derakhshandeh, Puran
Roxanne Varzi

Desalinization
Karim Hamdy
John F. Kolars (1996)

Deserts
John F. Kolars (1996)

Devrim, Izzet Melih
David Waldner (1996)

Dhahran
J. E. Peterson

Dhimma
Ilai Alon

Dhow
Malcolm C. Peck (1996)

Dhufar
Calvin H. Allen, Jr
Malcolm C. Peck (1996)

Dhufar Rebellion
Eric Hooglund
Malcolm C. Peck (1996)

Diaspora
Gabriel Sheffer

Diba, Farah
Haleh Vaziri

Dib, Mohammed
Phillip C. Naylor

Didouche, Mourad
Phillip C. Naylor (1996)

Dilmun
Emile A. Nakhleh (1996)

Dimona
Yehuda Gradus
Zachary Karabell (1996)

Dinka
Robert O. Collins (1996)

Dinshaway Incident (1906)
Arthur Goldschmidt (1996)

Diseases
Nancy Gallagher

Diwan
Mia Bloom (1996)

Diyarbakir
Eric Hooglund
Elizabeth Thompson (1996)

Djaout, Taher
Aida A. Bamia (1996)

Djebar, Assia
Marilyn Booth

Djemaʿa
Thomas G. Penchoen (1996)

Djerba
Laurence Michalak (1996)

Dlimi, Ahmed
Matthew S. Gordon (1996)

Doha
Anthony B. Toth
Malcolm C. Peck (1996)

Dolmabahçe Palace
Elizabeth Thompson (1996)

Dönme
Benjamin Braude

Dor Deʿa
Norman Stillman (1996)

Dorner, Dalia
Meron Medzini

Dost Mohammad Barakzai
Grant Farr (1996)

Douʿaji, Ali al-
Aida A. Bamia (1996)

Doughty, Charles
Benjamin Braude

Dowlatabadi, Mahmoud
Eric Hooglund

Dragomans
Zachary Karabell (1996)

Dreyfus Affair
Chaim I. Waxman

Drugs and Narcotics
W. Kenneth Thompson (1996)

Drummond–Wolff Convention
Arthur Goldschmidt (1996)

Druze
Samy S. Swayd
Robert Betts (1996)

Druze Revolts
As'ad AbuKhalil (1996)

Dual Containment
Eric Hooglund
F. Gregory Gause III (1996)

Dual Control
Arthur Goldschmidt (1996)

Dubai
Anthony B. Toth
Malcolm C. Peck (1996)

Dubs, Adolph
Grant Farr (1996)

Dufferin Report (1883)
David Waldner (1996)

Dukan Dam
Albertine Jwaideh (1996)

Dulles, John Foster
Neil Caplan
Zachary Karabell (1996)

Durand Line
Grant Farr

Durrani Dynasty
Ashraf Ghani

E

Eastern Desert
Arthur Goldschmidt (1996)

Eastern Orthodox Church
Elizabeth Thompson (1996)

Eastern Question
J. C. Hurewitz (1996)

East India Company
Jenab Tutunji (1996)

Ebadi, Shirin
Ziba Mir-Hosseini

Eban, Abba (Aubrey)
Gregory S. Mahler (1996)

Ebtekar, Maʿsumeh
Nayereh Tohidi

Ecevit, Bülent
Burçak Keskin-Kozat
Nermin Abadan-Unat (1996)

Ecevit, Rahşan
Burçak Keskin-Kozat

Economic and Military Aid
Paul Rivlin
Marvin G. Weinbaum (1996)

Economics
Jean-François Seznec

Eddé, Emile
Sami A. Ofeish

Eddé, Raymond
Michael R. Fischbach
Guilain P. Denoeux (1996)

Eden, Anthony
Zachary Karabell (1996)

Edirne
Eric Hooglund

Education
Linda Herrera

Efflatoun, Inji
Jessica Winegar

Ege University
Burçak Keskin-Kozat
I. Metin Kunt (1996)

Egypt
Arthur Goldschmidt
Ali E. Hillal Dessouki (1996)

Egyptian Feminist Union
Marilyn Booth

Egyptian Geographical Society
Donald Malcolm Reid (1996)

Egyptian–Israeli Peace Treaty (1979)
Laurie Z. Eisenberg

Egyptian Museum
Donald Malcolm Reid

Egyptian Women's Union
Arthur Goldschmidt (1996)

8 Mars Newspaper
Laurie King-Irani

Eisenhower, Dwight David
Zachary Karabell (1996)

Eitan, Rafael
Martin Malin (1996)

Eldem, Sedad Hakki
Elizabeth Thompson (1996)

Elites
Donald Maolcolm Reid (1996)

Emergency Regulations
Benjamin Joseph (1996)

Entebbe Operation
Zev Maghen (1996)

Ente Nazionale Idrocarboni (ENI)
Dirk Vandewalle (1996)

Enver Paşa
Hasan Kayali (1996)

Eqbal, Manouchehr
Neguin Yavari

Erbakan, Necmeddin
M. Hakan Yavuz
Frank Tachau (1996)

Erbil, Leyla
David Waldner (1996)

Erdoğan, Tayyip
M. Hakan Yavuz

Eretz Yisrael
Chaim I. Waxman

Ersoy, Mehmet Akif
Elizabeth Thompson (1996)

Ertuğrul, Muhsin
Elizabeth Thompson (1996)

Erzurum
Eric Hooglund
Elizabeth Thompson (1996)

Erzurum Congress (1919)
Elizabeth Thompson (1996)

Erzurum, Treaty of (1823)
Eric Hooglund
Zachary Karabell (1996)

Esendal, Memduh Şevket
Elizabeth Thompson (1996)

Esfandiary, Fereydun
Eric Hooglund
Michael C. Hillmann (1996)

Eshkol, Levi
Martin Malin (1996)

Eskinazi, Roza
Stavros Frangos

Esmati-Wardak, Masuma
Senzil Nawid

Etemadi, Saleha Faruq
Senzil Nawid

Ethiopian Jews
Emanuela Trevisan Semi
Shalvah Weil (1996)

Euphrates Dam
John R. Clark (1996)

Evian Accords (1962)
Phillip C. Naylor

Evren, Kenan
M. Hakan Yavuz
David Waldner (1996)

Exodus (1947)
Rachel Weissbrod

Eyüboğlu, Bedri Rahmi
Elizabeth Thompson (1996)

Ezra and Nehemiah Operations
Nissim Rejwan (1996)

F

Fadlallah, Shaykh Husayn
As'ad AbuKhalil

Fahd ibn Abd al-Aziz Al Saʿud
Anthony B. Toth
Malcolm C. Peck (1996)

Fahd Plan (1981)
Jenab Tutunji (1996)

Fahmi, Mahmud Pasha
Maysam J. al Faruqi

Faisal ibn Abd al-Aziz Al Saʿud
Malcolm C. Peck (1996)

Faisal I ibn Hussein
Reeva S. Simon (1996)

Faisal II ibn Ghazi
Peter Sluglett (1996)

Faisal–Weizmann Agreements
Neil Caplan (1996)

Falconry
Elizabeth Thompson (1996)

Fanon, Frantz
John Ruedy (1996)

Fao Peninsula
Albertine Jwaideh (1996)

Faqir, Fadia
Elise Salem

Faraj, Maysaloun
Jessica Winegar

Faraj, Murad
Michael M. Laskier (1996)

Farʾa, Wahiba
Susanne Dahlgren

Farès, Nabile
Laurie King-Irani

Farhad, Ghulam Muhammad
Grant Farr (1996)

Farhat al-Zawi
Rachel Simon (1996)

Farhi Family
Michael M. Laskier (1996)

Farhud
Sylvia G. Haim (1996)

Farid, Nagwa Kamal
Carolyn Fluehr-Lobban

Farmanfarma, Abd al-Hoseyn Mirza
Mansoureh Ettehadieh (1996)

Farmanfarmian, Settareh
Cherie Taraghi

Farouk
Robert L. Tignor (1996)

Farrokhzad, Forugh
Michael C. Hillmann (1996)

Fashoda Incident (1898)
Zachary Karabell (1996)

Fasi, Allal al-
C. R. Pennell (1996)

Fasi, Muhammad al-
C. R. Pennell (1996)

Fassih, Ismail
Pardis Minuchehr (1996)

Fatah, al-
Michael R. Fischbach
Michael Dunn (1996)

Fatat, al-
Muhammad Muslih (1996)

Fath Ali Shah Qajar
Mansoureh Ettehadieh (1996)

Fatwa
Maysam J. al Faruqi
Wael B. Hallaq (1996)

Fawwaz, Zaynab
Marilyn Booth

Fayruz
Christopher Reed Stone

Faysal ibn Turki Al Saʿud
Malcolm C. Peck (1996)

Faysal, Tujan
Curtis R. Ryan

Fedaʾiyan-e Islam
Ervand Abrahamian

Fedaʾiyan-e Khalq
Ervand Abrahamian

Female Genital Mutilation
Carolyn Fluehr-Lobban

Feraoun, Mouloud
Phillip C. Naylor (1996)

Ferit, Damat Mehmet
Elizabeth Thompson (1996)

Ferman
Elizabeth Thompson (1996)

Fertile Crescent
Zachary Karabell (1996)

Fertile Crescent Unity Plans
H. G. Balfour-Paul (1996)

Fes, Treaty of (1912)
Matthew S. Gordon (1996)

Fez, Morocco
Donna Lee Bowen (1996)

Fezzan
John L. Wright (1996)

Fidaʾiyyun
Philip Mattar
Lawrence Tal (1996)

Film
Roxanne Varzi

Fiqh
Maysam J. al Faruqi

Fish and Fishing
Eric Hooglund

Flapan, Simha
Gregory S. Mahler
Zachary Karabell (1996)

Fly Whisk Incident (1827)
Kenneth J. Perkins (1996)

Food: Ash
Neguin Yavari (1996)

Food: Baklava
Clifford A. Wright (1996)

Food: Borek
Cyrus Moshaver (1996)

Food: Bulgur
Clifford A. Wright (1996)

Food: Chelow
Clifford A. Wright (1996)

Food: Coffee
Clifford A. Wright (1996)

Food: Couscous
Clifford A. Wright (1996)

Food: Dolma
Clifford A. Wright (1996)

Food: Felafel
Zachary Karabell (1996)

Food: Ful
Clifford A. Wright (1996)

Food: Hummus
Zachary Karabell (1996)

Food: Kufta
Clifford A. Wright (1996)

Food: Mansaf
Zachary Karabell (1996)

Food: Mazza
Jenab Tutunji (1996)

Food: Muhammara
Jenab Tutunji (1996)

Food: Mujaddara
Jenab Tutunji (1996)

Food: Mulukhiyya
Tayeb El-Hibri (1996)

Food: Olives
Jenab Tutunji (1996)

Food: Pilaf
Clifford A. Wright (1996)

Food: Shashilik
Clifford A. Wright (1996)

Food: Shawarma
Clifford A. Wright (1996)

Food: Shish Kebab
Clifford A. Wright (1996)

Food: Tabbula
Jenab Tutunji (1996)

Food: Tahina
Zachary Karabell (1996)

Food: Tajin
Clifford A. Wright (1996)

Foreign Office, Great Britain
Roger Adelson

Forqan
Ervand Abrahamian

Forughi, Mirza Mohammad Ali Khan Zaka al-Molk
Neguin Yavari (1996)

Foucauld, Charles Eugène de
Phillip C. Naylor (1996)

Fourth Shore, The
George Joffe (1996)

France and the Middle East
John P. Spagnolo (1996)

Franco–Tunisian Conventions
Zachary Karabell (1996)

Franjiyya Family
Michael R. Fischbach

Franjiyya, Sulayman
Michael R. Fischbach
As'ad AbuKhalil (1996)

Freedom Movement (Nezhat-e Azadi Iran)
Eric Hooglund
Neguin Yavari (1996)

Freedom Party
Frank Tachau (1996)

Free French Mandate
Fred H. Lawson (1996)

Freemasons
Reeva S. Simon (1996)

Free Officers, Egypt
Ali E. Hillal Dessouki (1996)

Free Officers, Yemen
Robert D. Burrowes (1996)

Free Republican Party
Frank Tachau (1996)

Free Yemenis
Robert D. Burrowes (1996)

Freier, Recha
George R. Wilkes

French Foreign Legion
Kenneth J. Perkins (1996)

Frischmann, David
Ann Kahn (1996)

Front de Libération Nationale (FLN)
John Ruedy (1996)

Front for the Liberation of South Yemen
Robert D. Burrowes (1996)

Front Islamique du Salut (FIS)
Bradford Dillman (1996)

Front pour la Défense des Institutions Constitutionelles (FDIC)
Bruce Maddy-Weitzman (1996)

Fu'ad
Robert L. Tignor (1996)

Fujayra
Anthony B. Toth
Malcolm C. Peck (1996)

Fujayra–Sharjah Conflict
Malcolm C. Peck (1996)

Fundamental Pact
Matthew S. Gordon (1996)

Futuwwa
Guilain P. Denoeux (1996)

G

Gafsa Incident (1980)
Matthew S. Gordon (1996)

Gailani, Ahmad
Grant Farr

Galata
Elizabeth Thompson (1996)

Galatasaray Lycée
Anthony B. Toth
I. Metin Kunt (1996)

Galilee
Zev Maghen (1996)

Galilee, Sea of
Bryan Daves (1996)

Gallei Tzahal
Ann Kahn (1996)

Gallipoli
Sara Reguer (1996)

Gamal, Samiyah
Roberta L. Dougherty

Ganim, Halil
Elizabeth Thompson (1996)

Ganji, Akbar
Babak Rahimi

Garang, John
Carolyn Fluehr-Lobban
Paul Martin (1996)

Gardanne Mission
Daniel E. Spector (1996)

Gaspirali, Ismail Bey
Uli Schamiloglu (1996)

Gaza (City)
Mallika Good

Gaza Strip
Sara M. Roy

Geagea, Samir
As'ad AbuKhalil
Guilain P. Denoeux (1996)

Gebeyli, Claire
Mona Takieddine Amyuni

Gecekondu
Eric Hooglund

Gencer, Leyla
Filiz Ali

Genç Kalemler
Elizabeth Thompson (1996)

Gender: Gender and the Economy
Khaled Islaih

Gender: Gender and Education
Rachel Christina

Gender: Gender and Law
Laurie King-Irani

Gender: Gender and Politics
Wanda C. Krause

Gender: Study of
Laura Rice

General Directorate on the Status and Problems of Women
Burçak Keskin-Kozat

General Federation of Iraqi Women
Elizabeth Fernea

General People's Committees
Lisa Anderson (1996)

General People's Congress (GPC)
Lisa Anderson (1996)

General Tunisian Union of Students (UGTE)
Larry A. Barrie (1996)

General Union of Palestinian Women's Committees (GUPWC)
Mallika Good

General Women's Union of Syria
Mirna Lattouf

Geneva Peace Conference (1973)
Benjamin Joseph (1996)

Geography
John F. Kolars (1996)

Germany and the Middle East
Philip Mattar
Reeva S. Simon (1996)

Gezira Scheme
Ann M. Lesch (1996)

Gezira Sporting Club
Jean-Marc R. Oppenheim (1996)

Ghab, al-
Abdul-Karim Rafeq (1996)

Ghali, Boutros
Arthur Goldschmidt (1996)

Ghallab, Abd al-Karim
Aida A. Bamia

Ghanim, al-
Mary Ann Tétreault

Ghanim, Fathi
Maysam J. al Faruqi

Ghanmi, Azza
Laura Rice

Ghannouchi, Rached
Matthew S. Gordon (1996)

Gharb
Rahma Bourqia (1996)

Gharbzadegi
Michael C. Hillmann (1996)

Ghashmi, Ahmad Husayn
Robert D. Burrowes

Ghassemlou, Abdul Rahman
Amir Hassanpour

Ghazali, Muhammad al-
George R. Wilkes

Ghazali, Zaynab al-
Marilyn Booth

Ghazi ibn Faisal
Peter Sluglett (1996)

Ghorbal, Ashraf
George R. Wilkes
David Waldner (1996)

Ghoussoub, Mai
Jessica Winegar

Ghozali, Ahmed
Phillip C. Naylor

Ghuri, Emile al-
Philip Mattar
Muhammad Muslih (1996)

GIA (Armed Islamic Groups)
Azzedine G. Mansour

Giado Concentration Camp
Norman Stillman (1996)

Gibran, Khalil
As'ad AbuKhalil (1996)

Gilboa, Amir
Zvia Ginor (1996)

Giza
Arthur Goldschmidt (1996)

Glawi Family, al-
Rahma Bourqia (1996)

Glubb, John Bagot
Avi Shlaim (1996)

Gökalp, Ziya
Taha Parla (1996)

Golan Heights
Yehuda Gradus
Muhammad Muslih (1996)

Goldberg, Leah
Ann Kahn (1996)

Golden Square
Reeva S. Simon (1996)

Goldmann, Nahum
Gregory S. Mahler
Neil Caplan

Golestan, Ebrahim
Eric Hooglund

Golestan Palace
Parvaneh Pourshariati (1996)

Golpayagani, Mohammad Reza
Hamid Algar (1996)

Golshiri, Houshang
Eric Hooglund
Pardis Minuchehr (1996)

Golsorkhi, Khosrow
Afshin Matin-asgari

Gordon, Aaron David
Donna Robinson Divine

Gordon, Charles
Jean-Marc R. Oppenheim (1996)

Gorst, John Eldon
Peter Mellini (1996)

Government
Oliver Benjamin Hemmerle
Bernard Reich (1996)

Gozanski, Tamar
Laurie King-Irani

Grand Mosque
Anthony B. Toth
Malcolm C. Peck (1996)

Graziani, Rodolfo
George Joffe (1996)

Greater Syria
Abdul-Karim Rafeq (1996)

Greater Syria Plan
Zachary Karabell (1996)

Great Game, The
Zachary Karabell (1996)

Greco–Turkish War (1897)
Eric Hooglund
Alexander Kitroeff (1996)

Greeks in the Middle East
Alexander Kitroeff (1996)

Greek War of Independence
Alexander Kitroeff (1996)

Greenberg, Uri Zvi
Ann Kahn (1996)

Green Book
Lisa Anderson (1996)

Green Line
David Newman
Bryan Daves (1996)

Green March
Matthew S. Gordon (1996)

Griboyedov Incident
Parvaneh Pourshariati (1996)

Grivas, Georgios Theodoros
Zachary Karabell (1996)

Grobba, Fritz Konrad Ferdinand
Francis R. Nicosia (1996)

Grossman, Haika
George R. Wilkes

Gruenbaum, Yizhak
Zachary Karabell (1996)

Guest Workers
Eric Hooglund

Guilds
Richard W. Bulliet (1996)

Guinness, Walter Edward
Jenab Tutunji (1996)

Gülbenkian, Calouste
David Waldner (1996)

Gülen, Fetullah
M. Hakan Yavuz

Gulf Cooperation Council
Anthony B. Toth
Emile A. Nakhleh (1996)

Gulf Crisis (1990–1991)
Philip Mattar (1996)

Gulf of Oman
J. E. Peterson

Gulf of Suez
Arthur Goldschmidt (1996)

Gulf War (1991)
Daniel E. Spector

Gülhane Imperial Edict (1839)
Cemil Aydin

Güney, Yilmaz
Elizabeth Thompson (1996)

Guri, Chaim
Adina Friedman
Ann Kahn (1996)

Gur, Mordechai
Gregory S. Mahler
Zachary Karabell (1996)

Gürpinar, Hüseyin Rahmi
Elizabeth Thompson (1996)

Gürsel, Cemal
David Waldner (1996)

Gush Emunim
David Newman

H

Ha-avarah Agreement
Michael R. Marrus

Habash, George
George R. Wilkes
Mouin Rabbani (1996)

Habibi, Emile
Michael R. Fischbach

Habibollah Khan
Grant Farr (1996)

Habib, Philip Charles
Zachary Karabell (1996)

Habous
Vanesa Casanova-Fernandez

Hacene, Farouk Zehar
Aida A. Bamia

Hacettepe University
Burçak Keskin-Kozat
I. Metin Kunt (1996)

Ha-Cohen, Mordechai
Maurice M. Roumani (1996)

Hadassah
Mia Bloom (1996)

Haddad, Malek
Phillip C. Naylor (1996)

Haddad, Saʿd
David Waldner (1996)

Haddad, Wadi
Michael R. Fischbach
Lawrence Tal (1996)

Hadith
Maysam J. al Faruqi
Wael B. Hallaq (1996)

Hadj, Messali al-
Phillip C. Naylor (1996)

Hadramawt
Sumit Mandal (1996)

Hafiz, Abd al-Halim
Virginia Danielson (1996)

Hafiz, Amin al-
Michael R. Fischbach
Muhammad Muslih (1996)

Haganah
Pierre M. Atlas

Haggiag Family
Maurice M. Roumani (1996)

Ha-Halutz
Donna Robinson Divine

Haifa
Philip Mattar

Haifa University
Zachary Karabell (1996)

Haigazian College
George E. Irani (1996)

Haik
Rhimou Bernikho-Canin (1996)

Hajir, Abd al-Hoseyn
Neguin Yavari (1996)

Hajji Baba of Ispahan
Michael C. Hillmann (1996)

Hajri, Abdullah al-
Robert D. Burrowes (1996)

Hakim, Adnan al-
As'ad AbuKhalil (1996)

Hakim Family
Amatzia Baram (1996)

Hakim, Tawfiq al-
Roger Allen (1996)

Halakhah
Ephraim Tabory
Samuel C. Heilman (1996)

Halukka
Chaim I. Waxman

Hama
Geoffrey D. Schad
Abdul-Karim Rafeq (1996)

Hamadan
Parvaneh Pourshariati

Hamadi, Sabri
As'ad AbuKhalil (1996)

Hamama, Faten
Andrew Flibbert
David Waldner (1996)

Hama Massacre
Fred H. Lawson

HAMAS
Michael R. Fischbach

Hamas (Movement for a Peaceful Society)
Emad Eldin Shahin

Hamdi, Ibrahim al-
Manfred W. Wenner (1996)

Hamid al-Din Family
Robert D. Burrowes (1996)

Hamina, Mohammed Lakhdar
Phillip C. Naylor (1996)

Hammarskjöld, Dag
Brian Urquhart

Hammer, Zevulun
Gregory S. Mahler
Martin Malin (1996)

Hamra Riots
Michael R. Fischbach (1996)

Hamrouche, Mouloud
Phillip C. Naylor

Hamzawi, Rashid al-
Aida A. Bamia

Hanafi, Hasan
As'ad AbuKhalil

Hanafi School of Law
Wael B. Hallaq (1996)

Hananu, Ibrahim
Michael R. Fischbach
Muhammad Muslih (1996)

Hanbali School of Law
Wael B. Hallaq (1996)

Hand of Fatima
Laurence Michalak (1996)

Hanoune, Louisa
Robert Mortimer

Haq, al-
Michael R. Fischbach

Harel, Isser
Ian Black
Zev Maghen (1996)

Harem
Carolyn Fluehr-Lobban

Hareven, Shulamit
Adina Friedman
Nili Gold (1996)

Hariri, Rafiq Baha'uddin al-
As'ad AbuKhalil
Bassam Namani (1996)

Harkabi, Yehoshafat
Mordechai Bar-On
Martin Malin (1996)

Harkis
Phillip C. Naylor (1996)

Harratin
Rahma Bourqia (1996)

Harriman, W. Averell
Zachary Karabell (1996)

Hasa, al-
Anthony B. Toth
Malcolm C. Peck (1996)

Hasan, Fa'iq
Amatzia Baram (1996)

Hasan, Hani al-
Michael R. Fischbach
Lawrence Tal (1996)

Hasani, Taj al-Din al-
George E. Irani (1996)

Hasan, Khalid al-
Michael R. Fischbach
Lawrence Tal (1996)

Hashemi, Faezeh
Azadeh Kian-Thiébaut

Hashim, Ibrahim
Jenab Tutunji (1996)

Hashimi, Taha al-
Ayad al-Qazzaz (1996)

Hashimite House (House of Hashim)
Michael R. Fischbach

Hashimi, Yasin al-
Michael R. Fischbach
Mamoon A. Zaki (1996)

Ha-Shomer
Elizabeth Thompson (1996)

Ha-Shomer Ha-Tza'ir
Chaim I. Waxman

Hasidim
Chaim I. Waxman

Haskalah
Martin Malin (1996)

Hass, Amira
Khaled Islaih

Hassan I
Rémy Leveau (1996)

Hassan II
Rémy Leveau

Ha-Tikva
George R. Wilkes

Hatim Sultans of Hamdan
Robert D. Burrowes

Hatoum, Mona
Jessica Winegar

Hawatma, Nayif
Michael R. Fischbach

Hawi, George
Guilain P. Denoeux (1996)

Hawi, Khalil
Guilain P. Denoeux (1996)

Hawrani, Akram al-
Muhammad Muslih (1996)

Haycraft Commission (1921)
Philip Mattar

Hayim, Yusef
Sylvia G. Haim (1996)

Haykal, Muhammad Hasanayn
Ahmad S. Moussalli
Arthur Goldschmidt (1996)

Haykal, Muhammad Husayn
Arthur Goldschmidt (1996)

Haza, Ofra
Laurie King-Irani

Hazara
Grant Farr

Hazaz, Hayyim
Ann Kahn (1996)

Hazzan, Elijah Bekhor
Norman Stillman (1996)

Hebrew
Ruth Raphaeli (1996)

Hebrew University of Jerusalem
Pierre M. Atlas

Hebron
Michael R. Fischbach
Benjamin Joseph (1996)

Hedayat, Sadegh
Eric Hooglund
Michael C. Hillmann (1996)

Hekmatyar, Golbuddin
Grant Farr

Helmand River
Grant Farr

Herat
Grant Farr

Herzl, Theodor
Shimon Avish (1996)

Herzog, Chaim
Meron Medzini

Herzog, Izhak Halevi
Chaim I. Waxman (1996)

Herzog, Ya'acov David
Meron Medzini

Heskayl, Sasson
Sasson Somekh (1996)

Hess, Moses
Zachary Karabell (1996)

Hezb-e Islami
Grant Farr

Hibbat Zion
Donna Robinson Divine (1996)

High Commissioners (Palestine)
Philip Mattar

High State Council (Algeria)
John Ruedy

Hijab
Laurie King-Irani

Hijaz
Anthony B. Toth
Khalid Y. Blankinship (1996)

Hijaz Railroad
David Waldner (1996)

Hikma University, al-
John J. Donohue (1996)

Hilal, al-
Thomas Philipp (1996)

Hillel, Shlomo
Meron Medzini

Hilmi, Ahmad
Lawrence Tal (1996)

Hilu, Charles
As'ad AbuKhalil (1996)

Hilu, Pierre
As'ad AbuKhalil

Hindu Kush Mountains
Zachary Karabell (1996)

Hinnawi, Sami al-
Abdul-Karim Rafeq (1996)

Hirawi, Ilyas al-
As'ad AbuKhalil

Histadrut
Paul Rivlin (1996)

Historiography
John T. Chalcraft

Hizbullah
As'ad AbuKhalil

Hobeika, Elie
As'ad AbuKhalil
George E. Irani (1996)

Hodeida
Manfred W. Wenner

Hoffman, Yoel
Adina Friedman
Nili Gold (1996)

Holocaust
Dan Michman

Holy Land
Michael R. Fischbach
Reeva S. Simon (1996)

Holy Sepulchre, Church of the
Michael R. Fischbach
Jenab Tutunji (1996)

Homs
Fred H. Lawson (1996)

Hope-Simpson Commission (1930)
Philip Mattar

Hoss, Salim al-
As'ad AbuKhalil

Hostage Crises
Eric Hooglund

Hourani, Albert
Peter Sluglett

Hoveyda, Amir Abbas
Afshin Matin-asgari
Neguin Yavari (1996)

Hula Swamps
Donna Robinson Divine

Human Rights
Lynn Welchman
Paul Martin (1996)

Humphreys, Francis
Zachary Karabell (1996)

Hunchak Party
As'ad AbuKhalil (1996)

Hunkar-Iskelesi, Treaty of (1833)
Zachary Karabell (1996)

Hürriyet
Stephanie Capparell (1996)

Husari, Sati al-
Rita Stephan

Husayni, Abd al-Qadir al-
Muhammad Muslih (1996)

Husayn ibn Ali
Michael R. Fischbach
Zachary Karabell (1996)

Husayni Family, al-
Muhammad Muslih (1996)

Husayni, Hind al-
Ellen L. Fleischmann

Husayni, Husayn al-
As'ad AbuKhalil

Husayni, Jamal al-
Muhammad Muslih (1996)

Husayni, Muhammad Amin al-
Philip Mattar

Husayni, Musa Kazim al-
Michael R. Fischbach
Muhammad Muslih (1996)

Husayn–McMahon Correspondence (1915–1916)
Philip Mattar

Husayn, Taha
Roger Allen (1996)

Hussein ibn Talal
Michael R. Fischbach
Peter Gubser (1996)

Husseini, Rana
Isis Nusair

Hussein, Saddam
Louay Bahry

Hut, Shafiq al-
George R. Wilkes
Mouin Rabbani (1996)

I

Ibadiyya
Tayeb El-Hibri (1996)

Ibn Musa, Ahmad
Bruce Maddy-Weitzman (1996)

Ibn Tulun Mosque
Jonathan M. Bloom (1996)

Ibrahim, Abdullah
Ana Torres-Garcia
C. R. Pennell (1996)

Ibrahim, Fatima Ahmed
Sondra Hale

Ibrahimi, Ahmed Taleb
Phillip C. Naylor

Ibrahimi, Bashir
Phillip C. Naylor (1996)

Ibrahim ibn Muhammad Ali
Ali E. Hillal Dessouki (1996)

Ibrahimi, Lakhdar al-
Ana Torres-Garcia
Elizabeth Thompson (1996)

Ibrahim, Izzat
Ayad al-Qazzaz (1996)

Ibrahim, Muhammad Hafiz
Kenneth S. Mayers (1996)

Ibrahim, Saʿad al-Din
Rita Stephan

İdadi Schools
Elizabeth Thompson (1996)

Idlibi, Ulfat al-
Marilyn Booth

Idlib Province
Abdul-Karim Rafeq (1996)

Idris al-Sayyid Muhammad al-Sanusi
Julie Zuckerman (1996)

Idrisids
Manfred W. Wenner (1996)

Idris, Yusuf
Roger Allen (1996)

Ifni
Bruce Maddy-Weitzman

Ignatiev, Nikolas Pavlovich
Zachary Karabell (1996)

Ikha al-Watani Party
Peter Sluglett (1996)

Ikhlassi, Walid
Sabah Ghandour (1996)

Ikhwan
Anthony B. Toth
Malcolm C. Peck (1996)

Ilaysh, Muhammad
Khalid Blankinship

İlmiyye
Elizabeth Thompson (1996)

Imperialism in the Middle East and North Africa
John Ruedy
Richard C. Bulliet (1996)

Incense
Malcolm C. Peck (1996)

Industrialization
Waleed Hazbun
Rodney J. A. Wilson (1996)

Infitah
Arthur Goldschmidt (1996)

İnönü, Erdal
M. Hakan Yavuz
David Waldner (1996)

İnönü, İsmet
Walter F. Weiker (1996)

Institut d'Égypte
Donald Malcolm Reid

Institute for Palestine Studies
Michael R. Fischbach (1996)

Institute for Women's Studies in the Arab World (Lebanon)
Mirna Lattouf

Institute of Women's Studies of Bir Zeit University
Mona Ghali

Intelligence Organizations
Maria F. Curtis
Dale F. Eickelman (1996)

International, Dana
Yael Ben-zvi

International Debt Commission
Donald Malcolm Reid (1996)

International Monetary Fund
Khalil Gebara
David Waldner (1996)

Intifada (1987–1991)
Don Peretz

İpekci, Abdi
Elizabeth Thompson (1996)

Iqbal, Muhammad
Maysam J. al Faruqi

Iradeh-ye Melli Party
Parvaneh Pourshariati (1996)

Iran
Ahmad Ashraf

Iran–Contra Affair
Oliver Benjamin Hemmerle
Bryan Daves (1996)

Iranian Bureau of Women's Affairs
Azadeh Kian-Thiébaut

Iranian Languages
P. Oktor Skjaervo (1996)

Iranian Revolution (1979)
Eric Hooglund

Iran–Iraq War (1980–1988)
Eric Hooglund
Efraim Karsh (1996)

Iran Novin Party
Parvaneh Pourshariati (1996)

Iraq
Ayad Al-Qazzaz
Reeva S. Simon (1996)

Iraqi National Congress
Kristian P. Alexander

Iraqi Women's Union
Jacqueline Ismael

Iraq Petroleum Company (IPC)
Mary Ann Tétreault (1996)

Irbid
Michael R. Fischbach (1996)

Irgun Zvaʾi Leʾumi (IZL)
Chaim I. Waxman

Irshad An-Niswaan
Senzil Nawid

Iryani, Abd al-Rahman al-
Robert D. Burrowes

Isa Family, al-
Elizabeth Thompson (1996)

Isawiyya Brotherhood
Rahma Bourqia (1996)

Isfahan
Eric Hooglund
Farhad Arshad (1996)

Isfahan University
Parvaneh Pourshariati

Ishaaq, Kamala Ibrahim
Jessica Winegar

Ishaq, Adib
Zachary Karabell (1996)

Islah Party
Robert D. Burrowes
Jillian Schwedler (1996)

Islah Taleban Party
Parvaneh Pourshariati (1996)

Islam
Maysam J. al Faruqi
Tayeb El-Hibri (1996)

Islamic Action Front
Curtis R. Ryan

Islamic Congresses
Charles E. Butterworth
Martin Kramer (1996)

Islamic Countries Women Sport Solidarity Games (1992 and 1997)
Cherie Taraghi

Islamic Jihad
Michael R. Fischbach

Islamic Salvation Army (AIS)
Yahia Zoubir

Islamic University of Medina
Anthony B. Toth

Ismaʿil, Abd al-Fattah
Robert D. Burrowes (1996)

Ismaʿil ibn Ibrahim
Arthur Goldschmidt (1996)

Ismaʿili Shiʿism
Jenab Tutunji (1996)

Israel: Overview
Bernard Reich

Israel: Military and Politics
Mordechai Bar-On

Israel: Overview of Political Parties in
Gregory S. Mahler
Walter F. Weiker (1996)

Israel: Political Parties in
Gregory S. Mahler

Israeli Settlements
David Newman

Istanbul
Eric Hooglund
I. Metin Kunt (1996)

Istanbul Technical University
Niyazi Dalyanci (1996)

Istanbul University
Eric Hooglund
I. Metin Kunt (1996)

Istiqlal Party: Libya
John L. Wright (1996)

Istiqlal Party: Morocco
Bruce Maddy-Weitzman

Istiqlal Party: Palestine
Muhammad Muslih (1996)

Istiqlal Party: Syria
Abdul-Karim Rafeq (1996)

Italy in the Middle East
George Joffe (1996)

İzmir
Burçak Keskin-Kozat
I. Metin Kunt (1996)

İzmir Economic Congress
Frank Tachau (1996)

J

Jababdi, Latifa
Maria F. Curtis

Jabal al-Akhdar, Libya
Laurence Michalak (1996)

Jabal al-Akhdar, Oman
Anthony B. Toth

Jabal al-Khalil
Yehuda Gradus
Elizabeth Thompson (1996)

Jabal, Badawi al-
Abdul-Karim Rafeq (1996)

Jabal Druze
Abdul-Karim Rafeq (1996)

Jabal Nablus
Elizabeth Thompson (1996)

Jabal Shammar
Anthony B. Toth
Eleanor Abdella Doumato (1996)

Jaʿbari Family
Elizabeth Thompson (1996)

Jabarti, Abd al-Rahman al-
Walter Armbrust (1996)

Jabha al-Wataniyya, al-
Lisa Anderson (1996)

Jabotinsky, Vladimir Zeʾev
Pierre M. Atlas

Jabr, Salih
Ayad al-Qazzaz (1996)

Jacir, Emily
Jessica Winegar

Jadid, Salah
Michael R. Fischbach

Jaffa
Reeva S. Simon (1996)

Jallud, Abd al-Salam
Vanesa Casanova-Fernandez
Lisa Anderson (1996)

Jalluli Family
Larry A. Barrie (1996)

Jamahiriyya
Lisa Anderson (1996)

Jamali, Muhammad Fadhil al-
Michael R. Fischbach
Reeva S. Simon (1996)

Jamalzadeh, Mohammad Ali
Pardis Minuchehr (1996)

Jamiʿa al-Islamiyya, al-
Maria F. Curtis

Jamiʿat-e Islami
Grant Farr

Jangali
Neguin Yavari (1996)

Janissaries
Eric Hooglund
Avigdor Levy (1996)

Jarallah Family
Elizabeth Thompson (1996)

Jarash
Michael R. Fischbach

Jarring, Gunnar
Meron Medzini

Jawahiri, Muhammad Mahdi al-
Peter Sluglett (1996)

Jazeera, al-
Karim Hamdy

Jehad-e Sazandegi
Eric Hooglund

Jenin
Michael R. Fischbach

Jericho
Benjamin Joseph (1996)

Jericho Congress (1948)
Jenab Tutunji (1996)

Jerusalem
Michael R. Fischbach
Reeva S. Simon (1996)

Jewish Agency for Palestine
Donna Robinson Divine

Jewish Brigade
Bryan Daves (1996)

Jewish Colonial Trust
Jenab Tutunji (1996)

Jewish Colonization Association
Bryan Daves (1996)

Jewish Legion
Neil Caplan
Zachary Karabell (1996)

Jewish National Fund
Paul Rivlin

Jews in the Middle East
Harvey E. Goldberg
Norman Stillman (1996)

Jezreel Valley
Geremy Forman

Jibril, Ahmad
Michael R. Fischbach
Lawrence Tal (1996)

Jidda
J. E. Peterson

Jihad
Roxanne Varzi
Scott Alexander (1996)

Jinnah, Muhammad Ali
Hafeez Malik

Jizya
Elizabeth Thompson (1996)

Jmaʾa Tribal Council
Rahma Bourqia (1996)

Johnson–Crosbie Committee Report (1930)
Elizabeth Thompson (1996)

Johnson, Lyndon Baines
Zachary Karabell (1996)

Johnston Plan (1953)
Sara Reguer (1996)

John XIX
Donald Spanel (1996)

Joint Distribution Committee
Paul Rivlin
Bryan Daves (1996)

Jordan
Michael R. Fischbach
Peter Gubser (1996)

Jordanian Civil War (1970–1971)
Michael R. Fischbach
Peter Gubser (1996)

Jordanian Option
Avi Shlaim (1996)

Jordan River
Curtis R. Ryan
Sara Reguer (1996)

Joseph, Dov
Chaim I. Waxman

Jubayl, al-
J. E. Peterson

Judaism
Samuel C. Heilman (1996)

Judeo-Arabic
Norman Stillman (1996)

Jumayyil, Amin
Michael R. Fischbach
Majed Halawi (1996)

Jumayyil, Bashir
As'ad AbuKhalil

Jumayyil, Pierre
Majed Halawi (1996)

Jumblatt Family
Michael R. Fischbach
As'ad AbuKhalil (1996)

Jumblatt, Kamal
As'ad AbuKhalil (1996)

Jumblatt, Walid
Michael R. Fischbach
As'ad AbuKhalil (1996)

Justice Party
David Waldner (1996)

K

Ka'ba
Maysam J. al Faruqi

Kabak, Aaron Abraham
Ann Kahn (1996)

Kabul
Grant Farr

Kabul University
Grant Farr

Kabylia
Vanesa Casanova-Fernandez
Thomas G. Penchoen (1996)

Kadivar, Mohsen
Farzin Vahdat

Kadri, Mufide
Jessica Winegar

Kafr Qasim
Elizabeth Thompson (1996)

Kahan Commission (1983)
Laurie Z. Eisenberg
Jenab Tutunji (1996)

Kahane, Meir
Gregory S. Mahler
Walter F. Weiker (1996)

Kaid, Ahmed
Phillip C. Naylor (1996)

Kalemiyye
Elizabeth Thompson (1996)

Kalischer, Hirsch
Martin Malin (1996)

Kalvaryski, Chaim Margaliut-
Neil Caplan

Kamal, Ahmad
Donald Malcolm Reid (1996)

Kamal, Zahira
Rachel Christina

Kamil, Kibrish Mehmet
David Waldner (1996)

Kamil, Mustafa
Arthur Goldschmidt (1996)

Kanafani, Ghassan
Lawrence Tal (1996)

Kandahar
Grant Farr

Kaniuk, Yoram
Stephen Schecter
Zeva Shapiro (1996)

Kan, Suna
Filiz Ali

Karacan, Ali Naci
Elizabeth Thompson (1996)

Karaites
Samuel C. Heilman (1996)

Karak, al-
Michael R. Fischbach
Peter Gubser (1996)

Karama, Battle of (1968)
Lawrence Tal (1996)

Karame, Abd al-Hamid
Guilain P. Denoeux (1996)

Karame, Rashid
Guilain P. Denoeux (1996)

Karam, Yusuf
George E. Irani (1996)

Karbala
Scott Alexander (1996)

Karbaschi, Gholamhosain
Ali Akbar Mahdi

Kariyuka, Tahiya
Roberta L. Dougherty

Karmal, Babrak
Grant Farr

Kar, Mehrangiz
Ziba Mir-Hosseini

Karnouk, Liliane
Jessica Winegar

Karp Report (1984)
Gregory S. Mahler
Martin Malin (1996)

Karzai, Hamid
Robert L. Canfield

Kasap, Teodor
David Waldner (1996)

Kashani, Abu al-Qasem
Hamid Algar (1996)

Kashif al-Ghita Family
Michael Eppel (1996)

Kashwar Kamal, Meena
Senzil Nawid

Kasravi, Ahmad
Eric Hooglund (1996)

Kassallah
Robert O. Collins (1996)

Kasztner Affair
Zev Maghen (1996)

Kateb, Yacine
Yahia Zoubir

Kattani, Muhammad ibn Abd al-Kabir al-
Edmund Burke III (1996)

Kattaniya Brotherhood
Dale F. Eickelman (1996)

Katznelson, Berl
Donna Robinson Divine (1996)

Kawakibi, Abd al-Rahman al-
Fred H. Lawson (1996)

Kaylani, Abd al-Rahman al-
Michael Eppel (1996)

Kaylani, Rashid Ali al-
Peter Sluglett (1996)

Keban Dam
Elizabeth Thompson (1996)

Keinan, Amos
Donna Robinson Divine
Ann Kahn (1996)

Kemalettin Bey
Eric Hooglund
David Waldner (1996)

Kemalism
Taha Parla (1996)

Kenaz, Yehoshua
Stephen Schecter
Zeva Shapiro (1996)

Kennedy, John Fitzgerald
Michael R. Fischbach
Zachary Karabell (1996)

Kenter, Yildiz
David Waldner (1996)

Keren Hayesod
Chaim I. Waxman

Kerman
Parvaneh Pourshariati

Kessar, Israel
Gregory S. Mahler
Martin Malin (1996)

KGB
Charles C. Kolb

Khaddam, Abd al-Halim
Michael R. Fischbach
Fred H. Lawson (1996)

Khader, Asma
Isis Nusair

Khalaf, Abdulhadi
Eric Hooglund
Emile A. Nakhleh (1996)

Khalaf, Salah
Elizabeth Thompson (1996)

Khaldunniyya
Kenneth J. Perkins (1996)

Khaled, Leila
Frances Hasso

Khal, Helen
Jessica Winegar

Khalidi, Ahmad al-Samih al-
Michael R. Fischbach

Khalid ibn Abd al-Aziz Al Saʿud
Anthony B. Toth
Malcolm C. Peck (1996)

Khalidi, Husayn Fakhri al-
Michael R. Fischbach
Muhammad Muslih (1996)

Khalidi, Wahida al-
Ellen L. Fleischmann

Khalidi, Walid
Muhammad Muslih (1996)

Khalid, Khalid Muhammad
Maysam J. al Faruqi

Khalifa, Sahar
Laurie King-Irani

Khalil, Samiha Salama
Laurie King-Irani

Khalis, Mohammad Unis
Grant Farr (1996)

Khal, Yusuf al-
Guilain P. Denoeux (1996)

Khamenehi, Ali
Roxanne Varzi
Hamid Algar (1996)

Kharg Island
Eric Hooglund
Neguin Yavari (1996)

Kharrazi, Kamal
Ali Akbar Mahdi

Khartoum
Ann M. Lesch

Khatami, Mohammad
Eric Hooglund

Khatibi, Abdelkabir
Aida A. Bamia

Khattabi, Muhammad ibn Abd al-Karim al-
C. R. Pennell (1996)

Khayr al-Din
Larry A. Barrie (1996)

Khazʿal Khan
John R. Perry (1996)

Khaznader, Mustafa
Larry A. Barrie (1996)

Khemir, Sabiha
Jessica Winegar

Khider, Mohamed
Phillip C. Naylor (1996)

Khidhir, Zahra
Jacqueline Ismael

Khomeini, Ruhollah
Eric Hooglund
Neguin Yavari (1996)

Khorasan
Parvaneh Pourshariati

Khraief, Bechir
Aida A. Bamia (1996)

Khrimian, Mkrtich
Rouben P. Adalian (1996)

Khrushchev, Nikita S.
Oles M. Smolansky (1996)

Khubar, al-
Eric Hooglund
Les Ordeman (1996)

Khuri, Bishara al-
Guilain P. Denoeux (1996)

Khutba
Elizabeth Thompson (1996)

Khuzistan
Parvaneh Pourshariati

Khyber, Mir Akbar
Grant Farr

Khyber Pass
Grant Farr

Kianuri, Nur al-Din
Ervand Abrahamian

Kiarostami, Abbas
Roxanne Varzi

Kibbutz
Chaim I. Waxman

Kibbutz Movement
Donna Robinson Divine (1996)

Kikhya Family
John L. Wright (1996)

Kikhya, Rushdi al-
George E. Irani (1996)

Kimche, David
Ian Black
Ann Kahn (1996)

King–Crane Commission (1919)
Philip Mattar (1996)

King David Hotel
Mordechai Bar-On

King Saʿud University
Anthony B. Toth

Kirkbride, Alec Seath
Joseph Nevo
Jenab Tutunji (1996)

Kirkuk
Reeva S. Simon (1996)

Kiryat Arba
David Newman
Elizabeth Thompson (1996)

Kisakürek, Necip Fazil
Elizabeth Thompson (1996)

Kisch, Frederick Hermann
Neil Caplan (1996)

Kissinger, Henry
Paola Olimpo
David Waldner (1996)

Kitchener, Horatio Herbert
Peter Mellini (1996)

Kléber, Jean-Baptiste
Zachary Karabell (1996)

Knesset
Gregory S. Mahler
Walter F. Weiker (1996)

Koç, Vehbi
Elizabeth Thompson (1996)

Kollek, Teddy
Gregory S. Mahler

Kol, Moshe
Gregory S. Mahler
Martin Malin (1996)

Konya
Eric Hooglund

Konya, Battle of
Elizabeth Thompson (1996)

Kook, Abraham Isaac Hacohen
Chaim I. Waxman (1996)

Kook, Zvi Yehuda
Chaim I. Waxman (1996)

Koor Industries
Paul Rivlin (1996)

Koprülü, Mehmet Fuat
Uli Schamiloglu (1996)

Kordofan
Robert O. Collins

Kosher
Zachary Karabell (1996)

Kovner, Abba
George R. Wilkes
Zev Maghen (1996)

Krim, Belkacem
Phillip C. Naylor (1996)

Kuchek Khan-e Jangali
Neguin Yavari (1996)

Kudsi, Nazim al-
Michael R. Fischbach
Muhammad Muslih (1996)

Kurd Ali, Muhammad
William L. Cleveland (1996)

Kurdish Autonomous Zone
Chris Kutschera

Kurdish Revolts
Amir Hassanpour

Kurdistan
Chris Kutschera

Kurdistan Workers Party (PKK)
Martin Van Bruinessen

Kurds
Chris Kutschera

Kütahya, Peace of
Zachary Karabell (1996)

Kut al-Amara
Karen Pinto (1996)

Kuttab
Elizabeth Thompson (1996)

Kuwait
Mary Ann Tétreault
Malcolm C. Peck (1996)

Kuwait City
Mary Ann Tétreault
Malcolm C. Peck (1996)

Kuwait Fund for Arab Economic Development
Mary Ann Tétreault
Emile A. Nakhleh (1996)

Kuwait Petroleum Corporation
Mary Ann Tétreault

Kuwait University
Anthony B. Toth
Malcolm C. Peck (1996)

L

Laabi, Abdellatif
Aida A. Bamia

Laayounne
Bruce Maddy-Weitzman

Labor and Labor Unions
Ellis Goldberg

Labor Zionism
Donna Robinson Divine

Lacheraf, Mostefa
Phillip C. Naylor

Lacoste, Robert
Phillip C. Naylor (1996)

Ladino
Norman Stillman (1996)

Lado Enclave
Robert O. Collins (1996)

Lahad, Antoine
As'ad AbuKhalil
Guilain P. Denoeux (1996)

Lahhud, Emile
As'ad AbuKhalil

Lahiji, Shahla
Cherie Taraghi

Lahouel, Hocine
Vanesa Casanova-Fernandez
Phillip C. Naylor (1996)

Lamari, Mohamed
Azzedine G. Mansour

La Marsa Convention
Matthew S. Gordon (1996)

Lamrani, Muhammad Karim
Ana Torres-Garcia
Matthew S. Gordon (1996)

Land Code of 1858
David Waldner (1996)

Land Day
Lawrence Tal (1996)

Land Reform
Martin Bunton
Alan R. Richards (1996)

Landsmannschaften
Zev Maghen (1996)

Langer, Felicia
Carolyn Fluehr-Lobban

Lansdowne, Henry Charles Keith Petty Fitzmaurice
Zachary Karabell (1996)

Laraki, Ahmad
Matthew S. Gordon (1996)

Lata'if al-Musawwara Magazine
Mona Russell

Latakia
Abdul-Karim Refaq (1996)

La Tunisie Martyre
Matthew S. Gordon (1996)

Lausanne Conference (1949)
Michael R. Fischbach

Lausanne, Treaty of (1923)
Eric Hooglund
Daniel E. Spector (1996)

Lavon Affair
Mordechai Bar-On
Amos Perlmutter (1996)

Lavon, Pinhas
Meron Medzini
Reeva S. Simon (1996)

Law, Modern
Nathan J. Brown
Ann E. Mayer (1996)

Law of Return
Chaim I. Waxman
Zev Maghen (1996)

Lawrence, T. E.
Zouhair Ghazzal
Benjamin Braude (1996)

League of Arab States
Charles G. MacDonald

Lebanese Arab Army
As'ad AbuKhalil (1996)

Lebanese Civil War (1958)
Irene Gendzier (1996)

Lebanese Civil War (1975–1990)
As'ad AbuKhalil (1996)

Lebanese Crises of the 1840s
Tayeb El-Hibri (1996)

Lebanese Forces
Michael R. Fischbach
As'ad AbuKhalil (1996)

Lebanese Front
George E. Irani (1996)

Lebanese National Movement (LNM)
George E. Irani (1996)

Lebanese University
Michael R. Fischbach
As'ad AbuKhalil (1996)

Lebanese Women's Council
Lara Deeb

Lebanon
As'ad AbuKhalil

Lebanon, Mount
Guilain P. Denoeux (1996)

Legislative Council (Palestine)
Philip Mattar

Leibowitz, Yeshayahu
Chaim I. Waxman

Lemsine, Aicha
Aida A. Bamia

Lend-Lease Program
Zachary Karabell (1996)

Leskofcali Galip
David Waldner (1996)

Lesseps, Ferdinand de
David Waldner (1996)

Levantine
Philip Mattar
Jean-Marc R. Oppenheim (1996)

Levinger, Moshe
David Newman

Levin, Hanoch
Donna Robinson Divine
Ann Kahn (1996)

Levin, Shmaryahu
Martin Malin (1996)

Levin, Yizhak Meir
Ann Kahn (1996)

Levontin, Zalman
Bryan Daves (1996)

Levy, David
Gregory S. Mahler
Bryan Daves (1996)

Liberal Constitutionalist Party
David Waldner (1996)

Liberation Rally
David Waldner (1996)

Liberty, USS
Ian Black
Jenab Tutunji (1996)

Libya
Ronald Bruce St John
Lisa Anderson (1996)

LICA
Norman Stillman (1996)

Ligue Tunisienne pour la Défense des Droits de l'Homme (LTDH)
Ana Torres-Garcia
Larry A. Barrie (1996)

Likud
Walter F. Weiker (1996)

Lilienblum, Moses Leib
Walter F. Weiker (1996)

Litani Operation (1978)
Laurie Z. Eisenberg
Elizabeth Thompson (1996)

Litani River
Sara Riguer (1996)

Literature: Arabic
Pierre Cachia

Literature: Arabic, North African
Aida A. Bamia

Literature: Hebrew
Nili Gold (1996)

Literature: Persian
Eric Hooglund
Michael C. Hillmann (1996)

Literature: Turkish
Kyle T. Evered
Kathleen R. F. Burrill (1996)

Livnat, Limor
Meron Medzini

Lloyd George, David
Bernard Wasserstein

Lohamei Herut Yisrael
Pierre M. Atlas

Loi Cadre
Phillip C. Naylor (1996)

London Conference (1956)
Mordechai Bar-On

London Convention
Arnold Blumberg (1996)

London (Roundtable) Conference (1939)
Neil Caplan

London, Treaty of (1871)
Zachary Karabell (1996)

London, Treaty of (1913)
Zachary Karabell (1996)

Lotz, Wolfgang
Zev Maghen (1996)

Luke, Harry
Jenab Tutunji (1996)

Lurs
Eric Hooglund

Luxor
Paul Rowe
Arthur Goldschmidt (1996)

Luz, Kadish
Zev Maghen (1996)

Lyautey, Louis-Hubert Gonzalve
Remy Leveau (1996)

Lydda
Yehuda Gradus
Elizabeth Thompson (1996)

M

Ma al-Aynayn
Edmund Burke III (1996)

Maʿa lot
Yehuda Gradus
Zev Maghen (1996)

Maʿariv
Ann Kahn (1996)

Maʿbarah
Shlomo Deshen

Mabarrat Muhammad Ali
Nancy Gallagher

Maccabi
Norman Stillman (1996)

MacDonald, Malcolm
Joseph Nevo
Jenab Tutunji (1996)

MacDonald, Ramsay
Jenab Tutunji (1996)

MacMichael, Harold
Jenab Tutunji (1996)

Madani, Abassi al-
Robert Mortimer

Madani, Abdullah al-
Emile A. Nakhleh (1996)

Madani, Tawfiq al-
Phillip C. Naylor

Madkour, Ibrahim
Charles E. Butterworth

Madrasa
Denise A. Spellberg (1996)

Madrid Conference (1991)
Kenneth W. Stein

Magen David Adom (MDA)
Neil Caplan
Miriam Simon (1996)

Maghrib
Elizabeth Thompson (1996)

Magic Carpet Operation
Norman Stillman (1996)

Magnes, Judah
Chaim I. Waxman
Neil Caplan
Bryan Daves (1996)

Mahalla al-Kubra, al-
Ellis Goldberg (1996)

Mahalle Schools
Elizabeth Thompson (1996)

Mahdawi, Fadil Abbas al-
Louay Bahry (1996)

Mahd-e Ulya, Malek Jahan Khanum
Mansoureh Ettehadieh (1996)

Mahdi
Denise A. Spellberg

Mahdist State
Ann M. Lesch (1996)

Mahfuz, Najib
Roxanne Varzi
Pierre Cachia (1996)

Mahir, Ahmad
Roger Allen (1996)

Mahir, Ali
Roger Allen (1996)

Mahmud II
Eric Hooglund
Avigdor Levy (1996)

Mahmud Durrani
Grant Farr (1996)

Mahmudiyya Canal
Arthur Goldschmidt (1996)

Mahmud, Muhammad
Arthur Goldschmidt
Roger Allen (1996)

Mahmud, Mustafa
Arthur Goldschmidt

Mahmud of Sulaymaniya
Chris Kutschera (1996)

Maimon, Yehudah Leib Hacohen
Chaim I. Waxman (1996)

Majali Family
Michael R. Fischbach

Majali, Hazza al-
Jenab Tutunji (1996)

Majles al-Shura
Eric Hooglund
Neguin Yavari (1996)

Majlis Shura al-Nuwwab
Arthur Goldschmidt (1996)

Makdashi, Hesna
Caroline Seymour-Jorn

Makhmalbaf Family
Roxanne Varzi

Makhmalbaf, Mohsen
Roxanne Varzi

Makki, Hasan Muhammad
Robert D. Burrowes

Maksoud, Clovis
George E. Irani

Maktum Family, al-
M. Morsy Abdullah (1996)

Malaʾika, Nazik al-
Elise Salem

Malik, Charles Habib
Michael R. Fischbach
George E. Irani (1996)

Maliki School of Law
Wael B. Hallaq (1996)

Malkom Khan, Mirza
Mansoureh Ettehadieh (1996)

Maʿlouf, Amin
George E. Irani

Mamluks
Albertine Jwaideh (1996)

Manama
Fred H. Lawson

Mandaeans
Mamoon A. Zaki (1996)

Mandate System
Daniel E. Spector (1996)

Manifesto of the Algerian Muslim People
John Ruedy (1996)

Mansura, al-
Arthur Goldschmidt (1996)

Mansure Army
Elizabeth Thompson (1996)

Manufactures
Charles Issawi (1996)

Maqarin Dam
Michael R. Fischbach (1996)

Marabout
Dale F. Eickelman (1996)

Maratghi, Mustafa al-
David Waldner (1996)

Mardam, Jamil
Muhammad Muslih (1996)

Mardom Party
Parvaneh Pourshariati (1996)

Mareth Line
Larry A. Barrie (1996)

Ma'rib
Robert D. Burrowes

Mariette, Auguste
Donald Malcolm Reid (1996)

Mar'i, Mariam
Isis Nusair

Marine Barracks Bombing (Lebanon)
George E. Irani (1996)

Maritime Peace in Perpetuity, Treaty of (1853)
Anthony B. Toth

Marja al-Taqlid
Eric Hooglund
Neguin Yavari (1996)

Mark VIII
Donald Spanel (1996)

Marmara University
Burçak Keskin-Kozat
I. Metin Kunt (1996)

Maronites
As'ad AbuKhalil

Marrakech
Edmund Burke III (1996)

Marriage and Family
Rita Stephan

Marsh Arabs
Albertine Jwaideh (1996)

Ma'rufi, Abbas
Eric Hooglund
Pardis Minuchehr (1996)

Marzouki, Moncef
George R. Wilkes

Masada
Benjamin Kedar

Mas'adi, Mahmoud al-
Aida A. Bamia

Mashhad
Eric Hooglund
Cyrus Moshaver (1996)

Masira Island
Anthony B. Toth
Robert G. Landen (1996)

Masmoudi, Muhammad
Vanesa Casanova-Fernandez
Matthew S. Gordon (1996)

Maspéro, Gaston
Donald Malcolm Reid

Masri, Mai
Laurie King-Irani

Matrah
Robert G. Landen (1996)

Matzpen
George R. Wilkes

Maude, Frederick Stanley
Zachary Karabell (1996)

Mauritania
Naomi Zeff
Bradford Dillman (1996)

Mawdudi, Abu al-A'la al-
Maysam J. al Faruqi

Maysalun
Fred H. Lawson (1996)

Mazar-e Sharif
Grant Farr

Maziq, Husayn
Ronald Bruce St John

McMahon, Henry
David Waldner (1996)

Meah She'arim
Chaim I. Waxman

Mecca
Anthony B. Toth
Khalid Y. Blankinship (1996)

Meddeb, Abdelwahhab
Aida A. Bamia

Medicine and Public Health
Evelyn A. Early (1996)

Medina
Anthony B. Toth

Mediterranean Sea
Vanesa Casanova-Fernandez
Elizabeth Thompson (1996)

Meged, Aharon
George R. Wilkes
Ann Kahn (1996)

Mehmet Rauf
David Waldner (1996)

Mehmet V Reşat
Eric Hooglund
Zachary Karabell (1996)

Meir, Golda
Zaki Shalom
Gregory S. Mahler (1996)

Meknes
Rahma Bourqia (1996)

Meknes, Treaty of (1836)
C. R. Pennell (1996)

Melilla
Bruce Maddy-Weitzman

Memmi, Albert
Stefanie Wichhart
Will D. Swearingen (1996)

Menderes, Adnan
Eric Hooglund
Walter F. Weiker (1996)

Menou, Jacques François
David Waldner (1996)

Mernissi, Fatema
Laura Rice

Mesopotamia Campaign (1914–1918)
Zachary Karabell (1996)

Messianism
David Waldner (1996)

Mestiri, Ahmad
Ana Torres-Garcia
Kenneth J. Perkins (1996)

Meushi, Paul Peter
George E. Irani (1996)

Mevlevi Brotherhood
Rita Stephan
Tayeb El-Hibri (1996)

MI-6
Zachary Karabell (1996)

Michael, Sami
Nancy Berg
Zvia Ginor (1996)

Middle East
Karen Pinto (1996)

Middle East Defense Organization (MEDO)
Zachary Karabell (1996)

Middle East Supply Center (MESC)
Daniel E. Spector (1996)

Middle East Technical University
Eric Hooglund
I. Metin Kunt (1996)

Midfaʿi, Jamil al-
Peter Sluglett (1996)

Midhat Paşa
Roderic H. Davison (1996)

Mihrab
Scott Alexander (1996)

Milani, Tahmineh
Roxanne Varzi

Military in the Middle East
Daniel E. Spector

Millet System
Benjamin Braude (1996)

Milli Görüş Hareketi
M. Hakan Yavuz
Nermin Abadan-Unat (1996)

Milli İstihbarat Teşkilati
Elizabeth Thompson (1996)

Millspaugh, Arthur
Daniel E. Spector (1996)

Milner Mission
Arthur Goldschmidt (1996)

Mimouna Festival
Harvey E. Goldberg

Mimouni, Rachid
Rabia Bekkar
Phillip C. Naylor (1996)

Minaret
Elizabeth Thompson (1996)

Minorities
Benjamin Braude (1996)

Minz, Benjamin
Ann Kahn (1996)

Misri, Aziz Ali al-
Arthur Goldschmidt (1996)

Missionary Schools
John J. Donohue (1996)

Mission Civilisatrice
Zachary Karabell (1996)

Mixed Armistice Commissions
Neil Caplan (1996)

Mixed Courts
Donald Malcolm Reid (1996)

Mizrahi Movement
Chaim I. Waxman (1996)

Moadda, Mohamed
George R. Wilkes

Moda'i, Yitzhak
Gregory S. Mahler
Zev Maghen (1996)

Modernization
Charles Issawi (1996)

Mogannam, Matiel
Ellen L. Fleischmann

Moghaizel, Laure
Elise Salem

Mohajerani, Ataollah
Ali Akbar Mahdi

Mohammad Ali Shah Qajar
Eric Hooglund
Neguin Yavari (1996)

Mohammadi, Maulawi Mohammad Nabi
Grant Farr

Mohilever, Samuel
Martin Malin (1996)

Mojaddedi, Sebghatullah
Grant Farr

Mojahedin
Grant Farr

Mojahedin-e Khalq
Ervand Abrahamian

Mojtahed-Shabestari, Mohammad
Farzin Vahdat

Mollet, Guy
Zachary Karabell (1996)

Moltke, Helmuth von
Zachary Karabell (1996)

Monastir
Matthew S. Gordon (1996)

Mond, Alfred Moritz
Zachary Karabell (1996)

Montazeri, Hosayn Ali
Eric Hooglund
Hamid Algar (1996)

Montefiore, Moses
Zachary Karabell (1996)

Montgomery, Bernard Law
Zachary Karabell (1996)

Montreux Convention (1936)
Zachary Karabell (1996)

Moroccan–Algerian War
Phillip C. Naylor (1996)

Moroccan Question
Edmund Burke III (1996)

Morocco: Overview
Henri Lauzière
Larry A. Barrie (1996)

Morocco: Constitution
Henri Lauzière

Morocco: Political Parties in
Bruce Maddy-Weitzman

Morrison–Grady Plan (1946)
Zachary Karabell (1996)

Moshav
Paul Rivlin (1996)

Mosque
Scott Alexander (1996)

Mossad
Mordechai Bar-On

Mossadegh, Mohammad
Mansoor Moaddel (1996)

Mostaghanemi, Ahlam
Michelle Hartman

Mosul
Reeva S. Simon (1996)

Mosul, Anglo–Turkish Dispute over
Ayad al-Qazzaz (1996)

Motahhari, Mortaza
Hamid Algar (1996)

Motherland Party
M. Hakan Yavuz
Frank Tachau (1996)

Mouʿawwad, Naila
Elise Salem

Moudawana, al-
Laura Rice

Mourou, Abdelfattah
Emad Eldin Shahin

Mouvement de l'Unité Populaire (MUP)
Ana Torres-Garcia
Larry A. Barrie (1996)

Mouvement National Algérien
John Ruedy (1996)

Mouvement Populaire (MP)
Bruce Maddy-Weitzman

Mouvement pour le Triomphe des Libertés Démocratiques
John Ruedy (1996)

Movement for Unity and Reform (MUR)
Emad Eldin Shahin

Movement of Renewal
Vanesa Casanova-Fernandez
Larry A. Barrie (1996)

Mozaffar al-Din Qajar
Mansoureh Ettehadieh (1996)

M'Rabet, Fadela
Aida A. Bamia

Muʿalla Family, al-
Anthony B. Toth

Muasher, Marwan
Michael R. Fischbach

Mubarak, Husni
Arthur Goldschmidt

Mufide Kadri
David Waldner (1996)

Muhammad
Tayeb El-Hibri (1996)

Muhammad V
Rémy Leveau (1996)

Muhammad VI
Michael M. Laskier

Muhammad Ali
Fred H. Lawson (1996)

Muhammad Ali Mosque
Donald Malcolm Reid (1996)

Muhammad al-Sadiq
Larry A. Barrie (1996)

Muhammad, Aziz
Michael R. Fischbach
Michael Eppel (1996)

Muharram
Peter Chelkowski (1996)

Muharraq
Fred H. Lawson (1996)

Muhsin, Zuhayr
Elizabeth Thompson (1996)

Muhtar, Gazi Ahmet
Elizabeth Thompson (1996)

Muhyi al-Din, Khalid
Maysam J. al Faruqi
David Waldner (1996)

Muhyi al-Din, Zakariyya
George R. Wilkes
David Waldner (1996)

Mukhtar, Umar al-
George Joffe (1996)

Mukrani Family
Peter von Sivers (1996)

Munif, Abdel Rahman
Caroline Seymour-Jorn

Muntada al-Adabi, al-
Muhammad Muslih (1996)

Muntasir Family
George Joffe (1996)

Murabitun
Bassam Namani (1996)

Musa Dagh
Rouben P. Adalian (1996)

Musa Kazim
Zachary Karabell (1996)

Musa, Nabawiyya
Linda Herrera

Musa, Salama
David Waldner (1996)

Musavi-Ardebili, AbdolKarim
Eric Hooglund
Neguin Yavari (1996)

Musavi, Mir-Hosain
Ali Akbar Mahdi

Muscat
Anthony B. Toth
Robert G. Landen (1996)

Music
Virginia Danielson (1996)

Muslim Brotherhood
Maysam J. al Faruqi

Muslim Sisters Organization
Carolyn Fluehr-Lobban

Muslim World League
Khalid Y. Blankinship (1996)

Mustafa Fazil
Elizabeth Thompson (1996)

Mustafa Reşid
David Waldner (1996)

Mustafa Suphi
Elizabeth Thompson (1996)

Muwahhidun
Maria F. Curtis
Bassam Namani (1996)

Mzab
Thomas G. Penchoen (1996)

Mzali, Mohammed
Ana Torres-Garcia
Lisa Anderson (1996)

N

Naʿamaat
Paul Rivlin

Nabavi, Behzad
Ali Akbar Mahdi

Nabi Musa Pilgrimage
Emma Aubin Boltanski
Benjamin Joseph (1996)

Nabi Salih, al-
Fred H. Lawson (1996)

Nabizade Nazim
David Waldner (1996)

Nablus
Michael R. Fischbach
Benjamin Joseph (1996)

Nabulsi, Sulayman al-
Jenab Tutunji (1996)

Nadir Barakzai, Mohammad
Grant Farr (1996)

Nadi, Yunus
Elizabeth Thompson (1996)

Nafud Desert
Eleanor Abdella Doumato (1996)

Naguib, Muhammad
David Waldner (1996)

Nahal
Zev Maghen (1996)

Nahalal
Donna Robinson Divine (1996)

Nahda, al-
Emad Eldin Shahin

Nahhas, Mustafa al-
Michael R. Fischbach (1996)

Nahnah, Mahfoud
Emad Eldin Shahin

Nahum, Halfallah
Maurice M. Roumani (1996)

Nahum, Hayyim
Michael M. Laskier (1996)

Najaf, al-
Michael R. Fischbach
Mamoon A. Zaki (1996)

Najd
Eleanor Abdella Doumato (1996)

Najibullah
Grant Farr

Najjada, al-
Elizabeth Thompson (1996)

Nakba, al- (1948–1949)
Philip Mattar

Namik Kemal
Eric Hooglund
Zachary Karabell (1996)

Namir, Mordekhai
Zev Maghen (1996)

Namir, Orah
Meron Medzini

Naqshbandi
JoAnn Gross (1996)

Naser al-Din Shah
Eric Hooglund

Nashashibi Family
Michael R. Fischbach
Muhammad Muslih (1996)

Nasir, Ahmed Sayf al-
John L. Wright (1996)

Nasir, Hanna
Michael R. Fischbach
Jenab Tutunji (1996)

Nasir, Najib
Elizabeth Thompson (1996)

Nasrallah, Emily
Elise Salem

Nasrallah, Hasan
As'ad AbuKhalil

Nasruddin Hoca
Burçak Keskin-Kozat
Kathleen R. F. Burrill (1996)

Nassar, Sadhij
Ellen L. Fleischmann

Nasser, Gamal Abdel
Raymond William Baker (1996)

Nasser, Lake
Gregory B. Baecher
Arthur Goldschmidt (1996)

Nassif, Malak Hifni
Caroline Seymour-Jorn

Nateq-Nuri, Ali Akbar
Farhad Arshad (1996)

National Bloc
Michael R. Fischbach
George E. Irani (1996)

National Congress Party
Lisa Anderson (1996)

National Democratic Front (NDF)
Robert D. Burrowes

National Democratic Front for the Liberation of Oman and the Arab Gulf
Malcolm C. Peck (1996)

National Democratic Party (Iraq)
Reeva S. Simon (1996)

National Front for the Liberation of South Yemen
Manfred W. Wenner

National Front for the Salvation of Libya
Lisa Anderson (1996)

National Front, Iran
Afshin Matin-asgari

National Front, Lebanon
George E. Irani (1996)

Nationalism
Richard W. Bulliet (1996)

Nationalist Action Party
M. Hakan Yavuz
Frank Tachau (1996)

National Liberal Party
George E. Irani (1996)

National Liberation Front (Bahrain)
Fred H. Lawson

National Oil Corporation (Libya)
Mary Ann Tétreault (1996)

National Pact (Lebanon)
As'ad AbuKhalil (1996)

National Party (Egypt)
Arthur Goldschmidt

National Party (Syria)
Mahmoud Haddad (1996)

National Progressive Front (Syria)
Khalil Gebara

National Progressive Unionist Party
Raymond William Baker (1996)

National Salvation Front (Lebanon)
As'ad AbuKhalil (1996)

National Salvation Party
Eric Hooglund
Nermin Abadan-Unat (1996)

National Security Council (Turkey)
M. Hakan Yavuz

National Union (Egypt)
Raymond William Baker (1996)

National Unity Committee (Turkey)
Frank Tachau (1996)

National Water System (Israel)
Sara Reguer (1996)

National Women's Committee (Yemen)
Susanne Dahlgren

Natural Gas: Economic Exploitation of
Mary Ann Tétreault

Natural Gas: Middle East Reserves of
Jean-François Seznec (1996)

Navon, Yizhak
Gregory S. Mahler
Miriam Simon (1996)

Nawfal, Hind
Marilyn Booth

Nazareth
Laurie King-Irani
Benjamin Joseph (1996)

Nazif, Süleyman
David Waldner (1996)

Nazmi, Ziya
David Waldner (1996)

Ne'eman, Yuval
Mordechai Bar-On

Negev
Yehuda Gradus
Elizabeth Thompson (Negev Desert) (1996)

Nerval, Gérard de
Maysam J. al Faruqi

Neshat, Shirin
Jessica Winegar

Nesin, Nüsret Aziz
Elizabeth Thompson (1996)

Netanyahu, Benjamin
Eric Silver
Julie Zuckerman (1996)

Neturei Karta
Chaim I. Waxman (1996)

Neutral Zone
Emile A. Nakhleh (1996)

Newspapers and Print Media: Arab Countries
William A. Rugh

Newspapers and Print Media: Iran
Eric Hooglund

Newspapers and Print Media: Israel
Dov Shinar

Newspapers and Print Media: Turkey
Brian Silverstein

New Wafd
George R. Wilkes
Raymond William Baker (1996)

Nezzar, Khaled
Phillip C. Naylor

Nhaisi, Elia
Maurice M. Roumani (1996)

Niati, Houria
Jessica Winegar

Nile River
Gregory B. Baecher
Arthur Goldschmidt (1996)

Nimr, Faris
Guilain P. Denoeux (1996)

Nissim, Isaac
Chaim I. Waxman (1996)

Nixon, Richard Milhous
Zachary Karabell (1996)

Nizam al-Jadid, al-
Fred H. Lawson (1996)

Nizamiye Courts
Elizabeth Thompson (1996)

Nizip, Battle of (1839)
Fred H. Lawson (1996)

Noor al-Hussein (Queen Noor)
Curtis R. Ryan

Nordau, Max
Martin Malin (1996)

North Atlantic Treaty Organization (NATO)
Andrew Flibbert
Zachary Karabell (1996)

Northern Tier
Zach Levey

Nouakchott
Naomi Zeff

Nouira, Hedi
Matthew S. Gordon (1996)

Nuʿaymi Family, al-
Anthony B. Toth

Nubar, Boghos
Rouben P. Adalian (1996)

Nubar Pasha
Arthur Goldschmidt (1996)

Nubians
Carolyn Fluehr-Lobban
Aleya Rouchdy (1996)

Nuclear Capability and Nuclear Energy
Robert E. Harkavy

Nuer
Carolyn Fluehr-Lobban
Robert O. Collins (1996)

Numeiri, Muhammad Jaʿfar
Robert O. Collins

Numismatics
Michael L. Bates (1996)

Nuqrashi, Mahmud Fahmi al-
Arthur Goldschmidt (1996)

Nuri, Abd al-Malik
Sasson Somekh (1996)

Nuri, Fazlollah
Hamid Algar (1996)

Nursi, Said
M. Hakan Yavuz
Nico Landman (1996)

Nusayba Family
Michael R. Fischbach
Lawrence Tal (1996)

Nuun Magazine
Vanesa Casanova-Fernandez

O

Oasis Group
Mary Ann Tétreault

Occidental Petroleum
Mary Ann Tétreault

Oil Embargo (1973–1974)
Bryan Daves (1996)

Oman
Calvin H. Allen, Jr.
Robert G. Landen (1996)

Omar, Muhammad (Mullah)
Charles E. Butterworth

Omar Mukhtar Club
John L. Wright (1996)

Omdurman
Khalid M. El-Hassan
Robert O. Collins (1996)

Opium
Ana Torres-Garcia
Karen Pinto (1996)

Oran
Peter von Sivers (1996)

Ordinances on Veiling
Senzil Nawid

Organisation Armée Secrète (OAS)
John Ruedy (1996)

Organisation Marocaine des Droits de l'Homme
Vanesa Casanova-Fernandez
Larry A. Barrie (1996)

Organization for the Liberation of the Occupied South
Manfred W. Wenner

Organization of African Unity (OAU)
Zachary Karabell (1996)

Organization of Arab Petroleum Exporting Countries (OAPEC)
Karim Hamdy
Emile A. Nakhleh (1996)

Organization of Petroleum Exporting Countries (OPEC)
Mary Ann Tétreault

Organization of the Islamic Conference
Vanesa Casanova-Fernandez
Scott Alexander (1996)

Orientalism
John Lundquist

Orientalists, International Congress of
Vanesa Casanova-Fernandez
Richard W. Bulliet (1996)

Ormanian, Maghakia
Rouben P. Adalian (1996)

Ormsby-Gore, William George Arthur
Elizabeth Thompson (1996)

Ortaoyunu
Kathleen R. F. Burrill (1996)

Osirak
Ronen Zeidel (1996)

Oslo Accord (1993)
Philip Mattar

Osman, House of
I. Metin Kunt (1996)

Ottoman Empire: Overview
Donald Quataert (1996)

Ottoman Empire: Civil Service
Carter V. Findley (1996)

Ottoman Empire: Debt
Donald Quataert (1996)

Ottomanism
Hasan Kayali (1996)

Ottoman Liberal Union Party
Elizabeth Thompson (1996)

Ottoman Military: Army
Avigdor Levy (1996)

Ottoman Military: Navy
Avigdor Levy (1996)

Ottoman Parliament
Hasan Kayali (1996)

Ouary, Malek
Ana Torres-Garcia
Phillip C. Naylor (1996)

Ouazzani, Mohamed Hassan
Bruce Maddy-Weitzman (1996)

Oufkir, Muhammad
Matthew S. Gordon (1996)

Oujda Group
John Ruedy (1996)

Ould Sidʾ Ahmed Taya, Maʿouiya
Naomi Zeff

Ouled Sidi Cheikh
Phillip C. Naylor (1996)

Ouziel, Ben Zion Meir Hai
Chaim I. Waxman (1996)

OYAK (Ordu Yardimlasma Kurumu)
Elizabeth Thompson (1996)

Özal, Turgut
David Waldner (1996)

Oz, Amos
Adina Friedman
Zvia Ginor (1996)

Oz ve Shalom (Netivot shalom)
Mordechai Bar-On
Walter F. Weiker (1996)

P

Pachachi, Muzahim al-
Mamoon A. Zaki (1996)

Pagis, Dan
Adina Friedman
Julie Zuckerman (1996)

Pahlavi, Mohammad Reza
Ahmad Ashraf (1996)

Pahlavi, Reza
Ahmad Ashraf

Pakistan and the Middle East
Rasul Bakhsh Rais (1996)

Palestine
Neil Caplan
Ann M. Lesch
Don Peretz (1996)

Palestine Arab Revolt (1936–1939)
Rashid Khalidi (1996)

Palestine Economic Corporation
Elizabeth Thompson (1996)

Palestine Exploration Fund
Elizabeth Thompson (1996)

Palestine Land Development Company
Elizabeth Thompson (1996)

Palestine Liberation Organization (PLO)
Philip Mattar

Palestine National Charter (1968)
Muhammad Muslih (1996)

Palestine National Council
Maria F. Curtis
Mouin Rabbani (1996)

Palestine National Covenant (1964)
Muhammad Muslih (1996)

Palestine Research Center
Michael R. Fischbach
Jenab Tutunji (1996)

Palestinian Arab Congresses
Philip Mattar
Ann M. Lesch (1996)

Palestinian Authority
Michael R. Fischbach

Palestinian Citizens of Israel
Don Peretz

Palestinians
Philip Mattar
Muhammad Muslih (1996)

Palin Commission Report (1920)
Ann M. Lesch (1996)

Palmah
Pierre M. Atlas
Amos Perlmutter (1996)

Palmerston, Lord Henry John Temple
Eric Hooglund
Arnold Blumberg (1996)

Palmyra
Elizabeth Thompson (1996)

Pamir Mountains
Grant Farr

Pan-Arabism
Ronald Bruce St John

Pan-Turkism
Hasan Kayali (1996)

Parcham
Grant Farr (1996)

Paris Peace Settlements (1918–1923)
Eric Hooglund
Fawaz A. Gerges (1996)

Paris, Treaty of (1857)
Farhad Shirzad (1996)

Parliamentary Democratic Front
Michael R. Fischbach
As'ad AbuKhalil (1996)

Parsipur, Shahrnush
Michael C. Hillmann (1996)

Parti de l'Avant-Garde Socialiste (PAGS)
Yahia Zoubir
Phillip C. Naylor (1996)

Parti Démocratique Constitutionnel (PDC)
Bruce Maddy-Weitzman (1996)

Parti Démocratique de l'Indépendance (PDI)
Bruce Maddy-Weitzman

Parti d'Unité Populaire (PUP)
Ana Torres-Garcia
Matthew S. Gordon (1996)

Parti du Peuple Algérien (PPA)
John Ruedy (1996)

Parti National
Bruce Maddy-Weitzman (1996)

Parti National Démocratique (PND)
Bruce Maddy-Weitzman

Partition Plans (Palestine)
Avi Shlaim (1996)

Patriarch
Zachary Karabell (1996)

Patriarchs, Tomb of the
Chaim I. Waxman (1996)

Patriotic Union of Kurdistan (PUK)
Chris Kutschera

Peace and Amity, Treaty of (1805)
Larry A. Barrie (1996)

Peace Corps
Christopher Reed Stone
Zachary Karabell (1996)

Peace Now
Mordechai Bar-On

Peake, Frederick Gerard
Jenab Tutunji (1996)

Pearl Diving (Bahrain)
Fred H. Lawson (1996)

Peel Commission Report (1937)
Ann M. Lesch

Peled, Mattityahu
Mordechai Bar-On
Bryan Daves (1996)

Pelt, Adrian
Ronald Bruce St John

People's Assembly
Raymond William Baker (1996)

People's Democratic Party of Afghanistan
Grant Farr (1996)

People's Democratic Republic of Yemen
Robert D. Burrowes (1996)

People's Houses
Paul J. Magnarella (1996)

People's Socialist Party
Manfred W. Wenner

Pera
I. Metin Kunt (1996)

Peres, Shimon
Gregory S. Mahler

Pérez de Cuéllar, Javier
Ronald Bruce St John
Bryan Daves (1996)

Perim
Robert D. Burrowes

Permanent Mandates Commission
Elizabeth Thompson (1996)

Persian
M. A. Jazayary (1996)

Persian (Arabian) Gulf
Eric Hooglund
Elizabeth Thompson (1996)

Persian Cats
Eric Hooglund

Persian Script
Roxanne Varzi

Petah Tikvah
Chaim I. Waxman

Peter VII
Donald Spanel (1996)

Petra
Peter Gubser (1996)

Petrochemicals
Jean-François Seznec
Mary Ann Tétreault (1996)

Petroleum, Oil, and Natural Gas
Mary Ann Tétreault

Petroleum Reserves and Production
Jean-François Seznec

PETROMIN
Jean-Francois Seznec (1996)

Phalange
Michael R. Fischbach
As'ad AbuKhalil (1996)

Pharaonicism
James Jankowski (1996)

Pharaon, Rashad
George R. Wilkes
Les Ordeman (1996)

Philae
John Lundquist
David Waldner (1996)

Philby, Harry St. John
Neil Caplan
Benjamin Braude (1996)

Phoenicianism
As'ad AbuKhalil (1996)

Phosphates
Karim Hamdy

Pinsker, Leo
Martin Malin (1996)

Plague
Jenab Tutunji (1996)

Plumer, Herbert Charles Onslow
Ann M. Lesch (1996)

Pogrom
Jon Jucovy (1996)

Point Four
Elizabeth Thompson (1996)

POLISARIO
Bruce Maddy-Weitzman

Politi, Elie
George R. Wilkes
Michael M. Laskier (1996)

Pollard Affair
Ian Black

Polygamy
Jenab Tutunji (1996)

Popular Front
Charles U. Zenzie (1996)

Popular Front for the Liberation of Palestine
Maria F. Curtis
Mouin Rabbani (1996)

Popular Front for the Liberation of Palestine–General Command
George R. Wilkes
Mouin Rabbani (1996)

Popular Front for the Liberation of the Occupied Arabian Gulf
Malcolm C. Peck (1996)

Population
Paul Rivlin
Justin McCarthy (1996)

Port Sa'id
Charles C. Kolb
David Waldner (1996)

Postage Stamps
Donald Malcolm Reid

Potash Industry
Chaim I. Waxman
Peter Gubser (1996)

Potsdam Convention
Zachary Karabell (1996)

Powell, Colin L.
Michael R. Fischbach

Princess Basma Women's Resource Center
Isis Nusair

Progressive Socialist Party
As'ad AbuKhalil
George E. Irani (1996)

Protectorate States
Robert D. Burrowes (1996)

Protestantism and Protestant Missions
Eleanor Abdella Doumato

Protocols of the Elders of Zion
Michael R. Marrus
Jane Gerber (1996)

Pushtun
Eric Hooglund
Ashraf Ghani (1996)

Pyramids
Donald Malcolm Reid

Q

Qabbani, Nizar
Michael R. Fischbach
Bassam Namani (1996)

Qaddafi, Muammar al-
Ronald Bruce St John
Lisa Anderson (1996)

Qaddumi, Faruq
Michael R. Fischbach

Qadi
Scott Alexander (1996)

Qadiriyya Order
Laurence Michalak (1996)

Qafih, Yihye ben Solomon
Michael M. Laskier (1996)

Qaʿida, al-
As'ad AbuKhalil

Qairawan
Matthew S. Gordon (1996)

Qajar, Abdullah Mirza
Mansoureh Ettehadieh (1996)

Qajar, Agha Mohammad
Mansoureh Ettehadieh (1996)

Qajar Dynasty
Eric Hooglund
John Foran (1996)

Qalqiliya
Michael R. Fischbach

Qanun
Elizabeth Thompson (1996)

Qaradawi, Yusuf al-
Abdin Chande

Qaramanli Dynasty
Rachel Simon (1996)

Qarawiyyin, al-
Rahma Bourqia (1996)

Qasim, Abd al-Karim
Louay Bahry (1996)

Qasimi Family of Raʾs al-Khayma, al-
Anthony B. Toth

Qasimi Family of Sharjah, al-
Anthony B. Toth

Qassam, Izz al-Din al-
Philip Mattar

Qatar
Anthony B. Toth
Malcolm C. Peck (1996)

Qatar Petroleum
Anthony B. Toth
Mary Ann Tétreault (1996)

Qaʿwar, Widad
Laurie King-Irani

Qawuqji, Fawzi al-
Ann M. Lesch (1996)

Qiyomijian, Ohannes
As'ad AbuKhalil (1996)

Qom
Parvaneh Pourshariati

Qotbzadeh, Sadeq
Neguin Yavari (1996)

Queen Surraya
Senzil Nawid

Qurai, Ahmad Sulayman
George R. Wilkes
Mouin Rabbani (1996)

Qur'an
Maysam J. al Faruqi
Elizabeth Thompson (1996)

Qusayr, al-
Donald Malcolm Reid
Arthur Goldschmidt (1996)

Qutb, Sayyid
Ahmad S. Moussalli
Jean-Marc R. Oppenheim (1996)

Quwatli, Shukri al-
Muhammad Muslih (1996)

R

Raab, Esther
Shibolet Zait (1996)

Raad, In'am
Michael R. Fischbach
George E. Irani (1996)

Rabat
Donna Lee Bowen (1996)

Rabbani, Burhanuddin
Grant Farr

Rabbi
Samuel C. Heilman (1996)

Rabi, Mubarak
Aida A. Bamia

Rabin, Yitzhak
Gregory S. Mahler

Rabiyya Ali, Salim
Robert D. Burrowes

Radio and Television: Arab Countries
William A. Rugh

Radio and Television: Israel
Dov Shinar

Radio and Television: Turkey
Brian Silverstein

Rafsanjani, Ali Akbar Hashemi
Eric Hooglund
Hamid Algar (1996)

Rahnavard, Zahra
Janet Afary

Rajavi, Masud
Ervand Abrahamian

Rajub, Jibril
Michael R. Fischbach

Ramadan, Taha Yasin
Michael R. Fischbach
Amatzia Baram (1996)

Ramallah
Michael R. Fischbach
Lawrence Tal (1996)

Ramgavar Azadagan Party
As'ad AbuKhalil (1996)

Ramla
Yehuda Gradus
Elizabeth Thompson (1996)

Ramses College for Girls
Linda Herrera

Rania al-Abdullah (Queen Rania)
Curtis R. Ryan

Rasafi, Ma'ruf al-
Sasson Somekh (1996)

Ra's al-Khayma
Anthony B. Toth
Malcolm C. Peck (1996)

Rassemblement National Démocratique (RND)
Azzedine G. Mansour

Rassemblement National des Indépendants (RNI)
Bruce Maddy-Weitzman

Rassemblement pour la Culture et la Démocratie (RCD)
Azzedine G. Mansour

Rateb, Aisha
Maria F. Curtis

Ratebzad, Anahita
Grant Farr

Ratosh, Yonatan
Bryan Daves (1996)

Rauf Ezzat, Heba
Marilyn Booth

Ravikovitch, Dahlia
Zafrira Lidovsky-Cohen
Nili Gold (1996)

Reagan Plan (1982)
Laurie Z. Eisenberg

Reagan, Ronald
Michael R. Fischbach

Recaizade Mahmud Ekrem
David Waldner (1996)

Red Crescent Society
Vanesa Casanova-Fernandez

Red Line Agreement
Mary Ann Tétreault (1996)

Refah Partisi
Nermin Abadan-Unat

Refugees: Afghan
Grant Farr

Refugees: Balkan Muslim
Noah Butler
Justin McCarthy (1996)

Refugees: Jewish
Meron Medzini
Michael M. Laskier (1996)

Refugees: Kurdish
Chris Kutschera

Refugees: Palestinian
Philip Mattar
Don Peretz (1996)

Rejection Front
Michael R. Fischbach
Elizabeth Thompson (1996)

Republican Brotherhood
Carolyn Fluehr-Lobban

Republican People's Party (RPP)
Nermin Abadan-Unat

Revolutionary Association of the Women of Afghanistan (RAWA)
Senzil Nawid

Revolutionary Command Council (Egypt)
Matthew S. Gordon (1996)

Revolutionary Command Council (Libya)
Ronald Bruce St John

Revolutionary Guards
Eric Hooglund

Richmond, Ernest T.
Jenab Tutunji (1996)

Rida, Rashid
Donald Malcolm Reid (1996)

Rif
C. R. Pennell (1996)

Rifaat, Alifa
Caroline Seymour-Jorn

Rifaʿi, Samir al-
Jenab Tutunji (1996)

Rifaʿi, Zaid al-
Michael R. Fischbach

Rif War
C. R. Pennell (1996)

Rishon le-Zion
Yehuda Gradus
Bryan Daves (1996)

Riyadh
J. E. Peterson

Riyad, Mahmud
George E. Irani (1996)

Riyad, Mustafa al-
Arthur Goldschmidt (1996)

Rockefeller Museum
Michael R. Fischbach
Mia Bloom (1996)

Rogers, William Pierce
Ahmed H. Ibrahim
Zachary Karabell (1996)

Rolo Family
Michael M. Laskier (1996)

Roman Catholicism and Roman Catholic Missions
John J. Donohue (1996)

Romanization
Kathleen R. F. Burrill (1996)

Rome, Treaty of (1935)
Zachary Karabell (1996)

Rommel, Erwin
Daniel E. Spector (1996)

Roosevelt, Franklin Delano
Daniel E. Spector (1996)

Roosevelt, Kermit
Neguin Yavari

Rothschild, Edmond de
Reeva S. Simon (1996)

Royal Dutch Shell
Jean-François Seznec (1996)

Rub al-Khali
J. E. Peterson
Eleanor Abdella Doumato (1996)

Rubinstein, Amnon
Gregory S. Mahler
Bryan Daves (1996)

Rumelia
Karen Pinto (1996)

Ruppin, Arthur
Donna Robinson Divine (1996)

Ruşdiye Schools
Elizabeth Thompson (1996)

Rusk, Dean
Charles C. Kolb

Russia and the Middle East
Robert O. Freedman
Oles M. Smolansky (1996)

Russian–Ottoman Wars
Eric Hooglund
Oles M. Smolansky (1996)

Rutenberg, Pinhas
Neil Caplan
Sara Reguer (1996)

S

Saʿada, Antun
Sami A. Ofeish
Charles U. Zenzie (1996)

Saadawi, Nawal al-
Rita Stephan
David Waldner (1996)

Saade, George
Michael R. Fischbach
George E. Irani (1996)

Saba Family
Elizabeth Thompson (1996)

Sabah, Rasha al-
Mary Ann Tétreault

Sabah, Suad al-
Rita Stephan

Sabbagh, Hasib
George R. Wilkes
Mouin Rabbani (1996)

Sabbagh, Salah al-Din al-
Reeva S. Simon (1996)

Sabbath
Samuel C. Heilman

Sabra
Bryan Daves (1996)

Sabra and Shatila Massacres
Philip Mattar

Sabri, Ali
David Waldner (1996)

Sadat, Anwar al-
Fred H. Lawson (1996)

Sadat, Jihan al-
Arthur Goldschmidt

Sadawi, Bashir
John L. Wright (1996)

Sadiqi College
Aida A. Bamia (1996)

Sadi, Said
Yahia Zoubir

Sadr, Muhammad Baqir al-
Ayad al-Qazzaz (1996)

Sadr, Muhsin
Neguin Yavari (1996)

Sadr, Sitt Rabab al- (Charafeddine)
Rula Jurdi Abisaab

Saʿdun, Abd al- Muhsin al-
Albertine Jwaideh (1996)

Saʿdun Family, al-
Albertine Jwaideh (1996)

Saʿedi, Gholamhossein
Pardis Minuchehr (1996)

Safed
Bryan Daves (1996)

Safveti Ziya
Elizabeth Thompson (1996)

Sagues, Albert
Michael M. Laskier (1996)

Sahara
Bruce Maddy-Weitzmann (1996)

Saharan Arab Democratic Republic (SADR)
Bruce Maddy-Weitzman

Sahnoun, Ahmed
Emad Eldin Shahin

Saʿid, Amina al-
Linda Herrera

Said, Edward
John M. Lundquist

Saʿid, Nuri al-
Louay Bahry (1996)

Saʿid Pasha
Donald Malcolm Reid

Saʿidzadeh, Seyyed Mohsen
Ziba Mir-Hosseini

Saint Catherine's Monastery
Thomas Stransky

Saint Joseph University
As'ad AbuKhalil (1996)

Saint Mark's Cathedral
Raymond William Baker (1996)

Saʿiqa, al-
George R. Wilkes
Mouin Rabbani (1996)

Saison
Pierre M. Atlas

Sakakini, Khalil al-
Elizabeth Thompson (1996)

Salafiyya Movement
Mahmoud Haddad (1996)

Salam Family
Michael R. Fischbach

Salam, Saʾib
Michael R. Fischbach
As'ad AbuKhalil (1996)

Salant, Samuel
Chaim I. Waxman (1996)

Salih, Ali Abdullah
Manfred W. Wenner

Salih, Teyib
Khalid M. El-Hassan

Salim Hasan
Donald Malcolm Reid (1996)

Salim, Ali
Nancy Berg
Roger Allen (1996)

Salim, Jawad
Sasson Somekh (1996)

Sallal, Abdullah al-
Robert D. Burrowes

Salonika
Eric Hooglund
Elizabeth Thompson (1996)

Salt, al-
Jenab Tutunji (1996)

Samaritans
Benyamim Tsedaka

Samarra
Paul S. Rowe
Nazar al-Khalaf (1996)

Samar, Sima
Senzil Nawid

Samman, Ghada
Elise Salem

Samuel, Herbert Louis
Bernard Wasserstein

San'a
Robert D. Burrowes

San'a University
Robert D. Burrowes

Sanctions, Iraqi
Peter Sluglett

Sane'i, Yusef
Azadeh Kian-Thiébaut

San Remo Conference (1920)
Zachary Karabell (1996)

San Stefano, Treaty of (1878)
Oles M. Smolansky (1996)

Sant Egidio Platform
George R. Wilkes

Sanusi, Muhammad ibn Ali al-
Rachel Simon (1996)

Sanusi Order
Rachel Simon (1996)

Sanu, Ya'qub
David Waldner (1996)

Sapir, Pinhas
Martin Malin (1996)

Sarid, Yossi
Mordechai Bar-On
Bryan Daves (1996)

Sarkis, Ilyas
Bassam Namani (1996)

Sartawi, Issam
Benjamin Joseph (1996)

Sasson, Eliyahu
Itamar Rabinovich
Neil Caplan

Sassoon Family
Sylvia G. Haim (1996)

Satellite Cities Development
Maria F. Curtis
Hani Fakhouri (1996)

Saudi Arabia
J. E. Peterson

Saudi, Mona
Jessica Winegar

Saunders, Harold
George R. Wilkes

Saygun, Ahmed Adnan
David Waldner (1996)

Sayyab, Badr Shakir al-
Kamal abu-Deeb (1996)

Sayyida Zaynab Mosque
Raymond William Baker (1996)

Sayyidna Husayn Mosque
Raymond William Baker (1996)

School for Hakīmāt
Nancy Gallagher

Science and Technology
Antoine Benjamin Zahlan

Scouts
Guilain P. Denoeux (1996)

Sebastiani, Horace
Zachary Karabell (1996)

Sebbar, Leila
Aida A. Bamia

Sediq, Sohaila
Senzil Nawid

Sefrioui, Ahmed
Aida A. Bamia

Şeker Ahmet
David Waldner (1996)

Selçuk, Munir Nurettin
David Waldner (1996)

Selim III
I. Metin Kunt (1996)

Semitic Languages
David Waldner (1996)

Sepehri, Sohrab
Eric Hooglund
Pardis Minuchehr (1996)

September 11th, 2001
As'ad AbuKhalil

Seri, Dan-Benaya
Zvia Ginor (1996)

Setif
Phillip C. Naylor (1996)

Setif Revolt (1945)
Phillip C. Naylor (1996)

Şevket, Mahmut
Elizabeth Thompson (1996)

Sèvres Protocol (1956)
S. Ilan Troen

Sèvres, Treaty of (1920)
Sara Reguer (1996)

Sezer, Ahmet
M. Hakan Yavuz

Sfar, Bashir
Laurence Michalak (1996)

Sfar, Tahar
Vanesa Casanova-Fernandez
Matthew S. Gordon (1996)

Sfax
Matthew S. Gordon (1996)

Sfeir, Nasrallah
As'ad AbuKhalil

Shabʿa Farms
As'ad AbuKhalil

Shabbi, Abu al-Qasim al-
Larry A. Barrie (1996)

Shaʿbi Family
Manfred W. Wenner

Shader, Joseph
Guilain P. Denoeux (1996)

Shafiʿi School of Law
Wael B. Hallaq (1996)

Shafiq, Durriyya
David Waldner (1996)

Shahada, George
Michael R. Fischbach
Guilain P. Denoeux (1996)

Shahbandar, Abd al-Rahman
Charles U. Zenzie (1996)

Shahin, Tanyos
As'ad AbuKhalil (1996)

Shahin, Yusuf
Roxanne Varzi
David Waldner (1996)

Shaltut, Muhammad
Crystal Procyshen
Raymond William Baker (1996)

Shalvi, Alice
George R. Wilkes

Shami, Ahmad Muhammad al-
Robert D. Burrowes

Shamikh, Mubarak Abdullah al-
Ronald Bruce St John

Shami, Muhammad Abdullah al-
Robert D. Burrowes

Shamir, Moshe
Donna Robinson Divine
Ann Kahn (1996)

Shamir, Yitzhak
Charles Enderlin
Yaakov Shavit (1996)

Shamlu, Ahmad
Eric Hooglund
Michael C. Hillmann (1996)

Shammas, Anton
Michael R. Fischbach
Ann Kahn (1996)

Shapira, Hayyim Moshe
Bryan Daves (1996)

Sharabati, Ahmad al-
Abdul-Karim Rafeq (1996)

Shaʿrawi, Huda al-
Marilyn Booth
David Waldner (1996)

Shaʿrawi, Muhammad Mutwalli al-
As'ad AbuKhalil

Sharef, Zeʾev
Gregory S. Mahler
Bryan Daves (1996)

Sharett, Moshe
Gregory S. Mahler (1996)

Shariʿa
Wael B. Hallaq (1996)

Shariʿati, Ali
Hamid Algar (1996)

Shariatmadari, Kazem
Neguin Yavari (1996)

Sharif
Scott Alexander (1996)

Sharif, Aziz
Michael R. Fischbach
Marion Farouk-Sluglett (1996)

Sharif-Emami, Jaʿfar
Neguin Yavari

Sharifian Dynasties
Edmund Burke III (1996)

Sharif of Mecca
Khalid Y. Blankinship (1996)

Sharif, Omar
Roxanne Varzi
David Waldner (1996)

Sharjah
Eric Hooglund
Malcolm C. Peck (1996)

Sharm al-Shaykh
Arthur Goldschmidt
Zachary Karabell (1996)

Sharon, Ariel
Eric Silver
Yaakov Shavit (1996)

Sharqi Family, al-
Anthony B. Toth
M. Morsy Abdullah (1996)

Shatt al-Arab
Neguin Yavari

Shaʾul, Anwar
Sasson Somekh

Shawa, Laila
Jessica Winegar

Shaw Commission
Philip Mattar (1996)

Shawqi, Ahmad
Irfan Shahîd

Shaykh
Marilyn Higbee (1996)

Shaykh al-Islam
Scott Alexander (1996)

Shaykh, Hanan al-
Elise Salem

Shaykhi
Juan R. I. Cole

Shazar, Shneour Zalman
Bryan Daves (1996)

Shazli, Saʿd al-Din
David Waldner (1996)

Shekel
Bryan Daves (1996)

Shenhar, Yitzhak
Bryan Daves (1996)

Shenouda III
Arthur Goldschmidt
Donald Spanel (1996)

Shepheard's Hotel
Zachary Karabell (1996)

Sheshbesh
Cyrus Moshaver (1996)

Shiberghan
Grant Farr

Shid, Nahid
Azadeh Kian-Thiébaut

Shidyaq, Ahmad Faris al-
Guilain P. Denoeux (1996)

Shihabi, Zlikha al-
Ellen L. Fleischmann

Shiʿism
Roxanne Varzi
Tayeb El-Hibri (1996)

Shilluk
David Waldner (1996)

Shiloah, Reuven
Ian Black

Shimʿun, Mar
Peter Sluglett (1996)

Shin Bet
Ian Black
Julie Zuckerman (1996)

Shiraz
Eric Hooglund
Neguin Yavari (1996)

Shirazi, Mirza Hasan
Farhad Arshad (1996)

Shiraz University
Parvaneh Pourshariati

Shitreet, Bekhor
Bryan Daves (1996)

Shlonsky, Avraham
Mordechai Bar-On

Shochat, Manya
George R. Wilkes

Shorfa
Rahma Bourqia (1996)

Shuf
Michael R. Fischbach
As'ad AbuKhalil (1996)

Shufman, Gershon
Ann Kahn (1996)

Shukri, Mohammad
Aida A. Bamia

Shultz, George
Oliver Benjamin Hemmerle

Shumayyil, Shibli
Elizabeth Thompson (1996)

Shuqayri, Ahmad
Michael R. Fischbach

Shuqayri Family
Elizabeth Thompson (1996)

Shura
Elizabeth Thompson (1996)

Shuster, W. Morgan
Daniel E. Spector (1996)

Sib, Treaty of (1920)
Robert G. Landen (1996)

Sidera, Zineb
Jessica Winegar

Sidon
Charles C. Kolb
George E. Irani (1996)

Sidqi, Bakr
Peter Sluglett (1996)

Sidqi, Ismaʿil
David Waldner (1996)

Sidra, Gulf of
Stuart J. Borsch (1996)

Silk
Elizabeth Thompson (1996)

Silver, Abba Hillel
Mark A. Raider
Mia Bloom (1996)

Simavi, Sedat
Elizabeth Thompson (1996)

Sinai Peninsula
Paul S. Rowe
Elizabeth Thompson (1996)

Şinasi, İbrahim
Zachary Karabell (1996)

Şirket-i Hayriye
Elizabeth Thompson (1996)

Sirry, Gazbia
Jessica Winegar

Sisco, Joseph
George R. Wilkes

Sistan and Baluchistan
Parvaneh Pourshariati

Sistani, Ali al-
Michael R. Fischbach

Sitra
Fred H. Lawson (1996)

Sivas Conference (1919)
Ahmet Kuyas (1996)

Siwa Oasis
Arthur Goldschmidt

Slave Trade
Ehud R. Toledano (1996)

Smilansky, Moshe
George R. Wilkes
Ann Kahn (1996)

Sneh, Moshe
Gregory S. Mahler
Walter F. Weiker (1996)

Sobol, Yehoshua
Donna Robinson Divine
Julie Zuckerman (1996)

Social Democratic Party of Azerbaijan
Audrey L. Altstadt (1996)

Social Democratic Populist Party
M. Hakan Yavuz
Frank Tachau (1996)

Socotra
Robert D. Burrowes

Soheyli, Ali
Neguin Yavari (1996)

Sokolow, Nahum
Pierre M. Atlas

Soltani, Abdellatif
Emad Eldin Shahin

Somikh, Abdullah
Michael R. Fischbach
Sasson Somekh (1996)

SONATRACH
Ana Torres-Garcia
Dirk Vandewalle (1996)

Soroush, AbdolKarim
Afshin Matin-asgari

Sousse
Matthew S. Gordon (1996)

Soustelle, Jacques
Zachary Karabell (1996)

South Arabian Armed Forces
Robert D. Burrowes (1996)

South Arabian League
Manfred W. Wenner (1996)

Southeastern Anatolia Project
David Waldner (1996)

South Lebanon Army
Laurie Z. Eisenberg
Elizabeth Thompson (1996)

South Persia Rifles
Eric Hooglund
Jack Bubon (1996)

Spain and the Middle East
Vanesa Casanova-Fernandez

Spanish Morocco
Bruce Maddy-Weitzman (1996)

Special Forces of the Levant
As'ad AbuKhalil (1996)

Sphinx
Donald Malcolm Reid (1996)

Sprinzak, Joseph
Bryan Daves (1996)

Srvantziants, Garegin
Rouben P. Adalian (1996)

Stack, Lee
Oles M. Smolansky (1996)

Stanhope, Hester
Marilyn Booth

Stark, Freya
Ronald Bruce St John

Star of North Africa
John Ruedy (1996)

State Planning Organization (SPO)
Nermin Abadan-Unat

Stern, Abraham
Julie Zuckerman (1996)

Stock Market
Jean-François Seznec

Storrs, Ronald
Michael R. Fischbach (1996)

Straits Convention
Daniel E. Spector (1996)

Straits, Turkish
J. C. Hurewitz (1996)

Struma
Miriam Simon (1996)

Students in the Line of the Imam
Eric Hooglund
Neguin Yavari (1996)

Suarès Family
Michael M. Laskier (1996)

Sublime Porte
Zachary Karabell (1996)

Sudan
Ann M. Lesch

Sudanese Civil Wars
Ann M. Lesch

Sudanese Women's Union
Sondra Hale

Sudd
Robert O. Collins

Suez Canal
Jean-François Seznec
Arthur Goldschmidt (1996)

Suez Canal University
Donald Malcolm Reid

Suez Crisis (1956–1957)
Mordechai Bar-On

Suez–Mediterranean Pipeline
Jean-François Seznec

Sufism and the Sufi Orders
Maysam J. al Faruqi

Suissa, Albert
Donna Robinson Divine
Zvia Ginor (1996)

Sulayman, Hikmat
Peter Sluglett (1996)

Sulaymaniya
Nazar al-Khalaf (1996)

Suleiman, Mulay
Matthew S. Gordon (1996)

Sulh, Kazem al-
Guilain P. Denoeux (1996)

Sulh, Rashid al-
Michael R. Fischbach
Guilain P. Denoeux (1996)

Sulh, Riyad al-
Guilain P. Denoeux (1996)

Sulh, Sami al-
As'ad AbuKhalil (1996)

Sulh, Taki al-Din al-
Michael R. Fischbach
Guilain P. Denoeux (1996)

Sultan
I. Metin Kunt (1996)

Sultan Ahmet Mosque
Aptullah Kuran (1996)

Sultan Hasan Mosque
Raymond William Baker (1996)

Sultani Schools
Elizabeth Thompson (1996)

Sumud
Elizabeth Thompson (1996)

Sunay, Cevdet
Elizabeth Thompson (1996)

Sun Language Theory
Elizabeth Thompson (1996)

Sunna
Maysam J. al Faruqi
Scott Alexander (1996)

Sunni Islam
Maysam J. al Faruqi
Tayeb El-Hibri (1996)

Suphi Ezgi
David Waldner (1996)

Supreme Muslim Council
Philip Mattar

Sursock, Lady Cochrane
Mona Takieddine Amyuni

Sursuq Family
Elizabeth Thompson (1996)

Suwaydi Family
Ayad al-Qazzaz (1996)

Suwaydi, Tawfiq al-
Ayad al-Qazzaz (1996)

Suwaydiya Oil Fields
Abdul-Karim Rafeq

Suwayhli, Ramadan al-
George Joffe (1996)

Sykes, Mark
Roger Adelson
Zachary Karabell (1996)

Sykes–Picot Agreement (1916)
Zachary Karabell (1996)

Syria
Ronald Bruce St John
Fred H. Lawson (1996)

Syrian Desert
Abdul-Karim Rafeq (1996)

Syrian Social Nationalist Party
Ronald Bruce St John

Syrkin, Nachman
Donna Robinson Divine (1996)

Szold, Henrietta
Mia Bloom (1996)

T

Taba
Philip Mattar
Ann M. Lesch (1996)

Taba Negotiations (1995, 2001)
Philip Mattar

Tabaqa Dam
John R. Clark (1996)

Tabataba'i, Mohammad
Eric Hooglund
Hamid Algar (1996)

Tabataba'i, Ziya
Hamid Algar (1996)

Tabriz
Neguin Yavari

Tabriz University
Parvaneh Pourshariati
Neguin Yavari (1996)

Tagger, Sioneh
Julie Zuckerman (1996)

Taha, Mahmud Muhammad
Carolyn Fluehr-Lobban

Tahir, Kemal
David Waldner (1996)

Tahtawi, Rifa'a al-Rafi al-
Abdel Aziz EzzelArab (1996)

Ta'if Accord
George E. Irani
Bryan Daves (1996)

Ta'if, al-
J. E. Peterson

Ta'if, Treaty of al-
Anthony B. Toth
F. Gregory Gause, III (1996)

Ta'iz
Robert D. Burrowes

Tajiks
Grant Farr

Takfir wa al-Hijra, al-
Ahmad S. Moussalli
David Waldner (1996)

Talabani, Jalal
Chris Kutschera

Talal ibn Abdullah
Jenab Tutunji (1996)

Talat, Mehmet
Zachary Karabell (1996)

Taleqani, Azam
Azadeh Kian-Thiébaut

Talfa, Adnan Khayr Allah
Amatzia Baram (1996)

Taliban
Hafeez Malik

Tallal, Chaibia
Jessica Winegar

Tall al-Zaʿtar Refugee Camp
Elizabeth Thompson (1996)

Tall, Mustafa Wahbi al-
Michael R. Fischbach (1996)

Tall, Wasfi al-
Jenab Tutunji (1996)

Talmud
Ephraim Tabory
Benjamin Joseph (1996)

Tamimahs
Calvin H. Allen, Jr. (1996)

Tamimi, Amin al-
Elizabeth Thompson (1996)

Tamir, Shmuel
Gregory S. Mahler
Julie Zuckerman (1996)

Tammuz, Benyamin
Ann Kahn (1996)

Tanburi Cemil
David Waldner (1996)

Taner, Haldun
Elizabeth Thompson (1996)

Tangier, Treaty of
Kenneth J. Perkins (1996)

Tanpinar, Ahmed Hamdi
David Waldner (1996)

Tantawi, Muhammad Sayyid al-
Ahmad S. Moussalli

Tanzimat
Elizabeth Thompson (1996)

Taqla, Philippe
Khalil Gebara
Guilain P. Denoeux (1996)

Tarhan, Abdülhak Hamit
David Waldner (1996)

Tarikh Tolana
Grant Farr

Tariki, Abdullah
Anthony B. Toth
Les Ordeman (1996)

Tashilhit Language
Rahma Bourqia (1996)

Taurus Mountains
John R. Clark (1996)

Tax Farming
Ariel Salzmann (1996)

Tchernichovsky, Saul
Ann Kahn (1996)

Tea
Eric Hooglund
Clifford A. Wright (1996)

Technion-Israel Institute of Technology
Miriam Simon (1996)

Tehran
Eric Hooglund
Mansoureh Ettahedieh (1996)

Tekeli, Şirin
Yesim Arat

Tekke
Scott Alexander (1996)

Tel Aviv
Donna Robinson Divine (1996)

Tel Aviv University
Miriam Simon (1996)

Tel Hai
Donna Robinson Divine

Templars
Michael R. Fischbach

Terrorism
Eric Hooglund
Richard W. Bulliet (1996)

Tetuan
Bruce Maddy-Weitzman (1996)

Tevfik Fikret
David Waldner (1996)

Textile Industry
Charles Issawi (1996)

Thaalbi, Abd al-Aziz
Kenneth J. Perkins (1996)

Tharthar Project
Albertine Jwaideh (1996)

Tharwat, Abd al-Khaliq
David Waldner (1996)

Theater
Dina Amin

Tiberias
Bryan Daves (1996)

Tigris and Euphrates Rivers
John R. Clark (1996)

Tikrit
Michael R. Fischbach
Amatzia Baram (1996)

Tikriti Families
Ayad Al-Qazzaz

Tikriti, Hardan al-
Michael R. Fischbach
Amatzia Baram (1996)

Timar
Eric Hooglund
Elizabeth Thompson (1996)

Tindouf
David Gutelius

Tiran, Strait of
Anthony B. Toth

Tlas, Mustafa
Michael R. Fischbach

Tlatli, Moufida
Laura Rice

Tlemcen
Laurence Michalak (1996)

Tlili, Mustafa
Aida A. Bamia

Tobacco Revolt
Eric Hooglund
Roshanak Malek (1996)

Tobruk
Daniel E. Spector (1996)

Topkapi Palace
Eric Hooglund
Aptullah Kuran (1996)

Toumi, Khalida
Yahia Zoubir

Tourism
Anthony B. Toth

Trade
Mary Ann Tétreault
Charles Issawi (1996)

Trad, Petro
As'ad AbuKhalil (1996)

Trans-Arabian Pipeline
Mary Ann Tétreault

Trans-Iranian Railway
Jack Bubon (1996)

Transjordan Frontier Force
Jenab Tutunji (1996)

Transport
Anthony B. Toth
Charles Issawi (1996)

Trans-Turkey Pipeline
Niyazi Dalyanci (1996)

Treaty of 1815
Eric Hooglund

Treaty of Protection (1886)
Robert D. Burrowes (1996)

Tribes and Tribalism: Arabian Peninsula
Eleanor Abdella Doumato (1996)

Tribes and Tribalism: Butayna Tribe
Abdul-Karim Rafeq (1996)

Tribes and Tribalism: Dawasir Tribe
Eleanor Abdella Doumato (1996)

Tribes and Tribalism: Fadan Kharasa Tribe
Abdul-Karim Rafeq (1996)

Tribes and Tribalism: Guish Tribes
Rahma Bourqia (1996)

Tribes and Tribalism: Hassana Tribe
Abdul-Karim Rafeq (1996)

Tribes and Tribalism: Matawirah Tribe
Abdul-Karim Rafeq (1996)

Tribes and Tribalism: Muntafiq Tribe
Albertine Jwaideh (1996)

Tribes and Tribalism: Murrah, al-
Eleanor Abdella Doumato (1996)

Tribes and Tribalism: Mutayr Tribe
Eleanor Abdella Doumato (1996)

Tribes and Tribalism: Qashqa'i
Lois Beck (1996)

Tribes and Tribalism: Quraysh Tribe
Eleanor Abdella Doumato (1996)

Tribes and Tribalism: Shammar
Eleanor Abdella Doumato (1996)

Tribes and Tribalism: Tebu Tribe
Stuart J. Borsch (1996)

Tribes and Tribalism: Utayba Tribe
Eleanor Abdella Doumato (1996)

Tribes and Tribalism: Yazidis
Reeva S. Simon (1996)

Tribes and Tribalism: Yemeni
Robert D. Burrowes (1996)

Tripartite Treaty of Alliance
Eric Hooglund

Tripoli
John L. Wright (1996)

Tripoli Conference (1977)
Elizabeth Thompson (1996)

Tripoli Programme (1962)
Phillip C. Naylor (1996)

Tripolitania
Ronald Bruce St John

Trucial Coast
Malcolm C. Peck (1996)

True Path Party
M. Hakan Yavuz
Frank Tachau (1996)

Truman, Harry S.
Antonio Donno

Trumpeldor, Yosef
Donna Robinson Divine

Tsemel, Leah
Mona Ghali

Tubi, Tawfiq
Bryan Daves (1996)

Tudeh Party
Ervand Abrahamian

Tuhami al-Glawi
Edmund Burke III (1996)

Tuman Bey
Bassam Namani (1996)

Tunb Islands
Eric Hooglund
Malcolm C. Peck (1996)

Tunis
Larry A. Barrie (1996)

Tunisia: Overview
Angel M. Foster
Larry A. Barrie (1996)

Tunisia: Personal Status Code
Mounira Charrad

Tunisia: Political Parties in
Ana Torres-Garcia
Larry A. Barrie (1996)

Tunisi, Bayram al-
David Waldner (1996)

Tuqan, Fadwa
Michael R. Fischbach
Abla M. Amawi (1996)

Tuqan Family
Michael R. Fischbach
Elizabeth Thompson (1996)

Turabi, Hasan al-
Ahmad S. Moussalli
Jillian Schwedler (1996)

Turabi, Wisal al-Mahdi
Carolyn Fluehr-Lobban

Türkes, Alparslan
M. Hakan Yavuz
Frank Tachau (1996)

Turkey
Eric Hooglund
David Waldner (1996)

Turki, Fawaz
Michael R. Fischbach
Jenab Tutunji (1996)

Turkish–Afghan Treaty (1928)
David Waldner (1996)

Turkish Grand National Assembly
Nermin Abadan-Unat

Turkish Hearth Association
Paul J. Magnarella (1996)

Turkish Historical Society
Uli Schamiloglu (1996)

Turkish–Italian War (1911–1912)
Eric Hooglund
Rachel Simon (1996)

Turkish Language
Eric Hooglund
Erika Gilson (1996)

Turkish Law on the Protection of the Family (1998)
Burçak Keskin-Kozat

Turkish Linguistic Society
Uli Schamiloglu (1996)

Turkish National Pact
Frank Tachau (1996)

Turkish Script
Noah Butler

Turkish Workers Party
Frank Tachau (1996)

Turkism
Elizabeth Thompson (1996)

Turkmanchai, Treaty of (1828)
Eric Hooglund
Farhad Shirzad (1996)

Turko–Iranian War (1821–1823)
Daniel E. Spector (1996)

Turkology
Uli Schamiloglu (1996)

Turks
Eric Hooglund

Twareg
Thomas G. Penchoen (1996)

Twayni, Ghassan
Michael R. Fischbach
Guilain P. Denoeux (1996)

Twin Pillars Policy
Eric Hooglund
Zachary Karabell (1996)

Tyre
George E. Irani (1996)

U

Uganda Project
Chaim I. Waxman

Ulama
Denise A. Spellberg

Umar, Madiha
Jessica Winegar

Umayyad Mosque
Muhammad Muslih (1996)

Umm al-Qaywayn
Anthony B. Toth
Malcolm C. Peck (1996)

Umm al-Qura University
Khalid Y. Blankinship (1996)

Umma Party
Robert O. Collins

Umm Kulthum
Virginia Danielson (1996)

Umm Naʿsan
Fred H. Lawson (1996)

Union Démocratique du Manifeste Algérien (UDMA)
John Ruedy (1996)

Union Générale des Travailleurs Marocains (UGTM)
Ana Torres-Garcia
Larry A. Barrie (1996)

Union Générale des Travailleurs Tunisiens (UGTT)
Ana Torres-Garcia
Larry A. Barrie (1996)

Union Marocaine du Travail (UMT)
Ana Torres-Garcia
Bradford Dillman (1996)

Union Nationale des Etudiants Marocains (UNEM)
Bruce Maddy-Weitzman

Union Nationale des Forces Populaires (UNFP)
Vanesa Casanova-Fernandez
Bradford Dillman (1996)

Union of Tunisian Women
Angel M. Foster

Union Socialiste des Forces Populaires (USFP)
Vanesa Casanova-Fernandez

Union Tunisienne des Industrialistes, Compagnies, Artisans (UTICA)
Vanesa Casanova-Fernandez
Larry A. Barrie (1996)

United Arab Emirates
Anthony B. Toth
Malcolm C. Peck (1996)

United Arab Republic (UAR)
Michael R. Fischbach (1996)

United Jewish Appeal (UJA)
Paul Rivlin

United Nations and the Middle East
Thomas G. Weiss
F. T. Liu (1996)

United Nations Conciliation Commission for Palestine (UNCCP)
Neil Caplan
Fred J. Khouri (1996)

United Nations Economic Survey Mission (1949)
Zach Levey

United Nations Emergency Force
F. T. Liu (1996)

United Nations Interim Force in Lebanon
Brian Urquhart
As'ad AbuKhalil (1996)

United Nations Relief and Works Agency for Palestine Refugees in the Near East (UNRWA)
Michael R. Fischbach
F. T. Liu (1996)

United Nations Special Commission (UNSCOM)
Ayad Al-Qazzaz

United Nations Special Committee on Palestine, 1947 (UNSCOP)
Joseph Nevo
F. T. Liu (1996)

United Nations Truce Supervision Organization (UNTSO)
Neil Caplan
Charles U. Zenzie (1996)

United States of America and the Middle East
Don Peretz

Unity Party
Frank Tachau (1996)

University of Jordan
Michael R. Fischbach
Jenab Tutunji (1996)

University of Khartoum
Robert O. Collins

University of Tehran
Eric Hooglund
Mansoureh Ettehadieh (1996)

Urabi, Ahmad
Arthur Goldschmidt (1996)

Urbanization
Anthony B. Toth
John R. Clark (1996)

Urban Planning
Eric Hooglund
Hooshang Amirahmadi (1996)

Urwa al-Wuthqa, al-
Nikki Keddie (1996)

Uşakliğil, Halit Ziya
Elizabeth Thompson (1996)

Üsküdar
Elizabeth Thompson (1996)

Ussishkin, Menahem
Donna Robinson Divine

Usuli
Neguin Yavari

Utaybi, Juhayman al-
Eric Hooglund
Abdel Aziz EzzelArab (1996)

Uthman, Muhammad Ali
Robert D. Burrowes

Uthman, Uthman Ahmad
Arthur Goldschmidt

Uzbeks
M. Nazif Shahrani (1996)

V

Vaʿad Leʾumi
Neil Caplan

Vaka-i Hayriye
Eric Hooglund
Avigdor Levy (1996)

Valensi, Alfred
Norman Stillman

Vance, Cyrus
Daniel E. Spector

Van, Lake
John R. Clark

Vanunu Affair
Gregory S. Mahler
Julie Zuckerman (1996)

Varlik Vergisi
Elizabeth Thompson

Vatican and the Middle East
George E. Irani

Vazhapetian, Nerses
Rouben P. Adalian

Vazir Afkham, Soltan Ali Khan
Neguin Yavari

Vaziri, Qamar al-Moluk
Parvaneh Pourshariati

Velayat-e Faqih
Eric Hooglund
Hamid Algar (1996)

Velayati, Ali Akbar
Ali Akbar Mahdi

Versailles, Treaty of (1920)
Daniel E. Spector

Victoria College
William L. Cleveland
Alain Silvera (1996)

Village Institutes
Paul J. Magnarella

Volpi, Giuseppe
George Joffe

Vozuq al-Dowleh, Mirza Hasan Khan
Neguin Yavari

W

Wadi Hadramawt
Robert D. Burrowes (1996)

Wadi Natrun
Arthur Goldschmidt
Raymond William Baker (1996)

Wafd
J. Janice Terry

Wafdist Women's Central Committee
Maria F. Curtis

Wahrhaftig, Zerah
Gregory S. Mahler
Bryan Daves (1996)

Wallach, Yona
Nili Gold (1996)

Waqf
Imad-ad-Dean Ahmad
Denise A. Spellberg (1996)

War in Iraq (2003)
Michael R. Fischbach

Warnier Law
Peter von Sivers (1996)

War of Attrition (1969–1970)
Arthur Goldschmidt
Benjamin Joseph (1996)

Water
David B. Brooks

Wattar, al-Taher
Azzedine G. Mansour
Aida A. Bamia (1996)

Wauchope, Arthur
Bernard Wasserstein
Karen A. Thornsvard (1996)

Wavell, Archibald Percival
Daniel E. Spector (1996)

Wazir, Intisar al- (Umm Jihad)
Khaled Islaih

Wazir, Khalil al-
Mouin Rabbani (1996)

Wazzani, Muhammad Hassan al-
Bruce Maddy-Weitzman (1996)

Weizman, Ezer
Gregory S. Mahler

Weizmann, Chaim
Bernard Wasserstein

Weizmann Institute of Science
Miriam Simon (1996)

West Bank
David Newman
Geoffrey Aronson (1996)

Westernization
Peter Sluglett

Western Sahara
Ana Torres-Garcia
Bruce Maddy-Weitzman (1996)

Western Sahara War
Bruce Maddy-Weitzman

Western Wall
Samuel C. Heilman (1996)

Western Wall Disturbances
Philip Mattar (1996)

West German Reparations Agreement
Paul Rivlin

Wheelus Air Force Base
Stuart J. Borsch (1996)

White Flag League
Kenneth S. Mayers (1996)

White Papers on Palestine
Ann M. Lesch

White Revolution (1961–1963)
Eric Hooglund

Wifaq, al-
Norman Stillman (1996)

Wilson, Arnold T.
Peter Sluglett (1996)

Wilson, Woodrow
Lawrence Davidson
Zachary Karabell (1996)

Wingate, Charles Orde
Reeva S. Simon (1996)

Wingate, Reginald
Janice J. Terry (1996)

Wise, Stephen S.
Mark Raider

Wolff, Henry Drummond
Parvaneh Pourshariati (1996)

Women and Family Affairs Center
Islah Jad

Women in Black
George R. Wilkes

Women's Affairs Center (Gaza)
Islah Jad

Women's Centre for Legal Aid and Counseling
Islah Jad

Women's Forum for Research and Training (Yemen)
Susanne Dahlgren

Women's International Zionist Organization
Shimon Avish

Women's Library and Information Center (Istanbul)
Yesim Arat

Women's Organization of Iran (WOI)
Haleh Vaziri

Women's People's Party (1923)
Burçak Keskin-Kozat

Women's Religious Rituals
Sabine Kalinock

Women's Renaissance Club
Jacqueline Ismael

Women's Services
Nermin Abadan-Unat (1996)

Women's Studies Center (Jerusalem)
Islah Jad

Woodhead Commission (1938)
Pierre M. Atlas
Benjamin Joseph (1996)

World Bank
Jean-François Seznec

World Federation of Sephardi Communities
Mia Bloom (1996)

World Organization of Jews from Arab Countries (WOJAC)
Michael M. Laskier

World War I
Sara Reguer (1996)

World War II
Daniel E. Spector (1996)

World Zionist Organization (WZO)
Bernard Wasserstein

Y

Ya'ari, Me'ir
Bryan Daves (1996)

Yacine, Abdessalame
Henri Lauzière

Yacoubi, Rachida
Rabia Bekkar

Yadin, Yigael
Gregory S. Mahler
Mia Bloom (1996)

Yad Mordekhai
Jon Jucovy

Yad Vashem
Jon Jucovy (1996)

Yahya ibn Muhammad Hamid al-Din
Manfred W. Wenner (1996)

Yamani, Ahmad Zaki
Anthony B. Toth

Yanbu
J. E. Peterson

Yariv, Aharon
Julie Zuckerman (1996)

Yarmuk River
Elizabeth Thompson (1996)

Yarmuk University
Jenab Tutunji (1996)

Yasar Kemal
Chris Kutschera
Kathleen R. F. Burrill (1996)

Yasin, Ahmad Ismaʿil
As'ad AbuKhalil

Yata, Ali
C. R. Pennell (1996)

Yazd
Eric Hooglund

Yazdi, Ibrahim
Neguin Yavari

Yaziji, Ibrahim
Guilain P. Denoeux (1996)

Yaziji, Nasif
Mark Mechler (1996)

Yehoshua, Avraham B.
Stephen Schecter
Ann Kahn (1996)

Yellin-Mor, Natan
Pierre M. Atlas
Bryan Daves (1996)

Yemen
Manfred W. Wenner

Yemen Arab Republic
Robert D. Burrowes (1996)

Yemen Civil War
Robert D. Burrowes (1996)

Yemen Dynasties
Manfred W. Wenner (1996)

Yemen Hunt Oil Company
Robert D. Burrowes

Yemeni Socialist Party
Manfred W. Wenner

Yemeni Women's Union
Susanne Dahlgren

Yeshiva
Samuel C. Heilman (1996)

Yiddish
Neil Caplan
Reeva S. Simon (1996)

Yildirim Army
Elizabeth Thompson (1996)

Yishuv
Donna Robinson Divine

Yizhar, S.
Donna Robinson Divine
Bryan Daves (1996)

Yosef, Ovadiah
Ephraim Tabory
Julie Zuckerman (1996)

Young Algerians
John Ruedy (1996)

Young Egypt
James Jankowski (1996)

Young Ottomans
Hasan Kayali (1996)

Young Tunisians
O. W. Abi-Mershed

Young Turks
Hasan Kayali (1996)

Youssef, Mulay
Matthew S. Gordon (1996)

Youssoufi, Abderrahmane
Henri Lauzière

Youth Aliyah
Donna Robinson Divine

Youth Movements
Guilain P. Denoeux (1996)

Yücel, Hasan Ali
Elizabeth Thompson (1996)

Yüksek Öğretim Kurulu (YOK)
Burçak Keskin-Kozat
I. Metin Kunt (1996)

Yunis Jabir, Abu Bakr
Ronald Bruce St John

Yurdakul, Mehmet Emin
David Waldner (1996)

Yusufian, Boghos
Rouben P. Adalian (1996)

Yusuf, Yusuf Salman
Marion Farouk-Sluglett (1996)

Z

Zab Rivers
John R. Clark (1996)

Zabul
Grant Farr

Zach, Natan
Adina Friedman
Yaron Peleg (1996)

Zaghlul, Saʿd
Janice J. Terry (1996)

Zagros
Parvaneh Pourshariati (1996)

Zahawi, Jamil Sidqi al-
Jacqueline Ismael

Zahedan
Eric Hooglund

Zahir Shah
M. Nazif Shahrani

Zahla
George E. Irani (1996)

Zaʿim, Husni al-
Eyal Zisser
Charles U. Zeznie (1996)

Zamzam
Scott Alexander (1996)

Zana, Leyla
Shahrzad Mojab

Zanan Magazine
Nayereh Tohidi

Zangwill, Israel
Miriam Simon (1996)

Zanzibar
Malcolm C. Peck (1996)

Zaqaziq University
Donald Malcolm Reid

Zaraniq Confederation
Robert D. Burrowes (1996)

Zarqa, al-
Abla M. Amavi (1996)

Zaydan, Jurji
Thomas Philipp (1996)

Zaydism
Robert D. Burrowes (1996)

Zaytuna University
Aida A. Bamia (1996)

Zayyat, Latifa
Marilyn Booth

Zbiri, Tahar
Phillip C. Naylor

Zeid, Fahralnissa
Jessica Winegar

Zelda
Donna Robinson Divine
Zvia Ginor (1996)

Zell al-Soltan, Masʿud Mirza
Lawrence G. Potter (1996)

Zeroual, Liamine
Yahia Zoubir
Mia Bloom (1996)

Ziadeh, May
Elise Salem

Zikhron Yaʿakov
Bryan Daves (1996)

Zili, Ridha
Aida A. Bamia

Zionism
Neil Caplan
Donna Robinson Divine (1996)

Zionist Commission for Palestine
Donna Robinson Divine (1996)

Zionist Organization of America
Jerry Kutnick
Bryan Daves (1996)

Zionist Revisionist Movement
Yaakov Shavit (1996)

Ziwaj Mutʿa
Rula Jurdi Abisaab

Ziya, Abdülhamit
Elizabeth Thompson (1996)

Zohar, Uri
Chaim I. Waxman

Zohrab, Krikor
Rouben P. Adalian (1996)

Zonnenfeld, Yosef Hayyim
Chaim I. Waxman (1996)

Zoroastrianism
Eric Hooglund
Jamsheed K. Choksky (1996)

Zubayri, Qaʾid Muhammad Mahmud al-
Manfred W. Wenner (1996)

Zuʿbi, Mahmud al-
Michael R. Fischbach
Charles U. Zenzie (1996)

Zurayk, Constantine
Michael R. Fischbach
Charles U. Zenzie (1996)

List of Contributors

Nermin Abadan-Unat
Bogazici University, Istanbul
Çiller, Tansu
Civil Code of 1926
Demirel, Süleyman
Ecevit, Bülent
Milli Görüş Hareketi
National Salvation Party
Refah Partisi
Republican People's Party (RPP)
State Planning Organization (SPO)
Turkish Grand National Assembly
Women's Services

M. Morsy Abdullah
Centre for Documentation and Research, Abu Dhabi
Abu Musa Island
Al Nahayyan Family
Maktum Family, al-
Sharqi Family, al-

O. W. Abi-Mershed
Georgetown University
Clemenceau, Georges
Young Tunisians

Rula Jurdi Abisaab
University of Akron, Ohio
Sadr, Sitt Rabab al- (Charafeddine)
Ziwaj Mutʿa

Ervand Abrahamian
City University of New York, Baruch College
Fedaʾiyan-e Islam
Fedaʾiyan-e Khalq
Forqan
Kianuri, Nur al-Din
Mojahedin-e Khalq
Rajavi, Masud
Tudeh Party

Kamal Abu-Deeb
Centre of Near and Middle Eastern Studies
Adonis
Sayyab, Badr Shakir al-

Asʿad AbuKhalil
California State University, Stanislaus
AMAL
American University of Beirut (AUB)

Aoun, Michel
Arkoun, Mohammed
Arslan Family
Asʿad, Ahmad
Asʿad Family
Asʿad, Kamil
Asʿad Wali
Ashmawi, Muhammad Saʿid al-
Azm, Sadiq al-
Beirut
Berri, Nabi
Bin Ladin, Osama
Bishara, Suha
Chehab, Bashir
Chehab Family
Chehab, Fuʾad
Constitutional Bloc
Council for Development and Reconstruction (CDR)
Daʾud Pasha
Dabbas, Charles
Druze Revolts
Eddé, Emile
Fadlallah, Shaykh Husayn
Franjiyya, Sulayman
Geagea, Samir
Gibran, Kahlil
Hakim, Adnan al-
Hamadi, Sabri
Hanafi, Hasan
Hariri, Rafiq Bahaʾuddin al-
Hilu, Charles
Hilu, Pierre
Hirawi, Ilyas al-
Hizbullah
Hobeika, Elie
Hoss, Salim al-
Hunchak Party
Husayni, Husayn al-
Jumayyil, Bashir
Jumblatt Family
Jumblatt, Kamal
Jumblatt, Walid
Lahad, Antoine
Lahhud, Emile
Lebanese Arab Army
Lebanese Civil War (1975–1990)
Lebanese Forces
Lebanese University
Lebanon
Maronites
Nasrallah, Hasan
National Pact (Lebanon)
National Salvation Front (Lebanon)
Parliamentary Democratic Front
Phalange
Phoenicianism
Progressive Socialist Party
Qaʿida, al-
Qiyomijian, Ohannes
Ramgavar Azadagan Party
Saint Joseph University
Salam, Saʾib
September 11th, 2001
Sfeir, Nasrallah
Shabʿa Farms
Shahin, Tanyos
Shaʿrawi, Muhammad Mutwalli al-
Shuf
Special Forces of the Levant
Sulh, Sami al-
Trad, Petro
Yasin, Ahmad Ismaʿil

Rouben P. Adalian
Armenian National Institute
Alishan, Ghevond
Armenian Community of Jerusalem
Armenian Genocide
Armenian Millet
Armenian Revolutionary Movement
Armenians in the Middle East
Balyan Family
Cemal Paşa
Chamchian, Mikayel
Chrakian, Artin
Dashnak Party
Khrimian, Mkrtich
Musa Dagh
Ormanian, Maghakia
Srvantziants, Garegin
Vazhapetian, Nerses
Yusufian, Boghos
Zohrab, Krikor

Roger Adelson
Arizona State University
Arab Bureau (Cairo)
Foreign Office, Great Britain
Sykes, Mark

Janet Afary
Purdue University
Dabbagh, Marzieh
Rahnavard, Zahra

Imad-ad-Dean Ahmad
Minaret of Freedom, Bethesda, MD
Waqf

Karen Hunt Ahmed
University of Chicago
Ajman

Kristian Alexander
University of Utah
Iraqi National Congress

Scott Alexander
Catholic Theological Union
Allah
Jihad
Karbala
Mihrab
Mosque
Organization of the Islamic Conference
Qadi
Sharif
Shaykh al-Islam
Sunna
Tekke
Zamzam

Hamid Algar
University of California, Berkeley
Akhondzadeh, Mirza Fath Ali
Beheshti, Mohammad
Golpayagani, Mohammad Reza
Kashani, Abu al-Qasem
Khamenehi, Ali
Montazeri, Hosayn Ali
Motahhari, Mortaza
Nuri, Fazlollah
Rafsanjani, Ali Akbar Hashemi
Shariʿati, Ali
Sufism and the Sufi Orders
Tabatabaʾi, Mohammad
Tabatabaʾi, Ziya
Velayat-e Faqih

Filiz Ali
Mimar Sinan University
Biret, Idil
Gencer, Leyla
Kan, Suna

Calvin H. Allen, Jr.
Shenandoah University
Dhufar
Oman
Tamimahs

Roger Allen
University of Pennsylvania
Hakim, Tawfiq al-
Husayn, Taha
Idris, Yusuf
Mahir, Ahmad
Mahir, Ali
Mahmud, Muhammad
Salim, Ali

Ilai Alon
Tel Aviv University
Dhimma

Audrey L. Altstadt
University of Massachusetts, Amherst
Democratic Party of Azerbaijan
Social Democratic Party of Azerbaijan

Abla M. Amavi
Georgetown University
Tuqan, Fadwa
Zarqa, al-

Dina Amin
University of Pennsylvania
Theater

Hooshang Amirahmadi
Rutgers University, New Brunswick
Urban Planning

Mona Takieddine Amyuni
American University of Beirut
Gebeyli, Claire
Sursock, Lady Cochrane

Lisa Anderson
Columbia University
Bourguiba, Habib
General People's Committees
General People's Congress (GPC)
Green Book
Jabha al-Wataniyya, al-
Jallud, Abd al-Salam
Jamahiriyya
Libya

Mzali, Mohammed
National Congress Party
National Front for the Salvation of Libya
Qaddafi, Muammar al-

Yesim Arat
Bogaziçi University
Tekeli, Şirin
Women's Library and Information Center (Istanbul)

Walter Armbrust
St. Anthony's College
Jabarti, Abd al-Rahman al-

Geoffrey Aronson
Hebrew University
West Bank

Farhad Arshad
Columbia University
Isfahan
Nateq-Nuri, Ali Akbar
Nuri, Abd al-Malik
Shirazi, Mirza Hasan

Ahmad Ashraf
Columbia University
Bazaars and Bazaar Merchants
Iran
Pahlavi, Reza

Pierre M. Atlas
Marian College
Haganah
Hebrew University of Jerusalem
Jabotinsky, Vladimir Ze'ev
Lohamei Herut Yisrael
Palmah
Saison
Sokolow, Nahum
Woodhead Commission (1938)
Yellin-Mor, Natan

Shimon Avish
Columbia University
Herzl, Theodor

Cemil Aydin
Ohio State University
Gülhane Imperial Edict (1839)
Islamic Congresses

Gregory B. Baecher
University of Maryland
Aswan High Dam
Delta Barrages
Nasser, Lake
Nile River

Louay Bahry
Washington, DC
Hussein, Saddam
Mahdawi, Fadil Abbas al-
Qasim, Abd al-Karim
Sa'id, Nuri al-

Raymond William Baker
Trinity College
Nasser, Gamal Abdel
National Progressive Unionist Party
National Union (Egypt)
New Wafd
People's Assembly
Saint Mark's Cathedral
Sayyida Zaynab Mosque
Sayyidna Husayn Mosque
Shaltut, Muhammad
Sultan Hasan Mosque
Wadi Natrun

H. G. Balfour-Paul
Devon, England
Fertile Crescent Unity Plans

Aida A. Bamia
University of Florida
Bannis, Mohammad
Berrada, Mohammed
Bin Diyaf, Muhsen
Chraibi, Driss
Ghallab, Abd al-Karim
Hacene, Farouk Zehar
Hamzawi, Rashid al-
Khatibi, Abdelkabir
Laabi, Abdellatif
Lemsine, Aicha
Literature: Arabic, North African
Mas'adi, Mahmoud al-
Meddeb, Abdelwahhab
M'Rabet, Fadela
Rabi, Mubarak
Sebbar, Leila
Sefrioui, Ahmed

Shukri, Mohammad
Tlili, Mustafa
Zili, Ridha

Mordechai Bar-On
Yad Itzhak Ben-Zvi Institute
Anglo–Egyptian Treaty (1954)
Arab–Israeli General Armistice Agreements (1949)
Avnery, Uri
Barak, Ehud
Harkabi, Yehoshafat
Israel: Military and Politics
King David Hotel
Lavon Affair
London Conference (1956)
Mossad
Ne'eman, Yuval
Oz ve Shalom (Netivot shalom)
Peace Now
Peled, Mattityahu
Sarid, Yossi
Shlonsky, Avraham
Suez Crisis (1956–1957)

Larry A. Barrie
Fayetteville, NC
Ahmad Bey Husayn
Bayram V, Muhammad
General Tunisian Union of Students (UGTE)
Jalluli Family
Khayr al-Din
Khaznader, Mustafa
Ligue Tunisienne pour la Défense des Droits de l'Homme (LTDH)
Mareth Line
Morocco: Overview
Mouvement de l'Unité Populaire (MUP)
Movement of Renewal
Muhammad al-Sadiq
Organisation Marocaine des Droits de l'Homme
Peace and Amity, Treaty of (1805)
Shabbi, Abu al-Qasim al-
Tunis
Tunisia: Overview
Tunisia: Political Parties in
Union Générale des Travailleurs Marocains (UGTM)
Union Générale des Travailleurs Tunisiens (UGTT)
Union Tunisienne des Industrialistes, Compagnies, Artisans (UTICA)

Michael L. Bates
American Numismatic Society, New York
Numismatics

Vincent Battesti
Centre d'Études et de Documentation Économiques, Cairo, Egypt
Agriculture

Yehuda Bauer
Yad Vashem
Holocaust

Mangol Bayat
Independent Scholar, Cambridge, MA, and Brauningshof, Germany
Constitutional Revolution, Impact on Women

Lois Beck
Washington University
Marriage and Family

Joel S. Beinin
Stanford University
Communism in the Middle East

Rabia Bekkar
Georgetown University
Aicha, Lalla
Algerian Family Code (1984)
Arabization Policies
Ben Bouali, Hassiba
Bouhired, Jamila
Mimouni, Rachid
Yacoubi, Rachida

Yael Ben-zvi
Ben-Gurion University
International, Dana

Nancy Berg
Washington University
Michael, Sami
Salim, Ali

Elizabeth M. Bergman
Columbia University
Arabic Script

Rhimou Bernikho-Canin
Tarzana, CA
Haik

Robert Betts
American University of Beirut
Druze

Dale L. Bishop
National Council of the Churches of Christ in the USA
Christians in the Middle East

Ian Black
Guardian Newspaper, *London*
Harel, Isser
Kimche, David
Liberty, USS
Pollard Affair
Shiloah, Reuven
Shin Bet

Khalid Blankinship
Temple University
Hijaz
Ilaysh, Muhammad
Mecca
Muslim World League
Sharif of Mecca
Umm al-Qura University

Jonathan M. Bloom
Boston College
Ibn Tulun Mosque

Mia Bloom
Princeton University
Algiers Agreement (1975)
American Jewish Committee
American Jewish Congress
Camels
Carter, Jimmy
Crane, Charles R.
Dead Sea Scrolls
Diaspora
Diwan
Hadassah
Rockefeller Museum
Silver, Abba Hillel
Szold, Henrietta
World Federation of Sephardi Communities
Yadin, Yigael
Zeroual, Liamine

Arnold Blumberg
Towson State University
Ashkenazim
Berlin, Congress and Treaty of
London Convention
Palmerston, Lord Henry John Temple

Emma Aubin Boltanski
London, U.K.
Nabi Musa Pilgrimage

Jerome Bookin-Wiener
Bentley College
Barbary States
Barbary Wars
Corsairs

Marilyn Booth
University of Illinois, Urbana-Champaign
Abu Zeid, Layla
Ashour, Radwa
Djebar, Assia
Egyptian Feminist Union
Fawwaz, Zaynab
Ghazali, Zaynab al-
Idlibi, Ulfat al-
Nawfal, Hind
Rauf Ezzat, Heba
Shaʿrawi, Huda al-
Stanhope, Hester
Zayyat, Latifa

Iris Borowy
University of Rostock, Historical Institute
Alpha, Operation

Stuart J. Borsch
Columbia University
Sidra, Gulf of
Wheelus Air Force Base

Nabil Boudraa
Oregon State University
Chédid, Andrée

Kamal Boullatta
Rabat, Morocco
Darwish, Mahmud

Rahma Bourqia
Mohamed V University, Rabat
Azib
Gharb
Glawi Family, al-
Harratin
Isawiyya Brotherhood
Jmaʾa Tribal Council

Meknes
Qarawiyyin, al-
Shorfa
Tashilhit Language

Donna Lee Bowen
Brigham Young University
Alawite Dynasty
Ben Barka, Mehdi
Birth Control
Fez, Morocco
Rabat

Henry S. Bradsher
Arlington, VA
Afghanistan: Soviet Intervention in

Benjamin Braude
Boston College
Burckhardt, Johann Ludwig
Burton, Richard Francis
Canning, Stratford
Dönme
Doughty, Charles
Lawrence, T. E.
Millet System
Minorities
Philby, Harry St. John

David B. Brooks
Friends of the Earth, Canada
Water

Nathan J. Brown
George Washington University
Law, Modern

Jack Bubon
Fairfax, VA
Cossack Brigade
South Persia Rifles
Trans-Iranian Railway

Richard W. Bulliet
Columbia University
Alcohol
Cotton
Guilds
Historiography
Imperialism in the Middle East and North Africa
Nationalism
Orientalists, International Congress of
Terrorism

Martin Bunton
University of Victoria
Land Reform

Edmund Burke III
University of California, Santa Cruz
Abd al-Aziz ibn al-Hassan
Abd al-Hafid ibn al-Hassan
Abd al-Rahman ibn Hisham
Abu Himara
Ahmad Hibat Allah
Ahmad ibn Muhammad al-Raysuni
Kattani, Muhammad ibn Abd al-Kabir al-
Ma al-Aynayn
Marrakech
Moroccan Question
Sharifian Dynasties
Tuhami al-Glawi

Kathleen R. F. Burrill
Columbia University
Adivar, Abdulhak Adnan
Adivar, Halide Edib
Boratav, Pertev Naili
Dağlarca, Fazil Hüsnü
Literature: Turkish
Nasruddin Hoca
Ortaoyunu
Romanization
Yasar Kemal

Robert D. Burrowes
University of Washington
Abd al-Ghani, Abd al-Aziz
Ali Nasir Muhammad al-Hasani
Amri, Hasan al-
Antar, Ali Ahmad Nasir
Attas, Haydar Abu Bakr al-
Bab al-Mandab
Baydh, Ali Salim al-
Free Officers, Yemen
Free Yemenis
Front for the Liberation of South Yemen
Ghashmi, Ahmad Husayn
Hajri, Abdullah al-
Hamid al-Din Family
Hatim Sultans of Hamdan
Iryani, Abd al-Rahman al-
Islah Party

Ismaʿil, Abd al-Fattah
Maʾrib
Makki, Hasan Muhammad
National Democratic Front (NDF)
People's Democratic Republic of Yemen
Perim
Protectorate States
Rabiyya Ali, Salim
Sallal, Abdullah al-
Sanʿa
Sanʿa University
Shami, Ahmad Muhammad al-
Shami, Muhammad Abdullah al-
Socotra
South Arabian Armed Forces
Taʿiz
Treaty of Protection (1886)
Uthman, Muhammad Ali
Wadi Hadramawt
Yemen Arab Republic
Yemen Civil War
Yemen Hunt Oil Company
Zaraniq Confederation
Zaydism

Noah Butler
Northwestern University
Alexandretta
Refugees: Balkan Muslim
Turkish Script

Charles Butterworth
University of Maryland, Department of Government and Politics
Anawati, Georges Chehata
Awad, Louis
Madkour, Ibrahim
Omar, Muhammad (Mullah)

Pierre Cachia
Columbia University
Literature: Arabic
Mahfuz, Najib

Robert L. Canfield
Washington University
Afghanistan: Soviet Intervention in
Karzai, Hamid

Byron Cannon
University of Utah
Abd al-Qadir

Neil Caplan
Vanier College
Antisemitism
Biltmore Program (1942)
Binationalism
Dulles, John Foster
Faisal–Weizmann Agreements
Jewish Legion
Kalvaryski, Chaim Margaliut-
Kisch, Frederick Hermann
London (Roundtable) Conference (1939)
Magen David Adom (MDA)
Mixed Armistice Commissions
Palestine
Philby, Harry St. John
Rutenberg, Pinhas
United Nations Conciliation Commission for Palestine (UNCCP)
United Nations Truce Supervision Organization (UNTSO)
Vaʿad Leʾumi
Yiddish
Zionism

Stephanie Capparell
The Wall Street Journal, *New York*
Hürriyet

Vanesa Casanova-Fernandez
Georgetown University
Achour, Habib
B'nai B'rith
Constitutional Democratic Rally
Habous
Jallud, Abd al-Salam
Kabylia
Lahouel, Hocine
Masmoudi, Muhammad
Mediterranean Sea
Movement of Renewal
Nuun Magazine
Organisation Marocaine des Droits de l'Homme
Organization of the Islamic Conference
Orientalists, International Congress of
Red Crescent Society
Sfar, Tahar
Spain and the Middle East
Union Nationale des Forces Populaires (UNFP)
Union Socialiste des Forces Populaires (USFP)

Union Tunisienne des Industrialistes, Compagnies, Artisans (UTICA)

John T. Chalcraft
University of Edinburgh
Historiography

Abdin Chande
Sidwell Friends School
Qaradawi, Yusuf al-

Mounira Charrad
University of Texas, Austin
Tunisia: Personal Status Code

Peter Chelkowski
Kevorkian Center for Middle Eastern Studies
Muharram

Jamsheed K. Choksky
Indiana University, Bloomington
Zoroastrianism

Rachel Christina
RAND Education, University of Pittsburgh
Gender: Gender and Education
Kamal, Zahira

Kathleen M. Christison
Santa Fe, NM
Central Intelligence Agency (CIA)

John R. Clark
Columbia University
Adana
Aegean Sea
Alexandretta
Ankara
Euphrates Dam
Tabaqa Dam
Taurus Mountains
Tigris and Euphrates Rivers
Urbanization
Van, Lake
Zab Rivers

William L. Cleveland
Simon Fraser University
Antonius, George
Arslan, Shakib
Baghdad Pact (1955)
Crane, Charles R.
Kurd Ali, Muhammad
Victoria College

Juan R. I. Cole
University of Michigan
Ahsaʿi, Ahmad al-
Amin, Qasim
Bab, al-
Babis
Bahaʾi Faith
Shaykhi

Robert O. Collins
University of California, Santa Barbara
Abd al-Rahman al-Mahdi
Abdullahi, Muhammad Turshain
Azhari, Ismaʿil
Bahr al-Abyad
Bahr al-Arab
Bahr al-Ghazal
Bahr al-Jabal
Beja
Dinka
Kassallah
Kordofan
Lado Enclave
Nuer
Numeiri, Muhammad Jaʿfar
Omdurman
Sudd
Umma Party
University of Khartoum

Robyn Creswell
New York University
Darwish, Mahmud

Maria F. Curtis
University of Texas, Austin
Adham, Soraya
Arab Feminist Union
Bektashis
Ben Ali, Zayn al-Abidine
Bodrum
Bouih, Fatna el-
Central Intelligence Agency (CIA)
Communication
Dance
Intelligence Organizations
Jababdi, Latifa
Jamiʿa al-Islamiyya, al-

Muwahhidun
Palestine National Council
Popular Front for the Liberation of Palestine
Rateb, Aisha
Satellite Cities Development
Sistani, Ali al-
Wafdist Women's Central Committee

Susanne Dahlgren
University of Helsinki, Finland
Al-Suswa, Amat al-Alim
Far'a, Wahiba
National Women's Committee (Yemen)
Women's Forum for Research and Training (Yemen)
Yemeni Women's Union

Niyazi Dalyanci
Istanbul, Turkey
Istanbul Technical University
Trans-Turkey Pipeline

Virginia Danielson
Harvard University
Asmahan
Atrash, Farid al-
Darwish, Sayyid
Hafiz, Abd al-Halim
Music
Umm Kulthum

Bryan Daves
Columbia University
Ard, al-
Boutros-Ghali, Boutros
De Haan, Ya'akov Yisrael
Galilee, Sea of
Green Line
Iran–Contra Affair
Jewish Brigade
Jewish Colonization Association
Joint Distribution Committee
Levontin, Zalman
Levy, David
Oil Embargo (1973–1974)
Pérez de Cuéllar, Javier
Peled, Mattityahu
Ratosh, Yonatan
Rishon le-Zion
Rubinstein, Amnon
Sabra
Safed
Sarid, Yossi
Shapira, Hayyim Moshe
Sharef, Ze'ev
Shazar, Shneour Zalman
Shekel
Shenhar, Yitzhak
Shitreet, Bekhor
Sprinzak, Joseph
Ta'if Accord
Tiberias
Tubi, Tawfiq
Wahrhaftig, Zerah
Ya'ari, Me'ir
Yellin-Mor, Natan
Yizhar, S.
Zikhron Ya'akov
Zionist Organization of America

Lawrence Davidson
West Chester University
Wilson, Woodrow

Roderic H. Davison
Deceased
Midhat Paşa

C. Ernest Dawn
University of Illinois, Urbana
Aflaq, Michel
Arslan, Adil
Arsuzi, Zaki al-

Lara Deeb
Harvard University, Harvard Academy for International and Area Studies
Lebanese Women's Council

Richard Dekmejian
University of Southern California
Muslim Brotherhood

Walter Denny
University of Massachusetts, Amherst
Architecture
Art

Guilain P. Denoeux
Colby College
Aql, Sa'id
Ba'albak
Bliss, Daniel
Chamoun, Camille

Chamoun, Dany
Chehab, Khalid
Eddé, Raymond
Futuwwa
Geagea, Samir
Hawi, George
Hawi, Khalil
Karame, Abd al-Hamid
Karame, Rashid
Khal, Yusuf al-
Khuri, Bishara al-
Lahad, Antoine
Lebanon, Mount
Nimr, Faris
Scouts
Shader, Joseph
Shahada, George
Shidyaq, Ahmad Faris al-
Sulh, Kazem al-
Sulh, Rashid al-
Sulh, Riyad al-
Sulh, Taki al-Din al-
Taqla, Philippe
Twayni, Ghassan
Yaziji, Ibrahim
Youth Movements

Shlomo Deshen
Tel Aviv University
Black Panthers
Maʿbarah

Bradford Dillman
American University
Madani, Abassi al-
Mauritania
Union Marocaine du Travail (UMT)
Union Nationale des Forces Populaires (UNFP)

Donna Robinson Divine
Smith College
Ben-Zvi, Yizhak
Gordon, Aaron David
Ha-Halutz
Hibbat Zion
Hula Swamps
Jewish Agency for Palestine
Katznelson, Berl
Keinan, Amos
Kibbutz Movement
Labor Zionism
Levin, Hanoch
Nahalal
Ruppin, Arthur
Shamir, Moshe
Sobol, Yehoshua
Suissa, Albert
Syrkin, Nachman
Tel Aviv
Tel Hai
Trumpeldor, Yosef
Uganda Project
Ussishkin, Menahem
Yishuv
Yizhar, S.
Youth Aliyah
Zelda
Zionism
Zionist Commission for Palestine

Antonio Donno
Universita Degli Studi
Truman, Harry S.

John J. Donohue
University of Saint Joseph, Beirut
Baghdad University
Hikma University, al-
Missionary Schools
Roman Catholicism and Roman Catholic Missions

Roberta L. Dougherty
Moreton-in-Marsh, U.K.
Gamal, Samiyah
Kariyuka, Tahiya

Eleanor Abdella Doumato
University of Rhode Island
Jabal Shammar
Nafud Desert
Najd
Protestantism and Protestant Missions
Rub al-Khali
Tribes and Tribalism: Arabian Peninsula

Michael Dumper
University of Exeter
Haram al-Sharif

Michael Dunn
International Estimate, Arlington
Arafat, Yasir
Fatah, al-

Ayse Durakbasa Tarhan
Mugla Universitesi, Sosyoloji Botl
Aliyer, Fatimah
Araz, Nezihe

Evelyn A. Early
U.S. Department of State
Medicine and Public Health

Dale F. Eickelman
Dartmouth College
Berber Dahir
Intelligence Organizations
Kattaniya Brotherhood
Marabout

Laurie Z. Eisenberg
Carnegie Mellon University
Camp David Accords (1978)
Carter, Jimmy
Egyptian–Israeli Peace Treaty (1979)
Kahan Commission (1983)
Litani Operation (1978)
Reagan Plan (1982)
South Lebanon Army

Emad Eldin Shahin
American University in Cairo
Belhadj, Ali
Ben Salah, Ahmed
Hamas (Movement for a Peaceful Society)
Mourou, Abdelfattah
Movement for Unity and Reform (MUR)
Nahda, al-
Nahnah, Mahfoud
Sahnoun, Ahmed
Soltani, Abdellatif

Charles Enderlin
Jerusalem, Israel
Shamir, Yitzhak

Michael Eppel
Haifa University
Kashif al-Ghita Family
Kaylani, Abd al-Rahman al-
Muhammad, Aziz

Mansoureh Ettehadieh
University of Tehran
Abbas Mirza, Naʾeb al-Saltaneh
Ahmad Qajar
Bayat, Mortaza Qoli
Farmanfarma, Abd al-Hoseyn Mirza
Fath Ali Shah Qajar
Mahd-e Ulya, Malek Jahan Khanum
Malkom Khan, Mirza
Mozaffar al-Din Qajar
Qajar, Abdullah Mirza
Qajar, Agha Mohammad
Tehran
University of Tehran

Kyle T. Evered
Illinois State University
Literature: Turkish

Abdel Aziz EzzelArab
McGill University
Tahtawi, Rifaʿa al-Rafi al-
Utaybi, Juhayman al-

Hani Fakhouri
University of Michigan, Flint
Satellite Cities Development

Marion Farouk-Sluglett
Deceased
Sharif, Aziz
Yusuf, Yusuf Salman

Grant Farr
Portland State University
Afghanistan: Political Parties in
Afghanistan: U.S. Intervention in
Ahmad Shah Masʿud
Amin, Hafizullah
Amu Darya
Anglo–Afghan Treaty (1855)
Awakened Youth
Bamyan
Bost
Dar al-Moʿallamin
Dost Mohammad Barakzai
Dubs, Adolph
Durand Line
Farhad, Ghulam Muhammad
Gailani, Ahmad
Habibollah Khan
Hazara
Hekmatyar, Golbuddin
Helmand River
Herat
Hezb-e Islami
Jamiʿat-e Islami

Kabul
Kabul University
Kandahar
Karmal, Babrak
Khalis, Mohammad Unis
Khyber, Mir Akbar
Khyber Pass
Mahmud Durrani
Mazar-e Sharif
Mohammadi, Maulawi Mohammad Nabi
Mojaddedi, Sebghatullah
Mojahedin
Nadir Barakzai, Mohammad
Najibullah
Pamir Mountains
Parcham
People's Democratic Party of Afghanistan
Rabbani, Burhanuddin
Ratebzad, Anahita
Refugees: Afghan
Shiberghan
Tajiks
Tarikh Tolana
Zabul

Maysam J. al Faruqi
Georgetown University
Ahmar, Abdullah ibn Husayn al-
Daʿwa al-Islamiyya, al-
Fahmi, Mahmud Pasha
Fatwa
Fiqh
Ghanim, Fathi
Hadith
Iqbal, Muhammad
Islam
Kaʿba
Khalid, Khalid Muhammad
Mawdudi, Abu al-Aʿla al-
Muhyi al-Din, Khalid
Muslim Brotherhood
Nerval, Gérard de
Qurʾan
Sufism and the Sufi Orders
Sunna
Sunni Islam

Elizabeth Fernea
Austin, TX
General Federation of Iraqi Women

Carter V. Findley
Ohio State University
Bureau of Translation
Cevdet, Ahmet
Ottoman Empire: Civil Service

Michael R. Fischbach
Randolph-Macon College
Abbas, Mahmud
Abdullah II ibn Hussein
Abu al-Huda, Tawfiq
Abu Nuwwar, Ali
Adenauer, Konrad
Ahali Group
Amman
Annan, Kofi A.
Antun, Farah
Aqaba, Gulf of
Aql, Saʿid
Arab Boycott
Arafat, Yasir
Archaeology in the Middle East
Ard, al-
Arif, Arif al-
Atasi, Nur al-Din al-
Aziz, Tariq
Baghdad Summit (1978)
Baker, James A.
Banna, Sabri al-
Barghuthi Family
Barghuthi, Marwan
Barzani Family
Basma bint Talal
Bethlehem
Black September
Bush, George Herbert Walker
Bush, George Walker
Clinton, William Jefferson
Cox, Percy
Dahlan, Muhammad
Damascus Affair (1840)
Darwaza, Muhammad Izzat
Eddé, Raymond
Fatah, al-
Franjiyya Family
Franjiyya, Sulayman
Habibi, Emile
Haddad, Wadi
Hafiz, Amin al-
HAMAS

Hamra Riots
Hananu, Ibrahim
Hasan, Hani al-
Hasan, Khalid al-
Hashimi, Yasin al-
Hashimite House (House of Hashim)
Hawatma, Nayif
Hebron
Holy Land
Holy Sepulchre, Church of the
Husayn ibn Ali
Husayni, Musa Kazim al-
Hussein ibn Talal
Institute for Palestine Studies
Irbid
Islamic Jihad
Jadid, Salah
Jamali, Muhammad Fadhil al-
Jarash
Jenin
Jerusalem
Jibril, Ahmad
Jordan
Jordanian Civil War (1970–1971)
Jumayyil, Amin
Jumblatt Family
Jumblatt, Walid
Karak, al-
Kennedy, John Fitzgerald
Khaddam, Abd al-Halim
Khalidi, Ahmad al-Samih al-
Khalidi, Husayn Fakhri al-
Kudsi, Nazim al-
Lausanne Conference (1949)
Lebanese Forces
Lebanese University
Majali Family
Malik, Charles Habib
Maqarin Dam
Muasher, Marwan
Muhammad, Aziz
Nablus
Nahhas, Mustafa al-
Najaf, al-
Nashashibi Family
Nasir, Hanna
National Bloc
Nusayba Family
Palestine Research Center
Palestinian Authority
Parliamentary Democratic Front
Phalange
Powell, Colin L.
Qabbani, Nizar
Qaddumi, Faruq
Qalqiliya
Raad, Inʿam
Rajub, Jibril
Ramadan, Taha Yasin
Ramallah
Reagan, Ronald
Rejection Front
Rifaʿi, Zaid al-
Rockefeller Museum
Saade, George
Salam Family
Salam, Saʾib
Shahada, George
Shammas, Anton
Sharif, Aziz
Shuf
Shuqayri, Ahmad
Somikh, Abdullah
Storrs, Ronald
Sulh, Rashid al-
Sulh, Taki al-Din al-
Tall, Mustafa Wahbi al-
Templars
Tikrit
Tikriti, Hardan al-
Tlas, Mustafa
Tuqan Family
Tuqan, Fadwa
Turki, Fawaz
Twayni, Ghassan
United Arab Republic (UAR)
United Nations Relief and Works Agency for Palestine Refugees in the Near East (UNRWA)
University of Jordan
War in Iraq (2003)
Zuʿbi, Mahmud al-
Zurayk, Constantine

Ellen L. Fleischmann
University of Dayton

Abd al-Hadi, Tarab
Arab Women's Association of Palestine
Arab Women's Congress
Arab Women's Executive Committee

Husayni, Hind al-
Khalidi, Wahida al-
Mogannam, Matiel
Nassar, Sadhij
Shihabi, Zlikha al-

Andrew Flibbert
Trinity College
Hamama, Faten
North Atlantic Treaty Organization (NATO)

Carolyn Fluehr-Lobban
Rhode Island College
Arab
Farid, Nagwa Kamal
Female Genital Mutilation
Garang, John
Harem
Langer, Felicia
Muslim Sisters Organization
Nubians
Nuer
Republican Brotherhood
Taha, Mahmud Muhammad
Turabi, Wisal al-Mahdi

John Foran
University of California, Santa Barbara
Qajar Dynasty

Geremy Forman
University of Haifa
Jezreel Valley

Angel M. Foster
Ibis Reproductive Health
Birth Control
Cairo Family Planning Association
Democratic Women's Association (Tunisia)
Medicine and Public Health
Tunisia: Overview
Union of Tunisian Women

Steve Frangos
Round Lake, IL
Eskinazi, Roza

Robert O. Freedman
Baltimore Hebrew University
Communism in the Middle East
Russia and the Middle East

Adina Friedman
George Mason University
Guri, Chaim
Hareven, Shulamit
Hoffman, Yoel
Oz, Amos
Pagis, Dan
Zach, Natan

Nancy Gallagher
University of California, Santa Barbara
Diseases
Mabarrat Muhammad Ali
School for Hakīmāt

F. Gregory Gause, III
University of Vermont
Aden
Al Thani, Hamad ibn Khalifa
Ayni, Muhsin al-
Dual Containment
Ta'if, Treaty of al-

Khalil Gebara
University of Exeter
Attar, Nejat al-
International Monetary Fund
National Progressive Front (Syria)
Taqla, Philippe

Irene Gendzier
Boston University
Lebanese Civil War (1958)

Jane Gerber
City University of New York
Damascus Affair (1840)

Fawaz A. Gerges
Sarah Lawrence College
Paris Peace Settlements (1918–1923)

Mona Ghali
Richmond Hill, ON
Institute of Women's Studies of Bir Zeit University
Tsemel, Leah

Sabah Ghandour
University of Balamand
Bint al-Shati
Ikhlassi, Walid

Zouhair Ghazzal
Loyola University, Chicago
Alawi
Lawrence, T. E.

Martin Gilbert
University of Oxford
Churchill, Winston S.

Erika Gilson
Princeton University
Turkish Language

Zvia Ginor
Jewish Theological Seminary of America
Alterman, Natan
Baron, Dvora
Gilboa, Amir
Michael, Sami
Oz, Amos
Seri, Dan-Benaya
Suissa, Albert
Zelda

Nili Gold
University of Pennsylvania
Amichai, Yehuda
Appelfeld, Aharon
Bialik, Hayyim Nahman
Hareven, Shulamit
Hoffman, Yoel
Literature: Hebrew
Ravikovitch, Dahlia
Wallach, Yona

Ellis Goldberg
University of Washington
Labor and Labor Unions
Mahalla al-Kubra, al-

Harvey E. Goldberg
Indiana University, Bloomington
Jews in the Middle East
Mimouna Festival

Arthur Goldschmidt
Pennsylvania State University
Abbas Hilmi I
Abbas Hilmi II
Abd al-Maguid, Esmat
Abd al-Raziq, Ali
Abduh, Muhammad
Arab
Arab Socialist Union
Aswan
Baghdadi, Abd al-Latif al-
Bahariya
Baring, Evelyn
Buhayra
Communication
Damanhur
Delta
Dinshaway Incident (1906)
Drummond–Wolff Convention
Dual Control
Eastern Desert
Egypt
Egyptian Women's Union
Ghali, Boutros
Giza
Gulf of Suez
Haykal, Muhammad Hasanayn
Haykal, Muhammad Husayn
Infitah
Isma'il ibn Ibrahim
Kamil, Mustafa
Luxor
Mahmudiyya Canal
Mahmud, Muhammad
Mahmud, Mustafa
Majlis Shura al-Nuwwab
Mansura, al-
Milner Mission
Misri, Aziz Ali al-
Mubarak, Husni
Nasser, Lake
National Party (Egypt)
Nile River
Nubar Pasha
Nuqrashi, Mahmud Fahmi al-
Qusayr, al-
Riyad, Mustafa al-
Sadat, Jihan al-
Sharm al-Shaykh
Shenouda III
Siwa Oasis
Suez Canal
Urabi, Ahmad
Uthman, Uthman Ahmad
Wadi Natrun
War of Attrition (1969–1970)

Mallika Good
Foundation for Middle East Peace
Gaza (City)
General Union of Palestinian Women's Committees (GUPWC)

Jane E. Goodman
Indiana University
Amrouche, Fadhma At Mansour
Amrouche, Mary Louise (a.k.a. Marguerite Taos)

Matthew S. Gordon
Miami University
Achour, Habib
Ahardane, Majoub
Algiers, Battle of (1956–1957)
Amin Bey, al-
Arfa, Muhammad ibn
Baccouche, Hedi
Balafrej, Ahmed
Ben Ali, Zayn al-Abidine
Ben Ammar, Tahar
Black Thursday (1978)
Bouabid, Abderrahim
Boucetta, Muhammad
Bu Hamara
Chenik, Muhammad
Dlimi, Ahmed
Fes, Treaty of (1912)
Fundamental Pact
Gafsa Incident (1980)
Ghannouchi, Rached
Green March
La Marsa Convention
Lamrani, Muhammad Karim
Laraki, Ahmad
La Tunisie Martyre
Masmoudi, Muhammad
Monastir
Nouira, Hedi
Oufkir, Muhammad
Parti d'Unité Populaire (PUP)
Qairawan
Revolutionary Command Council (Egypt)
Sfar, Tahar
Sfax
Sousse
Suleiman, Mulay
Youssef, Mulay

Yehuda Gradus
Ben-Gurion University
Dimona
Golan Heights
Jabal al-Khalil
Lydda
Maʿa lot
Negev
Ramla
Rishon le-Zion

JoAnn Gross
Trenton State University
Naqshbandi

Peter Gubser
American Near East Refugee Aid, Washington, DC
Amman
Dead Sea
Hussein ibn Talal
Jordan
Jordanian Civil War (1970–1971)
Karak, al-
Petra
Potash Industry

David Gutelius
Stanford University
Arab Maghreb Union
Tindouf

Mahmoud Haddad
University of Balamund (Northern Lebanon)
Abu al-Timman, Jaʿfar
Ahd, al-
Azzam, Abd al-Rahman al-
Bustani, Sulayman
National Party (Syria)
Salafiyya Movement

Sylvia G. Haim
Middle Eastern Studies, England
Farhud
Hayim, Yusef
Sassoon Family

Majed Halawi
New York, NY
Alawi
Jumayyil, Amin
Jumayyil, Pierre

Sondra Hale
University of California, Los Angeles
Ibrahim, Fatima Ahmed
Sudanese Women's Union

Wael B. Hallaq
McGill University
Fatwa
Fiqh
Hadith
Hanafi School of Law
Hanbali School of Law
Maliki School of Law
Shafiʿi School of Law
Shariʿa

Karim Hamdy
Oregon State University
Chalabi, Ahmad
Desalinization
Jazeera, al-
Organization of Arab Petroleum Exporting Countries (OAPEC)
Phosphates

Milad Hanna
al-Ahram *Newspaper*
Copts

Robert E. Harkavy
Penn State
Nuclear Capability and Nuclear Energy

Michelle Hartman
McGill University
Mostaghanemi, Ahlam

Khalid M. El-Hassan
University of Kansas
Beja
Omdurman
Salih, Teyib

Amir Hassanpour
University of Toronto
Ghassemlou, Abdul Rahman
Kurdish Revolts

Frances Hasso
Oberlin College
Khaled, Leila

Waleed Hazbun
Johns Hopkins University
Akkad, Mustafa
Industrialization

Samuel Heilman
City University of New York, Queens College
Halakhah
Judaism
Karaites
Rabbi
Sabbath
Western Wall
Yeshiva

Oliver Benjamin Hemmerle
Baden, Germany
Government
Iran–Contra Affair
Shultz, George

Clement M. Henry
University of Texas at Austin
Banking

Linda Herrera
Leiden University
Education
Musa, Nabawiyya
Ramses College for Girls
Saʿid, Amina al-

Tayeb El-Hibri
University of Massachusetts, Amherst
Ibadiyya
Islam
Lebanese Crises of the 1840s
Mevlevi Brotherhood
Muhammad
Shiʿism
Sunni Islam

Marilyn Higbee
Columbia University
Shaykh

Michael C. Hillmann
University of Texas, Austin
Al-e Ahmad, Jalal
Bahar, Mohammad Taqi
Baraheni, Reza
Carpets, Persian

Daneshvar, Simin
Dashti, Ali
Dehkhoda, Ali Akbar
Esfandiary, Fereydun
Farrokhzad, Forugh
Gharbzadegi
Ghassemlou, Abdul Rahman
Hajji Baba of Ispahan
Hedayat, Sadegh
Literature: Persian
Parsipur, Shahrnush
Shamlu, Ahmad

Eric Hooglund
Institute for Palestine Studies, Washington, DC
Abbas Mirza, Na'eb al-Saltaneh
Abdülmecit II
Abu Musa Island
Afghanistan: Islamic Movements in
Alavi, Bozorg
Algiers Agreement (1975)
Amir-Entezam, Abbas
Anatolia
Anglo–Iranian Agreement (1919)
Anglo–Persian War (1856)
Anglo–Russian Agreement (1907)
Ankara
Ankara University
Antakya
Arfa, Hasan
Azerbaijan Crisis
Bakhtiari
Baraheni, Reza
Barakzai Dynasty
Behrangi, Samad
Constitutional Revolution
Curzon, George Nathaniel
Daneshvar, Simin
D'Arcy Concession (1901)
Dashti, Ali
Dhufar Rebellion
Diyarbakir
Dowlatabadi, Mahmoud
Dual Containment
Edirne
Erzurum
Erzurum, Treaty of (1823)
Esfandiary, Fereydun
Fish and Fishing
Freedom Movement (Nezhat-e Azadi Iran)
Gecekondu
Golestan, Ebrahim
Golshiri, Houshang
Greco–Turkish War (1897)
Guest Workers
Hedayat, Sadegh
Hostage Crises
Iranian Revolution (1979)
Iran–Iraq War (1980–1988)
Isfahan
Istanbul
Istanbul University
Janissaries
Jehad-e Sazandegi
Kasravi, Ahmad
Kemalettin Bey
Khalaf, Abdulhadi
Kharg Island
Khatami, Mohammad
Khomeini, Ruhollah
Khubar, al-
Konya
Lausanne, Treaty of (1923)
Literature: Persian
Lurs
Ma'rufi, Abbas
Mahmud II
Majles al-Shura
Marja al-Taqlid
Mashhad
Mehmet V Reşat
Menderes, Adnan
Middle East Technical University
Mohammad Ali Shah Qajar
Montazeri, Hosayn Ali
Musavi-Ardebili, AbdolKarim
Namik Kemal
Naser al-Din Shah
National Salvation Party
Newspapers and Print Media: Iran
Palmerston, Lord Henry John Temple
Paris Peace Settlements (1918–1923)
Persian (Arabian) Gulf
Persian Cats
Pushtun
Qajar Dynasty
Rafsanjani, Ali Akbar Hashemi
Revolutionary Guards
Russian–Ottoman Wars
Salonika

Sepehri, Sohrab
Shamlu, Ahmad
Sharjah
Shiraz
South Persia Rifles
Students in the Line of the Imam
Tabataba'i, Mohammad
Tea
Tehran
Terrorism
Timar
Tobacco Revolt
Topkapi Palace
Treaty of 1815
Tripartite Treaty of Alliance
Tunb Islands
Turkey
Turkish–Italian War (1911–1912)
Turkish Language
Turkmanchai, Treaty of (1828)
Turks
Twin Pillars Policy
University of Tehran
Urban Planning
Utaybi, Juhayman al-
Vaka-i Hayriye
Velayat-e Faqih
White Revolution (1961–1963)
Yazd
Zahedan
Zoroastrianism

J. C. Hurewitz
Columbia University
Britain and the Middle East up to 1914
Eastern Question
Straits, Turkish

Ahmed H. Ibrahim
Southwest Missouri State University
Abd al-Rahman, Umar
Bakhtiar, Shapur
Rogers, William Pierce

Amitzur Ilan
Hebrew University
Bernadotte, Folke

George E. Irani
Royal Roads University
Arab Socialism
Atasi, Jamal al-
Beitaddin Declaration
Christians in the Middle East
Council for Development and Reconstruction (CDR)
Haigazian College
Hasani, Taj al-Din al-
Hobeika, Elie
Karam, Yusuf
Kikhya, Rushdi al-
Lebanese Front
Lebanese National Movement (LNM)
Maksoud, Clovis
Malik, Charles Habib
Ma'louf, Amin
Marine Barracks Bombing (Lebanon)
Meushi, Paul Peter
National Bloc
National Front, Lebanon
National Liberal Party
Progressive Socialist Party
Raad, In'am
Riyad, Mahmud
Saade, George
Sidon
Ta'if Accord
Tyre
Vatican and the Middle East
Zahla

Khaled Islaih
Jerusalem, Israel
Gender: Gender and the Economy
Hass, Amira
Wazir, Intisar al- (Umm Jihad)

Jacqueline Ismael
University of Calgary
Iraqi Women's Union
Khidhir, Zahra
Women's Renaissance Club
Zahawi, Jamil Sidqi al-

Charles Issawi
Princeton University
Manufactures
Modernization
Textile Industry
Trade
Transport

Islah Jad
London, U.K.
Women and Family Affairs Center
Women's Affairs Center (Gaza)
Women's Centre for Legal Aid and Counseling
Women's Studies Center (Jerusalem)

James Jankowski
University of Colorado, Boulder
Pharaonicism
Young Egypt

M. A. Jazayary
University of Texas, Austin
Persian

George Joffe
University of London
Aozou Strip
Balbo, Italo
Bevin–Sforza Plan
Bilhayr, Abd al-Nabi
Fourth Shore, The
Graziani, Rodolfo
Italy in the Middle East
Mukhtar, Umar al-
Muntasir Family
Suwayhli, Ramadan al-
Volpi, Giuseppe

Benjamin Joseph
Philadelphia, PA
Bethlehem
Emergency Regulations
Geneva Peace Conference (1973)
Haycraft Commission (1921)
Hebron
Jericho
Nabi Musa Pilgrimage
Nablus
Nazareth
Sartawi, Issam
Talmud
War of Attrition (1969–1970)
Woodhead Commission (1938)

Jon Jucovy
Ramaz Upper School
Agadir Crisis
Algeciras Conference (1906)
Allenby, Edmund Henry
Amiens, Treaty of
Bund
Dreyfus Affair
Masada
Pogrom
Yad Mordekhai
Yad Vashem

Sabine Kalinock
University of Frankfurt, Germany
Women's Religious Rituals

Zachary Karabell
Harvard University
Acheson, Dean
Adana Conference
Adenauer, Konrad
Ahmet Vefik
Alexandria Convention
Ali Suavi
Antun, Farah
Arish, Convention of al- (1800)
Austria–Hungary and the Middle East
Aya Sofya
Baghdad Pact (1955)
Balta Liman, Convention of (1838)
Bandung Conference (1955)
Behar, Nissim
Bell, Gertrude
Ben-Aharon, Yitzhak
Benvenisti, Meron
Beyoglu Protocol
Black Sea
British–French Oil Agreement
Bucharest, Treaty of (1812)
Budapest Convention (1877)
Burg, Yosef
Cairo Conference (1921)
Central Treaty Organization (CENTO)
Clark–Darlan Agreement (1942)
Clemenceau, Georges
Compagnie Française des Pétroles (CFP)
Cyprus Convention (1878)
Darülfünün
De Bunsen, Maurice
Declaration of La Celle St. Cloud
Dimona
Dragomans
Dulles, John Foster

Eden, Anthony
Eisenhower, Dwight David
Erzurum, Treaty of (1823)
Fashoda Incident (1898)
Fertile Crescent
Flapan, Simha
Franco–Tunisian Conventions
Greater Syria Plan
Great Game, The
Grivas, Georgios Theodoros
Gruenbaum, Yizhak
Gur, Mordechai
Habib, Philip Charles
Haifa University
Harriman, W. Averell
Hess, Moses
Hijab
Hindu Kush Mountains
Humphreys, Francis
Hunkar-Iskelesi, Treaty of (1833)
Husayn ibn Ali
Ignatiev, Nikolas Pavlovich
Ishaq, Adib
Jewish Legion
Johnson, Lyndon Baines
Kennedy, John Fitzgerald
Kléber, Jean-Baptiste
Kosher
Kütahya, Peace of
Lansdowne, Henry Charles Keith Petty Fitzmaurice
Lend-Lease Program
London, Treaty of (1871)
London, Treaty of (1913)
Maude, Frederick Stanley
Medina
Mehmet V Reşat
Mesopotamia Campaign (1914–1918)
MI-6
Middle East Defense Organization (MEDO)
Mission Civilisatrice
Mollet, Guy
Moltke, Helmuth von
Mond, Alfred Moritz
Montefiore, Moses
Montgomery, Bernard Law
Montreux Convention (1936)
Musa Kazim
Namik Kemal
Nixon, Richard Milhous
North Atlantic Treaty Organization (NATO)
Organization of African Unity (OAU)
Patriarch
Peace Corps
Potsdam Convention
Rogers, William Pierce
Rome, Treaty of (1935)
San Remo Conference (1920)
Sebastiani, Horace
Sharm al-Shaykh
Shepheard's Hotel
Şinasi, İbrahim
Soustelle, Jacques
Sublime Porte
Sykes, Mark
Sykes–Picot Agreement (1916)
Talat, Mehmet
Twin Pillars Policy
Wilson, Woodrow

Efraim Karsh
King's College
Iran–Iraq War (1980–1988)

Hasan Kayali
La Jolla, CA
Balkan Wars (1912–1913)
Caliphate
Cemal Paşa
Committee for Union and Progress
Decentralization Party
Enver Paşa
Ottomanism
Ottoman Parliament
Pan-Turkism
Young Ottomans
Young Turks

Benjamin Kedar
Institute for Advanced Studies, The Hebrew University of Jerusalem
Masada

Nikki Keddie
University of California, Los Angeles
Afghani, Jamal al-Din al-
Anjoman
Urwa al-Wuthqa, al-

Burçak Keskin-Kozat
University of Michigan, Ann Arbor
Abdülmecit I
Ankara, Treaty of (1930)

Bilkent University
Boğaziçi (Bosporus) University
Boratav, Pertev Naili
Bursa
Çiller, Tansu
Demirel, Süleyman
Ecevit, Bülent
Ecevit, Rahşan
Ege University
General Directorate on the Status and Problems of Women
Hacettepe University
İzmir
Marmara University
Nasruddin Hoca
Turkish Law on the Protection of the Family (1998)
Women's People's Party (1923)
Yüksek Öğretim Kurulu (YOK)

Nazar al-Khalaf
Montreal, Canada
Basra
Samarra
Sulaymaniya

Rashid Khalidi
University of Chicago
Arab Nationalism
Palestine Arab Revolt (1936–1939)

Fred J. Khouri
Villanova University
United Nations Conciliation Commission for Palestine (UNCCP)

Azadeh Kian-Thiébaut
University of Paris 8 and Monde Iraniene, CNRS
Amini, Fatemeh
Hashemi, Faezeh
Iranian Bureau of Women's Affairs
Sane'i, Yusef
Shid, Nahid
Taleqani, Azam

Carolyn Killean
University of Chicago
Arabic

Laurie King-Irani
University of Victoria
Ba'albakki, Layla
8 Mars Newspaper
Farès, Nabile
Gender: Gender and Law
Gozanski, Tamar
Haza, Ofra
Hijab
Khalifa, Sahar
Khalil, Samiha Salama
Masri, Mai
Nazareth
Qa'war, Widad

Alexander Kitroeff
New York University
Cyprus
Greco–Turkish War (1897)
Greeks in the Middle East
Greek War of Independence

John F. Kolars
University of Michigan, Ann Arbor
Climate
Desalinization
Deserts
Geography

Charles C. Kolb
National Endowment for the Humanities
Assyrians
Baluchis
Ceramics
KGB
Port Sa'id
Rusk, Dean
Sidon

C. Max Kortepeter
New York University
Capitulations
Crimean War

Martin Kramer
Tel Aviv University
Islamic Congresses

Wanda Krause
American University of Sharjah
Gender: Gender and Politics

P. R. Kumaraswamy
Jawaharlal Nehru University
China and the Middle East

I. Metin Kunt
Sabanci University
Abdülmecit I
Ankara University
Atatürk University
Barkan, Ömer Lutfi
Bilkent University
Boğaziçi (Bosporus) University
Bursa
Ege University
Galatasaray Lycée
Hacettepe University
Istanbul
Istanbul University
İzmir
Marmara University
Middle East Technical University
Osman, House of
Pera
Selim III
Sultan
Yüksek Öğretim Kurulu (YOK)

Aptullah Kuran
University of the Bosphorus
Balyan Family
Sultan Ahmet Mosque
Topkapi Palace

Jerry Kutnick
Gratz College
American Jewish Committee
American Jewish Congress
Zionist Organization of America

Chris Kutschera
Paris, France
Barzani Family
Kurdish Autonomous Zone
Kurdistan
Kurds
Mahmud of Sulaymaniya
Patriotic Union of Kurdistan (PUK)
Refugees: Kurdish
Talabani, Jalal
Yasar Kemal

Ahmet Kuyas
Galatasaray Üniversitesi
Atatürk, Mustafa Kemal

Lisa M. Lacy
University of Texas, Austin
Arabian Horses

Robert G. Landen
Virginia Polytechnic Institute
Anglo–Omani Treaties
Masira Island
Matrah
Muscat
Oman
Sib, Treaty of (1920)

Nico Landman
Universiteit Utrecht
Nursi, Said

Michael M. Laskier
Bar-Ilay University, Israel
Alawite Dynasty
Algeria: Political Parties in
Alliance Israélite Universelle (AIU)
Bourguiba, Habib
Curiel Family
De Menasce Family
Faraj, Murad
Farhi Family
Muhammad VI
Nahum, Hayyim
Politi, Elie
Qafih, Yihye ben Solomon
Refugees: Jewish
Rolo Family
Sagues, Albert
Suarès Family
World Organization of Jews from Arab Countries (WOJAC)

Mirna Lattouf
Arizona State University, Tempe
AISHA: Arab Women's Forum
Beirut College for Women (BCW)
General Women's Union of Syria
Institute for Women's Studies in the Arab World (Lebanon)

Henri Lauzière
Georgetown University
Adl wa al-Ihsan, al-
Bouyali, Moustafa
Morocco: Overview

Morocco: Constitution
Yacine, Abdessalame
Youssoufi, Abderrahmane

Fred Lawson
Mills College
Al Khalifa Family
Arab Academy of Damascus
Bahrain
Bahraini–Qatari Wars
Bahrain Nationalist Movement
Belgrave, Charles Dalrymple
Biqa Valley
Damascus
Free French Mandate
Hama Massacre
Homs
Kawakibi, Abd al-Rahman al-
Khaddam, Abd al-Halim
Manama
Maysalun
Muhammad Ali
Muharraq
Nabi Salih, al-
National Liberation Front (Bahrain)
Nizam al-Jadid, al-
Nizip, Battle of (1839)
Pearl Diving (Bahrain)
Sadat, Anwar al-
Sitra
Syria
Umm Naʿsan

Ann M. Lesch
Villanova University
Abbud, Ibrahim
Abd al-Hadi Family
Alami Family, al-
Ansar, al-
Arab Higher Committee (Palestine)
Gezira Scheme
Khartoum
Mahdist State
Palestinian Arab Congresses
Palin Commission Report (1920)
Peel Commission Report (1937)
Plumer, Herbert Charles Onslow
Qawuqji, Fawzi al-
Sudan
Sudanese Civil Wars
Taba
White Papers on Palestine

Rémy Leveau
Institut d'Études Politiques de Paris
Cambon–Lansdowne Agreement (1904)
Hassan I
Hassan II
Lyautey, Louis-Hubert Gonzalve
Muhammad V

Zach Levey
University of Haifa
Arms and Armaments in the Middle East
Northern Tier
Tripartite Declaration (1950)
United Nations Economic Survey Mission (1949)

Avigdor Levy
Brandeis University
Janissaries
Mahmud II
Ottoman Military: Army
Ottoman Military: Navy
Vaka-i Hayriye

Zafrira Lidovsky-Cohen
Stern College, Yeshiva University
Ravikovitch, Dahlia

F. T. Liu
International Peace Academy, New York
United Nations and the Middle East
United Nations Emergency Force
United Nations Relief and Works Agency for Palestine Refugees in the Near East (UNRWA)
United Nations Special Committee on Palestine, 1947 (UNSCOP)

John Lundquist
Asian and Middle Eastern Division, New York Public Library
Orientalism
Philae
Said, Edward

Charles G. MacDonald
Florida International University
League of Arab States

Bruce Maddy-Weitzman
Tel Aviv University
Ben Jelloun, Umar
Ben Seddiq, Mahjoub
Comité d'Action Marocaine (CAM)
Confédération Démocratique du Travail (CDT)
Daddah, Mokhtar Ould
Front pour la Défense des Institutions Constitutionelles (FDIC)
Ibn Musa, Ahmad
Ifni
Istiqlal Party: Morocco
Laayounne
Melilla
Morocco: Political Parties in
Morrison–Grady Plan (1946)
Mouvement Populaire (MP)
Ouazzani, Mohamed Hassan
Parti Démocratique Constitutionnel (PDC)
Parti Démocratique de l'Indépendance (PDI)
Parti National
Parti National Démocratique (PND)
POLISARIO
Rassemblement National des Indépendants (RNI)
Sahara
Saharan Arab Democratic Republic (SADR)
Spanish Morocco
Tetuan
Union Nationale des Etudiants Marocains (UNEM)
Wazzani, Muhammad Hassan al-
Western Sahara
Western Sahara War

Zev Maghen
Bar-Ilay University, Israel
Entebbe Operation
Galilee
Harel, Isser
Kasztner Affair
Kovner, Abba
Landsmannschaften
Law of Return
Lotz, Wolfgang
Luz, Kadish
Ma'a lot
Moda'i, Yitzhak
Nahal
Namir, Mordekhai

Paul J. Magnarella
University of Florida
People's Houses
Turkish Hearth Association
Village Institutes

Ali Akbar Mahdi
Ohio Wesleyan University
Karbaschi, Gholamhosain
Kharrazi, Kamal
Mohajerani, Ataollah
Musavi, Mir-Hosain
Nabavi, Behzad
Velayati, Ali Akbar

Gregory S. Mahler
Kalamazoo College
Allon, Yigal
Ben-Aharon, Yitzhak
Ben-Gurion, David
Ben-Porat, Mordechai
Burg, Avraham
Burg, Yosef
Cohen, Ge'ula
Eban, Abba (Aubrey)
Flapan, Simha
Goldmann, Nahum
Gur, Mordechai
Hammer, Zevulun
Israel: Overview of Political Parties in
Israel: Political Parties in
Kahane, Meir
Karp Report (1984)
Kessar, Israel
Knesset
Kol, Moshe
Kollek, Teddy
Levy, David
Moda'i, Yitzhak
Navon, Yizhak
Peres, Shimon
Rabin, Yitzhak
Rubinstein, Amnon
Sharef, Ze'ev
Sharett, Moshe
Sneh, Moshe
Tamir, Shmuel
Vanunu Affair

Wahrhaftig, Zerah
Weizman, Ezer
Yadin, Yigael

Roshanak Malek
New York, NY
Tobacco Revolt

Hafeez Malik
Villanova University
Jinnah, Muhammad Ali
Taliban

Martin Malin
American Academy of Arts and Sciences
Abuhatzeira, Aharon
Alkalai, Judah ben Solomon Hai
Amit, Meir
Arens, Moshe
Avnery, Uri
Bar-Lev, Haim
Ben-Yehuda, Eliezer
Eitan, Rafael
Eshkol, Levi
Hammer, Zevulun
Haskalah
Kalischer, Hirsch
Karp Report (1984)
Kessar, Israel
Kol, Moshe
Levin, Shmaryahu
Mohilever, Samuel
Nordau, Max
Pinsker, Leo
Sapir, Pinhas

Sumit Mandal
Ithaca, NY
Hadramawt

Ruth Mandel
Bethesda, MD
Alevi

Azzedine G. Mansour
Laval University
Arch
Architecture
GIA (Armed Islamic Groups)
Lamari, Mohamed
Rassemblement National Démocratique (RND)
Rassemblement pour la Culture et la Démocratie (RCD)
Wattar, al-Taher

Abraham Marcus
University of Texas, Austin
Aleppo

Michael R. Marrus
University of Toronto, School of Graduate Studies
Ha-avarah Agreement
Protocols of the Elders of Zion

Paul Martin
Columbia University
Garang, John
Human Rights

Afshin Matin-asgari
University of California, Los Angeles
Confederation of Iranian Students
Golsorkhi, Khosrow
Hoveyda, Amir Abbas
National Front, Iran
Soroush, AbdolKarim

Philip Mattar
United States Institute of Peace
Advisory Council (Palestine)
Aqsa Intifada, al-
Arab College of Jerusalem
Arabic
Arab–Israel War (1982)
Arab League Summits
Asmar, Fawzi al-
Balfour Declaration (1917)
Camp David Summit (2000)
Cattan, Henry
Churchill White Paper (1922)
Fahd Plan (1981)
Fida'iyyun
Germany and the Middle East
Ghuri, Emile al-
Gulf Crisis (1990–1991)
Haifa
Haycraft Commission (1921)
High Commissioners (Palestine)
Hope-Simpson Commission (1930)
Husayni, Muhammad Amin al-
Husayn–McMahon Correspondence (1915–1916)

Institute for Palestine Studies
King–Crane Commission (1919)
Legislative Council (Palestine)
Levantine
Nakba, al- (1948–1949)
Oslo Accord (1993)
Palestine Liberation Organization (PLO)
Palestinian Arab Congresses
Palestinians
Qassam, Izz al-Din al-
Refugees: Palestinian
Sabra and Shatila Massacres
Shaw Commission
Supreme Muslim Council
Taba
Taba Negotiations (1995, 2001)

Ann E. Mayer
Wharton School, University of Pennsylvania
Law, Modern

Kenneth S. Mayers
University of California, Los Angeles
Ibrahim, Muhammad Hafiz
White Flag League

Justin McCarthy
University of Louisville
Abdülaziz
Abdülhamit II
Population
Refugees: Balkan Muslim

Mark Mechler
Washington, DC
Yaziji, Nasif

Meron Medzini
Rothberg International School, The Hebrew University, Mt. Scopus
Aloni, Shulamit
Amit, Meir
Bar-Lev, Haim
Ben-Zvi, Rahel Yanait
Dayan, Yael
Dorner, Dalia
Herzog, Chaim
Herzog, Ya'acov David
Hillel, Shlomo
Jarring, Gunnar
Lavon, Pinhas
Livnat, Limor
Namir, Orah
Refugees: Jewish

Peter Mellini
Sonoma State University
Gorst, John Eldon
Kitchener, Horatio Herbert

Paul Mendes-Flohr
University of Chicago
Buber, Martin

Garay Menicucci
University of California, Santa Barbara
Bakdash, Khalid

John Micgiel
Columbia University
Balkan Crises (1870s)
Balkans
Bulgarian Horrors

Laurence Michalak
University of California, Berkeley
Djerba
Hand of Fatima
Jabal al-Akhdar, Libya
Qadiriyya Order
Sfar, Bashir
Tlemcen

Dan Michman
Bar-Ilan University
Holocaust

Pardis Minuchehr
Columbia University
Akhavan-Saless, Mehdi
Chubak, Sadeq
Fassih, Ismail
Golshiri, Houshang
Jamalzadeh, Mohammad Ali
Ma'rufi, Abbas
Sa'edi, Gholamhossein
Sepehri, Sohrab

Ziba Mir-Hosseini
University of London
Ahl-e Haqq
Ebadi, Shirin
Kar, Mehrangiz
Sa'idzadeh, Seyyed Mohsen

Mansoor Moaddel
Eastern Michigan University
Adamiyat, Abbasquli
Adamiyat, Fereydun
Anglo–Iranian Agreement (1919)
Anglo–Iranian Oil Company
Bazargan, Mehdi
Mossadegh, Mohammad

Mohamed Hassan Mohamed
State University of New York, Fredonia
Tribes and Tribalism: Yemeni

Shahrzad Mojab
Institute for Women's Studies and Gender Studies, University of Toronto
Zana, Leyla

Robert Mortimer
Haverford college
Coordination des Archs (Algeria)
Hanoune, Louisa
Madani, Abassi al-

Cyrus Moshaver
Columbia University
Dar al-Islam
Mashhad
Sheshbesh

Ahmad S. Moussalli
American University of Beirut
Ashmawi, Muhammad Abd al-Rahman Salih al-
Banna, Hasan al-
Haykal, Muhammad Hasanayn
Qutb, Sayyid
Takfir wa al-Hijra, al-
Tantawi, Muhammad Sayyid al-
Turabi, Hasan al-

Muhammad Muslih
C. W. Post College of Long Island University
Abu Risha, Umar
Arab Club
Asad, Hafiz al-
Atasi, Hashim al-
Atasi, Nur al-Din al-
Atrash, Sultan Pasha al-
Azuri, Najib
Fatat, al-
Ghuri, Emile al-
Golan Heights
Hafiz, Amin al-
Hananu, Ibrahim
Hawrani, Akram al-
Husayni, Abd al-Qadir al-
Husayni Family, al-
Husayni, Jamal al-
Husayni, Musa Kazim al-
Istiqlal Party: Palestine
Khalidi, Husayn Fakhri al-
Khalidi, Walid
Kudsi, Nazim al-
Mardam, Jamil
Muntada al-Adabi, al-
Nashashibi Family
Palestine National Charter (1968)
Palestine National Covenant (1964)
Palestinians
Quwatli, Shukri al-
Umayyad Mosque

Amikam Nachmani
Bar-Ilan University
Anglo–American Committee of Inquiry (1946)

Emile A. Nakhleh
Mount St. Mary's College
Ahmar, Abdullah ibn Husayn al-
Awali, al-
Badr, Muhammad al-
Baharina
Bahrain National Oil Company (BANOCO)
Bahrain Order in Council
Bubiyan Island
Dilmun
Gulf Cooperation Council
Khalaf, Abdulhadi
Kuwait Fund for Arab Economic Development
Madani, Abdullah al-
Neutral Zone
Organization of Arab Petroleum Exporting Countries (OAPEC)

Bassam Namani
Embassy of Lebanon, Washington, DC
Beaufort, Charles-Marie-Napoléon d'Hautpoul de
Dentz, Henri-Fernand
Hariri, Rafiq Baha'uddin al-
Murabitun

Muwahhidun
Qabbani, Nizar
Sarkis, Ilyas
Tuman Bey

Hisham Nashabi
Makassed Philanthropic Islamic Association, Beirut
Arab College of Jerusalem

Senzil Nawid
Tucson, AZ
Afghan Women's Council
Association for the Protection of Women's Rights (Afghanistan)
Democratic Organization of Afghan Women (1965)
Esmati-Wardak, Masuma
Etemadi, Saleha Faruq
Irshad An-Niswaan
Kashwar Kamal, Meena
Ordinances on Veiling
Queen Surraya
Revolutionary Association of the Women of Afghanistan (RAWA)
Samar, Sima
Sediq, Sohaila

Phillip C. Naylor
Marquette University
Abbas, Ferhat
Abdelghani, Mohamed Benahmed
Abdesselam, Belaid
Ait Ahmed, Hocine
Algeria: Constitution
Amis du Manifeste et de la Liberté
Amrouche, Jean
Argoud, Antoine
Belkacem, Cherif
Bellounis, Muhammad
Ben Badis, Abd al-Hamid
Ben Bella, Ahmed
Ben Boulaid, Moustafa
Ben Khedda, Ben Youssef
Ben M'hidi, Muhammad Larbi
Bendjedid, Chadli
Benflis, Ali
Bitat, Rabah
Blum–Viollette Plan
Boudiaf, Mohamed
Boudjedra, Rachid
Bouteflika, Abdelaziz
Brahimi, Abdelhamid
Bureaux Arabes
Camus, Albert
Catroux, Georges
Challe, Maurice
Code de l'Indigénat
Delouvrier, Paul
Dib, Mohammed
Didouche, Mourad
Evian Accords (1962)
Feraoun, Mouloud
Foucauld, Charles Eugène de
Ghozali, Ahmed
Haddad, Malek
Hadj, Messali al-
Hamina, Mohammed Lakhdar
Hamrouche, Mouloud
Harkis
Ibrahimi, Ahmed Taleb
Ibrahimi, Bashir
Kaid, Ahmed
Khider, Mohamed
Krim, Belkacem
Lacheraf, Mostefa
Lacoste, Robert
Lahouel, Hocine
Loi Cadre
Mimouni, Rachid
Moroccan–Algerian War
Nezzar, Khaled
Ouary, Malek
Ouled Sidi Cheikh
Parti de l'Avant-Garde Socialiste (PAGS)
Setif
Setif Revolt (1945)
Tripoli Programme (1962)
Uqbi, Tayyib al-
Zbiri, Tahar

Joseph Nevo
University of Haifa
Attlee, Clement
Bludan Conferences (1937, 1946)
Kirkbride, Alec Seath
MacDonald, Malcolm
United Nations Special Committee on Palestine, 1947 (UNSCOP)

David Newman
Ben-Gurion University of the Negev
Green Line

Gush Emunim
Israeli Settlements
Kiryat Arba
Levinger, Moshe
West Bank

Francis R. Nicosia
Saint Michael's College
Berlin–Baghdad Railway
Grobba, Fritz Konrad Ferdinand

John D. Norton
University of Durham, England
Bektashis

Isis Nusair
Saint Mary's College
Husseini, Rana
Khader, Asma
Marʿi, Mariam
Princess Basma Women's Resource Center

Pierre Oberling
City University of New York, Hunter College
Denktash, Rauf

Sami Ofeish
University of Balamand
Eddé, Emile
Saʿada, Antun

Paola Olimpo
University of Lecce
Kissinger, Henry

Jean-Marc R. Oppenheim
Fordham University
Alexandria
Alexandria University
Balaclava, Battle of
Bonaparte, Napoléon
Gezira Sporting Club
Gordon, Charles
Levantine
Qutb, Sayyid

Les Ordeman
Columbia University
Bishara, Abdullah
Khubar, al-
Pharaon, Rashad
Tariki, Abdullah

Ibrahim M. Oweiss
Georgetown University
British–French Oil Agreement

Taha Parla
Bogazici University, Istanbul
Gökalp, Ziya
Kemalism

Malcolm C. Peck
Meridian International Center
Abd al-Aziz ibn Saʿud Al Saʿud
Abu Dhabi
Al al-Shaykh Family
Al Rashid Family
Al Saʿud, Saʿud ibn Abd al-Aziz
Al Sudayri Family
Al Sudayri, Hassa bint Ahmad
Al Thunayyan Family
Arabian Mission
Arab National Movement (ANM)
Buraymi Oasis Dispute
Dhow
Dhufar
Dhufar Rebellion
Doha
Dubai
Fahd ibn Abd al-Aziz Al Saʿud
Faisal ibn Abd al-Aziz Al Saʿud
Faysal ibn Turki Al Saʿud
Fujayra
Fujayra–Sharjah Conflict
Grand Mosque
Hasa, al-
Ikhwan
Incense
Khalid ibn Abd al-Aziz Al Saʿud
Kuwait
Kuwait City
Kuwait University
National Democratic Front for the Liberation of Oman and the Arab Gulf
Popular Front for the Liberation of the Occupied Arabian Gulf
Qatar
Raʾs al-Khayma
Sharjah
Trucial Coast
Tunb Islands
Umm al-Qaywayn

United Arab Emirates
Zanzibar

Yaron Peleg
Brandeis University
Agnon, Shmuel Yosef
Amir, Eli
Bejerano, Maya
Zach, Natan

Thomas G. Penchoen
University of California, Los Angeles
Berber
Djemaʿa
Kabylia
Mzab
Twareg

C. R. Pennell
University of Melbourne, Victoria
Bled al-Siba/Bled al-Makhzan
Casablanca
Ceuta
Fasi, Allal al-
Fasi, Muhammad al-
Ibrahim, Abdullah
Khattabi, Muhammad ibn Abd al-Karim al-
Meknes, Treaty of (1836)
Rif
Rif War
Yata, Ali

Don Peretz
State University of New York
Arab–Israel Conflict
Arab–Israel War (1948)
Arab–Israel War (1956)
Arab–Israel War (1967)
Arab–Israel War (1973)
Arab Revolt (1916)
Camp David Accords (1978)
Dayr Yasin
Intifada (1987–1991)
Palestine
Palestinian Citizens of Israel
Refugees: Palestinian
United States of America and the Middle East

Kenneth J. Perkins
University of South Carolina, Columbia
Ben Salah, Ahmed
Ben Yousouf, Salah
Bizerte
Bizerte Crisis (1961)
Bugeaud de la Piconnerie, Thomas-Robert
Crémieux Decree
Fly Whisk Incident (1827)
French Foreign Legion
Khaldunniyya
Mestiri, Ahmad
Tangier, Treaty of
Thaalbi, Abd al-Aziz

Amos Perlmutter
American University
Lavon Affair
Palmah

John R. Perry
University of Chicago
Browne, Edward Granville
Khazʿal Khan

J. E. Peterson
Tucson, AZ
Al al-Shaykh Family
Al Bu Saʿid Family and Tribe of Oman
Al Bu Saʿid, Qabus ibn Saʿid
Al Bu Saʿid, Saʿid ibn Taymur
Al Sudayri Family
Al Thunayyan Family
Dammam, al-
Dhahran
Gulf of Oman
Jidda
Jubayl, al-
Riyadh
Rub al-Khali
Saudi Arabia
Taʾif, al-
Yanbu

Thomas Philipp
Friedrich-Alexander Universität, Erlangen
Hilal, al-
Zaydan, Jurji

Karen Pinto
American University of Beirut
Archaeological Museum (Istanbul)
Bliss, Howard
Bodrum

Kut al-Amara
Middle East
Opium
Rumelia

Lawrence G. Potter
Columbia University
Amin al-Dowleh, Mirza Ali Khan
Amin al-Soltan, Ali-Asghar
Amin al-Zarb, Mohammad Hasan
Amir Kabir, Mirza Taqi Khan
Zell al-Soltan, Masʿud Mirza

Parvaneh Pourshariati
Ohio State University
Abadan
Adalat Party
Ahvaz
Dar al-Fonun
Democratic Party of Kurdistan (Iran)
Democratic Party of Kurdistan (Iraq)
Golestan Palace
Griboyedov Incident
Hamadan
Iradeh-ye Melli Party
Iran Novin Party
Isfahan University
Islah Taleban Party
Kerman
Khorasan
Khuzistan
Mardom Party
Qom
Shiraz University
Sistan and Baluchistan
Tabriz University
Vaziri, Qamar al-Moluk
Wolff, Henry Drummond
Zagros

Crystal Procyshen
International Christian University
Shaltut, Muhammad

Ayad al-Qazzaz
California State University, Sacramento
Ahali Group
Baghdad
Bazzaz, Abd al-Rahman al-
Daʿwa al-Islamiyya, al-
Hashimi, Taha al-
Ibrahim, Izzat
Iraq
Jabr, Salih
Mosul, Anglo–Turkish Dispute over
Sadr, Muhammad Baqir al-
Suwaydi Family
Suwaydi, Tawfiq al-
Tikriti Families
United Nations Special Commission (UNSCOM)

Donald Quataert
State University of New York, Birmingham
Ottoman Empire: Overview
Ottoman Empire: Debt
Westernization

Mouin Rabbani
University of Oxford
Habash, George
Hut, Shafiq al-
Palestine National Council
Popular Front for the Liberation of Palestine
Popular Front for the Liberation of Palestine–General Command
Qurai, Ahmad Sulayman
Sabbagh, Hasib
Saʿiqa, al-
Wazir, Khalil al-

Itamar Rabinovich
Tel Aviv University
Sasson, Eliyahu

Ali Jihad Racy
University of California, Los Angeles
Abd al-Wahhab, Humannad ibn

Abdul-Karim Rafeq
College of William and Mary
Akrad, Hayy al-
Ayn, Ras al-
Damascus University
Dayr al-Zawr Province
Ghab, al-
Greater Syria
Hama
Hinnawi, Sami al-
Idlib Province
Istiqlal Party: Syria
Jabal, Badawi al-
Jabal Druze
Latakia

Sharabati, Ahmad al
Syrian Desert

Babak Rahimi
Lake Forest, CA
Alizadeh, Ghazaleh
Ganji, Akbar

Mark Raider
State University of New York, Albany
American Israel Public Affairs Committee
Silver, Abba Hillel
Wise, Stephen S.

Rasul Bakhsh Rais
Columbia University
Pakistan and the Middle East

Ruth Raphaeli
Columbia University
Hebrew

Sara Reguer
City University of New York, Brooklyn College
Gallipoli
Johnston Plan (1953)
Jordan River
Litani River
National Water System (Israel)
Rutenberg, Pinhas
Sèvres, Treaty of (1920)
World War I

Bernard Reich
George Washington University
Government
Israel: Overview

Donald Malcolm Reid
Georgia State University
Adli
Ahram Center for Political and Strategic Studies, al-
Ain Shams University
Alexandria
Alexandria University
American University in Cairo (AUC)
Azhar, al-
Baghdadi, Abd al-Latif al-
Cairo
Cairo University
Champollion, Jean-François
Coptic Museum
Dar al Daʿwa wa al-Irshad
Dar al-Kutub al-Misriyya
Dar al-Ulum
Egyptian Geographical Society
Egyptian Museum
Elites
Institut d'Égypte
International Debt Commission
Kamal, Ahmad
Mariette, Auguste
Maspéro, Gaston
Mixed Courts
Muhammad Ali Mosque
Postage Stamps
Pyramids
Qusayr, al-
Rida, Rashid
Saʿid Pasha
Salim Hasan
Sphinx
Suez Canal University
Zaqaziq University

Nissim Rejwan
Hebrew University of Jerusalem
Ben-Porat, Mordechai
Ezra and Nehemiah Operations

Laura Rice
Oregon State University
Amari, Raja
Association des Femmes Tunisiennes pour la Recherche et le Développement (AFTURD)
Bakkar, Jalillah
Centre de Recherches, d'Études, de Documentation et d'Information sur la Femme (CREDIF)
Gender: Study of
Ghanmi, Azza
Mernissi, Fatema
Moudawana, al-
Tlatli, Moufida

Paul Rivlin
Tel Aviv University
Bar-Ilan University
Economic and Military Aid
Histadrut
Jewish National Fund
Joint Distribution Committee
Koor Industries

Moshav
Naʿamaat
Population
United Jewish Appeal (UJA)
West German Reparations Agreement

Aleya Rouchdy
Wayne State University
Nubians

Maurice M. Roumani
Ben-Gurion University of the Negev
Ha-Cohen, Mordechai
Haggiag Family
Nahum, Halfallah
Nhaisi, Elia

Paul Rowe
University of Western Ontario
Constantinople
Luxor
Samarra
Sinai Peninsula

Sara M. Roy
Harvard University
Gaza Strip

Barnett R. Rubin
BESA Center for Stategic Studies
Ahmad Shah Masʿud

John Ruedy
Georgetown University
Algeria: Overview
Algerian War of Independence
Algiers Charter
Arabization Policies
Armée de Libération Nationale (ALN)
Association of Algerian Muslim Ulama (AUMA)
Colons
Comité de Coordination et d'Exécution
Comité Révolutionnaire d'Unité et d'Action (CRUA)
Conseil National de la Révolution Algérienne (CNRA)
Fanon, Frantz
Front de Libération Nationale (FLN)
High State Council (Algeria)
Imperialism in the Middle East and North Africa
Manifesto of the Algerian Muslim People
Mouvement National Algérien
Mouvement pour le Triomphe des Libertés Démocratiques
Organisation Armée Secrète (OAS)
Oujda Group
Parti du Peuple Algérien (PPA)
Star of North Africa
Union Démocratique du Manifeste Algérien (UDMA)
Young Algerians

William A. Rugh
Georgetown University
Newspapers and Print Media: Arab Countries
Radio and Television: Arab Countries

Mona Russell
Massachusetts Institute of Technology
Abu Zayd, Hikmat
Anis Al-Jalis Magazine
Lata'if al-Musawwara Magazine

Curtis R. Ryan
Appalachian State University
Arab Legion
Faysal, Tujan
Islamic Action Front
Jordan River
Noor al-Hussein (Queen Noor)
Rania al-Abdullah (Queen Rania)

Elise Salem
Fairleigh Dickinson University
Adnan, Etel
Bahithat al-Lubnaniyyat, al-
Barakat, Hoda
Faqir, Fadia
Malaʾika, Nazik al-
Moghaizel, Laure
Mouʿawwad, Naila
Nasrallah, Emily
Samman, Ghada
Shaykh, Hanan al-
Ziadeh, May

Ariel Salzmann
New York University
Tax Farming

Geoffrey D. Schad
Shippensburg University
Hama

Uli Schamiloglu
University of Wisconsin, Madison
Azeri Language and Literature
Gaspirali, Ismail Bey
Koprülü, Mehmet Fuat
Turkish Historical Society
Turkish Linguistic Society
Turkology

Stephen Schecter
Université du Québec à Montréal
Kaniuk, Yoram
Kenaz, Yehoshua
Yehoshua, Avraham B.

Jillian Schwedler
University of Maryland, College Park
Islah Party
Turabi, Hasan al-

Emanuela Trevisan Semi
Ca' Foscari University of Venice
Ethiopian Jews

Caroline Seymour-Jorn
University of Wisconsin, Milwaukee
Bakr, Salwa
Makdashi, Hesna
Munif, Abdel Rahman
Nassif, Malak Hifni
Rifaat, Alifa

Pamela Dorn Sezgin
Marietta, GA
Music

Jean-François Seznec
Lafayette Group
Economics
Natural Gas: Middle East Reserves of
Petrochemicals
Petroleum Reserves and Production
PETROMIN
Royal Dutch Shell
Stock Market
Suez Canal
Suez–Mediterranean Pipeline
World Bank

A. Shapur Shahbazi
Eastern Oregon State College
Bisitun

Irfan Shahîd
Washington, DC
Shawqi, Ahmad

M. Nazif Shahrani
Indiana University, Bloomington
Afghanistan: Overview
Afghanistan: Islamic Movements in
Daud, Muhammad
Uzbeks
Zahir Shah

Zaki Shalom
Ben-Gurion Research Center
Meir, Golda

Seteney Shami
Social Science Research Council
Circassians

Zeva Shapiro
New York, NY
Kaniuk, Yoram
Kenaz, Yehoshua

Yaakov Shavit
Tel Aviv University
Altalena
Cohen, Ge'ula
Irgun Zva'i Le'umi (IZL)
Shamir, Yitzhak
Sharon, Ariel

Gabriel Sheffer
The Hebrew University of Jerusalem
Diaspora

William Shepard
University of Canterbury
Amin, Ahmad

Dov Shinar
Ben-Gurion University of the Negev
Newspapers and Print Media: Israel
Radio and Television: Israel

Faegheh Shirazi
University of Texas, Austin
Clothing

Farhad Shirzad
New York, NY
Paris, Treaty of (1857)
Turkmanchai, Treaty of (1828)

Avi Shlaim
Oxford University
All-Palestine Government
Glubb, John Bagot
Jordanian Option
Partition Plans (Palestine)

Eric Silver
Jerusalem, Israel
Begin, Menachem
Netanyahu, Benjamin
Sharon, Ariel

Alain Silvera
Bryn Mawr College
Victoria College

Brian Silverstein
University of California, Los Angeles
Newspapers and Print Media: Turkey
Radio and Television: Turkey

Paul Silverstein
Reed College
Berber Spring
Black Spring

Miriam Simon
Interreligious Coordinating Council in Israel
Bar-Ilan University
Ben-Gurion University of the Negev
Exodus (1947)
Ha-Tikva
Magen David Adom (MDA)
Navon, Yizhak
Saison
Struma
Technion-Israel Institute of Technology
Tel Aviv University
Weizmann Institute of Science
Zangwill, Israel

Rachel Simon
Princeton University Library
Farhat al-Zawi
Qaramanli Dynasty
Sanusi, Muhammad ibn Ali al-
Sanusi Order
Turkish–Italian War (1911–1912)

Reeva S. Simon
Columbia University
Arab–Israel War (1956)
Archaeology in the Middle East
Baʿth, al-
Faisal I ibn Hussein
Freemasons
Germany and the Middle East
Golden Square
Holy Land
Iraq
Jaffa
Jamali, Muhammad Fadhil al-
Jerusalem
Kirkuk
Lavon, Pinhas
Mosul
National Democratic Party (Iraq)
Rothschild, Edmond de
Sabbagh, Salah al-Din al-
Wingate, Charles Orde
Yiddish

Peter von Sivers
University of Utah
Ahmad Bey of Constantine
Algiers
Mukrani Family
Oran
Warnier Law

P. Oktor Skjaervo
Harvard University
Iranian Languages

Peter Sluglett
University of Utah
Abd al-Ilah ibn Ali
Anglo–Iraqi Treaties
Baʿth, al-
Colonialism in the Middle East
Cox, Percy
Faisal II ibn Ghazi
Ghazi ibn Faisal
Hourani, Albert
Ikha al-Watani Party
Jawahiri, Muhammad Mahdi al-
Kaylani, Rashid Ali al-
Midfaʿi, Jamil al-
Sanctions, Iraqi
Shimʿun, Mar
Sidqi, Bakr
Sulayman, Hikmat
Westernization
Wilson, Arnold T.

Oles M. Smolansky
Lehigh University
Brezhnev, Leonid Ilyich
Khrushchev, Nikita S.
Russia and the Middle East
Russian–Ottoman Wars
San Stefano, Treaty of (1878)
Stack, Lee

Sasson Somekh
Tel Aviv University
Heskayl, Sasson
Rasafi, Maʿruf al-
Salim, Jawad
Shaʾul, Anwar
Somikh, Abdullah

Tamara Sonn
The College of William and Mary
Alia, Queen

John P. Spagnolo
Simon Fraser University
De Gaulle, Charles
France and the Middle East

Donald Spanel
Credit Suisse First Boston
Coptic Museum
Copts
Cyril IV
Cyril V
Cyril VI
Demetrius II
John XIX
Mark VIII
Peter VII
Shenouda III

Daniel E. Spector
Troy State University
Alamayn, al-
Allied Middle East Command
D'Arcy Concession (1901)
Dardanelles, Treaty of the (1809)
Gardanne Mission
Gulf War (1991)
Lausanne, Treaty of (1923)
Mandate System
Middle East Supply Center (MESC)
Military in the Middle East
Millspaugh, Arthur
Rommel, Erwin
Roosevelt, Franklin Delano
Shuster, W. Morgan
Straits Convention
Tobruk
Vance, Cyrus
Versailles, Treaty of (1920)
Wavell, Archibald Percival
World War II

Denise A. Spellberg
University of Texas, Austin
Madrasa
Mahdi
Ulama
Waqf

Kenneth W. Stein
Emory University
Madrid Conference (1991)

Rita Stephan
University of Texas, Austin
Arab Women's Solidarity Association International
Husari, Sati al-
Ibrahim, Saʿad al-Din
Marriage and Family
Mevlevi Brotherhood
Saadawi, Nawal al-
Sabah, Suad al-

Norman Stillman
University of Oklahoma
Baqri Family
Ben Simeon, Raphael Aaron
B'nai B'rith
Busnach Family
Club National Israelite
Comité Juif Algérien d'études Sociales
Corcos Family
Dor Deʿa
Giado Concentration Camp
Hazzan, Elijah Bekhor
Jews in the Middle East
Judeo-Arabic
Ladino
LICA
Maccabi
Magic Carpet Operation
Valensi, Alfred

Ronald Bruce St John
Independent Scholar, Illinois
Asad, Bashshar al-
Asad, Hafiz al-
Cyrenaica
Libya
Maziq, Husayn
Pan-Arabism
Pelt, Adrian
Pérez de Cuéllar, Javier
Qaddafi, Muammar al-
Revolutionary Command Council (Libya)
Shamikh, Mubarak Abdullah al-
Stark, Freya
Syria
Syrian Social Nationalist Party
Tripolitania
Yunis Jabir, Abu Bakr

Christopher Reed Stone
Middlebury College
Fayruz
Peace Corps

Thomas Stransky
Tantur Ecumenical Institute, Jerusalem, Israel
Saint Catherine's Monastery

Samy S. Swayd
San Diego State University
Druze

Will D. Swearingen
Montana State University
Atlas Mountains
Memmi, Albert

Ephraim Tabory
Bar-Ilan University, Israel
Circumcision
Halakhah
Talmud
Yosef, Ovadiah

Frank Tachau
University of Illinois, Chicago
Confederation of Turkish Trade Unions
Erbakan, Necmeddin
Freedom Party
Free Republican Party
İzmir Economic Congress
Motherland Party
Nationalist Action Party
National Unity Committee (Turkey)
Social Democratic Populist Party
True Path Party
Türkes, Alparslan
Turkish National Pact
Turkish Workers Party
Unity Party

Kazuo Takahashi
University of the Air, Tokyo
China and the Middle East

Lawrence Tal
Admiral House, London, England
Bevin, Ernest
Bir Zeit University
Cattan, Henry
Fida'iyyun
Haddad, Wadi
Hasan, Hani al-
Hasan, Khalid al-
Hilmi, Ahmad
Jibril, Ahmad
Kanafani, Ghassan
Karama, Battle of (1968)
Land Day
Nusayba Family
Ramallah

Steve Tamari
Institute of Jerusalem Studies
Abbas, Mahmud
Ahmad al-Jazzar
Anglo–American Committee of Inquiry (1946)
Aqqad, Umar Abd al-Fattah al-
Arab Liberation Army
Arab Women's Congress
Arif, Arif al-
Banna, Sabri al-
Barghuthi Family
Beersheba
Black September

Cherie Taraghi
Üsküdar, Istanbul, Turkey
Behrouzi, Maryam
Farmanfarmian, Settareh

Islamic Countries Women Sport Solidarity Games (1992 and 1997)
Lahiji, Shahla

Abraham Terian
Andrews University
Armenian Community of Jerusalem

Janice J. Terry
Eastern Michigan University
Wafd
Wingate, Reginald
Zaghlul, Saʿd

Mary Ann Tetréault
Iowa State University
Al Sabah Family
Al Sabah, Mubarak
Al Saqr Family
Arabian American Oil Company (ARAMCO)
As-Is Agreement
Awadhi, Badria A. al-
Bishara, Abdullah
Ghanim, al-
Iraq Petroleum Company (IPC)
Kuwait
Kuwait City
Kuwait Fund for Arab Economic Development
Kuwait Petroleum Corporation
National Oil Corporation (Libya)
Natural Gas: Economic Exploitation of
Oasis Group
Occidental Petroleum
Organization of Petroleum Exporting Countries (OPEC)
Petrochemicals
Petroleum, Oil, and Natural Gas
Qatar Petroleum
Red Line Agreement
Sabah, Rasha al-
Trade
Trans-Arabian Pipeline

Elizabeth Thompson
University of Virginia
Abdülmecit II
Agop, Gullu
Ahmet Izzet
Ahmet Riza
Akçura, Yusuf
Altinay, Ahmed Refik
Ankara, Treaty of (1930)
Aqaba Incident
Arab Liberation Front
Aral, Öğuz
Arseven, Celal Esat
Atay, Salih Rifki
Bayrakdar, Mustafa
Bedel-i Askeri
Bludan Conferences (1937, 1946)
Bogazköy
Churchill, William
Cilicia
Darwish, Ishaq
Deedes, Wyndham
Diyarbakir
Dolmabahçe Palace
Eastern Orthodox Church
Eldem, Sedad Hakki
Ersoy, Mehmet Akif
Ertuğrul, Muhsin
Erzurum
Erzurum Congress (1919)
Esendal, Memduh Şevket
Eyüboğlu, Bedri Rahmi
Falconry
Ferit, Damat Mehmet
Ferman
Güney, Yilmaz
Gürpinar, Hüseyin Rahmi
Galata
Ganim, Halil
Genç Kalemler
Ha-Shomer
Ibrahimi, Lakhdar al-
İdadi Schools
İlmiyye
İpekci, Abdi
Isa Family, al-
Jabal al-Khalil
Jabal Nablus
Jaʿbari Family
Jarallah Family
Jizya
Johnson–Crosbie Committee Report (1930)
Kafr Qasim
Kalemiyye
Karacan, Ali Naci
Keban Dam
Khalaf, Salah

Khutba
Kiryat Arba
Kisakürek, Necip Fazil
Koç, Vehbi
Konya, Battle of
Kuttab
Litani Operation (1978)
Lydda
Maghrib
Mahalle Schools
Mansure Army
Mediterranean Sea
Milli İstihbarat Teşkilati
Minaret
Muhsin, Zuhayr
Muhtar, Gazi Ahmet
Mustafa Fazil
Mustafa Suphi
Nadi, Yunus
Najjada, al-
Nasir, Najib
Negev
Nesin, Nüsret Aziz
Nizamiye Courts
Ormsby-Gore, William George Arthur
OYAK (Ordu Yardimlasma Kurumu)
Palestine Economic Corporation
Palestine Exploration Fund
Palestine Land Development Company
Palmyra
Permanent Mandates Commission
Persian (Arabian) Gulf
Point Four
Qanun
Qur'an
Ramla
Rejection Front
Ruşdiye Schools
Saba Family
Safveti Ziya
Sakakini, Khalil al-
Salonika
Şevket, Mahmut
Shumayyil, Shibli
Shuqayri Family
Shura
Silk
Simavi, Sedat
Sinai Peninsula
Şirket-i Hayriye
South Lebanon Army
Sultani Schools
Sunay, Cevdet
Sun Language Theory
Sursuq Family
Tamimi, Amin al-
Taner, Haldun
Tanzimat
Timar
Tripoli Conference (1977)
Tuqan Family
Turkism
Uşakliğil, Halit Ziya
Üsküdar
Varlik Vergisi
Yarmuk River
Yildirim Army
Yücel, Hasan Ali
Ziya, Abdülhamit

W. Kenneth Thompson
U.S. Department of State, Washington, DC
Drugs and Narcotics

Karen A. Thornsvard
Madison, WI
Amir, Abd al-Hakim
Wauchope, Arthur

Robert L. Tignor
Princeton University
Baring, Evelyn
Farouk
Fu'ad

Nayereh Tohidi
California State University, Northridge
Ebtekar, Ma'sumeh
Zanan Magazine

Ehud R. Toledano
Tel Aviv University
Slave Trade

Ana Torres-Garcia
Universidad de Sevilla
Ahardane, Majoub
Baccouche, Hedi
Bouabid, Abderrahim
Ibrahim, Abdullah
Ibrahimi, Lakhdar al-
Lamrani, Muhammad Karim

Ligue Tunisienne pour la Défense des Droits de l'Homme (LTDH)
Mestiri, Ahmad
Mouvement de l'Unité Populaire (MUP)
Mzali, Mohammed
Opium
Ouary, Malek
Parti d'Unité Populaire (PUP)
SONATRACH
Tunisia: Political Parties in
Union Générale des Travailleurs Marocains (UGTM)
Union Générale des Travailleurs Tunisiens (UGTT)
Union Marocaine du Travail (UMT)
Western Sahara

Anthony B. Toth
Arlington, VA
Abdul-Aziz Bin Baz, Shaykh
Abu Dhabi
Al Nahayyan Family
Al Rashid Family
Al Saʿud Family
Al Thani Family
Ayn, al-
Baharina
Buraymi Oasis Dispute
Committee for the Defense of Legitimate Rights
Doha
Dubai
Fahd ibn Abd al-Aziz Al Saʿud
Fujayra
Galatasaray Lycée
Grand Mosque
Gulf Cooperation Council
Hasa, al-
Hijaz
Ikhwan
Islamic University of Medina
Jabal al-Akhdar, Oman
Jabal Shammar
Khalid ibn Abd al-Aziz Al Saʿud
King Saʿud University
Kuwait University
Maritime Peace in Perpetuity, Treaty of (1853)
Masira Island
Mecca
Medina
Muʿalla Family, al-
Muscat
Nuʿaymi Family, al-
Qasimi Family of Raʾs al-Khayma, al-
Qasimi Family of Sharjah, al-
Qatar
Qatar Petroleum
Raʾs al-Khayma
Sharqi Family, al-
Taʾif, Treaty of al-
Tariki, Abdullah
Tiran, Strait of
Tourism
Transport
Umm al-Qaywayn
United Arab Emirates
Urbanization
Yamani, Ahmad Zaki

S. Ilan Troen
Brandeis University
Ben-Gurion University of the Negev
Sèvres Protocol (1956)

Benyamim Tsedakah
Holon, Israel
Samaritans

Jenab Tutunji
George Washington University
Abdullah I ibn Hussein
Abu al-Huda, Tawfiq
Abu Nuwwar, Ali
Aqaba
Aqaba, Gulf of
Arab Legion
Asmar, Fawzi al-
Attlee, Clement
Badran, Mudar
Brookings Report (1975)
Clayton, Gilbert
East India Company
Fahd Plan (1981)
Guinness, Walter Edward
Hashim, Ibrahim
Holy Sepulchre, Church of the
Ismaʿili Shiʿism
Jericho Congress (1948)
Jewish Colonial Trust
Kahan Commission (1983)
Kirkbride, Alec Seath

Liberty, USS
Luke, Harry
MacDonald, Malcolm
MacDonald, Ramsay
MacMichael, Harold
Majali, Hazza al-
Nabulsi, Sulayman al-
Nasir, Hanna
Palestine Research Center
Peake, Frederick Gerard
Plague
Polygamy
Richmond, Ernest T.
Rifaʿi, Samir al-
Salt, al-
Talal ibn Abdullah
Tall, Wasfi al-
Transjordan Frontier Force
Turki, Fawaz
University of Jordan
Yarmuk University

Brian Urquhart
New York, NY
Bunche, Ralph J.
Hammarskjöld, Dag
United Nations Interim Force in Lebanon

Farzin Vahdat
Harvard University
Kadivar, Mohsen
Mojtahed-Shabestari, Mohammad

Martin Van Bruinessen
Universiteit Utrecht
Kurdistan Workers Party (PKK)

Dirk Vandewalle
Dartmouth College
Annaba
Bidonville
Boumédienne, Houari
Cantonnement/Refoulement
Constantine
Ente Nazionale Idrocarboni (ENI)
SONATRACH

Roxanne Varzi
New York University
Bani-Etemad, Rakhsan
Behbehani, Simin
Derakhshandeh, Puran
Film
Jihad
Khamenehi, Ali
Kiarostami, Abbas
Mahfuz, Najib
Makhmalbaf Family
Makhmalbaf, Mohsen
Milani, Tahmineh
Persian Script
Shahin, Yusuf
Sharif, Omar
Shiʿism

Haleh Vaziri
Intermedia Survey Institute, Washington, DC
Diba, Farah
Women's Organization of Iran (WOI)

Peter von Sivers
University of Utah
Algiers

David Waldner
University of Virginia
Abd al-Quddus, Ihsan
Abd al-Sabur, Salah
Abidin, Dino
Abu Qir, Battle of (1798)
Ahmet Ihsan Toʾkgoz
Ahmet Rasim
Akbulut, Ahmet Ziya
Ali Riza
Ararat, Mount
Aswan High Dam
Awad, Louis
Başiretci, Ali
Bekir, Fahri
Caylak
Çerkes Hasan Incident
Cevdet, Abdullah
Civil Service School (Ottoman)
Clot, Antoine Barthélémy
Commercial and Navigation Treaties
Congress of Ottoman Liberals (1902)
Dede Zekai
Dellalzade İsmail
Delta Barrages
Democrat Party
Devrim, Izzet Melih
Dufferin Report (1883)
Erbil, Leyla
Evren, Kenan

Gülbenkian, Calouste
Gürsel, Cemal
Ghanim, Fathi
Ghorbal, Ashraf
Haddad, Saʿd
Hamama, Faten
Hijaz Railroad
İnönü, Erdal
International Monetary Fund
Justice Party
Kamil, Kibrish Mehmet
Kasap, Teodor
Kemalettin Bey
Kenter, Yildiz
Khalid, Khalid Muhammad
Kissinger, Henry
Land Code of 1858
Leskofcali Galip
Lesseps, Ferdinand de
Liberal Constitutionalist Party
Liberation Rally
Maratghi, Mustafa al-
McMahon, Henry
Mehmet Rauf
Menou, Jacques François
Messianism
Mufide Kadri
Muhyi al-Din, Khalid
Muhyi al-Din, Zakariyya
Musa, Salama
Mustafa Reşid
Nabizade Nazim
Naguib, Muhammad
Nazif, Süleyman
Nazmi, Ziya
Özal, Turgut
Philae
Port Saʿid
Recaizade Mahmud Ekrem
Saadawi, Nawal al-
Sabri, Ali
Sanu, Yaʿqub
Saygun, Ahmed Adnan
Şeker Ahmet
Selçuk, Munir Nurettin
Semitic Languages
Shafiq, Durriyya
Shahin, Yusuf
Shaʿrawi, Huda al-
Sharif, Omar
Shazli, Saʿd al-Din
Shilluk
Sidqi, Ismaʿil
Southeastern Anatolia Project
Suphi Ezgi
Tahir, Kemal
Takfir wa al-Hijra, al-
Tanburi Cemil
Tanpinar, Ahmed Hamdi
Tarhan, Abdülhak Hamit
Tevfik Fikret
Tharwat, Abd al-Khaliq
Tunisi, Bayram al-
Turkey
Turkish–Afghan Treaty (1928)
Yurdakul, Mehmet Emin

Bernard Wasserstein
University of Chicago
Britain and the Middle East from 1914 to the Present
Bentwich, Norman
Colonial Office, Great Britain
Creech Jones, Arthur
Crossman, Richard
Lloyd George, David
Samuel, Herbert Louis
Wauchope, Arthur
Weizmann, Chaim
World Zionist Organization (WZO)

Chaim I. Waxman
Rutgers University
Aaronsohn Family
Agudat Israel
Aliyah
Arlosoroff, Chaim
Borochov, Ber
Bund
Dreyfus Affair
Eretz Yisrael
Halukka
Ha-Shomer Ha-Tzaʿir
Hasidim
Herzog, Izhak Halevi
Irgun Zvaʾi Leʾumi (IZL)
Joseph, Dov
Keren Hayesod
Kibbutz
Kook, Abraham Isaac Hacohen
Kook, Zvi Yehuda

Law of Return
Leibowitz, Yeshayahu
Magnes, Judah
Maimon, Yehudah Leib Hacohen
Meah She'arim
Mizrahi Movement
Neturei Karta
Nissim, Isaac
Ouziel, Ben Zion Meir Hai
Patriarchs, Tomb of the
Petah Tikvah
Potash Industry
Salant, Samuel
Uganda Project
Zohar, Uri
Zonnenfeld, Yosef Hayyim

Walter F. Weiker
Rutgers University
Ahdut ha-Avodah
Bayar, Celal
İnönü, İsmet
Israel: Overview of Political Parties in
Kahane, Meir
Knesset
Likud
Lilienblum, Moses Leib
Menderes, Adnan
Oz ve Shalom (Netivot shalom)
Sneh, Moshe

Shalvah Weil
Hebrew University of Jerusalem
Ethiopian Jews

Marvin G. Weinbaum
University of Illinois, Urbana
Economic and Military Aid

Thomas G. Weiss
Graduate Center, City University of New York
United Nations and the Middle East

Rachel Weissbrod
Bar-Ilan University, Israel
Exodus (1947)

Lynn Welchman
School of Oriental and African Studies, University of London
Crimes of Honor
Human Rights

Manfred W. Wenner
Prescott, AZ
Ahmad ibn Yahya Hamid al-Din
Bakil Tribal Confederation
Hamdi, Ibrahim al-
Hodeida
Idrisids
National Front for the Liberation of South Yemen
Organization for the Liberation of the Occupied South
People's Socialist Party
Salih, Ali Abdullah
Sha'bi Family
South Arabian League
Yahya ibn Muhammad Hamid al-Din
Yemen
Yemen Dynasties
Yemeni Socialist Party
Zubayri, Qa'id Muhammad Mahmud al-

Stephanie Wichhart
University of Texas, Austin
Memmi, Albert

George R. Wilkes
University of Cambridge
American Council for Judaism
Badr, Liana
Bialik, Hayyim Nahman
Bitton, Simone
Brenner, Yosef Hayyim
Brookings Report (1975)
Burton, Richard Francis
Chazan, Naomi
Cole, USS
Dentz, Henri-Fernand
Freier, Recha
Ghazali, Muhammad al-
Ghorbal, Ashraf
Grossman, Haika
Habash, George
"Ha-Tikva"
Hut, Shafiq al-
Kovner, Abba
Marzouki, Moncef
Matzpen
Meged, Aharon
Moadda, Mohamed
Muhyi al-Din, Zakariyya
New Wafd
Pharaon, Rashad
Politi, Elie
Popular Front for the Liberation of Palestine–General Command

Qurai, Ahmad Sulayman
Sabbagh, Hasib
Saʿiqa, al-
Sant Egidio Platform
Saunders, Harold
Shalvi, Alice
Shochat, Manya
Sisco, Joseph
Smilansky, Moshe
Women in Black

Rodney J. A. Wilson
University of Durham, England
Industrialization

Jessica Winegar
New York University
Ali, Wijdan
Amer, Ghada
Ani, Jannane al-
Art
Attar, Suad al-
Baya
Caland, Huguette
Efflatoun, Inji
Faraj, Maysaloun
Ghoussoub, Mai
Hatoum, Mona
Ishaaq, Kamala Ibrahim
Jacir, Emily
Kadri, Mufide
Karnouk, Liliane
Khal, Helen
Khemir, Sabiha
Neshat, Shirin
Niati, Houria
Saudi, Mona
Shawa, Laila
Sidera, Zineb
Sirry, Gazbia
Tallal, Chaibia
Umar, Madiha
Zeid, Fahralnissa

Clifford A. Wright
Arlington, MA
Tea

John L. Wright
Surrey, England
Baida
Basic People's Congresses
Benghazi
Cyrenaica
Fezzan
Istiqlal Party: Libya
Kikhya Family
Nasir, Ahmed Sayf al-
Omar Mukhtar Club
Sadawi, Bashir
Tripoli

Nathan Yanai
Haifa University
Dayan, Moshe

Neguin Yavari
Columbia University
Akhbari
Ala, Hoseyn
Alam, Amir Asadollah
Amini, Ali
Amir-Entezam, Abbas
Atabat
Ayn al-Dowleh, Abd al-Majid Mirza
Azerbaijan
Bakhtiari, Najaf Qoli Khan Samsam al-Soltaneh
Bakhtiar, Timur
Baluchistan
Bani Sadr, Abolhasan
Bast
Borujerdi, Hosayn
Chamran, Mostafa
Committee for Defense of Freedom and Human Rights
Daftari, Ahmad Matin
Eqbal, Manouchehr
Forughi, Mirza Mohammad Ali Khan Zaka al-Molk
Freedom Movement (Nezhat-e Azadi Iran)
Hajir, Abd al-Hoseyn
Hoveyda, Amir Abbas
Jangali
Kharg Island
Khomeini, Ruhollah
Kuchek Khan-e Jangali
Majles al-Shura
Marja al-Taqlid
Mohammad Ali Shah Qajar
Musavi-Ardebili, AbdolKarim
Qotbzadeh, Sadeq
Roosevelt, Kermit

Sadr, Muhsin
Shariatmadari, Kazem
Sharif-Emami, Jaʿfar
Shatt al-Arab
Shiraz
Soheyli, Ali
Students in the Line of the Imam
Tabriz
Tabriz University
Usuli
Vazir Afkham, Soltan Ali Khan
Vozuq al-Dowleh, Mirza Hasan Khan
Yazdi, Ibrahim

M. Hakan Yavuz
University of Utah
AKP (Justice and Development Party)
Erbakan, Necmeddin
Erdoğan, Tayyip
Evren, Kenan
Gülen, Fetullah
İnönü, Erdal
Milli Görüş Hareketi
Motherland Party
Nationalist Action Party
National Security Council (Turkey)
Nursi, Said
Sezer, Ahmet
Social Democratic Populist Party
True Path Party
Türkes, Alparslan

Shibolet Zait
Columbia University
Raab, Esther

Muhammad Zakariya
Arlington, VA
Calligraphy

Mamoon A. Zaki
LeMoyne-Owen College
Baban Family
Hashimi, Yasin al-
Mandaeans
Najaf, al-
Pachachi, Muzahim al-

Naomi Zeff
Somerville, MA
Mauritania
Nouakchott
Ould Sidʾ Ahmed Taya, Maʿouiya

Ronen Zeidel
Haifa University
Osirak

Charles U. Zenzie
U.S.-Indonesia Society, Washington, DC
Popular Front
Saʿada, Antun
Shahbandar, Abd al-Rahman
United Nations Truce Supervision Organization (UNTSO)
Zaʿim, Husni al-
Zuʿbi, Mahmud al-
Zurayk, Constantine

Steven Zipperstein
Hebrew University of Jerusalem
Ahad Ha-Am

Eyal Zisser
Tel Aviv University
Zaʿim, Husni al-

Yahia Zoubir
Thunderbird Europe/Centre Universitaire
Bennabi, Malek
Islamic Salvation Army (AIS)
Kateb, Yacine
Parti de l'Avant-Garde Socialiste (PAGS)
Sadi, Said
Toumi, Khalida
Zeroual, Liamine

Julie Zuckerman
Jerusalem, Israel
Goldmann, Nahum
Idris al-Sayyid Muhammad al-Sanusi
Netanyahu, Benjamin
Pagis, Dan
Shin Bet
Sobol, Yehoshua
Stern, Abraham
Tagger, Sioneh
Tamir, Shmuel
Vanunu Affair
Yariv, Aharon
Yosef, Ovadiah

GENEALOGIES

In the following genealogies and lines of succession, an asterisk preceding a name indicates that the Encyclopedia contains an entry for that individual. The names of those who ruled are indicated by boldfaced type. The following genealogies are not exhaustive, including only well-known figures and those in the direct line of succession. Where possible, the existence of additional family members has been indicated with arrows. With a few exceptions, female descendants are not included because they are typically denied inheritance of a throne and, consequently, little information is available about them.

FIGURE 1

Alawite Dynasty of Morocco, 1666–

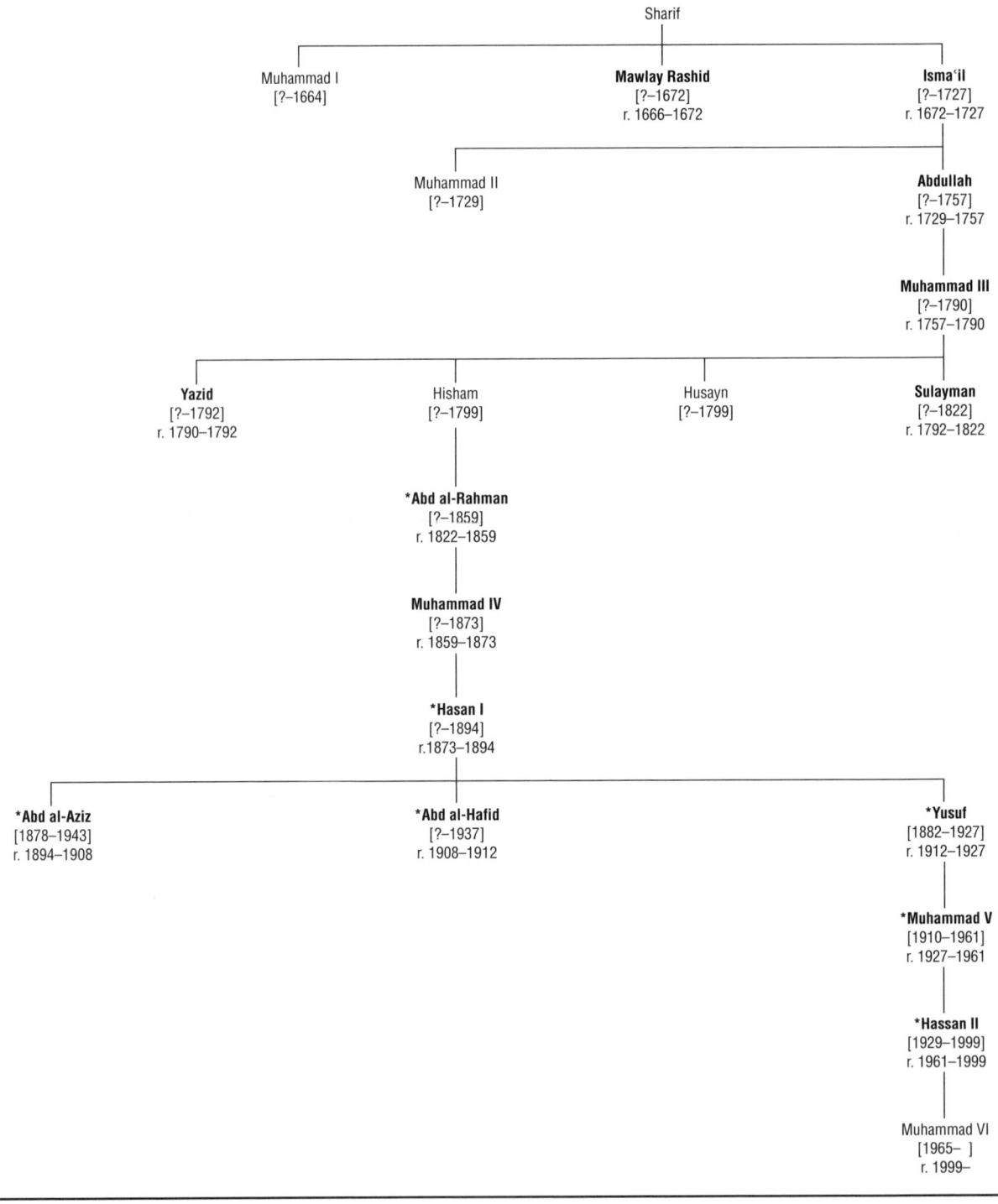

FIGURE 2

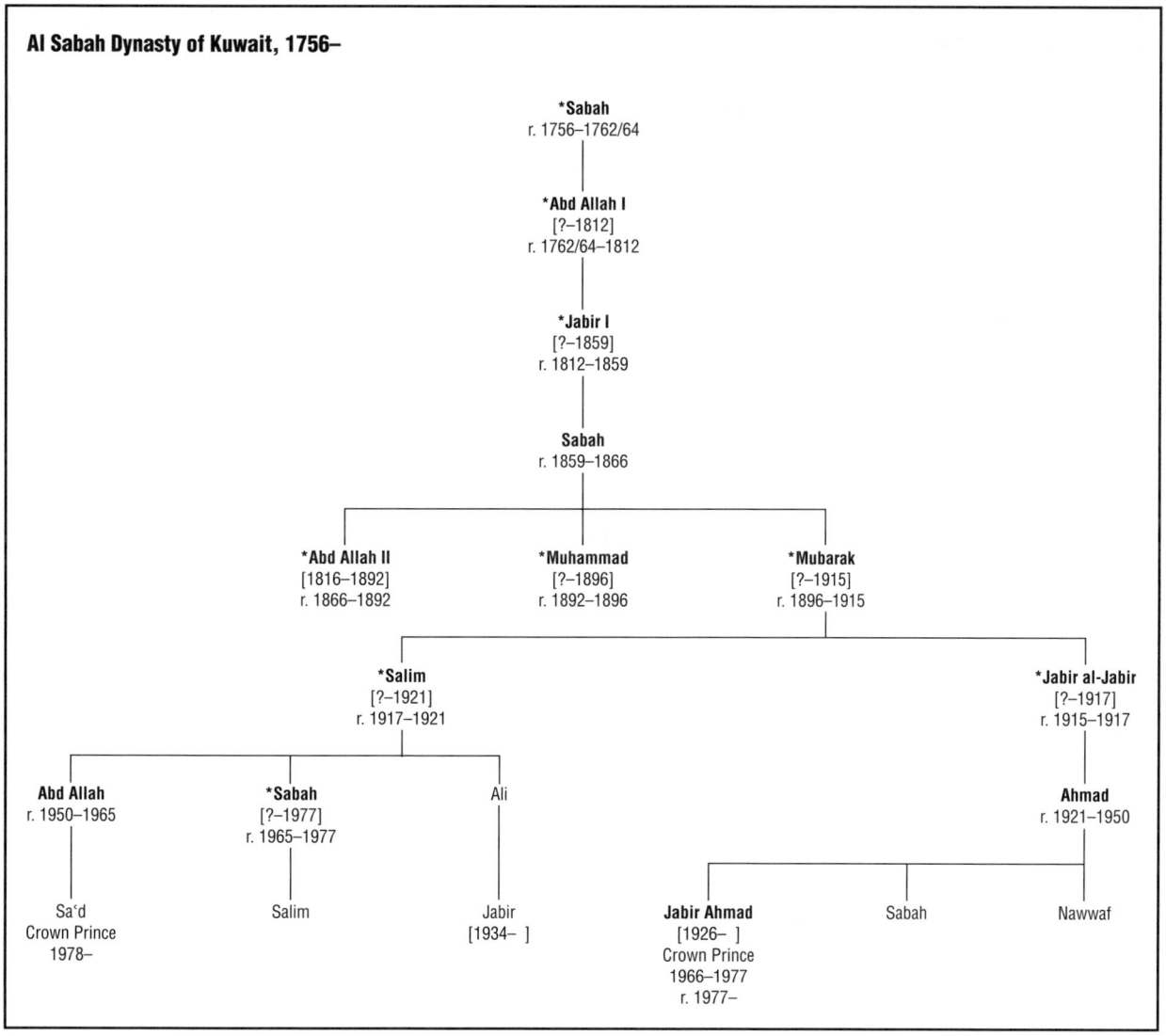
Al Sabah Dynasty of Kuwait, 1756–
*Sabah
r. 1756–1762/64
*Abd Allah I
[?–1812]
r. 1762/64–1812
*Jabir I
[?–1859]
r. 1812–1859
Sabah
r. 1859–1866
*Abd Allah II
[1816–1892]
r. 1866–1892
*Muhammad
[?–1896]
r. 1892–1896
*Mubarak
[?–1915]
r. 1896–1915
*Salim
[?–1921]
r. 1917–1921
*Jabir al-Jabir
[?–1917]
r. 1915–1917
Abd Allah
r. 1950–1965
*Sabah
[?–1977]
r. 1965–1977
Ali
Ahmad
r. 1921–1950
Sa'd
Crown Prince
1978–
Salim
Jabir
[1934–]
Jabir Ahmad
[1926–]
Crown Prince
1966–1977
r. 1977–
Sabah
Nawwaf

FIGURE 3

Al Saʿud Dynasty of Saudi Arabia, 1735–

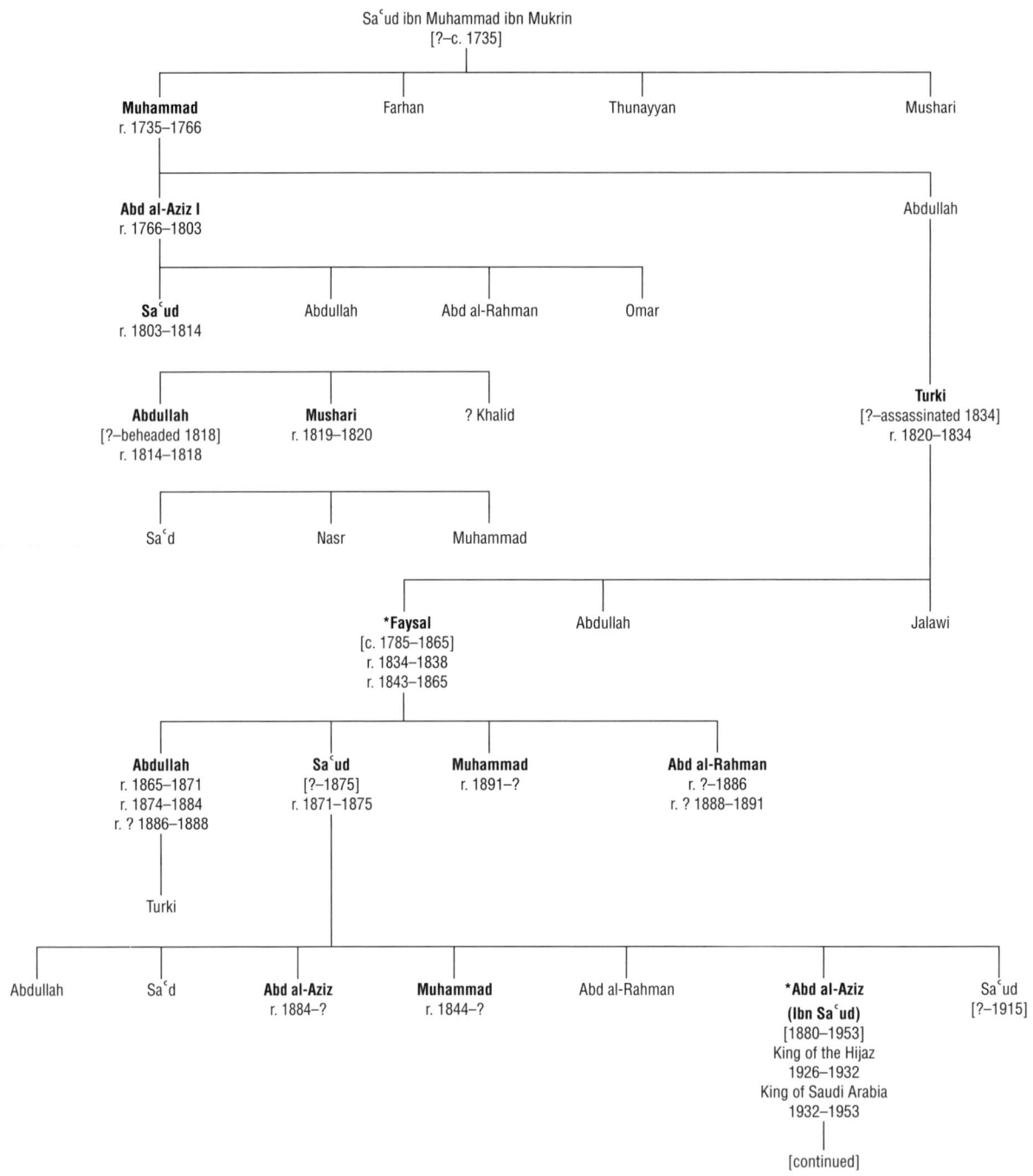

FIGURE 3 (*continued*)

Al Saʿud Dynasty of Saudi Arabia, 1735– [CONTINUED]

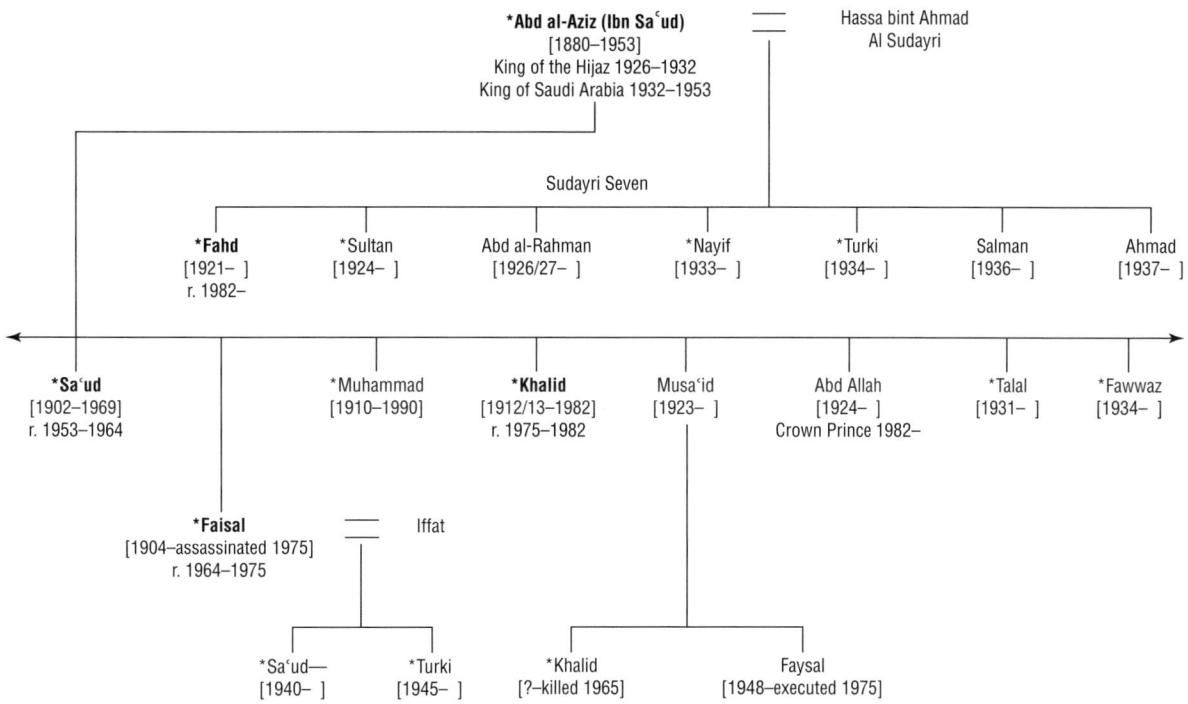

Note: Abd al-Aziz ibn Saʿud Al Saʿud (1880–1953) fathered forty-five sons and as many daughters by at least twenty-three different women. His wife Hassa gave birth to seven sons known as the Sudayri Seven, a reference to Hassa's descent from the Al Sudayri tribe. The descendants of Muhammad ibn Saʿud, the founder of the Al Saʿud dynasty, number in the tens of thousands and include the current king, Fahd, one of the Sudayri Seven.

FIGURE 4

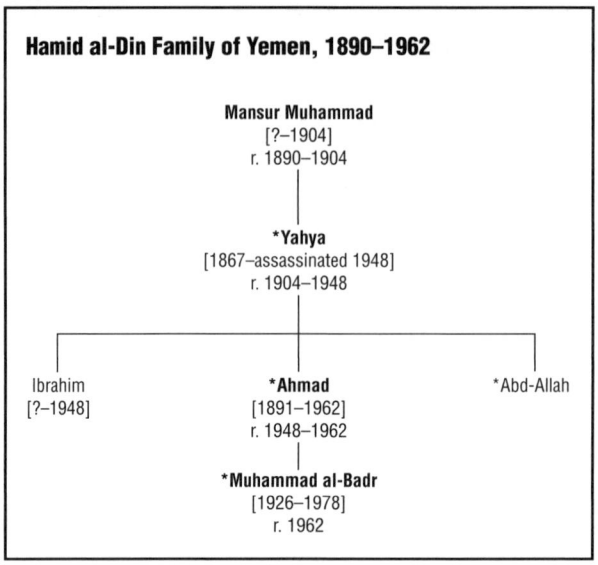
Hamid al-Din Family of Yemen, 1890–1962
Mansur Muhammad
[?–1904]
r. 1890–1904
*Yahya
[1867–assassinated 1948]
r. 1904–1948
Ibrahim
[?–1948]
*Ahmad
[1891–1962]
r. 1948–1962
*Abd-Allah
*Muhammad al-Badr
[1926–1978]
r. 1962

FIGURE 5

Hashimite Family of the Hijaz, 1828–

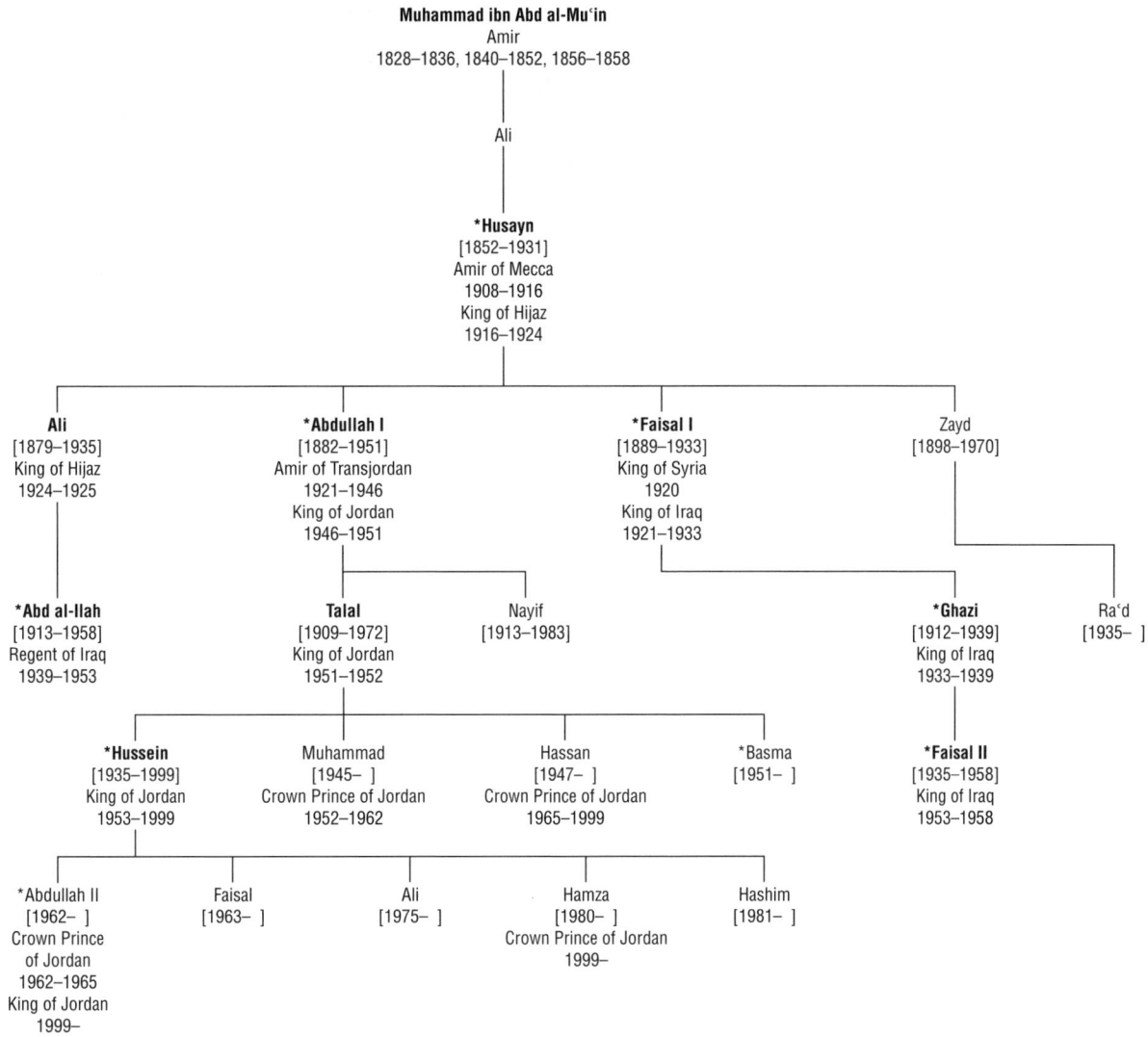

FIGURE 6

Khalifa Family of Bahrain, 1782–

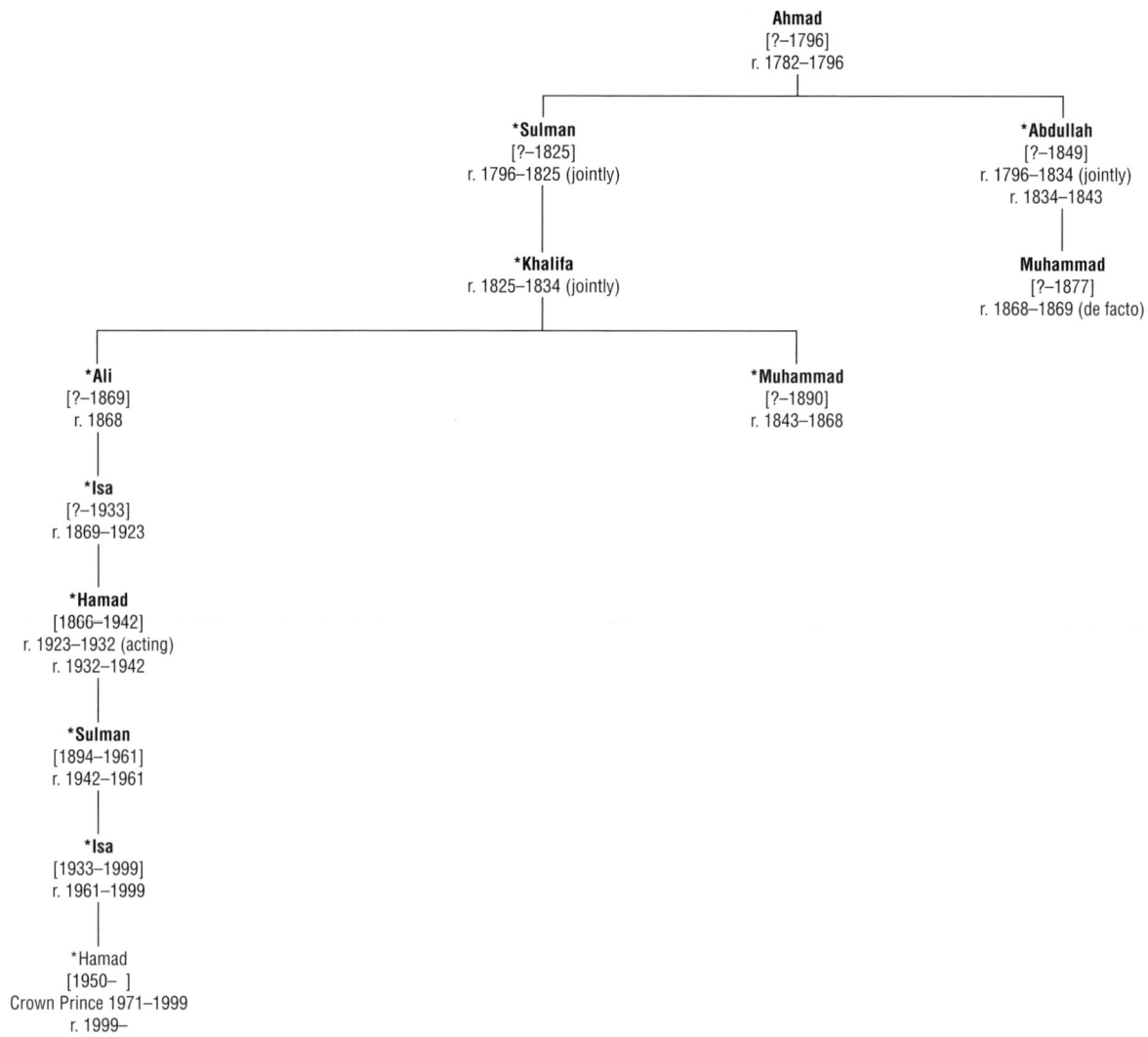

FIGURE 7

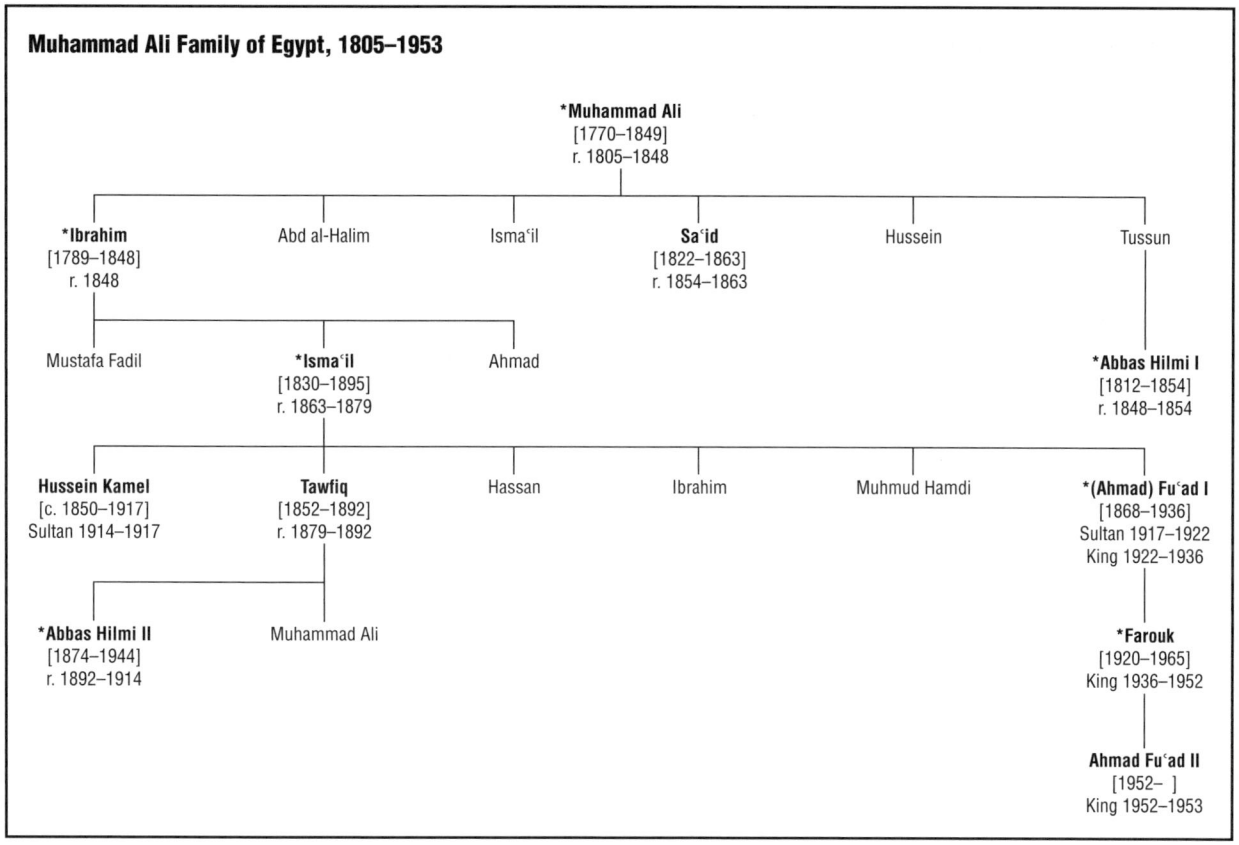
Muhammad Ali Family of Egypt, 1805–1953
*Muhammad Ali
[1770–1849]
r. 1805–1848
*Ibrahim
[1789–1848]
r. 1848
Abd al-Halim
Isma'il
Sa'id
[1822–1863]
r. 1854–1863
Hussein
Tussun
Mustafa Fadil
*Isma'il
[1830–1895]
r. 1863–1879
Ahmad
*Abbas Hilmi I
[1812–1854]
r. 1848–1854
Hussein Kamel
[c. 1850–1917]
Sultan 1914–1917
Tawfiq
[1852–1892]
r. 1879–1892
Hassan
Ibrahim
Muhmud Hamdi
*(Ahmad) Fu'ad I
[1868–1936]
Sultan 1917–1922
King 1922–1936
*Abbas Hilmi II
[1874–1944]
r. 1892–1914
Muhammad Ali
*Farouk
[1920–1965]
King 1936–1952
Ahmad Fu'ad II
[1952–]
King 1952–1953

FIGURE 8

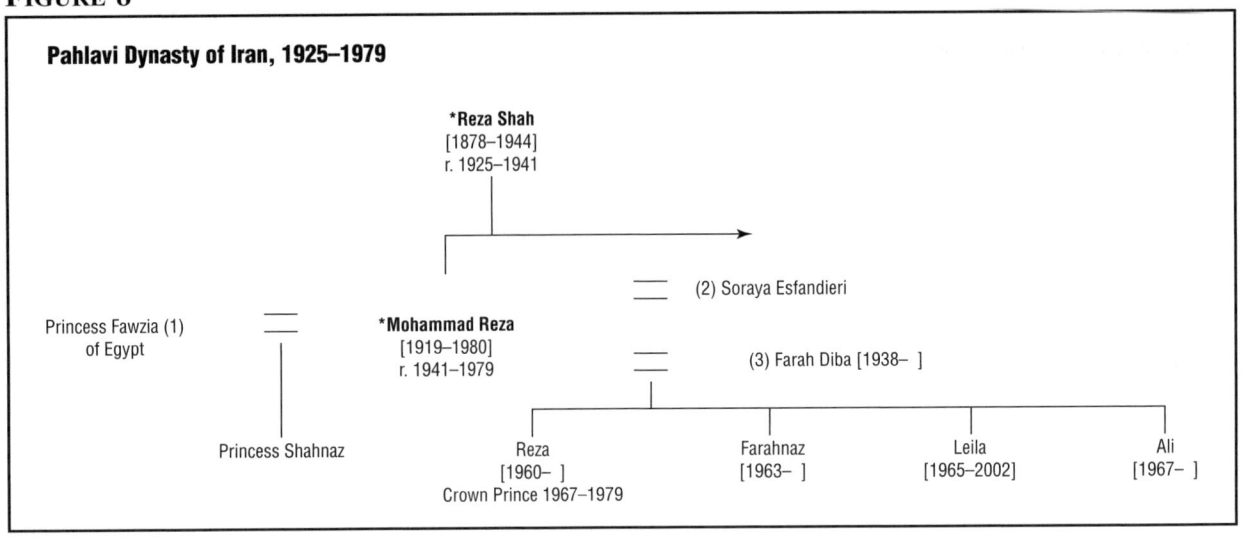
Pahlavi Dynasty of Iran, 1925–1979
*Reza Shah
[1878–1944]
r. 1925–1941
(2) Soraya Esfandieri
Princess Fawzia (1)
of Egypt
*Mohammad Reza
[1919–1980]
r. 1941–1979
(3) Farah Diba [1938–]
Princess Shahnaz
Reza
[1960–]
Crown Prince 1967–1979
Farahnaz
[1963–]
Leila
[1965–2002]
Ali
[1967–]

FIGURE 9

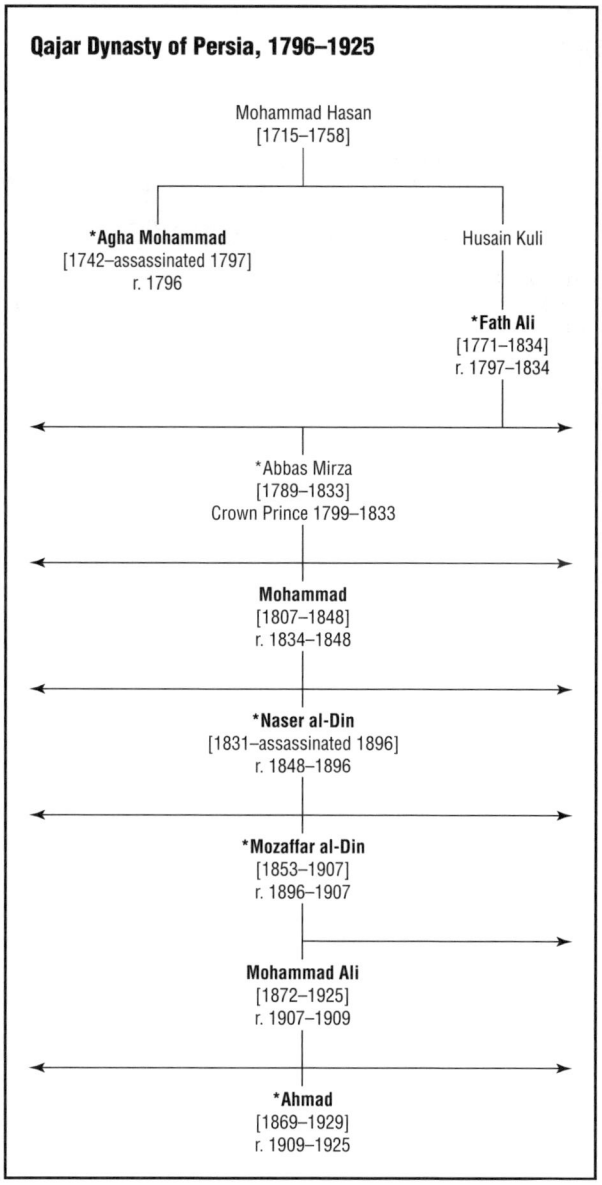
Qajar Dynasty of Persia, 1796–1925
Mohammad Hasan
[1715–1758]
*Agha Mohammad
[1742–assassinated 1797]
r. 1796
Husain Kuli
*Fath Ali
[1771–1834]
r. 1797–1834
*Abbas Mirza
[1789–1833]
Crown Prince 1799–1833
Mohammad
[1807–1848]
r. 1834–1848
*Naser al-Din
[1831–assassinated 1896]
r. 1848–1896
*Mozaffar al-Din
[1853–1907]
r. 1896–1907
Mohammad Ali
[1872–1925]
r. 1907–1909
*Ahmad
[1869–1929]
r. 1909–1925

FIGURE 10

Sultans of the Ottoman Empire, 1757–1922

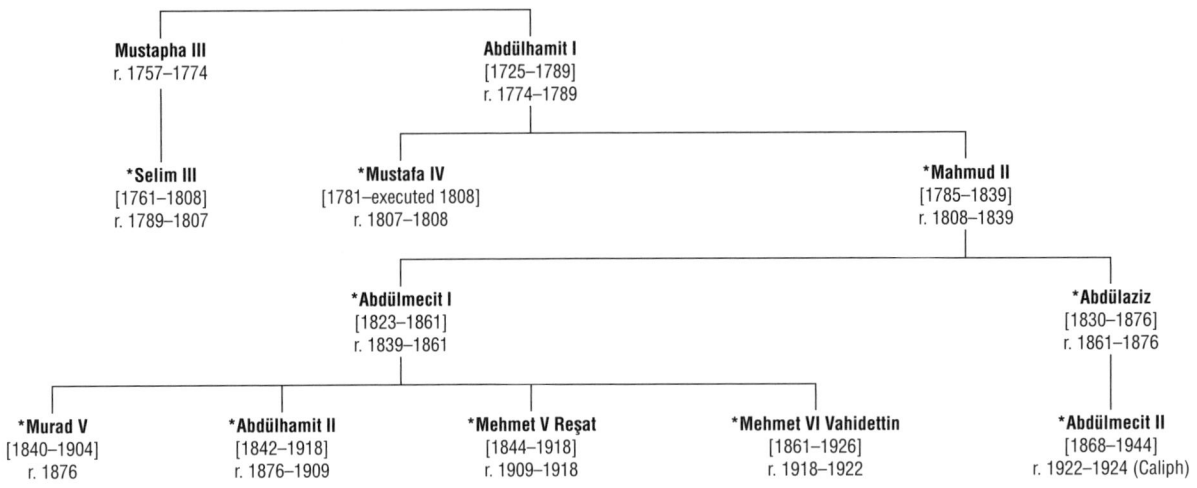

Twelve Imams of Shiʿa Islam

Ali ibn Abi Talib (d. 661, al-Najaf)
Hasan (d. 669, Medina)
Husayn (d. 680, Karbala)
Ali Zayn al-Abidin (d. 712, Medina)
Muhammad al-Baqir (d. 731, Medina)
Jaʿfar al-Sadiq (d. 765, Medina)
Musa al-Kazin (d. 799, Baghdad)
Ali al-Rida (d. 818, Mashhad)
Muhammad al-Taqi al-Jawad (d. 835, Baghdad)
Muhammad al-Naqi (d. 868, Samarra)
Hasan al-Askari (d. 873, Samarra)
Muhammad al-Mahdi al-Muntazar (the Hidden Imam, 873)

GLOSSARY

A

Abd: *Arabic for "slave."* Abd means slave. It is also often seen as part of Islamic male names. In such cases, "abd" is always followed by one of the 99 names of God, and denotes "servant of." For example, Abd al-Rahman ("servant of the Forgiving One"), or Abd al-Jabbar ("servant of the Almighty"). Abdullah means "servant of God."

Abu: *Form of the Arabic word* ab *("father").* When it is followed by a first name—usually, the name of a man's first-born son—it means "father of ___." "Abu so-and-so" is used in lieu of calling a man by his first name.

Agha: *Socio-political title of authority.* Agha ("chief," "master") was associated with certain administrators in the Ottoman empire. It is also used in other settings, such as among Kurds.

Allah: *Arabic word for "God."* Allah is simply Arabic for "God"; It is not the name of God. Both Christian and Muslim Arabs use the word Allah in their scriptures.

Amir: *Political title.* Amir (also emir) is derived from the Arabic word *amara* ("to command"), and is a title given to a person of high political rank. It is often translated as "prince."

Ashur: *Islamic tithe.* Also called zakah or zakat, ashur (from the Arabic word for "ten") is a charitable tithe prescribed in Islam. In North Africa, ashur also denotes the tenth month of the Islamic calendar, Muharram.

Ayatullah: *Shi'ite religious title.* Ayatullah (also ayatollah) is a title denoting a very high level *mujtahid* cleric. It is the highest rank a Shi'ite cleric can attain. See also "mujtahid."

B

Baraka: *Arabic, "blessing."* Baraka means a blessing from God, and can also refer to good luck in general. It is also the spiritual benefit that can be bestowed on someone by a saintly figure, and can also refer to a donation to some charitable institution.

Bedouin: *Arab nomads.* The term comes from the Arabic word *badu,* meaning "those who live in the *badiya,* (desert)." Bedouin formerly lived as pastoral nomads in the desert regions of the Arab world, although by the twentieth century, few true nomads remained. The term is still used, however, to denote those tribes and families who are of bedouin origin.

Bey: *Political title.* Bey is a Turkish term often translated as "prince." In the Ottoman empire's administration and military, it was given to mid-level officers. In modern Turkey, it is often used as a suffix to a man's first name as a polite form of address.

Bilharzia: *See Schistosomiasis.*

Bint: *Arabic, "girl."* Female children in the Arab world sometimes are referred to by making reference to their father. Thus, "so-and-so, bint [daughter] so-and-so." See also "ibn."

C

Casbah: *Old quarters of an Arabic city.* From the Arabic *qasaba* ("divide," "cut up"; also, "citadel" or "capital"), it is a term often used by Europeans to denote the older, native quarters of a town, as distinct from the newer areas in which foreigners lived.

D

Derb: *Street or neighborhood.* Moroccan cities were made up of various streets and neighborhoods. Each of these was referred to as a derb, from the Arabic *darb* ("street" or "path").

Dey: *Political title.* The Turkish word for maternal uncle, the position of dey originally was military, but came to denote administrative power in as well. Deys were found in North Africa, especially Tunisia and Algeria, from the late seventeenth through the early nineteenth centuries.

Dinar: *Monetary unit.* Dinar is derived from the Greek "dinarion" and the Latin "denarius." During the early Islamic period, it was a type of gold coin. Currently it serves as the currency of Algeria, Bahrain, Iraq, Jordan, Kuwait, Libya, Tunisia, and parts of the former Yugoslavia.

Dirham: *Monetary unit.* During the early Islamic period, the dirham was a type of silver coin. Currently it is used in Morocco, Libya, the United Arab Emirates, and Jordan.

Dunum: *Unit of surface area.* The dunum is used to measure surface area in parts of the Fertile Crescent. During the late Ottoman period, it equaled 919 square meters. In the 1920s, it was enlarged to 1,000 square meters (about 0.25 acre) in Lebanon, Syria, Palestine, and Transjordan. In Iraq, the dunum is 0.618 acre.

E

Effendi: *Honorific title.* The origins of this title are Greek, and refer to a man of property or education. During the late Ottoman period, it was used as a sign of respect for middle class males as well as for some bureaucratic positions. Another form of the word, effendum, is still used in Egypt to mean "mister" or "sir."

F

Feddan: *Unit of surface area.* Deriving from an Arabic term for a yoke of oxen, it referred to the amount of land such animals could farm. Thus the actual surface area called a feddan varied from region to region. In Egypt, where it remains the standard unit of surface area today, it equals 4,200.883 square meters, slightly more than one acre.

Fellagha: *Term denoting outlaws.* Fellagha (also fallak) derives from colloquial Tunisian Arabic. It was widely used by the French press to refer to Tunisian guerrilla groups fighting colonial rule, and was eventually used by the fighters themselves. It was also used in reference to anti-French fighters during the early days of the Algerian war of independence.

Fellah: *Peasant.* Fellah (also fallah; plural: fallahun, but more commonly fallahin following colloquial usage) derives from the Arabic verb *falaha* ("cultivate"). It refers to small scale, subsistence level cultivators in Arab countries, but can be used, often derisively, by urbanites to refer to the rural population generally.

G

Ghazel: *Type of poetic form.* The word is Arabic (ghazal; "flirtation" or "love poem"), and is also seen as gazel or ghazal. A lyrical poetic mode often expressing romantic love or eroticism, the form passed into Turkish, Persian, and Urdu poetry as well.

Ghorfa: *Arabic for "room."* The Arabic *ghurfa* refers to a room. In southern Tunisia, seminomadic peoples, usually Berbers, built fortress-like, multistoried structures to store grain. Examples still exist near Tataouine, Ksar Haddada, and Médenine.

H

Hajj: *Islamic pilgrimage.* Hajj (with a short "a" sound) is one of the "Five Pillars of Islam," and refers to a Muslim's obligation to make a pilgrimage to the holy sites in the cities of Mecca and Medina, in today's Saudi Arabia. Islam requires all Muslims who are physically and financially able to make the hajj at least once in their lifetime. The title "hajj" or sometimes "hajji" (with a long "a" sound) is the title given to a man who has completed the hajj. The female equivalent is "hajja."

Halal: *Arabic for "lawful."* In Islamic usage, it refers to aspects of life that are religious acceptable or lawful. It is especially used to refer to meat that has been slaughtered and prepared in accordance with Islamic law. See also "haram."

Haram: *Arabic for "forbidden."* Haram refers to aspects of life, including acts, food, etc., that are forbidden by Islamic law. See also "halal."

Hezbollahi: *"One of the Party of God."* It comes from an Arabic term *hizbullah,* found in the Qur'an that stems from *hizb* ("party") and *Allah* ("God"). In Iran, a hezbollahi came to mean a zealous and sometimes violent supporter of the concept of an Islamic state.

Hoca: *Honorific title.* Hoca is a Turkish word derived from the Persian *khwaja.* In the Turkish speaking parts of the Ottoman empire, it denoted religious scholars and certain administrative bureacrats. It is still used in modern Turkey to refer to teachers and religious scholars. See also "khawaja."

Hosainiyeh: *Place of a certain type of religious ceremony.* In Iran, it is a place where the martyrdom of the Imam Husayn ibn Ali is commemorated, especially on Ashura, the tenth day of the Islamic month of Muharram. It refers to the death of Husayn, grandson of the prophet Muhammad, in 680 at the hands of the Umayyads at Karbala, in Iraq. Traditionally, a hosainiyeh was a different structure than a mosque, and was a populist institution rather than one under the control of the Islamic clerics.

I

Ibn: *"Son."* Male children in the Arab world sometimes are referred to by making reference to their father. Thus, "so-and-so, ibn [son] so-and-so." See also "bint."

Iltizam: *Tax farm.* The Arabic term *iltizam* refers to a duty or obligation. During the Ottoman empire, it referred to a type of taxation whereby the authorities auctioned the rights to collect taxes to an individual, who became known as a *multazim.* The multazim paid the auction amount to the government, and was free to extract as much in taxation as possible from those living within the iltizam. It usually denoted the right to collect taxes from a specific area, but sometimes referred to taxes collected from a certain trade or profession. It was also called *muqata'a* in some areas. The Ottoman government tried on several occasions in the late nineteenth century to abolish the practice, but it remained in parts of the empire until the early twentieth century.

Imam: *Religious title.* The term derives from the Arabic *amma,* "to lead." Among Sunni Muslims, and imam refers to the leader of the prayers in a mosque. For Shi'ite Muslims, however, the term refers to the legitimate leader of the Muslim community, a position extending back to the first imam, Ali ibn Abi Talib, the cousin and son-in-law of the prophet Muhammad who also became the fourth caliph. Following Ali's death, the imamate devolved to his sons Hasan and Husayn, and thereafter to their descendants.

The Shiʿite concept of imam involves considerably greater power and influence than for Sunnis, for the Shiʿite imams possessed special spiritual powers to interpret the will of God.

Imamzadeh: *Persian term referring to the descendant of an imam or the tomb of such a person.* Among Twelver Shiʿa in Iran, the term is used to denote the descendant of one of the first eleven imams, as well as the tomb built over the burial place of such a person. Visiting such tombs is considered a meritorious act than can impart a special spiritual blessing, or baraka, to the visitor. See also "baraka."

Inqilab: *Revolution or uprising.* In modern Arabic political usage, the term inqilab is usually used to connote a sudden seizure of political power, often via a military coup d'état. In Persian, the term means "revolution," such as the 1979 revolution in Iran.

Izlane: *Berber songs.* The singular is izli. These are short (usually no longer than two lines) poetic songs among Berbers in the Middle Atlas mountains. The songs are sung at festive occasions, accompanied by drums and clapping, and often speak of love. They are also a vehicle for social and political commentary.

J

Jihad: *"Struggle" in the service of Islam.* Jihad derives from the Arabic verb *jahada,* "to struggle" or "to endeavor." In Islam it can refer to a number of sacred endeavors, from an individual's personal attempts to live his/her life properly according to Islamic principles, to armed struggle in the defense of Islam or Islamic territory. The term mujtahid derives from *jahada* as well. See also "mujtahid."

K

Karakul: *Afghani sheep.* Karakul is the name of a breed of short-tailed sheep raised in northern Afghanistan, largely by Turkmen and Uzbeks. The fleece is used for making hats.

Kaza: *Ottoman administrative unit.* Kaza is a Turkish word derived from the Arabic *qada.* By the late Ottoman empire, a province (*vilayet*; Arabic: *wilaya*) was divided into governorates called *sanjaks* (Arabic singular: *sanjaq*) or *livas* (Arabic singular: *liwa*). These in turn were divided into smaller units called kazas. Kaza can also refer to the judgment of a *qadi,* or judge. See also "liwa," "qaʾimmaqam," and "vilayet."

Khan: *Highway inn for travelers, or a warehouse for merchandise.* Khans were built as rest stops for travelers and caravans. A khan was also an urban complex for storing merchandise and hosting merchants.

Khanjar: *Type of Arabic dagger.* A khanjar usually refers to a slightly curved, double edged dagger that tapers to a point. The hilt is often decorated.

Khatib: *Islamic preacher.* A khatib is the religious official who delivers the sermon during Friday prayers in a mosque, usually from a raised pulpit called a *minbar.* See also "minbar."

Khawaja: *Honorific title of Persian origin.* In Egypt and parts of the Fertile Crescent, khawaja was a title used to denote a non-Muslim, both foreigners as well as native Christians and Jews. The term comes from the Persian *khwaja.* See also "hoca."

Khawr: *Natural harbor; also part of place names.* The term is used in the Persian/Arabian Gulf region.

Khedive: *High-level title used in Egypt from 1867–1914.* Khedive is a Persian word for a high prince that was used by the governors of Ottoman Egypt from 1867–1914 to replace the title "pasha" carried by other governors in the empire. It was first used by Ismaʿil Pasha, grandson of Muhammad Ali, who secured this right from the Ottoman sultan in order to differentiate and elevate himself from other provincial governors. The term was replaced with "sultan" by the British, who occupied Egypt starting in1882. See also "pasha" and "sultan."

Koran: *See Qurʾan.*

Kochi: *Afghani pastoral nomads.* Derived from the Pushtu term koch ("pack"), kochi referes to pastoral nomads, mostly Baluchis and Pushtuns, in Afghanistan.

Komiteh: *Armed Islamic revolutionary group in Iran.* Prior to merging with the official armed forces in 1991, the Komitehs (Islamic Revolutionary Committees) developed out of mosque-based revolutionaries in Tehran in 1978. Ayatollah Ruhollah Khomeini gave them official status in 1979, as did the Iranian majles (legislature) in 1983. The Komitehs served as a type of police force, combating drug trafficking, "immoral" behavior, as well as working against groups opposing the new regime.

L

Laz: *Ethnic group in Turkey.* The Laz live on the Black Sea, near Turkey's border with Georgia. The Laz language belongs to the Kartvelian language family, and is related to Georgian.

Lazma: *Plot of land in Iraq.* Tribes living in Iraq would distribute irrigated land to cultivators, called lazma, who then obtained prescriptive rights to that land by virtue of their ongoing cultivation of it. This came despite the fact that the land was not formally registered to the tribe.

Leff: *Type of political coalition in North Africa.* Coming from the Arabic word *laffa* ("to wrap"), a leff refers to political coalition whose members assist one another during disputes with other leffs. It is also called *saff* in some parts of North Africa and the Fertile Crescent.

Lira: *Ottoman monetary unit.* The lira, or pound, was named after an Italian silver coin, and was the currency used in the Ottoman empire. Modern Turkey, Syria, and Lebanon continue to use the lira as their national currencies.

Liwa: *Ottoman administrative unit.* During the late Ottoman empire, a province (*vilayet*; Arabic: *wilaya*) was divided into liwas (called liva in Turkish). A liwa was also called a *sanjak* (Arabic: *sanjaq*). These in turn were divided into smaller units called qadas or kazas. See also "kaza," "mutassarif," and "vilayet."

Luti: *Term implying deviation from moral standards.* In Iran during the late nineteenth and early twentieth centuries, the term originally referred to a member of a chivalrous brotherhood. It later assumed more negative connotations implying drunkenness and moral deviation. In parts of the modern Arab world, luti is a term used for a homosexual. Some surmise that the term derives from the biblical figure Lot, son of Noah.

M

Madrasa: *Arabic for "school."* Madrasa is the Arabic word for school. In Sunni Islam it referred to a school for teaching Islamic law, or shariʿa. It retains that meaning in parts of the contemporary Islamic world, although in modern Arab countries, the term is more broadly used to denote schools in general.

Majles: *Legislature or parliament.* Majles is the Persian form of the Arabic *majlis* (in Turkish, *meclis*), which is derived from the verb *jalasa* ("to sit"). It can mean a meeting, or sitting, in a number of senses, both private and public. In the public realm, it became the term used for legislatures in the Middle East and North Africa once these began to emerge in the nineteenth century. It can also refer to an appointed consultative body.

Malik: *"King" in Arabic.* Malik derives from the Arabic verb *malaka* ("to own"). It has been used in the modern Arab world to mean king.

Maʿpalim: *Illegal Jewish immigrants to Palestine.* Maʿpalim (Hebrew, "the daring ones") were Jewish immigrants who entered Palestine in violation of immigration quotas established by the British Mandate in Palestine, especially after the 1939 White Paper. The Zionist community in Palestine established the clandestine organization Mossad le-Aliyah Bet in 1938 to assist Jews fleeing Nazi persecution in Europe in reaching Palestine. British forces intercepted many maʿpalim and interned them in camps in Cyprus, including the 4,515 passengers aboard the ship *Exodus,* whose detainment in 1947 helped turn international sentiment against British rule in Palestine.

Mellah: *Jewish quarter of Moroccan towns.* Mellah derives from the Arabic word for salt. It stems from the forced resettlement of the Jewish community in Fez to an outlying saline area, and came to denote Jewish areas throughout Morocco. In urban areas, mellahs were gated quarters of cities. In rural areas, they were separate Jewish villages.

Minbar: *Pulpit in a mosque.* In a mosque, the sermon (*khitab*) is delivered by the preacher (*khatib*) from a raised pulpit called a minbar, derived from the Arabic *nabara* ("to raise the voice"). See also "khatib."

Mizrahim: *Jews from Islamic countries.* Mizrahim means "the easterners" in Hebrew. It is a term used in modern Israel to denote Jews whose origins extend back to North African, Middle Eastern, and West or South Asian Jewish communities. Some of these communities were quite ancient, especially those in Iraq, Iran, Syria, and Yemen. Most of these communities moved to Israel after its creation in 1948. The term Mizrahim has started to replace "Sephardim," which for a long time was loosely used to denote all Jews who were not European ("Ashkenazim"), but which in a strict sense only refers to the Jews who were expelled from Spain in 1492. See also "Sephardim" and the encyclopedia entry "Adot ha-Mizrah."

Moslem *See Muslim.*

Muezzin: *The one who calls Muslims to pray.* A muezzin (Arabic: *muʾadhdhin*) calls the Muslim faithful to pray, usually from a minaret. The call to prayer must be in Arabic, even though most of the world's Muslims do not speak Arabic.

Mufti: *Type of Islamic cleric.* A mufti is an expert in Islamic law empowered to given religious opinions on various matters. Such an opinion is called a fatwa. See the encyclopedia entry "fatwa."

Mujtahid: *Type of Shiʿite Muslim cleric.* A mujtahid is a Shiʿite religious scholar who is authorized to practice *ijtihad,* or interpretation. While the "door of interpretation" was closed for Sunni Muslims approximately 1,000 years ago, high level Shiʿite clerics called mujtahids still practice *ijtihad.*

Mukhtar: *Chief or headman.* Deriving from the Arabic word *khatara* ("to choose" or "select"), a mukhtar ("selected one") was an official appointed by the Ottoman authorities to serve as a go-between between the government and a tribe, village, or urban quarter. The function was part of the Ottomans' centralization efforts, efforts that included attempts to undercut traditional religious figures who had maintained levels of local influence. The position is still found in parts of the Arab world.

Mulai: *Title and form of address.* In Arabic, "my lord." Also mawlai, mawlay. A form of address formerly used when speaking to a king, sultan, or caliph. It is still used in Morocco when referring to the crown prince.

Muslim: *Follower of the Islamic religion.* Muslim (sometimes rendered Moslem) is someone who follows the religion of Islam.

Mutasarrif: *Ottoman provincial official.* A mutasarrif was the recipient of taxes from sub-provincial governorates in the Ottoman empire. By the late Ottoman era, the term denoted the government-appointed head of a governorate, or sanjak (also liwa). See also "liwa."

N

Narghila: *Water pipe.* A narghila (also called *arghila, qalyan,* and *shisha*) is a water pipe used in the Middle East and North Africa to smoke tobacco, usually flavored tobacco called *tombac.* They are commonly seen in all-male coffee houses.

O

Oasis: *Watered area surrounded by desert.* An oasis is a fertile area, watered by wells, that is found in the midst of a desert. They can be small or large.

Oglu: *Turkish for "son of."* When used as part of a male name, it means "son of. . ." For example, Süleimanoglu ("son of Süleiman"). In 1935, the Turkish government obliged Turks to adopt Western-style last, or family, names. Many Turks used this form to create family names.

P

Pasha: *Ottoman administrative and military title.* The Ottomans introduced the title "pasha" (modern Turkish, *paşa*) in the fourteenth century. It was used for the governors of sanjaks, or liwas, but later was bestowed upon other men of high military or governmental rank. With the reorganization of the Ottoman administration in 1864, governors of provinces (vilayets) were given the title pasha. The term remained in use in Turkey and some Arab countries, although it was banned in most of these in the twentieth century. It is still sometimes used, but only to refer to a man in an honorific fashion. See also "liwa" and "vilayet."

Pesh Merga: *Kurdish, "those who face death."* Modern term used to denote armed Kurdish fighters. It first appeared during the Kurdish war against the Iraqi government that began in 1962.

Q

Qa'id: *Arabic for "leader."* Arabic term denoting political leadership.

Qa'immaqam: *Ottoman provincial official.* The term itself is Arabic, and was the title given by Ottoman authorities to the official appointed to head a subgovernorate called a kaza (also qada). See also "kaza," "liwa," and "vilayet." It was also used to denote a low ranking military officer.

Qanat: *Canal.* A qanat (also qana) can mean an underground water channel for irrigating fields, but can also denote a surface level canal, both small and large (such as the Suez Canal).

Qat: *Plant with mildly stimulant effect.* The leaves of the qat (also khat) plant, Catha edulis, are chewed in southwestern Arabia and eastern Africa for their mildly stimulant effect. Similar to the stimulant qualities of caffeine, qat is chewed in the company of others as an important form of social gathering. In this regard, gathering together to chew qat is akin to gathering in a coffee house to drink coffee or tea. Qat chewing is a major activity in Yemen, whose economic as well as social impact on the country is profound. It is also chewed in African countries like Somalia.

Qibla: *Direction of Islamic prayer.* The qibla is the direction in which Muslims must pray. The first qibla was Jerusalem, but this was quickly changed in the seventh century to the direction of Mecca. Muslims around the globe all pray in the direction of Mecca.

Qirsh: *Monetary unit.* The Arabic word qirsh, and Turkish word ghurush or kuruş, is translated as piastre, itself the Italian name for the medieval peso duro. The qirsh was introduced into the Middle East in the early seventeenth century and became a unit of Ottoman currency equivalent to one-hundredth of a lira. It is still used as a small unit of currency in parts of the Middle East.

Qur'an: *Holy book of Islam.* The Qur'an (also Koran) is the holy book of Islam. It consists of *suras* (roughly, chapters) containing *ayas* (verses), and is believed by Muslims to be the literal word of God, as revealed in Arabic to the prophet Muhammad through the medium of the Angel Gabriel. The Qur'an was redacted within several generations of the Prophet's death in 632, and is read and revered by Muslims worldwide as God's final and definitive message (Arabic: *risala*) to humanity.

R

Re'aya: *Subjects of the Ottoman government.* Ottoman society was divided into two segments: rulers and ruled. The latter were called the re'aya, from the Arabic word denoting "flock." The ruling institution—the sultan and his government—were obliged to protect the re'aya, who in return paid taxes.

Reuter Concession: *Exclusive economic concession proposed by the Shah of Iran to Baron Julius de Reuter.* In July 1872, Nasir al-Din Shah, ruler of Iran, granted Baron Julius de Reuter, a British subject, a sweeping and exclusive seventy-year concession to carry out a number of business ventures within Iran. Among these were the construction of a railroad linking the Caspian Sea and the Persian Gulf, construction of streetcar lines, and operation of mines, among other ventures. Reuter, owner of a news agency, would have been granted an amazingly large amount of economic power with Iran. Opposition to the deal grew, both within Iran and in Europe (particularly Russia, which also had interests in Iran), and the concession was withdrawn in November

1873. Reuter did eventually maintain certain mining and banking rights in Iran, which led to the creation of the Imperial Bank of Persia.

Riyal: *Monetary unit.* The word *riyal* is of Spanish and French origin. The coin was introduced into the Ottoman empire in the nineteenth century, and first used in Iran in 1930, where it was popularly known as the kran. It is the basic currency unit of several Middle Eastern countries today, including Saudi Arabia, Iran, Oman, Yemen, and Qatar.

Roshanfekr: *Persian word for intellectuals.* Roshankekr (Persian, "enlightened thinker") is the Persian word for intellectual.

Ruzname: *Ottoman treasury offices and its registers.* The term comes from the Persian words *ruz* ("day"), and *name* ("book"). The Ottoman government used to term to denote a financial journal or ledger, and referred both to these and the Ottoman treasury offices as ruzname.

S

Salname: *Ottoman government yearbook.* Salname comes from the Persian words *sal* ("year"), and *name* ("book"). Salnames were statistical, geographical, and biographical yearbooks that were first published by the central Ottoman government in 1847 and later, beginning in 1865, by provincial authorities as well. Salnames contained information on population, expenditures, and education. They were discontinued after1922.

Sanjak: *See liwa.*

SAVAK: *Imperial Iranian intelligence agency.* SAVAK was the Persian acronym for the State Security and Intelligence Organization, and was formed by Mohammad Reza Pahlavi, Shah of Iran, in 1967. SAVAK was originally designed to ferret out communist activity, but grew to monitor all forms of internal dissent and external opposition and to censor the press. It was attached to the prime ministry. SAVAK became a feared organization within Iran and among Iranian exiles abroad, and was abolished after the 1979 revolution.

Sayyid: *Arabic word for "master," "lord," "chief," or "mister."* Prior to the coming of Islam, *sayyid* (plural: *sada* or *asyad*) was used in Arabia to denote a tribal chief. After the coming of Islam, it assumed a particular meaning: descendants and certain relatives of the prophet Muhammad. The term *sayyid* thereafter came to denote the direct descendants of the Prophet through his two grandsons, Hasan and Husayn, the sons of the union of the Prophet's daughter, Fatima, and his son-in-law (and cousin), Ali. In some part of the Arab world, notably in the Hijaz region of Arabia and parts of the Fertile Crescent, *sayyid* came to denote those who were part of the lineage of Husayn, while the term *sharif* denoted those descendant from Hasan. *Sayyids* were held in high social esteem. However, the terms *sayyid* or *sid* (also, "sidi": "my lord") have also been used in a variety of Islamic societies as a form of address for holy men and religious figures. It also is the modern Arabic equivalent of "mister." See also the encyclopedia entry "sharif."

Schistosomiasis: *Disease carried by small worms.* Also called bilharzia, the disease is spread by a small worm, known as the blood fluke, that attaches onto snails. Countries such as Egypt have witnessed the spread of the disease thanks to the development of dams, irrigation canals, and other such developmental projects. The medication that kills the snails that carry the disease is both expensive and unsuitable for use without close medical scrutiny. The result is that the disease has spread considerably, and constitutes one of the modern world's most significant parasitic infections.

Sefaretname: *Ottoman diplomatic report.* Derived from the Arabic word *safara* ("trip" or "journey") and the Persian word *name* ("book"), a sefaretname was a report written by an Ottoman diplomat upon his return from a foreign assignment.

Semites: *Members of the Semitic language family.* Semite (adjective: semitic) stems from the Hebrew *Shem,* the name of one of the sons of the Biblical figure Noah. Semites are peoples in the Middle East and Africa who speak one of the Semitic languages, which are branches of the Afro-Asiatic family. Examples of such languages are Amharic, Arabic, Aramaic, and Hebrew.

Sephardim: *Jews in medieval Spain and their modern descendants.* The term comes from the Biblical Hebrew word *Sepharad,* which while probably referring to the city of Sardis in Asia Minor, came to refer to the Iberian peninsula by the time of the Dark Ages in Europe. Sephardim thus referred to the Jews of Spain, who participated in the glittering civilization of Islamic Spain. However, with the Roman Catholic conquest of the final remaining Islamic part of Spain, Granada, in 1492, the Sephardim expelled or forced to convert. The exiles settled in a number of places, including the New World, European regions such as Italy and the Netherlands, and the Ottoman empire. In the latter, they established communities in the Balkans, Egypt, the Fertile Crescent, and North Africa. In their exile, they continued to speak Ladino, a form of medieval Castilian Spanish written in Hebrew letters. The term Sephardim eventually came to be used in an imprecise manner to mean all non-Ashkenazic Jews (Yiddish speaking Jews from central and eastern Europe), including those in Islamic regions like Iraq, Yemen, and Iran, whose ancestors never had lived in Spain. Increasingly, the term "Mizrahim" is being used to denote the Jews of North Africa, the Middle East, and west and south Asia, some of whom were descendants of the Spanish exiles but most of whom were not. See also "Mizrahim" and the encyclopedia article "Ashkenazim."

Serasker: *Highest Ottoman military rank in the nineteenth century.* Created in 1826, the officer of serasker represented the head of the Ottoman military. During the Tanzimat reorganization of government from 1839–1876, the serasker became a powerful figure, in control of his own treasury. The power of the serasker was reduced by Sultan Abdülhamit II, and was renamed minister of war in the early twentieth century. See also "seyfiyye."

Seven Sisters: *Group of Western oil companies in the Middle East.* The Seven Sisters were a cartel of Western oil companies that dominated the Middle Eastern oil industry from 1930–1970. They were: Standard Oil of New Jersey (Exxon), British Petroleum, Royal Dutch Shell, Chevron, Texaco, Mobil, and Gulf Oil. They increasingly lost power starting in the 1950s and 1960s as Middle Eastern countries began nationalizing their oil industries. With the merger of Chevron and Gulf in 1986, the number of "sisters" dropped to six, which remain important companies in the fields of oil refining and distribution.

Seyfiyye: *Ottoman military bureaucracy.* Derived from the Arabic term *sayf* ("sword"), the Ottomans used the term seyfiyye, "men of the sword," to refer to the various types of troops in the Ottoman military. The seyfiyye was replaced by the serasker in 1826, who unified the various types of military forces (with the exception of the navy). See also "serasker."

Shah: *Persian word for "king."* Shah is a title used by several different dynasties that ruled Iran.

Shuttle Diplomacy: *Term denoting a diplomatic intermediary shuttling back and forth between countries in an effort to arrange an agreement among contending countries.* The term was first raised to the level of public discourse to describe the efforts of American Secretary of State Henry Kissinger to bring about a disengagement of forces after the October 1973 Arab–Israeli war. Kissinger had to shuttle back and forth between the capitals of Egypt, Syria, and Israel, carrying his proposals, because the parties could not agree to meet together.

Sidara: *Type of cap used in Iraq.* The sidara was a type of cap introduced in Iraq in the 1920s that resembled a Western military cap that is called a variety of names, including side cap, for-and-aft cap, or overseas cap. Commonly black velvet, it became the emblem of the Iraqi governing and professional classes. It is no longer in use in Iraq, although a similar type of black cap is used by Muslims elsewhere, especially in south and southeast Asia.

Sitt: *Arabic for "lady."* Sitt is often used in female royal titles.

T

Taqlid: *Islamic legal term.* In Sunni Islam, the term taqlid came to mean "deference" or "imitation," in the sense that religious jurisprudents were obliged to defer to the doctrinal precedents of their respective schools of law (the

Shafiʿi, Hanbali, Hanafi, and Maliki schools). This, then, reduces the realm of individual interpretation (*ijtihad*). In Shiʿite Islam, however, the position of marja al-taqlid is quite different, and denotes an elite jurist who is spiritually empowered to employ *ijtihad.* See the encyclopedia article "Marja al-Taqlid."

Tariqa: *Sufi order or brotherhood.* Tariqa is an Arabic word derived from the term meaning "the way." It is used to denote sufi mystical orders. See the encyclopedia entry "Sufism and the Sufi Orders."

Tell: *Hill or mound.* The Arabic word *tall* means a hill, and is used to describe such geographical features. In archeological parlance, however, it refers to a mound containing ancient archeological remains. Finally, it also refers to a large region of North Africa from Morocco to Tunisia.

Thalweg Line: *Maritime boundary.* The thalweg principle of international law, whereby a river or some other body of water constitutes an international border, was most notably used in the Middle East in the case of the border between Iraq and Iran. While at one point in history, the thalweg of the Shatt al-Arab river between the two left the entire river in Iraqi hands, a 1975 treaty moved the thalweg to the midpoint of the river. Overturning this treaty was one of the motivating factors that led Iraq to attack Iran in 1980.

Tishrin: *Arabic term for the tenth and eleventh months of the Gregorian calendar.* In the modern Arab world, Tishrin al-Awwal ("First Tishrin") refers to the Gregorian (Western) month of October, while Tishrin al-Thani ("Second Tishrin") refers to November. Some Arab countries, notably Saudi Arabia, do not use the Gregorian calendar but only the Islamic (hijri) calendar. It is also the name of a newspaper in Syria, named after the initial Arab victories in the October 1973 Arab–Israeli war.

Tiwizi: *Community agricultural support in Berber societies.* Tiwizi is a principle whereby Berbers provide agricultural workers to assist families who need more hands in the fields, and is a socially-mandated obligation.

Toman: *Iranian monetary unit.* Toman is a word of Tatar origin referring to a military unit of 10,000 men, and refers to a gold coin worth ten silver krans (riyals), or 10,000 dinars. It first appeared in Iran ca. 1600. See also "dinar" and "riyal."

Turkmen: *Turkic peoples in Turkmenistan, Iran, and Afghanistan.* The Turkmen are speakers of Western Oghuz Turkic, and were originally pastoral nomads. They lived east of the Caspian Sea and west of the Amu Darya (Oxus) River. In addition, Turkmen minorities today reside in Iraq, Syria, and Turkey.

U

Umma: *Arabic word for community, especially the Islamic community.* The Arabic word umma, derived from *umm* ("mother"), is a term used in Islam to denote the worldwide community of the faithful. In the twentieth century, the term was sometimes used by Arabs to mean "nation" in a political sense, both in global terms (the pan-Arab umma) and local terms (a specific nation).

Urf: *Arabic customary law.* Urf refers to largely unwritten tribal or customary codes that govern social relations, in contradistinction to Islamic law (*shariʿa*) or state legal codes (qanun).

Ustadh: *Arabic for "teacher" or "master."* This term (also ostad or ustaz) is used to denote a teacher or professor, but can also be used as a polite form of address for any educated person.

Uzi: *Type of Israeli firearm.* The uzi is a short submachine gun designed by the Israeli army office Maj. Uziel Gal, after whom it is named.

V

Vali: *Ottoman provincial governor.* The term vali is the Turkish and Persian rendition of the Arabic *wali,* referring to someone who has been deputized to exercise authority. It meant "governor." The Mamluks assigned valis to their smallest administrative units, whereas in Iran and later in the Ottoman empire, a vali was the governor of the largest type of administrative unit. In the Ottoman empire, a vali was head of a *vilayet,* or province. See also "kaza," "liwa," and "vilayet."

Vilayet: *Ottoman Turkish term for province.* A vilayet, from the Arabic word *wilaya,* was the largest administrative unit within the Ottoman empire. See also "vali."

Vizier: *Type of government official; "minister."* Under the Ottomans, the vizier (Arabic: *wazir;* Turkish: *vezir*) served as a government minister. The vezir-i azam, or grand vizier, was the functional equivalent of a prime minister under the sultan. The Ottomans replaced the term with *vekil* (Arabic: *wakil*) in the 1830s, although *wazir* is still in use to denote a government minister in the Arab world.

Y

Yarmulke: *Jewish skullcap.* Jewish males have long worn a skullcap to indicate their submission to a higher authority, that is, God. The very religious wear one at all times, while more secular Jews only don them for religious ceremonies. The Hebrew term for this cap is *kippa.* Some speculate that the term yarmulke is an acronym for *yarai m'Elohim,* "one who is in awe of God."

Z

Zaʿim: *Arabic for "boss" or "leader."* Usually used in an informal manner to denote a strong leader. It is also used as a military rank in some Arab countries.

Zakat: *Islamic tithe, or almsgiving.* Zakat (also zaka) is one of the "Five Pillars of Islam," and is an important religious obligation for Muslims. It requires the giving of an individual's wealth. Historically, it was levied in Islamic countries as a tax upon adult Muslims.

Zawiya: *Islamic religious compound.* From the Arabic word for "corner" or "place of seclusion," a zawiya refers to the compound housing a Sufi brotherhood or the residence of a prominent Sufi master. See the encyclopedia article "Sufism and the Sufi Orders."

INDEX

Page numbers in boldface refer to the major entries on the subject. Page numbers in italics refer to illustrations, figures, and tables.

Volume 1: pp. 1–658
Volume 2: pp. 659–1354
Volume 3: pp. 1355–2028
Volume 4: pp. 2029–2632

A

AAC. *See* Anglo–American Committee of Inquiry
Aachen Congress (1818), 739
Aaronsohn, Aaron, 1–2
Aaronsohn, Alexander, 1
Aaronsohn, Ephraim Fishel, 1
Aaronsohn family, **1–2**
Aaronsohn, Malka, 1
Aaronsohn, Sarah, 1
Aba (garment), 611
Ababda clan, 433
Abadan (Iran), **2**
  Anglo–Iranian Oil Company in, 2, *201*, 518
  in Iran–Iraq War (1980–1988), 2, 1127
  urban planning in, 2300
Abadan Institute of Technology, 812
Abadan-Unat, Nermin, *as contributor*, 598, 601–602, 691–693, 745–746, 1545, 1665–1666, 1910–1911, 1918–1920, 2089–2090, 2243–2246, 2362
Aba Island
  Ahmad (Muhammad) on, 87
  Ansar on, 209, 210
Aba, Noureddine, 1426
Abasiyanik, Sait Faik, 784, 1437, 1440
Abassi, Madani. *See* Madani, Abassi al-
Abaya. *See Aba*
Abbas I (Safavi ruler), Isfahan under, 1141
Abbas, Ferhat, **2–4**, *3*
  in Amis du Manifeste et de la Liberté, 3, 189–190, 1804–1805
  Ben Badis (Abd al-Hamid) and, 441
  De Gaulle (Charles) and, Amrouche (Jean) as intermediary, 193
  in Front de Libération Nationale, 3–4, 2263, 2264
  and Hadj (Messali al-), 969
  Manifesto of the Algerian Muslim People by (1943), 3, 189, 1480
  "New Appeal to the Algerian People" by (1976), 4, 1365
  as president of provisional government, 3–4, 138
  in Union Démocratique du Manifeste Algérien, 3, 2263–2264
Abbas Hilmi I (viceroy of Egypt), **4–5**
  Chrakian (Artin) and, 588, 589
  deposition of, 2366
  government of, Clot (Antoine Barthélémy) in, 607
  and National Party, 1663
  Riyad (Mustafa al-) and, 1928
  uncle of, 1970
Abbas Hilmi II (viceroy of Egypt), *5*, **5–6**
  challenging British authority, 405
  court poet of, 2045
  and Gorst (John Eldon), 931
  government of, Ghali (Boutros) in, 6, 909
  Kamil (Mustafa) supported by, 1267
  Kawakibi (Abd al-Rahman al-) in service of, 1282
  Kitchener (Horatio Herbert) and, 5, 6, 1329
  removal of, 6, 509, 858
  and Urabi (Ahmad), 2297
Abbasi al-Mahdi, Muhammad al-, Ilaysh (Muhammad) opposition to, 1086
Abbas ibn Ali (imam), burial site of, as Atabat, 328
Abbasid dynasty, 662, 1131–1132, 2053
  decline of, 1132
  Islam under, 1147
  rise of, 1131–1132
  turbans during, 609
Abbas II (Baring), 407
Abbas, Ihsan, 1791
Abbas Khalili, 427
Abbas, Mahmud (Abu Mazin), **6–7**
  at Aqaba meeting (2003), 32
  Arafat (Yasir) and
    as political strategist, 6
    power struggle between, 7, 814, 997, 1900
  in al-Fatah, 6
  government of, Dahlan (Muhammad) in, 661
  at Oslo Accords (1993), 6
  in Palestinian Authority, as prime minister, 7, 1775, 1785

Abbas, Mahmud (Abu Mazin) *(continued)*
Qaddumi's (Faruq) opposition to, 1863
Sharon (Ariel) negotiating with, 2026
Abbas Mirza, Na'eb al-Saltaneh (crown prince of Iran), **7**
Amir Kabir (Mirza Taqi Khan) and, 189
grandson of, 809, 1643
military reforms of, 1117
in Napoleonic Wars, 816
in Russo–Persian wars, 7
in Turko–Iranian War, 2252
Abbas Mosque (Karbala), *2053*
Abbas, Ra'uf, 1036
Abbud, Ibrahim, **7–8**
Azhari (Isma'il) opposed to, 349
coup against (1964), 8, 2101
Ibrahim (Fatima Ahmed) in, 1075
Numeiri (Muhammad Ja'far) in, 1699
coup by (1958), 8, 2101
military rule of, 2101, 2103
Umma Party under, 2261
ABC Africa (film), 1318
Abcarius, Michael, in All-Palestine Government, 154
ABCFM. *See* American Board of Commissioners for Foreign Missions
Abd, 2209
Abda (section of Shammar tribe), 2211, 2214
Abd al-Azim shrine (Rayy)
bast taken at, 411
ulama sanctuary in, 1591
Abd al-Aziz ibn Abd al-Rahman, 1997, 1999
Abd al-Aziz ibn al-Hassan (sultan of Morocco), **8–9**
Abd al-Hafid ibn al-Hassan under, rebellion by (1907), 8, 14
Abu Himara rebellion and (1902–1909), 8, 37
acquiescence to French claims, 1566
Act of Algeciras (1906) signed by, 8, 827
Ibn Musa (Ahmad) as regent to, 8, 1074
Kattani (Muhammad ibn Abd al-Kabir al-) opposing, 1281
Marrakech under, 1493
in Moroccan crisis, 8
overthrow of, 8, 14
Ahmad ibn Muhammad al-Raysuni in, 86
Abd al-Aziz ibn Sa'ud Al Sa'ud (Ibn Sa'ud) (ruler of Saudi Arabia), *9,* **9–12,** *163, 165,* 1997
advisors to, 10, 515
Al Rashid family ousted by, 1999, 2214
in Arab–Israel War (1948), 1626
British negotiations with, 515
Antonius (George) in, 213–214
Churchill (Winston S.) and, 597
as caliph candidate, 557
Council of Ministers created by, 12
death of, 12, 164, 1626
exile during youth, 9, 10, 163
family power restored by, 1625
against Fertile Crescent unity, 825
foreign policy of, 11
as founder of Saudi Arabia, 9, 10, 163, 515, 1625–1626
government of
Al Sa'ud (Sa'ud ibn Abd al-Aziz) in, 164, 167–168
Al Thunayyan (Ahmad) in, 172
grandfather of, 819
Husayn ibn Ali conflict with, 646, 1000, 1053, 1626
Ikhwan led by, 1626, 2213
Ikhwan revolt against (1927–1929), 10, 1085, 1626
Islamic congress held by, 1152
Medina captured by, 1511, 1625–1626
mother of, 168
Mussolini (Benito) and, 515
oil concessions granted by, 11, 229, 1626
opposition to, within Al Sa'ud family, 163
on Palestine partition plan, 11
Philby (Harry St. John) and, 10, 1833
pragmatism of, 10
religion of, 9, 1625–1626
and Rida (Rashid), financial support for, 1923
and Riyadh, restoration of Saudi control over, 1928
sons and grandsons of, 11, *163,* 164–167, 168, 794, 796, 797, 1294
successors to, 164, 167
designation of, 11, 167
and al-Ta'if Treaty (1934), 2149
territorial expansion under, 9–10, 614, 2204
titles used by, 10, 11
tribal relations under, 10, 1085
U.S. relations with
oil in, 11, 1626
Roosevelt (Franklin Delano) assurances to, 1936
Roosevelt (Franklin) meeting (1945) and, 1626
during World War II, 1935–1936
Wahhabi Islam spread by, 9, 990, 1085, 1625–1626
wives of, 168
favorite, 168, 169, 794, 798
in World War I, neutrality of
Alusi (Mahmud Shukri al-) and, 173
Cox (Percy) and, 646
in World War II, neutrality of, 516
Abd al-Aziz, Muhammad, 1964
in POLISARIO, 1837
Abd al-Ghani, Abd al-Aziz, **12**
Abd al-Hadi, Amin, 13
Abd al-Hadi, Awni, 13, 2061
in Arab Executive, 1783
and Arab Higher Committee (AHC), 1030
in Istiqlal Party, 13, 1764
Abd al-Hadi family, **12–13**
in Nablus (West Bank), 1631
Abd al-Hadi, Majid, 13
Abd al-Hadi, Ra'uf, 13
Abd al-Hadi, Ruhi, 12–13
Abd al-Hadi, Rushdi, 13
Abd al-Hadi, Tahsin, 13
Abd al-Hadi, Tarab, **13**
Abd al-Hafid ibn al-Hassan (sultan of Morocco), **13–14**
abdication of, 14, 827, 1448
Ahmad Hibat Allah after, 86
Abu Himara rebellion and, 14, 37
acquiescence to French claims, 1566
Act of Algeciras opposed by, 14, 827
Bu Hamara executed by, 542
foreign policy of, 14
French relations with, 14
Glawi (Madani al-) supporting, 921
Kattani (Muhammad ibn Abd al-Kabir al-) and, 14, 1281
Marrakech under, 1493
nephew of, 1597–1598
rebellion led by (1907), 8, 14
Treaty of Fes signed by (1912), 14, 826–827

Abd al-Hamid Shoman, 390
Abd al-Ilah ibn Ali (regent of Iraq), **14–16,** *15,* 1968
in Anglo–Iraqi treaty negotiations, 203
assassination of, 15, 802
British support for, 14, 15, 1132
coup against (1958), 15
education of
at Arab College of Jerusalem, 226
at Victoria College, 2316
in Hashimite house, 1000
during revolt against Britain (1941), 15
Abd al-Jabbar, 195, 1457
Abd al-Karim. *See* Khattabi, Muhammad ibn Abd al-Karim al-
Abdallah Pasha (Mamluk ruler), 1478
Abd al-Maguid, Esmat, **16**
Abd al-Majid, Ismat. *See* Abd al-Maguid, Esmat
Abd al-Malik, Anwar, 1036
Abd al Nasir, Jamal. *See* Nasser, Gamal Abdel
Abd al-Qadir (Algerian leader), **16–18,** *17*
defeating French forces, 542
as freemason, 852
French occupation opposed by, 16–18
as outlaw according to Tangier Treaty, 2160
school established by, 759
Tafna Treaty (1837) and, 542
treaties signed by (1834), 17
Abd al-Qadir al-Jilani (Sufi teacher), 1863–1864, 2113
buried in Baghdad, 362
Qadiriyya Order founded by, 1863–1864
teachings of, 1864
works of, 1864
Abd al-Qadir, Khaled ibn Hasimi ibn Hajj, in Young Algerians, 2405
Abd al-Quddus, Ihsan, **18**
film based on stories by, 971
Abd al-Rahman I (Umayyad ruler), 2084
Abd al-Rahman III (Umayyad ruler), 2084
Abd al-Rahman, Aisha. *See* Bint al-Shati
Abd al-Rahman al-Mahdi (Sudanese leader) (b. 1885–1959), **18–19**
Ahmad (Muhammad) as father of, 18, 87
al-Ansar and, 209–210
British relations with, 18–19, 209–210
sons of, 210
in Umma Party, 19, 210, 2101, 2260–2261
Abd al-Rahman al-Rafiʾi, 1035
Abd al-Rahman ibn Hisham (sultan of Morocco), **19,** 2038
Casablanca under, 568
economic policies of, 19
and French occupation of Algeria, 19
al-Qarawiyyin under, 1871
Spanish conflict under, 19
Abd al-Rahman Khan (ruler of Afghanistan), **19–20**
Amin (Hafizullah) compared with, 186
in Anglo–Afghan wars, 19–20, 197
British support for, 19–20, 56, 197, 400, 536
centralizing policies of, 19, 20, 56
Durand Line agreement by, 400, 536, 734
in exile, 19
foreign policy power surrendered by, 19–20, 174, 197, 536
Hazara during reign of, 1015
son of, 20, 963–964
Abd al-Rahman, Mohammad Ali, 475
Abd al-Rahman, Salim, in Istiqlal Party, 1198
Abd al-Rahman, Umar, **20–21**
arrest of
in Egypt, 20, 21
in United States, 21
at al-Azhar, 20, 349
Mubarak (Husni) criticized by, 21
Nasser (Gamal Abdel) criticized by, 20
in Sadat (Anwar al-) assassination, 20, 349
Sadat (Anwar al-) criticized by, 20
Sadat (Anwar al-) granting amnesty to, 20
in World Trade Center bombing (1993), 21
Abd al-Raziq, Ali, **21–22**
vs. Amin (Ahmad), 183
on caliphate, 1923
Abd al-Raziq, Mustafa, 21
Abd al-Sabur, Salah, **22**
Abd al-Shafi, Haydar, in Palestinian Authority, resignation of, 1785
Abd al-Wahhab, Muhammad ibn (Islamic reformer)
Al al-Shaykh family descended from, 101
Al Saʿud (Muhammad ibn Saʿud) alliance with, 101, 162, 1998–1999
Al Thunayyan family support for, 172
Ibn Taymiyya's thought and, 990
Sufism criticized by, 2114
and Taliban, Deobandi movement among, 61
Abd al-Wahhab, Muhammad ibn (musician), **22,** 1618
Atrash (Farid al-) compared to, 336
Hafiz (Abd al-Halim) and, 970, 971
Umm Kulthum collaboration with, 2263
Abdelghani, Mohamed Benahmed, **22–23**
Abd el-Kader. *See* Abd al-Qadir
Abdelkadir (amir in Algeria), 122
Abdesselam, Belaid, **23,** 917, 1026, 2079
Abdi Pasha (Mamluk ruler), 1478
Abd Rabbo, Yasir, 357, 1009
at Madrid Peace Conference (1991), 1266
Abduh, Muhammad, **23–24**
Alusi (Mahmud Shukri al-) defense of, 173
Antun (Farah) compared with, 215
at al-Azhar, 24, 347, 1150, 2258
Ben Badis (Abd al-Hamid) influenced by, 440
commentary on Qurʾan by, 24, 1883
and Dar al-Daʿwa wa al-Irshad, 669
as disciple of Afghani (Jamal al-Din al-), 23, 51, 52, 1150
as freemason, 852
Kurd Ali (Muhammad) influenced by, 1338
Maratghi (Mustafa al-) and, 1485
Rida (Rashid) and, 1922, 1923
in Salafiyya movement, 1973, 1974
schools established by, 759
and *Urwa al-Wuthqa,* 1923, 2302
on women's issues, 187, 890

Abdülaziz (Ottoman sultan), **24–26**
army under, 1738–1739
brother of, 34
bureaucracy under, 24
and Çerkes Hasan incident, 575
death of, 25, 1525
debt under, 25
deposition of, 25, 26, 1525
foreign policy of, 25
Midhat Paşa and, 1525
palace of, 719
son of, 34
and Tanzimat reforms, 2161
Abdul-Aziz Bin Baz, Shaykh, **26**
Abdu'l-Baha, 365
Abdülhamit I (Ottoman sultan)
navy under, 1740
nephew of, 2009
Abdülhamit II (Ottoman sultan), **26–29,** *27*
Afghani (Jamal al-Din al-) invited by, 52
Armenians under, 299, 2311
Dashnak Party and, 676
army under, 1739
Azuri (Najib) criticism of, 351
and Berlin–Baghdad railway, 464, 532–533
in Berlin Treaty (1878), 26–27
Bursa developing under, 547
Bustani (Sulayman) criticizing, 550
censorship by, 28
Cevdet (Abdullah) and, 576
civil service under, 1735
Committee for Union and Progress opposing, 28
court system under, 1690
deposition of, 28, 2240
domestic policies of, 27–28
and Drummond-Wolff Convention (1885), 726
economic policy of, 27–28
education under, 757
foreign policy of, 26–27
and German relations, 742, 903–904
government of
Ahmet İzzet in, 90
Ahmet Vefik in, 92
Ali Suavi in, 144
in Greco–Turkish War (1897), 937
and Husayn ibn Ali, 1052
İlmiyye under, 1086
Jerusalem under, 1223
Kamil (Mustafa) supported by, 1267
Kasap (Teodor) pardoned by, 1277
masonic lodges under, 852
Midhat Paşa and, 1525
and Muhtar (Gazi Ahmet), 1607–1608
navy under, 1741
Nursi (Said) and, 1704
oppressive regime of, 1909
Ottoman Union Society opposing, 622–623
Palestine under, 1760
parliament under, 1742
Rida (Rashid) opposition to, 1923
in Russian-Ottoman War (1877-1878), 1946
territorial losses under, 26–27
theater closed by, 72
Zionism and, 2433
Abdullah, as son of Muhammad, 1595
Abdullah, Crown Prince. *See* Abdullah ibn Abd al-Aziz
Abdullah ibn Abd al-Aziz Al Saʿud (crown prince of Saudi Arabia), 795, 796, 798
as de facto ruler, 164, 1997
opposition to, within Al Saʿud family, 164
peace plan of, *1387*
Abdullah I ibn Hussein (king of Jordan), **29–31,** *30, 2152*
All-Palestine Government and, 154
Amman as capital of, 191
in Arab–Israel War (1948), 31, 242
General Armistice Agreement on (1949), 240
Arab Legion under, 1810
duties of, 257
and Arab nationalism, 1053
in Arab Revolt, 29
as architect of League of Arab States, 1386
assassination of, 31, 936, 1062, 1244, 2151–2152
Abu al-Huda (Tawfiq) after, 35
Husayni (Da'ud al-) and, 1054
Kirkbride (Alec Seath) after, 1325
British relations with
Kirkbride (Alec Seath) in, 1325
Kisch (Frederick Hermann) in, 1326
British support for, 29–31, 512, 800, 1244
Cairo Conference on (1921), 554
and Fertile Crescent unity, 825–826
government of
Abu al-Huda (Tawfiq) in, 35
Arslan (Adil) in, 306
Glubb (John Bagot) in, 923
Majali (Habis) in, 1470
grandson of, 1061
Greater Syria plan by, 936
and Hashim (Ibrahim), 999
in Hashimite house, 1000
Jericho Congress on rule of, 31, 1221
and Jewish Agency for Palestine, agreement between, 1058
and Jordanian Option, 1247
Peake (Frederick Gerard) as advisor to, 1810
Roosevelt (Franklin Delano) assurances to, 1936
Rutenberg (Pinhas) and, 1946
Shahbandar (Abd al-Rahman) supporting, 2021
Storrs (Ronald) meeting with, 2092
threat of attack on French mandate in Syria by, 512
West Bank annexed by (1950), 2339–2340
and West Bank unification, 1244
Abdullah II ibn Hussein (king of Jordan), **31–32,** *32*
accession of, 31, 1246
children of, 32
as crown prince, 31, 1064
domestic policies of, 32
foreign policy of, 32
Hamza as successor to, 1692
in Hashimite house, 1000
military under, 259
supporting women in parliament, 820
wife of, 1902
Abdullah ibn Rashid, 818
Abdullah, Ibrahim ibn. *See* Burckhardt, Johann Ludwig
Abdullahi, Khalifa. *See* Abdullahi, Muhammad Turshain
Abdullahi, Muhammad Turshain, **32–33,** 1463–1464
under Ahmad (Muhammad), 32–33
al-Ansar and, 209
in Omdurman, 33, 1712
as successor to Ahmad (Muhammad), 33, 87
Abdullah, M. Morsy, *as contributor,* 156, 1474–1475, 2042–2043
Abdullah Pasha (Mamluk ruler), 1478

Abdülmecit I (Ottoman sultan), **33–34**
accession of, 33
on Armenians in Jerusalem, 291
and Beyoglu Protocol (1861), 469
British support for, 33–34, 648–649
on Damascus affair (1840), 665
death of, 34
Dolmabahçe Palace built by, 719
education under, 757
government of, Mustafa Reşid in, 33
Gülhane Imperial Edict (1839) by, 954
Muslim opposition to, 34
Mustafa Reşid under, 1624
reform efforts of, 2161 (*See also* Tanzimat era)
reinforcing Paris Peace (1856) with Islahat Fermani, 740
Abdülmecit II (Ottoman sultan), **34**
Atatürk (Mustafa Kemal) giving residual powers to, 1376
in exile, 34, 1728
and Tanzimat reforms, 2161
Turkish Grand National Assembly election of, 34, 557
Abdul Qader. *See* Abd al-Qadir
Abdur Rahman, 1468
Abdut, ha- (journal), 507
Abha (Saudi Arabia), 1081
Abidin, Dino, **34**
Abi-Mershed, O. W., *as contributor,* 603–604, 2407–2408
Abi o Rabi (film), 832
Abir sarir (Mostaghanemi), 1581
Abisaab, Rula Jurdi, *as contributor,* 1960–1961, 2438–2439
Abnudi, Abd al-Rahman al-, 971
Abolqasem, Akhund Molla, Khomeini (Ruhollah) taught by, 1310
Abortion, 480, 1510–1511
Aboulker, Henri, in Comité Juif Algérien d'Études Sociales, 619
Abouzeid, Leila. *See* Abu Zeid, Layla
Abovian, Khachatur, 303
Abraham, Muhammad compared with, 1597
Abraham Fund (Israel), Navon (Yizhak) as chairman of, 1672
Abrahamian, Ervand
as contributor, 820, 821, 842, 1318, 1562–1563, 1900, 2222–2223
as historiographer, 1036
Abrika, Belaid, in Coordination des Archs, 638
Abu, definition of, 2621
Abu Abdullah ibn Muqla, calligraphy of, 558
Abu Ala. *See* Qurai, Ahmad Sulayman
Abu al-Hawl. *See* Sphinx
Abu al-Huda, Tawfiq, **35**
in Arab–Israel War (1948), 35
Jericho Congress resolutions approved by, 1221
opposition to, 1471
Nabulsi (Sulayman al-) in, 1632
as prime minister, 35, 2152
Rifaʿi (Samir al-) and, 1925
Abu al-Ilah Muhammad, 2262
Abu Ali Mustafa. *See* Zibri, Mustafa
Abu al-Lutf. *See* Qaddumi, Faruq
Abu al-Timman, Jaʿfar, **35–36**
in Ahali group, 35, 80
coup opposed by (1936), 80
Abu Ammar. *See* Arafat, Yasir
Abu Arish (Saudi Arabia), 1081, 1082
Abu-Assad, Hany, 833
Abu Bakr
as companion of Muhammad, 1596
as successor to Muhammad, 1597, 1641
Abu Bakr al-Siddiq. *See* Abdullahi, Muhammad Turshain
Abu-Deeb, Kamal
Adonis's poetry translated by, 48
as contributor, 47–48, 2002
Abu Dhabi (United Arab Emirates), **36–37,** 2219
Al Nahayyan family in, 156
British military withdrawal from, 521
British relations with, 36
Buraymi oasis claimed by, 517, 544
cities of, 343
oil reserves in, 36, 2270–2271
tribes in, 2210
Abu Dhabi Oil Company, 2110
Abu Faraj al-Isfahan, 666
Abu Hanafi al-Nuʿman ibn Thabit, 988
Abuhatzeira, Aharon, **37**
Abu Haytham. *See* Bakr, Ahmad Hasan al-
Abu Himara, **37**
Abd al-Hafid ibn al-Hassan and, 14, 37
rebellion led by (1902–1909), 8, 37
Abu Iyad. *See* Khalaf, Salah
Abu Jihad. *See* Wazir, Khalil al-
AbuKhalil, Asʿad, *as contributor,* 173–174, 180–181, 215–216, 289, 307, 314, 315–316, 320–321, 322, 350–351, 429–431, 467–468, 474–475, 481, 583–585, 633–634, 645, 660, 680, 730, 793–794, 849–850, 871, 920, 976–977, 981–982, 988, 994, 1031–1033, 1037–1039, 1045, 1050, 1055, 1253, 1254–1256, 1364, 1389, 1391–1393, 1394–1395, 1395–1396, 1396–1401, 1491–1492, 1647, 1662–1663, 1665, 1802, 1830–1831, 1833–1834, 1852–1853, 1865–1866, 1880, 1901, 1971, 1975–1976, 2011–2012, 2016–2017, 2021, 2031, 2059–2060, 2086, 2119, 2202, 2286–2287, 2381
Abu Layla, 355
Abu-Lughod, Lila, 897, 1037
Abu Luhum clan, 376
Abu Lutf. *See* Qaddumi, Faruq
Abu Marquz, Musa, 983
Abu Mazin. *See* Abbas, Mahmud
Abu Musa. *See* Musa Muragha, Saʿid
Abu Musa Island (Iran/UAE), **37–38,** 2040
Abu Naddara. *See* Sanu, Yaʿqub
Abu Nahleh, Lamis, in Institute of Women's Studies at Bir Zeit University, 1100
Abu Nasr, Julinda, in Institute for Women's Studies in the Arab World, 1100
Abu Nazzara Zarqa (newspaper), 1990
Abu Nidal. *See* Banna, Sabri al-
Abu Nidal group
Argov (Shlomo) attempted assassination by, 252
PLO opposed by, 252
Abu Nuwwar, Ali, **38–39**
in Arab Legion, 38–39, 257–258
in attempted coup (1957), 39, 258, 1632
Abu Qir, Battle of (1798), **39**

Abu Risha, Umar, **39**
Abu Saʿid. *See* Hasan, Khalid al-
Abu Shanab, Ismaʿil, assassination of, 983
Abu Sharif, Bassam, *1778*
  Mossad attack against, 1267
Abu Simbel, flooding by Lake Nasser, 1652
Abu Talib, Muhammad as nephew of, 1595
Abu Yusuf, 988
Abu Zaʿbal (Egypt), 2003
Abu Zant, Abd al-Munʿim, 1151
Abu Zayd, Hamza, Khalaf (Salah) killed by, 1292
Abu Zayd, Hikmat, **39–40**
Abu Zayd, Nasr, 769
Abu Zeid, Layla, **40**
Abwab (magazine), 916
AC. *See* Advisory council
Académie Ranson (Paris), 2429
Academy of Arabic Languages, 1456–1457
Academy of Fine Arts (Istanbul), 2429
Academy of the Hebrew Language (Jerusalem), 1018
Achdut (periodical), 456
Acheson, Dean, **40–41**
  on Dulles (John Foster), 733
  Middle East Defense Organization supported by, 1523
Achour, Habib, **41,** 486
  in Union Générale des Travailleurs Tunisiens, 41, 2264–2265
ACJ. *See* American Council for Judaism
Acquired immune deficiency syndrome. *See* AIDS/HIV
Acre Arab Women's Association, 1488
Acre Prison, Irgun Zvaʾi Leʾumi breaking into (1947), 1140
ACT. *See* Action of the Churches Together
Action of the Churches Together (ACT), 1855
Active defense doctrine, Wingate (Charles Orde) implementing, 2353
Adair, Robert, and Dardanelles Treaty (1809), 672
Adalat-khaneh, 2142
Adalat party (Iran), **41.** *See also* Communist Party of Iran
Adala wa al-Tanmiya (Morocco), 1601
Adalet ve Kalkınma Partisi. *See* Justice and Development Party
Adalian, Rouben P., *as contributor,* 143–144, 195–196, 290–304, 386, 571–572, 579, 588–589, 675–678, 1314, 1612–1613, 1694–1695, 1723, 2087, 2310–2311, 2414–2415, 2439–2440
Adamah, ha- (periodical), 507
Adamiyat, Abbasquli, **41–42**
Adamiyat, Fereydun, **42**
Adamiyat society (Iran), Mossadegh (Mohammad) in, 1580
Adana (city, Turkey), **42,** 2237
  Armenian defense of, *300*
  gecekondus on outskirts of, 872
  textile mills in, 2181
Adana (province, Turkey)
  Armenians massacred in, 571
    relief efforts following, 1694
  Cemal Paşa as governor of, 571
Adana Conference (1943), **42**
Adawiyya, Rabiʿa al-, 1149, 2111
Adb, 2621
Addis Ababa (Ethiopia), 2369–2370
Addis Ababa Accords (1972), 868, 1918, 2103
  Numeiri (Muhammad Jaʿfar) repudiating, 1701
  Sudanese civil war ended by, 1700
Ad Elat (Shamir), 2024
Adel Shah, 1867
Adelson, Roger, 841–842
  as contributor, 225, 2127–2128
Aden (Yemen), **42–43**
  annual rent paid by Britain for, 527
  British occupation of (1839–1967), 43, 534–535, 614, 2390
    area of, 534
    Colonial Office administration of, 514, 617
    end of, 520–521, 1813
    Foreign Office administration of, 534
    India Office administration of, 534
    indirect rule in, 514
    protectorate states during, 1853
    South Arabian League fighting, 2081–2082
    Treaty of Protection (1886) and security of, 2208
  as capital, 43, 2386
  Cole attack in (2000), 613, 2077
  Jewish exodus from, Magic Carpet Operation for (1948–1950), 1460
  Jewish refugees from, 1913
  legal system of, British influences on, 1380
  National Liberation Front control of, 1813, 1814
  port of, 527, 1039, 2206
Adenauer, Konrad, **43**
  reparations under, 43
Aden Trade Union Congress, Ayni (Muhsin al-) in, 343
Aden University, *vs.* Sanʿa University, 1985
ADF. *See* Arab Deterrent Force
Adham, Kamal
  Al Saʿud (Turki ibn Faisal) and, 167
  Al Saʿud (Saʿud ibn Faisal) influenced by, 166
  and security establishments, 798
Adham, Soraya, **43–44**
Adhani, Sulayman al-, 105
Adivar, Abdulhak Adnan, **44–45**
Adivar, Halide Edib, 44, **45–46,** 1437, 1439, 1440
Adiv, Ehud "Udi," 1500
Adler (numismatic scholar), 1702
Adli, **46**
Adl wa al-Ihsan, al- (Morocco), **46–47,** 1569, 1574
  and Union Nationale des Etudiants Marocains, 2266
  Yacine (Abdessalame) in, 46–47, 1569, 1574, 2375–2376
Admi, Lahbib, in Nahda, al-, 1635
Admoni, Nahum, as Mossad director, 1578
Adnan, Etel, **47**
Adnan tribe, 2210
Adonis (Ali Ahmad Saʿid), **47–48**
  Adnan (Etel) on, 47
  Shiʿr and, 1298
Adoption, in Tunisia, 2230
Adot ha-mizrah (Middle Eastern Jews), **48–50**
  Black Panthers and, 485

by country of origin, 49
definition of, 48
improving social and economic conditions of, 1417
intermarriage with European Jews, 48
maʿbarah experiences of, 1452
vs. mizrahim, 48
number of, 48, 49, 1234
political power of, 48–49
Adrianople. *See* Edirne
Adrianople, Treaty of (1829), 940, 1945
ADS. *See* Arab Development Society
Adultery, honor killings for, 649–650
Advanced warning and air control aircraft (AWACS), 796
Advertising, in Egyptian magazines, 206, 1375
Advisory council (AC) (Palestine), **50,** 1762
Kalvaryski (Chaim Margaliut-) in, 1265
Adwar (guerilla bands), in Italo–Sanusi War, 1609–1610
AE. *See* Arab Executive
Aegean Sea, **50–51,** 2236
waterway joining Black Sea and (*See* Straits, Turkish)
Aegean University. *See* Ege University
Afaq (journal), 467
AFARD. *See* Association des Femmes Africaines pour la Recherche et le Développement
Afary, Janet, *as contributor,* 659, 1899–1900
Afghan Academy of Science, 2166
Afghan Alphabet (Iranian film), 1473
Afghan Communist Party
Afghan Islamic movement conflict with, 60, 61
coup by (1978), 53, 58
establishment of, 57
mojahedin opposition to, 53, 1561
Soviet support for, 65
Afghan Historical Society. *See* Tarikh Tolana
Afghani, Ali Mohammad, 1436–1437
Afghani, Jamal al-Din al-, **51–53**
Abduh (Muhammad) as disciple of, 23, 51, 52, 1150
Alusi (Mahmud Shukri al-) defense of, 173
Başiretci (Ali) popularizing, 409
as freemason, 852
in modernist movements, 1149–1150
Naser al-Din Shah and, 1644
Rida (Rashid) admiration for, 1923
Riyad (Mustafa al-) and, 1928
in Salafiyya movement, 1973, 1974
Sanu (Yaʿqub) influenced by, 1990
and Tabataba'i (Mohammad), 2141
and *Urwa al-Wuthqa,* 1923, 2302
on women's issues, 890
Afghan Interim Government (AIG), 63
Mojaddedi (Sebghatullah) as president of, 1561
Afghanistan, **53–68,** *54. See also specific cities, organizations, people, and regions*
agriculture in, 55
in Anglo–Persian War (1856), 204
archaeological artifacts destroyed in, 279
Baluchis in, 385–386
Barakzai dynasty of, 399–401
bin Ladin (Osama) in, 474–475, 1865
border with Pakistan
Durand Line as, 400, 536, 734
pass between, 1317
British power in, over foreign policy, 19–20, 174, 197, 536
British protectorate in, 536
British–Russian rivalry over, 205, 536, 1942
British wars with (*See* Anglo–Afghan wars)
cities of, 53, 386–387, 494–495, 1020–1021, 1505, 2050
capital, 1260, 1268
civil wars in, 58–59
political parties in, 63–64
climate of, 54
constitution of (1964), 786
constitution of (1987), 59
cotton industry in, 644
coup in (1973), 57, 401, 679, 2421
coup in (1978), 53, 58, 62, 401, 680, 1813
Parcham in, 1801
Soviet role in, 65
coup in (1979), 58, 186
Parcham in, 1801
Soviet role in, 1274, 1801
coup in (1992), 59, 66
coup in (1996), 61
defense costs as percentage of GNP or GDP, *1530*
democratic experimentation in, 57
Durrani dynasty in, 55–56, 734–736, 1468
economic and military aid to, 748
economy of, 54–55
education in, 55
Taliban and, 2154–2155
elections of 2004 in, 53
ethnic groups in, 55, 1014–1015
factionalism in, 58–59
freshwater withdrawals by, *2331*
geography of, 53–54, 901
German relations with, Grobba (Fritz Konrad Ferdinand) and, 944
government of, 55 (*See also* Taliban)
interim, 64, 66
Interim Authority in, 53, 55, 2280
Jamiʿat-e Islami in, 1215
Loya Jerga in (*See* Loya Jerga)
Transitional Authority/Administration in, 53, 55, 67
U.S. role in, 67
guerrillas in
CIA support for, 572
under Hekmatyar (Golbuddin), 1020
in Hindu Kush Mountains, 1032
leadership of, 89
Reagan (Ronald) support for, 1908
during Soviet intervention, 65–66
guest workers from, 946
health care in, 2007–2008
higher education in, 55
at Kabul University, 1260
human rights violations in, 67
independence declared by, 56, 174
Iranian films on, 1473
Iranian invasion of (1857), 204, 1117
Treaty of Paris on, 1802
Iran invaded by, Isfahan siege in (1722), 1141
Islamic movements in, **60–62,** 1215 (*See also specific groups*)
factionalism in, 61, 63
goals of, 60–61
origins of, 60
political parties of, 62–63
student branch of, 60, 63
journals of, women's, 1140
languages in, 55

Afghanistan *(continued)*
Iranian, 1124–1125
Persian, 55, 1124, 1819–1820
Pushtun, 55, 1124, 1857
Turkmen, 2248
military of
equipment of, *1534*
force levels of, *1528–1529*
force structure of, *1532–1533*
reorganization of, 20
modernization of, 57, 174
mojahedin in (*See* Mojahedin)
monarchy of, 963–964, 2420–2421
mountains of, 53, 1032, 1799
Musahiban oligarchy in, 2420–2421
natural resources of, 54–55, 2050
in Northern Tier, 1692–1693
opium production in, 67, 494, 725, *725*, 1713
Herat and, 1021
Pakistani conflict with, United Nations in, 2279–2280
political parties in, **62–64** (*See also specific parties*)
population of, 53
postage stamps of, 1849–1850
president of, 1888–1889
press freedom in, 175
Protestant missions in, 1856
provinces of, 2417
Pushtun tribes in, 1857
al-Qaʿida in
presence of, 66
U.S. strikes against (1998), 606, 1865
U.S. strikes against (2001), 66
railways in, 20
refugees from (*See under* Refugees)
religions in, 55
Shiʿism, 2052
Sufism, 863
resistance war in (1978–1992)
Marxist government in, 1505
Mohammadi (Maulawi Mohammad Nabi) in, 1559
Mojaddedi (Sebghatullah) in, 1561
mojahedin in, *1561*, 1561–1562
Naqshbandi in, 1642
Saudi Arabian aid in, 1627
rivers of, 53–54, 193, 1020
Russian relations with, post-Soviet, 1944
science and technology in, 2004
socialism in, 62
Soviet intervention in (1979–1989), **65–66**, 1943
bin Ladin and, 1865, 2178
Brezhnev Doctrine and, 508
casualties of, 65, 66
failure of, 59, 66
Hezb-e Islami and, 1024
initial invasion in, 58, 65
mojahedin opposition to, 53, 59, 65–66, 474
number of troops in, 65
political conflict as cause of, 53, 65
president installed during, 58, 65, 1274
resistance to, *56*, 65–66, 89, 1021, 1024, 1540, 1920
Revolutionary Association of the Women of Afghanistan and, 1920
United Nations in, 2279–2280
U.S. policies during, 1908
U.S. role in, 66
withdrawal of troops from, 59, 66, 1943, 2280
Soviet relations with, 679–680
Tajiks in, 2150
taxes in, 175
teachers in
persecution of, 55
training at Dar al-Moʿallamin, 670–671
in trade, 55, 400
transportation in, 67
tribes in, 385–386
United Nations forces in, 2282
U.S. intervention in, **66–68**
from 1950s through 1970s, 66
alliance with tribal and paramilitary forces in, 1535
bombing campaign of (2001), 66
Bush (George W.) and, 549
and Bush's (George W.) resolve against Iraq, 2324
casualties of, 67
CIA in, 573
diplomatic relations during, 66
and elimination of Taliban, 2155
failure of, 67–68
hunt for Taliban/al-Qaida in, 66–67
Powell (Colin) in, 1852
reconstruction efforts in, 66–67, 68
United Nations and, 2282
U.S. *vs.* Russian spheres of influence in, 1032
Uzbeks in, 2306
women in, *58*
education for, 880, 1881
in government, 1906
journals for, 1140
in politics, 786, 894, 1981–1982
Queen Surraya's impact on, 1881
veiling for, *61*, 1715
women's organizations in
humanitarian, 68
Marxist, 693
protecting rights, 325, 1920
women's rights in, 786, 874, 881, 894, 1981–1982
Afghanistan (journal), 2166
Afghan Millat. *See* Afghan Nation
Afghan Nation, 807
socialist-nationalist model for, 62
spin-offs of, 62
Afghan Women's Council (AWC), **68**, 786
Afife Jale (Araz), 274
Afilal, Abd al-Razzak, in Istiqlal Party, 1198
Afilal, Abderrazak, in Union Générale des Travailleurs Marocains, 2264
Aflalo, Albert, in al-Wifaq, 2352
Aflam al-Alam al-Arabi (film company), 971
Aflam Sawt al-Fann (film company), 971
Aflaq, Michel, **68–70**
Arsuzi (Zaki al-) and, 308
in Baʿth party, 69, 412, 590, 2134
Bitar (Salah al-Din al-) and, 68–69, 482
controversy associated with, 69
Hafiz (Amin al-) and, 972
al-Tali published by, 68
tomb complex of, 70
African Americans, in Dimona (Israel), 708
African Charter on Human and People's Rights, 1048
African Network for Prevention of Child Abuse, 1496
Afrika Korps, 516
in al-Alamayn battle (1942), 102
Afro-Asiatisme, L' (Bennabi), 451
Afterlife
in Islam, 1146–1147
Zoroastrian belief in, 2442
After the Holidays (Kenaz), 1288
AFTURD. *See* Association des Femmes Tunisiennes pour la

Recherche et le Développement
Ağaç (journal), Kisakürek (Necip Fazil) in, 1326
Agadati, Baruch, 668
Agadir (Morocco), 1567
Agadir crisis (1911), **70**
Algeciras Conference leading to (1906), 70, 120
Aga Khan, on caliphate, 557
Aga Khan Awards, 283, 284
Agal, 610
Ağa, Mehmet Ali, 1109
Agam, Yaacov, **70–71**
Ağaoğlu, Ahmed, 1800
Age of Stone, An (Langer), 1374
Aggadah, in Jerusalem Talmud, 2158
Aggav Orha (Brenner), 507
Agha, 2621
Aghbalian, Nigol, 676
Aghlabid dynasty, 2228
Aghlabids (Tunisia), 2427
Ağitlar, Türküler, Destanlar (Boratav), 493
Agnon, Shmuel Yosef, *71,* **71–72,** 956, 1431
Nobel Prize for Literature to, 1164, 1431
Agop, Gullu, **72**
Agranat Commission, on Arab–Israel War (1973), 252
Agricultural cooperatives
in Egypt, 1372
in People's Democratic Republic of Yemen, 1373
in Tunisia, 1372
Agricultural runoff, 2331
Agriculture, **72–77.** *See also* Food
in Afghanistan, 55
in Algeria, 124
Kabylia, 1261
in Atlas Mountains, 335
Berber, 459
cotton, 643–645
date palms, 678–679
in deserts, 605, 701
dry-farming techniques in, 75
in Egypt, *753,* 754
Bahariya, 366
child labor in, 1358
cotton, 404, 405, 643–644, 2180, 2181, *2181*
and disease, 710
grain, 75, 76
grapes, 109–110
high-yield, 76
increasing demands for, 72–74
in Iran, 902, 1115
in Iraq
Basra, 410
dates in, 678–679
irrigation in (*See* Irrigation)
in Israel, *753, 1161,* 1162, 2200–2201
on kibbutzim, 1319, *1319,* 1320
moshavim and, 1576–1577
by Palestinian citizens, 1786
in Jordan, 1240, 1243
laborers in, 76
in Labor Zionism philosophy, 1359–1360, *1361*
land ownership and, 75–76
in Lebanon, 2255
in Libya, 1410
mechanization of, 76
in Morocco, *753,* 754, 913
tax on *(tartib),* 8
along Nile River, 690
in Oman, 1204, 1711
in Ottoman Empire, 1729–1730
after Land Code of 1858, 1367–1369
before Land Code of 1858, 1367
tax farming and, 1367, 2167–2168
in Palestine, 1760
and population growth, 1844
precipitation and, 74, 75
in Qatar, 1876
rice, *75*
in Saudi Arabia, 1996
water resources in, 702
sharecropping in, 1371
slaves in, 2072, 2073
in Sudan, 75, 2099
Gezira Scheme and, 908
in Syria, 909
Idlib province, 1080
in Syrian Desert, 2136
tax farming as means of managing revenues from, 2167–2168
trade deficits in, 72–74
in Tunisia, 2227
in Turkey, 902, 2238–2239
Anatolia, 194
Cilicia, 598
in West Bank
Jenin, 1220, 1221
Qalqiliya, 1869
in Yemen, 2319, 2387, 2388
Agudat Israel, **77–78,** 1178, 1554
domestic policy of, 77–78, 1178
foreign policy of, 77, 1178
internal rifts in, 77
Levin (Yizhak Meir) in, 1407–1408
Neturei Karta leaving, 1677
Po'alei Agudat Israel and, 1187
SHAS break with, 77, 1178, 1188
in Torah Religious Front, 1178, 1189
in United Religious Front, 1178, 1190
in United Torah Judaism, 1190
Zonnenfeld (Yosef Hayyim) and, 2440
Ahabat Zion (Mapu), 1430
Ahad Ha-Am, **78–79,** *79,* 470, 930, 1430, 2075
Nordau (Max) opposing cultural Zionism of, 1692
Ahaggar Mountains, 120, 901
Ahali, al- (newspaper), 79–80, 1654–1655
Ahali group (Iraq), **79–81**
Abu al-Timman (Ja'far) in, 35, 80
coup by (1936), 2065
leadership of, 79
National Democratic Party as outgrowth of, 1654
Ahardane, Majoub, **81**
in Mouvement Populaire, 1588
Aharonian, Avetis, 303, 676
Ahavat David (Kaniuk), 1268
AHC. *See* Arab Higher Committee
Ahd, al- (Arab nationalist society), **81**
and Faisal I ibn Hussein, 800
and al-Fatat, 815
Hashimi (Taha al-) in, 999
Hashimi (Yasin al-) in, 1001
Istiqlal Party members from, 1199
Misri (Aziz Ali al-) in, 1550
Sa'id (Nuri al-) in, 1967
Ahdut (newspaper), 446
Ahdut ha-Avodah (Israel), **81–82,** 1178
Ben-Zvi (Rahel Yanait) in, 456
establishment of, 1185
and Haganah, 972
in Ha-Shomer ha-Tza'ir, 82, 1178
in Israel Labor Party, 82, 1178
Katznelson (Berl) in, 1281
in MAPAI, 82, 1178, 1185
in MAPAM, 82, 1178
Namir (Mordekhai) in, 1641
ha-Po'el ha-Tza'ir merging with, 1362
Rabin (Yitzhak) in, 1891
Ahkam, 2033

Ahl, 2209
Ahl al-Hawa (Barakat), 398
Ahl al-Sunna wa al-jamaʿa, 2122, 2123
Ahl-e Haqq sect of Shiʿism, **82**
vs. Alevis, 113
Ahli (Egypt), 908
Ahliyya (Egyptian national court), 1553
Ahlul Bayt World Assembly, Velayati (Ali Akbar) in, 2314
Ahmad, Abd al-Rahim, in Arab Liberation Front, 259
Ahmad al-Jazzar (Bosnian governor), **82–83,** 807
Chehab (Bashir) under, 583–584
Ahmad, Ayn al-Hayat (princess of Egypt), 1452–1453
Ahmad Bey Husayn (of Tunisia), **83–85**
government of, Khaznader (Mustafa) in, 1308
Khayr al-Din and, 1306
military reforms of, 83–84
Ahmad Bey of Constantine, **85**
Ahmad Durrani (ruler of Afghanistan), **85–86**
dynasty established by, 85, 734–735
election of, 85, 734
Qandahar as capital of, 55–56
Ahmad, Faiz, 1278
Ahmad, Fathiyya, 2262
Ahmad Hibat Allah, **86**
father of, Ma al-Aynayn as, 1451
Ahmad ibn Muhammad al-Raysuni, **86,** 1927
Ahmad ibn Mustafa. *See* Ahmad Bey Husayn
Ahmad ibn Saʿid, Al Bu Saʿid dynasty founded by, 107, 1710
Ahmad ibn Tulun (governor of Egypt)
Damascus under, 662
Ibn Tulun Mosque constructed by, 1074
Ahmad ibn Yahya Hamid al-Din (imam of Yemen), **86–87**
attempted coup against (1955), 2391
Ayni (Muhsin al-) exiled by, 343
in emergence of North Yemen, 2391
in Hamid al-Din family, 985
son of, 358
and Zaydism, 2427
Ahmad, Ibrahim, 695
Ahmad, Imad-ad-Dean, *as contributor,* 2323
Ahmad, Jabir al-, 1952
Ahmad Khani, 1345
Ahmad Khan, Sayyid, 1150
on *hadith,* 968
Ahmad, Muhammad (al-Mahdi), **87–88,** 1463
Abdullahi (Muhammad Turshain) under, 32–33
followers of (*See* Ansar, al-)
in Omdurman, 87, 1301, 1712
revolt led by, 931
son of, Abd al-Rahman al-Mahdi as, 18, 87
successor to, Abdullahi (Muhammad Turshain) as, 33, 87
Ahmad, Muhammad Sulayman al-. *See* Jabal, Badawi al-
Ahmad Pasha (Mamluk ruler), 1478
Ahmad Qajar (ruler of Iran), **88–89**
British–Russian relations under, 88
coup against (1921), 88, 1755, 1869
father of, Mohammad Ali Shah Qajar as, 88, 637
majles under, 88, 1868
reign of, 88, 1868–1869
succession of, 1559
in World War I, 88, 1869
Ahmad Shah (Afghan court minister), daughter of, 2420
Ahmad Shah Masʿud (Afghan leader), **89,** 1505
assassination of, 89
as defense minister, under Rabbani (Burhanuddin), 89
guerrilla wars led by, 89
vs. Hekmatyar (Golbuddin), 1020
in Jamiʿat-e Islami, 89, 1215
Kabul surrounded by, 59
and Shura-i Nizar, 64
Taliban opposed by, 89
Ahmad, Zakariyya, 2263
Ahmar, Abdullah ibn Husayn al-, **89–90**
in Islah Party, 90, 1143, 2389
Ahmar, Husayn al-, execution of, 89
Ahmed, Karen Hunt, *as contributor,* 96
Ahmed, Leila, 1037
Ahmed, Mourad Sid, 919
Ahmet (Turkish writer), 1439
Ahmet III (Ottoman sultan), and education, 757
Ahmet İhsan Toʾkgoz, **90**
Ahmet İzzet, **90**
Ahmet Rasim, **90–91**
education of, 91, 687
Ahmet Riza, **91–92,** 867, *2409*
as Chamber of Deputies president, 91
in Committee for Union and Progress, 91, 623
at Congress of Ottoman Liberals, 91, 631
at *Meşveret,* 91, 623, 2408
in Young Turks, 91, 623, 2408
Ahmet Sefik. *See* Midhat Paşa
Ahmet Vefik, **92**
and Turkish nationalism, 2251
Ahram, al- (newspaper), 1474, 1678
Abd al-Quddus (Ihsan) in, 18
Awad (Louis) in, 341
Bint al-Shati in, 475
Haykal (Muhammad Hasanayn) and, 1012
Idris (Yusuf) in, 1082
Sadat (Anwar al-) opposed by, 1956
Ahram al-Iqtisadi, al- (weekly), 505
Ahram Center for Political and Strategic Studies, al- (Cairo), **92–93**
Ibrahim (Saʿad al-Din) at, 92, 1079
Ahrar, al- (periodical), 2332
Ahreman (Zoroastrian deity). *See* Angra Mainyu
Ahsa, al- (oasis), 1995, 1996, 1997
Ahsaʿi, Ahmad al-, **93,** 2046, 2047
Ahu Khanom's Husband (Afghani), 1436–1437
Ahundzade, Mirza Feth-Ali, 347
Ahura Mazda (Zoroastrian deity), 2441, 2442
Ahuzat Bayit (Israel), 2171
Ahvaz (Iran), **93**
Ahwal shakhsiyya, 833
Aicha, Lalla, **94**
Aid. *See* Economic and military aid
AIDS/HIV (Acquired immune deficiency syndrome/Human immunodificiency virus), 480, 713–714, 1508
Israeli attitudes about, 1014
AIG. *See* Afghan Interim Government
Ain Shams University (Egypt), **94,** 2425

Bakr (Salwa) at, 378
Bint al-Shati at, 475
Zayyat (Latifa) at, 2428
AIOC. *See* Anglo–Iranian Oil Company
AIPAC. *See* American Israel Public Affairs Committee
Air France airplane hijacking (1976). *See* Entebbe Operation
Airplane bombings. *See also* Pan Am flight 103 bombing
of French airliner over Africa (1989), Libyan settlement for, 1862
of Swiss airliner (1970), PFLP–GC in, 1841
Airplane hijackings
in Black September, 2176
by French military (1956), 1563, 1598
by PFLP
Air France (1976) (*See* Entebbe Operation)
El Al airplane (1970), attempted, 1293
Haddad (Wadi) and, 967
Khaled (Leila) in, 1293
multiple (1970), 270, 962, 967, 1246, 1840
PLO expelled from Jordan after, 270
Sabena at Lod Airport (1972), 398, 1677, 1839
TWA (1969), 1293
Air transport, 2207, *2207*
AIS. *See* Islamic Salvation Army
AISHA: Arab Women's Forum, **95,** 894
Ait Ahmed, Hocine, **95–96,** 1905
in Comité Révolutionnaire d'Unité et d'Action, 620
French skyjacking of, 442, 1309
Aït-Débrouville, Les (Mernissi), 1518
AIU. *See* Alliance Israélite Universelle
Aix-la-Chapelle, Treaty of (1821), 401
Aja'ib al-Athar fi al-Tarajim wa al-Akhbar (Jabarti), 1207
Aja Mountains, 1206
Ajansi, Bağimsiz Basin, 1051
AJAX, Operation, 733
AJC. *See* American Jewish Congress
Ajman (United Arab Emirates), **96,** 2219
economy of, 96
Nuʿaymi family, al- in, 1694
population of, 96
Ajman tribe, 2209
Ajwad tribe, 2212
Akaley, Lotfi, 1428
Akatli, Füsun, in Women's Library and Information Center, 2358
Akayla, Abdullah, 1151
Akbari, Mania, *831*
Akbulut, Ahmet Ziya, **96**
Akbulut, Yildirim, in Motherland Party, 1584
Akçura, Yusuf, **96–97**
pan-Turkism of, 97, 1800
Akçuroğlu, Yusuf, 1439, 2251
Akhar Saʿa (newspaper), 911
Akhavan-Saless, Mehdi, **97,** 1436
Akhbar, al- (newspaper), 1678
Haykal (Muhammad Hasanayn) and, 1012
Akhbar al-Yawm (newspaper), Abd al-Quddus (Ihsan) at, 18
Akhbari Shiʿism, **97–98,** 2055
vs. Usuli, 2303
Akhir al-Dunya (Idris), 1082
Akhir Saʿa (newspaper), Haykal (Muhammad Hasanayn) and, 1012
Akhondzadeh, Mirza Fath Ali, **98**
Akhshav Uvgyamim Ha-aherim (Amichai), 182
Akhtar (newspaper), 1682
Akif, Muhammad Mahdi, in Muslim Brotherhood, 1622
Akin, Güiten, 1440
Akkad (ancient), 824
Akkad, Mustafa, **98–99**
Akkas-Bashi, Mirza Ebrahim, 832
Akkash, Midhat, 1205
Akk tribe (Yemen), 2426
AKP. *See* Justice and Development Party
Akrad, Hayy al- (Syria), **100**
Akrama, Treaty of (1917), first Italo–Sanusi War ended by, 1609
Akrami, Jamsheed, *as contributor,* 831–833
Akşam (newspaper), Karacan (Ali Naci) in, 1269
Aksariyat faction (Fedaʾiyan-e Khalq), 821
Akud (Suissa), 2114–2115
Al Abu Nasir tribe, 2189
Ala, Hoseyn, **100–101**
attempted assassination of, 101, 820
government of, Arfa (Hasan) in, 286
as prime minister, 100–101
Alaini, Muhsin. *See* Ayni, Muhsin al-
Al al-Shaykh, Abdullah ibn Muhammad ibn Ibrahim, 101
Al al-Shaykh family, **101–102**
Al Saʿud family connection to, 101–102
Al al-Shaykh, Salih ibn Abd al-Aziz ibn Muhammad, 101
Alam (in Muharram rite), 1605
Alam, al- (newspaper), 910, 1197
Ibrahim (Abdullah) in, 1075
Alam al-Adabi, al- (journal), 1428
Alam al-Kitaba an Ahzan al-Manfa (Aʿraj), 273
Alam, Amir Asadollah, **102,** 1487
as prime minister, 102, 1753
response to riots (1963), 1753
Ala marfa al-ayyam (Mostaghanemi), 1581
Alamayn, al- (Egypt), **102–103**
battle at (1942), 102–103, 516, 1041, 1934, 2370
Montgomery (Bernard Law) at, 1565
Alami family, al-, **103–104**
Alami, Faydi al-, 103
Alami, Lamis, in Women's Centre for Legal Aid and Counseling, 2356
Alami, Muhammad al-, 103
Alami, Musa al-, 103
and Arab Information Offices, 1053
and Husayni (Jamal al-), 1056
Alam, Showkat al-Molk, 102
Alamut (Iran), Ismaʿili Shiʿism in, 1159
Alanya (Turkey), *2238*
Alavi, Bozorg, **104,** 1435
Alavi, Mortezar, 104
Alawi, Ahmed, 1904
Alawi Shiʿism, **104–105**
in Morocco, 2059, 2115
in Syria, 2129
in politics, 412–413
Alawite dynasty (Morocco), **105–107,** *106,* 1004, 1569, 2039

Alawite dynasty (Morocco) *(continued)*
Bu Hamara in, 542
corsairs used by, 643
Jews under, 1548
Marrakech under, 1493
Muhammad VI in, 1599–1600
political success of, 1549
al-Qarawiyyin under, 1871
as Sharifian dynasty, 2037, 2038
Alawite tribal confederation, 2212
Albania
Austro-Hungarian support for, 339
independence of, 384
Albanians, 383
Albayrak, Izzet, Kan (Suna) taught by, 1269
Albert Camus Prize, Gebeyli (Claire) awarded with, 872
Albert, Lake, 372
Albert Nile. *See* Bahr al-Jabal
Alborz. *See* Elburz Mountains
Albright, Madeleine, *2291*
Albright, William Foxwell, 277
Al Bu Falasa dynasty (Dubai), 1474
Al Bu Saʿid dynasty, **107–108,** 1710–1711
Dhufar under, 705–706
founder of, 107, 1710
Muscat under, 1616
Al Bu Saʿid, Faysal ibn Turki (sultan of Oman)
British relations with, 107, 204
Anglo–Omani treaties in, 204, 531–532
Cox (Percy) in, 645–646
reign of, 107
Al Bu Saʿid, Majid, 107
Al Bu Saʿid, Qabus (Qaboos) ibn Saʿid, **108,** *1710,* 1711
coup by (1970), 107, 108
NDFLOAG in, 1654
development under, 108
Dhufar under, 108, 705–706, 1842
foreign policy of, 108
Masira Island under, 1499
Muscat under, 1616
reign of, 108
Al Bu Saʿid, Saʿid ibn Sultan (sultan of Oman and Zanzibar), 107, 1710
emigration under, 2425
Al Bu Saʿid, Saʿid ibn Taymur (sultan of Oman), **109,** 1710–1711
coup against (1970), 107, 108, 109, 705
NDFLOAG in, 1654
Dhufar rebellion against (1965–1975), 108, 109, 705, 1842
reign of, 108, 109, 1710–1711
Al Bu Saʿid, Tariq ibn Taymur, 107, 108
Al Bu Saʿid, Thuwayni, 107
Alcohol, **109–110**
Al-e Ahmad, Jalal, **110,** 668, 913, 1435, 1437, 2342
anti-Westernism of, 1091
Alef, Muhammad. *See* Atif, Muhammad
Aleichem, Sholem, 464
Alemdar. *See* Bayrakdar, Mustafa
Aleppine People's Party, 825
Aleppo (Syria), *111,* **111–112**
Armenian Catholics of, under millet system, 1544
commercial activity in, 111–112
French mandate in, 111
guilds in, 947
Hananu (Ibrahim) entry into, 989
music in, 112
in Ottoman Empire, 111–112
Sykes-Picot Agreement (1916) on, 2128
Aleppo College, 1551–1552
Alessandra, Jacques, 1356
Alevi sect of Shiʿism, **112–115**
Bektashis and, 113, 435
beliefs of, 113, 114
language of, 113
origins of, 112–113
persecution of, 114
in Turkey, 2238
and Unity Party (Turkey), 2295
Alexander I (czar of Russia), and Bucharest Treaty (1812), 541
Alexander II (czar of Russia)
in Crimean War, 649
and London Treaty (1871), 1446
pogroms following assassination of, 2432
ultimatum of, after Bulgarian Horrors, 382
Alexander, Harold R. L. G., in Allied Middle East Command, 153
Alexander, Kristian P., *as contributor,* 1136–1137
Alexander, Scott, *as contributor,* 150, 1236, 1272, 1526, 1577, 1721–1722, 1863, 2036–2037, 2045–2046, 2122, 2171, 2422–2423
Alexander the Great (king of Macedonia)
Alexandretta founded by, 115
Alexandria Ariorum founded by, 1021
Alexandria founded by, 116
in Khorasan (Iran), 1312
Alexandretta (Turkey), **115–116**
in French mandate, 115
in Ottoman Empire, 115
territorial conflict over, 115
Arslan (Adil) in, 306
Arsuzi (Zaki al-) in, 308
Turkish control of, 115
Alexandria (Egypt), *116,* **116–118**
Alexandria University in, 119
Arab League summit (1964) in, *1387*
architecture of, 118, 282
banking in, 389
Bibliotheca in, *117,* 118
B'nai B'rith lodge in, 489
British occupation of, 117, 118, 2297
commercial activity in, 116–117
De Menasce family in, 691
foreign population of, 117, 118
Institut Egyptien in, 1099
Jewish community in, 1016, 1930
patriarchate of
claims to, 590
Eastern Orthodox, 590–591
petroleum industry in, 1824
port of, 116, 117, 2206
textile mills in, 2181
Victoria College in, 118, 2315–2316
water supply of, 1468
Alexandria Ariorum, 1021
Alexandria Conference of Arab States. *See* League of Arab States
Alexandria Convention (1840), **118–119**
Alexandria Protocol (1944), 1386. *See also* League of Arab States
Nahhas (Mustafa) and, 1636
Alexandria–Suez railroad, 528
Alexandria University, **119**
Shahin (Yusuf) at, 2021–2022
Alexandria Why? (film), 2022
ALF. *See* Arab Liberation Front
Al Fahd (Sudayri Seven), 794
Al Sudayri family link to, 168

government positions held by, 165, 166, 168
members of, 165, 166
Algar, Hamid, *as contributor,* 98, 427–428, 929, 1277–1278, 1299–1300, 1564–1565, 1583, 1704, 1898–1899, 2035–2036, 2141–2143, 2311–2313
Algeciras, Act of (1906), 827
Abd al-Aziz ibn al-Hassan signing of, 8
Casablanca port in, 568
Germany on revisions to, 70
leading to Agadir crisis (1911), 70, 120
opposition to, 8, 14
Algeciras Conference (1906), **119–120,** 827
and Agadir crisis (1911), 70, 120
Moroccan defeat at, 8
Algemeyner Yidisher Arbeiter-Bund in Rusland und Poylen. *See* Bund
Algeria, **120–135,** *121. See also specific cities, organizations, people, and regions*
agriculture in, 124
alcohol in, 109, 110
Arabic culture in, Zaytuna University and, 2428
Arabic language in
Arabization policies on, 124, 254–256
declared as foreign language, 1422
literature in, 273, 1424, 1425, 1426
as official language, 122, 255
prevalence of, 121
Arabization policies in, 124, 254–256
in Arab Maghreb Union, 260
Arabs in, number of, 121
Arafat (Yasir) in, 270
art of, 414, 2064
installation, 1687
painting, 1687
by women, 1687
banking in, 390, 392, *393*
Berber dialects in, 458, 1422, 2253
Berbers in (*See under* Berbers)
borders of, 120
with Morocco, conflict over, 4, 1566
Catholics in, 1932
censorship in, of Berber culture, 1261
charitable *waqfs* in, 2323
cities of, 632, 1713–1715, 2013
border, 2192
capital, 139–140
port, 208
Saharan, 2190–2191
Civil Concord policy in, 127, *133,* 135, 504, 1156
civil war in (1990s)
amnesty in, 127, 135, 1156
casualties of, 126, 130, 135
causes of, 126, 130
GIA in, 917, 919
Islamic groups in, 126, 135
climate of, 120
communism in, 626, 627
Constituent Assembly of, 3, 4
constitutions of, **128–131**
(1963), 124, 128–129, 437, 857
(1976), 124, 129–130, 132, 857
(1989), 125, 130, 132, 445, 857, 1383
(1996), 127, *129,* 130
Council of the Nation of, 127, 130, 132
coup in (1965), 23, 124, 129, 442, 499, 503, 1537, 1744
coup in (1967), attempted, 500
coup in (1992), 126, 134, 504, 858
Nezzar (Khaled) in, 1686
defense costs as percentage of GNP or GDP, *1530*
demographics in, 120
deserts of, 120, *125*
economic aid to, 749
economy of, 127–128, 752, 753, *753*
under Ben Bella (Ahmed), 442
under Bendjedid (Chadli), 444
under Boumédienne (Houari), 499–500
under Bouteflika (Abdelaziz), 445
education in, 122
access to, 122, 124
Arabization of, 124, 255
under Ben Bella (Ahmed), 442
during French occupation, 123–124
upbringing aspect of, 760
elections in (1990), 858
Family Code of (1984) (*See* Algerian Family Code)
feminism in, 894, 2195
film of, 716, 985
French language in, 122, 124, 255, 1424, 1425, 1428
French occupation of (1830–1962), 122–124, *845*
beginning of, 613
Blum–Viollette Plan in, 489
bureaux arabes in administration of, 545–546
cantonnement/refoulement policies for, 564
Catroux (Georges) in, 570
Challe (Maurice) in, 579
colons during (*See* Colons)
Constantine plan for (1958), 632
Crémieux Decree in (1870), 647–648
De Gaulle (Charles) and, 688
Delouvrier (Paul) in, 689
education during, 123–124
Fly Whisk incident (1827) and, 397, 835–836
Hadj (Messali al-) criticism of, 969
intelligence operations during, 1101
land ownership in, 1371
legal code during, Code de l'Indigénat in, 612
and literature, 1422
Moroccan response to, 19
Mukrani's (Muhammad al-) revolt against, 1610
Organisation Armée Secrète support for, 1715
Ouled Sidi Cheikh in, 1745
treaties in (1834), 17
tribal resistance to, 16–18
Young Algerians and, 2404–2405
French relations with
Bendjedid (Chadli) and, 444
Bouteflika (Abdelaziz) and, *504,* 505
Evian Accords (1962) and, 788–789
French settlers in, 617–618 (*See also* Colons)
against Crémieux Decree (1870), 647–648
independence movement and, 615, 618
geography of, 901
guest workers from, 946
in Gulf Crisis (1990–1991), 951
higher education in, 122
High State Council in, 1025–1026
hydrocarbon industry in, 23, 127, 2079–2080
IMF agreement with, 917
independence of (*See also* Algerian War of Independence)
celebrations of, *138*

Algeria *(continued)*
impact on Morocco, 1004
movement leading to, 615
Star of North Africa calling for, 2089
Tripoli Programme defining identity and direction for, 2217
industrialization of, 1095
Italian relations with, Ente Nazionale Idrocarboni and, 777–778
Jews in
antidefamation organization for, 619
French citizenship for, Crémieux Decree on, 647–648
immigration to Israel, 1914
during World War II, 1234
labor unions in, 1358
land purchases in, Warnier Law (1873) on, 2327
land reforms in, 1372
languages in, 121–122, 124 (*See also specific languages as subheads*)
in League of Arab States, 1387, 1388
legal system of, 1382–1383
legislative body in, 932
literature of, 483, 496–497, 563, 707, 715–716, 803–804, 806, 822–823, 965, 1280, 1403, 1422–1427, 2007
in Arabic, 273, 1581
Berber, 192, 193, 1426
"Generation of 1954," 965
novels and short stories, 1547, 1581, 2332–2333
poetry, 1581, 1687
by women, 1581, 1687
local/provincial elections in (1990), 125, 133
mahdi-inspired uprising in (1849), 1463
manufacturing in, 127, 128
map of, *121*
marriage in
Family Code on (1984), 136
minimum age for, Khemisti Law on (1963), 132
Mauritanian relations with, Bendjedid (Chadli) and, 444
military of
coup by (1992), 126, 134
elections influenced by, 126, 127
equipment of, *1534*
force levels of, *1528–1529*
force structure of, *1532–1533*
in multiparty system, 132–133
revolt by (1962), 1537
Moroccan relations with (*See also* Moroccan–Algerian War; Western Sahara War)
Ben Bella (Ahmed) and, 442
Bouteflika (Abdelaziz) and, 503
causes of strain in, 260
POLISARIO and, 503, 2190–2191
mountains of, 120, 335–336
Mukrani family in, **1610**
music of, 1617, 1714
National Assembly of, 127, 132
elections to, 127
power of, 129
prime minister selected by, 128
nationalism in, 496, 497
Boudiaf (Mohamed) and, 496
Bouhired (Jamila) and, 497
Hadj (Messali al-) and, 968–969
in literature, 1425–1426
strains of, 124
natural gas in, 1671, *1671*
newspaper and print media of, 1678
French-language, 1681–1682
government-controlled, 1680
transitional press, 1681
nuclear capability of, 1698
oil production in, 752
Italian interest in, 777–778
in OPEC, 1719
in Ottoman Empire, 122, 1713
parliamentary elections in
of 1991–1992, 95, 125–126, 130, 134–135, 984
of 1997, 1904, 2429
of 2002, 135, 1904
phosphate industry in, 1834
poetry of, 193, 716
POLISARIO supported by, 503, 1837, 2190–2191
political parties in, **131–135**, 1904
Berber, 134
dominant, 127, 134
Islamist, 126, 133–134, 984
multiple, legalization of, 125, 130, 132–133
number of, 133
secular, 1905
single-party system of, 125, 129
political system of, 127
population of, 120, 752, *753*
postage stamps of, 1850
presidential elections in
of 1995, 127, 130, 135, 984, 2430
of 1999, 135, 984
presidential powers in, 127, 132
press freedom in, 125
provisional government of (*See* Gouvernement Provisoire de la République Algérienne)
radio and television in, 1894, *1895*
reforms in, 933
under Bendjedid (Chadli), 445
regions of, 120, 1261
religions in, 122, 124
Isawiyya Brotherhood, 1141
Sunni Islam, 122
riots in (1988), casualties of, 132
Sahara in, *1963*
science and technology in, 2004
scout movement in, 2006
secularism in, 1965
socialism in
Soltani (Abdellatif) criticizing, 2079
and SONATRACH, 2079–2080
Soviet relations with, 1943
steel industry in, 208
Tamazight language in
after independence, 124
as official language, 122, 130, 1261
teachers in, foreign, 255, 256
terrorism in, 919
theater of, 1280
tourism in, 2196
in trade, 835
Baqri family and, 396–397
Busnach family and, 549–550
tribes in, 458, 459, 2253–2254
political power of, 122
at Tripoli Conference, 2217
Tunisian relations with, 444
Twareg in, 2253–2254
water resources of
freshwater withdrawals, *2331*
quantity of, 2330
Western Saharan relations with, 1005, 1006, 1837
Bendjedid (Chadli) and, 444
in Western Sahara War, Sahrawi exodus to, 1837
women in
as artists, 1687, 2064
constitution on, 129, 130
economic status of, *877*
Family Code on (1984), 130, 136, 1905
M'Rabet (Fadela) on, 1592
as painters, 414
as political activists, 990
in politics, 443, 497, 892, 894, 2195
rights of, 892, 2195

under single-party system, 131–132
as writers, 483, 1424, 1425, *1425*, 2007
World Bank and
capital stock and voting power in, *2363*
loans from, *2364*
relative voting strength in, *2364*
in World War II, 516, 2370
British attack on French fleet (1940), 2369
Algerian Association of Reformist Ulama, Madani (Tawfiq al-) in, 1456
Algerian Communist Party (PCA)
ban on, 1803
Parti de l'Avant-Garde Socialiste as successor to, 1803
Algerian Family Code (1984), **136**
Bouhired (Jamila) against, 497
constitution contradicted by, 130
on marriage, 136
Toumi (Khalida) opposing, 2195
on women, 130, 136, 1905
Algerian Human Rights League, 990
Algerianists, *vs. salafists*, 1155
Algerian Jewish Committee for Social Studies. *See* Comité Juif Algérien d'Études Sociales
Algerian League of Human Rights, 2195
Algerian National Movement. *See* Mouvement National Algérien
Algerian People's Party. *See* Parti du Peuple Algérien
Algerian People's Union. *See* Union Populaire Algérien
Algerian Radio, Wattar (al-Taher) in, 2332
Algerian War of Independence (1954–1962), **136–139**, 847, 848, 1460. *See also* Comité Révolutionnaire d'Unité et d'Action
Abbas (Ferhat) in, 3–4
Ait Ahmed (Hocine) in, 95
Algerian attempts to avoid, 136–137
Amrouche (Jean) in, 193
Argoud (Antoine) in, 287
Armée de Libération Nationale in, 290, 969
Battle of Algiers in, 141–142
Belkacem (Cherif) in, 437
Ben Bella (Ahmed) in, 442
Ben Boulaid (Moustafa) in, 443
Bendjedid (Chadli) in, 444
Ben M'hidi (Muhammad Larbi) in, 451
Boudiaf (Mohamed) in, 496
Boudjedra (Rachid) in, 496
Boumédienne (Houari) in, 498
Bouteflika (Abdelaziz) in, 503
Bouyali (Moustafa) in, 506
Brahimi (Abdelhamid) in, 506
casualties of, 124, 137, 139, 615
civilians targeted in, 137, 141
colons (foreign settlers) in, 139, 615, 618
Conseil National de la Révolution Algérienne in, 138, 632
Didouche (Mourad) in, 707–708
Evian Accords ending (1962), 139
colon rights in, 124, 618
Fanon (Frantz) as ideologue of, 803–804
French foreign legion in, 856
French initiative in (*See* Loi Cadre)
French military in, 137–138
French opposition to, 141–142, 615, 1715
among colons, 139, 618, 1715
French skyjacking of leaders of, 442, 496, 1362
Front de Libération Nationale in, 131, 138, 615, 857
Ibrahimi (Ahmed Taleb) in, 1076
international opinion on, 138–139, 141–142
Kabylia region in, 1261
Khider (Mohamed) in, 1309
Krim (Belkacem) in, 1336–1337
Lacheraf (Mostefa) in, 1362
leaders of, 136–137
as literary catalyst, 1426
in literature, 273, 716
Mollet (Guy) in, 1563
Mouvement National Algérien in, 969
Muhammad V in, 1598
national strike during (1956), 141
Nezzar (Khaled) in, 1686
number of fighters in, 137, 138
Organisation Armée Secrète in, 1715
Oujda Group in, 1743–1744
Philippeville massacres in, 137
pro-French Algerians during, 995
resident minister during, 1363
Sahnoun (Ahmed) in, 1965
Sections Administrative Spécialisées during, 545
start of, 124, 136, 137
Tripoli Programme defining independent Algeria, 2217
urban warfare in, 138, 141
women in, 136, 1592
Zbiri (Tahar) in, 2429
Algerian White (Djebar), 716, 1427
Algérie, nation et société, L' (Lacheraf), 1362
Algérie-actualité (periodical), Djaout (Taher) at, 715
Algérie des illusions, l' (M'Rabet), 1592
Algérie: Échec à une régression programmée (Nezzar), 1686
Algérie: Femmes et écritures (Mostaghanemi), 1581
Algériennes, les (M'Rabet), 1592
Alger-Républicain (newspaper), 1592
Algiers (Algeria), **139–140**
Arab League summit (1973) in, *1387*
as Barbary state, 401
Berbers in, 122, 139
Catholics in, 1932
during civil war, 140
corsairs in, 139, 643
French conquest of, 835
French military revolt in (1961), 287, 579
French occupation of, 122, 139–140
French settlers in, 139, 140
riot by (1956), *137*
industrial activity in, 139, 140
Organisation Armée Secrète coup attempt in, 1715
Spanish occupation of, 2084
Treaty of 1815 with United States, 2208
in War of Independence, 140, 141–142
Algiers Agreement (1975), **140–141**, 1066–1067, 1119, 2043
Nabavi (Behzad) and, 1630
Algiers, Battle of (1956–1957), **141–142**
Ben Bouali (Hassiba) killed in, 443
Ben M'hidi (Muhammad Larbi) in, 451
French foreign legion in, 856
impact on visibility of war, 138, 141–142
urban warfare strategy in, 138, 141
Algiers Charter, **142**
Tripoli Programme completed by, 2217

Algiers, Regency of, 122
Alhucemas (Spanish possession), 1567
Alia (queen of Jordan), **142–143**
Ali Agha (Mamluk ruler), 1478
Ali Akbar (imam), tomb of, as Atabat, 328
Ali al-Naqi, tomb of, as Atabat, 328
Ali Baba, Operation, 1913
Alier, Abel, in Addis Ababa Accords (1972), 1700
Ali, Filiz, *as contributor,* 476–477, 872–873, 1269
Alignment (Maʿarakh) party (Israel), 1178
  Burg (Avraham) in, 546
  Grossman (Haika) in, 945
  Middle Eastern Jewish opposition to, 49
Alihah al-mamsukha, al- (Baʿalbakki), 354
Ali ibn Abi Talib (caliph)
  assassination of, 2052
  burial place of, 1505
  as companion of Muhammad, 2053
  as founder of Shiʿism, 2052
  Kharijite break with, Ibadiyya branch after, 1073
  vs. Muʿawiya, 2052
  right to caliphate, 104
  as Shiʿite imam
    vs. caliph, 104
    tomb of, as Atabat, 328
  shrine to, 1637
  sons of, 2052
  as successor to Muhammad, 1597
Ali ibn Hilal, calligraphy of, 558
Ali ibn Yusuf (sultan of Fez), 828
Alija, al- (Morocco), 828
Al-Ilm wa al-Iman (Egyptian television show), 1469
Ali-nabi (Prophet), Muhammad as, 1595
Ali Nasir Muhammad al-Hasani, **143,** 1814
  Antar (Ali Ahmad Nasir) and, 211
Ali Pasha (Mamluk ruler), 1478
Ali-Rachedi, Louise. *See* Bittari, Zoubida
Ali, Rashid. *See* Kaylani, Rashid Ali al-
Ali Riza, **143**
  students of, 96
Ali, Salim Rabiyya. *See* Rabiyya Ali, Salim
Alishan, Ghevond, **143–144**
Ali Suavi, **144**
  newspapers edited by, 2406
  pan-Turkist influence on, 1800
  in Young Ottomans, 2405, 2406, 2407
Ali, Wijdan, **144–145**
Aliyah (Jewish immigration to Palestine), **145–148,** *147,* 2171
  Balfour Declaration (1917) and, 146, 614, 1223
  Balfour Declaration (1917) on, 381, 803, 1402
  British limits on, 1011
  by children, through Youth Aliyah, 2411
  Faisal–Weizmann Agreements on, 800, 803
  fifth wave of (1930s), 146–147
  financial support for *(halukka),* 980
  first wave of (1881–1903), 145–146
  fourth wave of (1924–1930), 146
  Germany opposing, 906
  Israel be-Aliyah on, 1182
  Labor Zionism and, 1360–1362
  literature of, 1431
  London Conference (1939) on, 1445
  motivations for, 145–148, *147*
  from Russia and Eastern Europe, 145–146, 508–509, 1361
  second wave of (1903–1914), 146
  Shaw Commission on, 2044
  third wave of (1919–1924), 146
Aliyah Bet, 147
Aliye, Fatma, 578
Aliyer, Fatimah, **148**
Alizadeh, Ghazaleh, **148–149**
Alkalai, Judah ben Solomon Hai, **149**
Al-Khalaf, Nazar, *as contributor,* 1980–1981, 2115
Al Khalifa, Abdullah ibn Ahmad, 149
Al Khalifa, Ahmad bin, Al Khalifa dynasty founded by, 149
Al Khalifa family, **149–150,** 1479
  Al Sabah family and, 158
  asylum to, 531
  in Bahrain, 149–150, 367–368, 369
  in Qatar, 149, 1875–1876
  in Zubara, 370
Al Khalifa, Hamad bin Isa, 150, *369,* 370, 2263
Al Khalifa, Isa, 150
Al Khalifa, Isa bin Ali, 149–150
  British appointment of, 149
  British exile of, 150
Al Khalifa, Isa bin Sulman, 150, 368
Al Khalifa, Khalifa ibn Hamad, 150
Al Khalifa, Khalifa ibn Sulman, 149
Al Khalifa, Muhammad ibn Khalifa, 149
Al Khalifa, Sulman ibn Ahmad, 149
Al Khalifa, Sulman ibn Hamad, 150, 436
Allah, **150,** 1145, 1596, 2621
Allah Khan, Ehsan, 1216
Allah, Rashid al-Din Fazl, 2144
Allah wa al-insan (Mahmud), 1469
All-Arab Federation of Women, 227
Alleg, Henri, 141
Allel, Mohamed, 918
Allenby Declaration (1922), 151
Allenby, Edmund Henry, **151**
  and benevolent paternalism, 514
  Clayton (Gilbert) under, 603
  Egyptian rebellion (1919) repressed by, 512
  Faisal I ibn Hussein's troops under, 800
  as high commissioner of Egypt, 2354
  Jabotinsky (Vladimir Ze'ev) under, 1208
  Jerusalem occupied by, 151, *263,* 509–510, *510,* 1223
  Jewish Legion with, 1230
  Mogannam (Matiel) and, 1557
  on NILI spy ring, 1
  Palestine Exploration Fund maps used by, 1772
  Palestine occupied by, 151, 1761
  protests against Palestine visit of (1933), 13
  Rothschild (James Armand de) and, 1937
  in Sudanese revolt (1924), 2349
  Tharwat (Abd al-Khaliq) negotiating with, 2183
  Wavell (Archibald Percival) and, 2334
  in World War I, 2367, 2368
  against Yildirim Army, 2400
Allen, Calvin H., Jr., *as contributor,* 705, 1709–1711, 2158
Allende, Salvador, death of, Kissinger (Henry) in, 1327
Allen, Roger, *as contributor,* 978–979, 1061, 1082–1083, 1465–1466, 1468–1469, 1977–1978

Alliance Israélite Universelle (AIU) (Jewish organization), **151–152,** 758
Behar (Nissim) at, 427
and Dor De'a movement, 720
establishment of, 151
Hayim (Yusef) and, 1012
influence of, 152, 1231–1232
Kalischer (Hirsch) and, 1265
leadership of, 151
need for, 151, 665
objectives of, 151–152
Sagues (Albert) at, 1963
schools of, 151, 152, 1265
Sha'ul (Anwar) at, 2043
Somikh (Abdullah) sending his son to, 2079
Alliance of Fidelity (Ottoman Empire), 2406
Allied Islamic Association, Rafsanjani (Ali Akbar Hashemi) in, 1898
Allied Middle East Command, **152–153**
All North Africa Association, 1005
Allon Plan, 153–154, 1191
Allon, Yigal, **153–154**
Israeli settlements under, 153–154, 1191
ministry position of, 1174
in Palmah, 153, 1795
Wingate (Charles Orde) and, 972
Allouache, Merzak, 2192
All-Palestine Government, **154–156**
Arab Higher Committee in, 154, 228
Arab recognition of, 155–156
end of, 156
Hilmi (Ahmad) in, 1030
Husayni (Jamal al-) in, 1056
Jericho Congress rejection of, 1221
Nusayba (Anwar) in, 1705
Almah (Sobol), 2076
Al-majlis al-baladi, 2224
Almog, Ruth, 1433
Almohads, 460, 2224, 2228
Marrakech conquered by, 1493
in Morocco, 1569
Almoravids, 2228
in Morocco, 1569
Western Sahara origins of, 2343
Alms, 2167
ALN. *See* Armée de Libération Nationale
Al Nahayyan family, **156,** 2040
Aloni, Bezalel, 1014
Alon, Ilia, *as contributor,* 703–704
Aloni, Nessim, 2185
Aloni, Shulamit, **156–157,** 893
in Citizens' Rights Movement, 157, 1180
Alphabet Reform (1928), 2248
Alpha, Operation, **157**
Dulles (John Foster) in, 157, 733
Alp, Tekin, 1800
Alpujarras uprising (1568–1571), 2084
Al-Qiyam (Algeria), 1455
Al Rashid, Abdullah ibn, 157
Al Rashid family, **157–158**
Al Sa'ud family conflict with, 162–163, 1626, 1999
in Jabal Shammar, 818
in Muwahhidun reform movement, 2214
Shammar tribe led by, 2214
Al Rashid, Muhammad ibn, 158
Al Rashid, Talal ibn Abdullah ibn, 158
Al Sabah, Abdullah, 158
Al Sabah, Abdullah II, 158
Al Sabah, Abdullah al-Salim (crown prince of Kuwait), 160
Al Sabah, Abdullah al-Salim (ruler of Kuwait), 159, 161–162
Al Sabah, Ahmad, 159, 161
Al Sabah family, **158–160,** 1348
constitution under, 159, 160
merchant opposition to, 159, 161
parliament under, 159, 160
Al Sabah, Jabir, 158
Al Sabah, Jabir II, 159
Al Sabah, Jabir al-Ahmad, 159–160
Al Sabah, Jarrah, 158, 160
Al Sabah, Mubarak, **160–161**
British agreements with, 1348
British support for, 159, 160, 161
coup by, 158, 160
foreign policy of, 159, 160
merchant relations with, 158–159, 160, 161
Al Sabah, Sabah, 158
Al Sabah, Sabah II, 158
Al Sabah, Sabah al-Salim III, 159
Al Sabah, Salim, 159
Al Saqr, Abd al-Aziz, 162
Al Saqr, Abdullah Hamid, 161
Al Saqr family, **161–162**
Al Saqr, Hamid, 161
Al Saqr, Jasim Hamid, 162
Al Saqr, Mohammad Jasim, 162
Al Sa'ud, Abd al Rahman, government positions held by, 168
Al Sa'ud, Ahmad, government positions held by, 166, 168
Al Sa'ud, Badr, 166
Al Sa'ud, Fahd ibn Abd al-Aziz. *See* Fahd ibn Abd al-Aziz Al Sa'ud
Al Sa'ud, Faisal ibn Abd al-Aziz. *See* Faisal ibn Abd al-Aziz Al Sa'ud
Al Sa'ud family, **162–167,** 1997–1998. *See also specific people*
Abd al-Wahhab (Muhammad ibn) alliance with, 101, 162
Al al-Shaykh family connection to, 101–102
Al Fahd (Sudayri Seven) of (*See* Al Fahd)
Al Rashid family conflict with, 162–163, 1626, 1999
Al Sudayri family alliance with, 168–169
Al Thunayyan branch of, 172
Free Princes' public split with, 798
government positions held by, 164–167
internal conflict in, 163, 164, 166
as muwahhidun (Wahhabi followers), 1625–1626
Najd controlled by, 101, 1638
oath of allegiance to, 798
original seat of, 1927
origins of, 162–163
Pharaon (Rashad) under, 1832
Quraysh tribe challenging legitimacy of, 2213
Riyadh as base for, 1625, 1928
Saudi Arabia unified under, 1625–1626
Shammar intermarriage with, 2214
al-Ta'if occupied by, 2148
tribes affiliated with, 2211
Al Sa'ud, Fawwaz ibn Abd al-Aziz (prince of Saudi Arabia), 166
Al Sa'ud, Faysal ibn Turki. *See* Faysal ibn Turki Al Sa'ud
Al Sa'ud, Khalid ibn Abd al-Aziz. *See* Khalid ibn Abd al-Aziz Al Sa'ud
Al Sa'ud, Mishal (princess of Saudi Arabia), execution of, 165

Al Saʿud, Muhammad ibn Abd al-Aziz (prince of Saudi Arabia), 164–165
brother of, 164, 1294
Al Saʿud, Muhammad ibn Saʿud (founder of dynasty)
Abd al-Wahhab (Muhammad ibn) alliance with, 101, 162, 172, 1998–1999
Al Thunayyan family related to, 172
in Wahhabism, 1625
Al Saʿud, Nawwaf (prince of Saudi Arabia), 166
Al Saʿud, Nayif ibn Abd al-Aziz (prince of Saudi Arabia), 166
government positions held by, 166, 168
Al Saʿud, Salman
government positions held by, 168
as potential successor, 168–169
Al Saʿud, Saʿud ibn Abd al-Aziz (king of Saudi Arabia), *165*, **167–168**
abdication by, forced, 11, 164, 168
Al Saʿud (Muhammad ibn Abd al-Aziz) opposing, 164–165
as crown prince, 167
government of
Al Saʿud (Talal ibn Abd al-Aziz) in, 164, 165–166, 167
Sultan ibn Abd al-Aziz Al Saʿud in, 165
and Husayni (Jamal al-), 1056
incompetence of, 11, 164, 167, 1999
power yielded to Faisal by, 164, 165–166, 167
reign of (1953–1964), 164, 167–168, 1999
as viceroy of Najd, 167
Al Saʿud, Saʿud ibn Faisal (prince of Saudi Arabia), 166
Al Saʿud, Talal ibn Abd al-Aziz (prince of Saudi Arabia), 165–166
government criticized by, 166
King Saʿud alliance with, 164, 165–166, 167
Al Saʿud, Turki ibn Abd al-Aziz (prince of Saudi Arabia), 166
Al Saʿud, Turki ibn Abdullah, 818, 1999
Al Saʿud, Turki ibn Faisal (prince of Saudi Arabia), 167–168
Al Sinjara (section of Shammar tribe), 2214
Al Sudayri, Ahmad al-Kabir, 168
Al Sudayri, Ahmad bin Muhammad, 168
Al Sudayri family, **168–169**
Al Saʿud family alliance with, 168–169
tribal origin of, 2211
Al Sudayri, Hassa bint Ahmad, **169**
as favorite wife of Ibn Sa'ud, 168, 169, 794, 798
sons of, 168, 169
Al Sudayri, Haya, 168
Al Sudayri, Jawhara, 168
Al Sudayri, Sultana bint Ahmad, 168
Al-Suswa, Amat al-Alim, **169**
Altaic language family, 2247
Altai language, 2247, 2252
Altalena (ship), **169–171**, *170*, 425
owned by Irgun Zva'i Le'umi, 169–171, 1140
Palmah in destruction of, 1795
Alteneuland (Herzl), 2172
Alterman, Natan, **171**, 956, 1432, *1433*
Alternance government (Morocco), 1573–1574, 1575
Al Thani, Abdullah ibn Khalid, 172
Al Thani, Abdullah ibn Khalifa, 172
Al Thani, Abdullah ibn Qasim (ruler of Qatar), 1876
Al Thani, Ahmad ibn Ali (ruler of Qatar), 172
Al Thani family, **171–172**, 1876, 2210
Al Thani, Hamad ibn Khalifa (amir of Qatar), **172**
coup by (1995), 172, 1876
foreign policy of, 1877
political reform under, 172, 1876–1877
Al Thani, Jassem, 172
Al Thani, Khalifa ibn Hamad (ruler of Qatar), 172
coup against (1995), 172, 1876
Al Thani, Muhammad. *See* Muhammad ibn Thani
Al Thani, Qasim ibn Muhammad (ruler of Qatar), 1876
Al Thunayyan, Abdullah ibn Thunayyan, 172
Al Thunayyan, Ahmad, 172
Al Thunayyan family, **172–173**
Al-tibb al-nabawi (prophetic medicine), 1508
Altinay, Ahmed Refik, **173**
Altındağ Women's Solidarity Foundation (Turkey), 894, 2249
Altman, Israel, 2147
Altneuland (Herzl), 1851
Altstadt, Audrey L., *as contributor*, 693–694, 2076
Altunian, Aristakes, 588
Alusi, Mahmud Shukri al-, **173**
Amal (Islamic normative practice), 1476
Amal, al- (newspaper), 1831
Am al-fil (Abu Zeid), 40
Amal Ghayr al-Kamila, al- (Samman), 1982
AMAL movement (Lebanon), **173–174**
Berri (Nabi) in, 174, 467
Chamran (Mostafa) in, 582
vs. Hizbullah, 1037, 1038
Husayni (Husayn al-) in, 1055
Islamic faction of, 1647
Nasrallah (Hasan) in, 1647
in National Front, 1657
PLO rivalry with, 174
political success of, 174
Shiʿite support for, 173–174
Amama. See Turbans
Amanah settlement movement, 957
Amanat, Abbas, 1036
Aman, Muhammad al-. *See* Muhammad (prophet of Islam)
Amanollah Khan (king of Afghanistan), **174–175**
abdication by, forced, 56, 175, 400
in Anglo–Afghan war of 1919, 174, 198
Dar al-Moʿallamin under, 670
foreign policy of, 174–175
independence declared by, 56, 174
modernization programs of, 56, 174
Musahiban brothers during rule of, 2420
Nadir Barakzai (Mohammad) freed by, 1633
political reforms of, 56, 175
rebellion against, 56, 175
wife of, 325, 1881
women's rights under, 325
Amanullah Barakzai. *See* Amanollah Khan
Amaoui, Noubir, 630
Amarar clan, 433

Amari, Raja, **175**
Amar, Licco, Kan (Suna) taught by, 1269
Amawi, Abla M., *as contributor,* 2233, 2426
Amazigh, 457, 458, 461
Amazigh Cultural Movement (Algeria), 1905
Am Ehad Party (Israel), 1178
  ideology of, 1178
Amerada Hess, in Oasis Group, 1707–1708
Ameran Dilemma, An: The Negro Problem and Modern Democracy (Myrdal), 543
Amer, Ghada, **176**
American-Arab Anti-Discrimination Committee, 1975
American Board of Christian Missions (ABCM), 1551
American Board of Commissioners for Foreign Missions (ABCFM), 1854
  schools established by, 758
American College for Girls. *See* Ramses College for Girls
American Council for Judaism (ACJ), **176–177**
American Israel Public Affairs Committee (AIPAC), **177**
American Jewish Committee, **177–178**
  accord with Israel (1950), 178
  vs. American Council for Judaism, 176
  Magnes (Judah) in, 1460
  objectives of, 177
  at Paris peace settlements, 177–178
American Jewish Congress (AJC), **178–179**
  vs. American Council for Judaism, 176
  Wise (Stephen S.) in, 2354
American–Jewish Joint Distribution Committee
  Magic Carpet Operation run by (1948–1950), 1460
  Magnes (Judah) in, 1460
American Jewish Relief Committee, Joint Distribution Committee established by, 1239
American Junior Women's College, 431
American Mission for Lebanon and Syria, 431
American Numismatic Society, 1702
American Petroleum Institute (API)
  gravity, 1828–1829, *1829*
  natural gas study of, 1670
American Protestant Mission, 1552
American Red Cross, support for Magen David Adom, 1459
American School for Girls, 431
American University Hospital (Beirut), 180
American University in Cairo (AUC), **179–180,** 758, 1551–1552
  gender studies at, 896
  Ibrahim (Saʿad al-Din) at, 1079
American University of Beirut (AUB), **180–181,** *181,* 429, 758, 1551–1552
  Arab National Movement at, 262
  Azm (Sadiq al-) at, 351
  Beirut College of Women as member college of, 431–432
  Bliss (Daniel) as president of, 487
  Bliss (Howard) at, 487
  Geagea (Samir) at, 871
  Ghoussoub (Mai) at, 916
  Hawi (Khalil) at, 1010
  Hoss (Salim al-) at, 1045
  Hourani (Albert) at, 1046
  Hut (Shafiq al-) at, 1070
  Khal (Yusuf al-) at, 1298
  Khaled (Leila) at, 1293
  vs. Lebanese University, 1396
  Maksoud (Hala Salaam) at, 1975
  Malik (Charles Habib) at, 1475
  Saba (Fawzi) at, 1951
  Sabbagh (Hasib) at, 1952
  Salam (Saʾib) at, 1975
  Salam (Salim) at, 1975
  Samman (Ghada) at, 1982
  Sharabati (Ahmad al-) at, 2030
  Shuqayri (Ahmad) at, 2061
  Sprinzak (Joseph) at, 2087
  students of, as SSNP members, 1949
  Sulh (Taki al-Din al-) at, 2119
  Tall (Wasfi al-) at, 2156
  Twayni (Ghassan) at, 2254
  Zurayk (Constantine) at, 2443
American University of Kuwait, 181
American Zionist Emergency Council, Wise (Stephen S.) on, 2354
American Zionist Public Affairs Committee. *See* American Israel Public Affairs Committee
America, USS, 1409
Amharic language, 787
  Arabic relationship to, 232
Amichai, Yehuda, **182,** 1432, 1433
Amiens, Treaty of (1802), **182–183**
Amin, Abd al-Munʿim, as Free Officer, 853
Amin, Ahmad, **183–184**
  Khalid (Khalid Muhammad) influenced by, 1296
Amin al-Dowleh, Mirza Ali Khan, **184**
  Amin al-Soltan (Ali-Asghar) rivalry with, 184, 1591
  nephew of, 2318
  in Qajar dynasty, 184, 1591
  son of, 186
Amin al-Soltan, Ali-Asghar, **184**
  Afghani (Jamal al-Din al-) and, 52
  Amin al-Dowleh (Mirza Ali Khan) rivalry with, 184, 1591
  Amin al-Zarb (Mohammad Hasan) and, 185
  dismissal of, 1591
  Zell al-Soltan and, 2430
Amin al-Zarb, Mohammad Hasan, **185**
Amin Bey, al- (ruler of Tunisia), **185**
Amin, Dina, *as contributor,* 2183–2188
Amin, Hafizullah, **185–186**
  assassination by Soviet troops, 58, 65, 186, 1274
  coup by (1979), 58, 186
  Durand Line challenged by, 734
  in People's Democratic Party of Afghanistan, 62, 185–186
    Khalq faction of, 62, 185, 1813
  presidency of, 186
  as prime minister, 186
  Soviet opposition to, 65, 186
Amini, Ali, **186–187**
  appointment of, U.S. role in, 1118, 1753
  dismissal of, 1753
Amin, Idi, 777
Amini, Fatemeh, **187**
Amin Izz al-Din, 1036
Amin Khan, Muhammad Bey, 187

Amin, Qasim, **187**
on Cairo University, 555
on women's issues, 187, 875, 890
Amin, Samir, 1036
Amir, 2621
Amir, Abd al-Hakim, **188**
Baghdadi (Abd al-Latif al-) as rival of, 363
in Revolutionary Command Council, 1921
as vice president of UAR, 2273
Amirahmadi, Hooshang, *as contributor,* 2299–2302
Amir Ali, on caliphate, 557
Amir al-mu'minin (commander of the faithful), 2155
Moroccan king as, 1568, 1572, 1586, 1599–1600
Amiras class, 297–298
Amira, Yeghiazar, 2415
Amir, Aziza, 832
Amir, Eli, **188,** 1452
Amir-Entezam, Abbas, **188–189**
Amir Kabir, Mirza Taqi Khan, **189**
assassination of, 189
Dar al-Fonun founded by, 189, 669, 1867
military reforms of, 1117
modernization under, 1476–1477
mother-in-law of, 1462
Naser al-Din Shah and, 189, 669, 1643–1644, 1867
newspaper founded by, 1682
Amir, Yigal, 403
Rabin (Yitzhak) assassinated by, 1168
Amis du Manifeste et de la Liberté (AML) (Algeria), **189–190**
Abbas (Ferhat) in, 3, 189–190, 1804–1805
establishment of, 3, 189
Hadj (Messali al-) in, 3, 189–190, 969
Parti du Peuple Algérien members in, 1805
Amital, Yehuda, 1749
Amit, Meir, **190**
and Harel (Isser), 992
as Mossad director, 1578
Amity and Commerce, Draft Treaty of (1535), 620
Ami viendra vous voir, un (Chraibi), 588
AML. *See* Amis du Manifeste et de la Liberté
Amma, 774
Amma Dedhahaba (Tchernichovsky), 2169
Amman (Jordan), **190–192,** *191*
Arab League summit (1980) in, *1387*
Arab League summit (1987) in, *1387*
Arab League summit (2001) in, *1387*
Arafat (Yasir) in, headquarters of, 270
as capital, 191
Circassians in, 190, 600
climate of, 1240
commercial activity in, 190–191
Fahralnissa Zeid Institute of Fine Arts in, 2429
infrastructure of, 191–192
origins of, 190
population of, 191, 1243
University of Jordan in, 2295
Ammar, Ben, 2192
Ammum, Iskandar, in Decentralization Party, 686
Ammush, Bassam, 1151
Amnesty International
advertisement for, International (Dana) in, 1105
on human-rights abuses of gay people, 888
Khader (Asma) work with, 1292
on Morocco, 1716
on Sabra and Shatila massacres, 254, 1955
Amor, Mohamed Belhaj, 2232
in Parti d'Unité Populaire, 1587, 1804
Amour, la fantasie, l' (Djebar), 716, 1424
Amour bilingue (Khatibi), 1303
Amour de loin, l' (Love from Afar) (opera, Ma'louf), 1478
Amr, Ali, in Arab–Israel War (1956), 245
Amri, Hasan al-, **192**
Amrouche, Belkacemou, 192
Amrouche, Fadhma At Mansour, **192,** 193, 1426
Amrouche, Jean, **193,** 1426
mother of, 192
Amrouche, Mary Louise (Marguerite Taos), **193,** 1426
mother of, 192, 193
AMU. *See* Arab Maghreb Union
Amu Darya River, 54, **193,** 1032
Amurath to Amurath (Bell), 437
Amyuni, Mona Takieddine, *as contributor,* 872, 2125
Ana Ahya (Ba'albakki), 354
An al-ruh allati suriqat tadrijiyyan (Bakr), 378
ANAP (Anavatan Partisi). *See* Motherland Party
Anatolia (Turkey), **193–194,** *194,* 2236
agriculture in, 194
Alevi Shi'ism in, 113
ancient history of, 2239
archaeology in, 278
Berlin Treaty (1878) on, 528
Circassians in, 599
cities of, 194, 207, 547–548, 1332
colonialism in, attempted, 614
cotton industry in, 644
development plan in (*See* Southeastern Anatolia Project)
geography of, 193–194
Greek invasion of (1922), 513
Lausanne Treaty (1923) on, 514
literature of, 1439–1440
London Treaty (1913) on, 511
mortality rates in, 1845
nationalism in, 2251
in Ottoman Empire
administrative changes to, 27
Land Code of 1858 effects, 1368, 1369
land ownership in, 1370–1371
population of, 1843, 1845
railways in, 2206
in Russian–Ottoman War (1877–1878), 2311
San Stefano Treaty (1878) and, 1988
Sèvres Treaty (1920) and, 512, 1376
Sykes-Picot Agreement (1916) on, 2128
Anatolian Left, 1919
Anatolian Plateau (Turkey), 194
Anatolian Railway Company, 464
Anatolian Turkish language, 2248
Anavatan Partisi (ANAP). *See* Motherland Party
Anawati, Georges Chehata, **194–195,** 1457
Anaza tribal confederation, 2211, 2213
Ancient and Modern Imperialism (Baring), 407
Ancient Egypt (Baikie), 1464

An V de la Révolution Algérienne, L' (Fanon), 804
Andalus, al-, 2084
Anday, Melih Cevdet, 1440
Anderson, Lisa, *as contributor,* 500–503, 898–899, 899, 941, 1207, 1212–1213, 1410–1415, 1627–1628, 1653, 1655, 1860–1863
Anderson, Robert, 2291
in Operation Alpha, 157
Andish-e Islami (journal), 1563
Andranik Ozanian, **195–196,** 303
Andrássy, Gyula, at Berlin Congress, 465
Andrássy, Julius, 339
Ane, l' (Chraibi), 588
Anfas (journal), 1355
Angel Gabriel (Jabril), appearance to Muhammad, 1595
Angioxyl, Terufah Nedirah (Tammuz), 2159
Angleton, James Jesus, in Israeli–Egyptian peace negotiations, 573
Anglican Christianity, 523
Anglo–Afghan Treaty (1855), **196**
Anglo–Afghan wars, **196–198**
of 1839–1842, 196
Dost Mohammad Barakzai in, 56, 196, 400, 721
Durrani dynasty and, 196, 735
of 1878–1880, 196–197, *197*
Abd al-Rahman Khan after, 19–20, 197
of 1919, for independence, 197–198
Amanollah Khan in, 174, 198
Anglo–Afghan Treaty and (1855), 196
Anglo–American Committee of Inquiry (AAC) (1946), **198–199**
Attlee (Clement) in, 338
Bevin (Ernest) in, 468
on binationalism, 473
at Bluden Conference (1946), 488
Buber (Martin) testifying before, 540–541
Cattan (Henry) in, 570
Creech Jones (Arthur) in, 647
Crossman (Richard) in, 650
on potash industry, 1851
report by, 199
Anglo–American Middle East Supply Center, 1483
Anglo–Dutch Shell, Thatcher (Margaret) selling off government shares in, 522
Anglo–Egyptian Bank, 389
Anglo–Egyptian convention (1877), on suppression of slave trade, 2074
Anglo–Egyptian Treaty (1936), 616
abrogation of (1951), 1635–1636
on British troops, 766
Eden (Anthony) and, 755
Egyptian nationalists demanding renegotiation of, 518
mixed courts under, 1553
Muslim Brotherhood opposing, 766
Nahhas (Mustafa) and, 1635–1636, 2320
and political autonomy of Egypt, 810, 859
Wafd and, 810
Anglo–Egyptian Treaty (1954), **199–200**
Abd al-Maguid (Esmat) in, 16
on British troops, 519
Anglo–French Agreement (1899), 216
Anglo–French Entente (1904). *See* Cambon–Lansdowne Agreement (1904)
Anglo–French Public Debt Commission. *See* Egyptian Public Debt Commission
Anglo–Iranian Agreement (1919), **200**
Curzon (George Nathaniel) in, 652
Vozuq al-Dowleh (Mirza Hasan Khan) and, 2318
Anglo–Iranian Oil Company (AIOC), **200–202.** *See also* Anglo–Persian Oil Company (APOC); British Petroleum
in Abadan, 2, *201,* 518
British government in, 201, 518, 671, 742
establishment of, 201, 671
Iran concession to, 200–202
nationalization of, 202, 518, 996, 1752
Eden (Anthony) opposing, 755
foreign response to, 1825
National Front and, 1655–1656
Qatar concession to, 1876
Anglo–Iraqi treaties, 202–203
Abd al-Ilah ibn Ali in, 15
British presence in Iraq based on, revolt against (1941), 36
Cox (Percy) in, 202, 646
Faisal I ibn Hussein in, 202
and Fertile Crescent unity, 825
Humphreys (Francis) in, 1050
Iraqi opposition to, 15, 203
Ikha al-Watani Party in, 1084, 1283
Jabr (Salih) in, 203, 1210
Kaylani (Abd al-Rahman al-) in, 1283
Kaylani (Rashid Ali al-) in, 1283
League of Nations membership in, 203
Saʿdun (Abd al-Muhsin al-) and, 1961
Saʿid (Nuri al-) in, 203, 1283, 1967
Anglo–Jordanian treaty (1948)
abrogation of (1957), 1632
Nabulsi (Sulayman al-) opposing, 1632
Anglo–Libyan Alliance Treaty (1953), 517
Anglo–Moroccan commercial agreement (1856), 19
Anglo–Omani treaties, **203–204,** 525–526, 531–532
Anglo–Ottoman treaty (1838), 1481
Anglo–Palestine Bank, 1229, 1408
Anglo–Persian Agreement (1919), Mossadegh (Mohammad) opposed to, 1580
Anglo–Persian Oil Company (APOC). *See also* Anglo–Iranian Oil Company; British Petroleum
British government as shareholder in, 537
foundation of, 537
al-Ghanim family in, 911
Wilson (Arnold T.) in, 2352–2353
Anglo–Persian War (1856), **204,** 1117
Treaty of Paris ending (1857), 204
Anglo–Russian Agreement (1907), **205**
Curzon (George Nathaniel) opposing, 651–652
Iranian response to, 205
Anglo–Saxon Oil Company, 537
Anglo–Turkish commercial convention (1838). *See* Balta Liman, Convention of (1838)
Anglo–Turkish Convention (1913)
Kuwaiti borders in, 159, 1678

Anglo–Turkish Convention *(continued)*
Ottoman relations with Kuwait in, 161
Angora (Turkey). *See* Ankara
Angra Mainyu (Zoroastrian deity), 2441, 2442
Anielewitz, Mordekhai, in Warsaw Ghetto uprising, 1001, 2377
Ani, Jananne al-, **205–206**
photographs by, *310, 311*
Animal Farm (Orwell), 46
Anis Al-Jalis (magazine), **206**
Anis, Muhammad, 1035
Ani, Yusuf al-, 2184
Aniza tribe, 2209
Anjoman (assembly), **206–207,** 947
in Iran, 1591
Anjoman-e Pulad, 2142
Ankara (Turkey), **207–208,** 2237
Ankara University in, 208
architecture of, 207, 282
Atatürk (Mustafa Kemal) in, 207, 331, *331*
Bilkent University in, 472
as capital, selection of, 1194
civil service school in, 602
gecekondus on outskirts of, 872
historical significance of, 194, 207
theaters in, 2187
Ankara–Istanbul railway, 2206
Ankara Language, History, and Geography School, 2160
Ankara State Opera, 872
Ankara, Treaty of (1930), **208**
Ankara University, **208,** 965
architecture of, 774
Boratav (Pertev Naili) at, 492
Ecevit (Bülent) at, 745
Güney (Yilmaz) at, 955
vs. Istanbul University, 1196
Kurdistan Workers Party at, 1343
Sezer (Ahmet) at, 2015
Women's Studies Center of, 2362
ANM. *See* Arab National Movement
Annaba (Algeria), **208**
French occupation of, 208
steel industry in, 208
Annan, Kofi A., **208–209**
and Economic and Social Commission for Western Asia, 2277
envoy sent to U.S.-occupied Iraq by, 2326
on Shabʿa Farms, 2017
on U.S. war in Iraq (2003), 2325
in Western Sahara peace process, 2344
Annunciation, Nazareth as site of, 1673
Annunciation, Greek Orthodox Church of the (Nazareth), 1673
Annunciation, Roman Catholic Church of the (Nazareth), 1673
ANP. *See* Armée Nationale Populaire
ANPA. *See* Armée Nationale Populaire Algérienne
Anqa, al- (Awad), 341
Ansar, al- (Sudan), **209–210**
Abd al-Rahman al-Mahdi and, 209–210
during Anglo–Egyptian period, 209–210
Baggara Arabs as, 1335
in independent Sudan, 2101
Numeiri (Muhammad Jaʿfar) attack on, 210, 2261
Numeiri (Muhammad Jaʿfar) opposed by, 1699–1701
during Turko–Egyptian period, 209
in Umma Party, 210, 2260, 2261
Ansar, al- (Medinese helpers), 1595
Ansari, Shaykh Morteza, 1490
Antakya (Turkey), **210–211**
French occupation of, 210
Antar, Ali Ahmad Nasir, **211**
Anti-Atlas Mountains, 901
Anti-Defamation League, and Bʾnai Bʾrith, 489
Antioch (Turkey). *See also* Antakya (Turkey)
patriarchate of, 590, 591
textile mills in, 2181
Antioch Orthodox Church, 738
Antisemitism, **211–213**
in Algeria
antidefamation organization against, 619
Crémieux Decree and (1870), 648
anti-Zionism and, 212, 1233
Christianity and, 211–212
definition of, 211
in France, 1021, 2433
Dreyfus affair and (1894), 723
and German nationalism, Hess (Moses) on, 1024
in Germany
LICA against, 1415–1416
LISCA against, 1416
in Iraq, Farhud (1941), 807–808
Islam and, 212
Labor Zionism as answer to, 1360
motivations for, 211–212
origin of term, 211
in Ottoman Empire, of Azuri (Najib), 352
in *Protocols of the Elders of Zion,* 1856
in Syria, in Damascus affair (1840), 212, 664–665
during World War I, American Jewish Congress work against, 178
and Zionism, development of, 2432
Anti-Taurus Mountains, 902, 2167
Anti-Zionism
of American Council for Judaism, 176
antisemitism and, 212, 1233
in British government, 518
of Bund, 544
of Israeli Communist Party, 1373
of Matzpen, 1500–1501, 2221
in Meah Sheʿarim, 1506
Muntada al-Adabi, al- in, 1611
Muslim Brotherhood in, 1621
Nasir (Najib) in, 1646
Neturei Karta in, 1677
in Palestine, under British rule, 1761–1762
of Palestinian Arab Congresses, 1782
among Palestinians, origins of, 1789
riots during Nabi Musa Pilgrimage (1920), 1630
Antonius, Albert, 213
Antonius, Constantine, 213
Antonius, George, **213–215,** 1460–1461
and Fertile Crescent unity, 825
and historiography, 1035
in Institute for Current World Affairs, 214, 647
at London Conference (1939), 214, 1766
at Victoria College, 213, 2315
Antonius, Habib, 213
Antonius, Katy Nimr, 214
Antonius, Michael, 213
Antun, Farah, **215**
Anya-Nya, 2103
Anzimat al-Taʿlim wa al-Hukm fi rif Filastin (Khalidi), 1294

Aoun, Michel, **215–216**
Chamoun (Dany) supporting, 581
Eddé (Raymond) supporting, 754
in exile, 215, 1492
as interim president, 215, 1393, 1394, 1400
in Lebanese Civil War, 215
as prime minister, appointment of, 1253
Sfeir (Nasrallah) persecuting, 2016
Syrian ejection of, 215
Ta'if Accord and, 2148
Aozou Strip, **216**
API. *See* American Petroleum Institute
APN. *See* Assemblée Populaire Nationale
APOC. *See* Anglo–Persian Oil Company
Apocrypha, Biblical Hebrew in, 1017
Apollonius, 116
Apostasy, 2049
Apostu, George, 556
Appelfeld, Aharon, *216*, **216–217**, 1433
Apple, The (Iranian film), 1473
APSAD. *See* Association for the Protection of Natural Sites and Ancient Buildings
Aqaba (Jordan), **217**
in Arab Revolt (1916), 510
map of, *217*
peace negotiations at (2003), 32
port of, 217
tourism in, 217–218
Aqaba, Gulf of, **217–218**, 901, 1675
aerial view of, *901*
in Arab–Israel War (1967), 1651
map of, *218*
Strait of Tiran connecting Red Sea and, 2191
Aqaba incident (1906), **218**
Aqalliyat faction (Feda'iyan-e Khalq), 821
Aqayl tribe, 2209
Aql (reason), 834
Kadivar (Mohsen) on, 1262
Aql, Sa'id, **218–219**
Phoenicianism of, 1834
Aqqad, Abbas Mahmud al-, 1419
Aqqad, Umar Abd al-Fattah al-, **219**
Aqsa Fida'iyyun Front, al-. *See* Popular Front for the Liberation of Palestine–General Command
Aqsa Intifada, al- (2000), **219–220**, 871
Arafat (Yasir) in, 219, 272, 1727
and Barak's (Ehud) political defeat, 399
Barghuthi (Marwan) supporting, 402
benefits related to, 1793
casualties of, 220, 1793
causes of, 219, 1793
civilians targeted in, 219
economic impact of, 220, 1162
and Gaza City's economy, 869
and Gaza Strip's economy, 870
HAMAS in, 219, 2381
impact on peace process, 220
Islamic Jihad in, 1155
Israeli response to, 219–220, 1793
military *vs.* political, 1174
occuping Nablus, 1631
occupying Bethlehem, 468
Jenin in, 1221
League of Arab States on, *1387*
Mossad failure to anticipate, 1579
Nabi Musa Pilgrimage forbidden during, 1630
in Nazareth, 1673
nonviolence in, 219
PFLP in, 1840
al-Qassam Brigades during, 983
Ramallah during, 1901
start of, 2178
demonstrations in, 219
Sharon's visit to Haram al-Sharif in, 219, 992, 1226–1227, 1727, 1793
suicide bombings in, 219, 1169, 1793
United Nations in, 2284
Vatican and, 2310
in West Bank, 2340–2341
Aqsa Martyrs Brigade, al- (Palestine), suicide bombings by, 219
Aqsa Martyrs of the World Islamic Front for Liberation, al- (Egypt), 1215
suicide bombings by, 814
Aqsa Mosque, al- (Jerusalem), 991, *991*
Abdullah I ibn Hussein assassination at, 31
arson in, 1226
construction of, 1222
Aquifers, 2329
in deserts, 702
drawing down of, 2330, *2331*
equity in use of, 2332
Israeli, 1668–1669, 2329
Aqura (Lebanon), *1397*
Arab(s), **220–223**
definition of, 220, 221
Islamic, 220, 221
nationalism among (*See* Arab nationalism)
vs. Turks, 221
Arab Academy of Damascus, **223–224**
Kurd Ali (Muhammad) and, 223, 1338
Arab Afghans, al-Takfir wa al-Hijra in, 2151
Arab Americans, in film industry, 98–99
Arab Apocalypse, The (Adnan), 47
Arab Army. *See* Arab Legion
Arab Association for Human Rights, Khader (Asma) in, 1291
Arab Awakening, The (Antonius), 213, 214, 647
Arab Bank, 390
Arab Banking Corporation, 390
Arab boycott, **224–225**
Arab Bulletin, 225
Arab Bureau (Cairo), **225**
Sykes (Mark) in, 2127
Arab Charter on Human Rights (1994), 1385
Arab Club (Palestinian nationalist organization), **225–226**
Club National Israélite and, 612
Habash (George) and, 962
Husayni (Muhammad Amin al-) in, 1056
Arab Collective Security Pact (1952), Jordan accepting, 2152
Arab College of Jerusalem, **226–227**
Khalidi (Ahmad al-Samih al-) at, 226–227, 1294
Sabbagh (Hasib) at, 1952
Arab Commission of Human Rights, Marzouki (Moncef) in, 1497
Arab Congresses. *See also* Palestinian Arab Congresses
first (1913), Darwaza (Muhammad Izzat) in, 673
Arab Contractors (firm), 2305
Arab Convention for the Suppression of Terrorism (1998), 1385
Arab Convention on Human Rights, 1048

Arab Council for Childhood and Development, 1952
Arab Cultural Establishment, 1952
Arab Democratic Party (Israel), 1178–1180
Arab Democratic Party (Lebanon), in National Front, 1656–1657
Arab Deterrent Force (ADF)
  countries contributing troops to, 432
  establishment of, *1387*
  Sarkis (Ilyas) attempting to disarm, 1992
  sent to Lebanon, 1387
Arab Development Society (ADS), Alami (Musa al-) in, 103
Arabeshot (Shammas), 2029
Arabesques (Shammas), 2029
Arab Executive (AE) (Palestine), 1402, 1973
  Arab Club and, 226
  election by Palestinian Arab Congress, 1782, 1783
  end of, 1764, 1783
  establishment of, 1762
  Husayni (Musa Kazim al-) in, 1224, 1764, 1782, 1783
  leadership of, 1224, 1764, 1782, 1783
  Palestine Arab Party and, 1765
Arab Federation, cabinet of, Hashim (Ibrahim) in, 999
Arab Federation (weekly), 917
Arab Feminist Union, **227–228,** 2031
Arab film, 832, 833
Arab Film Company, 832
"Arab Government of Moab," 1470
Arab Higher Committee (AHC) (Palestine), **228–229**
  and All-Palestine Government, 154, 228
  British ban on, 1766
  Cattan (Henry) in, 570
  Darwaza (Muhammad Izzat) in, 673
  Darwish (Ishaq) in, 673
  establishment of, 228, 1765
  Ghuri (Emile al-) on, 917
  Hilmi (Ahmad) in, 1030
  Husayni (Jamal al-) in, 1055
  information offices under, Alami (Musa al-) and, 103
  Khalidi (Husayn Fakhri al-) in, 1295
  at Lausanne Conference (1949), 1375
  Nashashibi (Raghid al-) on, 1645
  Palestine Arab Revolt led by (1936–1939), 1765–1766, 1770
  Peel Commission partition plan rejected by, 228, 1811
  revival of, 1766
  Saba (Fuʾad) as secretary to, 1951
  UN partition plan rejected by, 1766, 2274
Arab Higher Front, Arab Higher Committee opposed by, 1766
Arab Human Development Report
  gender imbalance initiatives by, 879
  on importance of education of women, 879
  on women in labor force, 877
Arab Human Rights Organization, 1952
Arabi, al- (journal), 1682
Arabia Felix. *See* Yemen
Arabia Insurance Company, 1951
Arabian American Oil Company (ARAMCO), **229–230**
  company towns established by, 2300
  establishment of, 229
    Abd al-Aziz ibn Saʿud Al Saʿud in, 11
  Saudi relations with, 229–230
  Saudi takeover of, 230, 1830
  success of, 229
  Trans-Arabian Pipeline of, 2202–2203
  TV programs broadcast by, 1895
  during World War II, 1935
Arabian Desert, subdivisions of, 701
Arabian Gulf. *See* Persian Gulf
Arabian horses, **230–231**
Arabian Mission, **231,** 1551, 1854
"Arabian Nights, The," Burton (Richard Francis) translating, 548
Arabian Peninsula, **231–232**. *See also* Persian Gulf
  under British control, 526–527, 530–534
  geography of, 231, 970
  Greeks in, 938
  Islam in, origins of, 1144
  oil production in, 231
  tribes of, 231–232, 2209–2215 (*See also specific tribes*)
    consolidation of, 231–232
    warfare between, 232
Arabian Sea, 231
Arabic alphabet, 234, *234*, 235, 2250
Arabic coffee, 837
Arabic folk culture, 1419, 1421
Arabic language, **232–234**
  in Algeria
    Arabization policies on, 124, 254–256
    declared as foreign language (1938), 1422
    literature in, 273, 1424, 1425, 1426
    as official language, 122, 255
    prevalence of, 121
  Arabization policies on, 124, 254–256
  and Arab nationalism, 261
  Arab unity based on, Husari (Sati al-) on, 1051
  Beja using, 433
  Berber languages borrowing from, 463
  classical style of *(Fusha)*, 232, 233
  development of, 233–234
  dialects of, 232–233
  in Egypt, 233, 763
  emergence of Islam and, 221, 232, 1419
  in Gaza Strip, 870
  Hebrew relationship to, 232
  in Iraq, 233
  in Israel, 1163
  in Jordan, 1242
  journalism in, 1419
  in Judeo-Arabic language, 1252
  modernization of, 1556
  in Morocco, 1567
    Arabization policies on, 254–256
    literature in, 1424, 1425, 1428
  origins of, 233–234
  in Ottoman Empire, translation by dragomans, 723
  on postage stamps, 1850
  prevalence of, 232, 234
  Qurʾan and, 232, 233–234, 1419
Rasafi (Maʿruf al-) study of, 1903
  reformation of modern usage of, 920
  in Saudi Arabia, 1997
  as Semitic language, 220, 232, 2010
  spread of, 232
    among non-Arabs, 221
    and trade, 2197
  in Sudan, 2099

in Syria, at Arab Academy of Damascus, 223–224
Tahtawi (Rifaʿa al-Rafi al-) translating works into, 2146–2148
in Tunisia, 717, 1422, 2226
Arabization policies on, 254–256
literature in, 1424, 1425, 1428
in Turkey, Alevi Shiʿites of, 113
written, in calligraphy, 558–559
in Yemen, 2388
Arabic literature. *See* Literature, Arabic
Arabic music, 324, 336, 1617–1620
Arabic script, **234–235**
alphabet of, 234, *234*, 235
ambiguity of, 234–235
as art, 232, 235
Azeri language in, 347
in calligraphy, 232, 235, 558–559
diacritical marks in, 234, 235
vs. Hebrew, 232, 234
in Persian script, 1820, 1821–1822
on postage stamps, 1850
in Qurʾan, 234
and Turkish language, 1932, 1933
types of, 235, 558
Arab identity, Ishaq (Adib) on, 1143
Arabi, Muhyi al-Din ibn al-, 2112
Arab Information Office, 2062
Arab Intellect Forum, 1952
Arab Investment Company, Aqqad (Umar Abd al-Fattah al-) at, 219
Arab–Israel conflict, **235–239**
al-Aqsa Intifada impact on, 220
antisemitism in, 212
Arafat (Yasir) in, 270–272
Israel recognized by, 271, 1725
archaeological sites in, 278–279
CIA involvement in, 573
during Cold War, 2175–2176
al-Fatah in, 813–814
fidaʾiyyun in, 831, 2176
films on, 833
France and, 846–847
Haganah in, 972
Hizbullah in, 2177
Holocaust imagery and, 1042
Institute for Palestine Studies on, 1099
Israel in, 1165–1168
before Israeli statehood, 235–236
in Jenin, 1221
Jordan in
Abdullah II ibn Hussein representing, 32
under Hussein ibn Talal, 1064
Land Day (strike), 1369
land-for-peace principle in
in Camp David Accords (1978), 560, 561
Rogers Peace Initiative (1970) and, 1930
Lausanne Conference (1949) held to resolve, 1375–1376
mutual recognition in, 271, 1167, 1725–1726, 1768
Operation Alpha in, 157
Organization of African Unity on, 1718
origins of, 235
Palestinian refugee question in, 1915, 1916
partition plans in (*See* Partition plans)
peace negotiations in, 238, 1166–1168, 2177–2178 (*See also specific events*)
Allon (Yigal) in, 153
Arafat (Yasir) in, 271–272
Baker Plan, 374
Barak (Ehud) and, 399
Barghuthi (Marwan) supporting, 402
Bernadotte (Folke) and, 466, 2274
bilateral, 319, 1768
Bourguiba (Habib) and, 502
Brookings Report (1975) and, 539
Bush (George Walker) and, 549
Clinton (Bill) in, 606
Dayan (Moshe) in, 682–683
Dulles (John Foster) in, 733
Fahd Plan, 795, 796, *1387*, 1388
Gulf Crisis and (1990–1991), 1792–1793
HAMAS opposition to, 983
Hammarskjöld (Dag) in, 986
Islamic Jihad opposing, 1155
Jarring (Gunnar) in, 1219
Jordan in, 1245–1246
Kennedy (John F.) in, 1288–1289
Kissinger (Henry) in, 1689
Mossad in, 1579
Muasher (Marwan) in, 1593
Mubarak (Husni) in, 1594
Netanyahu (Benjamin) in, 1677
Nixon (Richard Milhous) in, 1689
Nusayba (Sari) in, 1706
Powell (Colin) in, 1852
Qaddumi (Faruq) opposing, 1863
Qurai (Ahmad Sulayman) in, 661
Reagan Plan (1982) and, 1907–1908
Rogers (William) in, 1689
Sartawi (Issam) in, 1992–1993
Sasson (Eliyahu) in, 1993
Saudi Peace Plan of Crown Prince Abdullah, *1387*
Spain as mediator in, 2084
Taba negotiations (1995, 2000), 2140
war on terrorism hurting, 2178
women in, 893
PLO in, 2175–2176
political solution to
agreement on need for, 1725
failure of, 1726
groups opposing, 1917
on postage stamps, 1850
press coverage of, Israeli *vs.* Palestinian, *1679*
Shamir (Yitzhak) in, 1725
Soviet policies on, 1943
terrorism in, 2175–2178
and trade, 2201
Tripartite Declaration (1950) and, 2215
two-state solution to
PFLP support for, 1840
PLO support for, 1774
public support for, 1793
in Road Map (2003), 1170
United Nations in, 2274–2277, 2284
U.S. policies on
Baker (James A.) and, 374
under Clinton, 606
under Eisenhower, 2291
under Johnson, 1238
under Kennedy, 2291–2292
under Nixon, 2292
Vatican agreement on, 2310
water resources in, 1248–1249
Arab–Israeli General Armistice Agreements (1949), 236, **239–242**, 244, 1165
declared null and void by Israel (1974), 1553
duration of, 239
Egypt in, 239–240, 244
Jordan in, 240–241
Lebanon in, 240
Mixed Armistice Commissions supervising, 1552–1553
Syria in, 241
UN Truce Supervision Organization monitoring of, 236, 241, 244, 1552–1553

Arab–Israel War (1948), 236, **242–244,** 1537
Alami (Musa al-) during, 103
Arafat (Yasir) in, 269
Avnery (Uri) on, 340
Bar-Lev (Haim) in, 407
Ben-Gurion (David) in, 448
Ben-Porat (Mordechai) in, 452
Bethlehem during, 468
Britain in, 518
casualties of, 242, 244, 1795
Dayan (Moshe) in, 681
Egypt in, 242
defeat of, 236, 243, 766, 810
Eitan (Rafael) in, 774
Galilee in, 865
Gaza City in, 869
Gaza Strip in, 870
General Armistice Agreements ending (1949), 236, 239–242, 244, 1165, 2274
Gilboa (Amir) in, 920
Glubb (John Bagot) in, 922
and Green Line, 942
Grossman (Haika) in, 944
Guri (Chaim) in, 956
Haganah in, 973
Haifa during, 974
Harkabi (Yehoshafat) during, 995
Hawrani (Akram al-) in, 1010
Hebrew University of Jerusalem after, 1018
Hebron after, 1019
Herzog (Chaim) in, 1022
Husayni (Abd al-Qadir al-) in, 1054
impact on Arab world, 244
Iraq in, 242–243
Qasim (Abd al-Karim) from, 1872
Israel in, 1165
arms of, 304
military forces of, 242, 243, 1770, 1790, 1795
Palmah of, 1795
reasons for victory of, 1767, 1790
territorial expansion by, 236, 242, 243–244
Jaffa in, 1141
Jenin in, 1220–1221
Jerusalem in, 31, 681, 1224
King David Hotel of, 1324
Jordan in, 35, 242–243, 518, 1224, 1244
Arab Legion of, 31, 243, 257, 1224
Nablus (West Bank) occupation by, 1631
League of Arab States in, Arab Liberation Army of, 259, 1879–1880
Majali (Habis) in, 1470
military resources in, Palestine Arab Revolt and (1936–1939), 1770, 1790
Mount Scopus during, 966
Muslim Brotherhood in, 395, 1621
Naguib (Muhammad) in, 1634
Najjada in, 1638
Namir (Orah) in, 1641
Nazareth in, 1672–45
Ne'eman (Yuval) in, 1674
Negev in, 1675
Nuqrashi (Mahmud Fahmi al-) in, 1701
oil pipelines damaged in, 1138
Palestinian citizens of Israel after, 1785
Palestinian refugees from, 236, *243,* 244, 1639–1640, 1767, 1790, 1915, *1915,* 2287
Truman administration on, 2220
potash industry after, 1851
Qalqiliya (West Bank) after, 1869
Rabin (Yitzhak) in, 1891
Ramla in, 1901
Safed in, 1962
Saudi Arabia in, 1626
Shamir (Moshe) in, 2024
Sharon (Ariel) in, 2041
Shenouda III in, 2048
Shiloah (Reuven) in, 681
start of, 242, 1165
Syria in, 242
action-oriented politics after, 1486
Tiberias during, 2188
Transjordan after, 1061–1062
truces called in, 243, 244
UNCCP mediating between parties in, 1375–1376, 2274
United Nations in, 2274
mediation by, 2274
partition plan of (1947), 1790
Yad Mordekhai in, battle at, 2377
Arab–Israel War (1956), 237, **244–246,** 1537
Bar-Lev (Haim) in, 407
Britain in, 244–246
British *vs.* U.S. role in region after, 246
casualties of, 246
causes of, 244–245
cease-fire in, 246
Dulles (John Foster) and, 733
Eden (Anthony) in, 755
Egypt in, 236–237, 244–246
military forces of, 245–246
Nasser (Gamal Abdel) and, 1650
National Union as outgrowth of, 1667
Suez Canal and, 244–245, 1650
events leading up to, 2291
France in, 244–246, 847
Gaza Strip in, 871
Israel in, 244–246, 1165
Sharm al-Shaykh captured by, 2040
Kafr Qasim massacre before, 1262
Mixed Armistice Commissions weakened by, 1553
Ne'eman (Yuval) in, 1674
oil pipelines destroyed in, 1138
oil production during, 2203
Qalqiliya (West Bank) in, 1869
Sharon (Ariel) in, 2041
Soviet Union and, 245, 246
start of, 245–246, 2014
United Nations in
Emergency Force of, 246, 1165
truces called for by, 245
United States in, 245–246
Arab–Israel War (1967), 237, **246–250,** 1537
Amit (Meir) in, 190
Arab demands after, reduction of, 249
Arab League summit after, *1387*
Arab nationalism in, 248, 249
Ben-Gurion (David) in, 449
Britain in, 521
buildup to, 248
casualties of, 249
causes of, 246–248
cease-fire in, 249, 2275
Dayan (Moshe) in, 682
effects of, 237, 249
Egypt in, 237, 248–249
Eshkol (Levi) in, 785
fall of Libyan government after, 1506
al-Fatah in, 270
and fida'iyyun, 831
Gaza City in, 869
Gaza Strip in, 871
Ghorbal (Ashraf) in, 915
Golan Heights in, 925
and Green Line, 942
Guri (Chaim) in, 956
Gur (Mordechai) in, 956
Hebrew University of Jerusalem after, 1018
Hebron after, 1019
Herzog (Chaim) on eve of, 1022

Iraq in, 248, 287
Israel in, 246–249, 1165–1166, 1225
internal politics after, 249
preemptive strikes by, 237, 248–249
seizure of West Bank by, 1651, 2339, 2340
Sharm al-Shaykh captured by, 2040
territories conquered by, *247*, 248–249, 1166, 1417, 1791
victory of, 237, 249
in Jerusalem, 249, 1224–1225
Jordan in, 237, 248–249, 1224–1225, 2157
Arab Legion of, 258, 1225
Jordan River in, 248
Leibowitz (Yeshayahu) on, 1403
Likud on, 1417
Majali (Habis) in, 1470
map of, *247*
Moda'i (Yitzhak) in, 1555
Mossad in, 1578
Nasser (Gamal Abdel) in, 1651
Nezzar (Khaled) in, 1686
Palestinian citizens of Israel after, 1787
Palestinian refugees from, 1270, 1791, 1916
Palestinian refugees in, 248
in Qalqiliya (West Bank), 1869
Rabin (Yitzhak) in, 1891
Ramallah in, 1901
and Saudi Arabia, 799
Sharon (Ariel) in, 2041
Soviet Union in, 248, 508
Syria in, 237, 248–249
United Nations in, 249, 2275
U.S. neutrality in, 1238
MacNamara (Robert) and, 190
U.S. response to, Rusk (Dean) and, 1941
water resources after, 1248–1249
Arab–Israel War (1973), 237–238, **250–252,** 1537
Abdelghani (Mohamed Benahmed) in, 23
agreements ending, 238
Allon (Yigal) in, 153
Arab League summit on, *1387*
Barak (Ehud) in, 398
Bar-Lev (Haim) in, 408
Britain in, 522
casualties of, 250, 251, 252
causes of, 250
cease-fire in, 250, 1166, 2275
Dayan (Moshe) in, 682
Egypt in, 237–238, 250–252, 1957
Geneva Peace Conference (1973) ending, 900
Hareven (Shulamit) in, 993
Hebrew literature after, 1433–1434
Israel in, 250–252, 1166
attitude toward concessions after, 252
equipment used by, 1527
internal politics after, 252
territorial gains by, 250–251, 1166
territorial losses of, 238, 250, 251
Jordan in, 258
Meir (Golda) in, 1514–1515
Mixed Armistice Commissions ended after, 1553
Mossad warning about, 1579
Mubarak (Husni) in, 1593
and oil prices, 522, 2201
Palestinians in, attitude toward diplomacy after, 1792
peace negotiations in, 251–252, 1166
disengagement agreements in, 251–252, 1166, 1291
Kissinger (Henry) in, 251–252, 1328, 1957
al-Sa'iqa in, 1972
Saudi response to, 251
Sharon (Ariel) in, 2041
Shazli (Sa'd al-Din al-) in, 2048
Soviet Union in, 250
economic support to Egypt by, 748
supporting Arabs, 508
start of, 250
Syria in, 237–238, 250–252, 2135
Asad (Hafiz al-) and, 250, 251, 318
United Nations in, 250, 2275
United States in, 250, 1689
economic support to Israel by, 748
weapons supplied to Israel by, 250, 251, 799
U.S.–Soviet relations during, 2292
victory claims in, 251
Arab–Israel War (1982), 238, **252–254,** 1537
and Begin (Menachem), 426
Beirut in, *429*, 430
border disputes in, 240, 252
casualties of, 254, 1393, 1400, 1792
causes of, 252
cease-fires in, Habib (Philip Charles) and, 964
effects of, 254
Eitan (Rafael) in, 774
Hizbullah created in reaction to, 1037
Israel in, 252–254, 1166–1167
invasion by, 252–253
Lebanon in, 238, 252–254, 1537
General Armistice Agreement and (1949), 238
MAPAM opposing, 1185
Palestinians in, 1792
peace agreement in, 253–254, 1167
failure of, 240, 254, 1167
Habib (Philip Charles) and, 964
Kimche (David) in, 1322
Syrian opposition to, 318
Peace Now opposing, 1809
Phalange in, 252–254
PLO in, 238, 252–254, 426, 1166–1167, 2176
Arab Liberation Front of, 259
Arafat (Yasir) and, 270–271
Sabra and Shatila massacres in, 254, 1039, 1954–1955
Sharon (Ariel) in, 1537, 2042
planning of, *1392*, 2042
Syria in, 252, 964
United States in, 253–254
Arabiyya, al- (TV station), and Arab nationalism, 223
Arabiyyat, Abd al-Latif, in parliament, 1151
Arabiyyat, Ghazi, in Karama, Battle of (1968), 1270
Arabization policies, **254–256**
in Algeria, 124
Arab League. *See* League of Arab States
Arab League summits, **256–257,** *1387*
Alexandria (1964), *1387*
Algiers (1973), *1387*
Amman (1980), *1387*
Amman (1987), *1387*
Amman (2001), *1387*
Baghdad (1978), 363–364, *1387*, 2121
Baghdad (1990), *1387*
Beirut (2002), *1387*
Cairo (1948), *155*
Cairo (1964), *1387*, 1777
Cairo (1976), *1387*
Cairo (1995), *1387*
Cairo (2000), *1387*
Casablanca (1965), *1387*

Arab League summits *(continued)*
Casablanca (1985), *1387*
Casablanca (1988), *1387*
Casablanca (1989), *1387*
Fez (1981, 1982), 796, *1387*
Khartoum (1967), *1387*
Nasser (Gamal Abdel) at, 1651
Rabat (1969), *1387*
Rabat (1974), *1387*
Sharm al-Sheikh (2003), *1387*
summary of outcomes, *256*
Tunis (1979), *1387*
Arab Legion (Jordan), **257–259**
under Abdullah I ibn Hussein, 257, 1810
Abu Nuwwar (Ali) in, 38–39, 257–258
in Arab–Israel War (1948), 31, 243, 257, 1224
in Arab–Israel War (1967), 258, 1225
bedouins in, 922
under British mandate, 257, 1810
Camel Corps of, *258*
decline in importance of, 258
Druzes in, 729
equipment of, *1534*
establishment of, 257, 1810
force levels of, *1528–1529*, 1529
force structure of, *1532–1533*
Glubb (John Bagot) in, 257, 519, 921–922, 1810, 2204
under Hussein ibn Talal, 257–258, 519
in Karama, Battle of (1968), 258, 1270–1271, 1773
Majali (Habis) in, 1470
Peake (Frederick Gerard) in, 257, 922, 1810
vs. Transjordan Frontier Force, 2204
in World War II, 257
Arab Liberation Army (Arab League), **259**
in Arab–Israel War (1948), 259, 1879–1880
Husayni (Abd al-Qadir al-) in, 1052
Qawuqji (Fawzi al-) in, 259, 1879–1880
Arab Liberation Front (ALF) (PLO faction), **259–260**, 1773
in Rejection Front, 1917
Arab Maghreb Union (AMU), **260**, 439, 2343
formation of, 1566
Mauritania's alignment with, 1503
Arab Monetary Fund, 749
Arab Movement for Renewal. *See* TAʿAL
Arab National Bank, founding of, 1030
Arab nationalism, 221–223, **260–262**, 1658–1659, 1659. *See also* Pan-Arabism
of Abd al-Hadi (Awni), 13
of Aflaq (Michel), 68, 69–70
Allenby (Edmund Henry) support for, 151
anti-Zionism in, 1233
in Arab Feminist Union, 227–228
Arabic language and, 261
in Arab–Israel War (1967), 248, 249
in Arab Revolt (1916), 221, 262–264
barriers to, 222, 261–262
current status of, 222–223, 262
of Darwaza (Muhammad Izzat), 673
decline of, 260–261, 262
definition of, 222, 260
in Egypt, Suez Canal nationalization and, 222, 1065
al-Fatat and, 815
Fertile Crescent unity plans, 824–826
French support for, in Popular Front, 1839
Husari (Sati al-) and, 1051
Husayn ibn Ali and, 1052–1053
in Iraq, 801
and Qasim (Abd al-Karim), 1873
in Jordan, 1244
of Kawakibi (Abd al-Rahman al-), 261, 1282
in Libya, 1412
Revolutionary Command Council and, 1921
during mandate system, 261–262
Misri (Aziz Ali al-) in, 1550
Muntada al-Adabi, al- in, 1611
Nabulsi (Sulayman al-) in, 1632
of Nasser (Gamal Abdel), 222, 260, 1648, 1659
vs. nation-state nationalism, 261–262, 1549, 1660
origins of, 221, 260, 261
in Ottoman Empire, 261
al-Ahd society of, 81
of Azuri (Najib), 351–352
crackdown on, 264
of Qaddafi (Muammar), 1860
qawmiyya vs. wataniyya in, 1659
of Qawuqji (Fawzi al-), 1879–1880
of Quwatli (Shukri al-), 1885–1886
in Saudi Arabia, 799, 2166
of Shaʿbi family, 2018
Shumayyil (Shibli) criticizing, 2061
spread of, 260
Suez Canal nationalization and, 1065
in Syria, Damascus, 663
vs. traditional religious or ethnic identities, 1549
vs. Turkish nationalism, 261, 263
during World War I, 1384, 2367–2368
of Yaziji (Ibrahim), 2383
vs. Zionism, 1549
in Arab–Israel conflict, 235
Arab Nationalist Congress, Mardam (Jamil) in, 1486
Arab Nationalist Party (Syria), Arsuzi (Zaki al-) in, 308
Arab National Movement (ANM), **262**
Habash (George) in, 962, 1267
Haddad (Wadi) in, 967
Hawatma (Nayif) in, 1008
Kanafani (Ghassan) in, 1267
Khaled (Leila) in, 1293
Arab National Party, 402
in United Arab List, 1189
Arab News Network, 1895
Arab Oil Congress, first meeting of, 1718
Araboui, Omar, Belhadj (Ali) under, 436
Arab Radio and Television Network (ART), 1895
Arab Regional Center for Environmental Law, 341
Arab Resurrection. *See* Baʿth party
Arab Resurrection (magazine), 482
Arab Revolt (1916), **262–265**
Abdullah I ibn Hussein in, 29
Arslan (Shakib) criticism of, 307
Askari (Jaʿfar al-) in, 324
Ayyubi (Ali Jawdat al-) in, 345
British support for, 263–264, 510, 799–800
as foreign intervention, 1103
causes of, 263, 264
Faisal I ibn Hussein in, 29, 264, 799–800, 1384
Haganah's response to, 972
Hananu (Ibrahim) in, 989
Hijaz Railroad during, 1029

Husayni (Muhammad Amin al-) in, 1056
Husayn ibn Ali in, 221, 263–264, 324, 510, 1000, 1053, 2039, 2368
Lawrence (T. E.) in, 264, 324, 510, *511*, 513, 1384
McMahon (Henry) in, 1506
Midfaʿi (Jamal al-) in, 1524
Misri (Aziz Ali al-) in, 1550
nationalism in, 221, 262–264
Qawuqji (Fawzi al-) in, 1879
Quwatli (Shukri al-) in, 1885
Storrs (Ronald) in, 2092
Wingate (Reginald) in, 2354

Arab Revolts (1936–1939). *See* Palestine Arab Revolt (1936–1939)

Arab socialism, **265–266**
Hakim (Muhsin al-) on, 977
Hanoune (Louisa) and, 990

Arab Socialist Baʿth party (Syria), 1010

Arab Socialist List (Israel), 285

Arab Socialist Party
Baʿth party merging with, 412
in National Progressive Front, 1665

Arab Socialist Renaissance Party. *See* Baʿth party

Arab Socialist Union (ASU) (Egypt), **266–267,** 767
left faction of (National Progressive Unionist Party), 1665
Nasser (Gamal Abdel) and, 1650
Sabri (Ali) in, 1955
Sadat (Anwar al-) in, 1956
Sadat's (Anwar al-) dissolution of, 1665
as successor to National Union, 1667

Arab Socialist Union (Lebanon), in National Front, 1656–1657

Arab Socialist Union (Syria)
Atasi (Jamal al-) in, 329
in National Progressive Front, 1665

Arab states, definition of, 221

Arab Studies Society, 1226

Arab summit conferences. *See* Arab League summits

Arab theater. *See* Theater, Arabic

Arab Unified Military Command, 1387

Arab unity. *See* Pan-Arabism

Arab Woman and the Palestine Problem, The (Mognnam), 1557

Arab Women's Association of Palestine (AWA), **267–268**
Arab Women's Executive Committee and, 268
Mogannam (Matiel) in, 1557

Arab Women's Conference (1944)
Abd al-Hadi (Tarab) at, 13
Shihabi (Zlikha al-) at, 2052

Arab Women's Congress (Palestine), **268**
1929 meeting of, 268

Arab Women's Council, 1975

Arab Women's Development Society (AWDS), 893

Arab Women's Executive Committee (AWE) (Palestine), **268**
Abd al-Hadi (Tarab) in, 13
Khalidi (Wahida al-) in, 268, 1296
Mogannam (Matiel) in, 1557
Shihabi (Zlikha al-) in, 2051

Arab Women's Federation, 894

Arab Women's Forum. *See* AISHA

Arab Women's Network, Women's Studies Center in, 2363

Arab Women's Solidarity Association International (AWSA), **268–269**
magazine published by, 1706
Saadawi (Nawal al-) in, 894, 1950

Arab Women's Summit, 1902

Arab Women's Union, 267
Nassar (Sadhij) in, 1648
Shihabi (Zlikha al-) in, 2051

Arab Women Writers, 805

Arafa, Muhammad ibn, 2427

Arafat Daily (Bitton), 483

Arafat, Yasir, **269–272,** *270, 813, 1784, 1861*
Abbas (Mahmud) under
as political strategist, 6
power struggle between, 7, 814, 997, 1900
as prime minister, 7
and Albright (Madeleine), *2291*
in Algeria, training for, 270
in Aqsa Intifada, 219, 272, 1727
in Arab–Israel War (1948), 269
in Arab–Israel War (1982), 270–271
Asad (Hafiz al-) in conflict with, 413
assassination of, attempted, by PFLP–GC, 1842
authoritarian rule of, 1785
Avnery (Uri) meeting with, 340, 1187
Barghuthi (Marwan) in conflict with, 402
Bush (George W.) refusing to deal with, 549
at Camp David Summit (2000), 561–563, 606, 1775
blame attributed to, 562, 1168
offer rejected by, 399, 1727
clothing of, *kaffiya* in, 610
coalition building by, 271, 1774
Dahlan (Muhammad) and, power struggle between, 661
daughter of, 272
decline in power of, 270, 271
education of, 269, 270
in Egypt, as youth, 269
Egyptian intelligence meetings with, *1103*
engineering firm of, 270
in exile, 814
in al-Fatah, 270, 813, 814, 1773
vs. Habash (George), 962
Habib (Philip) meeting with, 1975
Hasan (Hani al-) and, 997
Hasan (Khalid al-) and, 998
Hawatma (Nayif) opposition to, 1009
headquarters of, moves of, 270, 271
Husayni (Abd al-Qadir al-) aided by, 269
Hussein ibn Talal relations with, 1063
signing agreement with (1970), 2157
in Intifada (1987–1991), 271
Islamic Jihad and, 272, 1155
Israeli peace movement meetings with, Peled (Mattityahu) in, 1812
Israeli rejection of, 1169
Israel recognized by, 271, 1725
in Jericho, 272, 1775
Jordanian peace accord with, 1247
and Karama, Battle of (1968), 1271
Khalaf (Salah) work with, 270, 1292
Khalil (Samiha Salama) run against (1996), 1297
in Lebanese Civil War (1975–1990), 270
in Muslim Brotherhood, 269, 272
Nobel Peace Prize to, *1817*
in Oslo Accords (1993), 271, 1725–1726
signing of, 271, 606, *1726*
terrorism renounced by, 219

Arafat, Yasir *(continued)*
as Palestinian Authority head, 272, 1775, 1784–1785
parents of, 269
in peace negotiations, 271–272
in plane crash (1992), 271, 272
as PLO leader, 1767
election of, 270, 1773
Qurai (Ahmad) in power struggle with, 814
Rabin (Yitzhak) peace agreement with, 1892
Rajub (Jibril) as advisor to, 1900
in Ramallah compound, Israeli siege of, 272, 1775
refugee camps visited by, *1773*
Sabbagh (Hasib) supporting, 1953
Said (Edward) opposing, 1966
al-Saʿiqa rebelling against, 1972
Sartawi (Issam) as adviser of, 1992
Sharon (Ariel) relations with, 272, 1169, 2026
successors to, potential, Qaddumi (Faruq) as, 1863
suicide bombings tolerated by, 1793
as Sunni Muslim, 272
in Syria, for training, 270
terrorism denounced by, 219, 1768
terrorist actions condoned by, 2178
Tlas (Mustafa) in conflict with, 2192
UN General Assembly address by (1974), 270, 1774
U.S. relations with, 271
Wazir (Khalil al-) as aide to, 270, 2334–2336
wealth of, personal, 270
wife of, 271, 272
at Wye River Accords (1998), 606
Arafat, Zahwa, 272
Aʿraj, Wasini al-, **272–273**
Aral, Oğuz, **273**
Aramaic language, 1017, 2010
ARAMCO. *See* Arabian American Oil Company
Arani, Taqi, 104
imprisonment of, death during, 1757
Ararat, Mount (Turkey), 194, **273–274**, 2237
Khorvirap cathedral on, *297*
Ararat revolt (1927–1931), 1340
Arat, Yeşim, *as contributor,* 2170–2171, 2358
Aravah Valley (Israel), 1675
Arazi Kanunnamesi. See Land Code of 1858
Araz, Nezihe, **274**
Arch (Kabyle tribal structure), **274**
in Coordination des Archs, 638
Archaeological Museum (Istanbul), **275**
Archaeology, **275–280**
in Afghanistan, 279
biblical, 275–276, 277–278
Palestine Exploration Fund and, 1771–1772
ceramics in, 574–575
in Egypt, 275, 276
Aswan High Dam and, 327
and Egyptian Museum, 771–772
by Egyptians, 276
hieroglyphics in, 275, 581–582
Mariette (Auguste) and, 1488
Maspéro (Gaston) and, 1499
by European countries, 275–279
in Iran, 276, 277
in Iraq, 276, 277, 279
Islamic numismatics in, 1701
in Israel, 278–279, 1164, 2376
Rockefeller Museum and, 1929
in Jerusalem, 275, 278–279, 1226
in Jordan, 1218
in Kuwait, 279
in Lebanon, 276–277
by Middle Eastern countries, 276, 277
in Palestine, 275–276, 277
pan-Arabism use of, 276–277
politics of, 278–279
in Saudi Arabia, 278
in Syria, 276–277
threats to artifacts, 278–279
in Turkey, 278
museums of, 275
in United Arab Emirates, 343
Architecture, **280–284**
Aga Khan Awards for, 283, 284
in Algeria, Algiers, 139–140
Berber, 459
colonial influences on, 280–282
cost of, 284
curricula for, 284
in Egypt, 281, 282
Alexandria, 118, 282
Cairo, 282, 1074
at Muhammad Ali Mosque, 1603
ideology of, 283–284
in Iran, 282
Isfahan, 1141, 1142
in Iraq, 282
Islamic influence on, 280, 282–284
Islamic Revival, 282
in Kuwait City, *1350,* 1351
major *vs.* minor, 280
in Morocco, 282, 283–284
Casablanca, 282, 283–284
nationalist, 282
in Ottoman Empire, 280, 281, 282
Ottoman Revival, 282, 1285
in Saudi Arabia, 284
in Soviet Union, 282
in Sudan, Omdurman, 1301–1302
in Tunisia, 284
in Turkey, 284, 774, 1285
Ankara, 207, 282
Istanbul, 1193, 1194–1195
Ard, al- (Israel), **284–285**
Ardahan (Russia), 2367
Ard Habibati, Al- (Ghallab), 910
Ardsvi Vaspurakan (periodical), 1314
Arel, Sadeddin, 2124
Arens, Moshe, **285**
Are You a Transhumanist? (Esfandiary), 784
ARF (Armenian Revolutionary Federation). *See* Dashnak Party
Arfa al-Dowleh, Reza Khan, 285
Arfa, Hasan, **285–286**
Arfa, Leila, 286
Arfa, Muhammad ibn, **286–287**
as ruler of Morocco
removal of, 287
selection of, 286–287
Argentina, Jewish settlements in, 1229
Joint Distribution Committee aid to, 1239
Arghoon, Fahkr Azami, 427
Argoud, Antoine, **287**
Argov, Shlomo, attempted assassination of, 252
Aridisols, 701
Arif, Abd al-Rahman, **287,** 288
Bazzaz (Abd al-Rahman al-) under, 422
Shiʿites under, 977
Arif, Abd al-Salam, **287–288**
Arif (Abd al-Rahman) as successor to, 287, 288
Bakr (Ahmad Hasan al-) associated with, 377
Bazzaz (Abd al-Rahman al-) under, 422
in coup (1958), 15, 288
in coup (1963), 413, 1066, 1134

as deputy prime minister, 288, 1872
presidency of, 288, 1873
Qasim (Abd al-Karim) and, 287–288, 1872, 1873
Shiʿites under, 977
Arif, Arif al-, **288,** 1224
historiography of, 1791
Arish, Convention of al- (1800), **288–289**
Aristidi Paşa, 2408
Arkhas Layali (Idris), 1082
Arkoun, Mohammed, **289**
Arlosoroff, Chaim, **289–290**
Armbrust, Walter, *as contributor,* 1206–1207
Armed Islamic Group (Algeria). *See* GIA
Armée de Libération Nationale (ALN) (Algeria), **290**
Belkacem (Cherif) in, 437
Ben Bella (Ahmed) in, 442
Bendjedid (Chadli) in, 444
Boudjedra (Rachid) in, 496
Boumédienne (Houari) in, 498, 1743–1744
Bouteflika (Abdelaziz) in, 503
Brahimi (Abdelhamid) in, 506
establishment of, 131
Evian Accords (1962), 788
French campaign against, Challe (Maurice) in, 579
Hamrouche (Mouloud) in, 987
Islamic Salvation Army modeled after, 1156
Kaid (Ahmed) in, 1264
Lamari (Mohamed) in, 1365–1366
Mélouza massacre (1957) by, 438
Mouvement National Algérien and, 438, 969
Nezzar (Khaled) in, 1686
structure of, 290
Zbiri (Tahar) in, 2428–2429
Zeroual (Liamine) in, 2430
Armée Islamique du Salut (Algeria). *See* Islamic Salvation Army (AIS)
Armée Nationale Populaire (ANP) (Algeria)
Zbiri (Tahar) in, 2429
Zeroual (Liamine) in, 2430
Armée Nationale Populaire Algérienne (ANPA) (Algeria), 438
Armenia
economy of, 303
industrialization of, 303
language of, official, 302
Lausanne Treaty (1923) and, 514, 1376
population of, 302
Russian control over, 1941
Sèvres Treaty (1920) and, 1376
territory of, 301
Turkish settlement of, 301
Armenian Apostolic Church, 302
in Oriental Orthodox family, 591
origins of, 302
Ormanian (Maghakia) in, 1723
Vazhapetian (Nerses) in, 2311
Armenian Catholic Church, 592
Armenian community of Jerusalem, **290–292**
Armenian folklore, 2087
Armenian General Benevolent Union (AGBU), Nubar (Boghos) in, 1694–1695
Armenian genocide (1915–1923), **292–296,** 1613, 2440
Andranik Ozanian against, 195
Armenian resistance to, 295
Cemal Paşa in, 293, 295, 571
confiscation of wealth in, 294–295
deportations in, 294, 295
Musa Dagh resistance of, 1612–1613
in Erzurum, 783
in Iraq, 294
killing techniques used in, 294
Nubar's (Boghos) philanthropy during, 1694–1695
punishment for, 295
in Syria, 294
World War I and, 2368
Armenian language, 301–302
dialects of, 301–302
grammar of, 579
Armenian millet, **296–299,** 1543–1545
Balyan family in, 386
constitution in (1860), 298
French support for, 1544
Vazhapetian (Nerses) in, 2310
Armenian nationalism, 299–301, 1659
Armenian Orthodox Church, in Turkey, 2238
Armenian Popular Songs Translated into English (Alishan), 144
Armenian Revolutionary Federation (ARF). *See* Dashnak Party
Armenian revolutionary movement, **299–301**
leadership of, 299, 303
origin of, 299, 2311
Armenians, **301–304**
demographics of, 302
distribution of, 302
economic livelihood of, 302–303
in Egypt, under Muhammad Ali, 2415
history of
Alishan (Ghevond) on, 144
Chamchian (Mikayel) on, 303, 579
major figures in, 303
in Iran, 1548
in Jerusalem, 290–292
languages of, 301–302 (*See also* Armenian language)
in Lebanon, 975
political parties of, 1050, 1901
manuscripts of, 291, 295
migration by, 1846–1847
nationalism of, 299–301, 1659
in Ottoman Empire
Dashnak Party and, 676–677
genocide against (*See* Armenian genocide)
millet system of (*See* Armenian millet)
Nubar's (Boghos) philanthropy toward, 1694
resistance by, 195, 299–301
revolutionary movement of, 299–301, 303
poetry of, 144
population of, 302
Protestant missions and, 1854
religion of, 302
royalty of, 303
in Russia, Dashnak Party and, 676–677
in Russian–Ottoman War (1877–1878), 2311
in Syria, 2129
in Turkey, 2238
Atatürk (Mustafa Kemal) and, 1549
in World War I, 195, 2367–2368
Armenian Social Democratic Party, 299
Arms and armaments, **304–305**
in Middle East military, *1534,* 1535
NEACC and, 2215
nonconventional, 305
in China, 586
Arms control
in Arab–Israel War (1948), 304
lack of agreements on, 305

Arms industry
of Egypt, 1483
of Israel, 305, 1483
Arms races, 304
Egypt and Israel in, 236
Arms sales, 304, 1535, 2201
by Britain, 750
for balancing oil imports, 523
to Iran, 523
to Iraq, 523
to Jewish forces, 1770, 1790
NEACC and, 2215
by China, 750
to Iran, 586
to Iraq, 586
to Saudi Arabia, 586, 1535
by Czechoslovakia, to Israel, 304
by Eastern Europe
to Egypt, 412
to Syria, 412
by France, 750
to Irgun Zva'i Le'umi, 170
to Israel, 304, 2109, 2215
NEACC and, 2215
by Germany, 907
to Iran, 2201
to Iraq, 2201
regulation of, 304
to Saudi Arabia, 796, 2201
by Soviet Union, 750, 1943
to Egypt, 304, 412, 2215
to Iraq, 304, 1535, 1969
to Syria, 304, 318, 412
by United States, 750
to Afghanistan, 66
in Arab–Israel War (1973), 250, 251, 799
to Egypt, 304, 1238
to Iran, 304, 1119, 1122–1123
in Iran–Contra affair, 1119, 1122–1123
to Israel, 250, 251, 304, 799, 1238, 1288, 1331
under Johnson, 1238
to Jordan, 304
under Kennedy, 1288
Kollek (Teddy) in, 1331
to Saudi Arabia, 304
to Turkey, 304
Arnon, Yaacov, Arafat (Yasir) meeting with, 1187
Arnove, Robert, 760
Aronson, Geoffrey, *as contributor,* 2339–2341
Arrows of Islam (Soltani), 2079
Arsanjani, Hassan, appointment of, U.S. role in, 1118, 1753
Arseven, Celal Esat, **305**
Arshad, Farhad, *as contributor,* 1141–1142, 1652–1653, 2057
Arslan, Adil, **305–306**
Arslan family, **307,** 729
Jumblatt rivalry with, 307, 1255
Arslan, Majid, 307
Arslan, Shakib, **307–308**
German support for, 906
and Hadj (Messali al-), 969
Islamic congress held by, 1152
Arslan, Talal, 307
Arsuzi, Muhammad Najib al-, 308
Arsuzi, Zaki al-, **308–309**
in al-Ba'th al-Arabi, 68–69
Asad (Hafiz al-) as follower of, 316
in Ba'th party, 412
ART. *See* Arab Radio and Television Network
Art, **309–314**
abstract, 312
of Algeria, 414, 2064
installation, 1687
painting, 1687
by women, 1687
Arab women in, Niati's (Houria) depiction of, 1687
avant-garde, 313
Lebanese, 47
Palestinian, 1211
Berber, 459
calligraphy as, 145, 232, 235, 558–559
modern, 312, 2259
ceramics, 574–575
cultural identity in, 313
of Egypt, 762, 1275, 2069
Coptic, 640
cultural identity in, 313
multimedia, 176
fine, 311
folk, 311
Palestinian, 1878–1879
government support for, 313–314
Hebrew, 469–470
historical, influence of, 310–311
installation, 312, 313, 1676, 1687
institutions of, 312
of Iran, 2011
carpets as, 566
multimedia, 1676
Musavi (Mir-Hosain) and, 1615–1616
by women, 1676
of Iraq, 1978–1979
avant-garde, 997
cultural identity in, 313
exhibition on, 805
exhibitions on, 337
multimedia, 205–206
by women, 337
Islamic
historical, 310
modern, 312
representations in, 311–312
of Israel, 70–71, 1163–1164, 2144
of Jordan, 144–145, 2001
of Lebanon, 47, 556, 916, 1294
of Morocco, 2155
museums of, 312
Orientalism in, 311, 1722
of Ottoman Empire, 143, 2008–2009
Palestinian, 1007–1008, 2044
patronage of, 312, 313–314
of Sudan, 1142
Sufism and, 2113
of Syria, 2259
trends in, 312–313
of Tunisia, 1308–1309
Turkish, 34, 96, 305, 790, 1262
cultural identity in, 313
painting, 1595, 1674
Western exposure to, 313–314
Western influences on, 310, 313–314
Artawiya, al- (Ikhwan settlement), 2213, 2214
Arts Academy (Cairo), Zayyat (Latifa) at, 2428
Aruch, 1960
Arusa, al- (magazine), 1374
Aruz, 2180
Arvandrud. *See* Shatt al-Arab
Aryana (journal), 2166
Asadabadi, Jamal al-Din, 411
As'ad, Ahmad, **314,** 315, 320
As'ad, Ali Bey al-, 817
Asad, Bashshar al-, **314–315,** *413*
antisemitic statements by, 212
in Ba'th party, 413
domestic policies of, 315
election to presidency, 315, 320
foreign policy of, 315
government of, Khaddam (Abd al-Halim) in, 1291
military under, *1531*
modernization under, 315
as president, 2130, 2135
as successor to Asad (Hafiz al-), *vs.* Khaddam (Abd al-Halim), 1291
As'ad family, **315–316,** 933
leader of, 314

Asad, Hafiz al-, **316–320,** *317*
Alawi origins of, 105, 316
in Arab–Israel War (1973), 250, 251, 318
disengagement agreement after (1974), 319, 1291
in Arab–Israel War (1982), refusal to withdraw from Lebanon, 964
Arafat (Yasir) in conflict with, 413
Atasi (Jamal al-) opposition to, 329
Bakdash (Khalid) supporting, 373
in Baʿth party, 316, 317, 412–413, 1211, 2130
Clinton (Bill) meeting with, 1168
Correction Movement of, National Progressive Front established after, 1665
in coup (1963), 316, 2130, 2134
coup by (1970), 317, 330
death of, 320, 1168
and Jumayyil (Amin), 1253
domestic policies of, 317
economic policies of, 317, 319
election of, 317
foreign policy of, 317–320, 2135
government of
Attar (Nejat al-) in, 337
Khaddam (Abd al-Halim) in, 1291
guerrilla warfare banned by, 319
Hafiz (Amin al-) opposition to, 972
and Hawrani (Akram al-), 1011
Hussein (Saddam) rivalry with, 318
on Iran–Iraq War (1980–1988), 318
Jadid (Salah) and, 316, 1211
Jewish emigration promised by, 2365
and Jordanian civil war, 1247
Jumani (Dafi) ousted by, 1972
Khaddam (Abd al-Halim) friendship with, 1290, 1291
in Military Committee, 316, 1211, 2134–2135
in peace negotiations, 319, 926
on postage stamps, 1850
rise of, 316–317
sons of, 314, 320
successor to, options for, 1291
Syro-centric Arabism of, 2137
Tlas (Mustafa) and, 2191–2192
and Zuʿbi (Mahmud al-), 2443
Asʿad, Kamil, **320**
in parliament, 314, 315, 320
Asʿad Pasha (Ottoman official), 320
Asad, Rifʿat al-
ambitions of, 1291
in Hama massacre, 982
intelligence organization headed by, 1102
Asʿad, Umm Kamil, 314
Asʿad Wali, **320–321**
Asali, Sabri al-
in National Party, 1664
as vice president of UAR, 2273
Asbiʿa tribe, 2211
Asceticism, in Islam, 1149
Asefat ha-Nivharim, Zionist Revisionist Movement and, 2437
Ash, 836
Ashan (Appelfeld), 217
"Ashara al-Tayyiba, al-" (play), 675
Ashʿariyya school, 1148
Ashiqqa Party (Sudan), Azhari (Ismaʿil) in, 349, 2261
Ashira, 2210
Ashkenazic Jews (Ashkenazim), **321,** *1761*
and Halakhah, 979
Hebrew language used by, 321
in Israel, 1162–1163
first chief rabbi of, 1022
Jerusalem, 1223
number of, 321
vs. Sephardic Jews, customs of, 1251
yarmulke *(kippah)* of, 611
Yiddish language of, 321, 1163, 2399
Yosef (Ovadiah) dismissed by, 2404
Ashmawi, Muhammad Abd al-Rahman Salih al-, **321–322**
Ashmawi, Muhammad Saʿid al-, **322**
Ashour, Radwa, **322**
Ashqar, Nidal al-, 2184
Ashraf, Ahmad, *as contributor,* 418–421, 1110–1122, 1752–1757
Ashraf Musa, al- (Asadi ruler), 1044
Ashrawi, Hanan, 875, 893, *893, 1048,* 1500
Ashtiani, Mirza Hasan
and Tabatabaʾi (Mohammad), 2141
in Tobacco Revolt, 2193–2194
Ashur, 2621
Ashura (tenth of Muharram), 1605–1606
armed resistance to U.S. occupation in Iraq on, 2326
Ashurkhanah (place for storyteller), 1606
Ashur, Nuʿman, 2184
Asia, Central, oil production in, 1720
Asia Minor. *See* Anatolia
Asian and North African Studies, International Congress of, 1723
Asifa, al- (military wing of al-Fatah), 813, 814
Wazir (Khalil al-) in, 2335
Asimi, Malika al-, 1428
Asim, Necib, 2251
Asir (Saudi Arabia)
conflicting claims to, 1081–1082
political significance of, 1081
al-Taʾif Treaty (1934) on, 2149
As-Is Agreement (1928), **323**
British Petroleum attempts to break, 1719
principles of, 323
signatories of, 323
Askari, Hasan al-, 1981
Askari, Jaʿfar al-, **323–324**
at Cairo Conference (1921), 554, 1023
as defense minister, 324, 801, 1967
Askaris, 775
Asl, 2209
Aslam (section of Shammar tribe), 2214
Aslawi, Leila, 1427
Asmahan, **324,** 336
Asmak al-Barr al-Mutawahhish (Aʿraj), 273
Asmar, Fawzi al-, **324–325**
Asnaf, 419
Asnaj, Abdullah Ali
in Organization for the Liberation of the Occupied South, 857, 1717
in People's Socialist Party, 1816
Asquith, H. H., 509, 686, 1329
Asre Ma (newspaper), 1630
Assaf, Roger, 2184
Assal, Fathiyya al-, 2184
Assassins, 1159
as subdivision of Ismaʿili Shiʿism, 1158

Assemani (numismatic scholar), 1702
Assemblée Populaire Nationale (APN) (Algeria)
establishment of, in constitution of 1976, 129
expanded role of, in constitution of 1989, 130
Assembly of Experts, 428, 1987
Assembly of French–Muslim Algerians. *See* Rassemblement Franco–Musulman Algérien
Assem, Medhat, 336
Association against Imperialism (Iraq), 627
Association des Femmes Africaines pour la Recherche et le Développement (AFARD), 325
Association des Femmes Tunisiennes pour la Recherche et le Développement (AFTURD), **325**, 894
Association for Equality before the Law of Men and Women, 990
Association for Equality between Men and Women (Algeria), 2195
Association for National Defense (Turkey), 832
Association for Promoting the Discovery of Africa, 545
Association for the Defense of the Rights of Anatolia and Rumelia, 2071
Association for the Protection of Natural Sites and Ancient Buildings (APSAD), 2125
Association for the Protection of Women's Rights (Afghanistan), **325–326**
Associationism, 1144, 1259
Kaʿba in, 1259
as precursor to Islam, 1144
Association Marocaine des Droits de l'Homme, 1716
Association of Algerian Muslim Ulama (AUMA), **326**
Amis du Manifeste et de la Liberté supported by, 190
Ben Badis (Abd al-Hamid) in, 440–441, 1425
Front de Libération Nationale supported by, 326, 1076
Ibrahimi (Bashir) in, 1076
Association of Algerian Scholars, 1965, 2078
Association of Arab-American University Graduates, 1975
Association of Brotherhood and Purity. *See* Jamʿiyyat al-Ikha wa al-Afaf
Association of Lebanese Women Researchers, 367
Association of Muslim North African Students, 450
Association of Sudanese Women, 2105
Association of the Islamic Call, 1965
Association of the Islamic Future (Morocco), 1590
Association of Women Writers and Journalists, 1364
Association Tunisienne des Femmes Démocrates (ATFD). *See* Democratic Women's Association
Assyria (ancient), 326, 824
Assyrian Christians, in Turkey, 2238
Assyrian Church of the East, 326
Assyrians, **326–327**
distribution of, 326
genocide against, 326, 515
in Iraq, 2056
languages of, 326
number of, 326
patriarchs of, 2056
religion of, 326
in Turkey, 2056
Astaire, Fred, 1273
Astarabadi, Bibi Khanoum, 891
ASU. *See* Arab Socialist Union
Aswan (Egypt), **327**
Aswan High Dam, **327–328**
construction of, 327, 405, *406*, 2098
Uthman (Uthman Ahmad) and, 2305
and disease, 710, 711
environmental impact of, 327
and fertility of Nile Delta, 1688
financing for
European aid in, 327
Soviet aid in, 327
Suez Canal nationalization in, 327, 1650
irrigation from, 327
Lake Nasser created by, 1651–1652
Nubian relocation for, 1652, 1696
Philae island submerged by, 1832
power generation at, 327
U.S. support for, 327
Dulles (John Foster) and, 327, 733, 773
Eisenhower (Dwight D.) veto of, 773
refusal to provide aid, 2291
Aswat Hanjara Mayyita (al-Asimi), 1428
Atabat (Iraqi holy places), **328**
Atallah, Sanizade, 712
Ataman, Kutlug, 832
Atash-e Khamush (Daneshvar), 668
Atasi, Hashim al-, **328–329**
cabinet of, Kikhya (Rushdi al-) in, 1322
government of, Hawrani (Akram al-) in, 1010
Hinnawi (Sami al-) coup and, 1032
in negotiations for Syrian independence, 328–329, 2132
presidency of, 329
Atasi, Jamal al-, **329**
Atasi, Nur al-Din al-, **329–330**
in coup (1963), 330
in coup (1966), 330
coup against (1970), by Asad (Hafiz al-), 317, 330
Atatürk Dam, 788, 1284, 2082, 2188, *2329*
Atatürk, Mustafa Kemal, **330–334**, *332*, *333*, *2241*
in Ankara, 207, 331, *331*
assassination plot against, 332
Atay (Salih Rifki) association with, 335
authoritarian rule by, 1287
Bayar (Celal) under, 415
Bektashis supporting, 435
on caliphate, 21, 34, 332, 556, 557
in Chanak crisis (1922), 513, 1441–1442
colonialism rejected by, 614
cultural reforms of, Nazmi (Ziya) in, 1674
death of, 2240
at Dolmabahçe Palace, 719
democracy as goal of, 334
as dictator, 933
domestic policies of, 332–333
Dönme and, 720
education policies of
Village Institutes in, 2316
Yücel (Hasan Ali) and, 2413
as elite, 776
Ertuğul (Muhsin) supported by, 782
at Erzurum Congress (1919), 783
Free Republican Party founded by, 854

government of, İnönü (İsmet) in, 1097
Grand National Assembly under, 331–334, 1287
Greek relations with, in Treaty of Ankara (1930), 208
Gürsel (Cemal) supporting, 957
and Hananu (Ibrahim) revolt, 989
Hashimi (Yasin al-) influenced by, 1001
industrialization under, 1094
Islamic congress held by, 1152
at İzmir Economic Congress (1923), 1202
and Kemalism, 1285–1288
rejection of concept by, 333
and language reform, 1932–1933
at Lausanne Conference (1923), 1376
legal reform under, civil codes in, 601–602
Mevlevi Brotherhood distrusted by, 1521
military career of, 330–331, 1527
minorities redefined or eliminated by, 1549
names of, origin of, 330, 332, *332*
in nationalist movement, 1659
nation building by, 333
newspapers and print media under, 1685
Nursi (Said) and, 1705
political opposition suppressed by, 332
portrait of, 1674
on postage stamps, 1850
as president, 2240
and Republican People's Party, 1918, 2077, 2240
Republic of Turkey declared by, 332
Salonika as birthplace of, 1979
secularization by, 332, 333, 891
of law, 1383
motivations for, 333
state feminism under, 892
supporting sun language theory, 2122
tekkes closed by, 2171
theater supported by, 2187
in Turkish–Italian War, 2247
Turkish Language Academy founded by, 2250
and Turkish National Pact, 2240, 2250
in war of independence, 331–332
Adivar (Abdulhak Adnan) and, 44
Adivar (Halide Edib) and, 45
legitimacy derived from, 1285–1286
wife of, 274
in World War I, 331, 509, 2367
in World War II, 2370–2371
in Yildirim Army, 2400
Youth Day created by, dance in, 668
Yurdakul (Mehmet Emin) and, 2414
Atatürk University (Erzurum), **334**
Atay, Salih Rifki, **334–335**, 1269
Ateşten Gömlek (Adivar), 46
Ateuf, al- (Algeria), 1627
ATFD (Association Tunisienne des Femmes Démocrates). *See* Democratic Women's Association
Athanasius (Coptic patriarch), 657
Atif, Muhammad, death of, 1866
Atlas Mountains, 120, *335*, **335–336**, 901, 1567, *1568*
Atlas, Pierre M., *as contributor*, 972–973, 1018–1019, 1208–1209, 1442–1443, 1795–1796, 1972–1973, 2078, 2363, 2384–2385
At Night (Erbil), 780
A toi (Benchkroun), 1428
Atrash, Amal al-. *See* Asmahan
Atrash, Fahd al-, 324, 336
Atrash, Farid al-, **336–337**
sister of, 324, 336
Atrash, Fu'ad al-, 324, 336
Atrash, Hasan al-, 324
Atrash, Sultan Pasha al-, **337**
in exile, 337
political career of, 729
revolt led by (1925–1927), 337, 729, 1206
Attarin (herbal pharmacists), 1508
Attar, Nejat al-, **337**
Attar, Suad al-, **337–338**
Attas, Haydar Abu Bakr al-, **338**
Attiya, Abdullah bin Hamad al-, 1878
Attlee, Clement, **338**
under Churchill (Winston S.), 338
Creech Jones (Arthur) under, 338, 647
as prime minister, 338
Atuot, 1699
Atyaf (Ashour), 322
AUB. *See* American University of Beirut
AUC. *See* American University in Cairo
Auchinleck, Claude J. E., *596*
in Allied Middle East Command, 153
AUMA. *See* Association of Algerian Muslim Ulama
Auschwitz-Birkenau concentration camp, 1041
joint Arab-Jewish pilgrimage to, 1043
Australia
guest workers in, 945
in U.S. invasion of Iraq (2003), 2325
Zoroastrianism in, 2441
Austria
in Crimean War, 739
in Eastern Question, 739, 741
guest workers in, 945
Hungarian union with (1867), 339
Karlowitz Treaty (1699) and, 739
at London Convention (1840), 1444, 2093
in Peace of Paris (1856), 649
in Syrian War (1839), 741
in Vienna Congress (1814–1815), 739
Austria-Hungary, **339–340**
Balkan refugees fleeing to, 382
Berlin Treaty (1878) and, 383, 465, 528, 1989
at Budapest Convention (1877), 541
Middle East policy of, 339
Ottoman alliance with, 534
against San Stefano Treaty, 382, 465, 1989
in World War I, 742
Authoritarian form of government, 933
Autobiographie du voleur de feu (al-Bayati), 1356
Autobiography of Jurji Zaydan, The. See Mudhakkirat Jurji Zaydan (Zaydan)
Autoemancipation: A Warning of a Russian Jew to His Brethren (Pinsker), 1835
Autogestion, 442, 1372
Automobile industry, in Egypt, *1482*, 1484
Autre, l' (Chédid), 583
Aventures de Télémaque, Les (Fénelon), 2148

Averoff (battleship), 939
Averoff, George, 939
Averroes, 195, 1457, 1493
Avesta (Zoroastrian text), 2441
  Herat in, 1021
Avestan language, 1125
Avicenna, 1457
  Anawati (Georges Chehata) on, 194, 195
Avidan, David, 1432
Avierino, Alexandra, 206
Avierino, Miltiades di, 206
Avish, Shimon, *as contributor,* 1021–1022, 2357
Avnery, Uri, **340–341**
  Arafat (Yasir) meeting with, 340, 1187
Avni (magazine), 273
Avni, Hüseyin
  assassination of, 575
  military improvements under, 24
AWA. *See* Arab Women's Association of Palestine
AWACS. *See* Advanced warning and air control aircraft
Awadhi, Badria A. al-, **341**
Awad, Louis, **341**
Awakened Youth (Afghanistan), **341**
  establishment of, 62, 341
Awali, al- (Bahrain), **342**
Awali hydroelectric power station (Lebanon), 1418
Awartani, Hisham, 2121
Awazim tribe, 2209
AWC. *See* Afghan Women's Council
Awda, Abd al-Aziz
  in Islamic Jihad, 1155
  in Palestinian Authority, 1155
Awdat al-Waʿy (Hakim), 978
AWDS. *See* Arab Women's Development Society
AWE. *See* Arab Women's Executive Committee
Awlad, al- (magazine), 1374
Awlad al-balad, in mahdist state of Sudan, 1463
Awlad Sidi Shaykh. *See* Ouled Sidi Cheikh
Awn, Michel. *See* Aoun, Michel
Aws, Muhammad and, 1596
AWSA. *See* Arab Women's Solidarity Association International
"Axis of Evil," in Bush's (George W.) state of union address, 1069, 1121, 2324
Ayalon Institute, 1030
Ayan (notable people), **342**
  collecting taxes, 1367, 1368
  imposing will on sultan, 1367
  Mahmud II asserting control over, 342, 1367
Aya Sofya (Hagia Sophia) (Istanbul), **342–343**, *1730*
  rebuilding of, 342, 633
Ayatullah, 2621
Ayatullah uzma, 2070
Aydin, Cemil, *as contributor,* 954–955
Aydin, Ozgur, 477
Ayin-i cem (ritual), 113–114
Ayn (notable person). *See Ayan*
Ayn, al- (United Arab Emirates), 36, **343**
Ayn al-Dowleh, Abd al-Majid Mirza, **343**
  dismissal of, 343
    Tabatabaʾi (Mohammad) demanding, 2142
Ayn al-Rimmani incident (1975), Phalange party in, 1254
Ayni Hospital, 1958
Ayni, Muhsin al-, **343–344**
Ayn, Qurrat al-, 891
Ayn, Ras al- (Syria), **344**
Ayn Shams University. *See* Ain Shams University
Ayrarat (Alishan), 144
Aysel, Daughter of the Marshy Village (film), 782
Ayyam, Al- (Husayn), 1060
Ayyam min hayati (al-Ghazali), 915
Ayyub, Dhu al-Nun, **344**
Ayyubi, Ali Jawdat al-, **345**
  opposition to, 1283
Ayyubid dynasty (Yemen), 2397
Ayyubi, Salah al-Din ibn al-, 663
  birthplace of, 2189
  Homs captured by, 1044
Azal, Mirza Yahya Sobh-i, 356
Azar, mah-e akhar-e payiz (Golestan), 928
Azerbaijan (former Soviet republic), 345
  Azeri language in, 347
  territory ceded by Iran, 345
Azerbaijan (Iranian province), **345–346**
  autonomy movement in, 345, 346
    Democratic Party of Azerbaijan in, 346, 693–694
    Soviet support for, 345, 346
  fishing industry of, 834
  industrial activity in, 345
  languages used in, 345, 346
  literacy in, 345–346
  music of, 1617
  Naser al-Din Shah in, 1643
  pishkars of, and Mozaffar al-Din Qajar, 1591
  population of, 345
Azerbaijan crisis (1945–1946), **346**
Azeri folk culture, 428
Azeri language, **347**, 2252
  in Azerbaijan, 345, 347, 2248
  in Iran, 347, 1111
  prevalence of, 347
  written, 347
Azeri literature, 98, **347**
Azeri people, 2253
Azgaptum (Ormanian), 1723
Az Gittik Uz Gittik (Boratav), 493
Azhar, al- (Egyptian university and mosque), **347–348**, *348, 552*
  Abd al-Rahman (Umar) at, 20, 349
  Abduh (Muhammad) at, 24, 347, 1150, 2258
  Academy of Islamic Research at, 349, 1153
  and Afghan Islamic movements, 60, 63
  Banna (Hasan al-) at, 395
  Boumédienne (Houari) at, 498
  caliphate restoration opposed by, 1486
  curriculum of, 347
    criticism of, 347
    reform of, 347–348, 1457–1458
  establishment of, 347, 551, 2054
  Ghazali (Muhammad al-) at, 914
  Ilaysh (Muhammad) at, 1086
  Khalid (Khalid Muhammad) and, 1296, 1297
  leadership of, 347, 1086
  legal authority of, challenges to, 2259
  on *The Message* (film), 98
  organizational structure of, 348–349
  Qaradawi (Yusuf al-) at, 1870
  schools associated with, *1145*
  Shaltut (Muhammad) at, 2022
  Shaʿrawi (Muhammad Mutwalli al) at, 2031

Tantawi (Muhammad Sayyid al-) at, 2161
Azhari, Ismaʿil, **349–350**
in Ashiqqa Party, 349, 2261
in National Unionist Party, 349, 2261
Azib (land ownership system), 350
Aziza (film), 2192
Aziz, Shah Abd al- (India), in Naqshbandi, 1642
Aziz, Tariq, **350**
Azl (coitus interruptus), 479, 1510
Azm, Abd al-Qadir al-, in Istiqlal Party, 1198
Azm, Khalid al-, Zaʿim coup and, 2422
Azm, Rafiq al-, in Decentralization Party, 686
Azm, Sadiq al-, **350–351**
Aznar, Jose Maria, Spain's African enclaves supported by, 1516
Aznar, José María, 2084
Azodanlou, Maryam, 1900
Azov, Sea of, 739
Azuri, Najib, **351–352**
Azzabim (Brenner), 507
Azzam, Abd al-Rahman al-, **352**
as secretary-general of League of Arab States, 352, 1386
Azzam, Abdullah
bin Ladin influenced by, 474, 1865
death of, 1865
Azzan ibn Qays, 1710
Azziman, Omar, in Organisation Marocaine des Droits de l'Homme, 1716
Azzouz, Hind, 1424, 1429

B

Baader–Meinhoff group (Germany), PFLP ties with, 1839
Ba Ahmad. *See* Ibn Musa, Ahmad
Baʿalbak (Lebanon), **353**, 1044, *1399*
Baʿalbak Festival, 353
Lebanese music at, 817
Baʿalbaki, Layla, **353–354**
Baʿal Shem Tov (Besht), 1002
Ba-Aretz (Frischmann), 856
Bab, al-, **354–355**
disciples of, 354, 355
education of, 354
execution of, 355, 356
pilgrimage of, 354
Baba, 435
Baba Amine (film), 2022
Babaghanush, 841
Bab al-Aziziyya (Libya), attack on military barracks at (1984), 1655
Bab al-maftuh, al- (Zayyat), 2428
Bab al-Mandab, **355**, 527
Baban, Mufti Ahmad, 355
Babi-i Ali Tercüme Odasi. *See* Bureau of Translation
Babi movement, 354–356, **355–356**, 1548
attempting assassination of Naser al-Din Shah, 356
Baha'i faith stemming from, 356, 364
Browne (Edward Granville) interested in, 540
in Constitutional Revolution, 356
founder of, 354, 355–356
persecution of, 354–355, 356
Shaykhis becoming, 2047
Babylon, archaeological work in, 276, 277
Babylonian Jewry Heritage Center, 452
Babylonian Talmud, 2158
Bacchus Temple (Baʿalbak), 353
Baccouche, Hedi, **356–357**
in Destourian Socialist Party, 356
in Neo-Destour Party, 356
as prime minister, 356–357
Baccouche, Taieb, in Union Générale des Travailleurs Tunisiens, 2265
Backgammon, 2050
Back, Gilbert, Kan (Suna) taught by, 1269
Bactrian language, 1125
Badakhshi, Taher, in Setem-e Melli, 62
Badawi, Ahmad al-, 2113
Badawiyya (Sufi order), 2113
Badayat al-Sham al-Kubra, 2136
Bad az tabestan (Alizadeh), 149
Badeau, John, at American University in Cairo, 179
Badiya, Bahithat al-, 2431
Badiyat al-Jazira, 2136
Badiyat al-Sham. See Syrian Desert
Badoglio, Pietro, 935
and Jewish community in Libya, 974
under Volpi (Giuseppe), 2317
Badr, battle of (624), Muhammad's victory in, 1596
Badran, Mudar, **357**
Badr Khan (Kurdish amir), 1345
Badr, Liana, **357–358**
Badr, Muhammad al- (imam of Yemen), **358**
in civil war, 2396
coup (1962) deposing, 358
death of, 2390
education of, 358
exile after civil war, 2390
father of, 87
in Hamid al-Din family, 985
Jordan and Saudi Arabia supporting, 2156
reforms of, 358
reign of, 358
Badu (bedouin), in Italo-Sanusi wars, 1609–1610
Baecher, Gregory B., *as contributor*, 327–328, 690, 1651–1652, 1687–1688
Baer, Gabriel, 1035
Baggala (sailing vessel), 704
Baggara Arabs, in Kordofan, 1335
Baghdad (Iraq), **358–362**, *359*, *361*
Aflaq (Michel) tomb complex in, 70
Arabic language in, 233
Arab League summit (1978) in, **363–364**, *1387*, 2121
Arab League summit (1990) in, *1387*
area of, 361
British occupation of (1917), 361, 509
as burial place, 362
as capital of Iraq, 359, 361–362
Cemal Paşa as governor of, 571
climate of, 359
destruction of
by Hülegü Khan, 360
by Timur Lenk, 360
early history of, 359–360, 1131–1132
establishment of, 359–360, 1131–1132
Golden Age of, 360
al-Hikma University in, 1029
improvement of
by Da'ud Paşa, 360
by Madhat Paşa, 360

Baghdad (Iraq) *(continued)*
Jewish community in, 1023
Jewish quarter of, in works by Michael (Sami), 1522
location of, 359, 360
Mamluk rulers of, 1478–1479
marketplace in, *361*
modern, 361–362
origin of name of, 359
under Ottoman rule, 360
administration of, 173
Midhat Paşa and, 1525
under Persian rule, 360
population of, 360, 361, 1131, *1843*
as trade center, 360
UN headquarters in, attack on (2003), 2283
U.S. bombing of (1991), 362, *950*
U.S. capture of (2003), 2325
U.S. occupation of, 1070
Women's Museum in, 898
in World War I, 2367
in World War II, 1968
Baghdad–Basra railroad, 533–534
Baghdad–Berlin railway. *See* Berlin–Baghdad Railway
Baghdad Club, 80
Baghdad–Damascus caravan, 2205
Baghdad Group for Modern Art, 1978
Baghdadi, Abd al-Latif al-, **362–363**
as vice president of UAR, 2273
Baghdad Law College
Bazzaz (Abd al-Rahman al-) at, 421
Sharif (Aziz) at, 2037
Baghdad Military College, 1953
Baghdad Pact (1955), **363,** 826, 1693, 1942
Iran in, 363, 519, 1693
Ala (Hoseyn) representing, 100–101
Iraq in, 363, 519, 1693
under Qasim (Abd al-Karim), 1872, 1969
Saʿid (Nuri al-) supporting, 363, 1969
withdrawal of, 363, 573, 1133
Jordan in, 1470, 1471
refusing membership, 363
Lebanon refusing membership to, 363
MEDO aspects included in, 1523, 1693
member states of, 363, 519
opposition to, 363, 519
Pakistan in, 363, 519, 1693
protests against, 1925
renaming of (*See* Central Treaty Organization)
Syria refusing membership to, 363, 373
Turkey in, 1693
support for, 363, 519, 696
U.S. support for, 2291
Dulles (John Foster) in, 733
Baghdad Railway, Lansdowne (Lord) supporting, 1374
Baghdad Railway Company, 464
Baghdad Times (newspaper), 2088
Baghdad University, **364,** 1551–1552
Bagram (Afghanistan), U.S. military base in, 67
Baha al-Din al-Samuqi, 727, 728
Baha'i faith, **364–366,** *365*
Abdu'l-Baha as leader of, 365
Browne (Edward Granville) interested in, 540
on education, 365
in Egypt, 365
headquarters of, 365
holy place for, *365*
in Iran, 364, 365, 1548
in Iraq, 365
in Libya, 365
persecution of
by Islamic Republic of Iran, 365
by Pahlavi regime, 365
by Shiʿites, 365
principles of, 364–365
Rabbani (Shoghi Effendi) as leader of, 365
stemming from Babi movement, 356, 364
on women, 365
Ba-Halomi (Tchernichovsky), 2168
Baharina, **366**
Bahariya, **366**
Bahar, Malek al-Shoara, 1757
Bahar, Mohammad Taqi, **366–367,** 1436
on universal male suffrage, 1144
Baha'ullah, Hosayn Ali
and Babis, 364
Baha'i faith founded by, 364
beliefs of, 364–365
in exile, 356, 364
Bahçeli, Devlet, in Nationalist Action Party, 1661
Bahithat (Lebanon), Moghaziel (Laure) in, 1557
Bahithat (publication), 367
Bahithat al-Badiya. *See* Nassif, Malak Hifni
Bahithat al-Lubnaniyyat al-, **367**
Bahonar, Mohammad Javad, bombing against, 1119
Ba-Horef (Brenner), 507
Bahrain, *367,* **367–370,** *370. See also specific cities, organizations, people, and regions*
Al Khalifa family in, 149–150, 367–368, 369
Arabian Mission in, 231
Arab National Movement in, 262
area of, 367
Baharina in, 366
banking in, 390, *393*
border with Qatar, dispute over, 370–371, 1877
British military withdrawal from, 521
British protectorate in, 368
Al Khalifa family in, 149–150
Belgrave (Charles Dalrymple) as advisor in, 436
nationalist opposition to, 368, 371
Order in Council establishing, 372
Zubara dispute, 370
British treaties with, 149, 531, 614
Catholics in, 1931
cities of, 342, 1607
capital, 367, 1479
clothing in, women's, *610*
constitution of (1973), 368–369
revision of, 150
defense costs as percentage of GNP or GDP, *1530*
dhows in, 705
Dilmun society in, 708
economy of, 752, *753*
education in, 436, 759
elections in (2002), 370
government of, 368–369
in Gulf Cooperation Council, 949
in Gulf Crisis (1990–1991), 950
higher education in, 1292
human rights in, 1048
independence of, 368, 371, 2219
United Nations in, 2279
Iranian Revolution (1979) supported by, 368
Islamic opposition movement in, 369–370
islands of, 2071, 2263
labor unions illegal in, 368, 1358
in League of Arab States, 1387, 1388

legal system of, British influences on, 1380
legislative body in, 932
location of, 367
map of, *368*
military of
equipment of, *1534*
force levels of, *1529*
force structure of, *1532–1533*
National Assembly of, Khalaf (Abdulhadi) in, 1292
nationalism in, 368, 371, **371**
natural gas production and reserves in, *1671*
newspapers and print media in, 1678–1679
loyalist approach of, 1681
oil production in, 752, 1482, 2199
by Bahrain National Oil Company, 371–372
Belgrave (Charles Dalrymple) and, 436
Britain and, 537
by Standard Oil of California, 229
pearling industry in, 1810
penal code of (1974), repealed, 150
in Persian Gulf, 1820
petroleum industry in, 1824
political parties illegal in, 368
political reforms in, 150
population of, 367, *753*
Protestant missions in, 1854
public health in, 436
radio and television in, *1895*
religions in, 368
Shiʿism, 366, 368, 369, 370, 371, 2052
Sunni Islam, 368, 371
Shiʿa religious bloc in, 1456
stock market in, 2091
strike in (1954), National Liberation Front and, 1661
tourism in, 2196
tribes in, 2210
water resources of
desalinization of, *700*
freshwater withdrawals, *2331*
women's clothing in, *610*
women's rights in, 893
World Bank and, capital stock and voting power in, *2363*
Bahraini–Qatari Wars, **370–371**
Bahrain National Oil Company (BANOCO), **371–372**
Bahrain Order in Council, **372**
Bahrain Petroleum Company (BAPCO)
al-Awali built by, 342
and Bahrain National Oil Company, 371
on Sitra, 2071
Texaco agreement with, 229
Bahr al-Abyad (White Nile), **372,** 373, 901–902, 1688, 2328
in Khartoum, 1301
Bahr al-Arab, **372**
Bahr al-Ghazal, **372,** 373
Lado Enclave of, 1363
Bahr al-Jabal, **372–373**
Bahry, Louay, *as contributor,* 1065–1070, 1462, 1872–1873, 1967–1970
Bahth an aʾida, al- (film), 376
Baida (Libya), **373**
Baikie, James, 1464
Baji, Ibn Khalaf al-, 1476
Bakdash, Khalid, **373**
in Communist Party of Syria, 373, 412, 626
in Hayy al-Akrad, 100
in Progressive National Front, 373
Baker, James A., III, **373–374**
Arab–Israel peace plan of, 374
under Bush (George H. W.), 374
in Gulf Crisis (1990–1991)
Aziz (Tariq) meeting with, 350
in negotiations, 374
at King David Hotel, 1324
at Madrid Peace Conference, 1458–1459, 1725
PLO leaders meeting with, 374
as secretary of state, 374
in U.S. occupation of Iraq, 2325
in Western Sahara peace process, 2344, 2346–2347
in Western Sahara War, 1837
Baker Plan, 374
Baker, Raymond William, *as contributor,* 1648–1651, 1665, 1667, 1685–1686, 1812, 1971–1972, 2002–2003, 2022, 2120–2121, 2319–2320
Bakhtiari, **374**
constitutionalists supported by, 1559
Bakhtiari, Najaf Qoli Khan Samsam al-Soltaneh, **374–375**
Bakhtiari, Sardar Muʿazzam, 375
Bakhtiari, Soraya Esfandiari, marriage to Pahlavi (Mohammad Reza), 1752
Bakhtiar, Shapur, **375**
in Committee for Defense of Freedom and Human Rights, 622
education of, 375
government of
establishment of, 1126
fall of, 1127, 1311
opposition to, 1126–1127
murder of, 375
in National Front Party, 375
in National Resistance Movement, 375
as prime minister, 375, 1311
Bakhtiar, Timur, **375–376**
Bakil tribal confederation, **376**
Bakkar, Jalillah, **376**
Baklava, 836
Bakr, Ahmad Hasan al-, *377,* **377–378**
Aziz (Tariq) support for, 350
in al-Baʿth party, 377, 413
birthplace of, 2189
in coup (1963), 377
in coup (1968), 377
as defense minister, 378
forced resignation of, 1067
and Hussein (Saddam), 378, 414, 1066
as president, 1066
as prime minister, 377–378
Tikriti (Hardan al-) in power struggle with, 2190
Bakri, Fawzi al-, in Istiqlal Party, 1198
Bakri, Taher, 1428
Bakr, Salwa, **378–379,** 1924
Baku, in World War I, 2367
Balaclava, Battle of, **379**
Balad. *See* National Democratic Assembly
Baladhuri, al- (numismatic scholar), 1701
Baladiyya, 373
Balafrej, Ahmed, **379**
arrest of, 1197
education of, 379
in Istiqlal Party, 379, 1196–1197, 1805
in nationalist movement, 618, 1598
as prime minister, 379
Balagha Shiʿriyya fi al-Rafd wa al-Huriyya wa al-Rasas (al-Kasrawi), 1429
Balalin (theater troupe), 2184
Balamand University, Twayni (Ghassan) at, 2254

Balas, Shimon, 1452
Balbo, Italo, **380,** 935
Balcony over the Fakahani (Badr), 357
Balfour, A. J., 381, *381*
as foreign secretary, 380, 842
Lansdowne (Lord) under, 1374
visit to Palestine, Arab College of Jerusalem protests and, 226
Weizmann's (Chaim) meeting with, 2337
Balfour Declaration (1917), **380–382,** 511, 1479, 2368
Arab College of Jerusalem opposed to, 226
Ben-Gurion (David) on, 447
British issuance of, 2435, 2436
in British mandate in Palestine, 538, 614, 743, 1763, 1802
British reaffirmation of (1931), 2338
British retreat from, 1763, 1790
British support for, 380, 1724
Churchill White Paper on (1922), 594, 2350
drafters of, 379
Jewish immigration under, 146, 381, 614, 803, 1223, 1402
Jewish support for, 1233
Lloyd George (David) and, 380, 381, 1441
London Conference (1939) on, 1445
as long-term causes of Nakba, 1639
Palestinian opposition to, 1011, 1789
Palin Commission report on (1920), 1794, 1795
and Paris peace conferences, 2315
phraseology of, 380–381
as political victory for Zionism, 2435
on rights of Palestinians, 381, 1763
Samuel (Herbert Louis) and, 380
Sokolow (Nahum) chairing committee drafting, 2078
Storrs (Ronald) and, 2092
text of, 379
U.S. support for, Wise (Stephen S.) and, 2354
Weizmann (Chaim) and, 380, 446–447, 2337
Ahad Ha-Am aid to, 78
on Western Wall, 381
white papers on Palestine modifying (1939), 515, 1790
and Zionism, 1165
and Zionist Organization of America, 2436
Balfour-Paul, H. G., *as contributor,* 824–826
"Balikçilar" (Tevfik Fikret), 2180
Balikh River, 2129
Balkan Crises (1870s), **382–383**
Balkan League, 384
Balkan nationalism, Austria-Hungary and, 339
Balkan Pact (1934), Treaty of Ankara and (1930), 208
Balkans, **383–384**
ethnic groups in, 383
Jewish immigration to, 383
Muslim refugees from, 1913
in Ottoman Empire, 1732
nationalist movement against, 382–383, 542–543, 1089, 1946, 2163–2164
Balkan Wars (1912–1913), **384,** 2247
Armenians in, Andranik Ozanian in, 195
and Bucharest Treaty (1913), 384
causes of, Agadir crisis in (1911), 70
Greece in, 384, 939
and Istanbul Treaty (1913), 384
and London Conference (1913), 384
Ottoman navy in, 1741
Ottoman territory loss due to, 384
Salonika in, 1979
states involved in, 384
Balkar language, 2252
Ballad of Ali from Keshan, The (Taner), 2160
Balliol College, 1983
Baltaji, Ibrahim al-Sayyid al-, 2262
Balta Liman, Convention of (1838), **385,** 621, 1481, 2163
Balthasar's Odyssey (Maʿlouf), 1478
Baluchi language, 385, 1124
Baluchis, **385,** 386
autonomy movement of, suppression of, 1922
in Zahedan, 2420
Baluchistan (Iran), **385–386,** 2070
cities of, 385, 2070, 2420
climate of, 2070
idea of unified, 386
location of, 385
population of, 385, 2070
Balyan family, **386**
architecture by, 280, 281, 298
Bamia, Aida A., *as contributor,* 272–273, 396, 466–467, 474, 483, 588, 715–716, 721–722, 910–911, 965, 987–988, 1303–1304, 1313–1314, 1355–1356, 1403, 1422–1430, 1498, 1507, 1592, 1890, 1959, 2007, 2008, 2060, 2192–2193, 2332–2333, 2427–2428, 2431
Ba-Mishʿol Ha-Ẓar (Kabak), 1260
Bamyan, **386–387**
Bamyan valley, 387
Bandung Conference (1955), **387**
Ait Ahmed (Hocine) at, 95
Bangladesh, women in, as head of state, 808, 875
Bani-Etemad, Rakhsan, **387–388,** 833
Bani Malik tribe, 2212
Bani Sadr, Abolhasan, **388–389**
Beheshti (Mohammad) as adversary of, 388, 428
education of, 388
election to presidency, 1119
as finance minister, 388
as foreign minister, 388
government of, Qotbzadeh (Sadeq) in, 1881
in hostage crisis, 388
impeachment of, 1119, 1472
Khamenehi (Ali) opposing, 1299
Khomeini (Ruhollah) and, 1119, 1311
in Mojahedin-e Khalq, 389
in National Front, 388, 389
in National Resistance Council, 389
opposition movement led by, Qotbzadeh (Sadeq) in, 1881
as president, 388–389
Bani Saʿid tribe, 2212
Bank al-Maghrib (Morocco), Islamic numismatics in, 1702–1703
Bank Control Commission (Lebanon), 390
Bank Hapoalim (Israel), 1033, 1034
Banking/banks, **389–394**
in Algeria, 392, *393*
in Bahrain, 390, *393*
in Egypt, 389, 390, 392, *393,* 394, 1838, 2031, 2096–2097
Farhi family in, 807
history of, 389–390
in Iran, 390, 392, *393,* 535–536, 1115, 1756

Wolff (Henry Drummond) and, 2355
in Iraq, 390, *393*
Islamic finance, 394
in Israel, 390, *393*
Histadrut and, 1033, 1034
Jews in, and antisemitism, 212
in Jordan, 390, *393*
in Kuwait, 159, 162, *393*
in Lebanon, 390–392, *393*
liberalization of, 392–394
in Libya, *393*
and manufacturing, 1482
market penetration of, 390–392
in Mauritania, *393*
in Morocco, 389, 390, *393*, 394
national, 390
in Oman, *393*
in Ottoman Empire, 389, 740, 2163
in Palestine
Hilmi (Ahmad) and, 1030
by Jewish Colonial Trust, 1229
Levontin (Zalman) and, 1408
in People's Democratic Republic of Yemen, *393*
in Qatar, *393*
in Saudi Arabia, 219, 390, *393*, 394
in Sudan, *393*, 394
in Syria, 390, *393*
top 100, *391–392*
in Tunisia, 389, 390, 392, *393*, 394
in Turkey, 389, 390, 392, *393*, 415
in United Arab Emirates, *393*
by women, 874, 878
in Yemen, *393*, 394
Bank Misr (Egypt), 1482
Bank of Istanbul, 389
Banks. *See* Banking/banks
Banna, Hasan al-, **394–395**
and Afghan Islamic movements, 60
assassination of, 321, 395, 1621
Belhadj (Ali) influenced by, 436
education of, 394–395
Institute for the Mothers of the Believers established by, 892
in Muslim Brotherhood, 394–395, 1620–1621
Ashmawi (Muhammad Abd al-Rahman Salih al-) and, 321
al-Qaradawi (Yusuf) and, 1870
Rida (Rashid) and, 1924
as teacher, 395
Wahhabi influence on, 1626
Banna, Sabri al-, **396**
Bannis, Mohammad, **396**, 1428
Bannounah, Khanatha, 1424
BANOCO. *See* Bahrain National Oil Company
Banque de Prêts, 535
Banque d'Escompte de Perse, 535
Banque du Liban, 390
Banque Franco-Tunisienne, 390
Banque Impériale Ottomane, 390
Banque Suarès, 2096
Banu Hajir tribe, 2209
Banu Iyad tribe, 2189
Banu Ka'b, 1316
Banu Khalid tribe, 2209
Banu Lam, 1316
Banu Malik tribe, 912
Banu Tamim tribe, 2209, 2210
Banu Waryaghal tribe, 1304, 1305
Banu Yam tribe, 2209
Banu Yas tribal confederation, 36, 2040, 2209, 2210
Maktum family, al- in, 1474
Banyas River, 241
Bany, William, 868
Baouab, Ouidad, 497
BAPCO. *See* Bahrain Petroleum Company
Baptême chacaliste, Le (Laabi), 1355
Baqa, 2111
Baqai, Mozaffar, Arfa (Hasan) and, 286
Baq'a refugee camp, *1245*
Baqdunis, Rashid, in Arab Academy of Damascus, 223
Baqer, Seyyed Mohammed, 929
Baqillani, Abu Bakr al-, 2019
Baqir, Mohammad, 2070
Baqir, Tahir, 277
Baqqari, in mahdist state, 1463
Baqri family, **396–397**, 835
Baqri, Jacob, 397
Baqri, Joseph, 397, 550
Baraheni, Reza, **397**, 1436
Baraka (blessings), 460, 2359, 2621
Baraka Bank, 394
Barak, Aharon, in Kahan Commission, 1263
Barakat, Hidaya Afifi, 1453
Barakat, Hoda, **397–398**
Barak, Ehud, **398–399**
in Arab–Israel War (1973), 398
in assassination of PLO leaders, 398
at Camp David Summit (2000), 399, 561–563, 606, 1775
Clinton (Bill) and, 1168
election of, 1168, 1727
in Entebbe Operation, 398
government of, 1168
Levy (David) in, 1408
Peres (Shimon) in, 1818
Sarid (Yossi) in, 1991
in Israel Defense Force, 398, 1171
Israeli settlements under, 1192
in Labor Party, 398, 1183, 1818
Lebanese withdrawal by, 254, 1168
Meimad and, 1186
military service of, 398
Netanyahu (Benjamin) and, 1677
Oslo Accords (1993) implemented by, 398
peace process under, 926, 1168, 1727
political defeat of, 219, 399, 563, 1169, 1727
as prime minister, 399
under Rabin (Yitzhak), 398
resignation of, 1169
Syrian negotiations with, 319, 1168
testifying in front of Supreme Court, *1382*
and Zionist Organization of America, 2436
Barakzai, Afdal, Cemal Paşa and, 572
Barakzai, Amanullah. *See* Amanollah Khan
Barakzai dynasty, **399–401**, 1468
Mohammadzai lineage of, 400
Barakzai, Fateh Khan, 400
Barakzai Pashtun tribe (Afghanistan), 2420
Baram, Amatzia, *as contributor*, 173, 287–288, 344, 350, 377–378, 416, 977–978, 997, 1900–1901, 2154, 2189–2190
Baramki, Dmitri, 277
Baransi, Salih, in al-Ard movement, 285
Barbary pirates, 401. *See also* Corsairs
demise of, 2216
in Qaramanli dynasty, 1871
and Treaty of Fes, 827
U.S./European war against, 1871, 2290
Barbary states, **401**
corsairs of, 401, 643
Barbary wars, **401**
corsairs in, 401, 643

Barbir, Munira, 431
Bardo, Treaty of (1881), 484, 2229
French protectorate over Tunisia established by, 1604
Barenboim, Daniel, 1966
Barghouthi, Siham
in Women's Centre for Legal Aid and Counseling, 2356
in Women's Studies Center, 2362
Barghuthi, Bashir, 402
Barghuthi family, **401–402**
Barghuthi, Marwan, **402**
in Palestinian Authority, no-confidence motion by (1997), 1785
Barghuthi, Mustafa, 402
Barghuthi, Umar Salih, 402
Barid Bayrut (Shaykh), 2046
Bar-Ilan, Meir, 1554
Bar-Ilan University, **402–403**
Baring, Evelyn (Lord Cromer), *403*, **403–407**, 766
Abbas Hilmi II conflict with, 5, 405
books by, 406–407
Condominium Agreement by (1899), 405, 530, 629
dual control of Egypt and, 731
in Egyptian Public Debt Commission, 404
financial reform by, 404
Gorst (John Eldon) under, 931
irrigation development by, 404, 405, *406*
in Liquidation Commission, 404
military training of, 403–404
nationalist movements and, 405–406
National Party opposing, 1663
and negative moral coloration of *levantine*, 1405
retirement of
Cairo University after, 555
Dinshaway incident and, 406, 709
Sudan conquest by, 405, 530
wife of, 404
on Zaghlul (Saʿd), 2418
Barjot, Pierre, 2108
Barkan, Ömer Lutfi, **407**
as historiographer, 1035
Bar-Lev, Haim, **407–408**
in Arab–Israel War (1948), 407
in Arab–Israel War (1956), 407
in Arab–Israel War (1973), 408
in Israel Defense Force, 407–408, 1171
in Palmah, 1795
in War of Attrition, 408
Bar–Lev Line, 408
in Arab–Israel War (1973), 250, 1579
in War of Attrition (1969–1970), 2327
Barley, agricultural production of, 75
Barmada, Mustafa, in People's Party, 1322
Baron, Dvora, **408**, 1434
Bar-On, Mordechai, *as contributor*, 199–200, 239–242, 340–341, 398–399, 994–995, 1170–1174, 1323–1324, 1377–1378, 1444, 1577–1579, 1674–1675, 1748–1749, 1809–1810, 1811–1812, 1991, 2058–2059, 2107–2110
Barq (newspaper), 2142
Barrie, Larry A., *as contributor*, 83–85, 418, 899, 1213, 1306–1307, 1308, 1416, 1487, 1567–1572, 1587, 1590–1591, 1603–1604, 1716–1717, 1807–1808, 2017–2018, 2224–2230, 2231–2232, 2264–2265, 2268–2269
Bar-Tov, Hanoch, 2185
Barudi, Fakhri Bey al-, Nationalist Youth supported by, 1337
Barudi, Mahmud Sami al-
and dual control, 731
Rifqi (Uthman) replace with, 2297
Bar-Yosef, Yosef, 2185
Barzani, Abd Al-Salam II, 408
Barzani, Ahmad, 408
Barzani family, **408–409**
in Naqshbandi, 1642
Barzani, Idris, 408
Barzani, Masʿud al-, 408, *1642*
in Democratic Party of Kurdistan, 695
on Iraqi Governing Council, 2325–2326
in Kurdistan Front, 1339
Talabani (Jalal) and, 2151
Barzani, Mawlana Khalid, 408
Barzani, Muhammad, 408
Barzani, Muhammad Khalid, 408
Barzani, Mullah Mustafa (General Barzani), 408
autonomy agreement between Hussein (Saddam) and, 2151
in Democratic Party of Kurdistan, 694–695
revolt led by (1945), 1968
revolt led by (1960), 1341, 1873
collapse of, 1915
Talabani (Jalal) and, 2151
Barzani, Taj ad-Din, 408
Basaʾir, al- (Algeria), 1456
Basaʾir, al- (newspaper), 1425
ba-Shaʿar (Israeli journal), 1512
Bash Hamba, Ali, in Young Tunisians, 2408
Bashir. *See* Chehab, Bashir
Bashir II, 1393
in Druze revolts, 730
reign of, 729
Bashir III, 1394
Bashir, Munir, 1618, *1619*
Bashir, Umar Hasan Ahmad al-, 2234, 2296
coup by (1989), 2101, 2261
political parties under, 2261
Sadiq al-Mahdi and, 2261
Bashkir language, 2248, 2252
Bash mufti, 418
Basic Law of 1996 (Oman), 1711
Basic People's Congresses (Libya), **409**
on jamahiriyya, 409
Başiret (newspaper), 409
Başiretci, Ali, **409**
Basir, Rawda al-, in Women's Centre for Legal Aid and Counseling, 2356
Basle Program (Zionism), 1021, 1692
Basma bint Talal (princess of Jordan), **409–410**
in Princess Basma Women's Resource Center, 1852
Basra (Iraq), *410*, **410–411**
as administrative and commercial center, 410
agriculture in, 410
Arabian Mission in, 231
archaeological research in, 276
British capture of (2003), 2325
during British mandate, 411
climate of, 410
ethnic groups in, 410
during Gulf Crisis (1990–1991), 411
in Iran–Iraq War, 410, 411, *1128*
location of, 410
under Ottoman control, 411

population of, 410, 1131
port of, 1130
Sykes-Picot Agreement (1916) on, 2128
university of, 410
during World War I, 411

Basra–Baghdad railroad. *See* Baghdad–Basra railroad

Basri, Driss
dismissal of, 1356, 1600
and Hassan II, 1006
as interior minister of Morocco, 1575

Basri, Hasan al-, 2111

Basri, Muhammad al-
Union Nationale des Etudiants Marocains and, 2266
in Union Nationale des Forces Populaires, 1197, 2266

Bast, **411–412**

Batatu, Hanna, 1036

Bates, Michael L., *as contibutor,* **1699–1701**

Baʿth (newspaper)
editorship of, 69
start of, 69

Baʿth al-Arabi, al-. *See also* Baʿth party
of Aflaq (Michel) and Bitar (Salah al-Din al-), 68–69, 308–309
of Arsuzi (Zaki al-), 68–69, 308–309

Baʿth party, **412–414**. *See also* Baʿth party *by country below*
Arab socialism of, 265
foundation of, 412
ideology of, 412
pan-Arabism of, 1799
secularism of, 1659

Baʿth Party (Iraq), 412, 413–414
Aflaq (Michel) in, 69
archive of, in Baghdad, 70
Aziz (Tariq) in, 350
Bakr (Ahmad Hasan al-) in, 377, 413
Bayati (Abd al-Wahhab al-) as cultural adviser of, 416
Bazzaz (Abd al-Rahman al-) persecuted by, 422
citizens killed by, 1846
Communist Party's alliance with, 1605
in coup (1958), 413
in coup (1963), 413, 1134
in coup (1968), 413, 1134
Federation of Iraqi Youth in, 2412
Hafiz (Amin al-) in, 972
Hussein (Saddam) in, 413–414, 1065–1066
Ibrahim (Izzat) in, 1078
and Qasim (Abd al-Karim), 413, 1462, 1873
Ramadan (Taha Yasin) in, 1900
religious suppression by, al-Daʿwa al-Islamiyya and, 680
Rikali (Fuʾad al-) in, 413
separation from Syrian Baʿth party, 413
Sharif (Aziz) in, 2037
vs. Shiʿite religious establishment, 977–978
social and economic development under, 1066
state feminism under, 892
Tikriti (Hardan al-) in, 2190
Tlas (Mustafa) in, 2191–2192
in United National Front, 1654
women's organization under, 898

Baʿth Party (Jordan), 412

Baʿth Party (Lebanon), 412
in National Front, 1656–1657

Baʿth Party (Syria), 412–413, 2130
Aflaq (Michel) in, 69, 412, 590, 2134
Alawite support of, 1549
Arab Socialist Party and, 412, 1010
Arsuzi (Zaki al-) in, 412
Asad (Bashshar al-) in, 315, *413*
Asad (Hafiz al-) in, 316, 317, 412–413, 1211, 2130
Atasi (Jamal al-) in, 329
Atasi (Nur al-Din al-) in, 329–330
Bitar (Salah al-Din al-) in, 69, 412, 482
in coup (1961), 412
in coup (1966), 412
electoral success of, 2133
establishment of, 69, 412
Hafiz (Amin al-) in, 971–972
Hama resistance to, 980, 982
Hawrani (Akram al-) and, 412
Jadid (Ghassan) in, 412
Jadid (Salah) in, 1211
Khaddam (Abd al-Halim) in, 1290–1291
Muhsin (Zuhayr) in, 1607
and National Party decline, 1664
in National Progressive Front, 1665
neo-
in coup (1966), 482
leadership of, 330
officers' coup in (1963), 316, 330
regionalist group in, 971–972
al-Saʿiqa created by, 1972
separation from Iraqi Baʿth party, 413
size of, 69
Syrian Communist Party and, 412
Syrian Social Nationalist Party and, 2136
and United Arab Republic formation, 412, 2273

Baʿth University, al-, 2132

Battaglia di Algeri, la (film), 142

Battesti, Vincent, *as contributor,* 72–77

Battle of the alleys, The (Boudjedra), 497

Batum (Russia), in World War I, 2367

Baya, **414**

Bayan, al- (Rushd), 1476

Bayane, al- (newspaper), establishment of, Yata (Ali) in, 2382

Bayar, Celal, *415,* **415–416**
under Atatürk (Mustafa Kemal), 415
in Democrat Party, 415, 695
İnönü (İsmet) rivalry with, 415, 1097, 1098
political and criminal charges against, 416
presidency of, 415, 1098
as prime minister, 1097
and Turkish economy, 415

Bayati, Abd al-Wahhab al-, **416**
as Baʿth party cultural adviser, 416
Laabi (Abdellatif) translating works of, 1356

Bayat, Mangol, *as contributor,* 637

Bayat, Mortaza Qoli, **416–417**

Baybars (Mamluk sultan), 1044
Nazareth recaptured by, 1672

Baydas, Khalil, 1790

Baydh, Ali Salim al-, **417**
as vice president, 417, 2389
in Yemeni Socialist Party, 417, 2389

Bayhaqi, 2019

Baykal, Deniz, and Republican People's Party, 1919

Bayrakdar, Mustafa, **417**
death of, 1217
Janissary rebellion against, 417
under Mahmud II, 417
and *Nizam-i Cedit,* 1217
reforms by, 417

Bayram III, Muhammad, 418

Bayram IV, Muhammad, 418

Bayram V, Muhammad, **418**
under Khayr al-Din, 1307

Baysal, Jale, in Women's Library and Information Center, 2358
Bayt, 2209, 2211
Bayt al-Din (Lebanon), palace of Chehab (Bashir) at, *583,* 584
Bayt al-Hikma Academy, 360
establishment of, 1132
Bayt al-shiʿr, 1428
Baytjali, Iskandar al-Khuri al-, 1791
Bayya al-Khawatim (musical), 817
Bazaars and bazaar merchants, **418–421**
Iranian, 419–421
modern, 419
in Tobacco Revolt (1891–1892), 1644
traditional, 419
Bazargan, Mehdi, **421**
cabinet of
Khamenehi (Ali) in, 1299
Yazdi (Ibrahim) in, 2382–2383
in Committee for Defense of Freedom and Human Rights, 622
Forqan denouncing, 842
as Freedom Movement founder, 421, 850, 1117
Khomeini (Ruhollah) supported by, 1311
in National Front, 1656
as National Iranian Oil Company director, 421
provisional government of, 1119, 1126, 1311
Amir-Entezam (Abbas) in, 188
resignation of, 1899
and Revolutionary Guards, 1921–1922
Bazzaz, Abd al-Rahman al-, **421–423**
education of, 421
pan-Arabism of, 421
as prime minister, 422–423
BCW. *See* Beirut College for Women
Beans, 838–839
Beʾarvot Hanegev (Shamir), 2185
Beaufort, Charles-Marie-Napoléon d'Hautpoul de, **423**
Beauvoir, Simone de, 563
Becher, Kurt, 1280
Béchir, Zoubeida, 1424
Beckett, Samuel, 2020
Beck, Lois, *as contributor,* 374, 2213
Bedel-i askeri, **423–424**
jizya replaced by, 423, 1237
Bedford College, 2088
Bedir Khan, 1344
Bedjaoui, Mohamed, 2217
Bedouin tribes, *221,* 2210, 2622
under Abd al-Aziz ibn Saʿud Al Saʿud, 9, 10, 1085
in Arab Legion, 257, 922
in Ikhwan (*See* Ikhwan)
Kuwaiti relations with, under Al Sabah (Mubarak), 159, 161
in Najd, 1638
in Negev, 1675
in Rub al-Khali, 1938
in Saudi Arabia, 2213, 2214
as threat to unification, 1626
on Sinai Peninsula, 2068
in Tunisia, *2210,* 2226
in Yemen, 2215
Beer, 109
Beersheba (Israel), **424,** 1160, 1675
Beer, Yisrael, 992
Be-Fisat ha-Ariq u-ve-Helkat ha-Hevel (Greenberg), 941
Begag, Azouz, 1427
Beggar, The (Esfandiary), 784
Begin, Menachem, **424–427,** *425, 426*
in *Altalena* arms shipment, 170
in Arab–Israel War (1967), 248
in Arab–Israel War (1982), 252, 254, 1174, 1537
Ben-Gurion (David) opposition, 448
in Betar, 424
Burg (Yosef) under, 546
in Camp David Accords (1978), 426, 560, 561, 567, 771, 2293, *2293*
Vance (Cyrus) and, 2308
coalition government led by, 1417
Agudat Israel in, 1178
Likud party in, 1167
in Dayr Yasin massacre (1948), 684
Egyptian–Israeli Peace Treaty (1979) signed by, 771
Eretz Yisrael term used by, 781
Golan Heights under, 925
government of, 425–426
Abuhatzeira (Aharon) in, 37
Amit (Meir) in, 190
Dayan (Moshe) in, 682–683
Ehrlich (Simha) in, 1184
Kimche (David) in, 1322
Sharon (Ariel) in, 2042
Weizman (Ezer) in, 2336
Haganah issuing ultimatum to, 1973
in Hebrew Resistance Movement, 425
in Herut Party, 425, 1181
in Irgun Zvaʾi Leʾumi, 170, 424–425, 1139, 1209
revolt against British by (1944), 1139
Israeli settlements under, 957, 1192
Jabotinsky (Vladimir Zeʾev) and, 424, 1181, 1209
and Likud, 425, 1184
Modaʾi (Yitzhak) and, 1555
and Osirak nuclear facility (1981), bombing of, 426, 1042
peace movement's impact on, 1809
and PLO, 426
political stability caused by, 1165
Reagan Plan (1982) rejected by, 1908
resignation of, 426, 1167
in Revisionist Zionism, 424
in Sabra and Shatila massacres, 1263
Sadat (Anwar al-) negotiating with, 1957
Saunders (Harold) criticized by, 2001
Shamir (Yitzhak) under, 2026
against UN Resolution 242, 425
on West Bank, 426
West German reparations opposed by, 425, 2348–2349
Begin, Zeʾev, in Likud Party, 1184
Behar, Nissim, **427**
Behʿazin, 1435
Behbahani, Sayyed Abdollah, in Constitutional Revolution, 2141–2142
Behbehani, Simin, **427**
Behcet, Mustafa, 712
Beheira. *See* Buhayra
Beheshti, Mohammad, **427–428**
Bani Sadr (Abolhasan) in conflict with, 388, 428
government of, Musavi (Mir-Hosain) in, 1615
Khomeini (Ruhollah) supported by, 427, 428
against Pahlavi regime, 428
Beheshti, Sayyed (Sayyid Ali)
and Hazara ethnolinguistic group, 1015
in mojahedin resistance, 1561

in Shura-ye Ittifagh-e Islami, 63, 1561
Behrangi, Samad, **428**
Behrouzi, Maryam, **428**
Beijing Conference (2000), 480
Beijing International Women's Conference (1995), 480, 745, 822, 888–889, 1396, 1511
Beilin, Yossi, and Oslo negotiations, 1725
Beinin, Joel S.
as contributor, 625–628
as historiographer, 1036
Beirut (Lebanon), *429,* **429–431,** *430. See also* Green Line
American University of, 180–181
in Arab–Israel War (1982), 252–253, 254
Arab League summit (2002) in, *1387*
Arab nationalism in, 221
Arafat (Yasir) in, headquarters of, 270–271
B'nai B'rith lodge in, 489
education in, 429
ethnic groups in, 429
gay-pride events in, 888
in Greater Lebanon, 429
Institute for Palestine Studies in, 1099
Israeli invasion of, *429,* 430
during Lebanese Civil War (1975–1990), 430–431
newspapers of, 1678
origin of name of, 429
Palestine Research Center in, 1781–1782
PLO in, 429–430
PFLP–GC bombing against (1970), 1841
population of, 429
as port, 2206
"poverty belt" of, 429
reconstruction of, 431
textile mills in, 2181
theater in, 1421
university in, 1395–1396
U.S. facilities attacked in, 1908, 2294
casualties of, 254
CIA and, 573
after Israeli–Lebanese security agreement, 254
U.S. withdrawal after, 254
Beirut '75 (Samman), 1982
Beirut College for Women (BCW), **431–432**
Beirut–Damascus railway. *See* Damascus–Beirut railway
Beirut Nightmares (Samman), 1982
Beirut Reform Society, 2125
Beirut University College (BUC), 431
Institute for Women's Studies in the Arab World at, 1100
Beitaddin Declaration, **432**
Beja, **432–434,** *433,* 737, 2097
Bejerano, Maya, **434,** 1434
Béji, Hélé, 1424, 1425
Beji, Mounir, 2232
Bekir Fahri, **434**
Bekir, Latife, in Women's People's Party, 2359
Bekkar, Rabia, *as contributor,* 94, 136, 254–256, 443, 497, 1547, 2376
Bektashis, **434–436**
Alevis and, 113, 435
Atatürk (Mustafa Kemal) supported by, 435
Bel Evladi segment of, 113
Dönme and, 720
elements of, 435
Mahmud II suppressing, 435
vs. Mevlevi Brotherhood, 435
in Ottoman Empire, 435
vs. Sunnis, 435
as women, 435
Yol Evladi segment of, 113
Belghoul, Farida, 1427
Belgium
custom officials from, Iranian employment of, 1591
Palestine under, Churchill (Winston S.) on, 595
Belgrave, Charles Dalrymple, **436**
Belhadj, Ali, **436–437**
arrest of, 134
Bendjedid (Chadli) meeting with, 1965
Bouyali (Moustafa) and, 436, 506
as FIS leader, 125, 133, 134, 436, 857
Beli Kochav (Burla), 547
Belkacem, Cherif, **437**
in Algerian War of Independence, 437
in Armée de Libération Nationale, 437
in Front de Libération Nationale, 437
in Oujda Group, 1743
Bel Ksiri (Morocco), 913
Belleten (journal), 2246
Bell, Gertrude, **437**
in Arab Bureau, 225
at Cairo Conference (1921), 554
as explorer, 437, 513
Faisal I ibn Hussein supported by, 437
Wilson (Arnold T.) and, 2352
Bell Organization. *See* Hunchak Party
Bellounis, Muhammad, **437–438**
Belly dance, 668, *668*
"Belonging to a New Family" (Bannis), 396
Ben Abdallah, Mohammed, 1745
Benaïcha, Ahmed, in Islamic Salvation Army, 1155, 1156
Ben Ali, Fekar, in Young Algerians, 2405
Ben Ali, Zayn al-Abidine, **438–440,** *439, 2231*
Baccouche (Hedi) under, 356
under Bourguiba (Habib), 439, 503
Bourguiba (Habib) replaced by, 1628
Communist Party under, 1590–1591
in Constitutional Democratic Rally, 439, 635
coup by (1987), 439, *439,* 503, 635, 2229, 2231
in Destour Party, 439
Ghannouchi (Rached) pardoned by, 356–357, 912
LTDH under, 1416
Marzouki (Moncef) opposing, 1497
Mestiri (Ahmad) and, 1520
military training of, 439
Moadda (Mohamed) and, 1554
against Mouvement de Tendance Islamique, 439
national pact of, with opposition, 439
Parti d'Unité Populaire under, 1587
in Parti Socialiste Destourien, 439, 635
presidency of, 439–440, 635, 2229, *2231,* 2232
Ben Ammar, Tahar, **440**
Ben Arfa. *See* Arfa, Muhammad Ibn
Ben Ashour, al-Taher, 2428
Ben Ashour, Mohammad al-Fadel, 1423

Ben Ashour, Mohammad al-Taher, 1423
Ben Badis, Abd al-Hamid, **440–441**
in Association of Algerian Muslim Ulama, 326, 440–441, 1425
and Bennabi (Malek), 451
education of, 440
Ibrahimi (Bashir) as companion to, 1076
Uqbi (Tayyib al-) criticism of, 2297
zawiyas confronted by, 1423
Benbaibèche, Tahar, 1904
Ben Barka, Mehdi, **441**
assassination of, 1574
Ben Jelloun (Umar) supporting, 450
Bouabid (Abderrahim) and, 495
in Istiqlal Party, 441, 1197
murder of, 441, 2410
return from exile, 1600
Union Nationale des Etudiants Marocains supporting, 2266
in Union Nationale des Forces Populaires, 441, 1197, 2266–2267
Youssoufi (Abderrahmane) and, 2410
Ben Barka: The Moroccan Equation (Bitton), 483
Ben Bella, Ahmed, **441–443**, *442*
Abbas (Ferhat) opposing, 4
in Algerian War of Independence, 124, 442, 615
and Algiers Charter, 142
in Armée de Libération Nationale, 442
Bendjedid (Chadli) and, 442
and Ben Khedda (Ben Youssef), 450
Bitat (Rabah) and, 483
Boumédienne (Houari) and
cooperation by, 128, 442, 499
rivalry between, 129, 442, 499
in Comité Révolutionnaire d'Unité et d'Action, 620
constitution drafted under, 124, 128–129
coup against (1965), 124, 1537
Abdelghani (Mohamed Benahmed) in, 23
Boumédienne (Houari) in, 129, 442, 499, 503
executive powers of, 124, 129
as first president, 124
election of, 129, 1744
French skyjacking of (1956), 442, 1309, 1563
in Front de Libération Nationale, 131, 442
in Gouvernement Provisoire de la République Algérienne, 442
government of, 2217
Abdesselam (Belaid) in, 23
Belkacem (Cherif) in, 437
Bouteflika (Abdelaziz) in, 503
Madani (Tawfiq al-) in, 1456
Ibrahimi (Ahmed Taleb) opposing, 1076
Khider (Mohamed) falling out with, 1309
Krim (Belkacem) opposing, 1337
Moroccan border dispute considered by, 1566
in Mouvement pour la Démocratie en Algérie, 442
opposition to, 1744
punishment for, 124
in Organisation Spéciale, 441
Oujda Group on, 1744
overthrow of, 1744
in Parti du Peuple Algérien, 441
power seized by (1962), 128
presidency of, 442
as prime minister, 442
National Assembly selection of, 128
Sant Egidio Platform signed by, 443
Setif Revolt (1945) and, 441
Zbiri (Tahar) and, 2429
Benbitour, Ahmed
Benflis (Ali) opposing, 445
under Bouteflika (Abdelaziz), 504
Ben Bouali, Hassiba, **443**
in Algerian War of Independence, 136
in National Liberation Front, 443
Ben Boulaid, Moustafa, **443–444**
in Algerian War of Independence, 443
in Comité Révolutionnaire d'Unité et d'Action, 137, 443, 620
in Front de Libération Nationale, 443
Hadj (Messali al-) supported by, 443
and Zbiri (Tahar), 2429
Benchkroun, Siham, 1428
Bendjedid, Chadli, *444*, **444–445**
Abdesselam (Belaid) opposing, 23
in Algerian War of Independence, 444
in Armée de Libération Nationale, 444
Belhadj (Ali) meeting with, 1965
and Ben Bella (Ahmed), 442
under Boumédienne (Houari), 444
Bouteflika (Abdelaziz) and, 444, 445, 504
in Conseil National de la Révolution Algérienne, 444
constitution revised under, 125, 130, 132
coup deposing (1992), Nezzar (Khaled) in, 1686
decentralization process under, 2080
in Front de Libération Nationale, resignation of, 133
government of
Abdelghani (Mohamed Benahmed) in, 23
Bitat (Rabah) in, 483
Brahimi (Abdelhamid) in, 506
Ghazali (Muhammad al-) in, 914
Ghozali (Ahmed) in, 917
Hamrouche (Mouloud) in, 987
Ibrahimi (Ahmed Taleb) in, 1076
Nahnah (Mahfoud) meeting with, 1965
opposition to, 124–125
parliamentary elections of 1991 and, 1026
pluralism under, 1006
political parties legalized by, 125, 132
presidency of, 444–445
resignation of, forced, 126, 130, 445, 1537
Ait Ahmed (Hocine) opposed to, 95
Lamari (Mohamed) demanding, 1365
Sahnoun (Ahmed) meeting with, 1965
and Zbiri (Tahar), 2429
and Zeroual (Liamine), 2430
Bendjelloul, Mohammad Saleh, 3
Beneficial Affair. *See Vaka-i hayriye*
Ben Eliezer, Israel, movement founded by, 1002
Benenden School (Britain), Basma bint Talal at, 409
Benevolent Society school movement, 758–759
Benevolent Society School of Alexandria, 759
Benflis, Ali, **445**
under Bouteflika (Abdelaziz), 445, 504

in Front de Libération Nationale, 445
under Hamrouche (Mouloud), 445
in Ligue Algérien des Droits de l'Homme, 445
Benghazi (Libya), **446**, 1410
in Cyrenaica region, 655
development of, 446
foundation of, 446
Italian invasion of, 446, 2246
under Ottoman rule, 446
population of, 446
U.S. bombing of (1986), 1862
in World War II, 446, *2369*, 2369–2370
Ben-Gurion, David, **446–449**, *447*, *448*
Altalena arms shipment and, 170
American Jewish Committee accord with (1950), 178
in Arab–Israel War (1948), 448
in Arab–Israel War (1956), 245
in Arab–Israel War (1967), 449
on Balfour Declaration, 447
Begin (Menachem) opposing, 448
Ben-Zvi (Yizhak) friendship, 446, 456, 457
and Biltmore Program (1942), 472
on "consensus of transfer" for Palestinians, 1640
on Dayr Yasin massacre (1948), 684
as defense minister, 448, 449, 1174
education of, 446
Egyptian peace negotiations with, Operation Alpha in, 157
Eshkol (Levi) rivalry with, 1188–1189
government of
Dayan (Moshe) in, 681–682
Eban (Abba) in, 744
Navon (Yizhak) in, 1671
Peres (Shimon) in, 1817
and Haganah, 972, 973
in ha-Halutz, 446
and Hammarskjöld (Dag), 986
Harel (Isser) and, 992, 1578
and Harkabi (Yehoshafat), 995
and Herzog (Yaʿacov David), 1023
in Histadrut, 447
Histadrut support for, 2402
independence declared by, 448, *1163*, 2031, 2172
Irgun Zvaʾi Leʾumi and, 170
Israel Defense Force under, *1171*, 1173
Jabotinsky (Vladimir Zeʾev) and, 1947
meeting between, 1209
in Jewish Agency, 447, *1228*
in Jewish Legion, 447, 1230, 1281
Kennedy (John Fitzgerald) and, 1288
Kollek (Teddy) supporting, 1331
LEHI declared illegal by, 1443, 2026
at London Conference (1939), 1445
in MAPAI, 447, 1185, 1362, 2402
on Masada veneration, 1497
Medinat Yisrael term used by, 781
Meir (Golda) and, 1514, *1514*
Mossad established by, 1577
and Nahal, 1634
in Palestine under British mandate, 447–448
Palmah under, 1795
before Peel Commission, testimony of, 447
Peres (Shimon) mentored by, 1817
in Poʿalei Zion, 446
as prime minister, 448, 449
in RAFI Party, 1188, 1189
resignation of
Lavon affair and, 449, 1185, 1188, 1377–1378
reasons given for, 449, 1188
Saison authorized by, 1972–1973
Sèvres Protocol signed by, 2014, 2109
and Sharett (Moshe), 449, 2032, 2033
and Sinai campaign of 1956, 681
in State List, 1188–1189
Weizmann (Chaim) superseded by, 2338
and West German Reparations Agreement, 448
on white papers, 447
Zionism supported by, 447
Ben-Gurion University of the Negev, 424, **449–450**
Benhabylès, Chérif, in Young Algerians, 2405
Benhaddou, Halima, 2376
Benhadj, Ali, Islamic Salvation Army allegiance to, 1155
Beni Amir clan, 433
Beni-Mellal (Morocco), 1567
Ben Ish Hai (Hayim), 1012
Ben Jaafar, Mustapha, 2232
Benjamin, Ernest Frank, 1229
Ben Jelloun, Tahar, 1424, *1427*, 1428, 2376
Ben Jelloun, Umar, **450**
Ben Khedda, Ben Youssef, **450**
in Front de Libération Nationale, 450
in Gouvernement Provisoire de la République Algérienne, 450
military leaders fired by, 1744
in Mouvement pour le Triomphe des Libertés Démocratiques, 450
"New Appeal to the Algerian People" by (1976), 4, 1365
in Parti du Peuple Algérien, 450
presidency of, 450
as president of provisional government, 4
as social affairs minister, 450
Ben Mami, Laila, 1429
Ben Mansour, Latifa, 1427
Ben Mayim le-Mayim (Brenner), 507
Ben Mʾhidi, Muhammad Larbi, **450–451**
in Algerian War of Independence, 451
Algiers campaign organized by, 141
in Comité Révolutionnaire d'Unité et d'Action, 137, 451, 620
death of, 451
in Front de Libération Nationale, 451
interrogation of, torture during, 141
in Organisation Spéciale, 450
in Parti du Peuple Algérien, 450
Ben, Miriam, 1424
Bennabi, Malek, **451–452**
Bennani, Abdelaziz, in Organisation Marocaine des Droits de l'Homme, 1716
Ben Ner, Yizhak, 1433
Ben-Porat, Mordechai, **452**
Bensalah, Abdelkader, 1904
Ben Salah, Ahmed, **452–453**
and Bourguiba (Habib), 452, 502, 1587
education of, 452
exile of, 1587
expulsion of, 452–453, 634
imprisonment of, 1587
Mestiri (Ahmad) and, 1519–1520
as minister of planning, 452
in Mouvement de l'Unité Populaire, 452, 1587, 1804, 2231
in Union Générale des Travailleurs Tunisiens, 452, 2264

Ben Saleh, Mohammad al-Hadi, 1429
Ben Seddiq, Mahjoub, **453**
imprisonment of, 453
in Union Marocaine du Travail, 453, 2266
in Union Nationale des Forces Populaires, 453, 1197, 2266, 2267
Ben Shaikh, Abdel Qader, 1429
Ben Simeon, Raphael Aaron, **453–454**
Bentwich, Norman, **454**, 2124
Benvenisti, Meron, **454**
Kollek (Teddy) criticized by, 1331
"Benvenisti Prognosis," 454
Ben Yahia, Habib, 440
Benyahia, Mohamed, 2217
death of, Ibrahimi (Ahmed Taleb) after, 1076
Ben-Yehuda, Eliezer, 427, **454–455**
and Hebrew revival, 1018
Uganda Project supported by, 2257
Ben Yizhak, Avraham, 1431
Ben Yousouf, Salah, **455–456**
assassination of, 455, 501
Ben Salah (Ahmed) and, 452
and beylicate, abolition of, 185
Bourguiba (Habib) and, 455, 501
exile in Egypt, 634
as justice minister, 455
in Neo-Destour Party, 455, 634
Ben-Zvi Institute, 457
Ben-Zvi, Rahel Yanait, **456**
as founder of Naʿamat, **1629**
and Ha-Shomer, 1001
Ben-Zvi, Yael, *as contributor,* 1105–1106
Ben-Zvi, Yizhak, **456–457**, *457*
Ben-Gurion (David) friendship, 446, 456, 457
in Jewish Legion, 457, 1230, 1281
presidency of, 457
in Vaʿad Leʾumi, 457, 2307
wife of, 456
Berats, 565
Berber(s), **457–463**, *458, 461, 462,* 1963–1964
agriculture of, 459
in Algeria, 121–122, 458, 459, 463–464 (*See also* Kabylia)
Ait Ahmed (Hocine) as leader of, 95
Algiers, 122, 139
censorship of, 1261
identity movement among, 192
in Mouvement pour le Triomphe des Libertés Démocratiques (MTLD), 969
in Mzab region, 1627
number of, 121
political parties supported by, 134
revolt by (1963), 95
Tamazight language of, 121–122, 638, 1261
youth killed in detention (2001), 96, 274, 638
art of, 459
in Atlas Mountains, 335, 336
rebellion against French protectorate, 1570
Braber, 458
Chawia, 458, 459
Chleuch, 458
on Djerba island, 717
Djerbi, 459
in Egypt, 458, 2071
emigration of, for work, 459
invading Iberian Peninsula, 2084
Jmaʾa tribal councils of, 1237
Kabyles, 458, 459
in Libya, 458
in Mauritania, 458–459
as minorities or subdominant group, 1549
in Morocco, 458, 459, 463, 487, 1567, 1569
under French protectorate, 1570
in Mouvement Populaire (MP), 1588–1589
under Muhammad VI, 1601–1602
music of, 193
Mzabi, 459
and nomadism, 459, *462*
origin of term, 457
religion of, 460
repression of, 463–464, 486 (*See also* Berber Spring; Black Spring)
sedentary, 459
social organization of, 459–460
Sousi, 459
Tuareg, 458, 459, *462*
in Tunisia, 458, 2226, 2227–2228
in Western Sahara, 2342
women, *458,* 463
Berber culture, 806, 1426
censorship of, in Algeria, 1261
official Moroccan recognition of, 1601–1602
Berber Dahir, **463**
Fasi (Allal al-) protesting against, 812
Free School campaign against, Arslan (Shakib) influence on, 307–308
Moroccan nationalism after, 1570, 1598
Berber festivals, *458, 461*
Berber languages, 457, 458, 460–463, 1567
alphabet of, 461–462
vs. Arabic
Arabization policies on, 255, 256
Kateb (Yacine) on, 1280
borrowing from Arabic language, 463
characteristics of, 460–461
dialects of
in Algeria, 458, 1422, 2253
in Morocco, 458, 2166–2167
Moroccan recognition of, official, 1601–1602
repression of, 463–464
Siwan dialect as, 2071
survival of, 463
Berber literature, 192, 462, 464, 1426
Berber music, 462
Berber Spring (1980) (Algeria), **463–464**
ban on Berber poetry and, 464
National Charter (1976) and, 444
Sadi (Said) in, 1959
start of, in Tizi-Ouzou, 1261
2001 commemoration of (*See* Black Spring)
Berdyczewski, Micah Joseph, 1430
Bergen-Belsen concentration camp, 1041
Berger, Elmer, in American Council for Judaism, 176
Berger, Joseph, 626
Berger, Morrow, 539
Bergman, Elizabeth M., *as contributor,* 234–235
Bergman, Samuel Hugo, 1461
Berg, Nancy, *as contributor,* 1521–1522, 1977–1978
Berihah. *See* Brichah
Berk, Ilhan, 1440
Berkowitz, Yizhak, **464**
Berlin–Baghdad Railway, **464–465**, 532–533
in Ankara, 207

construction of, 464–465
Deutsche Bank in, 464, 533, 904
international controversy over, 2206
Potsdam Convention on (1911), 1851
Berlin Conference (1885), 2085
Berlin, Congress of (1878), **465,** 528
Armenian delegation at, 2311
Khrimian (Mkrtich) in, 1314
Austro-Hungarian delegation at, 339
Ottoman Empire in, British support for, 27
San Stefano Treaty revised at, 27, 654, 1989, 2311
Berlin Memorandum, 382
Berlin, Treaty of (1878), **465**
on Armenians, 299, 2311
and Austria-Hungary, 383, 465, 528, 1989
and Bosnia-Herzegovina, 383, 1989
cessions by Ottoman Empire in, 26–27, 382–383, 465, 528, 1989
and Germany, 465, 528, 903
and Greater Bulgaria, 382–383, 1989
and Montenegro, 383, 1989
and Romania, 1989
and Russian territories, 383, 465, 528, 1989
and Serbia, 383, 1989
Bernadotte, Folke, **465–466,** *2275*
in Arab–Israel War (1948), 2274
at King David Hotel, 1324
assassination of, 466, 1250, 1443, 2026, 2274, 2385
Bunche (Ralph J.) as assistant to, 543
Cattan (Henry) and, 570
Bernadotte Plan for Arab–Israeli settlement, 466
Bernikho-Canin, Rhimou, *as contributor,* 975
Berque, Jacques, 2035
Berrada, Hamid, in Union Nationale des Etudiants Marocains, 2266
Berrada, Mohammed, **466–467**
Berriane (Algeria), 1627
Berri, Nabi, **467–468**
in AMAL movement, 174, 467, 1037, 1647
education of, 467
electoral success of, 467
vs. Husayni (Husayn al-), 1055
in parliament, 174
in "salvation committee," 1647
Besht (Baʿal Shem Tov), 1002
Bessarabia, Russian-Ottoman wars and, 1945
Beta Israel. *See* Ethiopian Jews
Bet al-Hakham family, 1012
Betar (youth movement), 1209
Begin (Menachem) in, 424
in Poland
leaders of, *2437*
Yellin-Mor (Natan) in, 2384
and revisionist Zionism, 2412, 2437
Bet Hannan (Sephardic settlement), 2364
Bet ha-Tefutsot (Tel Aviv), 928
Bethlehem (West Bank), **468,** *2339,* 2340
during Arab–Israel War (1948), 468
under British mandate, 468
under Israeli control, 468
Jordan annexing, 468
location of, 468
under Ottoman rule, 468
pilgrims in, *1759*
population of, 468
sacred sites in, 468
Betts, Robert, *as contributor,* 726–730
Between Two Wars (Bitton), 483
Bet Zilkha (seminary), 2079
Beur (Sebbar), 2007
Beurs, 1427
Beverages, alcoholic, 109–110
Beverly Hills (Egypt), 1995
Bevin–Bidault agreement (1945), 468
Bevin, Ernest, **468–469**
and Anglo–American Committee of Inquiry, 198
Crossman (Richard) in, 650
as foreign secretary, 468–469, 518, 647, 842
Middle Eastern policy conducted by, 338
Bevin–Sforza Plan (1949), 468, **469**
Bevin–Sidqi agreement (1946), 468
Bewicke, Hilda, 286
Bey, 2622
Beyath, Yahya Kemal, 1439
Bey, Boghos. *See* Yusufian, Boghos
Beyoğlu, 864
Beyoğlu Protocol (1861), **469**
Beyzai, Bahram, 2186
Bezalel Academy of Arts and Design, **469–470**
Bezalel Museum, 470
BG militia (Lebanon), 1253
Bialik, Hayyim Nahman, **470,** 1164, 1430–1431
as Ahad Haʿam's disciple, 470
Alterman (Natan) compared with, 171
education of, 470
Shlonsky (Avraham) rivalry, 2058
Bibby, Geoffrey, 708
Bible
archaeological research on, 275–276, 277–278
Palestine Exploration Fund and, 1771–1772
Christian, 589
Hebrew
Dead Sea Scrolls and, 685
kosher in, 1335
Holy Land of, Palestine as, 1758
Mount Ararat in, 274
Tomb of the Patriarchs in, 1807
Biblical Hebrew (BH), 1017
Bibliotheca Alexandria, *117,* 118
Bibliothèque Nationale (Paris), Islamic coin collection of, 1702
Bicycle Run, The (Iranian film), 1473
Bidʿa (religious innovation), muwahhidun rejection of, 1625
Bidaya al-Mujtahid wa Nihaya al-Muqtasid (Hafidʾ al-), 1476
Bidonvilles, **470–471**
in Casablanca, 569
in Tripoli, 2216
Bidun, in Kuwait, 1347
Bieberstein, Marschall von, 904
Biggeh (Egypt), 1832
Bihayri, Niʿmat al-, 1924–1925, 1994
Bilad, al- (newspaper), 1679
Bilad al-Sham. *See* Greater Syria
Bilad al-siba (lands of dissidence), Western Sahara as, 2343
"Biladi, Biladi" (Darwish), 675
Bilharzia. *See* Schistosomiasis
Bilhayr, Abd al-Nabi, **471**
Bilkent University, **472,** 491
Billah, Muhammad al-Baqi, 2114
Billets (Gebeyli), 872

Biltmore Program (1942), **472–473**
BILU. *See* Aliyah
Binationalism, **473**
  Anglo–American Committee of Inquiry on, 473
  Kalvaryski (Chaim Margaliut-) support for, 473, 1265
Bin Ayad, Mahmud, 389
Bin Diyaf, Muhsen, **474**
Bin Ladin, Osama, *474*, **474–475**
  in Afghanistan, 474–475
  childhood of, 474
  in *Cole* attack (2000), 613
  education of, 474, 1865
  on Gulf Crisis, 475
  in Pakistan, 474
  in al-Qaʿida, 474–475, 1865–1866
  Saudi support for, 164, 474
  and September 11th attacks, 475, 2155, 2178
  in Sudan, 475
  Taliban and, 61, 475, 1712, 1865, 2155
  U.S. attempts to capture, 1866
  U.S. support for (1980s), 2178
  wanted poster for, *2177*
Bint, 2622
Bint al-Shati, **475–476**, 892
Binyamina (Israeli settlement), 1938
Biqa Valley (Lebanon), **476**, 901, 2422
Bira, al- (Palestine), 893
Biʾr al-Qamh (Salim), 1978
Birds of Shade (Seri), 2012
Biret, Idil, **476–477**
"Bir içim su" (Tevfik Fikret), 2180
Birnbaum, Nathan, 2432
Birth control, **477–480**, 1510–1511
  advocates of, 477
  controversy over, 477
  cultural, political, and religious opposition to, 478–480
  manipulating population growth with, 477–478
  methods of, 480
  use of term, 478–479
Birth-control pills, 480
Birth of Israel, The: Myths and Realities (Flapan), 835
Birth rates, 1508
Bir Zeit University, **481**, 1901
  Aqqad (Umar Abd al-Fattah al-) support for, 219
  Barghuthi (Marwan) at, 402
  gender studies at, 896
  Institute of Women's Studies (IWS) at, 1100–1101
  Matzpen beginnings at, 1500
  Nasir (Hanna) as founder of, 1646
  Nusayba (Sari) at, 1705
Bishara, Abdullah, **481**
Bishara, Azmi, in election of 2003, 1788
Bishara, Suha, **481**
Bisharin clan, 433
Bishop, Dale L., *as contributor*, 589–593
Bisitun (Iran), **481–482**
Bismarck, Otto von, at Berlin Congress, 465, 528, 903
Bistami, Abu Yazid al-, 2113
Bitar, Abd al-Razzaq al-, and Arab nationalism, 261
Bitar, Midhat al-, in Baʿth party, 69
Bitar, Salah al-Din al-, **482**
  Aflaq (Michel) and, 68–69, 482
  al-Tali published by, 68
  Arsuzi (Zaki al-) and, 308
  assassination of, 482
  in Baʿth party, 69, 412, 482
  in coup (1963), 482
  education of, 482
  in exile, 482
  as foreign minister, 482
  government of
    Atasi (Jamal al-) in, 329
    Hafiz (Amin al-) in, 971
  as prime minister, 482
Bitat, Rabah, **482–483**
  Ben Bella (Ahmed) and, 483
  under Bendjedid (Chadli), 483
  under Boumédienne (Houari), 483
  in Comité Révolutionnaire d'Unité et d'Action, 137, 620
  French skyjacking of, 1309
  in Front de Libération Nationale, 482
Bittari, Zoubida, **483**
Bitton, Simone, **483**
Bizerte (Tunisia), **483–484**, 2225
Bizerte Crisis (1961), **484–485**, 501
Bizri, Afif al-, 2133
Blackboards, The (Iranian film), 1473
Black Box (Oz), 1748
Black Friday (Iran)
  casualties of, 1126
  public response following, 1126
Black, Ian, *as contributor*, 992, 1322, 1409–1410, 1838, 2055–2056, 2056–2057
Black Jews, in Dimona (Israel), Kahane (Meir) on, 1263
Black olives, *837*, 840
Black Panthers, 483, **485**
  protests in Israel, 1500
Black Saturday, Jumayyil (Bashir) in, 1253
Black Sea, **485**, 2236
  area of, 485
  climate of, 605
  Ottoman access to, 485, 1446, 2093–2094
  Russian access to, 739–740
    Kuçuk Kaynara Treaty (1774) and, 485, 739, 2094–2095
    London Treaty (1871) on, 1446
    Paris Peace (1856) on, 1446
    and relations with Ottoman Empire, 1945
  Straits Convention (1841) on, 2092–2093, 2095
  Turkish control of, 485, 2095
  waterway joining Aegean Sea and (*See* Straits, Turkish)
Black September (1970), **485–486**, 1063, 1245
  airplane hijackings by, 2176
  establishment of, 485
  hostages at Saudi embassy in Sudan by, 486
  Israeli athletes killed at Munich Olympics by, 485, 2176
  Khalaf (Salah) role in, 485, 1292
  Majali (Habis) in, 1470
  name of, 485
  parties dissolved after, 1257
  Salama (Ali Hasan) in, 485
  Tall (Wasfi al-) assassinated by, 485, 2157
  trigger for, 967
Black slaves, 2073, 2074
Black Spring (2001) (Algeria), 464, **486**
  Benflis (Ali) and, 445
  Bouteflika (Abdelaziz) and, 504
  casualties of, 274
  causes of, 1261
  Coordination des Arches created during, 274, 486, 638
Black Stone, 1259
Black Thursday (1978), **486–487**
  Union Générale des Travailleurs Tunisiens in, 41, 2265

Blair, Tony, in war against Iraq (2003), 2324
criticism for intelligence failures, 2326
Blake, William, critical studies on, 322
Blanc de l'Algérie, le (Djebar). *See Algerian White*
Blankinship, Khalid Y., *as contributor,* 1027–1028, 1086, 1506–1507, 1623, 2039, 2260
Blaustein, Jacob, in American Jewish Committee, 178
Blazing Sun, The (film), 2039
Bled al-Siba/Bled al-Makhzan, **487**
Blessure du Nom Propre, La (Khatibi), 396, 1304
Blida-Joinville Hospital, 804
Blindness, 712, *713*
Blind Owl, The (Hedayat), 1435
Bliss, Daniel, **487**
Bliss, Frederick, 487
Bliss, Howard, **487–488**
Blix, Hans, 1069, 1136
as UN weapons inspector, 2324
Bloc d'Action Nationale (Morocco). *See* Comité d'Action Marocaine
Bloc for Peace (Israel). *See* Gush Shalom
Bloc of the Faithful. *See* Gush Emunim (Israel)
Blood libel, 211. *See also* Antisemitism
in Damascus affair, 212, 664–665
Blood money
law on (Iran), 998
for men, 1987
for women, 1987, 2051
Bloom, Jonathan M., *as contributor,* 1074–1075
Bloom, Mia, *as contributor,* 140–141, 560, 567–568, 646–647, 685–686, 715, 966, 1929, 2066–2067, 2138, 2364–2365, 2376–2377, 2430
Bludan Conferences (1937, 1946), **488**
Blue Book (of al-Saʿid), 825
Blue Mosque (Istanbul). *See* Sultan Ahmet Mosque
Blue Mosque (Tabriz), 2144
Blue Nile, 372, 902, 1688, 2328. *See also* Nile River
in Khartoum, 1301
Blue Reason (Parsipur), 1803
Blue Shirts. *See* Wafd
Blue Stream natural gas pipeline, 1944
Blue Veil, The (film), 388
Blumberg, Arnold, *as contributor,* 321, 465, 1444–1445, 1796–1797
Blum, Léon, 489
Popular Front government under, 1839
in Syrian negotiations for independence, 328–329, 1839
Blum–Viollette Plan (1936), **489**
Abbas (Ferhat) support for, 3
Hadj (Messali al-) position on, 969
Blunt, Wilfrid, 52
and *Urwa al-Wuthqa, al-* (newspaper), 2302
B'nai B'rith, **489–490**
centers of, 489
in E.U., 489
formation of, 489
lodges of, 489
purpose of, 489
in U.S., 489
Bnei Akivah. *See* Gush Emunim
Board games, 2050
Boats. *See* Ships
Bodrum (Turkey), **490**
Boer War, 2127
Bogale, Yona, 787
Boğaziçi (Bosporus) University, **490–491,** 758, 1551–1552
Bogazköy (Turkey), **491**
Boir Ahmadi, 1447
Boîte à merveille, La (Sefrioui), 2008
Bols, Louis J., 1794, 1795
Boltanski, Emma Aubin, *as contributor,* 1630–1631
Bombay Marine, 526, 530
Bombay Presidency, 534
Bombing, The (Bitton), 483
Bona (Algeria). *See* Annaba
Bonaparte, Napoléon, **491–492**
and archaeological research, 275
in Battle of Abu Qir (1798), 39
Egypt invaded by (1798–1801), 183, *847*
administration during, 491
alienation of Egyptians during, 845
Anglo–Ottoman force ending, 491, 766
as British threat, 524, 525
Convention of al-Arish on (1800), 288–289
historical accounts of, 1207
impact of, 492
Kléber (Jean-Baptiste) in, 1330
Menou (Jacques François) in, 1517
Muhammad Ali in campaign against, 1602
Institut d'Égypte founded by, 1099
Saint Catherine's Monastery protected by, 1971
Sebastiani (Horace) under, 2006
in Treaty of Amiens (1802), 182–183
and Westernization, 2341
Bonn Conference (2001), 1121, 1275, 1365, 2421
interim government formed at, 66
Karzai (Hamid) appointed by, 1276
United Nations at, 2280
Bonyad-e Mostaz'afan (Iran), 1615
Bookin-Weiner, Jerome, *as contributor,* 401, 643
Book of Algeria (Madani), 1456
Boom (sailing vessel), 704
Booth, Marilyn, *as contributor,* 40, 322, 716, 769–770, 817, 914–915, 1080, 1672, 1906–1907, 2030–2031, 2088, 2428
Boqqali, Abdessalam al-, 1428
Boratav, Pertev Naili, **492–493**
Border guard (Israel), 1536
Borek, 836
Borochov, Ber, 456, **493**
Uganda Project opposed by, 2257
Borowy, Iris, *as contributor,* 157
Borsch, Stuart J., *as contributor,* 2066, 2214, 2349
Borujerdi, Hosayn, **493–494,** 929
death of, 1310
Khomeini (Ruhollah) under, 1310
Montazeri (Hosayn Ali) and, 1564
Musavi-Ardebili (AbdolKarim) and, 1614
Bosnia-Herzegovina
Austria-Herzegovina annexing, 384
Austro-Hungarian relations with, 339–340
Berlin Treaty (1878) and, 383, 465, 1989

Bosnia-Herzegovina *(continued)*
Budapest Convention (1877) and, 541
Muslim refugees from, 1913
nationalist movement in, 542
San Stefano Treaty (1878) and, 382, 1988
Bosporus, 2094, 2236
ferryboat company for, 2069
international status of, London Convention (1840) on, 1444, 2094
Turkish sovereignty over, under Montreux Convention (1936), 1565
Bosporus University, 2242
Bosquet, Pierre-Jean-François, 379
Bost (Afghanistan), **494–495**
Boston Female Society for Promoting Christianity amongst the Jews, 1854
Boston Symphony Orchestra, 477
Botta, Paul Emile, 276
Bouabid, Abderrahim, **495**
in Union Nationale des Forces Populaires, 2266, 2267
in Union Socialiste des Forces Populaires, 2268
Bouazza, Tayyib, in Union Marocaine du Travail, 453
Boucetta, Fatiha, 2376
Boucetta, Muhammad, **495**
in Istiqlal Party, 1197
Bouchiha, Mohamed, in Parti d'Unité Populaire, 1804, 2232
Boucs, les (Chraibi), 588
Bouderba, Omar, in Young Algerians, 2405
Boudiaf, Fatiha, 496
Boudiaf, Mohamed, **495–496**
in Algerian War of Independence, 496
assassination of, 496, 506, 917, 1026
in Comité d'Etat, 496
in Comité Révolutionnaire d'Unité et d'Action, 137, 496, 620
Didouche (Mourad) collaboration with, 708
French skyjacking of, 442, 496, 1309
in Front de Libération Nationale, 496
Hadj (Messali al-) supported by, 496
in High State Council, 1026
in Mouvement pour le Triomphe des Libertés Démocratiques, 496
in Organisation Spéciale, 496
in Parti de la Révolution Socialiste, 496
Boudjedra, Rachid, **496–497**, 1426
Boudraa, Nabil, *as contributor,* 582–583
Boughedir, Fédir, 2192
Bouhired, Jamila, **497**
in Algerian War of Independence, 136
Bou Hmara. *See* Abu Himara
Bouih, Fatna el-, **497–498**
imprisonment of, 1203
Bouillon, Gabriel, Kan (Suna) taught by, 1269
Boujemaʿa, Zoulaika, in Algerian War of Independence, 136
Boukhari, Khadija, 497
Boukharouba, Mohammed Ben Brahim. *See* Boumédienne, Houari
Boukhedenna, Sakina, 1427
Boukrouh, Nourredine, 451
Boulahia, Ismail, Moadda (Mohamed) and, 1554
Boulahya, Ismaïl, 2232
Boulam, Benaissa, 995
Boulanger, Nadia, 476
Boullatta, Kamal, *as contributor,* 673–675
Boumédienne, Houari, **498–500**, *499*
agricultural policies of, 124
in Algerian War of Independence, 498
in Armée de Libération Nationale, 498
Ben Bella (Ahmed) and
cooperation by, 128, 442, 499
rivalry between, 129, 442, 499, 503
Ben Khedda (Ben Youssef) and, 450
constitution revised under, 129–130
coup by (1965), 124, 129, 442, 499, 503, 1537
Abdelghani (Mohamed Benahmed) in, 23
educational reform by, 124
education of, 498
executive powers of, 129
in exile, 498
in Gouvernement Provisoire de la République Algérienne, 498
government of, 1744
Abbas (Ferhat) rejection of, 4
Abdelghani (Mohamed Benahmed) in, 23
Abdesselam (Belaid) in, 23
Belkacem (Cherif) in, 437
Bendjedid (Chadli) in, 444
Bitat (Rabah) in, 483
Bouteflika (Abdelaziz) in, 503
Hamrouche (Mouloud) in, 987
Ibrahimi (Ahmed Taleb) in, 1076
Kaid (Ahmed) in, 1264
Krim (Belkacem) opposing, 1337
Lacheraf (Mostefa) as advisor to, 1362
Nahnah's (Mahfoud) criticism of, 1636
in Oujda Group, 1743–1744
Parti de l'Avant-Garde Socialiste under, 1803
in Parti du Peuple Algérien, 498
presidency of, 499–500
in Setif Revolt (1945), 498
Wattar's (al-Taher) optimism for and disillusionment with, 2333
Zbiri (Tahar) and, 2429
Bou Noura (Algeria), 1627
Bouraoui, Hédi, 1424
Bouraoui, Nina, 1424
Bourgès-Maunoury, Maurice
and Loi Cadre, 1443
and Sèvres Protocol (1956), 2109
Bourguiba, Habib, **500–503**, *501, 2227*
Achour (Habib) pardoned by, 41
arrest of, 586
autonomy negotiations with France, 849
Ben Ali (Zayn al-Abidine) under, 439, 503
Ben Salah (Ahmed) and, 452, 502, 1587
Ben Yousouf (Salah) and, 455, 501
and beylicate, abolition of, 185
and Communist Party, 1590
in Constitutional Democratic Rally, 2231
coup against (1987), 503, 635, 1537, 2229
in Destour Party, 501
economic policies of, Union Générale des Travailleurs Tunisiens opposing, 2265

education of, 500–501, 1307
family planning supported by, 478
and Franco–Tunisian Convention, 455
in Gafsa incident (1980), 863
government of
Masmoudi (Muhammad) in, 1499
Mestiri (Ahmad) in, 1519–1520
Mzali (Mohammed) in, 1627–1628
Nouira (Hedi) in, 1693–1694
habous during government of, 964
ideological independence of, 502
Mouvement de L'Unité Populaire opposing, 1587
Mzali (Mohammed) opposing, 1628
nationalist movement led by, 615
in Neo-Destour Party, 501, 502, 634, 2229
in Parti Socialiste Destourien, 634, 635
and Personal Status Code, 912
presidency of, 501–503, 634–635, 2229
Marzouki (Moncef) on, 1496–1497
Sfar (Tahar) and, 2016
weakening influence of, 502–503
Bourguiba, Habib, Jr., 501
Bourguibisme, 502
Bourqia, Rahma, *as contributor,* 350, 912–913, 921, 996, 1141, 1237, 1515, 1871, 2059, 2166–2167, 2212
Boussouf, Abd al-Hafid, 498
Bouteflika, Abdelaziz, **503–505,** *504,* 2430
agenda of, 135
in Algerian War of Independence, 503
amnesty (Civil Concord) policy of, 127, 135, 504
for Islamic Salvation Army, 1156
poster for, *133*
in Armée de Libération Nationale, 503
Belkacem (Cherif) criticizing, 437
Ben Bella (Ahmed) and, 442, 503
Bendjedid (Chadli) and, 444, 445, 504
under Boumédienne (Houari), 503
Chérif (Hachemi) opposing, 1803
education policies of, Tamazight language in, 1261
election to presidency, 127, 135, 984
in exile, 504
as foreign minister, 503
in Front de Libération Nationale, 503–504
government of
Benbitour (Ahmed) in, 504
Benflis (Ali) in, 445, 504
Berber youth killed by, 96
Hanoune (Louisa) criticism of, 990
Nahnah (Mahfoud) in, 1636
Haut Comité d'Etat and, 504
in Oujda Group, 1743
Pouvoir supporting, 504
presidency of, 504–505
Sadi (Said) supporting, 1960
Toumi (Khalida) supporting, 2195
Boutros-Ghali, Boutros, **505**
at Ahram Center for Political and Strategic Studies, 92
in Arab–Israeli peace negotiations, 505
Basma bint Talal as advisor of, 409
education of, 505
Bouyali, Moustafa, **505–506**
in Algerian War of Independence, 506
Belhadj (Ali) and, 436, 506
in Front de Libération Nationale, 506
in Mouvement Islamique Armé, 505–506, 918
Bowen, Donna Lee, *as contributor,* 105–107, 441, 477–480, 828–829, 1888
Bowen, Harold, 1035
Bowie, Robert, 539
Bowles, Paul, 2060
Boycott I (Iranian film), 1473
Boy Scouts, 2006
Bozkir guzellemesi (Araz), 274
Bozkurt, Mahmut Esat, and civil codes, 602
Braber, 458
Bradsher, Henry S., *as contributor,* 65–66
Brahimi, Abdelhamid, **506**
Brahimi, Lakhdar
at Bonn Conference (2001), 2280
as UN envoy in U.S.-occupied Iraq, 2326
Brahuis (people), 385
"Brain drain," 761
Brami, Joseph, Valensi (Alfred) and, 2308
Brandeis, Louis, 2436
on Keren Hayesod, 1289
in Palestine Economic Corporation, 1771
Weizmann's (Chaim) quarrel with, 2338
Wise (Stephen S.) and, 2354
Brandt, Willy, Peled (Mattityahu) dialogue with, 1812
Braude, Benjamin, *as contributor,* 545, 548, 563–564, 719–720, 722, 1384–1385, 1543–1545, 1547–1550, 1832–1833
Braudel, Ferdinand, 407
Brazil, Jewish settlements in, 1229
Bread and Alley (Iranian film), 1473
"Bread, Hashish, and a Moon" (Qabbani), 1859
Breasted, James Henry, 772
Breast-feeding, 1508
Bremer, Paul L., III, 681
in U.S. occupation of Iraq, 2325–2326
Brenner, Yosef Hayyim, **506–507,** 1431
Breton, André, 414, 2020
Brezhnev Doctrine, 508
Brezhnev, Leonid Ilyich, **507–508,** *508*
in Afghanistan invasion, 65
in Communist Party, Khrushchev (Nikita S.) ousted by, 1314
under Khrushchev (Nikita), 507
and Nasser (Gamal Abdel), *1942*
Brichah, **508–509**
Kovner (Abba) in, 1336
Bridal Canopy, The (Agnon), 71
Bridge Party. *See* Gesher Party
Bringing Water from the Fountain Has Nothing Romantic about It (Niati), 1687
Britain, **509–538.** *See also* Anglo *entries; specific cities, organizations, people, and regions*
Aden occupied by (*See under* Aden)
Afghanistan protectorate of, 536
Afghan relations with
Durand Line in, 400, 536, 734
foreign policy control in, 19–20, 174, 197, 536
Afghan wars with (*See* Anglo–Afghan wars)
in Agadir crisis (1911), 70
in Anglo–Persian Oil Company, 537, 671
Arab Bureau of, 225

Britain *(continued)*
Arabian Peninsula under control of, 526–527
Arab independence promised by, 1059
in Arab–Israel War (1948), 518
in Arab–Israel War (1956), 244–246
in Arab–Israel War (1967), 521
in Arab–Israel War (1973), 522
Arab Revolt supported by (1916), 263–264, 510, 799–800, 1053
Arab unity support promised by, 380, 510–511, 517, 742–743, 815
archaeological research by, 275, 276, 277
Palestine Exploration Fund and, 1771–1772
arms sales by, 750
for balancing oil imports, 523
to Iran, 523
to Iraq, 523
to Jewish forces, 1770, 1790
NEACC and, 2215
Bahrain and, treaties between, 149, 531, 614
Bahrain protectorate of (*See under* Bahrain)
and Balfour Declaration (1917) (*See* Balfour Declaration)
Canning Award (1861), 2425
in Central Treaty Organization, 573
in Cold War, 517–518
and Baghdad Pact (1955), 363, 519
colonialism of, 613–616
Colonial Office of, 514, 518, 617
communications infrastructure by, 624
corsairs and, 526
in Crimean War, 648–649, 739
Cyprus under (*See under* Cyprus)
in Damascus affair (1840), 664–665
in Dardanelles Treaty (1809), 621, 671–672
as dominant power in Middle East (1914–1956), 509
in Eastern Question, 509, 739–743
economic and military aid from, 747
economy of
oil prices and, 522
Suez Canal closure of (1967–1975) and, 521
as EEC member, 522
Egyptian relations with (*See under* Egypt)
Egypt occupied by (*See under* Egypt)
espionage by, 1521
in European Economic Community, 522
and Fertile Crescent unity, 743, 824–825
Foreign Office of (*See* Foreign Office)
foreign policy of
Crimean War and, 648
De Bunsen (Maurice) and, 686
French relations with
Berlin Treaty (1878) and, 528
Cambon–Lansdowne Agreement in (1904), 529, 559–560, 1374
Moroccan claim supported in, 119–120
French rivalry with, 524, 846
over Egypt, 527–528, 529, 742
over India, 525, 526
over Iraqi oil, 2199
over Lado Enclave, 1363
and Lebanese independence, 1399
over Trucial Coast, 531
Germany as threat to, 533
in Greek War of Independence, 940
in Gulf Crisis (1990–1991), 523, 953
Hashimites supported by, 510, 515, 520, 801
imperialism of, 1089–1090
in India (*See under* India)
India Office of, 514, 526, 532, 534, 617
Iranian relations with, 1117 (*See also* Anglo–Persian War)
Curzon (George Nathaniel) in, 651–652
economic privileges in, Anglo–Iranian Agreement on (1919), 200
Jangali and, 1216
under Naser al-Din Shah, 1644
Treaty of Paris (1857) in, 1802
Wilson (Arnold T.) and, 2352–2353
Iraqi mandate of (*See under* Iraq)
in Iraq, U.S. war in (2003), 1136, 1539–1540, 2324–2325
prewar intelligence failures and, 2326
Italy under Mussolini (Benito) as threat to, 515
Jordanian mandate of (*See under* Jordan)
Kuwait and
bond between, 1348–1349
British troops as deterrent against Iraqi invasion of, 520
foreign policy of, 160
Kuwaiti treaty with (1899), 531, 614, 1348
Kuwait protectorate of, 534
Lebanese relations with, 512
legacy of, 523
legal system of, influencing law in Middle East, 886, 1380
Levant Company of, 525
Libyan relations with, 1415
Anglo–Libyan Alliance Treaty (1953) and, 517
and Libyan independence, 615
military withdrawal from, 521
mandates of, 512, 614, 1479–1480 (*See also under specific countries*)
education in, 758
indirect rule of, 514–515
King–Crane Commission on (1919), 1323
Paris peace settlements on, 1802
reduction of military presence in, 512–514
San Remo Conference (1920) on, 1988
Sèvres Treaty (1920) on, 2015
Sykes–Picot Agreement on, 2128, 2315
maritime truce in Persian Gulf (1853), 1489
masonic lodges set up by, 852
Middle East Defense Organization proposed by, 519
military of
after Arab–Israel War (1967), 521
Crossman (Richard) in, 650
on Cyprus, 519, 521, 529
in mandates, 512–514
after Suez Crisis (1956–1957), 520
Morocco and
reaction to Treaty of Meknes (1836), 1515
trade agreement between (1856), 19, 1515
Najd treaty with (1915), 531
in Napoleonic wars (*See* Napoleonic wars)
navy of
conversion to oil fuel, 671
Ottoman navy and, 1741

Northern Tier interests of, 1692–1693
oil imports to, 517, 522–523
from Bahrain, 537
from Iran, 526
from Iraq, 526
from Kuwait, 537
OPEC and, 522
oil production by, 1824–1825
Anglo–Iranian Oil Company of, 200–202, 518, 742
D'Arcy Concession and (1901), 200, 536–537, 671
in North Sea, 522
Saudi Arabia favoring U.S. companies and, 515
Oman and, 1710
in Dhufar rebellion, 705, 1842
treaties between, 203–204, 614
Operation Alpha of, 157
Ottoman Empire and (*See under* Ottoman Empire)
Palestine Arab Revolt (1936–1939) suppressed by, 381, 515
Palestinian mandate of (*See under* Palestine)
Palestinian policy of (*See also* White papers on Palestine)
Churchill (Winston S.) and, 595–597
in Churchill White Paper (1922), 594, 2349–2350
MacDonald Letter on (1931), 1454, 2350
in MacDonald White Paper (1939), 1454, 2350–2351, 2363
in Passfield White Paper (1930), 1453, 2350
Woodhead Commission (1938) on, 2350, 2363
Parliament of, Crossman (Richard) in, 650
Persian cats in, 1821
Persian Gulf interventions by, 1820
Persian Gulf under (*See under* Persian Gulf)
postage stamps of, 1849
Protestant missions from, 1796, 1797, 1854, 1855
Qatar intervention by, 1876
Qatar treaty with (1916), 531, 614
Russian–Ottoman War (1877–1878) and, 528
Russian relations with
Anglo–Russian Agreement on (1907), 205
Constantinople and, 511, 528, 529
Iran in, 88, 205, 651–652
rivalry over Afghanistan, 536
rivalry over Persia, 535–536
rivalry over southern central Asia, 936–937
Russo–Japanese War (1904–1905) and, 536
spheres of influence in Central Asia, 1032
Suez Canal and, 529
Turkish Straits and, 528, 529, 2093
against San Stefano Treaty, 382, 465, 1989
Saudi relations with
under Abd al-Aziz ibn Saʿud Al Saʿud, 11, 515
Faysal ibn Turki Al Saʿud and, 819
Treaty of Protection (1886) and, 2208
Sudan under (*See under* Sudan)
and Suez Canal (*See* Suez Canal; Suez Crisis)
Syrian relations with, 801, 824, 825
in Syrian War (1831–1833), 1346
Syria occupied by (1918), 510
terrorism and, 521, 522
in trade
Balta Liman, Convention of (1838) and, 385, 2163
with Ottoman Empire, 525–526, 742
Transjordanian mandate of (*See under* Jordan)
and Tripartite Declaration (1950), 2215
Trucial Coast controlled by, 531, 2218–2219
and Tunb Islands, 2224
Turkish relations with
Adana Conference in (1943), 42
dispute over Mosul oil deposits (1920–1928), 1582–133
Uganda Project proposed by, 2257
in United Arab Emirates (*See under* United Arab Emirates)
U.S. relations with, oil concessions after World War I and, 514
in Vienna Congress (1814–1815), 739
in World War I (*See under* World War I)
in World War II (*See under* World War II)
in Yemen
Aden occupied by, 2390
South Yemen under, 2390
withdrawal of, 2390
Zanzibar under, 2425
Zionists in, 2424–2425
Zoroastrianism in, 2441
Brit ha-Hayyal, 2437
British East India Company. *See* East India Company
British–French Oil Agreement (1920), **538–539**, 1988
on French share of oil, 628
on Turkish Petroleum Company, 538, 1988
British–Indian Steam Navigation Company, 1474
British Museum, Islamic coin collection of, 1702
British Oil Company, 200
British Petroleum. *See also* Anglo–Iranian Oil Company
in As-Is Agreement (1928), 323
attempts to break, 1718
Heskayl (Sasson) and, 1023
Iraq nationalizing, 410
in Kuwait Oil Company, 1349
prices set by, in Venezuela *vs.* Middle East, 1718–1719
Thatcher (Margaret) selling off government shares in, 522
and Turkish Petroleum Company, 1909
Brit Shalom
binationalism supported by, 473
Ruppin (Arthur) and, 1940
Brockelmann, Carl, in Arab Academy of Damascus, 224
Brookings Institution, 539
Brookings Report (1975), **539**
Brooks, David B., *as contributor,* 2327–2332
Browne, Edward Granville, **539–540**
Brown, George, 521
Brown, Nathan J., *as contributor,* 1379–1384
Brugsch, Heinrich K., Kamal (Ahmad) studies under, 1265
Bruit dort, Le (Tlili), 2193
Brûlure des interrogations, La (Laabi), 1356
Bruno, Armando, 145
Brushers (Nesin), 1676
Brussels Act (1980), 2074
Brzezinski, Zbigniew, 539
B'Tselem (Israel), 1809

Bu. *See* Abu Himara
Buber, Martin, **540–541,** 1461
Ahad Ha-Am and, 78
on Arab–Israel conflict, 540
binationalism supported by, 473
and Ha-Shomer ha-Tzaʿir, influence on, 1001
Bubiyan Island, **541,** 804, 949
Bubonic plague, 1835, 1845
Bubon, Jack, *as contributor,* 643, 2083, 2203–2204
BUC. *See* Beirut University College
Bucharest, Treaty of (1812), **541,** 1945
Canning (Stratford) in, 563
Bucharest, Treaty of (1913), 384
Büchner, Ludwig, 576, 2061
Buckley, William, kidnapping of, 1122
Budapest Convention (1877), **541–542**
Bududa mat (Hamzawi), 987
Buf-e Kur (Hedayat), 1019
Buffeh, al- (Salim), 1978
Bugeaud de la Piconnerie, Thomas-Robert, **542**
bureaux arabes created by, 545
Morocco attacked by, 19
Ouled Sidi Cheikh and, 1745
in Treaty of Tafna (1837), 17, 542
Bu Hamara, **542**
Buhayra (Egypt), **542**
cities of, 662
capital, 542, 662
under Mamluk rule, 542
under Ottoman rule, 542
Buhturis, 728
Bu Janah family. *See* Busnach family
Bukhari, Muhammad ibn Ismaʿil al-, *Sahih* of, 968
Bukhari, Sahih, *hadith* of, 1026
Bula, 2050
Bulaq, battle of (1517), 2223
Bulgaria. *See also* Greater Bulgaria
in Balkan League, 384
in Balkan wars, 384
expansion of, 339
independence of, 384
languages of, 2248
in Ottoman Empire, Midhat Paşa and, 1524–1525
Bulgarian Horrors, **542–543**
lack of British action after, 382
ultimatum of Alexander II after, 382
Bulgarian millet, 1544
Bulgarians, 383
Bulgur, 836–837, 841
Bullard, Reader, 540
Bulliet, Richard W., *as contributor,* 109–110, 643–645, 946–947, 1087–1091, 1723
Bülow, Bernhard von, Moroccan policy of, 119
Bulukbash, 2228
Bu Mariyam, Accord of (1921), in Italo–Sanus conflict, 1609
Bunche, Ralph J., 466, **543–544**
as adviser to Hammarskjöld (Dag), 543
as assistant to Bernadotte (Folke), 543
education of, 543
in General Armistice Agreement negotiations (1949), 239, *240,* 244, 2274
as mediator during Suez Crisis, 543
Nobel Peace Prize awarded to, 543, 2274
on U.S. race problem, 543
Bund, **544**
Bundahishn (Zoroastrian text), 2441
Bunton, Martin, *as contributor,* 1369–1373
Buraymi Oasis Dispute (1952–1974), 517, **544**
al-Ayn after, 343
Burckhardt, Johann Ludwig, **545**
Petra discovered by, 275, *1240*
Bureau for National Propaganda (Syria), 1486
Bureau of Translation, **545**
Bureaux arabes, **545–546**
Burg, Avraham, **546**
Burghul, Ali, 1871
Burg, Yosef, **546**
Burke, Edmund, III
as contributor, 8–9, 13–14, 19, 37, 86, 1280–1281, 1451, 1492–1493, 1566, 2037–2039, 2223
as historiographer, 1036
Burkina Faso, Berbers in, 458
Burla, Yehuda, **547**
Burma, at Bandung Conference, 387
Burma Oil, D'Arcy Concession assigned to, 671
Burnoose, 611
Burns, E. L. M., 2110
in United Nations Emergency Force, 2286
Burqa, *61*
Burrill, Kathleen R. F., *as contributor,* 44–46, 492–493, 661, 1437–1440, 1648, 1724, 1932–1933, 2380–2381
Burrowes, Robert D., *as contributor,* 12, 143, 192, 211, 338, 355, 417, 854, 855, 857, 913, 976, 985, 1007, 1140–1141, 1143, 1157, 1474, 1487–1488, 1653–1654, 1813–1815, 1819, 1853, 1892, 1979, 1983–1985, 2023, 2024, 2077–2078, 2081, 2149–2150, 2208, 2215, 2304–2305, 2319, 2391–2396, 2397, 2425–2426, 2427
Bursa (Turkey), **547–548,** 2237
gecekondus on outskirts of, 872
grape cultivation in, 110
manufacturing in, 194
as Ottoman capital, 547
population of, 547
textile mills in, 2181
as trade center, 547
during World War I, 547
Burton, Richard Francis, 513, **548**
Bush Doctrine, 2012
Bushehr (Iranian nuclear reactor), 1698
Bush, George Herbert Walker, **548–549**
Baker (James A.) under, 374
in Gulf Crisis (1990–1991), 548, 950, 951
in Iran–Contra affair, 1123
and Kurdish Autonomous Zone, 1339
at Madrid Peace Conference (1991), 549, 1725
Middle East policy of, 2294
and PLO, 548
son of, 2323–2324
Bush, George Walker, **549**
and Afghanistan, U.S. invasion of, 549
at Aqaba meeting (2003), 32
Arafat (Yasir) relations with, 272, 549
"axis of evil" speech of (2002), 1069, 2324
Iran in, 1121
Iraq in, 2324

on democratization in Middle East, 934
dual containment policy and, 730
government of, veterans of Gulf War in, 2324
on intelligence failures, 573
Iraqi National Congress funding from, 1137
in Iraq invasion (2003), 2323–2325
criticism for intelligence failures, 2326
Iraqi policy of, 1136
Middle East policy of, 2294
military response to September 11 by, Congressional authorization of, 66
Occidental Petroleum ties to, 1708
in peace process, 549
neglect of, 220
September 11th, 2001 changing presidency of, 549, 2011–2012
on two-state solution, 1170
war on terrorism by, 549, 2294
Iranian support for, 1121
Jordanian support for, 32
Bushnaq, Yusuf, Muhammad Ali Mosque constructed by, 1603
Bushruʾi, Molla Hosyan, 354, 356
Busnach family, **549–550**, 835
Busnach, Naphtali, 397, 550
Bustani, Antoine, 2422
Bustani, Butrus al-, 1658
Bustani, Fuʿad, 1395
Bustani, Sulayman, **550**
Bus, The (film), 832
Butayna tribe, 2211
Butler, Noah, *as contributor,* 115–116, 1913, 2250–2251
Butler, Richard, 1069, 2288
UN inspections team headed by, 1135
Butterworth, Charles E., *as contributor,* 194–195, 341, 1152–1154, 1456–1457
Buwayti, al-, 2019
Buyid dynasty, 2054
Büyük Birlik Partisi. *See* Great Unity Party
Büyük Doğu (magazine), Kisakürek (Necip Fazil) in, 1326
Buyuk Millet Meclisi. *See* Turkish Grand National Assembly
Bu Zian, 1463
Buzuq (Lebanese music), 1617
By the Pen (Al-e Ahmad), 110
Byzantine Empire, 2239
Constantinople in, 633, 1193
Damascus occupied by, 662
Eastern Orthodox Church in, 589, 738
Byzantine State Church, 737–738

C

Cabarets, 1619
Cachia, Pierre, *as contributor,* 1418–1422, 1464–1465
CADC. *See* Coordination des Archs
Çagetay, Ali Rifat, 2009
Cairo (Egypt), **551–554**, *553*
Ahram Center for Political and Strategic Studies in, 92
Ain Shams University in, 94
Allied Middle East Command in, 152–153
American University in, 179–180
Arabic language in, 233
Arab League summit (1948) in, *155*
Arab League summit (1964) in, *1387*
Arab League summit (1976) in, *1387*
Arab League summit (1990) in, *1387*
Arab League summit (1995) in, *1387*
Arab League summit (2000) in, *1387*
architecture of, 282, 1074
bazaars in, 419
Bʾnai Bʾrith lodge in, 489
under British rule, 552–553, 766
Arab Bureau in, 225
Caliphate Congress in (1926), 557
College of Fine Arts in, 312
Coptic Museum in, 638
disease in, 551
establishment of, 551
Fatimids in, 551, 1158
family planning in, 555
as Fatimid capital, 2054
Gezira Sporting Club in, *908,* 908–909
guilds in, 947
Ibn Tulun Mosque in, 1074
IDF placing explosives in, 1377, 1378
infrastructure of, 552–554
Institut d'Égypte in, 1099
Islamic congresses in, 1152
under Ismaʿil ibn Ibrahim, 552, 1157–1158
newspapers of, 1678
population of, 551, 552, 553, 554, *1845,* 1994
preservation movement in, 552
Radio and Television Building in, *1893*
Ramses College for Girls in, 1902
riots in (1981), 642
satellite cities development on outskirts of, 1994–1995
Sayyida Zaynab Mosque in, 2002
Sayyidna Husayn Mosque in, 2002–2003
Shepheard's Hotel in, 2050
Suez Canal and, 552
Sultan Hasan Mosque in, 2120–2121
textile mills in, 2181
transportation in, 553, 554
urban planning in, 2299
Cairo Agreement (1960), between Lebanon and PLO, 1653
Cairo Caliphate Conference (1926), Maratghi (Mustafa al-) at, 1485–1486
Cairo Conference (1921), **554–555**, 801, *1088*
Askari (Jaʿfar al- at), 1023
capitulations at, 566
Churchill (Winston S.) at, 512, 554, 596, 617, 801, 1023, *1088*
Heskayl (Sasson) at, 1023
Cairo conference on population (1994), 1511
Cairo Convention of Human Rights in Islam, 1049
Cairo–Damascus railway. *See* Damascus–Cairo railway
Cairo Family Planning Association (CFPA), **555**
Cairo Station (film), 832, 2022
Cairo Trilogy (Mahfuz), 1464
Cairo University, **555–556**
vs. American University in Cairo, 179
Amin (Ahmad) at, 183
archaeology at, 1266
Awad (Louis) at, 341
Balafrej (Ahmed) at, 379
Bint al-Shati at, 475
Boutros-Ghali (Boutros) at, 505
Dar al-Ulum school in, 671
Fuʾad supporting, 859

Cairo University *(continued)*
Ghallab (Abd al-Karim) at, 910
Ghanim (Fathi) at, 911
historiography at, 1035
Husayn (Taha) at, 1060
Rateb (Aisha) at, 1905
Saadawi (Nawal al-) at, 1950
Sabah (Suad al-) at, 1952
Sadat (Jihan al-) at, 1958
Saʿid (Amina al-) at, 1965
Salim Hasan at, 1978
vs. Sanʿa University, 1985
Shazli (Saʿd al-Din al-) at, 2048
Shenouda III at, 2048
Caisse de la Dette Publique, La. *See* International Debt Commission
Çakmak, Fevzi, 2413
Caland, Huguette, **556**
Caliphate, **556–558**
end of, 557
Islamic congresses on, 1152
Musa Kazim as defender of, 1613
nationalism and, 556–557
political authority taken from, 21, 557
restoration of proposed, 1485–1486
by Kawakibi (Abd al-Rahman al-), 1659
Shiʿite rejection of, 104
Turkish abolition of, 21, 34, 332, 557
Caliphate Congress (1926), 557
Calligraphy, **558–559**
as art, 145, 232, 235, 558–559
modern, 312, 2259
Persian, 1822
Qur'an in, 558, *558*, 1883
Callimachus, 116
CALTEX, establishment of, 229
CAM. *See* Comité d'Action Marocaine
Cama, Bhikaji, and women's participation in Wafd, 2321
Cambon–Lansdowne Agreement (1904), 529, **559–560**, 1374
Cambon, Paul, 1366
Cambridge University
Bentwich (Norman) at, 454
Browne (Edward Granville) at, 539
Eban (Abba) at, 744
Gorst (John Eldon) at, 931
Shalvi (Alive) at, 2023
Strorrs (Ronald) at, 2092
Camel Corps, of Arab Legion, *258*
Camels, *73*, **560**, 1964, 2205
in United Arab Emirates, *2270*
Camel Transport Corps of the British Army, 454
Cameri theater (Israel), 2418
Campaign Against Illiteracy Association (Iraq), 80
Campbell-Bannerman, Henry, Lansdowne (Lord) under, 1374
Camp David Accords (1978), **560–561**, 2293. *See also* Egyptian–Israeli Peace Treaty (1979)
Arab states rejecting, 770, *1387*, 1388
Baghdad Summit (1978) as response to, 363–364
Begin (Menachem) in, 426, 560, 561, 567, 771, 2293, *2293*, 2308
Boutros-Ghali (Boutros) and, 505
Carter (Jimmy) in, 238, 539, 560, 567, 770, 1166, 2293, *2293*
conflicting interpretations of, 238
Dayan (Moshe) in, 683
failure of, Israeli peace movement after, 1809
Franjiyya (Sulayman) against, 1395
Ghorbal (Ashraf) in, 916
Knesset vote on, 285, 561
land-for-peace principle in, 560, 561
League of Arab States condemning, *1387*, 1388
PLO excluded from, 1774
Qaddafi's condemnation of, 1861
and Reagan Plan, 1908
Sadat (Anwar al-) in, 426, 560, 567, 770, 1166, 1957, 2293, *2293*, 2308
Abd al-Rahman (Umar) opposed to, 20
Boutros-Ghali (Boutros) and, 505
and Saudi Arabia, 794, 796
Saunders (Harold) in, 2001
Shuqayri (Ahmad) opposing, 2062
on Sinai Peninsula, 2068
Syrian acceptance of, 319
Tehiyah party opposing, 1189
U.S. economic aid as incentive for, 748
Vance (Cyrus) in, 2308–2309
Camp David Summit (2000), **561–563**
Arafat (Yasir) in, 561–563, 1775
blame attributed to, 562, 1168
offer rejected by, 399, 1727
Barak (Ehud) in, 399, 561–563, 1775
Clinton (Bill) in, 399, 561–563, 606, 1168, 1727, 1775
failure of, 238, 1775
blame for, 562, 1168, 1727
intifada following, 2294
on Gaza Strip, 871
topics of discussion at, 561–562
Campi misti (mixed camps), in Italo–Sanusi conflict, 1609
Camus, Albert, **563**, 1425
Camus Prize, Gebeyli (Claire) awarded with, 872
Canaanite movement, 1432
Keinan (Amos) influenced by, 1284
Canaanites, in Palestine, 1758
Canaan, Tawfiq, 277
Canada, Zoroastrianism in, 2441
Canfield, Robert L., *as contributor*, 65–66, 1276
Cannes Film Festival (1976), 1977
Cannes Film Festival (1982), 955
Cannes Film Festival (1997), 2022
Cannes Film Festival (2002), *831*
Canning Award (1861), 2425
Canning, George, 563, 648
Canning, Stratford, **563–564**
Cannon, Byron, *as contributor*, 16–18
Cansever, Edip, 1440
Cantate pour l'oiseau mort (Gebeyli), 872
Cantine, James, in Arabian Mission, 231
Cantonnement/refoulement policies, **564**
Cantonnements, 471
Capaz, Osvaldo, Ifni occupied by, 1083
Cape Blanca, under Spanish control, 2085
Capitalism
imperialism and, 1089
industrialization and, 1093
Kemalism and, 1286
Capitulations, **564–566**, 2198
and Balta Liman, Convention of (1838), 385
at Cairo Conference (1921), 566
granted by Ottoman Empire, 564–566, 620–621

to Britain, 565, 621
end of, 566, 621
to France, 565, 620, 844–845
to Venice (1517), 564–565
Lausanne Treaty (1923) restoring, 1376
Levantines benefiting from, 1405
masonic lodge protection under, 852
Caplan, Neil, *as contributor,* 211–213, 289–290, 472–473, 733–734, 803, 927–928, 1230, 1265, 1326–1327, 1445–1446, 1459, 1460–1461, 1758–1769, 1832–1833, 1946–1947, 1993, 2284–2285, 2290, 2307–2308, 2399–2400, 2431–2436
Capparell, Stephanie, *as contributor,* 831–833, 1050–1051
Capsali, Moses, Jewish millet granted to, 1543
Caracalla (Roman emperor), Palmyra under, 1797
Carasso, Albert, 1232
Caravans, 2197, 2205
Cardigan, Lord, 379
Caribbean, Muharram rites in, 1606
Carioca dance, 1273
Carlebach, Ezriel, 1452
Carmel, Mount, *365*
Carmel Plan, 2371
Carmel wine cellars (Israel), 1927
Carnets de Shérazade, Les (Sebbar), 2007
Carpets
in Iran, 2181
Persian, **566–567**
in Kerman, 566, 1290
in Turkey, 2181
Carter, Ben Ami Ben Israel, 708
Carter Center, 1953
Carter, Jimmy, *425,* **567–568**
Asad's (Hafiz al-) promise to, regarding Jewish emigration, 2365
in Camp David Accords (1978), 238, 539, 560, 567, 770, 1166, 2293, *2293*
foreign policy of, 567
government of
Saunders (Harold) in, 2001
Vance (Cyrus) in, 2308–2309
in Iran hostage crisis (1979), 567, 1119
and Iranian Revolution, 1119, 1754
in peace process, 2292, 2293
political defeat of, 567
public service by, 567–568
Carthage (ancient kingdom), 2227
Cartoons, in Turkey, 273
Casablanca (Morocco), **568–570,** *569,* 828, 1567
Arab League summit (1965) in, *1387*
Arab League summit (1985) in, *1387*
Arab League summit (1988) in, *1387*
Arab League summit (1989) in, *1387*
architecture of, 282, 283–284
bombings in (2003), 1569
impact on elections, 2268
city plan for, 569
French protectorate in, 569
after independence, 569
massacre in (1947), 569
newspapers of, 1678
population of, 568, 569
riots in, 569
strikes in, 569
Casablanca Conference, Muhammad V and, 1598
Casanova-Fernandez, Vanesa, *as contributor,* 41, 489–490, 634–635, 964–965, 1212–1213, 1261, 1365, 1499, 1512, 1590–1591, 1706, 1716–1717, 1721–1722, 1723, 1909, 2016, 2083–2085, 2266–2267, 2268–2269
Casbah, 2622
of Algiers, 139, 140
CASOC, in Saudi Arabia, 229
Caspian sturgeon, 834
Castel-Bloom, Orli, 1434
Castro, Fidel, PFLP modeled on, 1839
Castro, Léon, 1233, 1416
Casus (film), 832
Cat(s), Persian, 1821, *1821*
Cathedral of St. Mark (al-Azbakiyya), 1490
Catherine II (empress of Russia), 739
Catholicism
Eastern-rite, 592–593
in Ottoman Empire, under millet system, 1543–1545
Roman (*See* Roman Catholicism)
Catholic missions, schools of, 1551
Catroux, Georges, **570**
and Free French mandate, 851
Cattan, Henry, **570**
Cattaoui, Jacob, 691
Cattaoui, Joseph Aslan, 1233
Cattle, of Dinka people, 709
Caucasian slaves, 2073, 2074
Caucasus, Muslims from, dominance over Arab-speaking majority, 1547
Cavafy, Constantine, 117
Antonius (George) and, 213, 938
Cave paintings, neolithic, *830*
Caviar, 834
Caylak, **570–571**
CCAR. *See* Central Conference of American Rabbis
CCC. *See* Consolidated Contractors Company
CCDH. *See* Conseil Consultatif des Droits de l'Homme
CCE. *See* Comité de Coordination et d'Exécution
CCI. *See* Compagnie de Constructions Internationales
CCN. *See* Conseil Consultatif National
CDLR. *See* Committee for the Defense of Legitimate Rights
CDR. *See* Council for Development and Reconstruction
CDT. *See* Confédération Démocratique du Travail
CEDAW. *See* Convention on the Elimination of all forms of Discrimination against Women
Cehdi, Ibrahim. *See* Nazif, Süleyman
Celaleddin Rumi, tomb of, 1332
Çelebis, 113
Cemal Paşa, Ahmet, **571–572,** 1880
in Armenian genocide, 293, 295, 571
assassination of, 572
and Baghdad province, Alusi (Mahmud Shukri al-) in, 173
in Committee for Union and Progress, 571–572
in Decentralization Party, 686
Faisal I ibn Hussein and, 799, 800
Nashashibi (Is'af) execution ordered by, 1645

Cemal Paşa, Ahmet *(continued)*
pan-Turkism of, 1800–1801
Syria under, 571–572, 2366, 2368
Damascus, 663
petition for independence of, 2202
Talat (Mehmet) and, 2153
in World War I, 905, 2366–2367, 2368
Cem, Cemil, 305
Censorship
in Algeria, of Berber culture, 1261
during conflicts, on all communications, 624–625
of education, 759, 761
in Egypt
of books, 1296
of Munif's (Abdel Rahman) books, 1611
of film industry, 98–99
in Iran, 1683
of education, 761
of film industry, 832
of literature, 1435, 1436–1437, 1803
of press, 1120, 1121, 1299
of theater, 2186
in Israel, 1683, 1897
in Ottoman Empire, 28
in Saudi Arabia, of books, 1611
in Turkey, of film industry, 832
Census. *See* Population
Center for Arab Women for Training and Research, 894
Center for Community Action, 489
Center for Community Medicine (Tunisia), 1496
Center for Human Rights and Public Policy (CHRPP), 489
Center for Islamic Study and Publication, 2036
Center for Jewish Identity, 489
Center for Muslim–Christian Encounter, 1953
Center for Senior Services, 489
Center for the Global South, Maksoud (Clovis) in, 1474
Center for Women's Participation (Iran), 1123
Center for Women's Studies and Research (Iran), 745
CENTO. *See* Central Treaty Organization
Central Bank of Tunisia, Nouira (Hedi) as head of, 1693
Central Committee of the Free Officers (Iraq), 1872
Central Conference of American Rabbis (CCAR), political Zionism affirmed by, opposition to, 176
Central Dialects, 1124
Central Intelligence Agency (CIA), **572–573**
in Chilean coup, 1327
communist parties destroyed by, 627
in Egyptian–Israeli peace negotiations, 157, 573
failures of, 573
foreign intelligence organizations influenced by, 1102
functions of, 572
in Iranian coup (1953), 572, 1118, 1752
Iraqi National Congress funding from, 1137
KGB compared to, 1290
Mossad relations with, 1578
operations of, 572–573
organizational structure of, 572
Roosevelt (Kermit) in, 1937
Central Relief Committee, Joint Distribution Committee established by, 1239
Central Treaty Organization (CENTO), 363, **573–574**. *See also* Baghdad Pact
Iran in, impact on country infrastructure, 2420
members of, 573
Central University (Madrid), 1951
Centre de Recherches, d'Études, de Documentation et d'Information sur la Femme (CREDIF) (Tunisia), **574**
Centre for Global Energy Studies, 2378
Centre National de la Recherche Scientifique (Paris), 492
Century Corporation, 2063
Ceramics, **574–575**
Cercle des représailles, le (Kateb), 1280
Ceride-i Havadis (newspaper), 1684
Churchill (William) at, 595
establishment of, 595
Ceriha (Mehmet Rauf), 1513
Çerkes Hasan incident (1876), **575**
CESA. *See* Comité Juif Algérien d'Études Sociales
Ceuta (Spanish possession), **575–576**, 1516, 1567, 2085
Cevdet, Abdullah, **576–577**
Nizamiye courts organized by, 1690
in Ottoman Union Society, 622
Cevdet, Ahmet, **577–578**
and Darülfünün university, 672
daughter of, Aliyer (Fatimah) as, 148
drafting Land Code of 1858, 1367
legal career of, 577–578
Osmanh published by, 2409
Ceylon, at Bandung Conference, 387
Ceyrekgil, Hasanzade Ibrahim, 872
CFP. *See* Compagnie Française des Pétroles
CFPA. *See* Cairo Family Planning Association
Chaabani, Mohammed, 442
Chabouti, Abdelkader, 919
Chad
Libyan border with, Aozou Strip in, 216
Libyan invasion of, CIA support for, 572
Chadirchi, Kamil, 1210
in Ahali group, 80–81
coup opposed by (1936), 80
as National Democratic Party leader, 1654–1655
Chador, 611
Chaghatai, descendants of, 1015
Chahine, Yusef, 497, 583, 832, 833
Chalabi, Ahmad, **578**
exile of, 578
on Iraqi Governing Council, 2325–2326
in Iraqi National Congress, 578, 1137
return to Iraq, 578
Chalabi, Fadhil al-, 1720
Chalcedon, Council of (451), 589, 639
Chalcraft, John T., *as contributor,* 1035–1037
Chaldaean Catholic church, 592–593
Chalhoub, Michel. *See* Sharif, Omar
Challe, Maurice, **579**
in Organisation Armée Secrète, 1715
and Sèvres Protocol (1956), 2109
Challe Plan, 579

Chamberlain, Neville, Eden (Anthony) in conflict with, 755
Chambi, Mount (Tunisia), 2225
Chamchian, Mikayel, 303, **579**
Chamedan (Alavi), 104
Chamoun, Camille, *580,* **580–581**
  attempt at monopolizing fishing in Lebanon, 1391
  as civil war (1958) catalyst, 1389–1391, 1399
  as Eisenhower Doctine (1957) advocate, 773, 1390
  election of, 580
  foreign policy of, 580
  government of
    Chehab (Khalid) in, 585
    Shader (Joseph) in, 2018
  in al-Hilf al-Thulathi, 1254
  Hilu (Charles) and, 1031
  Jumblatt (Kamal) opposing, 1255
  Karame (Rashid) opposing, 1271
  Khuri (Bishara al-) opposed by, 580, 1315
  in Lebanese Front, 1395
  Meushi (Paul Peter) opposing, 1520
  vs. al-Najjada, 977
  Nasser (Gamal Abdel) opposed by, 1399
  National Liberal Party of, 1661
  opposition to, 580–581
    Chehab (Fu'ad) response to, 585
  regime of, 1389–1391, 1399
  Salam (Sa'ib) opposing, 1975
  Sulh (Sami al-) supporting, 2119
  Syrian Social Nationalist Party supporting, 2137
  Taqla (Philippe) opposing, 2165
  Tigers militia of, in Lebanese Forces, 1394
  U.S. assistance to, 2291
Chamoun, Dany, **581**
  assassination of, 581, 871, 1661
  as leader of National Liberal Party, 1661
Chamoun, Jean Khalil, 1500
"Champagne spy." *See* Lotz, Wolfgang
Champollion-Figeac, Jacques-Joseph, 582
Champollion, Jean-François, 275, 492, **581–582**
Chamran, Mostafa, **582**
  Kharrazi (Kamal) and, 1300
  Khomeini (Ruhollah) supported by, 1311
  Qotbzadeh (Sadeq) and, 582, 1881
Chanak crisis (1922), 513, 1441–1442
Chancellor, John, 1402
  as high commissioner of Palestine, 1025
Chande, Abdin, *as contributor,* 1870
Chants anciens des femmes au Maroc (al-Fasi), 812
Chaouch, Ali, 2232
Chaouias, Berber language of, 122
Chapelet d'ambre, Le (Sefrioui), 2008
Characteristics of the Path Facing the Working Woman (report), 40
Charef, Mehdi, 1427
Charents, Yeghishe, 303
"Charge of the Light Brigade, The" (Tennyson), 379
Charitable organizations
  in Egypt, women's role in, 39–40
  in Iraq, for women, 2361–2362
  in United States, women's, 966
Charity. *See also* Philanthropy
  habous as, 964–965
Charles V (king of Spain), 2084
Charles X (king of France), 835
Charrad, Mounira M., *as contributor,* 2230–2231
Charter for National Action (Egypt), 1650
Châtillon, Renauld de, 1270
Chauvel, Harry, 510
Chawia, 458, 459
Chawqi Lycée, 497
Chazan, Naomi, **582**
Chebbi, Nejib, 2232
Chechens, *vs.* Circassians, in Jordan, 600
Checkbook diplomacy, in Kuwait, 1350–1351
Chédid, Andrée, **582–583**
Chédid, Louis, 582
Chefs historiques, 443, 451
Chehab, Bashir, **583–584**
  palace at Bayt al-Din, *583*
Chehab family, **584**
  Ahmad al-Jazzar and, 83, 583–584
Chehab, Fu'ad, **584–585**
  army under, 584
  Chamoun (Camille) opposing, 581
  domestic policies of, 585
  Eddé (Raymond) in conflict with, 754
  election to presidency, 585, 1391
  government of, Karame (Rashid) in, 1271
  Hamadi (Sabri) and, 981
  al-Hilf al-Thulathi opposing, 581, 1254
  Hilu (Charles) and, 1031
  Jumayyil (Pierre) opposing, 1254
  as president, 1399
  as prime minister, appointment of, 584–585
  Salam (Sa'ib) criticizing, 1975
  Sarkis (Ilyas) under, 1991
  Taqla (Philippe) under, 2165
Chehabi dynasty, 1398
  Druze-Maronite conflict over, 1491
Chehabism, 585, 1399
Chehab, Khalid, **585–586**
  as prime minister, 585
Chelkowski, Peter, *as contributor,* 1605–1607
Chelow, 837
Chemical industry, 1483
Chemical weapons, 305
  in Iran, 1535
  in Iran–Iraq War, 1067, 1128, 1129, 1538
  in Iraq, 1535
    UN inspections for, 1539
Chemin des ordalies, Le (Laabi), 1355
Chemins qui montent, Les (Feraoun), 823
Cheney, Richard (Dick), in Gulf War (1990–1991), 2324
Chenik, Muhammad, **586**
Cherati, Ikhlef, 919
Cherbourg (France), Mossad operation in (1969), 1578–1579
Chercheurs d'os, les (Djaout), 716
Chérif, Hachemi, in Parti de l'Avant-Garde Socialiste, 1803
Cherifi, Hanifa, 289
Cherkes. *See* Circassians
Cheshmahayesh (Alavi), 104
Chevron Oil Company, 2099–2100
Chich Khan (film), 376
Chickpeas, 838, 839
Chicly, Shemama, 832
Chided, Andre, 2184
Chikhi, Omar, 918
Child custody. *See* Custody
Child labor, in Egypt, 1358
Children
  in cotton industry, *644*

Children *(continued)*
health care for, 1509–1510
importance in marriage and family, 1494
in Iraq, impact of sanctions on, 1136
preference for girls or boys, 1494
as slaves, 2072
Children of Divorce (film), 1526
Children of Fire (film), 1500
Children of Gebalawi (Mahfuz), 1464
Children of Shatila (film), 1500
Children of the Ghetto (Zangwill), 2424
Child survival, 1509–1510
Chile, coup in, CIA role in, 1327
Chimères, Les (Nerval), 1675
China, **586–587**
arms proliferation by, 586
arms sales by, 750
to Saudi Arabia, 1535
Iraqi relations with, 586, 587
Israeli relations with, 586–587
Namir (Orah) and, 1641
Middle East policy of, 586–587
Naqshbandi in, 1642–1643
Palestinian relations with, Wazir (Khalil al-) and, 2335
Saudi relations with, 586, 587
silk from, 2066
U.S. relations with, Kissinger (Henry) in, 1327
U.S. war in Iraq opposed by (2003), 2324
Chinese Gordon. *See* Gordon, Charles
Chirac, Jacques, *504*, 505
Stasi Commission of, Arkoun (Mohammed) in, 289
Chirol, Valentine, Middle East designation and term popularized by, 1522
Chishti, Muʿin al-Din, 2113
Chishtiyya (Sufi order), 2113
Chleuh language, 1567
Chleuh people, 458
Choksy, Jamsheed K., *as contributor,* 2440–2442
Cholera, 711–712, 1508
in Iraq, 714
and population growth, 1843, 1845
"Cholera" (Iraqi poem), 1475
Chorasmian language, 1125
Chou En-Lai, 986
Chouf Le Look (Bitton), 483
Chraibi, Driss, **588,** 1423, 1427
women in novels of, 588, 2376
Chrakian, Artin, **588–589**
in educational reform, 588–589
education of, 588
Yusufian (Boghos) and, 2415
Chrakian, Khosrov, 588
Chrakian, Sukias, 588
Christ. *See* Jesus
Christian Democratic Union (Germany), Adenauer (Konrad) in, 43
Christianity. *See also specific denominations*
antisemitism and, 211–212
on birth control, 478, 479
and education for women, 882–883
Holy Land in, 1043
in imperialism, 1089
Jerusalem in, 1222
messianism in, 1519
in Ottoman Empire, 589–590, 1731
Palestine in, 1758
Sabbath in, 1954
secular nationalism and, 590
spread of, 589–590
theology of, 589
Christian missions, schools of, 1550–1552
Christian–Muslim alliance, in Lebanon, 2116, 2118
Christians, **589–593**
in Algeria, 122
Arab
in Jordan, 1242
Protestant missionary work with, 1854
in Arab nationalism, 1659
in Barbary wars, fighting corsairs, 401
in Bethlehem, 468
in Damascus affair (1840), 664–665
in Egypt, 1971 (*See also* Copts)
emigration of, 590
in Gaza Strip, 870
in guilds, 947
in Iran, 1548
in Iraq, 738
in Israel, 1163, *1164*
in Lebanon (*See also* Maronites)
in crises of 1840s, 1393–1394
Lebanese Front of, 1395
militias of, 1394
Orthodox, 738
as Levantines, 1405–1406
as minorities or subdominant groups, 1548
in nationalist movement, 1549
number in Middle East, 590
Orthodox
number of, 738
in Ottoman Empire, 738
in Ottoman Empire
and Balkan crises, 382–383
and Bulgarian Horrors, 543
millet system of, 1543–1545
Orthodox, 738
in Sudan, 523, 2099
in Syria, 738, 2130
in Tunisia, 2226
women, religious rituals of, 2360
Christian Union Congregational Church in New Jersey, 488
Christina, Rachel, *as contributor,* 879–884, 1266
Christison, Kathleen M., *as contributor,* 572–573
Chronicle of a Disappearance (film), 833
Chroniques de la citadelle d'exil (Laabi), 1355
CHRPP. *See* Center for Human Rights and Public Policy
Chrysalide, La (Lemsine), 1403
Chubak, Sadeq, **593–594,** 1435
Churches for Middle East Peace, 1855
Churchill, Alfred, 595
Churchill White Paper (1922), **594,** 2349–2350
Palestinian Arab Congress and, 1782
Samuel (Herbert Louis) and, 1983
Churchill, William, **594–595**
newspaper established by, 1684
Churchill, Winston S., **595–597,** *596*
on Allied Middle East Command, 153
at Cairo Conference (1921), 512, 554, 596, 617, 801, 1023, *1088*
in Colonial Office, 617
Egyptian policy of, *vs.* Allenby (Edmund Henry), 151
foreign policy of, 595
government of
Attlee (Clement) in, 338
Eden (Anthony) in, 755
and Husayni (Amin al-), 1057
and Jordan, Abdullah I ibn Hussein in, 29, 1244

at King David Hotel, 1323
on Middle East as designation and term, 1522
Muhammad V meeting with, 1598
on oil needs of Britain, 537
Pahlavi (Mohammad Reza) advised by, 1752
Palestinian policy of, 595–597
in Churchill White Paper (1922), 594
vs. white papers on Palestine (1939), 1770
and Roosevelt (Franklin Delano), 1935, *1935*
Turkish relations with, 516, 597
at Adana Conference (1943), 42
Weizmann's (Chaim) meeting with, 2337
white paper issued by, 1011
in World War I, 509, 2366
Gallipoli campaign, 866
in World War II, 515, 516
Church Missionary Society (CMS), 1551, 1854
schools established by, 758
Church of England, 523
Church World Service, 1981
Churgin, Pinhas, 403
Chuvash language, 2248, 2252
CIA. *See* Central Intelligence Agency
CID. *See* Criminal Investigation Division
Cidal (Mehmet Rauf), 1513
Ciel de porphyre (Lemsine), 1403
Cilicia (Turkey), **598**
Armenian state in, 301
Sykes-Picot Agreement (1916) on, 2128
Cilician Gates, 2167
Çiller, Tansu, **598**
as prime minister, 891, 2242
as True Path Party leader, 2220
Cinécrit (periodical), Amari (Raja) in, 175
Cingirakli Tatar (magazine), 1277
Cintra, under Spanish control, 2085
Circassians, **599–600**
in Jordan
Amman, 190, 600
Jarash, 1218
language of, 599
migration by, 599, 1846
as minorities, 599–600
number of, 600
as slaves, 2074
in Turkey, 2238
Circolo Sion (Zionist club), 966, 1686
Circumcision, **600–601**
female (*See* Female genital mutilation)
male, 600–601
performed by Samaritans, 1980
CIS. *See* Confederation of Iranian Students
CISNU. *See* Confederation of Iranian Students, National Union
Citibank, 390
Cities. *See* Urbanization; Urban planning; *specific cities*
Citizen Bishara (Bitton), 483
Citizens' Rights Movement (CRM) (Israel), 157, 1180, 1891
in Meretz Party, 1180, 1186
on racism in Knesset, 1184
City of Many Days (Hareven), 993
City Theater (Istanbul), 2187
Civic Caravan (Morocco), 1518
Civic Notions for the Citizens (Atatürk), 333
Civic Rights Movement (Israel), Aloni (Shulamit) in, 157
Civic Synergy (Morocco), 1518
Civil code(s)
of Egypt, 1382
of Iran, 1383
of Iraq, 1382
of Jordan, 1382
of Kuwait, 1382
of Libya, 1382
of Ottoman Empire, 577–578, 601
of Sudan, 1382
of Syria, 1382
of Turkey (1926), 332, **601–602**
of United Arab Emirates, 1382
Civilisation, ma mère, la (Chraibi), 588
Civilisées (film), 376
Civilization
vs. culture, Husari (Sati al-) on, 1051
Islamic, 1035
Civil law, 1380
Civil liberties, intelligence services and, 1104
Civil service, in Ottoman Empire, 602, 1734–1735
Civil Service School (Ottoman Empire), **602**
Claisse de la Dette Publique. *See* Egyptian Public Debt Commission
Clandestins, Les (Elalamy), 1425
Clapp, Gordon R., 2285
Clark–Darlan Agreement (1942), **602**
Clark, John R., *as contributor,* 42, 50–51, 115–116, 207–208, 788, 2140–2141, 2167, 2188–2189, 2298–2299, 2309, 2417
Clark, Mark, 602
Clark, Peter, works of Idlibi (Ulfat al-) translated by, 1080
"Clash of Civilizations, The" (Huntington), 1091
Claw, The (film), 2067
Clayton, Gilbert, **602–603**
Antonius (George) as secretary to, 213
in Arab Bureau, 225
Richmond (Ernest T.) as assistant to, 1922
Clemenceau, Georges, **603–604**
Algeria under, 603, 2405
foreign policy of, 603
and Sèvres Treaty (1920), 2014
at Versailles conference (1919), 801
Clerides, Glafkos, presidency of, 654
Cleveland, William L., *as contributor,* 213–215, 307–308, 363, 646–647, 1338, 2315–2316
Clientelism, in Lebanon, 1663
Clifford, Clark, 2220
Climate, **604–606**
of Afghanistan, 54
of Algeria, 120
desert, 604–605, 701, 702
of Iran, 1110–1111, 1316
of Iraq, 1130
of Israel, 1160–1161
of Jordan, 1240–1241
of Kuwait, 1347
of Oman, 705, 1710
of Ottoman Empire, 1729
of Palestine, 1758
of Qatar, 1875
of Turkey, 604, 605
of United Arab Emirates, 2269
of Yemen, 2386–2387
Clinton proposals (2000), 562
Clinton, William Jefferson, **606–607**
at Camp David Summit (2000), 399, 561–563, 606, 1168, 1727, 1775, 2294

Clinton, William Jefferson *(continued)*
dual containment policy of, 730
foreign policy of, 606
Iraqi policy of, 2323
Occidental Petroleum ties to, 1708
at Oslo Accords signing (1993), 606, *1726*
in peace process, 606, 1168
failure of, 606, 1727
at PLO meeting (1998), 1775
in Taba negotiations (2000), 2140
and Wye River Accords (1998), 1064
Clitoridectomy. *See* Female genital mutilation
Cloire des sables (Tlili), 2193
Closed Districts Act (1925), 2102
Close-Up (film), 1318, 1473
Clot, Antoine Barthélémy, **607**, 2003
in public health reform, 710
Clothing, **607–612**. *See also specific types*
cotton, 644–645
haik, 611, 975
headgear, 332, *607*, 608–611, 2240
hijab, 1026–1027
jallabiya, 433
jillaba, 612
men's, 607–612
on postage stamps of rulers, 1850
tawb, 433
Westernization of, 608
women's, 607–611 (*See also* Veiling)
Clown and His Daughter, The (Adivar), 46
Club d'Etude de la Condition de la Femme (Tunisia), 912
Club National Israélite (Zionist group), **612**
Club Tahar Haddad (Tunisia), 325
Club d'Etude de la Condition de la Femme at, 912
CMS. *See* Church Missionary Society
CNDR. *See* Comité National de Défense de la Révolution
CNRA. *See* Conseil National de la Révolution Algérienne
Coalition for Peace, 1809
Coalition of Islamic Societies, 820
Coalition Provisional Authority (Iraq), 2325
Coca-Cola Company, in League of Arab States boycott, 224
Cochrane, Desmond, 2125
Cocteau, Jean, 2020
Çocuklara Mahsus Gazete (Devrim), 702
Code de l'Indigénat (Algeria), **612**
Young Algerians on, 2405
Code of Personal Status (CPS) (Tunisia). *See* Personal Status Code
Coffee, 837
Beja tribe and, 433
trade of, 2198
in Yemen, 2390
Cohen–Baqri family, 396–397
Cohen, Eli, as Mossad agent in Syria, 1578
Cohen, Ge'ula, **612–613**
Cohen, Ran, in Peace Now, 1809
Cohen, Samuel, 1007
Cohen, Yaron. *See* International, Dana
Cohen, Zafrira Lidovsky, *as contributor*, 1907
Coins, Islamic, study of (numismatics), 1701–1703
Cold War
Arab–Israel conflict during, 2175–2176
Baghdad Pact (1955) during, 363, 519
Brezhnev (Leonid Ilyich) and, 507
Britain in, 517
Germany in, 907
Israel during, 2033
League of Arab States during, 1388
Middle East during, 1942–1943, 2290–2291
as arena of conflict, 2174–2175
start of, Azerbaijan crisis in (1945–1946), 346
twin pillars policy during, 2255
U.S. policies in, Kissinger (Henry) and, 1327
Cole, Juan R. I.
as contributor, 93, 187, 354–355, 355–356, 364–366, 2046–2047
as historiographer, 1036
Cole, USS, attack on (2000), **613**
Islamists in Yemen and, 2077, 2391
al-Qa'ida in, 613, 2391
Collectif féminin (Algeria), 2195
College of Christian Brothers, 2116
College of Fine Arts (Cairo), 312
College of Petroleum and Minerals, 2378
Colleges and universities. *See also specific schools*
art, 312
madrasa system of, 1457–1458
Protestant missions founding, 1855
College Tribune (newspaper), 431
Collins, Robert O., *as contributor*, 18–19, 32–33, 349–350, 372–373, 432–434, 709, 1279–1280, 1335, 1363, 1699–1701, 1712–1713, 2105–2106, 2260–2261, 2296
Colombia, Occidental Petroleum in, 1708
Colonialism, **613–617**. *See also* Imperialism; Mandate system; *specific countries*
and Arabic literature, 1419
Bandung Conference on, 387
and banking, 389–390
and education, 758–759, 880
and elites, 775
industrialization and, 1093
intelligence services in, 1101
labor union development in context of, 1357
and land ownership, 1370–1371
and legal systems, 1380
Said (Edward) on, 1966
and urban planning, 2299–2300
and women's rights, 885–886
Colonial Office (Britain), 514, 518, **617**
Colons (settlers in Algeria), **617–618**
Algerian independence opposed by, 139, 618, 1715
after Algerian War of Independence
emigration of, 124
rights for, 124, 618
in Algerian War of Independence, 139, 615, 618
in Organisation Armée Secrète, 139, 618, 1715
political power of, 123
riot by (1956), *137*
Columbia (space shuttle), Israeli astronaut on, 169
Columbia College and Law School, 2063
Columbia University
Bar-Lev (Haim) at, 407
Boutros-Ghali (Boutros) at, 505

Eisenhower (Dwight D.) at, 773
Said (Edward) at, 1966
COMESSA. *See* Community of Sahel–Saharan States
Comintern, and Communist Party of Palestine, 626
Comité d'Action Marocaine (CAM) (Morocco), **618–619,** 1574
establishment of, 618
French dissolution of, 619
Parti National formed after, 1805
Ouazzani (Mohamed Hassan) in, 618, 1743, 2336
platform of, 618
size of, 619
Comité de Coordination et d'Exécution (CCE) (Algeria), **619**
establishment of, 138
French offer rejected by, 138
functions of, 138
Comité d'Etat (HCE), Boudiaf (Mohamed) in, 496
Comité Juif Algérien d'Études Sociales (CESA) (Algeria), **619**
Comité National de Défense de la Révolution (CNDR), 496
Comité Révolutionnaire d'Unité et d'Action (CRUA) (Algeria), **619–620,** 1589
Ben Boulaid (Moustafa) in, 443
Ben M'hidi (Muhammad Larbi) in, 451
Boudiaf (Mohamed) in, 496
Didouche (Mourad) in, 708
establishment of, 136–137
Front de Libération Nationale established by, 138, 620, 1589
Krim (Belkacem) in, 137, 620, 1336
leadership of, 137, 620
planning for war by, 137, 620
Commercial and navigation treaties (Ottoman Empire), **620–622,** 1482. *See also specific treaties*
Commercial Bank of Egypt, Politi (Elie) in, 1838
Commercial code, in Ottoman Empire, 1381
Commercial procedure code, in Ottoman Empire, 1381
Commission of Inquiry for the International War Crimes Tribunal (1992), Saadawi (Nawal al-) on, 1950
Committee for Defense of Freedom and Human Rights (Iran), **622**
Committee for the Defense of Legitimate Rights (CDLR) (Saudi Arabia), **622**
Committee for the Defense of National Culture (Egypt), 2428
Committee for Union and Progress (CUP) (Ottoman Empire), **622–624**
Abdülhamit II opposed by, 28
Abdullah I ibn Hussein opposed by, 29
Ahmet İhsan To'kgoz in, 90
Ahmet Riza in, 91, 623
in Armenian genocide, 293, 294, 295
Armenian Revolutionary Federation cooperation with, 300
Atatürk (Mustafa Kemal) in, 331
Atay (Salih Rifki) in, 335
Cemal Paşa in, 571–572
Cevdet (Abdullah) in, 576
coup by (1908), 1659, 2240
coup by (1913), 384, 623, 2410
and Armenian genocide, 293
Damascus branch of, 2132
and Decentralization Party, 686
dissolution of, 623
Dönme and, 720
electoral success of, 623, 1737, 1742, 2409
Enver Paşa in, 778
Esendal (Memduh Şevket) in, 783
establishment of, 622–623, 2408
Freedom and Accord Party opposing, 823
freemason members of, 852
Genç Kalemler and, 873
Gökalp (Ziya) in, 924
Husari (Sati al-) in, 1051
Mehmet V as figurehead for, 1513
Misri (Aziz Ali al-) in, 1550
Muhtar (Gazi Ahmet) and, 1608
Nadi (Yanus) in, 1633
Nahum (Hayyim) and, 1637
Ottoman Liberal Union Party opposition to, 1737, 2409
and Şevket (Mahmut), 2013
Shaykh al-Islam's power transferred to Ministry of Justice by, 2046
Talat (Mehmet) in, 2153
Turkish nationalism of, *vs.* Arab nationalism, 261
Young Turks and, 622–623, 2408–2410
Committee of Coordination and Implementation. *See* Comité de Coordination et d'Exécution
Committee of National Unity (Bahrain), 371, 1661
Committee of Sa'dist Women (Egypt), 2321
Committee to Save the Fatherland (Iran), Arfa (Hasan) in, 286
Common law, 1380
Communication(s), **624–625**
expansion of infrastructure, 624–625
restrictions on, 624–625
women employed in, 877–878
Communism, **625–628.** *See also specific parties and countries*
decline of, 627–628
origins of, 625–626
Soviet efforts to spread, 1942–1943
spread of, 626–627
in Turkish literature, 1439
Communist Party (Afghanistan). *See* Afghan Communist Party
Communist Party (Cyprus), Vasileiou (George) in, 654
Communist Party (France), 626
Communist Party (Iraq)
alliance with Ba'th party, 1605
Muhammad (Aziz) in, 1604–1605
in United National Front, 1654
Communist Party (Israel), 628, 1182–1183
Palestinian citizens' support for, 1787
Communist Party (Lebanon)
leaders of, 1009
in National Front, 1656–1657
Communist Party (Morocco), Yata (Ali) in, 2382
Communist Party (Sudan), in attempted coup against Numeiri (Muhammad Ja'far) (1971), 1699–1700
Communist Party (Syria), in National Progressive Front, 1665
Communist Party (Tunisia), 1590–1591. *See also* Movement of Renewal
legalization of, 1627
Communist Party (Turkey)
Mustafa Suphi in, 1625
Yasar Kemal in, 2381
Communist Party of Algeria, 627

Communist Party of Egypt (CPE)
Adham (Soraya) in, 43–44
establishment of, 626, 627
women in, 43–44
Communist Party of Iran. *See also* Tudeh Party
attempted insurrection by, 41, 626
establishment of, 41, 626
Communist Party of Iraq (CPI), 627
Ayyub (Dhu al-Nun) in, 344
CIA-facilitated massacre and (1963), 627
vs. Hakim (Muhsin al-) followers, 977
Qasim (Abd al-Karim) lenience toward, 1873
Yusuf (Yusuf Salman) in, 627, 2415
Communist Party of Palestine (PCP), 626
Communist Party of Soviet Union (CPSU), Khrushchev (Nikita S.) in, 1314
Communist Party of Syria, 626
Communist Party of Syria and Lebanon (CPSL), 626
Bakdash (Khalid) in, 373, 412
Community of Sahel–Saharan States (COMESSA), establishment of, Libya in, 1414–1415, 1862
Comoros, in League of Arab States, 1388
Compagnie de Constructions Internationales (CCI), 2106
Compagnie Française des Pétroles (CFP), **628–629**
Compass for the Sunflower, A (Badr), 357
Comte, Auguste
and Ahmet Riza, 91
and Gökalp (Ziya), 924
Iqbal (Muhammad) on, 1110
Concert of Europe, 739–742
Concordia Company, 2126
Conder, Claude Reignier, 1772
Conditions de la renaissance, Les: Problème d'une civilisation (Bennabi), 451
Condominium, 629
Condominium Agreement (1899), 518, **629**
Baring (Evelyn) and, 405, 530
British troops imposing, 2100
Lado Enclave incorporated into, 1363
Condoms, 480
Confédération Démocratique du Travail (CDT) (Morocco), **629–630**
Union Générale des Travailleurs Marocains and, 2264
Union Marocaine du Travail and, 453, 629, 2266
Union Socialiste des Forces Populaires and, 2268
Confederation of Iranian Students (CIS), **630–631**
Amir-Entezam (Abbas) in, 188
Rahnavard (Zahra) in, 1899
Confederation of Iranian Students, National Union (CISNU), 630–631
Confederation of Revolutionary Trade Unions (Turkey). *See* Revolutionary Confederation of Labor Unions
Confederation of Turkish Trade Unions, 631, 1358–1359
Confessional System (Lebanon), 1662–1663
Congo, UN peacekeeping operation in, 986
Congo Free State, 1363
Congo River, Lado Enclave connecting Nile River with, 1363
Congregational Church, missions supported by, 1854
Congress (Iraqi political party), 344
Congress for the Republic (Tunisia), Marzouki (Moncef) in, 1497
Congress of Ottoman Liberals (1902), **631**
Ahmet Riza at, 91
Congress of Ottoman Liberals (1907), 631
Ahmet Riza at, 91, 631
Congress, U.S.
American Israel Public Affairs Committee lobbying of, 177
Iraq Liberation Act by (1998), 578, 1136
military response to September 11th authorized by, 66
ConocoPhillips, in Oasis Group, 1707–1708
Conorada Group. *See* Oasis Group
Conseil Consultatif des Droits de l'Homme (CCDH), 1716
Conseil Consultatif National (CCN), 496
Conseil National de la Révolution Algérienne (CNRA), **632**
Abbas (Ferhat) in, 2264
Bendjedid (Chadli) in, 444
establishment of, 138, 632
on FLN, 857
Consistoire Central des Israélites de France, 151
Consolidated Contractors Company (CCC), 1953
Constantine (Algeria), *126*, **632**
Catholics in, 1932
French occupation of, 122
Constantine (Roman emperor)
Aya Sofya (Hagia Sophia) built by, 342, 633
capital moved to Constantinople by, 589, 632, 1193
and pilgrimage to Holy Land, 1043
Constantinople (Turkey), **632–633**. *See also* Istanbul
Armenian genocide in, *293*
Armenian patriarchate of, 1723
Armenian millet and, 296–298
origins of, 296–297
British and French forces evacuating from (1922), 513–514
and British–Russian relations, 511, 528
as Byzantine capital, 633, 1193
Canning (Stratford) in, 563, 564
Christianity in, 589, 633
Eastern Orthodox patriarchate of, 590–591, 633
establishment of, 632, 1193, 2239
harbor of, *1740*
İdadi schools in, 1080
as Ottoman capital, 633, 1193–1194, 1729, 2253
Protestant missions in, 1854
as Roman capital, 589, 632, 1193
Constantinople Agreement (1915), 1942
Constantinople, Plan of (1958), 632
and Oran, 1714
Constantius (Roman emperor), Constantinople under, 633
Constant, Joseph, 2144
Constitution(s). *See under specific countries*
Constitutional and Democratic Popular Movement (MPCD) (Morocco), 1590
Constitutional Bloc (Lebanon), **633–634**
Chamoun (Camille) in, 580

Chehab (Khalid) in, 585
establishment of, 633
Hamadi (Sabri) in, 981
Khuri (Bishara al-) in, 633–634, 1315
Taqla (Philippe) in, 2165
Constitutional Democratic Rally (RCD) (Tunisia), **634–635**, 2231–2232
Ben Ali (Zayn al-Abidine) in, 439
Bourguiba (Habib) in, 2231
breaking away from Destour Party, 2231
conflict within, 634–635
foundation of, 2231
leadership of, 634–635
seeking control of LTDH, 1416
size of, 615
Constitutional government, 932
Constitutional Liberty Party (Egypt), Haykal (Muhammad Husayn) and, 1013
Constitutional Revolution (Iran) (1905–1909), **635–637**, 2430
Adamiyat (Abbasquli) in, 42
Adamiyat (Fereydun) on, 42
Akhbari school in, 98
anjoman (assembly) in, 207
Babis in, 356
Baha'is in, 365
Bakhtiari in, 374
bast taken during, 411
Bayat (Mortaza Qoli) in, 416
bazaar as political base during, 419, 420
Behbahani (Sayyed Abdollah) in, 2141–2142
Browne (Edward Granville) supporting, 540
constitution written during, 636, 1868
dates of, disagreement over, 636
Dehkhoda (Ali Akbar) in, 689
guilds in, 947
Jangali in, 1216
journalistic writing by leaders of, 1435
majles (parliament) formed in, 636, 1471–1472, 1868
Malkom Khan's *Qanun* and, 1477
Mossadegh (Mohammad) in, 1580
Mozaffar al-Din Qajar in, 635–636, 1868
newspapers and print media after, 1682
opposed by Mohammad Ali Shar Qajar, 1559
opposed by Nuri (Fazlollah), 1704
origins of, 635, 1868
political implications of, 1868–1869
protests in, 635–636
Sadr (Muhsin) in, 1960
Shaykhis in, 2047
Shi'ite *ulama* in, 2303
Tabataba'i (Mohammad) as leader of, 2141–2142
Tabriz during, 2144
women in, 891
impact on, **637**
Construction Crusade. *See* Jehad-e Sazandegi
Constructive socialism, 1362
Containment policy
Acheson (Dean) associated with, 40
Carter's (Jimmy) rejection of, 567
Contes Fassis (al-Fassi), 812
Contes Turcs (Boratav), 492
Continental. *See* ConocoPhillips
Contraception, 480. *See also* Birth control
rates of usage, 1844
Contra rebels (Nicaragua), in Iran–Contra affair, 1123
Convention Against Torture, 1048
Convention on the Elimination of all forms of Discrimination against Women (CEDAW) (1996), 887, 891, 896, 897, 912, 1048, 1396, 2357
Convention on the Rights of the Child (CRC), 1048
Conventions. *See under geographic term associated with the convention or under its popular name*
Conversos, 2084
Cooking, in religious rituals, 2360
Cook, Thomas, 2196
Cooperatives. *See* Agricultural cooperatives
Coordination des Archs (CADC) (Algeria), **638**
establishment of, events leading to, 274, 486, 638
platform of, 274, 638
Copeland, Miles, in Israeli–Egyptian peace negotiations, 573
Coptic Catholic Church, 592, 640
under Mark VIII, 1490
Coptic Community Council
Cyril V and, 656
Cyril VI and, 657
John XIX and, 1239
Coptic Evangelical Church, 640
Coptic language, 640
Coptic Legion, 1490
Coptic monasteries, in Wadi Natrun, 2319
Coptic Museum (Cairo), **638**
Coptic Orthodox Church
establishment of, 639
Ethiopic Orthodox Church and, 639, 657
laity of, enfranchisement of, 656
in Oriental Orthodox family, 591, 639
patriarchs of, 656–657, 691, 1239, 2048–2049
theology of, 639
Copts, **638–642**
in al-Mansura, 1480–1481
art of, 640
definition of, 639
in Egypt, 763–764, 1971–1972, 2048–2049
language of, 640
Milner Mission boycotted by, 1546
Musa (Salama) on, 1614
Muslim relations with, 640–642, 658
Muslim violence against, 641–642, 2049
in nationalist movement, 640–641, 1549
in New Wafd, 2321
New Wafd supported by, 1686
number of, 638–639
origin of term, 639
under Ottoman rule, 1544
in parliament, 641, 642
Protestant missions and, 1854
Saint Mark's Cathedral of, 1971–1972
in Wafd, 2320
Corcos family, **642–643**
Cordova, 2084
Cordovez, Diego, 2279
Cornwallis, Kinahan, 808
at Cairo Conference (1921), 554
Corpus Nummorum Saeculorun IX–XI (Tornberg), 1702
Correction Movement (Syria), National Progressive Front established after, 1665
Correction movement (Yemen), 2393
Corsairs, 401, **643**
Aix-la-Chapelle Treaty (1821) outlawing, 401

Corsairs *(continued)*
in Algiers, 139, 643
and Bizerte, 484
Britain fighting, 526
Bugeaud de la Piconnerie (Thomas-Robert) fighting, 542
in Morocco, 1515
Treaty of 1815 protecting from, 2208
in Tunis, 2224
Cortot, Alfred, 476
Cossack Brigade (Iran), **643**
authorized by Mohammad Ali Shar Qajar, 1559
in coup (1921), 643
in coup against majles (1908), 636–637, 643
Pahlavi (Reza) in, 643, 1755
Cotton, **643–645**, 1484
in Egypt, 116–117, 404, 405, 643–644, 645, *1092*, 1158, 1461, 2180, 2181, *2181*
in Iran, *2181*
in Iraq, *2181*
in Israel, 2180
in Lebanon, *2181*
in Palestine, *2181*
in Sudan, 908, 2180
in Syria, 2131, 2180, *2181*
in Turkey, 42, 644, 645, 2180, *2181*, 2198, 2238
Council for Development and Reconstruction (CDR) (Lebanon), **645**
Council for Israeli-Palestinian Peace (Israel), Peled (Mattityahu) in, 1812
Council for the Unity of the Southern Sudan, 1701
Council of Four, 471
U.S. proposal for Allied commission at, 1323
Council of Guardians (Iran), 1987
Council of Judicial Regulations (Ottoman Empire), 1690
Council of Justice (Egypt), 1472
Council of the Nation (Algeria), 127, 130
Council on Foreign Relations (U.S.), 1953
Count of Monte Cristo, The (Dumas), Turkish translation of, 1277
Courier services, 624
Court of Cassation (Ottoman Empire), 1690
Couscous, 837–838
Covering Islam: How the Media and the Experts Determine How We See the Rest of the World (Said), 1966
Cow, The (film), 832
Cox, Percy, **645–646**
and Abd al-Aziz ibn Saʿud Al Saʿud, 10
Abdullah I ibn Hussein and, 30
in Anglo–Iraqi Treaty (1922), 202, 646
Bell (Gertrude) as secretary of, 437
and benevolent paternalism, 514
at Cairo Conference (1921), 554
Kaylani (Abd al-Rahman al-) supported by, 1282
Wilson (Arnold T.) and, 2352
CPE. *See* Communist Party of Egypt
CPI. *See* Communist Party of Iraq
CPS. *See* Personal Status Code (Tunisia)
CPSL. *See* Communist Party of Syria and Lebanon
CPSU. *See* Communist Party of Soviet Union
Crabbs, Jack, 1207
Cranborne, Lord, 514
Crane, Charles R., **646–647**
Institute for Current World Affairs founded by, 214, 647
in King–Crane Commission (1919), 646, 1323
Shahbandar (Abd al-Rahman) friendship, 2021
CRC. *See* Convention on the Rights of the Child
CREDIF. *See* Centre de Recherches, d'Études, de Documentation et d'Information sur la Femme
Creech Jones, Arthur, 338, **647**
Crémieux, Adolphe, 647
in Alliance Israélite Universelle, 151
Crémieux, Albert, in Damascus affair (1840), 664–665
Crémieux Decree (1870), **647–648**
Creswell, Robyn, *as contributor*, 673–675
Crete
in Aegean Sea, 51
independence of, 937
Crime(s). *See also* Law, modern; *Shariʿa* (Islamic law)
of honor, **649–650**, 1495 (*See also* Honor killings)
Crimean Tatar language, 2252
Crimean War (1853–1856), **648–649**, 1945
Austria in, 739
Balaclava battle (1854) in, 379
Britain in, 648–649, 739
causes of, 648–649, 1222
and Eastern Question, 739
Egypt in, 1970
France in, 649, 739, 846
Gordon (Charles) in, 931
Nightingale (Florence) during, 2302
Ottoman Empire in, 33–34, 739, 2162
debt of, 33
navy of, 1741
Peace of Paris ending, 649
Russia in, 648–649, 739, 2162
Sardinia in, 739
Criminal code
of Egypt, 1382
in Ottoman Empire, 1381
Criminal Investigation Division (CID) (Britain), Stern (Abraham) killed by, 1443
Cripps, Stafford, 1237
"Crisis between Islam and Politics, The" (Ghanim), 911
Critique of Religious Thought (Azm), 351
CRM. *See* Citizens' Rights Movement
Croats, 383
Cromer, Lord. *See* Baring, Evelyn
Crosbie, Robert, 1238
Crossman, Richard, **650–651**
CRUA. *See* Comité Révolutionnaire d'Unité et d'Action
Crusaders, 1930
Arab resistance to, Homs in, 1044
and Church of the Holy Sepulchre (Jerusalem), 1043
French, 844
Jerusalem conquered by, 1930
Muslim defeat of, 1147
Nazareth captured by, 1672
Crusades Through Arab Eyes, The (Maʿlouf), 1478
Crystal Manifesto, Ishaaq (Kamala Ibrahim) in, 1142
Cukurova. *See* Cilicia
Culhane, Hind Rassam, *as contributor*, 831–833
Culi, Jacob, 1363

Cultural elites, 775
Cultural identity, in art, 313
Cultural imperialism, 1090–1091
Cultural property
in Armenian genocide, 295
conflict over, 278–279
ownership of, 279
protection of, 278–279
Culture and Imperialism (Said), 1966
Cumali, Necati, 2187
Cumhuriyet (newspaper), 1633, 1685
Yasar Kemal at, 2381
Cuneiform
Egyptian, deciphering of, 276
Persian, 1124
Cunningham, Alan Gordan, as high commissioner of Palestine, 1025
Cuno, Kenneth, 1036, 1207
CUP. *See* Committee for Union and Progress
Curiel family, **651**
Curiel, Henry
assassination of, 651
communism of, 627, 651
Curtis, Maria F., *as contributor,* 43–44, 227–228, 434–436, 438–440, 490, 497–498, 666–668, 1101–1105, 1203–1204, 1214–1215, 1625–1627, 1776–1781, 1839–1841, 1905–1906, 1994–1995, 2321–2322
Curzon, George Nathaniel, **651–652**
Abdullah I ibn Hussein restrained by, 512
as foreign secretary, 652, 842
political career of, Kitchener (Horatio Herbert) and, 1329
Custody
in Iran, 891
personal status laws on, 887
in Tunisia, 2230
Cyber AWSA, 269
Cyclist, The (Iranian film), 1473
Cyprus, **652–654**. *See also specific cities, organizations, people, and regions*
in Arab–Israel War (1956), 245
British rule in, 528–529, 652–653
Berlin Treaty (1878) and, 528, 1989
British military forces on, 519, 521, 529
Cyprus Convention on (1878), 654
cities of, major, 652
constitution of, 697
economy of, 652
geography of, 652
independence of (1960), 652, 653, 696–697, 943
legislative elections in, of 1960, 653
in Ottoman Empire, 652, 653
Palestine Research Center move to, 1782
political system of, 652
population of, 652
presidential elections in, of 1959, 653
Turkish–Greek dispute over, 1531–1535
Ecevit (Bülent) in, 1666
Erbakan (Necmeddin) in, 1666
Turkish occupation of (1974–), 652, 654
unification with Greece (enosis)
internal conflict over, 653–654, 697
opposition to, 696
support for, 653, 943
United Nations on, 653, 654, 697, 2277–2278
Cyprus Convention (1878), **654–655**
Cyrenaica (Libya), **655–656,** 1410, 2217
cities of, 446
Idris al-Sayyid Muhammad al-Sanusi as amir of, 655, 1081, 1321
independence for, 1321
Italian occupation of, 655, 935, 1321
Mukhtar (Umar al-) in guerilla war against, 1609–1610
Kikhya family in, 1321
Sanusi order in, 446, 1609
during World War II, 516
Cyrenaican National Congress, 1321
Cyrene (Libya), 655
Cyril I (Coptic patriarch), 657
Cyril IV (Coptic patriarch), **656**
Coptic Church revival under, 640, 656
educational reforms of, 656
murder of, Saʿid Pasha in, 656, 691
Peter VII and, 1822
Cyril V (Coptic patriarch), **656–657**
educational reforms of, 656
exile of, 656–657
John XIX as successor of, 1239
Cyril VI (Coptic patriarch), **657–658,** 2048
Cyrillic alphabet, 235
Czechoslovakia, arms sales by
to Egypt, 1650
to Israel, 304
Czech Republic, in U.S. invasion of Iraq (2003), 2325

D

Daʾan, Treaty of (1919), 2378
Dabbagh, Farajollah. *See* Soroush, AbdolKarim
Dabbagh, Marzieh, **659**
Dabbas, Charles, **660**
presidency of, 660
Dabka. *See* Debka
"D'abord, ce n'est pas la guerre" (Sebbar), 2007
Dacians, 383
Daddah, Ahmed, 660
Daddah, Mokhtar Ould, **660,** 1503
coup against (1978), 660
POLISARIO and, 2345
foreign policy of, 660
presidency of, 660
Dafanna al-Madi (Ghallab), 910
Dafatir Thaqafiyya (periodical), 357
Daftari, Ahmad Matin, **660**
Daftari, Hedayatollah Matin, 660
Dagan, Meir, as Mossad director, *1578,* 1579
Daghestan, Naqshbandi in, 1642–1643
Daghestani, Farah, in Princess Basma Women's Resource Center, 1852
Daghir, Asʿad, in Istiqlal Party, 1198
Dağlarca, Fazil Hüsnü, **661,** 1437, 1439
Dahab, Nefla, 1429
Dahlab, Saad, 788
Dahlan, Muhammad, **661–662**
Arafat (Yasir) and, power struggle between, 661
in Palestinian Authority, 1900
in Preventative Security Forces, 1785
Dahlgren, Susanne, *as contributor,* 169, 806, 1669, 2357, 2398–2399
Dahna, al- (desert), 1638
Dahruj, Faruq, 1009

Daʿi, Mirza Mehdi, Khomeini (Ruhollah) taught by, 1310
Daʾirat al-maʿarif (Arabic encyclopedia), 550
Dajla fi arajiniha, al- (Khraief), 1313
Dalyanci, Niyazi, *as contributor,* 1195, 2208
Damad Mahmud Paşa, 2409
Damages (section in Talmud), 2157
Damanhur (Buhayra), 542, **662**
Damascus (Syria), **662–664,** *2134*
  Arab Academy of, 223–224
  Arab Club in, 225–226
  Arab nationalism in, 663
  in Arab Revolt (1916), 510
  bazaars in, 419
  blood libel in (*See* Damascus affair)
  Circassians in, 600
  defense against Second Crusade, 1044
  Faisal I ibn Hussein controlling, 29, 800, 2132
  French mandate in, 664, 2132
  Great Mosque in, *2129*
  Jewish financiers in, 807
  and Medina, railroad connecting, 1028
  newspapers of, 1678
  in Ottoman Empire, 663, 1759
  Palestinian Arab Congress in (1920), 1782
  PFLP hijacking of TWA flight in (1969), 1293
  Protestant missions in, 1854
  Sykes-Picot Agreement (1916) on, 2128
  textile mills in, 2181
  Umayyad dynasty in, 662
  Umayyad Mosque in, 2259–2260
  in World War I, 2368
Damascus affair (1840), 212, **664–665**
Damascus–Baghdad caravan, 2205
Damascus–Beirut railway, 2206
Damascus–Cairo railway, 2206
Damascus Committee for the Defense of Palestine, 488
Damascus Museum, Islamic numismatics in, 1702
Damascus Protocol, 799, 815
Damascus Resolution (1920), 538
Damascus Spring (Syria), 315
Damascus Ten, Palestinian Democratic Union in, 1009
Damascus Tripartite Agreement, 1039
Damascus University, 664, **665–666,** 2132
  Bitar (Salah al-Din al-) at, 482
  Samman (Ghada) at, 1982
Damask, 644
Damavand, Mount, 901
Damen, Arham el-, in Women's Centre for Legal Aid and Counseling, 2356
Damietta branch of Nile River, 1688
Dammam, al- (Saudi Arabia), **666**
Damnés de la Terre, Les (Fanon), 804
Damour (Lebanon), in Arab–Israel War (1982), *253*
Dams. *See also specific dams*
  and water resources, 2329, *2329*
Damur (Lebanon), Saʿiqa attack on (1976), 1607
Dance, **666–668**. *See also* Music
  diversity of, 666
  Egyptian, 866, 1273
  in religious rituals, 2360
  role in celebrations, 667
  by women *vs.* men, 667
Daneshian, Karamat, 930
Daneshvar, Simin, **668–669,** 1435, 1803
Daney/Sanbar: North-South Conversation (Bitton), 483
Danielson, Virginia, *as contributor,* 324, 336–337, 675, 970–971, 1617–1620, 2261–2263
Dante Alighieri, 1208
Dar al-Daʿwa wa al-Irshad (Egypt), **669**
Dar al-Fonun (Iran), **669,** 757, 1477, 1643
  establishment of, Amir Kabir (Mirza Taqi Khan) in, 189, 669, 1867
  photography at, 1867
Dar al-Hajar (Yemen), *2392*
Dar al-Harb (abode of war), 670, 2155
Dar al-Islam (abode of Islam), **670,** 2154–2155
Dar al-Kutub al-Misriyya (Egyptian national library), **670**
  Ibrahim (Muhammad Hafiz) at, 1078
Dar al-Mal, 389
Dar al-Moʿallamin (Afghanistan), **670–671,** 1973
Dar al-Tifl al-Arabi (Israel), 1488
Dar al Ulum (Egypt), **671,** 757
  Banna (Hasan al-) at, 395
Dar al-Ulum (India), 2154
Darawshe, Abdul Wahab, in Arab Democratic Party, 1178–1180
Darazi, al-, 726
D'Arcy Concession (1901), 200–201, 536–537, **671**
D'Arcy, William Knox, 200, 536–537, 671
Dardaʾim movement, Qafih (Yihye ben Solomon) and, 1864
Dardanelles, 2094, 2236
  international status of, London Convention (1840) on, 1444, 2094
  Turkish sovereignty over, under Montreux Convention (1936), 1565
  in World War I, 509, 1194, 2365–2366
Dardanelles, Treaty of the (1809), **671–672**
  capitulations reaffirmed in, 621, 672
  Turkish Straits free passage in, 621, 672
Dari language, 1124, 1820, 1857
Darius the Great, 482
  Persian language of, 1124
Darkhei Noʾam (Alkalai), 149
Darlan, Jean François, in Clark–Darlan Agreement (1942), 602
Darnah (Libya). *See* Derna (Libya)
Darqawi, Abd al-Rahman al-, 1927
Darülfünün (university), **672–673**
Darwaza, Muhammad Izzat, **673**
  historiography of, 1791
  in Istiqlal Party, 673, 1198, 1764
Darwin, Charles, 2061
Darwish, Ali al-, 112
Darwish, Faysal al-, in Ikhwan movement, 1085
Darwish, Ishaq, **673**
Darwish, Mahmud, **673–675,** *674, 1778*
  Laabi (Abdellatif) translating works of, 1356
  themes of, 1791, 1792
Darwish, Sayyid, **675**
Darwish, Yusuf, in New Dawn group, 627
Dashnak Party (Armenia), **675–678**

accomplishments of, 676–677
Andranik Ozanian in, 195
Committee for Union and Progress cooperation with, 300
establishment of, 299, 675
and Hunchak Party (Lebanon), 1050
platform of, 299–300, 676
popularity of, 301
vs. Ramgavar Azadagan Party, **1901**

Dasht-e Kavir, 701

Dasht-e Lut, 701

Dashti, Ali, **678**

Dasin. *See* Yazidis

Dastgaha (music), 1617

"Data Processing" (Bejerano), 1434

Dates, 410, **678–679,** 2198
in Saudi Arabia, 1511

Daud, Muhammad, **679–680**
in Awakened Youth, 341
communist movement and, 57, 58, 61, 679, 680
coup against (1975), attempted, 61
coup against (1978), 58, 401, 680
coup by (1973), 57, 401, 679
Etemadi (Saleha Faruq) under, 786
Islamic movement under, 63
and Jamiʿat-e Islami, 1215
political parties under, 63
presidency of, 57–58, 679–680
and Zahir Shah, 57, 400, 679, 2421

Daʾud Pasha (Mamluk ruler), **680,** 1478
Baghdad improved by, 360

Daughter of Isis: The Autobiography of Nawal El Saadawi (al-Saadawi), 1950

Daughters of the Prophet, The (Bint al-Shati), 476

Davar (newspaper), 1512, 1683
Alterman (Natan) in, 1432
Goldberg (Leah) in, 927
Greenberg (Uri Zvi) in, 941
Guri (Chaim) in, 956
Katznelson (Berl) in, 1281
Sharett (Moshe) in, 2032
Shazar (Shneour Zalman) in, 2047
Shlonsky (Avraham) in, 2058

Davar, Ali Akbar, 1757

Daves, Bryan, *as contributor,* 284–285, 505, 688–689, 865–866, 942, 1122–1123, 1229–1230, 1239, 1408, 1460–1461, 1709, 1818–1819, 1906, 1927, 1938–1939, 1954, 1962, 1991, 2029–2030, 2031–2032, 2047, 2048, 2058, 2086–2087, 2148, 2188, 2221–2222, 2322, 2375, 2384–2385, 2403–2404, 2431, 2436

David (king of Israel), Muhammad compared with, 1597

Davidson, Lawrence, *as contributor,* 2353

David S. Sassoon (firm), 1993–1994

David's Stranger (Shamir), 2024

Davis, Eric, 1036

Davison, Roderic H., *as contributor,* 1524–1526

Daʿwa, al- (journal), 1682
Ashmawi (Muhammad Abd al-Rahman Salih al-) in, 321
Ghazali (Zaynab al-) in, 915

Daʿwa (mission), 2054

Daʿwa al-Islamiyya, al- (Iraq), **680–681**
Hakim (Muhsin al-) and, 977
Hizbullah and, 793
Sadr (Muhammad Baqir al-) in, 1960
violence by, 1067

Daw al-Harib, al- (Berrada), 467

Dawasin. *See* Yazidis

Dawasir tribe, 2209, 2211
in al-Khubar, 1315

Dawla (state), Husari (Sati al-) on, 1051

Dawlatli, 2224

Dawn, C. Ernest
as contributor, 68–70, 305–306, 308–309
as historiographer, 1037

Dayan, Moshe, **681–683,** *682*
in Arab–Israel War (1956), 245
Dayan (Yael) as daughter of, 683
as defense minister, 785
opposition of Meir (Golda) to, 1514
in General Armistice Agreement (1949), 240
and Harkabi (Yehoshafat), 995
in Israel Defense Force, 681, 682, 973, 1173
Lavie File adopted under, 1674
ministry position of, 1174
in Palmah, 1795
Peres (Shimon) alliance with, 1817
on poetry of Tuqan (Fadwa), 2233
in RAFI Party, 682, 1188
Sapir (Pinhas) criticizing, 1991
and Sèvres Protocol (1956), 2109
at St. Germain Conference (1956), 2109
Wingate (Charles Orde) and, 972

Dayan, Rahel, 683

Dayan, Yael, **683**

Day I Became Woman, The (Iranian film), 1473

Day of Darkness, The (Erbil), 781

Day of Sacrifice (Esfandiary), 784

Dayr Abu Maqar (Coptic monastery), 2319

Dayr al-Baramus (Coptic monastery), 2319

Dayr al-Qamar
Druze *vs.* Christian conflicts at, 1394
Ottoman siege of (1841), Karam (Yusuf) against, 1272

Dayr al-Surian (Coptic monastery), 2319

Dayr al-Zawr (Syria), 683–684, **683–684**
Armenian genocide in, 294

Dayr Anba Bishoi (Coptic monastery), 2319

Dayr Yasin (Israel), **684**
in Arab–Israel War (1948), attack on, 242, 684, 1443, 1850
orphans after massacre at, 1055

Days to Come, The (Sobol), 2076

Dead Sea, **684–685,** *685,* 901, 2328, *2328*
elevation of, 684, 685, 1240, 1248
Jordan River and, 685, 1248
potash industry in, 685, 1851
salinity of, 685

Dead Sea Scrolls, **685–686**
Biblical Hebrew in, 1017
content of, 278, 685–686
discovery of, 685
publication of, 686
Yadin (Yigael) and, 686, 2376

Dead Sea Works Ltd., 1851

Dean, Patrick, Sèvres Protocol signed by, 2014, 2109

Death rates, 1508

Debbas, Charles. *See* Dabbas, Charles

De Bellefonds Pasha, Linant, 690

Debka, 667

De Bono, Emilio, 2317

De Bunsen, Maurice, **686**

Decapolis, Irbid in, 1139
Decatur, Stephen, 2208
Decentralization Party (Ottoman Empire), **686–687**
  Cevdet (Abdullah) in, 576
Declaration of Barcelona (1995), 1512
Declaration of La Celle St. Cloud (1955), **687**, 849
Declaration of Principles on Interim Self-Government Arrangements (DOP) (1993). *See also* Oslo Accords
  Gulf Crisis and (1990–1991), 1792–1793
  Palestine National Charter superseded by (1968), 1776
  PFLP rejection of, 1840
  provisions of, 1726, 1775
  signing of, 1726
Declaration of the Establishment of the People's Authority (1977), 1413
Dedebaba, 435
Dede Zekai, **687**
Dédicace à l'année qui vient (Khatibi), 1304
Deeb, Katrin, in Arab Women's Executive Committee, 268
Deeb, Lara Z., *as contributor,* 1396
Deedes, Wyndham Henry, **687**
  Kirkbride (Alec Seath) and, 1324
  replacement for, 603
  Richmond (Ernest T.) as assistant to, 1922
Defense Emergency Regulations, 777
Defense Regulations (Jordan, 1954), 35
Defensive Shield, Operation (Israel), 1169
Defterdar, 823
Defterhane, 1367
Deganya (kibbutz), 865, 1361
  establishment of, 1319, 1320
De Gaulle, Charles, **688**
  and Algerian independence, 138–139, 142, 848
    Amrouche (Jean) as intermediary, 193
  Algeria under, 688
    Challe (Maurice) in, 579
    Code de l'Indigénat in, 612
    Delouvrier (Paul) in, 689
    and Evian Accords (1962), 788
    ordinance (7 March 1944) on, 3
  and Free French mandate, 688, 851
    Catroux (Georges) and, 570
  government of
    Delouvrier (Paul) in, 689
    Soustelle (Jacques) in, 2081
  on Hammarskjöld (Dag), 986
  Loi Cadre discarded by, 1443
  Muhammad V and, 1598
Degel HaTorah (Israel), 1180
  break with Agudat Israel, 77
  in United Torah Judaism, 1190
De Haan, Ya'akov Yisrael, **688–689**
  anti-Zionism of, 688–689
  assassination of, 688, 689
Dehkhoda, Ali Akbar, 540, **689**, 1435
Dehydration, with diarrhea in children, 1509–1510
"De la barbarie en général et de l'intégrisme en particulier" (Mimouni), 1547
Delcassé, Théophile, 119
  and Moroccan Question, 1566
Delacroix, Eugène, Niati's (Houria) work as critique of, 1687
Dellalzade Ismail, **689**
  Dede Zekai and, 687
Delouvrier, Paul, **689–690**
Delta Barrages, **690**
Delta, Nile, **690**
  and disease, 710, 711
Demain (publication), 1717
Démantèlement, Le (Boudjedra), 497
De Menasce, Béhor Levi, 691
De Menasce family, **690–691**
De Menasce, Félix Béhor, 691
De Menasce, Jacob, 690–691
De Menasce, Jacques Béhor, 691
Demetrius II (Coptic patriarch), **691**
  Cyril V compared with, 656
Demirel, Süleyman, **691–693**, *692*
  as chief of state, 2219–2220
  coup against (1980), 789
  government of, 691–692, 1257, 2241
    Çiller (Tansu) in, 598
    Erbakan (Necmeddin) in, 780
    İnönü (Erdal) in, 1097
    National Salvation Party in, 1666
    Türkes (Alparslan) in, 2236
  in Justice Party, 691, 1257, 2242
  in Nationalist Front, 692, 1257
  National Security Council banning from politics, 2219
  Özal (Turgut) and, 692, 1584, 1746, 1747
  presidency of, 692
  as prime minister, 691–692, 1746, 1747, 2242, 2244
    resignation of, 691, 1257
  in True Path Party, 2219
  True Path Party supported by, 1584
Demirjian, Stepan, 588
De Mirmono Tolena (Afghanistan), 786
Democratic Bloc (Morocco), 1574–1575
Democratic Constitutional Rally (RCD) (Tunisia). *See* Constitutional Democratic Rally
Democratic Faction (Zionist group), 2434
  Weizmann (Chaim) and, 2337
Democratic Forum for Labor and Freedoms. *See* Forum Démocratique pour le Travail et les Libertés
Democratic Front for Peace and Equality (DFPE) (Israel), 1180–1181, 1183, 1673, 1787
Democratic Front for the Liberation of Palestine (DFLP), 1008, 1009
  attack on Ma'alot by, 1452
  Kamal (Zahira) in, 1266
  Matzpen and, 1500
  in PLO, 1773
  split from PFLP, 1839
Democratic Left Party (Turkey)
  Ecevit (Bülent) in, 746, 2245
  Ecevit (Rahşan) in, 746, 747
  Motherland Party in coalition with, 746
  National Action Party in coalition with, 746
Democratic Movement for Change (DMC) (Israel), 1181
  Amit (Meir) in, 190
  and Citizens' Rights Movement, 1180
  establishment of, 1181, 2376
  foreign policy of, 1181
  Free Center in, 1181
  platform of, 1181
  Rubinstein (Amnon) in, 1181
  Shinui Party in, 1181, 1188
  Yadin (Yigael) in, 1181, 2376

Democratic Movement for National Liberation (HADITU) (Egypt), 627, 651, 853
Democratic Organization of Afghan Women (DOAW), **693,** 1920
vs. Revolutionary Association of the Women of Afghanistan, 1279
Democratic Party (Cyprus), Kyprianou (Spyros) in, 654
Democratic Party (Iran), Mossadegh (Mohammad) in, 1580
Democratic Party (Lebanon), Moghaizel (Laure) in, 1557
Democratic Party of Azerbaijan (DPA), **693–694**
Azerbaijan crisis caused by, 346, 693–694
Democratic Party of Kurdistan (KDP) (Iran), **694**
government established by, 1341
Democratic Party of Kurdistan (KDP) (Iraq), **694–695**
Iraqi National Congress meeting with, 1137
in Kurdish revolts, 1341
Patriotic Union of Kurdistan and, 1339, 1807
Democratic Popular Front for the Liberation of Palestine (DPFLP), in Intifada (1987–1991), 1108
Democratic Republic of Afghanistan (DRA), establishment of, 58
Democratic Socialist Party (Lebanon), As'ad (Kamil) in, 320
Democratic Unionist Party (DUP) (Sudan), 2101
Umma Party rivalry with, 2261
Democratic Women's Association (ATFD) (Tunisia), **695,** 912
Democrat Party (DP) (Turkey), **695–696,** 1918–1919
abolition of, 1667
coup against (1960), 696
dissolution of, 1919
economic policies of, 695–696
electoral success of, 1098, 2241
establishment of, 415, 695, 1098
foreign policy of, 696
Justice Party and, 1257, 2241
Koprülü (Mehmet Fuat) in, 695, 1335
Menderes (Adnan) in, 1517
newspapers and print media under, 1685
Nursi's (Said) return under, 1705
People's Houses opposed by, 1816
Turkish Grand National Assembly headed by, 2243
Demokrasy-i Now (Afghanistan), 2421
Demokratik Sol Partisi. *See* Democratic Left Party
Demolins, Edmond, 2409
Deng Xiaoping, foreign policy of, 586
Denktash, Rauf, 654, **696–697**
Denny, Walter, *as contributor,* 280–284, 309–314
Denoeux, Guilain P., *as contributor,* 218–219, 353, 487, 580–581, 585–586, 754–755, 860–861, 871, 1009–1010, 1271–1272, 1298–1299, 1315, 1364, 1401, 1688–1689, 2006, 2018, 2019–2021, 2051, 2115–2120, 2165, 2254–2255, 2383–2384, 2411–2413
Dentz, Henri-Fernand, **697–698**
Deny, Jean, 492–493
Deobandi movement, influence on Taliban, 61
Derakhshandeh, Puran, **698**
Derb, 2622
Deri, Arye, 2439
Derishat Tziyon (Kalischer), 1265
Derna (Libya), 1410, 2246
in Treaty of Peace and Amity (1805), 1807
Dersan, Kazim Şinasi, 1269
Dershanes, 948
Dersim (Turkey)
Alevis in, 113, 114
Kurdish revolt in, 1340
Der Tag (newspaper), 1460
Desalinization, **698–700,** 2330
cost of, 698, 700
distribution of technique, 699, *699*
environmental impacts of, 700
process of, 698, 699–700
Description de l'Egypte, 492
Desert(s), **700–702,** 902–903. *See also specific deserts*
boundaries of, 700–701
camels in, 560
climate of, 604–605, 701, 702
definition of, 701
plants in, 604–605, 701–702
precipitation in, 604–605, 701, 702
water resources in, 702
winds in, 605
Desert and the Sown, The (Bell), 437
Desert Fox, Operation (United States), 1069, 1135, 2288
Desertification, 1963
Desert Mobile Force. *See* Arab Legion
Desert Shield, Operation. *See* Gulf War (1991)
Desert Storm, Operation. *See* Gulf War (1991)
Deshen, Shlomo, *as contributor,* 48–50, 485, 1452
Désordre des choses, Le (Boudjedra), 497
Dessouki, Ali al-Din Hilal, at Ahram Center for Political and Strategic Studies, 92
Dessouki, Ali E. Hillal, *as contributor,* 266–267, 394–395, 629, 763–769, 853–854, 1077
Destiny (film), 833, 2022
Destourian Socialist Party (Tunisia). *See* Socialist Destour Party
Destour Party (Tunisia). *See also* Neo-Destour Party
Achour (Habib) in, 41
Ben Ali (Zayn al-Abidine) in, 439
Bourguiba (Habib) in, 501
Constitutional Democratic Rally breaking away from, 2231
establishment of, 634, 1456
Sfar (Tahar) in, 2016
splintering of, 634
Thaalbi (Abd al-Aziz) founding, 2182
Determined Path, Operation (Israel), 1169
Deutsche Bank, 464, 533, 534, 537, 904
Deuxième Bureau. *See* Intelligence Apparatus
Deval, Pierre, in Fly Whisk incident (1827), 835–836
Devarim (Wallach), 2322
Devekusu Kabare Tiyatrosu, 2160
Development Alternatives with Women for a New Era, 894
Development of Capitalism in Palestine, The (Gozanski), 934
Development Planning in an Oil Economy and the Role of the Woman (al-Sabah), 1952
Devrim, Izzet Melih, **702**

Devşirme, 2072
Dey, 2622
DFL. *See* Dhufar Liberation Front
DFLP. *See* Democratic Front for the Liberation of Palestine
DFPE. *See* Democratic Front for Peace and Equality
D Group (Turkey), 2429
Kisakürek (Necip Fazil) in, 1326
Dhafir tribe, 2209, 2212
Dhahran (Saudi Arabia), **703,** 2300
Dhakirat al-jasad (Mostaghanemi), 1424, 1581
Dhikr (silent invocation), 1641, 2113
musical occasions of, 1619
Dhimma (legal status of non-Muslims), **703–704,** 1543
Dhows (sailing vessels), **704–705**
Dhufar (Oman), **705,** 1709–1710
under Al Bu Saʿid dynasty, 108, 109, 705–706
climate of, 705, 1710
incense in, 1091
Dhufar Liberation Front (DFL) (Oman), 705, 1842
Dhufar rebellion (1965–1975), 108, 109, **705–706**
British forces in, 521, 705, 1842
PFLOAG in, 705, 1842
Soviet Union supporting, 2174
Dhu Nun, 2113
Dhuyul al-Kharif (Nuri), 1704
Diabetes, 713
Dialogue with an Atheist (Mahmud), 1469
Diamond industry, in Israel, 1095, 1483
Diana Sabbagh Foundation, 1953
Diarrheal diseases, 714
in children, 1509–1510
Diaspora, **706**
characteristics of, 706
definition of, 706
Gordon (Aaron David) on, 930
impact on Judaism, 1251
of Jews, 706
of Palestinians, 1791
vs. Zionism, 2432
Magnes (Judah) on, 1460
Diba, Farah (queen of Iran), **706–707,** 998
Diba, Sohrab, 706
Dib, Mohammed, **707,** 1426
in "Generation of 1954," 967
DiCassano, Donna Maria Theresa Serra, 2125
Dicle. See Tigris River
Dicran Pasha d'Abro, 2415
Didouche, Mourad, **707–708**
in Comité Révolutionnaire d'Unité et d'Action, 137, 620
Dienar, Baruch, 833
Diet, kosher, 1335–1336
Dighenis. *See* Grivas, Georgios Theodoros
Diglossia, 232
Dikar, Muhammad al-, Ahmad (Muhammad) educated by, 87
Dillman, Bradford, *as contributor,* 857–858, 1501–1503, 2265–2266, 2266–2267
Dilmen, Gunger, 2187
Dilmen, Ibrahim Necmi, 2122
Dilmun, **708**
Dimona (Israel), **708–709**
Black Jews in, Kahane (Meir) on, 1263
Dimona nuclear reactor (Israel), 708, 1696–1697, *1697*
Kennedy (John Fitzgerald) and, 1288
in Vanunu affair, 708, 1697, 2309
Dinar (Jordanian currency), 2622
devaluation of, 1243
Di Naye Velt (newspaper), 464
Dine, Thomas A., in American Israel Public Affairs Committee, 177
Dinka people, **709,** 867–868, 2098
Dino, Abidine, 2381
Dino, Arif, 2381
Dinshaway incident (Egypt) (1906), **709**
Abbas Hilmi II response to, 6
Ghali (Boutros) in, 909–910
National Party reconciliation after, 1663
and retirement of Baring (Evelyn), 406
Din wa al-Islam aw al-Daʿwa al-Islamiyya, al- (Kashif al-Ghita), 1278
Dirham, 2622
Dirʿiyya, al- (Saudi Arabia), 1998–1999
Dirty nuclear weapons, 1696
Diseases, **709–714.** *See also specific diseases*
and population growth, 1845
Disengagement agreements, ending Arab–Israel War (1973), 251–252, 1166
Kissinger (Henry) in, 1328
Syria in, 241, 319, 1166
Khaddam (Abd al-Halim) representing, 1291
Dishdasha, 611–612
Disinherited, The: Journal of a Palestinian in Exile (Turki), 2242
DISK. *See* Revolutionary Confederation of Labor Unions
Dis Oualla (Begag), 1427
Disraeli, Benjamin
at Berlin Congress, 465, 528
against Berlin Memorandum, 382
as foreign secretary, 842
San Stefano Treaty opposed by, 654
Di Tat (newspaper), 2384
Diuzian, Mikayel Chelebi, 579
Divan (Leskofcali), 1404
Divan poetry, 367, 1439
Divan şiiri, 1438
Divine Beginning, The (Abd al-Qadir), 1864
Divine, Donna Robinson
as contibutor, **1634–1635**
as contributor, 456–457, 930–931, 974, 1024–1025, 1047, 1227–1228, 1281, 1284–1285, 1320–1321, 1359–1362, 1407, 1939–1940, 2024–2025, 2076, 2114–2115, 2138, 2171–2172, 2172–2173, 2220–2221, 2303, 2400–2404, 2411, 2429–2430, 2431–2436, 2436
Divine Intervention (film), 833
Divorce, 1495
in Iran, 891, 2051
in Israel, 887
in Lebanon, 887
personal status laws on, 887
in Tunisia, 2230–2231
Diwan, 416, 491, **715,** 2045, 2228
Diwan (Rasafi), 1903
Diwan Faraj (Faraj), 805
Diwaniyya, 1952
Diyarbakir (Turkey), **715**
gecekondus on outskirts of, 872

as Kurdistan capital, 1342
Kurds in, 2423
Diyojen (magazine), Kasap (Teodor) in, 1277
Diz River, 1316
Diz River Dam, *1316*, 1316–1317
Djabali, Hawa, 1424
Djaout, Taher, **715–716**, 1426
Djats (people), 385
Djebar, Assia, **716**, 1424, *1425*, 1427
Djefel, Farida, *2175*
Djeghloul, Abdelkader, 1362
Djemaʿa, 459, **716–717**
Djerba (Tunisia), **717–718**, *718*
Djerbi, 459
Djerijian, Yeghya, 1050
Djibouti
in Gulf Crisis (1990–1991), 951
labor unions in, 1358
in League of Arab States, 1388
Djibouti Agreement (1999), 2261
Djilani, Hédi, in Union Tunisienne des Industrialistes, Compagnies, Artisans, 2268
Djurdjura Mountains, 1261
Dlimi, Ahmed, **718**
attempted coup by, 1005
involved in murder of Ben Barka (Mehdi), 441
DMC. *See* Democratic Movement for Change
DOAW. *See* Democratic Organization of Afghan Women
Doctor Ibrahim (Ayyub), 344
Doctor Zhivago (film), 2039
Dodecanese Islands, 742
Doestam, Abd al-Rashid, 1505
Dog and the Long Winter (Parsipur), 1802
Dogan Group, 1051
Doğramaci, Ihsan, 472, 965
Doğru Yol Partisi. *See* True Path Party (Turkey)
Doha (Qatar), **719**, *1877*
Al Khalifa attack against, 1876
population of, 719, 1875
Doha Declaration (2000), 1721–1722
Doing Daily Battle (Mernissi), 1518
Dokhtar-e Lor (film), 832
Dokoohaki, Parastu, 2424
"Dolarat" (Berrada), 467
Dolgan language, 2252
Dolma, 838
Dolmabahçe Palace, **719**, 2194
Do manzare (Alizadeh), 149
Dome of the Rock (Jerusalem), 991, *991*
attacks in, 1226
construction of, 1222
consulting architect for, 1922
on postage stamps, 1850
Domestic slaves, 2072, 2073
Domestic violence
in Afghanistan, Association for the Protection of Women's Rights and, 325
in Turkey, 894, 2249
Donatism, 460
Döner kebab, 840
Donglowai (Nubian dialect), 1696
Dönme (Turkey), **719–720**
Donno, Antonio, *as contributor*, 2220
Donohue, John J., *as contributor*, 364, 1029, 1550–1552, 1930–1932
Donya (periodical), 2222
Dor Ba-Arez, 1432–1433
Dor Deʿa, **720**
Dori, Yaʿakov
and Haganah, 972
in Israel Defense Force, 973
Dorner, Dalia, **720–721**
Dorsale massif, 2225
Dost Mohammad Barakzai (amir of Afghanistan), 400, **721**
in Anglo–Afghan wars, 56, 196, 400, 721
grandson of, Abd al-Rahman Khan as, 19
Dostum, Rashid, in Jambish-i-Melli, 64
Douʿaji, Ali al-, **721–722**
Double entendre, in Arabic literature, 1419
Douek, Raymond, in New Dawn group, 627
Dougherty, Roberta L., *as contributor*, 866–867, 1273–1274
Doughty, Charles, 513, **722**
Doumani, Beshara, 1036
Doumato, Eleanor Abdella, *as contributor*, 1206, 1633–1634, 1637–1638, 1853–1856, 1938, 2209–2211, 2213, 2214
Douz Festival of the Sahara, *458*
Dowaitir, Ziad, 833
Dowlatabadi, Mahmoud, **722–723**, 1436–1437
Dowlatabadi, Siddiqeh, 891
Dowleh, Nosrat al-, 809
Dowleh, Qavam al-, 2143
Dowry, 2051
Dozy, Reinhart, 576
DP. *See* Democrat Party
DPA. *See* Democratic Party of Azerbaijan
DPFLP. *See* Democratic Popular Front for the Liberation of Palestine
DRA. *See* Democratic Republic of Afghanistan
Dragomans, **723**
"Dreamer, The" (Bint al-Shati), 476
Dreamland (Egypt), 1995
Dreams of Hind and Camilla, The (film), 833
Dreams of Trespass (Mernissi), 1518
Dreyfus affair (1894), **723–724**, 846, 1021
and Azuri (Najib), 352
and Zionism, 2433
Dreyfus, Alfred, 723
Dried fruits, trade of, 2198, *2199*
Drif, Zohra
in Algerian War of Independence, 136
husband of, 483
Drinking the Sea at Gaza: Days and Nights in a Land under Siege (Hass), 1003
Drinking water, 2330
Drinks. *See also* Coffee; Tea
alcoholic, 109–110
Drip irrigation, 74–75, 2331
Drobles Plan. *See* Israeli settlements
Drori, Amir, in Sabra and Shatila massacres, 1263
Droshak (journal), 676
Drought, in Morocco, 1569
Druckman, Chaim, in Morashah Party, 1186
Drugs and narcotics, **724–726**. *See also specific types*
production of, 724–726
trade in, 724, 725
Drummond-Hay, E. W. A., reaction to Treaty of Meknes (1836), 1515
Drummond-Wolff Convention (1885), **726**

Drums, 1617
Druze, **726–730**
Arslan family of, 307, 729, 1255
under Chehab (Bashir), 583–584
communities of, 726–727
at Jabal Druze, 1205
divorce among, 1495
economic activities of, 726
emergence of, 727–728
emirates of, 728–729
in Golan Heights, 926
Jumblatt family of, 729, 1254–1255
leadership of, 727–729
in Lebanon, 729
in civil war (1975–1990), 1400
in crises of 1840s, 1393–1394
Maronite relations with, 1491–1492, 1548
under Ottoman rule, 469, 1398, 1548
Progressive Socialist Party of, 1853
strikes against Qulaylat (Ibrahim), 1612
in Mount Lebanon, 1397, 1398, 1401
Maronite conflict with, 320–321, 2021
mulukhiyya (food) prohibition, 840
in Ottoman Empire, 728–729
in Palestine, 729
spiritual initiation of, 727
in Syria, 469, 729, 2129–2130
under Ottoman Empire, 1548
Druze revolts (1830s), **730**
Duʿa (prayers of petition), 2359
Duʿaji, Ali al-, 1428
Dual containment policy, **730**
Dual control, of Egypt, 528, **730–731**, 1158
Dubai (United Arab Emirates), **731**, *2271*. *See also* United Arab Emirates
port of, 2271
ruling family of (Maktum family, al-), 1474
tourism in, 2196
as trade center, *2198*
Dubs, Adolph, **731–732**
assassination of, 66, 731–732
Amin (Hafizullah) in, 186
Dufferin, Lord, 732
Dufferin Report (1883), **732**
Duha al-Islam (Amin), 183
Dukan Dam, **732–733**, 2115
Dukhan (Qatar), oil production in, *1875*
Dukkali, Abu Shuʿayb al-, 14
Dulcimers, 1617
Dulles, Allen X., 733
Dulles, John Foster, **733–734**
on Aswan High Dam, 327, 733, 773
under Eisenhower (Dwight D.), 773
at London Conference (1956), 1444, 2108
in Operation Alpha, 157, 733
on Palestinian refugee issue, 1941
Suez Crisis and, 1937
Dulzin, Arie, in Liberal Party, 1184
Dumain (publication), 1717
Dumas, Alexandre, 1277
Kasap (Teodor) play based on, 1277
Dumper, Michael, *as contributor*, 991–992
Dunant, Jean-Henri, 1909
Dungeon of Ghosts (Ganji), 867
Dunn, Michael, *as contributor*, 269–272, 812–815
Dunum, 2622
Dünya (newspaper), Atay (Salih Rifki) in, 335
DUP. *See* Democratic Unionist Party
Durand Line, 400, 536, **734**
Durand, Mortimer, 536, 734
Durkheim, Emile, 924
Durr al-manthur fi tabaqat rabbat al-khudur, al- (Fawwaz), 817
Durra, Muhanna, 145
Durrani dynasty, 55–56, **734–736**, 1468
in Anglo–Afghan wars, 196, 735
collapse of, 400
establishment of, 85, 734–735
in Kandahar, 55–56, 85
Durrell, Lawrence, 118
Düstur (law volumes), 577
Dusturiyya school (Jerusalem), 1973
"Dutch disease," 2200
Dutch Reformed Church, Arabian Mission of, 231, 1854
Duwish, Faysal al-, 2213
Duzdar, Shahinda, in Arab Women's Executive Committee, 268
Duzhab (Iran), 2420
DYP. *See* True Path Party (Turkey)

E

"Each Person Has a Name" (Zelda), 2429
Early, Evelyn A., *as contributor*, 1508–1511
Earthquakes, 901
East, as designation and term, 1522
Eastern Desert, **737**, 763
area of, 737
population of, 737
regions of, 737
Eastern Europe. *See also specific countries*
Jewish Enlightenment movement in, 1017 (*See also* Haskalah)
Jews immigrating from, 145–146, 508–509, 1361
pan-Turanism in, 1800
socialism in, 1360
weapons sold by
to Egypt, 412
to Syria, 412
Zionism in, 1025
Eastern Music Group, 2009
Eastern (Greek) Orthodox Church, 590–591, *591*, **737–738**, *938*, 939
in Balkan Peninsula, 383
in Byzantine Empire, 589
churches in, 738
in Cyprus, 652, 653
establishment of, 590–591, 738
in Lebanon, deputy prime ministership reserved for members of, 1663
in Ottoman Empire, millet system of, 1543–1545
patriarch of, 917, 1806
principles of, 738
Protestant missions targeting of, 1854
theology of, 639
in Turkey, 2238
Eastern Province. *See* Hasa, al-
Eastern Question, **738–743**, 1522
Aachen Congress (1818) on, 739
Austria in, 739, 741
Britain in, 509, 739–743
Crimean War (1853–1856) and, 739
economy in, 741–742
Egypt in, 740–741, 742
France in, 739–743, 846
Italy in, 739, 742
Lausanne Treaty (1923) resolving, 743
Prussia in, 739, 741, 903
Russia in, 739–742

Turkish Straits in, 739–740
Vienna Congress (1814–1815) on, 739
World War I and, 742–743
Eastern-rite Catholic churches, 592–593
Eastern Women's Conference on the Palestine Problem (1938), 13
Arab Women's Association of Palestine after, 267
Khalidi (Wahida al-) at, 1296
Shihabi (Zlikha al-) at, 2052
East Germany, 906–907
East India Company (EIC), 525–526, 548, **743**, *2205*
in Anglo–Omani treaties, 203, 204, 525–526
Arabian Peninsula controlled by, 526–527, 530
and British–Persian relations, 526
changing commercial residencies into political residencies, 526, 527
and conquest of India, 525–526
in Omani trade, 525
Persian Gulf controlled by, 526–527, 530, 743
in Persian Gulf trade, 525
in South Asian trade, 525
East Jerusalem
in Arab–Israel War (1967), *248*, 249, 1224–1225
Arab residents of, 1160
Arif (Arif al-) as mayor of, 288
in Camp David Summit (2000), 561
as capital of future Palestinian state, 2340
establishment of, 1224
Israel extending law to, 426
Israeli annexation of, 249, 2340
impact on Palestinians, 1791
lack of international recognition of, 1788
Jordanian rule of, 1224
Palestinian citizens of Israel in, 1787–1788
unification with West Jerusalem, 1225
Easton, David, 2170
East West Divan (orchestra), 1966
Ebadi, Shirin, **743–744**, 875, 894
Nobel Peace Prize for, 1121
Eban, Abba (Aubrey), **744–745**
under Ben-Gurion (David), 744
education of, 744
under Eshkol (Levi), 744
in Jewish Agency, 744
Kollek (Teddy) work with, 1331
Shiloah (Reuven) under, 2056
Eberhard, Wolfram, 492
Ebtehar, Maryam, 2096
Ebtekar, Maʿsumeh, **745**
in Iranian Bureau of Women's Affairs, 1123
Eccel, A. Chris, *as contributor*, 347–349
Ecevit, Bülent, **745–746**, *746*
in Cyprus crisis, 1666
in Democratic Left Party, 746, 2245
education of, 745
Erbakan (Necmeddin) in conflict with, 746
government of, 692, 746
Nationalist Action Party in, 1661
National Salvation Party in, 1666
Keban Dam opened by, 1284
Motherland Party support for, 1584
in Republican People's Party, 745–746, 1098, 1666, 1919
resignation of, 746, 1666
wife of, 746, 747
Ecevit, Rahşan, 746, **747**
École des Langues Orientales (Paris), 812, 2146
École des Ponts et Chausées (Paris), 916
École Militaire–École de Guerre (Paris), 956
École Normale Supérieure
Bakkar (Jalillah) at, 376
Toumi (Khalida) at, 2195
École Supérieure des Beaux Arts (Paris), 2001
École Supérieure des Lettres (Paris), 2020
Economic and military aid, **747–752**
to Afghanistan, 748
to Algeria, 749
from Arab countries, *748*, 749–750, 751
bilateral, 747–749, 750
from Britain, 747
criticism of, 750–751
decline of, 751
dependence on, 751
effects of, 750–751
to Egypt, 747
from Arab countries, 749, 765
Camp David Accords (1978) and, 748, 771
dependence on, 751
from IMF, 749
role in Gulf War (1990–1991) and, 749
from Soviet Union, 748, 765
from United States, 748–749, 750, 765, 771
from France, 747
goals of, 747
for humanitarian needs, 750
from International Monetary Fund, 747, 749, 1106
to Iraq, 748
to Israel, 747
in Arab–Israel War (1973), 748
Camp David Accords (1978) and, 748
from United States, 748–749, *749*, 750, *750*
from Japan, 747
to Jordan, 747
from Arab countries, *748*, 749
dependence on, 751
from IMF, 749
from United States, 748, 749, 750
from Kuwait, 1349–1350, 1352
to Libya, 748
to Morocco, 748
from IMF, 749
from United States, 750
multilateral, 749–750, 750
from Palestine Economic Corporation, to Jews in Palestine, 1771
politics of, 747–749
to South Yemen, 748
from Soviet Union, 747, 748
to Sudan
from Arab countries, 749
from IMF, 749
to Syria, 747, 748
from Arab countries, 749
dependence on, 751
to Tunisia, 749
to Turkey, 747
from United States, 748, 750
from United States, 747, 748, 750
in Arab–Israel War (1973), 748
Camp David Accords (1978) and, 748, 771
through Economic Support Fund, 748
in Gulf War (1990–1991), 749
under Marshall Plan, 1836
under Point Four program, 1836

Economic and military aid *(continued)*
from World Bank, 747, 749
to Yemen Arab Republic, 749
Economic and Social Commission for Western Asia (ESCWA), 878, 2277
Economic and Social Council (ECOSOC), 2277
Economic Community of West Africa (ECOWAS), Mauritania's withdrawal from, 1503
Economic Council, 1387
Economic elites, 775
Economic Independence: How? (Gozanski), 934
Economics, **752–754**
of imperialism, 1087, 1088–1090
of industrialization, 1091–1094
Economic sanctions
against Iraq, by United Nations (*See* Sanctions, Iraqi)
against Libya
by United Nations, 522, 1414, 1415, 1707, 1708
by United States, 1707–1708
Economic Support Fund (ESF), 748
ECOSOC. *See* Economic and Social Council
ECP. *See* Executives of Construction Party
Ecuador, in OPEC, 1720
Eddé, Carlos, 1653
Eddé, Emile, **754**
Aoun (Michel) supported by, 754
Khuri (Bishara al-) rivalry with, 1315, 2202
Muslim prime minister appointed by, 1653
in National Bloc, 1653
opposition to, in Constitutional Bloc, 634
Phalange party and, 1254
as president, 754
as prime minister, 754
son of, 754
Sulh (Riyad al-) and, 2117
Trad (Petro) supporting, 2202
Eddé, Raymond, **754–755**
Chehab (Fu'ad) in conflict with, 754
exile of, 1653
in al-Hilf al-Thulathi, 581, 1254
Khuri (Bishara al-) opposed by, 1315
in Lebanese Civil War (1975–1990), 754
in National Bloc, 1653
in Socialist Front, 580
against Ta'if Accord, 754
Edebiyat-i Cedide, 1439
Eden, Anthony, **755**
and Anglo–Egyptian Treaty (1936), 755
in Arab–Israel War (1956), 755
Chamberlain (Neville) in conflict with, 755
under Churchill (Winston S.), 755
and Fertile Crescent unity, 825
as foreign secretary, 755, 842
and "Gentlemen's agreement" (1937), 755
Iranian oil nationalization opposed by, 755
and League of Arab States establishment, 517
at Montreux Convention (1936), 755, 1565
Nasser (Gamal Abdel) opposed by, 755
in Operation Alpha, 157
as prime minister, 755
resignation of, 520
Sèvres Protocol shredded by, 2014
on Suez Canal nationalization, 520, 755, 2108
on Suez Canal Users Association, 1444
Eder, Edith, in Women's International Zionist Organization, 2357
Edip, Halide, 1800
Edirne (Turkey), **755–756**
Balkan wars over, 384
B'nai B'rith lodge in, 489
foundation of, 755
tourism in, 755
Edirne, Treaty of (1713), 739
Edot Ha-Mizrah. *See* Adot Ha-Mizrah
Educated Girls' Association (Sudan), 2105
Education, **756–762**. *See also specific colleges, universities, and countries*
in 9th–16th century, 756
in 18th century, 756
in 19th century, 757
architecture, 284
art, 312
and "brain drain," 761
censorship of, 759, 761
centralization of, 759–760
colonialism and, 758–759, 880
European model and, 756, 757
in foreign schools, 758
gender and (*See* Gender, and education)
global policies on, 760–761
growth of press and, 759
madrasa system of, 1457–1458
in Mahalle Schools, 1461
missionary schools in, 1550–1552
modernization and, 880, 1556
nationalization and, 760
new schooling in (*See* New schooling)
in private schools, 761
in religious schools, 756, 757, 760, 761
vs. schooling, 756
in science and technology, 2004
upbringing aspect of, 759–760
of women, 760, 761, 879–884 (*See also* Gender, and education)
women's studies, 1100–1101
Education Regulation (1869) (Ottoman Empire), 758
EEC. *See* European Economic Community
Efendi, Agha, in Young Ottomans, 2405
Efendi, Ali Riza, 330
Efendi, Mehmet Esad, on *vaka-i hayriye*, 2308
Efendi, Süleyman Fehim, and Cevdet (Ahmet), 577
Effendi, 2622
Efflatoun, Inji, **762**
Efrat, Yona, in Kahan Commission, 1263
EFU. *See* Egyptian Feminist Union
Ege University, **762–763**
Egypt, **763–769**. *See also specific cities, organizations, people, and regions*
20th-century achievements of, Haykal (Muhammad Hasanayn) on, 1013
agriculture in, *753*, 754
in Bahariya, 366
child labor in, 1358
cotton, 404, 405, 643–644, 2180, 2181, *2181*
and disease, 710
alcohol in, 110
All-Palestine Government supported by, 154, 155, 156
in Arab boycott against Israel, 224
Arabia invaded by (1811–1818), 818
Arabian horses in, 230, 231
in Arab–Israel War (1948), 242, 810, 1537

defeat of, 236, 243, 766
General Armistice Agreement on (1949), 239–240, 244
in Arab–Israel War (1956), 236–237, 244–246
foreign policy of, 245
military forces of, 245–246
Nasser (Gamal Abdel) and, 1650
National Union as outgrowth of, 1667
in Arab–Israel War (1967), 237, 248–249, 1537
Nasser (Gamal Abdel) and, 1651
in Arab–Israel War (1973), 237–238, 250–252, 1537, 1957
Arab socialism in, 265
archaeology in, 275, 276, *276*
Aswan High Dam and, 327
and Egyptian Museum, 771–772
hieroglyphics in, 275, 581–582
Mariette (Auguste) and, 1488
Maspéro (Gaston) and, 1499
architecture in, 281, 282, 1603
armament levels of, 304
Armenians in, 2415
arms industry of, 1483
arms sales to
by Czechoslovakia, 1650
by Soviet Union, 304, 412, 2215
by United States, 304, 1238
army crisis in (1927), Antonius (George) in, 214
art of, 762, 1275, 2069
Coptic, 640
cultural identity in, 313
multimedia, 176
automobile industry in, *1482*, 1484
banking in, 389, 390, 392, *393*, 394, 1838, 2031, 2096–2097
Berbers in, 458, 2071
at Bludan Conference (1937), 488
borders of, 763
British–French rivalry over, 527–528, 742
British occupation of (1882–1922), 529, 613–614, *1561*
Abbas Hilmi II in, 5–6, 509, 858
Allenby (Edmund Henry) in, 151, 512
Baring (Evelyn) as consul (*See* Baring, Evelyn)
British withdrawal from, draft treaty for (1946), failure of, 338
Cambon–Lansdowne Agreement on (1904), 529, 559–560, 1374
Churchill (Winston S.) on, 595
Clayton (Gilbert) in, 603
Dinshaway incident in (1906), 406, 709, 909–910
and disease, 710, 711
Drummond-Wolff Convention on (1885), 726
dual control during, 528, 730–731, 1158
Dufferin report on (1883), 732
Europeans in, 614
financial reasons for, 1089–1090
French support for, 119
Gezira Sporting Club for British civil servants during, 908
Kamil (Mustafa) opposing, 1267
Kitchener (Horatio Herbert) in, 1329
land ownership in, 1371
McMahon (Henry) in, 1506
Milner Mission during, 1546
national movement against, 512, 616, 2418–2419
National Party opposing, 1663–1664
and Russian–French alliance, 742
Shepheard's Hotel as British gathering place during, 2050
as veiled protectorate, 766
during World War I, 509
British occupation of (1940s), Muslim Brotherhood opposing, 1620–1621
British relations with
Alexandria Convention in (1840), 118–119
Anglo–Egyptian Treaty (1936) and, 518, 766, 810, 859
under Farouk government, 516, 810
indirect British rule, 514, 515
Nahhas (Mustafa al-) and, 1635–1636
under Nasser (Gamal Abdel), 1649–1650
Sèvres Treaty (1920) and, 2015
Suez Canal and, 519–520, 2014
trade deficits and, 404, 2198–2199
Wafd party and, 2320–2321
Catholics in, 1931
censorship of books in, 1296
child labor in, 1358
Christians in, 1971 (*See also* Copts)
Circassians in, 599
cities of
capital, 551–554
delta, 1461, 1480–1481
port, 102–103, 116–118, 1848–1849, 1884
provincial capital, 327
satellite, 1994–1995
tourist center, 1447–1448
clothing in, 611–612
communication in, 624
communism in, 43–44, 625–626, 627, 651
constitution of, 766
Fu'ad and, 858–859
Liberal Constitutionalist Party and, 1409
religious equality in, 642
replacement of, 2065
cotton industry in, 116–117, 404, 405, 643–644, 645, *1092*, 1158, 2180, 2181, *2181*
coup in (1952), 776, 1537
CIA in, 572
Copts in, lack of, 641
by Free Officers, 518, 767, 810, 853–854, 1409
government supervision of charities after, 1453
Mahir (Ali) in, 1465
Misri (Aziz Ali al-) in, 1550
Muslim Brotherhood in, 1621
Nasser (Gamal Abdel) in, 1649
political parties abolished after, 1664
Sadat (Anwar al-) in, 1956
Wafd party disbanded after, 2321
court system of, mixed, 1553
in Crimean War, 1970
Curiel family in, 651
Damascus under, 662
dance in, 866, 1273
Dar al-Kutub al-Misriyya library of, 670
debt of, 117, 766, 1158
cancellation after Gulf War, 1594
International Debt Commission for, 1106, 1158
under Isma'il ibn Ibrahim, 404, 528
defense costs as percentage of GNP or GDP, *1530*
De Menasce family in, 690–691
democratization in, 767–769
Islamist groups obstructing, 768–769
under Mubarak (Husni), 768

Egypt *(continued)*
and multiparty elections, 768
under Sadat (Anwar al-), 767
disease in, 710–711, 712, 1845
Eastern Desert in, 737, 763
in Eastern Question, 740–741, 742
economic and military aid to, 747
from Arab countries, 749, 765
Camp David Accords (1978) and, 748, 771
dependence on, 751
from IMF, 749
role in Gulf War (1990–1991) and, 749
from Soviet Union, 748, 765
from United States, 748–749, 750, 765, 771
economy of, 752, 753–754, 765–766
in 1990s, 766
foreign investment in, 1096
Greeks and, 938, 939
under Mubarak (Husni), 1594
under Sadat (Anwar al-), 765–766, 1957
September 11th attacks and, 766
statistics on, *753*
women in labor force, 874, 875
education in, *765*
administrative bodies of, 757–758
Banna (Hasan al-) and, 395
at Dar al-Da'wa wa al-Irshad, 669
al-Maqasid schools, 759
Muslim Brotherhood schools, 759
new schooling, 756, 757
reform of, 588–589, 656
in religious schools, 761
Tahtawi (Rifa'a al-Rafi al-) and, 2146–2147
upbringing aspect of, 760
at Victoria College, 2315–2316
elections in, monitoring of, 1079
elites in, 776
female genital mutilation in, 822
feminism in (*See* Egyptian Feminist Union; Feminism, in Egypt)
film industry of, 970–971
films of, 324, 336–337, 832, 866, 1273, 2021–2022, 2039
documentary, 1079
fishing industry of, 834
France in, dual control by, 730–731, 1158
freemasonry in, 852
French–British rivalry over, 527–528
French occupation of (1798–1801), 766
administration during, 491
alienation of Egyptians during, 845
Anglo–Ottoman force ending, 491, 766
as British threat, 524, 525
Convention of al-Arish on (1800), 288–289
historical accounts of invasion, 1207
impact of, 492
Kléber (Jean-Baptiste) in, 1330
Menou (Jacques François) in, 1517
in Treaty of Amiens (1802), 183
French relations with
dual control by, 528
Suez Canal and, 2014
futuwwa in, 860
Gaza City occupied by, 869
Gaza Strip occupied by, 870–871
at Geneva Peace Conference (1973), 900
German relations with, 906
government of, 933
Greeks in, 938–939
in Greek War of Independence, 939, 940
guest workers from, 946
guilds in, 947
in Gulf Crisis (1990–1991), 951, 953, 1594
hieroglyphics of, deciphering of, 275, 581–582
higher education in, 761, 2425
at Ain Shams University, 94
at Alexandria University, 119
at American University in Cairo, 179–180
at al-Azhar, 347–349, 1457–1458
at Cairo University, 555–556
in *madrasa* system, 1457–1458
medical, 607
missionaries and, 1551–1552
at Suez Canal University, 2107
human rights in, for gay people, 888
independence from Britain (1922), 515, 2419
Allenby Declaration granting, 151
Milner Mission on, 1546
national movement for, 616
Tharwat (Abd al-Khaliq) supporting, 2183
Wafd and, 766, 858
industrialization of, 1094
industry of
in 19th century, 1357
textile, 1461
intelligence services of, 1102, *1103*
Iraqi relations with
agreement on unification, 288
Qasim (Abd al-Karim) and, 1872
irrigation in, 74, 763
Baring (Evelyn) developing, 404, 405, *406*
Islamic congresses held by, 1153
Islamic fundamentalism in
Ashmawi (Muhammad Sa'id al-) against, 322
Sha'rawi (Muhammad Mutwalli al-) and, 2031
al-Takfir wa al-Hijra and, 2150–2151
islands of, 1832
Isma'ili Shi'ism in, 1158
Israeli espionage agent in, 1446–1447
Israeli peace negotiations with, 1166 (*See also* Egyptian–Israeli Peace Treaty (1979))
after Arab–Israel War (1973), 251–252, 1166, 1328
Boutros-Ghali (Boutros) and, 505
at Camp David Accords (1978), 363, 560–561, 2293
Carter (Jimmy) in, 539, 567, 770
CIA in, 157, 573
Crossman (Richard) in, 650
in General Armistice Agreements (1949), 239–240
Israeli peace movement's impact on, 1809
Jarring (Gunnar) in, 1219
Kissinger (Henry) in, 1328
in Operation Alpha, 157
opposition to, 363, 561, 771
Sadat (Anwar al-) and, 426, 770, 1957
Saunders (Harold) and, 2001
Israeli relations with
arms race in, 236
deterioration of, 236
Lavon affair and, 449, 785, 1377–1378
Mossad in, 1579
under Mubarak (Husni), 1593–1594
under Nasser (Gamal Abdel), 1649–1650

Sinai peninsula and, 1957, 2068
Taba dispute, 2139, 2140
Tiran Strait blockades and, 2191
Jews in
immigration to Israel, 1913–1914
leaders of, 1016
LICA formation, 1415–1416
LISCA formation, 1416
Nahum (Hayyim) as chief rabbi of, 1637
Rolo family, 1930
during World War II, 1234
Jordanian relations with
Palestinian claims in, 154, 155
pledge of financial aid to Jordan (1957), 1632
journalism in, 1012, 1419, 1838
judiciary in, 768, 769
in Konya, Battle of (1832), 1333
labor unions in, 1358
Land Law (1858) of, 1970
land reforms in, *1370*, 1371–1372
languages in
Arabic, 233, 763, 1456–1457
Coptic, 640
at Lausanne Conference (1949), 1375
in League of Arab States, 1386, 1388
member-state dues of, 1387
readmission of, *1387*, 1388
suspension of membership of, 364, 771, *1387*, 1388
legal system of
French influences on, 1380
mixed courts, 939, 1382
reforms in, 1382
legislative body in, 932
literary criticism in, 341
literature of, 18, 475–476, 805, 911, 914–915, 978–979, 1060–1061, 1419, 1420, *1420*, 1421, 1950–1951, 1977–1978, 1990, 2019, 2044–2045, 2233, 2428
literary criticism, 1060, 1061
memoirs, 1013
novels, 1464–1465
short stories, 1082–1083, 1464–1465
by women, 322, 1472–1473, 1924–1925, 2431
location of, 763
at London Conference (1939), 1445
London Convention (1840) and, 1445, 1602, 1691, 2093–2094
majlis (assembly) of, 1472
manufacturing in, 1481–1484, *1482*, *1483*
map of, *764*
medical care in
Mabarrat Muhammed Ali and, 1452–1453
Mahmud (Mustafa) in, 1469
for women, 1510
on Middle East Defense Organization, 519
military dictatorships in, 767, 776
military of
conscripted by Muhammad Ali (nizam al-jadid, al-), 1690
equipment of, *1534*
force levels of, *1528–1529*, 1529, 1531
force structure of, *1532–1533*, 1535
role of, 1540–1541
modernization in, 1157–1158
and decline of bazaars, 419
under Muhammad Ali, 766
Mount Lebanon occupied by, 1393
music of, 22, 324, 336, 675, 970–971, 1617, 1619, 2261–2263
Muslim-Christian riots in, 986–987
Napoleonic expedition to, 1490
national anthem of, 675
nationalist movement in, 405–406
1919 uprisings, 1664, 2320, 2418
during British occupation, 405–406, 512
Copts in, 640–641, 1549
demanding renegotiation of Condominium Agreement, 518
Jews in, 1549
Nasser (Gamal Abdel) and, 1648, 1650–1651
National Party in, 1663–1664
Pharaonicism in, 1831–1832
during World War II, 516
Zaghlul (Sa'd) and, 2418–2419
natural gas reserves and production in, *1671*
newspaper and print media of, 1012, 1013, 1374–1375, 1474, 1678
English-language, 1682
French-language, 1682
government-controlled, 1680
magazines, 1682
privately controlled, 1680
transitional press, 1681
women's, 206
Nile Delta in, 690, 763
Nile Valley union with, 349
Nubians in, 1696
oases in, 2071–2072
open door policy of, 1094
infitah as, 1096
Orthodox Church in (*See* Copts)
in Ottoman Empire, 741
Buhayra, 542
defeat of Tuman Bey and, 2223
Ottoman invasion of
in Aqaba incident (1906), 218
Muhammad Ali in campaign against, 1602
Ottoman navy surrendered to, 1741
Ottoman relations with
during Greek rebellion (1825-1827), 1466
over Syrian control, 1466–1467
pan-Arabism in, 1799
parliament of, Copts in, 641, 642
People's Assembly of, weakness of, 1812
Pharaonicism in, 1831–1832
phosphate industry in, 1834–1835
PLO relations with, under Mubarak (Husni), 1593–1594
poetry of, 22, 1078–1079
political parties in, 768 (*See also specific parties*)
legalization of multiple, 267, 767
single system of, 266–267, 767
population censuses in, 1848
population growth in, 763, 764–765, 1843, 1845
population of, 752, *753*, 763–765, 1843, 1844, 1845
postage stamps of, 1849, 1850, 1858
pronatalist policies of, 478
Protestant missions in, 1854, 1856
Protocols of the Elders of Zion in, 1856
provinces of, 327, 921
public health in, 710
in 19th century, 2003
pyramids of, 1850, 1857–1858
radio and television in, *1893*, 1893–1894, *1895*
railways in, 4, 2206, *2206*
regions of, 763
religions in, 763–764
Baha'i faith, 365
Shi'ism, 2054
rivers of, 1688
Sahara in, 1963

Egypt *(continued)*
Saudi Arabian relations with, 795–796, 798
under Faisal (ibn Abd al-Aziz Al Saʿud), 1626
Sadat (Anwar al-) and, 1957
during Yemen Civil War, 1650
science and technology in, 2004, 2005
scout movement in, 2006
secularism in
Ghazali (Muhammad al-) opposing, 914
Tahtawi (Rifaʿa al-Rafi al-) and, 2147
slaves in, 2073, 2074
socialism in, 265, 266–267, 767
Soviet relations with, 1942, 1943
after Arab–Israel War (1967), 2292
in Arab–Israel War (1956), 245
in Arab–Israel War (1973), 250
under Brezhnev (Leonid Ilyich), 508, *508*
friendship treaty (1971), Baghdadi (Abd al-Latif al-) against, 363
Sadat (Anwar al-) ordering Soviet military advisers to leave, 508, 1957
stock market in, 2091, *2091*
Sudanese relations with, under Nasser (Gamal Abdel), 1649–1650
Sudan invaded by (1822), 1077
Sudan under, 529–530
Condominium Agreement on (1899), 405, 518, 530, 629, 1363, 2100
Fashoda incident (1898), 405, 529–530, 811
Foreign Office in, 530
Gezira Scheme under, 908
Mahdist movement in, 404–405
nationalist movement against, 2100
Suez Canal in (*See* Suez Canal)
Syrian relations with
Asad (Hafiz al-) and, 2135
entente in, 319
improvement of, 318
invasion under Muhammad Ali, 2093–2094
Sadat (Anwar al-) and, 1957
Syrian union with (*See* United Arab Republic)
in Syrian War (1831–1833), 740–741, 2093
in Syrian War (1839), 740–741, 2093
taxes in, poll *(jizya)*, Coptic exemption from, 640
tax farming in, 2167
teacher training in, at Dar al-Ulum, 671
terrorist attacks in, 278, 768–769
textile industry in, 404, 405, 2180, 2181, *2181*, 2182
theater in, 675, 1083, 1421, 1977–1978, 1990, 2184
Tiran Strait claimed by, 2191
tourism in, 2195–2196
Giza Pyramids, 2196
Luxor, 1447
security issues, 2196
Sharm al-Shaykh, 2040
in trade, 2200, *2200*, 2201
transport in, modern means of, *2207*
tribes in, 458
Urabi rebellion (1881–1882), 404, 766
Fahmi (Mahmud Pasha) in, 797
orator of, 1419
U.S. relations with
after Arab–Israel War (1973), 2292
Dulles (John Foster) and, 733
under Johnson, 1238
under Kennedy, 1288
under Mubarak (Husni), 1593
under Nasser (Gamal Abdel), 1650
Sadat (Anwar al-) and, 767, 1957
in War of Attrition (1969–1970), 2327
water resources of, 1468
freshwater withdrawals, *2331*
Lake Nasser and, 1651–1652
from Nile River, 1688
quantity of, 2330
Western Desert in, 763
Westernization of, 2341
women in
as activists, 1614, 1652, 1906–1907, 2428
as artists, 762, 2069
birth control clinic for, *479*
as cabinet members, 39
charitable organizations run by, 39–40, 1452–1453
as communists, 43–44
as dancers, 866
economic status of, 877, *877*
education for, 1902
as judges, 808, 1905
in labor force, 874, 875, 878
as landholders, 878
magazine on, 206
participation in civil society, 1905
physicians for, 2003
in politics, 762, 890–891, 892, 894, 914–915, 1950–1951, 1958, 1965–1966, 2019, 2030–2031
rejecting veiling, 772
religious rituals of, 2360, 2361
in Wafd party, 2320, 2321–2322
as writers, 378–379, 475–476, 914–915, 1950–1951, 2019
women's rights in, 762, 770, 772, 1958, 2019
limitations on, 874
organizations for, 268–269
World Bank and
capital stock and voting power in, *2363*
loans from, *2364*
in World War I, 2366–2368
British-Ottoman fighting in, 509–510
National Party opposing Britain in, 1664
in World War II, 515–516, 2369–2370
al-Alamayn battle in (1942), 102–103, 516, 1565, 2370
Farouk government, 810, 956
German troops in, 906
in Yemen Arab Republic, 2392, 2393, 2396
Yemen military revolt supported by (1965), 1531, 1537
Young Egypt movement in, 2405
Egyptian Antiquities Service
Mariette (Auguste) as founder of, 1488
Mariette (Auguste) in, 1970
Maspéro (Gaston) as director of, 1499
Salim Hasan in, 1978
Egyptian Feminist Union (EFU), **769–770**, 2030, 2321–2322
agenda of, 770
communist women in, absence of, 43
establishment of, 227, 769
goals of, 227
journals of, 770
Musa (Nabawiyya) in, 1614
Nabarawi (Sayza) in, 770
Saʿid (Amina al-) in, 1965

Shaʿrawi (Huda al-) in, 227, 770, 890
Egyptian Gazette, The (newspaper), 1682
Egyptian Geographical Society, **770**
Egyptian–Israeli Peace Treaty (1979), *425*, **770–771**, 2139
Arab–Israel War (1973) experiences and, 1537
Arab rejection of, Khaddam (Abd al-Halim) lobbying for, 1291
Arab states rejecting, 771
arms sales after, 304
Begin (Menachem) signing, 771
Camp David Accords leading to (1978), 238, 560, 561, 567, 770, 1166
conflicting interpretations of, 238
content of, 771
Dayan (Moshe) in, 683
on Israeli access to Suez Canal, 771
Sadat (Anwar al-) signing, 770
on Sinai Peninsula, 771, 2068
terms of, 1166
on United Nations Emergency Force (UNEF), 2276
Egyptian Movement for National Liberation (MELN), Curiel (Henry) in, 627, 651
Egyptian Museum (Cairo), **771–772**
Amir (Mustafa) as director of, 772
establishment of, 275, 771
Mariette (Auguste) in, 771, 1488
Maspéro (Gaston) as director of, 771, 1499
Tutankhamen Collection at, 772
Egyptian Organization for Human Rights (EOHR), on tuberculosis, 712
Egyptian Public Debt Commission, 404, 528
Egyptian Trade Union Federation, 1358
Egyptian University. *See* Cairo University
Egyptian Woman (magazine), 227
Egyptian Women's Union, **772**
Muslim Women's Association and, 914
Egyptian Writers Union, 1978
Egyptienne, L' (journal), 2030
Égyptiens, les (Amin), 187
Egyptology, 492, 581–582, 1978
Egyptian interest in, 276, 1265–1266
European involvement in, 275
Mariette (Auguste) in, 1488
Maspéro (Gaston) in, 1499
Egypt's Destiny (Naguib), 1634
Ehrlich, Simha, in Liberal Party, 1184
EIC. *See* East India Company
Eichmann, Adolf, 956, 992, 1042
capture of, impact on Holocaust survivors, 1751
in Kasztner affair (1954–1955), 1280
Mossad kidnapping of, 1578
trial of, Kovner (Abba) testimony at, 1336
Eickelman, Dale F.
as contributor, 463, 1101–1105, 1281, 1485
on education, 756
8 Mars (newspaper), **772–773**
Jababdi (Latifa) as editor of, 1203
Eighth Brigade (Lebanon), 215
81st Blow, The (documentary), 956
Eighty Million Women with Us (Efflatoun), 762
Eimah Gedolah ve-Yareʾah (Greenberg), 941
Eisenberg, Laura Z., *as contributor*, 560–561, 567–568, 770–771, 1262–1263, 1417–1418, 1907–1908, 2083
Eisenhower Doctrine, 773, 1942, 2110, 2291
Chamoun (Camille) advocating, 580, 773, 1390
Dulles (John Foster) and, 734
Jordanian aid under, 1632–1633
Eisenhower, Dwight David, **773**
in Allied Middle East Command, 153
in Arab–Israel War (1956), 246
on Aswan High Dam, 773
and Baghdad Pact (1955), 363
calling for cease-fire during Suez Crisis, 755, 773, 2109
government of
Dulles (John Foster) in, 733–734, 773
Rogers (William Pierce) in, 1929
Middle East policy under, 2291
in Operation Alpha, 157
Pahlavi (Mohammad Reza) advised by, 1752
in World War II, 516, 773
Eitan, Rafael, **774**
in Arab–Israel War (1948), 774
in Arab–Israel War (1982), 252, 254, 774
Gush Emunim supporting, 958
in Israel Defense Force, 1171
in Pollard affair, 1838
in Sabra and Shatila massacres, 254, 774, 1263, 1954
in Tzomet Party, 774
Ekeus, Rolf, 1135, 2288
Ekrem, Mahmut, Cevdet (Abdullah) influenced by, 576
El Al airplane, PFLP attempted hijacking of (1970), 1293
Elalamy, Yousouf Amin, 1425
Elat (Israel), 1675, 2191
Elazar, David
Middle Eastern origin of, 49
in Palmah, 1795
El-Baradei, Muhammad, 1136
as UN weapons inspector, 2324
Elburz Mountains, 901, 902, 1110, 1312, 2419
Eldad, Israel, in Lohamei Herut Yisrael, 1443, 2025, 2385
Eldem, Sedad Hakki, **774**
Ottoman Revival architecture of, 282
El-Din, Ibrahim Sayf, in General Armistice Agreements (1949), 239
Electricity. *See* Hydropower
El-Hassan, Khalid M., *as contributor*, 432–434, 1712–1713, 1977
El-Hibri, Tayeb, *as contributor*, 840, 1073, 1393–1394, 1521, 2052–2055, 2122–2124
Eliahu Hanabi Lodge (Alexandria), 489
Elieser, Ben. *See* Syrkin, Nachman
Eliot, T. S., 1422
Elites, **774–776**, *775*, *776*
analysis of, 774–775
colonialism and, 775
cultural, 775
early, 774
economic, 775
in Egypt, 776
in Iran, 776, *776*
in Iraq, 776
in Jordan, 776
in Libya, 776
military, 775–776
in Morocco, 776
in nineteenth century, 775
in Ottoman Empire, 775, *775*, 1734

Elites *(continued)*
political, 775
in Saudi Arabia, 776
slaves as, 775
social, 775
in Syria, 776
in Turkey, 776
ulama as, 2258
women as, 775
after World War II, 775
Elivar, Emre, 477
El-Kseur Platform (2001), 638
El-Okbi, Tayeb. *See* Uqbi, Tayyib al-
Elon, Benny, 958
El Ouezzani, Hassan, in nationalist movement, 1598
Eluard, Paul, 2020
Elysée Palace, Agam (Yaacov) commissioned for, 70
Emami, Sayyid Hoseyn, 976
Emami, Sayyid Mohammad, 2037
Embroidery
Palestinian, 1878–1879
women making, *875*, *881*
Emeç, Cetin, 1050
Emergency Measures (1945) (Israel), 1683
Emergency regulations, **776–777**
Emigré de Brisbane, L' (Shahada), 2020
Emmanuel, Taamrat, 787
Empire, definition of, 1087
Employment, migration for, 1847
Emre, Süleyman Arif, 1910
Emunah (Israel), 893
ENA (Etoile Nord-Africaine). *See* Star of North Africa
Encyclopedia Judaica, 927
Encyclopedia of Islam, Turkish edition of, Adivar (Abdulhak Adnan) in, 45
Enderlin, Charles, 1727
as contributor, 2025–2026
Engels, Friedrich, and Hess (Moses), 1024
English language, 523
on postage stamps, 1850
in Saudi Arabia, 1997
English-language newspapers
in Arab countries, 1681–1682
in Israel, 1683
ENI. *See* Ente Nazionale Idrocarboni
Enquête au pays, une (Chraibi), 588
Entebbe Operation (1976), **777,** 967, 1839
Barak (Ehud) in, 398
Gur (Mordechai) in, 956
Netanyahu (Yonatan) killed in, 1677
Ente Nazionale Idrocarboni (ENI), **777–778**
Entente (newspaper), Abbas (Ferhat) in, 3
Entente National (Morocco), 1574, 1588
Enver Paşa, *778,* **778–779,** *904,* 1540
Arabic script modified by, 1933
Cemal Paşa and, 571, 572
Churchill (Winston S.) and, 595
in Committee for Union and Progress, 778
coup by (1913), 778
Mehmet V and, 1513
Misri (Aziz Ali al-) and, 1550
Mustafa Suphi assassinated by supporters of, 1625
negotiating with Germany, 905
pan-Turkism of, 1800–1801
Talat (Mehmet) and, 2153
in Turkish–Italian War, 2247
in World War I, 2365, *2367*
Yildirim Army organized by, 2400
in Young Turk Revolution, 778
EOHR. *See* Egyptian Organization for Human Rights
EOKA. *See* Ethniki Organosis Kipriakou Agonos
EOKA-B (Cyprus), 654
Epoch of Stones, and Rage, and Hope, The (Langer), 1374
Eppel, Michael, *as contributor,* 1278, 1282–1283, 1604–1605
Eqbal, Manouchehr, **779–780**
Equal and More Equal (Michael), 1522
Equality Now, 887
Equate, 1353
Eratosthenes, 116
Erbakan, Necmeddin, **780,** *1666*
in Cyprus crisis, 1666
Ecevit (Bülent) in conflict with, 746
education of, 780
Milli Görüs Hareketti and, 1545
in National Order Party, 780, 1257, 1910
in National Salvation Party, 1665–1666
as prime minister, 780, 1911, 2242
in Refah Partisi, 598, 1911, 2236
in Virtue Party, 2236
Erbil, Leyla, **780–781**
Erciyas, Mount, 2237
Erdoğan, Tayyip, *99,* **781**
as Istanbul mayor, 781
in Justice and Development Party, 99, 100, 781, 1911, 2245
as prime minister, 100, 781
in Refah Partisi, 781
in Virtue Party, 781
Eretz-Israel under Ottoman Rule (Ben-Zvi), 457
Eretz Yisrael, **781–782**
Begin (Menachem) using term, 781
Borochov (Ber) on, 493
Buber (Martin) on, 540
in foundations of Zionism, 2432
haredi Jews using term, 781
literature of, 1431, 1432
origin of term, 781
settlers to, Ha-Shomer ha-Tzaʿir and, 1001
Eretz Yisrael ha-Shelema (Israel)
development of, 781
supporting Levinger (Moshe), 1407
Erez, Yalim, *2244*
Erg, 700
Erich Maria Remarque Peace Prize, Golshiri (Houshang) awarded with, 929
Eritrea
Italian control of, 1200, 1463–1464
as observer in League of Arab States, 1388
during World War II, 516
Erosion, in deserts, 702
Er Ramleh. *See* Ramla (Israel)
Ersoy, Mehmet Akif, **782,** 1439
Ertuğrul, Muhsin, **782,** 2187
Ertug-Yaras, Füsun, in Women's Library and Information Center, 2358
Erzincan earthquake (1992), 901
Erzurum (Turkey), **782–783**
Atatürk University in, 334
in World War I, 2367, 2368
Erzurum, battle of (1821), 2252
Erzurum Congress (1919), **783**
Erzurum, Treaty of (1823), **783,** 2252
Erzurum, Treaty of (1849), 783
Escargot entêté, L' (Boudjedra), 497
ESCWA. *See* Economic and Social Commission for Western Asia

Esek ha-Bish. See Lavon affair
Esendal, Memduh Şevket, **783–784**
ESF. *See* Economic Support Fund
Esfandiari, Soraya, 375
Esfandiary, Fereydun, **784**
Eshkol, Levi, **784–785**
in Arab–Israel War (1967), 785
Ben-Gurion (David) rivalry with, 1188–1189
death of, Allon (Yigal) as acting prime minister after, 153
as defense minister, 785
government of
Dayan (Moshe) in, 682
Eban (Abba) in, 744
Meir (Golda) in, 1514
Weizman (Ezer) in, 2336
in Haganah, 784
and Harel (Isser), 992
and Herzog (Yaʿacov David), 1023
in Jewish Agency, 784
in Jewish Legion, 1230
in Labor Party, 784, 1183
in Lavon affair, 785, 1377
as prime minister, 449, 784–785, 1378
Sapir (Pinhas) as deputy of, at Mekorot Water Company, 1991
Eskinazi, Roza, **785**
Eskinciyan (Ottoman Empire), 1466–1467
Esmati-Wardak, Masuma, **786**
Espace Tanassof (Tunisia), 325
Espérance trahie, L' (Bani Sadr), 389
Espionage
by British, 1521
Lotz (Wolfgang) as Israeli agent, 1446–1447
by NILI ring, 1
in Pollard affair, 1838
by Shin Bet, 2056–2057
Esprit libérale du Coran, L' (Thaalbi), 2182
Essaouira (Morocco), 2038
Esterhazy, Walsin, 723
Etatism, 415
Été à Stockholm, un (Khatibi), 1304
Eʿtedali Party, Bayat (Mortaza Qoli) in, 416
Eʿtemad al-Dowleh, Mirza Ebrahim Khan, 816
Etemadi, Saleha Faruq, **786**
Eternal Flame (Afghanistan). *See* Sholay-e Jawid
Eʿtesami, Parvin, 1436, 1803
E'tezad al-Dowleh Qajar Qovanlu, daughter of, Mahd-e Ulya, Malek Jahan Khanum as, 1462
Ethics, in Islam, 1145–1147
Ethiopia
conflict with mahdist state in Sudan, 1463–1464
Copts in, 657
female genital mutilation in, 822
Italian claims on, 1933
Italian occupation of, attempted, 1200
Jewish refugees from, *1914*
in World War II, 2368–2370
Ethiopian Jews, **786–788,** *787*
children of, 787
immigration to Israel, 147–148, 786
Israeli airlift of (1991), 786, 1239
Mossad involvement in, 1579
jobs of, 787
language of, 787
number of, 786
religion of, 787
vs. Judaism, 787
Ethiopic Orthodox Church, 639, 787
Coptic Orthodox Church and, 639, 657
Ethniké Hetairia (Greece), 937
Ethniki Organosis Kipriakou Agonos (EOKA) (Cyprus), 653, 943
Ethno-linguistic-regional identity, 1549
Eti bank (Turkey), 1482
Etoile Nord-Africaine (ENA). *See* Star of North Africa
Ettahadi (Algeria), 1803
Ettehad-e Eslam (Iran), 1216
Ettehadieh, Mansoureh, *as contributor,* 7, 88–89, 416–417, 809, 815–816, 1462, 1476–1477, 1591–1592, 1867, 2169–2170, 2296–2297
Etzel. *See* Irgun Zvaʾi Leʾumi (IZL)
Euclid, 116
Eulmi, Omar, 919
Eunuchs, 2074
Euphrates Dam, **788,** 2129, 2188
Euphrates River, **2188–2189,** 2237, 2328
Atatürk Dam on, 1284, *2329*
Basra on, 410
Keban Dam on, 1284
in Kurdistan, 1342
origin of, 902, 2188
origins in Turkey, 194
sediments from, 901
shipping on, 2205
Southeastern Anatolia Project and, 2082
in Syria, 2129
Tabaqa Dam on, 788, 2140–2141
tribes of, 2212
Euro-Mediterranean Partnership, 1415
Europe. *See also specific countries*
Orientalism in, 1722–1723
trade with, 2197–2199
European Community, Turkey in, 1747
European Convention on Human Rights, 1048
European Economic Community (EEC)
Britain as member of, 522
Spain as member of, 2084
European Parliament, Sakharov Prize for Freedom of Thought, for Zana (Leyla), 2423
European Union
Arab Maghreb Union modeled on, 260
Bʾnai Bʾrith in, 489
Germany in, 907
Libyan relations with, 1415
Moroccan relations with, 1601, 1602
Turkey in
AKP support for, 99
Erdoğan (Tayyip) on, 781
Europe, Concert of. *See* Concert of Europe
Eustache, Daniel, numismatic studies of, 1702–1703
Evangelical Protestant missions, 1855–1856
Evapotranspiration, 604
Ever Victorious Army, 931
Evian Accords (1962), **788–789**
chapters of, 788–789
colons in, rights for, 124, 618
Krim (Belkacem) in, 1337
signing of, 139, 788
Evliyaoğlu, Gökhan, 1257
Evolué, 1552
Evolution politique et culturelle au Maroc, L' (al-Fasi), 812

Evren, Kenan, **789**
Social Democratic Party restricted by, 1097
Examination of the World of Islam from a Historical and Philosophical Viewpoint, An (Cevdet), 576
Excommunication and Emigration (Egypt), in al-Jamiʿa al-Islamiyya, 1215
Executive Intelligence Review, 438
Executives of Construction Party (ECP) (Iran), Karbaschi (Gholamhosain) in, 1273
Exercices de tolérance (Laabi), 1355
Exile and the Redeemed (Ben-Zvi), 457
Exile's Return (Turki), 2242
Exodus (ship) (1947), **789–790,** 2289
Expediency Council (Iran)
Musavi (Mir-Hosain) on, 1615
Mustavi-Ardebili (AbdolKarim) on, 1615
Exploration and production-sharing agreements (EPSAs), with Libyan National Oil Corporation, 1662
Export-Import Bank of New York, 2082
Exproprié, l' (Djaout), 716
Extinguished Fire, The (Daneshvar), 1435
Exxon, in construction of Trans-Arabian Pipeline, 2202
Exxon Mobil, 2202
Eye diseases, 712
Eye of the Mirror, The (Badr), 357
Eylul (Mehmet Rauf), 1513
Eytan, Rachel, 1434
Eytan, Walter, in General Armistice Agreements (1949), 239
Eyüboğlu, Bedri Rahmi, **790**
Ezgi, Subhi, 687
Ezra and Nehemiah Operations, **790–791**
Ben-Porat (Mordechai) in, 452
Ezzat, Heba Raʾuf, 892
EzzelArab, Abdel Aziz, *as contributor,* 2146–2148, 2304

F

Fabianism, Musa (Salama) in, 1614
Facing the Dictators (Eden), 755
Fadan Kharasa tribe, 2212
Fadan Waʿad tribe, 2212
Fadel, Mohammad al-, 1423
Fadija (Nubian dialect), 1696
Fadiliyya Sufi (Mauritania), 1451
Fadlallah, Shaykh Husayn, **793–794**
CIA attack against, 573, 793
in Hizbullah, 793, 794, 1037
Fadwa, A Tale of a Palestinian Poetess (Badr), 357
Fadwa Tuqan (Badr), 357
Fahd ibn Abd al-Aziz Al Saʿud (king of Saudi Arabia), *794,* **794–796,** *795,* 1997
brothers of, 165–166
economic reforms of, 164, 795
as education minister, 794
and foreign affairs, 795–796
government of
Al Saʿud (Nayif ibn Abd al-Aziz) in, 166
Al Saʿud (Saʿud ibn Faisal) in, 166
Sultan ibn Abd al-Aziz Al Saʿud in, 165
government reforms by, 796
as interior minister, 794, 798
mother of, 169
peace plan of (*See* Fahd Plan)
reign of, 164, 795–796, 1999–2000
as second deputy prime minister, 794–795, 798
Fahd Plan (1981), 795, **796,** *1387,* 1388
two-state solution in, PLO support for, 1774
Fahmi, Abd al-Rahmin, numismatic studies of, 1702
Fahmi, Mahmud Pasha, **797**
Islamic Revival architecture of, 282
Fahmi, Mustafa, daughter of, 2418
Fahmy, Khaled, 1037
Fahralnissa Zeid Institute of Fine Arts (Amman), 2429
Faisal ibn Abd al-Aziz Al Saʿud (king of Saudi Arabia), **797–799,** 1997
as Al al-Shaykh descendant, 101
in Arab–Israel War (1967), 1626
in Arab–Israel War (1973), 1626
assassination of, 164, 1295, 1999
at Bandung Conference, 387
economic policies of, 164
education of, 797
and finances, 164, 798
and foreign affairs, 797, 798–799
government of
Al Saʿud (Fawwaz ibn Abd al-Aziz) in, 166
Al Saʿud (Muhammad ibn Abd al-Aziz) in, 164
Al Thunayyan (Ahmad) in, 172
Khalid ibn Abd al-Aziz Al Saʿud in, 1294–1295
Pharaon (Rashad) in, 1832
Sultan ibn Abd al-Aziz Al Saʿud in, 165
government reforms by, 798
Islamic congresses of, 1153
Muslim World League founded under auspices of, 1623
Nasser (Gamal Abdel) and, 167, 1626
as prime minister, 164, 794, 1999
reign of, 164, 1999
under Saʿud, power yielded to, 164, 165–166, 167
social reforms of, 164, 1999
sons of, 166–167
successor to, Khalid ibn Abd al-Aziz Al Saʿud as, 1295
as successor to Saʿud, 11, 164
U.S. visit of, *1998*
wives of, 168, 172
favorite, 166, 172
Faisal I ibn Hussein (king of Iraq), **799–802,** *800*
Abd al-Hadi (Awni) and, 13
in Anglo–Iraqi Treaty (1922), 202
and Arab nationalism, 801, 825, 1053
in Arab Revolt (1916), 29, 264, 799–800, 1384
British support for, 29, 35, 202, 801, 824–825, 1132, 1441
Allenby (Edmund Henry) in, 151
Bell (Gertrude) in, 437
Cox (Percy) in, 646
Glubb (John Bagot) in, 921
as Syrian king, 151, 512, 1504–1505
Cairo Conference on (1921), 554, 1023
at Conference of Paris, 2314
in Damascus, 663–664
death of, *800,* 802
education of, 799
and Faisal–Weizmann Agreements, 800, 803
al-Fatat and, 801, 815
French ejection of, 512, 801
government of
Askari (Jaʿfar al-) in, 324
Ayyubi (Ali Jawdat al-) in, 345

Hasani (Taj al-Din al-) in, 998
Kaylani (Abd al-Rahman al-) in, 1282
Hananu (Ibrahim) and, 989
Hashimi (Yasin al-) and, 1001
in Hashimite house, 1000
Husari (Sati al-) and, 1051
and Iraqi admission to League of Nations, 802
and Iraqi independence, 802
Jawahiri (Muhammad Mahdi al-) and, 1219
Jordan under, 1244
at King David Hotel, 1323
Mosul inclusion in Iraq sought by, 1582
pan-Arabism of, 800, 802, 824–825
at Paris peace settlements (1919), 511
Sabbagh (Salah al-Din al-) under, 1953
Sakakini (Khalil al-) admiring, 1973
Shahbandar (Abd al-Rahman) under, 2021
and Syrian independence, 800, 802
as Syrian king, 221, 512, 801, 1924
Allenby (Edmund Henry) on, 151
Arslan (Adil) under, 306
Askari (Jaʿfar al-) under, 324
Atasi (Hasim al-) and, 2132
British support for, 151, 512, 1504–1505
French ejection of, 221, 512, 801, 1244, 1504–1505
Istiqlal Party under, 1198, 1199
Khalidi (Husayn Fakhri al-) under, 1295
Tamimi (Amin al-) as adviser of, 2158
tribal support for, 1527
at Versailles conference (1919), 800–801
in World War I, 151
Faisal II ibn Ghazi (king of Iraq), **802,** 1968
assassination of, 15, 520, 802
coup against (1958), 15, 520
education of, 802
at Victoria College, 2316
in Hashimite house, 1000
and Hussein ibn Talal, 1062
regent for (*See* Abd al-Ilah ibn Ali)
Faisal Islamic Bank of Sudan, 394
Faisal, Muhammad al-, 394
Faisal–Weizmann Agreements, 800, **803**
Faitlovitch, Jacques, 787
Faizani, Mowlawi, in Afghan Islamic movement, 60
Fajiʾat al-Layla al-Sabiʿa Baʿda al-Alf (Aʿraj), 273
Fajr al-Islam (Amin), 183
Fakhd, 2210
Fakhouri, Hani, *as contributor,* 1994–1995
Fakhr al-Din I
reign of, 728
and Selim I, 728
Fakhr al-Din II al-Maʿhi
Jumblatt family and, 1254
Ottoman Empire and, 728
in Palmyra, 728, 1798
Fakhr al-Dowleh, 186
Fakhri, Sabah, 112, 1618
Falahi stitch, 1879
Falaj irrigation system, 1204
Falashas. *See* Ethiopian Jews
Falconry, **803**
Falkenhayn, Erich von, 905
in Yildirim Army, 2400
Fall, The (Camus), 563
Falluja (Iraq), armed resistance to U.S. occupation in, 2326
Falsafat al-thawra (Nasser), 1012
Falsafi, Abu Al-Qasem, 494
Familia (production company), 376
Family, **1493–1496,** *1494, 1495*
honor of, 1495
loyalty to, 1493
modernization and, 1556
Family codes. *See* Algerian Family Code; Moudawana; Ottoman Law of Family Rights (1917); Personal Status Code (Tunisia)
Family law, in Morocco (Moudawana, al-), 1585–1586
Family planning, 477–480, 1510–1511. *See also* Birth control
advocates of, 477
Cairo Family Planning Association and, 555
controversy over, 477
cultural, political, and religious opposition to, 478–480
in Iran, 1111
manipulating population growth with, 477–478
methods of, 480
use of term, 479
Family Planning Association of Iran, 809
Famine
in Ottoman Empire (1916), 264
after plague, 710
Famous Forty (Yemen), 1474
Fana, 2111
Fan al-Sinemaʾi, al- (magazine), 1374
Fanon, Frantz, **803–804**
Fantasia: An Algerian Cavalcade (Djebar), 716
Fao Peninsula (Iraq), **804**
in Iran–Iraq War (1980–1988), 1128
Faqir, Fadia, **804–805**
Farafir, al- (Idris), 1083
Farag, Alfred, 2184
Farah, Bulus, in National Liberation League, 626
Faraj, Maysaloun, **805**
Faraj, Muhammad Abd al-Salam
Islamic Jihad inspired by, 1154
in al-Jihad, 1214
Faraj, Murad, **805–806**
Faramush-Khaneh (Iran), 1477
Farʾa, Wahiba, **806**
Far East, as designation and term, 1522
Farès, Nabile, **806–807,** 1426
Farewell Baghdad (Amir), 188
Far from Medina (Djebar), 716
Farhad, Ghulam Muhammad, **807**
in Afghan Nation, 62
Farhan, Ishaq, in Islamic Action Front, 1151
Farhat al-Zawi, **807**
Farhi family, **807**
Farhi, Hayyim, 807
Farhud, **807–808,** 1233
Farid, Muhammad, in National Party, 1267
Farid, Nagwa Kamal, **808–809**
Farid, Wahid, 971
Farmanfarma, Abd al-Hoseyn Mirza, **809**
Farmanfarma, Nasrat al-Dowleh, 1318
Farmanfarmian, Settareh, **809–810**
"Farm corporation" concept, in Iran, 1372

Farokhzad, Furugh, 832
films of, 1318
Faroqhi, Suraiya, 1036
Farouk (king of Egypt), **810–811**
abdication by, 1465–1466
Azzam (Abd al-Rahman al-) support for, 352
and British relations, 516, 810
coup deposing, 767, 810, 853–854, 1409, 1537
Muhyi al-Din (Khalid) in, 1608
Muhyi al-Din (Zakariyya) in, 1608
Muslim Brotherhood in, 1621
Naguib (Muhammad) in, 1634
Nasser (Abdel Nasser) in, 1649
Wafd party disbanded after, 2321
education of, 810
in exile, 810–811
Mahir (Ali) and, 1465
Mahmud (Muhammad) and, 1468–1469
Maratghi (Mustafa al-) and, 1486
Muslim Brotherhood opposition, 810
reign of, 810
Wafd installed by, 810
Wafd removed by, 767, 810
Farouk-Sluglett, Marion, *as contributor,* 2037, 2415
Farouk University. *See* Alexandria University
Farra, Ibn al-, 990
Farr, Grant, *as contributor,* 62–64, 66–68, 89, 185–186, 193, 196, 341, 386–387, 494–495, 670–671, 721, 731–732, 734, 807, 863–864, 963–964, 1014–1015, 1020–1021, 1024, 1215–1216, 1260–1261, 1268, 1274, 1298, 1317–1318, 1468, 1505, 1559–1560, 1561–1562, 1633, 1638, 1799, 1801, 1812–1813, 1888–1889, 1906, 1912–1913, 2050, 2150, 2166, 2417–2418
Farrokhzad, Forugh, **811,** 928, 1436, 1803
Farsi, Abu Ishaq al-, 1344
Farsi language, 1820
Farsi, Mustaf al-, 1429
Faruqi, Ismaʿil, 284
Faruqi, Maysam J. al-, *as contributor,* 89–90, 680–681, 797, 816–817, 833–834, 911, 968, 1109–1110, 1144–1150, 1259–1260, 1296–1297, 1503–1504, 1608, 1620–1622, 1675–1676, 1882–1883, 2111–2114, 2122–2124
Farzaneh: Journal of Women's Studies (journal), 745
Fas al-Bali, 828–829
Fas al-Jadid, 828
Fascination (Boudjedra), 497
Fascist Italianization program. *See* Fourth Shore, The
Fashion, Lebanese, 556
Fashoda Incident (1898), 405, 529–530, **811**
Fasht al-Dibal reef, 370, 371
Fasi, Abbas al-, in Istiqlal Party, 1198
Fasi, Allal al-, **811–812**
death of, 1197
education of, 811
imprisonment of, 619
in Istiqlal Party, 812, 1196–1197, 1805
in nationalist movement, 618, 812, 1598
Ouazzani (Mohamed Hassan) conflict with, 1803
in Salafiyya movement, 811, 1423, 1974
Fasih, Esmaʿil, 1436
Fasi, Muhammad al-, **812**
Fassih, Ismail, **812**
Fatah, al-, **812–815**
Abbas (Mahmud) in, 6
in Arab–Israel conflict, 813–814
after Arab–Israel War (1967), increased attacks by, 1772
in Arab–Israel War (1967), 270
Arafat (Yasir) in, 270, 813, 814, 1773
Banna (Sabri al-) in, 396
Barghuthi (Marwan) in, 402
Black September established by, 485
central committee of, 813
establishment of, 6, 270, 813
full name of, 813
guerrilla groups of, 813, 814
Hasan (Hani al-) in, 997
Hasan (Khalid al-) in, 998
Hut (Shafiq al-) and, 1071
ideology of, 813–814
and Intifada, 814, 1108
Jordan and, 2156
in Karama, Battle of (1968), 270, 1270–1271, 1772–1773
Khalaf (Salah) in, 1292, 1773
Khaled (Leila) in, 1293
Lebanese Arab Army supported by, 1389
magazine of, 813
Mardam (Jamil) in, 1486
in massacre at Munich Olympics (1972), Israeli retaliation for, 1578
military wing of, 813, 814
Murabitun alliance with, 1612
Nusayba (Sari) supporting, 1705–1706
PFLP rivalry with, 962, 1773, 1840
and PLO, 813, *813,* 814
PLO controlled by, 1773
power struggle in, 814
Qaddumi (Faruq) in, 1863
Qurai (Ahmad Sulayman) in, 1881
Rajub (Jibril) in, 1900
revolutionary council of, 813, 814
rise in popularity of, 270
Sartawi (Issam) in, 1992
training camps of, 813
Wazir (Intisar al-) as first female member of, 2334
Wazir (Khalil al-) in, 2334–2335
youth movement of (*See* Shabiba)
Fatah Mosque (Bahrain), *370*
Fatat, al-, **815**
and al-Ahd, 815
Arab Club as offshoot of, 225
on Arabic language, 263
Darwaza (Muhammad Izzat) in, 673
and Faisal I ibn Hussein, 801, 815
Hananu (Ibrahim) in, 989
and Husayn ibn Ali, 815
Istiqlal Party members from, 1198
original aim of, 815
Quwatli (Shukri al-) in, 1885
during World War I, 815
Fatat, al- (newspaper), 1672
Fatemi, Husayn, attempted assassination of, 820
Fath (newspaper), censorship of, 1121
Fath al-Ali al-Malik (Ilaysh), 1086
Fath Ali Shah Qajar, **815–816,** 1868
Ahsaʿi (Ahmad al-) summoned by, 93
East India Company and, 526
granddaughter of, Mahd-e Ulya, Malek Jahan Khanum as, 1462
Mahmud II attacking (1821), 783
and modernization, 816
Russo–Persian treaties signed by, 816

Russo–Persian wars under reign of, 815–816
son of, Abbas Mirza (Na'eb al-Saltaneh) as, 7
Tehran developing under, 2169
Fatherland and Freedom (Ottoman Empire), Atatürk (Mustafa Kemal) in, 331
Fatherland party (Afghanistan), 1813
Fatherland party (Iran), 1110, 2143. *See also* Iradeh-ye Melli Party
Fathy, Hassan, 283
Fatima, as daughter of Muhammad, 1595, 1597
Fatimids
Cairo founded by, 551, 1158, 2054
Ibn Tulun Mosque restored by, 1074
as subdivision of Isma'ili Shi'ism, 1158
in Tunisia, 2228
in Tyre, 2255
Fatwa, 798, **816–817**
by Abd al-Rahman (Umar), 21
by Abdul-Aziz Bin Baz, 26
by Alusi (Mahmud Shukri al-), 173
on family planning, 1510
on female circumcision, 822
by Ilaysh (Muhammad), 1086
in Maliki school of law, 1476
muftis issuing, 816
against Rushdie (Salman)
by Khomeini (Ruhallah), 1300
Mohajerani (Ataollah) reaction to, 1558
by Shaltut (Muhammad), 2022
Shaykh al-Islam issuing, 2045
by Shirazi (Mirza Hasan), 2057, 2193
by Tantawi (Muhammad Sayyid al-), 2161
Faust (Goethe), Nerval's (Gérard de) translation of, 1675
Fava beans, 838–839
Fawda al-Ashya (Boudjedra), 497
Fawda al-Hawas (Mostaghanemi), 1424
Fawwaz, Zaynab, **817,** 890
Fawzia (princess of Egypt), marriage to Pahlavi (Mohammad Reza), 1752
Fawzi, Husayn, 927
Fawzi, Mahmud
and Hammarskjöld (Dag), 986
in Suez Crisis (1956–1957), 2108
Fax services, 625
Fayd al-Khatir (Amin), 183
Fayruz, **817–818,** 1617
Faysal Bank, 2031
Faysal ibn Turki Al Bu Sa'id. *See* Al Bu Sa'id, Faysal ibn Turki
Faysal ibn Turki Al Sa'ud (ruler of central Arabia), **818–819**
and foreign affairs, 819
imprisonment of, 818
in Najd, Al Thunayyan (Abdullah ibn Thunayyan) defeated by, 172
reign of, 819, 1999
in Wahhabi Islamic reform movement, 819
Faysal, Tujan, **819–820,** 894
Fayum oasis, *1370*
Fayz, Mulla Muhsin, Ahsa'i (Ahmad al-) on, 93
FAZ. *See* Federation of American Zionists
Fazilet Partisi. *See* Islamist Virtue Party
Fazy, Edmond, 352
FBI. *See* Federal Bureau of Investigation
FDA. *See* Front Démocratique Algérien
FDIC. *See* Front pour la Défense des Institutions Constitutionelles
FDTL. *See* Forum Démocratique pour le Travail et les Libertés
Fecr-i Ati, 1439
Feda'iyan-e Islam (Iran), **820**
Ala (Hoseyn) assassination attempted by, 101, 820
Borujerdi (Hosayn) denouncing, 494
Fatemi (Husayn) assassination attempted by, 820
as fida'iyyun, 831
Hajir (Abd al-Hoseyn) assassinated by, 976
Kashani (Abu al-Qasem) collaboration with, 1277
Kasravi (Ahmad) assassinated by, 820, 1279
Muslim Brotherhood and, 820
Razmara (Ali) assassinated by, 100, 820
on *shari'a,* 820
Feda'iyan-e Khalq (Iran), **821**
Feddan, 1371
Federal Bureau of Investigation (FBI), in Pollard affair, 1838
Federal Republic of Germany. *See* West Germany
Fédération de France du Front de Libération Nationale (FF-FLN) (Algeria), Ibrahimi (Ahmed Taleb) in, 1076
Fédération des Elus indigènes (Algeria), 3
Federation of American Zionists (FAZ), 2436
Magnes (Judah) in, 1460
Wise (Stephen S.) in, 2354
Federation of South Arabia, army of, 2081
Federation of Turkish Cypriot Associations, 696
Feis, Herbert, 229
Felafel, 838
Felicity Party (Turkey), establishment of, 99, 1911
Fellagha, 2622
Fellah, 2622
Fellata, 2099
Feluccas (sailboats), *605*
Female genital mutilation (FGM), 600–601, **822,** 1511
in Egypt, 822
in Ethiopia, 822
opposition to, 601
by Cairo Family Planning Association, 555
origins of, 601
Tantawi (Muhammad Sayyid al-) on, 2161
women's rights movement protesting, 822
Feminism
in Algeria, 894, 2195
M'Rabet (Fadela) and, 1592
colonial, 1037
in Egypt, 227, 2321–2322 (*See also* Egyptian Feminist Union)
Amin (Qasim) as father of, 875, 890
among communists, 43, 44
Islamic, 892
leading figures of, 890–891, 1958, 1965–1966, 2019, 2030–2031
Musa (Nabawiyya) in, 1614
Nassif (Malak Hifni) in, 1652
and historiography, 1037
in Iran, 428, 745, 892
Women's Organization of Iran in, 2358
in Iraq, 892

Feminism *(continued)*
Islamic, *Zanan* (magazine) and, 2423
in Israel, 1629, 2023
and peace protests, 2356
in Jordan, 819
in Lebanon, 817, 1396
in literature, 1475
Mernissi (Fatema) on, 1518
Nuun (magazine) in, 1706
in Ottoman Empire, 148
in Palestine, 1629
religious, 891–892
secular, 891–892
state, 892–893
in Tunisia, 912, 2230
in Turkey, 891, 892, 2170–2171, 2249
Women's Library and Information Center and, 2358
Women's People's Party and, 2359
Ziadeh (May) and, 2431
Femme algérienne, la (M'Rabet), 1592
"Femme Egyptienne et l'Islam, La" (Shafiq), 2019
Femme sans sepulture, La (Djebar), 1424
Femmes Démocrates (Tunisia), 912
Fenton, Roger, *649*
Répudiation, La (Boudjedra), 1426
Ferahfeza Saz Semaisi (Tanburi), 2160
Feraoun, Mouloud, **822–823**
Camus (Albert) and, 1425
death of, 823
in Generation of 1954, 707, 823, 967
Ferdowsi University, 1498
Ferhat, the Mountain Lover (Taner and Kemal), 2160
Feridun (Saygun), 2002
Ferit, Damat Mehmet, **823**
and Ottoman Liberal Union Party, 1737
Ferman, **823**
by Abdülmecit I, on Damascus affair, 665
Fernea, Elizabeth, *as contributor,* 898
Fertile Crescent, **824**
ancient civilizations of, 824
sanjaks, 824
vilayets, 824
Fertile Crescent unity plans, 743, **824–826**
Fertility rates, 1844, *1845*
Fery, Madame, 2003
Festivals (section in Talmud), 2157
Fes, Treaty of (1912), **826–828,** *827,* 1566, 2038
Abd al-Hafid ibn al-Hassan in, 14
crises leading to, 827
diplomatic maneuvers of, 827
French and Spanish protectorates under, 1570
implementation under Youssef (Mulay), 827, 2038, 2410
Lyautey (Louis-Hubert Gonzalve) and, 1448
monarchy powers under, 1599
Spain after, 1926
Spanish acquisition of Tarfaya under, 1567
Fevzi Pasha, Ahmet, 1741
Feyziyeh seminary
Borujerdi (Hosayn) at, 493–494, 1310
Ha'eri (Abd al-Karim) at, 1310
Khomeini (Ruhollah) at, 1310
Fez (hat), 332, 611, 2240
Fez (Morocco), **828–829,** *829,* 1567
Arab League summit (1981, 1982) in, 796, *1387*
economy of, 828
ethnic diversity in, 828
foundation of, 828
French occupation of, in Agadir crisis (1911), 70
guilds in, 947, *947*
historical monuments of, 828–829
Istiqlal Party in, 1196
Lyautey (Louis-Hubert Gonzalve) freeing from *makhzen* system, 1448
predecessors of, 828
al-Qarawiyyin university in, 1422, 1871
tourism in, 2196
Fez Festival of World Sacred Music, 667
Fez Plan, *1387,* 1908
PNC on, 1779
Fezzan (Libya), **829–830,** 1410, 2217
French administration of, Nasir (Ahmed Sayf al-) and, 1646
Italian conquest of, 830, 935
neolithic cave paintings in, *830*
oil production in, 830
under Ottoman rule, 830
during World War II, 516
FFFLN. *See* Fédération de France du Front de Libération Nationale
FFS. *See* Front des Forces Socialistes
FGM. *See* Female genital mutilation
Fi al-Darb al-Tawili (Azzouz), 1429
"Fi al-Islah al-Qarawi" (Ghallab), 910
FIDA. *See* Palestinian Democratic Union
Fida'iyyun, **830–831,** 2176. *See also* Suicide bombings
Fifteenth of Khordad Foundation, 1987
Fifteenth of May City (Egypt), 1995
Fighters List (Israel), 2026
Fighting Vanguard (Syria), 982
Figs, *2199*
Fikr, al- (journal), 1428
Khraief (Bechir) in, 1313
Fikret, Tevfik, 1439
Filali, Abdellatif, 1366
Filal, Souad, 2376
Filastin (al-Ghuri), 917
Filastin (newspaper), 1030, 2233
published by al-Isa family, 1141
Filastin Ibr Sittin Aman (al-Ghuri), 917
Filastinuna (magazine), 813
Filling the Gap (Shamir), 2025
Film, *831,* **831–833,** *832*
Algerian, 716, 985
American, Musa Dagh movie shelved by, 1613
Arab, 832, 833
Arab-American, 98–99
censorship of, 98–99, 832
Egyptian, 324, 336–337, 832, 866, 970–971, 1079, 1273, 2021–2022, 2039
Iranian, 387–388, 698, 832, 833, 928, 929–930, 1318, 1437, 1473, 1526
new wave in, 1318
Israeli, 483, 833, 956
Lebanese, 1499–1500
Moroccan, 483
Palestinian, 833
Tunisian, 175, 376, 2192
Turkish, 782, 832, 955, 2067
Film Farsi, 832
Fils du pauvre, Le (Feraoun), 823, 1425
Findley, Carter V., *as contributor,* 545, 577–578, 1734–1735
Fineshriber, William, in American Council for Judaism, 176
Finkenstein Treaty (1807), 869
Finn, James, 1223, 1797

Finten (Tarhan), 2165
Fiqh (Muslim jurisprudence), **833–834**, 2033, 2154
development of, 1148
Ilaysh (Muhammad) on, 1086
in Morocco, 1585
Firat. See Euphrates River
Firdawsi, 207
Fire, A (film), 928
Firqa-ye Ijtimaʿiyun-e Ammiyun. *See* Social Democratic Party of Azerbaijan
Firqeh-ye Komunist-e Iran. *See* Communist Party of Iran
First Century after Beatrice, The (Maʿlouf), 1478
Firuz, Maryam, 1318
Firuz Mirza, 809
FIS. *See* Front Islamique du Salut
Fischbach, Michael R.
as contributor, 6–7, 31–32, 35, 38–39, 43, 79–81, 190–192, 208–209, 215, 217–219, 224–225, 269–272, 275–280, 284–285, 288, 329–330, 350, 363–364, 373–374, 396, 401–402, 408–409, 409–410, 468, 485–486, 548–549, 572–573, 606–607, 624–625, 645–646, 661–662, 664–665, 673, 754–755, 812–815, 849–850, 963, 967–968, 971–972, 982–984, 986–987, 989, 991, 997, 998, 1000–1001, 1008–1009, 1019, 1043–1044, 1052–1053, 1058–1059, 1061–1065, 1099, 1139, 1154–1155, 1211, 1213–1214, 1218, 1220–1221, 1222–1227, 1235, 1239–1247, 1253, 1254–1255, 1256, 1270, 1288–1289, 1290–1291, 1294, 1295–1296, 1337, 1375–1376, 1394–1395, 1395–1396, 1470–1471, 1475–1476, 1485, 1593, 1604–1605, 1631–1632, 1636, 1637, 1644–1645, 1646, 1653, 1705–1706, 1751, 1781–1782, 1784–1785, 1802, 1830–1831, 1851–1852, 1859–1860, 1863, 1869, 1888, 1900–1901, 1901, 1908, 1917, 1926, 1929, 1951, 1975–1976, 2019–2021, 2029, 2037, 2059–2060, 2061–2062, 2070–2071, 2079, 2092–2093, 2116–2117, 2119–2120, 2156, 2173, 2189–2190, 2191–2192, 2233–2234, 2242, 2254–2255, 2273, 2287–2288, 2295, 2323–2327, 2442–2443, 2443
on Nakba, al-, 1639
FIS de la Haine (Boudjedra), 497, 1426
Fishing industry, **834**
in Azerbaijan, 834
in Egypt, 834
in Lake Nasser, 1651–1652
in Iran, 834
in Israel, 865
in Lebanon, Chamoun's (Camille) attempt at monopolizing, 1391
in Mauritania, 1503
in Morocco, 834, 1569
in Oman, 834, 1711, *1711*
in Russia, 834
in Saudi Arabia, 1996
in Syria, 2065
in Tunisia, 834
in Turkey, 834
in United Arab Emirates, 834
water resources for, 2330
Fiver Shiʿa, 2427. *See* also Zaydism
"Five, The" (generation of composers), 2002
Fi Zjham al-Madina (Shaʾul), 2043
Flame in the Ashes (documentary), 956
Flapan, Simha, **834–835**
Flax, 2180
Fleischmann, Ellen L., *as contributor,* 13, 267–268, 1055, 1296, 1556–1557, 1648, 2051–2052
Fleuve détourné, le (Mimouni), 1547
Flibbert, Andrew, *as contributor,* 982, 1692
FLM. *See* Free Lebanon Militia
FLN. *See* Front de Libération Nationale
Flogging, for alcohol consumption, 110
Flooding
in deserts, 702
in Iraq, of Little Zab River, 732–733
FLOSY. *See* Front for the Liberation of South Yemen
Flowers of Fire (Guri), 1432
Fluehr-Lobban, Carolyn, *as contributor,* 220–223, 808–809, 822, 867–869, 992–993, 1373–1374, 1622–1623, 1695–1696, 1699, 1917–1918, 2144–2145, 2235–2236
Flying Down to Rio (film), 1273
Fly Whisk Incident (1827), 397, **835–836**
FM2030. *See* Esfandiary, Fereydun
Foggaras (tunnels), water transport via, 2328
Folk arts and crafts, 311
Palestinian, 1878–1879
on postage stamps, 1850
Folk culture
Arabic, 1419, 1421
Armenian, 2087
Azeri, 428
Berber, 1426
Moroccan, 2008
Palestinian, 1878–1879
Turkish, 428, 492–493, 1438, 1439, 2002, 2251
Fond de la jarre, Le (Laabi), 1355
Food, **836–841**, *841*
ash, 836
baklava, 836
borek, 836
bulgur, 836–837, 841
chelow, 837
coffee, 837
cost of, 73
couscous, 837–838
dates, 678–679
dolma, 838
felafel, 838
fish, 834
ful, 838–839
hummus, 839, 841
increasing demand for, 72–73
kosher, 1335–1336
kufta, 839
mansaf, 839
mazza, 839
muhammara, 839–840
mujaddara, 840
mulukhiyya, 840
olives, *837,* 840
pilaf, 840
in religious rituals, 2360
rice, *838,* 840
shashlik, 840
shawarma, 840
shish kebab, 840–841
tabbula, 841
tahina, 841
tajin, 841
Food processing, 1483, *1483*

Foote, Hugh, 653
For and Against (Shamir), 2025
Foran, John, *as contributor,* 1868–1869
For Bread Alone (Shukri), 2060
Force et Matière (Buchner), 576
Forces of the Thunderbolt. *See* Saʿiqa, al-
Ford Foundation, 432
Ford, Gerald, government of, Kissinger (Henry) in, 1328
Ford, Henry, *Protocols of the Elders of Zion* and, 1856
Foreign Affairs (journal), "The Clash of Civilizations" (Huntington) in, 1091
Foreign Office (Britain), 514, **841–842**
  in Aden, 534
  Bevin (Ernest) in, 468–469, 647, 842
  vs. Colonial Office, 617
  in Persia, 526
  salaries paid by, 525
  in Sudan, 530
  Trucial States as responsibility of, 532, 2219
Forgotten Queens of Islam (Mernissi), 1518
Forman, Geremy, *as contributor,* 1234–1235
Forqan (Iran), **842**
Forqan (journal), 842
Forster, E. M., Antonius (George) and, 213
Forsyth, John, in Damascus affair (1840), 664
Fortna, Benjamin, 756–757
Forty Days of Musa Dagh (Werfel), 1613
Forugh–e Elm (journal), 2382
Forughi, Mirza Mohammad Ali Khan Zaka al-Molk, **842**
Forum Démocratique pour le Travail et les Libertés (FDTL) (Tunisia), 2231, 2232
Foster, Angel M., *as contributor,* 555, 695, 2267–2268
Foucauld, Charles Eugène de, **843**
Foucault, Michel, 289
  and historiography, 1037
Fou de Shérazade, Le (Sebbar), 2007
Fou d'espoir, Le (Laabi), 1355
Foule, la (Chraibi), 588
Fountain of Orthodoxy (journal), 782
Four Mothers movement (Israel), 2356
Fournier, Piérre, Kan (Suna) performance with, 1269
Fourteen Points, 2014, 2314, 2353
Fourth Shore, The, 380, **843**
Fraehn, C. M. (numismatic scholar), 1702
France, **843–849**. *See also* Franco *entries;* French foreign legion; Vichy government; *specific cities, organizations, people, and regions*
  Algerian independence from (*See* Algerian War of Independence)
  Algerian occupation by (*See under* Algeria)
  Algerian relations with
    Bendjedid (Chadli) and, 444
    Bouteflika (Abdelaziz) and, *504,* 505
    Evian Accords (1962) and, 788–789
  Algerians in *(harkis),* 995
  antisemitism in, 1021, 2433
    Dreyfus affair and (1894), 723
  in Arab–Israel conflict, 846–847
    and Tripartite Declaration (1950), 2215
  in Arab–Israel War (1956), 244–246
  Arab nationalism supported in, 1839
  archaeological research by, 275, 276, 277
  arms sales by, 750
    to Irgun Zvaʾi Leʾumi, 170
    to Israel, 304, 2109
    NEACC and, 2215
  bled al-siba/bled al-makhzan theory of, 487
  Bonaparte (Napoléon) ventures (*See* Napoleonic Wars)
  British relations with
    Berlin Treaty (1878) and, 528
    Cambon–Lansdowne Agreement in (1904), 529, 559–560, 1374
    Egyptian occupation supported in, 119
  British rivalry with, 524, 846
    and Lebanese independence, 1399
    over Egypt, 527–528, 529, 742
    over India, 525, 526
    over Iraqi oil, 2199
    over Lado Enclave, 1363
    over Trucial Coast, 531
  colonialism of, 613–616, *1087*
    habous under, 964
    mission civilisatrice of, 1552
  in Crimean War, 649, 739, 846
  in Dardanelles Treaty (1809), 671–672
  Dreyfus affair, 846
  in Eastern Question, 739–743, 846
  economic and military aid from, 747
  education in, religious symbols banned in (2003), 289
  Egyptian relations with, Suez Canal and, 2014
  Egypt invaded by (*See under* Egypt)
  Faisal I ibn Hussein ejected by, 801
  Free French mandate, 570, 688, 851, 856, 2086
  Golan Heights mandate of, 925
  in Greek War of Independence (1821–1930), 940
  guest workers in, 945, 946
  in Gulf War (1991), 953
  imperialism of, 1090
  intelligence services of, 1101
  Iranian relations with, Gardanne Mission and, 869
  in Iraq, Faisal I ibn Hussein ejected by, 1244
  Iraqi relations with
    under Hussein (Saddam), 1066
    in World War II, 697
  Israeli relations with, 847
    and Dimona reactor, 1696
    in Sinai campaign of 1956, 1817
  Italian agreements with
    on Libya, 1200
    Treaty of Rome, 1933
  Jewish organizations in, 151
  in Lebanese Civil War (1975–1990), 1393
  Lebanese expedition (1860–1861), 423
  Lebanese mandate of (*See under* Lebanon)
  legal system of, influencing law in Middle East, 886, 1380, 1382–1383
  Libyan relations with, Aozou Strip in, 216
  mandates of, 614, 1479–1480 (*See also specific countries*)
    education in, 758
    King–Crane Commission on (1919), 1323
    Paris peace settlements on, 1802
    San Remo Conference (1920) on, 1988

Sèvres Treaty (1920) on, 2015
Sykes–Picot Agreement on, 2128, 2315
masonic lodges set up by, 852
in Middle Ages, 844
and modernization, 844
Moroccan protectorate of (*See under* Morocco)
Morocco attacked by (1844), 19, 2038
in Napoleonic wars (*See* Napoleonic wars)
Ottoman relations with
Azuri (Najib) and, 351–352
capitulations granted to, 565, 620, 844–845
Muhammad Ali and, 846
Sebastiani (Horace) and, 2006–2007
during Tanzimat era, 2162–2163
at Paris peace conference, 2314
Popular Front government in, 1839
public schools and buildings in, religious symbols banned in (2003), 289
Russian alliance with, 742
Spanish alliance with, 2085
Spanish rivalry with, 2084
Sudan and, Fashoda incident (1898), 405, 529–530, 811
and Suez Canal (*See under* Suez Canal; Suez Crisis)
Syrian mandate of (*See under* Syria)
in Syrian War (1831–1833), 740–741, 1346, 2093
terrorism in, 919
Tunisian protectorate of (*See under* Tunisia)
U.S. war in Iraq opposed by (2003), 2324
in Western Sahara War, aid to Morocco, 2345
in World War I, 742, 846
Gallipoli campaign, 856, 866
in World War II, 2368–2372
Iraq supported by, 697
Mareth Line designated by, 1487
and Zionism, 846–847
Franciscan Brothers, in Jerusalem, 1930
Franco–British agreement (1904). *See* Cambon–Lansdowne Agreement (1904)
Franco, Francisco, 2084, 2086
Franco–Libyan Treaty (1955), 216
Franco–Moroccan agreement. *See* Tangier, Treaty of (1844)
Franco–Syrian Treaty (1936), 329, 1839
Franco–Tunisian Common Protocol (1950), 2227
Franco–Tunisian Conventions, 455, **849**
Frangos, Stavros, *as contributor,* 785
Franjiyya family, **849,** 1394
Franjiyya, Hamid, 849
Franjiyya, Sulayman, **849–850**
against Camp David peace accord, 1395
election of, 1254
Chamoun (Camille) in, 581
Hamadi (Sabri) and, 981–982
Karame (Rashid) under, 1271
in Lebanese Front, 1395
in National Salvation Front, 1665
presidency of, 1392, 1400
Salam (Sa'ib) under, 1975
Sarkis (Ilyas) rivalry with, 1992
Sulh (Rashid al-) under, 2117
Sulh (Taki al-Din al-) under, 2120
Twayni (Ghassan) under, 2254
Franjiyya, Tony, 849, 850, 871, 1394
Frank, Adolph, in potash industry, 1851
Frankfurter, Felix, Wise (Stephen S.) and, 2354
Frankincense, in incense, 1091
Franklin-Bouillon Agreement (1921), 989
Franz Ferdinand (Austrian archduke), assassination of, 340
Frederick II, 1672
Frederick the Great (kaiser of Prussia), 903
Free Center (Israel), 1181
in Likud, 1181, 1184, 1416–1417
Freedman, Robert O., *as contributor,* 1941–1944
Freedom and Accord party (Ottoman Empire), 1737
Ferit (Damat Mehmet) founding, 823
Freedom and Democracy Congress of Kurdistan (KADEK) (Turkey), 1341
establishment of, 1341, 1344
"Freedom Fighter and the Land, The" (Tuqan), 2233
Freedom-Liberal Bloc. *See* GAHAL
Freedom Movement (Iran), **850–851**
Amir-Entezam (Abbas) in, 188
Bazargan (Mehdi) in, 421, 850
founders of, 1117
government closure of (2001), 1121
imprisonment of leaders of, 850, 851
in Iranian Revolution (1979), 421, 850, 1126
Sahabi (Yadollah) in, 850
Taleqani (Mahmud) in, 850
Freedom Party (Israel). *See* Herut Party
Freedom Party (Turkey), **851**
Free French mandate, **851,** 856, 2086
Catroux (Georges) in, 570
De Gaulle (Charles) in, 570, 688
Free Lebanon Militia (FLM), 2083
Freemasons, **852–853,** 2037
Free Officers (Egypt), *853,* **853–854**
Aswan High Dam planned by, 327
Baghdadi (Abd al-Latif al-) in, 362
coup by (1952), 518, 767, 810, 853–854, 1409
CIA in, 572
Copts in, lack of, 641
government supervision of charities after, 1453
Misri (Aziz Ali al-) and, 1550
formation of, 853
Haykal (Muhammad Hasanayn) and, 1012
leader of, 853
Liberation Rally supporting, 1409
Muhyi al-Din (Khalid) in, 1608
Muhyi al-Din (Zakariyya) in, 1608
Muslim Brotherhood liaison with, 1621
Naguib (Muhammad) in, 1634
Nasser (Abdel Nasser) in, 1649
and National Union, 1667
organization of, 853
pension for, 853
and Revolutionary Command Council, 1921
Sabri (Ali) supporting, 1955
Sadat (Anwar al-) in, 1956
"six principles" of, 853
Free Officers (Iraq)
Arif (Abd al-Rahman) in, 287
Arif (Abd al-Salam) in, 288
Bakr (Ahmad Hasan al-) in, 377
coup by (1958), 15, 413, 1133, 1969
Free Officers (Jordan), Abu Nuwwar (Ali) and, 38

Free Officers (Yemen), 358, **854**
Free Princes (Saudi Arabia), public split with Al Saʿud family, 166, 798
Free Republican Party (Turkey), **854–855**
Free School Movement (Morocco), 811
  Arslan (Shakib) influence on, 307–308
  campaign against Berber Dahir, 307–308
Free Synagogue (New York), Wise (Stephen S.) in, 2354
Free Unionist Officers (Libya), 1860
Free Yemeni movement, **855**
  origins of, 2391
  Shami (Ahmad Muhammad al-) in, 2023
  Zubayri (Qaʾid Muhammad Mahmud al-) in, 2442
Freier, Recha, **855**
  Youth Aliyah established by, 2411
French foreign legion, **855–856**
  creation of, 855
  headquarters of, 855
  during World War I, 856
  during World War II, 856
French language
  in Algeria, 122, 124, 255
    literature in, 1424, 1425, 1426
  among Jews, 1252
  in Morocco, 255
    literature in, 1424, 1425, 1428
  on postage stamps, 1850
  in Tunisia, 255, 1959, 2226
    literature in, 1424, 1425, 1428, 2193
French-language newspapers, in Arab countries, 1681–1682
French–Lebanese treaty (1936), 2202
French Muslims. *See* Harkis
Frenkel, Naomi, 1434
Freshwater. *See also* Water resources
  withdrawals of, 2330, *2331*
Freylekhs, 667
Friedman, Adina, *as contributor,* 955–956, 993, 1039–1040, 1747–1748, 1751–1752, 2418
Friends of the Manifesto and of Liberty. *See* Amis du Manifeste et de la Liberté
Frischmann, David, **856,** 1430
From Durham to Tehran (Hillman), 1803
From Here We Know (Ghazali), 1297
From Here We Start (Khalid), 1296
Front de l'Algérie Française, 139
Front de Libération Nationale (FLN) (Algeria), **857**
  Abbas (Ferhat) in, 3–4, 2263, 2264
  Abdesselam (Belaid) in, 23
  Ait Ahmed (Hocine) in, 95
  in Algerian War of Independence, 857, 969
  Algiers Charter by, 142
  army of (*See* Armée de Libération Nationale)
  Association of Algerian Muslim Ulama support for, 326, 1076
  attempted coup (1967) and, 500
  Belkacem (Cherif) in, 437
  Ben Badis's (Abd al-Hamid) legacy of, 441
  Ben Bella (Ahmed) in, 442
  Ben Bouali (Hassiba) in, 443
  Ben Boulaid (Moustafa) in, 443
  Benflis (Ali) in, 445
  Ben Khedda (Ben Youssef) in, 450
  Ben Mʾhidi (Muhammad Larbi) in, 451
  Bitat (Rabah) in, 482
  Boudiaf (Mohamed) in, 496
  Boudjedra (Rachid) in, 496
  Bouhired (Jamila) in, 497
  Bouteflika (Abdelaziz) in, 503–504
  Bouyali (Moustafa) in, 506
  CNRA created by, 138, 632
  CNRA on, 857
  Comité de Coordination et d'Exécution of, 138, 619
  in constitution
    of 1963, 128–129, 131
    of 1976, 129
    of 1989, 132
  decline in popularity of, 132
  electoral success of, 127, 135, 918
  establishment of, by Comité Révolutionnaire d'Unité et d'Action, 138, 620, 1589
  in Evian Accords (1962), 788
  factional divisions in, 1743–1744
  Fanon (Frantz) in, 804
  French foreign legion breaking up, 856
  French hijacking of plane carrying leaders of (1956), 1563, 1598
  Front Islamique du Salut and, 506
  Haddad (Malek) in, 967
  Hadj (Messali al-) and, 969
  Hamrouche (Mouloud) in, 987
  Ibrahimi (Ahmed Taleb) in, 1076
  Kaid (Ahmed) in, 1264
  Kateb (Yacine) in, 1280
  Khider (Mohamed) in, 1309
  Lacheraf (Mostefa) in, 1362
  Lahouel (Hocine) in, 1365
  Madani (Tawfiq al-) in, 1456
  Mattei (Enrico) promising arms to, 777–778
  military's relationship with, 132–133
  Mouvement National Algérien and, 438, 1587–1588, 1589
  Muhammad V supporting, 1598
  Nezzar (Khaled) in, 1686
  Organisation Armée Secrète cease-fire with, 1715
  Parti de l'Avant-Garde Socialiste banned by, 1803
  political monopoly of, 131–132
    multiparty system ending, 130, 132–133
  Proclamation of 1 November 1954 by, 708
  as ruling party, 131–132
  Setif Revolt and, 2013
  Soustelle (Jacques) repressing, 2081
  and Tripoli Programme, 2217
  after War of Independence, 128–129
  in War of Independence, 131, 138, 615
    urban warfare by, 141
  Wattar (al-Taher) in, 2332
  on women's rights, 136
  Zbiri (Tahar) and, 2429
Front Démocratique Algérien (FDA), 917
Front des Forces Socialistes (FFS) (Algeria)
  Ait Ahmed (Hocine) in, 95
  elections of 2002 boycotted by, 135
  electoral success of, 127, 133
  Sadi (Said) in, 1959
  split in, 1905
Front for the Liberation of South Yemen (FLOSY), **857**
  National Liberation Front in, 857
  Organization for the Liberation of the Occupied South in, 857, 1717
Front for the Scholars of al-Azhar, on Tantawi (Muhammad Sayyid al-), 2161

Front Islamique du Salut (FIS) (Algeria), 506, **857–858**
Arab support for, 134
armed wing of (*See* Islamic Salvation Army)
banned by military, 126, 135
Belhadj (Ali) in, 436, 857
Bennabi (Malek) inspiring, 451
in elections
of 1990, 125, 130, 133
of 1991–1992, 95, 125–126, 130, 134–135, 917, 1025–1026
Front de Libération Nationale and, 506
government repression of, 918
Hachani (Abdel-kader) in, 857
Hamrouche (Mouloud) opposition to, 987
Islamist parties competing with, 134
leaders of, 125, 1455–1456
Madani (Abassi al-) in, 857
in opposition, 1989
platform of, 134
popularity of, 984
reasons for, 133–134
structure of, 857
Toumi (Khalida) opposing, 2195
violence by, 134
on women's issues, 892
Front pour la Défense des Institutions Constitutionelles (FDIC) (Morocco), **858,** 1574, 1588
Parti Démocratique Constitutionnel in, 1803
Parti Démocratique de l'Indépendance in, 1804
Frumkin, Israel Dov, 2401
FUA. *See* Union de L'Action Feminine
Fua, Albert, 2408
Fu'ad (king of Egypt), **858–859**
Cairo University and, 555
as caliph candidate, 21, 557, 1152
and constitution of 1923, 2419
Milner Mission meeting with, 1546
Nahum (Hayyim) named chief rabbi by, 1637
reign of, 766, 858–859
Rolo (Robert S.) as advisor to, 1930
Sidqi (Isma'il) under, 2065
son of, 810–811
Tharwat (Abd al-Khaliq) opposed by, 2183
Fu'ad, Abu Ahmad, in PFLP, 1840
Fu'ad I University. *See* Cairo University
Fu'ad Sarraj al-Din, New Wafd organized by, 1685
Fujayra (United Arab Emirates), **859,** 2219
economy of, 859
independence from Sharjah, 2270
population of, 859
al-Sharqi family in, 2042–2043
Fujayra–Sharjah Conflict, **859–860**
Ful, 838–839
Fulbe, 1503
Full Circle (Eden), 755
Fundamentalism, Islamic. *See also* Islamism
in Afghanistan (*See also* Taliban)
Kashwar Kamal (Meena) opposing, 1279
in Egypt
Ashmawi (Muhammad Sa'id al-) argument against, 322
Sha'rawi (Muhammad Mutwalli al-) and, 2031
al-Takfir wa al-Hijra and, 2150–2151
in Intifada (1987–1991), 1108
in Jordan, 1243
in Sudan, 2101, 2234–2235
and women's rights, 874
Fundamental Law (1921), 557
Fundamental Pact (1857), **860**
Khaznader (Mustafa) supporting, 1308
Muhammad al-Sadiq and, 1604
Fundamental Principles and Precepts of Islamic Government, The (Bani Sadr), 389
Fund for the Public Debt (Egypt), 766
Funerary ceremonies, in Zoroastrianism, 2442
Funny Girl (film), 2039
Fur (tribe), 2098
Furat. See Euphrates River
al- (newspaper), Kawakibi (Abd al-Rahman al-) in, 1282
Furness, Robin, Antonius (George) and, 213
Furqan, al- (journal), 1590
Furqan (Iran), Motahhari (Mortaza) assassinated by, 1583
Fursan al-Uruba fi al-Iraq (al-Sabbagh), 1953
Furu, 833, 2019, 2033
Fusha (classical Arabic), 232, 233
in literature, 1704
Futuhat al-Makiyya, al- (Arabi), 1457
Future (satellite station), 1895
Futuwwa, **860–861**
in Egypt, 860
in Iraq, 860–861
neighborhood defense by, 2411

G

Gabbeh (Iranian film), 1473
Gabès, Gulf of, 2016
Gabra, Gawdat, *as contributor,* 638–642
Gabrielli, Léon, 1305
Gad, Nehad, 2184
Gadser, Abdul, *60*
Gafsa (Tunisia), 2225
Gafsa incident (1980), **863**
Nouria (Hedi) in, 1694
Gagauz language, 2248, 2252
GAHAL Party (Israel), 1181, 1184
Weizman (Ezer) in, 2336
Gahiz, Minhajuddin, in Afghan Islamic movement, 60
Gailani, Ahmad, **863–864**
in Mahaz-e Islami, 63, 1561
in mojahedin resistance, 1561
Gailani, Fatana, in Afghan Women's Council, 68
Galata, **864**
Galatasaray Lycée, 757, 864, **864–865,** 2121
foundation of, 864
girls admitted to, 864
location of, 864
Simavi (Sedat) in, 2067
Tahir (Kemal) in, 2145
Taner (Haldun) in, 2160
Tevfik Fikret in, 2179–2180
Galatasaray University, 864
Galil assault rifle (Israel), 1535
Galilee, **865**
ancient history of, 865
under British control, 865
Circassians in, 600
cities of, 1451–1452
all-Arab, 1672–1673
Hula swamps in, 1047
Israeli conquest of (1948), 865
location of, 865
map of, *865*
in Ottoman Empire, 865

Galilee, Sea of, **865–866,** 925, 1668, 2328
under British rule, 865
draining of Hula swamps and, 1047
Jordan River and, 865, 1248
as water resource, 866, 1248–1249
for Israel, 1668–1669
in Johnston Plan, 1238
Galilee Social Research Center, 1488
Gallagher, John, 2198
Gallagher, Nancy, *as contributor,* 709–714, 1452–1453, 2003
Gallei Tzahal, **866**
Gallipoli, *844,* **866,** 1540, 2366, *2366*
Ottoman army at, 1527
in World War I, 866, 905
British-Ottoman fighting in, 509
French foreign legion in, 856
Gamaʿa al-Islamiyya, al-. *See* Jamiʿa al-Islamiyya, al-
Gamal, Samiyah, 175, **866–867,** 1273
Gandhi, Mohandas K., 541
Ganim, Halil, **867**
Ganj–e Shayegan (journal), 2382
Ganji, Akbar, **867**
imprisonment of, 1121
GAP. *See* Southeastern Anatolia Project
Garang, John, **867–869,** *868*
Gardanne, Claude-Matthew, 869
Gardanne Mission, **869**
Gardenia Park (Egypt), 1995
Gardens of Light, The (Maʿlouf), 1478
Gardet, Louis, Anawati (Georges Chehata) collaboration with, 194
Gardiner, Antoinette Avril, 1062
Gardoon (literary journal), 1496
Garip (Veli, Rifat, and Anday), 1440
Garmadi, Salah, 1428
Garner, Jay, in U.S. occupation of Iraq, 2325
Gaspirali (Gasprinski), Ismail Bey, **869,** 1800
Islamic congress attempted by, 1152
Gastroenteritis, 1508
Gathas (Zoroastrian text), 2441
Gaudibert, Pierre, 2155
Gault, Palmyre, 2003
Gause, F. Gregory, III, *as contributor,* 42–43, 172, 343–344, 730, 2149
Gauze, 644
Gay rights, 888
International (Dana) involvement in, 1105
Gaza (City), **869–870,** 870
ancient history of, 869
in Arab–Israel War (1948), 869
in Arab–Israel War (1967), 869
under British rule, 869
economy of, 869
Egyptian occupation of, 869
and HAMAS, 982
Israeli occupation of, 869
population of, 869
refugees in, 869
Women's Affair Center in, 2356
Gaza–Jericho Agreement (1994), Palestinian Authority created by, 1784
Gaza Strip, **870–871,** *871. See also* Occupied territories
All-Palestine Government in, 154–156
ancient history of, 870
in Arab–Israel War (1948), 870
in Arab–Israel War (1956), 871
in Arab–Israel War (1967), 871
area of, 870
borders of, 870
2000, *1768*
Camp David Accords and (1978), 561
Camp David Summit on (2000), 871
Christians in, 870
cities of, 870
economy of, 870
al-Fatah in, 814
industry of, 870
Israeli journalist in, 1003
Israeli seizure of
in Arab–Israel War (1967), 249, 871, 1159–1160, 1651
Germany criticizing, 907
Israeli settlements in, 957–959
increase in number of, 426
labor unions in, 1358
languages in, 870
location of, 870
map of, *870*
natural resources in, 870
Oslo Accords (1993) on, 871
in Ottoman Empire, 870
Palestinian Authority control of, 1784
Palestinian refugees in, 870, 1639
Palestinian resistance in, *1172*
Palestinian self-rule in, 1726, 1775
Palestinian state proposed in, 1640
Palestinian uprising in, Wazir (Khalil al-) and, 2335
population of, 870
Reagan Plan (1982) on, 1908
religions in, 870
water in, 870
Women in Black protests in, 2356
Gazelle Eye (film), 832
Gazelle River. *See* Bahr al-Ghazal
GCC. *See* Gulf Cooperation Council
GDP. *See* Gross domestic product
Geagea, Samir, **871**
arrest and trial of, 871, 2016
vs. Hobeika (Elie), 1039
imprisonment of, 1492
in Lebanese Civil War (1975–1990), 871
in Lebanese Forces, 871, 1394
in Phalange party, 871
role in Franjiyya (Tony) murder, 871
Gebali, Tahani al-, 1905
Gebara, Khalil, *as contributor,* 337, 1106, 1665, 2165
Gebeyli, Claire, **872**
Gece (Karasu), 1438
Gecekondu houses, **872**
in Ankara, 207
in Istanbul, 1194
Gelim, 567
Gelvin, James, 1037
Gemara, 2158
Gemayel family. *See under* Jumayyil
Gencer, Ibrahim, 872
Gencer, Leyla, **872–873**
Genç Kalemler (Turkey), **873,** 1439, 2251
Genç Kiz Kalbi (Mehmet Rauf), 1513
Gender, **873–897.** *See also* Women
and economy, **873–879**
access to assets, 878
in Algeria, *877*
education and, 875
in Egypt, 874, 877, *877,* 878
income discrimination, 878–879
initiatives, 879
international comparisons, 877
in Iran, *877*
in Iraq, *877*

in Israel, 876–877, *877*
in Jordan, *877*, 877–878, 878
in Kuwait, *877*
in Lebanon, *877*
modernization and, 874–876, 883, 885–886
in Morocco, 874, *877*
oil boom and, 874
private sector, 878
public sector, 878
restrictive environment and, 873–874
in Saudi Arabia, *877*
status of women, 876–878, *877*
in Syria, *877*
textile industry and, *875*, *876*
in Tunisia, 874, *877*
in Turkey, 877, *877*
in United Arab Emirates, 877
urbanization and, 875–876
in Yemen, 877, *877*
and education, 760, 761, **879–884**
in Afghanistan, 880
in Bahrain, 759
Christian influence, 882–883
curriculum, 880
in Egypt, 757, 761, 2003
Fawwaz (Zaynab) on, 817
fields of study, 878, 880
formal schooling, 880, 881, 882
illiteracy, 880
importance of, 879
improvements in, 876
informal schooling, 880, 881–882
initiatives, 883
international comparisons, 880
in Iran, 761, 880, *882*
Islamic influence, 880–882
in Israel, 880
in Kuwait, 761
participation, 880
in Qatar, 761
in Saudi Arabia, 759, 761
in Turkey, 880
and women in labor force, 875
and health
birth control, 477–480
improvements in, 876
and historiography, 1037
and law, **884–890** (*See also* Women's rights)
citizenship rights, 874, 884, 887
colonialism and, 885–886
gay, lesbian, and transgendered rights, 888
in Iran, 1970
in Israel, 887
in Jordan, 887
in Kuwait, 884
in Lebanon, 884, 887, 1396
patriarchy and, 886
personal status laws, 874, 886–888
regional and international perspectives, 888–889
right to vote (*See* Suffrage)
in Saudi Arabia, 884
in Tunisia, 325, 2230–2231
in Turkey, 2249
in United Arab Emirates, 884
and literature, 1472–1473, 1475
and politics, **890–895** (*See also* Feminism)
in Afghanistan, 786, 894, 1981–1982
in Algeria, 443, 497, 892, 894, 2195
in Egypt, 762, 890–891, 892, 894, 914–915, 1950–1951, 1958, 1965–1966, 2019, 2030–2031
in Iran, 428, 745, 891, 892, 894, 1364–1365, 2153
in Iraq, 892
in Israel, 893, 934–935, 1440, 1441, 2023, 2059
in Jordan, 819–820, 893, 894
in Kuwait, 1951–1952
in Lebanon, 481, 894, 1396, 1960–1961, 1975
in Morocco, 497–498, 894
nationalism and, 892–893
in Palestine, 893, 899, 2051–2052
reforms, 890–891
right to vote (*See* Suffrage)
in Sudan, 894
in Syria, 893, 899–900
in Tunisia, 894, 912
in Turkey, 747, 891, 892, 894, 2170–2171
women's organizations in, 893–894
preference for children, 1494
study of, **895–897** (*See also* Women's studies)
contemporary, 896
development of, 895–896
institutionalized, 895, 896–897
international conferences on, 895
passivity paradigm in, 896
religious paradigm in, 896
rescue paradigm in, 896
Gendzier, Irene, *as contributor*, 1389–1391
General Directorate on the Status and Problems of Women (Turkey), **897–898**, 2249
General Education Law (Ottoman Empire, 1869), 24, 2162
General Federation of Iraqi Women, **898**
General Federation of Labor (Israel). *See* Histadrut
General Intelligence Service (Egypt), Muhyi al-Din (Zakariyya) as founder of, 1608
General People's Committees (Libya), **898–899**
General People's Congress (GPC) (Libya), 409, **899**, 1413
establishment of, 899
on jamahiriyya, 899, 1213
on al-Manghusha government, 2024
Shamikh (Mubarak Abdullah al-) in, 2023–2024
General People's Congress (GPC) (Yemen), 806
in civil war (1994), 2390
crackdown on Islamists by, 2391
electoral success of, 1977, 2389
Islah Party coalition with, 1143
Islah Party opposing, 1143
leadership of, 2389
Salih (Ali Abdullah) in, 1976
in Yemen Arab Republic, 2394
General Petroleum and Mineral Organization. *See* PETROMIN
General Petroleum Company, 2110
General Refugee Congress, at Lausanne Conference (1949), 1375
General Security Service (GSS) (Israel). *See* Shin Bet
General Syrian Congress (1920), 538
General Treaty of Peace (1820), 526, 2040, 2218
General Tunisian Union of Students (UGTE), **899**
General Union for Palestinian Women (GUPW), Wazir (Intisar al-) in, 2334
General Union of Algerian Workers. *See* Union Générale des Travailleurs Algériens

General Union of Palestinian Women's Committees (GUPWC), 893, **899**
goal of, 899
Shihabi (Zlikha al-) in, 2052
General Union of Tunisian Workers. *See* Union Générale des Travailleurs Tunisiens
General Union of Yemeni Women, 2398
General Women's Union of Syria, **899–900**
General Zionist (Israel), 1181
"Generation of 1954," 823
Amrouche (Jean) influence on, 193
Feraoun (Mouloud) in, 707
Haddad (Malek) in, 707, 967
Genesis (Meged), 1512
Genesis of Nations, The (Saʿada), 1949
Geneva Accords (1988), 59, 2279–2280
Geneva Peace Conference (1973), **900**
chairmanship of, 251
failure of, 251
Kissinger (Henry) in, 1328
participants at, 1328
purpose of, 900
United Nations in, 1328, 2275
Genghis Khan, descendants of, 1015
Gennadios Scholarios (Greek Orthodox patriarch), millet granted to, 1543
Genocide. *See also* Armenian genocide; Holocaust
against Assyrians, 326, 515
"Gentlemen's agreement" (1937), 755
Geography, **900–903**
George II (king of Greece), at King David Hotel, 1323
George Mason University, Maksoud (Hala Salaam) at, 1975
Georgetown University, Maksoud (Hala Salaam) at, 1975
Georgette (Belghoul), 1427
Georgia, Russian annexation of, 1941
Georgians, in Turkey, 2238
Gerber, Jane, *as contributor,* 664–665
Gerges, Fawaz A., *as contributor,* 1801–1802
Gerhard, Walter, Kan (Suna) taught by, 1269
Gerizim, Mount, 1980
German Democratic Republic (GDR). *See* East Germany
German-language newspapers, in Israel, 1683
Germany, **903–907**. *See also* Prussia; West Germany; *specific cities, organizations, people, and regions*
Afghan relations with, Grobba (Fritz Konrad Ferdinand) and, 944
antisemitism in, 2371
LICA against, 1415–1416
LISCA against, 1416
archaeological research by, 276
arms sales by, 907
Berlin Treaty (1878) and, 465, 528, 903
as British threat, 533
in Cold War, 907
conference on future of Iran (2000) in (*See* Bonn Conference)
in Eastern Question, 903
economy of, 907
Egyptian relations with, 906
in European Union, 907
guest workers in, *945,* 945–946, *946*
in Gulf Crisis (1990–1991), 907
Haskalah movement in, 1430
Iranian relations with, 906
Iraqi relations with
German support for pan-Arab groups, 906
Grobba (Fritz Konrad Ferdinand) and, 944
Jamali (Muhammad Fadhil al-) and, 1213
Islamic numismatics in, 1702
Jews in
Ashkenazic, 321
emigration to Palestine, 146–147, 906, 961
Haskalah movement among, 1002–1003
in League of Nations, 906
LICA boycott of, 1416
mandates for former territories of, 1479–1480
masonic lodges set up by, 852
Moroccan interests of, 827
against French claim, 8, 70, 119–120
Nazi (*See also* Holocaust)
Africa Korps of, 1934
Arlosoroff (Chaim) negotiations with, 290
Husayni (Amin al-) cooperation with, 1042, 1057
oil needs of, 907
Ottoman relations with
Abdülhamit II and, 742, 903–904
and Berlin–Baghdad railway, 464, 532–533
concessions granted to Germany, 904
German military advisers in Ottoman army, 903, 904, 905
German–Ottoman alliance, 532–533, 742, 903–904
Ottoman–German convention (1914) on, 534
under Wilhelm II, 903, *904, 905*
Pahlavi (Mohammad Reza) visit to, student opposition to, 630
and Palestine, Ha-avarah Agreement with Jewish officials in, 961
pan-Arabism supported by, 906
Road Map (2003) supported by, 907
Russian relations with, Potsdam Convention in (1911), 1851
against San Stefano Treaty (1878), 1989
Saudi Arabian relations with, Grobba (Fritz Konrad Ferdinand) and, 944
Syrian relations with, 906
Templars from, 904, 2173
Turkish relations with, 906
U.S. war in Iraq opposed by (2003), 2324
in World War I, 742, 905–906, 2365–2368
Gallipoli campaign, 866, 905
Iran, 906
Versailles Treaty on, 906, 2314
in World War II, 906–907, 2368–2372
al-Alamayn battle in (1942), 516
Egypt, 906
Husayni (Hajj Muhammad Amin al-) supported by, 944
Kaylani revolt (1941) supported by, 516, 944
retreat from Mareth Line, 1487
Tobruk siege (1941), 516, 2194
Gesher ("Bridge") Party, 1181
Levy (David) in, 1408
Getreide - wirtschaft Syriens und Palästinas seit Beginn des Weltkrieges, Die (Grobba), 944

Gevul, ha- (Shamir), 2024
Gezira Scheme, **908**
Gezira Sporting Club, *908*, **908–909**
Ghab, al-, **909**
Ghachem, Moncef, 1425
Ghadjar, Aqa Mohammad. *See* Qajar, Agha Mohammad
Ghad wa al-Ghadab, al- (Bannounah), 1424
Ghali, Boutros, **909–910**
in Abbas Hilmi II cabinet, 6, 909
assassination of, 6, 640, 910, 1664
Condominium Agreement by (1899), 629
as deputy justice minister, 909
in Dinshaway Incident, 909–910
as finance minister, 909
as foreign minister, 909
under Nubar Pasha, 909
as prime minister, 910, 932
Ghali, Louise Majorelle Wasif, on Wafdist Women's Central Committee, 2321
Ghali, Mona, *as contributor,* 1100–1101, 2221
Ghallab, Abd al-Karim, **910–911**
Ghandhi, Mohandas (Mahatma), 1237
Ghandour, Sabah, *as contributor,* 475–476, 1084
Ghani, Ashraf, *as contributor,* 19–20, 85–86, 174–175, 196–198, 399–401, 734–736, 1857
Ghanim, Ahmad al-, 911
Ghanim family, al-, **911**
Ghanim, Fathi, **911**
Ghanim, Faysal al-, 911
Ghanim Industries, 911
Ghanim, Khalil, 2408
Ghanim, Shukri, 2024
Ghanim, Thunayan Faysal al-, 911
Ghanim, Wahib, in Baʿth party, 69, 309
Ghanim, Yusuf al-, 911
Ghanmi, Azza, **912**
Ghannouchi, Rached, **912**
Ben Ali (Zayn al-Abidine) against, 439
in exile, 912
imprisonment of, 912
in Islamic Tendency Movement, 1586
in Mouvement de Tendance Islamique, 912, 2226
pardoned by Ben Ali government, 356–357, 912
in Renaissance Party, 2231
against Socialist Destour Party, 912
in Society for the Preservation of the Qur'an, 912
Gharam wa Intiqam (film), 324
Gharb plains (Morocco), **912–913**, 1567
Gharbzadegi (Westoxification), **913**, 1091, 2342
Ghardaïa (Algeria), 1627
Gharian, Jewish community of, 973
Gharnata (Ashour), 322
Ghashmi, Ahmad Husayn, **913**
assassination of, 913, 1892, 1976
as Ismaʿili, 1007
as president, 913
tribal relations with, 90
Ghassemlou, Abdul Rahman, **914**
assassination of, 694, 914
in exile, 914
in Kurdish Democratic Party of Iran, 914
in Tudeh Party, 914
Ghayba, 2054
Ghayr muqallidin, 2124
Ghazal, 427
Ghazali, 2019
Ghazali, Ahmad Abdullah al-, 1923
Ghazali, Janbirdi al-, 663, 1907
Ghazali, Muhammad al-, **914**
on Khalid (Khalid Muhammad), 1297
Ghazali, Nazim al-, 1618
Ghazali, Zaynab al-, **914–915**
imprisonment of, 892, 915
in Muslim Women's Association, 892, 914
Ghazan Khan, 2144
Ghazel, 2623
Ghazi Ibn Faisal (king of Iraq), **915**
in Hashimite house, 1000
tutor to, Hashimi (Taha al-) as, 999
Ghazzali, Abu Hamid al-, 1148, 2113
Ghazzal, Zouhair, *as contributor,* 104–105, 1384–1385
Ghetto (Sobol), 2076
Ghibli wind, 605
Ghiwayat al-Shahrur al-Abyad (Shukri), 2060
Ghorbal, Ashraf, **915–916**
in Arab–Israel War (1967), 915
Ghorfa, 2623
Ghotbi, Farideh, 707
Ghoulabzouri, Mohammed el-, 2060
Ghoussoub, Mai, **916**
Ghozali, Ahmed, **916–917**
Hamrouche (Mouloud) replaced by, 987
Ghriba synagogue (Djerba), *717*
Ghubari script, 235
Ghuri, Emile al-, **917**
on Arab Higher Committee, 917
education of, 917
at London Conference (1946–1947), 917
in Palestine Arab Party, 917, 1765
Ghusn, Farid, 336
Ghuta, al- (oasis), Damascus near, 662
Ghuzz Turks, 2239
GIA (Armed Islamic Groups) (Algeria), **917–920**, *918*
in Algerian civil war, 917, 919
Allel (Mohamed) in, 918
amnesty offer rejected by, 135, 504
Bouyali (Moustafa) in, 506
decline of, 919
establishment of, 135, 918
groups in, 918
insurrection against military by, 126
and Islamic Salvation Army, 919, 1155, 1156
Layada (Abdelhak) in, 918, 919
Miliani (Mansouri) in, 918
organization of, 919
Rachid (Ouakali) in, 919
Sant Egidio Platform and, 1989
terrorist activities of, 919
Zitouni (Djamel) in, 919
Zouabri (Antar) in, 919
Giacaman, Rita
in Women and Family Affairs Center, 2355
in Women's Affair Center, 2356
Giado Concentration Camp, **920**
Gibb, Hamilton, 1035
and Husayni (Ishaq Musa al-), 1054
Gibli, Benjamin, 1377
Gibran, Khalil, **920**, 1421, *1421*
critical studies on, 322
Ziadeh (May) and, 2431

Gide, André, 68
Gilan, textile mills in, 2181
Gilbert, Martin, *as contributor,* 595–597
Gilboa, Amir, **920–921,** 1432
Gilels, Emil, 476
Gilgul (Pagis), 1752
Gilsenan, Michael, 1036
Gilson, Erika, *as contributor,* 2247–2249
Gimaret, Daniel, 1457
Ginor, Zvia, *as contributor,* 171, 408, 920–921, 1521–1522, 1747–1748, 2012, 2114–2115, 2429–2430
Ginzberg, Asher. *See* Ahad Ha-Am
Giraudeau, Bernard, 583
Giraud, Henri, 570
Girgir (magazine), Aral (Oğuz) in, 273
Girl Scouts, 2006
Givʿat Haviva (education center), 945
Givʿati Brigade (Israel), 407
  Kovner (Abba) in, 1336
  Neʾeman (Yuval) in, 1674
Givli, Binyamin, 1173
Giza (Egypt), **921,** 2086
  population of, 921
  pyramids of, 921, 1857
Gizuli, Muhammad al-, 808
Gladstone, William Ewart, 543
Glaser, Edouard, and Dor Deʿa movement, 720
Glaspie, April, 950
Glassware, trade of, 2197, 2198
Glawa tribe, 921
Glawi family, al-, **921**
Glawi, Madani al-, 921, 2223
Glawi, Thami al-, 921
Glawi, Tuhami al-, 2223
  Arfa (Muhammad ibn) selected by, 286–287
Globalization, lack of preparation for, 1094
Global Ministries, 1855
Globes (newspaper), 1684
Glorieuse Etoile (Algeria), Hadj (Messali al-) and, 969
Glorious Star. *See* Glorieuse Etoile (Algeria)
Glubb, John Bagot, *921,* **921–923**
  Abu Nuwwar (Ali) and, 38–39
  in Arab–Israel War (1948), 922
  in Arab Legion, 257, 519, 921–922, 1810, 2204
  and bedouins, 30, 922
  deposition of, 39
  on Talal ibn Abdullah, 2153
Glubb Pasha. *See* Glubb, John Bagot
Glubb, Sir Frederick, 921
GMMR. *See* Great Man-Made River
Gnessin, Uri Nissan, 1431
Gnostic baptists, in Iraq and Iran, 1479
Godfrey of Bouillon, 1930
God's Shadow: Prison Poems (Baraheni), 397
Gökalp, Tevfik, 923
Gökalp, Ziya, **923–925**
  Adivar (Halide Edib) influenced by, 45
  Atatürk (Mustafa Kemal) influenced by, 1659
  Atay (Salih Rifki) influenced by, 335
  in Committee for Union and Progress, 924
  education of, 923–924
  Erdoğan (Tayyip) reciting poem of, 781
  in exile, 924
  fascist movement using thoughts of, 924
  in Genç Kalemler, 873
  and Kemalism, 1286
  on nationalism, 1659
  promoting Turkish culture, 1439, 2251
  "social idealism" of, 924
  in Turkish Hearth Association, 2246
  in *Türk Yurdu,* 97
Golan Heights, **925–926,** *926. See also* Occupied territories
  in Arab–Israel War (1967), 249, 925
  in Arab–Israel War (1973), 250, 251
  area of, 925
  Circassians in, 600
  Druze in, 926
  French mandate in, 925
  Israel extending law to, 426, 925, 1160
  under Israeli control, 925
  Israeli seizure of, in Arab–Israel War (1967), 1651
  Israeli settlements in, 926
  location of, 925
  map of, *925*
  military importance of, 926
  origin of term, 925
  in Ottoman Empire, 925
  population of, 925–926
  under Syrian control, 925
  UN peacekeeping force in, 1166
  water sources in, 926
Golani Infantry Brigade (Israel), Amit (Meir) in, 190
Goldberg, Arthur, 1238
Goldberg, Ellis, *as contributor,* 1357–1359, 1461
Goldberg, Harvey E., *as contributor,* 1231–1234, 1546–1547
Goldberg, Leah, **926–927,** 1432
Gold Book of Algerian Jewry, 619
Golden Chariot, The (Bakr), 379
Golden Hell (Badr), 357
Golden Square, **927**
  Hashimi (Taha al-) and, 999
  Husayni (Hajj Muhammad Amin al-) supported by, 927
  in revolt against Britain (1941), 15, 927, 1283
    and Abd al-Ilah ibn Ali, 15
  Sabbagh (Salah al-Din al-) in, 927, 1953
  Saʿid (Fahmi) in, 927
  Saʿid (Nuri al-) opposed by, 927
  Salman (Mahmud) in, 927
  Shabib (Kamil) in, 927
Goldmann, Nahum, **927–928**
Gold, Nili, *as contributor,* 182, 216–217, 470, 993, 1039–1040, 1430–1434, 1907, 2322–2323
Goldschmidt, Arthur, Jr., *as contributor,* 4–6, 16, 21–22, 23–24, 220–223, 266–267, 327, 362–363, 366, 403–407, 542, 624–625, 662, 690, 709, 726, 730–731, 737, 763–769, 772, 909–910, 921, 952, 1012–1013, 1013–1014, 1096–1097, 1157–1158, 1267, 1447–1448, 1468–1469, 1472, 1480–1481, 1546, 1550, 1593–1594, 1651–1652, 1663–1664, 1687–1688, 1695, 1701, 1703, 1884, 1928–1929, 1958, 2040, 2048–2049, 2071–2072, 2106–2107, 2297–2298, 2305, 2319–2320, 2327
Goldstein, Baruch, massacre by (1994), 1325

Goldziher, Ignaz, in Arab Academy of Damascus, 224
Golestan, Ebrahim, **928,** 1435
Golestan, Kaveh, 928
Golestan Palace (Tehran), **928–929**
Golestan, Treaty of (1813), 816, 1117
  cessions by Iran in, 7, 345
Golomb, Eliahu
  and Haganah, 972
  in Jewish Legion, 1230
Golpayagani, Mohammad Reza, **929**
Golshiri, Houshang, **929–930,** 1435, 1436
Golsorkhi, Khosrow, **930**
Goltz, Kolmar von der, 1739
  as military adviser in Ottoman military, 904
  in World War I, 905
Gone du chaâba, Le (Begag), 1427
Good, Mallika, *as contributor,* 869–870, 899
Goodman, Jane E., *as contributor,* 192, 193
Goodman, Romana, in Women's International Zionist Organization, 2357
Gorbachev, Mikhail
  Afghan intervention ended by, 66
  Jewish immigration to Israel under, 1163
  Middle East policy of, 1943
Gorchakov, Alexsandr, 1446
  Ignatiev (Nikolas Pavlovich) compared to, 1084
Gordon, Aaron David, **930–931,** *1360*
  and Ha-Shomer ha-Tzaʿir, influence on, 1001
  Katznelson (Berl) friendship with, 1281
Gordon, Charles, 405, **931,** 2296
  death of, 1301
  rescue effort for, Kitchener (Horatio Herbert) in, 1329
Gordonia-Pioneer Youth Movement (Israel), 1378
Gordon, Judah Leib, 1430
Gordon, Matthew S., *as contributor,* 41, 81, 141–142, 185, 286–287, 356–357, 379, 438–440, 486–487, 495, 542, 586, 718, 826–828, 860, 863, 912, 942–943, 1366, 1374, 1375, 1499, 1564, 1693–1694, 1743, 1804, 1866, 1921, 2016, 2081, 2115, 2410
Gordon Memorial College (Sudan), 1301, 2100, 2144, 2296. *See also* University of Khartoum
Gordon, Yehudah Leib, 507
Gore, Albert, 549
Gören, Şerif, 955
Goren, Shlomo, 2404
Gorji, Monireh, 428
Gorky, Maksim, 470
Gorst, John Eldon, **931–932**
  death of, Kitchener (Horatio Herbert) after, 1329
  education of, 931
  in Egypt, 931–932
    Abbas Hilmi II and, 6, 931
    under Baring (Evelyn), 931
    as financial adviser, 931
    naming Ghali (Boutros) as prime minister, 910, 932
  and National Party, 1664
Gort, John, as high commissioner of Palestine, 1025
Göttingen collection, of Islamic coins, 1702
Gouraud, Henri-Joseph-Eugène, 801
Gousmi, Cherif, 919
Gouvernement Provisoire de la République Algérienne (GPRA), 1456
  Abdesselam (Belaid) in, 23
  Ben Bella (Ahmed) in, 442
  Ben Khedda (Ben Youssef) in, 450
  Boumédienne (Houari) in, 498
  campaign for independence by, 138
  Comité de Coordination et d'Exécution dissolved for, 619
  creation of, 138, 857
  French relations with, Evian Accords (1962) and, 788–789
  Krim (Belkacem) in, 1337
  Moroccan border dispute considered by, 1566
  president of, 138
    FLN appointment of, 3–4
Government, **932–934**
  authoritarian form of, 933
  constitutional, 932
  Islamic, 934
  legislative bodies in, 932–933
  parliamentary democracy, 932
  political pluralism in, 933–934
  republican form of, 933
  Shiʿite Islam on, *velayat-e faqih* (governance of jurists) in, 2311–2313
Government Law School (Jerusalem), 402
Gozanski, Tamar, **934–935**
GPC. *See* General People's Congress
GPRA. *See* Gouvernement Provisoire de la République Algérienne
Graduates Congress (Sudan), Azhari (Ismaʿil) in, 349
Gradus, Yehuda, *as contributor,* 708–709, 925–926, 1204–1205, 1450, 1451–1452, 1675, 1901–1902, 1927
Grady, Henry, 1576
Grady–Morrison Plan (1946). *See* Morrison–Grady Plan (1946)
Graham, Franklin, 1856
Grain
  agricultural production of, 75
    taxes on, 76
  bulgur, 836–837, 841
  couscous, 837–838
  trade of, 2198
Granada, 2084
Grand Bazaar of Istanbul, 419
Grand Bazaar of Tehran, 419
Grande maison, La (Dib), 1426
Grandhara empire, 387
Grandma Sultana's Salty Biscuits (Seri), 2012
Grand Mosque (Mecca), **935,** *1146,* 1507
  seizure of (1979)
    Al Saʿud family response to, 166, 167, 1295
    factors leading to, 1295
    Ikhwan in, 1085
    Utaybi (Juhaiman al-) in, 2214
Grand National Assembly (Turkey). *See* Turkish Grand National Assembly
Granforte, Apollo, 872
Gran, Peter, 1207
Grapes, for wine, 109–110
Grapes of Wrath, Operation (Israel), 1168
Graziani, Rodolfo, **935**
  in Cyrenaica campaign, 1610
  in Egyptian invasion (1940), 2369
  under Volpi (Giuseppe), 2317
  Wavell (Archibald) fighting against, 516

Great Britain. *See* Britain
Greater Bulgaria
Berlin Treaty and, 382–383, 465, 1989
San Stefano Treaty and, 382, 465, 1988–1989
Greater Israel. *See Eretz Yisrael*
Greater Land of Israel movement. *See* Eretz Yisrael ha-Shelema
Greater Lebanon
Beirut in, 429
creation of, 1398
Greater Morocco, 942
Greater Syria, **936**, 948
Greater Syria plan, 824–826, **936**
by Abdullah I ibn Hussein, 936
Quwatli (Shukri al-) opposing, 936
Saʿada (Antun) and, 936, 1950
Saʿid (Nuri al-) supporting, 936
Syrian Social Nationalist Party supporting, 2136–2137, *2137*
Zaʿim (Husni al-) opposing, 936
Greater Tunb, 2223–2224
Great Game, The, **936–937**
Great Man-Made River (GMMR), *1412*, 2329
Great Mosque (Damascus), *2129*
Great September Revolution (Libya), Muntasir family after, 1612
Great Socialist People's Libyan Arab Jamahiriyya. *See* Jamahiriyya (Libya)
Great Unity Party (Turkey), 2245
Great Voices of Arabic Music: Um Kulthum, Muhammad Abdel Wahab, and Farid al-Atrache (Bitton), 483
Great Zab River, 2417
Greco–Turkish War (1897), **937**
Greece. *See also specific cities, organizations, people, and regions*
Aegean Sea controlled by, 51
in Balkan League, 384
in Balkan Wars (1912–1913), 384, 939
dragomans (translators) from, 723
in Greco–Turkish War (1897), 937, *937*
independence of (1830), 1466 (*See also* Greek War of Independence)
Adrianople Treaty (1829) and, 940
London Treaty (1827) and, 940
İzmir (Turkey) occupied by, 1201
music of, 785
nationalism in, 1657–1658
Megali Idea in, 1657–1658
Ottoman war with (1897), 27
rebellion against Ottoman Empire, 1466
Turkey invaded by (1919), 2240
Turkish relations with
Chanak crisis (1922), 513, 1441–1442
in dispute over Cyprus, 1531–1535
Treaty of Ankara in (1930), 208
unification with Cyprus (enosis)
opposition to, 696
support for, 653, 943
U.S. economic and military aid to, 1836
Greek Catholic church, 592
Greek Catholic Synagogue Church (Nazareth), 1673
Greek Cypriot National Guard, 943
Greek millet, 1543–1545
Armenian millet compared to, 296
Greek Orthodox Church. *See* Eastern Orthodox Church
Greeks, **938–939**
in Arabian Peninsula, 938
in Egypt, 938–939
influence of, 938, 939
in mixed courts system, 939
as entrepreneurs, 938
in Palestine, 938
in Sudan, 938
in Turkey, 2238
Atatürk (Mustafa Kemal) and, 1549
Greek War of Independence (1821–1930), **939–940**
Britain in, 940
and Eastern Question, 738
Egypt in, 939, 940, 1077
France in, 940
Ipsilanti uprising (1821) in, 939
janissaries in, 1217
Mustafa Reşid influenced by, 1623
nationalism as result of, 1657–1658
Ottoman Empire in, 939–940, 2093
dismissal of Greek translators during, 545
Muhammad Ali supporting, 2093
Ottoman navy in, 1741
Peloponnese uprising (1821) in, 939–940
Russia in, 940
Green Army, in Turkish war of independence, Nadi (Yunus) in, 1633
Greenberg, Uri Zvi, **940–941**, 1432
Green Bird (Badr), 357
Green Book (Qaddafi), **941**, 1413, 1860
Green, David. *See* Ben-Gurion, David
Green Line, 430–431, **942**
closure of, 942
map of, *942*
opening of, 942
Tsemel (Leah) supporting, 2221
West Bank demarcated by, 2339, *2340*
Green March, **942–943**, 2084, *2085*, 2086
in Western Sahara War, 1566, 1571, 2345
Green Mosque (Fez), *829*
Green olives, *837*, 840
Green perestroika (Libya), 1414
Green Place, The (Shamir), 2025
"Green Pol Pot." *See* Zitouni, Djamel
Greffe (Boudjedra), 497
Greki, Anna, 1424
Grey, Edward
and Fashoda incident, 529
as foreign secretary, 842
Griboyedov Incident, **943**
Grigor V (Armenian patriarch), 291
Grigor VI (Armenian patriarch), 291
Grinnell College, Garang (John) at, 868
Grivas, Georgios Theodoros (Dighenis), **943**
British rule opposed by, 653, 943
enosis movement supported by, 653, 654, 696, 943
Makarios III opposed by, 654
Grobba, Fritz Konrad Ferdinand, 906, **943–944**
Gromaire, Marcel, 2069
Gross domestic product (GDP)
of Algeria, 127, *753*
of Bahrain, *753*
of Egypt, *753*
of Iran, *753*, 1115, 1753
of Iraq, *753*
of Israel, *753*, 1162, 1169
of Jordan, *753*
of Kuwait, *753*
of Lebanon, *753*

of Libya, *753*
of Morocco, *753*
of Oman, *753*
of Qatar, *753*
of Saudi Arabia, *753*
of Syria, *753*
of Tunisia, *753*
of Turkey, *753*
of United Arab Emirates, *753*
of Yemen, *753*
Gross, JoAnn, *as contributor,* 1641–1643
Grossman, David, 1433
Grossman, Haika, **944–945**
Grotefend, Georg Friedrich, 276
Grots u brots (Srvantziants), 2087
Groundwater, irrigation with, 74
Groupe Islamique Armée. *See* GIA
Groupe Salafiste pour la Prédication et le Combat (GSPC) (Algeria), 504
amnesty offer rejected by, 135
establishment of, 135
government fight against, Islamic Salvation Army in, 1156
al-Qaʿida links to, 1156
Groupes Islamiques Armés (Algeria). *See* GIA (Armed Islamic Groups)
Group for Defense Against the Illicit, 506
Group of Liberating Officers, 1737
Group of Modern Art, 2069
Gruenbaum, Yizhak, **945**
Gruen, David. *See* Ben-Gurion, David
Gruen, George E., *as contributor,* 224–225
Gruenwald Cross, Grossman (Haika) awarded with, 944
Grunwald, Malkiel, 2159
in Kasztner affair (1954–1955), 1280
Grunzweig, Emil, 1809
GSPC. *See* Groupe Salafiste pour la Prédication et le Combat
GSS. *See* Shin Bet
Guardian of German Property, 2173
Guardians of Cedars (Lebanon), 1395
Aql (Saʿid) and, 219
Gubser, Peter, *as contributor,* 190–192, 684–685, 1061–1065, 1239–1247, 1270, 1822–1823
Gudeira, Ahmad Rida, as FDIC founder, 858
Guenzetin assault (1955), 438
Guermah, Massinissa, 486, 638
Guerrara (Algeria), 1627
Guerrilla movements
fidaʾiyyun, 830–831, 2176
in PLO, 237, 1972
Palestine National Council of, 1778
Guerrilla warfare
in Afghanistan
CIA support for, 572
led by Ahmad Shah Masʿud, 89
during Soviet intervention, 65–66
in Algeria, by Islamic Salvation Army, 1156
Guest for the Night, A (Agnon), 71
Guest workers, *945,* **945–946,** *946*
Guevara, Che, Wazir's (Khalil al-) meeting with, 2335
Guilds, **946–947**
Guindi, Aida, 1902
Guinness, Walter Edward (Lord Moyne), **947–948**
on Greater Syria, 948
murder of, 515, 948, 1443, 1973, 2025
and Churchill (Winston S.), 597
Guish tribes, 2212
Gül, Abdullah, in AKP, 99, 100
Gülbenkian, Calouste, 537, 538, **948**
and Red Line Agreement, 1910
and Turkish Petroleum Company, 1909
Gülbenkian Foundation, 948
Gülen, Fetullah, **948**
Gulf Cooperation Council (GCC), 371, 796, **948–949,** 2200
Bishara (Abdullah) as secretary-general of, 481
establishment of, 949
Khalid ibn Abd al-Aziz Al Saʿud in, 1295
money held in banks in, 390
Peninsula Shield Force of, 949
Unified Economic Agreement (1981) of, 949
United Arab Emirates in, 2272
Gulf Crisis (1990–1991), **949–952,** 1538–1539. *See also* Gulf War (1991)
anti-Iraq countries in, 950–951
Aziz (Tariq) representing Iraq in, 350
Basra during, 411
bin Laden supporting Iraq in, 475
Bush (George H.W.) and, 548, 950, 951
causes of, 1134
China in, 587
consequences of, 951–952
Egypt in, 1594
Germany in, 907
Hussein (Saddam) and, 1067–1068
Ibrahim (Izzat) in, 1078
as impetus for Madrid Conference, 1458
Iran–Iraq War and, 1985
Iraqi invasion of Kuwait in
Arab League condemning, 951
events of, 950
Moroccan response to, 1006
reasons for, 949–950
Sabah (Suad al-) opposing, 1952
and UN economic sanctions, 951, 1985
Iraqi losses and casualties in, 1539
Iraqi military in, 1527, *1527,* 1538–1539
Jordan during, 1064
Kuwait in
Al Sabah family of, 160
archaeological artifacts taken from, 279
economic impact of, 1349, 1352
Kuwait City, 1351
liberation of, *1348*
oil wells damaged in, 1353
League of Arab States in, *1387,* 1388
Mauritania in, 1744–1745
Morocco during, 1006
oil prices and, 949
and OPEC, 1720
Pakistan in, 1758
PLO position on, 1775, 1792–1793
pro-Iraq countries in, 951
Qatar in, 1877
satellite television broadcasting during, 1895
Saudi Arabia in, 1627
Soviet involvement in, absence of, 66
Soviet weapons used in, 1943
and status of military in Middle East, 1539
United Nations in, 2281–2282
U.S. involvement in, 950, 951, 953, 2294
Gulf of Aqaba. *See* Aqaba, Gulf of

Gulf of Gabès, 2016
Gulf of Hammamet, 2081
Gulf of Oman, **952**, 2040
Gulf of Sidra, 2066
Gulf of Suez, **952**
Gulf Oil, 1910
Gulf Oil Corporation, in Kuwait Oil Company, 1349
Gulf War (1980–1988). *See* Iran–Iraq War
Gulf War (1991), 951, **953–954**, *1527*. *See also* Gulf Crisis (1990–1991)
  and Baghdad, 361
  Baker (James A.) negotiating, 374
  Ben Bella (Ahmed) supporting Iraq during, 443
  bombing of Iraqi cities during, 1985
  Britain in, 523, 953
  Egypt in, 951, 953
    and U.S. economic aid, 749
  France in, 953
  Iraq in, 1134–1135
    destruction of infrastructure of, 1135
  Karbala damaged in, 1272
  Operation Desert Shield in, 951, 953, 1538
  Operation Desert Storm in, *950*, 951, 953, 1538–1539
    Egypt in, 1594
  Saudi Arabia in, 796, 950, 951, 953, 2000
  Syria in, 951, 953
  United Nations in, 2281–2282
  U.S. in, 1134–1135
    military force used by, 1134–1135
Gülhane Hatt-ī Hümayunu. *See* Gülhane Imperial Edict (1839)
Gülhane Imperial Edict (1839), 885, **954–955**, 1735, 2162, 2163, 2164
  equality and citizenship in, 2341
  Tanzimat introduced by, 1624
Gümüspala, Ragip, in Justice Party, 1257
Günaydin (newspaper), 2067
Güney Anadolu Projesi (GAP). *See* Southeastern Anatolia Project
Güney, Yilmaz, **955**
Güntekin, Reşat Nuri, 1439
GUPWC. *See* General Union of Palestinian Women's Committees
Guri, Chaim, **955–956**
Guri, Haim, 1432
Gur, Mordechai, **956**
  in Arab–Israel War (1948), 956
  in Arab–Israel War (1967), 956
  education of, 956
  in Haganah, 956
  in Israel Defense Force, 973, 1171
  in Labor Party, 956
  in Palmah, 1795
Gürpinar, Hüseyin Rahmi, **956–957**
Gürsel, Cemal, **957**
  government of, İnönü (İsmet) in, 1098
  in National Unity Committee, 1667
Gürüz, Kemal, 2414
Gusaysa, Rabab Muhammad Mustafa Abu, 808
Gush Emunim (Israel), **957–959**, 958, *958*
  under Begin (Menachem), 957
  formation of, 957
  and Hebron, Israeli settlements in, 1019
  ideology of, 958
  influence on nationalism, 2412
  Kook (Zvi Yehuda) in, 1334
  Levinger (Moshe) as leader of, 958, 1407
  membership of, 958
  Porat (Hanan) as leader of, 958
  purpose of, 957
  settlements promoted by, 1191–1192
  terrorist activities of, 958
Gush Herut-Liberalim. *See* GAHAL
Gush Shalom (Israel), Avnery (Uri) in, 340
Gutelius, David, *as contributor*, 260, 2190–2191
Gutman, David, in Petah Tikvah, 1822
Gypsies, 383
Gyrfalcons, 803
Gyro, 840

H

Haaretz (newspaper), 934, 1683, 1684, 1991, 2159
  Keinan (Amos) in, 1284
  Kenaz (Yehoshua) in, 1288
Ha-Avarah Agreement, **961**
  and Jewish immigration to Palestine, 1041
Habash, George (al-Hakim), **961–963**, *2335*
  airplane hijackings by (1970), 1246
  American University of Beirut criticized by, 180
  in Arab National Movement, 1267
  death of, 1158
  followers of (*See* Druze)
  and Haddad (Wadi), 967
  and Hawatma (Nayif), 1008
  in PFLP, 1773, 1839, 1840
Habbabi, Mohammad Aziz al-, 1428
Habbub, Saniyya, 431
Habibi, Emile, **963**
Habibi, Shahla, in Iranian Bureau of Women's Affairs, 1123
Habibollah II, 57
Habibollah Khan (amir of Afghanistan), **963–964**, 2420
  in Anglo–Afghan wars, 197–198
  assassination of, 56, 174, 198
  Dar al-Moʿallamin under, 670
  Nadir Barakzai (Mohammad) and, 1633
  school established by, 56
  son of, 174
  as successor to Abd al-Rahman Khan, 20, 56, 197, 198, 400
Habib, Philip Charles, **964**, 1907
  Arafat (Yasir) meeting with, 1975
  PLO–Israeli cease-fire negotiated by (1981), 252, 1166
Habib, Zachary, as leader of Jewish community in Tripoli, 1637
Habl al-Matin (newspaper), 1682
Habous, **964–965**
Habshush, Hayyim, in Dor Deʿa movement, 720
Hacene, Farouk Zehar, **965**
Hacettepe University, **965–966**
Hachani, Abdel-kader, as FIS leader, 857
Hached, Ferhat
  Achour (Habib) work with, 41
  assassination of, 41, 2264
  in Union Générale des Travailleurs Tunisiens, 1358, 2264
Haci Bektaş Köyü (Syria), 113, 114–115
Haci Bektaş Veli, 113
Ha-Cohen, Mordechai, **966**
  on Haggiag family, 973
Ha-Cohen, Yehuda, 966

HADASH. *See* Democratic Front for Peace and Equality
Hadassah, **966**
Szold (Henrietta) in, 2138
Hadda Agreement (1925), Clayton (Gilbert) in, 603
Haddadin tribe, 2212
Haddad, Mahmoud, *as contributor,* 35–36, 81, 352, 550, 1664, 1973–1975
Haddad, Malek, **967**
in Generation of 1954, 707
Haddad, Robert, at American University of Beirut, 181
Haddad, Saʿd, **967**
Israeli authority over, 254
South Lebanon Army after death of, 1364
South Lebanon Army under, 2083
Haddad, Wadi, **967–968**
airplane hijacking by (1976), 777
Haddam, Anouar, in GIA, 1155
Haddam, Tedjini, in High State Council, 1026
Haddatha Abu Hurayra Qala . . . (Masʿadi), 1498
Hadd punishments, Taha (Mahmud Muhammad) against, 2145
Hadendowa clan, 433
Hadha al-Wajh Aʿrafuhu! (Ghallab), 910
Hadha Huwa al-Dustur (Ghallab), 910
Hadi al-Mahdi, al- (Sudanese leader), 210, 2261
Hadi, Asi al-, 1981
Hadi Bey, Osman, 275
Hadid, Muhammad
in Ahali group, 80–81
coup opposed by (1936), 80
in National Democratic Party, 1654
Hadira, al- (newspaper), 2016
Hadith (Islamic traditions), **968,** 1476, 2033
Amin (Ahmad) questioning of, 183
on female circumcision, 822
on *hijab* (veiling), 1026
Muhammad in, 1597
muwahhidun adherence to, 1625
patriarchal interpretations of, Mernissi (Fatema) on, 1518
in Shafiʿi school of law, 2018
in Sufism, 2112
Sunna extracted from, 2122
in Taliban curriculum, 2154
on turbans, 609
Hadithat Sharaf (Idris), 1082
Hadith Isa ibn Hisham (al-Muwaylihi), 1420
HADITU. *See* Democratic Movement for National Liberation
Hadj, Ali Ben, 1455
Hadjerès, Sadek, in Parti de l'Avant-Garde Socialiste, 1803
Hadj, Messali al-, **968–970**
in Amis du Manifeste et de la Liberté, 3, 189–190
banning from Algeria, 1589
Bellounis (Muhammad) supporting, 438
Ben Badis (Abd al-Hamid) and, 441
Ben Boulaid (Moustafa) supporting, 443
Boudiaf (Mohamed) supporting, 496
Comité Révolutionnaire d'Unité et d'Action opposing, 620
deportation of, 3
and Setif Revolt (1945), 2013
Front de Libération Nationale rejected by, 138, 1587–1588
imprisonment of, 1804, 1805
in Mouvement National Algérien, 131, 1587–1588
in Mouvement pour le Triomphe des Libertés Démocratiques, 1589, 1805
in Parti du Peuple Algérien, 1589, 1804
in Star of North Africa, 2089
and Zbiri (Tahar), 2428
Hadramawt (Yemen), **970**
British governance of, 1853
incense in, 1091
Jewish exodus from, Magic Carpet Operation for (1948–1950), 1460
tribes in, 2215
Hadrumetum. *See* Sousse (Tunisia)
Haʿeri, Abd al-Karim, 929
death of, 1310
Khomeini (Ruhollah) under, 1310
Haffar, Lutfi al-, in National Party, 1664
Hafid, Mulay. *See* Abd al-Hafid ibn al-Hassan
Hafiz, Abd al-Halim, **970–971**
Hafiz, Amin al-, **971–972**
Hafsid dynasty, 2224, 2228
Haganah (Zionist military group), **972–973**
Allon (Yigal) in, 153
Amit (Meir) in, 190
in Arab–Israel War (1948), 242
vs. Arab Liberation Army, 1052
Begin (Menachem) issued ultimatum by, 1973
Ben-Porat (Mordechai) in, 452
Ben-Zvi (Rahel Yanait) in, 456
Dayan (Moshe) in, 681
and Dayr Yasin massacre (1948), 684
in De Haan (Yaʿakov Yisrael) assassination, 688
elite forces of (*See* Palmah)
Eshkol (Levi) in, 784
Gur (Mordechai) in, 956
Guri (Chaim) in, 955
Harel (Isser) in, 992
Hareven (Shulamit) in, 993
Hillel (Shlomo) in, 1030
illegal immigration sponsored by, 147
Irgun Zvaʾi Leʾumi break from, 1139
Irgun Zvaʾi Leʾumi opposed by, 1140
in Israel Defense Force, 972
Kaniuk (Yoram) in, 1268
leadership of, 1172
LEHI members kidnapped by, 1442
as literary catalyst, 1432
Lotz (Wolfgang) in, 1447
military doctrine of, 972
Najjada, al- as Sunni counterpart of, 1638
Namir (Mordekhai) in, 1641
Neʾeman (Yuval) in, 1674
Palmach unit of, 153
Peres (Shimon) in, 1817
Qawuqji's (Fawzi al-) encounters with, 1879
Sharef (Zeʿev) in, 2031
Sharon (Ariel) in, 2041
Shiloah (Reuven) in, 2055
Shochat (Manya) in, 2059
Sneh (Moshe) in, 2075
Stern (Abraham) in, 2090
Yadin (Yigael) in, 2376
Yariv (Aharon) in, 2379
Haggiag family, **973–974**
Haggiag, Hmani (Rahmin), 973
Haggiag, Khalifa, 973
Haggiag, Nessim, 973
Haggiag, Simeone, 973
Hagia Sophia. *See* Aya Sofya

Hague Conventions, cultural property protected by, 278
ha-Hai Al ha-Met (Meged), 1512
Ha-Halutz (youth movement), **974,** 2412, 2434
Ben-Gurion (David) in, 446
Ben-Porat (Mordechai) in, 452
Sapir (Pinhas) in, 1991
Shenhar (Yitzhak) in, 2048
Trumpeldor (Yosef) affiliated with, 2221
Haider, Ghulam, Anglo–Afghan Treaty signed by (1855), 196
Haifa (Israel), **974–975,** 1160
as Baha'i faith headquarters, 365
Jewish refugees in, *145, 146, 1041, 2401*
Palestinian Arab Congress in (1920), 1782
reclaimed wastewater from, 1668
Templars establishing, 2173
Haifa Municipal Theater, 2076
Haifa–Tel Aviv highway assault, 1417
Haifa University, **975**
Zach (Natan) at, 2418
Haig, Alexander, on Arab–Israel War (1982), 253
Haigazian College, **975**
Haig, Douglas, 1994
Haik, 611, **975**
Ha'il (Saudi Arabia), 1206, 1638
Al Rashid family in, 157–158
overthrown by Al Sa'ud family (1921), 1626
tribes in, 2214
Ha'il, Abd al-Hamid, Khalaf (Salah) killed at villa of, 1292
Haile Selassie
at King David Hotel, 1323
restored to throne by Britain, 1200
Haim, Sylvia G., *as contributor,* 807–808, 1012, 1993–1994
Ha'iri, Kazim al-, al-Da'wa al-Islamiyya and, 681
Hajar al-Duhk (Barakat), 397–398
Hajir, Abd al-Hoseyn, **975–976**
Hajj (pilgrimage), 1506–1507, 1996, *1997,* 2623
Hijaz Railroad and, 1029
influence on Hijaz, 1028
Hajjar Mountains, 1903
Hajji Baba of Ispahan, **976**
Hajji Bektash, 434–435
Hajj, Munir al-, in Phalange party, 1831
Hajri, Abdullah al-, **976**
Hakawati (theater troupe), 2184
Hakawati, al-, 2184
Haketía. *See* Ladino
Hakim, Adnan al-, **976–977**
in Najjada, al-, 1638
Hakim, al-. *See* Habash, George
Hakim, al-Uzma Muhsin ibn Mahdi, 977
Hakim bi-Amr Allah, al-, 727–728
Hakim family, **977–978**
Hakimiyet-i Milliye (newspaper), 1685
Hakimiyya, 2151
Hakim, Mahdi al-, 978
Hakim, Mohammad Bager al-, *977*
Hakim, Muhammad Baqir al-, 978, 2071
assassination of, 1637, 2326
Hakim, Muhsin, 977
in al-Da'wa al-Islamiyya, 680
Hakim, Tawfiq al-, **978–979,** 1421, 2184
Ha-Kotel Ha-Ma'aravi. *See* Western Wall
Halaby, Elizabeth Najeeb. *See* Noor al-Hussein (Queen Noor)
Halaby, Najeeb, 539
Halakhah (Jewish religious law), **979–980,** 1554
Herzog (Izhak Halevi) and, 1022
in Israel, 1890
in Jerusalem Talmud, 2158
Leibowitz (Yeshayahu) on, 1403
scholarship on, by Qafih (Yihye ben Solomon), 1864
Halal, 2623
Halaoui, Muhammad, in Union Nationale des Etudiants Marocains, 2266
Halaqa, 2111
Halas (Mehmet Rauf), 1513
Halawi, Majed, *as contributor,* 104–105, 1253–1254
Hale, Sondra, *as contributor,* 1075–1076, 2105
Halevi, Benjamin, 2159
Halevy, Ephraim, as Mossad director, 1578, *1578,* 1579
Halévy, Joseph, and Dor De'a movement, 720
Halfaouine (film), 2192
Halfawi (Nubian dialect), 1696
Halicarnassos (ancient city), 490
Halife, 435
Halil Paşa, in World War I, 2367
Halim (prince of Egypt), 852
and National Party, 1663
Halk Bilgisi Haberleri (periodical), 492
Halk Evleri. See People's Houses
Halkin Sesi (newspaper), 696
Hallaq, Wael B., *as contributor,* 816–817, 968, 988–989, 989–990, 1476, 2018–2019, 2033–2035
Halliday, Denis, 1136
Halloween (film), 99
Halpulaar, 1503
Halukka, **980,** 2400
Halutz. *See* Ha-Halutz
Hama (Syria), **980–981,** 982, 1010
Arab revolt in (1925), 1879
Hamada, 700
Hamadan (Iran), **981**
Hamadani, Yusuf, in Naqshbandi, 1641–1642
Hamadhani, Badi al-Zaman al-, 1420
Hamadi, Sabri, **981–982**
Hamadish Brotherhood, Meknes as sacred city of, 1515
Hamama, Faten, **982**
Hama Massacre, 981, **982**
Hamami, Sa'id, Avnery (Uri) contact with, 340
HAMAS, **982–984**
in al-Aqsa Intifada (2000), 219, 983, 2381
Arafat (Yasir) and, 272
arrests of leaders of, 983
establishment of, 983, 2381
and fida'iyyun, 831
ideology of, 2381
in Intifada (1987–1991), 2177, 2381
Islamic Jihad rivalry with, end of, 1155
Mash'al (Khalil al-) in, Mossad assassination attempt against, 1579
and PLO, 983
Qassam (Izz al-Din al-) and, 1875
suicide bombings by, 219, 2177
and election of Netanyahu (Benjamin), 983
in Jerusalem, 1226, 1227
Palestinian support for, 983
Yasin (Ahmad Isma'il) in, 2381

Hamas (Movement for a Peaceful Society) (Algeria), **984**
Nahnah (Mahfoud) as founder of, 1636
Hamasat al-Zaman (Sha'ul), 2043
Hama uprising (1982), 2135
Hamburg–Amerika steamship line, 533, 904
Hamdani, Rashida al-, on National Women's Committee, 1669
Hamdan tribe, 913
Hamdi, Baligh, 971
Hamdi Bey, Osman, Kadri (Mufide) trained by, 1262
Hamdi, Ibrahim al-, **984–985**
assassination of, 89, 913, 2393
coup by (1974), 1140
Ghashmi (Ahmad Husayn) supporting, 913
government of, Hajri (Abdullah al-) in, 976
political reform under, 2392, 2393
Salih (Ali Abdullah) supporting, 1976
state-building by, 2393
and tribal power, 89, 2393
Hamdullah, Şeyh, calligraphy of, 559
Hamdy, Karim, *as contributor,* 578, 698–700, 1219–1220, 1717–1718, 1834–1835
Hamid al-Din family, **985**
Shami (Ahmad Muhammad al-) and, 2023
Hamid, Dina bint Abd al-, 1062
Hamilton, Lloyd N., 229
Hamina, Mohammed Lakhdar, **985**
Hamit, Abdulhak, 2187
Hamlin, Cyrus, 490
Hammada (plateaus), 1963
of Western Sahara, 2342
Hammamet, Gulf of, 2081
Hammami, Rema
in Institute of Women's Studies at Bir Zeit University, 1100
in Women and Family Affairs Center, 2355
in Women's Affair Center, 2356
Hammarskjöld, Dag, **985–986**
Bunche (Ralph J.) as adviser to, 543
Six Points of, 2108
in Suez Crisis (1956–1957), 1444, 2108, 2275, 2286
Hammer, Armand, Occidental Petroleum purchased by, 1708
Hammer, Zevulun, **986**
Hammuda, Yahya, as PLO leader, 1772
Hammurabi, 1131
Hamm, Zübeyde, 330
Hamov-hotov (Srvantziants), 2087
Hamra Riots, **986–987**
Hamrouche, Mouloud, **987**
Benflis (Ali) under, 445
Ghozali (Ahmed) under, 917
Hamshahri (newspaper), Karbaschi (Gholamhosain) in, 1273
Hamshbir (retail cooperative), 1034
Hamuda, Ibrahim, and Atrash (Farid al-), 336
Hamula, 2209
Hamza (crown prince of Jordan), 1692
Hamza ibn Ali al-Zawzani, 727–728
Hamza, Si, 1745
Hamzawi, Rashid al-, **987–988**
Hanafi, Hasan, **988**
Hanafi School of Law, **988–989,** 2034, 2035, 2123
on alcohol consumption, 109
and Hanbali School of Law, 990
Hananu, Ibrahim, **989**
Ha-Nasi, Yehuda, 2157
Hanbal, Ahmad ibn, 989, 1625
Hanbali School of Law, **989–990,** 1997, 2123
muwahhidun as followers of, 1625
Rida (Rashid) and, 1923
Handbook of Palestine, A (Luke), 1447
Handbook of Palestine and Trans-Jordan, The (Luke), 1447
Hande (weekly), 2067
Hand of Fatima, **990**
Hanegbi, Haim, 1501
Hang glider attack, on Israel, by PFLP–GC (1987), 1841, 1842
Hanifa, Abu, buried in Baghdad, 362
Hanifism, 1144
Hanim, Fatma Aliye, 1440
Hanim, Latife, biography of, 274
Hannah Szenes (Meged), 1512
Hanna, Milad, *as contributor,* 638–642
Hannibal, 2227
Hannibal (Madani), 1456
Hanoune, Louisa, **990**
Haouz plain (Morocco), 1567
Hapsburgs, support for Catholics under Ottoman Empire, 1544
Haq, al- (human rights organization), **991**
Haq, Gad al-Haq Ali Gad al-, 822
Haqiqa, 2111
Haraka al-Dimuqratiya lil-Taharrur al-Watani. *See* Democratic Movement for National Liberation
Haraka al-Misriyya lil-Taharrur al-Watani. *See* Egyptian Movement for National Liberation
Haraka al-Wataniyya fi al-Maghrib al-Arabi al- (al-Fasi), 812
Harakat al-Afwaj al-Islamiyya (political movement), 978
Harakat al-Mujtama al-Islamiyya (Algeria). *See* Mouvement de la Société pour la Paix
Harakat al-Muqawama al-Islamiyya. *See* HAMAS
Harakat al-Nahda. *See* Islamic Tendency Movement (Tunisia)
Harakat al-Nasiriyyan al-Mustaqillin (Lebanon), 1612
Harakat al-Qawmiyya al-Arabiyya (al-Ghuri), 917
Harakat al-Qawmiyyin al-Arab. *See* Arab National Movement (ANM)
Harakat al-Tajdid. *See* Movement of Renewal
Harakat-e Inqilab-e Islami (Afghanistan), 63
Mohammadi (Maulawi Mohammad Nabi) in, 1559
in mojahedin resistance, 1561
Harakat-e Islami (Afghanistan), 63
in mojahedin resistance, 1561
Haram, al- (Idris), 1083
Haram al-Ibrahimi, al- (Hebron), 1019
Haram al-Sharif (Temple Mount), *991,* **991–992**
administrative control of, 1225
archaeological sites in, conflict over, 279, 1226
attacks against, 1226, 2178
in Camp David Summit (2000), 562
construction of, 1222
Sharon's visit to, and al-Aqsa Intifada, 219, 1226–1227, 1727, 1793

Haramayn, al-, 2019
Hara Sghira (Tunisia), 718
Harb al-Watan (Faraj), 805
Harb, Talʿat, Asmahan and, 324
Harb tribe, 2209
Hardinge, Lord, 437
Haredi Jews
in Agudat Israel, 77
Eretz Yisrael term used by, 781
in Jerusalem, 1226
and Sabbath, 1954
Yiddish language of, 2399
Harel, Isser, **992**
as Mossad director, 1577–1578
resignation of, 1578
Shiloah (Reuven) in conflict with, 2056
in Shin Bet, 2056
Harem Days (Mernissi), 1518
Harems, **992–993**
Circassians in, 599
Shaʿrawi (Huda al-) on, 2030
slaves in, 2072, 2073, 2074
Harem Years (al-Shaʿrawi), 2030
Hareven, Shulamit, **993**, 1433, 1434
Har Homa Israeli settlement, 1226
Haridi, Gamal Farghali, al-Jamiʿa al-Islamiyya established by, 1214
Harim, 2030
Hariri Foundation, tuition loans by, for American University of Beirut, 181
Hariri, Rafiq Bahaʾuddin al-, *994*, **994**
Council for Development and Reconstruction under, 645
in Hariri Foundation, 181
Hirawi (Ilyas al-) and, 1033
vs. Hoss (Salim al-), 1045
Husayni (Husayn al-) opposition to, 1055
Lahhud (Emile) in conflict with, 1364, 1401
as prime minister, 1400–1401
reconstructing Beirut, 431
Hari Rud River, 54
Harissa, church at (Lebanon), May procession at, 2360
Harith al-Miyah (Barakat), 398
Harkabi, Yehoshafat, **994–995**
Harkavy, Robert E., *as contributor*, 1696–1699
Harkis, **995**
Harlech, Lord. *See* Ormsby-Gore, William George Arthur
Harmala, 2019
Harmel, Mohammed, 2232
in Movement of Renewal, 1590
Haroun, Mohamed Ali, in High State Council, 1026
Harratin, **996**
Harriman, W. Averell, **996**
Harrison, Earl G., 198
Harthama ibn Aʿyan, Monastir founded by, 1564
Hartman, Michelle, *as contributor*, 1581
Harvard University
Bunche (Ralph J.) at, 543
Bush (George W.) at, 549
Ecevit (Bülent) at, 745
Gur (Mordechai) at, 956
Kissinger (Henry) at, 1327
Said (Edward) at, 1966
Twayni (Ghassan) at, 2254
Hasa, al- (Saudi Arabia), **996–997**
Ottoman Empire reabsorbing (1871), 531
Shiʿite uprisings in (1979–1980), Khalid ibn Abd al-Aziz Al Saʿud response to, 164, 1295
tribes in, 2210, 2213
Hasan (Ali ibn Abi Tabin's son), 2052
Hasan, Ahmad Fuʾad, 971
Hasan al-Askari, 1489
tomb of, as Atabat, 328
Hasan al-Attar, 2146
Hasanayn, Ahmad, Asmahan and, 324
Hasan, Faʾiq, **997**
Hasan, Hani al-, **997**
Hasani, Abd al-Razzaq al-, 808
Hasan-i-Sabbah, Assassins founded by, 1159
Hasani, Taj al-Din al-, **997–998**
Hasaniyya dialect, 2342
Hasan, Khalid al- (Abu Saʿid), **998**
as al-Fatah founder, 813
in PLO, 814
Hasan Pasha (Mamluk ruler) (1704–1724), 1478
Hasan Pasha (Mamluk ruler) (1778–1780), 1478
Hashashiyyun, 831
Hashemi, Faezeh, 428, **998–999**
in women's sporting event, 1154
Hashem, Muhammad, 400
Hashid tribal confederation, 376, 1976
in Islah Party, 1143
Ha-Shiloah (journal), 78
Hashim, Hanan, 142
Hashim, Ibrahim, **999**
government of, Rifaʿi (Samir al-) in, 1925
Hashimi, Taha al-, 927, **999–1000**
Hashimite House (House of Hashim), **1000**
in Arab Revolt (1916), 221
British patronage, 510, 515, 520, 801
and Fertile Crescent unity, 824, 825, 826
Husayn ibn Ali as descendant of, 1052
Hussein ibn Talal as descendant of, 1061
Majali family service to, 1470–1471
Philby (Harry St. John) and, 1833
Hashimi, Yasin al-, **1000–1001**
in al-Ahd, 81, 1001
cabinet of, Kaylani (Abd al-Rahman al-) in, 1283
coup against (1936), 999, 1001
coup against (1946), 2065
and Hashimi (Taha al-), 999
in Ikha al-Watani Party, 1084, 1283
Sulayman (Hikmat) and, 2115
Hashish, 725–726
Assassins' use of, 1159
Ha-Shomer (Jewish defense organization), **1001**, 1172
Ha-Shomer ha-Tzaʿir (Israel), **1001–1002**, 1361
Ahdut ha-Avodah in, 82, 1178
Ben-Aharon (Yitzhak) in, 438
binationalism supported by, 473
Grossman (Haika) in, 944
Gush Emunim formed by, 957
in Kibbutz Artzi movement, 1319
Kovner (Abba) in, 1336
principles of, 1321
Yaʾari (Meʾir) in, 2375
Ha-Shomer Self-Defense Organization
Ben-Zvi (Rahel Yanait) in, 456
Shochat (Manya) in, 2059
Hasid, al- (magazine), 2043
Hasidic Jews. *See* Hassidic Jews
Haşim, Ahmet, 1439
Hasim Khan, Muhammad, 2420
Haskalah (Israel), **1002–1003**
and foundations of Zionism, 2432
and Hebrew language, 1003, 1018

Lilienblum (Moses Leib) on, 1417
and literature, 1430
Weizmann (Chaim) in, 2337
Hasneh (insurance company), 1034
Hass, Amira, **1003**
Hassan (prince of Jordan)
education of, at Victoria College, 2316
removed from post of crown prince, 31, 1246
Hassan I (sultan of Morocco), **1003–1004,** 2038
Marrakech under, 1493
sons of, 8, 14
Hassan II (king of Morocco), **1004–1006,** *1005,* 2039
in Alawite dynasty, 106–107
as *amir al-mu'minin* (commander of the faithful), 1586
ascension to throne, 1570, 1599
attempted coup against (1971), 1374, 1570–1571, 1573
Ouazzani (Mohamed Hassan) and, 1743
Oufkir (Muhammad) and, 1743
attempted coup against (1972), 1570–1571
authority over parliament, 1572–1573
Bouabid (Abderrahim) opposing, 495
coalition government of, 1573–1574, 1575
Ahardane (Majoub) in, 81
Aicha (Lalla) in, 94
Dlimi (Ahmed) in, 718
Ouazzani (Mohamed Hassan) in, 1743, 2336
Oufkir (Muhammad) in, 1743
Youssoufi (Abderrahmane) in, 1573–1574, 1575, 2268, 2411
constitutions influenced by, 1572–1573
domestic policies of, 107
economic adviser of, 1366
emergency powers of, 1572, 1588
foreign policy of, 107
Green March organized by, 942–943, 2084, *2085*
human rights under, 1573, 1716
Istiqlal Party and, 1197
moudawana reform under, 1203
Mouvement Populaire and, 1588
political opponents of, 1574–1575
punishment for, 107
political parties supporting, 1574
political reforms under, 1571, 1573, 1600
as prime minister, 1599
as prince, 1599
on reform of al-Moudawana, 1586
sister of, Aicha (Lalla) as, 94
tutor of, 812
Union Nationale des Forces Populaires opposing, 2267
Western Sahara expansion sought by, 1571, 1574, 1600, 2343, 2345–2346
Yacine (Abdessalame) criticism of, 2375
Hassan II Mosque (Casablanca), *568,* 570
architecture of, 283–284
Hassan, Amal Muhammad, 808
Hassana tribe, 2212
Hassaniya dialect, 1503
Hassanpour, Amir, *as contributor,* 914, 1339–1342
Hassidic Jews (Hasidim), **1002**
in Jerusalem, 1223
literature of, *71, 79*
in Safed, 1962
Yiddish language of, 2399
Hasso, Frances, *as contributor,* 1293
Hasson, Israel, as director of Shin Bet, 1579
Hassoun, Jacques, 1304
Hassuna, Abd al-Khaliq, as secretary-general of League of Arab States, 352, 1386
"Hasta çocuk" (Tevrik Fikret), 2180
Hatay province (Turkey), capital city of, 210–211
Ha-Tehiyah. *See* Tehiyah party
"Ha-Tikva" (Zionist anthem), **1007,** 2425
Hatim dynasty (Yemen), 2397
Hatim Sultans of Hamdan (North Yemen), **1007**
Hatiri, Rafiq, 2117
HATM (Movement for Reform and Renewal in Morocco). *See* Movement for Unity and Reform (MUR)
Hatoum, Mona, **1007–1008**
Hatt-i Hümayun (1856), 423, 823, 885, 1732–1733, 2162. *See also* Tanzimat era
Hatt-i Serif of Gülhane (1839), 1732–1733, 2073, 2162, 2163, 2164. *See also* Tanzimat era
Hattushash. *See* Bogazköy (Turkey)
Hatzfeld, Baron, 903
Haussmann, Georges, 552
and urban planning, 2299
Haut Comité d'Etat (HCE) (Algeria)
Abdesselam (Belaid) appointed by, 23, 1026
and Bouteflika (Abdelaziz), 504
dissolution of, 130
elections canceled by (1992), 95, 126
establishment of, 126, 130, 1026
Ghozali (Ahmed) in, 917
Nezzar (Khaled) establishing, 1686
Zeroual (Liamine) appointed by, 130, 1026
Hawa (journal), 1965
Hawadith, al- (newspaper), 1681, 1982
Hawari, Muhammad Nimr al-, in Najjada, al-, 1638
Hawar Islands, 370, 371
Hawash, Samar, in Women's Centre for Legal Aid and Counseling, 2356
Hawatma, Nayif, **1008–1009,** 1452
in Democratic Front for the Liberation of Palestine, 1773
influence on PLO, 1008, 1009
Marxist-Leninist faction led by, 962
Hawa wa al-wafa, al- (Fawwaz), 817
Hawi, George, **1009–1010**
Hawi, Khalil, **1010**
Shi'r and, 1298
Hawi, William, death of, 1253
Hawrani, Akram al-, **1010–1011**
in Ba'th party, 69, 412
as vice president of UAR, 2273
Hawwari, Muhammad Nimr al-, 1375
Hawwat wa al-Qasr, al- (Wattar), 2333
Hayal (magazine), 1277
Hayapatum (Alishan), 144
Hayat, al- (newspaper), 1681
Hayat, Nina, 1427
Haycraft Commission (1921), **1011–1012,** 2349
Haycraft, Thomas, 1011
Haydari, Buland al-, 344
Haydar, Sa'id, in Istiqlal Party, 1198
Hayim, Yusef, **1012**
Haykal, Muhammad Hasanayn, **1012–1013**
and Ahram Center for Political and Strategic Studies, 92
Sabri (Ali) in conflict with, 1956

Haykal, Muhammad Husayn, **1013–1014**
Abd al-Raziq (Ali) supported by, 21
Zaynab by, 1420
Hayy al-Ashgar (Egypt), 1995
Haza, Ofra, **1014**
Hazara, **1014–1015**
in Afghanistan, language of, 55
in Bamyan, 387
Hazaragi language, 55
Hazarajat region (Afghanistan), political parties in, 63–64
Hazaz, Hayyim, **1015–1016,** 1431
Hazbun, Waleed, *as contributor,* 98–99, 1091–1096
Ha-Zohar, 2437, 2438. *See also* Zionist Revisionist Movement
Hazrat Ali, Shrine of (Najaf), *1147*
Hazzan, Elijah Bekhor, 453, **1016**
HCE. *See* Comité d'Etat; Haut Comité d'Etat
Headgear, *607,* 608–611
in Turkey, declared illegal, 2240
Heakhzuyot (holding settlements), 1634
Healing cults, 2360
Health barbers, 2003
Heath, Edward, 521
Heavily Indebted Poor Country Initiative, Mauritania qualified for relief under, 1503
Hebrew alphabet, in Judeo-Arabic language, 1252
Hebrew art, 469–470
Hebrew Authors' Association, 547
Hebrew Bible
Dead Sea Scrolls and, 685
language of, 1016
Hebrew education, 427
Hebrew Encyclopedia, 1403
Hebrew Gymnasium (Jerusalem), 456
Hebrew Immigrant Aid Society, Jewish Colonization Association and, 1229
Hebrew Israelites, in Dimona (Israel), 708
Hebrew language, **1016–1018**
alphabet of, *1017*
Arabic relationship to, 232
vs. Arabic script, 232, 234
Ashkenazic use of, 321
Behar (Nissim) and, 427
Biblical, 1017
Haskalah movement and, 1003, 1018
Institute for Palestine Studies promotion of, 1099
in Israel, 1163
modernization of, 1556
poetry in, 1252
on postage stamps, 1850
preservation and growth of, 1017–1018
Rabbinic, 1017
revival of, 2399, 2432
Ben-Yehuda (Eliezer) and, 454–455
Bialik (Hayyim Nahman) and, 470
as Semitic language, 2010
Sephardic use of, 321
as symbol of Jewish independence, 1430
in Yiddish language, 2399
Hebrew literature. *See* Literature, Hebrew
Hebrew press, 1683–1684
Hebrew Resistance Movement
Begin (Menachem) in, 425
Haganah in, 973
Lohamei Herut Yisrael in, 1443
Hebrews, in Palestine, 1758
Hebrew theater. *See* Theater, Israeli
Hebrew Union College, Silver (Abba Hillel) at, 2066
Hebrew University of Jerusalem, **1018–1019,** 1224
archaeological department of, 277
Barak (Ehud) at, 398
Bentwich (Norman) at, 454
binationalism supported by, 473
bombing of student cafeteria in (2002), 1018
Burg (Yosef) at, 546
Goldberg (Leah) at, 927
Gur (Mordechai) at, 956
Guri (Chaim) at, 955
and Haifa University, 975
Harkabi (Yehoshafat) at, 995
Leibowitz (Yeshayahu) at, 1403
Magnes (Judah) as first president of, 1460–1461
Shamir (Yitzhak) at, 2025
Shammas (Anton) at, 2029
Stern (Abraham) at, 2090
Tsemel (Leah) at, 2221
Zach (Natan) at, 2418
Hebrew University of Tel Aviv, Ben-Porat (Mordechai) at, 452
Hebrew Writers Union, 470
Hebron (West Bank), **1019,** 2340
Israeli settlements in, 1019, 1325
expansion of, 2432
Gush Emunim movement and, 1019
Levinger (Moshe) leading, 1325, 1407
violence associated with, 1325
Israeli withdrawal from, 1677
Jabal al-Khalil mountains around, 1204–1205
Ja'bari family in, 1206
massacre in (1929), 2159
massacre of Palestinians in (1994), 1325
Tomb of the Patriarchs in, 1807
in Western Wall disturbances (1929), 2348
Hebron Agreement (1997), Kiryat Arba settlement in, 1325
HEC. *See* Higher Executive Committee; High Executive Council
Hedayat, Sadegh, **1019**
Alavi (Bozorg) and, 104
Pahlavi (Reza) alienating, 1757
plays by, 2186
short stories by, 1435
Hefetz (Levin), 1407
Hegel, Georg Wilhelm Friedrich, 1110
Heidelberg University
Goldmann (Nahum) at, 927
Taner (Haldun) at, 2160
Heikal, Muhammad Hasanayn. *See* Haykal, Muhammad Hasanayn
Heilman, Samuel C., *as contributor,* 979–980, 1250–1252, 1269–1270, 1889–1890, 1953–1954, 2347–2348, 2399
Hejaz Railway (Palestine/Israel), 974
Hekmatyar, Golbuddin, *60,* **1020**
in Afghan Interim Government, 63
communists opposed by, 61
and Hezb-e Islami, 1024
in Hezb-e Islami, 63, 1298
Kabul attacked by, 59
in Kashwar Kamal (Meena) assassination, 1279
Heliographs, 624
Hellenism, *vs.* Islam, 1148
Helmand-Arghandab River, 54
Helmand River, **1020,** 2070
Helmand Valley Project, 494
Helwan Railway (Egypt), 1930

Hemmerle, Oliver Benjamin, *as contributor,* 932–934, 1122–1123, 2061
Hendel, Yehudit, 1433, 1434
Henry, Clement Moore, *as contributor,* 389–394
Hepatitis A, 712
Hepatitis B, 712
Hepatitis C, 712–713
Herat (Afghanistan), 59, **1020–1021**
  Iranian cession of, 1313
  Iranian seizure of
    in Anglo–Persian War (1856), 204, 1117
    Naser al-Din Shah and, 1644
  Naqshbandi order in, 1642
Herbal medicine, 1508
Her Eyes (Alavi), 1435
Hermitage (St. Petersburg), Islamic coin collection of, 1702
Hermon, Mount, 926
Hermopolis Parva. *See* Damanhur
Herod Antipas, 2188
Herodotus, 490
Heroes of the Return (guerrilla group), Hut (Shafiq al-) and, 1071
Heroin, 724–725
Herrera, Linda, *as contributor,* 756–762, 1614, 1902, 1965–1966
Herut-Liberal Bloc. *See* GAHAL
Herut Party (Israel), 1181–1182
  Arens (Moshe) in, 285
  Begin (Menachem) in, 425, 1181
  Free Center split from, 1181
  in GAHAL, 1181, 1184
  Greenberg (Uri Zvi) in, 941
  in Kasztner affair (1954–1955), 1280
  in Likud, 1181–1182, 1184, 1416, 2041
  in national unity government, during Arab–Israel War (1967), 248
  platform of, 1182
  Shamir (Yitzhak) in, 2026
  union with Liberal Party, 1555
  Weizman (Ezer) in, 2336
Herzen, Alexander, 299
Herzlian Zionism, Ahad Ha-Am criticism of, 78
Herzliya Gymnasium (Tel Aviv)
  Shlonsky (Avraham) in, 2058
  Tagger (Sioneh) in, 2144
Herzl, Theodor, **1021–1022,** *2434*
  Borochov (Ber) opposing, 493
  and Hess (Moses), 1024
  Jabotinsky (Vladimir Ze'ev) on, 1208
  Levontin (Zalman) as associate of, 1408
  Mohilever (Samuel) and, 1560
  Nordau (Max) supporting, 1692
  on potash industry, 1851
  Sokolow (Nahum) supporting, 2078, 2172
  Uganda Project supported by, 2257
  in World Zionist Organization, 1165, 2372
  and Zangwill (Israel), 2424
  Zionism of, 470, 904, 1021, 2433–2434, 2437
    Dreyfus affair and, 723
  at Zionist Congress, *2433*
Herzog, Chaim, **1022**
  Shin Bet officers pardoned by, 2056
Herzog, Izhak Halevi, **1022,** 1023
Herzog, Ya'acov David, 1022, **1023**
Heshbon Over (Guri), 956
Heskayl, Hakam, 1023
Heskayl, Sasson (Sasun Effendi), **1023,** 1233
  at Cairo Conference (1921), 554
Hesse, Hermann, 149
Hess, Moses, **1023–1024,** 1359
  Rome and Jerusalem, 1024
Hetata, Sherif, 1950
Hevrat Ovdim (The Workers Company), 1033, 1034
He Walked through the Fields (Shamir), 2024
Hezb-e Asadollah Alam (Iran), 779
Hezb-e Islami (Afghanistan)
  in Afghan Interim Government, 63, **1024**
  factionalism of, 63
  Hekmatyar (Golbuddin) in, 63, 1020, 1298
  Khalis (Mohammad Unis) in, 63, 1298
  in mojahedin resistance, 1561
Hezb-e Mellet-e Iran. *See* Nation of Iran Party
Hezb-e melliyun (Iran), 779
Hezb-e Tudeh-ye Iran. *See* Tudeh Party
Hezb-e Wahadat (Afghanistan)
  establishment of, 64
  Hazara ethnolinguistic group and, 1015
  in interim government, 64
  in mojahedin resistance, 1561
Hezb-e Watan (Afghanistan), 1801
Hezbollahi, 2623
Hezyonot U-Manginot (Tchernichovsky), 2168
Hibat al-Faragh (Bannis), 396
Hibbat Zion, **1024–1025,** 2432
  Ahad Ha-Am in, 78
  early settlements of, 2431
  establishment of, 1430
  Lilienblum (Moses Leib) in, 1417
  Mohilever (Samuel) as founder of, 1560
  opposition to, 2434
  and Orthodox rabbis, 2432–2433
  Pinsker (Leo) in, 1835
  Ussishkin (Menahem) in, 2303
Hibri, Tayeb al-, *as contributor,* 1144–1150
Hicazkar Saz Semaisi (Tanburi), 2160
Hidden Face of Eve: Women in the Arab World (al-Saadawi), 1950
Hidden Half, The (film), 1526
Hieroglyphics, deciphered by Champollion (Jean-François), 275, 492, 581–582
Higbee, Marilyn, *as contributor,* 2045
High Commissioners (Palestine), **1025**
  duties of, 1762
Higher Executive Committee (HEC) (Bahrain), 371, 1661
High Executive Council (HEC) (Sudan), 2103
High State Council (Algeria), **1025–1026,** 2430
Hijab (veil), 611, **1026–1027**. *See also* Veiling
Hijab, Tantawi (Muhammad Sayyid al-) on, 2161
Hijaz (Saudi Arabia), **1027–1028,** 1995
  Al Sa'ud control of, 1999
  in Arab Revolt (1916), 221, 264
  cities of, 2148–2149
  delegation from, at Paris peace conference, 511, 2314
  Hashimite rule in, 1000
  Husayn ibn Ali as king of, 1052
  Kingdom of, 1000
  tribes in, 2214
  unification with Najd, 1626
  writing styles in, 558

Hijazi school, 1476
Hijaz, Kingdom of, 1507
Hijaz Railroad, 904, *1028*, **1028–1029**, 2206
in Amman, 190–191
southern terminus of, 1511
Hijra, al-, 2151
Hijra (migration)
of Ikhwan, 1085, 1626
of Muhammad, 1511, 1596, 1597
and Wahhabi movement, 1626
Hikayat Zahra (Shaykh), 2046
Hikma University, al-, **1029**
Hikmet, Nazim, 1437, 1439, 2145
Hilal, al- (magazine), **1029–1030**, 1420
Zaydan (Jurji) and, 2426
Hilf al-Thulathi, al- (Lebanon), 581, 1254
Eddé (Raymond) in, 754
Hillel, Ayin, 1432
Hillel, Shlomo, **1030**
Hillmann, M., on Al-e Ahmad (Jalal), 110
Hillmann, Michael C.
as contributor, 110, 366–367, 397, 566–567, 668–669, 678, 689, 784, 811, 913, 976, 1019, 1434–1437, 1802–1803, 2027
on Parsipur (Shahrnush), 1803
Hilmi (Abd al-Baqi), Ahmad, **1030–1031**
in All-Palestine Government, 154
Hilu, Charles, **1031**
amnesty by, 1888
government of, Karame (Rashid) in, 1271
Jumayyil (Pierre) and, 1254
as Phalange Party founder, 1031, 1400
as president, 1399–1400
Sarkis (Ilyas) under, 1991–1992
Taqla (Philippe) under, 2165
Twayni (Ghassan) under, 2254
Hilu, Henri, 1032
Hilu, Pierre, **1031–1032**
Hilu, Radwan al-, in Communist Party of Palestine, 626
Himmish, Bensalem, 1425, 1428
Hindiya River, 1316
Hindu Kush Mountains, 53, **1032**
Hinnawi, Sami al-, **1032**, 2422
coup against (1949), 329
government of, Aflaq (Michel) in, 69
Hira, Muhammad's retreats in, 1595
Hirawi, Ilyas al-, **1032–1033**
government of, Hoss (Salim al-) in, 1045
as president, 1400–1401
Hirfa, 947
Hiro, Dilip, 2289
Hirsch, Maurice de, 1229
Hirsch, Samson Raphael, followers of, in Agudat Israel, 77
Hirshfeld, Yair, in Oslo negotiations, 1725
Hisad al-Awwal, al- (Sha'ul), 2043
Histadrut (labor organization), **1033–1035**
Ben-Aharon (Yitzhak) in, 438
Ben-Gurion (David) in, 447
Brenner (Yosef Hayyim) in, 507
Burla (Yehuda) in, 547
controlling economic resources, 1358
elections in, 1176
foundation of, 1361
Haganah under, 972
headquarters of, *1033*, 2172
Katznelson (Berl) in, 1281
Kessar (Israel) in, 1290
Kol (Moshe) in, 1332
Koor Industries founded by, 1334
Labor Zionism as basis of, 1357
Lavon (Pinhas) as secretary-general of, 1377, 1378
Luz (Kadish) in, 1448
Meir (Golda) in, 1513
military controlled by, 1172
Na'amat's affiliation with, 1629
Shazar (Shneour Zalman) in, 2047
Sprinzak (Joseph) in, 2087
state-building by, 2402
Histoire, culture et société (Lacheraf and Djeghloul), 1362
Histoire des Musselmans (Dozy), 576
Historical Society of Afghanistan. *See* Tarikh Tolana
Historiography, **1035–1037**
Hourani (Albert) and, 1035, 1046–1047
Marxism and, 1036
nationalism and, 1035, 1036–1037
women and, 1037
Zaydan (Jurji) and, 1035, 2426
History (Cevdet), 577, 578
History of the Arab Peoples, A (Hourani), 1047
Hitler, Adolf
on al-Alamayn battle (1942), 102
Atatürk (Mustafa Kemal) compared to, 333–334
and Holocaust, 1040
Husayni (Amin al-) and, 1042
and Jewish immigration to Palestine, 961
opposing Jewish immigration to Palestine, 906
Philby (Harry St. John) praise for, 1833
Protocols of the Elders of Zion and, 1856
and Rommel (Erwin), 1934
Hitti, Philip, 488, 1397
HIV. *See* AIDS/HIV
Hizb al-Ahd al-Urdunni. *See* Jordanian Covenant Party
Hizb al-Ahrar al-Dusturiyyin (Egypt). *See* Constitutional Liberty Party (Egypt)
Hizb al-Islah (Palestine). *See* Reform Party
Hizb al-Istiqlal (Palestine). *See* Istiqlal Party
Hizb al-Nahda (Tunisia). *See* Renaissance Party
Hizb al-Shaʿb. *See* People's Party (Syria)
Hizb al-Tahrir (Syria), 998
Hizb al-Umma al-Ishtiraki (National Socialist Party) (Iraq), establishment of, 1210
Hizb al-Watani, al- (Egypt). *See* National Party
Hizb En Nahda. *See* Renaissance Party (Tunisia)
Hizb-e Wadat, 387
Hizb-i Iʿtidal (Iraq), Mossadegh (Mohammad) in, 1580
Hizb Misr al-Ishtiraki. *See* Socialist party (Egypt)
Hizbullah (Lebanon), **1037–1038**
vs. AMAL, 174, 1037, 1038
CIA attack against leadership of, 573
and al-Daʿwa al-Islamiyya, 793
Fadlallah (Shaykh Husyan) as spiritual guide of, 793, 794
formation of, 2177
Iran supporting, 2175
on Israeli withdrawal from Lebanon, 2017
lack of superpower patron for, 2177
Lahhud (Emile) supporting, 1364

Nasrallah (Hasan) in, 1647
South Lebanon Army fighting, 2083
suicide bombings by, 2177
terrorist activities of, 1038
Hnots yev norots (Srvantziants), 2087
Hobeika, Elie, **1038–1039**
in Lebanese Forces, 1394
Tripartite Accord (1985) signed by, 871
Hoca, 2623
Hodeida (Yemen), **1039,** 2386
al-Ta'if Treaty (1934) on, 2149
Hoffman, Yoel, **1039–1040,** 1434
Hoffner, Dan, 470
Hofi, Yitzhak
in Mossad, Kimche (David) under, 1322
as Mossad director, 1578
Hogarth, David G., Kirkbride (Alec Seath) and, 1324
Hojjatieh group (Iran), Velayati (Ali Akbar) in, 2313
Hok ha-Shvut. See Law of Return
Holland. *See* Netherlands
Holocaust, **1040–1043**
aliyah during, 147
documentary on, 956
history of, 1040–1041
Husayni (Amin al-) during, 1057
impact on Middle East, 1041–1043
and Israeli national identity, 1042
Jewish resistance to, 1041
in Kasztner affair (1954–1955), 1280
Kovner (Abba) in, 1336
literature on, 216–217, 1336, 1433, 1751–1752
survivors of
Anglo–American Committee of Inquiry on (1946), 198–199
on *Exodus* (ship), 789–790
at Haifa Port, *1041*
Jewish Brigade assistance to, 1229
transfer to Palestine, 920
West German reparations to, 43, 2348–2349
Yad Vashem and, 2377
and Zionism, 2435
Zionist Organization of America during, 2436
Holod, Renata, 283
Holy Land, **1043**
of Bible
Palestine as, 1758
Palestine Exploration Fund research on, 1771–1772
tourism in, 2195
Holy Sepulchre, Church of the, **1043–1044**
Nusayba family holding keys of, 1705
Holy war, 1236. *See also* Jihad
Holy War Army
Jordanian opposition to, 155
revival of, 154
Homeland Party (Afghanistan). *See* Hezb-e Watan
Homeland Party (Israel). *See* Moledet Party
Homer
Iliad, 275
Odyssey, 717
Homme du livre, l' (Chraibi), 588
Homosexual rights, 888
Homs (Syria), **1044**
Honein, Edward, 1395
Honor, crimes of, 649–650
Honor killings, 649–650, 1495
in Jordan, 887, 894
women's activism against, 1065, 1902
in Lebanon, 887
Noor al-Hussein in campaign against, 1691
Hooglund, Eric, *as contributor,* 7, 34, 37–38, 53–62, 104, 140–141, 188–189, 193–194, 200, 204, 205, 207–208, 210–211, 285–286, 346, 374, 397, 399–401, 428, 635–637, 651–652, 668–669, 671, 678, 705–706, 715, 722–723, 730, 755–756, 782–783, 783, 784, 834, 850–851, 872, 928, 929–930, 937, 945–946, 1019, 1046, 1125–1129, 1141–1142, 1193–1196, 1216–1218, 1220, 1279, 1285, 1292, 1300, 1303, 1310–1312, 1315, 1332, 1376–1377, 1434–1437, 1447, 1466–1468, 1471–1472, 1489–1490, 1496, 1498, 1513, 1517, 1524, 1558–1559, 1564–1565, 1614–1615, 1640–1641, 1643–1644, 1665–1666, 1682–1683, 1796–1797, 1801–1802, 1820–1821, 1857, 1868–1869, 1898–1899, 1921–1922, 1945–1946, 1979, 2011, 2027, 2039–2040, 2057, 2083, 2096, 2141–2142, 2169–2170, 2174–2179, 2190, 2193–2194, 2194, 2208, 2216, 2223–2224, 2236–2242, 2246–2247, 2247–2249, 2251–2252, 2253, 2255, 2296–2297, 2299–2302, 2304, 2308, 2311–2313, 2351–2352, 2382, 2420–2421, 2440–2442
Hookworm, 710
Hoover Institute, 492
Hope (film), 955
Hope-Simpson Commission (1930), **1044–1045,** 1454, 2044, 2350
Hope-Simpson, John, 1044, 2350
on space restrictions for Jewish settlers, 1789
Hopkins, Harry, 1404
Hora (dance), 667, 668
Hormuz, Strait of, 952
Horses, Arabian, 230–231
Hosayniyeh, 2623
Hosayniyeh-ye Ershad (Tehran), 2035
Hos, Dov, in Jewish Legion, 1230
Hoseyn Khan, Mirza(spelling), Malkom Khan (Mirza) and, 1477
Hoseyn Khan, Mohammad(spelling), 1867
Hossayn, Mohammad(spelling), Karmal (Babrak) in family of, 1274
Hosseini, Ezz al-Din, 694
Hoss, Salim al-, **1045**
as prime minister, 994, 1401
Sulh (Rashid al-) and, 2117
Hostage crises, **1046**
Entebbe Operation (1976), 777
Iran (1979), 567, 1046, *1113,* 1119, 2096, 2293
Algiers Agreement ending (1981), Nabavi (Behzad) and, 1630
Bani Sadr (Abolhasan) opposing, 388
Ebtekar (Ma'sumeh) in, 745
and Iran–Contra affair, 1119, 1122
and Iran–Iraq War, 1127
Lebanon (1984), 1046, 1908
in Iran–Contra affair, 1119, 1122–1123

Houari, Leila, 2376
Hourani, Albert, 1046–1047, 1406
as historiographer, 1035
House if Black, The (film), 832
Houssi, Majid el-, 1424
Hovevei Zion. *See* Hibbat Zion
Hoveyda, Amir Abbas, **1047**
in Iran Novin Party, 1129
as prime minister, 1129
Hovhannes Kolot (Armenian patriarch), 297
Howard, Richard, 1303
"How Do Our Literary Figures View Women?" (Bint al-Shati), 476
HRCAP. *See* Human Rights Center for the Assistance of Prisoners
Hubayqa, Elie. *See* Hobeika, Elie
Hubus (religious trust), 418
in Tunisia, 1604
Huda, al- (magazine), Khal (Yusuf al-) in, 1298
Huda, Sharif Murtada Alam al-, 2055
Hudaybi, Hasan al-, in Muslim Brotherhood, 321
Hudaybi, Ma'mun al-, in Muslim Brotherhood, *1621*, 1622
Hudaybiyya, al-, Mecca–Medina peace in, 1597
Hudayda (Yemen). *See* Hodeida (Yemen)
Hüdevendigar (Barkan), 407
Hudud (boundaries), 833
on bodily presentation, 1026–1027
Hufschmidt, G. H., King David Hotel decorated by, 1323
Hu Halah Basdot (Shamir), 2024, 2185
Huhu, Ahmad Reda, 1423, 1425
Hujar (agricultural colonies), in Wahhabi movement, 1626
Hukumat-e Velayi (Kadivar), 1262
Hula Swamps, **1047**
Hülegü Khan, 360
Human Development Report. *See* Arab Human Development Report; United Nations Human Development Report
Human figures, representations of
in Islamic art, 311–312
on postage stamps, 1849–1850
Humanism, 756
Humanitarian aid, 750
Human rights, **1047–1049**
in Afghanistan, violations of, 67
in Egypt, of gay people, 888
intelligence organizations' violations of, 1102
in Iran, 744
in Iranian Revolution (1979), 1119, 1754
organizations for, 622
public demands for, 1119
in Israel, 1373–1374, 2221
for Jews, Alliance Israélite Universelle on violations of, 152
in Jordan, 1065
activism for, 1291–1292
in Lebanon, 1396, 1960–1961
of gay people, 888
Moghaizel (Laure) as activist for, 1557–1558
in Libya, 1414, 1415
in Morocco
in constitution of 1992, 1573
Mohammad VI and, 1600
organizations for, 1716–1717
in Palestine, organizations for, 991
political use of, 1049
in Tunisia, 439–440, 1416
campaign on behalf of Moadda (Muhamed), 1554
Marzouki (Moncef) and, 1496–1497
in Turkey, Republican People's Party on, 1919
universality *vs.* cultural relativity of, 1049
war on terrorism causing concern for, 2178–2179
in Yemen, 806, 2357
Human Rights Award of French Republic, to Tsemel (Leah), 2221
Human Rights Center for the Assistance of Prisoners (HRCAP), on tuberculosis, 712
Human Rights League, Sadi (Said) in, 1959
Human Rights Watch
on human-rights abuses of gay people, 888
on human rights in Tunisia, 440
Khader (Asma) in, 1292
on Sabra and Shatila massacres, 254, 1955
Human Rights Watch Award, to Ebadi (Shirin), 744
Hummus, 839, 841
Humoral medicine, 1508
Humphrey Freedom Award, Samar (Sima) awarded with, 1982
Humphrey, Hubert H., American Israel Public Affairs Committee work for, 177
Humphreys, Francis, **1050**
Hunchak (publication), 299
Hunchak Party, **1050**
establishment of, 299
ideology of, 299
platform of, 299
Hungary
Austrian rule in, 339
Austrian union with (1867), 339 (*See also* Austria-Hungary)
Hunkar-Iskelesi, Treaty of (1833), **1050**, 1945, 2093
and Crimean War, 648
Hunter, F. Robert, 1036
Hunting, 803
Huntington, Samuel, 1091
Hunt Oil Company, 2397
Hurewitz, J. C., *as contributor*, 524–538, 738–743, 2094–2095
Hurgronje, Snouck, in Arab Academy of Damascus, 224
Hürriyet (newspaper), 41, **1050–1051**, 1685, 2067, 2406
vs. Milliyet, 1269
Hurriyya, al- (Salim), 1979
Hurvitz, Yair, 1434
Husari, Sati al-, **1051–1052**
curriculum instituted by, 801
and Fertile Crescent unity, 825
and Jam'iyyat al-Urwa al-Wuthqa (Society of the Firm Tie), 962
pan-Arabism of, 1799
Husayn (imam), Muharram commemoration of, 1605–1607
Husayn, Ahmad, in Young Egypt, 2405
Husayn, Aliya, 324, 336
Husayn Dey (ruler of Algeria), in Fly Whisk incident (1827), 397, 835–836
Husayni, Abd al-Qadir al-, **1052**, 1054
in Arab–Israel War (1948), 259, 1879
Arafat (Yasir) as aide to, 269
Palestinian guerrillas led by, Qawuqji (Fawzi al-) coordination with, 1879

Husayni, Amin al-. *See* Husayni, Muhammad Amin al- (Hajj Amin)
Husayn ibn Ali (Hashimite leader), **1052–1053,** 2052–2053
Abd al-Aziz ibn Saʿud Al Saʿud conflict with, 646
Arab Bureau collaboration with, 225
in Arab Revolt (1916), 221, 263–264, 510, 1000, 1506, 2039, 2368
Askari (Jaʿfar al-) under, 324
Hijaz Railroad in strategy of, 1029
Arslan (Shakib) criticism of, 307
as caliph candidate, 557
death in Karbala, 1272
al-Fatat and, 815
in Hashimite family, 1000
Islamic congress held by, 1152
martyrdom of, plays on, 2186
and McMahon, correspondence with, 263–264, 1053, 1059–1060, 1506
overthrown by Al Saʿud (Abd al-Aziz) (1924), 1625–1626
Saʿid (Nuri al-) supporting, 1967
sons of
Abdullah I ibn Hussein as, 29
and Arab nationalism, 1053
tomb of, as Atabat, 328, 1131, 1272
in World War I, 2366
Husayn ibn Ali Turki (bey of Tunisia), 2229
Husayni, Daʾud al-, 1054
Husaynid dynasty, 2229
Husayni family, al-, **1053–1054**
in Arab Club, 225–226
influence of, 1053
Jarallah family rivalry with, 1218
Nashashibi family rivalry with, 1224, 1644–1645, 1764, 1766
wealth of, 1053
Husayni, Faysal al-, 1054
and Arab Studies Society, 1226
secret talks with Israelis, 1705–1706
Husayni, Hind al-, **1055**
Husayni, Husayn al-, **1055,** 1058
in AMAL movement, 174
in parliament, 320
Husayni, Ishaq Musa al-, 1053–1054
Husayni, Jamal al-, 1053, **1055–1056**
Alami (Musa al-) and, 103
in All-Palestine Government, 154, 1030
in Arab Executive, 1783
in Arab Higher Committee, 1766
at London Conference (1939), 1766
Muslim–Christian Association guided by, 1761
in Palestine Arab Party, 1765, 1766
Husayni, Muhammad Amin al- (Hajj Amin), 1053, *1054,* **1056–1058**
in All-Palestine Government, 154, 155
antisemitic statement by, 212
Antonius (George) as advisor to, 214
appointment as mufti of Jerusalem, 1922
in Arab Club, 226
in Arab Higher Committee, 228
Arslan (Adil) opposition to, 306
assassination of, plans for, 1947
and Bludan Conferences, 488
under British mandate, 1056–1057
British relations with, 1764
Darwish (Ishaq) as nephew of, 673
exile of, 1057
German support for, 906, 944
Ghuri (Emile al-) supporting, 917
Golden Square supporting, 927
Husayni (Jamal al-) and, 1055, 1056
Islamic congress held by, 1152
as Jerusalem mufti, 1218, 1224, 1764
on Jews during World War II, 1234
Kaylani revolt (1941) supported by, 516
Muslim Brotherhood meeting with, 1621
Mussolini (Benito) supporting, 515
Nabi Musi Pilgrimage led by, 1630
Nashashibi family rivalry with, 1644–1645
and Nazi Germany, 1042, 1057
power of, 1764
revolt suggested to, by Qassam (Izz al-Din al-), 1874
Sabbagh (Salah al-Din al-) and, 1953
Samuel (Herbert Louis) supporting, 1983
in Supreme Muslim Council, 1011, 1224, 1764, 2124–2125
in Syria, Arif (Arif al-) with, 288
on UN Resolution 181, 1057, 1058
in World War II, 2371
Husayni, Munif al-, 1053
Husayni, Musa Kazim al-, 1053, **1058–1059**
antisemitism of, 212
in Arab Executive, 1224, 1764, 1782, 1783
death of, 1764, 1783
as Jerusalem mayor, 1224
dismissal of, 1645
Storrs (Ronald) dismissing, 2092
in Muslim–Christian Association, 1761
son of, 1052, 1054
Husayni, Raja al-, 1053
in All-Palestine Government, 154
Husayni, Rana. *See* Husseini, Rana
Husayni, Tahir Shuqri al-, daughter of, 1055
Husayniyya (place for storyteller), 1606
Husayn, Kamal al-Din, 853
Husayn Kamil, 509, 858
Husayn–McMahon correspondence (1915–1916), 263–264, 1053, **1059–1060,** 1506, 2368
Abdullah I ibn Hussein in, 29
in *The Arab Awakening* (Antonius), 214
British promise of support of Arab nation in, 380, 511, 742–743
Clayton (Gilbert) and, 603
conflicting interpretations of, 264
London Conference (1939) on, 1445
Husayn Mosque, al- (Karbala), *1131*
Husayn Muslim, Abu al-, *Sahih* of, 968
Husayn, Rashid, 2418
Husayn, Sharif, 511, 514–515
Husayn, Taha, **1060–1061,** 1419, 1420
Abd al-Raziq (Ali) supported by, 21
Amin (Ahmad) compared to, 183
at Cairo University, 556
on pre-Islamic Arabic poetry, 1923
Hüseyinzade, Ali, 1800
Husn al-awaqib aw Ghada al-zahira (Fawwaz), 817
Husni, Daud, 324, 336
Husni, Fikriyya, on Wafdist Women's Central Committee, 2321

Husri, Sate al-. *See* Husari, Sati al-
Hussein I, *1061*
government of, Majali (Abd al-Salam) in, 1471
Hussein, Aziza, 1902
Hussein, Barzan, 1070
Hussein ibn Talal (king of Jordan), **1061–1065,** *1062*
accession of, 1062, 1244
in Arab–Israel War (1967), 249, 258
Arab Legion under, 257–258, 519
and Arafat (Yasir), 1063
signing agreement with (1970), 2157
children of, *1062,* 1063
in civil war (1970–1971), 1246–1247
coup against (1957), attempted, 258
Abu Nuwwar (Ali) in, 39, 258
Nabulsi (Sulayman al-) suspected of role in, 1632–1633
crackdown on leftist activism, 1008
death of, 31, 1064, 1246
democratization process under, 1063
education of, at Victoria College, 2316
financial aid sought by
from Arab nations, 1632
from U.S., under Eisenhower Doctrine, 1632
funeral of, 1009, 1064
government of
Abu al-Huda (Tawfiq) in, 35
Abu Nuwwar (Ali) in, 38–39, 257–258
Majali (Hazza al-), 1470–1471
in Hashimite house, 1000
and Herzog (Ya'acov David), 1023
Jerusalem visited by, 1246
and Jordanian Option, 271, 1247
and Karama, Battle of (1968), 1270, 1271
marriages of, 1062–1063
moderation and centrism of, 1063–1064
periods of reign of, 1244–1245
PFLP expelled by, 1840
and PLO
peace accord between, 1247
refusing cooperation with, 2156
strained relations with, 1063
and Rabin (Yitzhak), *1063,* 1892
reign of, 2152–2153
historical periods in, 1063
Rifa'i (Samir al-) and, 1925
Rifa'i (Zaid al-) and, 1926
and Saudi Arabian relations, 2156
sons of, 31, 142
successor to, Abdullah II ibn Hussein as, 31
U.S. support for, 2291
wife of, 142–143, 409, 1691–1692, 1975, 2234
Husseini, Rana, **1065**
Hussein, Mahmud, 1036
Hussein Mosque (Karbala), *2054*
Hussein, Qusay, 1067, 1068
killing of, 1070, 2325
U.S. demand for departure from Iraq, 2325
Hussein, Sabawi, 1070
Hussein, Saddam, **1065–1070,** *1066*
Algiers Agreement (1975) signed by, 2043
allied coalition against, Turkish support for, 1747
archaeology supported by, 277
and architecture, 282
Asad (Hafiz al-) rivalry with, 318
autonomy agreement between Barzani (Mustafa) and, 2151
Aziz (Tariq) under, 350
Bakr (Ahmad Hasan al-) under, 378, 414
in Ba'th party, 413–414, 1065–1066
birthplace of, 2189
brother-in-law of, 2154
Bush (George H. W.) and, 2323–2324
Bush (George W.) and, 2324
capture by U.S. forces (2003), 1070, 1540, 2325
Chalabi (Ahmad) opposition to, 578
constitutional successor to, Ibrahim (Izzat) as, 1078
al-Da'wa al-Islamiyya and, 680, 681
as dictator, 933
election for president, 1067
entourage of, Ramadan (Taha Yasin) in, 1900
exile in Egypt, 1065
Fahd ibn Abd Al-Aziz Al Sa'ud passive toward, during Gulf Crisis, 796
family of, 1068, 2189
in Gulf War (1990–1991), 1539
and Hakim family, persecution of, 978
in Iran–Iraq War, 1067, 1134
and Iraqi debt, 949
Iraqi National Congress opposing, 1137
Israel threatened by (1990), 949–950
Khomeini (Ruhollah) expelled by, 1311
Kurdish revolts under, 1134, 1135
Kurdistan Front negotiations with, 1339
Kuwaiti territories claimed by, 541
liberation of Iraqi people from, as rationale for U.S. invasion, 2324
Moroccan public opinion on, 1006
nuclear capability of, 1698
personality cult of, 1068
PLO support for, 1775, 1793
Hasan (Khalid al-) opposition to, 998
police state under, 1066
political dominance of, 1134
on postage stamps, 1850
presidency assumed by, 1134
as president, 2189
purges under, 1067
removal from power, 549, 2189
rise of, 1134
September 11, 2001, and, 1069
Shi'ite revolt against, 1135
social and economic development under, 1066
sons of, 1067
Tel Aviv bombed by, 951
Tikriti (Hardan al-) in power struggle with, 2190
uprisings against, after Gulf War, 1068
U.S. position on
Bush (George W.) efforts to overthrow, 2294
demand for departure, 2325
opposition to and attack against (2003), 1539–1540, 2323–2327
Reagan (Ronald) support for, 1908
as vice president, 1134, 2189
wife of, 1067
Hussein, Taha, 475
Hussein, Uday, 1067
assassination attempt on, 1068
killing of, 1070, 2325
U.S. demand for departure from Iraq, 2325
wife of, 1078
Hussein, Watban, 1070

Huston, Nancy, 2007
Hutaym tribe, 2209
Hut, Shafiq al-, **1070–1071**
Hydrocarbon industry, in Algeria, 23, 127, 2079–2080
Hydropolitics, 1248–1249
Hydropower
  at Aswan High Dam, 327
  in Southeastern Anatolia Project, Keban Dam in, 1284
  water resources for, 2330
  on Yarmuk and Jordan Rivers, 2379

I

IAEA. *See* International Atomic Energy Agency
IAF. *See* Islamic Action Front
I and Thou (Buber), 540
IAW. *See* International Alliance of Women
IBA. *See* Israel Broadcasting Authority
Ibadat, 833
Ibadiyya (branch of Islam), **1073**
  in Algeria, 122
  in Libya, 1410
  in Oman, 1710
Ibbish, Yusuf, 306
Iberian Peninsula, 2084
Ibn, 2623
Ibn al-Arabi, 1457
Ibn al-Farra, 990
Ibn al-Jawzi, Abu al-Faraj, 990
Ibn amm, 2209
Ibn Arabi, and Sufism, 1149
Ibn Battuta, 838
Ibn Battuta (Akaley), 1428
Ibn Hanbal, 2019
Ibn Khaldun (Egyptian historian), 1701
  Khaldunniyya named for, 1293
  Muqaddima by, Ottoman translation of, 577, 578
Ibn Khaldun, Abd al-Rahman, at Zaytuna University, 2427
Ibn Khaldun Center for Development Studies (Cairo), Ibrahim (Saʿad al-Din) in, 1079
Ibn Musa, Ahmad (regent of Morocco), **1074**
  death of, 8, 1074
  reforms undermined by, 8
Ibn Nujaym, 988
Ibn Qayyim al-Jawziyya, 990
Ibn Rushd wa Falsafatuhu (Antun), 215
Ibn Saʿud. *See* Abd al-Aziz ibn Saʿud Al Saʿud
Ibn Surayj, 2019
Ibn Taymiyya, 101, 1148, 1625
Ibn Taymiyya, Taqi al-Din, 990
Ibn Tulun Mosque (Cairo), **1074–1075**
Ibrahim, Abd al-Fattah, 1210
Ibrahim, Abdullah, **1075**
  in Union Nationale des Forces Populaires, 1075, 1197, 2266–2267
Ibrahim, Ahmed H., *as contributor,* 20–21, 375, 1929–1930
Ibrahim al-Sharif, 2229
Ibrahim, Fatah, in Ahali group, 79
Ibrahim, Fatima Ahmed, 894, **1075–1076,** 2105
Ibrahim, Hafiz, 1061
Ibrahimi, Ahmed Taleb, **1076**
Ibrahimi, Bashir, **1076**
  son of, 1076
Ibrahim ibn Muhammad Ali (viceroy of Egypt), **1077**
  Battle of Nizip, 1690–1691
  death of, 1077
  Druze revolts under (1830s), 730
  government of, Chrakian (Artin) in, 589
  in Greek War of Independence, 940, 2093
  and Homs, 1044
  Jerusalem under, 1222
  missionary schools under, 1551
  Ottoman Empire attacked by, 1050
  son of, Mustafa Fazil as, 1623
  successor to, Abbas Hilmi I as, 4
  as Syrian governor, 1077
  in Syrian War (1831–1833), 1346, 2093
    Battle of Konya (1832), 1333
  in Syrian War (1839), 2093
Ibrahimi, Lakhdar al-, **1077–1078**
Ibrahim, Izzat, **1078,** *1527*
Ibrahim, Muhammad Hafiz, **1078–1079,** 1421
Ibrahim, Muhsin, Marxist-Leninist faction led by, 962
Ibrahim Pasha. *See* Ibrahim ibn Muhammad Ali
Ibrahim, Saʿad al-Din, 769, **1079**
  at al-Ahram Center for Political and Strategic Studies, 92, 1079
Ibra wa Dhikra aw al-Dawla al-Uthmaniyya Qabla al-Dustur wa Baʿdahu (Bustani), 550
Ibsen, Henrik, translation into Arabic, 22
ICA. *See* Jewish Colonization Association
Ich und Du (Buber), 540
Icon collection, 1971
ICPD. *See* International Conference on Population and Development
ICWA. *See* Institute for Current World Affairs
Idadi, 757
İdadi schools (Ottoman Empire), **1079–1080,** 1940
Identités meutrieres, Les (Maʿlouf), 1478
Identity
  cultural, in art, 313
  Ishaq (Adib) on, 1143
Identity Card (Esfandiary), 784
IDF. *See* Israel Defense Force
Idhaʾat al-Quds (radio station), 1842
IDHEC. *See* Institut des Hautes Études Cinématographiques
Idlibi, Ulfat al-, **1080**
Idlib province (Syria), **1080–1081**
Idris I ibn Abdallah (Fez founder), 828
Idris II (al-Aliya founder), 828
Idris al-Sayyid Muhammad al-Sanusi (Idris I) (king of Libya), **1081,** *2111*
  as amir of Cyrenaica, 655, 1081, 1321
  British support for, 615, 1081
  coup against (1969), 1081, 1860, 2218
    Yunis Jabir (Abu Bakr) in, 2414
  in exile in Egypt, 655, 1081
  Italian relations with, Kikhya (Umar Mansur al-) in, 1321
  as leader of Sanusi Order, 1081, 1412
  Nasir (Ahmed Sayf al-) and, 1646
  return from exile (1944), 615
  Sadawi (Bashir) supporting, 1959
  and Wheelus Air Force Base, 2349
  in World War I, 1081
  in World War II, 1081

Idrisids, **1081–1082,** 2059
in Morocco, 1569
Idrisi, Muhammad ibn Ali al- (leader of Idrisids), 1081–1082
Idris, Muhammad ibn, 2114
Idris, Yusuf, **1082–1083,** 2184
Iffat (wife of King Faisal), 166, 172
Iflas aw hubbak darbani (Khraief), 1313–1314
IFLB. *See* Islamic Front for the Liberation of Bahrain
Ifni (Morocco), **1083**
conflicting claims to, 1083
under Moroccan control, 2086
Spanish claim to, 1567
under Spanish control, 2085
Ifrikiya, ma pensée (Zili), 2431
IGADD. *See* Intergovernmental Authority on Drought and Desertification
Ignatiev, Nikolas Pavlovich, **1083–1084**
as advisor to Ottoman Empire, 25
and San Stefano Treaty (1878), 654
Ihqaqi family, 2047
Ihsanoğlu, Ekmeleddin, 757
Ihud
binationalism supported by, 473
Buber (Martin) in, 540–541
Ihud ha-Kibbutzim, 1319
Ihud Leʾumi (Israel). *See* National Union
Ihud movement (Israel), 1461
Ijaza, 1457
Ijma (consensus), 1148
vs. ijtihad, 1149
Iqbal (Muhammad) on, 1109
reform movements rejecting, 2124
society and, 2234
as source of law, 834, 2034
in Sunni Islam, 2123
validity of, 2151
Ijtihad (newspaper), 576
Ijtihad (reasoning from faith), 1490
Abd al-Aziz (ibn Saʿud Al Saʿud) permitting, 1626
vs. ijma, 1149
Iqbal (Muhammad) on, 1109
muftis trained in, 816
qiyas as form of, 1148, 2123
Salafiyya movement on, 1974
Saneʿi (Yusef) obtaining, 1987
Shaltut (Muhammad) on, 2022
in Shiʿism, 2055
society and, 2234
for solving gender problems, 892
for solving modern issues, 834
in Sunni Islam, 2124
validity of, 2151
Zanan (magazine) on, 2423
Ikdam (newspaper), Karacan (Ali Naci) in, 1269
Ikha al-Watani Party (Iraq), **1084**
Hashimi (Yasin al-) in, 1084, 1283
Kashif al-Ghita (Muhammad Husayn) and, 1278
Kaylani (Rashid Ali al-) in, 1084, 1283
Sulayman (Hikmat) in, 80, 1084
Ikham al-Fusul (Baji, al-), 1476
Ikhlassi, Walid, **1084,** 2184
Ikhtilaf, 1148, 2123
Ikhwan (Sanusi brotherhood), 1609–1610
Ikhwan (Saudi Arabia), **1085–1086**
under Abd al-Aziz ibn Saʿud Al Saʿud, 9, 10, 1085, 1626, 2213
ideology of, 1085–1086, 1626
military conquests by, 1085, 1626
Mutayr tribe in, 2213
revolt by (1927–1929), 10, 1085, 1626
sedentarization in, 1085
al-Taʾif occupied by, 1085, 2148
Utayba tribe in, 2214
Wahhabi Islam of, 9, 1085, 1626
Ikhwan al-Muslimin, al- (journal)
Ashmawi (Muhammad Abd al-Rahman Salih al-) in, 321
Qutb (Sayyid) in, 1884
Ikhwan al-Muslimun, al- (organization). *See* Muslim Brotherhood
Ikhwan al-Qassam (Palestinian youth group), 1874
Ikla Aks al Zaman, al- (Nasrallah), 1647
Ila al-Amam (periodical), 1842
Ila Asi (record), 818
Iʿlam, al- (newspaper), 418
Ilan, Amitzur, *as contributor,* 465–466
Ilaysh, Muhammad, **1086**
Iliad (Homer), 275
Arabic translation of, 550
I Like Mike (Meged), 1512
Ilj, Ahmad al-, 2184
Illah, 2123
Illyrians, 383
Ilm, 2146
Ilm al-kalam, 2033, 2154
Ilm al-tawhid, 2033
İlmiyye (Ottoman Empire), **1086–1087,** 1264
ILP. *See* Israel Labor Party
Iltizam (tax farming), 1367, 2623
in Afghanistan, 175
"Image of Women in our Literature, The" (Bint al-Shati), 476
Images from the Qajar Dynasty (Iranian film), 1473
Imaleyene, Fatima Zohra. *See* Djebar, Assia
Imam(s)
belief in authority of, 1148
burial sites of, as Atabat, 328
conflict over succession of, 105, 1148, 1158
definition of, 2623–2624
in Ibadiyya, 1073
as Shiʿite leaders, 104–105
Imama. See Turbans
Imam al-Sadr Foundation, 1961
Imambarah (place for storyteller), 1606
Imam Hatip schools, 761
Imamis. *See* Twelver Shiʿism
Imam jomeh, 2142
Imam Reza shrine, 1498
Imamzadeh, 2624
Iman al-Hadi, Numeiri (Muhammad Jaʿfar) opposed by, 1699
Iman Hatip schools (Turkey), 1545
Iman University, al-, closure of, 2388
Imazighen, 458
Imbabi, Muhammad al-, Ilaysh (Muhammad) as advisor to, 1086
Imber-Goldstein, Martha, *as contributor,* 231–232
Imber, Naphtali Herz, 2424–2425
and Israeli national anthem, 1927
and Zionist anthem, 1007
IMF. *See* International Monetary Fund
Immutability of the Qurʾan, The (Bint al-Shati), 476
Imperial Bank of Persia, 535, 2355
Imperialism, **1087–1091.** *See also* Colonialism
characteristics of, 1088
Christianity in, 1089

cultural, 1090–1091
definition of, 1087, 1088
direct, 1089
decline of, 1090–1091
economic effects of, 1087, 1088–1090
European
in Ottoman Empire, 2162–2163
vs. Ottoman Empire expansion, 1087–1089
forms of, 1089–1090
intelligence services in, 1101
loans leading to financial control in, 1089–1090
motivations for, 1088
origins of, 1087
resistance to, 1090, 1091
Imperial Ottoman Bank, 534
Imperial Ottoman University. *See* Darülfünün
Imperial Service school, 409
Imperial Tobacco Corporation, 2193
Import substitution industrialization (ISI), 1093
in Turkey, 1094
Inalcik, Halil, 1035
Inʿash al-Usra Society (Palestine), 893
Khalil (Samiha Salama) in, 1297–1298
I, Nasruddin Hoca, Never Shall Die (Boratav), 493
INC. *See* Iraqi National Congress
Incendie, L' (Dib), 1426
Incense, **1091**
Inci (magazine), 2067
Income
per capita
in Afghanistan, 54
growth rate of, 73
in Iran, 1115
in Qatar, 1876
of women, 878
Indépendance confisquée, l' (Abbas), 4
Independence Movements in Arab North Africa (al-Fasi), 812
Independence Party. *See* Istiqlal Party
Independence Party (Iraq), 1654
Independent Association for the Triumph of Women's Rights (Algeria), 894, 2195
Independent Bloc (Lebanon), Karame (Abd al-Hamid) in, 1271
Independent Human Rights Commission, 1982
Independent Liberal Party (Israel), 1181, 1184
Kol (Moshe) in, 1332
India
at Bandung Conference, 387
British–French rivalry over, 525
British rule in
and communication, 624
Cox (Percy) in, 645, 646
Curzon (George Nathaniel) in, 651
East India Company as primary instrument for conquering, 525–526
end of (1947), 517
India Office of, 514, 526, 617
Oman impacted by, 203–204
and Pakistani statehood, 1237
and railways, 2420
security in, 513, 524
and Trucial Coast control, 531
and caliphate, 556, 557
freemasonry in, 852
guest workers from, 946
Islam in, Iqbal (Muhammad) on, 1109
Muharram rites in, 1606
National Congress of
Jinnah (Muhammad Ali) and, 1236–1237
separate electorates in, 1236–1237
nuclear capability of, 1696
Pakistan conflict over Kashmir, nuclear threat in, 1696
and Pakistani statehood, 1237
Shiʿism in, 2052
silk from, 2066
Zoroastrianism in, 2440, 2442
Indian Expeditionary Force (IEP), 437
in Mesopotamia Campaign, 1518–1519
Indian Ocean trade, 2197
India Office (Britain), 514, 526, 532, 534, 617
Indo-European Telegraph Company, 624
Indonesia
at Bandung Conference, 387
needle exchange programs in, 714
women in
as head of state, 808
as judges, 808
Indus River, 1032
Industrialization, **1091–1096**. *See also* Modernization
of Algeria, 1095
Oran, 1714
of Armenia, 303
economic liberalization and, 1093, 1094
of Egypt, 1094
failure of, reasons for, 1092–1093
of Iran, 1095
of Iraq, 1094–1095
of Israel, 1095
of Jordan, 1095
of Morocco, 1095–1096
nationalism and, 1093
of Ottoman Empire, 1730
of Qatar, 752
of Saudi Arabia, 752, 1094, 1997
state-led, 1092, 1093
of Tunisia, 1095–1096
of Turkey, 1094
of United Arab Emirates, 752
of Yemen, 2388
Industrial Revolution, and trade, 2198
Indyk, Martin, *749*
Infante maure, L' (Dib), 1426
Infant mortality, 1509, 1845
Infernal Days of Mr. Ayaz, The (Baraheni), 397
Inferno (Dante), 1208
Infibulation, 822
Infitah policy (Egypt), 765–766, **1096–1097**, 1957
Inheritance, of women, 878
in Iraq, 898
in Lebanon, 887
personal status laws on, 887
Shiʿism on, 887
Sunni Islam on, 887
in Tunisia, 2230–2231
In Malkhus fun Tselem (Greenberg), 941
Innocence of the Devil, The (al-Saadawi), 1950
"Innocent, The" (Bint al-Shati), 476
INOC. *See* Iraq National Oil Company
İnönü, Erdal, **1097**, 1098–1099
in Republican People's Party, 2242
in Social Democratic Populist Party, 2077
İnönü, İsmet, **1097–1099**, *1098*
at Adana Conference (1943), 42
as Atatürk's (Mustafa Kemal) successor, 2240

İnönü, İsmet *(continued)*
Bayar (Celal) rivalry with, 415, 1097, 1098
and caliphate, 557
at Lausanne Conference (1923), 1376–1377
multiple political parties legalized by, 1097–1098
political reforms by, 2241
presidency of, 1097–1098
as prime minister, 1097, 1098
in Republican People's Party, 1098, 1918, 1919, 2077
sons of, 1097, 1098–1099
Turkish language reform under, 2413
in World War II, 2371
Inqilab, 2624
Insaniyat society (Iran), Mossadegh (Mohammad) in, 1580
In Search of Omar Khayyam (Dashti), 678
Insolation, L' (Boudjedra), 496
Installation art, 312, 313, 1676, 1687
Institut d'Égypte (Cairo), 492, **1099**
Institut des Hautes Études Cinématographiques (IDHEC) (Paris), 2192
Institut des Hautes Études Marocaines (Morocco), 812
Institute for Current World Affairs (ICWA), 647
Antonius (George) in, 214, 647
Institute for Palestine Studies, **1099**
Khalidi (Walid) in, 1296
Zurayk (Constantine) and, 2443
Institute for the Mothers of the Believers, 892
Institute for the Study of Jewish Communities in the Middle East, 457
Institute for Women's Studies in the Arab World (IWSAW) (Lebanon), 432, **1100**
Institut Egyptien (Alexandria), 1099
Institute of Arab Studies, 421
Institute of Palestine Studies, 1953
Institute of Scientific Information (ISI), 2004
Institute of Turkish Economic History, 407
Institute of Women's Studies (IWS) of Bir Zeit University, **1100–1101**
Intellectual Association of Egyptian Women, 2030
Intelligence Apparatus (Deuxième Bureau) (Lebanon), 1399, 1400
Intelligence organizations, **1101–1105**. *See also specific organizations*
and civil liberties, 1104
in colonial era, 1101
covert operations by, 1103
foreign intervention by, 1103
functions of, 1102–1103
list of, 1104–1105
public knowledge about, 1103–1104
U.S., Bush (George W.) on failures of, 573
Intergovernmental Authority on Drought and Desertification (IGADD), 2104
Interim Agreement (1995). *See* Oslo II
International Alliance of Women (IAW), Egyptian Feminist Union ties with, 227
International Alliance of Women for Suffrage and Equal Citizenship, 2031
International Atomic Energy Agency (IAEA)
inspections in Iraq, 2288
on Iran, 1121
in Iraq, weapons inspections by, 1135, 1136
on Israel, Dimona reactor of, 708
International Bank for Reconstruction and Development (IBRD), 2363–2364
Tharthar Project of, 2183
International Bill of Human Rights, 1048
International Centre for Dialogue Among Civilizations (ICDC), Mohajerani (Ataollah) as director of, 1558
International Commission, on Sabra and Shatila massacres, 1954–1955
International Confederation of Free Trade Unions, 452
International Conference on Population and Development (ICPD), 480
International Congress of Asian and North African Studies, 1723
International Congress of Orientalists, **1723**
International Council for Women, Moghaziel (Laure) on, 1557
International, Dana, **1105–1106**
International Debt Commission, 766, 909, **1106**, 1158
Khayr al-Din in, 1306
International Development Agency (IDA), 2363–2364
International Exhibition Centre (Bahrain), 2196
International Financial Commission
La Marsa Convention ending, 1366
in Tunisia, 1604
in Tunisian financial crisis, 1308
International Islamic News Agency, 1721
International Labor Organization, Awadhi (Badria A. al-) as advisor to, 341
International League against German Antisemitism, 1416
International Monetary Fund (IMF), **1106**
Algeria's agreement with, 917
economic aid from, 747, 749
education measured by, 760
establishment of, 1106
on Iranian economy, 1114–1115
and Morocco, privatization program in, 1569
objectives of, 1106
Tunisia aided by, 2269
International oil companies (IOCs)
competition among, start of, 1825–1826
coordination by, 1824
in joint ventures, 1824–1825
one company/one country pattern of, 1824–1825
posted price system of, 1718
price cuts by, 1718, 1719, 1826
International Olympic Committee, Mzali (Mohammed) on, 1628
International Security Assistance Force (ISAF), in Afghanistan, 2282
International Straits Commission, 2095
International Woman Suffrage Alliance (IWSA), 770, 2031
International Women's Tribune Center, 896
International Women's Year Conference (Mexico City) (1975), 1958

Internet access, 625
"In the City of Slaughter" (Bialik), 470
In the House of Silence: Autobiographical Essays by Arab Women Writers (Faqir), 805
In the Shadows of the City (film), 1500
Intifada (1987–1991), 871, **1106–1109**, *1107, 1108. See also* Aqsa Intifada, al-
  Arafat (Yasir) in, 271
  Bir Zeit University during, 481
  casualties of, 1108
  causes of, 238, 1107, 1792
  escalation of, 238, 1108
  al-Fatah role in, 814, 1108
  and Gaza City's economy, 869
  and Gaza Strip's economy, 870
  and Green Line closure, 942
  HAMAS in, 2177, 2381
    creation of, 983
  Hareven (Shulamit) in, 993
  impact on Israel, 1108
  Islamic Jihad in, 1108, 1155, 2177
  League of Arab States on, *1387*
  objectives of, 1108
  PFLP in, 1108, 1840
  PLO coordination of, 2177
    Dahlan (Muhammad) in, 661
  Rajub (Jibril) in, 1900
  Shamir (Yitzhak) opposing, 2026
  start of, 1107
    PFLP–GC in, 1235
  tactics used in, 1107, 1108
  Wazir (Khalil al-) and, 2335
  in West Bank, 2340
  Women in Black protests in, 2355–2356
  youth movements in, 1108, 2412
Intifada 2000. *See* Aqsa Intifada, al-
Intisar al-Shabab (film), 324
Intrauterine devices (IUDs), 480
Introduction to Muslim Theology (Anawati and Gardet), 194
Invention du désert, l' (Djaout), 716
Investment, foreign
  in Egypt, infitah policy promoting, 1096
  industrialization limited by, 1093
IOCs. *See* International oil companies
Iowa State University, Garang (John) at, 868
IPC. *See* Iraq Petroleum Company
İpekci, Abdi, **1109**
  in *Milliyet*, 1109, 1269
IPRP. *See* Islamic People's Republican Party
Ipsilanti, Alexander, 939
Iqbal, Muhammad, **1109–1110**
  in modernist movements, 1150
  two-nation theory of, 1109
    and Jinnah (Muhammad Ali), 1236
Iqta, 2167
IRA. *See* Irish Republican Army
Irada, 479
Irade (sultan's will), 823
Iradeh-ye Melli Party (Iran), **1110**
Irak (Grobba), 944
Iran, **1110–1122**. *See also specific cities, organizations, people, and regions*
  Abu Musa Island claimed by, 37–38, 2040
  Afghanistan invaded by (1857), 204, 1117
    Treaty of Paris on, 1802
  and Afghan political parties, 64
  Afghan refugees in, 1912
  agriculture in, 902, 1115
  alcohol in, 110
  Anglo–Russian Agreement on (1907), 205
  archaeology in, 276, 277, 481–482
  architecture in, 282
  arms sales to, 2201
    from Britain, 523
    by China, 586
    by United States, 304, 1119, 1122–1123, 1689
  art of, 566, 1615–1616, 1676, 2011
    multimedia, 1676
    Musavi (Mir-Hosain) and, 1615–1616
    by women, 1676
  in Baghdad Pact (1955), 363, 519, 1693, 2291
  Baha'is persecuted by, 365
  Bahrainis supporting, 369
  Bakhtiari in, 374
  Baluchis in, 385–386
  banking in, 390, 392, *393*, 535–536
    Wolff (Henry Drummond) and, 2355
  bast in, 411–412
  bazaars in, 419–421
  blood money law in, 998
  border with Iraq, 140–141, 2043
  British relations with, 1117 (*See also* Anglo–Persian War (1856))
    Curzon (George Nathaniel) in, 651–652
    East India Company and, 526
    economic privileges in, Anglo–Iranian Agreement on (1919), 200
    Jangali and, 1216
    under Mozaffar al-Din Qajar, 1591
    under Naser al-Din Shah, 1644
    oil nationalization and, 518
    Russian rivalry in, 88, 205, 535–536, 1942
    Shuster (W. Morgan) as financial adviser and, 2063–2064
    Tabataba'i (Ziya) supporting British policies, 2142, 2143
    Tobacco Revolt (*See* Tobacco Revolt)
    Tripartite Treaty of Alliance (1942) and, 2216
    Wilson (Arnold T.) and, 2352–2353
    during World War I, 809
  British sphere of influence in, 205, 1118
  bureaucracy of, 1119
  carpets in, 566–567
  Catholics in, 1932
  censorship in
    of education, 761
    of film industry, 832, 833
    of literature, 397, 1435, 1436–1437, 1803
    of press, 1120, 1121, 1299
    of theater, 2186
  in Central Treaty Organization, 573
  chemical and biological weapons of, 1535
  Christians in, 1548
  cities of, 2, 1498, 2070, 2420
    capital, 2169–2170
    desert, 2382
    provincial capitals, 93, 1289–1290, 2057, 2143–2144
    shrine, 1880
  climate of, 902, 1110–1111
  clothing in
    aba, 611
    turbans, 609, 610
  colonialism in, 614
  communication in, 624, 625
  communism in, 41, 625, 626–627
  constitutional revolution in (*See* Constitutional Revolution)
  constitution of (1876), 758
  constitution of (1906), 1383, 1435
    drafting of, 636, 1868
    signing of, 636, 1118

Iran *(continued)*
constitution of (1907), 1383
suspension of (1908), 637
constitution of (1979), 1383
approved in national referendum, 1119
legislative branch in, 1116
velayat-e faqih in, 1311, 1312, 2312, 2313
constitution of, Mozaffar al-Din Qajar and, 1591–1592
cotton industry in, 644, 645, *2181*
Council of Guardians in, 1116
coup in (1908), 1704
coup in (1921), 88, 1118, 1755, 1869, 2143
British role in, 88
Cossack Brigade in, 643
Mossadegh (Mohammad) in, 1580
Tabataba'i (Ziya) in, 1682
coup in (1950), 1536
coup in (1953), 375, 1682
CIA role in, 1937
foreign intervention in, 572, 733, 1103, 1118, 1752
and Iranian Revolution (1979), 1125
National Front influence before and after, 1655–1656
coup in (February 1963), 1065
coup in (November 1963), 1066
coup in (1982), 2036
currency of, reforms in, 185
custody in, 891
defense costs as percentage of GNP or GDP, 1529–1530, *1530*
division into zones (1907), 88, 1118
divorce in, 891, 2051
economy of, 752, 753, *753*, 1114–1115
education in, 756, 1112–1114, 1756
administrative bodies of, 758
first secular school, 1643
monopoly of *ulama* on, 757
new schooling in, 757, 758
under Pahlavi regime, 760
upbringing aspect of, 760
for women, 637, 1113, *1114*
elites in, 776, *776*
ethnic groups in, 1111–1112, 2420
expatriates from, 1117
family planning in, 1111, 1510–1511
feminism in, 428, 745, 892
film industry of, 387–388, 698, 832, 833, 928, 929–930, 1318, 1437
Makhmalbaf family in, 1473
Milani (Tahmineh) in, 1526
new wave in, 1318
fishing industry of, 834
foreign policy of, ideology in, 1300
freemasonry in, 852, 2037
French relations with, Gardanne Mission and, 869
future of, conference in Germany (2000) on, 1121, 1275, 1365
Gardanne Mission in, 869
geography of, 901, 1110
German relations with, 906
gharbzadegi in, 913
government of, 933, 934
guest workers from, 946
guilds in, 947
in Gulf War (1991), neutrality of, 951
higher education in, 761, 2296
Cultural Revolution in, 1114
at Dar al-Fonun, 669, 1867
at Ferdowsi University, 1498
at Isfahan University, 1142
madrasa system of, 1457–1458
at Shiraz University, 2057–2058
at Tabriz University, 2144
at Tehran University, 668–669
history of, Adamiyat (Fereydun) on, 42
hostage crisis in (1979), 567, 1046, *1113*, 1119, 2096, 2293
Bani Sadr (Abolhasan) opposing, 388
Ebtekar (Ma'sumeh) in, 745
and Iran–Contra affair, 1119, 1122
and Iran–Iraq War, 1127
human rights in, 744, 1048
organizations for, 622
public demands for, 1119
immunization programs in, *1509*
industrialization of, 1095, 1115
industry of, in nineteenth century, 1357
infrastructure of, 1756
intelligence organization of (*See* SAVAK)
in Iran–Iraq War (*See* Iran–Iraq War)
and Iraqi Kurds, support for, 1066
Iraqi relations with (*See also* Iran–Iraq War)
Algiers Agreement on (1975), 140–141, 1066–1067, 1119
Bazzaz (Abd al-Rahman al-) and, 423
war (*See* Iran–Iraq War (1980–1988))
on Iraq, U.S. war in (2003), 1301
irrigation in, 74
Islamic coin collections in, 1703
islands of, 1300
Jangali movement in, 1216
Jewish quarters in, 1231
Jews in, 1548
emigration of, 1234
Kurdish revolts in, 1340, 1341
Kurdish revolts supported by, in Iraq, 1134
Kurds in, 694, 914, 1111–1112
military action against, 1536
refugees from Turkey, 1915
labor unions in, 1359, 2222
land reforms in, *1371*, 1372, 1753
languages in, 1111, 1124–1125
Azeri, 347, 1111, 2248
Persian, 1111, 1819–1820
Qashqa'i, 2248
Sistani, 2070
in Lebanese Civil War (1975–1990), 1391
and Lebanon, Hizbullah in, 1037–1038
legal system of, 1116, 1383
reforms to, 1756
legislative body in, 932
literature of (*See* Literature, Persian)
Lurs in, 1447
magazines in, for women, 2423–2424
manufacturing in, 1481–1483, *1483*
map of, *1112*
Marxist guerrilla movements in, 821
military of, 1116
Cossack Brigade in, 643
equipment of, *1534*, 1535
force levels of, *1528–1529*
force structure of, *1532–1533*
in internal conflicts, 1536
reforms to, 1117
minorities or subdominant groups in, 1548, 1549
modernization of, 1756
Malkom Khan (Mirza) in, 1476–1477
under Naser al-Din Shah, 1643–1644
mountains of, 1110, 1316, 2419

Muharram rites in, 1605–1606
music of, 1617–1618, 1619, 2311
in Napoleonic Wars, 816
Naqshbandi order in, 1642
national assembly of (*See* Majles)
nationalism in, 1659–1660
anti-Western aspect of, 205
under Mozaffar al-Din Qajar, 1591
national referenda in, 1118–1119
natural gas production in, *1671*
natural gas reserves in, 1115, *1671*
needle exchange programs in, 714
newspapers and print media of, 1682–1683
newspapers of, 867, 2142, 2143
in Northern Tier, 1692–1693
nuclear capability of, 1698
Pakistan and, 1696
U.S. accusations regarding, 1121
oil nationalization in, 100, 202, 1118, 1752
foreign response to, 1825
Kuwaiti oil after, 1349
Mossadegh (Mohammad) and, 1581
National Front and, 1655–1656
nullification of, 186
oil production in, 752, 1482
by Anglo–Iranian Oil Company, 200–202, 518, 742
Compagnie Française des Pétroles in, 628
Consortium Oil Agreement on (1954), 186
D'Arcy Concession for, 200, 536–537, 671
economic role of, 1115
in Mosul, Anglo–Turkish dispute over (1920–1928), 1582–1583
start of, 2199
oil reserves in, 1115
Oman and, in Dhufar rebellion, 705, 1842
in OPEC, 1719, 1720
opium production in, 725
Ottoman relations with, Zuhab region and, 783
Pakistani alliance with, 1758
parliament of (*See* Majles)
Peace Corps in, 1808
Persian cats in, 1821
and Persian Gulf States, current strains between, 1903
PFLP–GC links with, 1841
PFLP supported by, 1840
poetry of, 97
political ideologies in, 1116–1117
political parties in
suppression of, 1117
women in, 1129
political system of, 1115–1117
clergy in, criticism of, 1262
population growth in, 1111, 2420
population of, 752, *753*, 1110, 1111, 1844, 1845–1846
postage stamps of, 1849, 1850
presidential elections in, 1119, 1120, 1121, 2424
pronatalist policies of, 478, 479
Protestant missions in, 1854
provinces of, 345–346, 1116, 1289–1290, 1312–1313, 1316–1317, 2070
Prussian relations with, 903
Qajar dynasty in (*See* Qajar dynasty (Iran))
radio and television in, *1896*
railways in, *2206*
reform movement in, 1117, 1119–1122, 1303
religions in, 1112 (*See also* Shiʿite Islam *subhead*)
Babi movement, 354–356
Bahaʾi faith, 364, 365
Islam, 1111, 1112
Ismaʿili Shiʿism, 1159
revolutions in (*See* Constitutional Revolution; Iranian Revolution)
riots in (1963), 1118, 1753
riots in (1999), 1120–1121
rivers of, 1316, 2417
rural development in, by Jehad-e Sazandegi, 1220
Russian relations with, 1117 (*See also* Russo–Persian treaties; Russo–Persian wars)
British rivalry in, 88, 205, 535–536
Griboyedov Incident and, 943
under Mozaffar al-Din Qajar, 1591
under Naser al-Din Shah, 1644
post-Soviet, 1944
Shuster (W. Morgan) and, 2063–2064
Turkmanchai Treaty (1828) and, 2251–2252
Russian sphere of influence in, 205, 1118
Saudi relations with, 1999–2000
Mecca riots (1988) and, 1627
science and technology in, 2004, 2005, 2006
secularization in, 891, 1756
Shaykhis persecuted in, 2047
Shiʿite Islam in, 2052, 2054
Akhbari school of, 97–98
conflict with Sunni Islam, 1548
during Ottoman Empire, 1548
as unifying force, 1549
social services in, 809–810
Soroush (AbdolKarim) as advocate of, 2080
Soviet invasion of (1920), 1216
Soviet invasion of (1941), 516, 2144
Soviet occupation of (1941–1946), 346, 1118, 1752
Azerbaijan crisis in, 346
end of, 346, 1118
Soviet relations with
during Cold War, 517
and Iran–Iraq War, 1127
Tripartite Treaty of Alliance (1942) and, 2216
Tudeh Party supported by, 2222
as state sponsor of terrorism, 2175
stock market in, 2091, *2091*
student activism in, 630–631, 1120
suffrage in, universal male, 1144
Syrian relations with, 318, 1291
temporary marriage (*ziwaj mutʿa*) in, 2438
textile industry in, 2066, 2180, 2181, *2181*
theater in (*See* Theater, Persian)
Tobacco Revolt in (*See* Tobacco Revolt)
in trade, 1115, 2198, 2199, *2200*
concessions for, 1117–1118
East India Company and, 525
Trans-Iranian railway in, 2057, 2203–2204
transport in, modern means of, *2207*
tribes in, 374, 385–386, 2213
Tudeh Party supporting, 2222
Tunb Islands controlled by, 2223–2224
ulama in, 2259
United Arab Emirates relations with, 38
Tunb Islands and, 2223–2224
U.S. military personnel in, diplomatic immunity for, 1310–1311
U.S. policy toward
as "Axis of Evil," 1121
dual containment as, 730
Dulles (John Foster) and, 733
under Nixon (Richard Mihous), 1689
Truman Doctrine and, 2291

Iran *(continued)*
U.S. relations with
after September 11 attacks, 1121
twin pillars policy and, 2255
U.S. war on terrorism supported by, 1121
velayat-e faqih in, 2311–2313
water resources in
foggaras (tunnels) for, 2328
freshwater withdrawals, *2331*
quantity of, 2330
Westernization in, 1118, 2341
White Revolution in (1961–1963), 2351–2352
women in
activist organizations of, 2358
as activists, 1899
advocate for rights of, 998
as artists, 1676, 1899
Constitutional Revolution impact on, 637
economic status of, *877*
education for, 637, 880, *882*, 1113, *1114*
as filmmakers, 387–388
government bureau on, 1123
hijab (veil) worn by, 1027
Islamic Revolution and, 1922
as judges, 744
as lawyers, 2051
magazine for, 2423–2424
in political parties, 1129
in politics, 428, 745, 891, 892, 894, 1364–1365, 2153
religious rituals of, 2360
seminary for, 187
in sporting events, 1154
suffrage for, 1471
in universities, 2296
as writers, 427, 811, 1435, 1899
women's rights in, *890*, 891
limitations on, 874
Sane'i (Yusef) on, 1987
within *shari'a* framework, 1970
World Bank and, capital stock and voting power in, *2363*
in World War I, 88, 1118, 1869
and British sympathies, 809
German troops in, 906
South Persia Rifles in, 2083
in World War II
Allied occupation of, 2216
Allies removing Pahlavi (Reza), 2143
neutrality of, 1757
in (Franklin Delano) recognition of contributions of, 1935
Zoroastrianism in, 2382, **2440–2441**
Iran–Contra affair, 1046, **1122–1123**, 1908
arms sales in, 1119, 1122–1123
covert intelligence activities in, 1103
Israel in, 1322
Kimche (David) in, 1322
Iran-e Novin Party, Hoveyda (Amir Abbas) in, 1047
Iran-e now (newspaper), 1682
Iran Freedom Movement. *See* Freedom Movement (Iran)
Iranian Bureau of Women's Affairs, **1123**
Iranian Family Protection Act (1967), 1383
Iranian Islamic Women's Institute, 2153
Iranian languages, **1124–1125**
geographic distribution of, 1124–1125
grammar of, 1125
Iranian Nationality and the Persian Language (Meskoob), 1437
Iranian New Wave, 833
Iranian Revolution (1979), **1125–1127**, 1536
Al-e Ahmad (Jalal) in, 110
Amini (Ali) in, 186
anjoman (assembly) in, 207
Bahrain supporting, 368
Bakhtiar (Shapur) in, 1126–1127
bazaar as political base during, 420
Carter (Jimmy) and, 1119, 1754
casualties of, 1119
causes of, 1125
Committee for Defense of Freedom and Human Rights in, 622
and education, 1552
Feda'iyan-e Khalq in, 821
Freedom Movement in, 421, 850, 1126
Ganji (Akbar) in, 867
guilds in, 947
human rights in, 1119, 1754
and Iran–Iraq War, 1127
Khomeini (Ruhollah) in, 1125–1126, 1311
land ownership after, 1372
legal system after, 1383
majles (parliament) after, 1471–1472
marja al-taqlid in, 1490
martial law declared before, 1126
Mojahedin-e Khalq in, 1562
monarchy ended by, 1125
Montazeri (Hosayn Ali) in, 1564
Motahhari (Mortaza) in, 1583
Muharram and, 1605, 1606
and music, 1618
National Front in, 1126, 1656
nationalism in, 1660
newspapers and print media in, 1682–1683
and oil prices, 1719
origins of, 1125
Pahlavi (Mohammad Reza) in, 1125–1126
actions leading to, 1125
fall of, 1126, 1311
response to uprisings by, 1126
Rahnavard (Zahra) in, 1899
Revolutionary Guards as guardians of, 1921–1922
rural development after, 1220
start of, 1119, 1311
Taleqani (Azam) in, 2153
Tehran in, 2170
Tudeh Party in, 2222
ulama in, 2259
velayat-e faqih (governance of jurists) in, 1490, 2312
violence in Qom leading to, 1119, 1126, 1880
women in, 891
worker strikes in, 1126
Iranian Students' Association in the United States (ISAUS), 630
Irani, George E., *as contributor*, 265–266, 329, 432, 589–593, 645, 975, 997–998, 1038–1039, 1272, 1322, 1395, 1474, 1475–1476, 1477–1478, 1488–1489, 1520–1521, 1653, 1656–1657, 1661, 1852–1853, 1888, 1928, 1951, 2065, 2148, 2255, 2310, 2422
Iran–Iraq War (1980–1988), **1127–1129**, 1538
Abadan (Iran) during, 2, 1127
air power in, 1128
arms sales during
by China, 586
by Germany, 907
and Baghdad, 361
Bani Sadr (Abolhasan) in, 388
Basra during, 410, 411, *1128*
casualties of, 1120, 1128, 1129, 1134, 1538, 1845–1846
causes of, 1127
cease-fires in, 1127
chemical weapons in, 1067, 1128, 1129, 1538

cities attacked in, 1120, 1127
costs of, 1538
economic impact of, 1134
Fao Peninsula occupation, 804, 1128
and Gulf Crisis (1990–1991), 1985
Gulf of Oman in, 952
Hussein (Saddam) in, 1067, 1134
industrialization after, 1095
international isolation of Iran in, 1127
Iraqi debt after, 949
Iraqi Kurdish resistance in aftermath of, 1915
Jordan in, 357
Kharg Island bombed during, 1300
Khorramshahr (Iran) in, 1127
Khuzistan province (Iran) in, 1317
land mines laid during, 1510
League of Arab States on, *1387*, 1388
as literary catalyst, 1429
Marzouki (Moncef) on, 1496
Mojahedin-e Khalq's alliance with Iraq in, 1562
Nabavi (Behzad) in, 1630
and oil trade, 2201
and OPEC, political divisions in, 1720
Pakistani neutrality in, 1758
pronatalist policies during, 479
Revolutionary Guards in, 1922
as sacred defense *vs.* jihad, 1236
and Saudi Arabia, 795, 796, 2000
Shatt al-Arab control during, 411, 2043
Shiʿite opposition during, 978
siege warfare in, 1120
Soviet policy during, 1943
start of, 1120, 1127
Syria in, 2135
Syrian position on, 318
Talfa (Adnan Khayr Allah) in, 2154
tanker war in, 1128
Tehran in, 2170
Tudeh Party in, 2222
Tunisia and, LTDH against pro-Iraqi stance of, 1416
United Nations in, 2280
UN Resolution 598 ending, 1120, 1128–1129, 2280
Pérez de Cuéllar (Javier) and, 1818
U.S. in
intelligence provided by, 1103
oil tankers escorted by, 1120
policy during, 1908
as war of attrition, 1128
Iran Novin Party, **1129**
dissolution of, 1129
platform of, 1129
women in, 1129
Iranology, 539–540
Iranshahr (Baluchistan), 385, 2070
Iran–United States Claims Tribunal, Nabavi (Behzad) as Iranian representative to, 1630
Iraq, **1129–1136**. *See also specific cities, organizations, people, and regions*
agriculture in, 410
dates in, 678–679
ancient civilizations of, 1131
anti-Saddam uprisings in, after Gulf War, 1068
antisemitism in, Farhud (1941), 807–808
in Arab–Israel War (1948), 242–243, 1537
in Arab–Israel War (1967), 248, 287
Arab nationalism in, 801
archaeology in, 276, 277, 279
architecture in, 282
Armenian genocide in, 294
arms sales to, 2201
by Britain, 523
by China, 586
by Soviet Union, 304, 1535, 1969
by United States (1954), 1693
art of, 1978–1979
avant-garde, 997
cultural identity in, 313
exhibitions on, 337, 805
multimedia, 205–206
by women, 337
Assyrians in, 326, 2056
Atabat (holy places) in, 328
in Baghdad Pact (1955), 363, 519, 1693, 1872, 2291
withdrawal of, 363, 573, 1133
banking in, 390, *393*
Baʿth party in (*See* Baʿth party (Iraq))
at Bludan Conference (1937), 488
borders of
with Iran, 140–141, 2043
with Saudi Arabia, 10, 1678
Uqayr Treaty on (1922), 159
British mandate in (1920–1932), 512, 514, 1132, 1480
Abu al-Timman (Jaʿfar) against, 35
Anglo–Iraqi treaties on, 202–203
Arabs in, 222
Baghdad, 361
Basra, 411
Cairo Conference on (1921), 554
Colonial Office administration of, 514, 617
Cox (Percy) in, 202, 646
end of (1932), 35, 515, 802, 1967
Faisal I ibn Hussein in, 35, 202, 646, 801–802, 824–825, 1441
Farhud, 808
Glubb (John Bagot) in, 921–922
land ownership in, 1371
League of Nations recommendation for, 1583
monarchic form of government during, 933
and oil concessions, 538
Saʿdun (Abd Al-Muhsin al-) opposing, 1961
San Remo Conference (1920) on, 1988
"second occupation," 999
Sèvres Treaty (1920) on, 2015
Sykes-Picot Agreement (1916) on, 2128
withdrawal of, 615
British occupation of, in World War I, 1132
and British Petroleum, negotiations with, 1023
British power in, 515
reestablishment in 1941, 1132
revolt against (1920), 35, 512
revolt against (1941), 15, 35–36, 1205, 1210 (*See under* Kaylani, Rashid Ali al-)
chemical and biological weapons of, 1535, 1539–1540
chemical weapons used by, in Iran–Iraq War, 1128, 1129
Chinese relations with, 586, 587
cholera in, 714
cities of, 1131, 1325, 1346, 1582, 1980–1981, 2189
bombing, during Gulf Crisis (1990–1991), 1985
capital, 358–362
holy, 1637
Kurdish, 2115
port, 410–411, 1130
climate of, 1130
clothing in
sidara, 611
women's, *609*, 610

Iraq *(continued)*
communication in, 624, 625
communism in, 625, 626, 627
constitution of, provisional (2004), 2071, 2326
cotton industry in, *2181*
coup in (1936), 35, 776, 999, 2065, 2115
Ahali group in, 80
coup in (1941), 35–36, 999
coup in (1958), 15, 288, 413, 520, 776, 1133, 1872, 1969
Hashimite monarchy overthrown in, 1000
Mala'ika (Nazik al-) on, 1475
National Democratic Party in, 1654
coup in (1959), attempted, 1133, 1873
coup in (1963), 288, 377, 412, 413, 422, 1134, 1873, 2189
coup in (1968), 377, 413, 1134, 2189
coup in (1979), 378
debt of, after Iran–Iraq War (1980–1988), 949
defense costs as percentage of GNP or GDP, *1530*
disease in, 714
economic and military aid to, 748
economy of, 752, 753
Bazzaz (Abd al-Rahman al-) and, 422
Iran–Iraq War and, 1134
Sa'id (Nuri al-) and, 1968
sanctions and, 1987
statistics on, *753*
during World War II, 1968
education in
economic sanctions and, 1986
expansion of, 1132, 1133
under Faisal I ibn Hussein, 801
missionary schools in, 1552
Sa'id (Nuri al-) and, 1968
for women, 1310
Egyptian relations with, Qasim (Abd al-Karim) and, 1872
Egyptian unification with, agreement on, 288
elites in, 776
emigration from, 1068
establishment of, after World War I, 1129
ethnic groups in, 1130–1131
family planning in, 478
feminism in, 892
foreign policy of, 1872
nonalliance, 1133
French relations with, 1066
futuwwa in, 860–861
geography of, 902–903, 1130
German relations with
German support for pan-Arab groups, 906
Grobba (Fritz Konrad Ferdinand) and, 944
Jamali (Muhammad Fadhil al-) and, 1213
in Greater Syria plan, 824–826
guest workers from, 946
in Gulf Crisis (1990–1991) (*See* Gulf Crisis)
in Gulf War (1980–1988) (*See* Iran–Iraq War)
Hashimite monarchy in, 1000
higher education in, 1029
at Baghdad University, 364
in *madrasa* system, 1458
human rights in, 1048
immunization rate in, 1510
independence of (1932), 515, 802, 1132, 1480, 1967
industrialization of, 1094–1095
infant mortality rate in, 1509
infrastructure of, 1134
after Gulf War (1990–1991), 1135
inheritance in, 898
intelligence services of, 1102
Iranian relations with
Algiers Agreement on (1975), 140–141, 1066–1067, 1119
Bazzaz (Abd al-Rahman al-) and, 423
war (*See* Iran–Iraq War (1980–1988))
in Iran–Iraq War (*See* Iran–Iraq War)
irrigation in, 74
Tharthar project for, 2182–2183
Islamic movement in, 1068
Israeli relations with
Hussein (Saddam) threatening Israel (1990), 949–950
Osirak reactor destruction and, 426
Jesuits in, 1029
Jews in, 1232, *1232*, 2079
immigration to Israel, 49, 188, 790, 1030, 1913
leadership of, 1023
during World War II, 807–808, 1233
Jordan federation, 826, 999, 1925, 1969
Jordanian relations with
Aqaba in, 217
Badran (Mudar) and, 357
Kurdish revolts in, 1134, 1340–1341
by Barzani (Mustafa), 1341, 1873
Talabani (Jalal) in, 2151
Kurds in (*See under* Kurd(s))
Kuwait claimed by
British troops as deterrent against, 520
Bubiyan Island, 541, 949
under Qasim (Abd al-Karim), 1873
al-Warba Island, 541, 949
Kuwaiti negotiations with, Ibrahim (Izzat) in, 1078
Kuwait invaded by (*See* Gulf War (1990–1991))
labor unions in, 1358
land mines in, 1510
land reforms in, 1372
languages in, 1131
Arabic, 233
Iranian, 1124
Turkmen, 2248
in League of Arab States, 1386, 1387, 1388
in League of Nations
admission of, 35, 802, 1132
and Anglo–Iraqi treaties, 203
in Lebanese Civil War (1975–1990), 1391
legal system of, 886
civil code, 1382
French influences on, 1380
Majalla, 1381, 1382
legislative body in, 932
literature of, 344, 416, 1421–1422, 1475, 1703–1704, 1903, 2002, 2043–2044, 2419
at London Conference (1939), 1445
malnutrition in, due to economic sanctions, 1136, 1986
Mamluk rulers of, 1478–1479
manufacturing in, 1481–1483, *1483*
map of, *1133*
Marsh Arabs of, 1496
Mauritania and, 1744–1745
as Mesopotamia, 1129–1130
military of, 949, 953, *1527*
equipment of, *1534*, 1535
force levels of, *1528–1529*, 1530–1531
force structure of, *1532–1533*
in internal conflicts, 1530–1531, 1536
Jordanian civil war and, 1246, 1247

organization of, 1527
role of, 1541
mountains of, 1325
music of, 1617–1618, 1619, *1619*
natural gas production and reserves in, *1671*
neutral zone shared with Saudi Arabia, 1678
newspapers of, 1525
government-controlled, 1680
No-Fly Zone of, creation of, 1135, 1339
nuclear capability of, 305, 1535, 1696, 1698
Osirak reactor and, 1535, 1698
and U.S. invasion (2003), 1698, 2324
nuclear weapons of, Osirak reactor and, 1724
Oil-for-Food Program in, 1069, 1135, 1339, 1720, 1986–1987
oil nationalization in, 1134, 1139
oil production in, 752, 1131, 1482
in Basra, 410
French–British rivalry over control of, 2199
after Gulf War, 1720
by Iraq Petroleum Company, 1131, 1138–1139
oil reserves in, 1131
oil revenues in, 1968
and Gulf War, 1134
in OPEC, 1138, 1719, 1720
origin of name, 1129
in Ottoman Empire, 1132
administration of, 1132
Baghdad, 360
Basra, 411
Land Code of 1858 effects, 1368, 1369
pan-Arabism in, 1799
plains of, 1272
PLO support for, 1775, 1793
population of, *753*, 1130–1131, 1844, 1845–1846
postage stamps of, 1849, 1850
prison camps in, *1089*
pronatalist policies of, 479
public health in, economic sanctions and, 1986
Qasim regime in, people's courts under, 1462
radio and television in, 1894, *1895*
railways in, 2206, *2206*
Ramadan Revolution (1963) in, Tikriti (Hardan al-) in, 2190
reforms in, Bazzaz (Abd al-Rahman al-) and, 422
refusing to attend Lausanne Conference (1949), 1375
regions of, 804
religions in, 1130
Baha'i faith, 365
Catholicsm, 1931–1932
Christianity, *592*, 738
Salafiyya movement, 1974
Sufism, *2112*
rivers of, 2188, 2328, 2417
dams on, 732–733
Rumaytha Rebellion (1935) in, 2065
Russian relations with, post-Soviet, 1944
Saudi Arabian relations with, 796
oil export, 2203
science and technology in, 2004, 2006
scout movement in, 2006
Shawwaf uprising (1959) in, 421
Shi'ite Islam in, 1548, 2052, 2054, 2070–2071
Shi'ite population in, Iranian Revolution and, 1067
Shi'ites in, 410
Soviet relations with, 1943
under Hussein (Saddam), 1066
under Qasim (Abd al-Karim), 1872, 1969
stock market in, *752*
Sunni Islam in, 1981
Shi'ite resistance to, Najaf, al- as center of, 1637
traditional dominance of, 1547
Sunni–Shi'ite conflict in, 1530–1531
Syrian relations with, 318
Baghdad Summit (1978) and, 364
Hussein (Saddam) and, 378
proposed union, 1032
Tabaqa Dam dispute, 788, 2141
terrorism in, 1540
textile industry in, 2066, *2181*
theater in, 2184
in trade, 2198, *2200*
Baghdad as center of, 360
Basra and, 410
transport in, modern means of, *2207*
tribes in, 1961–1962, 2212, 2214
at Tripoli Conference, 2217
Turkish relations with
Bazzaz (Abd al-Rahman al-) and, 423
dispute over dams, 788, 2082
oil pipelines in, 115–116
UN economic sanctions against (*See* Sanctions, Iraqi)
United Arab Emirates relations with, 2272
United Arab Republic and, 288, 826, 1969, 2273
UN relations with
under Annan (Kofi A.), 209
economic sanctions, 1068
Oil-for-Food Program, 1069
weapons inspections, 1069, 1539, 1698, 2288–2289, 2323, 2324
UN Resolution 1441 on, 2324–2325
U.S. attack on (1998), 2323
U.S. bombing of (1993), 1135
U.S. bombing of (1996), 1135
U.S. bombing of (1998), 1135
U.S. describing state terrorism in, 2175
U.S. dual containment policy toward, 730
U.S. relations with, Operation Desert Fox, 1069, 2288
U.S. war in (2003), 549, 1069–1070, 1136, 1539–1540, 1540, **2323–2327**, 2325–2326
Annan (Kofi A.) and, 209
and Arab nationalism, 222–223
archaeological artifacts in, 279
armed resistance to, 2326
Baghdad surrendering in, 362
Bendjedid (Chadli) criticizing, 445
British support for, 2324
Bush (George W.) in, 2323–2325
Chalabi (Ahmad) and, 578
China on, 587
CIA in, 573
coalition forces in, 2325
al-Da'wa al-Islamiyya after, 681
direct elections proposed in, 2326
Germany opposing, 907
global opposition to, 2324
and Hussein (Saddam) removed from power, 2189
Ibrahim (Izzat) in, 1078
Iranian reaction to, 1301
Iraqi National Congress in, 1137
al-Jazeera coverage of, 1219
Jordanian support for, 32
Kurdish forces in, 1339, 1341
League of Arab States on, *1387*, 1388–1389
looting during, 2325

Iraq *(continued)*
military operations in, 2325
neoconservatives in, 1136
Powell (Colin) in, 1852
prewar intelligence failures and, 2326
Protestant missions in, 1855
Qatar in, 1877
Russian position on, 1944
Samarra, 1981
search for weapons in, 1070
shifting rationale for, 2324
Shiʿite Islam under, 1637
Sistani (Ali al-) on, 2071
sovereignty transfer in, 2326
Spain supporting, 2084
start of, 1136
United Nations in, 2282–2283
UN on legality of, 1136
UN weapons inspections before, 1136
violence following, 1070
war crimes in, commission investigating, 1950
water resources in, 2328
freshwater withdrawals, *2331*
quantity of, 2330
under Sumerians, 2328
Wathba uprising in, 1210
weapons of mass destruction in, 1987
German involvement in, 907
identification and elimination of, as principal condition for lifting sanctions, 1135, 1985
UN inspections of, 1135, 1136, 1986, 2282–2283
U.S. unable to find, 2283
women in
charitable organization for, 2361–2362
economic status of, *877*
education for, 1310
improving situation of, 898
as judges, 808
umbrella organization for, 1137–1138
World Bank and, capital stock and voting power in, *2363*
in World War I, 2367
Basra, 411
British occupation of, 1132
British-Ottoman fighting in, 509
in World War II, 15
Arab Legion and, 257
British troops in, 1968
and economy, 1968
Kaylani revolt (1941) in (*See* Kaylani, Rashid Ali al-)

Iraqi Arabic language, 233
Iraqi Governing Council, 2325–2326
Chalabi (Ahmad) in, 578
Pachachi (Adnan) in, 1751
Iraqi Museum, 1978
Iraqi National Congress (INC), **1136–1137**
Chalabi (Ahmad) in, 578, 1137
platform of, 1137
U.S. role in, 1137
Iraqi National Museum (Baghdad), 277, 279
Iraqi Women's Federation. *See* General Federation of Iraqi Women
Iraqi Women's Union, **1137–1138**
objectives of, 1137
projects of, 1137–1138
Iraq Liberation Act (U.S., 1998), 578, 1136
Iraq Museum, Islamic numismatics in, 1702
Iraq National Oil Company (INOC), 410
establishment of, 1138
Iraq Petroleum Company (IPC), 538, **1138–1139**
concessions to, 1131, 1138
creation of, 1910
establishment of, 1131, 1138
Iraqi conflicts with, 1138
nationalization of, 1066, 1139
oil pipelines of, 1138
pipeline protection for, 2353
in Red Line Agreement (1928), 1824
Saʿid (Nuri al-) and, 1968
territory taken from, by Law Number 80, 1133, 1138, 1872–1873
Iraq–Turkey pipeline. *See* Trans-Turkey Pipeline
Iraq War (2003). *See* Iraq, U.S. war in
Irbid (Jordan), **1139**
under Ottoman rule, 1139
population of, 1139
Yarmuk University in, 1138, 2380
Ireland, Jews in, 1022
Irgun Zvaʾi Leʾumi (IZL), **1139–1140**, 2438
Acre Prison broken into by (1947), 1140
Altalena of, sinking of (1948), 169–171, 425, 1140
in Arab–Israel War (1948), 242
Avnery (Uri) in, 340
Begin (Menachem) in, 170, 424–425, 1139, 1209
British execution of militants of, 424–425, 1140
cooperating with Britain, 1442
Dayr Yasin massacre by (1948), 684, 1443
disbanding of, 1140
establishment of, 972, 1139, 1209
French arms sales to, 170
Greenberg (Uri Zvi) supporting, 941
Haganah opposing, 1140
incorporation into Israel Defense Force, 170, 1140
Israeli military action against, 1536
Israeli recognition of, 1140
Jabotinsky (Vladimir Zeʾev) in, 1209
King David Hotel bombing by (1946), 1140, 1324
Lohamei Herut Yisrael split from, 1139
Mossad operations against, 992
revolt against Britain, 1139–1140, 1443
Saison against, 1973
Shamir (Yitzhak) in, 2025
Stern (Abraham) in, 1442, *1442*, 2090
Tamir (Shmuel) in, 2159
terrorist acts of, 424–425, 1139–1140
Weizman (Ezer) in, 2336
in World War II, 1139
Yellin-Mor (Natan) in, 2384
Irish Republican Army (IRA), PFLP ties with, 1839
Iron-clad warships, origins of, 1741
Iron Hand (Syria), 2021
IRP. *See* Islamic Republican Party
Irrigation
drip, 74–75, 2331
in Egypt, 74, 763
from Aswan High Dam, 327
Baring (Evelyn) developing, 404, 405, *406*
environmental impact of, 74
falaj system of, 1204
in Iran, 74
in Iraq, 74
Tharthar project for, 2182–2183
in Israel, 1248, 1668–1669, 2331
in Jordan, 1240, 1243
from Jordan River, 1248

land area using, 74
in Morocco, 74, 913
from Nile River, 690, 763
recycled sewage for, 1668, 2329–2330
in Saudi Arabia, 702
in Sudan, 908
in Syria, 787, 909, 2140–2141
in Turkey, 74, 787, 2082, 2141
Irshad An-Niswaan (journal), **1140**
Ir Shalem (Israel), 1809
Irtihalat al-Lu'lu (al-Bihayri), 1994
Irtihal wa Zafir al-Mawj, al- (Bin Diyaf), 474
Irwell, Henrietta, in Women's International Zionist Organization, 2357
Iryani, Abd al-Rahman al-, **1140–1141**
Ahmar (Abdullah ibn Husayn al-) supporting, 89
coup against, 984, 1140
exile of, 1141, 2393
government of, Amri (Hasan al-) in, 192
republican-royalist reconciliation under, 1140, 2392, 2393
state-building by, 2393
Isa, Elias al-, 1141
Isa, Emile al-, 1141
ISAF. *See* International Security Assistance Force
Isa family, al-, **1141**
Isa ibn Ali (ruler of Bahrain), 531
Isa, Isa Da'ud al-, 1141
Isa, Michel al-, 1141
Isa, Raja al-, 1141
Isa, Raymond al-, 1141
ISAUS. *See* Iranian Students' Association in the United States
Isawiyya Brotherhood, Meknes as sacred city of, 1515
Isawiyya Brotherhood (Isawa), **1141**
Isa, Yusuf al-, 1141
Is Bank (Turkey), 1482
Isfahan (Iran), **1141–1142**
Afghan siege of (1722), 1141
architecture of, 1141, 1142
bazaars of, 420
as capital, 1141, 1142
carpet weaving in, 566
Catholics in, 1932
Isfahan University in, 1142
Karbaschi (Gholamhosain) as governor of, 1273
manufacturing in, 1093, 1142
population of, 1142
Protestant missions in, 1854
Tobacco Revolt in, 2193
Zell al-Soltan as governor of, 2430
Isfahan Is Half the World (Jamalzadeh), 1214
Isfahan University, **1142**
Isfara'ini, Abu Ishaq al-, 2019
Ishaaq, Kamala Ibrahim, **1142–1143**
Ishaq, Adib, **1143**
Ishq wa al-Mawt fi al-Zaman al-Harrashi, al- (Wattar), 2333
Ishtiraki, al- (magazine), Aziz (Tariq) in, 350
Ishto ha-Senu'ah (Burla), 547
ISI. *See* Import substitution industrialization; Institute of Scientific Information
Isis temple, on Philae island, 1832
Iskandari, Iraj, 2222
Iskat ha-Shokolada (Guri), 956
Iskenderun (Syria), 2129
Iskilli Memo (Kasap), 1277
Iskra (Egypt), 627, 651
Islahat Fermani (Reform Edict) (1856), reinforcing Paris Peace (1856), 740
Islah Party (YIP) (Yemen), **1143**
Ahmar (Abdullah ibn Husayn al-) in, 90, 1143, 2389
after civil war (1994), 1143, 2390
as coalition, member groups in, 1143
electoral success of, 90, 1143, 2389
leadership of, 2389
al-Qa'ida links to, 1143
Islah Taleban Party (Iran), **1144**
Islaih, Khaled, *as contributor,* 873–879, 1003, 2334
Islam, **1144–1150**. *See also* Shi'ite Islam; Sunni Islam
Allah in, 150, 1145
antisemitism and, 212
and Arabic language, 221, 232, 1419
among Arabs, 220, 221
in architecture, 280, 282–284
art of
historical, 310
modern, 312
representations in, 311–312
in Balkan Peninsula, 383
beginning of, 1595–1596
beliefs of, 1145
on birth control, 478, 479–480
circumcision in, 601
conversion to, requirement for, 1145
cradle of, Hijaz as, 1028
cultural history of, 1147–1148
Amin (Ahmad) on, 183
preservation and publication by Madkour (Ibrahim), 1456–1457
divorce or widowhood in, 1495
education in, *madrasa* system for, 1457–1458
and education women, 880–882
ethics of, 1145–1147
five pillars of, 1145
fundamentalist (*See* Fundamentalism)
vs. Hellenism, 1148
holy cities of, 1511–1512
Mecca, 1506–1507
and Holy Land, 1043
imams in, belief in authority of, 1148
in India, Iqbal (Muhammad) on, 1109
in Iran, 1111, 1112
in Israel, 1163
in Jordan, 1242–1243
Kharijite sect of
Azariqa branch of, 1073
Ibadiyya branch of, 1073
law of (*See Fiqh; Shari'a*)
mahdi in, 1462–1463, 1519
Mecca as spiritual center of, 1597
modernist movements in, 1149–1150
in Morocco, 1567–1569
mysticism in, 1149
and nationalism, 1659, 1660
origins of, 221
in Ottoman Empire, 1731
as unifying factor, 1089
Palestine in, 1758
philosophical developments in, 1148
polygamy in, 1839
in postage stamps, 1850
prayer in, 222
progressive, 2145
prohibitions of, 1144
Protestant missions targeting, 1854–1856
Qur'an in, role of, 1145, 1883
radical (*See* Islamism)
reform movements in, 1149
rise of, 1144
and trade, 2197

Islam *(continued)*
ruler of, caliphate as, 556–557
in Saharan Arab Democratic Republic, 1964
Salafiyya movement in, 1923
schisms in, 1148
science and, Mahmud (Mustafa) on, 1469
Second Message of, 1917
vs. secularism, 2342
Shaltut (Muhammad) on principles of, 2022
spread of, 221, 1144
Sufi orders and, 2113, 2114
theology of, 1145
in Tunisia, 2226
in Turkey, 2238
in United Arab Emirates, 2270
on Western interventions, 1150
women in
access to mosques restricted, 2359, *2360*
religious rituals of, 2359–2361
in Yemen, 2388
in San'a, 1983
Zaydan (Jurji) on, 2426
Islam (newspaper), 1682
Islam and Democracy (Mernissi), 1518
Islam and the State (Khalid), 1297
Islamic Action Front (IAF) (Jordan), **1150–1151**
electoral success of, 1151
Muslim Brotherhood and, 1150–1151
Islamic Association of Afghanistan. *See* Jami'at-e Islami (Afghanistan)
Islamic canon, *Zanan* (magazine) on, 2423–2424
Islamic Center (Hamburg), 427
Khatami (Mohammad) in, 1303
Islamic Character (Bint al-Shati), 476
Islamic civilization, 1035
Islamic coins, study of (numismatics), 1701–1703
Islamic Conference of Foreign Ministers
establishment of, 1721
Kuala Lumpur Declaration on International Terrorism by (2002), 1722
and Organization of the Islamic Conference, 1722
Islamic Conference of Kings and Heads of State, first (1969), 1721
Islamic congresses, **1152–1154**
in Jerusalem (1931), Rida (Rashid) in, 1923
Islamic Council (Afghanistan). *See* Shura-ye Ittifagh-e Islami
Islamic Countries' Solidarity Sport Council, 998
Islamic Countries Women Sport Solidarity Games (1992, 1997), **1154**
Islamic Development Bank, 749, 1153, 1721
Islamic Educational, Scientific, and Cultural Organization, 1721
Islamic feminism, 891–892
Zanan (magazine) and, 2423
Islamic finance, 394
Islamic Front (Afghanistan). *See* Mahaz-e Islami
Islamic Front for the Combat of Jews and Crusaders. *See also* Qa'ida, al-
establishment of, 1865
Islamic Front for the Liberation of Bahrain (IFLB), 369–370
Islamic governments, 934
Islamic Guidance Society (Bahrain), 369
Islamic Jihad, 983, **1154–1155**
Arafat (Yasir) and, 272, 1155
assassinations of militants from, 983
attacks by, 1155
and HAMAS, 983
HAMAS rivalry with, end of, 1155
internal conflict in, 1155
in Intifada (1987–1991), 1108, 1155, 2177
origins of, 1154–1155
Palestinian Authority crackdown on, 1155
peace process opposed by, 1155
suicide bombings by, 219, 1155
in Jerusalem, 1226, 1227
Islamic law. *See Shari'a*
Islamic Liberation Organization (Egypt), in al-Jami'a al-Islamiyya, 1215
Islamic Medical Organization (IMO), 1508
Islamic medicine, 1508
Islamic Movement (Israel), in United Arab List, 1189
Islamic movements. *See also* Islamism; *specific groups*
in Afghanistan, 60–62, 1215
political parties of, 62–63
in Algeria
political parties of, 126, 133–134
and women's rights, 136
in Bahrain, 369–370
Islamic Muhammad Union (Turkey), Nursi (Said) in, 1704
Islamic Nationalist party (Egypt), 2405
Islamic Party (Afghanistan). *See* Hezb-e Islami
Islamic People's Republican Party (IPRP), 2036
Islamic Republican Party (IRP) (Iran)
Beheshti (Mohammad) in, 428
Khamenehi (Ali) in, 1299
Musavi-Ardebili (AbdolKarim) in, 1615
Musavi (Mir-Hosain) in, 1615
Rafsanjani (Ali Akbar Hashemi) and, 1899
Islamic Republic of Mauritania. *See* Mauritania
Islamic Research Academy, 2022
Islamic Resistance Movement. *See* HAMAS
Islamic Revolutionary Movement (Afghanistan). *See* Harakat-e Inqilab-e Islami
Islamic Salvation Army (AIS) (Algeria), **1155–1156**
amnesty for members, 1156
disbanding, 504, 1156
establishment of, 134, 135, 1155
evolution of, *1156*
and GIA, 919, 1155, 1156
guerrilla warfare by, 1156
insurrection against military by, 126
in negotiations with government, 1156
in truce with government, 1156
Islamic Salvation Front (Algeria). *See* Front Islamique du Salut
Islamic Society (Afghanistan). *See* Jami'at-e Islami
Islamic Society (Egypt). *See* Jami'a al-Islamiyya, al-
Islamic Society (Iran). *See* Jam'iat Motalefeh Islami
Islamic State Movement (MEI) (Algeria), 919
Islamic States Broadcasting Organization, 1721

Islamic Student Association
Kharrazi (Kamal) in, 1300
Qotbzadeh (Sadeq) in, 1881
Islamic Tendency Movement. *See* Mouvement de Tendance Islamique
Islamic Union (Afghanistan). *See* Harakat-e Islami; Ittihad-e Islami
Islamic University of Medina, **1156–1157**, 1511
Islamic Vanguard (Egypt), in al-Jamiʿa al-Islamiyya, 1215
Islamic Women Sport Solidarity Council, 1154
Islamic Youth (Afghanistan). *See* Javanan-e Muslimin
Islamism. *See also* Fundamentalism
in Algeria, rise of, after military takeover (1992), 126
art as counterweight to, 314
cultural imperialism and, 1091
in Egypt
at Cairo University, 556
and Copts, 641–642
in Jordan, electoral success of, 1151
in Kuwait, 1350
in Morocco, 2266, 2268
pan-Arabism replaced by, 1799–1800
as political use of Islam, 223
in Turkey, publications of, 1326
vs. Turkism, 1800
in Yemen, Islah Party of, 1143
Islamist Virtue Party (Turkey), 2245
Islamist Welfare Party (Turkey). *See* Refah Partisi
"Islam or the Deluge" (Yacine), 2375
Islam Sharq (newspaper), 2142
Islam wa usul al-hukm, al- (Abd al-Raziq), 21
Isly, Battle of (1844), 2160
Ismael, Jacqueline, *as contributor,* 1137–1138, 1309–1310, 2361–2362, 2419
Ismaʿil (imam), as successor to Jaʿfar al-Sadiq, conflict over, 105, 1158
Ismaʿil (khedive of Egypt)
banishing freemasons from politics, 852
brother of, Mustafa Fazil as, 1623
education under, 757
Egyptian Geographical Society founded by, 770
Egyptian Museum inaugurated by, 771
European cabinet of, Nubar Pasha in, 1695
majlis (assembly) established by, 1472
Midhat Paşa and, 1525
mixed courts under, 1553
and Riyad (Mustafa al-), 1928
Tahtawi (Rifaʿa al-Rafi al-) under, 2146, 2147
and urban planning, 2299
and *Urwa al-Wuthqa, al-* (newspaper), 2302
Ismaʿil I (shah of Iran), 2144
Ismaʿil, Abd al-Fattah, **1157**
Rabiyya Ali (Salim) and, 1892
Rabiyya Ali (Salim) power struggle with, 1157, 1814
Antar (Ali Ahmad Nasir) in, 211
Ismaʿil, Abd al-Qadir, in Ahali group, 79
Ismaʿil ibn Ibrahim (viceroy of Egypt), *1157,* **1157–1158**
Afghani (Jamal al-Din al-) opposing, 52
architectural tastes of, 281
bankruptcy under, 404, 528
Cairo under, 552, 1157–1158
in Crimean War, *649*
debt under, 1158
International Debt Commission and, 1106
deposition of (1879), National Party in, 1663
dual control and, 528, 731, 1158
modernization by, 1157–1158
Ismaʿil ibn Muhammad Ali, 1077
Ismaʿilis. *See* Sevener Shiʿism
Ismaʿili Shiʿism, **1158–1159**
Alawi break with, 104–105
break with Shiʿite Imamis, 105
subdivisions of, 1158
in Yemen, 2388
Ismaʿil Kemal, as Chamber of Deputies president, 91
Ismaʿil Khan
in Herat, 1021
in Jamiʿat-e Islami, 1215
Ismaʿil, Mulay (sultan of Morocco), Meknes as capital under, 1515
Ismail, Namik, 2429
Ismet Pasha, *740, 741*
Isnards, Felix, 576
Ispartali Ali Paşa, nephew of, Mustafa Reşid as, 1623–1624
Israel, **1159–1190**. *See also specific cities, organizations, people, and regions*
administrative districts of, 1161
agriculture in, *753, 1161,* 1162, 1576–1577, 2200–2201
by Palestinian citizens, 1786
al-Alami family in, 103
American Jewish Committee support for, 177, 178
American Jewish Congress support for, 179
anthem of, 1927
Arab boycott against, 224–225
Arab conflict with (*See* Arab–Israel conflict)
Arabs in (*See* Palestinian citizens of Israel)
Arab wars with (*See* Arab–Israel War)
archaeology in, 278–279, 1164, 2376
armament levels of, 304, 305
British role in, 1770, 1790
arms industry of, 305, 1483
arms sales to
by Czechoslovakia, 304
by France, 304, 2109, 2215
by United States, 250, 251, 304, 1238, 1331, 1689
army of (*See* Israel Defense Force)
art in, 70–71, 1163–1164, 2144
Ashkenazic Jews in, 321, 1162–1163
assassinations sponsored by, 983
attack on USS *Liberty,* 1409–1410
banking in, 390, *393*
Bethlehem controlled by, 468
borders of, 1159, 1160
1949, *1760, 2279*
2000, *1159, 1768*
censorship in, 1897
Chinese relations with, 586–587
Namir (Orah) and, 1641
Christians in, 1163, *1164*
Circassians in, 600
cities of, 424, 1450, 1962, 2188
capital, 1222–1227
capital (1948-1950), 2171–2172
"development towns," 1160
frontier, 708
Galilean, 1451–1452
Jewish settlement, 1822
major, 1160
only all-Arab, 1672–1673
Orthodox quarters of, 1506
Palestinian, 684, 1262

Israel *(continued)*
port, 1211–1212
Zionist, 1927
citizenship in, laws on, 1162
climate of, 1160–1161, 1668
clothing in, yarmulke *(kippah)*, 611
during Cold War, 2033
collective communities in (*See* Kibbutz)
communism in, 628, 963, 1182–1183, 1373
confiscating Arab land in Palestine, Land Day as answer to, 1369
constitution of, 448
lack of written, 1164
cotton industry in, 644, 2180
currency of (*See* Shekel)
dance in, 667–668
Dead Sea and, 684–685
Declaration of Independence, Wahrhaftig (Zerah) as signer of, 2322
defense costs as percentage of GNP or GDP, *1530*
deserts of, 1160
divorce in, 887
Druzes in, 729
economic and military aid to, 747
in Arab–Israel War (1973), 748
Camp David Accords (1978) and, 748
from United States, 748–749, *749*, 750, *750*
economy of, *753*, 1161–1162, 1169
Arab boycott and, 224
growth in, 1162, 1169
education in, 1163
in religious schools, 760, 761
at Tel Aviv University, 2172
Egyptian peace negotiations with, 1166 (*See also* Egyptian–Israeli Peace Treaty (1979))
after Arab–Israel War (1973), 251–252, 1166, 1328
Boutros-Ghali (Boutros) and, 505
at Camp David Accords (1978), 363, 560–561, 2293
Carter (Jimmy) in, 539, 567, 770
CIA in, 157, 573
Crossman (Richard) in, 650
in General Armistice Agreements (1949), 239–240
Israeli peace movement's impact on, 1809
Jarring (Gunnar) in, 1219
Kissinger (Henry) in, 1328
in Operation Alpha, 157
opposition to, 363, 561, 2428
Sadat (Anwar al-) and, 426, 770, 1957
Saunders (Harold) and, 2001
Egyptian relations with
arms race in, 236
deterioration of, 236
Lavon affair and, 449, 785, 1377–1378
under Mubarak (Husni), 1593–1594
under Nasser (Gamal Abdel), 1649–1650
Sinai peninsula and, 1957, 2068
Suez Canal and, 2014
Taba dispute, 2139, 2140
Tiran Strait blockades and, 2191
electoral system of, 1164, 1175–1176
changes to, 1168, 1170, 1175
emergency regulations issued by, 776–777
espionage by, against U.S., in Pollard affair, 1838
espionage of, Mossad in, 1577–1579
establishment of state, 2435
Balfour Declaration (1917) and, 380–381, 381, 511
Bevin (Ernest) on, 468–469
Biltmore Program (1942) on, 472
Bludan Conferences against, 488
British mandate ending and, 517–518, 616
Churchill (Winston S.) on, 596, 597
Churchill White Paper on (1922), 594
as fundamental cause of Nakba, al, 1639–1640
Guinness (Walter Edward) on, 948
Holocaust and, 1042
international support for, 1165
Jericho Congress after (1948), 1221–1222
Lloyd George (David) supporting, 1441
Neturei Karta opposing, 1677
Roosevelt (Eleanor) support for, 1935
Sharett (Moshe) lobbying for, in United Nations, 2032
Stalin (Joseph) support for, 1943
Truman (Harry S.) supporting, 2220
United Nations and, 518, 1165
U.S. supporting, 517
white papers on Palestine (1939) on, 515
World Zionist Organization and, 2372–2373
Ethiopian Jews airlifted by (1991), 786, 1239
ethnic groups in, 1162–1163
feminism in, 2023
film industry of, 483, 833, 956
fishing in, 865
foreign policy of, Jordanian Option in, 1247
French relations with, 847
and Dimona reactor, 1696
Gaza City occupied by, 869
Gaza Strip occupied by, 870, 871
at Geneva Peace Conference (1973), 900
geography of, 902–903, 1159–1160
government of, 932, 933
in Gulf War (1991), 951
Halakhah in, 979
higher education in, 975, 1018–1019, 1163
Bar-Ilan University, 402–403
at Ben-Gurion University of the Negev, 449–450
at Bezalel Academy of Arts and Design, 469–470
Magnes (Judah) in, 1460–1461
at Technion-Israel Institute of Technology, 2169
history of, Flapan (Simha) challenging myths about, 835
human rights in, 2221
independence of (1948), 1362
Ben-Gurion (David) proclaiming, 448, 2172
as literary catalyst, 1432
industrialization of, 1095
intelligence agencies of (*See* Mossad)
in Iran–Contra affair, 1322
Iraqi Jews in, emigration of, 1030
Iraqi relations with
Hussein (Saddam) threatening Israel (1990), 949–950
Osirak reactor destruction and, 426
irrigation in, 1248
Jewish immigration to, *1231*, 1234 (*See also Aliyah;* Jew(s), immigration of)
from Arab countries, 2365
Law of Return allowing citizenship for, 787, 1384

Magic Carpet Operation for (1948–1950), 1460
residential transit camps for, 1452
from Soviet Union, 1943
Jewish refugees in, 1913–1914
Jews in
number of, 1162, *1164*
religious practices of, 1163
Jezreel Valley in, 1234–1235
Jordan and
attempted assassination of Mashʿal (Khalil al-) and, 1579
General Armistice Agreement between (1949), 240–241
Jordanian Option and, 1247
peace negotiations with, Khalidi (Walid) in, 1296
peace treaty between (1994) (*See* Jordanian–Israeli peace treaty)
journalism in, by women, 1003
Karaites in, 1270
Kasztner affair in (1954–1955), 1280
kibbutzim of, 2377
establishment of first, 855, 1361
Kurdish revolts supported by, in Iraq, 1134
labor and labor unions in, 1357, 1358, 1361, 1362 (*See also* Histadrut; Labor Zionism)
umbrella organization for, 1033–1035
landsmannschaften in, 1373
languages in, 1163
Arabic, 1163
Hebrew, 1163
at Lausanne Conference (1949), 1375–1376
Lavon affair in, 449, 785, 1377–1378, 1577–1578, 1991
League of Arab States on, boycott by, 224–225
in Lebanese Civil War (1975–1990), 1103, 1391, 1393, 1400
as Lebanese Forces ally, 1393, 1394
Lebanese Front collaborating with, 1395
Lebanese internal security maintained by, 1536
Lebanese occupation by, withdrawal from (2000), 254, 1168, 2017
Lebanon and, 1166–1167
agreement with Jumayyil (Amin) (1983), 1665
General Armistice Agreement between (1949), 240
peace treaty between (1983), 318, 1393
security agreement between, 254, 1253
Lebanon invaded by (1978), 240, 1166, 1417–1418
and Beitaddin Declaration (1978), 432
League of Arab States on, *1387*
PLO and, 2176
UN response to, 1393, 1400, 1417–1418
Lebanon invaded by (1982) (*See* Arab–Israel War (1982))
legal system of, 886, 1383
Halakhah in, 1890
legislative body of, 933 (*See also* Knesset)
literature of, 188, 408, 434, 547, 834–835, 855, 920–921, 926–927, 940–941, 955–956, 1164, 1268, 1288, 1407, 1432–1434, 2012, 2024–2025, 2029, 2058–2059, 2060, 2075, 2076, 2114–2115, 2159–2160, 2384, 2403, 2418, 2429 (*See also* Literature, Hebrew)
Arabic-language, 963
avant-garde, 1040
"Generation of the State" revolution in, 182, 1040
maʿbarah experiences in, 1452
novels and short stories, 1521–1522
poetry, 2322–2323
satire, 1284
by women, 993, 1907
Lotz (Wolfgang) as espionage agent of, 1446–1447
manufacturing in, *1162*, 1483, *1483*
medicine and public health in, 1459
military of (*See* Israel Defense Force)
Mizrahi Jews in, 1162
modern means of transport in, *2207*
and Morocco, 1006
moshavim of, 1576–1577
mountains of, 1160, 1206
museums of, 1164
music of, 1014, 1105–1106, 1164, 1618
Muslims in, 1163, *1164*
national identity in, Holocaust and, 1042
newspapers and print media of, 1164, *1679*, 1683–1684
English-language, 1683
German-language, 1683
Hebrew, 1683
party-owned, 1683
privately owned, 1683
nuclear capability of, 1696–1698, *1697*
Dimona reactor in, 708, 1288, 1697, 2309
rationale for, 1697–1698
occupied territories of (*See* Occupied territories)
and oil embargo (1973–1974), 1709
Orthodox Jews in, 1163
in Oslo Accord, 1724–1727
in Oslo II Interim Agreement (1995), 1726, 1775, 1784
Palestinian citizens of (*See* Palestinian citizens of Israel)
peace movement in (*See* Peace movement; *specific groups*)
"periphery doctrine" of, 992
Phalange Party supported by, 1954
plains of, 1234–1235
PLO cease-fire with (1981), 252, 1166
PLO mutual recognition with, 271, 928, 1167, 1725–1726, 1775
PLO negotiations, 2177–2178
PLO proclaimed as terrorist group by, 2176
political parties of, **1175–1190** (*See also specific parties*)
center/right, 1176
in coalition governments, 1164, 1175
electoral system and, 1175–1176
far left, 1177
influence of, 1176
left, 1176
Palestinian, 1178–1180, 1787, 1788
political issue complexity and, 1176–1177
reform, 1177
religious, 1176–1177, 1186
role of, 1175–1177
single-issue, 1177, 1182
political system of, 1164–1165
population of, 426, *753*, 1159, 1162–1163, 1844
by religion, 1162–1163, *1164*
postage stamps of, 1850
potash industry in, 1851
press control by, *1679*, 1681
prime minister of
cabinet of, 1164, 1330

Israel *(continued)*
election of, 1164, 1168, 1169, 1175, 1330
powers of, 1164
pronatalist policies of, 478
rabbinate in, 1890
radio and television in, 866, 1896–1897
railways in, *2206*
regions of, 1047, 1206
religion in, 1163
population by, 1162–1163, *1164*
rivers of, 1248–1249, 1668, 2379–2380
development of, 1238, 1248
Russian relations with, post-Soviet, 1944
Sabbath in, 1954
science and technology in, 2004, 2005
scout movement in, 2006
security in, influence of considerations of, 1171
security policy of, Lavie File and, 1674
Sephardic Jews in, 1162
settlements in, 2431
size of, 1159
society of, military influence on, 1171
South Lebanon Army supported by, 1364
Soviet Jews in, 48, 147, 1162, 1163, 1169
Soviet relations with, 1943
Soviet Union describing state terrorism in, 2175
Spanish relations with, 2084
stock market in, 2090, 2091, *2091*
Suez Canal access of, Egyptian–Israeli Peace Treaty (1979) on, 771
in Suez Crisis (1956–1957), 520, 2108–2110
suicide bombings in, by al-Aqsa Martyrs of the World Islamic Front for Liberation, 814
Supreme Court of, 721
Syrian peace negotiations with, 1168, 2135
after Arab–Israel War (1973), 251–252, 319
bilateral, start of, 319
collapse of, 238, 319, 1168
disengagement agreement in (1974), 241, 319, 1166, 1291
General Armistice Agreement in (1949), 241
Kissinger (Henry) in, 1328
Syrian relations with
Barak (Ehud) and, 399
Golan Heights and, 925
Shabʿa Farms and, 2017
during Zaʿim's rule, 2422
Templar property seized by, 2173
terrorism in, 958, 2176, 2178
Democratic Front for the Liberation of Palestine (DFLP) and, 1009
Irgun Zvaʾi Leʾumi and, 424–425
Lohamei Herut Yisrael and, 1442, 1443
Maʿalot attack (1974), 1452
textile industry in, 2180, *2181*, 2182
theater in (*See* Theater, Israeli)
tourism in, 2196
in Tiberias, 2188
in trade, 1161–1162, *2200*, 2200–2201
Arab boycott on, 224–225
limitations on, 1095
in United Nations, *2278*
U.S. relations with
after Arab–Israel War (1967), 2292
economic and military assistance, 2291
under Kennedy, 1288
Pollard affair and, 1838
Shultz (George) and, 2061
Vatican diplomatic relations with, 2310
walls built by (2004), 220
criticism of, 1169
in Jerusalem, 1227
in Qalqiliya, 1869
in War of Attrition (1969–1970), 2327
water resources of, 866, 1248–1249, 2379–2380
amount annually available, 1668
from aquifers, 1668–1669, 2329
freshwater withdrawals, *2331*
National Water System and, *1668*, 1668–1669
pricing policy for, 1668
quantity of, 2330
Water Law (1959) on, 1668
welfare programs in, 1786
West Bank occupied by (*See* West Bank)
West German reparations to, 43, 2348–2349
West Jerusalem controlled by, 1224
women in
economic status of, 876–877, *877*
education for, 880
as head of state, 875, 891
in journalism, 1003
in labor force, 877
organizations for, **1629**
peace activities of, 2355–2356
in politics, 893, 934–935, 944–945, 1440, 1441, 2023, 2059
as writers, 408, 434, 926–927, 1433, 1887, 1907
women's rights movement in, 1440
World Bank and, capital stock and voting power in, *2363*
and Zionist Organization of America, 2436
Israel (newspaper), 1686
Israel be-Aliyah, 1182
Israel Beiteinu, 1182
in National Union, 1187
Israel Broadcasting Authority (IBA), 866, 1897
Israel Communist Party (MAKI), 1182–1183
in Moked, 1182, 1188
RAKAH and, 1182–1183, 1188
SHELI Party created by, 1188
Israel Composers Fund, 855
Israel Consumers' Council, 157
Israel Defense Force (IDF), **1170–1174**
Allon (Yigal) in, 153
Altalena sunk by (1948), 169–171
Amichai (Yehuda) in, 182
Amit (Meir) in, 190
in al-Aqsa Intifada (2000), 1174
in Arab–Israel War (1973), 251, 252
in Arab–Israel War (1982), 252–253, 254
Barak (Ehud) in, 398, 1171
Bar-Lev (Haim) in, 407–408, 1171
Beirut under siege by (1982), 1954
under Ben-Gurion (David), *1171*, 1173
Burg (Avraham) in, 546
civilian control of, 1172–1173
civilian tasks by, 1173
Dayan (Moshe) in, 681, 682, 1173
depoliticization of, 1173
Eitan (Rafael) in, 1171
equipment of, 1527, *1534*, 1535

fighting South Lebanon Army (1999), 399
force levels of, *1528–1529*, 1529
force structure of, 1535
as formative common experience for citizens, 1541
Gur (Mordechai) in, 956, 1171
Haganah in, 972, 973
Harkabi (Yehoshafat) in, 995
Herzog (Chaim) in, 1022
immigrants in, 1173
Intelligence Division of (Aman), 1577
in internal conflicts, 1536
invading Lebanon (1978), 1417–1418
Irgun Zva'i Le'umi incorporation into, 170, 1140
Judge Advocate General Corps of, Dorner (Dalia) in, 721
in Karama, Battle of (1968), 1270–1271
Lavie File and, 1674
in Lavon affair, 1377, 1378
Lebanon invaded by (1978), 1166
Lipkin-Shahak (Amnon) in, 1171
Lotz (Wolfgang) in, 1447
Moda'i (Yitzhak) in, 1555
Nahal in, 1634
Namir (Orah) in, 1641
Ne'eman (Yuval) in, 1674
organization of, 1527–1528
Palestinian citizens in, 1786–1787
Palmah merged with, 1173, 1795–1796
Peled (Mattityahu) in, 1811
political activity after, 1174
political leaders' service in, 1171, 1174
politicization of, 1173–1174
Rabin (Yitzhak) in, 1171, 1173
radio of, 993
reservists in, 1527–1528
retreating from Security Zone (1999), 399
Revisionist Zionist groups disarmed by, 1536
under Sharett (Moshe), 1173
Sharon (Ariel) in, 2041
societal impact of, 1171
and South Lebanon Army, 399, 2083
Unit 101 and, 2041
universal conscription for, 1171, 1173
in West Bank, 2340
West Bank raids by, 1169
Yariv (Aharon) in, 2379
Israel Electric Corporation, 2379
Israel Gymnastics Club, 1453
Israeli, definition of, 236, 1785
Israeli–Arab conflict. *See* Arab–Israel conflict
Israeli Communist Party
Gozanski (Tamar) in, 934–935
Habibi (Emile) in, 963
Langer (Felicia) in, 1373
Israeli League for Human Rights, 1373
Israeli settlements, **1191–1193**
Allon (Yigal) plan for, 153–154, 1191
in al-Aqsa Intifada, causes of, 219, 1107
under Begin (Menachem), 957
in Camp David Summit (2000), 562
defense as reason for, 1191
Eshkol (Levi) and, 784
in Golan Heights, 926
government freeze on, 1192
continuing construction despite, 1192
government support for, 1191–1192
Gush Emunim plan for, 1191–1192
in Hebron, 1325
Levinger (Moshe) as leader of, 1325, 1407
impact on peace process, 562, 1193
international law on, 1192
around Jabal al-Khalil, 1205
legality of, 1192
Likud Party supporting, 1184
local government in, 1192
location of, *1191, 1192*
MAPAM opposing, 1185
in Negev, 1675
number of, *1191*
in Oslo Accords (1993), 1193
Peace Now and, 1809
population of, 1191, *1191*
security for, 1192–1193
Sephardic, 2364–2365
Sharon (Ariel) on, 2041–2042
in Tel Hai, 2172–2173
violence against Palestinians by, Karp Report on (1984), 1275–1276
in West Bank, 957–959, 2340
increase in number of, 426
Israeli Socialist Organization. *See* Matzpen
Israelites, in Palestine, 1759
Israeli Women's Network, 2023
Israel Labor List. *See* Rafi Party
Israel Labor Party (ILP), 1183
Ahdut ha-Avodah in, 82, 1178
Aloni (Shulamit) in, 157
in Arab–Israel War (1973), 250, 252
Barak (Ehud) in, 398, 1183, 1818
Bar-Lev (Haim) in, 408
Ben-Aharon (Yitzhak) in, 438
Ben-Porat (Mordechai) in, 452
Citizens' Rights Movement and, 1180
conflicts within, 1183
Dayan (Moshe) in, 682
Dayan (Yael) in, 683
decline in popularity of, 1891
domestic policy of, 1183
electoral success of, 1167, 1168, 1169, 1170, 1183
Eshkol (Levi) in, 784
establishment of, 682, 1183
foreign policy of, 1183
Jordanian Option in, 1247
GAHAL and, 1181
Greenberg (Uri Zvi) in, 941
Gur (Mordechai) in, 956
Gush Emunim opposed by, 957
Histardut and, 1034
Lavon affair causing split in, 1378
leaders of, 1183
election by members, 1175
and Likud, 1417
Likud coalition government with, 1167, 1184, 1817–1818
MAPAI in, 1185
Meir (Golda) in, 1514
Mitzna (Amram) in, 1170
moshav affiliated with, 1576
Namir (Mordekhai) in, 1641
Navon (Yizhak) in, 1671–1672
on occupied territory, 1183
need for keeping, 250
in peace process, 1183
Peres (Shimon) in, 1183, 1817–1818, 1892
platform of, 1183
political crisis within (1960s), 1377
political stability aided by, 1165
Rabin (Yitzhak) in, 1167, 1183
Sapir (Pinhas) in, 1991
Sarid (Yossi) in, 1991
in Sharon (Ariel) government, 1169, 1170
Shinui Party alliance with, 1188
Third Way Party split from, 1189
Weizman (Ezer) in, 2337
Israel, Marcel, 627
Israel Museum, 278, 279, 1164

Israel National Police, 1536
Israel Philharmonic Orchestra, 1164
Israel Prize
Aloni (Shulamit) awarded with, 157
Alterman (Natan) awarded with, *1433*
Amichai (Yehuda) awarded with, 182
Appelfeld (Aharon) awarded with, 217
Cohen (Ge'ula) awarded with, 613
Freier (Recha) awarded with, 855
Gilboa (Amir) awarded with, 920
Greenberg (Uri Zvi) awarded with, 941
Kaniuk (Yoram) awarded with, 1268
Kollek (Teddy) awarded with, 1332
Kovner (Abba) awarded with, 1336
Shlonsky (Avraham) awarded with, 2058
Shufman (Gershon) awarded with, 2060
Israel Water Planning Corporation, 1668
Issawi, Charles
as contributor, 1481–1485, 1555–1556, 2180–2182, 2197–2202, 2204–2208
as historiographer, 1035
Issues (journal), 2233
Istanbul (Turkey), **1193–1195,** 2237. *See also* Constantinople
Archaeological Museum in, 275
architecture of, 1193, 1194–1195
Aya Sofya in, 342
bazaars in, 419
Beyoğlu district of, 864
B'nai B'rith lodge in, 489
Erdoğan (Tayyip) as mayor of, 781
European part of, 1939
Galata district of, 864
gecekondus on outskirts of, 872
infrastructure of, 1194
Istanbul Technical University in, 1195
Istanbul University in, 1195–1196
names given to, 1193
newspapers and print media of, 1685
origins of, 1193
Pera district of, 1193, 1816–1817
population of, 1194, *1846*
as port, 2206
Ruşdiye Schools in, 1940
Russian emigration to, 1194
Suleimaniye Mosque in, *2237*
Sultan Ahmet Mosque in, *1194,* 2120, 2196
theaters in, 2187
tourism in, 2196, *2196*
transportation in, 1194, *1195*
Üsküdar district in, 2302–2303
Westernization of, 1193
in World War I, 1194, 2240
Allied occupation after, 1194
Istanbul–Ankara railway. *See* Ankara–Istanbul railway
Istanbul Conference (1876), 541
Istanbul Conservatory, 2009
Istanbul Fine Arts Academy, 790
Istanbul Hilton Hotel, 774
Istanbul Lycée, 492
Istanbul Municipal Theater, 782
Istanbul Technical University (ITU), 491, **1195**
Erbakan (Necmeddin) at, 780
Istanbul, Treaty of (1913), 384
Istanbul University, **1195–1196**
vs. Ankara University, 1196
architecture of, 774
Baraheni (Reza) at, 397
Barkan (Ömer Lutfi) at, 407
Ben-Gurion (David) at, 446
Darülfünün renamed, 672
Sharett (Moshe) at, 2032
Sulh (Riyad al-) at, 2117
Tanpinar (Ahmed Hamdi) at, 2160
Tekeli (Şirin) at, 2170
Women's Studies Center of, 2362
Istanbul–Vienna railway. *See* Vienna–Istanbul railway
Isthmus of Suez, 952
Istidd'af, 2151
Istihsan, 2034
Istikbal (magazine), 1277
Istiqlal Party (Iraq), in United National Front, 1654
Istiqlal Party (Libya), **1196**
Istiqlal Party (Morocco), **1196–1198,** 1574–1575
Balafrej (Ahmed) in, 1196–1197, 1805
Balafrey (Ahmed) in, 379
Ben Barka (Mehdi) in, 441, 1197
Ben Jelloun (Umar) in, 450
Bouabid (Abderrahim) in, 495
Boucetta (Muhammad) in, 495, 1197
elections of 1963 boycotted by, 1588
electoral success of, 1197–1198
establishment of, 1196, 1570, 1598
Fasi (Abbas al-) in, 1198
Fasi (Allal al-) in, 812, 1196–1197, 1805
Fasi (Muhammad al-) in, 812
FDIC opposing, 858
Ghallab (Abd al-Karim) in, 910
human rights organization of, 1716
Ibrahim (Abdullah) in, 1075
Islamists role in government opposed by, 1601
Mouvement Populaire opposing, 1588
Muhammad V and, 1004, 1570, 1598–1599
Parti Démocratique Constitutionnel cooperation with, 1803
Parti Démocratique de l'Indépendance and, 1804
Parti National reestablished as, 1196, 1805
platform of, 1197
Union Générale des Travailleurs Marocains as labor branch of, 1197, 2264
Union Marocaine du Travail affiliated with, 453, 2265
Union Nationale des Etudiants Marocains and, 2266
Union Nationale des Forces Populaires and, 1197, 2266
Union Socialiste des Forces Populaires and, 1197–1198, 2268
and al-Wifaq, 2352
Youssoufi (Abderrahmane) in, 2410
Istiqlal Party (Palestine), **1198**
Abd al-Hadi (Awni) in, 13, 1764
Darwaza (Muhammad Izzat) in, 673, 1764
Darwish (Ishaq) in, 673
decline of, 1198
establishment of, 1198, 1764
Hilmi (Ahmad) in, 1030
platform of, 1198
Shuqayri (Ahmad) in, 2061
Istiqlal Party (Syria), **1198–1199**
Darwaza (Muhammad Izzat) in, 673, 1198, 1764
establishment of, 1198
and independence of Syria, 801
Quwatli (Shukri al-) in, 1885
Istiqlal tamm (independence), 2320
Istislah, 834
ISWAW. *See* Institute for Women's Studies in the Arab World

Italo–Sanusi wars
first
Mukhtar (Umar al-) in, 1609
Treaty of Akrama ending (1917), 1609
second, Mukhtar (Umar al-) in, 1609–1610
Italy, **1199–1201**
Algerian relations with, Ente Nazionale Idrocarboni and, 777–778
as British threat, 515
in Eastern Question, 739, 742
empire sought by, 1199–1200
Ethiopia conquered by (1935), 515
Fezzan occupied by, 830, 935
and France, Treaty of Rome between, 1933
French relations with, 1200
legal system of, influencing law in Middle East, 1382
Libyan colonization by (*See under* Libya)
Libyan relations with, 1415
masonic lodges set up by, 852
Ottoman relations with (*See* Turkish–Italian War (1911–1912))
Sykes–Picot Agreement (1916) on, 742
Tripolitania occupied by, 935, 2218, 2247
Tunisia claims of, 1199
in World War I, 742
Gallipoli campaign, 866
and London Treaty (1913), 511
in World War II, 906, 1200, 2368–2372
Kaylani revolt (1941) supported by, 516
Ittihad, al- (periodical), 2222
Darwish (Mahmud) in, 674
Habibi (Emile) and, 963
Ittihad al-nisa'i al-misri al-. *See* Egyptian Feminist Union
Ittihad-e Islami (Afghanistan), 63
in mojahedin resistance, 1561
Ittihad Nisa al-Yaman. *See* Yemeni Women's Union
Ittijahat al-Tarbiyya wa al-Ta'lim fi Al-maniya wa Inkiltira wa Faransa (Jamali), 1213
ITU. *See* Istanbul Technical University
I Want the Day (Badr), 357
IWS. *See* Institute of Women's Studies
IWSA. *See* International Woman Suffrage Alliance
IWSAW. *See* Institute for Women's Studies in the Arab World
IZL. *See* Irgun Zva'i Le'umi
Izlane, 2624
İzmir (Turkey), *1201,* **1201–1202,** 2237
banks in, 389
Catholics in, 1932
Ege University in, 762–763
gecekondus on outskirts of, 872
Greek occupation of, 1201
Lausanne Treaty (1923) and, 1376
newspapers of, 2302
origins of, 1201
in Ottoman Empire, 1201
Kamil (Kibrish Mehmet) as governor of, 1266
population of, 1201, 1202
port of, 194, 1201, 2206
Protestant missions in, 1854
Sèvres Treaty (1920) and, 1376
textile mills in, 2181
trade in, 1201
İzmir Economic Congress (1923), 1201, **1202**
and Turkish alphabet, 1933
Izmirlian, Matteos, 298
Izz al-Din, 2019

J

Jaafari, Shaban, Arfa (Hasan) and, 286
Jababdi, Latifa, 497, 498, **1203–1204**
imprisonment of, 1203
and moudawana reform, 1203–1204
Jabal, al- (Ghanim), 911
Jabal al-Akhdar (Libya), 655, **1204**
Jabal al-Akhdar (Oman), **1204**
Jabal al-Ansariyya, 909
Jabal Ali (Saudi Arabia), 1094
Jabal Ali Port, *2198*
Jabal al-Khalil (West Bank), **1204–1205**
Jabal al-Zawiya, 909
Jabal Awliya Dam, 372
Jabal, Badawi al-, **1205**
Jabal Druze (Mount Lebanon), 1205
Jabal Druze (Syria), **1205–1206**
revolt in (1925–1927), 337, 729, 1206
Jabal Hafit (United Arab Emirates), 343
Jabali, Tahani al-. *See* Gebali, Tahani al-
Jaballah, Abdallah, as founder of Nahda, al-, 1635
Jabal Nablus (Israel), **1206**
Jabal Nafusa (Libya), 2218
Jabal Nuqum, 1983
Jabal Shammar (Saudi Arabia), **1206,** 1638
Al Rashid family in, 818
tribes in, 2214
Ja'bari family, **1206**
Ja'bari, Muhammad Ali, at Jericho Congress (1948), 1221
Jabarti, Abd al-Rahman al-, **1206–1207**
Jabha, al- (periodical), 1842
Jabha al-Wataniyya, al- (United National Front) (Tripolitania), **1207**
Jabhat al-Amal al-Islami. *See* Islamic Action Front
Jabiri, Ihsan al-, 307
Jabotinsky, Vladimir Ze'ev, *1208,* **1208–1209,** 1432, *2437*
Altalena named after, 170
Begin (Menachem) and, 424, 1181, 1209
and Ben-Gurion (David), 1209, 1947
death of, 1209
Irgun Zva'i Le'umi agreement with, 1139
in Jewish Legion, 1208, 1230
Netanyahu (Benzion) as disciple of, 1676–1677
in New Zionist Organization, 2372
program and ideology of, 2438
Revisionist movement formed by, 1362
and Rutenberg (Pinhas), 1946
on Tel Hai, 2173
Uganda Project opposed by, 2257
Weizmann's (Chaim) quarrel with, 2338
in Zionist Revisionist Movement, 1208–1209, 2372, 2435, 2437, 2438
Jabri, Ihsan, 103
Jabr, Salih, **1209–1211**
in Anglo–Iraqi treaty negotiations, 203, 1210

Jabr, Salih *(continued)*
death of, 1210
on Ezra and Nehemiah Operations, 790
as prime minister, 1210
Jacir, Emily, **1211**
Jacob, home of, 1631
Jacobites, under Ottoman rule, 1544
Jadid, al- (periodical), Darwish (Mahmud) in, 674
Jadid, Ghassan, 1211
in Baʿth party, 412
in coup (1966), 412
Jadidi, Muhammad Arslane, 1904
in Parti National Démocratique, 1805
Jadid, Salah, **1211**
Asad (Hafiz al-) and, 316, 1211
Atasi (Nur al-Din al-) support for, 330
economy under, 2131
Hafiz (Amin al-) and, 971–972
and Hawrani (Akram al-), 1011
in Military Committee, 1211
Jad, Islah
as contributor, 2355, 2356–2357, 2362–2363
in Institute of Women's Studies at Bir Zeit University, 1100
in Women and Family Affairs Center, 2355
in Women's Affair Center, 2356
Jaʿfar al-Sadiq (sixth imam), conflict over successor to, 1158
Jaʿfar, Aqa, Khomeini (Ruhollah) taught by, 1310
Jaʿfar ibn Khidr al-Najafi, 1278
Jaffa (Israel), **1211–1212**. *See also* Tel Aviv
anti-Zionist violence in, 1011
in Arab–Israel War (1948), 1141
Jews in, as Yishuv, 2402
Palestinian Arab Congress in (1921), 1782
Palestinians in, al-Isa family of, 1141
as part of Tel Aviv, 2171–2172
Templars in, 2173
Jaffa Riots (1921), 1447
Jahidhiya, al- (Algeria), 2332
Jahili, 2151
Jahiliyya, 2150
Jahlawan (people), 385
Jaïbi, Fadhel, 376
Jalboot (sailing vessel), 704
Jalil, al-. *See* Galilee
Jali script, 235
Jallabiya, 433
Jallud, Abd al-Salam, **1212–1213**
as prime minister, 1212
Qaddafi (Muammar) and, 1212
Jalluli family, **1213**
Jalluli, Hassuna, 1213
Jalluli, Mahmud, 1213
Jalluli, Muhammad, 1213
Jamaʿa, 947
Jamaʿat al Adl wa al Ihsan (Morocco), 1601
prisoners affiliated with freed by Muhammad VI, 1600
Jamaʿat al Islamiyya (Algeria), 1635
Jamaʿat al-Muslimin. *See* Takfir wa al-Hijra al-
Jamaʿat al-Ruwwad (Société Primitive), 997
Jamaʿat i-Islami (Pakistan), Mawdudi (Abu al-aʿla, al-) as founder and leader of, 1503–1504
Jamaʿat Taht al-Sur (Below the wall group), 721, 1428
Jamahir, al- (newspaper), 2332
Atasi (Jamal al-) in, 329
Aziz (Tariq) in, 350
Jamahiriyya (Libya), 409, 899, 941, **1213,** 1410, 1413, 2217
Jamali, Badr al-, Ibn Tulun Mosque restored by, 1074
Jamali, Muhammad Fadhil al-, **1213–1214**
at Bandung Conference, 387
Doctor Ibrahim (Ayyub) modeled after, 344
and Fertile Crescent unity, 826
Jamal, Samiya. *See* Gamal, Samiyah
Jamalzadeh, Mohammad Ali, **1214,** 1435
Jambish-i-Melli (Afghanistan), in interim government, 64
Jameʿeh (newspaper), 1970
Jameʿe Zainab, 428
Jamhuriyin. *See* Republican Brotherhood
Jamiʿa, al- (periodical), Antun (Farah) in, 215
Jamiʿa al-Arabiyya, al (newspaper), Hudayni (Munif al-) and, 1053
Jamiʿa al-Islamiyya, al- (Egypt), 768, **1214–1215**
Abd al-Rahman (Umar) in, 20
establishment of, 1214
government crackdown on, 1215
member groups in, 1214–1215
vs. Muslim Brotherhood, 1214
violence linked to, 1214–1215
Jami, Abd al-Rahman, 1642
Jamʿiat Demokrate-ye Mottaraqi (Afghanistan), 62
Jamiʿat-e Islami (Afghanistan), **1215–1216**
Ahmad Shah Masʿud in, 89, 1215
establishment of, 60, 63, 1215
factions split from, 63
in government, 64, 1215
Hekmatyar (Golbuddin) in, 1020
and Herat, 1021
and Hezb-e Islami, 1024
leadership of, 60, 63, 1215
and mojahedin, 61
in mojahedin resistance, 1561
objectives of, 1215
Rabbani (Burhanuddin) in, 60, 63, 64, 1215, 1888–1889
Jamiʿat-e Islami (Pakistan), 1215
Jamʿiat-e Social Demokrat (Afghanistan). *See* Afghan Nation
Jamʿiat Motalefeh Islami (JME) (Iran), Velayati (Ali Akbar) in, 2313
Jamila the Algerian (film), 497
Jamil, Husayn, in Ahali group, 79, 80
Jamʿiyat al-Maqasid al-Khayriyya, 759
Jamʿiyya, al-, 2147
Jamʿiyyat al-Ikha wa al-Afaf, 1218
Jamʿiyyat al-ikhwan al-muslimin. See Muslim Brotherhood
Jamʿiyyat al-Irshad wa al-Islah (Algeria), 984, 1636
Jamʿiyyat al-Sayyidat al-Muslimat (Egypt). *See* Muslim Women's Association
Jamʿiyyat al-Urwa al-Wuthqa (Society of the Firm Tie), 962
Jamr al-Ghafi, al- (Nasrallah), 1647
Jangal (newspaper), 1216, 1337
Jangali (Iran), **1216**
Communist Party of Iran and, 41
destruction of, 1216
establishment of, 1216
objectives of, 1216
Janin. *See* Jenin
Janissaries, **1216–1218,** *1217*
in Algeria, 122

decline of, 1216–1217
end of *(vaka-i hayriye)* (1826), 1217, 1467, 2308
establishment of, 1216
rebellions by, 417, 1217
under Mahmut II, 1466–1467
recruiting for, 1216
reform of, 1217

Jankowski, James, *as contributor,* 1831–1832, 2405

Jansen, Hermann, 207

Japan
in Arab boycott against Israel, 224, 225
economic and military aid from, 747
in World War II, 1935

Japanese Red Army, PFLP ties with, 1839

Jarallah family, **1218**

Jarallah, Hasan, 1218

Jarallah, Husam al-Din, 1218

Jarash (Jordan), **1218**
ruins at, 1218

Jarash Festival, 1218
Noor al-Hussein and, 1691

Jarba. *See* Djerba

Jardin des sortilèges ou le parfum des légendes, Le (Sefrioui), 2008

Jarida, al- (newspaper), 805

Jarra, Abu Ubayda ibn al-, 662

Jarring, Gunnar, **1218–1219**
and UN Resolution 242, 1166, 1219, 2275

Jashaʿam tribe, 2212

Jasmund, A., 1285

Jassy Peace (1792), 739

Jauziyya, Ibn Taimiyya Ibn Qayim al-, 436

Javanan-e Muslimin (Afghanistan), 63

Jawahiri, Muhammad Mahdi al-, **1219**

Jawaʾib, al- (newspaper), 2051

Jawlatun bayna Hanat al-Bahr al-Abyad al-Mutawassit (Douʿaji), 721–722

Jayyusi, Salma al-Khadra, 1792

Jazaʾiri, Ahmad al-, al-Takfir wa al-Hijra led by, 2151

Jazaʾiri, Tahir al-
and Arab nationalism, 261
Kurd Ali (Muhammad) studying under, 1338

Jazayery, M. A., *as contributor,* 1819–1820

Jazeera, al- (TV station), **1219–1220,** *1894,* 1896
and Arab nationalism, 223
criticism of, 1219
establishment of, 1219, 1877
expansion of, 1219–1220
al-Qaradawi (Yusuf) on, 1870

Jazira, al- (newspaper), 1679

Jazrawi, Taha al-. *See* Ramadan, Taha Yasin

JCT. *See* Jewish Colonial Trust

JDC. *See* Joint Distribution Committee

JDL. *See* Jewish Defense League

Jean Genet et Tennessee Williams à Tangier (Shukri), 2060

Jebana, 433

Jebhe-ye Melli. *See* National Front (Iran)

Jebhe-ye Nejat-e Milli (Afghanistan)
Mojaddedi (Sebghatullah) in, 1561
in mojahedin resistance, 1561

Jebhe-ye Nejat Milli (Afghanistan), 63

Jebusites, in Jerusalem, 1222

Jehad-e Sazandegi (Iran), **1220**
Nateq-Nuri (Ali Akbar) in, 1653

Jelve, Mirza Abul-Hasan, 2141

Jenin (West Bank), **1220–1221,** 2340
agriculture in, 1220, 1221
in Arab–Israel War (1948), 1220–1221
Israeli occupation of, 1221
refugee camp near
Israeli assault on (2002), 1221, 2284
UN tour of, *2281*

Jerad, Abdessalem, in Union Générale des Travailleurs Tunisiens, 2265

Jericho (West Bank), **1221,** 2340
Arafat (Yasir) return to, 272, 1775
Biblical accounts of, 1221
British rule in, 1221
Jordanian rule in, 1221
Palestinian refugee camps near, 1221
Palestinian self-rule in, 1221, 1726, 1775

Jericho Congress (1948), 31, **1221–1222**

Jeroboam's Rebellion, 1631

Jerusalem, 1160, **1222–1227.** *See also* East Jerusalem; West Jerusalem
al-Alami family in, 103
Arab Club in, 225–226
Arab College of, 226–227
in Arab–Israel War (1948), 31, 681, 1224
in Arab–Israel War (1967), 249, 1224–1225
Arab Women's Association of Palestine in, 267
archaeology in, 275, 278–279, 1226
Armenian community of, 290–292
Armenian patriarchate of, 291–292
Bezalel Academy of Arts and Design in, 469–470
during British mandate, 1223–1224
British occupation of (1917), 509–510, 1223
in Camp David Summit (2000), 561
as capital of Israel, 1224, 1225
as capital of Palestine, 1223, 1226
in Christianity, 1222
Christian Quarter of, *1223*
Christians in
institutions of, 590
number of, 590
Church of the Holy Sepulchre in, 1043–1044
city plan of, 1222–1223
Crusaders' conquest of, 1930
division of (1948), 1224
Eastern Orthodox patriarchate of, 590–591
expansion of, 1223, 1225
expansion of Jewish community in, 2432
Hadassah Hospital in, 1224
Haram al-Sharif (Temple Mount) in, *991,* 991–992
Hebrew University in, 1224
in Holy Land, 1043
al-Husayni family in, 1053–1054
infrastructure of, 1223
Islamic Jihad attacks in, 1155, 1226, 1227
Israeli jurisdiction over, Neturei Karta opposing, 1677
Israeli seizure of, in Arab–Israel War (1967), 1651
Jarallah family in, 1218
Jewish immigration into, 1223
Jewish Quarter of, 1224, 1225, *1225*

Jerusalem *(continued)*
Jews in
Arab attacks on (1920), 1794
as Yishuv, 2401–2402
in Judaism, 1222, 1226, 1251
Khalidi (Husayn Fakhri al-) as mayor of, 1224, 1295
King David Hotel in, 1323–1324
Kollek (Teddy) as mayor of, 1225, 1331–1332
Mandelbaum Gate in, 1224
mayors of, 1224, 1225, 1226
Mount Scopus in, 966
Nashashibi family in, 1644–1645
Nusayba family in, 1705–1706
Orthodox quarter of, 1506
Oslo Accord and, 1226
in Ottoman Empire, 1222–1223
British citizens in, 1796
in Palestine Arab Revolt (1936–1939), 1224
Palestinian Arab Congress in (1919), 1782
Palestinian nationalism in, 1224
Palestinians in
residency status of, 1225, 1226
threats to, 1226
Pisgat Ze'ev settlement in, 1225
population of, 1223–1224, 1225
religious-secular competition among Jews in, 1225–1226
riots in (1929), 235
Roman destruction of, 1165
Sadat (Anwar al-) visit to, 238
Saint James Monastery in, 291–292
suicide bombings in, 1226
Templars in, 2173
unification by Israel (1967), 1225
UN Resolution 181 (II) on, 1224, 1225
violence in, 1226
wall dividing (2004), 1227
Western Wall in (*See* Western Wall)
in World War I, 151, 1223, 2368
Zionism in, 1224
Jerusalem Center for Performing Arts, *2185*
Jerusalem Foundation, 1331
Jerusalem Girls College (JGC), 1055
Jerusalem Link, 1266
Jerusalem Post, 1683, 1684
Kimche (David) in, 1322
Jerusalem Star (periodical), 1141
Jerusalem Symphony, 1164
Jerusalem Talmud, 2158
Jervis, Ludmilla, 285
Jesuits
in Iraq, 1029
in Ottoman Empire, 1931
and Saint Joseph University, 1971
Jesus, 1519
in Christianity, 589
Qur'an on, 1145
tomb of, 1043
Je t'aime au gré de la mort (al-Qassim), 1356
Jettou, Driss
Istiqlal Party and, 1198
as prime minister,1575, 2268, 2411
Jeune Algérien, le: De la colonie vers la province (Abbas), 3
Jeune Turquie, La (newsletter), 867
Jew(s), **1231–1234**. *See also* Anti-semitism; Judaism
Aaronsohn family of, 1–2
in Algeria
antidefamation organization for, 619
French citizenship for, Crémieux Decree on, 647–648
during World War II, 1234
Ashkenazic (*See* Ashkenazic Jews)
benevolent associations of, 1373
Biblical accounts of, 1231
circumcision among, 601
citizenship status of, 1232
clothing of, yarmulke *(kippah), 608,* 611
communism among, 626, 627
in Damascus affair (1840), 664–665
definition of, 1251
diaspora of, 706
economic mobility of, 1232
education of
Dor De'a movement in, 720
opportunities for, 1231–1232
at yeshivas, 2399
in Egypt, during World War II, 1234
European, Haskalah movement among, 1002–1003
in France
denial of protection to, under Vichy government, 846
organizations for, 151
French language among, 1252
in Germany, Haskalah movement among, 1002–1003
in guilds, 947
immigration of
to Balkan Peninsula, 383
from Ethiopia, 786
from Iraq, 790
to Palestine (*See Aliyah*)
in Iran, 1234
in Iraq, 1232, *1232,* 2079
during World War II, 807–808, 1233
in Jerusalem, as Yishuv, 2401–2402
Judeo-Arabic language of, 1252
Karaites as, 1270
Ladino language used by, 1363
in Libya, 1410
in Giado concentration camp, 920
during World War II, 1233
of Middle Eastern origin (*See* Adot ha-mizrah)
migration of, 1232, 1234, 1847
into Israel, *1231,* 1234
into Jerusalem, 1223
into Palestine, 1233
as minorities or subdominant groups, 1548
in Morocco, 1234
Corcos family of, 642
under Muslim rule, 1231–1232
in nationalist movement, 1549
newspapers of, 1233
origins of, 1231
Orthodox (*See* Orthodox Jews)
in Ottoman Empire, 383, 1231–1232
British support of, 1544
as financiers, 807
Herzl (Theodor) proposal regarding, 1021
millet system of, 1543–1545
in Palestine (*See* Yishuv)
immigration to (*See Aliyah*)
political activism among, before Zionism, 1233
Protestant missions targeting, 1854
refugees, 1913–1914
on *Exodus,* 2289
Roosevelt (Franklin Delano) policies toward, 1935, 1936
in Russia, 1360
Sabras as, 1954
vs. Samaritans, 1980
Soviet, immigration to Israel, 48, 147, 1162, 1163, 1169
in Spain, converting to Christianity *(conversos),* 2084
Spanish expulsion of (*See* Sephardim)
in Syria, *1233,* 2129

in Tunisia, 1234, 2226
Djerba, 718
in Turkey, 1233, 1234, 2238
in U.S., organizations for, 176–179, 2273–2274
during World War II (*See also* Holocaust)
aliyah by, 147
in Giado concentration camp, 920
Joint Distribution Committee aid to, 1239
Levin (Yizhak Meir) rescuing, 1408
in Middle East, 1233–1234
Shapira (Hayyim Moshe) rescuing, 2030
Youth Aliyah aid to, 2411
in Yemen, 1231, 2388
Yiddish language of, 2399
Jewelry, Berber, 459
Jewish Agency for Palestine, **1227–1228**
and Abdullah I ibn Hussein, agreement between, 1058
Agudat Israel agreement with, 77
airlift operations of, 1913
Arlosoroff (Chaim) in, 289–290
Ben-Gurion (David) in, 447
Biltmore Program (1942) on, 472
Burg (Avraham) in, 546
Eban (Abba) in, 744
elections in, 1176
Eshkol (Levi) in, 784
establishment of
American Jewish Committee in, 178, 1227
call for, 1227
Churchill (Winston S.) on, 596
World Zionist Organization in, 178
Goldmann (Nahum) in, 927
Gruenbaum (Yizhak) in, 945
and Haganah, 972
headquarters in Jerusalem, 1224
on Israeli immigration from Arab countries, 2365
Joseph (Dov) in, 1250
and Keren Hayesod, 1289
Kol (Moshe) in, 1332
Kollek (Teddy) in, 1331
leadership of, 1227
MacDonald (Malcolm) as liaison to, 1453
MacDonald (Ramsay) Letter to (1931), 1454, 2350
MacMichael (Harold) on, 1455
Magic Carpet Operation run by (1948–1950), 1460
Maimon (Yehudah Leib Hacohen) in, 1470
Meir (Golda) in, 1513
members of, 1227–1228
military controlled by, 1172
Nashashibi family and, 1644
non-Zionists in, 1227–1228
offices of, 1224, 1228
on Peel Commission partition plan, 1811
precursor of, 2436
Rothschild (Edmond de) as honorary president of, 1938
Samuel (Herbert Louis) and, 1983
Sasson (Eliyahu) in, 1993
Sharef (Ze'ev) in, 2031
Shazar (Shneour Zalman) in, 2047
Shiloah (Reuven) in, 2056
Sneh (Moshe) in, 2075
status of, law on (1952), 2373
and Supreme Muslim Council, 1922
United Hebrew Resistance Movement arranged by, 1140
on UN partition plan (1947), 2274
Weizmann's resignation from presidency of, 1454, 2338
West German reparations sought by, 2348
World Zionist Organization and, 2372–2373
and Youth Aliyah, 2411
Zionist Revisionist Movement and, 2438
Jewish Brigade, **1229**
Amichai (Yehuda) in, 182
Holocaust and creation of, 1041
in World War II, 1540
Jewish Chronicle, 152
Jewish Colonial Trust (JCT), **1229,** 2372
Levontin (Zalman) as director of, 1408
Jewish Colonization Association (ICA), **1229–1230,** 1937–1938
establishment of, 1229, 1937
Kalvaryski (Chaim Margaliut-) in, 1265
Nasir (Najib) in, 1646
Jewish Colonization Corporation, donation from Mond (Alfred Moritz), 1564
Jewish Cultural Club (Libya), 1686
Jewish Defense League (JDL), Kahane (Meir) in, 1263
Jewish Enlightenment. *See* Haskalah
Jewish Institute of Religion, Wise (Stephen S.) as founder of, 2354
Jewish Legion, **1230**
Ben-Gurion (David) in, 447, 1281
Ben-Zvi (Rahel Yanait) and, 456
Ben-Zvi (Yizhak) in, 457, 1230, 1281
disbanding of, 1208, 1230
establishment of, 1208, 1230
Ha-Shomer members in, 1001
Jabotinsky (Vladimir Ze'ev) in, 1208, 1230
Joseph (Dov) in, 1250
Katznelson (Berl) in, 1230, 1281
Trumpeldor (Yosef) lobbying for creation of, 2221
Zionist Revisionist Movement and, 2438
Jewish Legion, The: Letters (Ben-Zvi), 457
Jewish Material Claims Against Germany, Conference on, 2348
Jewish Mule Corps, at Gallipoli, 1540
Jewish National Fund (JNF), **1230,** 2372
establishment of, 1230
Hope-Simpson's (John) criticism of, 2350
and Hula swamps, restoration of, 1047
land purchased by, 616, 1229, 1230
Palestine Land Development Company funded by, 1772
Ussishkin (Menahem) in, 2303
Jewish National Home, 2172
Jewish nationalism. *See* Zionism
Jewish Peril, The. See Protocols of the Elders of Zion
"Jewish Problem and the Socialist Jewish State, The" (Syrkin), 2138
Jewish religious schools, 760, 761
Jewish settlements. *See also* Israeli settlements
in South America, 1229
Jewish State, The (Herzl). *See Judenstaat, Der* (Herzl)
Jewish State Party, 2437
Jewish Territorial Organization for the Settlement of the Jews within the British Empire, 2425

Jewish Yishuv in Peki'in Village, The (Ben Zvi), 457
Jew's mallow, 840
Jezreel Valley (Israel), **1234–1235**
kibbutz in, 1321
Palestine Land Development Company purchases in, 1772
JHFHD. *See* Jordanian Hashemite Fund for Human Development
Jibril, Ahmad, **1235,** *1841*
in PFLP, 1235
in PFLP–GC, 1235, 1773, 1841
Jibril, Jihad, 1841
Jidda (Saudi Arabia), **1235–1236,** 1995
malaria in, 711
Jifri, Muhammad Ali, in Organization for the Liberation of the Occupied South, 1717
Jihad, **1236,** 2624
Afghan resistance war as, 1561
against Dar al-Harb (abode of war), 670
justifications for, 1236
meaning of term, 1236
Muslim Brotherhood and, 983
objectives of, 1236
Shaltut (Muhammad) on, 2022
al-Takfir wa al-Hijra on, 2151
Tantawi (Muhammad Sayyid al-) on, 2161
Jihad, al- (Egypt group), 768
in al-Jami'a al-Islamiyya, 1214–1215
in Sadat assassination, 1214
violence linked to, 1214–1215
Jihad, al- (periodical), Khalidi (Husayn Fakhri al-) in, 1295
Jihad, Islamic (Palestinian organization). *See* Islamic Jihad
Jihan's Laws, 1958
Jillaba, 612
Jinnah, Muhammad Ali, **1236–1237**
at Bandung Conference, 387
in establishment of Pakistan, 1236, 1237
in Indian National Congress, 1236–1237
Jiryis, Sabri
in al-Ard movement, 285
at Palestine Research Center, 1782
Jisr al-Qamar (musical), 817
Jisr, Muhammad al-, 660
Jiza. *See* Giza
Jizan (Saudi Arabia), al-Ta'if Treaty (1934) on, 2149
Jizi, al-Rabi ibn Sulayman al-, 2019
Jizya (poll tax), 423, **1237,** 2167
in Egypt, Coptic exemption from, 640
for non-Muslims, in Ottoman Empire, 1543
Jlasi, Zahra al-, 1424
Jma'a tribal council, **1237**
JME. *See* Jam'iat Motalefeh Islami
JNF. *See* Jewish National Fund
Joachim (Armenian bishop), millet granted to, 1543
Joffe, George, *as contributor,* 216, 380, 469, 471, 843, 935, 1199–1201, 1609–1610, 1611–1612, 2127, 2317
John XIX (Coptic patriarch), **1239**
John Humphrey Freedom Award, Samar (Sima) awarded with, 1982
John Paul II, Pope
appeal against U.S. war in Iraq (2003), 2324
attempted assassination of, 1109
in Bethlehem, 468
and Lebanese Civil War (1975–1990), 2310
Middle East visit by, 2310
Johnson–Crosbie Committee Report (1930), **1238**
Johnson, Joseph E., 1288–1289
Johnson, Lyndon Baines, **1238**
foreign policy of, 1238
government of
Kissinger (Henry) in, 1327
Vance (Cyrus) in, 2308
Johnson, Penny
in Institute of Women's Studies at Bir Zeit University, 1100
in Women's Studies Center, 2362
Johnson, William, 1238
Johnston, Eric, 2291
Johnston Plan by, 1238, 1248
Johnston Plan (1953), **1238–1239,** 1248, 1668
Joint Defense Council, 1387
Joint Distribution Committee (JDC), **1239**
establishment of, 1239
Jewish Colonization Association's work with, 1229
in United Jewish Appeal, 2273
Jolivet, Jean, 1457
Jomhury-ye Eslami (newspaper), 388
Jonathan Institute (Israel), 1677
Jong-e Isfahan (magazine), 929
Jonglei Canal, 2106
Jönler (Bekir Fahri), 434
Jonnart Law (1919), 603
Joppa. *See* Jaffa
Jordan, **1239–1246,** *1241. See also specific cities, organizations, people, and regions*
agriculture in, 1240, 1243
in Arab boycott against Israel, 224
Arab Collective Security Pact (1952) accepted by, 2152
Arab–Israel conflict and, 1064
after Arab–Israel War (1948), 1061–1062
in Arab–Israel War (1948), 35, 242–243, 518, 1224, 1244, 1537
General Armistice Agreement on (1949), 240–241
in Arab–Israel War (1967), 237, 248–249, 1063, 1224–1225, 1537, 2157
in Arab–Israel War (1973), 258
Arab Legion of (*See* Arab Legion)
Arab nationalism in, 1244
Arab National Movement in, 962
archaeological sites in, 1218
arms sales to, by United States, 304
art of, 144–145, 2001, 2429
in Baghdad Pact (1955), 1470, 1471
Baghdad Pact (1955) membership refused by, 363
Baghdad Summit (1978) on financial support to, 364
banking in, 390, *393*
Ba'th party in, 412
Bethlehem annexed by (1948), 468
Black September civil war in (1970), 1063, 1245
at Bludan Conference (1937), 488
borders of, with Saudi Arabia, 10
British mandate in (1922–1946), 512, 514, 1244, 1441, 1480
Abdullah I ibn Hussein in, 29–31, 512, 1244
Arab Legion during, 257
Cairo Conference on (1921), 554
Colonial Office administration of, 514, 617
end of, 518
Glubb (John Bagot) in, 922

Kirkbride (Alec Seath) in, 1324–1325
map of, *1762*
monarchic form of government during, 933
Peake (Frederick Gerard) in, 257, 1810
Transjordan Frontier Force defending, 2204
under Wauchope (Arthur), 2333
cabinet of ministers in, first, 35
and Camp David Accords (1978), 561
Catholics in, 1932
charitable *waqfs* in, 2323
children in, health care for, 1510
Circassians in, 600, 1218
cities of, 1218, 1243, 1979–1980
ancient, 1822–1823
capital, 190–192
northern, 1139
port, 217
provincial capital, 1270
civil war in (*See* Jordanian Civil War)
climate of, 1240–1241
constitution of (1952), 35, 2152
coup in (1957), 1925
attempted, 39, 258, 1632–1633
currency of (dinar), devaluation of, 1243
Dead Sea and, 684–685
defense costs as percentage of GNP or GDP, *1530*
democratization in, 1245
Hussein ibn Talal and, 1063
deserts of, 1240
East Jerusalem controlled by, 1224
economic and military aid to, 747
from Arab countries, *748*, 749
dependence on, 751
from IMF, 749
from United States, 748, 749, 750
economy of, 752, *753*, 753–754, 1243–1244
education in, in religious schools, 761
Egyptian relations with
Palestinian claims in, 154, 155
pledge of financial aid (1957), 1632
elites in, 776
and al-Fatah, 2156
feminism in, 819
at Geneva Peace Conference (1973), 900
geography of, 902–903, 1240
government of, 933
during Gulf Crisis (1990–1991), 951, 1064
Gulf of Aqaba in, 217
higher education in, 761, 2295
at Yarmuk University, 2380
honor killings in, 649, 887, 894
Noor al-Hussein in campaign against, 1691
women's activism against, 1065, 1902
human rights activism in, 1291–1292
human rights in, 1065
under Hussein ibn Talal, 1061–1065
immunization rate in, 1510
independence of, 30, 518, 1480
industrialization of, 1095
in Iran–Iraq War (1980–1988), 357
and Iraq, federation of, 999, 1925
Iraqi federation, 826, 1969
Iraqi relations with, 217
Badran (Mudar) and, 357
Islamic coin collections in, 1703
Islam in, 1242–1243
Islamism in, electoral success of, 1151
Israel and
attempted assassination of Mashʿal (Khalil al-) and, 1579
General Armistice Agreement between (1949), 240–241
Jordanian Option and, 1247
Khalidi (Walid) and, 1296
Mossad and, 1579
peace treaty between (1994) (*See* Jordanian–Israeli peace treaty)
Jericho under, 1221
journalism in, 1065
labor unions in, 1358
land ownership in, 1371
languages in, 1242
at Lausanne Conference (1949), 1375
in League of Arab States, 1386, 1388
legal system of, 886
civil code, 1382
French influences on, 1380
Majalla, 1381
legislative body in, 932
literacy in, 1291
literature of, 804–805, 1422, 2001, 2156
at London Conference (1939), 1445
Majali (Rufayfan) in, 1470
Majali family in, 1470–1471
manufacturing in, 1483, *1483*
military of (*See* Arab Legion)
minorities in, 1242
modern means of transport in, *2207*
Nabi Musi Pilgrimage banned by, 1630
national charter of, 1245
nationalism in, 520
nationalist movement in, 520
natural resources of, 1240
newspapers and print media in, transitional press, 1681
and Oman, in Dhufar rebellion, 705–706
in Ottoman Empire, 1244
overpopulation in, 1243
and Palestine Liberation Organization, 1063
Palestinians in, 1241–1242, 1916
activists, 1008
civil war by, 1246–1247
from Nakba, al-, 1639
number of, 1241
and population growth, 2426
refugee camps for, *1245*
parliament of
dissolution of (1954), 35
elections for, 1151, 1245
Palestinians in, 1222
recalling of (1984), 1245
in peace process, 1245–1246
PFLP in, 1840
airplane hijackings by (1970), 270, 1246, 1840
government challenged by, 1773
philanthropy in, 409
phosphate industry in, 1834–1835
and PLO, 270, 2156
political system of, 30
population of, *753*, 1844
postage stamps of, 1849
potash industry in, 1851
prime minister of, 999, 1925
radio and television in, *1895*
railways in, *2206*
religious freedom in, 1242
rivers of, 1248–1249, 2379–2380
development of, 1238, 1248
Saudi Arabian relations with
Hussein ibn Talal and, 2156
pledge of financial aid (1957), 1632
Talal ibn Abdullah and, 2152
security in, 357
stock market in, 2091, *2091*

Jordan *(continued)*
Sumud Fund by, 2121
Syrian Desert in, 2136
Syrian relations with
Asad (Hafiz al-) and, 2135
Badran (Mudar) and, 357
pledge of financial aid (1957), 1632
Talal ibn Abdullah reign, 2151–2153
textile industry in, *2181*
in trade, 2201
transit through, 1239
U.S. relations with, 1925
Free Trade Agreement in, 1593
military support in, 258
U.S. war on terrorism supported by, 32
Vatican relations with, 2310
war in Iraq supported by (2003), 32
water resources in, 1240, 1243, 1249, 2379–2380
from aquifers, 2329
freshwater withdrawals, *2331*
quantity of, 2330
West Bank unified with, 31, 1244
annexation by Abdullah I ibn Hussein (1950), 2339–2340
Jericho Congress on, 1221–1222
women in
activists, 1065, 1902
economic status of, *877*
in labor force, 877–878
literature on, 805
Noor al-Hussein as advocate for, 1691
in politics, 819–820, 893, 894
resource center for, 1852
rights for, 1291–1292
as students, 878
as writers, 804–805, 2001
women's rights in, 887
World Bank and
capital stock and voting power in, *2363*
loans from, *2364*
Yemeni relations with, coup (1962) and, 2156
Jordanian Civil War (1970–1971), **1246–1247**
Arab Legion in, 258
PFLP in, 1773
PLO in, 1246–1247, 1773
trigger for, 967
Jordanian Covenant Party, Majali (Abd al-Hadi) in, 1471
Jordanian Hashemite Fund for Human Development (JHFHD), 409
Jordanian–Israeli peace treaty (1994), 1168, 1246
Clinton (Bill) and, 606
Muasher (Marwan) and, 1593
and U.S. economic aid, 749
water resources in, 1249
Jordanian National Committee for Women, 409, 1852
Jordanian National Women's Forum, 1852
Jordanian Option, **1247**
Arafat (Yasir) in negotiations, 271
PNC rejection of, 1779
Jordan National Gallery of Fine Arts, 144–145
Jordan Phosphate Mines Company, 1851
Jordan River, 901, **1247–1250**, 2328, *2328*
and agriculture, 1248
aquifer of, 1249
conflict over, 237, 1248–1249
in Arab–Israel War (1967), 248
Dead Sea and, 685, 1248
development of
Johnston Plan for, 1238, 1248
Rutenburg plan for, 1248
draining of Hula Swamps and, 1047
in General Armistice Agreement (1949), 241
hydroelectric plan for, 1946
Israeli use of, 237, 1248–1249
salinity of, 1248
sources of water for, 1248, 1249, 2379
as water resource, 1668, 2328, 2330
Yarmuk River and, 1248, 2379
Jordan River Foundation, 32
Jordan University, Majali (Abd al-Salam) as president of, 1471
Joseph, tomb of, 1631
Joseph, Benjamin, *as contributor,* 468, 776–777, 900, 1019, 1221, 1630–1631, 1631–1632, 1672–1673, 1992–1993, 2157–2158, 2327, 2363
Joseph Conrad and the Fiction of Autobiography (Said), 1966
Joseph, Dov, **1250**
Josephus Flavius, 278, 1497
Jouhaud, Edmond, in Organisation Armée Secrète, 1715
Jour, Le (newspaper), 2254
Journal and "nationalité: immigré(e)" (Boukhedenna), 1427
Journal d'une femme insomniaque (Boudjedra), 497
Journalism. *See also* Newspapers and print media
in Arab countries, 1680
in Arabic language, 1419
in Egypt, 1012, 1419, 1838
in Iran, crackdown on, 1121
in Israel, 1683–1684
by women, 1003
in Jordan, by women, 1065
Palestinians in, 325
Persian, 1435
in Turkey, 1109, 1269, 1684–1685
Turkish, 1438
Journal 1955-1962 (Feraoun), 823
Journal Palestinien (Boudjedra), 497
Journey through the Qur'an (al-Ghazali), 914
Jours de Kabyle (Feraoun), 823
Jowzjan (Afghanistan), 2050
Joxe, Louis, 788
JP. *See* Justice Party
Jua'aba, Amal al-, in Women's Centre for Legal Aid and Counseling, 2356
Jua'abeh, Amal el-, in Women's Studies Center, 2362
Juba (Sudan), 2100
Juba Conference (1947), 2100
Jubayl, al- (Saudi Arabia), **1250**, 1997
housing for immigrant workers in, 2301
in Second Five-Year Development Plan, 1250, 2378
Jubilee Celebrations Committee (Israel), Moda'i (Yitzhak) as chairman of, 1555
Jubran, Salim, 1791
Jucovy, Jon, *as contributor,* 70, 119–120, 151, 182–183, 723–724, 1836, 2377
Judaean (publication), 1250
Judaism, **1250–1252**. *See also* Jew(s)
on birth control, 478, 479
conversion to, 1251
custom variations within, 1251
denominations within, determinant of, 979

in Diaspora, 1251
vs. Ethiopian Jews, 787
future of, 1252
Halakhah, 979
Hasidim in, 1002
Holy Land in, 1043
Jerusalem in, 1222, 1226, 1251
kosher in, 1335–1336
messianism in, 1519
origins of, 1250–1251
Palestine in, 1758
principles of, 1251–1252
Sabbath in, 1954
Talmud and, 2157–2158
Judea and Samaria. *See* West Bank
Judenstaat, Der (Herzl), 1021, 2433
Judeo-Arabic language, **1252–1253**
Judeo-Spanish language. *See* Ladino
Judezmo. *See* Ladino
Jufayr, al- (Bahrain), 369, *370*
Juha (Arabic character), 1648
Julien, Charles-André, 489
July Revolution (Egypt), 1465
Jumaʿa, Nuʿman, as New Wafd leader, 1686, 2321
Jumani, Dafi, 1972
Jumayyil, Amin, **1253**
appointing Aoun (Michel) as interim president, 1394
Geagea (Samir) challenging, 871
government of
Aoun (Michel) in, 215
Hoss (Salim al-) in, 1045
Karame (Rashid) in, 1272
vs. Hobeika (Elie), 1039
Israeli agreement of (1983)
nullification of, 1665
opposition to, 1665
Jumblatt (Walid) and, 1253, 1256
Karame (Rashid) opposing, 1272
National Salvation Front opposing, 1665
in parliament, 1253, 1831
in Phalange Party, 1400, 1831
presidency of, 1253, 1400, 1831
successor to, 1031
against Tripartite Declaration (1950), 1394
Twayni (Ghassan) under, 2254
U.S. support for, 1488
Jumayyil, Bashir, **1253**
in Arab–Israel War (1982), 253, 254
assassination of, 254, 1253, 1393, 1394, 1400, 1831, 1908, 1954
election of, 254, 1393, 1400
Franjiyya family rivalry, 849, 1394
Geagea (Samir) supporting, 871
Hirawi (Ilyas al-) and, 1033
Hobeika (Elie) and, 1038
Israeli support for, 253, 254, 1831
Israeli treaty rejected by, 254, 1103
in Lebanese Civil War, 581, 1253, 1661
in Lebanese Forces, 1253, 1393, 1394, 1400, 1831
presidency of, 1253, 1831
on "salvation committee," 1647
under Sarkis (Ilyas), 1992
Jumayyil, Nadim, 1253
Jumayyil, Pierre, **1253–1254**
death of, 1831
in al-Hilf al-Thulathi, 581, 1254
Khuri (Bishara al-) opposed by, 1315
in Lebanese Front, 1395
on National Pact, 1399
in Phalange party, 1254, 1831
Saade (George) as adviser of, 1951
in Socialist Front, 580
Jumblatt, Bashir, murder of, Chehab (Bashir) in, 584
Jumblatt family, 729, **1254–1255**
Arslan rivalry with, 307, 1255
Chehab (Bashir) crackdown on, 584
Jumblatt, Fuʾad, 1255
Jumblatt, Kamal, 729, **1255–1256**
assassination of, 729, 1255, 1256, 1853
Khuri (Bishara al-) opposed by, 1255, 1315
in Lebanese Civil War, 1255, 1256, 1853
in Lebanese National Movement, 1255, 1395, 1853
in Parliamentary Democratic Front, 1802
political power of, 1255–1256
in Progressive Socialist Party, 1255, 1852–1853
in Socialist Front, 580
Sulh (Rashid al-) and, 2117
Jumblatt, Nazira, 1255
Jumblatt, Walid, *727*, **1256**
attempted assassination of, 1256
and Damascus Tripartite Agreement, 1039
as Druze leader, 2059–2060
as family leader, 729, 1255, 1256
Jumayyil (Amin) and, 1253, 1256
in Lebanese National Movement, 1395
in National Salvation Front, 1665
in Progressive Socialist Party, 1256, 1853
Jumhuriyya, al- (newspaper), 911, 1678, 1956
Idris (Yusuf) in, 1082
Junayd, Abu al-Qasim al-, 2113
Jundi, Ahmad Sidqi Bey al-, in General Armistice Agreement (1949), 240
Jung, Eugène, 352
Junun (Bakkar), 376
Jurnal al-Iraq (newspaper), 1678, 1680
Jurnal al-Khadyu (newspaper), 1680
Jurshi, Salah Eddin al-, in Islamic Tendency Movement, 1586
Justice and Benevolence. *See* Adl wa al-Ihsan, al-
Justice and Charity. *See* Adl wa al-Ihsan, al-
Justice and Development Party (AKP) (Turkey), **99–100**, 2236
electoral success of, 99–100, 2245
Erdoğan (Tayyip) in, 781, 2245
establishment of, 99, 1911
ideology of, 100
Justice and Development Party (PJD) (Morocco), 2268
Justice Party (Iran), Dashti (Ali) in, 678
Justice Party (JP) (Turkey), **1257–1258**
coalition governments formed by, 2241
Confederation of Turkish Trade Unions relations with, 631
Demirel (Süleyman) in, 691, 1257, 2242
electoral success of, 691, 1257
establishment of, 1257
Gümüspala (Ragip) in, 1257
Nationalist Action Party and, 1257
organization of, 1257
Republican People's Party coalition with, 1257, 2241
State Planning Organization opposed by, 2089
True Path Party established by former members of, 2219
Justice sociale et développement en économie islamique (Brahimi), 506
Justinian
Aya Sofya (Hagia Sophia) rebuilt by, 342, 633
Constantinople under, 632–633

Juwayni, Abu Muhammad al-, 2019
Jwaideh, Albertine, *as contributor,* 678–679, 732–733, 804, 1478–1479, 1496, 1961–1962, 2182–2183, 2213

K

Kaʿba (Mecca), 935, **1259–1260,** 1507, 1595, 1597, *1997,* 2422
  Utaybi (Juhayman al-) occupation of, 2304
  as *waqf,* 2323
Kabaağaçlu, Cevatsakir, 490
Kabak, Aaron Abraham, **1260**
Kabediya, Abd al-Rahman, in coup (1958), 1699
Kabir, Maliki al-Amir al-, 1086
Kabir, Saʿud al-, Abd al-Aziz ibn Saʿud Al Saʿud treatment of, 10
Kabir, Sulayman Pasha al-. *See* Abu Layla
Kabul (Afghanistan), **1260**
  in Anglo–Afghan wars, 196–197
  as capital, 53, 56, 1260
  in civil war, 59, 1260
  Kabul University in, 1260
  under Karzai (Hamid), 1260
  mayor of, 807
  population of, 1260
  refugees in, 1260
  Taliban capture of, 1561
  Taliban in, 61
  Taliban occupying (1996), 2154
  Timur Durrani in, 56
Kabul River, 54
Kabul University, **1260–1261**
  Islamic movements at, 60, 63
  political parties at, 62, 1260
  Samar (Sima) at, 1981
Kabul Women's College, 786
Kabyle Revolt (1963), 442
Kabyles, 458, 459
Kabyle unrest (1980). *See* Berber Spring
Kabyle unrest (1985), 444
Kabyle unrest (2001). *See* Black Spring
Kabylia (Algeria), 458, **1261**
  agriculture in, 1261
  Arch tribal structure in, 274
  Berbers in, 121–122
    disorders among (2001), Coordination des Archs in, 638
    literature of, 192
    number of, 1261
    Tamazight language of, 121–122, 1261
    youth killed in detention (2001), 96, 274, 638
  disorders in (2001), Sadi (Said) resignation due to, 1960
  elections boycott in (2002), 1261
  Guenzetin assault (1955) in, 438
  population of, 1261
Kacemi, Abdel Hamid, 1904
  in Parti National Démocratique, 1805
Kach Party (Israel), 1184
  attacks by, 1264
  banned for racism, 1184, 1263
  Kahane (Meir) in, 1184, 1263
  in Kiryat Arba settlement, 1325
KADEK. *See* Freedom and Democracy Congress of Kurdistan
KADER (Turkey), 2171
Kadesh, Operation (Israel), 245
Kadha Ana Ya Dunya: Yawmiyyat Khalil Sakakini (al-Sakakini), 1973
Kadi-asker, 823
Kadiköy Girls School, 780
Kadīn Adaylarī Destekleme ve Eğitme Derneği, 2171
Kadīncīk Ana, 434
Kadin erenler (Araz), 274
Kadīn Eserleri Kütüphanesi ve Bilgi Merkezi. *See* Women's Library and Information Center (Istanbul)
Kadinlara Mahsus Gazete (newspaper), 148
Kadīnlar Halk Firkasi. *See* Women's People's Party (Turkey)
Kadinlar ve Siyasal-Toplumsal Hayat (Tekeli), 2170
Kadivar, Mohsen, **1261–1262**
Kadri, Mufide, **1262**
Kaffiya, 610–611
Kafi, Ali, in High State Council, 1026
Kafka, Franz, 216
Kafr Qasim (Israel), **1262**
  massacre of Palestinians in (1956), 1262
Kahana-Carmon, Amalia, 1433, 1434
Kahan Commission (1983), **1262–1263**
  on Eitan's (Rafael) role in Sabra and Shatila massacres, 774
  findings of, 254, 1263
  Shamir (Yitzhak) reprimanded by, 1263, 2026
  on Sharon's (Ariel) role, 254, 1263, 2026
Kahane, Binyamin, 1263–1264
Kahane Hai (Israel), 1263–1264
Kahane, Meir, **1263–1264**
  assassination of, 1263
  in Kach Party, 1184, 1263
Kahan, Yitzhak, 1954
  in Kahan Commission, 1263
Kahil, Mary, 1453
Kahn, Ann, *as contributor,* 70–71, 464, 469–470, 506–507, 508–509, 547, 856, 866, 926–927, 940–941, 955–956, 1015–1016, 1260, 1284–1285, 1322, 1407–1408, 1452, 1512–1513, 1550, 2024–2025, 2029, 2060, 2075, 2159–2160, 2168–2169, 2384
Kaid, Ahmed, **1264**
  in Oujda Group, 1743, 1744
Kairouan. *See* Qairawan
Kalam schools, 1148
Kalat (Afghanistan), 2417
Kalbiyya tribe, 2212
Kalem (magazine), Arseven (Celal Esat) in, 305
Kalemiyye (Ottoman Empire), **1264–1265**
Kalimat ala Jidar al-Samt (Bin Diyaf), 474
Kalimat Haqq (Abd al-Rahman), 21
Kalinock, Sabine, *as contributor,* 2359–2361
Kalischer, Hirsch, **1265**
Kalvaryski, Chaim Margaliut-, **1265**
  binationalism supported by, 473, 1265
  Kisch (Frederick Hermann) support for, 1326
  in Zionist Executive, 1265, 2402–2403
Kamal, Ahmad, **1265–1266**
  in Egyptology, 276, 1265–1266
Kamal, Zahira, **1266**
  at Madrid Peace Conference (1991), 1266
  in Women's Centre for Legal Aid and Counseling, 2356
  in Women's Studies Center, 2362

Kama Sutra, Burton (Richard Francis) translating, 548
Kamil, Kibrish Mehmet, **1266–1267**
Kamil, Mustafa (Egyptian nationalist, 1874–1908), **1267**
in Aqaba incident (1906), 218
Baring (Evelyn) criticized by, 406
British occupation of Egypt opposed by, 1267
Coptic response to, 640
death of, 1267
in National Party, 1267, 2297
speeches of, 1267
Darwish (Sayyid) adaptation of, 675
"What the National Party Wants," 1267
Kamil, Mustafa (Ottoman grand vizier)
in Balkan wars, 384
coup (1913) against, 384, 778, 1737
Kamil, Shaykh al-. *See* Mukhtari, Muhammad bin Isa al-Sufyani al-
Kamil, Shaykh Salih, 394
KAMPSAX, 2203
Kamran Durrani, 735
Kanafani, Ghassan, **1267–1268**
critical studies on, 322
Kanafi, Harwan, *1778*
Kanayan, Drastamard, 676
Kandahar (Afghanistan), **1268**
as capital, 1268
Durrani dynasty in, 55–56, 85
Omar (Muhammad) in, 1711, 1712, 2974
Taliban in, 61, 64, 1268
Kandehar (Iranian film), 1473
Kaniuk, Yoram, **1268–1269**
Kan, Suna, **1269**
Kant, Immanuel, 351
Kanun. *See* Qanun
Kanunlar (Barkan), 407
Kaplan, Mordecai, Ahad Ha-Am and, 78
Kapodistrias, Ioannes, 940
Karababa Dam, 788, 2141
Karabell, Zachary, *as contributor,* 40–41, 42, 43, 92, 118–119, 143–144, 215, 288–289, 339–340, 342–343, 363, 385, 387, 427, 437, 438, 454, 469, 485, 538–539, 541–542, 546, 554–555, 573–574, 602, 603–604, 628–629, 654–655, 672–673, 686, 687, 708–709, 723, 733–734, 755, 773, 783, 811, 824, 834–835, 838, 839, 841, 849, 936–937, 943, 945, 956, 964, 975, 996, 1023–1024, 1032, 1050, 1052–1053, 1083–1084, 1143, 1230, 1238, 1288–1289, 1330, 1335–1336, 1346, 1374, 1403–1404, 1446, 1501, 1513, 1518–1519, 1521, 1523, 1552, 1563–1564, 1565, 1575–1576, 1613–1614, 1640–1641, 1689, 1692, 1717–1718, 1806–1807, 1808, 1851, 1929–1930, 1933, 1988, 2006–2007, 2040, 2050, 2068–2069, 2081, 2097, 2127–2129, 2153, 2255, 2353
"Kara Bibik" (Nabizade Nazim), 1631
Karabisi, al-, 2019
Karacan, Ali Naci, **1269**
Karacan, Ercüment, 1269
Karachay language, 2252
Karagoz, 2187
Karaim language, 2252
Karaites, **1269–1270**
Karak, al- (Jordan), **1270**
Karakalpak language, 2252
Karakul, 2624
Karama, al- (magazine), 1716
Karama, Battle of (1968), **1270–1271**
Arab Legion in, 258, 1270–1271, 1773
al-Fatah in, 270, 1270–1271, 1772–1773
Karamanli dynasty. *See* Qaramanli dynasty
Karame, Abd al-Hamid, **1271**
Karame, Rashid, **1271–1272**
assassination of, 1272
government of, Jumayyil (Pierre) in, 1254
killing of, 871
in National Salvation Front, 1665
and PLO, refusal to deal with, 1031
as prime minister, 1271, 1272
resignation of, 1271, 1272
Karami, Umar, 1055, 2117
Karam, Yusuf, **1272**
Karanfil ve Yaseman (Mehmet Rauf), 1513
Karaosmanoğlu, Yakup Kadri, 1439
Karari, Battle of (1898), 1712
Kitchener (Horatio Herbert) in, 1712
Karasu, Bilge, 1438
Karbala (Iraq), **1272,** *2053, 2054*
armed resistance to U.S. occupation in, 2326
battle of
Muharram commemoration of, 1605–1607
retelling of *(majalis al-aza),* 1606
Husayn ibn Ali tomb in, as Atabat, 328, 1131, 1272
al-Husayn Mosque in, *1131*
U.S. capture of (2003), 2325
Wahhabi sacking of, 1625
Karbaschi, Gholamhosain, **1273**
Karikatür (magazine), 1676
Karimi-Majd, Roya, 2424
Karim Khan Zand, 1867
Karine-A (ship), 1169
Kariyuka, Tahiya, 866, **1273–1274**
Karkh, al- (Iraq), 361
Karkheh River, 1316
Karkhi, Abu al-Hasan al-, 988
Karkhi, Maʿruf al-, buried in Baghdad, 362
Karlowitz, Treaty of (1699), 339, 739
Karmal, Babrak, **1274**
factionalism under, 58
imprisonment of, 1274
Khyber (Mir Akbar) and, 1317
Najibullah (Mohammed) and, 1638
in People's Democratic Party of Afghanistan, 62, 1274, 1812
Parcham faction of, 62, 1274, 1801, 1813
political activism of, 1274
as president, Soviet installation of, 58, 65, 1274
Ratebzad (Anahita) and, 1906
Sediq (Sohaila) under, 2008
Kar, Mehrangiz, 894, **1274–1275,** 1365
and *Zanan* (magazine), 1274, 2423
Karmil, al- (newspaper), 1646, 1648
Karmil, al- (journal), Darwish (Mahmud) as editor of, 674
Karmi, Saʿid al-, in Arab Academy of Damascus, 223

Karnouk, Liliane, **1275**
Karo, Joseph, 979, 1962
Karoui, Hamed, 357
Karp, Judith, 1275–1276
Karp Report (1984), **1275–1276**
Karrubi, Mehdi, 1472
Kars (Russia), in World War I, 2367
Karsh, Efraim, *as contributor,* 1127–1129
Karst springs, in Ras al-Ayn (Syria), 344
Karun River, 93, 1316
  international navigation of, 2355
  sediments from, 901
Karzai, Hamid, *63, 400,* **1276**
  attempted assassination of, 1276
  British support for, 1276
  as deputy foreign minister, 1276
  Gailani (Ahmad) supporting, 864
  government of
    interim status of, 64, 1276
    Ismaʿil Khan in, 1021
    Jamiʿat-e Islami in, 64, 1215
    Loya Jerga confirmation of, 64, 1276
    Mojaddedi (Sebghatullah) in, 1561
    mojahedin in, 1561
    refugee situation under, 1912
    Samar (Sima) in, 1982
    Sediq (Sohaila) in, 2007
    Tajiks in, 67, 2150
  Hazara support for, 1015
  vs. Hekmatyar (Golbuddin), 1020
  Kabul under, 1260
  as president, 549, 1276
  Rabbani (Burhanuddin) and, 1889
  Taliban relations with, 1276
  U.S. support for, 67, 1276
  Zahir Shah and, 2421
Kasaba, Resat, 1036
Kasani, al-, 988
Kasap, Teodor, **1276–1277**
Kashan (Iran), bazaars of, 420
Kashani, Abu al-Qasem, **1277–1278**
  Arfa (Hasan) and, 286
  Borujerdi (Hosayn) opposing, 494
Kashf, 2112
Kashgari, Saʿd al-Din, 1642
Kashif al-Ghita (textbook), 1278
Kashif al-Ghita, Ali ibn Jaʿfar, 1278
Kashif al-Ghita family, **1278**
Kashif al-Ghita, Hasan ibn Jaʿfar, 1278
Kashif al-Ghita, Muhammad Husayn, 1278
Kashif al-Ghita, Musa ibn Jaʿfar, 1278
Kashmir, India–Pakistan conflict over, nuclear threat in, 1696
Kashrut (dietary laws), 1554
Kashwar Kamal, Meena, **1278–1279**
  assassination of, 1920
  and Revolutionary Association of the Women of Afghanistan (RAWA), 1920
Kasravi, Ahmad, **1279**
  assassination of, 820
  on women's issues, 891
Kasrawi, Samira al-, 1429
Kassala (Sudan), 2100
Kassallah (Sudan), **1279–1280**
Kasserine Pass, in World War II, 2370
Kasztner affair (1954–1955), 1042, **1280,** 2159
Kasztner, Reszo, 2159
Kasztner, Rudolf, 1280
Kataʾib, al-. *See* Phalange
Kataʾib al-Fida al-Arabi (Partisans of Arab Sacrifice), 962
Kataʾib Youth Organization, Moghaizel (Laure) in, 1557
Katatib, 761, 2147
Kateb, Yacine, **1280**
  in "Generation of 1954," 967
Katkov, Mikhail, 52
Katsav, Moshe, Modaʾi (Yitzhak) and, 1555
Katsnelson, Shmuel. *See* Tamir, Shmuel
Kattani, Muhammad Abd al-Hayy al-, 1281
Kattani, Muhammad ibn Abd al-Kabir al-, **1280–1281**
  Abd al-Hafid ibn al-Hassan crackdown on, 14, 1281
Kattaniya Brotherhood, **1281**
  Kattani (Muhammad ibn Abd al-Kabir al-) in, 1280–1281
Katznelson, Berl, **1281**
  in Jewish Legion, 1230, 1281
  in MAPAI, 1185, 1281
  social-democratic principles promoted by, 1362
Kavakci, Merve, *1381*
Kaveh (journal), 104, 1214
Kawakibi, Abd al-Rahman al-, **1282**
  and Arab nationalism, 261, 1282
  attack on Abdülhamit II, 1923
  and Islamic congresses, 1152
  revival of caliphate urged by, 1659
  treatises by, 1282
    Umm al-Qura, 1152, 1282
Kayali, Hasan, *as contributor,* 384, 556–558, 571–572, 622–624, 686–687, 778–779, 1737, 1742, 1800–1801, 2405–2407, 2408–2410
Kay, David, 1070
Kaye, Danny, 224
Kayhan Publishing Group, Yazdi (Ibrahim) in, 2383
Kaylani, Abd al-Rahman al-, **1282–1283**
  and Hawrani (Akram al-), 1010
  as prime minister, 1282–1283
  in Qadiriyya Order, 1282
Kaylani, Rashid Ali al-, **1283–1284**
  in Anglo–Iraqi treaties, 1283
  Arslan (Adil) opposition to, 306
  Arsuzi (Zaki al-) opposition to, 308
  and Fertile Crescent unity, 825
  French support for, 697
  German support for, 906, 944
  Hashimi (Taha al-) and, 999
  in Ikha al-Watani Party, 1084, 1283
  as interior minister, 1283
  and Jews in Iraq, 807, 1233
  as prime minister, 1283
  revolt against British by (1941), 516, 1283–1284
    Abd al-Ilah ibn Ali in, 15
    Abu al-Timman (Jaʿfar) support for, 35–36
    Arab Legion in response to, 257
    Arif (Abd al-Salam) support for, 287
    Bazzaz (Abd al-Rahman al-) in, 421
    defeat of, 1284
    Golden Square in, 927
    Husayni (Abd al-Qadir al-) in, 1052
    Husayni (Hajj Amin al-) supporting, 516
    Jabal (Badawi al-) in, 1205
    Jabr (Salih) in, 1210
    Syrian support for, 69
    Tamimi (Amin al-) in, 2158
  Sabbagh (Salah al-Din al-) and, 1953
  Sulayman (Hikmat) and, 2115

Kaza (Ottoman court), 1690, 2624
Kazakh language, 2247, 2252
Kazakhs, 2253
Kazan Tatar language, 2252
Kazimayn Mosque (Baghdad), *359*
Kazim Paşa, and Hijaz Railroad, 1029
Kazim, Safinaz, 1907
KDP. *See* Democratic Party of Kurdistan; Kurdistan Democratic Party
KDPI. *See* Kurdish Democratic Party of Iran
Keban Dam, 788, **1284**, 2082, 2141
Kedar, Benjamin, *as contributor,* 1497
Keddie, Nikki, *as contributor,* 51–53, 206–207, 2302
Kedourie, Elie, 1406
Kefar (Sobol), 2076
Kéfi, Ridha, 1429
Keightley, Charles, 2108
Keilberth, Joseph, 476
Keinan, Amos, **1284–1285**
Kemalettin Bey, **1285**
  Ottoman Revival style of, 282, 1285
Kemalism, **1285–1288**
  Atatürk (Mustafa Kemal) rejection of concept, 333
  definition of, 1285, 1815
  Gökalp's (Ziya) thoughts in, 924
  ideology of, 1286, 1287–1288
  and National Security Council, 1666–1667
  Ottoman opposition to, 823
  in People's Houses, 1815
  reforms of, 1286
  repression in, 1286–1287
  secularization in, 1286, 1287
  six principles of, 1918
  themes of, 2240
  Westernization in, 1285–1286
  and women's rights, 2359
Kemal, Namik. *See* Namik Kemal
Kemal, Orhan, 2160
Kemal, Yahya, 2160
Kemençe, 2160
Kempff, Wilhelm, 476
Kenaz, Yehoshua, **1288**, 1433
Kenen, Isaiah L., in American Israel Public Affairs Committee, 177
Keneset (periodical), 470
Kenitra (Morocco), 913, 1567
Kenitra Civil Prison, 497
Kennedy, John Fitzgerald, **1288–1289**
  American Israel Public Affairs Committee work for, 177
  Egyptian relations with, 1288
  "flexible response" strategy of, 1327
  government of, Kissinger (Henry) in, 1327
  Iranian relations with, 1118, 1753, *1753*
  Middle East policy under, 2291–2292
  Peace Corps established by, 1808
  presidency of, 1288–1289
  and White Revolution in Iran, 2351
Kent Actors, 1289
Kenter, Musfik, 1289
Kenter, Yildiz, **1289**
Kenuz (Nubian dialect), 1696
Kenya
  in Uganda Project, 2257
  U.S. embassy bombing in, 1865, *2177*
Kenyon, Kathleen, 277
  Palestine Economic Corporation funding for, 1772
Kerakanutiun Haykazian Lezvi (Chamchian), 579
Kerem (opera), 782
Kerem (Saygun), 2002
Keren Hayesod (World Zionist Organization), **1289**
Keren Kayemet le-Yisrael. *See* Jewish National Fund
Kerensky, Aleksandr, 1946
Kerman (Iran), **1289–1290**
  bazaars of, 420
  carpet weaving in, 566, 1290
Kermani, Karim Khan, 2047
Kermanshah (Iran), bazaars of, 420
Kerman Shaykhis, 2047
Kerr, Malcolm, assassination of, 181
Keskesi, 838
Keskin-Kozat, Burçak, *as contributor,* 33–34, 208, 472, 490–491, 492–493, 547–548, 598, 691–693, 745–746, 747, 762–763, 897–898, 965–966, 1201–1202, 1491, 1648, 2249, 2359, 2413–2414
Kesksou, 838
Kessar, Israel, **1290**
Ketabcheh-ye Ghaybi (Malkom Khan), 1477
Ketab-e Jomʿeh (weekly), 2027
Ketuvim, 2058, 2157
Keyhan Publishing Company, Khatami (Mohammad) in, 1303
KFAED. *See* Kuwait Fund for Arab Economic Development
Kfar Habad (Israel), Lubavitcher Hasidim in, 1002
Kfar Hittim (Sephardic settlement), 2364
KGB (Soviet Union), **1290**
  functions of, 1290
  organization of, 1290
Khabur River, 344, 2129
Khad (Afghanistan secret police), Najibullah (Mohammed) as president of, 1638
Khaddam, Abd al-Halim, **1290–1291**
Khader, Asma, 894, **1291–1292**
Khadija (wife of Muhammad), 1595–1596
Khadiri, 2209
Khaiber, Mir Akbar, 1801
Khair-Eddine, Mohammed, 1355, 1427–1428
Khakas language, 2247
Khalaf, Abdulhadi (Abd al-Hadi), **1292**
Khalaf, Muna, in Institute for Women's Studies in the Arab World, 1100
Khalaf, Nazar al-, *as contributor,* 410–411
Khalaf, Rima, 820
Khalaf, Salah (Abu Iyad), **1292–1293**
  as aide to Arafat (Yasir), 270
  Arafat (Yasir) work with, 1292
  assassination of, 814, 1292
  and Black September, 485, 1292
  as al-Fatah founder, 813, 1292, 1773
  Hasan (Hani al-) and, 997
  in PLO, 814, 1292, 2335
Khalas fi al-Mafhum al-Urthuduksi, al- (Shenouda III), 2049
Khaldunniyya (Tunisia), **1293**
  establishment of, 1293, 2408

Khaled, Leila, 521, *521*, **1293**
airplane hijackings by, 1293
in PFLP, 1293
released in prisoner exchange, 1293
Khal, Helen, **1294**
Khalid Baghdadi, Mawlana, 1642
Khalidi, Ahmad al-Samih al-, **1294**
at Arab College of Jerusalem, 226–227, 1294
wife of, 1975
Khalid ibn Abd al-Aziz Al Saʿud (king of Saudi Arabia), **1294–1295**, 1997
accession of, 1295
brother of, Al Saʿud (Muhammad ibn Abd al-Aziz) as, 164, 1294
as crown prince, 1295
education of, 1294
under Faisal ibn Abd al-Aziz Al Saʿud, 1294–1295
government of, Sultan ibn Abd al-Aziz Al Saʿud in, 165
and Hariri (Rafiq Bahaʾuddin al-), 994
partnership with Fahd ibn Abd al-Aziz Al Saʿud, 794–795, 798
reign of (1975–1982), 164, 1295, 1999
response to uprising (1979–1980), 164, 1295
Khalid ibn al-Walid, 662, 1044
Palmyra conquered by, 1798
Khalidi branch of Naqshbandi order, 1642
Khalidi, Husayn Fakhri al-, **1295–1296**
deportation of (1937), 1295, 1296
as Jerusalem mayor, 1224, 1295
as Jordan prime minister, 1295
Nashashibi family rivalry with, 1645
wife of, 1296
Khalidi, Mustafa al-, as Jerusalem mayor, 1224
Khalidi, Rashid, 1037
as contributor, 260–262, 1769–1771
Khalidi, Wahida al-, **1296**
in Arab Women's Executive Committee, 268, 1296
Khalidi, Walid, **1296**
PLO strategy influenced by, 1296
writings of, 1296, 1792
Khalid, Khalid Muhammad, **1296–1297**
Khalifa family. *See* Al Khalifa family
Khalifa group (Algeria), Zbiri (Tahar) and, 2429
Khalifa, Sahar, **1297**
Women and Family Affairs Center established by, 2355
in Women's Affair Center, 2356
on women's rights, 1792
Khalifa, Sulman ibn Ahmad, National Liberation Front and, 1661
Khalifeh, Sahar. *See* Khalifa, Sahar
Khalil, Fatima bint Asʿad, 817
Khalili, Mohammad Karim
Hazara ethnolinguistic group and, 1015
in Hezb-i-Wahadat, 64
Khalili, Ustad Karim, in Unity Party, 64
Khalil, Samiha Salama, 893, **1297–1298**
presidential campaign by, against Arafat (Yasir), 1297
Khalis, Mohammad Unis, **1298**
and Hezb-e Islami, 63, 1024, 1298, 1561
in mojahedin resistance, 1561
Khalis, Mowlana, in Afghan Islamic movement, 60
Khalq (Afghanistan), 58, 62, 1813
Amin (Hafizullah) in, 58, 62
in coup (1978), 1813
Najibullah (Mohammed) sent out of country by, 1638
rivalry with Parcham faction, 58, 62, 1801
Khal, Yusuf al-, **1298–1299**
Khamenehi, Ali, *1299*, **1299–1300**, *2258*
education of, 1299
election to presidency, 1119, 1299
as *faqih*, religious qualifications questioned by Montazeri (Hosayn Ali), 1564
government of, Musavi (Mir-Hosain) in, 1615
Khomeini (Ruhollah) and, 1299
Mohajerani (Ataollah) and, 1558
as president, 1899
as supreme spiritual guide, 1120, 1299
velayat-e faqih and, 2313
Velayati (Ali Akbar) under, 2313
Khamr (grape wine), 109
Khamsa. See Hand of Fatima
Khamsin wind, 605, 1161
Khan, 2120, 2624
Khandaq, al-, battle of (626), 1596
Khaneh Edrisi (Alizadeh), 149
Khangah, 2171
Khanjar, 2624
Khan Yunis, 870
Kharaj, 2167
Kharg Island (Iran), **1300**
in Anglo–Persian War (1856), 204
British occupation of (1838), 1300
in Iran–Iraq War (1980–1988), bombing of, 1300
Kharidjite Idabites, in Mzab region, 1627
Kharijite sect of Islam, 460
Azariqa branch of, 1073
Ibadiyya branch of, 1073
in Tunisia, 2226
Kharrazi, Kamal, **1300–1301**
foreign policy under, 1300–1301
internal criticism of, 1300–1301
Khartoum (Sudan), **1301–1303**, *1302*, 2100
Ahmad (Muhammad) in, 87
under Anglo–Egyptian control, 405, 1301
Arab League summit (1967) in, 1166, *1387*
Camboni School in, *1931*
Catholics in, 1932
infrastructure of, 1301, 1302
population of, 1301
under Turko–Egyptian control, 1301
university of, 2296
White and Blue Nile confluence at, 372, 902, 1301
Khartoum North (Sudan), 1302, 2100
Khartoum School, Ishaaq (Kamala Ibrahim) in, 1142
Khartoum University
Bint al-Shati at, 475
Salih (Teyib) at, 1977
Khashab wa Mukhmal (Nuri), 1704
Khassa, 774
Khasseki sultan, 2120
Khatami, Mohammad, **1303**
conservative constraints on, 1120, 1121, 1303
Ebtekar (Maʿsumeh) under, 745
election to presidency, 1120, 1121, 1303
Karbaschi (Gholamhosain) in, 1273
foreign policy of, 1300
and Freedom Movement, 850

government of
Kharrazi (Kamal) in, 1300
Mohajerani (Ataollah) in, 1558
Musavi (Mir-Hosain) in, 1615
Nabavi (Behzad) in, 1630
and Nasrallah (Hasan), *1038*
PFLP supported by, 1840
political reform by, lack of, 1121, 1303
reform movement launched by, 1303
Soroush (AbdolKarim) under, 2081
women's votes for, 998, 2424
Khatib, Abdelkarim, in Mouvement Populaire, 1588
breakaway faction of, 1588
Khatib, Ahmad al-, in Arab National Movement, 262
Khatibi, Abdelkabir, 396, **1303–1304**
Khatib, Muhibb al-Din al-, in Decentralization Party, 686
Khatib, Ruhi al-, 1224
Khatibs (preachers), 2624
khutba sermons by, 1315–1316
Khatisian, Alexander, 303, 676
Khatmiyya (Sudan), 2099, 2101
in Khartoum North, 1302
Khatmiyya Brotherhood (Sudan), in National Unionist Party, 2261
Khattabi, Muhammad ibn Abd al-Karim al-, **1304–1306,** *1305*
in exile, 1305
rebellion of (1921), 856, 1305–1306, 1450
Ahmad ibn Muhammad al-Raysuni in, 86
failure of, 1305, 1306
ideology of, 1305
Spanish–French forces fighting in, 2085
in Rif War, 1926–1927
Khattab, Umar ibn al-
on Armenians in Jerusalem, 290
conflict over election of, 1148
Khawaja, 2624
Khawar al-Udayd, tribes in, 2210
Khawr, 2624
Khayma, 2211
Khaymah shab bazi (Chubak), 593
Khayr al-Din, 860, **1306–1307**
Bayram V (Muhammad) under, 418, 1307
financial crisis arbitration by, 84, 1308
Khaznader (Mustafa) in conflict with, 1306, 1308
as Ottoman grand vizier, 1307
reforms by, 1307
reforms under, 1604
replacing Khaznader (Mustafa), 1604
resignation of, 1604
Sadiqi College founded by, 1307, 1959
as Tunisian prime minister, 1306, 1308
Khayr Eddin Pasha (Tunisia), Sadiki College established by, 1586
Khayri, Badi, Darwish (Sayyid) and, 675
Khayyatin tribe, 2212
Khayyat, Regina Habib, on Wafdist Women's Central Committee, 2321
Khazʿal Khan, **1307–1308**
Khaznader, Mustafa, **1308**
financial crisis under, 1308
Khayr al-Din in conflict with, 1306, 1308
Khayr al-Din replacing, 1604
Muhammad al-Sadiq and, 1603–1604
taxes under, 1604
Khazraj, Muhammad and, 1596
Khedive, 2624
Kheireddine, Mohamed, "New Appeal to the Algerian People" by (1976), 4, 1365
Khemir, Sabiha, **1308–1309**
Khemisti Law (Algeria, 1963), 132
Khider, Mohamed, **1309**
assassination of, 1309
in Comité Révolutionnaire d'Unité et d'Action, 620
in Etoile Nord-Africaine, 1309
French skyjacking of, 442, 1309
in Front de Libération Nationale, 1309
Khidhir, Zahra, **1309–1310**
Khilafat Congress (India), 556, 557
Khiraqi, Abu Qasim al-, 989, 990
Khiva, Khanate of, 1941
Khleifi, Michel, 833
Khlut tribe, 912
Khobar, al-. *See* Khubar, al-
Khoʾi, Abd al-Majid al-, 2071
Khoʾi, Abu al-Qasim al-, 2070
Khoʾi, Esmaʿil, 1436
Khojas, 1159
Khoma (Libya), 2246
Khomeini, Ruhollah, **1310–1312,** *1311, 1312*
anti-Western sentiment of, 1310–1311
arrest of, 850, 1310, 1311
and Iranian Revolution (1979), 1125
protests after, 1118, 1310, 1753
assassination of, planned, Qotbzadeh (Sadeq) in, 1880, 1881
Bakhtiar (Timur) supporting, 375
Bani Sadr (Abolhasan) and, 388, 1311
dismissal of, 1119
Beheshti (Mohammad) supporting, 427, 428
Borujerdi (Hosayn) associated with, 494
children of, 1310
criticism of Pahlavi (Mohammad Reza), 1606
Dabbagh (Marzieh) and, 659
death of, 1120, 1299, 1312, 1899, 2313
disciples of, Rafsanjani (Ali Akbar Hashemi) as, 1898
education of, 1299, 1310
education under, 761
in exile in Najaf, 328, 1311
fatwa issued by, 522
on Rushdie (Salman), 1300, 1558
Forqan denouncing, 842
Golpayagani (Mohammad Reza) supporting, 929
guilds supporting, 947
headquarters in Qom, 1880
in Iranian Revolution (1979), 1125–1126, 1311
Iranian supporters of, 1126, 1311
Islamic Jihad inspired by, 1155
Karbaschi (Gholamhosain) representing, 1273
Khamenehi (Ali) and, 1299
as *marja al-taqlid,* 1490
Montazeri (Hosayn Ali) and, 1564
Motahhari (Mortaza) and, 1583
Muharram influences on, 1606
and Musavi (Mir-Hosain), 1615
Musavi-Ardebili (AbdolKarim) and, 1614–1615
Nabavi (Behzad) and, 1630
Nateq-Nuri (Ali Akbar) and, 1653
National Front leaders purged by, 1656
opposition to, by Mojahedin-e Khalq in, 1562
political role of, 1311

Khomeini, Ruhollah *(continued)*
regime of, 934
return to Tehran (1979), 1119, 1126, 1311
Sane'i (Yusef) as student of, 1987
Shariatmadari (Kazem) opposing, 2036
Students in the Line of the Imam supporting, 2096
successor to, 1312
velayat-e faqih doctrine of, 793, 1311, 2311–2313
wife of, 1310
women's rights under, 892
Yazdi (Ibrahim) and, 2382, 2383

Khorasan (Iran), **1312–1313**
climate of, 1312
Naqshbandi in, 1642
population of, 1313

Khorasani, Akhund Molla Mohammad Kazem, 494

Khorde Avesta (Zoroastrian text), 2441

Khorramshahr (Iran), 1307–1308, 1317
in Iran–Iraq War (1980–1988), 1127

Khorvirap cathedral (Turkey), *297*

Khotanese language, 1125

Khouri, Fred J., *as contributor,* 2284–2285

Khraief, Bechir, **1313–1314**

Khrimian, Mkrtich (Armenian patriarch), 298, **1314,** 2087
at Congress of Berlin (1878), 1314
influence of, 303, 1314

Khrushchev, Nikita S., **1314**
Brezhnev (Leonid Ilyich) under, 507
on Hammarskjöld (Dag), 986
Mossad acquisition of speech delivered by, 1578

Khubar, al- (Saudi Arabia), **1315**
U.S. military apartments attacked in (1996), 1315

Khubz al-Hafi Sira Riwa'iyya, 1935-1956, al- (Shukri), 2060

Khufu, pyramids of, 1857

Khurasani, Akhund, 977

Khuri, Bishara al-, **1315**
and Christian–Muslim alliance, 2118
in Constitutional Bloc, 633–634, 981, 1315
Eddé (Emile) in feud with, 2202
Eddé (Emile) rivalry with, 1315
government of
Chamoun (Camille) in, 580
Chehab (Khalid) in, 585
Karame (Abd al-Hamid) in, 1271
Sulh (Riyad al-) in, 1315
and Hamadi (Sabri), 981
and National Pact, 1315, 1662–1663
opposition to, 1315
Chamoun (Camille) in, 580, 1315
Chehab (Fu'ad) response to, 584
Jumblatt (Kamal) in, 1255, 1315
Karame (Abd al-Hamid) in, 1271
Shader (Joseph) in, 2018
by Socialist Front, 580
Phalange party and, 1254
as president, 1315, 1399
as prime minister, 1315
resignation of, 580, 1315
Sulh (Kazem al-) and, 2116
and Sulh (Riyad al-), 1315, 2118

Khuri, Faris al-
in Arab Academy of Damascus, 223
in National Party, 1664

Khuri, Khalil al-, in Constitutional Bloc, 634

Khuruj al-Arabi, al- (Khalidi), 1295

Khusraw, Mulla, 988

Khutba, **1315–1316**

Khuzistan province (Iran), **1316–1317**
cities of, 2
capital, 93
climate of, 1316
in Iran–Iraq War (1980–1988), 1317
Khaz'al Khan in, 1307
map of, *1317*
population of, 1317
tribes in, 1316

Khyber, Mir Akbar, **1317**

Khyber Pass (Pakistan), 536, **1317–1318**

Kian (magazine), 1630, 2423

Kian-Thiébaut, Azadeh, *as contributor,* 187, 998–999, 1123, 1987–1988, 2051, 2153

Kianuri, Nur al-Din, **1318**
in Tudeh Party, 2222

Kiarostami, Abbas, *831,* 833, **1318,** 1473

Kibbutz, **1318–1320**
age segregation in, 1319
agriculture in, 1319, *1319,* 1320
dance in, 668
decline of, 1320
education in, 1320
elite status of, 1319, 1320
establishment of first, 855, 1319, 1320, 1361
jobs in, 1319, 1320, *1320*
as literary catalyst, 1432
Meir (Golda) and, 1513
Mizrahi movement and, 1554
Nahal and, 1634
origins of, 1320–1321
population of, 1319
age structure of, 1320
tenets of, 1319, 1320
Youth Aliyah and, 2411

Kibbutz Artzi movement, 1319

Kibbutz En Gev, Kollek (Teddy) in, 1331

Kibbutz Ha-Dati, 1321

Kibbutz ha-Me'uhad movement, 1178, 1319

Kibbutz movement, 1319–1320, **1320–1321**
establishment of, 1319
federations included in, 1319, 1320
and Histardut, 1034
Luz (Kadish) as leader of, 1448
number of kibbutzim in, 1319
religious, 1319–1320
secular, 1319
Shochat (Manya) in, 2059

Kidnappings, by al-Takfir wa al-Hijra, 2150

Kifak inta? (record), 818

Kikhya family, **1321–1322**

Kikhya, Fathi, 1321

Kikhya, Rashid al-, 1321

Kikhya, Rushdi al-, **1322**
in People's Party, 1322

Kikhya, Umar Mansur al-, 1321

Killean, Carolyn, *as contributor,* 232–234

Kilometer 56 (Shamir), 2024

Kimche, David, **1322**

King Abd al-Aziz University. *See* Umm al-Qura University

King–Crane Commission (1919), **1322–1323,** 2290, 2353
Crane (Charles R.) in, 646, 1323
creation of, Wilson (Woodrow) in, 1323, 2314
on Lebanon, 1323
on Palestine, 1323
on reunification of Syria, 824–825
Shahbandar (Abd al-Rahman) as interpreter for, 2021
on Syria, 1323
King David Hotel (Jerusalem), **1323–1324**
architecture of, 1323
bombing of (1946), 425, 1324
Churchill (Winston S.) on, 597
by Irgun Zva'i Le'umi, 1140, 1324
King Fahd Causeway, 367, *367,* 370
King Faisal International Prize for Islamic Studies, Ghazali (Muhammad al-) awarded with, 914
King Faisal University, 666
King, Henry C., in King–Crane Commission (1919), 1323
King-Irani, Laurie, *as contributor,* 353–354, 477–480, 773–774, 806–807, 884–890, 934–935, 1014, 1026–1027, 1297–1298, 1499–1500, 1672–1673, 1878–1879
King of Flesh and Blood, The (Shamir), 2024
King of the Benighted (Golshiri), 929, 1436
King Sa'ud University (Riyadh), **1324**
women at, 1324
Kingslake, Charles, 2088
Kinneret, Lake. *See* Galilee, Sea of
Kinneret, Lake (Israel), 1668
Kiouane, A., 1365
Kipling, Rudyard, 227, 936
Kippah. *See* Yarmulke
Kirghiz language, 2252
Kirkbride, Alan Logan, 1324
Kirkbride, Alec Seath, **1324–1325**
Kirkuk (Iraq), **1325**
oil production in, 1138, 1139, 1325
population of, 1325
U.S. capture of (2003), 2325
Kirmani, Mirza Agha Khan, 891
Kiryat Arba settlement (West Bank), 1019, **1325–1326**
establishment of, 1325
Levinger (Moshe) in, 1325
size of, 1325
Kiryat Shmona (Israel), PFLP–GC attack in, 1235, 1841
Kisakürek, Necip Fazil, **1326**
Kisas-i Enbiya ve Tevarih-i Hülefa (Cevdet), 578
Kisch, Frederick Hermann, **1326–1327**
Kishon, Ephraim, 2185
Kishon River, as Israeli water source, 1668
Kissinger, Henry, *1327,* **1327–1329,** *1328*
Carter's (Jimmy) rejection of policies of, 567
foreign policy of, 1327–1328
at King David Hotel, 1324
as national security advisor, 1327
in peace process, 1689
after Arab–Israel War (1973), 251–252, 1328, 1957, 2292
Rabin (Yitzhak) and, 1891
in realist school of international relations, 1327
Saunders (Harold) working with, 2001
as secretary of state, 1327–1328
in "Separation of Forces" agreement (1974), 241
shuttle diplomacy of, 1327–1328
Sisco (Joseph) as adviser to, 2070
Kitab, al-, 2018
Kitab al-Abyad li Huquq al-Mar'a al-Misriyya, al- (Shafiq), 2019
Kitab al-Aghrani (Abu Faraj al-Isfahan), 666
Kitab al-Hubb (Bannis), 396
Kitab al-Jilwa, 2214
Kitab al-Majmu (Adhani), 105
Kitab al-Milal wa al-Nihal (al-Shahrastani), 1457
Kitab al-Shifa (Avicenna), 1457
Kitab al-Tabikh fi al-Maghrib wa al-Andalus (cookery book), 838
Kitab al-Tih (Misbahi), 1429
Kitabat Kharij Aswar al-Alam (al-Asimi), 1428
Kitasato, Shibasaburo, 710
Kitchener, Henry Horatio, 1329
Kitchener, Horatio Herbert, *513,* **1329**
Abbas Hilmi II and, 5, 6, 405, 1329
Abdullah I ibn Hussein meeting with, 29
and Arab Revolt (1916), 263
Clayton (Gilbert) under, 603
defeat of mahdist state, 1464
in Egypt, 1329
in Fashoda incident (1898), 405, 529–530, 811
and Gordon Memorial College, 2296
in Karari, Battle of (1898), 1712
and National Party, 1664
Strorrs (Ronald) as secretary of, 2092
in Sudan, as governor-general, 629, 1329
Sykes (Mark) under, 2127
Wingate (Reginald) and, 2354
in World War I, 2366
Gallipoli campaign, 866
Kitroeff, Alexander, *as contributor,* 652–654, 937, 938–939, 939–940
Kivsat ha-Rash (Shamir), 2024
Klausner, Amos. *See* Oz, Amos
Kléber, Jean-Baptiste, **1330**
in Convention of al-Arish (1800), 289
Klein, Morton A., 2436
Klibi, Chadli, as secretary-general of League of Arab States, 1386
Klidar (Dowlatabadi), 722
Klutznick, Philip, 539
Knesset (Israeli parliament), **1330**
Abuhatzeira (Aharon) in, 37
Allon (Yigal) in, 153
Aloni (Shulamit) in, 157
Amit (Meir) in, 190
Arens (Moshe) in, 285
Avnery (Uri) in, 340
"basic laws" passed by, 1330
as substitute for constitution, 1164
cabinets approved by, 1164, 1330
on Camp David Accords (1978), 285, 561
Chazan (Naomi) in, 582
Cohen (Ge'ula) in, 612–613
Dayan (Moshe) in, 681
Dayan (Yael) in, 683
elections for, 1330
racism prohibited in, 1184
results of, 1167–1168, *1179–1180*
threshold for, 1175–1176, 1330

Knesset (Israeli parliament) *(continued)*
voting system used in, 1164, 1168, 1170, 1175–1176, 1330
formation of, 448
Habibi (Emile) in, 963
Hillel (Shlomo) in, 1030
Kahane (Meir) in, 1263
Kessar (Israel) in, 1290
Kol (Moshe) in, 1332
legislative process in, 1330
Navon (Yizhak) in, 1671–1672
Ne'eman (Yuval) in, 1674–1675
Netanyahu (Benjamin) in, 1677
Palestinian citizens represented in, 1786, 1788
Peled (Mattityahu) in, 1812
Peres (Shimon) in, 1817–1818
powers of, 1164, 1330
prime minister elected by, 1164, 1330
Rabin (Yitzhak) in, 1891
Rubinstein (Amnon) in, 1938–1939
Wahrhaftig (Zerah) in, 2322
Weizman (Ezer) in, 2337
Ya'ari (Me'ir) in, 2375
Yadin (Yigael) in, 2376
Yariv (Aharon) in, 2379
Yellin-Mor (Natan) in, 2385
Yizhar (S.) in, 2404
Knights of the Sinai, 1971
Kobra (princess of Afghanistan), in Association for the Protection of Women's Rights, 325
KOC. *See* Kuwait Oil Company
Kocharian, Robert
Jerusalem visited by, 292
presidency of, 303
Kochi, 2624
Koç Holding A.S., 1331
Koch, Robert, 712
Koç, Rehmi, M., 1331
Koç, Vehbi, **1331**
Kodashim, 2157
Kohn, Hans, 1461
Kohn, Leo, 448
Kokand, Khanate of, 1941
Kokar film trilogy, 1318
Kokoschka, Oskar, 2044
Kolars, John F., *as contributor,* 604–606, 698–702, 900–903
Kolb, Charles C., *as contributor,* 326–327, 385, 574–575, 1290, 1848–1849, 1940–1941, 2065
Koleyni, Abu Ja'far Mohammad, 1489
Kol ha-Am (newspaper), 1683
Kol Kitvei David Frischmann u-Mivhar Tirgumav (Frischmann), 856
Kollek, Teddy, **1331–1332**
as Jerusalem mayor, 1225, 1331–1332
Kol, Moshe, **1332**
Kol Shirei Shaul Tchernichovsky (Tchernichovsky), 2168–2169
Komedi-e Iran (theater), 2186
Komele, 1341
Komiteh, 2625
Königliche Museum (Berlin), Islamic coin collection of, 1702
Konya (Turkey), **1332,** 2237
Sufism in, 1332
Konya, Battle of (1832), **1332–1333**
Egyptian victory in, 1077, 1333
Konya Lycée, 492
Kook, Abraham Isaac Hacohen, **1333**
education of, 1333
Maimon (Yehudah Leib Hacohen) and, 1470
Qafih (Yihye ben Solomon) and, correspondence between, 1864
son of, 1333, 1334
successor of, 1022
Zonnenfeld (Yosef Hayyim) and, 2440
Kook, Zvi Yehuda, **1334**
Levinger (Moshe) influenced by, 1407
at Merkaz ha-Rav, 1333, 1334
Koor Industries, 1034, **1334–1335**
Amit (Meir) in, 190
Kopet Mountains, 901
Koprülü, Mehmet Fuat, **1335,** 1439
in Democrat Party, 695, 1335
Koraltan, Refik, in Democrat Party, 695
Koran. *See* Qur'an
Kordofan (Sudan), **1335**
Koren, Yeshayahu, 1433
Köroğlu (Saygun), 2002
Kortepeter, C. Max, *as contributor,* 564–566, 648–649
Kosher, **1335–1336,** 2360
Kosovo Liberation Army, 1913
Kosygin, Alexei, *1942*
Kotelawala, Sir John, at Bandung Conference, 387
Kotku, Mehmet Zahid, 780
Kovner, Abba, 508, **1336,** 1432
Koyi, Hajji Qadiri, 1340
KPC. *See* Kuwait Petroleum Corporation
KPC International, 1353
KPI. *See* Kuwait Petroleum International
Kramer, Martin, *as contributor,* 1152–1154
Krause, Wanda C., *as contributor,* 890–895
Kreisky, Bruno, Peled (Mattityahu) dialogue with, 1812
Kressenstein, Friedrich Kress von, 905
Krig oyf der Erd (Greenberg), 941
Krim, Belkacem, **1336–1337**
assassination of, 1337
in Comité Révolutionnaire d'Unité et d'Action, 137, 620, 1336
and Evian Accords (1962), 788, 1337
Kriyat Shmona (Israel), terrorism in, 2176
Ksars, 459
Ktubim (journal), 1431
Kuala Lumpur Declaration on International Terrorism (2002), 1722
Kub'a, Taysir, in PFLP, 1840
Kuchek Khan-e Jangali, 1216, **1337**
Küçük, Fazil, 697
Halkin Sesi founded by, 696
at London Conference (1959), 696
as vice president, election of, 653
Kuçuk Kaynara Treaty (1774), 485, 739, 2094–2095
Kücük Said Paşa, public defender introduced by, 1690
Küçük Sait, Kamil (Kibrish Mehmet) rivalry with, 1266
Kudsi, Nazim al-, **1337**
in People's Party, 1322, 1337
Küeli Incident (1859), 2164
Kufa (Iraq), 2052–2053, 2054
Kufar (unbelief), muwahhidun rejection of, 1625
Kufic writing, 558
Kufi script, 235
Kufrah (Libya), 1410
Kufta, 839

Kuhgiluyeh, 1447
Kuh-i Taftan (volcano), 385
Kulayni, Abu Jaʿfar al-, 2055
Kul system, 2072
Kultermann, Udo, 280
Kumaraswamy, P. R., *as contributor,* 586–587
Kumidiya Udib: Int Illi Qatalt al-Wahsh (Salim), 1978
Kumik language, 2252
Kumkapi French School (Istanbul), 492
Kum Ombo (Egyptian agricultural company), 1930
Kunt, I. Metin, *as contributor,* 33–34, 208, 334, 407, 472, 490–491, 547–548, 762–763, 864–865, 965–966, 1193–1196, 1201–1202, 1491, 1524, 1728, 1816–1817, 2009–2010, 2120, 2413–2414
Kupat Holim Kelalit (health fund), 1034
Kuran, Aptullah, *as contributor,* 386, 2120, 2194
Kurashi, Muhammad Abdullah al-, at al-Azhar, 347
Kurd(s), *1341,* **1344–1346**
  in cities, 1345
  culture of, 1344–1345
  international concern for, 1342
  in Iran, 694, 914, 1111–1112
    autonomy movement of, suppression of, 1922
    Azerbaijan province of, 345
    military action against, 1536
    Sunni faith of, 1548
  in Iraq, 1130
    Baʿth Party and, 1066
    CIA support for, 572
    after Gulf War, 1068
    Iranian support for, 1066
    during Iran–Iraq War, 1129, 1130
    Iraqi military action against, 1530, 1536, 1539
    Kirkuk, 1325
    Kurdish Autonomous Zone of, 1135, 1339
    in Mosul, 1469–1470, 1582
    no-fly zones and, 1069
    political parties of, 1807
    resistance in aftermath of Iran–Iraq War, 1915
    twelve-point agreement with, 422–423
    United Nations on, 1339, 2282
    U.S. invasion (2003) supported by, 2325
    in U.S. occupation, 2325–2326
    U.S. supporting, 2174
    in U.S. war (2003), 1339, 1341
  languages of (*See* Kurdish languages)
  literature of, 1345
  as minorities or subdominant group, 1549
  music of, *1618*
  in Naqshbandi, 1642–1643
  nationalism of, 1659
  number of, 1342, 1344
  origins of, 1344
  refugees, 1914–1915
  religion of, 1345
  revolts by (*See* Kurdish revolts)
  society of, 1345
  in Syria, Hayy al-Akrad quarter, 100
  in Turkey, 2238
    Atatürk (Mustafa Kemal) and, 1549
    Diyarbakir, 715
    imprisonment of political activists, 2423
    infiltration of, 1545
    military action against, 1536
    pocu of, 610–611
    and Refah Partisi, 1911
    Republican People's Party and, 1919
    revolt of 1922-1925, 1914
  Yasar Kemal as, 2381
  Yazidis as, 2214
Kurd Ali, Muhammad, **1338**
  in Arab Academy of Damascus, 223, 1338
  education of, 1338
Kurdish Autonomous Zone (Iraq), **1339,** 2151
  establishment of, 1135
  Patriotic Union of Kurdistan in, 1807
  power sharing in, 1339, 1807
  regional division of, 1339
  Washington Agreement on (1998), 1339, 1807
Kurdish Democratic Party of Iran (KDPI), 914
Kurdish languages, 1344, 2238
  in Alevi Shiʿism, 113
  dialects of, 1124, 1342, 1344
  written, 1344
Kurdish nationalism, 1340. *See also* Kurdish revolts
Kurdish Regional Government, 2151
Kurdish revolts, **1339–1342**
  foreign intervention in, 1340
  in Iran, 1340, 1341
  in Iraq, 1134, 1340–1341
    Arif (Abd al-Salam) failure to end, 288
    Barzani (Mustafa) in, 1341, 1873
    Hussein (Saddam) and, 1134, 1135
    international support for, 1127, 1134
    Mossad support for, 1578
    Pahlavi (Mohammad Reza) supporting, 1127
    Talabani (Jalal) in, 2151
  in Turkey, 1340, 1341
    by Kurdistan Workers Party, 1341, 1342, 1343
Kurdish Workers Party (Turkey), 1944
Kurdistan, **1342**
  autonomy movement of, 1469–1470
  Barzani family in, 408–409
  boundaries of, 1342
  cities of, 1342, 2115
  Iranian, 1342
  Iraqi, 1339, 1342
  Lausanne Treaty (1923) and, 1376
  mountains of, 1342
  rivers in, 1342
  Sèvres Treaty (1920) and, 1376
  Shiʿite Islam in, Ahl-e Haqq sect of, 82
  Turkish, 1342
Kurdistan Democratic Party (KDP), *1642,* 2151
Kurdistan Front of Iraq, 1339, 1807
Kurdistan Workers Party (PKK) (Turkey), **1342–1344**
  Alevis in, 114
  dissolution of, 1344
  establishment of, 1343
  ideology of, 1342, 1343
  origins of, 1342–1343
  revolt by (1984–1999), 1341, 1342, 1343
  violent tactics of, 1342, 1343
Kurdufan. *See* Kordofan
Kuria Muria islets, 527
Kurmandji dialect, 1344
Kush (Nubian kingdom), 1695
Kütahya Convention (1833), 2093

Kütahya, Peace of (1833), **1346**
Syria in, 1077
Kut al-Amara (Iraq), **1346**
battle of (1916), 1346
British surrender at, 509, 1346
Kashani (Abu al-Qasem) in, 1277
Maude (Frederick Stanley) at, 1501, 2367
World War I battles for, 1519, 2367
Kutan, Recai, 1911
Kutaysh, Umar, in PFLP, 1840
Kutla, al- (Morocco), 1574–1575
Kutla al-Wataniyya, al- (Libya), in national movement, 615–616
Kutnick, Jerry, *as contributor,* 177–179, 2436
Kutschera, Chris, *as contributor,* 408–409, 694–695, 1339, 1342, 1344–1346, 1469–1470, 1807, 1914–1915, 2151, 2380–2381
Kuttab, 475, 756, **1346–1347,** 2224
Kuttab, Eileen, 1100
Kuttab, Jonathan, 991
Kutubchi, Mullah Khidhir al-, 1309
Kutubiyya mosque (Morocco), 1568
Kuvayi milliye kadinlari (Araz), 274
Kuwait, **1347–1351**. *See also specific cities, organizations, people, and regions*
Abd al-Aziz ibn Saʿud Al Saʿud in exile in, 9, 10
Al Sabah family in, 158–160, 1348
Al Saqr family in, 161–162
Arabian Mission in, 231
archaeological artifacts taken from, 279
architecture of, *1350*
banking in, 159, 162, *393*
and Beitaddin Declaration (1978), 432
borders of
ambiguity of, 1349
Anglo–Turkish convention on (1913), 159, 1678
with Saudi Arabia, 1678
Uqayr Treaty on (1922), 159, 1349
Britain and, bond between, 1348–1349
British control of, in foreign policy, 160
British protectorate in, 534
British treaty with (1899), 531, 614, 1348
cities of, capital, 1351–1352
citizenship in, 1351
climate of, 1347
constitution of, 159, 160, 162
mineral resource ownership in, 1353
constitution of (1962), 1350
defense costs as percentage of GNP or GDP, *1530*
economic aid from, 749, 1349–1350, 1352
economy of, 752, *753,* 1349–1350, 1352
family planning in, 478
foreign policy of, 1350–1351
economic aid in, 1350–1351, 1352
geography of, 1347
in Gulf Cooperation Council, 949
in Gulf War (1990–1991), economic impact of, 1349
higher education in
at American University of Kuwait, 181
at Kuwait University, 1353–1354
women in, 1353–1354
immigrants in, 1347
independence of, 520
infant mortality rate in, 1509
Iraqi claim to
British troops as deterrent against, 520
Bubiyan Island, 541, 949
Qasim (Abd al-Karim) on, 1873
al-Warba Island, 541, 949
Iraqi invasion of (*See* Gulf Crisis (1990–1991))
Iraqi negotiations with, Ibrahim (Izzat) in, 1078
labor unions in, 1358
in League of Arab States, 1387, 1388
legal system of
civil code, 1382
French influences on, 1380
Majalla, 1382
reforms in, 1380
legislative body in, 932
liberation of (1991), 951
literature of, 1952
manufacturing in, 1483, *1483*
map of, *1347*
merchant opposition in, 159, 161
military of
equipment of, *1534*
force levels of, *1528–1529*
force structure of (army, air force, and navy), *1532–1533*
modern means of transport in, *2207*
natural gas production and reserves in, *1671*
neutral zone shared with Saudi Arabia, 1678
newspapers and print media in, 1679
diversity in, 1681
English-language, 1681
oil in, 537, 2199
oil nationalization in, 1349
oil production in, 752, 1349
concessions for, 1349
al-Ghanim family in, 911
after Iranian nationalization, 1349
by Kuwait Oil Company, 1349, 1824–1825
by Kuwait Petroleum Corporation, 1352–1353
oil revenues in, 1349
in OPEC, 1349, 1719
Ottoman alliance with, 158, 160, 161
Palestinians in, 1793
number of, 1347
persecution of, after Gulf War, 952
parliament of, 159, 160, 162
architecture of building, *1350,* 1351
elections for, 1350
power of, 1350
suspension of, 1350
political parties in, 1350
political system of, 1350
population of, *753,* 1347, 1844
prime minister of, monopoly on, 1350
Protestant missions in, 1854
radio and television in, *1895*
religion in, 1348
ruler succession in, 1350
Sanʿa University (Yemen) supported by, 1985
science and technology in, 2005
Shiʿism in, 2052
social services in, 1349
stock market in, 2091, *2091*
in trade, *2200*
tribes in, 2213
U.S. support for, dependence on, 1351
water resources in, 1347
women in
economic status of, *877*

higher education for, 1353–1354
in politics, 1350, 1951–1952
as writers, 1952
women's rights in, 884, 1951–1952
World Bank and
capital stock and voting power in, *2363*
relative voting strength in, *2364*
Kuwait: Anatomy of a Crisis Economy (al-Sabah), 1952
Kuwait, Bay of, 1347
Kuwait City, **1351–1352**
architecture of, 1351
in Gulf War (1990–1991), 1351
National Assembly building in, *1350*, 1351
population of, 1352
traffic in, 1352
urban sprawl in, 1351–1352
walls around, 1351
Kuwait Foreign Petroleum Exploration Company, 1353
Kuwait Fund for Arab Economic Development (KFAED), 1349, **1352**
recipients of, 1352
Kuwait Museum, 1351
Kuwait Natural Petroleum Company, 1353
Kuwait Oil Company (KOC), 1349, 1824–1825
al-Ghanim family in, 911
as Kuwait Petroleum Corporation subsidiary, 1353
Kuwait Oil Tanker Company, 1353
Kuwait Petroleum Corporation (KPC), **1352–1353**
establishment of, 1349, 1353
Kuwait Petroleum International (KPI), 1353
Kuwait Stock Exchange, 1952
Kuwait University, **1353–1354**
Awadhi (Badria A. al-) at, 341
in Gulf War (1990–1991), 1353
Sabah (Rasha al-) at, 1952
vs. San'a University, 1985
Kuyas, Ahmet, *as contributor*, 330–334, 2071
Kvergic, H. F., 2122
Kwanyin, Kerubino, 868
Kyle, Ella, 1902
Kyprianos (Eastern Orthodox archbishop), 652
Kyprianou, Spyros, presidency of, 654, 697
Kyrgyz language, 2247
Kyrgyz people, 2253

L

Laabi, Abdellatif, **1355–1356**, 1428
Laayounne (Western Sahara), **1356**, 2342
Labor Alignment (Israel)
MAPAI in, 1185
MAPAM in, 1185
Labor and labor unions, **1357–1359**. *See also* Child labor
in Algeria, 1358
development of, 1357
in Djibouti, 1358
in Egypt, 1358
illegal, 1358
imperialism's impact on indigenous, 1088–1089
in Iran, 1359, 2222
in Iraq, 1358
in Israel, 1357, 1358, 1361, 1362 (*See also* Histadrut; Labor Zionism)
in Jordan, 1358
in Kuwait, 1358
in Lebanon, 1358
in Libya, 1358
Marxism and "scientific socialism" and, 1357
in Mauritania, 1358
in Morocco, 453, 1358, 2264, 2265–2266
confederation of, 629–630
strikes by, 2264
privatization creating conflicts with, 1359
in Somalia, 1358
structure of, 1358
in Syria, 1358
in Tunisia, 41, 486, 1358, 2227, 2264–2265
for employers, 2268–2269
strike by, 2265
in Turkey, 1358–1359, 1359
confederation of, 631, 1358–1359
Koç (Vehbi) on, 1331
women in (*See* Gender, and economy)
in Yemen, 1358
Labor Party (Israel). *See* Israel Labor Party
Labor rights, films on, 832
Labor Zionism, **1359–1362**, *1360*, *1361*, 2372, 2434
as basis of Histadrut, 1357
Ben-Zvi (Yizhak) supporting, 456, 457
Borochov (Ber) and, 493
Gordon (Aaron David) as philosopher of, 930
origins of, 1359–1360
in Palestine, 1357, 1360–1362
Revisionist Movement's conflict with, 1209, 1973
spread of, 1361
Lacheraf, Mostefa, **1362**
Lacoste, Robert, **1362–1363**, 1443
as Catroux (Georges) replacement, 570
Lacy, Lisa M., *as contributor*, 230–231
LADH. *See* Ligue Algérien des Droits de l'Homme
Ladino language, 1231, **1363**
Lado Enclave, **1363**
Laenser, Mohand, in Mouvement Populaire, 1588
Lagaillarde, Pierre, in Organisation Armée Secrète, 1715
Lagin (Mamluk sultan), 1074
La Guera, under Spanish control, 2085
Lahad, Antoine, **1364**
attempted assassination of, 481
as South Lebanon Army leader, 1364, 2083
Lahathat min Umri (al-Sabah), 1952
Lahhud, Emile, **1364**
government of, Hoss (Salim al-) in, 1045
Hariri (Rafiq) in conflict with, 994, 1364, 1401
as leader of Lebanese Army, 1364
as president, 1364, 1401
supporting Hizbullah, 1364
Lahiji, Shahla, 894, **1364–1365**
Lahm mishwi, 841
Lahouel, Hocine, **1365**
"New Appeal to the Algerian People" by (1976), 4, 1365
Lahrani, Sid Ahmed, 918
Lakes. *See specific lakes*
Lalluh, Abd al-Rahim, in PFLP, 1840
Lamari, Mohamed, **1365–1366**
La Marsa Convention, **1366**, 2229
French protectorate over Tunisia confirmed by, 1604
Lamartine, Albert, 2068
Lamartine, Alphonse de, 1421, 2088

Lamb, 839, 840
Lamdan, Isaac, 1432
Lamdan, Yitzhak, 1497
Lamerhav (Israeli newspaper), 1512
Lampson, Miles (Lord Killearn), 810
  and Wafd party, 2320
Lamrani, Muhammad Karim, **1366**
  as economic adviser, 1366
  as prime minister, 1366, 1374
Land Code of 1858 (Ottoman Empire), **1366–1369**
  aim of, 1366
  Cevdet (Ahmed) in, 577, 1367
  content of, 1366–1367
  land ownership and taxation after, 1367–1369
  land ownership and taxation before, 1367
  and social structures, 885–886
Land Day, **1369**
Landen, Robert G., *as contributor,* 203–204, 1498–1499, 1500, 1616, 1709–1711, 2064
Land Law (1858) (Egypt), 1970
Landman, Nico, *as contributor,* 1704–1705
Land mines
  campaign to ban, Noor al-Hussein in, 1691
  laid during Gulf War, 1510
Land of Israel Movement
  Hazaz (Hayyim) and, 1015
  in Likud, 1184, 1417
Land ownership. *See also* Property rights
  and agriculture, 75–76
  colonialism and, 1370–1371
  in Iran, after Iranian Revolution (1979), 1372
  in Israel, by Palestinian citizens, 1786
  in Morocco, Azib system of, 350
  in Ottoman Empire, 1370–1371
    after Land Code of 1858, 1367–1369
    before Land Code of 1858, 1367
    of *shaykh,* 1368, 1369
  of women, 878
Land reform, **1369–1373**
  and agriculture, 76
  in Algeria, 1372
  in Arab socialism, 265
  in Egypt, *1370,* 1371–1372
  in Iran, *1371,* 1372, 1753
    in White Revolution, 2351–2352
  in Iraq, 1372
  in People's Democratic Republic of Yemen, 1372–1373
  phases of, 1370
  in Syria, 1372, 2131
  in Tunisia, 1372
Land registration, in Ottoman Empire, 1367, 1368
Landsdowne, Lord, 734
Landsmannschaften, **1373**
Lane-Poole, Stanley, Islamic coin catalog, 1702
Langer, Felicia, **1373–1374**
Langer, Moshe, 1373
Language(s). *See also specific languages*
  and nationalism, 1657
  written, in calligraphy, 558–559
  Zaydan (Jurji) on, 2426
Lansdowne, Henry Charles Keith Petty Fitzmaurice, 533, **1374**
Lansing, John G., in Arabian Mission, 231
Lap of the Beautiful Lady, The (Ikhlassi), 1084
La Pointe, Ali, 141
Laqqani, Ibrahim al-, Afghani (Jamal al-Din al-) and, 51
Laraki, Ahmad, **1374**
  as foreign affairs minister, 1374
  as prime minister, 1374
Laroui, Abdallah, 1091
Lashemesh (Tchernichovsky), 2168
Lashkar Gah. *See* Bost (Afghanistan)
Laskier, Michael M., *as contributor,* 105–107, 131–135, 151–152, 500–503, 651, 690–691, 805–806, 807, 1599–1602, 1637, 1838, 1864, 1913–1914, 1930, 1963, 2096–2097, 2365
Laskov, Haim, in Israel Defense Force, 1173
Last Sea, The (documentary), 956
Lata'if, al-Muqtataf, al- (publication), 1374
Lata'if al-Musawwara (magazine), **1374–1375**
Latakia, **1375**
Latif, Ali Abd al-, White Flag League founded by, 2349
Latin alphabet
  Arabic alphabet relation to, 234
  in Turkish language, 235, 332
Latin Catholic church, 593
Latin script
  in Azeri language, 347
  in Tajiki language, 1820
Lattouf, Mirna, *as contributor,* 95, 431–432, 899–900, 1100
Lausanne Conference (1949), **1375–1376**
  Shiloah (Reuven) at, 2056
  Turkish representation at, 331–332, *740, 741*
  United Nations Conciliation Commission for Palestine at, 2285
Lausanne Protocol, 1376
Lausanne, Treaty of (1923), 514, **1376–1377,** 1565
  Armenian genocide ended by, 295
  capitulations ended by, 566, 621
  civil codes required by, 601, 602
  and Dönme, 720
  Eastern Question resolved in, 743
  Nahum (Hayyim) and, 1637
  Turkish sovereignty in, 1802
  Turkish Straits free passage in, 621
Lausanne University, Tekeli (Şirin) at, 2170
Lauzière, Henri, *as contributor,* 46–47, 505–506, 1572–1573, 2375–2376, 2410–2411
Laval, Peirre, 1933
Lavie File (Israel), 1674
Lavi, Yoel, 1901
Lavoix (numismatic scholar), 1702
Lavon affair, 449, 785, **1377–1378,** 1991
  Ben-Gurion (David) resigning over, 1185, 1188
  Mossad in, 1577–1578
  RAFI Party on handling of, 1188
Lavon, Pinhas, **1378**
  in Lavon affair, 1377–1378
  and military politicization, 1173
  as secretary-general of Histadrut, 1377, 1378
Lavta, 2160
Law, modern, **1379–1384**
  advantages of, 1379
  British influences on, 886, 1380
  French influences on, 886, 1380, 1382–1383
  gender and (*See* Gender, and law)
  Italian influences on, 1382
  movements against, 1379

political pressures on, 1379–1380
reforms leading to, 2034–2035
distinctive paths of, 1383
progress of, 1380–1383
shariʿa-based, 1379, 1382, 1383
Law in the Service of Man. *See* Haq, al-
Law, Islamic. *See Shariʿa; specific schools of law*
Law of Return (Israel), 787, **1384**
and *aliyah,* 147
impact on population, 1162
Law on the Protection of the Family. *See* Turkish Law on the Protection of the Family (1998)
Lawrence, John, Anglo–Afghan Treaty signed by (1855), 196
Lawrence of Arabia. *See* Lawrence, T. E.
Lawrence of Arabia (film), 2039
Lawrence, T. E., **1384–1385**
in Arabian Peninsula, 232
in Arab Revolt (1916), 264, 510, *511,* 513, 1384
Askari (Jaʿfar al-) under, 324
at Cairo Conference (1921), 554
in Churchill–Abdullah I negotiations, 29
Doughty (Charles) and, 722
and Faisal-Weizmann Agreements, 800, 803
Kirkbride (Alec Seath) and, 1324
at Paris peace settlements (1919), 511
Storrs (Ronald) and, 2092
in World War I, 151, 1527, 2368
Lawson, Fred H., **1479**
as contributor, 149–150, 223–224, 367–371, 436, 476, 662–664, 851, 982, 1044, 1282, 1290–1291, 1504–1505, 1602–1603, 1607, 1631, 1661–1662, 1690, 1810, 1955–1958, 2071, 2129–2135, 2263
Layada, Abdelhak, in GIA, 918, 919
Layard, Austen Henry, 276
Layeq, Sulaiman, 1801
Layla (film), 832
Laylat imraʾa Ariqa (Boudjedra), 497
Laz, 2625
Laz, al- (Wattar), 1426
Lazaron, Morris, in American Council for Judaism, 176
Lazma, 2625
LDA. *See* Local Development Association
League against German Antisemitism. *See* LICA (Egypt)
League for Jewish–Arab Rapprochement and Cooperation, binationalism supported by, 473
League for National Liberation, Tubi (Tawfiq) in, 2221
League of Arab States, **1385–1389**
Abdullah I ibn Hussein as architect of, 1386
Algeria in, 1387, 1388
Ibrahimi (Lakhdar al-) representing, 1078
All-Palestine Government proposed by, 154–156
and Arab Convention on Human Rights, 1048
Arab Liberation Army of, 259, 1052
in Arab–Israel War (1948), 259, 1879–1880
Bahrain in, 1387, 1388
at Bluden Conference (1946), 488
boycott against Israel by, 224–225
Charter of (1945), nation-state nationalism in, 262
committees of, 1386
Comoros in, 1388
conference establishing (1944), Alami (Musa al-) at, 103
council of, 1386
delegations of, 1385
Djibouti in, 1388
Egypt in, 1386, 1388
Abd al-Maguid (Esmat) representing, 16
member-state dues of, 1387
readmission of, *1387,* 1388
suspension of membership of, 364, 771, *1387,* 1388
Eritrea as observer in, 1388
establishment of, 222, 517, 825, 1385–1386
financing, 1387–1388
headquarters of, 364, 503, 771, 1385
Iraq in, 1386, 1387, 1388
condemned for invasion of Kuwait, 951
on Israel, normalization of relations with, 220
Jordan in, 1388
on Jordan River diversion, 237
Kuwait in, 1387, 1388
Lebanon in, 1386, 1388
Libya in, 1387, 1388, 2218
withdrawal of membership, 1388
Maksoud (Clovis) in, 1474
Mauritania in, 1388
membership of, 1388
Morocco in, 1387, 1388
Nahhas (Mustafa al-) as architect of, 1386, 1636
negotiations establishing, Rifaʿi (Samir al-) in, 1925
Oman in, 1388
organization of, 1386–1387
on Palestine
civil administration in, 154
multiple partition plans for, 154
Palestine in, 1385, 1388
and PLO, 813, *1387,* 1388, 1774
policy of, 1388
POLISARIO not accepted by, 1964
prospects of, 1388–1389
purpose of, 1385
Qatar in, 1388
Riyad (Mahmud) as secretary general of, 1928
Saʿid (Nuri al-) as architect of, 1386, 1968
Sasson (Eliyahu) contacting, 1993
satellite organizations of, 1388
Saudi Arabia in, 1386, 1387, 1388
secretary-general of, 352, *1385,* 1386
Shuqayri (Ahmad) as secretary of, 2062
Somalia in, 1388
Sudan in, 1388
summits of (*See* Arab League summits)
Syria in, 1386, 1388
trade boycott by, 2200–2201
Transjordan in, 1386
and Tunisia, 1388, 2428
United Arab Emirates in, 1387, 1388
on water resources
from Jordan River, 237, 1238, 1248
from Yarmuk River, 2380
Women's Committee of, 894
Yemen in, 1385, 1386, 1387, 1388
League of Christian Sects, 2202
League of Human Rights, 439
League of National Action (Syria), Arsuzi (Zaki al-) in, 308

League of Nations
in Anglo–Turkish dispute over Mosul, 1583
Article 22 of, 1479
covenant of, consideration of territories' wishes in, 1323
establishment of, 2314
Fertile Crescent mandates, 824
Germany in, 906
Iraq in
admission of, 35, 203, 802, 1132
Pachachi (Muzahim al-) representing, 1751
Italy in, ostracism of, 1200
mandate system of, 514, 1479–1480, 1988, 2314
Permanent Mandates Commission overseeing, 1819
Turkey in, Treaty of Ankara and (1930), 208
League of Red Cross Societies, Magen David Adom denied recognition by, 1459
League of Women Students and Graduates from the University and Egyptian Institutes, 43
Lear, Tobias, 1807
Leaves of Olive (Darwish), 674
Leaving Beirut: Women and the Wars Within (Ghoussoub), 916
Lebanese American University, Institute for Women's Studies in the Arab World at, 894
Lebanese Arab Army, **1389**
Lebanese Army
budget for, 1364
Lahhud (Emile) as leader of, 1364
Special Forces of the Levant in, 2086
Lebanese Association for Human Rights, 1557
Lebanese Broadcasting Company, 1895
Lebanese Civil War (1958), **1389–1391,** *1390*
Chamoun (Camille) as catalyst of, 580, 1389–1391, 1399
Druze in, *728*
external parties in, 1389, 1390–1391
as failure of National Pact, 1663
Hakim (Adnan al-) in, 976
Hunchak Party during, 1050
League of Arab States investigating, 1391
Malik (Charles Habib) in, 1475
Meushi (Paul Peter) in, 1520
al-Najjada's role in, 977, 1638
National Liberal Party in, 1661
Phalange party in, *1390,* 1831
Ramgavar Azadagan Party during, 1901
Syrian Social Nationalist Party supporting, 2137
United Arab Republic and, 2277
United Nations on, 2277
Lebanese Civil War (1975–1990), **1391–1393,** *1392,* 1400–1401
AMAL movement in, 173–174
American University of Beirut during, 180
Aoun (Michel) in, 215
and banking, 390
Beirut in, 430–431
and Beirut College of Women, 432
Beitaddin Declaration (1978) attempting to end, 432
Biqa valley during, 476
Black Saturday of, 1253
causes of, 1391, 1400
Chamoun (Camille) in, 581
Council for Development and Reconstruction in, 645
depiction in film, 1500
Druze in, 729, 1400
Eddé (Raymond) in, 754
external parties in, 1391, 1393, 1400, 2176
as failure of National Pact, 1663
female scholars meeting informally during, 367
Franjiyya family in, 849–850
Free Lebanon Militia in, 2083
Geagea (Samir) in, 871
Haddad (Saʿd) in, 967
Israeli intervention in, 1103
Jumayyil (Bashir) in, 581, 1253, 1661
Jumayyil (Pierre) in, 1254
Jumblatt (Kamal) in, 1255, 1256, 1853
Khalaf (Salah) in, 1292
League of Arab States, 1387, *1387*
Lebanese Front in, 1395
Lebanese University during, 1396
as literary theme, 1982
LNM in, 1395
Malik (Charles Habib) in, 1475
Maronite displacement in, 1492
Maronite militias in, 1389, 1391, 1400
Moghaziel (Laure) in, 1557
Muhsin (Zuhayr) in, 1607
Murabitun in, 1612
Nasrallah's (Emily) writings on, 1647
orphans of, 1961
Palestinian refugees killed in, 426, 1393, 1954–1955, 2155–2156, 2176
Phalange party in, 430, 1103, 1254, 1391, 1831
phases of, 1393
PLO in, 270, 1391–1393, 1395, 1400, 1774, 2083, 2156
AMAL rivalry with, 174
Shiʿite support for, 174
Sadr (Musa al-) in, 173
Salam (Saʾib) in, 1975
sectarian power distribution and, 1391–1392
Syrian intervention in, Khaddam (Abd al-Halim) in, 1291
Syrian Social Nationalist Party in, 2137
Taʾif Accord ending, 2148
Tigers militia in, 1661
Vatican and, 2310
Lebanese Communist Party, Bishara (Suha) in, 481
Lebanese Crises of the 1840s, **1393–1394**
Lebanese Forces (LF), **1394–1395**
establishment of, 1253, 1394
Geagea (Samir) in, 871, 1394
Hobeika (Elie) in, 1394
Israel as ally of, 1393, 1394
Jumayyil (Bashir) in, 1253, 1393, 1394, 1400, 1831
murder of Franjiyya (Tony) family by, 849, 850, 871, 1394
National Liberal Party attacked by, 581
Phalange party attacked by, 1831
Tigers militia in, 1394, 1661
Lebanese Front, **1395**
establishment of, 1395
Israeli collaboration with, 1395
Malik (Charles Habib) in, 1475–1476
Phalange party in, 1831
purpose of, 1395
Lebanese language, Aql (Saʿid) on, 218
Lebanese nationalism, Phoenicianism in, 1833–1834

Lebanese National Movement (LNM), **1395**
Jumblatt (Kamal) in, 1255, 1395, 1853
Jumblatt (Walid) in, 1395
Progressive Socialist Party in, 1853
Lebanese Resistance Detachments. *See* AMAL movement
Lebanese University, **1395–1396**
Azm (Sadiq al-) at, 351
Berri (Nabi) at, 467
Lebanese Women's Council (LWC), **1396**
Lebanese Workers' Party, 626
Lebanon, **1396–1401**. *See also specific cities, organizations, people, and regions*
agriculture in, 2255
in Arab–Israel War (1948), General Armistice Agreement on (1949), 240
in Arab–Israel War (1982), 238, 252–254, 1537
archaeology in, 276–277
Armenian community in
college for, 975
political parties of, 1050, 1901
army of, reform after French mandate, 584
Arslan family in, 307, 1255
art of, 47, 556, 916, 1294
As'ad family of, 314, 315
Baghdad Pact (1955) membership refused by, 363
banking in, 390–392, *393*
Ba'th party in, 412
Biqa valley in, 476
at Bludan Conference (1937), 488
British relations with, 512
Catholics in, 1932
census (1932), 1392, 1397, 1398–1399
Chamoun (Camille) presidency, 1389–1391, 1399
charitable *waqfs* in, 2323
Chehab family in, 584
Chehabism in, 1031
Chehab (Fu'ad) presidency, 1399
Christians in (*See also* Maronites)
in crises of 1840s, 1393–1394
Lebanese Front of, 1395
militias of, 1394
number of, 590
Orthodox, 738
CIA activity in, 572–573
cities of, 353, 2422
capital, 429–431
historic coastal, 2255
civil wars in (*See* Lebanese Civil War; Lebanese Civil War (1958); Lebanese Civil War (1975–1990))
communism in, 626
constitution of, presidential term limits in, 580
constitution of (1926), 1398
cotton industry in, *2181*
Council for Development and Reconstruction of, 645
coup attempt in (1961), 1888
defense costs as percentage of GNP or GDP, *1530*
divorce in, 887
Druze in (*See* Druze)
economy of, *753*
women in labor force, 875
education in, 2254
missionary schools in, 1552
feminism in, 817, 1396
film industry of, Masri (Mai) in, 1499–1500
foreign debt of, 994
Franjiyya family in, 849–850, 1394
Franjiyya (Sulayman) presidency, 1392, 1400
Free French mandate, 851, 2086
French expedition to (1860-1861), 423
French mandate in, 846, 1398–1399, 1441, 1480
Arabs in, 221
Christian–Muslim alliance fighting, 2116, 2118
De Gaulle (Charles) and, 688
French foreign legion in, 856
General Syrian Congress (1920) on, 538
Jumblatt family during, 1255
Lebanese presidency under, 660
San Remo Conference (1920) on, 1988
Special Forces of the Levant in, 2086
Sulh (Riyad al-) opposing, 2117
Sykes-Picot Agreement (1916) on, 2128
Syrian opposition to, 1504–1505
geography of, 901, 902
government of, 933
Greater Lebanon creation, 1398
ground-to-air missiles in, removal of, 964
guest workers from, 946
in Gulf Crisis (1990–1991), 951
hashish production in, 725, 726
higher education in, 761
at American University of Beirut, 180–181
at Beirut College for Women, 431–432
at Lebanese University, 1395–1396
missionaries and, 1551–1552
at Saint Joseph University, 1971
Hilu (Charles) presidency, 1399–1400
Hirawi (Ilyas al-) presidency, 1400–1401
historical myth of, 1397
honor killings in, 887
hostage crisis in, in Iran–Contra affair, 1119, 1122–1123
hostage crisis in (1984), 1046, 1908
human rights in, 1960–1961
of gay people, 888
human rights organizations in, 1396
Moghaizel (Laure) in, 1557–1558
hydroelectric power station in, 1418
independence of, 801, 1399–1400, 1480
Maronites supporting, 1549
industry of, manufacturing, 1482
inheritance in, 887
Institute for Women's Studies in the Arab World in, 1100
and Iran, 1037–1038
Israel and, 1166–1167
agreement under Jumayyil (Amin) (1983), 1665
General Armistice Agreement between (1949), 240
internal security maintained by, 1536
Mossad and, 1579
peace treaty (1983), 318, 1393
security agreement between, 254, 1253
Israeli invasion of (1978), 240, 1166, 1417–1418
and Beitaddin Declaration (1978), 432
League of Arab States on, *1387*
PLO and, 2176
UN response to, 1393, 1400, 1417–1418, 2276
Israeli invasion of (1982) (*See* Arab–Israel War (1982))
Israeli occupation of, withdrawal from (2000), 254, 1038, 1168, 2017

Lebanon *(continued)*
Israeli security zone in (*See* Security Zone)
Jewish refugees from, 1914
Jumayyil family in, 1253–1254
Jumayyil (Amin) presidency, 1400
Jumblatt family in, 1254–1255
Khuri (Bishara al-) presidency, 1399
King–Crane Commission on (1919), 1323
labor unions in, 1358
Lahhud (Emile) presidency, 1364, 1401
at Lausanne Conference (1949), 1375
in League of Arab States, 1386, 1388
legal system of, 884, 886
Majalla, 1382
literature of, 47, 397–398, 817, 872, 916, 920, 1010, 1419, 1420, 1421, *1421*, 1975, 1982, 2019–2021, 2046, 2051
novels, 1477–1478
popular, 1646–1647
map of, *1398*
Marine barracks bombing in, **1488–1489**
Maronites in, 429, 1392, 1397, 1491–1492 (*See also* Phalange (Kataʾib) party)
in French mandate system, 1398
as largest sect, 1392, 1397, 1398–1399
Muslim–Christian alliance of, against French mandate, 2116, 2118
National Pact on, 1399, 2116, 2118
under Ottoman rule, 1398
Sfeir (Nasrallah) leading, 2016–2017
military of
equipment of, *1534*
force levels of, *1528–1529*, 1530
force structure of (army, air force, and navy), *1532–1533*
militias in, 1536
modern means of transport in, *2207*
mountains of, *1397*
music of, 1617–1618, 1619
nationalism in, 2115–2119
Maronites and, 1492
minority groups supporting, 1549
National Pact of, 933, 1399, 1662–1663, 2116, 2118
Taʾif Accord (1989) revision of, 1663
newspapers and print media of, 1678–1679, 2254
diversity in, 1681
English-language, 1682
French-language, 1682
government-controlled, 1680
magazines, 1682
offshore publishing of, 1681
privately controlled, 1680
opium production in, 725
in Ottoman Empire, 1397–1398, 1401
Beyoglu Protocol (1861) and, 469
crises of 1840s, 1393–1394
under Daʾud Pasha, 680
French support for Catholics in, 1544
mutasarrif system in, 1394, 1398
under Qiyomijian (Ohannes), 1880
subgovernorates in, 1394
Palestinian refugee camps in
AMAL siege of, 174
Nakba, al- and, 1639
Palestinians in, 1393, 1792, 1916
mass killing of, 426, 1393, 1792, 1954–1955, 2155–2156, 2176
Phalange conflict with, 1254, 2156
parliament of
1957 elections for, 580
1972 elections for, 1802
Asʿad (Ahmad) in, 314, 315
Asʿad (Kamil) in, 314, 315, 320
Husayn (Husayn al-) in, 320
peasant revolt in (1858), 2021
PFLP in, 1840
PLO in, 1774, 2176
in Arab–Israel War (1982), 238, 252–254
in Beirut, 429–430
Cairo Agreement between (1969), 1653
expulsion of, 1907
Franjiyya (Sulayman) opposing, 850, 1400
poetry of, 47–48, 307, 1298–1299
political parties in, Communist, 1009
population censuses in, 1848
population of, *753*, 1397, 1844, 1845
postage stamps of, 1850
prime minister of, 994, 1253
pronatalist policies of, 478
Protestant missions in, 1854, 1856
radio and television in, 1894, 1895, *1895*
railways in, 2206, *2206*
rivers in, 1418, *1418*
Roman ruins in, 353, *1399*
Sarkis (Ilyas) presidency, 1400
Saudi Arabian relations with, 795
science and technology in, 2005
scout movement in, 2006
sectarianism in, 1662–1663
Shiʿism in, 429, 1392, 1397, 1548, 2052
and AMAL movement, 173–174
and Hizbullah, 1037
leaders of, 1055
National Pact on, 1399
Shuf in, 2059–2060
Somalia and, 1388
songs and music of, 817–818
stock market in, 2091
Sunni Islam in, 429, 580, 2123
National Pact on, 2116
traditional dominance of, 1547
Sunnis in, 1392
leader of, 1045
Syrian relations with
Damascus Tripartite Agreement and, 1039
Franjiyya (Sulayman) and, 1395
internal security maintained by, 1536
Jumblatt (Kamal) and, 1256
Jumblatt (Walid) and, 1256
Lahhud (Emile) and, 1364
Shabʿa Farms and, 2017
Syrian Social Nationalist Party and, 2137
Taʿif Accord and, 2148
temporary marriage *(ziwaj mutʿa)* in, 2438
terrorism in (*See* Hizbullah)
terrorist ring in, Geagea (Samir) as leader of, 1394
textile industry in, 2066, 2181, *2181*, 2182
theater in, 1421, 2019–2021, 2046, 2184
in trade, 2198, 2201
United Nations in, *2283* (*See also* United Nations Interim Force in Lebanon)
Vatican's position on, 2310
water resources of
freshwater withdrawals, *2331*
quality of, 1510
quantity of, 2330

women in
activists and advocates for, 1557, 1584–1585
as artists, 916
college for, 431–432
as cultural officials, 2125
disease and, 714
economic status of, *877*
in labor force, 875
as political activists, 481
political and legal rights for, 1396, 1557
in politics, 894, 1960–1961, 1975
religious rituals of, 2360, 2361
as scholars, 367
as writers, 397–398, 817, 872, 916, 1646–1647, 1975, 1982, 2046
women's rights in, 884, 887
organizations in, 1396
World Bank and
capital stock and voting power in, *2363*
loans from, *2364*
in World War II, 2370
Special Forces of the Levant of, 2086
Lebanonism, Aql (Saʿid) support for, 218
Lebanon, Mount, **1401**
Druze in, 728–729, 1397, 1398, 1401
Druze–Maronite violence in, 1398, 2021
Asʿad Wali attempted reconciliation of, 320–321
Egyptian occupation of, 1393
Maronites in, 846, 1397, 1398, 1401
in Ottoman Empire, 1398, 1401
mutasarrif system in, 1394, 1398
subgovernorates in, 1394
peasant revolt in (1858), 2021
Shiʿite Muslims in, 1397
Shuf as part of governorate of, 2059–2060
Lebensohn, Micah Joseph, 1430
Leff, 2625
"Legend" (Yushij), 1435
Legge Fondamentale, 2127
Legislative bodies, 932–933
Legislative Council (Palestine), **1402–1403**
as advisory council replacement, 50, 1762–1763
elections for, of 1923, 50, 1763
original proposal for, 50, 1762–1763
Palestinian rejection of, 50, 1763
Qurai (Ahmad Sulayman) as speaker at, 1882
revival of idea, 1763
LEHI. *See* Lohamei Herut Yisrael
Lehren, Zvi Hirsch, 2400
Leib, James, 1515
Leibowitz, Yeshayahu, **1403**
Leipzig University
Burckhardt (Johann Ludwig) at, 545
Burg (Yosef) at, 546
Leisendorf, Erich, 477
Leishmaniasis, 1508
Lekem (Israel), in Pollard affair, 1838
Leland, Mickey, 868
Lemsine, Aicha, **1403,** 1424
Lend-lease program, U.S., **1403–1404,** 1934, 2290
and Middle East Supply Center, 1523
Saudi Arabia included in, 1936
Turkish eligibility for, after Adana Conference (1943), 42
Leninakan earthquake, Armenian relief efforts in, 1695
Lenin, Vladimir, pogroms under, 1836
Lenokhah Pesel Apollo (Tchernichovsky), 2168
Leopold (king of Belgium), 1363
Leo the African (Maʿlouf), 1478
Le Play, Frédéric, 2409
Leptis Magna (ancient city), 2217–2218
Lesbian rights, 888
Lesch, Ann M., *as contributor,* 7–8, 12–13, 87–88, 103–104, 209–210, 228–229, 908, 1301–1303, 1463–1464, 1758–1769, 1782–1784, 1794–1795, 1810–1811, 1835–1836, 1879–1880, 2097–2105, 2139, 2349–2351
Leskofcali Galip, **1404**
Lesseps, Ferdinand de, 528, **1404,** 1970, 2106, *2205*
Lesser Tunb, 2223–2224
Lettre ouverte à Habib Bourguiba (Mzali), 1628
Lettres algériennes (Boudjedra), 497
Lettres Parisiennes, autopsie de l'exil (Sebbar), 2007
Lettres persanes (Montesquieu), 1675
Levaddah (Kabak), 1260
"Levadi" (Bialik), 470
Levant
Catholics of, French support for, 1544
as designation and term, 1522
Special Forces of (*See* Special Forces of the Levant)
Levant Company, 525, 563, 621
Levantine, **1404–1406**
bourgeoisie, 1405
origin of term, 1404–1405
twentieth-century evolution of term, 1405–1406
Levantinism, 1406
Levant Trilogy (Manning), 908
Leveau, Rémy, *as contributor,* 559–560, 1003–1004, 1004–1006, 1448–1450, 1597–1599
Leveilly, Moh, 918
Levey, Zach, *as contributor,* 304–305, 1692–1693, 2215–2216, 2285
Levinger, Moshe, **1406–1407**
Kiryat Arba established by, 1325
Levin, Hanoch, **1407,** 2186
Levin, Shmaryahu, **1407**
Levin, Yizhak Meir, **1407–1408**
Levontin, Zalman, **1408**
and Rishon Le-Zion, founding of, 1927
Levy, Avigdor, *as contributor,* 1216–1218, 1466–1468, 1737–1741, 2308
Levy, David, **1408**
in Gesher Party, 1181
in Likud Party, 1184
Middle Eastern origin of, 49
Levy, Moshe, Middle Eastern origin of, 49
Levy, Walter J., 1827
Lewis, Bernard, 1 035
LF. *See* Lebanese Forces
Lias, Charles, 2315
Liʿbat al-sitt (film), 1273

Liberal Constitutionalist Party (Egypt), **1408–1409**
Adli supporters in, 46
coalition with Wafd, 1486
former Wafd members in, 1408
foundation of, 1408
Mahmud (Muhammad) in, 1468
newspaper of, 1409
Sidqi (Isma'il) in, 2065
Tharwat (Abd al-Khaliq) founding, 2183
Liberal Party (Egypt), Muslim Brotherhood alliance with, 1622
Liberal Party (Israel), 1181, 1184
in GAHAL, 1181, 1184
Kol (Moshe) in, 1332
in Likud, 425, 1184, 1416, 2041
Moda'i (Yitzhak) in, 1555
Sharon (Ariel) in, 2041
union with Herut Party, 1555
Liberal party (Yemen), 2442
Liberation List, 467
Liberation Movement of Iran, Yazdi (Ibrahim) in, 2382, 2383
Liberation of Women, The (Amin), 875, 890
Liberation Rally (Egypt), 767, **1409**
clash with Muslim Brotherhood, 1409
in coup (1952), 1409
Nasser (Gamal Abdel) supported by, 1409, 1649
National Union as succesor to, 1667
Liberty and Socialism party (Morocco), Yata (Ali) in, 2382
Liberty, USS, **1409–1410**
Libya, **1410–1415**. *See also specific cities, organizations, people, and regions*
agriculture in, 1410
alcohol in, 110
Arab–Israel War (1967) effects in, 1506
in Arab Maghreb Union, 260
Arab nationalism in, 1412
banking in, *393*
Berbers in, 458
Bevin–Sforza Plan (1949) on, 469
border with Chad, Aozou Strip in, 216
British relations with, 1415
Anglo–Libyan Alliance Treaty (1953) and, 517
military withdrawal from, 521
Catholics in, 1932
Chad invaded by, CIA support for, 572
chemical weapons of, 305
cities of, 446, 1410
de facto capital, 2216–2217, 2218
seaport, 2194
climate of, 1410
constitution of (1951), 1812
coup in (1969), 1081, 1412, 2218
Jallud (Abd al-Salam) in, 1212
Qaddafi (Muammar) in, 1081, 1860
Yunis Jabir (Abu Bakr) in, 2414
culture of, 1410
defense costs as percentage of GNP or GDP, *1530*
economic aid to, 748
economic sanctions against
by United Nations, 522, 1414, 1415, 1707, 1708
by United States, and oil production, 1707–1708
economy of, 752, *753*
in 1960s, 1412
European trade and investment and, 1415
green perestroika, 1414
reforms in, 1413–1414, 1861, 1862
resources and, 1410
elites in, 776
European Union relations, 1415
family planning in, 478
Fezzan region of, Nasir (Ahmed Sayf al-) in, 1646
foreign policy of, 1414–1415, 1862
French relations with, Aozou Strip in, 216
geography of, 901
government of, 933
in Gulf Crisis (1990–1991), 951
Gulf of Sidra on coast of, 2066
human rights in, 1414, 1415
Ibadi Islam in, 1410
independence of, 1411, 1460, 2216, 2218
British role in, 517, 615
UN role in, 1812
Italian colonization of, 615, 1200, 1411, 2246–2247
Accord of Mariyam (1921) and, 1609
Benghazi, 446
Fourth Shore, 380, 843
French agreement to, 1200
Graziani (Rodolfo) in, 935
Nasir (Ahmed Sayf al-) opposing, 1646
problems with, 1200
resistance to, 615, 807, 1321, 1609–1610
sfollamento in, 920
Treaty of Akrama and (1917), 1609
Tripoli, 2216, 2246
Tripolitania, 935, 2218, 2247
Volpi (Giuseppe) in, 2317
Jabal al-Akhdar region of, 1204
jamahiriyya in, 409, 899, 941, 1213, 1410, 1413, 2217
Jews in, 1410
in Giado concentration camp, 920
immigration to Israel, 1914
Nhaisi (Elia) and, 1686–1687
during World War II, 1041, 1233
Kikhya family in, 1321
labor unions in, 1358
in League of Arab States, 1387, 1388, 2218
withdrawal of membership, 1388
legal system of
civil code, 1382
Majalla, 1382
reforms in, 1383, 1414
map of, *1413*
Masmoudi (Muhammad) and, 1499
military of
equipment of, *1534*
force levels of, *1528–1529*
force structure of (army, air force, and navy), *1532–1533,* 1535
as monarchy, 1921, 2218
and Morocco, 1006
Muntasir family in, 1611–1612
national assembly of, establishment of, 1812
natural gas reserves and production in, *1671*
newspapers and print media of, 1678
mobilization approach of, 1680
nuclear capability of, 1698
program cessation announced by (2003), 1698
official name of country, 1410, 1413, 2217
oil concessions in, competition for, 1826
oil production in, 752, 1410, *1411*
during Arab–Israel War (1956), 2203
Fezzan region, 830

Law 24 and, 1662
National Oil Corporation in, 1662
by Oasis Group, 1707–1708
by Occidental Petroleum, 1708
and Tripoli, 2216
oil revenues of, 1410
in OPEC, 1719
in Ottoman Empire, 1410–1411, 2246–2247
Benghazi, 446
pan-Arabism in, 1799
PFLP–GC links with, 1841
PFLP supported by, 1840
POLISARIO supported by, 1837, 2190–2191
political organizations in, Omar Mukhtar Club, 1711
political system in, 1410, 1413
political system of, 1860, 1861
population of, *753*, 1410
postage stamps of, 1850
Qaddafi (Muammar al-) regime, 1410, 1412–1415, 2218
radio and television in, 1894–1895, *1895*
reforms in, 933
regions of
mountainous, 1204
traditional, 655, 829–830, 1410, 2217–2218
religions in, Baha'i faith, 365
resources of, 1410
revolutionary committees in, 1861
Sahara in, 1963
Sanusi Order in (*See* Sanusi Order)
social reform in, 1860
as state sponsor of terrorism, 2175
Sudan relations with, under Numeiri (Muhammad Ja'far), *1700*
Sunni Islam in, 1410
terrorism sponsored by, 1861, 1862 (*See also* Pan Am flight 103 bombing; UTA flight 772 bombing)
in trade, 1415
tribes in, 458
at Tripoli Conference, 2217
Tunisian relations with, Gafsa incident (1980) and, 863
United Nations in, 1812
U.S. bombing of (1986), 1414, 1862, 2217
U.S. relations with
after September 11th, 2001, 1415
water resources of
aquifers as, 702
freshwater withdrawals, *2331*
from Great Man-Made River, 2329
quantity of, 2330
weapons program of
German involvement in, 907
renouncement of, 1862
welfare benefits in, 1410
Wheelus Air Force Base turned over to, 2349
women in, 1410
in World War II, 516–517, 1200, 1411–1412, 2368–2370, *2369*, *2370*
Benghazi, 446
Cyrenaica, 516
Tobruk siege (1941), 516, 2194
Tripoli, 2216
Zionism in, 966
Libyan Independence and the United Nations (Pelt), 1812
LICA (Egypt), **1415–1416**
Lichtenstien, Aharon, 1749
Lidd, al-. *See* Lydda
Lieberman, Avigdor, in Israel Beiteinu, 1182
Life as a Fable (Sadeh), 1433
Life Beyond Them (Bitton), 483
Life expectancies, 876, 1508, *1844*
Light of Lost Suns, The (Gilboa), 921
Ligue Algérien des Droits de l'Homme (LADH) (Algeria), Benflis (Ali) in, 445
Ligue contre l'Antisémitisme Allemand. *See* LICA (Egypt)
Ligue Internationale Scolaire contre l'Antisémitisme. *See* LISCA
Ligue Marocaine de Défense des Droits de l'Homme, 1716
Ligue Tunisienne pour la Défense des Droits de l'Homme (LTDH), **1416**, 2265
Marzouki (Moncef) in, 1496–1497
Likud Party (Israel), 1184–1185, **1416–1417**
Abuhatzeira (Aharon) in, 37
accommodative stance toward religious tradition, 1554
Begin (Menachem) and, 425, 1184
Ben-Porat (Mordechai) in, 452
Burg (Yosef) in, 546
Cohen (Ge'ula) in, 612–613
creation of, 1555
Democratic Movement for Change and, 1181
electoral success of, 1167, 1168, 1169, 1170, 1184
suicide bombings and, 1226
establishment of, 1184
Arab–Israel War and (1967), 249
foreign policy of, Jordanian Option in, 1247
Free Center in, 1181, 1184
GAHAL and, 1181
Herut Party in, 1181–1182, 1184, 1416, 2041
internal conflicts in, 1184
Labor Party and, 1417
in coalition government, 1167, 1184, 1817–1818
Land of Israel Movement in, 1184
leaders of, election by members, 1175
Levy (David) in, 1184, 1408
Liberal Party in, 425, 1184, 1416, 2041
members of, 1416–1417
Middle Eastern Jewish support for, 48–49
Moda'i (Yitzhak) in, 1555
Netanyahu (Benjamin) in, 1184, 1677
on occupied territories, 1184
Oslo Accords rejected by, 1185, 1726, 1727
in peace negotiations, 1184
PLO rejected by, 271
platform of, 1184–1185
purpose of, 1417
on racism in Knesset, 1184
rise of, 1891
Shamir (Yitzhak) as leader of, 1184, 1417, 2026
Shamir (Moshe) in, 2024
Sharon (Ariel) in, *1176*, 1184, 2041
State List in, 1184
TAMI in, 1189
Tzomet Party in, 1189
Weizman (Ezer) in, 2336
Lilienblum, Moses Leib, **1417**
Liman von Sanders, Otto, 1739
Yildirim Army under, 2400
Limpus, Arthur H., 1741
Linen, 2180
Lion of the Desert (film), 99
Lipkin-Shahak, Amnon, in Israel Defense Force, 1171

Liqa lam yatimm (al-Rimawi), 1422
Liquefied natural gas (LNG), in Qatar, 1876
Liquidation Commission (Egypt), 404
Lira, 2625
LISCA, 1416
Liss wa al-Kilab, al (Mahfuz), 1464
Litani Operation (1978), **1417–1418**. *See also under* Lebanon
  Gur (Mordechai) in, 956
Litani River, *1418*, **1418**
Literacy
  in Algeria, 122
  female, 880
  in Iran, 1113
    Azerbaijan, 345–346
    White Revolution and, 2351
  in Israel, 1163
  in Jordan, 1291
  in Kuwait, 1349
  modernization and, 1556
  in Morocco, 1567, 1600
Literary criticism, in Egypt, 341
Literary essays, Persian, 1437
Literary History of Persia, A (Browne), 540
Literary Society (Palestine), 1645
Literature, **1418–1440**. *See also* Poetry; Theater; *specific authors*
  Algerian, 483, 496–497, 563, 707, 715–716, 803–804, 806, 822–823, 965, 1280, 1403, 1422–1427, 1547, 1581, 1687, 2007, 2332–2333
    in Arabic, 273, 1581
    Berber, 192, 193
    "Generation of 1954," 967
    by women, 1581, 1687
  Arabic, **1418–1422**, 1475, 2426
    colonialism and, 1419
    first autobiography, 2426
    first modern novel, 1013
    folk culture and, 1419, 1421
    in French, 582–583
    fusha language in, 1704
    new direction of, 1419–1420
    19th-century revival of, 2383, 2384
    preservation and promotion by Madkour (Ibrahim), 1456–1457
    pun and double entendre in, 1419
    roots of, 1419
    socialism and, 1422
    symbolist movement in, 218
    women's, 1472–1473, 1475
  Berber, 462, 464, 1426
  Egyptian, 18, 378–379, 475–476, 805, 911, 914–915, 978–979, 1013, 1060–1061, 1082–1083, 1419, 1420, *1420*, 1421, 1464–1465, 1950–1951, 1977–1978, 1990, 2019, 2044–2045, 2233, 2428
    literary criticism, 1060, 1061
    by women, 322, 1472–1473, 1924–1925
    women in, 2431
  Hebrew, 71–72, 408, 434, 464, 470, 506–507, 547, 834–835, 855, 856, 920–921, 926–927, 940–941, 955–956, 1407, **1430–1434**, 2012, 2024–2025, 2029, 2043–2044, 2048, 2058–2059, 2060, 2075, 2076, 2114–2115, 2159–2160, 2168–2169
    Aliyah period, 1431
    after Arab–Israel War (1973), 1433–1434
    Canaanite movement, 1432
    Dor Ba-Arez, 1432–1433
    in Eretz Yisrael, 1016, 1431, 1432
    expressionist, 1432
    Haskalah era, 1430
    Hibbat Zion school, 1430
    historical, 1260
    Holocaust in, 216–217, 1336, 1751–1752
    by Jewish immigrants in England, 2424–2425
    modern, 1018
    modernist, 1430–1431
    in Palestine under British mandate, 1431–1432
    postmodernist, 182
    from Russia, 1015–1016, 1906
    socialism and, 1432
    by women, 1887
    Zionist, 78–79, 1260
  Iranian (*See* Literature, Persian)
  Iraqi, 344, 416, 1421–1422, 1475, 1703–1704, 1903, 2002, 2043–2044, 2419
  Israeli, 188, 408, 434, 547, 834–835, 855, 920–921, 926–927, 940–941, 955–956, 1164, 1268, 1288, 1407, 1432–1434, 1521–1522, 2012, 2024–2025, 2029, 2058–2059, 2060, 2075, 2076, 2114–2115, 2159–2160, 2322–2323, 2384, 2403, 2418, 2429 (*See also* Literature, Hebrew)
    Arabic-language, 963
    avant-garde, 1040
    "Generation of the State" revolution in, 182, 1040
    ma'barah experiences in, 1452
    satire, 1284
    by women, 993, 1907
  Jordanian, 804–805, 1422, 2001, 2156
  Kurdish, 1345
  Kuwaiti, 1952
  Ladino, 1363
  Lebanese, 47, 353–354, 397–398, 817, 872, 916, 920, 1010, 1419, 1420, 1421, *1421*, 1477–1478, 1646–1647, 1975, 1982, 2019–2021, 2046, 2051
  modernization and, 1556
  Moroccan, 40, 396, 466–467, 497–498, 588, 910–911, 1355–1356, 1422–1425, *1424*, *1427*, 1427–1428, 1890, 2008, 2060
    in French language, 1303–1304
    in French *vs.* Arabic, 40
    women in, 588, 2376
  North African, **1422–1430**
    in Arabic language, 1424, 1425, 1426, 1428
    in French language, 1424, 1425, 1426, 1428
    women in, 1424, 1425, 1428
  orientalism in, 1675–1676
  Ottoman, 2439
    New Literature School and, 1909
  Palestinian, 357–358, 1297, 1790, 1791, 1792, 1973, 2029, 2233, 2234, 2242
  Persian (Iranian), 366–367, 397, 427, 428, 593, 668–669, 678, 722, 784, 811, 812, 928, 929–930, 930, **1434–1437**, 1496, 1802–1803, 1962, 2011, 2027
    allegorical realist, 149
    Azeri, 98, 347
    censorship of, 397, 1435, 1436–1437, 1803
    culture and history in, 1019
    literary essays, 1437
    nonestablishment, 110

Persian culture and history in, 1019
satirical, 976
20th-century, 104, 148–149
by women, 1803, 1899
Saudi Arabian, 1611
Sudanese, 1977
Sufism and, 2113
Syrian, 1084, 1982
women in, 1080
Tunisian, 474, 721–722, 987–988, 1313–1314, 1422–1425, *1423*, 1428–1429, 1498, 1507, 1516–1517, 2017–2018, 2192–2193, 2431
existentialism in, 1498
Turkish, 45–46, 661, 702, 780–781, 782, 783–784, 790, 955, 956–957, **1437–1440**, 1513, 1673–1674, 1676, 2145–2146, 2160–23, 2165–2166, 2179–2180, 2380–2381, 2414
Edebiyat-i Cedide, 1439
Fecr-i Ati, 1439
folk culture and, 428, 492–493, 1438, 1439, 2251
Genç Kalemler, 1439, 2251
Ottoman, 434, 1404, 1438–1439, 1962–1963, 2068–2069
realism in, 1631
realist village literature, 1439–1440
Second New Movement, 1440
Servet-i Fünun, 957, 1439, 1963, 2302
Tahiris, 2145
Türk Deneği, 2251
Yiddish, 464, 506–507
"Little Black Fish, The" (Behrangi), 428
Little Zab River, 2417
Liu, F. T., *as contributor*, 2274–2284, 2286, 2287–2288, 2289–2290
Livnat, Limor, **1440–1441**
Livni, Talia, as leader of Na'amat, 1629
Livre de sang, le (Khatibi), 1304
Liwa, al- (UAE oases), 36
tribes in, 2210
Liwa, al- (newspaper), 1663
Kamil (Mustafa) in, 218, 1267
Lloyd George, David, **1441–1442**
in Agadir crisis (1911), 70
and Balfour Declaration (1917), 380, 381, 1441
Chanak crisis (1922) causing downfall of, 513, 1441–1442
at Paris peace conference, 1441
as prime minister, 1441
and Sèvres Treaty (1920), 2014
Weizmann (Chaim) and, 2337
Lloyd, Selwyn
in Arab–Israel War (1956), 245
at London Conference (1956), 1444
and Sèvres Protocol (1956), 2109
in Suez Crisis (1956–1957), 2108
LNG. *See* Liquefied natural gas
LNM. *See* Lebanese National Movement
Local Development Association (LDA) movement (Yemen), 2393
Lockerbie (Scotland), airplane bombing over (1988). *See* Pan Am flight 103 bombing
Lockhart, Laurence, 540
Lockman, Zachary, 1036
Lod. *See* Lydda
Lod Airport (Israel), PFLP attack at (1972), 1839
Loghat'nameh, 689
Lohamei Herut Yisrael (LEHI), **1442–1443**
in Arab–Israel War (1948), 242
Bernadotte (Folke) assassinated by, 466, 1250, 1443, 2026, 2274, 2385
Cohen (Ge'ula) in, 612
and Dayr Yasin, 684, 1443
Eldad (Israel) in, 2025
establishment of, 1139
Guinness (Walter Edward) assassinated by, 948, 1443, 1973, 2025
Haganah kidnapping members of, 1442
in Hebrew Resistance Movement, 1443
ideology of, 1442
Israeli military action against, 1536
Mossad operations against, 992
radio broadcasts of, 612
Shamir (Yitzhak) in, 2025–2026
Stern (Abraham) founding, 1139, 1442, 2090, 2384
viewed as terrorist group, 1442, 2026
in World War II, 2371
Yellin-Mor (Natan) in, 2025, 2384–2385
Loi Cadre, **1443–1444**
De Gaulle (Charles) discarding, 1443
Lacoste (Robert) drafting, 1363, 1443
purpose of, 1443
Loin de Medine (Djebar), 716
Lola and Billy the Kid (film), 832
Lombardi, Giannina Arangi, 872
London Conference (1913), 384
London Conference (1946–1947), Ghuri (Emile al-) at, 917
London Conference (1956), **1444**, 2108
London Conference (1959), 653
Denktash (Rauf) at, 696
Küçük (Fazil) at, 696
London Convention (1840), **1444–1445**, 1602, 1691, 2093–2094
ending Egyptian control of Syria, 1077, 1691
territory ceded by Egypt in, 1796
London (Roundtable) Conference (1939), **1445–1446**, 2350, 2363
MacDonald (Malcolm) at, 1453–1454
Palestinian delegation at
Antonius (George) representing, 214, 1766
Arab Higher Committee in, 228
conflict within, 1766
Khalidi (Husayn Fakhri al-) representing, 1295
reasons for holding, 1766, 1790
London School of Economics, Sharett (Moshe) at, 2032
London Society for Promoting Christianity amongst the Jews, 1854
London Sunday Times (newspaper), in Vanunu affair, 2309
London Symphony Orchestra, 477
London, Treaty of (1827), 940
London, Treaty of (1840), 1393, 1945, 2068, 2094
London, Treaty of (1871), **1446**
London, Treaty of (1913), 511, **1446**
London University
Bazzaz (Abd al-Rahman al-) at, 421
Salih (Teyib) at, 1977
Long–Berenger Agreement (1919), 628

"Loser, The" (Bint al-Shati), 476
Lost in the Crowd (Al-e Ahmad), 1437
"Lost Woman, The" (Bint al-Shati), 476
Lotf Ali Khan Zand, 1867
Lotz, Wolfgang, **1446–1447**
Louhichi, Taieb, 2192
Love Across Frontiers (film), 698
Love in Two Languages (Khatibi), 1303
Loya Jerga (Afghanistan)
  under Amanollah Khan, 175
  Karzai government affirmed by, 64, 1276
  Rabbani (Burhanuddin) and, 59
  Transitional Authority created by, 55
  U.S. support for, 67
  women in, Association for the Protection of Women's Rights on, 325
  Zahir Shah and, 2421
Loyalist press, 1680–1681
Loyalties: Mesopotamia, 1914–1917 (Wilson), 2353
LTDH. *See* Ligue Tunisienne pour la Défense des Droits de l'Homme
Lu ʿbat al-Nisyan (Berrada), 467
Lubavitcher Hasidim, 1002
Lucan, Lord, 379
Ludo, 2050
Lughat al-Ay-Ay (Idris), 1082
Luizard, Pierre-Jean, 1987
Luke, Harry, **1447**
LUKOIL, 1944
Lunah (Burla), 547
Lundquist, John M., *as contributor,* 1722–1723, 1832, 1966–1967
Lunt, James, 923
Lupolianski, Uri, as Jerusalem mayor, 1226
Luria, Isaac, 1962
Luri language, 1447
Lurs, **1447**
Lutes, 1617
Lutfi al-Sayyid, Ahmad, 1408
  at Cairo University, 556
  and Haykal (Muhammad Husayn), 1013
  and Husayn (Taha), 1060
  on women's issues, 187
Luti, 2625
Luxor (Egypt), **1447–1448**
  temple at, terrorist attack on (1997), 278
Luz, Kadish, **1448**
LWC. *See* Lebanese Women's Council
Lyautey, Louis-Hubert Gonzalve, **1448–1450,** *1449*
  administration of, 1448–1450
  Casablanca under, 569
  and Fes Treaty (1912), 1448
  and Rabat, plan for, 1888
  Youssef (Mulay) and, 827, 1448, 2410
Lyazidi, Ahmad Muhammad
  imprisonment of, 619
  in nationalist movement, 618
  in Parti National, 1805
Lycée Chawqi, 497
Lydda (Israel), **1450**
  expulsion of Palestinian population from, 962

M

Maʿabarah, **1452**
Ma al-Aynayn, **1451**
  son of, 86
Maʿale Adumim (Israeli settlement), 2340
Maʿalim fi al-Tariq (Qutb), 1884
Maʿalot, **1451–1452**
  terrorism in, 2176
Maalouf, Amin, 583
Maʿarakh party. *See* Alignment party
Maʿarak zuqag (Boudjedra), 497
Maʿariv (newspaper, Israel), **1452,** 1684
Maʿarri, Abu al-Ala al-, study of, 1060, 1061
Maʿaziba tribe (Yemen), 2426
Mabahith, al- (Masʿadi), 1498
Mabarrat Muhammad Ali, **1452–1453**
Mabda, al- (newspaper), Abu al-Timman (Jaʿfar) in, 35
Mabior, John Garang de, 2103, 2106
  in Sudanese civil war, 1701
MacBride, Sean, 254
  International Commission chaired by, 1954–1955
Maccabean Pilgrimage to Palestine, 2424
Maccabeans (society), 2424
Maccabi, **1453**
MacDonald, Charles G., *as contributor,* 1385–1389
MacDonald, Malcolm, **1453–1454**
  at London Conference (1939), 1445–1446, 1453–1454, 1766, 1790
  Peel Commission plan retracted by, 1766
  white paper by (*See* White papers on Palestine (1939))
MacDonald, Ramsay, **1454–1455**
  Balfour Declaration reaffirmed by, 2338
  and Hope-Simpson Commission, 1044, 1045
  letter on British policy in Palestine (1931), 1454, 2350
  on Wauchope (Arthur), 2333
MacDonald white paper. *See* White papers on Palestine
Macdonogh, George, on NILI spy ring, 1
Macedonia
  Balkan wars over, 384
  Berlin Treaty (1878) and, 465, 1989
Macedonians, 383
Macération, La (Boudjedra), 497
Machino, Maurice T., 1592
Machover, Moshe, 1501
Machpelah, Cave of the. *See* Patriarchs, Tomb of the
MacMichael, Harold, **1455**
  as high commissioner of Palestine, 1025
MacMillan, Harold, 755
MacNamara, Robert, 190
Maʾdan (Marsh Arabs), 1496
Madani, Abassi al-, **1455–1456**
  arrest of, 134
  control of Marrakech, 1493
  criticizing secular policies, 1965
  as FIS leader, 125, 133, 134, 857
  Islamic Salvation Army allegiance to, 1155
  "Statement of Advice, The" issued by, 2079
Madani, Abdullah al-, **1456**
Madani al-Glawi, 2223
Madani, Izz al-Din al-, 1428, 2184
Madani, Tawfiq al-, **1456**
Madda, al-, 1879

Maddy-Weitzman, Bruce, *as contributor,* 450, 453, 618–619, 629–630, 660, 858, 1074, 1083, 1196–1198, 1356, 1588–1589, 1743, 1803–1804, 1805, 1836–1838, 1904–1905, 1963–1965, 2085–2086, 2179, 2266, 2336, 2342–2344, 2344–2347
Madhhab, 2018
muwahhidun as followers of, 1625
Madina, al- (Saudi Arabia), 1995
Madina, al- (newspaper), 1679
Madinat al-Salam (Egypt), 1995
Madinat Nasr (Egypt), 1994–1995
Madkour, Ibrahim, **1456–1457**
Madrasa, 360, 756, **1457–1458,** 2154, 2192, 2625
and Istanbul University, 1196
ulama teaching at, 2258
Madrasat al-Alsun, 2146
Madrasat al-Jamʿiyya al-Khayriyya al-Islamiyya bi al-Iskandariyya, 759
Madrasat al-Mushaghibin (Salim), 1978
Madrid Accords (1975), Spanish protectorate in Western Sahara ended by, 2345
Madrid Agreements (1975), 942, 943, 2084, 2086
Madrid Conference (1880), 1004
Madrid Peace Conference (1991), 238, **1458–1459,** 1725, 2084, 2294
bilateral negotiations at, between Palestinians and Israel, 1768
Bush (George H. W.) at, 549
failure of, 1775
framework for, PLO rejection of, 1775
Hawatma (Nayif) opposition to, 1009
Intifada as catalyst for (1987–1991), 1107
Netanyahu (Benjamin) at, 1677
Nusayba (Sari) at, 1706
and Oslo Accord (1993), 1793
Palestinian delegation at
Abd Rabbo (Yasir) in, 1266
Kamal (Zahira) in, 1266
PLO representatives at, 271, 1458–1459
refugee issue at, 1916
Shamir (Yitzhak) at, 2026
Syria at, 319, 2135
U.S. role in, bias in, 1775
Mafdal (Israel). *See* National Religious Party
Maftul, 838
Magarief, Yusuf al-, as leader of National Front for the Salvation of Libya, 1655
Magazines, 1682. *See also* Newspapers and print media; *specific magazines*
Magen David Adom (MDA), **1459**
Maghariba tribe, 2023
Maghen, Zev, *as contributor,* 777, 865, 992, 1280, 1336, 1373, 1446–1447, 1448, 1451–1452, 1555, 1634, 1641
Maghreb pluriel (Khatibi), 1303
Maghrib, **1459–1460**
labor unions in, 1358
literature on, 588 (*See also* Literature, North African)
Union of the Maghrib treaty, 1006
Maghrib (periodical), 379
Comité d'Action Marocaine platform in, 618
Magic Carpet Operation, **1460,** 1913
Magiciens (film), 376
Magnarella, Paul J., *as contributor,* 1815–1816, 2246, 2316–2317
Magnes, Judah, 540, **1460–1461**
Ahad Ha-Am and, 78
binationalism supported by, 473
and Hebrew University of Jerusalem, 1018
Philby (Harry St. John) and, 1833
Magsaysay Award for Community Leadership, Samar (Sima) awarded with, 1982
Mahabad (Iran), in Azerbaijan crisis (1945–1946), 346
Mahalla al-Kubra, al-, **1461**
Mahalle Schools, **1461–1462**
Tunisian abolition of, 1604
Mahan, Alfred Thayer, Middle East designation and term used by, 1522
Mahaz-e Islami (Afghanistan), 63
in mojahedin resistance, 1561
Mahaz-e Milli-e Islami-e Afghanistan, 863
Mahbubi, Sadr al-Shariʿa al-Thani al-, 988
Mahbusa, 2050
Mahdawi, Fadil Abbas al-, **1462**
Mahd-e Ulya, Malek Jahan Khanum, **1462**
son of, Naser al-Din Shah as, 1462, 1643
Mahdi, **1462–1463,** 1519, 2123
Mahdi, al. *See* Ahmad, Muhammad
Mahdi, Ali Akbar, *as contributor,* 1273, 1300–1301, 1558, 1615–1616, 1629–1630, 2313–2314
Mahdi, Amin al-, 2262
Mahdi, Sadiq al-, Numeiri (Muhammad Jaʿfar) and, 1700–1701
Mahdist(s), Numeiri (Muhammad Jaʿfar) opposed by, 1699–1701
Mahdist movement, in Sudan, 404–405
Khartoum, 1301
in Umma Party, 2261
Mahdist state, **1463–1464**
under Abdullahi (Muhammad Turshain), 32–33, 87
under Ahmad (Muhammad), 87
defeat of
in Karari, Battle of (1898), 1712
Kitchener (Horatio Herbert) in, 1329, 1712
Omdurman as capital of, 1301, 1712
Mahdiya (ancient city), 2228
Mahdiyya, Munira al-, 2262
Mahfuz, Isam, 2184
Mahfuz, Najib, 553, 1420, *1420,* **1464–1465**
Khemir (Sabiha) art on covers of, 1309
Ma Himar al-Hakim (Huhu), 1423
Mahir, Ahmad, 1465, **1465**
government of, Misri (Aziz Ali al-) in, 1550
Nuqrashi (Mahmud Fahmi al-) and, 1701
Mahir, Ali, **1465–1466**
Azzam (Abd al-Rahman al-) support for, 352
Mahmud (Muhammad) and, 1468–1469
Mahjar (émigré) writers, Ziadeh (May) and, 2431
Mahjub, Abd al-Khaliq, Ibrahim (Fatima Ahmed) influenced by, 1075
Mahjub, Rifʿat al-, assassination of, 1215

Mahler, Gregory S., *as contributor,* 153–154, 438, 446–449, 452, 546, 612–613, 744–745, 834–835, 927–928, 956, 986, 1175–1190, 1263–1264, 1275–1276, 1290, 1330, 1331–1332, 1344–1346, 1408, 1513–1515, 1555, 1671–1672, 1817–1818, 1890–1892, 1938–1939, 2031–2033, 2075, 2159, 2309, 2322, 2336–2337, 2376–2377
Mahlul, 1368
Mahmud II (Ottoman sultan), **1466–1468,** *1467*
on Armenians in Jerusalem, 290–291
asserting control over *ayan,* 1367
ayan undermined by, 342
Bayrakdar (Mustafa) under, 417
Bektashis suppressed by, 435
civil service under, 1734–1735
declaring war on Iran (1821), 783
Dolmabahçe Palace and, 719
education under, 757
Egyptian threat to, 1050, 1945
military under, 2162
army in, 1466–1467, 1738
janissaries in, 1217, 1466–1467, 2308
vaka-i hayriye (end of janissaries) under, 1467, 2308
modernization under, 1555
Muhammad Ali in conflict with, 2007
Mustafa Reşid under, 1623
reform efforts of, 954, 2161
and Ruşdiye Schools, 1940
Russian assistance to, 1050, 1945
son of, Abdülmecit I as, 33
in Syrian War (1831–1833), 1346
Konya, Battle of (1832), 1333
Mahmoud Darwish: As the Land Is the Language (Bitton), 483
Mahmud Durrani, 400, 735, **1468**
Mahmud ibn Ayad, 84
financial scam by
Khayr al-Din against, 1306
Khaznader (Mustafa) in, 1308
Mahmudi, Rahim, in Sholay-e Jawid, 62
Mahmudiyya Canal, 116, **1468**
Mahmud Khan, 2421
Mahmud, Muhammad, **1468**
Mahmud, Mustafa, **1469**
Mahmud Nedim Paşa, Midhat Paşa and, 1525
Mahmud, Nur al-Din, 663
defense of Damascus against Second Crusade, 1044
Mahmud of Sulaymaniyya, **1469–1470**
Mahmud, Shah, 400, 735
Mahmut II, 545
Mahrusa, al- (newspaper), 2431
Mahur Peşrevi (Tanburi), 2160
Maimonides, 979, 1231, 1251, 1403
at al-Azhar, 347
Maimonides Lodge (Cairo), 489
Maimon, Yehudah Leib Hacohen, **1470**
Maison de servitude, La (Sefrioui), 2008
Maiwand, battle of (1880), 197
Maiwandwal, Mohammad Hashim, in Jamʿiat Demokrate-ye Mottaraqi, 62
Majali, Abd al-Hadi, 1471
Majali, Abd al-Salam, 1471
Majali family, **1470–1471**
Majali, Habis, 1470
Majali, Hazza al-, 1470–1471, **1471**
Nabulsi (Sulayman al-) as rival of, 1471, 1632
Majali, Rufayfan, 1270, 1470
Majalis al-aza (retelling of Karbala), 1606
Majalla, al- (magazine), 1681
Ayyub (Dhu al-Nun) in, 344
Majalla al-Jadida (journal), 1614
Majallat al-Sayyidat al-Muslimat (journal), 914
Majallat Bint al-Nil (magazine), 2019
Majallot al-Fata (journal), 1614
Majani, Taghrid, father of, Majali (Hazza al-) as, 1470
Majba (Tunisian tax), 1604
Majid, Ahmad Ismat Abd al-, 1386
Majid al Ali (Umm al-Qaywayn ruler), 1592
Majles (Bahrain parliament), 371
Majles al-Shura (Iranian parliament), 411, 416, 1116, 1372, **1471–1472,** 2142, 2625
under Ahmad Qajar, 88, 1868
Amini (Ali) in, 186
Bani Sadr (Abolhasan) impeached by, 1119
coup against (1908)
Cossack Brigade in, 636–637, 643
Mohammad Ali Shah Qajar in, 636–637
Dabbagh (Marzieh) in, 659
dissolution of (1908), 637
elections to, 1116
of 2000, 1120
first, 636
establishment of, 1868
in Constitutional Revolution, 636, 1471, 1559, 1868
Mozaffar al-Din Qajar in, 1591–1592
opposition of Mohammad Ali to, 1559
after Iranian revolution (1979), 1471–1472
Kashani (Abu al-Qasem) in, 1277
Khamenehi (Ali) in, 1299
Khatami (Mohammad) in, 1303
Millspaugh (Arthur) as financial adviser to, 1546
Musavi (Mir-Hosain) endorsed by, 1119
Qajar dynasty deposed by, 88
Rafsanjani (Ali Akbar Hashemi) in, 1899
women's votes for, 2424
Majles al-Shura-ye Islami, 1471–1472
Majles al-Shura-ye Melli, 1471–1472
Majlisi, al-, 2055
Majlis Shura al-Nuwwab (Egyptian assembly), **1472**
establishment of, 1158
Majma-el Adamiyat (Iran), Adamiyat (Abbasquli) in, 42
Majnun al-Hukm (Himmish), 1428
Majnun al-Ward (Shukri), 2060
Majnun Islands, in Iran–Iraq War (1980–1988), 1128
Majzum bi lam, al- (al-Zanad), 1429
Makal, Mahmut, 2317
Makam (music), 1617
Makan al-Wathaniyy, al- (Bannis), 396
Makarios III (Eastern Orthodox archbishop), *653*
death of, 654
enosis movement supported by, 653, 696, 697
exiled by British, 653
internal opposition to, 654, 697
presidency of, 653–654
Makarius, Iskandar Shahin, 1374

Makatib al-Milla, 2147
Makawi, Abd al-Qawi, in Organization for the Liberation of the Occupied South, 857
Makdashi, Hesna, **1472–1473**
Makdisi, George, 756
Makdisi, Ussama, 1036
Makhmalbaf family, **1473**
Makhmalbaf Film House, 1473
Makhmalbaf, Hana, 1473
Makhmalbaf, Maysem, 1473
Makhmalbaf, Mohsen, 833, **1473**
in *Close-Up,* 1318
Makhmalbaf, Samira, 1473
Makhus, Ibrahim, Atasi (Nur al-Din al-) and, 329
Makhzan, 487, 542
Makhzaniya cities, 1515
Makhzen system, 1448, 1449
MAKI. *See* Israel Communist Party
Makki, Hasan Muhammad, **1474**
Makleff, Mordekhai
in General Armistice Agreements (1949), 240, 241
in Israel Defense Force, 1173
Makruh, 2033
Maksoud, Clovis, **1474**
wife of, 1975
Maksoud, Hala Salaam, 1975
Maktab, 756
Maktab-e Islam (journal), 1563, 1614
Maktum family, al-, **1474–1475**
and Dubai (United Arab Emirates), 731
Maktum ibn Buti, 1474
Maktum ibn Hashr, 1474
Maktum, Maktum al-, 2271
Maktum, Rashid ibn Saʿid al-, 1474
as prime minister of UAE, 2271
as vice president of UAE, 2270, 2271
Maktum, Saʿid ibn, 1474
Malaʾika, Nazik al-, 416, 1421–1422, **1475**
Malaʾika wa Shayatin (Bayati), 416
Malaria, 1508, 1509
in Egypt, 710–711
in Ottoman Empire, Alexandretta, 115
in Saudi Arabia, 711
Male circumcision, Samaritans performing, 1980
Malédiction, La (Mimouni), 1426, 1547
Malek al-shoʿara, 366
Maleki, Khalil, 928
Malek, Redha, 1026, 2217
Malek, Roshanak, *as contributor,* 2193–2194
Malekzadeh Khanum, 1462
Malhamat al-Mawt wa al-Milad fi Shaʿbi (al-Kasrawi), 1429
Malik, 2625
Malikane, 1367, 1368
Malikane mukataa, 2168
Malik, Charles Habib, **1475–1476**
at Bandung Conference, 387
in Lebanese Front, 1395
Malik, Hafeez, *as contributor,* 1236–1237, 2154–2155
Malik ibn Anas, 1476
Maliki School of Law, **1476,** 2123
habous in, 964
Ibadiyya on, 1073
Ilaysh (Muhammad) in, 1086
Malik Kurush awwal muluk al-Fars, al- (Fawwaz), 817
Malin, Martin, *as contributor,* 37, 149, 190, 285, 340–341, 407–408, 454–455, 774, 784–785, 986, 1002–1003, 1265, 1275–1276, 1290, 1332, 1407, 1560, 1835, 1991
Malkat ha-Ambatya (Levin), 1407
Malkom Khan, Mirza, **1476–1477**
Adamiyat (Abbasquli) work with, 42
Akhondzadeh (Mirza Fath Ali) and, 98
masonic lodge set up by, 852
Naser al-Din Shah and, 1644
Malley, Robert, 1727
Malnutrition, 714
in Iraq, due to economic sanctions, 1986
Maʿlouf, Amin, **1477–1478**
Maʿlouf, Rushdi, 1477
Maloumian, K., Congress of Ottoman Liberals (1907), 631
Malta, in Arab–Israel War (1956), 245
Maʿluf, Isa al-, in Arab Academy of Damascus, 223
Malwiyya Mosque, al- (Samarra), 1981
Mamasani, 1447
Mamluks, **1478–1479**
Buhayra ruled by, 542
in Egypt, 1547
Muhammad Ali's suppression of, 1602
in Iraq, 1478
and Muntafiq tribe, 2212
in Syria, 1547
Tuman Bey as last independent Egyptian sultan, 2223
in Tunisia, Muhammad al-Sadiq and, 1603–1604
Tyre occupied by, 2255
in Yemen, 2397
Mammeri, Mouloud, 464, 707, 1423, 1426
in "Generation of 1954," 967
Maʾmun, al- (Abbasid caliph), 360, 989
prosperity under, 1132
Maʿna al-Nakba (Zurayk), 1639, 2443
Manabir, 1957
Manahij al-Alhab al-Misriyya fi Mabahij al-Adab al-Asriyya (Tahtawi), 2147
Manama (Bahrain), 367, **1479**
Manana (Srvantziants), 2087
Manar, al- (journal)
Abduh (Muhammad) in, 24
Islamic congresses supported by, 1152
Khattabi (Muhammad ibn Abd al-Karim al-) interviewed in, 1305–1306
Rida (Rashid) as founder of, 1923–1924
Umm al-Qura in, 1282
Manasir tribe, 2209, 2210
Mandaeans, **1479**
Mandal, Sumit, *as contributor,* 970
Mandate system, 514, **1479–1480**. *See also specific countries*
Arab nationalism frustrated by, 261–262, 2353
Arabs in, 221–222
Class A in, 1479
Class B in, 1479–1480
Class C in, 1480
establishment of, 614
in Versailles Treaty, 2314, 2315
guiding principle of, 614
imperialism extended by, 1090, 2353
and Pan-Arabism, 1799
Permanent Mandates Commission overseeing, 1819

Mandate system *(continued)*
San Remo Conference (1920) on, 1988
Sèvres Treaty (1920) and, 2015
Sykes–Picot Agreement (1916) on, 2128
Wilson's (Woodrow) acceptance of, 2353
Mandelbaum Gate, 1224
Mandel, Ruth, *as contributor,* 112–115
Mandub, 2033
Mandur, Muhammad, 1061
Manescalo, Alfonso, 282
Manetti, Fernando, 556
Manfaluti, Mustafa Lutfi al-, 1419
Manghusha, Muhammad Ahmad al-, 2024
Maʿnids, 2059
Manifesto of the Algerian Muslim People (1943), 3, **1480**
Abbas (Ferhat) writing of, 3, 189, 1480
Parti du Peuple Algérien approval of, 1804
supplement to, 3
Maʿnis, 728
Mankur Palace, al- (Samarra), 1981
Männer und Mächte im Orient: 25 Jahre diplomatischer Tätigkeit im Orient (Grobba), 944
Manning, Olivia, 908
Manoogian, Aram, 676
Manor, Amos, 2056
Mansaf, 839
Mansour, Azzedine G., *as contributor,* 274, 280–284, 917–920, 1365–1366, 1904, 1905, 2332–2333
Mansur, al-, 359–360
Mansura, al-, **1480–1481**
Mansur, Abu Jaʿfar al- (Abbasid caliph), 1131–1132, *1132*
Mansur, Ahmad al-, 2038
Mansure Army, **1481**
Mansur, Hamza, 1151
Mansur, Hasan Ali
assassination of, 1129, 1898
and Iran-e Novin Party, 1047
in Iran Novin Party, 1129
Manufacturers-Hanover Trust, 2082
Manufactures, **1481–1485,** 1555
low productivity in, factors for, 1484
1900-1945, 1481–1482
post-1945, 1482–1484
pre-1900, 1481
Manufacturing. *See also* Industrialization
in Algeria, 127, 128
in Iran, Isfahan, 1093, 1142
in Israel, *1162*
preindustrial, 1092–1093
in Turkey, Bursa, 194
Manukian, Aram, 303
Man Who Lost His Shadow, The (Ghanim), 911
Many, Moshe, Middle Eastern origin of, 49
MAPAI (Israel), 1185
Ahdut ha-Avodah in, 82, 1178, 1185
Arlosoroff (Chaim) in, 289
Ben-Gurion (David) in, 447, 1185, 2402
Dayan (Moshe) in, 681–682
establishment of, 1185
foundation of, 1362
Gruenbaum (Yizhak) supporting, 945
Ha-Poʿel ha-Tzaʿir in, 1185
in Israel Labor Party, 1185
Katznelson (Berl) in, 1185, 1281
Lavon affair and, 1185, 1188
Lavon (Pinhas) as ideologist of, 1378
Luz (Kadish) in, 1448
and Palestinian citizens' political parties, 1786
platform of, 1185
prime ministers from, 1185
RAFI Party split from, 1187–1188
Shazar (Shneour Zalman) in, 2047
Shitreet (Bekhor) in, 2058
Sprinzak (Joseph) in, 2087
MAPAM (Israel), 1185
Ahdut ha-Avodah in, 82, 1178
Arab members of, 1185
Ben-Aharon (Yitzhak) in, 438
establishment of, 1185
Flapan (Simha) in, 835
and Ha-Shomer ha-Tzaʿir, 1002
in Labor Alignment, 1185
in Meretz Party, 1185, 1186
military influenced by, 1173
Mossad surveillance of, 1578
platform of, 1185
Sneh (Moshe) in, 2075
split in, 1185
Yaʾari (Meʾir) in, 2375
Maʿpilim, 2625
Mapu, Abraham, 1430
Maqam (music), 1617, 1618
Maqama, 1420, 2184
Maqamat, 2113
Maqam, Mirza Bozorg Qaʾem, 7
Maqarin (Widha) Dam, 1249, **1485,** 2379, 2380
Maqasi College al-, 2116
Maqasid al- schools, 759
Maqasid al-Shariʿa, 834
Maqasid School of Maqasid Benevolent Society, 759
Maqrizi, al- (numismatic scholar), 1701
Maqwar, Ahmad, in Parti National, 1805
Marʾa al-Jadida, al- (Amin), 187
Marʾa al-Misriyya min al-Faraʿina ila al-Yawm, al- (Shafiq), 2019
Maraʾa wa al-Amal, al- (Musa), 1614
Marabout (saint or holy person), **1485,** 2359
Maraboutic traditions, in Algeria, 122
Maraboutism, 460
Marabtin al-sadqan (clients for protection), 1609
Marada Brigade, 1394
Maʿrakatuna al-Arabiyya fi Muwajahat al-Istiʿmar wa al-Sahyuniyya (Ghallab), 910
Maratghi, Mustafa al-, **1485–1486**
Marathon, in Oasis Group, 1707–1708
Marchand, Jean-Baptiste, 405, 529–530, 811
Marconi Company, 1893
Marcus, Abraham, *as contributor,* 111–112
Mardam, Jamil, **1486**
in National Party, 1664
Mardin, Asli Davaz, in Women's Library and Information Center, 2358
Mardom Party (Iran), **1487**
Alam (Amir Asadollah) in, 102, 1487
Mareth Line, **1487**
Margalit, Dan, 1452
Marghinani, al-, 988
"Marginal Notes on the Book of the Relapse" (Qabbani), 1859
Marguerite Taos Kabyle. *See* Amrouche, Mary Louise

Ma'rib, **1487–1488**
Mariette, Auguste, **1488**
archaeological research by, 275
as director of Egyptian Museum, 771
in Egyptian Antiquities Service, 1970
in Institut d'Égypte, 1099
Ma'rifa, 2053, 2111
Marijuana, 725–726
production of, 724, 725–726
Mar'i, Mariam, **1488**
Marine Barracks Bombing (Lebanon), **1488–1489**
Marinids, 828
decline of Marrakech under, 1493
in Morocco, *1570*
Mar'i, Sayyid, in Arab Socialist Union, 267
Maristan, 2224
Maritime Peace in Perpetuity, Treaty of (1853), **1489**
Mariya al-Mayyita (Kéfi), 1429
Marja al-taqlid, 493–494, 929, **1489–1490,** 1960, 2036, 2071
Marja al-Taqlid, Hakim (Muhsin al-) after death of, 977
Marj Dabiq, battle of (1516), 2223
Mark VIII, **1490**
Peter VII chosen by, 1822
Markaz Ahl al-Bayt (Shi'ite cultural center), 978
Markov (numismatic scholar), 1702
Marmara, Sea of, 2094
Turkish sovereignty over, under Montreux Convention (1936), 1565
Marmara University, **1491**
Erdoğan (Tayyip) at, 781
Women's Labor Force and Employment Center of, 2362
Marne, First Battle of (1914), 2365
Maronite church, 593
establishment of, 593
under Meushi (Paul Peter), 1520
Maronite College, 1492
Maronite militias, in Lebanese Civil War (1975–1990), 1389, 1391, 1400
Maronites, **1491–1492**
Druze relations with, 1491–1492, 1548
Franjiyya family, 849–850, 1394
French support for, 845, 846, 1491–1492
Israeli relations with, Mossad in, 1579
in Lebanese Civil War (1975–1990), Murabitun expulsion of, 1612
in Lebanon, 429 (*See also* Phalange (Kata'ib) party)
Aql (Sa'id) influence on, 218–219
"Arab face of Lebanon" accepted by, 1662
in French mandate system, 1398
as largest sect, 1392, 1397, 1398–1399
under millet system, 1544
Muslim–Christian alliance of, against French mandate, 2116, 2118
nationalism of, 1834
National Pact on, 1399, 1662–1663, 2116, 2118
under Ottoman rule, 1398
presidency reserved for, 1662–1663
Sfeir (Nasrallah) leading, 2016–2017
support for independence, 1549
in Mount Lebanon, 846, 1397, 1398, 1401
Druze conflict with, 320–321, 2021
in National Liberal Party, 1661
in South Lebanon Army, 2083
Marrakech, **1492–1493,** 1567
Tuhami al-Glawi as pasha of, 2223
Marriage, **1493–1496,** *1494*
in Algeria
Family Code on (1984), 136
Khemisti Law on (1963), 132
civil ceremonies, 884
harem's role in arranging, 993
Islamic law in regard to, Republican Brothers' call for reform in, 1917–1918
personal status laws on, 887
polygamous, 1838–1839
between *qabila* and *khadiri* status, 2209
temporary (*ziwaj mut'a),* **2438–2439**
in Tunisia, 2230–2231
Marriage of the Blessed, The (Iranian film), 1473
Marrus, Michael R., *as contributor,* 961, 1856–1857
Marr, Wilhelm, 211
Marshall, George, 1936
Sharett (Moshe) negotiating with, 2032
Marshall, Louis, in American Jewish Committee, 178
Marshall Plan (1947), U.S. economic and military aid under, 1836
Marsh Arabs, **1496**
Mart, al- (Boudjedra), 497
Martin, Helen T., 1902
Martino, Giacomo di, 1321
Martin, Paul, *as contributor,* 867–869, 1047–1049
Ma'rufi, Abbas, **1496**
Marun, Anton, in Socialist party, 626
Marun, Yuhanna (of Antioch), 1491
Marun, Yuhanna (of Homs), 1491
Marx, Ester, 71
Marxism. *See also* Communism
and Arab National Movement, 1008
class analysis in, 774–775
on economics of imperialism, 1088–1089
Forqan denouncing, 842
and Ha-Shomer ha-Tza'ir, 1001
and historiography of Middle East, 1036
in Iran, synthesis with Islam, by Mojahedin-e Khalq, 1562
and labor movement in Middle East, 1357
and Popular Front for the Liberation of Palestine, 962
and Zionism, 2434
Marxism and Islam (Mahmud), 1469
Marxist guerrilla movements, in Iran, 821
Marx, Karl, and Hess (Moses), 1024
Maryama, wa al-rahil (Ashour), 322
Marzouki, Moncef, **1496–1497**
imprisonment of, 439
as LTDH leader, 1416
Masada, **1497**
archaeological finds at, 278
designation as World Heritage Site, 1497
"Masada complex," 1497
Mas'ad, Bulus, 2021
Mas'adi, Mahmoud al-, **1498**
Mas'ala al-Sharqiyya, al- (Kamil), 1267
Mas'ari, Muhammad al-, in Committee for the Defense of Legitimate Rights, 622

Masbuta (baptism), 1479
Mashaf Rash, 2214
Mash ala al-khuffayn al-, 2055
Mashʿal, Khalid, 983, 1579
Mashhad (Iran), **1478**
bazaars of, 420
as provincial capital, 1312
Shrine of Imam Reza in, *1313*
Mashhur, Huriya, on National Women's Committee, 1669
Mashiah, 1519
Mashmum al-full (Khraief), 1313
Mashriq Financial Investment Company, al-, 1951
Masie, A. M., 2168
Masira Island, **1498–1499**
Masjid (place of prostration), 1577, 2224. *See also* Mosques
Masjid al-Haram al-. See Grand Mosque (Mecca)
Masjid al-jami (central mosque), 1577
Maskukat, al- (journal), 1702
Maslaha, 834, 1974, 2022
Maslaha mursala, 834
Masmoudi, Muhammad, **1499**
Masorti movement, 2023
Masoud, Ahmad Shah, 2150
Maspéro, Gaston, **1499**
in archaeological research, 275
as director of Egyptian Museum, 771
Masri, Aziz Ali al-
in al-Ahd, 81
arrest of, Arab nationalist opposition to, 263
Masri, Mai, **1499–1500**
Massa (Israeli journal), 1512
Massachusetts Institute of Technology (MIT)
Sharabati (Ahmad al-) at, 2030
Shultz (George) at, 2061
Massad, Joseph, 1037
Massignon, Louis, 2035
in Arab Academy of Damascus, 224
Massu, Jacques, 138, 141
Master of the Estate (Bint al-Shati), 476
Masʿud, Ahmad Shah. *See* Ahmad Shah Masʿud
Masʿud, Wali, in Nizat-i-Milli, 64
Ma Tabaqqa min Sirat Lakhdar Hamrouche (Aʿraj), 273
Matawirah tribe, 2212
Materi, Mahmoud
presidency of, 634
in Socialist Destour Party, 634
Maternal health, 1509–1510
Maternity leave, in Iraq, 898
Matin-Asgari, Afshin, *as contributor,* 630–631, 930, 1047, 1655–1656, 2080–2081
"Matmid, ha-" (Bialik), 470
Matni, Nasib, assassination of, 1390
Matrah (Oman), **1500,** 1616
Mattar, Philip, *as contributor,* 50, 219–220, 252–254, 256–257, 324–325, 380–382, 561–563, 570, 594, 830–831, 903–907, 917, 949–952, 974–975, 1011–1012, 1025, 1044–1045, 1056–1058, 1059–1060, 1322–1323, 1402–1403, 1639–1640, 1724–1728, 1772–1776, 1782–1784, 1788–1794, 1874–1875, 1954–1955, 2044, 2124–2125, 2140, 2348
Mattei, Enrico, 777–778
Matzpen, **1500–1501**
Bitton (Simone) in, 483
Tsemel (Leah) in, 2221
Maude Declaration, 1501
Maude, Frederick Stanley, **1501,** 1519, 2367
Maures, 1503
Mauritania, **1501–1503,** *1502. See also specific cities, organizations, people, and regions*
Algerian relations with, Bendjedid (Chadli) and, 444
in Arab Maghreb Union, 260
banking in, *393*
Berbers in, 458–459
borders of, 1501
cities of
capital, 1501, 1693
maritime, 1501
climate and resources of, 1502–1503
constitution of, 1503, 1744
coup in (1978), 660
coup in (1984), 1744
culture of, 1503
debt relief for, 1503
drought in, *1501*
elections in
of 1992, 1744
of 1997, 1745
fishing in, 1503
foreign policy of, 660
French protectorate over (1901–1912), 1503
in Gulf Crisis (1990–1991), 951
during Gulf War, 1744–1745
harratin population of, 996
history of, 1503
independence of, 1503
Iraq and, 1744–1745
labor unions in, 1358
in League of Arab States, 1388
Morocco and, 660, 1388
nationalism in, 1503
oil discovered in, 1502
population of, 1501, 1503
rivers of, 1502
Senegal conflict with (1989–1991), 1503
Spain ceding territory to, 2084, 2086
Western Sahara in, 660, 1502, 1571, 1837, 2344, 2345
ceding of claims (1979), 2343, 2345
POLISARIO seizure of, 1503
withdrawal from ECOWAS, 1503
Mauritanian Regroupment Party, 1503
Ma vie, mon cri (Yacoubi), 2376
Mawali tribe, 2212
Mawaqif, al- (magazine), 1456
Adonis in, 48
Mawardi, al-, 2019
Mawasim al-Sharq (Bannis), 396
Mawdudi, Abu al-Aʿla al-, **1503–1504**
and Afghan Islamic movements, 60
commentary on Qurʾan by, 1883
Mawlawiyya (Sufi order), 2113
Mawlay Ismaʿil, 106
Mawlay Rashid, 106
Mawlid al-Nisyan (Masʿadi), 1498
Mawsil. *See* Mosul
Mayer, Ann E., *as contributor,* 1379–1384
Mayers, Kenneth S., *as contributor,* 1078–1079, 2349
May Lady, The (film), 388
May processions, 2360
Maysalun, **1504–1505**

Mazalim (courts), 2034
ijtihad permitted in, 1626
Mazar-e Sharif (Afghanistan), *57*, **1505**
fall to Taliban, 2421
massacre of Hazara civilians in, 1015
Mazdaqism Is the Origin of Socialism (Soltani), 2079
Mazini, Ibrahim Abd al-Qadir al-, 1420
Maziq, Husayn, **1505–1506**
Mazza, 839
Mazzini, Giuseppe, 1199
MBC. *See* Middle East Broadcasting
MCA. *See* Militant Clergy Association
McCarthy, Justin, *as contributor*, 24–29, 1842–1848, 1913
McFarlane, Robert, 964
in Iran–Contra affair, 1123
McMahon, Henry, **1506**
and Husayn ibn Ali, correspondence with, 263–264, 511, 1053, 1059–1060
MDA. *See* Mouvement pour la Démocratie en Algérie
MDS (Algeria). *See* Social and Democratic Movement
MDS (Tunisia). *See* Mouvement des Démocrates Socialistes
Meah Sheʿarim, **1506**
establishment of, 2440
in Western Wall disturbances (1929), 2348
Meʾam Loʾez (Culi), 1363
Meʾasef, Ha- (periodical), 1430
Measles, 1508
Meat, lamb as cuisine staple, 839, 840
Mecca (Saudi Arabia), **1506–1507**, 1995
architecture in, 284
bazaars in, 418
beginning of Islam religion in, 1595–1596
cholera in, 712
conflict with Muhammad-led Medina (624–628), 1596–1597
Grand Mosque of (*See* Grand Mosque)
Hashimite family of, 1052
in Hijaz, 1028
Husayn ibn Ali in, 1052
Islamic conquest of (630), 1597
Islam in, origins of, 1144
Kaʿba in, 935, 1259, *1997*
malaria in, 711
mihrab indicating direction toward, 1526
Muhammad preaching in, 1144
Muhammad's birth in, 1507, 1595
Muhammad's early life in, 1595
Muhammad's message rejected in, 1596
Muhammad's migration from, 1596
Muhammad's pilgrimage to, 1597
newspapers of, 1678
pilgrimage to (*See* Hajj)
rioting by Iranian pilgrims to (1988), 1627
sharifs of, 2039
as spiritual center of Islam, 1597
tribe of, 2213
Wahhabi occupation of, 1625
well of (Zamzam), 1595, **2422–2423**
Mecelle-i Ahkam-i Adliye, 578, 601
Mecelle law code (Ottoman Empire), 988
Mechler, Mark, *as contributor*, 2384
Mecili, André-Ali, murder of, 95
Meclis-i Vala, 2162, 2164
Meddahs, 2187
Meddeb, Abdelwahhab, *1423*, 1424, **1507**
Medeghri, Ahmed
Ben Bella (Ahmed) and, 442
death of, Abdelghani (Mohamed Benahmed) after, 23
in Oujda Group, 1743
Media. *See* Newspapers and print media
Median language, 1124
Medicine and public health, **1508–1511**. *See also* Diseases
child survival and maternal health in, 1509–1510
cosmopolitan, 1508–1509
curative options in, 1508–1509
in Egypt
Mabarrat Muhammed Ali and, 1452–1453
Mahmud (Mustafa) in, 1469
for women, 1510
humoral, 1508
improvements in
and mortality rates, 1845
and population growth, 1843, 1844
for women, 876
in Israel, Magen David Adom (MDA) in, 1459
local practices in, 1508–1509
politics of population, body, and food in, 1510–1511
prophetic, 1508
Protestant missions and, 1855
in Tunisia, Marzouki (Moncef) and, 1496
Western, 1508–1509
Medina (Saudi Arabia), **1511–1512**
Abd al-Aziz's (ibn Saʿud Al Saʿud) capture of, 1511, 1625–1626
architecture in, 284
as capital of Islamic state, 1597
conflict with Mecca (624–628), 1596–1597
Constitution of, 1596
and Damascus, railroad connecting, 1028
Islamic University of, 1156–1157
Muhammad's acceptance and leadership in, 1596–1597
Muhammad seeking refuge in, 1144
rise of Islamic state in, 1596–1597
Medinan school, 1476
Medinat Yisrael, 781
Mediterranean Sea, 902, **1512**
American shipping in, 2208
pollution of, 1512
Suez–Mediterranean Pipeline linking Red Sea and, 2110–2111
Medjerda River, 2225
MED-TV (television station), 1343
Medzini, Meron, *as contributor*, 156–157, 190, 407–408, 456, 683, 720–721, 1022, 1023, 1030, 1218–1219, 1378, 1440–1441, 1641, 1913–1914
Megali Idea, 1657–1658
Meged, Aharon, 1432, **1512–1513**
Megiddo, battle of (1918), 510
"Megillat ha-Esh" (Bialik), 470
Megnodichian, Armenouchic, 431
Mehasin (magazine), 1513
Mehdi, Aqa Sayyed, 2141
Mehmed Emin Ali Paşa, Midhat Paşa and, 1525
Mehmedkuhzade, Celil, 347
Mehmet II (Ottoman sultan)
Istanbul conquered by, 1193
millet system under, 1543
qanun of, 1870

Mehmet V Reşat, **1513**
in Konya, Battle of (1832), 1333
Mehmet VI Vahidettin, 1513
Atatürk (Mustafa Kemal) exiling, 1376
and caliphate, 556–557
decline of, 556–557
Osman dynasty under, 1728
Mehmet Ali Paşa (Ottoman military officer), and Hijaz Railroad, 1028, 1029
Mehmet Asat Yesari, calligraphy of, 559
Mehmet Bey, in Alliance of Fidelity, 2406
Mehmet Emin Ali Paşa, as Mustafa Reşid's protégé, 1624
Mehmet Fuad Paşa
Midhat Paşa and, 1524
as Mustafa Reşid's protégé, 1624
Mehmet Koja Husrev Paşa, 1481
appeasement of Muhammad Ali by, 1624
Mustafa Reşid rivalry with, 1624
Mehmet Rauf, **1513**
Mehmet Reşid, in Ottoman Union Society, 622
Mehmet Vedat, 282
Mehmet Zahid Kotku, in National Salvation Party, 1665
Mehrjui, Daryush, 832
Meimad Party (Israel), 1185–1186
platform of, 1186
Meinertzhagen, Richard, on NILI spy ring, 1
Meir, Golda, 891, **1513–1515,** *1514*
Abdullah I ibn Hussein meeting with, 30–31
Aloni (Shulamit) opposed by, 157
in Arab–Israel War (1973), 682, 1514–1515
confidence vote for, 153
in conflict with Ben-Gurion (David), 1514
over Lavon affair, 1378
as foreign minister, *448,* 449, 2033
government of
Allon (Yigal) in, 153
Hillel (Shlomo) in, 1030
Peres (Shimon) in, 1817
Rabin (Yitzhak) in, 1891
Yariv (Aharon) in, 2379
and Herzog (Ya'acov David), 1023
at Histadrut headquarters, *1033*
in Labor Party, 1183
resignation of, 252, 682, 744, 1513, 1514–1515
at St. Germain Conference (1956), 2109
Shiloah (Reuven) as adviser to, 2056
Meissner, Heinrich, and Hijaz Railroad, 1029
Mejelle, 2034
Meknes (Morocco), 828, **1515,** 1567
Isawiyya Brotherhood in, 1141
Meknes Prison, 497
Meknes, Treaty of (1836), **1515–1516**
Mekorot Water Company, 784, 1991
Mekteb-i Harbiye, 757, 778
Mekteb-i Mülkiye, 757, 864, 2163
Mekteb-i Sultani, 757, 864
Melekh Basar Va-Dam (Shamir), 2024
Melilla (Spanish possession), **1516,** 1567, 2085
Melkite Catholics, under millet system, 1544
Melkite Church, 738
Melkites, 1930
Mellah (Moroccan Jewish quarters), 1231, 2625–2626
Mellini, Peter, *as contributor,* 931–932, 1329
Melliyun Party. *See* National Party
Mello, Sergio Vieira de, killing of, 2326
MELN. *See* Egyptian Movement for National Liberation
Melos, 1431
Mélouza massacre (1957), 438
Meltem wind, 605
Même livre, le (Khatibi), 1304
Memmi, Albert, 1423, 1428, **1516–1517**
Mémoires du général Khaled Nezzar (Nezzar), 1686
Memoire tatotée, la (Khatibi), 1304
Memoirs from the Women's Prison (al-Saadawi), 1950
Memoirs of an Unrealistic Woman (Khalifa), 1297
Memory for Forgetfulness (Darwish), 674
Memory in the Flesh (Mostaghanemi), 1581
Mem o Zin (Ahmad Khani), 1345
Mendelssohn, Moses, 1430
and Haskalah movement, 1002
Menderes, Adnan, **1517**
coup against (1960), 1517
in Democrat Party, 695
execution of, 696
Freedom Party opposition, 851
in Free Republican Party, 854
Gürsel (Cemal) opposing, 957
U.S. support for, Dulles (John Foster) in, 733
Mendes-Flohr, Paul, *as contributor,* 540–541
Mendès-France, Pierre, 687
Peled (Mattityahu) dialogue with, 1812
Mendjli, Ali, in Oujda Group, 1743, 1744
Menicucci, Garay, *as contributor,* 373
Menou, Jacques François, 491, **1517**
Menuhin, Yehudi, Kan (Suna) performance with, 1269
Menzies Mission. *See* Suez Crisis
Menzies, Robert, at London Conference (1956), 1444, 2108
Merbah, Kasdi, 445
Ghozali (Ahmed) under, 917
successor to, 987
Mère du printemps, le (Chraibi), 588
Meretz Party (Israel), 1186
Aloni (Shulamit) in, 157, 893
Chazan (Naomi) in, 582
Citizens' Rights Movement members in, 1180, 1186
Dayan (Yael) in, 683
electoral success of, 1186
MAPAM in, 1185, 1186
platform of, 1186
Sarid (Yossi) in, 1991
Shinui Party in, 1186, 1188
Merhav, la- (paper), 956
Merkava battle tank (Israel), 1535
Merkaz ha-Rav school, 1333, 1334
Merkaz ruhani (spiritual center), 1553–1554
Mernissi, Fatema, **1518**
research on women by, 894, 2376
Meroe (Nubian kingdom), 1695
Mes'adi, Mahmoud al-, 1428
Mesekhtot, 2157
Mesfouf, 838
Meshkini, Marziyeh, 1473
Meskoob, Shahrokh, 1437
Mesopotamia. *See* Iraq
Mesopotamia Campaign (1914–1918), **1518–1519,** 2367

Maude (Frederick Stanley) in, 1501, 2367
Mesopotamia, 1917–1920: A Clash of Loyalties (Wilson), 2353
Message, The (film), 98–99
Messaoudi, Khalida. *See* Toumi, Khalida
Messiah, 1519
Messianic Regime: The End of the Road (Ben-Aharon), 438
Messianism, **1519**
Messick, Brinkley, 756
Mestiri, Ahmad, **1519–1520**
in Mouvement des Démocrates Socialistes, 2232
Meşveret (journal), 867
Ahmet Riza at, 91, 623, 2408
Metaphysics (Avicenna), 1457
"Metei Midbar" (Bialik), 470
Métier à tisser, Le (Dib), 1426
Metropolitan Museum of Art (New York), 279
Metruk, 1368
Metternich, Klemens von
in Damascus affair (1840), 664
and Mustafa Reşid, 1624
territorial expansionism under, 339
Me'uharim (Guri), 956
Meushi, Paul Peter, **1520–1521**
Mevat, 1368
Mevlevi Brotherhood, **1521**
Atatürk (Mustafa Kemal) closing, 2171
vs. Bektashis, 435
Mevlevis, 2113
Mezrag, Madani, in Islamic Salvation Army, 1155, 1156
MFO. *See* Multinational Force and Observers
M'hammas, 838
MHP. *See* Nationalist Action Party (Turkey)
MI-5, 1521
MI-6 (Britain), **1521**
in Iranian coup (1953), 1118, 1752
KGB compared to, 1290
MIA. *See* Mouvement Islamique Armé
Mi'ari, Muhammad
in al-Ard movement, 285
in Progressive List for Peace, 1187
Michael, Sami, 1452, **1521–1522**
Michalak, Laurence, *as contributor,* 717–718, 990, 1204, 1863–1864, 2015–2016, 2192
Michman, Dan, *as contributor,* 1040–1043
Middle East, as designation and term, **1522–1523**
Middle East Airlines, 1975
Middle East Broadcasting (MBC), 1895
Middle East Command (1951), 1692–1693
Middle East Defense Organization (MEDO), 519, **1523,** 1692–1693
Middle Eastern Jews. *See* Adot hamizrah
Middle East Society of Associated Accountants, 1951
Middle East Supply Center (MESC), **1523–1524**
Middle East Technical University, 491, **1524**
Women's Studies Graduate Program of, 2362
Midfa'i, Jamil al-, 927, **1524,** 1968
opposition to, 1283
Midhat, Ahmed, on Aliyer (Fatimah), 148
Midhat Paşa, **1524–1526,** 2407
Baghdad improved by, 360
in Çerkes Hasan incident (1876), 575
Damascus under, 663
Iraq improved by, 1132
and Kuwait alliance, 158
Namik Kemal and, 1641
Midrash, Rabbinic Hebrew in, 1017
Midwives, 2003
Miflagah Komunistit Yisraelit. *See* Israel Communist Party (MAKI)
MIFTAH. *See* Palestinian Initiative for the Promotion of Global Dialogue and Democracy
Miggiel, John, *as contributor,* 382–384, 542–543
Migration, 1846–1847
Mihrab, 1074, **1526,** 1577
Mikayelian, Kristapor, 676
Mikdamot (Yizhar), 2403
Miklat (newspaper), 464
Mikou, Mohamed, 1716
Mikoyan, Anastas, *1942*
Mikunis, Shmu'el, in Communist Party of Palestine, 626
Milani, Tahmineh, **1526**
Miles, George, in Islamic numismatics, 1702
Miliana River, 2225
Miliani, Mansouri, 918
Militant Clergy Association (MCA) (Iran), Karbaschi (Gholamhosain) opposing, 1273
Military, **1526–1543**
active force levels of, *1528–1529,* 1529–1531
in arbitrator regime, *1536*
in conflict between states, 1537–1540
in conflicts with and among Great Powers, 1540
defense costs as percentage of GNP or GDP, 1529–1530, *1530*
equipment of, *1534,* 1535
force structure of (army, air force, and navy), *1532–1533,* 1535
future of, 1541
in internal affairs of other countries, 1530–1531
in internal conflicts, 1530–1531, 1536–1537
modernization of, 1535
nontraditional, 1535
organization of, 1527–1535
participation in revolutions and coups, 1536–1537
role of, 1540–1541
in ruler regime, *1539*
as school of nation, 1541
Westernization of, 1527–1528
Military-administrative slaves, 2072–2073
Military aid. *See* Economic and military aid
Millat (Afghanistan), 62
Millet, 886
Millet Meclisi. *See* National Assembly
Millet system. *See also* Armenian millet
missionaries under, 1551
in Ottoman Empire, 1461, **1543–1545,** 1548, 1732 (*See also* Armenian millet)
Christians in, 590, 1543–1545
Cyprus in, 652
in eighteenth–nineteenth century, 1544–95
in fifteenth–seventeenth century, 1543–94
Milli Birlik Komitesi. *See* National Unity Committee (Turkey)

Milli Görüs. *See* National Outlook Movement (Turkey)
Milli Görüs Hareketti, **1545**, 1910
Milli Güvenlik Kurulu. *See* National Security Council (Turkey)
Milli Istihbarat Teşkilati (MIT) (Turkey), **1545**
Milli Nizam Partisi. *See* National Order Party (Turkey)
Milli Selamet Partisi (NSP). *See* National Salvation Party (Turkey)
Milliyet (newspaper), 746, 1685
İpekci (Abdi) in, 1109, 1269
Karacan (Ali Naci) in, 1269
Milliyetci Hareket Partisi (MHP). *See* Nationalist Action Party (Turkey)
Millspaugh, Arthur, **1545–1546**
Milner, Alfred, 1546
Milner Mission, **1546**
Milosevic, Slobodan, 1913
Milton, John, 144
Mimar: Architecture in Development (periodical), 283
Mimouna Festival, **1546–1547**
Mimouni, Rachid, 1426, **1547**
Minah al-Jalil (Ilaysh), 1086
Mina, Hanna, 1356
Minakovska, Alexandra Angela, 872
Minaret, **1547**
of Ibn Tulun Mosque, 1074
Mina Sulman, 1479
Minbar, 2626
Minbar (pulpit), 1577, 1606
Mines de rien (Boudjedra), 497
Min ha-Hakhlil ve-el ha-Kakhol (Greenberg), 941
Min ha-Metzar (Brenner), 507
Minhat Yehudah (Alkalai), 149
Minorities, **1547–1550**
bases for defining, 1547–1548, 1549
ethnic and linguistic, 1548–1549
non-Muslim, as *dhimmis*, 703
religious, 1548
vs. subdominant or subordinate groups, 1547
Mintaqas, 1375
Mint tea, 2169
Minuchehr, Pardis, *as contributor*, 97, 593–594, 812, 929–930, 1214, 1496, 1962, 2011
MINURSO. *See* United Nations Mission for the Referendum in Western Sahara
Minz, Benjamin, **1550**
Miramar (Mahfuz), 1464
Mirʿat al-Sharq (newspaper), 2063
Mirghani, Ali al-, in National Unionist Party, 2261
Mirghani, Muhammad Uthman al-, 2101
Mir-Hosseini, Ziba, *as contributor*, 82, 743–744, 1274–1275, 1970–1971
Miri, 1367, 1368
Mirjaveh (Iran), 2420
Mirliton du Ciel, l' (Memmi), 1517
Mirmon (magazine), 786
Miró Award, Attar (Suad al-) won by, 337
Mirza Hedayatollah Vazir Daftar, son of, Mossadegh (Mohammad) as, 1580
Mirza, Jahangir, 1867
Mirza Mohammad Khan. *See* Mossadegh, Mohammad
Mirza Mohammad Taqi Khan Amir Kabir, grandson of, Mohammad Ali Shah Qajar as, 1559
Misbah, al- (weekly), 2043
Misbahi, Hassouna, 1429
Miser, The (Molière), 1421
Mishael (Seri), 2012
Mishʿal, Khalid, attempted assassination of, 2381
Mishkovsky, Zelda. *See* Zelda (Israeli poet)
Mishlei Baqbuqim (Tammuz), 2160
Mishmar, ha- (publication), 927
Mishmar ha-Gvul (Israel), 1536
Mishna, Rabbinic Hebrew in, 1017
Mishnayot, 2157–2158
Mishne Torah (Maimonides), 979
Mishpahat ha-Adamah (Smilansky), 2075
Misir Carsisi, *839*
Misr (Egyptian journal), Ishaq (Adib) in, 1143
Misr al-Fatat. *See* Young Egypt
Misri, al- (Egyptian newspaper)
closure of, 1838
establishment of, 1838
Politi (Elie) in, 1838
Misri, Aziz Ali al-, **1550**
and al-Ahd, 999
German support for, 906
Misriyya, al- (journal), 2030
Misr Spinning and Weaving Company, 1461
Missiles
Chinese sale of, 586
U.S. sale of, to Afghan guerrillas, 66
Missionary Schools, **1550–1552**, *1551*
for women, 882–883
Mission civilisatrice, **1552**
Misurata (Libya), 1410
MIT. *See* Massachusetts Institute of Technology
Mitchell, Timothy, 756, 1037
Mithaq al-Watani, al- *See* National Pact (Lebanon)
Mithla Sayfin lan yatakarrar (Berrada), 467
Mithra (Zoroastrian deity), 2442
Mitla Pass, in Arab–Israel War (1956), 245
Mitterrand, François, 864
Kashwar Kamal (Meena) and, 1279
Mitzna, Amram, 1170
Mixed Armistice Commissions, **1552–1553**
Nusayba (Anwar) on, 1705
Mixed courts, **1553**
in Egypt, 939, 1382, 1553
in Tunisia, Fundamental Pact (1857) establishing, 860
Miʾyar al-Mughrib wa al-Jami al-Muʾrib (Wansharisi, al-), 1476
Mizan (periodical), 2408
Mizan: The Law Group for Human Rights in Jordan, Khader (Asma) in, 1291
Mizrahi Jews
definition of, 2626
in Israel, 1162
Jerusalem, 1223
leadership of, Yosef (Ovadiah) in, 2404
origin of term, 48
Mizrahi movement (Zionist group), **1553–1554**, 2372, 2433
De Haan (Yaʿakov Yisrael) in, 688
establishment of, 1022
Maimon (Yehudah Leib Hacohen) in, 1470
and Mizrahi Party, 1186
Mizrahi Party (Israel), 1186
electoral success of, 1186
platform of, 1186

Po'alei Mizrahi and, 1186, 1187
in United Religious Front, 1190
Mizrahi, Tawfiq, in Club National Israélite, 612
MNA. *See* Mouvement National Algérien
MNR. *See* Mouvement National pour la Réforme
Moadda, Mohamed, **1554–1555**
as successor to Mestiri (Ahmad), 1520
Moaddel, Mansoor, *as contributor,* 41–42, 200–202, 421, 1580–1581
"Mobile Identity and the Focal Distance of Memory" (Khemir), 1309
Mobilization press, 1680, 1685
Moda'i, Yitzhak, **1555**
in Liberal Party, 1184
Modarres, Hasan, 1757
Moderate Liberal Party (Jordan), founder of, 1470
Modern Egypt (Baring), 406–407
Modernization, **1555–1556**. *See also* Industrialization
and decline of bazaars, 419, 420
economic aspects of, 1555
and education, 880
in Egypt, 1157–1158
and decline of bazaars, 419
under Muhammad Ali, 766
France and, 844
intellectual/psychological aspects of, 1556
in Iran, 1756
of law (*See* Law, modern)
in Morocco, Lyautey (Louis-Hubert Gonzalve) and, 1448
Persian, under Fath Ali Shah Qajar, 816
political aspects of, 1556
social aspects of, 1556
in Syria, 315
in Turkey, 2240
vs. Westernization, 2341
and women's status, 874–876, 883, 885–886
Modern Language Association, 1966
Mo'ed, 2157
Mofaz, Sha'ul, *750*
as defense minister, 1174
Mogannam, Matiel, **1556–1557**
in Arab Women's Executive Committee, 268
Moghaizel Foundation (Lebanon), 1557–1558
Moghaizel, Laure, 894, 1396, **1557–1558**
Mogul Empire, 525, 526
Mohajerani, Ataollah, **1558**
Mohamed Khan, 833
Mohammad VI (king of Morocco), 933
Mohammad Ali Shah Qajar (ruler of Iran), **1558–1559**
abdication of, 1559
constitutional supplement signed by, 636
constitution opposed by, 636–637, 1559
coup against, 1868, 2430
as crown prince, 7, 1559
deposition of, 88, 374, 637
father of, Mozaffar al-Din Qajar as, 1592
government of, Amin al-Soltan (Ali-Asghar) in, 184
Kuchek Khan-e Jangali opposing, 1337
majles opposed by, 636–637, 1559
reign of (1907–1909), 636–637, 1868–1869
masonic lodges allowed under, 852
Sadr (Muhsin) supporting, 1960
son of
Ahmad Qajar as, 88, 637
Naser al-Din Shah as, 1643
Vazir Afkham (Soltan Ali Khan) under, 2311
Mohammadi, Maulawi Mohammad Nabi, **1559–1560**
in Harakat-e Inqilab-e Islami, 63, 1561
in mojahedin resistance, 1561
Mohammad Shah Qajar (ruler of Iran)
reign of (1834–1848), 1868
wife of, Mahd-e Ulya, Malek Jahan Khanum as, 1462
Mohammadzai dynasty, 721, 2007
Mohilever, Samuel, **1560**
and Zionism, 2432
Mohseni, Asaf
in Harakat-e Islami, 63, 1561
in mojahedin resistance, 1561
Mojab, Shahrzad, *as contributor,* 2423
Mojaddedi, Sebghatullah, **1561**
election as president, by Afghan Interim Government, 63, 1561
in Jebhe-ye Nejat-e Milli, 63, 1561
in mojahedin resistance, 1561
Mojahed (newspaper), 1562
Mojahedin (Afghanistan), *1561,* **1561–1562**
communists opposed by, 53, 1561
coup by (1992), 66, 1561
external support for, 59
government of, 1561
Hazara and, 1015
infighting among, 1561
in Karzai interim government, 1561
Najibullah opposed by, 59, 66, 1561
under Omar (Muhammad), 1712, 1713
origins of, Islamic movement in, 61
parties involved in, 1561
in resistance war, 1561–1562
Saudi Arabian aid to, 1627
Soviet intervention opposed by, 53, 59, 65–66, 474
Taliban opposition to, 61, 1561
U.S. supporting, 2174
Mojahedin-e Khalq (Iran), **1562–1563**
alliance with Iraq, 1562
Bani Sadr (Abolhasan) in, 389
categorized as terrorist organization, 1562
Feda'iyan-e Khalq influence on, 821
Rafsanjani (Ali Akbar Hashemi) and, 1899
Rajavi (Masud) in, 1900
uprising by, suppression of, 1922
U.S. occupation of Iraq and, 1562
Mojtahed-Shabestari, Mohammad, **1563**
Moked (Israel)
Israel Communist Party in, 1182, 1188
RAKAH in, 1182, 1188
Moldavia, languages of, 2248
Moldavian Soviet Socialist Republic, 507
Moledet Party (Israel), 1186
electoral success of, 1186
in National Union, 1187
platform of, 1186
Ze'evi (Rehavam) in, 1186

Molière, 1421
Kasap (Teodor) plays based on, 1277
translation of, 92, 171
Mollet, Guy, **1563**
in Arab–Israel War (1956), 245
and Sèvres Protocol (1956), 2109
in Suez Crisis (1956–1957), 2108
visit to Algeria, French riots protesting (1956), *137*
Moltke, Helmuth von, 903, **1563–1564**
Moment of Innocence (Iranian film), 1473
Monarchic form of government, 933
Monastero, Alberto, and Jewish community in Tripoli, 974
Monasticism, 787
Coptic, 640, *641*
Monastir, **1564**
Mond, Alfred Moritz, **1564**
Monde, Le (newspaper), 477
Monnet, Jean, 689
Monnot, Georges, 1457
Monophysite, 639
Monophysite churches, 738
Monotheism, of Islam, 1596, 1597
Monroe, Elizabeth, 1323
Monsieur Bob'le (Shahada), 2020
Montagne du lion, La (Tlili), 2193
Montazeri, Hosayn Ali, **1564–1565**
Kadivar (Mohsen) studying under, 1262
Khamenehi's mistreatment of, Yazdi (Ibrahim) on, 2383
religious qualifications of Khamendi as *faqih* questioned by, 1564
as successor-designate to Khomeini
confirmation of, 1564
resignation of, 1564
as successor to Khomeini (Ruhollah), 1312
Montefiore, Moses, **1565,** 1976
in Damascus affair (1840), 664–665
and expansion of Jerusalem, 1223
and Zionism, 2432
Montenegro
in Balkan League, 384
Balkan refugees fleeing to, 382
in Balkan wars, 384
independence of
Berlin Treaty (1878) and, 383, 1989
San Stefano Treaty (1878) and, 382, 1988
nationalist movement in, 542
Monteux, Pierre, 477
Montgomery, Bernard Law, **1565,** 2194
at al-Alamayn battle (1942), 102, 516, 1565, 2370
Montjoie Palestine (Aba), 1426
Montreux Convention (1936), 485, **1565**
capitulations under abandoned (1939), 1636
Eden (Anthony) at, 755
mixed courts ended by, 1553
on Turkish Straits, Turkish control of, 621, 743, 2095
Moore, Clement Henry, 450
Moore, Henry, 1978
Moors, 1964
Morad, Gowhar, 1962
Morashah Party (Israel), 1186
Mor Çatī Kadīn Sīğīnağī, 2171
Morgenthau, Henry, Jr., 1936
Morier, James Justinian, 976
Moriscos, 2084
Morley College (London), Ghoussoub (Mai) at, 916
Morning Herald (newspaper), 594
Moroccan–Algerian War, **1566**
Moroccan Association of Human Rights. *See* Association Marocaine des Droits de l'Homme
Moroccan crises (1905–1906, 1911)
Act of Algeciras on (1906), 8
Agadir crisis (1911), 70
Algeciras Conference on (1906), 119–120
British support for, 119–120
Cambon–Lansdowne Agreement on (1904), 559–560
financial aspect of, 14
German opposition to, 8, 70, 119–120
Moroccan Family Legal Code. *See* Moudawana, al-
Moroccan folk culture, 2008
Moroccan–Franco agreement. *See* Tangier, Treaty of (1844)
Moroccan Free Schools, 759
Moroccan Human Rights Organization. *See* Organisation Marocaine des Droits de l'Homme (OMDH)
Moroccan Institute of Higher Studies. *See* Institut des Hautes Études Marocaines
Moroccan Labor Union. *See* Union Marocaine du Travail
Moroccan League for the Defense of Human Rights. *See* Ligue Marocaine de Défense des Droits de l'Homme
Moroccan National Front
Parti Démocratique Constitutionnel in, 1803
Parti Démocratique de l'Indépendance in, 1804
Moroccan Observatory of Prisons (OMP), 498
Moroccan Question (1900–1912), **1566,** 2038
Abd al-Aziz ibn al-Hassan policies in, 8, 14
Abd al-Hafid ibn al-Hassan on, 14
Abu Himara's rebellion and, 37
Marrakech during, 1493
Morocco, **1567–1575**. *See also specific cities, organizations, people, and regions*
agriculture in, *753,* 754, 913
drought and, 1569
tax on *(tartib),* 8
AIDS action plan in, 713–714
Alawite dynasty in, 105–107, 1569
Algerian relations with (*See also* Moroccan–Algerian War; Western Sahara War)
Ben Bella (Ahmed) and, 442
Bouteflika (Abdelaziz) and, 503
causes of strain in, 260
POLISARIO and, 503, 2190–2191
Arabic language in, 1422, 1567
Arabization policies on, 254–256
Arabization policies in, 254–256
in Arab Maghreb Union, 260, 1566
architecture in, 282, 283–284
art in, 2155
banking in, 389, 390, *393,* 394
as Barbary state, 401
Berber dialect in, 2166–2167
Berbers in, 458, 459, 463, 487
border with Algeria
conflict over, 1566
dispute settled in, 4
Britain and, 1569

reaction to Treaty of Meknes (1836), 1515
trade agreement between (1856), 19, 1515
Catholics in, 1932
cities of, 1515, 1567
capital, 1888
historical capital, 828–829
port, 568–570, *1571*
provincial capital, 2179
second largest, 1492–1493
city planning in, 2299
communism in, 626
constitution of, **1572–1573**
first (1962), 1572
second (1970), 1572–1573
third (1972), 1573
fourth (1992), 1573
fifth (1996), 1573
article 35 of (state of emergency), 1572
equal rights under, 1585
Corcos family in, 642
corsairs in, 643
dance in, 667
defense costs as percentage of GNP or GDP, *1530*
economic and military aid to
from IMF, 749
from United States, 748, 750
economic liberalization reforms in, 1366
economy of, 752, *753*, 753–754, 1569
women in labor force, 874, *875*
education in, 756
low access to, 1600
upbringing aspect of, 760
elites in, 776
emigration from, as economic safety valve, 1569
ethnic groups of, 1567
European rivalry over (*See* Moroccan Question)
European Union relations with, 1601, 1602
family code in (*See* Moudawana, al-)
film industry of, 483
fishing industry of, 834
French attack on (1844), 19, 2038
French claim to (*See also* Moroccan crises)
Cambon–Lansdowne Agreement on (1904), 529, 827, 1374
French intelligence operations in, 1101
French language in, 255
French protectorate over (1912–1956), 848, 1460, 1567, 1569–1570
Agadir crisis leading to (1911), 70
Catroux (Georges) in, 570
Declaration of La Celle St. Cloud on (1953), 687
Fes Treaty (1912) and, 826–828, 1448, 2038–2039
French foreign legion in, 856
Khattabi rebellion (1921) in, 856, 1450
and literature, 1422
Lyautey administration, 1448–1450
Marrakech in, 1493
Muhammad V in, 1598
nationalist opposition to, 615, 618–619
pacification campaign during, 1570
resistance to, 1304–1306
Treaty of Fes (1912) and, 1570
Tuhami al-Glawi supporting, 2223
geography of, 1567, *1568*
government of, 933
guest workers from, 946
guilds in, 946, 947
in Gulf Crisis (1990–1991), 951
habous in, 964, 965
harratin population of, 996
hashish production in, 725, 726
higher education in, 1888
at al-Qarawiyyin, 1871
history of, 1569–1571
human rights in
in constitution of 1992, 1573
Mohammad VI and, 1600
organizations in, 1716–1717
immigrants from, to Israel, 485
immunization rate in, 1510
independence of, 812, 827–828, 1004, 1460, 1570
Declaration of La Celle St. Cloud on (1953), 687
industrialization of, 1095–1096
intelligence services in, 1101, 1104
irrigation in, 74, 913
Islamism in, 2266, 2268
Jewish quarters in *(mellah)*, 1231
Jews in, 1234, 1568
Corcos family of, 642
immigration to Israel, 49, 1546–1547, 1914
Mimouna Festival celebrated by, 1546–1547
Muhammad V and, 1598
Muhammad VI and, 1600
status and treatment of, 1548
support from Montefiore (Moses), 1565
al-Wifaq and, 2352
king as *amir al-mu'minin* (commander of the faithful) in, 1568, 1572, 1586, 1599–1600
labor unions in, 453, 1358, 2264, 2265–2266
confederation of, 629–630
strikes by, 2264
land ownership in, Azib system of, 350
languages of
Arabic, 1424, 1425, 1428
Berber dialects, 458, 2166–2167
French, 1424, 1425, 1428
in League of Arab States, 1387, 1388
legal system of, 1383
legislative body in, 932
literature of, 40, 396, 466–467, 497–498, 588, 910–911, 1355–1356, 1422–1425, *1424*, *1427*, 1427–1428, 1890, 2008, 2060
in French language, 1303–1304
women in, 588, 2376
Ma al-Aynayn and, 1451
manufacturing in, 1569
Mauritania and, 660, 1388, 1451
military of
equipment of, *1534*
force levels of, *1528–1529*
force structure of (army, air force, and navy), *1532–1533*
minorities or subdominant groups in, 1548
modernization in, Lyautey (Louis-Hubert Gonzalve) and, 1448
monarchy of, 1003–1006
Moroccan Question colonialism in, 8
moudawana in, reform of, 1203–1204
mountains of, 335–336, 1924
music of, 1617, 1619
nationalism in, 495, 1570, 1572, 2039
Comité d'Action Marocaine in, 1574
Istiqlal Party in, 1574
Muhammad V in, 1570, 1598–1599
organizations of, 618–619
newspapers and print media of, 1678, 1680

Morocco *(continued)*
diversity in, 1681
French-language, 1681–1682
overview of, **1567–1572**
parliamentary elections in, of 1993, 1904
parliament of
establishment of, 1572–1573
lack of power vis-à-vis monarchy, 1572–1573
Peace Corps in, 1808
personal status, family, and inheritance in (*See* Moudawana, al-)
phosphate industry in, 1834
political parties in, **1573–1575**, 1904
fractionalization by monarchy, 1570
population of, 752, *753*, 1567
prisoners' rights in, 1716, 1717
pronatalist policies of, 478
radio and television in, 1894, *1895*
rebellion in (1902–1909), 8, 37
reforms in, 933
regions of, 912–913
religion of, 1567–1569
Isawiyya Brotherhood, 1141
Salafiyya movement, 1974
rivers of, 1567, *1568*
ruling dynasties of, 1569
Sahrawi population of, 1356
Salafiyya Movement in, 811
science and technology in, 2004
Sharifian dynasties in, 2037–2039
Spain ceding territory to, 2084, 2086
Spanish claims to, 1567
Ifni ceded in, 1083
Spanish defeat of (1860), 1569
Spanish enclaves in, 1516, 1567
Spanish protectorate in (1912–1956), *1926*, 1926–1927, 2084 (*See also* Spanish Morocco)
Ahmad ibn Muhammad al-Raysuni in, 86
capital of, 2179
Fes Treaty (1912) and, 826–828, 1570, 2038–2039
resistance to, 1304–1306
Sufism in, Qadiriyya Order of, 1864
teachers in, foreign, 255
terrorism in, attack in Casablanca (2003), 1569
theater of, 2060
tourism in, 2196
in trade, 568, 569, 2038, 2198
with Tunisia, 2269
tribes in, 458, 459, 912, 2212
United States relations with, under Treaty of Meknes (1836), 1515
water resources of
freshwater withdrawals, *2331*
quantity of, 2330
and Western Sahara, 660, 1005, 1006, 1566, 1571, 1600, 1837, *2343*, 2343–2344 (*See also* Green March, Western Sahara War)
sand barrier built by, 718
women in
constitutional rights of, 1585
economic status of, *877*
government positions held by, 1601
health care for, 1510
in labor force, 874, *875*
literature on, 2376
Mernissi (Fatema) on, 1518
al-Moudawana on, 94, 1585–1586, 1601
National Plan of Action for, 1586, 1601
in politics, 497–498, 894
as writers, 497–498, 1424, 1428
women's rights in, 772–773, 892
World Bank and
capital stock and voting power in, *2363*
loans from, *2364*
privatization program of, 1569
in World War II, 516, 2370
Morris, Benny, 1037
on Zionist attacks on Palestinians, 1639
Morrison–Grady Plan (1946), **1575–1576**
Morrison, Herbert, 1576
Mortality rates, 1843, *1845*, 1845–1846
Mortara, Edgardo, 151
Mort au Canada (Chraibi), 588
Mort des artistes, la (Khatibi), 1303
Mortimer, Robert, *as contributor*, 638, 990, 1455–1456
Mosca, G., 774
Moses
burial site of, 1630–1631
Muhammad compared with, 1597
Moses, Operation (1984–1985), 786
Moshav, **1576–1577**
first, establishment of, 1576
Mizrahi movement and, 1554
Nahalal as first, 1361, **1634–1635**
Nahal and, 1634
Moshaver, Cyrus, *as contributor*, 670, 836, 1498, 2050
Moshav shitufi, 1576–1577
"Moshkele Hazir" (Berkowitz), 464
Moslem. *See* Muslim
Mosques, **1577**
architecture of, 1074
in Morocco, 1568
women's access to, 2359, *2360*
Mosquitoes, malaria transmitted by, 711
Mossad (Israel), **1577–1579**
Abu Sharif (Bassam) targeted by, 1267
Amit (Meir) in, 190
in Arab–Israeli War (1973), 1579
assassination attempt on Mashʿal (Khalid al-) by, 1579
assassination of Wazir (Khalil al-) by, 1578
directors of, identities kept secret, 1577
failures of, 1579
Harel (Isser) in, 992
international relations and operations of, 1578–1579
Kanafani (Ghassan) assassinated by, 1267
Kimche (David) in, 1322
in Lavon Affair (1954), 1577–1578
leadership of, 1577–1578
main functions and departments of, 1579
responsibilities of, 1577–1578
retaliation for Munich Olympics massacre by, 1578
Shamir (Yitzhak) in, 2026
Shiloah (Reuven) in, 2056
successes and prestige of, 1578–1579
Mossadegh, Mohammad, *1580*, **1580–1581**
Anglo–Persian Agreement (1919) opposed by, 1580
Arfa (Hasan) opposition to, 286
Borujerdi (Hosayn) opposing, 494
coup against (1953), 1581
CIA in, 572, 1118, 1752
Dulles (John Foster) in, 733
foreign intervention in, 1103, 1118, 1752

Daftari (Ahmad Matin) as son-in-law of, 660
fall of, 518
CIA in, 1937
government of
Amini (Ali) in, 186
Bakhtiar (Shapur) in, 375
Bakhtiar (Timur) in, 375
Bazargan (Mehdi) in, 421
guilds supporting, 947
Harriman (W. Averell) negotiations with, 996
imprisonment of, 1580, 1581
Kashani (Abu al-Qasem) and, 1277
in National Front, 1118, 1581, 1655–1656
in nationalism movement, 1660
negotiations with, Acheson (Dean) in, 40
oil nationalization by, 202, 417, 518, 1118, 1581, 1752
Eden (Anthony) opposing, 755
foreign response to, 1825
Kashani (Abu al-Qasem) in, 1277
Kuwaiti oil after, 1349
Yazdi (Ibrahim) on, 2382
Pahlavi (Reza) opposed by, 1580–1581
Pahlavi (Mohammad Reza) power struggle with, 1118, 1752
as prime minister, 1118
Tabataba'i (Ziya) opposing, 2143
Tudeh Party opposition to, 1118
Mossad Harav Kook, 1470
Mossad le-Ailiya Bet
airlift operations of, 1913
Hillel (Shlomo) in, 1030
Mosseri, Ezra, King David Hotel established by, 1323
Mossinsohn, Yigal, 1432, 2185
Mostaghanemi, Ahlam, 1424, **1581**
Mostashar al-Dowleh, Mirza Yousuf Khan, Adamiyat (Abbasquli) work with, 42
Mosul (Iraq), **1582**
British control of, under San Remo Conference, 1582
as French zone, under Sykes-Picot Agreement (1916), 1582
inclusion in Iran *vs.* Turkey, 1582–1583
Kurds in, 1582
autonomy movement of, 1469–1470
oil deposits in
Anglo–Turkish dispute over (1920-1928), **1582–1583**
royalties from given to Turkey, 1583
oil production in, 1138
population of, 1131
U.S. capture of (2003), 2325
in World War I, 2367
Motahhari, Mortaza, **1583**
Khomeini (Ruhollah) supported by, 1311
Motherland Party (Turkey), **1583–1584,** 2241–2242
Democratic Left Party in coalition with, 746
electoral success of, 2245
establishment of, 1746
Özal (Turgut) in, 1583–1584, 1746–1747, 2241
Social Democratic Populist Party opposing, 2077
True Path Party challenge to, 1584
True Path Party coalition with, 598, 1584, 2220
Yilmaz (Mesut) in, 746, 2242
Mother of the Prophet, The (Bint al-Shati), 476
Mothers (Bitton), 483
Mother State (Tahir), 2145–2146
Motor vehicles, 2207, *2207*
Mottahedeh, Roy, 756
Mou'awwad, Naila, **1584–1585**
Mou'awwad, René
assassination of, 1584
wife of, 1584–1585
Moudawana, al- (Moroccan family legal code), 1518, **1585–1586**
reform of, 1585–1586
Bouih (Fatna el-) in, 498
8 Mars newsletter on, 772–773
Jababdi (Latifa) in, 1203
on women, 94, 1585–1586, 1601
Moudjahid, al- (newspaper), 450, 804
Djebar (Assia) at, 716
Mountain River. *See* Bahr al-Jabal
Mount Lebanon. *See* Lebanon, Mount
Mount Scopus (Jerusalem), 966
Mount Tubkal (Morocco), 1567, *1568*
Mt. Zion School (Jerusalem), 2221
Mourners of Siyavosh (Daneshvar). *See Savushun*
Mourning, Muharram as period of, 1605–1606
Mourou, Abdelfattah, **1586–1587,** 2226
defamation campaign against, 1587
in Islamic Tendency Movement, 1586–1587
Mousa, Amr
on late member-state dues to League of Arab States, 1387
as secretary-general to League of Arab States, *1385,* 1386, *1387,* 1388–1389
Mousavi, Mir Hossein, government of, Nabavi (Behzad) in, 1630
Moussalli, Ahmad S., *as contributor,* 321–322, 394–395, 1012–1013, 1884–1885, 2150–2151, 2161, 2234–2235
Mouvement de la Réforme Nationale (MRN) (Algeria)
electoral success of, 135
platform of, 134
Mouvement de la Société pour la Paix (MSP) (Algeria), 1636
electoral success of, 127, 135
platform of, 134
Mouvement de l'Unité Populaire (MUP) (Tunisia), **1587,** 2231
Ben Salah (Ahmed) in, 452, 1804
Parti d'Unité Populaire branch of, 1804
Mouvement des Démocrates Socialistes (MDS) (Tunisia), 2231, 2232
as Ben Ali (Zayn al-Abidine) opposition, 439
Mestiri (Ahmad) in, 1520
Moadda (Mohamed) in, 1554
Mouvement de Tendance Islamique (MTI) (Tunisia), 2226, 2229
Ben Ali (Zayn al-Abidine) against, 439
and General Tunisian Union of Students, 899
Ghannouchi (Rached) in, 912
loosening restrictions on, by Ben Ali government, 356–357
Mouvement Ettajdid (Tunisia), 2232
Mouvement Ettajid. *See* Movement of Renewal
Mouvement Islamique Armé (MIA) (Algeria), Bouyali (Moustafa) in, 505–506, 918

Mouvement National Algérien (MNA), **1587–1588,** 1589
in Algerian War of Independence (1954–1962), 969
Bellounis (Muhammad) in, 438
Front de Libération Nationale challenged by, 131, 1587–1588, 1589
Hadj (Messali al-) and, 969
Mouvement National Populaire (Morocco), Ahardane (Majoub) in, 81
Mouvement National pour la Réforme (MNR) (Algeria), electoral success of, 127
Mouvement of Socialist Democrats. *See* Mouvement des Démocrates Socialistes
Mouvement Populaire (MP) (Morocco), 858, 1574–1575, **1588–1589**
Ahardane (Majoub) in, 81, 1588
Berbers in, 1588–1589
breakaway faction led by Khatib (Abdeldarim), 1588
Mouvement Populaire Démocratique et Constitutionnel (MPDC) (Morocco), 1575
Khatib (Abdelkarim) in, 1588
Mouvement pour la Démocratie en Algérie (MDA), Ben Bella (Ahmed) in, 442
Mouvement pour le Triomphe des Libertés Démocratiques (MTLD) (Algeria), **1589–1590**
Ait Ahmed (Hocine) in, 95
Bellounis (Muhammad) in, 438
Ben Khedda (Ben Youssef) in, 450
Berbers in, 969
Boudiaf (Mohamed) in, 496
conflict within
and Comité Révolutionnaire d'Unité et d'Action, 620
Hadj (Messali al-) and, 1589
direct action *vs.* political participation by, 1589
as front for Parti du Peuple Algérien, 1805
Hadj (Messali al-) in, 969, 1805
Lacheraf (Mostefa) in, 1362
Lahouel (Hocine) in, 1365
Mouvement National Algérien as continuation of, 1587, 1589
Movement for Civil Rights and Peace (RATZ) (Israel), 1991
Movement for Social Zionist Renewal, 452
Movement for the Liberation of the Sahara, 1837
Movement for the Triumph of Democratic Liberties. *See* Mouvement pour le Triomphe des Libertés Démocratiques
Movement for Unity and Reform (MUR) (Morocco), **1590**
Movement of Reform and Renewal (HATM) (Morocco), 1590
Movement of Renewal (Tunisia), **1590–1591,** 2231, 2232
Movement of the Disinherited (Lebanon), 173
Movement of the Triumph of Democratic Liberties. *See* Mouvement pour le Triomphe des Libertés Démocratiques
Movies. *See* Film
Moyne, Lord. *See* Guinness, Walter Edward
Mozaffar al-Din Qajar (ruler of Iran), **1591–1592**
Anglo–Russian rivalry and, 1591
Belgium custom officials employed by, 1591
constitution signed by, 636, 1591–1592, 1868
bast and, 411
daughter of, 186
government of
Amin al-Dowleh (Mirza Ali Khan) in, 184
Ayn al-Dowleh (Abd al-Majid Mirza) in, 343
Qajar (Abdullah Mirza) in, 1867
Vazir Afkham (Soltan Ali Khan) in, 2311
loans under, 184, 1591
motto honoring ("Adl-e Mozaffar"), 1592
national assembly formed by, 636, 1868
opposition to, in Constitutional Revolution, 635–636, 1868
reign of (1896–1906), 635–636, 1868
son of, Mohammad Ali Shah Qajar as, 1559, 1591
Zell al-Soltan and, 2430
Moznayim (weekly), 464
MP. *See* Mouvement Populaire
Mrabet, Ali, imprisonment of, opposition to, 1717
M'Rabet, Fadela (Fatma Abda), **1592**
Mr. Ibrahim (film), 2039
Mr. Mani (Yehoshua), 2384
MRN. *See* Mouvement de la Réforme Nationale
MSP. *See* Mouvement de la Société pour la Paix
MTI. *See* Mouvement de Tendance Islamique
MTLD. *See* Mouvement pour le Triomphe des Libertés Démocratiques
Mualem, Walid, in peace negotiations, 926
Muʿalla, Ahmad ibn Rashid al-, 1592, 2260
Muʿalla family, al-, **1592–1593,** 2260
Muʿalla, Rashid, 1592
Muʿalla, Rashid ibn Ahmad, 2260
Muʿallim Ali, Al- (Ghallab), 910
Muʿamalat, 833, 1974
Muasher, Marwan, **1593**
Muʾassasat al-Sahhab, 1866
Muʿawiya (founder of Umayyad dynasty), 2052
Muʿawiya ibn Abi Sufyan, 662
Ali ibn Abi Talib conflict with, arbitration of, 1073
Muʿawwad, Naʾila, 1055
Muʿawwad, René
acting president before election of, 1045
assassination of, 1033
Muʿayita, Mahmud, 1972
Muʾayyad, al- (newspaper), 805
Kamil (Mustafa) in, 1267
Kurd Ali (Muhammad) in, 1338
Mubah, 2033
Mubarak, Ali
Dar al-Ulum founded by, 671
municipal improvements in Cairo by, 552
national library founded by, 670
Mubarak, Gamal, at American University in Cairo, 180
Mubarak, Husni, *768, 795,* **1593–1594,** *1594*
Abd al-Rahman (Umar) criticism of, 21

American University in Cairo and, 179–180
in Arab–Israel War (1973), 1593
attempted assassination of, 1215, 1594
Cairo University and, 556
Egyptian–Israeli Peace Treaty (1979) and, 771
in Gulf War (1990–1991), 1594
Haykal (Muhammad Hasanayn) during regime of, 1012
industrialization under, 1094
infitah policy of, 1096
on al-Jamiʿa al-Islamiyya, 1214
military career of, 1537, 1593
and Muslim Brotherhood, 1621–1622
Muslim Brotherhood under, 1214
in National Democratic Party, 768
New Wafd under, 1685–1686
opposition to, 1594
on postage stamps, 1850
presidency of, 768
and satellite cities development, 1995
Syrian alliance with, 319
Mubarak, Suzanne
at American University in Cairo, 180
and libraries, 670
Mubashir, al- (newspaper), 1680
Mudanya, Treaty of (1923), 2240
Mudawana al-Kubra, al- (Saʿid), 1585
Mudawwana. See Moudawana, al-
Mudawwana al-Kubra, al- (Sahnun), 1476
Mudhakkirat Abd al-Latif al-Baghdadi (al-Baghdadi), 363
Mudhakkirat Jurji Zaydan (Zaydan), 2426
Mud hut, *2099*
Mudros Armistice (1918), 90, 2095, 2367, 2368
Muezzin, 2626
minarets used by, 1547
Mufide Kadri, **1595**
Mufid, Shaykh al-, 2055
Mufti, 816, 2034, 2626
chief (*See* Shaykh al-Islam)
Mugam (music), 1617
Mughaizel, Laure, 889
Mughannam, Matiel, speech by (1933), 13
Mughannam, Mughannam Ilyas al-, in Arab Executive, 1783
Mughn, al- (Abd al-Jabbar), 1457
Mughrabiyya, 838
Muhabizun, al-, 2184
Muhafidh, 1981
Muhafiz, 410
Muhajirun, al- (Meccan emigrants), 1596
Muhammad (prophet of Islam), **1595–1597**
as *ali-nabi* (Prophet), 1595
as bazaar merchant, 418–419
birthday celebrated, 2360
birthplace of, 1507, 1595
charitable *waqfs* established by, 2323
cousin of (*See* Ali ibn Abi Talib)
daughters of, 1595
death of, 1144
descendants of (*See Sharif;* Shorfa)
early life of, 1595
hadith about, 968
al-Husayni family as descendants of, 1053
immunity decree to Saint Catherine's Monastery by, 1971
invocation following appellation for, 1595
Islamic religion begun by, 1595–1596
Khadija as wife of, 1595–1596
pilgrimage to Mecca, 1597
preaching in Mecca, 1144
Qurʾan revealed by, 1595–1596, 1881–1882
as *rasul allah* (messenger of God), 1595
and rise of Islamic state, 1596–1597
Salafiyya movement on, 1974
sons of, 1595
successor of
Abu Bakr regarded as, 1597, 1641
Ali regarded as, 1597
Sunna of, 2122
tomb of, 1511
tribe of, 2213
turban of, 609
victory at battle of Badr (624), 1596
wives of, 418, 993
Muhammad III (king of Morocco), 2038
in Alawite dynasty, 106
Casablanca rebuilt by, 568
Muhammad IV (king of Morocco), *106*
Spanish defeat of (1860), 1569
Muhammad V (Sidi Muhammad bin Yusuf) (king of Morocco), **1597–1598**, *1598*, 2038–2039
in Alawite dynasty, 106
in Algerian War of Independence, 1598
Arfa (Muhammad ibn) as replacement for, 287
Ben Barka (Mehdi) under, 441
Churchill's (Winston) meeting with, 1598
constitution promised by, 1572, 1599
daughter of, Aicha (Lalla) as, 94
death of, 1599
and Declaration of La Celle St. Cloud (1953), 687
French exile of (1953–1955), 687, 1570, 1598
khutbas after, 1315
nationalism after, 615
Kattaniya Brotherhood opposing, 1281
monarchy's authority asserted by, 1570, 1572, 1574, 1598–1599
on Moudawana, al-, 1585
movement to depose (1953), Tuhami al-Glawi in, 2223
nationalism supported by, 1570, 1598–1599
political parties under, 1570, 1574, 1598–1599
al-Qarawiyyin under, 1871
return of, 1598
Catroux (Georges) in, 570
Roosevelt's (Franklin) meeting with, 569, 1598
son of, 1004
as symbol of independence and modernity, 1599
tomb complex of, architecture of, 282
Muhammad VI (king of Morocco), 1567, **1599–1602**, *1600*
in Alawite dynasty, 107, 1599–1600
as *amir al-muʾminin* (commander of the faithful), 1568, 1599–1600
Berbers and, 1601–1602
challenges facing, 1600
on democracy, 1600
on "disappeared" and victims of "arbitrary arrest," 1600

Muhammad VI (king of Morocco) *(continued)*
European Union relations with, 1601
human rights under, 1600, 1716
Islamists role in government opposed by, 1601
as king of the poor, 1568
moudawana reform under, 1204
Plan of Action by, 1586, 1601
political reforms under, 1571
promising regional development in Laayoune, 1356
religious tolerance under, 1600
in Western Sahara, *2343*
Yasine (Abdsalem) imprisoned by, 1574
Muhammad, Abd al-Zahra Uthman, 681
Muhammad Ali (viceroy of Egypt), **1602–1603**
in Alexandria Convention (1840), 118–119
Alexandria under, 116
Arabia invaded by, 818, 1602
Arabian horses of, 231
architectural tastes of, 281
army conscripted by (nizam al-jadid, al-), 1690
Balta Liman Convention (1838) weakening power of, 385
British relations with, 2007
burial site of, 1603
Cairo under, 551–552
Chehab (Bashir) supported by, 584
collusion with Bashir II, 1393
Copts under, 640
Peter VII and, 1822
cotton industry under, 643–644
in Damascus affair (1840), 665
and Delta Barrages, 690
descendants of, wali and khedive titles assumed by, 1602
education under, 757
in expedition against Napoléon, 1602
French relations with, 846
London Convention and (1840), 1796
government of
Chrakian (Artin) in, 589
Clot (Antoine Barthélémy) in, 607
Mustafa Reşid in, 1623–1624
Yusufian (Boghos) in, 2415
grandsons of, 4, 1157
Greeks in Egypt under, 938
in Greek War of Independence, 2093
hospitals opened by, 2003
irrigation developed by, 404
London Convention and (1840), 1445, 1602, 1691, 2094
Mahmud II and, 1466, 2007
Mamluks suppressed by, 1602
medical school under, 607
missionary schools under, 1551
modernization by, 766
and decline of bazaars, 419
modernization under, 1555
Ottoman navy surrendered to, 33, 1741
Ottoman relations with, 1050, 1945
Palestine invaded by, 1602
Palmerston (Lord Henry John Temple) and, 1346
as patron of Armenians, 2415
plague and, 710
public health policies of, 710
sons of, 1077, 1970
Sudan invaded by, 1602
syphilis and, 710
Syria invaded by, 118, 648, 1077, 1602
attempted appeasement by Mehmet Koja Husrev Paşa, 1624
Battle of Nizip in, 1690–1691
in Syrian War (1831–1833), 1346
Battle of Konya (1832), 1333
Syria under, 2093
Tahtawi (Rifaʿa al-Rafi al-) under, 2146
territorial expansion by, European intervention against, 33, 741
Palmerston (Lord) in, 1796
textile industry under, 2181
Muhammad Ali Mosque, **1603**
Muhammad al-Sadiq (bey of Tunisia), 860, **1603–1604**
constitution proclaimed by, 1603–1604
and Fundamental Pact (1857), 860, 1604
government of
Khayr al-Din in, 1306, 1307, 1308
Khaznader (Mustafa) in, 1308
Jalluli family and, 1213
Khaznader (Mustafa) and, 1603–1604
Tunis under, 2224
Muhammad al-Taqi, tomb of, as Atabat, 328
Muhammad, Aziz, **1604–1605**
Muhammad Fadil, son of, Ma al-Aynayn as, 1451
Muhammad Farid, in National Party, 1663–1664
Muhammad ibn Muqla, calligraphy of, 558
Muhammad ibn Talal (prince of Jordan), father-in-law of, Majali (Hazza al-) as, 1470
Muhammad ibn Thani, 171–172, 1876
Muhammad ibn Yahya, 2377
Muhammad ibn Yahya Hamid al-Din (imam of Yemen), 985
Muhammad Mandur wa Tandhir al-Naqd al-Arabi (Berrada), 467
Muhammad, Saqr ibn, 1903
Muhammad's Youth (Egypt), in al-Jamiʿa al-Islamiyya, 1215
Muhammad V University
Bannis (Mohammad) at, 396
Berrada (Mohammed) at, 467
Muhammadzai royal clan (Afghanistan), 2420
Muhammara (Iran), 839–840
Khazʿal Khan in, 1307–1308
Muhammed Sharif (Egyptian premier), in National Party, 1663
Muhanna, Iʿtimad, in Women's Affair Center, 2356
Muhaqqaq script, 558
Muharram, **1605–1607**
during Iranian Revolution (1979), 1126
rituals of
ambulatory, 1605–1606
stationary, 1605–1606
Muharram, Decree of (1881), 27
Muharraq (Bahrain), **1607**
Muharrir, al- (newspaper), 450
Muhaysin tribe, Khazʿal Khan as chief of, 1307
Muhayyer Saz Semaisi (Tanburi), 2160
Muhazarat (Aliyer), 148
Muhbir (newspaper), 2406
Muhi al-Din, Sabir, in PFLP, 1840
Muhittin, Nezihe, in Women's People's Party, 2359
Muhsin, Zuhayr, **1607**
assassination of, 1607
in al-Saʿiqa, 1972

Muhtar, Gazi Ahmet, **1607–1608**
government of, as "grand cabinet," 1608
Muhyi al-Din (leader of Qadiriyya), **1608**
son of, 16
Muhyi al-Din, Khalid
as Free Officer, 853
in National Progressive Unionist Party, 768, 1608
in Revolutionary Command Council, 1921
Muhyi al-Din, Zakariyya
as possible successor to Nasser, 1608
Sadat (Anwar al-) opposed by, 1608
Mujaddara, 840
Mujaddedi, Sebghatullah, 59
Gailani (Ahmad) under, 863
Mujaddidi branch of Naqshbandi order, 1642
Mujahedin. See Mojahedin
Mujahid. See Social Democratic Party of Azerbaijan
Mujahidin, 498, 508, 529
Mujamma Al-Islami, Al-, Yasin (Ahmad Ismaʿil) in, 2381
Muji, Muhammad al-, 971
Mujtahid, 816, 1463, 1987, 2055, 2070, 2626
Mukhtar, 2626
Mukhtari, Muhammad bin Isa al-Sufyani al-, Isawiyya Brotherhood founded by, 1141
Mukhtar, Umar al-, **1609–1610**
capture and hanging of, 1610
execution of, 935
film based on life of, 99
in Italo–Sanusi wars, 1609–1610
Mukhtasar, al- (Khalil), 1476
Mukrani family (Algeria), **1610**
Mulai, 2626
Mulay Idris College (Fez), 2008
Mulay Ismaʿil (sultan of Morocco), 996
Mulazimiyya (Sudan), 1463
Mülk, 1367, 1368
Mülkiyye, 1264
Mulqi, Fawzi al-, cabinet of, Khalidi (Husayn Fakhri al-) in, 1295
Mul Ta ha-Zekhukhit (Guri), 956
Multaqa (journal), 2357
Multilateral Guarantee Agency (MIGA), 2363–2364
Multinational Force and Observers (MFO), on Sinai Peninsula, 2068
Mulukhiyya, 840
Muna (princess of Jordan), 31
Munʿaraj, al- (al-Farsi), 1429
Munbir (newspaper), 144
Munich Olympics, Israeli athletes killed at, 485, 2176
Munif, Abdel Rahman, **1611**
Munsif Bey, Tayyib Brahim, overthrow of, 185
Munsif, Muhammad al-, Chenik (Muhammad) and, 586
Muntada al-Adabi, al-, **1611**
Muntafiq tribe, 1961–1962, 2213
Muntaqid, al- (periodical), 440
Muntasir, Abd al-Qasim, 2127
Muntasir family, **1611–1612**
Muntasir, Mahmud Bey, 1612
government of, Maziq (Husayn) in, 1506
Muntasir, Salim al-, in Istiqlal Party, 1196
Muntasir, Umar, 1612
MUP. *See* Mouvement de l'Unité Populaire
Muqaddam, 397, 550
Muqaddima (Ibn Khaldun), Ottoman translation of, 577, 578
Muqattam, al- (newspaper), 1374, 1688
Muqtabas, al- (journal), Kurd Ali (Muhammad) in, 1338
Muqtataf, al- (magazine), 550, 1688, 2426
Kurd Ali (Muhammad) in, 1338
MUR. *See* Movement for Unity and Reform
Murabbih Rabbuh, 86
Murabitun (Lebanon), **1612**
Murad I, 2190
Salonika captured by, 1979
Muradi, Al-Rabi ibn Sulayman al-, 2019
Murad, Layla, *vs.* Asmahan, 324
Mural (Darwish), 674–675
Murat I (Ottoman sultan), 1939
Murat III (Ottoman sultan), monogram of, *559*
Murat V (Ottoman sultan), 852
attempted coup to restore (1878), 144
Çerkes Hasan incident and (1876), 575
deposition of, 26
Midhat Paşa and, 1525
Murat, Mehmet (Murat Bey)
in Committee for Union and Progress, 2408–2409
in Young Turks, 623, 2408–2409
Murders, honor killings, 649–650, 1495
Noor al-Hussein in campaign against, 1691
Murex marine snail *(Murex brandaris),* 2065
Murrah, al- (tribe), 2209, 2211, 2213
Murshid al-Amin fi Tarbiyyat al-Banat wa al-Banin, al- (Tahtawi), 2147
Murshid amm (supreme guide), 1621
Muruʾa (magnanimity), 1595
Musa, Abdal, 434
Musa al-Alami, 1460–1461
Musa Dagh
in Armenian genocide, 295
Armenian resistance at, **1612–1613**
Musa, Hamid Majid, in Communist Party, 1605
Musahiban oligarchy (Afghanistan), 57, 2420–2421
Musa Kazim, **1613–1614**
as successor to Jaʿfar al-Sadiq, 1158
tomb of, as Atabat, 328
Musa, Khawaja. *See* Smilansky, Moshe
Musa Muragha, Saʿid (Abu Musa), revolt by (1983), 1774
Musa, Nabawiyya, **1614**
Musa, Salama, 1464, **1614**
Musavi-Ardebili, AbdolKarim, **1614–1615**
Musavi, Mir-Hosain, **1615–1616**
as prime minister, majles endorsement of, 1119
and Rahnavard (Zahra), 1899
Musawi, Abbas al-
Israeli assassination of, 1038, 1647
Nasrallah (Hasan) and, 1647
Musawi, Husayn al-, Islamic AMAL movement founded by, 1647
Musawwar, al- (magazine), 1682, 1965
Musaymi, Haya al-, 1151

Muscat (Oman), **1616**
British influence in, 204, 1710
Protestant missions in, 1854
Muscat and Oman. *See* Oman
Museum of Islamic Art (Cairo), Islamic coin collection of, 1702
Museum of the Jewish diaspora (Tel Aviv), 928
Musha'sha tribe, 1316
Music, **1617–1620**, *1618, 1619*. *See also* Dance
Arabic, 324, 336
of Beja, 433
Berber, 193, 462
East West Divan and, 1966
Egyptian, 22, 324, 336, 675, 970–971, 2261–2263
at Fez Festival of World Sacred Music, 667
Greek, 785
Iranian, 2311
Israeli, 1014, 1105–1106, 1164
Lebanese, 817–818
overarching genres of, 1617
processes and issues in, 1619–1620
regional distinctions in, 1617–1618
religious, of Alevis, 113–114
Sufism and, 2113
Syrian, 112
Turkish, 476–477, 687, 689, 872–873, 1269, 2002, 2009, 2124, 2160
Western influences on, 1619
Musical instruments, 1617
Musical occasions, 1619
Musketeer, Operation (Britain), 245, 2108–2109
Muslih, Muhammad
as contributor, 39, 225–226, 316–320, 328–330, 337, 351–352, 815, 917, 925–926, 971–972, 989, 1010–1011, 1052, 1053–1054, 1055–1056, 1058–1059, 1198, 1295–1296, 1296, 1337, 1486, 1611, 1644–1645, 1758–1769, 1776, 1781, 1788–1794, 1885–1886, 2259–2260
on Palestinian Arab Congress of 1920, 1782
Muslim, 2626
Muslim Brotherhood, **1620–1622**
against Anglo–Egyptian Treaty (1936), 766
in Arab–Israel War (1948), 395, 1621
Banna (Hasan al-) as founder of, 1620–1621, 1924
organization after assassination of, 1621–1622
in Egypt, 768, 1620–1622
abolition of, 767
and Afghan Islamic movements, 60, 63
alliance with Socialist Labor and Liberal parties, 1622
alliance with Wafd, 1622
Arafat (Yasir) in, 269, 272
armed wing of, 1214
Ashmawi (Muhammad Abd al-Rahman Salih al-) in, 321
assassinations by, 1214
Banna (Hasan al-) in, 394–395
clash with Liberation Rally, 1409
in coup (1952), 1621
Farouk opposing, 810
Free Officers and, 853
Ghazali (Muhammad al-) in, 914
and Hamas (Movement for a Peaceful Society), 984
Hudaibi (Mamoun al-) as leader of, *1621*, 1622
Hudaybi (Hasan al-) in, 321
and Islamic Jihad, 1154
vs. al-Jami'a al-Islamiyya, 1214
Khalid (Khalid Muhammad) opposing, 1297
Mubarak (Husni) and, 1621–1622
Nasser (Gamal Abdel) and, 1621, 1649, 1650
New Wafd and, 1685–1686, 2321
Nuqrashi (Mahmud Fahmi al-) and, 1701
outlawed by Nasser (Gamal Abdel), 987, 1214
outlawed for opposing Palestine partition plans (1948), 1621
parliament seats held by, 1622
al-Qaradawi (Yusuf) in, 1870
Qutb (Sayyid) in, 321, 1884
vs. Revolutionary Command Council, 1921
Sadat (Anwar al-) and, 321, 1214, 1621, 1955–1956
schools established by, 759
Tilmisani (Umar al-) in, 321, 1621
Feda'iyan-e Islam and, 820
Ghazali (Zaynab al-) in, 914
and HAMAS, 982–983
Hanbali School of Law and, 990
headquarters of, 395
influence of
on Nahda, al-, 1635
on Nahnah (Mahfoud), 1636
in Iraq, 395
Jami'at-e Islami and, 1215
and jihad, 983
in Jordan
electoral success of, 1150–1151
and Islamic Action Front, 1150–1151
murshid amm (supreme guide) of, 1621
objective of, 395
in Palestine Arab Revolt (1936–1939), 1620–1621
vs. PLO, 983
radical Muslim defectors from, 1621
Society for Islamic Culture merging with, 395
spread of, youth movements and, 2411
in Sudan, 395
Turabi (Hasan al-) in, 2234
women's participation in, 1622–1623
in Syria, 357, 395
amnesty for members of, 315
Attar (Isam al-) in, 337
and Hama rebellion, 980–981
suppression of, 317, 2135
Wahhabi influence on, 1626
Wazir (Khalil al-) and, 2334–2335
in Yemen, in Islah Party, 1143
Muslim–Christian Association (Palestine)
Arab Club and, 226
Darwish (Ishaq) in, 673
establishment of, 1761
leadership of, 1761
Palestinian nationalism promoted by, 1761–1762
Zionism opposed by, 1761
Muslim Sisters Organization, **1622–1623**
Muslim Students Association
Amir-Entezam (Abbas) in, 188
establishment of, 582
Kharrazi (Kamal) in, 1300
Muslim Women's Association, 892, 914
Muslim (Islamic) world, *vs.* Middle East, 1523
Muslim World League, **1623**

Saudi Arabian sponsorship of, 1153
Mussolini, Benito, *1199*
Atatürk (Mustafa Kemal) compared to, 333–334
as British threat, 515
Fourth Shore vision of, 843
Husayni (Hajj Amin al-) supported by, 515
Lyautey (Louis-Hubert Gonzalve) as admirer of, 1450
and Treaty of Rome, 1933
Mussolini–Laval Treaty (1935), 216
Mustafa III, son of, 2009
Mustafa, Amir, 772
Mustafa Çelebi Sabunci, Mosul under, 1582
Mustafa Efendi, son of, Mustafa Reşid as, 1623
Mustafa Fazil Paşa, **1623**
exclusion from line of succession, 1623
Young Ottomans supported by, 1623, 2405, 2406
Mustafa Kamil, in National Party, 1663–1664
Mustafa Reşid, **1623–1625**
under Abdülmecit I, 33, 1624
Cevdet (Abdullah) and, 577
commercial code of, 1624
Darülfünün proposed by, 672
dismissal of, 1624
and Gülhane Imperial Edict (1839), 954
in *kalemiyye*, 1264
in Kütahya, Peace of (1833), 1346
under Mahmud II, 1623–1624
Muhammad Ali and, 1623–1624
recruits and protégés of, 1624
rivalry with Mehmet Koja Husrev Paşa, 1624
Tanzimat program introduced by, 33, 1623–1624, 2161, 2163
and Tanzimat reforms, 2069, 2161
Mustafa, Shukri
in Muhammad's Youth, 1215
Qutb's (Sayyid) influence on, 1884
in al-Takfir wa al-Hijra, 2150
Mustafa Suphi, **1625**
Mustayr tribe, 2209
mut'a, 2055
Mutahhari, Morteza, on jihad, 1236
Mutanabbi, Abu al-Tayyib al-, 1061
Mutasarrif, 2626
in Mount Lebanon, 1394, 1398
Mutasarrif, 469
Muʿtasim, al- (Abbasid caliph), and Zaytuna University, 2427
Mutawakkil, al- (Abbasid caliph), Karbala destroyed by, 1272
Mutawakkil alla Allah, al-. *See* Zahir Shah, Mohammad
Mutawwʿun (Ikhwan enforcers), 1626
Mutayr tribe, 2213
in Ikhwan movement, 1085
Muʿtazila (school of religious thought), opposition to, 989
Muʿtazila school, 1148
Müteferrika, Ibrahim, Turkish-language works published by, 1684
Muttalib, Abd al-, grandson of, Muhammad as, 1595
Muwafaqat (Shatibi, al-), 1476
Muwahhidun (Wahhabi followers), **1625–1627**, 1636
Al Rashid family and, 2214
Al Sabah family conflict with, 158, 159
Deobandi movement and, 61
Hassan tribe pushed by, 2212
Ikhwan as, 1626
Muntafiq tribe defending Iraq against, 2213
in Najd, 1638
Saʿud family, al- in, 1625–1626
state of (Saudi Arabia), 1625–1627
Uqbi (Tayyib al-) in, 2297
Utaybi (Juhayman al-) in, 2304
Muwashshah (song), 112
Muwashshahat (music), 1618
Muwatta (Malik), 1476
Muwaylihi, Muhammad al-, 1420
Muzani, 2019
Müzei Humayun (Imperial Museum), Islamic coin catalog of, 1702
Muzhir al-Taqdis bi Dhahab Dawlat al-Faransis (Jabarti), 1207
Myerson, Golda. *See* Meir, Golda
Myerson, Morris, 1513
My Home, My Land (Khalaf and Rouleau), 1292
My Life Story (Amrouche), 192
My People Shall Live (Khaled), 1293
Myrdal, Gunnar, 543
Myrrh, in incense, 1091
Mysticism, 1403. *See also* Sufism
in Islam, 1149
Myth of Arab Piracy in the Gulf, The (Qasimi), 1874
Myth of Sisyphus, The (Camus), 563
Myths & Facts (guidebook), 177
My Travels around the World (al-Saadawi), 1950
My Turn to Speak: Iran, the Revolution, and Secret Deals with the U.S. (Bani Sadr), 389
Mzab, **1627**
Mzabis, 459
Berber language of, 122
Mzali, Mohammed, **1627–1628**
dismissal of, 1628
exile of, 1628
government of
labor movement tensions with, 41
Mestiri (Ahmad) in, 1520
as Nouira's (Hedi) successor, 1627
as prime minister, 502
return of (2002), 1628

N

Naamane-Guessous, Soumaya, 2376
Naʿamat (Israel), 893, **1629**
Namir (Orah) in, 1641
Nab (gold), 1695
Nabadat Fikr (Ghallab), 910
Nabarawi, Sayza, 770
Nabavi, Behzad, **1629–1630**
Nabi Musa Pilgrimage, **1630–1631**
anti-British riots during (1920), Jerusalem mayoral post before and after, 1645
Nabi Salih, al-, **1631**
Nabizade Nazim, **1631**
Nablus (West Bank), **1631–1632**, 2340
archaeological sites in, destruction of, 279
Israeli occupation of, 1631
Jordanian occupation of, 1631
Palestinian Arab Congress in (1922), 1782
Tuqan family in, 2233–2234
Women and Family Affairs Center in, 2355
Nablus Muslim–Christian Association, Tamimi (Amin al-) in, 2158
Nabulsi, Sulayman al-, **1632–1633**
Anglo–Jordanian treaty opposed and abrogated by, 1632

Nabulsi, Sulayman al- *(continued)*
dismissal of, Khalidi (Husayn Fakhri al-) after, 1295
government of
as first "popular front" government of Arab world, 1632
formation of, 1925
government purging by, Abu Nuwwar (Ali) and, 39
Hussein regime challenged by, 1244, 1632–1633
Majali (Hazza al-) and, 1471, 1632
Nachmani, Amikam, *as contributor,* 198–199
Naci, Muallim, 1439, 2180
Naciri, Khalid, in Organisation Marocaine des Droits de l'Homme, 1716
Naderi, Amir, 593
Naderpur, Nader, 1436
Nadhr (pledges), 2360
Nadi al-Arabi, al-. *See* Arab Club
Nadim, Abdullah al-, 1419
school established by, 759
Nadir Barakzai, Mohammad, **1633**
assassination of, 57, 679
Daud (Muhammad) and, 679
Nadir, Fu'ad Abu, 1394
Nadir Khan, Mohammad, 2420
Nadir Shah Afshar
assassination of, 85, 400
and Durrani dynasty, 85, 735
and Qajar family, 1867
and trade, 400
Nadir Shah, Muhammad, 2420
Nadi, Yunus, **1633**
Nadwa, al- (newspaper), 1679
Nady, Lutfia, 1902
Nafud Desert, 701, **1633–1634,** 1638
tribes in, 2214
Nageur d'un seul amour, Le (Shahada), 2020
Nag Hammadi Gospels, in Coptic Museum, 638
Naguib, Muhammad, 1465–1466, **1634**
Baghdadi (Abd al-Latif al-) under, 362
in coup against Farouk (1952), 1537, 1634
Free Officers electing, 854, 1634, 1649
military dictatorship of, 767
Misri (Aziz Ali al-) *vs.*, 1550
Muhyi al-Din (Khalid) supporting, 1608
Nasser (Gamal Abdel) in conflict with, 1409, 1634, 1649, 1921
in Revolutionary Command Council, 1921
Nahal, **1634**
Nahalal, 1361, **1634–1635**
Nahar, al- (newspaper), 1477, 2254
Nahar Weekly, al-, 1474
Nahayyan, Shakhbut ibn Dhiyah Al, 156
Nahayyan, Shakhbut ibn Sultan, 156
Nahayyan, Zayid ibn Khalifah, 156
Nahayyan, Zayid ibn Sultan al-
centralization favored by, 2272
in establishment of UAE, 156
infrastructure development under, 36
as president of UAE, 2270, 2271
as ruler of Abu Dhabi, 156
Nahda, al- (Algeria), 912, **1635**
al-Hilal (magazine) and, 1029
Khal (Yusuf al-) and, 1298
magazines associated with, 2426
Nahda, 1428
Nahda al-nisa'iyya (women's awakening), 1652
Nahda Party (Tunisia), Moadda (Mohamed) and, 1554
Nahda Urthuduksiyya movement, 1973
Nahhas, Maryam al-, 890
Nahhas, Mustafa al-, **1635–1636**
Anglo–Egyptian Treaty (1936) signed by, 2320
as architect of League of Arab States, 1386, 1636
British exile of, 1635
and Fertile Crescent unity, 825
Khalid (Khalid Muhammad) criticizing, 1296
Nuqrashi (Mahmud Fahmi al-) and, 1701
as prime minister, 516
as Wafd leader, *2320,* 2320–2321
Nahiqas, 1375
Nahiye (Ottoman court), 1690
Nahnah, Mahfoud, **1636**
Bendjedid (Chadli) meeting with, 1965
and Hamas (Movement for a Peaceful Society), 984
Nahum, Halfallah, **1636–1637**
vs. Haggiag (Simeone), 973
Nahum, Hayyim (Nahum Effendı), **1637**
Nahzat-e Azadi-ye Iran. *See* Freedom Movement
Naiba tribe, 2212
Naifar, Hemida al-, in Islamic Tendency Movement, 1586
Na'if ibn Abdullah, 2152
Na'im, al- (tribe), 2210
Naimi, Ali al-, 230
Na'ini, Muhammad Husayn, 977
Naissance du cinéma algérien (Boudjedra), 497
Najaf, al- (Iraq), **1637**
as Atabat (holy site), 328, 1131
Fadlallah (Shaykh Husayn) teaching in, 793
Kashif al-Ghita family in, 1278
Khomeini (Ruhollah) exiled in, 328, 1311
as place of pilgrimage for Shi'ites, 2052
Shrine of Hazrat Ali in, *1147*
Najafi, Aqa, Khomeini (Ruhollah) taught by, 1310
Najah University, al- (West Bank), 1631
Najd (Saudi Arabia), **1637–1638**
Al Sa'ud control of, 101, 162, 167, 818, 1638, 1928, 1999
Al Thunayyan control of, 172
British treaty with (1915), 531
tribes in, 2212, 2213, 2214
unification with Hijaz, 1626
Najd Desert, 701
Naj Hamadi power station (Egypt), Israeli destruction of, 2327
Najibullah, Mohammed, **1638**
coup against (1992), 59, 66, 1561
Esmati-Wardak (Masuma) under, 786
Etemadi (Saleha Faruq) under, 786
Karmal (Babrak) and, 1274
national unity promoted by, 58–59, 1801
Parcham and, 1801
in People's Democratic Party of Afghanistan, 1813
presidency of, 58–59
Soviet support for, 65, 66
Taliban killing, 1638, 2154
Najim, Lamis, 1267
Najjada, al-, **1638–1639**
Hakim (Adnan al-) and, 976–977
in Lebanon, 1638
in Palestine, 1638

Najmabadi, Hadi, 2141
Najran (Saudi Arabia)
al-Ta'if Treaty (1934) on, 2149
tribes in, 2213
Najun min an-Nar, al-. *See* Saved from the Inferno
Nakba, al- (1948–1949), **1639–1640**
homes lost in, 1639
land lost in, 1639
legacy of, 1640
long-term or fundamental causes of, 1639
reasons for occurrence of, 1767
refugees of, 1767, 1790
responsibility for, 1767
Nakhl (date palm in Muharram rite), 1605–1606
Nakhleh, Emile A., *as contributor,* 342, 358, 366, 371–372, 541, 708, 948–949, 1292, 1352, 1456, 1678, 1717–1718
Nalbandian, Mikayel, 303
Nalouti, Aroussia, 1424, 1429
Namadha-ye dasht-e moshavvash (Fassih), 812
Namani, Bassam, *as contributor,* 423, 994, 1612, 1625–1627, 1859–1860, 1991–1992, 2223
Nameh-ye Mardom (biweekly), 2222
Namik Kemal, 1438, **1640–1641,** 2186
Ali Suavi and, 144
Cevdet (Abdullah) influenced by, 576
in *Diyojen,* 1277
and language reform, 1933
Nazif (Süleyman) influenced by, 1674
newspapers edited by, 2406
and Ottoman constitution, 2407
Recaizade Mahmud Ekrem and, 1909
Vatan yahut Silistre by, 72, 1641, 1658
in Young Ottomans, 2405, 2406
and Ziya (Abdülhamit), 2439
Namir, Mordekhai, **1641**
Namir, Orah, **1641**
Napier, Charles, 118
Napoléon I. *See* Bonaparte, Napoléon
Napoléon III (emperor of France)
Abd al-Qadir released by, 17
and Lebanese expedition, 423
Palmerston (Lord) and, 1797
support for Maronites, 846
Napoleonic wars
Battle of Abu Qir in (1798), 39
Persian involvement in, 816
Treaty of Amiens in (1802), 182–183
Treaty of the Dardanelles in (1809), 671–672
Naqd al-Dhati, al- (al-Fasi), 812
Naqib, Abd al-Rahman al-, Heskayl (Sasson) and, 1023
Naqid Award, to Barakat (Hoda), 397
Naqim, Abdullah, Afghani (Jamal al-Din al-) and, 51
Naqqash, Marun al-, 1421, 2184
Naqshabandi, Muhammad Baha' al-Din al, 2113
Naqshbandi, **1641–1643**
branches of, 1642
Mojaddedi (Sebghatullah) in, 1561
National Salvation Party supported by, 1665–1666
political participation by, 1641–1642
Naqshbandi, Nasir al-, numismatic school founded by, 1702
Naqshbandiyya (Sufi order), 2113
Narcotics. *See* Drugs and narcotics
Narges (film), 388
Narghila, 2626
Nar wa al-Ikhtiyar, al- (Bannounah), 1424
nas, al- (people), 1596
Nasafi, Abu al-Barakat al-, 988
Nas al-Ghiwan (musical group), 1617
Nas al-Mu'annath, al- (al-Jlasi), 1424
Naser al-Din Shah Qajar, *1643,* **1643–1644**
accession to throne, 1643
Afghanistan invaded by, 204
assassination of, 52, 1591, 1644, 1868
Babis attempting assassination of, 356
and censorship, 1435
Cossack Brigade established by, 643
as crown prince, 1643
economic reforms of, 1868
education under, 757
Golestan Palace built by, 928
government of
Afghani (Jamal al-Din al-) in, 1644
Amin al-Dowleh (Mirza Ali Khan) in, 184
Amin al-Soltan (Ali-Asghar) in, 184
Amin al-Zarb (Mohammad Hasan) in, 185
Amir Kabir (Mirza Taqi Khan) in, 189, 669, 1643–1644, 1867
Ayn al-Dowleh (Abd al-Majid Mirza) in, 343
Malkom Khan (Mirza) in, 1644
Sadr (Muhsin) in, 1960
Isfahan under, 1142
modernization under, 1643–1644
mother of, Mahd-e Ulya, Malek Jahan Khanum as, 1462, 1643
newspapers under, 1682
Persian cats of, 1821
photography by, 1867
reign of, 1868
sons of, 2430
Mozaffar al-Din Qajar as, 1591
and Tabataba'i (Mohammad), 2141
Tehran developing under, 2169
and Tobacco Revolt, 1118, 1644, 1868, 2057, 2193–2194, 2355
Nashabi, Hisham, *as contributor,* 226–227
Nashashibi, Amal
in Women and Family Affairs Center, 2355
in Women's Affair Center, 2356
Nashashibi, Fakhri, 1645
Nashashibi family, **1644–1645**
Husayni family rivalry with, 1224, 1644–1645, 1764, 1766
in Muntada al-Adabi, al-, 1611
Nashashibi, Is'af, 1645
execution of, 1645
in Muntada al-Adabi, al-, 1611
Nashashibi, Muhammad Is'af al-, 1790
Nashashibi, Muhammad Zuhdi, 1645, *1645*
Nashashibi, Naser al-Din, 1645
Nashashibi, Raghib al-, 1645
as Jerusalem mayor, 1224, 1645
in National Defense Party, 1765, 1766
Nashashibi, Rana, in Women's Centre for Legal Aid and Counseling, 2356
Nashashibi, Uthman al-, 1644
Nashid al-Ard (Nuri), 1704
Nashim, 2157
Nas Illi fi al-Sama al-Thamina, al- (Salim), 1978

Nasir, Ahmed Sayf al-, **1646**
Nasir, Elizabeth, 1055
Nasir, Hanna, 1055, **1646**
Nasirian, Ali, 2186
Nasir Khan, 386
Nasir, Najib, **1646**
Nasir, Sayf al-Nasir family (Libya), 1646
Nasir, Victoria, 1055
Naskhi script, 235, 558, 559
Nasr (Afghanistan), 64
Nasr al-Din (Iranian character), 1648
Nasrallah, Emily, **1646–1647**
Nasrallah, Hasan, 1038, **1647**
  eldest son of slain by Israelis, 1647
  in Hizbullah, 1647
  and Khatami (Mohammad), *1038*
Nasr, Sayyed Ali, 2186
Nasruddin Hoca, **1648**
  stories by, Caylak's collection of, 571
Nass, 834, 1974
Nassar, Najib, 1648
Nassar, Riyad, in Institute for Women's Studies in the Arab World, 1100
Nassar, Sadhij, **1648**
Nasseef, Abdullah O., *1153*
Nasser, Gamal Abdel, *767,* 1465–1466, **1648–1651,** *1649, 1861*
  Abd al-Rahman (Umar) criticism of, 20
  admirers on, 1649
  and Ahram Center for Political and Strategic Studies, 92
  in Alexandria, speech by (1956), 118
  All-Palestine Government formally ended by, 156
  American University in Cairo and, 179
  in Arab–Israel War (1956), 236–237, 244–246, 1650
  in Arab–Israel War (1967), 237, 248, 1165, 1651
  and Arab nationalism, 222, 260, 1648, 1650–1651, 1659
  Arab Nationalist Movement on, 962
  and Arab socialism, 265
  and Arab Socialist Union, *266,* 266–267, 1650
  at Arab summit conferences, 1651
  al-Ard movement support for, 285
  attempted assassination of, 1621, 1650
    Qutb (Sayyid) and, 1884
  al-Azhar reforms under, 348
  Badr (Muhammad al-) admiring, 358
  Baghdadi (Abd al-Latif al-) under, 362
  Baghdad Pact (1955) opposed by, 363
  at Bandung Conference, 387
  Cairo under, 554
  Cairo University and, 556
  Chamoun (Camille) opposing, 1399
  charitable organizations under, 39–40
  Charter for National Action of, 266, 1650
  and Coptic patriarchate, 657
  Copts under, 641
  in coup against Farouk (1952), 1537, 1649
  critics on, 1649
  death of, 1651
  domestic affairs under, early, 1649
  Eden (Anthony) opposing, 755
  education of, 1648–1649
  Efflatoun (Inji) imprisoned by, 762
  and Faisal ibn Abd al-Aziz Al Saʿud, 167
  Faisal ibn Abd al-Aziz Al Saʿud challenging, 798
  Faisal (ibn Abd al-Aziz Al Sauʿd) in conflict with, 1626
  family planning supported by, 478
  and Fertile Crescent unity, 826
  foreign policy of
    early, 1649–1650
    European opposition to, 244
  as Free Officers leader, 810, 853, 1537, 1649
  Ghazali (Zaynab al-) arrested under, 892
  government of, 767, 933
    Abu Zayd (Hikmat) in, 39–40
    Amir (Abd al-Hakim) in, 188
    Ashmawi (Muhammad Abd al-Rahman Salih al-) invited to join, 321
    Hawrani (Akram al-) in, 1011
    Muhyi al-Din (Zakariyya) in, 1608
    Sidqi (Aziz) in, 1650
  and Haykal (Muhammad Hasanayn), 1012
  industrialization under, 1094
  infitah policy of, 1096
  and Institut d'Égypte, 1099
  Iraqi relations with, Qasim (Abd al-Karim) and, 1872
  Islamic congresses held by, 1152, 1153
  Israeli peace negotiations with
    Crossman (Richard) in, 650
    in Operation Alpha, 157
    U.S. peace plan and (1969), 1328
  Israeli relations with, deterioration of, 236
  and Karama, Battle of (1968), 1270
  Kennedy (John Fitzgerald) supporting, 1288
  Khalid (Khalid Muhammad) influence on, 1296
  Liberation Rally supporting, 1409, 1649
  Middle East Defense Organization opposed by, 1523
  military career of, 1537, 1540–1541, 1649
  Muhyi al-Din (Khalid) marginalized by, 1608
  and Muslim Brotherhood, 1621, 1649, 1650
  Muslim Brotherhood outlawed by, 1214
  Naguib (Muhammad) in conflict with, 1409, 1634, 1649, 1921
  al-Najjada and, 977
  National Bank of Egypt nationalized by, 390
  nationalizing Suez Canal, and UN peacekeeping force, 986
  Numeiri's (Muhammad Jaʿfar) admiration for, 1699
  Organization of African Unity and, 1718
  Palestinian citizens of Israel support for, 1787
  pan-Arabism of, 1799
  PLO created by, 1767
  in PLO-Jordanian peace accord, 1247
  on postage stamps, 1850
  Qaddafi's admiration of, 1860
  Qulaylat (Ibrahim) and, 1612
  and radio broadcasting, 1894
  resignation and return of (1967), 1651
  and Revolutionary Command Council, 1921
  rise to power, 1921
  Sabri (Ali) under, 1955
  Sadat (Anwar al-) as successor of, 1651

Sadat (Anwar al-) friendship, 1955, 1956
Sadat (Anwar al-) on, 1649
Sallal (Abdullah al-) and, 1979
Shafiq (Durriyya) opposing, 2019
Shuqayri (Ahmad) and, 2062
and Soviet help, 508, *508*
and Soviet Union
arms deal with, 1937
Kremlin meeting, *1942*
state feminism under, 892
Suez Canal nationalized by, 519–520, 2106, 2107–2108
and Arab–Israel War (1956), 245, 1650
to finance Aswan High Dam, 327, 1650
and London Conference (1956), 1444, 2108
in Suez Crisis (1956–1957), 2109, 2110
Tariki (Abdullah) supporting, 2166
as United Arab Republic president, 412, 1650, 1886, 2273
and Urabi (Ahmad), rehabilitation of, 2297
U.S. relations with
Dulles (John Foster) and, 733–734
during Suez Crisis, 1650
during Yemen Civil War, 1650
Victoria College nationalized by, 2316
Wafd party outlawed by (1953), 1685
in War of Attrition (1969–1970), 1651, 2327
and Yemen Civil War, 1650–1651, 2396
Nasser, Kamal, *813*
Nasser, Lake, **1651–1652**
Nubian relocation for, 327, 1652
size of, 327, 1651
water capacity of, 1651
Nassif, Malak Hifni, **1652**
Nateq-Nuri, Ali Akbar, 1472, **1652–1653**
in presidential election of 1997, 1120
Nath. *See* Nuer
Nation (magazine), 1966
National Action League, 2030
National Action Party (Turkey)
Democratic Left Party in coalition with, 746
Türkes (Alparslan) in, 2236
National Appeal. *See* Nida al-Qawmi al-
National Assembly (Algeria), Belkacem (Cherif) in, 437
National Assembly (Bahrain), 368–369, 370
National Assembly (Turkey), 2243
National Association (Greece). *See* Ethniké Hetairia (Greece)
National Association for the Families of Terrorism Victims (Algeria), *2175*
National Association of Journalists (Israel), 1684
National Authority for Ladino (Israel), Navon (Yizhak) in, 1672
National Bank of Egypt, 390
National Bank of Kuwait, 159, 162
National Bloc (Lebanon), 754, **1653**
National Bloc (Syria)
Atasi (Hashim al-) in, 328
Damascus branch of (National Party), 1664
and Fertile Crescent unity, 825
Hananu (Ibrahim) in, 989
Mardam (Jamil) in, 1486
vs. People's Party, 1322
Quwatli (Shukri al-) in, 328, 1885
Shahbandar (Abd al-Rahman) in conflict with, 2021
National Brotherhood (Iraq). *See* Ikha al-Watani Party
National Charter
Bendjedid (Chadli) and, 444
Tripoli Programme completed by, 2217
National Committee for Liberties (CNLT) (Tunisia), Marzouki (Moncef) in, 1497
National Committee for the Defense of Arab Lands (Palestine), 1369
National Committee for the Defense of Prisoners of Conscience (Tunisia), Marzouki (Moncef) in, 1496
National Committee of Students and Workers (Egypt), 2428
National Congress (India), 1236–1237
National Congress Party (Libya), **1653**
National Constitutional Party (Jordan), establishment of, 1471
National Council for the Liberation of Libya, 1959
National Council of Peace and Democracy of Afghanistan, 64
National Council of Resistance (Iran), 1562
National Council of the Algerian Revolution. *See* Conseil National de la Révolution Algérienne
National Defense Council (Iraq), 422
National Defense Party (Palestine), 1764–1765
decline of, 1766
establishment of, 1765
Mogannam (Matiel) in, 1557
Nashashibi (Raghib al-) as founder of, 1645
Peel Commission plan accepted by, 1766
National Democratic Alliance (NDA) (Sudan), 2101, 2104
establishment of, 2261
Garang (John) in, 868
Sadiq al-Mahdi in, 2261
National Democratic and Islamic Front (Palestine), 1009
peace process opposed by, 1155
National Democratic Assembly (Israel), 1187, 1787, 1788
platform of, 1187
National Democratic Front (NDF) (Yemen), **1653–1654**
establishment of, 2393
Hamdi's modernization programs opposed by, 985
uprising by, political-military defeat of, 2394
National Democratic Front for the Liberation of Oman and the Arab Gulf (NDFLOAG), **1654**
in Dhufar rebellion, 705
merger with PFLOAG, 706, 1842
National Democratic Party (Egypt), 768, 1664, 1957
Mubarak (Husni) in, 768
Mubarak nominated by, 1593
in People's Assembly, 1812
National Democratic Party (Iraq), **1654–1655**
Ahali group and, 80
establishment of, 80
in United National Front, 1654
National Dialogue Committee, Taqla (Philippe) in, 2165
National Economic Mobilization Headquarters (Iran), 1630

National Front (Iran), **1655–1656**. *See also* Second National Front (Iran)
Bani Sadr (Abolhasan) in, 388, 389
Bazargan (Mehdi) in, 1656
Confederation of Iranian Students and, 630
and Feda'iyan-e Khalq, 821
former Tudeh Party members in, 2222
vs. Hajir (Abd al-Hoseyn), 975
in Iranian Revolution (1979), 1126
Mossadegh (Mohammad) in, 1581, 1655–1656
Nabavi (Behzad) in, 1630
National Resistance Movement and, 1656, 2382
and oil nationalization, 1118, 1655–1656
origins of, 1117
youth movement of, 630
National Front (Jordan), Nabulsi (Sulayman al-) in, 1632
National Front (Lebanon), **1656–1657**
National Front (Morocco), Ouazzani (Mohamed Hassan) in, 2336
National Front (Turkey), National Salvation Party in, 1666
National Front for the Liberation of Palestine, establishment of, 962
National Front for the Liberation of South Yemen, **1655**, 2390
emergence of, 2398
National Front for the Salvation of Libya, **1655**
National Front Party (Iran), Bakhtiar (Shapur) in, 375
Nation Algérienne, La (Algeria), foundation of, 1365
National Guards (Saudi Arabia), 2211, 2213
National Intelligence and Counterintelligence Agency. *See* SAVAK
National Iranian Oil Company (NIOC)
Bazargan (Mehdi) as director of, 421
Eqbal (Manouchehr) as chairman of, 779
establishment of, 202
Fassih (Ismail) at, 812
foreign shares in, 1825
National Islamic Front (Afghanistan). *See* Mahaz-e Milli-e Islami-e Afghanistan
National Islamic Front (NIF) (Sudan), 808, 1701
government of, University of Khartoum under, 2296
Turabi (Hasan al-) in, 1622, 2101, 2234
women's movement supported by, 2235
Nationalism, **1657–1661**. *See also* Arab nationalism; Palestinian nationalism; *specific countries*
architecture influenced by, 282
caliphate and, 556–557
definition of, 1657
and education, 760
European influence on, 1658
Greek model of, 1657–1658
and historiography, 1035, 1036–1037
industrialization and, 1093
Islam and, 1659, 1660
and Labor Zionism, 1359–1360
and modernization, 1556
nation-state, *vs.* Arab nationalism, 261–262, 1549, 1660
qawmiyya vs. wataniyya in, 1659
in reaction to imperialism, 1090, 1091
religion and, 1659, 1660
religious, 1660
rise of, 1659–1660
secular, 1659
Christianity and, 590
and state feminism, 892–893
ulama resistance to, 2258
Nationalist Action Party (Turkey), **1660–1661**, 2245
closure after coup (1980), 1661
Gökalp's (Ziya) thoughts interpreted by, 924
Justice Party and, 1257
reemergence in 1990s, 1661
Nationalist Bloc Party (Iraq), 1000
Nationalist Front (Turkey), Demirel (Süleyman) in, 692, 1257
Nationalist Party (Iran). *See* Hezb-e melliyun (Iran)
Nationalist Work Party (Turkey), Gökalp's (Ziya) thoughts interpreted by, 924
Nationalist Youth (Syria), Kudsi (Nazim al-) in, 1337
Nationality Law (Israel), 1162
Nationalization policies, in Arab socialism, 265
National Liberal Immigration League, 427
National Liberal Party (Lebanon), **1661**
in Lebanese Front, 1395
National Liberal Party (NLP) (Algeria)
Chamoun (Camille) in, 581
Chamoun (Dany) in, 581
establishment of, 581
Tigers militia of, in Lebanese Civil War
Lebanese Forces attack on, 581
led by Chamoun (Dany), 581
National Liberation Army (Algeria). *See* Armée de Libération Nationale (ALN)
National Liberation Front (Afghanistan). *See* Jebhe-ye Nejat Milli
National Liberation Front (Algeria). *See* Front de Libération Nationale (FLN)
National Liberation Front (Bahrain), 371, **1661–1662**
National Liberation Front (NLF) (Yemen)
Aden controlled by, 1813, 1814
Ali Nasir Muhammad al-Hasani in, 143
Organization for the Liberation of the Occupied South and, 857, 1717
Rabiyya Ali (Salim) in, 1892
National Liberation League (NLL) (Palestine), 626
National Military Organization. *See* Irgun Zva'i Le'umi
National Movement (Iran), Arfa (Hasan) in, 286
National Movement Party (Turkey), Kisakürek (Necip Fazil) in, 1326
National Museum (Iraq), looting during U.S. invasion (2003), 2325
National Negro Congress, 543
National Network for Poverty Alleviation (Jordan), 1291
National Oil Corporation (Libya), **1662**
exploration and production-sharing agreements (EPSAs) of, 1662

National Oppression (Afghanistan). *See* Setem-e Melli
National Order Party (Turkey), 1910
Erbakan (Necmeddin) in, 780
Justice Party competition with, 1257
National Salvation Party as successor to, 1665
National Organization of Cypriot Fighters. *See* Ethniki Organosis Kipriakou Agonos
National Outlook Movement (Turkey), 1666
Milli Görüs Hareketti in, 1545
National Pact (Lebanon), 933, 1399, **1662–1663,** 2116, 2118
civil wars as failure of, 1663
Khuri (Bishara al-) in, 1315
Sulh (Riyad al-) in, 1315
Ta'if Accord (1989) revision of, 1663
National Pact (Tunisia), 1554
Communist Party in, 1590
National Pact (Turkey). *See* Turkish National Pact
National Party (Egypt), 406, **1663–1664**
Abbas Hilmi II in, 5–6
Copts in, 640
emergence of (1879), 1663
Kamil (Mustafa) in, 1267
origins as secret society, 1267
revival of (1893), 1663
rise of, Dinshaway incident and (1906), 406, 709
Urabi (Ahmad) and, 2297
National Party (Iran), Iran Novin Party replacing, 1129
National Party (Iraq), Abu al-Timman (Ja'far) in, 35
National Party (Morocco). *See* Parti National
National Party (Syria), **1664,** 2132
rivalry with People's Party, 1664
National Plan of Action (Morocco), 1586, 1601
National Popular Army (Algeria). *See* Armée Nationale Populaire (ANP) (Algeria)
National Progressive Front (Syria), **1665**
Atasi (Jamal al-) in, 329
National Progressive Unionist Party (Egypt), 768, **1665,** 1957
Muhyi al-Din (Khalid) in, 1608
National Reform Movement (MRN) (Algeria), 1635
National Refugee Service, in United Jewish Appeal, 2273
National Religious Party (NRP) (Israel), 1187, 1554
Abuhatzeira (Aharon) in, 37
Burg (Yosef) in, 546
and Citizens' Rights Movement, 1180
decline of, 1186
electoral success of, 1186, 1187
Gush Emunim formed by, 957
Mizrahi Party in, 1186
Morashah Party in, 1186
Nissim (Isaac) in, 1689
platform of, 1187
Po'alei Mizrahi in, 1186, 1187
Wahrhaftig (Zerah) in, 2322
National Resistance Council (Iran), Bani Sadr (Abolhasan) in, 389
National Resistance Movement (Iran), 1656
Amir-Entezam (Abbas) in, 188
Bakhtiar (Shapur) in, 375
Chamran (Mostafa) in, 582
Yazdi (Ibrahim) in, 2382
National Review (London), Middle East designation and term used by, 1522
National Salvation Front (Lebanon), **1665**
Karame (Rashid) in, 1272
National Salvation Party (NSP) (Turkey), 780, **1665–1666,** 1910
Erbakan (Necemetin) in, 1665–1666
Kisakürek (Necip Fazil) in, 1326
National Order Party as predecessor of, 1665
Refah Partisi as successor to, 1666, 2242
Republican People's Party in coalition with, 746
National School (Beirut), 550
National Security College (Israel), Eitan (Rafael) at, 774
National Security Council (Turkey), **1666–1667,** 2237–2238
Evren (Kenan) in, 789
National Security Organization (Turkey), Milli Istithbarat Teşkilati as successor to, 1545
National Socialist Party (Iraq). *See* Hizb al-Umma al-Ishtiraki
National Socialist Party (Jordan)
establishment of, 1471
Nabulsi (Sulayman al-) in, 1632
National Sports Club (Egypt), 908
National Syrian Women's Strategy, 900
National Textile Society (Algeria), 1365
National Turkish party, Yurdakul (Mehmet Emin) in, 2414
National Union (Egypt), 767, **1667**
in United Arab Republic, 2273
National Union (Israel), 1187
National Unionist Party (NUP) (Sudan)
Azhari (Isma'il) in, 349, 2261
vs. Umma Party, 2261
National Union of Algerian Students. *See* Union Nationale des Etudiants Algériens
National Union of Algerian Women. *See* Union Nationale des Femmes Algériennes
National Union of Algerian Youth. *See* Union Nationale de la Jeunesse Algérienne
National Union of Popular Forces. *See* Union Nationale des Forces Populaires
National Union of Tunisian Workers. *See* Union Nationale des Travailleurs Tunisiens
National Unity Committee (NUC) (Turkey), **1667–1668**
in coup (1960), 1667
formation of, 2241
infighting and purges in, 1667
Türkes (Alparslan) in, 2236
National Unity Government (Israel), 1417
Arens (Moshe) in, 285
Weizman (Ezer) in, 2336–2337
National Unity Party (Ottoman Empire), Ahmet Riza in, 91
National Water Carrier (Israel), 1668
National Water System (Israel), *1668,* **1668–1669**
National Will party (Iran), 2143
National Women's Committee (NWC) (Yemen), **1669**
Al-Suswa (Amat al-Alim) in, 169
Nation Arabe, La (journal), 307
Nation of Iran Party, 1117
NATO. *See* North Atlantic Treaty Organization

Natural gas, **1669–1671, 1824–1827**
associated, 1669
demand for
vs. coal, 1670
vs. oil, 1670
for desalinization process, 2330
economic exploitation of, **1669–1671**
exporters of, 1670
future of, 1827
liquefaction process for, 1671
modern uses of, 1670
OPEC policies on, 1670
Natural gas deposits
in Afghanistan, 2050
in Sahara, 1963
in Tunisia, 2225
in United Arab Emirates, Sharjah, 2040
in Yemen, 2390
Natural gas liquids, 1669
Natural gas production
in Middle East, 1671, *1671*
in Qatar, 1876
North Field of, 1876, 1878
Natural gas reserves
in Iran, 1115
in Middle East, 1671, *1671*
in Qatar, 1875
in United Arab Emirates, 2271
Natzerat Illit (Jewish development town), 1673
Navarino, Battle of (1927), 940
Navarra, André, Kan (Suna) performance with, 1269
Navigation treaties. *See* Commercial and navigation treaties
Navon, Yizhak, **1671–1672**
as first modern Israeli president, 1672
Middle Eastern origin of, 49, 1671
in RAFI Party, 1188
Sabra and Shatila massacre inquiry requested by, 1672
as Sephardic spokesman, 1672
Nawal El Saadawi Reader, The (al-Saadawi), 1950
Nawawi, Muhyi al-Din al-, 2019
Nawba (musical genre), 1617
Nawfal, Hind, **1672**
Nawfal, Maryam Nahhas, 1672
Nawfal, Nasim, 1672
Nawfal, Sara, 1672
Nawid, Senzil, *as contributor,* 68, 325–326, 693, 786, 1140, 1278–1279, 1715, 1881, 1920, 1981–1982, 2007–2008
Naylor, Phillip C., *as contributor,* 2–4, 22–23, 95–96, 128–131, 189–190, 193, 287, 437–438, 440–441, 441–443, 443–445, 450–451, 482–483, 489, 495–497, 503–505, 506, 545–546, 563, 570, 579, 612, 689–690, 707–708, 788–789, 822–823, 843, 916–917, 967, 968–970, 985, 987, 995, 1076, 1264, 1309, 1336–1337, 1362–1363, 1365, 1443–1444, 1456, 1547, 1566, 1686, 1743, 1745, 2013, 2217, 2297, 2428–2429
Nazareth (Israel), **1672–1673**
in Arab–Israel War (1948), 1672–45
under British mandate (1922–1948), 1672
as capital of Arabs in Israel, 1673
conflict with Natzerat Illit, 1673
as only all-Arab city in Israel, 1672–45
as site of Annunciation, 1673
Nazari ve ameli Türk musikisi (Suphi), 2124
Nazariyeha-ye Dulat dar Fiqh-e Shi (Kadivar), 1262
Nazerbekian, Avetis, in Armenian Social Democratic Party, 299
Nazerbekian, Maro, in Armenian Social Democratic Party, 299
Nazif, Süleyman, **1673–1674**
Nazi Party
Silver (Abbas Hillel) denouncing, 2067
Templars supporting, 2173
Nazir, al- (journal), Ashmawi (Muhammad Abd al-Rahman Salih al-) in, 321
Nazmi, Ziya, **1674**
NDA. *See* National Democratic Alliance
NDF. *See* National Democratic Front
NDFLOAG. *See* National Democratic Front for the Liberation of Oman and the Arab Gulf
NEACC. *See* Near East Arms Coordinating Committee
Near East, *vs.* Middle East, 1522–1523
Near East Air Transport Company, 1460
Near East Arms Coordinating Committee (NEACC), 304, 2215
Near East Report (bulletin), 177
Neda-ye Iran-e Novin (periodical), 1129
Nedim, Mahmut, 25
Nedjma (Kateb), 1280
Needle exchange programs, 714
Ne'eman, Yuval, **1674–1675**
Lavie File written by, 1674
as nuclear scientist, 1674–1675
Nefertari (queen of Egypt), tomb of, *276*
Negev (Israel), 1160, **1675**
in Arab–Israel War (1948), 243
climate of, 1161
Israeli settlements in, 1675
proposed Jewish settlement in, Churchill (Winston S.) on, 595
Negev Desert, 1248, 1758
Negev Hills (Israel), 1675
Negev Institute for Arid Zone Research, 424
Nehar Mitzrayim (Ben Simeon), 454
Nehemiah Operation, 790
Nehru, Jawaharlal, at Bandung Conference, 387
Nelson, Horatio, in Battle of Abu Qir (1798), 39
Neo-Baʿth party (Syria)
in coup (1966), 482
leadership of, 330
Neo-Destour Party (Tunisia), 634–635, 2427. *See also* Constitutional Democratic Rally
Baccouche (Hedi) in, 356
Ben Yousouf (Salah) in, 455
Bourguiba (Habib) in, 501, 502, 2229
labor union links to, 1358
Masmoudi (Muhammad) in, 1499
Mestiri (Ahmad) in, 1519–1520
monopoly held by broken, 1627
Sfar (Tahar) in, 2016
and Tunisian independence, 849
Union of Tunisian Women and, 2267
Neolithic cave paintings, *830*
Nerval, Gérard de, **1675–1676**
Neshat, Shirin, **1676**
Nesher, 1334
Nesin, Nüsret Aziz, 1437, 1440, **1676**
Nestorian Church, 738

Nestorians, 2056
in Iran, 1548
under Ottoman rule, 1544
Nestren (Tarhan), 2165
Netanyahu, Benjamin, **1676–1677**
Barak (Ehud) and, 1677
coalition government of, 1168
election of, 1168, 1184, 1727
HAMAS suicide bombings and, 983
in Hebron Agreement (1997), 1325
Levy (David) and, 1408
in Likud Party, 1184
Livnat (Limor) supporting, 1441
Lubavitcher Hasidim support for, 1002
at Madrid Peace Conference (1991), 1677
Mashʿal (Khalil al-) saved from assassination by, 1579
Oslo Accord rejected by, 1677
Palestinian "reciprocity" urged by, 1677
peace process under, 1168, 1727
Oslo Accord rejected by, 1726, 1793
at Wye River Accords (1998), 606, 1677
political defeat of, 1168
Sharon (Ariel) under, 2026
Netanyahu, Benzion, 1676–1677
Netanyahu, Yonatan, 777
Netherlands
oil embargo against (1973–1974), 1709
and trade, 2197
Netivot Shalom. *See* Oz ve Shalom
Neturei Karta, **1677–1678**
Neutral Zone, **1678**
oil production in, 1678
partitioning of, 1678
Neviʾim, 2157
Nevo, Joseph, *as contributor*, 338, 488, 1324–1325, 1453–1454, 2289–2290
"New Appeal to the Algerian People" (1976), 4, 1365
New Communist List (Israel). *See* RAKAH
New Dawn group (Egypt), 627
New Democracy (Afghanistan). *See* Demokrasy-i Now; Demokrasy-i Now (Afghanistan)
New Group (artistic movement), 34
New International Economic Order, 500
New Iran Party. *See* Iran Novin Party
New Islamic Jihad (Egypt), in al-Jamiʿa al-Islamiyya, 1215
New Islamic Mission, 1917. *See also* Republican Brotherhood
New Israeli shekel (NIS), 2048
Newman, David, *as contributor*, 942, 957–959, 1191–1193, 1325–1326, 1406–1407, 2339–2341
New Ottomans. *See* Young Ottomans
New Palace. *See* Topkapi Palace
New Persian studies, 540
New schooling, 756–757
administrative bodies of, 757–758
in Egypt, 756, 757
for ethnic minorities, 758
in Iran, 757, 758
in Ottoman Empire, 757, 758
vs. religious schooling, 756, 757
in Yemen, 756
Newspapers and print media, **1678–1685**
in Afghanistan, 1140
in Arab countries, **1678–1682**
common characteristics of, 1679–1680
cultural content of, 1680
diversity in, 1681
economic base for, 1680
first (*Jurnal al-Iraq*), 1678
fragmentation of, 1680
historical development of, 1678–1679
loyalist press, 1680–1681
mobilization, 1680
non-Arabic and specialized, 1681–1682
offshore publishing of, 1681
organization of, 1680–1681
political ties of, 1680
transitional press, 1681
UNESCO standard for, 1679
Arab–Israel conflict coverage in, *1679*
in Egypt, 206, 1012, 1013, 1374–1375
growth of, and education, 759
Hebrew, 1431, 1683–1684
in Iran, 867, 1682–1683, 2142, 2143, 2423–2424
in Iraq, 1525, 1678
in Israel, 1164, 1683–1684
in Lebanon, 2254
in Ottoman Empire, 409
in Tunisia, 439–440, 2016
in Turkey, 1050–1051, *1684*, 1684–1685, 2067
Nadi (Yanus) and, 1633
New Valley Project (Egypt), 1652
New Wafd (Egypt), 768, **1685–1686**, 2321
election boycott (1990) by, 1685–1686
Mubarak (Husni) and, 1685–1686
and Muslim Brotherhood, 1685–1686, 2321
Sadat (Anwar al-) and, 1685
secularism of, 1686
New Woman Research and Study Centre (Egypt), 894
New Women Society (Egypt), 2321
New York University Newman Prize, Gilboa (Amir) awarded with, 920–921
New Zionist Organization (NZO), 2372
establishment of, 1209, 2437
Nezer, Ahmet Necdet, presidency of, 2244
Nezhat-e Azadi Iran. *See* Freedom Movement
Nezib, battle of (1839), Moltke (Helmuth von) at, 1563
Nezikin, 2157
Nezzar, Khaled, **1686**
Ait Ahmed (Hocine) opposed to, 96
attempted assassination of (1993), 1686
in coup deposing Bendjedid (Chadli) (1992), 1686
defamation suit against Souaidia (Habib), 1686
as defense minister, 1686
Ghozali (Ahmed) supporting, 917
in High State Council, 1026
repression and torture charges against, 1686
and Zeroual (Liamine), 1026, 1365, 2430
Nhaisi, Elia, **1686–1687**
power struggle with Nahum (Halfallah), 1636–1637
Niati, Houria, **1687**
Nicaragua, Contra rebels of, in Iran–Contra affair, 1123
Nicholas I (czar of Russia)
British relations with, 648–649
in Syrian War (1831–1833), 1346
war against Ottoman Empire, 1945

Nicholas II (czar of Russia), 937
Nicolas Sursock Museum (Beirut), 2125
Nicosia (Cyprus), 652, 653
Nicosia, Francis R., *as contributor,* 464–465, 943–944
Nida al-Qawmi al- (Lebanon), 2116, 2119
Niebuhr, Karsten, 276
NIF. *See* National Islamic Front
Niger, Berbers in, 458
Niger River, 1963
Nightclubs, 1619
Nightingale, Florence, 649, 2302
Night of the Twentieth (Sobol), 2076
Nihal, Süküfe, in Women's People's Party, 2359
Nihayat al-Ijaz fi Sirat Sakin al-Hijaz (Tahtawi), 2148
Nihm tribe, 376
Nil, al- (newspaper), 817
Nile Basin, water availability in, 1687–1688
Nile River, **1687–1688,** 1963
  agriculture along, 690
  Alexandria linked to, by Mahmudiyya Canal, 116
  Aswan High Dam on (*See* Aswan High Dam)
  Bahr al-Abyad (White Nile), 372, 373, 901–902
  Bahr al-Ghazal as tributary of, 372
  Bahr al-Jabal as tributary of, 372–373
  Blue Nile, 372, 902
  bridges across, at Cairo, 553
  Delta Barrages on, 690
  delta of, 690
    and disease, 710, 711
  Dinka people along, 709
  disease transmission through, 710, 711
  drainage area of, 1687
  irrigation in Egypt from, 763
    Baring (Evelyn) developing, 404, 405, *406*
  Lado Enclave connecting Congo River with, 1363
  length of, 1687
  Philae island submerged in, 1832
  shipping on, 2205
  swamps of, 2105–2106
  as water resource, 1651–1652, 1687, 2328–2329
Niles, David, 2220
Nile Valley, 763
  Nubians in, 1695–1696
NILI spy ring, 1
Niʿmatullah (Sufi order), 2113
Niʿmatullah bin ʿAbdullah, 2113
Nimr, Faris, **1688–1689**
  daughter of, 214
Nimrud, archaeological research in, 276
Nimsawi, Umar al-, 1394
Nimule, 372
Nine Lights, doctrine of, 2236
Nine Lights of Türkes, 1661
Nineveh, archaeological research in, 276
NIOC. *See* National Iranian Oil Company
NIS. *See* New Israeli shekel
Nisa, al- (Qurʾanic verse), 2153
NISAA Web site, 95
Nisaʾiyyat, al- (Nassif), 1652
Nisanit (Faqir), 805
Nissa (journal), 912
Nissaboury, Mustafa, 1355
Nissim and Cherie (Bitton), 483
Nissim, Isaac, **1689**
Nissim, Moshe
  in Liberal Party, 1184
  Middle Eastern origin of, 49
Nisvan-I Islam (Aliyer), 148
Nixon, John, 1518–1519
Nixon, Richard Milhous, **1689**
  and Arab–Israel War (1973), 799, 1689
  Faisal ibn Abd al-Aziz Al Saʿud welcomed by, *1998*
  government of
    Kissinger (Henry) in, 1327–1328
    Rogers (William Pierce) in, 1929
    Shultz (George) in, 2061
  Middle East policy of, 1689, 2292
  in OPEC oil embargo (1973), 1689
  resignation of, 1689
Niyabat-e amma (general deputyship of jurists), 2312
Niyazi, Ghulam Muhammad
  in Afghan Islamic movement, 60
  in Jamiʿat-e Islami, 60
Nizam al-Jadid, al-, **1690**
Nizam al-Jadid program, 757
Nizam al-Mulk, 1457
Nizami (Tunisian military corps), 83–84
Nizam-i Cedit (Ottoman military corps), 1217
Nizamiye. *See* Ottoman military
Nizamiye courts, **1690**
  development of, Cevdet (Ahmed) in, 577
Nizamud-Din, Mullah, 2154
Nizari Ismaʿilis, 1158, 1159
Nizari tribe. *See* Adnan tribe
Nizat-i-Milli (Afghanistan), 64
Nizip, Battle of (1839), **1690–1691**
NLF. *See* National Liberation Front
NLL. *See* National Liberation League
NLP. *See* National Liberal Party
Nobel Peace Prize
  Annan (Kofi A.) awarded with, 209
  Arafat (Yasir) awarded with, *1817*
  Begin (Menachem) awarded with, 426
  Bunche (Ralph J.) awarded with, 239, 543, 2274
  Ebadi (Shirin) awarded with, 1121
  Freier (Recha) nominated for, 855
  Ibrahim (Saʿad al-Din) nominated for, 1079
  Peres (Shimon) awarded with, *1817*
  Rabin (Yitzhak) awarded with, *1817*
  Sadat (Anwar al-) awarded with, 426
  Zana (Leyla) nominated for, 2423
Nobel Prize for Literature
  to Agnon (Shmuel Yosef), 1164, 1431
  to Mahfuz (Najib), 1420, *1420,* 1464–1465
Noghay language, 2252
No, Lake, 372, 373
Nomadism, 902, 1410, 2209, 2211. *See also* Tribes and Tribalism
  in Algeria, 2253–2254
  Baluchis and, 385
  Berbers, 459, *462*
  in Eastern Desert, 737
  in Iran, 374, 2213
  Kurdish, 2214
  in Sahara, 1964
  in Saudi Arabia, 1996, 2213, 2214
  on Sinai Peninsula, 2068
  in Sudan, 433
  in Syrian Desert, 2136
  in Turkey, 2253
  in Yemen, 2209

Non-Governmental Committee for the Follow-Up of Woman Issues (Lebanon), 1396
Nongovernmental organizations (NGOs)
and human rights movement, 1049
Mernissi (Fatema) on, 1518
Non-Violence Movement (Lebanon), 1557
Noon (magazine), 269
Noor al-Hussein (Queen Noor), *1062*, 1063, **1691–1692**
Noor al-Hussein Foundation, 1691
Nordau, Max, **1692**
Uganda Project supported by, 2257
Valensi (Alfred) and, 2308
Zionism of, Dreyfus affair and, 723
North African Mission, 1551
North African Star. *See* Star of North Africa
North Atlantic Treaty Organization (NATO), **1692**
Article 5 invoked after September 11, 2001, 1692
Bandung Conference on, 387
Eisenhower (Dwight D.) as supreme commander of, 773
establishment of, Acheson (Dean) support for, 40
France in, Challe (Maurice) representing, 579
in Turkey, facilities of, 42
Turkey in, 696
Alexandretta, 115
Erdoğan (Tayyip) on, 781
military commitment of, 1527, 1531–1535, 1535
security assured during U.S. invasion of Iraq (2003), 1692
Northbrook, Lord, 404
Northern Alliance (Afghanistan), *67*
Ahmad Shah Masʿud in, 89
formation of, 1889
in interim government, 64
Iranian support for, 1121
Tajiks in, 2150
Northern Tier, **1692–1693**
North Korea
Pakistan's transfer of nuclear technology to, 1696
Palestinian relations with, Wazir (Khalil al-) and, 2335
North, Oliver, in Iran–Contra affair, 1123
Northrop Corporation, 1937
North Sea, oil production in, 522
Northwest Semitic languages, 2010
North Yemen. *See* Yemen Arab Republic
Norton, John D., *as contributor*, 434–436
Notes on the Bedouins and Wahabys (Burckhardt), 545
Not of This Time, Not of This Place (Amichai), 182, 1433
No to Torture (Niati), 1687
Notre Révolte (Challe), 579
Nouadhibou (Mauritania), 1501
Nouakchott (Mauritania), 1501, **1693**
Nouba des femmes du Mont Chenoua, la (film), 716
Nouira, Hedi, **1693–1694**
Mzali (Mohammed) as successor to, 1627
as prime minister, 502
Nour (magazine), 1472
Nouveau Théâtre de Tunis, 376
Novomeysky, Moshe, in potash industry, 1851
NRP. *See* National Religious Party
NSP. *See* National Salvation Party
Nuʿaymi family, al-, **1694**
Nuʿaymi, Humayd bin Rashid Al, Ajman ruled by, 96
Nuʿaymi, Rashid ibn Humayd al-, 1694
Nuba Mountains, 1335
Nuba people, in Kordofan, 1335
Nubar, Arakel Bey, 2415
Nubar, Boghos, **1694–1695**
Nubar Pasha, **1695**
Ghali (Boutros) under, 909
in Institut d'Égypte, 1099
and mixed courts, 1553
as prime minister of Egypt, 2415
son of, Nubar (Boghos) as, 1694
Nubians, **1695–1696**, 2097–2098
language and dialects of, 1696
relocation for Aswan High Dam, 1652, 1696
relocation of, for Aswan High Dam, 327, 2098
NUC. *See* National Unity Committee
Nuclear capability and nuclear energy, **1696–1699**
delivery systems for weapons, proliferation of, 1696
of Iran, U.S. accusations on, 1121
of Iraq, 305, 1535, 1696, 1698
Osirak reactor and, 1535, 1698, 1724
of Israel, 1696–1698, *1697*
at Dimona reactor, 708, 1288, 1696–1697, *1697*, 2309
in World War II, 1935
Nuer, **1699**, 2098
Nuer Settlement, 1699
Nuit sacrée, La (Ben Jelloun), 376, 1428
Nuit sacrée, La (film), 376
Nuit sauvage, La (Dib), 1426
Nuit tombe sur Alger la blanche, La (Hayat), 1427
Nuʿman, Muhammad Ahmad
Free Yemenis founded by, 855
government reform sought by, 2442
in Organization for the Liberation of the Occupied South, 1717
Numaylatiyya clan, 2212
Numeiri, Muhammad Jaʿfar, 808, **1699–1701**
and Addis Ababa Accords
negotiation of (1972), 1700
repudiation of (1981), 1701
agricultural policy under, 1700
Ansar attacked by, 210, 2261
Ansar (Mahdist) opposition to, 1699–1701
in coup (1958), 1699
in coup (1964), 1699
coup against, attempted (1971), 1699–1700
coup against (1985), 1701
Ibrahim (Fatima Ahmed) in, 1075
coup by (1969), 2101, 2103
coup installing (1969), 1699
education of, 1699
exile of (1985–1999), 1701
Garang (John) in conflict with, 868
government of, Turabi (Hasan al-) in, 1622
Islamic ideology of, 1701
Libyan relations under, *1700*
military career of, 1699
military revolution of, Azhari (Ismaʿil) after, 349
Nasser (Gamal Abdel) admired by, 1699
opposition to, Republican Brotherhood and, 1918
return of (1999), 1701
Taha (Mahmud Muhammad) tried by, 2145
Umma Party under, 2261

Numismatics, **1701–1703**
NUP. *See* National Unionist Party
Nuqrashi, Mahmud Fahmi al-, **1701**
in Arab–Israel War (1948), 1701
assassination of, 1701
Khalid (Khalid Muhammad) influenced by, 1296
in Sa'dist party, 1701
Nurcu. *See* Nursi, Said
Nurcus (followers of Nursi), 1705
National Salvation Party supported by, 1666
Nuri, Abd al-Malik, **1703–1704**
Nuri, Ali Akbar Nateq, 428
Nuri, Fazlollah, **1704**
bast taken by, 411
constitutionalism opposed by, 1704
in coup (1908), 1704
execution of, 1704
grandson of, 1318
on women's rights, 637
Nuri, Hojatoleslam Abdolah, 1558
Nur, Riza, 1737
Nursi, Said, 948, **1704–1705**
Nusair, Isis, *as contributor,* 1065, 1291–1292, 1488, 1852
Nusayba, Anwar, 1705
in All-Palestine Government, 154, 1705
Nusayba family, **1705–1706**
keys of Church of Holy Sepulchre held by, 1705
and keys to Church of the Holy Sepulchre, 1044
Nusayba, Hazem, 1705
Nusayba, Sari, 1705–1706
in Coalition for Peace, 1809
Nusayri. *See* Alawi
Nuseibeh, Ahuzen Zaki, 812
Nuseibeh family. *See* Nusayba family
Nuteg-Nuri, Ali Akbar. *See* Nateq-Nuri, Ali Akbar
Nützel (numismatic scholar), 1702
Nuun (magazine), **1706**
Nuwayhid, Bayan, 1071
NWC. *See* National Women's Committee
NZO. *See* New Zionist Organization

O

OADP. *See* Organization of Democratic and Popular Action
OAPEC. *See* Organization of Arab Petroleum Exporting Countries
OAS. *See* Organisation Armée Secrète
Oasis(es), 903, 1964
definition of, 2626
in Egypt, 2071–2072
in Saudi Arabia, 1995, 1996, 1997
Oasis Group, **1707–1708**
OAU. *See* Organization of African Unity
Oberling, Pierre, *as contributor,* 696–697
Ocak, 2228
Öcalan, Abdullah
abduction of, 1341, 1343
in Freedom and Democracy Congress of Kurdistan, 1344
in Kurdistan Workers Party, 1343
on trial for treason, 1343–1344
Occidental Petroleum, **1708–1709**
in Colombia, 1708
in Libya, 1708
Occidentosis: A Plague from the West (Gharbzadegi), 913
Occupied territories. *See also* Gaza Strip; Golan Heights; West Bank
Israeli seizure of, in Arab–Israel War (1967), 249, 1159–1160, 1791
Israeli settlements in (*See* Israeli settlements)
Israeli withdrawal from
in Gaza–Jericho Agreement (1994), 1784
Israeli attitudes toward, 249, 252
Kook (Zvi Yehuda) against, 1334
in Oslo Accords (1993), 1768, 1784
in Oslo II Interim Agreement (1995), 1726, 1775, 1784
Likud policy on, 1184
Palestinians in
number of, 1789
violence against, Karp Report on (1984), 1275–1276
Third Way Party on, 1189
Tzomet Party on, 1189
Ocean of Dreams, An (Saudi), 2001
October 6 University (Egypt), 1995
"October Paper" (1974), 1096
Odyssey (Homer), 717
Oea (ancient city), 2216, 2217
Oeil de la nuit, L' (Laabi), 1355
Oeil du jour, L' (Béji), 1424
Ofeish, Sami A., *as contributor,* 754, 1949–1950
Office Chérifien des Phosphates (Morocco), 1569
Office de la Radiodiffusion-Télévision Française (ORTF), 2192
Office for Reconstruction and Humanitarian Assistance (Iraq), 2325
Office of Dual Financial Control (Egypt), 766
Offshore publishing, 1681
Oflazoglu, Turan, 2187
Of Man Thou Art, and Unto Man Shalt Thou Return (Amichai), 182
Oghuz tribe, 434
Oglu, 2626
Ohalim movement, 2023
Ohel theater (Israel), 2418
Ohio University, Sartawi (Issam) at, 1992
Ohnet, George, 148
Ohrmazd (Zoroastrian deity). *See* Ahura Mazda
OIC. *See* Organization of the Islamic Conference
Oil, **1824–1827**
Oil companies. *See* International oil companies; *specific companies*
Oil concessions
of Gülbenkian (Calouste), 948
in Iran, 1825
D'Arcy Concession, 200, 671
in Iraq, 538
in Kuwait, 1824–1825
in Libya, competition for, 1826
one company/one country pattern of, 1824–1825
in Persia, 536–537
Red Line Agreement and, 1909–1910
after World War I, 514
Oil Consultation Commission, end of, political conflicts in, 1719
Oil dependence
and industrialization, 1093
of OPEC, 1721
Oil deposits, 901
in Yemen, 2390
Oil development
and urban planning, 2300–2301
U.S. investments in, 2290

Oil embargo (1973–1974), **1709**, 1718, 2292
ARAMCO support for, 230
Nixon (Richard Mihous) in, 1689
Saudi Arabia in, 1626
Oil-for-Food Program (Iraq), 1069, 1135, 1339, 1720, 1986–1987
Oil nationalization
in Iran
bazaar as political base during, 419
Bazargan (Mehdi) in, 421
Eden (Anthony) opposing, 755
foreign response to, 1825
Kuwaiti oil after, 1349
by Mossadegh (Mohammad), 417, 518
in Iraq, 1134, 1139
in Kuwait, 1349
OPEC in, participation strategy of, 1826
success of, 1826
Oil pipelines, 1830. *See also specific pipelines*
in Iraq, by Iraq Petroleum Company, 1138
from Iraq to Turkey, 115–116, 1830
Oil prices, 1828–1830
API gravity and, 1828–1829, *1829*
during Arab–Israel War (1973), 251, 522, 2201
As-Is Agreement on (1928), 323
benchmarks for, 1828
collapse in (1986), 522
in contracts, 1828
distance of transport and, 1829
and Gulf Crisis (1990–1991), 949
Gulf War and (1990–1991), 1720
of international oil companies, 1718, 1719
Iranian Revolution and, 1719
in Libya, government manipulation of, 1707, 1708
during oil embargo (1973–1974), 1709
under OPEC, 1718–1721, 1826
posted system of 1950s for, 1718–1719
revolution in (1970s), Occidental Petroleum in, 1708
Oil production, 1555, 1827–1830
in Algeria, 752
Italian interest in, 777–778
during Arab–Israel War (1956), 2203
in Bahrain, 752, 1482, 2199
by Bahrain National Oil Company, 371–372
Belgrave (Charles Dalrymple) and, 436
Britain and, 537
by Standard Oil of California, 229
contracts for, 1828
geographic distribution of, *1828*
and industrialization, 1094
in Iran, 752, 1482, 2199
Abadan, 2
by Anglo–Iranian Oil Company, 200–202, 518, 742
Compagnie Française des Pétroles in, 628
Consortium Oil Agreement on (1954), 186
D'Arcy Concession for, 200, 536–537, 671
economic value of, 1115
Kharg Island, 1300
nationalization of, 100, 186, 202, 1118, 1581, 1752
in Iraq, 752, 1131, 1482
in Basra, 410
French-British rivalry over control of, 2199
after Gulf War, 1720
by Iraq Petroleum Company, 1131, 1138–1139
Kirkuk, 1138, 1139, 1325
Mosul, 1138
in Kuwait, 537, 752, 1349, 2199
al-Ghanim family in, 911
by Kuwait Oil Company, 1349, 1824–1825
by Kuwait Petroleum Corporation, 1352–1353
in Libya, 752, 1410, *1411*
Cyrenaica region of, 655
Fezzan region, 830
Law 24 and, 1662
National Oil Corporation in, 1662
by Oasis Group, 1707–1708
by Occidental Petroleum, 1708
and Tripoli, 2216
and low female participation in work force, 874
in Mauritania, 1502
natural gas in, economic exploitation of, 1669–1671
in neutral zone, 1678
in North Sea, 522
by OAPEC, 1718
during oil embargo (1973–1974), 1709
in Oman, 752
by OPEC
mandatory quota system for, 1720
voluntary sharing plan for, 1719–1720
as percentage of gross domestic product, 1483–1484
in Qatar, 752
by foreign companies, Anglo–Iranian Oil Company, 1876
by Qatar Petroleum, 1878
in Saudi Arabia, 752, 1995, 1996–1997, 2199
Abd al-Aziz (ibn Saʿud Al Saʿud) and, 1626
by Arabian American Oil Company, 229–230
and end of Red Line Agreement, 1910
nationalization of, 230
by Standard Oil of California, 11, 229
Tariki (Abdullah) and, 2166
U.S. companies favored in, 515
Yamani (Ahmad Zaki) and, 2378
in Sudan, 2099–2100
in Syria, 752, 2126–2127
in Tunisia, 2225
in Turkey, 2239
in United Arab Emirates, 752
Sharjah, 2040
in Yemen, 752
by Yemen Hunt Oil Company, 2397
in Yemen Arab Republic, 2395, 2397
in Maʾri/al-Jawf basin, 1487–1488
Oil reserves, *752*, 1827–1830
geographic distribution of, 1828, *1828*
in Iran, 1115
in Iraq, 1131
in Qatar, 1875
size of, 1827
in United Arab Emirates, 2270–2271
Abu Dhabi, 36, 2270–2271
Oil revenues
in Bahrain, 436
investment outside oil industry, 1349, 1827
in Iraq, 1968
and Gulf War (1990–1991), 1134
in Kuwait, 1349
of Libya, 1410
of Saudi Arabia, 795, 799

Oil spills, 952
Oil tankers, 2107
Oil trade, 2199–2200, 2201
  Britain in, 517
    OPEC and, 522
  Persian Gulf in, 1820
Oil transport, 2207
  through pipelines (*See* Oil pipelines)
  in pricing, 1829
  Suez–Mediterranean Pipeline, 2110–2111
  Trans-Arabian Pipeline for, 2202–2203
  Trans-Turkey Pipeline for, 2208
Ojrat-ol misl, 2051
Okyar, Fethi, 854
Olam, ha- (newspaper), 2078
Olama, Mirza Mahmud Eftekhar, Khomeini (Ruhollah) taught by, 1310
Olam ha-Zeh, ha- (magazine), Avnery (Uri) in, 340
Old Lover, The (Erbil), 780
Olimpo, Paola, *as contributor,* 1327–1329
Olive oil, *837,* 840
Olives, *837,* 840
Olmert, Ehud, as Jerusalem mayor, 1332
  Haredi Jews and, 1226
OLOS. *See* Organization for the Liberation of the Occupied South
Olympic Games
  of 1972, Israelis murdered at, 1792
  of 1996, Palestinian Authority team at, 1784
Olympus, Mount, 937
Oman, **1709–1711**. *See also specific cities, organizations, people, and regions*
  agriculture in, 1204, 1711
  Al Bu Saʿid dynasty in, 107, 1710–1711
  in Arab boycott against Israel, 224
  Baluchis in, 385
  banking in, *393*
  borders of, with Yemen, 2385
  British relations with
    Anglo–Omani treaties in, 203–204, 525–526, 531–532, 614
    Cox (Percy) in, 645–646
    as de facto protectorate, 204
    in Dhufar rebellion, 521, 705, 1842
    military forces in, 521
    telegraph service and, 527
  Buraymi oasis claimed by, 517, 544
  cities of
    capital, 1616
    port, 1500, 1616
  climate of, 705, 1710
  coup in (1970), 107, 108
  defense costs as percentage of GNP or GDP, *1530*
  Dhufar rebellion in (1965–1975), 705–706
    Soviet Union supporting, 2174
  economy of, 752, *753*
  fishing industry of, 834, 1711, *1711*
  governates of, 705
  in Gulf Cooperation Council, 949
  in Gulf Crisis (1990–1991), 950
  human rights in, 1048
  labor unions illegal in, 1358
  in League of Arab States, 1388
  legal system of
    British influences on, 1380
    reforms in, 1380
  legislative body in, 932
  manufacturing in, 1483, *1483*
  military of
    equipment of, *1534*
    force levels of, *1528–1529*
    force structure of (army, air force, and navy), *1532–1533*
  natural gas production and reserves in, 1671, *1671*
  newspapers and print media of, 1678–1679
    loyalist approach of, 1681
  oil production in, 752
  political system of, 1711
  population of, *753,* 1844
  radio and television in, *1895*
  regions of, 705
    mountainous, 1204
  sand deserts of, 1938
  Sib Treaty (1920) in, 2064
  tamimahs in, 2158
  in trade, East India Company and, 525
  tribes in, 385, 2210
    Al Bu Saʿid family in, 107
  water resources of, freshwater withdrawals, *2331*
  World Bank and, capital stock and voting power in, *2363*
  and Zanzibar, 2425
Oman, Gulf of, **952,** 2040
Omar Gatlato (film), 2192
Omar, Mohamed Bel Haj, 452
Omar, Muhammad (Mullah), **1711–1712**
  election of, 2155
  in Kandahar, 1711, 1712, 2974
  Mohammadi (Maulawi Mohammad Nabi) and, 1559
  in Taliban, 64, 1712, 1767
Omar Mukhtar Club, **1712**
  Kikhya (Umar Mansur al-) conflict with, 1321
Ombre de la terre, L' (film), 2192
Ombres japonaises (Khatibi), 1304
Ombre sultane (Djebar), 1424
OMDH. *See* Organisation Marocaine des Droits de l'Homme
Omdurman (Sudan), **1712–1713,** *2097,* 2100
  Ahmad (Muhammad) in, 87, 1301, 1712
  architecture of, 1301–1302
  as Mahdist capital, 1301, 1712
  population of, 1301
Omdurman, Battle of (1898), Abdullahi (Muhammad Turshain) in, 33
Omega, Operation, 157
O Mes Soeurs Musulmanes, Pleurez! (Bittari), 483
Omid. *See* Akhavan-Saless, Mehdi
Omnium Nord-African (ONA), 1005
OMP. *See* Moroccan Observatory of Prisons
OMV, Occidental Petroleum and, 1708
ONA. *See* Omnium Nord-African
Onay, Gulsin, 477
Once upon a Time (collection), 1435
Once Upon a Time Cinema (Iranian film), 1473
Once upon a Time on the Nile (film), 2022
100 Soruda Türk Folkloru (Boratav), 493
100 Soruda Türk Halk edebiyata (Boratav), 493
One Israel Party, Meimad in, 1186
One Man with His Gun (Chubak), 593
One Nation. *See* Am Ehad Party
1001 années de la nostalgie, Les (Boudjedra), 497
Only in London (Shaykh), 2046
Only Yesterday (Agnon), 71
On the Bridge (Bint al-Shati), 476

On the Edge (film), 1288
"On the Slaughter" (Bialik), 470
On the Steps (Freier), 855
On the Trails of My Fancy (Chédid), 583
OPEC. *See* Organization of Petroleum Exporting Countries
OPEC Fund for International Development, 749–750
Open door policies, 1093
  in Egypt, 1094
    infitah as, 1096
Open Door, The (Zayyat). *See Bab al-maftuh, al-* (Zayyat)
Opera, 872–873
Operation Desert Fox (1998), 2323
Operation on Wings of Eagles, 1460
Opinion, l' (newspaper), 1197
Opium, 724–725, **1713**
  international initiative regarding, 1713
  from Iran, 2198
  medical use of, 724, 1713
  narcotic use of, 1713
  processing of, in Iran, 2420
  production of, 724–725
    in Afghanistan, 67, 494, 725, 1713
    in Iran, 725
    in Lebanon, 725
    in Turkey, 724–725
  rise of, 1713
  sale of, *724*
  trade of, in Afghanistan, 1021
Oppenheim, Jean-Marc R., *as contributor,* 116–118, 379, 491–492, 908–909, 931, 1404–1406, 1884–1885
Oppenheim, Max von, 905–906, 906
Optimism One (Esfandiary), 784
Oral rehydration therapy, 714
  for diarrhea, 1509–1510
Oran (Algeria), **1713–1715,** *1714*
  British attack on French fleet in (1940), 2369
  Catholics in, 1932
  French occupation of, 16, 122, 1713–1714
  housing in, 1714
  industrialization of, 1714
  under Ottoman Empire, 1713
  Spanish occupation of, 2084
  violence in, 1715
Oran, langue morte (Djebar), 1427
Orbit (satellite company), 1895
Orbits of Desire (Adonis), 48
Ordalie des voix (Lemsine), 1403
Ordeman, Les, *as contributor,* 481, 1219–1220, 1315, 1832, 2166
Ordered Troops, 1481
Ordinances, on veiling, **1715**
Ordu Yardimlasma Kurumu. *See* OYAK
Orfy, Wadad, 832
Organic Law (Egypt, 1913), 6
Organic Law (Lebanon), 469
Organisation Armée Secrète (OAS) (Algeria), 788, **1715**
  Argoud (Antoine) in, 287
  colons in, 139, 618, 1715
  Feraoun (Mouloud) murdered by, 823
Organisation Marocaine des Droits de l'Homme (OMDH), **1716–1717**
  accomplishments of, 1716–1717
  establishment of, 1716
  goals of, 1716
  government response to, 1716
Organisation pour l'Action Democratique et Populaire (OADP) (Morocco), 1574
Organisation Spéciale (OS) (Algeria), 1589
  Ait Ahmed (Hocine) in, 95
  Ben Bella (Ahmed) in, 441
  Ben M'hidi (Muhammad Larbi) in, 450
  Boudiaf (Mohamed) in, 496
  Krim (Belkacem) in, 1336
  Lahouel (Hocine) in, 1365
  and Mouvement pour le Triomphe des Libertés Démocratiques (MTLD), 969
  Setif Revolt and, 2013
Organisme de Coopération Industrielle, 506
Organization for the Liberation of the Occupied South (OLOS) (Yemen), **1717**
  National Liberation Front and, 857
Organization of Action for the Liberation of Palestine, 1992
Organization of African Unity (OAU), **1717–1718**
  on Israel, 1718
  Mubarak assassination attempt at meeting of (1995), 1594
  POLISARIO in, 1005
  SADR accepted by, 1964
  Saharan Arab Democratic Republic in, 1837
  in Western Sahara War
    as mediator, 1566, 2344, 2346
    recognition of Saharan Arab Democratic Republic (SADR), 2345
Organization of American States, 489
Organization of Arab Palestine, 1841
Organization of Arab Petroleum Exporting Countries (OAPEC), **1718**
  establishment of, 1718, 2378
  goals of, 1718
  members of, 1718
  oil embargo by (1973–1974), 1709, 1718
    ARAMCO support for, 230
  Yamani (Ahmad Zaki) in, 2378
Organization of Democratic and Popular Action (OADP), 498
Organization of Iranian Moslem Students (United States), Musavi (Mir-Hosain) in, 1615
Organization of Muslim Youth. *See* Sazman-i Javanani Musalman
Organization of People's Mujahedin of Iran (OPMI), Nabavi (Behzad) in, 1630
Organization of Petroleum Exporting Countries (OPEC), **1718–1721**
  during Arab–Israel War (1973), 251, 522
  Bazzaz (Abd al-Rahman al-) as secretary-general of, 422
  establishment of, 1718–1719
  Faisal ibn Abd al-Aziz Al Saʿud and, 799
  Iraq in, 1138, 1719
  Kuwait in, 1349, 1719
  leapfrogging tactic of, 1826
  market control by, As-Is Agreement as model for (1928), 323
  members of, 1719
  natural gas policies of, 1670
  North Sea oil production and, 522
  oil dependence of, 1721
  oil embargo imposed by (1973)
    Nixon (Richard Milhous) in, 1689
    Saudi Arabia in, 1626
  oil production in, 1719–1720
    mandatory quota system for, 1720

Organization of Petroleum Exporting Countries (OPEC) *(continued)*
sharing strategy for, 1719–1720
Organization of Arab Petroleum Exporting Countries and, 1718
Pahlavi (Mohammad Reza) in, 1753
and pan-Arabism, 824
participation strategy of, 1719, 1826
political divisions within, 1720–1721
power of, 522
prices under, 522, 1718–1721, 1826, 2200, 2201
Tariki (Abdullah) as cofounder of, 2166
trade influenced by, 2199–2200
U.S. opposition to, 1719
wealth generated by, and Islamic numismatics, 1703
Organization of the Islamic Conference (OIC), 799, **1721–1722**
and Cairo Convention of Human Rights in Islam, 1049
charter of, 1153, 1721
establishment of, 1153, 1721
functions of, 1153
goals of, 1721
membership in, 1722
Organization of the Mujahedin of Islamic Revolution (Iran), 1630
Organization of the Vanguards of the Popular Liberation War. *See* Saʿiqa, al-
Oriental, as designation and term, 1522
Orientalism, 492, **1722–1723**
in art, 311, 1722
on collection of Qur'an, 1883
in literature, 1675–1676
origin of concept, 1722
in postage stamps, 1850
Orientalism (Said), 1036, 1722, 1966
Orientalists, International Congress of, **1723**
Oriental Jews. *See* Adot ha-mizrah; Mizrahi Jews
Oriental Orthodox Churches, 591–592
member churches in, 591, 639
theology of, 589
Oriental Studies, 1035
Orient Express (Vienna–Istanbul railway), 464, 2206
Orient House, 1226, 1227
Orient, L'-Le jour (newspaper), 872, 2254
Orlogin (publication), 2058
Ormanian, Maghakia, 298, **1723**
Ormsby-Gore, William George Arthur, **1723–1724**
Orontes River, 909, 980, 2129
Orr, Akiva, 1501
Ortaoyunu, **1724**
Kasap (Teodor) plays based on, 1277
Ortaoyunus, 2187
ORTF. *See* Office de la Radiodiffusion-Télévision Française
Orthodox Christians
number of, 738
in Ottoman Empire, 738
Orthodox churches. *See* Eastern Orthodox Church; Oriental Orthodox churches
Orthodox Islam. *See* Sunni Islam
Orthodox Jews
in Israel, 1163
Neturei Karta of, 1677–1678
in Palestine, in 19th century, 1760
political party of, Agudat Israel as, 77–78
and Sabbath, 1954
Orwell, George, 46
Or Yehuda Local Council, 452
OS. *See* Organisation Spéciale
Osirak nuclear reactor, **1724**
in Iraq, Israeli strike against, 1535, 1698
Israel destroying (1981), 426
Oslo Accord (1993), **1724–1728**. *See also* Declaration of Principles
Abbas (Mahmud) in, 6
accomplishments of, 1727
American Jewish Congress support for, 179
archaeological sites in, 278
Barak (Ehud) implementing, 398
and Camp David Summit (2000), 562
collapse of, 1726–1727
blame for, 1727
context for, 1725
al-Fatah and, 814
on Gaza Strip, 871
Habash (George) on, 962
and Haram al-Sharif, future of, 992
Hawatma (Nayif) criticism of, 1009
Hebron after, 1019
Hut (Shafiq al-) protest against, 1071
Islamic Jihad opposing, 1155
Israeli settlements in, 1193
Israeli withdrawals in, 1768, 1784
and Jerusalem, 1226
Khaled (Leila) opposing, 1293
Likud Party rejecting, 1185, 1726, 1727
Livnat (Limor) opposing, 1440
Madrid Peace Conference leading to (1991), 1793
mutual recognition in, 238, 1167, 1725–1726, 1768, 1775
Palestinian Authority based on, 1784
Palestinian self-rule in, 238, 1775, 2340–2341
Peres (Shimon) in, 1725, 1818
PFLP opposing, 1840
Rabin (Yitzhak) legacy and, 1892
reception of, 1725–1727
Said (Edward) opposing, 1966
Salim (Ali) in, 1978
Sarid (Yossi) supporting, 1991
secret negotiations in, 1725
Qurai (Ahmad Sulayman) at, 1725, 1881–1882
Sharon (Ariel) opposing, 2177–2178
signing of, *1726*
by Arafat (Yasir), 271, 606, *1726*
Clinton (Bill) in, 606, *1726*
by Rabin (Yitzhak), 271, 606, *1726*
terrorism renounced in, 219, 1167
United Nations in, 2276–2277
Vatican and, 2310
West Bank under, 2340–2341
Zionist Organization of America on, 2436
Oslo II Interim Agreement (1995)
Israeli withdrawal in, from West Bank, 1727, 1775, 1784
provisions of, 1727
signing of, 1727
United Nations in, 2277
Osman I (Turkish ruler), 1728
Osman, Ahmed, 1904
Osman, House of, **1728**
Osmanli (journal), 576
Osmanli Bankasi, 390
Ossetic language, 1124
Ostermann, Helmut. *See* Avnery, Uri
Ostrich (Bejerano), 434
Otayba tribe. *See* Utayba tribe

Other, The (Chédid). *See Autre, l'*
Ottoman Bank. *See* Osmanli Bankasi
"Ottoman Bill of Rights." *See* Hatt-i Hümayun (1856)
Ottoman Bureau of Translation. *See* Bureau of Translation
Ottoman Debt Commission, 2199
Ottoman Empire, **1728–1737**. *See also specific cities, organizations, people, and regions*
Abd al-Hadi family in, 12–13
administrative divisions of, 1729
Aegean Sea in, 51
agriculture in, 1729–1730
after Land Code of 1858, 1367–1369
before Land Code of 1858, 1367
tax farming and, 1367, 2167–2168
alcohol in, 109–110
Algeria under, 122, 1713
Anatolia in, Land Code of 1858 effects, 1368, 1369
Arabian relations with, Faysal ibn Turki Al Saʿud and, 819
Arab nationalism in, 261
crackdown on, 264
Arab Revolt against (1916), 262–264, 510, 799–800
McMahon (Henry) in, 1506
architects in, 386
architecture in, 280, 281, 282
archives of, 407
Armenians in
Dashnak Party and, 676–677
genocide against (*See* Armenian genocide)
millet of, 296–298, 1543–1545
resistance by, 195, 299–301, 1612–1613
revolutionary movement of, 299–301, 303
art of, 143, 2008–2009
Austria-Hungary and, 534
Austro-Hungarian relations with, 339–340
Balkans in, nationalist movement in, 382–383, 542–543, 2163–2164
in bankruptcy, 2199
banks in, 389, 740, 2163
Bektashis in, 435
Black Sea access of, 485, 1446, 2093–2094
Britain and
in Aqaba incident (1906), 218
Berlin Treaty (1878) and, 528
British–Ottoman alliance, 491, 527–528, 530, 740, 846
Bulgarian Horrors and, 382
Canning (Stratford) and, 563–564
capitulations granted to, 565, 621
commercial convention, 2163
Drummond-Wolff Convention between (1885), 726
East India Company and, 525–526
Levant Company and, 525
Persian Gulf politics and, 531
Sinai Peninsula and, 2068
during Tanzimat era, 2162–2163
during World War I, 509–511
and Bulgarian Horrors (*See* Bulgarian Horrors)
in caliphate, 556
capitulations, 564–566, 620–621, 844–845
Catholic missionaries in, 1931
censorship in, 28
Çerkes Hasan incident in (1876), 575
cholera in, 712
Christians in, 589–590, 1731
Orthodox, 738
Circassians in, 599
cities of, 1979
capital, 547, 1729, 2253
civil code in, 577–578, 601
civil service in, **1734–1735**
Civil Service School for, 602
climate of, 1729
commercial and navigation treaties of, 620–621
communication in, 28, 624
constitution of, 1742, 2407
Midhat Paşa as father of, 1524–1526
constitution of (1876), 27, 1381
Namik Kemal as framer of, 1641
constitution of (1908), 2240
constitution of (1909), 1381
corsairs in, 643
coup in (1826), attempted, 1466–1467
coup in (1878), attempted, 144
coup in (1908), 1659, 2240
coup in (1913), 384, 623, 778, 2410
and Armenian genocide, 293
court system of, Nizamiye, 1690
in Crimean War, 739, 2162
Cyprus in, 652, 653
in Dardanelles Treaty (1809), 621, 671–672
debt of, 25, 614, 1732, **1735–1737**
under Abdülaziz, 25
under Abdülhamit II, 27–28
under Abdülmecit I, 33
in Crimean War, 33
decline of, 1466, 1728
and Eastern Question, 738–743
dissolution of, 1728, 2240, 2250
Druze in, 469, 728–729, 1398
economy of, 741–742, 1729–1730
Germany and, 904
reform of, 2162–2163
education in
administrative bodies of, 758
for civil servants, 602
European model in, 757, 864
Gaspirali (Ismail Bey) and, 869
at İdadi schools, 1079–1080
in Mahalle Schools, 1461
middle, 1940
new schooling in, 757, 758
primary, 1940
reform of, 24, 92, 757, 758, 2162
state schools in, 757
sultani lycées in, 864, 2121
Egypt in, 741
Buhayra, 542
in Convention of al-Arish (1800), 288–289
defeat of Tuman Bey and, 2223
Egypt invaded by, in Aqaba incident (1906), 218
elites in, 775, *775*
ethnic diversity in, 1731–1732, 2253
vs. European imperialism, 1087–1089
European imperialism in, 2162–2163
European part of (Rumelia), 1939
Fertile Crescent under, 824
Fezzan occupied by, 830
freemasonry in, 852
French relations with
Muhammad Ali and, 846
Sebastiani (Horace) and, 2006–2007
during Tanzimat era, 2162–2163
Gaza Strip in, 870
geography of, 1729
German relations with
Abdülhamit II and, 742, 903–904
and Berlin–Baghdad railway, 464, 532–533
concessions granted to Germany, 904

Ottoman Empire *(continued)*
German military advisers in Ottoman army, 903, 904, 905
German–Ottoman alliance, 532–533, 742, 903–904
Ottoman–German convention (1914) on, 534
under Wilhelm II, 903, *904*, *905*
Golan Heights in, 925
government seat of, 2194
in Greco–Turkish War (1897), 937
in Greek War of Independence, 939–940, 2093
Greek war with (1897), 27
guilds in, 946
Hadramawt in, 970
Hanafi school of law in, 988
higher education in, 1458
at Darülfünün, 672
Hijaz in, 1028
Hijaz Railroad in, 1028
historiography of, 1035
history of, Altinay (Ahmed Refik) on, 173
al-Husayni family under, 1053
İlmiyye in, 1086–1087, 1264
industrialization of, 1730
industry of, 1357
intelligence gathering in, 1100
Iranian relations with, Zuhab region and, 783
Iraq in, 1132
Baghdad, 360
Basra, 411
Land Code of 1858 effects, 1368, 1369
Islamic congresses in, 1152
Islamic numismatics in, 1702
Islam in, as unifying factor, 1089
Italian relations with (*See* Turkish–Italian War (1911–1912))
Jerusalem in, 1222–1223
Jews in, 383, 1231–1232
as financiers, 807
Herzl (Theodor) proposal regarding, 1021
Jordan in, 1244
Irbid, 1139
kalemiyye in, 1264
in Konya, Battle of (1832), 1333
Kuwait alliance with, 158, 160, 161
land ownership in, 1370–1371
after Land Code of 1858, 1367–1369
before Land Code of 1858, 1367
of *shaykh*, 1368, 1369
land registration in, 1367, 1368
languages in, 1731
Ladino, 1363
translation by dragomans of, 723
Turkish, 577, 1731
law code of Mecelle in, 988
Lebanon in, 1397–1398, 1401
Beyoglu Protocol (1861) and, 469
crises of 1840s, 1393–1394
under Da'ud Pasha, 680
mutasarrif system in, 1394, 1398
under Qiyomijian (Ohannes), 1880
subgovernorates in, 1394
legal system of, 2034
family code, 2035
Majalla, 1381
qanun in, 1870
reforms in, 954–955, 1381, 2034–2035
Libya in, 1410–1411, 2246–2247
Benghazi, 446
literature of, 434, 1404, 1438–1439, 1962–1963, 2068–2069, 2439
New Literature School and, 1909
at London Convention (1840), 1444, 1602, 2093
malaria in, 115
mandates for former territories of, 1479–1480
middle class in, 2240
military of (*See* Ottoman military)
millet system of (*See* Millet system)
modernization of
under Mahmud II, 1466–1467
Mustafa Reşid in, 1623–1624
music of, 2160
natural resources of, 1729
newspapers and print media in, 1684–1685
newspapers in, 409
non-Muslim groups in (*See* Millet system)
Osman dynasty in, 1728
Ottomanism in, 1737
Palestine in, *1733*, 1759–1761
Bethlehem, 468
courts in, 2124
Land Code of 1858 effects, 1368, 1369
land ownership in, 1371
Yishuv in, 2400–2402
Palestinians in, 1789
pan-Turkism in, 1800
parliament of, **1742**
elections to, 1737, 1742, 2409
organization of, 1742
reinstatement of, 28
suspension of, 27, 1742
plague in, 710
population censuses in, 1848
postage stamps of, 1849, *1849*, 1850
Qatar in, 1876
railways in, 28, 207, 464–465, 2206
Reform Decree in (1856), 1544
reform in (*See* Tanzimat era)
religion in, 1731
rise of, 1728
rivals of, 1087–1088
in 19th century, 2239–2240
Russian relations with, 25 (*See also* Russian–Ottoman wars)
Hunkar-Iskelesi Treaty (1833), 1050, 2093
in Syrian War (1831–1833), 2093
Sanusi order in, 1990
prosperity of, 1411
Saudi Arabia in, 1999
Sinai Peninsula in, 2068
slave trade in, 2072–2074
abolition of, 2074
during Tanzimat era, 2073–2074
Spanish rivalry, 2084
sultans in, 2120
power of, 1732
Sunni Islam in, 1147, 2123
Syria in, 936, *1733*, 2132
Aleppo, 111–112
Damascus, 663
Egyptian claim to, 1466
Land Code of 1858 effects, 1368–1369, 2132
land ownership in, 1371
Muhammad Ali invading, 2093
petition for independence of, 2202
in Syrian War (1831–1833), 740–741, 2093
in Syrian War (1839), 740–741, 2093
taxes in (*See* Taxes, in Ottoman Empire)
tax farming in, 1367, 2167–2168
tekkes in, 2171
territories of
Balkan wars (1912-1913) and, 384
Berlin Treaty (1878) and, 382–383, 465, 528, 1989

Eastern Question on, 738–743
Edirne Treaty (1713) and, 739
Jassy Treaty (1792) and, 739
Karlowitz Treaty (1699) and, 739
Kuçuk Kaynara Treaty (1774) and, 485, 739, 2094–2095
San Stefano Treaty (1878) and, 382, 1988–1989
in seventeenth century, 738
after World War I, 511
territory of, 1087, 1728
textile industry in, 2066
theater in, 72, 1277, 1724, 2068–2069
theater of, 1438
timar system in, 1367, 2190
trade in
Balta Liman, Convention of (1838) and, 385, 2163
with Britain, 525–526, 742
Bursa, 547
during Tanzimat era, 2163
Tunisia in, 2228–2229
Turkish nationalism in, Akçura (Yusuf) on, 97
in Turko–Iranian War, 2252
waqf in, 1368
Westernization of, 1732–1733, 1735, 2341
Young Ottomans opposition to, 2405–2407
women in
rights movement for, 148
as writers, 1440
in World War I, 742, 905, 2240, 2365–2368
Bursa, 547
Gallipoli campaign, 509, 866, 905
Kemalism, 823
Lausanne Treaty (1923) and, 514, 743, 1376–1377
military successes of, 1527
Mudros Armistice in, 90, 2367, 2368
Paris peace conference (1919) and, 511, 1441
Sèvres Treaty (1920) and, 512, 1376, 2014–2015
Sivas Conference (1919) and, 2071
Yemen in, 2390
pre-World War I revolt against, 2377–2378, 2391
San'a, 1983
Young Turks in (*See* Young Turks)
Ottoman Family Law (1917), 1382
Ottoman Freedom Society, Atatürk (Mustafa Kemal) in, 331
Ottoman–German convention (1914), 534
Ottoman Imperial Bank, 390, 740
Ottomanism, **1737**
vs. Turkism, 1800
of Young Turks, 1737, 2410
Ottoman Land Code of 1858. *See* Land Code of 1858
Ottoman Law of Family Rights (1917), 2035
Ottoman Liberal Union Party, **1737**
Committee for Union and Progress opposed by, 1737, 2409
establishment of, 1737
platform of, 1737
Ottoman Liberty and Entente party, 2409
suppression of, by Cemal Paşa, 571
Ottoman Liberty Society, 778
Ottoman military, 1527, **1737–1741**. *See also* Janissaries
under Abdülaziz, 24–25, 1738–1739
army of, **1737–1739**, *1738*
al-Ahd society in, 81
and Armenian genocide, 294
Cemal Paşa in, 571
at Gallipoli, 1527
Mansure, 1481
in World War I, 1527
German advisers in, 903, 904, 905
German training of, 1563
under Mahmud II, 1466–1467
navy of, **1739–1741**
surrendered to Egypt, 33, 1741
Nizam-i Cedit in, 1217
reform of, 417, 2162
under Selim III, 2009–2010
tax paid by non-Muslims for exemption from (*See Bedel-i askeri*)
as training for Arab leaders, 1527
Yildirim Army in, 2400
Ottoman Military College (Istanbul), Sabbagh (Salah al-Din al-) at, 1953
Ottoman Public Debt Administration, 27, 614, 1736
Ottoman Revival architecture, 282, 1285
Ottoman Turkish language. *See under* Turkish language
Ottoman Union Society, 622–623. *See also* Committee for Union and Progress
Ouali, Mustapha Sayed al-, in POLISARIO, 1837
Oualladi, Abdellah, in Organisation Marocaine des Droits de l'Homme, 1716
Ouary, Malek, **1743**
Ouazzani, Mohamed Hassan, **1743, 2336**
in Bloc d' Action Nationale, 2336
in Comité d'Action Marocaine, 618, 1743, 2336
imprisonment of, 619, 1743, 2336
in Parti Démocratique Constitutionnel, 619, 1743, 1803, 2336
in Parti Démocratique de l'Indépendance, 1804
Ouchy, Treaty of (1912), 2127
Oufkir, Muhammad, **1743**
involved in murder of Ben Barka (Mehdi), 441
Oujda (Morocco), 1567
Oujda Group, **1743–1744**
Ould Haidallah, Mohamed Khouna, coup against (1984), 1744
Ould Hamida, Benthami, in Young Algerians, 2405
Ould Sid'Ahmed Taya, Ma'ouiya, 1503, **1744–1745**
coup led by (1984), 1744
election of, 1744
presidency of, 1744–1745
Ouled Sidi Cheikh, **1745**
Oum al-Rbi'a River, 1567
Oumlil, Ali, in Organisation Marocaine des Droits de l'Homme, 1716
Oumma (Algeria), 450
Outremer (overseas), 1522
Ouyahia, Ahmed, 1904
Ouziel, Ben Zion Meir Hai, **1745**
Overfishing, 834
Oweiss, Ibrahim M., *as contributor,* 538–539
Owen, Roger, 1036, 2162
Oxford University
Basma bint Talal at, 409
Burton (Richard Francis) at, 548
Samuel (Herbert Louis) at, 1983
OYAK (Ordu Yardimlasma Kurumu), **1745–1746**

Özal, Turgut, *1746,* **1746–1747**
death of, 692, 1747, 2219
Demirel (Süleyman) and, 692, 1584, 1746, 1747
as deputy prime minister, 1746
in Keban Dam project, 1284
in Motherland Party, 1583–1584
presidency of, 1747, 2241–2242, 2244
as prime minister, 1746–1747
at State Planning Organization, 1746
Oz, Amos, 1164, 1433, **1747–1748**
Ozanian, Andranik. *See* Andranik Ozanian
Ozpetek, Ferzan, 832
Oz ve Shalom (Netivot Shalom), **1748–1749**
establishment of, 1748
objectives of, 1748

P

PA. *See* Palestinian Authority
Pachachi, Adnan, 1751
on Iraqi Governing Council, 2325–2326
Pachachi, Muzahim al-, **1751**
Pact of Alliance. *See* Sened-i Ittafak
Pact of the League of Arab States, 1385
Padishah, 2120
Pages from the Calendar (Ben-Aharon), 438
Pagis, Dan, 1432–1433, **1751–1752**
PAGS. *See* Parti de l'Avant-Garde Socialiste
Pahlavi, Ashraf (princess of Iran), women's rights supported by, 2358
Pahlavi Foundation, 2037
Pahlavi Guards Cavalry Regiment, Arfa (Hasan) in, 286
Pahlavi language
alphabet of, 1124, 1821
Zoroastrian texts written in, 1124, 2441
Pahlavi, Mohammad Reza (shah of Iran), *1658,* **1752–1755,** *1753, 1754*
accession of, foreign intervention in, 1118, 1752
administrative policies under, 2420
Algiers Agreement (1975) signed by, 2043
Allies installing, 2370
archaeology under, 277
assassination of, attempted, 1118, 1752
Kashani (Abu al-Qasem) in, 1277
autocratic rule by, 1119, 1753–1754
and Baha'i persecution, 365
Bakhtiar (Shapur) opposing, 375
Bakhtiar (Timur) opposing, 375
Bakhtiar (Timur) supporting, 375
bazaars under, 420
Beheshti (Mohammad) against, 428
Borujerdi (Hosayn) opposing, 494
and censorship, 1436
character flaws of, 1754–1755
children of, 1752
after coup (1953)
increased power of, 1118, 1752–1753
reinstatement of, 1752
coup reinstalling (1953), 1655–1656
death of, 707, 1754
demonstrations against (1963), 1119, 1753
demonstrations against (1978), 1126
educational policies of, 760, 761
in exile, 707, 1119, 1126, 1752, 1754
foreign relations under, 1119, 1753
Freedom Movement leaders imprisoned by, 850
government of
Alam (Amir Asadollah) in, 102, 1753
Amini (Ali) in, 186, 1118, 1753
Arfa (Hasan) in, 286
Arsanjani (Hassan) in, 1118, 1753
Soheyli (Ali) in, 2078
Hoveyda (Amir Abbas) and, 1047
human rights under, 622
Iran hostage crisis and, 1046
in Iranian Revolution (1979), 1125–1126
actions leading to, 1125
fall of, 1125, 1311
response to uprisings by, 1126
Iran Novin Party created by, 1129
Khomeini (Ruhollah) opposing, 1125–1126, 1310–1311
Khomeini's (Ruhollah) criticism of, 1606
Kurdish revolts in Iraq supported by, 1127
land deeds granted by, *1371*
land reforms of, 1753
majles power over, 1118, 1752
Mossadegh (Mohammad) power struggle with, 1118, 1752
and National Front, 1655–1656
newspapers and print media under, 1682
oil pricing strategy under, 1719, 1753
oil production under, 1825
opposition to
Mardom Party and appearance of, 1487
Mojahedin-e Khalq in, 1562
Nabavi (Behzad) in, 1630
Rafsanjani (Ali Akbar Hashemi) and, 1898–1899
University of Tehran and, 2296
overthrow of, 2293
Pakistani relations with, 1758
power of
decline of, 1754–1755
rise of, 1118, 1752–1753
price hikes by, Daftari (Ahmad Matin) opposition to, 660
regime of, as literary theme, 1435, 1436
revolutionary coalition against (*See also* Iranian Revolution)
formation of, 1119, 1754
Shariatmadari (Kazem) criticizing, 2036
during Soviet occupation, 1752
student activists opposing, 630–631
Students in the Line of the Imam demanding U.S. extradition of, 2096
traditional supporters of, 1119, 1753–1754
ulama opposing, 2259
and University of Tehran, 2296
and urban planning, 2299
U.S. support for, 996, 1937
and *velayat-e faqih* (governance of jurists), 2312
Western support for, 1118, 1752
White Revolution of, 2351–2352
wives of, 707, 1752
Pahlavi, Reza (crown prince of Iran), 1752
Pahlavi, Reza (shah of Iran), **1755–1757**
abdication by, forced, 1118, 1752, 1757
accession of, 1756
Allies removing, 2143, 2370

Anglo–Iranian Agreement nullified by, 200
and architecture, 282
Arfa (Hasan) and, 285–286
as army commander, 1755
Cossack Brigade under, 643
army reforms of, 1756
and Baha'i persecution, 365
Baraheni (Reza) opposing, 397
Bayat (Mortaza Qoli) under, 417
British support for, 1755
and censorship, 1436
character flaws of, 1756–1757
communist movement and, 41, 626
in Cossack Brigade, 643, 1755
in coup (1921), 88, 1118, 1755, 1869
Cossack Brigade in, 643
coup led by (1921), 1580, 2143
death of, 1757
Dowleh (Nosrat al-) executed by, 809
educational policies of, 760, 1756
as elite, 776
government of
Ala (Hoseyn) in, 100–101
Alam (Amir Asadollah) in, 102
Arfa (Hasan) in, 286
Daftari (Ahmad Matin) in, 660
Dashti (Ali) in, 678
Millspaugh (Arthur) as financial adviser to, 1546
Tabataba'i (Ziya) in, 1110
guilds under, 947
Islah Taleban Party supporting, 1144
Jangalis destroyed by, 1216
Khaz'al Khan arrested by, 1307
Kurdish revolts against, 1340
legal reforms of, 1756
as minister of war, 88
modernization by, 1756
nationalism of, 1659–1660
newspapers and print media under, 1682
oil concession under, to Anglo–Iranian Oil Company, 202
opposition to, Mossadegh (Mohammad) in, 1580–1581
as prime minister, 88, 1755
pro-German sympathies of, 906
Qajar dynasty ended by, 1869, 2143
regime of
Eqbal (Manouchehr) in, 779
as literary theme, 1435, 1436
Luri tribes during, 1447
Tabataba'i (Ziya) denouncing, 2143
secularization by, 1756
South Persia Rifles disbanded by, 2083
state feminism under, 892
surname chosen by, 1659–1660
Tabataba'i (Ziya) and, 1682
Tehran developing under, 2170
and theater, 2186
Trans-Iranian railway commissioned by, 2203
tribal opposition to, 1756
tribal policy of, 374
U.S. support for
CIA in, 572
Dulles (John Foster) in, 733
veiling banned by, 891
Vozuq al-Dowleh (Mirza Hasan Khan) under, 2318
Westernization by, 1118
Pahlavi, Shahnaz, 1752
Pahlavi University (Shiraz). *See also* Shiraz University
Alam (Amir Asadollah) at, 102
PAI. *See* Po'alei Agudat Israel
Paicovitch, Yigal. *See* Allon, Yigal
Pakhtun. *See* Pushtun
Pakistan, **1757–1758**
Afghani conflict with, United Nations in, 2279–2280
Afghan refugees in, 1912
Afghan Women's Council in, 68
in Baghdad Pact (1955), 363, 519, 1693, 2291
Baluchis in, 385–386
at Bandung Conference, 387
bin Ladin in, 474, 1865
border with Afghanistan
as Durand Line, 400, 536, 734
pass between, 1317
in Central Treaty Organization, 573
establishment of state (1947)
Iqbal (Muhammad) in, 1109
Jinnah (Muhammad Ali) in, 1236, 1237
guest workers from, 946
in Gulf War (1990–1991), 1758
India conflict over Kashmir, nuclear threat in, 1696
Iranian alliance with, 1758
Iran's border with, 2420
Islamic state in, Mawdudi (Abu al-a'la, al-) as advocate of, 1503–1504
Jami'at-e Islami headquarters in, 1215
languages in, Iranian, 1124–1125
Middle East policy of, 1757–1758
military of, 1758
mountains of, 1799
pass through, 1317
Muharram rites in, 1606
in Northern Tier, 1692–1693
nuclear capability of, 1696
as "Islamic bomb," 1696
technology shared by, 1696
Palestinians supported by, 1758
Saudi relations with, 1758
Shi'ism in, 2052
Sunni Islam in, 2123
Taliban supported by, 64
in trade, with Tunisia, 2269
tribes in, 385–386
turbans in, 609
women in
as head of state, 808, 875
religious rituals of, 2360
workers from, 1758
Zoroastrianism in, 2441, 2442
Pakistan Resolution (1942), 1237
Pakradouni, Karim, in Phalange party, 1831
Palestine, **1758–1769**. *See also* Arab–Israel conflict; *specific cities, organizations, people, and regions*
before 20th century, 1758–1761
agriculture in, 1760
All-Palestine Government proposed for, 154–156, 1030
Anglo–American Committee of Inquiry on (1946), 198–199
antisemitism in, 212
archaeology in, 275–276, 277
art of, 1007–1008, 2044
banking in, Levontin (Zalman) and, 1408
at Bludan Conference (1937), 488
borders of
1949, *1760*
2000, *1768*
under British mandate, 1758, *1762*
Jews and Christians on, 1758
British administration and mandate in (1917–1948), 512, 514, 614, 616, 1441, 1480, 1761–1767
Abd al-Hadi family in, 13
advisory council during, 50, 1762
Allenby (Edmund Henry) in, 151, 1761

Palestine *(continued)*
anti-Zionism in, 1761–1762, 1763
anti-Zionist violence during, 1011
Antonius (George) in, 213
Arabs in, 222, 1763, 1789–1790
Balfour Declaration in (1917), 538, 614, 743, 1763, 1802
Bethlehem, 468
Bevin (Ernest) in, 647
binationalism in, 473
Churchill (Winston S.) and, 595–597
Churchill White Paper on (1922), 594
collapse of, 517–518
Colonial Office administration of, 514, 518, 617
Creech Jones (Arthur) in, 647
dual obligation of, 1763
education in, 1294
emergency regulations issued in, 776–777
Galilee in, 865
Galilee Sea in, 865
Gaza City, 869
government system of, 1761, 1762–1763
Haifa during, 974
Hebrew literature in, 1431–1432
Hebrew name for, 781
high commissioner of, 1762
High Commissioners during, 1025
Hilmi (Ahmad) during, 1030–1031
Histadrut during, 1033
Hope-Simpson Commission during, 1044–1045
Husayni (Muhammad Amin al-) during, 1056–1057
Husayni (Musa Kazim al-) during, 1058–1059
al-Husayni family during, 1053
imperialism of, 1090
Irgun Zvaʾi Leʾumi revolt against, 1139–1140
Jewish forces armed by, 1770, 1790
Jewish immigration to, 1057, 1361
Jewish political organization in, 1764
Jewish sports organizations in, 1453
Kisch (Frederick Hermann) in, 1326
legislative council, 1402
legislative council during, 50, 1762–1763
London Conference (1939) on future of, 1445
MacMichael (Harold) on, 1455
map of, *1762*
Nashashibi family in, 1644–1645
Palestinian Arab Congress opposition to, 1782–1783
Palestinian political organization in, 1761–1762, 1764–1765
Palin Commission report on (1920), 1794–1795
Pan-Arabism in, 1799
Plumer (Herbert Charles Onslow) in, 1836
population growth during, 1763–1764
Qassam (Izz al-Din al-) against, 1874
restrictions to Jewish immigration under, 1045
revolt during (*See* Palestine Arab Revolt)
Richmond (Ernest T.) in, 1922
riots in, 512, 1763
rivalries during, intercommunal, 1763–1764
Saison in, 1972–1973
San Remo Conference (1920) on, 1988
self-government in, failure of, 1762–1763
Sèvres Treaty (1920) on, 2015
Special Night Squads during, 972
Supreme Muslim Council in, 2124–2125
Sykes-Picot Agreement (1916) on, 2128
termination of, UNSCOP support for, 2289
Transjordan Frontier Force defending, 2204
under Wauchope (Arthur), 2333
Weizmann (Chaim) and, 2338
Yishuv during, 1454, 1763–1764, 2402–2403
and Zionist movement, 2436, 2438
Zionist Revisionist Movement's policy regarding, 2438
British policy regarding
in Churchill White Paper (1922), 2349–2350
MacDonald Letter on (1931), 1454, 2350
in MacDonald White Paper (1939), 1454, 2350–2351, 2363
in Passfield White Paper (1930), 1453, 2350
white papers on, 2349–2351
Woodhead Commission (1938) on, 2350, 2363
in Christianity, 1758
civil administration in, temporary, 154
climate of, 1758
communism in, 626
constitution of (1988), 1966
cotton industry in, *2181*
dance in, 668
disease in, 714
Druze in, 729
economy of
19th-century, 1760
expansion of, 1789
education in, in religious schools, 761
fidaʾiyyun in, 831, 2176
film industry of, 833
flight and expulsion of Palestinians from (*See* Nakba, al-)
folk poems of, Hebrew translation of, 2418
Greeks in, 938
guest workers from, 946
higher education in, 1901
at Arab College of Jerusalem, 226–227
at Bir Zeit University, 481
as Holy Land of Bible, 1758
human rights organizations in, 991
hydroelectrification of, 1946
independence of, 801
in Islam, 1758
Israeli settlements in, Tel Hai, 2172–2173
Israeli statehood and status of, 1767
Jewish community in (*See* Yishuv)
Jewish immigration to, 2171 (*See also Aliyah*)
Anglo–American Committee of Inquiry on (1946), 198–199
Balfour Declaration (1917) on, 381, 614, 803, 1223, 1402
British limits on, 1011
by children through Youth Aliyah, 2411
Churchill White Paper (1922) on, 2350
Faisal–Weizmann Agreements on, 800, 803

financial support for *(halukka)*, 980
Germany opposing, 906
Hope-Simpson Commission (1930) on, 2350
Labor Zionism and, 1360–1362
London Conference (1939) on, 1445
as long-term causes of Nakba, al-, 1639
MacDonald (Ramsay) Letter on (1931), 1454
MacDonald (Malcolm) White Paper on (1939), 1454, 2350–2351
MacMichael (Harold) on, 1455
Mohilever (Samuel) and, 1560
Morrison–Grady Plan for (1946), 1576
Nazi rise to power and, 1041
Palestinian opposition to, 235, 1790
Passfield White Paper on (1930), 2350
Roosevelt (Franklin Delano) policy on, 1936
Ruppin (Arthur) and, 1940
from Russia and Eastern Europe, 508–509, 1361
Shaw Commission on, 2044
white papers on Palestine on (1939), 1766
Young Turk Revolution and, 1940
Zionist Revisionist Movement and, 2437
Johnson–Crosbie Committee Report on (1930), 1238
in Judaism, 1758
King–Crane Commission on (1919), 1323
Labor Zionism in, 1357, 1360–1362
Land Day in, as answer to Israeli confiscation of Arab land, 1369
in League of Arab States, 1385, 1388
legal system of, 886
literature of, 357–358, 1973, 2029, 2233, 2234, 2242
Maccabean Pilgrimage to, 2424
Morrison–Grady Plan (1946) for, 1576
Muhammad Ali's invasion of, 1602
names given to, 1759
newspapers and print media in, 1683–1684
in Ottoman Empire, *1733*, 1759–1761
Bethlehem, 468
courts in, 2124
Land Code of 1858 effects, 1368, 1369
land ownership in, 1371
Yishuv in, 1760, 2400–2402
philanthropy in, 1953
population censuses in, 1848
population growth in, 1763–1764
population of, 1759, 1843, 1845
potash industry in, 1851
Protestant missions in, 1796, 1797
question of, and human rights, 1049
railways in, 2206, *2206*
resistance movement in, leaders of, 1008–1009
rivers of, 1758
Templars in, 904, 2173
textile industry in, *2181*
theater in, 2184
tourism in, 2196
in trade, 2198
UN partition plan for (1947)
Holocaust and, 1042
Roosevelt (Eleanor) and, 1935
Stalin (Joseph) support for, 1943
water resources of, quantity of, 2330
women in
activists and leaders, 1556–1557, 1648
as artists, 2044
organizations for, 227–228, 267, 268, 1629
in politics, 893, 899, 2051–2052
as writers, 357–358, 2233, 2234
in World War I, 2366
British-Ottoman fighting in, 509–510
in World War II, 2371
Palestine and Transjordan (weekly), 917
Palestine Arab Executive. *See* Arab Executive
Palestine Arab Party, 1764–1765
establishment of, 1764
Ghuri (Emile al-) in, 917
Husayni (Jamal al-) in, 1055
leadership of, 1765
"national demands" of, 1765
in Palestine Arab Revolt (1936–1939), 1765
revival of, 1766
Palestine Arab Revolt (1936–1939), 1454, **1769–1771**
Arab Higher Committee in, 1765–1766, 1770
British and Zionist forces suppressing, 381, 515
British authority opposed in, 515
British forces suppressing, 236, 1766, 1770, 1771, 1790
British policy impacted by, 1770
casualties of, 1766, 1770, 1790
causes of, 235, 1770, 1790
communism during, 626
Darwaza (Muhammad Izzat) in, 673
economic impact of, 1770
emergency regulations issued during, 777
end of, 236, 1766, 1771
failure of, 1770
general strike in, 1765, 1770
Husayni (Abd al-Qadir al-) in, 1052
Husayni (Amin al-) in, 1057
Husayni (Da'ud al-) in, 1054
internal conflict in, 1766
Istiqlal Party (Syria) supporting, 1199
Jerusalem occupied during, 1224
military resources in, 1770
Muslim Brotherhood supporting, 1620–1621
opposition to, Nashashibi (Fakhri) in, 1645
Palestinian leadership drained by, 1766, 1770
partition plan rejected during, 236, 1766, 1790
start of, 1765, 1770
attacks against Jews in, 1874
Wauchope (Arthur) in, 2333
Wavell (Archibald Percival) in, 2334
Wingate (Charles Orde) in, 2353
Palestine Arab Women's Congress (1929), 13
Arab Women's Association of Palestine founded at, 267
Shihabi (Zlikha al-) at, 2051
Palestine Broadcasting Service, 1896
Palestine Communist Organization, in Intifada (1987–1991), 1108
Palestine Communist Party, Habibi (Emile) in, 963
Palestine Conciliation Commission, 466
Palestine Diary (Kisch), 1326
Palestine Economic Corporation, **1771**
Palestine Electric Corporation, 1946, 2379. *See also* Israel Electric Corporation

Palestine Exploration Fund, **1771–1772**
Palestine Foundation Fund. *See* Keren Hayesod
Palestine Jewish Colonization Association (PICA). *See* Jewish Colonization Association
Palestine Land Development Company (PLDC), 1047, **1772**
Palestine Liberation Army, 814
Palestine Liberation Front (PLF)
establishment of, 1235, 1841
Jibril (Ahmad) in, 1235
in Rejection Front, 1917
revival of, 1841
Palestine Liberation Organization (PLO), **1772–1776**
Abu Nidal opposition to, 252
in Arab boycott against Israel, 224
in Arab–Israel War (1982), 238, 252–254, 259, 270–271, 1166–1167
Arab Liberation Front faction of, 259, 1773
on Arab unity, 1781, 1791
Arafat (Yasir) as leader of, 1767
election of, 270, 1773
on armed struggle, 1776, 1781, 1791
Avnery (Uri) contacts with, 340
at Baghdad Summit (1978), 363, 364
Baker (James A.) meeting leaders of, 374
Banna (Sabri al-) in, 396
Barak (Ehud) leading assassination of leaders of, 398
cease-fire agreement with Israel, Habib (Philip Charles) and, 964
Central Committee of
functions of, 1778
members of, 1778
Chinese recognition of, 587
Darwish (Mahmud) in, 674
diplomatic approach of, 1767–1768, 1774–1775
after Arab–Israel War (1973), 1792
Intifada and, 1792
Egyptian relations with, under Mubarak (Husni), 1593–1594
establishment of, 1767, 1772, 1777, 1791
Executive Committee of
establishment of, 1772
PNC election of, 1772, 1778
and al-Fatah, 813, *813*, 814, 1773
and fida'iyyun, 831, 2176
formation of, 813, 2062
Free Lebanon Militia fighting, 2083
General Union of Palestinian Women's Committees under, 893, 899
goal of, 2062
statehood as, 1775, 1791
groups within, 1773–1774
criticism of PLO by, 1773
lack of coordination among, 1773–1774
guerrilla factions in, 237, 1972
power of, 1772–1773
in Gulf Crisis (1990–1991), 951
on Gulf Crisis (1990–1991), 1775, 1792–1793
Haifa–Tel Aviv highway assault by, 1417
and HAMAS, 983
Hammuda (Yahya) as leader of, 1772
Hasan (Khalid al-) in, 814, 998
Hawatma (Nayif) influence on, 1008, 1009
Husayni (Da'ud al-) in, 1054
Hussein ibn Talal relations with, 1063, 2156
Hut (Shafiq al-) in, 1071
institutional organizations of, 1774
international recognition of, 587, 1774
in Intifada, 2177
coordination of, 661
and diplomatic efforts, 1792
Islamic Jihad and, 1155
Israel aiming to destroy, 426, 2176
Israeli cease-fire with (1981), 252, 1166
Israeli mutual recognition with, 271, 1167, 1725–1726, 1775
Israeli negotiations with, 2177–2178
Weizman (Ezer) calling for, 2337
Israeli recognition of, 928
Israel proclaiming as terrorist group, 2176
Jericho under, 1221, 1726
and Jerusalem, 1226
Jerusalem Award for Culture and Arts of, awarded to Tuqan (Fadwa), 2233
in Jordan, expulsion after PFLP airplane hijackings (1970), 270
in Jordanian Civil War, 1008, 1246–1247, 1773
Jordanian peace accord with, 1247
after Karama, Battle of (1968), 1271
Khalaf (Salah) in, 814, 1292, 2335
League of Arab States and, 813, *1387*, 1388
League of Arab States recognition of, 1774
Lebanese agreement with (1969), 1653
Lebanese Arab Army supported by, 1389
in Lebanese Civil War (1975–1990), 270, 1774, 2083
AMAL rivalry with, 174
Shi'ite support for, 174
in Lebanon, 1774, 2176
in Arab–Israel War (1982), 238, 252–254
in Beirut, 429–430
in civil war (1975–1990), 1391–1393, 1395, 1400, 2156
Franjiyya (Sulayman) opposing, 850, 1400
setbacks for, 1774
at Madrid Conference (1991), 1458–1459
Matzpen and, 1500
members of, 2062
Muhsin (Zuhayr) in, 1607
vs. Muslim Brotherhood, 983
Nashashibi (Muhammad Zuhdi) in, 1645
Nasir (Hanna) in, 1646
Nasser (Gamal Abdel) and, 1767
as national liberation movement, 2176
in Oslo Accord, 1724–1727
in Oslo II Interim Agreement (1995), 1726, 1775, 1784
Palestinian Authority eclipsing, 1775
Palestinian rights campaign by, 1767–1768
parliament of (*See* Palestine National Council)
PFLP–GC opposition to, 1235, 1841–1842
PFLP in, 1773, 1840
Qaddumi (Faruq) in, 814, 1863

Qurai (Ahmad Sulayman) in, 1881–1882
vs. Rejection Front, 1917
Sartawi (Issam) in, 1992–1993
as security force *vs.* terrorist group, 1104
on self-determination, 1776, 1781
Sharon (Ariel) destroying infrastructure of, 2042
shifting toward peace initiative, 1953
Shuqayri (Ahmad) as leader of, 814, 1767, 1772, 1791, 2062
Soviet recognition of, 1943
Soviet Union supporting, 2176
strategy of, Khalidi (Walid) influence on, 1296
Sumud Fund by, 2121
Syrian attempts to control, 1774
Syria opposing, Tlas (Mustafa) and, 2192
at Tripoli Conference, 2217
in Tunisia, 2177
Bourguiba (Habib) and, 503
two-state solution supported by, 1774
U.S. relations with
under Bush (George H.W.), 548
CIA in, 572–573
opening of dialogue in, 271, 1768, 1774
Vatican relations with, 2310
Wazir (Khalil al-) in, 814, 2334–2336
Palestine Martyrs Works Society (SAMED), 1774
Palestine National Charter (1968), 814, **1776**
amendment of, 1772, 1773, 1776
DOP superseding, 1776
Fundamental Law in, 1777
Palestinian Authority eclipsing, 1779
principles of, 1776
armed struggle in, 1776, 1791
elimination of Israel in, 1772, 1775, 1776
restoration of Palestine in, 1772, 1773
self-determination in, 1776
sovereignty in, 1776
Palestine National Council (PNC), 814, **1776–1781,** *1777*
in All-Palestine Government, 155
Clinton (Bill) address to, 606
diversity in membership of, 1774, 1778
election to, process for, 1777, 1778
establishment of, 1777
Executive Committee elected by, 1772, 1778
al-Fatah in, rise of, 270
functions of, 1776, 1777
goals of, 1772
moderation of, 1774
guerrilla control of, 1778
HAMAS and, 983
Hut (Shafiq al-) in, 1070
Khaled (Leila) in, 1293
leadership of, 1778
limitations of, 1779
Palestinian independence declared by (1988), 1768, 1774, 1779–1780
resolutions by, summary of, 1779–1780
Sabbagh (Hasib) in, 1953
Said (Edward) in, 1966
sessions of
list of, 1779–1780
regulations for, 1777, 1778
Shuqayri (Ahmad) in, 2062
size of, 1778
UN Resolution 242 endorsed by, 1768, 1792
voting practices of, 1778
Wazir (Khalil al-) on, 2335, *2335*
Palestine National Covenant (1964), **1781**
adoption by Palestine National Council, 1772, 1781
amendment of, Palestine National Charter produced by (1968), 1776, 1781
principles of, 1781
Arab unity in, 1781
Palestine National Liberation Movement. *See* Fatah, al-
Palestine Popular Struggle Front, in Rejection Front, 1917
Palestine Potash Company, 1851
Palestine Prize for Poetry, awarded to Tuqan (Fadwa), 2233
Palestine Research Center, **1781–1782**
Palestine Royal Commission Report (1937), on Vaʿad Leʾumi, 2307
Palestine: Story of a Land (Bitton), 483
Palestine Telecommunications, *625*
Palestine Zionist Executive (PZE). *See also* Zionist Executive
Kisch (Frederick Hermann) in, 1326
Palestinian Arab Club, 800
Palestinian Arab Congresses, **1782–1784**
Arab Executive elected by, 1782, 1783
leadership of, 1764, 1782
Muslim–Christian Association in, 1762–1763
national charter by (1919), 1782
Zionism opposed by, 1782
Palestinian Arab National Party, 402
Nashashibi (Raghib al-) in, 1645
Palestinian Arabs
al-Husayni family as leaders of, 1053–1054
Jordanian relations with, 1063
organizations representing, 228
refugees, *1915,* 1915–1916
U.S. policy on, 1941
Sabra and Shatila massacres of, 1039
Zionist Revisionist Movement on, 2438
Palestinian Authority (PA), **1784–1785**
Abbas (Mahmud) in, 7, 1775, 1785
Arafat (Yasir) as head of, 272, 1775, 1784–1785
no-confidence motion against (1997), 1785
Ashrawi (Hanan al-) in, 893
Barghuthi (Bashir) in, 402
bureaucracy of, 1784–1785
Clinton (Bill) visit with, 606
Dahlan (Muhammad) in, 661
elections for, 1784
establishment of, 1768–1769, 1784
financial reform in, 1793
Gaza Strip controlled by, 1784
and HAMAS, 983
Hasan (Hani al-) in, 997
headquarters of, 869
intelligence agencies of, 1784–1785
as interim governing body, 1769, 1779, 1784
Islamic Jihad and
conflict between, 1155
crackdown on, 1155
Kamal (Zahira) in, 1266
Nabi Musi Pilgrimage organized by, 1630
Nashashibi (Muhammad Zuhdi) in, 1645
in Nazareth conflict, 1673
Oslo Accord (1993) and, 814
Oslo II (1995) and, 1784

Palestinian Authority (PA) *(continued)*
Palestinian opposition to, Qaddumi (Faruq) in, 1863
PLO eclipsed by, 1775, 1779
press control by, *1679*, 1681
prime minister of, creation of position, 7, 220, 1785, 1793
Qurai (Ahmad Sulayman) in, 1775, 1784, 1882
radio and television under, 1896
Rajub (Jibril) in, 1900
in Ramallah, 1901
reform of, 220
representing Palestine in League of Arab States, 1385
security forces of, 1784–1785
under Abbas (Mahmud), 7
Wazir (Intisar al-) in, 2334
in West Bank, 2340–2341
West Bank controlled by, discontinuity of area of, 1784
Women's Centre for Legal Aid and Counseling and, 2357
Palestinian citizens of Israel, 1163, **1785–1788**
after Arab–Israel War (1967), 1787
al-Ard movement among, 284–285
distribution of, 1785, 1786
emergency regulations restricting, 1785
government policy on, 1785, 1786, 1787
opposition to, 1787
in Haifa, 974
human rights of, 1373–1374, 2221
Israeli relations with
mistrust in, 1785–1786
segregation in, 1163
tensions in, 1788
jobs held by, 1786–1787, 1788
in Kafr Qasim, massacre of (1956), 1262
land ownership by, 1786
leaders of, 963
MAPAM support for, 1185
migrant labor by, Eban (Abba) against, 744
military service by, 1786–1787
nationalism among, 1787, 1788
in Nazareth, 1672–45
number of, 1785, 1787, 1789
political parties of, 1178–1180, 1786, 1787
poverty among, 1788
religion of, 1787
Sumud Fund for, 2121
in West Bank, 2339–2341
Palestinian Costumes (Weir), 608
Palestinian Democratic Union (FIDA), 1009
Kamal (Zahira) in, 1266
Palestinian Girl, The (Sobol), 2076
Palestinian Initiative for the Promotion of Global Dialogue and Democracy (MIFTAH), 1953
Palestinian Legislative Council (PLC), Wazir (Intisar al-) on, 2334
Palestinian Liberation Front–Path of Return (PLF–PR), Hut (Shafiq al-) in, 1070
Palestinian Liberation Movement. *See* Fatah, al-
Palestinian National Council, Wazir (Intisar al-) on, 2334
Palestinian National Fund, 1951
Palestinian nationalism
Arab Club promotion of, 225–226
of Darwish (Ishaq), 673
in Jerusalem, 1224
Muslim–Christian Association promotion of, 1761–1762
origins of, 1760–1761
among Palestinian citizens of Israel, 1787, 1788
Palestinian newspapers and print media, *1679*
loyalist approach of, 1681
offshore publishing of, 1681
unique characteristics of, 1681
Palestinian People's Party, Barghuthi (Bashir) in, 402
Palestinian refugees. *See* Refugees, Palestinian
Palestinians, **1788–1794**
Abd al-Hadi family of, 12–13
antisemitism among, 212
Arab states and
dependence of refugees on, 1791
tensions over approaches of, 1792
art of, 1211
folk, 1878–1879
Balfour Declaration (1917) on rights of, 381
under British rule, 1789–1790
societal changes during, 1789–1790
and Camp David Accords (1978), 561
Chinese support for, 587
classes of, societal, 1789
clothing of, *kaffiya* in, 610
culture of, stages of, 1789
definition of, 1788
after Israeli statehood, 236
before Israeli statehood, 1762, 1785
in Palestine National Covenant (1964), 1781
distribution of, 1789, 1791
education of, early childhood, 1488
in exile
distribution of, 1791
Palestinian state as goal of, 1767
folk culture of, 1878–1879
intellectual life of, 1790
al-Isa family of, 1141
as Israeli citizens (*See* Palestinian citizens of Israel)
in Jerusalem
residency status of, 1225, 1226
threats to, 1226
in Jordan, 1241–1242
civil war by, 1246–1247
number of, 1241
in Kuwait, 1793
number of, 1347
persecution of, after Gulf War, 952
Latin Catholicism among, 593
in Lebanon, 1393, 1792
mass killing of, 1792
Phalange conflict with, 1254
literature of, 1297, 1790, 1791, 1792
in occupied territories, number of, 1789
on Oslo Accord, 1726
in Ottoman Empire, 1789
Pakistani support for, 1758
poetry of, 673–675, 1791, 1792
population size of, 1788
radicalization of, 1791–1792
refugees (*See under* Refugees)
religion of, 1788–1789
right of return for, in Camp David Summit (2000), 561–562
rights of
Balfour Declaration (1917) on, 1763
Peace Now defense of, 1809
UN recognition of, 1767–1768
self-determination by
in national charter, 1776, 1781
progress toward, 1793
setbacks in, 1793
women
activists and advocates for, 1556–1557, 1648, 2334

legal aid and counseling for, 2357
organizations for, 2334, 2355, 2356, 2357
status in Israel, 1488
Zionism opposed by, origins of, 1789
Palestinian state
international support for, decline in, 1793
as PLO goal, 1775, 1791
PLO on
borders of, 1767
symbolic declaration of (1988), 1768, 1774, 1779–1780
in two-state solution
PFLP support for, 1840
public support for, 1793
UN support for, 1768
Palestinian Students Fund, 1953
Palestinian Talmud, 2158
Palin Commission report (1920), **1794–1795**, 2349
Palin, P. C., 1794
Palmah (Haganah elite force), **1795–1796**
Allon (Yigal) in, 153, 1795
Amichai (Yehuda) in, 182
British relations with, 1795
creation of, 972
Eitan (Rafael) in, 774
expansion of, 973
Guri (Chaim) in, 956
merged into Israel Defense Force, 1173, 1795–1796
Nahal as continuation of, 1634
Peled (Mattityahu) in, 1811
Rabin (Yitzhak) in, 1891
Shamir (Moshe) in, 2024
Palme, Olof, in Iran–Iraq peace settlement, 2280
Palmer, Sir Elwin, 931
Palmerston, Lord Henry John Temple, **1796–1797**
Asad (Hafiz al-) compared with, 320
and British–Ottoman alliance, 527–528, 530, 740, 1796–1797
and Crimean War, 648
in Damascus affair (1840), 664
delaying Suez Canal building, 528, 741
as foreign secretary, 527, 842, 1796
and international status of Bosporus and Dardanelles, 1444
at London Convention (1840), 2093–2094
and Muhammad Ali, 1346, 2007
and Mustafa Reşid, 1624
as prime minister, 527, 1796
Palmyra (Syria), **1797–1798**, *1798*
Stanhope (Hester) visit to, 275
Pamir mountains, **1799**
Pamuk, Orhan, 1437, *1438*
Panahi, Jafr, 833
Pan Am flight 103 bombing (Lockerbie), 522, 1414
and economic sanctions against Libya, 522, 1414, 1415
Libya failing to extradite defendants in, 522, 1414
Libyan compensation for, 1415, 1862
Libyan role in, Arab Maghreb Union on, 260
PFLP–GC in, 1841
Pan-Arab Feminist Union, 1965
Pan-Arabism, **1799–1800**. *See also* Arab nationalism; League of Arab States
of Aflaq (Michel), 68–69
archaeology and, 276–277
of al-Ard, 284–285
of Azzam (Abd al-Rahman al-), 352
of Bakr (Ahmad Hasan al-), 377
of Bazzaz (Abd al-Rahman al-), 421
of Darwaza (Muhammad Izzat), 673
decline of, 1799–1800
definition of, 1799
and education, 760
of Faisal I ibn Hussein, 800, 802, 824–825
Fertile Crescent unity and, 824–826
Germany supporting, 906
of Ghallab (Abd al-Karim), 910
of Ghanim (Fathi), 911
Hakim (Muhsin al-) reservations about, 977
Husari (Sati al-) conception of, 1051
Islamism supplanting, 1152–1153, 1799–1800
Nabulsi (Sulayman al-) in, 1632
of Nasser (Gamal Abdel), 1799
Nasser (Gamal Abdel) and, 1649, 1650–1651
of National Action League, 2030
vs. nation-state nationalism, 262
Numeiri's (Muhammad Jaʿfar) admiration for, 1699
OPEC and, 824
origins of, 1799
peak of, 1799
of PFLP, 1839
of PLO, 1781, 1791
of Quwatli (Shukri al-), 1885
of Sabbagh (Salah al-Din al-), 1953
of Saʿid (Amina al-), 1965
of Saʿid (Nuri al-), 825–826, 1967
of al-Saʿiqa, 1972
of Sakakini (Khalil al-), 1973
Salafiyya movement and, 1974
of Samman (Ghada), 1982
of Shawqi (Ahmad), 2045
of Shuqayri (Ahmad), 2061
Soviet support for, 517
of Zaydan (Jurji), 2426–2427
Paniagua, Valentín, 1818
Pan-Islamism
of Afghani (Jamal al-Din al-), 52, 2302
of Azzam (Abd al-Rahman al-), 352
Islamic congress promoting, 1152–1153
of Kuchek Khan-e Jangali, 1337
Panjah-o-seh nafar (Alavi), 104
Pan-Syrianism. *See* Syrian Social Nationalist Party
Panther (German gunboat), 70
Pan-Turanism, 1800, 2253
Pan-Turkism, **1800–1801**
of Akçura (Yusuf), 97, 1800
origins of, 1800
Papaver somniferum. See Opium
Papen, Franz von, 905
Paper trade, 2198
Pappé, Ilan, 1037
Paradise Lost (Milton), Armenian translation of, 144
Parallels and Paradoxes: Explorations in Music and Society (Said and Barenboim), 1966
Para Meselesi (Kasap), 1277
Paramilitary organizations, 1535
Para-statal foundations, in Iran, 1120
Parcham (Afghanistan), **1801**, 1813
collapse of government, 1801
in coup (1973), 57
in coup (1978), 1801, 1813
in coup (1979), 1801
Daud (Muhammad) and, 57, 58, 61, 679

Parcham (Afghanistan) *(continued)*
establishment of, 62, 1801
Karmal (Babrak) in, 62, 1274, 1801, 1813
Khyber (Mir Akbar) in, 1317
Najibullah (Mohammed) in, 1638
rivalry with Khalq faction, 58, 62, 1801
Soviet support for, 58, 1801
Parcham (newspaper), 1801
Khyber (Mir Akbar) in, 1317
Pardes, Ha- (Tammuz), 2159
Pareto, V., 774
Pariente, Moses, 389
Paris (France)
Delouvrier (Paul) and, 689
United Nations Conciliation Commission for Palestine meeting in (1951), 2285
Young Turks conference in (1902), 2409
Paris Conservatory, 476
Paris Peace (1856), 649, 1446
Islahat Fermani of Abdülmecit I reinforcing, 740
San Stefano Treaty (1878) infringing upon, 382
Paris Peace Conference (1919)
Mardam (Jamil) at, 1486
Nubar (Boghos) at, 1694
Weizmann (Chaim) at, 2338
Wilson (Woodrow) at, 2353
Wise (Stephen S.) at, 2354
Paris peace settlements (1918–1923), 511, **1801–1802**. *See also* Lausanne, Treaty of (1923); San Remo Conference (1920); Sèvres, Treaty of (1920)
British delegation at, 511, 1802
Allenby (Edmund Henry) in, 151
Egyptian nationalist case at, 2419
Faisal I ibn Hussein at, 511
French delegation at, 1802
Clemenceau (Georges) in, 603
geographic impact of, 1801–1802
Hijaz delegation at, 511, 2314
Iranian delegation at, Ala (Hoseyn) in, 100
Lawrence (T. E.) at, 511
on Libya, 2218
Lloyd George (David) at, 1441
mandate system in, 1802, 2314, 2315
political impact of, 1801–1802
Sèvres Treaty (1920) in, 2014–2015
Sokolow (Nahum) at, 2078
U.S. delegation at, Jewish community in, 177–178
Versailles Treaty in, 2314–2315
Weizmann (Chaim) at, 511
Zionists at, 511
Paris, Treaty of (1857), **1802**, 1945–1946
Palmerston (Lord) in, 1797
terms of, 204, 1802
Parla, Taha, *as contributor,* 923–925, 1285–1288
Parle mon fils, parle à ta mère (Sebbar), 2007
Parliamentary democracy, 932
Parliamentary Democratic Front (Lebanon), **1802**
Parsipur, Shahrnush, 1436, **1802–1803**
Parsis (Parsees), 2440
Parthian language, 1124
Parti Communiste Tunisien (PCT) (Tunisia), 2232
Parti de la Justice et du Developpement (PJD) (Morocco), 1575
Parti de la Révolution Socialiste (PRS) (Algeria), Boudiaf (Mohamed) in, 496
Parti de l'Avant-Garde Socialiste (PAGS) (Algeria), **1803**
Parti Démocrate Progressiste (PDP) (Tunisia), 2231, 2232
Parti Démocratique Constitutionnel (PDC) (Morocco), **1803–1804**
establishment of, 619, 1743, 1803
Ouazzani (Mohamed Hassan) in, 619, 1743, 1803, 2336
Parti Démocratique de l'Indépendance and, 1803, 1804
Parti Démocratique de l'Indépendance (PDI) (Morocco), **1804**
electoral success of, 1804
Parti Démocratique Constitutionnel and, 1803, 1804
Parti des Indépendants Démocrates. *See* Parti National Démocratique
Parti d'Unité Populaire (PUP) (Tunisia), 452, 1587, **1804**, 2231, 2232
Parti du Peuple Algérien (PPA), **1804–1805**
Ait Ahmed (Hocine) in, 95
Bellounis (Muhammad) in, 438
Ben Bella (Ahmed) in, 441
Ben Khedda (Ben Youssef) in, 450
Ben M'hidi (Muhammad Larbi) in, 450
Boumédienne (Houari) in, 498
government ban on, 1804
Hadj (Messali al-) in, 969, 1589
Khider (Mohamed) in, 1309
Krim (Belkacem) in, 1336
Lahouel (Hocine) in, 1365
as Star of North Africa successor, 2089
underground activities of, 1804–1805
Parti du Progres et du Socialisme (PPS) (Morocco), 1574
Parties Law (1977) (Egypt), 1957
Parti National (Morocco), **1805**
establishment of, 619, 1805
French crackdown on, 1805
platform of, 1805
reestablished as Istiqlal Party, 1196, 1805
Parti National Démocratique (PND) (Morocco), 1574–1575, **1805**
electoral success of, 1805
establishment of, 1805
formation of, 1904
Parti Ouvrier Communiste Tunisien (POCT) (Tunisia), 2231
Parti Populaire Syrien (PPS). *See* Syrian Social Nationalist Party
Parti Républicain Démocratique et Social (PRDS) (Mauritania), 1503, 1744
Partisans of Arab Sacrifice (Kata'ib al-Fida al-Arabi), 962
Partisans of Peace, 2037
Parti Socialist Destourien (PSD). *See* Socialist Destour Party
Parti Socialiste Démocratique (Morocco), 858
Parti Socialiste Destourien (PSD) (Tunisia). *See* Socialist Destour Party
Parti Socialiste Liberale (PSL) (Tunisia), 2231, 2232
Partition plans (Palestine), **1806**
All-Palestine Government in, 154–156
of Peel Commission (1937), 1766, 1790, 1806, 1811, 2350–2351
Abdullah I ibn Hussein acceptance of, 30
Arab Higher Committee rejection of, 228, 1811

Arab opposition to, 236, 1790, 1806
British retraction of, 1766, 1811
Jewish acceptance of, 1806
Jewish Agency on, 1811
Jewish opposition to, 236
Jewish *vs.* Palestinian area in, 1790, 1811
map of, *1765*
National Defense Party acceptance of, 1766
Weizmann (Chaim) and, 2338
Woodhead Commission (1938) response to, 2350, 2363
of United Nations (1947), 236, 1480, 1790, 1806, 2274
Arab Higher Committee rejection of, 1766, 2274
and Arab–Israel War (1948), 236, 242
Arab opposition to, 236, 242, 1639–1640, 1767, 1790, 1806
border proposed in, 1806
Israeli statehood in, 1165
Jewish acceptance of, 236, 242, 1790, 1806, 2274
Jewish *vs.* Palestinian area in, 1790, *2276*
map of, *2276*
Muslim Brotherhood opposition to, 1621
Negev under, 1675
Saudi response to, 11
timetable of, 1806
UN vote on, 1767, 1806, 2274
violence after announcement of, 1767
Party of God. *See* Hizbullah
Party of Justice and Development (PJD) (Morocco), 1569, 1590
Party of Liberation and Socialism (PLS) (Morocco), Jababdi (Latifa) in, 1203
Party of Popular Unity (Tunisia). *See* Parti d'Unité Populaire
Party of the Algerian People. *See* Parti du Peuple Algérien
Party of the Iranian Masses. *See* Tudeh Party
Parvaresh, 759–760
Pasadena Playhouse (California), 2022
Pasandideh, Morteza, Khomeini (Ruhollah) taught by, 1310
Paşa, Ziya, 1438
Pasdaran (Afghanistan), rise of, 64
Pasha, 2626–2627
Pasha, Adli, 1465
Pashtun. *See* Pushtun
Pasolini, Pier Paolo, 175
Passage, Pulse, and Possessed (Neshat), 1676
Passé simple, Le (Chraibi), 588, 1423
Passfield White Paper (1930), 1044–1045, 1453, 2350
Passivity paradigm of gender inequality, 896
Passport, Le (Begag), 1427
Passport, women attaining, 874
Past Continuous (Shabtai), 1433
Pasteurella pestis, 1835
Patient Stone, The (Chubak), 593, 1435
Patmutiun Hayots i Skzbane Ashkharhi Minchev tsam diarn 1784 (Chamchian), 579
Patriarch, **1806–1807**
definition of, 1806
and legal status of women, 886
in personal status laws, 887
Patriarch of Antioch and the East (Maronite), 1492
Patriarchs, Tomb of the, 1019, **1807**
Patriarchy
family, 1493–1494
in *hadith* (Islamic traditions), Mernissi (Fatema) on, 1518
Moudawana, al- (Morocco) on, 1585
Patriotic Alliance. *See* Alliance of Fidelity
Patriotic Union of Kurdistan (PUK), **1807,** 2151
Democratic Party of Kurdistan and, 1339, 1807
Iraqi National Congress meeting with, 1137
in Kurdish revolts, 1341
Patterson, John Henry, in Jewish Legion, 1230
Paul VI, Pope
and Lebanese Civil War (1975–1990), 2310
Shenouda III meeting with, 2049
Payam-i Hajar (magazine), 2153
Paykar (Combat) organization (Iran), 1562
Pazdawi (Sunni legal theorist), 988
Pazyryk Carpet, 566
PCA. *See* Algerian Communist Party
PCG. *See* People General Congress
PCP. *See* Communist Party of Palestine
PCT. *See* Parti Communiste Tunisien
PDC. *See* Parti Démocratique Constitutionnel
PDI. *See* Parti Démocratique de l'Indépendance
PDP. *See* Parti Démocrate Progressiste
PDPA. *See* People's Democratic Party of Afghanistan
PDRY. *See* People's Democratic Republic of Yemen
Peace and Amity, Treaty of (1805), **1807–1808**
"Peace Bands," in Palestine Arab Revolt (1936–1939), 1645
Peace, Commerce, and Secret Alliance, Treaty of. *See* Dardanelles, Treaty of
Peace Corps (U.S.), **1808**
Peace for Israel. *See* SHELI Party
Peace movement, in Israel. *See also specific organizations*
Avnery (Uri) in, 340
Harkabi (Yehoshafat) in, 995
impact of, 1809
Peled (Mattityahu) in, 1812
Peace Now (Israel), **1809–1810**
attacks against, 1809
Chazan (Naomi) in, 582
demonstrations by, 1809
establishment of, 1809
Hareven (Shulamit) in, 993
Meged (Aharon) in, 1512
Oz (Amos) in, 1748
secularism of, 1749
size of, 1809
Peace of Kütahaya (1833), 1466
Peacock Throne (jewel), 928
Peake, Frederick Gerard, **1810**
in Arab Legion, 257, 922, 1810
Pearling industry
in Bahrain, **1810**
dhows used in, 704
in Qatar, 1876
in United Arab Emirates, 36
Pearson, Lester, 2110
Peau Noire, Masques Blancs (Fanon), 804
PEC Israel Economic Corporation, 1771
Peckinpah, Sam, 98
Peck, Malcolm C., *as contributor,* 9–12, 36–37, 101–102, 157–158, 167–169, 172–173, 231, 262,

Peck, Malcolm C. *(continued)*
544, 704–706, 719, 731, 794–796, 797–799, 818–819, 859–860, 935, 996–997, 1085–1086, 1091, 1294–1295, 1347–1352, 1353–1354, 1654, 1842, 1875–1878, 1903–1904, 2039–2040, 2218–2219, 2223–2224, 2260, 2269–2272, 2425
Peddler, The (Iranian film), 1473
Peel Commission, 2350–2351
Arab Higher Committee presentation to, 228
Ben-Gurion (David) testifying before, 447
MacMichael (Harold) on, 1455
mission of, 1765–1766, 1810
Weizman (Chaim) and, 2338
Woodhead Commission (1938) response to, 2350, 2363
Peel Commission Report (1937), 1445, **1810–1811**
Alami (Musa al-) fired after, 103
Bludan Conferences against, 488
on causes of unrest, 1806, 1811
Husayni (Amin al-) rejection of, 1057
partition plan in, 1766, 1790, 1806, 1811
Abdullah I ibn Hussein acceptance of, 30
Arab Higher Committee rejection of, 228, 1811
Arab opposition to, 236, 1790, 1806
British retraction of, 1766, 1811
Jewish Agency on, 1811
Jewish opposition to, 236
Jewish *vs.* Palestinian area in, 1790, 1811
map of, *1765*
National Defense Party acceptance of, 1766
revisionists' opposition to, 2438
Zionist acceptance of, 1806
Peel, William Robert Wellesley, 1810–1811
Peindre L'Orient (Boudjedra), 497
Peker, Recep, Atay (Salih Rifki) and, 335
Peled, Mattityahu, **1811–1812**
in Progressive List for Peace, 1187, 1812
Peleg, Yarom, *as contributor,* 71–72, 188, 434, 2418
Pellagra, 712
Pelletreau, Robert, in peace negotiations, 271
Peloponnese uprising (1821), 939–940
Pelt, Adrian, **1812**
Pembroke College
Browne (Edward Granville) at, 539
Strorrs (Ronald) at, 2092
Penal code
of Morocco, 1383
in Ottoman Empire, 1381
of Tunisia, 1383
Penal procedure code, in Ottoman Empire, 1381
Penchoen, Thomas G., *as contributor,* 457–463, 716–717, 1261, 1627, 2253–2254
Pene (film), 832
Penguin Book of Turkish Verse, The (Menemencioğlu and İz), 1440
Peninsula Shield Force, 949
Pennell, C. R., *as contributor,* 487, 568–570, 575–576, 811–812, 1075, 1304–1306, 1515–1516, 1924, 1926–1927, 2382
Penon de Velez de la Gomera (Spanish possession), 1567
Pen's League, 920
Pentagon, terrorist attack on (2001). *See* September 11th
Pentateuch, 1980
People General Congress (PCG) (Yemen)
Al-Suswa (Amat al-Alim) in, 169
Islah Party coalition with, 90
People's Assembly (Egyptian legislature), **1812**
People's Bloc (Bahrain), 369
People's Democratic Party of Afghanistan (PDPA), **1812–1813**
Amin (Hafizullah) in, 62, 185–186
collapse of, 1889
coup by (1978), 62, 65, 1813
Democratic Organization of Afghan Women in, 693
establishment of, 62, 1812
factions of, 58, 62, 1813 (*See also* Khalq; Parcham)
ideology of, 62, 1812–1813
Islamic opposition to, 1813
Karmal (Babrak) in, 62, 1274, 1812
Najibullah (Mohammed) in, 1638
Parcham faction *vs.* Khalq faction of, 1638
Ratebzad (Anahita) in, 1906
Revolutionary Association of the Women of Afghanistan (RAWA) opposition to, 1920
social reforms by, 1813
Soviet support for, 58, 65
Taraki (Nur Mohammed) in, 58, 1812
People's Democratic Republic of Yemen (PDRY) (South Yemen), **1813–1815**
Aden as capital of, 43, 2386
banking in, *393*
border with North Yemen, 2377, 2390
British occupation of, 2390
and Dhufar rebellion, 705, 1842
economic and military aid to, 748
economy of, 1814, 2385
establishment of, 1813
independence for, 520, 1813, 2390
Soviet Union supporting, 2174
infrastructure of, 1814
land reforms in, 1372–1373
merger into Yemen (1990), 417, 1814, 1976, 2385, 2390
National Front/Socialist Party in, 1655
political system of, 2385, 2387
president of, 338, 1892
prime minister of, 143, 338
protectorate states comprising, 1853
Socotra in, 2077
Soviet relations with, 1815
at Tripoli Conference, 2217
U.S. describing state terrorism in, 2175
Yemeni Socialist Party in, 2398
People's Houses (Turkey), **1815–1816,** 2246
People's Liberation Movement (Sudan), Nuer in, 1699
People's Mojahedin of Iran, 1117
People's Party (Iran). *See* Hezb-e Asadollah Alam (Iran)
People's Party (Iraq), Sharif (Aziz) in, 2037
People's Party (Syria), 2133
Kikhya (Rushdi al-) in, 1322
Kudsi (Nazim al-) in, 1322, 1337
National Party rivalry with, 1664
People's Relief Committee, Joint Distribution Committee established by, 1239

People's Rooms (Turkey), 1816
People's Socialist Party (PSP) (Yemen), **1816**
Pepsi Cola Company, League of Arab States boycott and, 224
Pera district (Istanbul), 1193, **1816–1817**
Perakim be-Toledot ha-Yishuv (Smilansky), 2075
Perdicaris, Ian, kidnapping of, 86
Peres, Shimon, *1817*, **1817–1818**
  in Arab–Israel War (1956), 245
  Burg (Avraham) under, 546
  government of
    Moda'i (Yitzhak) in, 1555
    Namir (Orah) in, 1641
    Navon (Yizhak) in, 1672
  Kollek (Teddy) supported by, 1331
  in Labor–Likud coalition government, 1167, 1818
  in Labor Party, 1183, 1817–1818
  Labor Party under, 1892
  Mauritania visited by, 1745
  military background of, 1171
  Nobel Peace Prize to, *1817*
  in Oslo negotiations, 1725, 1818
  peace process under, 1168, 1725, 1726, 1818
  political defeat of, 1167, 1168, 1727, 1817, 1818
  vs. Rabin (Yitzhak), 1891
  Rabin (Yitzhak) and, 1183, 1817, 1818
  in RAFI Party, 1188, 1817
  at St. Germain Conference (1956), 2109
  visit to Morocco, 1006
Peretz, Don, *as contributor,* 235–239, 242–252, 262–265, 560–561, 684, 1106–1109, 1758–1769, 1785–1788, 1915–1916, 2290–2295
Peretz, Isaac Leib, 1430
Pérez Alfonso, Juan Pablo, 2166
Pérez de Cuéllar, Javier, **1818–1819**
  on Afghanistan, 2279
  Boutros-Ghali (Boutros) as successor of, 505
  in hostage negotiations, 2280
  and Iran–Iraq War (1980–1988), 1818
  and Western Sahara War, 2280–2281
Pericles, Demetrius, Antonius (George) and, 213
Perim, islet of, 527
Perim (Yemen), **1819**
Perkins, Kenneth J., *as contributor,* 452–453, 455–456, 483–485, 542, 647–648, 835–836, 855–856, 1293, 1519–1520, 2160, 2182
Perlmutter, Amos, *as contributor,* 1795–1796
Permanent Congress of the Lebanese Orders of Monks, 1395
Permanent Mandates Commission, 1480, **1819**
  Ormsby-Gore (William) in, 1724
Permanent Military Commission, 1387
Perry, John R., *as contributor,* 539–540, 1307–1308
Persepolis, archaeological work at, *278*
Perse, St.-John, 2020
Persia. *See* Iran
Persia and the Persian Question (Curzon), 651
Persia Committee, 540
Persian Bank Mining Rights Corporation, 536
Persian carpets. *See* Carpets
Persian cats, *1821*, **1821**
Persian Cossack Brigade, 535
Persian (Arabian) Gulf, **1820–1821**, 2328. *See also* Arabian Peninsula
  abolition of slavery in, 2074
  British–Arab maritime truce in (1853), 1489
  British interventions in, 1820
  under British control, 530–534
    East India Company and, 526–527, 530, 743
    General Treaty of Peace (1820) and, 526, 2040, 2218–2219
    India Office responsible for, 514, 532
  geography of, 901
  oil in, 517
  shipbuilding in, 2198
  tourism in, 2196
  trade in, East India Company and, 525
  trade routes through, 1820
  Tunb Islands in, 2223–2224
Persian Gulf War. *See* Gulf War
Persian language, 1124, **1819–1820**
  in Afghanistan, 55, 1124, 1819–1820
  alphabet of, 1820
  Hazaragi dialect of, 1015
  in Iran, 1819–1820
    prevalence of, 1111
  vs. Kurdish language, 1344
  modernization of, 1556
  and nationalism, 1659–1660
  origins of, 1124
  script of, 1820, 1821–1822
  in Tajikistan (*See* Tajiki language)
  translation of, by dragomans, 723
  variants of, 1124, 1820
Persian literature. *See* Literature, Persian
Persian script, 1820, **1821–1822**
Persian theater. *See* Theater, Persian
Personal Narrative of a Pilgrimage to Al-Madinah and Meccah (Burton), 548
Personal Status Code (Tunisia), 502, 912, **2230–2231**
Personal status laws, 874, 886–888
Personal View (Shamir), 2025
Perspectives Judéo-Arabes, 483
Peshawar (Pakistan), as base for Afghan resistance, 1561
Peshawar parties (Afghanistan), in interim government, 64
Pesh Merga, 2627
Pesyan, Mohammad Taqi Khan, 375
Petah Tikvah, 1025
  Raab (Esther) childhood in, 1887
Petah Tikvah (Israel), **1822**
Pétain, Henri-Philippe, 1450
Pétain, Philippe, 697
Peter I (tsar of Russia), 739
Peter VII (Coptic patriarch), **1822**
Peterson, J. E., *as contributor,* 101–102, 107–108, 109, 168–169, 172–173, 666, 703, 952, 1235–1236, 1250, 1927–1928, 1938, 1995–2001, 2148–2149, 2378–2379
Petit musé portatif (Laabi), 1355
Petra (Jordan), **1822–1823**
  ruins of, *277*
    rediscovery of, 275, *1240*
Petrie, Flinders, archaeological research by, 275
Petrie, W. M. F., Palestine Economic Corporation funding for, 1772
Petrochemical Industries Company, 1353

Petrochemicals, 752, 1483, **1823**
natural gas and, 1669–1670, 1671
Petroleum, **1824–1827**. *See also* Natural gas; Oil
origins of industry, 1824
in Sahara, 1963
in Syrian Desert, 2136
in Tunisia, 2225
Petroleum production, **1827–1830**. *See also* Oil production
by OAPEC, 1717, 1718
in Oman, 1711
Petroleum reserves, **1827–1830**. *See also* Natural gas reserves; Oil reserves
Petroline, 2203
PETROMIN, **1830**
establishment of, 1830, 2378
as SUMED owner, 2110
Peykar-e Farhad (Maʿrufi), 1496
PFLOAG. *See* Popular Front for the Liberation of the Occupied Arabian Gulf
PFLP. *See* Popular Front for the Liberation of Palestine
PFLP–GC. *See* Popular Front for the Liberation of Palestine–General Command
PFLP–GC (B), 1841
Phalange (Kataʾib) party (Lebanon), **1830–1831**
in Arab–Israel War (1982), 252–254
massacre by, 254
decline of, 1831
electoral success of, 1831
establishment of, 1254, 1830–1831
French relations with, 1831
Geagea (Samir) in, 871
Hilu (Charles) founding, 1031, 1400
Hirawi (Ilyas al-) and, 1033
ideology of, 1831
Israeli support of, 1954
Jumayyil (Amin) in, 1400, 1831
Jumayyil (Bashir) in, 1253
Jumayyil (Pierre) in, 1254, 1831
in Lebanese Civil War (1958), *1390*, 1831
clash with Najjada, al-, 1638
in Lebanese Civil War (1975–1990), 430, 1103, 1254, 1391, 1831
siege of Tal al-Zaʿtar refugee camp, 1607
murder of Franjiyya (Tony) family by, 849, 850, 871, 1394
Najjada, al- as Sunni counterpart to, 1638
opposition to, National Salvation Front in, 1665
Palestinian conflict with, 1254, 2156
Palestinian refugees killed by, 1954
in Sabra and Shatila massacres, 1262, 1263
Saade (George) as leader of, 1394, 1831, 1951
Shader (Joseph) in, 2018
size of, 1831
SSNP attacked by, 1950
Phantasia (Meddeb), 1507
Pharaonic circumcision, 822
Pharaonicism, **1831–1832**
Pharaon, Rashad, **1832**
Pharmaceuticals industry, in Jordan, 1095
Pheraios, Rhigas, in nationalist movement, 1657
Philadelphia, USS, prisoners of war from, in Treaty of Peace and Amity (1805), 1807
Philae (Egypt), **1832**
Philanthropy. *See also* Charitable organizations
of Basma bint Talal, 409
of Gülbenkian (Calouste), 948
Hariri (Rafiq Bahaʾuddin al-) and, 994
Husayni (Hind al-) and, 1055
of Sabbagh (Hasib), 1953
of Sadr (Sitt Rabab al-), 1961
Philby, Harry St. John, **1832–1833**
and Abd al-Aziz ibn Saʿud Al Saʿud, 10, 515, 1833
Abdullah I ibn Hussein and, 30
Philby, Kim, 1833
Philike Hetairia (Greece), 1657
Philippe, Louis, 855
Philippeville massacres, 137
Philipp, Thomas, *as contributor,* 1029–1030, 2426–2427
Philistines, in Palestine, 1758–1759
Phillip III (king of Spain), 2084
Philologiae Turcicae Fundamenta (Deny), 492–493
Philosophical Matters (Russell), 45
Phoenicia company, 1334
Phoenicianism, **1833–1834**
in Phalange party, 1831
Phoenicians, in Morocco, 1569
Phosphates, **1834–1835**
in Morocco, 1569
in Syrian Desert, 2136
Photography
in Egypt, in magazines, 1374–1375
in Persia, 1867
PICA (Palestine Jewish Colonization Association). *See* Jewish Colonization Association
Picasso, Pablo, 414
Picot, Georges François, 2127, 2128
Pilaf, 840
Pilgrimage, 2195
to Karbala, 1272
to Mashhad, 1498
to Mecca (*See* Hajj)
to Nabi Musa, 1630–1631
to Naqshbandi shrines, 1643
to Nazareth, 1673
by women, 2359
Pillar of Salt (Memmi), 1517
Pillars of Salt (Faqir), 805
Pinay, Antoine, 687
Pineau, Christian
Sèvres Protocol signed by, 2014, 2109
in Suez Crisis (1956–1957), 2108
Pinon, René, 352
Pinsker, Leo, **1835**
and Hibbat Zion, 1024, 1025
Pinti Hamit (Kasap), 1277
Pinto, Karen, *as contributor,* 275, 487–488, 490, 1346, 1522–1523, 1713, 1939
Pipelines. *See* Oil pipelines; *specific pipelines*
Piracy. *See also* Barbary pirates; Corsairs
Britain condemning, in General Treaty of Peace (1820), 526, 2218
on Trucial Coast, 2218
Piraeus (Greece), British naval bombardment of, 1796
Pirate Coast. *See* Trucial Coast
Pisgah, Ha- (newspaper), 2168
Pishevari, Jaʿfar, 2144
in Azerbaijan autonomy movement, 345, 693
death of, 694
Pishkars (Azerbaijan), 1591
Pita bread, 838, 839
Pitch (petroleum), 1824
Pittsburgh Platform (1885), American Council for Judaism support for, 176

Pitt, William, the Younger, 648
Piyano (journal), 434
PJD. *See* Justice and Development Party
PKK. *See* Kurdistan Workers Party
Plague, 710, **1835**
  and population growth, 1845
Plague, The (Camus), 563
Plakato, 2050
"Plan of Reforms" (manifesto), 812
Plants, in deserts, 604–605, 701–702
Plastics industry, in Saudi Arabia, 1094
Platform of Rome, 990
Playboys (Shamir), 2025
Plaza Lasso, Galo, in Cyprus problem, 2278
PLDC. *See* Palestine Land Development Company
PLF. *See* Palestine Liberation Front
PLFO. *See* Popular Front for the Liberation of Oman
PLF–PR. *See* Palestinian Liberation Front–Path of Return
PLO. *See* Palestine Liberation Organization
PLO: the Dialogue Desk (Bitton), 483
PLS. *See* Party of Liberation and Socialism
Plugot Mahatz. *See* Palmah
Plumer, Herbert Charles Onslow, **1835–1836**
  as high commissioner of Palestine, 1025, 2204
Plutoland (Awad), 341
PNC. *See* Palestine National Council
PND. *See* Parti National Démocratique
Pneumonic plague, 1835
Poaching, 834
Poʿalei Agudat Israel (PAI), 1187
  Agudat Israel and, 1187
  kibbutzim of, 1320
  Minz (Benjamin) in, 1550
  platform of, 1187
  in Torah Religious Front, 1178, 1189
  in United Religious Front, 1190
Poʿalei Mizrahi (Israel), 1187
  in National Religious Party, 1186
  in United Religious Front, 1190
Poʿalei Zion (Israel), 1361
  Ben-Gurion (David) in, 446
  Ben-Zvi (Rahel Yanait) in, 456
  Ben-Zvi (Yizhak) in, 456
  binationalism supported by, 473
  Shazar (Shneour Zalman) in, 2047
Poʿalei Zion (Labor Zionist party), 2434
POCT. *See* Parti Ouvrier Communiste Tunisien
Pocu, 610–611
Poʿel ha-Mizrahi, 1554, 2030
Poʿel ha-Tzaʿir, ha- (Israel)
  Ahdut ha-Avodah merging with, 1362
  Arlosoroff (Chaim) in, 289
  formation of, 1361
  in MAPAI, 1185
Poʿel ha-Tzaʿir, ha- (journal), 507
Poésie palestinienne de combat, La (Laabi), 1355
Poésies I (Shahada), 2020
Poetry. *See also* Literature; *specific poets*
  Algerian, 193, 716, 806, 1424, 1426
  Arabic, 1421–1422
    beliefs expressed in, 220–221
    modern, 1475
    pre-Islamic, Husayn (Taha) on, 1923
    symbolist movement in, 218
  Armenian, 144
  Egyptian, 22, 805, 1078–1079, 2044–2045
  Hebrew, 171, 182, 470, 920–921, 926–927, 941, 955–956, 1252, 1430–1432, *1433,* 1752, 1906, 2048, 2058–2059, 2418, 2429
    by women, 1887
  Iranian, 97, 2027
  Iraqi, 416, 1421–1422, 1475, 2002
  Israeli, 1336
  Kuwaiti, 1952
  Lebanese, 47–48, 307, 817, 872, 920, 1298–1299, 1421, *1421,* 2019–2021
  Moroccan, 396, 1355–1356, *1427,* 1428
  Ottoman, 1438, 1439, 1909, 2068
  Palestinian, 673–675, 1791, 1792, 2029, 2233, 2234
  Persian, 366–367, 397, 811, 929–930, 930, 1435–1436
  resistance, 674
  Sufism and, 2113
  sung, 1617–1618
  Syrian, 39
  Tunisian, *1423,* 1428, 1429, 2017–2018
  Turkish, 576, 661, 780, 782, 790, 1440, 2161, 2165–2166, 2179–2180, 2414
  Yiddish, 941
Pogroms, **1836**
  aliyah caused by, 145–146
  definition of, 1836
  U.S. Jewish defense organizations after, 177
  and Zionism, 1024, 2432
Poindexter, John, in Iran–Contra affair, 1123
Point Four program (U.S.), **1836**
Poirier, Richard, 1966
Poland
  Betar in, leaders of, *2437*
  Haskalah movement in, 1430
  Holocaust in, 1040
  Jews from, in Palestine, 146
  Jews immigrating from, 508–509
  Karlowitz Treaty (1699) and, 739
  in U.S. invasion of Iraq (2003), 2325
POLISARIO, 1005, **1836–1838**
  Algerian support for, 2343–2344, 2345
  Algeria supporting, 503, 1837, 2190–2191
  diplomatic recognition of, 2345
  establishment of, 1571
  executive committee of, 1964
  guerrilla war against Morocco (1976–1991), 1571, 1600, 2342, 2343–2347
    UN diplomatic efforts in, 2344–2345, 2346–2347
  League of Arab States not accepting, 1964
  Libya supporting, 1837, 2190–2191
  Mauritania territory ceded to, 2345
  SADR as government-in-exile of, 1964
  Sahrawi (Saharan) Arab Democratic Republic established by, 2343
  Spain opposing, 2084
  territory in Mauritania seized by, 1503
  war of national liberation against Spain, 1571, 2343
  in Western Sahara War, 1837
Political and Literary Essays (Baring), 407

Political elites, 775
Political pluralism, 933
Politics of Dispossession, The: The Struggle for Palestinian Self-Determination, 1969–1994 (Said), 1966
Politi, Elie, **1838**
Pollard affair (1985), **1838**
Pollard, Jonathan, 1838
Poll taxes, 2167
Pollution, of Mediterranean Sea, 1512
Polo, Marco, Kerman visited by, 1290
Polygamy, *1494*, 1495, **1838–1839**
in Tunisia, law on, 2230
Polytheism
Islam's rejection of, 1596, 1597
muwahhidun rejection of, 1625
Pompidou, Georges, Agam (Yaacov) commissioned by, 70
Pontecorvo, Gillo, 142
Pontic Mountains, 901
Pontus Mountains, 194
Popular Democratic Front for the Liberation of Palestine, 1008
Popular Front (Bahrain), 1662
Popular Front (France), **1839**
Popular Front for the Liberation of Oman (PLFO)
in Bahrain, 368
establishment of, 706, 1008, 1842
Popular Front for the Liberation of Oman and the Arab Gulf, 1662
establishment of, 706, 1842
Popular Front for the Liberation of Palestine (PFLP), **1839–1841**
airplane hijackings by
Air France (1976) (*See* Entebbe Operation)
El Al airplane (1970), attempted, 1293
multiple (1970), 270, 962, 1246, 1840
Sabena at Lod Airport (1972), 398, 1839
TWA (1969), 1293
in al-Aqsa Intifada (2000), 1840
establishment of, 1839
al-Fatah rivalry with, 1773, 1840
funding for, 1840
groups merged into, 1235, 1839, 1841
groups split from, 1839, 1841
Habash (George) in, 962, 1773, 1839, 1840
Haddad (Wadi) in, 967
ideology of, 1839
in Intifada (1987–1991), 1108, 1840
Jibril (Ahmad) in, 1235
in Jordan, 1773, 1840
Kanafani (Ghassan) in, 1267
Khaled (Leila) in, 1293
in Lebanon, 1840
military and terrorist tactics of, 962
Mossad targeting leaders of, 1268
in PLO, 1773, 1840
and Rejection Front, 1917
Soviet support for, 1840
terrorist attacks by, 1839–1840
Popular Front for the Liberation of Palestine–External Operations, Haddad (Wadi) and, 967
Popular Front for the Liberation of Palestine–General Command (PFLP–GC), **1841–1842**
establishment of, 1235, 1841
guerrilla tactics of, 1841
ideology of, 1841
in Intifada (1987–1991), 1235
Jibril (Ahmad) in, 1235, 1773, 1841
in PLO, 1773, 1841
PLO opposed by, 1235, 1841–1842
prisoner exchange with Israel (1985), 1842
in Rejection Front, 1917
split from PFLP, 1839, 1841
terrorist attacks by, 1235, 1841–1842
Popular Front for the Liberation of Saguia al-Hamra and Rio de Oro. *See* POLISARIO
Popular Front for the Liberation of the Occupied Arabian Gulf (PFLOAG) (Oman), 1654, **1842**
in Dhufar rebellion, 705, 1842
merger with NDFLOAG, 706, 1842
Popular Movement (Morocco). *See* Mouvement Populaire
Popular Reform Society (Iraq), 80
Popular Socialist Party (Yemen), Ayni (Muhsin al-) in, 343
Popular Unity Movement. *See* Mouvement de l'Unité Populaire
Popular Unity Party. *See* Parti D'Unité Populaire
Popular Unity Party (Tunisia). *See* Mouvement de L'Unité Populaire
Population, **1842–1848**
Population censuses, 1847–1848, *1848*
Population control, 1510–1511
Population density, 1843
Population growth, 1842–1846, *1844*
in Egypt, 763, 764–765, 1843, 1845
fertility and, 1844
and food production, 73, 1844
in Iran, 1111
mortality and, 1843, 1845–1846
in Palestine, among Jews, 1763–1764
projections for, 1846
regional rates of, 73
in Turkey, 1843, 1844
and urban planning, 2301
in Yemen, 2385
Population migration, 1846–1847
Populist Party (Turkey), merger with Social Democratic Party, in Social Democratic Populist Party, 1097
Port Fouad (Egypt), 1849
"Portrait du colonisé" (Memmi), 1517
Portraits of Women in the Work of Bahram Beizaie, Filmmaker and Scriptwriter (Lahiji), 1364–1365
Port Saʿid (Egypt), **1848–1849**, 1970
Portsmouth Treaty (1947), signing of, 1210
Port Sudan (Sudan), 2100
Portugal, and trade, 2197
Postage stamps, **1849–1851**
pyramids on, 1850, 1858
Postal services, expansion of, 624
Post-Mortem (Kaniuk), 1268
Potash industry, **1851**
Dead Sea in, 685, 1851
Potsdam Convention (1911), **1851**
Potter, Lawrence G., *as contributor*, 184, 185, 189, 2430
Poulenc, Francis, 873
Pour changer l'Algérie (Boukrouh), 451

Pour la Révolution Africaine (Fanon), 804
Pour ne plus rêver (Boudjedra), 497
Pourshariati, Parvaneh, *as contributor,* 2, 41, 93, 669, 694, 928–929, 943, 981, 1110, 1129, 1142, 1144, 1289–1290, 1312–1313, 1316–1317, 1487, 1880, 2057–2058, 2070, 2144, 2311, 2355, 2419
Pourzand, Siyamak, 1275
Pouvoir (Algeria)
  Bouteflika (Abdelaziz) supported by, 504
  Brahimi (Abdelhamid) criticizing, 506
  Nezzar (Khaled) in, 1686
Powell, Colin L., **1851–1852**
  in Gulf War (1990–1991), 2324
  Security Council address of (2003), 2324
  in U.S. war in Iraq (2003), 2324
Powell Doctrine, 1852
Power generation. *See* Hydropower
Poyraz wind, 605
PPA. *See* Parti du Peuple Algérien
Prague School of Economics, 914
Prayer niche. *See Mihrab*
PRDS. *See* Parti Républicain Démocratique et Social
Precipitation. *See also* Climate
  and agriculture, 74, 75
  processes of, 605
  seasonal patterns of, 74
  and water resources, 2328
Preil, Gabriel, 1432
Presbyterian Church of America in New York, Beirut College for Women established by, 431
Presbyterian missionaries, 1854
  Coptic Evangelical Church established by, 640
Present at the Creation (Acheson), 40
Press, freedom of. *See also* Censorship
  in Afghanistan, 175
  in Algeria, 125
  in Iran, restraints on, 1120, 1121, 1299
Press and Poetry of Modern Persia, The (Browne), 540
Press Cooperative S.A.L., 2254
Press Council (1963) (Israel), 1684
Press Law (Egypt, 1881), 6
Press Ordinance (1933) (Palestine), 1683
Preventative Security Forces (Palestinian Authority), leadership of, 1785
Prière de la peur (Ben Mansour), 1427
Primary School Regulation (1836) (Egypt), 757–758
Primrose, Archibald (Lord Rosebery), 405
Prince Ehtejab (Golshiri), 1435
Princess Basma Women's Resource Center (Jordan), 409, 893, **1852**
Princeton University
  Said (Edward) at, 1966
  Shultz (George) at, 2061
Printemps Berbère. See Berber Spring
Prise de Gibraltar, La (Boudjedra), 497
Prison Days (Dashti), 678
Privatization, creating conflicts with labor unions, 1359
Privy Council (Egypt), 1472
Problème des idées dans le monde musulman, Le (Bennabi), 451
Procyshen, Crystal, *as contributor,* 2022
Progrès Egyptien, le (newspaper), 1682
Progress and Socialism party (Morocco), Yata (Ali) in, 2382
Progressive Democratic Party (Afghanistan). *See* Jamʿiat Demokrate-ye Mottaraqi
Progressive Democratic Party (Tunisia). *See* Parti Démocrate Progressiste
Progressive Islam, 2145
Progressive List for Peace (Israel), 285, 1187
  Arafat (Yasir) meeting with members, 1187
  electoral success of, 1187
  Peled (Mattityahu) in, 1187, 1812
  platform of, 1187
Progressive National Front (Syria), 315
  Bakdash (Khalid) in, 373
Progressive National Movement (Israel). *See* Progressive List for Peace
Progressive Party (Israel), 1181
  Kol (Moshe) in, 1332
Progressive Republican Party (Turkey), 44, 332
Progressive Socialist Party (PSP) (Lebanon), **1852–1853**
  establishment of, 1255
  ideology of, 1853
  Jumblatt (Kamal) in, 1255, 1852–1853
  Jumblatt (Walid) in, 1256, 1853
  in National Front, 1656–1657
  reorganization of, 1256
  strikes against Qulaylat (Ibrahim), 1612
Pro-Jerusalem Society, 2092
Pronatalist policies, 478, 479
Property rights. *See also* Land ownership
  distribution of, 1370
  individualized, 1370
  use of law for restructuring, 1379
Prophète voilé, le (Khatibi), 1304
Prophetic medicine, 1508
Prophet, The (Gibran), 920, *1421*
Prost, Henri, 569
Protectorate states (South Yemen), **1853**
Protestantism
  in Balkan Peninsula, 383
  Bliss (Daniel) and, 487
  Bliss (Howard) and, 487–488
  denominations of, 1854
  influence of, 593
  in Ottoman Empire, British support of, 1544
  prevalence of, 1854
  theology of, 1854
Protestant missions, **1853–1856**
  in 19th century, 590, 1854–1855, 2290
  achievements of, 1854–1855
  from Britain, 1854, 1855
    in Palestine, 1796, 1797
  conservative evangelical, 1855–1856
  educational institutions of, 1854, 1855
  goals of, 1854
  influence of, 1853–1854
  mainline, 1855, 1856
  problems with, 1854, 1856
  schools of, 1551
  from U.S., 231, 1854–1856
Protocols of the Elders of Zion, **1856–1857**
  antisemitism based on, 212, 1856
  as forgery, 212, 1856
Provide Comfort, Operation, 1339
Provisional Council of State (Israel), Wahrhaftig (Zerah) in, 2322

Provisional Government of the Algerian Republic. *See* Gouvernement Provisoire de la République Algérienne
Provisional Sahrawi National Council, 1964
Prudent socialism, 422
Prussia. *See also* Germany
in Eastern Question, 739, 741, 903
Iranian relations with, 903
at London Convention (1840), 1444, 2093
in Syrian War (1839), 741, 2093
in Vienna Congress (1814–1815), 739
PSD. *See* Socialist Destour Party
PSL. *See* Parti Socialiste Liberale
PSP. *See* People's Socialist Party; Progressive Socialist Party; Social Party for Progress
Ptolemy I, in Alexandria, 116
Ptolemy, Claudius, 116
Public Action Committee against Torture in Israel, 2221
Public Agenda (nonprofit organization), 2308
Public health. *See also* Medicine and public health
child survival and maternal health in, 1509–1510
politics of population, body, and food in, 1510–1511
Public Security Law (Bahrain), 369
Publishing industry
in Israel, 1164
offshore, 1681
in Turkey, 1326
PUK. *See* Patriotic Union of Kurdistan
Pulitzer Prize, for Acheson (Dean), 40
Pun, in Arabic literature, 1419
Pundago Shel Yirmiyahu (Tammuz), 2160
Pundak, Ron, in Oslo negotiations, 1725
Punic Wars, 2227
Punishment, in *shariʿa*, 2033–2034
PUP. *See* Parti D'Unité Populaire; Parti d'Unité Populaire
Purifications (section in Talmud), 2157
Purple Roof Women's Shelter, 894, 2171, 2249
Pushtun language (Pushto), 1857
in Afghanistan, 55, 1124, 1857
grammar of, 1125
in Iranian family of languages, 1125, 1857
in Pakistan, 1124
Pushtun people, **1857**
ambiguous genealogy of, 1857
Barakzai tribe, 2420
Durand Line and, 734
and Durrani dynasty, 85, 734–736
in Karzai government, 67
major clans of, 1857
in Zabul province, 2417
Pushtun tribes, Durand Line and, 400
Pustunwali (code of behavior), 1857
Pyramids, 921, **1857–1858**
on postage stamps, 1850, 1858
PZE. *See* Palestine Zionist Executive

Q

Qabbani, Abu Khalil al-, 2184
Qabbani, Nizar, **1859–1860**
songs based on poetry of, 971
Qabbas, Al- (newspaper), Al Saqr family in, 162
Qabila, 2209
Qaboos, Sultan. *See* Al Bu Saʿid, Qabus ibn Saʿid
Qada, 2059
Qadarif (Sudan), 2100
Qadasr, Suʿad al-, as women and human rights activist, 2357
Qaddafi, Muammar al-, *1414,* **1860–1863,** *1861, 1862*
changing legal system, 1383
coup against, attempted (1970), 1506
coup by (1969), 1081, 1860
economic reforms of, 1413–1414, 1861, 1862
education of, 1860
Fezzan as home of, 830
foreign policy of, 1862
formal position of, lack of, 1860
in Gafsa incident (1980), 863
General People's Committees established by, 898
Green Book by, 941, 1413, 1860
Jallud (Abd al-Salam) and, 1212
on jamahiriyya, 941, 1213
Maziq (Husayn) exiled under, 1506
opposition to, National Front for the Salvation of Libya in, 1655
pan-Arabism of, 1799
POLISARIO supported by, 1837
political reform under, 1410, 1413, 1860, 1861
regime of, 1410, 1412–1415, 2218
rise of, 1860
Shamikh (Mubarak Abdullah al-) in, 2024
social reform under, 1860
Sudan relations under, *1700*
terrorism sponsored by, 1861
and U.S. bombing of Libya (1986), 1414, 1862
Yunis Jabir (Abu Bakr) and, 2414
Qaddumi, Faruq (Abu Lutf), **1863**
Palestinian state proposed by (1967), 1863
peace process opposed by, 1863
in PLO, 814
Qaddurah, Ibtihaj, 1396
Qadi (judge), **1863,** 2024
jurisdiction of, 1863
qualifications for, 1863
Qadi, Isam al-, 1972
Qadimayn (Iraq), as Atabat (holy site), 328
Qadir al-Jili, Abd al-, 990
Qadir al-Maghribi, Abd al-, in Arab Academy of Damascus, 223
Qadir, Hadj Ali Abd al-, 2089
Qadiriyya Order (Sufism), **1863–1864,** 2113
Abd al-Qadir al-Jilani in, 1863–1864
Abd al-Qadir in, 16
Gailani (Ahmad) as head of, 863
Kaylani (Abd al-Rahman al-) in, 1282
Muhyi al-Din in, 16
origins of, 1864
spread of, 1864
Qadi, Yunis al-, 675
Qaeda. *See* Qaʿida, al-
Qafih, Yihye ben Solomon, **1864**
in Dor Deʿa movement, 720
Qahtaniya, al- (secret society), 263
Misri (Aziz Ali al-) as founder of, 1550
Qahtan tribe, 2132, 2209, 2210
Qahwaji, Habib, in al-Ard movement, 285
Qaʾid, 2627
Qaʿida, al-, 1526, **1865–1866**
in Afghanistan
presence of, 66
U.S. hunt for, 66–67

U.S. strikes against (1998), 606, 1865
U.S. strikes against (2001), 66
archaeological sites targeted by, 278
bin Ladin in, 474–475, 1865–1866
in *Cole* attack (2000), 613, 2391
communications in, 1866
cultural imperialism and, 1091
establishment of, 1865
GSPC links to, 1156
ideology of, 1865, 1866
and Iraq, possible links as rationale for U.S. invasion (2003), 2324
in Iraq, 1540
Islah Party links to, 1143
Khubar attacked by, U.S. military apartments in (1996), 1315
links to Casablanca terrorism (2003), 1569
nuclear acquisition by feared, 1696
objectives of, 1865
organizational structure of, 1865
propaganda by, 1866
Qatar links to, 172
Taliban supporting, 2155, 2178
terrorist attacks by, 1865–1866, 2177 (*See also* September 11th)
training by, 1865
U.S. war against (2001), 66, 549, 1866, 2178
Zawahiri (Ayman) in, 1865

Qa'immaqam, 2627

Qa'immaqam, 409, 1981

Qa'im maqamiyatayn, 1394

Qairawan (Tunisia), **1866,** 2225, 2228

Qajar, Abdullah Mirza, **1867**

Qajar, Agha Mohammad, 1462, **1867,** 1868
assassination of, 815

Qajar dynasty (Iran), **1868–1869**
Amin al-Soltan (Ali-Asghar) under, 184
Amin al-Zarb (Mohammad Hasan) under, 185
Babis persecuted by, 356
British relations with, 526
carpets of, 566
end of, 1869, 2143
Cossack Brigade in, 643
Islah Taleban Party in, 1144
majles in, 88
Farmanfarma (abd al-Hoseyn Mirza) in, 809
Fath Ali Shah Qajar in, 815–816
and industry, 1357
Mahd-e Ulya, Malek Jahan Khanum in, 1462
minorities or subdominant groups under, 1548
Naser al-Din Shah in, 1643–1644
satirical look into Persian society under, 976
Shaykhis in, 2047
Tabriz during, 2144
tobacco monopoly granted to Britain, 2193
in Turko–Iranian War, 2252
Zell al-Soltan and, 2430

Qalam al-Tarjama, 2146

Qalqiliya (West Bank), **1869**
agriculture in, 1869
in Arab–Israel conflict, 1869

Qanat, 2627

Qanats (tunnels), water transport via, 2328

Qandalaft, Dimitri, in Arab Academy of Damascus, 223

Qanooni, Younus, in Nizat-i-Milli, 64

Qanum, 2034

Qanun (Malkom Khan), 1477

Qanun (newspaper), 1682

Qanun (secular law), 1367, **1869–1870**

Qapudan, Salim, 2105

Qaradawi, Yusuf al-, **1870**
education of, 1870
in Muslim Brotherhood, 1870

Qarafi, al-, 1476

Qaramanli, Ahmed, 1870
Treaty of Peace and Amity on (1805), 1807

Qaramanli, Ali, 1870–1871

Qaramanli dynasty (Tripolitania), **1870–1871**

Qaramanli, Mehmed, 1870

Qaramanli, Yusuf, 1871
U.S. conflict with, 1871
Treaty of Peace and Amity ending (1805), 1807–1808

Qarawiyin mosque (Morocco), 1568

Qarawiyyin, 2008

Qarawiyyin, al- (university), 828, 1422, **1871**
Bint al-Shati at, 475
Fasi (Allal al-) at, 811
Fasi (Muhammad al-) at, 812
Ghallab (Abd al-Karim) at, 910
Khattabi (Muhammad ibn Abd al-Karim al-) at, 1304

Qardawsh, Mansur, in al-Ard movement, 285

Qar'un reservoir (Lebanon), 1418

Qasabji, Muhammad al-, 2263

Qasba, 2224

Qasemlu, Abd al-Rahman. *See* Ghassemlou, Abdul Rahman

Qashqa'i language, 2248

Qashqa'i tribal confederation, 2083, 2213

Qasideh, 366

Qasim, al-, as son of Muhammad, 1595

Qasim (Saudi Arabia), 1638

Qasim, Abd al-Karim, *1872,* **1872–1873**
Arif (Abd al-Salam) and, 287–288, 1872, 1873
attempted assassination of (1958), 413, 1065, 1133
Bakr (Ahmad Hasan al-) dismissed from army by, 377
Bazzaz (Abd al-Rahman al-) in conflict with, 421
in coup (1958), 15, 288, 413, 1133, 1872
coup against (1959), 1582, 1873
coup against (1963), 288, 1873
domestic policy of, 1872–1873
execution of, 1873
foreign policy of, 1872
government of
Ayyub (Dhu al-Nun) in, 344
Hadid (Muhammad) in, 1654
Hakim (Muhsin al-) during regime of, 977
housing projects built by, 361
Kaylani (Rashid Ali al-) opposing, 1284
National Democratic Party and, 1654–1655
people's courts under, 1462
presidency of, 1872–1873
as prime minister, 1872–1873, 1969
Salim (Jawad) commissioned by, 1978–1979
Tall (Wasfi al-) against, 2156

Qasimi family of Ra's al-Khayma, al-, **1873,** 1903, 2040

Qasimi family of Sharjah, al-, **1873–1874**

Qasimi, Humayd ibn Abdullah al-, 1873

Qasimi, Jamal al-Din al-, and Arab nationalism, 261
Qasimi, Khalid, 1873
Qasimi, Khalid ibn Muhammad al-, 1874, 2040
Qasimi, Muhammad bin Salim al-, 1873
Qasimi, Rashid ibn Mattar bin Rahman, 1874
Qasimi, Saqr, 1873
Qasimi, Saqr bin Sultan al-, 1874, 2040
Qasimi, Sultan bin Muhammad al-, 1874
Qasimi, Sultan bin Saqr bin Rashid al-, 1874
Qasimi, Sultan ibn Salim al-, 1873
Qasim, Samih al-, 1791
Qasr al-Ayni (school for boys), 757
Qasr al-Ayni Hospital, 1958
Qassam Brigades, al-, 831, 983
  assassinations of militants from, 983
Qassamite Brotherhood. *See* Ikhwan al-Qassam
Qassam, Izz al-Din al-, **1874–1875**
  attacks against Israelis by, 1874
  death of, 831, 1771, 1874
    impact on Palestinian community, 1057
  Islamic Jihad inspired by, 1154
  and Palestine Arab Revolt (1936–1939), 1771
Qassim, Samih al-, 1356
Qassrawi, Mukarram, in Women's Centre for Legal Aid and Counseling, 2356
Qat (plant), 2627
  in Yemen, 2387, 2388
Qatar, **1875–1878**. *See also specific cities, organizations, people, and regions*
  agriculture in, 1876
  Al Khalifa family in, 149, 1875–1876
  Al Thani family in, 171–172, 1876
  in Arab boycott against Israel, 224
  banking in, *393*
  and Beitaddin Declaration (1978), 432
  border with Bahrain, dispute over, 370–371, 1877
  border with Saudi Arabia, dispute over, 1877
  British intervention in, 1876
  British treaty with (1916), 531, 614
  cities of, capital, 719
  climate of, 1875
  constitution of, 1876
  coup in (1995), 1876
  defense costs as percentage of GNP or GDP, *1530*
  Doha as capital of, 719
  economy of, 752, *753*, 1876
  elections in, 1877
  foreign policy of, 1877
  foreign population of, 1875
  geography of, 1875
  in Gulf Cooperation Council, 949
  in Gulf Crisis (1990–1991), 950
  in Gulf War (1990–1991), 1877
  human rights in, 1048
  independence for (1971), 1876
  independence of, 2219
  industrialization in, 752
  Iranians in, 1875
  Islam in, 1875
  al-Jazeera in, 1219
  labor unions illegal in, 1358
  in League of Arab States, 1388
  legislative body in, 932
  military of
    equipment of, *1534*
    force levels of, *1529*
    force structure of (army, air force, and navy), *1532–1533*
  natural gas production and reserves in, 1671, *1671*
  natural gas production in, 1876
    in North Field, 1876, 1878
  natural gas reserves of, 1875
  newspapers and print media of, 1678–1679
    loyalist approach of, 1681
  oil production in, 752
    by foreign companies, Anglo–Iranian Oil Company, 1876
    by Qatar Petroleum, 1878
  oil reserves of, 1875
  in Ottoman Empire, 1876
  pearling industry in, 1876
  political system of, 1876–1877
  population of, 752, *753*, 1844, 1875
  al-Qaʿida links to, 172
  radio and television in, *1895*, 1895–1896
  tribes in, 2210
  in war in Iraq (2003), 1877
  water resources in, 1875
  World Bank and, capital stock and voting power in, *2363*
Qatar General Petroleum Company (QGPC). *See* Qatar Petroleum
Qatar Petroleum (QP), **1878**
  establishment of, 1878
  nationalization of, 1878
  as SUMED owner, 2110
Qatif, al- (oasis), 1995, 1996, 1997
Qavam, Ahmad
  and Azerbaijan autonomy movement, 345, 346
  crackdown on British influence by, 1110
  Eqbal (Manouchehr) under, 779
  government of, Mossadegh (Mohammad) in, 1580
  as prime minister
    appointment of, 1118
    Arfa (Hasan) opposed by, 286
    resignation of, 1118
  in Soviet withdrawal, 1118, 1752
Qavam al-Saltaneh, Ahmad, brother of, 2318
Qavam, Malektaj, 102
Qaʿwar, Kamil Amin, 1878
Qaʿwar, Widad, **1878–1879**
Qawasim tribe, 2209, 2218
Qawmiyya, in nationalism, 1659
Qawqa, Ibrahim, deportation of, 983
Qawuqji, Fawzi al-, **1879–1880**
  in Arab Liberation Army, 259, 1052, 1879–1880
  and Hawrani (Akram al-), 1010
Qayrawan, al-. *See* Qairawan
Qaysis, 728
Qazvini, Mohammad, 540
Qazzaz, Ayad al-, *as contributor*, 79–81, 358–362, 421–423, 999–1000, 1078, 1129–1136, 1209–1211, 1582–1583, 1960, 2125–2126, 2189, 2288–2289
Qeshm Island, 527, 530, 532
  in Persian Gulf, 1820
QGPC (Qatar General Petroleum Company). *See* Qatar Petroleum
Qibla, 2627
Qina Taht al-jild, al- (Kéfi), 1429
Qirsh, 2627
Qiryat Arba. *See* Kiryat Arba
Qisas shamiyya (Idlibi), 1080
"Qissat al-Ra's al-Maqtuʿa" (Berrada), 467
Qissat Hayati fi Wadi al-Rafidayn (Shaʾul), 2043
Qitʿa al-musiqiyya, al- (music), 1618
Qiyam, al-, 451, 1965
Qiyas, 1148, 2123

Qiyomijian, Ohannes, **1880**
QIZs. *See* Qualified Industrial Zones
Qom (Iran), **1880**
carpet weaving in, 566
in Constitutional Revolution (1905–1909), 636
in Iranian Revolution (1979), 1119, 1126, 1880
Montazeri (Hosayn Ali) at, 1564
religious institution in, 929
seminary for women in, 187
as Shiʿite center, 2054–2055
ulamas leaving Tehran for (1904), 1591
Qom Law School, 1970
Qotbzadeh, Sadeq, **1880–1881**
Chamran (Mostafa) and, 582, 1880
Khomeini (Ruhollah) supported by, 1311
QP. *See* Qatar Petroleum
Qualified Industrial Zones (QIZs), in Jordan, 1244
Quandt, William, 539
Quarta Sponda. *See* Fourth Shore, The
Quataert, Donald
as contributor, 1728–1734, 1735–1737
as historiographer, 1036
Quba mosque (Medina), 2323
Qubbanji, Muhammad al-, 1618
Qubbat al-Sakhra (Jerusalem). *See* Dome of the Rock (Jerusalem)
Qubbat Talha Mosque (Sanʿa, Yemen), *2387*
Quds al Arabi, al- (newspaper), 1681
Quds Committee, al-, Muhammad VI as chairman of, 1602
Qudsi, Nazim al-. *See* Kudsi, Nazim al-
Quds University, al-, Nusayba (Sari) as president of, 1705
Quduri, al-, 988
Queen Alia Fund for Social Development, 409
Queen Arwa University, Farʾa (Wahiba) founding, 806
Queen Surraya. *See* Surraya
Queen Zein Al-Sharaf Institute for Development, 409
Quest for Identity: The Image of Iranian Women in Prehistory and History, The (Lahiji and Kar), 1365
Question irakienne, La (Luizard), 1987
Quetta (Baluchistan), 385
Quetta (Pakistan), Revolutionary Association of the Women of Afghanistan (RAWA) in, 1920
Quinn, Anthony, 98
Qui se souvient de la mer (Dib), 1426
Qulaylat, Ibrahim, Murabitun founded by, 1612
Qum. *See* Qom
Qumisyun al-Taʿlim, 2146
Quneitra (Golan Heights), in Arab–Israel War (1973), *251*
Qurai, Ahmad Sulayman (Abu Ala), *1784,* **1881–1882**
Arafat (Yasir) in power struggle with, 814
in Oslo negotiations, 1725, 1881–1882
as PA prime minister, 1775, 1882
as PA speaker of council, 1784
in PLO, 1881–1882
as prime minister, 2042
Qurʾan, **1882–1883**
on alcohol consumption, 109
on Allah, 1145
and Arabic language, 232, 233–234, 1419
on birth control, 480
calligraphy of, 558, *558,* 1883
collection of, 1883
definition of, 2627
ethics in, 1145–1147
fiqh derived from, 1148
FIS on establishment of Islamic state based on, 857
and *hadith,* 968
on *hijab* (veiling), 1026
Husayn (Taha) at, 1060
interpretation of, 1882–1883
on Jews, and antisemitism, 212
in *madrasa* education system, 1457–1458
Mawdudi (Abu al-aʿla, al-) commentary on, 1504
muwahhidun adherence to, 1625
Nursi (Said) on, 1705
on polygamy, 1839
revealed by Muhammad, 1595–1596, 1882
role in Islam, 1145, 1883
on *shariʿa,* 2033, 2034
structure of, 1882
Sufi interpretation of, 2111, 2112
Sunna in, 2122
themes of, 1882–1883
on women, 808, 1987, 2153
Mernissi (Fatema) on, 1518
women's reading of, 2359–2360
Qurʾan and Issues of Human Condition, The (Bint al-Shati), 476
Qurʾanic Phenomenon, The (Bennabi), 451
Quray, Ahmad Sulayman. *See* Qurai, Ahmad Sulayman
Quraysh tribe, 2213
and Hashimite house, 1000
Qurei, Ahmad Sulayman. *See* Qurai, Ahmad Sulayman
Qusaybi, Ghazi al-, 798
Qusayr, al- (Egypt), **1884**
Qusi, Ihsan al-, on Wafdist Women's Central Committee, 2321
Qutbiyyan, al- (Egypt), in al-Jamiʿa al-Islamiyya, 1215
Qutb, Sayyid, **1884–1885**
and Afghan Islamic movements, 60
Belhadj (Ali) influenced by, 436
bin Ladin studying works of, 474
commentary on Qurʾan by, 1883
execution of, 1215, 1621, 1884
Islamic Jihad inspired by, 1154
in Muslim Brotherhood, 1621, 1884
Ashmawi (Muhammad Abd al-Rahman Salih al-) and, 321
Nasser (Gamal Abdel) and, 1884
and al-Qutbiyyan, 1215
Rida (Rashid) and, 1924
in al-Takfir wa al-Hijra, 2150
writings of, 1883, 1884–1885
Quttineh, Lamia, in Women's Centre for Legal Aid and Counseling, 2356
Qutuz (Mamluk sultan), 1044
Quwatli, Shukri al-, *1885,* **1885–1886**
coup against (1949), 1886, 2422
in exile, 1885–1886, 1886
French occupation opposed by, 1885
government of, Arslan (Adil) in, 306
against Greater Syria plan, 936
in National Bloc, 328, 1885
in National Party, 1664
presidency of, 1886, 2133
United Arab Republic supported by, 1886, 2273

R

Raab, Esther, 1431, **1887**
Raʿad, al- (newspaper), 1682
Raad, Inʿam, **1888,** 2137

Ra'anan, Natan, at Merkaz ha-Rav, 1333
Rababa, 433
Rabat (Morocco), 828, 1567, *1570,* **1888**
  Arab League summit (1969) in, *1387*
  Arab League summit (1974) in, *1387*
  Catholics in, 1932
  numismatic center in, 1702–1703
Rabbani, Burhanuddin, **1888–1889**
  communists opposed by, 61
  coup against (1996), 61
  government of
    Ahmad Shah Mas'ud in, 89
    Hekmatyar (Golbuddin) in, 1020
    Karzai (Hamid) in, 1276
  in Jami'at-e Islami, 60, 63, 64, 1215, 1561, 1888–1889
  in mojahedin resistance, 1561
  presidency of, 59, 1215, 1889
  veiling ordinances under, 1715
Rabbani, Mouin, *as contributor,* 961–963, 1070–1071, 1776–1781, 1839–1842, 1881–1892, 1952–1953, 1972, 2334–2336
Rabbani, Shoghi Effendi, 365
Rabbi(s), *1889,* **1889–1890**
  criteria for becoming, 1889
  women as, 1889
  and Zionist organizations, 1024–1025, 2432–2433
Rabbinic Hebrew (RH), 1017
Rabi, Mubarak, *1424,* 1425, **1890**
Rabinovich, Itamar
  as contributor, 1993
  in peace negotiations, 926
Rabin, Yitzhak, **1890–1892,** *1891*
  after Arab–Israel War (1973), 252
  and Arafat (Yasir), 1892
  assassination of, 403, 1168, 1726, 1793, 1892, 2177
  Barak (Ehud) under, 398
  election of, 1725
  financial scandal involving, 1891
  funeral of, Hussein ibn Talal at, 1246
  on Golan Heights, 926
  government of, 1891
    Allon (Yigal) in, 153
    Aloni (Shulamit) in, 157
    Gur (Mordechai) in, 956
    Hillel (Shlomo) in, 1030
    Namir (Orah) in, 1641
    Peres (Shimon) in, 1818
    Sarid (Yossi) in, 1991
    Sharon (Ariel) in, 2041
    Yariv (Aharon) in, 2379
  Harkabi (Yehoshafat) and, 995
  and Hussein ibn Talal, *1063,* 1892
  in Israel Defense Force, 1171, 1173
  Israeli settlements under, 1192
  Kissinger (Henry) and, *1328*
  in Labor Party, 1167, 1183
  legacy of, 1892
  military career of, 1891
  Nobel Peace Prize to, *1817*
  in Oslo Accords (1993), 1725–1726
    signing of, 271, 606, *1726*
  in Palmah, 1795
  and peace agreements, 1892
  Peres (Shimon) and, 1183, 1817, 1818
  political career of, 1891
  and Zionist Organization of America, 2436
Rabita al-Qalamiyya al- (Pen's League), 920
Rabiyya Ali, Salim, **1892**
  Isma'il (Abd al-Fattah) power struggle with, 1157, 1814
    Antar (Ali Ahmad Nasir) in, 211
Rachel's tomb (Bethlehem), 2359
Rachid, Ouakali, 919
Racine, translation of, 171
Racy, Ali Jihad, *as contributor,* 22
Ra'd (newspaper), 1110, 2142
Radd ala al-dahriyyin, al- (Afghani), 23
Ra'd-e Emruz (newspaper), 2143
Radfan Rebellion, Antar (Ali Ahmad Nasir) in, 211
Radif (Iranian music), 1617, 1618
Ra'd, In'am. *See* Raad, In'am
Radio and television, **1893–1898**
  in Algeria, M'Rabet (Fadela) on, 1592
  al-Jazeera, 1219–1220
  in Arab countries, 1893–1896
    audiences for, 1895
    ownership and control of, 1895–1896
  and Arab nationalism, 222–223
  Christian station, 1856
  in Egypt, 1469
  in Israel, 866, 1896–1897
  and music, 1619
  PFLP–GC radio stations, 1842
  Protocols of the Elders of Zion on, 1856
  in Saudi Arabia, 164, 798, 1894
  spread of, 624–625, 625
  in Turkey, 1897–1898, 2245
Radio Jerusalem. *See* Idha'at al-Quds
Radio Lebanon, 817, 818
Radubis (Mahfuz), 1464
Rafah, 870
Rafeq, Abdul-Karim, *as contributor,* 100, 344, 665–666, 683–684, 909, 936, 980–981, 1032, 1080–1081, 1198–1199, 1205–1206, 1375, 2030, 2126–2127, 2136, 2211, 2212
Rafi'i, 2019
RAFI Party (Israel), 1187–1188, 1378
  Ben-Gurion (David) in, 1188, 1189
  Ben-Porat (Mordechai) in, 452
  Dayan (Moshe) in, 682, 1188
  establishment of, 1187–1188
  Kollek (Teddy) in, 1331
  on Lavon affair, 1188
  Navon (Yizhak) in, 1671
  Peres (Shimon) in, 1188, 1817
  platform of, 1188
Rafsanjani, Ali Akbar Hashemi, 1472, **1898–1899**
  Bani Sadr (Abolhasan) in conflict with, 388
  daughter of, 998
  election to presidency, 1120
  government of
    Mohajerani (Ataollah) in, 1558
    Musavi (Mir-Hosain) in, 1615
  and Iranian Bureau of Women's Affairs, 1123
  radicals' relationship with, 1120
  and Revolutionary Guards, 1922
  rural development under, 1220
  Tehran under, Karbaschi (Gholamhosain) as mayor of, 1273
Rafto Prize for Human Rights, to Ebadi (Shirin), 744
Rage aux tripes, La (Tlili), 2193
Raghib, Ali Abu al-, 820
Raghif Yanbud ka al-Qalb, al- (Samman), 1982
Rahbani, Asi al-, 817
Rahbani brothers, plays by, 1617
Rahbani, Mansur al-, 817
Rahbani, Ziyad al-, 818
Rah-e Now (journal), 867
Rahhal, Husayn al-, communism of, 625
Rahimi, Babak, *as contributor,* 148–149, 867

Rahmani, Slimane, 918
Rahnavard, Zahra, 1615–1616, **1899–1900**
Ra'i, al- (newspaper), 1520
Ra'i (Algerian music), 1617, 1687
in Oran, 1714
Ra'ida, al- (journal), 432, 1100
Ra'id al-Tunisi, al- (newspaper), 418, 1307, 1680, 2051
Raider, Mark A., *as contributor,* 177, 2066–2067, 2354–2355
Railroad, 2206, *2206*
Ankara–Istanbul, 2206
Berlin–Baghdad, 464–465, 532–533, 2206
Damascus–Beirut, 2206
Damascus–Cairo, 2206
Hijaz, 2206
Trans-Iranian, 2057, 2203–2204
Vienna–Istanbul (Orient Express), 2206
during World War I, 2206
Rainfall. *See* Precipitation
Rais, Rasul Bakhsh, *as contributor,* 1757–1758
Raja'i, Muhammad Ali, 388
assassination of, 1119, 1299
election to presidency, 1119
government of
Musavi (Mir-Hosain) in, 1615
Nabavi (Behzad) in, 1630
Rajavi, Maryam, 1900
Rajavi, Masud, **1900**
Bani Sadr (Abolhasan) and, 389
in Mojahedin-e Khalq, 1562
"Raji'un" (resistance song), 818
Rajub, Jibril, **1900**
Dahlan (Muhammad) in conflict with, 661
in Preventative Security Forces, 1785
RAKAH (New Communist List) (Israel), 1188, 1369
electoral success of, 1787
establishment of, 1182, 1188, 1787
Habibi (Emile) in, 963
Israel Communist Party and, 1182–1183, 1188
in Moked, 1182, 1188
Palestinian citizens in, 1188, 1787
Progressive List for Peace challenging, 1187
Raki (beverage), 110
Rakweh, 837
Ralliement Constitutionnel Démocratique (RCD). *See* Constitutional Democratic Rally
Rally for Culture and Democracy. *See* Rassemblement pour la Culture et la Démocratie
Ramadan
fasting during, *1130*
Muhammad's revelation of Qur'an during, 1595–1596
in Tunisia, 2226
women's religious rituals during, 2359–2360
Ramadan City (Egypt), 1995
Ramadan, Hafiz, in National Party, 1664
Ramadan Revolution (1963)
Bakr (Ahmad Hasan al-) in, 377
Tikriti (Hardan al-) in, 2190
Ramadan, Taha Yasin, **1900–1901**
Ramadan War. *See* Arab–Israel War (1973)
Ramallah (West Bank), **1901,** 2340
Arafat (Yasir) compound in, Israeli siege of, 272, 1775
Ramat Gan (Israel), 402–403
Rambam. *See* Maimonides
Ramgavar Azadagan Party, **1901**
Rami, Ahmad, 2262, 2263
Ramirez, Ilyich Sanchez, 777
Ramla (Israel), **1901–1902**
Ramon, Ilan, 1169
Ramon Magsaysay Award for Community Leadership, Samar (Sima) awarded with, 1982
Ramses College for Girls (Egypt), 758, **1902**
Rana's Wedding (film), 357, 833
Randolph, A. Philip, 543
Rania al-Abdullah (Queen Rania), **1902**
marriage to Abdullah II, 32
philanthropic activities of, 32
Rantisi, Abd al-Aziz
assassination of, 983
deportation of, 983
Raphaeli, Ruth, *as contributor,* 1016–1018
Rapture (Neshat), 1676
Raqaba, 1367, 1368
Rasafi, Ma'ruf al-, **1903**
Rasa'il al-Zaynabiyya, al- (Fawwaz), 817
Ra's al-Khayma (United Arab Emirates), **1903–1904,** 2219
claiming sovereignty over Tunb Islands, 2224
al-Qasimi family of, 1873
secession from Sharjah, 2270
Sharjah united with, 1873, 2040
tribes in, 2210
Rashayda tribe, 2209
Rashi, 1251
Rashid, Harun al-, 360, 1132
as founder of Najaf, al-, 1637
Rashid ibn Ahmad (Umm al-Qaywayn ruler), 1592
Rashi script, 1017
Rashnu (Zoroastrian deity), 2442
Rashti, Sayyid Kazim
al-Bab studying under, 354
and Shaykhism, 2047
Raşit Paşa, assassination of, 575
Ra's Khatib (Yemen), 1039
Rasmiyya, Asma, in *Irshad An-Niswaan,* 1140
Rassemblement Franco–Musulman Algérien, 3
Rassemblement National Démocratique (RND) (Algeria), **1904**
creation of, 127, 135, 2430
electoral success of, 135
Rassemblement National des Indépendants (RNI) (Morocco), 1574–1575, **1904–1905**
Parti National Démocratique split from, 1805
Rassemblement Patriotique National (RPN), 496
Rassemblement pour la Culture et la Démocratie (RCD) (Algeria), **1905**
elections of 2002 boycotted by, 135
electoral success of, 127, 133, 134
Sadi (Said) in, 1959–1960
Toumi (Khalida) in, 2195
Rassid dynasty, 358
Rastakhiz party (Iran), 1487
Ras Tanura (Saudi Arabia), oil production in, 229
Rasul allah (messenger of God), Muhammad as, 1595
Rasulid dynasty, 2397
Rateb, Aisha, **1905–1906**
Ratebzad, Anahita, **1906**
in Democratic Organization of Afghan Women, 693
Ratib, A'isha. *See* Rateb, Aisha
Ratib, Ulfat, on Wafdist Women's Central Committee, 2321
Ratio legis, 2123

Ratosh, Yonatan, 1432, **1906**
RATZ. *See* Movement for Civil Rights and Peace
Ratz. *See* Citizens' Rights Movement
Rauf Ezzat, Heba, **1906–1907**
Raʾuf Izzat, Hiba. *See* Rauf Ezzat, Heba
Rauf, Mehmet, 1439
Ravikovitch, Dahlia, 1433, **1907**
Ravitzky, Avi, 1749
RAWA. *See* Revolutionary Association of the Women of Afghanistan
Rawda khwan (storyteller), 1606
Rawda khwani (retelling of Karbala), 1606
Rawdat al-Madaris al-Misriyya (journal), 2146, 2148
Rawlinson, Henry Creswicke, 276
Raʾy, al- (periodical), Kanafani (Ghassan) in, 1267
Raʾy al-Amm, al- (newspaper), on *Cole* attack (2000), 613
Raydaniyya, battle of (1517), 2223
Raymond, André, 1035, 1036
Rayy (Iran), *bast* taken in, 411
Raziel, David, in Irgun Zvaʾi Leʾumi, 1139
Razi, Fakhr al-Din al-, 2019
Razi, Muhammad ibn Zakariyya al-, 837
Razmara, Ali
  Arfa (Hasan) opposed to, 286
  assassination of, 100, 286, 820
RCC. *See* Revolutionary Command Council
RCD (Algeria). *See* Rassemblement pour la Culture et la Démocratie
RCD (Tunisia). *See* Constitutional Democratic Rally
Reagan Plan (1982), **1907–1908**, 2294
  announcement of, 253
  opposition to, 253–254
  PLO excluded in, 1774
  PNC rejection of, 1779
  Shultz (George) and, 2061
  terms of, 253
Reagan, Ronald, **1908**
  election of, and formation of National Front (Lebanon), 1656
  government of, Rogers (William Pierce) in, 1929
  in Iran–Contra affair, 1046, 1123
  Marine barracks bombing under, 1488–1489
  Middle East policy of, 2294
  special envoy to Middle East, 964
  war against terrorism by
    bombing of Libya (1986), 1414
    economic sanctions against Libya in, 1707
Reʿaya, 775, 2627
"Rebellious, The" (Bint al-Shati), 476
Rebel, The (Camus), 563
Rebetika, 785
Recaizade Mahmud Ekrem, 1438–1439, **1909**, 2180
  Ahmet İhsan Toʾkgoz and, 90
Reckoning, The (Eden), 755
Reconnaissance au Maroc, 1883-84 (Foucauld), 843
Reconstruction of Religious Thought in Islam, The (Iqbal), 1109
Recording industry, 1619
Red Crescent Society, **1909**
  Adivar (Abdulhak Adnan) in, 44
  functions of, 1774
Red Eagles
  establishment of, 1840
  in Intifada (1987–1991), 1840
Redjam, Abderrezak, in GIA, 1155
Red Line Agreement (1928), **1909–1910**, 2199
  As-Is Agreement and (1928), 323
  cancellation of, Arabian American Oil Company after, 229
  Compagnie Française des Pétroles in, 628
  and construction of Trans-Arabian Pipeline, 2202
  impact on Middle East countries, 1824
  terms of, 1824
Red Sea, 2102
  formation of, 901
  islands in, 1819
    dispute over ownership of, 2385
  Strait of Tiran connecting Gulf of Aqaba and, 2191
  Suez–Mediterranean Pipeline linking Mediterranean Sea and, 2110–2111
"Red Shaykh." *See* Tariki, Abdullah
Red Thread, The (Shamir), 2025
Reed, R. W. G., 2316
Refah Partisi (Turkey), **1910–1911**
  as continuation of National Salvation Party, 2242
  electoral success of, 2245
  Erbakan (Necmeddin) in, 2236
  Erdoğan (Tayyip) in, 781
  as successor to National Salvation Party, 1666
  True Path Party coalition with, 598, 2220
Reform and Reconstructionist movement (Judaism), and Halakhah, 979
Reform Bloc (Lebanon), Karame (Abd al-Hamid) in, 1271
Reform Decree (1856, Ottoman Empire), 1544
Reform Grouping (Yemen). *See* Islah Party
Reform Party (Palestine), Khalidi (Husayn Fakhri al-) in, 1295
Refoulement policy, **564**
Refuge (Michael), 1522
Refugees, **1911–1916**
  Afghan, 1847, *1847*, 1912–1913
    in Iran, 1847, 2420
    in Kabul, 1260
    number of, 53
    from Soviet intervention, 65
    women, 68, 1920
  Armenian
    from Armenian genocide, 295
    Nubar's (Boghos) philanthropy toward, 1694–1695
  Balkan Muslim, 1913
  Jewish, 1913–1914
    from Arab countries, 2365
    death of, on *Struma*, 2095–2096
    on *Exodus*, 2289
    in Haifa (Israel), *145*, *146*, *2401*
    maʿbarah experiences of, 1452
    Roosevelt (Franklin Delano) policies toward, 1935, 1936
  Kurdish, *1340*, 1914–1915
  migration by, 1846–1847
  Palestinian, *1915*, 1915–1916
    in Amman, 191
    from Arab–Israel War (1948), 236, *243*, 244, 1639–1640, 1767, 1790, 2287
    from Arab–Israel War (1967), 1270, 1791
    in Arab–Israel War (1967), 248
    in Arab–Israel War (1982), 254
    in Camp David Summit (2000), 561–562
    after establishment of Israel, 381
    flight and expulsion of (al-Nakba), 1639–1640
    Lausanne Conference (1949) discussing issues of, 1375, 1376

in Lebanon, mass killing of, 426, 1393, 1954–1955, 2155–2156, 2176 (*See also* Sabra and Shatila massacres)
on postage stamps, 1850
properties of, 381
right to return, 1916
Taba negotiations (2000) on, 2140
United Nations and, 2284–2285, 2287
UN Resolution 194 on, 466
U.S. policy on, 1941
Sahrawi, from Western Sahara War, 1837
Western Sahara, 2343, 2345, *2346*
"Refutation of the Materialists" (Afghani), 52
Reg, 700
Regime change
student activism for, 2412
U.S. calls for, 1121, 1136
Règlement Organique (1861), 1401
Regnault, Eugene, 826
Règne de barbarie, et d'autres poèmes, Le (Laabi), 1355
Regroupements, 471
Reguer, Sara, *as contributor,* 866, 1238–1239, 1247–1250, 1418, 1946–1947, 2014–2015, 2365–2368
Regulation for Public Instruction (1869, Ottoman Empire), 1461
Rehovot (Palestine), Mohilever (Samuel) as founder of, 1560
Rehovot ha-Nahar-Sefer ha-Ilyot ve-ha-Ko'ah (Greenberg), 941
Reich, Bernard, *as contributor,* 932–934, 1159–1170
Reid, Donald Malcolm, *as contributor,* 46, 92–93, 94, 116–118, 119, 179–180, 347–349, 362–363, 551–554, 555–556, 581–582, 638, 669, 670, 671, 770, 771–772, 774–776, 1099, 1106, 1265–1266, 1488, 1499, 1553, 1603, 1849–1851, 1857–1858, 1884, 1922–1924, 1970, 1978, 2086, 2107, 2425
Reines, Isaac Jacob
Maimon (Yehudah Leib Hacohen) and, 1470
Uganda Project supported by, 2257
and Zionism, 1553–1554, 2432
Reinwald, Georg, 872
Reis ül-küttap (Ottoman Empire), 1264
Rejection Front, **1917**
Arab Liberation Front in, 259
Jibril (Ahmad) in, 1235
PFLP–GC in, 1841
Rejuvenation of the Family. *See* In'ash al-Usra
Rejwan, Nissim, *as contributor,* 452, 790–791
Religious Bloc (Bahrain), 369
Religious Institute for Islamic Affairs, *370*
Religious Kibbutz movement, 1319–1320
Religious nationalism, 1660
Religious paradigm of gender inequality, 896
Religious Rescue Project in Europe, 546
Religious rituals, women's, **2359–2361**
at home and outside home, 2359–2360
vows, cults, and holy women in, 2360–2361
Religious schools, 756, 757, 760, 761
Remarque Peace Prize, Golshiri (Houshang) awarded with, 929
Remide, Nimet, in Women's People's Party, 2359
Renaissance Movement. *See* Islamic Tendency Movement (Tunisia)
Renaissance Party (Algeria). *See* Nahda, al-
Renaissance Party (Tunisia), 2231
Ben Ali (Zayn al-Abidine) banning, 439
Renan, Joseph Ernest, 52, 215, 2068
René Mou'awwad Foundation, 1584–1585
Rentier economies, 1093
Repose and Meditation (Egypt), Muhammad's Youth absorbed into, 1215
Representations. *See* Human figures
Representatives of the People (Bahrain), 371
Republican Brotherhood, **1917–1918**
Taha (Mahmud Muhammad) founding, 2144–2145
Republican form of government, 933
Republican Guard (Iraq), *1527*
Republican Peasants Nation Party (Turkey), 1660, 2236
Republican People's Party (RPP) (Turkey), 1666, **1918–1920**
as agent of central government rule, 2240
Atatürk (Mustafa Kemal) and, 2077, 2240
Democrat Party opposition to, 695
dissolution of, 1919
Ecevit (Bülent) in, 745–746, 1098
electoral success of, 99, 1098, 2245
Esendal (Memduh Şevket) in, 784
Freedom Party opposition, 851
İnönü (Erdal) in, 2242
İnönü (İsmet) in, 1098, 2077
Justice Party coalition with, 1257, 2241
Koç (Vehbi) in, 1331
Menderes (Adnan) in, 1517
National Salvation Party in coalition with, 746
and National Unity Committee, 2241
People's Houses established by, 1815–1816
political reforms initiated by, 2241, 2243
press as mobilization tool of, 1685
principles of, 1918
Social Democratic Populist Party merging with, 2077
Turkish Workers Party and, 2251
Republican Senate (Turkey), 2243
Republican Sisters, 1917
Répudiation, La (Boudjedra), 496
Requim Le Na'aman (Tammuz), 2159
Rescue paradigm of gender inequality, 896
Reserve Fund for Future Generations (RFFG) (Kuwait), 159, 1349
Reserve Mobile Force (Jordan)
Peake (Frederick Gerard) establishing, 1810
reorganization into Arab Legion, 257, 1810
Reshumot (periodical), 470
Resource for Seekers of the Path of Wisdom, The (Abd al-Qadir), 1864
Respiratory infections, acute, 1509, 1510

Responsa, 453, 454
Rets de l'oiseleur, les (Djaout), 715
Return of Consciousness, The (Hakim). *See Awdat al-Waʿy* (Hakim)
Return of the Prodigal Son, The (film), 2022
Return to Childhood (Abu Zeid). *See Ruju ila al-tufula*
Reuter Concession, 2627–2628
  Wolff (Henry Drummond) and, 2355
Reuter, Julius de, 535, 536
Réveil de la nation arabe, le (Azuri), 351
Revelation of the Hidden, The (Abd al-Qadir), 1864
Revisionist Movement. *See* Zionist Revisionist Movement
Revivim (periodical), 507
Revolution africaine (magazine), 497
Revolutionary Association of the Women of Afghanistan (RAWA), 894, **1920**
  Kashwar Kamal (Meena) in, 1279
  Samar (Sima) in, 1981
Revolutionary Command Council (Egypt), **1921**
  Baghdadi (Abd al-Latif al-) in, 362
  Muhyi al-Din (Zakariyya) on, 1608
  Naguib (Muhammad) as head of, 1634
Revolutionary Command Council (RCC) (Iraq), 413
  Aziz (Tariq) in, 350
  Ibrahim (Izzat) in, 1078
Revolutionary Command Council (RCC) (Libya), 1413, **1921**
  establishment of, 1860
Revolutionary Command Council (Sudan), 1699–1700
Revolutionary Committee for Unity and Action. *See* Comité Révolutionnaire d'Unité et d'Action
Revolutionary Confederation of Labor Unions (DISK) (Turkey), 631, 1359
Revolutionary Council (al-Fatah)
  Banna (Sabri al-) in, 396
  Barghuthi (Marwan) in, 402
Revolutionary Guards (Afghanistan). *See* Pasdaran
Revolutionary Guards (Iran), 934, 1116, **1921–1922**
Revolutionary Military Council (Iraq), 422
Revolutionary Organization of the Toilers of Kurdistan. *See* Komele
Revolutionary Organization of the Tudeh Party of Iran, 2222
Reward, in *shariʿa,* 2033–2034
Reza (imam), in Khorasan, 1313, *1313*
Reza Khan. *See* Pahlavi, Reza
RFFG. *See* Reserve Fund for Future Generations
Rhazes, 837
Ribat (fortified religious center), 2113
  at Monastir (Tunisia), 1564
Rice, *75, 838,* 840
Rice, Laura, *as contributor,* 175, 325, 376, 574, 895–897, 912, 1518, 1585–1586, 2192
Richards, Alan R., *as contributor,* 72–77, 1369–1373
Rich, Claudius James, 276
Richmond, Ernest T., **1922**
  Arab authority expanded by, 603
Rida. See Aba
Rida, Rashid, **1922–1924**
  Abduh (Muhammad) and, 24
  Alusi (Mahmud Shukri al-) defense of, 173
  Antun (Farah) compared with, 215
  and Arab nationalism, 261
  Ben Badis (Abd al-Hamid) influenced by, 440
  biography of, by Arslan, Shakib, 307
  call for compromise by, 1150
  Dar al-Daʿwa wa al-Irshad run by, 669
  in Decentralization Party, 686
  Hanbali School of Law and, 990
  Kurd Ali (Muhammad) friendship with, 1338
  al-Manar published by, 1152
  in Salafiyya movement, 1973, 1974
Rida, Sayyid al-Hasan al-, as guerilla leader, 1610
Riddle, Frederick, Kan (Suna) performance with, 1269
Rides du lion, Les (Laabi), 1355
Rien qu'une autre année (Darwish), 1356
Rif (Morocco), **1924**
  Khattabi (Muhammad ibn Abd al-Karim al-) in, 1304–1306
Rifaat, Alifa, **1924–1925**
  Khemir (Sabiha) art on covers of, 1309
Rifaʿi, Ahmad al-, 2113
Rifaʿi, Samir al-, **1925**
  cabinet of, Khalidi (Husayn Fakhri al-) in, 1295
  son of, 1926
Rifaʿiyya (Sufi order), 2113
Rifaʿi, Zaid al-, **1926**
Rifat, Oktay, 1440
Rif Mountains (Morocco)
  rebellion in, 1570
  Spanish protectorate in, 1570
Rifqi, Uthman, 797
  protests against, 2297
Rif rebellion (1921). *See* Khattabi, Muhammad ibn Abd al-Karim al-, rebellion of
Rif War, *1926,* **1926–1927**
Right Livelihood Award, Langer (Felicia) awarded with, 1373
Rig Veda, Kabul in, 1260
Rihani, Amin, 1278
Rihani, Najib al-, 866, 1273
Rihla ila Israʾil (Salim), 1978
Rihla Jabaliyya, Rihla Saʿba (Tuqan), 2233
Rihlate min al-shakk ila al-iman (Mahmud), 1469
Rijal fi al-Shams (Kanafani), 1267
Rikabi, Fuʾad al-, 413
Rimawi, Mahmud al-, 1422
Rimbaud et Shéhérazade (Laabi), 1355
Rires de l'arbre à palabre (Zrika), 1355
Risafa, al- (Iraq), 361
Risala, al-, 2018
Risala, al- (magazine), 1924
Risala, al- (Qayrawani, al-), 1476
Risalat al-Ghufran (Bint al-Shati), 476
Risalat al-Tawhid (Abduh), 24
Risalatu Fikr (Ghallab), 910
Risale-i Nur (Nursi), 1705
Rishama (rite of ablution), 1479
Rishon le-Zion (Israel), **1927**
  Levontin (Zalman) as founder of, 1408
  Rothschild (Edmond de) support for, 1937
Ritter, Scott, 2289
Rivlin, Paul, *as contributor,* 402–403, 747–752, 1033–1035, 1230, 1239, 1334–1335, 1576–1577, 1629, 1842–1848, 2273–2274, 2348–2349

Rivlin, Yosef, 2401
Riyad, Abd al-Munʿim, death in War of Attrition, 2327
Riyadh, al- (newspaper), 1679
Asmar (Fawzi al-) in, 325
Riyadh (Saudi Arabia), 1638, **1927–1928,** 1995
under Al Saʿud rule, 1625, 1999
bank in, *393*
King Saʿud University in, 1324
Riyad, Mahmud, **1928**
Abd al-Maguid (Esmat) work with, 16
as secretary-general of League of Arab States, 1386
Riyad, Mustafa al- (Riyaz Pasha), **1928–1929**
as prime minister, conflict over appointment of, 5
Riyad, Sharifa, on Wafdist Women's Central Committee, 2321
Riyal, 2628
Riyaz Pasha. *See* Riyad, Mustafa al-
Rizq, 479
RND. *See* Rassemblement National Démocratique
RNI. *See* Rassemblement National des Indépendants
Road Map (2003), 220, 1170, 1793, 1852, 2341
Germany supporting, 907
two-state solution in, 1170
United Nations in, 2284
Roadways, 2207, *2207*
Robert, Christopher Rheinlander, 490
Robert College, 758, 1551–1552. *See also* Boğaziçi (Bosporus) University
Ecevit (Bülent) at, 745
Ecevit (Rahşan) at, 747
Tarhan (Abdülhak Hamit) at, 2165
Tevfik Fikret at, 2180
Robinson, Edward, in biblical archaeology, 275
Robinson, Ronald, 2198
Roches, Leon, 860
Rock, Alfred, in Palestine Arab Party, 1765
Rockefeller Foundation, 710, 711
Rockefeller, John D., 772
Rockefeller Museum (Jerusalem), **1929**
biblical artifacts in, 277
Israeli control of, 279
Rock of Tanios, The (Maʿlouf), 1478
Rogan, Eugene, 1036
Rogers, Ginger, 1273
Rogers Peace Initiative (1970), 1930, 1941, 2292
Rogers Plan
for Arab–Israeli peace, 1689, 2327
Begin (Menachem) against, 425
Rogers, William Pierce, **1929–1930**
peace plan of (1969), Kissinger (Henry) rejecting, 1328
in peace process, 1689
Rogue states, 1526
Rolo family, **1930**
Rolo, Giacomo, 1930
Rolo, Robert J., 1930
Rolo, Robert S., 1930
Rolo, Ruben, 1930
Rolo, Simon, 1930
Roman alphabet. *See* Latin alphabet
Roman Catholicism, **1930–1932**. *See also* Vatican
in Balkan Peninsula, 383
split with Eastern churches, 589
Roman Catholic missions, Foucauld (Charles) hermitage, 843
Roman Empire
capital of, 589, 632
Christianity in, 589
Jerusalem destroyed by, 1165
in Morocco, 1569
Palestine in, 1759
Palmyra (Syria) in, 1797–1798
Romania
in Balkan wars, 384
Berlin Treaty (1878) and, 1989
and Nazi Germany, 1040
San Stefano Treaty (1878) and, 382, 1988
Romanian Jews, settlement in Israel, 2431
Romanians, 383
Romanization, of Turkish language, **1932–1933**
Romanovs, support for Orthodox religions under Ottoman Empire, 1544
Roman ruins
in Lebanon, 353, *1399*
in Tripolitania, 2218
Romdhane, Ali, in Union Générale des Travailleurs Tunisiens, 2265
Rome, Christianity in, 589
Rome and Jerusalem (Hess), 1024, 1359
Rome Group (Afghanistan), in interim government, 64
Rome Platform. *See* Sant Egidio Platform (1995)
Rome Statute, 2179
Rome, Treaty of (1935), **1933**
Rommel, Erwin, **1933–1934,** *1934*
advancing in western desert (1942), 810, 906
at al-Alamayn battle (1942), 102–103, 516, 1041, 1565, 1934, 2370
Allied Middle East Command against, 153
defeat of Wavell (Archibald Percival), 2334
as Desert Fox, *2370*
fighting against British forces in Tobruk (1941), 516, 2194
and Jews of Palestine, 1041
in Libyan campaign, 2370, *2370*
Roosevelt, Anna Eleanor, 1934
at United Nations, 1935
Roosevelt, Franklin Delano, **1934–1936,** *1935*
Abd al-Aziz ibn Saʿud Al Saʿud meeting with, 1626
on security alliance, 11
early career of, 1934
Lend-Lease program of, 1403–1404, 1934, 1936
Muhammad V meeting with, 569, 1598
policies toward Jewish refugees, 1935, 1936
Saudi Arabia relations under, 1935–1936
Silver (Abbas Hillel) and, 2067
Wise (Stephen S.) and, 2354–2355
during World War II, 1934–1935
Roosevelt, Kermit, **1937**
in CIA, 1937
in Israeli–Egyptian peace negotiations, 573
Roosevelt, Theodore
Bliss (Howard) friendship, 487
opium trade under, 1713
and Ramses College for Girls (Egypt), 1902
Rosebery, Lord. *See* Primrose, Archibald
Rose Garden. *See* Golestan Palace (Tehran)
Rosellini, Ippolito, 582

Rosen, Pinhas, in Lavon affair, 1377
Rosenthal, Joseph, in Socialist party, 625–626
Rosetta branch of Nile River, 1688
Rosetta Stone, 275, 276, 482, 492, 581
Roshanfekr, 2628
Roshangaran Publishing, 1364
Ross, Edward, in Anglo–Omani treaties, 204
Rotana (Nubian language), 1696
Rothschild, Edmond de, **1937–1938**
as Balfour Declaration (1917) drafter, 380
Behar (Nissim) and, 427
Israeli settlements supported by, 145–146, 1822, 1927, 2431
Jewish immigration to Palestine supported by, 1560
response to *Der Judenstaat* (Herzl), 1021
trying to regain Western Wall for Jewish community, 427
and Zionism, 2432
Rothschild Foundation, and Israel Television, 1897
Rothschild-Hadassah University Hospital (Palestine), 966
Rothschild, James Armand de, 1937
death of, 1938
Rouchdy, Aleya, *as contributor,* 1695–1696
Rouleau, Eric, 1292
Roumani, Maurice M., *as contributor,* 966, 973–974, 1636–1637, 1686–1687
Rousseau, Henri, 2044
Rowe, Paul S., *as contributor,* 632–633, 1447–1448, 1980–1981, 2067–2068
Royal Air Maroc (Morocco), 1569
Ben Seddiq (Mahjoub) at, 453
French skyjacking of, 1309, 1362
Lamrani (Muhammad Karim) as director of, 1366
Royal Asiatic Society, 540
Royal Dutch Shell, **1938**
in As-Is Agreement (1928), 323
in price wars, 323
and Turkish Petroleum Company, 1909
Royal Military College (England)
Farouk at, 810
Talal ibn Abdullah at, 2153
Roy, Sara M., *as contributor,* 870–871
RPN. *See* Rassemblement Patriotique National
RPP. *See* Republican People's Party
RSP. *See* Socialist Progressive Rally
Rub al-Khali (Saudi Arabia), 701, 1638, **1938,** 1995
tribes in, 2213, 2215
Rubashov, Shneour Zalman. *See* Shazar, Shneour Zalman
Rubʿe Rashidi (Tabriz), 2144
Rubin, Barnett R., *as contributor,* 89
Rubinstein, Amnon, **1938–1939**
in Democratic Movement for Change, 1181
Rubiyya, Salim Ali. *See* Rabiyya Ali, Salim
Ruedy, John, *as contributor,* 120–128, 136–139, 142, 254–256, 290, 326, 617–618, 619–620, 632, 803–804, 857, 1025–1026, 1087–1091, 1480, 1587–1588, 1589–1590, 1715, 1743–1744, 1804–1805, 2089, 2263–2264, 2404–2405
Rugh, William A., *as contributor,* 1678–1682, 1893–1896
Ruhab (magazine), 434
Ruhafza, in *Irshad An-Niswaan,* 1140
Ruhi, Shaykh Ahmad, 891
Ruju ila al-tufula (Abu Zeid), 40
Ruman, Mikhaʾil, 2184
Rumaytha Rebellion (1935) (Iraq), 2065
Rumelia, **1939**
Rumi, Jalal al-Din, 434–435, 1149, 2113
Rumi, Mevlana Celalledina (Jalal al-Din), 1521
Runic alphabet, 2250
Ruppin, Arthur, 1461, **1939–1940**
Palestine Land Development Company founded by, 1772
Ruqiyya, as daughter of Muhammad, 1595
Rüşdiye, 757
Ruşdiye Schools, 1461, **1940**
Rush, Alan, 158
Rushani, Laila Sarahat, in *Irshad An-Niswaan,* 1140
Rushdie, Salman, 351, 522
fatwa against
Kharrazi (Kamal) rejecting, 1300
Mohajerani (Ataollah) reaction to, 1558
Rusk, Dean, **1940–1941**
Russell, Bertrand, 45
Russell, Francis, in Operation Alpha, 157
Russell, Mona, *as contributor,* 39–40, 206, 1374–1375
Russia, **1941–1944**. *See also* Russo *entries;* Soviet Union
and Armenian revolutionary movement, 299, 300
Armenians in
Dashnak Party and, 676–677
edict confiscating churches of, 300–301
Black Sea access of, 739–740
Kuçuk Kaynara Treaty (1774) and, 485, 739, 2094–2095
London Treaty (1871) on, 1446
Paris Peace (1856) on, 1446
British relations with
Constantinople and, 511, 528, 529
Iran in, 88, 205, 651–652
perceived threat to India and, 1941
rivalry over Afghanistan, 536
rivalry over Persia, 535–536
rivalry over southern central Asia, 936–937
Russo–Japanese War (1904–1905) and, 536
spheres of influence, 1032, 1941–1942
Suez Canal and, 529
Turkish Straits and, 528, 529, 2093
Circassians in, 599
Cossacks of, and Iranian Cossack Brigade, 643
cotton exported to, 644
in Crimean War, 648–649, 739, 2162
and Dardanelles Treaty (1809), 671, 672
in Eastern Question, 739–742
fishing industry of, 834
French relations with,
Russian–French alliance, 742
German relations with, Potsdam Convention in (1911), 1851
in Greek War of Independence (1821–1930), 940
Haskalah movement in, 1430
Hebrew literature from, 1015–1016
Iranian relations with, 1117
Griboyedov Incident and, 943
under Naser al-Din Shah, 1644

Shuster (W. Morgan) and, 2063–2064
Turkmanchai Treaty (1828) and, 2251–2252
Islamic numismatics in, 1702
Jews in, 1360
emigration of, 146, 508–509, 1361, 2432
Libyan relations with, 1415
at London Convention (1840), 1444, 2093
Middle East policy of, 1944
migrations caused by, 1846–1847
Ottoman relations with, 25 (*See also* Russian–Ottoman wars)
Hunkar-Iskelesi Treaty (1833) and, 1050, 2093
in Syrian War (1831–1833), 2093
pogroms in, 1836
and Zionism, 1024, 2432
Protocols of the Elders of Zion in, 1856
socialism in, 1360
and Sykes–Picot Agreement (1916), 2128
in Syrian War (1831–1833), 740–741, 1346, 2093
territory of
Berlin Treaty (1878) and, 383, 465, 528, 1989
San Stefano Treaty (1878) and, 382, 1988–1989
Turks in, pan-Turkism among, 1800
U.S. war in Iraq opposed by (2003), 2324
Uzbeks under, 2306
in Vienna Congress (1814–1815), 739
in World War I, 742, 2365–2368, 2367
Zionism in, 2432, 2435
Russian Orthodox Church, 738
Russian–Ottoman wars, **1945–1946**
of 1696, 739
of 1710–1711, 739
of 1768–1774, 739
Kuçuk Kaynara Treaty (1774) ending, 739, 2094–2095
of 1787–1792, 739
of 1806–1812, 1466
Bucharest Treaty (1812) ending, 541
Midhat Paşa and, 1525
of 1828–1829, 1466
of 1877–1878, 2164
Abdülhamit II in, 26
Austro-Hungarian role in, 339
Berlin Treaty (1878) ending, 465, 1989
and British interests, 528
Budapest Convention (1877) before, 541
Bulgarian Horrors and, 382
Ignatiev (Nikolas Pavlovich) in, 1084
Muhtar (Gazi Ahmet) in, 1607
San Stefano Treaty (1878) ending, 465, 1988–1989
Vazhapetian (Nerses) in, 2311
and Muslim refugees, 1913
Ottoman navy in, 1740
Russo–Japanese War (1904–1905)
and British–Russian relations, 536
Trumpeldor (Yosef) in, 2220–2221
Russo–Persian treaties
Golestan, Treaty of (1813), 816, 1117
Turkmanchai, Treaty of (1828), 816, 1117
Russo–Persian wars, 1117, 1941
of 1804–1813, Abbas Mirza (Na'eb al-Saltaneh) in, 7
of 1824–1828, Abbas Mirza (Na'eb al-Saltaneh) in, 7
under Fath Ali Shah Qajar's reign, 815–816
Russo–Turkish wars. *See* Russian–Ottoman wars
Rusul al-Insaniyya (Nuri), 1703–1704
Rutenberg, Pinhas, **1946–1947**
in Jewish Legion, 1230
Jordan River development by, 1248
Ru'us al-Jibal (Oman), 1709
Ruwwad, al-, 2002
Ruz al-Yusuf (weekly), Abd al-Quddus (Ihsan) at, 18
Ruzname, 2628
Ruznameh-e vaqa-ye ittifaqiyeh (newspaper), 1682
Ryan, Curtis R., *as contributor,* 257–259, 819–820, 1150–1151, 1247–1250, 1691–1692, 1902

S

Sa'ada, al- (Shukri), 2060
Sa'ada, Antun, **1949–1950**
execution of, 826, 1950
in exile, 1950
on Fertile Crescent unity, 825, 826
and Greater Syria plan, 936, 1950
in Syrian Social Nationalist Party, 1949–1950, 2136–2137
and Za'im (Husni al-), 2422
Za'im (Husni al-) betraying, 1950
Sa'ada, Khalil, 1949
Sa'adat, Ahmad, in PFLP, 1840
Saadawi, Nawal al-, **1950–1951**, 2184
in Arab Women's Solidarity Association International, 268, 1950
education of, 1950
imprisonment of, 1950
Sa'aday Gaon, 1231
Saade, George, 1394, **1951**
in Phalange party, 1831
Saadet Partisi (Turkey). *See* Felicity Party
Sa'adis, in Morocco, 1569
Saadi, Yusef, 497
Saalam Cinema (Iranian film), 1473
Saba & Co., 1951
Saba family, **1951**
Saba, Fawzi, 1951
Saba, Fu'ad, 1951
Sabah al-Khayr (newspaper), 911
Sabahettin
Ahmet Riza rivalry with, 91
Congress of Ottoman Liberals organized by (1902), 631
decentralist followers of, 2409
and Young Turks, 2409
Sabah family. *See* Al Sabah family
Sabah, Marc, in al-Wifaq, 2352
Sabah Publishing and Distribution House, 1952
Sabah, Rasha al-, **1951–1952**
Sabah, Suad al-, **1952**
Sabahun wa Yazhafu al-Layl (Ghallab), 910
Sabanci University, 491
Sab'at Abwab (Ghallab), 910
Sabbagh Foundation, 1953
Sabbagh, Hasib, **1952–1953**
Sabbagh, Randa Shahhal, 481
Sabbagh, Salah al-Din al-, 927, **1953**
Sabbagh, Tawfiq al-, 112
Sabbah, Michel, as Latin Catholic patriarch, 593
Sabbath, **1953–1954**
Sabena airliner hijacking, at Lod Airport (1972), 398, 1839
Netanyahu (Benjamin) in storming of, 1677

Sabha (Libya), 1410
SABIC. *See* Saudi Basic Industries Corporation
Sabil al-Rashid (journal), 2182
Sabir, Mirza Ali-Ekber, 347
Sabkshenasi, 367
Sabra, **1954**
Sabra and Shatila massacres (Lebanon), 1774, **1954–1955**
  Eitan (Rafael) role in, 254, 774, 1263, 1954
  Hobeika (Elie) in, 1039
  investigation of (*See* Kahan Commission)
  Navon (Yizhak) requesting inquiry into, 1672
  Shamir (Yitzhak) role in, 1263, 2026
  Sharon (Ariel) role in, 254, 1039, 1263, 1954, 2026
Sabratah (ancient city), 2217
Sabri, Ali, **1955**
  Haykal (Muhammad Hasanayn) in conflict with, 1956
Sacred Things (section in Talmud), 2157
Saʿda (Yemen), Zaydi population in, 2427
Saʿd, Ahmad Sadiq, in New Dawn group, 627
Sadat, Anwar al-, *425,* **1955–1958,** *1956*
  Abd al-Rahman (Umar) granted amnesty by, 20
  and Ahram Center for Political and Strategic Studies, 92
  American University in Cairo and, 179
  in Arab–Israel War (1973), 250, 1957
  and Arab Socialist Union, 267, 1665
  army under, 767
  assassination of, 768, 771, –1593, 1957
    Abd al-Rahman (Umar) in, 20, 349
  Begin (Menachem) negotiating with, 1957
  Cairo University and, 556
  in Camp David Accords (1978), 426, 560, 567, 770, 1166, 1957, 2293, *2293*
    Boutros-Ghali (Boutros) and, 505
    PLO excluded by, 1774
    Vance (Cyrus) and, 2308
  Copts under, 641–642
  in coup (1952), 1956
  education of, 1955
  Egyptian–Israeli Peace Treaty (1979) signed by, 770
  Faisal (ibn Abd al-Aziz Al Saʿud) and, 1626
  in Free Officers movement, 1956
  and Gezira Sporting Club, 908
  Ghorbal (Ashraf) as security adviser to, 915–916
  Haykal (Muhammad Hasanayn) during regime of, 1012
  imprisonment of, 1956
  industrialization under, 1094
  infitah economic policy of, 765–766, 1096, 1957
  Jerusalem trip of, 238, 1957
    King David Hotel in, 1324
    Tripoli Conference as response to, 2217
  Kissinger (Henry) meeting with, *1327*
  military experience of, 1537, 1540–1541
  Mubarak (Husni) under, 1593
  Muhyi al-Din (Khalid) opposing, 1608
  Muhyi al-Din (Zakariyya) opposing, 1608
  and Muslim Brotherhood, 1621, 1955–1956
    crackdown on, 321, 1956
    revitalization of, 1214
  on Nasser (Gamal Abdel), 1649
  Nasser (Gamal Abdel) friendship, 1955, 1956
  as Nasser's (Gamal Abdel) successor, 1651
  New Wafd under, 1685, 2321
  normalization policy toward Israel, opposition to, 2428
  ordering Soviet military advisers to leave, 508, 1957
  in peace process, 2292–2293
  and pension for Free Officers, 853
  on postage stamps, 1850
  as president, 767, 1956–1957
  in Revolutionary Command Council, 1921
  Sabri (Ali) and, 1955
  satellite cities development by, 1994, 1995
  Shaʿrawi (Muhammad Mutwalli al-) under, 2031
  Shazli (Saʿd al-Din al-) criticizing, 2048
  Shenouda III accused by, 2048–2049
  Sheounda III exiled by, 2319
  Suez Canal University founded by, 2107
  and U.S. relations, 2292
  Uthman (Uthman Ahmad) and, 2305
  as vice president, 1956
  Wafd leadership arrested by, 1957
  wife of, 1958
Sadat City (Egypt), 1995
Sadat, Jihan al-, **1958**
Sadawi, Bashir, **1958–1959**
  in National Congress Party, 1653
Saʿdawi, Nawwal al-, 875, 894
Sadd al-Wahda. *See* Maqarin (Widha) Dam
Saddam City. *See* Baghdad (Iraq)
Saddiq (holy person), 1485
Sadeh, Pinhas, 1433
Sadeh, Yitzhak
  in Haganah, 972
  in Palmah, 1795
Sadeq, Sayyed, 2141
Saʿdians, 2037 2038, 2059
  Marrakech under, 1493
Sadi family, 105
Sadiki College (Tunisia), Mourou (Abdelfattha) at, 1586
Sadiq al-Mahdi, al- (Sudanese leader), 210, 2103
  Baggara Arabs supporting, 1335
  imprisonment of, 2261
  in National Democratic Alliance, 2261
  as prime minister, 210, 2261
  sister of, 2235–2236
  Turabi (Hasan al-) under, 2234
  in Umma Party, 210, 2261
Sadiqi College (Tunis), 84, 1428, **1959**
  Ben Salah (Ahmed) at, 452
  Bourguiba (Habib) at, 500
  establishment of, 1307, 1604
  Sfar (Tahar) at, 2016
  vs. Zaytuna University, 1959
Sadiq, Ismaʿil al-, 2053
Sadiq, Jafar al-, 2053
Sadiq, Yusuf, as Free Officer, 853
Sadi, Said, **1959–1960**
  in Berber Spring (1980), 1959
  Bouteflika (Abdelaziz) supported by, 1960
  in Front des Forces Socialistes, 1959
  in Human Rights League, 1959

and interruption of electoral process, 1905
in Rassemblement pour la Culture et la Démocratie, 1959–1960
Toumi (Khalid) in disagreement with, 2195
Saʿdist party (Egypt)
establishment of, 1465
Nuqrashi (Mahmud Fahmi al-) in, 1701
Saʿd, Maʿruf, 1391
SADR. *See* Saharan Arab Democratic Republic
Sadr City. *See* Baghdad (Iraq)
Sadr Foundation, 1961
Sadr, Muhammad Baqir al-, **1960**
in al-Daʿwa al-Islamiyya, 680, 1960
execution of, 1960
and Hakim (Muhsin al-), 977
Sadr, Muhsin, **1960**
Sadr, Musa al-
abduction of
impact on Shiʿites, 174
Jallud (Abd al-Salam) and, 1212
Qotbzadeh (Sadeq) in, 1881
in AMAL movement, 173
Husayni (Husayn al-) and, 1055
paramilitary training by, Dabbagh (Marzieh) and, 659
sister of, 1960–1961
social vision of, 1960–1961
Sadr, Shadi, 2424
Sadr, Sitt Rabab al- (Charafeddine), **1960–1961**
"Sad, The" (Bint al-Shati), 476
Saʿdun, Abd al- Muhsin al-, **1961**
Saʿdun, Ahmad al-, 162
Saʿdun family, al-, **1961–1962**
Muntafiq tribe led by, 2212
Saduq, Ibn Babawayh al-, 2055
Saʿedi, Gholamhossein, 1435, 1437, **1962**, 2186
Saʾeedi, Nubians in Egypt as, 1696
Safar-e nagozashtani (Alizadeh), 149
Safavid dynasty (Iran), 1548, 2054
Akhbari school in, 97
British relations with, 526
carpets of, 566
guilds in, 946
Isfahan as capital of, 1141
Islam spread by, 1147
as Ottoman Empire rival, 1087–1088
rise of Qajar dynasty during, 1868
turbans during, 609
Safavid Shiʿism, 2054
Safavi, Navab, 820
Safawi, Ismaʿil al-, 2054
Safawiyya (Sufi order), 2113
Safed (Israel), **1962**
expansion of Jewish community in, 2432
in Western Wall disturbances (1929), 2348
Safi (Morocco), 1567
Safinat hanan ila al-qamar (Baʿalbakki), 354
Safiy al-Din, 2113
Safveti Ziya, **1962–1963**
Sagues, Albert, **1963**
Saguy, Yehoshua, in Sabra and Shatila massacres, 1263
Sahabi, Yadollah, as Freedom Movement founder, 850
Sahara Desert, *1963*, **1963–1964**. *See also* Western Sahara
in Algeria, 120, *125*, *1963*
oases of, *123*
and war of independence, 139
area of, 1963
climate of, 1963
in Egypt, 1963
harratin in, 996
in Libya, 1963
minerals in, 1963
oases of, *123*, 1964
population of, 1964
rivers of, 1963
subdivisions of, 700
Taghit Oasis of, *604*
trade in, 1964
tribes in, 458, 459, *462*, 1963–1964, 2214
Saharan Arab Democratic Republic (SADR), 503, **1964–1965**, 2343
constitution of (1976), 1964
diplomatic recognition of, 2345, 2347
establishment of, 1837, 1964
international recognition of, 1837
Islam in, 1964
Organization of African Unity accepting, 1964
president of, 1837
Sahb al-Javaher, 1489
Sahbani, Ismail, 2227
in Union Générale des Travailleurs Tunisiens, 2265
Sahel (Mauritania), 1502
Sahel (Tunisia), 2225
Sahib, Pirizade, 577
Sahih (Bukhari, al-), 1508
Sahirtu minhu al-Layali (Douʿaji), 721
Sahnoun, Ahmed, **1965**
in Algerian War of Independence, 1965
in Association of the Islamic Call, 1965
Belhadj (Ali) under, 436
Bendjedid (Chadli) meeting with, 1965
criticizing secular policies, 1965
imprisonment of, 1965
"The Statement of Advice" issued by, 2079
Sahrawi (Western Sahara people), 2342
in Laayoune, 1356
refugees, 2343, 2345, *2346*
struggle for independence by, 1836–1837
in Western Sahara War, 1571, 1600, 2343–2347
exodus to Algeria by, 1837
Sahrawi Popular Liberation Army, 1837
Sahul tribe, 2209
Saʿid, Ali Ahmad. *See* Adonis
Saʿid, Amina al-, **1965–1966**
Said, Edward, 1091, **1966–1967**
Arafat (Yasir) opposed by, 1966
on colonialism, 1966
and East West Divan, 1966
education of, 1966
Orientalism, 1036, 1722, 1966
resignation from PNC, 1780
topics addressed by, 1792
Saʿid, Fahmi, 927
Saidi, Ayatollah, Dabbagh (Marzieh) and, 659
Saïd, Makhloufi, in GIA, 1155
Saʿid, Nuri al-, **1967–1970**
Abd al-Ilah ibn Ali and, 15
in al-Ahd, 1967
in Anglo–Iraqi treaty negotiations, 203, 1283, 1967
as architect of League of Arab States, 1386, 1968
Baghdad Pact (1955) supported by, 363, 1969
Barzani revolt (1945) crushed by, 1968
British influence on, 1132

Saʿid, Nuri al- *(continued)*
coup against (1958), 15, 1969
assassination of, 520, 1133, 1872
education of, 1967
in exile, 1968
Faisil I ibn Hussein supported by, 800
Golden Square opposing, 927
government of, Midfaʿi (Jamal al-) in, 1524
Greater Syria plan supported by, 936
Husayn ibn Ali supported by, 1967
involved in Ghazi ibn Faisal's death, 915
as Iraqi army chief of staff, 801, 1967
Jabr (Salih) opposing, 1210
Magnes (Judah) and, 1460–1461
military career of, 1527
and National Democratic Party, 1654
pan-Arabism of, 825–826, 1967
as prime minister, 1967–1969
pro-British stance of, 1967–1968
in revolt against Britain (1941), 15
Saʿid Pasha (Mamluk ruler), 1478
Saʿid Pasha (viceroy of Egypt), **1970**
in Crimean War, 1970
in Cyril IV's murder, 656, 691
Egyptian Museum commissioned by, 771
de Lesseps (Ferdinand) under, 1404, 1970
Port Saʿid named for, 1849
and Suez Canal building, 766, 1970
Saʿid revolt, Shaykh (1925), 1340
Saʿid, Rida, 665
Saʿid, Sahnun ben, 1585
Saʿid, Shaykh Sayyid (king of Oman), 2425
Saʿidzadeh, Seyyed Mohsen, **1970–1971**
and *Zanan* (magazine), 2423
Saint Catherine's Monastery (Mount Sinai), **1971**
Saint George's School (Jerusalem), 917
St. Germain Conference (1956), 2109
Saint James Cathedral (Jerusalem), 291
Saint James Monastery (Jerusalem), 291–292
St. John, Ronald Bruce, *as contributor,* 314–315, 316–320, 655–656, 1410–1415, 1505–1506, 1799–1800, 1812, 1818–1819, 1860–1863, 1921, 2023–2024, 2088–2089, 2129–2135, 2136–2138, 2217–2218, 2414
St. John Philby, Harry, 1460–1461
Saint Joseph University, 429, 758, 1551–1552, **1971**
Eddé (Raymond) at, 754
establishment of, 1971
vs. Lebanese University, 1396
Sarkis (Ilyas) at, 1991
Sulh (Rashid al-) at, 2116
Sulh (Riyad al-) at, 2117
Saint Mark's Cathedral (Egypt), **1971–1972**
St. Paul's School, 454
St. Peter's fish, 865
Saʿiqa, al-, **1972**
Muhsin (Zuhayr) as leader of, 1607
in PLO, 1773
Saʿiqa, al- (bulletin), 1972
SAIRI. *See* Supreme Assembly of the Islamic Revolution in Iraq
Saison, **1972–1973**
Palmah in, 1795
Saison des hommes, La (film), 2192
Sakakini, Khalil al-, **1973**
at Arab College of Jerusalem, 226
literary style of, 1790
Sakarya, battle of (1921), Atatürk (Mustafa Kemal) in, 331
Sakkah, Ahmad, 1375
Saladin, 2189
Salafis, 1973
Salafist Group for Preaching and Combat (Algeria). *See* Groupe Salafiste pour la Prédication et le Combat
Salafists, 451
vs. Algerianists, 1155
Salafiyya movement, **1973–1975**
Abduh (Muhammad) in, 1973, 1974
Afghani (Jamal al-Din al-) in, 1973, 1974
Ben Badis (Abd al-Hamid) influenced by, 440
in Egypt, as part of Muslim Brotherhood, 1620
Fasi (Allal al-) in, 811, 1423, 1974
in Iraq, 1974
Khattabi (Muhammad ibn Abd al-Karim al-) influenced by, 1304
legal reforms of, 1974
members of, 1973
in Morocco, 1974
and pan-Arabism, 1974
on Prophet Muhammad, 1974
Rida (Rashid) in, 1923, 1973, 1974
vs. Sunni Islam, 1974
in Syria, 1974
teachings of, 1973–1974
Wahhabi influence on, 1626
zawiyas challenged by, 1423
Salam (newspaper), closure of (1999), 1120
Salama, Ali Hasan al-
in Black September, 485
CIA and, 573
Salama, Mary, 1902
Salam, Anbara, 1975
Salama, Reda, 1902
Salam family, **1975**
Salam, Ghida, 1975
Salam, Saʾib, 1392, **1975–1976**
Salam, Salah, in Revolutionary Command Council, 1921
Salam, Salim, 1975
Salam, Salim Ali, 1975
Salam, Tammam, 1975
Salan, Raoul
Massu (Jacques) under, 141
in Organisation Armée Secrète, 1715
Salant, Samuel, **1976**
Salat al-jumʿa (Friday noon prayer), 1577
Salé (Morocco), 1888
Sal-e Bala (Maʿrufi), 1496
Sale guerre, la (Souaidia), 1686
Salem, Elise, *as contributor,* 47, 367, 397–398, 804–805, 1475, 1557–1558, 1584–1585, 1646–1647, 1982, 2046, 2430–2431
Salibi, Kamal, 1397
Salih (pious one), 1485
Salih, Ali Abdullah, **1976–1977**
Ali Nasir Muhammad al-Hasani and, 143
amnesty granted by, to Attas (Haydar Abu Bakr al-), 338
crackdown on Islamists by, 2391
in General People's Congress, 1976, 2389, 2394

Hamdi (Ibrahim al-) supported by, 1976
Islah Party connection to, 1143
as president of Yemen, 1976, 2385
election of, 2388–2389
as president of Yemen Arab Republic, 1976, 2392, 2394–2395
economy under, 1976, 2395
infrastructure development by, 2395
state-building by, 1976, 2394
tribal relations with, 90
Yemeni Socialist Party opposing, 1655
Salih, Teyib, **1977**
Salim, Afif, 1791
Salim, Ali, **1977–1978**
Salim Hasan, **1978**
Salim, Jawad, **1978–1979**
Salim, Mamduh, 1956
Salim, Tawfiq, in General Armistice Agreement (1949), 240
Salisbury, Robert, 726
Lansdowne (Lord) under, 1374
Sallal, Abdullah al-, **1979**
Amri (Hasan al-) and, 192
Egyptian influence on, 2396
in exile, 1979
military training in Iraq for, 192, 1979
Nasser (Gamal Abdel) and, 1979
overthrow of, 2393, 2396
Ahmar (Abdullah ibn Husayn al-) in, 89
presidency of, 1979, 2391–2392
republic declared by, 358
Zubayri (Qa'id Muhammad Mahmud al-) and, 2442
Sallum, Anis, in Arab Academy of Damascus, 223
Salma Mountains, 1206
Salman, Mahmud, 927
Salname (Ottoman yearbook), 1848, 2211, 2212, 2628
Salomon, Yoel Moshe, 2401
in Petah Tikvah, 1822
Salonika (Greece), **1979**
Dönme in, 720
in Ottoman Empire, 1979
as trade and cultural center, 1979
Salon Köşelerinde (Safveti Ziya), 1963
Salt, al- (Jordan), **1979–1980**
Saltana, Shoa al-, 2064
Saltaneh, Mirza Mohammad Ali Khan Ala al-, 100
Saltaneh, Najm al- (Shahzadeh Khanom), son of, Mossadegh (Mohammad) as, 1580
Saltaneh, Taj, 891
Salzmann, Ariel, *as contributor,* 2167–2168
Sam'a (communal rite), 1521
Samaritans, **1980**
holidays celebrated by, 1980
vs. Judaism, 1980
language of, 1980
male circumcision performed by, 1980
number of, 1980
principles of faith of, 1980
symbols of identification for, 1980
Samaritan's Purse (SP), 1856
Samarqandi, Abu al-Layth al-, 988
Samarra (Iraq), **1980–1981**
as Atabat (holy site), 328
climate of, 1981
development of, 1981
historic sites in, 1981
location of, 1981
mosques in, architecture of, 1074
population of, 1981
U.S. invasion of (2003), 1981
Samar, Sima, **1981–1982**
Samawiyya (Egypt), in al-Jami'a al-Islamiyya, 1215
Sambuk (sailing vessel), 704
SAMED. *See* Palestine Martyrs Works Society
Samfoni-ye Mordegan (Ma'rufi), 1496
Samid, Qurai (Ahmad Sulayman) in, 1881
Sami, Mahmud, 797
Samir, al-, 2184
Samman, Ghada, **1982**
Sampson, Nikos, dictatorship headed by, 654
Samson the Nazarite (Jabotinsky), 1208
Samt (Dahab), 1429
Samuel, Herbert Louis, **1982–1983**
advisory council of, 50, 1762
and Balfour Declaration (1917), 380
Churchill White Paper written by (1922), 594, 1983
Deedes (Wyndham) and, 687
education of, 1983
Fertile Crescent unity plan supported by, 825
and Haycraft Commission, 1011
as high commissioner of Palestine, 1025, 1402, 1441, 1762, 1982–1983, 2124
and Husayni (Muhammad Amin al-), 1056, 1983
Jabotinsky (Vladimir Ze'ev) granted amnesty by, 1208
and Jewish Agency for Palestine, 1983
legislative council proposed by, 1762–1763
Nashashibi (Fakhri) as aide-de-camp to, 1645
Supreme Muslim Council created by, 1983, 2124
Weizmann (Chaim) and, 2337
Zionist sympathies of, 1763, 1983
San'a (Yemen), **1983–1984,** *1984, 2389*
architecture of, 1984
as capital, 1983–1984, 2385–2386
Hatim sultans in, 1007
historical significance of, 2385–2386
location of, 1983–1984
newspapers of, 1678
population of, 1984
Qubbat Talha Mosque in, *2387*
siege of (1968), 1983
Amri (Hasan al-) in, 192
Makki (Hasan Muhammad) in, 1474
Ta'iz compared to, 2149
as World Heritage Site, 1984
San'a Mutiny (1968, Yemen), 1653
Sanandaj (Iran), as Kurdistan capital, 1342
San'a University, **1984–1985**
vs. Aden University, 1985
vs. Cairo University, 1985
Far'a (Wahiba) at, 806
Kuwait supporting, 1985
vs. Kuwait University, 1985
Makki (Hasan Muhammad) as president of, 1474
Sanctions, Iraqi, 362, 951, 1135, **1985–1987,** *1986,* 2323
consequences of, 1135–1136, 1510, 1986–1987, 2282
end of, 2282, 2283
lifted in U.S. occupation, 2325
and Oil-for-Food Program, 1720, 1986–1987
requirements for ending, 2282
dismantling weapons programs as, 1135
UN Resolution 661 and, 1135, 1985

Sanctions, Iraqi *(continued)*
UN Resolution 687 and, 1135, 1985
UN Resolution 986 and, 1135, 1985–1986
UN Resolution 1483 and, 1987, 2283
Sand dunes, 700
Sanders, Otto Liman von, 905
in World War I, 2365
Sane'i, Hassan, 1987
Sane'i, Yusef, **1987–1988**
San Francisco Conference (1945), 543
Sang-e sabur (Chubak), 593
Sanhan tribe, 1976
Sanhuri, Abd Al-Razzaq al-, 1382
Saniyya School al-, 757
Sanjak. *See* liwa
Sanjak (Ottoman court), 824, 1450, 1690
San Remo Agreement (1920). *See* British–French Oil Agreement (1920)
San Remo Conference (1920), *1988,* **1988**
Mosul control transferred to British in, 1582
results of, 1802, 1988, 2315
Sansar (Mehmet Rauf), 1513
San Stefano, Treaty of (1878), 465, *1945,* 1946, **1988–1989**
and Austria-Hungary, 339, 382, 465, 1989
and Bosnia-Herzegovina, 382, 1988
British criticism of, 382, 1989
and Cyprus Convention (1878), 654
and Germany, 1989
and Greater Bulgaria, 382, 465, 1988–1989
Ignatiev (Nikolas Pavlovich) in, 1084
and Montenegro, 382, 1988
revision of, at Congress of Berlin, 27, 654, 1989, 2311
and Romania, 382, 1988
and Serbia, 382, 1988
Vazhapetian (Nerses) and, 2311
Santa Fe Braun, 1353
Sant Egidio Platform (1995), **1989–1990**
Ait Ahmed (Hocine) support for, 96
Ben Bella (Ahmed) signing, 443
Sanusi, Muhammad ibn Ali al-, **1990**
grandson of, 1081
Sanusi Order founded by, 655, 1990
Sanusi Order, **1990**
in Cyrenaica (Libya), 446, 655, 1609
Idris al-Sayyid Muhammad al-Sanusi as leader of, 1081, 1412
leadership of, 1081
in Ottoman Empire, 1990
prosperity of, 1411
principles of, 1990
Sanusi (Muhammad ibn Ali al-) founding, 1990
in Siwa oasis, 2071
Tebu tribe influenced by, 2214
war against Italian colonization, Mukhtar (Umar al-) in, 1609–1610
zawiyas in, 1990
Sanu, Ya'qub (Abu Naddara), 852, **1990–1991,** 2184
prominence of, 1232
Sapir, Pinhas, **1991**
Saqafi, Khadijeh, 1310
Saqi Books, 916
Sarakhsi, Shams al-A'imma al-, 988
Sarawan (people), 385
Saray-Cedid. *See* Topkapi Palace
Sardar, 385
Sardines, 834
Sardinia, in Crimean War, 739
Sarid, Yossi, **1991**
Sari Guilford University (U.K.), Sabah (Suad al-) at, 1952
Sarkis, Ilyas, **1991–1992**
and Arab Deterrent Force, 1992
under Chehab (Fu'ad), 1991
education of, 1991
Franjiyya (Sulayman) rivalry with, 981, 1992
government of, Hirawi (Ilyas al-) in, 1033
under Hilu (Charles), 1991–1992
Hoss (Salim al-) and, 1045
Jumayyil (Bashir) under, 1992
as president, 1400, 1992
in presidential election of 1970, 1031
"salvation committee" formed by, 1647
Twayni (Ghassan) under, 2254
Sar-o tah yek karbas (Jamalzadeh), 1214
Sarraflar, 389
Sarraj, Abd al-Hammid, *vs.* Hussein ibn Talal, 1925
Sarraut, Albert, Syrian negotiations with, for independence, 328–329
Sarruf, Ya'qub, Nimr (Faris) and, 1688
Sartawi, Issam, **1992–1993**
assassination of, 1993
Avnery (Uri) contact with, 340
education of, 1992
in al-Fatah, 1992
Peled (Mattityahu) dialogue with, 1812
in PLO, 1992–1993
Sartre, Jean-Paul, 563
SAS. *See* Sections Administrative Spécialisées
Sasna Tsrrer (Srvantziants), 2087
Sassanian dynasty, 2057
Sasson, Eliyahu, **1993**
Sassoon ben Salih, 1993
Sassoon, David, 1993–1994
Sassoon, Edward Albert, 1994
Sassoon, Elias David, 1994
Sassoon family, **1993–1994**
Sassoon, Philip, 1994
Sassoon, Siegfried, 1994
Sassoon, Solomon David, 1994
Sastroamidjojo, Ali, at Bandung Conference, 387
"Sasuntsi Davit kam Mheri tur" (Srvantziants), 2087
Sat-7 (television station), 1856
Satanic Verses, The (Rushdie), 522, 1300
Satellite cities development, **1994–1995**
conditions of, 1994
goal of, 1994
industrial, 1995
investors in, 1994
Mubarak (Husni) and, 1995
names of cities in, 1995
population of cities in, 1995
residential, 1994–1995
Sadat (Anwar al-) and, 1994, 1995
Satellite dishes, 625
Satellite television broadcasting, 1895
Satin rouge (film), 175
Satire
in Azeri literature, 347
in Israeli literature, 1284

Satmar Hasidim, 1002
Satmar Hassidic sect, Neturei Karta supported by, 1677
Saʿud family, al-. *See under* Al Saʿud
Saudi American Bank, 390
Saudi Arabia, **1995–2001**. *See also specific cities, organizations, people, and regions*
agriculture in, 1511, 1996
Al al-Shaykh family in, 101–102
alcohol in, 110
Al Rashid family in, 157–158
Al Saʿud family in (*See* Al Saʿud family)
Al Sudayri family in, 168–169
in Arab–Israel War (1948), 1626
in Arab–Israel War (1967), 799, 1626
in Arab–Israel War (1973), 251, 1626
Arab nationalism in, 799, 2166
archaeology in, 278
architecture in, 284
area of, 1995
armament levels of, 304
arms sales to, 796, 2201
by China, 586, 1535
by United States, 304
Asir region claimed by, 1081
banking in, 219, 390, *393*, 394
and Beitaddin Declaration (1978), 432
bin Laden (Osama) in, 474
bin Ladin (Osama) supported by, 164
at Bludan Conference (1937), 488
borders of, 1995
Anglo–Turkish convention on (1913), 1678
with Iraq, 10, 1678
with Jordan, 10
with Kuwait, 1678
with Qatar, 1877
Uqayr Treaty on (1922), 159
with Yemen, 10, 2385
British relations with
under Abd al-Aziz ibn Saʿud Al Saʿud, 515
under Faysal ibn Turki Al Saʿud, 819
Treaty of Protection (1886) and, 2208
Buraymi oasis claimed by, 517, 544
Camp David Accords (1978) and, 794, 796
Chinese relations with, 586, 587
cities of, 703, 1995, 2148–2149
capital, 1638, 1927–1928, 1995
holy, 1506–1507, 1511–1512, 1995, 1997, *1997*
port, 666, 1235–1236, 1250, 1315, 1995, 2378–2379
climate of, 1996
communication in, 625
Council of Ministers in, establishment of, 12
defense costs as percentage of GNP or GDP, *1530*
deserts of, 1938, 2136
economic aid from, 749
economy of, 752, *753*, 795, 1996–1997
education in, 759, 794, 798, 1997
Egyptian relations with, 795–796, 798
under Faisal (ibn Abd al-Aziz Al Saʿud), 1626
Sadat (Anwar al-) and, 1957
elites in, 776
establishment of, 9, 10–11, 515, 1998–1999
family planning in, 478
fishing in, 1996
German relations with, Grobba (Fritz Konrad Ferdinand) and, 944
government of, 934
in Gulf Cooperation Council, 949
in Gulf Crisis (1990–1991), 796, 950, 951, 953, 1067, 1538, 1627, 2000
Hanbali School of Law in, 990
higher education in, 1928, 1997
at Islamic University of Medina, 1156–1157, 1511
at King Faisal University, 666
at King Saʿud University, 1324
at Umm al-Qura University, 2260
women in, 1324
Hijaz in, 1028
human rights in, 1048
industrialization in, 752, 1094, 1997
in International Monetary Fund, 1106
Iranian relations with, 1999–2000
Mecca riots (1988) and, 1627
Iran–Iraq War (1980–1988) and, 795, 796, 2000
Iraqi relations with, 796
oil export, 2203
Islamic congresses held by, 1152–1153
Jordanian relations with
Hussein ibn Talal and, 2156
pledge of financial aid to Jordan (1957), 1632
Talal ibn Abdullah and, 2152
labor unions illegal in, 1358
languages in, 1997
in League of Arab States, 1386, 1387, 1388
Lebanese relations with, 795
legal system of, 1380–1381
reforms in, 1380
legislative body in, 932
literature of, 1611
location of, 1995
at London Conference (1939), 1445
malaria in, 711
manufacturing in, 1483, *1483*
map of, *1996*
military of
equipment of, *1534*, 1535
force levels of, *1528–1529*
force structure of, *1532–1533*
mountains of, 1995–1996
muwahhidun (Wahhabi followers) in, 1625–1627
natural gas production and reserves in, 1671, *1671*
neutral zone of
shared with Iraq, 1678
shared with Kuwait, 1678
newspapers and print media of, 1678–1679
loyalist approach in, 1681
offshore publishing of, 1681
oases in, 1995, 1996, 1997
in oil embargo (1973), 1626
oil production in, 752, 1995, 1996–1997, 2199
Abd al-Aziz (ibn Saʿud Al Saʿud) and, 1626
by Arabian American Oil Company, 229–230
and end of Red Line Agreement, 1910
nationalization of, 230
by Standard Oil of California, 11, 229
Tariki (Abdullah) and, 2166
U.S. companies favored in, 515
Yamani (Ahmad Zaki) and, 2378
oil revenues of, 795, 799
in OPEC, 1719
production quota for, 1720
in Ottoman Empire, 1999
Ottoman relations with, Faysal ibn Turki Al Saʿud and, 819
Pakistani relations with, 1758

Saudi Arabia *(continued)*
on Palestine, partition plans for, 11
pan-Islamism promoted by, 1152–1153
political structure of, 1997–1998
population of, *753*, 1844, 1995
postage stamps of, 1849, 1850
al-Qaʿida and, 1866
radio and television in, 164, 798, 1894, 1895, *1895*
railways in, 2206, *2206*
regions of, 996–997, 1027–1028, 1206, 1995–1996
religions in, 1997
Catholicism, 1931
Shiʿism, 1997, 2052
Sunni Islam, 1997
Wahhabi Islam, 1997
royal family of
al-Qaʿida and, 1866
succession in, rules of, 11
science and technology in, 2004, 2005
Second Five-Year Development Plan of
al-Jubayl in, 1250, 2378
Yanbu in, 1250, 2378
and September 11th attacks, 164
social welfare in, 1997
stock market in, 2090, *2091*, 2091–2092
Syrian relations with, Asad (Hafiz al-) and, 2135
terrorism in, 2000
tourism in, 1996
in trade, 1996, *2200*
transport in, modern means of, *2207*
tribes in, 2209–2211, 2211, 2213, 2214
Tunisian relations of, Masmoudi (Muhammad) as mediator in, 1499
unification of, 1625–1627
U.S. relations with, 517, 796, 799, 1998, *1998*, 2000
under Abd al-Aziz ibn Saʿud Al Saʿud, 515
during Gulf War (1990–1991), 1627
under Nixon (Richard Milhous), 1689
oil in, 11
Plan 1002–90 for defense of, 1538
security alliance in, 11
after September 11th, 2000
twin pillars policy and, 2255
water resources in
for agriculture, 702
desalinization of, *698*, 699, *699*, 700
freshwater withdrawals, *2331*
in Western Sahara War, aid to Morocco, 2345
women in
economic status of, *877*
religious rituals of forbidden, 2361
women's rights in, 874, 884
World Bank and
capital stock and voting power in, *2363*, 2364
relative voting strength in, *2364*
in World War I, neutrality of, 173, 646
in World War II, 1935
neutrality of, 516
in Yemen Civil War, 2277, 2396
conflict with Egypt over, 1650
Yemeni relations with, 798–799
coup (1962) and, 2156
Salih (Ali Abdullah) and, 1976
al-Taʾif Treaty (1934) and, 2149
Saudi Arabia Bank, *393*
Saudi Arabian Monetary Agency, 2092
Saudi Arabian Oil Company, 230
Saudi Aramco. *See* Saudi Arabian Oil Company
Saudi Bank, Aqqad (Umar Abd al-Fattah al-) at, 219
Saudi Basic Industries Corporation (SABIC), 1094
Saʿud ibn Abd al-Aziz Al Saʿud. *See* Al Saʿud, Saʿud ibn Abd al-Aziz
Saudi British Bank, Aqqad (Umar Abd al-Fattah al-) at, 219
Saudi, Mona, **2001**
Saudi Peace Plan of Crown Prince Abdullah, *1387*
Saudi Research and Marketing Group, 1681
Saunders, Harold, **2001**
Saur Revolution (Afghanistan), Mojaddedi (Sebghatullah) in, 1561
Sausser-Hall, G., 602
SAVAK (Iranian intelligence), 1102, 2628
Bakhtiar (Timur) in, 375
under Eqbal (Manouchehr), 779
establishment of, 1118
and Iranian Revolution (1979), 1125
Mossad relations with, 1578
political show trial concocted by, 930
Saved from the Inferno (Egypt)
in al-Jamiʿa al-Islamiyya, 1215
Muhammad's Youth absorbed into, 1215
Savushun (Daneshvar), 669, 1435
Sawakin (Sudan), 2100
Sawmaʿa Tahtariq (Ben Mami), 1429
Sawt al-Marʾa (publication), 2105
Sayeret Matkal (Israel), Netanyahu (Benjamin) in, 1677
Say, Fazil, 477
Sayfettin, Ömer, 873, 1909
Saygun, Ahmed Adnan, **2002**
Sayigh, Fayez, on Nakba, al-, 1639
Sayrafi, Abu Bakr al-, 2019
Sayyab, Badr Shakir al-, 416, 1421–1422, **2002**
Shiʿr and, 1298
Sayyad, Parviz, 1437, 2186
Sayyaf, Abdul Rasul
in Ittihad-e Islami, 63, 1561
in Jamiʿat-e Islami, 63
in mojahedin resistance, 1561
Sayyid, 2036
definition of, 2628
Sayyida, 808
Sayyid Ali, Fatima Makki al-, 808
Sayyidat al-Maqam (Wasini), 1427
Sayyida Zaynab Mosque (Cairo), **2002**
construction of, Abbas Hilmi I in, 4
Sayyid, Jalal al-, in Baʿth party, 69
Sayyidna Husayn Mosque (Cairo), **2002–2003**
Sazanov, Sergei, 2128
Sazman-e Engelab-e Hezb-e Tudeh-ye Iran, 2222
Sazman-e Ettelaʿat va Zed-e Ettelaʿat-e Keshvar. *See* SAVAK
Sazman-e Mojahedin-e Khalq-e Iran. *See* Mojahedin-e Khalq (Iran)
Sazman-i Javanani Musalman (Afghanistan), 60
Sbaï, Nafissa, 2376
Scapegoat (Amir), 188
Scarves. *See also* Veiling
in Turkey, ban on, *1381*

Schachar, David, 1432
Schach, Eliezer, 2404
Schad, Geoffrey D., *as contributor,* 980–981
Schamiloglu, Uli, *as contributor,* 347, 869, 1335, 2246, 2249–2250, 2252–2253
Schatz, Boris, 469
Schechter Institute of Jewish Studies (Jerusalem), 2023
Schecter, Stephen, *as contributor,* 1268–1269, 1288, 2384
Schemes, 2099
Scherherazade Goes West (Mernissi), 1518
Schistosomiasis (bilharzia), 710, 711, 712–713, 1508, 1509, 2628
Schliemann, Heinrich, 278
Schlonsky, Avraham, *1431,* 1431–1432
Schneersohn, Menachem Mendel, 1002
Scholasticism, 756
Scholem, Gershom, 1461
School for Hakīmāt, **2003**
Schooling
  vs. education, 756
  new (*See* New schooling)
  religious, 756, 757
School of Fine Arts (Baghdad), 1978
School of Oriental Languages. *See* École des Langues Orientales
School Principal, The (Al-e Ahmad), 110, 1435
Schulzinger, Robert, 1327
Schwab, Raymond, 1722
Schwartz, Hillel, in Iskra, 627, 651
Schwarzkopf, Norman, 951
Schwedler, Jillian, *as contributor,* 1143, 2234–2235
Science and Philosophy (Cevdet), 576
Science and technology, **2003–2006**
  in Afghanistan, 2004
  in Algeria, 2004
  application of, 2004, 2005
  education in, 2004
    female students in, 878, 880
  in Egypt, 2004, 2005
  institutional framework of, 2005
  in Iran, 2004, 2005, 2006
  in Iraq, 2004, 2006
  in Israel, 1095, 2004, 2005
  in Kuwait, 2005
  in Lebanon, 2005
  manpower development in, 2004
  in Morocco, 2004
  national policies on, 2005–2006
  research and development in, 2004–2005
  in Saudi Arabia, 2004, 2005
  in Syria, 2004
  in Turkey, 2004, 2005, 2006
  women employed in, 877–878
"Scientific socialism," 1357
Scipio Africanus, 2227
Scott, C. P., Weizmann (Chaim) and, 2337
Scouts, **2006**
SCP. *See* Sudanese Communist Party
Scribes, in Ottoman Empire, 1734
SCUA. *See* Suez Canal Users Association
Scud missiles, 1535
SDP. *See* Social Democratic Party
Seager, Basil, 2024
Searching (al-Saadawi), 1950
Searchlight to the Depth (Shamir), 2025
Season of Migration to the North (Salih), 1977
SEATO. *See* Southeast Asia Treaty Organization
Sebastatsi, Mekhitar, 303
Sebastiani, Horace, **2006–2007**
Sebbar, Leila, 1424, **2007**
Sebha (Libya). *See* Sabha (Libya)
Second Message of Islam, 1917
Second National Front (Iran), 850, 1656
Second New Movement (Turkey), 1440
Secret Army Organization (OAS). *See* Organisation Armée Secrète
Secret Labor Union (Bahrain), 371
Secret Life of Saeed, the Ill-Fated Pessoptimist, The: A Palestinian Who Became a Citizen of Israel (Habibi), 963
Secrets of My Land (Baraheni), 1436
Sections Administrative Spécialisées (SAS), 545
Secular feminism, 891–892
Secularism
  in Algeria, 1965
  in Egypt
    Ghazali (Muhammad al-) opposing, 914
    Tahtawi (Rifa'a al-Rafi al-) and, 2147
  in Iran, 891
  vs. Islam, 2342
  in nationalism movement, 1659
  in Turkey, 415, 891, *1381,* 1383, 2240
    Gökalp (Ziya) and, 924
    Sezer (Ahmet) and, 2015
  ulama resistance to, 2258
Security Council resolutions. *See under* United Nations Security Council
Security Service (Israel). *See* Shin Bet
Security Zone (Lebanon), 1400
  establishment of, 238, 1167
  IDF retreating from (1999), 399
Sedad, Ali, 578
Sedarim, 2157
Seda-ye Pa-ye Ab (Sepehri), 2011
Seddiki, Nourredine, 918
Seddiqi, Marziyeh, in Iranian Bureau of Women's Affairs, 1123
Sediq, Sohaila, **2007–2008**
Seeckt, Hans von, 905
Seed Carriers, The (Shamir), 2025
Seeds (section in Talmud), 2157
Seetzen, Ulrich J., 1218
Sefaretname, 2628
Sefarim, Mendele Mokher, 507, 1430
  and Hebrew revival, 1018
Sefer ha-Kitrug ve-ha-Emunah (Greenberg), 941
Sefer Ha-Munahim Li-Refuah U-Lemadaei Ha-Tev'a (Tchernichovsky), 2168
Sefrioui, Ahmed, 1427, **2008**
Sehabettin, Cenap, 1439
Sehim kaimesi, 389
Şeker Ahmet, **2008–2009**
Sekrou, 838
Selaiha, Nehad, 2184
Selçuk, Munir Nurettin, **2009**
Self-Criticism After the Defeat (Azm), 351
Selim I, 1728
  death of, Damascus after, 663
  Druze and, 728
  Venice treaty with (1517), 564
Selim III (Ottoman sultan), *2009,* **2009–2010**
  civil service under, 1734
  education under, 757
  foreign policy of, 2009–2010
  friendship with French, 845, 2006–2007
  military under, 2009–2010
    janissaries in, 1217

Selim III (Ottoman sultan) *(continued)*
navy in, 1740
Nizam-i Cedit established by, 1217
modernization under, 1555
overthrow of, 2010
ayan in, 342
janissaries in, 1217
Seljuk dynasty, Isfahan as capital of, 1141
Seljuk Empire, 2239
Semaʿa, 666
Semah, 435
Semaphores, 624
Semiarid regions, climate of, 605
Semi, Emanuela Trevisan, *as contributor,* 786–788
Seminomadism, 459
Semites, 2628
Semitic languages, 460, **2010–2011**
Arabic as, 220
character-defining features of, 2010–2011
Northwest group of, 2010
South group of, 2010
Semiye, Emine, 578
Semolina, 837, 838
Sened-i Itaʿat (Deed of Obedience), 1217
Sened-i Ittafak (Pact of Alliance) (1808), 342, 417
Senegal
Berbers in, 458
Mauritania conflict with (1989–1991), 1503
Senegal River, 1502
Sepahsalar, Mirza Hosayn Khan, military reforms of, 1117
"Separation of Forces" agreement (1974), 241
Sepehri, Sohrab, 1436, **2011**
Sephardic Jews (Sephardim), 2629
as adot ha-mizrah, 48
arrival in Middle East, 1231
vs. Ashkenazic Jews, customs of, 1251
books on, 2012
definition of, 48
and Halakhah, 979
Hebrew language used by, 321
influence of, 1231
in Israel, 1162
Israeli settlements of, 2364–2365
Ladino language used by, 1363
as Levantines, 1405
Navon (Yizhak) in, 1671–1672
Nissim (Isaac) as chief rabbi of, 1689
Yosef (Ovadiah) and, 2404
Sephardi Torah Guardians party (Israel). *See* SHAS
September 11th, 2001, terrorist attack, **2011–2012,** *2012,* 2178
Ahmad Shah Masʿud assassination linked to, 89
American University of Beirut enrollment after, 181
anti-U.S. sentiment increasing after, 2012
bin Laden (Osama) and, 475, 2155
Bush (George W.) presidency after, 549, 2011–2012
call for extradition of Renaissance Party leaders after, 440
CIA activities after, 573
crackdown on money laundering after, 394
and Egyptian economy, 766
events on, 2011
hijackers in
Egyptian origin of, 769
Saudi origin of, 1866, 2000
intelligence services after, 1104
Iranian response to, 1121
and Iraq
Bush's (George W.) resolve against, 2324
U.S. policy toward, 1136
Iraqi response to, 1069
media attention on terrorism after, 2174
NATO Article 5 invoked after, 1692
purpose of, 2011
Saudi Arabia and, 164
Tajik political role in Afghanistan after, 2150
United Nations on, 2282
U.S.-Libyan relations after, 1415
U.S. military response to, 2294
Congressional authorization of, 66
U.S. neoconservative agenda after, 1136
U.S.-Saudi Arabian relations after, 2000
Yemen cooperating with U.S. after, 2196
Septicemic plague, 1835
Septimius Odaenathus, 1797
Seraggedddin, as New Wafd leader, 1686
Serasker, 2162, 2629
Serbia
in Balkan League, 384
Balkan refugees fleeing to, 382
in Balkan wars, 384
independence of
Berlin Treaty (1878) and, 383, 1989
San Stefano Treaty (1878) and, 382, 1988
nationalist movement in, 542
in Ottoman Empire, 1728
revolt in (1803–1805), by *ayan,* 342
Serbs, 383
Serfaty, Abraham, return from exile, 1600
Serf's Daughter, The (Behʿazin), 1435
Serhane, Abdelhak, 2376
Seri, Dan-Benaya, **2012**
Serir, 700
Sermet, Huseyin, 477
Serra, Francesco, 2125
Servet-i Fünun, 957, 1439, 1963, 2302
Servet-i Fünun (journal), 1513, 1631, 1674
Ahmet İhsan Tokgoz at, 90
Servet-i Fünun (newspaper), 2180
Servet-i Fünun (Tarhan), 2165
Setem-e Melli (Afghanistan), 62
Setif (Algeria), **2013**
Setif Revolt (1945), **2013**
Amis du Manifeste et de la Liberté in, violence blamed on, 190
Ben Bella (Ahmed) affected by, 441
Boumédienne (Houari) in, 498
cause of, 2013
Parti du Peuple Algérien in, 969, 1805
Settimana Israelitica, La (newspaper), 1686
Settlement policy (Israel). *See* Israeli settlements
Sevak, Paruyr, 303
Sevener Shiʿism, 1548, 2054
Seven Pillars of Wisdom (Lawrence), 1384
Seven Sisters, 2629
Seventh Army. *See* Yildirim Army
Şevket, Mahmut, **2013**
assassination of, 623, 1737, 2013
Committee for Union and Progress and, 2013
as grand vizier, 2013
military training of, 2013

Sèvres Protocol (1956), 520, **2013–2014,** 2109
Sèvres, Treaty of (1920), 512, **2014–2015,** *2015*
Jewish Agency for Palestine in, 1227
and Lausanne, Treaty of (1923), 1802
partition plans for Turkey in, 1802
as political victory for Zionism, 2435
Turkish opposition to, 1802
Sewage
recycled, as water resource, 1668, 2329–2330
and water pollution, 2331–2332
Sexual activity, honor killings for, 649–650, 1495
Noor al-Hussein in campaign against, 1691
Sexually transmitted diseases (STDs), 480
Seyfettin, Ömer, 1439, 1800
Seyfiyye, 1264, 2629
Seymour-Jorn, Caroline, *as contributor,* 378–379, 1472–1473, 1611, 1652, 1924–1925
Seyun (Yemen), Old Sultan's Palace in, *1813*
"Seyyire-i Tesamüh" (Nabizade Nazim), 1631
Sezer, Ahmet, **2015**
Seznec, Jean-François, *as contributor,* 752–754, 1671, 1823, 1827–1830, 1938, 2090–2092, 2106–2107, 2110–2111, 2363–2364
Sfar, Bashir, **2015–2016**
in Young Tunisians, 2408
Sfar, Rachid, Mzali (Mohammed) replaced by, 1628
Sfar, Tahar, **2016**
Sfax (Tunisia), **2016,** 2225
Jalluli family in, 1213
Sfayr, Salil, 2021
Sfeir, Nasrallah, 1492, **2016–2017**
as political leader, 593
Sfez, Batto (Samuel), 860
Sfollamento, 920
Sforza, Carlo, 469
Shaʿabi, Najib Qahtan al-, in 1999 presidential elections, 2389, 2398
Shaʿb, al- (newspaper), 1906
Shabab, al- (weekly), 917
Shabab imraʾa (film), 1273
Shabab Muhammad. *See* Muhammad's Youth
Shabʿa Farms, **2017**
Israeli occupation of, 254
Nasrallah (Hasan) opposing, 1647
Shabak. *See* Shin Bet
Shabak affair, 2056
Shabazi, Shalom, 1014
Shabbetai Tzevi, 719–720
Shabbi, Abu al-Qasim al-, 1428, **2017–2018**
Shaʿbi (music), 1687
Shabiba (Fatah youth movement)
Barghuthi (Marwan) in, 402
Dahlan (Muhammad) in, 661
Shabib, Kamil, 927
Shaʿbi family, **2018**
Shaʿbi, Faysal Abd al-Latif al-, 2018
Shaʿbi, Najib Qahtan, 2018
Shabin Karahissar, Armenian resistance at, 1613
Shaʿbi, Qahtan al-, 2018
in National Liberation Front, 1814
Shaʿbiyya doctrine, of Ahali group, 80
Shabtai, Aharon, 1434
Shabtai, Yaacov, 1433
Shach, Eliezer, break with Agudat Israel, 77
Shadaba, al- (newspaper), Kawakibi (Abd al-Rahman al-) in, 1282
Shadhili, Abu al-Hassan al-, 2113
Shadhiliyya (Sufi order), 2113
Ilaysh (Muhammad) in, 1086
Shafaq-e Sorkh (newspaper), 678
Shafiʿi, Muhammad ibn Idris al-, 2018
Shafiʿi school of law, **2018–2019,** 2123
foundation of, 2018
and Hanbali School of Law, 990
influence of, 2019
principles of, 2018
scholars of, 2019
students of, 2019
Shafik, Doria, 890–891
Shafi, Mirza, 816
Shafiq, Durriyya, **2019**
Shafra, al-, 2210
Shaftesbury, Anthony Ashley Cooper, 1796
Shaghmoum, al-Miloudi, 1428
Shah, 2629
Shahab Sayyiduna Muhammad, 1621
Shahada (witnessing), 1145, 2113
Shahada, George, **2019–2021**
Shaham, Nathan, 1432
Shahbandar, Abd al-Rahman, **2021**
in Arab Academy of Damascus, 223
assassination of, 2021
and Abdullah I ibn Hussein, 30
Atrash (Sultan Pasha al-) and, 337
education of, 2021
under Faisal I ibn Hussein, 2021
National Bloc in conflict with, 2021
Shahbazi, A. Shapur, *as contributor,* 481–482
Shah-e siyah pushan (Golshiri), 929
Shahid (martyr), in Afghan resistance war, 1561
Shahid Beheshti University, Ebtekar (Maʿsumeh) at, 745
Shahîd, Irfan, *as contributor,* 2044–2045
Shahin, Emad Eldin, *as contributor,* 436–437, 452–453, 984, 1586–1587, 1590, 1635, 1636, 1965, 2078–2079
Shahin, Tanyos, **2021**
Shahin, Yusuf, 818, **2021–2022**
Shahnameh (Ferdowsi), 207, 2027
Shahrani, M. Nazif, *as contributor,* 53–62, 679–680, 2305–2306, 2420–2421
Shahrastani, al, 1457
Shai (Haganah intelligence service), Harel (Isser) in, 992
Shair Evlenmesi (Shinasi), 2187
Shakespeare, William, translation of, 171
Shakespear, William (British captain), Abd al-Aziz ibn Saʿud Al Saʿud and, 10
Shallah, Ramadan Abdullah, in Islamic Jihad, 1155
Shalom, Avraham, 2056
Shalom Yerushalayim (Alkalai), 149
Shalom, Zaki, *as contributor,* 1513–1515
Shaltut, Muhammad, **2022**
at al-Azhar, 348
on jihad, 1236
Shalvi, Alice, **2023**
Shamali, Fuʾad al-, in Lebanese Workers' Party, 626

Shamʿa wa ad-Dahalib, al- (Wattar), 2333
Shami, Abdullah al-
imprisonment by Palestinian Authority, 1155
in Islamic Jihad, 1155
Shami, Ahmad Muhammad al-, **2023**
Shamikh, Mubarak Abdullah al-, **2023–2024**
Shami, Muhammad Abdullah al-, **2024**
Shamir, Moshe, 956, **2024–2025**, 2185
Shamir, Yitzhak, *2025*, **2025–2026**
in Arab–Israel War (1982), 252
under Begin (Menachem), 2026
education of, 2025
election of, and formation of National Front (Lebanon), 1656
government of, Modaʾi (Yitzhak) in, 1555
imprisonment of, 2025
against Intifada (1987–1991), 2026
in Irgun Zvaʾi Leʾumi, 2025
Karp committee appointed by, 1275
in Labor–Likud coalition government, 1167, 1818
as Likud leader, 466, 1184, 1417, 2026
in Lohamei Herut Yisrael, 1443, 2025–2026, 2385
peace process under, 271, 1725, 2026
in Sabra and Shatila massacres, 1263, 2026
Sharon (Ariel) under, 2026
Shami, Seteney, *as contributor*, 599–600
Shamiyya al-, 2136
Shamlu, Ahmad, 1436, **2027**
Shammar tribe, 2209, 2214
Shammas, Anton, **2029**
Shamʿun, Camille. *See* Chamoun, Camille
Shanah Ahat (Brenner), 507
Shant, Levon, 676
Shantytowns. *See* Bidonvilles
Shapira, Hayyim Moshe, **2029–2030**
Shapiro, Zeva, *as contributor*, 1268–1269, 1288
Sharabati, Ahmad al-, **2030**
Sharabati, Uthman al-, 2030
Sharab-e kham (Fassih), 812
Sharabi, Hisham, 1792
Shara, Faruk al-, Israeli negotiations with, 1168
Sharafkandi, Sadegh, death of, 694
Sharaf, Layla, 820
Sharaif, 361
Sharansky, Natan, in Israel be-Aliyah, 1182
Shaʿrawi, Ali al-, 227
Shaʿrawi, Huda al-, 1652, **2030–2031**
in Arab Feminist Union, 227
in Egyptian Feminist Union, 227, 770, 890
in Egyptian Women's Union, 772
and *hijab*, removal of, 1027
and Rateb (Aisha), 1905
Saʿid (Amina al-) as protégé of, 1965
on Wafdist Women's Central Committee, 2321
in Wafd party, 2320
and Ziadeh (May), 2431
Shaʿrawi, Muhammad Mutwalli al-, **2031**
Sharecropping, 1371
Sharef, Zeʾev, **2031–2032**
Sharett, Moshe, *2032*, **2032–2033**
Ben-Gurion (David) and, 449, 2032, 2033
Egyptian peace negotiations with, in Operation Alpha, 157
as foreign minister, 449, 2032
and Harkabi (Yehoshafat), 995
and Herzog (Yaʿacov David), 1023
investigating Lavon affair, 1377
Israel Defense Force under, politicization of, 1173
Joseph (Dov) and, 1250
Kasztner affair and (1954–1955), 1280
Meir (Golda) and, 1513–1514
Navon (Yizhak) and, 1671
negotiating with Marshall (George), 2032
negotiating with UNSCOM, 2032
as prime minister, 449, 2033
"principle of nonidentification" of, 2032–2033
Sasson (Eliyahu) supporting, 1993
Shiloah (Reuven) under, 2056
in West German reparations agreement, 43
Sharh Tanqih al-Fusul (Qarafi, al-), 1476
Shariʿa (Islamic law), **2033–2035**
administration of, by qadi, 1863
Berber Dahir (1930) removing Berbers from, 463
challenges to, *Zanan* (magazine) and, 2423
code system and, 2034–2035
components of, 2033–2034
Convention on the Elimination of all forms of Discrimination against Women (CEDAW) (1996) and, 1048
Dar al-Harb in, 670
Dar al-Islam in, 670
definition of, 2033
development of, 2034–2035
in Egypt, 1553
in Salafiyya movement, 1620
Shenouda III opposing, 2049
fatwa (legal opinion), 816–817
Fedaʾiyan-e Islam on, 820
on female circumcision, 822
fiqh (knowledge of), 833–834, 2033, 2154
gender equality within framework of, 1970
hadith in, 968
on *hijab* (veiling), 1026
in Iran, Nuri's (Fazlollah) insistence on, 1704
in Iraq, in provisional constitution (2004), 2326
in Morocco, 1585, 1598
Musa Kazim on, 1613
Naqshbandi adherence to, 1641–1642
in Ottoman Empire
Gülhane Imperial Edict (1839) on, 954
vs. Nizamiye, 1690
on personal status matters, 1380
on polygamy, 1839
vs. qanun, 1870
Qurʾan on, 2033, 2034
Qutb (Sayyid) on, 1884
reward and punishment in, 2033–2034
Salafiyya movement reinterpreting, 1974
in Saudi Arabia, 934
secular organs of justice and, 2034
as source of modern law, 1379, 1382, 1383
spread of, and trade, 2197
in Sudan, 1622
Garang (John) opposing, 868
under Numeiri (Muhammad Jaʿfar), 1701
Sufism and, 2112

Sunni schools of law and, 2034
Taha (Mahmud Muhammad) on, 1917, 2145
Tahtawi (Rifaʿa al-Rafi al-) on, 2147
in Tunisia, Ghannouchi (Rached) supporting, 912
Turabi (Hasan al-) on, 2234
in Wahhabism, 1625
on women and marriage, Republican Brothers' call for reform in, 1917–1918
women appointed to, 808
Shariʿa College, 364
Shariʿati, Ali, **2035–2036**
Rahnavard (Zahra) and circle of, 1899
Shariʿati, Mohammad Taqi, 2035
Shariatmadari, Kazem, **2036**
women's seminary established under, 187
Sharif, **2036–2037**
in Hashimite family, 1000
Sharif, Aziz, **2037**
Sharif-Emami, Jaʿfar, **2037**
Sharifian dynasties, **2037–2039**
legitimacy of, 2213
Sharifism
Alawi in, 2037, 2038
establishment of, 2037
Saʿdians in, 2037–2038
Sufism in, 2037
Sunni Islam in, 2037
Sharif, Ismaʿil al-, 2038
Sharif, Muhammad al-, 2038, 2297
Sharif of Mecca, **2039**
Sharif, Omar, **2039**
Sharif, Rashid al-, 2038
Sharif (noble) tribe, 2213, 2214
Sharjah (United Arab Emirates), **2039–2040**, 2219
Abu Musa Island claimed by, 38, 2040
climate of, 2040
coup attempt in (1972), 2040
Fujayra conflict, 859–860
Fujayra independence from, 2270
oil and gas in, 2040
population of, 2040
prosperity of, 2040
al-Qasimi family of, 1873–1874
Ra's al-Khayma secession from, 2270
Ra's al-Khayma united with, 1873, 2040
tourism in, 2040
trade in, 2040
tribes in, 2210
Sharm al-Shaykh (Egypt), **2040**
in Arab–Israel War (1956), 245
Arab League summit (2003) in, *1387*
Israel capturing (1956), 2040
Israel capturing (1967), 2040
peace summit at (2000), 606
Sharon, Ariel, *1392, 2041*, **2041–2042**
Abbas (Mahmud) negotiating with, 2026
in al-Aqsa Intifada (2000), 219–220, 992, 1174, 1793
reoccupation of West Bank during, 2341
at Aqaba meeting (2003), 32
in Arab–Israel War (1948), 2041
in Arab–Israel War (1956), 2041
in Arab–Israel War (1967), 2041
in Arab–Israel War (1973), 2041
in Arab–Israel War (1982), 252, 253, 254, 1174, 1537, 2042
on Arafat (Yasir) condoning terrorist actions, 2178
Arafat (Yasir) relations with, 272, 1169, 2042
under Begin (Menachem), 2042
Bush (George W.) support for, 220
Bush (George W.) willing to work with, 549
Dagan (Meir) appointed Mossad director by, *1578*, 1579
as defense minister, 1174
removal of, 1263
election of, 219, 1169, 1726
government of, 1169, 1170
Gush Emunim under, 958
Labor Party in, 1169, 1170
Netanyahu (Benjamin) in, 1677
Peres (Shimon) in, 1818
in Haganah, 2041
Haram al-Sharif visited by, and al-Aqsa Intifada, 219, 1226–1227, 1727
in Israel Defense Force, 973, 1171, 2041
Israeli settlements under, 1192, 2041–2042
Israel's invasion of Lebanon (1982) planned by, *1392*, 2042
Levy (David) under, 1408
in Liberal Party, 2041
in Likud Party, *1176*, 1184, 2041
Livnat (Limor) under, 1441
under Netanyahu (Benjamin), 2026
Oslo Accord rejected by, 1726, 1793, 2177–2178
peace process under, 1169, 1726, 1775
PLO infrastructure destroyed by, 2042
as prime minister, 2026
under Rabin (Yitzhak), 2041
and relocation of Ethiopian Jews, *787*
resignation of, 2026
in Sabra and Shatila massacres, 254, 1039, 1263, 1954, 2026
security under, 1169
under Shamir (Yitzhak), 2026
in Shlomzion, 2041
in Unit 101, 2041
Sharq, al- (journal), 2029
Kurd Ali (Muhammad) in, 1338
Sharq al-Awsat, al- (newspaper), 1681
Asmar (Fawzi al-) in, 325
Sharqi family, al-, **2042–2043**
Sharqi, Hamad ibn Abdullah al-, 2042
Sharqi, Hamad ibn Muhammad al-, 859, 2043
Sharqiyyin tribe, 2042
SHAS (Israel), 1188, 1554
Aloni (Shulamit) opposed by, 157
break with Agudat Israel, 77, 1178, 1188
electoral success of, 77, 1188
National Religious Party criticized by, 1187
platform of, 1188
vs. United Torah Judaism, 1190
Yosef (Ovadiah) in, 1188, 2404
Shashi, Abu Bakr al-, 2019
Shashi, al-Qaffal al-, 2019
Shashlik, 840
Shatibi, Abu Ishaq al-, 1476
Shatila massacres. *See* Sabra and Shatila massacres
Shatt al-Arab, 804, **2043**
Basra situated at head of, 410
control of, during Iran–Iraq War, 411, 2043
oil in, 537
Shatt al-Arab River, 902, 2328
as border between Iran and Iraq
Algiers Agreement on (1975), 140–141
conflict over, and Iran–Iraq War (1980–1988), 1538

Shatt al-Jarid (Tunisia), 2225
Shatt Dijla. See Tigris River
Shatts, 2225
Shaʾul, Anwar, **2043–2044**
Shavit, Shabtai, as Mossad director, 1578
Shavit, Yaakov, *as contributor,* 169–171, 612–613, 2025–2026, 2041–2042, 2437–2438
Shawa, Laila, **2044**
Shawarma, 840
Shaw Commission, 1044, 1454, **2044,** 2350
  on Western Wall disturbances, 2348, 2350
Shawqi, Ahmad, 1421, **2044–2045,** 2184
  Abd al-Wahhab (Muhammad ibn) and, 22
  biography of, by Arslan, Shakib, 307
  Husayn (Taha) study of, 1061
  Ibrahim (Muhammad Hafiz) compared with, 1078
  Umm Kulthum and, 2263
Shawqi, Inshirah, gender preventing delivery of appeal for independence, 2321
Shawqiyyat, al-, 2045
Shaw, Standord, 1035
Shawwaf uprising (1959), 421
Shaw, Walter, 2044
Shawwa, Sami al-, 112
Shaybani, Muhammad ibn al-Hasan al-, 988
Shaykh, **2045**
  in Baghdad *vilayet* of Ottoman Empire, 1525
  land ownership of, 1368, 1369
Shaykh al-Islam, **2045–2046**
  CUP transferring power of, to Ministry of Justice, 2046
  decline of, 1086, 1087
  fatwa issued by, 2045
  in İlmiyye, 1086, 1087
  in Twelver Shiʿism, 2046
  use of title, 2045
Shaykh al-madina, 2224
Shaykh, Hanan al-, **2046**
Shaykhi(s), 354, **2046–2047**
  Ahsaʿi (Ahmad al-) and, 93, 2046, 2047
  becoming Babis, 2047
  in Constitutional Revolution, 2047
  Kerman, 2047
  Mozaffar al-Din Shah as, 2047
  persecuted in Islamic Republic of Iran, 2047
  in Qajar dynasty, 2047
  in Shiʿism, 2047
  Tabriz, 2047
Shaykh, Muhammad al-, 2038
Shaykhukha wa qisas ukhra (Zayyat), 2428
Shayʾun fi Nafsika (al-Tabayniyy), 1429
Shazar, Shneour Zalman, **2047**
  Irgun Zvaʾi Leʾumi recognized by, 1140
Shazdeh Ehtejab (Golshiri), 929
Shazli, Saʿd al-Din, **2048**
Shedadeh, Aziz, 1375
Sheffer, Gabriel, *as contributor,* 706
Shehadeh, Raja, 991
Shekel, **2048**
SHELI Party (Israel), 1188
Shell. *See* Royal Dutch Shell
Shelley, Percy Bysshe, 1421
Shelomo Molkho (Kabak), 1260
Shelton, Hugh, *750*
Shemali, Fuad, 1395
Shemer, Naomi, 956
Shenhar, Yitzhak, **2048**
Shenouda III (Coptic pope), *639,* **2048–2049**
  in Arab–Israel War (1948), 2048
  dismissal of (1981), 987
  Easter celebrations canceled by (1981), 642
  in exile, 2048–2049
  under house arrest, 642
  Monophysite rejected by, 639
  Pope Paul VI meeting with, 2049
  Sadat (Anwar al-) accusing, 2048–2049
  Sadat (Anwar al-) exiling, 2319
  Tantawi (Muhammad Sayyid al-) meeting with, 2161
  UNESCO prize for tolerance awarded to, 2049
Shepard, William, *as contributor,* 183–184
Shepheard's Hotel (Cairo), **2050**
Sheraga tribe, 2212
Sher Ali (amir of Afghanistan), 19, 400
Sherarda tribe, 2212
Shérazade, 17 ans, brune, frisée, les yeux verts (Sebbar), 2007
Sherkat, Shahla, 894, 2423
Shertok, Moshe. *See* Sharett, Moshe
Sheshbesh, **2050**
Shiʿat Ali, 2052
Shibam (Yemen), *701, 1814*
Shiberghan (Afghanistan), **2050**
Shiber, Saba George, 1351
Shid, Nahid, **2051**
Shidyaq, Ahmad Faris al-, 1419, **2051**
Shihab, al- (newspaper), 440, 1425
Shihab family. *See* Chehab family
Shihabi, Amir Bashir al-, 2088
Shihabi, Faʾiz al-, in Istiqlal Party, 1198
Shihabi, Hikmat, in peace negotiations, 926
Shihabis, 728–729
Shihabi, Zlikha al-, **2051–2052**
Shiʿite Islam, **2052–2055**. *See also specific sects*
  in Afghanistan, 2052
    Interim Government of, exclusion from, 63
    resistance war in, 1561
  Ali as successor to Muhammad in, 1597
  Ali ibn Abi Talib as founder of, 2052
  Bahaʾis persecuted by, 365
  in Bahrain, 366, 368, 369, 370, 371, 2052
    pool on Nabi Salih, al- revered by, 1631
  caliph rejected by, 104
  in Egypt, 2054
  growth of, 2054
  imams of, 104–105
    belief in authority of, 1148
    conflict in succession of, 105, 1148, 1158
  in India, 2052
  in Iran, 2052, 2054
    Babi movement rejected by, 354, 355, 356
    Babi movement stemming from, 354, 355
    conflict with Sunnis, 1548
    in Mojahedin-e Khalq, 1562
    under Ottoman Empire, 1548
    as unifying force, 1549
  in Iraq, 410, 1548, 2052, 2054, 2070–2071
    Atabat (holy places) of, 328
    Hakim family, 977–978
    Iranian Revolution and, 1067
    resistance to Sunni rulers, Najaf, al- as center of, 1637

Sadr (Muhammad Baqir al-) inspiring, 1960
U.S. occupation (2003–) and, 1637, 2326
judicial system of, 2046
jurisprudence in
Akhbari school of, 97–98
Usuli school of, 2303
jurists in
niyabat-e amma (general deputyship) and, 2311–2313
velayat-e faqih (governance) and, 2311–2313
Kashif al-Ghita family in, 1278
in Kuwait, 2052
in Lebanon, 429, 1392, 1397, 1548, 1662–1663, 2052
AMAL supported by, 173–174
Fadlallah (Shaykh Husyan) as teacher of, 793–794
National Pact on, 1399
speakership of parliament reserved for members of, 1662–1663
madrasa education system in, 1458
mahdi in, 1462–1463
marja al-taqlid in, **1489–1490**
as minorities or subdominant groups, 1548
Muharram in, 1605–1607
Najaf as place of pilgrimage for, 2052
origin of term, 2052
origins of, 1148, 2052–2053
in Pakistan, 2052
political parties of, 63–64
Qashqa'i following, 2213
in Qatar, 1875
Rassid dynasty of, 358
Safavid, 2054
Samarra as holy city of, 1981
in Saudi Arabia, 1997, 2052
scholars of, 2054–2055
Shaykhism in, 2047
in South Lebanon Army, 2083
on *Sunna,* 2123
vs. Sunni Islam, 104–105, 1148, 2055, 2122–2123
in Syria, 2129
and temporary marriage (*ziwaj mut'a),* 2438–2439
theology of, 2053–2054
Ahsa'i (Ahmad al-) on, 93
in Turkey, 112–115, 2238
ulama of, role of, 2259
on women, inheritance of, 887
women in, religious rituals of, 2360
in Yemen, 2052, 2388
Shi'ite Party of the Islamic Call (Bahrain), 369
Shikara, Ahmad Abdul A. R., *as contributor,* 323–324, 345
Shilluk, **2055,** 2098
Shilo'ah, Ha- (periodical), 470, 1430
Shiloah, Reuven, **2055–2056**
in Arab–Israel War (1948), 681
General Armistice Agreement on (1949), 240
under Eban (Abba), 2056
in Haganah, 2055
Harel (Isser) in conflict with, 2056
in Jewish Agency, 2056
at Lausanne Conference (1949), 2056
in Mossad, 1577, 2056
successor to, 992
Shimoni, Yuval, 1434
Shim'un, Mar, **2056**
Shinar, Dov, *as contributor,* 1683–1684, 1896–1897
Shin Bet (Israel), 1577, 1579, **2056–2057**
Harel (Isser) in, 992, 2056
and Shabak affair, 2056
torture used by, 2056
Shinui Party (Israel), 1188
in Democratic Movement for Change, 1181, 1188
in Meretz Party, 1186, 1188
platform of, 1188
Rubinstein (Amnon) and, 1938
in Sharon (Ariel) government, 1170
Ships, 2069, 2205
dhows, 704–705
feluccas (sailboats), *605*
iron-clad warships, origins of, 1741
modern, 2207, *2207*
steam-powered, 2198
and trade, 2197, 2198
Shiqaqi, Fathi Abd al-Aziz, in Islamic Jihad, 1155
Sh'ir (magazine)
Adonis in, 48
Darwish (Mahmud) in, 674
Khal (Yusuf al-) in, 1298
Shira (Agnon), 71–72
Shirak (Alishan), 144
Shi'r al-hurr, al-, 2002
Shiraz (Iran), **2057**
bazaars of, 420
Shirazi, Abu Ishaq al-, 2019
Shirazi, Faegheh, *as contributor,* 607–612
Shirazi, Mirza Hasan, **2057**
residence in Samarra, 328
Tabataba'i (Mohammad) studying under, 2141
in Tobacco Revolt, 2057, 2141, 2193
Shirazi, Mulla Sadra, Ahsa'i (Ahmad al-) on, 93
Shirazi, Sayyid Ali Mohammad. *See* Bab, al-
Shiraz University, **2057–2058**
Shirdel, Kamran, films of, 1318
Shirim (Amichai), 182
Shirk (polytheism), muwahhidun rejection of, 1625
Shirzad, Farhad, *as contributor,* 1802, 2251–2252
Shishakli, Adib
and Atasi (Hashim al-) as titular president, 329
conspiracy against (1951), 2030
coup by (1949), 329, 1032, 2133
government of, Hawrani (Akram al-) in, 1010
overthrow of, 1886, 2133
resistance to government of, 980
and Za'im (Husni al-), 2422
Shish kebab, 840–841
Shitreet, Bekhor, **2058**
Shlaim, Avi
as contributor, 154–156, 921–923, 1247, 1806
as historiographer, 1037
Shlomzion, Sharon (Ariel) in, 2041
Shlonsky, Avraham, **2058–2059**
Shneurson, Zelda. *See* Zelda (Israeli poet)
Shoah. *See* Holocaust
Shobat, Ella, 1036
Shochat, Manya, **2059**
Shojaie, Zahra, in Iranian Bureau of Women's Affairs, 1123
Sholay-e Jawid (Afghanistan), 62
Shooting Magda (Sobol), 2076
Shorfa, 996, **2059**
Shor language, 2252
Short stories
in Arabic literature, 1082–1083, 1419, 1420
of Egypt, 1082–1083
Palestinian, 1297

Short stories *(continued)*
in Persian literature, 1435, 1802–1803
of Syria, 1084
of Tunisia, 1313
SHP. *See* Social Democratic Populist Party
Shuckburgh, Evelyn, in Operation Alpha, 157
Shuf (Lebanon), **2059–2060**
Jumblatt family in, 1254
Shufman, Gershon, **2060**
Shuhada Foundation, 1982
Shuhuda Ya'udun Hatha al-Usbu (Wattar), 2333
Shuja Durrani, 196, 735
brother of, 1468
Shukri, Ibrahim, 768
Shukri, Mohammad, 1425, **2060**
Shulkhan Arukh (Karo), 979, 1962
Shultz, George, **2061**
education of, 2061
in Israeli–Lebanese security agreement, 254, 318
at King David Hotel, 1324
under Nixon (Richard M.), 2061
and Reagan Plan (1982), 2061
Shumayyil, Shibli, **2061**
Shuqayri, Ahmad, **2061–2062**
against Camp David Accords (1978), 2062
education of, 2061
in exile, 2062
expulsion from Jordan, 2156
vs. Hut (Shafiq al-), 1071
in Istiqlal Party, 2061
and Nasser (Gamal Abdel), 2062
as PLO founder, 813, 1777, 2062
as PLO leader, 814, 1767, 1772, 1791, 2062
Shuqayri, Anwar al-, 2063
Shuqayri, As'ad al-, 2061, 2062–2063
Shuqayri family, **2062–2063**
Shura, 1145, **2063,** 2234
in Afghanistan, establishment of, 63
vs. anjoman (assembly), 207
in Iran, 1359
Shura Council (Hizbullah, Lebanon), Nasrallah (Hasan) on, 1647
Shura-i Nizar (Afghanistan), in interim government, 64
Shura-i-Zanan-i-Afghanistan, 786
Shura-ye Ittifagh-e Islami (Afghanistan), 63
in mojahedin resistance, 1561
Shuster, W. Morgan, **2063–2064**
Russian demand for dismissal of, 88
Shuttar, Al- (Shukri), 2060
Shutters (Freier), 855
Shuttle diplomacy, 2070
definition of, 2629
Kissinger (Henry) as architect of, 1327–1328
Shu'un Filastiniyya (journal), 1782
Darwish (Mahmud) as editor of, 674
Siba'a tribe, 2212
Sibay tribe, 2209
Sibila, battle of (1929), 1085
Sib, Treaty of (1920), 1710, **2064**
Sidara, 611, 2629
Siddiq al-Mahdi (Sudanese leader), 210
Siddiqi, al-Tayyib al-, 2184
Sidera, Zineb, **2064–2065**
Sidi Barrani (Egypt), 2369
Sidi Ifni (Morocco), 1083
Sidi Muhammad ibn Abdullah, favorite son of, 1003
Sidi Muhammad ibn Abdullah University, 828
Sidi Muhammad, Mulay (sultan of Morocco), Montefiore (Moses) and, 1565
Sidi Sliman (Morocco), 913
Sidi Yahya (Morocco), 913
Sidon (Lebanon), **2065**
As'ad Wali in, 320–321
fishermen strike (1975) at, 1391
fishing in, 2065
Hariri (Rafiq Baha'uddin al-) and, 994
Jewish financiers in, 807
Sidqi, Aziz, 1650
Sidqi, Bakr, **2065**
in Ahali group, 80
coup led by (1936), 999, 1001
Abu al-Timman (Ja'far) supported by, 35
Ahali group in, 80
crackdown on opposition by, 43
Sulayman (Hikmat) friendship, 2115
Sidqi, Isma'il, **2065–2066**
in exile, 2065
under King Fu'ad, 2065
in Liberal Constitutionalist Party, 2065
Mahmud (Muhammad) and, 1468
Maratghi (Mustafa al-) opposing, 1486
as prime minister of Egypt, 859, 2066
in Wafd, 2065
Wafd opposing, 2066
Zaghlul (Sa'd) and, 2065
Sidra, Gulf of, **2066**
Sieff, Rebecca, in Women's International Zionist Organization, 2357
Siemens, Georg von, 533
Sifr al-Naqla wa al-Tasawwur (Ben Saleh), 1429
Sifriyat ha-Po'alim (Shlonsky), 2058
Sihab, al- (turban of Muhammad), 609
Silence (Iranian film), 1473
Silences du palais, Les (film), 2192
Silences of the Palace (film), 833
Silk, **2066,** 2180, 2197, 2198
Silk Road, 2066
Silo, Fawzi, in General Armistice Agreement (1949), 241
Silsila (initiatic chain), 1641, 2113
Silvera, Alain, *as contributor,* 2315–2316
Silver, Abba Hillel, **2066–2067**
during Holocaust, 2436
Wise (Stephen S.) conflict with, 2355
Silver, Eric, *as contributor,* 424–427, 1676–1677, 2041–2042
"Silver Platter, The" (Alterman), 171
Silverstein, Brian, *as contributor,* 1684–1685, 1897–1898
Silverstein, Paul, *as contributor,* 463–464, 485–486
Simaika, Marcus, Coptic Museum founded by, 638
"Siman-Tov's Thousand Wives" (Seri), 2012
Simavi, Erol, 1051, 2067
Simavi, Sedat, **2067**
and *Hürriyet* (newspaper), 1051
Simeon bar Yohai, *717*
Simit bread, *841*
Simko, Isma'il Agha, 1340, 1345
Simond, Paul Lewis, 710

Simon, Miriam, *as contributor,* 402–403, 449–450, 1459, 1671–1672, 2095–2096, 2169, 2172, 2339, 2424–2425
Simon, Rachel, *as contributor,* 807, 1870–1871, 1990, 2246–2247
Simon, Reeva S., *as contributor,* 244–246, 275–280, 412–414, 799–802, 852–853, 903–907, 927, 1043, 1211–1212, 1213–1214, 1222–1227, 1325, 1378, 1582, 1654–1655, 1937–1938, 1953, 2173, 2214–2215, 2353–2354, 2399–2400
Simoon wind, 605
Sinai (Israeli periodical), 1470
Sinai campaign of 1956, 681, 1537
  Amit (Meir) in, 190
  Anglo–Egyptian Treaty nullified by, 200
  Dayan (Moshe) in, 681
  Israeli-French negotiations before, Peres (Shimon) in, 1817
  Operation Alpha and, 157
Sinai I disengagement agreement (1974), Kissinger (Henry) in, 1328
Sinai II disengagement agreement (1975), Kissinger (Henry) in, 1328
Sinai, Mount, 1971, 2067–2068
Sinai Peninsula, **2067–2068**
  Bedouin tribes on, 2068
  British occupation of, during World War I, 509
  British–Ottoman rivalry over, 2068
  Camp David Accords (1978) on, 2068
  climate of, 2067
  Egyptian–Israeli Peace Treaty (1979) on, 771, 2068
  Egypt trying recapture of (1972–1973), 1957, 2068
  Israeli evacuation of (1982), 1166
    military action against opponents of, 1536
  Israeli seizure of, in Arab–Israel War (1967), 249, 1537, 1651, 2068
  location of, 763, 2067
  London Treaty (1840) on, 2068
  origin of term, 2067
  under Ottoman control, 2068
  withdrawal of UN forces from, Nasser's (Gamal Abdel) request for, 1651
Şinasi, İbrahim, **2068–2069**
  as pioneer of modernism, 1438
  newspaper edited by, 1684
  in Young Ottomans, 2069, 2405, 2406, 2407
  and Ziya (Abdülhamit), 2439
Sinatra, Frank, 224
Sinekli Bakkal (Adivar), 46
Sinf, 947
Siniora, Randa, in Women's Studies Center, 2362
Sion (journal), 292
Sion, Dov, 683
Sira al-Madhhab wa al-Aqida fi al-Qur'an (Ghallab), 910
Siraj al-Akhbar (newspaper), 56
  Young Afghan Party and, 62
Siraj al-Din, Fu'ad, as New Wafd leader, 2321
Sirat al-Mustaqim, al- (Straight Path), terrorist attack in Casablanca, 1569
Sirhindi, Ahmad, 1642, 2114
Şirket-i Hayriye, **2069**
Sirry, Gazbia, **2069**
Sisakan (Alishan), 144
Sisco Associates, 2070
Sisco, Joseph, **2069–2070**
Sistan (Iran), **2070**
Sistani, Ali al-, **2070–2071**
  al-Da'wa al-Islamiyya and, 681
  direct elections urged by, 2326
Sistani language, 2070
Sistanis, in Zahedan (Iran), 2420
Sisters of Zion School (Jerusalem), 2051
Sivan (Alishan), 144
Sitra (Bahrain), **2071**
Sitt, 2629
Sitt, al-. See Stanhope, Hester
Sitt Marie Rose (Adnan), 47
Siuni, Papken, 676
Sivas Conference (1919), **2071**
  Atatürk (Mustafa Kemal) in, 331
Sivers, Peter von, *as contributor,* 85, 139–140, 1610, 1713–1715, 2327
Siwa oasis, **2071–2072**
Sixième jour, le (Chédid), 583
Six-Point Agreement (1973), Kissinger (Henry) in, 1328
Six Points (Hammarskjöld), 2108
Sixth Day, The (Chédid). *See Sixième jour, le*
Sixth of October City (Egypt), 1995
Siyah Inciler (Mehmet Rauf), 1513
Siyahkal incident (1971), 821
Siyasa, al- (journal)
  Abd al-Raziq (Ali) in, 21
  Haykal (Muhammad Husayn) and, 1013
Siyasa al-Dawliyya, al- (journal), 505, 1682
Skif, Hamid, 1426
Skin and the Gown, The (Appelfeld), 217
SLA. *See* South Lebanon Army
Slade School of Art (London)
  Salim (Jawad) at, 1978
  Sirry (Gazbia) at, 2069
Slave(s)
  agricultural, 2072, 2073
  black, 2073, 2074
  Caucasian, 2073, 2074
  children as, 2072
  definition of, 2072
  domestic, 2072, 2073
  in Egypt, 2073, 2074
  in harems, 2072, 2073, 2074
  harratin as, 996
  military-administrative, 2072–2073
  social mobility of, 775
  women as, 2072, 2073
  in Yemen, 2073
Slave trade, **2072–2075,** 2197
  Anglo–Egyptian convention (1877) on suppression of, 2074
  Brussels Act (1980) against, 2074
  Christian sailors sold in, 542
  Circassians in, 599, 2074
  in Ottoman Empire, 2072–2074
    abolition of, 2074
    during Tanzimat era, 2073–2074
  route of, 2073
  in Tunisia, abolition of, 84
  volume of, 2073
Slavic languages, in Ottoman Empire, 1731
Slavic nationalism, and Austria-Hungary, 339
Slavs, 383
Slim, Fatima, 1429

Slouschz, Nahum, 277
Haggiag (Khalifa) poems in books of, 973
Slovakia, in U.S. invasion of Iraq (2003), 2325
Slovenes, 383
Sluglett, Peter, *as contributor,* 14–16, 202–203, 412–414, 613–617, 645–646, 802, 915, 1046–1047, 1084, 1219, 1283–1284, 1524, 1985–1987, 2056, 2065, 2115, 2341–2342, 2352–2353
Smallpox vaccine, 1508, 2003
Smara, under Spanish control, 2085
SMC. *See* Supreme Muslim Council
Smetana, Bedrich, and Zionist anthem, 1007
Smilansky, Moshe, **2075,** 2403
Smith, Sidney, 1330
Smithsonian Institution, 279
Smolansky, Oles M., *as contributor,* 507–508, 1314, 1941–1944, 1945–1946, 1988–1989, 2087–2088
Smolenskin, Perez, 507
Smyrna. *See* İzmir
Sneh, Moshe, **2075**
Soap industry, in Idlib province (Syria), 1080
Sobhe Emruz (newspaper), 867
Sobol, Yehoshua, **2076,** 2186
SOCAL. *See* Standard Oil of California
Social and Democratic Movement (MDS) (Algeria), 1803
Social Democratic Party (Egypt), 1957
Social Democratic Party (SDP) (Turkey)
electoral success of, 1097
establishment of, 1097
İnönü (Erdal) in, 1097
merger with Populist Party, in Social Democratic Populist Party, 1097
Motherland Party challenged by, 1747
Social Democratic Party of Azerbaijan, **2076**
Social Democratic Populist Party (SHP) (Turkey), 1919, **2076–2077,** 2219, 2242
establishment of, 1097, 2077
İnönü (Erdal) in, 1097, 1098–1099, 2077
Motherland Party opposition, 2077
Republican People's Party merging with, 2077
True Path Party merging with, 2077
Social Democratic Society (Afghanistan). *See* Afghan Nation
Social elites, 775
"Social idealism," 924
Social injustice, films on, 832
Socialism, 776
in Afghanistan, 62
in Algeria
constitution on, 128, 130
Soltani (Abdellatif) criticizing, 2079
and SONATRACH, 2079–2080
Arab, 265
Hakim (Muhsin al-) on, 977
Hanoune (Louisa) and, 990
and Arabic literature, 1422
constructive, 1362
in Egypt, 265, 266–267, 767
and Hebrew literature, 1432
and Labor Zionism, 1359–1360, 1361–1362
prudent, 422
in Russia and Eastern Europe, 1360
"scientific," 1357
and use of law for restructuring property rights, 1379
and Zionism, 289, 1281, 2434
Socialist Destour Party (PSD) (Tunisia), 634, 2229, 2231
Baccouche (Hedi) in, 356
Ben Ali (Zayn al-Abidine) in, 439
Ghannouchi (Rached) opposing, 912
and LTDH, 1416
Mestiri (Ahmad) in, 1519–1520
Socialist Forces Front (Algeria). *See* Front des Forces Socialistes
Socialist Front (Lebanon)
Chamoun (Camille) in, 580
establishment of, 580
Socialist International, Republican People's Party in, 1919
Socialist Labor Party (Egypt), 768
Muslim Brotherhood alliance with, 1622
Socialist Liberal Party. *See* Parti Socialiste Liberale
Socialist National Front (Lebanon), Twayni (Ghassan) as candidate of, 2254
Socialist Party (Egypt), 626, 2405
Musa (Salama) on, 1614
Socialist Party (France), 1563
Socialist Party (Yemen). *See* Yemeni Socialist Party
Socialist People's Libyan Arab Jamahiriyya. *See* Jamahiriyya (Libya)
Socialist Progressive Rally (RSP) (Tunisia), 2232
Socialist Unionist Democratic Party (Syria), in National Progressive Front, 1665
Socialist Union of Popular Forces. *See* Union Socialiste des Forces Populaires
Socialist Union Party (Syria), in National Progressive Front, 1665
Socialist Vanguard Party (Algeria). *See* Parti de l'Avant-Garde Socialiste
Socialist Workers Organization (Algeria), 990
Social Party for Progress (PSP) (Tunisia), 2232
Social services
in Iran, 809–810
in Kuwait, 1349
Société Nationale de Transport et de Commercialisation des Hydrocarbures. *See* SONATRACH
Société Primitive (Jamaʿat al-Ruwwad), 997
Society for Islamic Culture (Egypt), 395
Muslim Brotherhood merger with, 1620
Society for Protecting the Rights of the Child (Iran), 744
Society for the Defense of Liberty and National Sovereignty of the Iranian Nation, 1117
Society for the Preservation of the Qurʾan, 2229
Ghannouchi (Rached) in, 912
Society for the Study of the Turkish Language. *See* Turkish Linguistic Society
Society for the Study of Turkish History, 2246
Society for Women's Development (Sudan), 1622

Society of Free Youth (Bahrain), 371
Society of Israel. *See* Agudat Israel
Society of Mothers of the Future (Egypt), 2321
Society of Muslim Brothers. *See* Muslim Brotherhood
Society of Muslims. *See* Takfir wa al-Hijra al-
Society of the Firm Tie (Jamʿiyyat al-Urwa al-Wuthqa), 962
Society of the Renaissance of the Egyptian Woman, 2321
Socony Vacuum
  Arabian American Oil Company partnership with, 229
  in construction of Trans-Arabian Pipeline, 2202
Socotra (Yemen), **2077–2078**
Sofreh (ritual meal), 2360, 2361
Soft Link Com, Nezzar (Khaled) in, 1686
Sogdian language, 1125
Soheyli, Ali, **2078**
Soif, la (Djebar), 716
Soirée des proverbes, La (Shahada), 2020
Sokolow, Nahum, **2078**
Solange Giraud, Born Tache (Bitton), 483
Soldier with the Arabs, A (Glubb), 923, 2153
Soleil en instance (Darwish), 1356
Solel Boneh (construction and industrial group), 1034, 1334
Solomon Grup (Levin), 1407
Solomon, Operation (1991), 786
Solomon's Stables (Jerusalem), 991
Solstice barbelé (Djaout), 716
Soltam, 1334
Soltani, Abdellatif, **2078–2079**
  Belhadj (Ali) under, 436
  criticizing secular policies, 1965
Somalia
  camels in, 560
  female genital mutilation in, 822
  in Gulf Crisis (1990–1991), 951
  human rights in, 1048
  Italian presence in, 1200
  labor unions in, 1358
  in League of Arab States, 1388
  Lebanon and, 1388
Somekh, Sasson, *as contributor,* 1023, 1703–1704, 1903, 1978–1979, 2043–2044, 2079
Somikh, Abdullah, **2079**
  and Hayim (Yusef), 1012
Somikh, Yehuda, 1012
Sommeil du juste (Mammeri), 1423
SONATRACH (Algerian hydrocarbon enterprise), **2079–2080**
  Abdesselam (Belaid) in, 23, 2079
  Brahimi (Abdelhamid) in, 506
  Ghozali (Ahmed) as director-general of, 916–917
Song of Birds (Bejerano), 434
Song of the Slain (Baraheni), 1436
Songs of Life (al-Shabbi), 2018
Soninké, 1503
Sonnetot Krim (Tchernichovsky), 2168
Sonn, Tamara, *as contributor,* 142–143
Sontag, Deborah, 1727
Son Yildiz (Mehmet Rauf), 1513
Sorani dialect, 1344
Sorayya in a Coma (Fasih), 1436
Sorbonne (university)
  Baccouche (Hedi) at, 356
  Bakhtiar (Shapur) at, 375
  Balafrej (Ahmed) at, 379
  Berrada (Mohammed) at, 467
  Boucetta (Muhammad) at, 495
  Bourguiba (Habib) at, 501
  Fasi (Muhammad al-) at, 812
  Guri (Chaim) at, 955
  Shafiq (Durriyya) at, 2019
  Sobol (Yehoshua) at, 2076
  Tlili (Mustafa) at, 2192–2193
  Turabi (Hasan al-) at, 2234
Sorek River, as Israeli water source, 1668
Soroush, AbdolKarim, **2080–2081**
SOS Children's Villages International, 1958
Sosyal Demokrat Halkci Parti (SHP). *See* Social Democratic Populist Party
Souaidia, Habib, Nezzar's (Khaled) defamation suit against, 1686
Souchon, Wilhelm, in World War I, 2365
Souffles (magazine), 1355, 1356
Souk (market), in Matrah (Oman), 1616
Soul of a Jew (Sobol), 2076
Soummamm Congress Platform, 450
Souroush, Albolkarim, publications by supporters of, 1630
Sousi, 459
Sous River valley (Morocco), 1567
Sousse (Tunisia), **2081,** 2225
Soustelle, Jacques, **2081**
South Arabian Armed Forces, **2081**
South Arabian League, **2081–2082**
Southeast Asia Treaty Organization (SEATO), Bandung Conference on, 387
Southeastern Anatolia Project (Turkey), **2082,** 2090
  Keban Dam in, 1284
  loans for, 2082
  total cost of, 2090
  and Turkish–Iraqi relations, 2082
  and Turkish–Syrian relations, 2082
Southern Baptist Convention, 1855
Southern Defense Force (Sudan), 2103
Southern Gates of Arabia, The (Stark), 2088
South Lebanon Army (SLA), **2083**
  under Haddad (Saʿd), 2083
  Hizbullah fighting, 2083
  IDF and, 399, 2083
  Lahad (Antoine) as leader of, 1364, 2083
  Maronites in, 2083
  Shiʿites in, 2083
South Persia Rifles, **2083**
South Semitic languages, 2010
South Slavs, 383
South-West Persia: A Political Officer's Diary, 1940 (Wilson), 2352
South Yemen. *See* People's Democratic Republic of Yemen
So Vast Is the Prisona (Djebar), 716
Soviet Socialist Republic of Iran, 41, 626
Soviet Union, 1942–1944
  Afghanistan invaded by (*See under* Afghanistan)
  Afghan relations with, Daud (Muhammad) and, 679–680
  Arab–Israel conflict and, 1943
  in Arab–Israel War (1956), 245, 246
  in Arab–Israel War (1967), 248, 508
    U.S. conflict with, 237
  in Arab–Israel War (1973), 250, 508
    economic support to Egypt by, 748
  Arab nationalism supported by, 517
  architecture of, 282
  arms sales by, 304, 750, 1943

Soviet Union *(continued)*
to Egypt, 412, 2215
to Iraq, 304, 1535, 1969
to Syria, 304, 318, 412
in Azerbaijan autonomy movement, 345, 346
during Cold War, 517
Baghdad Pact (1955) against, 363
and communist parties, 627
Dhufar rebellion in Oman supported by, 2174
economic and military aid from, 747, 748, 765
education in, of Afghans, 55
Egyptian relations with, 1942
in Arab–Israel War (1956), 245
in Arab–Israel War (1973), 250
and Aswan High Dam, 327
under Brezhnev (Leonid Ilyich), 508, *508*
friendship treaty (1971), Baghdadi (Abd al-Latif al-) against, 363
Sadat (Anwar al-) ordering Soviet military advisers to leave, 508, 1957
in Gulf Crisis (1990–1991), 951
intelligence agency of (*See* KGB)
intelligence services influenced by, 1102
and Iranian Kurds, 694
Iranian relations with
during Cold War, 517
and Iran–Iraq War, 1127
Tripartite Treaty of Alliance (1942) and, 2216
Tudeh Party supported by, 2222
Iran invaded by (1941), 516, 1216, 2144
during Iran–Iraq War, 1943
Iraqi relations with
under Hussein (Saddam), 1066
under Qasim (Abd al-Karim), 1872, 1969
Jews from, immigration to Israel, 48, 147, 1162, 1163, 1169
pan-Turkism in, 1801
PFLP supported by, 1840
PLO supported by, 2176
South Yemen independence movement supported by, 2174
state terrorism term used by, 2175
submarine base of, on Socotra, 2077
Syrian relations with, 318, 373
Turkish Straits claim by, 621, 2095
U.S. policy toward
under Carter, 567
Dulles (John Foster) in, 733
Kissinger (Henry) in, 1327
U.S. relations with, Brezhnev (Leonid Ilyich) and, 507
during World War II, 1942
SP. *See* Samaritan's Purse
Spagnolo, John P., *as contributor,* 688, 843–849
Spain, **2083–2085**. *See also specific cities, organizations, people, and regions*
Alpujarras uprising (1568–1571) in, 2084
Ceuta as possession of, 575–576
as EEC member, 2084
French alliance with, 2085
French rivalry with, 2084
Islamic numismatics in, 1702
Israeli relations with, 2084
Jews converting to Christianity *(conversos),* 2084
Jews expelled from (*See* Sephardim)
Madrid Agreements (1975) and cessions by, 942, 2084, 2086
medieval, Hebrew poets of, 1017
Moroccan enclaves of, 1516, 1567
Moroccan protectorate of (*See under* Morocco)
Muslims converting to Christianity *(moriscos),* 2084
Ottoman rivalry with, 2084
in peace process, 2084
POLISARIO opposed by, 2084
U.S. relations with, 2084
U.S. war in Iraq (2003) supported by, 2324
Western Sahara protectorate of (*See under* Western Sahara)
Morocco occupying (*See* Green March)
Spanel, Donald, *as contributor,* 638–642, 656–658, 691, 1239, 1490, 1822, 2048–2049
Spanish–French Treaty (1912), on Spanish control of Ifni, 1083
Spanish–Moroccan Treaty (1956), on Ifni, 1083
Spanish Morocco, 1516, 2084, *2085,* **2085–2086**
Berlin Conference (1885) on, 2085
cities in, 2085
Spanish Sahara. *See* Western Sahara
Spanyol. *See* Ladino
Sparks of Ashes (Iraqi poetry), 1475
Special Forces of the Levant, **2086**
Chehab (Fu'ad) in, 584
in Free French forces, 2086
in Lebanese Army, 2086
under Vichy government, 2086
Special Organization. *See* Organisation Spéciale
Spector, Daniel E., *as contributor,* 102–103, 152–153, 671–672, 869, 953–954, 1376–1377, 1479–1480, 1523–1524, 1526–1543, 1545–1546, 1933–1934, 1934–1936, 2063–2064, 2093–2094, 2194, 2252, 2308–2309, 2314–2315, 2334, 2368–2372
Speke, John, 548
Spellberg, Denise A., **1462–1463** *as contributor,* 1457–1458, 2258–2259, 2323
Spencer, Herbert, 2061
Sphinx (Egypt), 921, **2086**
on postage stamps, 1850
Spice market, *839*
Spice trade, 2197
Spies. *See* Espionage
Spirit possession cults, 2360
Spiritualisme et Matérialisme (Isnards), 576
Spiritual Zionism, 470
SPLA. *See* Sudan People's Liberation Army
Spleen de Casablanca, Le (Laabi), 1355
SPLM. *See* Sudan People's Liberation Movement
SPO. *See* State Planning Organization
Sponeck, Han von, 1136
Sports, women's, 1154
advocacy for, 998
Springs, karst, in Ras al-Ayn (Syria), 344
Sprinzak, Joseph, **2086–2087**
Spy, The (film), 2067
Sraosha (Zoroastrian deity), 2442
Srvantziants, Garegin, **2087**
SSNP. *See* Syrian Social Nationalist Party
Stack, Lee, 1465, **2087–2088**
assassination of, 2349
and Egyptian government crisis, 2419
Nuqrashi (Mahmud Fahmi al-) implicated and cleared in, 1701

Staff College, 1953
Stalin, Josef, 485
  ambitions in Middle East, 1942
  death of, MAPAM after, 1185
  vs. Khrushchev (Nikita S.), 1314
  and Palestinian partition, support for, 1943
Stampfer, Yehoshua, in Petah Tikvah, 1822
Standard Oil of California (SOCAL)
  in Bahrain, 229
  in construction of Trans-Arabian Pipeline, 2202
  Red Line Agreement and, 1910
  in Saudi Arabia, 11, 229
Standard Oil of New Jersey. *See also* Exxon
  Arabian American Oil Company partnership with, 229
  in As-Is Agreement (1928), 323
  in construction of Trans-Arabian Pipeline, 2202
  Red Line Agreement and, 1910
Standard Oil of New York
  in price wars, 323
  Red Line Agreement and, 1910
Stanford University
  Barak (Ehud) at, 398
  Turkish collection at, 492
Stanhope, Hester, **2088**
  Palmyra visited by, 275
Stanley, Ethel, 404
Star Enterprises, 230
Stark, Freya, 513, **2088–2089**
Star of North Africa (Algeria), **2089**
  growth of, 1426
  Hadj (Messali al-) in, 969
  Khider (Mohamed) in, 1309
  Lahouel (Hocine) in, 1365
  Parti du Peuple Algérien as extension of, 1804
  Parti du Peuple Algérien as successor of, 2089
Starrett, Gregory, 759
Stars of Jericho (Badr), 357
Stars Outside (Alterman), 171, 1432
Stasi Commission (France), Arkoun (Mohammed) in, 289
State feminism, 892–893
State List (Israel), 1188–1189
  Ben-Gurion (David) in, 1188–1189
  in Likud, 1184, 1417
"Statement of Advice, The," 2079
State Planning Organization (SPO) (Turkey), **2089–2090,** 2241
Statue de sel, La (Memmi), 1423, 1517
Status of Women in Yemen, The (National Women's Committee), 1669
Stavsky, Avraham, 290
Steadfastness Fund. *See* Sumud Fund
Steamships, 2198, *2205,* 2205–2206
Steam: The Turkish Bath (film), 832
Steel industry
  in Algeria, 208
  in Turkey, 1482, 1484
Stein, Kenneth W., *as contributor,* 1458–1459
Stekel, Wilhelm, Arabic translation of, 1294
Stephan, Rita, *as contributor,* 268–269, 1051–1052, 1079, 1493–1496, 1521, 1950–1951, 1952
Stephan, Stephen Hanna, 277
Stern, Abraham, *1442,* 1442–1443, **2090**
  and Bernadotte (Folke) assassination, 1250
  CID killing, 1443
  Di Tat edited by, 2384
  in Haganah, 2090
  in Irgun Zvai Le'umi, 1442, *1442,* 2090
  in Lohamei Herut Yisrael, 972, 1139, 1442, 2090, 2384
  against white papers on Palestine (1939), 2090
  in World War II, 2371
  Yellin-Mor (Natan) and, 2384
Stern Gang. *See* Lohamei Herut Yisrael
Stettinius, Edward, 1404
Stillman, Norman, *as contributor,* 396–397, 453–454, 549–550, 612, 619, 642–643, 720, 920, 1016, 1231–1234, 1252–1253, 1363, 1415–1416, 1453, 1460, 2308, 2352
Stinger antiaircraft missiles, sold by U.S. to Afghan guerrillas, 66
Stockholm (Sweden), Islamic numismatics in, 1702
Stock market, **2090–2092,** *2091*
  in Bahrain, 2091
  in Egypt, 2091, *2091*
  foreign investors in, 2091
  in Iran, 2091, *2091*
  in Iraq, *752*
  in Israel, 2090, 2091, *2091*
  in Jordan, 2091, *2091*
  in Kuwait, 2091, *2091*
  in Lebanon, 2091
  in Saudi Arabia, 2090, *2091,* 2091–2092
  size of, 2090
  in Turkey, 2090, *2091,* 2092, *2092*
Stokes, C. B., 2063
Stone, Christopher Reed, *as contributor,* 817–818, 1808
Stone on a Grave, A (Al-e Ahmad), 1437
Stories of Love and Pursuit (Badr), 357
Storrs, Ronald, 513, **2092–2093**
  Abdullah I ibn Hussein meeting with, 29, 2092
  in Arab Revolt, 2092
  and Balfour Declaration (1917), 2092
  and Husayni (Musa Kazim al-), 1058
  and Nashashibi (Raghib al-), 1645
  in Pro-Jerusalem Society, 2092
  Weizmann (Chaim) meeting with, 2092
Story of a Warrior, A (Cohen), 613
Story of Tou, The (Ghanim), 911
Straight Path, The (journal), 782
Strait of Hormuz, 952
Straits Convention (1841), 1691, 1945, **2093–2094,** 2095
  Turkish opposition to, 621
Straits, Turkish, 902, *2094,* **2094–2095**. *See also* Black Sea; Bosporus; Dardanelles
  and British–Russian relations, 528, 529, 2093
  in Eastern Question, 739–740
  importance to Russia, 1945
  international control of, under Lausanne Treaty (1923), 1565
  passage through
    Dardanelles Treaty restricting, 621
    Laussanne Treaty reestablishing, 621
    Montreux Convention (1936) on, 743, 2095
    Soviet claim to, 621, 2095
    Straits Convention (1841) on, 2093–2094, 2095
    Turkish control of, 621
  Turkish sovereignty over, under Montreux Convention (1936), 1565
  in World War I, 2365–2366

"Stranger, The" (Bint al-Shati), 476
Stranger, The (Camus), 563
Strange Woman, A (Erbil), 780
Stransky, Thomas, *as contributor*, 1971
Stratétegies de développement pour l'Algerie: 1962-1991 (Brahimi), 506
Stratford de Redcliffe, Viscount. *See* Canning, Stratford
Street Children Phenomenon in Yemen (WFRT), 2357
Strike the Whore (film), 832
Strokes of Genius: Contemporary Iraqi Art (exhibition), 805
Struma (ship), **2095–2096**
Student activism. *See also* Youth movements
  in Afghanistan, Islamic movement in, 60, 63
  in Iran, 630–631, 1120
  in Lebanon, at American University of Beirut, 180
  for regime change, 2412
Students in the Line of the Imam, 850, **2096**
Sturgeon, 834
Suad al-Sabah Publishing and Distribution House, 1952
"Su'al wa jawab" (leaflet), 2357
Suarès della Pegna, Menachem, 2096
Suarès, Edgar, 2096–2097
Suarès family, **2096–2097**
Suarès, Félix, 2096
Suarès, Isaac, 2096
Suarès, Joseph, 2096
Suarès, Raphael, 2096
Suarès Square (Cairo), 2096
Subbi (baptizers), 1479
Sublime Porte (Ottoman Empire), **2097**
  fermans issued by, 823
  Mustafa Reşid as representative of, 1624
Succession ouverte (Chraibi), 588, 1423
Sudan, **2097–2102**. *See also specific cities, organizations, people, and regions*
  agriculture in, 2099
    dry-farming techniques of, 75
    Gezira Scheme and, 908
  area of, 2097
  art of, 1142
  assassination of Stack (Sir Lee) in (1924), 1465, 2349
  banking in, *393*, 394
  and Beitaddin Declaration (1978), 432
  Beja in, 432–434, 2097
  bin Ladin (Osama) in, 475, 1865
  British–Egyptian dominion over, 529–530, 2100, 2102–2103
    Abd al-Rahman al-Mahdi in, 18–19, 209–210
    al-Ansar during, 209–210
    Baring (Evelyn) and, 405, 530
    Condominium Agreement on (1899), 405, 518, 530, 629, 1363, 2100, 2349
    education under, 2296
    fall of mahdist state to, 1463–1464
    Fashoda incident (1898), 405, 529–530, 811
    Foreign Office in, 530
    Gezira Scheme under, 908
    Kitchener (Horatio Herbert) in, 629, 1329
    Lado Enclave incorporated into, 1363
    Mahdist movement in, 404–405
    nationalist movement against, 2100
    revolt against (1924), 2349
    Wingate (Reginald) and, 2354
  cities of, 1279–1280, 2100
    capital, 1301–1302, 1712
  climate of, 2099
  communism in, 627
  constitution of (1999), 2101
  cotton industry in, 644, 908, 2180
  coup in (1958), 8, 2101
    Numeiri (Muhammad Ja'far) in, 1699
  coup in (1964), 8, 1075, 2101
    Numeiri (Muhammad Ja'far) in, 1699
  coup in (1969), 210, 2101, 2103
    Numeiri (Muhammad Ja'far) installed in, 1699
  coup in (1985), 1075, 2101, 2103
    Numeiri (Muhammad Ja'far) deposed in, 1701
  coup in (1989), 210, 2101, 2104, 2261, 2296
  defense costs as percentage of GNP or GDP, *1530*
  Dinka people of, 709, 867–868, 2098
  economic aid to
    from Arab countries, 749
    from IMF, 749
  economy of, 2099–2100, 2101
  Egyptian invasion of (1822), 1077, 1602
  Egyptian relations with, under Nasser (Gamal Abdel), 1649–1650
  Egyptian union with, proposal for, 349
  ethnic groups in, 2097–2099, 2103
  Fur tribe in, 2098
  geography of, 2099
  Greeks in, 938
  in Gulf Crisis (1990–1991), 951
  higher education in, 2296
  human rights in, 1048
  independence of, 519, 1917, 2101, 2102
    declaration of, 349
  irrigation in, 908
  Islamic fundamentalism in, 2101, 2234–2235
  languages in, 2099
    Arabic, 2099
    TaBedawie, 433
  in League of Arab States, 1388
  legal system of, 2104
    British influences on, 1380
    civil code, 1382
  Libyan relations with, under Numeiri (Muhammad Ja'far), *1700*
  literature of, 1977
  location of, 2102
  mahdist state in, 1463–1464
  map of, *2098*
  military of
    equipment of, *1534*
    force levels of, *1528–1529*
    force structure of, *1532–1533*
  Muslim Brotherhood in, 395, 2234
  nationalism in, 87, 2296
  natural resources in, 2099–2100
  newspapers and print media in, mobilization approach of, 1680
  Nubians in, 1696, 2097–2098
  Nuer in, 1699, 2098
  October Revolution in (1964), 1917
  oil production in, 2099–2100
  parliament of, Ibrahim (Fatima Ahmed) in, 1075
  political parties in, legalization of, 2261
  population of, 2097
  Protestant missions in, 1856
  provinces of, administrative, 1335
  pyramids in, 1857–1858

al-Qaʿida in, U.S. strikes against (1998), 606
radio and television in, *1895*
railways in, *2206*
regions of, 1335
religions in, 2099
Catholicism, 1931, *1931*, 1932
Christianity, 523, 2099
Sufism, 2099
Republican Brotherhood in, 1917
rivers of, 372, 1688
sharīʿa in
campaign against imposition of, 1918
women appointed to, 808
Shilluk in, 2055, 2098
terrorism in, by Black September, 486
textile industry in, 908, 2180
transport in, modern means of, *2207*
tribes in, 432–434, 2055, 2097–2099
Turko–Egyptian control of, 2100
al-Ansar during, 209
end of (1885), 209
water resources of
freshwater withdrawals, *2331*
from Nile River, 1688
quantity of, 2330
women in, 1917
in Muslim Sisters Organization, 1622–1623
in politics, 894
religious rituals of, 2360
Turabi, Hassan al- on, 1622–1623
women's rights in, 2105, 2235–2236
in World War II, 2369–2370
Sudanese Civil Wars, **2102–2105**, 2103
Abdullahi (Muhammad Turshain) in, 32–33
Addis Ababa Accords (1972) ending, 1700
famine during, 1511
Nuer people in, 1699
Numeiri (Muhammad Jaʿfar) in, 1700
revival of (1983), 1701, 2103–2104, 2106
Garang (John) in, 868
Sudanese Communist Party (SCP), 627, 2105
Ibrahim (Fatima Ahmed) in, 1075
Sudanese National Radio, 1977
Sudanese Socialist Union (SSU), 1700, 1701
Sudanese Women's Union (SWU), 894, 1622, **2105**
ban on, 1075
Ibrahim (Fatima Ahmed) in, 1075
Sudan People's Liberation Army (SPLA), 1701, 2100, 2103–2104, *2104*, 2106
Garang (John) in, 868
Sudan People's Liberation Movement (SPLM), 2101, 2103–2104, 2106
Garang (John) in, 868, *868*
Sudan Socialist Union, 2101
Sudayri Seven. *See* Al Fahd
Sudd, **2105–2106**
Dinka people in, 709
Sudd, al- (Masʿadi), 1498
Sudd swamps (Sudan), 1688, 2329
Suez, as port, 2206
Suez–Alexandria railroad. *See* Alexandria–Suez railroad
Suez Canal, 902, 1512, **2106–2107**
in Arab–Israel War (1973), 250
British interests in, 519–520, 529
Egyptian nationalization and, 519–520, 2014
importance of, 519, 528, 2106
security of, 517, 529
during World War II, 515–516
British occupation of, 2199
Anglo–Egyptian Treaty ending (1954), 199–200, 519, 1650
closure of (1967–1975), 521, 2107
Egyptian nationalization of, 519–520, 2106, 2107–2108 (*See also* Suez Crisis (1956–1957))
in Arab–Israel War (1956), 245, 1650
and Arab nationalism, 222
Eden (Anthony) opposing, 520, 755, 2108
to finance Aswan High Dam, 327, 1650
legality of, 1444
and London Conference (1956), 1444, 2108
Nasser speech on (1956), 118
reasons for, 519
and Sèvres Protocol, 520, 2014, 2109
volume of traffic before, 2207
enlargement of, 2107
free transit through, 529
French building of, 2106, *2106*, *2205*
Britain delaying, 528, 741
British opposition to, 740
and Egyptian state debt, 766
French advantage due to, 524, 846
Lesseps (Ferdinand de) in, 528, 1404, 1970, 2106, *2205*
Palmerston (Lord) and, 1797
Saʿid Pasha and, 766, 1970
impact on Cairo, 552
under Ismaʿil ibn Ibrahim, 1158
Israeli access to
Egyptian–Israeli Peace Treaty (1979) on, 771
in General Armistice Agreements (1949), 239
and Ottoman Empire, in Yemen, 2390
Port Saʿid on, 1848–1849
return to Egypt, Anglo–Egyptian Treaty on (1954), 199–200, 1650
security of, 517, 529
statistics on, *2107*
transit fees for using, 2107
UN peacekeeping force in area of, 986
in War of Attrition (1969–1970), 2327
in World War I, 2106
in World War II, 515–516, 2106, 2369–2370
Suez Canal Authority, 2107
Suez Canal Company, 1444, 2106
Britain as shareholder in, 528
nationalization of (*See* Suez Canal, Egyptian nationalization of)
Suez Canal University, **2107**
Suez Canal Users Association (SCUA), 1444, 2108
Suez caravan, 2205
Suez Crisis (1956–1957), **2107–2110**
Britain in, 520, 2108–2110
Bahrainis opposing, 371
and London Conference (1956), 1444
Bunche (Ralph J.) as mediator during, 543
China in, 587
diplomatic measures preceding, 2108
Dulles (John Foster) and, 733, 1937
Eisenhower (Dwight D.) calling for cease-fire in, 755, 773, 2109
Fawzi (Mahmud) in, 2108

Suez Crisis (1956–1957) *(continued)*
France in, 847, 2108–2110
French foreign legion, 856
Lacoste (Robert) supporting, 1363
and London Conference (1956), 1444
Mollet (Guy) and, 1563
Nasser regime opposition and, 520
Hammarskjöld (Dag) in, 1444, 2108
Harkabi (Yehoshafat) during, 995
international pressure for cease-fire in, 2109–2110
Iraqi stand during, Bazzaz (Abd al-Rahman al-) critical of, 421
Israel in, 520, 2108–2110
Lloyd (Selwy) in, 2108
London Conference (1956) in, 1444, 2108
Mollet (Guy) in, 2108
Musketeer Operation in, 2108–2109
Nasser (Gamal Abdel) in, 1650, 2109, 2110
Pineau (Christian) in, 2108
Roosevelt (Kermit) involvement in, 1937
Sèvres Protocol (1956) and, 520, 2013–2014, 2109
United Nations in, 1444, 2108, 2109–2110, 2275
Emergency Force of, 2275, 2286
U.S. against use of force in, 2108
U.S. response to, 2291
Suez, Gulf of, **952**
Suez, Isthmus of, 952
Suez–Mediterranean Pipeline (SUMED), 1830, **2110–2111**
Suffrage
in Saudi Arabia, 884
in United Arab Emirates, 884
for women, 887
in Bahrain, 893
in Egypt, 891
in Iran, *890*
in Kuwait, 884, 893
Sufism, **2111–2114**
Abd al-Wahhab (Muhammad ibn) criticizing, 2114
abolishment of, in Turkey, 2171
in Afghanistan, 863
art influenced by, 312, 2113
Banna (Hasan al-) and, 394, 1620
Bektashis and, 434–436
interpretation of Qur'an in, 2111, 2112
in Iraq, *2112*
Kattaniya Brotherhood of, 1281
Khalidi, 1642
Mevlevi Brotherhood of, 1521
Musa Kazim in, 1613
mysticism of, 1149
Naqshbandi in, 1641–1643
orders of, 2113–2114 (*See also specific orders*)
establishment of, 2113
and spread of Islam, 1149, 2113, 2114
origin of term, 2111
orthodox opposition to, 1149
philosophical expression of, 1149
reform movements in, 1149
restoring orthodoxy in, 1149, 2114
and *shariʿa*, 2112
in Sharifism, 2037
spread of, 1149
in Sudan, 2099
Suleiman (Mulay) suppressing, 2115
tekke (headquarters) of, 2171
theological and philosophical basis of, 2111–2113
women in, 2360
and Yacine (Abdessalame), 2375
Sufiyan tribe, 912
Sugar trade, 2198
Suha: Surviving Hell (documentary), 481
Suhravardi, and Ahsaʿi (Ahmad al-), 93
Suhrawardi al-, 2113
Suhrawardi, Chihab al-Din Yahya: Récites de l'exil occidental (Meddeb), 1507
Suhrawardiyya (Sufi order), 2113
Suicide bombings
in al-Aqsa Intifada, 219, 1169, 1793
by al-Aqsa Martyrs Brigade, 219
by al-Aqsa Martyrs of the World Islamic Front for Liberation, 814
Arafat (Yasir) toleration for, 1793
by HAMAS, 2177
by Hizbullah, 2177
by Islamic Jihad, 219, 1155, 1226, 1227
in Israel, 2178
Israeli response to, 1169
in Jerusalem, 1226, 1227
at Suez Canal, against British forces, 200
Suissa, Albert, **2114–2115**
Sukenik, E. L., 2376
and Dead Sea Scrolls, 686
at Hebrew University, archaeological department of, 277
Sukot (Nubian dialect), 1696
Suksukaniyya, 838
Süküti, İshak
in Committee for Union and Progress, 2409
in Ottoman Union Society, 622
Sulayhid dynasty (Yemen), 2397
weakening of, 1007
Sulayman, Abdullah, oil concession by, 229
Sulayman Abu Layla (Mamluk ruler), 1478
Sulayman Agha (Sulayman the Great) (Mamluk ruler), 1478
Sulayman, Ali, 316
Sulayman, Hikmat, **2115**
in Ahali group, 80
in coup (1936), 80, 2065, 2115
government of, Abu al-Timman (Jaʿfar) in, 35
Hashimi (Yasin al-) and, 2115
in Ikha al-Watani Party, 80, 1084
Kaylani (Rashid Ali al-) and, 2115
Sidqi (Bakr) friendship, 2115
Sulaymaniya (Iraq), **2115**
Kurdish Regional Government established in, 2151
as Kurdistan capital, 1342
Mahmud of, 1469–1470
Sulayman, Omar, *1103*
Sulayman, Shakir Abu, 1395
Sulayman the Little (Mamluk ruler), 1478
Suleiman, Elia, 833
Suleimaniye Mosque (Istanbul), *2237*
Suleiman, Mulay, **2115**
Süleyman I (the Magnificent), 1728
Iraq under, 1132
as Shaykh al-Islam, 2046
Süleymaniye Library. *See* Süleymaniye Mosque
Süleymaniye Mosque (Istanbul), *283*
Aya Sofya as inspiration for, 342
Sulh, Kazem al-, **2115–2116**, 2118, 2119
and National Pact, 1662–1663
Sulh, Rashid al-, **2116–2117**
Sulh, Riyad al-, *2117*, **2117–2119**
assassination of, 2118
daughter of, 165

Eddé (Emile) and, 2117
education of, 2117
in exile, 2117
Khuri (Bishara al-) cooperation with, 1315
in National Pact, 1315
as prime minister, 1399, 2118
Sulh, Sami al-, 2116, **2119**
Chamoun (Camille) supported by, 2119
Shader (Joseph) under, 2018
Sulh, Taki al-Din al-, 2116, 2118, **2119–2120**
Sultan, **2120**
ayan imposing will on, 1367
residence of, 2097
tughra (signature) of, 823
Sultan Ahmet Mosque (Istanbul), *1194*, **2120**, 2196
Aya Sofya as inspiration for, 342
Sultan Hasan Mosque (Cairo), **2120–2121**
Sultan ibn Abd al-Aziz Al Saʿud (prince of Saudi Arabia), 165, 795, 798
as de facto successor, 165, 168
government positions held by, 165, 168
mother of, 169
Sultan ibn Ahmad (ruler of Oman), in Anglo–Omani treaty, 204
Sultani schools, 864, **2121**
İdadi schools renamed as, 1080
Sultans ottomans, Les (Ganim), 867
Sulubba tribe, 2209
SUMED. *See* Suez–Mediterranean Pipeline
Sumer (ancient), 824, 902, 2188
Sümer bank (Turkey), 1482
Sumud, **2121**
Sumud Fund, 2121
Sunay, Cevdet, **2121–2122**
Sunbati, Riyad al-
and Atrash (Farid al-), 336
Umm Kulthum and, 2263
Sunday School movement, 2048
Sun language theory, **2122**
Sunna (record of Prophet), 1476, 2034, **2122**
definition of, 2122
extracted from *hadith*, 2122
on female circumcision, 822
FIS on establishment of Islamic state based on, 857
Shiʿism on, 2123
Sunna fasting, 2122
Sunna of the Prophet, The (al-Ghazali), 914
Sunna prayers, 2122
Sunni Islam, **2122–2124**. *See also specific sects*
Abu Bakr as successor to Muhammad in, 1597
in Afghanistan, resistance war in, 1561
in Algeria, 122
in Bahrain, 368, 371
of Baluchis, 385
vs. Bektashism, 435
of Berbers, 460
"fifth school" of, Zaydism as, 2427
Hanafi school of law in, 988–989, 2034, 2035, 2123
Hanbali school of law in, 989–990, 1997, 2123
historical and modern developments of, 2123–2124
vs. Ibadiyya, 1073
in Iran, conflict with Shiʿites, 1548
in Iraq
conflict with Shiʿites, 1530–1531
in Samarra, 1981
Shiʿite resistance against, Najaf as center of, 1637
traditional dominance of, 1547
in Jordan, 1242
among Kurds, 1345
in Lebanon, 429, 580, 1392, 2123
National Pact on, 1662–1663, 2116
in al-Nida al-Qawmi, 2116
prime ministership reserved for members of, 1662–1663
traditional dominance of, 1547
in Libya, 1410
madrasa education system in, 1457–1458
mahdi in, 1463
Maliki school of law in, 1476, 2123
in Mauritania, 1503
as minority or subdominant groups, 1548
in Morocco, 1568
muwahhidun in, 1625–1627
Naqshbandi in, 1641–1643
origin of name, 2123
in Ottoman Empire, 1147, 2123
in Pakistan, 2123
in Qatar, 1875
reform movements in, 2123, 2124
vs. Salafiyya movement, 1974
in Saudi Arabia, 1997
scholarship on
by Alusi (Mahmud Shukri al-), 173
by al-Qaradawi (Yusuf), 1870
Shafiʿi school of law in, 2018–2019, 2123
shariʿa system provided by, 2034
in Sharifism, 2037
Shiʿite Islam compared with, 104–105, 1148, 2055, 2122–2123
spread of, 1147
in Syria, 2129
Aleppo, 111
and temporary marriage (*ziwaj mutʿa*), 2438
in Tunisia, 2226
in Turkey, 2238
ulama of, powers of, 2258, 2259
on women, inheritance of, 887
in Yemen, 2388
Sunni Social Reform Society (Bahrain), 369
Sunni Triangle, armed resistance to U.S. occupation in, 2326
Supermarket (film), 833
Supervielle, Jules, 2020
Suphi Ezgi, **2124**
Supporters of the Call (Bahrain), 369
Supreme Advisory Assembly, Bishara (Abdullah) in, 481
Supreme Assembly of the Islamic Revolution in Iraq (SAIRI), 978
Supreme Council for Women's Affairs (Yemen), 1669
Supreme Council of Culture (Egypt), 1457
Supreme Council of Judicial Ordinances (Ottoman Empire), 1467
Supreme Defense Council (Iran), 388
Supreme Muslim Council (SMC), **2124–2125**
authority of, expansion of, 603
creation of, 1011
Husayni (Muhammad Amin al-) in, 1056, 1224, 1764, 1922, 2124–2125
against legislative council, 1402
Samuel (Herbert Louis) creating, 1983, 2124
Tamimi (Amin al-) in, 2158
Supreme National Committee for Human Rights (Yemen), 806

Supreme Opposition Council (Yemen), 2398
Suq al-Dakhili, al- (Shukri), 2060
Suqutra. *See* Socotra (Yemen)
Surest Path to Knowledge Concerning the Condition of Countries, The (Khayr), 1306
Süreya, Cemal, 1440
Suriya (newspaper), 1680
Suriyya al-Janubiyya (newspaper), Arif (Arif al-) in, 288
Surp Karapet (monastery), 2087
Surraya (queen of Afghanistan), **1881**
  in Association for the Protection of Women's Rights, 325
Sursock, Alfred Bey, 2125
Sursock, Lady Cochrane, **2125**
Sursock Museum (Beirut), 2125
Sursuq, Albert, 2125
Sursuq family, **2125**
Sursuq, Michel, 2125
Surur, Najib, 2184
Survivre comme l'espoir (Aslawi), 1427
Süs (magazine), 1513
Susa. *See* Sousse (Tunisia)
Susini, Jean-Jacques, in Organisation Armée Secrète, 1715
Suspended Dreams (film), 1500
Suswa, Amat al-Alim al-, on National Women's Committee, 1669
Suwayd, Amin, in Arab Academy of Damascus, 223
Suwaydi family, **2125–2126**
Suwaydi, Naji al-, 2126
Suwaydi, Shaykh Abdullah al-, 2125
Suwaydi, Tawfiq al-, **2126**
  Jabr (Salih) under, 1210
Suwaydiya oil fields, **2126–2127**
Suwaydi, Yusuf al-, 2126
Suwayhli, Ramadan al-, 471, **2127**
Suyuti, 2019
Swayd, Samy, *as contributor,* 726–730
Swearingen, Will D., *as contributor,* 335–336, 1516–1517
Sweden
  guest workers in, 945
  Islamic numismatics in, 1702
Switzerland, civil code of, in Turkish codes, 602
SWU. *See* Sudanese Women's Union
Sykes, Mark, 1501, **2127–2128**
  in Arab Bureau, 225
  in Boer War, 2127
  Clayton (Gilbert) and, 603
  in World War I, 2127
Sykes, Percy Molesworth, 2083
Sykes–Picot Agreement (1916), 846, 1479, 1504, 2127, *2128,* **2128–2129,** 2368
  and British–French Oil Agreement (1920), 538
  British promises in, 380, 511
  criticism of
    by Clayton (Gilbert), 603
    by Clemenceau (Georges), 603
  and Damascus, 800
  on Italian territories, 742
  and mandate system, 2128, 2315
  in San Remo Conference (1920), 1802
"Sylvie" (Nerval), 1675
Syphilis, 710
  in Egypt, 2003
Syria, **2129–2135**. *See also specific cities, organizations, people, and regions*
  administrative divisions in
    of 1952, 1080
    of 1982, 1080–1081
  agriculture in, 909
  Alawis in, 105, 2129
    in politics, 412–413
  antisemitism in, 212, 664–665
  Arab Club in, 225–226
  in Arab–Israel War (1948), 242, 1537
    General Armistice Agreement on (1949), 241
  in Arab–Israel War (1967), 237, 248–249, 1537
  in Arab–Israel War (1973), 237–238, 250–252, 1537, 2135
    as political victory, 318
  in Arab–Israel War (1982), 252, 964
  Arafat (Yasir) in, 270
  archaeology in, 276–277
  area of, 2129
  armament levels of, 304
  Armenian genocide in, 294, 571
  Armenians in, 2129
  arms sales to
    from Soviet bloc, 412
    by Soviet Union, 304, 318
  art of, 2259
  Assyrians in, 326
  Baghdad Pact (1955) membership refused by, 363, 373
  Baghdad Summit (1978) on financial support to, 364
  banking in, 390, *393*
  and Beitaddin Declaration (1978), 432
  at Bludan Conference (1937), 488
  British occupation of (1918), 510
  British relations with, 801, 824, 825
    withdrawal from mandate, 1504
  Cemal Paşa as governor of, 571–572, 2366, 2368
  chemical weapons of, 305
  Circassians in, 600
  cities of, 1044
    ancient, 1797–1798
    border, 344
    capital, 662–664
    northern, 111–112
    port, 1375, 2065
  communication in, 625
  communism in, 373, 626
  constitution of (1950), 2133
  constitution of (1973), 2130
  cotton industry in, 644, 645, 2131, 2180, *2181*
  coup in (1949), 329, 776, 826, 1886, 2133, 2137, 2422
    CIA in, 572
    Hinnawi (Sami al-) in, 1032
  coup in (1954), 2133
  coup in (1961), 412
  coup in (1963), 316, 330, 482, 971, 1011, 2130, 2134, 2191
  coup in (1966), 330, 412, 482, 2191
  coup in (1970), 317, 330, 2191–2192
  dams in, 787, 2129, 2140–2141, 2188
  dance in, 667
  defense costs as percentage of GNP or GDP, *1530*
  demilitarized zones in
    after Arab–Israel War (1973), 251
    disputes over (1967), 248
    in General Armistice Agreement (1949), 241
  Druze in, 469, 729, 2129–2130
    under Ottoman Empire, 1548
  Druze revolts in (1830s), 730
  economic aid to, 747, 748
    from Arab countries, 749
    dependence on, 751
  economy of, 752, *753,* 2131
    crisis in (1985–1990), 319
    growth in, 317
    under Jadid (Salah), 2131

liberalization of, 317
reforms in, 315, 319
education in, 2131–2132
missionary schools in, 1552
Egyptian control of
Battle of Nizip in, 1690–1691
battles with Ottoman Empire over, 1466–1467
Ibrahim ibn Muhammad Ali as governor during, 1077
London Convention ending (1840), 1077, 1691
Mehmet Koja Husrev Paşa and, 1624
under Muhammad Ali, 1602, 1624, 1690–1691
nizam al-jadid, al- in, 1690
treaties granting, 648, 1077, 1466
Egyptian invasion of, under Muhammad Ali, 118, 648, 1077, 1602, 2093–2094
Egyptian relations with
Asad (Hafiz al-) and, 2135
entente in, 319
improvement of, 318
Sadat (Anwar al-) and, 1957
Egyptian union with (*See* United Arab Republic)
elites in, 776
ethnic groups in, 2129
fishing in, 2065
foreign policy of, stages in late 20th century, 317–320
Free French mandate in, 851
French mandate in, 801, 824, 846, 1441, 1480, 2132
Abdullah I ibn Hussein threatening attack of, 512
Antakya (Turkey) in, 210
Arabs in, 221
armed conflict at Maysalun over (1920), 1504–1505
Atasi (Hashim al-) cooperation with, 328
Faisal I ibn Hussein ousted for, 151, 221, 512, 801, 1504–1505
French foreign legion in, 856
General Syrian Congress (1920) on, 538
"honorable cooperation" with, 1486
national movement during, 615–616, 989, 1486
Palestinian Arab Congress rejection of, 1782
Qassam (Izz al-Din al-) against, 1874
Qawuqji (Fawzi al-) against, 1879
Quwatli (Shukri al-) against, 1885
revolt against (1925–1927), 337, 729, 1206
San Remo Conference (1920) on, 1988
Sèvres Treaty (1920) on, 2015
Sykes-Picot Agreement (1916) on, 2128
general strike in (1936), 1885
geography of, 902
German relations with, 906
government of, 933, 2130–2131
Zuʿbi (Mahmud al-) in, 2442–2443
Greater Syria plan, 824–826, 1950, 2136–2137, *2137*, 2353
guilds in, 947
in Gulf Crisis (1990–1991), 951, 953
higher education in, 761, 1044
at Arab Academy of Damascus, 223–224
at Damascus University, 664, 665–666, 2132
at Tishrin University, 2132
at University of Aleppo, 666, 2132
at University of the Baʿth, 666
at University of Tishrin, 666
independence of, 801, 1480, 2132–2133
General Syrian Congress (1920) proclaiming, 538
nationalist struggle for, 328, 615–616, 2132
negotiations for (1936), 328–329, 1839
Versailles conference (1919) and, 800
intelligence services of, 1102
Iranian relations with, 318, 1291
in Iran–Iraq War (1980–1988), 318, 2135
Iraqi relations with, 318
Baghdad Summit (1978) and, 364
Hussein (Saddam) and, 378
proposed union, 1032
irrigation in, 787, 909, 2129, 2140–2141
Israeli peace negotiations with, 1168, 2135
after Arab–Israel War (1973), 251–252, 319
bilateral, start of, 319
collapse of, 238, 319, 1168
disengagement agreement in (1974), 241, 319, 1166, 1291
General Armistice Agreement in (1949), 241
Kissinger (Henry) in, 1328
at Madrid Conference, 1458–1459
Israeli relations with
Barak (Ehud) and, 399
Golan Heights and, 925
Shabʿa Farms and, 2017
Jews in, *1233*, 2129
emigration of, 2365
immigration to Israel, 1914
in Jordanian civil war, 1247
Jordanian relations with
Asad (Hafiz al-) and, 2135
Badran (Mudar) and, 357
pledge of financial aid to Jordan (1957), 1632
and Jordan River development, 1248
King–Crane Commission on (1919), 1323
Kurdistan Workers Party supported by, 1343
labor unions in, 1358
land reforms in, 1372, 2131
language in, Arabic, 223–224
at Lausanne Conference (1949), 1375
in League of Arab States, 1386, 1388
in Lebanese Civil War (1975–1990), 432, 1291, 1391, 1393, 1400
strikes against Qulaylat (Ibrahim), 1612
Lebanese internal security maintained by, 1536
Lebanese relations with
Damascus Tripartite Agreement and, 1039
Franjiyya (Sulayman) and, 1395
Jumblatt (Kamal) and, 1256
Jumblatt (Walid) and, 1256
Lahhud (Emile) and, 1364
Shabʿa Farms and, 2017
Syrian Social Nationalist Party and, 2137
Taʿif Accord and, 2148
legal system of, 886
civil code, 1382
Majalla, 1382
legislative body in, 932
literature of, 1084, 1982
women in, 1080
location of, 2129
at Madrid Peace Conference (1991), 319

Syria *(continued)*
manufacturing in, 1482, 1483, *1483*
map of, *2130*
markets in, *2133*
military of, *1531*
equipment of, *1534*
force levels of, *1528–1529*, 1529
force structure of, *1532–1533*, 1535
role of, 1541
modernization of, 315
under Muhammad Ali, 2093–2094
Muhammad's journeys in, 1595
music of, 112, 1617–1618
nationalism in, 1659, 2021, 2132, 2137
minority groups supporting, 1549
National Party in, 1664
nationalization program in, 972
newspapers and print media of, 1678
mobilization approach of, 1680
privately controlled, 1680
oil pipelines through, 1138
oil production in, 752, 2126–2127
origin of term, 936
in Ottoman Empire, 936, *1733*, 2132
French support for Catholics in, 1544
Land Code of 1858 effects, 1368–1369, 2132
land ownership in, 1371
petition for independence of, 2202
Palestinians in, 1916
from Nakba, al-, 1639
pan-Arabism in, 1799
parliament of
Arslan (Adil) in, 306
establishment of, 317
PFLP–GC links with, 1841
PFLP supported by, 1840
PLO control sought by, 1774
PLO opposition, Tlas (Mustafa) and, 2192
poetry of, 39
political reform in, 317
population of, *753*, 1843, 1844, 2129–2130
postage stamps of, 1849–1850
presidential elections in, 315
president of, 997–998
provinces of, 683–684, 1080–1081
radio and television in, *1895*
railways in, 2206, *2206*
regions of, 909, 1205–1206
religions in, 2129–2130
Catholicism, 1931
Christianity, 738, 2130
Qadiriyya Order, 1864
Salafiyya movement, 1974
Shiʿism, 2129
Sunni Islam, 2129
rivers in, 2129, 2188, 2328, 2379–2380
al-Saʿiqa supported by, 1972
Saudi Arabian relations with, Asad (Hafiz al-) and, 2135
science and technology in, 2004
scout movement in, 2006
Soviet relations with, 318, 373, 1943
after Arab–Israel War (1967), 2292
Suwaydiya oil fields in, 2126–2127
textile industry in, 2131, 2180, 2181, *2181*
theater in, 2184
tourism in, 2196
in trade, 2131, 2132, 2198, 2201
Trans-Arabian Pipeline security concerns in, 2203
transport in, modern means of, *2207*
tribes in, 2211, 2212–2213
at Tripoli Conference, 2217
Turkish relations with, dispute over dams, 2082, 2141
in United Arab Republic, 1011
U.S. covert operations in, 1103
U.S. describing state terrorism in, 2175
U.S. relations with, 319
Wahhabi raids in, 1625
water resources in, 344, 1249, 2129, 2379–2380
freshwater withdrawals, *2331*
qanats (tunnels) for, 2328
quantity of, 2330
women in
as cabinet members, 337
economic status of, *877*
in politics, 893, 899–900
voting rights for, 1032
as writers, 1982
World Bank and, capital stock and voting power in, *2363*
in World War I, 2366, 2368
in World War II, 2370
Yazidis in, 2130
Syriac language, 2010
Syriac Orthodox Church, 326
Syrian Catholic church, 592
Syrian Communist Party
Bakdash (Khalid) in, 373, 412
Baʿth party and, 412
Syrian Computer Society, 315
Syrian Congress, Rida (Rashid) in, 1924
Syrian Conserves Company, 1885
Syrian Desert, 701, **2136**
agriculture in, 2136
area of, 2136
climate of, 2136
in Iraq, 2136
in Jordan, 1240, 2136
natural resources in, 2136
parts of, 2136
in Saudi Arabia, 2136
in Syria, 2136
Syrian National Party, 1949
Syrian Orthodox church, 590, 591–592
dialect of, 592
in Oriental Orthodox family, 591
size of, 591
Syrian Petroleum Authority, 2126
Syrian Protestant College (Beirut), 758. *See also* American University of Beirut
Nimr (Faris) at, 1688
Shahbandar (Abd Al-Rahman) at, 2021
Shumayyil (Shibli) at, 2061
Syrian Revolt, Great (1925–1927)
Atrash (Sultan Pasha al-) in, 337, 729, 1206
Hama during, 980
Mardam (Jamil) in, 1486
Quwatli (Shukri al-) in, 1885
Syrian Scientific Society, 2383
Syrian Social Nationalist Party (SSNP), 825, 826, 1659, *2136*, **2136–2138**, *2137*
Adonis (Ali Ahmad Saʿid) in, 47
establishment of, 2136
Greater Syria plan supported by, 2136–2137, *2137*
ideology of, 2136–2137
impact on Baʿth party, 2136
in Lebanese Civil War (1958), 2137
in Lebanese Civil War (1975–1990), 2137
members of, 1949
in National Front, 1656–1657
Orthodox Christians in, 2136
Phalange Party attacking, 1950
Raad (Inʿam) in, 1888

Sa'ada (Antun) in, 1949–1950, 2136–2137
Sulh (Riyad al-) assassinated by, 2118
Tall (Wasfi al-) supporting, 2156
Syrian University, 665, 666
Arab Academy of Damascus merger with, 223–224
Syrian War (1831–1833), 740–741, 2093
Battle of Konya in (1832), 1332–1333
Britain in, 1346
Egypt in, 740–741, 1346, 2093
France in, 740–741, 1346, 2093
Kütahya Convention (1833) ending, 2093
Ottoman Empire in, 740–741, 2093
Peace of Kütahya (1833) ending, 1346
Russia in, 740–741, 1346, 2093
Syrian War (1839), 740–741, 2093
Syris, Protestant missions in, 1854
Syrkin, Nachman, **2138**
Uganda Project supported by, 2257
Szold, Henrietta, **2138**
in Hadassah, 966, 2138
in Youth Aliyah, 855, 2138, 2411

T

TA'AL (Israel), 1787, 1788
Taba (Egypt), **2139**
in Aqaba incident (1906), 218
Taba Accords. *See* Taba negotiations (1995, 2001)
Taba'i al-Istibdad wa Masari al-Isti'bad (Kawakibi), 1282
Taba'i, Muhammad al-, Asmahan and, 324
Taba incident. *See* Aqaba incident (1906)
Taba negotiations (1995, 2001), **2140**
Palestinian rights in, 1640
Tabaqa Dam, 788, 2129, **2140–2141**
Tabari, Ehsan, 2222
Tabataba'i, Mohammad, **2141–2142**
in Constitutional Revolution, 2141–2142
imprisonment of, 2142
studying under Shirazi (Mirza Hasan), 2141
Tabataba'i, Ziya, **2142–2143**
Anglo–Iranian Agreement nullified by, 200
coup by (1921), 88, 1118, 1682, 1755
denouncing Pahlavi dictatorship, 2143
in exile, 2143
Fatherland party of, 1110, 2143
in Iradeh-ye Melli Party, 1110
Mossadegh (Mohammad) opposed to, 1580
newspapers of, 1682, 2142, 2143
opposing Mossadegh (Mohammad), 2143
as prime minister, 2143
appointment of, 1755
Pahlavi (Reza) ousting, 1755
supporting British policy in Iran, 2142, 2143
Tabayniyy, Natila al-, 1429
Tabbe ot Ashan (Goldberg), 927
Tabbula, 841
TaBedawie language, 433
Tabenkin, Yitzhak, 956
Tabi, Shakir Sahib al-, 83
Tables reales, 2050
Tabory, Ephraim, *as contributor,* 600–601, 979–980, 2157–2158, 2404
Tabriz (Iran), **2143–2144**
in Azerbaijan crisis (1945–1946), 346, 693
bazaars of, 420
carpet weaving in, 566
in Constitutional Revolution, 636
industrial activity in, 345
in Russo–Persian wars, 7
Tabriz Shaykhis, 2047
Tabriz–Trabzon caravan, 2205
Tabriz University, **2144**
Eqbal (Manouchehr) at, 779
Tachau, Frank, *as contributor,* 631, 780, 851, 854–855, 1202, 1583–1584, 1657–1661, 1660–1661, 1667–1668, 2076–2077, 2219–2220, 2236, 2250, 2251, 2295
Tachelhit language, 1567
Tadiran, 1334
Tadja (in Muharram rite), 1606
Tadla plain (Morocco), 1567
Tadmur (Syria), 1797–1798
Tafakkuk, al- (Boudjedra), 497, 1426
Tafkir wa al-Hijra, al-. *See* Excommunication and Emigration
Tafna, Treaty of (1837), 17, 542
Tafsir, 2154
Tafsut n Imazighen. See Berber Spring
Tagger, Sioneh, **2144**
Tagger, Sulayman, in Club National Israélite, 612
Tahaddi, al- (Bin Diyaf), 474
Taha, Mahmud Muhammad, **2144–2145**
execution of, 1918
and Republican Brotherhood, 1917–1918
Taharut Sehiya (Tammuz), 2160
Tahdhib, al- (Baradhi, al-), 1476
Tahdid al-nasl. See Birth control
Taher, Abdal Hadi, in PETROMIN, 1830
Tahina, 841
Tahirid dynasty (Yemen), 2397
Tahiris, 2145
Tahir, Kemal, **2145–2146**
Tahkim, al-, 2052
Tahmasp, 2054
Tahrir al-Mar'a (Amin et al.), 187
Tahrira stitch, 1879
Tahtawi, Rifa'a al-Rafi al-, 1419, **2146–2148**
in archaeology, 276
educational agenda and influence of, 2146–2147
education of, 2146
in Institut d'Égypte, 1099
institutional career of, 2146
on liberation of women, 890
political perspective of, 2147
Sa'id Pasha rehabilitating, 1970
as translation movement founder, 2146–2148
Ta'if, al-, **2148–2149**
Ikhwan occupation of, 1085
Muhammad's message rejected in, 1596
Taifa, 618, 947
Ta'if Accord (1989), **2148**
Council for Development and Reconstruction after, 645
Eddé (Raymond) opposing, 754
Geagea (Samir) supporting, 871
Hariri (Rafiq Baha'uddin al-) and, 994
Husayni (Husayn al-) and, 1055
National Pact revised by, 1663
Ta'if, Treaty of al- (1934), **2149**
on claims to Asir, 1082

Ta'iz (Yemen), **2149–2150**, 2386
as capital, 2386
San'a compared to, 2149
Tajammu. *See* National Progressive Unionist Party (Egypt)
Tajdid, al- (newspaper), 1590
Tajiki language, 1820, 2150
grammar of, *vs.* standard Persian, 1124
script of, 1820
Tajikistan
cease-fire in, 1944
Tajiks in, 2150
Uzbeks in, 2306
Tajiks, **2150**
in Jami'at-e Islami, 1215
in Karzai government, 67
Tajin, 841
Takahaski, Kazuo, *as contributor,* 586–587
TAKAM. *See* Kibbutz Movement
Takeover in Tehran: The Inside Story of the 1979 U.S. Embassy Capture (Ebtekar), 745
Takfir, al-, 2151
Takfir wa al-Hijra al-, **2150–2151**
Takhlis al-Ibriz fi Talkhis Bariz (Tahtawi), 2146
Takht-e nard, 2050
Takhtit al-a'ila. See Family planning
Takiya (place for storyteller), 1606
Takrit. *See* Tikrit
Takvim-i Vekayi (newspaper), 1684
Ceride-i Havadis in competition with, 595
Talabani, Jalal, 695, **2151**
in exile, 2151
on Iraqi Governing Council, 2325–2326
Kurdish Regional Government established by, 2151
in Kurdish revolt (1960–1963), 2151
in Kurdistan Front, 1339
in Patriotic Union of Kurdistan, 1807
Patriotic Union of Kurdistan founded by, 2151
Talal ibn Abdullah (king of Jordan), **2151–2153**, *2152*
accession of, 1244
daughter of, 409
in Hashimite house, 1000
mental health of, 1062, 2152
parliament deposing, 2152–2153
Regency Council following abdication of, Hashim (Ibrahim) in, 999
reign of, 2152
removal of, 1244
son of, 1061
Tal al-Za'tar refugee camp, in Lebanese Civil War, 1607
Talat, Mehmet, **2153**
Cemal Paşa and, 571, 572
in Committee for Union and Progress, 2153
as grand vizier, 2153
murder of, 2153
Musa Kazim under, 1613
negotiating with Germany, 905
in Young Turk revolution (1908), 2153
Zohrab (Krikor) and, 2440
Talbot, G. F., 2193
Taleqani, Azam, **2153**
Taleqani, Mahmud, 2153
as Freedom Movement founder, 850
Khomeini (Ruhollah) supported by, 1311
Talfah, Adnan Khayr Allah, **2154**
Talfiq, 1974
Tali, al- (periodical), 402, 1972
Aflaq (Michel) in, 68
Taliban (Afghanistan), **2154–2155**
archaeological artifacts destroyed by, 279
bin Ladin and, 61, 475, 1712, 1865, 2155, 2178
coup by (1996), 61, 1561, 2280
and education, 2154–2155
education of leaders of, 2154
elimination of, 2155
establishment of, 61
Hazara opposition to, 1015
in Herat, 1021
vs. Hezb-e Islami, 1024
Hizb-e Wadat fighting with, 387
ideology of, 1712
in Kandahar, 61, 64, 1268
Karzai (Hamid) relationship with, 1276
Mohammadi (Maulawi Mohammad Nabi) and, 1559
vs. Northern Alliance, 1889
Omar (Muhammad) in, 64, 1712, 1767
opposition to
Ahmad Shah Mas'ud in, 89
Gailani (Ahmad) in, 864
Jami'at-e Islami in, 1215
Mazar e-Sharif in, 1505
Northern Alliance in, 1535
post-Soviet Russia and, 1944
tribal and paramilitary forces in, 1535
origin of term, 2154
Pakistani support for, 64
policies of, 2154
al-Qa'ida supported by, 2155, 2178
refugee flight under, 1912
rise of, 53, 59, 61, 64
U.S. defeat of, *59,* 61–62, 64, 66, 549, 1712, 2155
Iran in, 1121
women's rights limited by, 874, 881, 894
in Zabul province, 2417
Zahir Shah's welcome to, 2421
Talib, Fatima, 1622, 2105
Talismano (Meddeb), 1507
Tallal, Chaibia, **2155**
Tall al-Za'tar refugee camp, **2155–2156**
in Lebanese Civil War, 1253
Talla Society, 1958
Tal, Lawrence, *as contributor,* 468–469, 481, 570, 830–831, 967–968, 997, 998, 1030–1031, 1235, 1267–1268, 1270–1271, 1369, 1705–1706, 1901
Tall, Mustafa Wahbi al-, **2156**
Tall, Wasfi al-, **2156–2157**
assassination of, 485, 2157
as prime minister, 2156–2157
Talmud, **2157–2158**
kosher in, 1335
Rabbinic Hebrew in, 1017
yeshiva study of, 2399
Talmud Bavli, 2158
Talmud Yerushalmi, 2158
Talqa al-Akhira, al- (Shukri), 2060
Tamahak, 843
Tamari, Steve, *as contributor,* 6–7, 82–83, 198–199, 219, 259, 268, 288, 396, 401–402, 424, 485–486
Tamas (Nalouti), 1429
Tamasha (rite of ablution), 1479
Tamazight, 457, 461
Tamazight language, 1567, 2167
after independence, 124, 1261
in Kabylia region (Algeria), 121
Coordination des Archs on, 638
as official language, 122, 130, 1261

TAMI (Israel), 1189
Abuhatzeira (Aharon) in, 37
electoral success of, 1189
establishment of, 37, 1189
in Likud, 1189
National Religious Party criticized by, 1187
platform of, 1189
Tamimahs, **2158**
Tamimi, Abdallah ibn Ibad al-Murri al-, Ibadiyya founded by, 1073
Tamimi, Adnan al-, 2158
Tamimi, Amin al-, **2158–2159**
Tamir, Shmuel, **2159**
in Kasztner affair (1954–1955), 1280
Tamir, Ya'el, in Peace Now, 1809
Tamiyya, 838
Tamkin, 2151
Tammuz, Benyamin, 1432, **2159–2160**
Tan (newspaper), 1676
Tanbur, 2160
Tanburi Cemil, **2160**
Taner, Haldun, **2160,** 2187
Tanganyika, and Zanzibar, union of, 2425
Tangier (Morocco), 827, 1567, *1571*
Catholics in, 1932
under Spanish control, 2085
Tangier, Treaty of (1844), **2160**
Tangsir (Chubak), 593, 1435
Tanin (newspaper), 2180
Tannenberg, Battle of (1914), 2365
Tanpinar, Ahmed Hamdi, **2160–2161**
Tantawi, Muhammad Sayyid al-, **2161**
on female circumcision, 822
Tanuhi, Izz al-Din al-, in Arab Academy of Damascus, 223
Tanukhis, 728
Tanzania, U.S. embassy bombing in, 1865, *2177*
Tanzim, al-, 1395
Tanzim al-usra. See Family planning
Tanzimatcilar (men of Tanzimat), 1624
Tanzimat era (1839–1876) (Ottoman Empire), **2161–2165**
administration during, 2063, 2162, 2163, 2164
Ahmet Vefik in, 92
Armenian millet in, 298
army in, 1737
assessment of, 2164
civil service in, Civil Service School and, 602
in Cyprus, 652
defense and international affairs during, 2162
design and implementation of reforms, 2164
dragomans in, 723
early opposition to, 2406
economy during, 2162–2163
education in, 757, 758, 2162
end of, 1735, 2164
and equal rights, 885
European influences and internal motivations of, 2163–2164
Gülhane Imperial Edict (1839) and, 954–955
Hatt-i Serif of Gülhane (1839) initiating, 2073, 2162, 2163, 2164
initiation under Abdülmecit I, 33–34, 2161
and joint-stock companies, 2069
Land Code of 1858 in, 1366–1369
literature of, 1438–1439
Malkom Khan (Mirza) in, 1477
masonic lodges in, 852
millet system during, 1544
Mustafa Fazil in, 1623
Mustafa Reşid introducing, 1623–1624
navy in, 1741
order and justice in, 2162
Ottomanism in, 1737
purpose of, 2161, 2164
rise of, 1735
slave trade during, 2073–2074
in Tunisia, 83
Westernization in, 2341
Young Ottoman opposition to, 2163, 2405–2407
Tapline. *See* Trans-Arabian Pipeline
Taqaddum Party, al- (Iraq), 1961
Taqasim (music), 1618
Taqiyya (caution), 1548
Taqla, Philippe, **2165**
Taqla, Salim, 2165
Taqlid (imitation), 1149, 1504, 2022, 2124, 2154, 2629–2630
Iqbal (Muhammad) on, 1109
Taqrib bayna al-madhabib, al-, 2022
Taraghi, Cherie, *as contributor,* 428, 809–810, 1154, 1364–1365
Taraki, Lisa
in Institute of Women's Studies at Bir Zeit University, 1100
in Women's Studies Center, 2362
Taraki, Nur Mohammed, 58
assassination of, 58
coup against (1979), 58, 186
Durand Line challenged by, 734
government of, Amin (Hafizullah) in, 186
in People's Democratic Party of Afghanistan, 62, 1812
Khalq faction of, 62, 1813
presidency of, 186–187
Soviet support for, 58, 65
Tarbiat Modarres University, Ebtekar (Ma'sumeh) at, 745
Tarbiya, 759–760
Tarbush, 611
Tarfaya (Morocco)
under Moroccan control, 2086
Spanish claim to, 1567
under Spanish control, 2085
Tarhan, Abdülhak Hamit, 1438, **2165–2166**
Cevdet (Abdullah) influenced by, 576
Tarhan, Ayse Durakbasa, *as contributor,* 148, 274
Tarifit language, 2167
Tarih-i Cevdet, 577, 578
Tarikh, al- (Algeria), 1456
T'arikh Muddah al-Faransis bi Misr (Jabarti), 1207
Tarikh Tolana, **2166**
Tariki, Abdullah, **2166**
Tariqa, 2630
Tariqa, 2099, 2113, 2114
Tariq al-Jadid, al- (journal), 1590–1591
Tariqa Muhammadiyya, 2114
Tarrifit language, 1567
Tarsus, 2167
Tartib (Moroccan tax on agriculture), 8
Tarzi, Mahmud, 1881
in *Irshad An-Niswaan,* 1140
Young Afghan Party and, 62
Tasarruf, 1367
TASE index, 2091
Tashilhit language, **2166–2167**
TASI index, 2092
Ta'silan likayan (Mas'adi), 1498
Taste of Cherry (film), 1318
Tasvir-i Efkar (newspaper), 1438, 1640, 1673, 1684–1685, 2068, 2406, 2407
Karacan (Ali Naci) in, 1269
Recaizade Mahmud Ekrem and, 1909

Taswir (representational art), ban on, 311–312
Tatar language, 2248, 2252
Tatars, 2253
Tatawi, Nawal al-, 1902
Tatawwur al-Dusturi wa al-Niyabi bi al-Maghrib min sanat 1908 ila sanat 1978 (Ghallab), 910
Taurus Mountains, 194, 901, 902, 1342, **2167**, 2188
Tavallali, Faridun, 1436
Tawali, 2050
Tawaqqufwa al-Tabayyun, al-. *See* Repose and Meditation
Tawb, 433
Tawfiq, Ahmad al-, 1425
Tawfiq, Amin, daughter of, 187
Tawfiq Mosque (Tunis), 2224
Tawfiq, Muhammad (khedive of Egypt), *1157*
  Afghani (Jamal al-Din al-) deported by, 52
  banishing freemasons from politics, 852
  British restoring to power, 404
  European support for, 1158
  father of, 1158
  Ilaysh (Muhammad) opposition to, 1086
  and Urabi (Ahmad), 2297
Tawhid (unity of Allah), 1625, 2111, 2112
  as cornerstone of Islam, 1145
Tawil, Kamal al-, 971
Tawil, Suha, 272
Tawlat al-zahr, 2050
Taxes
  in Afghanistan, 175
  on agricultural products, 76
  guilds paying, 947
  in Morocco, on agriculture *(tartib)*, 8
  in Ottoman Empire
    bedel-i askeri, 423–424, 1237
    jizya, 423, 1237, 2167
    after Land Code of 1858, 1367–1369
    before Land Code of 1858, 1367
    reform of, 2162, 2163
  poll *(jizya)*, 1237
    on *dhimmis*, 703
    in Egypt, Coptic exemption from, 640
    in Ottoman Empire, 423, 1237, 2167
  in Tunisia, 1308
  in Turkey, Varlik Vergisi, 2309–2310
Tax farming, **2167–2168**
  advantages of, 2167
  in Egypt, 2167
  in Ottoman Empire, 1367, 2167–2168
  power of, 2167
Tax fief, 2167
Tayebi, Mohamed, in Oujda Group, 1743
Taymiyya, Hanbali ibn, 2124
Taymiyya, Taqiyy al-Din ibn, 2114
Taymur, A'isha, 2431
Taymuriyya, A'isha al-, 890
Taymur, Mahmud (Muhammad), 675, 1420
  Qisas shamiyya (Idlibi) introduction by, 1080
Tayyibis, as subdivison of Isma'ili Shi'ism, 1158
Tazi, Ezzeddine, 1425, 1428
Ta'zir, 833
Ta'ziya (Iranian Muharram ritual), 1606
Ta'ziyeh, 2186
Tazmamart (Moroccan prison), 1600
Tchernichovsky, Saul, 1164, **2168–2169**
Tea, **2169**
Teachers
  in Afghanistan
    persecution of, 55
    training for, 670–671
  in Algeria, foreign, 255, 256
  in Egypt, training for, 671
  in Morocco
    foreign, 255
    at al-Qarawiyyin, 1871
  in Tunisia, foreign, 255
  in Turkey, training for, 2316–2317
  ulama as, 2258
Tebu tribe, 2214
Technical Military Academy Group (TMA). *See* Islamic Liberation Organization
Technion-Israel Institute of Technology, **2169**
Technology industry. *See also* Science and technology
  in Israel, 1095
Tehiyah party (Israel), 1189
  Ben-Porat (Mordechai) in, 452
  Cohen (Ge'ula) in, 613
  electoral success of, 1189
  Ne'eman (Yuval) in, 1674
  platform of, 1189
  Shamir (Moshe) in, 2024
  Tzomet Party merging with, 774
  Tzomet Party split from, 1189
Tehran (Iran), *1111*, **2169–2170**
  bast taken in, 411
  bazaars in, 419, 420
  in Constitutional Revolution, 636
  development of, 2169–2170
  Golestan Palace in, 928–929
  in Iranian Revolution, 2170
    demonstrations leading to, 1126
  in Iran–Iraq War, 1120, 2170
  Karbaschi (Gholamhosain) as mayor of, 1273
  modernization of, 1273
  oil production in, *1825*
  population of, 2169, 2170
  textile mills in, 2181
  as Trans-Iranian railway hub, 2203
  urban planning in, 2299
  U.S. embassy seized in, 2096
    and Amir-Entezam (Abbas), 188
    Bani Sadr (Abolhasan) opposing, 388
    Ebtekar (Ma'sumeh) in, 745
Tehran Conference (1943), 1935
Tehran School of Social Work, 809
Tehran University
  Bani Sadr (Abolhasan) at, 388
  Baraheni (Reza) at, 397
  Daneshvar (Simin) at, 668–669
  Ebadi (Shirin) at, 743
  Eqbal (Manouchehr) at, 779
  Kianuri (Nur al-Din) at, 1318
  Mojtahed-Shabestari (Mohammad) at, 1563
  Motahhari (Mortaza) at, 1583
  Sa'edi (Gholamhossein) at, 1962
  Sepehri (Sohrab) at, 2011
  Shid (Nahid) at, 2051
  Soroush (AbdolKarim) at, 2080
  student demonstrations at, militia attack during, 1120
Tekdal, Ahmet, 1910
Tekeli, Şirin, **2170–2171**
  in Women's Library and Information Center, 2358
Tekke, **2171**
Tekumah Party (Israel), in National Union, 1187
Tel Aviv (Israel), 1160, *1160*, **2171–2172**. *See also* Jaffa (Israel)

Ahuzat Bayit in, 2171–2172
Altalena sinking at, 170
Bet ha-Tefutsot in, 928
building of, 2299
embassies in, 1225
foundation of, 2171
gay-pride events in, 888
ha-Tikva Theater group in, 1014
Hussein (Saddam) bombing, 951
metropolitan area of, 1927
name of, 2172
as political, economic, and cultural center, 2172
population of, 2172
reclaimed wastewater from, 1668
Tel Aviv Circle of Poets, 2322
Tel Aviv Museum of Art, Amer (Ghada) exhibition at, 176
Tel Aviv University, **2172**
Eitan (Rafael) at, 774
Livnat (Limor) at, 1440
Ne'eman (Yuval) at, 1674
Zach (Natan) at, 2418
Telegraph service, 624
and British–Omani relations, 527
Tel El-Zaatar s'est tu à la tombée de la nuit (Aba), 1426
Telephone service, 624
mobile, 625
Telespheres (Esfandiary), 784
Television. *See* Radio and television
Tel Hai, **2172–2173**
Trumpeldor (Yosef) organizing defenses of, 2221
Tell, 2630
Tell (Tunisia), 2225
Tell Mountains, 120
Telrad, 1334
Temimi Foundation for Scientific Research and Information (Tunisia), 1499
Temo, Ibrahim, in Ottoman Union Society, 622
Templars, 904, **2173**
Temple, Henry John. *See* Palmerston, Lord Henry John Temple
Temple Mount. *See* Haram al-Sharif
Temporary marriage. *See* Ziwaj Mut'a
Ten (film), 1318
Tenet, George, on Arab–Israel conflict, 573
Tengour, Habib, 1424
Tennyson, Alfred, 379
Tensift River, 1567
Tent City (film), 833
Teper, Elie, 626
Tercüman (newspaper), 869, 2160
Tercüman-i Hakikat (newspaper), 2180
Tercünab-i Ahvâl (newspaper), 1684–1685
Terian, Abraham, *as contributor,* 290–292
Ter-Petrossian, Levon
Jerusalem visited by, 292
presidency of, 303
Terre et le sang, La (Feraoun), 823
Terrorism, **2174–2179**. *See also* Airplane hijackings; Guerrilla movements; Hostage crises; Kidnappings; Suicide bombings; *specific terrorist organizations*
age of participants in, 1215
in Algeria, 919
in Arab–Israel conflict, 2175–2178
Arafat (Yasir) denouncing, 219, 1768
archaeological sites targeted by, 278
British reactions to, 521, 522
and decline in tourism, *2196,* 2196–2197
defining, 2174–2175
effective ways of reducing, 2179
in Egypt, 768–769
Luxor, 278
in France, 919
in Iran–Contra affair, 1122–1123
in Iraq, U.S.-occupied, 1540
in Israel, 958, 2176, 2178
Democratic Front for the Liberation of Palestine (DFLP) and, 1009
HAMAS and, 983
Hebrew University of Jerusalem cafeteria bombing (2002), 1018
Hizbullah and, 1038
by Irgun Zva'i Le'umi, 424–425, 1139–1140, 1140, 1324
King David Hotel bombing (1946), 1140, 1324
Lohamei Herut Yisrael and, 1442, 1443
retaliatory acts for, 972, 983
Jewish, Weizmann (Chaim) denouncing, 2338
in Lebanon, Geagea (Samir) as leader of ring, 1394
by Libya, 1861, 1862 (*See also* Pan Am flight 103 bombing; UTA flight 772 bombing)
and U.S. bombing (1986), 1414
media attention on, after September 11th, 2001, 2174
Mojahedin-e Khalq categorized as, 1562
in Morocco, Casablanca (2003), 1569, 2268
at Munich Olympics (1972), 2176
Israeli retaliation for, 1578
nontraditional military forces for, 1535
Organization of the Islamic Conference on, 1722
by PFLP, 1839–1840
by PFLP–GC, 1235, 1841–1842
by al-Qa'ida, 1865–1866, *2177* (*See also* September 11th)
in Saudi Arabia, 2000
in Sudan, by Black September, 486
in Tunisia, at *Ghriba* synagogue (Djerba), *717*
U.S. war on, 2174, 2178–2179
Arab–Israel peace process unresolved due to, 2178
Bush (George W.) and, 549
civilians as primary victims of, 2178–2179
Iranian support for, 1121
Jordanian support for, 32
vocabulary of, 2175
Terror-Neged-Terror (Israel), 958
Terry, Janice J., *as contributor,* 2320–2321, 2354, 2418–2419
Testimonium, 855
Tethyan Sea, 901
Tétreault, Mary Ann, *as contributor,* 158–162, 229–230, 323, 341, 481, 911, 1138–1139, 1347–1353, 1662, 1669–1671, 1707–1709, 1718–1721, 1823, 1824–1827, 1878, 1909–1910, 1951–1952, 2197–2202, 2202–2203
Tetuan (Morocco), **2179**
Tetuan, Treaty of (1860), on Spanish control of Ifni, 1083
Tevfik, Ebüzziya
in *Diyojen,* 1277
Nazif (Süleyman) and, 1673
Tevfik Fikret, **2179–2180**
Ahmet İhsan To'kgoz and, 90
Tevfik, Mehmet. *See* Caylak

Texaco
Bahrain Petroleum Company agreement with, 229
in construction of Trans-Arabian Pipeline, 2202
Texas Company. *See* Texaco
Textile industry, 1482, 1483, *1483*, 1484, *2180*, **2180–2182**, *2181*
Berber, 459
carpets in, 566–567, 2181
cotton in (*See* Cotton)
in Egypt, 404, 405, 1461, 2180, 2181, *2181*, 2182
in Iran, 2066, 2180, 2181, *2181*
Yazd, 2382
in Iraq, 2066, *2181*
in Israel, 2180, *2181*, 2182
in Jordan, *2181*
in Lebanon, 2066, 2181, *2181*, 2182
linen in, 2180
mills in, 2181–2182
in Ottoman Empire, 1730, 2066
output of, 2180–2181, *2181*
in Palestine, *2181*
silk in, 2066, 2180, 2197, 2198
in Sudan, 908, 2180
in Syria, 2131, 2180, 2181, *2181*
trade in, 2066, 2180–2181, 2197, 2198
in Turkey, 2180, 2181, *2181*, 2182, 2238
Bursa, 547
women working in, *875*, *876*
wool in, 2180, 2181
Textiles, Palestinian, 1879
Teymurtash, Abdul Hussein, 1757
TGNA. *See* Turkish Grand National Assembly
Thaalbi, Abd al-Aziz al-, **2182**, 2229
in Destour Party, 634, 2182
education of, 2182
La Tunisie Martyre by, 1375
in Young Tunisians, 2182, 2408
at Zaytuna University, 2427
Tha'am, 838
Thaʿirat, Al- (Barakat), 397
Thalweg, 2043
Thalweg Line, 2630
Thamer, Nadjia, 1424
Thameur, Habib
presidency of, 634
in Socialist Destour Party, 634
Thant, U
and Bahrain, independence for, 2279
Bunche (Ralph J.) as adviser to, 543
in Yemen Civil War (1962–1970), 2277
Thaqafa al-Jadida, al- (magazine), 416
Thaqafa wa al-Fikr fi Muwajahat al-Tahaddi (Ghallab), 910
Tharthar Dam, 1981
Tharthar Project (Iraq), 1000, **2182–2183**
Tharwat, Abd al-Khaliq, **2183**
Thatcher, Margaret, selling off government shares in British Petroleum, 522
Thawr, Abu, 2019
Thawra City, al- (Iraq), 361
Theater, **2183–2188**
Algerian, 1280
Arabic, 1421, 2183–2184
golden age of, 2184
Hakim (Tawfiq al-) and, 979
premodern performance arts and, 2184
women in, 2184
Egyptian, 675, 1083, 1421, 1977–1978, 1990, 2184
Iraqi, 2184
Israeli, 2076, 2184–2186
national movement and, 2184–2185
non-mimetic experimental, 2185
realism in, 2185
self-reflective, 2185–2186
Lebanese, 1421, 2019–2021, 2046, 2184
Moroccan, 2060
Ottoman, 1277, 1438, 2068–2069
ortaoyunu, 1724
Turkish-language, 72
Palestinian, 2184
Persian, 1437, 1962, 2186
censorship of, 2186
diasporic, 2186
modern, 2186
traditional, 2186
Syrian, 2184
Tunisian, 376, 1428
Turkish, 274, 305, 782, 872–873, 1289, 2160, 2165, 2186–2187
government support for, 2187
traditional, 2187
Western-style, 2186–2187
Theater of the Absurd, 2020, 2185, 2186
Théâtre des Champs-Elysées, 476
Thé au harem d'Archi Ahmed, Le (Charef), 1427
Theocracies, 934
Theocritus, 116
These Are My Brothers (Langer), 1374
Thessalonika. *See* Salonika (Greece)
"They Kill Teachers" (Sebbar), 2007
Third International Theory, 941
Third National Front (Iran), 1656
Third Way Party (Israel), 1189
platform of, 1189
Third World Conference on Women (Nairobi) (1985), 745
Thomas, Bertram, 227, 1833
Thompson, Elizabeth
as contributor, 34, 72, 90, 91–92, 96–97, 173, 208, 218, 259–260, 273, 305, 334–335, 342, 417, 423–424, 488, 491, 574–575, 594–595, 598, 673, 687, 715, 719, 737–738, 774, 782–783, 783–784, 790, 803, 823, 864, 867, 873, 955, 956–957, 1001, 1077–1078, 1079–1080, 1086–1087, 1109, 1141, 1204–1205, 1206, 1218, 1237, 1238, 1262, 1264–1265, 1269, 1284, 1292–1293, 1315–1316, 1325–1326, 1331, 1332–1333, 1346–1347, 1417–1418, 1450, 1459–1460, 1461–1462, 1481, 1512, 1545, 1547, 1607–1608, 1623, 1625, 1633, 1638–1639, 1646, 1675, 1676, 1690, 1723–1724, 1737, 1745–1746, 1771–1772, 1797–1798, 1819, 1820–1821, 1836, 1869–1870, 1901–1902, 1917, 1940, 1951, 1962–1963, 1973, 1979, 2013, 2061, 2062–2063, 2066, 2067–2068, 2069, 2083, 2121–2122, 2125, 2155–2156, 2158–2159, 2160, 2161–2165, 2190, 2217, 2233–2234, 2251, 2302–2303, 2309–2310, 2379–2380, 2400, 2413, 2439
as historiographer, 1037
Thompson, W. Kenneth, *as contributor*, 724–726
Thon, Yaakov, in Vaʿad Leʾumi, 2307
Thornsvard, Karen A., *as contributor*, 188, 2333–2334

Thousand Nights and a Night, The, Burton (Richard Francis) translating, 548
Thrace
  Balkan wars over, 384
  land ownership in, 1370
Thracians, 383
Three Emperors' League, 382
Three Kinds of Policy (Akçura), 1800
Thuluth script, 558, 559
Thunayyan, Abdullah, 819
Thunderbolt Army. *See* Yildirim Army
Thutmoses III (Egyptian pharaoh), 662
Tibawi, Abd al-Latif, 1791
Tiberias (Israel), **2188**
  expansion of Jewish community in, 2432
Tiberias, Lake. *See* Galilee, Sea of
Tiberius (Roman emperor), Palmyra under, 1797
Tibesti Mountains, 901
Tibet, British–Russian rivalry over, 205
Tibi, Ahmad, in election of 2003, 1788
Tibu, 1964
Tifinagh, 461–462, 2167
Tigers militia, 1394
  in Lebanese Civil War (1975–1990), 1661
Tignor, Robert L., *as contributor,* 403–407, 810–811, 858–859
Tigris River, **2188–2189,** 2237, 2328
  Basra on, 410
  in Kurdistan, 1342
  Kut al-Amara on, 1346
  origin of, 194, 902, 2188
  Samarra on, 1981
  sediments from, 901
  shipping on, 2205
  Southeastern Anatolia Project and, 2082
  Tikrit on, 2189
  tributaries of, 2188, 2417
  in Turkey, 194
Tihana (Yemen), 2425–2426
Tijani, Ahmad al-, 2113
Tijaniyya (Sufi order), 2113
Tikrit (Iraq), **2189**
  armed resistance to U.S. occupation in, 2326
  Ayyubi (Salah al-Din ibn al-) from, 2189
  Bakr (Ahmad Hasan al-) from, 2189
  foundation of, 2189
  Hussein (Saddam) from, 2189
  population of, 2189
Tikriti families, **2189**
Tikriti, Hardan al-, **2189–2190**
Tilmisani, Umar al-
  in Muslim Brotherhood, 321, 1621
  release by Sadat (Anwar al-), 1621
Tilsit, Treaty of (1807), 869
Timar, 1367, **2190**
Time, Great Tranquility (Amichai), 182
Time of Short Migrations, The (Ikhlassi), 1084
Timimoun (Boudjedra), 497
Timinhur. *See* Damanhur
Timur Durrani, 735
  in Kabul, 56
  son of, Mahmud Durrani as, 1468
Timur Lenk, 360
Timur the Lame (Tamerlane), descendents of, 1015
Tindouf (Algeria), **2190–2191**
Tiran, Strait of, 2040, **2191**
  in Arab–Israel War (1956), 245, 1165
  in Arab–Israel War (1967), 237, 1165
Tiris al-Gharbia (Western Sahara), Mauritania ceding of (1979), 2345
Tishrin, 2630
Tishrin University, 2132
Tithes, 2167
Tiwizi, 2630
Tizi-Ouzou (Algeria), demonstrations in (1980). *See* Berber Spring
TJFF. *See* Transjordan Frontier Force
Tlas, Mustafa, **2191–2192**
Tlatli, Moufida, 833, **2192**
Tlemcen (Algeria), **2192**
Tlili, Abderrahmane, 2232
Tlili, Mustafa, 1424, **2192–2193**
Tliq tribe, 912
TMA (Technical Military Academy Group). *See* Islamic Liberation Organization
Tnu'ah Ha-Kibbutzit Ha-Meuhedet, Ha- (TAKAM). *See* Kibbutz Movement
Tobacco concessions
  Naser al-Din Shah's granting of, 1644, 2355
  Wolff (Henry Drummond) obtaining, 2355
Tobacco industry, 1483
Tobacco Revolt (1891–1892), 1118, 1659, 1868, **2193–2194**
  Afghani (Jamal al-Din al-) in, 52
  Amin al-Soltan (Ali-Asghar) and, 184
  Ashtiani (Mirza Hasan) in, 2193–2194
  bazaar as political base during, 419, 420
  mass participation in, 1868
  Naser al-Din Shah and, 1644, 1665, 2057, 2193–2194
  Shirazi (Mirza Hasan) in, 2057, 2141, 2193
  ulama in, 2193
  Wolff (Henry Drummond) and, 2355
  women in, 891
Tobacco trade, 2198
To Be an Arab in Israel (Asmar), 325
Tobruk (Libya), 516, **2194**
Tofalar language, 2252
Toghril Beg, Isfahan as capital under, 1141
Tohidi, Nayereh, *as contributor,* 745, 2423–2424
Tohorot, 2157
To Know a Woman (Oz), 1748
Toledano, Ehud R., *as contributor,* 2072–2075
Toledano, Ya'acov Moshe, rivalry with Nissim (Isaac), 1689
Toman, 2630
Tombeau d'ibn Arabi (Meddeb), 1507
Tombéza (Mimouni), 1547
Tomer, Ben-Zion, 2185
To Neo Hanoumaki (Eskinazi), 785
Tonguç, Ismail Hakki, 2316
Topkapi Palace, 864, **2194**
Topographie idéale pour une agression caractérisée (Boudjedra), 496–497
Torah, 1250, 1251, 1980, 2157
Torah Flag (Israel). *See* Degel Ha-Torah
Torah Religious Front (Israel), 1189
  Agudat Israel in, 1178, 1189
  Po'alei Agudat Israel in, 1178, 1189

Torch, Operation (World War II), 516
Toren, Ha- (newspaper), 464
Torit mutiny (1955) (Sudan), 2103
Tornberg (numismatic scholar), 1702
Torres, Carlos, 760
Torres-Garcia, Ana, *as contributor,* 81, 356–357, 495, 1075, 1077–1078, 1366, 1416, 1519–1520, 1587, 1627–1628, 1713, 1743, 1804, 2079–2080, 2231–2232, 2264–2265, 2265–2266, 2342–2344
Torture
  in Algeria, during War of Independence, 141
  of gays and lesbians, 888
  in Morocco, human rights organizations and, 1715, 1716
  used by Shin Bet, 2056
Totah, Khalil, at Arab College of Jerusalem, 226
Toth, Anthony B., *as contributor,* 26, 36–37, 156, 157–158, 162–167, 171–172, 343, 366, 544, 622, 719, 731, 794–796, 859, 864–865, 935, 948–949, 996–997, 1085–1086, 1156–1157, 1204, 1206, 1294–1295, 1324, 1353–1354, 1489, 1498–1499, 1506–1507, 1511–1512, 1592–1593, 1616, 1694, 1873–1874, 1875–1878, 1903–1904, 2042–2043, 2149, 2166, 2191, 2195–2197, 2204–2208, 2260, 2269–2272, 2298–2299, 2378
To the End (Shamir), 2025
Toumi, Khalida, 894, **2195**
Tourism, **2195–2197**
  in Algeria, 2196
  art and, 313
  in Bahrain, 2196
  decline in, terrorism and, *2196,* 2196–2197
  definition of, 2195
  in Egypt, 2195–2196
    Giza Pyramids, 2196
    Luxor, 1447
    security issues, 2196
    Sharm al-Shaykh, 2040
  in Holy Land, 2195
  in Israel, 2196
    Tiberias, 2188
  in Morocco, 1569, 2196
    Fez, 2196
  in Palestine, 2196
  pilgrimage as, 1996, 2195
  in Saudi Arabia, 1996
  in Syria, 2196
  in Tunisia, 2196
  in Turkey, 2196
    Edirne, 755
    Istanbul, 2196, *2196*
  in United Arab Emirates, 2196
    Sharjah, 2040
  in Yemen, 2196–2197
Tous les horizons, de (Chraibi), 588
Toward Islamic Doctrine (Soltani), 2079
Tower, John, in Iran–Contra investigation, 1123
Townshend, Charles, 509, 1518–1519
  in Kut al-Amara, battle of (1916), 1346
  in World War I, 2367
Toynbee, Arnold, *vs.* Herzog (Ya'acov David), 1023
TPC. *See* Turkish Petroleum Company
Trabzon–Tabriz caravan, 2205
Trachoma, *711,* 712, 1508
Trade, **2197–2202**. *See also* Bazaars and bazaar merchants
  in 16th century, 2197
  in 18th century, 2198
  in 19th century, 2198–2199
  Afghanistan in, 55
    Nadir Shah and, 400
  agricultural deficit in, 72–74, 124
  Algeria in, 124, 127, 835
    Baqri family and, 396–397
    Busnach family and, 549–550
  ancient, 2197
  Arab–Israel conflict and, 2201
  Arab Maghreb Union goals for, 260
  capitulations in treaties on, 564–566, 620–621
  coffee, 2198
  cotton, 2198, 2238
  dates, 2198
  dried fruits, 2198, *2199*
  Egypt in, 2200, *2200,* 2201
    cotton of, 643–644
  with Europe, 2197–2199
  figs, *2199*
  glassware, 2197, 2198
  grain, 2198
  Iran in, 1115, 2198, 2199, *2200*
    concessions for, 1117–1118
  Iraq in, 2198, *2200*
    Baghdad as center of, 360
    Basra and, 410
  Israel in, 1161–1162, *2200,* 2200–2201
    Arab boycott on, 224–225
    limitations on, 1095
  Jordan in, 1243–1244, 2201
  Kuwait in, *2200*
  Lebanon in, 2198, 2201
  Libya in, 1415
  modern, 2199–2201
  Morocco in, 568, 569, 2038, 2198
    with Tunisia, 2269
  oil (*See* Oil trade)
  opium, 2198
  Ottoman Empire in, 1481, 1730
    Balta Liman, Convention of (1838) and, 385, 2163
    with Britain, 525–526
    Bursa, 547
    commercial and navigation treaties on, 620–621
    during Tanzimat era, 2163
  Pakistan in, with Tunisia, 2269
  Palestine in, 2198
  paper, 2198
  through Persian Gulf, 1820
  pre-1900, 1481
  Saudi Arabia in, 1996, *2200*
  silk, 2197, 2198
  slave (*See* Slave trade)
  spices, 2197
  sugar, 2198
  Syria in, 2131, 2132, 2198, 2201
  tea, 2169
  Templars and, 2173
  textile, 2066, 2180–2181, 2197, 2198
  tobacco, 2198
  trans-Saharan, 1964
  Tunisia in
    with Morocco, 2269
    with Pakistan, 2269
  Turkey in, 2198, *2199,* 2200, *2200,* 2201
  United Arab Emirates in, *2198, 2200,* 2272
  weapons, 2201
  during World War I, 2198
  during World War II, 2199
  Yemen in, 2198, 2201, 2388, 2389–2390
Trade unions. *See* Labor and labor unions
Trad, Petro, **2202**
Trained Victorious Soldiers Muhammad. *See* Mansure Army

"Train, The" (al-Rimawi), 1422
Trans-Anatolian railroad. *See* Berlin–Baghdad Railway
Trans-Arabian Pipeline, 1830, **2202–2203**
  advantage of, 2203
  capacity of, 2203
  construction of, 2202
  route of, 2202
  sabotaging of, PFLP and, 962
  security concerns of, 2203
Transgendered rights, 888
Transhumance, 459
Trans-Iranian Railway, 2057, **2203–2204**
  Ahvaz along, 93
Transitional Military Council (Sudan), 2101
Transitional press, 1681
Transjordan. *See* Jordan
Transjordan Frontier Force (TJFF), **2204**
  and Arab Legion, 257
Translation movement, Tahtawi (Rifaʿa al-Rafi al-) as founder of, 2146–2148
Transoxiana, Naqshbandi in, 1642
Transport, **2204–2208**
  on camels, 560
  caravans, 2197, 2205
  modern means of, 2207, *2207*
  of oil (*See* Oil transport)
  railroad, 2206, *2206*
  ships and shipping, 2069, 2205
    modern, 2207, *2207*
    steamships, 2198, *2205*, 2205–2206
    and trade, 2197, 2198
Transsexuality, 1105
Trans–Turkey Pipeline, **2208**
Travels in Arabia (Burckhardt), 545
Travels in Arabia Deserta (Doughty), 722
Travels in Syria and the Holy Land (Burckhardt), 545
"Travels of a Latter-Day Benjamin of Tudela" (Amichai), 182
Treaty of 1815, **2208**
Treaty of Adrianople (1829), 1466
Treaty of Bucharest (1812), 1466
Treaty of Joint Defense and Economic Cooperation (1950), 1386–1387
Treaty of Peace (1912), 2247
Treaty of Protection (1886), **2208**
Treeville. *See* Hayy al-Ashgar (Egypt)
Tribal armies or militia, 1527, 1535
Tribes and tribalism, **2208–2215**. *See also* Nomadism; *specific tribes*
  in Afghanistan, 385–386
  in Algeria, 458, 459, 2253–2254
  in Arabian Peninsula, 231–232, 2209–2212
    lineage, 2209–2210
    nomadic, *2210*, 2211
    superior *vs.* inferior tribes, 2209
  in Bahrain, 2210
  in Burkina Faso, 458
  definition of, 2209
  in Egypt, 458
  in Iran, 374, 385–386, 2213
  in Iraq, 1961–1962, 2212, 2214
  in Kuwait, 2213
  in Libya, 458
  in Mauritania, 458
  in Morocco, 458, 459, 912, 2212
  in Niger, 458
  in Oman, 385, 2210
  in Pakistan, 385–386
  polygamy in, 1839
  in Qatar, 2210
  of Sahara, 458, 459, *462*, 1963–1964, 2214
  in Saudi Arabia, 2209–2211, 2211, 2213, 2214
  in Senegal, 458
  in Sudan, 432–434, 2055, 2097–2099
  in Syria, 2211, 2212–2213
  in Tunisia, *2210*, 2226
  in Turkey, 2214, 2253
  in United Arab Emirates, 385, 2210, 2270
  in Yemen, 376, 2215
Tric-trac, 2050
Trifi, Mokhtar, 1416
Trilateral Commission, 2070
Trinidad, Muharram rites in, 1606
Trinity College
  Bentwich (Norman) at, 454
  Gorst (John Eldon) at, 931
Tripartite Accord (1985), Hobeika (Elie) signing, 871
Tripartite Alliance (Lebanon). *See* Hilf al-Thulathi, al-
Tripartite Committee, *1387*
  resolving Lebanese Civil War (1975–1990), 2148
Tripartite Declaration (1950), **2215–2216**
  arms control in, 304
  Hobeika (Elie) signing, 1394
Tripartite Treaty of Alliance (1942), **2216**
  Soviet breach of, 346
Tripoli (Lebanon), French control of, Karame (Abd al-Hamid) opposing, 1271
Tripoli (Libya), 1410, **2216–2217**, 2218
  as Barbary state, 401
  corsairs in, 643, 2216
  as de facto capital, 2216–2217, 2218
  drinking water of, *1412*
  economy of, 2216
  foundation of, 2216
  independence of, 2216
  during Italian invasion, 2216, 2246
  Jewish community of, 973
    Nahum (Halfallah) as president of, 1636–1637
    Nhaisi (Elia) and, 1686–1687
  Muntasir family in, 1611–1612
  newspapers of, 1678
  oil boom and, 2216
  origin of name of, 2216
  population of, 2216
  prosperity of, 2216
  Spanish occupation of, 2084
  U.S. bombing of (1986), 1862, 2217
  U.S. conflict with, Treaty of Peace and Amity ending (1805), 1807–1808
  during World War II, 2216
  Zionism in, 966
Tripoli Conference (1977), **2217**
Tripoli Programme (1962), 789, **2217**
  Conseil National de la Révolution Algérienne adoption of, 632
  drafting of, Ait Ahmed (Hocine) in, 95
  Lacheraf (Mostefa) drafting, 1362
Tripoli Republic (1918-1923), 2218
Tripolitania (Libya), 1410, **2217–2218**
  ancient cities of, 2217–2218
  foundation of, 2217
  Idris al-Sayyid Muhammad al-Sanusi as amir of, 1081
  Istiqlal Party and, 1196
  during Italian invasion, 935, 2218, 2247
  Jewish community in, 1016
  migration from, to Tunisia, 2218
  nationalist movement in, 807, 1207

Tripolitania (Libya) *(continued)*
population of, 2217
Qaramanli dynasty in, 1870–1871
Roman ruins in, 2218
Suwayhli (Ramadan al-) and, 2127
during World War II, 516
Tripolitanian National Congress Party, 1959
Triptyque de Rabat (Khatibi), 1304
TRNC. *See* Turkish Republic of Northern Cyprus
Troen, S. Ilan, *as contributor,* 2013–2014
Troupes Spéciales du Levant. *See* Special Forces of the Levant
TRT. *See* Turkish Radio and Television
Trucial Coast, **2218–2219**
British control of, 531, 2218–2219, 2270
origin of name, 2219
Trucial Council, 2270
Trucial Oman Levies, 2219
Trucial States, 1489
Trucial States Council, 2219
Trucial States Rulers' Council, Muʿalla (Ahmad bin Rashid al-) on, 1592
True Path Party (DYP) (Turkey), **2219–2220,** 2242
Çiller (Tansu) in, 598
in coalition government with Motherland Party, 1584, 2220
in coalition government with Refah Party, 2220
in coalition government with SHP, 2219
Demirel (Süleyman) support for, 692, 1584
establishment of, 1257, 2219
Motherland Party challenged by, 1584, 1747
Social Democratic Populist Party merging with, 2077
Truffaut, François, 175
Truman Doctrine (1947), 517, 1942, 2290–2291
Acheson (Dean) support for, 40
Point Four program under, 1836
Truman, Harry S, **2220**
American Israel Public Affairs Committee work for, 177
and Anglo–American Committee of Inquiry (1946), 338
and displaced persons after World War II, 198
establishment of Israel supported by, 2220
inaugural speech by (1949), Point Four in, 1836
Middle East Defense Organization supported by, 1523
on Palestine partition plans, Saudi response to, 11
on Palestinian refugees of Arab–Israel War (1948), 2220
Soviet containment strategy of, 2095
special envoy to Iran under, 996
Trans-Arabian Pipeline supported by, 2202
Weizmann, Chaim and, 2338, *2338*
during World War II, 1935
Trumpeldor, Yosef, **2220–2221**
assassination of, 1448, 2173
and ha-Halutz, 974, 2221
and Jewish Legion, 2221
in Russo–Japanese War (1904–1905), 2220–2221
and Tel Hai defense, 2221
Tschernichovsky, Saul, 1431
Tsedaka, Benyamim, *as contributor,* 1980
Tsemel, Leah, 1501, **2221**
Tsirkas, Stratis, 938
Tuareg, 458, 459, *462*
Tuareg language, 463
alphabet of, 461–462
Tuba and the Meaning of Night (Parsipur), 1436, 1803
Tubal ligations, 480
Tuberculosis, 712, 1508, 1510
vaccine for, 1508
Tübingen University (Germany), Islamic numismatics at, 1702
Tubi, Tawfiq, **2221–2222**
Tucker, Judith, 1037
Tudeh Party (Iran), **2222–2223**
Alavi (Bozorg) in, 104
Bakhtiar (Timur) supporting, 375
ban on, 779, 1118, 2222
CIA in destruction of, 627
Confederation of Iranian Students and, 630
and Democratic Party of Azerbaijan, 693
establishment of, 627, 2222
and Fedaʾiyan-e Khalq, 821
Ghassemlou (Abdul Rahman) in, 914
Golestan (Ebrahim) in, 928
growth of, 2222
guild members in, 947
in Iranian Revolution, 2222
in Iran–Iraq War, 2222
Kianuri (Nur al-Din) in, 1318, 2222
oil nationalization opposed by, 1118
rise of, 627
setbacks suffered by, 2222
size of, 627
Soviet support of, 2222
Tabatabaʾi (Ziya) and, 2143
torture of members of, 2222
Tughra (signature), 823
Tuhami al-Glawi, **2223**
control of Marrakech, 1493
in rebellion (1907), 8, 14
Tuhfa al-Maktabiyya li-Taqrib al-Lughat al-Arabiyya, al- (Tahtawi), 2148
Tujjar, 419
Tuman (section of Shammar tribe), 2214
Tuman Bey (sultan of Egypt), **2223**
Tunb Islands, **2223–2224**
Iran's occupation of, 1903
Tunis (Tunisia), **2224–2225,** 2225, *2228*
Algerian government in exile in, 615
under Almohad dynasty, 2224, 2228
Arab League summit (1979) in, *1387*
Arafat (Yasir) in, headquarters of, 271, 1774
as Barbary state, 401
Catholics in, 1932
corsairs in, 643
during French protectorate, 2224–2225
guest workers from, 946
under Hafsid dynasty, 2224, 2228
mosques in, 2224
newspapers of, 1678
under Ottoman control, 2228–2229
PLO in, after Arab–Israel War (1982), 253
population of, 2224
quarter system in, 2224
Spanish occupation of, 2084
wealth of, 2224
Zaytuna University in, 1422
Tunisia, **2225–2230.** *See also specific cities, organizations, people, and regions*

abortion in, 480
under Aghlabid dynasty, 2228
agriculture in, 2227
Algerian relations with, Bendjedid (Chadli) and, 444
under Almohad dynasty, 2224, 2228
Almoravids in, 2228
ancient history of, 2227–2228
Arabization policies in, 254–256
in Arab Maghreb Union, 260
architecture in, 284
art of, 1308–1309
banking in, 392, *393*, 394
banks in, 389, 390
Berbers in, 458, 2226, 2227–2228
beylicate abolished in, 185
Catholics in, 1932
children in, health care for, 1510
Christians in, 2226
cities of, 1866, 2081, 2225
capital, 2224–2225, *2228*
port, 483–484, 1564, 2016
climate of, 2225
communism in, 626
constitution of (1861), 1383
bill of rights in, 1604
power of ministers in, 1308
proclaimed by Muhammad al-Sadiq, 1603–1604
coup in (1987), 439, *439*, 503, 635, 2229, 2231
defense costs as percentage of GNP or GDP, *1530*
economic aid to, 749
economic policy of, 634
during French protectorate, 2229
economy of, 752, *753*, 2226–2227
under Ben Ali (Zayn al-Abidine), 440
under Bourguiba (Habib), 503
liberalization of, 2269
women in labor force, 874
education in, Khaldunniyya in, 1293
ethnic groups in, 2226
family laws in, 502, 2230–2231
Fatimids in, 2228
feminism in, 912, 2230
films in, 175, 376, 2192
financial crisis in, 84, 1308
fishing industry of, 834
French control of, Ottoman challenges to, 1467
French invasion of (1881), 1604
French protectorate over (1881–1956), 848, 1460
Bardo Treaty (1881) and, 484, 2229
Berlin Treaty (1878) on, 528
and Bizerte naval base, 484, 501
economic development during, 2229
imposition of, 1603–1604
under La Marsa Convention (1883), 1366, 1604, 2229
and literature, 1422
Muhammad al-Sadiq and, 1603–1604
nationalism during, 615, 1375, 2016, 2229
Thaalbi (Abd al-Aziz) opposing, 2182, 2229
under Treaty of Bardo (1881), 1604
Tunis under, 2224–2225
Young Tunisians during, 2229, 2407–2408
Zaytuna University during, 2428
Fundamental Pact (1857), 860
Muhammad al-Sadiq and, 1604
geography of, 2225
in Gulf Crisis (1990–1991), 951
habous in, 964–965
under Hafsid dynasty, 2224, 2228
higher education in, 2427–2428
in *madrasa* system, 1457–1458
at Sadiqi College, 1959
at Zaytuna University, 1422, 1428
human rights in, 439–440, 1416
campaign on behalf of Moadda (Mohammed), 1554
Marzouki (Moncef) and, 1496–1497
under Husaynid dynasty, 2229
independence of, 849, 1460, 2229
Bourguiba (Habib) and, 501
Masmoudi (Muhammad) in, 1499
movement leading to, 615, 2229
industrialization of, 1095–1096
industry of, in 19th century, 1357
intelligence services of, 1102
islands of, 717–718
Italian claims to, 1199
Jews in, 1234, 2226
Haggiag family, 973
immigration to Israel, 1914
Nazi occupation and, 1041
labor code in, 2269
labor unions in, 41, 486, 1358, 2227, 2264–2265
for employers, 2268–2269
strike by, 2265
land reforms in, 1372
languages in
Arabic, 254–256, 1422, 1424, 1425, 1428, 2226
Bedouin dialect, 2226
French, 255, 1424, 1425, 1428, 1959, 2193, 2226
in League of Arab States, 1388
legal system of, 886
mixed courts, 860
reforms in, 1383
legislative body in, 932
Libyan relations with, Gafsa incident (1980) and, 863
literature of, 474, 721–722, 987–988, 1313–1314, 1422–1425, *1423*, 1428–1429, 2017–2018, 2431
existentialism in, 1498
novels and short stories, 1498, 1507, 1516–1517
plays, 1498
poetry, 1507
map of, *2226*
medical care in, Marzouki (Moncef) and, 1496
migration to, from Tripolitania, 2218
military of
academy for, 84
equipment of, *1534*
force levels of, *1528–1529*
force structure of, *1532–1533*
nizami in, 83–84
reforms in, 83–84
mountains of, 335–336
music of, 1617
nationalism in, 1375, 2016, 2229
Nouira (Hedi) in, 1693–1694
natural resources of, 2225
newspapers and print media of, 1678, 2016
French-language, 1681–1682
government-controlled, 1680
laws on, 439–440
transitional press, 1681
oil production in, 2225
in Ottoman Empire, 2228–2229
Tanzimat reforms in, 83
Peace Corps in, 1808
Personal Status Code of, 502, 912, **2230–2231**
phosphate industry in, 1834
PLO in, 2177
Bourguiba (Habib) and, 503
political parties in, **2231–2232**
(*See also specific parties*)
under Ben Ali (Zayn al-Abidine), 356–357

Tunisia *(continued)*
population of, *753*, 2225–2226
pronatalist policies of, 478
radio and television in, 1894, *1895*
reforms in, 933
Mayram V (Muhammad) and, 418
religion in, 2226
revolt in (1864), 1604
rivers of, 2225
Saudi Arabian relations of, Masmoudi (Muhammad) as mediator in, 1499
scout movement in, 2006
slave trade in, abolition of, 84
taxes in, 1308
teachers in, foreign, 255
theater in, 376, 1428
tourism in, 2196
in trade
Jalluli family in, 1213
with Morocco, 2269
with Pakistan, 2269
tribes in, *2210*, 2226
water resources of
freshwater withdrawals, *2331*
quantity of, 2330
women in
economic status of, *877*
as feminists, 2230
as judges, 808
in labor force, 874
organizations for, 325, 695, 2267–2268
in politics, 894, 912
research on, 574
in workforce, 2227
as writers, 1424, 1428–1429
women's rights in, 325, 892, 912, 2230–2231
World Bank loans to, *2364*
in World War I, 2229
in World War II, 2229, 2370
Mareth Line protecting, 1487
Zirids in, 2228
Tunisian Communist Party. *See* Parti Communiste Tunisien
Tunisian Communist Workers Party. *See* Parti Ouvrier Communiste Tunisien
Tunisian General Labor Union, Achour (Habib) in, 41
Tunisian League for the Defense of Human Rights. *See* Ligue Tunisienne pour la Défense des Droits de l'Homme
Tunisian Union of Industrialists, Businessmen, and Artisans. *See* Union Tunisienne des Industrialistes, Compagnies, Artisans
Tunisian Zionist Federation, Valensi (Alfred) in, 2308
Tunisi, Bayram al-, **2233**, 2263
Tunisie Martyre, La (manifesto), **1375**
Tunisie martyre, La (Thaalbi), 2182
Tunisien, Le (journal), 2182, 2408
Tuqan, Ahmad, 2234
Tuqan, Alia Baha al-Din, 1062–1063
Tuqan, Aliya, 2234
Tuqan, Baha al-Din, 142
Tuqan, Fadwa, **2233**, 2234
on liberation of Palestine, 1791
on women's rights, 1792
Tuqan family, **2233–2234**
in Jabal Nablus region, 1206
in Nablus (West Bank), 1631
Tuqan, Hafiz, 2234
Tuqan, Ibrahim, 2233, 2234
Tuqan, Qadri, 2234
Tuqan, Sulayman, 2234
Turabi, Hasan al-, **2234–2235**, *2235*
and banking, 394
bin Laden and, 475
on emancipation of women, 1622–1623
as fundamentalist Islamic thinker, 2234–2235
and imposition of *shariʿa*, 868
in Muslim Brotherhood, 2234
in National Islamic Front, 1622, 2101, 2234
and Numeiri (Muhammad Jaʿfar), 1701
on *ulama*, 2259
wife of, 2235–2236
Turabi, Wisal al-Mahdi, **2235–2236**
Turath (musical poetry), 1617–1618
Turbans, 608–610
color of, 609–610
significance of, 608–610
for women, 610
Turim (journal), 1431, 2058
Türkçe. *See* Turkish language
Türkçe Şiirler (Yurdakul), 2414
Türk Dili (journal), 2250
Türk Dili Araştirma Kurumu. *See* Turkish Linguistic Society
Türk Dili Tetkik Cemiyeti. *See* Turkish Linguistic Society
Türkes, Alparslan, 957, **2236**
Kisakürek (Necip Fazil) and, 1326
as leader of Nationalist Action Party, 1660–1661
Nine Lights of, 1661
purged from National Unity Committee, 1667
Turkey, **2236–2242**. *See also* Ottoman Empire; *specific cities, organizations, people, and regions*
Aegean Sea controlled by, 51
agriculture in, 598, 902, 2238
Alawis in, 105
alcohol in, 110
ancient history of, 2239
archaeology in, 275, 278
architecture in, 284, 774, 1285
armament levels of, 305
Armenians in, 571, 2238, 2440
arms sales to, by United States, 304
art of, 34, 96, 305, 790, 1262, 1595, 1674, 2429
cultural identity in, 313
Assyrians in, 326, 2056
in Baghdad Pact (1955), 363, 519, 696, 1693, 2291
Balkan Muslim refugees in, 1913
banking in, 389, 390, 392, *393*, 415
Black Sea controlled by, 485, 2095
British relations with
Adana Conference in (1943), 42
dispute over Mosul oil deposits (1920–1928), 1582–133
caliphate in, 556
abolition of, 21, 34, 332, 557
restoration of proposed, 1659
cartoons in, 273
censorship in, of film industry, 832
in Central Treaty Organization, 573
charitable *waqfs* in, 2323
Circassians in, 600, 2238
cities of, 42, 490, 491, 547–548, 632–633, 715, 1193–1195, 2237
capital, 207, 2237
gecekondus in, 872
port, 115–116, 1201–1202
provincial capitals, 210–211, 755–756, 782–783, 1332
Civil Code of (1926), 332, 601–602
climate of, 604, 605, 902, 2237
clothing in, 332, 611
communism in, 625
constitutional amendments in (1928), 332

constitution of (1921), 1383
constitution of (1924), 924, 1383, 2240
constitution of (1960), provisional, 1667
constitution of (1961), 1383, 1667, 2241, 2243
constitution of (1982), 789, 1383, 1667, 2237, 2241, 2244–2245
higher education in, 2413
religion in, 1287
trade unions in, 631
cotton industry in, 42, 644, 645, 2180, *2181*, 2198, 2238
coup in (1960), 696, 957, 1098, 1537, 1919, 2236, 2241, 2243
Menderes (Adnan) ousted in, 1517
National Unity Committee in, 1667
and press liberalization, 1685
coup in (1971), 1537, 1898, 2241
coup in (1980), 746, 789, 1537, 1898, 1919, 2236, 2241, 2243
Nationalist Action Party closed after, 1661
political parties disbanded after, 1666
Cyprus occupied by (1974–), 652, 654
dams in, 787, 2082, 2141, 2188
dance in, 667, 668
defense costs as percentage of GNP or GDP, *1530*
earthquakes in, 901
economic and military aid to, 747
from U.S., 748, 750, 1836
economy of, 752, *753*, 753–754, 2240, 2241, 2242
24 January Measures for, 1746
Bayar (Celal) and, 415
Democrat Party policies on, 695–696
liberalization of, 1094
Özal's reform of, 1746–1747
summit meeting on (1923), 1202
women in labor force, 875
education in, 760
kuttabs banned in, 1347
religious schools in, 761
Village Institutes and, 2316–2317, 2413
Yüksek Öğretim Kurulu and, 2413–2414
elections in, 2244, 2245
Democrat Party in, 695
Justice Party in, 691, 1257
elites in, 776
ethnic groups of, 2238
in European Community, 1747
in European Union
AKP support for, 99
military as impediment to, 1667
feminism in, 891, 892, 2170–2171, 2249
fertility rates in, 1844
film industry of, 782, 832, 955, 2067
fishing industry of, 834
geography of, 901, 2236–2237
Georgians in, 2238
German relations with, 906
government of, 932, 933–934, 2237–2238, 2244
Greek invasion of (1919), 2240
Greek relations with
Chanak crisis (1922), 513, 1441–1442
in dispute over Cyprus, 1531–1535
Treaty of Ankara in (1930), 208
Greeks in, 2238
guest workers from, *945*, 945–946, *946*
in Gulf War (1991), 951
heroin production in, 724–725
higher education in, 761, 965–966
at Ankara University, 208
at Atatürk University, 334
at Bilkent University, 472
at Boğaziçi (Bosporus) University, 490–491
at Ege University, 762–763
at Istanbul Technical University, 1195
at Istanbul University, 1195–1196
at Marmara University, 1491
at Middle East Technical University, 1524
missionaries and, 1551–1552
women studies in, 2362
hijab (veiling) in, debate on, 1027
honorific titles banned in, 332
human rights in, 1048
Republican People's Party on, 1919
independence for, 2240, *2241*
declaration of (1923), 557
industrialization of, 1094
industry of, 2238–2239, 2240
intelligence organization of, 1545
Iraqi relations with
Bazzaz (Abd al-Rahman al-) and, 423
dispute over dams, 2082
oil pipelines in, 115–116
irrigation in, 74, 787, 2082, 2141
Islamist publications in, 1326
Jews in, 1233, 2238
Ashkenazic, 321
emigration of, 1234
Nahum (Hayyim) as chief rabbi of, 1637
journalism in, 1109, 1269, 1684–1685
journalists imprisoned in, 1685
Kemalism in, 1285–1288
Kurdish revolts in, 1340, 1341, 1914
Kurds in, 2238
imprisonment of political activists, 2423
military action against, 1536
pocu of, 610–611
Republican People's Party and, 1919
labor unions in, 1358–1359, 1359
confederation of, 631, 1358–1359
lakes of, 194, 2309
languages in, 2238 (*See also* Turkish language)
alphabet used in, 235, 332
Iranian, 1124
Lausanne Treaty (1923) gains, 514, 1376
in League of Nations, Treaty of Ankara and (1930), 208
legal system of, 886, 1379, 1383
legislative body of (*See* Turkish Grand National Assembly)
literature of (*See* Literature, Turkish)
manufacturing in, 1481–1484
map of, *2239*
Mevlevi Brotherhood in, 1521
on Middle East Defense Organization, 519
migration into, 1846–1847
military of
equipment of, *1534*
force levels of, *1528–1529*
force structure of, *1532–1533*, 1535
governmental influence of, 1667
in internal conflicts, 1536
National Security Council role curtailed (2001), 1667
navy, 1535
organization of, 1527
participation in coups, 1537
minorities or subdominant groups in, Atatürk (Mustafa Kemal) and, 1549
modernization in, 2240

Turkey *(continued)*
mountains of, 194, 273–274, 2167, 2237
museums in, 275, 342
music of, 476–477, 687, 689, 872–873, 1269, 1617, 2002, 2009, 2124, 2160
Naqshbandi order in, 1642–1643
nationalism in (*See* Turkish nationalism)
National Security Council of, 1666–1667
in NATO, 696, 1692
facilities of, 42
military commitment to, 1527, 1531–1535, 1535
security assured during U.S. invasion of Iraq (2003), 1692
newspapers and print media in, 1050–1051, *1684*, 1684–1685, 2067
mobilization press, 1685
Nadi (Yanus) and, 1633
in Northern Tier, 1692–1693
oil in, 2239
oil pipelines through, 115–116, 1830
opera in, 872–873
OYAK in, 1745–1746
pan-Turkism in, 1801
parliamentary elections in, 99–100
patronyms required in, 332
Peace Corps in, 1808
poetry of, 576, 661, 2414
political parties in, 2241–2242, 2243, 2245 (*See also specific parties*)
first, 1918–1919
leftist, 2295
multiple, legalization of, 1097–1098
pro-Islamic, 1910–1911
political reforms in, 2240–2241, 2243–2246
population censuses in, 1848, 2236
population growth in, 1843, 1844
population of, 752, *753*, 1843, 1844, 1845, 1848, 2236
postage stamps of, 1850
pronatalist policies of, 478
Protestant missions in, 1854
provinces of, 715, 2237
publishing industry in, 1326
radio and television in, 1897–1898
railways in, 2206, *2206*
regions of, 193–194, 598
religions in, 2238
Alevi Shiʿism, 112–115
Catholicism, 1932
Christianity, 590
Sufism, 2171
rivers of, 194, 2188, 2237, 2328–2329, 2417
Russian relations with, post-Soviet, 1944
scarves in, ban on, *1381*
science and technology in, 2004, 2005, 2006
secularism in, 332, 333, 415, 891, 1286, *1381*, 1383, 2240
Gökalp (Ziya) and, 924
Romanization of language and, 1933
Sezer (Ahmet) and, 2015
Sèvres Treaty (1920) losses, 512, 1376
Soviet Union describing state terrorism in, 2175
State Planning Organization of, 1746, 2089–2090, 2241
stock market in, 2090, *2091*, 2092, *2092*
Syrian relations with, dispute over dams, 2082, 2141
teacher training in, at Village Institutes, 2316–2317
television in, 2245
textile industry in, 547, 2180, 2181, *2181*, 2182
theater in (*See* Theater, Turkish)
tourism in, 2196
Edirne, 755
Istanbul, *2196*
in trade, 2198, *2199*, 2200, *2200*, 2201
trade treaties in, 621
tribes in, 2214, 2253
U.S. policy toward, Truman Doctrine and, 2291
U.S. relations with, Bayar (Celal) and, 415
Varlik Vergisi taxes in, 2309–2310
vatan (fatherland) in, 1641, 1658
veiling in, ban on, 891, 2240, 2413
war of independence in
Adivar (Abdulhak Adnan) in, 44
Adivar (Halide Edib) in, 45
Atatürk (Mustafa Kemal) in, 44, 45, 331–332
İnönü (İsmet) in, 1097
Nadi (Yunus) in, 1633
Sunay (Cevdet) in, 2121
water resources of, 2328–2329
Atatürk Dam and, *2329*
freshwater withdrawals, *2331*
Lake Van as, *2330*
quantity of, 2330
Westernization of, 1285–1286
opposition to, 1545
women in
as artists, 1595, 2429
economic status of, 877, *877*
education for, 880
governmental services for, 2362
as head of state, 808, 875, 891, 2220, 2242
Kurdish activists, 2423
in labor force, 875, 877
library and information resources for, 2358
as musicians, 476–477
in politics, 747, 891, 894, 2170–2171
in Refah Partisi, 1911
religious rituals of, 2360
as singers, 872–873
as writers, 780–781, 1440
women's rights in, 897–898, 2249
in World War II, 2370–2371
Adana Conference on (1943), 42
Churchill (Winston S.) and, 42, 516, 597
neutral stance of, 516, 2240
Roosevelt (Franklin Delano) recognition of contributions of, 1935
Varlik Vergisi tax and, 2309–2310
Turkey–Iraq pipeline. *See* Trans–Turkey Pipeline
Turkic language group, 2247–2248, 2252
Turki, Fawaz, **2242**
on liberation of Palestine, 1791
Türk İs. *See* Confederation of Turkish Trade Unions
Turkish–Afghan Treaty (1928), **2243**
Turkish Club, 2250
Turkish coffee, 837
Turkish Council of Higher Education. *See* Yüksek Öğretim Kurulu
Turkish folk culture, 1438, 1439, 2002, 2251
Turkish Grand National Assembly (TGNA), 2237, **2243–2246**, *2244*
Abdülmecit II as caliph chosen by, 34, 557
Adivar (Abdulhak Adnan) in, 44

Adivar (Halide Edib) in, 45
Ahmet Rasim in, 91
in Ankara, 207
architecture of building housing, 1285
Arseven (Celal Esat) in, 305
under Atatürk (Mustafa Kemal), 331–334, 1287
bicameral, 2243
Demirel (Süleyman) voted as chief of state by, 2219–2220
Democrat Party heading, 2243
foundation of, 2243
functions of, 2244
İnönü (İsmet) in, 1098
Koprülü (Mehmet Fuat) in, 1335
Nationalist Action Party in, 1661
National Salvation Party in, 1665–1666
unicameral, 2244

Turkish Hearth Association, **2246**
Adivar (Halide Edib) in, 45
Akçura (Yusuf) in, 1800
People's Houses as successor to, 1815

Turkish Historical Committee of the Turkish Hearth, 2246

Turkish Historical Society, 407, **2246**

Turkish Homeland Society. *See* Türk Yurdu Cemiyati

Turkish–Italian War (1911–1912), 742, 1200, **2246–2247**

Turkish Labor Bank, 415

Turkish language, **2247–2249**
academic study of, 2252
in Afghanistan, 55
alphabet of (*See* Turkish script)
Azerbaijani (*See* Azeri language)
features of, 2248–2249
modern, 2248
modern dictionary of, 92
modernization of, 1556
old Anatolian, 2248
organization devoted to study of, 2249–2250
in Ottoman Empire, 1731, 2248, 2250
reform of, 577
theater of, 72
translation by dragomans, 723
on postage stamps, 1850
reform movement for, 577, 873
Atay (Salih Rifki) in, 335
pan-Turkism and, 1800
Yücel (Hasan Ali) in, 2413
Romanization of, 1932–1933
sun language theory of, 2122
Tahtawi (Rifaʿa al-Rafi al-) translating works into, 2146–2148
in Turkey, among Alevi Shiʿites, 113
vocabulary of, 2248

Turkish Language Academy, 2250

Turkish Law on the Protection of the Family (1998), **2249**

Turkish Linguistic Society, **2249–2250**

Turkish nationalism, 924, 1658–1659, 1918, 2236, 2246, 2251. *See also* Pan-Turkism
vs. Arab nationalism, 261, 263
Mustafa Suphi in, 1625
Romanization of language and, 1933

Turkish National Pact (1920), 2240, **2250**
Atatürk (Mustafa Kemal) and, 331

Turkish Petroleum Company (TPC), 537, 742. *See also* Iraq Petroleum Company
British–French Oil Agreement (1920) on, 538, 1988
French share of Compagnie Française des Pétroles for, 628
in Paris peace settlements, 1802
post–World War I reorganization of, 1909–1910
San Remo Conference (1920) and, 1582
Sèvres Treaty (1920) on, 2015

Turkish Radio and Television (TRT), 1898

Turkish Republic of Northern Cyprus (TRNC), 652, 654, 697
international recognition of, 2278

Turkish Riviera, 490

Turkish script, 2240, 2248, **2250–2251**
alphabet of, 235, 332
Arabic as, 1932, 1933
Latin alphabet in, 1932–1933

Turkish Society, 1800

Turkish Straits. *See* Straits, Turkish

Turkish Union of Writers, 781

Turkish Workers Party, **2251**
outlawing of, 2295

Turkish Writers Syndicate, 1676

Turkism, **2251**. *See also* Pan-Turkism
vs. Islamism, 1800
vs. Ottomanism, 1800

Türkiye Büyük Millet Meclisi. *See* Turkish Grand National Assembly

Turkmanchai, Treaty of (1828), 816, 943, 1117, 1941, **2251–2252**
cessions by Iran in, 7, 345

Turkmenistan, language of, 2248

Turkmen language, 2248, 2252

Turkmen people, 2253, 2630
in Iran, autonomy movement of, suppression of, 1922

Türk Ocaği. *See* Turkish Hearth Association

Turko–Iranian War (1821–1823), **2252**

Turkology, 492, **2252–2253**

Turks, 383, 2238, **2253**
vs. Arabs, 221
migration by, 1846–1847

Türk Tarih Kurumu. *See* Turkish Historical Society

Türk Yurdu (periodical)
Akçura (Yusuf) in, 97
Gökalp (Ziya) in, 97

Türk Yurdu Cemiyati, Akçura (Yusuf) in, 97

Tushka canal (Egypt), 1652

Tusun ibn Muhammad Ali, 1077

Tutankhamen Collection (Egyptian Museum), 772

Tutunji, Jenab, *as contributor,* 29–31, 35, 38–39, 217–218, 257–259, 324–325, 338, 357, 602–603, 743, 796, 839–840, 841, 947–948, 999, 1043–1044, 1158–1159, 1221–1222, 1229, 1262–1263, 1324–1325, 1409–1410, 1447, 1453–1454, 1454–1455, 1471, 1632–1633, 1646, 1781–1782, 1810, 1835, 1838–1839, 1922, 1925, 1979–1980, 2151–2153, 2156–2157, 2204, 2242, 2295, 2380

Tutush, Duqaq ibn, 1044

Tuvan language, 2252

Tuv Mitzrayim (Ben Simeon), 454

Tuwayrani, Hasan Husni Pasha al-, 817

Tuyur Aylul (Nasrallah), 1646

TWA airplane, PFLP hijacking of (1969), 1293

Twareg language, 843

Twareg people, 1964, **2253–2254**
Berber language of, 122

Twayni, Ghassan, **2254–2255**
Twelver Shiʿism, 1463, 1489–1490, 2054
hostility toward non-Muslims, 1548
Husayn ibn Ali in, 1272
Ismaʿili Shiʿism split with, 1158
pilgrimage centers for, Karbala as, 1272
Shaykh al-Islam in, 2046
in Syria, 2129
Twenty-Three Years: A Study of the Prophetic Career of Mohammad (Dashti), 678
Twin pillars policy, **2255**
Two Women (film), 1526
Typen Türkischer Volksmörchen (Boratav and Eberhard), 492
Typhoid fever, 1508
Typhus, 1508
Tyre (Lebanon), **2255**
Tzaddik (holy person), 1485
Tzeʾirei Zion, 2086
Tzfira, al- (newspaper), 2078
Tzofeh, ha- (newspaper), 1683
Tzomet Party (Israel), 774, 1189
electoral success of, 1189
platform of, 1189
Tzur Moshe (Sephardic settlement), 2364
Tzur, Zvi, in Israel Defense Force, 1173
Tzvi, Ha- (periodical), 454

U

UAE. *See* United Arab Emirates
UAF. *See* Union de L'Action Feminine, L'
UAR. *See* United Arab Republic
Ubayd, Makram, in Wafd, 2320
Ubaydullah, Kurdish revolts led by, 1340
Ubayyad al- (Sudan), 2100
UC. *See* Union Constitutionelle
Udayay tribe, 2212
Udayd, al- (airbase), 1877
UDHR. *See* Universal Declaration of Human Rights
UDMA. *See* Union Démocratique du Manifeste Algérien
UDU. *See* Union Démocratique Unioniste
Uganda, hostage crisis in. *See* Entebbe Operation
Uganda Project, **2257**
Borochov (Ber) opposing, 493, 2257
British proposal for, 2257
opposition to, 2257
support for, 2257
Zangwill (Israel) and, 2425
Ugaritic language, 2010
UGEMA. *See* Union Générale des Etudiants Musulmans Algériens
UGTE. *See* General Tunisian Union of Students
UGTM. *See* Union Générale des Travailleurs Marocains
UGTT. *See* Union Générale des Travailleurs Tunisiens
UIA. *See* United Israel Appeal
Uighur language, 2252
UJA. *See* United Jewish Appeal
UJC. *See* United Jewish Communities
Ukaz (newspaper), 1679
Ulama (religious scholars), **2258–2259**
in Afghanistan, 2154, 2155
in Algeria, 1456
bazaar lifestyle and, 420
Bonaparte (Napoléon) appointing, 491
in Egypt, Milner Mission boycotted by, 1546
as elites, 775, *775*, 776, 2258
family values stance of, 1511
on female circumcision, 822
in Iran, 2259
and monopoly on education, 757
under Mozaffar al-Din Qajar, 1591
and Naser al-Din Shah, 1644
Islamic People's Republican Party on, 2036
madrasa education system supported by, 1457
marja al-taqlid as, 1490
in Morocco, al-Moudawana reviewed by, 1585–1586
nationalism resisted by, 2258
origins of, 2258
in Ottoman Empire, Nizamiye opposed by, 1690
political authority of, 2258
power of
challenges to, 2259
reduction in, 2258
role of, 2258–2259
in Saud Arabia, Faisal ibn Abd al-Aziz and, 798
secularism resisted by, 2258
socioeconomic class of, 2258
Tahtawi (Rifaʿa al-Rafi al-) resented by, 2147
as teachers, 756, 757, 2258
in Tobacco Revolt, 2193
Turabi (Hasan al-) on, 2235
Ülkü (newspaper), 1685
Uludağ University, 548
Ulus (newspaper), 745
Atay (Salih Rifki) in, 335
Umar I (caliph), 411
charitable *waqfs* under, 2323
Nusayba family given control over Church of Holy Sepulchre by, 1705
on temporary marriage, 2438
Umar II (caliph), poll taxes under, 1237
Umari, Amin al-, 927
Umar, Madiha, **2259**
paintings of, *309*, 2259
Umar Pasha (Mamluk ruler), 1478
Umar, Sidi Fadil Bu, as guerilla leader, 1610
Umayyad dynasty, 662
elites in, 774
governorate of, on Iberian Peninsula, 2084
Islam spread by, 1144
Muʿawiya as founder of, 2052
and *shari'a*, 2034
Umayyad Mosque (Damascus), 662, *663*, **2259–2260**
Umi-Zur Devash (Ben Simeon), 454
Umm, al- (Shafiʿi), 2018
Umma, al- (newspaper), 2260
Umma (community), 1145, 2213, 2630
Husari (Sati al-) on, 1051
of Medina, Muhammad's declaration of, 1596
vs. nationalism, 1660
Rida (Rashid) on, 1923
Umm al-Qaywayn (United Arab Emirates), 2219, **2260**
geography of, 2260
Muʿalla family, al- in, 1592
population of, 2260
Umm al-Qura (Kawakibi), 1152, 1282
Umm al-Qura University, **2260**
Umma Party (Sudan), 406, **2260–2261**

Abd al-Rahman al-Mahdi in, 19, 210, 2101, 2260–2261
al-Ansar in, 210, 2260, 2261
conflict within, 2261
electoral success of, 2261
leadership of, 210
parties opposing, 2261
platform of, 2260–2261
Sadiq al-Mahdi in, 210, 2261
women's movement supported by, 2235
Umm Kulthum, 1618, **2261–2263**, *2262*
Asmahan compared to, 324
as daughter of Muhammad, 1595
Umm Naʿsan (Bahrain), **2263**
Umm Qasr (Iraq), port of, 1130
Umm Said (Qatar), 2301
Ümran (journal), 90
Umran, Muhammad, Asad (Hafiz al-) and, 316
UMT. *See* Union Marocaine du Travail
UN. *See* United Nations
Unas, pyramids of, 1857
Unayza (Saudi Arabia), 1638
UNCCP. *See* United Nations Conciliation Commission for Palestine
UNCU. *See* Unified National Command of the Uprising
Under the Rubble (film), 1500
Under the Skin of the City (film), 388
UNDOF. *See* United Nations Disengagement and Observer Force
UNDP. *See* United Nations Development Programme
UNEA. *See* Union Nationale des Etudiants Algériens
Une enfance algérienne (Sebbar), 2007
Une enfance outremer (Sebbar), 2007
Une enfance singulière (M'Rabet), 1592
UNEF. *See* United Nations Emergency Force
UNEM. *See* Union Nationale des Etudiants Marocains
UNESCO. *See* United Nations Educational, Scientific, and Cultural Organization
UNFA. *See* Union Nationale des Femmes Algériennes
UNFICYP. *See* United Nations Peacekeeping Force in Cyprus
UNFP. *See* Union Nationale des Forces Populaires
UNFT. *See* Union of Tunisian Women
UNGOMAP. *See* United Nations Good Offices Mission in Afghanistan and Pakistan
Uniate Christians
in Bulgaria, millet system of, 1544
under French mandate, 1480
Uniate churches, 589–590, 738
UNICEF. *See* United Nations Children's Fund
UNIFEM. *See* United Nations Development Fund for Women
Unified Economic Agreement (1981), 949
Unified National Command of the Uprising (UNCU), HAMAS and, 983
Unified National Leadership of the Uprising (UNLU), in Intifada (1987–1991), 1108
UNIFIL. *See* United Nations Interim Force in Lebanon
UNIFSA. *See* United National and Islamic Front for the Salvation of Afghanistan
UNIIMOG. *See* United Nations Iran–Iraq Military Observer Group
Union(s). *See* Labor and labor unions
Union and Progress Society (Turkey), 415
Union Constitutionelle (UC) (Morocco), 1574–1575
Union de L'Action Feminine, L' (UAF) (Morocco)
Bouih (Fatna el-) and, 498
establishment of, 1203
Jababdi (Latifa) in, 1203
newspaper of, 772–773
reform of al-Moudawana urged by, 1586
Union Démocratique du Manifeste Algérien (UDMA), **2263–2264**
Abbas (Ferhat) in, 3, 2263–2264
establishment of, 3, 2263
Kaid (Ahmed) in, 1264
objectives of, 2263–2264
Union Démocratique Unioniste (UDU) (Tunisia), 2231, 2232
Union du Maghreb Arabe. *See* Arab Maghreb Union
Union Générale des Etudiants Musulmans Algériens (UGEMA), Abdesselam (Belaid) in, 23
Union Générale des Étudiants Tunisiens (UGET). *See* General Tunisian Union of Students
Union Générale des Travailleurs Algériens (UGTA), under Front de Libération Nationale control, 131
Union Générale des Travailleurs Marocains (UGTM), **2264**
Confédération Démocratique du Travail and, 629, 2264
as Istiqlal Party labor branch, 1197, 2264
Union Marocaine du Travail and, 453, 2264, 2265
Union Générale des Travailleurs Tunisiens (UGTT), 1358, 2227, **2264–2265**
Achour (Habib) in, 41, 486, 2264–2265
Ben Salah (Ahmed) in, 452, 2264
in Black Thursday (1978), 2265
crackdown after, 41, 2265
Black Thursday riots by, 486–487
conflict within, 2265
decline of, 2265
economic policies opposed by, 2264–2265
establishment of, 2264
Hached (Ferhat) in, 1358
Neo-Destour Party collaboration with, 634
strike by, 2265
Tunisian General Labor Union merger with, 41
Union Démocratique Unioniste and, 2232
Union Nationale des Travailleurs Tunisiens and, 2265
Unionist Democratic Union. *See* Union Démocratique Unioniste
Union Marocaine du Travail (UMT), **2265–2266**
Ben Seddiq (Mahjoub) in, 453, 2266
Bouazza (Tayyib) in, 453
Confédération Démocratique du Travail and, 453, 629, 2266
conflict within, 2265–2266

Union Marocaine du Travail (UMT) *(continued)*
Istiqlal Party affiliated with, 453, 2265
Union Générale des Travailleurs Marocains and, 453, 2264, 2265
Union Nationale des Forces Populaires affiliated with, 2265, 2267
Union Socialiste des Forces Populaires and, 453
Union Nationale de la Jeunesse Algérienne (UNJA), under Front de Libération Nationale control, 131
Union Nationale des Etudiants Algériens (UNEA)
dissolution of, 131
under Front de Libération Nationale control, 131
Union Nationale des Etudiants Marocains (UNEM), **2266**
agenda of, 2266
government crackdown on, 2266
Islamists in, 2266
Union Nationale des Femmes Algériennes (UNFA), under Front de Libération Nationale control, 131–132
Union Nationale des Femmes Tunisiennes (UNFT). *See* Union of Tunisian Women
Union Nationale des Forces Populaires (UNFP) (Morocco), 1574, **2266–2267**
Basri (Muhammad al-) in, 1197, 2266
Ben Barka (Mehdi) in, 441, 1197, 2266–2267
Ben Jelloun (Umar) in, 450
Ben Seddiq (Mahjoub) in, 453, 1197, 2266, 2267
Bouabid (Abderrahim) in, 495, 2266, 2267
Casablanca section of, 2266
conflicts within, 2266–2267
constitution boycotted by (1962), 1572
elections of 1963 boycotted by, 1588
establishment of, 1570
FDIC opposing, 858
government crackdown on, 2266
Ibrahim (Abdullah) in, 1075, 1197, 2266–2267
leadership structure of, 2267
platform of, 2267
Rabat section of, 2266–2267
split with Istiqlal Party, 812, 1197, 2266
Union Marocaine du Travail and, 2265, 2267
Union Nationale des Etudiants Marocains and, 2266
Youssoufi (Abderrahmane) in, 2266, 2410
Union Nationale des Musulmans Nord-Africans, 969
Union Nationale des Travailleurs Tunisiens (UNTT), Union Générale des Travailleurs Tunisiens and, 2265
Union of Academies of Arabic Language, 1457
Union of General Zionists, 2338
Union of Moroccan Writers, 467
Union of Palestinian Medical Relief Committee, 402
Union of Palestinian Students (Egypt), Arafat (Yasir) in, 269
Union of the Daughter of the Nile, 2019
Union of the Maghrib treaty, 1006
Union of Tunisian Women (UNFT), **2267–2268**
membership of, 2267
objectives of, 2267–2268
Union of Zionist Revisionists. *See* Zionist Revisionist Movement
Union Populaire Algérien (UPA), 3
Union Socialiste des Forces Populaires (USFP) (Morocco), 1574–1575, 1601, **2268**
Bouabid (Abderrahim) in, 495, 2268
electoral success of, 2268
establishment of, 2267, 2268
government led by, 1904
human rights organization of, 1716
Ibrahim (Abdullah) in, 1075
Islamists role in government opposed by, 1601
Istiqlal Party and, 1197–1198, 2268
platform of, 2268
Union Marocaine du Travail and, 453
Youssoufi (Abderrahmane) in, 2268, 2411
Union Theological Seminary, Bliss (Howard) at, 487
Union Tunisienne des Industrialistes, Compagnies, Artisans (UTICA), 2227, **2268–2269**
Union Universelle de la Jeunesse Juive, 1453
Unit 101 (Israel), 2041
Unitarians. *See* Muwahhidun
United Arab Emirates (UAE), **2269–2272**. *See also specific cities, organizations, people, and regions; specific emirates*
Abu Musa Island claimed by, 37–38, 2040
Al Nahayyan family in, 156
archaeology in, 343
assassination of Majali (Hazza al-) by, 1470–1471
Baluchis in, 385
banking in, *393*
and Beitaddin Declaration (1978), 432
borders of, 2269
British control of, 36, 2270
Abu Musa Island dispute in, 38
treaties on, 36, 614, 2270
Catholics in, 1931
cities of, 36, 343, 2270
climate of, 2269
constitution of, 2271
defense costs as percentage of GNP or GDP, *1530*
economic aid from, 749
economy of, 752, *753*, 2270–2271
education in, upbringing aspect of, 760
emirates of, 36, 96, 731, 1903, 2219, 2260 (*See also specific emirates*)
establishment of, 36, 521, 2219
fishing industry of, 834
foreign relations of, 2270, 2272
Fujayra–Sharjah conflict in (1972), 859–860
geography of, 2269
in Gulf Cooperation Council, 949
in Gulf Crisis (1990–1991), 950
human rights in, 1048
industrialization in, 752
Iranian relations with, 38
Tunb Islands and, 2223–2224
on Iraq, 2272
Islam in, 2270
labor unions illegal in, 1358
in League of Arab States, 1387, 1388
legal system of
Majalla, 1382
reforms in, 1380
legislative body in, 932
manufacturing in, 1483, *1483*
map of, *2272*

military of
equipment of, *1534*
force levels of, *1528–1529*
force structure of, *1532–1533*
Muʿalla family, al- in, 1592
natural gas production in, *1671*
natural gas reserves in, *1671*, 2271
newspapers and print media of, 1679
loyalist approach of, 1681
Nuʿaymi family, al- in, 1694
oil production in, 752
oil reserves in, 2270–2271
pearling industry of, 36
political system of, 2271–2272
population of, 752, *753*, 1844, 2270
radio and television in, *1895*
ruling family of (Maktum family, al-), 1474
sand deserts of, 1938
tourism in, 2196
in trade, *2198*, *2200*, 2272
tribes in, 385, 2210, 2270
Trucial Coast as colonial precursor of, 2218–2219
Tunb Islands claimed by, 2223–2224
U.S. relations with, 2272
women in, economic status of, 877
women's rights in, 884
World Bank and, capital stock and voting power in, *2363*
United Arab List (Israel), 1189–1190, 1787
platform of, 1189–1190
United Arab Party (Israel), in United Arab List, 1189
United Arab Republic (UAR), 2133–2134, **2273**
Bakr (Ahmad Hasan al-) supporting, 377
Bazzaz (Abd al-Rahman al-) opposing, 423
Bitar (Salah al-Din al-) role in creation of, 482
collapse of, 1886, 2273
establishment of, 2273
governmental institutions of, 2273
Hawrani (Akram al-) as advocate of, 1011
Iraq and, 288, 826, 1969, 2273
Jordan and, 826, 1925
and Lebanese Civil War (1958), 1389, 1390–1391, 2277
Nasser (Gamal Abdel) as president of, 412, 1650–1651, 1886, 2273
pan-Arabism in, 1799
political parties in, 2273
Quwatli (Shukri al-) supporting, 1886, 2273
Sarraj (Abd al-Hammid) and, 1925
Syrian support for, 2273
Western opposition to, 2273
United Arab States, 2273
United Front (Afghanistan). *See also* Northern Alliance
establishment of, 1215
after overthrow of Taliban, 1215
United Hebrew Resistance Movement
member groups in, 1140
violent actions by, 1140
United Israel Appeal (UIA), 2273
United Jewish Appeal (UJA), 1913, **2273–2274**
Keren Hayesod as part of, 1289
United Jewish Communities (UJC), 2274
United Kibbutz Movement, 1319
United Kingdom of Libya, 2218
United National and Islamic Front for the Salvation of Afghanistan (UNIFSA), 1889
United National Front (Iraq), 1654
United National Front (Tripolitania). *See* Jabha al-Wataniyya, al-
United Nations (UN), **2274–2284**
on Afghanistan, Soviet intervention in (1979–1989), 2279–2280
Annan (Kofi A.) as secretary-general of, 208–209
in al-Aqsa Intifada (2000), 2284
in Arab–Israel negotiations, 2274–2277, 2284
Bernadotte (Folke) in, 465–466, 2274
General Armistice Agreements (1949), 239, 241
Jarring (Gunnar) as special envoy in, 1219, 2275
in Arab–Israel War (1948), 2274
call for truce by, 243, 244
in Arab–Israel War (1956), call for truce by, 245
in Arab–Israel War (1967), 249, 2275
call for cease-fire by, 249
in Arab–Israel War (1973), 2275
call for cease-fire by, 250
on Bahrain, independence for, 2279
Boutros-Ghali (Boutros) as secretary-general of, 505
China's admission to, foreign policy after, 586
Conference on Women (1995), Platform of Action of, 1852
Convention on Torture, Moroccan ratification of, 1716
on Cyprus, 653, 654, 697, 2277–2278
Dulles (John Foster) in, 733
Economic and Social Commission for Western Asia of, 2277
economic sanctions by
against Iraq (*See* Sanctions, Iraqi)
against Libya, 522, 1414, 1415, 1707, 1708
education measured by, 760
establishment of, 1935
gender imbalance initiatives by, 879
at Geneva Peace Conference (1973), 1328, 2275
in Gulf Crisis (1990–1991), 2281–2282
and Gulf War, 1067
under Hammarskjöld (Dag), 985–986
human rights treaties under, 1048
Ibrahimi (Lakhdar al-) in, 1078
in Iran–Iraq War (1980–1988), 2280
in Iraq, U.S. war in (2003), 2282–2283
Iraqi policy of
disarmament operations, 1069
economic sanctions in, 1068, 1510, 2323, 2325
Oil-for-Food Program, 1069
Powell's (Colin L.) address on (2003), 2324
Resolution 1441 on, 2324–2325
U.S. efforts on thwarted, 2324–2325
weapons inspections in, 1539, 1698, 2323, 2324
and Israel, establishment of, 518
Israel as member of, *2278*
on Israeli invasion of Lebanon (1978), 1393, 1400, 1417–1418, 2276
League of Arab States as regional alternative to, 1388
Lebanese Civil War (1958) investigated by, 1391, 2277
Organization of the Islamic Conference and, 1721

United Nations (UN) *(continued)*
in Oslo Accords (1993), 2276–2277
Palestine partition plan of (1947) (*See under* Partition plans)
Palestinian refugee problem and, 1915
Palestinians' rights recognized by, 1767–1768
Pérez de Cuéllar (Javier) as secretary-general of, 1818
PLO in, observer status of, 1774
population growth projections by, 1846
Roosevelt (Eleanor) at, 1935
on September 11th terrorist attack, 2282
on Soviet invasion of Afghanistan, 66
in Suez Crisis (1956–1957), 1444, 2108, 2109–2110, 2275
Universal Declaration of Human Rights by (*See* Universal Declaration of Human Rights)
and U.S. war in Iraq (2003), 209
in Western Sahara War, 1837, 2280–2281, 2344–2345, 2346–2347
Women's Program in Africa and the Middle East of, 1950
in Yemen Civil War (1962–1970), 2277

United Nations Children's Fund (UNICEF), disease prevention and treatment by, 712, 714

United Nations Commission on Human Rights, 1935

United Nations Committee on Palestine, Eban (Abba) in, 744

United Nations Conciliation Commission for Palestine (UNCCP), **2284–2285**
accomplishments of, 2285
establishment of, 236, 2274, 2284
Kennedy (John F.) and, 1289
Lausanne Conference (1949) held by, 1375–1376, 2285
members of, 2284–2285
mission of, 2284

United Nations Development Fund for Women (UNIFEM), 894

United Nations Development Programme (UNDP)
Basma bint Talal and, 409
Gebeyli (Claire) in, 872
Maksoud (Clovis) in, 1474
Poverty Strategy Initiative of, 1291

United Nations Disengagement and Observer Force (UNDOF), 1166, 2277

United Nations Economic Survey Mission (1949), **2285**
establishment of, 2285
Lausanne Conference establishing, 1376

United Nations Educational, Scientific, and Cultural Organization (UNESCO)
Algeria's delegate to, 1362
Amer (Ghada) awarded by, 176
Basma bint Talal at, 409
daily newspaper standards of, 1679
Eqbal (Manouchehr) in, 779
and Grand Egyptian Museum, 772
Pérez de Cuéllar (Javier) in, 1818
Philae island temples moved by, 1832
prize for tolerance of, awarded to Shenouda III, 2049
Salih (Teyib) in, 1977
World Heritage Sites of (*See* World Heritage Site)

United Nations Emergency Force (UNEF), **2286**
Bunche (Ralph J.) and, 543
in Egypt
Annan (Kofi A.) and, 209
in Arab–Israel War (1973), 2275
Egyptian–Israeli Peace Treaty ending (1979), 2276
entry after Arab–Israel War (1956), 237, 246, 1165
and General Armistice Agreements (1949), 239
in Suez Crisis, 2110, 2275, 2286
withdrawal before Arab–Israel War (1967), 237, 248, 1165, 2286
establishment of, 237, 2275, 2286
at Sharm al-Shaykh, 2040
troops of, 2286

United Nations General Assembly
Arab Higher Committee before, Cattan (Henry) in, 570
Arafat (Yasir) address to (1974), 270, 1774
on Ifni, Spanish *vs.* Moroccan control of, 1083
on Libyan independence, 1812
Istiqlal Party testimony before, 1196
Resolution 181 (II) of, 1806, 2289
Husayni (Amin al-) rejection of, 1057, 1058
on Jerusalem, 1224, 1225
PLO endorsement of, 1774
Resolution 194 of, in Camp David Summit (2000), 562
Resolution 302 of, 2285, 2287
Resolution 1141 of, 1136
Resolution 1284 of, 2288
Resolution 3236 of, 1767–1768
Resolution 3379 of, Herzog (Chaim) response to, 1022
Resolution on the Granting of Independence to Colonial Countries and Peoples, 2174

United Nations Good Offices Mission in Afghanistan and Pakistan (UNGOMAP), 2280

United Nations Human Development Report
and education of women, 883
on status of women, 876–877

United Nations Institute for Training and Research, 2193

United Nations Interim Force in Lebanon (UNIFIL), 1417–1418, **2286–2287**
current status of, 2277, 2287
establishment of, 1166, 2276, 2286
failure of, 2276, 2286

United Nations Iran–Iraq Military Observer Group (UNIIMOG), 2280

United Nations Mission for the Referendum in Western Sahara (MINURSO), 2281, 2344, 2346

United Nations Monitoring, Verification, and Inspection Commission (UNMOVIC), 1069, 2288
Iraqi weapons inspections by, 1136, 2282–2283, 2324

United Nations Observation Group in Lebanon (UNOGIL), 2277

United Nations Observation Mission in Yemen (UNYOM), 2277

United Nations Peacekeeping Force in Cyprus (UNFICYP), 2278

United Nations Relief and Works Agency for Palestine Refugees in the Near East (UNRWA), 1916, **2287–2288**
budget of, 2287
current status of, 2277, 2287
establishment of, 2274, 2285, 2287
mission of, 2287

number of refugees aided by, 2287
programs of, 2287
Tall al-Zaʿtar refugee camp built by, 2155
United Nations Security Council
Azerbaijan crisis considered by, 346
Resolution 128 of, 2277
Resolution 181 of, 502
Resolution 186 of, 2278
Resolution 194 of, 466, 502
Resolution 242 of
adoption of, 249, 1166, 2275
and Arab–Israel War (1973), 250
Begin (Menachem) against, 425
and Brookings Report, 539
in Camp David Accords (1978), 560
conflicting interpretations of, 237
implementation of, failure in, 250
Jarring (Gunnar) and, 242, 1166, 1219, 2275
land-for-peace principle in, 1792
Madrid Conference based on (1991), 1458
Palestine National Council endorsement of, 1768, 1792
PLO acceptance of, 1725, 1774
Sisco (Joseph) and, 2070
Syrian acceptance of, 318, 2135
terms of, 237, 249, 1166, 2275
U.S. support for, 1238, 2292
Resolution 338 of
adoption of, 251, 2275
and Geneva Peace Conference (1973), 900
Madrid Conference based on (1991), 1458
Syrian acceptance of, 2135
terms of, 251, 1166, 2275
Resolution 425 of, 1166, 2286
Israeli compliance with, 1168
Resolution 479 of, 2280
Resolution 497 of, 925
Resolution 598, 2043
Resolution 598 of, 1120, 1128–1129, 2280
Resolution 660 of, 907
Resolution 661 of, 1135, 1985
Resolution 678 of, 2281, 2288
China on, 587
Germany supporting, 907
Resolution 687 of, 1135, 1985, 2282
Resolution 688 of, 1339, 2282
Resolution 707 of, 2288
Resolution 713 of, 1135
Resolution 986 of, 1069, 1135, 1339, 1985–1986
Resolution 1368 of, 2282
Resolution 1373 of, 2282
Resolution 1441 of, 2282
Resolution 1483 of, 1136, 1987, 2283
Resolution 1511 of, 1136, 2283
United Nations Special Commission (UNSCOM), 1986, **2288–2289**
infiltration by U.S. intelligence agencies, 2289
Iraqi weapons inspections by, 1135, 2282, 2323
and Iraq's disarmament operations, 1069, 2288
Sharott (Moshe) negotiating with, 2032
United Nations Special Committee on Palestine (UNSCOP) (1947), **2289–2290**
Arab Higher Committee boycott of, 228
establishment of, 2274
on "Exodus Affair," 790
partition plan recommended by, 2274
United Nations Special Committee on Palestine, 1947 (UNSCOP), 447
Bunche (Ralph J.) writing proposal for, 543
United Nations Truce Supervision Organization (UNTSO), 236, 241, 244, 543, 2274, **2290**
current status of, 2277
Mixed Armistice Commissions under, 1552–1553
United Palestine Appeal (UPA), 2273, 2274
Wise (Stephen S.) in, 2354
United Partisans Organization, Kovner (Abba) in, 1336
United Political Organization of the National Front (Yemen), 2397–2398
United Popular Front (Iraq), 1654
United Religious Front (Israel), 1190
Agudat Israel in, 1178, 1190
United States, **2290–2295**
in Afghanistan
intervention of (*See under* Afghanistan)
during Soviet intervention, 66, 2174
in Arab–Israel conflict
Baker (James A.) and, 374
and Tripartite Declaration (1950), 2215
in Arab–Israel War (1956), 245–246
in Arab–Israel War (1967)
neutrality of, 1238
Soviet conflict with, 237
in Arab–Israel War (1973), 250, 1689
economic support to Israel by, 748
weapons supplied to Israel by, 250, 251, 799
in Arab–Israel War (1982), 253–254
in arms control efforts, 304
arms sales by, 750
to Afghanistan, 66
to Egypt, 304, 1238
to Iran, 304, 1119, 1122–1123, 1689
to Israel, 250, 251, 304, 1238, 1288, 1331, 1689
under Johnson, 1238
to Jordan, 304
to Saudi Arabia, 304
to Turkey, 304
B'nai B'rith in, 489
British relations with, oil concessions after World War I and, 514
in Central Treaty Organization, 573, 574
Chinese relations with, Kissinger (Henry) in, 1327
Circassians in, 600
Civil War in, and cotton trade, 116–117, 644
during Cold War, and Baghdad Pact (1955), 363, 519
as dominant power, 517
economic and military aid from, 747, 2290–2291
in Arab–Israel War (1973), 748
Camp David Accords (1978) and, 748, 771
through Economic Support Fund, 748
to Egypt, 748–749, 750, 765, 771
Gulf War (1990–1991) and, 749
to Israel, 748–749, *749*, 750, *750*
to Jordan, 748, 749, 750, 1244
under Marshall Plan, 1836
to Morocco, 748, 750
under Point Four program, 1836
to Turkey, 748, 750

United States *(continued)*
Egyptian relations with
under Mubarak (Husni), 1593
under Nasser (Gamal Abdel), 1650
Sadat (Anwar al-) and, 767, 1957
embassies of, al-Qaʿida bombing of, 1865, *2177*
in Gulf War (1990–1991) (*See* Gulf War)
and hostage crises, 1046
Iran and
dual containment policy toward, 730
Nixon (Richard Milhous) and, 1689
twin pillars policy and, 2255
U.S. military in, diplomatic immunity for, 1310–1311
in Iran–Iraq War (1980–1988), intelligence provided by, 1103
Iraq and, Operation Desert Fox, 1069
Iraq attack in Operation Desert Fox (1998), 2323
Iraqi Kurdish revolts supported by, 1134, 2174
Iraq invaded by (2003), 549, 1069–1070, 1539–1540, 2323–2327
al-Jazeera coverage of, 1219
and Baghdad surrendering, 362
Bendjedid (Chadli) criticizing, 445
British support for, 2324–2325
Bush (George W.) and, 2323–2325
coalition forces in, 2325
Germany opposing, 907
global opposition to, 2324
Hussein (Saddam) removed from power, 2189
League of Arab States on, *1387*, 1388–1389
looting during, 2325
military operations in, 2325
prewar intelligence failures and, 2326
Samarra, 1981
shifting rationale for, 2324
Sistani (Ali al-) on, 2071
Spain supporting, 2084
traditional allies opposing, 2324
Iraqi policy of
dual containment, 730
September 11 attacks and, 1136
weapons inspections and, 1135
Iraq occupation by (2003–), 1540, 2325–2326
armed resistance to, 2326
direct elections proposed in, 2326
sovereignty transfer in, 2326
Islamic numismatics in, 1702
Israeli attacking ship of, 1409–1410
Israeli relations with
Kollek (Teddy) in, 1331
under Nixon (Richard Milhous), 1689
Pollard affair in, 1838
Shultz (George) and, 2061
U.S. support for statehood, 517
Jewish immigration to, restrictions on, 146
Jewish organizations in, 176–179, 966, 2273–2274
Jordanian relations with
Free Trade Agreement in, 1593
military support in, 258
trade between, 1244
Kuwaiti dependence on, 1351
in Lebanese Civil War (1958), military intervention in, 1391
in Lebanese Civil War (1975–1990), 1393
Libyan relations with
economic sanctions in, and oil production, 1707–1708
after September 11th, 2001, 1415
U.S. bombings and (1986), 1414, 1862, 2217
Middle East Defense Organization proposed by, 519
military of
headquarters for navy's Fifth Fleet, 1479
lease on Masira Island, 1499
Marine barracks bombing (Lebanon), 1488–1489
Morocco relations with, under Treaty of Meknes (1836), 1515
Northern Tier interests of, 1692–1693
oil embargo against (1973–1974), 1709
oil imports to, quota on, 1826
oil production by, 1824–1826
OPEC opposed by, 1719
and opium trade, 1713
Ottoman treaties with, 621
Pahlavi (Mohammad Reza) visit to, student opposition to, 630
in peace process
at Camp David Accords (1978), 560–561
under Johnson, 1238
Kissinger (Henry) in, 1327–1328
at Madrid Peace Conference, 1725
Operation Alpha of, 157
PLO talks with, 271
Road Map by (2003), 220, 1170, 1793, 1852
on UN Resolution 242, 1238
petrochemical industry in, 1823
and PLO
under Bush (George H.W.), 548
opening of dialogue between, 271, 1768, 1774
al-Qaʿida targets bombed by (1998), 606, 1865
regime changes called for by, 1121, 1136
Saudi relations with, 517, 796, 799, 1998, *1998*, 2000
under Abd al-Aziz ibn Saʿud Al Saʿud, 11, 515, 1626
during Gulf War (1990–1991), 1627
under Nixon (Richard Milhous), 1689
oil in, 11, 1626
security alliance in, 11
after September 11th, 2001, 2000
twin pillars policy and, 2255
Soviet policy of
under Carter, 567
Dulles (John Foster) in, 733
Soviet relations with, Brezhnev (Leonid Ilyich) and, 507
Spanish relations with, 2084
state terrorism term used by, 2175
in Suez Crisis, 520
against use of force, 2108
Syrian relations with, 319
Treaty of 1815 with Algiers, 2208
Tripoli conflict with, 1871
Treaty of Peace and Amity ending (1805), 1807–1808
Turkish relations with, Bayar (Celal) and, 415
United Arab Emirates relations with, 2272
and United Nations Special Commission (UNSCOM), 2288–2289
in War of Attrition (1969–1970), 1689
war on terrorism by, 2174, 2178–2179
Arab–Israel peace process unresolved due to, 2178

Bush (George W.) and, 549
civilians as primary victims of, 2178–2179
Jordanian support for, 32
in Western Sahara War, aid to Morocco, 2345
and World Bank, 2363–2364
in World War II, 1934–1935
emergence as premier power, 2372
Lend-Lease program of, 1403–1404, 1523, 1934
Operation Torch, 516
Yemeni relations with
Cole attack and, 2077
after September 11th, 2001, 2196
Zionism in, 2434, 2436
organizations against, 176
Zoroastrianism in, 2441

United States Agency for International Development (USAID), in Afghan reconstruction efforts, 67

United States for Pioneer Women, 456

United States of Africa, 1415

United Syrian Kingdom, Jordan in, 1244

United Torah Judaism Party, 1190
platform of, 1190

"Uniting for Peace" (1956), 2109

Unity of Labor. *See* Ahdut ha-Avodah

Unity Party (Afghanistan). *See* Hezb-e Wahadat

Unity Party (Turkey), **2295**

Universal Declaration of Human Rights (UDHR), 1048
LTDH adopting, 1416

Universal House of Justice, 365

Universal Maritime Suez Canal Company, 2106

Universal Union of Jewish Youth, 1453

University of Aleppo, 666, 2132

University of Algiers
Ben Bouali (Hassiba) at, 443
disciples of Bennabi (Malek) establishing mosque at, 451
student riots at, 1965, 2079
Toumi (Khalida) at, 2195

University of Azerbaijan, 2144

University of Basra, 410

University of Berlin, 943

University of Birmingham (U.K.), Sabah (Rasha al-) at, 1951

University of Cairo. *See* Cairo University

University of California (Berkeley)
Esfandiary (Fereydun) at, 784
Shamlu (Ahmad) at, 2027

University of California (Los Angeles)
Bunche (Ralph J.) at, 543
Esfandiary (Fereydun) at, 784

University of Chicago
Shultz (George) at, 2061
Sisco (Joseph) at, 2070

University of Cincinnati
Ghuri (Emile al-) at, 917
Silver (Abba Hillel) at, 2066

University of Deoband, 2154

University of Essex (England), Zach (Natan) at, 2418

University of Gar Younis, 446

University of Istanbul. *See* Istanbul University

University of Jordan, **2295**

University of Khartoum, 1301, **2296**
Garang (John) at, 868
Turabi (Hasan al-) at, 2234

University of London
Salam (Sa'ib) at, 1975
Turabi (Hasan al-) at, 2234

University of Lyons
Fanon (Frantz) at, 804
and Saint Joseph University, 1971

University of Mashdad, 2035

University of Paris
Ben Salah (Ahmed) at, 452
Boutros-Ghali (Boutros) at, 505
Trad (Petro) at, 2202

University of Rabat, Bannis (Mohammad) at, 396

University of Riyadh. *See* King Saʿud University

University of Strasbourg, Barkan (Ömer Lutfi) at, 407

University of Tehran, **2296–2297**
Golestan (Ebrahim) at, 928

University of the Baʿth, 666

University of Tishrin, 666

University of Tizi-Ouzou, 464

University of Tunis, *shariʿa* school of, 2427

UNJA. *See* Union Nationale de la Jeunesse Algérienne

UNLU. *See* Unified National Leadership of the Uprising

UNMOVIC. *See* United Nations Monitoring, Verification, and Inspection Commission

UNOGIL. *See* United Nations Observation Group in Lebanon

UNRWA. *See* United Nations Relief and Works Agency for Palestine Refugees in the Near East

UNSCOM. *See* United Nations Special Commission

UNSCOP. *See* United Nations Special Committee on Palestine

UNTSO. *See* United Nations Truce Supervision Organization

UNTT. *See* Union Nationale des Travailleurs Tunisiens

UNYOM. *See* United Nations Observation Mission in Yemen

UPA. *See* United Palestine Appeal

Upbringing aspect of schooling, 759–760

Up-Wingers (Esfandiary), 784

Uqayr, Treaty of (1922), 159
on Kuwaiti borders, 159, 1349

Uqbi, Tayyib al-, **2297**

Uqla, Adnan, 982

Uqsur, al-. *See* Luxor

Urabi, Ahmad, 797, **2297–2298**
rebellion by (*See* Urabi rebellion)
vs. Riyad (Mustafa al-), 1929

Urabi, Mahmud Husni al-, in Socialist party, 626

Urabi rebellion (1881–1882), 404, 766
Abduh (Muhammad) support for, 23
Alexandria in, 117
British suppression of, economic motivations for, 1089–1090
causes of, debt supervision in, 117
Fahmi (Mahmud Pasha) in, 797
Ilaysh (Muhammad) in, 1086
majlis (assembly) in, 1472
National Party in, 1663
orator of, 1419

Uralic languages, 2247

Urban II, Pope, 1930

Urbanization, **2298–2299**
and internal migration, 1847
in Jordan, 1243

Urban planning, **2299–2302**
in colonial period, 2299–2300
in oil-boom era, 2300–2301
in transitional period, 2300

Urf, 463, 2630

Urfa, Armenian resistance at, 1613
Urmia, Lake (Iran), 1342
Urquhart, Brian, *as contributor,* 543–544, 985–986, 2286–2287
Urs Baghl (Wattar), 2333
Urwa al-Wuthqa, al- (society), 23
Urwa al-Wuthqa, al- (newspaper), 1923, **2302**
  Abduh (Muhammad) in, 23, 1923, 2302
  Afghani (Jamal al-Din al-) in, 52, 1923, 2302
USAID. *See* United States Agency for International Development
Uşakliğil, Halit Ziya, 1439, **2302**
USA Patriot Act, 2011
Usba, Ahmad Abu, on Wafdist Women's Central Committee, 2321
USFP. *See* Union Socialiste des Forces Populaires
Ush, Muhammad Abu al-Faraj al-, numismatic studies of, 1702
Ushr, 1990, 2167
Üsküdar (Istanbul), **2302–2303**
Usrat at-Ta'akhi (Lebanon), 793
Ussishkin, Menahem, **2303**
  and ha-Halutz, 974
  Uganda Project opposed by, 2257
USS *Liberty. See Liberty,* USS
U.S.S.R. *See* Russia
Usta, al- (Salim), 1978
Ustadh, 2630
Usul, 2033, 2055
Usul al-fiqh, 833–834, 1148, 2019, 2154
  in Maliki school of law, 1476
Usul-i cedid, 869
Usuli school of law, 2047, **2303–2304**
Usuli Shi'ism, 2055
Üşür, 1367
UTA flight 772 bombing (Niger)
  Libyan compensation for, 1415
  Libyan involvement in, 1414
Utayba tribe, 2209, 2214
  attempted coup by (1979), 10
Utaybi, Juhayman al-, 2214, **2304**
  in Grand Mosque seizure (1979), 1085
Utbiyya, al- (Utbi), 1476
Uthman ibn Affan, official version of Qur'an under, 1883
Uthman, Muhammad Ali, **2304–2305**
Uthman Shakyh al-Din, 1463
Uthman, Uthman Ahmad, **2305**
UTICA. *See* Union Tunisienne des Industrialistes, Compagnies, Artisans
Utub tribe, al-, 1348
Utzon, Jørn, *1350*
Uygur language, 2247
Uzal. *See* San'a
Uzbekistan, 2306
  Tajiks in, 2150
Uzbek language, 2247, 2252
Uzbeks, 2253, **2305–2306**
  in Afghanistan, 1505
Uzi, 2630
Uzi submachine gun, 1535

V

Va'ad ha-Lashon, 454
Va'ad Le'umi (VL), **2307–2308**
  Ben-Zvi (Yizhak) in, 457
  functions of, 2307, 2402
  Kalvaryski (Chaim Margaliut-) in, 1265
  leadership of, 2307
  Rutenberg (Pinhas) in, 1946, 1947
  and Youth Aliyah, 2411
Vaccinations, *1509*
  Egyptian programs for, 1453
  for hepatitis, 712
  percent of children receiving full, 1510
  for smallpox, 2003
  for tuberculosis, 712
Vahdat, Farzin, *as contributor,* 1261–1262, 1563
Vahidettin (Ottoman sultan), Ferit (Damat Mehmet) in alliance with, 823
Vainqueur de coupe, Le (Boudjedra), 497
Vaka-i hayriye (1826), 1217, 1467, **2308**
  casualties of, 2308
  popular reception of, 1217, 2308
Vakit (newspaper), Karacan (Ali Naci) in, 1269
Valensi, Alfred, **2308**
Valerian (Roman emperor), 1797
Vali, 1993, 2630
Valide sultan, 2120
Vali-ye faqih, vs. marja al taqlid, 1490
Valleys of the Assassins, The (Stark), 2088
Van (Turkey)
  Armenian genocide in, 294, 295
  Armenian political society in, 299
  Armenian resistance at, 1613
  in World War I, 2367, 2368
Van Bruinessen, Martin, *as contributor,* 1342–1344
Vance, Cyrus, **2308–2309**
Vandals, 2227
  in Morocco, 1569
Vandewalle, Dirk, *as contributor,* 208, 470–471, 498–500, 564, 632, 777–778, 2079–2080
Vanguard (magazine), 482
Van, Lake (Turkey), 194, 1342, **2309,** *2330*
Vanunu affair, 708, 1697, **2309**
Vanunu, Mordechai, 708, 2309
  Israeli nuclear capability disclosed by, 1697
Varaq parehha-ye zendan (Alavi), 104
Varlik Vergisi, **2309–2310**
Varzi, Roxanne, *as contributor,* 427, 698, 831–833, 1236, 1299–1300, 1318, 1464–1465, 1473, 1526, 1821–1822, 2021–2022, 2039, 2052–2055
Vasileiou, George, presidency of, 654
Vasmer (numismatic scholar), 1702
Vaste est la prison (Djebar). *See So Vast Is the Prisona*
Vatan (newspaper), 1685
Vatan (Turkish fatherland), 1641, 1658
Vatan yahut Silistre (Kemal), 72, 1438, 1641, 1658, 2186
Vatican, **2310**
  diplomatic goals of, 2310
  Israeli diplomatic relations with, 2310
  on Jews in death of Jesus, 211
  in Nazareth conflict, 1673
Vatican Council, Second (1962–1965), 2310
Vazhapetian, Nerses, 298, **2310–2311**
  Ormanian (Maghakia) ordained by, 1723
  and Srvantziants (Garegin), 2087

Vazir Afkham, Soltan Ali Khan, **2311**
Vaziri, Haleh, *as contributor,* 706–707, 2358–2359
Vaziri, Qamar al-Moluk, **2311**
Vegetables, 838
Vegetation. *See* Plants
Veil and the Male Elite, The (Mernissi), 1518
Veiling, 611, **1026–1027**
in Afghanistan, *61*
ordinances on, 1715
in Egypt, women rejecting, 772
in Iran
during Constitutional Revolution, 637
during Pahlavi regime, 891
in Turkey, ban on, 891, 2240, 2413
Veils Up (newspaper), 431
Velayat-e faqih (governance of jurists), **2311–2313**
in Iranian constitution (1979), 1311, 1312, 2312, 2313
Kadivar (Mohsen) criticism of, 1262
Khomeini (Ruhollah) formulation of, 793, 1311, 2311–2313
Mojtahed-Shabestari (Mohammad) and, 1563
Montazeri (Hosayn Ali) and, 1564
Velayat-e motlaqaye faqih (absolute governance of jurists), 2312
Velayati, Ali Akbar, **2313–2314**
as Iranian foreign minister, 2313
Veli, Ornan, 1440
Velt, Di (weekly), 941
Venery, Salvatore, Kadri (Mufide) trained by, 1262
Venezuela
oil production in, Middle East competition with, 1718–1719
in OPEC, 1719
Venice, Ottoman Empire treaty with (1517), capitulations in, 564–565
Venice Declaration (1980), 522
Venizelos, Eleutherios, in Treaty of Ankara (1930), 208
Verges, Jacques, 497
Versailles conference (1919)
Clemenceau (Georges) at, 801
Faisal I ibn Hussein at, 800–801
Versailles, Treaty of (1920), 906, **2314–2315**
Husayn ibn Ali on, 1053
ratification of, 2314
signing of, 2314
terms of, 2314
Vezirli, Necef Beg, 347
Vichy government
denial of protection to Jews under, 846
establishment of, 2368–2369
Free French troops overthrowing, 851, 856
Special Forces of the Levant under, 2086
Victoria (Michael), 1522
Victoria (queen of England)
Abdülmecit I supported by, 33–34
in Damascus affair (1840), 664
Persian cats of, 1821
on postage stamp, 1849
Victoria College, **2315–2316**
Antonius (George) at, 213, 2315
establishment of, 118, 2315
nationalization of, 2316
student body of, 2315–2316
Victoria, Lake, 1688
"Victory City." *See* Madinat Nasr (Egypt)
Vie à l'endroit, La (Boudjedra), 497
Vieille, Paul, 388
Vieira de Mello, Sergio, 2283
Vienna Congress (1814–1815), 739
Vienna Human Rights Conference (1993), 822
Vienna–Istanbul railway (Orient Express), 464, 2206
Vienot, Pierre, 489
in Syrian negotiations for independence, 329
Vie Quotidienne en Algérie, La (Boudjedra), 497
Vietnam, Palestinian relations with, Wazir (Khalil al-) and, 2335
Vietnam Savaşimiz (Dağlarca), 661
Vietnam War, Kissinger (Henry) in, 1327
Vigiles, les (Djaout), 716
Vikings, Islamic coins buried by, 1702
Vilayet (Ottoman court), 411, 824, 1524, 1690, 2631
of Damascus, 663
Vilayet Law of 1864 (Ottoman Empire), Palestine after, 1759
Vilayet Law of 1867 (Ottoman Empire), 24, 2162
Villa Cisneros, under Spanish control, 2085
Village Institutes (Turkey), **2316–2317**
Yücel (Hasan Ali) and, 2413
Villeneuve, 471
Vilna ghetto, Kovner (Abba) in, 1336
Vincennes (U.S. warship), in Iran–Iraq War (1980–1988), 1120
Violence, Zionist Revisionist Movement and, 2437
Viollette, Maurice, 489
Virgin Mary, veneration by Christian women, 2360
Virtue Party (Turkey)
closure of, 99
creation of, 1911
Erbakan (Necmeddin) in, 2236
Erdoğan (Tayyip) in, 781
Vives (numismatic scholar), 1702
Vizier, 823, 2631
VL. *See* Vaʿad Leʾumi
Vlachs, 383
Vocation de l'Islam, La (Bennabi), 451
Vogel, David, 1431, 1432
Vogt, Emile, King David Hotel designed by, 1323
Voice of Jerusalem (radio station), 1896
Voice of the Arabs (radio program), 818, 1894
Volcanism, 901
Volksocialismus, 289
Volonte (Ohnet), 148
Volozhin Yeshiva (Orthodox academy), 470
Volpi, Giuseppe, **2317**
Vomito blanco (Khatibi), 1304
Von Sivers, Peter. *See* Sivers, Peter von
Voting. *See* Suffrage
Voyage en Orient (Nerval), 1675
Voyage, Le (Shahada), 2020
Vozuq al-Dowleh, Mirza Hasan Khan, **2318**
Vratsian, Simon, 303, 676
Vu, lu, entendu (Chraibi), 588

W

Wa Akhrajaha min al-Janna (Ghallab), 910
Wa Bazagha Fajr Jadid (Shaʾul), 2043

Waʿd, 479
Wadi Araba, 1249
Wadi Dhahr (Yemen), Dar al-Hajar in, *2392*
Wadi Hadramawt (Yemen), **2319**
economy of, 1814
tribes in, 2215
Wadi Natrun, **2319–2320**
Wadi Run (Jordan), *1242*
Wad Madani (Sudan), 2100
Wafa Party (Algeria), Ibrahimi (Ahmed Taleb) in, 1076
Wafa wa al-Amal, al- (al-Sadat), 1958
Wafd, al- (newspaper), 2321
Wafd (Egypt), **2320–2321**
abolition of, 767
Adli split with, 46
Copts in, 640–641
disbanding of, 2321
and Egypt's independence, 766, 858
establishment of, 640
Farouk installing, 810
Farouk removing, 767, 810
Haykal (Muhammad Husayn) and, 1013
Khalid (Khalid Muhammad) influenced by, 1296
leadership of, 2418–2419
Liberal Constitutionalist Party coalition with, 1486
Mabarrat Muhammad Ali opposed by, 1453
Mahir (Ahmad) in, 1465
Mahir (Ali) in, 1465
Mahmud (Muhammad) in, 1468–1469
members of, forming Liberal Constitutionalist Party, 1408
Milner Mission boycotted by, 1546
Muslim Brotherhood alliance with, 1622
Nahhas (Mustafa al-) in, 1635, *2320,* 2320–2321
Nasser (Gamal Abdel) outlawing (1953), 1685
National Party support for, 1664
New Wafd as successor to, 1685–1686, 2321
Nuqrashi (Mahmud Fahmi al-) in, 1701
organization of, 2320
origin of name, 2320
power of, 859
Sadat (Anwar al-) ordering arrest of, 1957
Sidqi (Ismaʿil) in, 2065
Sidqi (Ismaʿil) opposed by, 2066
in uprisings (1919), 1664, 2320
Wingate's (Reginald) meeting with, 2354
women's rights in, 227, 2320, 2321–2322
critique of and dissatisfaction with, 2321–2322
in World War II, 2320–2321
Young Egypt opposition to, 2405
youth organization of, 2320
Zaghlul (Saʿd) in, 640–641, 766, 2320
Wafdist Women's Central Committee, 770, **2321–2322**
work on Zaghlul's (Saʿid) behalf, 2321
Wahadat (Afghanistan). *See* Unity Party
Wahda Dam, al-. *See* Maqarin Dam
Wahdat al-shuhud, 2114
Wahdi ma al-Ayyam (Tuqan), 2233
Wahhabi Islam, 1625–1627. *See also* Muwahhidun
Abd al-Aziz ibn Saʿud Al Saʿud promotion of, 9, 1085
Faysal ibn Turki Al Saʿud as follower of, 819
origins of, in Arabian Peninsula, 232
vs. politically motivated neo-fundamentalism, 1627
in Saudi Arabia, 1997
Saudi Arabia as state of, 1625–1626
spread of, 2123
Wahhab, Muhammad ibn Abd al-, 1625
Wahrhaftig, Zerah, **2322**
Wailing Wall. *See* Western Wall
Wajib, 2033
Wakhi language, 1125
Waldheim, Kurt
on Afghanistan, Soviet intervention in (1979–1989), 2279
at Geneva Peace Conference (1973), 1328, 2275
Pérez de Cuéllar (Javier) and, 1818
Waldner, David, *as contributor,* 18, 22, 34, 39, 90–91, 96, 143, 273–274, 327–328, 341, 409, 434, 570–571, 575, 576–577, 602, 607, 620–622, 631, 687, 689, 690, 695–696, 702, 732, 780–781, 789, 915–916, 948, 957, 967, 982, 1028–1029, 1097, 1106, 1257–1258, 1266–1267, 1276–1277, 1285, 1289, 1327–1329, 1366–1369, 1404, 1408–1409, 1485–1486, 1506, 1513, 1517, 1519, 1595, 1608–1609, 1614, 1623–1625, 1631, 1634, 1673–1674, 1746–1747, 1832, 1848–1849, 1909, 1950–1951, 1955, 1990–1991, 2002, 2008–2009, 2010–2011, 2019, 2021–2022, 2030–2031, 2039, 2048, 2055, 2065–2066, 2082, 2124, 2145–2146, 2150–2151, 2160–2161, 2165–2166, 2179–2180, 2183, 2233, 2236–2242, 2243, 2414
Wali (guardian or tutor), for Moroccan women, 1585
Wali al-Tahir yaʿudu ila makamihi al-zaki, al- (Wattar), 1427, 2333
Walid ibn Abd al-Malik, 662, 2259
Waliyy, 2053
Walking through Fire: A Life of Nawal al Saadawi (al-Saadawi), 1950
Wallach, Yona, 1434, **2322–2323**
Wallerstein, Immanuel, 1089
Walls of Gaza (Shawa), 2044
Wamdatt Bakira (al-Sabah), 1952
Wa Nasibi min al-Ufuq (Ben Shaikh), 1429
Wangenheim, Hans von, 904
Wanisi, Zuhur, 1425
Wannus, Saʿdallah, 2184
Waqaʾi al-Misriyya, al- (newspaper), 1680
Abduh (Muhammad) at, 23
Waqaʾi al-Misriyya al- (newspaper), 2146, 2148
Waq al-Ahdhiya al-Khashina (Aʿraj), 273
Waqf (Islamic endowment), 407, **2323**
in Coptic Orthodox Church, 657–658
madrasa education system supported by, 1457
in Ottoman Empire, 1368
Shaʿrawi (Muhammad Mutwalli al-) as minister of, 2031
Warba Island al-, 541, 949
War between the Whistlers, The (Nesin), 1676
Wardak, Firuza, 693

Wardani, Nasif al-, 910
Warfalla tribe, 471
War Generation–Beirut (film), 1500
War in Iraq (2003). *See* Iraq, U.S. war in
War injuries, to women and children, 1509–1510
Warnier Law, **2327**
War of Attrition (1969–1970), **2327**
  Bar-Lev (Haim) in, 408
  as impetus for Israel's nuclear acquisition, 1697
  Israel in, 1166
  Nasser (Gamal Abdel) and, 1651
  Rogers Plan in, 2327
  United States in, 1689
War of the Mountains (1983), Jumblatt (Walid) and, 1256
War of Three Hundred Years Between Algeria and Spain, The (Madani), 1456
War Refugee Board (U.S.), 1936
Warren, Charles, 1771
Warsaw Ghetto uprising, 1041, 2377
  Ha-Shomer ha-Tzaʿir members during, 1001
Warsaw Treaty Organization, 1692
Warsaw University, Begin (Menachem) at, 424
Warschawski, Michel, 1501, 2221
Washington Agreement (1998), 2151
  fighting ended by, 1339, 1807
  implementation of, 1807
Washington Pact (1935), 278
Wasif, Wissa, on Wafdist Women's Central Committee, 2321
Wasini, Laraj, 1427
Wasla stitch, 1879
Wasserstein, Bernard, *as contributor,* 454, 509–524, 617, 647, 650–651, 1441–1442, 1982–1983, 2333–2334, 2337–2339, 2372–2373
Wassmuss, Wilhelm, 906
Watan, 2147
Wataniyya, in nationalism, 1659
Waterbury, John, at American University of Beirut, 181
Water Kissing Water (Michael), 1522
Water resources, **2327–2332**. *See also* Desalinization
  for agriculture (*See* Irrigation)
  from aquifers, 1668–1669, 2329
  climate and, 2328
  dams and, 2329, *2329*
  in deserts, 702
  equity for, 2332
  freshwater, drawing down of, 2331, *2331*
  in Gaza Strip, 870
  in Golan Heights, 926
  harvesting of, 2330
  history and, 2328
  in Israel, 866, 1248–1249, 2379–2380
  in Jordan, 1240, 1243, 1249, 2379–2380
  from Jordan River, 2328
    conflict over, 237, 248, 1248–1249
    development of, 1238, 1248–1249
    Johnston Plan for, 1238, 1248
  in Kuwait, 1347
  in Libya, aquifers as, 702
  from Nile River, 1651–1652, 1687, 2328–2329
  political conflict over, 237, 1248–1249, 2332, 2379–2380
  pollution of, 2331–2332
  population growth and, 478
  problems with, 2330–2331
  in Qatar, 1875
  quality of, 2331–2332
  quantity of, 2330–2331, *2331*
  from rivers, 2328–2329
  scarcity of, 2327
  sewage as, recycled, 1668, 2329–2330
  sources of, 2328–2330
  in Syria, 344, 1249, 2379–2380
  uses of, 2330
  in West Bank, 1249
  from Yarmuk River, 1485, 2379–2380
Wathba uprising (Iraq), 1210
Watson, Charles R., at American University in Cairo, 179
Wattar, al-Taher, 1426, 1427, **2332–2333**
Wattle-and-daub structures, *2099*
Wauchope, Arthur, **2333–2334**
  as high commissioner of Palestine, 1025
Wavell, Archibald Percival, **2334**
  in Allied Middle East Command, 152–153, 2369
  fighting against Graziani (Rodolfo), 516
  fighting against Rommel (Erwin) in Tobruk (1941), 516, 2194
  Wingate (Charles Orde) and, 2353
Waxman, Chaim I., **1553–1554**
  as contributor, 1–2, 77–78, 145–148, 289–290, 493, 544, 781–782, 980, 1001–1002, 1002, 1022, 1139–1140, 1250, 1289, 1318–1320, 1333, 1334, 1384, 1403, 1460–1461, 1470, 1506, 1677–1678, 1689, 1745, 1807, 1822, 1851, 1976, 2257, 2439, 2440
Wazir, Intisar al- (Umm Jihad), **2334**
  as first female member of Fatah, al-, 2334
  in General Union for Palestinian Women, 2334
  as wife of Wazir (Khalil al-), 2334, 2335
Wazir, Khalil al- (Abu Jihad), **2334–2336**, *2335*
  as aide to Arafat (Yasir), 270, 2334–2336
  assassination of, 814, 2335
    Abbas (Mahmud) after, 6
    by Mossad agents, 1578
  in al-Fatah, 6, 813, 1773, 2334–2335
  in PLO, 814, 2334–2336
  Rajub (Jibril) as deputy to, 1900
  wife of, Wazir (Intisar al-) as, 2334, 2335
Wazzani, Muhammad Hassan al-, **2336**. *See also* Ouazzani, Mohamed Hassan
Wazzani, Thami al-, in Parti Démocratique de l'Indépendance, 1804
WCC. *See* World Council of Churches
Weapons. *See* Arms
Weapons of mass destruction (WMD), 1526
  in Iraq, 1987
    identification and elimination of, as principal condition for lifting sanctions, 1135, 1985
    UN efforts to eliminate, 1986, 2288–2289
    and U.S. invasion (2003), 1539–1540
We are immigrating (Ben-Zvi), 456
"We Are No More Evil than Men" (Bint al-Shati), 476
We Are Not Your Slave Girls Anymore (Khalifa), 1297
Wedding in Galilee (film), 833
Wedding of Zein and Other Sudanese Stories, The (Salih), 1977

Wedding of Zein, The (film), 1977
Weddings, Palestinian, women's garments in, 1879
We Egyptian Women (Efflatoun), 762
Weiker, Walter F., *as contributor,* 81–82, 415–416, 1097–1099, 1175–1177, 1263–1264, 1330, 1416–1417, 1517, 1748–1749, 2075
Weil, Shalavah, *as contributor,* 786–788
Weimar Republic, 906
Weinbaum, Marvin G., *as contributor,* 747–752
Weir, Shelagh, 608
Weissbrod, Rachel, *as contributor,* 789–790
Weiss, Thomas G., *as contributor,* 2274–2284
Weizman, Ezer, **2336–2337**
  Hawatma (Nayif) and, 1009
  in Israel Defense Force, 1171
  modern presidency of, 2337
  negotiations with PLO urged by, 2337
  resignation of, 2337
  scandal involving, 2337
Weizmann, Chaim, **2337–2339,** *2338*
  Arlosoroff (Chaim) support for, 289
  and Balfour Declaration (1917), 380, 446–447, 2337
    Ahad Ha-Am aid to, 78
  Ben-Gurion (David) superseding, 2338
  and Biltmore Program (1942), 472
  biography of, started by Crossman (Richard), 650
  borders proposed by, Yarmuk River in, 2379
  British–Zionism alliance as "Rock of Gibraltar" of, 2338
  Churchill (Winston S.) and, 595, 597, 2337
  De Menasce (Félix Béhor) and, 691
  and Democratic Faction, 2337, 2434
  Faisal agreement on Jewish immigration, 800, 803
  as first president of Israel, 2338–2339
  and Hebrew University of Jerusalem, 1018
  Jabotinsky (Vladimir Ze'ev) on, 1208
  in Jewish Agency for Palestine establishment of, 178, 1227
    resignation from presidency, 1454, 2338, 2350
  Jewish terrorism denounced by, 2338
  on Keren Hayesod, 1289
  Kisch (Frederick Hermann) supported by, 1326
  Levin (Shmaryahu) supporting, 1407
  on London Conference (1939) proposals, 1445–1446
  MacDonald Letter sent to, 1454, 2350
  and Negev settlement, Churchill (Winston S.) on, 595
  nephew of, Weizman (Ezer) as, 2336
  NILI criticized by, 1
  Nordau (Max) opposing practical Zionism of, 1692
  in Paris Peace Conference (1919), 511, 2338
  Passfield White Paper (1932) opposed by, 2350
  and Peel Commission, 2338
    testimony by, 1811
  scientific institute named for, 2339
  Storrs (Ronald) meeting with, 2092
  and Truman (Harry S.), 2338, *2338*
  West German reparations sought by, 2348
  in World Zionist Organization, 2372
  and Zionist Commission for Palestine, 2338, 2436
Weizmann Institute of Science (Israel), 744, 2031, **2339**
Weizmann, Vera, in Women's International Zionist Organization, 2357
Welchman, Lynn, *as contributor,* 649–650, 1047–1049
Welfare Association for Palestinians, 1953
Welfare benefits, in Libya, 1410
Welfare Party (Turkey). *See* Refah Partisi
Wells, overpumping of, 2331
We Moderns (Zangwill), 2425
Wenner, Manfred W., *as contributor,* 86–87, 376, 984–985, 1039, 1081–1082, 1655, 1717, 1816, 1976–1977, 2018, 2081–2082, 2377–2378, 2385–2391, 2396–2398, 2442
Werfel, Franz, 1613
West, Orientalism in, 1721–1722
West Bank, **2339–2341,** *2340. See also* Occupied territories
  in al-Aqsa Intifada, 2341
  Areas A, B, and C of, 2340–2341
  Baker Plan for, 374
  Begin (Menachem) on, 426
  borders of, 2339
    in 2000, *1768*
  Cairo and, bridges between, 553
  Camp David Accords and (1978), 561
  Camp David Summit and (2000), 562
  Catholics in, 1932
  cities of, 468, 1631, 1869, 2340
    Israeli, 2340
    Palestinian, 1220–1221, 1901
  Dead Sea and, 684–685
  economic troubles in, 2340
  al-Fatah in, 814
  Green Line demarcating, 2339, *2340*
  Israel Defense Force raids on, 1169
  Israeli checkpoints in, *2339*
  Israeli occupation of, 2178, 2340–2341
    Germany criticizing, 907
    as literary theme, 2233
    Matzpen protests of, 1500–1501
  Israeli reoccupation of, 2341
  Israeli seizure of, in Arab–Israel War (1967), 249, 1063, 1159–1160, *1191,* 1651, 2339, 2340
  Israeli withdrawal from, 2340–2341
    in Oslo II (1995), 1727, 1775, 1784
    Wye River Accords (1998) and, 1677
  Jewish settlements in (*See* Israeli settlements)
  under Jordan, 31, 1244
    annexation by Abdullah I ibn Hussein (1950), 2339–2340
    Jericho Congress on, 1221–1222
  labor unions in, 1358
  mountains of, 1204–1205
  Nashashibi (Raghid al-) as governor of, 1645
  Oslo Accords (1993) and, 2340

Palestinian Authority control in, discontinuity of area under, 1784
Palestinian refugees in, 1639
Palestinian self-determination in, 2340–2341
Palestinian state proposed in, 1640
Palestinian uprising in, Wazir (Khalil al-) and, 2335
Reagan Plan (1982) on, 1908
sovereignty over East Jerusalem in, 2340
Taba negotiations (1995) on, 2140
total area of, 2339
water resources in, 1249
Women in Black protests in, 2356
West Bank Data Project, 454
West Beirut (film), 833
Western Desert, 763
Westernization, **2341–2342**
Ahmad (Jalal Al-e) on, 2342
anti-Western reactions to, 1091
of clothing, 608
intellectual/psychological aspects of, 1556
of Iran, 1118
of military, 1527–1528
vs. modernization, 2341
of Ottoman Empire, 1732–1733, 1735
Young Ottomans opposition to, 2405–2407
of Turkey, 1285–1286
opposition to, 1545
Western Sahara, 1963, **2342–2344**. *See also* POLISARIO
Algerian–Moroccan rivalry related to, 1005, 1006
Algerian relations with, 1837
Bendjedid (Chadli) and, 444
as *bilad al-siba* (lands of dissidence), 2343
borders of, 2342
cities of, 1356
capital, 2342
geography of, 2342–2343
independence of, struggle for, 1836–1837
under Mauritania, 660, 1502, 1571, 1837, 2343, 2344, 2345
claims ceded (1979), 2343, 2345
Moroccan–Spanish agreement on (1976), 1516
under Morocco, 660, 1451, 1571, 1837, *2343*, 2343–2344
sand barrier built by, 718
nationalism in, 1571
political history of, 2343
population of, 2342–2343
self-determination in
delay of referendum on, 1571, 2344, 2346–2347
Hassan II's acceptance of, 2346
Sahrawi support for, 2343
voter identification for, 2344, 2347
Spanish protectorate in, 1356, 1571, 2084, 2085, 2343
Madrid Accords (1975) ending, 2345
Morocco occupying (*See* Green March)
natural resources in, 2086
struggle against, 1836–1837
Western Sahara War, 2086, 2342, 2343–2344, **2344–2347**
Baker (James A., III) in, 2344, 2346–2347
cease-fire in, 2281
foreign aid to Morocco in, 2345
Green March in, 1566, 1571, 2345
Mauritania territory seized in, 1503, 2345
Moroccan–Algerian conflict in, 1566, 1600, 2345
Moroccan–POLISARIO conflict in, 1571, 1600, 1837, 2343–2347
Organization of African Unity mediation in, 2344
outbreak of, 2345–2346
refugees from, 2343, 2345, *2346*
sand walls built in, 2345
United Nations in, 2280–2281, 2344–2345, 2346–2347
Western Wall (Jerusalem), 991, **2347–2348**
after Arab–Israel War (1967), 1225
Balfour Declaration (1917) on, 381
under British mandate, 2347
under Jordanian rule, 2347
Rothschild (Edmond de) trying to regain for Jewish community, 427
significance of, 235, 1222
for Jews, 2347
to Muslims, 2348
white papers on (1928, 1930), 2350
Western Wall disturbances (1929), 991, **2348**
Arab Women's Association of Palestine founded after, 267
causes of, 235, 1224
and Hebron massacre, 2159
Hope-Simpson Commission after, 1044
Husayni (Musa Kazim al-) during, 1059
revival of legislative council derailed by, 1402
Shaw Commission inquiring into, 2044, 2348, 2350
West German Reparations Agreement (1952), 43, 907, **2348–2349**
Begin (Menachem) protesting, 425
Ben-Gurion (David) and, 448
Goldmann (Nahum) and, 928
West Germany, 906–907
constitution of, 43
Israeli occupation of West Bank and Gaza Strip criticized by, 907
West Jerusalem
in Arab–Israel War (1967), 1224–1225
establishment of, 1224
Jewish residents of, 1160
unification with East Jerusalem, 1225
"Weststruck." *See Gharbzadegi*
Weststruckness (Al-e Ahmad), 1437
"What the National Party Wants" (Kamil), 1267
Wheat. *See* Grain
Wheelus Air Force Base, **2349**
Where the Jackals Howl (Oz), 1748
White Fathers, 1931, 1932
White Flag League (Sudan), **2349**
White Nile. *See* Bahr al-Abyad
White papers on Palestine (1939), **2349–2351**
Abdullah I ibn Hussein acceptance of, 30
and *aliyah*, 147
Arab Higher Committee opposing, 228, 1030
Balfour Declaration modified by, 515, 1790
Ben-Gurion (David) on, 447
Bevin (Ernest) following, 468
Biltmore Program (1942) denouncing, 472
Churchill (Winston S.) opposing, 597, 1770
Haganah immigration operations to circumvent, 972
Husayni (Amin al-) rejection of, 1057

White papers on Palestine (1939) *(continued)*
Jewish expansion restricted in, 1766
on legislative council, 1402
London Conference (1939) failure and, 1446
by MacDonald (Malcolm), 1454, 1766, 1790, 2350–2351, 2363
MacDonald (Ramsay) Letter overriding (1931), 1454, 2350
opposition to, after outbreak of World War II, 1041
Palestine Arab Revolt and (1936–1939), 1770
Passfield (1930), 1453, 2350
Peel Commission plan retracted by, 1766, 1811
precursors to, 2349
proposals contained in, 1766
Stern (Abraham) opposing, 2090
on Western Wall claims (1928, 1930), 2350
White Revolution (1961–1963) (Iran), **2351–2352**
Alam (Amir Asadollah) in, 102, 1753
Amini (Ali) policies in, 186
criticism of viewed as disloyalty to shah, 2352
unfulfilled expectations in, 2351–2352
U.S. role in, 1118
White Sisters, 1931
Whitney Biennial exhibition, Amer (Ghada) in, 176
WHO. *See* World Health Organization
Wichhart, Stefanie K., *as contributor,* 1516–1517
Widowhood, 1495
Wieseltier, Meir, 1434
Wifaq, al- (Morocco), **2352**
Wigoder, Geoffrey, *as contributor,* 831–833
Wihda Dam. *See* Maqarin Dam
Wijdan. *See* Ali, Wijdan
Wilaya V, 498
Wilber, Donald, 1937
Wild Flowers (film), 1500
Wild Thorns (Khalifa), 1297
Wilhelm II (kaiser of Germany)
and Algeciras Conference (1906), 119
Jerusalem visited by, 1223
and Ottoman relations, 903, *904, 905*
Wilkes, George R., *as contributor,* 176–177, 357–358, 470, 483, 506–507, 539, 548, 582, 613, 697–698, 855, 914, 915–916, 944–945, 961–963, 1007, 1070–1071, 1336, 1496–1497, 1500–1501, 1512–1513, 1554–1555, 1608–1609, 1685–1686, 1832, 1838, 1841–1842, 1881–1882, 1952–1953, 1972, 1989–1990, 2001, 2023, 2059, 2069–2070, 2075, 2355–2356
"Will a Woman Become a Shaykh in al-Azhar?" (Bint al-Shati), 476
Will You Let Me Love My Country? (al-Sabah), 1952
Wilson, Arnold T., **2352–2353**
Bell (Gertrude) as secretary of, 437
at Cairo Conference (1921), 554
Iraqi revolt (1920) repressed by, 512
Wilson, C. C., 2368
Wilson, Harold
in Arab–Israel War (1967), 521
Crossman (Richard) under, 650
Wilson, Rodney J. A., *as contributor,* 1091–1096
Wilson, Woodrow, **2353**
Crane (Charles R.) support for, 646
Fourteen Points of, 2014, 2314, 2353
and King–Crane Commission (1919), 1323, 2290, 2314
mandate system accepted by, 2353
at Paris Peace Conference (1919), 2353
and rise of nationalism, 1659, 2353
and Roosevelt (Franklin Delano), 1934
on Sykes-Picot Agreement (1916), 2128
Wise (Stephen S.) and, 2354
in World War I, 2353
Winckler, Hugo, 278
Winds, 605, 1161
Wine, 109–110
Winegar, Jessica, *as contributor,* 144–145, 176, 205–206, 309–314, 337–338, 414, 556, 762, 805, 916, 1007–1008, 1142–1143, 1211, 1262, 1275, 1294, 1308–1309, 1676, 1687, 2001, 2044, 2064–2065, 2069, 2155, 2259, 2429
Wingate, Charles Orde, **2353–2354**
active defense doctrine of, 2353
in Arab revolt, Dayan (Moshe) under, 681
and Special Night Squads, 972
Zionist sympathies of, 2353
Wingate, Reginald, 603, **2354**
in Arab Bureau, 225
Egyptian delegation to, 2418
as governor-general of Sudan, 2354
as high commissioner of Egypt, 2354
Wafd meeting with, 2354
in World War I, 2368
Winter in Arabia (Stark), 2088
Winter of the Dry Sea, A (Ikhlassi), 1084
Wise, Stephen S., 2067, **2354–2355**
Silver (Abba Hillel) conflict with, 2355
Wissa, Ester Fahmi, on Wafdist Women's Central Committee, 2321
With My Own Eyes (Langer), 1374
With the Chosen (Bint al-Shati), 476
Wives of the Prophet, The (Bint al-Shati), 476
WIZO. *See* Women's International Zionist Organization
Wolff, Henry Drummond, 726, **2355**
Wolffsohn, David, Nordau (Max) and, 1692
Wolof, 1503
Wolsey, Louis, in American Council for Judaism, 176
Woman and Sex (al-Saadawi), 1950
Woman Artist in Lebanon, The (Khal), 1294
Woman at Point Zero (al-Saadawi), 1950
Woman in Islamic Teachings, The (Turabi, al-), 1622
Woman Named Rachid, A (Bouih), 498
Woman of Her Time, A (television show), 1500
Woman's Voice, The (periodical), 1075
Women. *See also* Gender; Women's rights
in Afghanistan, *58*
education for, 880, 1881
in government, 1906

journals for, 1140
organizations for, 68, 325, 693
in politics, 786, 894, 1981–1982
Queen Surraya's impact on, 1881
veiling for, *61*, 1715
in Alevi Shiʿism, 114
in Algeria
as artists, 1687, 2064
constitution on, 129, 130
economic status of, *877*
Family Code on (1984), 130, 136, 1905
M'Rabet (Fadela) on, 1592
as painters, 414
as political activists, 990
in politics, 443, 497, 892, 894, 2195
under single-party system, 131–132
as writers, 483, 1424, 1425, *1425*, 2007
in Arab theater, 2184
Baha'i faith on, 365
in Bahrain, as students, 759
in Bangladesh, as head of state, 808, 875
bank accounts of, 874, 878
Bektashi, 435
Berber, *458*, 463
birth control for (*See* Birth control)
blood money for, 1987, 2051
Circassian, in slave trade, 599
clothing for, 607–611
haik, 975
hijab, 1026–1027
crimes of honor against, 649–650, 887, 1495
Noor al-Hussein in campaign against, 1691
dance by, 667
dependence on men, 874, 888
education for, 760, 761
through Protestant missions, 1855
in Egypt
as activists, 1906–1907
activists and advocates for, 1614, 1652
as artists, 762, 2069
birth control clinic for, *479*
as cabinet members, 39
charitable organizations run by, 39–40, 1452–1453
as communists, 43–44
as dancers, 866
economic status of, 877, *877*
education for, 1902
as judges, 808, 1905
in labor force, 874, 875, 878
as landholders, 878
magazine on, 206
participation in civil society, 1905
physicians for, 2003
in politics, 762, 890–891, 892, 894, 914–915, 1950–1951, 1958, 1965–1966, 2019, 2030–2031
as students, 761
in Wafd party, 2320, 2321–2322
as writers, 378–379, 475–476, 914–915, 1924–1925, 1950–1951, 2019, 2431
as elites, 775
as explorers, 437
in family life, 1493–1496
fertility of, 1844
in *harem*, 992–993
health care for, 1509–1510
and historiography, 1037
in Indonesia
as head of state, 808
as judges, 808
in Iran
activist organizations of, 2358
as artists, 1676, 1899
Constitutional Revolution impact on, 637
economic status of, *877*
education for, 637, 880, *882*, 1113, *1114*
as filmmakers, 387–388
government bureau on, 1123
higher education for, 2296
hijab (veil) worn by, 1027
Islamic Revolution and, 1922
as judges, 744
as lawyers, 2051
magazine for, 2423–2424
in political parties, 1129
in politics, 428, 745, 891, 892, 894, 1364–1365, 2153
seminary for, 187
in sporting events, 1154
as students, 761
suffrage for, 1471
as writers, 427, 811, 1435, 1899
in Iraq
charitable organization for, 2361–2362
economic status of, *877*
education for, 1310
improving situation of, 898
as judges, 808
umbrella organization for, 1137–1138
UN economic sanctions and, 1510
Islamic law regarding, Republican Brothers' call for reform in, 1917–1918
in Israel
economic status of, 876–877, *877*
education for, 880
as head of state, 875, 891
journalists, 1003
in labor force, 877
peace activities of, 2355–2356
as poets, 2429–2430
in politics, 893, 934–935, 944–945, 1440, 1441, 2023, 2059
as writers, 408, 434, 926–927, 1433, 1887, 1907
Jewish, as rabbis, 1889
in Jordan
as activists, 1065
economic status of, *877*
in labor force, 877–878
literature on, 805
Noor al-Hussein as advocate for, 1691
in politics, 819–820, 893, 894
resource center for, 1852
as students, 878
as writers, 804–805, 2001
in Kuwait
economic status of, *877*
higher education for, 1353–1354
in politics, 1350, 1951–1952
as students, 761
as writers, 1952
in labor force (*See* Gender, and economy)
in Lebanon
activists and advocates for, 1557, 1584–1585
as artists, 916
college for, 431–432
as cultural officials, 2125
disease and, 714
economic status of, *877*
in labor force, 875
as political activists, 481
in politics, 894, 1960–1961, 1975
religious rituals of, 2360, 2361
as scholars, 367
as writers, 397–398, 817, 872, 916, 1646–1647, 1975, 1982, 2046

Women *(continued)*
in Libya, 1410
life expectancy of, 876
in marriage, 1493–1496
modernization and, 1556
in Morocco
economic status of, *877*
government positions held by, 1601
health care for, 1510
in labor force, 874, *875*
literature on, 2376
al-Moudawana on, 94, 1585–1586, 1601
National Plan of Action for, 1586, 1601
in politics, 497–498, 894
as writers, 497–498, 1424, 1428
in Oman, 1711
in Pakistan, as head of state, 808, 875
in Palestine
activists and leaders, 1556–1557, 1648
as artists, 2044
organizations for, 227–228, 267, 268, 1629
in politics, 893, 899, 2051–2052
as writers, 357–358, 2233, 2234
Palestinian
activists and advocates for, 1556–1557, 1648, 2334
as artists, 1007–1008
legal aid and counseling for, 2357
organizations for, 2334, 2355, 2356, 2357
philanthropists, 1055
status in Israel, 1488
passports attained by, 874
in Qatar, as students, 761
Qur'an on, 808, 1987, 2153
Mernissi (Fatema) on, 1518
religious rituals of, 2359–2361
at home and outside home, 2359–2360
vows, cults, and holy women in, 2360–2361
in Saudi Arabia
economic status of, *877*
higher education for, 1324
as students, 759, 761
in *shariʿa*, 808
as slaves, 2072, 2073
in sports, 1154
advocacy for, 998
status of, modernization and, 874–876, 883, 885–886
in Sudan, 1917
in Muslim Sisters Organization, 1622–1623
in politics, 894
religious rituals of, 2360
Turabi, Hassan al- on, 1622–1623
in Syria
as cabinet members, 337
economic status of, *877*
in politics, 893, 899–900
as writers, 1982
in temporary marriage *(ziwaj mutʿa)*, 2439
traveling alone, 874, 887
in Tunisia
economic status of, *877*
as judges, 808
in labor force, 874
organizations for, 325, 695, 2267–2268
in politics, 894, 912
research on, 574
in workforce, 2227
as writers, 1424, 1428–1429
in Turkey
as artists, 1595, 2429
economic status of, 877, *877*
education for, 880
as feminists, 2170–2171
governmental services for, 2362
as head of state, 808, 875, 891, 2220, 2242
Kurdish activists, 2423
in labor force, 875, 877
library and information resources for, 2358
as musicians, 476–477
in politics, 747, 891, 894, 2170–2171
in Refah Partisi, 1911
religious rituals of, 2360
as singers, 872–873
as writers, 780–781, 1440
in United Arab Emirates, economic status of, 877
in United States, Jewish organizations for, 966
veils for (*See* Veiling)
in Yemen
as cabinet members, 169
economic status of, 877, *877*
forum for mobilizing, 2357
in labor force, 877
organizations of, 1669
religious rituals of, 2360
Yemeni Women's Union for, 2398–2399
Women (section in Talmud), 2157
Women and Family Affairs Center (Palestinian), **2355**
"Women between the Extremes of Passivity and Ethical Choice" (Iraqi essay), 1475
Women for Women's Human Rights (Turkey), 894
Women for Women's Rights, 2249
Women in Black (Israel), 893, **2355–2356**
Women in Green (Israel), 2356
Women in Publishing Award, Lahiji (Shahla) awarded with, 1365
Women Living Under Muslim Laws, 887
Women's Affairs (journal), 2355
Women's Affairs Center (Gaza), **2356**
Women's Association, 786
Women's Central Committee (Egypt), 2030
Women's Centre for Legal Aid and Counseling (Jerusalem), **2356–2357**
Women's Committee for Popular Resistance (Egypt), 44
Women's Committee of the Arab League, 894
Women's Contributions to Pashtu Oral Tradition (Esmati-Wardak), 786
Women's Coordination Committee of India, 786
Women's Federation Society (Palestine), 893
Women's Forum for Research and Training (Yemen), **2357**
Women's Grouping (Algeria), 2195
Women's International Zionist Organization (WIZO), 893, **2357**
Women's Library and Information Center (Istanbul), 894, **2358**, 2362
Tekeli (Şirin) founding, 2171
Women's Lobby (Israel), 1440
Women's Museum (Baghdad), 898
Women's Organization of Iran (WOI), **2358–2359**
Women's People's Party (Turkey), **2359**
Women's Program in Africa and the Middle East (UN), 1950
Women's Rebellion and Islamic Memory (Mernissi), 1518

Women's Renaissance Club (Iraq), **2361–2362**
Women's rights. *See also* Gender, and law
in Afghanistan, 786, 874, 881, 894, 1981–1982
in Algeria, 892, 2195
in Bahrain, 893
Chazan (Naomi) on, 582
colonialism and, 885–886
in Egypt, 762, 770, 772, 1958, 2019
limitations on, 874
organizations for, 268–269
vs. female genital mutilation, 822
films on, 832
international convention on, 1048
in Iran, *890*, 891, 1970
advocates for, 998
limitations on, 874
Sane'i (Yusef) on, 1987
within *shari'a* framework, 1970
in Jordan, 887, 1291–1292
in Kuwait, 884, 1951–1952
in Lebanon, 884, 887, 1396, 1557
in Morocco, 772–773, 892
constitutional, 1585
network of organizations for, 95
in Ottoman Empire, movement for, 148
personal status laws limiting, 874, 886–888
in Saudi Arabia, 874, 884
in Sudan, 2105, 2235–2236
in Syria, to vote, 1032
Taha (Mahmud Muhammad) arguing for, 2145
in Tunisia, 892, 912, 2230–2231
legal, 325
in Turkey, 897–898, 2249
in United Arab Emirates, 884
violation of, legal responses to, 885
in Yemen, 806
Women's Services (Turkey), **2362**
Women's Solidarity Society, 1055
Women's studies, institutes for, 1100–1101
in Lebanon, 1100
Palestinian, 1100–1101
in Turkey, 2362
Women's Studies Center (Iran), 1364
Women's Studies Center (Jerusalem), **2362–2363**
Women's Tribunal, 888
Women's Union (Syria), 893
Women without Men (Parsipur), 1436, 1803
Woodhead Commission (1938), 2350, **2363**
on Peel partition plan, 1790, 1811
Woodhead, John, 2363
Wood, Kenneth, 1978
Wood, Richard, 860
Woodworth, Robert Sessions, Arabic translation of, 1294
Wool, 2180, 2181
Wool Carder, The (Erbil), 780
Woolley, Leonard, 276, 2050
Workers' and Peasants' Communist Party (Egypt), 627
Workers' and Peasants' Party (Turkey), 625
Workers of Zion. *See* Po'alei Zion
Workers Party (Algeria), 990
World Bank, **2363–2364**
capital stock and voting power in, *2363*, 2364
economic aid from, 747, 749
education measured by, 760
and education of women, 883
and Egypt, *2363*, *2364*
infitah policy of, 1096
gender imbalance initiatives by, 879
goals in Middle East, 2364
loans to Middle East countries, *2364*
and Morocco, *2363*, *2364*
privatization program in, 1569
relative voting strength of Middle East countries in, *2364*
Southeastern Anatolia Project loans from, 2082
Tunisia aided by, 2269
United States power in, 2364
on wages of women, 878
World Center, 489
World Council of Churches (WCC), 1855
World Economic Forum
2003 meeting of, 1244
Rania al-Abdullah in, 1902
World Federation for Women, 894
World Federation of Sephardi Communities, **2364–2365**
World Health Organization (WHO)
Annan (Kofi A.) in, 209
Basma bint Talal at, 409
and diarrheal diseases, 714
and malaria, 711
and tuberculosis, 712
World Heritage Site
Masada designated as, 1497
San'a as, 1984
World Jewish Congress, 928
Wise (Stephen S.) in, 2354
women in, 2357
World Medical Association, on female genital mutilation, 601
World Mizrahi Movement, 546
World Muslim Women Organization for South East Asia, 1952
World Organization of Jews from Arab Countries (WOJAC), 1914, **2365**
Ben-Porat (Mordechai) in, 452
World Organization of the Scout Movement, 2006
World Peace Movement, 2058
World Trade Center (New York)
1993 bombing of, 2178
Abd al-Rahman (Umar) in, 21
2001 attacks on (*See* September 11th)
World Union of Poalei Zion, 493
World War I, **2365–2368**
antisemitism in, American Jewish Congress work against, 178
Arab nationalism during, 1384, 2367–2368
Arab Revolt (1916) during (*See* Arab Revolt)
Armenians in, 195, 2367–2368
Austria-Hungary in, 340, 742
Britain in, 509–511, 742, 2365–2368
in Egypt, 509
Gallipoli campaign, 509, 866
Jewish Legion of, 1208, 1230
London Treaty (1913), 511, 1446
Maude (Frederick Stanley) and, 1501, 2367
Mesopotamia Campaign of, 1501, 1518–1519, 2367
NILI spy ring and, 1–2
vs. Ottoman Empire, 509–511
Sèvres Treaty (*See* Sèvres, Treaty of)
South Persia Rifles organized by, 2083
Sykes–Picot Agreement (*See* Sykes–Picot Agreement)
Dardanelles front in, 509, 1194
and Eastern Question, 742–743
Egypt in, 509, 2366–2368
National Party opposition to Britain in, 1664

World War I *(continued)*
Egypt–Palestine front in, 509–510
end of (*See* Paris peace settlements)
espionage in, by NILI spy ring, 1
al-Fatat during, 815
France in, 742, 846
French foreign legion, 856
Gallipoli campaign, 856, 866
Germany in, 742, 905–906
Gallipoli campaign, 866, 905
Iran, 906
Hijaz Railroad during, 1029
Iran in, 88, 1118, 1869
and British sympathies, 809
German troops in, 906
South Persia Rifles in, 2083
Iraq in, 2367
Basra, 411
British occupation of, 1132
British-Ottoman fighting in, 509
Italy in, 742
Gallipoli campaign, 866
and London Treaty (1913), 511
Jerusalem in, 151, 1223
Kut al-Amara, battle of (1916), 1346
as literary theme, 1439
mandate system after (*See* Mandate system)
Mareth Line in, 1487
Middle East military in, 1540
Ottoman Empire in, 742, 905, 2240, 2365–2368
army of, 1739
vs. Britain, 509–511
Bursa, 547
capitulations of, 566
Gallipoli campaign, 509, 866, 905
Kemalism, 823
Lausanne Treaty (1923) and, 514, 743, 1376–1377
military successes of, 1527
Mudros Armistice in, 90, 2367, 2368
navy of, 1741
Paris peace conference (1919) and, 511, 1441
Sèvres Treaty (1920) and, 512, 1376, 2014–2015
Sivas Conference (1919) and, 2071
Yildirim Army of, 2400
Palestine–Egypt front in, 509–510
Palestine's Jews during, 1940
and population growth, 1843
railroads during, 2206
roadways during, 2207
Russia in, 742
Saudi Arabia in, neutrality of, 173, 646
textile industry during, 2181
trade during, 2198
Tunisia in, 2229
Wilson (Woodrow) in, 2353
Yemen in, 2378
World War II, **2368–2372**
Africa Korps in, 1934
Algeria in, 516
Allied Middle East Command in, 152–153
Arab support for Axis in, 2371
Britain in, 515–517, 2368–2372
in al-Alamayn battle (1942), 516
in Allied Middle East Command, 152–153
assault on Mareth Line, 1487
Egypt, 515–516
Iraq, 1968
Irgun Zva'i Le'umi fighting with, 1139
Jewish Brigade of, 1229
Palestine Regiment of, 1229
refugee policy of, and *Struma* tragedy, 2095–2096
Tobruk siege (1941), 516, 2194
East African invasion in, 2369–2370
Egypt in, 515–516, 2369–2370
in al-Alamayn battle (1942), 1565, 2370
El Alamein battle in (1942), 102–103, 516
Farouk government, 516, 810
German troops in, 906
France in, 2368–2372
denial of protection to Jews under Vichy government, 846
French foreign legion, 856
Iraq supported by, 697
Germany in, 906–907
in al-Alamayn battle (1942), 516
Egypt, 906
Husayni (Hajj Muhammad Amin al-) supported by, 944
Kaylani revolt (1941) supported by, 516, 944
Tobruk siege (1941), 516, 2194
Ha-Shomer ha-Tza'ir members during, 1001
Iran in
Allied occupation of, 2216
Allies removing Pahlavi (Reza), 2143
neutrality of, 1757
Iraq in, 15, 257
British troops in, 1968
and economy, 1968
Kaylani revolt (1941) in (*See under* Kaylani, Rashid Ali al-)
Italy in, 906, 1200
Kaylani revolt (1941) supported by, 516
Jewish Agency during, 1228
Jews during
aliyah by, 147
British relations with, 2371
Carmel Plan for defense of Palestine, 2371
Joint Distribution Committee aid to, 1239
Levin (Yizhak Meir) rescuing, 1408
in Middle East, 807–808, 1233–1234, 2371
U.S. policy on, 1935
Youth Aliyah aid to, 2411
Jordan in, Arab Legion of, 257
land reforms after, 1370, 1371
Lebanon in, Special Forces of the Levant of, 2086
Libya in, 516–517, 1200, 1411–1412
Benghazi, 446
Cyrenaica, 516
Tobruk siege (1941), 516, 2194
Tripoli, 2216
Middle East at beginning of, 2368
Middle East at end of, 2371–2372
Middle East military in, 1540
Morocco in, 516
North African invasion in, 2369–2370
Clark–Darlan Agreement after (1942), 602
and population growth, 1844
roadways during, 2207
Saudi Arabia in, neutral stance of, 516
Southwest Asia in, 2370–2371
Soviet Union in, 1942
Suez Canal in, 515–516
textile industry during, 2181–2182
trade during, 2199
Tunisia in, 2229
Turkey in, 2370–2371
Adana Conference on (1943), 42
Churchill (Winston S.) and, 42, 516, 597
neutral stance of, 516, 2240
Varlik Vergisi tax and, 2309–2310
U.S. in
emergence as premier power, 2372

Lend-Lease program of, 1403–1404, 1523, 1934, 2290
Operation Torch, 516
World Zionist Congress
of 1897, 470
Basle Program formulated at, 1692, 1789
Mohilever (Samuel) and, 1560
of 1898, Wise (Stephen S.) at, 2354
of 1903, Uganda Project proposed at, 2257
Dayan (Moshe) at, 681
De Menasce (Félix Béhor) at, 691
World Zionist Organization (WZO), **2372–2373**
activities of, 2434
British recognition of, 1764
Burg (Avraham) in, 546
Churchill White Paper criticized by, 2350
establishment of, 1021–1022, 1165, 1229, 2433
and Faisal-Weizmann Agreements, 803
Goldmann (Nahum) in, 928
Herzl (Theodor) in, 1022, 1165, 2433
Jabotinsky (Vladimir Ze'ev) and, 1208, 1209
Jewish Agency for Palestine established by, 178, 1227
Jewish Colonial Trust of, 1229
Jewish immigrants ignoring policies of, 1361
Jewish National Fund of, 1229, 1230
Joseph (Dov) and, 1250
Keren Hayesod fundraising division of, 1289
Kol (Moshe) in, 1332
legislative council accepted by, 50
Maimon (Yehudah Leib Hacohen) in, 1470
Mizrahi in, 1553–1554
Namir (Mordekhai) in, 1641
NILI criticized by, 1
Nordau (Max) and, 1692
Palestine Land Development Company of, 1772
Palestine office of, 2436
Ruppin (Arthur) in, 1939
Sokolow (Nahum) in, 2078
status of, law on (1952), 2373
Syrkin (Nachman) in, 2138
on Uganda Project, 2257
Weizmann's (Chaim) in, 2337–2338
women in, 2357
and Yishuv, 2402
and Zionist Organization of America, 2436
Wright, Clifford A., *as contributor,* 836–841, 2169
Wright, John L., *as contributor,* 373, 409, 446, 655–656, 829–830, 1196, 1321–1322, 1646, 1712, 1958–1959, 2216–2217
Wye River Accords (1998)
Clinton (Bill) in, 606
Hussein ibn Talal in, 1064
Netanyahu (Benjamin) in, 1677
WZO. *See* World Zionist Organization

X

Xakas language, 2252
Xerophthalmia, *713*
Xerophytes, 701
Xerxes, Persian language of, 1124

Y

Ya'akobi ve-Ledental (Levin), 1407
Ya'alon, Moshe, 1174
Ya'ariba dynasty (Oman), Muscat under, 1616
Ya'ari, Me'ir, **2375**
Yabiah Omer (Yosef), 2404
Yacef, Saadi, in Algerian War of Independence, 141, 142
Yacine, Abdessalame, **2375–2376**
in al-Adl wa al-Ihsan, 46–47, 1569, 1574, 2375–2376
imprisonment of, 1569, 1574, 2375
release of, 1569, 1574
Yacine, Kateb, 707
Yacob, Tadesse, 787
Yacoubi, Rachida, **2376**
"Yadigarlarm" (Nabizade Nazim), 1631
Yadin, Yigael, **2376–2377**
archaeological finds of, 278
and Dead Sea Scrolls, 686, 2376
in Democratic Movement for Change, 1181, 2376
in Israel Defense Force, 973, 1173
Yad Mordekhai (kibbutz), **2377**
Yad Vashem, **2377**
Yaffe, Eliezer, on moshavim, 1576
Yaghnobi language, 1125
Yahad (Israel), Weizman (Ezer) in, 2337
Yahia, pas de chance (Farès), 806
Yahudiyya farahiyya, 2050
Yahya, Gholam, in Azerbaijan autonomy movement, 345
Yahya ibn Hussein, al-Hadi ila al-Haqq (imam of Yemen), 2396, 2427
Yahya ibn Muhammad Hamid al-Din (imam and king of Yemen), **2377–2378**
Asir claims by, 1082
assassination of, 2378
campaigns against tribes of, 376
in emergence of North Yemen, 2391
in Hamid al-Din family, 985
and Makki (Hasan Muhammad), 1474
military training in Iraq under, 192
palace of (Dar al-Hajar), *2392*
policy goals of, 2378
in revolt against Ottoman Empire, 2377–2378
son of, 86
and al-Ta'if Treaty (1934), 2149
and Zaraniq Confederation, 2425
and Zaydism, 2427
Ya'ir Avraham Shtern (Shamir), 2025
Yakut language, 2247, 2252
Yalçin, Hüseyin Cahit, 2180
Yale University
Bush (George H. W.) at, 548
Bush (George W.) at, 549
Sabah (Rasha al-) at, 1951
Saunders (Harold) at, 2001
Yalkut Moreshet (journal), Kovner (Abba) in, 1336
Yalman, Ahmed Emin, 720
Yalova Termal Hotel (Turkey), 774
Yamani, Ahmad Zaki, 798, **2378**
participation strategy of, 1826
Tariki (Abdullah) replaced by, 2166
Yamanis, 728
Yamani tribe. *See* Qahtan tribe
Yamaniyya, al- (newspaper), 1669
Yamit (Jewish settlement), evacuation of, 1536
Yam tribe (North Yemen), 1007
Yamulki, Aziz, 927

Yanai, Nathan, *as contributor,* 681–683
Yanbu (Saudi Arabia), **2378–2379**
in Second Five-Year Development Plan, 1250, 2378
Yankelovich, Daniel, 2308
Yaʿqub, General, 1490
Yaʿqub Khan (regent of Kabul), 536
Yaʿqub, Mirza, son of, Malkom Khan (Mirza) as, 1476
Yaʿqub, Talʿat, in PLF, 1841
Yaqut al-Musta'simi, calligraphy of, 558
YAR. *See* Yemen Arab Republic
Yariv, Aharon, **2379**
Yarkon River, as Israeli water source, 1668
Yarmouk Numismatics (journal), 1703
Yarmuk River, 925, 2129, **2379–2380**
canals on, 2379, 2380
conflict over, 1249, 2379–2380
dam on, 1485
development of, 2379–2380
hydroelectric plan for, 1946
Israeli control of, 1249, 2379–2380
Jordanian access to, 1249, 2379
and Jordan River, 1248, 2379
Maqarin (Widha) Dam on, 1249, 2379, 2380
Yarmuk University (Jordan), 1138, **2380**
numismatic research at, 1703
Yarmulke *(kippah), 608,* 611, 2631
Yaron, Amos, in Sabra and Shatila massacres, 1263
Yarzi, Roxanne, *as contributor,* 387–388
Yasar Kemal, 1437, 1439, **2380–2381**
Yasar, Neither Dead nor Alive (Nesin), 1676
Yasavi, Ahmed, 1642
Yasavi branch of Naqshbandi order, 1642
Yasawiyya (Sufi order), 2113
Yasin, Ahmad Ismaʿil, **2381**
arrest of, 983
assassination of, 983, 2381
in HAMAS, 2381
health problems of, 2381
imprisonment of, 2381
in Muslim Brotherhood, 983
release of, 2381
Yasin, Rania al-. *See* Rania al-Abdullah
Yasin, Sayyid, at Ahram Center for Political and Strategic Studies, 92
Yasin, Subhi, 1874
Yata, Ali, **2382**
in Casablanca politics, 569–570
Yatom, Dani, as Mossad director, 1578, 1579
Yatom, Danny, *1102*
Yavari, Neguin, *as contributor,* 97–98, 100–101, 102, 186–187, 188–189, 328, 343, 345–346, 374–375, 375–376, 385–386, 388–389, 411–412, 493–494, 582, 622, 660, 779–780, 836, 842, 850–851, 976–977, 1047, 1216, 1300, 1310–1312, 1337, 1471–1472, 1489–1490, 1558–1559, 1614–1615, 1880–1881, 1937, 1960, 2036, 2037, 2043, 2057, 2078, 2096, 2143–2144, 2303–2304, 2311, 2318, 2382–2383
Yavnieli, Shmuel, in Jewish Legion, 1230
Yavuz, M. Hakan, *as contributor,* 99–100, 780, 781, 788–789, 948, 1097, 1545, 1583–1584, 1657–1661, 1660–1661, 1666–1667, 1704–1705, 2015, 2076–2077, 2219–2220, 2236
Yawm, al- (newspaper), 1679
Yawm min al-Umr (Bin Diyaf), 474
Yazbak, Yusuf, 626
Yazd (Iran), **2382**
bazaars of, 420
Zoroastrianism in, 2382
Yazdi, Farrokhi, 1757
Yazdi, Ibrahim, 851, **2382–2383**
Chamran (Mostafa) and, 582
Kharrazi (Kamal) and, 1300
Khomeini (Ruhollah) supported by, 1311
Qotbzadeh (Sadeq) and, 1881
Yazdi, Muhammad Kazim, 977
Yazid ibn Abi Sufyan, 662
Yazid ibn Muʿawiya (caliph), Husayn ibn Ali killed by, 1272
Yazidis, 2130, 2214
Yazid, Mulay, 2115
Yaziji, Ibrahim, **2383–2384**
Yaziji, Nasif, 2383, **2384**
Yaziji, Warda al-, 2431
Year amongst the Persians, A (Browne), 539
Year of the Elephant (Abu Zeid). *See Am al-fil*
Yedigün (magazine), Kisakürek (Necip Fazil) in, 1326
Yediot Aharonot (newspaper), 934, 1683, 1684
Keinan (Amos) in, 1284
Yediot Hadahot (newspaper), 1683
Yeghishe I (Armenian patriarch), 291
Yehoshua, Avraham B., 1164, 1433, 2185, **2384**
Yeki bud yeki nabud (Jamalzadeh), 1214
Yekta Bey, Rauf, 687, 2124
Yellin, David, in Vaʿad Leʾumi, 2307
Yellin-Mor, Natan, **2384–2385**
in Bernadotte (Folke) assassination, 2385
in Lohamei Herut Yisrael, 1443, 2025, 2384–2385
Yellow Canary, The (film), 388
Yemen, **2385–2391,** *2386. See also* People's Democratic Republic of Yemen; *specific cities, organizations, people, and regions*
agriculture in, 2319, 2387, 2388
alcohol in, 110
Asir region claimed by, 1081
banking in, *393,* 394
borders of, 2385
demarcation of, 2385
between North and South, 2390
with Oman, 2385
with Saudi Arabia, 10, 2385
British occupation of, 2390
cities of, 2149–2150, 2385–2386
capital, 1983–1984
port, 42–43
civil wars in (*See* Yemen Civil War)
climate of, 2386–2387
colonialism in, 614
communications in, 647
constitution of, 1140, 1977, 2388
coup (1962), 358
culture of, 2388
defense costs as percentage of GNP or GDP, *1530*
Dor Deʿa movement in, 720
dynasties in, 2396–2397
economy of, 752, *753,* 2388
Badr (Muhammad al-) and, 358

education in, 2388
for Famous Forty, 1474
new schooling, 756
in religious schools, 761
elections (1993), 1976
elections (1997), 1976–1977
elections (1999), 1977
elections (2003), 1977
geography of, 2386–2387
government of, 933
efforts to reform, 2442
guest workers from, 946
in Gulf Crisis (1990–1991), 951
Hadramawt in, 970
higher education in, 2388
at San'a University, 1984–1985
human rights in, 806, 2357
immunization rate in, 1510
industrialization of, 2388
infant mortality rate in, 1509
Islamists in, 2391
islands of, 1819, 2077
Jewish exodus from, Magic Carpet Operation for (1948–1950), 1460
Jews from, 1913
in Israel, 49
in Palestine, 146
Jews in, 2388
Jewish quarters for, 1231
labor unions in, 1358
language in, Arabic, 2388
in League of Arab States, 1385, 1386, 1387, 1388
legal reforms in, 1380
legislative body in, 932
at London Conference (1939), 1445
marriage in, *1494*
military of
equipment of, *1534*
force levels of, *1528–1529*
force structure of, *1532–1533*
military revolt in (1965), Egyptian support for, 1531, 1537
natural gas in, *1671*, 2390
natural resources of, 2388, 2390
newspapers and print media in, 1679
diversity in, 1681
oil deposits in, 2390
oil production in, 752
by Yemen Hunt Oil Company, 2397
Organization for the Liberation of the Occupied South in, 1716
in Ottoman Empire, 2390
pre-World War I revolt against, 2377–2378, 2391
San'a, 1983
parliamentary elections in, 90, 1140, 1143, 2389
political system of, 2387–2389
population of, *753*, 1844, 1845, 1848, 2385
ports of, 1039
postage stamps of, 1849, 1850
presidential elections in, 2388–2389, 2398
Protestant missions in, 1856
radio and television in, *1895*
religions in
Islam, 2388
Shi'ism, 2052
revolution of 1962 in, 2427
sand deserts of, 1938
Saudi Arabian relations with, 798–799
Salih (Ali Abdullah) and, 1976
al-Ta'if Treaty (1934) and, 2149
slaves in, 2073
social reforms in, Badr (Muhammad al-) and, 358
tourism in, 2196–2197
in trade, 2198, 2201, 2388, 2389–2390
tribes in, 376, 2215, 2378
unification of, 2385, 2390, 2395
National Democratic Front and, 1653–1654
in United Arab Republic, 2273
United Nations observation mission in, 2277
U.S. relations with
Cole attack and, 2077
after September 11th, 2001, 2196
water resources of, freshwater withdrawals, *2331*
women in
as cabinet members, 169
economic status of, 877, *877*
forum for mobilizing, 2357
in labor force, 877
organizations for, 1669, 2398–2399
religious rituals of, 2360
rights of, 806
World Bank loans to, *2364*
in World War I, 2378
Zaraniq Confederation in, 2425–2426
Zaydism in, 358, 2388, 2396, 2397, **2427**
Yemen Arab Republic (YAR) (North Yemen), **2391–2395**
attempted coup in (1955), 2391
border with South Yemen, 2377, 2390
Catholics in, 1931
cities of
ancient, 1487–1488
capital, 1983
civil war in (*See* Yemen Civil War)
constitution of, 2393, 2394
coup in (1974), 913, 1140
creation of, 2427
defense costs as percentage of GNP or GDP, *1530*
economic aid to, from Arab countries, 749
economy of, 2385, 2394–2395
Salih (Ali Abdullah) and, 1976
Egyptian influence on, 2392, 2393, 2396
higher education in, at San'a University, 1984–1985
independence for, 2390
infrastructure development in, 2395
major eras of, 2391–2392
Makki (Hasan Muhammad) in, 1474
manufacturing in, 1483, *1483*
merger into Yemen (1990), 417, 1976, 2385, 2390, 2395
military of, 2394
equipment of, *1534*
force levels of, *1528–1529*
force structure of, *1532–1533*
National Pact of, 2394
oil production in, 2395, 2397
in Ma'ri/al-Jawf basin, 1487–1488
in Ottoman Empire, 2390
pre-World War I revolt against, 2377–2378, 2391
Peace Corps in, 1808
political parties in
ban on, 2393
General People's Congress as, 2394
political system of, 2385, 2387–2388, 2392–2393
president of, 984–985
prime minister of, 12, 343
radio and television in, 1894
republican-royalist reconciliation in, 343, 1140, 2392, 2393, 2396
ruling dynasty of, 985
socioeconomic development in, 2393–2394
state-building efforts in, 2391, 2392–2393, 2394
tribes in
Hatim sultans of Hamdan, 1007
political power of, 2392, 2393

Yemen Civil War (1962–1970), **2395–2396**
Ahmar (Abdullah ibn Husayn al-) in, 89
Amri (Hasan al-) in, 192
Free Officers in, 854
Free Yemenis in, 855
Hajri (Abdullah al-) in, 976
Nasser (Gamal Abdel) in, 1650–1651
objectives of, 2390
republican-royalist reconciliation in, 343, 1140, 2392, 2393, 2396
Saudi Arabia in, 2277, 2396
Shami (Ahmad Muhammad al-) in, 2023
Shami (Muhammad Abdullah al-) in, 2024
state-building efforts during, 2392, 2393, 2396
tribes in, 2396
United Nations in, 2277
Yemen Civil War (1994), 1976
General People's Congress in, 2390
origins of, 2390
Yemeni Socialist Party in, 2389, 2390
Yemen dynasties, **2396–2397**
Yemen Hunt Oil Company (YHOC), **2397**
Yemeni Islah Party (YIP). *See* Islah Party
Yemen International Language Institute, 806
Yemeni Socialist Party (YSP), 1655, **2397–2398**
Ali Nasir Muhammad al-Hasani in, 143
Antar (Ali Ahmad Nasir) in, 211
Baydh (Ali Salim al-) in, 417
in civil war (1994), 2389, 2390
electoral success of, 2389, 2398
establishment of, 1814, 2397
Islah Party coalition with, 1143
Ismaʿil (Abd al-Fattah) in, 1157
leadership of, 2389
Yemeni Women's Association (YWA), 2398
Yemeni Women's Union (YWU), **2398–2399**
Al-Suswa (Amat al-Alim) in, 169
Yeme Ziklag (Yizhar), 2403
Yeni Gün (newspaper), 1633
Yeni Turan (Adivar), 45–46
Yerevan (Armenia), 676
Yeridah (emigration from Israel), 145
Yersin, Alexander, 710
Yesayi III (Armenian patriarch), 291
Yesevi, Ahmet, influence on Alevis, 113
Yesha Council (Israel), 958
Yesh Gvul (Israel), 546
Yeshiva, **2399**
of Kook (Abraham Isaac Hacohen), 1333
Yeshurun, Avoth, 1434
Yeshurun, Zelda, 1434
YHOC. *See* Yemen Hunt Oil Company
Yiddish language, **2399–2400**
Ashkenazic use of, 321, 1163, 2399
Bund as advocate of, 544
evolution of, 321
Hebrew in, 2399
in Israel, 1163
poems in, 941
Yiddish literature, 464, 506–507
Yilderim Operation (World War I), 2367
Yildirim Army (Ottoman Empire), **2400**
Yilmaz, Mesut, 598
in Motherland Party, 746, 1584, 2242
YIP (Yemeni Islah Party). *See* Islah Party
Yisavi, Ahmad al-, 2113
Yishuv (Jews in Palestine), 469, **2400–2403**
in 19th century, 145–146, 1760, 2400–2402
binationalism supported by, 473
British policy on
in Churchill White Paper (1922), 594
crackdown (1946), 973
in MacDonald (Ramsay) Letter (1931), 1454
in white papers on Palestine (1939), 1766
defense force of, 2403
definition of, 2400
financial support for, 2400
from Keren Hayesod, 1289
from U.S., 1771
Holocaust and, 1041
housing projects of, 2401–2402
Kisch (Frederick Hermann) as advisor to, 1326
main armed force of, 972
manufacturing in, 1481–1482
Minz (Benjamin) and, 1550
Nazi Germany and, 961
Old *vs.* New, 2400–2402
origins of, 2400
political structures of, 1764, 2402–2403
population growth of, 1763–1764
response to Nazi policies, 1041
in urban areas, 1763, 1764
U.S. economic aid to, 1771
Vaʿad Leʾumi of, 2307, 2402
Zionist, 2400–2403
Zionist efforts toward establishing, 2434
Zionist Revisionist Movement and, 2437
Yiyha, Isaac, Dor Deʿa movement opposed by, 720
Yizhar, S., 1432, **2403–2404**
YOK. *See* Yüksek Öğretim Kurulu
Yol (film), 955
Yom Kippur War. *See* Arab–Israel War (1973)
Yonah Be-Hazer Zarah (Shamir), 2024
Yonathan, Nathan, 1432
Yoredet (Bitton), 483
Yosef, Ovadiah, **2404**
in SHAS, 1188, 2404
Yost, Charles, 539
Young Afghan Party, 62
Young Algerians, **2404–2405**
agenda of, 2405
Clemenceau (Georges) support for, 603
Young Egypt, 853, **2405**
Young Guard. *See* Ha-Shomer ha-Tzaʿir
Young Men's Muslim associations
establishment of, 1874, 2411
Qassam (Izz al-Din al-) in, 1874
Young Ottomans, 2240, **2405–2407**
Ali Suavi in, 144
decline of, 2407
influence of, 2407
leadership of, 2405–2406
Mustafa Faziz financing, 1623
Namik Kemal in, 1640–1641
opposing Tanzimat reforms, 2163
Ottomanism of, 1737
pan-Turkist influence on, 1800
publications of, 2406, 2407
Şinasi, İbrahim in, 2069
vs. Young Turks, 2405, 2408, 2410
Ziya (Abdülhamit) in, 2439

Young Tunisians, 2229, **2407–2408**
education at military academy, 84
Khaldunniyya founded by, 1293, 2408
Thaalbi (Abd al-Aziz) in, 2182
Young Turks, 776, 2240, **2408–2410**
Ahmet Riza in, 91, 623, 2408
vs. Arab nationalism, 261, 263
in Armenian genocide, 294
Musa Dagh resistance of, 1612–1613
army under, 1739
Bekir Fahri in, 434
Cemal Paşa and, 571
Committee for Union and Progress of, 622–623, 2408–2410
at Congress of Ottoman Liberals (1902), 631
constitution under, 1742
definition of, 2408
Egyptian National Party supporting, 1664
freemasonry and, 852
Ganim (Halil) in, 867
Husari (Sati al-) and, 1051
and Husayn ibn Ali, 1052, 1053
ideology of, 2410
İlmiyye decline under, 1086–1087
and Jewish settlement in Palestine, 1940
Mehmet V as figurehead for, 1513
Misri (Aziz Ali al-) in, 1550
Nahum (Hayyim) and, 1637
navy under, 1741
Nursi (Said) and, 1704
origins of, 2408
Ottomanism of, 1737, 2410
Paris conference of (1902), 2409
parliament under, 1742
revolution of (1908), 384, 2251
Churchill (Winston S.) and, 595
and civil service, 1735
Enver Paşa in, 778
newspapers and print media after, 1685
Ottoman army in, 1739
Talat (Mehmet) in, 2153
before revolution of (1908), 2408–2409
rivalries within, 623, 2408–2409
in Salonika, 1979
Shumayyil (Shibli) supporting, 2061
Turkism of, 2251
vs. Young Ottomans, 2405, 2408, 2410
Young, William Tanner, 1796
Young Women's Muslim Association (YWMA), Khidhir (Zahra) in, 1310
Young Worker, The. *See* Po'el ha-Tza'ir, ha-
Youssef, Mulay (sultan of Morocco), *1449,* 2038, **2410**
French selection of, 14
Glawi (Madani al-) under, 921
Lyautey (Louis-Hubert Gonzalve) putting on throne, 827, 1448
al-Qarawiyyin university under, 1871
Youssoufi, Abderrahmane, **2410–2411**
exile of, 2410–2411
Hassan II and, 1006, 1571, 1573–1574
labor strikes under, 2264
as prime minister, 1573–1574, 1575, 2268, 2411
Spanish enclaves disputed by, 1516
in Union Nationale des Forces Populaires, 2266, 2410
in Union Socialiste des Forces Populaires, 2268, 2411
Youth Aliyah (Israel), **2411**
establishment of, 855
Kol (Moshe) in, 1332
Szold (Henrietta) in, 855, 2138
Youth movements, **2411–2413**. *See also specific movements*
in 19th century, 2411
in 20th century, 2411–2412
Iraqi *futuwwa,* 860–861
as literary catalyst, 1432
paramilitary, 2411–2412
role of, 2411–2412
scouting, 2006
in Zionist Revisionist Movement, 1209
YSP. *See* Yemeni Socialist Party
Yücel, Hasan Ali, **2413**
Yu'firid dynasty (Yemen), 2397
Yuhanna, Mikha'il. *See* Aziz, Tariq
Yüksek Öğretim Kurulu (YOK) (Turkey), **2413–2414**
Afghani (Jamal al-Din al-) at, 51
Yunis Jabir, Abu Bakr, **2414**
Yunus Emre (Saygun), 2002
Yurdakul, Mehmet Emin, 1439, 1800, **2414**
Yusab II (Coptic patriarch), 657
Yushij, Nima, 427, 1435–1436
Alizadeh (Ghazaleh) compared with, 149
Yusuf (Ottoman grand vizier), in Convention of al-Arish (1800), 289
Yusuf (ruler of Lebanon), Chehab (Bashir) and, 583
Yusuf, Fatima al-, *Ruz al-Yusuf* founded by, 18
Yusufian, Boghos (Boghos Bey), **2414–2415**
death of, successor after, 589
nephew and protégé of, Nubar (Boghos) as, 1694
Yusuf, Muhammad, as prime minister, 57
Yusuf, Mulay, son of, Muhammad V as, 1597–1598
Yusuf, Yusuf Salman (Fahd), **2415**
in Communist Party of Iraq, 627, 2415
execution of, 627, 2415
YWA. *See* Yemeni Women's Association
YWMA. *See* Young Women's Muslim Association
YWU. *See* Yemeni Women's Union
Yzernitsky, Yitzhak. *See* Shamir, Yitzhak

Z

Za'ab tribe, 2209
Zaban-i Zanan (magazine), 891
Zabol (Iran), 2070
Zab Rivers, **2417**
Dukan Dam on, 732–733
Zabul (Afghan province), **2417–2418**
Zabul (Iranian city), **2417–2418**
Zach, Natan, 1432, **2418**
Zadig (Voltaire), 1675
Za'farani, al-, 2019
Zafzaf, Mohammad, 1428
Zaghlul, Sa'd, **2418–2419**
Abbas Hamli II and, 6
Abduh (Muhammad) and, 24
Adli and, 46
Afghani (Jamal al-Din al-) and, 51
British opposition to, 46
on Cairo University, 555
Copts and, 640–641
excluded from office, by Kitchener (Horatio Herbert), 1329
exile of, and Wafd, establishment of, 640

Zaghlul, Saʿd *(continued)*
government of, Nuqrashi (Mahmud Fahmi al-) in, 1701
Haykal (Muhammad Husayn) and, 1013
in Legislative Assembly, 6
Mahir (Ahmad) and, 1465
Mahir (Ali) and, 1465
Mahmud (Muhammad) and, 1468
Sidqi (Ismaʿil) and, 2065
Wafdist Women's Central Committee working on behalf of, 2321
as Wafd leader, 640–641, 766, 858, 2320
Zaghlul, Safia, 2418
Zaghlul, Safiyya, 2320
Zagros Mountains, 374, 901, 902, 1110, 1316, 1325, 1342, 2213, **2419**
Zahawi, Jamil Sidqi al-, **2419**
Zahedan (Iran), 2070, **2420**
Zahedi, Fazlollah
cabinet of, Amini (Ali) in, 186
in ouster of Mossadegh (Mohammad), 1581
as prime minister, 1118
Zahir al-Din Tughtaqin, 663
Zahiris, 2034
Zahir, Khalda, 2105
Zahir Shah, Mohammad (king of Afghanistan), *399, 400,* **2420–2421,** *2421*
accession of, 57
campaign to reinstate, Karzai (Hamid) in, 1276
coup against (1973), 57, 401, 679
foreign policy of, 57
government of, Daud (Muhammad) in, 57, 400, 679
modernization under, 57
political party development under, 62
reign of, 57, 400–401
Tarikh Tolana founded by, 2166
in U.S. intervention, 67
Zahla (Lebanon), **2422**
Zahla crisis (1981), Hirawi (Ilyas al-) as mediator in, 1033
Zahlan, Antoine Benjamin, *as contributor,* 2003–2006
Zahleh (Lebanon). *See* Zahla
Zahra, Al-, Rahnavard (Zahra) as president of, 1615–1616
Zaidan, Gurgi. *See* Zaydan, Jurji
Zaʿim, 2631
Zaʿim, Husni al-, **2422**
coup against (August 1949), 1032
coup by (1949), 826, 1886, 2133, 2137
CIA in, 572
government of, Arslan (Adil) in, 306
against Greater Syria plan, 936
overthrow of, 2137
Saʿada (Antun) betrayed by, 1950
Zainab Society. *See* Jameʿe Zainab
Zait, Shibolet, *as contributor,* 1887
Zajal, 2233
Zakariya, Muhammad, *as contributor,* 558–559
Zakat, 2167, 2631
Zaki, Mamoon A., *as contributor,* 355, 1000–1001, 1479, 1637, 1751
Zakir, Kasim Beg, 347
Zakiyya, Muhammad al-Nafs al-, 2053
Zaman al-Akhta (Shukri), 2060
Zaman Durrani, 735
brother of, 1468
Zaman Zaman Içinde (Boratav), 493
Zamir, Zvi, as Mossad director, 1578
Zamzam (Mecca), 1595, **2422–2423**
Zan (newspaper), 998
Zanad, Mohammad al-Habib al-, 1429
Zana, Leyla, **2423**
Zana, Mehdi, 2423
Zanan (magazine), 894, 1970, **2423–2424**
Kar (Mehrangiz) in, 1274
Zanan-i-Afghanistan (journal), 693
Zand (Zoroastrian text), 2441
Zand dynasty, 2057
Zangwill, Israel, **2424–2425**
Zan-i-Afghan (journal), 68
Zan-i Ruz (magazine), 2423
Zaʿnum, Salim, in Palestine National Council, 1780
Zanzibar, **2425**
Al Bu Saʿid sultanates in, 107, 1710
Zaqaziq University (Egypt), **2425**
Zaraniq Confederation, **2425–2426**
Zaranj (Afghanistan), 2417
Zarathushtra. *See* Zoroastrianism
Zarhuni, al-Jilali ibn Idris al-. *See* Bu Hamara
Zarhuni, Jilali ibn Idris al-Yusufi al-. *See* Abu Himara
Zarqa, al- (Jordan), **2426**
Zaʿrur, Ahmad, 1841
Zavarian, Simon, 676
Zawahiri, Ayman al-, bin Ladin and, 475, 1865
Zawahiri, Muhammad al-Ahmadi al-, 348
Zawiya, 373, 618, 1423, 1990, 2113, 2171, 2224, 2631
Zawiya al-Baidu. *See* Baida (Libya)
Zawra, al- (bookshop), 1309–1310
Zawra, al- (newspaper), 1525, 2419
Alusi (Mahmud Shukri al-) at, 173
Zayandeh River, 1141
Zaydan, Jurji, 1420, **2426–2427**
and *al-Hilal* (magazine), 1029
and historiography, 1035, 2426
Zaydan, Muhammad, in PLF, 1841
Zayd ibn Ali Zayn al-Abidin, 2427
Zayd ibn Thabit, 1883
Zaydism, **2427**
Free Officers overthrowing, 854
Hatim sultans and, 1007
in Yemen, 358, 2388, 2396, 2397
Hashid and Bakil tribal confederations, 376
in Sanʿa, 1983
Zaynab
as daughter of Muhammad, 1595
shrine of (Damascus), 2359
Zaynab (Haykal), 1420
Zaynab and the Throne (Ghanim), 911
Zaytuna Mosque (Tunis), 2224
Zaytunat (Badr), 357
Zaytuna University (Tunisia), 1422, 1428, **2427–2428**
Bayram V (Muhammad) at, 418
Ben Badis (Abd al-Hamid) at, 440
Khaldunniyya and, 1293
Khayr al-Din and, 1604
vs. Sadiqi College, 1959
Shabbi (Abu al-Qasim al-) at, 2017
Thaalbi (Abd al-Aziz) at, 2182
Zayyad, Tawfiq, 1791
Zayyat, Latifa, **2428**
Zaza dialect, 1344
Zbiri, Tahar, **2428–2429**
coup attempted by (1967), 500
Zeʾevi, Rehavam
assassination of, 1169
Saʿadat (Ahmad) in, 1840
in Moledet Party, 1186

Zeff, Naomi, *as contributor,* 1501–1503, 1693, 1744–1745
Zehra (Nabizade Nazim), 1631
Zeidel, Ronen, *as contributor,* 1724
Zeid, Fahralnissa, **2429**
Ze'irei ha-Mizrahi, 2029–2030
Zeitlin, Hillel, Qafih (Yihye ben Solomon) and, correspondence between, 1864
Zekai, Dede, 2124
Zeki, Salih, 45
Zelda (Israeli poet), **2429–2430**
Zell al-Soltan, Mas'ud Mirza, **2430**
Zeller, Marie-André, in Organisation Armée Secrète, 1715
Zeman, Ha- (newspaper), 464
Zemestan (Akhavan-Saless), 97
Zenobia (queen of Palmyra), 1797–1798
Zenzie, Charles U., *as contributor,* 1839, 1949–1950, 2021, 2290, 2422, 2442–2443
Zera'im, 2157
Zeroual, Liamine, **2430**
  Lamari (Mohamed) under, 1365–1366
  Nahnah's (Mahfoud) candidacy against, 1636
  political party of, 1904
  presidency of, 504
    appointment to, 127, 130, 1026
    election to, 127, 130, 135
    resignation of, 127
  replacing Nezzar (Khaled) as defense minister, 1365
Zerrouky, Hassane, 919
Zhou Enlai, *587*
Ziadeh, May, 1652, **2430–2431**
Zibri, Mustafa
  assassination of, 1840
  in PFLP, 1840
Zikhron Ya'akov (Israeli settlement), **2431**
  Aaronsohn family in, 1
  establishment of, 1
  Rothschild (Edmond de) support for, 1937, 1938
Zikr (ceremony of remembrance), 1521, 2360
Zili, Ridha, **2431**
Zilzal, al- (Wattar), 2333
Zinat in the President's Funeral Procession (Bakr), 378
Zindani, Abd al-Majid al-
  al-Iman University run by, 2388
  in *Cole* attack (2000), 613
Zionism, 1659, **2431–2436**. *See also* Labor Zionism
  Abdullah I ibn Hussein on, 30
  Ahad Ha-Am on, 78–79
  anthem of, 1007, 2425
  vs. Arab nationalism, 1549
    in Arab–Israel conflict, 235
  Balfour Declaration (1917) and, 1165, 2435
  Basle Program of, 1021, 1692
  Behar (Nissim) supporting, 427
  Ben-Gurion (David) supporting, 447
  Bentwich (Norman) supporting, 454
  Ben-Zvi (Rahel Yanait) supporting, 456
  Ben-Zvi (Yizhak) supporting, 456
  British policy on
    in Balfour Declaration (1917), 380
    Churchill (Winston S.) on, 595–596
    in Churchill White Paper (1922), 594
    impact on Palestinians, 1789
    Lloyd George (David) supporting, 1441
    in Palestine mandate, 1763
  British supporters of, 2424–2425
  Buber (Martin) supporting, 540
  cleansing or transfer policy of, 1640
  coining of name, 2432
  communism and, 626
  Congress in Basel, Switzerland, *2433*
  cultural, 1692, 2434
  vs. diaspora, 2432
    Magnes (Judah) on, 1460
  early support for, 1165, 1233
  in education, at yeshivas, 2399
  Faisal–Weizmann Agreements, 800, 803
  films on, 833
  foundations of, 2432
  French involvement in, 846–847
  goals of, 447
  on *halukka,* 980
  and Ha-Shomer ha-Tza'ir, 1001–1002
  Haskalah movement and, 1003
  and Hebrew University of Jerusalem, 1018
  Herzl (Theodor) and, 1021
  Hess (Moses) and, 1024
  Holocaust and, 1042, 2435
  Jabotinsky (Vladimir Ze'ev) on, 1208–1209
  in Jerusalem, 1224
  Jewish Colonial Trust and, 1229
  kibbutz movement in, 855, 1318–1320, 1361
  King–Crane Commission on (1919), 1323
  and land reclamation, 1047
  in Libya, 966
  Lilienblum (Moses Leib) supporting, 1417
  and literature, 78–79, 1430, 1432
  Maccabi clubs and, 1453
  Maimon (Yehudah Leib Hacohen) in, 1470
  Masada veneration in, 1497
  Meged (Aharon) in, 1512
  Minz (Benjamin) in, 1550
  Mizrahi movement in, 1553–1554
  Mohilever (Samuel) in, 1560
  Mond (Alfred Moritz) in, 1564
  Montefiore (Moses) in, 1565
  Namir (Mordekhai) in, 1641
  Nazi policies and, 1041
  in newspapers and print media, 1683
  Nhaisi (Elia) in, 1686–1687
  Nordau (Max) in, 1692
  opposition to, 1057, 1059 (*See also* Anti-Zionism)
    by American Council for Judaism, 176
    antisemitism and, 1233
    in Arab nationalism, 1233
    by De Haan (Ya'akov Yisrael), 688–689
    by Richmond (Ernest T.), 1922
  options considered by, 2435
  organizations of, 612, 2432–2434 (*See also specific organizations*)
  and Orthodox rabbis, 1024–1025
  Palestinian expulsion supported by, 1639–1640 (*See also* Nakba, al-)
  Palestinians massacred by supporters of, 1639
  Palestinian violence in response to, 1011
  at Paris peace settlements (1918–1923), 511
  Pinsker (Leo) supporting, 1835
  political, 1692, 2434, 2437
  practical, 1692
  revisionist movement within, 2437, 2438
  rise of, 1233–1234

Zionism *(continued)*
Roosevelt (Franklin Delano) support for, 1936
Rutenberg (Pinhas) and, 1946
Samman (Ghada) criticizing, 1982
Samuel (Herbert Louis) supporting, 1983
Sasson (Eliyahu) supporting, 1993
secular, Agudat Israel opposed to, 77
Shapira (Hayyim Moshe) supporting, 2030
socialism and, 289, 1281, 2434
Sokolow (Nahum) as spokesman of, 2078
spiritual, 470
today, 2435
Trumpeldor (Yosef) as advocate of, 2221
Ussishkin (Menahem) and, 2303
Weizmann (Chaim) in, 2337–2339
Wingate (Charles Orde) and, 2353
Wise (Stephen S.) in, 2354–2355
women in, 2357
after World War I, 2435
Yishuv in, 2400–2403
youth movements in, 974, 2412
Zionism and the Palestinians (Flapan), 835
Zionism: Its History, Object and Importance (Nasir), 1646
Zionist Actions Committee, 546
Zionist Commission for Palestine, **2436**
Ormsby-Gore (William) in, 1724
Palin Commission report criticizing (1920), 1795
Weizmann (Chaim) and, 2338
Zionist Executive
Jabotinsky (Vladimir Ze'ev) in, 1208
Kalvaryski (Chaim Margaliut-) in, 1265, 2402–2403
and Keren Hayesod, 1289
Shapira (Hayyim Moshe) in, 2030
Sokolow (Nahum) in, 2078
Zionist Organization of America (ZOA), **2436**
Wise (Stephen S.) in, 2354
Zionist Revisionist Movement, 2372, **2437–2438**
Arlosoroff (Chaim) opposed by, 290
Begin (Menachem) in, 424
Betar youth movement and, 2412, 2437
establishment of, 1209, 1362, 2435
Greenberg (Uri Zvi) in, 941
and Herut Party, 1181
Irgun Zva'i Le'umi as defense group for, 1139
Israeli military action against, 1536
Jabotinsky (Vladimir Ze'ev) in, 1208–1209, 2372, 2437
Labor Zionism's conflict with, 1209, 1973
Likud as descendant of, 1184
Netanyahu (Benzion) as founder of, 1676–1677
organization of, 1208–1209, 2437–2438
platform of, 1184, 1208, 2438
and violence, 2437
in Western Wall disturbances (1929), 2348
youth movement in, 1209, 2437
Zionist Right, 2437
Zionist Socialist Workers Union, 493
Zionist Workers movement, 1319
Zion Mule Corps, 2221
Zipperstein, Steven, *as contributor,* 78–79
Zirids, in Tunisia, 2228
Zirwal, al-Amin. *See* Zeroual, Liamine
Zisser, Eyal, *as contributor,* 2422
Zitouni, Djamel, 919
Zitouni, Jamel, 919
Ziwaj mut'a (temporary marriage), **2438–2439**
Ziyada, Marie. *See* Ziadeh, May
Ziyada, Nicola, 1791
Ziya Paşa, Abdülhamit, **2439**
Ali Suavi and, 144
newspaper edited by, 2406
and Ottoman constitution, 2407
in Young Ottomans, 2405, 2406, 2407
Ziyaret (visits to saints), muwahhidun rejection of, 1625
ZOA. *See* Zionist Organization of America
Zofeh, Ha- (newspaper), 464
Zohar, Uri, **2439**
Zohrab, Krikor, **2439–2440**
Zohrap, Grigor. *See* Zohrab, Krikor
Zola, Emile, on Dreyfus affair, 723
Zonnenfeld, Yosef Hayyim, **2440**
Zorian, Stepan, 676
Zoroastrianism, **2440–2442**
funerary ceremonies in, 2442
in India, 2440, 2442
initiation ceremony in, 2441, *2441*
in Iran, 1548, **2440–2441**
Yazd, 2382
Persian-language documents of, 1124
women in, religious rituals of, 2360, 2361
Zouabri, Antar, 919
Zoubir, Yahia, *as contributor,* 451–452, 1155–1156, 1280, 1803, 1959–1960, 2195, 2430
Zouini, Maria, 497
Zrika, Abdallah, 1355
Zu'ama (bosses), in Lebanon, 1663
Zu'ama al-Islah fi al-'Asr al-Hadith (Amin), 183
Zu'aytir, Akram, 1205
historiography of, 1791
in Istiqlal Party, 1764
Zu'ayyin, Yusuf
Atasi (Nur al-Din al-) and, 329
Hafiz (Amin al-) and, 972
Zubara, 370–371
Zubayri, Qa'id Muhammad Mahmud al-, **2442**
Free Yemenis founded by, 855
Zu'bi, Mahmud al-, **2442–2443**
Zuckerman, Julie, *as contributor,* 1081, 1676–1677, 1751–1752, 2056–2057, 2076, 2090, 2144, 2159, 2309, 2379, 2404
Zuhab, Treaty of (1639), 783
Zu Haderekh (Gozanski), 934
Zuhr al-Islam (Amin), 183
Zuray'id dynasty (Yemen), 2397
Zurayk, Constantine, **2443**
and Jam'iyyat al-Urwa al-Wuthqa, 962
on Nakba, al-, 1639
Zurayq, Qustantin. *See* Zurayk, Constantine
Zurich Agreement (1959), 653
"Zuruni Kull Sana Marra" (Darwish), 675
Zwemer, Samuel, in Arabian Mission, 231

Flagler College Library
P.O. Box 1027
St. Augustine, FL 32085